Table of Atomic Masses*

Element	Symbol	Atomic Number	Atomic Mass	Element	Symbol	Atomic Number	Atomic Mass	Element	Symbol	Atomic Number	Atomic Mass
Actinium	Ac	89	[227]§	Hafnium	Hf	72	178.5	Promethium	Pm	61	[145]
Aluminum	Al	13	26.98	Hassium	Hs	108	[265]	Protactinium	Pa	91	[231]
Americium	Am	95	[243]	Helium	He	2	4.003	Radium	Ra	88	226
Antimony	Sb	51	121.8	Holmium	Ho	67	164.9	Radon	Rn	86	[222]
Argon	Ar	18	39.95	Hydrogen	H	1	1.008	Rhenium	Re	75	186.2
Arsenic	As	33	74.92	Indium	In	49	114.8	Rhodium	Rh	45	102.9
Astatine	At	85	[210]	Iodine	I	53	126.9	Rubidium	Rb	37	85.47
Barium	Ba	56	137.3	Iridium	Ir	77	192.2	Ruthenium	Ru	44	101.1
Berkelium	Bk	97	[247]	Iron	Fe	26	55.85	Rutherfordium	Rf	104	[261]
Beryllium	Be	4	9.012	Krypton	Kr	36	83.80	Samarium	Sm	62	150.4
Bismuth	Bi	83	209.0	Lanthanum	La	57	138.9	Scandium	Sc	21	44.96
Bohrium	Bh	107	[264]	Lawrencium	Lr	103	[260]	Seaborgium	Sg	106	[263]
Boron	B	5	10.81	Lead	Pb	82	207.2	Selenium	Se	34	78.96
Bromine	Br	35	79.90	Lithium	Li	3	6.941	Silicon	Si	14	28.09
Cadmium	Cd	48	112.4	Lutetium	Lu	71	175.0	Silver	Ag	47	107.9
Calcium	Ca	20	40.08	Magnesium	Mg	12	24.31	Sodium	Na	11	22.99
Californium	Cf	98	[251]	Manganese	Mn	25	54.94	Strontium	Sr	38	87.62
Carbon	C	6	12.01	Meitnerium	Mt	109	[268]	Sulfur	S	16	32.07
Cerium	Ce	58	140.1	Mendelevium	Md	101	[258]	Tantalum	Ta	73	180.9
Cesium	Cs	55	132.90	Mercury	Hg	80	200.6	Technetium	Tc	43	[98]
Chlorine	Cl	17	35.45	Molybdenum	Mo	42	95.94	Tellurium	Te	52	127.6
Chromium	Cr	24	52.00	Neodymium	Nd	60	144.2	Terbium	Tb	65	158.9
Cobalt	Co	27	58.93	Neon	Ne	10	20.18	Thallium	Tl	81	204.4
Copper	Cu	29	63.55	Neptunium	Np	93	[237]	Thorium	Th	90	232.0
Curium	Cm	96	[247]	Nickel	Ni	28	58.69	Thulium	Tm	69	168.9
Dubnium	Db	105	[262]	Niobium	Nb	41	92.91	Tin	Sn	50	118.7
Dysprosium	Dy	66	162.5	Nitrogen	N	7	14.01	Titanium	Ti	22	47.88
Einsteinium	Es	99	[252]	Nobelium	No	102	[259]	Tungsten	W	74	183.9
Erbium	Er	68	167.3	Osmium	Os	76	190.2	Uranium	U	92	238.0
Europium	Eu	63	152.0	Oxygen	O	8	16.00	Vanadium	V	23	50.94
Fermium	Fm	100	[257]	Palladium	Pd	46	106.4	Xenon	Xe	54	131.3
Fluorine	F	9	19.00	Phosphorus	P	15	30.97	Ytterbium	Yb	70	173.0
Francium	Fr	87	[223]	Platinum	Pt	78	195.1	Yttrium	Y	39	88.91
Gadolinium	Gd	64	157.3	Plutonium	Pu	94	[244]	Zinc	Zn	30	65.38
Gallium	Ga	31	69.72	Polonium	Po	84	[209]	Zirconium	Zr	40	91.22
Germanium	Ge	32	72.59	Potassium	K	19	39.10				
Gold	Au	79	197.0	Praseodymium	Pr	59	140.9				

*The values given here are to four significant figures where possible.   §A value given in parentheses denotes the mass of the longest-lived isotope.

CHEMISTRY, FIFTH EDITION
by Steven S. Zumdahl and Susan A. Zumdahl
Copyright © 2000 by Houghton Mifflin Company. All rights reserved.

Senior Sponsoring Editor: Richard Stratton
Associated Editor: Marianne Stepanian
Senior Project Editor: Cathy Labresh Brooks
Senior Production/Design Coordinator: Jill Haber
Senior Manufacturing Coordinator: Marie Barnes
Marketing Manager: Andy Fisher

Photo credits: Student text/IAE: page A69; Alternate Edition: page A65

CHEMICAL PRINCIPLES, FOURTH EDITION
by Steven S. Zumdahl
Copyright © 2002 by Houghton Mifflin Company. All rights reserved.

Editor-in-Chief: Kathi Prancan
Senior Sponsoring Editor: Richard Stratton
Development Editor: Marianne Stepanian
Senior Production/Design Coordinator: Deborah Azerrad Savona
Manufacturing Manager: Florence Cadran
Executive Marketing Manager: Andy Fisher

Custom Publishing Editor: Dan Luciano
Custom Publishing Production Manager: Kathleen McCourt
Project Coordinator: Kayla Whittet

Cover Design: Joel Gendron

ISBN: 0-618-34301-6
N02121

1 2 3 4 5 6 7 8 9 – KP – 04 03 02

Houghton Mifflin
Custom Publishing

222 Berkeley Street • Boston, MA 02116

Address all correspondence and order information to the above address.

RUTGERS UNIVERSITY
GENERAL CHEMISTRY
GENERAL INFORMATION
FALL 2002-SPRING 2003

Welcome to General Chemistry 161-162 at Rutgers University. We sincerely hope that you will find this course to be both a valuable part of your education and an enjoyable experience. All the members of the instructional staff are committed to making General Chemistry as profitable and as painless as possible for you. Your success in the course will also be our success - but we will have to do it together.

This supplement provides important information about course organization, policies, procedures, and testing. The syllabus and details about grading will be provided separately by E-mail and/or on the General Chemistry web site.

COORDINATORS

Coordinators: Dr. Robert Boikess: Chemistry 161-162 fall 2002, spring 2003
[E-mail: boikess@rutchem.rutgers.edu]
Dr. Ramesh Agarwal: Chemistry 161 spring 2003
[E-mail: agarwal@rutchem.rutgers.edu]
Dr. Asbed Vassilian: Chemistry 161-162 (Solid Gems) fall 2002, spring 2003
[E-mail: asbed@rutchem.rutgers.edu]

REQUIRED MATERIALS

(1) *Chemistry* Fifth Edition, Rutgers University Custom Version by Zumdahl and Zumdahl (Houghton Mifflin). In general, lecture material and homework problems originate in this book. **Students are responsible for all assigned readings and problems, whether or not the material is explicitly discussed in lecture.**

(2) A scientific calculator (logarithms, exponentials, powers, roots, etc.). **Calculators with memories or graphing capabilities may not be used for exams.** An acceptable calculator will generally cost in the neighborhood of $10.

COURSE WEB SITE

The URL for the General Chemistry home page is

http://rutchem.rutgers.edu/generalchem.html

Once you get to the General Chemistry home page you will find your particular course listed and you should open its web page.

You will be able to find a great deal of the information you need and want about General Chemistry on the web page of the course in which you are enrolled. This web page will include the syllabus and any changes to the syllabus. It may also include some lecture notes and additional explanatory material, and practice exams with answers. As necessary, it will also list exam locations, information about conflict exams, exam topics, and answers to the exams just after you take them.

The web page will also provide any organizational or administrative details about the course that you need to know, such as the way your grade at the end of the semester will be calculated. When possible, we will also post cancellations due to weather or other emergencies.

You are responsible for checking and acting upon all information posted on the web page. You should check the web page regularly and of course you will also be responsible for all announcements made in lectures.

PREREQUISITES

The corequisite for Chemistry 161 and the prerequisite for 162 is 01:640:111 Precalculus I or 640:115 Precalculus College Mathematics, or their equivalent. You must have successfully completed one of these mathematics courses in order to register for Chemistry 162.

LABORATORY REQUIREMENT

Chemistry 161-162 has a one-semester (one-credit) laboratory corequisite, namely Chemistry 171 "Introduction to Experimentation". Students must have completed Chemistry 171 (or its equivalent) **before** or be registered for Chemistry 171 **at the same time** as Chemistry 162. Students may take Chemistry 171 in either the fall or spring semester. **Students who do not fulfill this requirement will not receive a course grade for Chemistry 162 until they do.**

The following information through Page 5 is applicable in all details only for those students who begin the study of General Chemistry in the fall semester. Variations in these instructions for students who are registered for 161 in the spring or summer session will be provided by the lecturer.

ALTERNATIVE COURSES

There are a number of different course options available   Chemistry 161-162 (Solid Gems) has longer meeting times and is designed for students who may benefit from more intensive instruction, extra testing, and evaluation. It meets for lecture three times a week for 80-minute periods and offers smaller recitation groups that meet twice weekly. Both versions of Chemistry 161-162 cover the same material and have a common final examination.

A more advanced course, Chemistry 163-164, Honors General Chemistry, is also offered by the department. It requires one year of high school chemistry as a prerequisite and Calculus I and II as corequisites for 163 and 164, respectively. Please see your lecturer as soon as possible for additional information, if you are interested in this alternative course sequence.

You have two options if you determine that you are unprepared for Chemistry 161-162. If you are enrolled in Chemistry 161 in the Fall semester, you may drop Chemistry 161 **NOW** and enroll in Introduction to Chemistry (Chemistry 134: 3 credits), a course that is designed to help you acquire the skills necessary for success in general chemistry. Chemistry 134 is offered only in the fall semester. Since Chemistry 161 is also offered in the spring semester, you may enter the 161-162 track immediately after completing Chemistry 134. Please consult your lecturer and/or college adviser before making this decision.

An alternative is to remain in Chemistry 161 and evaluate your situation after the first examination on October 2, 2002. If your performance at that time indicates your skills are weak, you may seek permission to switch into Preparation for General Chemistry (Chemistry 133: 2 credits). The simple procedure you need to follow to effect this course change will be announced in lecture and recitation after the first exam.

LECTURES

You will be assigned to a lecture section, attending either three 55-minute or two 80-minute lectures per week. The lecture schedule for **Chem 161** in the **fall of 2002** and **Chem 162** in the **spring of 2003** is as follows:

Day/Period	Time	Location
MWTh2*	10:05 - 11:00 AM	HCK 138 (Douglass)
MWF4*	1:25 - 2:20 PM	BE AUD (Livingston)
MW7	6:10 - 7:30 PM	BE AUD (Livingston)
Solid Gems MWF2	9:50 - 11:10 AM	SC 135 (College Ave)

The MWTh2* lectures in HCK-138 and the MWF4* lectures in BE-AUD are synchronized, and you may be able to pick up a missed daytime lecture by attending the other daytime section. The evening lectures are only partially synchronized with the daytime lectures. You may also wish to attend a lecture on a difficult topic more than once.

You are responsible for all material introduced in lecture, whether or not the corresponding topics are covered in the text, and for any announcements made in lecture (particularly important announcements will also be posted on the web site). Our experience has shown very clearly that students who attend lectures regularly tend to do better in the course than those who do not attend on a regular basis.

LECTURE EXTRA CREDIT

As an additional incentive to prepare for and attend lecture, there will be periodic opportunities to earn extra credit in class. On a random, unannounced basis, at least five times during the semester, the lecturer will present a problem, allow you five minutes to work on it, and then collect your paper. This lecture quiz is "open book" and you will also be permitted to work together with other students if you wish. Everyone making a reasonable effort to solve the problem will be awarded extra-credit points. Since your papers will be filed by recitation section, you **MUST include your section number and your instructor's name on your paper in order to get credit.** Many students have had their grades raised with these extra credit points, which demonstrate attendance in lectures and a commitment to putting in the effort needed to do as well as possible in the course. On the other hand, complaints about grades from students with low lecture quiz scores have not been well received.

RECITATIONS

You are scheduled for at least one 55-minute recitation per week. The purpose of the recitation meeting is to give you an opportunity to interact with a member of the instructional staff of the course in a relatively small group, to permit you to ask questions, and to provide additional problem-solving drill. Please be prepared and do not hesitate to ask questions. The questions need not be restricted to assigned problems; any material from the textbook or the lectures that is not clear to you can be discussed.

If you miss your scheduled recitation section, you should attend another recitation section during the same week. The time and place of all the recitations in General Chemistry can be found in the Schedule of Classes or on the Rutgers web site.

Your recitation instructor is available to provide you with significant extra help during office hours and by appointment. In addition, if your course grade is near a borderline at the end of the semester, you may benefit from your recitation instructor's positive evaluation or be hurt by your recitation instructor's negative evaluation of your attendance and participation. Specific details about how this evaluation is formulated will be provided in each course.

EXAMINATIONS

There will be three (four for the SG course) 80-minute "hour" examinations and a 3-hour final examination according to the schedule outlined in your syllabus and in the Rutgers Schedule of Classes. Formal lecture is canceled on the day of an hour exam. Instead the lecturers will conduct review sessions, and will answer questions.

Hour exams will consist of approximately 25 multiple-choice questions and the final exam will consist of approximately 55 multiple-choice questions. Edited copies of exams from previous years will be available for practice.

We do **not** expect you to memorize numbers such as physical constants or atomic weights. The periodic table and any necessary physical constants will always be given on the exam. In addition your lecturer will tell you which, if any, "formulas" will be given on the exam.

Bring an inexpensive scientific calculator that does not have a memory or graphing capabilities to the exam. Sharing calculators is not permitted. Also bring several #2 pencils, an eraser, and an **official photo ID** to the exam. Your photo ID will be checked during the exam; and students without a photo ID will not be permitted to take the exam

All common hour exams **must** be taken at the scheduled time unless an official conflict exists. The following situations may constitute an official conflict:

1. registration for another course that meets at the same time as the exam
2. another common hour exam at the same time
3. participation in intercollegiate athletic events
4. religious observances

For students who have official conflicts with common hour exams, **a conflict examination will be given on the same evening as the regularly scheduled exam.** A conflict and makeup exam for the final will be given before commencement. To request permission to attend the conflict exam, submit a **conflict request form**, which is available on the course web site or from the course coordinator, no later than 10 days before the scheduled exam along with appropriate documentation to the course coordinator, or if so instructed to:

Ms Donna Axelrod

Chemistry Undergraduate Secretary

Room 150 Wright Labs, e-mail: axelrod@rutchem, or Fax 5-5312

A list of students approved for the conflict exam will be posted on the web site by the Friday prior to each hourly. **Students whose names do not appear on this list will NOT be admitted to the conflict exam.**

If you miss an examination for unforeseen and verifiable medical or other serious reasons, contact the Course Coordinator by E-mail as soon as possible. You must provide to the course coordinator a **written explanation and appropriate supporting documents,** including a **letter from a Dean** verifying that your documentation is satisfactory (documents from non-Rutgers personnel without an accompanying letter from a Dean will not be sufficient) in order for your absence to be excused. In such cases, the final exam will be weighted more heavily to offset the missed exam. **There are no makeups for hour exams. An unexcused absence will be counted as a zero.**

If you miss the final exam you must provide acceptable written documentation (from a Dean) explaining your absence to Ms Axelrod by noon of the Friday immediately following the final exam in order to take the make-up final exam. You will be allowed to take the make-up final and be notified of its time and place, if we judge that your reasons for missing the final exam are valid ones.

ACADEMIC INTEGRITY

All University policies on academic integrity will be strictly enforced. We shall report promptly to the appropriate college authority any instance of suspected cheating or facilitating the academic dishonesty of others. If the charge is upheld through the Student Judicial System, there will be serious consequences ranging from reprimand to expulsion from the university. Furthermore, the instructional staff has the right to retest any student whose performance on a particular quiz or exam seems inconsistent with his/her other work.

CHAIN OF COMMAND

Routine questions regarding course material, homework, quizzes, exams, absences etc. should be directed first to your recitation instructor. If a question remains unanswered, ask your lecturer. If an issue is still unresolved, come and see your Course Coordinator, during his office hours or send him an E-mail message. Include a telephone number and an E-mail address at which you can be reached.

ADDITIONAL HELP

General Chemistry is considered by many students to be a difficult course. Such a conclusion is correct. When you look at the Syllabus, you will probably realize that there is a lot of work assigned. We expect that you will need to spend several hours per week studying outside of class for every hour of class time, just to achieve minimal mastery of the material. Putting in more study hours is therefore highly recommended. Moreover, chemistry is a cumulative subject, in which one principle builds upon another. Our experience shows that those students who fall behind, especially at the beginning, encounter great difficulty, and often do not catch up. On the other hand, if you work in a timely and conscientious way, and follow the study tips below, you should do fine.

If difficulties remain despite the efforts of the instructional staff and extensive studying on your own and with peers then seek help early! A list of office hours for all lecturers and recitation instructors will be posted on the web page. We will be glad to assist you, but you must take the initiative.

In addition, tutoring is provided by the Learning Resource Centers (**http://lrc.rutgers.edu**, 932-1443). The Math and Science Learning Centers (**http://mslc.rutgers.edu**, 445-3123, 932-8991) have old exams and other study aids on reserve.

SOME STUDY SUGGESTIONS

1. Do the assigned reading before each lecture.
2. Reread the assigned reading after lecture, focusing on the sections emphasized in the lecture and on those sections, if any, that you did not understand completely.
3. Understand the concepts. Problems on exams are rarely identical to homework problems. You cannot be effective in solving problems without understanding the technical concepts behind the problems.
4. Do the assigned homework problems. When you are done, check to make sure that you have done the problem correctly. Do not spend an excessive amount of time struggling with a problem you cannot do. Seek help with the problem in recitation and office hours. Once you understand a problem, make sure you can do it on your own later. The most common trap that students fall into is thinking that just because they understand (or think they understand) the book's or lecturer's solution to a problem, they will be able to do a similar problem on an exam. Success in this course requires **active knowledge**, the ability to understand concepts and have the skills to **use** them.
5. If, after doing all the assigned problems, you feel in need of more drill, do some of the unassigned problems. Do not hesitate to seek help from any of the instructional staff or at the Learning Centers.
6. Studying with one or more friends often proves beneficial if everyone participates actively.

Finally, please understand that the goal of the instructional staff in this course is the same as your goal: your mastery of all the knowledge and skills necessary for successful completion of the course. If we all do our share, this goal is readily attainable for everyone who should be pursuing a career in science.

So work hard and good luck.

Contents

To the Student

The major purpose of this book, of course, is to help you learn chemistry. However, this main thrust is closely linked to two other goals: to show how important and how interesting the subject is, and to show how to think like a chemist. To solve complicated problems the chemist uses logic, trial and error, intuition, and, above all, patience. A chemist is used to being wrong. The important thing is to learn from a mistake, recheck assumptions, and try again. A chemist thrives on puzzles that seem to defy solutions.

Many of you using this text do not plan to be practicing chemists. However, the nonchemist can benefit from the chemist's attitude. Problem solving is important in all professions and in all walks of life. The techniques you will learn from this book will serve you well in any career you choose. Thus, we believe that the study of chemistry has much to offer the nonmajor, including an understanding of many fascinating and important phenomena and a chance to hone problem-solving skills.

This book attempts to present chemistry in a manner that is sensible to the novice. Chemistry is not the result of an inspired vision. It is the product of countless observations and many attempts, using logic and trial and error, to account for these observations. In this book the concepts are developed in a natural way: The observations come first and then models are constructed to explain the observed behavior.

Models are a major focus in this book. The uses and limitations of models are emphasized, and science is treated as a human activity, subject to all the normal human foibles. Mistakes are discussed as well as successes.

A central theme of this book is a thoughtful, systematic approach to problem solving. Learning encompasses much more than simply memorizing facts. Truly educated people use their factual knowledge as a starting point—a base for creative approaches to solving problems.

Read through the material in the text carefully. For most concepts, illustrations or photos will help you visualize what is going on. To further help you visualize concepts by using animations, videos, and molecular models, we have packaged a CD-ROM, *General Chemistry: Interactive,* with your text. Blue CD icons in the text margin signal that there is companion material available on the CD.

Often a given type of problem is "walked through" in the text before the corresponding sample exercises appear. Strategies for solving problems are given throughout the text.

Thoroughly examine the sample exercises and the problem-solving strategies. The strategies summarize the approach taken in the text; the sample exercises follow the strategies step-by-step. The CD icons in the text will direct you to additional sample exercises found on *General Chemistry: Interactive.* Schematics in Chapter 15 also illustrate the logical pathways to solving aqueous equilibrium problems.

Throughout the text, we have used margin notes to highlight key points, to comment on an application of the text material, or to reference material in other parts of the book. **Chemical Impact,** the boxed feature that appears frequently throughout the text, discusses especially interesting applications of chemistry to the everyday world.

Each chapter has a summary and key terms list for review, and the glossary gives a quick reference for definitions.

Learning chemistry requires working the end-of-chapter exercises assigned by your professor. Answers to exercises denoted by blue question numbers are in the back of the book, and complete solutions to those exercises are in the *Partial Solutions Guide.* Additional exercises are available on the enclosed CD, and to help you assess your level of proficiency, the *student web site* (www.hmco.com/college) offers quizzes that feature instant grading results.

The *Study Guide* contains extra practice problems and many worked examples. The supplement, *Solving Equilibrium Problems with Applications to Qualitative Analysis,* reinforces in great detail the text's step-by-step approach to solving equilibrium problems and contains many worked examples and self-quiz questions.

It is very important to use the exercises to your best advantage. Your main goal should not be to simply get the correct answer but to *understand the process* for getting the answer. Memorizing the solutions for specific problems is not a very good way to prepare for an exam. There are too many pigeonholes required to cover every possible problem type. Look within the problem for the solution. Use the concepts you have learned along with a systematic, logical approach to find the solution. Learn to trust yourself to think it out. You will make mistakes, but the important thing is to learn from these errors. The only way to gain confidence is to do lots of practice problems and use these to diagnose your weaknesses.

Be patient and thoughtful and work hard to understand rather than simply memorize. We wish you an interesting and satisfying year.

Features of *Chemistry*
FIFTH EDITION

Each **Chapter Opener** includes a ▶
full-page photograph tied to the
chapter material.

The **Contents** gives students an
overview of the topics to come.
▼

CHAPTER 4

Types of Chemical Reactions and Solution Stoichiometry

Much of the chemistry that affects each of us occurs
among substances dissolved in water. For example, virtually all the chemistry
that makes life possible occurs in an aqueous environment. Also, various
medical tests involve aqueous reactions, depending heavily on analyses of
blood and other body fluids. In addition to the common tests for sugar,
cholesterol, and iron, analyses for specific chemical markers allow detection
of many diseases before obvious symptoms occur.

Aqueous chemistry is also important in our environment. In recent years,
contamination of the groundwater by substances such as chloroform and
nitrates has been widely publicized. Water is essential for life, and the
maintenance of an ample supply of clean water is crucial to all civilization.

To understand the chemistry that occurs in such diverse places as the
human body, the atmosphere, the groundwater, the oceans, the local water
treatment plant, your hair as you shampoo it, and so on, we must
understand how substances dissolved in water react with each other.

However, before we can understand solution reactions, we need to
discuss the nature of solutions in which water is the dissolving medium, or
solvent. These solutions are called **aqueous solutions.** In this chapter we will
study the nature of materials after they are dissolved in water and various
types of reactions that occur among these substances. You will see that the
procedures developed in Chapter 3 to deal with chemical reactions work
very well for reactions that take place in aqueous solutions. To understand
the types of reactions that occur in aqueous solutions, we must first explore
the types of species present. This requires an understanding of the nature
of water.

Contents

◀ The chapter begins with an engag-
ing introduction that demonstrates
how chemistry is related to everyday
life.

Yellow lead iodide is produced when lead nitrate is mixed with potassium iodide.

131

CHEMICAL IMPACT

The Chemistry of Air Bags

MOST EXPERTS AGREE that air bags represent a very important advance in automobile safety. These bags, which are stored in the auto's steering wheel or dash, are designed to inflate rapidly (within about 40 ms) in the event of a crash, cushioning the front seat occupants against impact. The bags then deflate immediately to allow vision and movement after the crash. Air bags are activated when a severe deceleration (an impact) causes a steel ball to compress a spring and electrically ignite a detonator cap, which, in turn, causes sodium azide (NaN₃) to decompose explosively, forming sodium and nitrogen gas:

$$2NaN_3(s) \longrightarrow 2Na(s) + 3N_2(g)$$

This system works very well and requires a relatively small amount of sodium azide (100 g yields 56 L N₂(g) at 25°C and 1.0 atm).

When a vehicle containing air bags reaches the end of its useful life, the sodium azide present in the activators must be given proper disposal. Sodium azide, besides being explosive, has a toxicity roughly equal to that of sodium cyanide. It also forms hydrazoic acid (HN₃), a toxic and explosive liquid, when treated with acid.

The air bag represents an application of chemistry that has already saved thousands of lives.

Inflated air bags.

◀ **Chemical Impact** boxes describe current applications of chemistry. These special interest boxes cover such topics as alternative fuels, night vision technology, and microchip laboratories.

A mixture of gases results whenever a gas is collected by displacement of water. For example, Fig. 5.13 shows the collection of oxygen gas produced by the decomposition of solid potassium chlorate. In this situation, the gas in the bottle is a mixture of water vapor and the oxygen being collected. Water vapor is present because molecules of water escape from the surface of the liquid and collect in the space above the liquid. Molecules of water also return to the liquid. When the rate of escape equals the rate of return, the number of water molecules in the vapor state remains constant, and thus the pressure of water vapor remains constant. This pressure, which depends on temperature, is called the *vapor pressure of water.*

Vapor pressure will be discussed in detail in Chapter 10. A table of water vapor pressure values is given in Section 10.8.

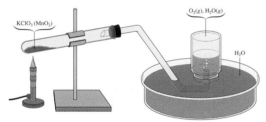

Figure 5.13
The production of oxygen by thermal decomposition of KClO₃. The MnO₂ is mixed with the KClO₃ to make the reaction faster.

07 g N
caffeine

02 g O
caffeine

8.001 mol C
mol caffeine

9.92 mol H
mol caffeine

4.002 mol N
mol caffeine

2.001 mol O
mol caffeine

lar formula for caffeine:

Computer-generated molecule of caffeine.

The methods for obtaining empirical and molecular formulas are summarized as follows:

Empirical Formula Determination

- Since mass percentage gives the number of grams of a particular element per 100 grams of compound, base the calculation on 100 grams of compound. Each percent will then represent the mass in grams of that element.
- Determine the number of moles of each element present in 100 grams of compound using the atomic masses of the elements present.
- Divide each value of the number of moles by the smallest of the values. If each resulting number is a whole number (after appropriate rounding), these numbers represent the subscripts of the elements in the empirical formula.
- If the numbers obtained in the previous step are not whole numbers, multiply each number by an integer so that the results are all whole numbers.

Numbers very close to whole numbers, such as 9.92 and 1.08, should be rounded to whole numbers. Numbers such as 2.25, 4.33, and 2.72 should not be rounded to whole numbers.

Molecular Formula Determination

Method One
- Obtain the empirical formula.
- Compute the mass corresponding to the empirical formula.
- Calculate the ratio

Important Rules and Steps ▶ appear in colored boxes so students can locate them easily.

The main acidic component of vinegar is acetic acid ($HC_2H_3O_2$). The formula is written to indicate that acetic acid has two chemically distinct types of hydrogen atoms. Formulas for acids are often written with the acidic hydrogen atom or atoms (any that will produce H^+ ions in solution) listed first. If any nonacidic hydrogens are present, they are written later in the formula. Thus the formula $HC_2H_3O_2$ indicates one acidic and three nonacidic hydrogen atoms. The dissociation reaction for acetic acid in water can be written as follows:

$$HC_2H_3O_2(aq) \underset{}{\overset{H_2O}{\rightleftharpoons}} H^+(aq) + C_2H_3O_2^-(aq)$$

Acetic acid is very different from the strong acids because only about 1% of its molecules dissociate in aqueous solutions at typical concentrations. For example, in a solution containing 0.1 mole of $HC_2H_3O_2$ per liter, for every 100 molecules of $HC_2H_3O_2$ originally dissolved in water, approximately 99 molecules of $HC_2H_3O_2$ remain intact (see Fig. 4.8). That is, only one molecule out of every 100 dissociates (to produce one H^+ ion and one $C_2H_3O_2^-$ ion).

Because acetic acid is a weak electrolyte, it is called a **weak acid.** Any acid, such as acetic acid, that *dissociates (ionizes) only to a slight extent in aqueous solutions is called a weak acid.* In Chapter 14 we will explore the subject of weak acids in detail.

The most common weak base is ammonia (NH_3). When ammonia is dissolved in water, it reacts as follows:

$$NH_3(aq) + H_2O(l) \longrightarrow NH_4^+(aq) + OH^-(aq)$$

The solution is *basic* because OH^- ions are produced. Ammonia is called a **weak base** because *the resulting solution is a weak electrolyte;* that is, very few ions are formed. In fact, in a solution containing 0.1 mole of NH_3 per liter, for every 100 molecules of NH_3 originally dissolved, only one NH_4^+ ion and one OH^- ion are produced; 99 molecules of NH_3 remain unreacted (see Fig. 4.9).

Molecular Model: $HC_2H_3O_2$

Many **Sample Exercises,** titled for easy reference, are located throughout the text. They model a thoughtful, step-by-step approach to solving problems. Cross-references to similar end-of-chapter exercises are provided at the end of each Sample Exercise. ▼

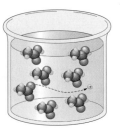

= Hydrogen

= Oxygen

= Carbon

Figure 4.8
Acetic acid ($HC_2H_3O_2$) [exists in] water mostly as undissoc[iated] molecules. Only a smal[l percent] of the molecules are ion[ized].

The art program has been updated for this edition. Molecular-level diagrams in particular have been increased in number and are now clearer and easier to comprehend.

Sample Exercise 6.4 **Enthalpy**

When 1 mole of methane (CH_4) is burned at constant pressure, 890 kJ of energy is released as heat. Calculate ΔH for a process in which a 5.8-g sample of methane is burned at constant pressure.

Solution

At constant pressure, 890 kJ of energy per mole of CH_4 is produced as heat:

$$q_P = \Delta H = -890 \text{ kJ/mol } CH_4$$

Note that the minus sign indicates an exothermic process. In this case, a 5.8-g sample of CH_4 (molar mass = 16.0 g/mol) is burned. Since this amount is smaller than 1 mole, less than 890 kJ will be released as heat. The actual value can be calculated as follows:

$$5.8 \text{ g } CH_4 \times \frac{1 \text{ mol } CH_4}{16.0 \text{ g } CH_4} = 0.36 \text{ mol } CH_4$$

and

$$0.36 \text{ mol } CH_4 \times \frac{-890 \text{ kJ}}{\text{mol } CH_4} = -320 \text{ kJ}$$

Thus, when a 5.8-g sample of CH_4 is burned at constant pressure,

$$\Delta H = \text{heat flow} = -320 \text{ kJ}$$

See Exercises 6.33 through 6.36.

Calorimetry

The device used experimentally to determine the heat associated with a chemical reaction is called a **calorimeter. Calorimetry,** the science of measuring heat, is based on observing the temperature change when a body absorbs or discharges energy as heat. Substances respond differently to being heated. One substance might require a great deal of heat energy to raise its temperature by one degree, whereas another will exhibit the same temperature change after absorbing relatively little heat. The **heat capacity** C of a substance, which is a measure of this property, is defined as

$$C = \frac{\text{heat absorbed}}{\text{increase in temperature}}$$

When an element or a compound is heated, the energy required will depend on the amount of the substance present (for example, it takes twice as much energy to raise the temperature of two grams of water by one degree than it takes to raise the temperature of one gram of water by one degree). Thus, in defining the heat capacity of a substance, the amount of substance must be specified. If the heat capacity is given *per gram* of substance, it is called the **specific heat capacity,** and its units are J/°C · g or J/K · g. If the heat capacity is given *per mole* of the substance, it is called the **molar heat capacity,** and it has the units J/°C · mol or J/K · mol. The specific

Specific heat capacity: the energy required to raise the temperature of one gram of a substance by one degree Celsius.

Molar heat capacity: the energy required to raise the temperature of one mole of a substance by one degree Celsius.

Each chapter has a **Summary** section to reinforce key concepts in the chapter. **Key Terms** are printed in bold type and are defined within the chapter where they first appear. They are also grouped at the end of the chapter and in the Glossary at the back of the text.

In-Class Discussion Questions are designed to promote discussion among groups of students in class.

For Review

Summary

Of the three states of matter, the gaseous state is the most easily understood experimentally and theoretically. A gas can be described quantitatively by specifying four properties: volume, pressure, temperature, and the amount of gas present.

Atmospheric pressure is measured with a barometer, and in the laboratory, gas pressure is usually measured with a manometer. Both devices employ columns filled with mercury, and the most commonly used units of pressure are based on the height of such a column in millimeters: 1 mm Hg equals 1 torr; 1 standard atmosphere equals 760 torr. In the SI system, the unit of pressure is the pascal (1 N/m^2).

Early experiments on the behavior of gases dealt with the relationship among the four characteristic properties. Boyle's law states that the volume of a given amount of a gas is inversely proportional to its pressure (at constant temperature). Charles's law states that for a given amount of gas at a constant pressure, the volume is directly proportional to the temperature in Kelvins. At a temperature of $-273.2°C$ (0 K), the volume of a gas extrapolates to zero, and this temperature is called absolute zero. Avogadro's law states that equal volumes of gases at the same temperature and pressure contain the same number of particles.

These three laws can be combined into the ideal gas law:

$$PV = nRT$$

where R is called the universal gas constant (0.08206 L · atm/K · mol). This equation allows calculation of any one of the characteristic properties, given the other three. The ideal gas law describes the limiting behavior approached by real gases at low pressures and high temperatures.

The molar volume (22.42 liters) is the volume of an ideal gas at STP (standard temperature and pressure) or 0°C and 1 atmosphere.

The pressure of a gaseous mixture is described by Dalton's law of partial pressures, which states that the total pressure of a mixture of gases in a container is the sum of the pressures that each gas would exert if it were alone (its partial pressure), that is,

$$P_{TOTAL} = P_1 + P_2 + P_3 + \cdots$$

The mole fraction of a given component in a mixture of gases can be calculated from the ratio of the partial pressure of that component to the total gas pressure.

The kinetic molecular theory of gases is a theoretical model constructed to account for ideal gas behavior. This model assumes that the volume of the gas particles is zero, that there are no interactions between particles, and that the particles are in constant motion, colliding with the container walls to produce pressure. In addition, this model shows that the average kinetic energy of the gas particles is directly proportional to the Kelvin temperature of the gas.

The root mean square velocity for the particles in a gas can be calculated from the temperature and the molar mass of the gas. Within any gas sample there is a range of velocities, since the gas particles collide and exchange kinetic energy. An increase in temperature increases the average velocity of the gas particles. The relative rates of diffusion, the mixing of gases, and effusion, the passage of a gas

Key Terms

Section 5.1
barometer
manometer
mm Hg
torr
standard atmosphere
pascal

Section 5.2
Boyle's law
ideal gas
Charles's law
absolute zero
Avogadro's law

Section 5.3
universal gas constant
ideal gas law

Section 5.4
molar volume
standard temperature and
  pressure (STP)

Section 5.5
Dalton's law of partial pressures
partial pressure
mole fraction

Section 5.6
kinetic molecular theory (KMT)
root mean square velocity
joule

Section 5.7
diffusion
effusion
Graham's law of effusion

Section 5.8
real gas
van der Waals equation

Section 5.9
atmosphere
air pollution
photochemical smog
acid rain

In-Class Discussion Questions

These questions are designed to be considered by groups of students in class. Often these questions work well for introducing a particular topic in class.

1. Consider the following apparatus: a test tube covered with a nonpermeable elastic membrane inside a container that is closed with a cork. A syringe goes through the cork.

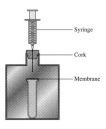

- Syringe
- Cork
- Membrane

   a. As you push down on the syringe, how does the membrane covering the test tube change?
   b. You stop pushing the syringe but continue to hold it down. In a few seconds, what happens to the membrane?

2. Figure 5.2 shows a picture of a barometer. Which of the following statements is the best explanation of how this barometer works?
   a. Air pressure outside the tube causes the mercury to move in the tube until the air pressure inside and outside the tube is equal.
   b. Air pressure inside the tube causes the mercury to move in the tube until the air pressure inside and outside the tube is equal.
   c. Air pressure outside the tube counterbalances the weight of the mercury in the tube.
   d. Capillary action of the mercury causes the mercury to go up the tube.

3.

---

   c. the law of multiple proportions

16. What refinements had to be made in Dalton's atomic theory to account for Gay-Lussac's results on the combining volumes of gases?

17. What evidence led to the conclusion that cathode rays had a negative charge?

18. What discoveries were made by J. J. Thomson, Henri Becquerel, and Lord Rutherford? How did Dalton's model of the atom have to be modified to account for these discoveries?

19. What is the distinction between atomic number and mass number? Between mass number and atomic mass?

20. Distinguish between the terms *family* and *period* in connection with the periodic table. For which of these terms is the term *group* also used?

21. When hydrogen is burned in oxygen to form water, the composition of water formed does not depend on the amount of oxygen. Interpret this in terms of the law of definite proportions.

22. The two most reactive families of elements are the halogens and the alkali metals. How do they differ in their reactivities?

Exercises

In this section similar exercises are paired.

Development of the Atomic Theory

23. When mixtures of gaseous H_2 and gaseous Cl_2 react, a product forms that has the same properties regardless of the relative amounts of H_2 and Cl_2 used.

measuring the mass of a substance that reacts with 1.00 g of oxygen. Given the following data and taking the atomic mass of hydrogen as 1.00, generate a table of relative atomic masses for oxygen, sodium, and magnesium.

Element	Mass That Combines with 1.00 g Oxygen	Assumed Formula
Hydrogen	0.126 g	HO
Sodium	2.875 g	NaO
Magnesium	1.500 g	MgO

How do your values compare with those in the periodic table? How do you account for any differences?

28. The mass of beryllium that combines with 1.000 g of oxygen to form beryllium oxide is 0.5633 g. When atomic masses were first being measured, it was thought that the formula of beryllium oxide was Be_2O_3. What would be the atomic mass of beryllium if this were the case? Assume that oxygen has an atomic mass of 16.00.

The Nature of the Atom

29. From the information in this chapter on the mass of the proton, the mass of the electron, and the sizes of the nucleus and the atom, calculate the densities of a hydrogen nucleus and a hydrogen atom.

30. If you wanted to make an accurate scale model of the hydrogen atom and decided that the nucleus would have a diameter of 1 mm, what would be the diameter of the entire model?

Questions test students' conceptual grasp of the material, **Exercises** (paired and organized by topic) reinforce students' understanding of each section; **Additional Exercises** (not keyed by topic) require students to identify and apply the appropriate concepts themselves; **Challenge Problems** involve students integrating a number of concepts and skills; and **Marathon Problems** are even more comprehensive and challenging.

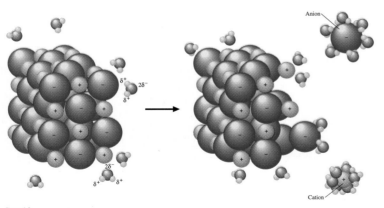

Anion

δ^+ $2\delta^-$
δ^+

$2\delta^-$
δ^+ δ^+

Cation

Figure 4.2
Polar water molecules interact with the positive and negative ions of a salt, assisting in the dissolving process.

Animation: The Dissolution of a Solid in a Liquid

The **solubility** of ionic substances in water varies greatly. For example, sodium chloride is quite soluble in water, whereas silver chloride (contains Ag^+ and Cl^- ions) is only very slightly soluble. The differences in the solubilities of ionic compounds in water typically depend on the relative attractions of the ions for each other (these forces hold the solid together) and the attractions of the ions for water molecules (which cause the solid to disperse [dissolve] in water). Solubility is a complex topic that we will explore in much more detail in Chapter 11. However, the most important thing to remember at this point is that when an ionic solid does dissolve in water, the ions become hydrated and are dispersed (move around independently).

Water also dissolves many nonionic substances. Ethanol (C_2H_5OH), for example, is very soluble in water. Wine, beer, and mixed drinks are aqueous solutions of ethanol and other substances. Why is ethanol so soluble in water? The answer lies in the structure of the alcohol molecules, which is shown in Fig. 4.3(a). The molecule contains a polar O—H bond like those in water, which makes it very compatible with water. The interaction of water with ethanol is represented in Fig. 4.3(b).

Many substances do not dissolve in water. Pure water will not, for example, dissolve animal fat, because fat molecules are nonpolar and do not interact effectively with polar water molecules. In general, polar and ionic substances are expected to be more soluble in water than nonpolar substances. "Like dissolves like" is a useful rule for predicting solubility. We will explore the basis for this generalization when we discuss the details of solution formation in Chapter 11.

Molecular Model: C_2H_5OH

What masses of calcium sulfate and phosphoric acid can be produced from the reaction of 1.0 kg calcium phosphate with 1.0 kg concentrated sulfuric acid (98% H_2SO_4 by mass)?

102. Hydrogen cyanide is produced industrially from the reaction of gaseous ammonia, oxygen, and methane:

$$2NH_3(g) + 3O_2(g) + 2CH_4(g) \longrightarrow 2HCN(g) + 6H_2O(g)$$

If 5.00×10^3 kg each of NH_3, O_2, and CH_4 are reacted, what mass of HCN and of H_2O will be produced, assuming 100% yield?

103. The reaction of ethane gas (C_2H_6) with chlorine gas produces C_2H_5Cl as its main product (along with HCl). In addition, the reaction invariably produces a variety of other minor products, including $C_2H_4Cl_2$, $C_2H_3Cl_3$, and others. Naturally, the production of these minor products reduces the yield of the main product. Calculate the percent yield of C_2H_5Cl if the reaction of 300. g of ethane with 650. g of chlorine produced 490. g of C_2H_5Cl.

104. A student prepared aspirin in a laboratory experiment using the reaction in Exercise 96. The student reacted 1.50 g salicylic acid with 2.00 g acetic anhydride. The yield was 1.50 g aspirin. Calculate the theoretical yield and the percent yield for this experiment.

105. Aluminum burns in bromine, producing aluminum bromide:

$$2Al(s) + 3Br_2(l) \longrightarrow 2AlBr_3(s)$$

In a certain experiment, 6.0 g aluminum was reacted with an excess of bromine to yield 50.3 g aluminum bromide. Calculate the theoretical and percent yields for this experiment.

106. Consider the following unbalanced reaction:

$$P_4(s) + F_2(g) \longrightarrow PF_3(g)$$

How many grams of F_2 are needed to produce 120. g of PF_3 if the reaction has a 78.1% yield?

Additional Exercises

107. Only one isotope of this element occurs in nature. One atom of this isotope has a mass of 9.123×10^{-23} g. Identify the element and give its atomic mass.

108. Chloral hydrate ($C_2H_3Cl_3O_2$) is a drug formerly used as a sedative and hypnotic. It is the compound used to make "Mickey Finns" in detective stories.
   a. Calculate the molar mass of chloral hydrate.
   b. How many moles of $C_2H_3Cl_3O_2$ molecules are in 500.0 g chloral hydrate?
   c. What is the mass in grams of 2.0×10^{-2} mol chloral hydrate?
   d. How many chlorine atoms are in 5.0 g chloral hydrate?
   e. What mass of chloral hydrate would contain 1.0 g Cl?
   f. What is the mass of exactly 500 molecules of chloral hydrate?

given below:
   a. 50 molecules of H_2 and 25 molecules of O_2
   b. 100 molecules of H_2 and 40 molecules of O_2
   c. 100 molecules of H_2 and 100 molecules of O_2
   d. 0.50 mol H_2 and 0.75 mol O_2
   e. 0.80 mol H_2 and 0.75 mol O_2
   f. 1.0 g H_2 and 0.25 mol O_2
   g. 5.00 g H_2 and 56.00 g O_2

99. When a mixture of silver metal and sulfur is heated, silver sulfide is formed:

$$16Ag(s) + S_8(s) \xrightarrow{\text{Heat}} 8Ag_2S(s)$$

   a. What mass of Ag_2S is produced from a mixture of 2.0 g Ag and 2.0 g S_8?
   b. What mass of which reactant is left unreacted?

100. Mercury and bromine will react with each other to produce mercury(II) bromide:

$$Hg(l) + Br_2(l) \longrightarrow HgBr_2(s)$$

   a. What mass of $HgBr_2$ can be produced from the reaction of 10.0 g Hg and 9.00 g Br_2? What mass of which reagent is left unreacted?
   b. What mass of $HgBr_2$ can be produced from the reaction of 5.00 mL mercury (density = 13.6 g/mL) and 5.00 mL bromine (density = 3.10 g/mL)?

101. Consider the following unbalanced equation:

$$Ca_3(PO_4)_2(s) + H_2SO_4(aq) \longrightarrow CaSO_4(s) + H_3PO_4(aq)$$

Chemistry's Multimedia Resources

You have purchased, along with this text, a wealth of multimedia resources designed to enhance the fifth edition of *Chemistry.* The CD-ROM *Chemistry Interactive,* 4.0 is located at the back of all new copies of this text, and your instructor will provide you with a password to access the web site located at www.hmco.com/college. As you read through the pages of *Chemistry,* a CD-ROM icon in the margin that looks like this ⬜ alerts you to material on the CD. The icon includes a label so that you can easily locate the file on the CD. Additionally, you can go to the free web site (www.hmco.com/college) and access *Chemistry's* chapter-by-chapter glossary, on-line quizzes, and media activities. The media activities are specifically designed to walk you through all the miltimedia material for each chapter in a way that is clear and easy to understand.

These text icons and labels will direct you to the General Chemistry Interactive CD, where additional content is available to deepen your understanding of important concepts and allow for additional opportunities to practice problem-solving skills.

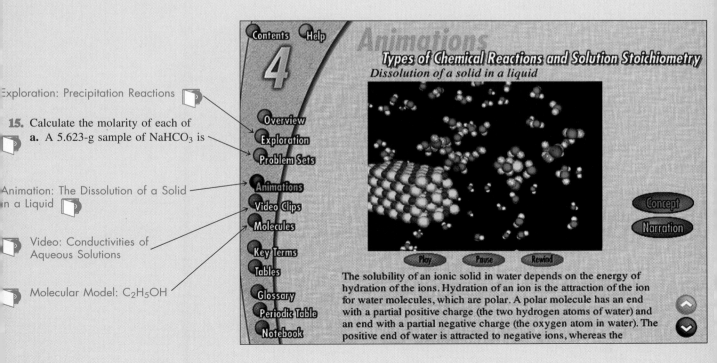

Chemical Foundations

Contents

When you start your car, do you think about chemistry? Probably not, but you should. The power to start your car is furnished by a lead storage battery. How does this battery work, and what does it contain? When a battery goes dead, what does that mean? If you use a friend's car to "jump start" your car, did you know that your battery could explode? How can you avoid such an unpleasant possibility? What is in the gasoline that you put in your tank, and how does it furnish the energy to drive to school? What is the vapor that comes out of the exhaust pipe, and why does it cause air pollution? Your car's air conditioner might have a substance in it that is leading to the destruction of the ozone layer in the upper atmosphere. What are we doing about that? And why is the ozone layer important anyway?

All these questions can be answered by understanding some chemistry. In fact, we'll consider the answers to all these questions in this text.

Chemistry is around you all the time. You are able to read and understand this sentence because chemical reactions are occurring in your brain. The food you ate for breakfast or lunch is now furnishing energy through chemical reactions. Trees and grass grow because of chemical changes.

Chemistry also crops up in some unexpected places. When archaeologist Luis Alvarez was studying in college, he probably didn't realize that the chemical elements iridium and niobium would make him very famous when they helped him solve the problem of the disappearing dinosaurs. For decades scientists had wrestled with the mystery of why the dinosaurs, after ruling the earth for millions of years, suddenly became extinct 65 million years ago. In studying core samples of rocks dating back to that period, Alvarez and his coworkers recognized unusual levels of iridium and niobium in these samples—levels much more characteristic of extraterrestrial bodies than of the earth. Based on these observations, Alvarez hypothesized that a large meteor hit the earth 65 million years ago, changing atmospheric

Sea anemones release a chemical alarm when attacked by a fish. This waterborne signal spreads through the dense colony of anemones, warning each individual to draw in its tentacles and close its mouth.

conditions so much that the dinosaurs' food couldn't grow, and they died—almost instantly in the geologic timeframe.

Chemistry is also important to historians. Did you realize that lead poisoning probably was a significant contributing factor to the decline of the Roman Empire? The Romans had high exposure to lead from lead-glazed pottery, lead water pipes, and a sweetening syrup called *sapa* that was prepared by boiling down grape juice in lead-lined vessels. It turns out that one reason for sapa's sweetness was lead acetate ("sugar of lead") that formed as the juice was cooked down. Lead poisoning with its symptoms of lethargy and mental malfunctions certainly could have contributed to the demise of the Roman society.

Chemistry is also apparently very important in determining a person's behavior. Various studies have shown that many personality disorders can be linked directly to imbalances of trace elements in the body. For example, studies on the inmates at Stateville Prison in Illinois link low cobalt levels with violent behavior. Lithium salts have been shown to be very effective in controlling the effects of manic depressive disease, and you've probably at some time in your life felt a special "chemistry" for another person. Studies suggest there is literally chemistry going on between two people who are attracted to each other. "Falling in love" apparently causes changes in the chemistry of the brain; chemicals are produced that give that "high" associated with a new relationship. Unfortunately, these chemical effects seem to wear off over time, even if the relationship persists and grows.

The importance of chemistry in the interactions of people should not really surprise us, since we know that insects communicate by emitting and receiving chemical signals via molecules called *pheromones*. For example, ants have a very complicated set of chemical signals to signify food sources, danger, and so forth. Also, various female sex attractants have been isolated and used to lure males into traps to control insect populations. It would not be surprising if humans also emitted chemical signals that we were not aware of on a conscious level. Thus chemistry is pretty interesting and pretty important. The main goal of this text is to help you understand the concepts of chemistry so that you can better appreciate the world around you and can be more effective in whatever career you choose.

This scientist reads conductivity values for mineral deposits from Chile's Atacama Desert.

1.1 Chemistry: An Overview

Although we will discuss all these things in much more detail as we proceed through this text, let's preview here what chemistry is about. Chemistry is fundamentally concerned with how one substance changes to another—how plants grow by absorbing water and carbon dioxide, how humans manufacture the proteins we need to live from the food we consume, how smog forms in areas with traffic congestion, how nylon for jackets and tents is made, and on and on.

Through processes we will discuss in this text scientists have learned that the matter of the universe is composed of atoms. It is hard to believe, but our universe with its incredible diversity is made of only a hundred or so different types of atoms. You can think of these approximately 100 atoms as the letters in an alphabet out of which all the "words" in the universe are made. It is the way the atoms are organized in a given substance that determines the properties of that substance. For example, water, one of the most common and important substances on earth, is composed of two types of atoms: hydrogen and oxygen. There are two hydrogen atoms and one oxygen atom bound together to form the water molecule:

A scientist studying the photosynthesis of wheat.

When an electric current passes through it, water is decomposed to hydrogen and oxygen. These *chemical elements* themselves exist naturally as diatomic (two-atom) molecules:

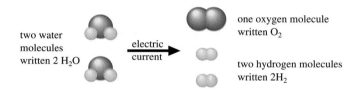

We can represent the decomposition of water to its component elements, hydrogen and oxygen, as follows:

Molecular Models: O_2, H_2, H_2O

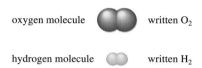

Notice that it takes two molecules of water to furnish the right number of oxygen and hydrogen atoms to allow for the formation of the two-atom molecules. This reaction explains why the battery in your car can explode if you jump start it improperly. When you hook up the jumper cables, current flows through the dead battery, which contains water (and other things), and causes hydrogen and oxygen to form by decomposition of some of the water. A spark can cause this accumulated hydrogen and oxygen to explode, forming water again.

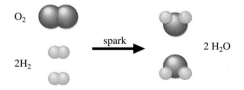

This example illustrates two of the fundamental concepts of chemistry: (1) matter is composed of various types of atoms, and (2) one substance changes to another by reorganizing the way the atoms are attached to each other.

These are core ideas of chemistry, and we will have much more to say about them.

Science: A Process for Understanding Nature and Its Changes

How do you tackle the problems that confront you in real life? Think about your trip to school. If you live in a city, traffic is undoubtedly a problem you confront daily. How do you decide the best way to drive to school? If you are new in town, you first get a map and look at the possible ways to make the trip. Then you might collect information from people who know the area about the advantages and disadvantages of various routes. Based on this information, you probably try to predict the best route. However, you can find the best route only by trying several of them and comparing the results. After a few experiments with the various possibilities, you probably will be able to select the best way. What you are doing in solving this everyday problem is applying the same process that scientists use to study nature. The first thing you did was collect relevant data. Then you made a prediction, and then you tested it by trying it out. This process contains the fundamental elements of science.

1. Making observations (collecting data)
2. Making a prediction (formulating a hypothesis)
3. Doing experiments to test the prediction (testing the hypothesis)

Scientists call this process the *scientific method.* We will discuss this in more detail in the next section. One of life's most important activities is solving problems—not "plug and chug" exercises, but real problems—problems that have new facets to them, that involve things you may have never confronted before. The more creative you are at solving these problems, the more effective you will be in your career and your personal life. Part of the reason for learning chemistry, therefore, is to become a better problem solver. Chemists are usually excellent problem solvers, because to master chemistry, you have to master the scientific approach. Chemical problems are frequently very complicated—there is usually no neat and tidy solution. Often it is difficult to know where to begin.

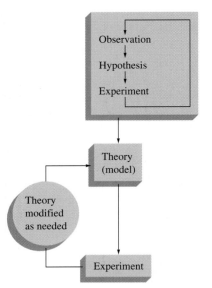

1.2 The Scientific Method

Science is a framework for gaining and organizing knowledge. Science is not simply a set of facts but is also a plan of action—a *procedure* for processing and understanding certain types of information. Scientific thinking is useful in all aspects of life, but in this text we will use it to understand how the chemical world operates. As we have said in our previous discussion, the process that lies at the center of scientific inquiry is called the **scientific method.** There are actually many scientific methods, depending on the nature of the specific problem under study and on the particular investigator involved. However, it is useful to consider the following general framework for a generic scientific method (see Fig. 1.1):

Figure 1.1
The fundamental steps of the scientific method.

Steps in the Scientific Method

1. *Making observations.* Observations may be *qualitative* (the sky is blue; water is a liquid) or *quantitative* (water boils at 100°C; a certain chemistry book weighs 2 kilograms). A qualitative observation does not involve a number. A quantitative observation (called a **measurement**) involves both a number and a unit.
2. *Formulating hypotheses.* A **hypothesis** is a *possible* explanation for an observation.
3. *Performing experiments.* An experiment is carried out to test a hypothesis. This involves gathering new information that enables a scientist to decide whether or not the hypothesis is valid—that is, whether it is supported by the new information learned from the experiment. Experiments always produce new observations, and this brings the process back to the beginning again.

To understand a given phenomenon, these steps are repeated many times, gradually accumulating the knowledge necessary to provide a possible explanation of the phenomenon.

Once a set of hypotheses that agrees with the various observations is obtained, the hypotheses are assembled into a theory. A **theory,** which is often called a **model,** is a set of tested hypotheses that gives an overall explanation of some natural phenomenon.

It is very important to distinguish between observations and theories. An observation is something that is witnessed and can be recorded. A theory is an *interpretation*—a possible explanation of *why* nature behaves in a particular way. Theories inevitably change as more information becomes available. For example, the motions of the sun and stars have remained virtually the same over the thousands of years during which humans have been observing them, but our explanations—our theories—for these motions have changed greatly since ancient times. (See the Chemical Impact on Observations, Theories, and the Planets on page 7.)

The point is that scientists do not stop asking questions just because a given theory seems to account satisfactorily for some aspect of natural behavior. They continue doing experiments to refine or replace the existing theories. This is generally done by using the currently accepted theory to make a prediction and then performing an experiment (making a new observation) to see whether the results bear out this prediction.

Robert Boyle (1627–1691) was born in Ireland. He became especially interested in experiments involving air and developed an air pump with which he produced evacuated cylinders. He used these cylinders to show that a feather and a lump of lead fall at the same rate in the absence of air resistance and that sound cannot be produced in a vacuum. His most famous experiments involved careful measurements of the volume of a gas as a function of pressure. In his book The Skeptical Chymist, *Boyle urged that the ancient view of elements as mystical substances should be abandoned and that an element should instead be defined as anything that cannot be broken down into simpler substances. This conception was an important step in the development of modern chemistry.*

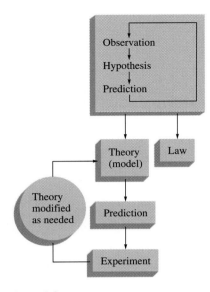

Figure 1.2

The various parts of the scientific method.

Always remember that theories (models) are human inventions. They represent attempts to explain observed natural behavior in terms of human experiences. A theory is actually an educated guess. We must continue to do experiments and to refine our theories (making them consistent with new knowledge) if we hope to approach a more nearly complete understanding of nature.

As scientists observe nature, they often see that the same observation applies to many different systems. For example, studies of innumerable chemical changes have shown that the total observed mass of the materials involved is the same before and after the change. Such generally observed behavior is formulated into a statement called a **natural law.** For example, the observation that the total mass of materials is not affected by a chemical change in those materials is called the **law of conservation of mass.**

Note the difference between a natural law and a theory. A natural law is a summary of observed (measurable) behavior, whereas a theory is an explanation of behavior. *A law summarizes what happens; a theory (model) is an attempt to explain why it happens.*

In this section we have described the scientific method as it might ideally be applied (see Fig. 1.2). However it is important to remember that science does not always progress smoothly and efficiently. For one thing, hypotheses and observations are not totally independent of each other, as we have assumed in the description of the idealized scientific method. The coupling of observations and hypotheses occurs because once we begin to proceed down a given theoretical path, our hypotheses are unavoidably couched in the language of that theory. In other words, we tend to see what we expect to see and often fail to notice things that we do not expect. Thus the theory we are testing helps us because it focuses our questions. However, at the very same time, this focusing process may limit our ability to see other possible explanations.

It is also important to keep in mind that scientists are human. They have prejudices; they misinterpret data; they become emotionally attached to their theories and thus lose objectivity; and they play politics. Science is affected by profit motives, budgets, fads, wars, and religious beliefs. Galileo, for example, was forced to recant his astronomical observations in the face of strong religious resistance. Lavoisier, the father of modern chemistry, was beheaded because of his political affiliations. And great progress in the chemistry of nitrogen fertilizers resulted from the desire to produce explosives to fight wars. The progress of science is often affected more by the frailties of humans and their institutions than by the limitations of scientific measuring devices. The scientific methods are only as effective as the humans using them. They do not automatically lead to progress.

1.3 Units of Measurement

Making observations is fundamental to all science. A quantitative observation, or *measurement,* always consists of two parts: a *number* and a scale (called a *unit*). Both parts must be present for the measurement to be meaningful.

In this textbook we will use measurements of mass, length, time, temperature, electric current, and the amount of a substance, among others. Scientists recognized long ago that standard systems of units had to be adopted if measurements were to be useful. If every scientist had a different set of units, complete chaos would result. Unfortunately, different standards were adopted in different parts of the world.

CHEMICAL IMPACT

Observations, Theories, and the Planets

HUMANS HAVE ALWAYS been fascinated by the heavens, by the behavior of the sun by day and the stars by night. Although more accurately measured now because of precise instruments, the basic *observations* of these events have remained the same over the past 4000 years. However, our *interpretations* of the events have changed dramatically. For example, about 2000 B.C. the Egyptians postulated that the sun was a boat inhabited by the god Ra, who daily sailed across the sky.

Over the years, patterns in the changes in the heavens were recognized and, through marvelous devices such as Stonehenge in England, were connected to the seasons of the year. People also noted that seven objects seemed to move against the background of "fixed stars." These objects, actually the sun, the moon, and the planets Mercury, Venus, Mars, Jupiter, and Saturn, were called the "wanderers." The planets appeared to move from west to east, except Mars, which seemed to slow down and even move backwards for a few weeks.

One of the first explanations for these observations came from Eudoxus, born in 400 B.C. He imagined the earth as fixed, with the planets attached to a nested set of transparent spheres that moved at different rates around the earth. The stars were attached to the outermost sphere. This model, although clever, still did not account for the strange behavior of Mars. Five hundred years later, Ptolemy, a Greek scholar, worked out a plan more complex than that of Eudoxus, in which the planets were attached to the edges of spheres that "rolled around" the spheres of Eudoxus (see time line). This model accounted for the behavior of all the planets, including the apparent reversals in the motion of Mars.

Because of human prejudice that the earth should be the center of the universe, Ptolemy's model was assumed to be correct for more than a thousand years, and its wide acceptance actually inhibited the advancement of astronomy. Finally, in 1543, a Polish cleric, Nicholas Copernicus, postulated that the earth was only one of the planets, all of which revolved around the sun. This "demotion" of the earth's status produced violent opposition to the new model, and in fact, Copernicus's writings were "corrected" by religious officials before scholars were allowed to use them.

The Copernican theory persisted and was finally given a solid mathematical base by Johannes Kepler. Kepler postulated elliptical rather than circular orbits for the planets in order to account more completely for their observed motions. Kepler's hypotheses were in turn further refined 36 years after his death by Isaac Newton, who recognized that the concept of gravitation could account for the positions and motions of the planets. However, even the brilliant models of Newton were found incomplete by Albert Einstein, who showed that Newton's mechanics was a special case of a much more general model.

Thus the same basic observations were made for several thousand years, but the explanations—the models—have changed remarkably from the Egyptians' boat of Ra to Einstein's relativity.

Our models will inevitably change, and we should expect them to do so. They can help us make scientific progress, or they can inhibit progress if we become too attached to them. Although the fundamental facts of chemistry will remain the same, the models in a chemistry text written a century from now will certainly be quite different from the ones presented here.

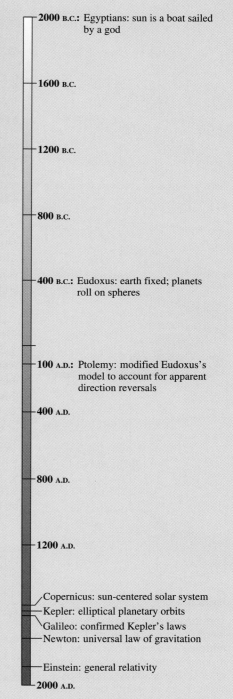

2000 B.C.: Egyptians: sun is a boat sailed by a god

1600 B.C.

1200 B.C.

800 B.C.

400 B.C.: Eudoxus: earth fixed; planets roll on spheres

100 A.D.: Ptolemy: modified Eudoxus's model to account for apparent direction reversals

400 A.D.

800 A.D.

1200 A.D.

Copernicus: sun-centered solar system
Kepler: elliptical planetary orbits
Galileo: confirmed Kepler's laws
Newton: universal law of gravitation

Einstein: general relativity

2000 A.D.

A time line showing how models of the solar system changed over 4000 years.

Scientists making measurements in a biomedical laboratory.

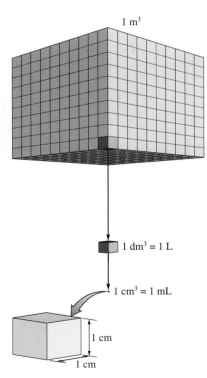

Figure 1.3

The largest cube has sides 1 m in length and a volume of 1 m³. The middle-sized cube has sides 1 dm in length and a volume of 1 dm³, or 1 L. The smallest cube has sides 1 cm in length and a volume of 1 cm³, or 1 mL.

The two major systems are the *English system* used in the United States (and a few African countries) and the *metric system* used by most of the rest of the industrialized world. This duality causes a good deal of trouble; for example, parts as simple as bolts are not interchangeable between machines built using the two systems. As a result, the United States has begun to adopt the metric system.

Most scientists in all countries have for many years used the metric system. In 1960, an international agreement set up a system of units called the *International System* (*le Système International* in French), or the **SI system.** This system is based on the metric system and units derived from the metric system. The fundamental SI units are listed in Table 1.1. We will discuss how to manipulate these units later in this chapter.

Because the fundamental units are not always convenient (expressing the mass of a pin in kilograms is awkward), prefixes are used to change the size of the unit. These are listed in Table 1.2. Some common objects and their measurements in SI units are listed in Table 1.3.

One physical quantity that is very important in chemistry is *volume,* which is not a fundamental SI unit but is derived from length. A cube that measures 1 meter (m) on each edge is represented in Fig. 1.3. This cube has a volume of $(1 \text{ m})^3 = 1 \text{ m}^3$.

Table 1.1 The Fundamental SI Units		
Physical Quantity	*Name of Unit*	*Abbreviation*
Mass	kilogram	kg
Length	meter	m
Time	second	s
Temperature	kelvin	K
Electric current	ampere	A
Amount of substance	mole	mol
Luminous intensity	candela	cd

Table 1.2 The Prefixes Used in the SI System (Those most commonly encountered are shown in blue.)

Prefix	Symbol	Meaning	Exponential Notation*
exa	E	1,000,000,000,000,000,000	10^{18}
peta	P	1,000,000,000,000,000	10^{15}
tera	T	1,000,000,000,000	10^{12}
giga	G	1,000,000,000	10^{9}
mega	M	1,000,000	10^{6}
kilo	k	1,000	10^{3}
hecto	h	100	10^{2}
deka	da	10	10^{1}
—	—	1	10^{0}
deci	d	0.1	10^{-1}
centi	c	0.01	10^{-2}
milli	m	0.001	10^{-3}
micro	μ	0.000001	10^{-6}
nano	n	0.000000001	10^{-9}
pico	p	0.000000000001	10^{-12}
femto	f	0.000000000000001	10^{-15}
atto	a	0.000000000000000001	10^{-18}

*See Appendix 1.1 if you need a review of exponential notation.

Table 1.3 Some Examples of Commonly Used Units

Length A dime is 1 mm thick. A quarter is 2.5 cm in diameter. The average height of an adult man is 1.8 m.

Mass A nickel has a mass of about 5 g. A 120-lb person has a mass of about 55 kg.

Volume A 12-oz can of soda has a volume of about 360 mL.

Recognizing that there are 10 decimeters (dm) in a meter, the volume of this cube is $(1 \text{ m})^3 = (10 \text{ dm})^3 = 1000 \text{ dm}^3$. A cubic decimeter, that is $(1 \text{ dm})^3$, is commonly called a *liter (L)*, which is a unit of volume slightly larger than a quart. As shown in Fig. 1.3, 1000 liters are contained in a cube with a volume of 1 cubic meter. Similarly, since 1 decimeter equals 10 centimeters (cm), the liter can be divided into 1000 cubes each with a volume of 1 cubic centimeter:

$$1 \text{ liter} = (1 \text{ dm})^3 = (10 \text{ cm})^3 = 1000 \text{ cm}^3$$

Also, since $1 \text{ cm}^3 = 1$ milliliter (mL),

$$1 \text{ liter} = 1000 \text{ cm}^3 = 1000 \text{ mL}$$

Thus 1 liter contains 1000 cubic centimeters, or 1000 milliliters.

Chemical laboratory work frequently requires measurement of the volumes of liquids. Several devices for the accurate determination of liquid volume are shown in Fig. 1.4 (see page 10).

An important point concerning measurements is the relationship between mass and weight. Although these terms are sometimes used interchangeably, they are *not* the same. **Mass** *is a measure of the resistance of an object to a change in its state of motion.* Mass is measured by the force necessary to give an object a certain acceleration. On earth we use the force that gravity exerts on an object to measure its mass. We call this force the object's **weight.** Since weight is the response of mass to gravity, it varies with the strength of the gravitational field. Therefore, your body mass is the same on the earth or on the moon, but your weight would be much less on the moon than on earth because of the moon's smaller gravitational field.

Because weighing something on a chemical balance (see Fig. 1.5) involves comparing the mass of that object to a standard mass, the terms *weight* and *mass* are sometimes used interchangeably, although this is incorrect.

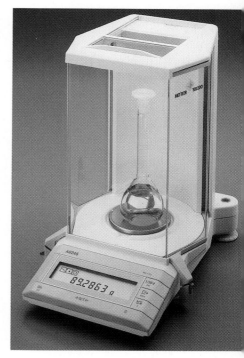

Figure 1.5
An electronic analytical balance.

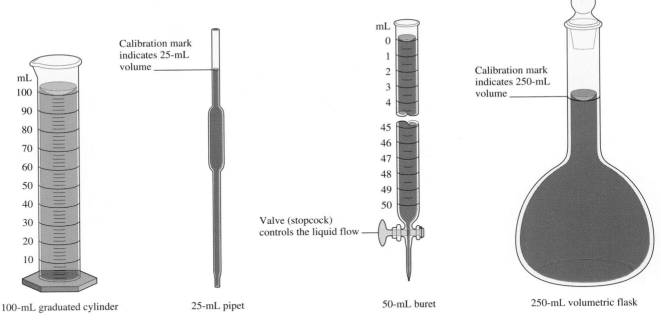

100-mL graduated cylinder   25-mL pipet   50-mL buret   250-mL volumetric flask

Figure 1.4

Common types of laboratory equipment used to measure liquid volume.

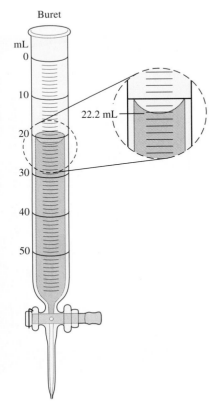

1.4 Uncertainty in Measurement

The number associated with a measurement is obtained using some measuring device. For example, consider the measurement of the volume of a liquid using a buret (shown in Fig. 1.6 with the scale greatly magnified). Notice that the meniscus of the liquid occurs at about 22.15 milliliters. This means that about 22.15 mL of liquid has been delivered from the buret (if the initial position of the liquid meniscus was 0.00 mL). Note that we must estimate the last number of the volume reading by interpolating between the 0.1-mL marks. Since the last number is estimated, its value may be different if another person makes the same measurement. If five different people read the same volume, the results might be as follows:

Person	Results of Measurement
1	22.15 mL
2	22.14 mL
3	22.16 mL
4	22.17 mL
5	22.16 mL

Figure 1.6

Measurement of volume using a buret. The volume is read at the bottom of the liquid curve (called the *meniscus*).

These results show that the first three numbers (22.1) remain the same regardless of who makes the measurement; these are called *certain* digits. However, the digit to the right of the 1 must be estimated and therefore varies; it is called an *uncertain* digit. We customarily report a measurement by recording all the certain digits plus the *first* uncertain digit. In our example it would not make any sense to try to record the volume of thousandths of a milliliter because the value for hundredths of a milliliter must be estimated when using the buret.

It is very important to realize that a *measurement always has some degree of uncertainty.* The uncertainty of a measurement depends on the precision of the measuring device. For example, using a bathroom scale, you might estimate the mass of a grapefruit to be approximately 1.5 pounds. Weighing the same grapefruit on a highly precise balance might produce a result of 1.476 pounds. In the first case, the uncertainty occurs in the tenths of a pound place; in the second case, the uncertainty occurs in the thousandths of a pound place. Suppose we weigh two similar grapefruits on the two devices and obtain the following results:

A measurement always has some degree of uncertainty.

	Bathroom Scale	Balance
Grapefruit 1	1.5 lb	1.476 lb
Grapefruit 2	1.5 lb	1.518 lb

Do the two grapefruits have the same mass? The answer depends on which set of results you consider. Thus a conclusion based on a series of measurements depends on the certainty of those measurements. For this reason, it is important to indicate the uncertainty in any measurement. This is done by always recording the certain digits and the first uncertain digits (the estimated number). These numbers are called the **significant figures** of a measurement.

Uncertainty in measurement is discussed in more detail in Appendix 1.5.

The convention of significant figures automatically indicates something about the uncertainty in a measurement. The uncertainty in the last number (the estimated number) is usually assumed to be ± 1 unless otherwise indicated. For example, the measurement 1.86 kilograms can be taken to mean 1.86 ± 0.01 kilograms.

Sample Exercise 1.1 *Uncertainty in Measurement*

In analyzing a sample of polluted water, a chemist measured out a 25.00-mL water sample with a pipet (see Fig. 1.4). At another point in the analysis, the chemist used a graduated cylinder (see Fig. 1.4) to measure 25 mL of a solution. What is the difference between the measurements 25.00 mL and 25 mL?

Solution

Even though the two volume measurements appear to be equal, they really convey different information. The quantity 25 mL means that the volume is between 24 mL and 26 mL, whereas the quantity 25.00 mL means that the volume is between 24.99 mL and 25.01 mL. The pipet measures volume with much greater precision than does the graduated cylinder.

See Question 1.19.

When making a measurement, it is important to record the results to the appropriate number of significant figures. For example, if a certain buret can be read to ±0.01 mL, you should record a reading of twenty-five milliliters as 25.00 mL, not 25 mL. This way at some later time when you are using your results to do calculations, the uncertainty in the measurement will be known to you.

Precision and Accuracy

Two terms often used to describe the reliability of measurements are *precision* and *accuracy*. Although these words are frequently used interchangeably in everyday life, they have different meanings in the scientific context. **Accuracy** refers to the agreement of a particular value with the true value. **Precision** refers to the degree of agreement among several measurements of the same quantity. Precision reflects the *reproducibility* of a given type of measurement. The difference between these terms is illustrated by the results of three different dart throws shown in Fig. 1.7.

Two different types of errors are illustrated in Fig. 1.7. A **random error** (also called an *indeterminate error*) means that a measurement has an equal probability of being high or low. This type of error occurs in estimating the value of the last digit of a measurement. The second type of error is called **systematic error** (or *determinate error*). This type of error occurs in the same direction each time; it is either always high or always low. Figure 1.7(a) indicates large random errors (poor technique). Figure 1.7(b) indicates small random errors but a large systematic error, and Figure 1.7(c) indicates small random errors and no systematic error.

In quantitative work, precision is often used as an indication of accuracy; we assume that the *average* of a series of precise measurements (which should "average out" the random errors because of their equal probability of being high or low) is accurate, or close to the "true" value. However, this assumption is valid only if systematic errors are absent. Suppose we weigh a piece of brass five times on a very precise balance and obtain the following results:

Weighing	Result
1	2.486 g
2	2.487 g
3	2.485 g
4	2.484 g
5	2.488 g

Normally, we would assume that the true mass of the piece of brass is very close to 2.486 grams, which is the average of the five results:

$$\frac{2.486 \text{ g} + 2.487 \text{ g} + 2.485 \text{ g} + 2.484 \text{ g} + 2.488 \text{ g}}{5} = 2.486 \text{ g}$$

However, if the balance has a defect causing it to give a result that is consistently 1.000 gram too high (a systematic error of +1.000 gram), then the measured value of 2.486 grams would be seriously in error. The point here is that high precision among several measurements is an indication of accuracy *only* if systematic errors are absent.

(a)

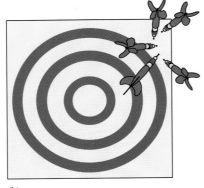
(b)

(c)

Figure 1.7

The results of several dart throws show the difference between *precise* and *accurate*. (a) Neither accurate nor precise (large random errors). (b) Precise but not accurate (small random errors, large systematic error). (c) Bull's-eye! Both precise and accurate (small random errors, no systematic error).

Sample Exercise 1.2 *Precision and Accuracy*

Precision is an indication of accuracy only if there are no systematic errors.

To check the accuracy of a graduated cylinder, a student filled the cylinder to the 25-mL mark using water delivered from a buret (see Fig. 1.4) and then read the volume delivered. Following are the results of five trials:

Trial	Volume Shown by Graduated Cylinder	Volume Shown by the Buret
1	25 mL	26.54 mL
2	25 mL	26.51 mL
3	25 mL	26.60 mL
4	25 mL	26.49 mL
5	25 mL	26.57 mL
Average	25 mL	26.54 mL

Is the graduated cylinder accurate?

Solution

The results of the trials show very good precision (for a graduated cylinder). The student has good technique. However, note that the average value measured using the buret is significantly different from 25 mL. Thus this graduated cylinder is not very accurate. It produces a systematic error (in this case, the indicated result is low for each measurement).

See Question 1.20.

1.5 Significant Figures and Calculations

Calculating the final result for an experiment usually involves adding, subtracting, multiplying, or dividing the results of various types of measurements. Since it is very important that the uncertainty in the final result is known correctly, we have developed rules for counting the significant figures in each number and for determining the correct number of significant figures in the final result.

Rules for Counting Significant Figures

1. *Nonzero integers.* Nonzero integers always count as significant figures.
2. *Zeros.* There are three classes of zeros:
  a. *Leading zeros* are zeros that *precede* all the nonzero digits. These do not count as significant figures. In the number 0.0025, the three zeros simply indicate the position of the decimal point. This number has only two significant figures.

Leading zeros are never significant figures.

Captive zeros are always significant figures.

Trailing zeros are sometimes significant figures.

Exact numbers never limit the number of significant figures in a calculation.

b. *Captive zeros* are zeros *between* nonzero digits. These always count as significant figures. The number 1.008 has four significant figures.

c. *Trailing zeros* are zeros at the *right end* of the number. They are significant only if the number contains a decimal point. The number 100 has only one significant figure, whereas the number 1.00×10^2 has three significant figures. The number one hundred written as 100. also has three significant figures.

3. *Exact numbers.* Many times calculations involve numbers that were not obtained using measuring devices but were determined by counting: 10 experiments, 3 apples, 8 molecules. Such numbers are called *exact numbers.* They can be assumed to have an infinite number of significant figures. Other examples of exact numbers are the 2 in $2\pi r$ (the circumference of a circle) and the 4 and the 3 in $\frac{4}{3}\pi r^3$ (the volume of a sphere). Exact numbers also can arise from definitions. For example, one inch is defined as *exactly* 2.54 centimeters. Thus, in the statement 1 in = 2.54 cm, neither the 2.54 nor the 1 limits the number of significant figures when used in a calculation.

Exponential notation is reviewed in Appendix 1.1.

Note that the number 1.00×10^2 above is written in **exponential notation.** This type of notation has at least two advantages: the number of significant figures can be easily indicated, and fewer zeros are needed to write a very large or very small number. For example, the number 0.000060 is much more conveniently represented as 6.0×10^{-5}. (The number has two significant figures.)

Sample Exercise 1.3 *Significant Figures*

Give the number of significant figures for each of the following results.

a. A student's extraction procedure on tea yields 0.0105 g of caffeine.
b. A chemist records a mass of 0.050080 g in an analysis.
c. In an experiment a span of time is determined to be 8.050×10^{-3} s.

Solution

a. The number contains three significant figures. The zeros to the left of the 1 are leading zeros and are not significant, but the remaining zero (a captive zero) is significant.
b. The number contains five significant figures. The leading zeros (to the left of the 5) are not significant. The captive zeros between the 5 and the 8 are significant, and the trailing zero to the right of the 8 is significant because the number contains a decimal point.
c. This number has four significant figures. Both zeros are significant.

See Exercises 1.25 and 1.26.

Caffeine, which occurs in such items as tea, coffee, and cola nuts, is a respiratory and cardiac stimulant.

Molecular Model: Caffeine

To this point we have learned to count the significant figures in a given number. Next, we must consider how uncertainty accumulates as calculations are carried out.

The detailed analysis of the accumulation of uncertainties depends on the type of calculation involved and can be complex. However, in this textbook we will employ the following simple rules that have been developed for determining the appropriate number of significant figures in the result of a calculation.

Rules for Significant Figures in Mathematical Operations*

1. *For multiplication or division,* the number of significant figures in the result is the same as the number in the least precise measurement used in the calculation. For example, consider the calculation

$$4.56 \times 1.4 = 6.38 \xrightarrow{\text{Corrected}} 6.4$$

          ↑   ↑
Limiting term has   Two significant
two significant   figures
figures

The product should have only two significant figures, since 1.4 has two significant figures.

2. *For addition or subtraction,* the result has the same number of decimal places as the least precise measurement used in the calculation. For example, consider the sum

    12.11
    18.0   ← Limiting term has one decimal place
     1.013
    31.123 $\xrightarrow{\text{Corrected}}$ 31.1
                      ↑
           One decimal place

The correct result is 31.1, since 18.0 has only one decimal place.

Note that for multiplication and division, significant figures are counted. For addition and subtraction, the decimal places are counted.

In most calculations you will need to round numbers to obtain the correct number of significant figures. The following rules should be applied when rounding.

Rules for Rounding

1. In a series of calculations, carry the extra digits through to the final result, *then* round.
2. If the digit to be removed
   a. is less than 5, the preceding digit stays the same. For example, 1.33 rounds to 1.3.
   b. is equal to or greater than 5, the preceding digit is increased by 1. For example, 1.36 rounds to 1.4.

Rule 2 is consistent with the operation of electronic calculators.

---

*Although these simple rules work well for most cases, they can give misleading results in certain cases. For more information, see L. M. Schwartz, "Propagation of Significant Figures," *J. Chem. Ed.* **62** (1985): 693; and H. Bradford Thompson, Is 8°C equal to 50°F? *J. Chem. Ed.* **68** (1991): 400.

Although rounding is generally straightforward, one point requires special emphasis. As an illustration, suppose that the number 4.348 needs to be rounded to two significant figures. In doing this, we look *only* at the *first number* to the right of the 3:

$$4.348$$
↑
Look at this number to
round to two significant figures.

Do not round sequentially. The number 6.8347 rounded to three significant figures is 6.83, not 6.84.

The number is rounded to 4.3 because 4 is less than 5. It is incorrect to round sequentially. For example, do *not* round the 4 to 5 to give 4.35 and then round the 3 to 4 to give 4.4.

When rounding, *use only the first number to the right of the last significant figure.*

It is important to note that Rule 1 above usually will not be followed in the Sample Exercises in this text because we want to show the correct number of significant figures in *each step* of a problem. This same practice is followed for the detailed solutions given in the *Solutions Guide*. However, as stated in Rule 1, the best procedure is to carry extra digits throughout a series of calculations and round to the correct number of significant figures only at the end. This is the practice you should follow. The fact that your rounding procedures are different from those used in this text must be taken into account when you check your answer with the one given at the end of the book or in the *Solutions Guide*. Your answer (based on rounding only at the end of a calculation) may differ in the last place from that given here as the "correct" answer because we have rounded after each step. To help you understand the difference between these rounding procedures, we will consider them further in Sample Exercise 1.4.

Sample Exercise 1.4 *Significant Figures in Mathematical Operations*

Carry out the following mathematical operations, and give each result with the correct number of significant figures.

a. $1.05 \times 10^{-3} \div 6.135$
b. $21 - 13.8$
c. As part of a lab assignment to determine the value of the gas constant (R), a student measured the pressure (P), volume (V), and temperature (T) for a sample of gas, where

$$R = \frac{PV}{T}$$

The following values were obtained: $P = 2.560$, $T = 275.15$, and $V = 8.8$. (Gases will be discussed in detail in Chapter 5; we will not be concerned at this time about the units for these quantities.) Calculate R to the correct number of significant figures.

Solution

a. The result is 1.71×10^{-4}, which has three significant figures because the term with the least precision (1.05×10^{-3}) has three significant figures.

b. The result is 7 with no decimal place because the number with the least number of decimal places (21) has none.

c.
$$R = \frac{PV}{T} = \frac{(2.560)(8.8)}{275.15}$$

The correct procedure for obtaining the final result can be represented as follows:

$$\frac{(2.560)(8.8)}{275.15} = \frac{22.528}{275.15} = 0.0818753$$
$$= 0.082 = 8.2 \times 10^{-2} = R$$

The final result must be rounded to two significant figures because 8.8 (the least precise measurement) has two significant figures. To show the effects of rounding at intermediate steps, we will carry out the calculation as follows:

Rounded to two
significant figures
$\downarrow$

$$\frac{(2.560)(8.8)}{275.15} = \frac{22.528}{275.15} = \frac{23}{275.15}$$

Now we proceed with the next calculation:

$$\frac{23}{275.15} = 0.0835908$$

Rounded to two significant figures, this result is

$$0.084 = 8.4 \times 10^{-2}$$

Note that intermediate rounding gives a significantly different result than was obtained by rounding only at the end. Again, we must reemphasize that in *your* calculations you should round *only at the end*. However, because rounding is carried out at intermediate steps in this text (to always show the correct number of significant figures), the final answer given in the text may differ slightly from the one you obtain (rounding only at the end).

See Exercises 1.29 through 1.32.

There is a useful lesson to be learned from part c of Sample Exercise 1.4. The student measured the pressure and temperature to greater precision than the volume. A more precise value of R (one with more significant figures) could have been obtained if a more precise measurement of V had been made. As it is, the efforts expended to measure P and T very precisely were wasted. Remember that a series of measurements to obtain some final result should all be done to about the same precision.

1.6 *Dimensional Analysis*

It is often necessary to convert a given result from one system of units to another. The best way to do this is by a method called the **unit factor method,** or more commonly **dimensional analysis.** To illustrate the use of this method, we will consider

Table 1.4 English–Metric Equivalents

Length	1 m = 1.094 yd
	2.54 cm = 1 in
Mass	1 kg = 2.205 lb
	453.6 g = 1 lb
Volume	1 L = 1.06 qt
	1 ft³ = 28.32 L

several unit conversions. Some equivalents in the English and metric systems are listed in Table 1.4. A more complete list of conversion factors given to more significant figures appears in Appendix 6.

Consider a pin measuring 2.85 centimeters in length. What is its length in inches? To accomplish this conversion, we must use the equivalence statement

$$2.54 \text{ cm} = 1 \text{ in}$$

If we divide both sides of this equation by 2.54 cm, we get

$$\frac{2.54 \text{ cm}}{2.54 \text{ cm}} = 1 = \frac{1 \text{ in}}{2.54 \text{ cm}}$$

Note that the expression 1 in/2.54 cm equals 1. This expression is called a *unit factor*. Since 1 inch and 2.54 centimeters are exactly equivalent, multiplying any expression by this unit factor will not change its *value*.

The pin has a length of 2.85 centimeters. Multiplying this length by the appropriate unit factor gives

$$2.85 \text{ cm} \times \frac{1 \text{ in}}{2.54 \text{ cm}} = \frac{2.85}{2.54} \text{ in} = 1.12 \text{ in}$$

Note that the centimeter units cancel to give inches for the result. This is exactly what we wanted to accomplish. Note also that the result has three significant figures, as required by the number 2.85. Recall that the 1 and 2.54 in the conversion factor are exact numbers by definition.

Sample Exercise 1.5   Unit Conversions I

A pencil is 7.00 in long. What is its length in centimeters?

Solution

In this case we want to convert from inches to centimeters. Therefore, we must use the reciprocal of the unit factor used above to do the opposite conversion:

$$7.00 \text{ in} \times \frac{2.54 \text{ cm}}{1 \text{ in}} = (7.00)(2.54) \text{ cm} = 17.8 \text{ cm}$$

Here the inch units cancel, leaving centimeters, as requested.

See Exercises 1.37 and 1.38.

Note that two unit factors can be derived from each equivalence statement. For example, from the equivalence statement 2.54 cm = 1 in, the two unit factors are

$$\frac{2.54 \text{ cm}}{1 \text{ in}} \quad \text{and} \quad \frac{1 \text{ in}}{2.54 \text{ cm}}$$

Consider the direction of the required change to select the correct unit factor.

How do you choose which one to use in a given situation? Simply look at the *direction* of the required change. To change from inches to centimeters, the inches must cancel. Thus the factor 2.54 cm/1 in is used. To change from centimeters to inches, centimeters must cancel, and the factor 1 in/2.54 cm is appropriate.

Converting from One Unit to Another

- To convert from one unit to another, use the equivalence statement that relates the two units.
- Derive the appropriate unit factor by looking at the direction of the required change (to cancel the unwanted units).
- Multiply the quantity to be converted by the unit factor to give the quantity with the desired units.

Sample Exercise 1.6 Unit Conversion II

You want to order a bicycle with a 25.5-in frame, but the sizes in the catalog are given only in centimeters. What size should you order?

Solution

You need to go from inches to centimeters, so 2.54 cm/1 in is appropriate:

$$25.5 \text{ in} \times \frac{2.54 \text{ cm}}{1 \text{ in}} = 64.8 \text{ cm}$$

See Exercises 1.37 and 1.38.

To ensure that the conversion procedure is clear, a multistep problem is considered in Sample Exercise 1.7.

Sample Exercise 1.7 Unit Conversions III

A student has entered a 10.0-km run. How long is the run in miles?

Solution

This conversion can be accomplished in several different ways. Since we have the equivalence statement 1 m = 1.094 yd, we will proceed by a path that uses this fact. Before we start any calculations, let us consider our strategy. We have kilometers, which we want to change to miles. We can do this by the following route:

$$\text{kilometers} \longrightarrow \text{meters} \longrightarrow \text{yards} \longrightarrow \text{miles}$$

To proceed in this way, we need the following equivalence statements:

$$1 \text{ km} = 1000 \text{ m}$$
$$1 \text{ m} = 1.094 \text{ yd}$$
$$1760 \text{ yd} = 1 \text{ mi}$$

To make sure the process is clear, we will proceed step by step:

KILOMETERS TO METERS:

$$10.0 \; \cancel{km} \times \frac{1000 \; m}{1 \; \cancel{km}} = 1.00 \times 10^4 \; m$$

METERS TO YARDS:

$$1.00 \times 10^4 \; \cancel{m} \times \frac{1.094 \; yd}{1 \; \cancel{m}} = 1.094 \times 10^4 \; yd$$

Note that we should have only three significant figures in the result. Since this is an intermediate result, however, we will carry the extra digit. Remember, round off only the final result.

YARDS TO MILES:

$$1.094 \times 10^4 \; \cancel{yd} \times \frac{1 \; mi}{1760 \; \cancel{yd}} = 6.216 \; mi$$

Note in this case that 1 mi equals exactly 1760 yd *by designation.* Thus 1760 is an exact number.

Since the distance was originally given as 10.0 km, the result can have only three significant figures and should be rounded to 6.22 mi. Thus

$$10.0 \; km = 6.22 \; mi$$

Alternatively, we can combine the steps:

$$10.0 \; \cancel{km} \times \frac{1000 \; \cancel{m}}{1 \; \cancel{km}} \times \frac{1.094 \; \cancel{yd}}{1 \; \cancel{m}} \times \frac{1 \; mi}{1760 \; \cancel{yd}} = 6.22 \; mi$$

See Exercises 1.37 and 1.38.

Normally we round to the correct number of significant figures after each step. However, you should round only at the end.

In using dimensional analysis, your verification that everything has been done correctly is that you end up with the correct units. *In doing chemistry problems, you should always include the units for the quantities used.* Always check to see that the units cancel to give the correct units for the final result. This provides a very valuable check, especially for complicated problems.

Study the procedures for unit conversions in the following Sample Exercises.

Sample Exercise 1.8 *Unit Conversion IV*

The speed limit on many highways in the United States is 55 mi/h. What number would be posted in kilometers per hour?

Solution

Result obtained by rounding only at the end of the calculation

$$\frac{55 \; \cancel{mi}}{h} \times \frac{1760 \; \cancel{yd}}{1 \; \cancel{mi}} \times \frac{1 \; \cancel{m}}{1.094 \; \cancel{yd}} \times \frac{1 \; km}{1000 \; \cancel{m}} = 88 \; km/h$$

Note that all units cancel except the desired kilometers per hour.

See Exercises 1.43 and 1.44.

Sample Exercise 1.9 *Unit Conversions V*

A Japanese car is advertised as having a gas mileage of 15 km/L. Convert this rating to miles per gallon.

Solution

Result obtained by rounding only at the end of the calculation

$$\frac{15 \text{ km}}{\text{L}} \times \frac{1000 \text{ m}}{1 \text{ km}} \times \frac{1.094 \text{ yd}}{1 \text{ m}} \times \frac{1 \text{ mi}}{1760 \text{ yd}} \times \frac{1 \text{ L}}{1.06 \text{ qt}} \times \frac{4 \text{ qt}}{1 \text{ gal}} = 35 \text{ mi/gal}$$

See Exercises 1.45 and 1.46.

1.7 *Temperature*

Three systems for measuring temperature are widely used: the Celsius scale, the Kelvin scale, and the Fahrenheit scale. The first two temperature systems are used in the physical sciences, and the third is used in many of the engineering sciences. Our purpose here is to define the three temperature scales and show how conversions from one scale to another can be performed. Although these conversions can be carried out routinely on most calculators, we will consider the process in some detail here to illustrate methods of problem solving.

The three temperature scales are defined and compared in Fig. 1.8. Note that the size of the temperature unit (the *degree*) is the same for the Kelvin and Celsius scales. The fundamental difference between these two temperature scales is in their zero points. Conversion between these two scales simply requires an adjustment for the different zero points.

Temperature (Kelvin) = temperature (Celsius) + 273.15

$T_K = T_C + 273.15$

or   Temperature (Celsius) = temperature (Kelvin) − 273.15

$T_C = T_K - 273.15$

For example, to convert 300.00 K to the Celsius scale, we do the following calculation:

$$300.00 - 273.15 = 26.85°C$$

Note that in expressing temperature in Celsius units, the designation °C is used. The degree symbol is not used when writing temperature in terms of the Kelvin scale. The unit of temperature on this scale is called a *kelvin* and is symbolized by the letter K.

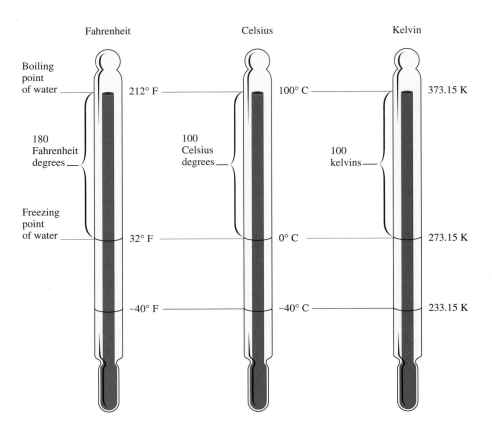

Figure 1.8

The three major temperature scales.

Converting between the Fahrenheit and Celsius scales is somewhat more complicated because both the degree sizes and the zero points are different. Thus we need to consider two adjustments: one for degree size and one for the zero point. First, we must account for the difference in degree size. This can be done by reconsidering Fig. 1.8. Notice that since 212°F = 100°C and 32°F = 0°C,

$$212 - 32 = 180 \text{ Fahrenheit degrees} = 100 - 0 = 100 \text{ Celsius degrees}$$

Thus 180° on the Fahrenheit scale is equivalent to 100° on the Celsius scale, and the unit factor is

$$\frac{180°\text{F}}{100°\text{C}} \quad \text{or} \quad \frac{9°\text{F}}{5°\text{C}}$$

or the reciprocal, depending on the direction in which we need to go.

Next, we must consider the different zero points. Since 32°F = 0°C, we obtain the corresponding Celsius temperature by first subtracting 32 from the Fahrenheit temperature to account for the different zero points. Then the unit factor is applied to adjust for the difference in the degree size. This process is summarized by the equation

$$(T_\text{F} - 32°\text{F})\frac{5°\text{C}}{9°\text{F}} = T_\text{C} \tag{1.1}$$

where T_F and T_C represent a given temperature on the Fahrenheit and Celsius scales, respectively. In the opposite conversion, we first correct for degree size and then correct for the different zero point. This process can be summarized in the following general equation:

$$T_F = T_C \times \frac{9°F}{5°C} + 32°F \qquad (1.2)$$

Equations (1.1) and (1.2) are really the same equation in different forms. See if you can obtain Equation (1.2) by starting with Equation (1.1) and rearranging.

At this point it is worthwhile to weigh the two alternatives for learning to do temperature conversions: You can simply memorize the equations, or you can take the time to learn the differences between the temperature scales and to understand the processes involved in converting from one scale to another. The latter approach may take a little more effort, but the understanding you gain will stick with you much longer than the memorized formulas. This choice also will apply to many of the other chemical concepts. Try to think things through!

> Understand the process of converting from one temperature scale to another; do not simply memorize the equations.

Sample Exercise **1.10** *Temperature Conversions I*

Normal body temperature is 98.6°F. Convert this temperature to the Celsius and Kelvin scales.

Solution

Rather than simply using the formulas to solve this problem, we will proceed by thinking it through. The situation is diagramed in Fig. 1.9. First, we want to convert 98.6°F to the Celsius scale. The number of Fahrenheit degrees between

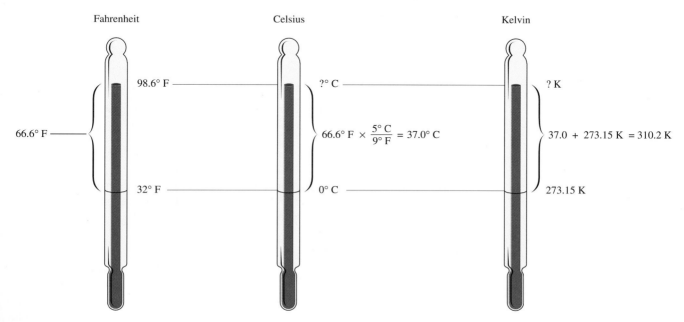

Figure 1.9
Normal body temperature on the Fahrenheit, Celsius, and Kelvin scales.

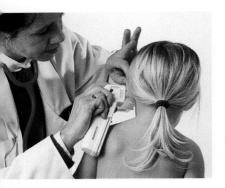

A physician taking the temperature of a patient.

32.0°F and 98.6°F is 66.6°F. We must convert this difference to Celsius degrees:

$$66.6°F \times \frac{5°C}{9°F} = 37.0°C$$

Thus 98.6°F corresponds to 37.0°C.

Now we can convert to the Kelvin scale:

$$T_K = T_C + 273.15 = 37.0 + 273.15 = 310.2 \text{ K}$$

Note that the final answer has only one decimal place (37.0 is limiting).

See Exercises 1.47 and 1.48.

Sample Exercise 1.11 *Temperature Conversions II*

One interesting feature of the Celsius and Fahrenheit scales is that −40°C and −40°F represent the same temperature, as shown in Fig. 1.8. Verify that this is true.

Solution

The difference between 32°F and −40°F is 72°F. The difference between 0°C and −40°C is 40°C. The ratio of these is

$$\frac{72°F}{40°C} = \frac{8 \times 9°F}{8 \times 5°C} = \frac{9°F}{5°C}$$

as required. Thus −40°C is equivalent to −40°F.

See Challenge Problem 1.86.

Since, as shown in Sample Exercise 1.11, −40° on both the Fahrenheit and Celsius scales represents the same temperature, this point can be used as a reference point (like 0°C and 32°F) for a relationship between the two scales:

$$\frac{\text{Number of Fahrenheit degrees}}{\text{Number of Celsius degrees}} = \frac{T_F - (-40)}{T_C - (-40)} = \frac{9°F}{5°C}$$

or

$$\frac{T_F + 40}{T_C + 40} = \frac{9°F}{5°C} \tag{1.3}$$

where T_F and T_C represent the same temperature (but not the same number). This equation can be used to convert Fahrenheit temperatures to Celsius and vice versa and may be easier to remember than Equations (1.1) and (1.2).

Sample Exercise 1.12 *Temperature Conversions III*

Liquid nitrogen, which is often used as a coolant for low-temperature experiments, has a boiling point of 77 K. What is this temperature on the Fahrenheit scale?

Solution

We will first convert 77 K to the Celsius scale:

$$T_C = T_K - 273.15 = 77 - 273.15 = -196°C$$

To convert to the Fahrenheit scale, we will use Equation (1.3):

$$\frac{T_F + 40}{T_C + 40} = \frac{9°F}{5°C}$$

$$\frac{T_F + 40}{-196°C + 40} = \frac{T_F + 40}{-156°C} = \frac{9°F}{5°C}$$

$$T_F + 40 = \frac{9°F}{5°C}(-156°C) = -281°F$$

$$T_F = -281°F - 40 = -321°F$$

See Exercises 1.49 and 1.50.

Liquid nitrogen is so cold that water condenses out of the surrounding air, forming a cloud as the nitrogen is poured.

1.8 Density

A property of matter that is often used by chemists as an "identification tag" for a substance is **density,** the mass of substance per unit volume of the substance:

$$\text{Density} = \frac{\text{mass}}{\text{volume}}$$

The density of a liquid can be determined easily by weighing an accurately known volume of liquid. This procedure is illustrated in Sample Exercise 1.13.

Sample Exercise 1.13 Determining Density

A chemist, trying to identify the main component of a compact disc cleaning fluid, finds that 25.00 cm³ of the substance has a mass of 19.625 g at 20°C. The following are the names and densities of the compounds that might be the main component:

Compound	Density in g/cm³ at 20°C
Chloroform	1.492
Diethyl ether	0.714
Ethanol	0.789
Isopropyl alcohol	0.785
Toluene	0.867

There are two ways of indicating units that occur in the denominator. For example, we can write g/cm³ or g cm⁻³. Although we will use the former system here, the other system is widely used.

Which of these compounds is the most likely to be the main component of the compact disc cleaner?

Because gold has a higher density than sand, it settles to the bottom of a prospector's pan.

Solution

To identify the unknown substance, we must determine its density. This can be done by using the definition of density:

$$\text{Density} = \frac{\text{mass}}{\text{volume}} = \frac{19.625 \text{ g}}{25.00 \text{ cm}^3} = 0.7850 \text{ g/cm}^3$$

This density corresponds exactly to that of isopropyl alcohol, which is therefore the most likely main component of the cleaner. However, note that the density of ethanol is also very close. In order to be sure that the compound is isopropyl alcohol, we should run several more density experiments. (In the modern laboratory, many other types of tests could be done to distinguish between these two liquids.)

See Exercises 1.55 and 1.56.

Besides being a tool for the identification of substances, density has many other uses. For example, the liquid in your car's lead storage battery (a solution of sulfuric acid) changes density because the sulfuric acid is consumed as the battery discharges. In a fully charged battery, the density of the solution is about 1.30 g/cm³. If the density falls below 1.20 g/cm³, the battery will have to be recharged. Density measurement is also used to determine the amount of antifreeze, and thus the level of protection against freezing, in the cooling system of a car.

The densities of various common substances are given in Table 1.5.

1.9 Classification of Matter

Before we can hope to understand the changes we see going on around us—the growth of plants, the rusting of steel, the aging of people, rain becoming more acidic—we must find out how matter is organized. **Matter,** best defined as anything occupying space and having mass, is the material of the universe. Matter is complex and has many levels of organization. In this section we introduce basic ideas about the structure of matter and its behavior.

We will start by considering the definitions of the fundamental properties of matter. Matter exists in three **states:** solid, liquid, and gas. A *solid* is rigid; it has a fixed volume and shape. A *liquid* has a definite volume but no specific shape; it assumes the shape of its container. A *gas* has no fixed volume or shape; it takes on the shape and volume of its container. In contrast to liquids and solids, which are only slightly compressible, gases are highly compressible; it is relatively easy to decrease the volume of a gas. Table 1.5 gives the states of some common substances at 20°C and 1 atmosphere of pressure.

Most of the matter around us consists of **mixtures** of pure substances. Wood, gasoline, wine, soil, and air are all mixtures. The main characteristic of a mixture is that it has *variable composition*. For example, wood is a mixture of many substances, the proportions of which vary depending on the type of wood and where it grows. Mixtures can be classified as **homogeneous** (having visibly indistinguishable parts) or **heterogeneous** (having visibly distinguishable parts).

Table 1.5 Densities of Various Common Substances* at 20°C		
Substance	*Physical State*	*Density (g/cm³)*
Oxygen	Gas	0.00133
Hydrogen	Gas	0.000084
Ethanol	Liquid	0.789
Benzene	Liquid	0.880
Water	Liquid	0.9982
Magnesium	Solid	1.74
Salt (sodium chloride)	Solid	2.16
Aluminum	Solid	2.70
Iron	Solid	7.87
Copper	Solid	8.96
Silver	Solid	10.5
Lead	Solid	11.34
Mercury	Liquid	13.6
Gold	Solid	19.32

*At 1 atmosphere pressure

A homogeneous mixture is called a **solution.** Air is a solution consisting of a mixture of gases. Wine is a complex liquid solution. Brass is a solid solution of copper and zinc. Sand in water and iced tea with ice cubes are examples of heterogeneous mixtures. Heterogeneous mixtures usually can be separated into two or more homogeneous mixtures or pure substances (for example, the ice cubes can be separated from the tea).

Mixtures can be separated into pure substances by physical methods. A **pure substance** is one with constant composition. Water is a good illustration of these ideas. As we will discuss in detail later, pure water is composed solely of H_2O molecules, but the water found in nature (groundwater or the water in a lake or ocean) is really a mixture. Seawater, for example, contains large amounts of dissolved minerals. Boiling seawater produces steam, which can be condensed to pure water, leaving the minerals behind as solids. The dissolved minerals in seawater also can be separated out by freezing the mixture, since pure water freezes out. The processes of boiling and freezing cause **physical changes:** When water freezes or boils, it changes its state but remains water; it is still composed of H_2O molecules. A physical change is a change in the form of a substance, not in its chemical composition. A physical change can be used to separate a mixture into pure compounds, but it will not break compounds into elements.

One of the most important methods for separating the components of a mixture is **distillation,** a process that depends on differences in the volatility (how readily substances become gases) of the components. In simple distillation, a mixture is heated in a device such as that shown in Fig. 1.10. The most volatile component vaporizes at the lowest temperature, and the vapor passes through a cooled tube (a condenser), where it condenses back into its liquid state.

The simple, one-stage distillation apparatus shown in Fig. 1.10 works very well when only one component of the mixture is volatile. For example, a mixture of water and sand is easily separated by boiling off the water. Water containing dissolved minerals behaves in much the same way. As the water is boiled off, the minerals remain behind as nonvolatile solids. Simple distillation of seawater using the sun

The term *volatile* refers to the ease with which a substance can be changed to its vapor.

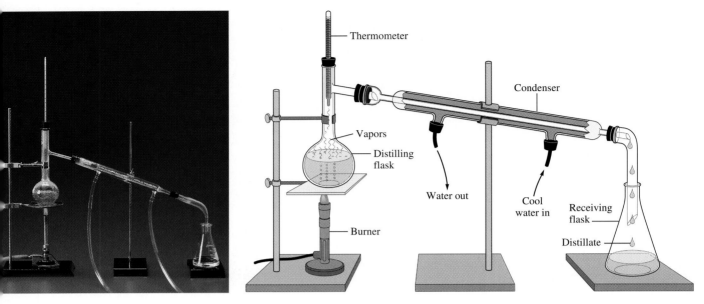

Figure 1.10

Simple laboratory distillation apparatus. Cool water circulates through the outer portion of the condenser, causing vapors from the distilling flask to condense into a liquid. The nonvolatile component of the mixture remains in the distilling flask.

as the heat source is an excellent way to desalinate (remove the minerals from) seawater.

However, when a mixture contains several volatile components, the one-step distillation does not give a pure substance in the receiving flask, and more elaborate methods are required.

Another method of separation is simple **filtration,** which is used when a mixture consists of a solid and a liquid. The mixture is poured onto a mesh, such as filter paper, which passes the liquid and leaves the solid behind.

A third method of separation is called **chromatography.** Chromatography is the general name applied to a series of methods that employ a system with two *phases* (states) of matter: a mobile phase and a stationary phase. The *stationary phase* is a solid, and the *mobile phase* is either a liquid or a gas. The separation process occurs because the components of the mixture have different affinities for the two phases and thus move through the system at different rates. A component with a high affinity for the mobile phase moves relatively quickly through the chromatographic system, whereas one with a high affinity for the solid phase moves more slowly.

One simple type of chromatography, **paper chromatography,** employs a strip of porous paper, such as filter paper, for the stationary phase. A drop of the mixture to be separated is placed on the paper, which is then dipped into a liquid (the mobile phase) that travels up the paper as though it were a wick (see Fig. 1.11). This method of separating a mixture is often used by biochemists, who study the chemistry of living systems.

It should be noted that when a mixture is separated, the absolute purity of the separated components is an ideal. Because water, for example, inevitably comes into

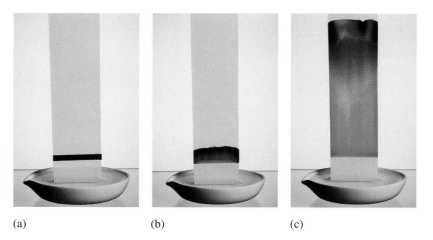

(a)   (b)   (c)

Figure 1.11

Paper chromatography of ink. (a) A line of the mixture to be separated is placed at one end of a sheet of porous paper. (b) The paper acts as a wick to draw up the liquid. (c) The component with the weakest attraction for the paper travels faster than those that cling to the paper.

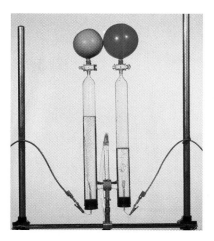

Figure 1.12

Electrolysis is an example of a chemical change. In this apparatus, water is decomposed to hydrogen gas (filling the red balloon) and oxygen gas (filling the blue balloon). This process will be discussed in detail in Chapter 17.

contact with other materials when it is synthesized or separated from a mixture, it is never absolutely pure. With great care, however, substances can be obtained in very nearly pure form.

Pure substances contain compounds (combinations of elements) or free elements. A **compound** is a substance with *constant composition* that can be broken down into elements by chemical processes. An example of a chemical process is the electrolysis of water (see Fig. 1.12), in which an electric current is passed through water to break it down into the free elements hydrogen and oxygen. This process produces a chemical change because the water molecules have been broken down. The water is gone, and in its place we have the free elements hydrogen and oxygen. A **chemical change** is one in which a given substance becomes a new substance or substances with different properties and different composition. **Elements** are substances that cannot be decomposed into simpler substances by chemical or physical means.

We have seen that the matter around us has various levels of organization. The most fundamental substances we have discussed so far are elements. As we will see in later chapters, elements also have structure: They are composed of atoms, which in turn are composed of nuclei and electrons. Even the nucleus has structure: it is composed of protons and neutrons. And even these can be broken down further, into elementary particles called *quarks*. However, we need not concern ourselves with such details at this point. Figure 1.13 summarizes our discussion of the organization of matter.

The element mercury (top left) combines with the element iodine (top right) to form the compound mercuric iodide (bottom). This is an example of a chemical change.

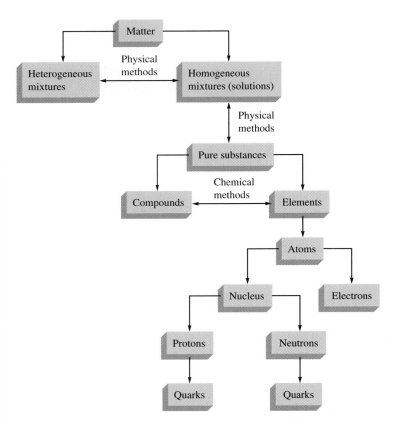

Figure 1.13
The organization of matter.

For Review

Summary

Ideally, the progress of any science occurs by use of the scientific method, which first makes observations of nature and then looks for patterns in the observations that often lead to the formulation of natural laws. A theory or model is then constructed to provide an interpretation of the behavior of nature. The theory is tested by further experiments and is modified as necessary.

Quantitative observations are called measurements and always consist of a number and a scale or unit. Measurement always involves some uncertainty. Drawing conclusions from the results of measurements requires that the extent of the uncertainty be known. This information is conveyed by using the correct number of significant figures. The preferred system of units among scientists is the SI system. Converting results from one set of units to another is accomplished with unit factors (dimensional analysis).

Matter can exist in three states—solid, liquid, and gas—and has many levels of organization. Mixtures of compounds can be separated by methods involving only physical changes, such as distillation, filtration, and various forms of chromatography. On the other hand, compounds can be broken down to elements only through chemical changes.

In-Class Discussion Questions

These questions are designed to be considered by groups of students in class. Often these questions work well for introducing a particular topic in class.

1. **a.** There are 365 days per year, 24 hours per day, 12 months per year, and 60 minutes per hour. Use these data to determine how many minutes are in a month.
   b. Now use the following data to calculate the number of minutes in a month: 24 hours per day, 60 minutes per hour, 7 days per week, and 4 weeks per month.
   c. Why are these answers different? Which (if any) is more correct? Why?

2. You go to a convenience store to buy candy and find the owner to be rather odd. He allows you to buy pieces in multiples of four, and to buy four, you need $0.23. He only allows you to do this by using 3 pennies and 2 dimes. You have a bunch of pennies and dimes, and instead of counting them, you decide to weigh them. You have 636.3 g of pennies, and each penny weighs 3.03 g. Each dime weighs 2.29 g. Each piece of candy weighs 10.23 g.
   a. How many pennies do you have?
   b. How many dimes do you need to buy as much candy as possible?
   c. How much should all these dimes weigh?
   d. How many pieces of candy could you buy? (number of dimes from part b)
   e. How much would this candy weigh?
   f. How many pieces of candy could you buy with twice as many dimes?

3. When a marble is dropped into a beaker of water, it sinks to the bottom. Which of the following is the best explanation?
   a. The surface area of the marble is not large enough to be held up by the surface tension of the water.
   b. The mass of the marble is greater than that of the water.
   c. The marble weighs more than an equivalent volume of the water.
   d. The force from dropping the marble breaks the surface tension of the water.
   e. The marble has greater mass and volume than the water.
   Justify your choice, and for choices you did not pick, explain what is wrong about them.

4. You have two beakers, one filled to the 100-mL mark with sugar (the sugar has a mass of 180.0 g) and the other filled to the 100-mL mark with water (the water has a mass of 100.0 g). You pour all the sugar and all the water together in a bigger beaker and stir until the sugar is completely dissolved.
   a. Which of the following is true about the mass of the solution? Explain.
   i. It is much greater than 280.0 g.
   ii. It is somewhat greater than 280.0 g.
   iii. It is exactly 280.0 g.
   iv. It is somewhat less than 280.0 g.
   v. It is much less than 280.0 g.
   b. Which of the following is true about the volume of the solution? Explain.
   i. It is much greater than 200.0 mL.
   ii. It is somewhat greater than 200.0 mL.
   iii. It is exactly 200.0 mL.
   iv. It is somewhat less than 200.0 mL.
   v. It is much less than 200.0 mL.

5. You may have noticed that when water boils, you can see bubbles that rise to the surface of the water.
   a. What is inside these bubbles?
   i. air
   ii. hydrogen and oxygen gas
   iii. oxygen gas
   iv. water vapor
   v. carbon dioxide gas
   b. Is the boiling of water a chemical or physical change? Explain.

6. If you place a glass rod over a burning candle, the glass appears to turn black. What is happening to each of the following (physical change, chemical change, both, or neither) as the candle burns? Explain each answer.
   a. the wax
   b. the wick
   c. the glass rod

7. Which characteristics of a solid, a liquid, and a gas are exhibited by each of the following substances? How would you classify each substance?
   a. a bowl of pudding
   b. a bucketful of sand

8. You have water in each graduated cylinder shown:

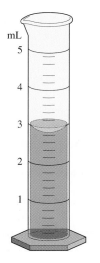 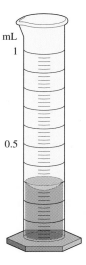

You then add both samples to a beaker. How would you write the number describing the total volume? What limits the precision of this number?

9. Paracelsus, a sixteenth-century alchemist and healer, adopted as his slogan: "The patients are your textbook, the sickbed is your study." Is this view consistent with using the scientific method?

10. What is wrong with the following statement?

"The results of the experiment do not agree with the theory. Something must be wrong with the experiment."

11. Why is it incorrect to say that the results of a measurement were accurate but not precise?

12. What data would you need to estimate the money you would spend on gasoline to drive your car from New York to Chicago? Provide estimates of values and a sample calculation.

13. Sketch two pieces of glassware: one that can measure volume to the thousandths place and one that can measure volume only to the ones place.

14. You have a 1.0-cm^3 sample of lead and a 1.0-cm^3 sample of glass. You drop each in separate beakers of water. How do the volumes of water displaced by each sample compare? Explain.

15. Sketch a magnified view (showing atoms/molecules) of each of the following and explain:
   a. a heterogeneous mixture of two different compounds
   b. a homogeneous mixture of an element and a compound

A blue question or exercise number indicates that the answer to that question or exercise appears at the back of this book and a solution appears in the *Solutions Guide*.

Questions

16. Define and explain the differences between the following terms.
   a. law and theory
   b. theory and experiment
   c. qualitative and quantitative
   d. hypothesis and theory

17. Is the scientific method suitable for solving problems only in the sciences? Explain.

18. Which of the following statements (hypotheses) could be tested by quantitative measurement?
   a. Ty Cobb was a better hitter than Pete Rose.
   b. Ivory soap is $99\frac{44}{100}\%$ pure.
   c. Rolaids consumes 47 times its weight in excess stomach acid.

19. Explain why the uncertainty of a measurement depends on the precision of the measuring device. Give an example to illustrate.

20. A student performed an analysis of a sample for its calcium content and got the following results:

$$14.92\% \quad 14.91\% \quad 14.88\% \quad 14.91\%$$

The actual amount of calcium in the sample is 15.70%. What conclusion can you draw about the accuracy and precision of these results?

21. Distinguish between physical changes and chemical changes.

22. Why is the separation of mixtures into pure or relatively pure substances so important when performing a chemical analysis?

Exercises

In this section similar exercises are paired.

Significant Figures and Unit Conversions

23. Which of the following are exact numbers?
   a. The elevation of Breckenridge, Colorado, is *9600* ft.
   b. There are *12* eggs in a dozen.
   c. One yard is equal to *0.9144* m.
   d. The announced attendance at a football game was *52,806*.
   e. In 1983, *1759* Ph.D.s in chemistry were awarded in the United States.
   f. The budget deficit of the U.S. government in fiscal year 1990 was *$269 billion*.

24. Which of the following are exact numbers?
   a. There are *100* cm in 1 m.
   b. One meter equals *1.094* yard.
   c. We can use the equation

$$°F = \tfrac{9}{5}°C + 32$$

to convert from Celsius to Fahrenheit temperature. Are the numbers $\frac{9}{5}$ and *32* exact or inexact?
   d. $\pi = 3.1415927$.

25. How many significant figures are in each of the following?
   a. 12
   b. 1098
   c. 2001
   d. 2.001×10^3
   e. 0.0000101
   f. 1.01×10^{-5}
   g. 1000.
   h. 22.04030

26. How many significant figures are in each of the following?
   a. 100
   b. 1.0×10^2
   c. 1.00×10^3
   d. 100.
   e. 0.0048
   f. 0.00480

g. 4.80×10^{-3}　　**h.** 4.800×10^{-3}

27. Round off each of the following numbers to three significant figures, and write the answer in standard exponential notation.
  a. 312.54
  b. 0.00031254
  c. 31,254,000
  d. 0.31254
  e. 31.254×10^{-3}

28. Use exponential notation to express the number 480 to
  a. one significant figure
  b. two significant figures
  c. three significant figures
  d. four significant figures

29. Perform the following mathematical operations, and express each result to the correct number of significant figures.
  a. $97.381 + 4.2502 + 0.99195$
  b. $171.5 + 72.915 - 8.23$
  c. $1.00914 + 0.87104 + 1.2012$
  d. $21.901 - 13.21 - 4.0215$

30. Perform the following mathematical operations, and express each result to the correct number of significant figures.
  a. $\dfrac{0.102 \times 0.0821 \times 273}{1.01}$

  b. $0.14 \times 6.022 \times 10^{23}$

  c. $4.0 \times 10^4 \times 5.021 \times 10^{-3} \times 7.34993 \times 10^2$

  d. $\dfrac{2.00 \times 10^6}{3.00 \times 10^{-7}}$

31. Perform the following mathematical operations, and express each result to the correct number of significant figures.
  a. $4.184 \times 100.62 \times (25.27 - 24.16)$

  b. $\dfrac{8.925 - 8.904}{8.925} \times 100$

  (This type of calculation is done many times in calculating a percentage error. Assume that this example is such a calculation; thus 100 can be considered to be an exact number.)

  c. $(9.04 - 8.23 + 21.954 + 81.0) \div 3.1416$

  d. $\dfrac{9.2 \times 100.65}{8.321 + 4.026}$

  e. $0.1654 + 2.07 - 2.114$

  f. $8.27(4.987 - 4.962)$

  g. $\dfrac{9.5 + 4.1 + 2.8 + 3.175}{4}$

  (Assume that this operation is taking the average of four numbers. Thus 4 in the denominator is exact.)

  h. $\dfrac{9.025 - 9.024}{9.025} \times 100$ (100 is exact)

32. Perform the following mathematical operations, and express the result to the correct number of significant figures.
  a. $6.022 \times 10^{23} \times 1.05 \times 10^2$

  b. $\dfrac{6.6262 \times 10^{-34} \times 2.998 \times 10^8}{2.54 \times 10^{-9}}$

  c. $1.285 \times 10^{-2} + 1.24 \times 10^{-3} + 1.879 \times 10^{-1}$

  d. $1.285 \times 10^{-2} - 1.24 \times 10^{-3}$

  e. $\dfrac{(1.00866 - 1.00728)}{6.02205 \times 10^{23}}$

  f. $\dfrac{9.875 \times 10^2 - 9.795 \times 10^2}{9.875 \times 10^2} \times 100$ (100 is exact)

  g. $\dfrac{9.42 \times 10^2 + 8.234 \times 10^2 + 1.625 \times 10^3}{3}$ (3 is exact)

33. Perform each of the following conversions.
  a. 8.43 cm to millimeters
  b. 2.41×10^2 cm to meters
  c. 294.5 nm to centimeters
  d. 1.445×10^4 m to kilometers
  e. 235.3 m to millimeters
  f. 903.3 nm to micrometers

34. a. How many kilograms are in one teragram?
  b. How many nanometers are in 6.50×10^2 terameters?
  c. How many kilograms are in 25 femtograms?
  d. How many liters are in 8.0 cubic decimeters?
  e. How many microliters are in one milliliter?
  f. How many picograms are in one microgram?

35. Many atomic dimensions are expressed in angstroms. (1 Å = 1×10^{-8} cm). What is the angstrom equal to in terms of the SI units nanometer (nm) and picometer (pm)?

36. Two atoms in a molecule are 134 pm apart. What is the distance in nanometers and angstroms?

37. Perform the following unit conversions.
  a. Congratulations! You and your spouse are the proud parents of a new baby, born while you are studying in a country that uses the metric system. The nurse has informed you that the baby weighs 3.91 kg and measures 51.4 cm. Convert your baby's weight to pounds and ounces and her length to inches (rounded to the nearest quarter inch).
  b. The circumference of the earth is 25,000 mi at the equator. What is the circumference in kilometers? in meters?
  c. A rectangular solid measures 1.0 m by 5.6 cm by 2.1 dm. Express its volume in cubic meters, liters, cubic inches, and cubic feet.

38. Perform the following unit conversions.
  a. 908 oz to kilograms
  b. 12.8 L to gallons
  c. 125 mL to quarts
  d. 2.89 gal to milliliters
  e. 4.48 lb to grams
  f. 550 mL to quarts

39. Use the following exact conversion factors to perform the stated calculations:

$$5\tfrac{1}{2} \text{ yards} = 1 \text{ rod}$$

$$40 \text{ rods} = 1 \text{ furlong}$$

$$8 \text{ furlongs} = 1 \text{ mile}$$

a. The Kentucky Derby race is 1.25 miles. How long is the race in rods, furlongs, meters, and kilometers?

b. A marathon race is 26 miles, 385 yards. What is this distance in rods, furlongs, meters, and kilometers?

40. Although the preferred SI unit of area is the square meter, land is often measured in the metric system in hectares (ha). One hectare is equal to 10,000 m^2. In the English system, land is often measured in acres (1 acre = 160 rod^2). Use the exact conversions and those given in Exercise 39 to calculate the following.

a. 1 ha = _____ km^2.

b. The area of a 5.5-acre plot of land in hectares, square meters, and square kilometers.

c. A lot with dimensions 120 ft by 75 ft is to be sold for $6500. What is the price per acre? What is the price per hectare?

41. Precious metals and gems are measured in troy weights in the English system:

$$24 \text{ grains} = 1 \text{ pennyweight (exact)}$$
$$20 \text{ pennyweight} = 1 \text{ troy ounce (exact)}$$
$$12 \text{ troy ounces} = 1 \text{ troy pound (exact)}$$
$$1 \text{ grain} = 0.0648 \text{ gram}$$
$$1 \text{ carat} = 0.200 \text{ gram}$$

a. The most common English unit of mass is the pound avoirdupois. What is one troy pound in kilograms and in pounds?

b. What is the mass of a troy ounce of gold in grams and in carats?

c. The density of gold is 19.3 g/cm^3. What is the volume of a troy pound of gold?

42. Apothecaries (druggists) use the following set of measures in the English system:

$$20 \text{ grains ap} = 1 \text{ scruple (exact)}$$
$$3 \text{ scruples} = 1 \text{ dram ap (exact)}$$
$$8 \text{ dram ap} = 1 \text{ oz ap (exact)}$$
$$1 \text{ dram ap} = 3.888 \text{ g}$$

a. Is an apothecary grain the same as a troy grain? (See Exercise 41.)

b. 1 oz ap = _____ oz troy

c. An aspirin tablet contains 5.00×10^2 mg of active ingredient. How many grains ap of active ingredient does it contain? How many scruples?

d. What is the mass of 1 scruple in grams?

43. In the United Kingdom, British Rail runs two types of modern high-speed passenger trains, the Intercity-125 and the Intercity-225. The Intercity-125 has a top speed of 125 mi/h, whereas the newer Intercity-225 has a top speed of 225 km/h. Which train is faster?

44. The world record for the hundred meter dash is 9.79 s. What is the corresponding average speed in units of m/s, km/h, ft/s,

and mi/h? At this speed, how long would it take to run 1.00×10^2 yards?

45. You're planning to buy a new car. One model that you're considering gets 32 miles to a gallon of gasoline in highway travel. The one that your spouse likes gets 14 kilometers to the liter. Which car has the better gas mileage?

46. You pass a road sign saying "New York 112 km." If you drive at a constant speed of 65 mi/h, how long should it take you to reach New York? If your car gets 28 miles to the gallon, how many liters of gasoline are necessary to travel 112 km?

Temperature

47. A person has a temperature of 102.5°F. What is this temperature on the Celsius scale? on the Kelvin scale?

48. If the temperature in a room is 74°F, what is this temperature on the Celsius scale? on the Kelvin scale?

49. Many chemical quantities are specified as being measured at 25°C. What is this temperature on the Fahrenheit scale? on the Kelvin scale?

50. Helium boils at about 4 K. What is this temperature in °F? in °C?

51. A thermometer gives a reading of 20.6°C ± 0.1°C. What is the temperature in °F? What is the uncertainty?

52. A thermometer gives a reading of 96.1°F ± 0.2°F. What is the temperature in °C? What is the uncertainty?

Density

53. The density of aluminum is 2.70 g/cm^3. Express this value in units of kilograms per cubic meter and pounds per cubic foot.

54. A material will float on the surface of a liquid if the material has a density less than that of the liquid. Given that the density of water is approximately 1.0 g/mL, will a block of material having a volume of 1.2×10^4 in^3 and weighing 350 lb float or sink when placed in a reservoir of water?

55. A star is estimated to have a mass of 2×10^{36} kg. Assuming it to be a sphere of average radius 7.0×10^5 km, calculate the average density of the star in units of grams per cubic centimeter.

56. A rectangular block has dimensions 2.9 cm × 3.5 cm × 10.0 cm. The mass of the block is 615.0 g. What are the volume and density of the block?

57. Diamonds are measured in carats, and 1 carat = 0.200 g. The density of diamond is 3.51 g/cm^3. What is the volume of a 5.0-carat diamond?

58. The volume of a diamond is found to be 2.8 mL. What is the mass of the diamond in carats? (See Exercise 57.)

59. A sample containing 33.42 g of metal pellets is poured into a graduated cylinder initially containing 12.7 mL of water, causing the water level in the cylinder to rise to 21.6 mL. Calculate the density of the metal.

60. The density of pure silver is 10.5 g/cm^3 at 20°C. If 5.25 g of pure silver pellets is added to a graduated cylinder containing 11.2 mL of water, to what volume level will the water in the cylinder rise?

61. In each of the following pairs, which has the greater mass? (See Table 1.5.)
  a. 1.0 kg of feathers or 1.0 kg of lead
  b. 1.0 mL of mercury or 1.0 mL of water
  c. 19.3 mL of water or 1.00 mL of gold
  d. 75 mL of copper or 1.0 L of benzene

62. In each of the following pairs, which has the greater volume?
  a. 1.0 kg of feathers or 1.0 kg of lead
  b. 100 g of gold or 100 g of water
  c. 1.0 L of copper or 1.0 L of mercury

Classification and Separation of Matter

63. What are some of the differences between a solid, a liquid, and a gas?

64. What is the difference between homogeneous and heterogeneous matter? Classify each of the following as homogeneous or heterogeneous.
  a. soil
  b. the atmosphere
  c. a carbonated soft drink
  d. gasoline
  e. gold
  f. a solution of ethanol and water

65. Classify each of the following as a mixture or a pure substance.
  a. water
  b. blood
  c. the oceans
  d. iron
  e. brass
  f. uranium
  g. wine
  h. leather
  i. table salt (NaCl)
  Of the pure substances, which are elements and which are compounds?

66. The properties of a mixture are typically averages of the properties of its components. The properties of a compound may differ dramatically from the properties of the elements that combine to produce the compound. For each process described below, state whether the material being discussed is most likely a mixture or a compound, and state whether the process is a chemical change or a physical change.
  a. An orange liquid is distilled, resulting in the collection of a yellow liquid and a red solid.
  b. A colorless, crystalline solid is decomposed, yielding a pale yellow-green gas and a soft, shiny metal.
  c. A cup of tea becomes sweeter as sugar is added to it.

Additional Exercises

67. A children's pain relief elixir contains 80. mg acetaminophen per 0.50 teaspoon. The dosage recommended for a child who weighs between 24 and 35 lb is 1.5 teaspoons. What is the range of acetaminophen dosages, expressed in mg acetaminophen/kg body weight, for children who weigh between 24 and 35 lb?

68. A mole of helium gas contains 6.02×10^{23} helium atoms. How many helium atoms are there in a millimole of helium? in a kilomole?

69. In Shakespeare's *Richard III,* the First Murderer says:
  "Take that, and that! [*Stabs Clarence*]
  If that is not enough, I'll drown you in a malmsey butt within!"
  Given that 1 butt = 126 gal, in how many liters of malmsey (a foul brew similar to mead) was the unfortunate Clarence about to be drowned?

70. You are in Paris and want to buy some peaches for lunch. The sign in the fruit stand indicates that peaches are 11.5 francs per kilogram. Given that there are approximately 5 francs to the dollar, calculate what a pound of peaches will cost in dollars.

71. The contents of one 40. lb bag of topsoil will cover 10. square feet of ground to a depth of 1.0 inch. How many bags are needed to cover a plot which measures 200. by 300. m to a depth of 4.0 cm?

72. Science fiction often uses nautical analogies to describe space travel. If the starship *U.S.S. Enterprise* is traveling at warp factor 1.71, what is its speed in knots? (Warp 1.71 = 5.00 times the speed of light; speed of light = 3.00×10^8 m/s; 1 knot = 2000 yd/h, exactly.)

73. Convert the following Celsius temperatures to Kelvin and to Fahrenheit degrees.
  a. the boiling-point temperature of ethyl alcohol, 78.1°C
  b. a cold wintery day, −25°C
  c. the lowest possible temperature, −273°C
  d. the melting-point temperature of sodium chloride, 801°C

74. In the opening scenes of the movie *Raiders of the Lost Ark,* Indiana Jones tries to remove a gold idol from a booby-trapped pedestal. He replaces the idol with a bag of sand of approximately equal volume. (Density of gold = 19.32 g/cm^3; density of sand ≈ 2 g/cm^3.)
  a. Did he have a reasonable chance of not activating the mass-sensitive booby trap?
  b. In a later scene he and an unscrupulous guide play catch with the idol. Assume that the volume of the idol is about 1.0 L. If it were solid gold, what mass would the idol have? Is playing catch with it plausible?

75. Mercury poisoning is a debilitating disease that is often fatal. In the human body, mercury reacts with essential enzymes leading to irreversible inactivity of these enzymes. If the amount of mercury in a polluted lake is 0.4 μg Hg/mL, what is the total mass in kilograms of mercury in the lake? (The lake has a surface area of 100 mi^2 and an average depth of 20 ft.)

76. Two spherical objects have the same mass. One floats on water; the other sinks. Which object has the greater diameter? Explain your answer.

77. One metal object is a cube with edges of 3.00 cm and a mass of 140.4 g. A second metal object is a sphere with a radius of 1.42 cm and a mass of 61.6 g. Are these objects made of the same or different metals? Assume that the calculated densities are accurate to $\pm 1.00\%$.

78. Assume that the following numbers are known to ± 1 in the last digit. Perform the following divisions and estimate the maximum uncertainty in each result. That is, determine the largest and smallest number that could occur for each case. (See Appendix 1.5.)
a. $103 \div 101$
b. $101 \div 99$
c. $99 \div 101$
Considering your calculated error limits, to how many significant figures should each result be expressed? Do any of these constitute an exception to the rule for division listed in Section 1.5? Rationalize any discrepancies.

79. According to the *Official Rules of Baseball,* a baseball must have a circumference not more than 9.25 in or less than 9.00 in and a mass not more than 5.25 oz or less than 5.00 oz. What range of densities can a baseball be expected to have? Express this range as a single number with an accompanying uncertainty limit.

80. The chemist in Sample Exercise 1.13 did some further experiments. She found that the pipet used to measure the volume of the cleaner is accurate to ± 0.03 cm^3. The mass measurement is accurate to ± 0.002 g. Are these measurements sufficiently precise for the chemist to distinguish between isopropyl alcohol and ethanol?

81. The density of an irregularly shaped object was determined as follows. The mass of the object was found to be 28.90 g $\pm$ 0.03 g. A graduated cylinder was partially filled with water. The reading of the level of the water was 6.4 cm^3 $\pm$ 0.1 cm^3. The object was dropped in the cylinder, and the level of the water rose to 9.8 cm^3 $\pm$ 0.1 cm^3. What is the density of the object with appropriate error limits? (See Appendix 1.5.)

Challenge Problems

82. Many times errors are expressed in terms of percentage. The percentage error is the absolute value of the difference of the true value and the experimental value, divided by the true value, and multiplied by 100.

$$\text{Percent error} = \frac{|\text{true value} - \text{experimental value}|}{\text{true value}} \times 100$$

Calculate the percent error for the following measurements.
a. The density of an aluminum block determined in an experiment was 2.64 g/cm^3. (True value 2.70 g/cm^3.)
b. The experimental determination of iron in iron ore was 16.48%. (True value 16.12%.)
c. A balance measured the mass of a 1.000-g standard as 0.9981 g.

83. A rule of thumb in designing experiments is to avoid using a result that is the small difference between two large measured quantities. In terms of uncertainties in measurement, why is this good advice?

84. A person weighed 15 pennies on a balance and recorded the following masses:

3.112 g	3.109 g	3.059 g
2.467 g	3.079 g	2.518 g
3.129 g	2.545 g	3.050 g
3.053 g	3.054 g	3.072 g
3.081 g	3.131 g	3.064 g

Curious about the results, he looked at the dates on each penny. Two of the light pennies were minted in 1983 and one in 1982. The dates on the 12 heavier pennies ranged from 1970 to 1982. Two of the 12 heavier pennies were minted in 1982.
a. Do you think the Bureau of the Mint changed the way they made pennies? Explain.
b. The person calculated the average mass of the 12 heavy pennies. He expressed this average as 3.0828 g $\pm$ 0.0482 g. What is wrong with the numbers in this result, and how should the value be expressed?

85. On October 21, 1982, the Bureau of the Mint changed the composition of pennies (see Exercise 84). Instead of an alloy of 95% Cu and 5% Zn by mass, a core of 99.2% Zn and 0.8% Cu with a thin shell of copper was adopted. The overall composition of the new penny was 97.6% Zn and 2.4% Cu by mass. Does this account for the difference in mass among the pennies in Exercise 84? Assume the volume of the individual metals that make up each penny can be added together to give the overall volume of the penny, and assume each penny is the same size. (Density of Cu = 8.96 g/cm^3; density of Zn = 7.14 g/cm^3.)

86. Ethylene glycol is the main component in automobile antifreeze. To monitor the temperature of an auto cooling system, you intend to use a meter that reads from 0 to 100. You devise a new temperature scale based on the approximate melting and boiling points of a typical antifreeze solution ($-45°$C and 115°C). You wish these points to correspond to 0°A and 100°A, respectively.
a. Derive an expression for converting between °A and °C.
b. Derive an expression for converting between °F and °A.

c. At what temperature would your thermometer and a Celsius thermometer give the same numerical reading?

d. Your thermometer reads 86°A. What is the temperature in °C and in °F?

e. What is a temperature of 45°C in °A?

87. Confronted with the box shown in the diagram, you wish to discover something about its internal workings. You have no tools and cannot open the box. You pull on rope B, and it moves rather freely. When you pull on rope A, rope C appears to be pulled slightly into the box. When you pull on rope C, rope A almost disappears into the box.*

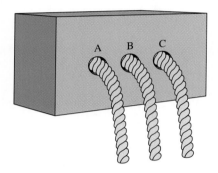

a. Based on these observations, construct a model for the interior mechanism of the box.

b. What further experiments could you do to refine your model?

88. An experiment was performed in which an empty 100-mL graduated cylinder was weighed. It was weighed once again after it had been filled to the 10.0-mL mark with dry sand. A 10-mL pipet was used to transfer 10.00 mL of methanol to the cylinder. The sand–methanol mixture was stirred until bubbles no longer emerged from the mixture and the sand looked uniformly wet. The cylinder was then weighed again. Use the data obtained from this experiment (and displayed at the end of this problem) to find the density of the dry sand, the density of methanol, and the density of sand particles. Does the bubbling that occurs when the methanol is added to the dry sand indicate that the sand and methanol are reacting?

Mass of cylinder plus wet sand	45.2613 g
Mass of cylinder plus dry sand	37.3488 g
Mass of empty cylinder	22.8317 g
Volume of dry sand	10.0 mL
Volume of sand + methanol	17.6 mL
Volume of methanol	10.00 mL

Marathon Problem†

This problem is designed to incorporate several concepts and techniques into one situation. Marathon Problems can be used in class by groups of students to help facilitate problem-solving skills.

89. A cylindrical bar of gold that is 1.5 in high and 0.25 in in diameter has a mass of 23.1984 g, as determined on an analytical balance. An empty graduated cylinder is weighed on a triple-beam balance and has a mass of 73.47 g. After pouring a small amount of a liquid into the graduated cylinder, the mass is 79.16 g. When the gold cylinder is placed in the graduated cylinder (the liquid covers the top of the gold cylinder), the volume indicated on the graduated cylinder is 8.5 mL. Assume that the temperature of the gold bar and the liquid are 86°F. If the density of the liquid decreases by 1.0% for each 10°C rise in temperature (over the range 0 to 50°C), determine

a. the density of the gold at 86°F.

b. the density of the liquid at 40°F.

Note: Parts a and b can be answered independently.

---

*From Yoder, Suydam, and Snavely, *Chemistry* (New York: Harcourt Brace Jovanovich, 1975), pp. 9–11.

†This Marathon Problem was developed by James H. Burness, Penn State University, York Campus. Reprinted with permission from the *Journal of Chemical Education,* Vol. 68, No. 11, 1991, pp. 919–922; copyright © 1991, Division of Chemical Education, Inc.

Atoms, Molecules, and Ions

Contents

Where does one start in learning chemistry? Clearly we must consider some essential vocabulary and something about the origins of the science before we can proceed very far. Thus, while Chapter 1 provided background on the fundamental ideas and procedures of science in general, Chapter 2 covers the specific chemical background necessary for understanding the material in the next few chapters. The coverage of these topics is necessarily brief at this point. We will develop these ideas more fully as it becomes appropriate to do so. A major goal of this chapter is to present the systems for naming chemical compounds to provide you with the vocabulary necessary to understand this book and to pursue your laboratory studies.

Because chemistry is concerned first and foremost with chemical changes, we will proceed as quickly as possible to a study of chemical reactions (Chapters 3 and 4). However, before we can discuss reactions, we must consider some fundamental ideas about atoms and how they combine.

A gold statue of the Goddess of Serket created by goldsmiths in ancient Egypt.

2.1 The Early History of Chemistry

Chemistry has been important since ancient times. The processing of natural ores to produce metals for ornaments and weapons and the use of embalming fluids are two applications of chemical phenomena that were utilized prior to 1000 B.C.

The Greeks were the first to try to explain why chemical changes occur. By about 400 B.C. they had proposed that all matter was composed of four fundamental substances: fire, earth, water, and air. The Greeks also considered the question of whether matter is continuous, and thus infinitely divisible into smaller pieces, or composed of small, indivisible particles. Supporters of the latter position were Demokritos* of Abdera (c. 460–c. 370 B.C.) and Leucippos, who used the term *atomos* (which later became *atoms*) to describe these ultimate particles. However, because the Greeks had no experiments to test their ideas, no definitive conclusion could be reached about the divisibility of matter.

The next 2000 years of chemical history were dominated by a pseudoscience called *alchemy*. Some alchemists were mystics and fakes who were obsessed with the idea of turning cheap metals into gold. However, many alchemists were serious scientists, and this period saw important advances: The alchemists discovered several elements and learned to prepare the mineral acids.

The foundations of modern chemistry were laid in the sixteenth century with the development of systematic metallurgy (extraction of metals from ores) by a German, Georg Bauer (1494–1555), and the medicinal application of minerals by a Swiss alchemist/physician known as Paracelsus (full name: Philippus Theophrastus Bombastus von Hohenheim [1493–1541]).

The first "chemist" to perform truly quantitative experiments was Robert Boyle (1627–1691), who carefully measured the relationship between the pressure and volume of air. When Boyle published his book *The Skeptical Chymist* in 1661, the quantitative sciences of physics and chemistry were born. In addition to his results on the quantitative behavior of gases, Boyle's other major contribution to chemistry consisted of his ideas about the chemical elements. Boyle held no preconceived notion about the number of elements. In his view, a substance was an element unless it could be broken down into two or more simpler substances. As Boyle's experimental definition of an element became generally accepted, the list of known elements began to grow, and the Greek system of four elements finally died. Although Boyle was an excellent scientist, he was not always right. For example, he clung to the alchemists' views that metals were not true elements and that a way would eventually be found to change one metal into another.

The phenomenon of combustion evoked intense interest in the seventeenth and eighteenth centuries. The German chemist Georg Stahl (1660–1734) suggested that a substance he called "phlogiston" flowed out of the burning material. Stahl postulated that a substance burning in a closed container eventually stopped burning because the air in the container became saturated with phlogiston. Oxygen gas, discovered by Joseph Priestley (1733–1804),† an English clergyman and scientist (Fig. 2.1), was found to support vigorous combustion and was thus supposed to be low in phlogiston. In fact, oxygen was originally called "dephlogisticated air."

Figure 2.1

The Priestley Medal is the highest honor given by the American Chemical Society. It is named for Joseph Priestley, who was born in England on March 13, 1733. He performed many important scientific experiments, among them the discovery that a gas later identified as carbon dioxide could be dissolved in water to produce *seltzer*. Also, as a result of meeting Benjamin Franklin in London in 1766, Priestley became interested in electricity and was the first to observe that graphite was an electrical conductor. However, his greatest discovery occurred in 1774 when he isolated oxygen by heating mercuric oxide.

Because of his nonconformist political views, he was forced to leave England. He died in the United States in 1804.

*Democritus is an alternate spelling.

†Oxygen gas was actually first observed by the Swedish chemist Karl W. Scheele (1742–1786), but because his results were published after Priestley's, the latter is commonly credited with the discovery of oxygen.

CHEMICAL IMPACT

There's Gold in Them There Plants!

GOLD HAS ALWAYS held a strong allure. For example, the alchemists were obsessed with finding a way to transform cheap metals into gold. Also, when gold was discovered in California in 1849, a frantic rush occurred to that area and other areas in the west. Although gold is still valuable, most of the high-grade gold ores have been exhausted. This leaves the low-grade ores—ores with low concentrations of gold that are expensive to process relative to the amount of gold finally obtained.

Now two scientists have come across a novel way to concentrate the gold from low-grade ores. Christopher Anderson and Robert Brooks of Massey University in Palmerston North, New Zealand, have found plants that accumulate gold atoms as they grow in soil containing gold ore [*Nature* 395 (1998): 553]. The plants brassica (of the mustard family) and chicory seem especially effective as botanical "gold miners." When these plants are dried and burned (after having grown in gold-rich soil), the resulting ash contains approximately 150 ppm (parts per million) of gold. (1 ppm gold represents 1 g of gold in 10^6 g of sample.)

The New Zealand scientists were able to double the amount of gold taken from the soil by the plants by treating the soil with ammonium thiocyanate (NH_4SCN). The thiocyanate, which reacts with the gold, making it more available to the plants, subsequently breaks down in the soil and therefore poses no environmental hazard.

This plant from the mustard family is a newly discovered source of gold.

Thus plants seem to hold great promise as gold miners. They are efficient and reliable and will never go on strike.

2.2 Fundamental Chemical Laws

By the late eighteenth century, combustion had been studied extensively; the gases carbon dioxide, nitrogen, hydrogen, and oxygen had been discovered; and the list of elements continued to grow. However, it was Antoine Lavoisier (1743–1794), a French chemist (Fig. 2.2), who finally explained the true nature of combustion, thus clearing the way for the tremendous progress that was made near the end of the eighteenth century. Lavoisier, like Boyle, regarded measurement as the essential operation of chemistry. His experiments, in which he carefully weighed the reactants and products of various reactions, suggested that *mass is neither created nor destroyed.* Lavoisier's verification of this **law of conservation of mass** was the basis for the developments in chemistry in the nineteenth century.

Lavoisier's quantitative experiments showed that combustion involved oxygen (which Lavoisier named), not phlogiston. He also discovered that life was supported by a process that also involved oxygen and was similar in many ways to combustion. In 1789 Lavoisier published the first modern chemistry textbook, *Elementary Treatise on Chemistry,* in which he presented a unified picture of the chemical knowledge assembled up to that time. Unfortunately, in the same year the text was published, the French Revolution broke out. Lavoisier, who had been associated with collecting taxes for the government, was executed on the guillotine as an enemy of the people in 1794.

Oxygen is from the French *oxygène,* meaning "generator of acid," because it was initially considered to be an integral part of all acids.

Antoine Lavoisier was born in Paris on August 26, 1743. Although Lavoisier's father wanted his son to follow him into the legal profession, young Lavoisier was fascinated by science. From the beginning of his scientific career, Lavoisier recognized the importance of accurate measurements. His careful weighings showed that mass was conserved in chemical reactions and that combustion involves reaction with oxygen. Also, he wrote the first modern chemistry textbook. It is not surprising that Lavoisier is often called the father of modern chemistry.

To help support his scientific work, Lavoisier invested in a private tax-collecting firm and married the daughter of one of the company executives. His connection to the tax collectors proved fatal, for radical French revolutionaries demanded his execution, which occurred on the guillotine on May 8, 1794.

After 1800, chemistry was dominated by scientists who, following Lavoisier's lead, performed careful weighing experiments to study the course of chemical reactions and to determine the composition of various chemical compounds. One of these chemists, a Frenchman, Joseph Proust (1754–1826), showed that *a given compound always contains exactly the same proportion of elements by mass.* For example, Proust found that the substance copper carbonate is always 5.3 parts copper to 4 parts oxygen to 1 part carbon (by mass). The principle of the constant composition of compounds, originally called "Proust's law," is now known as the **law of definite proportion.**

Proust's discovery stimulated John Dalton (1766–1844), an English schoolteacher (Fig. 2.3), to think about atoms as the particles that might compose elements. Dalton reasoned that if elements were composed of tiny individual particles, a given compound should always contain the same combination of these atoms. This concept explained why the same relative masses of elements were always found in a given compound.

But Dalton discovered another principle that convinced him even more of the existence of atoms. He noted, for example, that carbon and oxygen form two different compounds that contain different relative amounts of carbon and oxygen, as shown by the following data:

	Mass of Oxygen That Combines with 1 g of Carbon
Compound I	1.33 g
Compound II	2.66 g

Dalton noted that compound II contains twice as much oxygen per gram of carbon as compound I, a fact that could easily be explained in terms of atoms. Compound

I might be CO, and compound II might be CO_2.* This principle, which was found to apply to compounds of other elements as well, became known as the **law of multiple proportions:** *When two elements form a series of compounds, the ratios of the masses of the second element that combine with 1 gram of the first element can always be reduced to small whole numbers.*

To make sure the significance of this observation is clear, in Sample Exercise 2.1 we will consider data for a series of compounds consisting of nitrogen and oxygen.

Sample Exercise 2.1 *Illustrating the Law of Multiple Proportions*

The following data were collected for several compounds of nitrogen and oxygen:

	Mass of Nitrogen That Combines with 1 g of Oxygen
Compound A	1.750 g
Compound B	0.8750 g
Compound C	0.4375 g

Show how these data illustrate the law of multiple proportions.

Solution

For the law of multiple proportions to hold, the ratios of the masses of nitrogen combining with 1 gram of oxygen in each pair of compounds should be small whole numbers. We therefore compute the ratios as follows:

$$\frac{A}{B} = \frac{1.750}{0.875} = \frac{2}{1}$$

$$\frac{B}{C} = \frac{0.875}{0.4375} = \frac{2}{1}$$

$$\frac{A}{C} = \frac{1.750}{0.4375} = \frac{4}{1}$$

These results support the law of multiple proportions.

See Exercises 2.25 and 2.26.

Figure 2.3

John Dalton (1766–1844), an Englishman, began teaching at a Quaker school when he was 12. His fascination with science included an intense interest in meteorology, which led to an interest in the gases of the air and their ultimate components, atoms. Dalton is best known for his atomic theory, in which he postulated that the fundamental differences among atoms are their masses. He was the first to prepare a table of relative atomic weights.

Dalton was a humble man with several apparent handicaps: He was not articulate and he was color-blind, a terrible problem for a chemist. Despite these disadvantages, he helped to revolutionize the science of chemistry.

The significance of the data in Sample Exercise 2.1 is that compound A contains twice as much nitrogen (N) per gram of oxygen (O) as does compound B and that

---

*Subscripts are used to show the numbers of atoms present. The number 1 is understood (not written). The symbols for the elements and the writing of chemical formulas will be illustrated further in Sections 2.6 and 2.7.

compound B contains twice as much nitrogen per gram of oxygen as does compound C.

These data can be explained readily if the substances are composed of molecules made up of nitrogen atoms and oxygen atoms. For example, one set of possibilities for compounds A, B, and C is

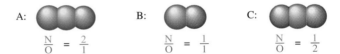

A: $\dfrac{N}{O} = \dfrac{2}{1}$ B: $\dfrac{N}{O} = \dfrac{1}{1}$ C: $\dfrac{N}{O} = \dfrac{1}{2}$

Now we can see that compound A contains 2 atoms of N for every atom of O, whereas compound B contains 1 atom of N per atom of O. That is, compound A contains twice as much nitrogen per given amount of oxygen as does compound B. Similarly, since compound B contains one N per O and compound C contains one N per *two* O's, the nitrogen content of compound C per given amount of oxygen is half that of compound B.

Another set of compounds that fits the data in Sample Exercise 2.1 is

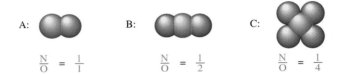

A: $\dfrac{N}{O} = \dfrac{1}{1}$ B: $\dfrac{N}{O} = \dfrac{1}{2}$ C: $\dfrac{N}{O} = \dfrac{1}{4}$

Verify for yourself that these compounds satisfy the requirements.

Still another set that works is

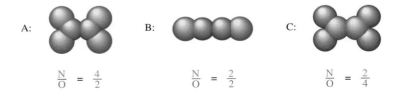

A: $\dfrac{N}{O} = \dfrac{4}{2}$ B: $\dfrac{N}{O} = \dfrac{2}{2}$ C: $\dfrac{N}{O} = \dfrac{2}{4}$

See if you can come up with still another set of compounds that satisfies the data in Sample Exercise 2.1. How many more possibilities are there?

In fact, an infinite number of other possibilities exists. Dalton could not deduce absolute formulas from the available data on relative masses. However, the data on the composition of compounds in terms of the relative masses of the elements supported his hypothesis that each element consisted of a certain type of atom and that compounds were formed from specific combinations of atoms.

2.3 *Dalton's Atomic Theory*

In 1808 Dalton published *A New System of Chemical Philosophy,* in which he presented his theory of atoms:

1. Each element is made up of tiny particles called atoms.

2. The atoms of a given element are identical; the atoms of different elements are different in some fundamental way or ways.

3. Chemical compounds are formed when atoms of different elements combine with each other. A given compound always has the same relative numbers and types of atoms.

4. Chemical reactions involve reorganization of the atoms—changes in the way they are bound together. The atoms themselves are not changed in a chemical reaction.

It is instructive to consider Dalton's reasoning on the relative masses of the atoms of the various elements. In Dalton's time water was known to be composed of the elements hydrogen and oxygen, with 8 grams of oxygen present for every 1 gram of hydrogen. If the formula for water were OH, an oxygen atom would have to have 8 times the mass of a hydrogen atom. However, if the formula for water were H_2O (two atoms of hydrogen for every oxygen atom), this would mean that each atom of oxygen is 16 times as massive as *each* atom of hydrogen (since the ratio of the mass of one oxygen to that of *two* hydrogens is 8 to 1). Because the formula for water was not then known, Dalton could not specify the relative masses of oxygen and hydrogen unambiguously. To solve the problem, Dalton made a fundamental assumption: He decided that nature would be as simple as possible. This assumption led him to conclude that the formula for water should be OH. He thus assigned hydrogen a mass of 1 and oxygen a mass of 8.

Using similar reasoning for other compounds, Dalton prepared the first table of **atomic masses** (sometimes called **atomic weights** by chemists, since mass is often determined by comparison to a standard mass—a process called *weighing*). Many of the masses were later proved to be wrong because of Dalton's incorrect assumptions about the formulas of certain compounds, but the construction of a table of masses was an important step forward.

Although not recognized as such for many years, the keys to determining absolute formulas for compounds were provided in the experimental work of the French chemist Joseph Gay-Lussac (1778–1850) and by the hypothesis of an Italian chemist named Amadeo Avogadro (1776–1856). In 1809 Gay-Lussac performed experiments in which he measured (under the same conditions of temperature and pressure) the volumes of gases that reacted with each other. For example, Gay-Lussac found that 2 volumes of hydrogen react with 1 volume of oxygen to form 2 volumes of gaseous water and that 1 volume of hydrogen reacts with 1 volume of chlorine to form 2 volumes of hydrogen chloride. These results are represented schematically in Fig. 2.4.

These statements are a modern paraphrase of Dalton's ideas.

Joseph Louis Gay-Lussac, a French physicist and chemist, was remarkably versatile. Although he is now known primarily for his studies on the combining of volumes of gases, Gay-Lussac was instrumental in the studies of many of the other properties of gases. Some of Gay-Lussac's motivation to learn about gases arose from his passion for ballooning. In fact, he made ascents to heights of over 4 miles to collect air samples, setting altitude records that stood for about 50 years. Gay-Lussac also was the codiscoverer of boron and the developer of a process for manufacturing sulfuric acid. As chief assayer of the French mint, Gay-Lussac developed many techniques for chemical analysis and invented many types of glassware now used routinely in labs. Gay-Lussac spent his last 20 years as a lawmaker in the French government.

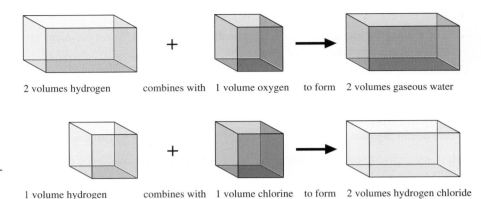

2 volumes hydrogen   combines with 1 volume oxygen to form 2 volumes gaseous water

1 volume hydrogen   combines with 1 volume chlorine to form 2 volumes hydrogen chloride

Figure 2.4

A representation of some of Gay-Lussac's experimental results on combining gas volumes.

In 1811 Avogadro interpreted these results by proposing that *at the same temperature and pressure, equal volumes of different gases contain the same number of particles.* This assumption (called **Avogadro's hypothesis**) makes sense if the distances between the particles in a gas are very great compared with the sizes of the particles. Under these conditions, the volume of a gas is determined by the number of molecules present, not by the size of the individual particles.

If Avogadro's hypothesis is correct, Gay-Lussac's result,

2 volumes of hydrogen react with 1 volume of oxygen

$\longrightarrow$ 2 volumes of water vapor

can be expressed as follows:

2 molecules* of hydrogen react with 1 molecule of oxygen

$\longrightarrow$ 2 molecules of water

These observations can best be explained by assuming that gaseous hydrogen, oxygen, and chlorine are all composed of diatomic (two-atom) molecules: H_2, O_2, and Cl_2, respectively. Gay-Lussac's results can then be represented as shown in Fig. 2.5.

The Italian chemist Stanislao Cannizzaro (1826–1910) cleared up the confusion in 1860 by doing a series of molar mass determinations that convinced the scientific community that the correct atomic mass of carbon is 12. For more information, see *From Caveman to Chemist* by Hugh Salzberg (American Chemical Society, 1991), p. 223.

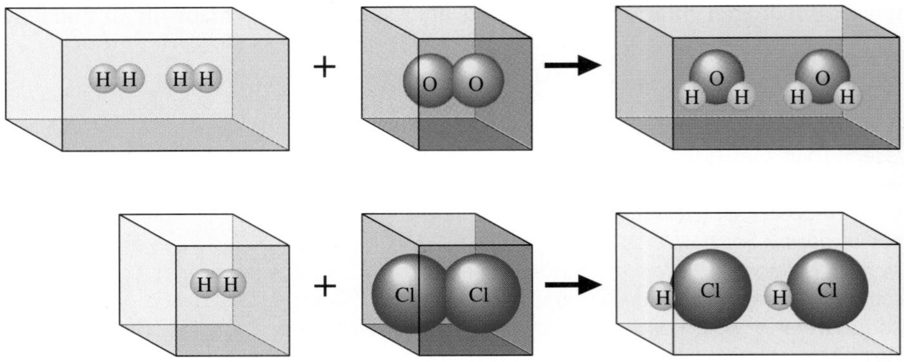

Figure 2.5

A representation of combining gases at the molecular level. The spheres represent atoms in the molecules.

*A *molecule* is a collection of atoms (see Sec. 2.6).

(Note that this reasoning suggests that the formula for water is H_2O, not OH as Dalton believed.)

Unfortunately, Avogadro's interpretations were not accepted by most chemists, and a half-century of confusion followed, in which many different assumptions were made about formulas and atomic masses.

During the nineteenth century, painstaking measurements were made of the masses of various elements that combined to form compounds. From these experiments a list of relative atomic masses could be determined. One of the chemists involved in contributing to this list was a Swede named Jöns Jakob Berzelius (1779–1848), who discovered the elements cerium, selenium, silicon, and thorium and developed the modern symbols for the elements used in writing the formulas of compounds.

2.4 Early Experiments to Characterize the Atom

On the basis of the work of Dalton, Gay-Lussac, Avogadro, and others, chemistry was beginning to make sense. The concept of atoms was clearly a good idea. Inevitably, scientists began to wonder about the nature of the atom. What is an atom made of, and how do the atoms of the various elements differ?

The Electron

The first important experiments that led to an understanding of the composition of the atom were done by the English physicist J. J. Thomson (Fig. 2.6), who studied electrical discharges in partially evacuated tubes called **cathode-ray tubes** (Fig. 2.7) during the period from 1898 to 1903. Thomson found that when high voltage was applied to the tube, a "ray" he called a *cathode ray* (because it emanated from the negative electrode, or cathode) was produced. Because this ray was produced at the negative electrode and was repelled by the negative pole of an applied electric field (see Fig. 2.8), Thomson postulated that the ray was a stream of negatively charged particles, now called **electrons.** From experiments in which he measured the

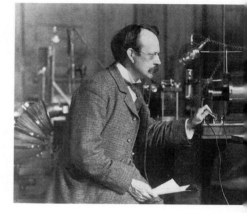

Figure 2.6
J. J. Thomson (1856–1940) was an English physicist at Cambridge University. He received the Nobel Prize in physics in 1906.

Video: Cathode Ray Tube

Figure 2.7
A cathode-ray tube. The fast-moving electrons excite the gas in the tube, causing a glow between the electrodes. The green color in the photo is due to the response of the screen (coated with zinc sulfide) to the electron beam.

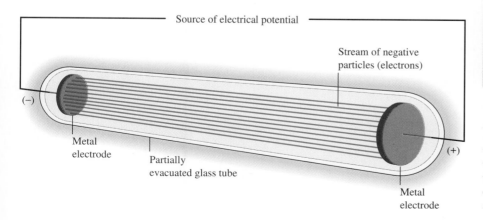

Source of electrical potential

Stream of negative particles (electrons)

(−)

Metal electrode

Partially evacuated glass tube

(+)

Metal electrode

CHEMICAL IMPACT

Berzelius, Selenium, and Silicon

JÖNS JAKOB BERZELIUS was probably the best experimental chemist of his generation and, given the crudeness of his laboratory equipment, maybe the best of all time. Unlike Lavoisier, who could afford to buy the best laboratory equipment available, Berzelius worked with minimal equipment in very plain surroundings. One of Berzelius's students described the Swedish chemist's workplace: "The laboratory consisted of two ordinary rooms with the very simplest arrangements; there were neither furnaces nor hoods, neither water system nor gas. Against the walls stood some closets with the chemicals, in the middle the mercury trough and the blast lamp table. Beside this was the sink consisting of a stone water holder with a stopcock and a pot standing under it. [Next door in the kitchen] stood a small heating furnace."

In these simple facilities Berzelius performed more than 2000 experiments over a 10-year period to determine accurate atomic masses for the 50 elements then known. His success can be seen from the data in the table below. These remarkably accurate values attest to his experimental skills and patience.

Besides his table of atomic masses, Berzelius made many other major contributions to chemistry. The most important of these was the invention of a simple set of symbols for the elements along with a system for writing the formulas of compounds to replace the awkward symbolic representations of the alchemists. Although some chemists, including Dalton, objected to the new system, it was gradually adopted and forms the basis of the system we use today.

In addition to these accomplishments, Berzelius also discovered the elements cerium, thorium, selenium, and silicon. Of these elements, selenium and silicon are particularly important in today's world. Berzelius discovered selenium in 1817 in connection with his studies of sulfuric acid. For years selenium's toxicity has

The Alchemists' Symbols for Some Common Elements and Compounds	
Substance	*Alchemists' Symbol*
Silver	☽
Lead	♄
Tin	♃
Platinum	☽⊙
Sulfuric acid	+⊕
Alcohol	∨
Sea salt	⊙

Comparison of Several of Berzelius's Atomic Masses with the Modern Values		
	Atomic Mass	
Element	*Berzelius's Value*	*Current Value*
Chlorine	35.41	35.45
Copper	63.00	63.55
Hydrogen	1.00	1.01
Lead	207.12	207.2
Nitrogen	14.05	14.01
Oxygen	16.00	16.00
Potassium	39.19	39.10
Silver	108.12	107.87
Sulfur	32.18	32.07

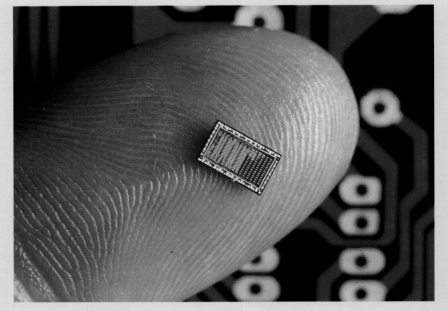

A silicon chip.

deflection of the beam of electrons in a magnetic field, Thomson determined the *charge-to-mass ratio* of an electron:

$$\frac{e}{m} = -1.76 \times 10^8 \text{ C/g}$$

where e represents the charge on the electron in coulombs (C) and m represents the electron mass in grams.

One of Thomson's primary goals in his cathode-ray tube experiments was to gain an understanding of the structure of the atom. He reasoned that since electrons could be produced from electrodes made of various types of metals, *all* atoms must contain electrons. Since atoms were known to be electrically neutral, Thomson further assumed that atoms also must contain some positive charge. Thomson postulated that an atom consisted of a diffuse cloud of positive charge with the negative electrons embedded randomly in it. This model, shown in Fig. 2.9, is often called the

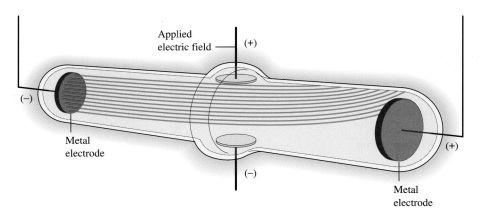

Figure 2.8

Deflection of cathode rays by an applied electric field.

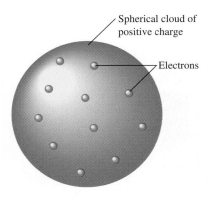

Figure 2.9

The plum pudding model of the atom.

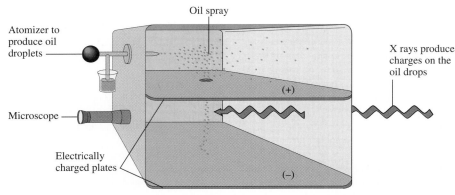

Figure 2.10

A schematic representation of the apparatus Millikan used to determine the charge on the electron. The fall of charged oil droplets due to gravity can be halted by adjusting the voltage across the two plates. This voltage and the mass of the oil drop can then be used to calculate the charge on the oil drop. Millikan's experiments showed that the charge on an oil drop is always a whole-number multiple of the electron charge.

plum pudding model because the electrons are like raisins dispersed in a pudding (the positive charge cloud), as in plum pudding, a favorite English dessert.[*]

In 1909 Robert Millikan (1868–1953), working at the University of Chicago, performed very clever experiments involving charged oil drops. These experiments allowed him to determine the magnitude of the electron charge (see Fig. 2.10). With this value and the charge-to-mass ratio determined by Thomson, Millikan was able to calculate the mass of the electron as 9.11×10^{-31} kilogram.

Radioactivity

In the late nineteenth century scientists discovered that certain elements produce high-energy radiation. For example, in 1896 the French scientist Henri Becquerel found accidentally that a piece of a mineral containing uranium could produce its image on a photographic plate in the absence of light. He attributed this phenomenon to a spontaneous emission of radiation by the uranium, which he called **radioactivity.** Studies in the early twentieth century demonstrated three types of radioactive emission: gamma (γ) rays, beta (β) particles, and alpha (α) particles. A γ ray is high-energy "light"; a β particle is a high-speed electron; and an α particle has a 2+ charge, that is, a charge twice that of the electron and with the opposite sign. The mass of an α particle is 7300 times that of the electron. More modes of radioactivity are now known, and we will discuss them in Chapter 21. Here we will consider only α particles because they were used in some crucial early experiments.

The Nuclear Atom

In 1911 Ernest Rutherford (Fig. 2.11), who performed many of the pioneering experiments to explore radioactivity, carried out an experiment to test Thomson's plum

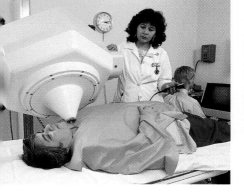

A technician using a scanner to monitor the uptake of radioactive iodine in a patient's thyroid.

[*]Although J. J. Thomson is generally given credit for this model, the idea was apparently first suggested by the English mathematician and physicist William Thomson (better known as Lord Kelvin and not related to J. J. Thomson).

pudding model. The experiment involved directing α particles at a thin sheet of metal foil, as illustrated in Fig. 2.12. Rutherford reasoned that if Thomson's model were accurate, the massive α particles should crash through the thin foil like cannonballs through gauze, as shown in Fig. 2.13(a). He expected the α particles to travel through the foil with, at the most, very minor deflections in their paths. The results of the experiment were very different from those Rutherford anticipated. Although most of the α particles passed straight through, many of the particles were deflected at large angles, as shown in Fig. 2.13(b), and some were reflected, never hitting the detector. This outcome was a great surprise to Rutherford. (He wrote that this result was comparable with shooting a howitzer at a piece of paper and having the shell reflected back.)

Rutherford knew from these results that the plum pudding model for the atom could not be correct. The large deflections of the α particles could be caused only by a center of concentrated positive charge that contains most of the atom's mass, as illustrated in Fig. 2.13(b). Most of the α particles pass directly through the foil because the atom is mostly open space. The deflected α particles are those that had a "close encounter" with the massive positive center of the atom, and the few

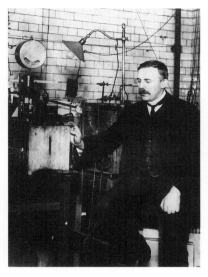

Figure 2.11

Ernest Rutherford (1871–1937) was born on a farm in New Zealand. In 1895 he placed second in a scholarship competition to attend Cambridge University but was awarded the scholarship when the winner decided to stay home and get married. As a scientist in England, Rutherford did much of the early work on characterizing radioactivity. He named the α and β particles and the γ ray and coined the term *half-life* to describe an important attribute of radioactive elements. His experiments on the behavior of α particles striking thin metal foils led him to postulate the nuclear atom. He also invented the name *proton* for the nucleus of the hydrogen atom. He received the Nobel Prize in chemistry in 1908.

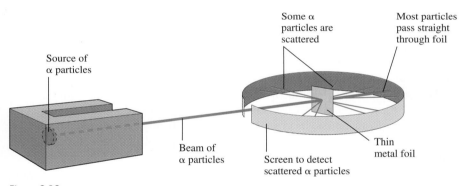

Figure 2.12

Rutherford's experiment on α-particle bombardment of metal foil.

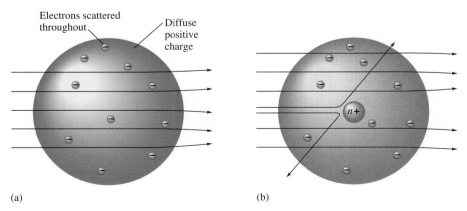

(a)   (b)

Figure 2.13

(a) The expected results of the metal foil experiment if Thomson's model were correct. (b) Actual results.

reflected α particles are those that made a "direct hit" on the much more massive positive center.

In Rutherford's mind these results could be explained only in terms of a **nuclear atom**—an atom with a dense center of positive charge (the **nucleus**) with electrons moving around the nucleus at a distance that is large relative to the nuclear radius.

2.5 The Modern View of Atomic Structure: An Introduction

In the years since Thomson and Rutherford, a great deal has been learned about atomic structure. Because much of this material will be covered in detail in later chapters, only an introduction will be given here. The simplest view of the atom is that it consists of a tiny nucleus (with a diameter of about 10^{-13} cm) and electrons that move about the nucleus at an average distance of about 10^{-8} cm from it (see Fig. 2.14).

As we will see later, the chemistry of an atom mainly results from its electrons. For this reason, chemists can be satisfied with a relatively crude nuclear model. The nucleus is assumed to contain **protons,** which have a positive charge equal in magnitude to the electron's negative charge, and **neutrons,** which have virtually the same mass as a proton but no charge. The masses and charges of the electron, proton, and neutron are shown in Table 2.1.

Two striking things about the nucleus are its small size compared with the overall size of the atom and its extremely high density. The tiny nucleus accounts for almost all the atom's mass. Its great density is dramatically demonstrated by the fact that a piece of nuclear material about the size of a pea would have a mass of 250 million tons!

An important question to consider at this point is, "*If all atoms are composed of these same components, why do different atoms have different chemical properties?*" The answer to this question lies in the number and the arrangement of the electrons. The electrons constitute most of the atomic volume and thus are the parts that "intermingle" when atoms combine to form molecules. Therefore, the number of electrons possessed by a given atom greatly affects its ability to interact with other atoms. As a result, the atoms of different elements, which have different numbers of protons and electrons, show different chemical behavior.

The forces that bind the positively charged protons in the nucleus will be discussed in Chapter 21.

The *chemistry* of an atom arises from its electrons.

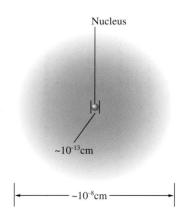

Nucleus

$\sim 10^{-13}$ cm

$\sim 10^{-8}$ cm

Figure 2.14

A nuclear atom viewed in cross section. Note that this drawing is not to scale.

Table 2.1 The Mass and Charge of the Electron, Proton, and Neutron

Particle	Mass	Charge*
Electron	9.11×10^{-31} kg	1 $-$
Proton	1.67×10^{-27} kg	1 $+$
Neutron	1.67×10^{-27} kg	None

*The magnitude of the charge of the electron and the proton is 1.60×10^{-19} C.

CHEMICAL IMPACT

Reading the History Bogs

SCIENTISTS OFTEN "READ" the history of the earth and its inhabitants using very different "books" than traditional historians. For example, the disappearance of the dinosaurs 65 million years ago in an "instant" of geological time was a great mystery until unusually high iridium and osmium levels were discovered at a position in the earth's crust corresponding to that time. These high levels of iridium and osmium suggested that an extraterrestrial object had struck the earth 65 million years ago with catastrophic results for the dinosaurs. Since then, the huge buried crater caused by the object has been discovered on the Yucatan Peninsula, and virtually everyone is now convinced that this is the correct explanation for the disappearing dinosaurs.

History is also being "read" by scientists studying ice cores from glaciers in Iceland. Now Swiss scientists have found that ancient peat bogs can furnish a reliable historical record. Geochemist William Shotyk of the University of Bern has found a 15,000-year window on history by analyzing the lead content of core samples from a Swiss mountainside peat bog [*Science* **281** (1998): 1635]. Various parts of the core samples were dated by ^{14}C dating techniques (see Chapter 21, Section 21.4 for more information) and analyzed for their scandium and lead contents. Also, the $^{206}Pb/^{207}Pb$ ratio was measured for each sample. These data are represented in the accompanying figure. Notice that the $^{206}Pb/^{207}Pb$ ratio remains very close to 1.20 (see the green band in the figure) from 14,000 years to 3200 years. The value of 1.20 is the same as the average $^{206}Pb/^{207}Pb$ ratio in the earth's soil.

The core also reveals that the total lead and scandium levels increased

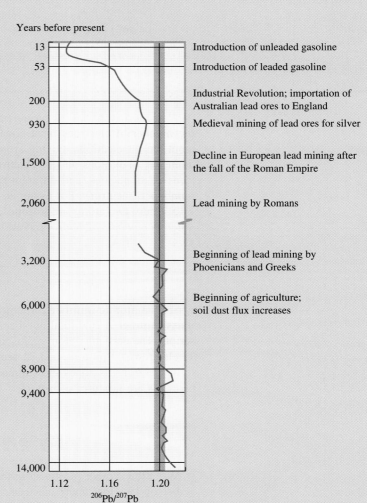

Years before present

Years	Event
13	Introduction of unleaded gasoline
53	Introduction of leaded gasoline
200	Industrial Revolution; importation of Australian lead ores to England
930	Medieval mining of lead ores for silver
1,500	Decline in European lead mining after the fall of the Roman Empire
2,060	Lead mining by Romans
3,200	Beginning of lead mining by Phoenicians and Greeks
6,000	Beginning of agriculture; soil dust flux increases

$^{206}Pb/^{207}Pb$

Geochemist William Shotyk's analysis of the lead content of ice core samples reveals a 15,000-year history of lead levels. (Note: Dates are based on calibrated radiocarbon dating. Because the core was retrieved in two segments, a break in data occurs between 2060 and 3200 years before present.)

simultaneously at the 6000-year mark but that the $^{206}Pb/^{207}Pb$ ratio remained close to 1.20. This coincides with the beginning of agriculture in Europe, which caused more soil dust to enter the atmosphere.

Significantly, about 3000 years ago the $^{206}Pb/^{207}Pb$ ratio decreased markedly. This also corresponds in the core sample to an increase in total lead content out of proportion to the increase in scandium. This indicates the lead no longer resulted from soil dust but from other activities of humans—lead mining had begun. Since the 3000-year mark, the $^{206}Pb/^{207}Pb$ ratio has remained well below 1.20, indicating that human use of lead ores has become the dominant source of airborne lead. This is confirmed by the sharp decline in the ratio beginning 200 years ago that corresponds to the importation into England of Australian lead ores having low $^{206}Pb/^{207}Pb$ ratios.

So far only lead has been used to read the history in the bog. However, Shotyk's group is also measuring the changes in the levels of copper, zinc, cadmium, arsenic, mercury, and antimony. More interesting stories are sure to follow.

A sodium atom has 11 protons in its nucleus. Since atoms have no net charge, the number of electrons must equal the number of protons. Therefore, a sodium atom has 11 electrons moving around its nucleus. It is *always* true that a sodium atom has 11 protons and 11 electrons. However, each sodium atom also has neutrons in its nucleus, and different types of sodium atoms exist that have different numbers of neutrons. For example, consider the sodium atoms represented in Fig. 2.15. These two atoms are **isotopes,** or *atoms with the same number of protons but different numbers of neutrons.* Note that the symbol for one particular type of sodium atom is written

where the **atomic number** Z (number of protons) is written as a subscript, and the **mass number** A (the total number of protons and neutrons) is written as a superscript. (The particular atom represented here is called "sodium twenty-three." It has 11 electrons, 11 protons, and 12 neutrons.) Because the chemistry of an atom is due to its electrons, isotopes show almost identical chemical properties. In nature most elements are mixtures of isotopes.

Sample Exercise 2.2 *Writing the Symbols for Atoms*

Write the symbol for the atom that has an atomic number of 9 and a mass number of 19. How many electrons and how many neutrons does this atom have?

Solution

The atomic number 9 means the atom has 9 protons. This element is called *fluorine,* symbolized by F. The atom is represented as

$$^{19}_{9}F$$

and is called "fluorine nineteen." Since the atom has 9 protons, it also must have 9 electrons to achieve electrical neutrality. The mass number gives the total number of protons and neutrons, which means that this atom has 10 neutrons.

See Exercises 2.43 through 2.46.

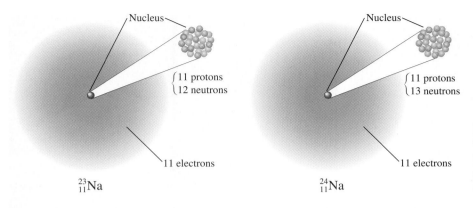

Figure 2.15
Two isotopes of sodium. Both have eleven protons and eleven electrons, but they differ in the number of neutrons in their nuclei.

2.6 *Molecules and Ions*

From a chemist's viewpoint, the most interesting characteristic of an atom is its ability to combine with other atoms to form compounds. It was John Dalton who first recognized that chemical compounds are collections of atoms, but he could not determine the structure of atoms or their means for binding to each other. During the twentieth century we have learned that atoms have electrons and that these electrons participate in bonding one atom to another. We will discuss bonding thoroughly in Chapters 8 and 9; here we will introduce some simple bonding ideas that will be useful in the next few chapters.

The forces that hold atoms together in compounds are called **chemical bonds.** One way that atoms can form bonds is by *sharing electrons.* These bonds are called **covalent bonds,** and the resulting collection of atoms is called a **molecule.** Molecules can be represented in several different ways. The simplest method is the **chemical formula,** in which the symbols for the elements are used to indicate the types of atoms present and subscripts are used to indicate the relative numbers of atoms. For example, the formula for carbon dioxide is CO_2, meaning that each molecule contains 1 atom of carbon and 2 atoms of oxygen.

Examples of molecules that contain covalent bonds are hydrogen (H_2), water (H_2O), oxygen (O_2), ammonia (NH_3), and methane (CH_4). More information about a molecule is given by its **structural formula,** in which the individual bonds are shown (indicated by lines). Structural formulas may or may not indicate the actual shape of the molecule. For example, water might be represented as

$$H—O—H \quad \text{or} \quad \begin{array}{c} O \\ \diagup \; \diagdown \\ H \qquad H \end{array}$$

The structure on the right shows the actual shape of the water molecule. Scientists know from experimental evidence that the molecule looks like this. (We will study the shapes of molecules further in Chapter 8.) The structural formula for ammonia is shown at right.

Molecular Models: H_2, H_2O, O_2, NH_3, CH_4

$$\begin{array}{c} N \\ H \; \Big| \; H \\ H \end{array}$$

Ammonia

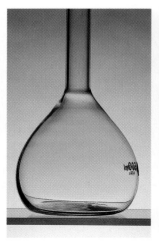

Sodium metal is soft enough to be cut easily with a knife (far left). Chlorine is a green gas (second from left). When sodium and chlorine are combined, they react vigorously (second from right) to form sodium chloride (far right).

Note that atoms connected to the central atom by dashed lines are behind the plane of the paper, and atoms connected to the central atom by wedges are in front of the plane of the paper.

In a compound composed of molecules, the individual molecules move around as independent units. For example, a molecule of methane gas can be represented in several ways. The structural formula for methane (CH_4) is shown in Fig. 2.16. The **space-filling model** of methane, which shows the relative sizes of the atoms as well as their relative orientation in the molecule, is given in Fig. 2.17. **Ball-and-stick models** are also used to represent molecules. The ball-and-stick structure of methane is shown in Fig. 2.18.

Methane

Figure 2.16

The structural formula for methane.

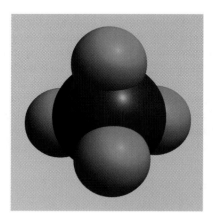

Figure 2.17

Space-filling model of methane. This type of model shows both the relative sizes of the atoms in the molecule and their spatial relationships.

Figure 2.18

Ball-and-stick model of methane.

A second type of chemical bond results from attractions among ions. An **ion** is an atom or group of atoms that has a net positive or negative charge. The best known ionic compound is common table salt, or sodium chloride, which forms when neutral chlorine and sodium react.

To see how the ions are formed, consider what happens when an electron is transferred from a sodium atom to a chlorine atom (the neutrons in the nuclei will be ignored):

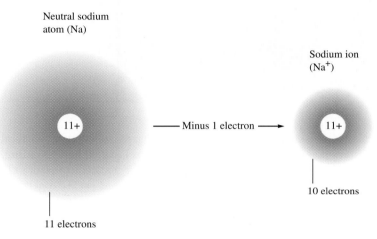

Neutral sodium atom (Na)

Sodium ion (Na$^+$)

11+   Minus 1 electron ⟶   11+

11 electrons

10 electrons

With one electron stripped off, the sodium, with its 11 protons and only 10 electrons, now has a net 1+ charge—it has become a *positive ion*. A positive ion is called a **cation.** The sodium ion is written as Na$^+$, and the process can be represented in shorthand form as

$$Na \longrightarrow Na^+ + e^-$$

If an electron is added to chlorine,

Na$^+$ is usually called the *sodium ion* rather than the sodium cation. Also Cl$^-$ is called the *chloride ion* rather than the chloride anion. In general, when a specific ion is referred to, the word *ion* rather than cation or anion is used.

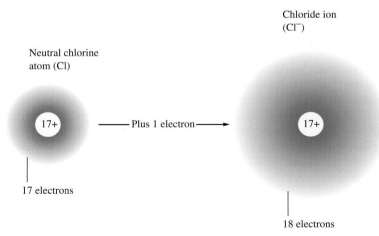

Chloride ion (Cl$^-$)

Neutral chlorine atom (Cl)

17+   Plus 1 electron ⟶   17+

17 electrons

18 electrons

the 18 electrons produce a net 1− charge; the chlorine has become an *ion with a negative charge*—an **anion.** The chloride ion is written as Cl$^-$, and the process is represented as

$$Cl + e^- \longrightarrow Cl^-$$

Figure 2.19

(a) The arrangement of sodium ions (Na$^+$) and chloride ions (Cl$^-$) in the ionic compound sodium chloride. (b) Cubic crystals of sodium chloride shown magnified 500 times.

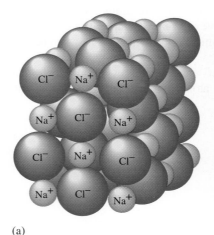

(a)   (b)

Because anions and cations have opposite charges, they attract each other. This *force of attraction between oppositely charged ions* is called **ionic bonding.** Sodium metal and chlorine gas (a green gas composed of Cl$_2$ molecules) react to form solid sodium chloride, which contains many Na$^+$ and Cl$^-$ ions packed together, as shown in Fig. 2.19(a). The solid forms the beautiful colorless cubic crystals shown in Fig. 2.19(b).

A solid consisting of oppositely charged ions is called an **ionic solid,** or a **salt.** Ionic solids can consist of simple ions, as in sodium chloride, or of **polyatomic** (many atom) **ions,** as in ammonium nitrate (NH$_4$NO$_3$), which contains ammonium ions (NH$_4^+$) and nitrate ions (NO$_3^-$). The ball-and-stick models of these ions are shown in Fig. 2.20.

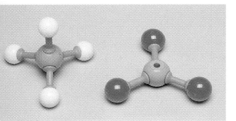

Figure 2.20

Ball-and-stick models of the ammonium ion (NH$_4^+$) and the nitrate ion (NO$_3^-$).

2.7 An Introduction to the Periodic Table

In a room where chemistry is taught or practiced, a chart called the **periodic table** is almost certain to be found hanging on the wall. This chart shows all the known elements and gives a good deal of information about each. As our study of chemistry progresses, the usefulness of the periodic table will become more obvious. This section will simply introduce it to you.

A simplified version of the periodic table is shown in Fig. 2.21. The letters in the boxes are the symbols for the elements; these abbreviations are based on the current element names or the original names* (see Table 2.2). The number shown above each symbol is the *atomic number* (number of protons) for that element. For example, carbon (C) has atomic number 6, and lead (Pb) has atomic number 82. Most of the elements are **metals.** Metals have characteristic physical properties such as efficient conduction of heat and electricity, malleability (they can be hammered into thin sheets), ductility (they can be pulled into wires), and (often) a lustrous appearance. Chemically, metals tend to *lose* electrons to form positive ions. For example, copper is a typical metal. It is lustrous (although it tarnishes readily); it is an excellent conductor of electricity (it is widely used in electrical wires); and it is

Gold is one of only a few metals that occur naturally as a free element, sometimes in spectacular form. The largest gold nugget ever mined in Colorado (found near Breckenridge) weighs 13 pounds.

*See David W. Ball, "Elemental Etymology: What's in a Name?" *J. Chem. Ed.* **62** (1985): 787.

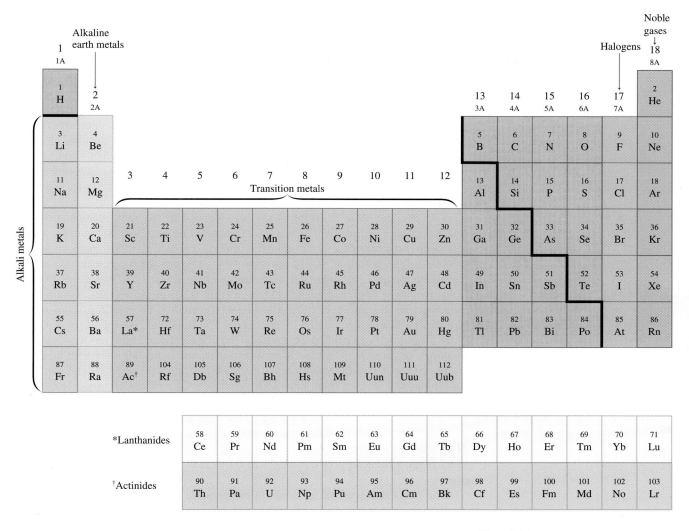

Figure 2.21
The periodic table.

Table 2.2 The Symbols for the Elements That Are Based on the Original Names

Current Name	Original Name	Symbol
Antimony	Stibium	Sb
Copper	Cuprum	Cu
Iron	Ferrum	Fe
Lead	Plumbum	Pb
Mercury	Hydrargyrum	Hg
Potassium	Kalium	K
Silver	Argentum	Ag
Sodium	Natrium	Na
Tin	Stannum	Sn
Tungsten	Wolfram	W

Metals tend to form positive ions; nonmetals tend to form negative ions.

Elements in the same vertical column in the periodic table form a *group* (or *family*) and generally have similar properties.

Three members of the halogen family: chlorine, bromine, and iodine (left to right).

Molecular Models: Br_2, Cl_2, F_2, I_2

Another format of the periodic table will be discussed in Section 7.11.

readily formed into various shapes, such as pipes for water systems. Copper is also found in many salts, such as the beautifully blue copper sulfate, in which copper is present as Cu^{2+} ions. Copper is a member of the transition metals—the metals shown in the center of the periodic table.

The relatively few **nonmetals** appear in the upper right-hand corner of the table (to the right of the heavy line in Fig. 2.21), except hydrogen, a nonmetal that resides in the upper left-hand corner. The nonmetals lack the physical properties that characterize the metals. Chemically, they tend to *gain* electrons in reactions with metals to form negative ions. Nonmetals often bond to each other by forming covalent bonds. For example, chlorine is a typical nonmetal. Under normal conditions it exists as Cl_2 molecules; it reacts with metals to form salts containing Cl^- ions (NaCl, for example); and it forms covalent bonds with nonmetals (for example, hydrogen chloride gas, HCl).

The periodic table is arranged so that elements in the same vertical columns (called **groups** or **families**) have *similar chemical properties*. For example, all the **alkali metals,** members of Group 1A—lithium (Li), sodium (Na), potassium (K), rubidium (Rb), cesium (Cs), and francium (Fr)—are very active elements that readily form ions with a 1+ charge when they react with nonmetals. The members of Group 2A—beryllium (Be), magnesium (Mg), calcium (Ca), strontium (Sr), barium (Ba), and radium (Ra)—are called the **alkaline earth metals.** They all form ions with a 2+ charge when they react with nonmetals. The **halogens,** the members of Group 7A—fluorine (F), chlorine (Cl), bromine (Br), iodine (I), and astatine (At)—all form diatomic molecules. Fluorine, chlorine, bromine, and iodine all react with metals to form salts containing ions with a 1− charge (F^-, Cl^-, Br^-, and I^-). The members of Group 8A—helium (He), neon (Ne), argon (Ar), krypton (Kr), xenon (Xe), and radon (Rn)—are known as the **noble gases.** They all exist under normal conditions as monatomic (single-atom) gases and have little chemical reactivity.

Note from Fig. 2.21 that alternate sets of symbols are used to denote the groups. The symbols 1A through 8A are the traditional designations, whereas the numbers 1 to 18 have been suggested recently. In this text the 1A to 8A designations will be used.

The horizontal rows of elements in the periodic table are called **periods.** Horizontal row one is called the *first period* (it contains H and He); row two is called the *second period* (elements Li through Ne); and so on.

We will learn much more about the periodic table as we continue with our study of chemistry. Meanwhile, when an element is introduced in this text, you should always note its position on the periodic table.

2.8 Naming Simple Compounds

When chemistry was an infant science, there was no system for naming compounds. Names such as sugar of lead, blue vitrol, quicklime, Epsom salts, milk of magnesia, gypsum, and laughing gas were coined by early chemists. Such names are called *common names.* As chemistry grew, it became clear that using common names for compounds would lead to unacceptable chaos. Nearly five million chemical compounds are currently known. Memorizing common names for these compounds would be an impossible task.

The solution, of course, is to adopt a *system* for naming compounds in which the name tells something about the composition of the compound. After learning the system, a chemist given a formula should be able to name the compound or, given a name, should be able to construct the compound's formula. In this section we will specify the most important rules for naming compounds other than organic compounds (those based on chains of carbon atoms).

We will begin with the systems for naming inorganic **binary compounds**—compounds composed of two elements—which we classify into various types for easier recognition. We will consider both ionic and covalent compounds.

Binary Ionic Compounds (Type I)

Binary ionic compounds contain a positive ion (cation) always written first in the formula and a negative ion (anion). In naming these compounds, the following rules apply:

1. The cation is always named first and the anion second.

2. A monatomic (meaning one-atom) cation takes its name from the name of the element. For example, Na^+ is called sodium in the names of compounds containing this ion.

   A monatomic cation has the same name as its parent element.

3. A monatomic anion is named by taking the root of the element name and adding *-ide*. Thus the Cl^- ion is called chloride.

Some common monatomic cations and anions and their names are given in Table 2.3.

The rules for naming binary ionic compounds are illustrated by the following examples:

In formulas of ionic compounds, simple ions are represented by the element symbol: Cl means Cl^-, Na means Na^+, and so on.

Compound	Ions Present	Name
NaCl	Na^+, Cl^-	Sodium chloride
KI	K^+, I^-	Potassium iodide
CaS	Ca^{2+}, S^{2-}	Calcium sulfide
Li_3N	Li^+, N^{3-}	Lithium nitride
CsBr	Cs^+, Br^-	Cesium bromide
MgO	Mg^{2+}, O^{2-}	Magnesium oxide

Table 2.3 Common Monatomic Cations and Anions

Cation	Name	Anion	Name
H^+	Hydrogen	H^-	Hydride
Li^+	Lithium	F^-	Fluoride
Na^+	Sodium	Cl^-	Chloride
K^+	Potassium	Br^-	Bromide
Cs^+	Cesium	I^-	Iodide
Be^{2+}	Beryllium	O^{2-}	Oxide
Mg^{2+}	Magnesium	S^{2-}	Sulfide
Ca^{2+}	Calcium	N^{3-}	Nitride
Ba^{2+}	Barium	P^{3-}	Phosphide
Al^{3+}	Aluminum		
Ag^+	Silver		

Sample Exercise 2.3 *Naming Type I Binary Compounds*

Name each binary compound.

a. CsF   **b.** $AlCl_3$ **c.** LiH

Solution

a. CsF is cesium fluoride.
b. $AlCl_3$ is aluminum chloride.
c. LiH is lithium hydride.

Notice that, in each case, the cation is named first, and then the anion is named.

See Exercise 2.61.

Binary Ionic Compounds (Type II)

Type II binary ionic compounds contain a metal that can form more than one type of cation.

In the binary ionic compounds considered above (type I), the metal present forms only a single type of cation. That is, sodium forms only Na^+, calcium forms only Ca^{2+}, and so on. However, as we will see in more detail later in the text, there are many metals that form more than one type of positive ion and thus form more than one type of ionic compound with a given anion. For example, the compound $FeCl_2$ contains Fe^{2+} ions, and the compound $FeCl_3$ contains Fe^{3+} ions. In a case such as this, the *charge on the metal ion must be specified.* The systematic names for these two iron compounds are iron(II) chloride and iron(III) chloride, respectively, where the *Roman numeral indicates the charge of the cation.*

Another system for naming these ionic compounds that is seen in the older literature was used for metals that form only two ions. *The ion with the higher charge has a name ending in -ic, and the one with the lower charge has a name ending in -ous.* In this system, for example, Fe^{3+} is called the ferric ion, and Fe^{2+} is called the ferrous ion. The names for $FeCl_3$ and $FeCl_2$ are then ferric chloride and ferrous chloride, respectively. In this text we will use the system that employs Roman numerals. Table 2.4 lists the systematic names for many common Type II cations.

Table 2.4 Common Type II Cations

Ion	Systematic Name
Fe^{3+}	Iron(III)
Fe^{2+}	Iron(II)
Cu^{2+}	Copper(II)
Cu^+	Copper(I)
Co^{3+}	Cobalt(III)
Co^{2+}	Cobalt(II)
Sn^{4+}	Tin(IV)
Sn^{2+}	Tin(II)
Pb^{4+}	Lead(IV)
Pb^{2+}	Lead(II)
Hg^{2+}	Mercury(II)
Hg_2^{2+}*	Mercury(I)
Ag^+	Silver†
Zn^{2+}	Zinc†
Cd^{2+}	Cadmium†

*Note that mercury(I) ions always occur bound together to form Hg_2^{2+} ions.
†Although these are transition metals, they form only one type of ion, and a Roman numeral is not used.

Sample Exercise 2.4 *Naming Type II Binary Compounds*

Give the systematic name of each of the following compounds.
a. CuCl   **b.** HgO   **c.** Fe_2O_3 **d.** MnO_2 **e.** $PbCl_2$

Solution

All these compounds include a metal that can form more than one type of cation; thus we must first determine the charge on each cation. This can be done by recognizing that a compound must be electrically neutral; that is, the positive and negative charges must exactly balance.

A compound must be electrically neutral.

a. In CuCl, for example, since the anion is Cl^-, the cation must be Cu^+. The name is copper(I) chloride, where the Roman numeral I indicates the 1+ charge on Cu^+.
b. In HgO, since the anion is oxide, O^{2-}, the mercury cation must be Hg^{2+} to give a net charge of zero as required. Thus the name is mercury(II) oxide.
c. In Fe_2O_3, the three O^{2-} ions carry a total charge of 6−, so the two iron cations must carry a total charge of 6+. Thus each iron ion is Fe^{3+}, and the name is iron(III) oxide.
d. In the compound MnO_2, the cation has a 4+ charge, and the name is manganese(IV) oxide.
e. In $PbCl_2$ the cation has a 2+ charge, so the name is lead(II) chloride.

See Exercise 2.62.

Note that the use of a Roman numeral in a systematic name is required only in cases where more than one ionic compound forms between a given pair of elements. This case most commonly occurs for compounds containing transition metals, which often form more than one cation. *Elements that form only one cation do not need to be identified by a Roman numeral.* Common metals that do not require Roman numerals are the Group 1A elements, which form only 1+ ions; the Group 2A elements, which form only 2+ ions; and aluminum, which forms only Al^{3+}. The element silver deserves special mention at this point. In virtually all its compounds silver is found as the Ag^+ ion. Therefore, although silver is a transition metal (and can potentially form ions other than Ag^+), silver compounds are usually named without a Roman numeral. Thus AgCl is typically called silver chloride rather than silver(I) chloride, although the latter name is technically correct. Also, a Roman numeral is not used for zinc compounds, since zinc forms only the Zn^{2+} ion.

As shown in Sample Exercise 2.4, when a metal ion is present that forms more than one type of cation, the charge on the metal ion must be determined by balancing the positive and negative charges of the compound. To do this you must be able to recognize the common cations and anions and know their charges (see Tables 2.3 and 2.5).

A compound containing a transition metal usually requires a Roman numeral in its name.

Crystals of copper(II) sulfate.

Sample Exercise 2.5 *Naming Binary Compounds*

Give the systematic name of each of the following compounds.
a. $CoBr_2$ b. $CaCl_2$ c. Al_2O_3 d. $CrCl_3$

Solution

Compound	Name	Comment
a. $CoBr_2$	Cobalt(II) bromide	Cobalt is a transition metal; the compound name must have a Roman numeral. The two Br^- ions must be balanced by a Co^{2+} ion.

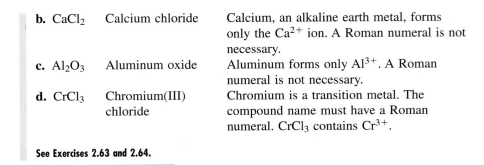

b. CaCl$_2$ Calcium chloride   Calcium, an alkaline earth metal, forms only the Ca^{2+} ion. A Roman numeral is not necessary.

c. Al$_2$O$_3$ Aluminum oxide   Aluminum forms only Al^{3+}. A Roman numeral is not necessary.

d. CrCl$_3$ Chromium(III) chloride   Chromium is a transition metal. The compound name must have a Roman numeral. CrCl$_3$ contains Cr^{3+}.

See Exercises 2.63 and 2.64.

The following flowchart is useful when you are naming binary ionic compounds:

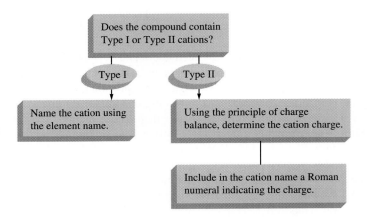

The common type I and type II ions are summarized in Fig. 2.22. Also shown in Fig. 2.22 are the common monatomic ions.

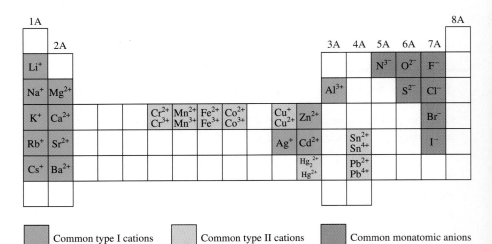

Figure 2.22

The common cations and anions.

CHEMICAL IMPACT

Buckminsterfullerene: A New Form of Carbon

A FAVORITE CHEMISTRY exam question—What are the forms of elemental carbon?—now has a new answer: diamond, graphite, and buckminsterfullerene. Buckminsterfullerene? This fascinating new form of elemental carbon containing C_{60} molecules was first identified by R. E. Smalley of Rice University, H. F. Kroto of the University of Sussex, England, and their collaborators. It has now been synthesized in large quantities using techniques developed by a team of physicists at the University of Arizona.

The structure of the C_{60} molecule resembles a soccer ball. It is an approximately spherical molecule with the carbon atoms arranged at the 60 vertices of 32 interconnecting pentagons (12) and hexagons (20). This molecule gets its name from the work of Buckminster Fuller, who proposed geodesic domes with frameworks similar to the arrangement of the carbon atoms in C_{60}.

Buckminsterfullerene was first synthesized in large quantities in the lab of Donald R. Huffman of the University of Arizona by vaporizing carbon from pure graphite electrodes in an atmosphere of helium gas at a pressure of 100 torr. This process was a team effort with Wolfgang Krätschmer

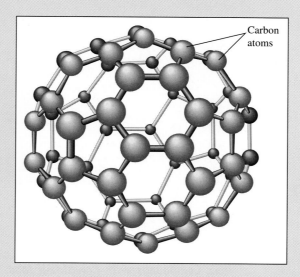

Carbon atoms

The structure of buckminsterfullerene.

of the Max Planck Institute for Nuclear Physics in Germany. The soot that forms in this environment is about 5% C_{60} by mass. The scientists also have found significant quantities of another "fullerene" in this soot that consists of C_{70} molecules. The C_{70} molecule is similar to the spherical C_{60} molecule except that the extra carbon atoms lead to an egg-shaped structure.

The discovery of fullerenes has led to a flurry of activity in labs around the world as chemists rush to characterize this new substance. Already scientists have produced the C_{60}^- and C_{60}^{2-} anions and have prepared C_{60} molecules with various substituents added. It's safe to say that a new branch of chemistry has been founded.

Molecular Model: C_{60}

Various chromium compounds dissolved in water. From left to right: $CrCl_2$, $K_2Cr_2O_7$, $Cr(NO_3)_3$, $CrCl_3$, K_2CrO_4.

Molecular Models: NH_4^+, NO_2^-, NO_3^-, SO_3^{2-}, SO_4^{2-}, HSO_4^-, PO_4^{3-}, HPO_4^{2-}, $H_2PO_4^-$, HCO_3^-, $C_2H_3O_2^-$

Table 2.5 Common Polyatomic Ions

Ion	Name	Ion	Name
Hg_2^{2+}	Mercury(I)	NCS^-	Thiocyanate
NH_4^+	Ammonium	CO_3^{2-}	Carbonate
NO_2^-	Nitrite	HCO_3^-	Hydrogen carbonate
NO_3^-	Nitrate		(bicarbonate is a widely
SO_3^{2-}	Sulfite		used common name)
SO_4^{2-}	Sulfate	ClO^-	Hypochlorite
HSO_4^-	Hydrogen sulfate	ClO_2^-	Chlorite
	(bisulfate is a widely	ClO_3^-	Chlorate
	used common name)	ClO_4^-	Perchlorate
OH^-	Hydroxide	$C_2H_3O_2^-$	Acetate
CN^-	Cyanide	MnO_4^-	Permanganate
PO_4^{3-}	Phosphate	$Cr_2O_7^{2-}$	Dichromate
HPO_4^{2-}	Hydrogen phosphate	CrO_4^{2-}	Chromate
$H_2PO_4^-$	Dihydrogen phosphate	O_2^{2-}	Peroxide
		$C_2O_4^{2-}$	Oxalate

Ionic Compounds with Polyatomic Ions

We have not yet considered ionic compounds that contain polyatomic ions. For example, the compound ammonium nitrate, NH_4NO_3, contains the polyatomic ions NH_4^+ and NO_3^-. Polyatomic ions are assigned special names that *must be memorized* in order to name the compounds containing them. The most important polyatomic ions and their names are listed in Table 2.5.

Polyatomic ion formulas must be memorized.

Note in Table 2.5 that several series of anions contain an atom of a given element and different numbers of oxygen atoms. These anions are called **oxyanions.** When there are two members in such a series, the name of the one with the smaller number of oxygen atoms ends in *-ite* and the name of the one with the larger number ends in *-ate,* for example, sulfite (SO_3^{2-}) and sulfate (SO_4^{2-}). When more than two oxyanions make up a series, *hypo-* (less than) and *per-* (more than) are used as prefixes to name the members of the series with the fewest and the most oxygen atoms, respectively. The best example involves the oxyanions containing chlorine, as shown in Table 2.5.

Sample Exercise 2.6 Naming Compounds Containing Polyatomic Ions

Give the systematic name of each of the following compounds.

a. Na_2SO_4 **b.** KH_2PO_4 **c.** $Fe(NO_3)_3$ **d.** $Mn(OH)_2$

e. Na_2SO_3 **f.** Na_2CO_3 **g.** $NaHCO_3$ **h.** $CsClO_4$

i. $NaOCl$ **j.** Na_2SeO_4 **k.** $KBrO_3$

Solution

Compound	Name	Comment
a. Na_2SO_4	Sodium sulfate	
b. KH_2PO_4	Potassium dihydrogen phosphate	
c. $Fe(NO_3)_3$	Iron(III) nitrate	Transition metal—name must contain a Roman numeral. Fe^{3+} ion balances three NO_3^- ions.
d. $Mn(OH)_2$	Manganese(II) hydroxide	Transition metal—name must contain a Roman numeral. Mn^{2+} ion balances two OH^- ions.
e. Na_2SO_3	Sodium sulfite	
f. Na_2CO_3	Sodium carbonate	
g. $NaHCO_3$	Sodium hydrogen carbonate	Often called sodium bicarbonate.
h. $CsClO_4$	Cesium perchlorate	
i. $NaOCl$	Sodium hypochlorite	
j. Na_2SeO_4	Sodium selenate	Atoms in the same group, like sulfur and selenium, often form similar ions that are named similarly. Thus SeO_4^{2-} is selenate, like SO_4^{2-} (sulfate).
k. $KBrO_3$	Potassium bromate	As above, BrO_3^- is bromate, like ClO_3^- (chlorate).

See Exercises 2.65 and 2.66.

Binary Covalent Compounds (Type III)

Binary covalent compounds are formed between *two nonmetals*. Although these compounds do not contain ions, they are named very similarly to binary ionic compounds.

In *binary covalent compounds,* the element names follow the same rules as for binary ionic compounds.

In the naming of binary covalent compounds, the following rules apply:

1. The first element in the formula is named first, using the full element name.
2. The second element is named as if it were an anion.
3. Prefixes are used to denote the numbers of atoms present. These prefixes are given in Table 2.6.
4. The prefix *mono-* is never used for naming the first element. For example, CO is called carbon monoxide, *not* monocarbon monoxide.

To see how these rules apply, we will now consider the names of the several covalent compounds formed by nitrogen and oxygen:

Compound	Systematic Name	Common Name
N_2O	Dinitrogen monoxide	Nitrous oxide
NO	Nitrogen monoxide	Nitric oxide
NO_2	Nitrogen dioxide	
N_2O_3	Dinitrogen trioxide	
N_2O_4	Dinitrogen tetroxide	
N_2O_5	Dinitrogen pentoxide	

Table 2.6 Prefixes Used to Indicate Number in Chemical Names

Prefix	Number Indicated
mono-	1
di-	2
tri-	3
tetra-	4
penta-	5
hexa-	6
hepta-	7
octa-	8
nona-	9
deca-	10

Notice from the preceding examples that to avoid awkward pronunciations, we often drop the final o or a of the prefix when the element begins with a vowel. For example, N_2O_4 is called dinitrogen tetroxide, *not* dinitrogen tetr*a*oxide, and CO is called carbon monoxide, *not* carbon mon*o*oxide.

Some compounds are always referred to by their common names. The two best examples are water and ammonia. The systematic names for H_2O and NH_3 are never used.

Molecular Models: N_2O, NO, NO_2, N_2O_3, N_2O_4, N_2O_5

Sample Exercise 2.7 Naming Type III Binary Compounds

Name each of the following compounds.

a. PCl_5 **b.** PCl_3 **c.** SF_6 **d.** SO_3 **e.** SO_2 **f.** CO_2

Solution

Compound	Name
a. PCl_5	Phosphorus pentachloride
b. PCl_3	Phosphorus trichloride
c. SF_6	Sulfur hexafluoride
d. SO_3	Sulfur trioxide
e. SO_2	Sulfur dioxide
f. CO_2	Carbon dioxide

The rules for naming binary compounds are summarized in Fig. 2.23. Prefixes to indicate the number of atoms are used only in type III binary compounds (those containing two nonmetals). An overall strategy for naming compounds is in Fig. 2.24.

Sample Exercise 2.8 Naming Various Types of Compounds

Give the systematic name for each of the following compounds.
a. P_4O_{10} **b.** Nb_2O_5 **c.** Li_2O_2 **d.** $Ti(NO_3)_4$

Solution

Compound	Name	Comment
a. P_4O_{10}	Tetraphosphorus decaoxide	Binary covalent compound (type III), so prefixes are used. The *a* in *deca-* is sometimes dropped.

b. Nb_2O_5 — Niobium(V) oxide — Type II binary compound containing Nb^{5+} and O^{2-} ions. Niobium is a transition metal and requires a Roman numeral.

c. Li_2O_2 — Lithium peroxide — Type I binary compound containing the Li^+ and O_2^{2-} (peroxide) ions.

d. $Ti(NO_3)_4$ — Titanium(IV) nitrate — Not a binary compound. Contains the Ti^{4+} and NO_3^- ions. Titanium is a transition metal and requires a Roman numeral.

See Exercise 2.69.

Formulas from Names

So far we have started with the chemical formula of a compound and decided on its systematic name. The reverse process is also important. For example, given the name calcium hydroxide, we can write the formula as $Ca(OH)_2$ because we know that calcium only forms Ca^{2+} ions and that, since hydroxide is OH^-, two of these anions will be required to give a neutral compound. Similarly, the name iron(II) oxide implies the formula FeO, since the Roman numeral II indicates the presence of Fe^{2+}, which is balanced by one oxide ion, O^{2-}.

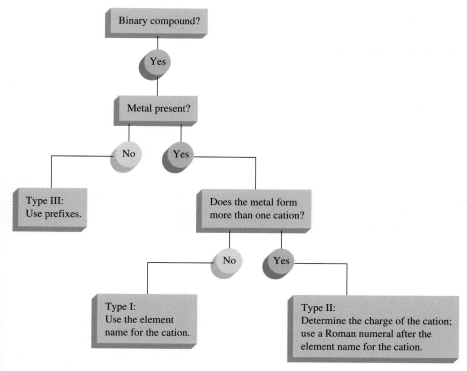

Figure 2.23
A flowchart for naming binary compounds.

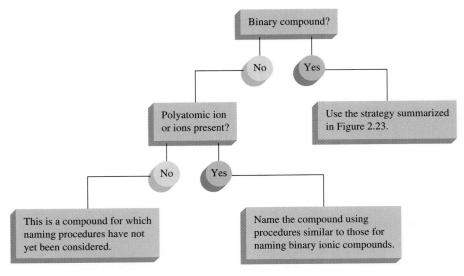

Figure 2.24
Overall strategy for naming chemical compounds.

Sample Exercise 2.9 Writing Compound Formulas from Names

Given the following systematic names, write the formula for each compound.

a. Vanadium(V) fluoride   **b.** Dioxygen difluoride
c. Rubidium peroxide   **d.** Gallium oxide

Solution

Name	Chemical Formula	Comment
a. Vanadium(V) fluoride	VF_5	The compound contains V^{5+} ions and requires five F^- ions for charge balance.
b. Dioxygen difluoride	O_2F_2	The prefix *di-* indicates two of each atom.
c. Rubidium peroxide	Rb_2O_2	Since rubidium is in Group 1A, it forms only $1+$ ions. Thus two Rb^+ ions are needed to balance the $2-$ charge on the peroxide ion (O_2^{2-}).
d. Gallium oxide	Ga_2O_3	Since gallium is in Group 3A, like aluminum, it forms $3+$ ions. Two Ga^{3+} ions are required to balance the charge on three O^{2-} ions.

See Exercises 2.71 and 2.72.

Acids

When dissolved in water, certain molecules produce a solution containing free H^+ ions (protons). These substances, **acids,** will be discussed in detail in Chapters 4, 14, and 15. Here we will simply present the rules for naming acids.

Acids can be recognized by the hydrogen that appears first in the formula.

An acid can be viewed as a molecule with one or more H^+ ions attached to an anion. The rules for naming acids depend on whether or not the anion contains oxygen. If the *anion does not contain oxygen,* the acid is named with the prefix *hydro-* and the suffix *-ic.* For example, when gaseous HCl is dissolved in water, it forms hydrochloric acid. Similarly, HCN and H_2S dissolved in water are called hydrocyanic and hydrosulfuric acids, respectively.

When the *anion contains oxygen,* the acidic name is formed from the root name of the anion with a suffix of *-ic* or *-ous,* depending on the name of the anion.

1. If the anion name ends in *-ate,* the suffix *-ic* is added to the root name. For example, H_2SO_4 contains the sulfate anion (SO_4^{2-}) and is called sulfuric acid; H_3PO_4 contains the phosphate anion (PO_4^{3-}) and is called phosphoric acid; and $HC_2H_3O_2$ contains the acetate ion ($C_2H_3O_2^-$) and is called acetic acid.

2. If the anion has an *-ite* ending, the *-ite* is replaced by *-ous.* For example, H_2SO_3, which contains sulfite (SO_3^{2-}), is named sulfurous acid; and HNO_2, which contains nitrite (NO_2^-), is named nitrous acid.

The application of these rules can be seen in the names of the acids of the oxyanions of chlorine:

Acid	**Anion**	**Name**
$HClO_4$	Perchlor*ate*	Perchlor*ic* acid
$HClO_3$	Chlor*ate*	Chlor*ic* acid
$HClO_2$	Chlor*ite*	Chlor*ous* acid
HClO	Hypochlor*ite*	Hypochlor*ous* acid

The names of the most important acids are given in Tables 2.7 and 2.8. An overall strategy for naming acids is shown in Fig. 2.25.

Table 2.7 Names of Acids* That Do Not Contain Oxygen

Acid	Name
HF	Hydrofluoric acid
HCl	Hydrochloric acid
HBr	Hydrobromic acid
HI	Hydroiodic acid
HCN	Hydrocyanic acid
H_2S	Hydrosulfuric acid

*Note that these acids are aqueous solutions containing these substances.

Table 2.8 Names of Some Oxygen-Containing Acids

Acid	Name
HNO_3	Nitric acid
HNO_2	Nitrous acid
H_2SO_4	Sulfuric acid
H_2SO_3	Sulfurous acid
H_3PO_4	Phosphoric acid
$HC_2H_3O_2$	Acetic acid

Molecular Models: H_2SO_3, H_2SO_4, H_3PO_4, HCl

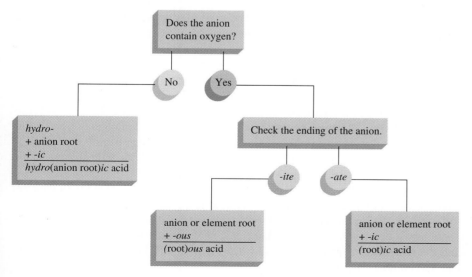

Figure 2.25

A flowchart for naming acids. An acid is best considered as one or more H^+ ions attached to an anion.

Key Terms

For Review

Summary

Three fundamental laws formed the basis for early chemistry: the law of conservation of mass (matter can be neither created nor destroyed), the law of definite proportion (a given compound always contains exactly the same proportion of elements by mass), and the law of multiple proportions (if two elements A and B form a series of compounds, the ratios of the masses of A that combine with 1 gram of B can always be represented by small whole numbers). Dalton accounted for these laws in his atomic theory. He postulated that all elements are composed of atoms; that all atoms of a given element are identical; that chemical compounds are formed when atoms combine; and that the atoms themselves are not changed in a chemical reaction but the way they are grouped (bound together) is changed.

Atoms consist of a dense nucleus containing protons and neutrons, surrounded by electrons that occupy a very large volume relative to the size of the nucleus. Electrons have a relatively small mass (1/1840 of the proton mass) and a negative charge. Protons have a positive charge equal in magnitude (but opposite in sign) to that on the electron. A neutron has virtually the same mass as a proton but no charge.

Isotopes are atoms with the same number of protons (thus constituting the same element) but different numbers of neutrons. That is, isotopes have the same atomic number but different mass numbers (total numbers of neutrons and protons).

Atoms can combine to form molecules by sharing electrons to form covalent bonds. A molecule can be described by a chemical formula showing the numbers and types of atoms involved, by a structural formula (showing which atoms are joined to each other), or by ball-and-stick or space-filling models that show the exact positions of the atoms in space. When an atom loses one or more electrons, it forms a positive ion called a cation. If an atom gains electrons, it becomes a negatively charged anion. The interaction of oppositely charged ions to form an ionic compound is called ionic bonding.

The periodic table arranges the elements in order of increasing atomic number, and elements that have similar chemical properties fall into vertical columns, or groups. Most of the elements are metals, which tend to form cations in ionic compounds with nonmetals. Nonmetals tend to form anions when they react with metals.

Compounds are named using systems of rules. These rules vary depending on the type of compound being named. For binary ionic compounds (those which contain a metal and a nonmetal), the metal is named first, followed by a name derived from the root name of the nonmetal. In a compound (type I) containing a metal that always forms the same cation (sodium always forms Na^+, magnesium always forms Mg^{2+}, and so on), the name of the metal is sufficient. In a compound (type II) that contains a metal that can form more than one cation (iron can form Fe^{2+} and Fe^{3+} and so on), the metal name is followed by a Roman numeral that indicates the cation charge.

Polyatomic ions have special names that must be memorized along with their net charges. In compounds containing polyatomic ions, the cation name is given first, followed by the anion name. For type III binary covalent compounds (those that contain two nonmetals), the first element is named using the entire element name and the second element is named as if it were an anion. Prefixes are used to indicate the numbers of atoms present.

Suggested Reading

1. Isaac Asimov, *A Short Story of Chemistry* (New York: Anchor Books, Doubleday and Co., Inc., 1965).

2. Robert P. Crease and Charles C. Mann, *The Second Creation,* Chapters 1 and 2 (New York: Macmillan Publishing Co., 1986).

3. Enid S. Lipeles, "The chemical contributions of Amadeo Avogadro," *J. Chem. Ed.* **60** (1983): 127.

4. Sir William Roscoe, *John Dalton and the Rise of Modern Chemistry,* 1896.

In-Class Discussion Questions

These questions are designed to be considered by groups of students in class. Often these questions work well for introducing a particular topic in class.

1. Which of the following is true about an individual atom? Explain.
   a. An individual atom should be considered to be a solid.
   b. An individual atom should be considered to be a liquid.
   c. An individual atom should be considered to be a gas.
   d. The state of the atom depends on which element it is.
   e. An individual atom cannot be considered to be a solid, liquid, or gas.
   Justify your choice, and for choices you did not pick, explain what is wrong with them.

2. You have gone back in time and are working with Dalton. He is working on a table of relative masses, and these are his data:

   0.602 g gas *A* reacts with 0.295 g gas *B*
   0.172 g gas *B* reacts with 0.401 g gas *C*
   0.320 g gas *A* reacts with 0.374 g gas *C*

   a. Assuming simplest formulas (*AB, BC,* and *AC*), construct a table of relative masses for Dalton.
   Knowing some history of chemistry, you tell Dalton that if he finds the volumes of the gases at equal temperature and pressure, he need not assume simplest formulas. You collect the following data:

   6 volumes gas *A* + 1 volume gas *B* → 4 volumes product
   1 volume gas *B* + 4 volumes gas *C* → 4 volumes product
   3 volumes gas *A* + 2 volumes gas *C* → 6 volumes product

   b. Write out the simplest balanced equations, and find the actual relative masses of the elements. Explain your reasoning.

3. How would you go about finding the number of "chalk molecules" it takes to write your name on the board? Provide an explanation of all you would need to do and a sample calculation.

4. These questions concern the work of J. J. Thomson.
   a. From Thomson's work, which particles do you think he would feel are most important for the formation of compounds (chemical changes) and why?
   b. Of the remaining two subatomic particles, which do you place second in importance for forming compounds and why?
   c. Propose three models that explain Thomson's findings and evaluate them. To be complete you should include Thomson's findings.

5. Heat is applied to an ice cube in a closed container until only steam is present. Draw a representation of this process, assuming you can see it at an extremely high level of magnification. What happens to the size of the molecules? What happens to the total mass of the sample?

6. You have a chemical in a sealed glass container filled with air. The system has a mass of 250.0 g. The chemical is ignited by means of a magnifying glass focusing sunlight on the reactant. After the chemical is completely burned, what is the mass of the setup? Explain your answer.

7. You take three compounds consisting of two elements and decompose them. In order to determine the relative masses of *X, Y,* and *Z,* you collect and weigh the elements, obtaining the following data:

Elements in Compound	Masses of Elements
X and *Y*	*X* = 0.4 g, *Y* = 4.2 g
Y and *Z*	*Y* = 1.4 g, *Z* = 1.0 g
X and *Y*	*X* = 2.0 g, *Y* = 7.0 g

   a. What are the assumptions in solving this problem?
   b. What are the relative masses of *X, Y,* and *Z*?
   c. What are the chemical formulas of the three compounds?
   d. If you decompose 21 g of compound *XY,* how much of each element is present?

8. The vitamin niacin (nicotinic acid, $C_6H_5NO_2$) can be isolated from a variety of natural sources such as liver, yeast, milk, and whole grain. It also can be synthesized from commercially available materials. Which source of nicotinic acid, from a nutritional view, is best for use in a multivitamin tablet? Why?

9. One of the best indications of a useful theory is that it raises more questions for further experimentation than it originally answered. Does this apply to Dalton's atomic theory? Give examples.

10. Dalton assumed that all atoms of the same element were identical in all their properties. Explain why this assumption is not valid.

11. Evaluate each of the following as an acceptable name for water:
    a. dihydrogen oxide
    b. hydroxide hydride
    c. hydrogen hydroxide
    d. oxygen dihydride

12. Why do we call $Ba(NO_3)_2$ barium nitrate, but we call $Fe(NO_3)_2$ iron(II) nitrate?

13. Why is calcium dichloride not the correct systematic name for $CaCl_2$?

14. The common name for NH_3 is ammonia. What would be the systematic name for NH_3? Support your answer.

A blue question or exercise number indicates that the answer to that question or exercise appears at the back of this book and a solution appears in the *Solutions Guide*.

Questions

15. Use Dalton's atomic theory to account for each of the following.
    a. the law of conservation of mass
    b. the law of definite proportion
    c. the law of multiple proportions

16. What refinements had to be made in Dalton's atomic theory to account for Gay-Lussac's results on the combining volumes of gases?

17. What evidence led to the conclusion that cathode rays had a negative charge?

18. What discoveries were made by J. J. Thomson, Henri Becquerel, and Lord Rutherford? How did Dalton's model of the atom have to be modified to account for these discoveries?

19. What is the distinction between atomic number and mass number? Between mass number and atomic mass?

20. Distinguish between the terms *family* and *period* in connection with the periodic table. For which of these terms is the term *group* also used?

21. When hydrogen is burned in oxygen to form water, the composition of water formed does not depend on the amount of oxygen. Interpret this in terms of the law of definite proportions.

22. The two most reactive families of elements are the halogens and the alkali metals. How do they differ in their reactivities?

Exercises

In this section similar exercises are paired.

Development of the Atomic Theory

23. When mixtures of gaseous H_2 and gaseous Cl_2 react, a product forms that has the same properties regardless of the relative amounts of H_2 and Cl_2 used.

a. How is this result interpreted in terms of the law of definite proportion?

b. When a volume of H_2 reacts with an equal volume of Cl_2 at the same temperature and pressure, what volume of product having the formula HCl is formed?

24. A reaction of 1 liter of chlorine gas (Cl_2) with 3 liters of fluorine gas (F_2) yields 2 liters of a gaseous product. All gas volumes are at the same temperature and pressure. What is the formula of the gaseous product?

25. Several compounds containing only sulfur (S) and fluorine (F) are known. Three of them have the following compositions:
    i. 1.188 g of F for every 1.000 g of S
    ii. 2.375 g of F for every 1.000 g of S
    iii. 3.563 g of F for every 1.000 g of S
    How do these data illustrate the law of multiple proportions?

26. Hydrazine, ammonia, and hydrogen azide all contain only nitrogen and hydrogen. The mass of hydrogen that combines with 1.00 g of nitrogen for each compound is 1.44×10^{-1} g, 2.16×10^{-1} g, and 2.40×10^{-2} g, respectively. Show how these data illustrate the law of multiple proportions.

27. Early tables of atomic weights (masses) were generated by measuring the mass of a substance that reacts with 1.00 g of oxygen. Given the following data and taking the atomic mass of hydrogen as 1.00, generate a table of relative atomic masses for oxygen, sodium, and magnesium.

Element	Mass That Combines with 1.00 g Oxygen	Assumed Formula
Hydrogen	0.126 g	HO
Sodium	2.875 g	NaO
Magnesium	1.500 g	MgO

How do your values compare with those in the periodic table? How do you account for any differences?

28. The mass of beryllium that combines with 1.000 g of oxygen to form beryllium oxide is 0.5633 g. When atomic masses were first being measured, it was thought that the formula of beryllium oxide was Be_2O_3. What would be the atomic mass of beryllium if this were the case? Assume that oxygen has an atomic mass of 16.00.

The Nature of the Atom

29. From the information in this chapter on the mass of the proton, the mass of the electron, and the sizes of the nucleus and the atom, calculate the densities of a hydrogen nucleus and a hydrogen atom.

30. If you wanted to make an accurate scale model of the hydrogen atom and decided that the nucleus would have a diameter of 1 mm, what would be the diameter of the entire model?

31. In an experiment it was found that the total charge on an oil drop was 5.93×10^{-18} C. How many negative charges does the drop contain?

32. A chemist in a galaxy far, far away performed the Millikan oil drop experiment and got the following results for the charges on various drops. Use these data to calculate the charge of the electron in zirkombs.

2.56×10^{-12} zirkombs $\quad$ 7.68×10^{-12} zirkombs
3.84×10^{-12} zirkombs $\quad$ 6.40×10^{-13} zirkombs

33. What are the symbols of the following elements: gold, silver, mercury, potassium, iron, antimony, tungsten?

34. What are the symbols of the following metals: sodium, beryllium, manganese, chromium, uranium?

35. What are the symbols of the following nonmetals: fluorine, chlorine, bromine, sulfur, oxygen, phosphorus?

36. What are the symbols of the following elements: titanium, selenium, plutonium, nitrogen, and silicon?

37. Give the names of the metals that correspond to the following symbols: Sn, Pt, Co, Ni, Mg, Ba, K.

38. Give the names of the nonmetals that correspond to the following symbols: As, I, Xe, He, C, Si.

39. List the noble gas elements. Which of the noble gases has only radioactive isotopes? (This situation is indicated on most periodic tables by parentheses around the mass of the element. See inside front cover.)

40. Which lanthanide element and which transition element have only radioactive isotopes? (See Exercise 39.)

41. In the periodic table, how many elements are found in
    a. the second period?   c. the fourth period?
    b. the third period?   d. Group 5A?

42. In the periodic table, how many elements are found in
    a. Group 2A?   c. the nickel group?
    b. the oxygen family?   d. Group 8A?

43. Give the number of protons and neutrons in the nucleus of each of the following atoms:
    a. $^{238}_{94}$Pu   d. $^{4}_{2}$He
    b. $^{65}_{29}$Cu   e. $^{60}_{27}$Co
    c. $^{52}_{24}$Cr   f. $^{54}_{24}$Cr

44. How many protons and neutrons are contained in the nucleus of each of the following atoms? In an atom of each element, how many electrons are present?
    a. $^{42}_{22}$Ti   c. $^{76}_{32}$Ge   e. $^{75}_{33}$As
    b. $^{64}_{30}$Zn   d. $^{86}_{36}$Kr   f. $^{41}_{19}$K

45. An atom has 9 protons and 10 neutrons in the nucleus. What is its symbol?

46. Write the atomic symbol ($^{A}_{Z}$X) for each of the isotopes described below.
    a. $Z = 8$, number of neutrons = 9
    b. the isotope of chlorine in which $A = 37$

c. $Z = 27$, $A = 60$
d. number of protons = 26, number of neutrons = 31
e. the isotope of I with a mass number of 131
f. $Z = 3$, number of neutrons = 4

47. What is the symbol for an ion with 63 protons, 60 electrons, and 88 neutrons?

48. An ion contains 50 protons, 68 neutrons, and 48 electrons. What is its symbol?

49. What is the symbol of an ion with 16 protons, 18 neutrons, and 18 electrons?

50. What is the symbol for an ion that has 16 protons, 16 neutrons, and 18 electrons?

51. Complete the following table:

Symbol	Number of protons in nucleus	Number of neutrons in nucleus	Number of electrons	Net charge
	33	42		3+
$^{128}_{52}$Te^{2-}			54	
	16	16	16	
	81	123		1+
$^{195}_{78}$Pt				

52. Complete the following table:

Symbol	Number of protons in nucleus	Number of neutrons in nucleus	Number of electrons	Net charge
$^{238}_{92}$U				
	20	20		2+
	23	28	20	
$^{89}_{39}$Y				
	35	44	36	
	15	16		3−

53. Classify the following elements as metals or nonmetals:

Mg $\quad$ Si $\quad$ Rn
Ti $\quad$ Ge $\quad$ Eu
Au $\quad$ B $\quad$ Am
Bi $\quad$ At $\quad$ Br

54. The distinction between metals and nonmetals is really not a clear one. Some elements, called *metalloids*, are intermediate

in their properties. Which elements in Exercise 53 would you reclassify as metalloids? What other elements in the periodic table would you expect to be metalloids?

55. Which of the following sets of elements are all in the same group in the periodic table?
    a. Fe, Ru, Os   **c.** Sn, As, S
    b. Rh, Pd, Ag   **d.** Se, Te, Po

56. Which of the following sets of elements are all in the same group in the periodic table?
    a. N, P, O   **c.** Rb, Sn
    b. C, Si, Ge   **d.** Mg, Ca

57. Consider the elements of Group 4A (the "carbon family"): C, Si, Ge, Sn, and Pb. What is the trend in metallic character as one goes down this group?

58. What is the trend in metallic character going from left to right across a period in the periodic table?

59. Would you expect each of the following atoms to gain or lose electrons when forming ions? What ion is the most likely in each case?
    a. Na   **c.** Ba   **e.** Al
    b. Sr   **d.** I   **f.** S

60. Would you expect each of the following atoms to gain or lose electrons when forming ions? What ion is the most likely in each case?
    a. Ra   **c.** P   **e.** Br
    b. In   **d.** Te   **f.** Rb

Nomenclature

61. Name each of the following compounds:
    a. NaCl   **c.** CaS
    b. Rb_2O **d.** AlI_3

62. Name each of the following compounds:
    a. Hg_2O **c.** CoS
    b. $FeBr_3$ **d.** $TiCl_4$

63. Name each of the following compounds:
    a. CrO_3 **c.** Al_2O_3 **e.** $CaBr_2$
    b. Cr_2O_3 **d.** NaH   **f.** $ZnCl_2$

64. Name each of the following compounds:
    a. CsF   **c.** Ag_2S **e.** TiO_2
    b. Li_3N **d.** MnO_2 **f.** Sr_3P_2

65. Name each of the following compounds:
    a. $KClO_4$ **c.** $Al_2(SO_4)_3$
    b. $Ca_3(PO_4)_2$ **d.** $Pb(NO_3)_2$

66. Name each of the following compounds:
    a. $BaSO_3$ **c.** $KMnO_4$
    b. $NaNO_2$ **d.** $K_2Cr_2O_7$

67. Name each of the following compounds:
    a. NI_3 **c.** SF_2
    b. PCl_3 **d.** N_2F_4

68. Name each of the following compounds:
    a. SO_2 **c.** P_2S_5
    b. ICl_3 **d.** N_2O_4

69. Name each of the following compounds:
    a. CuI   **f.** S_4N_4
    b. CuI_2 **g.** SF_6
    c. CoI_2 **h.** NaOCl
    d. Na_2CO_3 **i.** $BaCrO_4$
    e. $NaHCO_3$ **j.** NH_4NO_3

70. Name each of the following compounds:
    a. $HC_2H_3O_2$ **g.** H_2SO_4
    b. NH_4NO_2 **h.** Sr_3N_2
    c. Co_2S_3 **i.** $Al_2(SO_3)_3$
    d. ICl   **j.** SnO_2
    e. $Pb_3(PO_4)_2$ **k.** Na_2CrO_4
    f. KIO_3 **l.** HClO

71. Write the formula for each of the following compounds:
    a. cesium bromide   **e.** silicon tetrachloride
    b. barium sulfate   **f.** chlorine trifluoride
    c. ammonium chloride   **g.** beryllium oxide
    d. chlorine monoxide   **h.** magnesium fluoride

72. Write the formula for each of the following compounds:
    a. sulfur difluoride
    b. sulfur hexafluoride
    c. sodium dihydrogen phosphate
    d. lithium nitride
    e. chromium(III) carbonate
    f. tin(II) fluoride
    g. ammonium acetate
    h. ammonium hydrogen sulfate
    i. cobalt(III) nitrate
    j. mercury(I) chloride
    k. potassium chlorate
    l. sodium hydride

73. Write the formula for each of the following compounds:
    a. sodium oxide   **g.** lead(IV) sulfide
    b. sodium peroxide   **h.** copper(I) chloride
    c. potassium cyanide   **i.** gallium arsenide
    d. copper(II) nitrate   **j.** cadmium selenide
    e. silicon tetrachloride **k.** zinc sulfide
    f. lead(II) sulfide

74. Write the formula for each of the following compounds:
    a. ammonium hydrogen phosphate
    b. mercury(I) sulfide
    c. silicon dioxide
    d. sodium sulfite
    e. aluminum hydrogen sulfate
    f. nitrogen trichloride
    g. hydrobromic acid
    h. bromous acid
    i. perbromic acid
    j. potassium hydrogen sulfide

k. calcium iodide

l. cesium perchlorate

Additional Exercises

75. Insulin, a complex protein molecule produced by the pancreas in all vertebrates, is a hormone that regulates carbohydrate metabolism. Inability to produce sufficient insulin results in diabetes mellitus. Diabetes is treated by injections of insulin. Given the law of definite proportion, would you expect any differences in chemical activity between human insulin extracted from pancreatic tissue and human insulin produced by genetically engineered bacteria? Explain.

76. For each of the following ions, indicate the total number of protons and electrons in the ion. For the positive ions in the list, predict the formula of the simplest compound formed between each positive ion and the oxide ion. For the negative ions in the list, predict the formula of the simplest compound formed between each negative ion and the aluminum ion.

a. Fe^{2+} **e.** S^{2-}

b. Fe^{3+} **f.** P^{3-}

c. Ba^{2+} **g.** Br^-

d. Cs^+ **h.** N^{3-}

77. The formulas and common names for several substances are given below. Give the systematic names for these substances.

a.	sugar of lead	$Pb(C_2H_3O_2)_2$
b.	blue vitrol	$CuSO_4$
c.	quicklime	CaO
d.	Epsom salts	$MgSO_4$
e.	milk of magnesia	$Mg(OH)_2$
f.	gypsum	$CaSO_4$
g.	laughing gas	N_2O

78. Identify each of the following elements:

a. a member of the same family as oxygen whose most stable ion contains 54 electrons

b. a member of the alkali metal family whose most stable ion contains 36 electrons

c. a noble gas with 18 protons in the nucleus

d. a halogen with 85 protons and 85 electrons

79. How many hydrogen atoms are there in 1 molecule of $C_6H_{12}O_6$? in 2 molecules of C_2H_6? in 3 molecules of CH_4? in 4 molecules of H_3PO_4? in 6 molecules of H_2O?

80. An element's most stable ion forms an ionic compound with bromine, having the formula XBr_2. If the ion of element X has a mass number of 230 and has 86 electrons, what is the identity of the element, and how many neutrons does it have?

81. The designations 1A through 8A used for certain families of the periodic table are helpful for predicting the charges on ions in binary ionic compounds. In these compounds, the metals generally take on a positive charge equal to the family number, while the nonmetals take on a negative charge equal to the family number minus eight. Thus the compound between sodium and chlorine contains Na^+ ions and Cl^- ions and has the formula NaCl. Predict the formula and the name of the binary compound formed from the following pairs of elements.

a. Ca and N   **e.** Ba and I

b. K and O   **f.** Al and Se

c. Rb and F   **g.** Cs and P

d. Mg and S   **h.** In and Br

82. By analogy with phosphorous compounds, name the following: Na_3AsO_4, H_3AsO_4, $Mg_3(SbO_4)_2$.

Challenge Problems

83. The elements in one of the groups in the periodic table are often called the **coinage metals.** Identify the elements in this group based on your own experience.

84. A combustion reaction involves the reaction of a substance with oxygen gas. The complete combustion of any hydrocarbon (binary compound of carbon and hydrogen) produces carbon dioxide and water as the only products. Octane is a hydrocarbon that is found in gasoline. Complete combustion of octane produces 8 liters of carbon dioxide for every 9 liters of water vapor (both measured at the same temperature and pressure). What is the ratio of carbon atoms to hydrogen atoms in a molecule of octane?

85. Two elements, R and Q, combine to form two binary compounds. In the first compound, 14.0 g of R combines with 3.00 g of Q. In the second compound, 7.00 g of R combines with 4.50 g of Q. Show that these data are in accord with the law of multiple proportions. If the formula of the second compound is RQ, what is the formula of the first compound?

86. The early alchemists used to do an experiment in which water was boiled for several days in a sealed glass container. Eventually, some solid residue would appear in the bottom of the flask, which was interpreted to mean that some of the water in the flask had been converted into "earth." When Lavoisier repeated this experiment, he found that the water weighed the same before and after heating and the mass of the flask plus the solid residue equaled the original mass of the flask. Were the alchemists correct? Explain what really happened. (This experiment is described in the article by A. F. Scott in *Scientific American,* January 1984.)

87. Each of the statements given below is true, but Dalton might have had trouble explaining some of them with his atomic theory. Give explanations for the following statements.

a. Ethyl alcohol and dimethyl ether have the same composition by mass (52% carbon, 13% hydrogen, and 35% oxygen), yet the two have different melting points, boiling points, and solubilities in water.

b. Burning wood leaves an ash that is only a small fraction of the mass of the original wood.

c. Atoms can be broken down into smaller particles.

d. One sample of lithium hydride is 87.4% lithium by mass, while another sample of lithium hydride is 74.9% lithium by mass. However, the two samples have the same properties.

CHAPTER 3

Stoichiometry

Contents

Chemical reactions have a profound effect on our lives. There are many examples: Food is converted to energy in the human body; nitrogen and hydrogen are combined to form ammonia, which is used as a fertilizer; fuels and plastics are produced from petroleum; the starch in plants is synthesized from carbon dioxide and water using energy from sunlight; human insulin is produced in laboratories by bacteria; cancer is induced in humans by substances from our environment; and so on, in a seemingly endless list. The central activity of chemistry is to understand chemical changes such as these, and the study of reactions occupies a central place in this book. We will examine why reactions occur, how fast they occur, and the specific pathways they follow.

In this chapter we will consider the quantities of materials consumed and produced in chemical reactions. This area of study is called **chemical stoichiometry** (pronounced stoy·kē·om'·etry). To understand chemical stoichiometry, you must first understand the concept of relative atomic masses.

The violent chemical reaction of bromine and phosphorus.

3.1 Atomic Masses

As we saw in Chapter 2, the first quantitative information about atomic masses came from the work of Dalton, Gay-Lussac, Lavoisier, Avogadro, and Berzelius. By observing the proportions in which elements combine to form various compounds, nineteenth-century chemists calculated relative atomic masses. The modern system of atomic masses, instituted in 1961, is based on ^{12}C ("carbon twelve") as the standard. In this system, ^{12}C *is assigned a mass of exactly 12 atomic mass units* (amu), and the masses of all other atoms are given relative to this standard.

The most accurate method currently available for comparing the masses of atoms involves the use of the **mass spectrometer.** In this instrument, diagramed in Fig. 3.1, atoms or molecules are passed into a beam of high-speed electrons, which knock electrons off the atoms or molecules being analyzed and change them into positive ions. An applied electric field then accelerates these ions into a magnetic field. Because an accelerating ion produces its own magnetic field, an interaction with the applied magnetic field occurs, which tends to change the path of the ion. The amount of path deflection for each ion depends on its mass—the most massive ions are deflected the smallest amount—which causes the ions to separate, as shown in Fig. 3.1. A comparison of the positions where the ions hit the detector plate gives very accurate values of their relative masses. For example, when ^{12}C and ^{13}C are analyzed in a mass spectrometer, the ratio of their masses is found to be

$$\frac{\text{Mass } ^{13}C}{\text{Mass } ^{12}C} = 1.0836129$$

Since the atomic mass unit is defined such that the mass of ^{12}C is *exactly* 12 atomic mass units, then on this same scale,

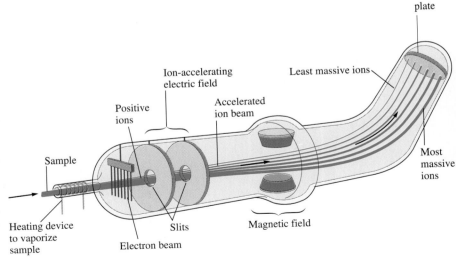

Figure 3.1

(left) A scientist injecting a sample into a mass spectrometer. (above) Schematic diagram of a mass spectrometer.

$$\text{Mass of } ^{13}\text{C} = (1.0836129)(12 \text{ amu}) = 13.003355 \text{ amu}$$

↑
Exact number
by definition

The masses of other atoms can be determined in a similar fashion.

The mass for each element is given in the table inside the front cover of this text. This value, even though it is actually a mass, is (for historical reasons) sometimes called the *atomic weight* for each element.

Look at the value of the atomic mass of carbon given in this table. You might expect to see 12, since we said the system of atomic masses is based on ^{12}C. However, the number given for carbon is not 12 but 12.01. Why? The reason for this apparent discrepancy is that the carbon found on earth (natural carbon) is a mixture of the isotopes ^{12}C, ^{13}C, and ^{14}C. All three isotopes have six protons, but they have six, seven, and eight neutrons, respectively. Because natural carbon is a mixture of isotopes, the atomic mass we use for carbon is an *average value* reflecting the average of the isotopes composing it.

The average atomic mass for carbon is computed as follows: It is known that natural carbon is composed of 98.89% ^{12}C atoms and 1.11% ^{13}C atoms. The amount of ^{14}C is negligibly small at this level of precision. Using the masses of ^{12}C (exactly 12 amu) and ^{13}C (13.003355 amu), we can calculate the average atomic mass for natural carbon as follows:

98.89% of 12 amu + 1.11% of 13.0034 amu =
$$(0.9889)(12 \text{ amu}) + (0.0111)(13.0034 \text{ amu}) = 12.01 \text{ amu}$$

This average atomic mass traditionally has been called the *atomic weight* of carbon. In this text we will call the average mass for an element the **average atomic mass** or, simply, the *atomic mass* for that element.

Even though natural carbon does not contain a single atom with mass 12.01, for stoichiometric purposes, we can consider carbon to be composed of only one type of atom with a mass of 12.01. This enables us to count atoms of natural carbon by weighing a sample of carbon.

To make sure that the idea of counting objects by weighing them is clear, consider the following situation. Suppose you work in a hardware store and someone comes in and requests 600 quarter-inch hex nuts. You could count out the nuts, but this would be a slow process. You have a scale available, and you realize that weighing out the nuts would be a much faster means of counting them. What information do you need to count the hex nuts by weighing them? The answer is *the average mass*. To determine the average mass of the nuts, you count out a sample of 10 and weigh them. Suppose the mass of the 10 nuts is 105 g. This result means the average mass of a nut is

$$\frac{105 \text{ g}}{10 \text{ nuts}} = 10.5 \text{ g/nut}$$

Now what size sample will contain 600 hex nuts? It's just

$$600 \text{ nuts} \times \frac{10.5 \text{ g}}{\text{nut}} = 6300 \text{ g} = 6.30 \text{ kg}$$

Therefore, you weigh out a sample of 6.30 kg of the hex nuts, put them in a bag, and assure the customer that the bag contains 600 hex nuts as requested.

Most elements occur in nature as mixtures of isotopes; thus atomic masses are usually average values.

It is much easier to weigh out 600 hex nuts than count them one by one.

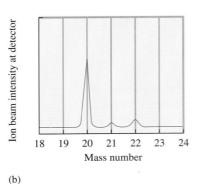

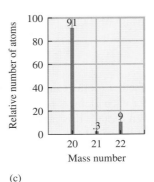

(b)

(c)

Figure 3.2

(a) Neon gas glowing in a discharge tube. The relative intensities of the signals recorded when natural neon is injected into a mass spectrometer, represented in terms (b) "peaks" and (c) a bar graph. The relative areas of the peaks are 0.9092 (^{20}Ne), 0.00257 (^{21}Ne), and 0.0882 (^{22}Ne); natural neon is therefore 90.92% ^{20}Ne, 0.257% ^{21}Ne, and 8.82% ^{22}Ne.

(a)

Notice that counting by weighing works if you know the *average* mass of the units being counted. In the preceding example, it's possible that not one of the hex nuts had a mass of exactly 10.5 g. All that matters is that the average mass is 10.5 g.

Counting by weighing works just the same for atoms as for hex nuts. For natural carbon with an average mass of 12.01 atomic mass units, to obtain 1000 atoms would require weighing out 12,010 atomic mass units of natural carbon (a mixture of ^{12}C and ^{13}C).

As in the case of carbon, the mass for each element listed in the table inside the front cover of the text is an average value based on the isotopic composition of the naturally occurring element. For instance, the mass listed for hydrogen (1.008) is the average mass for natural hydrogen, which is a mixture of ^{1}H and ^{2}H (deuterium). *No* atom of hydrogen actually has the mass 1.008.

In addition to being useful for determining accurate mass values for individual atoms, the mass spectrometer is also used to determine the isotopic composition of a natural element. For example, when a sample of natural neon is injected into a mass spectrometer, the mass spectrum shown in Fig. 3.2 is obtained. The areas of the "peaks" or the heights of the bars indicate the relative abundances of $^{22}_{10}$Ne, $^{21}_{10}$Ne, and $^{22}_{10}$Ne atoms.

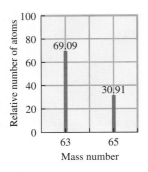

Figure 3.3

Mass spectrum of natural copper.

Sample Exercise 3.1 *The Average Mass of an Element*

When a sample of natural copper is vaporized and injected into a mass spectrometer, the results shown in Fig. 3.3 are obtained. Use these data to compute the average mass of natural copper. (The mass values for ^{63}Cu and ^{65}Cu are 62.93 amu and 64.93 amu, respectively.)

Solution

As shown by the graph, of every 100 atoms of natural copper, 69.09 are ^{63}Cu and 30.91 are ^{65}Cu. Thus the mass of 100 atoms of natural copper is

$$(69.09 \text{ atoms})\left(62.93 \frac{\text{amu}}{\text{atom}}\right) + (30.91 \text{ atoms})\left(64.93 \frac{\text{amu}}{\text{atom}}\right) = 6355 \text{ amu}$$

The *average mass* of a copper atom is

$$\frac{6355 \text{ amu}}{100 \text{ atoms}} = 63.55 \text{ amu/atom}$$

This mass value is used in doing calculations involving the reactions of copper and is the value given in the table inside the front cover of this book.

See Exercises 3.21 through 3.24.

3.2 *The Mole*

Because samples of matter typically contain so many atoms, a unit of measure called the *mole* has been established for use in counting atoms. For our purposes, it is most convenient to define the **mole** (abbreviated mol) as *the number equal to the number of carbon atoms in exactly 12 grams of pure ^{12}C*. Techniques such as mass spectrometry, which count atoms very precisely, have been used to determine this number as 6.02214×10^{23} (6.022×10^{23} will be sufficient for our purposes). This number is called **Avogadro's number** to honor his contributions to chemistry. *One mole of something consists of 6.022×10^{23} units of that substance.* Just as a dozen eggs is 12 eggs, a mole of eggs is 6.022×10^{23} eggs.

The magnitude of the number 6.022×10^{23} is very difficult to imagine. To give you some idea, 1 mole of seconds represents a span of time 4 million times as long as the earth has already existed, and 1 mole of marbles is enough to cover the entire earth to a depth of 50 miles! However, since atoms are so tiny, a mole of atoms or molecules is a perfectly manageable quantity to use in a reaction (see Fig. 3.4).

The SI definition of the mole is the amount of a substance that contains as many entities as there are in exactly 12 g of carbon-12.

Avogadro's number is 6.022×10^{23}. One mole of anything is 6.022×10^{23} units of that substance.

Figure 3.4

Proceeding clockwise from the top, samples containing one mole each of copper, aluminum, iron, sulfur, iodine, and (in the center) mercury.

Table 3.1 Comparison of 1-Mole Samples of Various Elements		
Element	*Number of Atoms Present*	*Mass of Sample (g)*
Aluminum	6.022×10^{23}	26.98
Copper	6.022×10^{23}	63.55
Iron	6.022×10^{23}	55.85
Sulfur	6.022×10^{23}	32.07
Iodine	6.022×10^{23}	126.9
Mercury	6.022×10^{23}	200.6

How do we use the mole in chemical calculations? Recall that Avogadro's number is defined as the number of atoms in exactly 12 grams of ^{12}C. This means that 12 grams of ^{12}C contain 6.022×10^{23} atoms. It also means that a 12.01-gram sample of natural carbon contains 6.022×10^{23} atoms (a mixture of ^{12}C, ^{13}C, and ^{14}C atoms, with an average atomic mass of 12.01). Since the ratio of the masses of the samples (12 g/12.01 g) is the same as the ratio of the masses of the individual components (12 amu/12.01 amu), the two samples contain the *same number* of atoms (6.022×10^{23}).

To be sure this point is clear, think of oranges with an average mass of 0.5 pound each and grapefruit with an average mass of 1.0 pound each. Any two sacks for which the sack of grapefruit weighs twice as much as the sack of oranges will contain the same number of pieces of fruit. The same idea extends to atoms. Compare natural carbon (average mass of 12.01) and natural helium (average mass of 4.003). A sample of 12.01 grams of natural carbon contains the same number of atoms as 4.003 grams of natural helium. Both samples contain 1 mole of atoms (6.022×10^{23}). Table 3.1 gives more examples that illustrate this basic idea.

Thus the mole is defined such that a sample of a natural element with a mass equal to the element's atomic mass expressed in grams contains 1 mole of atoms. This definition also fixes the relationship between the atomic mass unit and the gram. Since 6.022×10^{23} atoms of carbon (each with a mass of 12 amu) have a mass of 12 g, then

> The mass of 1 mole of an element is equal to its atomic mass in grams.

$$(6.022 \times 10^{23} \text{ atoms})\left(\frac{12 \text{ amu}}{\text{atom}}\right) = 12 \text{ g}$$

and

$$6.022 \times 10^{23} \text{ amu} = 1 \text{ g}$$

$\uparrow$
Exact
number

This relationship can be used to derive the unit factor needed to convert between atomic mass units and grams.

Sample Exercise 3.2 Determining the Mass of a Sample of Atoms

Americium is an element that does not occur naturally. It can be made in very small amounts in a device known as a *particle accelerator.* Compute the mass in grams of a sample of americium containing six atoms.

Solution

From the table inside the front cover of the text, we note that one americium atom has a mass of 243 amu. Thus the mass of six atoms is

$$6 \text{ atoms} \times 243 \frac{\text{amu}}{\text{atom}} = 1.46 \times 10^3 \text{ amu}$$

Using the relationship

$$6.022 \times 10^{23} \text{ amu} = 1 \text{ g}$$

we write the conversion factor for converting atomic mass units to grams:

$$\frac{1 \text{ g}}{6.022 \times 10^{23} \text{ amu}}$$

The mass of six americium atoms in grams is

$$1.46 \times 10^3 \text{ amu} \times \frac{1 \text{ g}}{6.022 \times 10^{23} \text{ amu}} = 2.42 \times 10^{-21} \text{ g}$$

See Exercise 3.29.

To do chemical calculations, you must understand what the mole means and how to determine the number of moles in a given mass of a substance. These procedures are illustrated in Sample Exercises 3.3 and 3.4.

CHEMICAL IMPACT

Elemental Analysis Catches Elephant Poachers

IN AN EFFORT to combat the poaching of elephants by controlling illegal exports of ivory, scientists are now using the isotopic composition of ivory trinkets and elephant tusks to identify the region of Africa where the elephant lived. Using a mass spectrometer, scientists analyze the ivory for the relative amounts of ^{12}C, ^{13}C, ^{14}N, ^{15}N, ^{86}Sr, and ^{87}Sr to determine the diet of the elephant and thus its place of origin. For example, because grasses use a different photosynthetic pathway to produce glucose than do trees, grasses have a slightly different $^{13}C/^{12}C$ ratio from that of trees. They have different ratios because each time a carbon atom is added in going from simpler to more complex compounds, the more massive ^{13}C is disfavored relative to ^{12}C because it reacts more slowly. Because trees use more steps to build up glucose, they end up with a smaller $^{13}C/^{12}C$ ratio in their leaves relative to grasses, and this difference is then reflected in the tissues of elephants. Thus scientists can tell whether a particular tusk came from a savanna-dwelling elephant (grass-eating) or from a tree-browsing elephant.

Similarly, because the ratios of $^{15}N/^{14}N$ and $^{87}Sr/^{86}Sr$ in elephant tusks also vary depending on the region of Africa the elephant inhabits, they also can be used to trace the elephant's origin. In fact, using these techniques, scientists have reported being able to discriminate between elephants living only about 100 miles apart.

There is now international concern about the dwindling elephant populations in Africa—their numbers have decreased by 40% over the past decade. This concern has led to bans in the export of ivory from many countries in Africa. However, a few nations still allow ivory to be exported. Thus, to enforce the trade restrictions, the origin of a given piece of ivory must be established. It is hoped that the "isotope signature" of the ivory can be used for this purpose.

(top) Pure aluminum. (bottom) Aluminum alloys are used for many high-quality bicycle components, such as this chain wheel.

Sample Exercise 3.3 *Determining Moles of Atoms*

Aluminum (Al) is a metal with a high strength-to-mass ratio and a high resistance to corrosion; thus it is often used for structural purposes. Compute both the number of moles of atoms and the number of atoms in a 10.0-g sample of aluminum.

Solution

The mass of 1 mole (6.022×10^{23} atoms) of aluminum is 26.98 g. The sample we are considering has a mass of 10.0 g. Since the mass is less than 26.98 g, this sample contains less than 1 mole of aluminum atoms. We can calculate the number of moles of aluminum atoms in 10.0 g as follows:

$$10.0 \text{ g Al} \times \frac{1 \text{ mol Al}}{26.98 \text{ g Al}} = 0.371 \text{ mol Al atoms}$$

The number of atoms in 10.0 g (0.371 mol) of aluminum is

$$0.371 \text{ mol Al} \times \frac{6.022 \times 10^{23} \text{ atoms}}{1 \text{ mol Al}} = 2.23 \times 10^{23} \text{ atoms}$$

See Exercise 3.30.

Sample Exercise 3.4 *Calculating Numbers of Atoms*

A silicon chip used in an integrated circuit of a microcomputer has a mass of 5.68 mg. How many silicon (Si) atoms are present in the chip?

Solution

The strategy for doing this problem is to convert from milligrams of silicon to grams of silicon, then to moles of silicon, and finally to atoms of silicon:

$$5.68 \text{ mg Si} \times \frac{1 \text{ g Si}}{1000 \text{ mg Si}} = 5.68 \times 10^{-3} \text{ g Si}$$

$$5.68 \times 10^{-3} \text{ g Si} \times \frac{1 \text{ mol Si}}{28.09 \text{ g Si}} = 2.02 \times 10^{-4} \text{ mol Si}$$

$$2.02 \times 10^{-4} \text{ mol Si} \times \frac{6.022 \times 10^{23} \text{ atoms}}{1 \text{ mol Si}} = 1.22 \times 10^{20} \text{ atoms}$$

See Exercise 3.31.

Always check to see if your answer is sensible.

It always makes sense to think about whether your answer is reasonable as you do a calculation. In Sample Exercise 3.4, 5.68 mg of silicon is clearly much less than 1 mol of silicon (which has a mass of 28.09 g), so the final answer of 1.22×10^{20} atoms (compared with 6.022×10^{23} atoms) is at least in the right direction. Paying careful attention to units and making sure the answer is reasonable can help you detect an inverted conversion factor or a number that was incorrectly entered in your calculator.

Sample Exercise 3.5 *Calculating the Number of Moles and Mass*

Cobalt (Co) is a metal that is added to steel to improve its resistance to corrosion. Calculate both the number of moles in a sample of cobalt containing 5.00×10^{20} atoms and the mass of the sample.

Solution

Note that the sample of 5.00×10^{20} atoms of cobalt is less than 1 mole (6.022×10^{23} atoms) of cobalt. What fraction of a mole it represents can be determined as follows:

$$5.00 \times 10^{20} \text{ atoms Co} \times \frac{1 \text{ mol Co}}{6.022 \times 10^{23} \text{ atoms Co}} = 8.30 \times 10^{-4} \text{ mol Co}$$

Since the mass of 1 mole of cobalt atoms is 58.93 g, the mass of 5.00×10^{20} atoms can be determined as follows:

$$8.30 \times 10^{-4} \text{ mol Co} \times \frac{58.93 \text{ g Co}}{1 \text{ mol Co}} = 4.89 \times 10^{-2} \text{ g Co}$$

See Exercise 3.32.

3.3 Molar Mass

A chemical compound is, ultimately, a collection of atoms. For example, methane (the major component of natural gas) consists of molecules that each contain one carbon and four hydrogen atoms (CH_4). How can we calculate the mass of 1 mole of methane; that is, what is the mass of 6.022×10^{23} CH_4 molecules? Since each CH_4 molecule contains one carbon atom and four hydrogen atoms, 1 mole of CH_4 molecules contains 1 mole of carbon atoms and 4 moles of hydrogen atoms. The mass of 1 mole of methane can be found by summing the masses of carbon and hydrogen present:

Mass of 1 mol C   =   12.01 g
Mass of 4 mol H   = 4 × 1.008 g
Mass of 1 mol CH_4 =   16.04 g

Molecular Model: CH_4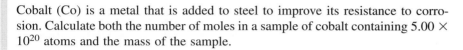

Note that in this case, the term 12.01 limits the number of significant figures.

Because 16.04 g represents the mass of 1 mole of methane molecules, it makes sense to call it the *molar mass* for methane. Thus the **molar mass** of a substance is *the mass in grams of one mole of the compound.* Traditionally, the term *molecular weight* has been used for this quantity. However, we will use molar mass exclusively in this text. The molar mass of a known substance is obtained by summing the masses of the component atoms as we did for methane.

A substance's molar mass is the mass in grams of 1 mole of the substance.

CHEMICAL IMPACT

Measuring the Masses of Large Molecules, or Making Elephants Fly

WHEN A CHEMIST produces a new molecule, one crucial property for making a positive identification is the molecule's mass. There are many ways to determine the molar mass of a compound, but one of the fastest and most accurate methods involves mass spectrometry. This method requires that the substance be put into the gas phase and ionized. The deflection that the resulting ion exhibits as it is accelerated through a magnetic field can be used to obtain a very precise value of its mass. One drawback of this method is that it is difficult to use with large molecules because they are difficult to vaporize. That is, substances that contain large molecules typically have very high boiling points, and these molecules are often damaged when they are vaporized at such high temperatures. A case in point

involves proteins, an extremely important class of large biologic molecules that are quite fragile at high temperatures. Typical methods used to obtain the masses of protein molecules are slow and tedious.

Mass spectrometry has not been used previously to obtain protein masses because proteins decompose at the temperatures necessary to vaporize them. However, a new technique called *matrix-assisted laser desorption* has been developed that allows mass spectrometric determination of protein molar masses. In this technique, the large "target" molecule is embedded in a matrix of smaller molecules. The matrix is then placed in a mass spectrometer and blasted with a laser beam, which causes its disintegration. Disintegration of the matrix frees the

large target molecule, which is then swept into the mass spectrometer. One researcher involved in this project likened this method to an elephant on top of a tall building: "The elephant must fly if the building is suddenly turned into fine grains of sand."

This technique allows scientists to determine the mass of huge molecules. So far researchers have measured proteins with masses up to 350,000 daltons (1 dalton is the mass of a hydrogen atom). This method, which makes mass spectrometry a routine tool for the determination of protein masses, probably will be extended to even larger molecules such as DNA and could be a revolutionary development in the characterization of biomolecules.

Sample Exercise 3.6 *Calculating Molar Mass I*

Juglone, a dye known for centuries, is produced from the husks of black walnuts. It is also a natural herbicide (weed killer) that kills off competitive plants around the black walnut tree but does not affect grass and other noncompetitive plants. The formula for juglone is $C_{10}H_6O_3$.

a. Calculate the molar mass of juglone.
b. A sample of 1.56×10^{-2} g of pure juglone was extracted from black walnut husks. How many moles of juglone does this sample represent?

Solution

a. The molar mass is obtained by summing the masses of the component atoms. In 1 mole of juglone there are 10 moles of carbon atoms, 6 moles of hydrogen atoms, and 3 moles of oxygen atoms:

$$
\begin{aligned}
10\ \text{C:} &\quad 10 \times 12.01\ \text{g} &= 120.1\ \text{g} \\
6\ \text{H:} &\quad 6 \times 1.008\ \text{g} &= 6.048\ \text{g} \\
3\ \text{O:} &\quad 3 \times 16.00\ \text{g} &= \underline{48.00\ \text{g}} \\
\text{Mass of 1 mol } C_{10}H_6O_3 &= 174.1\ \text{g}
\end{aligned}
$$

The mass of 1 mole of juglone is 174.1 g, which is the molar mass.

b. The mass of 1 mole of this compound is 174.1 g; thus 1.56×10^{-2} g is much less than a mole. The exact fraction of a mole can be determined as follows:

$$1.56 \times 10^{-2} \text{ g juglone} \times \frac{1 \text{ mol juglone}}{174.1 \text{ g juglone}} = 8.96 \times 10^{-5} \text{ mol juglone}$$

See Exercises 3.35 through 3.38.

Sample Exercise 3.7 *Calculating Molar Mass II*

Calcium carbonate ($CaCO_3$), also called *calcite,* is the principal mineral found in limestone, marble, chalk, pearls, and the shells of marine animals such as clams.

a. Calculate the molar mass of calcium carbonate.
b. A certain sample of calcium carbonate contains 4.86 moles. What is the mass in grams of this sample? What is the mass of the CO_3^{2-} ions present?

Solution

a. Calcium carbonate is an ionic compound composed of Ca^{2+} and CO_3^{2-} ions. In 1 mole of calcium carbonate there are 1 mole of Ca^{2+} ions and 1 mole of CO_3^{2-} ions. The molar mass is calculated by summing the masses of the components:

$$
\begin{aligned}
&1 \ Ca^{2+}: &1 \times 40.08 \text{ g} &= \ \ 40.08 \text{ g} \\
&1 \ CO_3^{2-}: \\
&1 \ C: &1 \times 12.01 \text{ g} &= \ \ 12.01 \text{ g} \\
&3 \ O: &3 \times 16.00 \text{ g} &= \ \ \underline{48.00 \text{ g}} \\
&\text{Mass of 1 mol } CaCO_3 &&= 100.09 \text{ g}
\end{aligned}
$$

Thus the mass of 1 mole of $CaCO_3$ (1 mol Ca^{2+} plus 1 mol CO_3^{2-}) is 100.09 g. This is the molar mass.

b. The mass of 1 mole of $CaCO_3$ is 100.09 g. The sample contains nearly 5 moles, or close to 500 g. The exact amount is determined as follows:

$$4.86 \text{ mol } CaCO_3 \times \frac{100.09 \text{ g } CaCO_3}{1 \text{ mol } CaCO_3} = 486 \text{ g } CaCO_3$$

To find the mass of carbonate ions (CO_3^{2-}) present in this sample, we must realize that 4.86 moles of $CaCO_3$ contains 4.86 moles of Ca^{2+} ions and 4.86 moles of CO_3^{2-} ions. The mass of 1 mole of CO_3^{2-} ions is

$$
\begin{aligned}
&1 \ C: &1 \times 12.01 &= 12.01 \text{ g} \\
&3 \ O: &3 \times 16.00 &= \underline{48.00 \text{ g}} \\
&\text{Mass of 1 mol } CO_3^{2-} &&= 60.01 \text{ g}
\end{aligned}
$$

Thus the mass of 4.86 moles of CO_3^{2-} ions is

$$4.86 \text{ mol } CO_3^{2-} \times \frac{60.01 \text{ g } CO_3^{2-}}{1 \text{ mol } CO_3^{2-}} = 292 \text{ g } CO_3^{2-}$$

See Exercises 3.39 through 3.42.

Isopentyl acetate is released when a bee stings.

Sample Exercise 3.8 *Molar Mass and Numbers of Molecules*

Isopentyl acetate ($C_7H_{14}O_2$), the compound responsible for the scent of bananas, can be produced commercially. Interestingly, bees release about 1 μg (1×10^{-6} g) of this compound when they sting. The resulting scent attracts other bees to join the attack. How many molecules of isopentyl acetate are released in a typical bee sting? How many atoms of carbon are present?

Solution

Since we are given a mass of isopentyl acetate and want to find the number of molecules, we must first compute the molar mass:

$$7 \text{ mol C} \times 12.01 \frac{\text{g}}{\text{mol}} = 84.07 \text{ g C}$$

$$14 \text{ mol H} \times 1.008 \frac{\text{g}}{\text{mol}} = 14.11 \text{ g H}$$

$$2 \text{ mol O} \times 16.00 \frac{\text{g}}{\text{mol}} = \frac{32.00 \text{ g O}}{130.18 \text{ g}}$$

This means that 1 mole of isopentyl acetate (6.022×10^{23} molecules) has a mass of 130.18 g.

To find the number of molecules released in a sting, we must first determine the number of moles of isopentyl acetate in 1×10^{-6} g:

$$1 \times 10^{-6} \text{ g } C_7H_{14}O_2 \times \frac{1 \text{ mol } C_7H_{14}O_2}{130.18 \text{ g } C_7H_{14}O_2} = 8 \times 10^{-9} \text{ mol } C_7H_{14}O_2$$

Since 1 mole is 6.022×10^{23} units, we can determine the number of molecules:

$$8 \times 10^{-9} \text{ mol } C_7H_{14}O_2 \times \frac{6.022 \times 10^{23} \text{ molecules}}{1 \text{ mol } C_7H_{14}O_2} = 5 \times 10^{15} \text{ molecules}$$

To determine the number of carbon atoms present, we must multiply the number of molecules by 7, since each molecule of isopentyl acetate contains seven carbon atoms:

$$5 \times 10^{15} \text{ molecules} \times \frac{7 \text{ carbon atoms}}{\text{molecule}} = 4 \times 10^{16} \text{ carbon atoms}$$

NOTE:

In keeping with our practice of always showing the correct number of significant figures, we have rounded after each step. However, if extra digits are carried throughout this problem, the final answer rounds to 3×10^{16}.

See Exercises 3.43 through 3.48.

To show the correct number of significant figures in each calculation, we round after each step. In your calculations, always carry extra significant figures through to the end; then round.

3.4 Percent Composition of Compounds

There are two common ways of describing the composition of a compound: in terms of the numbers of its constituent atoms and in terms of the percentages (by mass) of its elements. We can obtain the mass percents of the elements from the formula of the compound by comparing the mass of each element present in 1 mole of the compound to the total mass of 1 mole of the compound.

For example, for ethanol, which has the formula C_2H_5OH, the mass of each element present and the molar mass are obtained as follows:

Molecular Model: C_2H_5OH

$$\text{Mass of C} = 2\ \text{mol} \times 12.01\frac{\text{g}}{\text{mol}} = 24.02\ \text{g}$$

$$\text{Mass of H} = 6\ \text{mol} \times 1.008\frac{\text{g}}{\text{mol}} = 6.048\ \text{g}$$

$$\text{Mass of O} = 1\ \text{mol} \times 16.00\frac{\text{g}}{\text{mol}} = \underline{16.00\ \text{g}}$$

$$\text{Mass of 1 mol } C_2H_5OH = 46.07\ \text{g}$$

The **mass percent** (often called the *weight percent*) of carbon in ethanol can be computed by comparing the mass of carbon in 1 mole of ethanol to the total mass of 1 mole of ethanol and multiplying the result by 100:

$$\text{Mass percent of C} = \frac{\text{mass of C in 1 mol } C_2H_5OH}{\text{mass of 1 mol } C_2H_5OH} \times 100\%$$

$$= \frac{24.02\ \text{g}}{46.07\ \text{g}} \times 100\% = 52.14\%$$

The mass percents of hydrogen and oxygen in ethanol are obtained in a similar manner:

$$\text{Mass percent of H} = \frac{\text{mass of H in 1 mol } C_2H_5OH}{\text{mass of 1 mol } C_2H_5OH} \times 100\%$$

$$= \frac{6.048\ \text{g}}{46.07\ \text{g}} \times 100\% = 13.13\%$$

$$\text{Mass percent of O} = \frac{\text{mass of O in 1 mol } C_2H_5OH}{\text{mass of 1 mol } C_2H_5OH} \times 100\%$$

$$= \frac{16.00\ \text{g}}{46.07\ \text{g}} \times 100\% = 34.73\%$$

Notice that the percentages add up to 100.00%; this provides a check that the calculations are correct.

Sample Exercise 3.9 *Calculating Mass Percent I*

Carvone is a substance that occurs in two forms having different arrangements of the atoms but the same molecular formula ($C_{10}H_{14}O$) and mass. One type of carvone gives caraway seeds their characteristic smell, and the other type is responsible for the smell of spearmint oil. Compute the mass percent of each element in carvone.

Solution

The masses of the elements in 1 mole of carvone are

$$\text{Mass of C in 1 mol} = 10 \text{ mol} \times 12.01 \ \frac{g}{mol} = 120.1 \text{ g}$$

$$\text{Mass of H in 1 mol} = 14 \text{ mol} \times \ \ 1.008 \ \frac{g}{mol} = \ \ 14.11 \text{ g}$$

$$\text{Mass of O in 1 mol} = \ \ 1 \text{ mol} \times 16.00 \ \frac{g}{mol} = \ \ \underline{16.00 \text{ g}}$$

$$\text{Mass of 1 mol } C_{10}H_{14}O = 150.2 \text{ g}$$

Next we find the fraction of the total mass contributed by each element and convert it to a percentage:

$$\text{Mass percent of C} = \frac{120.1 \text{ g C}}{150.2 \text{ g } C_{10}H_{14}O} \times 100\% = 79.96\%$$

$$\text{Mass percent of H} = \frac{14.11 \text{ g H}}{150.2 \text{ g } C_{10}H_{14}O} \times 100\% = 9.394\%$$

$$\text{Mass percent of O} = \frac{16.00 \text{ g O}}{150.2 \text{ g } C_{10}H_{14}O} \times 100\% = 10.65\%$$

CHECK:

Sum the individual mass percent values—they should total to 100% within round-off errors. In this case, the percentages add up to 100.00%.

See Exercises 3.55 and 3.56.

Sample Exercise 3.10 *Calculating Mass Percent II*

Although Fleming is commonly given credit for the discovery of penicillin, there is good evidence that penicillium mold extracts were used in the nineteenth century by Lord Joseph Lister to cure infections.

Penicillin, the first of a now large number of antibiotics (antibacterial agents), was discovered accidentally by the Scottish bacteriologist Alexander Fleming in 1928, but he was never able to isolate it as a pure compound. This and similar antibiotics have saved millions of lives that might have been lost to infections. Penicillin F has the formula $C_{14}H_{20}N_2SO_4$. Compute the mass percent of each element.

Solution

The molar mass of penicillin F is computed as follows:

$$\text{C: } \ 14 \text{ mol} \times 12.01 \ \frac{g}{mol} = 168.1 \text{ g}$$

$$\text{H: } \ 20 \text{ mol} \times 1.008 \ \frac{g}{mol} = \ 20.16 \text{ g}$$

$$\text{N: } \ 2 \text{ mol} \times 14.01 \ \frac{g}{mol} = \ 28.02 \text{ g}$$

$$\text{S: } \ 1 \text{ mol} \times 32.07 \ \frac{g}{mol} = \ 32.07 \text{ g}$$

$$O: \quad 4 \text{ mol} \times 16.00 \ \frac{g}{\text{mol}} = 64.00 \text{ g}$$

$$\text{Mass of 1 mol } C_{14}H_{20}N_2SO_4 = 312.4 \text{ g}$$

$$\text{Mass percent of C} = \frac{168.1 \text{ g C}}{312.4 \text{ g } C_{14}H_{20}N_2SO_4} \times 100\% = 53.81\%$$

$$\text{Mass percent of H} = \frac{20.16 \text{ g H}}{312.4 \text{ g } C_{14}H_{20}N_2SO_4} \times 100\% = 6.453\%$$

$$\text{Mass percent of N} = \frac{28.02 \text{ g N}}{312.4 \text{ g } C_{14}H_{20}N_2SO_4} \times 100\% = 8.969\%$$

$$\text{Mass percent of S} = \frac{32.07 \text{ g S}}{312.4 \text{ g } C_{14}H_{20}N_2SO_4} \times 100\% = 10.27\%$$

$$\text{Mass percent of O} = \frac{64.00 \text{ g O}}{312.4 \text{ g } C_{14}H_{20}N_2SO_4} \times 100\% = 20.49\%$$

Penicillin is isolated from a mold that can be grown in large quantities in fermentation tanks.

CHECK:

The percentages add up to 99.99%.

See Exercises 3.57 through 3.60.

3.5 *Determining the Formula of a Compound*

When a new compound is prepared, one of the first items of interest is the formula of the compound. This is most often determined by taking a weighed sample of the compound and either decomposing it into its component elements or reacting it with oxygen to produce substances such as CO_2, H_2O, and N_2, which are then collected and weighed. A device for doing this type of analysis is shown in Fig. 3.5. The results of such analyses provide the mass of each type of element in the compound, which can be used to determine the mass percent of each element.

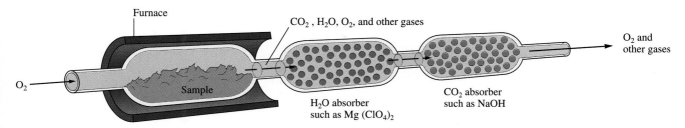

Figure 3.5

A schematic diagram of the combustion device used to analyze substances for carbon and hydrogen. The sample is burned in the presence of excess oxygen, which converts all its carbon to carbon dioxide and all its hydrogen to water. These products are collected by absorption using appropriate materials, and their amounts are determined by measuring the increase in masses of the absorbents.

Molecular Model: CO_2, H_2O, N_2

We will see how information of this type can be used to compute the formula of a compound. Suppose a substance has been prepared that is composed of carbon, hydrogen, and nitrogen. When 0.1156 gram of this compound is reacted with oxygen, 0.1638 gram of carbon dioxide (CO_2) and 0.1676 gram of water (H_2O) are collected. Assuming that all the carbon in the compound is converted to CO_2, we can determine the mass of carbon originally present in the 0.1156-gram sample. To do this, we must use the fraction (by mass) of carbon in CO_2. The molar mass of CO_2 is

$$\text{C:} \quad 1 \text{ mol} \times 12.01 \frac{\text{g}}{\text{mol}} = 12.01 \text{ g}$$

$$\text{O:} \quad 2 \text{ mol} \times 16.00 \frac{\text{g}}{\text{mol}} = \underline{32.00 \text{ g}}$$

$$\text{Molar mass of } CO_2 = 44.01 \text{ g/mol}$$

The fraction of carbon present by mass is

$$\frac{\text{Mass of C}}{\text{Total mass of } CO_2} = \frac{12.01 \text{ g C}}{44.01 \text{ g } CO_2}$$

Ball-and-stick model of CO_2.

This factor can now be used to determine the mass of carbon in 0.1638 gram of CO_2:

$$0.1638 \text{ g } CO_2 \times \frac{12.01 \text{ g C}}{44.01 \text{ g } CO_2} = 0.04470 \text{ g C}$$

Remember that this carbon originally came from the 0.1156-gram sample of unknown compound. Thus the mass percent of carbon in this compound is

$$\frac{0.04470 \text{ g C}}{0.1156 \text{ g compound}} \times 100\% = 38.67\% \text{ C}$$

The same procedure can be used to find the mass percent of hydrogen in the unknown compound. We assume that all the hydrogen present in the original 0.1156 gram of compound was converted to H_2O. The molar mass of H_2O is 18.02 grams, and the fraction of hydrogen by mass in H_2O is

$$\frac{\text{Mass of H}}{\text{Mass of } H_2O} = \frac{2.016 \text{ g H}}{18.02 \text{ g } H_2O}$$

Ball-and-stick model of H_2O.

Therefore, the mass of hydrogen in 0.1676 gram of H_2O is

$$0.1676 \text{ g } H_2O \times \frac{2.016 \text{ g H}}{18.02 \text{ g } H_2O} = 0.01875 \text{ g H}$$

And the mass percent of hydrogen in the compound is

$$\frac{0.01875 \text{ g H}}{0.1156 \text{ g compound}} \times 100\% = 16.22\% \text{ H}$$

The unknown compound contains only carbon, hydrogen, and nitrogen. So far we have determined that it is 38.67% carbon and 16.22% hydrogen. The remainder must be nitrogen:

$$100.00\% - (38.67\% + 16.22\%) = 45.11\% \text{ N}$$
$$\qquad\quad \uparrow \qquad\quad \uparrow$$
$$\qquad\quad \% \text{ C} \qquad \% \text{ H}$$

We have determined that the compound contains 38.67% carbon, 16.22% hydrogen, and 45.11% nitrogen. Next we use these data to obtain the formula.

Since the formula of a compound indicates the *numbers* of atoms in the compound, we must convert the masses of the elements to numbers of atoms. The easiest way to do this is to work with 100.00 grams of the compound. In the present case, 38.67% carbon by mass means 38.67 grams of carbon per 100.00 grams of compound; 16.22% hydrogen means 16.22 grams of hydrogen per 100.00 grams of compound; and so on. To determine the formula, we must calculate the number of carbon atoms in 38.67 grams of carbon, the number of hydrogen atoms in 16.22 grams of hydrogen, and the number of nitrogen atoms in 45.11 grams of nitrogen. We can do this as follows:

$$38.67 \text{ g C} \times \frac{1 \text{ mol C}}{12.01 \text{ g C}} = 3.220 \text{ mol C}$$

$$16.22 \text{ g H} \times \frac{1 \text{ mol H}}{1.008 \text{ g H}} = 16.09 \text{ mol H}$$

$$45.11 \text{ g N} \times \frac{1 \text{ mol N}}{14.01 \text{ g N}} = 3.219 \text{ mol N}$$

Thus 100.00 grams of this compound contains 3.220 moles of carbon atoms, 16.09 moles of hydrogen atoms, and 3.219 moles of nitrogen atoms.

We can find the smallest *whole-number ratio* of atoms in this compound by dividing each of the mole values above by the smallest of the three:

$$C: \quad \frac{3.220}{3.220} = 1.000 = 1$$

$$H: \quad \frac{16.09}{3.220} = 4.997 = 5$$

$$N: \quad \frac{3.219}{3.220} = 1.000 = 1$$

Thus the formula might well be CH_5N. However, it also could be $C_2H_{10}N_2$ or $C_3H_{15}N_3$, and so on—that is, some multiple of the smallest whole-number ratio. Each of these alternatives also has the correct relative numbers of atoms. That is, any molecule that can be represented as $(CH_5N)_n$, where n is an integer, has the **empirical formula** CH_5N. To be able to specify the exact formula of the molecule involved, the **molecular formula,** we must know the molar mass.

Suppose we know that this compound with empirical formula CH_5N has a molar mass of 31.06 g/mol. How do we determine which of the possible choices represents the molecular formula? Since the molecular formula is always a whole-number multiple of the empirical formula, we must first find the empirical formula mass for CH_5N:

Molecular formula = (empirical formula)$_n$, where n is an integer.

$$
\begin{array}{lll}
1 \text{ C:} & 1 \times 12.01 \text{ g} = & 12.01 \text{ g} \\
5 \text{ H:} & 5 \times 1.008 \text{ g} = & 5.040 \text{ g} \\
1 \text{ N:} & 1 \times 14.01 \text{ g} = & \underline{14.01 \text{ g}} \\
\end{array}
$$

Formula mass of CH_5N = 31.06 g/mol

This is the same as the known molar mass of the compound. Thus in this case the empirical formula and the molecular formula are the same; this substance consists

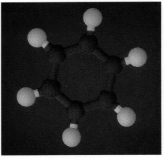

$C_6H_6 = (CH)_6$

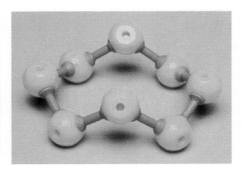

$S_8 = (S)_8$

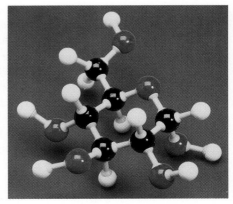

$C_6H_{12}O_6 = (CH_2O)_6$

Figure 3.6

Examples of substances whose empirical and molecular formulas differ. Notice that molecular formula = (empirical formula)$_n$, where n is an integer.

Molecular Model: glucose

of molecules with the formula CH_5N. It is quite common for the empirical and molecular formulas to be different; some examples where this is the case are shown in Fig. 3.6.

Sample Exercise 3.11 *Determining Empirical and Molecular Formulas I*

Determine the empirical and molecular formulas for a compound that gives the following analysis (in mass percents):

71.65% Cl   24.27% C   4.07% H

The molar mass is known to be 98.96 g/mol.

Solution

First, we convert the mass percents to masses in grams. In 100.00 g of this compound there are 71.65 g of chlorine, 24.27 g of carbon, and 4.07 g of hydrogen. We use these masses to compute the moles of atoms present:

$$71.65 \text{ g Cl} \times \frac{1 \text{ mol Cl}}{35.45 \text{ g Cl}} = 2.021 \text{ mol Cl}$$

$$24.27 \text{ g C} \times \frac{1 \text{ mol C}}{12.01 \text{ g C}} = 2.021 \text{ mol C}$$

$$4.07 \text{ g H} \times \frac{1 \text{ mol H}}{1.008 \text{ g H}} = 4.04 \text{ mol H}$$

Dividing each mole value by 2.021 (the smallest number of moles present), we obtain the empirical formula $ClCH_2$.

To determine the molecular formula, we must compare the empirical formula mass with the molar mass. The empirical formula mass is 49.48 g/mol (confirm this). The molar mass is known to be 98.96 g/mol.

$$\frac{\text{Molar mass}}{\text{Empirical formula mass}} = \frac{98.96 \text{ g/mol}}{49.48 \text{ g/mol}} = 2$$

$$\text{Molecular formula} = (ClCH_2)_2 = Cl_2C_2H_4$$

This substance is composed of molecules with the formula $Cl_2C_2H_4$.

Notice that the method we employ here allows us to determine the molecular formula of a compound but not its structural formula. The compound $Cl_2C_2H_4$ is called *dichloroethane*. There are two forms of this compound, shown in Fig. 3.7. The form on the right was formerly used as an additive in leaded gasoline.

See Exercises 3.71 and 3.72.

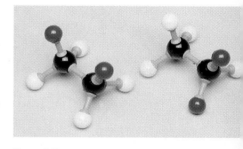

Figure 3.7
The two forms of dichloroethane.

Molecular Model:
$Cl_2C_2H_4$, a and b

Sample Exercise 3.12 **Determining Empirical and Molecular Formulas II**

A white powder is analyzed and found to contain 43.64% phosphorus and 56.36% oxygen by mass. The compound has a molar mass of 283.88 g/mol. What are the compound's empirical and molecular formulas?

Solution

In 100.00 g of this compound there are 43.64 g of phosphorus and 56.36 g of oxygen. In terms of moles, in 100.00 g of the compound we have

$$43.64 \text{ g P} \times \frac{1 \text{ mol P}}{30.97 \text{ g P}} = 1.409 \text{ mol P}$$

$$56.36 \text{ g O} \times \frac{1 \text{ mol O}}{16.00 \text{ g O}} = 3.523 \text{ mol O}$$

Dividing both mole values by the smaller one gives

$$\frac{1.409}{1.409} = 1 \text{ P} \quad \text{and} \quad \frac{3.523}{1.409} = 2.5 \text{ O}$$

This yields the formula $PO_{2.5}$. Since compounds must contain whole numbers of atoms, the empirical formula should contain only whole numbers. To obtain the simplest set of whole numbers, we multiply both numbers by 2 to give the empirical formula P_2O_5.

To obtain the molecular formula, we must compare the empirical formula mass to the molar mass. The empirical formula mass for P_2O_5 is 141.94.

$$\frac{\text{Molar mass}}{\text{Empirical formula mass}} = \frac{283.88}{141.94} = 2$$

The molecular formula is $(P_2O_5)_2$, or P_4O_{10}.

The structural formula of this interesting compound is given in Fig. 3.8.

See Exercises 3.73 and 3.74.

In Sample Exercises 3.11 and 3.12 we found the molecular formula by comparing the empirical formula mass with the molar mass. There is an alternate way to obtain the molecular formula. For example, in Sample Exercise 3.11 we know the molar mass of the compound is 98.96 g/mol. This means that 1 mole of the compound weighs 98.96 grams. Since we also know the mass percentages of each element, we can compute the mass of each element present in 1 mole of compound:

Chlorine: $\quad \dfrac{71.65 \text{ g Cl}}{100.0 \text{ g compound}} \times \dfrac{98.96 \text{ g}}{\text{mol}} = \dfrac{70.90 \text{ g Cl}}{\text{mol compound}}$

Carbon: $\quad \dfrac{24.27 \text{ g C}}{100.0 \text{ g compound}} \times \dfrac{98.96 \text{ g}}{\text{mol}} = \dfrac{24.02 \text{ g C}}{\text{mol compound}}$

Hydrogen: $\quad \dfrac{4.07 \text{ g H}}{100.0 \text{ g compound}} \times \dfrac{98.96 \text{ g}}{\text{mol}} = \dfrac{4.03 \text{ g H}}{\text{mol compound}}$

Now we can compute moles of atoms present per mole of compound:

Chlorine: $\quad \dfrac{70.90 \text{ g Cl}}{\text{mol compound}} \times \dfrac{1 \text{ mol Cl}}{35.45 \text{ g Cl}} = \dfrac{2.000 \text{ mol Cl}}{\text{mol compound}}$

Carbon: $\quad \dfrac{24.02 \text{ g C}}{\text{mol compound}} \times \dfrac{1 \text{ mol C}}{12.01 \text{ g C}} = \dfrac{2.000 \text{ mol C}}{\text{mol compound}}$

Hydrogen: $\quad \dfrac{4.03 \text{ g H}}{\text{mol compound}} \times \dfrac{1 \text{ mol H}}{1.008 \text{ g H}} = \dfrac{4.00 \text{ mol H}}{\text{mol compound}}$

Thus 1 mole of the compound contains 2 mol Cl atoms, 2 mol C atoms, and 4 mol H atoms, and the molecular formula is $Cl_2C_2H_4$, as obtained in Sample Exercise 3.11.

Figure 3.8

The structure of P_4O_{10}. Note that the oxygen atoms act as "bridges" between the phosphorus atoms. This compound has a great affinity for water and is often used as a desiccant, or drying agent.

Molecular Model: P_4O_{10}

Molecular Model: caffeine

Sample Exercise 3.13 *Determining a Molecular Formula*

Caffeine, a stimulant found in coffee, tea, and chocolate, contains 49.48% carbon, 5.15% hydrogen, 28.87% nitrogen, and 16.49% oxygen by mass and has a molar mass of 194.2 g/mol. Determine the molecular formula of caffeine.

Solution

We will first determine the mass of each element in 1 mole (194.2 g) of caffeine:

$$\frac{49.48 \text{ g C}}{100.0 \text{ g caffeine}} \times \frac{194.2 \text{ g}}{\text{mol}} = \frac{96.09 \text{ g C}}{\text{mol caffeine}}$$

$$\frac{5.15 \text{ g H}}{100.0 \text{ g caffeine}} \times \frac{194.2 \text{ g}}{\text{mol}} = \frac{10.0 \text{ g H}}{\text{mol caffeine}}$$

$$\frac{28.87 \text{ g N}}{100.0 \text{ g caffeine}} \times \frac{194.2 \text{ g}}{\text{mol}} = \frac{56.07 \text{ g N}}{\text{mol caffeine}}$$

$$\frac{16.49 \text{ g O}}{100.0 \text{ g caffeine}} \times \frac{194.2 \text{ g}}{\text{mol}} = \frac{32.02 \text{ g O}}{\text{mol caffeine}}$$

Now we will convert to moles:

Carbon: $\dfrac{96.09 \text{ g C}}{\text{mol caffeine}} \times \dfrac{1 \text{ mol C}}{12.01 \text{ g C}} = \dfrac{8.001 \text{ mol C}}{\text{mol caffeine}}$

Hydrogen: $\dfrac{10.0 \text{ g H}}{\text{mol caffeine}} \times \dfrac{1 \text{ mol H}}{1.008 \text{ g H}} = \dfrac{9.92 \text{ mol H}}{\text{mol caffeine}}$

Nitrogen: $\dfrac{56.07 \text{ g N}}{\text{mol caffeine}} \times \dfrac{1 \text{ mol N}}{14.01 \text{ g N}} = \dfrac{4.002 \text{ mol N}}{\text{mol caffeine}}$

Oxygen: $\dfrac{32.02 \text{ g O}}{\text{mol caffeine}} \times \dfrac{1 \text{ mol O}}{16.00 \text{ g O}} = \dfrac{2.001 \text{ mol O}}{\text{mol caffeine}}$

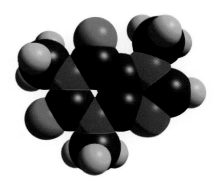

Computer-generated molecule of caffeine.

Rounding the numbers to integers gives the molecular formula for caffeine: $C_8H_{10}N_4O_2$.

See Exercises 3.73 and 3.74.

The methods for obtaining empirical and molecular formulas are summarized as follows:

Empirical Formula Determination

- Since mass percentage gives the number of grams of a particular element per 100 grams of compound, base the calculation on 100 grams of compound. Each percent will then represent the mass in grams of that element.
- Determine the number of moles of each element present in 100 grams of compound using the atomic masses of the elements present.
- Divide each value of the number of moles by the smallest of the values. If each resulting number is a whole number (after appropriate rounding), these numbers represent the subscripts of the elements in the empirical formula.
- If the numbers obtained in the previous step are not whole numbers, multiply each number by an integer so that the results are all whole numbers.

Numbers very close to whole numbers, such as 9.92 and 1.08, should be rounded to whole numbers. Numbers such as 2.25, 4.33, and 2.72 should not be rounded to whole numbers.

Molecular Formula Determination

Method One

- Obtain the empirical formula.
- Compute the mass corresponding to the empirical formula.
- Calculate the ratio

$$\frac{\text{Molar mass}}{\text{Empirical formula mass}}$$

- The integer from the previous step represents the number of empirical formula units in one molecule. When the empirical formula subscripts are multiplied by this integer, the molecular formula results. This procedure is summarized by the equation:

$$\text{Molecular formula} = (\text{empirical formula}) \times \frac{\text{molar mass}}{\text{empirical formula mass}}$$

Method Two

- Using the mass percentages and the molar mass, determine the mass of each element present in one mole of compound.
- Determine the number of moles of each element present in one mole of compound.
- The integers from the previous step represent the subscripts in the molecular formula.

Note that method two assumes that the molar mass of the compound is known accurately.

3.6 Chemical Equations

Chemical Reactions

A chemical change involves a reorganization of the atoms in one or more substances. For example, when the methane (CH_4) in natural gas combines with oxygen (O_2) in the air and burns, carbon dioxide (CO_2) and water (H_2O) are formed. This process is represented by a **chemical equation** with the **reactants** (here methane and oxygen) on the left side of an arrow and the **products** (carbon dioxide and water) on the right side:

$$CH_4 + O_2 \longrightarrow CO_2 + H_2O$$

Reactants   Products

Notice that the atoms have been reorganized. *Bonds have been broken, and new ones have been formed.* It is important to recognize that *in a chemical reaction, atoms are neither created nor destroyed. All atoms present in the reactants must be accounted for among the products.* In other words, there must be the same number of each type of atom on the product side and on the reactant side of the arrow. Making sure that this rule is obeyed is called **balancing a chemical equation** for a reaction.

The equation (shown above) for the reaction between CH_4 and O_2 is not balanced. We can see this from the following diagram:

Molecular Models: CH_4, O_2, CO_2, H_2O

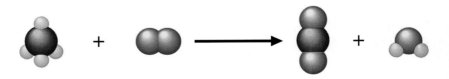

Notice that the number of oxygen atoms (in O_2) on the left of the arrow is two, while on the right there are three O atoms (in CO_2 and H_2O). Also, there are four hydrogen atoms (in CH_4) on the left and only two (in H_2O) on the right. Remember that a chemical reaction is simply a rearrangement of the atoms (a change in the way they are organized). Atoms are not created or destroyed in a chemical reaction. Thus the reactants and products must occur in numbers that give the same number of each type of atom among both the reactants and products. Simple trial and error will allow us to figure this out for the reaction of methane with oxygen. The needed numbers of molecules are

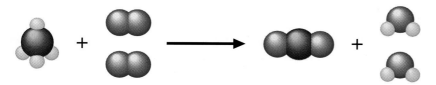

Notice that now we have the same number of each type of atom represented among the reactants and the products.

We can represent the preceding situation in a shorthand manner by the following chemical equation:

$$CH_4 + 2O_2 \longrightarrow CO_2 + 2H_2O$$

We can check that the equation is balanced by comparing the number of each type of atom on both sides:

$$CH_4 + 2O_2 \longrightarrow CO_2 + 2H_2O$$

1 C 4 H   4 O   1 C   2 O   4 H   2 O

To summarize, we have

Reactants	Products
1 C	1 C
4 H	4 H
4 O	4 O

The Meaning of a Chemical Equation

The chemical equation for a reaction gives two important types of information: the nature of the reactants and products and the relative numbers of each.

The reactants and products in a specific reaction must be identified by experiment. Besides specifying the compounds involved in the reaction, the equation often gives the *physical states* of the reactants and products:

State	Symbol
Solid	(s)
Liquid	(l)
Gas	(g)
Dissolved in water (in aqueous solution)	(aq)

Video: Oxygen, Hydrogen, Soap Bubbles, and Balloons

Table 3.2 Information Conveyed by the Balanced Equation for the Combustion of Methane

Reactants	$\longrightarrow$	Products
$CH_4(g) + 2O_2(g)$	$\longrightarrow$	$CO_2(g) + 2H_2O(g)$
1 molecule CH_4	$\longrightarrow$	1 molecule CO_2
+ 2 molecules O_2		+ 2 molecules H_2O
1 mol CH_4 molecules	$\longrightarrow$	1 mol CO_2 molecules
+ 2 mol O_2 molecules		+ 2 mol H_2O molecules
6.022×10^{23} CH_4 molecules	$\longrightarrow$	6.022×10^{23} CO_2 molecules
+ $2(6.022 \times 10^{23})$ O_2 molecules		+ $2(6.022 \times 10^{23})$ H_2O molecules
16 g CH_4 + 2(32 g) O_2	$\longrightarrow$	44 g CO_2 + 2(18 g) H_2O
80 g reactants	$\longrightarrow$	80 g products

Hydrochloric acid reacts with solid sodium hydrogen carbonate to produce gaseous carbon dioxide.

Exploration: Conservation of Mass and Balancing Equations

For example, when hydrochloric acid in aqueous solution is added to solid sodium hydrogen carbonate, the products carbon dioxide gas, liquid water, and sodium chloride (which dissolves in the water) are formed:

$$HCl(aq) + NaHCO_3(s) \longrightarrow CO_2(g) + H_2O(l) + NaCl(aq)$$

The relative numbers of reactants and products in a reaction are indicated by the *coefficients* in the balanced equation. (The coefficients can be determined because we know that the same number of each type of atom must occur on both sides of the equation.) For example, the balanced equation

$$CH_4(g) + 2O_2(g) \longrightarrow CO_2(g) + 2H_2O(g)$$

can be interpreted in several equivalent ways, as shown in Table 3.2. Note that the total mass is 80 grams for both reactants and products. We expect the mass to remain constant, since chemical reactions involve only a rearrangement of atoms. Atoms, and therefore mass, are conserved in a chemical reaction.

From this discussion you can see that a balanced chemical equation gives you a great deal of information.

3.7 Balancing Chemical Equations

An unbalanced chemical equation is of limited use. Whenever you see an equation, you should ask yourself whether or not it is balanced. The principle that lies at the heart of the balancing process is that atoms are conserved in a chemical reaction. The same number of each type of atom must be found among the reactants and products. It is also important to recognize that the identity of the reactants and products of a reaction are determined by experimental observation. For example, when liquid ethanol is burned in the presence of sufficient oxygen gas, the products are always carbon dioxide and water. When the equation for this reaction is balanced, the *identities* of the reactants and products must not be changed. *The formulas of the compounds must never be changed in balancing a chemical equation.* That is, the subscripts in a formula cannot be changed, nor can atoms be added or subtracted from a formula.

Most chemical equations can be balanced by inspection, that is, by trial and error. It is always best to start with the most complicated molecules (those containing the greatest number of atoms). For example, consider the reaction of ethanol with oxygen, given by the unbalanced equation

In balancing equations, start with the most complicated molecule.

$$C_2H_5OH(l) + O_2(g) \longrightarrow CO_2(g) + H_2O(g)$$

which can be represented by the following molecular models:

Molecular Models: C_2H_5OH, O_2, CO_2, H_2O

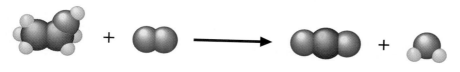

Notice that the carbon and hydrogen atoms are not balanced. There are two carbon atoms on the left and one on the right, and there are six hydrogens on the left and two on the right. We need to find the correct numbers of reactants and products so that we have the same number of all types of atoms among the reactants and products. We will balance the equation "by inspection" (a systematic trial-and-error procedure).

The most complicated molecule here is C_2H_5OH. We will begin by balancing the products that contain the atoms in C_2H_5OH. Since C_2H_5OH contains two carbon atoms, we place the coefficient 2 before the CO_2 to balance the carbon atoms:

$$\underset{\text{2 C atoms}}{C_2H_5OH(l)} + O_2(g) \rightarrow \underset{\text{2 C atoms}}{2CO_2(g)} + H_2O(g)$$

Since C_2H_5OH contains six hydrogen atoms, the hydrogen atoms can be balanced by placing a 3 before the H_2O:

$$\underset{(5+1)\text{ H}}{C_2H_5OH(l)} + O_2(g) \rightarrow 2CO_2(g) + \underset{(3 \times 2)\text{ H}}{3H_2O(g)}$$

Last, we balance the oxygen atoms. Note that the right side of the preceding equation contains seven oxygen atoms, whereas the left side has only three. We can correct this by putting a 3 before the O_2 to produce the balanced equation:

$$\underset{\underbrace{\underset{\text{1 O}}{C_2H_5OH(l)} + \underset{\text{6 O}}{3O_2(g)}}_{\text{7 O}}}{} \rightarrow \underset{\underbrace{\underset{(2\times2)\text{ O}}{2CO_2(g)} + \underset{\text{3 O}}{3H_2O(g)}}_{\text{7 O}}}{}$$

Now we check:

$$C_2H_5OH(l) + 3O_2(g) \rightarrow 2CO_2(g) + 3H_2O(g)$$

2 C atoms	2 C atoms
6 H atoms	6 H atoms
7 O atoms	7 O atoms

The equation is balanced.

The balanced equation can be represented as follows:

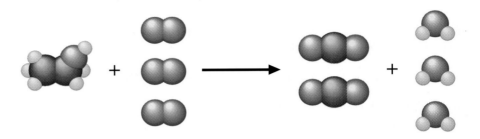

You can see that all the elements balance.

WRITING AND BALANCING THE EQUATION FOR A CHEMICAL REACTION

STEP 1

Determine what reaction is occurring. What are the reactants, the products, and the physical states involved?

STEP 2

Write the *unbalanced* equation that summarizes the reaction described in step 1.

STEP 3

Balance the equation by inspection, starting with the most complicated molecule(s). Determine what coefficients are necessary so that the same number of each type of atom appears on both reactant and product sides. Do not change the identities (formulas) of any of the reactants or products.

Sample Exercise 3.14 *Balancing a Chemical Equation I*

Chromium compounds exhibit a variety of bright colors. When solid ammonium dichromate, $(NH_4)_2Cr_2O_7$, a vivid orange compound, is ignited, a spectacular reaction occurs, as shown in the two photographs on page 105. Although the reaction is actually somewhat more complex, let's assume here that the products are solid chromium(III) oxide, nitrogen gas (consisting of N_2 molecules), and water vapor. Balance the equation for this reaction.

Solution

STEP 1

From the description given, the reactant is solid ammonium dichromate, $(NH_4)_2Cr_2O_7(s)$, and the products are nitrogen gas, $N_2(g)$, water vapor, $H_2O(g)$, and solid chromium(III) oxide, $Cr_2O_3(s)$. The formula for chromium(III) oxide

Chromate and dichromate compounds are carcinogens (cancer-inducing agents) and should be handled very carefully.

3.8 Stoichiometric Calculations: Amounts of Reactants and Products

As we have seen in previous sections of this chapter, the coefficients in chemical equations represent *numbers* of molecules, not masses of molecules. However, when a reaction is to be run in a laboratory or chemical plant, the amounts of substances needed cannot be determined by counting molecules directly. Counting is always done by weighing. In this section we will see how chemical equations can be used to determine the *masses* of reacting chemicals.

To develop the principles for dealing with the stoichiometry of reactions, we will consider the reaction of propane with oxygen to produce carbon dioxide and water. We will consider the question: *"What mass of oxygen will react with 96.1 grams of propane?"* In doing stoichiometry, the first thing we must do is *write the balanced chemical equation* for the reaction. In this case the balanced equation is

Before doing any calculations involving a chemical reaction, be sure the equation for the reaction is balanced.

$$C_3H_8(g) + 5O_2(g) \longrightarrow 3CO_2(g) + 4H_2O(g)$$

which can be visualized as

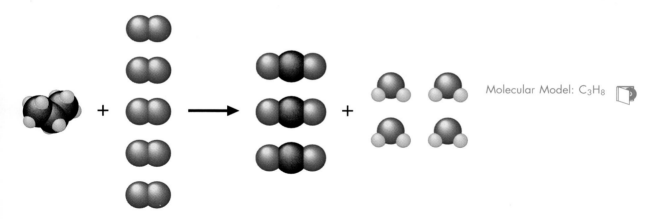

Molecular Model: C_3H_8

This equation means that 1 mole of C_3H_8 reacts with 5 moles of O_2 to produce 3 moles of CO_2 and 4 moles of H_2O. To use this equation to find the masses of reactants and products, we must be able to convert between masses and moles of substances. Thus we must first ask: *"How many moles of propane are present in 96.1 grams of propane?"* The molar mass of propane to three significant figures is 44.1 (that is, $3 \times 12.01 + 8 \times 1.008$). The moles of propane can be calculated as follows:

$$96.1 \text{ g } C_3H_8 \times \frac{1 \text{ mol } C_3H_8}{44.1 \text{ g } C_3H_8} = 2.18 \text{ mol } C_3H_8$$

Next we must take into account the fact that each mole of propane reacts with 5 moles of oxygen. The best way to do this is to use the balanced equation to construct a **mole ratio.** In this case we want to convert from moles of propane to moles of oxygen. From the balanced equation we see that 5 moles of O_2 is required for each mole of C_3H_8, so the appropriate ratio is

THE NEXT TIME that you visit a gas station, take a moment to note the octane rating that accompanies the grade of gasoline that you are purchasing. The gasoline is priced according to its octane rating—a measure of the fuel's antiknock properties. In a conventional internal combustion engine, gasoline vapors and air are drawn into the combustion cylinder on the downward stroke of the piston. This air-fuel mixture is compressed on the upward piston stroke (compression stroke), and a spark from the sparkplug ignites the mix. The rhythmic combustion of the fuel-air mix occurring sequentially in several cylinders furnishes the power to propel the vehicle down the road. Excessive heat and pressure (or poor-quality fuel) within the cylinder may cause the premature combustion

of the mixture—commonly known as engine "knock" or "ping." Over time, this engine knock can damage the engine, resulting in inefficient performance and costly repairs.

A consumer typically is faced with three choices of gasoline, with octane ratings of 87 (regular), 89 (midgrade), and 93 (premium). But if you happen to travel or live in the higher elevations of the Rocky Mountain states, you might be surprised to find different octane ratings at the gasoline pumps. The reason for this provides a lesson in stoichiometry. At higher elevations the air is less dense—the volume of oxygen per unit volume of air is smaller. Most engines are designed to achieve a 14:1 oxygen-to-fuel ratio in the cylinder prior to combustion. If less

oxygen is available, then less fuel is required to achieve this optimal ratio. In turn, the lower volumes of oxygen and fuel result in a lower pressure in the cylinder. Because high pressure tends to promote knocking, the lower pressure within engine cylinders at higher elevations promotes a more controlled combustion of the fuel-air mixture, and therefore, octane requirements are lower. While consumers in the Rocky Mountain states can purchase three grades of gasoline, the octane ratings of these fuel blends are different from those in the rest of the United States. In Denver, Colorado, regular gasoline is 85 octane, midgrade is 87 octane, and premium is 91 octane—2 points lower than gasoline sold in most of the rest of the country.

$$\frac{5 \text{ mol } O_2}{1 \text{ mol } C_3H_8}$$

Multiplying the number of moles of C_3H_8 by this factor gives the number of moles of O_2 required:

$$2.18 \text{ mol } C_3H_8 \times \frac{5 \text{ mol } O_2}{1 \text{ mol } C_3H_8} = 10.9 \text{ mol } O_2$$

Notice that the mole ratio is set up so that the moles of C_3H_8 cancel out, and the units that result are moles of O_2.

Since the original question asked for the mass of oxygen needed to react with 96.1 grams of propane, the 10.9 moles of O_2 must be converted to *grams*. Since the molar mass of O_2 is 32.0 g/mol,

$$10.9 \text{ mol } O_2 \times \frac{32.0 \text{ g } O_2}{1 \text{ mol } O_2} = 349 \text{ g } O_2$$

Therefore, 349 grams of oxygen is required to burn 96.1 grams of propane.

This example can be extended by asking: *"What mass of carbon dioxide is produced when 96.1 grams of propane is combusted with oxygen?"* In this case we must convert between moles of propane and moles of carbon dioxide. This can be accomplished by looking at the balanced equation, which shows that 3 moles of CO_2 is produced for each mole of C_3H_8 reacted. The mole ratio needed to convert from moles of propane to moles of carbon dioxide is

$$\frac{3 \text{ mol CO}_2}{1 \text{ mol C}_3\text{H}_8}$$

The conversion is

$$2.18 \text{ mol C}_3\text{H}_8 \times \frac{3 \text{ mol CO}_2}{1 \text{ mol C}_3\text{H}_8} = 6.54 \text{ mol CO}_2$$

Then, using the molar mass of CO_2 (44.0 g/mol), we calculate the mass of CO_2 produced:

$$6.54 \text{ mol CO}_2 \times \frac{44.0 \text{ g CO}_2}{1 \text{ mol CO}_2} = 288 \text{ g CO}_2$$

We will now summarize the sequence of steps needed to carry out stoichiometric calculations.

96.1 g C_3H_8 → $\dfrac{1 \text{ mol C}_3\text{H}_8}{44.1 \text{ g C}_3\text{H}_8}$ → 2.18 mol C_3H_8 → $\dfrac{3 \text{ mol CO}_2}{1 \text{ mol C}_3\text{H}_8}$ → 6.54 mol CO_2

$\dfrac{44.0 \text{ g CO}_2}{1 \text{ mol CO}_2}$ → 288 g CO_2

THE STEPS FOR CALCULATING MASSES OF REACTANTS AND PRODUCTS IN CHEMICAL REACTIONS

STEP 1
Balance the equation for the reaction.

STEP 2
Convert the known mass of the reactant or product to moles of that substance.

STEP 3
Use the balanced equation to set up the appropriate mole ratios.

STEP 4
Use the appropriate mole ratios to calculate the number of moles of the desired reactant or product.

STEP 5
Convert from moles back to grams if required by the problem.

Astronaut Sidney M. Gutierrez changes the lithium hydroxide cannisters on space shuttle Columbia. The lithium hydroxide is used to purge carbon dioxide from the air in the shuttle's cabin.

Sample Exercise 3.16 *Chemical Stoichiometry I*

Solid lithium hydroxide is used in space vehicles to remove exhaled carbon dioxide from the living environment by forming solid lithium carbonate and liquid water. What mass of gaseous carbon dioxide can be absorbed by 1.00 kg of lithium hydroxide?

Solution

STEP 1

Using the description of the reaction, we can write the unbalanced equation:

$$LiOH(s) + CO_2(g) \longrightarrow Li_2CO_3(s) + H_2O(l)$$

The balanced equation is

$$2LiOH(s) + CO_2(g) \longrightarrow Li_2CO_3(s) + H_2O(l)$$

STEP 2

We convert the given mass of LiOH to moles, using the molar mass of LiOH (6.941 + 16.00 + 1.008 = 23.95 g/mol):

$$1.00 \; \text{kg LiOH} \times \frac{1000 \; \text{g LiOH}}{1 \; \text{kg LiOH}} \times \frac{1 \; \text{mol LiOH}}{23.95 \; \text{g LiOH}} = 41.8 \; \text{mol LiOH}$$

STEP 3

Since we want to determine the amount of CO_2 that reacts with the given amount of LiOH, the appropriate mole ratio is

$$\frac{1 \; \text{mol CO}_2}{2 \; \text{mol LiOH}}$$

STEP 4

We calculate the moles of CO_2 needed to react with the given mass of LiOH using this mole ratio:

$$41.8 \; \text{mol LiOH} \times \frac{1 \; \text{mol CO}_2}{2 \; \text{mol LiOH}} = 20.9 \; \text{mol CO}_2$$

STEP 5

Next we calculate the mass of CO_2, using its molar mass (44.0 g/mol):

$$20.9 \; \text{mol CO}_2 \times \frac{44.0 \; \text{g CO}_2}{1 \; \text{mol CO}_2} = 9.20 \times 10^2 \; \text{g CO}_2$$

Thus 920. g of $CO_2(g)$ will be absorbed by 1.00 kg of LiOH(s).

See Exercises 3.89 and 3.90.

Sample Exercise 3.17 *Chemical Stoichiometry II*

Baking soda ($NaHCO_3$) is often used as an antacid. It neutralizes excess hydrochloric acid secreted by the stomach:

$$NaHCO_3(s) + HCl(aq) \longrightarrow NaCl(aq) + H_2O(l) + CO_2(aq)$$

Milk of magnesia, which is an aqueous suspension of magnesium hydroxide, is also used as an antacid:

$$Mg(OH)_2(s) + 2HCl(aq) \longrightarrow 2H_2O(l) + MgCl_2(aq)$$

Which is the more effective antacid per gram, $NaHCO_3$ or $Mg(OH)_2$?

Antacids contain bases for neutralizing excess stomach acid.

Solution

To answer the question, we must determine the amount of HCl neutralized per gram of $NaHCO_3$ and per gram of $Mg(OH)_2$. Using the molar mass of $NaHCO_3$ (84.01 g/mol), we can determine the moles of $NaHCO_3$ in 1.00 g of $NaHCO_3$:

$$1.00 \text{ g NaHCO}_3 \times \frac{1 \text{ mol NaHCO}_3}{84.01 \text{ g NaHCO}_3} = 1.19 \times 10^{-2} \text{ mol NaHCO}_3$$

Next we determine the moles of HCl using the mole ratio 1 mol HCl/1 mol $NaHCO_3$:

$$1.19 \times 10^{-2} \text{ mol NaHCO}_3 \times \frac{1 \text{ mol HCl}}{1 \text{ mol NaHCO}_3} = 1.19 \times 10^{-2} \text{ mol HCl}$$

Thus 1.00 g of $NaHCO_3$ will neutralize 1.19×10^{-2} mol HCl.

Using the molar mass of $Mg(OH)_2$ (58.32 g/mol), we determine the moles of $Mg(OH)_2$ in 1.00 g:

$$1.00 \text{ g Mg(OH)}_2 \times \frac{1 \text{ mol Mg(OH)}_2}{58.32 \text{ g Mg(OH)}_2} = 1.71 \times 10^{-2} \text{ mol Mg(OH)}_2$$

To determine the moles of HCl that will react with this amount of $Mg(OH)_2$, we use the mole ratio 2 mol HCl/1 mol $Mg(OH)_2$:

$$1.71 \times 10^{-2} \text{ mol Mg(OH)}_2 \times \frac{2 \text{ mol HCl}}{1 \text{ mol Mg(OH)}_2} = 3.42 \times 10^{-2} \text{ mol HCl}$$

Thus 1.00 g of $Mg(OH)_2$ will neutralize 3.42×10^{-2} mol HCl. It is a better antacid per gram than $NaHCO_3$.

See Exercises 3.91 and 3.92.

3.9 Calculations Involving a Limiting Reactant

When chemicals are mixed together to undergo a reaction, they are often mixed in **stoichiometric quantities,** that is, in exactly the correct amounts so that all reactants "run out" (are used up) at the same time. To clarify this concept, let's consider

The details of the Haber process are discussed in Section 19.2.

 Exploration: Limiting Reactants

the production of hydrogen for use in the manufacture of ammonia by the **Haber process.** Ammonia, a very important fertilizer itself and a starting material for other fertilizers, is made by combining nitrogen (from the air) with hydrogen according to the equation

$$N_2(g) + 3H_2(g) \longrightarrow 2NH_3(g)$$

Hydrogen can be obtained from the reaction of methane with water vapor:

$$CH_4(g) + H_2O(g) \longrightarrow 3H_2(g) + CO(g)$$

We can illustrate what we mean by stoichiometric quantities by first visualizing the balanced equation as follows:

Since this reaction involves one molecule of methane reacting with one molecule of water, to have stoichiometric amounts of methane and water we must have equal numbers of them, as shown in Fig. 3.9, where several stoichiometric mixtures are shown.

Suppose we want to calculate the mass of water required to react *exactly* with 2.50×10^3 kilograms of methane? That is, how much water will just consume all the 2.50×10^3 kilograms of methane, leaving no methane or water remaining?

To do this calculation, we need to recognize that we need equal numbers of methane and water molecules. Therefore, we first need to find the number of moles of methane molecules in 2.50×10^3 kg (2.50×10^6 g) of methane:

$$2.50 \times 10^6 \text{ g CH}_4 \times \frac{1 \text{ mol CH}_4}{16.04 \text{ g CH}_4} = 1.56 \times 10^5 \text{ mol CH}_4 \text{ molecules}$$

$$\uparrow$$
$$\text{molar mass of CH}_4$$

Ammonia is dissolved in irrigation water to provide fertilizer for a field of corn.

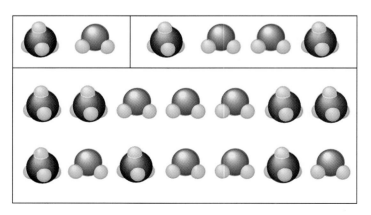

Figure 3.9

Three different stoichiometric mixtures of methane and water, which react one-to-one.

This same number of water molecules has a mass determined as follows:

$$1.56 \times 10^5 \text{ mol H}_2\text{O} \times \frac{18.02 \text{ g}}{\text{mol H}_2\text{O}} = 2.81 \times 10^6 \text{ g H}_2\text{O} = 2.81 \times 10^3 \text{ kg H}_2\text{O}$$

Thus, if 2.50×10^3 kilograms of methane is mixed with 2.81×10^3 kilograms of water, both reactants will "run out" at the same time. The reactants have been mixed in stoichiometric quantities.

If, on the other hand, 2.50×10^3 kilograms of methane is mixed with 3.00×10^3 kilograms of water, the methane will be consumed before the water runs out. The water will be in *excess*; that is, there will be more water molecules than methane molecules in the reaction mixture. What is the implication of this with respect to the number of product molecules that can form?

To answer this question, consider the situation on a smaller scale. Assume we mix 10 CH_4 molecules and 17 H_2O molecules and let them react. How many H_2 and CO molecules can form?

First picture the mixture of CH_4 and H_2O molecules as shown in Fig. 3.10.

Then imagine that groups consisting of one CH_4 molecule and one H_2O molecule (Fig. 3.10) will react to form 3 H_2 and one CO molecules (Fig. 3.11).

Notice that products can form only when both CH_4 and H_2O are available to react. Once the 10 CH_4 molecules are used up by reacting with 10 H_2O molecules, the remaining water molecules cannot react. They are in excess. Thus the number of products that can form is *limited* by the methane. Once the methane is consumed, no more products can be formed, even though some water still remains. In this situation the amount of methane *limits* the amount of products that can be formed. This brings us to the concept of the **limiting reactant** (or **limiting reagent**), which is the reactant that is consumed first and that therefore limits the amounts of products that can be formed. In any stoichiometry calculation involving a chemical reaction, it is essential to determine which reactant

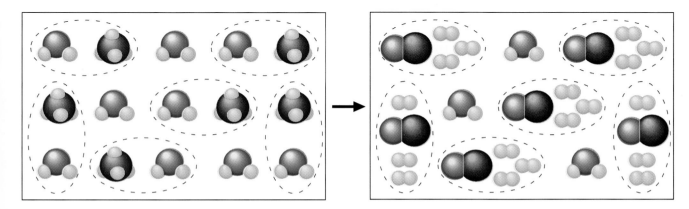

Figure 3.10
A mixture of CH_4 and H_2O molecules.

Figure 3.11
Methane and water have reacted to form products according to the equation $CH_4 + H_2O \longrightarrow 3H_2 + CO$.

is limiting in order to calculate correctly the amounts of products that will be formed.

To further explore the idea of a limiting reactant, consider the ammonia synthesis reaction:

$$N_2(g) + 3H_2(g) \longrightarrow 2NH_3(g)$$

Molecular Models: N_2, H_2, NH_3

Assume that 5 N_2 molecules and 9 H_2 molecules are placed in a flask. Is this a stoichiometric mixture of reactants, or will one of them be consumed before the other runs out? From the balanced equation we know that each N_2 molecule requires 3 H_2 molecules for the reaction to occur:

Thus the required H_2/N_2 ratio is $3H_2/1N_2$. In our experiment we have 9 H_2 and 5 N_2, or a ratio of $9H_2/5N_2 = 1.8H_2/1N_2$.

Since the actual ratio (1.8:1) of H_2/N_2 is less than the ratio required by the balanced equation (3:1), there is not enough hydrogen to react with all the nitrogen. That is, the hydrogen will run out first, leaving some unreacted N_2 molecules. We can visualize this as shown in Fig. 3.12.

Figure 3.12 shows that 3 of the N_2 molecules react with the 9 H_2 molecules to produce 6 NH_3 molecules:

$$3N_2 + 9H_2 \longrightarrow 6NH_3$$

This leaves 2 N_2 molecules unreacted—the nitrogen is in excess.

What we have shown here is that in this experiment the hydrogen is the limiting reactant. The amount of H_2 initially present determines the amount of NH_3 that can form. The reaction was not able to use up all the N_2 molecules because the H_2 molecules were all consumed by the first 3 N_2 molecules to react.

Another way to look at this is to determine how much H_2 would be required by 5 N_2 molecules. Multiplying the balanced equation

$$N_2(g) + 3H_2(g) \longrightarrow 2NH_3(g)$$

by 5 gives

$$5N_2(g) + 15H_2(g) \longrightarrow 10NH_3(g)$$

Thus 5 N_2 molecules would require 15 H_2 molecules and we only have 9. This tells us the same thing we learned earlier—the hydrogen is limiting.

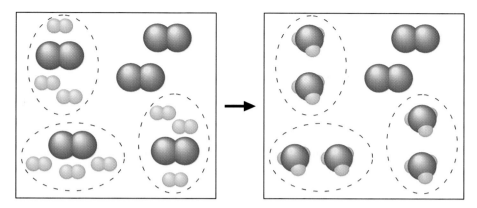

Figure 3.12
Hydrogen and nitrogen react to form ammonia according to the equation
$N_2 + 3H_2 \longrightarrow 2NH_3$.

The most important point here is this: *The limiting reactant limits the amount of product that can form.* The reaction that actually occurred was

$$3N_2(g) + 9H_2(g) \longrightarrow 6NH_3(g)$$

not

$$5N_2(g) + 15H_2(g) \longrightarrow 10NH_3(g)$$

Thus 6 NH_3 were formed, not 10 NH_3, because the H_2, not the N_2, was limiting.

In the laboratory or chemical plant we work with much larger quantities than the few molecules of the preceding example. Therefore, we must learn to deal with limiting reactants using moles. The ideas are exactly the same, except that we are using moles of molecules instead of individual molecules. For example, suppose 25.0 kilograms of nitrogen and 5.00 kilograms of hydrogen are mixed and reacted to form ammonia. How do we calculate the mass of ammonia produced when this reaction is run to completion (until one of the reactants is completely consumed)?

As in the preceding example, we must use the balanced equation

$$N_2(g) + 3H_2(g) \longrightarrow 2NH_3(g)$$

to determine whether nitrogen or hydrogen is the limiting reactant and then to determine the amount of ammonia that is formed. We first calculate the moles of reactants present:

$$25.0 \text{ kg N}_2 \times \frac{1000 \text{ g N}_2}{1 \text{ kg N}_2} \times \frac{1 \text{ mol N}_2}{28.0 \text{ g N}_2} = 8.93 \times 10^2 \text{ mol N}_2$$

$$5.00 \text{ kg H}_2 \times \frac{1000 \text{ g H}_2}{1 \text{ kg H}_2} \times \frac{1 \text{ mol H}_2}{2.016 \text{ g H}_2} = 2.48 \times 10^3 \text{ mol H}_2$$

Since 1 mol N_2 reacts with 3 mol H_2, the number of moles of H_2 that will react exactly with 8.93×10^2 mol N_2 is

$$8.93 \times 10^2 \text{ mol } N_2 \times \frac{3 \text{ mol } H_2}{1 \text{ mol } N_2} = 2.68 \times 10^3 \text{ mol } H_2$$

Always determine which reactant is limiting.

Thus 8.93×10^2 mol N_2 requires 2.68×10^3 mol H_2 to react completely. However, in this case, only 2.48×10^3 mol H_2 is present. This means that the hydrogen will be consumed before the nitrogen. Thus hydrogen is the *limiting reactant* in this particular situation, and we must use the amount of hydrogen to compute the quantity of ammonia formed:

$$2.48 \times 10^3 \text{ mol } H_2 \times \frac{2 \text{ mol } NH_3}{3 \text{ mol } H_2} = 1.65 \times 10^3 \text{ mol } NH_3$$

Converting moles to kilograms gives

$$1.65 \times 10^3 \text{ mol } NH_3 \times \frac{17.0 \text{ g } NH_3}{1 \text{ mol } NH_3} = 2.80 \times 10^4 \text{ g } NH_3 = 28.0 \text{ kg } NH_3$$

Note that to determine the limiting reactant, we could have started instead with the given amount of hydrogen and calculated the moles of nitrogen required:

$$2.48 \times 10^3 \text{ mol } H_2 \times \frac{1 \text{ mol } N_2}{3 \text{ mol } H_2} = 8.27 \times 10^2 \text{ mol } N_2$$

Thus 2.48×10^3 mol H_2 requires 8.27×10^2 mol N_2. Since 8.93×10^2 mol N_2 is actually present, the nitrogen is in excess. The hydrogen will run out first, and thus again we find that hydrogen limits the amount of ammonia formed.

A related but simpler way to determine which reactant is limiting is to compare the mole ratio of the substances required by the balanced equation with the mole ratio of reactants actually present. For example, in this case the mole ratio of H_2 to N_2 required by the balanced equation is

$$\frac{3 \text{ mol } H_2}{1 \text{ mol } N_2}$$

That is,

$$\frac{\text{mol } H_2}{\text{mol } N_2} \text{ (required)} = \frac{3}{1} = 3$$

In this experiment we have 2.48×10^3 mol H_2 and 8.93×10^2 mol N_2. Thus the ratio

$$\frac{\text{mol } H_2}{\text{mol } N_2} \text{ (actual)} = \frac{2.48 \times 10^3}{8.93 \times 10^2} = 2.78$$

Since 2.78 is less than 3, the actual mole ratio of H_2 to N_2 is too small, and H_2 must be limiting. If the actual H_2 to N_2 mole ratio had been greater than 3, then the H_2 would have been in excess and the N_2 would be limiting.

Sample Exercise 3.18 *Stoichiometry: Limiting Reactant*

Nitrogen gas can be prepared by passing gaseous ammonia over solid copper(II) oxide at high temperatures. The other products of the reaction are solid copper and water vapor. If a sample containing 18.1 g of NH_3 is reacted with 90.4 g of CuO, which is the limiting reactant? How many grams of N_2 will be formed?

Solution

From the description of the problem, we can obtain the following balanced equation:

$$2NH_3(g) + 3CuO(s) \longrightarrow N_2(g) + 3Cu(s) + 3H_2O(g)$$

Next we must compute the moles of NH_3 (molar mass = 17.03 g/mol) and of CuO (molar mass = 79.55 g/mol):

$$18.1 \text{ g NH}_3 \times \frac{1 \text{ mol NH}_3}{17.03 \text{ g NH}_3} = 1.06 \text{ mol NH}_3$$

$$90.4 \text{ g CuO} \times \frac{1 \text{ mol CuO}}{79.55 \text{ g CuO}} = 1.14 \text{ mol CuO}$$

To determine the limiting reactant, we use the mole ratio for CuO and NH_3:

$$1.06 \text{ mol NH}_3 \times \frac{3 \text{ mol CuO}}{2 \text{ mol NH}_3} = 1.59 \text{ mol CuO}$$

Thus 1.59 mol CuO is required to react with 1.06 mol NH_3. Since only 1.14 mol CuO is actually present, the amount of CuO is limiting; CuO will run out before NH_3 does. We can verify this conclusion by comparing the mole ratio of CuO and NH_3 required by the balanced equation

$$\frac{\text{mol CuO}}{\text{mol NH}_3} \text{ (required)} = \frac{3}{2} = 1.5$$

with the mole ratio actually present

$$\frac{\text{mol CuO}}{\text{mol NH}_3} \text{ (actual)} = \frac{1.14}{1.06} = 1.08$$

Since the actual ratio is too small (smaller than 1.5), CuO is the limiting reactant.

Because CuO is the limiting reactant, we must use the amount of CuO to calculate the amount of N_2 formed. From the balanced equation, the mole ratio between CuO and N_2 is

$$\frac{1 \text{ mol N}_2}{3 \text{ mol CuO}}$$

$$1.14 \text{ mol CuO} \times \frac{1 \text{ mol N}_2}{3 \text{ mol CuO}} = 0.380 \text{ mol N}_2$$

Using the molar mass of N_2 (28.0 g/mol), we can calculate the mass of N_2 produced:

$$0.380 \text{ mol } N_2 \times \frac{28.0 \text{ g } N_2}{1 \text{ mol } N_2} = 10.6 \text{ g } N_2$$

See Exercises 3.99 through 3.102.

The amount of a product formed when the limiting reactant is completely consumed is called the **theoretical yield** of that product. In Sample Exercise 3.18, 10.6 grams of nitrogen represents the theoretical yield. This is the *maximum amount* of nitrogen that can be produced from the quantities of reactants used. Actually, the amount of product predicted by the theoretical yield is seldom obtained because of side reactions (other reactions that involve one or more of the reactants or products) and other complications. The *actual yield* of product is often given as a percentage of the theoretical yield. This is called the **percent yield:**

Percent yield is important as an indicator of the efficiency of a particular laboratory or industrial reaction.

$$\frac{\text{Actual yield}}{\text{Theoretical yield}} \times 100\% = \text{percent yield}$$

For example, if the reaction considered in Sample Exercise 3.18 actually gave 6.63 grams of nitrogen instead of the predicted 10.6 grams, the percent yield of nitrogen would be

$$\frac{6.63 \text{ g } N_2}{10.6 \text{ g } N_2} \times 100\% = 62.5\%$$

Sample Exercise 3.19 *Calculating Percent Yield*

Methanol (CH_3OH), also called *methyl alcohol,* is the simplest alcohol. It is used as a fuel in race cars and is a potential replacement for gasoline. Methanol can be manufactured by combination of gaseous carbon monoxide and hydrogen. Suppose 68.5 kg $CO(g)$ is reacted with 8.60 kg $H_2(g)$. Calculate the theoretical yield of methanol. If 3.57×10^4 g CH_3OH is actually produced, what is the percent yield of methanol?

Molecular Model: CH_3OH

Solution

First, we must find out which reactant is limiting. The balanced equation is

$$2H_2(g) + CO(g) \longrightarrow CH_3OH(l)$$

Next we must calculate the moles of reactants:

$$68.5 \text{ kg } CO \times \frac{1000 \text{ g } CO}{1 \text{ kg } CO} \times \frac{1 \text{ mol } CO}{28.02 \text{ g } CO} = 2.44 \times 10^3 \text{ mol } CO$$

$$8.60 \text{ kg } H_2 \times \frac{1000 \text{ g } H_2}{1 \text{ kg } H_2} \times \frac{1 \text{ mol } H_2}{2.016 \text{ g } H_2} = 4.27 \times 10^3 \text{ mol } H_2$$

To determine which reactant is limiting, we compare the mole ratio of H_2 and CO required by the balanced equation

Methanol is used as a fuel in Indianapolis-type racing cars.

$$\frac{\text{mol H}_2}{\text{mol CO}} \text{ (required)} = \frac{2}{1} = 2$$

with the actual mole ratio

$$\frac{\text{mol H}_2}{\text{mol CO}} \text{ (actual)} = \frac{4.27 \times 10^3}{2.44 \times 10^3} = 1.75$$

Since the actual mole ratio of H_2 to CO is smaller than the required ratio, *H_2 is limiting.* We therefore must use the amount of H_2 and the mole ratio between H_2 and CH_3OH to determine the maximum amount of methanol that can be produced:

$$4.27 \times 10^3 \text{ mol } H_2 \times \frac{1 \text{ mol } CH_3OH}{2 \text{ mol } H_2} = 2.14 \times 10^3 \text{ mol } CH_3OH$$

Using the molar mass of CH_3OH (32.04 g/mol), we can calculate the theoretical yield in grams:

$$2.14 \times 10^3 \text{ mol } CH_3OH \times \frac{32.04 \text{ g } CH_3OH}{1 \text{ mol } CH_3OH} = 6.86 \times 10^4 \text{ g } CH_3OH$$

Thus, from the amount of reactants given, the maximum amount of CH_3OH that can be formed is 6.86×10^4 g. This is the *theoretical yield.*

The percent yield is

$$\frac{\text{Actual yield (grams)}}{\text{Theoretical yield (grams)}} \times 100 = \frac{3.57 \times 10^4 \text{ g } CH_3OH}{6.86 \times 10^4 \text{ g } CH_3OH} \times 100\% = 52.0\%$$

See Exercises 3.103 and 3.104.

STEPS FOR SOLVING A STOICHIOMETRY PROBLEM INVOLVING MASSES OF REACTANTS AND PRODUCTS

STEP 1

Write and balance the equation for the reaction.

STEP 2

Convert the known masses of substances to moles.

STEP 3

Determine which reactant is limiting.

STEP 4

Using the amount of the limiting reactant and the appropriate mole ratios, compute the number of moles of the desired product.

STEP 5

Convert from moles to grams, using the molar mass.

For Review

Key Terms

chemical stoichiometry

Section 3.1
mass spectrometer
average atomic mass

Section 3.2
mole
Avogadro's number

Section 3.3
molar mass

Section 3.4
mass percent

Section 3.5
empirical formula
molecular formula

Section 3.6
chemical equation
reactants
products
balancing a chemical
  equation

Summary

Stoichiometry deals with the quantities of materials consumed and produced in chemical reactions. It is, in effect, chemical arithmetic. The average atomic mass for each element is obtained by computing the average of the masses of the naturally occurring isotopes. All atomic masses are based on a mass scale that assigns exactly 12 atomic mass units to a ^{12}C atom.

A mole is a unit of measure equal to the number of carbon atoms in exactly 12 grams of pure ^{12}C. This number has been determined experimentally to be 6.02214×10^{23}, which is called Avogadro's number. One mole of any substance contains Avogadro's number of units. One mole of an element has a mass equal to the element's atomic mass in grams.

The molar mass (molecular weight) of a compound is the mass in grams of one mole of the compound and is computed by summing the average masses of its constituent atoms.

Percent composition represents the mass percent of each element in a compound:

$$\text{Mass percent} = \frac{\text{mass of element in 1 mole of substance}}{\text{mass of 1 mole of substance}} \times 100\%$$

The empirical formula is the simplest whole-number ratio of the various types of atoms in a compound and can be derived from the percent composition of the compound. The molecular formula is the exact formula of a molecule of a substance and is always an integer multiple of the empirical formula.

In a chemical reaction, atoms are neither created nor destroyed; they are merely reorganized. All atoms present in the reactants must be accounted for among the products. A chemical equation represents the chemical reaction showing reactants on the left side of an arrow and products on the right. A balanced equation gives the relative numbers of reactant and product molecules.

Amounts of reactants consumed and products formed can be calculated from the balanced equation for a reaction by using the mole ratios relating the reactants and products. The limiting reactant (reagent) is the one that is consumed first and thus determines how much product can be formed.

The theoretical yield of a product is the maximum amount that can be produced from a given amount of the limiting reactant. The actual yield, the amount of product actually obtained in a given experiment, is always less than the theoretical yield. The actual yield is usually represented as a percent yield: the percentage of the theoretical yield actually obtained.

Section 3.8
mole ratio

Section 3.9
stoichiometric quantities
Haber process
limiting reactant (reagent)
theoretical yield
percent yield

In-Class Discussion Questions

These questions are designed to be considered by groups of students in class. Often these questions work well for introducing a particular topic in class.

1. The following are actual student responses to the question: Why is it necessary to balance chemical equations?
   a. The chemicals will not react until you have added the correct mole ratios.
   b. The correct products will not be formed unless the right amount of reactants have been added.
   c. A certain number of products cannot be formed without a certain number of reactants.
   d. The balanced equation tells you how much reactant you need and allows you to predict how much product you'll make.
   e. A mole-to-mole ratio must be established for the reaction to occur as written.

   Justify the best choice, and for choices you did not pick, explain what is wrong with them.

2. What information do we get from a formula? From an equation?

3. You are making cookies and are missing a key ingredient—eggs. You have most of the other ingredients needed to make the cookies, except you have only 1.33 cups of butter and no eggs. You note that the recipe calls for 2 cups of butter and 3 eggs (plus the other ingredients) in order to make 6 dozen cookies. You call a friend and have him bring you some eggs.
   a. How many eggs do you need?
   b. If you use all the butter (and get enough eggs), how many cookies will you make?

   Unfortunately, your friend hangs up before you tell him how many eggs you need. When he arrives, he has a surprise for you—to save time, he has broken them all in a bowl for you.

You ask him how many he brought, and he replies, "I can't remember." You weigh the eggs and find that they weigh 62.1 g. Assuming that an average egg weighs 34.21 g,
   a. How much butter is needed to react with all the eggs?
   b. How many cookies can you make?
   c. Which will you have left over, eggs or butter?
   d. How much is left over?

4. Nitrogen (N_2) and hydrogen (H_2) react to form ammonia (NH_3). Consider the mixture of N_2 (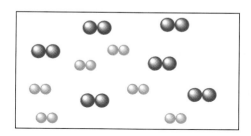) and H_2 ( ) in a closed container as illustrated below:

Assuming the reaction goes to completion, draw a representation of the product mixture. Explain how you arrived at this representation.

5. For the preceding question, which of the following equations best represents the reaction?
   a. $6N_2 + 6H_2 \longrightarrow 4NH_3 + 4N_2$
   b. $N_2 + H_2 \longrightarrow NH_3$
   c. $N + 3H \longrightarrow NH_3$
   d. $N_2 + 3H_2 \longrightarrow 2NH_3$
   e. $2N_2 + 6H_2 \longrightarrow 4NH_3$

   Justify your choice, and for choices you did not pick, explain what is wrong with them.

6. You know that chemical A reacts with chemical B. You react 10.0 g A with 10.0 g B. What information do you need to

determine the amount of product that will be produced? Explain.

7. A new grill has a mass of 30.0 kg. You put 3.0 kg of charcoal in the grill. You burn all the charcoal and the grill has a mass of 30.0 kg. What is the mass of the gases given off? Explain.

8. What happens to the weight of an iron bar when it rusts?
   a. There is no change, since mass is always conserved.
   b. The weight increases.
   c. The weight increases, but if the rust is scraped off, the bar has the original weight.
   d. The weight decreases.
   Justify your choice, and for choices you did not pick, explain what is wrong with them. Make sure to explain what it means for something to rust.

9. You may have noticed that water sometimes drips from the exhaust of a car as it is running. Is this evidence that there is at least a small amount of water originally present in the gasoline? Explain.

Questions 10 and 11 deal with the following situation: You react chemical A with chemical B to make one product. It takes 100 g of A to react completely with 20 g B.

10. What is the mass of the product?
    a. Less than 10 g.
    b. Between 20 and 100 g.
    c. Between 100 and 120 g.
    d. Exactly 120 g.
    e. More than 120 g.

11. What is true about the chemical properties of the product?
    a. The properties are more like chemical A.
    b. The properties are more like chemical B.
    c. The properties are an average of those of chemical A and chemical B.
    d. The properties are not necessarily like either chemical A or chemical B.
    e. The properties are more like chemical A or more like chemical B, but more information is needed.
    Justify your choice, and for choices you did not pick, explain what is wrong with them.

12. Is there a difference between a homogeneous mixture of hydrogen and oxygen in a 2:1 mole ratio and a sample of water vapor? Explain.

13. Chlorine exists mainly as two isotopes, ^{37}Cl and ^{35}Cl. Which is more abundant? How do you know?

14. The average mass of a carbon atom is 12.011. Assuming you could pick up one carbon atom, estimate the chance that you would randomly get one with a mass of 12.011. Support your answer.

15. Can the subscripts in a chemical formula be fractions? Explain. Can the coefficients in a balanced chemical equation be frac-

tions? Explain. Changing the subscripts of chemicals can balance the equations mathematically. Why is this unacceptable?

16. Consider the equation $2A + B \longrightarrow A_2B$. If you mix 1.0 mol of A with 1.0 mol of B, how many moles of A_2B can be produced?

17. According to the law of conservation of mass, mass cannot be gained or destroyed in a chemical reaction. Why can't you simply add the masses of two reactants to determine the total mass of product?

A blue question or exercise number indicates that the answer to that question or exercise appears at the back of the book and a solution appears in the *Solutions Guide*.

Questions

18. The atomic mass of boron (B) is given in the periodic table as 10.81, yet no single atom of boron has a mass of 10.81 amu. Explain.

19. What is the difference between the empirical and molecular formulas of a compound? Can they ever be the same? Explain.

20. Why is the actual yield of a reaction often less than the theoretical yield?

Exercises

In this section similar exercises are paired.

Atomic Masses and the Mass Spectrometer

21. The element magnesium (Mg) has three stable isotopes with the following masses and abundances:

Isotope	Mass (amu)	Abundance
^{24}Mg	23.9850	78.99%
^{25}Mg	24.9858	10.00%
^{26}Mg	25.9826	11.01%

Calculate the average atomic mass (the atomic weight) of magnesium from these data.

22. Assume that element Uus is synthesized and that it has the following stable isotopes:

^{284}Uus (283.4 amu)	34.60%
^{285}Uus (284.7 amu)	21.20%
^{288}Uus (287.8 amu)	44.20%

What is the value of the average atomic mass for Uus that would be listed on the periodic table?

23. An element is a mixture of two isotopes. One isotope of the element has an atomic mass of 34.96885 amu and has a rel-

ative abundance of 75.53%. The other isotope has an atomic mass of 36.96590 amu. Calculate the average atomic mass and identify the element.

24. An element consists of 1.40% of an isotope with mass 203.973 amu, 24.10% of an isotope with mass 205.9745 amu, 22.10% of an isotope with mass 206.9759 amu, and 52.40% of an isotope with mass 207.9766 amu. Calculate the average atomic mass and identify the element.

25. The element europium exists in nature as two isotopes: ^{151}Eu has a mass of 150.9196 amu, and ^{153}Eu has a mass of 152.9209 amu. The average atomic mass of europium is 151.96 amu. Calculate the relative abundance of the two europium isotopes.

26. The element rhenium (Re) has two naturally occurring isotopes, ^{185}Re and ^{187}Re, with an average atomic mass of 186.207 amu. Rhenium is 62.60% ^{187}Re, and the atomic mass of ^{187}Re is 186.956 amu. Calculate the mass of ^{185}Re.

27. The mass spectrum of bromine (Br_2) consists of three peaks with the following characteristics:

Mass (amu)	Relative size
157.84	0.2534
159.84	0.5000
161.84	0.2466

How do you interpret these data?

28. Naturally occurring tellurium (Te) has the following isotopic abundances:

Isotope	Abundance	Mass (amu)
^{120}Te	0.09%	119.90
^{122}Te	2.46%	121.90
^{123}Te	0.87%	122.90
^{124}Te	4.61%	123.90
^{125}Te	6.99%	124.90
^{126}Te	18.71%	125.90
^{128}Te	31.79%	127.90
^{130}Te	34.48%	129.91

Draw the mass spectrum of H_2Te, assuming that the only hydrogen isotope present is ^1H (mass 1.008).

Moles and Molar Masses

29. Calculate the mass of 500. atoms of iron (Fe).

30. How many Fe atoms and how many moles of Fe atoms are in 500.0 g of iron?

31. Diamond is a natural form of pure carbon. How many atoms of carbon are in a 1.00-carat diamond (1.00 carat = 0.200 g)?

32. A diamond contains 5.0×10^{21} atoms of carbon. How many moles of carbon and how many grams of carbon are in this diamond?

33. Aluminum metal is produced by passing an electric current through a solution of aluminum oxide (Al_2O_3) dissolved in molten cryolite (Na_3AlF_6). Calculate the molar masses of Al_2O_3 and Na_3AlF_6.

34. The Freons are a class of compounds containing carbon, chlorine, and fluorine. While they have many valuable uses, they have been shown to be responsible for depletion of the ozone in the upper atmosphere. In 1991, two replacement compounds for Freons went into production: HFC-134a (CH_2FCF_3) and HCFC-124 ($CHClFCF_3$). Calculate the molar masses of these two compounds.

35. Calculate the molar mass of the following substances.
    a. NH_3
    b. N_2H_4
    c. $(NH_4)_2Cr_2O_7$

36. Calculate the molar mass of the following substances.
    a. P_4O_6
    b. $Ca_3(PO_4)_2$
    c. Na_2HPO_4

37. How many moles of compound are present in 1.00 g of each of the compounds in Exercise 35?

38. How many moles of compound are present in 1.00 g of each of the compounds in Exercise 36?

39. How many grams of compound are present in 5.00 mol of each of the compounds in Exercise 35?

40. How many grams of compound are present in 5.00 mol of each of the compounds in Exercise 36?

41. How many grams of nitrogen are present in 5.00 mol of each of the compounds in Exercise 35?

42. How many grams of phosphorus are present in 5.00 mol of each of the compounds in Exercise 36?

43. How many molecules (or formula units) are present in 1.00 g of each of the compounds in Exercise 35?

44. How many molecules (or formula units) are present in 1.00 g of each of the compounds in Exercise 36?

45. How many atoms of nitrogen are present in 1.00 g of each of the compounds in Exercise 35?

46. How many atoms of phosphorus are present in 1.00 g of each of the compounds in Exercise 36?

47. Ascorbic acid, or vitamin C ($C_6H_8O_6$), is an essential vitamin. It cannot be stored by the body and must be present in the diet. What is the molar mass of ascorbic acid? Vitamin C tablets are taken as a dietary supplement. If a typical tablet contains 500.0 mg of vitamin C, how many moles and how many molecules of vitamin C does it contain?

48. The molecular formula of acetylsalicylic acid (aspirin), one of the most commonly used pain relievers, is $C_9H_8O_4$.
   a. Calculate the molar mass of aspirin.
   b. A typical aspirin tablet contains 500. mg of $C_9H_8O_4$. How many moles of $C_9H_8O_4$ molecules and how many molecules of acetylsalicylic acid are in a 500.-mg tablet?

49. How many moles are represented by each of these samples?
   a. 100 molecules (exactly) of H_2O
   b. 100.0 g H_2O
   c. 150 molecules (exactly) of O_2

50. How many moles are represented by each of these samples?
   a. 150.0 g Fe_2O_3 **c.** 1.5×10^{16} molecules of BF_3
   b. 10.0 mg NO_2

51. Determine the mass in grams of the following:
   a. 3.00×10^{20} N_2 molecules   **e.** 2.00×10^{-15} mol N_2
   b. 3.00×10^{-3} mol N_2 **f.** 18.0 picomoles of N_2
   c. 1.5×10^2 mol N_2 **g.** 5.0 nanomoles of N_2
   d. A single N_2 molecule

52. How many atoms of nitrogen are present in 5.00 g of each of the following?
   a. glycine, $C_2H_5O_2N$ **c.** calcium nitrate
   b. magnesium nitride   **d.** dinitrogen tetroxide

53. Aspartame is an artificial sweetener that is 160 times sweeter than sucrose (table sugar) when dissolved in water. It is marketed as Nutra-Sweet. The molecular formula of aspartame is $C_{14}H_{18}N_2O_5$.
   a. Calculate the molar mass of aspartame.
   b. How many moles of molecules are present in 10.0 g aspartame?
   c. Calculate the mass in grams of 1.56 mol aspartame.
   d. How many molecules are in 5.0 mg aspartame?
   e. How many atoms of nitrogen are in 1.2 g aspartame?
   f. What is the mass in grams of 1.0×10^9 molecules of aspartame?
   g. What is the mass in grams of one molecule of aspartame?

54. Humulone, $C_{21}H_{30}O_5$, is one of the flavor components that gives a bitter taste to the hops used in making beer.
   a. What is the molar mass of humulone?
   b. How many moles of $C_{21}H_{30}O_5$ molecules are in 275 mg of humulone?
   c. What is the mass of 0.600 mol of humulone?
   d. How many atoms of hydrogen are in 1.00 pg of humulone?
   e. What is the mass of 1.00×10^9 molecules of humulone?
   f. What is the mass of one molecule of humulone?

Percent Composition

55. Photocells use a semiconducting material that produces an electric current or a change in resistance on exposure to light. Compounds of cadmium (Cd) combined with an element from Group 6A of the periodic table are used in many common photocells. Calculate the mass percent of Cd in CdS, CdSe, and CdTe.

56. Calculate the percent composition by mass of the following compounds that are important starting materials for synthetic polymers:
   a. $C_3H_4O_2$ (acrylic acid, from which acrylic plastics are made)
   b. $C_4H_6O_2$ (methyl acrylate, from which Plexiglas is made)
   c. C_3H_3N (acrylonitrile, from which Orlon is made)

57. In 1987 the first substance to act as a superconductor at a temperature above that of liquid nitrogen (77 K) was discovered. The approximate formula of this substance is $YBa_2Cu_3O_7$. Calculate the percent composition by mass of this material.

58. There are several important compounds that contain only nitrogen and oxygen. Calculate the mass percent of nitrogen in each of the following:
   a. NO, a gas formed by the reaction of N_2 with O_2 in internal combustion engines
   b. NO_2, a brown gas mainly responsible for the brownish color of photochemical smog
   c. N_2O_4, a colorless liquid used as a fuel in space shuttles
   d. N_2O, a colorless gas sometimes used as an anesthetic by dentists (known as laughing gas)

59. Arrange the following substances in order of increasing mass percent of carbon.
   a. caffeine, $C_8H_{10}N_4O_2$
   b. sucrose, $C_{12}H_{22}O_{11}$
   c. ethanol, C_2H_5OH

60. Arrange the substances in Exercise 58 in order of the increasing mass percent of nitrogen.

61. Vitamin B_{12}, cyanocobalamin, is essential for human nutrition. It is concentrated in animal tissue but not in higher plants. Although nutritional requirements for the vitamin are quite low, people who abstain completely from animal products may develop a deficiency anemia. Cyanocobalamin is the form used in vitamin supplements. It contains 4.34% cobalt by mass. Calculate the molar mass of cyanocobalamin, assuming that there is one atom of cobalt in every molecule of cyanocobalamin.

62. Fungal laccase, a blue protein found in wood-rotting fungi, is 0.390% Cu by mass. If a fungal laccase molecule contains 4 copper atoms, what is the molar mass of fungal laccase?

Empirical and Molecular Formulas

63. Express the composition of each of the following compounds as the mass percents of its elements.
   a. formaldehyde, CH_2O
   b. glucose, $C_6H_{12}O_6$
   c. acetic acid, $HC_2H_3O_2$

64. Considering your answer to Exercise 63, which type of formula, empirical or molecular, can be obtained from elemental analysis that gives percent composition?

65. Give the empirical formula for each of the following compounds (for which the common names are given).
   a. vitamin C, $C_6H_8O_6$
   b. benzene, C_6H_6
   c. acetylene, C_2H_2
   d. phosphorus pentoxide, P_4O_{10}
   e. glucose, $C_6H_{12}O_6$
   f. acetic acid, $HC_2H_3O_2$

66. Determine the molecular formulas to which the following empirical formulas and molar masses pertain.
   a. SNH (188.35 g/mol)
   b. $NPCl_2$ (347.64 g/mol)
   c. CoC_4O_4 (341.94 g/mol)
   d. SN (184.32 g/mol)

67. One of the most commonly used white pigments in paint is a compound of titanium and oxygen that contains 59.9% Ti by mass. Determine the empirical formula of this compound.

68. The compound adrenaline contains 56.79% C, 6.56% H, 28.37% O, and 8.28% N by mass. What is the empirical formula for adrenaline?

69. There are two binary compounds of mercury and oxygen. Heating either of them results in the decomposition of the compound, with oxygen gas escaping into the atmosphere while leaving a residue of pure mercury. Heating 0.6498 g of one of the compounds leaves a residue of 0.6018 g. Heating 0.4172 g of the other compound results in a mass loss of 0.016 g. Determine the empirical formula of each compound.

70. A sample of urea contains 1.121 g N, 0.161 g H, 0.480 g C, and 0.640 g O. What is the empirical formula of urea?

71. A compound that contains only nitrogen and oxygen is 30.4% N by mass; the molar mass of the compound is 92 g/mol. What is the empirical formula of the compound? What is the molecular formula of the compound?

72. A compound containing only sulfur and nitrogen is 69.6% S by mass; the molar mass is 184 g/mol. What are the empirical and molecular formulas of the compound?

73. Benzene contains only carbon and hydrogen and is 7.74% H by mass; the molar mass of benzene is 78.1 g/mol. Determine the empirical and molecular formulas of benzene.

74. Adipic acid is an organic compound composed of 49.31% C, 43.79% O, and the rest hydrogen. If the molar mass of adipic acid is 146.1 g/mol, what are the empirical and molecular formulas for adipic acid?

75. Many homes in rural America are heated by propane gas, a compound that contains only carbon and hydrogen. Complete combustion of a sample of propane produced 2.641 g of carbon dioxide and 1.442 g of water as the only products. Find the empirical formula of propane.

76. A compound contains only C, H, and N. Combustion of 35.0 mg of the compound produces 33.5 mg CO_2 and 41.1 mg H_2O. What is the empirical formula of the compound?

77. Cumene is a compound containing only carbon and hydrogen that is used in the production of acetone and phenol in the chemical industry. Combustion of 47.6 mg cumene produces some CO_2 and 42.8 mg water. The molar mass of cumene is between 115 and 125 g/mol. Determine the empirical and molecular formulas.

78. A compound contains only carbon, hydrogen, and oxygen. Combustion of 10.68 mg of the compound yields 16.01 mg CO_2 and 4.37 mg H_2O. The molar mass of the compound is 176.1 g/mol. What are the empirical and molecular formulas of the compound?

Balancing Chemical Equations

79. Write a balanced chemical equation that describes each of the following.
   a. Iron metal reacts with oxygen to form rust, iron(III) oxide.
   b. Calcium metal reacts with water to produce aqueous calcium hydroxide and hydrogen gas.
   c. Aqueous barium hydroxide reacts with aqueous sulfuric acid to produce solid barium sulfate and water.

80. Give the balanced equation for each of the following chemical reactions:
   a. Glucose ($C_6H_{12}O_6$) reacts with oxygen gas to produce gaseous carbon dioxide and water vapor.
   b. Solid iron(III) sulfide reacts with gaseous hydrogen chloride to form solid iron(III) chloride and hydrogen sulfide gas.
   c. Carbon disulfide liquid reacts with ammonia gas to produce hydrogen sulfide gas and solid ammonium thiocyanate (NH_4SCN).

81. Balance the following equations:
   a. $Cu(s) + AgNO_3(aq) \rightarrow Ag(s) + Cu(NO_3)_2(aq)$
   b. $Zn(s) + HCl(aq) \rightarrow ZnCl_2(aq) + H_2(g)$
   c. $Au_2S_3(s) + H_2(g) \rightarrow Au(s) + H_2S(g)$

82. Balance the following equations:
   a. $Ca(OH)_2(aq) + H_3PO_4(aq) \rightarrow H_2O(l) + Ca_3(PO_4)_2(s)$
   b. $Al(OH)_3(s) + HCl(aq) \rightarrow AlCl_3(aq) + H_2O(l)$
   c. $AgNO_3(aq) + H_2SO_4(aq) \rightarrow Ag_2SO_4(s) + HNO_3(aq)$

83. Balance the following equations representing combustion reactions:
   a. $C_{12}H_{22}O_{11}(s) + O_2(g) \rightarrow CO_2(g) + H_2O(g)$
   b. $C_6H_6(l) + O_2(g) \rightarrow CO_2(g) + H_2O(g)$
   c. $Fe(s) + O_2(g) \rightarrow Fe_2O_3(s)$
   d. $C_4H_{10}(g) + O_2(g) \rightarrow CO_2(g) + H_2O(g)$
   e. $FeO(s) + O_2(g) \rightarrow Fe_2O_3(s)$

84. Balance the following equations:

a. $Cr(s) + S_8(s) \rightarrow Cr_2S_3(s)$

b. $NaHCO_3(s) \xrightarrow{\text{Heat}} Na_2CO_3(s) + CO_2(g) + H_2O(g)$

c. $KClO_3(s) \xrightarrow{\text{Heat}} KCl(s) + O_2(g)$

d. $Eu(s) + HF(g) \rightarrow EuF_3(s) + H_2(g)$

85. Silicon is produced for the chemical and electronics industries by the following reactions. Give the balanced equation for each reaction.

a. $SiO_2(s) + C(s) \xrightarrow[\text{arc furnace}]{\text{Electric}} Si(s) + CO(g)$

b. Silicon tetrachloride is reacted with very pure magnesium, producing silicon and magnesium chloride.

c. $Na_2SiF_6(s) + Na(s) \rightarrow Si(s) + NaF(s)$

86. Phosphorus occurs naturally in the form of fluorapatite, $CaF_2 \cdot 3Ca_3(PO_4)_2$, the dot indicating 1 part CaF_2 to 3 parts $Ca_3(PO_4)_2$. This mineral is reacted with an aqueous solution of sulfuric acid in the preparation of a fertilizer. The products are phosphoric acid, hydrogen fluoride, and gypsum, $CaSO_4 \cdot 2H_2O$. Write and balance the chemical equation describing this process.

87. Lead hydrogen arsenate, an inorganic insecticide used against the potato beetle, is a product in the following reaction:

$Pb(NO_3)_2(aq) + H_3AsO_4(aq) \longrightarrow$
$PbHAsO_4(s) + HNO_3(aq)$

Balance this equation.

88. The electrolysis of concentrated brine solutions is an important source of NaOH, H_2, and Cl_2 for the chemical industry. The reaction is

$NaCl(aq) + H_2O(l) \xrightarrow{\text{Electricity}}$
$Cl_2(g) + H_2(g) + NaOH(aq)$

Balance this equation.

Reaction Stoichiometry

89. Calculate the masses of Cr_2O_3, N_2, and H_2O produced from 10.8 g $(NH_4)_2Cr_2O_7$ in an ammonium dichromate volcano reaction as described in Sample Exercise 3.14.

90. Over the years, the thermite reaction has been used for welding railroad rails, in incendiary bombs, and to ignite solid-fuel rocket motors. The reaction is

$Fe_2O_3(s) + 2Al(s) \longrightarrow 2Fe(l) + Al_2O_3(s)$

What masses of iron(III) oxide and aluminum must be used to produce 15.0 g iron? What is the maximum mass of aluminum oxide that could be produced?

91. The reusable booster rockets of the U.S. space shuttle employ a mixture of aluminum and ammonium perchlorate for fuel. A possible equation for this reaction is

$3Al(s) + 3NH_4ClO_4(s) \longrightarrow$
$Al_2O_3(s) + AlCl_3(s) + 3NO(g) + 6H_2O(g)$

What mass of NH_4ClO_4 should be used in the fuel mixture for every kilogram of Al?

92. One of relatively few reactions that takes place directly between two solids at room temperature is

$Ba(OH)_2 \cdot 8H_2O(s) + NH_4SCN(s) \longrightarrow$
$Ba(SCN)_2(s) + H_2O(l) + NH_3(g)$

In this equation, the $\cdot 8H_2O$ in $Ba(OH)_2 \cdot 8H_2O$ indicates the presence of eight water molecules. This compound is called barium hydroxide octahydrate.

a. Balance the equation.

b. What mass of ammonium thiocyanate (NH_4SCN) must be used if it is to react completely with 6.5 g barium hydroxide octahydrate?

93. Coke is an impure form of carbon that is often used in the industrial production of metals from their oxides. If a sample of coke is 95% carbon by mass, determine the mass of coke needed to react completely with 1.0 ton of copper(II) oxide.

$2CuO(s) + C(s) \longrightarrow 2Cu(s) + CO_2(g)$

94. Bacterial digestion is an economical method of sewage treatment. The reaction

$5CO_2(g) + 55NH_4^+(aq) + 76O_2(g) \xrightarrow{\text{bacteria}}$
$C_5H_7O_2N(s) + 54NO_2^-(aq) + 52H_2O(l) + 109H^+(aq)$
bacterial tissue

is an intermediate step in the conversion of the nitrogen in organic compounds into nitrate ions. How much bacterial tissue is produced in a treatment plant for every 1.0×10^4 kg of wastewater containing 3.0% NH_4^+ ions by mass? Assume that 95% of the ammonium ions are consumed by the bacteria.

95. The compound cisplatin, $Pt(NH_3)_2Cl_2$, has been studied extensively as an antitumor agent.

a. Calculate the elemental percent composition by mass of cisplatin.

b. Cisplatin is synthesized as follows:

$K_2PtCl_4(aq) + 2NH_3(aq) \longrightarrow Pt(NH_3)_2Cl_2(s) + 2KCl(aq)$

What mass of cisplatin can be made from 100. g of K_2PtCl_4 and sufficient NH_3? What mass of KCl is also produced?

96. Aspirin ($C_9H_8O_4$) is synthesized by reacting salicylic acid ($C_7H_6O_3$) with acetic anhydride ($C_4H_6O_3$). The balanced equation is

$C_7H_6O_3 + C_4H_6O_3 \longrightarrow C_9H_8O_4 + HC_2H_3O_2$

a. What mass of acetic anhydride is needed to completely consume 1.00×10^2 g salicylic acid?

b. What is the maximum mass of aspirin (the theoretical yield) that could be produced in this reaction?

Limiting Reactants and Percent Yield

97. Consider the reaction

$$Mg(s) + I_2(s) \longrightarrow MgI_2(s)$$

Identify the limiting reagent in each of the reaction mixtures below:
  a. 100 atoms of Mg and 100 molecules of I_2
  b. 150 atoms of Mg and 100 molecules of I_2
  c. 200 atoms of Mg and 300 molecules of I_2
  d. 0.16 mol Mg and 0.25 mol I_2
  e. 0.14 mol Mg and 0.14 mol I_2
  f. 0.12 mol Mg and 0.08 mol I_2
  g. 6.078 g Mg and 63.46 g I_2
  h. 1.00 g Mg and 2.00 g I_2
  i. 1.00 g Mg and 20.00 g I_2

98. Consider the reaction

$$2H_2(g) + O_2(g) \longrightarrow 2H_2O(g)$$

Identify the limiting reagent in each of the reaction mixtures given below:
  a. 50 molecules of H_2 and 25 molecules of O_2
  b. 100 molecules of H_2 and 40 molecules of O_2
  c. 100 molecules of H_2 and 100 molecules of O_2
  d. 0.50 mol H_2 and 0.75 mol O_2
  e. 0.80 mol H_2 and 0.75 mol O_2
  f. 1.0 g H_2 and 0.25 mol O_2
  g. 5.00 g H_2 and 56.00 g O_2

99. When a mixture of silver metal and sulfur is heated, silver sulfide is formed:

$$16Ag(s) + S_8(s) \xrightarrow{\text{Heat}} 8Ag_2S(s)$$

  a. What mass of Ag_2S is produced from a mixture of 2.0 g Ag and 2.0 g S_8?
  b. What mass of which reactant is left unreacted?

100. Mercury and bromine will react with each other to produce mercury(II) bromide:

$$Hg(l) + Br_2(l) \longrightarrow HgBr_2(s)$$

  a. What mass of $HgBr_2$ can be produced from the reaction of 10.0 g Hg and 9.00 g Br_2? What mass of which reagent is left unreacted?
  b. What mass of $HgBr_2$ can be produced from the reaction of 5.00 mL mercury (density = 13.6 g/mL) and 5.00 mL bromine (density = 3.10 g/mL)?

101. Consider the following unbalanced equation:

$$Ca_3(PO_4)_2(s) + H_2SO_4(aq) \longrightarrow CaSO_4(s) + H_3PO_4(aq)$$

What masses of calcium sulfate and phosphoric acid can be produced from the reaction of 1.0 kg calcium phosphate with 1.0 kg concentrated sulfuric acid (98% H_2SO_4 by mass)?

102. Hydrogen cyanide is produced industrially from the reaction of gaseous ammonia, oxygen, and methane:

$$2NH_3(g) + 3O_2(g) + 2CH_4(g) \longrightarrow 2HCN(g) + 6H_2O(g)$$

If 5.00×10^3 kg each of NH_3, O_2, and CH_4 are reacted, what mass of HCN and of H_2O will be produced, assuming 100% yield?

103. The reaction of ethane gas (C_2H_6) with chlorine gas produces C_2H_5Cl as its main product (along with HCl). In addition, the reaction invariably produces a variety of other minor products, including $C_2H_4Cl_2$, $C_2H_3Cl_3$, and others. Naturally, the production of these minor products reduces the yield of the main product. Calculate the percent yield of C_2H_5Cl if the reaction of 300. g of ethane with 650. g of chlorine produced 490. g of C_2H_5Cl.

104. A student prepared aspirin in a laboratory experiment using the reaction in Exercise 96. The student reacted 1.50 g salicylic acid with 2.00 g acetic anhydride. The yield was 1.50 g aspirin. Calculate the theoretical yield and the percent yield for this experiment.

105. Aluminum burns in bromine, producing aluminum bromide:

$$2Al(s) + 3Br_2(l) \longrightarrow 2AlBr_3(s)$$

In a certain experiment, 6.0 g aluminum was reacted with an excess of bromine to yield 50.3 g aluminum bromide. Calculate the theoretical and percent yields for this experiment.

106. Consider the following unbalanced reaction:

$$P_4(s) + F_2(g) \longrightarrow PF_3(g)$$

How many grams of F_2 are needed to produce 120. g of PF_3 if the reaction has a 78.1% yield?

Additional Exercises

107. Only one isotope of this element occurs in nature. One atom of this isotope has a mass of 9.123×10^{-23} g. Identify the element and give its atomic mass.

108. Chloral hydrate ($C_2H_3Cl_3O_2$) is a drug formerly used as a sedative and hypnotic. It is the compound used to make "Mickey Finns" in detective stories.
  a. Calculate the molar mass of chloral hydrate.
  b. How many moles of $C_2H_3Cl_3O_2$ molecules are in 500.0 g chloral hydrate?
  c. What is the mass in grams of 2.0×10^{-2} mol chloral hydrate?
  d. How many chlorine atoms are in 5.0 g chloral hydrate?
  e. What mass of chloral hydrate would contain 1.0 g Cl?
  f. What is the mass of exactly 500 molecules of chloral hydrate?

109. The empirical formula of styrene is CH; the molar mass of styrene is 104.14 g/mol. How many H atoms are present in a 2.00-g sample of styrene?

110. Terephthalic acid is an important chemical used in the manufacture of polyesters and plasticizers. It contains only C, H, and O. Combustion of 19.81 mg terephthalic acid produces 41.98 mg CO_2 and 6.45 mg H_2O. The molar mass of terephthalic acid is 166 g/mol. Calculate the empirical and molecular formulas for terephthalic acid.

111. A binary compound between an unknown element E and hydrogen contains 91.27% E and 8.73% H by mass. If the formula of the compound is E_3H_8, calculate the atomic mass of E.

112. A 0.755-g sample of hydrated copper(II) sulfate

$$CuSO_4 \cdot xH_2O$$

was heated carefully until it had changed completely to anhydrous copper(II) sulfate ($CuSO_4$) with a mass of 0.483 g. Determine the value of x. (This number is called the *number of waters of hydration* of copper(II) sulfate. It specifies the number of water molecules per formula unit of $CuSO_4$ in the hydrated crystal.)

113. Calcium oxide, or lime, is produced by the thermal decomposition of limestone:

$$CaCO_3(s) \xrightarrow{\text{Heat}} CaO(s) + CO_2(g)$$

What mass of CaO can be produced from 2.00×10^3 kg limestone?

114. ABS plastic is a tough, hard plastic used in applications requiring shock resistance. The polymer consists of three monomer units: acrylonitrile (C_3H_3N), butadiene (C_4H_6), and styrene (C_8H_8).

    a. A sample of ABS plastic contains 8.80% N by mass. It took 0.605 g of Br_2 to react completely with a 1.20-g sample of ABS plastic. Bromine reacts 1:1 (by moles) with the butadiene molecules in the polymer and nothing else. What is the percent by mass of acrylonitrile and butadiene in this polymer?

    b. What are the relative numbers of each of the monomer units in this polymer?

115. Consider the reaction

$$4Al(s) + 3O_2(g) \longrightarrow 2Al_2O_3(s)$$

Identify the limiting reagent in each of the following reaction mixtures:

    a. 1.0 mol Al and 1.0 mol O_2
    b. 2.0 mol Al and 4.0 mol O_2
    c. 0.50 mol Al and 0.75 mol O_2
    d. 64.75 g Al and 115.21 g O_2
    e. 75.89 g Al and 112.25 g O_2
    f. 51.28 g Al and 118.22 g O_2

116. Methane (CH_4) is the main component of marsh gas. Heating methane in the presence of sulfur produces carbon disulfide and hydrogen sulfide as the only products.

    a. Write the balanced chemical equation for the reaction of methane and sulfur.

    b. Calculate the theoretical yield of carbon disulfide when 120. g of methane is reacted with an equal mass of sulfur.

117. An iron ore sample contains Fe_2O_3 plus other impurities. A 752-g sample of impure iron ore is heated with excess carbon, producing 453 g of pure iron by the following reaction:

$$Fe_2O_3(s) + 3C(s) \longrightarrow 2Fe(s) + 3CO(g)$$

What is the mass percent of Fe_2O_3 in the impure iron ore sample? Assume that Fe_2O_3 is the only source of iron and that the reaction is 100% efficient.

118. Commercial brass, an alloy of Zn and Cu, reacts with hydrochloric acid as follows:

$$Zn(s) + 2HCl(aq) \longrightarrow ZnCl_2(aq) + H_2(g)$$

(Cu does not react with HCl.) When 0.5065 g of a certain brass alloy is reacted with excess HCl, 0.0985 g $ZnCl_2$ is eventually isolated.

    a. What is the composition of the brass by mass?

    b. How could this result be checked without changing the above procedure?

119. Vitamin A has a molar mass of 286.4 g/mol and a general molecular formula of C_xH_yE, where E is an unknown element. If vitamin A is 83.86% C and 10.56% H by mass, what is the molecular formula of vitamin A?

Challenge Problems

120. Natural rubidium has the average mass 85.4678 and is composed of isotopes ^{85}Rb (mass = 84.9117) and ^{87}Rb. The ratio of atoms $^{85}Rb/^{87}Rb$ in natural rubidium is 2.591. Calculate the mass of ^{87}Rb.

121. A compound contains only carbon, hydrogen, nitrogen, and oxygen. Combustion of 0.157 g of the compound produced 0.213 g CO_2 and 0.0310 g H_2O. In another experiment, it is found that 0.103 g of the compound produces 0.0230 g NH_3. What is the empirical formula of the compound? *Hint:* Combustion involves reacting with excess O_2. Assume that all the carbon ends up in CO_2 and all the hydrogen ends up in H_2O. Also assume that all the nitrogen ends up in the NH_3 in the second experiment.

122. Nitric acid is produced commercially by the Ostwald process, represented by the following equations:

$$4NH_3(g) + 5O_2(g) \longrightarrow 4NO(g) + 6H_2O(g)$$
$$2NO(g) + O_2(g) \longrightarrow 2NO_2(g)$$
$$3NO_2(g) + H_2O(l) \longrightarrow 2HNO_3(aq) + NO(g)$$

What mass of NH_3 must be used to produce 1.0×10^6 kg HNO_3 by the Ostwald process, assuming 100% yield in each reaction?

123. In the production of printed circuit boards for the electronics industry, a 0.60-mm layer of copper is laminated onto an insulating plastic board. Next, a circuit pattern made of a chemically resistant polymer is printed on the board. The unwanted copper is removed by chemical etching, and the protective polymer is finally removed by solvents. One etching reaction is

$$Cu(NH_3)_4Cl_2(aq) + 4NH_3(aq) + Cu(s) \longrightarrow$$
$$2Cu(NH_3)_4Cl(aq)$$

A plant needs to manufacture 10,000 printed circuit boards, each 8.0×16.0 cm in area. An average of 80.% of the copper is removed from each board (density of copper = 8.96 g/cm^3). What masses of $Cu(NH_3)_4Cl_2$ and NH_3 are needed to do this? Assume 100% yield.

124. The aspirin substitute, acetaminophen ($C_8H_9O_2N$), is produced by the following three-step synthesis:

I. $C_6H_5O_3N(s) + 3H_2(g) + HCl(aq) \longrightarrow$
$$C_6H_8ONCl(s) + 2H_2O(l)$$

II. $C_6H_8ONCl(s) + NaOH(aq) \longrightarrow$
$$C_6H_7ON(s) + H_2O(l) + NaCl(aq)$$

III. $C_6H_7ON(s) + C_4H_6O_3(l) \longrightarrow$
$$C_8H_9O_2N(s) + HC_2H_3O_2(l)$$

The first two reactions have percent yields of 87% and 98% by mass, respectively. The overall reaction yields 3 mol of acetaminophen product for every 4 mol of $C_6H_5O_3N$ reacted.
a. What is the percent yield by mass for the overall process?
b. What is the percent yield by mass of step III?

125. An element X forms both a dichloride (XCl_2) and a tetrachloride (XCl_4). Treatment of 10.00 g XCl_2 with excess chlorine forms 12.55 g XCl_4. Calculate the atomic mass of X, and identify X.

126. When $M_2S_3(s)$ is heated in air, it is converted to $MO_2(s)$. A 4.000-g sample of $M_2S_3(s)$ shows a decrease in mass of 0.277 g when it is heated in air. What is the average atomic mass of M?

127. When aluminum metal is heated with an element from Group 6A of the periodic table, an ionic compound forms. When the experiment is performed with an unknown Group 6A element, the product is 18.56% Al by mass. What is the formula of the compound?

128. A sample of a mixture containing only sodium chloride and potassium chloride has a mass of 4.000 g. When this sample is dissolved in water and excess silver nitrate is added, a white solid (silver chloride) forms. After filtration and drying, the solid silver chloride has the mass 8.5904 g. Calculate the mass percent of each mixture component.

129. A 1.500-g sample of a mixture containing only Cu_2O and CuO was treated with hydrogen to produce 1.252 g pure copper metal. Calculate the percentage composition (by mass) of the mixture.

Marathon Problem*

This problem is designed to incorporate several concepts and techniques into one situation. Marathon Problems can be used in class by groups of students to help facilitate problem-solving skills.

130. From the information below, determine the mass of substance C that will be formed if 45.0 grams of substance A reacts with 23.0 grams of substance B. (Assume that the reaction between A and B goes to completion.)
a. Substance A is a gray solid that consists of an alkaline earth metal and carbon (37.5% by mass). It reacts with substance B to produce substances C and D. Forty million trillion formula units of A have a mass of 4.26 milligrams.
b. 47.9 grams of substance B contains 5.36 grams of hydrogen and 42.5 grams of oxygen.
c. When 10.0 grams of C is burned in excess oxygen, 33.8 grams of carbon dioxide and 6.92 grams of water are produced. A mass spectrum of substance C shows a parent molecular ion with a mass-to-charge ratio of 26.
d. Substance D is the hydroxide of the metal in substance A.

*This Marathon Problem was developed by James H. Burness, Penn State University, York Campus. Reprinted with permission from the *Journal of Chemical Education,* Vol. 68, No. 11, 1991, pp. 919–922; copyright © 1991, Division of Chemical Education, Inc.

Chapter 4

Types of Chemical Reactions and Solution Stoichiometry

Much of the chemistry that affects each of us occurs among substances dissolved in water. For example, virtually all the chemistry that makes life possible occurs in an aqueous environment. Also, various medical tests involve aqueous reactions, depending heavily on analyses of blood and other body fluids. In addition to the common tests for sugar, cholesterol, and iron, analyses for specific chemical markers allow detection of many diseases before obvious symptoms occur.

Aqueous chemistry is also important in our environment. In recent years, contamination of the groundwater by substances such as chloroform and nitrates has been widely publicized. Water is essential for life, and the maintenance of an ample supply of clean water is crucial to all civilization.

To understand the chemistry that occurs in such diverse places as the human body, the atmosphere, the groundwater, the oceans, the local water treatment plant, your hair as you shampoo it, and so on, we must understand how substances dissolved in water react with each other.

However, before we can understand solution reactions, we need to discuss the nature of solutions in which water is the dissolving medium, or *solvent*. These solutions are called **aqueous solutions.** In this chapter we will study the nature of materials after they are dissolved in water and various types of reactions that occur among these substances. You will see that the procedures developed in Chapter 3 to deal with chemical reactions work very well for reactions that take place in aqueous solutions. To understand the types of reactions that occur in aqueous solutions, we must first explore the types of species present. This requires an understanding of the nature of water.

Yellow lead iodide is produced when lead nitrate is mixed with potassium iodide.

4.1 Water, the Common Solvent

Molecular Model: H_2O

Water is one of the most important substances on earth. It is essential for sustaining the reactions that keep us alive, but it also affects our lives in many indirect ways. Water helps moderate the earth's temperature; it cools automobile engines, nuclear power plants, and many industrial processes; it provides a means of transportation on the earth's surface and a medium for the growth of a myriad of creatures we use as food; and much more.

One of the most valuable properties of water is its ability to dissolve many different substances. For example, salt "disappears" when you sprinkle it into the water used to cook vegetables, as does sugar when you add it to your iced tea. In each case the "disappearing" substance is obviously still present—you can taste it. What happens when a solid dissolves? To understand this process, we need to consider the nature of water. Liquid water consists of a collection of H_2O molecules. An individual H_2O molecule is "bent" or V-shaped, with an H—O—H angle of approximately 105 degrees:

$$H \overset{105°}{\diagdown \diagup} H$$
$$O$$

The O—H bonds in the water molecule are covalent bonds formed by electron sharing between the oxygen and hydrogen atoms. However, the electrons of the bond are not shared equally between these atoms. For reasons we will discuss in later chapters, oxygen has a greater attraction for electrons than does hydrogen. If the electrons were shared equally between the two atoms, both would be electrically neutral because, on average, the number of electrons around each would equal the number of protons in that nucleus. However, because the oxygen atom has a greater attraction for electrons, the shared electrons tend to spend more time close to the oxygen than to either of the hydrogens. Thus the oxygen atom gains a slight excess of negative charge, and the hydrogen atoms become slightly positive. This is shown in Fig. 4.1, where δ (delta) indicates a *partial* charge (*less than one unit of charge*). Because of this unequal charge distribution, water is said to be a **polar molecule.** It is this polarity that gives water its great ability to dissolve compounds.

A schematic of an ionic solid dissolving in water is shown in Fig. 4.2. Note that the "positive ends" of the water molecules are attracted to the negatively charged anions and that the "negative ends" are attracted to the positively charged cations. This process is called **hydration.** The hydration of its ions tends to cause a salt to "fall apart" in the water, or to dissolve. The strong forces present among the positive and negative ions of the solid are replaced by strong water–ion interactions.

It is very important to recognize that when ionic substances (salts) dissolve in water, they break up into the *individual* cations and anions. For instance, when ammonium nitrate (NH_4NO_3) dissolves in water, the resulting solution contains NH_4^+ and NO_3^- ions moving around independently. This process can be represented as

$$NH_4NO_3(s) \xrightarrow{H_2O(l)} NH_4^+(aq) + NO_3^-(aq)$$

where (*aq*) designates that the ions are hydrated by unspecified numbers of water molecules.

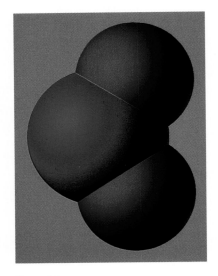

Figure 4.1

(top) The water molecule is polar. (bottom) A space-filling model of the water molecule.

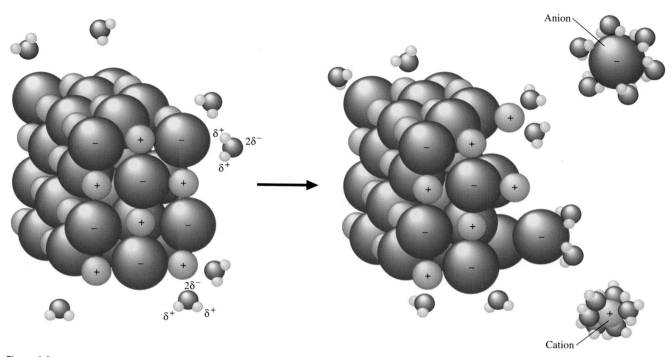

Figure 4.2

Polar water molecules interact with the positive and negative ions of a salt, assisting in the dissolving process.

Animation: The Dissolution of a Solid in a Liquid

The **solubility** of ionic substances in water varies greatly. For example, sodium chloride is quite soluble in water, whereas silver chloride (contains Ag^+ and Cl^- ions) is only very slightly soluble. The differences in the solubilities of ionic compounds in water typically depend on the relative attractions of the ions for each other (these forces hold the solid together) and the attractions of the ions for water molecules (which cause the solid to disperse [dissolve] in water). Solubility is a complex topic that we will explore in much more detail in Chapter 11. However, the most important thing to remember at this point is that when an ionic solid does dissolve in water, the ions become hydrated and are dispersed (move around independently).

Water also dissolves many nonionic substances. Ethanol (C_2H_5OH), for example, is very soluble in water. Wine, beer, and mixed drinks are aqueous solutions of ethanol and other substances. Why is ethanol so soluble in water? The answer lies in the structure of the alcohol molecules, which is shown in Fig. 4.3(a). The molecule contains a polar O—H bond like those in water, which makes it very compatible with water. The interaction of water with ethanol is represented in Fig. 4.3(b).

Molecular Model: C_2H_5OH

Many substances do not dissolve in water. Pure water will not, for example, dissolve animal fat, because fat molecules are nonpolar and do not interact effectively with polar water molecules. In general, polar and ionic substances are expected to be more soluble in water than nonpolar substances. "Like dissolves like" is a useful rule for predicting solubility. We will explore the basis for this generalization when we discuss the details of solution formation in Chapter 11.

Figure 4.3
(a) The ethanol molecule contains a polar O—H bond similar to those in the water molecule.
(b) The polar water molecule interacts strongly with the polar O—H bond in ethanol. This is a case of "like dissolving like."

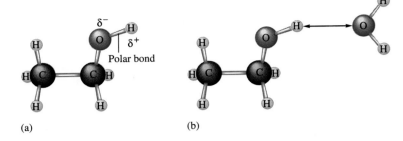

(a)   (b)

4.2 The Nature of Aqueous Solutions: Strong and Weak Electrolytes

As we discussed in Chapter 2, a solution is a homogeneous mixture. It is the same throughout (the first sip of a cup of coffee is the same as the last), but its composition can be varied by changing the amount of dissolved substances (one can make weak or strong coffee). In this section we will consider what happens when a substance, the **solute,** is dissolved in liquid water, the **solvent.**

One useful property for characterizing a solution is its **electrical conductivity,** its ability to conduct an electric current. This characteristic can be checked conveniently by using an apparatus like the ones shown in Figure 4.4. If the solution in the container conducts electricity, the bulb lights. Pure water is not an electrical conductor. However, some aqueous solutions conduct current very efficiently, and the bulb shines very brightly; these solutions contain **strong electrolytes.** Other solutions conduct only a small current, and the bulb glows dimly; these solutions contain **weak electrolytes.** Some solutions permit no current to flow, and the bulb remains unlit; these solutions contain **nonelectrolytes.**

The basis for the conductivity properties of solutions was first correctly identified by Svante Arrhenius (1859–1927), then a Swedish graduate student in physics, who carried out research on the nature of solutions at the University of Uppsala in the early 1880s. Arrhenius came to believe that the conductivity of solutions arose from the presence of ions, an idea that was at first scorned by the majority of the scientific establishment. However, in the late 1890s when atoms were found to contain charged particles, the ionic theory suddenly made sense and became widely accepted.

As Arrhenius postulated, the extent to which a solution can conduct an electric current depends directly on the number of ions present. Some materials, such as sodium chloride, readily produce ions in aqueous solution and thus are strong electrolytes. Other substances, such as acetic acid, produce relatively few ions when dissolved in water and are weak electrolytes. A third class of materials, such as sugar, form virtually no ions when dissolved in water and are nonelectrolytes.

Strong Electrolytes

Strong electrolytes are substances that are completely ionized when they are dissolved in water, as represented in Fig. 4.4(a). We will consider several classes of strong electrolytes: (1) soluble salts, (2) strong acids, and (3) strong bases.

Video: Conductivities of Aqueous Solutions

An *electrolyte* is a substance that when dissolved in water produces a solution that can conduct electricity.

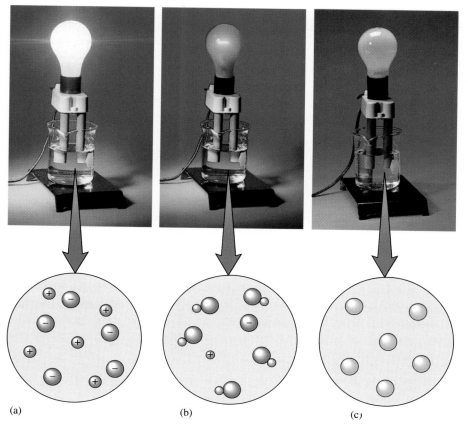

(a)　　　　　　　(b)　　　　　　　(c)

Figure 4.4
Electrical conductivity of aqueous solutions. The circuit will be completed and will allow current to flow only when there are charge carriers (ions) in the solution. (a) A hydrochloric acid solution, which is a strong electrolyte, contains ions that readily conduct the current and give a brightly lit bulb. (b) An acetic acid solution, which is a weak electrolyte, contains only a few ions and does not conduct as much current as a strong electrolyte. The bulb is only dimly lit. (c) A sucrose solution, which is a nonelectrolyte, contains no ions and does not conduct a current. The bulb remains unlit.

As shown in Fig. 4.2, a salt consists of an array of cations and anions that separate and become hydrated when the salt dissolves. For example, when $BaCl_2$ dissolves in water, it produces hydrated Ba^{2+} and Cl^- ions in the solution (see Fig. 4.5). Virtually no $BaCl_2$ units are present. Thus $BaCl_2$ is a strong electrolyte.

One of Arrhenius's most important discoveries concerned the nature of acids. Acidity was first associated with the sour taste of citrus fruits. In fact, the word *acid* comes directly from the Latin word *acidus,* meaning "sour." The mineral acids sulfuric acid (H_2SO_4) and nitric acid (HNO_3), so named because they were originally obtained by the treatment of minerals, were discovered around 1300.

Although acids were known for hundreds of years before the time of Arrhenius, no one had recognized their essential nature. In his studies of solutions, Arrhenius found that when the substances HCl, HNO_3, and H_2SO_4 were dissolved in water, they behaved as strong electrolytes. He postulated that this was the result of ionization reactions in water, for example:

$$HCl \xrightarrow{H_2O} H^+(aq) + Cl^-(aq)$$

$$HNO_3 \xrightarrow{H_2O} H^+(aq) + NO_3{}^-(aq)$$

$$H_2SO_4 \xrightarrow{H_2O} H^+(aq) + HSO_4{}^-(aq)$$

Thus Arrhenius proposed that an ***acid*** *is a substance that produces H+ ions (protons) when it is dissolved in water.*

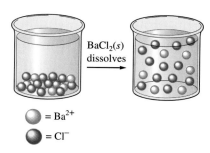

$BaCl_2(s)$ dissolves

○ $= Ba^{2+}$
● $= Cl^-$

Figure 4.5

When solid $BaCl_2$ dissolves, the Ba^{2+} and Cl^- ions are randomly dispersed in the water.

The Arrhenius definition of an acid is a substance that produces H^+ ions in solution.

Molecular Models: HCl, HNO₃, NO₃⁻, H₂SO₄, HSO₄⁻

Studies of conductivity show that when HCl, HNO₃, and H₂SO₄ are placed in water, *virtually every molecule ionizes.* These substances are strong electrolytes and are thus called **strong acids.** All three are very important chemicals, and much more will be said about them as we proceed. However, at this point the following facts are important:

> Sulfuric acid, nitric acid, and hydrochloric acid are aqueous solutions and should be written in chemical equations as $H_2SO_4(aq)$, $HNO_3(aq)$, and $HCl(aq)$, respectively, although they often appear without the (aq) symbol.

Perchloric acid, $HClO_4(aq)$, is another strong acid.

A strong acid is one that completely dissociates into its ions. Thus, if 100 molecules of HCl are dissolved in water, 100 H^+ ions and 100 Cl^- ions are produced. Virtually no HCl molecules exist in aqueous solutions (see Fig. 4.6).

Sulfuric acid is a special case. The formula H_2SO_4 indicates that this acid can produce two H^+ ions per molecule when dissolved in water. However, only the first H^+ ion is completely dissociated. The second H^+ ion can be pulled off under certain conditions, which we will discuss later. Thus an aqueous solution of H_2SO_4 contains mostly H^+ ions and HSO_4^- ions.

Strong electrolytes dissociate (ionize) completely in aqueous solution.

Another important class of strong electrolytes consists of the **strong bases,** soluble ionic compounds containing the hydroxide ion (OH^-). When these compounds are dissolved in water, the cations and OH^- ions separate and move independently. Solutions containing bases have a bitter taste and a slippery feel. The most common basic solutions are those produced when solid sodium hydroxide (NaOH) or potassium hydroxide (KOH) is dissolved in water to produce ions, as follows (see Fig. 4.7):

$$NaOH(s) \xrightarrow{\;H_2O\;} Na^+(aq) + OH^-(aq)$$

$$KOH(s) \xrightarrow{\;H_2O\;} K^+(aq) + OH^-(aq)$$

Weak Electrolytes

Weak electrolytes dissociate (ionize) only to a small extent in aqueous solution.

Weak electrolytes are substances that exhibit a small degree of ionization in water. That is, they produce relatively few ions when dissolved in water, as shown in Fig. 4.4(b). The most common weak electrolytes are weak acids and weak bases.

$\textcircled{+}$ = H^+
$\textcircled{-}$ = Cl^-

Figure 4.6
HCl(aq) is completely ionized.

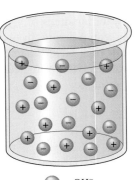

$\textcircled{-}$ = OH^-
$\textcircled{+}$ = Na^+

Figure 4.7
An aqueous solution of sodium hydroxide.

The main acidic component of vinegar is acetic acid ($HC_2H_3O_2$). The formula is written to indicate that acetic acid has two chemically distinct types of hydrogen atoms. Formulas for acids are often written with the acidic hydrogen atom or atoms (any that will produce H^+ ions in solution) listed first. If any nonacidic hydrogens are present, they are written later in the formula. Thus the formula $HC_2H_3O_2$ indicates one acidic and three nonacidic hydrogen atoms. The dissociation reaction for acetic acid in water can be written as follows:

Molecular Model: $HC_2H_3O_2$

$$HC_2H_3O_2(aq) \underset{}{\overset{H_2O}{\rightleftharpoons}} H^+(aq) + C_2H_3O_2^-(aq)$$

Acetic acid is very different from the strong acids because only about 1% of its molecules dissociate in aqueous solutions at typical concentrations. For example, in a solution containing 0.1 mole of $HC_2H_3O_2$ per liter, for every 100 molecules of $HC_2H_3O_2$ originally dissolved in water, approximately 99 molecules of $HC_2H_3O_2$ remain intact (see Fig. 4.8). That is, only one molecule out of every 100 dissociates (to produce one H^+ ion and one $C_2H_3O_2^-$ ion).

Because acetic acid is a weak electrolyte, it is called a **weak acid.** Any acid, such as acetic acid, that *dissociates (ionizes) only to a slight extent in aqueous solutions is called a weak acid.* In Chapter 14 we will explore the subject of weak acids in detail.

The most common weak base is ammonia (NH_3). When ammonia is dissolved in water, it reacts as follows:

$$NH_3(aq) + H_2O(l) \longrightarrow NH_4^+(aq) + OH^-(aq)$$

The solution is *basic* because OH^- ions are produced. Ammonia is called a **weak base** because *the resulting solution is a weak electrolyte;* that is, very few ions are formed. In fact, in a solution containing 0.1 mole of NH_3 per liter, for every 100 molecules of NH_3 originally dissolved, only one NH_4^+ ion and one OH^- ion are produced; 99 molecules of NH_3 remain unreacted (see Fig. 4.9).

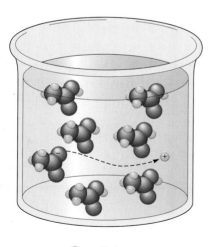

= Hydrogen

= Oxygen

= Carbon

Figure 4.8

Acetic acid ($HC_2H_3O_2$) exists in water mostly as undissociated molecules. Only a small percent of the molecules are ionized.

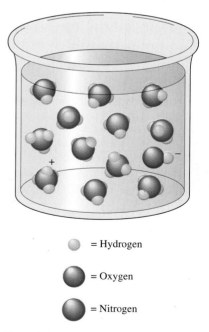

= Hydrogen

= Oxygen

= Nitrogen

Figure 4.9

The reaction of NH_3 in water.

CHEMICAL IMPACT

Arrhenius: A Man with Solutions

SCIENCE IS A human endeavor, subject to human frailties and governed by personalities, politics, and prejudices. One of the best illustrations of the often bumpy path of the advancement of scientific knowledge is the story of Swedish chemist Svante Arrhenius.

When Arrhenius began studies toward his doctorate at the University of Uppsala around 1880, he chose to investigate the passage of electricity through solutions, a mystery that had baffled scientists for a century. The first experiments had been done in the 1770s by Cavendish, who compared the conductivity of salt solution with that of rain water using his own physiologic reaction to the electric shocks he received! Arrhenius had an array of instruments to measure electric current, but the process of carefully weighing, measuring, and recording data from a multitude of experiments was a tedious one.

After his long series of experiments was performed, Arrhenius quit his laboratory bench and returned to his country home to try to formulate a model that could account for his data. He wrote, "I got the idea in the night of the 17th of May in the year 1883, and I could not sleep that night until I had worked through the whole problem." His idea was that ions were responsible for conducting electricity through a solution.

Back at Uppsala, Arrhenius took his doctoral dissertation containing the new theory to his advisor, Professor Cleve, an eminent chemist and the discoverer of the elements holmium and thulium. Cleve's uninterested response was what Arrhenius had expected. It was in keeping with Cleve's resistance to new ideas—he had not even accepted Mendeleev's periodic table, introduced 10 years earlier.

It is a long-standing custom that before a doctoral degree is granted, the dissertation must be defended before a panel of professors. Although this procedure is still followed at most universities today, the problems are usually worked out in private with the evaluating professors before the actual defense. However, when Arrhenius did it, the dissertation defense was an open debate, which could be rancorous and humiliating. Knowing that it would be unwise to antagonize his professors, Arrhenius downplayed his convictions about his new theory as he defended his dissertation. His diplomacy paid off: He was awarded his degree, albeit reluctantly, because the professors still did not believe his model and considered him to be a marginal scientist, at best.

Such a setback could have ended his scientific career, but Arrhenius was a crusader; he was determined to see his theory triumph. He promptly embarked on a political campaign, enlisting the aid of several prominent scientists, to get his theory accepted.

Ultimately, the ionic theory triumphed. Arrhenius's fame spread, and honors were heaped on him, culminating in the

Svante August Arrhenius.

Nobel Prize in chemistry in 1903. Not one to rest on his laurels, Arrhenius turned to new fields, including astronomy; he formulated a new theory that the solar system may have come into being through the collision of stars. His exceptional versatility led him to study the use of serums to fight disease, energy resources and conservation, and the origin of life.

Additional insight on Arrhenius and his scientific career can be obtained from his address on receiving the Willard Gibbs Award. See *Journal of the American Chemical Society* **36** (1912): 353.

Nonelectrolytes

Nonelectrolytes are substances that dissolve in water but do not produce any ions, as shown in Fig. 4.4(c). An example of a nonelectrolyte is ethanol (see Fig. 4.3 for the structural formula). When ethanol dissolves, entire C_2H_5OH molecules are dispersed in the water. Since the molecules do not break up into ions, the resulting solution does not conduct an electric current. Another common nonelectrolyte is table sugar (sucrose, $C_{12}H_{22}O_{11}$), which is very soluble in water but which produces no ions when it dissolves. The sucrose molecules remain intact.

Molecular Models: $C_2H_3O_2{}^-$, NH_3, $NH_4{}^+$, sucrose

4.3 *The Composition of Solutions*

Chemical reactions often take place when two solutions are mixed. To perform stoichiometric calculations in such cases, we must know two things: (1) the *nature of the reaction,* which depends on the exact forms the chemicals take when dissolved, and (2) the *amounts of chemicals* present in the solutions, usually expressed as concentrations.

The concentration of a solution can be described in many different ways, as we will see in Chapter 11. At this point we will consider only the most commonly used expression of concentration, **molarity** (M), which is defined as *moles of solute per volume of solution in liters:*

$$M = \text{molarity} = \frac{\text{moles of solute}}{\text{liters of solution}}$$

A solution that is 1.0 molar (written as 1.0 M) contains 1.0 mole of solute per liter of solution.

Sample Exercise 4.1 *Calculation of Molarity I*

Calculate the molarity of a solution prepared by dissolving 11.5 g of solid NaOH in enough water to make 1.50 L of solution.

Solution

To find the molarity of the solution, we first compute the number of moles of solute using the molar mass of NaOH (40.00 g/mol):

$$11.5 \text{ g NaOH} \times \frac{1 \text{ mol NaOH}}{40.00 \text{ g NaOH}} = 0.288 \text{ mol NaOH}$$

Then we divide by the volume of the solution in liters:

$$\text{Molarity} = \frac{\text{mol solute}}{\text{L solution}} = \frac{0.288 \text{ mol NaOH}}{1.50 \text{ L solution}} = 0.192 \ M \text{ NaOH}$$

See Exercises 4.15 and 4.16.

Sample Exercise 4.2 *Calculation of Molarity II*

Calculate the molarity of a solution prepared by dissolving 1.56 g of gaseous HCl in enough water to make 26.8 mL of solution.

Solution

First we calculate the number of moles of HCl (molar mass = 36.46 g/mol):

$$1.56 \text{ g HCl} \times \frac{1 \text{ mol HCl}}{36.46 \text{ g HCl}} = 4.28 \times 10^{-2} \text{ mol HCl}$$

Next we must change the volume of the solution to liters:

$$26.8 \text{ mL} \times \frac{1 \text{ L}}{1000 \text{ mL}} = 2.68 \times 10^{-2} \text{ L}$$

Finally, we divide the moles of solution by the liters of solution:

$$\text{Molarity} = \frac{4.28 \times 10^{-2} \text{ mol HCl}}{2.68 \times 10^{-2} \text{ L solution}} = 1.60 \ M \text{ HCl}$$

See Exercises 4.15 and 4.16.

It is important to realize that the conventional description of a solution's concentration may not accurately reflect the true composition of the solution. Solution concentration is always given in terms of the form of the solute *before* it dissolves. For example, when a solution is described as being 1.0 M NaCl, this means that the solution was prepared by dissolving 1.0 mole of solid NaCl in enough water to make 1.0 liter of solution; it does not mean that the solution contains 1.0 mole of NaCl units. Actually, the solution contains 1.0 mole of Na^+ ions and 1.0 mole of Cl^- ions. This situation is further illustrated in Sample Exercise 4.3.

Sample Exercise 4.3 *Concentrations of Ions I*

Give the concentration of each type of ion in the following solutions:

a. 0.50 M Co(NO$_3$)$_2$
b. 1 M Fe(ClO$_4$)$_3$

Solution

a. When solid Co(NO$_3$)$_2$ dissolves, the cobalt(II) cation and the nitrate anions separate:

$$\text{Co(NO}_3)_2(s) \xrightarrow{\text{H}_2\text{O}} \text{Co}^{2+}(aq) + 2\text{NO}_3{}^-(aq)$$

An aqueous solution of Co(NO$_3$)$_2$.

For each mole of $Co(NO_3)_2$ that is dissolved, the solution contains 1 mol Co^{2+} ions and 2 mol NO_3^- ions. Thus a solution that is 0.50 M $Co(NO_3)_2$ contains 0.50 M Co^{2+} and (2×0.50) M NO_3^- or 1.0 M NO_3^-.

b. When solid $Fe(ClO_4)_3$ dissolves, the iron(III) cation and the perchlorate anions separate:

$$Fe(ClO_4)_3(s) \xrightarrow{H_2O} Fe^{3+}(aq) + 3ClO_4^-(aq)$$

Thus a solution that is described as 1 M $Fe(ClO_4)_3$ actually contains 1 M Fe^{3+} ions and 3 M ClO_4^- ions.

See Exercise 4.17.

Often chemists need to determine the number of moles of solute present in a given volume of a solution of known molarity. The procedure for doing this is easily derived from the definition of molarity. If we multiply the molarity of a solution by the volume (in liters) of a particular sample of the solution, we get the moles of solute present in that sample:

$$\text{Liters of solution} \times \text{molarity} = \text{liters of solution} \times \frac{\text{moles of solute}}{\text{liters of solution}}$$

$$= \text{moles of solute}$$

$$M = \frac{\text{moles of solute}}{\text{liters of solution}}$$

This procedure is demonstrated in Sample Exercises 4.4 and 4.5.

Sample Exercise 4.4 *Concentration of Ions*

Calculate the number of moles of Cl^- ions in 1.75 L of 1.0×10^{-3} M $ZnCl_2$.

Solution

When solid $ZnCl_2$ dissolves, it produces ions as follows:

$$ZnCl_2(s) \xrightarrow{H_2O} Zn^{2+}(aq) + 2Cl^-(aq)$$

Thus a 1.0×10^{-3} M $ZnCl_2$ solution contains 1.0×10^{-3} M Zn^{2+} ions and 2.0×10^{-3} M Cl^- ions. To calculate the moles of Cl^- ions in 1.75 L of the 1.0×10^{-3} M $ZnCl_2$ solution, we must multiply the volume times the molarity:

$$\text{1.75 L solution} \times 2.0 \times 10^{-3} \, M \, Cl^- = \text{1.75 L solution} \times \frac{2.0 \times 10^{-3} \, \text{mol} \, Cl^-}{\text{L solution}}$$

$$= 3.5 \times 10^{-3} \, \text{mol} \, Cl^-$$

See Exercise 4.19.

Sample Exercise 4.5 *Concentration and Volume*

Typical blood serum is about 0.14 M NaCl. What volume of blood contains 1.0 mg NaCl?

Solution

We must first determine the number of moles represented by 1.0 mg NaCl (molar mass = 58.45 g/mol):

$$1.0 \; \text{mg NaCl} \times \frac{1 \; \text{g NaCl}}{1000 \; \text{mg NaCl}} \times \frac{1 \; \text{mol NaCl}}{58.45 \; \text{g NaCl}} = 1.7 \times 10^{-5} \; \text{mol NaCl}$$

Next, we must determine what volume of 0.14 M NaCl solution contains 1.7×10^{-5} mol NaCl. There is some volume, call it V, that when multiplied by the molarity of this solution will yield 1.7×10^{-5} mol NaCl, that is:

$$V \times \frac{0.14 \; \text{mol NaCl}}{\text{L solution}} = 1.7 \times 10^{-5} \; \text{mol NaCl}$$

We want to solve for the volume:

$$V = \frac{1.7 \times 10^{-5} \; \text{mol NaCl}}{\dfrac{0.14 \; \text{mol NaCl}}{\text{L solution}}} = 1.2 \times 10^{-4} \; \text{L solution}$$

Thus 0.12 mL of blood contains 1.7×10^{-5} mol NaCl or 1.0 mg NaCl.

See Exercises 4.21 and 4.22.

A **standard solution** is a *solution whose concentration is accurately known.* Standard solutions, often used in chemical analysis, can be prepared as shown in Fig. 4.10 and in Sample Exercise 4.6.

Sample Exercise 4.6 *Solutions of Known Concentration*

To analyze the alcohol content of a certain wine, a chemist needs 1.00 L of an aqueous 0.200 M $K_2Cr_2O_7$ (potassium dichromate) solution. How much solid $K_2Cr_2O_7$ must be weighed out to make this solution?

Solution

We must first determine the moles of $K_2Cr_2O_7$ required:

$$1.00 \; \text{L solution} \times \frac{0.200 \; \text{mol } K_2Cr_2O_7}{\text{L solution}} = 0.200 \; \text{mol } K_2Cr_2O_7$$

Winemaking has become a science as well as an art.

This amount can be converted to grams using the molar mass of $K_2Cr_2O_7$ (294.18 g/mol).

$$0.200 \text{ mol } K_2Cr_2O_7 \times \frac{294.20 \text{ g } K_2Cr_2O_7}{\text{mol } K_2Cr_2O_7} = 58.8 \text{ g } K_2Cr_2O_7$$

Thus, to make 1.00 L of 0.200 M $K_2Cr_2O_7$, the chemist must weigh out 58.8 g $K_2Cr_2O_7$, transfer it to a 1.00-L volumetric flask, and add distilled water to the mark on the flask.

See Exercises 4.23a and c and 4.24c and e.

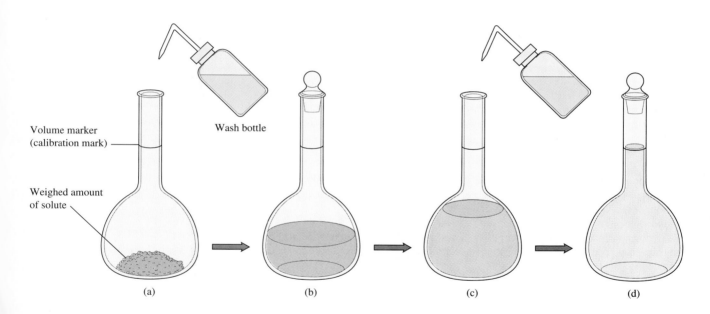

Volume marker
(calibration mark)

Wash bottle

Weighed amount
of solute

(a)   (b)   (c)   (d)

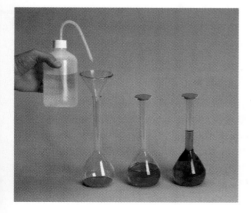

Figure 4.10

Steps involved in the preparation of a standard solution. (a) A weighed amount of a substance (the solute) is put into the volumetric flask, and a small quantity of water is added. (b) The solid is dissolved in the water by gently swirling the flask (*with the stopper in place*). (c) More water is added, until the level of the solution just reaches the mark etched on the neck of the flask (d).

CHEMICAL IMPACT

Tiny Laboratories

ONE OF THE major impacts of modern technology is to make things smaller. The best example is the computer. Calculations that 30 years ago required a machine the size of a large room now can be carried out on a hand-held calculator. This tendency toward miniaturization is also having a major impact on the science of chemical analysis. Using the techniques of computer chip makers, researchers are now constructing minuscule laboratories on the surface of a tiny chip made of silicon, glass, or plastic (see photo). Instead of electrons, 10^{-6} to 10^{-9} L of liquids move between reaction chambers on the chip through tiny capillaries. The chips typically contain no moving parts. Instead of conventional pumps, the chip-based laboratories use voltage differences to move liquids that contain ions from one reaction chamber to another.

Microchip laboratories have many advantages. They require only tiny amounts of sample. This is especially advantageous for expensive, difficult-to-prepare materials or in cases such as criminal investigations, where only small amounts of evidence may exist. The chip laboratories also minimize contamination because they represent a "closed system" once the material has been introduced to the chip. The chips also can be made to be disposable to prevent cross-contamination of different samples.

The chip laboratories present some difficulties not found in macroscopic laboratories. The main problem concerns the large surface area of the capillaries and reaction chambers relative to the sample volume. Molecules or biological cells in the sample solution encounter so much "wall" that they may undergo unwanted reactions with the wall materials. Glass seems to present the least of these problems, and the walls of silicon chip laboratories can be protected by formation of relatively inert silicon dioxide. Because plastic is inexpensive, it seems a good choice for disposable chips, but plastic also is the most reactive with the samples and the least durable of the available materials.

Caliper Technologies Corporation, Palo Alto, California, is working toward creating a miniature chemistry laboratory about the size of a toaster that can be used with "plug-in" chip-based laboratories. Various chips would be furnished with the unit that would be appropriate for different types of analyses. The entire unit would be connected to a computer to collect and analyze the data. There is even the possibility that these "laboratories" could be used in the home to perform analyses such as blood sugar and blood cholesterol and to check for the presence of bacteria such as *E. coli* and many others. This would revolutionize the health care industry.

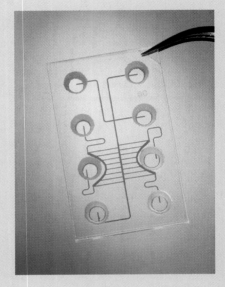

Plastic chips such as this one made by Caliper Technologies are being used to perform laboratory procedures traditionally done with test tubes.

Adapted from "The Incredible Shrinking Laboratory" by Corinna Wu, as appeared in *Science News,* Vol. 154, August 15, 1998, p. 104.

Dilution

Dilution with water does not alter the numbers of moles of solute present.

To save time and space in the laboratory, routinely used solutions are often purchased or prepared in concentrated form (called *stock solutions*). Water is then added to achieve the molarity desired for a particular solution. This process is called **dilution.** For example, the common acids are purchased as concentrated solutions and diluted as needed. A typical dilution calculation involves determining how much water must be added to an amount of stock solution to achieve a solution of the desired concentration. The key to doing these calculations is to remember that

Moles of solute after dilution = moles of solute before dilution

because only water (no solute) is added to accomplish the dilution.

For example, suppose we need to prepare 500. mL of 1.00 M acetic acid ($HC_2H_3O_2$) from a 17.4 M stock solution of acetic acid. What volume of the stock solution is required? The first step is to determine the number of moles of acetic acid in the final solution by multiplying the volume by the molarity (remembering that the volume must be changed to liters):

$$500. \text{ mL solution} \times \frac{1 \text{ L solution}}{1000 \text{ mL solution}} \times \frac{1.00 \text{ mol } HC_2H_3O_2}{\text{L solution}}$$
$$= 0.500 \text{ mol } HC_2H_3O_2$$

Thus we need to use a volume of 17.4 M acetic acid that contains 0.500 mol $HC_2H_3O_2$. That is,

$$V \times \frac{17.4 \text{ mol } HC_2H_3O_2}{\text{L solution}} = 0.500 \text{ mol } HC_2H_3O_2$$

Solving for V gives

$$V = \frac{0.500 \text{ mol } HC_2H_3O_2}{\dfrac{17.4 \text{ mol } HC_2H_3O_2}{\text{L solution}}} = 0.0287 \text{ L or } 28.7 \text{ mL solution}$$

Thus, to make 500 mL of a 1.00 M acetic acid solution, we can take 28.7 mL of 17.4 M acetic acid and dilute it to a total volume of 500 mL with distilled water.

A dilution procedure typically involves two types of glassware: a pipet and a volumetric flask. A *pipet* is a device for accurately measuring and transferring a given volume of solution. There are two common types of pipets: *volumetric* (or *transfer*) *pipets* and *measuring pipets,* as shown in Fig. 4.11. Volumetric pipets come in specific sizes, such as 5 mL, 10 mL, 25 mL, and so on. Measuring pipets are used to measure volumes for which a volumetric pipet is not available. For example, we would use a measuring pipet as shown in Fig. 4.12 to deliver 28.7 mL of 17.4 M acetic acid into a 500-mL volumetric flask and then add water to the mark to perform the dilution described above.

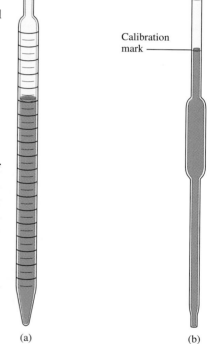

Calibration mark

(a)   (b)

Figure 4.11

(a) A measuring pipet is graduated and can be used to measure various volumes of liquid accurately. (b) A volumetric (transfer) pipet is designed to measure one volume accurately. When filled to the mark, it delivers the volume indicated on the pipet.

Sample Exercise 4.7 **Concentration and Volume**

What volume of 16 M sulfuric acid must be used to prepare 1.5 L of a 0.10 M H_2SO_4 solution?

Solution

We must first determine the moles of H_2SO_4 in 1.5 L of 0.10 M H_2SO_4:

$$1.5 \text{ L solution} \times \frac{0.10 \text{ mol } H_2SO_4}{\text{L solution}} = 0.15 \text{ mol } H_2SO_4$$

Next we must find the volume of 16 M H_2SO_4 that contains 0.15 mol H_2SO_4:

$$V \times \frac{16 \text{ mol } H_2SO_4}{\text{L solution}} = 0.15 \text{ mol } H_2SO_4$$

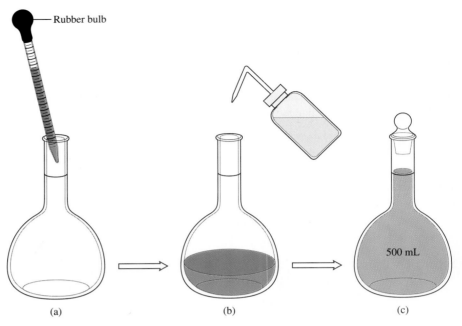

Figure 4.12
(a) A measuring pipet is used to transfer 28.7 mL of 17.4 M acetic acid solution to a volumetric flask. (b) Water is added to the flask to the calibration mark. (c) The resulting solution is 1.00 M acetic acid.

Solving for V gives

$$V = \frac{0.15 \text{ mol } H_2SO_4}{\dfrac{16 \text{ mol } H_2SO_4}{1 \text{ L solution}}} = 9.4 \times 10^{-3} \text{ L or } 9.4 \text{ mL solution}$$

Thus, to make 1.5 L of 0.10 M H_2SO_4 using 16 M H_2SO_4, we must take 9.4 mL of the concentrated acid and dilute it with water to 1.5 L. The correct way to do this is to add the 9.4 mL of acid to about 1 L of distilled water and then dilute to 1.5 L by adding more water.

In diluting an acid, "Do what you oughta, always add acid to water."

See Exercises 4.23b and d and 4.24a, b, and d.

As noted earlier, the central idea in performing the calculations associated with dilutions is to recognize that the moles of solute are not changed by the dilution. Another way to express this condition is by the following equation:

$$M_1V_1 = M_2V_2$$

where M_1 and V_1 represent the molarity and volume of the original solution (before dilution) and M_2 and V_2 represent the molarity and volume of the diluted solution. This equation makes sense because

$$M_1 \times V_1 = \text{mol solute before dilution}$$
$$= \text{mol solute after dilution} = M_2 \times V_2$$

Repeat Sample Exercise 4.7 using the equation $M_1V_1 = M_2V_2$. Note that in doing so

$$M_1 = 16\ M \qquad M_2 = 0.10\ M \qquad V_2 = 1.5\ L$$

and V_1 is the unknown quantity sought. The equation $M_1V_1 = M_2V_2$ always holds for a dilution. This equation will be easy for you to remember if you understand where it comes from.

4.4 Types of Chemical Reactions

Although we have considered many reactions so far in this text, we have examined only a tiny fraction of the millions of possible chemical reactions. In order to make sense of all these reactions, we need some system for grouping reactions into classes. Although there are many different ways to do this, we will use the system most commonly used by practicing chemists:

Types of Solution Reactions

- Precipitation reactions
- Acid–base reactions
- Oxidation–reduction reactions

Virtually all reactions can be put into one of these classes. We will define and illustrate each type in the following sections.

4.5 Precipitation Reactions

When two solutions are mixed, an insoluble substance sometimes forms; that is, a solid forms and separates from the solution. Such a reaction is called a **precipitation reaction,** and the solid that forms is called a **precipitate**. For example, a precipitation reaction occurs when an aqueous solution of potassium chromate, $K_2CrO_4(aq)$, which is yellow, is added to a colorless aqueous solution containing barium nitrate, $Ba(NO_3)_2(aq)$. As shown in Fig. 4.13, when these solutions are mixed, a yellow solid forms. What is the equation that describes this chemical change? To write the equation, we must know the identities of the reactants and products. The reactants have already been described: $K_2CrO_4(aq)$ and $Ba(NO_3)_2(aq)$. Is there some way we can predict the identities of the products? In particular, what is the yellow solid?

The best way to predict the identity of this solid is to think carefully about what products are possible. To do this, we need to know what species are present in the

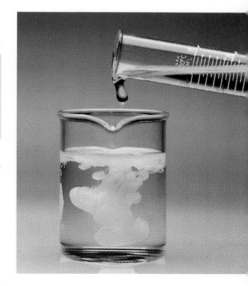

Figure 4.13
When yellow aqueous potassium chromate is added to a colorless barium nitrate solution, yellow barium chromate precipitates.

Exploration: Precipitation Reactions

When ionic compounds dissolve in water, the *resulting solution contains the separated ions.*

solution after the two reactant solutions are mixed. First, let's think about the nature of each reactant solution. The designation $Ba(NO_3)_2(aq)$ means that barium nitrate (a white solid) has been dissolved in water. Notice that barium nitrate contains the Ba^{2+} and NO_3^- ions. *Remember: In virtually every case, when a solid containing ions dissolves in water, the ions separate* and move around independently. That is, $Ba(NO_3)_2(aq)$ does not contain $Ba(NO_3)_2$ units; it contains separated Ba^{2+} and NO_3^- ions.

Similarly, since solid potassium chromate contains the K^+ and CrO_4^{2-} ions, an aqueous solution of potassium chromate (which is prepared by dissolving solid K_2CrO_4 in water) contains these separated ions.

We can represent the mixing of $K_2CrO_4(aq)$ and $Ba(NO_3)_2(aq)$ in two ways. First, we can write

$$K_2CrO_4(aq) + Ba(NO_3)_2(aq) \longrightarrow products$$

However, a much more accurate representation is

$$\underbrace{2K^+(aq) + CrO_4^{2-}(aq)}_{\substack{\text{The ions in} \\ K_2CrO_4(aq)}} + \underbrace{Ba^{2+}(aq) + 2NO_3^-(aq)}_{\substack{\text{The ions in} \\ Ba(NO_3)_2(aq)}} \longrightarrow products$$

Thus the mixed solution contains the ions:

$$K^+ \qquad CrO_4^{2-} \qquad Ba^{2+} \qquad NO_3^-$$

How can some or all of these ions combine to form a yellow solid? This is not an easy question to answer. In fact, predicting the products of a chemical reaction is one of the hardest things a beginning chemistry student is asked to do. Even an experienced chemist, when confronted with a new reaction, is often not sure what will happen. The chemist tries to think of the various possibilities, considers the likelihood of each possibility, and then makes a prediction (an educated guess). Only after identifying each product *experimentally* is the chemist sure what reaction has taken place. However, an educated guess is very useful because it provides a place to start. It tells us what kinds of products we are most likely to find. We already know some things that will help us predict the products of the above reaction.

1. When ions form a solid compound, the compound must have a zero net charge. Thus the products of this reaction must contain *both anions and cations.* For example, K^+ and Ba^{2+} could not combine to form the solid, nor could CrO_4^{2-} and NO_3^-.

2. Most ionic materials contain only two types of ions: one type of cation and one type of anion (for example, $NaCl$, KOH, Na_2SO_4, K_2CrO_4, $Co(NO_3)_2$, NH_4Cl, Na_2CO_3).

The possible combinations of a given cation and a given anion from the list of ions K^+, CrO_4^{2-}, Ba^{2+}, and NO_3^- are

$$K_2CrO_4 \qquad KNO_3 \qquad BaCrO_4 \qquad Ba(NO_3)_2$$

Which of these possibilities is most likely to represent the yellow solid? We know it's not K_2CrO_4 or $Ba(NO_3)_2$. They are the reactants. They were present (dissolved) in the separate solutions that were mixed. The only real possibilities for the solid that formed are

$$KNO_3 \quad and \quad BaCrO_4$$

To decide which of these most likely represents the yellow solid, we need more facts. An experienced chemist knows that the K^+ ion and the NO_3^- ion are both colorless. Thus, if the solid is KNO_3, it should be white not yellow. On the other hand, the CrO_4^{2-} ion is yellow (note in Fig. 4.13 that $K_2CrO_4(aq)$ is yellow). Thus the yellow solid is almost certainly $BaCrO_4$. Further tests show that this is the case.

So far we have determined that one product of the reaction between $K_2CrO_4(aq)$ and $Ba(NO_3)_2(aq)$ is $BaCrO_4(s)$, but what happened to the K^+ and NO_3^- ions? The answer is that these ions are left dissolved in the solution; KNO_3 does not form a solid when the K^+ and NO_3^- ions are present in this much water. In other words, if we took solid KNO_3 and put it in the same quantity of water as is present in the mixed solution, it would dissolve. Thus, when we mix $K_2CrO_4(aq)$ and $Ba(NO_3)_2(aq)$, $BaCrO_4(s)$ forms, but KNO_3 is left behind in solution (we write it as $KNO_3(aq)$). Thus the equation for this precipitation reaction is

$$K_2CrO_4(aq) + Ba(NO_3)_2(aq) \longrightarrow BaCrO_4(s) + 2KNO_3(aq)$$

As long as water is present, the KNO_3 remains dissolved. (See Fig. 4.14 to help visualize what is happening in this reaction. Note the solid $BaCrO_4$ on the bottom of the container, while the K^+ and NO_3^- ions remain dispersed in the solution.) If we removed the solid $BaCrO_4$ and then evaporated the water, white solid KNO_3 would be obtained; the K^+ and NO_3^- ions assemble themselves into solid KNO_3 when the water is removed.

Now let's consider another example. When an aqueous solution of silver nitrate is added to an aqueous solution of potassium chloride, a white precipitate forms. We can represent what we know so far as

$$AgNO_3(aq) + KCl(aq) \longrightarrow \text{unknown white solid}$$

Remembering that when ionic substances dissolve in water, the ions separate, we can write

$$\underbrace{Ag^+, NO_3^-}_{\substack{\text{In silver} \\ \text{nitrate} \\ \text{solution}}} + \underbrace{K^+, Cl^-}_{\substack{\text{In potassium} \\ \text{chloride} \\ \text{solution}}} \longrightarrow \underbrace{Ag^+, NO_3^-, K^+, Cl^-}_{\substack{\text{Combined solution,} \\ \text{before reaction}}} \longrightarrow \text{white solid}$$

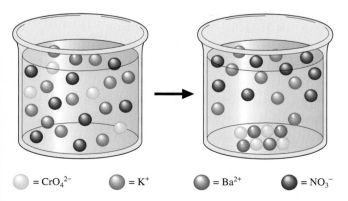

$\bigcirc$ = CrO_4^{2-} $\bullet$ = K^+ $\bullet$ = Ba^{2+} $\bullet$ = NO_3^-

Figure 4.14

The reaction of $K_2CrO_4(aq)$ and $Ba(NO_3)_2(aq)$.

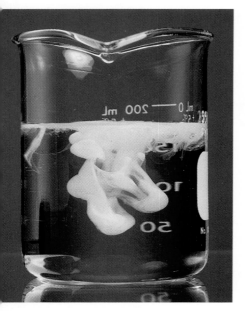

Figure 4.15

Precipitation of silver chloride by mixing solutions of silver nitrate and potassium chloride. The K^+ and NO_3^- ions remain in solution.

Since we know the white solid must contain both positive and negative ions, the possible compounds that can be assembled from this collection of ions are

$$AgNO_3 \quad KCl \quad AgCl \quad KNO_3$$

Since $AgNO_3$ and KCl are the substances dissolved in the two reactant solutions, we know that they do not represent the white solid product. Therefore, the only real possibilities are

$$AgCl \quad and \quad KNO_3$$

From the first example considered, we know that KNO_3 is quite soluble in water. Thus solid KNO_3 will not form when the reactant solids are mixed. The product must be $AgCl(s)$ (which can be proved by experiment to be true). The equation for the reaction now can be written

$$AgNO_3(aq) + KCl(aq) \longrightarrow AgCl(s) + KNO_3(aq)$$

Figure 4.15 shows the result of mixing aqueous solutions of $AgNO_3$ and KCl. Figure 4.16 shows a microscopic visualization of the reaction.

Notice that in these two examples we had to apply both concepts (solids must have a zero net charge) and facts (KNO_3 is very soluble in water, the CrO_4^{2-} is yellow, and so on). Doing chemistry requires both understanding ideas and remembering key information. Predicting the identity of the solid product in a precipitation reaction requires knowledge of the solubilities of common ionic substances. As an aid in predicting the products of precipitation reactions, some simple solubility rules are given in Table 4.1. You should memorize these rules.

The phrase *slightly soluble* used in the solubility rules in Table 4.1 means that the tiny amount of solid that dissolves is not noticeable. The solid appears to be insoluble to the naked eye. Thus the terms *insoluble* and *slightly soluble* are often used interchangeably.

Note that the information in Table 4.1 allows us to predict that AgCl is the white solid formed when solutions of $AgNO_3$ and KCl are mixed. Rules 1 and 2 indicate that KNO_3 is soluble, and Rule 3 states that AgCl is insoluble.

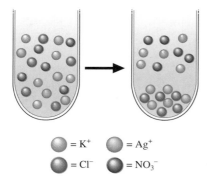

Figure 4.16

The reaction of KCl(aq) and $AgNO_3(aq)$.

Table 4.1 Simple Rules for the Solubility of Salts in Water
1. Most nitrate (NO_3^-) salts are soluble.
2. Most salts containing the alkali metal ions (Li^+, Na^+, K^+, Cs^+, Rb^+) and the ammonium ion (NH_4^+) are soluble.
3. Most chloride, bromide, and iodide salts are soluble. Notable exceptions are salts containing the ions Ag^+, Pb^{2+}, and Hg_2^{2+}.
4. Most sulfate salts are soluble. Notable exceptions are $BaSO_4$, $PbSO_4$, Hg_2SO_4, and $CaSO_4$.
5. Most hydroxide salts are only slightly soluble. The important soluble hydroxides are NaOH and KOH. The compounds $Ba(OH)_2$, $Sr(OH)_2$, and $Ca(OH)_2$ are marginally soluble.
6. Most sulfide (S^{2-}), carbonate (CO_3^{2-}), chromate (CrO_4^{2-}), and phosphate (PO_4^{3-}) salts are only slightly soluble.

When solutions containing ionic substances are mixed, it will be helpful in determining the products if you think in terms of *ion interchange.* For example, in the preceding discussion we considered the results of mixing $AgNO_3(aq)$ and $KCl(aq)$. In determining the products, we took the cation from one reactant and combined it with the anion of the other reactant:

$$Ag^+ \quad + \quad NO_3^- \quad + \quad K^+ \quad + \quad Cl^- \quad \longrightarrow$$

Possible
solid
products

The solubility rules in Table 4.1 allow us to predict whether either product forms as a solid.

The key to dealing with the chemistry of an aqueous solution is first to *focus on the actual components of the solution before any reaction occurs* and then to figure out how these components will react with each other. Sample Exercise 4.8 illustrates this process for three different reactions.

To begin, focus on the ions in solution before any reaction occurs.

Sample Exercise 4.8 Predicting Reaction Products

Using the solubility rules in Table 4.1, predict what will happen when the following pairs of solutions are mixed.

a. $KNO_3(aq)$ and $BaCl_2(aq)$
b. $Na_2SO_4(aq)$ and $Pb(NO_3)_2(aq)$
c. $KOH(aq)$ and $Fe(NO_3)_3(aq)$

Solution

a. $KNO_3(aq)$ stands for an aqueous solution obtained by dissolving solid KNO_3 in water to form a solution containing the hydrated ions $K^+(aq)$ and $NO_3^-(aq)$. Likewise, $BaCl_2(aq)$ is a solution formed by dissolving solid $BaCl_2$ in water to produce $Ba^{2+}(aq)$ and $Cl^-(aq)$. When these two solutions are mixed, the resulting solution contains the ions K^+, NO_3^-, Ba^{2+}, and Cl^-. All ions are hydrated, but the (aq) is omitted for simplicity. To look for possible solid products, combine the cation from one reactant with the anion from the other:

$$K^+ \quad + \quad NO_3^- \quad + \quad Ba^{2+} \quad + \quad Cl^- \quad \longrightarrow$$

Possible
solid
products

Note from Table 4.1 that the rules predict that both KCl and $Ba(NO_3)_2$ are soluble in water. Thus no precipitate forms when $KNO_3(aq)$ and $BaCl_2(aq)$ are mixed. All the ions remain dissolved in solution. No chemical reaction occurs.

Lead sulfate is a white solid.

Solid Fe(OH)₃ forms when aqueous KOH and Fe(NO₃)₃ are mixed.

b. Using the same procedures as in part a, we find that the ions present in the combined solution before any reaction occurs are Na^+, SO_4^{2-}, Pb^{2+}, and NO_3^-. The possible salts that could form precipitates are

$$Na^+ \quad + \quad SO_4^{2-} \quad + \quad Pb^{2+} \quad + \quad NO_3^- \quad \longrightarrow$$

The compound $NaNO_3$ is soluble, but $PbSO_4$ is insoluble (see Rule 4 in Table 4.1). When these solutions are mixed, $PbSO_4$ will precipitate from the solution. The balanced equation is

$$Na_2SO_4(aq) + Pb(NO_3)_2(aq) \longrightarrow PbSO_4(s) + 2NaNO_3(aq)$$

c. The combined solution (before any reaction occurs) contains the ions K^+, OH^-, Fe^{3+}, and NO_3^-. The salts that might precipitate are KNO_3 and $Fe(OH)_3$. The solubility rules in Table 4.1 indicate that both K^+ and NO_3^- salts are soluble. However, $Fe(OH)_3$ is only slightly soluble (Rule 5) and hence will precipitate. The balanced equation is

$$3KOH(aq) + Fe(NO_3)_3(aq) \longrightarrow Fe(OH)_3(s) + 3KNO_3(aq)$$

See Exercises 4.29 and 4.30.

4.6 Describing Reactions in Solution

In this section we will consider the types of equations used to represent reactions in solution. For example, when we mix aqueous potassium chromate with aqueous barium nitrate, a reaction occurs to form a precipitate ($BaCrO_4$) and dissolved potassium nitrate. So far we have written the **molecular equation** for this reaction:

$$K_2CrO_4(aq) + Ba(NO_3)_2(aq) \longrightarrow BaCrO_4(s) + 2KNO_3(aq)$$

Although the molecular equation shows the reactants and products of the reaction, it does not give a very clear picture of what actually occurs in solution. As we have seen, aqueous solutions of potassium chromate, barium nitrate, and potassium nitrate contain individual ions, not molecules, as implied by the molecular equation. Thus the **complete ionic equation**

> A strong electrolyte is a substance that completely breaks apart into ions when dissolved in water.

$$2K^+(aq) + CrO_4^{2-}(aq) + Ba^{2+}(aq) + 2NO_3^-(aq) \longrightarrow$$
$$BaCrO_4(s) + 2K^+(aq) + 2NO_3^-(aq)$$

better represents the actual forms of the reactants and products in solution. *In a complete ionic equation, all substances that are strong electrolytes are represented as ions.*

The complete ionic equation reveals that only some of the ions participate in the reaction. The K^+ and NO_3^- ions are present in solution both before and after the reaction. The ions that do not participate directly in the reaction are called **spectator ions.** The ions that participate in this reaction are the Ba^{2+} and CrO_4^{2-} ions, which combine to form solid $BaCrO_4$:

$$Ba^{2+}(aq) + CrO_4^{2-}(aq) \longrightarrow BaCrO_4(s)$$

This equation, called the **net ionic equation,** includes only those solution components directly involved in the reaction. Chemists usually write the net ionic equation for a reaction in solution because it gives the actual forms of the reactants and products and includes only the species that undergo a change.

Net ionic equations include only those components that undergo changes in the reaction.

Three Types of Equations Are Used to Describe Reactions in Solution:

- The **molecular equation** gives the overall reaction stoichiometry but not necessarily the actual forms of the reactants and products in solution.
- The **complete ionic equation** represents as ions all reactants and products that are strong electrolytes.
- The **net ionic equation** includes only those solution components undergoing a change. Spectator ions are not included.

Sample Exercise 4.9 Writing Equations for Reactions

For each of the following reactions, write the molecular equation, the complete ionic equation, and the net ionic equation.

a. Aqueous potassium chloride is added to aqueous silver nitrate to form a silver chloride precipitate plus aqueous potassium nitrate.
b. Aqueous potassium hydroxide is mixed with aqueous iron(III) nitrate to form a precipitate of iron(III) hydroxide and aqueous potassium nitrate.

Solution

a. Molecular Equation

$$KCl(aq) + AgNO_3(aq) \longrightarrow AgCl(s) + KNO_3(aq)$$

Complete Ionic Equation (*Remember:* Any ionic compound dissolved in water will be present as the separated ions.)

$$K^+(aq) + Cl^-(aq) + Ag^+(aq) + NO_3^-(aq) \longrightarrow AgCl(s) + K^+(aq) + NO_3^-(aq)$$

Spectator ion   Spectator ion   Solid, not written as separate ions   Spectator ion   Spectator ion

Canceling the spectator ions

$$\cancel{K^+}(aq) + Cl^-(aq) + Ag^+(aq) + \cancel{NO_3^-}(aq) \longrightarrow AgCl(s) + \cancel{K^+}(aq) + \cancel{NO_3^-}(aq)$$

gives the following net ionic equation.

Net Ionic Equation

$$Cl^-(aq) + Ag^+(aq) \longrightarrow AgCl(s)$$

b. Molecular Equation

$$3KOH(aq) + Fe(NO_3)_3(aq) \longrightarrow Fe(OH)_3(s) + 3KNO_3(aq)$$

Complete Ionic Equation

$$3K^+(aq) + 3OH^-(aq) + Fe^{3+}(aq) + 3NO_3^-(aq) \longrightarrow$$
$$Fe(OH)_3(s) + 3K^+(aq) + 3NO_3^-(aq)$$

Net Ionic Equation

$$3OH^-(aq) + Fe^{3+}(aq) \longrightarrow Fe(OH)_3(s)$$

See Exercises 4.31 through 4.36.

4.7 Stoichiometry of Precipitation Reactions

In Chapter 3 we covered the principles of chemical stoichiometry: the procedures for calculating quantities of reactants and products involved in a chemical reaction. Recall that in performing these calculations we first convert all quantities to moles and then use the coefficients of the balanced equation to assemble the appropriate mole ratios. In cases where reactants are mixed we must determine which reactant is limiting, since the reactant that is consumed first will limit the amounts of products formed. *These same principles apply to reactions that take place in solutions.* However, there are two points about solution reactions that need special emphasis. The first is that it is sometimes difficult to tell immediately what reaction will occur when two solutions are mixed. Usually we must do some thinking about the various possibilities and then decide what probably will happen. The first step in this process *always* should be to write down the species that are actually present in the solution, as we did in Section 4.5. The second special point about solution reactions is that to obtain the moles of reactants we must use the volume of the solution and its molarity. This procedure was covered in Section 4.3.

We will introduce stoichiometric calculations for reactions in solution in Sample Exercise 4.10.

Sample Exercise 4.10 Determining the Mass of Product Formed

Calculate the mass of solid NaCl that must be added to 1.50 L of a 0.100 M AgNO$_3$ solution to precipitate all the Ag$^+$ ions in the form of AgCl.

Solution

When added to the AgNO$_3$ solution (which contains Ag$^+$ and NO$_3^-$ ions), the solid NaCl dissolves to yield Na$^+$ and Cl$^-$ ions. Thus the mixed solution contains the ions

$$Ag^+ \qquad NO_3^- \qquad Na^+ \qquad Cl^-$$

Note from Table 4.1 that $NaNO_3$ is soluble and $AgCl$ is insoluble. Therefore, solid $AgCl$ forms according to the following net ionic equation:

$$Ag^+(aq) + Cl^-(aq) \longrightarrow AgCl(s)$$

In this case we must add enough Cl^- ions to react with all the Ag^+ ions present. Thus we must calculate the moles of Ag^+ ions present in 1.50 L of a 0.100 M $AgNO_3$ solution (remember that a 0.100 M $AgNO_3$ solution contains 0.100 M Ag^+ ions and 0.100 M NO_3^- ions):

$$1.50 \, \cancel{L} \times \frac{0.100 \text{ mol } Ag^+}{\cancel{L}} = 0.150 \text{ mol } Ag^+$$

Because Ag^+ and Cl^- react in a 1:1 ratio, 0.150 mol Cl^- ions and thus 0.150 mol $NaCl$ are required. We calculate the mass of $NaCl$ required as follows:

$$0.150 \text{ mol } \cancel{NaCl} \times \frac{58.45 \text{ g } NaCl}{\cancel{\text{mol } NaCl}} = 8.77 \text{ g } NaCl$$

See Exercise 4.39.

Notice from Sample Exercise 4.10 that the procedures for doing stoichiometric calculations for solution reactions are very similar to those for other types of reactions. It is useful to think in terms of the following steps for reactions in solution.

STOICHIOMETRY FOR REACTIONS IN SOLUTION

STEP 1

Identify the species present in the combined solution, and determine what reaction occurs.

STEP 2

Write the balanced net ionic equation for the reaction.

STEP 3

Calculate the moles of reactants.

STEP 4

Determine which reactant is limiting.

STEP 5

Calculate the moles of product or products, as required.

STEP 6

Convert to grams or other units, as required.

Sample Exercise 4.11 *Determining the Mass of Product Formed*

When aqueous solutions of Na_2SO_4 and $Pb(NO_3)_2$ are mixed, $PbSO_4$ precipitates. Calculate the mass of $PbSO_4$ formed when 1.25 L of 0.0500 M $Pb(NO_3)_2$ and 2.00 L of 0.0250 M Na_2SO_4 are mixed.

Solution

STEP 1

Identify the species present in the combined solution, and determine what reaction occurs. When the aqueous solutions of Na_2SO_4 (containing Na^+ and SO_4^{2-} ions) and $Pb(NO_3)_2$ (containing Pb^{2+} and NO_3^- ions) are mixed, the resulting solution contains the ions Na^+, SO_4^{2-}, Pb^{2+}, and NO_3^-. Since $NaNO_3$ is soluble and $PbSO_4$ is insoluble (see Rule 4 in Table 4.1), solid $PbSO_4$ will form.

STEP 2

Write the balanced net ionic equation for the reaction. The net ionic equation is

$$Pb^{2+}(aq) + SO_4^{2-}(aq) \longrightarrow PbSO_4(s)$$

STEP 3

Calculate the moles of reactants. Since 0.0500 M $Pb(NO_3)_2$ contains 0.0500 M Pb^{2+} ions, we can calculate the moles of Pb^{2+} ions in 1.25 L of this solution as follows:

$$1.25 \, L \times \frac{0.0500 \text{ mol } Pb^{2+}}{L} = 0.0625 \text{ mol } Pb^{2+}$$

The 0.0250 M Na_2SO_4 solution contains 0.0250 M SO_4^{2-} ions, and the number of moles of SO_4^{2-} ions in 2.00 L of this solution is

$$2.00 \, L \times \frac{0.0250 \text{ mol } SO_4^{2-}}{L} = 0.0500 \text{ mol } SO_4^{2-}$$

STEP 4

Determine which reactant is limiting. Because Pb^{2+} and SO_4^{2-} react in a 1:1 ratio, the amount of SO_4^{2-} will be limiting (0.0500 mol SO_4^{2-} is less than 0.0625 mol Pb^{2+}).

STEP 5

Calculate the moles of product. Since the Pb^{2+} ions are present in excess, only 0.0500 mol of solid $PbSO_4$ will be formed.

STEP 6

Convert to grams of product. The mass of $PbSO_4$ formed can be calculated using the molar mass of $PbSO_4$ (303.3 g/mol):

$$0.0500 \text{ mol PbSO}_4 \times \frac{303.3 \text{ g PbSO}_4}{1 \text{ mol PbSO}_4} = 15.2 \text{ g PbSO}_4$$

See Exercises 4.41 and 4.42.

4.8 Acid–Base Reactions

Earlier in this chapter we considered Arrhenius's concept of acids and bases: An acid is a substance that produces H^+ ions when dissolved in water, and a base is a substance that produces OH^- ions. Although these ideas are fundamentally correct, it is convenient to have a more general definition of a base, which includes substances that do not contain OH^- ions. Such a definition was provided by Johannes N. Brønsted (1879–1947) and Thomas M. Lowry (1874–1936), who defined acids and bases as follows:

An **acid** is a proton donor.

A **base** is a proton acceptor.

How do we know when to expect an acid–base reaction? One of the most difficult tasks for someone inexperienced in chemistry is to predict what reaction might occur when two solutions are mixed. With precipitation reactions, we found that the best way to deal with this problem is to focus on the species actually present in the mixed solution. This also applies to acid–base reactions. For example, when an aqueous solution of hydrogen chloride (HCl) is mixed with an aqueous solution of sodium hydroxide (NaOH), the combined solution contains the ions H^+, Cl^-, Na^+, and OH^-. The separated ions are present because HCl is a strong acid and NaOH is a strong base. How can we predict what reaction occurs, if any? First, will NaCl precipitate? From Table 4.1 we can see that NaCl is soluble in water and thus will not precipitate. Therefore, the Na^+ and Cl^- ions are spectator ions. On the other hand, because water is a nonelectrolyte, large quantities of H^+ and OH^- ions cannot coexist in solution. They react to form H_2O molecules:

$$H^+(aq) + OH^-(aq) \longrightarrow H_2O(l)$$

This is the net ionic equation for the reaction that occurs when aqueous solutions of HCl and NaOH are mixed.

Next, consider mixing an aqueous solution of acetic acid ($HC_2H_3O_2$) with an aqueous solution of potassium hydroxide (KOH). In our earlier discussion of conductivity we said that an aqueous solution of acetic acid is a weak electrolyte. This tells us that acetic acid does not dissociate into ions to any great extent. In fact, in $0.1\ M\ HC_2H_3O_2$ approximately 99% of the $HC_2H_3O_2$ molecules remain undissociated. However, when solid KOH is dissolved in water, it dissociates completely to produce K^+ and OH^- ions. Therefore, in the solution formed by mixing aqueous solutions of $HC_2H_3O_2$ and KOH, *before any reaction occurs,* the principal species are $HC_2H_3O_2$, K^+, and OH^-. What reaction will occur? A possible precipitation reaction could occur between K^+ and OH^-. However, we know that KOH is soluble,

Exploration: Acid–Base Reactions

The Brønsted–Lowry concept of acids and bases will be discussed in detail in Chapter 14.

so precipitation does not occur. Another possibility is a reaction involving the hydroxide ion (a proton acceptor) and some proton donor. Is there a source of protons in the solution? The answer is yes—the $HC_2H_3O_2$ molecules. The OH^- ion has such a strong affinity for protons that it can strip them from the $HC_2H_3O_2$ molecules. The net ionic equation for this reaction is

$$OH^-(aq) + HC_2H_3O_2(aq) \longrightarrow H_2O(l) + C_2H_3O_2^-(aq)$$

This reaction illustrates a very important general principle: *The hydroxide ion is such a strong base that for purposes of stoichiometric calculations it can be assumed to react completely with any weak acid that we will encounter.* Of course, OH^- ions also react completely with the H^+ ions in solutions of strong acids.

We will now deal with the stoichiometry of acid–base reactions in aqueous solutions. The procedure is fundamentally the same as that used previously for precipitation reactions.

PERFORMING CALCULATIONS FOR ACID–BASE REACTIONS

STEP 1

List the species present in the combined solution *before any reaction occurs,* and decide what reaction will occur.

STEP 2

Write the balanced net ionic equation for this reaction.

STEP 3

Calculate the moles of reactants. For reactions in solution, use the volumes of the original solutions and their molarities.

STEP 4

Determine the limiting reactant where appropriate.

STEP 5

Calculate the moles of the required reactant or product.

STEP 6

Convert to grams or volume (of solution), as required.

An acid–base reaction is often called a **neutralization reaction.** When just enough base is added to react exactly with the acid in a solution, we say the acid has been *neutralized.*

Sample Exercise 4.12 Neutralization Reactions I

What volume of a 0.100 *M* HCl solution is needed to neutralize 25.0 mL of 0.350 *M* NaOH?

Solution

STEP 1

List the species present in the combined solution before any reaction occurs, and decide what reaction will occur. The species present in the mixed solutions before any reaction occurs are

$$\underbrace{H^+ \quad Cl^-}_{\text{From HCl}(aq)} \qquad \underbrace{Na^+ \quad OH^-}_{\text{From NaOH}(aq)}$$

What reaction will occur? The two possibilities are

$$Na^+(aq) + Cl^-(aq) \longrightarrow NaCl(s)$$
$$H^+(aq) + OH^-(aq) \longrightarrow H_2O(l)$$

Since we know that NaCl is soluble, the first reaction does not take place (Na^+ and Cl^- are spectator ions). However, as we have seen before, the reaction of the H^+ and OH^- ions to form H_2O does occur.

STEP 2

Write the balanced net ionic equation. The balanced net ionic equation for this reaction is

$$H^+(aq) + OH^-(aq) \longrightarrow H_2O(l)$$

STEP 3

Calculate the moles of reactants. The number of moles of OH^- ions in the 25.0-mL sample of 0.350 *M* NaOH is

$$25.0 \text{ mL NaOH} \times \frac{1 \text{ L}}{1000 \text{ mL}} \times \frac{0.350 \text{ mol OH}^-}{\text{L NaOH}} = 8.75 \times 10^{-3} \text{ mol OH}^-$$

STEP 4

Determine the limiting reactant. This problem requires the addition of just enough H^+ ions to react exactly with the OH^- ions present. Thus we need not be concerned with determining a limiting reactant.

STEP 5

Calculate the moles of reactant needed. Since H^+ and OH^- ions react in a 1:1 ratio, 8.75×10^{-3} mol H^+ ions is required to neutralize the OH^- ions present.

STEP 6

Convert to volume required. The volume *V* of 0.100 *M* HCl required to furnish 8.75×10^{-3} mol H^+ ions can be calculated as follows:

$$V \times \frac{0.100 \text{ mol H}^+}{\text{L}} = 8.75 \times 10^{-3} \text{ mol H}^+$$

Solving for V gives

$$V = \frac{8.75 \times 10^{-3} \text{ mol } H^+}{\dfrac{0.100 \text{ mol } H^+}{L}} = 8.75 \times 10^{-2} \text{ L}$$

Thus 8.75×10^{-2} L (87.5 mL) of 0.100 M HCl is required to neutralize 25.0 mL of 0.350 M NaOH.

See Exercises 4.49 and 4.50.

Sample Exercise 4.13 *Neutralization Reactions II*

In a certain experiment, 28.0 mL of 0.250 M HNO$_3$ and 53.0 mL of 0.320 M KOH are mixed. Calculate the amount of water formed in the resulting reaction. What is the concentration of H$^+$ or OH$^-$ ions in excess after the reaction goes to completion?

Solution

The species available for reaction are

$$\underbrace{\text{H}^+ \quad \text{NO}_3{}^-}_{\substack{\text{From HNO}_3 \\ \text{solution}}} \qquad \underbrace{\text{K}^+ \quad \text{OH}^-}_{\substack{\text{From KOH} \\ \text{solution}}}$$

Since KNO$_3$ is soluble, K$^+$ and NO$_3{}^-$ are spectator ions, so the net ionic equation is

$$\text{H}^+(aq) + \text{OH}^-(aq) \longrightarrow \text{H}_2\text{O}(l)$$

We next compute the amounts of H$^+$ and OH$^-$ ions present:

$$28.0 \text{ mL HNO}_3 \times \frac{1 \text{ L}}{1000 \text{ mL}} \times \frac{0.250 \text{ mol H}^+}{\text{L HNO}_3} = 7.00 \times 10^{-3} \text{ mol H}^+$$

$$53.0 \text{ mL KOH} \times \frac{1 \text{ L}}{1000 \text{ mL}} \times \frac{0.320 \text{ mol OH}^-}{\text{L KOH}} = 1.70 \times 10^{-2} \text{ mol OH}^-$$

Since H$^+$ and OH$^-$ react in a 1:1 ratio, the limiting reactant is H$^+$. This means that 7.00×10^{-3} mol H$^+$ ions will react with 7.00×10^{-3} mol OH$^-$ ions to form 7.00×10^{-3} mol H$_2$O.

The amount of OH$^-$ ions in excess is obtained from the following difference:

$$\text{Original amount} - \text{amount consumed} = \text{amount in excess}$$
$$1.70 \times 10^{-2} \text{ mol OH}^- - 7.00 \times 10^{-3} \text{ mol OH}^- = 1.00 \times 10^{-2} \text{ mol OH}^-$$

The volume of the combined solution is the sum of the individual volumes:

$$\text{Original volume of HNO}_3 + \text{original volume of KOH} = \text{total volume}$$
$$28.0 \text{ mL} + 53.0 \text{ mL} = 81.0 \text{ mL} = 8.10 \times 10^{-2} \text{ L}$$

Thus the molarity of OH^- ions in excess is

$$\frac{\text{mol } OH^-}{\text{L solution}} = \frac{1.00 \times 10^{-2} \text{ mol } OH^-}{8.10 \times 10^{-2} \text{ L}} = 0.123 \; M \; OH^-$$

See Exercises 4.51 and 4.52.

Acid–Base Titrations

Volumetric analysis is a technique for determining the amount of a certain substance by doing a titration. A **titration** involves delivery (from a buret) of a measured volume of a solution of known concentration (the *titrant*) into a solution containing the substance being analyzed (the *analyte*). The titrant contains a substance that reacts in a known manner with the analyte. The point in the titration where enough titrant has been added to react exactly with the analyte is called the **equivalence point** or the **stoichiometric point.** This point is often marked by an **indicator,** a substance added at the beginning of the titration that changes color at (or very near) the equivalence point. The point where the indicator *actually* changes color is called the **endpoint** of the titration. The goal is to choose an indicator such that the endpoint (where the indicator changes color) occurs exactly at the equivalence point (where just enough titrant has been added to react with all the analyte).

Ideally, the endpoint and stoichiometric point should coincide.

The following three requirements must be met for a titration to be successful:

1. The exact reaction between titrant and analyte must be known (and rapid).
2. The stoichiometric (equivalence) point must be marked accurately.
3. The volume of titrant required to reach the stoichiometric point must be known accurately.

When the analyte is a base or an acid, the required titrant is a strong acid or strong base, respectively. This procedure is called an *acid–base titration.* An indicator very commonly used for acid–base titrations is phenolphthalein, which is colorless in an acidic solution and pink in a basic solution. Thus, when an acid is titrated with a base, the phenolphthalein remains colorless until after the acid is consumed and the first drop of excess base is added. In this case, the endpoint (the solution changes from colorless to pink) occurs approximately one drop of base beyond the stoichiometric point. This type of titration is illustrated in the three photos in Fig. 4.17 on page 162.

We will deal with the acid–base titrations only briefly here but will return to the topic of titrations and indicators in more detail in Chapter 15. The titration of an acid with a standard solution containing hydroxide ions is illustrated in Sample Exercise 4.15. In Sample Exercise 4.14 we show how to determine accurately the concentration of a sodium hydroxide solution. This procedure is called *standardizing the solution.*

(a)

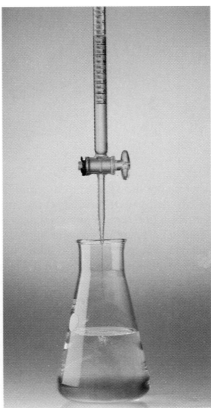

(b)

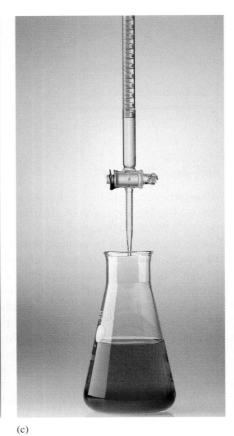

(c)

Figure 4.17

The titration of an acid with a base. (a) The titrant (the base) is in the buret, and the beaker contains the acid solution along with a small amount of indicator. (b) As base is added drop by drop to the acid solution in the beaker during the titration, the indicator changes color, but the color disappears on mixing. (c) The stoichiometric (equivalence) point is marked by a permanent indicator color change. The volume of base added is the difference between the final and initial buret readings.

Sample Exercise 4.14 *Neutralization Titration*

A student carries out an experiment to standardize (determine the exact concentration of) a sodium hydroxide solution. To do this, the student weighs out a 1.3009-g sample of potassium hydrogen phthalate ($KHC_8H_4O_4$, often abbreviated KHP). KHP (molar mass 204.22 g/mol) has one acidic hydrogen. The student dissolves the KHP in distilled water, adds phenolphthalein as an indicator, and titrates the resulting solution with the sodium hydroxide solution to the phenolphthalein endpoint. The difference between the final and initial buret readings indicates that 41.20 mL of the sodium hydroxide solution is required to react exactly with the 1.3009 g KHP. Calculate the concentration of the sodium hydroxide solution.

Solution

$KHC_8H_4O_4$ dissolves in water to give the K^+ and $HC_8H_4O_4^-$ ions. The net ionic acid–base reaction between aqueous sodium hydroxide (containing Na^+ and OH^- ions) and KHP is

$$HC_8H_4O_4^-(aq) + OH^-(aq) \longrightarrow H_2O(l) + C_8H_4O_4^{2-}(aq)$$

Since the reaction exhibits 1:1 stoichiometry, we know that 41.20 mL of the sodium hydroxide solution must contain exactly the same number of moles of OH^- as there are moles of $HC_8H_4O_4^-$ in 1.3009 g $KHC_8H_4O_4$.

We calculate the moles of $KHC_8H_4O_4$ in the usual way:

$$1.3009 \text{ g } \cancel{KHC_8H_4O_4} \times \frac{1 \text{ mol } KHC_8H_4O_4}{204.22 \text{ g } \cancel{KHC_8H_4O_4}} = 6.3701 \times 10^{-3} \text{ mol } KHC_8H_4O_4$$

This means that 6.3701×10^{-3} mol OH^- must be added to react with the 6.3701×10^{-3} mol $HC_8H_4O_4^-$. Thus 41.20 mL (4.120×10^{-2} L) of the sodium hydroxide solution must contain 6.3701×10^{-3} mol OH^- (and Na^+), and the concentration of the sodium hydroxide solution is

$$\text{Molarity of NaOH} = \frac{\text{mol NaOH}}{\text{L solution}} = \frac{6.3701 \times 10^{-3} \text{ mol NaOH}}{4.120 \times 10^{-2} \text{ L}}$$

$$= 0.1546 \ M$$

This standard sodium hydroxide solution can now be used in other experiments (see Sample Exercise 4.15).

See Exercises 4.53, 4.54, and 4.56.

Sample Exercise 4.15 *Neutralization Analysis*

An environmental chemist analyzed the effluent (the released waste material) from an industrial process known to produce the compounds carbon tetrachloride (CCl_4) and benzoic acid ($HC_7H_5O_2$), a weak acid that has one acidic hydrogen atom per molecule. A sample of this effluent weighing 0.3518 g was shaken with water, and the resulting aqueous solution required 10.59 mL of 0.1546 M NaOH for neutralization. Calculate the mass percent of $HC_7H_5O_2$ in the original sample.

Molecular Model: $HC_7H_5O_2$

Solution

In this case, the sample was a mixture containing CCl_4 and $HC_7H_5O_2$, and it was titrated with OH^- ions. Clearly, CCl_4 is not an acid (it contains no hydrogen atoms), so we can assume it does not react with OH^- ions. However, $HC_7H_5O_2$ is an acid that donates one H^+ ion per molecule to react with an OH^- ion as follows:

$$HC_7H_5O_2(aq) + OH^-(aq) \longrightarrow H_2O(l) + C_7H_5O_2^-(aq)$$

Although $HC_7H_5O_2$ is a weak acid, the OH^- ion is such a strong base that we can assume that each OH^- ion added will react with a $HC_7H_5O_2$ molecule until all the benzoic acid is consumed.

We must first determine the number of moles of OH^- ions required to react with all the $HC_7H_5O_2$:

$$10.59 \text{ mL NaOH} \times \frac{1 \text{ L}}{1000 \text{ mL}} \times \frac{0.1546 \text{ mol } OH^-}{\text{L NaOH}} = 1.637 \times 10^{-3} \text{ mol } OH^-$$

This number is also the number of moles of $HC_7H_5O_2$ present. The number of grams of the acid is calculated using its molar mass (122.12 g/mol):

$$1.637 \times 10^{-3} \text{ mol } HC_7H_5O_2 \times \frac{122.12 \text{ g } HC_7H_5O_2}{1 \text{ mol } HC_7H_5O_2} = 0.1999 \text{ g } HC_7H_5O_2$$

The mass percent of $HC_7H_5O_2$ in the original sample is

$$\frac{0.1999 \text{ g}}{0.3518 \text{ g}} \times 100 = 56.82\%$$

See Exercise 4.55.

In doing problems involving titrations, you must first decide what reaction is occurring. Sometimes this seems difficult because the titration solution contains several components. *The key to success is to first write down all the components in the solution and focus on the chemistry of each one.* We have been emphasizing this approach in dealing with the reactions between ions in solution. Make it a habit to write down the components of solutions before trying to decide what reaction(s) might take place as you attempt the end-of-chapter problems involving titrations.

The first step in the analysis of a complex solution is to write down the components and focus on the chemistry of each one.

4.9 Oxidation–Reduction Reactions

Exploration: Oxidation–Reduction Reactions

We have seen that many important substances are ionic. Sodium chloride, for example, can be formed by the reaction of elemental sodium and chlorine:

$$2Na(s) + Cl_2(g) \longrightarrow 2NaCl(s)$$

In this reaction, solid sodium, which contains neutral sodium atoms, reacts with chlorine gas, which contains diatomic Cl_2 molecules, to form the ionic solid NaCl, which contains Na^+ and Cl^- ions. This process is represented in Fig. 4.18. *Reactions like this one, in which one or more electrons are transferred, are called* **oxidation–reduction reactions** *or* **redox reactions.**

Many important chemical reactions involve oxidation and reduction. Photosynthesis, which stores energy from the sun in plants by converting carbon dioxide and water to sugar, is a very important oxidation–reduction reaction. In fact, most reactions used for energy production are redox reactions. In humans, the oxidation of sugars, fats, and proteins provides the energy necessary for life. Combustion reactions, which provide most of the energy to power our civilization, also involve oxidation and reduction. An example is the reaction of methane with oxygen:

$$CH_4(g) + 2O_2(g) \longrightarrow CO_2(g) + 2H_2O(g) + energy$$

Even though none of the reactants or products in this reaction is ionic, the reaction is still assumed to involve a transfer of electrons from carbon to oxygen. To explain this, we must introduce the concept of oxidation states.

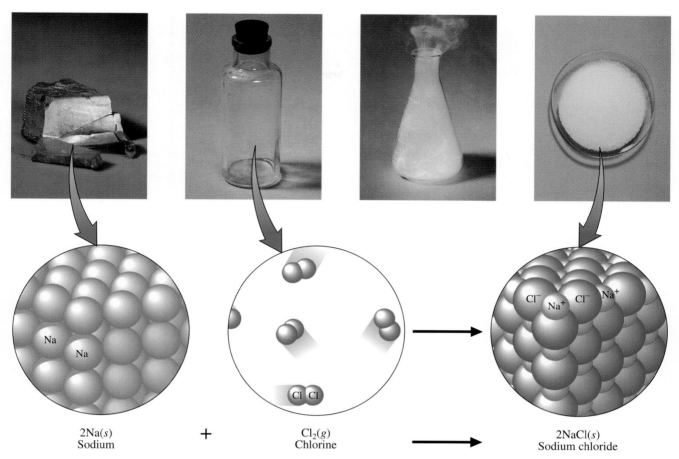

Figure 4.18
The reaction of solid sodium and gaseous chlorine to form solid sodium chloride.

Oxidation States

The concept of **oxidation states** (also called *oxidation numbers*) provides a way to keep track of electrons in oxidation–reduction reactions, particularly redox reactions involving covalent substances. Recall that electrons are shared by atoms in covalent bonds. The oxidation states of atoms in covalent compounds are obtained by arbitrarily assigning the electrons (which are actually shared) to particular atoms. We do this as follows: For a covalent bond between two identical atoms, the electrons are split equally between the two. In cases where two different atoms are involved (and the electrons are thus shared unequally), the shared electrons are assigned completely to the atom that has the stronger attraction for electrons. For example, recall from the discussion of the water molecule in Section 4.1 that oxygen has a greater attraction for electrons than does hydrogen. Therefore, in assigning the oxidation state of oxygen and hydrogen in H_2O, we assume that the oxygen atom actually possesses all the electrons. Recall that a hydrogen atom has one electron. Thus, in water, oxygen has formally "taken" the electrons from two hydrogen atoms. This

CHEMICAL IMPACT

Iron Zeroes in on Pollution

TREATING GROUNDWATER CONTAMINATED with pollutants is typically very complicated and very expensive. However, chemists have discovered a low-tech, economical method for treating the contaminated groundwater near a former semiconductor manufacturing plant in Sunnyvale, California. They have replaced the elaborate decontamination machinery used at the site for more than a decade with 220 tons of iron filings buried in a giant trough. Because there are no pumps to maintain and no electricity to purchase, this simple system will save approximately $300,000 per year. The property, which was thought to be unusable for the 30-year lifetime of the old clean-up process because of the need for constant monitoring and access, can now be used immediately.

A schematic of the iron treatment method is shown in the accompanying figure. At Sunnyvale, the iron barrier is 40 feet long, 4 feet wide, and 20 feet deep. In the 4 days it takes for contaminated water to seep through the wall of iron, the chlorinated organic contaminants are degraded into products that are then themselves decomposed to simpler substances. According to engineers on the site, the polluted water that seeps through the wall meets Environmental Protection Agency (EPA) standards when it emerges on the other side.

How does iron metal clean up contaminated groundwater? It's a result of the ability of iron metal (oxidation state = 0)

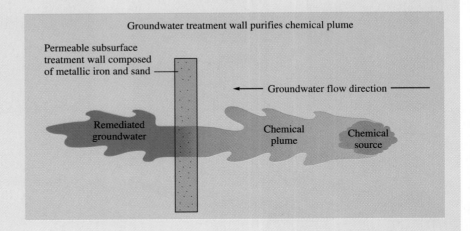

Groundwater treatment wall purifies chemical plume

Permeable subsurface treatment wall composed of metallic iron and sand

Groundwater flow direction

Remediated groundwater

Chemical plume

Chemical source

to act as a reducing agent toward the chlorine-containing organic pollutant molecules. The reaction can be represented as follows:

$$Fe(s) + RCl(aq) + H^+(aq) \longrightarrow Fe^{2+}(aq) + RH(aq) + Cl^-(aq)$$

where RCl represents a chlorinated organic molecule. The reaction appears to involve a direct reaction between the metal and an RCl molecule adsorbed on the metal surface.

In addition to decomposing chlorinated organic contaminants, iron appears to be useful against other pollutants as well. Iron can degrade dye wastes from textile mills and can reduce soluble Cr(VI) compounds to insoluble Cr(III) products, which are much less harmful. Iron's reducing abilities also appear useful in

removing radioactive technetium, a common pollutant at nuclear processing facilities. Iron also appears to be effective for removing nitrates from the soil.

Other metals, such as zinc, tin, and palladium, also have shown promise for use in groundwater clean-up. These metals generally react more quickly than iron but are more expensive and pose their own environmental hazards.

Inexpensive and environmentally benign, iron seems to be the metal of choice for most groundwater clean-up. It's cheap, it's effective, it's almost a miracle!

Figure reproduced with permission from *Chemical & Engineering News*, July 3, 1995, 73(27), p. 20. Copyright © 1995 American Chemical Society.

gives the oxygen an *excess* of two electrons (its oxidation state is −2) and leaves each hydrogen with no electrons (the oxidation state of each hydrogen is thus +1).

We define the *oxidation states* (or *oxidation numbers*) of the atoms in a covalent compound as the imaginary charges the atoms would have if the shared electrons were divided equally between identical atoms bonded to each other or, for different atoms, were all assigned to the atom in each bond that has the greater attraction for

Table 4.2 Rules for Assigning Oxidation States

	Summary
1. The oxidation state of an atom in an element is 0. For example, the oxidation state of each atom in the substances $Na(s)$, $O_2(g)$, $O_3(g)$, and $Hg(l)$ is 0.	Element: 0
2. The oxidation state of a monatomic ion is the same as its charge. For example, the oxidation state of the Na^+ ion is $+1$ and of the Cl^- ion is -1.	
3. In its compounds, fluorine is always assigned an oxidation state of -1.	Fluorine: -1
4. Oxygen is usually assigned an oxidation state of -2 in its covalent compounds, such as CO, CO_2, SO_2, and SO_3. Exceptions to this rule include peroxides (compounds containing the O_2^{2-} group), where each oxygen is assigned an oxidation state of -1, as in hydrogen peroxide (H_2O_2), and OF_2 in which oxygen is assigned a $+2$ oxidation state.	Oxygen: -2
5. In its covalent compounds with nonmetals, hydrogen is assigned an oxidation state of $+1$. For example, in the compounds HCl, NH_3, H_2O, and CH_4, hydrogen is assigned an oxidation state of $+1$.	Hydrogen: $+1$
6. The sum of the oxidation states must be zero for an electrically neutral compound. For an ion, the sum of the oxidation states must equal the charge of the ion. For example, the sum of the oxidation states for the hydrogen and oxygen atoms in water is 0; the sum of the oxidation states for the carbon and oxygen atoms in CO_3^{2-} is -2; and the sum of oxidation states for the nitrogen and hydrogen atoms in NH_4^+ is $+1$.	

electrons. Of course, for ionic compounds containing monatomic ions, the oxidation states of the ions are equal to the ion charges.

These considerations lead to a series of rules for assigning oxidation states that are summarized in Table 4.2. Application of these simple rules allows the assignment of oxidation states in most compounds. The principles are illustrated by Sample Exercise 4.16.

Although these rules do not cover every possible case, they will be sufficient for our purposes.

It is worthwhile to note at this point that the convention is to write actual charges on ions as $n+$ or $n-$, the number being written *before* the plus or minus sign. On the other hand, oxidation states (not actual charges) are written $+n$ or $-n$, the number being written *after* the plus or minus sign.

Sample Exercise 4.16 *Assigning Oxidation States*

Assign oxidation states to all atoms in the following.

a. CO_2
b. SF_6
c. NO_3^-

Solution

a. Since we have a specific rule for the oxidation state of oxygen, we will assign its value first. The oxidation state of oxygen is -2. The oxidation state of the carbon atom can be determined by recognizing that since CO_2 has no

Oxidation of copper metal by nitric acid. The copper atoms lose two electrons to form Cu^{2+} ions, which give a deep green color that becomes turquoise when diluted with water.

charge, the sum of the oxidation states for oxygen and carbon must be zero. Since each oxygen is -2 and there are two oxygen atoms, the carbon atom must be assigned an oxidation state of $+4$:

$$CO_2$$

$+4$ -2 for each oxygen

We can check the assigned oxidation states by noting that when the number of atoms is taken into account, the sum is zero as required:

$$1(+4) + 2(-2) = 0$$

No. of C   No. of O
atoms   atoms

b. Since we have no rule for sulfur, we first assign the oxidation state of each fluorine as -1. The sulfur must then be assigned an oxidation state of $+6$ to balance the total of -6 from the fluorine atoms:

$$SF_6$$

$+6$ -1 for each fluorine

CHECK: $+6 + 6(-1) = 0$

c. Oxygen has an oxidation state of -2. Because the sum of the oxidation states of the three oxygens is -6 and the net charge on the NO_3^- ion is $1-$, the nitrogen must have an oxidation state of $+5$:

$$NO_3^-$$

$+5$ -2 for each oxygen

CHECK: $+5 + 3(-2) = -1$

Note that in this case the sum must be -1 (the overall charge on the ion).

See Exercises 4.57 through 4.60.

Magnetite is a magnetic ore containing Fe_3O_4. Note that the compass needle points toward the ore.

We need to make one more point about oxidation states, and this can be illustrated by the compound Fe_3O_4, which is the main component in magnetite, an iron ore that accounts for the reddish color of many types of rocks and soils. To determine the oxidation states in Fe_3O_4, we first assign each oxygen atom its usual oxidation state of -2. The three iron atoms must yield a total of $+8$ to balance the total of -8 from the four oxygens. This means that each iron atom has an oxidation state of $+\frac{8}{3}$. A noninteger value for oxidation state may seem strange because charge is expressed in whole numbers. However, although they are rare, noninteger oxidation states do occur because of the rather arbitrary way that electrons are divided up by the rules in Table 4.2. For Fe_3O_4, for example, the rules assume that all the iron atoms are equal, when in fact this compound can best be viewed as containing four O^{2-} ions, two Fe^{3+} ions, and one Fe^{2+} ion per formula unit. (Note that the "average" charge on iron works out to be $\frac{8}{3}+$, which is equal to the oxidation state we determined above.) Noninteger oxidation states should not intimidate you. They are used in the same way as integer oxidation states—for keeping track of electrons.

The Characteristics of Oxidation–Reduction Reactions

Oxidation–reduction reactions are characterized by a transfer of electrons. In some cases, the transfer occurs in a literal sense to form ions, such as in the reaction

$$2Na(s) + Cl_2(g) \longrightarrow 2NaCl(s)$$

However, sometimes the transfer is less obvious. For example, consider the combustion of methane (the oxidation state for each atom is given):

$$CH_4(g) + 2O_2(g) \longrightarrow CO_2(g) + 2H_2O(g)$$

Oxidation state   −4   +1   0   +4   −2   +1 −2
(each H)   (each O) (each H)

Note that the oxidation state for oxygen in O_2 is 0 because it is in elemental form. In this reaction there are no ionic compounds, but we can still describe the process in terms of a transfer of electrons. Note that carbon undergoes a change in oxidation state from −4 in CH_4 to +4 in CO_2. Such a change can be accounted for by a loss of eight electrons (the symbol e^- stands for an electron);

$$CH_4 \longrightarrow CO_2 + 8e^-$$

$$-4 \qquad +4$$

On the other hand, each oxygen changes from an oxidation state of 0 in O_2 to −2 in H_2O and CO_2, signifying a gain of two electrons per atom. Since four oxygen atoms are involved, this is a gain of eight electrons:

$$2O_2 + 8e^- \longrightarrow CO_2 + 2H_2O$$

$$0 \qquad\qquad 4(-2) = -8$$

No change occurs in the oxidation state of hydrogen, and it is not formally involved in the electron-transfer process.

With this background, we can now define some important terms. **Oxidation** is an *increase* in oxidation state (a loss of electrons). **Reduction** is a *decrease* in oxidation state (a gain of electrons). Thus in the reaction

$$2Na(s) + Cl_2(g) \longrightarrow 2NaCl(s)$$

$$0 \qquad 0 \qquad\qquad +1 \quad -1$$

sodium is oxidized and chlorine is reduced. In addition, Cl_2 is called the **oxidizing agent (electron acceptor),** and Na is called the **reducing agent (electron donor).** These terms are summarized in Fig. 4.19.

Concerning the reaction

$$CH_4(g) + 2O_2(g) \longrightarrow CO_2(g) + 2H_2O(g)$$

$$-4 \; +1 \qquad 0 \qquad\qquad +4 \; -2 \qquad +1 \; -2$$

we can say the following:

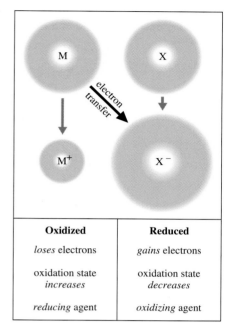

Oxidized	Reduced
loses electrons	*gains* electrons
oxidation state *increases*	oxidation state *decreases*
reducing agent	*oxidizing* agent

Figure 4.19
A summary of an oxidation–reduction process, in which M is oxidized and X is reduced.

Molecular Models: CH_4, O_2, CO_2, H_2O

Oxidation is an increase in oxidation state. *Reduction* is a decrease in oxidation state.

A helpful mnemonic device is OIL RIG (**O**xidation **I**nvolves **L**oss; **R**eduction **I**nvolves **G**ain). Another common mnemonic is LEO says GER. (**L**oss of **E**lectrons, **O**xidation; **G**ain of **E**lectrons, **R**eduction).

An oxidizing agent is reduced and a reducing agent is oxidized in a redox reaction.

Video: Zinc and Iodine

Carbon is oxidized because there has been an increase in its oxidation state (carbon has formally lost electrons).

Oxygen is reduced because there has been a decrease in its oxidation state (oxygen has formally gained electrons).

CH_4 is the reducing agent.

O_2 is the oxidizing agent.

Note that when the oxidizing or reducing agent is named, the *whole compound* is specified, not just the element that undergoes the change in oxidation state.

Sample Exercise 4.17 *Oxidation–Reduction Reactions I*

When powdered aluminum metal is mixed with pulverized iodine crystals and a drop of water is added to help the reaction get started, the resulting reaction produces a great deal of energy. The mixture bursts into flames, and a purple smoke of I_2 vapor is produced from the excess iodine. The equation for the reaction is

$$2Al(s) + 3I_2(s) \longrightarrow 2AlI_3(s)$$

For this reaction, identify the atoms that are oxidized and reduced, and specify the oxidizing and reducing agents.

Solution

The first step is to assign oxidation states:

Since each aluminum atom changes its oxidation state from 0 to +3 (an increase in oxidation state), aluminum is *oxidized*. On the other hand, the oxidation state of each iodine atom decreases from 0 to −1, and iodine is *reduced*. Since Al furnishes electrons for the reduction of iodine, it is the *reducing agent;* I_2 is the *oxidizing agent*.

See Exercises 4.61 and 4.62.

Finely ground aluminum and iodine are mixed and react vigorously to form aluminum iodide after a drop of water is added. The purple cloud is excess iodine vaporized by the heat of the reaction.

Sample Exercise 4.18 *Oxidation–Reduction Reactions II*

Metallurgy, the process of producing a metal from its ore, always involves oxidation–reduction reactions. In the metallurgy of galena (PbS), the principal lead-containing ore, the first step is the conversion of lead sulfide to its oxide (a process called *roasting*):

$$2PbS(s) + 3O_2(g) \longrightarrow 2PbO(s) + 2SO_2(g)$$

The oxide is then treated with carbon monoxide to produce the free metal:

$$PbO(s) + CO(g) \longrightarrow Pb(s) + CO_2(g)$$

For each reaction, identify the atoms that are oxidized and reduced, and specify the oxidizing and reducing agents.

Solution

For the first reaction, we can assign the following oxidation states:

$$2PbS(s) + 3O_2(g) \longrightarrow 2PbO(s) + 2SO_2(g)$$

+2 −2   0   +2 −2 +4 −2 (each O)

The oxidation state for the sulfur atom increases from −2 to +4. Thus sulfur is oxidized. The oxidation state for each oxygen atom decreases from 0 to −2. Oxygen is reduced. The oxidizing agent (that accepts the electrons) is O_2, and the reducing agent (that donates electrons) is PbS.

For the second reaction we have

$$PbO(s) + CO(g) \longrightarrow Pb(s) + CO_2(g)$$

+2 −2 +2 −2   0   +4 −2 (each O)

Lead is reduced (its oxidation state decreases from +2 to 0), and carbon is oxidized (its oxidation state increases from +2 to +4). PbO is the oxidizing agent, and CO is the reducing agent.

See Exercises 4.61 and 4.62.

4.10 Balancing Oxidation–Reduction Equations

Oxidation–reduction reactions in aqueous solutions are often complicated, which means that it can be difficult to balance their equations by simple inspection. In this section we will discuss a special technique for balancing the equations of redox reactions that occur in aqueous solutions. This is called the *half-reaction method*.

The Half-Reaction Method for Balancing Oxidation–Reduction Reactions in Aqueous Solutions

For oxidation–reduction reactions that occur in aqueous solution, it is useful to separate the reaction into two **half-reactions:** one involving oxidation and the other involving reduction. For example, consider the unbalanced equation for the oxidation–reduction reaction between cerium(IV) ion and tin(II) ion:

$$Ce^{4+}(aq) + Sn^{2+}(aq) \longrightarrow Ce^{3+}(aq) + Sn^{4+}(aq)$$

This reaction can be separated into a half-reaction involving the substance being *reduced,*

$$Ce^{4+}(aq) \longrightarrow Ce^{3+}(aq)$$

CHEMICAL IMPACT

Aging: Does It Involve Oxidation?

ALTHOUGH AGING IS supposed to bring wisdom, almost no one wants to get old. Along with wisdom, aging brings wrinkles, loss of physical strength, and greater susceptibility to disease.

Why do we age? No one knows for certain, but many scientists think that oxidation plays a major role. The oxygen molecule and other oxidizing agents in the body apparently can extract single electrons from the large molecules that make up cell membranes, thus making them very reactive. Subsequently, these activated molecules can link up, changing the properties of the cell membrane. At some point, enough of these reactions have occurred that the body's immune system comes to view the changed cell as an "enemy" and destroys it. This is particularly detrimental to the organism when the cells involved are irreplaceable. Nerve cells, for example, fall into this category. They rarely regenerate in an adult.

The body has defenses against oxidation, such as vitamin E, a well-known antioxidant. Studies have shown that red blood cells age much faster than normal when they are deficient in vitamin E. Based on studies such as these, some have suggested large doses of vitamin E as a preventative against aging, but there is no solid evidence that this practice has any impact on aging.

Another protective antioxidant found in our bodies is superoxide dismutase (SOD), which protects us from the superoxide ion O_2^-, a powerful oxidizing agent that is particularly damaging to vital enzymes. The importance of SOD in opposing the aging process is indicated from the results of a study by Dr. Richard Cutler at the Gerontology Research Center of the National Institutes of Health in Baltimore that showed a strong correlation between the life span of a dozen mammalian species and their levels of SOD. Human SOD is now being produced by the techniques of biotechnology in amounts that will enable scientists to carefully study its effects on aging and on various diseases such as rheumatoid arthritis and muscular dystrophy. Although SOD is available in health food stores in forms to be taken orally, this practice is useless because the SOD is digested (broken down into simpler substances) before it can reach the bloodstream.

Research does indicate that consuming certain foods may retard the aging process. For example, a recent study of 8000 male Harvard graduates found that chocolate and candy eaters live almost a year longer than those who abstain. Although the researchers from Harvard School of Public Health are not certain of the mechanism for this effect, they suggest that the antioxidants present in chocolate may provide the health benefits. For example, chocolate contains phenols, antioxidants that are also present in wine, another substance that seems to promote good health if used in moderation.

Oxidation is only one possible cause for aging. Research continues on many fronts to try to discover why we get "older" as time passes.

Can eating chocolate slow down the aging process?

and one involving the substance being *oxidized,*

$$\mathrm{Sn}^{2+}(aq) \longrightarrow \mathrm{Sn}^{4+}(aq)$$

The general procedure is to balance the equations for the half-reactions separately and then to add them to obtain the overall balanced equation. The half-reaction method for balancing oxidation–reduction equations differs slightly depending on whether the reaction takes place in acidic or basic solution.

STEPS IN THE HALF-REACTION METHOD FOR BALANCING EQUATIONS FOR OXIDATION–REDUCTION REACTIONS OCCURRING IN ACIDIC SOLUTION

STEP 1

Write separate equations for the oxidation and reduction half-reactions.

STEP 2

For each half-reaction,
a. Balance all the elements except hydrogen and oxygen.
b. Balance oxygen using H_2O.
c. Balance hydrogen using H^+.
d. Balance the charge using electrons.

STEP 3

If necessary, multiply one or both balanced half-reactions by an integer to equalize the number of electrons transferred in the two half-reactions.

STEP 4

Add the half-reactions, and cancel identical species.

STEP 5

Check that the elements and charges are balanced.
    We will illustrate this method by balancing the equation for the reaction between permanganate and iron(II) ions in acidic solution:

$$MnO_4^-(aq) + Fe^{2+}(aq) \xrightarrow{\text{Acid}} Fe^{3+}(aq) + Mn^{2+}(aq)$$

This reaction can be used to analyze iron ore for its iron content.

STEP 1

Identify and write equations for the half-reactions. The oxidation states for the half-reaction involving the permanganate ion show that manganese is reduced:

$$MnO_4^- \longrightarrow Mn^{2+}$$

$$\overset{\nearrow}{+7} \quad \overset{\uparrow}{-2 \text{ (each O)}} \quad \overset{\uparrow}{+2}$$

This is the *reduction half-reaction.* The other half-reaction involves the oxidation of iron(II) to iron(III) ion and is the *oxidation half-reaction:*

$$Fe^{2+} \longrightarrow Fe^{3+}$$

$$\overset{\uparrow}{+2} \qquad \overset{\uparrow}{+3}$$

STEP 2

Balance each half-reaction. For the reduction reaction, we have

$$MnO_4^-(aq) \longrightarrow Mn^{2+}(aq)$$

a. The manganese is balanced.
b. We balance oxygen by adding $4H_2O$ to the right side of the equation:

$$MnO_4^-(aq) \longrightarrow Mn^{2+}(aq) + 4H_2O(l)$$

c. Next, we balance hydrogen by adding $8H^+$ to the left side:

$$8H^+(aq) + MnO_4^-(aq) \longrightarrow Mn^{2+}(aq) + 4H_2O(l)$$

d. All the elements have been balanced, but we need to balance the charge using electrons. At this point we have the following overall charges for reactants and products in the reduction half-reaction:

$$8H^+(aq) + MnO_4^-(aq) \longrightarrow Mn^{2+}(aq) + 4H_2O(l)$$

$$\underbrace{8+ \quad + \quad 1-}_{7+} \qquad \qquad \underbrace{2+ \quad + \quad 0}_{2+}$$

We can equalize the charges by adding five electrons to the left side:

$$\underbrace{5e^- + 8H^+(aq) + MnO_4^-(aq)}_{2+} \longrightarrow \underbrace{Mn^{2+}(aq) + 4H_2O(l)}_{2+}$$

Both the *elements* and the *charges* are now balanced, so this represents the balanced reduction half-reaction. The fact that five electrons appear on the reactant side of the equation makes sense, since five electrons are required to reduce MnO_4^- (Mn has an oxidation state of $+7$) to Mn^{2+} (Mn has an oxidation state of $+2$).

For the oxidation reaction

$$Fe^{2+}(aq) \longrightarrow Fe^{3+}(aq)$$

the elements are balanced, and we must simply balance the charge:

$$\underbrace{Fe^{2+}(aq)}_{2+} \longrightarrow \underbrace{Fe^{3+}(aq)}_{3+}$$

One electron is needed on the right side to give a net $2+$ charge on both sides:

$$\underbrace{Fe^{2+}(aq)}_{2+} \longrightarrow \underbrace{Fe^{3+}(aq) + e^-}_{2+}$$

STEP 3

The number of electrons gained in the reduction half-reaction must equal the number of electrons lost in the oxidation half-reaction.

Equalize the electron transfer in the two half-reactions. Since the reduction half-reaction involves a transfer of five electrons and the oxidation half-reaction involves a transfer of only one electron, the oxidation half-reaction must be multiplied by 5:

$$5Fe^{2+}(aq) \longrightarrow 5Fe^{3+}(aq) + 5e^-$$

STEP 4

Add the half-reactions. The half-reactions are added to give

$$5e^- + 5Fe^{2+}(aq) + MnO_4^-(aq) + 8H^+(aq) \longrightarrow$$
$$5Fe^{3+}(aq) + Mn^{2+}(aq) + 4H_2O(l) + 5e^-$$

Note that the electrons cancel (as they must) to give the final balanced equation:

$$5Fe^{2+}(aq) + MnO_4^-(aq) + 8H^+(aq) \longrightarrow 5Fe^{3+}(aq) + Mn^{2+}(aq) + 4H_2O(l)$$

STEP 5

Check that elements and charges are balanced.

Elements balance: 5Fe, 1Mn, 4O, 8H $\longrightarrow$ 5Fe, 1Mn, 4O, 8H

Charges balance: $5(2+) + (1-) + 8(1+) = 17+ \longrightarrow$
$$5(3+) + (2+) + 0 = 17+$$

The equation is balanced.

Sample Exercise 4.19 *Balancing Oxidation–Reduction Reactions (Acidic)*

Potassium dichromate ($K_2Cr_2O_7$) is a bright orange compound that can be reduced to a blue-violet solution of Cr^{3+} ions. Under certain conditions, $K_2Cr_2O_7$ reacts with ethyl alcohol (C_2H_5OH) as follows:

$$H^+(aq) + Cr_2O_7{}^{2-}(aq) + C_2H_5OH(l) \longrightarrow Cr^{3+}(aq) + CO_2(g) + H_2O(l)$$

Balance this equation using the half-reaction method.

Solution

STEP 1

The reduction half-reaction is

$$Cr_2O_7{}^{2-}(aq) \longrightarrow Cr^{3+}(aq)$$

Chromium is reduced from an oxidation state of $+6$ in $Cr_2O_7{}^{2-}$ to one of $+3$ in Cr^{3+}.

The oxidation half-reaction is

$$C_2H_5OH(l) \longrightarrow CO_2(g)$$

Carbon is oxidized from an oxidation state of -2 in C_2H_5OH to $+4$ in CO_2.

STEP 2

Balancing all elements except hydrogen and oxygen in the first half-reaction, we have

$$Cr_2O_7{}^{2-}(aq) \longrightarrow 2Cr^{3+}(aq)$$

Balancing oxygen using H_2O, we have

$$Cr_2O_7{}^{2-}(aq) \longrightarrow 2Cr^{3+}(aq) + 7H_2O(l)$$

Balancing hydrogen using H^+, we have

$$14H^+(aq) + Cr_2O_7{}^{2-}(aq) \longrightarrow 2Cr^{3+}(aq) + 7H_2O(l)$$

Balancing the charge using electrons, we have

$$6e^- + 14H^+(aq) + Cr_2O_7{}^{2-}(aq) \longrightarrow 2Cr^{3+}(aq) + 7H_2O(l)$$

Next, we turn to the oxidation half-reaction

$$C_2H_5OH(l) \longrightarrow CO_2(g)$$

Balancing carbon, we have

$$C_2H_5OH(l) \longrightarrow 2CO_2(g)$$

Balancing oxygen using H_2O, we have

$$C_2H_5OH(l) + 3H_2O(l) \longrightarrow 2CO_2(g)$$

Balancing hydrogen using H^+, we have

$$C_2H_5OH(l) + 3H_2O(l) \longrightarrow 2CO_2(g) + 12H^+(aq)$$

(top) Acidified potassium dichromate is added to a beaker of ethyl alcohol. (bottom) Potassium dichromate is reduced to a blue-violet solution of Cr^{3+} ions by ethyl alcohol.

We then balance the charge by adding $12e^-$ to the right side:

$$\frac{C_2H_5OH(l) + 3H_2O(l) \longrightarrow 2CO_2(g) + 12H^+(aq) + 12e^-}{16H^+(aq) + 2Cr_2O_7{}^{2-}(aq) + C_2H_5OH(l) \longrightarrow 4Cr^{3+} + 11H_2O(l) + 2CO_2(g)}$$

STEP 3

In the reduction half-reaction there are 6 electrons on the left-hand side, and there are 12 electrons on the right-hand side of the oxidation half-reaction. Thus we multiply the reduction half-reaction by 2 to give

$$12e^- + 28H^+(aq) + 2Cr_2O_7{}^{2-}(aq) \longrightarrow 4Cr^{3+}(aq) + 14H_2O(l)$$

STEP 4

Adding the half-reactions and canceling identical species, we have

Reduction Half-Reaction

$$12e^- + 28H^+(aq) + 2Cr_2O_7{}^{2-}(aq) \longrightarrow 4Cr^{3+}(aq) + 14H_2O(l)$$

Oxidation Half-Reaction

$$\frac{C_2H_5OH(l) + 3H_2O(l) \longrightarrow 2CO_2(g) + 12H^+(aq) + 12e^-}{16H^+(aq) + 2Cr_2O_7{}^{2-}(aq) + C_2H_5OH(l) \longrightarrow 4Cr^{3+} + 11H_2O(l) + 2CO_2(g)}$$

STEP 5

Check that elements and charges are balanced.

Elements balance: 22H, 4Cr, 15O, 2C $\longrightarrow$ 22H, 4Cr, 15O, 2C

Charges balance: $+16 + 2(-2) + 0 = +12 \longrightarrow 4(+3) + 0 + 0 = +12$

See Exercises 4.63 and 4.64.

Oxidation–reduction reactions can occur in basic solutions (the reactions involve OH^- ions) as well as in acidic solution (the reactions involve H^+ ions). The half-reaction method for balancing equations is slightly different for the two cases.

THE HALF-REACTION METHOD FOR BALANCING EQUATIONS FOR OXIDATION–REDUCTION REACTIONS OCCURRING IN BASIC SOLUTION

STEP 1

Use the half-reaction method as specified for acidic solutions to obtain the final balanced equation *as if H^+ ions were present.*

STEP 2

To both sides of the equation obtained above, add a number of OH^- ions that is equal to the number of H^+ ions. (We want to eliminate H^+ by forming H_2O.)

STEP 3

Form H_2O on the side containing both H^+ and OH^- ions, and eliminate the number of H_2O molecules that appear on both sides of the equation.

STEP 4

Check that elements and charges are balanced.
We will illustrate how this method is applied in Sample Exercise 4.20.

Sample Exercise 4.20 Balancing Oxidation–Reduction Reactions (Basic)

Silver is sometimes found in nature as large nuggets; more often it is found mixed with other metals and their ores. An aqueous solution containing cyanide ion is often used to extract the silver using the following reaction that occurs in basic solution:

$$Ag(s) + CN^-(aq) + O_2(g) \xrightarrow{\text{Basic}} Ag(CN)_2^-(aq)$$

Balance this equation using the half-reaction method.

Solution

STEP 1

Balance the equation as if H^+ ions were present. Balance the oxidation half-reaction:

$$CN^-(aq) + Ag(s) \longrightarrow Ag(CN)_2^-(aq)$$

Balance carbon and nitrogen:

$$2CN^-(aq) + Ag(s) \longrightarrow Ag(CN)_2^-(aq)$$

Balance the charge:

$$2CN^-(aq) + Ag(s) \longrightarrow Ag(CN)_2^-(aq) + e^-$$

Balance the reduction half-reaction:

$$O_2(g) \longrightarrow$$

Balance oxygen:

$$O_2(g) \longrightarrow 2H_2O(l)$$

Balance hydrogen:

$$O_2(g) + 4H^+(aq) \longrightarrow 2H_2O(l)$$

Balance the charge:

$$4e^- + O_2(g) + 4H^+(aq) \longrightarrow 2H_2O(l)$$

Multiply the balanced oxidation half-reaction by 4:

$$8CN^-(aq) + 4Ag(s) \longrightarrow 4Ag(CN)_2^-(aq) + 4e^-$$

Add the half-reactions, and cancel identical species:

Oxidation Half-Reaction

$$8CN^-(aq) + 4Ag(s) \longrightarrow 4Ag(CN)_2^-(aq) + 4e^-$$

Reduction Half-Reaction

$$\frac{4e^- + O_2(g) + 4H^+(aq) \longrightarrow 2H_2O(l)}{8CN^-(aq) + 4Ag(s) + O_2(g) + 4H^+(aq) \longrightarrow 4Ag(CN)_2^-(aq) + 2H_2O(l)}$$

STEP 2

Add OH^- ions to both sides of the balanced equation to eliminate the H^+ ions. We need to add $4OH^-$ to each side:

$$8CN^-(aq) + 4Ag(s) + O_2(g) + \underbrace{4H^+(aq) + 4OH^-(aq)}_{4H_2O(l)} \longrightarrow$$
$$4Ag(CN)_2^-(aq) + 2H_2O(l) + 4OH^-(aq)$$

STEP 3

Eliminate as many H_2O molecules as possible:

$$8CN^-(aq) + 4Ag(s) + O_2(g) + 2H_2O(l) \longrightarrow 4Ag(CN)_2^-(aq) + 4OH^-(aq)$$

STEP 4

Check that elements and charges are balanced.

Elements balance: $8C, 8N, 4Ag, 4O, 4H \longrightarrow 8C, 8N, 4Ag, 4O, 4H$

Charges balance: $8(1-) + 0 + 0 + 0 = 8- \longrightarrow 4(1-) + 4(1-) = 8-$

See Exercises 4.65 and 4.66.

For Review

Key Terms

aqueous solution

Section 4.1
polar molecule
hydration
solubility

Section 4.2
solute
solvent
electrical conductivity
strong electrolyte
weak electrolyte

Summary

Many important chemical reactions occur in aqueous solutions. Water is a good solvent for ionic solids because the polar water molecules interact with the ions. This assists in the dissolving process. One characteristic property of a solution is its electrical conductivity. Solutions of strong electrolytes conduct current easily because there is 100% dissociation to ions. Weak electrolytes dissociate only to a small extent and their solutions exhibit low conductivity. Nonelectrolytes produce no ions when they dissolve and conduct no current.

The Arrhenius definition regards an acid as a substance that produces H^+ ions (protons) in solution; a base is a substance that produces OH^- ions. The Brønsted–Lowry concept defines an acid as a proton donor and a base as a proton acceptor. A strong acid dissociates completely in water, and a weak acid dissociates only very slightly.

One means of describing solution concentration is molarity:

$$\text{Molarity } (M) = \frac{\text{moles of solute}}{\text{liters of solution}}$$

Since molarity relates the volume of the solution and the moles of solute, it allows the principles of stoichiometry to be applied to reactions in solution. A standard solution is one in which the molarity is accurately known. When a solution is diluted, only solvent is added, which means that

Moles of solute after dilution = moles of solute before dilution

which leads to the relationship

$$M_1V_1 = M_2V_2$$

Three types of equations describe reactions in solution: molecular equations, which show reactants and products as if they were molecules; complete ionic equations, in which all reactants and products that are strong electrolytes are represented as ions; and net ionic equations, in which only those solution components undergoing a change are represented. Spectator ions (those ions remaining unchanged in a reaction) are not included in the net ionic equation.

General rules concerning solubility help to predict the outcomes of precipitation reactions.

Volumetric analysis involves the titration of a solution containing the substance to be determined. One type of volumetric analysis uses neutralization (acid–base) reactions; the unknown concentration of an acid is determined by titration with a base of known concentration (or vice versa). The point in the titration where just enough titrant has been added to react exactly with the substance being determined is called the stoichiometric (equivalence) point.

Oxidation–reduction (redox) reactions involve a transfer of electrons. One method for keeping track of electrons is to use oxidation states for atoms in compounds. A series of rules is used to assign these oxidation states. Oxidation is an increase in oxidation state (a loss of electrons). Reduction is a decrease in oxidation state (a gain of electrons). An oxidizing agent accepts electrons, and a reducing agent donates electrons.

Equations for oxidation–reduction reactions occurring in aqueous solution can be balanced using the half-reaction method, which splits a reaction into two parts (the oxidation half-reaction and the reduction half-reaction).

nonelectrolyte
acid
strong acid
strong base
weak acid
weak base

Section 4.3
molarity
standard solution
dilution

Section 4.5
precipitation reaction
precipitate

Section 4.6
molecular equation
complete ionic equation
spectator ions
net ionic equation

Section 4.8
acid
base
neutralization reaction
volumetric analysis
titration
stoichiometric (equivalence) point
indicator
endpoint

Section 4.9
oxidation–reduction (redox) reaction
oxidation state
oxidation
reduction
oxidizing agent (electron acceptor)
reducing agent (electron donor)

Section 4.10
half-reactions

In-Class Discussion Questions

These questions are designed to be considered by groups of students in class. Often these questions work well for introducing a particular topic in class.

1. Assume you have a highly magnified view of a solution of HCl that allows you to "see" the HCl. Draw this magnified view. If you dropped in a piece of magnesium, the magnesium would disappear and hydrogen gas would be released. Represent this change using symbols for the elements, and write out the balanced equation.

2. You have a solution of table salt in water. What happens to the salt concentration (increases, decreases, or stays the same) as the solution boils? Draw pictures to explain your answer.

3. You have a sugar solution (solution *A*) with concentration *x*. You pour one-fourth of this solution into a beaker, and add an equivalent volume of water (solution *B*).
 a. What is the ratio of sugar in solutions *A* and *B*?
 b. Compare the volumes of solutions *A* and *B*.
 c. What is the ratio of the concentrations of sugar in solutions *A* and *B*?

4. You add an aqueous solution of lead nitrate to an aqueous solution of potassium iodide. Draw highly magnified views of each solution individually, and the mixed solution including any product that forms. Write the balanced equation for the reaction.

5. Order the following molecules from lowest to highest oxidation state of the nitrogen atom: HNO_3, NH_4Cl, N_2O, NO_2, $NaNO_2$.

6. Why is it that when something gains electrons, it is said to be *reduced*? What is being reduced?

7. Consider separate aqueous solutions of HCl and H_2SO_4 with the same molar concentrations. You wish to neutralize an aqueous solution of NaOH. For which acid solution would you need to add more volume (in milliliters) to neutralize the base?
 a. the HCl solution
 b. the H_2SO_4 solution
 c. You need to know the acid concentrations to answer this question.
 d. You need to know the volume and concentration of the NaOH solution to answer this question.
 e. c and d
 Explain.

8. Draw molecular-level pictures to differentiate between concentrated and dilute solutions.

A blue question or exercise number indicates that the answer to that question or exercise appears at the back of this book and a solution appears in the *Solutions Guide*.

Questions

9. Distinguish between the terms *slightly soluble* and *weak electrolyte*.

10. How would you determine experimentally whether a substance is a strong or weak electrolyte?

Exercises

In this section similar exercises are paired.

Aqueous Solutions: Strong and Weak Electrolytes

11. Show how each of the following strong electrolytes "breaks up" into its component ions upon dissolving in water.

 a. NaBr **f.** $FeSO_4$
 b. $MgCl_2$ **g.** $KMnO_4$
 c. $Al(NO_3)_3$ **h.** $HClO_4$
 d. $(NH_4)_2SO_4$ **i.** $NH_4C_2H_3O_2$ (ammonium acetate)
 e. HI

12. Show how each of the following strong acids or strong bases "breaks up" into its component ions upon dissolving in water.
 a. HCl
 b. HNO_3
 c. $Ca(OH)_2$
 d. KOH

13. Calcium chloride is a strong electrolyte and is used to "salt" streets in the winter to melt ice and snow. Write a reaction to show how this substance breaks apart when it dissolves in water.

14. Commercial cold packs and hot packs are available for treating athletic injuries. Both types contain a pouch of water and a dry chemical. When the pack is struck, the pouch of water breaks, dissolving the chemical, and the solution becomes either hot or cold. Many hot packs use magnesium sulfate, and many cold packs use ammonium nitrate. Write reactions to show how these strong electrolytes break apart when they dissolve in water.

Solution Concentration: Molarity

15. Calculate the molarity of each of these solutions.
 a. A 5.623-g sample of $NaHCO_3$ is dissolved in enough water to make 250.0 mL of solution.
 b. A 184.6-mg sample of $K_2Cr_2O_7$ is dissolved in enough water to make 500.0 mL of solution.
 c. A 0.1025-g sample of copper metal is dissolved in 35 mL of concentrated HNO_3 to form Cu^{2+} ions and then water is added to make a total volume of 200.0 mL. (Calculate the molarity of Cu^{2+}.)

16. Calculate the molarity of each of the following solutions.
 a. A 16.45-g sample of NaCl is dissolved in enough water to make 1.000 L of solution.
 b. An 853.5-mg sample of KIO_3 is dissolved in enough water to make 250.0 mL of solution.
 c. A 0.4508-g sample of iron is dissolved in a small amount of concentrated nitric acid forming Fe^{3+} ions in solution and is diluted to a total volume of 500.0 mL. (Calculate the molarity of Fe^{3+}.)

17. Calculate the concentration of all ions present in each of the following solutions of strong electrolytes.
 a. 0.15 *M* $CaCl_2$
 b. 0.26 *M* $Al(NO_3)_3$
 c. 0.25 *M* $K_2Cr_2O_7$
 d. 2.0×10^{-3} *M* $Al_2(SO_4)_3$

18. Calculate the concentration of all ions present in each of the following solutions of strong electrolytes.
 a. 0.100 mol of $Ca(NO_3)_2$ in 100.0 mL of solution
 b. 2.5 mol of Na_2SO_4 in 1.25 L of solution

c. 5.00 g of NH_4Cl in 500.0 mL of solution

d. 1.00 g K_3PO_4 in 250.0 mL of solution

19. Which of the following solutions of strong electrolytes contains the largest number of moles of chloride ions: 100.0 mL of 0.30 M $AlCl_3$, 50.0 mL of 0.60 M $MgCl_2$, or 200.0 mL of 0.40 M NaCl?

20. Which of the following solutions of strong electrolytes contains the largest number of ions: 100.0 mL of 0.100 M NaOH, 50.0 mL of 0.200 M $BaCl_2$, or 75.0 mL of 0.150 M Na_3PO_4?

21. What volume of a 0.100 M solution of $NaHCO_3$ contains 0.350 g of $NaHCO_3$?

22. How many grams of NaOH are contained in 250.0 mL of a 0.400 M sodium hydroxide solution?

23. Describe how you would prepare 2.00 L of each of the following solutions.
a. 0.250 M NaOH from solid NaOH
b. 0.250 M NaOH from 1.00 M NaOH stock solution
c. 0.100 M K_2CrO_4 from solid K_2CrO_4
d. 0.100 M K_2CrO_4 from 1.75 M K_2CrO_4 stock solution

24. How would you prepare 1.00 L of a 0.50 M solution of each of the following?
a. H_2SO_4 from "concentrated" (18 M) sulfuric acid
b. HCl from "concentrated" (12 M) reagent
c. $NiCl_2$ from the salt $NiCl_2 \cdot 6H_2O$
d. HNO_3 from "concentrated" (16 M) reagent
e. Sodium carbonate from the pure solid

25. A solution is prepared by dissolving 10.8 g ammonium sulfate in enough water to make 100.0 mL of stock solution. A 10.00-mL sample of this stock solution is added to 50.00 mL of water. Calculate the concentration of ammonium ions and sulfate ions in the final solution.

26. Calculate the sodium ion concentration when 70.0 mL of 3.0 M sodium carbonate is added to 30.0 mL of 1.0 M sodium bicarbonate.

27. A standard solution is prepared for the analysis of fluoxymesterone ($C_{20}H_{29}FO_3$), an anabolic steroid. A stock solution is first prepared by dissolving 10.0 mg of fluoxymesterone in enough water to give a total volume of 500.0 mL. A 100.0-μL aliquot (portion) of this solution is diluted to a final volume of 100.0 mL. Calculate the concentration of the final solution in terms of molarity.

28. A stock solution containing Mn^{2+} ions was prepared by dissolving 1.584 g pure manganese metal in nitric acid and diluting to a final volume of 1.000 L. The following solutions were then prepared by dilution:

For solution A, 50.00 mL of stock solution was diluted to 1000.0 mL.

For solution B, 10.00 mL of solution A was diluted to 250.0 mL.

For solution C, 10.00 mL of solution B was diluted to 500.0 mL.

Calculate the concentrations of the stock solution and solutions A, B, and C.

Precipitation Reactions

29. When the following solutions are mixed together, what precipitate (if any) will form?
a. $BaCl_2(aq) + Na_2SO_4(aq)$
b. $Pb(NO_3)_2(aq) + KCl(aq)$
c. $AgNO_3(aq) + Na_3PO_4(aq)$
d. $NaOH(aq) + Fe(NO_3)_3(aq)$

30. When the following solutions are mixed together, what precipitate (if any) will form?
a. $FeSO_4(aq) + KCl(aq)$
b. $Al(NO_3)_3(aq) + Ba(OH)_2(aq)$
c. $CaCl_2(aq) + Na_2SO_4(aq)$
d. $K_2S(aq) + Ni(NO_3)_2(aq)$

31. For the reactions in Exercise 29, write the balanced molecular equation, complete ionic equation, and net ionic equation. If no precipitate forms, write "No reaction."

32. For the reactions in Exercise 30, write the balanced molecular equation, complete ionic equation, and net ionic equation. If no precipitate forms, write "No reaction."

33. Write net ionic equations for each of the following.
a. $AgNO_3(aq) + KI(aq) \rightarrow$
b. $CuSO_4(aq) + Na_2S(aq) \rightarrow$
c. $CoCl_2(aq) + NaOH(aq) \rightarrow$
d. $NiCl_2(aq) + KNO_3(aq) \rightarrow$

34. Write net ionic equations for each of the following.
a. $AgNO_3(aq) + BaCl_2(aq) \rightarrow$
b. $FeSO_4(aq) + K_2S(aq) \rightarrow$
c. $NaOH(aq) + K_2SO_4(aq) \rightarrow$
d. $Hg_2(NO_3)_2(aq) + CaCl_2(aq) \rightarrow$

35. Write net ionic equations for the reaction, if any, that occurs when aqueous solutions of the following are mixed.
a. Ammonium sulfate and barium nitrate
b. Lead(II) nitrate and sodium chloride
c. Sodium phosphate and potassium nitrate
d. Sodium bromide and rubidium chloride
e. Copper(II) chloride and sodium hydroxide

36. Write net ionic equations for the reaction, if any, that occurs when aqueous solutions of the following are mixed.
a. cobalt(III) chloride and sodium hydroxide
b. silver nitrate and ammonium carbonate
c. copper(II) sulfate and mercury(II) chloride
d. strontium nitrate and potassium iodide

37. A lake may be polluted with Pb^{2+} ions. What precipitation reaction might you use to test for the presence of Pb^{2+}?

38. A sample may contain any or all of the following ions: Hg_2^{2+}, Ba^{2+}, and Mn^{2+}. No precipitate formed when an aqueous solution of NaCl or Na_2SO_4 was added to the sample solution. A precipitate formed when the sample solution was made basic with NaOH. Which ion or ions are present in the sample solution?

39. What mass of NaCl is required to precipitate all the silver ions from 50.0 mL of a 0.0500 M solution of $AgNO_3$?

40. What volume of 0.100 M Na_3PO_4 is required to precipitate all the lead(II) ions from 150.0 mL of 0.250 M $Pb(NO_3)_2$?

41. What mass of solid aluminum hydroxide is produced when 50.0 mL of 0.200 M $Al(NO_3)_3$ is added to 200.0 mL of 0.100 M KOH?

42. What mass of barium sulfate is produced when 100.0 mL of a 0.100 M solution of barium chloride is mixed with 100.0 mL of a 0.100 M solution of iron(III) sulfate?

43. A 100.0-mL aliquot of 0.200 M aqueous potassium hydroxide is mixed with 100.0 mL of 0.200 M aqueous magnesium nitrate.
    a. Write a balanced chemical equation for any reaction that occurs.
    b. What precipitate forms?
    c. What mass of precipitate is produced?
    d. Calculate the concentration of each ion remaining in solution after precipitation is complete.

44. How many grams of silver chloride can be prepared by the reaction of 100.0 mL of 0.20 M silver nitrate with 100.0 mL of 0.15 M calcium chloride? Calculate the concentrations of each ion remaining in solution after precipitation is complete.

Acid–Base Reactions

45. Write the balanced molecular, complete ionic, and net ionic equations for each of the following acid–base reactions.
    a. $HClO_4(aq) + Mg(OH)_2(s) \rightarrow$
    b. $HCN(aq) + NaOH(aq) \rightarrow$
    c. $HCl(aq) + NaOH(aq) \rightarrow$

46. Write the balanced molecular, complete ionic, and net ionic equations for each of the following acid–base reactions.
    a. $HNO_3(aq) + Al(OH)_3(s) \rightarrow$
    b. $HC_2H_3O_2(aq) + KOH(aq) \rightarrow$
    c. $Ca(OH)_2(aq) + HCl(aq) \rightarrow$

47. Write the balanced molecular, complete ionic, and net ionic equations for the reactions that occur when the following are mixed.
    a. potassium hydroxide (aqueous) and nitric acid
    b. barium hydroxide (aqueous) and hydrochloric acid
    c. perchloric acid [$HClO_4(aq)$] and solid iron(III) hydroxide

48. Write the balanced molecular, complete ionic, and net ionic equations for the reactions that occur when the following are mixed.
    a. solid silver hydroxide and hydrobromic acid
    b. aqueous strontium hydroxide and hydroiodic acid
    c. solid iron(III) hydroxide and nitric acid

49. What volume of each of the following acids will react completely with 50.00 mL of 0.200 M NaOH?

a. 0.100 M HCl
b. 0.150 M HNO_3
c. 0.200 M $HC_2H_3O_2$ (1 acidic hydrogen)

50. What volume of each of the following bases will react completely with 25.00 mL of 0.200 M HCl?
    a. 0.100 M NaOH
    b. 0.0500 M $Ba(OH)_2$
    c. 0.250 M KOH

51. A solution is prepared by dissolving 15.0 g NaOH in 150.0 mL of 0.250 M nitric acid. Will the final solution be acidic, basic, or neutral? Calculate the concentrations of all the ions present in the solution after the reaction has occurred. Assume no volume change on addition of NaOH.

52. Hydrochloric acid (75.0 mL of 0.250 M) is added to 225.0 mL of 0.0550 M $Ba(OH)_2$ solution. What is the concentration of the excess H^+ or OH^- ions left in this solution?

53. A 25.00-mL sample of hydrochloric acid solution requires 24.16 mL of 0.106 M sodium hydroxide for complete neutralization. What is the concentration of the original hydrochloric acid solution?

54. What volume of 0.0200 M calcium hydroxide is required to neutralize 35.00 mL of 0.0500 M nitric acid?

55. A student titrates an unknown amount of potassium hydrogen phthalate ($KHC_8H_4O_4$, often abbreviated KHP) with 20.46 mL of a 0.1000 M NaOH solution. KHP (molar mass = 204.22 g/mol) has one acidic hydrogen. How many grams of KHP were titrated (reacted completely) by the sodium hydroxide solution?

56. The concentration of a certain sodium hydroxide solution was determined by using the solution to titrate a sample of potassium hydrogen phthalate (abbreviated as KHP). KHP is an acid with one acidic hydrogen and a molar mass of 204.22 g/mol. In the titration, 20.46 mL of the sodium hydroxide solution was required to react with 0.1082 g KHP. Calculate the molarity of the sodium hydroxide.

Oxidation–Reduction Reactions

57. Assign oxidation states for all atoms in each of the following compounds.
    a. $KMnO_4$ f. Fe_3O_4
    b. NiO_2 g. $XeOF_4$
    c. $K_4Fe(CN)_6$ (Fe only)   h. SF_4
    d. $(NH_4)_2HPO_4$ i. CO
    e. P_4O_6 j. $Na_2C_2O_4$

58. Assign oxidation states for all atoms in each of the following compounds.
    a. UO_2^{2+} f. $Mg_2P_2O_7$
    b. As_2O_3 g. $Na_2S_2O_3$
    c. $NaBiO_3$ h. Hg_2Cl_2
    d. As_4 i. $Ca(NO_3)_2$
    e. $HAsO_2$

59. Assign the oxidation state for chlorine in each of the following anions: OCl^-, ClO_2^-, ClO_3^-, and ClO_4^-

60. Assign the oxidation state for nitrogen in each of the following.
a. Li_3N
b. NH_3
c. N_2H_4
d. NO
e. N_2O
f. NO_2
g. NO_2^-
h. NO_3^-
i. N_2

61. Specify which of the following are oxidation–reduction reactions, and identify the oxidizing agent, the reducing agent, the substance being oxidized, and the substance being reduced.
a. $CH_4(g) + 2O_2(g) \rightarrow CO_2(g) + 2H_2O(g)$
b. $Zn(s) + 2HCl(aq) \rightarrow ZnCl_2(aq) + H_2(g)$
c. $Cr_2O_7^{2-}(aq) + 2OH^-(aq) \rightarrow 2CrO_4^{2-}(aq) + H_2O(l)$
d. $O_3(g) + NO(g) \rightarrow O_2(g) + NO_2(g)$
e. $2H_2O_2(l) \rightarrow 2H_2O(l) + O_2(g)$
f. $2CuCl(aq) \rightarrow CuCl_2(aq) + Cu(s)$

62. Specify which of the following are oxidation–reduction reactions, and identify the oxidizing agent, the reducing agent, the substance being oxidized, and the substance being reduced.
a. $Cu(s) + 2Ag^+(aq) \rightarrow 2Ag(s) + Cu^{2+}(aq)$
b. $HCl(g) + NH_3(g) \rightarrow NH_4Cl(s)$
c. $SiCl_4(l) + 2H_2O(l) \rightarrow 4HCl(aq) + SiO_2(s)$
d. $SiCl_4(l) + 2Mg(s) \rightarrow 2MgCl_2(s) + Si(s)$
e. $Al(OH)_4^-(aq) \rightarrow AlO_2^-(aq) + 2H_2O(l)$

63. Balance the following oxidation–reduction reactions that occur in acidic solution.
a. $Zn(s) + HCl(aq) \rightarrow Zn^{2+}(aq) + H_2(g)$
b. $I^-(aq) + ClO^-(aq) \rightarrow I_3^-(aq) + Cl^-(aq)$
c. $As_2O_3(s) + NO_3^-(aq) \rightarrow H_3AsO_4(aq) + NO(g)$
d. $Br^-(aq) + MnO_4^-(aq) \rightarrow Br_2(l) + Mn^{2+}(aq)$
e. $CH_3OH(aq) + Cr_2O_7^{2-}(aq) \rightarrow CH_2O(aq) + Cr^{3+}(aq)$

64. Balance the following oxidation–reduction reactions that occur in acidic solution using the half-reaction method.
a. $Cu(s) + NO_3^-(aq) \rightarrow Cu^{2+}(aq) + NO(g)$
b. $Cr_2O_7^{2-}(aq) + Cl^-(aq) \rightarrow Cr^{3+}(aq) + Cl_2(g)$
c. $Pb(s) + PbO_2(s) + H_2SO_4(aq) \rightarrow PbSO_4(s)$
d. $Mn^{2+}(aq) + NaBiO_3(s) \rightarrow Bi^{3+}(aq) + MnO_4^-(aq)$
e. $H_3AsO_4(aq) + Zn(s) \rightarrow AsH_3(g) + Zn^{2+}(aq)$

65. Balance the following oxidation–reduction reactions that occur in basic solution.
a. $Al(s) + MnO_4^-(aq) \rightarrow MnO_2(s) + Al(OH)_4^-(aq)$
b. $Cl_2(g) \rightarrow Cl^-(aq) + OCl^-(aq)$
c. $NO_2^-(aq) + Al(s) \rightarrow NH_3(g) + AlO_2^-(aq)$

66. Balance the following oxidation–reduction reactions that occur in basic solution.
a. $Cr(s) + CrO_4^{2-}(aq) \rightarrow Cr(OH)_3(s)$
b. $MnO_4^-(aq) + S^{2-}(aq) \rightarrow MnS(s) + S(s)$
c. $CN^-(aq) + MnO_4^-(aq) \rightarrow CNO^-(aq) + MnO_2(s)$

67. Chlorine gas was first prepared in 1774 by C. W. Scheele by oxidizing sodium chloride with manganese(IV) oxide. The reaction is

$$NaCl(aq) + H_2SO_4(aq) + MnO_2(s) \longrightarrow$$
$$Na_2SO_4(aq) + MnCl_2(aq) + H_2O(l) + Cl_2(g)$$

Balance this equation.

68. Gold metal will not dissolve in either concentrated nitric acid or concentrated hydrochloric acid. It will dissolve, however, in aqua regia, a mixture of the two concentrated acids. The products of the reaction are the $AuCl_4^-$ ion and gaseous NO. Write a balanced equation for the dissolution of gold in aqua regia.

Additional Exercises

69. Calcium metal will react with water as follows:

$$Ca(s) + 2H_2O(l) \longrightarrow Ca(OH)_2(aq) + H_2(g)$$

What is the molarity of hydroxide ions in the solution formed when 4.25 g calcium metal is dissolved in enough water to make a final volume of 225 mL?

70. A 230.-mL sample of a 0.275 M $CaCl_2$ solution is left on a hot plate overnight; the following morning, the solution is 1.10 M. What volume of water evaporated from the 0.275 M $CaCl_2$ solution?

71. Write balanced molecular equations, complete ionic equations, and net ionic equations for the following reactions. Write "NR" if there is no reaction. All reactants are aqueous solutions.
a. Silver nitrate + barium chloride $\rightarrow$
b. Ammonium nitrate + potassium chloride $\rightarrow$
c. Ammonium sulfide + iron(II) chloride $\rightarrow$
d. Potassium carbonate + copper(II) sulfate $\rightarrow$

72. A 20.0-mL sample of 0.200 M K_2CO_3 is added to 30.0 mL of 0.400 M $Ba(NO_3)_2$. Barium carbonate precipitates. Calculate the concentration of barium ions when precipitation is complete. Assume that the reaction is 100% efficient.

73. Rust stains can be removed by washing a surface with a dilute solution of oxalic acid ($H_2C_2O_4$). The reaction is

$$Fe_2O_3(s) + 6H_2C_2O_4(aq) \longrightarrow$$
$$2Fe(C_2O_4)_3^{3-}(aq) + 3H_2O(l) + 6H^+(aq)$$

a. Is this an oxidation–reduction reaction?
b. What mass of rust can be removed by 1.0 L of a 0.14 M solution of oxalic acid?

74. A 1.42-g sample of a pure compound, with formula M_2SO_4, was dissolved in water and treated with an excess of aqueous barium chloride, resulting in the precipitation of all the sulfate ions as barium sulfate. The precipitate was collected, dried, and found to weigh 2.33 g. Determine the atomic mass of M, and identify M.

75. Douglasite is a mineral with the formula $2KCl \cdot FeCl_2 \cdot 2H_2O$. Calculate the mass percent of douglasite in a 455.0-mg sample if it took 37.20 mL of a 0.1000 M $AgNO_3$ solution to precipitate all of the Cl^- as AgCl. Assume the douglasite is the only source of chloride ion.

76. Saccharin ($C_7H_5NO_3S$) is sometimes dispensed in tablet form. Ten tablets with a total mass of 0.5894 g were dissolved in water. They were oxidized to convert all the sulfur to sulfate ion, which was precipitated by adding an excess of barium chloride solution. The mass of $BaSO_4$ obtained was 0.5032 g. What is the average mass of saccharin per tablet? What is the average mass percent of saccharin in the tablets?

77. Chlorisondiamine ($C_{14}H_{18}Cl_6N_2$) is a drug used in the treatment of hypertension. A 1.28-g sample of a medication containing the drug was treated to destroy the organic material and to release all the chlorine as chloride ion. When the filtered solution containing chloride ion was treated with an excess of silver nitrate, 0.104 g silver chloride was recovered. Calculate the mass percent of chlorisondiamine in the medication, assuming the drug is the only source of chloride.

78. A mixture contains only NaCl and $Fe(NO_3)_3$. A 0.456-g sample of the mixture is dissolved in water, and an excess of NaOH is added, producing a precipitate of $Fe(OH)_3$. The precipitate is filtered, dried, and weighed. Its mass is 0.107 g. Calculate the following.
    a. the mass of iron in the sample
    b. the mass of $Fe(NO_3)_3$ in the sample
    c. the mass percent of $Fe(NO_3)_3$ in the sample

79. A 10.00-mL sample of vinegar, an aqueous solution of acetic acid ($HC_2H_3O_2$), is titrated with 0.5062 M NaOH, and 16.58 mL is required to reach the equivalence point.
    a. What is the molarity of the acetic acid?
    b. If the density of the vinegar is 1.006 g/cm^3, what is the mass percent of acetic acid in the vinegar?

80. When hydrochloric acid reacts with magnesium metal, hydrogen gas and aqueous magnesium chloride are produced. What volume of 5.0 M HCl is required to react completely with 3.00 g of magnesium?

81. A 2.20-g sample of an unknown acid (empirical formula = $C_3H_4O_3$) is dissolved in 1.0 L of water. A titration required 25.0 mL of 0.500 M NaOH to react completely with all the acid present. Assuming the unknown acid has one acidic proton per molecule, what is the molecular formula of the unknown acid?

82. Many oxidation–reduction reactions can be balanced by inspection. Try to balance the following reactions by inspection. In each reaction, identify the substance reduced and the substance oxidized.
    a. $Al(s) + HCl(aq) \rightarrow AlCl_3(aq) + H_2(g)$
    b. $CH_4(g) + S(s) \rightarrow CS_2(l) + H_2S(g)$
    c. $C_3H_8(g) + O_2(g) \rightarrow CO_2(g) + H_2O(l)$
    d. $Cu(s) + Ag^+(aq) \rightarrow Ag(s) + Cu^{2+}(aq)$

83. The Ostwald process for the commercial production of nitric acid involves the following three steps:
    $$4NH_3(g) + 5O_2(g) \longrightarrow 4NO(g) + 6H_2O(g)$$
    $$2NO(g) + O_2(g) \longrightarrow 2NO_2(g)$$
    $$3NO_2(g) + H_2O(l) \longrightarrow 2HNO_3(aq) + NO(g)$$
    a. Which reactions in the Ostwald process are oxidation–reduction reactions?
    b. Identify each oxidizing agent and reducing agent.

84. One of the classical methods for the determination of the manganese content in steel is to convert all the manganese to the deeply colored permanganate ion and then to measure the absorption of light. The steel is dissolved in nitric acid, producing the manganese(II) ion and nitrogen dioxide gas. This solution is then reacted with an acidic solution containing periodate ion; the products are the permanganate and iodate ions. Write balanced chemical equations for both these steps.

85. You are given a compound that is either iron(II) sulfate or iron(III) sulfate. How could you determine the identity of the compound using a dilute solution of potassium permanganate?

Challenge Problems

86. The units of parts per million (ppm) and parts per billion (ppb) are commonly used by environmental chemists. In general, 1 ppm means 1 part of solute for every 10^6 parts of solution. Mathematically, by mass:
    $$ppm = \frac{\mu g \text{ solute}}{g \text{ solution}} = \frac{mg \text{ solute}}{kg \text{ solution}}$$
    In the case of very dilute aqueous solutions, a concentration of 1.0 ppm is equal to 1.0 μg of solute per 1.0 mL, which equals 1.0 g solution. Parts per billion is defined in a similar fashion. Calculate the molarity of each of the following aqueous solutions.
    a. 5.0 ppb Hg in H_2O
    b. 1.0 ppb $CHCl_3$ in H_2O
    c. 10.0 ppm As in H_2O
    d. 0.10 ppm DDT ($C_{14}H_9Cl_5$) in H_2O

87. In most of its ionic compounds, cobalt is either Co(II) or Co(III). One such compound, containing chloride ion and waters of hydration, was analyzed, and the following results were obtained. A 0.256-g sample of the compound was dissolved in water, and excess silver nitrate was added. The silver chloride was filtered, dried, and weighed, and it had a mass of 0.308 g. A second sample of 0.416 g of the compound was dissolved in water, and an excess of sodium hydroxide was added. The hydroxide salt was filtered and heated in a flame, forming cobalt(III) oxide. The mass of cobalt(III) oxide formed was 0.145 g.
    a. What is the percent composition, by mass, of the compound?
    b. Assuming the compound contains one cobalt atom per formula unit, what is the molecular formula?
    c. Write balanced equations for the three reactions described.

88. A sample is a mixture of KCl and KBr. When 0.1024 g of the sample is dissolved in water and reacted with excess silver nitrate, 0.1889 g solid is obtained. What is the composition by mass percent of the original mixture?

89. You are given a solid that is a mixture of Na_2SO_4 and K_2SO_4. A 0.205-g sample of the mixture is dissolved in water. An excess of an aqueous solution of $BaCl_2$ is added. The $BaSO_4$ that is formed is filtered, dried, and weighed. Its mass is 0.298 g. What mass of SO_4^{2-} ion is in the sample? What is the mass percent of SO_4^{2-} ion in the sample? What are the percent compositions by mass of Na_2SO_4 and K_2SO_4 in the sample?

90. Complete and balance each acid–base reaction.
  a. $H_3PO_4(aq) + NaOH(aq) \rightarrow$
  Contains three acidic hydrogens
  b. $H_2SO_4(aq) + Al(OH)_3(s) \rightarrow$
  Contains two acidic hydrogens
  c. $H_2Se(aq) + Ba(OH)_2(aq) \rightarrow$
  Contains two acidic hydrogens
  d. $H_2C_2O_4(aq) + NaOH(aq) \rightarrow$
  Contains two acidic hydrogens

91. One of the harmful effects of acid rain is the deterioration of structures and statues made of marble or limestone, both essentially calcium carbonate. The reaction of calcium carbonate with sulfuric acid yields carbon dioxide, water, and calcium sulfate. Since calcium sulfate is soluble in water, part of the object is washed away by the rain. Write a balanced chemical equation for the reaction of sulfuric acid with calcium carbonate.

92. A 10.00-mL sample of sulfuric acid from an automobile battery requires 35.08 mL of 2.12 M sodium hydroxide solution for complete neutralization. What is the molarity of the sulfuric acid? The reaction is

$$H_2SO_4(aq) + 2NaOH(aq) \longrightarrow 2H_2O(l) + Na_2SO_4(aq)$$

93. Some of the substances commonly used in stomach antacids are MgO, $Mg(OH)_2$, and $Al(OH)_3$.
  a. Write a balanced equation for the neutralization of hydrochloric acid by each of these substances.
  b. Which of these substances will neutralize the greatest amount of 0.10 M HCl per gram?

94. Carminic acid, a naturally occurring red pigment extracted from the cochineal insect, contains only carbon, hydrogen, and oxygen. It was commonly used as a dye in the first half of the nineteenth century. It is 53.66% C and 4.09% H by mass. A titration required 18.02 mL of 0.0406 M NaOH to neutralize 0.3602 g carminic acid. Assuming that there is only one acidic hydrogen per molecule, what is the molecular formula of carminic acid?

95. Citric acid, which can be obtained from lemon juice, has the molecular formula $C_6H_8O_7$. A 0.250-g sample of citric acid dissolved in 25.0 mL of water requires 37.2 mL of 0.105 M NaOH for complete neutralization. How many acidic hydrogens per molecule does citric acid have?

96. Balance the following equations by the half-reaction method.
  a. $Fe(s) + HCl(aq) \rightarrow HFeCl_4(aq) + H_2(g)$
  b. $IO_3^-(aq) + I^-(aq) \xrightarrow{\text{Acid}} I_3^-(aq)$
  c. $Cr(NCS)_6^{4-}(aq) + Ce^{4+}(aq) \xrightarrow{\text{Acid}}$
  $Cr^{3+}(aq) + Ce^{3+}(aq) + NO_3^-(aq) + CO_2(g) + SO_4^{2-}(aq)$
  d. $CrI_3(s) + Cl_2(g) \xrightarrow{\text{Base}}$
  $CrO_4^{2-}(aq) + IO_4^-(aq) + Cl^-(aq)$
  e. $Fe(CN)_6^{4-}(aq) + Ce^{4+}(aq) \xrightarrow{\text{Base}}$
  $Ce(OH)_3(s) + Fe(OH)_3(s) + CO_3^{2-}(aq) + NO_3^-(aq)$
  f. $Fe(OH)_2(s) + H_2O_2(aq) \xrightarrow{\text{Base}} Fe(OH)_3(s)$

97. A solution is prepared by dissolving 0.150 ± 0.003 g NaCl in a volumetric flask. The volume of the flask is 100.0 ± 0.5 mL. What is the molarity of NaCl in the solution? What is the range of values for the molarity of NaCl? Express this as a value $\pm$ the uncertainty. (See Appendix 1.5.)

98. It took 25.06 ± 0.05 mL of a sodium hydroxide solution to titrate a 0.4016-g sample of KHP (see Exercise 55). Calculate the concentration and uncertainty in the concentration of the sodium hydroxide solution. (See Appendix 1.5.) Neglect any uncertainty in the mass.

99. You wish to prepare 1 L of a 0.02 M potassium iodate solution. You require that the final concentration be within 1% of 0.02 M and that the concentration must be known accurately to the fourth decimal place. How would you prepare this solution? Specify the glassware you would use, the accuracy needed for the balance, and the ranges of acceptable masses of KIO_3 that can be used.

Marathon Problem

This problem is designed to incorporate several concepts and techniques into one situation. Marathon Problems can be used in class by groups of students to help facilitate problem-solving skills.

100. Three students were asked to find the identity of the metal in a particular sulfate salt. They dissolved a 0.1472-g sample of the salt in water and treated it with excess barium chloride, resulting in the precipitation of barium sulfate. After the precipitate had been filtered and dried, it weighed 0.2327 g.

Each student analyzed the data independently and came to different conclusions. Pat decided that the metal was titanium. Chris thought it was sodium. Randy reported that it was gallium. What formula did each student assign to the sulfate salt?

Look for information on the sulfates of gallium, sodium, and titanium in this text and reference books such as the *CRC Handbook of Chemistry and Physics*. What further tests would you suggest to determine which student is most likely correct?

Gases

Contents

Matter exists in three distinct physical states: gas, liquid, and solid. Although relatively few substances exist in the gaseous state under typical conditions, gases are very important. For example, we live immersed in a gaseous solution. The earth's atmosphere is a mixture of gases that consists mainly of elemental nitrogen (N_2) and oxygen (O_2). The atmosphere both supports life and acts as a waste receptacle for the exhaust gases that accompany many industrial processes. The chemical reactions of these waste gases in the atmosphere lead to various types of pollution, including smog and acid rain. The gases in the atmosphere also shield us from harmful radiation from the sun and keep the earth warm by reflecting heat radiation back toward the earth. In fact, there is now great concern that an increase in atmospheric carbon dioxide, a product of the combustion of fossil fuels, is causing a dangerous warming of the earth.

In this chapter we will look carefully at the properties of gases. First we will see how measurements of gas properties lead to various types of laws—statements that show how the properties are related to each other. Then we will construct a model to explain why gases behave as they do. This model will show how the behavior of the individual particles of a gas leads to the observed properties of the gas itself (a collection of many, many particles).

The study of gases provides an excellent example of the scientific method in action. It illustrates how observations lead to natural laws, which in turn can be accounted for by models.

The Breitling Orbiter 3, shown over the Swiss Alps, recently completed a nonstop trip around the world.

5.1 Pressure

A gas uniformly fills any container, is easily compressed, and mixes completely with any other gas. One of the most obvious properties of a gas is that it exerts pressure on its surroundings. For example, when you blow up a balloon, the air inside pushes against the elastic sides of the balloon and keeps it firm.

As mentioned earlier, the gases most familiar to us form the earth's atmosphere. The pressure exerted by this gaseous mixture that we call air can be dramatically demonstrated by the experiment shown in Fig. 5.1. A small volume of water is placed in a metal can, and the water is boiled, which fills the can with steam. The can is then sealed and allowed to cool. Why does the can collapse as it cools? It is the atmospheric pressure that crumples the can. When the can is cooled after being sealed so that no air can flow in, the water vapor (steam) condenses to a very small volume of liquid water. As a gas, the water filled the can, but when it is condensed to a liquid, the liquid does not come close to filling the can. The H_2O molecules formerly present as a gas are now collected in a very small volume of liquid, and there are very few molecules of gas left to exert pressure outward and counteract the air pressure. As a result, the pressure exerted by the gas molecules in the atmosphere smashes the can.

A device to measure atmospheric pressure, the **barometer,** was invented in 1643 by an Italian scientist named Evangelista Torricelli (1608–1647), who had been a student of Galileo. Torricelli's barometer is constructed by filling a glass tube with liquid mercury and inverting it in a dish of mercury, as shown in Fig. 5.2. Notice that a large quantity of mercury stays in the tube. In fact, at sea level the height of this column of mercury averages 760 mm. Why does this mercury stay in the tube, seemingly in defiance of gravity? Figure 5.2 illustrates how the pressure exerted by the atmospheric gases on the surface of mercury in the dish keeps the mercury in the tube.

Atmospheric pressure results from the mass of the air being pulled toward the center of the earth by gravity—in other words, it results from the weight of the air. Changing weather conditions cause the atmospheric pressure to vary, so the height

As a gas, water occupies 1200 times as much space as it does as a liquid at 25°C and atmospheric pressure.

Soon after Torricelli died, a German physicist named Otto von Guericke invented an air pump. In a famous demonstration for the King of Prussia in 1663, Guericke placed two hemispheres together, pumped the air out of the resulting sphere through a valve, and showed that teams of horses could not pull the hemispheres apart. Then, after secretly opening the air valve, Guericke easily separated the hemispheres by hand. The King of Prussia was so impressed that he awarded Guericke a lifetime pension!

 Video: Collapsing Can

Figure 5.1

The pressure exerted by the gases in the atmosphere can be demonstrated by boiling water in a large metal can (a) and then turning off the heat and sealing the can. As the can cools, the water vapor condenses, lowering the gas pressure inside the can. This causes the can to crumple (b).

(a)

(b)

of the column of Hg supported by the atmosphere at sea level varies; it is not always 760 mm. The meteorologist who says a "low" is approaching means that the atmospheric pressure is going to decrease. This condition often occurs in conjunction with a storm.

Atmospheric pressure also varies with altitude. For example, when Torricelli's experiment is done in Breckenridge, Colorado (elevation 9600 feet), the atmosphere supports a column of mercury only about 520 mm high because the air is "thinner." That is, there is less air pushing down on the earth's surface at Breckenridge than at sea level.

Units of Pressure

Because instruments used for measuring pressure, such as the **manometer** (Fig. 5.3), often contain mercury, the most commonly used units for pressure are based on the height of the mercury column (in millimeters) that the gas pressure can support. The unit **mm Hg** (millimeter of mercury) is often called the **torr** in honor of Torricelli. The terms *torr* and *mm Hg* are used interchangeably by chemists. A related unit for pressure is the **standard atmosphere** (abbreviated atm):

$$1 \text{ standard atmosphere} = 1 \text{ atm} = 760 \text{ mm Hg} = 760 \text{ torr}$$

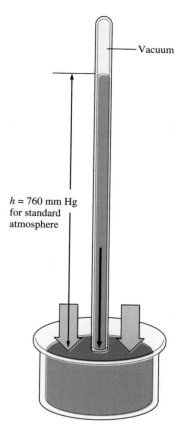

$h = 760$ mm Hg for standard atmosphere

Figure 5.2

A torricellian barometer. The tube, completely filled with mercury, is inverted in a dish of mercury. Mercury flows out of the tube until the pressure of the column of mercury (shown by the black arrow) "standing on the surface" of the mercury in the dish is equal to the pressure of the air (shown by the yellow arrows) on the rest of the surface of the mercury in the dish.

Mercury is used to measure pressure because of its high density. By way of comparison, the column of water required to measure a given pressure would be 13.5 times as high as a mercury column used for the same purpose.

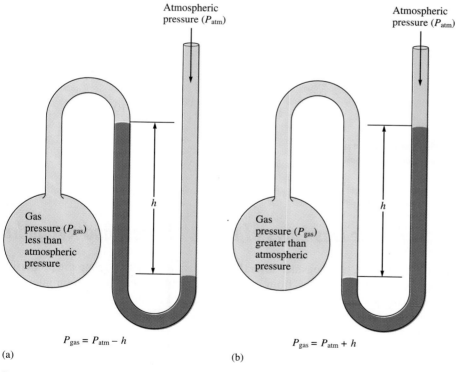

(a) $P_{gas} = P_{atm} - h$ (b) $P_{gas} = P_{atm} + h$

Figure 5.3

A simple manometer, a device for measuring the pressure of a gas in a container. The pressure of the gas is given by h (the difference in mercury levels) in units of torr (equivalent to mm Hg). (a) Gas pressure = atmospheric pressure − h. (b) Gas pressure = atmospheric pressure + h.

However, since pressure is defined as force per unit area,

$$\text{Pressure} = \frac{\text{force}}{\text{area}}$$

the fundamental units of pressure involve units of force divided by units of area. In the SI system, the unit of force is the newton (N) and the unit of area is meters squared (m²). (For a review of the SI system, see Chapter 1.) Thus the unit of pressure in the SI system is newtons per meter squared (N/m²) and is called the **pascal** (Pa). In terms of pascals, the standard atmosphere is

$$1 \text{ standard atmosphere} = 101{,}325 \text{ Pa}$$

Thus 1 atmosphere is about 10^5 pascals. Since the pascal is so small, and since it is not commonly used in the United States, we will use it sparingly in this book. However, converting from torrs or atmospheres to pascals is straightforward, as shown in Sample Exercise 5.1.

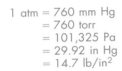

1 atm = 760 mm Hg
      = 760 torr
      = 101,325 Pa
      = 29.92 in Hg
      = 14.7 lb/in²

Sample Exercise 5.1 *Pressure Conversions*

The pressure of a gas is measured as 49 torr. Represent this pressure in both atmospheres and pascals.

Solution

$$49 \text{ torr} \times \frac{1 \text{ atm}}{760 \text{ torr}} = 6.4 \times 10^{-2} \text{ atm}$$

$$6.4 \times 10^{-2} \text{ atm} \times \frac{101{,}325 \text{ Pa}}{1 \text{ atm}} = 6.5 \times 10^{3} \text{ Pa}$$

See Exercises 5.23 and 5.24.

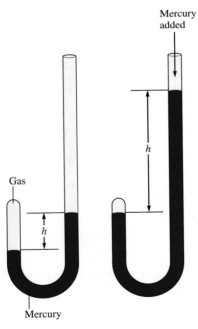

Mercury
added

h

Gas

h

Mercury

Figure 5.4

A J-tube similar to the one used by Boyle.

5.2 *The Gas Laws of Boyle, Charles, and Avogadro*

In this section we will consider several mathematical laws that relate the properties of gases. These laws derive from experiments involving careful measurements of the relevant gas properties. From these experimental results, the mathematical relationships among the properties can be discovered. These relationships are often represented pictorially by means of graphs (plots).

We will take a historical approach to these laws to give you some perspective on the scientific method in action.

Boyle's Law

The first quantitative experiments on gases were performed by an Irish chemist, Robert Boyle (1627–1691). Using a J-shaped tube closed at one end (Fig. 5.4), which he reportedly set up in the multistory entryway of his house, Boyle studied the relationship between the pressure of the trapped gas and its volume. Representative values from Boyle's experiments are given in Table 5.1. These data show that the product of the pressure and volume for the trapped air sample is constant within the accuracies of Boyle's measurements (note the third column in Table 5.1). This behavior can be represented by the equation

$$PV = k$$

which is called **Boyle's law** and where k is a constant for a given sample of air at a specific temperature.

It is convenient to represent the data in Table 5.1 by using two different plots. The first type of plot, P versus V, forms a curve called a *hyperbola* shown in Fig. 5.5(a). Looking at this plot, note that as the volume drops by about half (from 58.8 to 29.1), the pressure doubles (from 24.0 to 48.0). In other words, there is an *inverse relationship* between pressure and volume. The second type of plot can be obtained by rearranging Boyle's law to give

$$V = \frac{k}{P} = k\frac{1}{P}$$

which is the equation for a straight line of the type

$$y = mx + b$$

where m represents the slope and b the intercept of the straight line. In this case, $y = V$, $x = 1/P$, $m = k$, and $b = 0$. Thus a plot of V versus $1/P$ using Boyle's data gives a straight line with an intercept of zero, as shown in Fig. 5.5(b).

In the three centuries since Boyle carried out his studies, the sophistication of measuring techniques has increased tremendously. The results of highly accurate measurements show that Boyle's law holds precisely only at very low pressures. Measurements at higher pressures reveal that PV is not constant but varies as the pressure is varied. Results for several gases at pressures below 1 atm are shown in Fig. 5.6. Note the very small changes that occur in the product PV as the pressure is changed at these low pressures. Such changes become more significant at much higher pressures, where the complex nature of the dependence of PV on pressure becomes more obvious. We will discuss these deviations and the reasons for them in detail in Section 5.8. *A gas that strictly obeys Boyle's law is called an* **ideal gas.** We will describe the characteristics of an ideal gas more completely in Section 5.3.

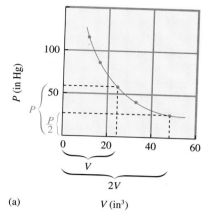

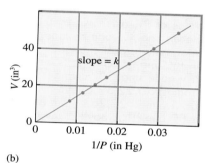

Figure 5.5

Plotting Boyle's data from Table 5.1. (a) A plot of P versus V shows that the volume doubles as the pressure is halved. (b) A plot of V versus $1/P$ gives a straight line. The slope of this line equals the value of the constant k.

Boyle's law: $V \propto 1/P$ at constant temperature.

Graphing is reviewed in Appendix 1.3.

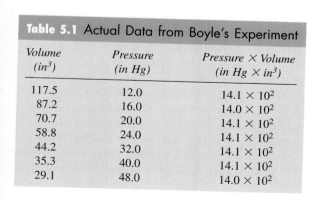

Table 5.1 Actual Data from Boyle's Experiment

Volume (in³)	Pressure (in Hg)	Pressure × Volume (in Hg × in³)
117.5	12.0	14.1×10^2
87.2	16.0	14.0×10^2
70.7	20.0	14.1×10^2
58.8	24.0	14.1×10^2
44.2	32.0	14.1×10^2
35.3	40.0	14.1×10^2
29.1	48.0	14.0×10^2

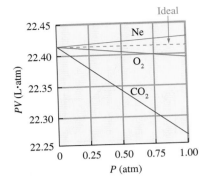

Figure 5.6
A plot of *PV* versus *P* for several gases at pressures below 1 atm. An ideal gas is expected to have a constant value of *PV*, as shown by the dotted line. Carbon dioxide shows the largest change in *PV*, and this change is actually quite small: *PV* changes from about 22.39 L · atm at 0.25 atm to 22.26 L · atm at 1.00 atm. Thus Boyle's law is a good approximation at these relatively low pressures.

Boyle's law also can be written as
$$P_1V_1 = P_2V_2$$

Always check that your answer makes physical (common!) sense.

One common use of Boyle's law is to predict the new volume of a gas when the pressure is changed (at constant temperature), or vice versa. Because deviations from Boyle's law are so slight at pressures close to 1 atm, in our calculations we will assume that gases obey Boyle's law (unless stated otherwise).

Sample Exercise 5.2 Boyle's Law I

Sulfur dioxide (SO_2), a gas that plays a central role in the formation of acid rain, is found in the exhaust of automobiles and power plants. Consider a 1.53-L sample of gaseous SO_2 at a pressure of 5.6×10^3 Pa. If the pressure is changed to 1.5×10^4 Pa at a constant temperature, what will be the new volume of the gas?

Solution

We can solve this problem using Boyle's law,

$$PV = k$$

which also can be written as

$$P_1V_1 = k = P_2V_2 \quad \text{or} \quad P_1V_1 = P_2V_2$$

where the subscripts 1 and 2 represent two states (conditions) of the gas (both at the same temperature). In this case,

$$P_1 = 5.6 \times 10^3 \text{ Pa} \qquad P_2 = 1.5 \times 10^4 \text{ Pa}$$
$$V_1 = 1.53 \text{ L} \qquad V_2 = ?$$

We can solve the preceding equation for V_2:

$$V_2 = \frac{P_1V_1}{P_2} = \frac{5.6 \times 10^3 \text{ Pa} \times 1.53 \text{ L}}{1.5 \times 10^4 \text{ Pa}} = 0.57 \text{ L}$$

The new volume will be 0.57 L.

See Exercise 5.29.

The fact that the volume decreases in Sample Exercise 5.2 makes sense because the pressure was increased. *To help eliminate errors, make it a habit to check whether an answer to a problem makes physical sense.*

We mentioned before that Boyle's law is only approximately true for real gases. To determine the significance of the deviations, studies of the effect of changing pressure on the volume of a gas are often done, as shown in Sample Exercise 5.3.

Sample Exercise 5.3 *Boyle's Law II*

In a study to see how closely gaseous ammonia obeys Boyle's law, several volume measurements were made at various pressures, using 1.0 mol NH_3 gas at a temperature of 0°C. Using the results listed below, calculate the Boyle's law constant for NH_3 at the various pressures.

Molecular Model: NH_3

Experiment	Pressure (atm)	Volume (L)
1	0.1300	172.1
2	0.2500	89.28
3	0.3000	74.35
4	0.5000	44.49
5	0.7500	29.55
6	1.000	22.08

Solution

To determine how closely NH_3 gas follows Boyle's law under these conditions, we calculate the value of k (in L · atm) for each set of values:

Experiment	1	2	3	4	5	6
$k = PV$	22.37	22.32	22.31	22.25	22.16	22.08

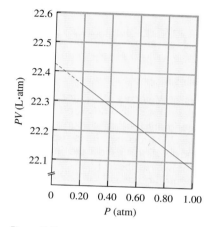

Figure 5.7
A plot of *PV* versus *P* for 1 mol of ammonia. The dashed line shows the extrapolation of the data to zero pressure to give the "ideal" value of *PV* of 22.41 L · atm.

Although the deviations from true Boyle's law behavior are quite small at these low pressures, note that the value of k changes regularly in one direction as the pressure is increased. Thus to calculate the "ideal" value of k for NH_3, we can plot *PV* versus *P*, as shown in Fig. 5.7, and extrapolate (extend the line beyond the experimental points) back to zero pressure, where, for reasons we will discuss later, a gas behaves most ideally. The value of k obtained by this extrapolation is 22.41 L · atm. Notice that this is the same value obtained from similar plots for the gases CO_2, O_2, and Ne at 0°C, as shown in Fig. 5.6.

See Question 5.19.

Charles's Law

In the century following Boyle's findings, scientists continued to study the properties of gases. One of these scientists was a French physicist, Jacques Charles (1746–1823), who was the first person to fill a balloon with hydrogen gas and who made the first solo balloon flight. Charles found in 1787 that the volume of a gas at constant pressure increases *linearly* with the temperature of the gas. That is, a plot of the volume of a gas (at constant pressure) versus its temperature (°C) gives a straight

Video: Liquid Nitrogen and Balloons

Animations: Charles's Law and Balloon Submersion in Liquid N_2

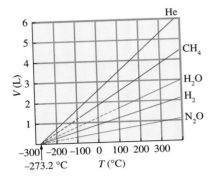

Figure 5.8

Plots of V versus T (°C) for several gases. The solid lines represent experimental measurements on gases. The dashed lines represent extrapolation of the data into regions where these gases would become liquids or solids. Note that the samples of the various gases contain different numbers of moles.

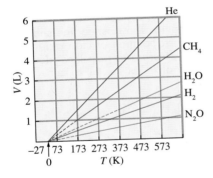

Figure 5.9

Plots of V versus T as in Fig. 5.8, except here the Kelvin scale is used for temperature.

Charles's law: $V \propto T$ (expressed in K) of constant pressure.

A snowmaking machine, in which water is blown through nozzles by compressed air. The mixture is cooled by expansion to form ice crystals of snow.

line. This behavior is shown for several gases in Fig. 5.8. A very interesting feature of these plots is that the volumes of all the gases extrapolate to zero at the same temperature, −273.2°C. On the Kelvin temperature scale this point is defined as 0 K, which leads to the following relationship between the Kelvin and Celsius scales:

$$K = °C + 273$$

When the volumes of the gases shown in Fig. 5.8 are plotted versus temperature on the Kelvin scale, the plots in Fig. 5.9 result. In this case, the volume of each gas is *directly proportional to temperature* and extrapolates to zero when the temperature is 0 K. This behavior is represented by the equation known as **Charles's law,**

$$V = bT$$

where T is in Kelvins and b is a proportionality constant.

Before we illustrate the uses of Charles's law, let us consider the importance of 0 K. At temperatures below this point, the extrapolated volumes would become negative. The fact that a gas cannot have a negative volume suggests that 0 K has a special significance. In fact, 0 K is called **absolute zero,** and there is much evidence to suggest that this temperature cannot be attained. Temperatures of approximately 0.000001 K have been produced in laboratories, but 0 K has never been reached.

Sample Exercise 5.4 *Charles's Law*

A sample of gas at 15°C and 1 atm has a volume of 2.58 L. What volume will this gas occupy at 38°C and 1 atm?

Solution

Charles's law, which describes the dependence of the volume of a gas on temperature at constant pressure, can be used to solve this problem. Charles's law in the form $V = bT$ can be rearranged to

$$\frac{V}{T} = b$$

An equivalent statement is

$$\frac{V_1}{T_1} = b = \frac{V_2}{T_2}$$

Charles's law also can be written as
$$\frac{V_1}{T_1} = \frac{V_2}{T_2}$$

where the subscripts 1 and 2 represent two states for a given sample of gas at constant pressure. In this case, we are given the following (note that the temperature values *must* be changed to the Kelvin scale):

$$T_1 = 15°C + 273 = 288 \text{ K} \qquad T_2 = 38°C + 273 = 311 \text{ K}$$
$$V_1 = 2.58 \text{ L} \qquad\qquad V_2 = ?$$

Solving for V_2 gives

$$V_2 = \left(\frac{T_2}{T_1}\right) V_1 = \left(\frac{311\,\cancel{K}}{288\,\cancel{K}}\right) 2.58 \text{ L} = 2.79 \text{ L}$$

CHECK

The new volume is greater than the initial volume, which makes physical sense because the gas will expand as it is heated.

See Exercise 5.30.

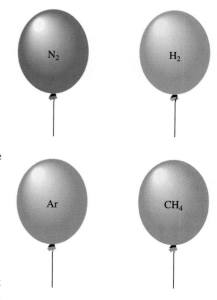

Figure 5.10
These balloons each hold 1.0 L of gas at 25°C and 1 atm. Each balloon contains 0.041 mol of gas, or 2.5×10^{22} molecules.

Avogadro's Law

In Chapter 2 we noted that in 1811 the Italian chemist Avogadro postulated that equal volumes of gases at the same temperature and pressure contain the same number of "particles." This observation is called **Avogadro's law,** which is illustrated by Fig. 5.10. Stated mathematically, Avogadro's law is

$$V = an$$

where V is the volume of the gas, n is the number of moles of gas particles, and a is a proportionality constant. This equation states that *for a gas at constant temperature and pressure, the volume is directly proportional to the number of moles of gas.* This relationship is obeyed closely by gases at low pressures.

Sample Exercise 5.5 *Avogadro's Law*

Suppose we have a 12.2-L sample containing 0.50 mol oxygen gas (O_2) at a pressure of 1 atm and a temperature of 25°C. If all this O_2 were converted to ozone

Molecular Models: O_2, O_3

(O_3) at the same temperature and pressure, what would be the volume of the ozone?

Solution

The balanced equation for the reaction is

$$3O_2(g) \longrightarrow 2O_3(g)$$

To calculate the moles of O_3 produced, we must use the appropriate mole ratio:

$$0.50 \text{ mol } O_2 \times \frac{2 \text{ mol } O_3}{3 \text{ mol } O_2} = 0.33 \text{ mol } O_3$$

Avogadro's law states that $V = an$, which can be rearranged to give

$$\frac{V}{n} = a$$

Avogadro's law also can be written as

$$\frac{V_1}{n_1} = \frac{V_2}{n_2}$$

Since a is a constant, an alternative representation is

$$\frac{V_1}{n_1} = a = \frac{V_2}{n_2}$$

where V_1 is the volume of n_1 moles of O_2 gas and V_2 is the volume of n_2 moles of O_3 gas. In this case we have

$$n_1 = 0.50 \text{ mol} \qquad n_2 = 0.33 \text{ mol}$$
$$V_1 = 12.2 \text{ L} \qquad V_2 = ?$$

Solving for V_2 gives

Animation: The Ideal Gas Law, $PV = nRT$

$$V_2 = \left(\frac{n_2}{n_1}\right)V_1 = \left(\frac{0.33 \text{ mol}}{0.50 \text{ mol}}\right) 12.2 \text{ L} = 8.1 \text{ L}$$

CHECK

Note that the volume decreases, as it should, since fewer moles of gas molecules will be present after O_2 is converted to O_3.

See Exercises 5.31 and 5.32.

5.3 The Ideal Gas Law

We have considered three laws that describe the behavior of gases as revealed by experimental observations:

Boyle's law:	$V = \dfrac{k}{P}$	(at constant T and n)
Charles's law:	$V = bT$	(at constant P and n)
Avogadro's law:	$V = an$	(at constant T and P)

These relationships, which show how the volume of a gas depends on pressure, temperature, and number of moles of gas present, can be combined as follows:

$$V = R\left(\frac{Tn}{P}\right)$$

where R is the combined proportionality constant called the **universal gas constant.** When the pressure is expressed in atmospheres and the volume in liters, R has the value 0.08206 L · atm/K · mol. The preceding equation can be rearranged to the more familiar form of the **ideal gas law:**

$$PV = nRT$$

$R = 0.08206 \dfrac{L \cdot atm}{K \cdot mol}$

The ideal gas law is an *equation of state* for a gas, where the state of the gas is its condition at a given time. A particular *state* of a gas is described by its pressure, volume, temperature, and number of moles. Knowledge of any three of these properties is enough to completely define the state of a gas, since the fourth property can then be determined from the equation for the ideal gas law.

It is important to recognize that the ideal gas law is an empirical equation—it is based on experimental measurements of the properties of gases. A gas that obeys this equation is said to behave *ideally.* The ideal gas equation is best regarded as a limiting law—it expresses behavior that real gases *approach* at low pressures and high temperatures. Therefore, an ideal gas is a hypothetical substance. However, most gases obey the ideal gas equation closely enough at pressures below 1 atm that only minimal errors result from assuming ideal behavior. Unless you are given information to the contrary, you should assume ideal gas behavior when solving problems involving gases in this text.

The ideal gas law can be used to solve a variety of problems. Sample Exercise 5.6 demonstrates one type, where you are asked to find one property characterizing the state of a gas, given the other three.

The ideal gas law applies best at pressures smaller than 1 atm.

Sample Exercise 5.6 *Ideal Gas Law I*

A sample of hydrogen gas (H_2) has a volume of 8.56 L at a temperature of 0°C and a pressure of 1.5 atm. Calculate the moles of H_2 molecules present in this gas sample.

Solution

Solving the ideal gas law for n gives

$$n = \frac{PV}{RT}$$

In this case $P = 1.5$ atm, $V = 8.56$ L, $T = 0°C + 273 = 273$ K, and $R = 0.08206$ L · atm/K · mol. Thus

$$n = \frac{(1.5 \ \cancel{atm})(8.56 \ \cancel{L})}{\left(0.08206 \ \dfrac{\cancel{L} \cdot \cancel{atm}}{\cancel{K} \cdot mol}\right)(273 \ \cancel{K})} = 0.57 \text{ mol}$$

See Exercises 5.33 through 5.38.

The reaction of zinc with hydrochloric acid to produce bubbles of hydrogen gas.

The ideal gas law is also used to calculate the changes that will occur when the conditions of the gas are changed.

Sample Exercise 5.7 Ideal Gas Law II

Suppose we have a sample of ammonia gas with a volume of 3.5 L at a pressure of 1.68 atm. The gas is compressed to a volume of 1.35 L at a constant temperature. Use the ideal gas law to calculate the final pressure.

Solution

The basic assumption we make when using the ideal gas law to describe a change in state for a gas is that the equation applies equally well to both the initial and the final states. In dealing with a change in state, we always *place the variables that change on one side of the equals sign and the constants on the other.* In this case the pressure and volume change, and the temperature and the number of moles remain constant (as does R, by definition). Thus we write the ideal gas law as

$$PV = nRT$$

$$\nearrow \qquad \nwarrow$$

Change   Remain constant

Since n and T remain the same in this case, we can write $P_1V_1 = nRT$ and $P_2V_2 = nRT$. Combining these gives

$$P_1V_1 = nRT = P_2V_2 \qquad \text{or} \qquad P_1V_1 = P_2V_2$$

We are given $P_1 = 1.68$ atm, $V_1 = 3.5$ L, and $V_2 = 1.35$ L. Solving for P_2 thus gives

$$P_2 = \left(\frac{V_1}{V_2}\right)P_1 = \left(\frac{3.5 \text{ L}}{1.35 \text{ L}}\right) 1.68 \text{ atm} = 4.4 \text{ atm}$$

CHECK

Does this answer make sense? The volume decreased (at constant temperature), so the pressure should increase, as the result of the calculation indicates. Note that the calculated final pressure is 4.4 atm. Most gases do not behave ideally above 1 atm. Therefore, we might find that if we *measured* the pressure of this gas sample, the observed pressure would differ slightly from 4.4 atm.

See Exercise 5.39.

Sample Exercise 5.8 Ideal Gas Law III

A sample of methane gas that has a volume of 3.8 L at 5°C is heated to 86°C at constant pressure. Calculate its new volume.

Solution

To solve this problem, we take the ideal gas law and segregate the changing variables and the constants by placing them on opposite sides of the equation. In this case, volume and temperature change, and the number of moles and pressure (and, of course, R) remain constant. Thus $PV = nRT$ becomes

$$\frac{V}{T} = \frac{nR}{P}$$

which leads to

$$\frac{V_1}{T_1} = \frac{nR}{P} \quad \text{and} \quad \frac{V_2}{T_2} = \frac{nR}{P}$$

Combining these gives

$$\frac{V_1}{T_1} = \frac{nR}{P} = \frac{V_2}{T_2} \quad \text{or} \quad \frac{V_1}{T_1} = \frac{V_2}{T_2}$$

We are given

$$T_1 = 5°C + 273 = 278 \text{ K} \qquad T_2 = 86°C + 273 = 359 \text{ K}$$
$$V_1 = 3.8 \text{ L} \qquad\qquad\qquad V_2 = ?$$

Thus

$$V_2 = \frac{T_2 V_1}{T_1} = \frac{(359 \, \cancel{K})(3.8 \text{ L})}{278 \, \cancel{K}} = 4.9 \text{ L}$$

CHECK

Is the answer sensible? In this case the temperature increased (at constant pressure), so the volume should increase. Thus the answer makes sense.

See Exercise 5.40.

The problem in Sample Exercise 5.8 could be described as a "Charles's law problem," whereas the problem in Sample Exercise 5.7 might be called a "Boyle's law problem." In both cases, however, we started with the ideal gas law. The real advantage of using the ideal gas law is that it applies to virtually any problem dealing with gases and is easy to remember.

Sample Exercise 5.9 Ideal Gas Law IV

A sample of diborane gas (B_2H_6), a substance that bursts into flame when exposed to air, has a pressure of 345 torr at a temperature of $-15°C$ and a volume of 3.48 L. If conditions are changed so that the temperature is 36°C and the pressure is 468 torr, what will be the volume of the sample?

Molecular Model: B_2H_6

Solution

Since, for this sample, pressure, temperature, and volume all change while the number of moles remains constant, we use the ideal gas law in the form

$$\frac{PV}{T} = nR$$

which leads to

$$\frac{P_1V_1}{T_1} = nR = \frac{P_2V_2}{T_2} \quad \text{or} \quad \frac{P_1V_1}{T_1} = \frac{P_2V_2}{T_2}$$

Then

$$V_2 = \frac{T_2P_1V_1}{T_1P_2}$$

We have

$$P_1 = 345 \text{ torr} \qquad\qquad P_2 = 468 \text{ torr}$$
$$T_1 = -15°C + 273 = 258 \text{ K} \qquad T_2 = 36°C + 273 = 309 \text{ K}$$
$$V_1 = 3.48 \text{ L} \qquad\qquad V_2 = ?$$

Thus

$$V_2 = \frac{(309 \cancel{K})(345 \cancel{\text{torr}})(3.48 \text{ L})}{(258 \cancel{K})(468 \cancel{\text{torr}})} = 3.07 \text{ L}$$

See Exercises 5.41 through 5.44.

Since the equation used in Sample Exercise 5.9 involves a *ratio* of pressures, it was unnecessary to convert pressures to units of atmospheres. The units of torrs cancel. (You will obtain the same answer by inserting $P_1 = \frac{345}{760}$ and $P_2 = \frac{468}{760}$ into the equation.) However, temperature *must always* be converted to the Kelvin scale; since this conversion involves *addition* of 273, the conversion factor does not cancel. Be careful.

One of the many other types of problems dealing with gases that can be solved using the ideal gas law is illustrated in Sample Exercise 5.10.

Always convert the temperature to the Kelvin scale when applying the ideal gas law.

Sample Exercise 5.10 Ideal Gas Law V

A sample containing 0.35 mol argon gas at a temperature of 13°C and a pressure of 568 torr is heated to 56°C and a pressure of 897 torr. Calculate the change in volume that occurs.

Solution

We use the ideal gas law to find the volume for each set of conditions:

State 1	State 2
$n_1 = 0.35$ mol	$n_2 = 0.35$ mol
$P_1 = 568 \text{ torr} \times \dfrac{1 \text{ atm}}{760 \text{ torr}} = 0.747$ atm	$P_2 = 897 \text{ torr} \times \dfrac{1 \text{ atm}}{760 \text{ torr}} = 1.18$ atm
$T_1 = 13°C + 273 = 286$ K	$T_2 = 56°C + 273 = 329$ K

Solving the ideal gas law for volume gives

$$V_1 = \frac{n_1 R T_1}{P_1} = \frac{(0.35 \text{ mol})(0.08206 \text{ L} \cdot \text{atm/K} \cdot \text{mol})(286 \text{ K})}{(0.747 \text{ atm})} = 11 \text{ L}$$

and

$$V_2 = \frac{n_2 R T_2}{P_2} = \frac{(0.35 \text{ mol})(0.08206 \text{ L} \cdot \text{atm/K} \cdot \text{mol})(329 \text{ K})}{(1.18 \text{ atm})} = 8.0 \text{ L}$$

Thus, in going from state 1 to state 2, the volume changes from 11 L to 8.0 L. The change in volume, ΔV (Δ is the Greek capital letter delta), is then

$$\Delta V = V_2 - V_1 = 8.0 \text{ L} - 11 \text{ L} = -3 \text{ L}$$

The *change* in volume is negative because the volume decreases. Note that for this problem (unlike Sample Exercise 5.9) the pressures must be converted from torrs to atmospheres, as required by the atmosphere part of the units for R, since each volume was found separately and the conversion factor does not cancel.

See Exercise 5.45.

5.4 Gas Stoichiometry

Suppose we have 1 mole of an ideal gas at 0°C (273.2 K) and 1 atm. From the ideal gas law, the volume of the gas is given by

$$V = \frac{nRT}{P} = \frac{(1.000 \text{ mol})(0.08206 \text{ L} \cdot \text{atm/K} \cdot \text{mol})(273.2 \text{ K})}{1.000 \text{ atm}} = 22.42 \text{ L}$$

This volume of 22.42 liters is the **molar volume** of an ideal gas (at 0°C and 1 atm). The measured molar volumes of several gases are listed in Table 5.2. Note that the molar volumes of some of the gases are very close to the ideal value, while others deviate significantly. Later in this chapter we will discuss some of the reasons for the deviations.

The conditions 0°C and 1 atm, called **standard temperature and pressure** (abbreviated **STP**), are common reference conditions for the properties of gases. For example, the molar volume of an ideal gas is 22.42 liters at STP (see Fig. 5.11).

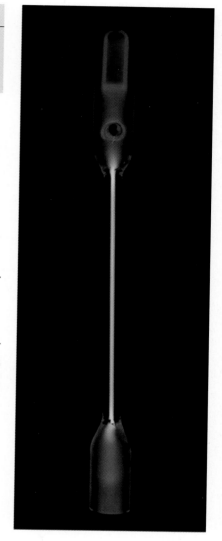

Argon glowing in a discharge tube.

When 273.15 K is used in this calculation, the molar volume obtained in Sample Exercise 5.3 is 22.41 L.

STP: 0°C and 1 atm

Table 5.2 Molar Volumes for Various Gases at 0°C and 1 atm

Gas	Molar Volume (L)
Oxygen (O_2)	22.397
Nitrogen (N_2)	22.402
Hydrogen (H_2)	22.433
Helium (He)	22.434
Argon (Ar)	22.397
Carbon dioxide (CO_2)	22.260
Ammonia (NH_3)	22.079

Sample Exercise 5.11 *Gas Stoichiometry I*

A sample of nitrogen gas has a volume of 1.75 L at STP. How many moles of N_2 are present?

Solution

We could solve this problem using the ideal gas equation, but we can take a shortcut by using the molar volume of an ideal gas at STP. Since 1 mole of an ideal gas at STP has a volume of 22.42 L, 1.75 L of N_2 at STP will contain less than 1 mole. We can find how many moles using the ratio of 1.75 L to 22.42 L:

$$1.75 \; L \, N_2 \times \frac{1 \; \text{mol} \; N_2}{22.42 \; L \, N_2} = 7.81 \times 10^{-2} \; \text{mol} \; N_2$$

See Exercises 5.47 and 5.48.

Many chemical reactions involve gases. By assuming ideal behavior for these gases, we can carry out stoichiometric calculations if the pressure, volume, and temperature of the gases are known.

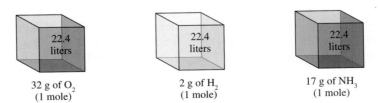

32 g of O_2 (1 mole)   2 g of H_2 (1 mole)   17 g of NH_3 (1 mole)

Figure 5.11
A mole of any gas occupies a volume of approximately 22.4 L at STP.

Sample Exercise 5.12 *Gas Stoichiometry II*

Quicklime (CaO) is produced by the thermal decomposition of calcium carbonate ($CaCO_3$). Calculate the volume of CO_2 at STP produced from the decomposition of 152 g $CaCO_3$ by the reaction

$$CaCO_3(s) \longrightarrow CaO(s) + CO_2(g)$$

Solution

We employ the same strategy we used in the stoichiometry problems earlier in this book. That is, we compute the number of moles of $CaCO_3$ consumed and the number of moles of CO_2 produced. The moles of CO_2 can then be converted to volume using the molar volume of an ideal gas.

Using the molar mass of $CaCO_3$ (100.09 g/mol), we can calculate the number of moles of $CaCO_3$:

$$152 \text{ g } CaCO_3 \times \frac{1 \text{ mol } CaCO_3}{100.09 \text{ g } CaCO_3} = 1.52 \text{ mol } CaCO_3$$

Since each mole of $CaCO_3$ produces a mole of CO_2, 1.52 mol CO_2 will be formed. We can compute the volume of CO_2 at STP by using the molar volume:

$$1.52 \text{ mol } CO_2 \times \frac{22.42 \text{ L } CO_2}{1 \text{ mol } CO_2} = 34.1 \text{ L } CO_2$$

Thus the decomposition of 152 g $CaCO_3$ produces 34.1 L CO_2 at STP.

See Exercises 5.49 through 5.52.

Note that in Sample Exercise 5.12 the final step involved calculation of the volume of gas from the number of moles. Since the conditions were specified as STP, we were able to use the molar volume of a gas at STP. If the conditions of a problem are different from STP, the ideal gas law must be used to compute the volume.

Remember that the molar volume of an ideal gas is 22.42 L when measured *at STP*.

Sample Exercise 5.13 *Gas Stoichiometry III*

A sample of methane gas having a volume of 2.80 L at 25°C and 1.65 atm was mixed with a sample of oxygen gas having a volume of 35.0 L at 31°C and 1.25 atm. The mixture was then ignited to form carbon dioxide and water. Calculate the volume of CO_2 formed at a pressure of 2.50 atm and a temperature of 125°C.

Solution

From the description of the reaction, the unbalanced equation is

$$CH_4(g) + O_2(g) \longrightarrow CO_2(g) + H_2O(g)$$

which can be balanced to give

$$CH_4(g) + 2O_2(g) \longrightarrow CO_2(g) + 2H_2O(g)$$

Next, we must find the limiting reactant, which requires calculating the numbers of moles of each reactant. We convert the given volumes of methane and oxygen to moles using the ideal gas law as follows:

$$n_{CH_4} = \frac{PV}{RT} = \frac{(1.65 \text{ atm})(2.80 \text{ L})}{(0.08206 \text{ L} \cdot \text{atm/K} \cdot \text{mol})(298 \text{ K})} = 0.189 \text{ mol}$$

$$n_{O_2} = \frac{PV}{RT} = \frac{(1.25 \text{ atm})(35.0 \text{ L})}{(0.08206 \text{ L} \cdot \text{atm/K} \cdot \text{mol})(304 \text{ K})} = 1.75 \text{ mol}$$

In the balanced equation for the combustion reaction, 1 mol CH_4 requires 2 mol O_2. Thus the moles of O_2 required by 0.189 mol CH_4 can be calculated as follows:

$$0.189 \text{ mol } CH_4 \times \frac{2 \text{ mol } O_2}{1 \text{ mol } CH_4} = 0.378 \text{ mol } O_2$$

Since 1.75 mol O_2 is available, O_2 is in excess. The limiting reactant is CH_4. The number of moles of CH_4 available must be used to calculate the number of moles of CO_2 produced:

$$0.189 \text{ mol } CH_4 \times \frac{1 \text{ mol } CO_2}{1 \text{ mol } CH_4} = 0.189 \text{ mol } CO_2$$

Since the conditions stated are not STP, we must use the ideal gas law to calculate the volume:

$$V = \frac{nRT}{P}$$

In this case $n = 0.189$ mol, $T = 125°C + 273 = 398$ K, $P = 2.50$ atm, and $R = 0.08206$ L $\cdot$ atm/K $\cdot$ mol. Thus

$$V = \frac{(0.189 \text{ mol})(0.08206 \text{ L} \cdot \text{atm/K} \cdot \text{mol})(398 \text{ K})}{2.50 \text{ atm}} = 2.47 \text{ L}$$

This represents the volume of CO_2 produced under these conditions.

See Exercises 5.53 and 5.54.

Molar Mass of a Gas

One very important use of the ideal gas law is in the calculation of the molar mass (molecular weight) of a gas from its measured density. To see the relationship between gas density and molar mass, consider that the number of moles of gas n can be expressed as

$$n = \frac{\text{grams of gas}}{\text{molar mass}} = \frac{\text{mass}}{\text{molar mass}} = \frac{m}{\text{molar mass}}$$

Substitution into the ideal gas equation gives

$$P = \frac{nRT}{V} = \frac{(m/\text{molar mass})RT}{V} = \frac{m(RT)}{V(\text{molar mass})}$$

However, m/V is the gas density d in units of grams per liter. Thus

$$P = \frac{dRT}{\text{molar mass}}$$

$$\text{Density} = \frac{\text{mass}}{\text{volume}}$$

or

$$\text{Molar mass} = \frac{dRT}{P} \qquad\qquad (5.1)$$

Thus, if the density of a gas at a given temperature and pressure is known, its molar mass can be calculated.

Sample Exercise 5.14 *Gas Density/Molar Mass*

The density of a gas was measured at 1.50 atm and 27°C and found to be 1.95 g/L. Calculate the molar mass of the gas.

Solution

Using Equation (5.1), we calculate the molar mass as follows:

$$\text{Molar mass} = \frac{dRT}{P} = \frac{\left(1.95\ \frac{\text{g}}{\cancel{\text{L}}}\right)\left(0.08206\ \frac{\cancel{\text{L}} \cdot \cancel{\text{atm}}}{\cancel{\text{K}} \cdot \text{mol}}\right)(300.\ \cancel{\text{K}})}{1.50\ \cancel{\text{atm}}} = 32.0\ \text{g/mol}$$

CHECK

These are the units expected for molar mass.

See Exercises 5.57 through 5.60.

You could memorize the equation involving gas density and molar mass, but it is better simply to remember the total gas equation, the definition of density, and the relationship between number of moles and molar mass. You can then derive the appropriate equation when you need it. This approach ensures that you understand the concepts and means one less equation to memorize.

5.5 *Dalton's Law of Partial Pressures*

Among the experiments that led John Dalton to propose the atomic theory were his studies of mixtures of gases. In 1803 Dalton summarized his observations as follows: *For a mixture of gases in a container, the total pressure exerted is the sum of the*

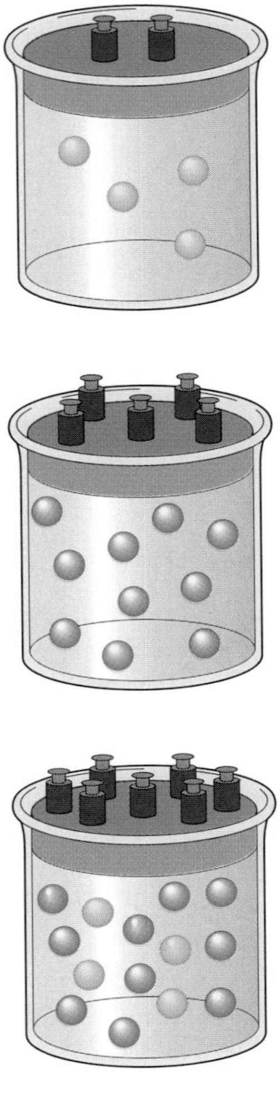

Figure 5.12
The partial pressure of each gas in a mixture of gases in a container depends on the number of moles of that gas. The total pressure is the sum of the partial pressures and depends on the total moles of gas particles present, no matter what they are.

pressures that each gas would exert if it were alone. This statement, known as **Dalton's law of partial pressures,** can be expressed as follows:

$$P_{\text{TOTAL}} = P_1 + P_2 + P_3 + \cdots$$

where the subscripts refer to the individual gases (gas 1, gas 2, etc.). The symbols P_1, P_2, P_3, and so on represent each **partial pressure,** that is, the pressure that a particular gas would exert if it were alone in the container.

Assuming that each gas behaves ideally, the partial pressure of each gas can be calculated from the ideal gas law:

$$P_1 = \frac{n_1RT}{V}, \qquad P_2 = \frac{n_2RT}{V}, \qquad P_3 = \frac{n_3RT}{V}, \qquad \cdots$$

The total pressure of the mixture P_{TOTAL} can be represented as

$$\begin{aligned} P_{\text{TOTAL}} = P_1 + P_2 + P_3 + \cdots &= \frac{n_1RT}{V} + \frac{n_2RT}{V} + \frac{n_3RT}{V} + \cdots \\ &= (n_1 + n_2 + n_3 + \cdots)\left(\frac{RT}{V}\right) \\ &= n_{\text{TOTAL}}\left(\frac{RT}{V}\right) \end{aligned}$$

where n_{TOTAL} is the sum of the numbers of moles of the various gases. Thus, for a mixture of ideal gases, it is the *total number of moles of particles* that is important, not the identity or composition of the involved gas particles. This idea is illustrated in Fig. 5.12.

This important observation indicates some fundamental characteristics of an ideal gas. The fact that the pressure exerted by an ideal gas is not affected by the identity (composition) of the gas particles reveals two things about ideal gases: (1) the volume of the individual gas particle must not be important, and (2) the forces among the particles must not be important. If these factors were important, the pressure exerted by the gas would depend on the nature of the individual particles. These observations will strongly influence the model that we will eventually construct to explain ideal gas behavior.

Sample Exercise 5.15 Dalton's Law I

Mixtures of helium and oxygen are used in scuba diving tanks to help prevent "the bends." For a particular dive, 46 L He at 25°C and 1.0 atm and 12 L O_2 at 25°C and 1.0 atm were pumped into a tank with a volume of 5.0 L. Calculate the partial pressure of each gas and the total pressure in the tank at 25°C.

Solution

The first step is to calculate the number of moles of each gas using the ideal gas law in the form:

$$n = \frac{PV}{RT}$$

$$n_{He} = \frac{(1.0 \text{ atm})(46 \text{ L})}{(0.08206 \text{ L} \cdot \text{atm}/\text{K} \cdot \text{mol})(298 \text{ K})} = 1.9 \text{ mol}$$

$$n_{O_2} = \frac{(1.0 \text{ atm})(12 \text{ L})}{(0.08206 \text{ L} \cdot \text{atm}/\text{K} \cdot \text{mol})(298 \text{ K})} = 0.49 \text{ mol}$$

The tank containing the mixture has a volume of 5.0 L, and the temperature is 25°C. We can use these data and the ideal gas law to calculate the partial pressure of each gas:

$$P = \frac{nRT}{V}$$

$$P_{He} = \frac{(1.9 \text{ mol})(0.08206 \text{ L} \cdot \text{atm}/\text{K} \cdot \text{mol})(298 \text{ K})}{5.0 \text{ L}} = 9.3 \text{ atm}$$

$$P_{O_2} = \frac{(0.49 \text{ mol})(0.08206 \text{ L} \cdot \text{atm}/\text{K} \cdot \text{mol})(298 \text{ K})}{5.0 \text{ L}} = 2.4 \text{ atm}$$

The total pressure is the sum of the partial pressures:

$$P_{TOTAL} = P_{He} + P_{O_2} = 9.3 \text{ atm} + 2.4 \text{ atm} = 11.7 \text{ atm}$$

See Exercises 5.61 and 5.62.

At this point we need to define the **mole fraction:** *the ratio of the number of moles of a given component in a mixture to the total number of moles in the mixture.* The Greek lowercase letter chi (X) is used to symbolize the mole fraction. For example, for a given component in a mixture, the mole fraction X_1 is

$$X_1 = \frac{n_1}{n_{TOTAL}} = \frac{n_1}{n_1 + n_2 + n_3 + \cdots}$$

From the ideal gas equation we know that the number of moles of a gas is directly proportional to the pressure of the gas, since

$$n = P\left(\frac{V}{RT}\right)$$

That is, for each component in the mixture,

$$n_1 = P_1\left(\frac{V}{RT}\right), \qquad n_2 = P_2\left(\frac{V}{RT}\right), \qquad \cdots$$

Therefore, we can represent the mole fraction in terms of pressures:

$$X_1 = \frac{n_1}{n_{TOTAL}} = \frac{\overbrace{P_1(V/RT)}^{n_1}}{\underbrace{P_1(V/RT)}_{n_1} + \underbrace{P_2(V/RT)}_{n_2} + \underbrace{P_3(V/RT)}_{n_3} + \cdots}$$

$$= \frac{(V/RT)P_1}{(V/RT)(P_1 + P_2 + P_3 + \cdots)}$$

$$= \frac{P_1}{P_1 + P_2 + P_3 + \cdots} = \frac{P_1}{P_{\text{TOTAL}}}$$

In fact, the mole fraction of each component in a mixture of ideal gases is directly related to its partial pressure:

$$\chi_2 = \frac{n_2}{n_{\text{TOTAL}}} = \frac{P_2}{P_{\text{TOTAL}}}$$

Sample Exercise 5.16 Dalton's Law II

The partial pressure of oxygen was observed to be 156 torr in air with a total atmospheric pressure of 743 torr. Calculate the mole fraction of O_2 present.

Solution

The mole fraction of O_2 can be calculated from the equation

$$\chi_{O_2} = \frac{P_{O_2}}{P_{\text{TOTAL}}} = \frac{156 \text{ torr}}{743 \text{ torr}} = 0.210$$

Note that mole fraction has no units.

See Exercise 5.65.

The expression for the mole fraction,

$$\chi_1 = \frac{P_1}{P_{\text{TOTAL}}}$$

can be rearranged to give

$$P_1 = \chi_1 \times P_{\text{TOTAL}}$$

That is, *the partial pressure of a particular component of a gaseous mixture is the mole fraction of that component times the total pressure.*

Sample Exercise 5.17 Dalton's Law III

The mole fraction of nitrogen in the air is 0.7808. Calculate the partial pressure of N_2 in air when the atmospheric pressure is 760. torr.

Solution

The partial pressure of N_2 can be calculated as follows:

$$P_{N_2} = \chi_{N_2} \times P_{\text{TOTAL}} = 0.7808 \times 760. \text{ torr} = 593 \text{ torr}$$

See Exercise 5.66.

CHEMICAL IMPACT

The Chemistry of Air Bags

MOST EXPERTS AGREE that air bags represent a very important advance in automobile safety. These bags, which are stored in the auto's steering wheel or dash, are designed to inflate rapidly (within about 40 ms) in the event of a crash, cushioning the front seat occupants against impact. The bags then deflate immediately to allow vision and movement after the crash. Air bags are activated when a severe deceleration (an impact) causes a steel ball to compress a spring and electrically ignite a detonator cap, which, in turn, causes sodium azide (NaN$_3$) to decompose explosively, forming sodium and nitrogen gas:

$$2NaN_3(s) \longrightarrow 2Na(s) + 3N_2(g)$$

This system works very well and requires a relatively small amount of sodium azide (100 g yields 56 L N$_2$(g) at 25°C and 1.0 atm).

When a vehicle containing air bags reaches the end of its useful life, the sodium azide present in the activators must be given proper disposal. Sodium azide, besides being explosive, has a toxicity roughly equal to that of sodium cyanide. It also forms hydrazoic acid (HN$_3$), a toxic and explosive liquid, when treated with acid.

The air bag represents an application of chemistry that has already saved thousands of lives.

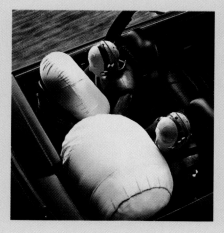

Inflated air bags.

A mixture of gases results whenever a gas is collected by displacement of water. For example, Fig. 5.13 shows the collection of oxygen gas produced by the decomposition of solid potassium chlorate. In this situation, the gas in the bottle is a mixture of water vapor and the oxygen being collected. Water vapor is present because molecules of water escape from the surface of the liquid and collect in the space above the liquid. Molecules of water also return to the liquid. When the rate of escape equals the rate of return, the number of water molecules in the vapor state remains constant, and thus the pressure of water vapor remains constant. This pressure, which depends on temperature, is called the *vapor pressure of water.*

Vapor pressure will be discussed in detail in Chapter 10. A table of water vapor pressure values is given in Section 10.8.

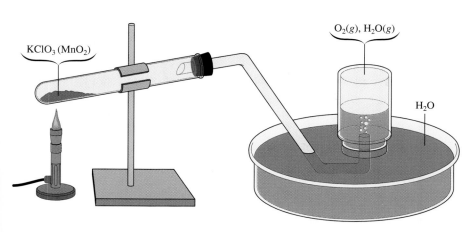

KClO$_3$ (MnO$_2$)

O$_2$(g), H$_2$O(g)

H$_2$O

Figure 5.13

The production of oxygen by thermal decomposition of KClO$_3$. The MnO$_2$ is mixed with the KClO$_3$ to make the reaction faster.

Sample Exercise 5.18 *Gas Collection over Water*

A sample of solid potassium chlorate ($KClO_3$) was heated in a test tube (see Fig. 5.13) and decomposed by the following reaction:

$$2KClO_3(s) \longrightarrow 2KCl(s) + 3O_2(g)$$

The oxygen produced was collected by displacement of water at 22°C at a total pressure of 754 torr. The volume of the gas collected was 0.650 L, and the vapor pressure of water at 22°C is 21 torr. Calculate the partial pressure of O_2 in the gas collected and the mass of $KClO_3$ in the sample that was decomposed.

Solution

First we find the partial pressure of O_2 from Dalton's law of partial pressures:

$$P_{TOTAL} = P_{O_2} + P_{H_2O} = P_{O_2} + 21 \text{ torr} = 754 \text{ torr}$$

Thus

$$P_{O_2} = 754 \text{ torr} - 21 \text{ torr} = 733 \text{ torr}$$

Now we use the ideal gas law to find the number of moles of O_2:

$$n_{O_2} = \frac{P_{O_2}V}{RT}$$

In this case,

$$P_{O_2} = 733 \text{ torr} = \frac{733 \text{ torr}}{760 \text{ torr/atm}} = 0.964 \text{ atm}$$

$$V = 0.650 \text{ L}$$

$$T = 22°C + 273 = 295 \text{ K}$$

$$R = 0.08206 \text{ L} \cdot \text{atm/K} \cdot \text{mol}$$

Thus

$$n_{O_2} = \frac{(0.964 \text{ atm})(0.650 \text{ L})}{(0.08206 \text{ L} \cdot \text{atm/K} \cdot \text{mol})(295 \text{ K})} = 2.59 \times 10^{-2} \text{ mol}$$

Next we will calculate the moles of $KClO_3$ needed to produce this quantity of O_2. From the balanced equation for the decomposition of $KClO_3$, we have a mole ratio of 2 mol $KClO_3$/3 mol O_2. The moles of $KClO_3$ can be calculated as follows:

$$2.59 \times 10^{-2} \text{ mol } O_2 \times \frac{2 \text{ mol } KClO_3}{3 \text{ mol } O_2} = 1.73 \times 10^{-2} \text{ mol } KClO_3$$

Using the molar mass of $KClO_3$ (122.6 g/mol), we calculate the grams of $KClO_3$:

$$1.73 \times 10^{-2} \text{ mol } KClO_3 \times \frac{122.6 \text{ g } KClO_3}{1 \text{ mol } KClO_3} = 2.12 \text{ g } KClO_3$$

Thus the original sample contained 2.12 g $KClO_3$.

See Exercises 5.67 through 5.69.

CHEMICAL IMPACT

Scuba Diving

OXYGEN IS ESSENTIAL to our existence, but surprisingly, it can be harmful under certain circumstances. At sea level the partial pressure of this life-sustaining gas is 0.21 atmosphere,* and in each normal breath we inhale about 0.02 mole of O_2 molecules. Our bodies operate very effectively under these conditions, but the situation changes if we subject ourselves to greater pressures—for example, by diving in deep water. A scuba diver at a depth of 100 feet experiences approximately 4 atmospheres of pressure, and at 300 feet the pressure is about 10 atmospheres. This increased pressure affects the ear canals and squeezes the lungs, but a more serious effect involves the increased partial pressure of oxygen in air breathed at these pressures. Elevated concentrations of oxygen are actually quite harmful for reasons that are not well understood. The symptoms of oxygen poisoning include confusion, impaired vision and hearing, and nausea. Clearly, it is possible to get too much of a good thing.

At a depth of 300 feet under the ocean's surface, the partial pressure of oxygen is about 2 atmospheres (0.21 × 10 atmospheres) for a diver inhaling compressed air. This is much too high, so the

Scuba diver.

oxygen must be diluted by another gas. Although it might seem to be an ideal candidate, nitrogen cannot be used. At elevated pressures, a large quantity of nitrogen dissolves in the blood, producing nitrogen narcosis, often called "rapture of the deep," which has an effect not unlike that from imbibing too many martinis. The

increased solubility of nitrogen in blood at high pressures is also responsible for an agonizing condition called "the bends," which results when a diver makes too rapid an ascent. The diver's joints become locked in a bent position—hence the name. Just as a bottle of soda fizzes when the pressure inside the bottle is released by opening the cap, the excess dissolved nitrogen in the bloodstream forms bubbles that can stop blood flow and impair the nervous system.

Helium is the diluting agent most often used in scuba tanks. It is inert, and its solubility in blood is much lower than that of oxygen or nitrogen. However, it has the effect of raising the pitch of the human voice, producing a "Donald Duck" effect. This effect occurs because the pitch of the voice depends on the density of the gas surrounding the vocal cords; lower density yields a higher pitch. Because the mass of a He atom is much smaller than the masses of N_2 and O_2, the density of helium gas is much lower than that of air.

* This result is obtained from Dalton's law. Since the mole fraction of O_2 in air is 0.21, the partial pressure of O_2 is 0.21 × 1 atm = 0.21 atm.

5.6 The Kinetic Molecular Theory of Gases

We have so far considered the behavior of gases from an experimental point of view. Based on observations from different types of experiments, we know that at pressures of less than 1 atm most gases closely approach the behavior described by the ideal gas law. Now we want to construct a model to explain this behavior.

Before we do this, let's briefly review the scientific method. Recall that a law is a way of generalizing behavior that has been observed in many experiments. Laws are very useful, since they allow us to predict the behavior of similar systems. For example, if a chemist prepares a new gaseous compound, a measurement of the gas density at known pressure and temperature can provide a reliable value for the compound's molar mass.

However, although laws summarize observed behavior, they do not tell us *why* nature behaves in the observed fashion. This is the central question for scientists. To try to answer this question, we construct theories (build models). The models in chemistry consist of speculations about what the individual atoms or molecules (microscopic particles) might be doing to cause the observed behavior of the macroscopic systems (collections of very large numbers of atoms and molecules).

A model is considered successful if it explains the observed behavior in question and predicts correctly the results of future experiments. It is important to understand that a model can never be proved absolutely true. In fact, *any model is an approximation* by its very nature and is bound to fail at some point. Models range from the simple to the extraordinarily complex. We use simple models to predict approximate behavior and more complicated models to account very precisely for observed quantitative behavior. In this text we will stress simple models that provide an approximate picture of what might be happening and that fit the most important experimental results.

An example of this type of model is the **kinetic molecular theory (KMT),** a simple model that attempts to explain the properties of an ideal gas. This model is based on speculations about the behavior of the individual gas particles (atoms or molecules). The postulates of the kinetic molecular theory as they relate to the particles of an ideal gas can be stated as follows:

Animations: Visualizing Molecular Motion (Single Molecule and Many Molecules)

1. The particles are so small compared with the distances between them that *the volume of the individual particles can be assumed to be negligible* (zero).

2. *The particles are in constant motion. The collisions of the particles with the walls of the container are the cause of the pressure exerted by the gas.*

3. *The particles are assumed to exert no forces on each other;* they are assumed neither to attract nor to repel each other.

4. *The average kinetic energy of a collection of gas particles is assumed to be directly proportional to the Kelvin temperature of the gas.*

Of course, the molecules in a real gas have finite volumes and do exert forces on each other. Thus *real gases* do not conform to these assumptions. However, we will see that these postulates do indeed explain *ideal gas* behavior.

The true test of a model is how well its predictions fit the experimental observations. The postulates of the kinetic molecular model picture an ideal gas as consisting of particles having no volume and no attractions for each other, and the model assumes that the gas produces pressure on its container by collisions with the walls.

Let's consider how this model accounts for the properties of gases as summarized by the ideal gas law: $PV = nRT$.

Pressure and Volume (Boyle's Law)

Animation: Microscopic Illustration of Boyle's Law

We have seen that for a given sample of gas at a given temperature (n and T are constant) that if the volume of a gas is decreased, the pressure increases:

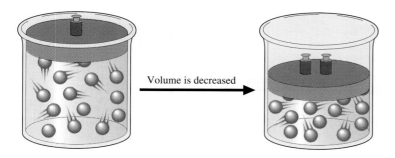

Volume is decreased

Figure 5.14
The effects of decreasing the volume of a sample of gas at constant temperature.

$$P = (nRT)\frac{1}{V}$$
$$\uparrow$$
Constant

This makes sense based on the kinetic molecular theory, since a decrease in volume means that the gas particles will hit the wall more often, thus increasing pressure, as illustrated in Fig. 5.14.

Pressure and Temperature

From the ideal gas law we can predict that for a given sample of an ideal gas at a constant volume, the pressure will be directly proportional to the temperature:

$$P = \left(\frac{nR}{V}\right)T$$
$$\uparrow$$
Constant

The KMT accounts for this behavior because when the temperature of a gas increases, the speeds of its particles increase, the particles hitting the wall with greater force and greater frequency. Since the volume remains the same, this would result in increased gas pressure, as illustrated in Fig. 5.15.

Volume and Temperature (Charles's Law)

The ideal gas law indicates that for a given sample of gas at a constant pressure, the volume of the gas is directly proportional to the temperature in kelvins:

$$V = \left(\frac{nR}{P}\right)T$$
$$\uparrow$$
Constant

Animation: Microscopic Illustration of Charles's Law

This can be visualized from the KMT, as shown in Fig. 5.16. When the gas is heated to a higher temperature, the speeds of its molecules increase and thus they hit the walls more often and with more force. The only way to keep the pressure constant in this situation is to increase the volume of the container. This compensates for the increased particle speeds.

Figure 5.15
The effects of increasing the temperature of a sample of gas at constant volume.

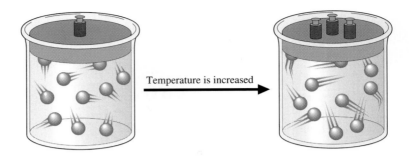

Figure 5.16
The effects of increasing the temperature of a sample of gas at constant pressure.

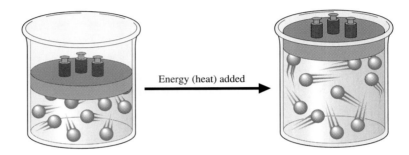

Volume and Number of Moles (Avogadro's Law)

The ideal gas law predicts that the volume of a gas at a constant temperature and pressure depends directly on the number of gas particles present:

$$V = \left(\frac{RT}{P}\right)n$$

Constant

This makes sense in terms of the KMT, because an increase in the number of gas particles at the same temperature would cause the pressure to increase if the volume were held constant (see Fig. 5.17). The only way to return the pressure to its original value is to increase the volume.

It is important to recognize that the volume of a gas (at constant P and T) depends only on the *number* of gas particles present. The individual volumes of the particles are not a factor because the particle volumes are so small compared with the distances between the particles (for a gas behaving ideally).

Mixture of Gases (Dalton's Law)

The observation that the total pressure exerted by a mixture of gases is the sum of the pressures of the individual gases is expected because the KMT assumes that all gas particles are independent of each other and that the volumes of the individual particles are unimportant. Thus the identities of the gas particles do not matter.

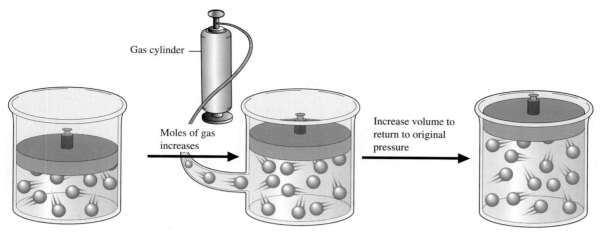

Figure 5.17
The effects of increasing the number of moles of gas particles at constant temperature and pressure.

Deriving the Ideal Gas Law

We have shown qualitatively that the assumptions of the KMT successfully account for the observed behavior of an ideal gas. We can go further. By applying the principles of physics to the assumptions of the KMT, we can in effect derive the ideal gas law.

As shown in detail in Appendix 2, we can apply the definitions of velocity, momentum, force, and pressure to the collection of particles in an ideal gas and *derive* the following expression for pressure:

$$P = \frac{2}{3}\left[\frac{nN_A\left(\frac{1}{2}m\overline{u^2}\right)}{V}\right]$$

where P is the pressure of the gas, n is the number of moles of gas, N_A is Avogadro's number, m is the mass of each particle, $\overline{u^2}$ is the average of the square of the velocities of the particles, and V is the volume of the container.

The quantity $\frac{1}{2}m\overline{u^2}$ represents the average kinetic energy of a gas particle. If the average kinetic energy of an individual particle is multiplied by N_A, the number of particles in a mole, we get the average kinetic energy for a mole of gas particles:

$$(KE)_{avg} = N_A\left(\frac{1}{2}m\overline{u^2}\right)$$

Using this definition, we can rewrite the expression for pressure as

$$P = \frac{2}{3}\left[\frac{n(KE)_{avg}}{V}\right] \quad \text{or} \quad \frac{PV}{n} = \frac{2}{3}(KE)_{avg}$$

The fourth postulate of the kinetic molecular theory is that the average kinetic energy of the particles in the gas sample is directly proportional to the temperature in Kelvins. Thus, since $(KE)_{avg} \propto T$, we can write

$$\frac{PV}{n} = \frac{2}{3}(KE)_{avg} \propto T \quad \text{or} \quad \frac{PV}{n} \propto T$$

Kinetic energy (KE) given by the equation $KE = \frac{1}{2}m\overline{u^2}$ is the energy due to the motion of a particle. We will discuss this further in Section 6.1.

Video: Liquid Nitrogen and Balloons

(a)　　　　　(b)　　　　　(c)

(a) A balloon filled with air at room temperature. (b) The balloon is dipped into liquid nitrogen at 77 K. (c) The balloon collapses as the molecules inside slow down due to the decreased temperature. Slower molecules produce a lower pressure.

 Animation: Balloon Submersion in Liquid N_2

Note that this expression has been *derived* from the assumptions of the kinetic molecular theory. How does it compare to the ideal gas law—the equation obtained from experiment? Compare the ideal gas law,

$$\frac{PV}{n} = RT \qquad \text{From experiment}$$

with the result from the kinetic molecular theory,

$$\frac{PV}{n} \propto T \qquad \text{From theory}$$

These expressions have exactly the same form if R, the universal gas constant, is considered the proportionality constant in the second case.

The agreement between the ideal gas law and the predictions of the kinetic molecular theory gives us confidence in the validity of the model. The characteristics we have assumed for ideal gas particles must agree, at least under certain conditions, with their actual behavior.

The Meaning of Temperature

We have seen from the kinetic molecular theory that the Kelvin temperature indicates the average kinetic energy of the gas particles. The exact relationship between temperature and average kinetic energy can be obtained by combining the equations:

$$\frac{PV}{n} = RT = \frac{2}{3}(\text{KE})_{\text{avg}}$$

which yields the expression

$$(\text{KE})_{\text{avg}} = \frac{3}{2}RT$$

This is a very important relationship. It summarizes the meaning of the Kelvin temperature of a gas: The Kelvin temperature is an index of the random motions of the particles of a gas, with higher temperature meaning greater motion. (As we will see in Chapter 10, temperature is an index of the random motions in solids and liquids as well as in gases.)

Root Mean Square Velocity

In the equation from the kinetic molecular theory, the average velocity of the gas particles is a special kind of average. The symbol $\overline{u^2}$ means the average of the *squares* of the particle velocities. The square root of $\overline{u^2}$ is called the **root mean square velocity** and is symbolized by u_{rms}:

$$u_{rms} = \sqrt{\overline{u^2}}$$

We can obtain an expression for u_{rms} from the equations

$$(KE)_{avg} = N_A(\tfrac{1}{2}m\overline{u^2}) \quad \text{and} \quad (KE)_{avg} = \frac{3}{2}RT$$

Combination of these equations gives

$$N_A(\tfrac{1}{2}m\overline{u^2}) = \frac{3}{2}RT \quad \text{or} \quad \overline{u^2} = \frac{3RT}{N_A m}$$

Taking the square root of both sides of the last equation produces

$$\sqrt{\overline{u^2}} = u_{rms} = \sqrt{\frac{3RT}{N_A m}}$$

In this expression m represents the mass in kilograms of a single gas particle. When N_A, the number of particles in a mole, is multiplied by m, the product is the mass of a *mole* of gas particles in *kilograms*. We will call this quantity M. Substituting M for $N_A m$ in the equation for u_{rms}, we obtain

$$u_{rms} = \sqrt{\frac{3RT}{M}}$$

Before we can use this equation, we need to consider the units for R. So far we have used 0.08206 L · atm/K · mol as the value of R. But to obtain the desired units (meters per second) for u_{rms}, R must be expressed in different units. As we will see in more detail in Chapter 6, the energy unit most often used in the SI system is the joule (J). A **joule** is defined as a kilogram meter squared per second squared (kg · m^2/s^2). When R is converted to include the unit of joules, it has the value 8.3145 J/K · mol. When R in these units is used in the expression $\sqrt{3RT/M}$, u_{rms} is obtained in the units of meters per second as desired.

$$R = 0.08206 \; \frac{L \cdot atm}{K \cdot mol}$$

$$R = 8.3145 \; \frac{J}{K \cdot mol}$$

Sample Exercise 5.19 *Root Mean Square Velocity*

Calculate the root mean square velocity for the atoms in a sample of helium gas at 25°C.

Animation: The Kinetic Molecular Theory and Heat Transfer

Solution

The formula for root mean square velocity is

$$u_{rms} = \sqrt{\frac{3RT}{M}}$$

In this case $T = 25°C + 273 = 298$ K, $R = 8.3145$ J/K · mol, and M is the mass of a mole of helium in kilograms:

$$M = 4.00\frac{g}{mol} \times \frac{1 \text{ kg}}{1000 \text{ g}} = 4.00 \times 10^{-3} \text{ kg/mol}$$

Thus

$$u_{rms} = \sqrt{\frac{3\left(8.3145 \dfrac{J}{K \cdot mol}\right)(298 \text{ K})}{4.00 \times 10^{-3} \dfrac{kg}{mol}}} = \sqrt{1.86 \times 10^6 \frac{J}{kg}}$$

Since the units of J are kg · m²/s², this expression becomes

$$\sqrt{1.86 \times 10^6 \frac{kg \cdot m^2}{kg \cdot s^2}} = 1.36 \times 10^3 \text{ m/s}$$

Note that the resulting units (m/s) are appropriate for velocity.

See Exercises 5.73 and 5.74.

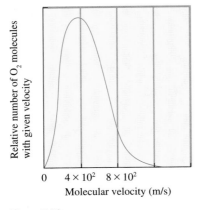

Figure 5.18

Path of one particle in a gas. Any given particle will continuously change its course as a result of collisions with other particles, as well as with the walls of the container.

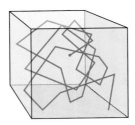

Figure 5.19

A plot of the relative number of O_2 molecules that have a given velocity at STP.

So far we have said nothing about the range of velocities actually found in a gas sample. In a real gas there are large numbers of collisions between particles. For example, as we will see in the next section, when an odorous gas such as ammonia is released in a room, it takes some time for the odor to permeate the air. This delay results from collisions between the NH_3 molecules and the O_2 and N_2 molecules in the air, which greatly slow the mixing process.

If the path of a particular gas particle could be monitored, it would look very erratic, something like that shown in Fig. 5.18. The average distance a particle travels between collisions in a particular gas sample is called the *mean free path*. It is typically a very small distance (1×10^{-7} m for O_2 at STP). One effect of the many collisions among gas particles is to produce a large range of velocities as the particles collide and exchange kinetic energy. Although u_{rms} for oxygen gas at STP is approximately 500 meters per second, the majority of O_2 molecules do not have this velocity. The actual distribution of molecular velocities for oxygen gas at STP is shown in Fig. 5.19. This figure shows the relative number of gas molecules having each particular velocity.

We are also interested in the effect of *temperature* on the velocity distribution in a gas. Figure 5.20 shows the velocity distribution for nitrogen gas at three temperatures. Note that as the temperature is increased, the curve peak moves toward higher values and the range of velocities becomes much larger. The peak of the curve reflects the most probable velocity (the velocity found most often as we sample the movement of the various particles in the gas). Because the kinetic energy increases with temperature, it makes sense that the peak of the curve should move to higher values as the temperature of the gas is increased.

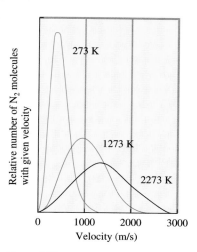

Figure 5.20

A plot of the relative number of N_2 molecules that have a given velocity at three temperatures. Note that as the temperature increases, both the average velocity (reflected by the curve's peak) and the spread of velocities increase.

5.7 Effusion and Diffusion

We have seen that the postulates of the kinetic molecular theory, when combined with the appropriate physical principles, produce an equation that successfully fits the experimentally observed behavior of gases as they approach ideal behavior. Two phenomena involving gases provide further tests of this model.

Diffusion is the term used to describe the mixing of gases. When a small amount of pungent-smelling ammonia is released at the front of a classroom, it takes some time before everyone in the room can smell it, because time is required for the ammonia to mix with the air. The rate of diffusion is the rate of the mixing of gases. **Effusion** is the term used to describe the passage of a gas through a tiny orifice into an evacuated chamber, as shown in Fig. 5.21. The rate of effusion measures the speed at which the gas is transferred into the chamber.

Effusion

Thomas Graham (1805–1869), a Scottish chemist, found experimentally that the rate of effusion of a gas is inversely proportional to the square root of the mass of its particles. Stated in another way, the relative rates of effusion of two gases at the same temperature and pressure are given by the inverse ratio of the square roots of the masses of the gas particles:

$$\frac{\text{Rate of effusion for gas 1}}{\text{Rate of effusion for gas 2}} = \frac{\sqrt{M_2}}{\sqrt{M_1}}$$

where M_1 and M_2 represent the molar masses of the gases. This equation is called **Graham's law of effusion.**

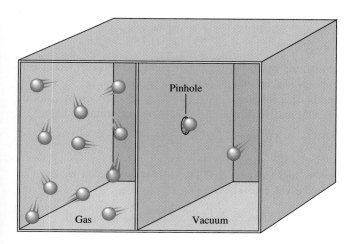

In Graham's law the units for molar mass can be g/mol or kg/mol, since the units cancel in the ratio $\sqrt{M_2}/\sqrt{M_1}$.

Figure 5.21

The effusion of a gas into an evacuated chamber. The rate of effusion (the rate at which the gas is transferred across the barrier through the pin hole) is inversely proportional to the square root of the mass of the gas molecules.

Sample Exercise 5.20 Effusion Rates

Calculate the ratio of the effusion rates of hydrogen gas (H_2) and uranium hexa-fluoride (UF_6), a gas used in the enrichment process to produce fuel for nuclear reactors (see Fig. 5.22).

Solution

First we need to compute the molar masses: Molar mass of H_2 = 2.016 g/mol, and molar mass of UF_6 = 352.02 g/mol. Using Graham's law,

$$\frac{\text{Rate of effusion for } H_2}{\text{Rate of effusion for } UF_6} = \frac{\sqrt{M_{UF_6}}}{\sqrt{M_{H_2}}} = \sqrt{\frac{352.02}{2.016}} = 13.2$$

The effusion rate of the very light H_2 molecules is about 13 times that of the massive UF_6 molecules.

See Exercises 5.81 through 5.84.

Figure 5.22

Uranium-enrichment converters from the Paducah gaseous diffusion plant in Kentucky.

Animation: The Effusion of a Gas

Does the kinetic molecular model for gases correctly predict the relative effusion rates of gases summarized by Graham's law? To answer this question, we must recognize that the effusion rate for a gas depends directly on the average velocity of its particles. The faster the gas particles are moving, the more likely they are to pass through the effusion orifice. This reasoning leads to the following *prediction* for two gases at the same pressure and temperature (T):

$$\frac{\text{Effusion rate for gas 1}}{\text{Effusion rate for gas 2}} = \frac{u_{rms} \text{ for gas 1}}{u_{rms} \text{ for gas 2}} = \frac{\sqrt{\dfrac{3RT}{M_1}}}{\sqrt{\dfrac{3RT}{M_2}}} = \frac{\sqrt{M_2}}{\sqrt{M_1}}$$

This equation is identical to Graham's law. Thus the kinetic molecular model does fit the experimental results for the effusion of gases.

Diffusion

Diffusion is frequently illustrated by the lecture demonstration represented in Fig. 5.23, in which two cotton plugs soaked in ammonia and hydrochloric acid are simultaneously placed at the ends of a long tube. A white ring of ammonium chloride (NH_4Cl) forms where the NH_3 and HCl molecules meet several minutes later:

$$NH_3(g) + HCl(g) \longrightarrow NH_4Cl(s)$$
$$\text{White solid}$$

As a first approximation we might expect that the distances traveled by the two gases are related to the relative velocities of the gas molecules:

$$\frac{\text{Distance traveled by } NH_3}{\text{Distance traveled by } HCl} = \frac{u_{rms} \text{ for } NH_3}{u_{rms} \text{ for } HCl} = \sqrt{\frac{M_{HCl}}{M_{NH_3}}} = \sqrt{\frac{36.5}{17}} = 1.5$$

Animation: Diffusion of Gases

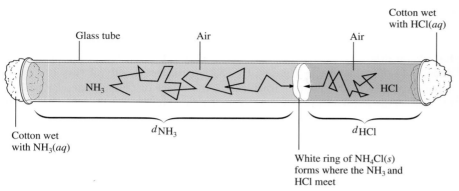

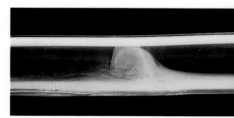

Figure 5.23

(right) When HCl(g) and NH$_3$(g) meet in the tube, a white ring of NH$_4$Cl(s) forms. (above) A demonstration of the relative diffusion rates of NH$_3$ and HCl molecules through air. Two cotton plugs, one dipped in HCl(aq) and one dipped in NH$_3$(aq), are simultaneously inserted into the ends of the tube. Gaseous NH$_3$ and HCl vaporizing from the cotton plugs diffuse toward each other and, where they meet, react to form NH$_4$Cl(s).

However, careful experiments produce an observed ratio of less than 1.5, indicating that a quantitative analysis of diffusion requires a more complex analysis.

The diffusion of the gases through the tube is surprisingly slow in light of the fact that the velocities of HCl and NH$_3$ molecules at 25°C are about 450 and 660 meters per second, respectively. Why does it take several minutes for the NH$_3$ and HCl molecules to meet? The answer is that the tube contains air and thus the NH$_3$ and HCl molecules undergo many collisions with O$_2$ and N$_2$ molecules as they travel through the tube. Because so many collisions occur when gases mix, diffusion is quite complicated to describe theoretically.

5.8 Real Gases

An ideal gas is a hypothetical concept. No gas *exactly* follows the ideal gas law, although many gases come very close at low pressures and/or high temperatures. Thus ideal gas behavior can best be thought of as the behavior *approached by **real gases*** under certain conditions.

We have seen that a very simple model, the kinetic molecular theory, by making some rather drastic assumptions (no interparticle interactions and zero volume for the gas particles), successfully explains ideal behavior. However, it is important that we examine real gas behavior to see how it differs from that predicted by the ideal gas law and to determine what modifications are needed in the kinetic molecular theory to explain the observed behavior. Since a model is an approximation and will inevitably fail, we must be ready to learn from such failures. In fact, we often learn more about nature from the failures of our models than from their successes.

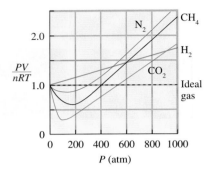

Figure 5.24

Plots of PV/nRT versus P for several gases (200 K). Note the significant deviations from ideal behavior ($PV/nRT = 1$). The behavior is close to ideal only at low pressures (less than 1 atm).

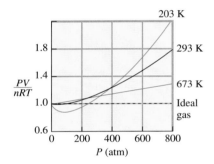

Figure 5.25

Plots of PV/nRT versus P for nitrogen gas at three temperatures. Note that although nonideal behavior is evident in each case, the deviations are smaller at the higher temperatures.

P' is corrected for the finite volume of the particles. The attractive forces have not yet been taken into account.

The attractive forces among molecules will be discussed in Chapter 10.

We will examine the experimentally observed behavior of real gases by measuring the pressure, volume, temperature, and number of moles for a gas and noting how the quantity PV/nRT depends on pressure. Plots of PV/nRT versus P are shown for several gases in Fig. 5.24. For an ideal gas, PV/nRT equals 1 under all conditions, but notice that for real gases, PV/nRT approaches 1 only at very low pressures (typically below 1 atm). To illustrate the effect of temperature, PV/nRT is plotted versus P for nitrogen gas at several temperatures in Fig. 5.25. Note that the behavior of the gas appears to become more nearly ideal as the temperature is increased. The most important conclusion to be drawn from these figures is that a real gas typically exhibits behavior that is closest to ideal behavior at *low pressures* and *high temperatures*.

How can we modify the assumptions of the kinetic molecular theory to fit the behavior of real gases? An equation for real gases was developed in 1873 by Johannes van der Waals (1837–1923), a physics professor at the University of Amsterdam who in 1910 received a Nobel Prize for his work. To follow his analysis, we start with the ideal gas law,

$$P = \frac{nRT}{V}$$

Remember that this equation describes the behavior of a hypothetical gas consisting of volumeless entities that do not interact with each other. In contrast, a real gas consists of atoms or molecules that have finite volumes. Therefore, the volume available to a given particle in a real gas is less than the volume of the container because the gas particles themselves take up some of the space. To account for this discrepancy, van der Waals represented the actual volume as the volume of the container V minus a correction factor for the volume of the molecules nb, where n is the number of moles of gas and b is an empirical constant (one determined by fitting the equation to the experimental results). Thus the volume *actually available* to a given gas molecule is given by the difference $V - nb$.

This modification of the ideal gas equation leads to the equation

$$P' = \frac{nRT}{V - nb}$$

The volume of the gas particles has now been taken into account.

The next step is to allow for the attractions that occur among the particles in a real gas. The effect of these attractions is to make the observed pressure P_{obs} smaller than it would be if the gas particles did not interact:

$$P_{obs} = (P' - \text{correction factor}) = \left(\frac{nRT}{V - nb} - \text{correction factor}\right)$$

This effect can be understood using the following model. When gas particles come close together, attractive forces occur, which cause the particles to hit the wall very slightly less often than they would in the absence of these interactions (see Fig. 5.26).

The size of the correction factor depends on the concentration of gas molecules defined in terms of moles of gas particles per liter (n/V). The higher the concentration, the more likely a pair of gas particles will be close enough to attract each other. For large numbers of particles, the number of interacting *pairs* of particles depends

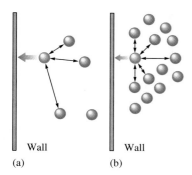

Wall   Wall

(a)   (b)

Figure 5.26

(a) Gas at low concentration—relatively few interactions between particles. The indicated gas particle exerts a pressure on the wall close to that predicted for an ideal gas. (b) Gas at high concentration—many more interactions between particles. The indicated gas particle exerts a much lower pressure on the wall than would be expected in the absence of interactions.

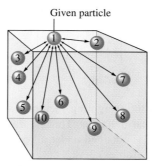

Given particle

Gas sample with ten particles

Figure 5.27

Illustration of pairwise interactions among gas particles. In a sample with 10 particles, each particle has 9 possible partners, to give $10(9)/2 = 45$ distinct pairs. The factor of $\frac{1}{2}$ arises because when particle 1 is the particle of interest we count the ① $\cdots$ ② pair, and when particle ② is the particle of interest we count the ② $\cdots$ ① pair. However, ① $\cdots$ ② and ② $\cdots$ ① are the same pair that we have counted twice. Therefore, we must divide by 2 to get the actual number of pairs.

on the square of the number of particles and thus on the square of the concentration, or $(n/V)^2$. This can be justified as follows: In a gas sample containing N particles, there are $N-1$ partners available for each particle, as shown in Fig. 5.27. Since the $1 \cdots 2$ pair is the same as the $2 \cdots 1$ pair, this analysis counts each pair twice. Thus, for N particles, there are $N(N-1)/2$ pairs. If N is a very large number, $N-1$ approximately equals N, giving $N^2/2$ possible pairs. Thus the pressure, corrected for the attractions of the particles, has the form

$$P_{\text{obs}} = P' - a\left(\frac{n}{V}\right)^2$$

where a is a proportionality constant (which includes the factor of $\frac{1}{2}$ from $N^2/2$). The value of a for a given real gas can be determined from observing the actual behavior of that gas. Inserting the corrections for both the volume of the particles and the attractions of the particles gives the equation

$$P_{\text{obs}} = \frac{nRT}{V - nb} - a\left(\frac{n}{V}\right)^2$$

Observed pressure   Volume of the container   Volume correction   Pressure correction

We have now corrected for both the finite volume and the attractive forces of the particles.

P_{obs} is usually called just P.

This equation can be rearranged to give the **van der Waals equation:**

$$\underbrace{\left[P_{obs} + a\left(\frac{n}{V}\right)^2\right]}_{\substack{\text{Corrected pressure} \\ P_{ideal}}} \times \underbrace{(V - nb)}_{\substack{\text{Corrected volume} \\ V_{ideal}}} = nRT$$

The values of the weighting factors a and b are determined for a given gas by fitting experimental behavior. That is, a and b are varied until the best fit of the observed pressure is obtained under all conditions. The values of a and b for various gases are given in Table 5.3.

Experimental studies indicate that the changes van der Waals made in the basic assumptions of the kinetic molecular theory correct the major flaws in the model. First, consider the effects of volume. For a gas at low pressure (large volume), the volume of the container is very large compared with the volumes of the gas particles. That is, in this case the volume available to the gas is essentially equal to the volume of the container, and the gas behaves ideally. On the other hand, for a gas at high pressure (small container volume), the volume of the particles becomes significant so that the volume available to the gas is significantly less than the container volume. These cases are illustrated in Fig. 5.28. Note from Table 5.3 that the volume correction constant b generally increases with the size of the gas molecule, which gives further support to these arguments.

The fact that a real gas tends to behave more ideally at high temperatures also can be explained in terms of the van der Waals model. At high temperatures the particles are moving so rapidly that the effects of interparticle interactions are not very important.

The corrections to the kinetic molecular theory that van der Waals found necessary to explain real gas behavior make physical sense, which makes us confident that we understand the fundamentals of gas behavior at the particle level. This is significant because so much important chemistry takes place in the gas phase. In fact, the mixture of gases called the atmosphere is vital to our existence. In the following section we consider some of the important reactions that occur in the atmosphere.

Table 5.3 Values of the van der Waals Constants for Some Common Gases

Gas	$a\left(\dfrac{atm \cdot L^2}{mol^2}\right)$	$b\left(\dfrac{L}{mol}\right)$
He	0.0341	0.0237
Ne	0.211	0.0171
Ar	1.35	0.0322
Kr	2.32	0.0398
Xe	4.19	0.0511
H_2	0.244	0.0266
N_2	1.39	0.0391
O_2	1.36	0.0318
Cl_2	6.49	0.0562
CO_2	3.59	0.0427
CH_4	2.25	0.0428
NH_3	4.17	0.0371
H_2O	5.46	0.0305

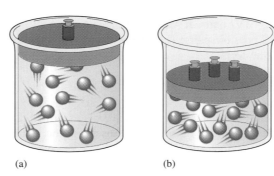

(a)　　　　　(b)

Figure 5.28

The volume taken up by the gas particles themselves is less important at (a) large container volume (low pressure) than at (b) small container volume (high pressure).

5.9 Chemistry in the Atmosphere

The most important gases to us are those in the **atmosphere** that surrounds the earth's surface. The principal components are N_2 and O_2, but many other important gases, such as H_2O and CO_2, are also present. The average composition of the earth's atmosphere near sea level, with the water vapor removed, is shown in Table 5.4. Because of gravitational effects, the composition of the earth's atmosphere is not constant; heavier molecules tend to be near the earth's surface, and light molecules tend to migrate to higher altitudes, with some eventually escaping into space. The atmosphere is a highly complex and dynamic system, but for convenience we divide it into several layers based on the way the temperature changes with altitude. (The lowest layer, called the *troposphere,* is shown in Fig. 5.29.) Note that in contrast to the complex temperature profile of the atmosphere, the pressure decreases in a regular way with increasing altitude.

The chemistry occurring in the higher levels of the atmosphere is mostly determined by the effects of high-energy radiation and particles from the sun and other sources in space. In fact, the upper atmosphere serves as an important shield to prevent this high-energy radiation from reaching the earth, where it would damage the relatively fragile molecules sustaining life. In particular, the ozone in the upper atmosphere helps prevent high-energy ultraviolet radiation from penetrating to the earth. Intensive research is in progress to determine the natural factors that control the ozone concentration and how it is affected by chemicals released into the atmosphere.

The chemistry occurring in the troposphere, the layer of atmosphere closest to the earth's surface, is strongly influenced by human activities. Millions of tons of gases and particulates are released into the troposphere by our highly industrial civilization. Actually, it is amazing that the atmosphere can absorb so much material with relatively small permanent changes (so far).

Significant changes, however, are occurring. Severe **air pollution** is found around many large cities, and it is probable that long-range changes in our planet's weather are taking place. We will discuss some of the long-range effects of pollution in Chapter 6. In this section we will deal with short-term, localized effects of pollution.

The two main sources of pollution are transportation and the production of electricity. The combustion of petroleum in vehicles produces CO, CO_2, NO, and NO_2, along with unburned molecules from petroleum. When this mixture is trapped close to the ground in stagnant air, reactions occur producing chemicals that are potentially irritating and harmful to living systems.

The complex chemistry of polluted air appears to center around the nitrogen oxides (NO_x). At the high temperatures found in the gasoline and diesel engines of cars and trucks, N_2 and O_2 react to form a small quantity of NO that is emitted into the air with the exhaust gases (see Fig. 5.30). This NO is immediately oxidized in air to NO_2, which, in turn, absorbs energy from sunlight and breaks up into nitric oxide and free oxygen atoms:

$$NO_2(g) \xrightarrow{\text{Radiant energy}} NO(g) + O(g)$$

Oxygen atoms are very reactive and can combine with O_2 to form *ozone:*

$$O(g) + O_2(g) \longrightarrow O_3(g)$$

Table 5.4 Atmospheric Composition Near Sea Level (Dry Air)*

Component	Mole Fraction
N_2	0.78084
O_2	0.20948
Ar	0.00934
CO_2	0.000345
Ne	0.00001818
He	0.00000524
CH_4	0.00000168
Kr	0.00000114
H_2	0.0000005
NO	0.0000005
Xe	0.000000087

*The atmosphere contains various amounts of water vapor depending on conditions.

Molecular Models: N_2, O_2, H_2O, CO_2, NO, NO_2, HNO_3

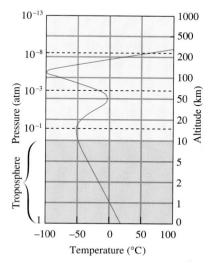

Figure 5.29

The variation of temperature and pressure with altitude. Note that the pressure steadily decreases with altitude, but the temperature increases and decreases.

Ozone is also very reactive and can react directly with other pollutants, or the ozone can absorb light and break up to form an energetically excited O_2 molecule (O_2^*) and an energetically excited oxygen atom (O^*). The latter species readily reacts with a water molecule to form two hydroxyl radicals (OH):

$$O^* + H_2O \longrightarrow 2OH$$

The hydroxyl radical is a very reactive oxidizing agent. For example, OH can react with NO_2 to form nitric acid:

$$OH + NO_2 \longrightarrow HNO_3$$

The OH radical also can react with the unburned hydrocarbons in the polluted air to produce chemicals that cause the eyes to water and burn and are harmful to the respiratory system.

The end product of this whole process is often referred to as **photochemical smog,** so called because light is required to initiate some of the reactions. The production of photochemical smog can be understood more clearly by examining as a group the reactions discussed above:

$$NO_2(g) \longrightarrow NO(g) + O(g)$$
$$O(g) + O_2(g) \longrightarrow O_3(g)$$
$$\underline{NO(g) + \tfrac{1}{2}O_2(g) \longrightarrow NO_2(g)}$$

Net reaction: $\qquad \tfrac{3}{2}O_2(g) \longrightarrow O_3(g)$

Note that the NO_2 molecules assist in the formation of ozone without being themselves used up. The ozone formed then leads to the formation of OH and other pollutants.

We can observe this process by analyzing polluted air at various times during a day (see Fig. 5.30). As people drive to work between 6 and 8 a.m., the amounts of NO, NO_2, and unburned molecules from petroleum increase. Later, as the decomposition of NO_2 occurs, the concentration of ozone and other pollutants builds up. Current efforts to combat the formation of photochemical smog are focused on cutting down the amounts of molecules from unburned fuel in automobile exhaust and designing engines that produce less nitric oxide.

The other major source of pollution results from burning coal to produce electricity. Much of the coal found in the Midwest contains significant quantities of sulfur, which, when burned, produces sulfur dioxide:

$$S \text{ (in coal)} + O_2(g) \longrightarrow SO_2(g)$$

A further oxidation reaction occurs when sulfur dioxide is changed to sulfur trioxide in the air*:

$$2SO_2(g) + O_2(g) \longrightarrow 2SO_3(g)$$

The production of sulfur trioxide is significant because it can combine with droplets of water in the air to form sulfuric acid:

$$SO_3(g) + H_2O(l) \longrightarrow H_2SO_4(aq)$$

Sulfuric acid is very corrosive to both living things and building materials. Another result of this type of pollution is **acid rain.** In many parts of the northeastern

The OH radical has no charge [it has one fewer electron than the hydroxide ion (OH^-)].

Although represented here as O_2, the actual oxidant for NO is OH or an organic peroxide such as CH_3COO, formed by oxidation of organic pollutants.

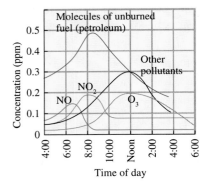

Figure 5.30

Concentration (in molecules per million molecules of "air") for some smog components versus time of day. (Reprinted by permission from P. A. Leighton, "Photochemistry of Air Pollution," in *Physical Chemistry: A Series of Monographs,* ed. Eric Hutchinson and P. Van Rysselberghe, Vol. IX, New York: Academic Press, 1961.)

---

*This reaction is very slow unless solid particles are present. See Chapter 12 for a discussion.

CHEMICAL IMPACT

Acid Rain: A Growing Problem

RAINWATER, EVEN IN pristine wilderness areas, is slightly acidic because some of the carbon dioxide present in the atmosphere dissolves in the raindrops to produce H^+ ions by the following reaction:

$$H_2O(l) + CO_2(g)$$
$$\longrightarrow H^+(aq) + HCO_3^-(aq)$$

This process produces only very small concentrations of H^+ ions in the rainwater. However, gases such as NO_2 and SO_2, which are by-products of energy use, can produce significantly higher H^+ concentrations. Nitrogen dioxide reacts with water to give a mixture of nitrous acid and nitric acid:

$$2NO_2(g) + H_2O(l)$$
$$\longrightarrow HNO_2(aq) + HNO_3(aq)$$

Sulfur dioxide is oxidized to sulfur trioxide, which then reacts with water to form sulfuric acid:

$$2SO_2(g) + O_2(g) \longrightarrow 2SO_3(g)$$
$$SO_3(g) + H_2O(l) \longrightarrow H_2SO_4(aq)$$

The damage caused by the acid formed in polluted air is a growing worldwide problem. Lakes are dying in Norway, the forests are under stress in Germany, and buildings and statues are deteriorating all over the world.

The Field Museum in Chicago contains more white Georgia marble than any other structure in the world. But nearly 70 years of exposure to the elements has taken such a toll on it that the building has recently undergone a multimillion-dollar renovation to replace the damaged marble with freshly quarried material.

What is the chemistry of the deterioration of marble by sulfuric acid? Marble is produced by geologic processes at high temperatures and pressures from limestone, a sedimentary rock formed by slow deposition of calcium carbonate from the shells of marine organisms. Lime-

The damaging effects of acid rain can be seen by comparing these photos of a decorative statue on the Field Museum in Chicago. The first photo was taken about 1920, the second in 1990.

stone and marble are chemically identical ($CaCO_3$) but differ in physical properties; limestone is composed of smaller particles of calcium carbonate and is thus more porous and more workable. Although both limestone and marble are used for buildings, marble can be polished to a higher sheen and is often preferred for decorative purposes.

Both marble and limestone react with sulfuric acid to form calcium sulfate. The process can be represented most simply as

$$CaCO_3(s) + H_2SO_4(aq)$$
$$\longrightarrow Ca^{2+}(aq) + SO_4^{2-}(aq)$$
$$+ H_2O(l) + CO_2(g)$$

In this equation the calcium sulfate is represented by separate hydrated ions because calcium sulfate is quite water soluble and dissolves in rainwater. Thus, in areas bathed by rainwater, the marble slowly dissolves away.

In areas of the building protected from the rain, the calcium sulfate can form the mineral gypsum ($CaSO_4 \cdot 2H_2O$). The $\cdot 2H_2O$ in the formula of gypsum indicates the presence of two water molecules (called *waters of hydration*) for each $CaSO_4$ formula unit in the solid. The smooth surface of the marble is thus replaced by a thin layer of gypsum, a more porous material that binds soot and dust.

What can be done to protect limestone and marble structures from this kind of damage? Of course, one approach is to lower sulfur dioxide emissions from power plants (see Fig. 5.32). In addition, scientists are experimenting with coatings to protect marble from the acidic atmosphere. However, a coating can do more harm than good unless it "breathes." If moisture trapped beneath the coating freezes, the expanding ice can fracture the marble. Needless to say, it is difficult to find a coating that will allow water, but not acid, to pass—but the search continues.

Figure 5.31

An environmental officer in Wales tests the pH of water.

Molecular Models: SO_2, SO_3, H_2SO_4

United States and southeastern Canada, acid rain has caused some freshwater lakes to become too acidic to support any life (Fig. 5.31).

The problem of sulfur dioxide pollution is made more complicated by the energy crisis. As petroleum supplies dwindle and the price increases, our dependence on coal will probably grow. As supplies of low-sulfur coal are used up, high-sulfur coal will be utilized. One way to use high-sulfur coal without further harming the air quality is to remove the sulfur dioxide from the exhaust gas by means of a system called a *scrubber* before it is emitted from the power plant stack. A common method of scrubbing is to blow powdered limestone ($CaCO_3$) into the combustion chamber, where it is decomposed to lime and carbon dioxide:

$$CaCO_3(s) \longrightarrow CaO(s) + CO_2(g)$$

The lime then combines with the sulfur dioxide to form calcium sulfite:

$$CaO(s) + SO_2(g) \longrightarrow CaSO_3(s)$$

To remove the calcium sulfite and any remaining unreacted sulfur dioxide, an aqueous suspension of lime is injected into the exhaust gases to produce a *slurry* (a thick suspension), as shown in Fig. 5.32.

Unfortunately, there are many problems associated with scrubbing. The systems are complicated and expensive and consume a great deal of energy. The large quantities of calcium sulfite produced in the process present a disposal problem. With a typical scrubber, approximately 1 ton of calcium sulfite per year is produced per person served by the power plant. Since no use has yet been found for this calcium sulfite, it is usually buried in a landfill. As a result of these difficulties, air pollution by sulfur dioxide continues to be a major problem, one that is expensive in terms of damage to the environment and human health as well as in monetary terms.

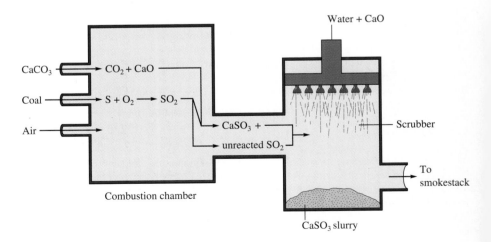

Figure 5.32

A schematic diagram of the process for scrubbing sulfur dioxide from stack gases in power plants.

For Review

Summary

Of the three states of matter, the gaseous state is the most easily understood experimentally and theoretically. A gas can be described quantitatively by specifying four properties: volume, pressure, temperature, and the amount of gas present.

Atmospheric pressure is measured with a barometer, and in the laboratory, gas pressure is usually measured with a manometer. Both devices employ columns filled with mercury, and the most commonly used units of pressure are based on the height of such a column in millimeters: 1 mm Hg equals 1 torr; 1 standard atmosphere equals 760 torr. In the SI system, the unit of pressure is the pascal (1 N/m^2).

Early experiments on the behavior of gases dealt with the relationship among the four characteristic properties. Boyle's law states that the volume of a given amount of a gas is inversely proportional to its pressure (at constant temperature). Charles's law states that for a given amount of gas at a constant pressure, the volume is directly proportional to the temperature in Kelvins. At a temperature of $-273.2°C$ (0 K), the volume of a gas extrapolates to zero, and this temperature is called absolute zero. Avogadro's law states that equal volumes of gases at the same temperature and pressure contain the same number of particles.

These three laws can be combined into the ideal gas law:

$$PV = nRT$$

where R is called the universal gas constant (0.08206 L · atm/K · mol). This equation allows calculation of any one of the characteristic properties, given the other three. The ideal gas law describes the limiting behavior approached by real gases at low pressures and high temperatures.

The molar volume (22.42 liters) is the volume of an ideal gas at STP (standard temperature and pressure) or 0°C and 1 atmosphere.

The pressure of a gaseous mixture is described by Dalton's law of partial pressures, which states that the total pressure of a mixture of gases in a container is the sum of the pressures that each gas would exert if it were alone (its partial pressure), that is,

$$P_{TOTAL} = P_1 + P_2 + P_3 + \cdots$$

The mole fraction of a given component in a mixture of gases can be calculated from the ratio of the partial pressure of that component to the total gas pressure.

The kinetic molecular theory of gases is a theoretical model constructed to account for ideal gas behavior. This model assumes that the volume of the gas particles is zero, that there are no interactions between particles, and that the particles are in constant motion, colliding with the container walls to produce pressure. In addition, this model shows that the average kinetic energy of the gas particles is directly proportional to the Kelvin temperature of the gas.

The root mean square velocity for the particles in a gas can be calculated from the temperature and the molar mass of the gas. Within any gas sample there is a range of velocities, since the gas particles collide and exchange kinetic energy. An increase in temperature increases the average velocity of the gas particles. The relative rates of diffusion, the mixing of gases, and effusion, the passage of a gas

Key Terms

Section 5.1
barometer
manometer
mm Hg
torr
standard atmosphere
pascal

Section 5.2
Boyle's law
ideal gas
Charles's law
absolute zero
Avogadro's law

Section 5.3
universal gas constant
ideal gas law

Section 5.4
molar volume
standard temperature and
  pressure (STP)

Section 5.5
Dalton's law of partial pressures
partial pressure
mole fraction

Section 5.6
kinetic molecular theory (KMT)
root mean square velocity
joule

Section 5.7
diffusion
effusion
Graham's law of effusion

Section 5.8
real gas
van der Waals equation

Section 5.9
atmosphere
air pollution
photochemical smog
acid rain

through a small orifice into an empty chamber, are inversely proportional to the square roots of the atomic or molar masses of the gases in question.

Real gases behave ideally only at high temperatures and low pressures. The van der Waals equation is a modification of the ideal gas equation that takes into consideration that real gas particles take up volume and interact with each other.

In-Class Discussion Questions

These questions are designed to be considered by groups of students in class. Often these questions work well for introducing a particular topic in class.

1. Consider the following apparatus: a test tube covered with a nonpermeable elastic membrane inside a container that is closed with a cork. A syringe goes through the cork.

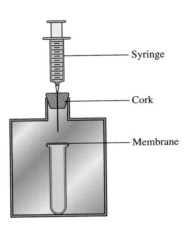

— Syringe

— Cork

— Membrane

   a. As you push down on the syringe, how does the membrane covering the test tube change?
   b. You stop pushing the syringe but continue to hold it down. In a few seconds, what happens to the membrane?

2. Figure 5.2 shows a picture of a barometer. Which of the following statements is the best explanation of how this barometer works?
   a. Air pressure outside the tube causes the mercury to move in the tube until the air pressure inside and outside the tube is equal.
   b. Air pressure inside the tube causes the mercury to move in the tube until the air pressure inside and outside the tube is equal.
   c. Air pressure outside the tube counterbalances the weight of the mercury in the tube.
   d. Capillary action of the mercury causes the mercury to go up the tube.

   e. The vacuum that is formed at the top of the tube holds up the mercury.
   Justify your choice, and for the choices you did not pick, explain what is wrong with them. Pictures help!

3. The barometer below shows the level of mercury at a given atmospheric pressure. Fill all the other barometers with mercury for that same atmospheric pressure. Explain your answer.

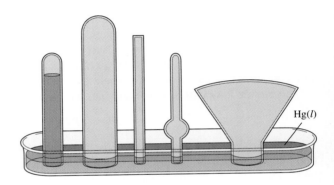

Hg(*l*)

4. As you increase the temperature of a gas in a sealed, rigid container, what happens to the density of the gas? Would the results be the same if you did the same experiment in a container with a piston at constant pressure? (See Figure 5.16.)

5. A diagram in a chemistry book shows a magnified view of a flask of air as follows:

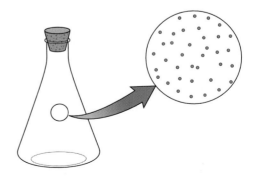

What do you suppose is between the dots (the dots represent air molecules)?

a. air
b. dust
c. pollutants
d. oxygen
e. nothing

6. If you put a drinking straw in water, place your finger over the opening, and lift the straw out of the water, some water stays in the straw. Explain.

7. A chemistry student relates the following story: I noticed my tires were a bit low and went to the gas station. As I was filling the tires, I thought about the kinetic molecular theory (KMT). I noticed the tires because the volume was low, and I realized that I was increasing both the pressure and volume of the tires. "Hmmm," I thought, "that goes against what I learned in chemistry, where I was told pressure and volume are inversely proportional." What is the fault in the logic of the chemistry student in this situation? Explain *why* we think pressure and volume to be inversely related (draw pictures and use the KMT).

8. Chemicals *X* and *Y* (both gases) react to form the gas *XY*, but it takes a bit of time for the reaction to occur. Both *X* and *Y* are placed in a container with a piston (free to move), and you note the volume. As the reaction occurs, what happens to the volume of the container? (See Fig. 5.17.)

9. Which statement best explains why a hot-air balloon rises when the air in the balloon is heated?
   a. According to Charles's law, the temperature of a gas is directly related to its volume. Thus the volume of the balloon increases, making the density smaller. This lifts the balloon.
   b. Hot air rises inside the balloon, and this lifts the balloon.
   c. The temperature of a gas is directly related to its pressure. The pressure therefore increases, and this lifts the balloon.
   d. Some of the gas escapes from the bottom of the balloon, thus decreasing the mass of gas in the balloon. This decreases the density of the gas in the balloon, which lifts the balloon.
   e. Temperature is related to the root mean square velocity of the gas molecules. Thus the molecules are moving faster, hitting the balloon more, and thus lifting the balloon.
   Justify your choice, and for the choices you did not pick, explain what is wrong with them.

10. Draw a highly magnified view of a sealed, rigid container filled with a gas. Then draw what it would look like if you cooled the gas significantly but kept the temperature above the boiling point of the substance in the container. Also draw what it would look like if you heated the gas significantly. Finally, draw what each situation would look like if you evacuated enough of the gas to decrease the pressure by a factor of 2.

11. If you release a helium balloon, it soars upward and eventually pops. Explain this behavior.

12. If you have any two gases in different containers that are the same size at the same pressure and same temperature, what is true about the moles of each gas? Why is this true?

13. Explain the following seeming contradiction: You have two gases, *A* and *B*, in two separate containers of equal volume and at equal pressure and temperature. Therefore, you must have the same number of moles of each gas. Because the two temperatures are equal, the average kinetic energies of the two samples are equal. Therefore, since the energy given such a system will be converted to translational motion (that is, move the molecules), the root mean square velocities of the two are equal, and thus the particles in each sample move, on average, with the same relative speed. Since *A* and *B* are different gases, they each must have a different molar mass. If *A* has higher molar mass than *B*, the particles of *A* must be hitting the sides of the container with more force. Thus the pressure in the container of gas *A* must be higher than that in the container with gas *B*. However, one of our initial assumptions was that the pressures were equal.

14. You have a balloon covering the mouth of a flask filled with air at 1 atm. You apply heat to the bottom of the flask until the volume of the balloon is equal to that of the flask.
   a. Which has more air in it, the balloon or the flask? Or do both have the same amount? Explain.
   b. In which is the pressure greater, the balloon or the flask? Or is the pressure the same? Explain.

15. How does Dalton's law of partial pressures help us with our model of ideal gases? That is, what postulates of the kinetic molecular theory does it support?

A blue question or exercise number indicates that the answer to that question or exercise appears at the back of the book and a solution appears in the *Solutions Guide*.

Questions

16. Rationalize the following observations.
   a. Aerosol cans will explode if heated.
   b. You can drink through a soda straw.
   c. A thin-walled can will collapse when the air inside is removed by a vacuum pump.
   d. Manufacturers produce different types of tennis balls for high and low elevations.

17. Show how Boyle's law and Charles's law are special cases of the ideal gas law.

18. Using the postulates of the kinetic molecular theory, give molecular interpretations of Boyle's law and Charles's law.

19. Figures 5.6 and 5.7 plot *PV* versus *P* for several different gases. Which gas in these two plots behaves more ideally? Explain.

20. At room temperature, water is a liquid with a molar volume of 18 mL. At 105°C and 1 atm pressure, water is a gas and has a molar volume of over 30 L. Explain the large difference in molar volumes.

21. Briefly describe two methods one might use to find the molar mass of a newly synthesized gas for which a molecular formula was not known.

22. Consider a sample of gas molecules for the following question.
   a. How is the average kinetic energy of the gas molecules related to temperature?
   b. How is the average velocity of the gas molecules related to temperature?
   c. How is the average velocity of the gas molecules related to the molar mass of the gas at constant temperature?

Exercises

In this section similar exercises are paired.

Pressure

23. Freon-12 (CF_2Cl_2) is commonly used as the refrigerant in central home air conditioners. The system is initially charged to a pressure of 4.8 atm. Express this pressure in each of the following units (1 atm = 14.7 psi).
   a. mm Hg   **c.** Pa
   b. torr   **d.** psi

24. A gauge on a compressed gas cylinder reads 2200 psi (pounds per square inch; 1 atm = 14.7 psi). Express this pressure in each of the following units.
   a. standard atmospheres
   b. megapascals (MPa)
   c. torr

25. A sealed-tube manometer (as shown below) can be used to measure pressures below atmospheric pressure. The tube above the mercury is evacuated. When there is a vacuum in the flask, the mercury levels in both arms of the U-tube are equal. If a gaseous sample is introduced into the flask, the mercury levels are different. The difference h is a measure of the pressure of the gas inside the flask. If h is equal to 6.5 cm, calculate the pressure in the flask in torr, pascals, and atmospheres.

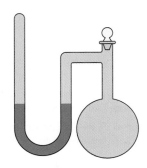
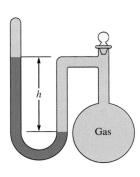

26. If the sealed-tube manometer in Exercise 25 had a height difference of 20.0 inches between the mercury levels, what is the pressure in the flask in torr and atmospheres?

27. A diagram for an open-tube manometer is shown below.

Atmosphere

If the flask is open to the atmosphere, the mercury levels are equal. For each of the following situations where a gas is contained in the flask, calculate the pressure in the flask in torr, atmospheres, and pascals.

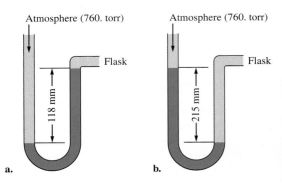

Atmosphere (760. torr)   Atmosphere (760. torr)

Flask   Flask

118 mm   215 mm

a.   **b.**

   c. Calculate the pressures in the flask in parts a and b (in torr) if the atmospheric pressure is 635 torr.

28. a. If the open-tube manometer in Exercise 27 contains a nonvolatile silicone oil (density = 1.30 g/cm³) instead of mercury (density = 13.6 g/cm³), what are the pressures in the flask as shown in parts a and b in torr, atmospheres, and pascals?

   b. What advantage would there be in using a less dense fluid than mercury in a manometer used to measure relatively small differences in pressure?

Gas Laws

29. An aerosol can contains 400. mL of compressed gas at 5.20 atm pressure. When all the gas is sprayed into a large plastic bag, the bag inflates to a volume of 2.14 L.

What is the pressure of gas inside the plastic bag? Assume temperature is constant.

30. A balloon is filled to a volume of 7.00×10^2 mL at a temperature of 20.0°C. The balloon is then cooled at constant pressure to a temperature of 1.00×10^2 K. What is the final volume of the balloon?

31. If 0.500 mol of nitrogen gas occupies a volume of 11.2 L at 0°C, what volume will 2.00 mol of nitrogen gas occupy at the same temperature and pressure?

32. Consider the following chemical equation.

$$2NO_2(g) \longrightarrow N_2O_4(g)$$

If 25.0 mL of NO_2 gas is completely converted to N_2O_4 gas under the same conditions, what volume will the N_2O_4 occupy?

33. Complete the following table for an ideal gas.

	P (atm)	V (L)	n (mol)	T
a.	5.00		2.00	155°C
b.	0.300	2.00		155 K
c.	4.47	25.0	2.01	
d.		2.25	10.5	75°C

34. Complete the following table for an ideal gas.

	P (atm)	V (L)	n (mol)	T
a.	7.74×10^3 Pa	12.2 mL		25°C
b.		43.0 mL	0.421 mol	223 K
c.	455 torr		4.4×10^{-2} mol	331°C
d.	745 mm Hg	11.2 L	0.401 mol	

35. The steel reaction vessel of a bomb calorimeter, which has a volume of 75.0 mL, is charged with oxygen gas to a pressure of 145 atm at 22°C. Calculate the moles of oxygen in the reaction vessel.

36. A 5.0-L flask contains 0.60 g O_2 at a temperature of 22°C. What is the pressure (in atm) inside the flask?

37. A 2.50-L container is filled with 175 g argon.
   a. If the pressure is 10.0 atm, what is the temperature?
   b. If the temperature is 225 K, what is the pressure?

38. What volume is occupied by 2.0 g of He at 25°C and a pressure of 775 mm Hg?

39. A particular balloon is designed by its manufacturer to be inflated to a volume of no more than 2.5 L. If the balloon is filled with 2.0 L of helium at sea level, is released, and

rises to an altitude at which the atmospheric pressure is only 500. mm Hg, will the balloon burst? (Assume temperature is constant.)

40. A balloon has a volume of 175 cm³ at 19°C. At what temperature will the volume of the balloon have increased by 25.0% (at constant pressure)?

41. A compressed gas cylinder, at 13.7 MPa and 23°C, is in a room where a fire raises the temperature to 450.°C. What is the new pressure in the cylinder?

42. A container is filled with an ideal gas to a pressure of 40.0 atm at 0°C.
   a. What will be the pressure in the container if it is heated to 45°C?
   b. At what temperature would the pressure be 1.50×10^2 atm?
   c. At what temperature would the pressure be 25.0 atm?

43. An ideal gas is contained in a cylinder with a volume of 5.0×10^2 mL at a temperature of 30.°C and a pressure of 710. torr. The gas is then compressed to a volume of 25 mL, and the temperature is raised to 820.°C. What is the new pressure of the gas?

44. A compressed gas cylinder contains 1.00×10^3 g of argon gas. The pressure inside the cylinder is 2050. psi (pounds per square inch) at a temperature of 18°C. How much gas remains in the cylinder if the pressure is decreased to 650. psi at a temperature of 26°C?

45. A sealed balloon is filled with 1.00 L of helium at 23°C and 1.00 atm. The balloon rises to a point in the atmosphere where the pressure is 220. torr and the temperature is −31°C. What is the change in volume of the balloon as it ascends from 1.00 atm to a pressure of 220. torr?

46. A hot-air balloon is filled with air to a volume of 4.00×10^3 m³ at 745 torr and 21°C. The air in the balloon is then heated to 62°C, causing the balloon to expand to a volume of 4.20×10^3 m³. What is the ratio of the number of moles of air in the heated balloon to the original number of moles of air in the balloon? (*Hint:* Openings in the balloon allow air to flow in and out. Thus the pressure in the balloon is always the same as that of the atmosphere.)

Gas Density, Molar Mass, and Reaction Stoichiometry

47. What mass of helium is required to fill a 1.5-L balloon at STP?

48. A student adds 4.00 g of dry ice (solid CO_2) to an empty balloon. What will be the volume of the balloon at STP after all the dry ice sublimes (converts to gaseous CO_2)?

49. Calculate the volume of O_2, at STP, required for the complete combustion of 125 g octane (C_8H_{18}) to CO_2 and H_2O.

50. The method used by Joseph Priestley to obtain oxygen made use of the thermal decomposition of mercuric oxide:

$$2HgO(s) \xrightarrow{\text{Heat}} 2Hg(l) + O_2(g)$$

What volume of oxygen gas, measured at 30.°C and 725 torr, can be produced from the complete decomposition of 4.10 g mercuric oxide?

51. In 1897 the Swedish explorer Andreé tried to reach the North Pole in a balloon. The balloon was filled with hydrogen gas. The hydrogen gas was prepared from iron splints and diluted sulfuric acid. The reaction is

$$Fe(s) + H_2SO_4(aq) \longrightarrow FeSO_4(aq) + H_2(g)$$

The volume of the balloon was 4800 m³ and the loss of hydrogen gas during filling was estimated at 20.%. What mass of iron splints and 98% (by mass) H_2SO_4 were needed to ensure the complete filling of the balloon? Assume a temperature at 0°C, a pressure of 1.0 atm during filling, and 100% yield.

52. Air bags are activated when a severe impact causes a steel ball to compress a spring and electrically ignite a detonator cap. This causes sodium azide (NaN_3) to decompose explosively according to the following reaction:

$$2NaN_3(s) \longrightarrow 2Na(s) + 3N_2(g)$$

What mass of $NaN_3(s)$ must be reacted in order to inflate an air bag to 70.0 L at STP?

53. Consider the reaction between 50.0 mL of liquid methyl alcohol, CH_3OH (density = 0.850 g/mL), and 22.8 L of O_2 at 27°C and a pressure of 2.00 atm. The products of the reaction are $CO_2(g)$ and $H_2O(g)$. Calculate the number of moles of H_2O formed if the reaction goes to completion.

54. Urea (H_2NCONH_2) is used extensively as a nitrogen source in fertilizers. It is produced commercially from the reaction of ammonia and carbon dioxide:

$$2NH_3(g) + CO_2(g) \xrightarrow[\text{Pressure}]{\text{Heat}} H_2NCONH_2(s) + H_2O(g)$$

Ammonia gas at 223°C and 90. atm flows into a reactor at a rate of 500. L/min. Carbon dioxide at 223°C and 45 atm flows into the reactor at a rate of 600. L/min. What mass of urea is produced per minute by this reaction assuming 100% yield?

55. Hydrogen cyanide is prepared commercially by the reaction of methane, $CH_4(g)$, ammonia, $NH_3(g)$, and oxygen, $O_2(g)$, at high temperature. The other product is gaseous water.
   a. Write a chemical equation for the reaction.
   b. What volume of $HCN(g)$ can be obtained from 20.0 L $CH_4(g)$, 20.0 L $NH_3(g)$, and 20.0 L $O_2(g)$? The volumes of all gases are measured at the same temperature and pressure.

56. Methanol, CH_3OH, can be produced by the following reaction:

$$CO(g) + 2H_2(g) \longrightarrow CH_3OH(g)$$

Hydrogen at STP flows into a reactor at a rate of 16.0 L/min. Carbon monoxide at STP flows into the reactor at a rate of 25.0 L/min. If 5.30 g of methanol is produced per minute, what is the percent yield of the reaction?

57. A gas consisting of only carbon and hydrogen has an empirical formula of CH_2. The gas has a density of 1.65 g/L at 27°C and 734 torr. Determine the molar mass and molecular formula of the gas.

58. A compound has the empirical formula CHCl. A 256-mL flask, at 373 K and 750. torr, contains 0.800 g of the gaseous compound. Give the molecular formula.

59. Silicon tetrachloride ($SiCl_4$) and trichlorosilane ($SiHCl_3$) are both starting materials for the production of electronics-grade silicon. Calculate the densities of pure $SiCl_4$ and pure $SiHCl_3$ vapor at 85°C and 758 torr.

60. Calculate the density of ammonia gas at 27°C and 635 torr.

Partial Pressure

61. A piece of solid carbon dioxide, with a mass of 7.8 g, is placed in a 4.0-L otherwise empty container at 27°C. What is the pressure in the container after all the carbon dioxide vaporizes? If 7.8 g solid carbon dioxide were placed in the same container but it already contained air at 740 torr, what would be the partial pressure of carbon dioxide and the total pressure in the container after the carbon dioxide vaporizes?

62. A mixture of 1.00 g H_2 and 1.00 g He is placed in a 1.00-L container at 27°C. Calculate the partial pressure of each gas and the total pressure.

63. Consider the flasks diagramed below. What are the final partial pressures of H_2 and N_2 after the stopcock between the two flasks is opened? (Assume the final volume is 3.00 L.) What is the total pressure (in torr)?

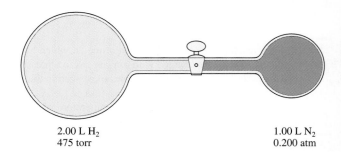

2.00 L H_2
475 torr

1.00 L N_2
0.200 atm

64. If the initial pressures of the H_2 and N_2 in the flasks in Exercise 63 were 360. torr and 240. torr, respectively, what would be the final pressure after the stopcock is opened?

65. The partial pressure of $CH_4(g)$ is 0.175 atm and that of $O_2(g)$ is 0.250 atm in a mixture of the two gases.

a. What is the mole fraction of each gas in the mixture?

b. If the mixture occupies a volume of 10.5 L at 65°C, calculate the total number of moles of gas in the mixture.

c. Calculate the number of grams of each gas in the mixture.

66. At 0°C a 1.0-L flask contains 5.0×10^{-2} mol N_2, 1.5×10^2 mg O_2, and 5.0×10^{21} molecules of NH_3. What is the partial pressure of each gas, and what is the total pressure in the flask?

67. A sample of nitrogen gas was collected over water at 20.°C and a total pressure of 1.00 atm. A total volume of 2.50×10^2 mL was collected. What mass of nitrogen was collected? (At 20.°C the vapor pressure of water is 17.5 torr.)

68. Helium is collected over water at 25°C and 1.00 atm total pressure. What total volume of gas must be collected to obtain 0.586 g of helium? (At 25°C the vapor pressure of water is 23.8 torr.)

69. At elevated temperatures, sodium chlorate decomposes to produce sodium chloride and oxygen gas. A 0.8765-g sample of impure sodium chlorate was heated until the production of oxygen gas ceased. The oxygen gas collected over water occupied 57.2 mL at a temperature of 22°C and a pressure of 734 torr. Calculate the mass percent of $NaClO_3$ in the original sample. (At 22°C the vapor pressure of water is 19.8 torr.)

70. The oxides of Group 2A metals (symbolized by M here) react with carbon dioxide according to the following reaction:

$$MO(s) + CO_2(g) \longrightarrow MCO_3(s)$$

A 2.85-g sample containing only MgO and CuO is placed in a 3.00-L container. The container is filled with CO_2 to a pressure of 740. torr at 20.°C. After the reaction has gone to completion, the pressure inside the flask is 390. torr at 20.°C. What is the mass percent of MgO in the mixture? Assume that only the MgO reacts with CO_2.

Kinetic Molecular Theory and Real Gases

71. Calculate the average kinetic energy of the CH_4 molecules in a sample of CH_4 gas at 273 K and at 546 K.

72. Calculate the average kinetic energy of the N_2 molecules in a sample of N_2 gas at 273 K and at 546 K.

73. Calculate the root mean square velocity of the CH_4 molecules in a sample of CH_4 gas at 273 K and at 546 K.

74. Calculate the root mean square velocity of the N_2 molecules in a sample of N_2 gas at 273 K and at 546 K.

75. Do all the molecules in a 1-mol sample of $CH_4(g)$ have the same energy at 273 K?

76. Do all the molecules in a 1-mol sample of $CH_4(g)$ have the same velocity at 546 K?

77. Consider a 1-mol sample of $CH_4(g)$ at 273 K. If the temperature is increased, what happens to the average kinetic energy and the average velocity of the CH_4 molecules? Explain.

78. Consider a 1.0-L container of neon gas at STP. Will the average kinetic energy, average velocity, and frequency of collisions of gas molecules with the walls of the container increase, decrease, or remain the same under each of the following conditions?

a. The temperature is increased to 100°C.

b. The temperature is decreased to $-50°C$.

c. The volume is decreased to 0.5 L.

d. The number of moles of neon is doubled.

79. Consider three identical flasks filled with different gases.

Flask A: CO at 760 torr and 0°C

Flask B: N_2 at 250 torr and 0°C

Flask C: H_2 at 100 torr and 0°C

a. In which flask will the molecules have the greatest average kinetic energy?

b. In which flask will the molecules have the greatest average velocity?

80. Consider separate 1.0-L gaseous samples of H_2, Xe, Cl_2, and O_2 all at STP.

a. Rank the gases in order of increasing average kinetic energy.

b. Rank the gases in order of increasing average velocity.

c. How can separate 1.0-L samples of O_2 and H_2 each have the same average velocity?

81. The effusion rate of an unknown gas is measured and found to be 31.50 mL/min. Under identical experimental conditions, the effusion rate of O_2 is found to be 30.50 mL/min. If the choices are CH_4, CO, NO, CO_2, and NO_2, what is the identity of the unknown gas?

82. The rate of effusion of a particular gas was measured and found to be 24.0 mL/min. Under the same conditions, the rate of effusion of pure methane (CH_4) gas is 47.8 mL/min. What is the molar mass of the unknown gas?

83. One way of separating oxygen isotopes is by gaseous diffusion of carbon monoxide. The gaseous diffusion process behaves like an effusion process. Calculate the relative rates of effusion of $^{12}C^{16}O$, $^{12}C^{17}O$, and $^{12}C^{18}O$. Name some advantages and disadvantages of separating oxygen isotopes by gaseous diffusion of carbon dioxide instead of carbon monoxide.

84. It took 4.5 minutes for 1.0 L helium to effuse through a porous barrier. How long will it take for 1.0 L Cl_2 gas to effuse under identical conditions?

85. Calculate the pressure exerted by 0.5000 mol N_2 in a 1.0000-L container at 25.0°C

a. using the ideal gas law.
b. using the van der Waals equation.
c. Compare the results.

86. Calculate the pressure exerted by 0.5000 mol N_2 in a 10.000-L container at 25.0°C
    a. using the ideal gas law.
    b. using the van der Waals equation.
    c. Compare the results.
    d. Compare the results with those in Exercise 85.

Atmosphere Chemistry

87. Use the data in Table 5.4 to calculate the partial pressure of NO in dry air assuming that the total pressure is 1.0 atm. Assuming a temperature of 0°C, calculate the number of molecules of NO per cubic centimeter.

88. Use the data in Table 5.4 to calculate the partial pressure of He in dry air assuming that the total pressure is 1.0 atm. Assuming a temperature of 25°C, calculate the number of He atoms per cubic centimeter.

89. A 10.0-L sample of air was collected at an altitude of 1.00×10^2 km. Estimate the volume of the sample at STP. (See Fig. 5.29.)

90. A 1.0-L sample of air is collected at 25°C at sea level (1.00 atm). Estimate the volume this sample of air would have at an altitude of 15 km (see Fig. 5.29).

91. Write reactions to show how nitric and sulfuric acids are produced in the atmosphere.

92. Write reactions to show how the nitric and sulfuric acids in acid rain react with marble and limestone. (Both marble and limestone are primarily calcium carbonate.)

Additional Exercises

93. Draw a qualitative graph to show how the first property varies with the second in each of the following (assume 1 mol of an ideal gas and T in Kelvin).
    a. PV versus V with constant T
    b. P versus T with constant V
    c. T versus V with constant P
    d. P versus V with constant T
    e. P versus $1/V$ with constant T
    f. PV/T versus P

94. At STP, 1.0 L Br_2 reacts completely with 3.0 L F_2, producing 2.0 L of a product. What is the formula of the product? (All substances are gases.)

95. A 2.747-g sample of manganese metal is reacted with excess HCl gas to produce 3.22 L of $H_2(g)$ at 373 K and 0.951 atm and a manganese chloride compound ($MnCl_x$). What is the formula of the manganese chloride compound produced in the reaction?

96. Equal moles of hydrogen gas and oxygen gas are mixed in a flexible reaction vessel and then sparked to initiate the formation of gaseous water. Assuming that the reaction goes to completion, what is the ratio of the final volume of the gas mixture to the initial volume of the gas mixture if both volumes are measured at the same temperature and pressure?

97. A 15.0-L tank is filled with H_2 to a pressure of 2.00×10^2 atm. How many balloons (each 2.00 L) can be inflated to a pressure of 1.00 atm from the tank? Assume that there is no temperature change and that the tank cannot be emptied below 1.00 atm pressure.

98. A bicycle tire is filled with air to a pressure of 100. psi at a temperature of 19°C. Riding the bike on asphalt on a hot day increases the temperature of the tire to 58°C. The volume of the tire increases by 4.0%. What is the new pressure in the bicycle tire?

99. Consider the three flasks in the diagram below. Assuming the connecting tubes have negligible volume, what is the partial pressure of each gas and the total pressure when all the stopcocks are opened?

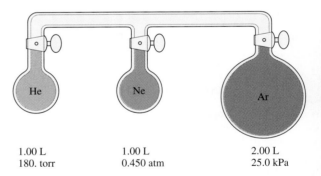

1.00 L	1.00 L	2.00 L
180. torr	0.450 atm	25.0 kPa

100. A spherical glass container of unknown volume contains helium gas at 25°C and 1.960 atm. When a portion of the helium is withdrawn and adjusted to 1.00 atm at 25°C, it is found to have a volume of 1.75 cm³. The gas remaining in the first container shows a pressure of 1.710 atm. Calculate the volume of the spherical container.

101. A 2.00-L sample of $O_2(g)$ was collected over water at a total pressure of 785 torr and 25°C. When the $O_2(g)$ was dried (water vapor removed), the gas had a volume of 1.94 L at 25°C and 785 torr. Calculate the vapor pressure of water at 25°C.

102. Acetylene gas, $C_2H_2(g)$, can be produced by reacting solid calcium carbide, CaC_2, with water. The products are acetylene and calcium hydroxide. What volume of wet acetylene is collected at 25°C and 715 torr when 5.20 g calcium carbide is reacted with an excess of water? (At 25°C the vapor pressure of water is 23.8 torr.)

103. In the "Méthode Champenoise," grape juice is fermented in a wine bottle to produce sparkling wine. The reaction is

$$C_6H_{12}O_6(aq) \longrightarrow 2C_2H_5OH(aq) + 2CO_2(g)$$

Fermentation of 750. mL grape juice (density = 1.0 g/cm³) is allowed to take place in a bottle with a total volume of 825 mL until 12% by volume is ethanol (C_2H_5OH). Assuming that the CO_2 is insoluble in H_2O (actually, a wrong assumption), what would be the pressure of CO_2 inside the wine bottle at 25°C? (The density of ethanol is 0.79 g/cm³.)

104. A 20.0-L stainless steel container was charged with 2.00 atm of hydrogen gas and 3.00 atm of oxygen gas. A spark ignited the mixture, producing water. What is the pressure in the tank at 25°C? at 125°C?

105. Uranium hexafluoride is a solid at room temperature, but it boils at 56°C. Determine the density of uranium hexafluoride at 60.°C and 745 torr.

106. One of the chemical controversies of the nineteenth century concerned the element beryllium (Be). Berzelius originally claimed that beryllium was a trivalent element (forming Be^{3+} ions) and that it gave an oxide with the formula Be_2O_3. This resulted in a calculated atomic mass of 13.5 for beryllium. In formulating his periodic table, Mendeleev proposed that beryllium was divalent (forming Be^{2+} ions) and that it gave an oxide with the formula BeO. This assumption gives an atomic mass of 9.0. In 1894, A. Combes (*Comptes Rendus* 1894, p. 1221) reacted beryllium with the anion $C_5H_7O_2^-$ and measured the density of the gaseous product. Combes's data for two different experiments are as follows:

	I	II
Mass	0.2022 g	0.2224 g
Volume	22.6 cm³	26.0 cm³
Temperature	13°C	17°C
Pressure	765.2 mm Hg	764.6 mm

If beryllium is a divalent metal, the molecular formula of the product will be $Be(C_5H_7O_2)_2$; if it is trivalent, the formula will be $Be(C_5H_7O_2)_3$. Show how Combes's data help to confirm that beryllium is a divalent metal.

107. A compound contains only nitrogen and hydrogen and is 87.4% nitrogen by mass. A gaseous sample of the compound has a density of 0.977 g/L at 710. torr and 100.°C. What is the molecular formula of the compound?

108. A compound contains only C, H, and N. It is 58.51% C and 7.37% H by mass. Helium effuses through a porous frit 3.20 times as fast as the compound does. Determine the empirical and molecular formulas of this compound.

109. The nitrogen content of organic compounds can be determined by the Dumas method. The compound in question is first reacted by passage over hot CuO(s):

$$\text{Compound} \xrightarrow[\text{CuO}(s)]{\text{Hot}} N_2(g) + CO_2(g) + H_2O(g)$$

The product gas is then passed through a concentrated solution of KOH to remove the CO_2. After passage through the KOH solution, the gas contains N_2 and is saturated with water vapor. In a given experiment a 0.253-g sample of a compound produced 31.8 mL N_2 saturated with water vapor at 25°C and 726 torr. What is the mass percent of nitrogen in the compound? (The vapor pressure of water at 25°C is 23.8 torr.)

110. A compound contains only C, H, and N. A chemist analyzes it by doing the following experiments.
  a. Complete combustion of 35.0 mg of the compound produced 33.5 mg CO_2 and 41.1 mg H_2O.
  b. A 65.2-mg sample of the compound was analyzed for nitrogen by the Dumas method (see Exercise 109), giving 35.6 mL of dry N_2 at 740. torr and 25°C.
  c. The effusion rate of the compound as a gas was measured and found to be 24.6 mL/min. The effusion rate of argon gas, under identical conditions, is 26.4 mL/min.
  What is the formula of the compound?

111. Consider the following diagram:

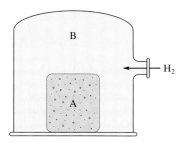

Container A (with porous walls) is filled with air at STP. It is then inserted into a large enclosed container (B) which is then flushed with $H_2(g)$. What will happen to the pressure inside container A? Explain your answer.

112. Without looking at tables of values, which of the following gases would you expect to have the largest value of the van der Waals constant b: H_2, N_2, CH_4, C_2H_6, or C_3H_8?

113. From the values in Table 5.3 for the van der Waals constant a for the gases H_2, CO_2, N_2, and CH_4, predict which of these gas molecules show the strongest intermolecular attractions.

Challenge Problems

114. An important process for the production of acrylonitrile (C_3H_3N) is given by the following reaction:

$$2C_3H_6(g) + 2NH_3(g) + 3O_2(g) \longrightarrow$$
$$2C_3H_3N(g) + 6H_2O(g)$$

A 150.-L reactor is charged to the following partial pressures at 25°C:

$$P_{C_3H_6} = 0.500 \text{ MPa}$$
$$P_{NH_3} = 0.800 \text{ MPa}$$
$$P_{O_2} = 1.500 \text{ MPa}$$

What mass of acrylonitrile can be produced from this mixture (MPa = 10^6 Pa)?

115. A chemist weighed out 5.14 g of a mixture containing unknown amounts of BaO(s) and CaO(s) and placed the sample in a 1.50-L flask containing $CO_2(g)$ at 30.0°C and 750. torr. After the reaction to form $BaCO_3(s)$ and $CaCO_3(s)$ was completed, the pressure of $CO_2(g)$ remaining was 230. torr. Calculate the mass percentages of CaO(s) and BaO(s) in the mixture.

116. A mixture of chromium and zinc weighing 0.362 g was reacted with an excess of hydrochloric acid. After all the metals in the mixture reacted, 225 mL of dry hydrogen gas was collected at 27°C and 750. torr. Determine the mass percent Zn in the metal sample. [Zinc reacts with hydrochloric acid to produce zinc chloride and hydrogen gas; chromium reacts with hydrochloric acid to produce chromium(III) chloride and hydrogen gas.]

117. Methane (CH_4) gas flows into a combustion chamber at a rate of 200. L/min at 1.50 atm and ambient temperature. Air is added to the chamber at 1.00 atm and the same temperature, and the gases are ignited.
   a. To ensure complete combustion of CH_4 to $CO_2(g)$ and $H_2O(g)$, three times as much oxygen as is necessary is reacted. Assuming air is 21 mole percent O_2 and 79 mole percent N_2, calculate the flow rate of air necessary to deliver the required amount of oxygen.
   b. Under the conditions in part a, combustion of methane was not complete as a mixture of $CO_2(g)$ and $CO(g)$ was produced. It was determined that 95.0% of the carbon in the exhaust gas was present in CO_2. The remainder was present as carbon in CO. Calculate the composition of the exhaust gas in terms of mole fraction of CO, CO_2, O_2, N_2, and H_2O. Assume CH_4 is completely reacted and N_2 is unreacted.

118. A sample of methane (CH_4) gas contains a small amount of helium. Calculate the volume percentage of helium if the density of the sample is 0.70902 g/L at 0.0°C and 1.000 atm.

119. The total mass that can be lifted by a balloon is given by the difference between the mass of air displaced by the balloon and the mass of the gas inside the balloon. Consider a hot-air balloon that approximates a sphere 5.00 m in diameter and contains air heated to 65°C. The surrounding air temperature is 21°C. The pressure in the balloon is equal to the atmospheric pressure, which is 745 torr.
   a. What total mass can the balloon lift? Assume that the average molar mass of air is 29.0 g/mol. (*Hint:* Heated air is less dense than cool air.)
   b. If the balloon is filled with enough helium at 21°C and 745 torr to achieve the same volume as in part a, what total mass can the balloon lift?
   c. What mass could the hot-air balloon in part a lift if it were on the ground in Denver, Colorado, where a typical atmospheric pressure is 630. torr?

120. We state that the ideal gas law tends to hold best at low pressures and high temperatures. Show how the van der Waals equation simplifies to the ideal gas law under these conditions.

121. Atmospheric scientists often use mixing ratios to express the concentrations of trace compounds in air. Mixing ratios are often expressed as ppmv (parts per million volume):

$$\text{ppmv of } X = \frac{\text{vol. of } X \text{ at STP}}{\text{total vol. of air at STP}} \times 10^6$$

On a recent autumn day, the concentration of carbon monoxide in the air in downtown Denver, Colorado, reached 3.0×10^2 ppmv. The atmospheric pressure at that time was 628 torr, and the temperature was 0°C.
   a. What was the partial pressure of CO?
   b. What was the concentration of CO in molecules per cubic centimeter?

122. Formaldehyde (CH_2O) is sometimes released from foamed insulation currently being used in homes. The federal standard for the allowable amount of CH_2O in air is 1.0 ppbv (parts per billion volume; similar to ppmv as defined in Exercise 121). How many molecules per cubic centimeter is this at STP? If the concentration of formaldehyde in a room is 1.0 ppbv, what total mass of formaldehyde is present at STP if the room measures 18.0 ft × 24.0 ft × 8.0 ft?

Marathon Problem*

This problem is designed to incorporate several concepts and techniques into one situation. Marathon Problems can be used in class by groups of students to help facilitate problem-solving skills.

123. Use the following information to identify element A and compound B, then answer questions a and b.
   An empty glass container has a mass of 658.572 g. It has a mass of 659.452 g after it has been filled with nitrogen gas at a pressure of 790. torr and a temperature of 15°C. When the container is evacuated and refilled with a certain element (A) at a pressure of 745 torr and a temperature of 26°C, it has a mass of 660.59 g.

*This Marathon Problem was developed by James H. Burness of Penn State University, York Campus. Reprinted with permission from the *Journal of Chemical Education,* Vol. 68, No. 11, 1991, pp. 919–922; copyright © 1991, Division of Chemical Education, Inc.

Compound B, a gaseous organic compound that consists of 85.6% carbon and 14.4% hydrogen by mass, is placed in a stainless steel vessel (10.68 L) with excess oxygen gas. The vessel is placed in a constant-temperature bath at 22°C. The pressure in the vessel is 11.98 atm. In the bottom of the vessel is a container that is packed with Ascarite and a desiccant. Ascarite is asbestos impregnated with sodium hydroxide; it quantitatively absorbs carbon dioxide:

$$2NaOH(s) + CO_2(g) \longrightarrow Na_2CO_3(s) + H_2O(l)$$

The desiccant is anhydrous magnesium perchlorate, which quantitatively absorbs the water produced by the combustion reaction as well as the water produced by the above reaction. Neither the Ascarite nor the desiccant reacts with compound B or oxygen. The total mass of the container with the Ascarite and desiccant is 765.3 g.

The combustion reaction of compound B is initiated by a spark. The pressure immediately rises, then begins to decrease, and finally reaches a steady value of 6.02 atm. The stainless steel vessel is carefully opened, and the mass of the container inside the vessel is found to be 846.7 g.

A and B react quantitatively in a 1:1 mole ratio to form one mole of the single product, gas C.

a. How many grams of C will be produced if 10.0 L of A and 8.60 L of B (each at STP) are reacted by opening a stopcock connecting the two samples?

b. What will be the total pressure in the system?

Thermochemistry

Contents

*E*nergy is the essence of our very existence as individuals and as a society. The food that we eat furnishes the energy to live, work, and play, just as the coal and oil consumed by manufacturing and transportation systems power our modern industrialized civilization.

Huge quantities of carbon-based fossil fuels have been available for the taking. This abundance of fuels has led to a world society with a voracious appetite for energy, consuming millions of barrels of petroleum every day. We are now dangerously dependent on the dwindling supplies of oil, and this dependence is an important source of tension among nations in today's world. In an incredibly short time we have moved from a period of ample and cheap supplies of petroleum to one of high prices and uncertain supplies. If our present standard of living is to be maintained, we must find alternatives to petroleum. To do this, we need to know the relationship between chemistry and energy, which we explore in this chapter.

There are additional problems with fossil fuels. The waste products from burning fossil fuels significantly affect our environment. For example, when a carbon-based fuel is burned, the carbon reacts with oxygen to form carbon dioxide, which is released into the atmosphere. Although much of this carbon dioxide is consumed in various natural processes such as photosynthesis and the formation of carbonate materials, the amount of carbon dioxide in the atmosphere is steadily increasing. This increase is significant because atmospheric carbon dioxide absorbs heat radiated from the earth's surface and radiates it back toward the earth. Since this is an important mechanism for controlling the earth's temperature, many scientists fear that an increase in the concentration of carbon dioxide will warm the earth, causing significant changes in climate. In addition, impurities in the fossil fuels react with components of the air to produce air pollution. We discussed some aspects of this problem in Chapter 5.

Just as energy is important to our society on a macroscopic scale, it is critically important to each living organism on a microscopic scale. The living cell is a miniature chemical factory powered by energy from chemical reactions. The process of cellular respiration extracts the energy stored in

When a match is struck, chemical reactions occur to produce heat.

sugars and other nutrients to drive the various tasks of the cell. Although the extraction process is more complex and more subtle, the energy obtained from "fuel" molecules by the cell is the same as would be obtained from burning the fuel to power an internal combustion engine.

Whether it is an engine or a cell that is converting energy from one form to another, the processes are all governed by the same principles, which we will begin to explore in this chapter. Additional aspects of energy transformation will be covered in Chapter 16.

6.1 The Nature of Energy

Although the concept of energy is quite familiar, energy itself is rather difficult to define precisely. We will define **energy** as the *capacity to do work or to produce heat*. In this chapter we will concentrate specifically on the heat transfer that accompanies chemical processes.

One of the most important characteristics of energy is that it is conserved. The **law of conservation of energy** states that *energy can be converted from one form to another but can be neither created nor destroyed*. That is, the energy of the universe is constant. Energy can be classified as either potential or kinetic energy. **Potential energy** is energy due to position or composition. For example, water behind a dam has potential energy that can be converted to work when the water flows down through turbines, thereby creating electricity. Attractive and repulsive forces also lead to potential energy. The energy released when gasoline is burned results from differences in attractive forces between the nuclei and electrons in the reactants and products. The **kinetic energy** of an object is energy due to the motion of the object and depends on the mass of the object m and its velocity v: $KE = \frac{1}{2}mv^2$.

Energy can be converted from one form to another. For example, consider the two balls in Fig. 6.1(a). Ball A, because of its higher position initially, has more potential energy than ball B. When A is released, it moves down the hill and strikes B. Eventually, the arrangement shown in Fig. 6.1(b) is achieved. What has happened in going from the initial to the final arrangement? The potential energy of A has decreased, but since energy is conserved, all the energy lost by A must be accounted for. How is this energy distributed?

Initially, the potential energy of A is changed to kinetic energy as the ball rolls down the hill. Part of this kinetic energy is then transferred to B, causing it to be raised to a higher final position. Thus the potential energy of B has been increased. However, since the final position of B is lower than the original position of A, some of the energy is still unaccounted for. Both balls in their final positions are at rest, so the missing energy cannot be due to their motions. What has happened to the remaining energy?

The answer lies in the interaction between the hill's surface and the ball. As ball A rolls down the hill, some of its kinetic energy is transferred to the surface of the hill as heat. This transfer of energy is called *frictional heating*. The temperature of the hill increases very slightly as the ball rolls down.

Before we proceed further, it is important to recognize that heat and temperature are decidedly different. As we saw in Chapter 5, *temperature* is a property that reflects the random motions of the particles in a particular substance. **Heat,** on the

The total energy content of the universe is constant.

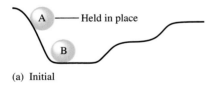

(a) Initial

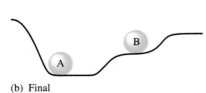

(b) Final

Figure 6.1

(a) In the initial positions, ball A has a higher potential energy than ball B. (b) After A has rolled down the hill, the potential energy lost by A has been converted to random motions of the components of the hill (frictional heating) and to the increase in the potential energy of B.

other hand, involves the *transfer* of energy between two objects due to a temperature difference. Heat is not a substance contained by an object, although we often talk of heat as if this were true.

Note that in going from the initial to the final arrangements in Fig. 6.1, ball B gains potential energy because work was done by ball A on B. **Work** is defined as force acting over a distance. Work is required to raise B from its original position to its final one. Part of the original energy stored as potential energy in A has been transferred through work to B, thereby increasing B's potential energy. Thus there are two ways to transfer energy: through work and through heat.

In rolling to the bottom of the hill shown in Fig. 6.1, ball A will always lose the same amount of potential energy. However, the way that this energy transfer is divided between work and heat depends on the specific conditions—the **pathway.** For example, the surface of the hill might be so rough that the energy of A is expended completely through frictional heating; A is moving so slowly when it hits B that it cannot move B to the next level. In this case, no work is done. Regardless of the condition of the hill's surface, the *total energy* transferred will be constant. However, the amounts of heat and work will differ. Energy change is independent of the pathway; however, work and heat are both dependent on the pathway.

This brings us to a very important concept: the **state function** or **state property.** A state function refers to a property of the system that depends only on its *present state*. A state function (property) does not depend in any way on the system's past (or future). In other words, the value of a state function does not depend on how the system arrived at the present state; it depends only on the characteristics of the present state. This leads to a very important characteristic of a state function: A change in this function (property) in going from one state to another state is independent of the particular pathway taken between the two states.

A worker using an oxyacetylene torch.

Of the functions considered in our present example, energy is a state function, but work and heat are not state functions.

Chemical Energy

The ideas we have just illustrated using mechanical examples also apply to chemical systems. The combustion of methane, for example, is used to heat many homes in the United States:

$$CH_4(g) + 2O_2(g) \longrightarrow CO_2(g) + 2H_2O(g) + energy\ (heat)$$

To discuss this reaction, we divide the universe into two parts: the system and the surroundings. The **system** is the part of the universe on which we wish to focus attention; the **surroundings** include everything else in the universe. In this case we define the system as the reactants and products of the reaction. The surroundings consist of the reaction container (a furnace, for example), the room, and anything else other than the reactants and products.

When a reaction results in the evolution of heat, it is said to be **exothermic** (*exo-* is a prefix meaning "out of"); that is, energy flows *out of the system.* For example, in the combustion of methane, energy flows out of the system as heat. Reactions that absorb energy from the surroundings are said to be **endothermic.** When the heat flow is *into a system,* the process is endothermic. For example, the formation of nitric oxide from nitrogen and oxygen is endothermic:

$$N_2(g) + O_2(g) + energy\ (heat) \longrightarrow 2NO(g)$$

Where does the energy, released as heat, come from in an exothermic reaction? The answer lies in the difference in potential energies between the products and the reactants. Which has lower potential energy, the reactants or the products? We know that total energy is conserved and that energy flows from the system into the surroundings in an exothermic reaction. This means that *the energy gained by the surroundings must be equal to the energy lost by the system.* In the combustion of methane, the energy content of the system decreases, which means that 1 mole of CO_2 and 2 moles of H_2O molecules (the products) possess less potential energy than do 1 mole of CH_4 and 2 moles of O_2 molecules (the reactants). The heat flow into the surroundings results from a lowering of the potential energy of the reaction system. This always holds true. *In any exothermic reaction, some of the potential energy stored in the chemical bonds is being converted to thermal energy (random kinetic energy) via heat.*

The energy diagram for the combustion of methane is shown in Fig. 6.2, where $\Delta(PE)$ represents the *change* in potential energy stored in the bonds of the products as compared with the bonds of the reactants. In other words, this quantity represents the difference between the energy required to break the bonds in the reactants and the energy released when the bonds in the products are formed. In an exothermic process, the bonds in the products are stronger (on average) than those of the reactants. That is, more energy is released by forming the new bonds in the products than is consumed to break the bonds in the reactants. The net result is that the quantity of energy $\Delta(PE)$ is transferred to the surroundings through heat.

For an endothermic reaction, the situation is reversed, as shown in Fig. 6.3. Energy that flows into the system as heat is used to increase the potential energy of the system. In this case the products have higher potential energy (weaker bonds on average) than the reactants.

The study of energy and its interconversions is called **thermodynamics.** The law of conservation of energy is often called the **first law of thermodynamics** and is stated as follows: *The energy of the universe is constant.*

The **internal energy** E of a system can be defined most precisely as the sum of the kinetic and potential energies of all the "particles" in the system. The internal energy of a system can be changed by a flow of work, heat, or both. That is,

$$\Delta E = q + w$$

Figure 6.2

The combustion of methane releases the quantity of energy $\Delta(PE)$ to the surroundings via heat flow. This is an exothermic process.

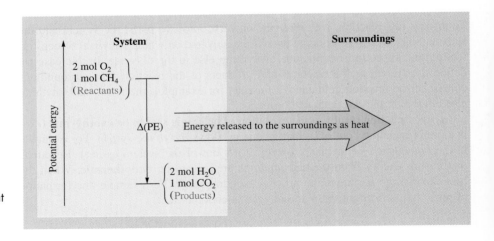

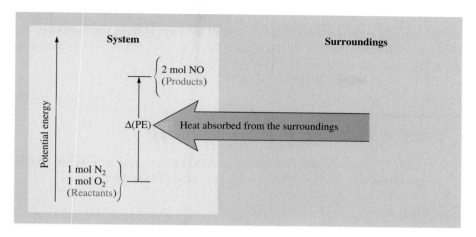

Figure 6.3

The energy diagram for the reaction of nitrogen and oxygen to form nitric oxide. This is an endothermic process: Heat [equal in magnitude to $\Delta(PE)$] flows into the system from the surroundings.

where ΔE represents the change in the system's internal energy, q represents heat, and w represents work.

Thermodynamic quantities always consist of two parts: a *number*, giving the magnitude of the change, and a *sign,* indicating the direction of the flow. *The sign reflects the system's point of view.* For example, if a quantity of energy flows *into* the system via heat (an endothermic process), q is equal to $+x$, where the *positive* sign indicates that the *system's energy is increasing.* On the other hand, when energy flows *out of* the system via heat (an exothermic process), q is equal to $-x$, where the *negative* sign indicates that the *system's energy is decreasing.*

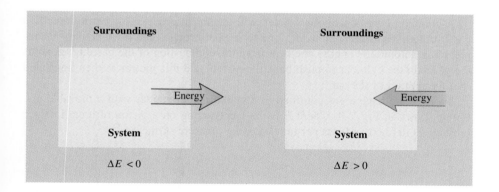

In this text the same conventions also apply to the flow of work. If the system does work on the surroundings (energy flows out of the system), w is negative. If the surroundings do work on the system (energy flows into the system), w is positive. We define work from the system's point of view to be consistent for all thermodynamic quantities. That is, in this convention the signs of both q and w reflect what happens to the system; thus we use $\Delta E = q + w$.

In this text we *always* take the system's point of view. This convention is not followed in every area of science. For example, engineers are in the business of designing machines to do work, that is, to make the system (the machine) transfer energy to its surroundings through work. Consequently, engineers define work from

The convention in this text is to take the system's point of view; $q = -x$ denotes an exothermic process, and $q = +x$ denotes an endothermic one.

the surroundings' point of view. In their convention, work that flows out of the system is treated as positive because the energy of the surroundings has increased. The first law of thermodynamics is then written $\Delta E = q - w'$, where w' signifies work from the surroundings' point of view.

Sample Exercise 6.1 Internal Energy

Calculate ΔE for a system undergoing an endothermic process in which 15.6 kJ of heat flows and where 1.4 kJ of work is done on the system.

Solution

We use the equation

$$\Delta E = q + w$$

where $q = +15.6$ kJ, since the process is endothermic, and $w = +1.4$ kJ, since work is done on the system. Thus

$$\Delta E = 15.6 \text{ kJ} + 1.4 \text{ kJ} = 17.0 \text{ kJ}$$

The system has gained 17.0 kJ of energy.

See Exercises 6.21 through 6.24.

The joule (J) is the fundamental SI unit for energy:

$$J = \frac{kg \cdot m^2}{s^2}$$

One kilojoule (kJ) $= 10^3$ J.

A common type of work associated with chemical processes is work done by a gas (through *expansion*) or work done to a gas (through *compression*). For example, in an automobile engine, the heat from the combustion of the gasoline expands the gases in the cylinder to push back the piston, and this motion is then translated into the motion of the car.

Suppose we have a gas confined to a cylindrical container with a movable piston as shown in Fig. 6.4, where F is the force acting on a piston of area A. Since pressure is defined as force per unit area, the pressure of the gas is

$$P = \frac{F}{A}$$

Work is defined as force applied over a distance, so if the piston moves a distance Δh, as shown in Fig. 6.4, then the work done is

$$\text{Work} = \text{force} \times \text{distance} = F \times \Delta h$$

Since $P = F/A$ or $F = P \times A$, then

$$\text{Work} = F \times \Delta h = P \times A \times \Delta h$$

Since the volume of a cylinder equals the area of the piston times the height of the cylinder (Fig. 6.4), the change in volume ΔV resulting from the piston moving a distance Δh is

$$\Delta V = \text{final volume} - \text{initial volume} = A \times \Delta h$$

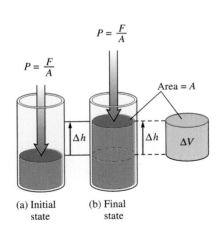

(a) Initial state (b) Final state

Figure 6.4

(a) The piston, moving a distance Δh against a pressure P, does work on the surroundings. (b) Since the volume of a cylinder is the area of the base times its height, the change in volume of the gas is given by $\Delta h \times A = \Delta V$.

Substituting $\Delta V = A \times \Delta h$ into the expression for work gives

$$\text{Work} = P \times A \times \Delta h = P\Delta V$$

This gives us the *magnitude* (size) of the work required to expand a gas ΔV against a pressure P.

What about the sign of the work? The gas (the system) is expanding, moving the piston against the pressure. Thus the system is doing work on the surroundings, so from the system's point of view the sign of the work should be negative.

For an *expanding* gas, ΔV is a positive quantity because the volume is increasing. Thus ΔV and w must have opposite signs, which leads to the equation

$$w = -P\Delta V$$

Note that for a gas expanding against an external pressure P, w is a negative quantity as required, since work flows out of the system. When a gas is *compressed,* ΔV is a negative quantity (the volume decreases), which makes w a positive quantity (work flows into the system).

w and $P\Delta V$ have opposite signs because when the gas expands (ΔV is positive), work flows into the surroundings (w is negative).

Sample Exercise 6.2 PV Work

Calculate the work associated with the expansion of a gas from 46 L to 64 L at a constant external pressure of 15 atm.

Solution

For a gas at constant pressure,

$$w = -P\Delta V$$

In this case $P = 15$ atm and $\Delta V = 64 - 46 = 18$ L. Hence

$$w = -15 \text{ atm} \times 18 \text{ L} = -270 \text{ L} \cdot \text{atm}$$

Note that since the gas expands, it does work on its surroundings. Energy flows out of the gas, so w is a negative quantity.

For an ideal gas, work can occur only when its volume changes. Thus, if a gas is heated at constant volume, the pressure increases but no work occurs.

See Exercises 6.25 and 6.26.

In dealing with "*PV* work," keep in mind that the *P* in $P\Delta V$ always refers to the external pressure—the pressure that causes a compression or that resists an expansion.

Sample Exercise 6.3 *Internal Energy, Heat, and Work*

A balloon is being inflated to its full extent by heating the air inside it. In the final stages of this process, the volume of the balloon changes from 4.00×10^6 L to 4.50×10^6 L by the addition of 1.3×10^8 J of energy as heat. Assuming that the balloon expands against a constant pressure of 1.0 atm, calculate ΔE for the process. (To convert between L · atm and J, use 1 L · atm = 101.3 J.)

Solution

To calculate ΔE, we use the equation

$$\Delta E = q + w$$

Since the problem states that 1.3×10^8 J of energy is *added* as heat,

$$q = +1.3 \times 10^8 \text{ J}$$

The work done can be calculated from the expression

$$w = -P\Delta V$$

In this case $P = 1.0$ atm and

$$\Delta V = V_{\text{final}} - V_{\text{initial}}$$
$$= 4.50 \times 10^6 \text{ L} - 4.00 \times 10^6 \text{ L} = 0.50 \times 10^6 \text{ L} = 5.0 \times 10^5 \text{ L}$$

Thus

$$w = -1.0 \text{ atm} \times 5.0 \times 10^5 \text{ L} = -5.0 \times 10^5 \text{ L} \cdot \text{atm}$$

Note that the negative sign for w makes sense, since the gas is expanding and thus doing work on the surroundings.

To calculate ΔE, we must sum q and w. However, since q is given in units of J and w is given in units of L · atm, we must change the work to units of joules:

$$w = -5.0 \times 10^5 \text{ L} \cdot \text{atm} \times \frac{101.3 \text{ J}}{\text{L} \cdot \text{atm}} = -5.1 \times 10^7 \text{ J}$$

Then

$$\Delta E = q + w = (+1.3 \times 10^8 \text{ J}) + (-5.1 \times 10^7 \text{ J}) = 8 \times 10^7 \text{ J}$$

Since more energy is added through heating than the gas expends doing work, there is a net increase in the internal energy of the gas in the balloon. Hence ΔE is positive.

See Exercises 6.27 and 6.28.

A propane burner is used to heat the air in a hot air balloon.

6.2   Enthalpy and Calorimetry

Enthalpy

So far we have discussed the internal energy of a system. A less familiar property of a system is its **enthalpy** H, which is defined as

$$H = E + PV$$

where E is the internal energy of the system, P is the pressure of the system, and V is the volume of the system.

Since internal energy, pressure, and volume are all state functions, *enthalpy is also a state function.* But what exactly is enthalpy? To help answer this question, consider a process carried out at constant pressure and where the only work allowed is pressure–volume work ($w = -P\Delta V$). Under these conditions, the expression

$$\Delta E = q_P + w$$

becomes

$$\Delta E = q_P - P\Delta V$$

or

$$q_P = \Delta E + P\Delta V$$

where q_P is the heat at constant pressure.

We will now relate q_P to a change in enthalpy. The definition of enthalpy is $H = E + PV$. Therefore, we can say

Change in H = (change in E) + (change in PV)

or

$$\Delta H = \Delta E + \Delta(PV)$$

Since P is constant, the change in PV is due only to a change in volume. Thus

$$\Delta(PV) = P\Delta V$$

and

$$\Delta H = \Delta E + P\Delta V$$

This expression is identical to the one we obtained for q_P:

$$q_P = \Delta E + P\Delta V$$

Thus, for a process carried out at constant pressure and where the only work allowed is that from a volume change, we have

$$\Delta H = q_P$$

At constant pressure (where only PV work is allowed), the change in enthalpy ΔH of the system is equal to the energy flow as heat. This means that for a reaction studied at constant pressure, the flow of heat is a measure of the change in enthalpy for the system. For this reason, the terms *heat of reaction* and *change in enthalpy* are used interchangeably for reactions studied at constant pressure.

For a chemical reaction, the enthalpy change is given by the equation

$$\Delta H = H_{products} - H_{reactants}$$

In a case in which the products of a reaction have a greater enthalpy than the reactants, ΔH will be positive. Thus heat will be absorbed by the system, and the reaction is endothermic. On the other hand, if the enthalpy of the products is less than that of the reactants, ΔH will be negative. In this case the overall decrease in enthalpy is achieved by the generation of heat, and the reaction is exothermic.

Enthalpy is a state function. A change in enthalpy does not depend on the pathway between two states.

Recall from the previous section that w and $P\Delta V$ have opposite signs:
$$w = -P\Delta V$$

$\Delta H = q$ *only* at constant pressure.

The change in enthalpy of a system has no easily interpreted meaning except at constant pressure, where ΔH = heat.

At constant pressure, exothermic means ΔH is negative; endothermic means ΔH is positive.

Sample Exercise 6.4 *Enthalpy*

When 1 mole of methane (CH_4) is burned at constant pressure, 890 kJ of energy is released as heat. Calculate ΔH for a process in which a 5.8-g sample of methane is burned at constant pressure.

Solution

At constant pressure, 890 kJ of energy per mole of CH_4 is produced as heat:

$$q_P = \Delta H = -890 \text{ kJ/mol } CH_4$$

Note that the minus sign indicates an exothermic process. In this case, a 5.8-g sample of CH_4 (molar mass = 16.0 g/mol) is burned. Since this amount is smaller than 1 mole, less than 890 kJ will be released as heat. The actual value can be calculated as follows:

$$5.8 \text{ g } CH_4 \times \frac{1 \text{ mol } CH_4}{16.0 \text{ g } CH_4} = 0.36 \text{ mol } CH_4$$

and

$$0.36 \text{ mol } CH_4 \times \frac{-890 \text{ kJ}}{\text{mol } CH_4} = -320 \text{ kJ}$$

Thus, when a 5.8-g sample of CH_4 is burned at constant pressure,

$$\Delta H = \text{heat flow} = -320 \text{ kJ}$$

See Exercises 6.33 through 6.36.

Calorimetry

The device used experimentally to determine the heat associated with a chemical reaction is called a **calorimeter. Calorimetry,** the science of measuring heat, is based on observing the temperature change when a body absorbs or discharges energy as heat. Substances respond differently to being heated. One substance might require a great deal of heat energy to raise its temperature by one degree, whereas another will exhibit the same temperature change after absorbing relatively little heat. The **heat capacity** C of a substance, which is a measure of this property, is defined as

$$C = \frac{\text{heat absorbed}}{\text{increase in temperature}}$$

Specific heat capacity: the energy required to raise the temperature of one gram of a substance by one degree Celsius.

Molar heat capacity: the energy required to raise the temperature of one mole of a substance by one degree Celsius.

When an element or a compound is heated, the energy required will depend on the amount of the substance present (for example, it takes twice as much energy to raise the temperature of two grams of water by one degree than it takes to raise the temperature of one gram of water by one degree). Thus, in defining the heat capacity of a substance, the amount of substance must be specified. If the heat capacity is given *per gram* of substance, it is called the **specific heat capacity,** and its units are J/°C · g or J/K · g. If the heat capacity is given *per mole* of the substance, it is called the **molar heat capacity,** and it has the units J/°C · mol or J/K · mol. The specific

Table 6.1 The Specific Heat Capacities of Some Common Substances

Substance	Specific Heat Capacity (J/°C · g)
$H_2O(l)$	4.18
$H_2O(s)$	2.03
$Al(s)$	0.89
$Fe(s)$	0.45
$Hg(l)$	0.14
$C(s)$	0.71

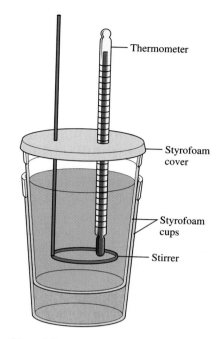

Figure 6.5

A coffee-cup calorimeter made of two Styrofoam cups.

heat capacities of some common substances are given in Table 6.1. Note from this table that the heat capacities of metals are very different from that of water. It takes much less energy to change the temperature of a gram of a metal by 1°C than for a gram of water.

Although the calorimeters used for highly accurate work are precision instruments, a very simple calorimeter can be used to examine the fundamentals of calorimetry. All we need are two nested Styrofoam cups with a cover through which a stirrer and thermometer can be inserted, as shown in Fig. 6.5. This device is called a "coffee-cup calorimeter." The outer cup is used to provide extra insulation. The inner cup holds the solution in which the reaction occurs.

The measurement of heat using a simple calorimeter such as that shown in Fig. 6.5 is an example of **constant-pressure calorimetry,** since the pressure (atmospheric pressure) remains constant during the process. Constant-pressure calorimetry is used in determining the changes in enthalpy (heats of reactions) for reactions occurring in solution. Recall that under these conditions, the change in enthalpy equals the heat.

For example, suppose we mix 50.0 mL of 1.0 M HCl at 25.0°C with 50.0 mL of 1.0 M NaOH also at 25°C in a calorimeter. After the reactants are mixed by stirring, the temperature is observed to increase to 31.9°C. As we saw in Section 4.8, the net ionic equation for this reaction is

$$H^+(aq) + OH^-(aq) \longrightarrow H_2O(l)$$

When these reactants (each originally at the same temperature) are mixed, the temperature of the mixed solution is observed to increase. Therefore, the chemical reaction must be releasing energy as heat. This released energy increases the random motions of the solution components, which in turn increases the temperature. The quantity of energy released can be determined from the temperature increase, the mass of solution, and the specific heat capacity of the solution. For an approximate result, we will assume that the calorimeter does not absorb or leak any heat and that the solution can be treated as if it were pure water with a density of 1.0 g/mL.

We also need to know the heat required to raise the temperature of a given amount of water by 1°C. Table 6.1 lists the specific heat capacity of water as 4.18 J/°C · g. This means that 4.18 J of energy is required to raise the temperature of 1 gram of water by 1°C.

From these assumptions and definitions, we can calculate the heat (change in enthalpy) for the neutralization reaction:

If two reactants at the same temperature are mixed and the resulting solution gets warmer, this means the reaction taking place is exothermic. An endothermic reaction cools the solution.

Energy released by the reaction

= energy absorbed by the solution

= specific heat capacity × mass of solution × increase in temperature

= $s \times m \times \Delta T$

In this case the increase in temperature $(\Delta T) = 31.9°C - 25.0°C = 6.9°C$, and the mass of solution $(m) = 100.0$ mL × 1.0 g/mL = 1.0×10^2 g. Thus

$$\text{Energy released} = s \times m \times \Delta T$$

$$= \left(4.18 \; \frac{J}{°C \cdot g}\right)(1.0 \times 10^2 \; g)(6.9°C)$$

$$= 2.9 \times 10^3 \; J$$

How much energy would have been released if twice these amounts of solutions had been mixed? The answer is that twice as much energy would have been produced. The heat of a reaction is an *extensive property;* it depends directly on the amount of substance, in this case on the amounts of reactants. In contrast, an *intensive property* is not related to the amount of a substance. For example, temperature is an intensive property.

Enthalpies of reaction are often expressed in terms of moles of reacting substances. The number of moles of H^+ ions consumed in the preceding experiment is

$$50.0 \; mL \times \frac{1 \; L}{1000 \; mL} \times \frac{1.0 \; mol}{L} \; H^+ = 5.0 \times 10^{-2} \; mol \; H^+$$

Thus 2.9×10^3 J heat was released when 5.0×10^{-2} mol H^+ ions reacted, or

$$\frac{2.9 \times 10^3 \; J}{5.0 \times 10^{-2} \; mol \; H^+} = 5.8 \times 10^4 \; J/mol$$

of heat released per 1.0 mol H^+ ions neutralized. Thus the *magnitude* of the enthalpy change per mole for the reaction

$$H^+(aq) + OH^-(aq) \longrightarrow H_2O(l)$$

is 58 kJ/mol. Since heat is *evolved,* $\Delta H = -58$ kJ/mol.

Notice that in this example we mentally keep track of the direction of the energy flow and assign the correct sign at the end of the calculation.

Sample Exercise 6.5 Constant-Pressure Calorimetry

When 1.00 L of 1.00 M $Ba(NO_3)_2$ solution at 25.0°C is mixed with 1.00 L of 1.00 M Na_2SO_4 solution at 25°C in a calorimeter, the white solid $BaSO_4$ forms and the temperature of the mixture increases to 28.1°C. Assuming that the calorimeter absorbs only a negligible quantity of heat, that the specific heat capacity of the solution is 4.18 J/°C · g, and that the density of the final solution is 1.0 g/mL, calculate the enthalpy change per mole of $BaSO_4$ formed.

Solution

The ions present before any reaction occurs are Ba^{2+}, NO_3^-, Na^+, and SO_4^{2-}. The Na^+ and NO_3^- ions are spectator ions, since $NaNO_3$ is very soluble in water and will not precipitate under these conditions. The net ionic equation for the reaction is therefore

$$Ba^{2+}(aq) + SO_4{}^{2-}(aq) \longrightarrow BaSO_4(s)$$

Since the temperature increases, formation of the solid $BaSO_4$ must be exothermic; ΔH will be negative.

Heat evolved by reaction

> = heat absorbed by solution
>
> = specific heat capacity × mass of solution × increase in temperature

Since 1.00 L of each solution is used, the total solution volume is 2.00 L, and

$$\text{Mass of solution} = 2.00 \, \cancel{L} \times \frac{1000 \, \cancel{mL}}{1 \, \cancel{L}} \times \frac{1.0 \, g}{\cancel{mL}} = 2.0 \times 10^3 \, g$$

$$\text{Temperature increase} = 28.1°C - 25.0°C = 3.1°C$$

$$\text{Heat evolved} = (4.18 \, J/°\cancel{C} \cdot \cancel{g})(2.0 \times 10^3 \, \cancel{g})(3.1°\cancel{C}) = 2.6 \times 10^4 \, J$$

Thus

$$q = q_P = \Delta H = -2.6 \times 10^4 \, J$$

Since 1.0 L of 1.0 M $Ba(NO_3)_2$ contains 1 mol Ba^{2+} ions and 1.0 L of 1.0 M Na_2SO_4 contains 1.0 mol $SO_4{}^{2-}$ ions, 1.0 mol solid $BaSO_4$ is formed in this experiment. Thus the enthalpy change per mole of $BaSO_4$ formed is

$$\Delta H = -2.6 \times 10^4 \, J/mol = -26 \, kJ/mol$$

See Exercises 6.45 through 6.48.

Calorimetry experiments also can be performed at **constant volume.** For example, when a photographic flashbulb flashes, the bulb becomes very hot, because the reaction of the zirconium or magnesium wire with the oxygen inside the bulb is exothermic. The reaction occurs inside the flashbulb, which is rigid and does not change volume. Under these conditions, no work is done (because the volume must change for pressure–volume work to be performed). To study the energy changes in reactions under conditions of constant volume, a "bomb calorimeter" (Fig. 6.6) is used. Weighed reactants are placed inside a rigid steel container (the "bomb") and ignited. The energy change is determined by measuring the increase in the temperature of the water and other calorimeter parts. For a constant-volume process, the change in volume ΔV is equal to zero, so work (which is $-P\Delta V$) is also equal to zero. Therefore,

$$\Delta E = q + w = q = q_V \qquad \text{(constant volume)}$$

Suppose we wish to measure the energy of combustion of octane (C_8H_{18}), a component of gasoline. A 0.5269-g sample of octane is placed in a bomb calorimeter known to have a heat capacity of 11.3 kJ/°C. This means that 11.3 kJ of energy is required to raise the temperature of the water and other parts of the calorimeter by 1°C. The octane is ignited in the presence of excess oxygen, and the temperature increase of the calorimeter is 2.25°C. The amount of energy released is calculated as follows:

Molecular Model: C_8H_{18}

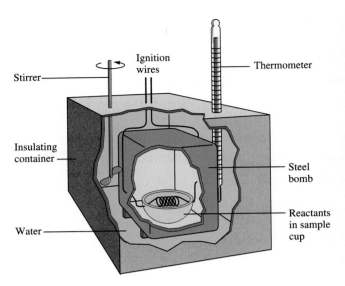

Figure 6.6

A bomb calorimeter. The reaction is carried out inside a rigid steel "bomb" (photo of actual disassembled "bomb" shown on right), and the heat evolved is absorbed by the surrounding water and other calorimeter parts. The quantity of energy produced by the reaction can be calculated from the temperature increase.

Energy released by the reaction

$$= \text{temperature increase} \times \text{energy required to change the temperature by } 1°C$$
$$= \Delta T \times \text{heat capacity of calorimeter}$$
$$= 2.25°C \times 11.3 \text{ kJ/}°C = 25.4 \text{ kJ}$$

This means that 25.4 kJ of energy was released by the combustion of 0.5269 g octane. The number of moles of octane is

$$0.5269 \text{ g octane} \times \frac{1 \text{ mol octane}}{114.2 \text{ g octane}} = 4.614 \times 10^{-3} \text{ mol octane}$$

Since 25.4 kJ of energy was released for 4.614×10^{-3} mol octane, the energy released per mole is

$$\frac{25.4 \text{ kJ}}{4.614 \times 10^{-3} \text{ mol}} = 5.50 \times 10^3 \text{ kJ/mol}$$

Since the reaction is exothermic, ΔE is negative:

$$\Delta E_{\text{combustion}} = -5.50 \times 10^3 \text{ kJ/mol}$$

Note that since no work is done in this case, ΔE is equal to the heat.

$$\Delta E = q + w = q \qquad \text{since } w = 0$$

Thus $q = -5.50 \times 10^3$ kJ/mol.

CHEMICAL IMPACT

Firewalking: Magic or Science?

A Hindu firewalking ceremony in the Fiji Islands.

FOR MILLENNIA PEOPLE have been amazed at the ability of Eastern mystics to walk across beds of glowing coals without any apparent discomfort. Even in the United States, thousands of people have performed feats of firewalking as part of motivational seminars. How is this possible? Do firewalkers have supernatural powers?

Actually, there are good scientific explanations, based on the concepts covered in this chapter, of why firewalking is possible. The first important factor concerns the heat capacity of feet. Because human tissue is mainly composed of water, it has a relatively large specific heat capacity. This means that a large amount of energy must be transferred from the coals to significantly change the temperature of the feet. During the brief contact between feet and coals, there is relatively little time for energy flow so the feet do not reach a high enough temperature to cause damage.

Second, although the surface of the coals has a very high temperature, the red hot layer is very thin. Therefore, the quantity of energy available to heat the feet is smaller than might be expected. This factor points to the difference between temperature and heat. Temperature reflects the *intensity* of the random kinetic energy in a given sample of matter. The amount of energy available for heat flow, on the other hand, depends on the quantity of matter at a given temperature—ten grams of matter at a given temperature contains ten times as much thermal energy as one gram of the same matter. This is why the tiny spark from a sparkler does not hurt when it hits your hand. The spark has a very high temperature but has so little mass that no significant energy transfer occurs to your hand. This same argument applies to the very thin hot layer on the coals.

Thus, although firewalking is an impressive feat, there are several sound scientific reasons why it is possible (with the proper training and a properly prepared bed of coals).

Sample Exercise 6.6 *Constant-Volume Calorimetry*

It has been suggested that hydrogen gas obtained by the decomposition of water might be a substitute for natural gas (principally methane). To compare the energies of combustion of these fuels, the following experiment was carried out using a bomb calorimeter with a heat capacity of 11.3 kJ/°C. When a 1.50-g sample of methane gas was burned with excess oxygen in the calorimeter, the temperature increased by 7.3°C. When a 1.15-g sample of hydrogen gas was burned with excess oxygen, the temperature increase was 14.3°C. Calculate the energy of combustion (per gram) for hydrogen and methane.

Hydrogen's potential as a fuel is discussed in Section 6.6.

Solution

We calculate the energy of combustion for methane using the heat capacity of the calorimeter (11.3 kJ/°C) and the observed temperature increase of 7.3°C:

$$\text{Energy } \textit{released} \text{ in the combustion of 1.5 g CH}_4 = (11.3 \text{ kJ/°C})(7.3°C)$$
$$= 83 \text{ kJ}$$

The direction of energy flow is indicated by words in this example. Using signs to designate the direction of energy flow:

$$\Delta E_{combustion} = -55 \text{ kJ/g}$$

for methane and

$$\Delta E_{combustion} = -141 \text{ kJ/g}$$

for hydrogen.

$$\text{Energy } \textit{released} \text{ in the combustion of 1 g CH}_4 = \frac{83 \text{ kJ}}{1.5 \text{ g}} = 55 \text{ kJ/g}$$

Similarly, for hydrogen

$$\text{Energy } \textit{released} \text{ in the combustion of 1.15 g H}_2 = (11.3 \text{ kJ/°C})(14.3°C)$$
$$= 162 \text{ kJ}$$

$$\text{Energy } \textit{released} \text{ in the combustion of 1 g H}_2 = \frac{162 \text{ kJ}}{1.15 \text{ g}} = 141 \text{ kJ/g}$$

The energy released in the combustion of 1 g hydrogen is approximately 2.5 times that for 1 g methane, indicating that hydrogen gas is a potentially useful fuel.

See Exercises 6.49 and 6.50.

6.3   Hess's Law

ΔH is not dependent on the reaction pathway.

Since enthalpy is a state function, the change in enthalpy in going from some initial state to some final state is independent of the pathway. This means that *in going from a particular set of reactants to a particular set of products, the change in enthalpy is the same whether the reaction takes place in one step or in a series of steps.* This principle is known as **Hess's law** and can be illustrated by examining the oxidation of nitrogen to produce nitrogen dioxide. The overall reaction can be written in one step, where the enthalpy change is represented by ΔH_1.

Molecular Models: N$_2$, O$_2$, NO$_2$

$$N_2(g) + 2O_2(g) \longrightarrow 2NO_2(g) \qquad \Delta H_1 = 68 \text{ kJ}$$

This reaction also can be carried out in two distinct steps, with enthalpy changes designated by ΔH_2 and ΔH_3:

$$N_2(g) + O_2(g) \longrightarrow 2NO(g) \qquad\qquad \Delta H_2 = 180 \text{ kJ}$$
$$2NO(g) + O_2(g) \longrightarrow 2NO_2(g) \qquad\qquad \Delta H_3 = -112 \text{ kJ}$$

$$\text{Net reaction:} \quad N_2(g) + 2O_2(g) \longrightarrow 2NO_2(g) \qquad \Delta H_2 + \Delta H_3 = 68 \text{ kJ}$$

Note that the sum of the two steps gives the net, or overall, reaction and that

$$\Delta H_1 = \Delta H_2 + \Delta H_3 = 68 \text{ kJ}$$

The principle of Hess's law is shown schematically in Fig. 6.7.

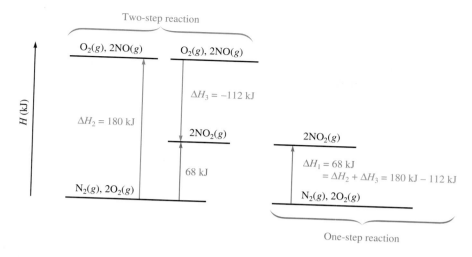

Two-step reaction

$\Delta H_2 = 180$ kJ

$\Delta H_3 = -112$ kJ

$O_2(g), 2NO(g)$ $O_2(g), 2NO(g)$

$2NO_2(g)$

$N_2(g), 2O_2(g)$

68 kJ

$2NO_2(g)$

$\Delta H_1 = 68$ kJ
$= \Delta H_2 + \Delta H_3 = 180$ kJ $- 112$ kJ

$N_2(g), 2O_2(g)$

One-step reaction

Figure 6.7

The principle of Hess's law. The same change in enthalpy occurs when nitrogen and oxygen react to form nitrogen dioxide, regardless of whether the reaction occurs in one (red) or two (blue) steps.

Characteristics of Enthalpy Changes

In order to use Hess's law to compute enthalpy changes for reactions, it is important to understand two characteristics of ΔH for a reaction:

1. If a reaction is reversed, the sign of ΔH is also reversed.

2. The magnitude of ΔH is directly proportional to the quantities of reactants and products in a reaction. If the coefficients in a balanced reaction are multiplied by an integer, the value of ΔH is multiplied by the same integer.

Both these rules follow in a straightforward way from the properties of enthalpy changes. The first rule can be explained by recalling that the *sign* of ΔH indicates the *direction* of the heat flow at constant pressure. If the direction of the reaction is reversed, the direction of the heat flow also will be reversed. To see this, consider the preparation of xenon tetrafluoride, which was the first binary compound made from a noble gas:

$$Xe(g) + 2F_2(g) \longrightarrow XeF_4(s) \qquad \Delta H = -251 \text{ kJ}$$

This reaction is exothermic, and 251 kJ of energy flows into the surroundings as heat. On the other hand, if the colorless XeF_4 crystals are decomposed into the elements, according to the equation

$$XeF_4(s) \longrightarrow Xe(g) + 2F_2(g)$$

the opposite energy flow occurs because 251 kJ of energy must be added to the system to produce this endothermic reaction. Thus, for this reaction, $\Delta H = +251$ kJ.

The second rule comes from the fact that ΔH is an extensive property, depending on the amount of substances reacting. For example, since 251 kJ of energy is evolved for the reaction

$$Xe(g) + 2F_2(g) \longrightarrow XeF_4(s)$$

then for a preparation involving twice the quantities of reactants and products, or

$$2Xe(g) + 4F_2(g) \longrightarrow 2XeF_4(s)$$

twice as much heat would be evolved:

$$\Delta H = 2(-251 \text{ kJ}) = -502 \text{ kJ}$$

Reversing the direction of a reaction changes the sign of ΔH.

Crystals of xenon tetrafluoride, the first reported binary compound containing a noble gas element.

Molecular Models: F_2, XeF_4

Molecular Models: graphite, diamond

Sample Exercise 6.7 *Hess's Law I*

Two forms of carbon are *graphite,* the soft, black, slippery material used in "lead" pencils and as a lubricant for locks, and *diamond,* the brilliant, hard gemstone. Using the enthalpies of combustion for graphite (-394 kJ/mol) and diamond (-396 kJ/mol), calculate ΔH for the conversion of graphite to diamond:

$$C_{graphite}(s) \longrightarrow C_{diamond}(s)$$

Solution

The combustion reactions are

$$C_{graphite}(s) + O_2(g) \longrightarrow CO_2(g) \qquad \Delta H = -394 \text{ kJ}$$
$$C_{diamond}(s) + O_2(g) \longrightarrow CO_2(g) \qquad \Delta H = -396 \text{ kJ}$$

Note that if we reverse the second reaction (which means we must change the sign of ΔH) and sum the two reactions, we obtain the desired reaction:

$$
\begin{array}{ll}
C_{graphite}(s) + O_2(g) \longrightarrow CO_2(g) & \Delta H = -394 \text{ kJ} \\
CO_2(g) \longrightarrow C_{diamond}(s) + O_2(g) & \Delta H = -(-396 \text{ kJ}) \\
\hline
C_{graphite}(s) \longrightarrow C_{diamond}(s) & \Delta H = 2 \text{ kJ}
\end{array}
$$

Thus 2 kJ of energy is required to change 1 mol graphite to diamond. This process is endothermic.

See Exercises 6.51 and 6.52.

Sample Exercise 6.8 *Hess's Law II*

Molecular Models: B₂H₆

Diborane (B_2H_6) is a highly reactive boron hydride, which was once considered as a possible rocket fuel for the U.S. space program. Calculate ΔH for the synthesis of diborane from its elements, according to the equation

$$2B(s) + 3H_2(g) \longrightarrow B_2H_6(g)$$

using the following data:

Reaction	ΔH
(a) $2B(s) + \frac{3}{2}O_2(g) \longrightarrow B_2O_3(s)$	-1273 kJ
(b) $B_2H_6(g) + 3O_2(g) \longrightarrow B_2O_3(s) + 3H_2O(g)$	-2035 kJ
(c) $H_2(g) + \frac{1}{2}O_2(g) \longrightarrow H_2O(l)$	-286 kJ
(d) $H_2O(l) \longrightarrow H_2O(g)$	44 kJ

Solution

To obtain ΔH for the required reaction, we must somehow combine equations (a), (b), (c), and (d) to produce that reaction and add the corresponding ΔH values. This can best be done by focusing on the reactants and products of the required reaction. The reactants are $B(s)$ and $H_2(g)$, and the product is $B_2H_6(g)$. How can we obtain the correct equation? Reaction (a) has $B(s)$ as a reactant, as needed in the required equation. Thus reaction (a) will be used as it is. Reaction (b) has $B_2H_6(g)$ as a reactant, but this substance is needed as a product. Thus reaction (b) must be reversed, and the sign of ΔH must be changed accordingly. Up to this point we have

$$
\begin{array}{lll}
\text{(a)} & 2B(s) + \tfrac{3}{2}O_2(g) \longrightarrow B_2O_3(s) & \Delta H = -1273 \text{ kJ} \\
-\text{(b)} & B_2O_3(s) + 3H_2O(g) \longrightarrow B_2H_6(g) + 3O_2(g) & \Delta H = -(-2035 \text{ kJ}) \\
\hline
\text{Sum:} & B_2O_3(s) + 2B(s) + \tfrac{3}{2}O_2(g) + 3H_2O(g) \longrightarrow B_2O_3(s) + B_2H_6(g) + 3O_2(g) & \Delta H = 762 \text{ kJ}
\end{array}
$$

Deleting the species that occur on both sides gives

$$2B(s) + 3H_2O(g) \longrightarrow B_2H_6(g) + \tfrac{3}{2}O_2(g) \qquad \Delta H = 762 \text{ kJ}$$

We are closer to the required reaction, but we still need to remove $H_2O(g)$ and $O_2(g)$ and introduce $H_2(g)$ as a reactant. We can do this using reactions (c) and (d). If we multiply reaction (c) and its ΔH value by 3 and add the result to the preceding equation, we have

$$
\begin{array}{lll}
& 2B(s) + 3H_2O(g) \longrightarrow B_2H_6(g) + \tfrac{3}{2}O_2(g) & \Delta H = 762 \text{ kJ} \\
3 \times \text{(c)} & 3[H_2(g) + \tfrac{1}{2}O_2(g) \longrightarrow H_2O(l)] & \Delta H = 3(-286 \text{ kJ}) \\
\hline
\text{Sum:} & 2B(s) + 3H_2(g) + \tfrac{3}{2}O_2(g) + 3H_2O(g) \longrightarrow B_2H_6(g) + \tfrac{3}{2}O_2(g) + 3H_2O(l) & \Delta H = -96 \text{ kJ}
\end{array}
$$

We can cancel the $\tfrac{3}{2}O_2(g)$ on both sides, but we cannot cancel the H_2O because it is gaseous on one side and liquid on the other. This can be solved by adding reaction (d), multiplied by 3:

$$
\begin{array}{lll}
& 2B(s) + 3H_2(g) + 3H_2O(g) \longrightarrow B_2H_6(g) + 3H_2O(l) & \Delta H = -96 \text{ kJ} \\
3 \times \text{(d)} & 3[H_2O(l) \longrightarrow H_2O(g)] & \Delta H = 3(44 \text{ kJ}) \\
\hline
& 2B(s) + 3H_2(g) + 3H_2O(g) + 3H_2O(l) \longrightarrow B_2H_6(g) + 3H_2O(l) + 3H_2O(g) & \Delta H = +36 \text{ kJ}
\end{array}
$$

This gives the reaction required by the problem:

$$2B(s) + 3H_2(g) \longrightarrow B_2H_6(g) \qquad \Delta H = +36 \text{ kJ}$$

Thus ΔH for the synthesis of 1 mol diborane from the elements is $+36$ kJ.

See Exercises 6.53 through 6.58.

HINTS FOR USING HESS'S LAW

Calculations involving Hess's law typically require that several reactions be manipulated and combined to finally give the reaction of interest. In doing this procedure you should work *backward* from the required reaction, using the reactants and products to decide how to manipulate the other given reactions at your disposal. Reverse any reactions as needed to give the required reactants and products, and then multiply reactions to give the correct numbers of reactants and products. This process involves some trial and error, but it can be very systematic if you always allow the final reaction to guide you.

6.4 Standard Enthalpies of Formation

For a reaction studied under conditions of constant pressure, we can obtain the enthalpy change using a calorimeter. However, this process can be very difficult. In fact, in some cases it is impossible, since certain reactions do not lend themselves to such study. An example is the conversion of solid carbon from its graphite form to its diamond form:

$$C_{graphite}(s) \longrightarrow C_{diamond}(s)$$

The value of ΔH for this process cannot be obtained by direct measurement in a calorimeter because the process is much too slow under normal conditions. However, as we saw in Sample Exercise 6.7, ΔH for this process can be calculated from heats of combustion. This is only one example of how useful it is to be able to *calculate* ΔH values for chemical reactions. We will next show how to do this using standard enthalpies of formation.

The **standard enthalpy of formation** (ΔH_f°) of a compound is defined as the *change in enthalpy that accompanies the formation of one mole of a compound from its elements with all substances in their standard states.*

A *degree symbol* on a thermodynamic function, for example, ΔH°, indicates that the corresponding process has been carried out under standard conditions. The **standard state** for a substance is a precisely defined reference state. Because thermodynamic functions often depend on the concentrations (or pressures) of the substances involved, we must use a common reference state to properly compare the thermodynamic properties of two substances. This is especially important because, for most thermodynamic properties, we can measure only *changes* in the property. For example, we have no method for determining absolute values of enthalpy. We can measure enthalpy changes (ΔH values) only by performing heat-flow experiments.

Recently, the International Union of Pure and Applied Chemists (IUPAC) has adopted 1 bar (100,000 Pa) as the standard pressure instead of 1 atm (101,305 Pa). Both standards are now in wide use.

Standard state is *not* the same as the standard temperature and pressure (STP) for a gas (discussed in Section 5.4).

Conventional Definitions of Standard States

For a Compound

- The standard state of a gaseous substance is a pressure of exactly 1 atmosphere.
- For a pure substance in a condensed state (liquid or solid), the standard state is the pure liquid or solid.
- For a substance present in a solution, the standard state is a concentration of exactly 1 M.

For an Element

- The standard state of an element is the form in which the element exists under conditions of 1 atmosphere and 25°C. (The standard state for oxygen is $O_2(g)$ at a pressure of 1 atmosphere; the standard state for sodium is $Na(s)$; the standard state for mercury is $Hg(l)$, and so on.)

Several important characteristics of the definition of the enthalpy of formation will become clearer if we again consider the formation of nitrogen dioxide from the elements in their standard states:

$$\tfrac{1}{2}N_2(g) + O_2(g) \longrightarrow NO_2(g) \qquad \Delta H_f^\circ = 34 \text{ kJ/mol}$$

Note that the reaction is written so that both elements are in their standard states, and 1 mole of product is formed. Enthalpies of formation are *always* given per mole of product with the product in its standard state.

The formation reaction for methanol is written as

$$C(s) + 2H_2(g) + \tfrac{1}{2}O_2(g) \longrightarrow CH_3OH(l) \qquad \Delta H_f^\circ = -239 \text{ kJ/mol}$$

The standard state of carbon is graphite, the standard states for oxygen and hydrogen are the diatomic gases, and the standard state for methanol is the liquid.

The ΔH_f° values for some common substances are shown in Table 6.2. More values are found in Appendix 4. The importance of the tabulated ΔH_f° values is that enthalpies for many reactions can be calculated using these numbers. To see how this is done, we will calculate the standard enthalpy change for the combustion of methane:

$$CH_4(g) + 2O_2(g) \longrightarrow CO_2(g) + 2H_2O(l)$$

Brown nitrogen dioxide gas.

Enthalpy is a state function, so we can invoke Hess's law and choose *any* convenient pathway from reactants to products and then sum the enthalpy changes along the chosen pathway. A convenient pathway, shown in Fig. 6.8, involves taking the reactants apart to the respective elements in their standard states in reactions (a) and (b) and then forming the products from these elements in reactions (c) and (d). This general pathway will work for any reaction, since atoms are conserved in a chemical reaction.

Note from Fig. 6.8 that reaction (a), where methane is taken apart into its elements, that is,

$$CH_4(g) \longrightarrow C(s) + 2H_2(g)$$

is just the reverse of the formation reaction for methane:

$$C(s) + 2H_2(g) \longrightarrow CH_4(g) \qquad \Delta H_f^\circ = -75 \text{ kJ/mol}$$

Video: Ammonium Chloride and Barium Hydroxide

Since reversing a reaction means changing the sign of ΔH but keeping the magnitude the same, ΔH for reaction (a) is $-\Delta H_f^\circ$, or 75 kJ. Thus $\Delta H^\circ_{(a)} = 75$ kJ.

Next we consider reaction (b). Here oxygen is already an element in its standard state, so no change is needed. Thus $\Delta H^\circ_{(b)} = 0$.

The next steps, reactions (c) and (d), use the elements formed in reactions (a) and (b) to form the products. Note that reaction (c) is simply the formation reaction for carbon dioxide:

Molecular Models: graphite, H_2, O_2, CH_3OH, CH_4, CO_2, H_2O

$$C(s) + O_2(g) \longrightarrow CO_2(g) \qquad \Delta H_f^\circ = -394 \text{ kJ/mol}$$

and

$$\Delta H^\circ_{(c)} = \Delta H_f^\circ \text{ for } CO_2(g) = -394 \text{ kJ}$$

Reaction (d) is the formation reaction for water:

$$H_2(g) + \tfrac{1}{2}O_2(g) \longrightarrow H_2O(l) \qquad \Delta H_f^\circ = -286 \text{ kJ/mol}$$

Table 6.2 Standard Enthalpies of Formation for Several Compounds at 25°C

Compound	ΔH_f° (kJ/mol)
$NH_3(g)$	−46
$NO_2(g)$	34
$H_2O(l)$	−286
$Al_2O_3(s)$	−1676
$Fe_2O_3(s)$	−826
$CO_2(g)$	−394
$CH_3OH(l)$	−239
$C_8H_{18}(l)$	−269

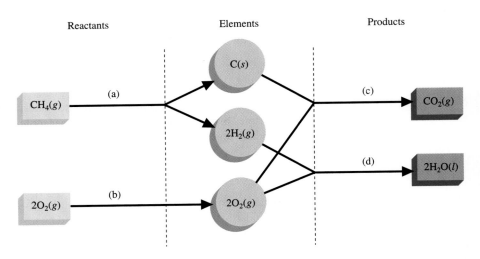

Figure 6.8

In this pathway for the combustion of methane, the reactants are first taken apart in reactions (a) and (b) to form the constituent elements in their standard states, which are then used to assemble the products in reactions (c) and (d).

However, since 2 moles of water are required in the balanced equation, we must form 2 moles of water from the elements:

$$2H_2(g) + O_2(g) \longrightarrow 2H_2O(l)$$

Thus

$$\Delta H^\circ_{(d)} = 2 \times \Delta H_f^\circ \text{ for } H_2O(l) = 2(-286 \text{ kJ}) = -572 \text{ kJ}$$

We have now completed the pathway from the reactants to the products. The change in enthalpy for the reaction is the sum of the ΔH values (including their signs) for the steps:

$\Delta H^\circ_{\text{reaction}}$

$$= \Delta H^\circ_{(a)} + \Delta H^\circ_{(b)} + \Delta H^\circ_{(c)} + \Delta H^\circ_{(d)}$$

$$= [-\Delta H_f^\circ \text{ for } CH_4(g)] + 0 + [\Delta H_f^\circ \text{ for } CO_2(g)] + [2 \times \Delta H_f^\circ \text{ for } H_2O(l)]$$

$$= -(-75 \text{ kJ}) + 0 + (-394 \text{ kJ}) + (-572 \text{ kJ})$$

$$= -891 \text{ kJ}$$

This process is diagramed in Fig. 6.9. Notice that the reactants are taken apart and converted to elements [not necessary for $O_2(g)$] that are then used to form products. You can see that this is a very exothermic reaction because very little energy is required to convert the reactants to the respective elements but a great deal of energy is released when these elements form the products. This is why this reaction is so useful for producing heat to warm homes and offices.

Let's examine carefully the pathway we used in this example. First, the reactants were broken down into the elements in their standard states. This process involved reversing the formation reactions and thus switching the signs of the enthalpies of formation. The products were then constructed from these elements. This involved formation reactions and thus enthalpies of formation. We can summarize this entire process as follows: *The enthalpy change for a given reaction can be calculated by*

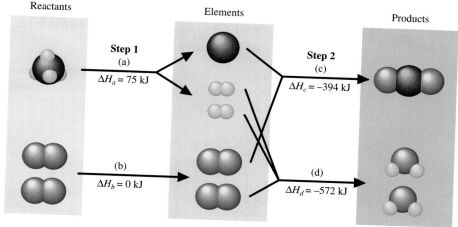

Figure 6.9

A schematic diagram of the energy changes for the reaction $CH_4(g) + 2O_2(g) \rightarrow CO_2(g) + 2H_2O(l)$.

subtracting the enthalpies of formation of the reactants from the enthalpies of formation of the products. Remember to multiply the enthalpies of formation by integers as required by the balanced equation. This statement can be represented symbolically as follows:

$$\Delta H°_{\text{reaction}} = \Sigma n_p \Delta H_f°(\text{products}) - \Sigma n_r \Delta H_f°(\text{reactants}) \qquad (6.1)$$

where the symbol Σ (sigma) means "to take the sum of the terms," and n_p and n_r represent the moles of each product or reactant, respectively.

Elements are not included in the calculation because elements require no change in form. We have in effect *defined* the enthalpy of formation of an element in its standard state as zero, since we have chosen this as our reference point for calculating enthalpy changes in reactions.

Subtraction means to reverse the sign and add.

Keep in Mind the Following Key Concepts When Doing Enthalpy Calculations:

- When a reaction is reversed, the magnitude of ΔH remains the same, but its sign changes.
- When the balanced equation for a reaction is multiplied by an integer, the value of ΔH for that reaction must be multiplied by the same integer.
- The change in enthalpy for a given reaction can be calculated from the enthalpies of formation of the reactants and products:

$$\Delta H°_{\text{reaction}} = \Sigma n_p \Delta H_f°(\text{products}) - \Sigma n_r \Delta H_f°(\text{reactants})$$

- Elements in their standard states are not included in the $\Delta H_{\text{reaction}}$ calculations. That is, $\Delta H_f°$ for an element in its standard state is zero.

Elements in their standard states are not included in enthalpy calculations using $\Delta H_f°$ values.

Sample Exercise 6.9 *Enthalpy from Standard Enthalpies of Formation I*

Using the standard enthalpies of formation listed in Table 6.2, calculate the standard enthalpy change for the overall reaction that occurs when ammonia is burned in air to form nitrogen dioxide and water. This is the first step in the manufacture of nitric acid.

$$4NH_3(g) + 7O_2(g) \longrightarrow 4NO_2(g) + 6H_2O(l)$$

Solution

We will use the pathway in which the reactants are broken down into elements in their standard states, which are then used to form the products (see Fig. 6.10).

STEP 1

Decomposition of NH₃(g) into elements (reaction (a) in Fig. 6.10). The first step is to decompose 4 moles of NH₃ into N₂ and H₂:

$$4NH_3(g) \longrightarrow 2N_2(g) + 6H_2(g)$$

The preceding reaction is 4 times the *reverse* of the formation reaction for NH₃:

$$\tfrac{1}{2}N_2(g) + \tfrac{3}{2}H_2(g) \longrightarrow NH_3(g) \qquad \Delta H_f^\circ = -46 \text{ kJ/mol}$$

Thus

$$\Delta H^\circ_{(a)} = 4 \text{ mol}[-(-46 \text{ kJ/mol})] = 184 \text{ kJ}$$

STEP 2

Elemental oxygen (reaction (b) in Fig. 6.10). Since O₂(g) is an element in its standard state, $\Delta H^\circ_{(b)} = 0$.

We now have the elements N₂(g), H₂(g), and O₂(g), which can be combined to form the products of the overall reaction.

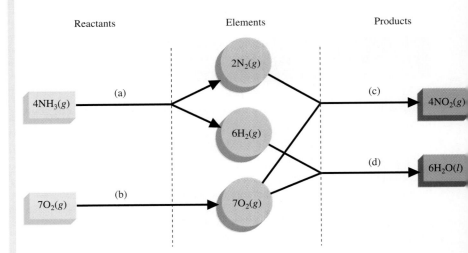

Figure 6.10
A pathway for the combustion of ammonia.

STEP 3

Synthesis of $NO_2(g)$ from elements (reaction (c) in Fig. 6.10). The overall reaction equation has 4 moles of NO_2. Thus the required reaction is 4 times the formation reaction for NO_2:

$$4 \times [\tfrac{1}{2}N_2(g) + O_2(g) \longrightarrow NO_2(g)]$$

and

$$\Delta H°_{(c)} = 4 \times \Delta H_f° \text{ for } NO_2(g)$$

From Table 6.2, $\Delta H_f°$ for $NO_2(g) = 34$ kJ/mol and

$$\Delta H°_{(c)} = 4 \text{ mol} \times 34 \text{ kJ/mol} = 136 \text{ kJ}$$

STEP 4

Synthesis of $H_2O(l)$ from elements (reaction (d) in Fig. 6.10). Since the overall equation for the reaction has 6 moles of $H_2O(l)$, the required reaction is 6 times the formation reaction for $H_2O(l)$:

$$6 \times [H_2(g) + \tfrac{1}{2}O_2(g) \longrightarrow H_2O(l)]$$

and

$$\Delta H°_{(d)} = 6 \times \Delta H_f° \text{ for } H_2O(l)$$

From Table 6.2, $\Delta H_f°$ for $H_2O(l) = -286$ kJ/mol and

$$\Delta H°_{(d)} = 6 \text{ mol} (-286 \text{ kJ/mol}) = -1716 \text{ kJ}$$

To summarize, we have done the following:

$$4NH_3(g) \xrightarrow{\Delta H°_{(a)}} \left[\begin{array}{l} 2N_2(g) + 6H_2(g) \\ 7O_2(g) \end{array} \right\} \xrightarrow[\Delta H°_{(d)}]{\Delta H°_{(c)}} \begin{array}{l} 4NO_2(g) \\ 6H_2O(l) \end{array}$$

$$7O_2(g) \xrightarrow{\Delta H°_{(b)}}$$

Elements in their
standard states

We add the $\Delta H°$ values for the steps to get $\Delta H°$ for the overall reaction:

$$\begin{aligned}
\Delta H°_{reaction} &= \Delta H°_{(a)} + \Delta H°_{(b)} + \Delta H°_{(c)} + \Delta H°_{(d)} \\
&= [4 \times -\Delta H_f° \text{ for } NH_3(g)] + 0 + [4 \times \Delta H_f° \text{ for } NO_2(g)] \\
&\quad + [6 \times \Delta H_f° \text{ for } (H_2O(l)] \\
&= [4 \times \Delta H_f° \text{ for } NO_2(g)] + [6 \times \Delta H_f° \text{ for } H_2O(l)] \\
&\quad - [4 \times \Delta H_f° \text{ for } NH_3(g)] \\
&= \Sigma n_p \Delta H_f°(\text{products}) - \Sigma n_r \Delta H_f°(\text{reactants})
\end{aligned}$$

Remember that elemental reactants and products do not need to be included, since $\Delta H_f°$ for an element in its standard state is zero. Note that we have again obtained Equation (6.1). The final solution is

$$\begin{aligned}
\Delta H°_{reaction} &= [4 \times (34 \text{ kJ})] + [6 \times (-286 \text{ kJ})] - [4 \times (-46 \text{ kJ})] \\
&= -1396 \text{ kJ}
\end{aligned}$$

See Exercises 6.61 and 6.62.

Now that we have shown the basis for Equation (6.1), we will make direct use of it to calculate ΔH for reactions in succeeding exercises.

The thermite reaction is one of the most energetic chemical reactions known.

Sample Exercise 6.10 Enthalpies from Standard Enthalpies of Formation II

Using enthalpies of formation, calculate the standard change in enthalpy for the thermite reaction:

$$2Al(s) + Fe_2O_3(s) \longrightarrow Al_2O_3(s) + 2Fe(s)$$

This reaction occurs when a mixture of powdered aluminum and iron(III) oxide is ignited with a magnesium fuse.

Solution

We use Equation (6.1):

$$\Delta H° = \Sigma n_p \Delta H_f°(\text{products}) - \Sigma n_r \Delta H_f°(\text{reactants})$$

where

$$\Delta H_f° \text{ for } Fe_2O_3(s) = -826 \text{ kJ/mol}$$
$$\Delta H_f° \text{ for } Al_2O_3(s) = -1676 \text{ kJ/mol}$$
$$\Delta H_f° \text{ for } Al(s) = \Delta H_f° \text{ for } Fe(s) = 0$$

Thus

$$\Delta H°_{\text{reaction}} = \Delta H_f° \text{ for } Al_2O_3(s) - \Delta H_f° \text{ for } Fe_2O_3(s)$$
$$= -1676 \text{ kJ} - (-826 \text{ kJ}) = -850. \text{ kJ}$$

This reaction is so highly exothermic that the iron produced is initially molten. This process is often used as a lecture demonstration and also has been used in welding massive steel objects such as ships' propellers.

See Exercises 6.65 and 6.66.

Sample Exercise 6.11 Enthalpies from Standard Enthalpies of Formation III

Methanol (CH_3OH) is often used as a fuel in high-performance engines in race cars. Using the data in Table 6.2, compare the standard enthalpy of combustion per gram of methanol with that per gram of gasoline. Gasoline is actually a mixture of compounds, but assume for this problem that gasoline is pure liquid octane (C_8H_{18}).

Solution

The combustion reaction for methanol is

$$2CH_3OH(l) + 3O_2(g) \longrightarrow 2CO_2(g) + 4H_2O(l)$$

Using the standard enthalpies of formation from Table 6.2 and Equation (6.1), we have

$$\Delta H^\circ_{reaction} = 2 \times \Delta H^\circ_f \text{ for } CO_2(g) + 4 \times \Delta H^\circ_f \text{ for } H_2O(l) -$$
$$2 \times \Delta H^\circ_f \text{ for } CH_3OH(l)$$
$$= 2 \times (-394 \text{ kJ}) + 4 \times (-286 \text{ kJ}) - 2 \times (-239 \text{ kJ})$$
$$= -1454 \text{ kJ}$$

Thus 1454 kJ of heat is evolved when 2 moles of methanol burn. The molar mass of methanol is 32.0 g/mol. This means that 1454 kJ of energy is produced when 64.0 g methanol burns. The enthalpy of combustion per gram of methanol is

$$\frac{-1454 \text{ kJ}}{64.0 \text{ g}} = -22.7 \text{ kJ/g}$$

The combustion reaction for octane is

$$2C_8H_{18}(l) + 25O_2(g) \longrightarrow 16CO_2(g) + 18H_2O(l)$$

Using the standard enthalpies of information from Table 6.2 and Equation (6.1), we have

$$\Delta H^\circ_{reaction} = 16 \times \Delta H^\circ_f \text{ for } CO_2(g) + 18 \times \Delta H^\circ_f \text{ for } H_2O(l) -$$
$$2 \times \Delta H^\circ_f \text{ for } C_8H_{18}(l)$$
$$= 16 \times (-394 \text{ kJ}) + 18 \times (-286 \text{ kJ}) - 2 \times (-269 \text{ kJ})$$
$$= -1.09 \times 10^4 \text{ kJ}$$

Video: Thermite Reaction

This is the amount of heat evolved when 2 moles of octane burn. Since the molar mass of octane is 114.2 g/mol, the enthalpy of combustion per gram of octane is

$$\frac{-1.09 \times 10^4 \text{ kJ}}{2(114.2 \text{ g})} = -47.8 \text{ kJ/g}$$

The enthalpy of combustion per gram of octane is approximately twice that per gram of methanol. On this basis, gasoline appears to be superior to methanol for use in a racing car, where weight considerations are usually very important. Why then is methanol in fact used in racing cars? The answer is that methanol burns much more smoothly than gasoline in high-performance engines, and this advantage more than compensates for its weight disadvantage.

See Exercise 6.71.

6.5 *Present Sources of Energy*

Woody plants, coal, petroleum, and natural gas provide a vast resource of energy that originally came from the sun. By the process of photosynthesis, plants store energy that can be claimed by burning the plants themselves or the decay products that have been converted over millions of years to **fossil fuels.** Although the United States currently depends heavily on petroleum for energy, this dependency is a relatively recent phenomenon, as shown in Fig. 6.11. In this section we discuss some sources of energy and their effects on the environment.

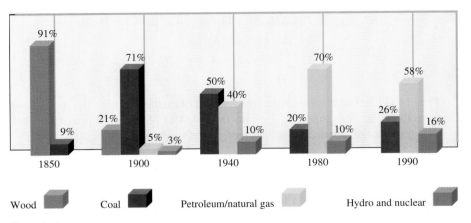

Figure 6.11
Energy sources used in the United States.

Table 6.3 Names and Formulas for Some Common Hydrocarbons	
Formula	*Name*
CH_4	Methane
C_2H_6	Ethane
C_3H_8	Propane
C_4H_{10}	Butane
C_5H_{12}	Pentane
C_6H_{14}	Hexane
C_7H_{16}	Heptane
C_8H_{18}	Octane

Table 6.4 Uses of the Various Petroleum Fractions	
Petroleum Fraction in Terms of Numbers of Carbon Atoms	*Major Uses*
C_5–C_{10}	Gasoline
C_{10}–C_{18}	Kerosene
	Jet fuel
C_{15}–C_{25}	Diesel fuel
	Heating oil
	Lubricating oil
$>C_{25}$	Asphalt

Petroleum and Natural Gas

Although how they were produced is not completely understood, petroleum and natural gas were most likely formed from the remains of marine organisms that lived approximately 500 million years ago. **Petroleum** is a thick, dark liquid composed mostly of compounds called *hydrocarbons* that contain carbon and hydrogen. (Carbon is unique among elements in the extent to which it can bond to itself to form chains of various lengths.) Table 6.3 gives the formulas and names for several common hydrocarbons. **Natural gas,** usually associated with petroleum deposits, consists mostly of methane, but it also contains significant amounts of ethane, propane, and butane.

The composition of petroleum varies somewhat, but it consists mostly of hydrocarbons having chains that contain from 5 to more than 25 carbons. To be used efficiently, the petroleum must be separated into fractions by boiling. The lighter molecules (having the lowest boiling points) can be boiled off, leaving the heavier ones behind. The commercial uses of various petroleum fractions are shown in Table 6.4.

The petroleum era began when the demand for lamp oil during the Industrial Revolution outstripped the traditional sources: animal fats and whale oil. In response to this increased demand, Edwin Drake drilled the first oil well in 1859 at Titusville, Pennsylvania. The petroleum from this well was refined to produce *kerosene* (fraction C_{10}–C_{18}), which served as an excellent lamp oil. *Gasoline* (fraction C_5–C_{10}) had limited use and was often discarded. However this situation soon changed. The development of the electric light decreased the need for kerosene, and the advent of the "horseless carriage" with its gasoline-powered engine signaled the birth of the gasoline age.

As gasoline became more important, new ways were sought to increase the yield of gasoline obtained from each barrel of petroleum. William Burton invented a process at Standard Oil of Indiana called *pyrolytic (high-temperature) cracking.* In this process, the heavier molecules of the kerosene fraction are heated to about 700°C, causing them to break (crack) into the smaller molecules of hydrocarbons in the gasoline fraction. As cars became larger, more efficient internal combustion engines were designed. Because of the uneven burning of the gasoline then available, these engines "knocked," producing unwanted noise and even engine damage. Intensive research to find additives that would promote smoother burning produced tetraethyl lead, $(C_2H_5)_4Pb$, a very effective "antiknock" agent.

The addition of tetraethyl lead to gasoline became a common practice, and by 1960, gasoline contained as much as 3 grams of lead per gallon. As we have discovered so often in recent years, technological advances can produce environmental problems. To prevent air pollution from automobile exhaust, catalytic converters have been added to car exhaust systems. The effectiveness of these converters, however, is destroyed by lead. The use of leaded gasoline also greatly increased the amount of lead in the environment, where it can be ingested by animals and humans. For these reasons, the use of lead in gasoline has been phased out, requiring extensive (and expensive) modifications of engines and of the gasoline refining process.

Coal

Coal was formed from the remains of plants that were buried and subjected to high pressure and heat over long periods of time. Plant materials have a high content of cellulose, a complex molecule whose empirical formula is CH_2O but whose molar mass is around 500,000 g/mol. After the plants and trees that flourished on the earth at various times and places died and were buried, chemical changes gradually lowered the oxygen and hydrogen content of the cellulose molecules. Coal "matures" through four stages: lignite, subbituminous, bituminous, and anthracite. Each stage has a higher carbon-to-oxygen and carbon-to-hydrogen ratio; that is, the relative carbon content gradually increases. Typical elemental compositions of the various coals are given in Table 6.5. The energy available from the combustion of a given mass of coal increases as the carbon content increases. Therefore, anthracite is the most valuable coal, and lignite, the least.

Coal is an important and plentiful fuel in the United States, currently furnishing approximately 20% of our energy. As the supply of petroleum dwindles, the share of the energy supply from coal could increase to as high as 30% by the year 2000. However, coal is expensive and dangerous to mine underground, and the strip mining of fertile farmland in the Midwest or of scenic land in the West causes obvious problems. In addition, the burning of coal, especially high-sulfur coal, yields air pollutants such as sulfur dioxide, which, in turn, can lead to acid rain, as we learned in Chapter 5. However, even if coal were pure carbon, the carbon dioxide produced when it was burned would still have significant effects on the earth's climate.

Coal has variable composition depending on both its age and location.

Coal being strip-mined.

Table 6.5 Elemental Composition of Various Types of Coal					
	Mass Percent of Each Element				
Type of Coal	*C*	*H*	*O*	*N*	*S*
Lignite	71	4	23	1	1
Subbituminous	77	5	16	1	1
Bituminous	80	6	8	1	5
Anthracite	92	3	3	1	1

Effects of Carbon Dioxide on Climate

The earth receives a tremendous quantity of radiant energy from the sun, about 30% of which is reflected back into space by the earth's atmosphere. The remaining energy passes through the atmosphere to the earth's surface. Some of this energy is absorbed by plants for photosynthesis and some by the oceans to evaporate water, but most of it is absorbed by soil, rocks, and water, increasing the temperature of the earth's surface. This energy is in turn radiated from the heated surface mainly as *infrared radiation*, often called *heat radiation*.

The atmosphere, like window glass, is transparent to visible light but does not allow all the infrared radiation to pass back into space. Molecules in the atmosphere, principally H_2O and CO_2, strongly absorb infrared radiation and radiate it back toward the earth, as shown in Fig. 6.12, so a net amount of thermal energy is retained by the earth's atmosphere, causing the earth to be much warmer than it would be without its atmosphere. In a way, the atmosphere acts like the glass of a greenhouse, which is transparent to visible light but absorbs infrared radiation, thus raising the temperature inside the building. This **greenhouse effect** is seen even more spectacularly on Venus, where the dense atmosphere is thought to be responsible for the high surface temperature of that planet.

Thus the temperature of the earth's surface is controlled to a significant extent by the carbon dioxide and water content of the atmosphere. The effect of atmospheric moisture (humidity) is apparent in the Midwest. In summer, when the humidity is high, the heat of the sun is retained well into the night, giving very high nighttime temperatures. On the other hand, in winter, the coldest temperatures always occur on clear nights, when the low humidity allows efficient radiation of energy back into space.

The atmosphere's water content is controlled by the water cycle (evaporation and precipitation), and the average remains constant over the years. However, as fossil fuels have been used more extensively, the carbon dioxide concentration has increased by about 16% from 1880 to 1980. Projections indicate that the carbon dioxide content of the atmosphere may be double in the twenty-first century what it was in 1880. This *could* increase the earth's average temperature by as much as 3°C, causing dramatic changes in climate and greatly affecting the growth of food crops.

How well can we predict long-term effects? Because weather has been studied for a period of time that is minuscule compared with the age of the earth, the factors that control the earth's climate in the long range are not clearly understood. For example, we do not understand what causes the earth's periodic ice ages. So it is difficult to estimate the impact of the increasing carbon dioxide levels.

In fact, the variation in the earth's average temperature over the past century is somewhat confusing. In the northern latitudes during the past century, the average

The electromagnetic spectrum, including visible and infrared radiation, is discussed in Chapter 7.

The average temperature of the earth's surface is 298 K. It would be 255 K without the "greenhouse gases."

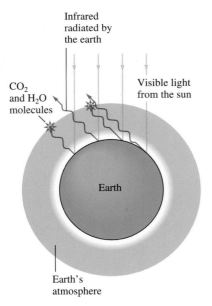

Figure 6.12

The earth's atmosphere is transparent to visible light from the sun. This visible light strikes the earth, and part of it is changed to infrared radiation. This infrared radiation from the earth's surface is strongly absorbed by CO_2, H_2O, and other molecules present in smaller amounts (for example, CH_4 and N_2O) in the atmosphere. In effect, the atmosphere traps some of the energy, acting like the glass in a greenhouse and keeping the earth warmer than it would otherwise be.

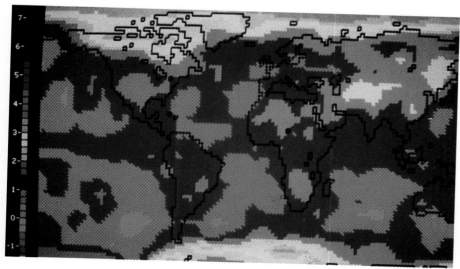

Changes in annual mean temperature between 1958 and (projected) 2010–2019.

temperature rose by 0.8°C over a period of 60 years, then cooled by 0.5°C during the next 25 years, and finally warmed by 0.2°C in the succeeding 15 years. Such fluctuations do not match the steady increase in carbon dioxide. However, in southern latitudes and near the equator during the past century, the average temperature showed a steady rise totaling 0.4°C. This figure is in reasonable agreement with the predicted effect of the increasing carbon dioxide concentration over that period. Another significant fact is that the past 10 years constitute the warmest decade on record.

Although the exact relationship between the carbon dioxide concentration in the atmosphere and the earth's temperature is not known at present, one thing is clear: The increase in the atmospheric concentration of carbon dioxide is quite dramatic (see Fig. 6.13). We must consider the implications of this increase as we consider our future energy needs.*

6.6 New Energy Sources

As we search for the energy sources of the future, we need to consider economic, climatic, and supply factors. There are several potential energy sources: the sun (solar), nuclear processes (fission and fusion), biomass (plants), and synthetic fuels. Direct use of the sun's radiant energy to heat our homes and run our factories and transportation systems seems a sensible long-term goal. But what do we do now? Conservation of fossil fuels is one obvious step, but substitutes for fossil fuels also must be found. We will discuss some alternative sources of energy here. Nuclear power will be considered in Chapter 21.

*For a review of this topic, see "Web of Interactions Makes It Difficult to Untangle Global Warming Data," by Bette Hileman, *Chemical and Engineering News* (April 27, 1992): 7.

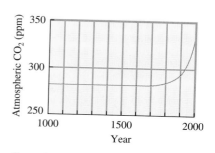

Figure 6.13

The atmospheric CO_2 concentration over the past 1000 years, based on ice core data and direct readings (since 1958). Note the dramatic increase in the past 100 years.

Coal Conversion

One alternative energy source involves using a traditional fuel—coal—in new ways. Since transportation costs for solid coal are high, more energy-efficient fuels are being developed from coal. One possibility is to produce a gaseous fuel. Substances like coal that contain large molecules have high boiling points and tend to be solids or thick liquids. To convert coal from a solid to a gas therefore requires reducing the size of the molecules; the coal structure must be broken down in a process called *coal gasification.* This is done by treating the coal with oxygen and steam at high temperatures to break many of the carbon–carbon bonds. These bonds are replaced by carbon–hydrogen and carbon–oxygen bonds as the coal fragments react with the water and oxygen. The process is represented in Fig. 6.14. The desired product is a mixture of carbon monoxide and hydrogen called *synthetic gas,* or **syngas,** and methane (CH_4) gas. Since all the components of this product can react with oxygen to release heat in a combustion reaction, this gas is a useful fuel.

One of the most important considerations in designing an industrial process is efficient use of energy. In coal gasification, some of the reactions are exothermic:

$$C(s) + 2H_2(g) \longrightarrow CH_4(g) \qquad \Delta H° = -75 \text{ kJ}$$
$$C(s) + \tfrac{1}{2}O_2(g) \longrightarrow CO(g) \qquad \Delta H° = -111 \text{ kJ}$$
$$C(s) + O_2(g) \longrightarrow CO_2(g) \qquad \Delta H° = -394 \text{ kJ}$$

Other gasification reactions are endothermic, for example:

$$C(s) + H_2O(g) \longrightarrow H_2(g) + CO(g) \qquad \Delta H° = 131 \text{ kJ}$$

A portable, solar-powered traffic speed reminder in Bishop, California.

Figure 6.14

Coal gasification. Reaction of coal with a mixture of steam and air breaks down the large hydrocarbon molecules in the coal to smaller gaseous molecules, which can be used as fuels.

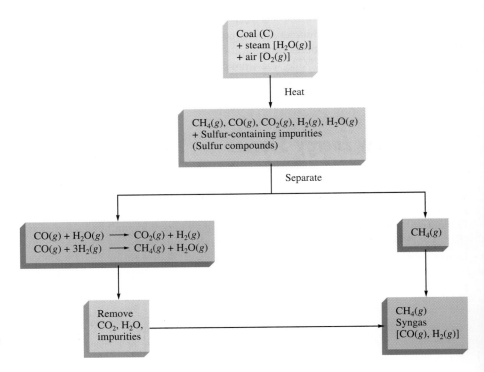

If such conditions as the rate of feed of coal, air, and steam are carefully controlled, the correct temperature can be maintained in the process without using any external energy source. That is, an energy balance is maintained.

An industrial process must be energy efficient.

As stated earlier, syngas can be used directly as a fuel, but it is also important as a raw material to produce other fuels. For example, syngas can be converted directly to methanol:

$$CO(g) + 2H_2(g) \longrightarrow CH_3OH(l)$$

Methanol is used in the production of synthetic fibers and plastics and also can be used as a fuel. In addition, it can be converted directly to gasoline. Approximately half of South Africa's gasoline supply comes from methanol produced from syngas.

In addition to coal gasification, the formation of *coal slurries* is another new use of coal. A slurry is a suspension of fine particles in a liquid, and coal must be pulverized and mixed with water to form a slurry. The slurry can be handled, stored, and burned in ways similar to those used for *residual oil,* a heavy fuel oil from petroleum accounting for almost 15% of U.S. petroleum imports. One hope is that coal slurries might replace solid coal and residual oil as fuels for electricity-generating power plants. However, the water needed for slurries might place an unacceptable burden on water resources, especially in the western states.

Hydrogen as a Fuel

If you have ever seen a lecture demonstration where hydrogen–oxygen mixtures were ignited, or if you have seen a newsfilm or an old photo of the Hindenburg disaster, you have witnessed a demonstration of hydrogen's potential as a fuel. The combustion reaction is

$$H_2(g) + \tfrac{1}{2}O_2(g) \longrightarrow H_2O(l) \qquad \Delta H^\circ = -286 \text{ kJ}$$

As we saw in Sample Exercise 6.6, the heat of combustion of $H_2(g)$ per gram is approximately 2.5 times that of natural gas. In addition, hydrogen has a real advantage over fossil fuels in that the only product of hydrogen combustion is water; fossil fuels also produce carbon dioxide. However, even though it appears that hydrogen is a very logical choice as a major fuel for the future, there are three main problems: the cost of production, storage, and transport.

First let's look at the production problem. Although hydrogen is very abundant on earth, virtually none of it exists as the free gas. Currently, the main source of hydrogen gas is from the treatment of natural gas with steam:

$$CH_4(g) + H_2O(g) \longrightarrow 3H_2(g) + CO(g)$$

We can calculate ΔH for this reaction using Equation (6.1):

$$
\begin{aligned}
\Delta H^\circ &= \Sigma n_p \Delta H_f^\circ(\text{products}) - \Sigma n_r \Delta H_f^\circ(\text{reactants}) \\
&= \Delta H_f^\circ \text{ for } CO(g) - \Delta H_f^\circ \text{ for } CH_4(g) - \Delta H_f^\circ \text{ for } H_2O(g) \\
&= -111 \text{ kJ} - (-75 \text{ kJ}) - (-242 \text{ kJ}) = 206 \text{ kJ}
\end{aligned}
$$

Note that this reaction is highly endothermic; treating methane with steam is not an efficient way to obtain hydrogen for fuel. It would be much more economical to burn the methane directly.

A virtually inexhaustible supply of hydrogen exists in the waters of the world's oceans. However, the reaction

$$H_2O(l) \longrightarrow H_2(g) + \tfrac{1}{2}O_2(g)$$

requires 286 kJ of energy per mole of liquid water, and under current circumstances, large-scale production of hydrogen from water is not economically feasible. However, several methods for such production are currently being studied: electrolysis of water, thermal decomposition of water, thermochemical decomposition of water, and biological decomposition of water.

Electrolysis will be discussed in Chapter 17.

Electrolysis of water involves passing an electric current through it, as shown in Fig. 1.12 in Chapter 1. The present cost of electricity makes the hydrogen produced by electrolysis too expensive to be competitive as a fuel. However, if in the future we develop more efficient sources of electricity, this situation could change.

Thermal decomposition is another method for producing hydrogen from water. This involves heating the water to several thousand degrees, where it spontaneously decomposes into hydrogen and oxygen. However, attaining temperatures in this range would be very expensive even if a practical heat source and a suitable reaction container were available.

In the thermochemical decomposition of water, chemical reactions, as well as heat, are used to "split" water into its components. One such system involves the following reactions (the temperature required for each is given in parentheses):

$$
\begin{array}{ll}
2HI \longrightarrow I_2 + H_2 & (425°C) \\
2H_2O + SO_2 + I_2 \longrightarrow H_2SO_4 + 2HI & (90°C) \\
\underline{H_2SO_4 \longrightarrow SO_2 + H_2O + \tfrac{1}{2}O_2} & \underline{(825°C)}
\end{array}
$$

Net reaction: $H_2O \longrightarrow H_2 + \tfrac{1}{2}O_2$

Note that the HI is not consumed in the net reaction. Note also that the maximum temperature required is 825°C, a temperature that is feasible if a nuclear reactor is used as a heat source. A current research goal is to find a system for which the required temperatures are low enough that sunlight can be used as the energy source.

But what about the organisms that decompose water without the aid of electricity or high temperatures? In the process of photosynthesis, green plants absorb carbon dioxide and water and use them along with energy from the sun to produce the substances needed for growth. Scientists have studied photosynthesis for years, hoping to get answers to humanity's food and energy shortages. At present, much of this research involves attempts to modify the photosynthetic process so that plants will release hydrogen gas from water instead of using the hydrogen to produce complex compounds. Small-scale experiments have shown that under certain conditions plants do produce hydrogen gas, but the yields are far from being commercially useful. At this point the economical production of hydrogen gas remains unrealized.

The storage and transportation of hydrogen also present problems. First, on metal surfaces the H_2 molecule decomposes to atoms. Since the atoms are so small, they can migrate into the metal, causing structural changes that make it brittle. This might lead to a pipeline failure if hydrogen were pumped under high pressure.

A second problem is the relatively small amount of energy that is available *per unit volume* of hydrogen gas. Although the energy available per gram of hydrogen is significantly greater than that per gram of methane, the energy available per given

Green plants, such as these wildflowers at the base of Torrey's Peak in Colorado, store energy from the sun.

volume of hydrogen is about one-third that available from the same volume of methane. This is demonstrated in Sample Exercise 6.12.

Sample Exercise 6.12 *Enthalpies of Combustion*

Compare the energy available from the combustion of a given volume of methane and the same volume of hydrogen at the same temperature and pressure.

Solution

In Sample Exercise 6.6 we calculated the heat released for the combustion of methane and hydrogen: 55 kJ/g CH_4 and 141 kJ/g H_2. We also know from our study of gases that 1 mol $H_2(g)$ has the same volume as 1 mol $CH_4(g)$ at the same temperature and pressure (assuming ideal behavior). Thus, for molar volumes of both gases under the same conditions of temperature and pressure,

$$\frac{\text{Enthalpy of combustion of 1 molar volume of } H_2(g)}{\text{Enthalpy of combustion of 1 molar volume of } CH_4(g)}$$

$$= \frac{\text{enthalpy of combustion per mole of } H_2}{\text{enthalpy of combustion per mole of } CH_4}$$

$$= \frac{(-141 \text{ kJ/g})(2.02 \text{ g } H_2/\text{mol } H_2)}{(-55 \text{ kJ/g})(16.04 \text{ g } CH_4/\text{mol } CH_4)}$$

$$= \frac{-285}{-882} \approx \frac{1}{3}$$

Thus about three times the volume of hydrogen gas is needed to furnish the same energy as a given volume of methane.

See Exercise 6.72.

Could hydrogen be considered as a potential fuel for automobiles? This is an intriguing question. The internal combustion engines in automobiles can be easily adapted to burn hydrogen. However, the primary difficulty is the storage of enough hydrogen to give an automobile a reasonable range. This is illustrated by Sample Exercise 6.13.

Sample Exercise 6.13 *Comparing Enthalpies of Combustion*

Assuming that the combustion of hydrogen gas provides three times as much energy per gram as gasoline, calculate the volume of liquid H_2 (density = 0.0710 g/mL) required to furnish the energy contained in 80.0 L (about 20 gal) of gasoline (density = 0.740 g/mL). Calculate also the volume that this hydrogen would occupy as a gas at 1.00 atm and 25°C.

Solution

The mass of 80.0 L gasoline is

$$80.0 \, L \times \frac{1000 \, mL}{1 \, L} \times \frac{0.740 \, g}{mL} = 59{,}200 \, g$$

Since H_2 furnishes three times as much energy per gram as gasoline, only a third as much liquid hydrogen is needed to furnish the same energy:

$$\text{Mass of } H_2(l) \text{ needed} = \frac{59{,}200 \, g}{3} = 19{,}700 \, g$$

Since density = mass/volume, then volume = mass/density, and the volume of $H_2(l)$ needed is

$$V = \frac{19{,}700 \, g}{0.0710 \, g/mL}$$

$$= 2.77 \times 10^5 \, mL = 277 \, L$$

Thus 277 L of liquid H_2 is needed to furnish the same energy of combustion as 80.0 L of gasoline.

To calculate the volume that this hydrogen would occupy as a gas at 1.00 atm and 25°C, we use the ideal gas law:

$$PV = nRT$$

In this case

$$P = 1.00 \text{ atm, } T = 273 + 25°C = 298 \text{ K, and } R = 0.08206 \text{ L} \cdot \text{atm/K} \cdot \text{mol.}$$

Also,

$$n = 19{,}700 \, g \, H_2 \times \frac{1 \text{ mol } H_2}{2.02 \, g \, H_2} = 9.75 \times 10^3 \text{ mol } H_2$$

Thus

$$V = \frac{nRT}{P} = \frac{(9.75 \times 10^3 \, mol)(0.08206 \text{ L} \cdot atm/K \cdot mol)(298 \, K)}{1.00 \, atm}$$

$$= 2.38 \times 10^5 \, L = 238{,}000 \, L$$

At 1 atm and 25°C, the hydrogen gas needed to replace 20 gal of gasoline occupies a volume of 238,000 L.

See Exercises 6.73 and 6.74.

You can see from Sample Exercise 6.13 that an automobile would need a huge tank to hold enough hydrogen gas (at 1 atm) to have a typical mileage range. Clearly, hydrogen must be stored as a liquid or in some other way. Is this feasible? Because of its very low boiling point (20 K), storage of liquid hydrogen requires a superinsulated container that can withstand high pressures. Storage in this manner would be both expensive and hazardous because of the potential for explosion. Thus storage of hydrogen in the individual automobile as a liquid does not seem practical.

CHEMICAL IMPACT

Heat Packs

A SKIER IS trapped by a sudden snowstorm. After building a snow cave for protection, she realizes her hands and feet are freezing; she is in danger of frostbite. Then she remembers the four small packs in her pocket. She removes the plastic cover from each one to reveal a small paper packet. She places one packet in each boot and one in each mitten. Soon her hands and feet are toasty warm.

These "magic" packets of energy contain a mixture of powdered iron, activated carbon, sodium chloride, cellulose (sawdust), and zeolite, all moistened by a little water. The paper cover is permeable to air.

The exothermic reaction that produces the heat is a very common one—the rusting of iron. The overall reaction can be represented as

$$4Fe(s) + 3O_2(g) \longrightarrow 2Fe_2O_3(s)$$
$$\Delta H° = -1652 \text{ kJ}$$

although in reality it is somewhat more complicated. When the plastic envelope is removed, O_2 molecules penetrate the paper and the reaction begins.

The oxidation of iron by oxygen occurs naturally. Any steel surface exposed to the atmosphere inevitably rusts, but this process is quite slow—much too slow to be useful in hot packs. However, if the iron is ground into a fine powder, the resulting increase in surface area causes the reaction with oxygen to be fast enough to warm hands and feet. Such packets can produce heat for up to 6 hours.

A popular brand of portable hot pack.

A much better alternative seems to be the use of metals that absorb hydrogen to form solid metal hydrides:

$$H_2(g) + M(s) \longrightarrow MH_2(s)$$

To use this method of storage, hydrogen gas would be pumped into a tank containing the solid metal in powdered form, where it would be absorbed to form the hydride, whose volume would be little more than that of the metal alone. This hydrogen would then be available for combustion in the engine by release of $H_2(g)$ from the hydride as needed:

$$MH_2(s) \longrightarrow M(s) + H_2(g)$$

Several types of solids that absorb hydrogen to form hydrides are being studied for use in hydrogen-powered vehicles. In fact, in 1992 Mazda unveiled a hydrogen-powered car that uses this technology. The 100-hp rotary-engined HR-X can exceed 90 mph and has a range of 120 miles on a tank of hydrogen gas.

Metal hydrides are discussed in Chapter 18.

Other Energy Alternatives

Many other energy sources are being considered for future use. The western states, especially Colorado, contain huge deposits of *oil shale,* which consists of a complex carbon-based material called *kerogen* contained in porous rock formations. These deposits have the potential of being a larger energy source than the vast

CHEMICAL IMPACT

Nature Has Hot Plants

THE VOODOO LILY is a beautiful, seductive—and foul-smelling—plant. The exotic-looking lily features an elaborate reproductive mechanism—a purple spike that can reach nearly 3 feet in length and is cloaked by a hoodlike leaf. But approach to the plant reveals bad news—it smells terrible!

Despite its antisocial odor, this putrid plant has fascinated biologists for many years because of its ability to generate heat. At the peak of its metabolic activity, the plant's blossom can be as much as 15°C above its ambient temperature. To generate this much heat, the metabolic rate of the plant must be close to that of a flying hummingbird!

What's the purpose of this intense heat production? For a plant faced with limited food supplies in the very competitive tropical climate where it grows, heat production seems like a great waste of energy. The answer to this mystery is that the voodoo lily is pollinated mainly by carrion-loving insects. Thus the lily prepares a malodorous mixture of chemicals characteristic of rotting meat, which it then "cooks" off into the surrounding air to attract flesh-feeding beetles and flies. Then, once the insects enter the pollination chamber, the high temperatures there (as high as 110°F) cause the insects to remain very active to better carry out their pollination duties.

The voodoo lily is only one of many such thermogenic (heat-producing) plants. These plants are of special interest to biologists because they provide opportunities to study metabolic reactions that are quite subtle in "normal" plants. For ex-

The voodoo lily attracts pollinating insects with its foul odor.

ample, recent studies have shown that salicylic acid, the active form of aspirin, is probably very important in producing the metabolic bursts in thermogenic plants.

Besides studying the dramatic heat effects in thermogenic plants, biologists are also interested in calorimetric studies of regular plants. For example, very precise calorimeters have been designed that can be used to study the heat produced, and thus the metabolic activities, of clumps of cells no larger than a bread crumb. Several scientists have suggested that a single calorimetric measurement taking just a few minutes on a tiny plant might be useful in predicting the growth rate of the mature plant throughout its lifetime. If true, this would provide a very efficient method for selecting the plants most likely to thrive as adults.

Because the study of the heat production by plants is an excellent way to learn about plant metabolism, this continues to be a "hot" area of research.

CHEMICAL IMPACT

Veggie Gasoline?

GASOLINE USAGE IS as high as ever, and world petroleum supplies will eventually dwindle. One possible alternative to petroleum as a source of fuels and lubricants is vegetable oil—the same vegetable oil we now use to cook french fries. Researchers believe that the oils from soybeans, corn, canola, and sunflowers all have the potential to be used in cars as well as on salads.

The use of vegetable oil for fuel is not a new idea. Rudolf Diesel reportedly used peanut oil to run one of his engines at the Paris Exposition in 1900. In addition, ethyl alcohol has been used widely as a fuel in South America and as a fuel additive in the United States.

Biodiesel, a fuel made by esterifying the fatty acids found in vegetable oil, has some real advantages over regular diesel fuel. Biodiesel produces fewer pollutants such as particulates, carbon monoxide, and complex organic molecules, and since vegetable oils have no sulfur, there is no noxious sulfur dioxide in the exhaust gases. Also, biodiesel can run in existing engines with little modification. In addition, biodiesel is much more biodegradable than petroleum-based fuels, so spills cause less environmental damage.

Of course, biodiesel also has some serious drawbacks. The main one is that it costs about three times as much as regular diesel fuel. Biodiesel also produces more nitrogen oxides in the exhaust than conventional diesel fuel and is less stable in storage. Biodiesel also can leave more gummy deposits in engines and must be "winterized" by removing com-

This promotion bus both advertises biodiesel and demonstrates its usefulness.

ponents that tend to solidify at low temperatures.

The best solution may be to use biodiesel as an additive to regular diesel fuel. One such fuel is known as B20 because it is 20% biodiesel and 80% conventional diesel fuel. B20 is especially attractive because of the higher lubricating ability of vegetable oils, thus reducing diesel engine wear.

Vegetable oils are also being looked at as replacements for motor oils and hydraulic fluids. Tests of a sunflower seed–based engine lubricant manufactured by Renewable Lubricants of Hartville, Ohio, have shown satisfactory lubricating ability while lowering particle emissions. In addition, Lou Honary and his colleagues at the University of Northern Iowa have de-

veloped BioSOY, a vegetable oil–based hydraulic fluid for use in heavy machinery.

Veggie oil fuels and lubricants seem to have a growing market as petroleum supplies wane and as environmental laws become more stringent. In Germany's Black Forest region, for example, environmental protection laws require that farm equipment use only vegetable oil fuels and lubricants. In the near future there may be veggie oil in your garage as well as in your kitchen.

Adapted from "Fill 'Er Up . . . with Veggie Oil," by Corinna Wu, as appeared in *Science News*, Vol. 154, December 5, 1998, p. 364.

petroleum deposits of the Middle East. The main problem with oil shale is that the trapped fuel is not fluid and cannot be pumped. To recover the fuel, the rock must be heated to a temperature of 250°C or higher to decompose the kerogen to smaller molecules that produce gaseous and liquid products. This process is expensive and yields large quantities of waste rock, which have a negative environmental impact.

Ethanol (C_2H_5OH) is another fuel with the potential to supplement, if not replace, gasoline. The most common method of producing ethanol is fermentation, a process in which sugar is changed to alcohol by the action of yeast. The sugar can come from virtually any source, including fruits and grains, although fuel-grade ethanol would probably come mostly from corn. Car engines can burn pure alcohol or *gasohol,* an alcohol–gasoline mixture (10% ethanol in gasoline), with little modification. Gasohol is now widely available in the United States. The use of pure alcohol as a motor fuel is not feasible in most of the United States because it does not vaporize easily when temperatures are low. However, pure ethanol could be a very practical fuel in warm climates. For example, in Brazil, large quantities of ethanol fuel are being produced for cars.

Methanol (CH_3OH), an alcohol similar to ethanol, which has been used successfully for many years in race cars, is now being evaluated as a motor fuel in California. A major gasoline retailer has agreed to install pumps at 25 locations to dispense a fuel that is 85% methanol and 15% gasoline for use in specially prepared automobiles. The California Energy Commission feels that methanol has great potential for providing a secure, long-term energy supply that would alleviate air-quality problems. Arizona and Colorado are also considering methanol as a major source of portable energy.

Another potential source of liquid fuels is oil squeezed from seeds (*seed oil*). For example, some farmers in North Dakota, South Africa, and Australia are now using sunflower oil to replace diesel fuel. Oil seeds, found in a wide variety of plants, can be processed to produce an oil composed mainly of carbon and hydrogen, which of course reacts with oxygen to produce carbon dioxide, water, and heat. It is hoped that oil-seed plants can be developed that will thrive under soil and climatic conditions unsuitable for corn and wheat. The main advantage of seed oil as a fuel is that it is renewable. Ideally, fuel would be grown just like food crops.

For Review

Key Terms

Section 6.1
energy
law of conservation of energy
potential energy
kinetic energy
heat

Summary

Energy can be defined as the capacity to do work or to produce heat. The law of conservation of energy (or the first law of thermodynamics) states that energy can be converted from one form to another, but it cannot be created or destroyed. Heat is a means for the transfer of energy. Chemical reactions can either evolve or absorb heat, depending on whether the potential energy stored in the bonds of the reactant molecules is greater or less than the energy stored in the bonds of the product molecules.

When a reaction evolves heat, it is said to be exothermic; a reaction that absorbs heat from its surroundings is endothermic. Energy is a state function; that is, a change in energy in going from one state to another is independent of the pathway.

Heat flow associated with a chemical reaction is measured by calorimetry, a technique that involves measuring temperature changes when a body absorbs or discharges heat. For a process carried out at constant pressure, the heat flow equals the change in enthalpy (ΔH).

Since enthalpy is a state function, the change in enthalpy in going from a given set of reactants to a given set of products is the same regardless of whether the reaction takes place in one step or in a series of steps (a principle known as Hess's law). We can therefore calculate the enthalpy change for an overall reaction by summing the ΔH values from a series of steps that yield that net reaction. Also, it is often convenient to calculate the ΔH° value for a reaction from values for the standard enthalpies of formation (ΔH_f°) of the reactants and products. The standard enthalpy of formation is the enthalpy change that accompanies the formation of one mole of a compound from its elements, where all substances are in their standard states. For a given reaction,

$$\Delta H^\circ_{\text{reaction}} = \Sigma n_\text{p} \Delta H_f^\circ(\text{products}) - \Sigma n_\text{r} \Delta H_f^\circ(\text{reactants})$$

The practical aspects of energy production from fossil fuels involve problems of supply and environmental impact. The combustion of carbon-based fuels produces carbon dioxide, which is involved, along with atmospheric water, in controlling the surface temperature of the earth. Increased carbon dioxide concentration in the atmosphere may produce gradual global warming due to the greenhouse effect. Alternative fuels, such as syngas from coal, hydrogen from breakdown of water, and ethanol from the fermentation of sugar, are being studied as replacements for petroleum products.

work
pathway
state function (property)
system
surroundings
exothermic
endothermic
thermodynamics
first law of thermodynamics
internal energy

Section 6.2
enthalpy
calorimeter
calorimetry
heat capacity
specific heat capacity
molar heat capacity
constant-pressure calorimetry
constant-volume calorimetry

Section 6.3
Hess's law

Section 6.4
standard enthalpy of formation
standard state

Section 6.5
fossil fuels
petroleum
natural gas
coal
greenhouse effect

Section 6.6
syngas

In-Class Discussion Questions

These questions are designed to be considered by groups of students in class. Often these questions work well for introducing a particular topic in class.

1. Objects placed together eventually reach the same temperature. When you go into a room and touch a piece of metal in that room, it feels colder than a piece of plastic. Explain.

2. What is meant by the term *lower in energy?* Which is lower in energy, a mixture of hydrogen and oxygen gases or liquid water? How do you know? Which of the two is more stable? How do you know?

3. A fire is started in a fireplace by striking a match and lighting crumpled paper under some logs. Explain all the energy transfers in this scenario using the terms *exothermic, endothermic, system, surroundings, potential energy,* and *kinetic energy* in the discussion.

4. Liquid water turns to ice. Is this process endothermic or exothermic? Explain what is occurring using the terms *system, surroundings, heat, potential energy,* and *kinetic energy* in the discussion.

5. Consider the following statements: "Heat is a form of energy, and energy is conserved. The heat lost by a system must be equal to the amount of heat gained by the surroundings. Therefore, heat is conserved." Indicate everything you think is correct in these statements. Indicate everything you think is incorrect. Correct the incorrect statements and explain.

6. Consider 5.5 L of a gas at a pressure of 3.0 atm in a cylinder with a movable piston. The external pressure is changed so that the volume changes to 10.5 L.
   a. Calculate the work done, and indicate the correct sign.
   b. Use the preceding data but consider the process to occur in two steps. At the end of the first step, the volume is 7.0 L. The second step results in a final volume of 10.5 L. Calculate the work done, and indicate the correct sign.
   c. Calculate the work done if after the first step the volume is 8.0 L and the second step leads to a volume of 10.5 L. Does the work differ from that in part b? Explain.

7. In Question 6 the work calculated for the different conditions in the various parts of the question was different even though the system had the same initial and final conditions. Based on this information, is work a state function?
   a. Explain how you know that work is not a state function.
   b. Why does the work increase with an increase in the number of steps?
   c. Which two-step process resulted in more work, when the first step had the bigger change in volume or when the second step had the bigger change in volume? Explain.

8. Photosynthetic plants use the following reaction to produce glucose, cellulose, and so forth:

$$6CO_2(g) + 6H_2O(l) \xrightarrow{\text{Sunlight}} C_6H_{12}O_6(s) + 6O_2(g)$$

How might extensive destruction of forests exacerbate the greenhouse effect?

A blue question or exercise number indicates that the answer to that question or exercise appears at the back of this book and a solution appears in the *Solutions Guide*.

Questions

9. Explain why ΔH is obtained directly from a coffee-cup calorimeter, whereas ΔE is obtained directly from a bomb calorimeter.

10. Explain why oceanfront areas generally have smaller temperature fluctuations than inland areas.

11. High-quality hi-fi power amplifiers generate large amounts of heat. To dissipate the heat and prevent damage to the electronic components, heat-radiating metal fins are used. Would it be better to make these fins out of iron or aluminum? Why? (See Table 6.1 for specific heat capacities.)

12. Why is it a good idea to rinse your thermos bottle with hot water before filling it with hot coffee?

13. What is a state function? Enthalpy and internal energy are state functions as a direct consequence of the first law of thermodynamics. Explain.

14. Hess's law is really just another statement of the first law of thermodynamics. Explain.

15. What is the purpose for defining standard enthalpies of formation?

16. Explain the advantages and disadvantages of hydrogen as an alternative fuel.

Exercises

In this section similar exercises are paired.

Potential and Kinetic Energy

17. Calculate the kinetic energy of a baseball (mass = 5.25 oz) with a velocity of 1.0×10^2 mi/h.

18. Calculate the kinetic energy of a 1.0×10^{-5}-g object with a velocity of 2.0×10^5 cm/s.

19. Which has the greater kinetic energy, an object with a mass of 2.0 kg and a velocity of 1.0 m/s or an object with a mass of 1.0 kg and a velocity of 2.0 m/s?

20. Consider the accompanying diagram. Ball A is allowed to fall and strike ball B. Assume that all of ball A's energy is transferred to ball B, at point I, and that there is no loss of energy to other sources. What is the kinetic energy and the potential energy of ball B at point II? The potential energy is given by PE = mgz, where m is the mass in kilograms, g is the gravitational constant (9.8 m/s^2), and z is the distance in meters.

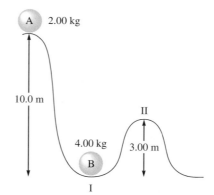

Heat and Work

21. Calculate ΔE for each of the following cases.
    a. $q = +51$ kJ, $w = -15$ kJ
    b. $q = +100.$ kJ, $w = -65$ kJ
    c. $q = -65$ kJ, $w = -20.$ kJ
    d. In which of these cases does the system do work on the surroundings?

22. Calculate ΔE for each of the following.
    a. $q = -47$ kJ, $w = +88$ kJ
    b. $q = +82$ kJ, $w = +47$ kJ
    c. $q = +47$ kJ , $w = 0$
    d. In which of these cases do the surroundings do work on the system?

23. A gas absorbs 45 kJ of heat and does 29 kJ of work. Calculate ΔE.

24. A system releases 125 kJ of heat while 104 kJ of work is done on it. Calculate ΔE.

25. The volume of an ideal gas is decreased from 5.0 L to 5.0 mL at a constant pressure of 2.0 atm. Calculate the work associated with this process.

26. Consider a mixture of air and gasoline vapor in a cylinder with a piston. The original volume is 40. cm^3. If the combustion of this mixture releases 950. J of energy, to what volume will the gases expand against a constant pressure of 650. torr if all the energy of combustion is converted into work to push back the piston?

27. A balloon filled with 39.1 mol helium has a volume of 876 L at 0.0°C and 1.00 atm pressure. The temperature of the balloon is increased to 38.0°C as it expands to a volume of 998 L, the pressure remaining constant. Calculate q, w, and ΔE for the helium in the balloon. (The molar heat capacity for helium gas is 20.8 J/°C · mol.)

28. One mole of $H_2O(g)$ at 1.00 atm and 100.°C occupies a volume of 30.6 L. When one mole of $H_2O(g)$ is condensed to one mole of $H_2O(l)$ at 1.00 atm and 100.°C, 40.66 kJ of heat is released. If the density of $H_2O(l)$ at this temperature and pressure is 0.996 g/cm^3, calculate ΔE for the condensation of one mole of water at 1.00 atm and 100.°C.

Properties of Enthalpy

29. The equation for the fermentation of glucose to alcohol and carbon dioxide is

$$C_6H_{12}O_6(aq) \longrightarrow 2C_2H_5OH(aq) + 2CO_2(g)$$

The enthalpy change for the reaction is -67 kJ. Is the reaction exothermic or endothermic? Is energy, in the form of heat, absorbed or evolved as the reaction occurs?

30. The reaction

$$SO_3(g) + H_2O(l) \longrightarrow H_2SO_4(aq)$$

is the last step in the commercial production of sulfuric acid. The enthalpy change for this reaction is -227 kJ. In designing a sulfuric acid plant, is it necessary to provide for heating or cooling of the reaction mixture? Explain.

31. Are the following processes exothermic or endothermic?
    a. When solid KBr is dissolved in water, the solution gets colder.
    b. Natural gas (CH_4) is burned in a furnace.
    c. When concentrated H_2SO_4 is added to water, the solution gets very hot.
    d. Water is boiled in a teakettle.

32. Are the following processes exothermic or endothermic?
    a. the combustion of gasoline in a car engine
    b. water condensing on a cold pipe
    c. $CO_2(s) \longrightarrow CO_2(g)$
    d. $F_2(g) \longrightarrow 2F(g)$

33. For the reaction

$$S(s) + O_2(g) \longrightarrow SO_2(g) \qquad \Delta H = -296 \text{ kJ/mol}$$

    a. How much heat is evolved when 275 g sulfur is burned in excess O_2?
    b. How much heat is evolved when 25 mol sulfur is burned in excess O_2?
    c. How much heat is evolved when 150. g sulfur dioxide is produced?

34. The overall reaction in commercial heat packs can be represented as

$$4Fe(s) + 3O_2(g) \longrightarrow 2Fe_2O_3(s) \qquad \Delta H = -1652 \text{ kJ}$$

    a. How much heat is released when 4.00 mol iron is reacted with excess O_2?
    b. How much heat is released when 1.00 mol Fe_2O_3 is produced?
    c. How much heat is released when 1.00 g iron is reacted with excess O_2?
    d. How much heat is released when 10.0 g Fe and 2.00 g O_2 are reacted?

35. Consider the combustion of propane:

$$C_3H_8(g) + 5O_2(g) \longrightarrow 3CO_2(g) + 4H_2O(l)$$
$$\Delta H = -2221 \text{ kJ}$$

Assume that all the heat in Sample Exercise 6.3 comes from the combustion of propane. What mass of propane must be burned to furnish this amount of energy assuming the heat transfer process is 60.% efficient?

36. Consider the following reaction:

$$CH_4(g) + 2O_2(g) \longrightarrow CO_2(g) + 2H_2O(l)$$
$$\Delta H = -891 \text{ kJ}$$

Calculate the enthalpy change for each of the following cases:
a. 1.00 g methane is burned in excess oxygen.
b. 1.00×10^3 L methane gas at 740. torr and 25°C is burned in excess oxygen.

Calorimetry and Heat Capacity

37. The specific heat capacity of aluminum is 0.900 J/°C · g.
 a. Calculate the energy needed to raise the temperature of a 8.50×10^2-g block of aluminum from 22.8°C to 94.6°C.
 b. Calculate the molar heat capacity of aluminum.

38. The specific heat capacity of silver is 0.24 J/°C · g.
 a. Calculate the energy required to raise the temperature of 150.0 g Ag from 273 K to 298 K.
 b. Calculate the energy required to raise the temperature of 1.0 mol Ag by 1.0°C (called the *molar heat capacity* of silver).
 c. It takes 1.25 kJ of energy to heat a sample of pure silver from 12.0°C to 15.2°C. Calculate the mass of the sample of silver.

39. It takes 78.2 J to raise the temperature of 45.6 g lead by 13.3°C. Calculate the specific heat capacity and molar heat capacity of lead.

40. It takes 585 J of energy to raise the temperature of 125.6 g mercury from 20.0°C to 53.5°C. Calculate the specific heat capacity and the molar mass capacity of mercury.

41. A 30.0-g sample of water at 280. K is mixed with 50.0 g of water at 330. K. Calculate the final temperature of the mixture assuming no heat loss to the surroundings.

42. A 15.0-g sample of nickel metal is heated to 100.0°C and dropped into 55.0 g of water, initially at 23.0°C. Assuming that all the heat lost by the nickel is absorbed by the water, calculate the final temperature of the nickel and water. (The specific heat of nickel is 0.444 J/°C · g.)

43. A 150.0-g sample of a metal at 75.0°C is added to 150.0 g of H₂O at 15.0°C. The temperature of the water rises to 18.3°C. Calculate the specific heat capacity of the metal, assuming that all the heat lost by the metal is gained by the water.

44. A 46.2-g sample of copper is heated to 95.4°C and then placed in a calorimeter containing 75.0 g water at 19.6°C. The final temperature of the metal and water is 21.8°C. Calculate the specific heat capacity of copper, assuming that all the heat lost by the copper is gained by the water.

45. In a coffee-cup calorimeter, 50.0 mL of 0.100 *M* AgNO₃ and 50.0 mL of 0.100 *M* HCl are mixed to yield the following reaction:

$$Ag^+(aq) + Cl^-(aq) \longrightarrow AgCl(s)$$

The two solutions were initially at 22.60°C, and the final temperature is 23.40°C. Calculate the heat that accompanies this reaction in kJ/mol of AgCl formed. Assume that the combined solution has a mass of 100.0 g and has a specific heat capacity of 4.18 J/°C · g.

46. In a coffee-cup calorimeter, 1.60 g of NH₄NO₃ is mixed with 75.0 g of water at an initial temperature of 25.00°C. After dissolution of the salt, the final temperature of the calorimeter contents is 23.34°C. Assuming the solution has a heat capacity of 4.18 J/°C · g and assuming no heat loss to the calorimeter, calculate the enthalpy change for the dissolution of NH₄NO₃ in units of kJ/mol.

47. Consider the dissolution of CaCl₂:

$$CaCl_2(s) \longrightarrow Ca^{2+}(aq) + 2Cl^-(aq) \qquad \Delta H = -81.5 \text{ kJ}$$

An 11.0-g sample of CaCl₂ is dissolved in 125 g of water, with both substances at 25.0°C. Calculate the final temperature of the solution assuming no heat lost to the surroundings and assuming the solution has a specific heat capacity of 4.18 J/°C · g.

48. Consider the reaction

$$2HCl(aq) + Ba(OH)_2(aq) \longrightarrow BaCl_2(aq) + 2H_2O(l)$$
$$\Delta H = -118 \text{ kJ}$$

Calculate the heat when 100.0 mL of 0.500 *M* HCl is mixed with 300.0 mL of 0.500 *M* Ba(OH)₂. Assuming that the temperature of both solutions was initially 25.0°C and that the final mixture has a mass of 400.0 g and a specific heat capacity of 4.18 J/°C · g, calculate the final temperature of the mixture.

49. Camphor (C₁₀H₁₆O) has an energy of combustion of −5903.6 kJ/mol. When a sample of camphor with mass 0.1204 g is burned in a bomb calorimeter, the temperature increases by 2.28°C. Calculate the heat capacity of the calorimeter.

50. A 0.1964-g sample of quinone (C₆H₄O₂) is burned in a bomb calorimeter that has a heat capacity of 1.56 kJ/°C. The temperature of the calorimeter increases by 3.2°C. Calculate the energy of combustion of quinone per gram and per mole.

Hess's Law

51. The enthalpy of combustion of solid carbon to form carbon dioxide is −393.7 kJ/mol carbon, and the enthalpy of combustion of carbon monoxide to form carbon dioxide is −283.3 kJ/mol CO. Use these data to calculate ΔH for the reaction

$$2C(s) + O_2(g) \longrightarrow 2CO(g)$$

52. Combustion reactions involve reacting a substance with oxygen. When compounds containing carbon and hydrogen are combusted, carbon dioxide and water are the products. Using the enthalpies of combustion for C_4H_4 (-2341 kJ/mol), C_4H_8 (-2755 kJ/mol), and H_2 (-286 kJ/mol), calculate ΔH for the reaction

$$C_4H_4(g) + 2H_2(g) \longrightarrow C_4H_8(g)$$

53. Given the following data:

$$S(s) + \tfrac{3}{2}O_2(g) \longrightarrow SO_3(g) \qquad \Delta H = -395.2 \text{ kJ}$$
$$2SO_2(g) + O_2(g) \longrightarrow 2SO_3(g) \qquad \Delta H = -198.2 \text{ kJ}$$

calculate ΔH for the reaction

$$S(s) + O_2(g) \longrightarrow SO_2(g)$$

54. Given the following data:

$$C_2H_2(g) + \tfrac{5}{2}O_2(g) \longrightarrow 2CO_2(g) + H_2O(l)$$
$$\Delta H = -1300. \text{ kJ}$$
$$C(s) + O_2(g) \longrightarrow CO_2(g) \qquad \Delta H = -394 \text{ kJ}$$
$$H_2(g) + \tfrac{1}{2}O_2(g) \longrightarrow H_2O(l) \qquad \Delta H = -286 \text{ kJ}$$

calculate ΔH for the reaction

$$2C(s) + H_2(g) \longrightarrow C_2H_2(g)$$

55. Given the following data:

$$2O_3(g) \longrightarrow 3O_2(g) \qquad \Delta H = -427 \text{ kJ}$$
$$O_2(g) \longrightarrow 2O(g) \qquad \Delta H = +495 \text{ kJ}$$
$$NO(g) + O_3(g) \longrightarrow NO_2(g) + O_2(g) \qquad \Delta H = -199 \text{ kJ}$$

calculate ΔH for the reaction

$$NO(g) + O(g) \longrightarrow NO_2(g)$$

56. The bombardier beetle uses an explosive discharge as a defensive measure. The chemical reaction involved is the oxidation of hydroquinone by hydrogen peroxide to produce quinone and water:

$$C_6H_4(OH)_2(aq) + H_2O_2(aq) \longrightarrow C_6H_4O_2(aq) + 2H_2O(l)$$

Calculate ΔH for this reaction from the following data:

$$C_6H_4(OH)_2(aq) \longrightarrow C_6H_4O_2(aq) + H_2(g)$$
$$\Delta H = +177.4 \text{ kJ}$$
$$H_2(g) + O_2(g) \longrightarrow H_2O_2(aq) \qquad \Delta H = -191.2 \text{ kJ}$$
$$H_2(g) + \tfrac{1}{2}O_2(g) \longrightarrow H_2O(g) \qquad \Delta H = -241.8 \text{ kJ}$$
$$H_2O(g) \longrightarrow H_2O(l) \qquad \Delta H = -43.8 \text{ kJ}$$

57. Given the following data:

$$H_2(g) + \tfrac{1}{2}O_2(g) \longrightarrow H_2O(l)$$
$$\Delta H = -285.8 \text{ kJ}$$
$$N_2O_5(g) + H_2O(l) \longrightarrow 2HNO_3(l)$$
$$\Delta H = -76.6 \text{ kJ}$$
$$\tfrac{1}{2}N_2(g) + \tfrac{3}{2}O_2(g) + \tfrac{1}{2}H_2(g) \longrightarrow HNO_3(l)$$
$$\Delta H = -174.1 \text{ kJ}$$

calculate the ΔH for the reaction

$$2N_2(g) + 5O_2(g) \longrightarrow 2N_2O_5(g)$$

58. Given the following data:

$$P_4(s) + 6Cl_2(g) \longrightarrow 4PCl_3(g) \qquad \Delta H = -1225.6 \text{ kJ}$$
$$P_4(s) + 5O_2(g) \longrightarrow P_4O_{10}(s) \qquad \Delta H = -2967.3 \text{ kJ}$$
$$PCl_3(g) + Cl_2(g) \longrightarrow PCl_5(g) \qquad \Delta H = -84.2 \text{ kJ}$$
$$PCl_3(g) + \tfrac{1}{2}O_2(g) \longrightarrow Cl_3PO(g) \qquad \Delta H = -285.7 \text{ kJ}$$

calculate ΔH for the reaction

$$P_4O_{10}(s) + 6PCl_5(g) \longrightarrow 10Cl_3PO(g)$$

Standard Enthalpies of Formation

59. Give the definition of the standard enthalpy of formation for a substance. Write separate reactions for the formation of NaCl, H_2O, $C_6H_{12}O_6$, and $PbSO_4$ that have $\Delta H°$ values equal to $\Delta H_f°$ for each compound.

60. Write reactions for which the enthalpy change will be
 a. $\Delta H_f°$ for solid aluminum oxide.
 b. The standard enthalpy of combustion of liquid ethanol, $C_2H_5OH(l)$.
 c. The standard enthalpy of neutralization of sodium hydroxide solution by hydrochloric acid.
 d. $\Delta H_f°$ for gaseous vinyl chloride, $C_2H_3Cl(g)$.
 e. The enthalpy of combustion of liquid benzene, $C_6H_6(l)$.
 f. The enthalpy of solution of solid ammonium bromide.

61. Use the values of $\Delta H_f°$ in Appendix 4 to calculate $\Delta H°$ for the following reactions.
 a. $2NH_3(g) + 3O_2(g) + 2CH_4(g) \longrightarrow 2HCN(g) + 6H_2O(g)$
 b. $Ca_3(PO_4)_2(s) + 3H_2SO_4(l) \longrightarrow 3CaSO_4(s) + 2H_3PO_4(l)$
 c. $NH_3(g) + HCl(g) \longrightarrow NH_4Cl(s)$

62. Use the values of $\Delta H_f°$ in Appendix 4 to calculate $\Delta H°$ for the following reactions.
 a. $C_2H_5OH(l) + 3O_2(g) \longrightarrow 2CO_2(g) + 3H_2O(g)$
 b. $SiCl_4(l) + 2H_2O(l) \longrightarrow SiO_2(s) + 4HCl(aq)$
 c. $MgO(s) + H_2O(l) \longrightarrow Mg(OH)_2(s)$

63. The Ostwald process for the commercial production of nitric acid from ammonia and oxygen involves the following steps:

$$4NH_3(g) + 5O_2(g) \longrightarrow 4NO(g) + 6H_2O(g)$$
$$2NO(g) + O_2(g) \longrightarrow 2NO_2(g)$$
$$3NO_2(g) + H_2O(l) \longrightarrow 2HNO_3(aq) + NO(g)$$

a. Use the values of ΔH_f° in Appendix 4 to calculate the value of ΔH° for each of the preceding reactions.
b. Write the overall equation for the production of nitric acid by the Ostwald process by combining the preceding equations. (Water is also a product.) Is the overall reaction exothermic or endothermic?

64. Calculate ΔH° for each of the following reactions using the data in Appendix 4:

$$4Na(s) + O_2(g) \longrightarrow 2Na_2O(s)$$
$$2Na(s) + 2H_2O(l) \longrightarrow 2NaOH(aq) + H_2(g)$$
$$2Na(s) + CO_2(g) \longrightarrow Na_2O(s) + CO(g)$$

Explain why a water or carbon dioxide fire extinguisher might not be effective in putting out a sodium fire.

65. The reusable booster rockets of the space shuttle use a mixture of aluminum and ammonium perchlorate as fuel. A possible reaction is

$$3Al(s) + 3NH_4ClO_4(s)$$
$$\longrightarrow Al_2O_3(s) + AlCl_3(s) + 3NO(g) + 6H_2O(g)$$

Calculate ΔH° for this reaction.

66. The space shuttle orbiter utilizes the oxidation of methyl hydrazine by dinitrogen tetroxide for propulsion:

$$4N_2H_3CH_3(l) + 5N_2O_4(l)$$
$$\longrightarrow 12H_2O(g) + 9N_2(g) + 4CO_2(g)$$

Calculate ΔH° for this reaction.

67. Consider the reaction

$$2ClF_3(g) + 2NH_3(g) \longrightarrow N_2(g) + 6HF(g) + Cl_2(g)$$
$$\Delta H^\circ = -1196 \text{ kJ}$$

Calculate ΔH_f° for $ClF_3(g)$.

68. The standard enthalpy of combustion of ethene gas, $C_2H_4(g)$, is -1411.1 kJ/mol at 298 K. Given the following enthalpies of formation, calculate ΔH_f° for $C_2H_4(g)$.

$CO_2(g)$	-393.5 kJ/mol
$H_2O(l)$	-285.9 kJ/mol

Energy Consumption and Sources

69. Water gas is produced from the reaction of steam with coal:

$$C(s) + H_2O(g) \longrightarrow H_2(g) + CO(g)$$

Assuming that coal is pure graphite, calculate ΔH° for this reaction.

70. Syngas can be burned directly or converted to methanol. Calculate ΔH° for the reaction

$$CO(g) + 2H_2(g) \longrightarrow CH_3OH(l)$$

71. Some automobiles and buses have been equipped to burn propane (C_3H_8). Compare the amounts of energy that can be obtained per gram of $C_3H_8(g)$ and per gram of gasoline, assuming that gasoline is pure octane, $C_8H_{18}(l)$. (See Sample Exercise 6.11.) Look up the boiling point of propane. What disadvantages are there to using propane instead of gasoline as a fuel?

72. Acetylene (C_2H_2) and butane (C_4H_{10}) are gaseous fuels with enthalpies of combustion of -49.9 kJ/g and -49.5 kJ/g, respectively. Compare the energy available from the combustion of a given volume of acetylene to the combustion energy from the same volume of butane at the same temperature and pressure.

73. Assume that 4.19×10^6 kJ of energy is needed to heat a home. If this energy is derived from the combustion of methane (CH_4), what volume of methane, measured at STP, must be burned? ($\Delta H^\circ_{combustion}$ for $CH_4 = -891$ kJ/mol)

74. The complete combustion of acetylene, $C_2H_2(g)$, produces 1300. kJ of energy per mole of acetylene consumed. How many grams of acetylene must be burned to produce enough heat to raise the temperature of 1.00 gal of water by 10.0°C if the process is 80.0% efficient? Assume the density of water is 1.00 g/cm³.

Additional Exercises

75. Consider the following changes:
a. $COCl_2(g) \longrightarrow CO(g) + Cl_2(g)$
b. $N_2(g) \longrightarrow N_2(l)$
c. $CO(g) + H_2O(g) \longrightarrow H_2(g) + CO_2(g)$
d. $Ca_3P_2(s) + 6H_2O(l) \longrightarrow 3Ca(OH)_2(s) + 2PH_3(g)$
e. $2CH_3OH(l) + 3O_2(g) \longrightarrow 2CO_2(g) + 4H_2O(l)$
f. $I_2(s) \longrightarrow I_2(g)$
At constant temperature and pressure, in which of these changes is work done by the system on the surroundings? by the surroundings on the system? In which of them is no work done?

76. Consider the following cyclic process carried out in two steps on a gas:

Step 1: 45 J of heat is added to the gas, and 10. J of expansion work is performed.

Step 2: 60. J of heat is removed from the gas as the gas is compressed back to the initial state.

Calculate the work for the gas compression in Step 2.

77. A sample of an ideal gas at 15.0 atm and 10.0 L is allowed to expand against a constant external pressure of 2.00 atm at a constant temperature. Calculate the work in units of kJ for the gas expansion.

78. A biology experiment requires the preparation of a water bath at 37.0°C (body temperature). The temperature of the cold tap water is 22.0°C, and the temperature of the hot tap water is 55.0°C. If a student starts with 90.0 g of cold water, what mass of hot water must be added to reach 37.0°C?

79. Calculate $\Delta H°$ for the reaction

$$2K(s) + 2H_2O(l) \longrightarrow 2KOH(aq) + H_2(g)$$

A 5.00-g chunk of potassium is dropped into 1.00 kg water at 24.0°C. What is the final temperature of the water after the preceding reaction occurs? Assume that all the heat is used to raise the temperature of the water. (Never run this reaction. It is very dangerous; it bursts into flame!)

80. The enthalpy of neutralization for the reaction of a strong acid with a strong base is −56 kJ/mol of water produced. How much energy will be released when 200.0 mL of 0.400 M HCl is mixed with 150.0 mL of 0.500 M NaOH?

81. In a bomb calorimeter, the reaction vessel is surrounded by water that must be added for each experiment. Since the amount of water is not constant from experiment to experiment, the mass of water must be measured in each case. The heat capacity of the calorimeter is broken down into two parts: the water and the calorimeter components. If a calorimeter contains 1.00 kg water and has a total heat capacity of 10.84 kJ/°C, what is the heat capacity of the calorimeter components?

82. The bomb calorimeter in Exercise 81 is filled with 987 g of water. The initial temperature of the calorimeter contents is 23.32°C. A 1.056-g sample of benzoic acid ($\Delta E_{comb} = -26.42$ kJ/g) is combusted in the calorimeter. What is the final temperature of the calorimeter contents?

83. The combustion of 0.1584 g benzoic acid increases the temperature of a bomb calorimeter by 2.54°C. Calculate the heat capacity of this calorimeter. (The energy released by combustion of benzoic acid is 26.42 kJ/g.) A 0.2130-g sample of vanillin ($C_8H_8O_3$) is then burned in the same calorimeter, and the temperature increases by 3.25°C. What is the energy of combustion per gram of vanillin? per mole of vanillin?

84. Given the following data:

$$Fe_2O_3(s) + 3CO(g) \longrightarrow 2Fe(s) + 3CO_2(g)$$
$$\Delta H° = -23 \text{ kJ}$$

$$3Fe_2O_3(s) + CO(g) \longrightarrow 2Fe_3O_4(s) + CO_2(g)$$
$$\Delta H° = -39 \text{ kJ}$$

$$Fe_3O_4(s) + CO(g) \longrightarrow 3FeO(s) + CO_2(g)$$
$$\Delta H° = +18 \text{ kJ}$$

calculate $\Delta H°$ for the reaction

$$FeO(s) + CO(g) \longrightarrow Fe(s) + CO_2(g)$$

85. The enthalpy change for the conversion of white phosphorus to red phosphorus is −17.6 kJ/mol. Will one mole of red phosphorus or one mole of white phosphorus give off more heat when burned in air?

86. Given the following data:

$$4CuO(s) \longrightarrow 2Cu_2O(s) + O_2(g) \qquad \Delta H° = 288 \text{ kJ}$$
$$Cu_2O(s) \longrightarrow Cu(s) + CuO(s) \qquad \Delta H° = 11 \text{ kJ}$$

calculate the standard enthalpy of formation for CuO(s).

87. Calculate $\Delta H°$ for each of the following reactions, which occur in the atmosphere.
   a. $C_2H_4(g) + O_3(g) \longrightarrow CH_3CHO(g) + O_2(g)$
   b. $O_3(g) + NO(g) \longrightarrow NO_2(g) + O_2(g)$
   c. $SO_3(g) + H_2O(l) \longrightarrow H_2SO_4(aq)$
   d. $2NO(g) + O_2(g) \longrightarrow 2NO_2(g)$

Challenge Problems

88. Consider 2.00 mol of an ideal gas that is taken from state A ($P_A = 2.00$ atm, $V_A = 10.0$ L) to state B ($P_B = 1.00$ atm, $V_B = 30.0$ L) by two different pathways:

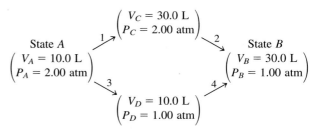

These pathways are summarized on the following graph of P versus V:

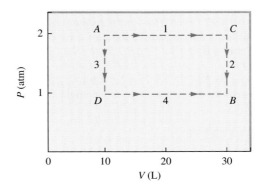

Calculate the work (in units of J) associated with the two pathways. Is work a state function? Explain.

89. Combustion of table sugar produces $CO_2(g)$ and $H_2O(l)$. When 1.46 g of table sugar is combusted in a constant volume (bomb) calorimeter, 24.00 kJ of heat is liberated.
    a. Assuming that table sugar is pure sucrose, $C_{12}H_{22}O_{11}(s)$, write the balanced equation for the combustion reaction.
    b. Calculate ΔE in kJ/mol $C_{12}H_{22}O_{11}$ for the combustion reaction of sucrose.
    c. Calculate ΔH in kJ/mol $C_{12}H_{22}O_{11}$ for the combustion reaction of sucrose at 25°C.

90. The sun supplies energy at a rate of about 1.0 kilowatt per square meter of surface area (1 watt = 1 J/s). The plants in an agricultural field produce the equivalent of 20. kg of sucrose $(C_{12}H_{22}O_{11})$ per hour per hectare (1 ha = 10,000 m²). Assuming that sucrose is produced by the reaction

$$12CO_2(g) + 11H_2O(l) \longrightarrow C_{12}H_{22}O_{11}(s) + 12O_2(g)$$
$$\Delta H = 5640 \text{ kJ}$$

calculate the percentage of sunlight used to produce the sucrose, that is, determine the efficiency of photosynthesis.

91. The best solar panels currently available are about 13% efficient in converting sunlight to electricity. A typical home will use about 40. kWh of electricity a day (1 kWh = 1 kilowatt hour; 1 kW = 1000 J/s). Assuming 8.0 hours of useful sunlight per day, calculate the minimum solar panel surface area necessary to provide all of a typical home's electricity. (See Exercise 90 for the energy rate supplied by the sun.)

92. On Easter Sunday, April 3, 1983, nitric acid spilled from a tank car near downtown Denver, Colorado. The spill was neutralized with sodium carbonate:

$$2HNO_3(aq) + Na_2CO_3(s)$$
$$\longrightarrow 2NaNO_3(aq) + H_2O(l) + CO_2(g)$$

    a. Calculate $\Delta H°$ for this reaction. Approximately 2.0×10^4 gal nitric acid was spilled. Assume that the acid was an aqueous solution containing 70.0% HNO_3 by mass with a density of 1.42 g/cm³. How much sodium carbonate was required for complete neutralization of the spill, and how much heat was evolved? ($\Delta H_f°$ for $NaNO_3(aq) = -467$ kJ/mol)
    b. According to *The Denver Post* for April 4, 1983, authorities feared that dangerous air pollution might occur during the neutralization. Considering the magnitude of $\Delta H°$, what was their major concern?

93. A piece of chocolate cake contains about 400 Calories. A nutritional Calorie is equal to 1000 calories (thermochemical calories), which is equal to 4.184 kJ. How many 8-in-high steps must a 180-lb man climb to expend the 400 Cal from the piece of cake? See Exercise 20 for the formula for potential energy.

94. The standard enthalpy of formation of $H_2O(l)$ at 298 K is -285.6 kJ/mol. Calculate the change in internal energy for the following reaction at 298 K and 1.00 atm:

$$2H_2O(l) \longrightarrow 2H_2(g) + O_2(g) \qquad \Delta E = ?$$

Hint: Using the ideal gas equation, derive an expression for work in terms of *n, R,* and *T.*

Marathon Problem*

This problem is designed to incorporate several concepts and techniques into one situation. Marathon Problems can be used in class by groups of students to help facilitate problem-solving skills.

95. A sample consisting of 22.7 g of a nongaseous, unstable compound X is placed inside a metal cylinder with a radius of 8.00 cm, and a piston is carefully placed on the surface of the compound so that, for all practical purposes, the distance between the bottom of the cylinder and the piston is zero. (A hole in the piston allows trapped air to escape as the piston is placed on the compound; then this hole is plugged so that nothing inside the cylinder can escape.) The piston-and-cylinder apparatus is carefully placed in 10.00 kg of water at 25.00°C. The barometric pressure is 778 torr.

    When the compound spontaneously decomposes, the piston moves up, the temperature of the water reaches a maximum of 29.52°C, and then it gradually decreases as the water loses heat to the surrounding air. The distance between the piston and the bottom of the cylinder, at the maximum temperature, is 59.8 cm. Chemical analysis shows that the cylinder contains 0.300 mol carbon dioxide, 0.250 mol liquid water, 0.025 mol oxygen gas, and an undetermined amount of a gaseous element A.

*This Marathon Problem was developed by James H. Burness of Penn State University, York Campus. Reprinted with permission from the *Journal of Chemical Education,* Vol. 68, No. 11, 1991, pp. 919–922; copyright © 1991, Division of Chemical Education, Inc.

It is known that the enthalpy change for the decomposition of X, according to the reaction described above, is −1893 kJ/mol X. The standard enthalpies of formation for gaseous carbon dioxide and liquid water are −393.5 kJ/mol and −286 kJ/mol, respectively. The heat capacity for water is 4.184 J/°C · g. The conversion factor between L · atm and J can be determined from the two values for the gas constant R, namely, 0.08206 L · atm/mol · K and 8.3145 J/mol · K. The vapor pressure of water at 29.5°C is 31 torr. Assume that the heat capacity of the pis-ton-and-cylinder apparatus is negligible and that the piston has negligible mass.

Given the preceding information, determine

a. The formula for X.

b. The pressure–volume work (in kJ) for the decomposition of the 22.7-g sample of X.

c. The *molar* change in internal energy for the decomposition of X and the approximate standard enthalpy of formation for X.

Atomic Structure and Periodicity

Contents

*I*n the past 200 years, a great deal of experimental evidence has accumulated to support the atomic model. This theory has proved to be both extremely useful and physically reasonable. When atoms were first suggested by the Greek philosophers Democritus and Leucippus about 400 B.C., the concept was based mostly on intuition. In fact, for the following 20 centuries, no convincing experimental evidence was available to support the existence of atoms. The first real scientific data were gathered by Lavoisier and others from quantitative measurements of chemical reactions. The results of these stoichiometric experiments led John Dalton to propose the first systematic atomic theory. Dalton's theory, although crude, has stood the test of time extremely well.

Once we came to "believe in" atoms, it was logical to ask: What is the nature of an atom? Does an atom have parts, and if so, what are they? In Chapter 2 we considered some of the experiments most important for shedding light on the nature of the atom. Now we will see how the atomic theory has evolved to its present state.

One of the most striking things about the chemistry of the elements is the periodic repetition of properties. There are several groups of elements that show great similarities in chemical behavior. As we saw in Chapter 2, these similarities led to the development of the periodic table of the elements. In this chapter we will see that the modern theory of atomic structure accounts for periodicity in terms of the electron arrangements in atoms.

However, before we examine atomic structure, we must consider the revolution that took place in physics in the first 30 years of the twentieth century. During that time, experiments were carried out, the results of which could not be explained by the theories of classical physics developed by Isaac Newton and many others who followed him. A radical new theory called *quantum mechanics* was developed to account for the behavior of light and atoms. This "new physics" provides many surprises for humans who are used to the macroscopic world, but it seems to account flawlessly (within the bounds of necessary approximations) for the behavior of matter.

Light refracted through a prism.

As the first step in our exploration of this revolution in science we will consider the properties of light, more properly called *electromagnetic radiation*.

Although the waves associated with light are not obvious to the naked eye, ocean waves provide a familiar source of recreation.

7.1 Electromagnetic Radiation

One of the ways that energy travels through space is by **electromagnetic radiation.** The light from the sun, the energy used to cook food in a microwave oven, the X rays used by dentists, and the radiant heat from a fireplace are all examples of electromagnetic radiation. Although these forms of radiant energy seem quite different, they all exhibit the same type of wavelike behavior and travel at the speed of light in a vacuum.

Waves have three primary characteristics: wavelength, frequency, and speed. **Wavelength** (symbolized by the lowercase Greek letter lambda, λ) is the *distance between two consecutive peaks or troughs in a wave,* as shown in Fig. 7.1. The **frequency** (symbolized by the lowercase Greek letter nu, ν) is defined as the *number of waves (cycles) per second that pass a given point in space.* Since all types of electromagnetic radiation travel at the speed of light, short-wavelength radiation must have a high frequency. You can see this in Fig. 7.1, where three waves are shown traveling between two points at constant speed. Note that the wave with the shortest wavelength (λ_3) has the highest frequency and the wave with the longest

Animation: Electromagnetic Wave

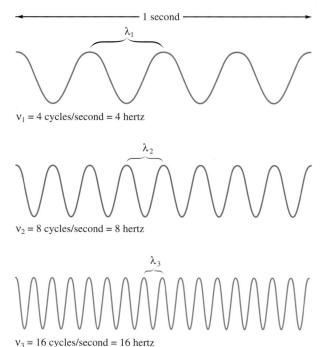

Figure 7.1

The nature of waves. Note that the radiation with the shortest wavelength has the highest frequency.

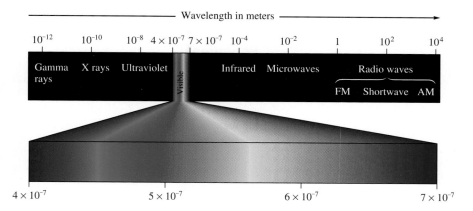

Figure 7.2
Classification of electromagnetic radiation. Spectrum adapted by permission from C. W. Keenan, D. C. Kleinfelter, and J. H. Wood, *General College Chemistry*, 6th ed. (New York: Harper & Row, 1980).

wavelength (λ_1) has the lowest frequency. This implies an inverse relationship between wavelength and frequency, that is, $\lambda \propto 1/\nu$, or

Wavelength λ and frequency ν are inversely related.

$$\lambda\nu = c$$

where λ is the wavelength in meters, ν is the frequency in cycles per second, and c is the speed of light (2.9979×10^8 m/s). In the SI system, cycles is understood, and the unit per second becomes 1/s, or s^{-1}, which is called the *hertz* (abbreviated Hz).

c = speed of light
= 2.9979×10^8 m/s

Electromagnetic radiation is classified as shown in Fig. 7.2. Radiation provides an important means of energy transfer. For example, the energy from the sun reaches the earth mainly in the form of visible and ultraviolet radiation, whereas the glowing coals of a fireplace transmit heat energy by infrared radiation. In a microwave oven the water molecules in food absorb microwave radiation, which increases their motions. This energy is then transferred to other types of molecules via collisions, causing an increase in the food's temperature. As we proceed in the study of chemistry, we will consider many of the classes of electromagnetic radiation and the ways in which they affect matter.

CHEMICAL IMPACT

Flies That Dye

MEDITERRANEAN AND MEXICAN fruit flies are formidable pests that have the potential to seriously damage several important fruit crops. Because of this, there have been several widely publicized sprayings of residential areas in southern California with the pesticide malathion to try to control fruit flies. Now there may be a better way to kill fruit flies—with a blend of two common dyes (red dye no. 28 and yellow dye no. 8) long used to color drugs and cosmetics. One of the most interesting things about this new pesticide is that it is activated by light. After an insect eats the blend of dyes, the molecules absorb light (through the insect's transparent body), which causes them to generate oxidizing agents that attack the proteins and cell membranes in the bug's body. Death occurs within 12 hours.

The sunlight that turns on the dye's toxicity after the fly ingests it also degrades the dye in the environment, making it relatively safe. It appears likely that in the near future the fruit fly will "dye" with little harm to the environment.

When a strontium salt is dissolved in methanol (with a little water) and ignited, it gives a brilliant red flame. The red color is produced by emission of light when electrons, excited by the energy of the burning methanol, fall back to their ground states.

Sample Exercise 7.1 *Frequency of Electromagnetic Radiation*

The brilliant red colors seen in fireworks are due to the emission of light with wavelengths around 650 nm when strontium salts such as $Sr(NO_3)_2$ and $SrCO_3$ are heated. (This can be easily demonstrated in the lab by dissolving one of these salts in methanol that contains a little water and igniting the mixture in an evaporating dish.) Calculate the frequency of red light of wavelength 6.50×10^2 nm.

Solution

We can convert wavelength to frequency using the equation

$$\lambda \nu = c \quad \text{or} \quad \nu = \frac{c}{\lambda}$$

where $c = 2.9979 \times 10^8$ m/s. In this case $\lambda = 6.50 \times 10^2$ nm. Changing the wavelength to meters, we have

$$6.50 \times 10^2 \ \text{nm} \times \frac{1 \ \text{m}}{10^9 \ \text{nm}} = 6.50 \times 10^{-7} \ \text{m}$$

and

$$\nu = \frac{c}{\lambda} = \frac{2.9979 \times 10^8 \ \text{m/s}}{6.50 \times 10^{-7} \ \text{m}} = 4.61 \times 10^{14} \ \text{s}^{-1} = 4.61 \times 10^{14} \ \text{Hz}$$

See Exercises 7.37 and 7.38.

When alternating current at 110 volts is applied to a dill pickle, a glowing discharge occurs. The current flowing between the electrodes (forks), which is supported by the Na^+ and Cl^- ions present, apparently causes some sodium atoms to form in an excited state. When these atoms relax to the ground state, they emit visible light at 589 nm, producing the yellow glow reminiscent of sodium vapor lamps.

7.2 The Nature of Matter

It is probably fair to say that at the end of the nineteenth century, physicists were feeling rather smug. Available theories could explain phenomena as diverse as the motions of the planets and the dispersion of visible light by a prism. Rumor has it that students were being discouraged from pursuing physics as a career because it was felt that all the major problems had been solved, or at least described in terms of the current physical theories.

At the end of the nineteenth century, the idea prevailed that matter and energy were distinct. Matter was thought to consist of particles, whereas energy in the form of light (electromagnetic radiation) was described as a wave. Particles were things that had mass and whose position in space could be specified. Waves were described as massless and delocalized; that is, their position in space could not be specified. It also was assumed that there was no intermingling of matter and light. Everything known before 1900 seemed to fit neatly into this view.

At the beginning of the twentieth century, however, certain experimental results suggested that this picture was incorrect. The first important advance came in 1900 from the German physicist Max Planck (1858–1947). Studying the radiation profiles emitted by solid bodies heated to incandescence, Planck found that the results

CHEMICAL IMPACT

Chemistry That Doesn't Leave You in the Dark

IN THE ANIMAL world, the ability to see at night provides predators with a distinct advantage over their prey. The same advantage can be gained by military forces and law enforcement agencies around the world through the use of recent advances in night vision technology.

All types of night vision equipment are electrooptical devices that amplify existing light. A lens collects light and focuses it on an image intensifier. The image intensifier is based on the photoelectric effect—materials that give off electrons when light is shined on them. Night vision intensifiers use semiconductor-based materials to produce large numbers of

electrons for a given input of photons. The emitted electrons are then directed onto a screen covered with compounds that phosphoresce (glow when struck by electrons). While television tubes use various phosphors to produce color pictures, night vision devices use phosphors that appear green, because the human eye can distinguish more shades of green than any other color. The viewing screen shows an image that otherwise would be invisible to the naked eye during nighttime viewing.

Current night vision devices use gallium arsenide (GaAs)–based intensifiers that can amplify input light as much as

50,000 times. These devices are so sensitive they can use starlight to produce an image. It is also now possible to use light (infrared) that cannot be sensed with the human eye to create an image.

This technology, while developed originally for military and law enforcement applications, is now becoming available to the consumer. For example, Cadillac is including night vision as an option on its cars for the year 2000. As night-imaging technology improves and costs become less prohibitive, a whole new world is opening up for the technophile—after the sun goes down.

could not be explained in terms of the physics of his day, which held that matter could absorb or emit any quantity of energy. Planck could account for these observations only by postulating that energy can be gained or lost only in *whole-number multiples* of the quantity $h\nu$, where h is a constant called **Planck's constant,** determined by experiment to have the value 6.626×10^{-34} J · s. That is, the change in energy for a system ΔE can be represented by the equation

$$\Delta E = nh\nu$$

where n is an integer (1, 2, 3, . . .), h is Planck's constant, and ν is the frequency of the electromagnetic radiation absorbed or emitted.

Planck's result was a real surprise. It had always been assumed that the energy of matter was continuous, which meant that the transfer of any quantity of energy was possible. Now it seemed clear that energy is in fact **quantized** and can occur only in discrete units of size $h\nu$. Each of these small "packets" of energy is called a *quantum*. A system can transfer energy only in whole quanta. Thus energy seems to have particulate properties.

> Energy can be gained or lost only in integer multiples of $h\nu$.

> Planck's constant = 6.626×10^{-34} J · s.

Sample Exercise 7.2 *The Energy of a Photon*

The blue color in fireworks is often achieved by heating copper(I) chloride (CuCl) to about 1200°C. Then the compound emits blue light having a wavelength of 450 nm. What is the increment of energy (the quantum) that is emitted at 4.50×10^2 nm by CuCl?

Solution

The quantum of energy can be calculated from the equation

$$\Delta E = h\nu$$

The frequency ν for this case can be calculated as follows:

$$\nu = \frac{c}{\lambda} = \frac{2.9979 \times 10^8 \text{ m/s}}{4.50 \times 10^{-7} \text{ m}} = 6.66 \times 10^{14} \text{ s}^{-1}$$

So

$$\Delta E = h\nu = (6.626 \times 10^{-34} \text{ J} \cdot \text{s})(6.66 \times 10^{14} \text{ s}^{-1}) = 4.41 \times 10^{-19} \text{ J}$$

A sample of CuCl emitting light at 450 nm can only lose energy in increments of 4.41×10^{-19} J, the size of the quantum in this case.

See Exercises 7.39 and 7.40.

The next important development in the knowledge of atomic structure came when Albert Einstein (see Fig. 7.3) proposed that electromagnetic radiation is itself quantized. Einstein suggested that electromagnetic radiation can be viewed as a stream of "particles" called **photons.** The energy of each photon is given by the expression

$$E_{\text{photon}} = h\nu = \frac{hc}{\lambda}$$

where h is Planck's constant, ν is the frequency of the radiation, and λ is the wavelength of the radiation.

In a related development, Einstein derived the famous equation

$$E = mc^2$$

in his *special theory of relativity* published in 1905. The equation points out the close relationship between energy and mass. In fact, we have learned that mass is a form of energy. When a system loses energy, it also loses mass. This is more apparent if we rearrange the equation in the following form:

$$\underset{\text{Mass}}{m} = \frac{E}{c^2} \quad \leftarrow \text{Energy}$$

Speed of light

Using this form of the equation, we can calculate the mass associated with a given quantity of energy.

If a beam of light can be considered to be a stream of "particles" (photons), do the photons have mass? The answer is no. Photons do not exhibit mass in the same

Figure 7.3

Albert Einstein (1879–1955) was born in Germany. Nothing in his early development suggested genius; even at the age of 9 he did not speak clearly, and his parents feared that he might be handicapped. When asked what profession Einstein should follow, his school principal replied, "It doesn't matter; he'll never make a success of anything." When he was 10, Einstein entered the Luitpold Gymnasium (high school), which was typical of German schools of that time in being harshly disciplinarian. There he developed a deep suspicion of authority and a skepticism that encouraged him to question and doubt—valuable qualities in a scientist. In 1905, while a patent clerk in Switzerland, Einstein published a paper explaining the photoelectric effect via the quantum theory. For this revolutionary thinking he received a Nobel Prize in 1921. Highly regarded by this time, he worked in Germany until 1933, when Hitler's persecution of the Jews forced him to come to the United States. He worked at the Institute for Advanced Studies at Princeton University until his death in 1955.

Einstein was undoubtedly the greatest physicist of our age. Even if someone else had derived the theory of relativity, his other work would have ensured his ranking as the second greatest physicist of his time. Our concepts of space and time were radically changed by ideas he first proposed when he was 26 years old. From then until the end of his life, he attempted unsuccessfully to find a single unifying theory that would explain all physical events.

Animations: Photoelectric Effect (Yellow and Blue)

way as classical particles do. However, Einstein's equations do predict that a photon has momentum, which is best thought of as an intrinsic property of the photon not dependent separately on mass and velocity as for a classical particle. In 1922 American physicist Arthur Compton (1892–1962) performed experiments involving collisions of X rays and electrons that showed that photons do exhibit the apparent mass calculated from the preceding equation.

We can summarize the important conclusions from the work of Planck and Einstein as follows:

Energy is quantized. It can occur only in discrete units called quanta.

Electromagnetic radiation, which was previously thought to exhibit only wave properties, seems to show certain characteristics of particulate matter as well. This phenomenon is sometimes referred to as the **dual nature of light** and is illustrated in Fig. 7.4.

Thus light, which previously was thought to be purely wavelike, was found to have certain characteristics of particulate matter. But is the opposite also true? That is, does matter that is normally assumed to be particulate exhibit wave properties? This question was raised in 1923 by a young French physicist named Louis de Broglie (1892–1987), who derived the following relationship for the wavelength of a particle with momentum mv:

$$\lambda = \frac{h}{mv}$$

This equation, called *de Broglie's equation*, allows us to calculate the wavelength for a particle, as shown in Sample Exercise 7.3.

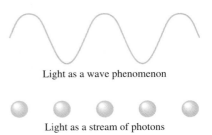

Light as a wave phenomenon

Light as a stream of photons

Figure 7.4

Electromagnetic radiation exhibits wave properties and particulate properties. The energy of each photon of the radiation is related to the wavelength and frequency by the equation $E_{photon} = h\nu = hc/\lambda$.

Do not confuse ν (frequency) with v (velocity).

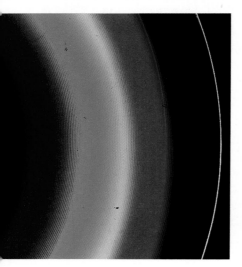

(top) Light diffracted by the closely spaced grooves on a compact disc shows the visible spectrum. (bottom) Prismatic diffraction.

Molecular Model: NaCl

Sample Exercise 7.3   Calculations of Wavelength

Compare the wavelength for an electron (mass = 9.11×10^{-31} kg) traveling at a speed of 1.0×10^7 m/s with that for a ball (mass = 0.10 kg) traveling at 35 m/s.

Solution

We use the equation $\lambda = h/mv$, where

$$h = 6.626 \times 10^{-34} \text{ J} \cdot \text{s} \quad \text{or} \quad 6.626 \times 10^{-34} \text{ kg} \cdot \text{m}^2/\text{s}$$

since

$$1 \text{ J} = 1 \text{ kg} \cdot \text{m}^2/\text{s}^2$$

For the electron,

$$\lambda_e = \frac{6.626 \times 10^{-34} \frac{\text{kg} \cdot \text{m} \cdot \text{m}}{\text{s}}}{(9.11 \times 10^{-31} \text{ kg})(1.0 \times 10^7 \text{ m/s})} = 7.27 \times 10^{-11} \text{ m}$$

For the ball,

$$\lambda_b = \frac{6.626 \times 10^{-34} \frac{\text{kg} \cdot \text{m} \cdot \text{m}}{\text{s}}}{(0.10 \text{ kg})(35 \text{ m/s})} = 1.9 \times 10^{-34} \text{ m}$$

See Exercises 7.45 through 7.48.

Notice from Sample Exercise 7.3 that the wavelength associated with the ball is incredibly short. On the other hand, the wavelength of the electron, although still quite small, happens to be on the same order as the spacing between the atoms in a typical crystal. This is important because, as we will see presently, it provides a means for testing de Broglie's equation.

Diffraction results when light is scattered from a regular array of points or lines. The diffraction of light from the ridges and grooves of a compact disc is shown in the photograph. The colors result because the various wavelengths of visible light are not all scattered in the same way. The colors are "separated," giving the same effect as light passing through a prism. Just as a regular arrangement of ridges and grooves produces diffraction, so does a regular array of atoms or ions in a crystal. For example, when X rays are directed onto a crystal of sodium chloride, with its regular array of Na^+ and Cl^- ions, the scattered radiation produces a **diffraction pattern** of bright spots and dark areas on a photographic plate, as shown in Fig. 7.5(a). This occurs because the scattered light can interfere constructively (the peaks and troughs of the beams are in phase) to produce a bright spot [Fig. 7.5(b)] or destructively (the peaks and troughs are out of phase) to produce a dark area [Fig. 7.5(c)].

A diffraction pattern can only be explained in terms of waves. Thus this phenomenon provides a test for the postulate that particles such as electrons have wavelengths. As we saw in Sample Exercise 7.3, an electron with a velocity of 10^7 m/s (easily achieved by acceleration of the electron in an electric field) has a wavelength of about 10^{-10} m, which is roughly the distance between the ions in a crystal such as sodium chloride. This is important because diffraction occurs most efficiently when the spacing between the scattering points is about the same as the wavelength of the wave being diffracted. Thus, if electrons really do have an associated wavelength, a crystal should diffract electrons. An experiment to test this idea was carried out in 1927 by C. J. Davisson and L. H. Germer at Bell Laboratories. When they directed a beam of electrons at a nickel crystal, they observed a diffraction pattern similar to that seen from the diffraction of X rays. This result verified de Broglie's relationship, at least for electrons. Larger chunks of matter, such as balls, have such small wavelengths (see Sample Exercise 7.3) that they are impossible to verify experimentally. However, we believe that all matter obeys de Broglie's equation.

Now we have come full circle. Electromagnetic radiation, which at the turn of the twentieth century was thought to be a pure waveform, was found to possess particulate properties. Conversely, electrons, which were thought to be particles, were found to have a wavelength associated with them. The significance of these results is that matter and energy are not distinct. Energy is really a form of matter, and all matter shows the same types of properties. That is, *all matter exhibits both particulate and wave properties.* Large pieces of matter, such as baseballs, exhibit predominantly particulate properties. The associated wavelength is so small that it is not observed. Very small bits of matter, such as photons, while showing some particulate properties, exhibit predominantly wave properties. Pieces of matter with intermediate mass, such as electrons, show clearly both the particulate and wave properties of matter.

7.3 The Atomic Spectrum of Hydrogen

As we saw in Chapter 2, key information about the atom came from several experiments carried out in the early twentieth century, in particular Thomson's discovery of the electron and Rutherford's discovery of the nucleus. Another important experiment was the study of the emission of light by excited hydrogen atoms. When a sample of hydrogen gas receives a high-energy spark, the H_2 molecules absorb energy, and some of the H—H bonds are broken. The resulting hydrogen atoms are *excited;* that is, they contain excess energy, which they release by emitting light of various wavelengths to produce what is called the *emission spectrum* of the hydrogen atom.

To understand the significance of the hydrogen emission spectrum, we must first describe the **continuous spectrum** that results when white light is passed through a prism, as shown in Fig. 7.6(a). This spectrum, like the rainbow produced when sunlight is dispersed by raindrops, contains *all* the wavelengths of visible light. In contrast, when the hydrogen emission spectrum in the visible region is passed through a prism, as shown in Fig. 7.6(b), we see only a few lines, each of which corresponds to a discrete wavelength. The hydrogen emission spectrum is called a **line spectrum.**

What is the significance of the line spectrum of hydrogen? It indicates that *only certain energies are allowed for the electron in the hydrogen atom.* In other words,

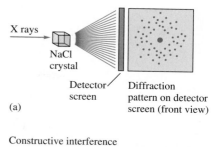

(a)

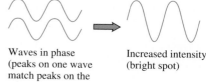

Constructive interference

Waves in phase (peaks on one wave match peaks on the other wave)

(b)

Increased intensity (bright spot)

Destructive interference

Trough

Peak

Waves out of phase (troughs and peaks coincide)

(c)

Decreased intensity (dark spot)

Figure 7.5

(a) Diffraction occurs when electromagnetic radiation is scattered from a regular array of objects, such as the ions in a crystal of sodium chloride. The large spot in the center is from the main incident beam of X rays. (b) Bright spots in the diffraction pattern result from *constructive interference* of waves. The waves are in phase; that is, their peaks match. (c) Dark areas result from *destructive interference* of waves. The waves are out of phase; the peaks of one wave coincide with the troughs of another wave.

Molecular Model: H_2

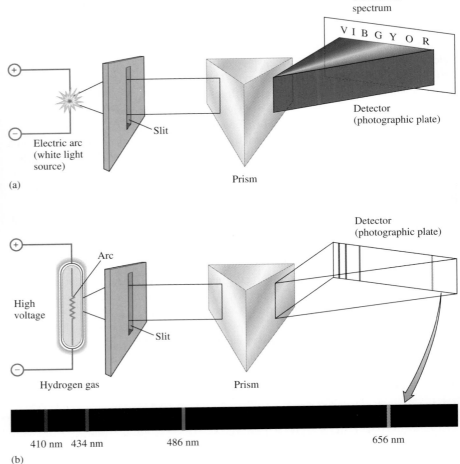

Continuous spectrum

V I B G Y O R

Detector (photographic plate)

Slit

Electric arc (white light source)

Prism

(a)

Detector (photographic plate)

Arc

High voltage

Slit

Hydrogen gas

Prism

410 nm   434 nm   486 nm   656 nm

(b)

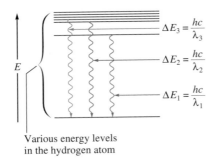

A rainbow over Vail, Colorado.

Figure 7.6

(a) A continuous spectrum containing all wavelengths of visible light (indicated by the initial letters of the colors of the rainbow). (b) The hydrogen line spectrum contains only a few discrete wavelengths. Spectrum adapted by permission from C. W. Keenan, D. C. Kleinfelter, and J. H. Wood, *General College Chemistry*, 6th ed. (New York: Harper & Row, 1980).

 Animations: Refraction of White Light and H$_2$ Line Spectrum

$\Delta E_3 = \dfrac{hc}{\lambda_3}$

$\Delta E_2 = \dfrac{hc}{\lambda_2}$

E

$\Delta E_1 = \dfrac{hc}{\lambda_1}$

Various energy levels in the hydrogen atom

Figure 7.7

A change between two discrete energy levels emits a photon of light.

the energy of the electron in the hydrogen atom is *quantized*. This observation ties in perfectly with the postulates of Max Planck discussed in Section 7.2. Changes in energy between discrete energy levels in hydrogen will produce only certain wavelengths of emitted light, as shown in Fig. 7.7. For example, a given change in energy from a high to a lower level would give a wavelength of light that can be calculated from Planck's equation:

$$\Delta E = h\nu = \frac{hc}{\lambda}$$

Change in energy

Frequency of light emitted

Wavelength of light emitted

The discrete line spectrum of hydrogen shows that only certain energies are possible; that is, the electron energy levels are quantized. In contrast, if any energy level were allowed, the emission spectrum would be continuous.

7.4 The Bohr Model

In 1913, a Danish physicist named Niels Bohr (1885–1962), aware of the experimental results we have just discussed, developed a **quantum model** for the hydrogen atom. Bohr proposed that the *electron in a hydrogen atom moves around the nucleus only in certain allowed circular orbits.* He calculated the radii for these allowed orbits by using the theories of classical physics and by making some new assumptions.

From classical physics Bohr knew that a particle in motion tends to move in a straight line and can be made to travel in a circle only by application of a force toward the center of the circle. Thus Bohr reasoned that the tendency of the revolving electron to fly off the atom must be just balanced by its attraction for the positively charged nucleus. But classical physics also decreed that a charged particle under acceleration should radiate energy. Since an electron revolving around the nucleus constantly changes its direction, it is constantly accelerating. Therefore, the electron should emit light and lose energy—and thus be drawn into the nucleus. This, of course, does not correlate with the existence of stable atoms.

Clearly, an atomic model based solely on the theories of classical physics was untenable. Bohr also knew that the correct model had to account for the experimental spectrum of hydrogen, which showed that only certain electron energies were allowed. The experimental data were absolutely clear on this point. Bohr found that his model would fit the experimental results if he assumed that the angular momentum of the electron (angular momentum equals the product of mass, velocity, and orbital radius) could only occur in certain increments. It was not clear why this should be true, but with this assumption, Bohr's model gave hydrogen atom energy levels consistent with the hydrogen emission spectrum. The model is represented pictorially in Fig. 7.8.

Although we will not show the derivation here, the most important equation to come from Bohr's model is the expression for the *energy levels available to the electron in the hydrogen atom:*

$$E = -2.178 \times 10^{-18} \text{ J}\left(\frac{Z^2}{n^2}\right) \qquad (7.1)$$

in which n is an integer (the larger the value of n, the larger is the orbit radius) and Z is the nuclear charge. Using Equation (7.1), Bohr was able to calculate hydrogen atom energy levels that exactly matched the values obtained by experiment.

The negative sign in Equation (7.1) simply means that the energy of the electron bound to the nucleus is lower than it would be if the electron were at an infinite distance ($n = \infty$) from the nucleus, where there is no interaction and the energy is zero:

The J in Equation (7.1) stands for joules.

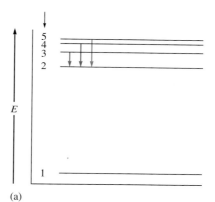

(a)

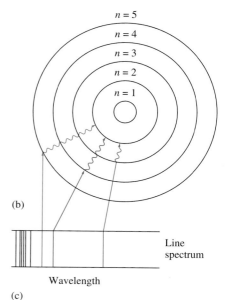

(b)

(c)

Figure 7.8

Electronic transitions in the Bohr model for the hydrogen atom. (a) An energy-level diagram for electronic transitions. (b) An orbit-transition diagram, which accounts for the experimental spectrum. (Note that the orbits shown are schematic. They are not drawn to scale.) (c) The resulting line spectrum on a photographic plate. Note that the lines in the visible region of the spectrum correspond to transitions from higher levels to the $n = 2$ level.

Niels Hendrik David Bohr (1885–1962) as a boy lived in the shadow of his younger brother Harald, who played on the 1908 Danish Olympic Soccer Team and later became a distinguished mathematician. In school, Bohr received his poorest marks in composition and struggled with writing during his entire life. In fact, he wrote so poorly that he was forced to dictate his Ph.D. thesis to his mother. Nevertheless, Bohr was a brilliant physicist. After receiving his Ph.D. in Denmark, he constructed a quantum model for the hydrogen atom by the time he was 27. Even though his model later proved to be incorrect, Bohr remained a central figure in the drive to understand the atom. He was awarded the Nobel Prize in physics in 1922.

$$E = -2.178 \times 10^{-18} \text{ J}\left(\frac{Z^2}{\infty}\right) = 0$$

The energy of the electron in any orbit is negative relative to this reference state.

Equation (7.1) can be used to calculate the change in energy of an electron when the electron changes orbits. For example, suppose an electron in level $n = 6$ of an excited hydrogen atom falls back to level $n = 1$ as the hydrogen atom returns to its lowest possible energy state, its **ground state.** We use Equation (7.1) with $Z = 1$, since the hydrogen nucleus contains a single proton. The energies corresponding to the two states are as follows:

For $n = 6$: $\quad E_6 = -2.178 \times 10^{-18} \text{ J}\left(\frac{1^2}{6^2}\right) = -6.050 \times 10^{-20} \text{ J}$

For $n = 1$: $\quad E_1 = -2.178 \times 10^{-18} \text{ J}\left(\frac{1^2}{1^2}\right) = -2.178 \times 10^{-18} \text{ J}$

Note that for $n = 1$ the electron has a more negative energy than it does for $n = 6$, which means that the electron is more tightly bound in the smallest allowed orbit.

The change in energy ΔE when the electron falls from $n = 6$ to $n = 1$ is

ΔE = energy of final state − energy of initial state

$= E_1 - E_6 = (-2.178 \times 10^{-18} \text{ J}) - (-6.050 \times 10^{-20} \text{ J})$

$= -2.117 \times 10^{-18} \text{ J}$

The negative sign for the *change* in energy indicates that the atom has *lost* energy and is now in a more stable state. The energy is carried away from the atom by the production (emission) of a photon.

The wavelength of the emitted photon can be calculated from the equation

$$\Delta E = h\left(\frac{c}{\lambda}\right) \quad \text{or} \quad \lambda = \frac{hc}{\Delta E}$$

where ΔE represents the change in energy of the atom, which equals the energy of the emitted photon. We have

$$\lambda = \frac{hc}{\Delta E} = \frac{(6.626 \times 10^{-34} \text{ J} \cdot \text{s})(2.9979 \times 10^8 \text{ m/s})}{2.117 \times 10^{-18} \text{ J}} = 9.383 \times 10^{-8} \text{ m}$$

Note that for this calculation the absolute value of ΔE is used (we have not included the negative sign). In this case we indicate the direction of energy flow by saying that a photon of wavelength 9.383×10^{-8} m has been *emitted* from the hydrogen atom. Simply plugging the negative value of ΔE into the equation would produce a negative value for λ, which is physically meaningless.

Sample Exercise 7.4 *Energy Quantization in Hydrogen*

Calculate the energy required to excite the hydrogen electron from level $n = 1$ to level $n = 2$. Also calculate the wavelength of light that must be absorbed by a hydrogen atom in its ground state to reach this excited state.*

*After this exercise we will no longer show cancellation marks. However, the same process for canceling units applies throughout this text.

Solution

Using Equation (7.1) with $Z = 1$, we have

$$E_1 = -2.178 \times 10^{-18} \text{ J}\left(\frac{1^2}{1^2}\right) = -2.178 \times 10^{-18} \text{ J}$$

$$E_2 = -2.178 \times 10^{-18} \text{ J}\left(\frac{1^2}{2^2}\right) = -5.445 \times 10^{-19} \text{ J}$$

$$\Delta E = E_2 - E_1 = (-5.445 \times 10^{-19} \text{ J}) - (-2.178 \times 10^{-18} \text{ J}) = 1.633 \times 10^{-18} \text{ J}$$

The positive value for ΔE indicates that the system has gained energy. The wavelength of light that must be *absorbed* to produce this change is

$$\lambda = \frac{hc}{\Delta E} = \frac{(6.626 \times 10^{-34} \text{ J} \cdot \text{s})(2.9979 \times 10^8 \text{ m/s})}{1.633 \times 10^{-18} \text{ J}}$$

$$= 1.216 \times 10^{-7} \text{ m}$$

Note from Fig. 7.2 that the light required to produce the transition from the $n = 1$ to $n = 2$ level in hydrogen lies in the ultraviolet region.

See Exercises 7.49 and 7.50.

At this time we must emphasize two important points about the Bohr model:

1. The model correctly fits the quantized energy levels of the hydrogen atom and postulates only certain allowed circular orbits for the electron.

2. As the electron becomes more tightly bound, its energy becomes more negative relative to the zero-energy reference state (corresponding to the electron being at infinite distance from the nucleus). As the electron is brought closer to the nucleus, energy is released from the system.

Using Equation (7.1), we can derive a general equation for the electron moving from one level (n_{initial}) to another level (n_{final}):

$$\Delta E = \text{energy of level } n_{\text{final}} - \text{energy of level } n_{\text{initial}}$$

$$= E_{\text{final}} - E_{\text{initial}}$$

$$= (-2.178 \times 10^{-18} \text{ J})\left(\frac{1^2}{n_{\text{final}}{}^2}\right) - (-2.178 \times 10^{-18} \text{ J})\left(\frac{1^2}{n_{\text{initial}}{}^2}\right)$$

$$= -2.178 \times 10^{-18} \text{ J}\left(\frac{1}{n_{\text{final}}{}^2} - \frac{1}{n_{\text{initial}}{}^2}\right) \tag{7.2}$$

Equation (7.2) can be used to calculate the energy change between *any* two energy levels in a hydrogen atom, as shown in Sample Exercise 7.5.

Sample Exercise 7.5 *Electron Energies*

Calculate the energy required to remove the electron from a hydrogen atom in its ground state.

Solution

Removing the electron from a hydrogen atom in its ground state corresponds to taking the electron from $n_{initial} = 1$ to $n_{final} = \infty$. Thus

$$\Delta E = -2.178 \times 10^{-18} \text{ J}\left(\frac{1}{n_{final}^2} - \frac{1}{n_{initial}^2}\right)$$

$$= -2.178 \times 10^{-18} \text{ J}\left(\frac{1}{\infty} - \frac{1}{1^2}\right)$$

$$= -2.178 \times 10^{-18} \text{ J}(0 - 1) = 2.178 \times 10^{-18} \text{ J}$$

The energy required to remove the electron from a hydrogen atom in its ground state is 2.178×10^{-18} J.

See Exercises 7.55 and 7.56.

Video: Flame Tests

CHEMICAL IMPACT

Fireworks

THE ART OF using mixtures of chemicals to produce explosives is an ancient one. Black powder—a mixture of potassium nitrate, charcoal, and sulfur—was being used in China well before 1000 A.D. and has been used subsequently through the centuries in military explosives, in construction blasting, and for fireworks. The du Pont Company, now a major chemical manufacturer, started out as a manufacturer of black powder. In fact, the founder, Eleuthère du Pont, learned the manufacturing technique from none other than Lavoisier.

Before the nineteenth century, fireworks were confined mainly to rockets and loud bangs. Orange and yellow colors came from the presence of charcoal and iron filings. However, with the great advances in chemistry in the nineteenth century, new compounds found their way into fireworks. Salts of copper, strontium, and barium added brilliant colors. Magnesium and aluminum metals gave a dazzling white light. Fireworks, in fact, have changed very little since then.

How do fireworks produce their brilliant colors and loud bangs? Actually, only

A fireworks competition in Montreal, Canada.

a handful of different chemicals are responsible for most of the spectacular effects. To produce the noise and flashes, an oxidizer (an oxidizing agent) and a fuel (a reducing agent) are used. A common mixture involves potassium perchlorate ($KClO_4$) as the oxidizer and aluminum

and sulfur as the fuel. The perchlorate oxidizes the fuel in a very exothermic reaction, which produces a brilliant flash, due to the aluminum, and a loud report from the rapidly expanding gases produced. For a color effect, an element with a colored emission spectrum is included. Recall that the electrons in atoms can be raised to higher-energy orbitals when the atoms absorb energy. The excited atoms can then release this excess energy by emitting light of specific wavelengths, often in the visible region. In fireworks, the energy to excite the electrons comes from the reaction between the oxidizer and fuel.

Yellow colors in fireworks are due to the 589-nm emission of sodium ions. Red colors come from strontium salts emitting at 606 nm and from 636 to 688 nm. This red color is familiar from highway safety flares. Barium salts give a green color in fireworks, due to a series of emission lines between 505 and 535 nm. A really good blue color, however, is hard to obtain. Copper salts give a blue color, emitting in the 420- to 460-nm region. But difficulties occur because another commonly used oxidizing agent, potas-

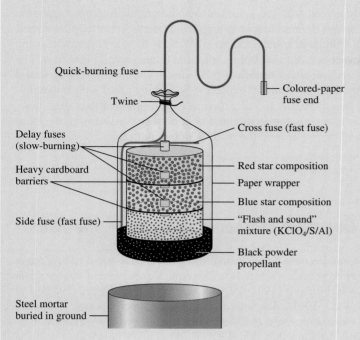

Quick-burning fuse

Twine

Colored-paper fuse end

Delay fuses (slow-burning)

Cross fuse (fast fuse)

Heavy cardboard barriers

Red star composition

Paper wrapper

Blue star composition

Side fuse (fast fuse)

"Flash and sound" mixture (KClO$_4$/S/Al)

Black powder propellant

Steel mortar buried in ground

A typical aerial shell used in fireworks displays. Time-delayed fuses cause a shell to explode in stages. In this case a red starburst occurs first, followed by a blue starburst, and finally a flash and loud report. Reproduced with permission from *Chemical & Engineering News*, June 29, 1981, *59* (26), p. 24. Copyright © 1981 American Chemical Society.

sium chlorate (KClO$_3$), reacts with copper salts to form copper chlorate, a highly explosive compound that is dangerous to store. Paris green, a copper salt containing arsenic, was once used extensively but is now considered to be too toxic.

A typical aerial shell is shown in the diagram. The shell is launched from a mortar (a steel cylinder) using black powder as the propellant. Time-delayed fuses are used to fire the shell in stages. A list of chemicals commonly used in fireworks is given in the table.

Although you might think that the chemistry of fireworks is simple, the achievement of the vivid white flashes and the brilliant colors requires complex combinations of chemicals. For example, because the white flashes produce high flame temperatures, the colors tend to wash out. Thus oxidizers such as KClO$_4$ are sometimes used with fuels that produce relatively low flame temperatures. An added difficulty, however, is that perchlorates are very sensitive to accidental ignition and are therefore quite hazardous. Another problem arises from the use of sodium salts. Because sodium produces an extremely bright yellow emission, sodium salts cannot be used when other colors are desired. Carbon-based fuels also give a yellow flame that masks other colors, and this limits the use of organic compounds as fuels. You can see that the manufacture of fireworks that produce the desired effects and are also safe to handle requires careful selection of chemicals. And, of course, there is still the dream of a deep blue flame.

Chemicals Commonly Used in the Manufacture of Fireworks

Oxidizers	Fuels	Special Effects
Potassium nitrate	Aluminum	Red flame: strontium nitrate, strontium carbonate
Potassium chlorate	Magnesium	Green flame: barium nitrate, barium chlorate
Potassium perchlorate	Titanium	Blue flame: copper carbonate, copper sulfate, copper oxide
Ammonium perchlorate	Charcoal	Yellow flame: sodium oxalate, cryolite (Na$_3$AlF$_6$)
Barium nitrate	Sulfur	White flame: magnesium, aluminum
Barium chlorate	Antimony sulfide	Gold sparks: iron filings, charcoal
Strontium nitrate	Dextrin	White sparks: aluminum, magnesium, aluminum–magnesium alloy, titanium
	Red gum	Whistle effect: potassium benzoate or sodium salicylate
	Polyvinyl chloride	White smoke: mixture of potassium nitrate and sulfur
		Colored smoke: mixture of potassium chlorate, sulfur, and organic dye

At first Bohr's model appeared to be very promising. The energy levels calculated by Bohr closely agreed with the values obtained from the hydrogen emission spectrum. However, when Bohr's model was applied to atoms other than hydrogen, it did not work at all. Although some attempts were made to adapt the model using elliptical orbits, it was concluded that Bohr's model is fundamentally incorrect. The model is, however, very important historically, because it showed that the observed quantization of energy in atoms could be explained by making rather simple assumptions. Bohr's model paved the way for later theories. It is important to realize, however, that the current theory of atomic structure is in no way derived from the Bohr model. Electrons do *not* move around the nucleus in circular orbits, as we shall see later in this chapter.

Although Bohr's model fits the energy levels for hydrogen, it is a fundamentally incorrect model for the hydrogen atom.

7.5 The Quantum Mechanical Model of the Atom

By the mid-1920s it had become apparent that the Bohr model could not be made to work. A totally new approach was needed. Three physicists were at the forefront of this effort: Werner Heisenberg (1901–1976), Louis de Broglie (1892–1987), and Erwin Schrödinger (1887–1961). The approach they developed became known as *wave mechanics* or, more commonly, *quantum mechanics.* As we have already seen, de Broglie originated the idea that the electron, previously considered to be a particle, also shows wave properties. Pursuing this line of reasoning, Schrödinger, an Austrian physicist, decided to attack the problem of atomic structure by giving emphasis to the wave properties of the electron. To Schrödinger and de Broglie, the electron bound to the nucleus seemed similar to a **standing wave,** and they began research on a wave mechanical description of the atom.

The most familiar example of standing waves occurs in association with musical instruments such as guitars or violins, where a string attached at both ends vibrates to produce a musical tone. The waves are described as "standing" because they are stationary; the waves do not travel along the length of the string. The motions of the string can be explained as a combination of simple waves of the type shown in Fig. 7.9. The dots in this figure indicate the nodes, or points of zero lateral (sideways) displacement, for a given wave. Note that there are limitations on the allowed wavelengths of the standing wave. Each end of the string is fixed, so there is always a node at each end. This means that there must be a whole number of *half* wavelengths in any of the allowed motions of the string (see Fig. 7.9).

A similar situation results when the electron in the hydrogen atom is imagined to be a standing wave. As shown in Fig. 7.10, only certain circular orbits have a circumference into which a whole number of wavelengths of the standing electron wave will "fit." All other orbits would produce destructive interference of the standing electron wave and are not allowed. This seemed like a possible explanation for the observed quantization of the hydrogen atom, so Schrödinger worked out a model for the hydrogen atom in which the electron was assumed to behave as a standing wave.

It is important to recognize that Schrödinger could not be sure that this idea would work. The test had to be whether or not the model would correctly fit the experimental data on hydrogen and other atoms. The physical principles for describing

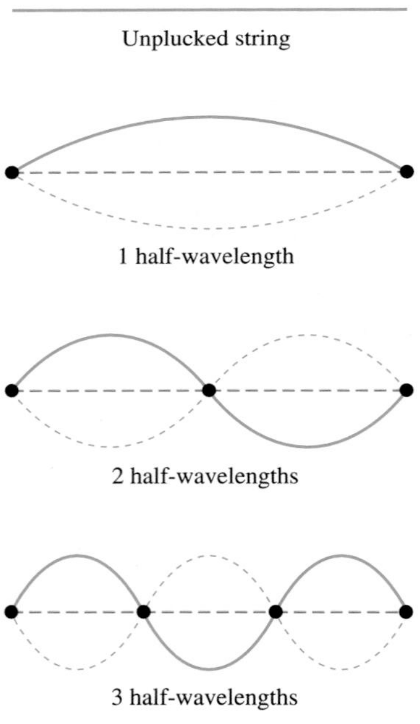

Unplucked string

1 half-wavelength

2 half-wavelengths

3 half-wavelengths

Figure 7.9

The standing waves caused by the vibration of a guitar string fastened at both ends. Each dot represents a node (a point of zero displacement).

standing waves were well known in 1925 when Schrödinger decided to treat the electron in this way. His mathematical treatment is too complicated to be detailed here. However, the form of Schrödinger's equation is

$$\hat{H}\psi = E\psi$$

where ψ, called the **wave function,** is a function of the coordinates (x, y, and z) of the electron's position in three-dimensional space and $\hat{H}$ represents a set of mathematical instructions called an *operator.* In this case, the operator contains mathematical terms that produce the total energy of the atom when they are applied to the wave function. E represents the total energy of the atom (the sum of the potential energy due to the attraction between the proton and electron and the kinetic energy of the moving electron). When this equation is analyzed, many solutions are found. Each solution consists of a wave function ψ that is characterized by a particular value of E. A specific wave function is often called an **orbital.**

To illustrate the most important ideas of the **quantum (wave) mechanical model** of the atom, we will first concentrate on the wave function corresponding to the lowest energy for the hydrogen atom. This wave function is called the $1s$ orbital. The first point of interest is to explore the meaning of the word *orbital.* As we will see, this is not a trivial matter. One thing is clear: An orbital is *not* a Bohr orbit. The electron in the hydrogen $1s$ orbital is not moving around the nucleus in a circular orbit. How, then, is the electron moving? The answer is quite surprising: *We do not know.* The wave function gives us no information about the detailed pathway of the electron. This is somewhat disturbing. When we solve problems involving the motions of particles in the macroscopic world, we are able to predict their pathways. For example, when two billiard balls with known velocities collide, we can predict their motions after the collision. However, we cannot predict the electron's motion from the $1s$ orbital function. Does this mean that the theory is wrong? Not necessarily: We have already learned that an electron does not behave much like a billiard ball, so we must examine the situation closely before we discard the theory.

To help us understand the nature of an orbital, we need to consider a principle discovered by Werner Heisenberg, one of the primary developers of quantum mechanics. Heisenberg's mathematical analysis led him to a surprising conclusion: *There is a fundamental limitation to just how precisely we can know both the position and momentum of a particle at a given time.* This is a statement of the **Heisenberg uncertainty principle.** Stated mathematically, the uncertainty principle is

$$\Delta x \cdot \Delta(mv) \geq \frac{h}{4\pi}$$

where Δx is the uncertainty in a particle's position, $\Delta(mv)$ is the uncertainty in a particle's momentum, and h is Planck's constant. Thus the minimum uncertainty in the product $\Delta x \cdot \Delta(mv)$ is $h/4\pi$. What this equation really says is that the more accurately we know a particle's position, the less accurately we can know its momentum, and vice versa. This limitation is so small for large particles such as baseballs or billiard balls that it is unnoticed. However, for a small particle such as the electron, the limitation becomes quite important. Applied to the electron, the uncertainty principle implies that we cannot know the exact motion of the electron as it moves around the nucleus. It is therefore not appropriate to assume that the electron is moving around the nucleus in a well-defined orbit, as in the Bohr model.

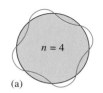

(a)

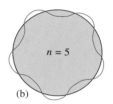

(b)

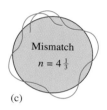

(c)

Figure 7.10

The hydrogen electron visualized as a standing wave around the nucleus. The circumference of a particular circular orbit would have to correspond to a whole number of wavelengths, as shown in (a) and (b), or else destructive interference occurs, as shown in (c). This is consistent with the fact that only certain electron energies are allowed; the atom is quantized. (Although this idea encouraged scientists to use a wave theory, it does not mean that the electron really travels in circular orbits.)

The Physical Meaning of a Wave Function

Given the limitations indicated by the uncertainty principle, what then is the physical meaning of a wave function for an electron? That is, what is an atomic orbital? Although the wave function itself has no easily visualized meaning, the square of the function does have a definite physical significance. *The square of the function indicates the probability of finding an electron near a particular point in space.* For example, suppose we have two positions in space, one defined by the coordinates x_1, y_1, and z_1 and the other by the coordinates x_2, y_2, and z_2. The relative probability of finding the electron at positions 1 and 2 is given by substituting the values of x, y, and z for the two positions into the wave function, squaring the function value, and computing the following ratio:

$$\frac{[\psi(x_1, y_1, z_1)]^2}{[\psi(x_2, y_2, z_2)]^2} = \frac{N_1}{N_2}$$

> Probability is the likelihood, or odds, that something will occur.

The quotient N_1/N_2 is the ratio of the probabilities of finding the electron at positions 1 and 2. For example, if the value of the ratio N_1/N_2 is 100, the electron is 100 times more likely to be found at position 1 than at position 2. The model gives no information concerning when the electron will be at either position or how it moves between the positions. This vagueness is consistent with the concept of the Heisenberg uncertainty principle.

The square of the wave function is most conveniently represented as a **probability distribution,** in which the intensity of color is used to indicate the probability value near a given point in space. The probability distribution for the hydrogen $1s$ wave function (orbital) is shown in Fig. 7.11(a). The best way to think about this diagram is as a three-dimensional time exposure with the electron as a tiny moving light. The more times the electron visits a particular point, the darker the negative becomes. Thus the darkness of a point indicates the probability of finding an electron at that position. This diagram is also known as an *electron density map; electron density* and *electron probability* mean the same thing. When a chemist uses the term *atomic orbital,* he or she is probably picturing an electron density map of this type.

Another way of representing the electron probability distribution for the $1s$ wave function is to calculate the probability at points along a line drawn outward in any direction from the nucleus. The result is shown in Fig. 7.11(b). Note that the probability of finding the electron at a particular position is greatest close to the nucleus and it drops off rapidly as the distance from the nucleus increases. We are also interested in knowing the *total* probability of finding the electron in the hydrogen atom at a particular *distance* from the nucleus. Imagine that the space around the hydrogen nucleus is made up of a series of thin spherical shells (rather like layers in an onion), as shown in Fig. 7.12(a). When the total probability of finding the electron in each spherical shell is plotted versus the distance from the nucleus, the plot in Fig. 7.12(b) is obtained. This graph is called the **radial probability distribution.**

The maximum in the curve occurs because of two opposing effects. The probability of finding an electron at a particular position is greatest near the nucleus, but the volume of the spherical shell increases with distance from the nucleus. Therefore, as we move away from the nucleus, the probability of finding the electron at a given position decreases, but we are summing more positions. Thus the total probability increases to a certain radius and then decreases as the electron probability at each position becomes very small. For the hydrogen $1s$ orbital, the maximum radial probability (the distance at which the electron is most likely to be found) occurs at a

(a)

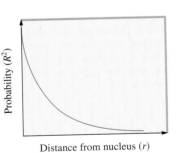

Probability (R^2)

Distance from nucleus (r)

(b)

Figure 7.11

(a) The probability distribution for the hydrogen $1s$ orbital in three-dimensional space. (b) The probability of finding the electron at points along a line drawn from the nucleus outward in any direction for the hydrogen $1s$ orbital.

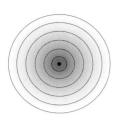

(a)

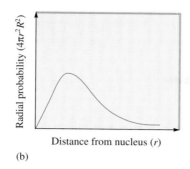

(b)

Figure 7.12

(a) Cross section of the hydrogen 1s orbital probability distribution divided into successive thin spherical shells. (b) The radial probability distribution. A plot of the total probability of finding the electron in each thin spherical shell as a function of distance from the nucleus.

distance of 5.29×10^{-2} nm or 0.529 Å from the nucleus. Interestingly, this is exactly the radius of the innermost orbit in the Bohr model. Note that in Bohr's model the electron is assumed to have a circular path and so is *always* found at this distance. In the quantum mechanical model, the specific electron motions are unknown, and this is the *most probable* distance at which the electron is found.

One more characteristic of the hydrogen 1s orbital that we must consider is its size. As we can see from Fig. 7.11, the size of this orbital cannot be defined precisely, since the probability never becomes zero (although it drops to an extremely small value at large values of *r*). So, in fact, the hydrogen 1s orbital has no distinct size. However, it is useful to have a definition of relative orbital size. *The definition most often used by chemists to describe the size of the hydrogen 1s orbital is the radius of the sphere that encloses 90% of the total electron probability.* That is, 90% of the time the electron is inside this sphere.

So far we have described only the lowest-energy wave function in the hydrogen atom, the 1s orbital. Hydrogen has many other orbitals, which we will describe in the next section. However, before we proceed, we should summarize what we have said about the meaning of an atomic orbital. An orbital is difficult to define precisely at an introductory level. Technically, an orbital is a wave function. However, it is usually most helpful to picture an orbital as a three-dimensional electron density map. That is, an electron "in" a particular atomic orbital is assumed to exhibit the electron probability indicated by the orbital map.

$1 \text{ Å} = 10^{-10}$ m; the angstrom is most often used as the unit for atomic radius because of its convenient size. Another convenient unit is the picometer:

$$1 \text{ pm} = 10^{-12} \text{ m}$$

7.6 Quantum Numbers

When we solve the Schrödinger equation for the hydrogen atom, we find many wave functions (orbitals) that satisfy it. Each of these orbitals is characterized by a series of numbers called **quantum numbers,** which describe various properties of the orbital:

The **principal quantum number** (*n*) has integral values: 1, 2, 3, ... The principal quantum number is related to the size and energy of the orbital. As *n* increases, the orbital becomes larger and the electron spends more time further from the nucleus. An increase in *n* also means higher energy, because the electron is less tightly bound to the nucleus, and the energy is less negative.

Table 7.1 The Angular Momentum Quantum Numbers and Corresponding Letters Used to Designate Atomic Orbitals

Value of ℓ	0	1	2	3	4
Letter Used	s	p	d	f	g

Number of Orbitals Per Subshell

$s = 1$
$p = 3$
$d = 5$
$f = 7$
$g = 9$

Table 7.2 Quantum Numbers for the First Four Levels of Orbitals in the Hydrogen Atom

n	ℓ	Orbital Designation	m_ℓ	Number of Orbitals
1	0	$1s$	0	1
2	0	$2s$	0	1
	1	$2p$	$-1, 0, +1$	3
3	0	$3s$	0	1
	1	$3p$	$-1, 0, 1$	3
	2	$3d$	$-2, -1, 0, 1, 2$	5
4	0	$4s$	0	1
	1	$4p$	$-1, 0, 1$	3
	2	$4d$	$-2, -1, 0, 1, 2$	5
	3	$4f$	$-3, -2, -1, 0, 1, 2, 3$	7

$n = 1, 2, 3, \ldots$
$\ell = 0, 1, \ldots (n - 1)$
$m_\ell = -\ell, \ldots 0, \ldots +\ell$

The **angular momentum quantum number** (ℓ) has integral values from 0 to $n - 1$ for each value of n. This quantum number is related to the shape of atomic orbitals. The value of ℓ for a particular orbital is commonly assigned a letter: $\ell = 0$ is called s; $\ell = 1$ is called p; $\ell = 2$ is called d; $\ell = 3$ is called f. This system arises from early spectral studies and is summarized in Table 7.1.

The **magnetic quantum number** (m_ℓ) has integral values between ℓ and $-\ell$, including zero. The value of m_ℓ is related to the orientation of the orbital in space relative to the other orbitals in the atom.

The first four levels of orbitals in the hydrogen atom are listed with their quantum numbers in Table 7.2. Note that each set of orbitals with a given value of ℓ (sometimes called a **subshell**) is designated by giving the value of n and the letter for ℓ. Thus an orbital where $n = 2$ and $\ell = 1$ is symbolized as $2p$. There are three $2p$ orbitals, which have different orientations in space. We will describe these orbitals in the next section.

Sample Exercise 7.6 *Electron Subshells*

For principal quantum level $n = 5$, determine the number of allowed subshells (different values of ℓ), and give the designation of each.

Solution

For $n = 5$, the allowed values of ℓ run from 0 to 4 ($n - 1 = 5 - 1$). Thus the subshells and their designations are

$\ell = 0$	$\ell = 1$	$\ell = 2$	$\ell = 3$	$\ell = 4$
$5s$	$5p$	$5d$	$5f$	$5g$

See Exercises 7.59 through 7.62.

7.7 Orbital Shapes and Energies

We have seen that the meaning of an orbital is represented most clearly by a probability distribution. Each orbital in the hydrogen atom has a unique probability distribution. We also saw that another means of representing an orbital is by the surface that surrounds 90% of the total electron probability. These two types of representations for the hydrogen 1s, 2s, and 3s orbitals are shown in Fig. 7.13. Note the characteristic spherical shape of each of the *s* orbitals. Note also that the 2s and 3s orbitals contain areas of high probability separated by areas of zero probability. These latter areas are called **nodal surfaces,** or simply **nodes.** The number of nodes increases as *n* increases. For *s* orbitals, the number of nodes is given by $n - 1$. For our purposes, however, we will think of *s* orbitals only in terms of their overall spherical shape, which becomes larger as the value of *n* increases.

The two types of representations for the 2p orbitals (there are no 1p orbitals) are shown in Fig. 7.14. Note that the *p* orbitals are not spherical like *s* orbitals but have two *lobes* separated by a node at the nucleus. The *p* orbitals are labeled according to the axis of the *xyz* coordinate system along which the lobes lie. For example, the 2p orbital with lobes centered along the *x* axis is called the $2p_x$ orbital.

As you might expect from our discussion of the *s* orbitals, the 3p orbitals have a more complex probability distribution than that of the 2p orbitals (see Fig. 7.15), but they can still be represented by the same boundary surface shapes. The surfaces just grow larger as the value of *n* increases.

There are no *d* orbitals that correspond to principal quantum levels $n = 1$ and $n = 2$. The *d* orbitals ($\ell = 2$) first occur in level $n = 3$. The five 3d orbitals have the shapes shown in Fig. 7.16. The *d* orbitals have two different fundamental shapes. Four of the orbitals (d_{xz}, d_{yz}, d_{xy}, and $d_{x^2-y^2}$) have four lobes centered in the plane indicated in the orbital label. Note that d_{xy} and $d_{x^2-y^2}$ are both centered in the *xy* plane; however, the lobes of the $d_{x^2-y^2}$ lie *along* the *x* and *y* axes, while the lobes of d_{xy} lie *between* the axes. The fifth orbital, d_{z^2}, has a unique shape with two lobes along the *z* axis and a belt centered in the *xy* plane. The *d* orbitals for levels $n > 3$ look like the 3d orbitals but have larger lobes.

The *f* orbitals first occur in level $n = 4$, and as might be expected, they have shapes even more complex than those of the *d* orbitals. Figure 7.17 shows representations of the 4f orbitals ($\ell = 3$) along with their designations. These orbitals are not involved in the bonding in any of the compounds we will consider in this text. Their shapes and labels are simply included for completeness.

So far we have talked about the shapes of the hydrogen atomic orbitals but not about their energies. For the hydrogen atom, the energy of a particular orbital is

n value
↓
$2p_x$ ← orientation in space
↑
ℓ value

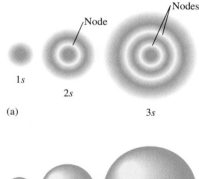

(a)

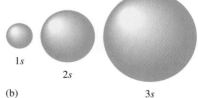

(b)

Figure 7.13

Two representations of the hydrogen 1s, 2s, and 3s orbitals. (a) The electron probability distribution. (b) The surface that contains 90% of the total electron probability (the size of the orbital, by definition).

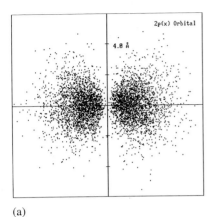

(a)

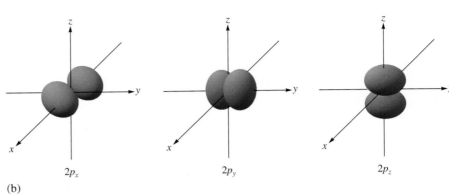

(b)

Figure 7.14

Representation of the 2p orbitals. (a) The electron probability distribution for a 2p orbital. Generated from a program by Robert Allendoerfer on Project SERAPHIM disk PC2402; printed with permission. (b) The boundary surface representations of all three 2p orbitals.

Animations: s-orbitals and Bonding and Antibonding, p-orbitals

Figure 7.15

A cross section of the electron probability distribution for a 3p orbital.

determined by its value of *n*. Thus *all* orbitals with the same value of *n* have the *same energy*—they are said to be **degenerate.** This is shown in Fig. 7.18, where the energies for the orbitals in the first three quantum levels for hydrogen are shown.

Hydrogen's single electron can occupy any of its atomic orbitals. However, in the lowest energy state, the *ground state,* the electron resides in the 1s orbital. If energy is put into the atom, the electron can be transferred to a higher-energy orbital, producing an *excited state.*

A Summary of the Hydrogen Atom

- In the quantum (wave) mechanical model, the electron is viewed as a standing wave. This representation leads to a series of wave functions (orbitals) that describe the possible energies and spatial distributions available to the electron.

- In agreement with the Heisenberg uncertainty principle, the model cannot specify the detailed electron motions. Instead, the square of the wave function represents the probability distribution of the electron in that orbital. This allows us to picture orbitals in terms of probability distributions, or electron density maps.

- The size of an orbital is arbitrarily defined as the surface that contains 90% of the total electron probability.

- The hydrogen atom has many types of orbitals. In the ground state, the single electron resides in the 1s orbital. The electron can be excited to higher-energy orbitals if energy is put into the atom.

7.8 Electron Spin and the Pauli Principle

The concept of **electron spin** was developed by Samuel Goudsmit and George Uhlenbeck while they were graduate students at the University of Leyden in the Netherlands. They found that a fourth quantum number (in addition to *n*, ℓ, and m_ℓ)

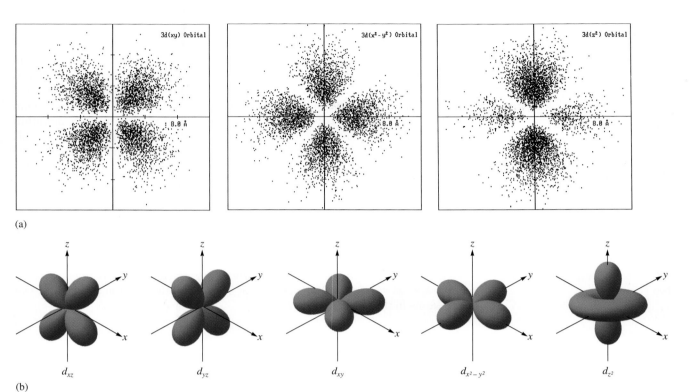

(a)

(b)

Figure 7.16

Representation of the 3d orbitals. (a) Electron density plots of selected 3d orbitals.   Generated from a program by Robert Allendoerfer on Project SERAPHIM disk PC2402; printed with permission.   (b) The boundary surfaces of all of the 3d orbitals.

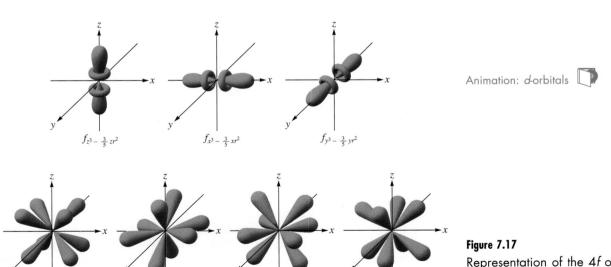

Animation: d-orbitals

Figure 7.17

Representation of the 4f orbitals in terms of their boundary surfaces.

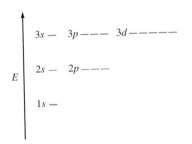

Figure 7.18

Orbital energy levels for the hydrogen atom.

$$m_s = +\frac{1}{2} \text{ or } -\frac{1}{2}$$

Each orbital can hold a maximum of two electrons.

was necessary to account for the details of the emission spectra of atoms. The spectral data indicate that the electron has a magnetic moment with two possible orientations when the atom is placed in an external magnetic field. Since they knew from classical physics that a spinning charge produces a magnetic moment, it seemed reasonable to assume that the electron could have two spin states, thus producing the two oppositely directed magnetic moments (see Fig. 7.19). The new quantum number adopted to describe this phenomenon, called the **electron spin quantum number** (m_s), can have only one of two values, $+\frac{1}{2}$ and $-\frac{1}{2}$. We can interpret this to mean that the electron can spin in one of two opposite directions, although other interpretations also have been suggested.

For our purposes, the main significance of electron spin is connected with the postulate of Austrian physicist Wolfgang Pauli (1900–1958): *In a given atom no two electrons can have the same set of four quantum numbers (n, ℓ, m_ℓ, and m_s).* This is called the **Pauli exclusion principle.** Since electrons in the same orbital have the same values of n, ℓ, and m_ℓ, this postulate says that they must have different values of m_s. Then, since only two values of m_s are allowed, *an orbital can only hold two electrons, and they must have opposite spins.* This principle will have important consequences as we use the atomic model to account for the electron arrangements of the atoms in the periodic table.

7.9 Polyelectronic Atoms

The quantum mechanical model gives a description of the hydrogen atom that agrees very well with experimental data. However, the model would not be very useful if it did not account for the properties of all the other atoms as well.

To see how the model applies to **polyelectronic atoms,** that is, atoms with more than one electron, let's consider helium, which has two protons in its nucleus and two electrons:

There are three energy contributions that must be considered in the description of the helium atom: (1) the kinetic energy of the electrons as they move around the nucleus, (2) the potential energy of attraction between the nucleus and the electrons, and (3) the potential energy of repulsion between the two electrons.

Although the helium atom can be readily described in terms of the quantum mechanical model, the Schrödinger equation that results cannot be solved exactly. The difficulty arises in dealing with the repulsions between the electrons. Since the electron pathways are unknown, the electron repulsions cannot be calculated exactly. This is called the *electron correlation problem.*

The electron correlation problem occurs with all polyelectronic atoms. To treat these systems using the quantum mechanical model, we must make approximations. Most commonly, the approximation used is to treat each electron as if it were moving in a *field of charge that is the net result of the nuclear attraction and the average repulsions of all the other electrons.*

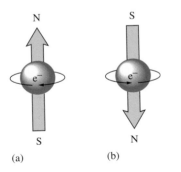

Figure 7.19

A picture of the spinning electron. Spinning in one direction, the electron produces the magnetic field oriented as shown in (a). Spinning in the opposite direction, it gives a magnetic field of the opposite orientation, as shown in (b).

For example, consider the sodium atom, which has 11 electrons:

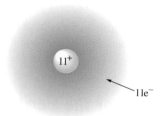

Now let's single out the outermost electron and consider the forces this electron feels. The electron clearly is attracted to the highly charged nucleus. However, the electron also feels the repulsions caused by the other 10 electrons. The net effect is that the electron is not bound nearly as tightly to the nucleus as it would be if the other electrons were not present. We say that the electron is *screened* or *shielded* from the nuclear charge by the repulsions of the other electrons.

This picture of polyelectronic atoms leads to *hydrogenlike orbitals* for these atoms. They have the same general shapes as the orbitals for hydrogen, but their sizes and energies are different. The differences occur because of the interplay between nuclear attraction and the electron repulsions.

One especially important difference between polyelectronic atoms and the hydrogen atom is that for hydrogen all the orbitals in a given principal quantum level have the same energy (they are said to be *degenerate*). This is not the case for polyelectronic atoms, where we find that for a given principal quantum level the orbitals vary in energy as follows:

$$E_{ns} < E_{np} < E_{nd} < E_{nf}$$

In other words, when electrons are placed in a particular quantum level, they "prefer" the orbitals in the order s, p, d, and then f. Why does this happen? Although the concept of orbital energies is a complicated matter, we can qualitatively understand why the $2s$ orbital has a lower energy than the $2p$ orbital in a polyelectronic atom by looking at the probability profiles of these orbitals (see Fig. 7.20). Notice that the $2p$ orbital has its maximum probability closer to the nucleus than for the $2s$. This might lead us to predict that the $2p$ would be preferable (lower energy) to the $2s$ orbital. However, notice the small hump of electron density that occurs in the $2s$ profile very near the nucleus. This means that although an electron in the $2s$ orbital spends most of its time a little further from the nucleus than does an electron in the $2p$ orbital, it spends a small but very significant amount of time very near the nucleus. We say that the $2s$ electron *penetrates* to the nucleus more than for the $2p$ orbital. This *penetration effect* causes an electron in a $2s$ orbital to be attracted to the nucleus more strongly than an electron in a $2p$ orbital. That is, the $2s$ orbital is lower in energy than the $2p$ orbitals in a polyelectronic atom.

The same thing happens in the other principal quantum levels as well. Figure 7.21 shows the radial probability profiles for the $3s$, $3p$, and $3d$ orbitals. Note again the hump in the $3s$ profile very near the nucleus. The innermost hump for the $3p$ is farther out, and this causes the energy of the $3s$ orbital to be lower than that of the $3p$. Notice that the $3d$ orbital has its maximum probability closer to the nucleus than for either the $3s$ or $3p$, but its absence of probability near the nucleus causes it to

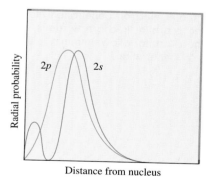

Figure 7.20

A comparison of the radial probability distributions of the $2s$ and $2p$ orbitals.

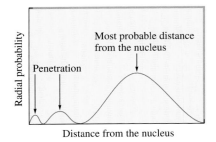

(a)

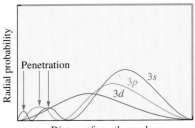

(b)

Figure 7.21

(a) The radial probability distribution for an electron in a 3s orbital. Although a 3s electron is mostly found far from the nucleus, there is a small but significant probability (shown by the arrows) of its being found close to the nucleus. The 3s electron penetrates the shield of inner electrons. (b) The radial probability distribution for the 3s, 3p, and 3d orbitals. The arrows indicate that the s orbital (blue arrow) allows greater electron penetration than the p orbital (red arrow) does; the d orbital allows minimal electron penetration.

be highest in energy of the three orbitals. The relative energies of the orbitals for $n = 3$ are

$$E_{3s} < E_{3p} < E_{3d}$$

In general, the more effectively an orbital allows its electron to penetrate the shielding electrons to be close to the nuclear charge, the lower is the energy of that orbital.

7.10   The History of the Periodic Table

The modern periodic table contains a tremendous amount of useful information. In this section we will discuss the origin of this valuable tool; later we will see how the quantum mechanical model for the atom explains the periodicity of chemical properties. Certainly the greatest triumph of the quantum mechanical model is its ability to account for the arrangement of the elements in the periodic table.

The periodic table was originally constructed to represent the patterns observed in the chemical properties of the elements. As chemistry progressed during the eighteenth and nineteenth centuries, it became evident that the earth is composed of a great many elements with very different properties. Things are much more complicated than the simple model of earth, air, fire, and water suggested by the ancients. At first, the array of elements and properties was bewildering. Gradually, however, patterns were noticed.

The first chemist to recognize patterns was Johann Dobereiner (1780–1849), who found several groups of three elements that have similar properties, for example, chlorine, bromine, and iodine. However, as Dobereiner attempted to expand this model of *triads* (as he called them) to the rest of the known elements, it became clear that it was severely limited.

The next notable attempt was made by the English chemist John Newlands, who in 1864 suggested that elements should be arranged in *octaves,* based on the idea that certain properties seemed to repeat for every eighth element in a way similar to the musical scale, which repeats for every eighth tone. Even though this model managed to group several elements with similar properties, it was not generally successful.

The present form of the periodic table was conceived independently by two chemists: the German Julius Lothar Meyer (1830–1895) and Dmitri Ivanovich Mendeleev (1834–1907), a Russian (Fig. 7.22). Usually Mendeleev is given most of the credit, because it was he who emphasized how useful the table could be in predicting the existence and properties of still unknown elements. For example, in 1872 when Mendeleev first published his table (see Fig. 7.23), the elements gallium, scandium, and germanium were unknown. Mendeleev correctly predicted the existence and properties of these elements from gaps in his periodic table. The data for germanium (which Mendeleev called "*ekasilicon*") are shown in Table 7.3. Note the excellent agreement between the actual values and Mendeleev's predictions, which were based on the properties of other members in the group of elements similar to germanium.

Using his table, Mendeleev also was able to correct several values for atomic masses. For example, the original atomic mass of 76 for indium was based on the assumption that indium oxide had the formula InO. This atomic mass placed indium, which has metallic properties, among the nonmetals. Mendeleev assumed the atomic mass

Figure 7.22

Dmitri Ivanovich Mendeleev (1834–1907), born in Siberia as the youngest of 17 children, taught chemistry at the University of St. Petersburg. In 1860 Mendeleev heard the Italian chemist Cannizzaro lecture on a reliable method for determining the correct atomic masses of the elements. This important development paved the way for Mendeleev's own brilliant contribution to chemistry—the periodic table. In 1861 Mendeleev returned to St. Petersburg, where he wrote a book on organic chemistry. Later Mendeleev also wrote a book on inorganic chemistry, and he was struck by the fact that the systematic approach characterizing organic chemistry was lacking in inorganic chemistry. In attempting to systematize inorganic chemistry, he eventually arranged the elements in the form of the periodic table.

Mendeleev was a versatile genius who was interested in many fields of science. He worked on many problems associated with Russia's natural resources, such as coal, salt, and various metals. Being particularly interested in the petroleum industry, he visited the United States in 1876 to study the Pennsylvania oil fields. His interests also included meteorology and hot-air balloons. In 1887 he made an ascent in a balloon to study a total eclipse of the sun.

was probably incorrect and proposed that the formula of indium oxide was really In_2O_3. Based on this correct formula, indium has an atomic mass of approximately 113, placing the element among the metals. Mendeleev also corrected the atomic masses of beryllium and uranium.

Because of its obvious usefulness, Mendeleev's periodic table was almost universally adopted, and it remains one of the most valuable tools at the chemist's disposal. For example, it is still used to predict the properties of elements yet to be discovered, as shown in Table 7.4.

TABELLE II

REIHEN	GRUPPE I. — R^2O	GRUPPE II. — RO	GRUPPE III. — R^2O^3	GRUPPE IV. RH^4 RO^2	GRUPPE V. RH^3 R^2O^5	GRUPPE VI. RH^2 RO^3	GRUPPE VII. RH R^2O^7	GRUPPE VIII. — RO^4
1	H = 1							
2	Li = 7	Be = 9,4	B = 11	C = 12	N = 14	O = 16	F = 19	
3	Na = 23	Mg = 24	Al = 27,3	Si = 28	P = 31	S = 32	Cl = 35,5	
4	K = 39	Ca = 40	— = 44	Ti = 48	V = 51	Cr = 52	Mn = 55	Fe = 56, Co = 59, Ni = 59, Cu = 63.
5	(Cu = 63)	Zn = 65	— = 68	— = 72	As = 75	Se = 78	Br = 80	
6	Rb = 85	Sr = 87	?Yt = 88	Zr = 90	Nb = 94	Mo = 96	— = 100	Ru = 104, Rh = 104, Pd = 106, Ag = 108.
7	(Ag = 108)	Cd = 112	In = 113	Sn = 118	Sb = 122	Te = 125	J = 127	
8	Cs = 133	Ba = 137	?Di = 138	?Ce = 140	—	—	—	— — — —
9	(—)		—	—	—	—	—	
10	—	—	?Er = 178	?La = 180	Ta = 182	W = 184	—	Os = 195, Ir = 197, Pt = 198, Au = 199.
11	(Au = 199)	Hg = 200	Tl = 204	Pb = 207	Bi = 208	—	—	
12	—	—	—	Th = 231	—	U = 240	—	— — — —

Figure 7.23

Mendeleev's early periodic table, published in 1872. Note the spaces left for missing elements with atomic masses 44, 68, 72, and 100. *From Annalen der Chemie und Pharmacie,* VIII, Supplementary Volume for 1872, page 511.

The Growing Periodic Table

THE PERIODIC TABLE of the elements has undergone significant changes since Mendeleev published his first version in 1869. In particular, in the past 60 years we have added 20 new elements beyond uranium. These so-called transuranium elements all have been synthesized using particle accelerators.

Edwin M. McMillan and Phillip H. Abelson succeeded in synthesizing the first transuranium element, neptunium (element 93), at the University of California, Berkeley, in 1940. In 1941, Glenn T. Seaborg synthesized and identified element 94 (plutonium), and over the next several years, researchers under his direction at UC Berkeley discovered nine other transuranium elements. In 1945 Seaborg suggested that the elements heavier than element 89 (actinium) were misplaced as transition metals and should be relocated on the periodic table in a series below the transition metals (the actinide series). Seaborg was awarded a Nobel Prize in chemistry in 1951 for his contributions.

In recent years, three major research facilities have taken the lead in synthesizing new elements. Along with UC Berkeley, Nuclear Research in Dubna, Russia, and GSI in Darmstadt, Germany, were responsible for synthesizing elements 104–112 by the end of 1996. In

Dr. Glenn Seaborg.

Atomic Number	Name	Symbol
104	Rutherfordium	Rf
105	Dubium	Db
106	Seaborgium	Sg
107	Bohrium	Bh
108	Hassium	Hs
109	Meitnerium	Mt

the spring of 1999 the elements 114, 116, and 118 were reported, with little doubt that more are on their way.

As it turned out, naming the new elements has caused more controversy than anything else connected with their discovery. Traditionally, the discoverer of an element is allowed to name it. However, because there is some dispute among the researchers at Berkeley, Darmstadt, and Dubna about who really discovered the various elements, competing names were submitted. After years of controversy, the International Union of Pure and Applied Chemistry (IUPAC) finally settled on the names listed in the accompanying table.

The name for element 106 in honor of Glenn Seaborg caused special controversy because an element had never before been named for a living person (Dr. Seaborg died in 1999). However, because of Seaborg's commanding stature in the scientific community, the name seaborgium was adopted.

Names for the elements beyond 109 have not been decided, and these elements are represented on many periodic tables with three letters that symbolize their atomic numbers. More traditional names will no doubt be assigned in due time (hopefully with a minimum of controversy).

Table 7.3 Comparison of the Properties of Germanium as Predicted by Mendeleev and as Actually Observed

Properties of Germanium	Predicted in 1871	Observed in 1886
Atomic weight	72	72.3
Density	5.5 g/cm^3	5.47 g/cm^3
Specific heat	0.31 J/(°C · g)	0.32 J/(°C · g)
Melting point	Very high	960°C
Oxide formula	RO_2	GeO_2
Oxide density	4.7 g/cm^3	4.70 g/cm^3
Chloride formula	RCl_4	$GeCl_4$
bp of chloride	100°C	86°C

Table 7.4 Predicted Properties of Elements 113 and 114

Property	Element 113	Element 114
Chemically like	Thallium	Lead
Atomic mass	297	298
Density	16 g/mL	14 g/mL
Melting point	430°C	70°C
Boiling point	1100°C	150°C

A current version of the periodic table is shown inside the front cover of this book. The only fundamental difference between this table and that of Mendeleev is that it lists the elements in order by atomic number rather than by atomic mass. The reason for this will become clear later in this chapter as we explore the electron arrangements of the atom. Another recent format of the table is discussed in the following section.

7.11 *The Aufbau Principle and the Periodic Table*

We can use the quantum mechanical model of the atom to show how the electron arrangements in the hydrogenlike atomic orbitals of the various atoms account for the organization of the periodic table. Our main assumption here is that all atoms have the same type of orbitals as have been described for the hydrogen atom. *As protons are added one by one to the nucleus to build up the elements, electrons are similarly added to these hydrogenlike orbitals.* This is called the **aufbau principle.**

Aufbau is German for "building up."

Hydrogen has one electron, which occupies the 1s orbital in its ground state. The configuration for hydrogen is written as $1s^1$, which can be represented by the following *orbital diagram:*

H (Z = 1)
He (Z = 2)
Li (Z = 3)
Be (Z = 4)
B (Z = 5)
etc.

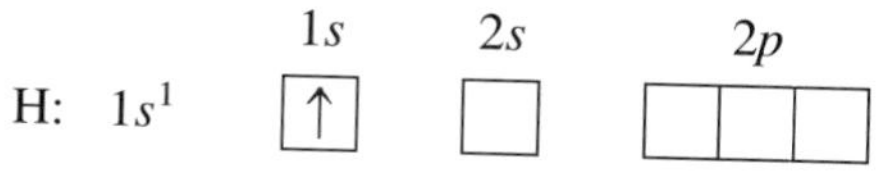

H: $1s^1$ | 1s | 2s | 2p |

The arrow represents an electron spinning in a particular direction.

The next element, *helium,* has two electrons. Since two electrons with opposite spins can occupy an orbital, according to the Pauli exclusion principle, the electrons for helium are in the 1s orbital with opposite spins, producing a $1s^2$ configuration:

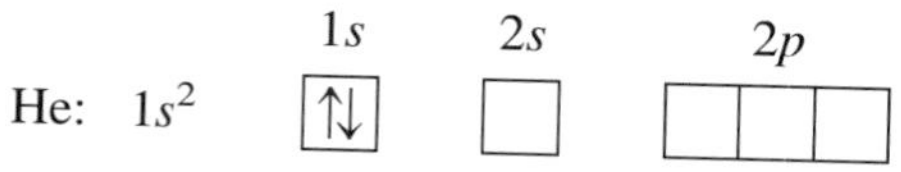

He: $1s^2$ | 1s | 2s | 2p |

Lithium has three electrons, two of which can go into the 1s orbital before the orbital is filled. Since the 1s orbital is the only orbital for $n = 1$, the third electron will occupy the lowest-energy orbital with $n = 2$, or the 2s orbital, giving a $1s^2 2s^1$ configuration:

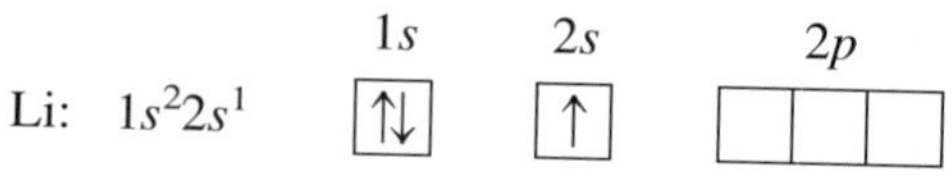

Li: $1s^2 2s^1$ | 1s | 2s | 2p |

The next element, *beryllium,* has four electrons, which occupy the 1s and 2s orbitals:

$$\text{Be:} \quad 1s^2 2s^2 \qquad \begin{array}{ccc} 1s & 2s & 2p \\ \boxed{\uparrow\downarrow} & \boxed{\uparrow\downarrow} & \boxed{\;|\;\;|\;} \end{array}$$

Boron has five electrons, four of which occupy the 1s and 2s orbitals. The fifth electron goes into the second type of orbital with $n = 2$, the 2p orbitals:

$$\text{B:} \quad 1s^2 2s^2 2p^1 \qquad \begin{array}{ccc} 1s & 2s & 2p \\ \boxed{\uparrow\downarrow} & \boxed{\uparrow\downarrow} & \boxed{\uparrow\;|\;\;|\;} \end{array}$$

Since all the 2p orbitals have the same energy (are degenerate), it does not matter which 2p orbital the electron occupies.

Carbon is the next element and has six electrons. Two electrons occupy the 1s orbital, two occupy the 2s orbital, and two occupy 2p orbitals. Since there are three 2p orbitals with the same energy, the mutually repulsive electrons will occupy *separate 2p orbitals.* This behavior is summarized by **Hund's rule** (named for the German physicist F. H. Hund), which states that *the lowest energy configuration for an atom is the one having the maximum number of unpaired electrons allowed by the Pauli principle in a particular set of degenerate orbitals.* By convention, the unpaired electrons are represented as having parallel spins (with spin "up").

> For an atom with unfilled subshells, the lowest energy is achieved by electrons occupying separate orbitals with parallel spins, as far as allowed by the Pauli exclusion principle.

The configuration for carbon could be written $1s^2 2s^2 2p^1 2p^1$ to indicate that the electrons occupy separate 2p orbitals. However, the configuration is usually given as $1s^2 2s^2 2p^2$, and it is understood that the electrons are in different 2p orbitals. The orbital diagram for carbon is

$$\text{C:} \quad 1s^2 2s^2 2p^2 \qquad \begin{array}{ccc} 1s & 2s & 2p \\ \boxed{\uparrow\downarrow} & \boxed{\uparrow\downarrow} & \boxed{\uparrow\;|\;\uparrow\;|\;} \end{array}$$

Note that the unpaired electrons in the 2p orbitals are shown with parallel spins.

The configuration for *nitrogen,* which has seven electrons, is $1s^2 2s^2 2p^3$. The three electrons in the 2p orbitals occupy separate orbitals with parallel spins:

$$\text{N:} \quad 1s^2 2s^2 2p^3 \qquad \begin{array}{ccc} 1s & 2s & 2p \\ \boxed{\uparrow\downarrow} & \boxed{\uparrow\downarrow} & \boxed{\uparrow\;|\;\uparrow\;|\;\uparrow} \end{array}$$

The configuration for *oxygen,* which has eight electrons, is $1s^2 2s^2 2p^4$. One of the 2p orbitals is now occupied by a pair of electrons with opposite spins, as required by the Pauli exclusion principle:

$$\text{O:} \quad 1s^2 2s^2 2p^4 \qquad \begin{array}{ccc} 1s & 2s & 2p \\ \boxed{\uparrow\downarrow} & \boxed{\uparrow\downarrow} & \boxed{\uparrow\downarrow\;|\;\uparrow\;|\;\uparrow} \end{array}$$

The orbital diagrams and electron configurations for *fluorine* (nine electrons) and *neon* (ten electrons) are as follows:

$$\text{F:} \quad 1s^2 2s^2 2p^5 \qquad \begin{array}{ccc} 1s & 2s & 2p \\ \boxed{\uparrow\downarrow} & \boxed{\uparrow\downarrow} & \boxed{\uparrow\downarrow\;|\;\uparrow\downarrow\;|\;\uparrow} \end{array}$$

$$\text{Ne:} \quad 1s^2 2s^2 2p^6 \qquad \begin{array}{ccc} 1s & 2s & 2p \\ \boxed{\uparrow\downarrow} & \boxed{\uparrow\downarrow} & \boxed{\uparrow\downarrow\;|\;\uparrow\downarrow\;|\;\uparrow\downarrow} \end{array}$$

With neon, the orbitals with $n = 1$ and $n = 2$ are now completely filled.

For *sodium,* the first ten electrons occupy the 1s, 2s, and 2p orbitals, and the eleventh electron must occupy the first orbital with $n = 3$, the 3s orbital. The elec-

Sodium metal is so reactive that it is stored under kerosene to protect it from the oxygen in the air.

tron configuration for sodium is $1s^22s^22p^63s^1$. To avoid writing the inner-level electrons, this configuration is often abbreviated as [Ne]$3s^1$, where [Ne] represents the electron configuration of neon, $1s^22s^22p^6$.

The next element, *magnesium*, has the configuration $1s^22s^22p^63s^2$, or [Ne]$3s^2$. Then the next six elements, *aluminum* through *argon*, have configurations obtained by filling the $3p$ orbitals one electron at a time. Figure 7.24 summarizes the electron configurations of the first 18 elements by giving the number of electrons in the type of orbital occupied last.

[Ne] is shorthand for $1s^22s^22p^6$.

At this point it is useful to introduce the concept of **valence electrons,** that is, *the electrons in the outermost principal quantum level of an atom.* The valence electrons of the nitrogen atom, for example, are the $2s$ and $2p$ electrons. For the sodium atom, the valence electron is the electron in the $3s$ orbital, and so on. Valence electrons are the most important electrons to chemists because they are involved in bonding, as we will see in the next two chapters. The inner electrons are known as **core electrons.**

Note in Fig. 7.24 that a very important pattern is developing: *The elements in the same group (vertical column of the periodic table) have the same valence electron configuration.* Remember that Mendeleev originally placed the elements in groups based on similarities in chemical properties. Now we understand the reason behind these groupings. Elements with the same valence electron configuration show similar chemical behavior.

The element after argon is *potassium*. Since the $3p$ orbitals are fully occupied in argon, we might expect the next electron to go into a $3d$ orbital (recall that for $n = 3$ the orbitals are $3s$, $3p$, and $3d$). However, the chemistry of potassium is clearly very similar to that of lithium and sodium, indicating that the last electron in potassium occupies the $4s$ orbital instead of one of the $3d$ orbitals, a conclusion confirmed by many types of experiments. The electron configuration of potassium is

A vial containing potassium metal.

$$\text{K:} \quad 1s^22s^22p^63s^23p^64s^1 \quad \text{or} \quad \text{[Ar]}4s^1$$

The next element is *calcium:*

$$\text{Ca:} \quad \text{[Ar]}4s^2$$

The next element, *scandium*, begins a series of 10 elements (scandium through zinc) called the **transition metals,** whose configurations are obtained by adding electrons to the five $3d$ orbitals. The configuration of scandium is

$$\text{Sc:} \quad \text{[Ar]}4s^23d^1$$

Calcium metal.

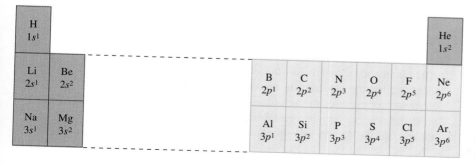

H $1s^1$								He $1s^2$
Li $2s^1$	Be $2s^2$		B $2p^1$	C $2p^2$	N $2p^3$	O $2p^4$	F $2p^5$	Ne $2p^6$
Na $3s^1$	Mg $3s^2$		Al $3p^1$	Si $3p^2$	P $3p^3$	S $3p^4$	Cl $3p^5$	Ar $3p^6$

Figure 7.24

The electron configurations in the type of orbital occupied last for the first 18 elements.

That of *titanium* is

$$\text{Ti:} \quad [Ar]4s^2 3d^2$$

And that of *vanadium* is

$$\text{V:} \quad [Ar]4s^2 3d^3$$

Chromium is the next element. The expected configuration is $[Ar]4s^2 3d^4$. However, the observed configuration is

$$\text{Cr:} \quad [Ar]4s^1 3d^5$$

The explanation for this configuration of chromium is beyond the scope of this book. In fact, chemists are still disagreeing over the exact cause of this anomaly. Note, however, that the observed configuration has both the 4s and 3d orbitals half-filled. This is a good way to remember the correct configuration.

The next four elements, *manganese* through *nickel,* have the expected configurations:

$$\text{Mn:} \quad [Ar]4s^2 3d^5 \qquad \text{Co:} \quad [Ar]4s^2 3d^7$$
$$\text{Fe:} \quad [Ar]4s^2 3d^6 \qquad \text{Ni:} \quad [Ar]4s^2 3d^8$$

The configuration for *copper* is expected to be $[Ar]4s^2 3d^9$. However, the observed configuration is

$$\text{Cu:} \quad [Ar]4s^1 3d^{10}$$

In this case, a half-filled 4s orbital and a filled set of 3d orbitals characterize the actual configuration.

Zinc has the expected configuration:

$$\text{Zn:} \quad [Ar]4s^2 3d^{10}$$

The configurations of the transition metals are shown in Fig. 7.25. After that, the next six elements, *gallium* through *krypton,* have configurations that correspond to filling the 4p orbitals (see Fig. 7.25).

The entire periodic table is represented in Fig. 7.26 in terms of which orbitals are being filled. The valence electron configurations are given in Fig. 7.27. From these two figures, note the following additional points:

1. The $(n + 1)s$ orbitals always fill before the *nd* orbitals. For example, the 5s orbitals fill in rubidium and strontium before the 4d orbitals fill in the second row of transition metals (yttrium through cadmium). This early filling of the s orbitals can be explained by the penetration effect. For example, the 4s orbital allows for so much more penetration to the vicinity of the nucleus that it becomes lower in energy than the 3d orbital. Thus the 4s fills before the 3d. The same things can be said about the 5s and 4d, the 6s and 5d, and the 7s and 6d orbitals.

2. After lanthanum, which has the configuration $[Xe]6s^2 5d^1$, a group of 14 elements called the **lanthanide series,** or the **lanthanides,** occurs. This series of elements corresponds to the filling of the seven 4f orbitals. Note that sometimes an electron occupies a 5d orbital instead of a 4f orbital. This occurs because the energies of the 4f and 5d orbitals are very similar.

Chromium is often used to plate bumpers and hood ornaments, such as this statue of Mercury found on a 1929 Buick.

The $(n + 1)s$ orbital fills before the *nd* orbitals.

Lanthanides are elements in which the 4f orbitals are being filled.

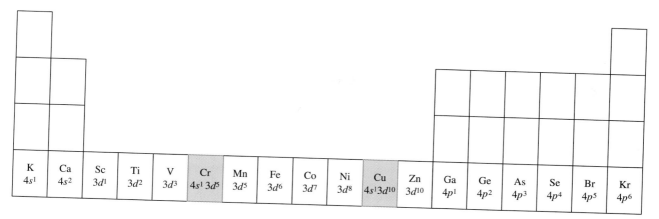

| K $4s^1$ | Ca $4s^2$ | Sc $3d^1$ | Ti $3d^2$ | V $3d^3$ | Cr $4s^1 3d^5$ | Mn $3d^5$ | Fe $3d^6$ | Co $3d^7$ | Ni $3d^8$ | Cu $4s^1 3d^{10}$ | Zn $3d^{10}$ | Ga $4p^1$ | Ge $4p^2$ | As $4p^3$ | Se $4p^4$ | Br $4p^5$ | Kr $4p^6$ |

Figure 7.25

Electron configurations for potassium through krypton. The transition metals (scandium through zinc) have the general configuration $[Ar]4s^2 3d^n$, except for chromium and copper.

3. After actinium, which has the configuration $[Rn]7s^2 6d^1$, a group of 14 elements called the **actinide series,** or the **actinides,** occurs. This series corresponds to the filling of the seven $5f$ orbitals. Note that sometimes one or two electrons occupy the $6d$ orbitals instead of the $5f$ orbitals, because these orbitals have very similar energies.

4. The group labels for Groups 1A, 2A, 3A, 4A, 5A, 6A, 7A, and 8A indicate the *total number* of valence electrons for the atoms in these groups. For example, all the elements in Group 5A have the configuration $ns^2 np^3$. (The d electrons fill one period late and are usually not counted as valence electrons.) The meaning of the group labels for the transition metals is not as clear as for the Group A elements, and these will not be used in this text.

Actinides are elements in which the $5f$ orbitals are being filled.

The group label tells the total number of valence electrons for that group.

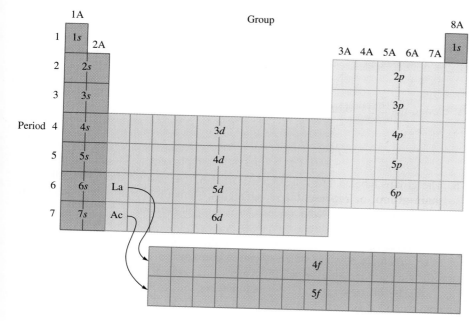

Figure 7.26

The orbitals being filled for elements in various parts of the periodic table. Note that in going along a horizontal row (a period), the $(n + 1)s$ orbital fills before the nd orbital. The group labels indicate the number of valence electrons (ns plus np electrons) for the elements in each group.

Representative Elements

d-Transition Elements

Representative Elements

Noble Gases

8A
ns^2np^6

1A ns^1 — Group numbers

2A ns^2

3A ns^2np^1

4A ns^2np^2

5A ns^2np^3

6A ns^2np^4

7A ns^2np^5

Period number, highest occupied electron level

Period 1

| 1 H $1s^1$ | | | | | | | | | | | | | | | | | 2 He $1s^2$ |

Period 2

| 3 Li $2s^1$ | 4 Be $2s^2$ | | | | | | | | | | 5 B $2s^22p^1$ | 6 C $2s^22p^2$ | 7 N $2s^22p^3$ | 8 O $2s^22p^4$ | 9 F $2s^22p^5$ | 10 Ne $2s^22p^6$ |

Period 3

| 11 Na $3s^1$ | 12 Mg $3s^2$ | | | | | | | | | | 13 Al $3s^23p^1$ | 14 Si $3s^23p^2$ | 15 P $3s^23p^3$ | 16 S $3s^23p^4$ | 17 Cl $3s^23p^5$ | 18 Ar $3s^23p^6$ |

Period 4

| 19 K $4s^1$ | 20 Ca $4s^2$ | 21 Sc $4s^23d^1$ | 22 Ti $4s^23d^2$ | 23 V $4s^23d^3$ | 24 Cr $4s^13d^5$ | 25 Mn $4s^23d^5$ | 26 Fe $4s^23d^6$ | 27 Co $4s^23d^7$ | 28 Ni $4s^23d^8$ | 29 Cu $4s^13d^{10}$ | 30 Zn $4s^23d^{10}$ | 31 Ga $4s^24p^1$ | 32 Ge $4s^24p^2$ | 33 As $4s^24p^3$ | 34 Se $4s^24p^4$ | 35 Br $4s^24p^5$ | 36 Kr $4s^24p^6$ |

Period 5

| 37 Rb $5s^1$ | 38 Sr $5s^2$ | 39 Y $5s^24d^1$ | 40 Zr $5s^24d^2$ | 41 Nb $5s^14d^4$ | 42 Mo $5s^14d^5$ | 43 Tc $5s^14d^6$ | 44 Ru $5s^14d^7$ | 45 Rh $5s^14d^8$ | 46 Pd $4d^{10}$ | 47 Ag $5s^14d^{10}$ | 48 Cd $5s^24d^{10}$ | 49 In $5s^25p^1$ | 50 Sn $5s^25p^2$ | 51 Sb $5s^25p^3$ | 52 Te $5s^25p^4$ | 53 I $5s^25p^5$ | 54 Xe $5s^25p^6$ |

Period 6

| 55 Cs $6s^1$ | 56 Ba $6s^2$ | 57 La* $6s^25d^1$ | 72 Hf $6s^25d^2$ | 73 Ta $6s^25d^3$ | 74 W $6s^25d^4$ | 75 Re $6s^25d^5$ | 76 Os $6s^25d^6$ | 77 Ir $6s^25d^7$ | 78 Pt $6s^15d^9$ | 79 Au $6s^15d^{10}$ | 80 Hg $6s^25d^{10}$ | 81 Tl $6s^26p^1$ | 82 Pb $6s^26p^2$ | 83 Bi $6s^26p^3$ | 84 Po $6s^26p^4$ | 85 At $6s^26p^5$ | 86 Rn $6s^26p^6$ |

Period 7

| 87 Fr $7s^1$ | 88 Ra $7s^2$ | 89 Ac** $7s^26d^1$ | 104 Rf $7s^26d^2$ | 105 Db $7s^26d^3$ | 106 Sg $7s^26d^4$ | 107 Bh $7s^26d^5$ | 108 Hs $7s^26d^6$ | 109 Mt $7s^26d^7$ | 110 Uun $7s^26d^8$ | 111 Uuu $7s^16d^{10}$ | 112 Uub $7s^26d^{10}$ |

f-Transition Elements

*Lanthanides

| 58 Ce $6s^24f^{1}5d^1$ | 59 Pr $6s^24f^35d^0$ | 60 Nd $6s^24f^45d^0$ | 61 Pm $6s^24f^55d^0$ | 62 Sm $6s^24f^65d^0$ | 63 Eu $6s^24f^75d^0$ | 64 Gd $6s^24f^75d^1$ | 65 Tb $6s^24f^95d^0$ | 66 Dy $6s^24f^{10}5d^0$ | 67 Ho $6s^24f^{11}5d^0$ | 68 Er $6s^24f^{12}5d^0$ | 69 Tm $6s^24f^{13}5d^0$ | 70 Yb $6s^24f^{14}5d^0$ | 71 Lu $6s^24f^{14}5d^1$ |

**Actinides

| 90 Th $7s^25f^06d^2$ | 91 Pa $7s^25f^26d^1$ | 92 U $7s^25f^36d^1$ | 93 Np $7s^25f^46d^1$ | 94 Pu $7s^25f^66d^0$ | 95 Am $7s^25f^76d^0$ | 96 Cm $7s^25f^76d^1$ | 97 Bk $7s^25f^96d^0$ | 98 Cf $7s^25f^{10}6d^0$ | 99 Es $7s^25f^{11}6d^0$ | 100 Fm $7s^25f^{12}6d^0$ | 101 Md $7s^25f^{13}6d^0$ | 102 No $7s^25f^{14}6d^0$ | 103 Lr $7s^25f^{14}6d^1$ |

Figure 7.27
The periodic table with atomic symbols, atomic numbers, and partial electron configurations.

5. The groups labeled 1A, 2A, 3A, 4A, 5A, 6A, 7A, and 8A are often called the **main-group,** or **representative, elements.** Remember that every member of these groups has the same valence electron configuration.

The International Union of Pure and Applied Chemistry (IUPAC), a body of scientists organized to standardize scientific conventions, has recommended a new form for the periodic table, which the American Chemical Society has adopted (see Fig. 7.28). In this new version the group number indicates the number of *s*, *p*, and *d* electrons added since the last noble gas. We will not use the new format in this

1	2	3	4	5	6	7	8	9	10	11	12	13	14	15	16	17	18
1 H																	2 He
3 Li	4 Be											5 B	6 C	7 N	8 O	9 F	10 Ne
11 Na	12 Mg											13 Al	14 Si	15 P	16 S	17 Cl	18 Ar
19 K	20 Ca	21 Sc	22 Ti	23 V	24 Cr	25 Mn	26 Fe	27 Co	28 Ni	29 Cu	30 Zn	31 Ga	32 Ge	33 As	34 Se	35 Br	36 Kr
37 Rb	38 Sr	39 Y	40 Zr	41 Nb	42 Mo	43 Tc	44 Ru	45 Rh	46 Pd	47 Ag	48 Cd	49 In	50 Sn	51 Sb	52 Te	53 I	54 Xe
55 Cs	56 Ba	57 La*	72 Hf	73 Ta	74 W	75 Re	76 Os	77 Ir	78 Pt	79 Au	80 Hg	81 Tl	82 Pb	83 Bi	84 Po	85 At	86 Rn
87 Fr	88 Ra	89 Ac**	104 Rf	105 Db	106 Sg	107 Bh	108 Hs	109 Mt	110 Uun	111 Uuu	112 Uub						

*Lanthanide series	58 Ce	59 Pr	60 Nd	61 Pm	62 Sm	63 Eu	64 Gd	65 Tb	66 Dy	67 Ho	68 Er	69 Tm	70 Yb	71 Lu
**Actinide series	90 Th	91 Pa	92 U	93 Np	94 Pu	95 Am	96 Cm	97 Bk	98 Cf	99 Es	100 Fm	101 Md	102 No	103 Lr

Figure 7.28

A form of the periodic table recommended by IUPAC.

book, but you should be aware that the familiar periodic table may be soon replaced by this or a similar format.

The results considered in this section are very important. We have seen that the quantum mechanical model can be used to explain the arrangement of the elements in the periodic table. This model allows us to understand that the similar chemistry exhibited by the members of a given group arises from the fact that they all have the same valence electron configuration. Only the principal quantum number of the valence orbitals changes in going down a particular group.

It is important to be able to give the electron configuration for each of the main-group elements. This is most easily done by using the periodic table. If you understand how the table is organized, it is not necessary to memorize the order in which the orbitals fill. Review Figs. 7.26 and 7.27 to make sure that you understand the correspondence between the orbitals and the periods and groups.

Predicting the configurations of the transition metals (3*d*, 4*d*, and 5*d* elements), the lanthanides (4*f* elements), and the actinides (5*f* elements) is somewhat more difficult because there are many exceptions of the type encountered in the first-row transition metals (the 3*d* elements). You should memorize the configurations of chromium and copper, the two exceptions in the first-row transition metals, since these elements are often encountered.

When an electron configuration is given in this text, the orbitals are listed in the order in which they fill.

Cr: $[Ar]4s^1 3d^5$
Cu: $[Ar]4s^1 3d^{10}$

A diagram that is often used to summarize the order in which the orbitals are filled in polyelectronic atoms is shown in Fig. 7.29. Note that this diagram is generated by listing horizontally the orbitals in a given principal quantum level and then drawing diagonal arrows to show the order of filling.

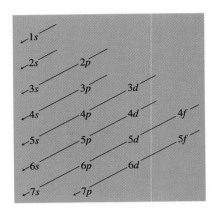

Figure 7.29

A diagram that summarizes the order in which the orbitals fill in polyelectronic atoms.

Sample Exercise 7.7 *Electron Configurations*

Give the electron configurations for sulfur (S), cadmium (Cd), hafnium (Hf), and radium (Ra) using the periodic table inside the front cover of this book.

Solution

Sulfur is element 16 and resides in Period 3, where the 3*p* orbitals are being filled (see Fig. 7.30). Since sulfur is the fourth among the "3*p* elements," it must have four 3*p* electrons. Its configuration is

$$\text{S:}\quad 1s^2 2s^2 2p^6 3s^2 3p^4 \quad \text{or} \quad [\text{Ne}]3s^2 3p^4$$

Cadmium is element 48 and is located in Period 5 at the end of the 4*d* transition metals, as shown in Fig. 7.30. It is the tenth element in the series and thus has 10 electrons in the 4*d* orbitals, in addition to the 2 electrons in the 5*s* orbital. The configuration is

$$\text{Cd:}\quad 1s^2 2s^2 2p^6 3s^2 3p^6 4s^2 3d^{10} 4p^6 5s^2 4d^{10} \quad \text{or} \quad [\text{Kr}]5s^2 4d^{10}$$

Hafnium is element 72 and is found in Period 6, as shown in Fig. 7.30. Note that it occurs just after the lanthanide series. Thus the 4*f* orbitals are already filled. Hafnium is the second member of the 5*d* transition series and has two 5*d* electrons. The configuration is

$$\text{Hf:}\quad 1s^2 2s^2 2p^6 3s^2 3p^6 4s^2 3d^{10} 4p^6 5s^2 4d^{10} 5p^6 6s^2 4f^{14} 5d^2 \quad \text{or} \quad [\text{Xe}]6s^2 4f^{14} 5d^2$$

Radium is element 88 and is in Period 7 (and Group 2A), as shown in Fig. 7.30. Thus radium has two electrons in the 7*s* orbital, and the configuration is

$$\text{Ra:}\quad 1s^2 2s^2 2p^6 3s^2 3p^6 4s^2 3d^{10} 4p^6 5s^2 4d^{10} 5p^6 6s^2 4f^{14} 5d^{10} 6p^6 7s^2 \quad \text{or} \quad [\text{Rn}]7s^2$$

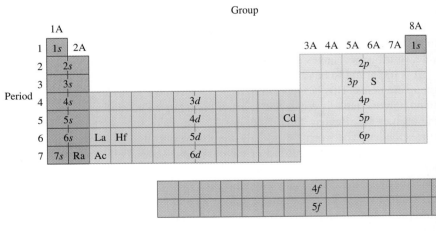

Figure 7.30

The positions of the elements considered in Sample Exercise 7.7.

See Exercises 7.69 through 7.72.

7.12 *Periodic Trends in Atomic Properties*

We have developed a fairly complete picture of polyelectronic atoms. Although the model is rather crude because the nuclear attractions and electron repulsions are simply lumped together, it is very successful in accounting for the periodic table of elements. We will next use the model to account for the observed trends in several important atomic properties: ionization energy, electron affinity, and atomic size.

Ionization Energy

Ionization energy is the energy required to remove an electron from a gaseous atom or ion:

$$X(g) \longrightarrow X^+(g) + e^-$$

where the atom or ion is assumed to be in its ground state.

To introduce some of the characteristics of ionization energy, we will consider the energy required to remove several electrons in succession from aluminum in the gaseous state. The ionization energies are

$$Al(g) \longrightarrow Al^+(g) + e^- \qquad I_1 = 580 \text{ kJ/mol}$$
$$Al^+(g) \longrightarrow Al^{2+}(g) + e^- \qquad I_2 = 1815 \text{ kJ/mol}$$
$$Al^{2+}(g) \longrightarrow Al^{3+}(g) + e^- \qquad I_3 = 2740 \text{ kJ/mol}$$
$$Al^{3+}(g) \longrightarrow Al^{4+}(g) + e^- \qquad I_4 = 11,600 \text{ kJ/mol}$$

Several important points can be illustrated from these results. In a stepwise ionization process, it is always the highest-energy electron (the one bound least tightly) that is removed first. The **first ionization energy** I_1 is the energy required to remove the highest-energy electron of an atom. The first electron removed from the aluminum atom comes from the $3p$ orbital (Al has the electron configuration $[Ne]3s^23p^1$). The second electron comes from the $3s$ orbital (since Al^+ has the configuration $[Ne]3s^2$). Note that the value of I_1 is considerably smaller than the value of I_2, the **second ionization energy.**

This makes sense for several reasons. The primary factor is simply charge. Note that the first electron is removed from a neutral atom (Al), whereas the second electron is removed from a $1+$ ion (Al^+). The increase in positive charge binds the electrons more firmly, and the ionization energy increases. The same trend shows up in the third (I_3) and fourth (I_4) ionization energies, where the electron is removed from the Al^{2+} and Al^{3+} ions, respectively.

The increase in successive ionization energies for an atom also can be interpreted using our simple model for polyelectronic atoms. The increase in ionization energy from I_1 to I_2 makes sense because the first electron is removed from a $3p$ orbital that is higher in energy than the $3s$ orbital from which the second electron is removed. The largest jump in ionization energy by far occurs in going from the third ionization energy (I_3) to the fourth (I_4). This is so because I_4 corresponds to removing a core electron (Al^{3+} has the configuration $1s^22s^22p^6$), and core electrons are bound much more tightly than valence electrons.

Table 7.5 gives the values of ionization energies for all the Period 3 elements. Note the large jump in energy in each case in going from removal of valence electrons to removal of core electrons.

Table 7.5 Successive Ionization Energies in Kilojoules per Mole for the Elements in Period 3

Element	I_1	I_2	I_3	I_4	I_5	I_6	I_7
Na	495	4560		Core electrons*			
Mg	735	1445	7730				
Al	580	1815	2740	11,600			
Si	780	1575	3220	4350	16,100		
P	1060	1890	2905	4950	6270	21,200	
S	1005	2260	3375	4565	6950	8490	27,000
Cl	1255	2295	3850	5160	6560	9360	11,000
Ar	1527	2665	3945	5770	7230	8780	12,000

*Note the large jump in ionization energy in going from removal of valence electrons to removal of core electrons.

General decrease ↑

General increase →

The values of the first ionization energies for the elements in the first six periods of the periodic table are graphed in Fig. 7.31. Note that in general as we go *across a period from left to right, the first ionization energy increases.* This is consistent with the idea that electrons added in the same principal quantum level do not completely shield the increasing nuclear charge caused by the added protons. Thus electrons in the same principal quantum level are generally more strongly bound as we

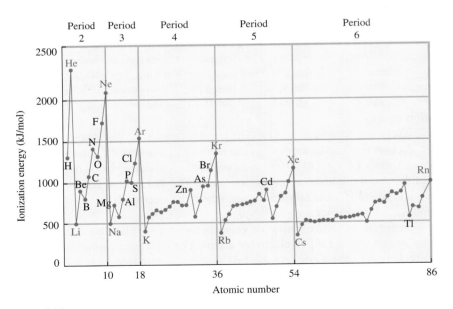

Figure 7.31
The values of first ionization energy for the elements in the first six periods. In general, ionization energy decreases in going down a group. For example, note the decrease in values for Group 1A and Group 8A. In general, ionization energy increases in going left to right across a period. For example, note the sharp increase going across Period 2 from lithium through neon.

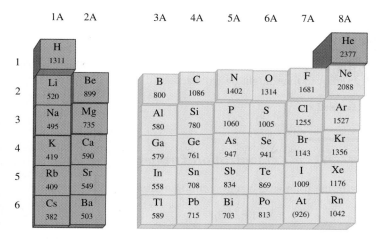

Figure 7.32

Trends in ionization energies for the representative elements.

Table 7.6 First Ionization Energies for the Alkali Metals and Noble Gases

Atom	I_1 (kJ/mol)
Group 1A	
Li	520
Na	495
K	419
Rb	409
Cs	382
Group 8A	
He	2377
Ne	2088
Ar	1527
Kr	1356
Xe	1176
Rn	1042

move to the right on the periodic table, and there is a general increase in ionization energy values as electrons are added to a given principal quantum level.

On the other hand, *first ionization energy decreases in going down a group.* This can be seen most clearly by focusing on the Group 1A elements (the alkali metals) and the Group 8A elements (the noble gases), as shown in Table 7.6. The main reason for the decrease in ionization energy in going down a group is that the electrons being removed are, on average, farther from the nucleus. As n increases, the size of the orbital increases, and the electron is easier to remove.

In Fig. 7.31 we see that there are some discontinuities in ionization energy in going across a period. For example, for Period 2, discontinuities occur in going from beryllium to boron and from nitrogen to oxygen. These exceptions to the normal trend can be explained in terms of electron repulsions. The decrease in ionization energy in going from beryllium to boron reflects the fact that the electrons in the filled $2s$ orbital provide some shielding for electrons in the $2p$ orbital from the nuclear charge. The decrease in ionization energy in going from nitrogen to oxygen reflects the extra electron repulsions in the doubly occupied oxygen $2p$ orbital.

The ionization energies for the representative elements are summarized in Fig. 7.32.

First ionization energy increases across a period and decreases down a group.

Sample Exercise 7.8 **Trends in Ionization Energies**

The first ionization energy for phosphorus is 1060 kJ/mol, and that for sulfur is 1005 kJ/mol. Why?

Solution

Phosphorus and sulfur are neighboring elements in Period 3 of the periodic table and have the following valence electron configurations: Phosphorus is $3s^2 3p^3$, and sulfur is $3s^2 3p^4$.

Ordinarily, the first ionization energy increases as we go across a period, so we might expect sulfur to have a greater ionization energy than phosphorus. However, in this case the fourth p electron in sulfur must be placed in an already occupied orbital. The electron–electron repulsions that result cause this electron to be more easily removed than might be expected.

See Question 7.30 and Exercise 7.93.

Sample Exercise 7.9 *Ionization Energies*

Consider atoms with the following electron configurations:

$$1s^2 2s^2 2p^6$$
$$1s^2 2s^2 2p^6 3s^1$$
$$1s^2 2s^2 2p^6 3s^2$$

Which atom has the largest first ionization energy, and which one has the smallest second ionization energy? Explain your choices.

Solution

The atom with the largest value of I_1 is the one with the configuration $1s^2 2s^2 2p^6$ (this is the neon atom), because this element is found at the right end of Period 2. Since the $2p$ electrons do not shield each other very effectively, I_1 will be relatively large. The other configurations given include $3s$ electrons. These electrons are effectively shielded by the core electrons and are farther from the nucleus than the $2p$ electrons in neon. Thus I_1 for these atoms will be smaller than for neon.

The atom with the smallest value of I_2 is the one with the configuration $1s^2 2s^2 2p^6 3s^2$ (the magnesium atom). For magnesium, both I_1 and I_2 involve valence electrons. For the atom with the configuration $1s^2 2s^2 2p^6 3s^1$ (sodium), the second electron lost (corresponding to I_2) is a core electron (from a $2p$ orbital).

See Questions 7.31 and 7.32 and Exercise 7.121.

Electron Affinity

Electron affinity *is the energy change associated with the addition of an electron to a gaseous atom:*

$$X(g) + e^- \longrightarrow X^-(g)$$

The sign convention for electron affinity values follows the convention for energy changes used in Chapter 6.

Because two different conventions have been used, there is a good deal of confusion in the chemical literature about the signs for electron affinity values. Electron affinity has been defined in many textbooks as the energy *released* when an electron is added to a gaseous atom. This convention requires that a positive sign be attached to an exothermic addition of an electron to an atom, which opposes normal thermodynamic conventions. Therefore, in this book we define electron affinity as a *change*

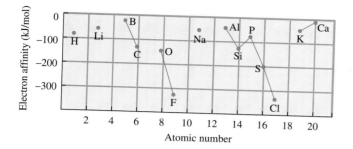

Figure 7.33
The electron affinity values for atoms among the first 20 elements that form stable, isolated X⁻ ions. The lines shown connect adjacent elements. The absence of a line indicates missing elements (He, Be, N, Ne, Mg, and Ar) whose atoms do not add an electron exothermically and thus do not form stable, isolated X⁻ ions.

in energy, which means that if the addition of the electron is exothermic, the corresponding value for electron affinity will carry a negative sign.

Figure 7.33 shows the electron affinity values for the atoms among the first 20 elements that form stable, isolated negative ions—that is, the atoms that undergo the addition of an electron as shown above. As expected, all these elements have negative (exothermic) electron affinities. Note that the *more negative* the energy, the greater is the quantity of energy released. Although electron affinities generally become more negative from left to right across a period, there are several exceptions to this rule in each period. The dependence of electron affinity on atomic number can be explained by considering the changes in electron repulsions as a function of electron configurations. For example, the fact that the nitrogen atom does not form a stable, isolated $N^-(g)$ ion, whereas carbon forms $C^-(g)$, reflects the difference in the electron configurations of these atoms. An electron added to nitrogen $(1s^2 2s^2 2p^3)$ to form the $N^-(g)$ ion $(1s^2 2s^2 2p^4)$ would have to occupy a $2p$ orbital that already contains one electron. The extra repulsion between the electrons in this doubly occupied orbital causes $N^-(g)$ to be unstable. When an electron is added to carbon $(1s^2 2s^2 2p^2)$ to form the $C^-(g)$ ion $(1s^2 2s^2 2p^3)$, no such extra repulsions occur.

In contrast to the nitrogen atom, the oxygen atom can add one electron to form the stable $O^-(g)$ ion. Presumably oxygen's greater nuclear charge compared with that of nitrogen is sufficient to overcome the repulsion associated with putting a second electron into an already occupied $2p$ orbital. However, it should be noted that a second electron *cannot* be added to an oxygen atom $[O^-(g) + e^- \not\rightarrow O^{2-}(g)]$ to form an isolated oxide ion. This outcome seems strange in view of the many stable oxide compounds (MgO, Fe_2O_3, and so on) that are known. As we will discuss in detail in Chapter 8, the O^{2-} ion is stabilized in ionic compounds by the large attractions that occur among the positive ions and the oxide ions.

When we go down a group, electron affinity should become more positive (less energy released), since the electron is added at increasing distances from the nucleus. Although this is generally the case, the changes in electron affinity in going down most groups are relatively small, and numerous exceptions occur. This behavior is demonstrated by the electron affinities of the Group 7A elements (the halogens) shown in Table 7.7. Note that the range of values is quite small compared with the changes that typically occur across a period. Also note that although chlorine, bromine, and iodine show the expected trend, the energy released when an electron is added to fluorine is smaller than might be expected. This smaller energy release has been attributed to the small size of the $2p$ orbitals. Because the electrons must

Table 7.7 Electron Affinities of the Halogens

Atom	Electron Affinity (kJ/mol)
F	−327.8
Cl	−348.7
Br	−324.5
I	−295.2

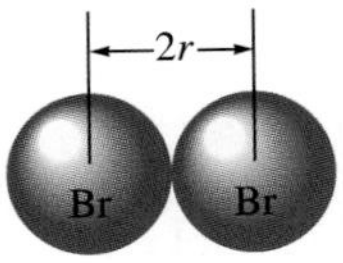

Figure 7.34

The radius of an atom (r) is defined as half the distance between the nuclei in a molecule consisting of identical atoms.

be very close together in these orbitals, there are unusually large electron–electron repulsions. In the other halogens with their larger orbitals, the repulsions are not as severe.

Atomic Radius

Just as the size of an orbital cannot be specified exactly, neither can the size of an atom. We must make some arbitrary choices to obtain values for **atomic radii.** These values can be obtained by measuring the distances between atoms in chemical compounds. For example, in the bromine molecule, the distance between the two nuclei is known to be 228 pm. The bromine atomic radius is assumed to be half this distance, or 114 pm, as shown in Fig. 7.34. These radii are often called *covalent atomic radii* because of the way they are determined (from the distances between atoms in covalent bonds).

For nonmetallic atoms that do not form diatomic molecules, the atomic radii are estimated from their various covalent compounds. The radii for metal atoms (called *metallic radii*) are obtained from half the distance between metal atoms in solid metal crystals.

The values of the atomic radii for the representative elements are shown in Fig. 7.35. Note that these values are significantly smaller than might be expected from the 90% electron density volumes of isolated atoms, because when atoms form bonds, their electron "clouds" interpenetrate. However, these values form a self-consistent data set that can be used to discuss the trends in atomic radii.

Note from Fig. 7.35 that the atomic radii decrease in going from left to right across a period. This decrease can be explained in terms of the increasing effective nuclear charge (decreasing shielding) in going from left to right. This means that the valence electrons are drawn closer to the nucleus, decreasing the size of the atom.

Atomic radius increases down a group, because of the increases in the orbital sizes in successive principal quantum levels.

Sample Exercise 7.10 *Trends in Radii*

Predict the trend in radius for the following ions: Be^{2+}, Mg^{2+}, Ca^{2+}, and Sr^{2+}.

Solution

All these ions are formed by removing two electrons from an atom of a Group 2A element. In going from beryllium to strontium, we are going down the group, so the sizes increase:

$$Be^{2+} < Mg^{2+} < Ca^{2+} < Sr^{2+}$$

↑ Smallest radius   ↑ Largest radius

See Exercises 7.83, 7.84, and 7.87.

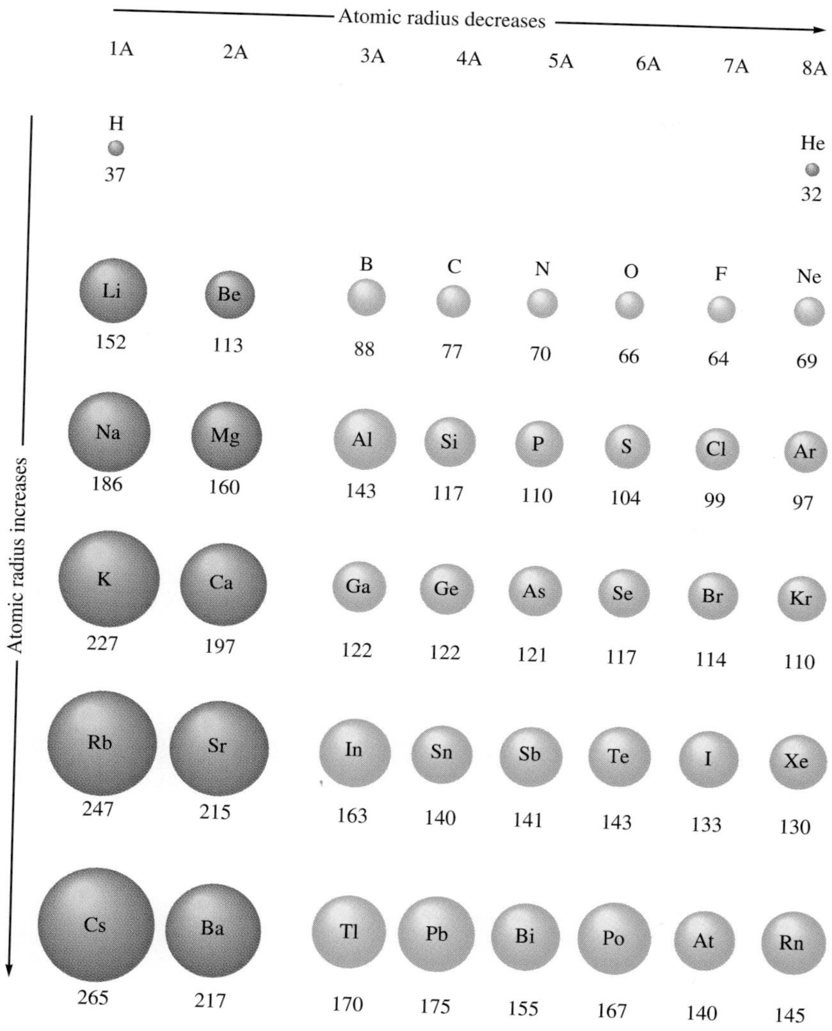

Figure 7.35

Atomic radii (in picometers) for selected atoms. Note that atomic radius decreases going across a period and increases going down a group. The values for the noble gases are estimated, because data from bonded atoms are lacking.

7.13 The Properties of a Group: The Alkali Metals

We have seen that the periodic table originated as a way to portray the systematic properties of the elements. Mendeleev was primarily responsible for first showing its usefulness in correlating and predicting the elemental properties. In this section we will summarize much of the information available from the table. We also will illustrate the usefulness of the table by discussing the properties of a representative group, the alkali metals.

Information Contained in the Periodic Table

1. The essence of the periodic table is that the groups of representative elements exhibit similar chemical properties that change in a regular way. The quantum

mechanical model of the atom has allowed us to understand the basis for the similarity of properties in a group—that each group member has the same valence electron configuration. *It is the number and type of valence electrons that primarily determine an atom's chemistry.*

2. One of the most valuable types of information available from the periodic table is the electron configuration of any representative element. If you understand the organization of the table, you will not need to memorize electron configurations for these elements. Although the predicted electron configurations for transition metals are sometimes incorrect, this is not a serious problem. You should, however, memorize the configurations of two exceptions, chromium and copper, since these $3d$ transition elements are found in many important compounds.

3. As we mentioned in Chapter 2, certain groups in the periodic table have special names. These are summarized in Fig. 7.36. Groups are often referred to by these names, so you should learn them.

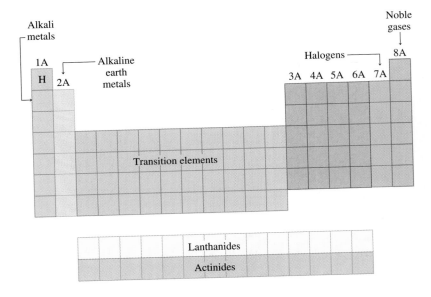

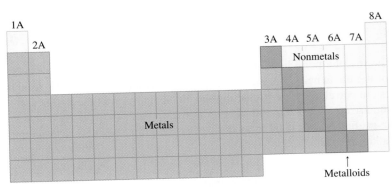

Figure 7.36

Special names for groups in the periodic table.

4. The most basic division of the elements in the periodic table is into metals and nonmetals. The most important chemical property of a metal atom is the tendency to give up one or more electrons to form a positive ion; metals tend to have low ionization energies. The metallic elements are found on the left side of the table, as shown in Fig. 7.36. The most chemically reactive metals are found on the lower left-hand portion of the table, where the ionization energies are smallest. The most distinctive chemical property of a nonmetal atom is the ability to gain one or more electrons to form an anion when reacting with a metal. Thus nonmetals are elements with large ionization energies and the most negative electron affinities. The nonmetals are found on the right side of the table, with the most reactive ones in the upper right-hand corner, except for the noble gas elements, which are quite unreactive. The division into metals and nonmetals shown in Fig. 7.36 is only approximate. Many elements along the division line exhibit both metallic and nonmetallic properties under certain circumstances. These elements are often called **metalloids,** or sometimes **semimetals.**

Metals and nonmetals were first discussed in Chapter 2.

The Alkali Metals

The metals of Group 1A, the alkali metals, illustrate very well the relationships among the properties of the elements in a group. Lithium, sodium, potassium, rubidium, cesium, and francium are the most chemically reactive of the metals. We will not discuss francium here because it occurs in nature in only very small quantities. Although hydrogen is found in Group 1A of the periodic table, it behaves as a nonmetal, in contrast to the other members of that group. The fundamental reason for hydrogen's nonmetallic character is its very small size (see Fig. 7.35). The electron in the small $1s$ orbital is bound tightly to the nucleus.

Hydrogen will be discussed further in Chapter 18.

Some important properties of the first five alkali metals are shown in Table 7.8. The data in Table 7.8 show that in going down the group, the first ionization energy decreases and the atomic radius increases. This agrees with the general trends discussed in Section 7.12.

The overall increase in density in going down Group 1A is typical of all groups. This occurs because atomic mass generally increases more rapidly than atomic size. Thus there is more mass per unit volume for each succeeding element.

Table 7.8 Properties of Five Alkali Metals

Element	Valence Electron Config- uration	Density at 25°C (g/cm³)	mp (°C)	bp (°C)	First Ionization Energy (kJ/mol)	Atomic (covalent) Radius (pm)	Ionic (M⁺) Radius (pm)
Li	$2s^1$	0.53	180	1330	520	152	60
Na	$3s^1$	0.97	98	892	495	186	95
K	$4s^1$	0.86	64	760	419	227	133
Rb	$5s^1$	1.53	39	668	409	248	148
Cs	$6s^1$	1.87	29	690	382	265	169

Other groups will be discussed in Chapters 18 and 19.

Oxidation–reduction reactions were discussed in Chapter 4.

 Molecular Models: Cl_2, NaCl

The smooth decrease in melting point and boiling point in going down Group 1A is not typical; in most other groups more complicated behavior occurs. Note that the melting point of cesium is only 29°C. Cesium can be melted readily using only the heat from your hand. This is very unusual—metals typically have rather high melting points. For example, tungsten melts at 3410°C. The only other metals with low melting points are mercury (mp −38°C) and gallium (mp 30°C).

The chemical property most characteristic of a metal is the ability to lose its valence electrons. The Group 1A elements are very reactive. They have low ionization energies and react with nonmetals to form ionic solids. A typical example involves the reaction of sodium with chlorine to form sodium chloride:

$$2Na(s) + Cl_2(g) \longrightarrow 2NaCl(s)$$

where sodium chloride contains Na^+ and Cl^- ions. This is an oxidation–reduction reaction in which chlorine oxidizes sodium. In the reactions between metals and nonmetals, it is typical for the nonmetal to behave as the oxidizing agent and the metal to behave as the reducing agent, as shown by the following reactions:

$$2Na(s) + S(s) \longrightarrow Na_2S(s)$$
Contains Na^+ and S^{2-} ions

$$6Li(s) + N_2(g) \longrightarrow 2Li_3N(s)$$
Contains Li^+ and N^{3-} ions

$$2Na(s) + O_2(g) \longrightarrow Na_2O_2(s)$$
Contains Na^+ and O_2^{2-} ions

For reactions of the types just shown, the relative reducing powers of the alkali metals can be predicted from the first ionization energies listed in Table 7.8. Since it is much easier to remove an electron from a cesium atom than from a lithium atom, cesium should be the better reducing agent. The expected trend in reducing ability is

$$Cs > Rb > K > Na > Li$$

Potassium reacts violently with water.

CHEMICAL IMPACT

Potassium—Too Much of a Good Thing Can Kill You

POTASSIUM IS WIDELY recognized as an essential element. In fact, our daily requirement for potassium is more than twice that for sodium. Because most foods contain potassium, serious deficiency of this element in humans is rare. However, potassium deficiency can be caused by kidney malfunction or by the use of certain diuretics. Potassium deficiency leads to muscle weakness, irregular heartbeat, and depression.

Potassium is found in the fluids of the body as the K^+ ion, and its presence is essential to the operation of our nervous system. The passage of impulses along the nerves requires the flow of K^+ (and Na^+) through channels in the membranes of the nerve cells. Failure of this ion flow prevents nerve transmissions and results in death. For example, the black mamba snake kills its victims by injecting a venom that blocks the potassium channels in the nerve cells.

Although a steady intake of potassium is essential to preserve life, ironically, too much potassium can be lethal. In fact, the deadly ingredient in the drug mixture used for executing criminals is potassium chloride. Injection of a large amount of a potassium chloride solution produces

The black mamba snake's venom kills by blocking the potassium channels in the nerve cells of victims.

an excess of K^+ ion in the fluids surrounding the cells and prevents the essential flow of K^+ out the cells to allow nerve impulses to occur. This causes the heart to stop beating. Unlike other forms of execution, death by lethal injection of potassium chloride does not harm the organs of the body. Thus condemned criminals who are executed in this manner can donate their organs for transplants.

This order is observed experimentally for direct reactions between the solid alkali metals and nonmetals. However, this is not the order for reducing ability found when the alkali metals react in aqueous solution. For example, the reduction of water by an alkali metal is very vigorous and exothermic:

$$2M(s) + 2H_2O(l) \longrightarrow H_2(g) + 2M^+(aq) + 2OH^-(aq) + \text{energy}$$

The order of reducing abilities observed for this reaction for the first three group members is

$$\text{Li} > \text{K} > \text{Na}$$

In the gas phase potassium loses an electron more easily than sodium, and sodium more easily than lithium. Thus it is surprising that lithium is the best reducing agent toward water.

Table 7.9 Hydration Energies for Li$^+$, Na$^+$, and K$^+$ Ions

Ion	Hydration Energy (kJ/mol)
Li$^+$	-510
Na$^+$	-402
K$^+$	-314

This reversal occurs because the formation of the M$^+$ ions in aqueous solution is strongly influenced by the hydration of these ions by the polar water molecules. The *hydration energy* of an ion represents the change in energy that occurs when water molecules attach to the M$^+$ ion. The hydration energies for the Li$^+$, Na$^+$, and K$^+$ ions (shown in Table 7.9) indicate that the process is exothermic in each case. However, nearly twice as much energy is released by the hydration of the Li$^+$ ion as for the K$^+$ ion. This difference is caused by size effects; the Li$^+$ ion is much smaller than the K$^+$ ion, and thus its *charge density* (charge per unit volume) is also much greater. This means that the polar water molecules are more strongly attracted to the small Li$^+$ ion. Because the Li$^+$ ion is so strongly hydrated, its formation from the lithium atom occurs more readily than the formation of the K$^+$ ion from the potassium atom. Although a potassium atom in the gas phase loses its valence electron more readily than a lithium atom in the gas phase, the opposite is true in aqueous solution. This anomaly is an example of the importance of the polarity of the water molecule in aqueous reactions.

There is one more surprise involving the highly exothermic reactions of the alkali metals with water. Experiments show that in water lithium is the best reducing agent, so we might expect that lithium should react the most violently with water. However, this is not true. Sodium and potassium react much more vigorously. Why is this so? The answer lies in the relatively high melting point of lithium. When sodium and potassium react with water, the heat evolved causes them to melt, giving a larger area of contact with water. Lithium, on the other hand, does not melt under these conditions and reacts more slowly. This illustrates the important principle (which we will discuss in detail in Chapter 12) that the energy change for a reaction and the rate at which it occurs are not necessarily related.

In this section we have seen that the trends in atomic properties summarized by the periodic table can be a great help in understanding the chemical behavior of the elements. This fact will be emphasized over and over as we proceed in our study of chemistry.

Key Terms

Section 7.1
electromagnetic radiation
wavelength
frequency

Section 7.2
Planck's constant
quantization
photon
$E = mc^2$
dual nature of light
diffraction
diffraction pattern

Section 7.3
continuous spectrum
line spectrum

Section 7.4
quantum model
ground state

Section 7.5
standing wave
wave function
orbital
quantum (wave) mechanical model
Heisenberg uncertainty principle
probability distribution
radial probability distribution

Section 7.6
quantum numbers
principal quantum number (n)
angular momentum quantum number (ℓ)

For Review

Summary

Energy can travel through space as electromagnetic radiation, which is characterized by wavelength (λ), frequency (ν), and speed ($c = 2.9979 \times 10^8$ m/s). These three properties are related by the equation $\lambda\nu = c$. Originally, energy was assumed to be continuous, but Planck showed that energy could be lost or gained only in quanta, which are whole-number multiples of $h\nu$ (h is Planck's constant, 6.626×10^{-34} J · s). Einstein postulated that electromagnetic radiation itself can be viewed as a stream of particles called photons, each with energy $h\nu$. Electromagnetic radiation therefore exhibits both wave and particulate properties. The postulate by de Broglie that particles possess wave characteristics was verified by diffraction experiments showing that all matter exhibits the same properties.

A continuous spectrum results from dispersing white light. However, when the emission spectrum produced by excited hydrogen atoms is dispersed, only selected wavelengths are seen, giving a line spectrum. This shows that only certain energies are allowed for the electron in the hydrogen atom.

The Bohr model of the hydrogen atom speculated that the electron in a hydrogen atom moves around the nucleus in certain allowed circular orbits and that the line spectrum was produced when an electron moved from one orbit to another. The Bohr model, however, was shown to be incorrect.

The quantum (wave) mechanical model for the hydrogen atom employs the concept of standing waves. The electron is described by a wave function, often called an orbital, which does not give the exact position for the electron at a given time. This is consistent with the Heisenberg uncertainty principle, which states that it is impossible to know both the position and the momentum of a particle accurately at a given time. However, we can give a physical meaning to the wave function: the square of the function is related to the probability of finding an electron near a particular point in space. Probability distribution (electron density maps) are used to define orbital shapes. Orbitals are characterized by the quantum numbers n, ℓ, and m_ℓ.

Another property of the electron is its spin. An electron appears to spin in two directions, giving rise to two values for the electron spin quantum number (m_s). This concept leads to the Pauli exclusion principle: no two electrons in a given atom can have the same set of four quantum numbers.

Using this principle along with the quantum mechanical model, we can predict the electronic configurations of the atoms in the periodic table. As protons are added one by one to the nucleus to build up the elements, electrons are added to the orbitals. This is called the aufbau principle.

The greatest triumph of the quantum mechanical model is its use to explain the observed periodic properties of the elements as summarized by the periodic table. The chemical properties of an atom are determined by the arrangement of the valence electrons (the electrons in the outermost principal quantum level). Elements in the same group of the periodic table have the same valence electron configurations, which explains why group members show similar chemical properties.

The periodic trends in atomic properties such as ionization energy, electron affinity, and atomic radius can be explained in terms of the concepts of nuclear attraction, electron repulsions, shielding, and penetration.

magnetic quantum number (m_ℓ)
subshell

Section 7.7
nodal surface
node
degenerate

Section 7.8
electron spin
electron spin quantum number
Pauli exclusion principle

Section 7.9
polyelectronic atoms

Section 7.11
aufbau principle
Hund's rule
valence electrons
core electrons
transition metals
lanthanide series
actinide series
main-group elements (representative elements)

Section 7.12
first ionization energy
second ionization energy
electron affinity
atomic radii

Section 7.13
metalloids (semimetals)

In-Class Discussion Questions

These questions are designed to be considered by groups of students in class. Often these questions work well for introducing a particular topic in class.

1. What does it mean for something to have wavelike properties? particulate properties? Electromagnetic radiation can be discussed in terms of both particles and waves. Explain the experimental verification for each of these views.

2. Defend and criticize Bohr's model. Why was it reasonable that such a model was proposed, and what evidence was there that it "works"? Why do we no longer "believe" in it?

3. The first four ionization energies for the elements X and Y are shown at the right. The units are not kJ/mol.

	X	Y
First	170	200
Second	350	400
Third	1800	3500
Fourth	2500	5000

Identify the elements X and Y. There may be more than one correct answer, so explain completely.

4. Compare the first ionization energy of helium to its second ionization energy, remembering that both electrons come from the $1s$ orbital. Explain the difference without using actual numbers from the text.

5. Which has the larger second ionization energy, lithium or beryllium? Why?

6. Explain why a graph of ionization energy versus atomic number (across a row) is not linear. Where are the exceptions? Why are there exceptions?

7. Without referring to your text, predict the trend of second ionization energies for the elements sodium through argon. Compare your answer with Table 7.5. Explain any differences.

8. Account for the fact that the line that separates the metals from the nonmetals on the periodic table is diagonal downward to the right instead of horizontal or vertical.

9. Explain *electron* from a quantum mechanical perspective, including a discussion of atomic radii, probabilities, and orbitals.

10. Choose the best response for the following. The ionization energy for the chlorine atom is equal in magnitude to the electron affinity for
   a. the Cl atom.
   b. the Cl^- ion.
   c. the Cl^+ ion.
   d. the F atom.
   e. none of these.
   Explain each choice. Justify your choice, and for the choices you did not select, explain what is incorrect about them.

11. Consider the following statement: "The ionization energy for the potassium atom is negative, because when K loses an electron to become K^+, it achieves a noble gas electron configuration." Indicate everything that is correct in this statement. Indicate everything that is incorrect. Correct the incorrect information and explain.

12. In going across a row of the periodic table, electrons are added and ionization energy generally increases. In going down a column of the periodic table, electrons are also being added but ionization energy decreases. Explain.

13. How does probability fit into the description of the atom?

14. What is meant by an *orbital?*

A blue question or exercise number indicates that the answer to that question or exercise appears at the back of the book and a solution appears in the *Solutions Guide.*

Questions

15. What experimental evidence supports the quantum theory for light?

16. What do we mean when we say that something is quantized? In the Bohr model of the hydrogen atom, what is quantized?

17. For what sizes of particles must one consider both wave and particle properties?

18. Summarize some of the evidence supporting the wave properties of matter.

19. Define each of the following terms.
   a. photon
   b. quantum number
   c. ground state
   d. excited state

20. In the hydrogen atom, what information do we get from the values of the quantum numbers n, ℓ, and m_ℓ?

21. How do the 2p orbitals differ from each other?

22. How do the 2p and 3p orbitals differ from each other?

23. What is a nodal surface in an atomic orbital?

24. Why can we not account exactly for the repulsions among electrons in a polyelectronic atom?

25. We define a spin quantum number, but do we know that an electron literally spins?

26. Explain what we mean when we say that a 4s electron is more penetrating than a 3d electron.

27. Why do we emphasize the valence electrons in an atom when discussing atomic properties?

28. What is the relationship between valence electrons and elements in the same group of the periodic table?

29. Many times the claim is made that subshells half filled with electrons are particularly stable. Can you suggest a possible physical basis for this claim?

30. Explain why the first ionization energy tends to increase as one proceeds from left to right across a period. Why is the first ionization energy of aluminum lower than that of magnesium and the first ionization energy of sulfur lower than that of phosphorus?

31. Why do the successive ionization energies of an atom always increase?

32. Note the successive ionization energies for silicon given in Table 7.5. Would you expect to see any large jumps between successive ionization energies of silicon as you removed all the electrons, one by one, beyond those shown in the table?

33. Why is it much harder to explain the line spectra of polyelectronic atoms and ions than it is to explain the line spectra of hydrogen and hydrogenlike ions?

34. Scientists use emission spectra to confirm the presence of an element in materials of unknown composition. Why is this possible?

35. Does the minimization of electron–electron repulsions correlate with Hund's rule?

36. In the hydrogen atom, what is the physical significance of the state for which $n = \infty$ and $E = 0$?

Exercises

In this section similar exercises are paired.

Light and Matter

37. The laser in an audio compact disc player uses light with a wavelength of 7.80×10^2 nm. Calculate the frequency of this light.
38. An FM radio station broadcasts at 99.5 MHz. Calculate the wavelength of the corresponding radio waves.

39. Microwave radiation has a wavelength on the order of 1.0 cm. Calculate the frequency and the energy of a single photon of this radiation. Calculate the energy of an Avogadro's number of photons (called an *einstein*) of this radiation.
40. A photon of ultraviolet (UV) light possesses enough energy to mutate a strand of human DNA. What is the energy of a single UV photon and a mole of UV photons having a wavelength of 25 nm?

41. The work function of an element is the energy required to remove an electron from the surface of the solid element. The work function for lithium is 279.7 kJ/mol (that is, it takes 279.7 kJ of energy to remove one mole of electrons from one mole of Li atoms on the surface of Li metal). What is the maximum wavelength of light that can remove an electron from an atom on the surface of lithium metal?
42. It takes 208.4 kJ of energy to remove 1 mole of electrons from an atom on the surface of rubidium metal. How much energy does it take to remove a single electron from an atom on the surface of solid rubidium? What is the maximum wavelength of light capable of doing this?

43. It takes 7.21×10^{-19} J of energy to remove an electron from an iron atom. What is the maximum wavelength of light that can do this?
44. The ionization energy of gold is 890.1 kJ/mol. Is light with a wavelength of 225 nm capable of ionizing a gold atom (removing an electron) in the gas phase?

45. Calculate the de Broglie wavelength for each of the following.
    a. a proton with a velocity 90.% of the speed of light
    b. a 150-g ball with a velocity of 10. m/s
46. Neutron diffraction is used in determining the structures of molecules.
    a. Calculate the de Broglie wavelength of a neutron moving at 1.00% of the speed of light.
    b. Calculate the velocity of a neutron with a wavelength of 75 pm (1 pm = 10^{-12} m).

47. Calculate the de Broglie wavelength of an electron moving with a velocity that is 1.0×10^{-3} times the speed of light.
48. Calculate the velocities of electrons with de Broglie wavelengths of 1.0×10^2 nm and 1.0 nm, respectively.

Hydrogen Atom: The Bohr Model

49. Calculate the wavelength of light emitted when each of the following transitions occur in the hydrogen atom.
    a. $n = 3 \rightarrow n = 2$
    b. $n = 4 \rightarrow n = 2$
    c. $n = 2 \rightarrow n = 1$
50. Calculate the wavelength of light emitted when each of the following transitions occur in the hydrogen atom.
    a. $n = 4 \rightarrow n = 3$
    b. $n = 5 \rightarrow n = 4$
    c. $n = 5 \rightarrow n = 3$

51. Using vertical lines, indicate the transitions from Exercise 49 on an energy-level diagram for the hydrogen atom (see Fig. 7.8).
52. Using vertical lines, indicate the transitions from Exercise 50 on an energy-level diagram for the hydrogen atom (see Fig. 7.8).

53. Does a photon of visible light ($\lambda \approx 400$ to 700 nm) have sufficient energy to excite an electron in a hydrogen atom from the $n = 1$ to the $n = 5$ energy state? from the $n = 2$ to the $n = 6$ energy state?
54. An excited hydrogen atom emits light with a frequency of 1.141×10^{14} Hz to reach the energy level for which $n = 4$. In what principal quantum level did the electron begin?

55. Calculate the maximum wavelength of light capable of removing an electron for a hydrogen atom from the energy state characterized by $n = 1$. by $n = 2$.
56. Calculate the maximum wavelength of light capable of removing an electron for a hydrogen atom from the energy state characterized by $n = 4$. by $n = 10$.

Quantum Mechanics, Quantum Numbers, and Orbitals

57. From the Heisenberg uncertainty principle, calculate Δx for an electron with $\Delta v = 0.100$ m/s. How does Δx compare with the size of a hydrogen atom?
58. From the Heisenberg uncertainty principle, calculate Δx for a baseball (mass = 145 g) with $\Delta v = 0.100$ m/s. How does Δx compare with the size of a baseball?

59. What are the possible values for the quantum numbers n, ℓ, and m_ℓ?

60. Which of the following orbital designations are incorrect: $1s$, $1p$, $7d$, $9s$, $3f$, $4f$, $2d$?

61. Which of the following sets of quantum numbers are not allowed in the hydrogen atom? For the sets of quantum numbers that are incorrect, state what is wrong in each set.
  a. $n = 2$, $\ell = 1$, $m_\ell = -1$
  b. $n = 1$, $\ell = 1$, $m_\ell = 0$
  c. $n = 8$, $\ell = 7$, $m_\ell = -6$
  d. $n = 1$, $\ell = 0$, $m_\ell = 2$

62. Which of the following sets of quantum numbers are not allowed in the hydrogen atom? For the sets of quantum numbers that are incorrect, state what is wrong in each set.
  a. $n = 3$, $\ell = 2$, $m_\ell = 2$
  b. $n = 4$, $\ell = 3$, $m_\ell = 4$
  c. $n = 0$, $\ell = 0$, $m_\ell = 0$
  d. $n = 2$, $\ell = -1$, $m_\ell = 1$

63. What is the physical significance of the value of ψ^2 at a particular point in an atomic orbital?

64. In defining the sizes of orbitals, why must we use an arbitrary value, such as 90% of the probability of finding an electron in that region?

Polyelectronic Atoms

65. How many orbitals in an atom can have the designation: $5p$, $3d_{z^2}$, $4d$, $n = 5$, $n = 4$?

66. How many electrons in an atom can have the designation $1p$, $6d_{x^2-y^2}$, $4f$, $7p_y$, $2s$, $n = 3$?

67. Give the maximum number of electrons in an atom that can have these quantum numbers:
  a. $n = 4$
  b. $n = 5$, $m_\ell = +1$
  c. $n = 5$, $m_s = +\frac{1}{2}$
  d. $n = 3$, $\ell = 2$
  e. $n = 2$, $\ell = 1$

68. Give the maximum number of electrons in an atom that can have these quantum numbers:
  a. $n = 0$, $\ell = 0$, $m_\ell = 0$
  b. $n = 2$, $\ell = 1$, $m_\ell = -1$, $m_s = -\frac{1}{2}$
  c. $n = 3$
  d. $n = 2$, $\ell = 2$
  e. $n = 1$, $\ell = 0$, $m_\ell = 0$

69. The elements Si, Ga, As, Ge, Al, Cd, S, and Se are all used in the manufacture of various semiconductor devices. Write the expected electron configuration for these atoms.

70. The elements Cu, O, La, Y, Ba, Tl, and Bi are all found in high-temperature ceramic superconductors. Write the expected electron configuration for these atoms.

71. Write the expected electron configurations for each of the following atoms: Sc, Fe, P, Cs, Eu, Pt, Xe, Br.

72. Write the expected electron configurations for each of the following atoms: Cl, As, Sr, W, Pb, Cf.

73. Using Fig. 7.27, list the elements (ignore the lanthanides and actinides) that have ground state electron configurations that differ from those we would expect from their positions in the periodic table.

74. The electron configurations in Fig. 7.27 are for atoms in the gas phase and are determined experimentally. Would you expect the electron configurations to be the same in the solid and liquid states as in the gas phase?

75. Write an electron configuration for each of the following.
  a. The lightest halogen atom
  b. The alkali metal with only $2p$ and $3p$ electrons.
  c. The three lightest alkaline earth metals
  d. The Group 3A element in the same period as Sn
  e. The nonmetallic elements in Group 4A
  f. The (as yet undiscovered) noble gas after radon

76. Using only the periodic table inside the front cover of the text, write the expected ground-state electron configurations for
  a. the third element in Group 5A.
  b. element number 116.
  c. an element with three unpaired $5d$ electrons.
  d. the halogen with electrons in the $6p$ atomic orbitals.

77. Give a possible set of values of the four quantum numbers for all the electrons in a boron atom and a nitrogen atom if each is in the ground state.

78. Give a possible set of values for the four quantum numbers of all the valence electrons in each of the following atoms if each is in its ground state: Mg, As, Xe.

79. A certain oxygen atom has the electron configuration $1s^2 2s^2 2p_x^2 2p_y^2$. How many unpaired electrons are present? Is this an excited state of oxygen? In going from this state to the ground state would energy be released or absorbed?

80. Which of the following electron configurations correspond to an excited state? Identify the atoms and write the ground-state electron configuration where appropriate.
  a. $1s^2 2s^2 3p^1$
  b. $1s^2 2s^2 2p^6$
  c. $1s^2 2s^2 2p^4 3s^1$
  d. $[Ar]4s^2 3d^5 4p^1$
  How many unpaired electrons are present in each of these species?

81. Cr, Mn, Fe, Co, Ni, Cu, and Zn are all first-row transition metals that are essential for human health (see Table 20.18). Rank these transition metals in order of increasing number of unpaired electrons in the ground state.

82. How many unpaired electrons are present in each of the following in the ground state: O, O^+, O^-, Os, Zr, S, F, Ar?

The Periodic Table and Periodic Properties

83. Arrange the following groups of atoms in order of increasing size.
   a. Be, Mg, Ca
   b. Te, I, Xe
   c. Ga, Ge, In
84. Arrange the following groups of atoms in order of increasing size.
   a. Rb, Na, Be
   b. Sr, Se, Ne
   c. Fe, P, O

85. Arrange the atoms in Exercise 83 in order of increasing first ionization energy.
86. Arrange the atoms in Exercise 84 in order of increasing first ionization energy.

87. In each of the following sets, which atom or ion has the smallest radius?
   a. Li, Na, K
   b. P, As
   c. O^+, O, O^-
   d. S, Cl, Kr
   e. Pd, Ni, Cu
88. In each of the following sets, which atom or ion has the smallest ionization energy?
   a. Cs, Ba, La
   b. Zn, Ga, Ge
   c. In, P, Ar
   d. Tl, Sn, As
   e. O, O^-, O^{2-}

89. In 1994 at an American Chemical Society meeting, it was proposed that element 106 be named seaborgium, Sg, in honor of Glenn Seaborg, discoverer of the first transuranium element.
   a. Write the expected electron configuration for element 106.
   b. What other element would be most like element 106 in its properties?
   c. Write the formula for a possible oxide and a possible oxyanion of element 106.
90. Predict some of the properties of element 117 (the symbol is Uus, following conventions proposed by the International Union of Pure and Applied Chemistry, or IUPAC).
   a. What will be its electron configuration?
   b. What element will it most resemble chemically?

   c. What will be the formula of the neutral binary compounds it forms with sodium, magnesium, carbon, and oxygen?
   d. What oxyanions would you expect Uus to form?

91. Using the element phosphorus as an example, write the equation for a process in which the energy change will correspond to the ionization energy.
92. Using the element phosphorus as an example, write the equation for a process in which the energy change will correspond to the electron affinity.

93. The first ionization energies of As and Se are 0.947 and 0.941 MJ/mol, respectively. Rationalize these values in terms of electron configurations.
94. The electron affinities of the elements from aluminum to chlorine are −44, −120, −74, −200.4, and −384.7 kJ/mol, respectively. Rationalize the trend in these values.

95. For each of the following pairs of elements

   (C and N)   (Ar and Br)

   pick the atom with
   a. more favorable (exothermic) electron affinity.
   b. higher ionization energy.
   c. larger size.
96. For each of the following pairs of elements

   (Mg and K)   (F and Cl)

   pick the atom with
   a. more favorable (exothermic) electron affinity.
   b. higher ionization energy.
   c. larger size.

97. Order the atoms in each of the following sets from the least exothermic electron affinity to the most.
   a. S, Se
   b. F, Cl, Br, I
98. Order the atoms in each of the following sets from the least exothermic electron affinity to the most.
   a. N, O, F
   b. Al, Si, P

99. The electron affinity for sulfur is more exothermic than that for oxygen. Account for this.
100. Which would have the more negative electron affinity, the oxygen atom or the O^- ion? Explain.

101. Use data in this chapter to determine
   a. the electron affinity of Mg^{2+}.
   b. the electron affinity of Al^+.
102. Use data in this chapter to determine
   a. the ionization energy of Cl^-.
   b. the ionization energy of Cl.
   c. the electron affinity of Cl^+.

Alkali and Alkaline Earth Elements

103. An ionic compound of potassium and oxygen has the empirical formula KO. Would you expect this compound to be potassium(II) oxide or potassium peroxide? Explain.

104. An ionic compound of magnesium and oxygen has the empirical formula MgO. Would you expect this compound to be magnesium(II) oxide or magnesium(I) peroxide? Explain.

105. Cesium was discovered in natural mineral waters in 1860 by R. W. Bunsen and G. R. Kirchhoff using the spectroscope they invented in 1859. The name came from the Latin *caesius* ("sky blue") because of the prominent blue line observed for this element at 455.5 nm. Calculate the frequency and energy of a photon of this light.

106. The bright yellow light emitted by a sodium vapor lamp consists of two emission lines at 589.0 and 589.6 nm. What are the frequency and the energy of a photon of light at each of these wavelengths? What are the energies in kJ/mol?

107. Give the name and formula of each of the binary compounds formed from the following elements.
    a. Li and N
    b. Na and Br
    c. K and S

108. Give the name and formula of each of the binary compounds formed from the following elements.
    a. Li and P
    b. Rb and H
    c. Na and O

109. Complete and balance the equations for the following reactions.
    a. $Li(s) + O_2(g) \rightarrow$
    b. $K(s) + S(s) \rightarrow$

110. Complete and balance the equations for the following reactions.
    a. $Cs(s) + H_2O(l) \rightarrow$
    b. $Na(s) + Cl_2(g) \rightarrow$

Additional Exercises

111. Photogray lenses incorporate small amounts of silver chloride in the glass of the lens. When light hits the AgCl particles, the following reaction occurs:

$$AgCl \xrightarrow{h\nu} Ag + Cl$$

The silver metal that is formed causes the lenses to darken. The enthalpy change for this reaction is 3.10×10^2 kJ/mol. Assuming all this energy must be supplied by light, what is the maximum wavelength of light that can cause this reaction?

112. Consider the following approximate visible light spectrum:

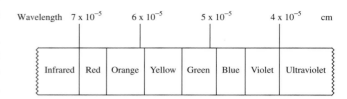

Barium emits light in the visible region of the spectrum. If each photon of light emitted from barium has an energy of 3.90×10^{-19} J, what color of visible light is emitted?

113. One of the visible lines in the hydrogen emission spectrum corresponds to the $n = 6$ to $n = 2$ electronic transition. What color light is this transition? See Exercise 112.

114. An electron is excited from the $n = 1$ ground state to the $n = 3$ state in a hydrogen atom. Which of the following statements are true? Correct the false statements to make them true.
    a. It takes more energy to ionize the electron from $n = 3$ than from the ground state.
    b. The electron is further from the nucleus on average in the $n = 3$ state than in the $n = 1$ state.
    c. The wavelength of light emitted if the electron drops from $n = 3$ to $n = 2$ will be shorter than the wavelength of light emitted if the electron falls from $n = 3$ to $n = 1$.
    d. The wavelength of light emitted when the electron returns to the ground state from $n = 3$ will be the same as the wavelength of light absorbed to go from $n = 1$ to $n = 3$.
    e. For $n = 3$, the electron is in the first excited state.

115. On which quantum numbers does the energy of an electron depend in each of the following?
    a. A one-electron atom or ion
    b. An atom or ion with more than one electron

116. Although no currently known elements contain electrons in g orbitals in the ground state, it is possible that these elements will be found or that electrons in excited states of known elements could be in g orbitals. For g orbitals, the value of ℓ is 4. What is the lowest value of n for which g orbitals could exist? What are the possible values of m_ℓ? How many electrons could a set of g orbitals hold?

117. In the ground state of cadmium, Cd,
    a. how many electrons have $\ell = 2$ as one of their quantum numbers?
    b. how many electrons have $n = 4$ as one of their quantum numbers?
    c. how many electrons have $m_\ell = -1$ as one of their quantum numbers?

d. how many electrons have $m_s = -\frac{1}{2}$ as one of their quantum numbers?

118. Total radial probability distributions for the helium, neon, and argon atoms are shown in the following graph. How can one interpret the shapes of these curves in terms of electron configurations, quantum numbers, and nuclear charges?

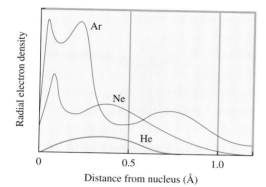

119. Predict the atomic number of the next alkali metal after francium, and give its ground-state electron configuration.

120. An ion having a 4+ charge and a mass of 49.9 amu has 2 electrons with principal quantum number $n = 1$, 8 electrons with $n = 2$, and 10 electrons with $n = 3$. Supply as many of the properties for the ion as possible from the information given. *Hint:* In forming ions, the $4s$ electrons are lost before the $3d$ electrons.

a. the atomic number
b. total number of s electrons
c. total number of p electrons
d. total number of d electrons
e. the number of neutrons in the nucleus
f. the ground-state electron configuration of the neutral atom

121. The successive ionization energies for an unknown element are
$I_1 = 896$ kJ/mol
$I_2 = 1752$ kJ/mol
$I_3 = 14,807$ kJ/mol
$I_4 = 17,948$ kJ/mol
To which family in the periodic table does the unknown element most likely belong?

122. An unknown element is a nonmetal and has a valence electron configuration of ns^2np^4.
a. How many valence electrons does this element have?
b. What are some possible identities for this element?
c. What is the formula of the compound this element would form with potassium?

d. Would this element have a larger or smaller radius than barium?
e. Would this element have a greater or smaller ionization energy than fluorine?

123. Elements with very large ionization energies also tend to have highly exothermic electron affinities. Explain. Which group of elements would you expect to be an exception to this statement?

124. The changes in electron affinity as one goes down a group in the periodic table are not nearly as large as the variations in ionization energies. Why?

125. Using data from this chapter, calculate the change in energy expected for each of the following processes.
a. $Na(g) + Cl(g) \rightarrow Na^+(g) + Cl^-(g)$
b. $Mg(g) + F(g) \rightarrow Mg^+(g) + F^-(g)$
c. $Mg^+(g) + F(g) \rightarrow Mg^{2+}(g) + F^-(g)$
d. $Mg(g) + 2F(g) \rightarrow Mg^{2+}(g) + 2F^-(g)$

126. Write equations corresponding to the following.
a. The fourth ionization energy of Se
b. The electron affinity of S^-
c. The electron affinity of Fe^{3+}
d. The ionization energy of Mg

127. The work function is the energy required to remove an electron from an atom on the surface of a metal. How does this definition differ from that for ionization energy?

128. Many more anhydrous lithium salts are hygroscopic (readily absorb water) than are those of the other alkali metals. Explain.

Challenge Problems

129. One of the emission spectral lines for Be^{3+} has a wavelength of 253.4 nm for an electronic transition that begins in the state with $n = 5$. What is the principal quantum number of the lower-energy state corresponding to this emission? (Hint: The Bohr model can be applied to electron ions. Don't forget the Z factor: Z = nuclear charge = atomic number.)

130. The figure below represents part of the emission spectrum for a one-electron ion in the gas phase. All the lines result from electronic transitions from excited states to the $n = 3$ state. (See Exercise 129.)

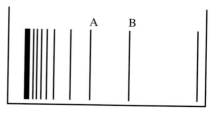

a. What electronic transitions correspond to lines A and B?

b. If the wavelength of line B is 142.5 nm, calculate the wavelength of line A.

131. The wave function for the $2p_z$ orbital in the hydrogen atom is

$$\psi_{2p_z} = \frac{1}{4\sqrt{2\pi}} \left(\frac{Z}{a_0}\right)^{3/2} \sigma e^{-\sigma/2} \cos \theta$$

where a_0 is the value for the radius of the first Bohr orbit in meters (5.29×10^{-11}), σ is $Z(r/a_0)$, r is the value for the distance from the nucleus in meters, and θ is an angle. Calculate the value of $\psi_{2p_z}^2$ at $r = a_0$ for $\theta = 0$ (z axis) and for $\theta = 90°$ (xy plane).

132. Answer the following questions assuming that m_s could have three values rather than two and that the rules for n, ℓ, and m_ℓ are the normal ones.

a. How many electrons would an orbital be able to hold?

b. How many elements would the first and second periods in the periodic table contain?

c. How many elements would be contained in the first transition metal series?

d. How many electrons would the set of $4f$ orbitals be able to hold?

133. Assume that we are in another universe with different physical laws. Electrons in this universe are described by four quantum numbers with meanings similar to those we use. We will call these quantum numbers p, q, r, and s. The rules for these quantum numbers are as follows:

$p = 1, 2, 3, 4, 5, \ldots$.

q takes on positive odd integer values and $q \le p$.

r takes on all even integer values from $-q$ to $+q$. (Zero is considered an even number.)

$s = +\frac{1}{2}$ or $-\frac{1}{2}$

a. Sketch what the first four periods of the periodic table will look like in this universe.

b. What are the atomic numbers of the first four elements you would expect to be least reactive?

c. Give an example, using elements in the first four rows, of ionic compounds with the formulas XY, XY_2, X_2Y, XY_3, and X_2Y_3.

d. How many electrons can have $p = 4$, $q = 3$?

e. How many electrons can have $p = 3$, $q = 0$, $r = 0$?

f. How many electrons can have $p = 6$?

134. We expect the atomic radius to increase going down a group in the periodic table. Can you suggest why the atomic radius of hafnium breaks this rule? (See data below.)

Atomic Radii, in pm			
Sc	157	Ti	147.7
Y	169.3	Zr	159.3
La	191.5	Hf	147.6

135. Consider the following ionization energies for aluminum:

$Al(g) \longrightarrow Al^+(g) + e^- \qquad I_1 = 580 \text{ kJ/mol}$

$Al^+(g) \longrightarrow Al^{2+}(g) + e^- \qquad I_2 = 1815 \text{ kJ/mol}$

$Al^{2+}(g) \longrightarrow Al^{3+}(g) + e^- \qquad I_3 = 2740 \text{ kJ/mol}$

$Al^{3+}(g) \longrightarrow Al^{4+}(g) + e^- \qquad I_4 = 11,600 \text{ kJ/mol}$

a. Account for the trend in the values of the ionization energies.

b. Explain the large increase between I_3 and I_4.

c. Which one of the four ions has the greatest electron affinity? Explain.

d. List the four aluminum ions given above in order of increasing size, and explain your ordering. (*Hint:* Remember that most of the size of an atom or ion is due to its electrons.)

136. While Mendeleev predicted the existence of several undiscovered elements, he did not predict the existence of the noble gases, the lanthanides, or the actinides. Propose reasons why Mendeleev was not able to predict the existence of the noble gases.

Marathon Problem*

This problem is designed to incorporate several concepts and techniques into one situation. Marathon Problems can be used in class by groups of students to help facilitate problem-solving skills.

137. From the information below, identify element X.

a. The wavelength of the radio waves sent by an FM station broadcasting at 97.1 MHz is 30 million (3.00×10^7) times greater than the wavelength corresponding to the energy difference between a particular excited state of the hydrogen atom and the ground state.

b. Let V represent the principal quantum number for the valence shell of element X. If an electron in the hydrogen atom falls from shell V to the inner shell corresponding to the excited state mentioned above in part a, the wavelength of light emitted is the same as the wavelength of an electron moving at a speed of 570. m/s.

c. The number of unpaired electrons for element X in the ground state is the same as the maximum number of electrons in an atom that can have the quantum number designations $n = 2$, $m_\ell = -1$, and $m_s = -\frac{1}{2}$.

d. Let A equal the charge of the stable ion that would form when the undiscovered element 120 forms ionic compounds. This value of A also represents the angular momentum quantum number for the subshell containing the unpaired electron(s) for element X.

*This Marathon Problem was developed by James H. Burness, Penn State University, York Campus. Reprinted with permission from the *Journal of Chemical Education,* Vol. 68, No. 11, 1991, pp. 919–922; copyright © 1991, Division of Chemical Education, Inc.

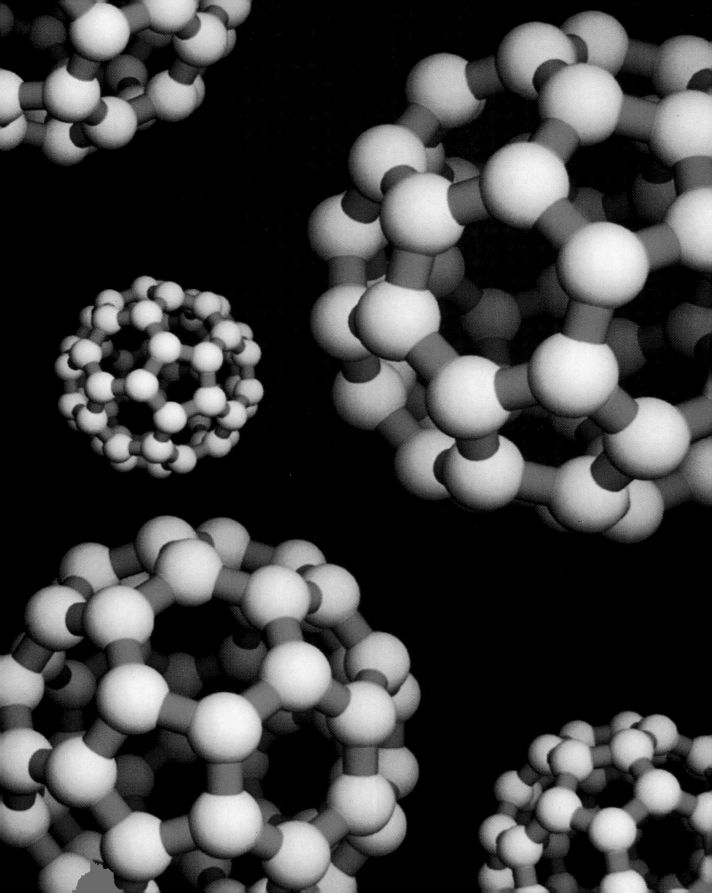

CHAPTER 8

Bonding: General Concepts

As we examine the world around us, we find it to be composed almost entirely of compounds and mixtures of compounds: Rocks, coal, soil, petroleum, trees, and human bodies are all complex mixtures of chemical compounds in which different kinds of atoms are bound together. Substances composed of unbound atoms do exist in nature, but they are very rare. Examples are the argon in the atmosphere and the helium mixed with natural gas reserves.

The manner in which atoms are bound together has a profound effect on chemical and physical properties. For example, graphite is a soft, slippery material used as a lubricant in locks, and diamond is one of the hardest materials known, valuable both as a gemstone and in industrial cutting tools. Why do these materials, both composed solely of carbon atoms, have such different properties? The answer, as we will see, lies in the bonding in these substances.

Silicon and carbon are next to each other in Group 4A of the periodic table. From our knowledge of periodic trends, we might expect SiO_2 and CO_2 to be very similar. But SiO_2 is the empirical formula of silica, which is found in sand and quartz, and carbon dioxide is a gas, a product of respiration. Why are they so different? We will be able to answer this question after we have developed models for bonding.

Molecular bonding and structure play the central role in determining the course of all chemical reactions, many of which are vital to our survival. Later in this book we will demonstrate their importance by showing how enzymes facilitate complex chemical reactions, how genetic characteristics are transferred, and how hemoglobin in the blood carries oxygen throughout the body. All of these fundamental biological reactions hinge on the geometric structures of molecules, sometimes depending on very subtle differences in molecular shape to channel the chemical reaction one way rather than another.

Many of the world's current problems require fundamentally chemical answers: disease and pollution control, the search for new energy sources, the development of new fertilizers to increase crop yields, the improvement

Contents

Carbon forms very stable spherical C_{60} molecules.

(left) Quartz grows in beautiful, regular crystals. (right) Graphite and diamond.

of the protein content in various staple grains, and many more. To understand the behavior of natural materials, we must understand the nature of chemical bonding and the factors that control the structures of compounds. In this chapter we will present various classes of compounds that illustrate the different types of bonds and then develop models to describe the structure and bonding that characterize materials found in nature. Later these models will be useful in understanding chemical reactions.

8.1   Types of Chemical Bonds

What is a chemical bond? There is no simple and yet complete answer to this question. In Chapter 2 we defined bonds as forces that hold groups of atoms together and make them function as a unit.

There are many types of experiments we can perform to determine the fundamental nature of materials. For example, we can study physical properties such as melting point, hardness, and electrical and thermal conductivity. We can also study solubility characteristics and the properties of the resulting solutions. To determine the charge distribution in a molecule, we can study its behavior in an electric field. We can obtain information about the strength of a bonding interaction by measuring the **bond energy,** which is the energy required to break the bond.

There are several ways in which atoms can interact with one another to form aggregates. We will consider several specific examples to illustrate the various types of chemical bonds.

Earlier, we saw that when solid sodium chloride is dissolved in water, the resulting solution conducts electricity, a fact that helps to convince us that sodium chloride is composed of Na^+ and Cl^- ions. Therefore, when sodium and chlorine react to form sodium chloride, electrons are transferred from the sodium atoms to the chlorine atoms to form Na^+ and Cl^- ions, which then aggregate to form solid sodium chloride. Why does this happen? The best simple answer is that *the system can achieve the lowest possible energy by behaving in this way.* The attraction of a chlorine atom for the extra electron and the very strong mutual attractions of the oppositely charged ions provide the driving forces for the process. The resulting solid sodium chloride is a very sturdy material; it has a melting point of approximately 800°C. The bonding forces that produce this great thermal stability result from the electrostatic attractions of the closely packed, oppositely charged ions. This is an example of **ionic bonding.** Ionic substances are formed when an atom that loses electrons relatively easily reacts with an atom that has a high affinity for electrons. That is, an **ionic compound** results when a metal reacts with a nonmetal.

The energy of interaction between a pair of ions can be calculated using **Coulomb's law** in the form

$$E = 2.31 \times 10^{-19} \text{ J} \cdot \text{nm} \left(\frac{Q_1 Q_2}{r} \right)$$

where E has units of joules, r is the distance between the ion centers in nanometers, and Q_1 and Q_2 are the numerical ion charges.

For example, in solid sodium chloride the distance between the centers of the Na^+ and Cl^- ions is 2.76 Å (0.276 nm), and the ionic energy per pair of ions is

$$E = 2.31 \times 10^{-19} \text{ J} \cdot \text{nm} \left[\frac{(+1)(-1)}{0.276 \text{ nm}} \right] = -8.37 \times 10^{-19} \text{ J}$$

where the negative sign indicates an attractive force. That is, the *ion pair has lower energy than the separated ions.*

Coulomb's law also can be used to calculate the repulsive energy when two like-charged ions are brought together. In this case the calculated value of the energy will have a positive sign.

We have seen that a bonding force develops when two different types of atoms react to form oppositely charged ions. But how does a bonding force develop between two identical atoms? Let's explore this situation from a very simple point of view by considering the energy terms that result when two hydrogen atoms are brought close together, as shown in Fig. 8.1(a). When hydrogen atoms are brought close together, there are two unfavorable potential energy terms, proton–proton repulsion and electron–electron repulsion, and one favorable term, proton–electron attraction. Under what conditions will the H_2 molecule be favored over the separated hydrogen atoms? That is, what conditions will favor bond formation? The answer lies in the strong tendency in nature for any system to achieve the lowest possible energy. A bond will form (that is, the two hydrogen atoms will exist as a molecular unit) if the system can lower its total energy in the process.

In this case, then, the hydrogen atoms will position themselves so that the system will achieve the lowest possible energy; the system will act to minimize the sum of the positive (repulsive) energy terms and the negative (attractive) energy term. The distance where the energy is minimum is called the **bond length.** The total energy of this system as a function of distance between the hydrogen nuclei is shown in Fig. 8.1(b). Note several important features of this diagram:

> A bond will form if the energy of the aggregate is lower than that of the separated atoms.

The energy terms involved are the net potential energy that results from the attractions and repulsions among the charged particles and the kinetic energy due to the motions of the electrons.

> Potential energy was discussed in Chapter 6.

The zero point of energy is defined with the atoms at infinite separation.

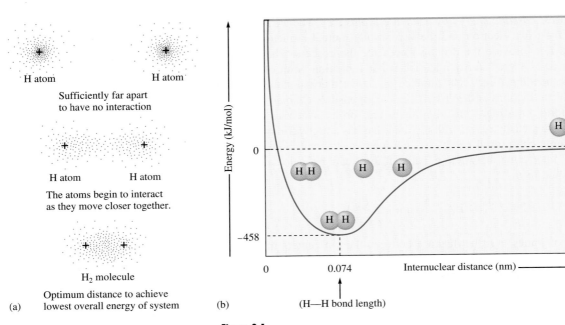

(a)

(b)

(H—H bond length)

Figure 8.1

(a) The interaction of two hydrogen atoms. (b) Energy profile as a function of the distance between the nuclei of the hydrogen atoms. As the atoms approach each other (right side of graph), the energy decreases until the distance reaches 0.074 nm (0.74 Å) and then begins to increase again due to repulsions.

At very short distances the energy rises steeply because of the importance of the repulsive forces when the atoms are very close together.

The bond length is the distance at which the system has minimum energy.

In the H_2 molecule, the electrons reside primarily in the space between the two nuclei, where they are attracted simultaneously by both protons. This positioning is precisely what leads to the stability of the H_2 molecule compared with two separated hydrogen atoms. The potential energy of each electron is lowered because of the increased attractive forces in this area. When we say that a bond is formed between the hydrogen atoms, we mean that the H_2 molecule is more stable than two separated hydrogen atoms by a certain quantity of energy (the bond energy).

We can also think of a bond in terms of forces. The simultaneous attraction of each electron by the protons generates a force that pulls the protons toward each other and that just balances the proton–proton and electron–electron repulsive forces at the distance corresponding to the bond length.

The type of bonding we encounter in the hydrogen molecule and in many other molecules in which *electrons are shared by nuclei* is called **covalent bonding.**

So far we have considered two extreme types of bonding. In ionic bonding the participating atoms are so different that one or more electrons are transferred to form oppositely charged ions, which then attract each other. In covalent bonding two identical atoms share electrons equally. The bonding results from the mutual attraction of the two nuclei for the shared electrons. Between these extremes are intermediate cases in which the atoms are not so different that electrons are completely trans-

Ionic and covalent bonds are the extreme bond types.

 Molecular Models: NaCl, H_2, HF

ferred but are different enough that unequal sharing results, forming what is called a **polar covalent bond.** An example of this type of bond occurs in the hydrogen fluoride (HF) molecule. When a sample of hydrogen fluoride gas is placed in an electric field, the molecules tend to orient themselves as shown in Fig. 8.2, with the fluoride end closest to the positive pole and the hydrogen end closest to the negative pole. This result implies that the HF molecule has the following charge distribution:

H—F

$\delta+$ $\delta-$

where δ (lowercase delta) is used to indicate a fractional charge. This same effect was noted in Chapter 4, where many of water's unusual properties were attributed to the polar O—H bonds in the H_2O molecule.

The most logical explanation for the development of the partial positive and negative charges on the atoms (bond polarity) in such molecules as HF and H_2O is that the electrons in the bonds are not shared equally. For example, we can account for the polarity of the HF molecule by assuming that the fluorine atom has a stronger attraction for the shared electrons than the hydrogen atom. Likewise, in the H_2O molecule the oxygen atom appears to attract the shared electrons more strongly than the hydrogen atoms do. Because bond polarity has important chemical implications, we find it useful to quantify the ability of an atom to attract shared electrons. In the next section we show how this is done.

8.2 Electronegativity

The different affinities of atoms for the electrons in a bond are described by a property called **electronegativity:** *the ability of an atom in a molecule to attract shared electrons to itself.*

The most widely accepted method for determining values of electronegativity is that of Linus Pauling (1901–1995), an American scientist who won the Nobel Prizes for both chemistry and peace. To understand Pauling's model, consider a hypothetical molecule HX. The relative electronegativities of the H and X atoms are determined by comparing the measured H—X bond energy with the "expected" H—X bond energy, which is an average of the H—H and X—X bond energies:

$$\text{Expected H—X bond energy} = \frac{\text{H—H bond energy} + \text{X—X bond energy}}{2}$$

The difference (Δ) between the actual (measured) and expected bond energies is

$$\Delta = (\text{H—X})_{\text{act}} - (\text{H—X})_{\text{exp}}$$

If H and X have identical electronegativities, $(\text{H—X})_{\text{act}}$ and $(\text{H—X})_{\text{exp}}$ are the same, and Δ is 0. On the other hand, if X has a greater electronegativity than H, the shared electron(s) will tend to be closer to the X atom. The molecule will be polar, with the following charge distribution:

H—X

$\delta+$ $\delta-$

Note that this bond can be viewed as having an ionic as well as a covalent component. The attraction between the partially (and oppositely) charged H and X atoms

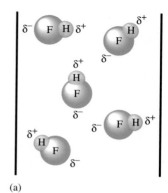

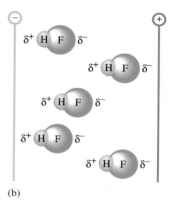

Figure 8.2
The effect of an electric field on hydrogen fluoride molecules. (a) When no electric field is present, the molecules are randomly oriented. (b) When the field is turned on, the molecules tend to line up with their negative ends toward the positive pole and their positive ends toward the negative pole.

Increasing electronegativity →

Decreasing electronegativity →

																H 2.1	
Li 1.0	Be 1.5											B 2.0	C 2.5	N 3.0	O 3.5	F 4.0
Na 0.9	Mg 1.2											Al 1.5	Si 1.8	P 2.1	S 2.5	Cl 3.0
K 0.8	Ca 1.0	Sc 1.3	Ti 1.5	V 1.6	Cr 1.6	Mn 1.5	Fe 1.8	Co 1.9	Ni 1.9	Cu 1.9	Zn 1.6	Ga 1.6	Ge 1.8	As 2.0	Se 2.4	Br 2.8
Rb 0.8	Sr 1.0	Y 1.2	Zr 1.4	Nb 1.6	Mo 1.8	Tc 1.9	Ru 2.2	Rh 2.2	Pd 2.2	Ag 1.9	Cd 1.7	In 1.7	Sn 1.8	Sb 1.9	Te 2.1	I 2.5
Cs 0.7	Ba 0.9	La–Lu 1.0–1.2	Hf 1.3	Ta 1.5	W 1.7	Re 1.9	Os 2.2	Ir 2.2	Pt 2.2	Au 2.4	Hg 1.9	Tl 1.8	Pb 1.9	Bi 1.9	Po 2.0	At 2.2
Fr 0.7	Ra 0.9	Ac 1.1	Th 1.3	Pa 1.4	U 1.4	Np–No 1.4–1.3										

Figure 8.3
The Pauling electronegativity values. Electronegativity generally increases across a period and decreases down a group.

will lead to a greater bond strength. Thus $(H—X)_{act}$ will be larger than $(H—X)_{exp}$. The greater the difference in the electronegativities of the atoms, the greater is the ionic component of the bond and the greater is the value of Δ. Thus the relative electronegativities of H and X can be assigned from the Δ values.

Electronegativity values have been determined by this process for virtually all the elements; the results are given in Fig. 8.3. Note that electronegativity generally increases going from left to right across a period and decreases going down a group for the representative elements. The range of electronegativity values is from 4.0 for fluorine to 0.7 for cesium.

The relationship between electronegativity and bond type is shown in Table 8.1. For identical atoms (an electronegativity difference of zero), the electrons in the bond are shared equally, and no polarity develops. When two atoms with very dif-

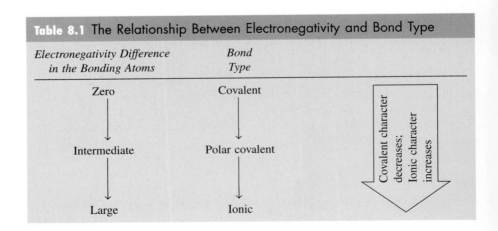

Table 8.1 The Relationship Between Electronegativity and Bond Type

Electronegativity Difference in the Bonding Atoms	*Bond Type*	
Zero	Covalent	Covalent character decreases; Ionic character increases
↓	↓	
Intermediate	Polar covalent	
↓	↓	
Large	Ionic	

ferent electronegativities interact, electron transfer can occur to form the ions that make up an ionic substance. Intermediate cases give polar covalent bonds with unequal electron sharing.

Sample Exercise 8.1 *Relative Bond Polarities*

Order the following bonds according to polarity: H—H, O—H, Cl—H, S—H, and F—H.

Solution

The polarity of the bond increases as the difference in electronegativity increases. From the electronegativity values in Fig. 8.3, the following variation in bond polarity is expected (the electronegativity value appears in parentheses below each element):

$$H—H < S—H < Cl—H < O—H < F—H$$
(2.1)(2.1) (2.5)(2.1)   (3.0)(2.1)   (3.5)(2.1)   (4.0)(2.1)

Electronegativity
difference   0   0.4   0.9   1.4   1.9

Covalent bond ─────────→ Polar covalent bond
Polarity increases

See Exercises 8.25 and 8.26.

8.3 *Bond Polarity and Dipole Moments*

We have seen that when hydrogen fluoride is placed in an electric field, the molecules have a preferential orientation (see Fig. 8.2). This follows from the charge distribution in the HF molecule, which has a positive end and a negative end. A molecule such as HF that has a center of positive charge and a center of negative charge is said to be **dipolar,** or to have a **dipole moment.** The dipolar character of a molecule is often represented by an arrow pointing to the negative charge center with the tail of the arrow indicating the positive center of charge:

$\delta+$ $\delta-$

Of course, any diatomic (two-atom) molecule that has a polar bond also will show a molecular dipole moment. Polyatomic molecules also can exhibit dipolar behavior. For example, because the oxygen atom in the water molecule has a greater electronegativity than the hydrogen atoms, the molecular charge distribution is that shown in Fig. 8.4(a). Because of this charge distribution, the water molecule behaves in an electric field as if it had two centers of charge—one positive and one negative—as shown in Fig. 8.4(b). The water molecule has a dipole moment. The

Molecular Models: H_2O, NH_3

Figure 8.4

(a) The charge distribution in the water molecule. (b) The water molecule in an electric field.

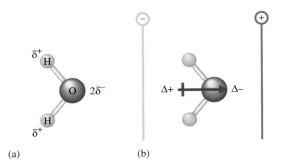

(a)   (b)

same type of behavior is observed for the NH_3 molecule (Fig. 8.5). Some molecules have polar bonds but do not have a dipole moment. This occurs when the individual bond polarities are arranged in such a way that they cancel each other out. An example is the CO_2 molecule, which is a linear molecule that has the charge distribution shown in Fig. 8.6. In this case the opposing bond polarities cancel out, and the carbon dioxide molecule does not have a dipole moment. There is no preferential way for this molecule to line up in an electric field. (Try to find a preferred orientation to make sure you understand this concept.)

There are many cases besides that of carbon dioxide where the bond polarities oppose and exactly cancel each other. Some common types of molecules with polar bonds but no dipole moment are shown in Table 8.2.

Molecular Models: CO_2, SO_3, CCl_4

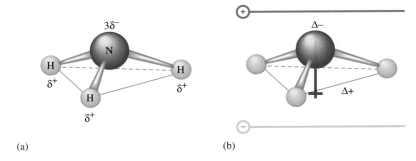

(a)   (b)

Figure 8.5

(a) The structure and charge distribution of the ammonia molecule. The polarity of the N—H bonds occurs because nitrogen has a greater electronegativity than hydrogen. (b) The dipole moment of the ammonia molecule oriented in an electric field.

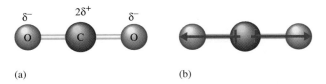

(a)   (b)

Figure 8.6

(a) The carbon dioxide molecule. (b) The opposed bond polarities cancel out, and the carbon dioxide molecule has no dipole moment.

Table 8.2 Types of Molecules with Polar Bonds but No Resulting Dipole Moment

Type		Cancellation of Polar Bonds	Example	Ball-and-Stick Model
Linear molecules with two identical bonds	B—A—B	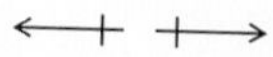 ←—+—+—→	CO_2	
Planar molecules with three identical bonds 120 degrees apart	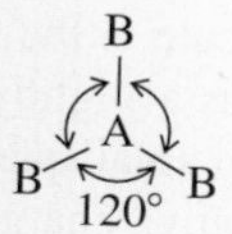 B B—A—B 120°	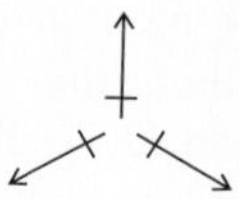	SO_3	
Tetrahedral molecules with four identical bonds 109.5 degrees apart	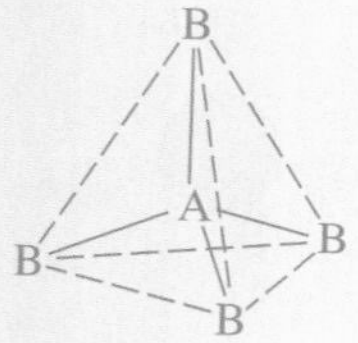 B⋯A⋯B	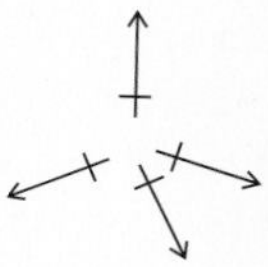	CCl_4	

Sample Exercise 8.2 *Bond Polarity and Dipole Moment*

For each of the following molecules, show the direction of the bond polarities and indicate which ones have a dipole moment: HCl, Cl_2, SO_3 (a planar molecule with the oxygen atoms spaced evenly around the central sulfur atom), CH_4 [tetrahedral (see Table 8.2) with the carbon atom at the center], and H_2S (V-shaped with the sulfur atom at the point).

Molecular Models: HCl, Cl_2, SO_3, H_2S

Solution

The HCl molecule: In Fig. 8.3, we see that the electronegativity of chlorine (3.0) is greater than that of hydrogen (2.1). Thus the chlorine will be partially negative, and the hydrogen will be partially positive. The HCl molecule has a dipole moment:

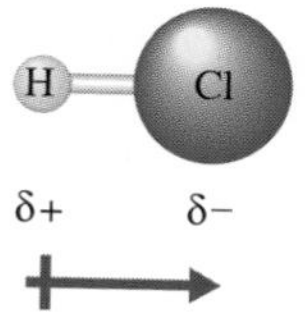

$\delta+$ $\delta-$

The Cl_2 molecule: The two chlorine atoms share the electrons equally. No bond polarity occurs, and the Cl_2 molecule has no dipole moment.

The SO_3 molecule: The electronegativity of oxygen (3.5) is greater than that of sulfur (2.5). This means that each oxygen will have a partial negative charge, and the sulfur will have a partial positive charge:

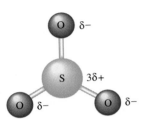

The presence of polar bonds does not always yield a polar molecule.

The bond polarities arranged symmetrically as shown cancel, and the molecule has no dipole moment. This molecule is the second type shown in Table 8.2.

    The CH₄ molecule: Carbon has a slightly higher electronegativity (2.5) than does hydrogen (2.1). This leads to small partial positive charges on the hydrogen atoms and a small partial negative charge on the carbon:

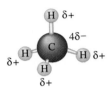

This case is similar to the third type in Table 8.2, and the bond polarities cancel. The molecule has no dipole moment.

    The H₂S molecule: Since the electronegativity of sulfur (2.5) is slightly greater than that of hydrogen (2.1), the sulfur will have a partial negative charge, and the hydrogen atoms will have a partial positive charge, which can be represented as

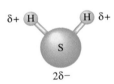

This case is analogous to the water molecule, and the polar bonds result in a dipole moment oriented as shown:

See Question 8.17.

8.4   *Ions: Electron Configurations and Sizes*

Atoms in stable compounds usually have a noble gas electron configuration.

The description of the electron arrangements in atoms that emerged from the quantum mechanical model has helped a great deal in our understanding of what constitutes a stable compound. In virtually every case the atoms in a stable compound have a noble gas arrangement of electrons. Nonmetallic elements achieve a noble gas electron configuration either by sharing electrons with other nonmetals to form covalent bonds or by taking electrons from metals to form ions. In the second case, the nonmetals form anions, and the metals form cations. The generalizations that apply to electron configurations in stable compounds are as follows:

- When *two nonmetals* react to form a covalent bond, they share electrons in a way that completes the valence electron configurations of both atoms. That is, both nonmetals attain noble gas electron configurations.

- When *a nonmetal and a representative-group metal* react to form a binary ionic compound, the ions form so that the valence electron configuration of the non-metal achieves the electron configuration of the next noble gas atom and the va-lence orbitals of the metal are emptied. In this way both ions achieve noble gas electron configurations.

These generalizations apply to the vast majority of compounds and are impor-tant to remember. We will deal with covalent bonds more thoroughly later, but now we will consider what implications these rules hold for ionic compounds.

Predicting Formulas of Ionic Compounds

At the beginning of this discussion it should be emphasized that when chemists use the term *ionic compound,* they are usually referring to the solid state of that compound. In the solid state the ions are close together. That is, solid ionic com-pounds contain a large collection of positive and negative ions packed together in a way that minimizes the $\ominus\cdot\cdot\ominus$ and $\oplus\cdot\cdot\oplus$ repulsions and maximizes the $\oplus\cdot\cdot\ominus$ attractions. This situation stands in contrast to the gas phase of an ionic substance, where the ions are quite far apart on average. In the gas phase, a pair of ions may get close enough to interact, but large collections of ions do not ex-ist. Thus, when we speak in this text of the stability of an ionic compound, we are referring to the solid state, where the large attractive forces present among oppo-sitely charged ions tend to stabilize (favor the formation of) the ions. For example, as we mentioned in the preceding chapter, the O^{2-} ion is not stable as an isolated, gas-phase species but, of course, is very stable in many solid ionic compounds. That is, $MgO(s)$, which contains Mg^{2+} and O^{2-} ions, is very stable, but the iso-lated, gas-phase ion pair $Mg^{2+}\cdot\cdot O^{2-}$ is not energetically favorable in comparison with the separate neutral gaseous atoms. Thus you should keep in mind that in this section, and in most other cases where we are describing the nature of ionic com-pounds, the discussion usually refers to the solid state, where many ions are si-multaneously interacting.

To illustrate the principles of electron configurations in stable, solid ionic com-pounds, we will consider the formation of an ionic compound from calcium and oxygen. We can predict what compound will form by considering the valence elec-tron configurations of the two atoms:

$$Ca:\quad [Ar]4s^2$$
$$O:\quad [He]2s^22p^4$$

From Fig. 8.3 we see that the electronegativity of oxygen (3.5) is much greater than that of calcium (1.0). Because of this large difference, electrons will be transferred from calcium to oxygen to form oxygen anions and calcium cations in the

In the solid state of an ionic com-pound the ions are relatively close to-gether, and many ions are simultane-ously interacting:

In the gas phase of an ionic sub-stance the ions would be relatively far apart and would not contain large groups of ions:

Exploration: Formation of Ionic Com-pounds from Ions

compound. How many electrons are transferred? We can base our prediction on the observation that noble gas configurations are generally the most stable. Note that oxygen needs two electrons to fill its $2s$ and $2p$ valence orbitals and to achieve the configuration of neon ($1s^2 2s^2 2p^6$). And by losing two electrons, calcium can achieve the configuration of argon. Two electrons are therefore transferred:

$$Ca + O \longrightarrow Ca^{2+} + O^{2-}$$
$$2e^-$$

To predict the formula of the ionic compound, we simply recognize that chemical compounds are always electrically neutral—they have the same quantities of positive and negative charges. In this case we have equal numbers of Ca^{2+} and O^{2-} ions, and the empirical formula of the compound is CaO.

The same principles can be applied to many other cases. For example, consider the compound formed between aluminum and oxygen. Because aluminum has the configuration $[Ne]3s^2 3p^1$, it loses three electrons to form the Al^{3+} ion and thus achieves the neon configuration. Therefore, the Al^{3+} and O^{2-} ions form in this case. Since the compound must be electrically neutral, there must be three O^{2-} ions for every two Al^{3+} ions, and the compound has the empirical formula Al_2O_3.

Table 8.3 shows common elements that form ions with noble gas electron configurations in ionic compounds. In losing electrons to form cations, metals in Group 1A lose one electron, those in Group 2A lose two electrons, and those in Group 3A lose three electrons. In gaining electrons to form anions, nonmetals in Group 7A (the halogens) gain one electron, and those in Group 6A gain two electrons. Hydrogen typically behaves as a nonmetal and can gain one electron to form the hydride ion (H^-), which has the electron configuration of helium.

There are some important exceptions to the rules discussed here. For example, tin forms both Sn^{2+} and Sn^{4+} ions, and lead forms both Pb^{2+} and Pb^{4+} ions. Also, bismuth forms Bi^{3+} and Bi^{5+} ions, and thallium forms Tl^+ and Tl^{3+} ions. There are no simple explanations for the behavior of these ions. For now, just note them as exceptions to the very useful rule that ions generally adopt noble gas electron configurations in ionic compounds. Our discussion here refers to representative met-

A bauxite mine. Bauxite contains Al_2O_3, the main source of aluminum.

Table 8.3 Common Ions with Noble Gas Configurations in Ionic Compounds

Group 1A	Group 2A	Group 3A	Group 6A	Group 7A	Electron Configuration
H^-, Li^+	Be^{2+}				[He]
Na^+	Mg^{2+}	Al^{3+}	O^{2-}	F^-	[Ne]
K^+	Ca^{2+}		S^{2-}	Cl^-	[Ar]
Rb^+	Sr^{2+}		Se^{2-}	Br^-	[Kr]
Cs^+	Ba^{2+}		Te^{2-}	I^-	[Xe]

als. The transition metals exhibit more complicated behavior, forming a variety of ions that will be considered in Chapter 20.

Sizes of Ions

Ion size plays an important role in determining the structure and stability of ionic solids, the properties of ions in aqueous solution, and the biologic effects of ions. As with atoms, it is impossible to define precisely the sizes of ions. Most often, ionic radii are determined from the measured distances between ion centers in ionic compounds. This method, of course, involves an assumption about how the distance should be divided up between the two ions. Thus you will note considerable disagreement among ionic sizes given in various sources. Here we are mainly interested in trends and will be less concerned with absolute ion sizes.

Various factors influence ionic size. We will first consider the relative sizes of an ion and its parent atom. Since a positive ion is formed by removing one or more electrons from a neutral atom, the resulting cation is smaller than its parent atom. The opposite is true for negative ions; the addition of electrons to a neutral atom produces an anion significantly larger than its parent atom.

It is also important to know how the sizes of ions vary depending on the positions of the parent elements in the periodic table. Figure 8.7 shows the sizes of the most important ions (each with a noble gas configuration) and their position in the periodic table. Note that ion size increases down a group. The changes that occur horizontally are complicated because of the change from predominantly metals on the left-hand side of the periodic table to nonmetals on the right-hand side. A given period thus contains both elements that give up electrons to form cations and ones that accept electrons to form anions.

One trend worth noting involves the relative sizes of a set of **isoelectronic ions**— *ions containing the same number of electrons.* Consider the ions O^{2-}, F^-, Na^+, Mg^{2+}, and Al^{3+}. Each of these ions has the neon electron configuration. How do the sizes of these ions vary? In general, there are two important facts to consider in predicting the relative sizes of ions: the number of electrons and the number of protons. Since these ions are isoelectronic, the number of electrons is 10 in each case. Electron repulsions therefore should be about the same in all cases. However, the number of protons increases from 8 to 13 as we go from the O^{2-} ion to the Al^{3+} ion. Thus, in going from O^{2-} to Al^{3+}, the 10 electrons experience a greater attraction as the positive charge on the nucleus increases. This causes the ions to become smaller. You can confirm this by looking at Fig. 8.7. In general, for a series of isoelectronic ions, the size decreases as the nuclear charge Z increases.

For isoelectronic ions, size decreases as Z increases.

Figure 8.7

Sizes of ions related to positions of the elements in the periodic table. Note that size generally increases down a group. Also note that in a series of isoelectronic ions, size decreases with increasing atomic number. The ionic radii are given in units of picometers.

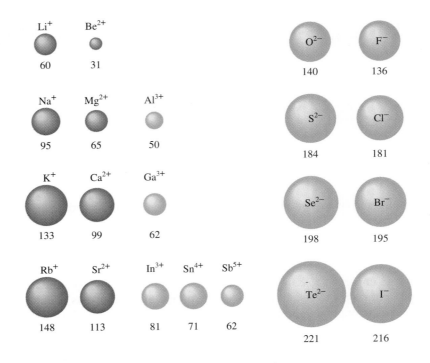

Sample Exercise 8.3 *Relative Ion Size I*

Arrange the ions Se^{2-}, Br^-, Rb^+, and Sr^{2+} in order of decreasing size.

Solution

This is an isoelectronic series of ions with the krypton electron configuration. Since these ions all have the same number of electrons, their sizes will depend on the nuclear charge. The Z values are 34 for Se^{2-}, 35 for Br^-, 37 for Rb^+, and 38 for Sr^{2+}. Since the nuclear charge is greatest for Sr^{2+}, it is the smallest of these ions. The Se^{2-} ion is largest:

$$Se^{2-} > Br^- > Rb^+ > Sr^{2+}$$

$$\underset{\text{Largest}}{\uparrow} \qquad\qquad\qquad \underset{\text{Smallest}}{\uparrow}$$

See Exercises 8.33 and 8.34.

Sample Exercise 8.4 *Relative Ion Size II*

Choose the largest ion in each of the following groups.

a. Li^+, Na^+, K^+, Rb^+, Cs^+

b. Ba^{2+}, Cs^+, I^-, Te^{2-}

Solution

a. The ions are all from Group 1A elements. Since size increases down a group (the ion with the greatest number of electrons is largest), Cs^+ is the largest ion.

b. This is an isoelectronic series of ions, all of which have the xenon electron configuration. The ion with the smallest nuclear charge is largest:

$$Te^{2-} > I^- > Cs^+ > Ba^{2+}$$
$$Z = 52 \quad Z = 53 \quad Z = 55 \quad Z = 56$$

See Exercises 8.35 and 8.36.

8.5 Formation of Binary Ionic Compounds

In this section we will introduce the factors that influence the stability and the structures of solid binary ionic compounds. We know that metals and nonmetals react by transferring electrons to form cations and anions that are mutually attractive. The resulting ionic solid forms because the aggregated oppositely charged ions have a lower energy than the original elements. Just how strongly the ions attract each other in the solid state is indicated by the **lattice energy**—*the change in energy that takes place when separated gaseous ions are packed together to form an ionic solid:*

$$M^+(g) + X^-(g) \longrightarrow MX(s)$$

The lattice energy is often defined as the energy *released* when an ionic solid forms from its ions. However, in this book the sign of an energy term is always determined from the system's point of view: negative if the process is exothermic, positive if endothermic. Thus, using this convention, the lattice energy has a negative sign.

The structures of ionic solids will be discussed in detail in Chapter 10.

We can illustrate the energy changes involved in the formation of an ionic solid by considering the formation of solid lithium fluoride from its elements:

$$Li(s) + \tfrac{1}{2}F_2(g) \longrightarrow LiF(s)$$

To see the energy terms associated with this process, we take advantage of the fact that energy is a state function and break this reaction into steps, the sum of which gives the overall reaction.

STEP 1

Sublimation of solid lithium. Sublimation involves taking a substance from the solid state to the gaseous state:

$$Li(s) \longrightarrow Li(g)$$

The enthalpy of sublimation for $Li(s)$ is 161 kJ/mol.

STEP 2

Ionization of lithium atoms to form Li^+ ions in the gas phase:

$$Li(g) \longrightarrow Li^+(g) + e^-$$

Lithium fluoride.

This process corresponds to the first ionization energy for lithium, which is 520 kJ/mol.

STEP 3

Dissociation of fluorine molecules. We need to form a mole of fluorine atoms by breaking the F—F bonds in a half mole of F_2 molecules:

$$\tfrac{1}{2}F_2(g) \longrightarrow F(g)$$

The energy required to break this bond is 154 kJ/mol. In this case we are breaking the bonds in a half mole of fluorine, so the energy required for this step is (154 kJ)/2, or 77 kJ.

STEP 4

Formation of F^- ions from fluorine atoms in the gas phase:

$$F(g) + e^- \longrightarrow F^-(g)$$

The energy change for this process corresponds to the electron affinity of fluorine, which is -328 kJ/mol.

STEP 5

Formation of solid lithium fluoride from the gaseous Li^+ and F^- ions:

$$Li^+(g) + F^-(g) \longrightarrow LiF(s)$$

This corresponds to the lattice energy for LiF, which is -1047 kJ/mol.

Since the sum of these five processes yields the desired overall reaction, the sum of the individual energy changes gives the overall energy change:

	Process	Energy Change (kJ)
	$Li(s) \rightarrow Li(g)$	161
	$Li(g) \rightarrow Li^+(g) + e^-$	520
	$\tfrac{1}{2}F_2(g) \rightarrow F(g)$	77
	$F(g) + e^- \rightarrow F^-(g)$	-328
	$Li^+(g) + F^-(g) \rightarrow LiF(s)$	-1047
Overall:	$Li(s) + \tfrac{1}{2}F_2(g) \rightarrow LiF(s)$	-617 kJ (per mole of LiF)

In doing this calculation, we have ignored the small difference between ΔH_{sub} and ΔE_{sub}.

This process is summarized by the energy diagram in Fig. 8.8. Note that the formation of solid lithium fluoride from its elements is highly exothermic, mainly because of the very large negative lattice energy. A great deal of energy is released when the ions combine to form the solid. In fact, note that the energy released when an electron is added to a fluorine atom to form the F^- ion (328 kJ/mol) is not enough to remove an electron from lithium (520 kJ/mol). That is, when a metallic lithium atom reacts with a nonmetallic fluorine atom to form *separated* ions:

$$Li(g) + F(g) \longrightarrow Li^+(g) + F^-(g)$$

the process is endothermic and thus unfavorable. Clearly, then, the main impetus for the formation of an ionic compound rather than a covalent compound results

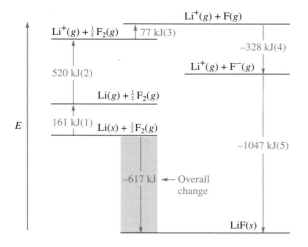

E

Li$^+$(g) + F(g)

Li$^+$(g) + $\frac{1}{2}$F$_2$(g) ↑ 77 kJ(3)

−328 kJ(4)

520 kJ(2)

Li$^+$(g) + F$^-$(g)

Li(g) + $\frac{1}{2}$F$_2$(g)

161 kJ(1) Li(s) + $\frac{1}{2}$F$_2$(g)

−1047 kJ(5)

−617 kJ ← Overall change

LiF(s)

Figure 8.8

The energy changes involved in the formation of solid lithium fluoride from its elements. The numbers in parentheses refer to the reaction steps discussed in the text.

from the strong mutual attractions among the Li$^+$ and F$^-$ ions in the solid. The lattice energy is the dominant energy term.

The structure of solid lithium fluoride is represented in Fig. 8.9. Note the alternating arrangement of the Li$^+$ and F$^-$ ions. Also note that each Li$^+$ is surrounded by six F$^-$ ions, and each F$^-$ ion is surrounded by six Li$^+$ ions. This structure can be rationalized by assuming that the ions behave as hard spheres that pack together in a way that both maximizes the attractions among the oppositely charged ions and minimizes the repulsions among the identically charged ions.

All the binary ionic compounds formed by an alkali metal and a halogen have the structure shown in Fig. 8.9, except for the cesium salts. The arrangement of ions shown in Fig. 8.9 is often called the *sodium chloride structure*, after the most common substance that possesses it.

Lattice Energy Calculations

In discussing the energetics of the formation of solid lithium fluoride, we emphasized the importance of lattice energy in contributing to the stability of the ionic solid. Lattice energy can be represented by a modified form of Coulomb's law:

$$\text{Lattice energy} = k\left(\frac{Q_1 Q_2}{r}\right)$$

where k is a proportionality constant that depends on the structure of the solid and the electron configurations of the ions, Q_1 and Q_2 are the charges on the ions, and r is the shortest distance between the centers of the cations and anions. Note that the lattice energy has a negative sign when Q_1 and Q_2 have opposite signs. This result is expected, since bringing cations and anions together is an exothermic process. Also note that the process becomes more exothermic as the ionic charges increase and as the distances between the ions in the solid decrease.

The importance of the charges in ionic solids can be illustrated by comparing the energies involved in the formation of NaF(s) and MgO(s). These solids contain the isoelectronic ions Na$^+$, F$^-$, Mg^{2+}, and O^{2-}. The energy diagram for the formation of the two solids is given in Fig. 8.10. Note several important features:

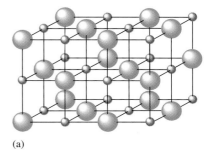

(a)

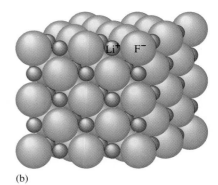

Li$^+$ F$^-$

(b)

Figure 8.9

The structure of lithium fluoride. (a) Represented by ball-and-stick model. Note that each Li$^+$ ion is surrounded by six F$^-$ ions, and each F$^-$ ion is surrounded by six Li$^+$ ions. (b) Represented with the ions shown as spheres. The structure is determined by packing the spherical ions in a way that both maximizes the ionic attractions and minimizes the ionic repulsions.

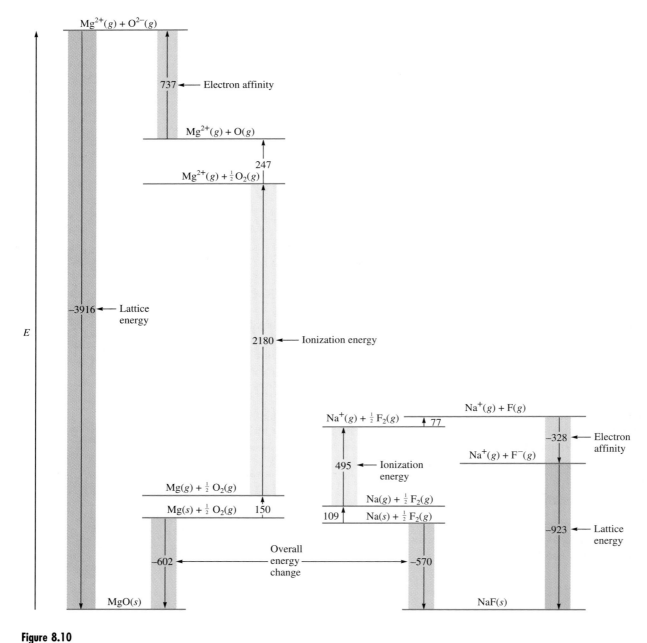

Figure 8.10

Comparison of the energy changes involved in the formation of solid sodium fluoride and solid magnesium oxide. Note the large lattice energy for magnesium oxide (where doubly charged ions are combining) compared with that for sodium fluoride (where singly charged ions are combining).

The energy released when the gaseous Mg^{2+} and O^{2-} ions combine to form solid MgO is much greater (more than four times greater) than that released when the gaseous Na^+ and F^- ions combine to form solid NaF.

The energy required to remove two electrons from the magnesium atom (735 kJ/mol for the first and 1445 kJ/mol for the second, yielding a total of 2180 kJ/mol) is much greater than the energy required to remove one electron from a sodium atom (495 kJ/mol).

Energy (737 kJ/mol) is required to add two electrons to the oxygen atom in the gas phase. Addition of the first electron is exothermic (-141 kJ/mol), but addition of the second electron is quite endothermic (878 kJ/mol). This latter energy must be obtained indirectly, since the $O^{2-}(g)$ ion is not stable.

In view of the facts that twice as much energy is required to remove the second electron from magnesium as to remove the first and that addition of an electron to the gaseous O^- ion is quite endothermic, it seems puzzling that magnesium oxide contains Mg^{2+} and O^{2-} ions rather than Mg^+ and O^- ions. The answer lies in the lattice energy. Note that the lattice energy for combining gaseous Mg^{2+} and O^{2-} ions to form MgO(s) is 3000 kJ/mol more negative than that for combining gaseous Na^+ and F^- ions to form NaF(s). Thus the energy released in forming a solid containing Mg^{2+} and O^{2-} ions rather than Mg^+ and O^- ions more than compensates for the energies required for the processes that produce the Mg^{2+} and O^{2-} ions.

If there is so much lattice energy to be gained in going from singly charged to doubly charged ions in the case of magnesium oxide, why then does solid sodium fluoride contain Na^+ and F^- ions rather than Na^{2+} and F^{2-} ions? We can answer this question by recognizing that both Na^+ and F^- ions have the neon electron configuration. Removal of an electron from Na^+ requires an extremely large quantity of energy (4560 kJ/mol) because a $2p$ electron must be removed. Conversely, the addition of an electron to F^- would require use of the relatively high energy $3s$ orbital, which is also an unfavorable process. Thus we can say that for sodium fluoride the extra energy required to form the doubly charged ions is greater than the gain in lattice energy that would result.

This discussion of the energies involved in the formation of solid ionic compounds illustrates that a variety of factors operate to determine the composition and structure of these compounds. The most important of these factors involve the balancing of the energies required to form highly charged ions and the energy released when highly charged ions combine to form the solid.

Since the equation for lattice energy contains the product Q_1Q_2, the lattice energy for a solid with 2+ and 2− ions should be four times that for a solid with 1+ and 1− ions. That is,

$$\frac{(+2)(-2)}{(+1)(-1)} = 4$$

For MgO and NaF, the observed ratio of lattice energies (see Fig. 8.10) is

$$\frac{-3916 \text{ kJ}}{-923 \text{ kJ}} = 4.24$$

8.6 *Partial Ionic Character of Covalent Bonds*

Recall that when atoms with different electronegativities react to form molecules, the electrons are not shared equally. The possible result is a polar covalent bond or, in the case of a large electronegativity difference, a complete transfer of one or more electrons to form ions. The cases are summarized in Fig. 8.11.

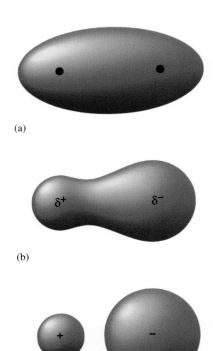

(a)

(b)

(c)

Figure 8.11

The three possible types of bonds: (a) a covalent bond formed between identical atoms; (b) a polar covalent bond, with both ionic and covalent components; and (c) an ionic bond with no electron sharing.

How well can we tell the difference between an ionic bond and a polar covalent bond? The only honest answer to this question is that there are probably no totally ionic bonds between *discrete pairs of atoms*. The evidence for this statement comes from calculations of the percent ionic character for the bonds of various binary compounds in the gas phase. These calculations are based on comparisons of the measured dipole moments for molecules of the type X—Y with the calculated dipole moments for the completely ionic case, X^+Y^-. The percent ionic character of a bond can be defined as

Percent ionic character of a bond =

$$\left(\frac{\text{measured dipole moment of X—Y}}{\text{calculated dipole moment of } X^+Y^-} \right) \times 100\%$$

Application of this definition to various compounds (in the gas phase) gives the results shown in Fig. 8.12, where percent ionic character is plotted versus the difference in the electronegativity values of X and Y. Note from this plot that ionic character increases with electronegativity difference, as expected. However, none of the bonds reaches 100% ionic character, even though compounds with the maximum possible electronegativity differences are considered. Thus, according to this definition, no individual bonds are completely ionic. This conclusion is in contrast to the usual classification of many of these compounds (as solids). All the compounds shown in Fig. 8.12 with more than 50% ionic character are normally considered to be ionic solids. Recall, however, the results in Fig. 8.12 are for the gas phase, where individual XY molecules exist. These results cannot necessarily be assumed to apply to the solid state, where the existence of ions is favored by the multiple ion interactions.

Another complication in identifying ionic compounds is that many substances contain polyatomic ions. For example, NH_4Cl contains NH_4^+ and Cl^- ions, and Na_2SO_4 contains Na^+ and SO_4^{2-} ions. The ammonium and sulfate ions are held together by covalent bonds. Thus, calling NH_4Cl and Na_2SO_4 ionic compounds is somewhat ambiguous.

We will avoid these problems by adopting an operational definition of ionic compounds: *Any compound that conducts an electric current when melted will be classified as ionic.*

Figure 8.12

The relationship between the ionic character of a covalent bond and the electronegativity difference of the bonded atoms.

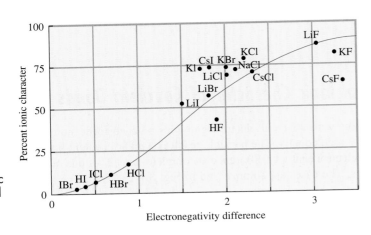

8.7 The Covalent Chemical Bond: A Model

Before we develop specific models for covalent chemical bonding, it will be helpful to summarize some of the concepts introduced in this chapter.

What is a chemical bond? Chemical bonds can be viewed as forces that cause a group of atoms to behave as a unit.

Why do chemical bonds occur? There is no principle of nature that states that bonds are favored or disfavored. Bonds are neither inherently "good" nor inherently "bad" as far as nature is concerned; *bonds result from the tendency of a system to seek its lowest possible energy.* From a simplistic point of view, bonds occur when collections of atoms are more stable (lower in energy) than the separate atoms. For example, approximately 1652 kJ of energy is required to break a mole of methane (CH_4) molecules into separate C and H atoms. Or, taking the opposite view, 1652 kJ of energy is released when 1 mole of methane is formed from 1 mole of gaseous C atoms and 4 moles of gaseous H atoms. Thus we can say that 1 mole of CH_4 molecules in the gas phase is 1652 kJ lower in energy than 1 mole of carbon atoms plus 4 moles of hydrogen atoms. Methane is therefore a stable molecule relative to its separated atoms.

We find it useful to interpret molecular stability in terms of a model called a *chemical bond.* To understand why this model was invented, let's continue with methane, which consists of four hydrogen atoms arranged at the corners of a tetrahedron around a carbon atom:

Given this structure, it is natural to envision four individual C—H interactions (we call them *bonds*). The energy of stabilization of CH_4 is divided equally among the four bonds to give an average C—H bond energy per mole of C—H bonds:

$$\frac{1652 \text{ kJ/mol}}{4} = 413 \text{ kJ/mol}$$

Next, consider methyl chloride, which consists of CH_3Cl molecules having the structure

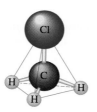

Experiments have shown that approximately 1578 kJ of energy is required to break down 1 mole of gaseous CH_3Cl molecules into gaseous carbon, chlorine, and hydrogen atoms. The reverse process can be represented as

$$C(g) + Cl(g) + 3H(g) \longrightarrow CH_3Cl(g) + 1578 \text{ kJ/mol}$$

Molecular Models: CH_4, CH_3Cl

A tetrahedron has four equal triangular faces.

Molten NaCl conducts an electric current, indicating the presence of mobile Na^+ and Cl^- ions.

A mole of gaseous methyl chloride is lower in energy by 1578 kJ than its separate gaseous atoms. Thus a mole of methyl chloride is held together by 1578 kJ of energy. Again, it is very useful to divide this energy into individual bonds. Methyl chloride can be visualized as containing one C—Cl bond and three C—H bonds. If we assume arbitrarily that a C—H interaction represents the same quantity of energy in any situation (that is, that the strength of a C—H bond is independent of its molecular environment), we can do the following bookkeeping:

$$1 \text{ mol C—Cl bonds plus 3 mol C—H bonds} = 1578 \text{ kJ}$$

$$\text{C—Cl bond energy} + 3(\text{average C—H bond energy}) = 1578 \text{ kJ}$$

$$\text{C—Cl bond energy} + 3(413 \text{ kJ/mol}) = 1578 \text{ kJ}$$

$$\text{C—Cl bond energy} = 1578 - 1239 = 339 \text{ kJ/mol}$$

These assumptions allow us to associate given quantities of energy with C—H and C—Cl bonds.

It is important to note that the bond concept is a human invention. Bonds provide a method for dividing up the energy evolved when a stable molecule is formed from its component atoms. Thus in this context a bond represents a quantity of energy obtained from the overall molecular energy of stabilization in a rather arbitrary way. This is not to say that the concept of individual bonds is a bad idea. In fact, the modern concept of the chemical bond, conceived by the American chemists G. N. Lewis and Linus Pauling, is one of the most useful ideas chemists have ever developed.

Models: An Overview

The framework of chemistry, like that of any science, consists of *models*—attempts to explain how nature operates on the microscopic level based on experiences in the macroscopic world. To understand chemistry, one must understand its models and how they are used. We will use the concept of bonding to reemphasize the important characteristics of models, including their origin, structure, and uses.

Models originate from our observations of the properties of nature. For example, the concept of bonds arose from the observations that most chemical processes involve collections of atoms and that chemical reactions involve rearrangements of the ways the atoms are grouped. Therefore, to understand reactions, we must understand the forces that bind atoms together.

In natural processes there is a tendency toward lower energy. Collections of atoms therefore occur because the aggregated state has lower energy than the separated atoms. Why? As we saw earlier in this chapter, the best explanations for the energy change involve atoms sharing electrons or atoms transferring electrons to become ions. In the case of electron sharing, we find it convenient to assume that individual bonds occur between pairs of atoms. Let's explore the validity of this assumption and see how it is useful.

In a diatomic molecule such as H_2, it is natural to assume that a bond exists between the atoms, holding them together. It is also useful to assume that individual bonds are present in polyatomic molecules such as CH_4. Therefore, instead of thinking of CH_4 as a unit with a stabilization energy of 1652 kJ per mole, we choose to think of CH_4 as containing four C—H bonds, each worth 413 kJ of energy per mole of bonds. Without this concept of individual bonds in molecules, chemistry would be hopelessly complicated. There are millions of different chem-

Bonding is a model proposed to explain molecular stability.

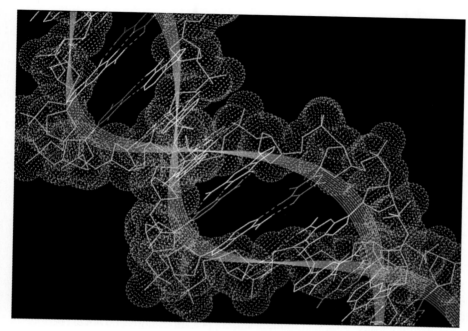

The concept of individual bonds makes it much easier to deal with complex molecules such as DNA. A small segment of a DNA molecule is shown here.

ical compounds, and if each of these compounds had to be considered as an entirely new entity, the task of understanding chemical behavior would be overwhelming.

The bonding model provides a framework to systematize chemical behavior by enabling us to think of molecules as collections of common fundamental components. For example, a typical biomolecule, such as a protein, contains hundreds of atoms and might seem discouragingly complex. However, if we think of a protein as constructed of individual bonds, C—C, C—H, C—N, C—O, N—H, and so on, it helps tremendously in predicting and understanding the protein's behavior. The essential idea is that we expect a given bond to behave about the same in any molecular environment. Used in this way, the model of the chemical bond has helped chemists to systematize the reactions of the millions of existing compounds.

In addition to being useful, the bonding model is also physically sensible. It makes sense that atoms can form stable groups by sharing electrons; shared electrons give a lower energy state because they are simultaneously attracted by two nuclei.

Also, as we will see in the next section, bond energy data support the existence of discrete bonds that are relatively independent of the molecular environment. It is very important to remember, however, that the chemical bond is only a model. Although our concept of discrete bonds in molecules agrees with many of our observations, some molecular properties require that we think of a molecule as a whole, with the electrons free to move through the entire molecule. This is called *delocalization* of the electrons, a concept that will be discussed more completely in the next chapter.

Fundamental Properties of Models

- Models are human inventions, always based on an incomplete understanding of how nature works. *A model does not equal reality.*

- Models are often wrong. This property derives from the first property. Models are based on speculation and are always oversimplifications.

- Models tend to become more complicated as they age. As flaws are discovered in our models, we "patch" them and thus add more detail.

- It is very important to understand the assumptions inherent in a particular model before you use it to interpret observations or to make predictions. Simple models usually involve very restrictive assumptions and can be expected to yield only qualitative information. Asking for a sophisticated explanation from a simple model is like expecting to get an accurate mass for a diamond using a bathroom scale.

    For a model to be used effectively, we must understand its strengths and weaknesses and ask only appropriate questions. An illustration of this point is the simple aufbau principle used to account for the electron configurations of the elements. Although this model correctly predicts the configuration for most atoms, chromium and copper, for example, do not agree with the predictions. Detailed studies show that the configurations of chromium and copper result from complex electron interactions that are not taken into account in the simple model. However, this does not mean that we should discard the simple model that is so useful for most atoms. Instead, we must apply it with caution and not expect it to be correct in every case.

- When a model is wrong, we often learn much more than when it is right. If a model makes a wrong prediction, it usually means we do not understand some fundamental characteristics of nature. We often learn by making mistakes. (Try to remember this when you get back your next chemistry test.)

8.8 Covalent Bond Energies and Chemical Reactions

In this section we will consider the energies associated with various types of bonds and see how the bonding concept is useful in dealing with the energies of chemical reactions. One important consideration is to establish the sensitivity of a particular type of bond to its molecular environment. For example, consider the stepwise decomposition of methane:

Process	Energy Required (kJ/mol)
$CH_4(g) \rightarrow CH_3(g) + H(g)$	435
$CH_3(g) \rightarrow CH_2(g) + H(g)$	453
$CH_2(g) \rightarrow CH(g) + H(g)$	425
$CH(g) \rightarrow C(g) + H(g)$	339

$$\text{Total} = 1652$$

$$\text{Average} = \frac{1652}{4} = 413$$

Although a C—H bond is broken in each case, the energy required varies in a nonsystematic way. This example shows that the C—H bond is somewhat sensitive to its environment. We use the *average* of these individual bond dissociation energies even though this quantity only approximates the energy associated with a C—H bond in a particular molecule. The degree of sensitivity of a bond to its environment also can be seen from experimental measurements of the energy required to break the C—H bond in the following molecules:

Molecule	Measured C—H Bond Energy (kJ/mol)
$HCBr_3$	380
$HCCl_3$	380
HCF_3	430
C_2H_6	410

These data show that the C—H bond strength varies significantly with its environment, but the concept of an average C—H bond strength remains useful to chemists. The average values of bond energies for various types of bonds are listed in Table 8.4.

So far we have discussed bonds in which one pair of electrons is shared. This type of bond is called a **single bond.** As we will see in more detail later, atoms sometimes share two pairs of electrons, forming a **double bond,** or share three pairs of electrons, forming a **triple bond.** The bond energies for these *multiple bonds* are also given in Table 8.4.

A relationship also exists between the number of shared electron pairs and the bond length. As the number of shared electrons increases, the bond length shortens. This relationship is shown for selected bonds in Table 8.5.

Table 8.4 Average Bond Energies (kJ/mol)

Single Bonds								Multiple Bonds	
H—H	432	N—H	391	I—I	149			C=C	614
H—F	565	N—N	160	I—Cl	208			C≡C	839
H—Cl	427	N—F	272	I—Br	175			O=O	495
H—Br	363	N—Cl	200					C=O*	745
H—I	295	N—Br	243			S—H	347	C≡O	1072
		N—O	201			S—F	327	N=O	607
C—H	413	O—H	467			S—Cl	253	N=N	418
C—C	347	O—O	146			S—Br	218	N≡N	941
C—N	305	O—F	190			S—S	266	C≡N	891
C—O	358	O—Cl	203					C=N	615
C—F	485	O—I	234			Si—Si	340		
C—Cl	339					Si—H	393		
C—Br	276	F—F	154			Si—C	360		
C—I	240	F—Cl	253			Si—O	452		
C—S	259	F—Br	237						
		Cl—Cl	239						
		Cl—Br	218						
		Br—Br	193						

*C=O(CO_2) = 799

Table 8.5 Bond Lengths for Selected Bonds			
Bond	*Bond Type*	*Bond Length (pm)*	*Bond Energy (kJ/mol)*
C—C	Single	154	347
C=C	Double	134	614
C≡C	Triple	120	839
C—O	Single	143	358
C=O	Double	123	745
C—N	Single	143	305
C=N	Double	138	615
C≡N	Triple	116	891

Bond Energy and Enthalpy

Bond energy values can be used to calculate approximate energies for reactions. To illustrate how this is done, we will calculate the change in energy that accompanies the following reaction:

$$H_2(g) + F_2(g) \longrightarrow 2HF(g)$$

This reaction involves breaking one H—H and one F—F bond and forming two H—F bonds. For bonds to be broken, energy must be *added* to the system—an endothermic process. Consequently, the energy terms associated with bond breaking have *positive* signs. The formation of a bond *releases* energy, an exothermic process, so the energy terms associated with bond making carry a *negative* sign. We can write the enthalpy change for a reaction as follows:

ΔH = sum of the energies required to break old bonds (positive signs) plus the sum of the energies released in the formation of new bonds (negative signs)

This leads to the expression

$$\Delta H = \underbrace{\Sigma D \text{ (bonds broken)}}_{\text{Energy required}} - \underbrace{\Sigma D \text{ (bonds formed)}}_{\text{Energy released}}$$

where Σ represents the sum of terms, and D represents the bond energy per mole of bonds. (D *always* has a positive sign.)

In the case of the formation of HF,

$$\Delta H = D_{H—H} + D_{F—F} - 2D_{H—F}$$

$$= 1 \text{ mol} \times \frac{432 \text{ kJ}}{\text{mol}} + 1 \text{ mol} \times \frac{154 \text{ kJ}}{\text{mol}} - 2 \text{ mol} \times \frac{565 \text{ kJ}}{\text{mol}}$$

$$= -544 \text{ kJ}$$

Thus when 1 mol $H_2(g)$ and 1 mol $F_2(g)$ react to form 2 mol $HF(g)$, 544 kJ of energy should be released.

This result can be compared with the calculation of ΔH for this reaction from the standard enthalpy of formation for HF (-271 kJ/mol):

$$\Delta H° = 2 \text{ mol} \times (-271 \text{ kJ/mol}) = -542 \text{ kJ}$$

Thus the use of bond energies to calculate ΔH works quite well in this case.

Sample Exercise 8.5 *ΔH from Bond Energies*

Using the bond energies listed in Table 8.4, calculate ΔH for the reaction of methane with chlorine and fluorine to give Freon-12 (CF_2Cl_2).

$$CH_4(g) + 2Cl_2(g) + 2F_2(g) \longrightarrow CF_2Cl_2(g) + 2HF(g) + 2HCl(g)$$

Molecular Models: CH_4, F_2, CF_2Cl_2, HF, HCl

Solution

The idea here is to break the bonds in the gaseous reactants to give individual atoms and then assemble these atoms into the gaseous products by forming new bonds:

$$\text{Reactants} \xrightarrow[\text{required}]{\text{Energy}} \text{atoms} \xrightarrow[\text{released}]{\text{Energy}} \text{products}$$

We then combine the energy changes to calculate ΔH:

ΔH = energy required to break bonds − energy released when bonds form

where the minus sign gives the correct sign to the energy terms for the exothermic processes.

Reactant bonds broken:

$$CH_4: \quad \text{4 mol C—H} \qquad 4 \text{ mol} \times \frac{413 \text{ kJ}}{\text{mol}} = 1652 \text{ kJ}$$

$$2Cl_2: \quad \text{2 mol Cl—Cl} \qquad 2 \text{ mol} \times \frac{239 \text{ kJ}}{\text{mol}} = 478 \text{ kJ}$$

$$2F_2: \quad \text{2 mol F—F} \qquad 2 \text{ mol} \times \frac{154 \text{ kJ}}{\text{mol}} = 308 \text{ kJ}$$

$$\text{Total energy required} = 2438 \text{ kJ}$$

Product bonds formed:

$$CF_2Cl_2: \quad \text{2 mol C—F} \qquad 2 \text{ mol} \times \frac{485 \text{ kJ}}{\text{mol}} = 970 \text{ kJ}$$

$$\text{and}$$

$$\text{2 mol C—Cl} \qquad 2 \text{ mol} \times \frac{339 \text{ kJ}}{\text{mol}} = 678 \text{ kJ}$$

$$HF: \quad \text{2 mol H—F} \qquad 2 \text{ mol} \times \frac{565 \text{ kJ}}{\text{mol}} = 1130 \text{ kJ}$$

$$HCl: \quad \text{2 mol H—Cl} \qquad 2 \text{ mol} \times \frac{427 \text{ kJ}}{\text{mol}} = 854 \text{ kJ}$$

$$\text{Total energy released} = 3632 \text{ kJ}$$

We now can calculate ΔH:

ΔH = energy required to break bonds − energy released when bonds form

  = 2438 kJ − 3632 kJ

  = −1194 kJ

Since the sign of the value for the enthalpy change is negative, this means that 1194 kJ of energy is released per mole of CF_2Cl_2 formed.

See Exercises 8.47 through 8.52.

8.9 *The Localized Electron Bonding Model*

So far we have discussed the general characteristics of the chemical bonding model and have seen that properties such as bond strength and polarity can be assigned to individual bonds. In this section we introduce a specific model used to describe covalent bonds. We need a simple model that can be applied easily even to very complicated molecules and that can be used routinely by chemists to interpret and organize the wide variety of chemical phenomena. The model that serves this purpose is the **localized electron (LE) model,** which assumes that *a molecule is composed of atoms that are bound together by sharing pairs of electrons using the atomic orbitals of the bound atoms.* Electron pairs in the molecule are assumed to be localized on a particular atom or in the space between two atoms. Those pairs of electrons localized on an atom are called **lone pairs,** and those found in the space between the atoms are called **bonding pairs.**

As we will apply it, the LE model has three parts:

1. Description of the valence electron arrangement in the molecule using Lewis structures (will be discussed in the next section).

2. Prediction of the geometry of the molecule using the valence shell electron pair repulsion (VSEPR) model (will be discussed in Section 8.13).

3. Description of the type of atomic orbitals used by the atoms to share electrons or hold lone pairs (will be discussed in Chapter 9).

8.10 *Lewis Structures*

The **Lewis structure** of a molecule shows how the valence electrons are arranged among the atoms in the molecule. These representations are named after G. N. Lewis (Fig. 8.13). The rules for writing Lewis structures are based on observations of thousands of molecules. From experiment, chemists have learned that the *most important requirement for the formation of a stable compound is that the atoms achieve noble gas electron configurations.*

We have already seen that when metals and nonmetals react to form binary ionic compounds, electrons are transferred and the resulting ions typically have noble gas electron configurations. An example is the formation of KBr, where the K^+ ion has the [Ar] electron configuration and the Br^- ion has the [Kr] electron configuration. In writing Lewis structures, the rule is that *only the valence electrons are included.* Using dots to represent electrons, the Lewis structure for KBr is

Lewis structures show only valence electrons.

No dots are shown on the K^+ ion because it has no valence electrons. The Br^- ion is shown with eight electrons because it has a filled valence shell.

Next we will consider Lewis structures for molecules with covalent bonds, involving elements in the first and second periods. The principle of achieving a noble gas electron configuration applies to these elements as follows:

- Hydrogen forms stable molecules where it shares two electrons. That is, it follows a **duet rule.** For example, when two hydrogen atoms, each with one electron, combine to form the H_2 molecule, we have

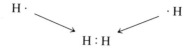

- By sharing electrons, each hydrogen in H_2, in effect, has two electrons; that is, each hydrogen has a filled valence shell.

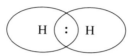

- Helium does not form bonds because its valence orbital is already filled; it is a noble gas. Helium has the electron configuration $1s^2$ and can be represented by the Lewis structure

$$He\,:$$

- The second-row nonmetals carbon through fluorine form stable molecules when they are surrounded by enough electrons to fill the valence orbitals, that is, the $2s$ and the three $2p$ orbitals. Since eight electrons are required to fill these orbitals, these elements typically obey the **octet rule;** they are surrounded by eight electrons. An example is the F_2 molecule, which has the following Lewis structure:

F atom with seven valence electrons F_2 molecule   F atom with seven valence electrons

- Note that each fluorine atom in F_2 is, in effect, surrounded by eight electrons, two of which are shared with the other atom. This is a *bonding pair* of electrons, as discussed earlier. Each fluorine atom also has three pairs of electrons not involved in bonding. These are the *lone pairs*.

- Neon does not form bonds because it already has an octet of valence electrons (it is a noble gas). The Lewis structure is

$$:Ne\,:$$

- Note that only the valence electrons of the neon atom ($2s^2 2p^6$) are represented by the Lewis structure. The $1s^2$ electrons are core electrons and are not shown.

From the preceding discussion we can formulate the following rules for writing the Lewis structures of molecules containing atoms from the first two periods.

Figure 8.13
G. N. Lewis (1875–1946).

Carbon, nitrogen, oxygen, and fluorine always obey the octet rule in stable molecules.

Rules for Writing Lewis Structures

- Sum the valence electrons from all the atoms. Do not worry about keeping track of which electrons come from which atoms. It is the *total* number of electrons that is important.
- Use a pair of electrons to form a bond between each pair of bound atoms.
- Arrange the remaining electrons to satisfy the duet rule for hydrogen and the octet rule for the second-row elements.

To see how these rules are applied, we will draw the Lewis structures of a few molecules. We will first consider the water molecule and follow the previous rules.

STEP 1

We sum the *valence* electrons for H_2O as shown:

$$1 + 1 + 6 = 8 \text{ valence electrons}$$
$$\nearrow \quad \nearrow \quad \nearrow$$
$$H \quad H \quad O$$

STEP 2

Using a pair of electrons per bond, we draw in the two O—H single bonds:

$$H—O—H$$

Note that *a line instead of a pair of dots is used to indicate each* pair *of bonding electrons.* This is the standard notation.

STEP 3

We distribute the remaining electrons to achieve a noble gas electron configuration for each atom. Since four electrons have been used in forming the two bonds, four electrons $(8 - 4)$ remain to be distributed. Hydrogen is satisfied with two electrons (duet rule), but oxygen needs eight electrons to have a noble gas configuration. Thus the remaining four electrons are added to oxygen as two lone pairs. Dots are used to represent the lone pairs:

$$H—\overset{..}{\underset{..}{O}}—H \qquad \text{Lone pairs}$$

H—O—H represents H:O:H

This is the correct Lewis structure for the water molecule. Each hydrogen has two electrons and the oxygen has eight, as shown below:

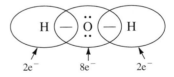

$$2e^- \qquad 8e^- \qquad 2e^-$$

As a second example, let's write the Lewis structure for carbon dioxide. Summing the valence electrons gives

$$4 + 6 + 6 = 16$$
$$\nearrow \quad \nearrow \quad \nearrow$$
$$C \quad O \quad O$$

After forming a bond between the carbon and each oxygen,

$$O—C—O$$

the remaining electrons are distributed to achieve noble gas configurations on each atom. In this case we have 12 electrons $(16 - 4)$ remaining after the bonds are drawn. The distribution of these electrons is determined by a trial-and-error process. We have 6 pairs of electrons to distribute. Suppose we try 3 pairs on each oxygen to give

$$:\overset{..}{\underset{..}{O}}—C—\overset{..}{\underset{..}{O}}:$$

Is this correct? To answer this, we need to check two things:

1. The total number of electrons. There are 16 valence electrons in this structure, which is the correct number.

2. The octet rule for each atom. Each oxygen has 8 electrons, but the carbon only has 4. This cannot be the correct Lewis structure.

How can we arrange the 16 available electrons to achieve an octet for each atom? Suppose there are 2 shared pairs between the carbon and each oxygen:

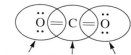

8 electrons   8 electrons   8 electrons

$O=C=O$ represents

$\ddot{O}::C::\ddot{O}$

Now each atom is surrounded by 8 electrons, and the total number of electrons is 16, as required. This is the correct Lewis structure for carbon dioxide, which has two double bonds and four lone pairs.

Finally, let's consider the Lewis structure of the CN^- (cyanide) ion. Summing the valence electrons, we have

$$CN^-$$

4 + 5 + 1 = 10

Note that the negative charge means an extra electron is present. After drawing a single bond (C—N), we distribute the remaining electrons to achieve a noble gas configuration for each atom. Eight electrons remain to be distributed. We can try various possibilities, for example:

$$\ddot{C}-\ddot{N}$$

This structure is incorrect because C and N have only six electrons each instead of eight. The correct arrangement is

$$[:C\equiv N:]^-$$

(Satisfy yourself that both carbon and nitrogen have eight electrons.)

Sample Exercise 8.6 *Writing Lewis Structures*

Give the Lewis structure for each of the following.

a. HF   d. CH_4
b. N_2 e. CF_4
c. NH_3 f. NO^+

Solution

In each case we apply the three rules for writing Lewis structures. Recall that lines are used to indicate shared electron pairs and that dots are used to indicate nonbonding pairs (lone pairs). We have the following tabulated results:

	Total Valence Electrons	Draw Single Bonds	Calculate Number of Electrons Remaining	Use Remaining Electrons to Achieve Noble Gas Configurations	Check Number of Electrons
a. HF	$1 + 7 = 8$	H—F	6	H—$\ddot{\text{F}}$:	H, 2 F, 8
b. N_2	$5 + 5 = 10$	N—N	8	:N≡N:	N, 8

c. NH_3	$5 + 3(1) = 8$	H—N—H
		     H
			2	H—$\ddot{\text{N}}$—H
				     H
					H, 2
					 N, 8

d. CH_4	$4 + 4(1) = 8$	H
		 H—C—H
		   H
			0	H
				 H—C—H
				   H
					H, 2
					 C, 8

e. CF_4	$4 + 4(7) = 32$	F
		 F—C—F
		   F
			24	:$\ddot{\text{F}}$:
				 :$\ddot{\text{F}}$—C—$\ddot{\text{F}}$:
				   :$\ddot{\text{F}}$:
					F, 8
					 C, 8

f. NO^+	$5 + 6 - 1 = 10$	N—O	8	$[:N≡O:]^+$	N, 8 O, 8

See Exercises 8.63 and 8.64.

When writing Lewis structures, do not worry about which electrons come from which atoms in a molecule. The best way to look at a molecule is to regard it as a new entity that uses all the available valence electrons of the atoms to achieve the lowest possible energy.[*] The valence electrons belong to the molecule, rather than to the individual atoms. Simply distribute all valence electrons so that the various rules are satisfied, without regard for the origin of each particular electron.

8.11 Exceptions to the Octet Rule

The localized electron model is a simple but very successful model, and the rules we have used for Lewis structures apply to most molecules. However, with such a simple model, some exceptions are inevitable. Boron, for example, tends to form compounds in which the boron atom has fewer than eight electrons around it—it does not have a complete octet. Boron trifluoride (BF_3), a gas at normal temperatures and pressures, reacts very energetically with molecules such as water and am-

[*]In a sense this approach corrects for the fact that the localized electron model overemphasizes that a molecule is simply a sum of its parts, that is, that the atoms retain their individual identities in the molecule.

monia that have available electron pairs (lone pairs). The violent reactivity of BF_3 with electron-rich molecules arises because the boron atom is electron-deficient. Boron trifluoride has 24 valence electrons. The Lewis structure often drawn for BF_3 is

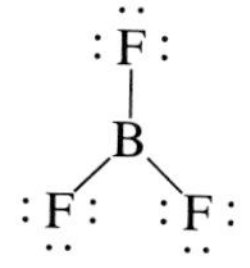

$$
\begin{array}{c}
:\!\ddot{F}\!: \\
| \\
B \\
\diagup \quad \diagdown \\
:\!\ddot{F}\!: \quad :\!\ddot{F}\!:
\end{array}
$$

Molecular Models: BF_3, SF_6, H_3NBF_3

Note that in this structure boron has only 6 electrons around it. The octet rule for boron can be satisfied by drawing a structure with a double bond, such as

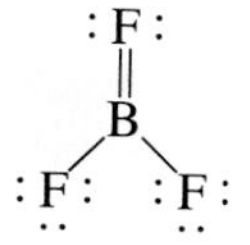

$$
\begin{array}{c}
:\!\ddot{F}\!: \\
\| \\
B \\
\diagup \quad \diagdown \\
:\!\ddot{F}\!: \quad :\!\ddot{F}\!:
\end{array}
$$

Recent studies indicate that double bonding may be important in BF_3. However, the boron atom in BF_3 certainly behaves as if it is electron-deficient, as indicated by the reactivity of BF_3 toward electron-rich molecules, for example, toward NH_3 to form H_3NBF_3:

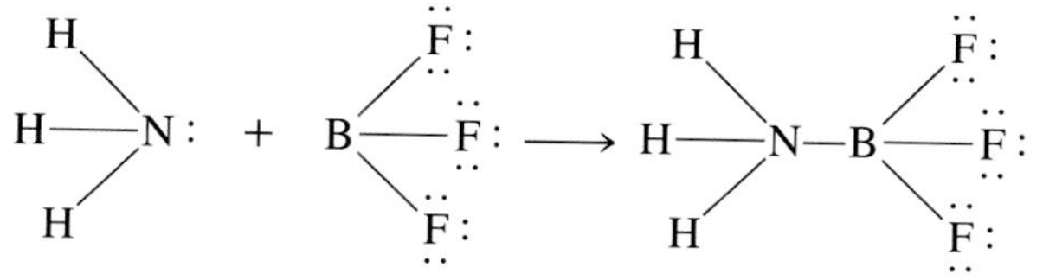

In this stable compound, boron has an octet of electrons.

It is characteristic of boron to form molecules in which the boron atom is electron-deficient. On the other hand, carbon, nitrogen, oxygen, and fluorine can be counted on to obey the octet rule.

Some atoms exceed the octet rule. This behavior is observed only for those elements in Period 3 of the periodic table and beyond. To see how this arises, we will consider the Lewis structure for sulfur hexafluoride (SF_6), a well-known and very stable molecule. The sum of the valence electrons is

$$6 + 6(7) = 48 \text{ electrons}$$

Indicating the single bonds gives the structure on the left below:

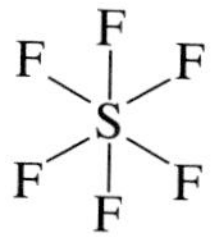

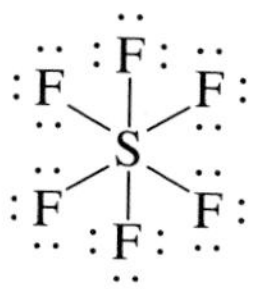

We have used 12 electrons to form the S—F bonds, which leaves 36 electrons. Since fluorine always follows the octet rule, we complete the six fluorine octets to give the structure on the right above. This structure uses all 48 valence electrons for SF_6, but sulfur has 12 electrons around it; that is, sulfur *exceeds* the octet rule. How can this happen?

To answer this question, we need to consider the different types of valence orbitals characteristic of second- and third-period elements. The second-row elements have $2s$ and $2p$ valence orbitals, and the third-row elements have $3s$, $3p$, and $3d$ orbitals. The $3s$ and $3p$ orbitals fill with electrons in going from sodium to argon, but the 3*d* orbitals remain empty. For example, the valence orbital diagram for a sulfur atom is

3*s*   3*p*   3*d*

Third-row elements can exceed the octet rule.

The localized electron model assumes that the empty 3*d* orbitals can be used to accommodate extra electrons. Thus the sulfur atom in SF_6 can have 12 electrons around it by using the 3*s* and 3*p* orbitals to hold 8 electrons, with the extra 4 electrons placed in the formerly empty 3*d* orbitals.

Lewis Structures: Comments About the Octet Rule

- The second-row elements C, N, O, and F should always be assumed to obey the octet rule.
- The second-row elements B and Be often have fewer than eight electrons around them in their compounds. These electron-deficient compounds are very reactive.
- The second-row elements never exceed the octet rule, since their valence orbitals (2*s* and 2*p*) can accommodate only eight electrons.
- Third-row and heavier elements often satisfy the octet rule but can exceed the octet rule by using their empty valence *d* orbitals.
- When writing the Lewis structure for a molecule, satisfy the octet rule for the atoms first. If electrons remain after the octet rule has been satisfied, then place them on the elements having available *d* orbitals (elements in Period 3 or beyond).

Whether the atoms that exceed the octet rule actually place the extra electrons in their *d* orbitals is a matter of controversy among theoretical chemists. We will not consider this issue in this text.

Sample Exercise 8.7 *Lewis Structures for Molecules That Violate the Octet Rule I*

Molecular Model: PCl_5

Write the Lewis structure for PCl_5.

Solution

We can follow the same stepwise procedure we used above for sulfur hexafluoride.

STEP 1

Sum the valence electrons.

$$5 + 5(7) = 40 \text{ electrons}$$

↑   ↑
P   Cl

STEP 2

Indicate single bonds between bound atoms.

$$
\begin{array}{c}
\text{Cl} \quad \text{Cl} \\
\text{Cl—P} \\
\text{Cl} \quad \text{Cl}
\end{array}
$$

STEP 3

Distribute the remaining electrons. In this case, 30 electrons ($40 - 10$) remain. These are used to satisfy the octet rule for each chlorine atom. The final Lewis structure is

$$
\begin{array}{c}
:\!\text{Cl}\!: \\
:\!\text{Cl—P} \\
:\!\text{Cl}\!:
\end{array}
\begin{array}{c}
\text{Cl}: \\
\text{Cl}:
\end{array}
$$

Note that phosphorus, which is a third-row element, has exceeded the octet rule by two electrons.

See Exercises 8.65 and 8.66.

In the PCl_5 and SF_6 molecules, the central atoms (P and S, respectively) must have the extra electrons. However, in molecules having more than one atom that can exceed the octet rule, it is not always clear which atom should have the extra electrons. Consider the Lewis structure for the triiodide ion (I_3^-), which has

Molecular Models: I_3^-, ICl_4^-

$$3(7) + 1 = 22 \text{ valence electrons}$$

$$\uparrow \qquad \uparrow$$
$$1 \qquad 1 - \text{charge}$$

Indicating the single bonds gives I—I—I. At this point, 18 electrons ($22 - 4$) remain. Trial and error will convince you that one of the iodine atoms must exceed the octet rule, but *which* one?

The rule we will follow is that *when it is necessary to exceed the octet rule for one of several third-row (or higher) elements, assume that the extra electrons should be placed on the central atom.*

Thus for I_3^- the Lewis structure is

$$\left[:\!\text{I}\!-\!\ddot{\text{I}}\!-\!\ddot{\text{I}}\!: \right]^-$$

where the central iodine exceeds the octet rule. This structure agrees with known properties of I_3^-.

Sample Exercise 8.8 *Lewis Structures for Molecules That Violate the Octet Rule II*

Write the Lewis structure for each molecule or ion.

a. ClF_3 **b.** XeO_3 **c.** $RnCl_2$ **d.** $BeCl_2$ **e.** ICl_4^-

Solution

a. The chlorine atom (third row) accepts the extra electrons.

b. All atoms obey the octet rule.

c. Radon, a noble gas in Period 6, accepts the extra electrons.

d. Beryllium is electron-deficient.

e. Iodine exceeds the octet rule.

See Exercises 8.65 and 8.66.

8.12 Resonance

Sometimes more than one valid Lewis structure (one that obeys the rules we have outlined) is possible for a given molecule. Consider the Lewis structure for the nitrate ion (NO_3^-), which has 24 valence electrons. To achieve an octet of electrons around each atom, a structure like this is required:

Molecular Model: NO_3^-

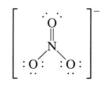

If this structure accurately represents the bonding in NO_3^-, there should be two types of N---O bonds observed in the molecule: one shorter bond (the double bond) and two identical longer ones (the two single bonds). However, experiments clearly show that NO_3^- exhibits only *one* type of N---O bond with a length and strength *between* those expected for a single bond and a double bond. Thus, although the structure we have shown above is a valid Lewis structure, it does *not* correctly represent the bonding in NO_3^-. This is a serious problem, and it means that the model must be modified.

Look again at the proposed Lewis structure for NO_3^-. There is no reason for choosing a particular oxygen atom to have the double bond. There are really three valid Lewis structures:

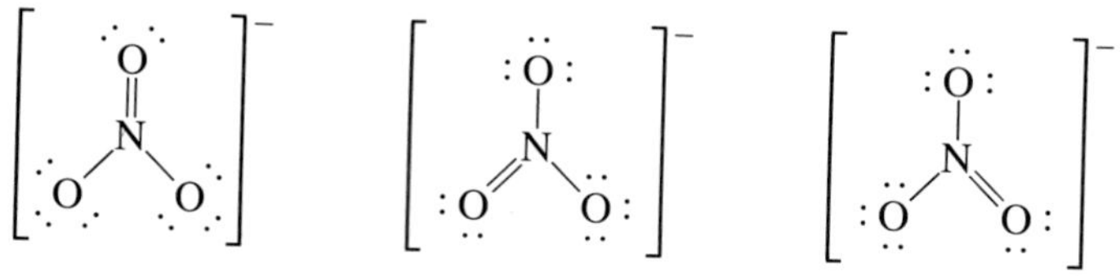

Is any of these structures a correct description of the bonding in NO_3^-? No, because NO_3^- does not have one double and two single bonds—it has three equivalent bonds. We can solve this problem by making the following assumption: The correct description of NO_3^- is *not given by any one* of the three Lewis structures but is given only by the *superposition of all three.*

The nitrate ion does not exist as any of the three extreme structures but exists as an average of all three. **Resonance** *occurs when more than one valid Lewis structure can be written for a particular molecule.* The resulting electron structure of the molecule is given by the average of these **resonance structures.** This situation is usually represented by double-headed arrows as follows:

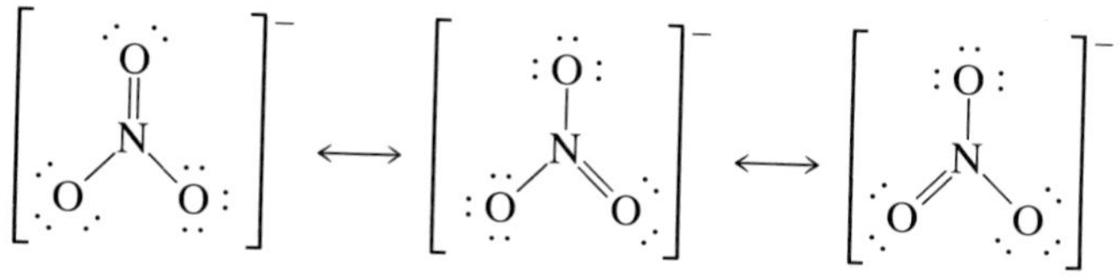

Note that in all these resonance structures the arrangement of the nuclei is the same. Only the placement of the electrons differs. The arrows do not mean that the molecule "flips" from one resonance to another. They simply show that the *actual structure is an average of the three resonance structures.*

The concept of resonance is necessary because the localized electron model postulates that electrons are localized between a given pair of atoms. However, nature does not really operate this way. Electrons are really delocalized—they can move around the entire molecule. The valence electrons in the NO_3^- molecule distribute themselves to provide equivalent N---O bonds. Resonance is necessary to compensate for the defective assumption of the localized electron model. However, this model is so useful that we retain the concept of localized electrons and add resonance to allow the model to treat species such as NO_3^-.

Sample Exercise 8.9 Resonance Structures

Describe the electron arrangement in the nitrite anion (NO_2^-) using the localized electron model.

Solution

We will follow the usual procedure for obtaining the Lewis structure for the NO_2^- ion. In NO_2^- there are $5 + 2(6) + 1 = 18$ valence electrons. Indicating the single bonds gives the structure

$$O—N—O$$

The remaining 14 electrons $(18 - 4)$ can be distributed to produce these structures:

This is a resonance situation. Two equivalent Lewis structures can be drawn. *The electronic structure of the molecule is correctly represented not by either resonance structure but by the average of the two.* There are two equivalent N---O bonds, each one intermediate between a single and a double bond.

See Exercises 8.67 through 8.72.

Odd-Electron Molecules

Relatively few molecules formed from nonmetals contain odd numbers of electrons. One common example is nitric oxide (NO), which is formed when nitrogen and oxygen gases react at the high temperatures in automobile engines. Nitric oxide is emitted into the air, where it immediately reacts with oxygen to form gaseous nitrogen dioxide (NO_2), another odd-electron molecule.

Since the localized electron model is based on pairs of electrons, it does not handle odd-electron cases in a natural way. To treat odd-electron molecules, a more sophisticated model is needed.

Formal Charge

Equivalent Lewis structures contain the same numbers of single and multiple bonds. For example, the resonance structures for O_3

are equivalent Lewis structures. These are equally important in describing the bonding in O_3. Nonequivalent Lewis structures contain different numbers of single and multiple bonds.

Molecules or polyatomic ions containing atoms that can exceed the octet rule often have many nonequivalent Lewis structures, all of which obey the rules for writing Lewis structures. For example, as we will see in detail below, the sulfate ion has a Lewis structure with all single bonds and several Lewis structures that contain double bonds. How do we decide which of the many possible Lewis structures best describes the actual bonding in sulfate? One method is to estimate the charge on each atom in the various possible Lewis structures and use these charges to select the most appropriate structure(s). We will see below how this is done, but first we must decide on a method to assign atomic charges in molecules.

In Chapter 4 we discussed one system for obtaining charges, called *oxidation states*. However, in assigning oxidation states, we always count *both* the shared electrons as belonging to the more electronegative atom in a bond. This practice leads to highly exaggerated estimates of charge. In other words, although oxidation states are useful for bookkeeping electrons in redox reactions, they are not realistic estimates of the actual charges on individual atoms in a molecule, so they are not suitable for judging the appropriateness of Lewis structures. Another definition of the charge on an atom in a molecule, the formal charge, can, however, be used to evaluate Lewis structures. As we will see below, the **formal charge** of an atom in a molecule is *the difference between the number of valence electrons on the free atom and the number of valence electrons assigned to the atom in the molecule.*

Therefore, to determine the formal charge of a given atom in a molecule, we need to know two things.

1. The number of valence electrons on the free neutral atom (which has zero net charge because the number of electrons equals the number of protons)
2. The number of valence electrons "belonging" to the atom in a molecule

We then compare these numbers. If in the molecule the atom has the same number of valence electrons as it does in the free state, the positive and negative charges just balance, and it has a formal charge of zero. If the atom has one more valence electron in a molecule than it has as a free atom, it has a formal charge of -1, and so on. Thus the formal charge on an atom in a molecule is defined as

Formal charge = (number of valence electrons on free atom)
  $-$ (number of valence electrons assigned to the atom in the molecule)

To compute the formal charge of an atom in a molecule, we assign the valence electrons in the molecule to the various atoms, making the following assumptions:

1. Lone pair electrons belong entirely to the atom in question.
2. Shared electrons are *divided equally* between the two sharing atoms.

Thus the number of valence electrons assigned to a given atom is calculated as follows:

(Valence electrons)$_{assigned}$ = (number of lone pair electrons)
  $+ \frac{1}{2}$ (number of shared electrons)

We will illustrate the procedure for calculating formal charges by considering two of the possible Lewis structures for the sulfate ion, which has 32 valence electrons. For the Lewis structure

$$\begin{bmatrix} & \overset{\displaystyle ..}{\underset{\displaystyle ..}{:O:}} & \\ :\overset{..}{\underset{..}{O}}\!-\!\overset{|}{\underset{|}{S}}\!-\!\overset{..}{\underset{..}{O}}: \\ & \overset{|}{\underset{\displaystyle ..}{:O:}} & \end{bmatrix}^{2-}$$

Molecular Model: $SO_4{}^{2-}$

each oxygen atom has 6 lone pair electrons and shares 2 electrons with the sulfur atom. Thus, using the preceding assumptions, each oxygen is assigned 7 valence electrons.

Valence electrons assigned to each oxygen = 6 *plus* $\frac{1}{2}(2) = 7$

            ↑   ↑

        Lone Shared

        pair electrons

     electrons

$$\text{Formal charge on oxygen} = 6 \; minus \; 7 = -1$$

Valence electrons
on a free O atom

Valence electrons
assigned to each O
in SO_4^{2-}

The formal charge on each oxygen is -1.

For the sulfur atom there are no lone pair electrons, and eight electrons are shared with the oxygen atoms. Thus, for sulfur,

$$\text{Valence electrons assigned to sulfur} = 0 \; plus \; \tfrac{1}{2}(8) = 4$$

Lone   Shared
pair   electrons
electrons

$$\text{Formal charge on sulfur} = 6 \; minus \; 4 = 2$$

Valence electrons
on a free S atom

Valence
electrons
assigned to S
in SO_4^{2-}

A second possible Lewis structure is

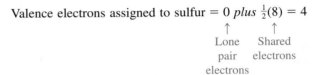

In this case the formal charges are as follows:

For oxygen atoms with single bonds:

$$\text{Valence electrons assigned} = 6 + \tfrac{1}{2}(2) = 7$$
$$\text{Formal charge} = 6 - 7 = -1$$

For oxygen atoms with double bonds:

$$\text{Valence electrons assigned} = 4 + \tfrac{1}{2}(4) = 6$$

Each double
bond has 4
electrons

$$\text{Formal charge} = 6 - 6 = 0$$

For the sulfur atom:

$$\text{Valence electrons assigned} = 0 + \tfrac{1}{2}(12) = 6$$
$$\text{Formal charge} = 6 - 6 = 0$$

We will use two fundamental assumptions about formal charges to evaluate Lewis structures:

1. Atoms in molecules try to achieve formal charges as close to zero as possible.
2. Any negative formal charges are expected to reside on the most electronegative atoms.

We can use these principles to evaluate the two Lewis structures for sulfate given previously. Notice that in the structure with only single bonds, each oxygen has a formal charge of -1, while the sulfur has a formal charge of $+2$. In contrast, in the structure with two double bonds and two single bonds, the sulfur and two oxygen atoms have a formal charge of 0, while two oxygens have a formal charge of -1. Based on the assumptions given above, the structure with two double bonds is preferred—it has lower formal charges and the -1 formal charges are on electronegative oxygen atoms. Thus, for the sulfate ion, we might expect resonance structures such as

to more closely describe the bonding than the Lewis structure with only single bonds.

Rules Governing Formal Charge

- To calculate the formal charge on an atom:
  1. Take the sum of the lone pair electrons and one-half the shared electrons. This is the number of valence electrons assigned to the atom in the molecule.
  2. Subtract the number of assigned electrons from the number of valence electrons on the free, neutral atom to obtain the formal charge.
- The sum of the formal charges of all atoms in a given molecule or ion must equal the overall charge on that species.
- If nonequivalent Lewis structures exist for a species, those with formal charges closest to zero and with any negative formal charges on the most electronegative atoms are considered to best describe the bonding in the molecule or ion.

Sample Exercise 8.10 *Formal Charges*

Give possible Lewis structures for XeO_3, an explosive compound of xenon. Which Lewis structure or structures are most appropriate according to the formal charges?

Solution

For XeO_3 (26 valence electrons) we can draw the following possible Lewis structures (formal charges are indicated in parentheses):

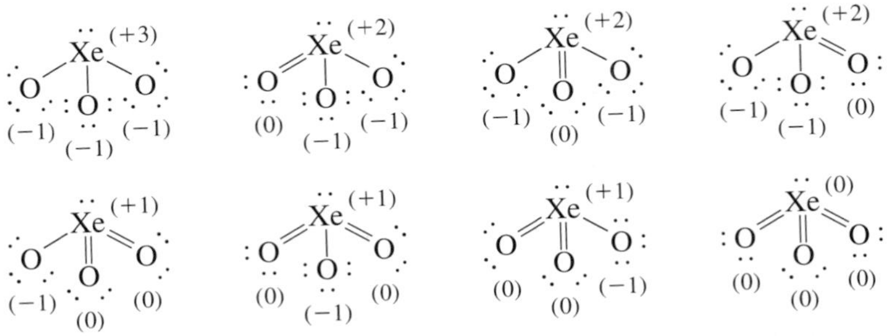

Based on the ideas of formal charge, we would predict that the Lewis structures with the lower values of formal charge would be most appropriate for describing the bonding in XeO_3.

See Exercises 8.75 through 8.78.

As a final note, there are a couple of cautions about formal charge to keep in mind. First, although formal charges are closer to actual atomic charges in molecules than are oxidation states, formal charges still provide only *estimates* of charge—they should not be taken as actual atomic charges. Second, the evaluation of Lewis structures using formal charge ideas can lead to erroneous predictions. Tests based on experiments must be used to make the final decisions on the correct description of the bonding in a molecule or polyatomic ion.

Exploration: The VSEPR Theory of Molecular Structure

8.13 Molecular Structure: The VSEPR Model

The structures of molecules play a very important role in determining their chemical properties. As we will see later, this is particularly important for biological molecules; a slight change in the structure of a large biomolecule can completely destroy its usefulness to a cell or may even change the cell from a normal one to a cancerous one.

Many accurate methods now exist for determining **molecular structure,** the three-dimensional arrangement of the atoms in a molecule. These methods must be used if precise information about structure is required. However, it is often useful to be able to predict the approximate molecular structure of a molecule. In this section we consider a simple model that allows us to do this. This model, called the **valence shell electron-pair repulsion (VSEPR) model,** is useful in predicting the geometries of molecules formed from nonmetals. The main postulate of this model is that *the structure around a given atom is determined principally by minimizing electron-pair repulsions.* The idea here is that the bonding and nonbonding pairs around a given atom will be positioned as far apart as possible. To see how this model works, we will first consider the molecule $BeCl_2$, which has the Lewis structure

$BeCl_2$ has only four electrons around Be and is expected to be very reactive with electron-pair donors.

$$:\ddot{C}l—Be—\ddot{C}l:$$

Note that there are two pairs of electrons around the beryllium atom. What arrangement of these electron pairs allows them to be as far apart as possible to minimize the repulsions? Clearly, the best arrangement places the pairs on opposite sides of the beryllium atom at 180 degrees from each other:

Molecular Models: $BeCl_2$, BF_3, CH_4

This is the maximum possible separation for two electron pairs. Once we have determined the optimal arrangement of the electron pairs around the central atom, we can specify the molecular structure of $BeCl_2$, that is, the positions of the atoms. Since each electron pair on beryllium is shared with a chlorine atom, the molecule has a **linear structure** with a 180-degree bond angle:

Cl—Be—Cl
180°

Next, let's consider BF_3, which has the Lewis structure

$$:\ddot{F}:$$
$$:\ddot{F}—B—\ddot{F}:$$

Here the boron atom is surrounded by three pairs of electrons. What arrangement will minimize the repulsions? The electron pairs are farthest apart at angles of 120 degrees:

Since each of the electron pairs is shared with a fluorine atom, the molecular structure will be

This is a planar (flat) and triangular molecule, which is commonly described as a **trigonal planar structure.**

Next, let's consider the methane molecule, which has the Lewis structure

H
|
H—C—H
|
H

There are four pairs of electrons around the central carbon atom. What arrangement of these electron pairs best minimizes the repulsions? First, let's try a square planar arrangement:

The carbon atom and the electron pairs are centered in the plane of the paper, and the angles between the pairs are all 90 degrees.

Is there another arrangement with angles greater than 90 degrees that would put the electron pairs even further away from each other? The answer is yes. The **tetrahedral arrangement** has angles of 109.5 degrees:

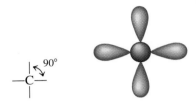

It can be shown that this is the maximum possible separation of four pairs around a given atom. This means that *whenever four pairs of electrons are present around an atom, they should always be arranged tetrahedrally.*

Now that we have the electron-pair arrangement that gives the least repulsion, we can determine the positions of the atoms and thus the molecular structure of CH_4. In methane, each of the four electron pairs is shared between the carbon atom and a hydrogen atom. Thus the hydrogen atoms are placed as in Fig. 8.14, and the molecule has a tetrahedral structure with the carbon atom at the center.

Recall that the main idea of the VSEPR model is to find the arrangement of electron pairs around the central atom that minimizes the repulsions. Then we can determine the molecular structure from knowing how the electron pairs are shared with the peripheral atoms. Use the following steps to predict the structure of a molecule using the VSEPR model.

STEP 1

Draw the Lewis structure for the molecule.

STEP 2

Count the electron pairs and arrange them in the way that minimizes repulsion (that is, put the pairs as far apart as possible).

STEP 3

Determine the positions of the atoms from the *way the electron pairs are shared.*

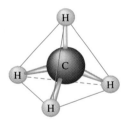

Figure 8.14

The molecular structure of methane. The tetrahedral arrangement of electron pairs produces a tetrahedral arrangement of hydrogen atoms.

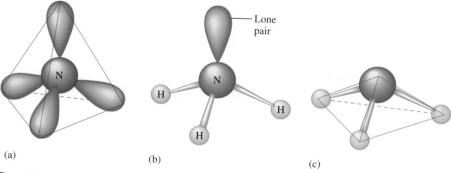

(a)   (b)   (c)

Figure 8.15

(a) The tetrahedral arrangement of electron pairs around the nitrogen atom in the ammonia molecule. (b) Three of the electron pairs around nitrogen are shared with hydrogen atoms as shown and one is a lone pair. Although the arrangement of *electron pairs* is tetrahedral, as in the methane molecule, the hydrogen atoms in the ammonia molecule occupy only three corners of the tetrahedron. A lone pair occupies the fourth corner. (c) Note that molecular geometry is trigonal pyramidal, not tetrahedral.

STEP 4

Determine the name of the molecular structure from the *positions of the atoms.*

We will predict the structure of ammonia (NH_3) using this stepwise approach.

STEP 1

Draw the Lewis structure:

$$H{-}\overset{..}{N}{-}H$$
$$\underset{H}{|}$$

STEP 2

Count the pairs of electrons and arrange them to minimize repulsions. The NH_3 molecule has four pairs of electrons: three bonding pairs and one nonbonding pair. From the discussion of the methane molecule, we know that the best arrangement of four electron pairs is a tetrahedral array, as shown in Fig. 8.15(a).

STEP 3

Determine the positions of the atoms. The three H atoms share electron pairs, as shown in Fig. 8.15(b).

STEP 4

Name the molecular structure. It is very important to recognize that the *name* of the molecular structure is always based on the *positions of the atoms.* The placement of the electron pairs determines the structure, but the name is based on the positions of the atoms. Thus it is incorrect to say that the NH_3 molecule is tetrahedral. It has a tetrahedral arrangement of electron pairs but not a tetrahedral arrangement of atoms. The molecular structure of ammonia is a **trigonal pyramid** (one side is different from the other three) rather than a tetrahedron, as shown in Fig. 8.15(c).

Figure 8.16
(a) The tetrahedral arrangement of the four electron pairs around oxygen in the water molecule. (b) Two of the electron pairs are shared between oxygen and the hydrogen atoms and two are lone pairs. (c) The V-shaped molecular structure of the water molecule.

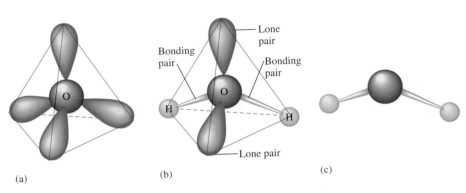

(a)

(b)

(c)

Sample Exercise 8.11 *Prediction of Molecular Structure I*

Describe the molecular structure of the water molecule.

Solution

The Lewis structure for water is

$$H—\overset{..}{\underset{..}{O}}—H$$

There are four pairs of electrons: two bonding pairs and two nonbonding pairs. To minimize repulsions, these are best arranged in a tetrahedral array, as shown in Fig. 8.16(a). Although H_2O has a tetrahedral arrangement of electron pairs, it is not a tetrahedral molecule. The atoms in the H_2O molecule form a V shape, as shown in Fig. 8.16(b) and (c).

See Exercises 8.83 and 8.84.

 Molecular Models: NH_3, H_2O

From Sample Exercise 8.11 we see that the H_2O molecule is V-shaped, or bent, because of the presence of the lone pairs. If no lone pairs were present, the molecule would be linear, the polar bonds would cancel, and the molecule would have no dipole moment. This would make water very different from the polar substance so familiar to us.

From the previous discussion we would predict that the H—X—H bond angle (where X is the central atom) in CH_4, NH_3, and H_2O should be the tetrahedral angle of 109.5 degrees. Experimental studies, however, show that the actual bond angles are those given in Fig. 8.17. What significance do these results have for the VSEPR model? One possible point of view is that we should be pleased to have the observed angles so close to the tetrahedral angle. The opposite view is that the deviations are significant enough to require modification of the simple model so that it can more accurately handle similar cases. We will take the latter view.

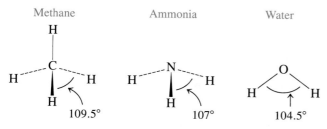

Methane

Ammonia

Water

109.5°

107°

104.5°

Figure 8.17

The bond angles in the CH_4, NH_3, and H_2O molecules. Note that the bond angle between bonding pairs decreases as the number of lone pairs increases.

Let us examine the following data:

	CH_4	NH_3	H_2O
Number of lone pairs	0	1	2
Bond angle	109.5°	107°	104.5°

One interpretation of the trend observed here is that lone pairs require more space than bonding pairs; in other words, as the number of lone pairs increases, the bonding pairs are increasingly squeezed together.

This interpretation seems to make physical sense if we think in the following terms. A bonding pair is shared between two nuclei, and the electrons can be close to either nucleus. They are relatively confined between the two nuclei. A lone pair is localized on only one nucleus, and both electrons will be close only to that nucleus, as shown schematically in Fig. 8.18. These pictures help us understand why a lone pair may require more space near an atom than a bonding pair.

As a result of these observations, we make the following addition to the original postulate of the VSEPR model: *Lone pairs require more room than bonding pairs and tend to compress the angles between the bonding pairs.*

So far we have considered cases with two, three, and four electron pairs around the central atom. These are summarized in Table 8.6. For five pairs of electrons, there are several possible choices. The one that produces minimum repulsion is a **trigonal bipyramid.** Note from Table 8.6 that this arrangement has two different angles, 90 degrees and 120 degrees. As the name suggests, the structure formed by this arrangement of pairs consists of two trigonal-based pyramids that share a common base. Six pairs of electrons can best be arranged around a given atom with 90-degree angles to form an **octahedral structure,** as shown in Table 8.6.

In order to use the VSEPR model to determine the geometric structures of molecules, you should memorize the relationships between the number of electron pairs and their best arrangement.

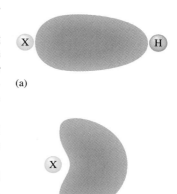

(a)

(b)

Figure 8.18

(a) In a bonding pair of electrons, the electrons are shared by two nuclei. (b) In a lone pair, both electrons must be close to a single nucleus and tend to take up more of the space around that atom.

Table 8.6 Arrangements of Electron Pairs Around an Atom Yielding Minimum Repulsion

Number of Electron Pairs	Arrangement of Electron Pairs		Example
2	Linear		
3	Trigonal planar		
4	Tetrahedral		
5	Trigonal bipyramidal		
6	Octahedral		

Molecular Models: PCl_5, PCl_4^+, PCl_6^-

Sample Exercise 8.12 *Prediction of Molecular Structure II*

When phosphorus reacts with excess chlorine gas, the compound phosphorus pentachloride (PCl_5) is formed. In the gaseous and liquid states, this substance consists of PCl_5 molecules, but in the solid state it consists of a 1:1 mixture of PCl_4^+ and PCl_6^- ions. Predict the geometric structures of PCl_5, PCl_4^+, and PCl_6^-.

Solution

The Lewis structure for PCl_5 is shown. Five pairs of electrons around the phosphorus atom require a trigonal bipyramidal arrangement (see Table 8.6). When the chlorine atoms are included, a trigonal bipyramidal molecule results:

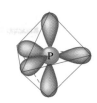

The Lewis structure for the PCl_4^+ ion $(5 + 4(7) - 1 = 32$ valence electrons) is shown below. There are four pairs of electrons surrounding the phosphorus atom in the PCl_4^+ ion, which requires a tetrahedral arrangement of the pairs. Since each pair is shared with a chlorine atom, a tetrahedral PCl_4^+ cation results.

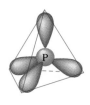 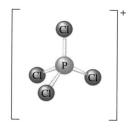

The Lewis structure for PCl_6^- $(5 + 6(7) + 1 = 48$ valence electrons) is shown below. Since phosphorus is surrounded by six pairs of electrons, an octahedral arrangement is required to minimize repulsions, as shown below in the center. Since each electron pair is shared with a chlorine atom, an octahedral PCl_6^- anion is predicted.

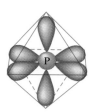 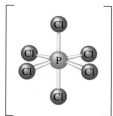

See Exercises 8.81, 8.82, 8.85, and 8.86.

Sample Exercise 8.13 *Prediction of Molecular Structure III*

Because the noble gases have filled *s* and *p* valence orbitals, they were not expected to be chemically reactive. In fact, for many years these elements were called *inert gases* because of this supposed inability to form any compounds. However, in the early 1960s several compounds of krypton, xenon, and radon were synthesized. For example, a team at the Argonne National Laboratory produced the stable colorless compound xenon tetrafluoride (XeF_4). Predict its structure and whether it has a dipole moment.

Solution   The Lewis structure for XeF_4 is

Crystals of xenon tetrafluoride.

The xenon atom in this molecule is surrounded by six pairs of electrons, which means an octahedral arrangement.

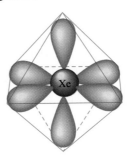

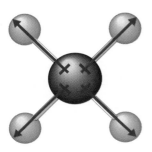

The structure predicted for this molecule will depend on how the lone pairs and bonding pairs are arranged. Consider the two possibilities shown in Fig. 8.19. The bonding pairs are indicated by the presence of the fluorine atoms. Since the structure predicted differs in the two cases, we must decide which of these arrangements is preferable. The key is to look at the lone pairs. In the structure in part (a), the lone pair–lone pair angle is 90 degrees; in the structure in part (b), the lone pairs are separated by 180 degrees. Since lone pairs require more room than bonding pairs, a structure with two lone pairs at 90 degrees is unfavorable. Thus the arrangement in Fig. 8.19(b) is preferred, and the molecular structure is predicted to be square planar. Note that this molecule is *not* described as being octahedral. There is an *octahedral arrangement of electron pairs,* but the *atoms* form a **square planar structure.**

Although each Xe—F bond is polar (fluorine has a greater electronegativity than xenon), the square planar arrangement of these bonds causes the polarities to cancel.

Thus XeF_4 has no dipole moment, as shown in the margin.

See Exercises 8.87 through 8.90.

We can further illustrate the use of the VSEPR model for molecules or ions with lone pairs by considering the triiodide ion (I_3^-).

$$\left[:\ddot{I} - \ddot{I} - \ddot{I}: \right]^-$$

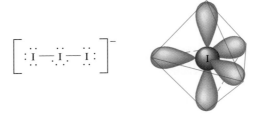

The central iodine atom has five pairs around it, which requires a trigonal bipyramidal arrangement. Several possible arrangements of lone pairs are shown in Fig. 8.20. Note that structures (a) and (b) have lone pairs at 90 degrees, whereas in (c) all lone pairs are at 120 degrees. Thus structure (c) is preferred. The resulting molecular structure for I_3^- is linear:

$$[I—I—I]^-$$

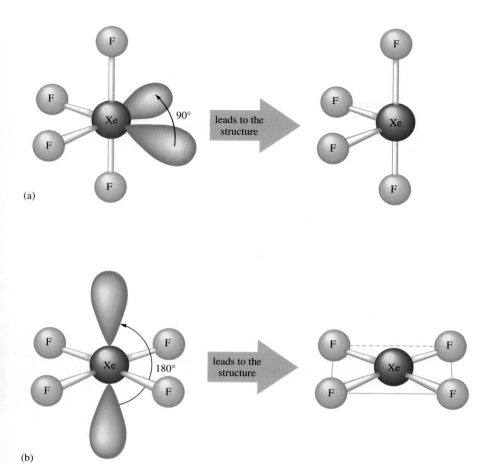

Figure 8.19

Possible electron pair arrangements for XeF$_4$. Since arrangement (a) has lone pairs at 90° from each other, it is less favorable than arrangement (b), where the lone pairs are at 180°.

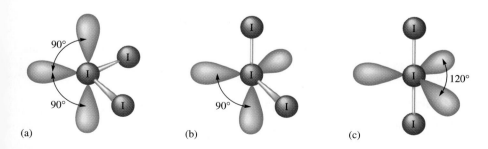

Figure 8.20

Three possible arrangements of the electron pairs in the I$_3^-$ ion. Arrangement (c) is preferred because there are no 90° lone pair–lone pair interactions.

The VSEPR Model and Multiple Bonds

So far in our treatment of the VSEPR model we have not considered any molecules with multiple bonds. To see how these molecules are handled by this model, let's consider the NO_3^- ion, which requires three resonance structures to describe its electronic structure:

The NO_3^- ion is known to be planar with 120-degree bond angles:

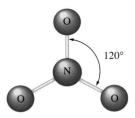

This planar structure is the one expected for three pairs of electrons around a central atom, which means that *a double bond should be counted as one effective pair* in using the VSEPR model. This makes sense because the two pairs of electrons involved in the double bond are *not* independent pairs. Both the electron pairs must be in the space between the nuclei of the two atoms in order to form the double bond. In other words, the double bond acts as one center of electron density to repel the other pairs of electrons. The same holds true for triple bonds. This leads us to another general rule: *For the VSEPR model, multiple bonds count as one effective electron pair.*

The molecular structure of nitrate also shows us one more important point: *When a molecule exhibits resonance, any one of the resonance structures can be used to predict the molecular structure using the VSEPR model.* These rules are illustrated in Sample Exercise 8.14.

Sample Exercise 8.14   *Structures of Molecules with Multiple Bonds*

Predict the molecular structure of the sulfur dioxide molecule. Is this molecule expected to have a dipole moment?

Solution

First, we must determine the Lewis structure for the SO_2 molecule, which has 18 valence electrons. The expected resonance structures are

Molecular Model: SO_2

To determine the molecular structure, we must count the electron pairs around the sulfur atom. In each resonance structure the sulfur has one lone pair, one pair in a single bond, and one double bond. Counting the double bond as one pair yields three effective pairs around the sulfur. According to Table 8.6, a trigonal planar arrangement is required, which yields a V-shaped molecule:

$$O \overset{120°}{\underset{S}{\curvearrowright}} O$$

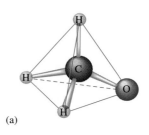

(a)

Thus the structure of the SO_2 molecule is expected to be V-shaped, with a 120-degree bond angle. The molecule has a dipole moment directed as shown:

$$O \overset{\uparrow}{\underset{S}{\diagup\diagdown}} O$$

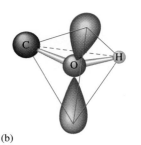

Since the molecule is V-shaped, the polar bonds do not cancel.

See Exercises 8.91 and 8.92.

(b)

It should be noted at this point that lone pairs that are oriented at least 120 degrees from other pairs do not produce significant distortions of bond angles. For example, the angle in the SO_2 molecule is actually quite close to 120 degrees. We will follow the general principle that *a 120-degree angle provides lone pairs with enough space so that distortions do not occur. Angles less than 120 degrees are distorted when lone pairs are present.*

(c)

Figure 8.21
The molecular structure of methanol. (a) The arrangement of electron pairs and atoms around the carbon atom. (b) The arrangement of bonding and lone pairs around the oxygen atom. (c) The molecular structure.

Molecules Containing No Single Central Atom

So far we have considered molecules consisting of one central atom surrounded by other atoms. The VSEPR model can be readily extended to more complicated molecules, such as methanol (CH_3OH). This molecule is represented by the following Lewis structure:

$$H-\overset{\overset{\displaystyle H}{|}}{\underset{\underset{\displaystyle H}{|}}{C}}-\overset{..}{\underset{..}{O}}-H$$

Molecular Model: CH_3OH

The molecular structure can be predicted from the arrangement of pairs around the carbon and oxygen atoms. Note that there are four pairs of electrons around the carbon, which requires a tetrahedral arrangement, as shown in Fig. 8.21(a). The oxygen also has four pairs, which requires a tetrahedral arrangement. However, in this case the tetrahedron will be slightly distorted by the space requirements of the lone pairs [Fig. 8.21(b)]. The overall geometric arrangement for the molecule is shown in Fig. 8.21(c).

CHEMICAL IMPACT

Chemical Structure and Communication: Semiochemicals

IN THIS CHAPTER we have stressed the importance of being able to predict the three-dimensional structure of a molecule. Molecular structure is important because of its effect on chemical reactivity. This is especially true in biological systems, where reactions must be efficient and highly specific. Among the hundreds of types of molecules in the fluids of a typical biological system, the appropriate reactants must find and react only with each other—they must be very discriminating. This specificity depends largely on structure. The molecules are constructed so that only the appropriate partners can approach each other in a way that allows reaction.

Another area where molecular structure is central is in the use of molecules as a means of communication. Examples of a chemical communication occur in humans in the conduction of nerve impulses across synapses, the control of the manufacture and storage of key chemicals in cells, and the senses of smell and taste. Plants and animals also use chemical communication. For example, ants lay down a chemical trail so that other ants can find a particular food supply. Ants also warn their fellow workers of approaching danger by emitting certain chemicals.

Molecules convey messages by fitting into appropriate receptor sites in a very specific way, which is determined by their structure. When a molecule occupies a receptor site, chemical processes are stimulated that produce the appropriate response. Sometimes receptors can be fooled, as in the use of artificial sweeteners—molecules fit the sites on the taste buds that stimulate a "sweet" response in the brain, but they are not metabolized in the same way as natural sugars. Similar deception is useful in insect control. If an area is sprayed with synthetic female sex attractant molecules, the males

The queen bee secretes a chemical that prevents the worker bees from raising a competitive sovereign.

of that species become so confused that mating does not occur.

A *semiochemical* is a molecule that delivers a message between members of the same or different species of plant or animal. There are three groups of these chemical messengers: allomones, kairomones, and pheromones. Each is of great ecological importance.

An *allomone* is defined as a chemical that somehow gives adaptive advantage to the producer. For example, leaves of the black walnut tree contain a herbicide, juglone, that appears after the leaves fall to the ground. Juglone is not toxic to grass or certain grains, but it is effective against plants such as apple trees that would compete for the available water and food supplies.

Antibiotics are also allomones, since the microorganisms produce them to inhibit other species from growing near them.

Many plants produce bad-tasting chemicals to protect themselves from plant-eating insects and animals. The familiar compound nicotine deters animals from eating the tobacco plant. The millipede sends an unmistakable "back off"

message by squirting a predator with benzaldehyde and hydrogen cyanide.

Defense is not the only use of allomones, however. Flowers use scent as a way to attract pollinating insects. Honeybees, for instance, are guided to alfalfa to flowers by a series of sweet-scented compounds.

Kairomones are chemical messengers that bring advantageous news to the receiver, and the floral scents are kairomones from the honeybees' viewpoint. Many predators are guided by kairomones emitted by their food. For example, apple skins exude a chemical that attracts the codling moth larva. In some cases kairomones help the underdog. Certain marine mollusks can pick up the "scent" of their predators, the sea stars, and make their escape.

Pheromones are chemicals that affect receptors of the same species as the donor. That is, they are specific within a species. *Releaser pheromones* cause an immediate reaction in the receptor, and *primer pheromones* cause long-term effects. Examples of releaser pheromones are sex attractants of insects, generated in some species by the males and in others by the females. Sex pheromones also have been found in plants and mammals.

Alarm pheromones are highly volatile compounds (ones easily changed to a gas) released to warn of danger. Honeybees produce isoamyl acetate ($C_7H_{14}O_2$) in their sting glands. Because of its high volatility, this compound does not linger after the state of alert is over. Social behavior in insects is character-ized by the use of *trail pheromones*, which are used to indicate a food source. Social insects such as bees, ants, wasps, and termites use these substances. Since trail pheromones are less volatile compounds, the indicators persist for some time.

Primer pheromones, which cause long-term behavioral changes, are harder to isolate and identify. One example, however, is the "queen substance" produced by queen honeybees. All the eggs in a colony are laid by one queen bee. If she is removed from the hive or dies, the worker bees are activated by the absence of the queen substance and begin to feed royal jelly to bee larvae in order to raise a new queen. The queen substance also prevents the development of the workers' ovaries so that only the queen herself can produce eggs.

Many studies of insect pheromones are now under way in the hope that they will provide a method of controlling insects that is more efficient and safer than the current chemical pesticides.

Summary of the VSEPR Model

The rules for using the VSEPR model to predict molecular structure are

- Determine the Lewis structure(s) for the molecule.
- For molecules with resonance structures, use any of the structures to predict the molecular structure.
- Sum the electron pairs around the central atom.
- In counting pairs, count each multiple bond as a single effective pair.
- The arrangement of the pairs is determined by minimizing electron-pair repulsions. These arrangements are shown in Table 8.6.
- Lone pairs require more space than bonding pairs. Choose an arrangement that gives the lone pairs as much room as possible. Recognize that the lone pairs may produce a slight distortion of the structure at angles less than 120 degrees.

The VSEPR Model—How Well Does It Work?

The VSEPR model is very simple. There are only a few rules to remember, yet the model correctly predicts the molecular structures of most molecules formed from nonmetallic elements. Molecules of any size can be treated by applying the VSEPR model to each appropriate atom (those bonded to at least two other atoms) in the molecule. Thus we can use this model to predict the structures of molecules with hundreds of atoms. It does, however, fail in a few instances. For example, phosphine (PH_3), which has a Lewis structure analogous to that of ammonia,

$$H-\overset{\displaystyle ..}{P}-H \qquad H-\overset{\displaystyle ..}{N}-H$$
$$\overset{|}{H} \qquad\qquad\quad \overset{|}{H}$$

Molecular Model: PH_3

would be predicted to have a molecular structure similar to that for NH_3, with bond angles of approximately 107 degrees. However, the bond angles of phosphine are actually 94 degrees. There are ways of explaining this structure, but more rules have to be added to the model.

This again illustrates the point that simple models are bound to have exceptions. In introductory chemistry we want to use simple models that fit the majority of cases; we are willing to accept a few failures rather than complicate the model. The amazing thing about the VSEPR model is that such a simple model predicts correctly the structures of so many molecules.

For Review

Key Terms

Section 8.1
bond energy
ionic bonding
ionic compound
Coulomb's law
bond length
covalent bonding
polar covalent bond

Section 8.2
electronegativity

Section 8.3
dipolar
dipole moment

Section 8.4
isoelectronic ions

Section 8.5
lattice energy

Section 8.8
single bond
double bond
triple bond

Section 8.9
localized electron (LE) model
lone pair
bonding pair

Section 8.10
Lewis structure
duet rule
octet rule

Section 8.12
resonance
resonance structure
formal charge

Summary

Chemical bonds hold groups of atoms together. Bonding occurs when a group of atoms can lower its total energy by aggregating. Bonds can be classified into several types. In an ionic bond there is a transfer of electrons to form ions; in a covalent bond electrons are shared. Between these extremes, in a polar covalent bond electrons are shared unequally. The percent ionic character of the bond in a diatomic molecule XY can be defined as

$$\text{Percent ionic character} = \left(\frac{\text{measured dipole moment of X—Y}}{\text{calculated dipole moment of X}^+\text{Y}^-} \right) \times 100\%$$

Electronegativity is defined as the relative ability of an atom in a molecule to attract the electrons shared in a bond. The electronegativity difference of the atoms involved in a bond determines the polarity of that bond. The spatial arrangement of polar bonds determines the overall polarity, or dipole moment, of a molecule.

Stable molecules usually contain atoms that have filled valence orbitals. Nonmetals bonding to each other achieve noble gas configurations in their valence orbitals by covalent bonding. A nonmetal and a representative-group metal achieve the same result by transferring electrons to form ions.

Ions have significantly different sizes from their parent atoms. Cations are smaller because the parent atom has lost electrons to become an ion. Anions, because they have more electrons than the parent atom, are larger. In general, ion size increases going down a group. Isoelectronic ions (having the same number of electrons) decrease in size with increasing Z values.

Lattice energy is the change in energy that takes place when separated gaseous ions are packed together to form an ionic solid. Bond energy, the energy necessary to break a covalent bond, varies with the number of shared electron pairs. A single bond involves one electron pair; a double bond, two electron pairs; and a triple bond, three electron pairs. Bond energies can be used to calculate the enthalpy change for a reaction.

The Lewis structure of a molecule shows how the valence electrons are arranged among the atoms. The duet rule for hydrogen and the octet rule for second-row elements reflect the observation that atoms tend to fill their valence orbitals. Elements in the third row and beyond can exceed the octet rule because of the availability of empty *d* orbitals.

Sometimes more than one valid Lewis structure can be drawn for the same molecule, which is accounted for by the concept of resonance. The actual electronic structure is represented by the superposition of the resonance structures in such cases.

When several nonequivalent Lewis structures can be drawn for a molecule, formal charge is often used to choose the most appropriate structure(s). The VSEPR model is very useful in predicting the geometries of molecules formed from nonmetals. The principal postulate of this model is that the structure around a given atom is determined by minimizing electron-pair repulsions.

> **Section 8.13**
> molecular structure
> valence shell electron pair repulsion (VSEPR) model
> linear structure
> trigonal planar structure
> tetrahedral structure
> trigonal pyramid
> trigonal bipyramid
> octahedral structure
> square planar structure

In-Class Discussion Questions

These questions are designed to be considered by groups of students in class. Often these questions work well for introducing a particular topic in class.

1. Explain the electronegativity trends across a row and down a column of the periodic table. Compare these trends with those of ionization energies and atomic radii. How are they related?

2. The ionic compound AB is formed. The charges on the ions may be +1, −1; +2, −2; +3, −3 or even larger. What are the factors that determine the charge for an ion in an ionic compound?

3. Using only the periodic table, predict the most stable ion for Na, Mg, Al, S, Cl, K, Ca, and Ga. Arrange these from largest to smallest radius, and explain why the radius varies as it does. Compare your predictions with Fig. 8.7.

4. The bond energy for a C—H bond is about 413 kJ/mol in CH_4 but 380 kJ/mol in $CHBr_3$. Although these values are relatively close in magnitude, they are different. Explain why they are different. Does the fact that the bond energy is lower in $CHBr_3$ make any sense? Why?

5. Consider the following statement: "Because oxygen wants to have a negative two charge, the second electron affinity is more negative than the first." Indicate everything that is correct in this statement. Indicate everything that is incorrect. Correct the incorrect statements and explain.

6. Which has the greater bond lengths: NO_2^- or NO_3^-? Explain.

7. The following ions are best described with resonance structures. Draw the resonance structures, and using formal charge arguments, predict the best Lewis structure for each ion.
   a. NCO^-
   b. CNO^-

8. Would you expect the electronegativity of titanium to be the same in the species Ti, Ti^{2+}, Ti^{3+}, and Ti^{4+}? Explain.

9. The second electron affinity values for both oxygen and sulfur are unfavorable (endothermic). Explain.

10. What is meant by a chemical bond? Why do atoms form bonds with each other? Why do some elements exist as molecules in nature instead of as free atoms?

11. Why are some bonds ionic and some covalent?

12. Does a Lewis structure tell which electrons come from which atoms? Explain.

A blue question or exercise number indicates that the answer to that question or exercise appears at the back of this book and a solution appears in the *Solutions Guide.*

Questions

13. Explain the difference between the following pairs of terms.
    a. electronegativity and electron affinity
    b. covalent bond and polar covalent bond
    c. polar covalent bond and ionic bond

14. Define the term *isoelectronic.* When comparing sizes of ions of elements in the same period in the periodic table, why is it advantageous to compare isoelectronic species?

15. Although the VSEPR model is correct in predicting that CH_4 is tetrahedral, NH_3 is pyramidal, and H_2O is bent, the model in its simplest form does not account for the fact that these molecules do not have exactly the same bond angles (∠HCH is 109.5 degrees, as expected for a tetrahedron, but ∠HNH is 107.3 degrees and ∠HOH is 104.5 degrees). Explain these deviations from the tetrahedral angle.

16. Explain the terms *resonance* and *delocalized electrons.*

17. What two requirements should be satisfied for a molecule to be polar?

18. Give a rationalization for the octet rule in terms of orbitals.

Exercises

In this section similar exercises are paired.

Chemical Bonds and Electronegativity

19. Without using Fig. 8.3, predict the order of increasing electronegativity in each of the following groups of elements.
    a. C, N, O
    b. S, Se, Cl
    c. Si, Ge, Sn
    d. Tl, S, Ge
20. Without using Fig. 8.3, predict the order of increasing electronegativity in each of the following groups of elements.
    a. Na, K, Rb
    b. B, O, Ga
    c. F, Cl, Br
    d. S, O, F

21. Without using Fig. 8.3, predict which bond in each of the following groups will be the most polar.
    a. C—F, Si—F, Ge—F
    b. P—Cl, S—Cl
    c. S—F, S—Cl, S—Br
    d. Ti—Cl, Si—Cl, Ge—Cl
22. Without using Fig. 8.3, predict which bond in each of the following groups will be the most polar.
    a. C—H, Si—H, Sn—H
    b. Al—Br, Ga—Br, In—Br, Tl—Br
    c. C—O or Si—O
    d. O—F or O—Cl

23. Repeat Exercises 19 and 21, this time using the values for the electronegativities of the elements given in Fig. 8.3. Are there differences in your answers?
24. Repeat Exercises 20 and 22, this time using the values for the electronegativities of the elements given in Fig. 8.3. Are there differences in your answers?

25. Hydrogen has an electronegativity value between boron and carbon and identical to phosphorus. With this in mind, rank the following bonds in order of decreasing polarity: P—H, O—H, N—H, F—H, C—H.
26. Rank the following bonds in order of increasing ionic character: N—O, Ca—O, C—F, Br—Br, K—F.

Ions and Ionic Compounds

27. Write electron configurations for the most stable ion formed by each of the elements Rb, Ba, Se, and I.
28. Write electron configurations for the most stable ion formed by each of the elements S, Br, Ra, and Cs.

29. Write electron configurations for
    a. the cations Mg^{2+}, K^+, and Al^{3+}.
    b. the anions N^{3-}, O^{2-}, F^-, and Te^{2-}.
30. Write electron configurations for
    a. the cations Sr^{2+}, Cs^+, In^+, and Pb^{2+}.
    b. the anions P^{3-}, S^{2-}, and Br^-.

31. Which of the following ions have noble gas electron configurations?
    a. Fe^{2+}, Fe^{3+}, Sc^{3+}, Co^{3+}
    b. Tl^+, Te^{2-}, Cr^{3+}
    c. Pu^{4+}, Ce^{4+}, Ti^{4+}
    d. Ba^{2+}, Pt^{2+}, Mn^{2+}
32. Which of the following ions have noble gas electron configurations?
    a. V^{3+}, V^{5+}, Ni^{2+}
    b. Ta^{2+}, Ta^{5+}, Cd^{2+}
    c. Rb^{2+}, Sr^{2+}, Sn^{2+}
    d. P^{3-}, S^{3-}, Br^{3-}

33. Give three ions that are isoelectronic with neon. Place these ions in order of increasing size.
34. Give three ions that are isoelectronic with argon. Place these ions in order of increasing size.

35. For each of the following groups, place the atoms and/or ions in order of decreasing size.
    a. Cu, Cu^+, Cu^{2+}
    b. Ni^{2+}, Pd^{2+}, Pt^{2+}
    c. O, O^-, O^{2-}
    d. La^{3+}, Eu^{3+}, Gd^{3+}, Yb^{3+}
    e. Te^{2-}, I^-, Cs^+, Ba^{2+}, La^{3+}
36. For each of the following groups, place the atoms and/or ions in order of decreasing size.
    a. V, V^{2+}, V^{3+}, V^{5+}
    b. Na^+, K^+, Rb^+, Cs^+
    c. Te^{2-}, I^-, Cs^+, Ba^{2+}
    d. P, P^-, P^{2-}, P^{3-}
    e. O^{2-}, S^{2-}, Se^{2-}, Te^{2-}

37. Predict the empirical formulas of the ionic compounds formed from the following pairs of elements. Name each compound.
    a. Li and N
    b. Ga and O
    c. Rb and Cl
    d. Ba and S
38. Predict the empirical formulas of the ionic compounds formed from the following pairs of elements. Name each compound.
    a. Al and Cl
    b. Na and O
    c. Sr and F
    d. Ca and S

39. Which compound in each of the following pairs of ionic substances has the most exothermic lattice energy? Justify your answers.
  a. NaCl, KCl
  b. LiF, LiCl
  c. $Mg(OH)_2$, MgO
  d. $Fe(OH)_2$, $Fe(OH)_3$
  e. NaCl, Na_2O
  f. MgO, BaS

40. Which compound in each of the following pairs of ionic substances has the most exothermic lattice energy? Justify your answers.
  a. LiF, CsF
  b. NaBr, NaI
  c. $BaCl_2$, BaO
  d. Na_2SO_4, $CaSO_4$
  e. KF, K_2O
  f. Li_2O, Na_2S

41. Use the following data to estimate ΔH_f° for sodium chloride.

$$Na(s) + \tfrac{1}{2}Cl_2(g) \longrightarrow NaCl(s)$$

Lattice energy	-786 kJ/mol
Ionization energy for Na	495 kJ/mol
Electron affinity of Cl	-349 kJ/mol
Bond energy of Cl_2	239 kJ/mol
Enthalpy of sublimation for Na	109 kJ/mol

42. Use the following data to estimate ΔH_f° for magnesium fluoride.

$$Mg(s) + F_2(g) \longrightarrow MgF_2(s)$$

Lattice energy	-3916 kJ/mol
First ionization energy of Mg	735 kJ/mol
Second ionization energy of Mg	1445 kJ/mol
Electron affinity of F	-328 kJ/mol
Bond energy of F_2	154 kJ/mol
Enthalpy of sublimation of Mg	150. kJ/mol

43. Consider the following energy changes:

	ΔH (kJ/mol)
$Mg(g) \rightarrow Mg^+(g) + e^-$	735
$Mg^+(g) \rightarrow Mg^{2+}(g) + e^-$	1445
$O(g) + e^- \rightarrow O^-(g)$	-141
$O^-(g) + e^- \rightarrow O^{2-}(g)$	878

Magnesium oxide exists as $Mg^{2+}O^{2-}$ and not as Mg^+O^-. Explain.

44. Using data from Exercise 43, calculate ΔH for the reaction

$$O(g) + 2e^- \longrightarrow O^{2-}(g)$$

45. Rationalize the following lattice energy values:

Compound	Lattice Energy (kJ/mol)
CaSe	-2862
Na_2Se	-2130
CaTe	-2721
Na_2Te	-2095

46. The lattice energies of $FeCl_3$, $FeCl_2$, and Fe_2O_3 are (in no particular order) -2631, -5359, and $-14,774$ kJ/mol. Match the appropriate formula to each lattice energy. Explain.

Bond Energies

47. Use bond energy values (Table 8.4) to estimate ΔH for each of the following reactions in the gas phase.
  a. $H_2 + Cl_2 \rightarrow 2HCl$
  b. $N \equiv N + 3H_2 \rightarrow 2NH_3$

48. Use bond energy values (Table 8.4) to estimate ΔH for each of the following reactions.
  a.
$$H{-}C{\equiv}N(g) + 2H_2(g) \longrightarrow H{-}\underset{\underset{H}{|}}{\overset{\overset{H}{|}}{C}}{-}\underset{\underset{H}{|}}{\overset{\overset{H}{|}}{N}}(g)$$

  b.
$$\underset{H}{\overset{H}{>}}N{-}N\underset{H}{\overset{H}{<}}(l) + 2F_2(g) \longrightarrow N{\equiv}N(g) + 4HF(g)$$

49. Use bond energies (Table 8.4) to predict ΔH for the isomerization of methyl isocyanide to acetonitrile:

$$CH_3N{\equiv}C(g) \longrightarrow CH_3C{\equiv}N(g)$$

50. Acetic acid is responsible for the sour taste of vinegar. It can be manufactured using the following reaction:

$$CH_3OH(g) + C{\equiv}O(g) \longrightarrow CH_3\overset{\overset{\displaystyle O}{\|}}{C}{-}OH(l)$$

Use tabulated values of bond energies (Table 8.4) to estimate ΔH for this reaction.

51. Use bond energies to predict ΔH for the combustion of ethanol:

$$C_2H_5OH(l) + 3O_2(g) \longrightarrow 2CO_2(g) + 3H_2O(g)$$

52. Estimate ΔH for the following reaction using bond energies.

$$H_2C=CH_2 + O_3(g) \longrightarrow CH_3CH(g) + O_2(g)$$

53. Use bond energies (Table 8.4) to estimate ΔH for the following reaction:

$$C_6H_{12}O_6(s) \longrightarrow 2CO_2(g) + 2CH_3CH_2OH(l)$$

The structure of glucose $(C_6H_{12}O_6)$ is

54. The space shuttle orbiter utilizes the oxidation of methyl hydrazine by dinitrogen tetroxide for propulsion:

$$5N_2O_4(l) + 4N_2H_3CH_3(l)$$
$$\longrightarrow 12H_2O(g) + 9N_2(g) + 4CO_2(g)$$

Use bond energies to estimate ΔH for this reaction. The structures for the reactants are:

55. Consider the following reaction:

$$H_2(g) + O_2(g) \longrightarrow H_2O_2(g) \qquad \Delta H = -153 \text{ kJ}$$

Given that the H_2 bond energy is 432 kJ/mol, the O_2 bond energy is 495 kJ/mol, and the OH bond energy is 467 kJ/mol, estimate the bond energy for the oxygen–oxygen single bond.

56. Consider the following reaction:

$$\Delta H = -549 \text{ kJ}$$

Estimate the carbon–fluorine bond energy given that the C—C bond energy is 347 kJ/mol, the C=C bond energy is 614 kJ/mol, and the F—F bond energy is 154 kJ/mol.

57. Compare your answers from parts a and b of Exercise 47 with ΔH values calculated for each reaction using standard enthalpies of formation in Appendix 4. Do enthalpy changes calculated from bond energies give a reasonable estimate of the actual values?

58. Compare your answer from Exercise 50 to the ΔH value calculated from standard enthalpies of formation in Appendix 4. Explain any discrepancies.

59. The standard enthalpies of formation for $S(g)$, $F(g)$, $SF_4(g)$, and $SF_6(g)$ are $+278.8$, $+79.0$, -775, and -1209 kJ/mol, respectively.
   a. Use these data to estimate the energy of an S—F bond.
   b. Compare your calculated values to the value given in Table 8.4. What conclusions can you draw?
   c. Why are the ΔH_f° values for $S(g)$ and $F(g)$ not equal to zero, since sulfur and fluorine are elements?

60. Use the following standard enthalpies of formation to estimate the N—H bond energy in ammonia: $N(g)$, 472.7 kJ/mol; $H(g)$, 216.0 kJ/mol; $NH_3(g)$, -46.1 kJ/mol. Compare your value to the one in Table 8.4.

61. The standard enthalpy of formation of $NH_3(g)$ is -46 kJ/mol. Use this and values for the $N\equiv N$ and H—H bond energies to estimate the N—H bond energy. Compare this result with the value in Table 8.4.

62. The standard enthalpy of formation of $N_2H_4(g)$ is 95.4 kJ/mol. Use this along with the data and the result in Exercise 60 to estimate the N—N single bond energy. Compare this with the value in Table 8.4.

Lewis Structures and Resonance

63. Write Lewis structures that obey the octet rule for each of the following.
   a. HCN
   b. PH_3
   c. $CHCl_3$
   d. NH_4^+
   e. H_2CO
   f. SeF_2
   g. CO_2
   h. O_2
   i. HBr
   Except for HCN and H_2CO, the first atom listed is the central atom. For HCN and H_2CO, carbon is the central atom.

64. Write Lewis structures that obey the octet rule for each of the following molecules and ions. (In each case the first atom listed is the central atom.)
   a. $POCl_3$, SO_4^{2-}, XeO_4, PO_4^{3-}, ClO_4^-
   b. NF_3, SO_3^{2-}, PO_3^{3-}, ClO_3^-

c. ClO_2^-, SCl_2, PCl_2^-

d. Considering your answers to parts a, b, and c, what conclusions can you draw concerning the structures of species containing the same number of atoms and the same number of valence electrons?

65. Write Lewis structures for the following molecules or ions, which have central atoms that do not obey the octet rule:

$$PF_5, \ BeH_2, \ BH_3, \ Br_3^-, \ SF_4, \ XeF_4, \ ClF_5, \text{ and } SF_6$$

66. ClF_3 and BrF_3 are both used to fluorinate uranium to produce UF_6 in the processing and reprocessing of nuclear fuel. Write Lewis structures for ClF_3 and BrF_3.

67. Write Lewis structures for the following. Show all resonance structures where applicable.
a. NO_2^-, NO_3^-
b. OCN^-, SCN^-, N_3^-
(Carbon is the central atom in OCN^- and SCN^-.)

68. Some of the important pollutants in the atmosphere are ozone (O_3), sulfur dioxide, and sulfur trioxide. Write Lewis structures for these three molecules. Show all resonance structures where applicable.

69. Benzene (C_6H_6) consists of a six-membered ring of carbon atoms with one hydrogen bonded to each carbon. Write Lewis structures for benzene, including resonance structures.

70. Borazine ($B_3N_3H_6$) has often been called "inorganic" benzene. Write Lewis structures for borazine. Borazine contains a six-membered ring of alternating boron and nitrogen atoms.

71. An important observation supporting the need for resonance in the localized electron model was that there are only three different structures of dichlorobenzene ($C_6H_4Cl_2$). How does this fact support the need for the concept of resonance (see Exercise 69)?

72. Consider the following bond lengths:

$$C—O \quad 143 \text{ pm} \qquad C{=}O \quad 123 \text{ pm} \qquad C{\equiv}O \quad 109 \text{ pm}$$

In the CO_3^{2-} ion, all three C—O bonds have identical bond lengths of 136 pm. Why?

73. Place the species below in order of shortest to longest nitrogen–nitrogen bond.

$$N_2 \qquad N_2F_4 \qquad N_2F_2$$

(N_2F_4 exists as $F_2N—NF_2$, and N_2F_2 exists as $FN—NF$.)

74. Order the following species with respect to carbon–oxygen bond length (longest to shortest).

$$CO, \qquad CO_2, \qquad CO_3^{2-}, \qquad CH_3OH$$

What is the order from the weakest to the strongest carbon–oxygen bond? (CH_3OH exists as $H_3C—OH$.)

Formal Charge

75. Use the formal charge arguments to rationalize why BF_3 would not follow the octet rule.

76. Use formal charge arguments to explain why CO has a much smaller dipole moment than would be expected on the basis of electronegativity.

77. Write Lewis structures that obey the octet rule for the following species. Assign the formal charge for each central atom.
a. $POCl_3$
b. SO_4^{2-}
c. ClO_4^-
d. PO_4^{3-}
e. SO_2Cl_2
f. XeO_4
g. ClO_3^-
h. NO_4^{3-}

78. Write Lewis structures for the species in Exercise 77 that involve minimum formal charges.

Molecular Structure and Polarity

79. Predict the molecular structure and bond angles for each molecule or ion in Exercises 63 and 67.

80. Predict the molecular structure and bond angles for each molecule or ion in Exercises 64 and 68.

81. There are several molecular structures based on the trigonal bipyramid geometry (see Table 8.6). Three such structures are

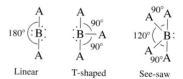

Linear   T-shaped   See-saw

Which of the compounds in Exercises 65 and 66 have these molecular structures?

82. Two variations of the octahedral geometry (see Table 8.6) are illustrated below.

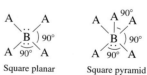

Square planar Square pyramid

Which of the compounds in Exercise 65 have these molecular structures?

83. Predict the molecular structure (including bond angles) for each of the following.
a. SeO_3
b. SeO_2

84. Predict the molecular structure (including bond angles) for each of the following.
   a. PCl_3
   b. SCl_2
   c. SiF_4

85. Predict the molecular structure (including bond angles) for each of the following. (See Exercises 81 and 82.)
   a. $XeCl_2$
   b. ICl_3
   c. TeF_4
   d. PCl_5

86. Predict the molecular structure (including bond angles) for each of the following. (See Exercises 81 and 82.)
   a. ICl_5
   b. $XeCl_4$
   c. $SeCl_6$

87. Which of the molecules in Exercise 83 have dipole moments (are polar)?

88. Which of the molecules in Exercise 84 have dipole moments (are polar)?

89. Which of the molecules in Exercise 85 have dipole moments (are polar)?

90. Which of the molecules in Exercise 86 have dipole moments (are polar)?

91. Write Lewis structures and predict the molecular structures of the following. (See Exercises 81 and 82.)
   a. OCl_2, KrF_2, BeH_2, SO_2
   b. SO_3, NF_3, IF_3
   c. CF_4, SeF_4, KrF_4
   d. IF_5, AsF_5
   Which of these compounds are polar?

92. Write Lewis structures and predict whether each of the following is polar or nonpolar.
   a. HOCN (exists as HO—CN)
   b. COS
   c. CO_2
   d. CF_2Cl_2
   e. SeF_6
   f. H_2CO (C is the central atom.)

93. The addition of antimony pentafluoride (SbF_5) to liquid hydrogen produces a solution called a *superacid*. Superacids are capable of acting as acids toward many compounds that we normally expect not to act as bases. For example, in the following reaction, HF acts as a base:

$$SbF_5 + 2HF \longrightarrow SbF_6^- + H_2F^+$$

Write Lewis structures for and predict the molecular structures of the reactants and products in this reaction. Predict the polarities of SbF_5 and HF.

94. Write a Lewis structure and predict the molecular structure and polarity for each of the following sulfur fluorides: SF_2, SF_4, SF_6, and S_2F_4 (exists as F_3S—SF). Predict the F—S—F bond angles in each molecule. (See Exercises 81 and 82.)

95. The molecules BF_3, CF_4, CO_2, PF_5, and SF_6 are all nonpolar, even though they all contain polar bonds. Why?

96. There are three possible structures of $PF_3(CH_3)_2$, where P is the central atom. Draw them and describe how measurements of dipole moments might be used to distinguish among them.

Additional Exercises

97. Arrange the following ions in order of increasing radius and in order of increasing ionization energy.
   a. O^{2-}, F^-, Na^+, Mg^{2+}
   b. P^{3-}, Ca^{2+}
   c. K^+, Cl^-, S^{2-}

98. Some of the important properties of ionic compounds are
   i. low electrical conductivity as solids and high conductivity in solution or when molten.
   ii. relatively high melting and boiling points.
   iii. brittleness.
   iv. solubility in polar solvents.

   How does the concept of ionic bonding discussed in this chapter account for these properties?

99. For each of the following, write an equation that corresponds to the energy given.
   a. lattice energy of NaCl
   b. lattice energy of NH_4Br
   c. lattice energy of MgS
   d. O==O double bond energy beginning with $O_2(g)$ as a reactant

100. What is the relationship between ΔH_f° for H(g) given in Exercise 60 and the H—H bond energy in Table 8.4?

101. Write Lewis structures for CO_3^{2-}, HCO_3^-, and H_2CO_3. When acid is added to an aqueous solution containing carbonate or bicarbonate ions, carbon dioxide gas is formed. We generally say that carbonic acid (H_2CO_3) is unstable. Use bond energies to estimate ΔH for the reaction (in the gas phase)

$$H_2CO_3 \longrightarrow CO_2 + H_2O$$

Specify a possible cause for the instability of carbonic acid.

102. Which member of the following pairs would you expect to be more energetically stable? Justify each choice.
   a. NaBr or $NaBr_2$
   b. ClO_4 or ClO_4^-

c. SO_4 or XeO_4

d. OF_4 or SeF_4

103. Lewis structures can be used to understand why some molecules react in certain ways. Write the Lewis structures for the reactants and products in the reactions described below.

a. Nitrogen dioxide dimerizes to produce dinitrogen tetroxide.

b. Boron trifluoride accepts a pair of electrons from ammonia, forming BF_3NH_3.

Give a possible explanation for why these two reactions occur.

104. Disulfur dinitride (S_2N_2) exists as a ring of alternating sulfur and nitrogen atoms. S_2N_2 will polymerize to polythiazyl, which acts as a metallic conductor of electricity along the polymer chain. Write a Lewis structure for S_2N_2.

105. Although both Br_3^- and I_3^- ions are known, the F_3^- ion has not been observed. Explain.

106. S_2Cl_2 and SCl_2 are important industrial chemicals used primarily in the vapor-phase vulcanization of certain rubbers. Draw Lewis structures for S_2Cl_2 and SCl_2. (S_2Cl_2 exists as Cl—S—S—Cl.)

107. Refer back to Exercises 77 and 78. Would you make the same prediction for the molecular structure for each case using the Lewis structure obtained in Exercise 77 as compared with the one obtained in Exercise 78?

108. The skeletal structure for dinitrogen tetroxide is

Write Lewis structures for dinitrogen tetroxide, including all resonance structures.

109. Two molecules exist with the formula N_2F_2. The Lewis structures are

a. What are the N—N—F bond angles in the two molecules?

b. What is the polarity of each molecule?

Challenge Problems

110. An alternative definition of electronegativity is

Electronegativity = constant (I.E. − E.A.)

where I.E. is the ionization energy and E.A. is the electron affinity using the sign conventions of this book. Use data in

Chapter 7 to calculate the (I.E. − E.A.) term for F, Cl, Br, and I. Do these values show the same trend as the electronegativity values given in this chapter? The first ionization energies of the halogens are 1678, 1255, 1138, and 1007 kJ/mol, respectively. (*Hint:* Choose a constant so that the electronegativity of fluorine equals 4.0. Using this constant, calculate relative electronegativities for the other halogens and compare to values given in the text.)

111. Look up the energies for the bonds in CO and N_2. Although the bond in CO is stronger, CO is considerably more reactive than N_2. Give a possible explanation.

112. Three processes that have been used for the industrial manufacture of acrylonitrile (CH_2CHCN), an important chemical used in the manufacture of plastics, synthetic rubber, and fibers, are shown below. Use bond energy values (Table 8.4) to estimate ΔH for each of the reactions.

b. $4CH_2\!\!=\!\!CHCH_3 + 6NO \xrightarrow[\text{Ag}]{700°C}$

$4CH_2\!\!=\!\!CHCN + 6H_2O + N_2$

The nitrogen–oxygen bond energy in nitric oxide (NO) is 630. kJ/mol.

c. $2CH_2\!\!=\!\!CHCH_3 + 2NH_3 + 3O_2 \xrightarrow[\text{425–510°C}]{\text{Catalyst}}$

$2CH_2\!\!=\!\!CHCN + 6H_2O$

d. Is the elevated temperature noted in parts b and c needed to provide energy to endothermic reactions?

113. Use the following data to estimate ΔH for the reaction $S^-(g) + e^- \rightarrow S^{2-}(g)$. Include an estimate of uncertainty.

	ΔH_f°	Lattice Energy	I.E. of M	ΔH_{sub} of M
Li_2S	−500	−2472	520	161
Na_2S	−365	−2203	495	109
K_2S	−381	−2052	419	90
Rb_2S	−361	−1949	409	82
Cs_2S	−360	−1850	382	78

$S(s) \longrightarrow S(g) \qquad \Delta H = 277$ kJ/mol

$S(g) + e^- \longrightarrow S^-(g) \qquad \Delta H = -200$ kJ/mol

Assume that all values are known to ± 1 kJ/mol.

114. Many times extra stability is characteristic of a molecule or ion in which resonance is possible. How could this be used to explain the acidities of the following compounds? (The acidic hydrogen is marked by an asterisk.) Part c shows resonance in the C_6H_5 ring.

a. H—C—OH* **b.** CH_3—C—CH=C—CH$_3$ **c.**

(structures with O, OH*, OH* and the benzene ring with OH*)

115. A promising new material with great potential as a fuel in solid rocket motors is ammonium dinitramide, $NH_4N(NO_2)_2$.
a. Draw Lewis structures (including resonance forms) for the dinitramide ion, $N(NO_2)_2{}^-$.
b. Predict the bond angles about each nitrogen in the dinitramide ion.

116. Draw a Lewis structure for the N,N-dimethylformamide molecule. The skeletal structure is

H—C—N—CH$_3$ with O above C and CH$_3$ below N

Various types of evidence lead to the conclusion that there is some double bond character to the C—N bond. Draw one or more resonance structures that support this observation.

117. Predict the molecular structure for each of the following. (See Exercises 81 and 82.)
a. $BrFI_2$
b. XeO_2F_2
c. $TeF_2Cl_3{}^-$

For each formula there are at least two different structures that can be drawn using the same central atom. Draw all possible structures for each formula.

118. The study of carbon-containing compounds and their properties is called *organic chemistry*. Besides carbon atoms, organic compounds also can contain hydrogen, oxygen, and nitrogen atoms (as well as other types of atoms). A common trait of simple organic compounds is to have Lewis structures

where all atoms have a formal charge of zero. Consider the following incomplete Lewis structure for an organic compound called *histidine* (an amino acid, which is the building block of all proteins found in our bodies):

(structure of histidine)

Draw a complete Lewis structure for histidine in which all atoms have a formal charge of zero. What should be the approximate bond angles about the carbon atom labeled 1 and the nitrogen atom labeled 2?

119. Nitrous oxide (N_2O) has three possible Lewis structures:

:N=N=O: ⟷ :N≡N—O: ⟷ :N—N≡O:

Given the following bond lengths,

N—N	167 pm	N=O	115 pm
N=N	120 pm	N—O	147 pm
N≡N	110 pm		

rationalize the observations that the N—N bond length in N_2O is 112 pm and that the N—O bond length is 119 pm. Assign formal charges to the resonance structures for N_2O. Can you eliminate any of the resonance structures on the basis of formal charges? Is this consistent with observation?

120. Which of the following molecules have dipole moments? For the molecules that are polar, indicate the polarity of each bond and the direction of the net dipole moment of the molecule.
a. CH_2Cl_2, $CHCl_3$, CCl_4
b. CO_2, N_2O
c. PH_3, NH_3

Marathon Problem

This problem is designed to incorporate several concepts and techniques into one situation. Marathon Problems can be used in class by groups of students to help facilitate problem-solving skills.

121. Identify the five compounds of H, N, and O described below. For each compound, write a Lewis structure that is consistent with the information given.

a. All the compounds are electrolytes, although not all of them are strong electrolytes. Compounds C and D are ionic and compound B is covalent.

b. Nitrogen occurs in its highest possible oxidation state in compounds A and C; nitrogen occurs in its lowest possible oxidation state in compounds C, D, and E. The formal charge on both nitrogens in compound C is +1; the formal charge on the only nitrogen in compound B is 0.

c. Compounds A and E exist in solution. Both solutions give off gases. Commercially available concentrated solutions of compound A are normally 16 M. The commercial, concentrated solution of compound E is 15 M.

d. Commercial solutions of compound E are labeled with a misnomer that implies that a binary, gaseous compound of nitrogen and hydrogen has reacted with water to produce ammonium ions and hydroxide ions. Actually, this reaction occurs to only a slight extent.

e. Compound D is 43.7% N and 50.0% O by mass. If compound D were a gas at STP, it would have a density of 2.86 g/L.

f. A formula unit of compound C has one more oxygen than a formula unit of compound D. Compounds C and A have one ion in common when compound A is acting as a strong electrolyte.

g. Solutions of compound C are weakly acidic; solutions of compound A are strongly acidic; solutions of compounds B and E are basic. The titration of 0.726 g of compound B requires 21.98 mL of 1.000 M HCl for complete neutralization.

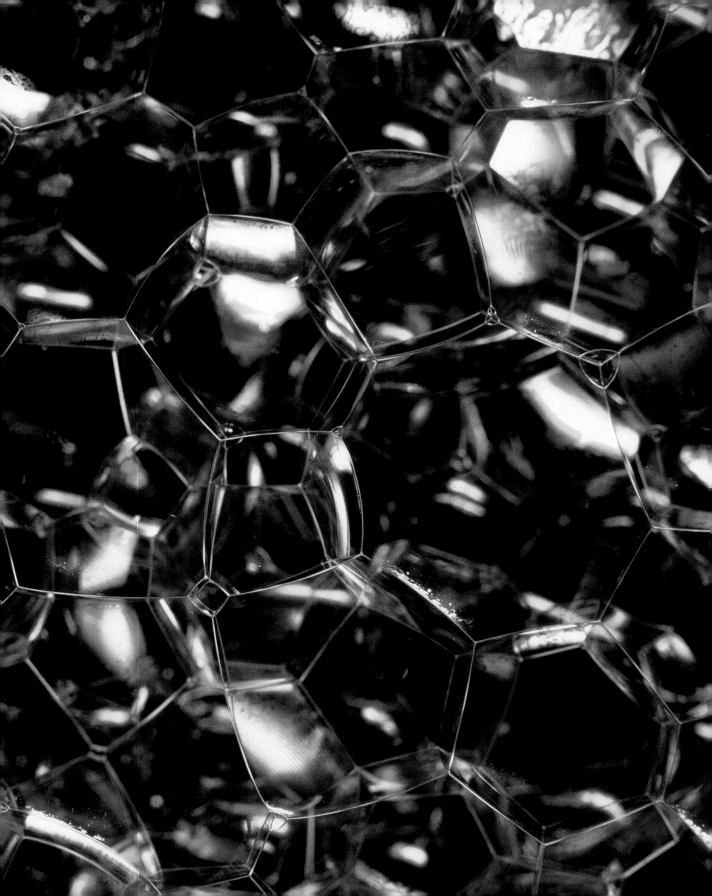

Covalent Bonding: Orbitals

Contents

*I*n Chapter 8 we discussed the fundamental concepts of bonding and introduced the most widely used simple model for covalent bonding: the localized electron model. We saw the usefulness of a bonding model as a means for systematizing chemistry by allowing us to look at molecules in terms of individual bonds. We also saw that molecular structure can be predicted by minimizing electron-pair repulsions. In this chapter we will examine bonding models in more detail, particularly focusing on the role of orbitals.

9.1 Hybridization and the Localized Electron Model

As we saw in Chapter 8, the localized electron model views a molecule as a collection of atoms bound together by sharing electrons between their atomic orbitals. The arrangement of valence electrons is represented by the Lewis structure (or structures, where resonance occurs), and the molecular geometry can be predicted from the VSEPR model. In this section we will describe the atomic orbitals used to share electrons and hence to form the bonds.

sp³ Hybridization

Let us reconsider the bonding in methane, which has the Lewis structure and molecular geometry shown in Fig. 9.1. In general, we assume that bonding involves only the valence orbitals. This means that the hydrogen atoms in methane use $1s$ orbitals. The valence orbitals of a carbon atom are the $2s$ and $2p$ orbitals shown in Fig. 9.2. In thinking about how carbon can use these orbitals to bond to the hydrogen atoms, we can see two related problems:

Animation: *sp³* Hybridization

Molecular Model: CH_4

A close-up of soap bubbles reveals their geometric shapes.

The valence orbitals are the orbitals associated with the highest principal quantum level that contains electrons on a given atom.

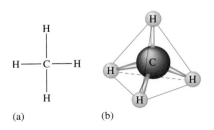

Figure 9.1

(a) The Lewis structure of the methane molecule. (b) The tetrahedral molecular geometry of the methane molecule.

Hybridization is a modification of the localized electron model to account for the observation that atoms often seem to use special atomic orbitals in forming molecules.

sp^3 hybridization gives a tetrahedral set of orbitals.

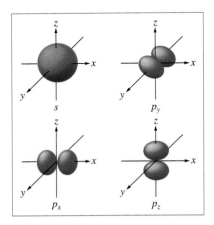

Figure 9.2

The valence orbitals on a free carbon atom: $2s$, $2p_x$, $2p_y$, and $2p_z$.

1. Using the $2p$ and $2s$ atomic orbitals will lead to two different types of C—H bonds: (a) those from the overlap of a $2p$ orbital of carbon and a $1s$ orbital of hydrogen (there will be three of these) and (b) those from the overlap of a $2s$ orbital of carbon and a $1s$ orbital of hydrogen (there will be one of these). This is a problem because methane is known to have four identical C—H bonds.

2. Since the carbon $2p$ orbitals are mutually perpendicular, we might expect the three C—H bonds formed with these orbitals to be oriented at 90-degree angles:

However, the methane molecule is known by experiment to be tetrahedral with bond angles of 109.5 degrees.

This analysis leads to one of two conclusions: Either the simple localized electron model is wrong or carbon adopts a set of atomic orbitals other than its "native" $2s$ and $2p$ orbitals to bond to the hydrogen atoms in forming the methane molecule. The second conclusion seems more reasonable. The $2s$ and $2p$ orbitals present on an *isolated* carbon atom may not be the best set of orbitals for bonding; a new set of atomic orbitals might better serve the carbon atom in forming molecules. To account for the known structure of methane, it makes sense to assume that the carbon atom has four equivalent atomic orbitals, arranged tetrahedrally. In fact, such a set of orbitals can be obtained quite readily by combining the carbon $2s$ and $2p$ orbitals, as shown schematically in Fig. 9.3. This mixing of the native atomic orbitals to form special orbitals for bonding is called **hybridization**. The four new orbitals are called sp^3 orbitals because they are formed from one $2s$ and three $2p$ orbitals (s^1p^3). We say that the carbon atom undergoes sp^3 **hybridization** or is sp^3 **hybridized**. The four sp^3 orbitals are identical in shape, each one having a large lobe and a small lobe (see Fig. 9.4). The four orbitals are oriented in space so that the large lobes form a tetrahedral arrangement, as shown in Fig. 9.3.

The hybridization of the carbon $2s$ and $2p$ orbitals also can be represented by an orbital energy-level diagram, as shown in Fig. 9.5. Note that electrons have been omitted because we do not need to be concerned with the electron arrangements on the individual atoms—it is the total number of electrons and the arrangement of these electrons in the *molecule* that are important. We are assuming that carbon's atomic orbitals are rearranged to accommodate the best electron arrangement for the molecule as a whole. The new sp^3 atomic orbitals on carbon are used to share electron pairs with the $1s$ orbitals from the four hydrogen atoms, as shown in Fig. 9.6 on page 418.

At this point let's summarize the bonding in the methane molecule. The experimentally known structure of this molecule can be explained if we assume that the carbon atom adopts a special set of atomic orbitals. These new orbitals are obtained by combining the $2s$ and the three $2p$ orbitals of the carbon atom to produce four identically shaped orbitals that are oriented toward the corners of a tetrahedron and are used to bond to the hydrogen atoms. Thus the four sp^3 orbitals on carbon in methane are postulated to account for its known structure.

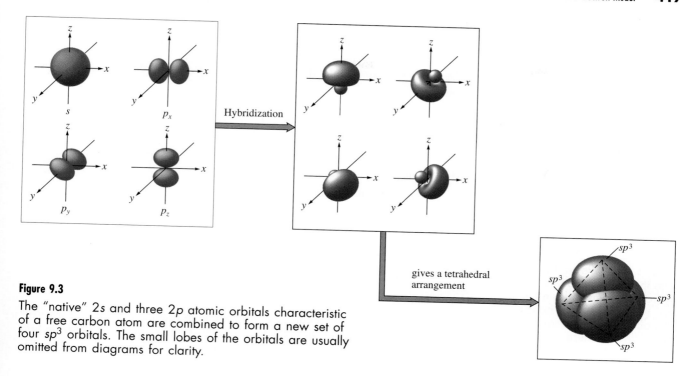

Figure 9.3

The "native" 2s and three 2p atomic orbitals characteristic of a free carbon atom are combined to form a new set of four sp^3 orbitals. The small lobes of the orbitals are usually omitted from diagrams for clarity.

gives a tetrahedral arrangement

Remember this principle: *Whenever a set of equivalent tetrahedral atomic orbitals is required by an atom, this model assumes that the atom adopts a set of sp^3 orbitals; the atom becomes sp^3 hybridized.*

It is really not surprising that an atom in a molecule might adopt a different set of atomic orbitals (called **hybrid orbitals**) from those it has in the free state. It does not seem unreasonable that to achieve minimum energy, an atom uses one set of atomic orbitals in the free state and a different set in a molecule. This is consistent with the idea that a molecule is more than simply a sum of its parts. What the atoms in a molecule were like before the molecule was formed is not as important as how the electrons are best arranged in the molecule. Therefore, this model assumes that the individual atoms respond as needed to achieve the minimum energy for the molecule.

Figure 9.5

An energy-level diagram showing the formation of four sp^3 orbitals.

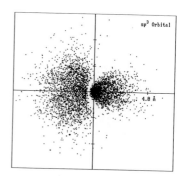

Figure 9.4

Cross section of an sp^3 orbital. Generated from a program by Robert Allendoerfer on Project SERAPHIM disk PC2402; printed with permission.

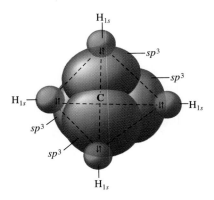

Figure 9.6

The tetrahedral set of four sp^3 orbitals of the carbon atom are used to share electron pairs with the four 1s orbitals of the hydrogen atoms to form the four equivalent C—H bonds. This accounts for the known tetrahedral structure of the CH_4 molecule.

Molecular Models: NH_3, C_2H_4

A double bond acts as one effective electron pair.

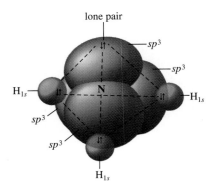

Figure 9.7

The nitrogen atom in ammonia is sp^3 hybridized.

Sample Exercise 9.1 *The Localized Electron Model I*

Describe the bonding in the ammonia molecule using the localized electron model.

Solution

A complete description of the bonding involves three steps:

1. Writing the Lewis structure
2. Determining the arrangement of electron pairs using the VSEPR model
3. Determining the hybrid atomic orbitals needed to describe the bonding in the molecule

The Lewis structure for NH_3 is

$$H-\overset{\displaystyle ..}{N}-H$$
$$\underset{\displaystyle H}{|}$$

The four electron pairs around the nitrogen atom require a tetrahedral arrangement to minimize repulsions. We have seen that a tetrahedral set of sp^3 hybrid orbitals is obtained by combining the 2s and three 2p orbitals. In the NH_3 molecule three of the sp^3 orbitals are used to form bonds to the three hydrogen atoms, and the fourth sp^3 orbital holds the lone pair, as shown in Fig. 9.7.

See Exercise 9.11.

---

sp² Hybridization

Ethylene (C_2H_4) is an important starting material in the manufacture of plastics. The C_2H_4 molecule has 12 valence electrons and the following Lewis structure:

We saw in Chapter 8 that a double bond acts as one effective pair, so in the ethylene molecule each carbon is surrounded by three effective pairs. This requires a trigonal planar arrangement with bond angles of 120 degrees. What orbitals do the carbon atoms in this molecule employ? The molecular geometry requires a set of orbitals in one plane at angles of 120 degrees. Since the 2s and 2p valence orbitals of carbon do not have the required arrangement, we need a set of hybrid orbitals.

The sp^3 orbitals we have just considered will not work because they are at angles of 109.5 degrees rather than the required 120 degrees. In ethylene the carbon atom must hybridize in a different manner. A set of three orbitals arranged at 120-degree angles in the same plane can be obtained by combining one s orbital and two p orbitals, as shown in Fig. 9.8. The orbital energy-level diagram for this arrangement is shown in Fig. 9.9. Since one 2s and two 2p orbitals are used to form these hybrid orbitals, this is called **sp² hybridization.** Note from Fig. 9.8 that the plane of the sp^2 hybridized orbitals is determined by which p orbitals are used. Since

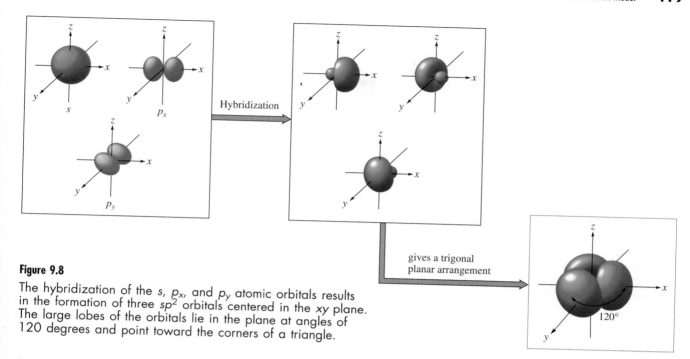

Figure 9.8

The hybridization of the s, p_x, and p_y atomic orbitals results in the formation of three sp^2 orbitals centered in the xy plane. The large lobes of the orbitals lie in the plane at angles of 120 degrees and point toward the corners of a triangle.

gives a trigonal planar arrangement

in this case we have arbitrarily decided to use the p_x and p_y orbitals, the hybrid orbitals are centered in the xy plane.

In forming the sp^2 orbitals, one $2p$ orbital on carbon has not been used. This remaining p orbital (p_z) is oriented perpendicular to the plane of the sp^2 orbitals, as shown in Fig. 9.10.

Now we will see how these orbitals can be used to account for the bonds in ethylene. The three sp^2 orbitals on each carbon can be used to share electrons, as shown in Fig. 9.11. In each of these bonds, the electron pair is shared in an area centered on a line running between the atoms. This type of covalent bond is called a **sigma (σ) bond.** In the ethylene molecule, the σ bonds are formed using sp^2 orbitals on each carbon atom and the $1s$ orbital on each hydrogen atom.

How can we explain the double bond between the carbon atoms? In the σ bond the electron pair occupies the space between the carbon atoms. The second bond must therefore result from sharing an electron pair in the space *above and below* the σ bond. This type of bond can be formed using the $2p$ orbital perpendicular to the sp^2 hybrid orbitals on each carbon atom (refer to Fig. 9.10). These parallel p orbitals can share an electron pair, which occupies the space above and below a line joining the atoms, to form a **pi (π) bond,** as shown in Fig. 9.12.

Note that σ bonds are formed from orbitals whose lobes point toward each other, but π bonds result from parallel orbitals. A *double bond always consists of one σ*

sp^2 hybridization gives a trigonal planar arrangement of atomic orbitals.

Note in Fig. 9.10 and the figures that follow that the orbital lobes are artificially narrowed to more clearly show their relative orientations.

Animation: sp^2 Hybridization

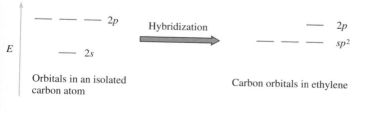

E

Orbitals in an isolated carbon atom

Hybridization

Carbon orbitals in ethylene

Figure 9.9

An orbital energy-level diagram for sp^2 hybridization. Note that one p orbital remains unchanged.

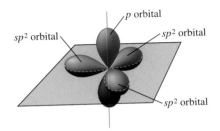

Figure 9.10
When an s and two p orbitals are mixed to form a set of three sp^2 orbitals, one p orbital remains unchanged and is perpendicular to the plane of the hybrid orbitals. Note that in this figure and those that follow, the orbitals are drawn with narrowed lobes to show their orientations more clearly.

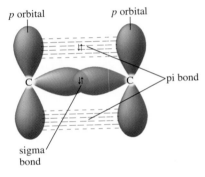

Figure 9.12
A carbon–carbon double bond consists of a σ bond and a π bond. In the σ bond the shared electrons occupy the space directly between the atoms. The π bond is formed from the unhybridized p orbitals on the two carbon atoms. In a π bond the shared electron pair occupies the space above and below a line joining the atoms.

 Molecular Model: CO_2

Figure 9.13
(a) The orbitals used to form the bonds in ethylene. (b) The Lewis structure for ethylene.

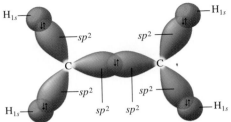

Figure 9.11
The σ bonds in ethylene. Note that for each bond the shared electron pair occupies the region directly between the atoms.

bond, where the electron pair is located directly between the atoms, *and one π bond*, where the shared pair occupies the space above and below the σ bond.

We can now completely specify the orbitals that this model assumes are used to form the bonds in the ethylene molecule. As shown in Fig. 9.13, the carbon atoms use sp^2 hybrid orbitals to form the σ bonds to the hydrogen atoms and to each other, and they use p orbitals to form the π bond with each other. Note that we have accounted fully for the Lewis structure of ethylene with its carbon–carbon double bond and carbon–hydrogen single bonds.

This example illustrates an important general principle of this model: *Whenever an atom is surrounded by three effective pairs, a set of sp^2 hybrid orbitals is required.*

sp Hybridization

Another type of hybridization occurs in carbon dioxide, which has the following Lewis structure:

$$\ddot{O}=C=\ddot{O}$$

In the CO_2 molecule the carbon atom has two effective pairs that will be arranged at an angle of 180 degrees. We therefore need a pair of atomic orbitals oriented in opposite directions. This requires a new type of hybridization, since neither sp^3 nor sp^2 hybrid orbitals will fit this case. To obtain two hybrid orbitals arranged at

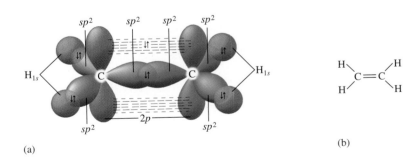

(a)

(b)

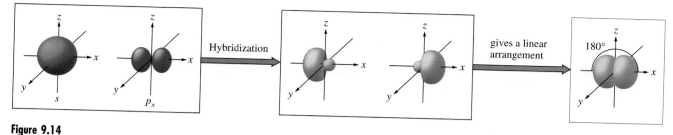

Figure 9.14
When one *s* orbital and one *p* orbital are hybridized, a set of two *sp* orbitals oriented at 180 degrees results.

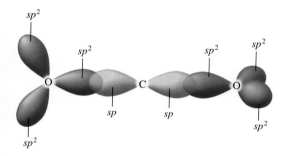

Figure 9.15
The hybrid orbitals in the CO_2 molecule.

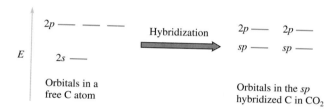

Figure 9.16
The orbital energy-level diagram for the formation of *sp* hybrid orbitals on carbon.

180 degrees requires **sp hybridization,** involving one *s* orbital and one *p* orbital, as shown in Fig. 9.14.

Animation: *sp* Hybridization

In terms of this model, *two effective pairs around an atom will always require sp hybridization of that atom.* The *sp* orbitals of carbon in carbon dioxide can be seen in Fig. 9.15, and the corresponding orbital energy-level diagram for their formation is given in Fig. 9.16. These *sp* hybrid orbitals are used to form the σ bonds between the carbon and the oxygen atoms. Note that two 2*p* orbitals remain unchanged on the *sp* hybridized carbon. These are used to form the π bonds with the oxygen atoms.

In the CO_2 molecule each oxygen atom has three effective pairs around it, requiring a trigonal planar arrangement of the pairs. Since a trigonal set of hybrid orbitals requires sp^2 hybridization, each oxygen atom is sp^2 hybridized. One *p* orbital on each oxygen is unchanged and is used for the π bond with the carbon atom.

Now we are ready to use our model to describe the bonding in carbon dioxide. The *sp* orbitals on carbon form σ bonds with the sp^2 orbitals on the two oxygen atoms (Fig. 9.15). The remaining sp^2 orbitals on the oxygen atoms hold lone pairs. The π bonds between the carbon atom and each oxygen atom are formed by the overlap of parallel 2*p* orbitals. The *sp* hybridized carbon atom has two unhybridized *p* orbitals, pictured in Fig. 9.17. Each of these *p* orbitals is used to form a π bond with an oxygen atom (see Fig. 9.18). The total bonding picture for the CO_2 molecule is shown in Fig. 9.19. Note that this picture of the bonding neatly explains the arrangement of electrons predicted by the Lewis structure.

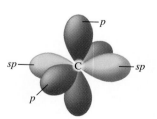

Figure 9.17
The orbitals of an *sp* hybridized carbon atom.

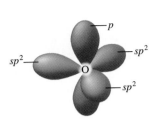

Figure 9.18
The orbital arrangement for an sp^2 hybridized oxygen atom.

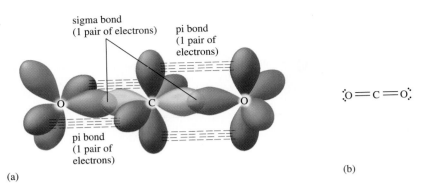

Figure 9.19
(a) The orbitals used to form the bonds in carbon dioxide. Note that the carbon–oxygen double bonds each consist of one σ bond and one π bond.
(b) The Lewis structure for carbon dioxide.

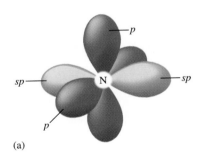

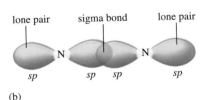

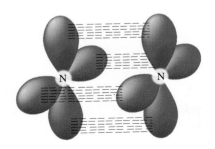

Figure 9.20
(a) An sp hybridized nitrogen atom. There are two sp hybrid orbitals and two unhybridized p orbitals. (b) The σ bond in the N_2 molecule. (c) The two π bonds in N_2 are formed when electron pairs are shared between two sets of parallel p orbitals.

Sample Exercise 9.2 *The Localized Electron Model II*

Describe the bonding in the N_2 molecule.

Solution

The Lewis structure for the nitrogen molecule is

$$: N \equiv N :$$

where each nitrogen atom is surrounded by two effective pairs. (Remember that a multiple bond counts as one effective pair.) This gives a linear arrangement (180 degrees) requiring a pair of oppositely directed orbitals. This situation requires sp hybridization. Each nitrogen atom in the nitrogen molecule has two sp hybrid orbitals and two unchanged p orbitals, as shown in Fig. 9.20(a). The sp orbitals are used to form the σ bond between the nitrogen atoms and to hold lone pairs, as shown in Fig. 9.20(b). The p orbitals are used to form the two π bonds [see Fig. 9.20(c)]; each pair of overlapping parallel p orbitals holds one electron pair. Such bonding accounts for the electron arrangement given by the Lewis structure. The triple bond consists of a σ bond (overlap of two sp orbitals) and two π bonds (each one from an overlap of two p orbitals). In addition, a lone pair occupies an sp orbital on each nitrogen atom.

See Exercises 9.13 and 9.14.

dsp³ Hybridization

To illustrate the treatment of a molecule in which the central atom exceeds the octet rule, consider the bonding in the phosphorus pentachloride molecule (PCl_5). The Lewis structure

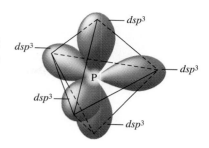

Figure 9.21

A set of *dsp³* hybrid orbitals on a phosphorus atom. Note that the set of five *dsp³* orbitals has a trigonal bipyramidal arrangement. (Each *dsp³* orbital also has a small lobe that is not shown in this diagram.)

shows that the phosphorus atom is surrounded by five electron pairs. Since five pairs require a trigonal bipyramidal arrangement, we need a trigonal bipyramidal set of atomic orbitals on phosphorus. Such a set of orbitals is formed by ***dsp³* hybridization** of one *d* orbital, one *s* orbital, and three *p* orbitals, as shown in Fig. 9.21.

The *dsp³* hybridized phosphorus atom in the PCl_5 molecule uses its five *dsp³* orbitals to share electrons with the five chlorine atoms. *Note that a set of five effective pairs around a given atom always requires a trigonal bipyramidal arrangement, which in turn requires dsp³ hybridization of that atom.*

The Lewis structure for PCl_5 shows that each chlorine atom is surrounded by four electron pairs. This requires a tetrahedral arrangement, which in turn requires a set of four *sp³* orbitals on each chlorine atom.

Now we can describe the bonding in the PCl_5 molecule. The five P—Cl σ bonds are formed by sharing electrons between a *dsp³* orbital* on the phosphorus atom and an *sp³* orbital on each chlorine.[†] The other *sp³* orbitals on each chlorine hold lone pairs. This is shown in Fig. 9.22.

Molecular Models: PCl_5, I_3^-

Sample Exercise 9.3 *The Localized Electron Model III*

Describe the bonding in the triiodide ion (I_3^-).

Solution

The Lewis structure for I_3^-

$$\left[\,:\ddot{I}\!-\!\ddot{I}\!-\!\ddot{I}: \, \right]^-$$

shows that the central iodine atom has five pairs of electrons (see Section 8.11). A set of five pairs requires a trigonal bipyramidal arrangement, which in turn requires a set of *dsp³* orbitals. The outer iodine atoms have four pairs of electrons, which calls for a tetrahedral arrangement and *sp³* hybridization.

Thus the central iodine is *dsp³* hybridized. Three of these hybrid orbitals hold lone pairs, and two of them overlap with *sp³* orbitals of the other two iodine atoms to form σ bonds.

See Exercise 9.21.

---

* There is considerable controversy about whether the *d* orbitals are as heavily involved in the bonding in these molecules as this model predicts. However, this matter is beyond the scope of this text.

[†] Although we have no way of proving conclusively that each chlorine is *sp³* hybridized, we assume that minimizing electron-pair repulsions is as important for peripheral atoms as for the central atom. Thus we will apply the VSEPR model and hybridization to both central and peripheral atoms.

(a)

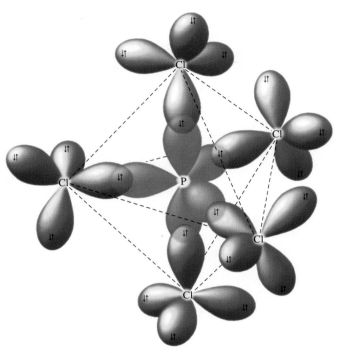

(b)

Figure 9.22

(a) The structure of the PCl₅ molecule. (b) The orbitals used to form the bonds in PCl₅. The phosphorus uses a set of five dsp^3 orbitals to share electron pairs with sp^3 orbitals on the five chlorine atoms. The other sp^3 orbitals on each chlorine atom hold lone pairs.

 Molecular Models: SF₆, XeF₄

d^2sp^3 hybridization gives six orbitals arranged octahedrally.

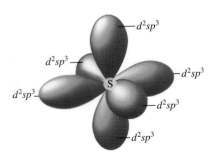

Figure 9.23

An octahedral set of d^2sp^3 orbitals on a sulfur atom. The small lobe of each hybrid orbital has been omitted for clarity.

d^2sp^3 Hybridization

Some molecules have six pairs of electrons around a central atom; an example is sulfur hexafluoride (SF₆), which has the Lewis structure

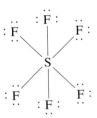

This requires an octahedral arrangement of pairs and in turn an octahedral set of six hybrid orbitals, or **d^2sp^3 hybridization,** in which two d orbitals, one s orbital, and three p orbitals are combined (see Fig. 9.23). Note that *six electron pairs around an atom are always arranged octahedrally and require d^2sp^3 hybridization of the atom.* Each of the d^2sp^3 orbitals on the sulfur atom is used to bond to a fluorine atom. Since there are four pairs on each fluorine atom, the fluorine atoms are assumed to be sp^3 hybridized.

Sample Exercise 9.4 *The Localized Electron Model IV*

How is the xenon atom in XeF₄ hybridized?

Solution

As seen in Sample Exercise 8.13, XeF_4 has six pairs of electrons around xenon that are arranged octahedrally to minimize repulsions. An octahedral set of six atomic orbitals is required to hold these electrons, and the xenon atom is d^2sp^3 hybridized.

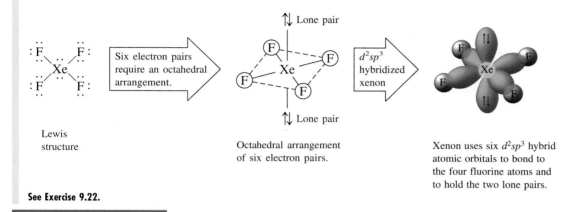

Lewis structure

Octahedral arrangement of six electron pairs.

Xenon uses six d^2sp^3 hybrid atomic orbitals to bond to the four fluorine atoms and to hold the two lone pairs.

See Exercise 9.22.

The Localized Electron Model: A Summary

The description of a molecule using the localized electron model involves three distinct steps:

- Draw the Lewis structure(s).
- Determine the arrangement of electron pairs using the VSEPR model.
- Specify the hybrid orbitals needed to accommodate the electron pairs.

It is important to do the steps in this order. For a model to be successful, it must follow nature's priorities. In the case of bonding, it seems clear that the tendency for a molecule to minimize its energy is more important than the maintenance of the characteristics of atoms as they exist in the free state. The atoms adjust to meet the "needs" of the molecule. When considering the bonding in a particular molecule, therefore, we always start with the molecule rather than the component atoms. In the molecule the electrons will be arranged to give each atom a noble gas configuration, where possible, and to minimize electron-pair repulsions. We then assume that the atoms adjust their orbitals by hybridization to allow the molecule to adopt the structure that gives the minimum energy.

In applying the localized electron model, we must remember not to overemphasize the characteristics of the separate atoms. It is not where the valence electrons originate that is important; it is where they are needed in the molecule to achieve stability. In the same vein, it is not the orbitals in the isolated atom that matter, but what orbitals the molecule requires for minimum energy.

The requirements for the various types of hybridization are summarized in Fig. 9.24 on the following page.

Number of Effective Pairs	Arrangement of Pairs		Hybridization Required

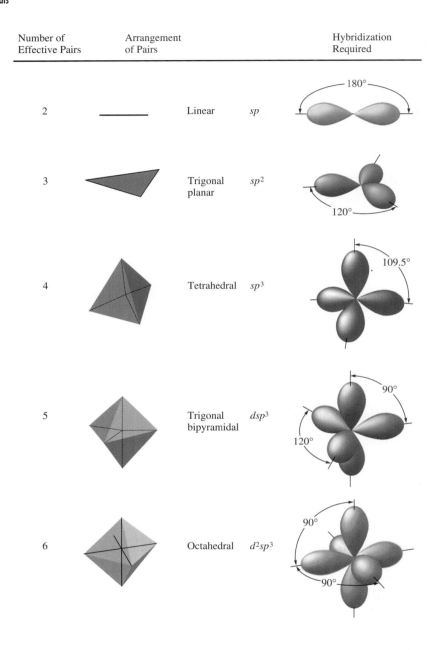

Figure 9.24
The relationship of the number of effective pairs, their spatial arrangement, and the hybrid orbital set required.

Molecular Models: CO, BF₄⁻, XeF₂

Sample Exercise 9.5 *The Localized Electron Model V*

For each of the following molecules or ions, predict the hybridization of each atom, and describe the molecular structure.
a. CO
b. BF₄⁻
c. XeF₂

Solution

a. The CO molecule has 10 valence electrons, and its Lewis structure is

$$: C \equiv O :$$

Each atom has two effective pairs, which means that both are *sp* hybridized. The triple bond consists of a σ bond produced by overlap of an *sp* orbital from each atom and two π bonds produced by overlap of $2p$ orbitals from each atom. The lone pairs are in *sp* orbitals. Since the CO molecule has only two atoms, it must be linear.

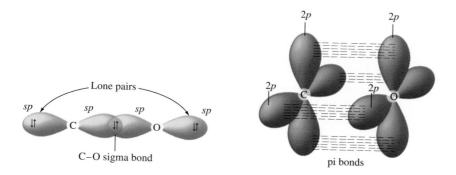

b. The BF_4^- ion has 32 valence electrons. The Lewis structure shows four pairs of electrons around the boron atom, which means a tetrahedral arrangement:

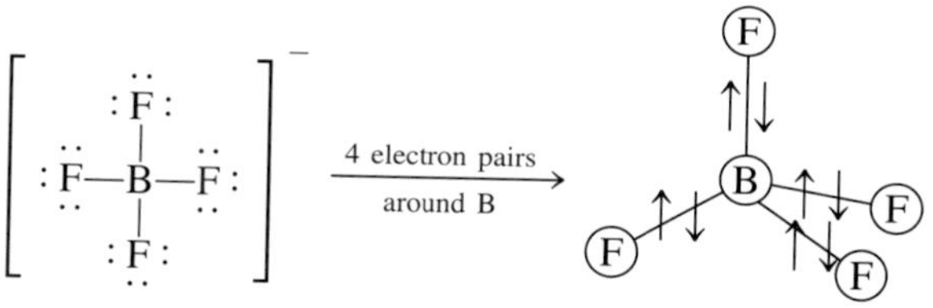

This requires sp^3 hybridization of the boron atom. Each fluorine atom also has four electron pairs and can be assumed to be sp^3 hybridized (only one sp^3 orbital is shown for each fluorine atom). The BF_4^- ion's molecular structure is tetrahedral.

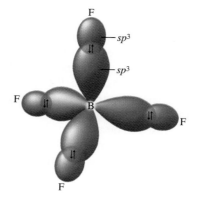

c. The XeF_2 molecule has 22 valence electrons. The Lewis structure shows five electron pairs on the xenon atom, which requires a trigonal bipyramidal arrangement:

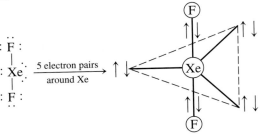

Note that the lone pairs are placed in the plane where they are 120 degrees apart. To accommodate five pairs at the vertices of a trigonal bipyramid requires that the xenon atom adopt a set of five dsp^3 orbitals. Each fluorine atom has four electron pairs and can be assumed to be sp^3 hybridized. The XeF_2 molecule has a linear arrangement of atoms.

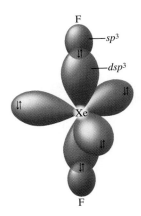

See Exercises 9.23 and 9.24.

Exploration: Molecular Orbitals in H_2

9.2 The Molecular Orbital Model

We have seen that the localized electron model is of great value in interpreting the structure and bonding of molecules. However, there are some problems with this model. For example, it incorrectly assumes that electrons are localized, and so the concept of resonance must be added. Also, the model does not deal effectively with molecules containing unpaired electrons. And finally, the model gives no direct information about bond energies.

Molecular orbital theory parallels the atomic theory discussed in Chapter 7.

Another model often used to describe bonding is the **molecular orbital model.** To introduce the assumptions, methods, and results of this model, we will consider the simplest of all molecules, H_2, which consists of two protons and two electrons. A very stable molecule, H_2 is lower in energy than the separated hydrogen atoms by 432 kJ/mol.

Since the hydrogen molecule consists of protons and electrons, the same components found in separated hydrogen atoms, it seems reasonable to use a theory similar to the atomic theory discussed in Chapter 7, which assumes that the electrons in an atom exist in orbitals of a given energy. Can we apply this same type of model to the hydrogen molecule? Yes. In fact, describing the H_2 molecule in terms of quantum mechanics is quite straightforward.

However, even though it is formulated rather easily, this problem cannot be solved exactly. The difficulty is the same as that in dealing with polyelectronic atoms—the electron correlation problem. Since we do not know the details of the electron movements, we cannot deal with the electron–electron interactions in a specific way. We need to make approximations that allow a solution of the problem but do not destroy the model's physical integrity. The success of these approximations can only be measured by comparing predictions based on theory with experimental observations. In this case we will see that the simplified model works very well.

Just as atomic orbitals are solutions to the quantum mechanical treatment of atoms, **molecular orbitals (MOs)** are solutions to the molecular problem. Molecular orbitals have many of the same characteristics as atomic orbitals. Two of the most important are that they can hold two electrons with opposite spins and that the square of the molecular orbital wave function indicates electron probability.

We will now describe the bonding in the hydrogen molecule using this model. The first step is to obtain the hydrogen molecule's orbitals, a process that is greatly simplified if we assume that the molecular orbitals can be constructed from the hydrogen $1s$ atomic orbitals.

When the quantum mechanical equations for the hydrogen molecule are solved, two molecular orbitals result, which can be represented as

$$MO_1 = 1s_A + 1s_B$$
$$MO_2 = 1s_A - 1s_B$$

where $1s_A$ and $1s_B$ represent the $1s$ orbitals from the two separated hydrogen atoms. This process is shown schematically in Fig. 9.25.

The orbital properties of most interest are size, shape (described by the electron probability distribution), and energy. These properties for the hydrogen molecular orbitals are represented in Fig. 9.26. From Fig. 9.26 we can note several important points:

1. The electron probability of both molecular orbitals is centered along the line passing through the two nuclei. For MO_1 the greatest electron probability is *between* the nuclei, and for MO_2 it is on *either side* of the nuclei. This type of electron distribution is described as *sigma* (σ), as in the localized electron model. Accordingly, we refer to MO_1 and MO_2 as **sigma (σ) molecular orbitals.**

2. In the molecule only the molecular orbitals are available for occupation by electrons. The $1s$ atomic orbitals of the hydrogen atoms no longer exist, because the H_2 molecule—a new entity—has its own set of new orbitals.

3. MO_1 is lower in energy than the $1s$ orbitals of free hydrogen atoms, while MO_2 is higher in energy than the $1s$ orbitals. This fact has very important implications for the stability of the H_2 molecule, since if the two electrons (one from each hydrogen atom) occupy the lower-energy MO_1, they will have lower energy than they do in the two separate hydrogen atoms. This situation favors molecule formation, because nature tends to seek the lowest energy state. That is, the driving force for molecule formation is that the molecular orbital available

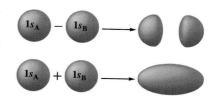

Figure 9.25

The combination of hydrogen $1s$ atomic orbitals to form molecular orbitals.

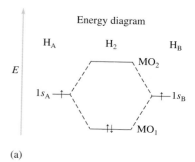

(a)

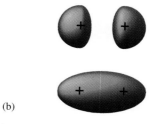

(b)

Figure 9.26

(a) The molecular orbital energy-level diagram for the H_2 molecule. (b) The shapes of the molecular orbitals are obtained by squaring the wave functions for MO_1 and MO_2.

Animation: s-orbitals and Bonding and Anti-Bonding

Bonding will result if the molecule has lower energy than the separated atoms.

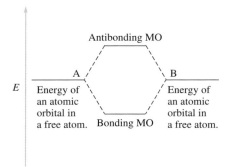

Figure 9.27

Bonding and antibonding molecular orbitals (MOs).

to the two electrons has lower energy than the atomic orbitals these electrons occupy in the separated atoms. This situation is favorable to bonding, or *probonding.*

On the other hand, if the two electrons were forced to occupy the higher-energy MO_2, they would be definitely *antibonding.* In this case, these electrons would have lower energy in the separated atoms than in the molecule, and the separated state would be favored. Of course, since the lower-energy MO_1 *is* available, the two electrons occupy that MO and the molecule is stable.

We have seen that the molecular orbitals of the hydrogen molecule fall into two classes: bonding and antibonding. A **bonding molecular orbital** is *lower in energy than the atomic orbitals of which it is composed.* Electrons in this type of orbital will favor the molecule; that is, they will favor bonding. An **antibonding molecular orbital** is *higher in energy than the atomic orbitals of which it is composed.* Electrons in this type of orbital will favor the separated atoms (they are antibonding). Figure 9.27 illustrates these ideas.

4. Figure 9.26 shows that for the bonding molecular orbital in the H_2 molecule the electrons have the greatest probability of being between the nuclei. This is exactly what we would expect, since the electrons can lower their energies by being simultaneously attracted by both nuclei. On the other hand, the electron distribution for the antibonding molecular orbital is such that the electrons are mainly outside the space between the nuclei. This type of distribution is not expected to provide any bonding force. In fact, it causes the electrons to be higher in energy than in the separated atoms. Thus the molecular orbital model produces electron distributions and energies that agree with our basic ideas of bonding. This fact reassures us that the model is physically reasonable.

5. The labels on molecular orbitals indicate their symmetry (shape), the parent atomic orbitals, and whether they are bonding or antibonding. Antibonding character is indicated by an asterisk. For the H_2 molecule, both MOs have σ symmetry, and both are constructed from hydrogen $1s$ atomic orbitals. The molecular orbitals for H_2 are therefore labeled as follows:

$$MO_1 = \sigma_{1s}$$
$$MO_2 = \sigma_{1s}*$$

6. Molecular electron configurations can be written in much the same way as atomic (electron) configurations. Since the H_2 molecule has two electrons in the σ_{1s} molecular orbital, the electron configuration is σ_{1s}^2.

7. Each molecular orbital can hold two electrons, but the spins must be opposite.

8. Orbitals are conserved. The number of molecular orbitals will always be the same as the number of atomic orbitals used to construct them.

Many of the above points are summarized in Fig. 9.28.

Now suppose we could form the H_2^- ion from a hydride ion (H^-) and a hydrogen atom. Would this species be stable? Since the H^- ion has the configuration $1s^2$ and the H atom has a $1s^1$ configuration, we will use $1s$ atomic orbitals to construct the MO diagram for the H_2^- ion, as shown in Fig. 9.29. The electron configuration for H_2^- is $(\sigma_{1s})^2(\sigma_{1s}*)^1$.

The key idea is that the H_2^- ion will be stable if it has a lower energy than its separated parts. From Fig. 9.29 we see that in going from the separated H^- ion and H atom to the H_2^- ion, the model predicts that two electrons are lowered in energy

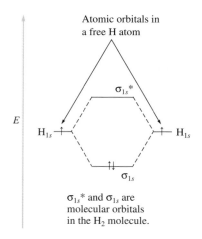

Figure 9.28

A molecular orbital energy-level diagram for the H_2 molecule.

and one electron is raised in energy. In other words, two electrons are bonding and one electron is antibonding. Since more electrons favor bonding, H_2^- is predicted to be a stable entity—a bond has formed. But how would we expect the bond strengths in the molecules of H_2 and H_2^- to compare?

In the formation of the H_2 molecule, two electrons are lowered in energy and no electrons are raised in energy compared with the parent atoms. When H_2^- is formed, two electrons are lowered in energy and one is raised, producing *a net lowering of the energy of only one electron.* Thus the model predicts that H_2 is *twice as stable* as H_2^- with respect to their separated components. In other words, the bond in the H_2 molecule is predicted to be about twice as strong as the bond in the H_2^- ion.

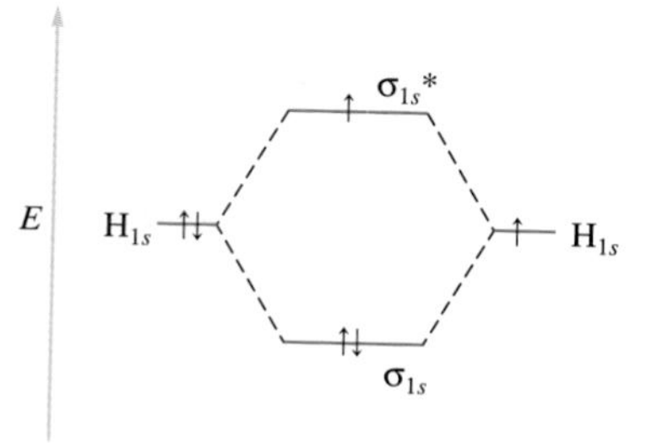

Figure 9.29

The molecular orbital energy-level diagram for the H_2^- ion.

Bond Order

To indicate bond strength, we use the concept of bond order. **Bond order** is *the difference between the number of bonding electrons and the number of antibonding electrons divided by two.*

$$\text{Bond order} = \frac{\text{number of bonding electrons} - \text{number of antibonding electrons}}{2}$$

We divide by 2 because, from the localized electron model, we are used to thinking of bonds in terms of *pairs* of electrons.

Since the H_2 molecule has two bonding electrons and no antibonding electrons, the bond order is

$$\text{Bond order} = \frac{2 - 0}{2} = 1$$

The H_2^- ion has two bonding electrons and one antibonding electron; the bond order is

$$\text{Bond order} = \frac{2 - 1}{2} = \frac{1}{2}$$

Although the model predicts that H_2^- should be stable, this ion has never been observed, again emphasizing the perils of simple models.

Bond order is an indication of bond strength because it reflects the difference between the number of bonding electrons and the number of antibonding electrons. *Larger bond order means greater bond strength.*

We will now apply the molecular orbital model to the helium molecule (He_2). Does this model predict that this molecule will be stable? Since the He atom has a $1s^2$ configuration, $1s$ orbitals are used to construct the molecular orbitals, and the molecule will have four electrons. From the diagram shown in Fig. 9.30 it is apparent that two electrons are raised in energy and two are lowered in energy. Thus the bond order is zero:

$$\frac{2 - 2}{2} = 0$$

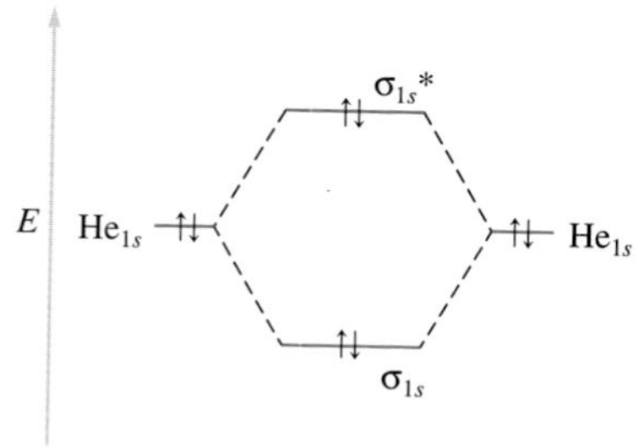

This implies that the He_2 molecule is *not* stable with respect to the two free He atoms, which agrees with the observation that helium gas consists of individual He atoms.

Figure 9.30

The molecular orbital energy-level diagram for the He_2 molecule.

9.3 Bonding in Homonuclear Diatomic Molecules

In this section we consider *homonuclear diatomic molecules* (those composed of two identical atoms) of elements in Period 2 of the periodic table. Since the lithium atom has a $1s^2 2s^1$ electron configuration, it would seem that we should use the Li $1s$ and $2s$ orbitals to form the molecular orbitals of the Li_2 molecule. However, the $1s$ orbitals on the lithium atoms are much smaller than the $2s$ orbitals and therefore do not overlap in space to any appreciable extent (see Fig. 9.31). Thus the two electrons in each $1s$ orbital can be assumed to be localized and not to participate in the bonding. *In order to participate in molecular orbitals, atomic orbitals must overlap in space.* This means that only the valence orbitals of the atoms contribute significantly to the molecular orbitals of a particular molecule.

The molecular orbital diagram of the Li_2 molecule and the shapes of its bonding and antibonding MOs are shown in Fig. 9.32. The electron configuration for Li_2 (valence electrons only) is σ_{2s}^2, and the bond order is

$$\frac{2 - 0}{2} = 1$$

The Li_2 is a stable molecule (has lower energy than two separated lithium atoms). However, this does not mean that Li_2 is the most stable form of elemental lithium. In fact, at normal temperature and pressure, lithium exists as a solid containing many lithium atoms bound to each other.

For the beryllium molecule (Be_2) the bonding and antibonding orbitals both contain two electrons. In this case the bond order is $(2 - 2)/2 = 0$, and since Be_2 is not more stable than two separated Be atoms, no molecule forms. However, beryllium metal contains many beryllium atoms bonded to each other and is stable for reasons we will discuss in Chapter 10.

Since the boron atom has a $1s^2 2s^2 2p^1$ configuration, we describe the B_2 molecule by considering how p atomic orbitals combine to form molecular orbitals. Recall that p orbitals have two lobes and that they occur in sets of three mutually perpendicular orbitals [see Fig. 9.33(a)]. When two B atoms approach each other, two pairs of p orbitals can overlap in a parallel fashion [Fig. 9.33(b) and (c)] and one pair can overlap head-on [Fig. 9.33(d)].

First, let's consider the molecular orbitals from the head-on overlap, as shown in Fig. 9.34(a). Note that the electrons in the bonding MO are, as expected, concentrated between the nuclei, and the electrons in the antibonding MO are concentrated outside the area between the two nuclei. Also, both these MOs are σ molecular orbitals. The p orbitals that overlap in a parallel fashion also produce bonding and

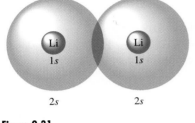

Figure 9.31

The relative sizes of the lithium $1s$ and $2s$ atomic orbitals.

Beryllium metal.

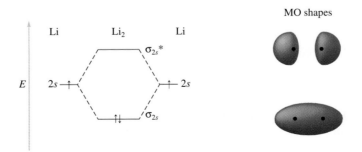

Figure 9.32

The molecular orbital energy-level diagram for the Li_2 molecule.

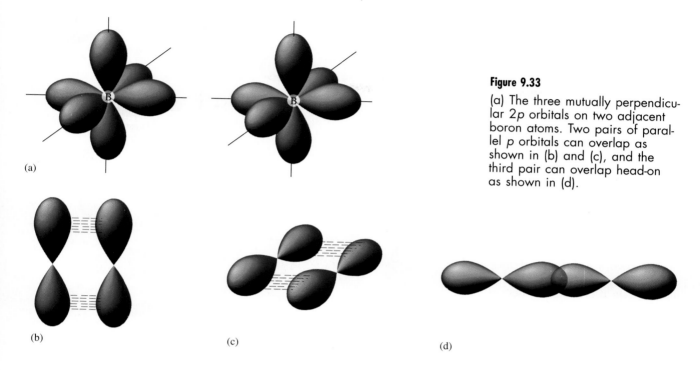

Figure 9.33
(a) The three mutually perpendicular 2p orbitals on two adjacent boron atoms. Two pairs of parallel p orbitals can overlap as shown in (b) and (c), and the third pair can overlap head-on as shown in (d).

antibonding orbitals [Fig. 9.34(b)]. Since the electron probability lies above and below the line between the nuclei, both the orbitals are **pi (π) molecular orbitals.** They are designated as π_{2p} for the bonding MO and $\pi_{2p}{}^*$ for the antibonding MO.

Let's try to make an educated guess about the relative energies of the σ and π molecular orbitals formed from the 2p atomic orbitals. Would we expect the electrons to prefer the σ bonding orbital (where the electron probability is concentrated in the area between the nuclei) or the π bonding orbital? The σ orbital would seem to have the lower energy, since the electrons are closest to the two nuclei. This agrees with the observation that σ interactions are stronger than π interactions.

Figure 9.35 gives the molecular orbital energy-level diagram *expected* when the two sets of 2p orbitals on the boron atoms combine to form molecular orbitals. Note that there are two π bonding orbitals at the same energy (degenerate orbitals) formed from the two pairs of parallel p orbitals, and there are two degenerate π antibonding orbitals. The energy of the π_{2p} orbitals is expected to be higher than that of the σ_{2p} orbital because σ interactions are generally stronger than π interactions.

To construct the total molecular orbital diagram for the B_2 molecule, we make the assumption that the 2s and 2p orbitals combine separately (in other words, there is no 2s–2p mixing). The resulting diagram is shown in Fig. 9.36. Note that B_2 has six *valence* electrons. (Remember the 1s orbitals and electrons are assumed not to participate in the bonding.) This diagram predicts the bond order:

$$\frac{4 - 2}{2} = 1$$

Therefore, B_2 should be a stable molecule.

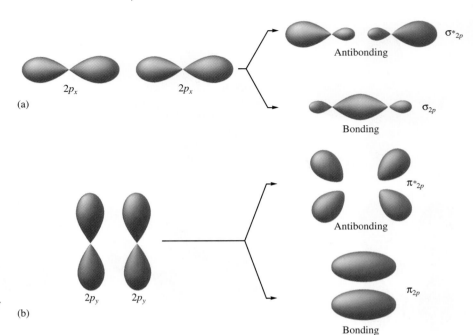

(a)

(b)

Figure 9.34

(a) The two *p* orbitals on the boron atom that overlap head-on produce two σ molecular orbitals, one bonding and one antibonding. (b) Two *p* orbitals that lie parallel overlap to produce two π molecular orbitals, one bonding and one antibonding.

Paramagnetism

At this point we need to discuss an additional molecular property—magnetism. Most materials have no magnetism until they are placed in a magnetic field. However, in the presence of such a field, magnetism of two types can be induced. **Paramagnetism** causes the substance to be attracted into the inducing magnetic field. **Diamagnetism** causes the substance to be repelled from the inducing magnetic field. Figure 9.37 illustrates how paramagnetism is measured. The sample is weighed with the electromagnet turned off and then weighed again with the electromagnet turned on. An increase in weight when the field is turned on indicates the sample is paramagnetic. Studies have shown that *paramagnetism is associated with unpaired electrons and diamagnetism is associated with paired electrons.* Any substance that has both paired and unpaired electrons will exhibit a net paramagnetism, since the effect of paramagnetism is much stronger than that of diamagnetism.

The molecular orbital energy-level diagram represented in Fig. 9.36 predicts that the B_2 molecule will be diamagnetic, since the MOs contain only paired electrons. However, experiments show that B_2 is actually paramagnetic with two unpaired electrons. Why does the model yield the wrong prediction? This is yet another illustration of how models are developed and used. In general, we try to use the simplest possible model that accounts for all the important observations. In this case, although the simplest model successfully describes the diatomic molecules up to B_2, it certainly is suspect if it cannot describe the B_2 molecule correctly. This means we must either discard the model or find a way to modify it.

Let's consider one assumption that we made. In our treatment of B_2, we have assumed that the *s* and *p* orbitals combine separately to form molecular orbitals. Calculations show that when the *s* and *p* orbitals are allowed to mix in the same molecular orbital, a different energy-level diagram results for B_2 (see Fig. 9.38). Note that even though the *s* and *p* contributions to the MOs are no longer separate,

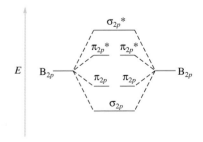

Figure 9.35

The *expected* molecular orbital energy-level diagram resulting from the combination of the 2*p* orbitals on two boron atoms.

we retain the simple orbital designations. The energies of π_{2p} and σ_{2p} orbitals are reversed by p–s mixing, and the σ_{2s} and the σ_{2s}^* orbitals are no longer equally spaced relative to the energy of the free $2s$ orbital.

When the six valence electrons for the B_2 molecule are placed in the modified energy-level diagram, each of the last two electrons goes into one of the degenerate π_{2p} orbitals. This produces a paramagnetic molecule in agreement with experimental results. Thus, when the model is extended to allow p–s mixing in molecular orbitals, it predicts the correct magnetism. Note that the bond order is $(4 - 2)/2 = 1$, as before.

The remaining diatomic molecules of the elements in Period 2 can be described using similar ideas. For example, the C_2 and N_2 molecules use the same set of orbitals as for B_2 (see Fig. 9.38). Because the importance of $2s$–$2p$ mixing decreases across the period, the σ_{2p} and π_{2p} orbitals revert to the order expected in the absence of $2s$–$2p$ mixing for the molecules O_2 and F_2, as shown in Fig. 9.39.

Several significant points arise from the orbital diagrams, bond strengths, and bond lengths summarized in Fig. 9.39 for the Period 2 diatomics:

1. There are definite correlations between bond order, bond energy, and bond length. As the bond order predicted by the molecular orbital model increases, the bond energy increases and the bond length decreases. This is a clear indication that the bond order predicted by the model accurately reflects bond strength, and it strongly supports the reasonableness of the MO model.

2. Comparison of the bond energies of the B_2 and F_2 molecules indicates that bond order cannot automatically be associated with a particular bond energy. Although both molecules have a bond order of 1, the bond in B_2 appears to be about twice as strong as the bond in F_2. As we will see in our later discussion of the halogens, F_2 has an unusually weak single bond due to larger than usual electron–electron repulsions (there are 14 valence electrons on the small F_2 molecule).

3. Note the very large bond energy associated with the N_2 molecule, which the molecular orbital model predicts will have a bond order of 3, a triple bond. The very strong bond in N_2 is the principal reason that many nitrogen-containing

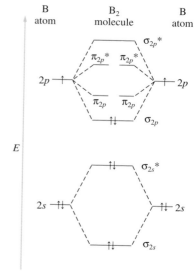

Figure 9.36

The *expected* molecular orbital energy-level diagram for the B_2 molecule.

Bond energy increases with increasing bond order; bond length decreases with increasing bond order.

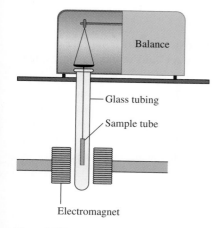

Figure 9.37

Diagram of the kind of apparatus used to measure the paramagnetism of a sample. A paramagnetic sample will appear heavier when the electromagnet is turned on because the sample is attracted into the inducing magnetic field.

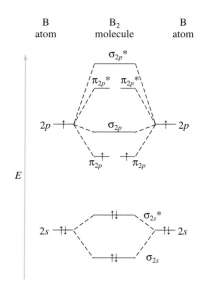

Figure 9.38

The *correct* molecular orbital energy-level diagram for the B_2 molecule. When p–s mixing is allowed, the energies of the σ_{2p} and π_{2p} orbitals are reversed. The two electrons from the B $2p$ orbitals now occupy separate, degenerate π_{2p} molecular orbitals and thus have parallel spins. Therefore, this diagram explains the observed paramagnetism of B_2.

	B_2	C_2	N_2	O_2	F_2
σ_{2p}^*	—	—	—	σ_{2p}^* —	—
π_{2p}^*	— —	— —	— —	π_{2p}^* ↑ ↑	↑↓ ↑↓
σ_{2p}	—	—	↑↓	π_{2p} ↑↓ ↑↓	↑↓ ↑↓
π_{2p}	↑ ↑	↑↓ ↑↓	↑↓ ↑↓	σ_{2p} ↑↓	↑↓
σ_{2s}^*	↑↓	↑↓	↑↓	σ_{2s}^* ↑↓	↑↓
σ_{2s}	↑↓	↑↓	↑↓	σ_{2s} ↑↓	↑↓
Magnetism	Para–magnetic	Dia–magnetic	Dia–magnetic	Para–magnetic	Dia–magnetic
Bond order	1	2	3	2	1
Observed bond dissociation energy (kJ/mol)	290	620	942	495	154
Observed bond length (pm)	159	131	110	121	143

Figure 9.39

The molecular orbital energy-level diagrams, bond orders, bond energies, and bond lengths for the diatomic molecules B_2 through F_2. Note that for O_2 and F_2 the σ_{2p} orbital is lower in energy than the π_{2p} orbitals.

compounds are used as high explosives. The reactions involving these explosives give the very stable N_2 molecule as a product, thus releasing large quantities of energy.

4. The O_2 molecule is known to be paramagnetic. This can be very convincingly demonstrated by pouring liquid oxygen between the poles of a strong magnet, as shown in Fig. 9.40. The oxygen remains there until it evaporates. Significantly, the molecular orbital model correctly predicts oxygen's paramagnetism, while the localized electron model predicts a diamagnetic molecule.

Sample Exercise 9.6 *The Molecular Orbital Model I*

For the species O_2, O_2^+, and O_2^-, give the electron configuration and the bond order for each. Which has the strongest bond?

Solution

The O_2 molecule has 12 valence electrons $(6 + 6)$; O_2^+ has 11 valence electrons $(6 + 6 - 1)$; and O_2^- has 13 valence electrons $(6 + 6 + 1)$. We will assume that the ions can be treated using the same molecular orbital diagram as for the neutral diatomic molecule:

	O_2	O_2^+	O_2^-
σ_{2p}^*	—	—	—
π_{2p}^*	↑ ↑	↑ —	↑↓ ↑
π_{2p}	↑↓ ↑↓	↑↓ ↑↓	↑↓ ↑↓
σ_{2p}	↑↓	↑↓	↑↓
σ_{2s}^*	↑↓	↑↓	↑↓
σ_{2s}	↑↓	↑↓	↑↓

The electron configuration for each species can then be taken from the diagram:

$$O_2: \quad (\sigma_{2s})^2(\sigma_{2s}^*)^2(\sigma_{2p})^2(\pi_{2p})^4(\pi_{2p}^*)^2$$
$$O_2^+: \quad (\sigma_{2s})^2(\sigma_{2s}^*)^2(\sigma_{2p})^2(\pi_{2p})^4(\pi_{2p}^*)^1$$
$$O_2^-: \quad (\sigma_{2s})^2(\sigma_{2s}^*)^2(\sigma_{2p})^2(\pi_{2p})^4(\pi_{2p}^*)^3$$

The bond orders are:

$$\text{For } O_2: \quad \frac{8 - 4}{2} = 2$$

$$\text{For } O_2^+: \quad \frac{8 - 3}{2} = 2.5$$

$$\text{For } O_2^-: \quad \frac{8 - 5}{2} = 1.5$$

Thus O_2^+ is expected to have the strongest bond of the three species.

See Exercises 9.35 through 9.38.

Video: Magnetic Properties of Liquid Nitrogen and Oxygen

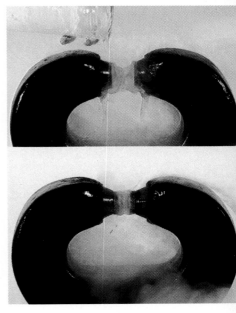

Figure 9.40
When liquid oxygen is poured into the space between the poles of a strong magnet, it remains there until it boils away. This attraction of liquid oxygen for the magnetic field demonstrates the paramagnetism of the O_2 molecule.

Sample Exercise 9.7 *The Molecular Orbital Model II*

Use the molecular orbital model to predict the bond order and magnetism of each of the following molecules.
a. Ne_2
b. P_2

Solution

a. The valence orbitals for Ne are $2s$ and $2p$. Thus we can use the molecular orbitals we have already constructed for the diatomic molecules of the Period 2 elements. The Ne_2 molecule has 16 valence electrons (8 from each atom).

Placing these electrons in the appropriate molecular orbitals produces the following diagram:

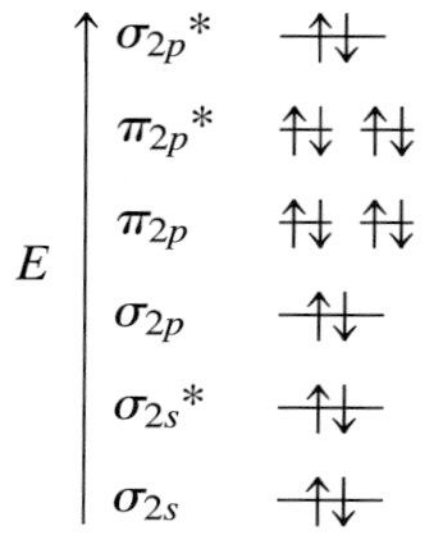

$$
E \uparrow
\begin{array}{ll}
\sigma_{2p}^* & \uparrow\downarrow \\[4pt]
\pi_{2p}^* & \uparrow\downarrow \quad \uparrow\downarrow \\[4pt]
\pi_{2p} & \uparrow\downarrow \quad \uparrow\downarrow \\[4pt]
\sigma_{2p} & \uparrow\downarrow \\[4pt]
\sigma_{2s}^* & \uparrow\downarrow \\[4pt]
\sigma_{2s} & \uparrow\downarrow
\end{array}
$$

The bond order is $(8 - 8)/2 = 0$, and Ne_2 does not exist.

b. The P_2 molecule contains phosphorus atoms from the third row of the periodic table. We will assume that the diatomic molecules of the Period 3 elements can be treated in a way very similar to that which we have used so far. Thus we will draw the MO diagram for P_2 analogous to that for N_2. The only change will be that the molecular orbitals will be formed from $3s$ and $3p$ atomic orbitals. The P_2 model has 10 valence electrons (5 from each phosphorus atom). The resulting molecular orbital diagram is

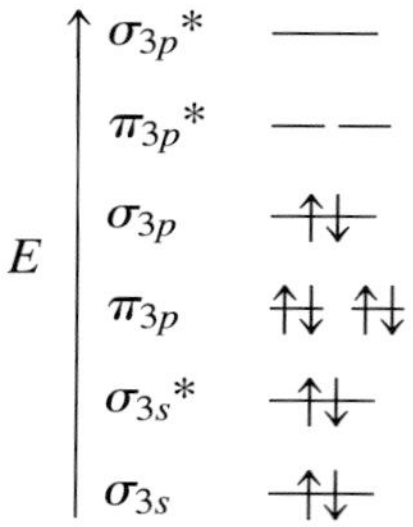

$$
E \uparrow
\begin{array}{ll}
\sigma_{3p}^* & \underline{\quad} \\[4pt]
\pi_{3p}^* & \underline{\quad} \; \underline{\quad} \\[4pt]
\sigma_{3p} & \uparrow\downarrow \\[4pt]
\pi_{3p} & \uparrow\downarrow \quad \uparrow\downarrow \\[4pt]
\sigma_{3s}^* & \uparrow\downarrow \\[4pt]
\sigma_{3s} & \uparrow\downarrow
\end{array}
$$

The molecule has a bond order of 3 and is expected to be diamagnetic.

See Exercises 9.39 and 9.40.

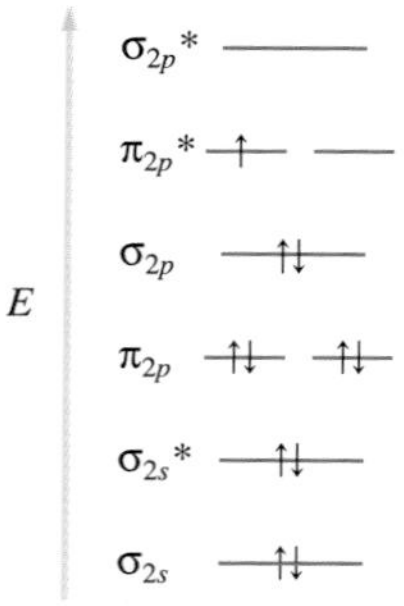

Figure 9.41

The molecular orbital energy-level diagram for the NO molecule. We assume that orbital order is the same as that for N_2. The bond order is 2.5.

9.4 Bonding in Heteronuclear Diatomic Molecules

In this section we will deal with selected examples of **heteronuclear** (different atoms) **diatomic molecules.** A special case involves molecules containing atoms adjacent to each other in the periodic table. Since the atoms involved in such a molecule are so similar, we can use the molecular orbital diagram for homonuclear molecules. For example, we can predict the bond order and magnetism of nitric oxide (NO) by placing its 11 valence electrons (5 from nitrogen and 6 from oxygen) in the molecular orbital energy-level diagram shown in Fig. 9.41. The molecule should be paramagnetic and has a bond order of

$$
\frac{8 - 3}{2} = 2.5
$$

Experimentally, nitric oxide is indeed found to be paramagnetic. Notice that this odd electron molecule is described very naturally by the MO model. In contrast, the localized electron model, in the simple form used in this text, cannot be used readily to treat such molecules.

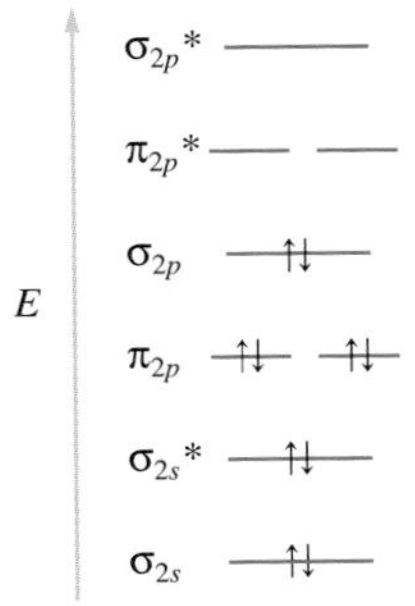

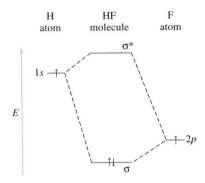

Figure 9.42

The molecular orbital energy-level diagram for both the NO^+ and CN^- ions.

Sample Exercise 9.8 The Molecular Orbital Model III

Use the molecular orbital model to predict the magnetism and bond order of the NO^+ and CN^- ions.

Solution

The NO^+ ion has 10 valence electrons $(5 + 6 - 1)$. The CN^- ion also has 10 valence electrons $(4 + 5 + 1)$. Both ions are therefore diamagnetic and have a bond order derived from the equation

$$\frac{8 - 2}{2} = 3$$

The molecular orbital diagram for these two ions is the same (see Fig. 9.42).

See Exercises 9.41 through 9.44.

When the two atoms of a diatomic molecule are very different, the energy-level diagram for homonuclear molecules can no longer be used. A new diagram must be devised for each molecule. We will illustrate this case by considering the hydrogen fluoride (HF) molecule. The electron configurations of the hydrogen and fluorine atoms are $1s^1$ and $1s^2 2s^2 2p^5$, respectively. To keep things as simple as possible, we will assume that fluorine uses only one of its $2p$ orbitals to bond to hydrogen. Thus the molecular orbitals for HF will be composed of fluorine $2p$ and hydrogen $1s$ orbitals. Figure 9.43 gives the partial molecular orbital energy-level diagram for HF, focusing only on the orbitals involved in the bonding. We are assuming that fluorine's other valence electrons remain localized on the fluorine. The $2p$ orbital of fluorine is shown at a lower energy than the $1s$ orbital of hydrogen on the diagram because fluorine binds its valence electrons more tightly. Thus the $2p$ electron on a free fluorine atom is at lower energy than the $1s$ electron on a free hydrogen atom. The diagram predicts that the HF molecule should be stable because both electrons are lowered in energy relative to their energy in the free hydrogen and fluorine atoms, and this is the driving force for bond formation.

Because the fluorine $2p$ orbital is lower in energy than the hydrogen $1s$ orbital, the electrons prefer to be closer to the fluorine atom. That is, the σ molecular orbital containing the bonding electron pair shows greater electron probability close to the fluorine (see Fig. 9.44). The electron pair is not shared equally. This causes the fluorine atom to have a slight excess of negative charge and leaves the hydrogen atom partially positive. This is *exactly* the bond polarity observed for HF. Thus the molecular orbital model accounts in a straightforward way for the different electronegativities of hydrogen and fluorine and the resulting unequal charge distribution.

Figure 9.43

A partial molecular orbital energy-level diagram for the HF molecule.

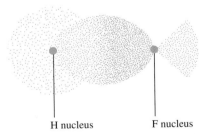

Figure 9.44

The electron probability distribution in the bonding molecular orbital of the HF molecule. Note the greater electron density close to the fluorine atom.

9.5 Combining the Localized Electron and Molecular Orbital Models

Molecular Models: O_3, NO_3^-, C_6H_6

One of the main difficulties with the localized electron model is its assumption that electrons are localized. This problem is most apparent with molecules for which several valid Lewis structures can be drawn. It is clear that none of these structures taken alone adequately describes the electronic structure of the molecule. The concept of resonance was invented to solve this problem. However, even with resonance included, the localized electron model does not describe molecules and ions such as O_3 and NO_3^- in a very satisfying way.

It would seem that the ideal bonding model would be one with the simplicity of the localized electron model but with the delocalization characteristic of the molecular orbital model. We can achieve this by combining the two models to describe molecules that require resonance. Note that for species such as O_3 and NO_3^- the double bond changes position in the resonance structures (see Fig. 9.45). Since a double bond involves one σ and one π bond, there is a σ bond between all bound atoms in each resonance structure. It is really the π bond that has different locations in the various resonance structures.

In molecules that require resonance, it is the π bonding that is most clearly delocalized.

We can conclude that the σ bonds in a molecule can be described as being localized with no apparent problems. It is the π bonding that must be treated as being delocalized. Thus, for molecules that require resonance, we will use the localized electron model to describe the σ bonding and the molecular orbital model to describe the π bonding. This allows us to keep the bonding model as simple as possible and yet give a more physically accurate description of such molecules.

We will illustrate the general method by considering the bonding in benzene, an important industrial chemical that must be handled carefully because it is a known carcinogen. The benzene molecule (C_6H_6) consists of a planar hexagon of carbon atoms with one hydrogen atom bound to each carbon atom, as shown in Fig. 9.46(a). In the molecule all six C—C bonds are known to be equivalent. To explain this fact, the localized electron model must invoke resonance [see Fig. 9.46(b)].

A better description of the bonding in benzene results when we use a combination of the models, as described above. In this description it is assumed that the σ bonds of carbon involve sp^2 orbitals, as shown in Fig. 9.47. These σ bonds are all centered in the plane of the molecule.

Since each carbon atom is sp^2 hybridized, a p orbital perpendicular to the plane of the ring remains on each carbon atom. These six p orbitals can be used to form π molecular orbitals, as shown in Fig. 9.48(a). The electrons in the resulting π molecular orbitals are delocalized above and below the plane of the ring, as shown in

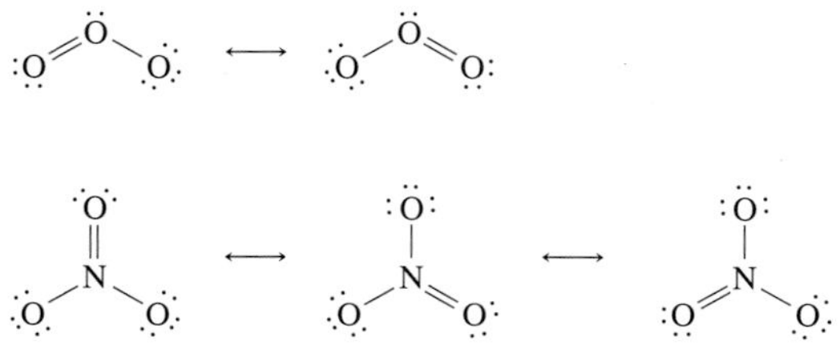

Figure 9.45

The resonance structures for O_3 and NO_3^-. Note that it is the double bond that occupies various positions in the resonance structures.

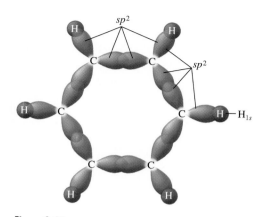

Figure 9.46

(a) The benzene molecule consists of a ring of six carbon atoms with one hydrogen atom bound to each carbon; all atoms are in the same plane. All the C—C bonds are known to be equivalent. (b) Two of the resonance structures for the benzene molecule. The localized electron model must invoke resonance to account for the six equal C—C bonds.

Figure 9.47

The σ bonding system in the benzene molecule.

Fig. 9.48(b). This gives six equivalent C—C bonds, as required by the known structure of the benzene molecule. The benzene structure is often written as

to indicate the **delocalized π bonding** in the molecule.

Very similar treatments can be applied to other planar molecules for which resonance is required by the localized electron model. For example, the NO_3^- ion can be described using the π molecular orbital system shown in Fig. 9.49. In this molecule each atom is assumed to be sp^2 hybridized, which leaves one p orbital on each atom perpendicular to the plane of the ion. These p orbitals can combine to form the π molecular orbital system.

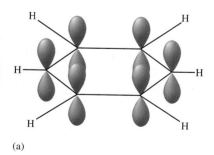

(a)

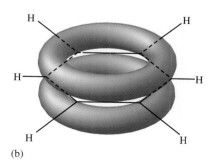

(b)

Figure 9.48

(a) The π molecular orbital system in benzene is formed by combining the six p orbitals from the six sp^2 hybridized carbon atoms. (b) The electrons in the resulting π molecular orbitals are delocalized over the entire ring of carbon atoms, giving six equivalent bonds. A composite of these orbitals is represented here.

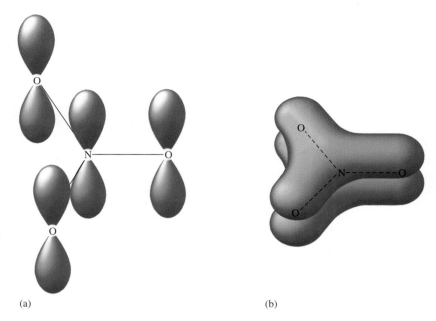

Figure 9.49

(a) The p orbitals used to form the π bonding system in the NO_3^- ion. (b) A representation of the delocalization of the electrons in the π molecular orbital system of the NO_3^- ion.

(a)   (b)

For Review

Summary

In this chapter we have emphasized the role of orbitals in the covalent bonding in molecules. The two most useful models are the localized electron model and the molecular orbital model.

In the localized electron model, a molecule is pictured as a group of atoms sharing electron pairs using atomic orbitals. Because the requirements of the molecule are different from those of separated atoms, the original atomic orbitals are combined to form new hybrid orbitals, which are used by the atoms in the molecule. The specific set of hybrid orbitals needed is determined by the arrangement of electron pairs that gives the minimum repulsion. For example, an atom surrounded by four electron pairs requires a tetrahedral arrangement and a set of sp^3 hybrid orbitals; a trigonal planar arrangement requires sp^2 hybridization, and a linear arrangement requires sp hybridization.

When an electron pair is shared in the area centered on a line joining the atoms, the covalent bond is called a σ bond. A π bond occurs when p orbitals overlap in a parallel fashion. The shared electron pair then occupies the space above and below the line joining the bonded atoms.

Multiple bonds involve σ and π bonds. A double bond consists of a σ bond and a π bond; a triple bond involves a σ bond and two π bonds.

In the molecular orbital model for covalent bonding, the molecule is assumed to be a new entity consisting of positively charged nuclei and electrons. We use calculations similar to those used for atoms to determine the allowed orbitals in the molecule. The molecular orbitals are constructed from the valence orbitals of the atoms involved in forming the molecule.

Molecular orbitals are classified in two ways:

1. MOs are classified according to their energy. A bonding MO is an orbital that is lower in energy than the original atomic orbitals. In going from the free atoms to the molecule, electrons occupying bonding MOs are lowered in energy. This favors formation of a stable molecule (bonds are formed). An antibonding MO is an orbital that is higher in energy than the original atomic orbitals. In going from the free atoms to the molecule, electrons in antibonding MOs are raised in energy. These electrons oppose bonding.

2. MOs are classified according to their shape (symmetry). Sigma (σ) molecular orbitals have their electron probability centered about a line passing through the two nuclei. Pi (π) molecular orbitals have their electron probability concentrated above and below the line passing through the nuclei.

Bond order is an index of bond strength:

$$\text{Bond order} = \frac{\text{number of bonding electrons} - \text{number of antibonding electrons}}{2}$$

The greater the difference between the number of electrons that are lowered in energy (bonding electrons) and the number of electrons that are raised in energy (antibonding electrons) when the molecule forms, the greater will be the stability of the molecule (the stronger the bonding).

The main strengths of the molecular orbital model are that it correctly predicts the relative bond strength and magnetism of simple diatomic molecules (the correct prediction of the paramagnetism of the oxygen molecule is an important example), it accounts for bond polarity, and it correctly portrays electrons as being delocalized in polyatomic molecules. The main disadvantage of the molecular orbital model is that it is difficult to apply qualitatively to polyatomic molecules.

The concept of resonance is required for certain molecules because the localized electron model incorrectly assumes that electrons are located between a given pair of atoms in a molecule. A more physically accurate description of these molecules can be given by combining the localized electron and molecular orbital models. The σ bonds in these molecules can be regarded as localized, while the π bonding is best described as delocalized.

In-Class Discussion Questions

These questions are designed to be considered by groups of students in class. Often these questions work well for introducing a particular topic in class.

1. What are molecular orbitals? How do they compare with atomic orbitals? Can you tell by the shape of the bonding and antibonding orbitals which is lower in energy? Explain.

2. Explain the difference between the σ and π MOs for homonuclear diatomic molecules. How are bonding and antibonding orbitals different? Why are there two π MOs and one σ MO? Why are the π MOs degenerate?

3. Compare Figs. 9.36 and 9.38. Why are they different? Because B_2 is known to be paramagnetic, the π_{2p} and σ_{2p} molecular orbitals must be switched from the first prediction. What is the rationale for this? Why might one expect the σ_{2p} to be lower in energy than the π_{2p}? Why can't we use diatomic oxygen to help us decide whether the σ_{2p} or π_{2p} is lower in energy?

4. Which of the following would you expect to be more favorable energetically? Explain.

a. An H_2 molecule in which enough energy is added to excite one electron from the bonding to the antibonding MO.

b. Two separate H atoms.

5. Draw the Lewis structure for HCN. Indicate the hybrid orbitals, and draw a picture showing all the bonds between the atoms, labeling each bond as σ or π.

6. Which is the more correct statement: "The methane molecule (CH_4) is a tetrahedral molecule because it is sp^3 hybridized" or "The methane molecule (CH_4) is sp^3 hybridized because it is a tetrahedral molecule"? What, if anything, is the difference between these two statements?

A blue question or exercise number indicates that the answer to that question or exercise appears at the back of this book and a solution appears in the *Solutions Guide*.

Questions

7. What are the relationships among bond order, bond energy, and bond length? Which of these quantities can be measured?

8. Electrons in σ bonding molecular orbitals are most likely to be found in the region between the two bonded atoms. Why does this arrangement favor bonding? In a σ antibonding orbital, where are the electrons most likely to be found in relation to the nuclei in a bond?

9. What type of experiment can be done to determine if a material is paramagnetic?

10. What type of molecules exhibit delocalized π bonding? Explain.

Exercises

In this section similar exercises are paired.

The Localized Electron Model and Hybrid Orbitals

11. Use the localized electron model to describe the bonding in H_2O.

12. Use the localized electron model to describe the bonding in CCl_4.

13. Use the localized electron model to describe the bonding in H_2CO (carbon is the central atom).

14. Use the localized electron model to describe the bonding in C_2H_2 (exists as HCCH).

15. Give the expected hybridization of the central atom for the molecules or ions in Exercises 63 and 67 from Chapter 8.

16. Give the expected hybridization of the central atom for the molecules or ions in Exercises 64 and 68 from Chapter 8.

17. Give the expected hybridization of the central atom for the molecules or ions in Exercise 65 from Chapter 8.

18. Give the expected hybridization of the central atom for the molecules in Exercise 66 from Chapter 8.

19. Give the expected hybridization of the central atom for the molecules or ions in Exercise 83 from Chapter 8.

20. Give the expected hybridization of the central atom for the molecules or ions in Exercise 84 from Chapter 8.

21. Give the expected hybridization of the central atom for the molecules or ions in Exercise 85 from Chapter 8.

22. Give the expected hybridization of the central atom for the molecules or ions in Exercise 86 from Chapter 8.

23. For each of the following molecules, write the Lewis structure(s), predict the molecular structure (including bond angles), give the expected hybrid orbitals on the central atom, and predict the overall polarity.

a. CF_4	**f.** TeF_4	**j.** SeF_6
b. NF_3	**g.** AsF_5	**k.** IF_5
c. OF_2	**h.** KrF_2	**l.** IF_3
d. BF_3	**i.** KrF_4	
e. BeH_2		

24. For each of the following molecules or ions that contain sulfur, write the Lewis structure(s), predict the molecular structure (including bond angles), and give the expected hybrid orbitals for sulfur.

a. SO_2

b. SO_3

c. $S_2O_3^{2-}$ $\begin{bmatrix} & O & \\ S-S-O \\ & O & \end{bmatrix}^{2-}$

d. $S_2O_8^{2-}$ $\begin{bmatrix} O & & & O \\ O-S-O-O-S-O \\ O & & & O \end{bmatrix}^{2-}$

e. SO_3^{2-}

f. SO_4^{2-}

g. SF_2

h. SF_4

i. SF_6

j. F_3S-SF

k. SF_5^+

25. Why must all six atoms in C_2H_4 be in the same plane?

26. The allene molecule has the following Lewis structure:

Are all four hydrogen atoms in the same plane? If not, what is their spatial relationship? Explain.

27. Biacetyl and acetoin are added to margarine to make it taste more like butter.

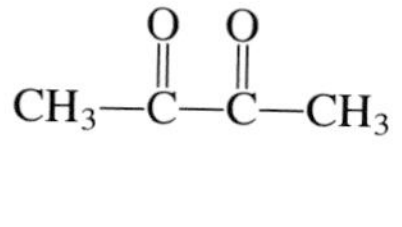

Biacetyl

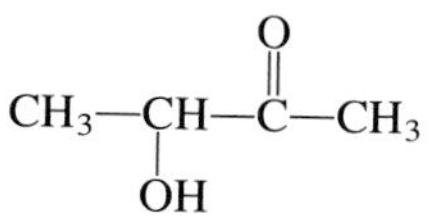

Acetoin

Complete the Lewis structures, predict values for all C—C—O bond angles, and give the hybridization of the carbon atoms in these two compounds. Are the four carbons and two oxygens in biacetyl in the same plane? How many σ bonds and how many π bonds are there in biacetyl and acetoin?

28. Many important compounds in the chemical industry are derivatives of ethylene (C_2H_4). Two of them are acrylonitrile and methyl methacrylate.

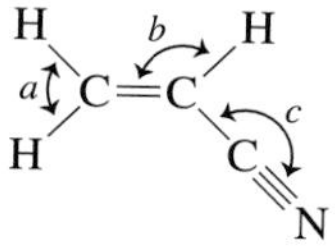

Acrylonitrile

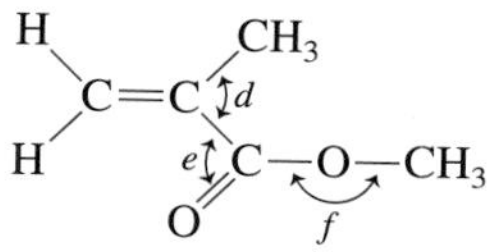

Methyl methacrylate

Complete the Lewis structures, showing all lone pairs. Give approximate values for bond angles *a* through *f*. Give the hybridization of all carbon atoms. In acrylonitrile, how many of the atoms in the molecule lie in the same plane? How many σ bonds and how many π bonds are there in methyl methacrylate and acrylonitrile?

29. One of the first drugs to be approved for use in treatment of acquired immune deficiency syndrome (AIDS) is azidothymidine (AZT). Complete the Lewis structure for AZT.

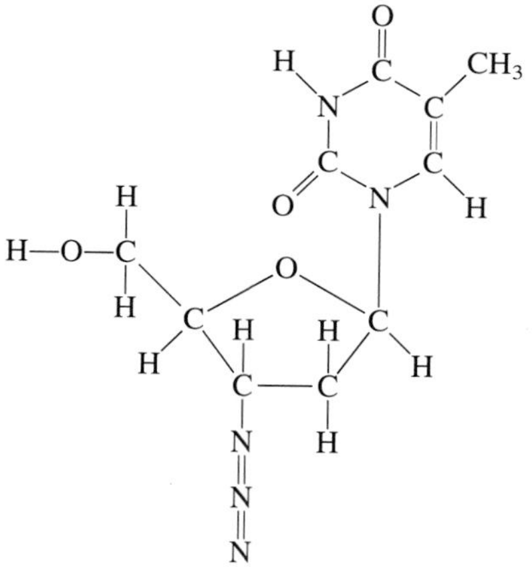

a. How many carbon atoms are sp^3 hybridized?
b. How many carbon atoms are sp^2 hybridized?
c. Which atom is *sp* hybridized?
d. How many σ bonds are in the molecule?
e. How many π bonds are in the molecule?

f. What is the N—N—N bond angle in the azide (—N_3) group?
g. What is the H—O—C bond angle in the side group attached to the five-membered ring?
h. What is the hybridization of the oxygen atom in the —CH_2OH group?

30. Hot and spicy foods contain molecules that stimulate pain-detecting nerve endings. Two such molecules are piperine and capsaicin:

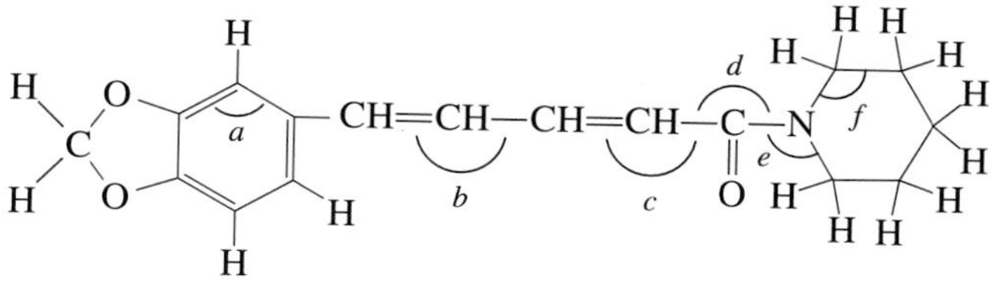

Piperine

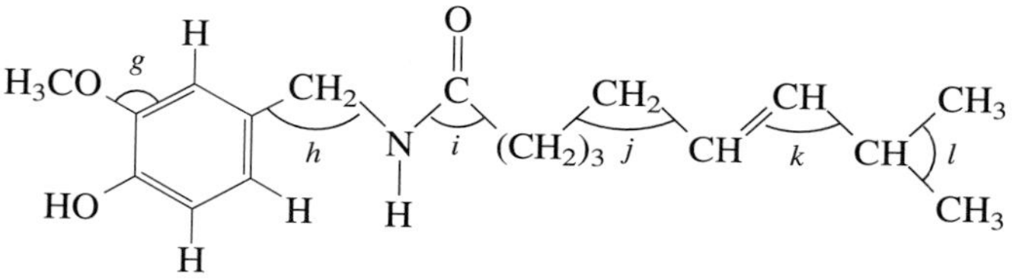

Capsaicin

Piperine is the active compound in white and black pepper, and capsaicin is the active compound in chili peppers. The ring structures in piperine and capsaicin are shorthand notation. Each point where lines meet represents a carbon atom.

a. Complete the Lewis structure for piperine and capsaicin showing all lone pairs of electrons.
b. How many carbon atoms are sp, sp^2, and sp^3 hybridized in each molecule?
c. Which hybrid orbitals are used by the nitrogen atoms in each molecule?
d. Give approximate values for the bond angles marked *a* through *l* in the above structures.

31. Minoxidil ($C_9H_{15}N_5O$) is a compound that has been approved as a treatment for some types of male-pattern baldness. An incomplete Lewis structure for minoxidil is

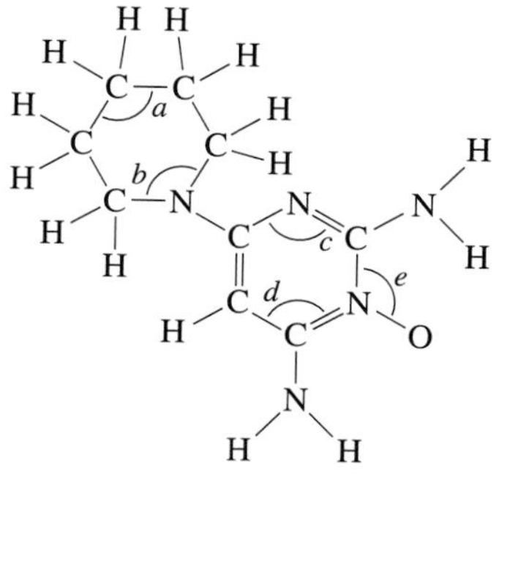

Complete the Lewis structure and answer the following questions.

a. Give the hybridization of the five nitrogen atoms in minoxidil.

b. Give the hybridization of each of the nine carbon atoms in minoxidil.

c. Give approximate values of the bond angles marked *a*, *b*, *c*, *d*, and *e*.

d. How many σ bonds exist in minoxidil?

e. How many π bonds exist in minoxidil?

32. The antibiotic thiarubin-A was discovered by studying the feeding habits of wild chimpanzees in Tanzania. The structure for thiarubin-A is

$$H_3C—C\equiv C—C \quad \begin{matrix} H & H \\ | & | \\ C—C \\ \end{matrix} \quad C—C\equiv C—C\equiv C—CH=CH_2$$
$$S—S$$

a. Complete the Lewis structure showing all lone pairs of electrons.

b. Indicate the hybrid orbitals used by the carbon and sulfur atoms in thiarubin-A.

c. How many σ and π bonds are present in this molecule?

The Molecular Orbital Model

33. Which of the following are predicted by the molecular orbital model to be stable diatomic species?

a. H_2^+, H_2, H_2^-, H_2^{2-}

b. He_2^{2+}, He_2^+, He_2

34. Which of the following are predicted by the molecular orbital model to be stable diatomic species?

a. N_2^{2-}, O_2^{2-}, F_2^{2-}

b. Be_2, B_2, Ne_2

35. Using the molecular orbital model, write electron configurations for the following diatomic species and calculate the bond orders. Which ones are paramagnetic?

a. Li_2

b. C_2

c. O_2

36. Using the molecular orbital model, write electron configurations for the following diatomic species and calculate the bond orders. Which ones are paramagnetic?

a. N_2

b. N_2^+

c. N_2^-

37. Using the molecular orbital model to describe the bonding in O_2^+, O_2, O_2^-, and O_2^{2-}, predict the bond orders and the relative bond lengths for these four species. How many unpaired electrons are present in each one?

38. Using the molecular orbital model to describe the bonding in F_2^+, F_2, and F_2^-, predict the bond orders and the relative bond lengths for these three species. How many unpaired electrons are present in each species?

39. Acetylene (C_2H_2) can be produced from the reaction of calcium carbide (CaC_2) with water. Use both the localized electron and molecular orbital models to describe the bonding in the acetylide anion (C_2^{2-}).

40. Construct a molecular orbital energy-level diagram for the Cl_2 molecule. Is Cl_2 expected to be paramagnetic?

41. Using the molecular orbital model, write electron configurations for the following diatomic species and calculate the bond orders. Which ones are paramagnetic?

a. CO

b. CO^+

c. CO^{2+}

42. Using the molecular orbital model, write electron configurations for the following diatomic species and calculate the bond orders. Which ones are paramagnetic?

a. NO^+

b. NO

c. NO^-

43. Place the species CO, CO^+, and CO^{2+} in order of increasing bond length and increasing bond energy. Use your results from Exercise 41.

44. Place the species NO^+, NO, and NO^- in order of increasing bond length and increasing bond energy. Use your results from Exercise 42.

45. Show how two $2p$ atomic orbitals can combine to form a σ or a π molecular orbital.

46. Show how a hydrogen $1s$ atomic orbital and a fluorine $2p$ atomic orbital overlap to form bonding and antibonding molecular orbitals in the hydrogen fluoride molecule. Are these molecular orbitals σ or π molecular orbitals?

47. Use Figs. 9.43 and 9.44 to answer the following questions.

a. Would the bonding molecular orbital in HF place greater electron density near the H or the F atom? Why?

b. Would the bonding molecular orbital have greater fluorine $2p$ character, greater hydrogen $1s$ character, or an equal contribution from both? Why?

c. Answer the previous two questions for the antibonding molecular orbital in HF.

48. The diatomic molecule OH exists in the gas phase. The bond length and bond energy have been measured to be 97.06 pm and 424.7 kJ/mol, respectively. Assume that the OH molecule is analogous to the HF molecule discussed in the chapter and that molecular orbitals result from the overlap of a lower-energy p_z orbital from oxygen with the higher-energy $1s$ orbital of hydrogen (the O—H bond lies along the z axis).

a. Which of the two molecular orbitals will have the greater hydrogen $1s$ character?

b. Can the $2p_x$ orbital of oxygen form molecular orbitals with the $1s$ orbital of hydrogen? Explain.

c. Knowing that only the $2p$ orbitals of oxygen will interact significantly with the $1s$ orbital of hydrogen, complete the molecular orbital energy-level diagram for OH. Place the correct number of electrons in the energy levels.

d. Estimate the bond order for OH.

e. Predict whether the bond order of OH^+ will be greater than, less than, or the same as that of OH. Explain.

49. Describe the bonding in the O_3 molecule and the NO_2^- ion using the localized electron model. How would the molecular orbital model describe the π bonding in these two species?

50. Describe the bonding in the CO_3^{2-} ion using the localized electron model. How would the molecular orbital model describe the π bonding in this species?

Additional Exercises

51. Draw the Lewis structures, predict the molecular structures, and describe the bonding (in terms of the hybrid orbitals for the central atom) for the following.

a. XeO_3 **d.** $XeOF_2$
b. XeO_4 **e.** XeO_3F_2
c. $XeOF_4$

52. $FClO_2$ and F_3ClO can both gain a fluoride ion to form stable anions. F_3ClO and F_3ClO_2 will both lose a fluoride ion to form stable cations. Draw the Lewis structures and describe the hybrid orbitals used by chlorine in these ions.

53. Vitamin B_6 is an organic compound whose deficiency in the human body can cause apathy, irritability, and an increased susceptibility to infections. Below is an incomplete Lewis structure for vitamin B_6. Complete the Lewis structure and answer the following questions. *Hint:* Vitamin B_6 can be classified as an organic compound (a compound based on carbon atoms). The majority of Lewis structures for simple organic compounds have all atoms with a formal charge of zero. Therefore, add lone pairs and multiple bonds to the structure below to give each atom a formal charge of zero.

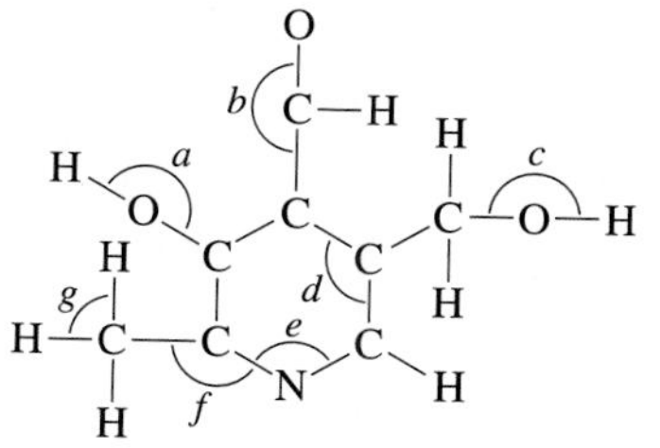

a. How many σ bonds and π bonds exist in vitamin B_6?
b. Give approximate values for the bond angles marked *a* through *g* in the structure.
c. How many carbon atoms are sp^2 hybridized?

d. How many carbon, oxygen, and nitrogen atoms are sp^3 hybridized?
e. Does vitamin B_6 exhibit delocalized π bonding? Explain.

54. Using bond energies from Table 8.4, estimate the barrier to rotation about a carbon–carbon double bond. To do this, consider what must happen to go from

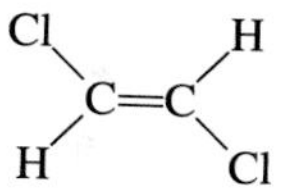

to

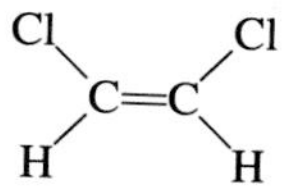

in terms of making and breaking chemical bonds; that is, what must happen in terms of the π bond?

55. Complete the Lewis structures of the following molecules. Predict the molecular structure, polarity, bond angles, and hybrid orbitals used by the atoms marked by asterisks for each molecule.

a. $COCl_2$

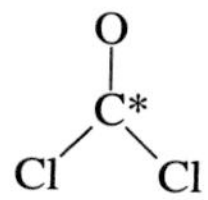

b. N_2F_2

$$F-N^*-N^*-F$$

c. COS

$$O-C^*-S$$

d. ICl_3

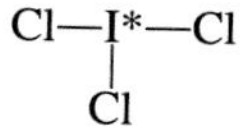

56. Complete the following resonance structures for $POCl_3$.

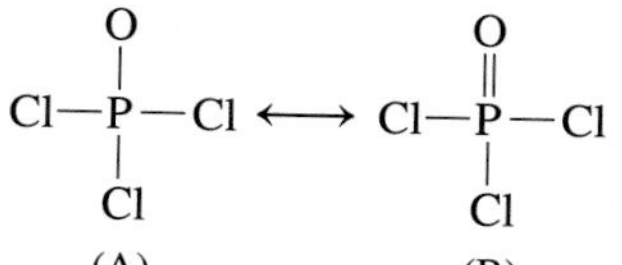

a. Would you predict the same molecular structure from each resonance structure?
b. What is the hybridization of P in each structure?
c. What orbitals can the P atom use to form the π bond in structure B?

d. Which resonance structure would be favored on the basis of formal charges?

57. The N_2O molecule is linear and polar.

 a. On the basis of this experimental evidence, which arrangement, NNO or NON, is correct? Explain your answer.

 b. On the basis of your answer to part a above, write the Lewis structure of N_2O (including resonance forms). Give the formal charge on each atom and the hybridization of the central atom.

 c. How would the multiple bonding in $:N{\equiv}N{-}\ddot{O}:$ be described in terms of orbitals?

58. Describe the bonding in NO^+, NO^-, and NO using both the localized electron and molecular orbital models. Account for any discrepancies between the two models.

59. Describe the bonding in the first excited state of N_2 (the one closest in energy to the ground state) using the molecular orbital model. What differences do you expect in the properties of the molecule in the ground state as compared to the first excited state? (An excited state of a molecule corresponds to an electron arrangement other than that giving the lowest possible energy.)

60. A Lewis structure obeying the octet rule can be drawn for O_2 as follows:

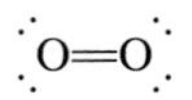

$$\ddot{O}{=}\ddot{O}$$

Use the molecular orbital energy-level diagram for O_2 to show that the above Lewis structure corresponds to an excited state.

Challenge Problems

61. Two structures can be drawn by cyanuric acid:

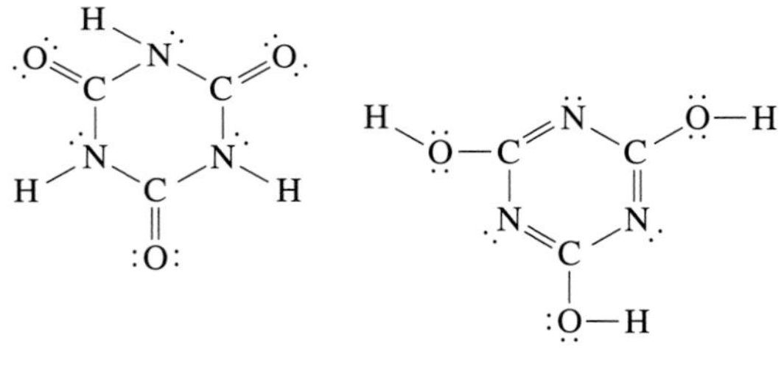

 a. Are these two structures the same molecule? Explain.

 b. Give the hybridization of the carbon and nitrogen atoms in each structure.

 c. Use bond energies (Table 8.4) to predict which form is more stable; that is, which contains the strongest bonds?

62. Cholesterol ($C_{27}H_{46}O$) has the following structure:

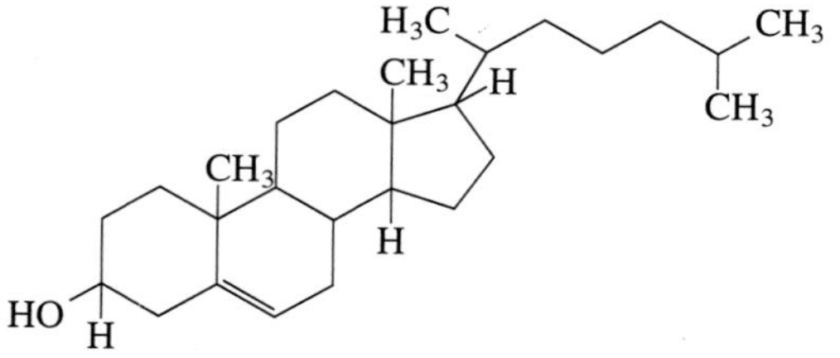

In such shorthand structures, each point where lines meet represents a carbon atom and most H atoms are not shown. Draw the complete structure showing all carbon and hydrogen atoms. (There will be four bonds to each carbon atom.) Indicate which carbon atoms use sp^2 or sp^3 hybrid orbitals. Are all carbon atoms in the same plane, as implied by the structure?

63. Cyanamide (H_2NCN), an important industrial chemical, is produced by the following steps:

$$CaC_2 + N_2 \longrightarrow CaNCN + C$$

$$CaNCN \xrightarrow{\text{Acid}} H_2NCN$$
$$\text{Cyanamide}$$

Calcium cyanamide (CaNCN) is used as a direct-application fertilizer, weed killer, and cotton defoliant. It is also used to make cyanamide, dicyandiamide, and melamine plastics:

$$H_2NCN \xrightarrow{\text{Acid}} NCNC(NH_2)_2$$
$$\text{Dicyandiamide}$$

$$NCNC(NH_2)_2 \xrightarrow[NH_3]{\text{Heat}}$$

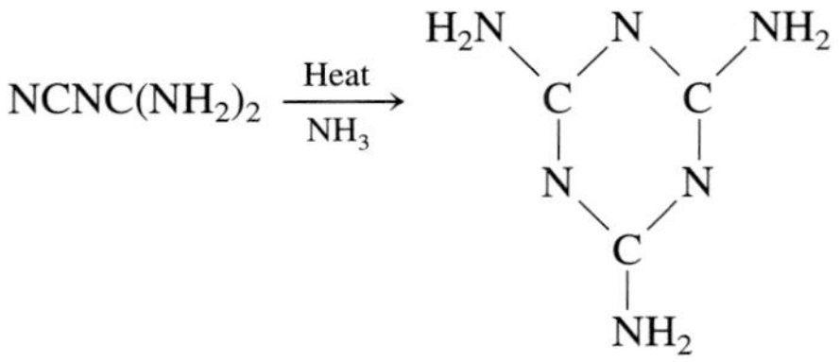

Melamine
(π bonds not shown)

 a. Write Lewis structures for NCN^{2-}, H_2NCN, dicyandiamide, and melamine, including resonance structures where appropriate.

 b. Give the hybridization of the C and N atoms in each species.

 c. How many σ bonds and how many π bonds are in each species?

 d. Is the ring in melamine planar?

 e. There are three different C—N bond distances in dicyandiamide, $NCNC(NH_2)_2$, and the molecule is nonlinear. Of all the resonance structures you drew for this molecule, predict which should be the most important.

64. In Exercise 69 in Chapter 8, the Lewis structures for benzene (C_6H_6) were drawn. Using one of the Lewis structures, estimate ΔH_f° for $C_6H_6(g)$ using bond energies and given that the standard enthalpy of formation of $C(g)$ is 717 kJ/mol. The experimental ΔH_f° value of $C_6H_6(g)$ is 83 kJ/mol. Explain the discrepancy between the experimental value and the calculated ΔH_f° value for $C_6H_6(g)$.

65. A flask containing gaseous N_2 is irradiated with 25-nm light.

 a. Using the following information, indicate what species can form in the flask during irradiation.

$$N_2(g) \longrightarrow 2N(g) \qquad \Delta H = 941 \text{ kJ/mol}$$
$$N_2(g) \longrightarrow N_2^+(g) + e^- \qquad \Delta H = 1501 \text{ kJ/mol}$$
$$N(g) \longrightarrow N^+(g) + e^- \qquad \Delta H = 1402 \text{ kJ/mol}$$

b. What range of wavelengths will produce atomic nitrogen in the flask but will not produce any ions?

c. Explain why the first ionization energy of N_2 (1501 kJ/mol) is greater than the first ionization energy of atomic nitrogen (1402 kJ/mol).

66. As compared with CO and O_2, CS and S_2 are very unstable molecules. Give an explanation based on the relative abilities of the sulfur and oxygen atoms to form π bonds.

67. Values of measured bond energies may vary greatly depending on the molecule studied. Consider the following reactions:

$$NCl_3(g) \longrightarrow NCl_2(g) + Cl(g) \qquad \Delta H = 375 \text{ kJ/mol}$$
$$ONCl(g) \longrightarrow NO(g) + Cl(g) \qquad \Delta H = 158 \text{ kJ/mol}$$

Rationalize the difference in the values of ΔH for these reactions, even though each reaction appears to involve only the breaking of one N—Cl bond. (*Hint:* Consider the bond order of the NO bond in ONCl and in NO.)

Liquids and Solids

Contents

You have only to think about water to appreciate how different the three states of matter are. Flying, swimming, and ice skating are all done in contact with water in its various forms. Clearly, the arrangements of the water molecules must be significantly different in its gas, liquid, and solid forms.

In Chapter 5 we saw that a gas can be pictured as a substance whose component particles are far apart, are in rapid random motion, and exert relatively small forces on each other. The kinetic molecular model was constructed to account for the ideal behavior that most gases approach at high temperatures and low pressures.

Solids are obviously very different from gases. A gas has low density and high compressibility and completely fills its container. Solids have much greater densities, are compressible only to a very slight extent, and are rigid—a solid maintains its shape irrespective of its container. These properties indicate that the components of a solid are close together and exert large attractive forces on each other.

The properties of liquids lie somewhere between those of solids and gases but not midway between, as can be seen from some of the properties of the three states of water. For example, compare the enthalpy change for the melting of ice at 0°C (the heat of fusion) with that for vaporizing liquid water at 100°C (the heat of vaporization):

$$H_2O(s) \longrightarrow H_2O(l) \qquad \Delta H°_{fus} = 6.02 \text{ kJ/mol}$$
$$H_2O(l) \longrightarrow H_2O(g) \qquad \Delta H°_{vap} = 40.7 \text{ kJ/mol}$$

These values show a much greater change in structure in going from the liquid to the gaseous state than in going from the solid to the liquid state. This suggests that there are extensive attractive forces among the molecules in liquid water, similar to but not as strong as those in the solid state.

The relative similarity of the liquid and solid states also can be seen in the densities of the three states of water. As shown in Table 10.1, the

A climber ascending an ice cave in Alaska.

Table 10.1 Densities of the Three States of Water

State	Density (g/cm^3)
Solid (0°C, 1 atm)	0.9168
Liquid (25°C, 1 atm)	0.9971
Gas (400°C, 1 atm)	3.26×10^{-4}

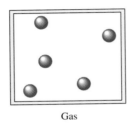
Gas

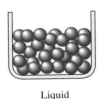
Liquid

Solid

Figure 10.1

Schematic representations of the three states of matter.

densities for liquid and solid water are quite close.* Compressibilities also can be used to explore the relationship among water's states. At 25°C, the density of liquid water changes from 0.99707 g/cm^3 at a pressure of 1 atm to 1.046 g/cm^3 at 1065 atm. Given the large change in pressure, this is a very small variation in the density. Ice also shows little variation in density with increased pressure. On the other hand, at 400°C, the density of gaseous water changes from 3.26×10^{-4} g/cm^3 at 1 atm pressure to 0.157 g/cm^3 at 242 atm—a huge variation.

The conclusion is clear. The liquid and solid states show many similarities and are strikingly different from the gaseous state, as shown schematically in Fig. 10.1. We must bear this in mind as we develop models for the structures of solids and liquids.

We will proceed in our study of liquids and solids by first considering the properties and structures of liquids and solids. Then we will consider the changes in state that occur between solid and liquid, liquid and gas, and solid and gas.

Exploration: Intermolecular Forces

10.1 Intermolecular Forces

In Chapters 8 and 9 we saw that atoms can form stable units called *molecules* by sharing electrons. This is called *intramolecular* (within the molecule) *bonding*. In this chapter we consider the properties of the **condensed states** of matter (liquids and solids) and the forces that cause the aggregation of the components of a substance to form a liquid or a solid. These forces may involve covalent or ionic bonding, or they may involve weaker interactions usually called **intermolecular forces** (because they occur between, rather than within, molecules).

It is important to recognize that when a substance such as water changes from solid to liquid to gas, *the molecules remain intact.* The changes in states are due to changes in the forces *among* the molecules rather than in those *within* the molecules. In ice, as we will see later in this chapter, the molecules are virtually locked in place, although they can vibrate about their positions. If energy is added, the motions of the molecules increase, and they eventually achieve the greater movement

Remember that temperature is a measure of the random motions of the particles in a substance.

* Although the densities of solid and liquid water are quite similar, as is typical for most substances, water is quite unusual in that the density of its solid state is slightly less than that of its liquid state. For most substances, the density of the solid state is slightly greater than that of the liquid state.

and disorder characteristic of liquid water. The ice has melted. As more energy is added, the gaseous state is eventually reached, with the individual molecules far apart and interacting relatively little. However, the gas still consists of water molecules. It would take much energy to overcome the covalent bonds and decompose the water molecules into their component atoms. This can be seen by comparing the energy needed to vaporize 1 mole of liquid water (40.7 kJ) with that needed to break the O—H bonds in 1 mole of water molecules (934 kJ).

Dipole–Dipole Forces

As we saw in Section 8.3, molecules with polar bonds often behave in an electric field as if they had a center of positive charge and a center of negative charge. That is, they exhibit a dipole moment. Molecules with dipole moments can attract each other electrostatically by lining up so that the positive and negative ends are close to each other, as shown in Fig. 10.2(a). This is called a **dipole–dipole attraction.** In a condensed state such as a liquid, where many molecules are in close proximity, the dipoles find the best compromise between attraction and repulsion. That is, the molecules orient themselves to maximize the ⊕---⊖ interactions and to minimize ⊕---⊕ and ⊖---⊖ interactions, as represented in Fig. 10.2(b).

Dipole–dipole forces are typically only about 1% as strong as covalent or ionic bonds, and they rapidly become weaker as the distance between the dipoles increases. At low pressures in the gas phase, where the molecules are far apart, these forces are relatively unimportant.

Particularly strong dipole–dipole forces, however, are seen among molecules in which hydrogen is bound to a highly electronegative atom, such as nitrogen, oxygen, or fluorine. Two factors account for the strengths of these interactions: the great polarity of the bond and the close approach of the dipoles, allowed by the very small size of the hydrogen atom. Because dipole–dipole attractions of this type are so unusually strong, they are given a special name—**hydrogen bonding.** Figure 10.3 shows hydrogen bonding among water molecules.

Dipole–dipole forces are forces that act between polar molecules.

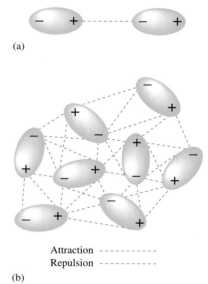

(a)

(b)

Attraction - - - - - - - -
Repulsion   - - - - - - - -

Figure 10.2

(a) The electrostatic interaction of two polar molecules. (b) The interaction of many dipoles in a condensed state.

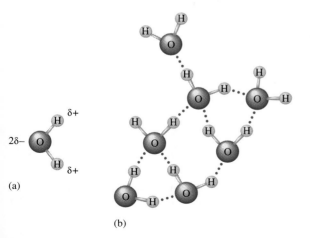

Figure 10.3

(a) The polar water molecule. (b) Hydrogen bonding among water molecules. Note that the small size of the hydrogen atom allows for close interactions.

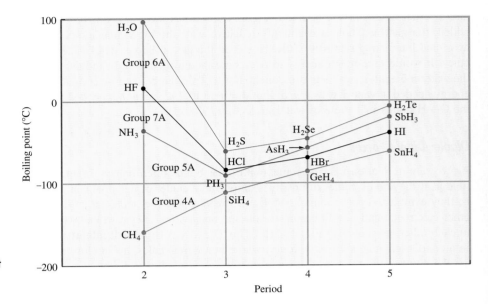

Figure 10.4

The boiling points of the covalent hydrides of the elements in Groups 4A, 5A, 6A, and 7A.

Boiling point will be defined precisely in Section 10.8.

Hydrogen bonding has a very important effect on physical properties. For example, the boiling points for the covalent hydrides of the elements in Groups 4A, 5A, 6A, and 7A are given in Fig. 10.4. Note that the nonpolar tetrahedral hydrides of Group 4A show a steady increase in boiling point with molar mass (that is, in going down the group), whereas, for the other groups, the lightest member has an unexpectedly high boiling point. Why? The answer lies in the especially large hydrogen bonding interactions that exist among the smallest molecules with the most polar X—H bonds. These unusually strong hydrogen bonding forces are due primarily to two factors. One factor is the relatively large electronegativity values of the lightest elements in each group, which leads to especially polar X—H bonds. The second factor is the small size of the first element of each group, which allows for the close approach of the dipoles, further strengthening the intermolecular forces. Because the interactions among the molecules containing the lightest elements in Groups 5A and 6A are so strong, an unusually large quantity of energy must be supplied to overcome these interactions and separate the molecules to produce the gaseous state. These molecules will remain together in the liquid state even at high temperatures; hence the very high boiling points.

London Dispersion Forces

Even molecules without dipole moments must exert forces on each other. We know this because all substances—even the noble gases—exist in the liquid and solid states under certain conditions. The forces that exist among noble gas atoms and nonpolar molecules are called **London dispersion forces.** To understand the origin of these forces, let's consider a pair of noble gas atoms. Although we usually assume that the electrons of an atom are uniformly distributed about the nucleus, this is apparently not true at every instant. As the electrons move about the nucleus, a momentary nonsymmetrical electron distribution can develop that produces a temporary dipolar arrangement of charge. The formation of this temporary dipole can, in

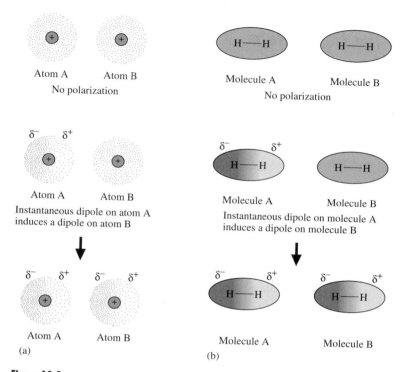

Table 10.2 The Freezing Points of the Group 8A Elements	
Element	*Freezing Point (°C)*
Helium*	−269.7
Neon	−248.6
Argon	−189.4
Krypton	−157.3
Xenon	−111.9

*Helium is the only element that will not freeze by lowering its temperature at 1 atm. Pressure must be applied to freeze helium.

Figure 10.5

(a) An instantaneous polarization can occur on atom A, creating an instantaneous dipole. This dipole creates an induced dipole on neighboring atom B. (b) Nonpolar molecules such as H_2 also can develop instantaneous and induced dipoles.

turn, affect the electron distribution of a neighboring atom. That is, this *instantaneous dipole* that occurs accidentally in a given atom can then *induce* a similar dipole in a neighboring atom, as represented in Fig. 10.5(a). This phenomenon leads to an interatomic attraction that is relatively weak and short-lived but that can be very significant especially for large atoms (see below). For these interactions to become strong enough to produce a solid, the motions of the atoms must be greatly slowed down. This explains, for instance, why the noble gas elements have such low freezing points (see Table 10.2).

Note from Table 10.2 that the freezing point rises going down the group. The principal cause for this trend is that as the atomic number increases, the number of electrons increases, and there is an increased chance of the occurrence of momentary dipole interactions. We describe this phenomenon using the term *polarizability,* which indicates the ease with which the electron "cloud" of an atom can be distorted to give a dipolar charge distribution. Thus we say that large atoms with many electrons exhibit a higher polarizability than small atoms. This means that the importance of London dispersion forces increases greatly as the size of the atom increases.

These same ideas also apply to nonpolar molecules such as H_2, CH_4, CCl_4, and CO_2 [see Fig. 10.5(b)]. Since none of these molecules has a permanent dipole moment, their principal means of attracting each other is through London dispersion forces.

The dispersion forces in molecules with large atoms are quite significant and are often actually more important than dipole–dipole forces.

Molecular Models: H_2, CH_4, CCl_4, CO_2

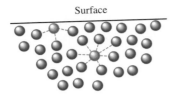

Figure 10.6
A molecule in the interior of a liquid is attracted by the molecules surrounding it, whereas a molecule at the surface of a liquid is attracted only by molecules below it and on each side.

For a given volume, a sphere has a smaller surface area than any other shape.

Surface tension: The resistance of a liquid to an increase in its surface area.

10.2 The Liquid State

Liquids and liquid solutions are vital to our lives. Of course, water is the most important liquid. Besides being essential to life, water provides a medium for food preparation, for transportation, for cooling in many types of machines and industrial processes, for recreation, for cleaning, and for a myriad of other uses.

Liquids exhibit many characteristics that help us understand their nature. We have already mentioned their low compressibility, lack of rigidity, and high density compared with gases. Many of the properties of liquids give us direct information about the forces that exist among the particles. For example, when a liquid is poured onto a solid surface, it tends to bead as droplets, a phenomenon that depends on the intermolecular forces. Although molecules in the interior of the liquid are completely surrounded by other molecules, those at the liquid surface are subject to attractions only from the side and from below (Fig. 10.6). The effect of this uneven pull on the surface molecules tends to draw them into the body of the liquid and causes a droplet of liquid to assume the shape that has the minimum surface area—a sphere.

To increase a liquid's surface area, molecules must move from the interior of the liquid to the surface. This requires energy, since some intermolecular forces must be overcome. The resistance of a liquid to an increase in its surface area is called the **surface tension** of the liquid. As we would expect, liquids with relatively large intermolecular forces, such as those with polar molecules, tend to have relatively high surface tensions.

Polar liquids typically exhibit **capillary action,** the spontaneous rising of a liquid in a narrow tube. Two different types of forces are responsible for this property: *cohesive forces,* the intermolecular forces among the molecules of the liquid, and

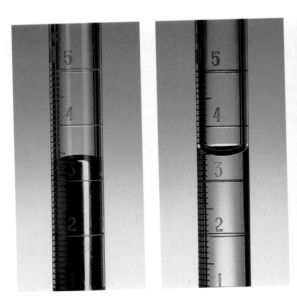

Figure 10.7
Nonpolar liquid mercury forms a convex meniscus in a glass tube, whereas polar water forms a concave meniscus.

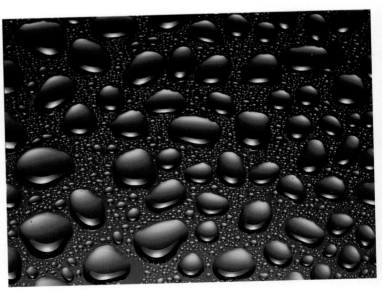

Beads of water on a waxed car finish.

adhesive forces, the forces between the liquid molecules and their container. We have already seen how cohesive forces operate among polar molecules. Adhesive forces occur when a container is made of a substance that has polar bonds. For example, a glass surface contains many oxygen atoms with partial negative charges that are attractive to the positive end of a polar molecule such as water. This ability of water to "wet" glass makes it creep up the walls of the tube where the water surface touches the glass. This, however, tends to increase the surface area of the water, which is opposed by the cohesive forces that try to minimize the surface. Thus, because water has both strong cohesive (intermolecular) forces and strong adhesive forces to glass, it "pulls itself" up a glass capillary tube (a tube with a small diameter) to a height where the weight of the column of water just balances the water's tendency to be attracted to the glass surface. The concave shape of the meniscus (see Fig. 10.7) shows that water's adhesive forces toward the glass are stronger than its cohesive forces. A nonpolar liquid such as mercury (see Fig. 10.7) shows a convex meniscus. This behavior is characteristic of a liquid in which the cohesive forces are stronger than the adhesive forces toward glass.

Another property of liquids strongly dependent on intermolecular forces is **viscosity,** a measure of a liquid's resistance to flow. As might be expected, liquids with large intermolecular forces tend to be highly viscous. For example, glycerol, whose structure is

$$
\begin{array}{c}
\quad\;\; H \\
\quad\;\; | \\
H\!-\!C\!-\!O\!-\!H \\
\quad\;\; | \\
H\!-\!C\!-\!O\!-\!H \\
\quad\;\; | \\
H\!-\!C\!-\!O\!-\!H \\
\quad\;\; | \\
\quad\;\; H
\end{array}
$$

has an unusually high viscosity due mainly to its high capacity to form hydrogen bonds using its O—H groups.

Molecular complexity also leads to higher viscosity because very large molecules can become entangled with each other. For example, gasoline, a nonviscous liquid, contains hydrocarbon molecules of the type $CH_3\!-\!(CH_2)_n\!-\!CH_3$, where n varies from about 3 to 8. However, grease, which is very viscous, contains much larger hydrocarbon molecules in which n varies from 20 to 25.

Structural Model for Liquids

In many respects, the development of a structural model for liquids presents greater challenges than developing such a model for the other two states of matter. In the gaseous state the particles are so far apart and are moving so rapidly that intermolecular forces are negligible under most circumstances. This means that we can use a relatively simple model for gases. In the solid state, although the intermolecular forces are large, the molecular motions are minimal, and fairly simple models are again possible. The liquid state, however, has both strong intermolecular forces *and* significant molecular motions. Such a situation precludes the use of really simple models for liquids. Recent advances in *spectroscopy,* the study of the manner in which substances interact with electromagnetic radiation, make it possible to follow the very rapid changes that occur in liquids. As a result, our models of liquids are becoming more accurate. As a starting point, a typical liquid might best be viewed

The composition of glass is discussed in Section 10.5.

Viscosity: A measure of a liquid's resistance to flow.

Molecular Models: glycerol, C_8H_{18}, $C_{22}H_{46}$

as containing a large number of regions where the arrangements of the components are similar to those found in the solid, but with more disorder, and a smaller number of regions where holes are present. The situation is highly dynamic, with rapid fluctuations occurring in both types of regions.

10.3 An Introduction to Structures and Types of Solids

There are many ways to classify solids, but the broadest categories are **crystalline solids,** those with a highly regular arrangement of their components, and **amorphous solids,** those with considerable disorder in their structures.

The regular arrangement of the components of a crystalline solid at the microscopic level produces the beautiful, characteristic shapes of crystals, such as those shown in Fig. 10.8. The positions of the components in a crystalline solid are usually represented by a **lattice,** a three-dimensional system of points designating the positions of the components (atoms, ions, or molecules) that make up the substance. The *smallest repeating unit* of the lattice is called the **unit cell.** Thus a particular lattice can be generated by repeating the unit cell in all three dimensions to form the extended structure. Three common unit cells and their lattices are shown in Fig. 10.9. Note from Fig. 10.9 that the extended structure in each case can be viewed as a series of repeating unit cells that share common faces in the interior of the solid.

Although we will concentrate on crystalline solids in this book, there are many important noncrystalline (amorphous) materials. An example is common glass, which is best pictured as a solution in which the components are "frozen in place" before they can achieve an ordered arrangement. Although glass is a solid (it has a rigid shape), a great deal of disorder exists in its structure.

Figure 10.8
Two crystalline solids: pyrite (left), amethyst (right).

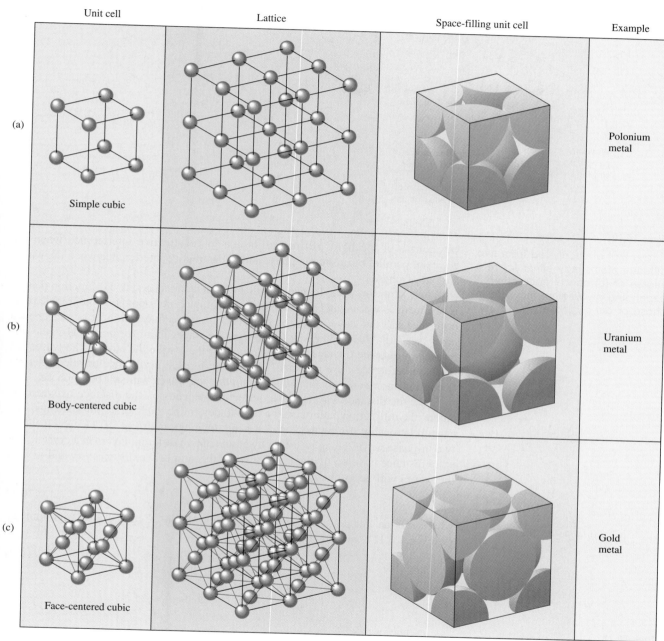

Unit cell	Lattice	Space-filling unit cell	Example
(a) Simple cubic			Polonium metal
(b) Body-centered cubic			Uranium metal
(c) Face-centered cubic			Gold metal

Animation: Unit Cells and Crystal Packing

Figure 10.9

Three cubic unit cells and the corresponding lattices. Note that only parts of spheres on the corners and faces of the unit cells reside inside the unit cell, as shown by the "cutoff" versions.

X-Ray Analysis of Solids

The structures of crystalline solids are most commonly determined by **X-ray diffraction.** Diffraction occurs when beams of light are scattered from a regular array of points in which the spacings between the components are comparable with the

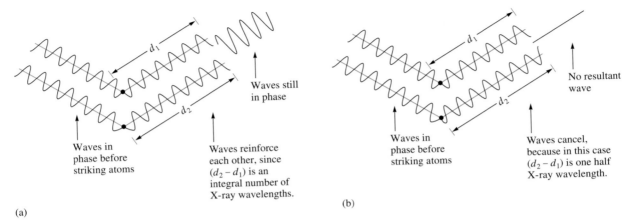

(a)

(b)

Waves in phase before striking atoms

Waves reinforce each other, since $(d_2 - d_1)$ is an integral number of X-ray wavelengths.

Waves in phase before striking atoms

No resultant wave

Waves cancel, because in this case $(d_2 - d_1)$ is one half X-ray wavelength.

Figure 10.10

X rays that are scattered from two different atoms may either (a) reinforce or (b) cancel each other, depending on whether they are in phase or out of phase.

wavelength of the light. Diffraction is due to constructive interference when the waves of parallel beams are in phase and to destructive interference when the waves are out of phase.

When X rays of a single wavelength are directed at a crystal, a diffraction pattern is obtained, as we saw in Fig. 7.5. The light and dark areas on the photographic plate occur because the waves scattered from various atoms may reinforce or cancel each other (see Fig. 10.10). The key to whether the waves reinforce or cancel is the difference in distance traveled by the waves after they strike the atoms. The waves are in phase before they are reflected, so if the difference in distance traveled after reflection is an *integral number of wavelengths,* the waves will still be in phase.

Since the distance traveled after reflection depends on the distance between the atoms, the diffraction pattern can be used to determine the interatomic spacings. The exact relationship can be worked out using the diagram in Fig. 10.11, which shows two in-phase waves being reflected by atoms in two different layers in a crystal. The extra distance traveled by the lower wave is the sum of the distances xy and yz, and the waves will be in phase after reflection if

$$xy + yz = n\lambda \tag{10.1}$$

where n is an integer and λ is the wavelength of the X rays. Using trigonometry (see Fig. 10.11), we can show that

$$xy + yz = 2d \sin \theta \tag{10.2}$$

Figure 10.11

Reflection of X rays of wavelength λ from a pair of atoms in two different layers of a crystal. The lower wave travels an extra distance equal to the sum of xy and yz. If this distance is an integral number of wavelengths ($n = 1, 2, 3, \ldots$), the waves will reinforce each other when they exit the crystal.

Incident rays

Reflected rays

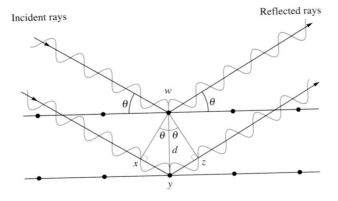

where d is the distance between the atoms and θ is the angle of incidence and reflection. Combining Equation (10.1) and Equation (10.2) gives

$$n\lambda = 2d \sin \theta \qquad (10.3)$$

Equation (10.3) is called the *Bragg equation* after William Henry Bragg (1862–1942) and his son William Lawrence Bragg (1890–1972), who shared the Nobel Prize in physics in 1915 for their pioneering work in X-ray crystallography.

A diffractometer is a computer-controlled instrument used for carrying out the X-ray analysis of crystals. It rotates the crystal with respect to the X-ray beam and collects the data produced by the scattering of the X rays from the various planes of atoms in the crystal. The results are then analyzed by computer.

The techniques for crystal structure analysis have reached a level of sophistication that allows the determination of very complex structures, such as those important in biological systems. For example, the structures of several enzymes have been determined, thus enabling biochemists to understand how they perform their functions. We will explore this further in Chapter 12. Using X-ray diffraction, we can gather data on bond lengths and angles and in so doing can test the predictions of our models of molecular geometry.

Sample Exercise 10.1 *Using the Bragg Equation*

X rays of wavelength 1.54 Å were used to analyze an aluminum crystal. A reflection was produced at $\theta = 19.3$ degrees. Assuming $n = 1$, calculate the distance d between the planes of atoms producing this reflection.

Solution

To determine the distance between the planes, we use Equation (10.3) with $n = 1$, $\lambda = 1.54$ Å, and $\theta = 19.3$ degrees. Since $2d \sin \theta = n\lambda$,

$$d = \frac{n\lambda}{2 \sin \theta} = \frac{(1)(1.54 \text{ Å})}{(2)(0.3305)} = 2.33 \text{ Å} = 233 \text{ pm}$$

See Exercises 10.47 and 10.48.

Types of Crystalline Solids

There are many different types of crystalline solids. For example, although both sugar and salt dissolve readily in water, the properties of the resulting solutions are quite different. The salt solution readily conducts an electric current, whereas the sugar solution does not. This behavior arises from the nature of the components in these two solids. Common salt (NaCl) is an ionic solid; it contains Na^+ and Cl^- ions. When solid sodium chloride dissolves in the polar water, sodium and chloride ions are distributed throughout the resulting solution and are free to conduct electric current. Table sugar (sucrose), on the other hand, is composed of neutral molecules that are dispersed throughout the water when the solid dissolves. No ions are present, and the resulting solution does not conduct electricity. These examples illustrate two

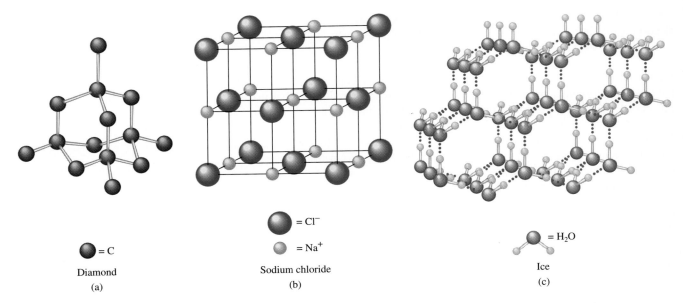

= Cl⁻

= Na⁺

= C

Diamond

(a)

Sodium chloride

(b)

= H₂O

Ice

(c)

Figure 10.12

Examples of three types of crystalline solids. Only part of the structure is shown in each case. (a) An atomic solid. (b) An ionic solid. (c) A molecular solid. The dotted lines show the hydrogen bonding interactions among the polar water molecules.

Buckminsterfullerene, C₆₀, is a particular member of the fullerene family.

 Molecular Models: graphite, diamond, C₆₀

The internal forces in a solid determine the properties of the solid.

important types of solids: **ionic solids,** represented by sodium chloride, and **molecular solids,** represented by sucrose. Ionic solids have ions at the points of the lattice that describes the structure of the solid. A molecular solid, on the other hand, has discrete covalently bonded molecules at each of its lattice points. Ice is a molecular solid that has an H_2O molecule at each point (see Fig. 10.12).

A third type of solid is represented by elements such as carbon (which exists in the forms graphite, diamond, and the fullerenes), boron, silicon, and all metals. These substances all have atoms at the lattice points that describes the structure of the solid. Therefore, we call solids of this type **atomic solids.** Examples of these three types of solids are shown in Fig. 10.12.

To summarize, we find it convenient to classify solids according to what type of component occupies the lattice points. This leads to the classifications *atomic solids* (atoms at the lattice points), *molecular solids* (discrete, relatively small molecules at the lattice points), and *ionic solids* (ions at the lattice points). In addition, atomic solids are placed into the following subgroups based on the bonding that exists among the atoms in the solid: *metallic solids, network solids,* and *Group 8A solids.* In metallic solids, a special type of delocalized nondirectional covalent bonding occurs. In network solids, the atoms bond to each other with strong directional covalent bonds that lead to giant molecules, or networks, of atoms. In the Group 8A solids, the noble gas elements are attracted to each other with London dispersion forces. The classification of solids is summarized in Table 10.3.

The markedly different bonding present in the various atomic solids leads to dramatically different properties for the resulting solids. For example, although argon, copper, and diamond all are atomic solids, they have strikingly different properties. Argon (a Group 8A solid) has a very low melting point ($-189°C$), whereas diamond (a network solid) and copper (a metallic solid) melt at high temperatures (about 3500 and 1083°C, respectively). Copper is an excellent conductor of electricity, whereas argon and diamond are both insulators. Copper can be easily changed in shape; it is both malleable (can be formed into thin sheets) and ductile (can be pulled into a wire). Diamond, on the other hand, is the hardest natural substance known. We will explore the structure and bonding of atomic solids in the next two sections.

Table 10.3 Classification of Solids

	Atomic Solids			Molecular Solids	Ionic Solids
	Metallic	Network	Group 8A		
Components that occupy the lattice points:	Metal atoms	Nonmetal atoms	Group 8A atoms	Discrete molecules	Ions
Bonding:	Delocalized covalent	Directional covalent (leading to giant molecules)	London dispersion forces	Dipole–dipole and/or London dispersion forces	Ionic

10.4 Structure and Bonding in Metals

Metals are characterized by high thermal and electrical conductivity, malleability, and ductility. As we will see, these properties can be traced to the nondirectional covalent bonding found in metallic crystals.

A metallic crystal can be pictured as containing spherical atoms packed together and bonded to each other equally in all directions. We can model such a structure by packing uniform, hard spheres in a manner that most efficiently uses the available space. Such an arrangement is called **closest packing.** The spheres are packed in layers, as shown in Fig. 10.13, in which each sphere is surrounded by six others. In the second layer the spheres do not lie directly over those in the first layer. Instead, each one occupies an indentation (or dimple) formed by three spheres in

The closest packing model for metallic crystals assumes that metal atoms are uniform, hard spheres.

(a) *abab* — Closest packing

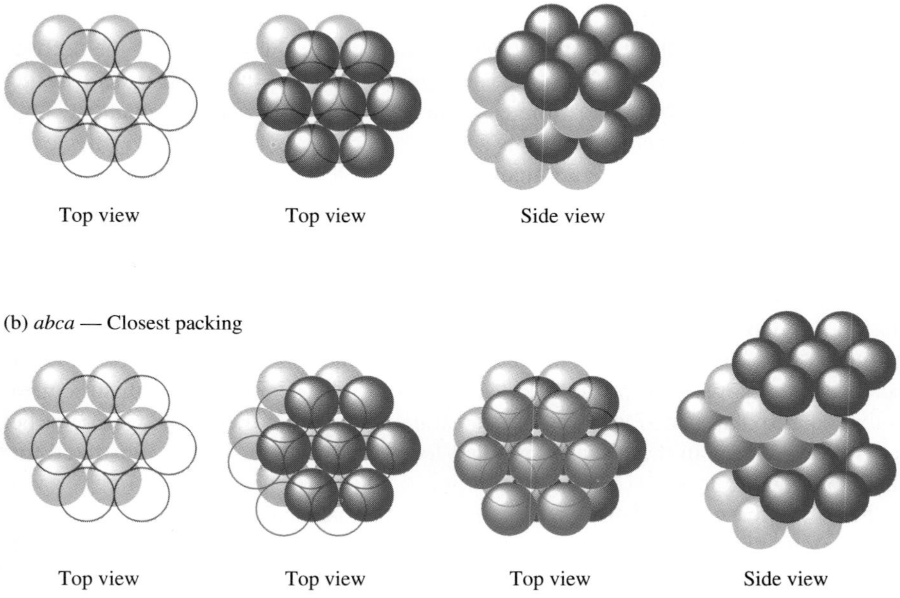

Top view   Top view   Side view

(b) *abca* — Closest packing

Top view   Top view   Top view   Side view

Figure 10.13
The closest packing arrangement of uniform spheres. In each layer a given sphere is surrounded by six others. (a) *aba* packing: The second layer is like the first, but it is displaced so that each sphere in the second layer occupies a dimple in the first layer. The spheres in the third layer occupy dimples in the second layer so that the spheres in the third layer lie directly over those in the first layer (*aba*). (b) *abc* packing: The spheres in the third layer occupy dimples in the second layer so that no spheres in the third layer lie above any in the first layer (*abc*). The fourth layer is like the first.

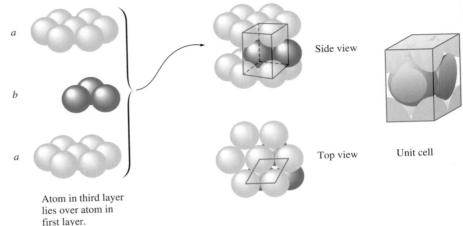

Figure 10.14

When spheres are closest packed so that the spheres in the third layer are directly over those in the first layer (aba), the unit cell is the hexagonal prism illustrated here in red.

Atom in third layer lies over atom in first layer.

Side view

Top view

Unit cell

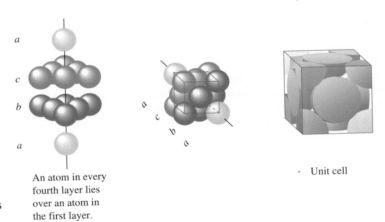

Figure 10.15

When spheres are packed in the abc arrangement, the unit cell is face-centered cubic. To make the cubic arrangement easier to see, the vertical axis has been tilted as shown.

An atom in every fourth layer lies over an atom in the first layer.

Unit cell

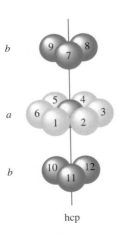

hcp

Figure 10.16

The indicated sphere has 12 nearest neighbors.

the first layer. In the third layer the spheres can occupy the dimples of the second layer in two possible ways: They can occupy positions so that each sphere in the third layer lies directly over a sphere in the first layer (the *aba* arrangement; Fig. 10.13a), or they can occupy positions so that no sphere in the third layer lies over one in the first layer (the *abc* arrangement; Fig. 10.13b).

The *aba* arrangement has the *hexagonal* unit cell shown in Fig. 10.14, and the resulting structure is called the **hexagonal closest packed (hcp) structure.** The *abc* arrangement has a *face-centered cubic* unit cell, as shown in Fig. 10.15, and the resulting structure is called the **cubic closest packed (ccp) structure.** Note that in the hcp structure the spheres in every other layer occupy the same vertical position (*ababab* · · ·), whereas in the ccp structure the spheres in every fourth layer occupy the same vertical position (*abcabca* · · ·). A characteristic of both structures is that each sphere has 12 equivalent nearest neighbors: 6 in the same layer, 3 in the layer above, and 3 in the layer below (that form the dimples). This is illustrated for the hcp structure in Fig. 10.16.

Knowing the *net* number of spheres (atoms) in a particular unit cell is important for many applications involving solids. To illustrate how to find the net number of spheres in a unit cell, we will consider a face-centered cubic unit cell (Fig. 10.17).

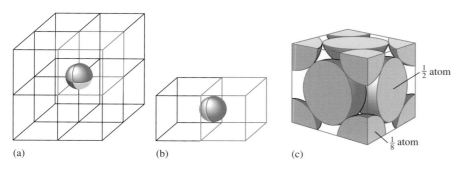

(a)   (b)   (c)

Figure 10.17
The net number of spheres in a face-centered cubic unit cell. (a) Note that the sphere on a corner of the colored cell is shared with 7 other unit cells (a total of 8). Thus $\frac{1}{8}$ of such a sphere lies within a given unit cell. Since there are 8 corners in a cube, there are 8 of these $\frac{1}{8}$ pieces, or 1 net sphere. (b) The sphere on the center of each face is shared by 2 unit cells, and thus each unit cell has $\frac{1}{2}$ of each of these types of spheres. There are 6 of these $\frac{1}{2}$ spheres to give 3 net spheres. (c) Thus the face-centered cubic unit cell contains 4 net spheres (all of the pieces can be assembled to give 4 spheres).

Note that this unit cell is defined by the *centers* of the spheres on the cube's corners. Thus 8 cubes share a given sphere, so $\frac{1}{8}$ of this sphere lies inside each unit cell. Since a cube has 8 corners, there are $8 \times \frac{1}{8}$ pieces, or enough to put together 1 whole sphere. The spheres at the center of each face are shared by 2 unit cells, so $\frac{1}{2}$ of each lies inside a particular unit cell. Since the cube has 6 faces, we have $6 \times \frac{1}{2}$ pieces, or enough to construct 3 whole spheres. Thus the net number of spheres in a face-centered cubic unit cell is

$$\left(8 \times \frac{1}{8}\right) + \left(6 \times \frac{1}{2}\right) = 4$$

Sample Exercise 10.2 *Calculating the Density of a Closest Packed Solid*

Silver crystallizes in a cubic closest packed structure. The radius of a silver atom is 144 pm. Calculate the density of solid silver.

Solution

Density is mass per unit volume. Thus we need to know how many silver atoms occupy a given volume in the crystal. The structure is cubic closest packed, which means the unit cell is face-centered cubic, as shown in the accompanying figure.

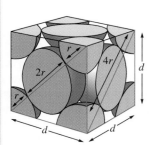

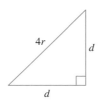

We must find the volume of this unit cell for silver and the net number of atoms it contains. Note that in this structure the atoms touch along the diagonals for each face and not along the edges of the cube. Thus the length of the diagonal

Crystalline silver contains cubic closest packed silver atoms.

is $r + 2r + r$, or $4r$. We use this fact to find the length of the edge of the cube by the Pythagorean theorem:

$$d^2 + d^2 = (4r)^2$$
$$2d^2 = 16r^2$$
$$d^2 = 8r^2$$
$$d = \sqrt{8r^2} = r\sqrt{8}$$

Since $r = 144$ pm for a silver atom,

$$d = (144 \text{ pm})(\sqrt{8}) = 407 \text{ pm}$$

The volume of the unit cell is d^3, which is $(407 \text{ pm})^3$, or 6.74×10^7 pm^3. We convert this to cubic centimeters as follows:

$$6.74 \times 10^7 \text{ pm}^3 \times \left(\frac{1.00 \times 10^{-10} \text{ cm}}{\text{pm}}\right)^3 = 6.74 \times 10^{-23} \text{ cm}^3$$

Since we know that the net number of atoms in the face-centered cubic unit cell is 4, we have 4 silver atoms contained in a volume of 6.74×10^{-23} cm^3. The density is therefore

$$\text{Density} = \frac{\text{mass}}{\text{volume}} = \frac{(4 \text{ atoms})(107.9 \text{ g/mol})(1 \text{ mol}/6.022 \times 10^{23} \text{ atoms})}{6.74 \times 10^{-23} \text{ cm}^3}$$
$$= 10.6 \text{ g/cm}^3$$

See Exercises 10.49 through 10.52.

Examples of metals that form cubic closest packed solids are aluminum, iron, copper, cobalt, and nickel. Magnesium and zinc are hexagonal closest packed. Calcium and certain other metals can crystallize in either of these structures. Some metals, however, assume structures that are not closest packed. For example, the alkali metals have structures characterized by a *body-centered cubic (bcc) unit cell* (see Fig. 10.9), where the spheres touch along the body diagonal of the cube. In this structure, each sphere has 8 nearest neighbors (count the number of atoms around the atom at the center of the unit cell), as compared with 12 in the closest packed structures. Why a particular metal adopts the structure it does is not well understood.

Bonding Models for Metals

Malleable: Can be pounded into thin sheets.

Ductile: Can be drawn to form a wire.

Any successful bonding model for metals must account for the typical physical properties of metals: malleability, ductility, and the efficient and uniform conduction of heat and electricity in all directions. Although the shapes of most pure metals can be changed relatively easily, most metals are durable and have high melting points. These facts indicate that the bonding in most metals is both *strong* and *nondirectional*. That is, although it is difficult to separate metal atoms, it is relatively easy to move them, provided the atoms stay in contact with each other.

The simplest picture that explains these observations is the *electron sea model*, which envisions a regular array of metal cations in a "sea" of valence electrons (see

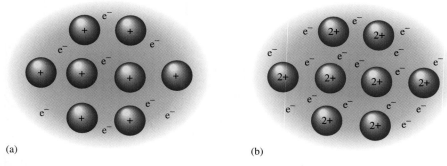

(a)　　　　　　　　　　　　　(b)

Figure 10.18

The electron sea model for metals postulates a regular array of cations in a "sea" of valence electrons. (a) Representation of an alkali metal (Group 1A) with one valence electron. (b) Representation of an alkaline earth metal (Group 2A) with two valence electrons.

Fig. 10.18). The mobile electrons can conduct heat and electricity, and the metal ions can be easily moved around as the metal is hammered into a sheet or pulled into a wire.

A related model that gives a more detailed view of the electron energies and motions is the **band model,** or **molecular orbital (MO) model,** for metals. In this model, the electrons are assumed to travel around the metal crystal in molecular orbitals formed from the valence atomic orbitals of the metal atoms (Fig. 10.19).

Recall that in the MO model for the gaseous Li_2 molecule (Section 9.3), two widely spaced molecular orbital energy levels (bonding and antibonding) result when two identical atomic orbitals interact. However, when many metal atoms interact, as in a metal crystal, the large number of resulting molecular orbitals become more closely spaced and finally form a virtual continuum of levels, called *bands,* as shown in Fig. 10.19.

As an illustration, picture a magnesium metal crystal, which has an hcp structure. Since each magnesium atom has one $3s$ and three $3p$ valence atomic orbitals, a crystal with n magnesium atoms has available $n(3s)$ and $3n(3p)$ orbitals to form the molecular orbitals, as illustrated in Fig. 10.20. Note that the core electrons are localized, as shown by their presence in the energy "well" around each magnesium atom. However, the valence electrons occupy closely spaced molecular orbitals, which are only partially filled.

The existence of empty molecular orbitals close in energy to filled molecular orbitals explains the thermal and electrical conductivity of metal crystals. Metals conduct electricity and heat very efficiently because of the availability of highly mobile electrons. For example, when an electric potential is placed across a strip of metal, for current to flow, electrons must be free to move. In the band model for metals, mobile electrons are furnished when electrons in filled molecular orbitals are excited into empty ones. These conduction electrons are free to travel throughout the metal crystal as dictated by the potential imposed on the metal. The molecular orbitals occupied by these conducting electrons are called *conduction bands.* These mobile electrons also account for the efficiency of the conduction of heat through metals. When one end of a metal rod is heated, the mobile electrons can rapidly transmit the thermal energy to the other end.

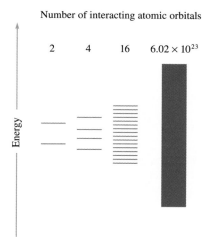

Number of interacting atomic orbitals

2　　4　　16　　6.02×10^{23}

Energy

Figure 10.19

The molecular orbital energy levels produced when various numbers of atomic orbitals interact. Note that for two atomic orbitals two rather widely spaced energy levels result. (Recall the description of H_2 in Section 9.2.) As more atomic orbitals are available to form molecular orbitals, the resulting energy levels are more closely spaced, finally producing a band of very closely spaced orbitals.

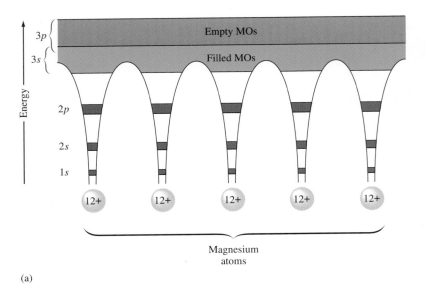

Figure 10.20

(a) A representation of the energy levels (bands) in a magnesium crystal. The electrons in the 1s, 2s, and 2p orbitals are close to the nuclei and thus are localized on each magnesium atom as shown. However, the 3s and 3p valence orbitals overlap and mix to form molecular orbitals. Electrons in these energy levels can travel throughout the crystal.
(b) Crystals of magnesium grown from a vapor.

Metal Alloys

Because of the nature of the structure and bonding of metals, other elements can be introduced into a metallic crystal relatively easily to produce substances called alloys. An **alloy** is best defined as *a substance that contains a mixture of elements and has metallic properties*. Alloys can be conveniently classified into two types.

In a **substitutional alloy** some of the host metal atoms are *replaced* by other metal atoms of similar size. For example, in brass, approximately one-third of the atoms in the host copper metal have been replaced by zinc atoms, as shown in Fig. 10.21(a). Sterling silver (93% silver and 7% copper), pewter (85% tin, 7% copper, 6% bismuth, and 2% antimony), and plumber's solder (95% tin and 5% antimony) are other examples of substitutional alloys.

An **interstitial alloy** is formed when some of the interstices (holes) in the closest packed metal structure are occupied by small atoms, as shown in Fig. 10.21(b). Steel, the best known interstitial alloy, contains carbon atoms in the holes of an iron crystal. The presence of the interstitial atoms changes the properties of the host metal. Pure iron is relatively soft, ductile, and malleable due to the absence of directional bonding. The spherical metal atoms can be rather easily moved with respect to each other. However, when carbon, which forms strong directional bonds, is introduced into an iron crystal, the presence of the directional carbon–iron bonds makes the resulting alloy harder, stronger, and less ductile than pure iron. The amount of carbon directly affects the properties of steel. *Mild steels,* containing less than 0.2% carbon, are ductile and malleable and are used for nails, cables, and chains.

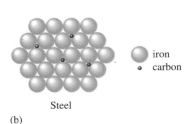

Brass

(a)

copper

zinc

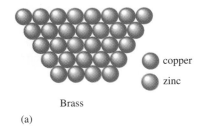

Steel

(b)

iron

carbon

Figure 10.21

Two types of alloys.

CHEMICAL IMPACT

What Sank the Titanic?

ON APRIL 12, 1912, the steamship *Titanic* struck an iceberg in the North Atlantic approximately 100 miles south of the Grand Banks of Newfoundland and within 3 hours was resting on the bottom of the ocean. Of her more than 2300 passengers and crew, over 1500 lost their lives. While the tragic story of the *Titanic* has never faded from the minds and imaginations of the generations that followed, the 1985 discovery of the wreck by a joint Franco-American expedition at a depth of 12,612 feet rekindled the world's interest in the "greatest ocean-going vessel" ever built. The discovery also would reveal important scientific clues as to why and how the *Titanic* sank so quickly in the frigid waters of the North Atlantic.

The *Titanic* was designed to be virtually "unsinkable," and even in the worst case scenario, a head-on collision with another ocean liner, the ship was engineered to take from one to three days to sink. Thus its quick trip to the bottom has puzzled scientists for years. In 1991, Steve Blasco, an ocean-floor geologist for the Canadian Department of Natural Resources, led a scientific expedition to the wreck. On one of 17 dives to the site, Blasco's team recovered a piece of steel that appeared to be a part of the *Titanic's* hull. Unlike modern steel, which would have shown evidence of bending in a collision, the steel recovered from the *Titanic* appeared to have shattered on impact with the iceberg. This suggested that the metal might not have been as ductile (*ductility* is the ability to stretch without breaking) as it should have been. In 1994,

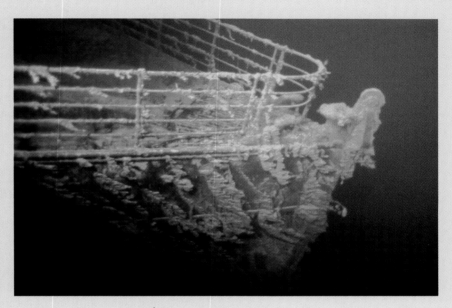

Bow of the Titanic *under* $2\frac{1}{2}$ *miles of water.*

tests were conducted on small pieces of metal, called *coupons,* cut from the recovered piece of hull. These samples shattered without bending. Further analysis showed that the steel used to construct the hull of the *Titanic* was high in sulfur content, and it is known that sulfur occlusions tend to make steel more brittle. This evidence suggests that the quality of the steel used to make the hull of the *Titanic* may very well have been an important factor that led to the rapid sinking of the ship.

But—not so fast. The *Titanic* continues to provoke controversy. A team of naval engineers and scientists recently have concluded that it was not brittle steel but faulty rivets that doomed the *Titanic.* During expeditions in 1996 and 1998 conducted by RMS Titanic, Inc., more samples of *Titanic's* steel and rivets were obtained for further study. Analysis of these samples by a team headed by Tim Foecke of the National Institute of Standards and Technology (NIST) shows that the rivets contain three times the expected amount of silicate slag. Foecke and his colleagues argue that the high slag content resulted in weak rivets that snapped in large numbers when the collision occurred, mortally wounding the ship.

What sank the *Titanic?* It hit an iceberg. The details remain to be figured out.

Medium steels, containing 0.2 to 0.6% carbon, are harder than mild steels and are used in rails and structural steel beams. *High-carbon steels,* containing 0.6 to 1.5% carbon, are tough and hard and are used for springs, tools, and cutlery.

Many types of steel also contain elements in addition to iron and carbon. Such steels are often called *alloy steels,* and they can be viewed as being mixed

Table 10.4 The Composition of the Two Brands of Steel Tubing Commonly Used to Make Lightweight Racing Bicycles

Brand of Tubing	% C	% Si	% Mn	% Mo	% Cr
Reynolds	0.25	0.25	1.3	0.20	—
Columbus	0.25	0.30	0.65	0.20	1.0

interstitial (carbon) and substitutional (other metals) alloys. Bicycle frames, for example, are constructed from a wide variety of alloy steels. The compositions of the two brands of steel tubing most commonly used in expensive racing bicycles are given in Table 10.4.

10.5 Carbon and Silicon: Network Atomic Solids

Many atomic solids contain strong directional covalent bonds to form a solid that might best be viewed as a "giant molecule." We call these substances **network solids.** In contrast to metals, these materials are typically brittle and do not efficiently conduct heat or electricity. To illustrate network solids, in this section we will discuss two very important elements, carbon and silicon, and some of their compounds.

The two most common forms of carbon, diamond and graphite, are typical network solids. In diamond, the hardest naturally occurring substance, each carbon atom is surrounded by a tetrahedral arrangement of other carbon atoms to form a huge molecule [see Fig. 10.22(a)]. This structure is stabilized by covalent bonds, which, in terms of the localized electron model, are formed by the overlap of sp^3 hybridized carbon atomic orbitals.

It is also useful to consider the bonding among the carbon atoms in diamond in terms of the molecular orbital model. Energy-level diagrams for diamond and a typical metal are given in Fig. 10.23. Recall that the conductivity of metals can be explained by postulating that electrons are excited from filled levels into the very near empty levels, or conduction bands. However, note that in the energy-level diagram for diamond there is *a large gap between the filled and the empty levels.* This means that electrons cannot be transferred easily to the empty conduction bands. As a result, diamond is not expected to be a good electrical conductor. In fact, this prediction of the model agrees exactly with the observed behavior of diamond, which is known to be an electrical insulator—it does not conduct an electric current.

Graphite is very different from diamond. While diamond is hard, basically colorless, and an insulator, graphite is slippery, black, and a conductor. These differences, of course, arise from the differences in bonding in the two types of solids. In contrast to the tetrahedral arrangement of carbon atoms in diamond, the structure of graphite is based on layers of carbon atoms arranged in fused six-membered rings, as shown in Fig. 10.22(b). Each carbon atom in a particular layer of graphite is surrounded by the three other carbon atoms in a trigonal planar arrangement with 120-degree bond angles. The localized electron model predicts sp^2 hybridization in this case. The three sp^2 orbitals on each carbon are used to form σ bonds with three other

Molecular Models: diamond, graphite

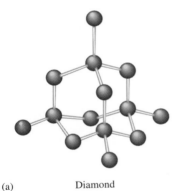

(a)   Diamond

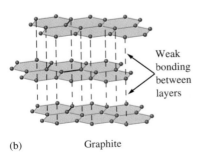

Weak bonding between layers

(b)   Graphite

Figure 10.22

The structures of diamond and graphite. In each case only a small part of the entire structure is shown.

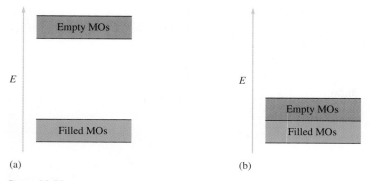

(a)   (b)

Figure 10.23

Partial representation of the molecular orbital energies in (a) diamond and (b) a typical metal.

carbon atoms. One $2p$ orbital remains unhybridized on each carbon and is perpendicular to the plane of carbon atoms, as shown in Fig. 10.24. These orbitals combine to form a group of closely spaced π molecular orbitals that are important in two ways. First, they contribute significantly to the stability of the graphite layers because of the π bond formation. Second, the π molecular orbitals with their delocalized electrons account for the electrical conductivity of graphite. These closely spaced orbitals are exactly analogous to the conduction bands found in metal crystals.

Graphite is often used as a lubricant in locks (where oil is undesirable because it collects dirt). The slipperiness that is characteristic of graphite can be explained by noting that graphite has very strong bonding *within* the layers of carbon atoms but little bonding *between* the layers (the valence electrons are all used to form σ and π bonds among carbons within the layers). This arrangement allows the layers

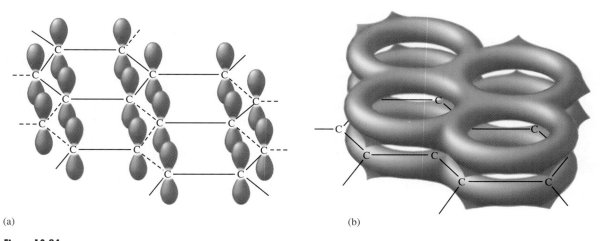

(a)   (b)

Figure 10.24

The p orbitals (a) perpendicular to the plane of the carbon ring system in graphite can combine to form (b) an extensive π-bonding network.

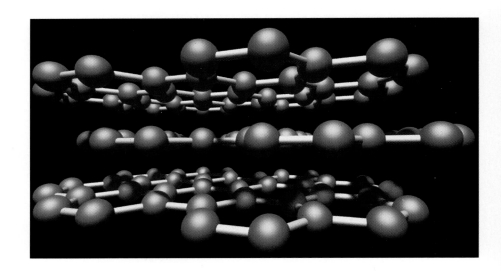

Figure 10.25

Graphite consists of layers of carbon atoms.

Molecular Models: Si, SiO_2, SiO_4^{4-}

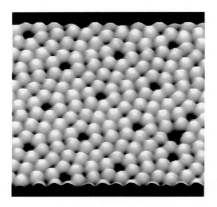

Computer-generated model of silicon.

The bonding in the CO_2 molecule was described in Section 9.1.

to slide past one another quite readily. Graphite's layered structure is shown in Fig. 10.25. This is in contrast to diamond, which has uniform bonding in all directions in the crystal.

Because of their extreme hardness, diamonds are used extensively in industrial cutting implements. Thus it is desirable to convert cheaper graphite to diamond. As we might expect from the higher density of diamond (3.5 g/cm^3) compared with that of graphite (2.2 g/cm^3), this transformation can be accomplished by applying very high pressures to graphite. The application of 150,000 atm of pressure at 2800°C converts graphite virtually completely to diamond. The high temperature is required to break the strong bonds in graphite so the rearrangement can occur.

Silicon is an important constituent of the compounds that make up the earth's crust. In fact, silicon is to geology as carbon is to biology. Just as carbon compounds are the basis for most biologically significant systems, silicon compounds are fundamental to most of the rocks, sands, and soils found in the earth's crust. However, although carbon and silicon are next to each other in Group 4A of the periodic table, the carbon-based compounds of biology and the silicon-based compounds of geology have markedly different structures. Carbon compounds typically contain long strings of carbon–carbon bonds, whereas the most stable silicon compounds involve chains with silicon–oxygen bonds.

The fundamental silicon–oxygen compound is **silica,** which has the empirical formula SiO_2. Knowing the properties of the similar compound carbon dioxide, one might expect silica to be a gas that contains discrete SiO_2 molecules. In fact, nothing could be further from the truth—quartz and some types of sand are typical of the materials composed of silica. What accounts for this difference? The answer lies in the bonding.

Recall that the Lewis structure of CO_2 is

$$\ddot{O}=C=\ddot{O}$$

and that each C=O bond can be viewed as a combination of a σ bond involving a carbon sp hybrid orbital and a π bond involving a carbon $2p$ orbital. On the contrary, silicon cannot use its valence $3p$ orbitals to form strong π bonds with oxygen, mainly because of the larger size of the silicon atom and its orbitals, which results in less effective overlap with the smaller oxygen orbitals. Therefore, instead of forming π bonds, the silicon atom satisfies the octet rule by forming single bonds with four oxygen atoms, as shown in the representation of the structure of quartz in Fig. 10.26. Note that each silicon atom is at the center of a tetrahedral arrangement of oxygen atoms, which are shared with other silicon atoms. Although the empirical formula for quartz is SiO_2, the structure is based on a *network* of SiO_4 tetrahedra with shared oxygen atoms rather than discrete SiO_2 molecules. It is obvious that the differing abilities of carbon and silicon to form π bonds with oxygen have profound effects on the structures and properties of CO_2 and SiO_2.

Compounds closely related to silica and found in most rocks, soils, and clays are the **silicates.** Like silica, the silicates are based on interconnected SiO_4 tetrahedra. However, in contrast to silica, where the O/Si ratio is 2:1, silicates have O/Si ratios greater than 2:1 and contain silicon–oxygen *anions*. This means that to form the neutral solid silicates, cations are needed to balance the excess negative charge. In other words, silicates are salts containing metal cations and polyatomic silicon–oxygen anions. Examples of important silicate anions are shown in Fig. 10.27.

When silica is heated above its melting point (about 1600°C) and cooled rapidly, an amorphous solid called a **glass** results (see Fig. 10.28). Note that a glass contains a good deal of disorder, in contrast to the crystalline nature of quartz. Glass more closely resembles a very viscous solution than it does a crystalline solid.

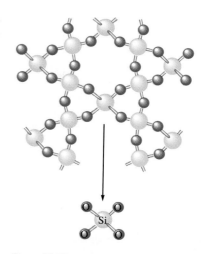

Figure 10.26

(top) The structure of quartz (empirical formula SiO_2). Quartz contains chains of SiO_4 tetrahedra (bottom) that share oxygen atoms.

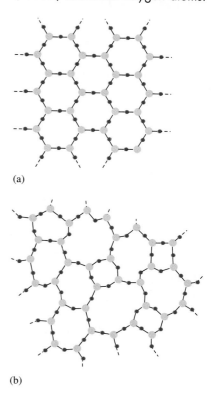

(a)

(b)

Figure 10.28

Two-dimensional representations of (a) a quartz crystal and (b) a quartz glass.

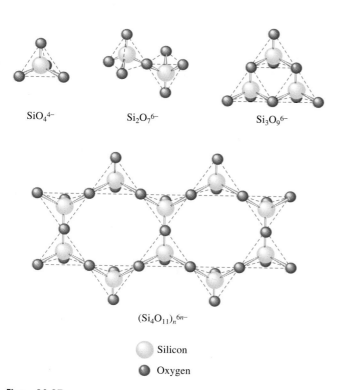

$SiO_4{}^{4-}$ $Si_2O_7{}^{6-}$ $Si_3O_9{}^{6-}$

$(Si_4O_{11})_n{}^{6n-}$

◯ Silicon

● Oxygen

Figure 10.27

Examples of silicate anions, all of which are based on $SiO_4{}^{4-}$ tetrahedra.

Table 10.5 Compositions of Some Common Types of Glass

Type of Glass	Percentages of Various Components						
	SiO_2	CaO	Na_2O	B_2O_3	Al_2O_3	K_2O	MgO
Window (soda-lime glass)	72	11	13	—	0.3	3.8	—
Cookware (aluminosilicate glass)	55	15	—	—	20	—	10
Heat-resistant (borosilicate glass)	76	3	5	13	2	0.5	—
Optical	69	12	6	0.3	—	12	—

A glass pitcher being manufactured.

An artist paints a ceramic vase before glazing.

Common glass results when substances such as Na_2CO_3 are added to the silica melt, which is then cooled. The properties of glass can be varied greatly by varying the additives. For example, addition of B_2O_3 produces a glass (called *borosilicate glass*) that expands and contracts little under large temperature changes. Thus it is useful for labware and cooking utensils. The most common brand name for this glass is Pyrex. The addition of K_2O produces an especially hard glass that can be ground to the precise shapes needed for eyeglass and contact lenses. The compositions of several types of glass are shown in Table 10.5.

Ceramics

Ceramics are typically made from clays (which contain silicates) and hardened by firing at high temperatures. Ceramics are nonmetallic materials that are strong, brittle, and resistant to heat and attack by chemicals.

Like glass, ceramics are based on silicates, but with that the resemblance ends. Glass can be melted and remelted as often as desired, but once a ceramic has been hardened, it is resistant to extremely high temperatures. This behavior results from the very different structures of glasses and ceramics. A glass is a *homogeneous,* noncrystalline "frozen solution," and a ceramic is *heterogeneous.* A ceramic contains two phases: minute crystals of silicates that are suspended in a glassy cement.

To understand how ceramics harden, it is necessary to know something about the structure of clays. Clays are formed by the weathering action of water and carbon dioxide on the mineral feldspar, which is a mixture of silicates with empirical formulas such as $K_2O \cdot Al_2O_3 \cdot 6SiO_2$ and $Na_2O \cdot Al_2O_3 \cdot 6SiO_2$. Feldspar is really an *aluminosilicate* in which aluminum as well as silicon atoms are part of the oxygen-bridged polyanion. The weathering of feldspar produces kaolinite, consisting of tiny thin platelets with the empirical formula $Al_2Si_2O_5(OH)_4$. When dry, the platelets cling together; when water is present, they can slide over one another, giving clay its plasticity. As clay dries, the platelets begin to interlock again. When the remaining water is driven off during firing, the silicates and cations form a glass that binds the tiny crystals of kaolinite.

Ceramics have a very long history. Rocks, which are natural ceramic materials, served as the earliest tools. Later, clay vessels dried in the sun or baked in fires served as containers for food and water. These early vessels were no doubt crude and quite porous. With the discovery of glazing, which probably occurred about 3000 B.C. in Egypt, pottery became more serviceable as well as more beautiful. Prized porcelain is essentially the same material as crude earthenware, but specially

CHEMICAL IMPACT

Golfing with Glass

YOU PROBABLY CAN guess what material traditionally was used to construct the "woods" used in golf. Modern technology has changed things. Like the bats used in college baseball, most "woods" are now made of metal. While bats are made of aluminum, golf club heads are often made of stainless steel or titanium.

Metals and their alloys usually form crystals that contain highly ordered arrangements of atoms. However, a company called Liquidmetal Golf of Laguna Niguel, California, has begun producing golf clubs containing glass—metallic glass. The company has found that when molten mixtures of titanium, zirconium, nickel, beryllium, and copper are cooled, they solidify, forming a glass. Unlike crystalline materials that contain a regular array of atoms, glasses are amorphous—the atoms are randomly scattered throughout the solid.

These golf clubs with metallic glass inserts have some unusual characteristics. Golfers who have tried the clubs say they combine hardness with a "soft feel." Stud-ies show that the glass transfers more of the energy of the golf swing to the ball with less impact to the golfer's hands than with regular metal woods.

One of the fortunate properties of this five-component metallic glass (invented in 1992 by William L. Johnson and Atakan Peker at the California Institute of Technology) is that it can be cooled relatively slowly to form the glass. This allows manufacture of relatively large glass objects such as inserts for golf club heads. Most mixtures of metals that form glasses must be cooled very rapidly to obtain the glass, which results in tiny particles of glass leading to powders.

David S. Lee, head of manufacturing at Liquidmetal Golf, says that golf clubs were an obvious first application for this five-component glass because golfers are used to paying high prices for clubs that employ new technology. Liquidmetal Golf is now looking for other applications of this new glass. How about glass bicycle frames?

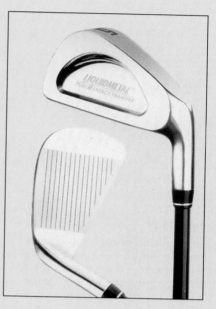

Golf clubs with a titanium shell and metallic glass inserts.

selected clays and glazings are used for porcelain and the clay object is fired at a very high temperature.

Although ceramics have been known since antiquity, they are not obsolete materials. On the contrary, ceramics constitute one of the most important classes of "high-tech" materials. Because of their stability at high temperatures and resistance to corrosion, ceramics seem an obvious choice for constructing jet and automobile engines in which the greatest fuel efficiencies are possible at very high temperatures. But ceramics are brittle—they break rather than bend—and this limits their usefulness. However, more flexible ceramics can be obtained by adding small amounts of organic polymers. Taking their cue from natural "organoceramics" such as teeth and shells of sea creatures that contain small amounts of organic polymers, materials scientists have found that incorporating tiny amounts of long organic molecules into ceramics as they form produces materials that are much less subject to fracture. These materials should be useful for lighter, more durable engine parts, as well as for flexible superconducting wire and microelectronic devices. In addition, these organoceramics hold great promise for prosthetic devices such as artificial bones.

Video: Magnetic Levitation by a Superconductor

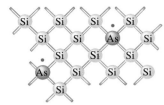

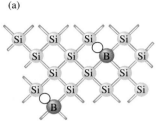

n-type semiconductor

(a)

p-type semiconductor

(b)

Figure 10.29

(a) A silicon crystal doped with arsenic, which has one more valence electron than silicon. (b) A silicon crystal doped with boron, which has one less electron than silicon.

Electrons must be in singly occupied molecular orbitals to conduct a current.

Semiconductors

Elemental silicon has the same structure as diamond, as might be expected from its position in the periodic table (in Group 4A directly under carbon). Recall that in diamond there is a large energy gap between the filled and empty molecular orbitals (see Fig. 10.23). This gap prevents excitation of electrons to the empty molecular orbitals (conduction bands) and makes diamond an insulator. In silicon the situation is similar, but the energy gap is smaller. A few electrons can cross the gap at 25°C, making silicon a **semiconducting element,** or **semiconductor.** In addition, at higher temperatures, where more energy is available to excite electrons into the conduction bands, the conductivity of silicon increases. This is typical behavior for a semiconducting element and is in contrast to that of metals, whose conductivity decreases with increasing temperature.

The small conductivity of silicon can be enhanced at normal temperatures if the silicon crystal is *doped* with certain other elements. For example, when a small fraction of silicon atoms is replaced by arsenic atoms, each having *one more* valence electron than silicon, extra electrons become available for conduction, as shown in Fig. 10.29(a). This produces an **n-type semiconductor,** a substance whose conductivity is increased by doping it with atoms having more valence electrons than the atoms in the host crystal. These extra electrons lie close in energy to the conduction bands and can be easily excited into these levels, where they can conduct an electric current [see Fig. 10.30(a)].

We also can enhance the conductivity of silicon by doping the crystal with an element such as boron, which has only three valence electrons, *one less* than silicon. Because boron has one less electron than is required to form the bonds with the surrounding silicon atoms, an electron vacancy, or *hole*, is created, as shown in Fig. 10.29(b). As an electron fills this hole, it leaves a new hole, and this process can be repeated. Thus the hole advances through the crystal in a direction opposite to movement of the electrons jumping to fill the hole. Another way of thinking about this phenomenon is that in pure silicon each atom has four valence electrons and the low-energy molecular orbitals are exactly filled. Replacing silicon atoms with boron atoms leaves vacancies in these molecular orbitals, as shown in Fig. 10.30(b). This means that there is only one electron in some of the molecular orbitals, and these unpaired electrons can function as conducting electrons. Thus the substance becomes a better conductor. When semiconductors are doped with atoms having fewer valence electrons than the atoms of the host crystal, they are called **p-type semiconductors,** so named because the positive holes can be viewed as the charge carriers.

Figure 10.30

Energy-level diagrams for (a) an n-type semiconductor and (b) a p-type semiconductor.

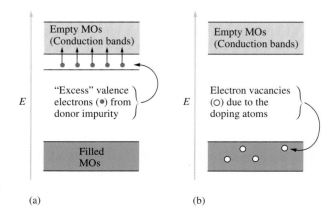

Most important applications of semiconductors involve connection of a p-type and an n-type to form a **p–n junction.** Figure 10.31(a) shows a typical junction; the red dots represent excess electrons in the n-type semiconductor, and the white circles represent holes (electron vacancies) in the p-type semiconductor. At the junction, a small number of electrons migrate from the n-type region into the p-type region, where there are vacancies in the low-energy molecular orbitals. The effect of these migrations is to place a negative charge on the p-type region (since it now has a surplus of electrons) and a positive charge on the n-type region (since it has lost electrons, leaving holes in its low-energy molecular orbitals). This charge buildup, called the *contact potential,* or *junction potential,* prevents further migration of electrons.

Now suppose an external electric potential is applied by connecting the negative terminal of a battery to the p-type region and the positive terminal to the n-type region. The situation represented in Fig. 10.31(b) results. Electrons are drawn toward the positive terminal, and the resulting holes move toward the negative terminal—exactly opposite to the natural flow of electrons at the p–n junction. The junction resists the imposed current flow in this direction and is said to be under *reverse bias.* No current flows through the system.

On the other hand, if the battery is connected so that the negative terminal is connected to the n-type region and the positive terminal is connected to the p-type region [Fig. 10.31(c)], the movement of electrons (and holes) is in the favored direction. The junction has low resistance, and a current flows easily. The junction is said to be under *forward bias.*

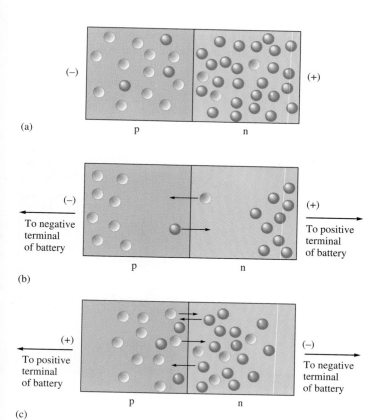

(a)

(b)

(c)

Figure 10.31

The p–n junction involves the contact of a p-type and an n-type semiconductor. (a) The charge carriers of the p-type region are holes (◯). In the n-type region the charge carriers are electrons (⬤). (b) No current flows (reverse bias). (c) Current readily flows (forward bias). Note that each electron that crosses the boundary leaves a hole behind. Thus the electrons and the holes move in opposite directions.

A p–n junction makes an excellent *rectifier,* a device that produces a pulsating direct current (flows in one direction) from alternating current (flows in both directions alternately). When placed in a circuit where the potential is constantly reversing, a p–n junction transmits current only under forward bias, thus converting the alternating current to direct current. Radios, computers, and other electronic devices formerly used bulky, unreliable vacuum tubes as rectifiers. The p–n junction has revolutionized electronics; modern solid-state components contain p–n junctions in printed circuits.

Printed circuits are discussed in the Chemical Impact feature on page 498.

10.6   *Molecular Solids*

So far we have considered solids in which atoms occupy the lattice positions. In some of these substances (network solids), the solid can be considered to be one giant molecule. In addition, there are many types of solids that contain discrete molecular units at each lattice position. A common example is ice, where the lattice positions are occupied by water molecules [see Fig. 10.12(c)]. Other examples are dry ice (solid carbon dioxide), some forms of sulfur that contain S_8 molecules [Fig. 10.32(a)], and certain forms of phosphorus that contain P_4 molecules [Fig. 10.32(b)]. These substances are characterized by strong covalent bonding *within* the molecules but relatively weak forces *between* the molecules. For example, it takes only 6 kJ of energy to melt 1 mole of solid water (ice) because only intermolecular (H_2O—H_2O) interactions must be overcome. However, 470 kJ of energy is required to break 1 mole of covalent O—H bonds. The differences between the covalent bonds within the molecules and the forces between the molecules are apparent from the comparison of the interatomic and intermolecular distances in solids shown in Table 10.6.

The forces that exist among the molecules in a molecular solid depend on the nature of the molecules. Many molecules such as CO_2, I_2, P_4, and S_8 have no di-

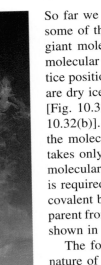

A "steaming" piece of dry ice.

Figure 10.32

(a) Sulfur crystals (yellow) contain S_8 molecules. (b) White phosphorus (containing P_4 molecules) is so reactive with the oxygen in air that it must be stored under water.

(a)

(b)

Table 10.6 Comparison of Atomic Separations Within Molecules (Covalent Bonds) and Between Molecules (Intermolecular Interactions)

Solid	Distance Between Atoms in Molecule*	Closest Distance Between Molecules in the Solid
P_4	220 pm	380 pm
S_8	206 pm	370 pm
Cl_2	199 pm	360 pm

*The shorter distances within the molecules indicate stronger bonding.

pole moment, and the intermolecular forces are London dispersion forces. Because these forces are often relatively small, we might expect all these substances to be gaseous at 25°C, as is the case for carbon dioxide. However, as the size of the molecules increases, the London forces become quite large, causing many of these substances to be solids at 25°C.

Molecular Models: P_4, S_8

When molecules do have dipole moments, their intermolecular forces are significantly greater, especially when hydrogen bonding is possible. Water molecules are particularly well suited to interact with each other because each molecule has two polar O—H bonds and two lone pairs on the oxygen atom. This can lead to the association of four hydrogen atoms with each oxygen: two by covalent bonds and two by dipole forces:

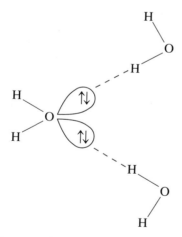

Note the two relatively short covalent oxygen–hydrogen bonds and the two longer oxygen–hydrogen dipole interactions that can be seen in the ice structure in Fig. 10.12(c).

10.7 Ionic Solids

Ionic solids are stable, high-melting substances held together by the strong electrostatic forces that exist between oppositely charged ions. The principles governing

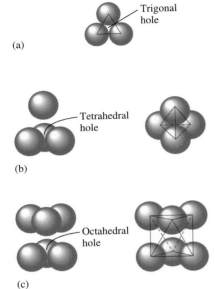

(a)

(b)

(c)

Figure 10.33

The holes that exist among closest packed uniform spheres. (a) The trigonal hole formed by three spheres in a given plane. (b) The tetrahedral hole formed when a sphere occupies a dimple formed by three spheres in an adjacent layer. (c) The octahedral hole formed by six spheres in two adjacent layers.

the structures of ionic solids were introduced in Section 8.5. In this section we will review and extend these principles.

The structures of most binary ionic solids, such as sodium chloride, can be explained by the closest packing of spheres. Typically, the larger ions, usually the anions, are packed in one of the closest packing arrangements (hcp or ccp), and the smaller cations fit into holes among the closest packed anions. The packing is done in a way that maximizes the electrostatic attractions among oppositely charged ions and minimizes the repulsions among ions with like charges.

There are three types of holes in closest packed structures:

1. Trigonal holes are formed by three spheres in the same layer [Fig. 10.33(a)].
2. Tetrahedral holes are formed when a sphere sits in the dimple of three spheres in an adjacent layer [Fig. 10.33(b)].
3. Octahedral holes are formed between two sets of three spheres in adjoining layers of the closest packed structures [Fig. 10.33(c)].

For spheres of a given diameter, the holes increase in size in the order

$$\text{trigonal} < \text{tetrahedral} < \text{octahedral}$$

In fact, trigonal holes are so small that they are never occupied in binary ionic compounds. Whether the tetrahedral or octahedral holes in a given binary ionic solid are occupied depends mainly on the *relative* sizes of the anion and cation. For example, in zinc sulfide the S^{2-} ions (ionic radius = 180 pm) are arranged in a cubic closest packed structure with the smaller Zn^{2+} ions (ionic radius = 70 pm) in the tetrahedral holes. The locations of the tetrahedral holes in the face-centered cubic unit cell of the ccp structure are shown in Fig. 10.34(a). Note from this figure that there are eight tetrahedral holes in the unit cell. Also recall from the discussion in Section 10.4 that there are four net spheres in the face-centered cubic unit cell. Thus there are *twice as many tetrahedral holes as packed anions* in the closest packed structure. Zinc sulfide must have the same number of S^{2-} ions and Zn^{2+} ions to achieve electrical neutrality. Thus in the zinc sulfide structure only *half* the tetrahedral holes contain Zn^{2+} ions, as shown in Fig. 10.34(c).

The structure of sodium chloride can be described in terms of a cubic closest packed array of Cl^- ions with Na^+ ions in all the octahedral holes. The locations of the octahedral holes in the face-centered cubic unit cell are shown in Fig. 10.35(a). The easiest octahedral hole to find in this structure is the one at the center of the cube. Note that this hole is surrounded by six spheres, as is required to form an

Figure 10.34

(a) The location (X) of a tetrahedral hole in the face-centered cubic unit cell. (b) One of the tetrahedral holes. (c) The unit cell for ZnS where the S^{2-} ions (yellow) are closest packed with the Zn^{2+} ions (red) in alternating tetrahedral holes.

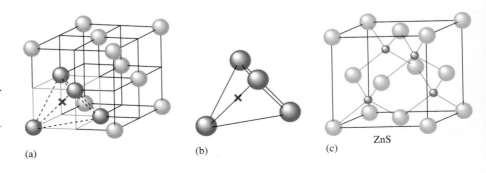

(a)

(b)

(c)

ZnS

CHEMICAL IMPACT

Gallium Arsenide Lasers

LASERS ARE AN essential part of modern life, providing the most efficient way to carry telephone communications by cable, the best quality music using compact disc players, and the most accurate method for reading grocery prices. The laser (the word *lase* is an acronym for "*light amplification by stimulated emission*") is a device for producing an intense, coherent beam of light that results when excited electrons release photons as they change to a lower energy state. Excited electrons can return to a lower energy level by spontaneous, random emission of light. However, there is another mechanism in which the emission process is actually stimulated by a passing photon that has the same energy as the emitted photon. This is the phenomenon on which the laser is based. We will have more to say about this presently.

Gallium arsenide is a prominent member of the so-called 3–5 class of semiconductors, those containing elements from Groups 3A and 5A of the periodic table. An n-type semiconductor results when the arsenic-to-gallium ratio is greater than 1. A p-type semiconductor results when gallium is in excess. By carefully controlling the conditions under which a Ga–As semiconductor is made, one can design p–n junctions into the material. At each p–n junction electrons from the n-type region are available to "fall into" holes in the p-type region, producing photons (see the accompanying figure). As the emitted photons travel through the solid, they *stimulate* the emission of additional photons. A mirror at the edge of the solid reflects these photons back through the substance, where they stimulate even more emission events. All these stimulated emissions produce photons with their waves in phase. Thus this process leads to a large number of coherent (in-phase) photons, which proceed out the other end of the solid where a "half-mirror" is placed. This mirror reflects

some of the photons and allows the rest to leave as an intense, coherent "laser beam" of light. A current driven through the substance by an applied potential difference provides a continuous supply of electrons (and removes electrons to make new holes) so that the process occurs continuously while the power is on.

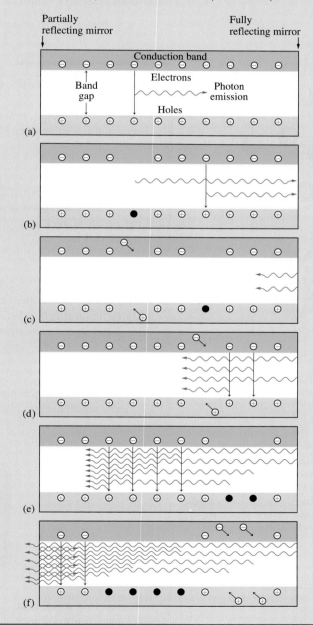

Closest packed structures contain twice as many tetrahedral holes as packed spheres. Closest packed structures contain the same number of octahedral holes as packed spheres.

octahedron. The remaining octahedral holes are shared with other unit cells and are more difficult to visualize. However, it can be shown that the number of octahedral holes in the ccp structure is the *same* as the number of packed anions. Figure 10.35(b) shows the structure for sodium chloride that results from Na^+ ions filling all the octahedral holes in a ccp array of Cl^- ions.

A great variety of ionic solids exists. Our purpose in this section is not to give an exhaustive treatment of ionic solids, but to emphasize the fundamental principles governing their structures. As we have seen, the most useful model for explaining the structures of these solids regards the ions as hard spheres that are packed to maximize attractions and minimize repulsions.

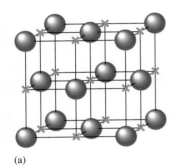

(a)

(b)

Figure 10.35

(a) The locations (gray X) of the octahedral holes in the face-centered cubic unit cell. (b) Representation of the unit cell for solid NaCl. The Cl^- ions (green spheres) have a ccp arrangement with Na^+ ions (gray spheres) in all the octahedral holes. Note that this representation shows the idealized closest packed structure of NaCl. In the actual structure, the Cl^- ions do not quite touch.

 Molecular Model: NaCl

Sample Exercise 10.3 *Determining the Number of Ions in a Unit Cell*

Determine the net number of Na^+ and Cl^- ions in the sodium chloride unit cell.

Solution

Note from Fig. 10.35(b) that the Cl^- ions are cubic closest packed and thus form a face-centered cubic unit cell. There is a Cl^- ion on each corner and one at the center of each face of the cube. Thus the net number of Cl^- ions present in a unit cell is

$$8(\tfrac{1}{8}) + 6(\tfrac{1}{2}) = 4$$

The Na^+ ions occupy the octahedral holes located in the center of the cube and midway along each edge. The Na^+ ion in the center of the cube is contained entirely in the unit cell, whereas those on the edges are shared by four unit cells (four cubes share a common edge). Since the number of edges in a cube is 12, the net number of Na^+ ions present is

$$1(1) + 12(\tfrac{1}{4}) = 4$$

We have shown that the net number of ions in a unit cell is 4 Na^+ ions and 4 Cl^- ions, which agrees with the 1:1 stoichiometry of sodium chloride.

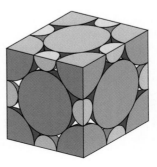

See Exercises 10.63 through 10.68.

In this chapter we have considered various types of solids. Table 10.7 summarizes these types of solids and some of their properties.

Sample Exercise 10.4 Types of Solids

Using Table 10.7, classify each of the following substances according to the type of solid it forms.

a. Gold
b. Carbon dioxide
c. Lithium fluoride
d. Krypton

Solution

a. Solid gold is an atomic solid with metallic properties.
b. Solid carbon dioxide contains nonpolar carbon dioxide molecules and is a molecular solid.
c. Solid lithium fluoride contains Li^+ and F^- ions and is a binary ionic solid.
d. Solid krypton contains krypton atoms that can interact only through London dispersion forces. It is an atomic solid but has properties characteristic of a molecular solid with nonpolar molecules.

See Exercises 10.71 and 10.72.

Table 10.7 Types and Properties of Solids

Type of solid:	Atomic			Molecular	Ionic
	Network	Metallic	Group 8A		
Structural unit:	Atom	Atom	Atom	Molecule	Ion
Type of bonding:	Directional covalent bonds	Nondirectional covalent bonds involving electrons that are delocalized throughout the crystal	London dispersion forces	Polar molecules: dipole–dipole interactions Nonpolar molecules: London dispersion forces	Ionic
Typical properties:	Hard High melting point Insulator	Wide range of hardness Wide range of melting points Conductor	Very low melting	Soft Low melting point Insulator	Hard High melting point Insulator
Examples:	Diamond	Silver Iron Brass	Argon(s)	Ice (solid H_2O) Dry ice (solid CO_2)	Sodium chloride Calcium fluoride

10.8 Vapor Pressure and Changes of State

Now that we have considered the general properties of the three states of matter, we can explore the processes by which matter changes state. One very familiar example of a change in state occurs when a liquid evaporates from an open container. This is clear evidence that the molecules of a liquid can escape the liquid's surface and form a gas, a process called **vaporization,** or **evaporation.** Vaporization is endothermic because energy is required to overcome the relatively strong intermolecular forces in the liquid. The energy required to vaporize 1 mole of a liquid at a pressure of 1 atm is called the **heat of vaporization,** or the **enthalpy of vaporization,** and is usually symbolized as ΔH_{vap}.

The endothermic nature of vaporization has great practical significance; in fact, one of the most important roles that water plays in our world is to act as a coolant. Because of the strong hydrogen bonding among its molecules in the liquid state, water has an unusually large heat of vaporization (40.7 kJ/mol). A significant portion of the sun's energy that reaches earth is spent evaporating water from the oceans, lakes, and rivers rather than warming the earth. The vaporization of water is also crucial to the body's temperature-control system through evaporation of perspiration.

Vapor is the usual term for the gas phase of a substance that exists as a solid or liquid at 25°C and 1 atm.

ΔH_{vap} for water at 100°C is 40.7 kJ/mol.

Vapor Pressure

When a liquid is placed in a closed container, the amount of liquid at first decreases but eventually becomes constant. The decrease occurs because there is an initial net transfer of molecules from the liquid to the vapor phase (Fig. 10.36). This evaporation process occurs at a constant rate at a given temperature (see Fig. 10.37). However, the reverse process is different. Initially, as the number of vapor molecules increases, so does the rate of return of these molecules to the liquid. The process by which vapor molecules re-form a liquid is called **condensation.** Eventually, enough vapor molecules are present above the liquid so that the rate of condensation equals the rate of evaporation (see Fig. 10.37). *At this point no further net change occurs in the amount of liquid or vapor because the two opposite processes exactly balance each other;* the system is at **equilibrium.** Note that this system is highly *dynamic* on the molecular level—molecules are constantly escaping from and entering the liquid at a high rate. However, there is no *net* change because the two opposite processes just *balance* each other.

A system at equilibrium is dynamic on the molecular level but shows no macroscopic changes.

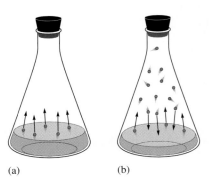

(a)   (b)

Figure 10.36

Behavior of a liquid in a closed container. (a) Initially, net evaporation occurs as molecules are transferred from the liquid to the vapor phase, so the amount of liquid decreases. (b) As the number of vapor molecules increases, the rate of return to the liquid (condensation) increases, until finally the rate of condensation equals the rate of evaporation. The system is at equilibrium, and no further changes occur in the amounts of vapor or liquid.

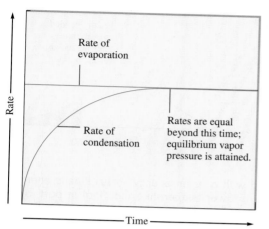

Figure 10.37

The rates of condensation and evaporation over time for a liquid sealed in a closed container. The rate of evaporation remains constant and the rate of condensation increases as the number of molecules in the vapor phase increases, until the two rates become equal. At this point, the equilibrium vapor pressure is attained.

The pressure of the vapor present at equilibrium is called the **equilibrium vapor pressure,** or more commonly, the **vapor pressure** of the liquid. A simple barometer can measure the vapor pressure of a liquid, as shown below in Fig. 10.38(a). The liquid is injected at the bottom of the tube of mercury and floats to the surface because the mercury is so dense. A portion of the liquid evaporates at the top of the column, producing a vapor whose pressure pushes some mercury out of the tube. When the system reaches equilibrium, the vapor pressure can be determined from the change in the height of the mercury column since

Molecular Model: C_2H_5OH

$$P_{\text{atmosphere}} = P_{\text{vapor}} + P_{\text{Hg column}}$$

Thus

$$P_{\text{vapor}} = P_{\text{atmosphere}} - P_{\text{Hg column}}$$

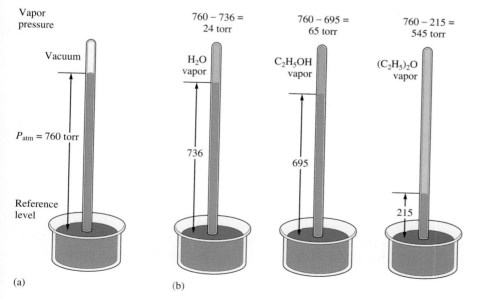

Figure 10.38

(a) The vapor pressure of a liquid can be measured easily using a simple barometer of the type shown here. (b) The three liquids, water, ethanol (C_2H_5OH), and diethyl ether [(C_2H_5)$_2$O], have quite different vapor pressures. Ether is by far the most volatile of the three. Note that in each case a little liquid remains (floating on the mercury).

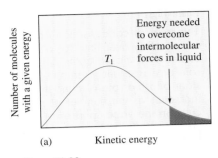
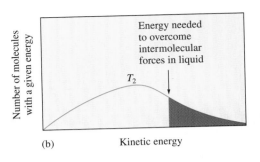

Figure 10.39

The number of molecules in a liquid with a given energy versus kinetic energy at two temperatures. Part (a) shows a lower temperature than that in part (b). Note that the proportion of molecules with enough energy to escape the liquid to the vapor phase (indicated by shaded areas) increases dramatically with temperature. This causes vapor pressure to increase markedly with temperature.

The vapor pressures of liquids vary widely [see Fig. 10.38(b)]. Liquids with high vapor pressures are said to be *volatile*—they evaporate rapidly from an open dish. The vapor pressure of a liquid is principally determined by the size of the *intermolecular forces* in the liquid. Liquids in which the intermolecular forces are large have relatively low vapor pressures because the molecules need high energies to escape to the vapor phase. For example, although water has a much lower molar mass than diethyl ether, the strong hydrogen-bonding forces that exist among water molecules in the liquid cause water's vapor pressure to be much lower than that of diethyl ether [see Fig. 10.38(b)]. In general, substances with large molar masses have relatively low vapor pressures, mainly because of the large dispersion forces. The more electrons a substance has, the more polarizable it is, and the greater are the dispersion forces.

Measurements of the vapor pressure for a given liquid at several temperatures show that *vapor pressure increases significantly with temperature.* Figure 10.39 illustrates the distribution of molecular kinetic energy present in a liquid at two different temperatures. To overcome the intermolecular forces in a liquid, a molecule must have sufficient kinetic energy. As the temperature of the liquid is increased, the fraction of molecules having the minimum energy needed to overcome these forces and escape to the vapor phase increases markedly. Thus the vapor pressure of a liquid increases dramatically with temperature. Values for water at several temperatures are given in Table 10.8.

The quantitative nature of the temperature dependence of vapor pressure can be represented graphically. Plots of vapor pressure versus temperature for water, ethanol, and diethyl ether are shown in Fig. 10.40(a). Note the nonlinear increase in vapor pressure for all the liquids as the temperature is increased. We find that a straight line can be obtained by plotting $\ln(P_{vap})$ versus $1/T$, where T is the Kelvin temperature, as shown in Fig. 10.40(b). We can represent this behavior by the equation

$$\ln(P_{vap}) = -\frac{\Delta H_{vap}}{R}\left(\frac{1}{T}\right) + C \qquad (10.4)$$

where ΔH_{vap} is the enthalpy of vaporization, R is the universal gas constant, and C is a constant characteristic of a given liquid. The symbol *ln* means that the natural logarithm of the vapor pressure is taken.

Table 10.8 The Vapor Pressure of Water as a Function of Temperature	
$T\,(°C)$	$P\,(torr)$
0.0	4.579
10.0	9.209
20.0	17.535
25.0	23.756
30.0	31.824
40.0	55.324
60.0	149.4
70.0	233.7
90.0	525.8

Natural logarithms are reviewed in Appendix 1.2.

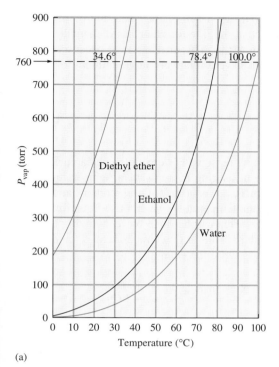

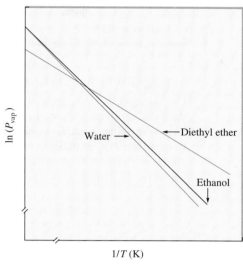

Figure 10.40
(a) The vapor pressure of water, ethanol, and diethyl ether as a function of temperature. (b) Plots of $\ln(P_{vap})$ versus $1/T$ (Kelvin temperature) for water, ethanol, and diethyl ether.

Equation (10.4) is the equation for a straight line of the form $y = mx + b$, where

$$y = \ln(P_{vap})$$

$$x = \frac{1}{T}$$

$$m = \text{slope} = -\frac{\Delta H_{vap}}{R}$$

$$b = \text{intercept} = C$$

Sample Exercise 10.5 Determining Enthalpies of Vaporization

Using the plots in Fig. 10.40(b), determine whether water or diethyl ether has the larger enthalpy of vaporization.

Solution

When $\ln(P_{vap})$ is plotted versus $1/T$, the slope of the resulting straight line is

$$-\frac{\Delta H_{vap}}{R}$$

Note from Fig. 10.40(b) that the slopes of the lines for water and diethyl ether are both negative, as expected, and that the line for ether has the smaller slope. Thus ether has the smaller value of ΔH_{vap}. This makes sense because the hydrogen bonding in water causes it to have a relatively large enthalpy of vaporization.

See Exercise 10.79.

Equation (10.4) is important for several reasons. For example, we can determine the heat of vaporization for a liquid by measuring P_{vap} at several temperatures and then evaluating the slope of a plot of $\ln(P_{vap})$ versus $1/T$. On the other hand, if we know the values of ΔH_{vap} and P_{vap} at one temperature, we can use Equation (10.4) to calculate P_{vap} at another temperature. This can be done by recognizing that the constant C does not depend on temperature. Thus at two temperatures T_1 and T_2 we can solve Equation (10.4) for C and then write the equality

$$\ln(P_{vap,T_1}) + \frac{\Delta H_{vap}}{RT_1} = C = \ln(P_{vap,T_2}) + \frac{\Delta H_{vap}}{RT_2}$$

This can be rearranged to

$$\ln(P_{vap,T_1}) - \ln(P_{vap,T_2}) = \frac{\Delta H_{vap}}{R}\left(\frac{1}{T_2} - \frac{1}{T_1}\right)$$

Equation 10.5 is called the Clausius–Clapeyron equation.

or

$$\ln\left(\frac{P_{vap,T_1}}{P_{vap,T_2}}\right) = \frac{\Delta H_{vap}}{R}\left(\frac{1}{T_2} - \frac{1}{T_1}\right) \tag{10.5}$$

Sample Exercise 10.6 Calculating Vapor Pressure

The vapor pressure of water at 25°C is 23.8 torr, and the heat of vaporization of water at 25°C is 43.9 kJ/mol. Calculate the vapor pressure of water at 50.°C.

Solution

We will use Equation (10.5):

$$\ln\left(\frac{P_{vap,T_1}}{P_{vap,T_2}}\right) = \frac{\Delta H_{vap}}{R}\left(\frac{1}{T_2} - \frac{1}{T_1}\right)$$

In solving this problem, we ignore the fact that ΔH_{vap} is slightly temperature dependent.

For water we have

$$P_{vap,T_1} = 23.8 \text{ torr}$$
$$T_1 = 25 + 273 = 298 \text{ K}$$
$$T_2 = 50. + 273 = 323 \text{ K}$$
$$\Delta H_{vap} = 43.9 \text{ kJ/mol} = 43,900 \text{ J/mol}$$
$$R = 8.3145 \text{ J/K mol}$$

Thus
$$\ln\left(\frac{23.8 \text{ torr}}{P_{\text{vap},T_2} \text{ (torr)}}\right) = \frac{43{,}900 \text{ J/mol}}{8.3145 \text{ J/K mol}}\left(\frac{1}{323 \text{ K}} - \frac{1}{298 \text{ K}}\right)$$

$$\ln\left(\frac{23.8}{P_{\text{vap},T_2}}\right) = -1.37$$

Taking the antilog (see Appendix 1.2) of both sides gives

$$\frac{23.8}{P_{\text{vap},T_2}} = 0.254$$

$$P_{\text{vap},T_2} = 93.7 \text{ torr}$$

See Exercises 10.81 through 10.84.

Like liquids, solids have vapor pressures. Figure 10.41 shows iodine vapor in equilibrium with solid iodine in a closed flask. Under normal conditions iodine **sublimes;** that is, it goes directly from the solid to the gaseous state without passing through the liquid state. **Sublimation** also occurs with dry ice (solid carbon dioxide).

Sublimation: A process in which a substance goes directly from the solid to the gaseous state.

Changes of State

What happens when a solid is heated? Typically, it will melt to form a liquid. If the heating continues, the liquid will at some point boil and form the vapor phase. This process can be represented by a **heating curve:** a plot of temperature versus time for a process where energy is added at a constant rate.

Exploration: Changes of State

Figure 10.41

Iodine being heated, causing it to sublime onto an evaporating dish cooled by ice.

Figure 10.42

The heating curve for a given quantity of water where energy is added at a constant rate. The plateau at the boiling point is longer than the plateau at the melting point because it takes almost seven times more energy (and thus seven times the heating time) to vaporize liquid water than to melt ice. The slopes of the other lines are different because the different states of water have different molar heat capacities (the energy required to raise the temperature of 1 mole of a substance by 1°C).

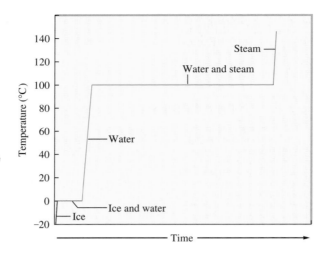

Phase changes of carbon dioxide are discussed in Section 10.9.

Ionic solids such as NaCl and NaF have very high melting points and enthalpies of fusion because of the strong ionic forces in these solids. At the other extreme is $O_2(s)$, a molecular solid containing nonpolar molecules with weak intermolecular forces.

The melting and boiling points will be defined more precisely later in this section.

The heating curve for water is given in Fig. 10.42. As energy flows into the ice, the random vibrations of the water molecules increase as the temperature rises. Eventually, the molecules become so energetic that they break loose from their lattice positions, and the change from solid to liquid occurs. This is indicated by a plateau at 0°C on the heating curve. At this temperature, called the *melting point,* all the added energy is used to disrupt the ice structure by breaking the hydrogen bonds, thus increasing the potential energy of the water molecules. The enthalpy change that occurs at the melting point when a solid melts is called the **heat of fusion,** or more accurately, the **enthalpy of fusion ΔH_{fus}.** The melting points and enthalpies of fusion for several representative solids are listed in Table 10.9.

The temperature remains constant until the solid has completely changed to liquid; then it begins to increase again. At 100°C the liquid water reaches its *boiling point,* and the temperature then remains constant as the added energy is used to vaporize the liquid. When the liquid is completely changed to vapor, the temperature again begins to rise. Note that changes of state are physical changes; although intermolecular forces have been overcome, no chemical bonds have been broken. If the water vapor were heated to much higher temperatures, the water molecules would

Table 10.9 Melting Points and Enthalpies of Fusion for Several Representative Solids

Compound	Melting Point (°C)	Enthalpy of Fusion (kJ/mol)
O_2	−218	0.45
HCl	−114	1.99
HI	−51	2.87
CCl_4	−23	2.51
$CHCl_3$	−64	9.20
H_2O	0	6.02
NaF	992	29.3
NaCl	801	30.2

break down into the individual atoms. This would be a chemical change, since covalent bonds are broken. We no longer have water after this occurs.

The melting and boiling points for a substance are determined by the vapor pressures of the solid and liquid states. Figure 10.43 shows the vapor pressures of solid and liquid water as functions of temperature near 0°C. Note that below 0°C the vapor pressure of ice is less than the vapor pressure of liquid water. Also note that the vapor pressure of ice has a larger temperature dependence than that of the liquid. That is, the vapor pressure of ice increases more rapidly for a given rise in temperature than does the vapor pressure of water. Thus, as the temperature of the solid is increased, a point is eventually reached where the *liquid and solid have identical vapor pressures*. This is the melting point.

These concepts can be demonstrated experimentally using the apparatus illustrated in Fig. 10.44, where ice occupies one compartment and liquid water the other. Consider the following cases.

Case 1. A temperature at which the vapor pressure of the solid is greater than that of the liquid. At this temperature the solid requires a higher pressure than the liquid does to be in equilibrium with the vapor. Thus, as vapor is released from the solid to try to achieve equilibrium, the liquid will absorb vapor in an attempt to reduce the vapor pressure to its equilibrium value. The net effect is a conversion from solid to liquid through the vapor phase. In fact, no solid can exist under these conditions. The amount of solid will steadily decrease and the volume of liquid will increase. Finally, there will be only liquid in the right compartment, which will come to equilibrium with the water vapor, and no further changes will occur in the system. This temperature must be above the melting point of ice, since only the liquid state can exist.

Case 2. A temperature at which the vapor pressure of the solid is less than that of the liquid. This is the opposite of the situation in case 1. In this case, the liquid requires a higher pressure than the solid does to be in equilibrium with the vapor, so the liquid will gradually disappear, and the amount of ice will increase. Finally, only the solid will remain, which will achieve equilibrium with

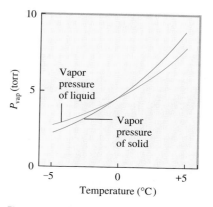

Figure 10.43

The vapor pressures of solid and liquid water as a function of temperature. The data for liquid water below 0°C are obtained from supercooled water. The data for solid water above 0°C are estimated by extrapolation of vapor pressure from below 0°C.

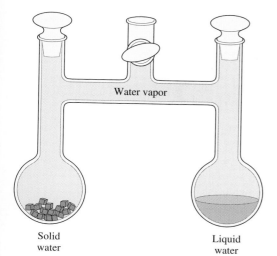

Figure 10.44

An apparatus that allows solid and liquid water to interact only through the vapor state.

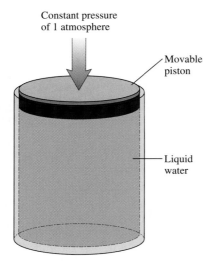

Constant pressure of 1 atmosphere

Movable piston

Liquid water

Figure 10.45

Water in a closed system with a pressure of 1 atm exerted on the piston. No bubbles can form within the liquid as long as the vapor pressure is less than 1 atm.

the vapor. This temperature must be *below the melting point* of ice, since only the solid state can exist.

Case 3. A temperature at which the vapor pressures of the solid and liquid are identical. In this case, the solid and liquid states have the same vapor pressure, so they can coexist in the apparatus at equilibrium simultaneously with the vapor. This temperature represents the *freezing point* where both the solid and liquid states can exist.

We can now describe the melting point of a substance more precisely. The **normal melting point** is defined as *the temperature at which the solid and liquid states have the same vapor pressure under conditions where the total pressure is 1 atmosphere.*

Boiling occurs when the vapor pressure of a liquid becomes equal to the pressure of its environment. The **normal boiling point** of a liquid is *the temperature at which the vapor pressure of the liquid is exactly 1 atmosphere.* This concept is illustrated in Fig. 10.45. At temperatures where the vapor pressure of the liquid is less than 1 atmosphere, no bubbles of vapor can form because the pressure on the surface of the liquid is greater than the pressure in any spaces in the liquid where the bubbles are trying to form. Only when the liquid reaches a temperature at which the pressure of vapor in the spaces in the liquid is 1 atmosphere can bubbles form and boiling occur.

However, changes of state do not always occur exactly at the boiling point or melting point. For example, water can be readily **supercooled;** that is, it can be cooled below 0°C at 1 atm pressure and remain in the liquid state. Supercooling occurs because, as it is cooled, the water may not achieve the degree of organization necessary to form ice at 0°C, and thus it continues to exist as the liquid. At some point the correct ordering occurs and ice rapidly forms, releasing energy in the exothermic process and bringing the temperature back up to the melting point, where the remainder of the water freezes (see Fig. 10.46).

A liquid also can be **superheated,** or raised to temperatures above its boiling point, especially if it is heated rapidly. Superheating can occur because bubble formation in the interior of the liquid requires that many high-energy molecules gather

Figure 10.46

The supercooling of water. The extent of supercooling is given by *S.*

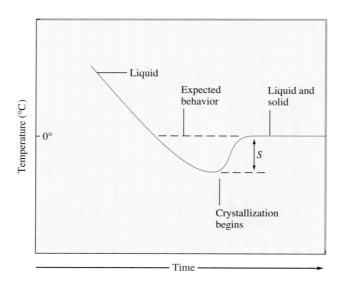

Liquid

Expected behavior

Liquid and solid

Temperature (°C)

0°

S

Crystallization begins

Time

in the same vicinity, and this may not happen at the boiling point, especially if the liquid is heated rapidly. If the liquid becomes superheated, the vapor pressure in the liquid is greater than the atmospheric pressure. Once a bubble does form, since its internal pressure is greater than that of the atmosphere, it can burst before rising to the surface, blowing the surrounding liquid out of the container. This is called *bumping* and has ruined many experiments. It can be avoided by adding boiling chips to the flask containing the liquid. Boiling chips are bits of porous ceramic material containing trapped air that escapes on heating, forming tiny bubbles that act as "starters" for vapor bubble formation. This allows a smooth onset of boiling as the boiling point is reached.

10.9 *Phase Diagrams*

A **phase diagram** is a convenient way of representing the phases of a substance as a function of temperature and pressure. For example, the phase diagram for water (Fig. 10.47) shows which state exists at a given temperature and pressure. It is important to recognize that a phase diagram describes conditions and events in a *closed* system of the type represented in Fig. 10.45, where no material can escape into the surroundings and no air is present. Notice that the diagram is not drawn to scale (neither axis is linear). This is done to emphasize certain features of the diagram that will be discussed below.

To show how to interpret the phase diagram for water, we will consider heating experiments at several pressures, shown by the dashed lines in Fig. 10.48.

Experiment 1. Pressure is 1 atm. This experiment begins with the cylinder shown in Fig. 10.45 completely filled with ice at a temperature of $-20°C$ and the piston exerting a pressure of 1 atm directly on the ice (there is no air space). Since at temperatures below $0°C$ the vapor pressure of ice is less than 1 atm—which is the constant external pressure on the piston—no vapor is present in the cylinder. As the cylinder is heated, ice is the only component until the temperature reaches $0°C$, where the ice changes to liquid water as energy is added. This is the normal melting point of water. Note that under these

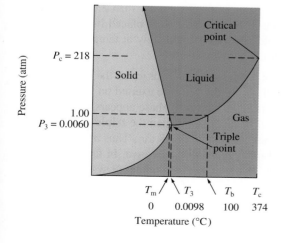

Figure 10.47
The phase diagram for water. T_m represents the normal melting point; T_3 and P_3 denote the triple point; T_b represents the normal boiling point; T_c represents the critical temperature; P_c represents the critical pressure. The negative slope of the solid/liquid line reflects the fact that the density of ice is less than that of liquid water. (Note that this line extends indefinitely, as indicated by the arrow.)

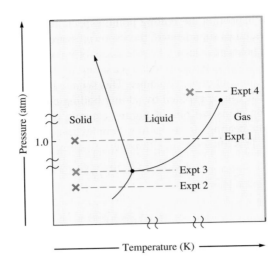

Figure 10.48

Diagrams of various heating experiments on samples of water in a closed system.

conditions no vapor exists in the system. The vapor pressures of the solid and liquid are equal, but this vapor pressure is less than 1 atm, so no water vapor can exist. This is true on the solid/liquid line everywhere except at the triple point (see Experiment 3 below). When the solid has completely changed to liquid, the temperature again rises. At this point, the cylinder contains only liquid water. *No vapor is present* because the vapor pressure of liquid water under these conditions is less than 1 atm, the constant external pressure on the piston. Heating continues until the temperature of the liquid water reaches 100°C. At this point, the vapor pressure of liquid water is 1 atm, and boiling occurs, with the liquid changing to vapor. This is the normal boiling point of water. After the liquid has been completely converted to steam, the temperature again rises as the heating continues. The cylinder now contains only water vapor.

Experiment 2. Pressure is 2.0 torr. Again, we start with ice as the only component in the cylinder at −20°C. The pressure exerted by the piston in this case is only 2.0 torr. As heating proceeds, the temperature rises to −10°C, where the ice changes directly to vapor, a process known as *sublimation.* Sublimation occurs when the vapor pressure of ice is equal to the external pressure, which in this case is only 2.0 torr. No liquid water appears under these conditions because the vapor pressure of liquid water is always greater than 2.0 torr, and thus it cannot exist at this pressure. If liquid water were placed in a cylinder under such a low pressure, it would vaporize immediately at temperatures above −10°C or freeze at temperatures below −10°C.

Experiment 3. Pressure is 4.58 torr. Again, we start with ice as the only component in the cylinder at −20°C. In this case the pressure exerted on the ice by the piston is 4.58 torr. As the cylinder is heated, no new phase appears until the temperature reaches 0.01°C (273.16 K). At this point, called the **triple point,** solid and liquid water have identical vapor pressures of 4.58 torr. Thus *at 0.01°C (273.16 K) and 4.58 torr all three states of water are present.* In fact, *only* under these conditions can all three states of water coexist in a closed system.

Experiment 4. Pressure is 225 atm. In this experiment we start with liquid water in the cylinder at 300°C; the pressure exerted by the piston on the water is

225 atm. Liquid water can be present at this temperature because of the high external pressure. As the temperature increases, something happens that we did not see in the first three experiments: the liquid gradually changes into a vapor but goes through an intermediate "fluid" region, which is neither true liquid nor vapor. This is quite unlike the behavior at lower temperatures and pressures, say at 100°C and 1 atm, where the temperature remains constant while a definite phase change from liquid to vapor occurs. This unusual behavior occurs because the conditions are beyond the critical point for water. The **critical temperature** can be defined as the temperature above which the vapor cannot be liquefied no matter what pressure is applied. The **critical pressure** is the pressure required to produce liquefaction *at* the critical temperature. Together, the critical temperature and the critical pressure define the **critical point.** For water the critical point is 374°C and 218 atm. Note that the liquid/vapor line on the phase diagram for water ends at the critical point. Beyond this point the transition from one state to another involves the intermediate "fluid" region just described.

Applications of the Phase Diagram for Water

There are several additional interesting features of the phase diagram for water. Note that the solid/liquid boundary line has a negative slope. This means that the melting point of ice *decreases* as the external pressure *increases.* This behavior, which is opposite to that observed for most substances, occurs because the density of ice is *less* than that of liquid water at the melting point. The maximum density of water occurs at 4°C; when liquid water freezes, its volume increases.

Molecular Model: H_2O

We can account for the effect of pressure on the melting point of water using the following reasoning. At the melting point, liquid and solid water coexist—they are in dynamic equilibrium, since the rate at which ice is melting is just balanced by the rate at which the water is freezing. What happens if we apply pressure to this system? When subjected to increased pressure, matter reduces its volume. This behavior is most dramatic for gases but also occurs for condensed states. Since a given mass of ice at 0°C has a larger volume than the same mass of liquid water, the system can reduce its volume in response to the increased pressure by changing to liquid. Thus at 0°C and an external pressure greater than 1 atm, water is liquid. In other words, the freezing point of water is less than 0°C when the pressure is greater than 1 atm.

Figure 10.49 illustrates the effect of pressure on ice. At the point X on the phase diagram, ice is subjected to increased pressure at constant temperature. Note that as the pressure is increased, the solid/liquid line is crossed, indicating that the ice melts. This phenomenon may be important in ice skating. The narrow blade of the skate exerts a large pressure, since the skater's weight is supported by the small area of the blade. Also, the frictional heating due to the moving skate contributes to the melting of the ice.* After the blade passes, the liquid refreezes as normal pressure and temperature return. Without this lubrication effect due to the thawing ice, ice skating would not be the smooth, graceful activity that many people enjoy.

Ice's lower density has other implications. When water freezes in a pipe or an engine block, it will expand and break the container. This is why water pipes are

---

* The physics of ice skating is quite complex, and there is disagreement about whether the pressure or the frictional heating of the ice skate is most important. See "Letter to the Editor," by R. Silberman, *J. Chem. Ed.* **65** (1988): 186.

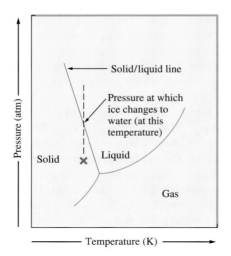

Figure 10.49

The phase diagram for water. At point x on the phase diagram, water is a solid. However, as the external pressure is increased while the temperature remains constant (indicated by the vertical dotted line), the solid/liquid line is crossed and the ice melts.

The effect of pressure on ice allows this skater to glide smoothly.

insulated in cold climates and antifreeze is used in water-cooled engines. The lower density of ice also means that ice formed on rivers and lakes will float, providing a layer of insulation that helps prevent bodies of water from freezing solid in the winter. Aquatic life can therefore continue to live through periods of freezing temperatures.

A liquid boils at the temperature where the vapor pressure of the liquid equals the external pressure. Thus the boiling point of a substance, like the melting point, depends on the external pressure. This is why water boils at different temperatures at different elevations (see Table 10.10), and any cooking carried out in boiling

Table 10.10 Boiling Point of Water at Various Locations

Location	Feet Above Sea Level	P_{atm} (torr)	Boiling Point (°C)
Top of Mt. Everest, Tibet	29,028	240	70
Top of Mt. McKinley, Alaska	20,320	340	79
Top of Mt. Whitney, Calif.	14,494	430	85
Leadville, Colo.	10,150	510	89
Top of Mt. Washington, N.H.	6,293	590	93
Boulder, Colo.	5,430	610	94
Madison, Wis.	900	730	99
New York City, N.Y.	10	760	100
Death Valley, Calif.	−282	770	100.3

CHEMICAL IMPACT

Making Diamonds at Low Pressures: Fooling Mother Nature

IN 1955 ROBERT H. WENTORF, JR., accomplished something that borders on alchemy—he turned peanut butter into diamonds. He and his coworkers at the General Electric Research and Development Center also changed roofing pitch, wood, coal, and many other carbon-containing materials into diamonds, using a process involving temperatures of $\approx 2000°C$ and pressures of $\approx 10^5$ atm. Although the first diamonds made by this process looked like black sand because of the impurities present, the process has now been developed to a point such that beautiful, clear, gem-quality diamonds can be produced. General Electric now has the capacity to produce 150 million carats (30,000 kg) of diamonds annually (virtually all of which is "diamond grit" used for industrial purposes such as abrasive coatings on cutting tools). The production of large, gem-quality diamonds by this process is still too expensive to compete with the natural sources of these stones. However, this may change as methods are developed for making diamonds at low pressures.

The high temperatures and pressures used in the GE process for making diamonds make sense if one looks at the accompanying phase diagram for carbon. Note that graphite—not diamond—is the most stable form of carbon under ordinary conditions of temperature and pressure. However, diamond becomes more stable than graphite at very high pressures (as one would expect from the greater density of diamond). The high temperature used in the GE process is necessary to disrupt the bonds in graphite so that diamond (the most stable form of carbon at the high pressures used in the process) can form. Once the diamond is produced, the elemental carbon is "trapped" in this form at normal conditions (25°C, 1 atm) because the reaction back to the graphite form is so slow. That is, even though graphite is more stable than diamond at 25°C and 1 atm, diamond can exist almost indefinitely because the conversion to graphite is a *very slow* reaction. As a result, diamonds formed at the high pressures found deep in the earth's crust can be brought to the earth's surface by natural geologic processes and continue to exist for millions of years.*

We have seen that diamond formed in the laboratory at high pressures is "trapped" in this form, but this process is very expensive. Can diamond be formed at low pressures? The phase diagram for carbon says no. However, researchers have found that under the right conditions diamonds can be "grown" at low pressures. The process used is called *chemical vapor deposition (CVD)*. CVD uses an energy source to release carbon atoms from a compound such as methane into a steady flow of hydrogen gas (some of which is dissociated to produce hydrogen atoms). The carbon atoms then deposit as a diamond film on a surface maintained at a temperature between 600 and 900°C. Why does diamond form on this surface rather than the favored graphite? Nobody is sure, but it has been suggested that at these relatively high temperatures the diamond structure grows faster than the graphite structure and so diamond is favored under these conditions. It also has been suggested that the hydrogen atoms present react much faster with graphite fragments than with diamond fragments, effectively removing any graphite from the growing film. Once it forms, of course, diamond is trapped. The major advantage of CVD is that there is no need for the extraordinarily high pressures used in the traditional process for synthesizing diamonds.

The first products with diamond films are already on the market. Audiophiles

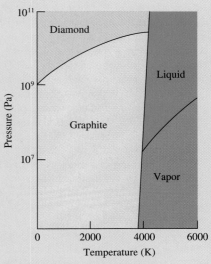

The phase diagram for carbon.

can buy tweeters that have diaphragms coated with a thin diamond film that limits sound distortion. Watches with diamond-coated crystals are planned, as are diamond-coated windows in infrared scanning devices used in analytical instruments and missile guidance systems. These applications represent only the beginning for diamond-coated products.

*In Morocco, a 50-km-long slab called Beni Bousera contains chunks of graphite that were probably once diamonds formed in the deposit when it was buried 150 km underground. As this slab slowly rose to the surface over millions of years, the very slow reaction changing diamond to graphite had time to occur. On the other hand, in the diamond-rich kimberlite deposits in South Africa, which rise to the surface much faster, the diamonds have not had sufficient time to revert to graphite.

CHEMICAL IMPACT

Transistors and Printed Circuits

TRANSISTORS HAVE HAD an immense impact on the technology of electronic devices for which signal amplification is needed, such as communications equipment and computers. Before the invention of the transistor at Bell Laboratories in 1947, amplification was provided exclusively by vacuum tubes, which were both bulky and unreliable. The first electronic digital computer, ENIAC, built at the University of Pennsylvania, had 19,000 vacuum tubes and consumed 150,000 watts of electricity. Because of the discovery and development of the transistor and the printed circuit, a hand-held calculator run by a small battery has the same computing power as ENIAC.

A *junction transistor* is made by joining n-type and p-type semiconductors so as to form an n–p–n or a p–n–p junction. The former type is shown in Fig. 10.50. In this diagram the input signal (to be amplified) occurs in circuit 1, which has a small resistance and a forward-biased n–p junction (junction 1). As the voltage of the input signal to this circuit varies, the current in the circuit varies, which means there is

a change in the number of electrons crossing the n–p junction. Circuit 2 has a relatively large resistance and is under reverse bias. The key to operation of the transistor is that current only flows in circuit 2 when electrons crossing junction 1 also cross junction 2 and travel to the positive terminal. Since the current in circuit 1 determines the number of electrons crossing junction 1, the number of electrons available to cross junction 2 is also directly proportional to the current in circuit 1. The current in circuit 2 therefore varies depending on the current in circuit 1.

The voltage V, current I, and resistance R in a circuit are related by the equation

$$V = IR$$

Since circuit 2 has a large resistance, a given current in circuit 2 produces a larger voltage than the same current in circuit 1, which has a small resistance. Thus a signal or variable voltage in circuit 1, such as might be produced by a human voice on a telephone, is reproduced in circuit 2, but with much greater voltage changes. That is, the input signal

has been *amplified* by the junction transistor. This device, which has replaced the large vacuum tube, is a tiny component of a printed circuit on a silicon chip.

Silicon chips are really "planar" transistors constructed from thin layers of n-type and p-type regions connected by conductors. A chip less than 1 cm wide can contain hundreds of printed circuits and be used in computers, radios, and televisions.

A printed circuit has many n–p–n junction transistors. Fig. 10.51 illustrates the formation of one transistor area. The chip begins as a thin wafer of silicon that has been doped with an n-type impurity. A protective layer of silicon dioxide is then produced on the wafer by exposing it in a furnace to an oxidizing atmosphere. The next step is to produce a p-type semiconductor. To do this, the surface of the oxide is covered by a light-sensitive wax, as shown in Fig. 10.51(a). A template that only allows light to shine through in selected areas is then placed on top [Fig. 10.51(b)], and light is shown on the chip. The wax that has been exposed to

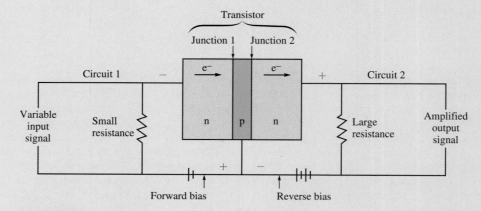

Figure 10.50

A schematic of two circuits connected by a transistor. The signal in circuit 1 is amplified in circuit 2.

light undergoes a chemical change that causes its solubility to be different from the unexposed wax. The exposed wax is dissolved using selective solvents [Fig. 10.51(c)], and the exposed area is treated with an etching solution to dissolve the oxide coating [Fig. 10.51(d)]. When the remaining wax is dissolved, the silicon wafer has its oxide coating intact except at the one spot (of diameter x), as shown in Fig. 10.51(d).

Exposing the wafer to a p-type impurity such as boron at about 1000°C causes a p-type semiconductor area to be formed in the exposed spot as the boron atoms diffuse into the silicon crystal [Fig. 10.51(e)]. Next, to form a small n-type area in the center of the p-type region, the wafer is again placed in the oxidizing furnace to be recoated over its entire surface with oxide. Then a new wax covering is applied, which is illuminated through a template with a transparent area indicated by y [Fig. 10.51(f)]. The wax and oxide are then removed from the illuminated area, and the wafer is exposed to an n-type impurity to form a small n-type region as shown in Fig. 10.51(g). Next, conductors are layered onto the chip giving the finished transistor [Fig. 10.51(h)], which has two circuits connected through an n–p–n junction (see Fig. 10.50). This transistor then becomes a part of a large circuit layered onto the chip and interconnected by conductors.

The method given here for producing a printed circuit does not represent the latest technology in this field. The manufacture of printed circuits is a highly competitive business, and changes in methodology occur almost daily.

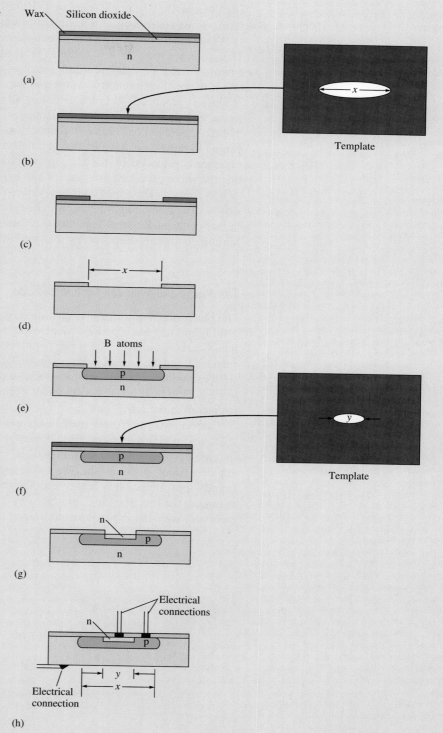

Figure 10.51

The steps for forming a transistor in a crystal of initially pure silicon.

Water boils at 89°C in Leadville, Colorado.

water will be affected by this variation. For example, it takes longer to hard-boil an egg in Leadville, Colorado (elevation: 10,150 ft), than in San Diego, California (sea level), since water boils at a lower temperature in Leadville.

As we mentioned earlier, the phase diagram for water describes a closed system. Therefore, we must be very cautious in using the phase diagram to explain the behavior of water in a natural setting, such as on the earth's surface. For example, in dry climates (low humidity), snow and ice seem to sublime—a minimum amount of slush is produced. Wet clothes put on an outside line at temperatures below 0°C freeze and then dry while frozen. However, the phase diagram (Fig. 10.47) shows that ice should *not* be able to sublime at normal atmospheric pressures. What is happening in these cases? Ice in the natural environment is not in a closed system. The pressure is provided by the atmosphere rather than by a solid piston. This means that the vapor produced over the ice can escape from the immediate region as soon as it is formed. The vapor does not come to equilibrium with the solid, and the ice slowly disappears. Sublimation, which seems forbidden by the phase diagram, does in fact occur under these conditions, although it is not the sublimation under equilibrium conditions described by the phase diagram.

The Phase Diagram for Carbon Dioxide

The phase diagram for carbon dioxide (Fig. 10.52) differs from that for water. The solid/liquid line has a positive slope, since solid carbon dioxide is more dense than liquid carbon dioxide. The triple point for carbon dioxide occurs at 5.1 atm and $-56.6°C$, and the critical point occurs at 72.8 atm and 31°C. At a pressure of 1 atm, solid carbon dioxide sublimes at $-78°C$, a property that leads to its common name, *dry ice*. No liquid phase occurs under normal atmospheric conditions, making dry ice a convenient refrigerant.

Carbon dioxide is often used in fire extinguishers, where it exists as a liquid at 25°C under high pressures. Liquid carbon dioxide released from the extinguisher into the environment at 1 atm immediately changes to a vapor. Being heavier than air, this vapor smothers the fire by keeping oxygen away from the flame. The liquid/vapor transition is highly endothermic, so cooling also results, which helps to put out the fire. The "fog" produced by a carbon dioxide extinguisher is not solid carbon dioxide but rather moisture frozen from the air.

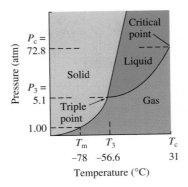

Figure 10.52

The phase diagram for carbon dioxide. The liquid state does not exist at a pressure of 1 atm. The solid/liquid line has a positive slope, since the density of solid carbon dioxide is greater than that of liquid carbon dioxide.

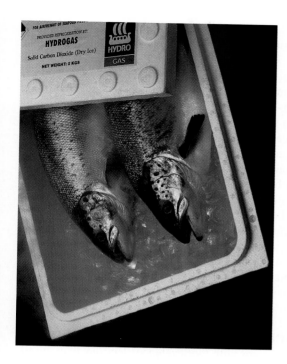

Fish packed in dry ice for shipping.

For Review

Summary

Liquids and solids are the two condensed states of matter; their formation is caused by intermolecular forces among the molecules, atoms, or ions. Dipole–dipole forces are attractions between molecules that have dipole moments. These forces are particularly strong for molecules containing hydrogen bonded to a highly electronegative element such as nitrogen, oxygen, or fluorine. In these cases the resulting dipole forces are called hydrogen bonds and account for the unusually high boiling points of the hydrides of the first elements in Groups 5A, 6A, and 7A. London dispersion forces caused by instantaneous dipoles are important in substances composed of nonpolar molecules. Liquids exhibit various properties—surface tension, capillary action, and viscosity—that depend on the strengths of the intermolecular forces.

The two broadest categories of solids are crystalline and amorphous solids. Crystalline solids have a regular arrangement, or lattice, of component particles, the smallest repeating unit of which is the unit cell. Crystalline solids can be classified according to what type of components occupy the lattice points: atoms (atomic solids), ions (ionic solids), or molecules (molecular solids). The arrangement of particles in a crystalline solid can be determined by X-ray diffraction techniques, and the interatomic distances in the crystal can be related to the wavelength and angle of reflection of the X rays by the Bragg equation.

Key Terms

Section 10.1
condensed states
intermolecular forces
dipole–dipole attraction
hydrogen bonding
London dispersion forces

Section 10.2
surface tension
capillary action
viscosity

Section 10.3
crystalline solid
amorphous solid
lattice
unit cell
X-ray diffraction
ionic solid
molecular solid
atomic solid

The structure of metals is modeled by assuming atoms to be uniform spheres and packing them as compactly as possible. There are two closest packing arrangements: hexagonal and cubic.

The bonding in metallic crystals can be described in terms of the electron sea model (valence electrons are assumed to move freely about the metal cations) or in terms of the band model (electrons are assumed to travel through the metal crystal in molecular orbitals formed from the valence atomic orbitals of the metal atoms). In the band model the large number of available atomic orbitals form closely spaced energy levels. Electricity can be readily conducted by electrons in conduction bands, which are molecular orbitals containing only a single electron.

Metals form alloys, which can be classified as substitutional or interstitial.

Carbon is a typical network solid containing strong directional covalent bonds. Diamond and graphite are two allotropes of carbon, with very different physical properties determined by their different bonding.

Silicon should be very similar in properties to carbon since carbon and silicon are next to each other in Group 4A, but in fact their compounds are markedly dissimilar. Silica, the fundamental silicon–oxygen compound, does not contain discrete SiO_2 molecules but rather a network of interconnected SiO_4 tetrahedra. Silicates, salts containing polyatomic anions of silicon and oxygen, are components of rocks, soil, clays, glass, and ceramics.

Semiconductors are formed when pure silicon is doped with other elements. An n-type semiconductor contains atoms with more valence electrons than the silicon atom, and a p-type semiconductor has atoms with fewer valence electrons than silicon. The modern electronics industry is based on devices with p–n junctions.

Molecular solids have small molecules at the lattice points and are held together by relatively weak intermolecular forces. Ice is an example. Ionic solids, on the other hand, are held together by strong electrostatic attractions. The crystal structure of ionic solids can often be described by fitting the smaller ions (usually cations) into holes in the closest packed structures formed by the larger ions (usually anions).

The phase change between liquid and vapor is called vaporization, or evaporation, and the energy required to change 1 mole of liquid to its vapor is the heat of vaporization (ΔH_{vap}). Condensation is the reverse process by which vapor molecules return to the liquid state. When the rates of evaporation and condensation exactly balance in a closed container, the system is at equilibrium, and the resulting pressure of the vapor is called the vapor pressure. The volatility of liquids depends on intermolecular forces. Liquids with strong intermolecular forces tend to have low vapor pressures.

The normal melting point of a solid is defined as the temperature at which the solid and its liquid have identical vapor pressures. The normal boiling point of a liquid occurs at a temperature where the vapor pressure of the liquid is 1 atmosphere.

A phase diagram for a substance shows which state exists at a given temperature and pressure. The triple point on a phase diagram represents the temperature and pressure where all three states coexist. The critical point is defined by the critical temperature and critical pressure. Critical temperature is that temperature above which the vapor cannot be liquefied no matter what pressure is applied. The critical pressure is the pressure required to produce liquefaction at the critical temperature.

In-Class Discussion Questions

These questions are designed to be considered by groups of students in class. Often these questions work well for introducing a particular topic in class.

1. It is possible to balance a paper clip on the surface of water in a beaker. If you add a bit of soap to the water, however, the paper clip sinks. Explain how the paper clip can float and why it sinks when soap is added.

2. Consider a sealed container half-filled with water. Which statement best describes what occurs in the container?
   a. Water evaporates until the air is saturated with water vapor; at this point, no more water evaporates.
   b. Water evaporates until the air is overly saturated (supersaturated) with water, and most of this water recondenses; this cycle continues until a certain amount of water vapor is present, and then the cycle ceases.
   c. Water does not evaporate because the container is sealed.
   d. Water evaporates, and then water evaporates and recondenses simultaneously and continuously.
   e. Water evaporates until it is eventually all in vapor form.
   Explain each choice. Justify your choice, and for choices you did not pick, explain what is wrong with them.

3. Explain the following: You add 100 mL of water to a 500-mL round-bottom flask and heat the water until it is boiling. You remove the heat, stopper the flask, and the boiling stops. You then run cool water over the neck of the flask, and the boiling begins again. It seems as though you are boiling water by cooling it.

4. Is it possible for the dispersion forces in a particular substance to be stronger than the hydrogen bonding forces in another substance? Explain your answer.

5. Does the nature of intermolecular forces change when a substance goes from a solid to a liquid, or from a liquid to a gas? What causes a substance to undergo a phase change?

6. Why do liquids have a vapor pressure? Do all liquids have vapor pressures? Explain. Do solids exhibit vapor pressure? Explain. How does vapor pressure change with changing temperature? Explain.

7. Water in an open beaker evaporates over time. As the water is evaporating, is the vapor pressure increasing, decreasing, or staying the same? Why?

8. What is the vapor pressure of water at 100°C? How do you know?

9. Refer to Fig. 10.42. Why doesn't temperature increase continuously over time? That is, why does the temperature stay constant for periods of time?

10. Which are stronger, intermolecular or intramolecular forces for a given molecule? What observation(s) have you made that support this? Explain.

11. Why does water evaporate?

Questions

A blue question or exercise number indicates that the answer to that question or exercise appears at the back of this book and a solution appears in the *Solutions Guide*.

12. Describe the relationship between the polarity of individual molecules and the nature and strength of intermolecular forces.

13. List the major types of intermolecular forces in order of increasing strength. Is there some overlap? That is, can the strongest London dispersion forces be greater than some dipole–dipole forces? Give an example of such an instance.

14. Describe the relationship between molecular size and the strength of London dispersion forces.

15. How do the following physical properties depend on the strength of intermolecular forces?
   a. surface tension
   b. viscosity
   c. melting point
   d. boiling point
   e. vapor pressure

16. How do typical dipole–dipole forces differ from hydrogen bonds? In what ways are they similar?

17. Distinguish between the following pairs.
   a. polarizability and polarity
   b. London dispersion forces and dipole–dipole forces
   c. intermolecular forces and intramolecular forces

18. In what ways are liquids similar to solids? In what ways are liquids similar to gases?

19. Atoms are assumed to touch in closest packed structures, yet every closest packed unit cell contains a significant amount of empty space. Why?

20. Define *critical temperature* and *critical pressure*. In terms of the kinetic molecular theory, why is it impossible for a substance to exist as a liquid above its critical temperature?

21. What is the relationship between critical temperature and intermolecular forces?

22. Use the kinetic molecular theory to explain why a liquid gets cooler as it evaporates from an insulated container.

23. Distinguish between the items in the following pairs.
   a. crystalline solid and amorphous solid
   b. ionic solid and molecular solid
   c. molecular solid and network solid
   d. metallic solid and network solid

24. Will a crystalline solid or an amorphous solid give a simpler X-ray diffraction pattern? Why?

25. Is it possible to generalize that amorphous solids always have weaker or stronger interparticle forces than crystalline solids? Explain.

26. Use the band model to describe differences among insulators, conductors, and semiconductors.

27. Use the band model to explain why each of the following increases the conductivity of a semiconductor.
    a. increasing the temperature
    b. irradiating with light
    c. adding an impurity

28. How do conductors and semiconductors differ as to the effect of temperature on electrical conductivity?

29. Define each of the following.
    a. condensation
    b. evaporation
    c. sublimation
    d. supercooled liquid

30. Describe what is meant by a dynamic equilibrium in terms of the vapor pressure of a volatile liquid.

31. How does each of the following affect the rate of evaporation of a liquid in an open dish?
    a. intermolecular forces
    b. temperature
    c. surface area

32. When wet laundry is hung on a clothesline on a cold winter day, it will freeze but eventually dry. Explain.

33. Why is a burn from steam typically much more severe than a burn from boiling water?

34. Why is the enthalpy of vaporization for water much greater than its enthalpy of fusion? What does this say about changes in intermolecular forces in going from solid to liquid to vapor?

Exercises

In this section similar exercises are paired.

Intermolecular Forces and Physical Properties

35. Identify the most important types of interparticle forces present in the solids of each of the following substances.
    a. Ar
    b. HCl
    c. HF
    d. $CaCl_2$
    e. CH_4
    f. CO
    g. $NaNO_3$

36. Identify the most important types of interparticle forces present in the solids of each of the following substances.
    a. NH_4Cl
    b. Teflon, $CF_3(CF_2CF_2)_nCF_3$
    c. Polyethylene, $CH_3(CH_2CH_2)_nCH_3$
    d. $CHCl_3$
    e. NH_3

f. NO
g. BF_3

37. Predict which substance in each of the following pairs would have the greater intermolecular forces.
    a. CO_2 or OCS
    b. PF_3 or PF_5
    c. SF_2 or SF_6
    d. SO_3 or SO_2

38. For which molecule in each of the following pairs would you expect greater intermolecular forces?
    a. $CH_3CH_2CH_2NH_2$ or $H_2NCH_2CH_2NH_2$
    b. CH_3CH_3 or H_2CO
    c. CH_3OH or H_2CO
    d. HF or HBr

39. Rationalize the difference in boiling points for each of the following pairs of substances:
    a. *n*-pentane $CH_3CH_2CH_2CH_2CH_3$ 36.2°C

    neopentane $H_3C-\underset{\underset{CH_3}{|}}{\overset{\overset{CH_3}{|}}{C}}-CH_3$ 9.5°C

    b. dimethyl ether CH_3OCH_3 −25°C
       ethanol CH_3CH_2OH 79°C
    c. HF   20°C
       HCl   −85°C
    d. HCl   −85°C
       LiCl   1360°C
    e. *n*-pentane $CH_3CH_2CH_2CH_2CH_3$ 36.2°C
       n-propane $CH_3CH_2CH_3$ −42°C
    f. *n*-propane $CH_3CH_2CH_3$ −42°C
       dimethyl ether CH_3OCH_3 −25°C

40. Rationalize the boiling points in the following organic compounds.

    $CH_3C\overset{\overset{O}{\diagup\diagdown}}{\underset{OH}{\diagdown}}$ 118°C

    $ClCH_2C\overset{\overset{O}{\diagup\diagdown}}{\underset{OH}{\diagdown}}$ 189°C

    $CH_3C\overset{\overset{O}{\diagup\diagdown}}{\underset{OCH_3}{\diagdown}}$ 57°C

41. In each of the following groups of substances, pick the one that has the given property. Justify your answer.
    a. highest boiling point: HCl, Ar, or F_2
    b. highest freezing point: H_2O, NaCl, or HF
    c. lowest vapor pressure at 25°C: Cl_2, Br_2, or I_2
    d. lowest freezing point: N_2, CO, or CO_2

e. lowest boiling point: CH_4, CH_3CH_3, or $CH_3CH_2CH_3$
f. highest boiling point: HF, HCl, or HBr

g. lowest vapor pressure at 25°C: $CH_3CH_2CH_3$, CH_3CCH_3,
   or $CH_3CH_2CH_2OH$

42. In each of the following groups of substances, pick the one that has the given property. Justify each answer.
a. highest boiling point: CCl_4, CF_4, or CBr_4
b. lowest freezing point: LiF, Cl_2, HBr
c. smallest vapor pressure at 25°C: CH_3OCH_3, CH_3CH_2OH, $CH_3CH_2CH_3$
d. greatest viscosity: H_2S, HF, H_2O_2
e. greatest heat of vaporization: H_2CO, CH_3CH_3, CH_4
f. smallest enthalpy of fusion: I_2, CsBr, CaO

Properties of Liquids

43. The shape of the meniscus of water in a glass tube is different from that of mercury in a glass tube. Why?

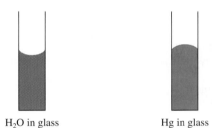

H₂O in glass   Hg in glass

What would be the shape of the meniscus of water in a polyethylene tube? (Polyethylene can be represented as $CH_3(CH_2)_nCH_3$, where n is a large number on the order of 1000.)

44. Will water rise to a greater height by capillary action in a glass tube or in a polyethylene tube of the same diameter?

45. Hydrogen peroxide (H_2O_2) is a syrupy liquid with a relatively low vapor pressure and a normal boiling point of 152.2°C. Rationalize the differences of these physical properties from those of water.

46. Carbon diselenide (CSe_2) is a liquid at room temperature. The normal boiling point is 125°C, and the melting point is −45.5°C. Carbon disulfide (CS_2) is also a liquid at room temperature with normal boiling and melting points of 46.5°C and −111.6°C, respectively. How do the strengths of the intermolecular forces vary from CO_2 to CS_2 to CSe_2? Explain.

Structures and Properties of Solids

47. X rays from a copper X-ray tube ($\lambda = 1.54$ Å) were diffracted at an angle of 14.22 degrees by a crystal of silicon. Assuming first-order diffraction ($n = 1$ in the Bragg equation), what is the interplanar spacing in silicon?

48. X rays of wavelength 2.63 Å were used to analyze a crystal. The angle of first-order diffraction ($n = 1$ in the Bragg equation) was 15.55 degrees. What is the spacing between crystal planes, and what would be the angle for second-order diffraction ($n = 2$)?

49. Calcium has a cubic closest packed structure as a solid. Assuming that calcium has an atomic radius of 197 pm, calculate the density of solid calcium.

50. Nickel has a face-centered cubic unit cell. The density of nickel is 6.84 g/cm³. Calculate a value for the atomic radius of nickel.

51. Iridium (Ir) has a face-centered cubic unit cell with an edge length of 383.3 pm. Calculate the density of solid iridium.

52. You are given a small bar of an unknown metal X. You find the density of the metal to be 10.5 g/cm³. An X-ray diffraction experiment measures the edge of the face-centered cubic unit cell as 4.09 Å (1 Å = 10^{-10} m). Identify X.

53. Titanium metal has a body-centered cubic unit cell. The density of titanium is 4.50 g/cm³. Calculate the edge length of the unit cell and a value for the atomic radius of titanium. (*Hint:* In a body-centered arrangement of spheres, the spheres touch across the body diagonal.)

54. Barium has a body-centered cubic structure. If the atomic radius of barium is 222 pm, calculate the density of solid barium.

55. What fraction of the total volume of a cubic closest packed structure is occupied by atoms? (*Hint:* $V_{sphere} = \frac{4}{3}\pi r^3$.)

56. Iron has a density of 7.86 g/cm³ and crystallizes in a body-centered cubic lattice. Show that only 68% of a body-centered lattice is actually occupied by atoms, and determine the atomic radius of iron.

57. How can an n-type semiconductor be produced from pure germanium?

58. How can a p-type semiconductor be produced from pure germanium?

59. Selenium is a semiconductor used in photocopying machines. What type of semiconductor would be formed if a small amount of indium impurity is added to pure selenium?

60. The Group 3A/Group 5A semiconductors are composed of equal amounts of atoms from Group 3A and Group 5A, for example, InP and GaAs. These types of semiconductors are used in light-emitting diodes and solid-state lasers. What would you add to make a p-type semiconductor from pure GaAs? How would you dope pure GaAs to make an n-type semiconductor?

61. The band gap in aluminum phosphide (AlP) is 2.5 electron-volts (1 eV = 1.6×10^{-19} J). What wavelength of light is emitted by an AlP diode?

62. An aluminum antimonide solid-state laser emits light with a wavelength of 730. nm. Calculate the band gap in joules.

63. The structures of some common crystalline substances are shown below. Show that the net composition of each unit cell corresponds to the correct formula of each substance.

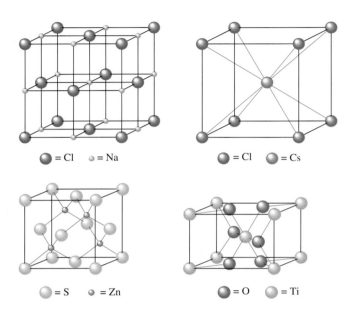

= Cl   = Na   = Cl   = Cs

= S   = Zn   = O   = Ti

64. The unit cell for nickel arsenide is shown below. What is the formula of this compound?

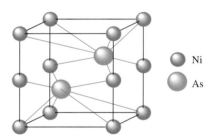

Ni

As

65. Cobalt fluoride crystallizes in a closest packed array of fluoride ions with the cobalt ions filling one-half of the octahedral holes. What is the formula of this compound?

66. The compounds Na_2O, CdS, and ZrI_4 all can be described as cubic closest packed anions with the cations in tetrahedral holes. What fraction of the tetrahedral holes is occupied for each case?

67. A certain metal fluoride crystallizes in such a way that the fluoride ions occupy simple cubic lattice sites, while the metal ions occupy the body centers of *half* the cubes. What is the formula of the metal fluoride?

68. The structure of manganese fluoride can be described as a simple cubic array of manganese ions with fluoride ions at the center of each edge of the cubic unit cell. What is the charge of the manganese ions in this compound?

69. Magnesium oxide has the same structure as sodium chloride and has a density of 3.58 g/cm³. Calculate the edge length of the unit cell using this information. The ionic radii of Mg^{2+} and O^{2-} are 65 and 140. pm, respectively. Calculate the edge length of the unit cell from these data and compare it with your first answer.

70. The CsCl structure is a simple cubic array of chloride ions with a cesium ion at the center of each cubic array (see Exercise 63). Given that the density of cesium fluoride is 3.97 g/cm³, and assuming that the chloride and cesium ions touch along the body diagonal of the cubic unit cell, calculate the distance between the centers of adjacent Cs^+ and Cl^- ions in the solid. Compare this value with the expected distance based on the sizes of the ions. The ionic radius of Cs^+ is 169 pm, and the ionic radius of Cl^- is 181 pm.

71. What type of solid will each of the following substances form?
   a. CO_2 e. Ru   i. NaOH
   b. SiO_2 f. I_2 j. U
   c. Si   g. KBr   k. $CaCO_3$
   d. CH_4 h. H_2O l. PH_3

72. What type of solid will each of the following substances form?
   a. diamond   e. KCl   i. Ar
   b. PH_3 f. quartz   j. Cu
   c. H_2 g. NH_4NO_3 k. $C_6H_{12}O_6$
   d. Mg   h. SF_2

73. The memory metal, nitinol, is an alloy of nickel and titanium. It is called a *memory metal* because after being deformed, a piece of nitinol wire will return to its original shape. The structure of nitinol consists of a simple cubic array of Ni atoms and an inner penetrating simple cubic array of Ti atoms. In the extended lattice, a Ti atom is found at the center of a cube of Ni atoms; the reverse is also true.
   a. Describe the unit cell for nitinol.
   b. What is the empirical formula of nitinol?
   c. What are the coordination numbers (number of nearest neighbors) of Ni and Ti in nitinol?

74. The unit cell for a pure xenon fluoride compound is shown below. What is the formula of the compound?

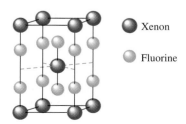

Xenon

Fluorine

75. Perovskite is a mineral containing calcium, titanium, and oxygen. Two different representations of the unit cell are shown below. Show that both these representations give the same formula and the same number of oxygen atoms around each titanium atom.

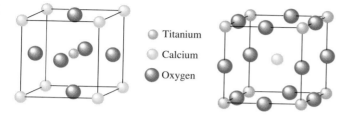

○ Titanium
○ Calcium
● Oxygen

76. A mineral crystallizes in a cubic closest packed array of sulfur ions with aluminum ions in one-half of the octahedral holes and zinc ions in one-eighth of the tetrahedral holes. What is the formula of this mineral?

77. Materials, containing the elements Y, Ba, Cu, and O, that are superconductors (electrical resistance equals zero) at temperatures above that of liquid nitrogen were recently discovered. The structures of these materials are based on the perovskite structure. Were they to have the ideal perovskite structure, the superconductor would have the structure shown in part (a) of the figure below.

a. What is the formula of this ideal perovskite material?
b. How is this structure related to the perovskite structure shown in Exercise 75?

These materials, however, do not act as superconductors unless they are deficient in oxygen. The structure of the actual superconducting phase appears to be that shown in part (b) of the figure.

c. What is the formula of this material?

78. The structures of another class of ceramic, high-temperature superconductors are shown in the figure below.

a. Determine the formula of each of these four superconductors.
b. One of the structural features that appears to be essential for high-temperature superconductivity is the presence of planar sheets of copper and oxygen atoms. As the number of sheets in each unit cell increases, the temperature for the onset of superconductivity increases. Order the four structures from lowest to the highest superconducting temperature.

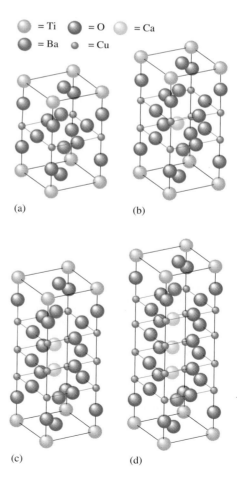

○ = Ti   ● = O   ○ = Ca
● = Ba   ● = Cu

(a)   (b)

(c)   (d)

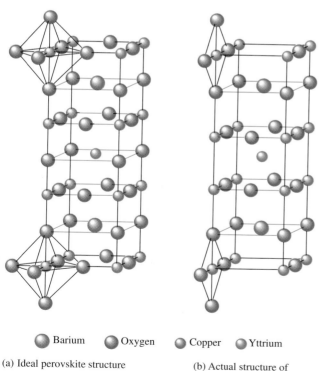

● Barium   ● Oxygen   ● Copper   ● Yttrium

(a) Ideal perovskite structure

(b) Actual structure of superconductor

c. Assign oxidation states to Cu in each structure assuming Tl exists as Tl^{3+}. The oxidation states of Ca, Ba, and O are assumed to be +2, +2, and −2, respectively.

d. It also appears that copper must display a mixture of oxidation states for a material to exhibit superconductivity. Explain how this occurs in these materials as well as in the superconductor in Exercise 77.

Phase Changes and Phase Diagrams

79. Plot the following data and determine ΔH_{vap} for magnesium and lithium. In which metal is the bonding stronger?

Vapor Pressure (mm Hg)	Temperature (°C)	
	Li	Mg
1.	750.	620.
10.	890.	740.
100.	1080.	900.
400.	1240.	1040.
760.	1310.	1110.

80. From the following data for liquid nitric acid, determine its heat of vaporization and normal boiling point.

Temperature (°C)	Vapor Pressure (mm Hg)
0	14.4
10.	26.6
20.	47.9
30.	81.3
40.	133
50.	208
80.	670.

81. In Breckenridge, Colorado, the typical atmospheric pressure is 520. torr. What is the boiling point of water ($\Delta H_{vap} = 40.7$ kJ/mol) in Breckenridge?

82. What pressure would have to be applied to steam at 350.°C to condense the steam to liquid water ($\Delta H_{vap} = 40.7$ kJ/mol)?

83. The enthalpy of vaporization of mercury is 59.1 kJ/mol. The normal boiling point of mercury is 357°C. What is the vapor pressure of mercury at 25°C?

84. The normal boiling point for acetone is 56.5°C. At an elevation of 5300 ft the atmospheric pressure is 630. torr. What would be the boiling point of acetone ($\Delta H_{vap} = 32.0$ kJ/mol) at this elevation? What would be the vapor pressure of acetone at 25.0°C at this elevation?

85. A substance has the following properties:

		Specific Heat Capacities	
ΔH_{vap}	20. kJ/mol	C(s)	3.0 J/g · °C
ΔH_{fus}	5 kJ/mol	C(l)	2.5 J/g · °C
bp	75°C	C(g)	1.0 J/g · °C
mp	−15°C		

Sketch a heating curve for the substance starting at −50°C.

86. Describe how a phase diagram can be constructed from the heating curve for a substance.

87. How much energy does it take to convert 0.500 kg ice at −20.°C to steam at 250.°C? Specific heat capacities: ice, 2.1 J/g · °C; liquid, 4.2 J/g · °C; steam, 2.0 J/g · °C, $\Delta H_{vap} = 40.7$ kJ/mol, $\Delta H_{fus} = 6.02$ kJ/mol.

88. What is the final temperature when 0.850 kJ of energy is added to 10.0 g ice at 0°C? (See Exercise 87.)

89. An ice cube tray contains enough water at 22.0°C to make 18 ice cubes that each have a mass of 30.0 g. The tray is placed in a freezer that uses CF_2Cl_2 as a refrigerant. The heat of vaporization of CF_2Cl_2 is 158 J/g. What mass of CF_2Cl_2 must be vaporized in the refrigeration cycle to convert all the water at 22.0°C to ice at −5.0°C? The heat capacities for $H_2O(s)$ and $H_2O(l)$ are 2.08 J/g · °C and 4.18 J/g · °C, respectively, and the enthalpy of fusion for ice is 6.02 kJ/mol.

90. A 0.250-g chunk of sodium metal is cautiously dropped into a mixture of 50.0 g of water and 50.0 g of ice, both at 0°C. The reaction is

$$2Na(s) + 2H_2O(l) \longrightarrow 2NaOH(aq) + H_2(g)$$
$$\Delta H = -368 \text{ kJ}$$

Will the ice melt? Assuming the final mixture has a specific heat capacity of 4.18 J/g · °C, calculate the final temperature. The enthalpy of fusion for ice is 6.02 kJ/mol.

91. Consider the phase diagram given below. What phases are present at points A through H? Identify the triple point, normal boiling point, normal freezing point, and critical point. Which phase is denser, solid or liquid?

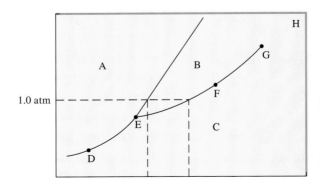

92. Sulfur exhibits two solid phases, rhombic and monoclinic. Use the accompanying phase diagram for sulfur to answer the following questions. (The phase diagram is not to scale.)
a. How many triple points are in the phase diagram?
b. What phases are in equilibrium at each of the triple points?
c. What is the stable phase at 1 atm and 100°C?
d. What are the normal melting point and the normal boiling point of sulfur?
e. Which is the densest phase?
f. At a pressure of 1.0×10^{-5} atm, can rhombic sulfur sublime?

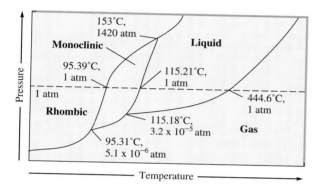

Additional Exercises

93. The nonpolar hydrocarbon $C_{25}H_{52}$ is a solid at room temperature. Its boiling point is greater than 400°C. Which has the stronger intermolecular forces, $C_{25}H_{52}$ or H_2O? Explain your answer.

94. Rationalize the differences in physical properties in terms of intermolecular forces for the following organic compounds. Compare the first three substances with each other, compare the last three with each other, and then compare all six. Can you account for any anomalies?

	bp (°C)	mp (°C)	ΔH_{vap} (kJ/mol)
Benzene, C_6H_6	80	6	33.9
Naphthalene, $C_{10}H_8$	218	80	51.5
Carbon tetrachloride	76	−23	31.8
Acetone, CH_3COCH_3	56	−95	31.8
Acetic acid, CH_3CO_2H	118	17	39.7
Benzoic acid, $C_6H_5CO_2H$	249	122	68.2

95. Many organic acids, such as acetic acid (CH_3CO_2H), whose structure is shown in Exercise 40, exist in the gas phase as hydrogen-bonded dimers (two molecule units). Draw a reasonable structure for such dimers.

96. Consider the following enthalpy changes:

$$F^- + HF \longrightarrow FHF^- \qquad \Delta H = -155 \text{ kJ/mol}$$
$$(CH_3)_2C{=}O + HF \longrightarrow (CH_3)_2C{=}O\text{---}HF$$
$$\Delta H = -46 \text{ kJ/mol}$$
$$H_2O(g) + HOH(g) \longrightarrow H_2O\text{---}HOH \text{ (in ice)}$$
$$\Delta H = -21 \text{ kJ/mol}$$

How do the strengths of hydrogen bonds vary with the electronegativity of the element to which hydrogen is bonded? Where in the preceding series would you expect hydrogen bonds of the following type to fall?

$$\overset{|}{N}\text{---}HO\text{---} \quad \text{and} \quad \overset{|}{N}\text{---}H\text{---}\overset{|}{N}$$

97. When a metal was exposed to X rays, it emitted X rays of a different wavelength. The emitted X rays were diffracted by a LiF crystal ($d = 201$ pm), and first-order diffraction ($n = 1$ in the Bragg equation) was detected at an angle of 34.68 degrees. Calculate the wavelength of the X ray emitted by the metal.

98. The radius of gold is 144 pm, and the density is 19.32 g/cm³. Does elemental gold have a face-centered cubic structure or a body-centered cubic structure?

99. How could you tell experimentally if TiO_2 is an ionic solid or a network solid?

100. Boron nitride (BN) exists in two forms. The first is a slippery solid formed from the reaction of BCl_3 with NH_3, followed by heating in an ammonia atmosphere at 750°C. Subjecting the first form of BN to a pressure of 85,000 atm at 1800°C produces a second form that is the second hardest substance known. Both forms of BN remain solids to 3000°C. Suggest structures for the two forms of BN.

101. A student was asked to calculate the final temperature of a mixture prepared by adding 20.0 g of ice, initially at −10.0°C, to 20.0 g of water, initially at 25°C. She assumed that all the heat lost in cooling the water would be used to warm the ice and concluded that the final temperature of the mixture would be 13°C. However, the correct answer is 0°C. What did the student neglect in her considerations? (See Exercise 87.)

102. A 20.0-g sample of ice at −10.0°C is mixed with 100.0 g of water at 80.0°C. Calculate the final temperature of the mixture assuming no heat loss to the surroundings. The heat capacities of $H_2O(s)$ and $H_2O(l)$ are 2.08 and 4.18 J/g·°C, respectively, and the enthalpy of fusion for ice is 6.02 kJ/mol.

103. In regions with dry climates, evaporative coolers are used to cool air. A typical electric air conditioner is rated at 1.00×10^4 Btu/h (1 Btu, or British thermal unit = amount of energy to raise the temperature of 1 lb of water by 1°F).

How much water must be evaporated each hour to dissipate as much heat as a typical electric air conditioner?

104. Use the accompanying phase diagram for carbon to answer the following questions.
   a. How many triple points are in the phase diagram?
   b. What phases can coexist at each triple point?
   c. What happens if graphite is subjected to very high pressures at room temperature?
   d. If we assume that the density increases with an increase in pressure, which is more dense, graphite or diamond?

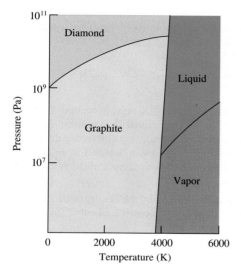

Challenge Problems

105. Using the heats of fusion and vaporization for water, calculate the change in enthalpy for the sublimation of water:

$$H_2O(s) \longrightarrow H_2O(g)$$

Using the ΔH value given in Exercise 96 and the number of hydrogen bonds formed with each water molecule, estimate what portion of the intermolecular forces in ice can be accounted for by hydrogen bonding.

106. Oil of wintergreen, or methyl salicylate, has the following structure:

mp = $-8°C$

Methyl-4-hydroxybenzoate is another molecule with exactly the same molecular formula; it has the following structure:

mp = $127°C$

Account for the large difference in the melting points of the two substances.

107. Consider the following melting point data:

Compound:	NaCl	MgCl₂	AlCl₃	SiCl₄	PCl₃	SCl₂	Cl₂
mp (°C):	801	708	190	−70	−91	−78	−101
Compound:	NaF	MgF₂	AlF₃	SiF₄	PF₅	SF₆	F₂
mp (°C):	997	1396	1040	−90	−94	−56	−220

Account for the trends in melting points in terms of interparticle forces.

108. Rubidium chloride has the sodium chloride structure at normal pressures but assumes the cesium chloride structure at high pressures (see Exercise 70). What ratio of densities is expected for these two forms? Does this change in structure make sense on the basis of simple models? The ionic radius of Rb^+ is 148 pm and the ionic radius of Cl^- is 181 pm.

109. Some ionic compounds contain a mixture of different charged cations. For example, some titanium oxides contain a mixture of Ti^{2+} and Ti^{3+} ions. Consider a certain oxide of titanium that is 28.31% oxygen by mass and contains a mixture of Ti^{2+} and Ti^{3+} ions. Determine the formula of the compound and the relative numbers of Ti^{2+} and Ti^{3+} ions.

110. Spinel is a mineral that contains 37.9% aluminum, 17.1% magnesium, and 45.0% oxygen, by mass, and has a density of 3.57 g/cm³. The edge of the cubic unit cell measures 809 pm. How many of each type of atom are present in the unit cell?

111. Mn crystallizes in the same type of cubic unit cell as Cu. Assuming that the radius of Mn is 5.6% larger than the radius of Cu and the density of copper is 8.96 g/cm³, calculate the density of Mn.

112. You are asked to help set up a historical display in the park by stacking some cannonballs next to a Revolutionary War cannon. You are told to stack them by starting with a triangle in which each side is composed of four touching cannonballs. You are to continue stacking them until you have a single ball on the top centered over the middle of the triangular base.
   a. How many cannonballs do you need?
   b. What type of closest packing is displayed by the cannonballs?

c. The four corners of the pyramid of cannonballs form the corners of what type of regular geometric solid?

113. Some water is placed in a sealed glass container connected to a vacuum pump (a device used to pump gases from a container), and the pump is turned on. The water appears to boil and then freezes. Explain these changes using the phase diagram for water. What would happen to the ice if the vacuum pump was left on indefinitely?

Marathon Problem

This problem is designed to incorporate several concepts and techniques into one situation. Marathon Problems can be used in class by groups of students to help facilitate problem-solving skills.

114. General Zod has sold Lex Luther what Zod claims to be a new copper-colored form of kryptonite, the only substance that can harm Superman. Lex, not believing in honor among thieves, decided to carry out some tests on the supposed kryptonite. From previous tests, Lex knew that kryptonite is a metal having a specific heat capacity of 0.082 J/g · °C and a density of 9.2 g/mL.

Lex Luther's first experiment was an attempt to find the specific heat capacity of kryptonite. He dropped a 10 g ± 3 g sample of the metal into a boiling water bath at a temperature of 100.0°C ± 0.2°C. He waited until the metal had reached the bath temperature and then quickly transferred it to 100 g ± 3 g of water that was contained in a calorimeter at an initial temperature of 25.0°C ± 0.2°C. The final temperature of the metal and water was 25.2°C. Based on these results, is it possible to distinguish between copper and kryptonite? Explain.

When Lex found that his results from the first experiment were inconclusive, he decided to determine the density of the sample. He managed to steal a better balance and determined the mass of another portion of the purported kryptonite to be 4 g ± 1 g. He dropped this sample into water contained in a 25-mL graduated cylinder and found that it displaced a volume of 0.42 mL ± 0.02 mL. Is the metal copper or kryptonite? Explain.

Lex was finally forced to determine the crystal structure of the metal General Zod had given him. He found that the cubic unit cell contained 4 atoms and had an edge length of 600. pm. Explain how this information enabled Lex to identify the metal as copper or kryptonite.

Will Lex be going after Superman with the kryptonite or seeking revenge on General Zod? What improvements could he have made in his experimental techniques to avoid performing the crystal structure determination?

CHAPTER 11

Properties of Solutions

Most of the substances we encounter in daily life are mixtures: Wood, milk, gasoline, champagne, seawater, shampoo, steel, and air are common examples. When the components of a mixture are uniformly intermingled—that is, when a mixture is homogeneous—it is called a *solution*. Solutions can be gases, liquids, or solids, as shown in Table 11.1. However, we will be concerned in this chapter with the properties of liquid solutions, particularly those containing water. As we saw in Chapter 4, many essential chemical reactions occur in aqueous solutions because water is capable of dissolving so many substances.

Table 11.1 Various Types of Solutions

Example	State of Solution	State of Solute	State of Solvent
Air, natural gas	Gas	Gas	Gas
Vodka in water, antifreeze	Liquid	Liquid	Liquid
Brass	Solid	Solid	Solid
Carbonated water (soda)	Liquid	Gas	Liquid
Seawater, sugar solution	Liquid	Solid	Liquid
Hydrogen in platinum	Solid	Gas	Solid

Opals are formed from colloidal suspensions of silica when the liquid evaporates.

11.1 Solution Composition

Because a mixture, unlike a chemical compound, has a variable composition, the relative amounts of substances in a solution must be specified. The qualitative terms *dilute* (relatively little solute present) and *concentrated* (relatively large amount of solute) are often used to describe solution content, but we need to define solution composition more precisely in order to perform calculations. For example, in dealing with the stoichiometry of solution reactions in Chapter 4, we found it useful to describe solution composition in terms of **molarity,** or the number of moles of solute per liter of solution (symbolized by M).

Other ways of describing solution composition are also useful. **Mass percent** (sometimes called *weight percent*) is the percent by mass of the solute in the solution:

$$\text{Mass percent} = \left(\frac{\text{mass of solute}}{\text{mass of solution}}\right) \times 100\%$$

Another way of describing solution composition is the **mole fraction** (symbolized by the Greek lowercase letter chi, X), the ratio of the number of moles of a given component to the total number of moles of solution. For a two-component solution, where n_A and n_B represent the number of moles of the two components,

$$\text{Mole fraction of component A} = X_A = \frac{n_A}{n_A + n_B}$$

Still another way of describing solution composition is **molality** (symbolized by m), the number of moles of solute per *kilogram of solvent:*

$$\text{Molality} = \frac{\text{moles of solute}}{\text{kilogram of solvent}}$$

A solute is the substance being dissolved. The solvent is the dissolving medium.

$$\text{Molarity} = \frac{\text{moles of solute}}{\text{liters of solution}}$$

When liquids are mixed, the liquid present in the largest amount is called the *solvent.*

In very dilute aqueous solutions, the magnitude of the molality and the molarity are almost the same.

Sample Exercise 11.1 *Various Methods for Describing Solution Composition*

A solution is prepared by mixing 1.00 g ethanol (C_2H_5OH) with 100.0 g water to give a final volume of 101 mL. Calculate the molarity, mass percent, mole fraction, and molality of ethanol in this solution.

Solution

Molarity: The moles of ethanol can be obtained from its molar mass (46.07 g/mol):

$$1.00 \text{ g } C_2H_5OH \times \frac{1 \text{ mol } C_2H_5OH}{46.07 \text{ g } C_2H_5OH} = 2.17 \times 10^{-2} \text{ mol } C_2H_5OH$$

$$\text{Volume} = 101 \text{ mL} \times \frac{1 \text{ L}}{1000 \text{ mL}} = 0.101 \text{ L}$$

Since molarity depends on the volume of the solution, it changes slightly with temperature. Molality is independent of temperature because it depends only on mass.

$$\text{Molarity of } C_2H_5OH = \frac{\text{moles of } C_2H_5OH}{\text{liters of solution}} = \frac{2.17 \times 10^{-2} \text{ mol}}{0.101 \text{ L}}$$
$$= 0.215 \ M$$

Mass percent:

$$\text{Mass percent } C_2H_5OH = \left(\frac{\text{mass of } C_2H_5OH}{\text{mass of solution}}\right) \times 100\%$$
$$= \left(\frac{1.00 \text{ g } C_2H_5OH}{100.0 \text{ g } H_2O + 1.00 \text{ g } C_2H_5OH}\right) \times 100\%$$
$$= 0.990\% \ C_2H_5OH$$

Mole fraction:

$$\text{Mole fraction of } C_2H_5OH = \frac{n_{C_2H_5OH}}{n_{C_2H_5OH} + n_{H_2O}}$$
$$n_{H_2O} = 100.0 \text{ g } H_2O \times \frac{1 \text{ mol } H_2O}{18.0 \text{ g } H_2O} = 5.56 \text{ mol}$$
$$\chi_{C_2H_5OH} = \frac{2.17 \times 10^{-2} \text{ mol}}{2.17 \times 10^{-2} \text{ mol} + 5.56 \text{ mol}}$$
$$= \frac{2.17 \times 10^{-2}}{5.58} = 0.00389$$

Molality:

$$\text{Molality of } C_2H_5OH = \frac{\text{moles of } C_2H_5OH}{\text{kilogram of } H_2O} = \frac{2.17 \times 10^{-2} \text{ mol}}{100.0 \text{ g} \times \frac{1 \text{ kg}}{1000 \text{ g}}}$$
$$= \frac{2.17 \times 10^{-2} \text{ mol}}{0.1000 \text{ kg}}$$
$$= 0.217 \ m$$

See Exercises 11.27 through 11.29.

Another concentration measure sometimes encountered is **normality** (symbolized by N). Normality is defined as the number of *equivalents* per liter of solution, where the definition of an equivalent depends on the reaction taking place in the solution. *For an acid–base reaction,* the equivalent is the mass of acid or base that can furnish or accept exactly 1 mole of protons (H^+ ions). In Table 11.2 note, for example, that the equivalent mass of sulfuric acid is the molar mass divided by 2, since each mole of H_2SO_4 can furnish 2 moles of protons. The equivalent mass of calcium hydroxide is also half the molar mass, since each mole of $Ca(OH)_2$ contains 2 moles of OH^- ions that can react with 2 moles of protons. Note that the equivalent is defined so that 1 equivalent of acid will react with exactly 1 equivalent of base.

For oxidation–reduction reactions, the equivalent is defined as the quantity of oxidizing or reducing agent that can accept or furnish 1 mole of electrons. Thus 1 equivalent of reducing agent will react with exactly 1 equivalent of oxidizing agent.

The definition of an equivalent depends on the reaction taking place in the solution.

The quantity we call *equivalent mass* here traditionally has been called *equivalent weight.*

Oxidation–reduction half-reactions were discussed in Section 4.10.

CHEMICAL IMPACT

Electronic Ink

THE PRINTED PAGE has been a primary means of communication for over 3000 years, and researchers at the Massachusetts Institute of Technology (MIT) believe they have discovered why. It seems that the brain responds positively to fixed images on a sheet of paper, particularly those areas of the brain that store and process "spatial maps." In comparison, information displayed on computer screens or TV screens seems to lack some of the visual signals that stimulate the learning centers of the brain to retain knowledge. While modern technology provides us with many other media by which we can communicate, the appeal of written words on a piece of paper remains. Surprisingly, the technology of printing has changed very little since the invention of the printing press—that is, until now.

In the past several years Joseph M. Jacobson and his students at MIT have developed a prototype of a self-printing page. The key to this self-printing "paper" is microencapsulation technology—the same technology that is used in "carbonless" carbon paper and "scratch-and-sniff" cologne and perfume advertisements in magazines. Jacobson's system involves the use of millions of transparent fluid-filled capsules containing microscopic particles. These particles are colored and positively charged on one side and white and negatively charged on the other. When an electric field is selectively applied to the capsules, the white side of the micro-particles can be oriented upward or the colored side can be caused to flip up. Appropriate application of an electric field can orient the particles in such a way as to produce words, and once the words have been created, virtually no more energy is needed to keep the particles in place. An image can be maintained on a page with consumption of only 50 millionths of an amp of power! The entire display is about 200 μm thick (2.5 times that of paper) and is so flexible and durable that it can be curled around a pencil and can operate at temperatures from −4 to 158°F. Presently, print resolution is not as good as a modern laser printer, but reduction of the microencapsulated particles from 50 to 40 μm should produce print that rivals the quality of the laser printer.

The first commercial applications of this technology will most likely appear in retail stores across the country before 2000 in the form of electronic signs that can be updated instantly from a central location. The present technology is a long way from being able to create electronic books, but this is the eventual goal of Jacobson's research team. It seems very likely that this electronic ink technology will contribute greatly to the evolution of the printed page over the next century.

The equivalent mass of an oxidizing or reducing agent can be calculated from the number of electrons in its half-reaction. For example, MnO_4^- reacting in acidic solution absorbs five electrons to produce Mn^{2+}:

$$MnO_4^- + 5e^- + 8H^+ \longrightarrow Mn^{2+} + 4H_2O$$

Table 11.2 The Molar Mass, Equivalent Mass, and Relationship of Molarity and Normality for Several Acids and Bases

Acid or Base	Molar Mass	Equivalent Mass	Relationship of Molarity and Normality
HCl	36.5	36.5	$1\,M = 1\,N$
H_2SO_4	98	$\dfrac{98}{2} = 49$	$1\,M = 2\,N$
NaOH	40	40	$1\,M = 1\,N$
$Ca(OH)_2$	74	$\dfrac{74}{2} = 37$	$1\,M = 2\,N$

Since the MnO_4^- ion present in 1 mole of $KMnO_4$ consumes 5 moles of electrons, the equivalent mass is the molar mass divided by 5:

$$\text{Equivalent mass of } KMnO_4 = \frac{\text{molar mass}}{5} = \frac{158 \text{ g}}{5} = 31.6 \text{ g}$$

Sample Exercise 11.2 *Calculating Various Methods of Solution Composition from the Molarity*

The electrolyte in automobile lead storage batteries is a 3.75 M sulfuric acid solution that has a density of 1.230 g/mL. Calculate the mass percent, molality, and normality of the sulfuric acid.

Solution

The density of the solution in grams per liter is

$$1.230 \frac{\text{g}}{\text{mL}} \times \frac{1000 \text{ mL}}{1 \text{ L}} = 1.230 \times 10^3 \text{ g/L}$$

Thus 1 liter of this solution contains 1230. g of the mixture of sulfuric acid and water. Since the solution is 3.75 M, we know that 3.75 mol H_2SO_4 is present per liter of solution. The number of grams of H_2SO_4 present is

$$3.75 \text{ mol} \times \frac{98.1 \text{ g } H_2SO_4}{1 \text{ mol}} = 368 \text{ g } H_2SO_4$$

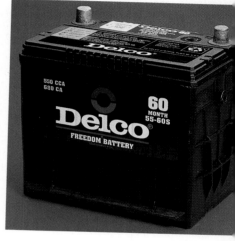

A modern 12-volt lead storage battery of the type used in automobiles.

The amount of water present in 1 liter of solution is obtained from the difference

$$1230. \text{ g solution} - 368 \text{ g } H_2SO_4 = 862 \text{ g } H_2O$$

$$862 \text{ g } H_2O \times \frac{1 \text{ mol } H_2O}{18.0 \text{ g } H_2O} = 47.9 \text{ mol } H_2O$$

Since we now know the masses of the solute and solvent, we can calculate the mass percent.

$$\text{Mass percent } H_2SO_4 = \frac{\text{mass of } H_2SO_4}{\text{mass of solution}} \times 100\% = \frac{368 \text{ g}}{1230. \text{ g}} \times 100\%$$

$$= 29.9\% \ H_2SO_4$$

From the moles of solute and the mass of solvent we can calculate the molality.

$$\text{Molality of } H_2SO_4 = \frac{\text{moles } H_2SO_4}{\text{kilogram of } H_2O}$$

$$= \frac{3.75 \text{ mol } H_2SO_4}{862 \text{ g } H_2O \times \frac{1 \text{ kg } H_2O}{1000 \text{ g } H_2O}} = 4.35 \ m$$

Since each sulfuric acid molecule can furnish two protons, 1 mol H_2SO_4 represents 2 equivalents. Thus a solution with 3.75 mol H_2SO_4 per liter contains $2 \times 3.75 = 7.50$ equivalents per liter, and the normality is 7.50 N.

See Exercise 11.33.

11.2 The Energies of Solution Formation

A brown pelican's egg in Everglades National Park, Florida. The presence of DDT in many birds causes their eggs' shells to become too thin.

Dissolving solutes in liquids is very common. We dissolve salt in the water used to cook vegetables, sugar in iced tea, stains in cleaning fluid, gaseous carbon dioxide in water to make soda water, ethanol in gasoline to make gasohol, and so on.

Solubility is important in other ways. For example, because the pesticide DDT is fat-soluble, it is retained and concentrated in animal tissues, where it causes detrimental effects. This is why DDT, even though it is effective for killing mosquitos, has been banned in the United States. Also, the solubility of various vitamins is important in determining correct dosages. The insolubility of barium sulfate means it can be used safely to improve X rays of the gastrointestinal tract, even though Ba^{2+} ions are quite toxic.

What factors affect solubility? The cardinal rule of solubility is *like dissolves like.* We find that we must use a polar solvent to dissolve a polar or ionic solute and a nonpolar solvent to dissolve a nonpolar solute. Now we will try to understand why this behavior occurs. To simplify the discussion, we will assume that the formation of a liquid solution takes place in three distinct steps.

Polar solvents dissolve polar solutes; nonpolar solvents dissolve nonpolar solutes.

STEP 1

Separating the solute into individual components of the solute (expanding the solute).

STEP 2

Overcoming intermolecular forces in the solvent to make room for the solute (expanding the solvent).

STEP 3

Allowing the solute and solvent to interact to form the solution.

These steps are illustrated in Fig. 11.1. Steps 1 and 2 require energy, since forces must be overcome to expand the solute and solvent. Step 3 usually releases energy. In other words, steps 1 and 2 are endothermic, and step 3 is often exothermic. The enthalpy change associated with the formation of the solution, called the **enthalpy (heat) of solution** (ΔH_{soln}), is the sum of the ΔH values for the steps:

The enthalpy of solution is the sum of the energies used in expanding both solvent and solute and the energy of solvent–solute interaction.

$$\Delta H_{soln} = \Delta H_1 + \Delta H_2 + \Delta H_3$$

where ΔH_{soln} may have a positive sign (energy absorbed) or a negative sign (energy released), as shown in Fig. 11.2.

To illustrate the importance of the various energy terms in the equation for ΔH_{soln}, we will consider two specific cases. First, we know that oil is not soluble in water. When oil tankers leak, the petroleum forms an oil slick that floats on the water and

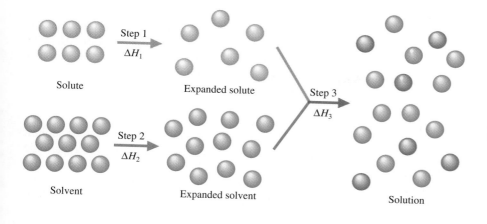

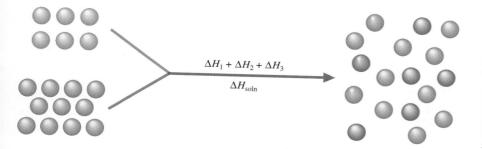

Animation: The Dissolution of a Solid in a Liquid

Figure 11.1

The formation of a liquid solution can be divided into three steps: (1) expanding the solute, (2) expanding the solvent, and (3) combining the expanded solute and solvent to form the solution.

is eventually carried onto the beaches. We can explain the immiscibility of oil and water by considering the energy terms involved. Oil is a mixture of nonpolar molecules that interact through London dispersion forces, which depend on molecule size. We expect ΔH_1 to be small for a typical nonpolar solute, but it will be relatively large for the large oil molecules. The term ΔH_3 will be small, since interactions between the nonpolar solute molecules and the polar water molecules will be

ΔH_1 is expected to be small for nonpolar solutes but can be large for large molecules.

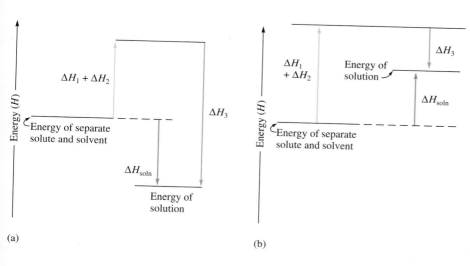

Figure 11.2

The heat of solution (a) ΔH_{soln} has a negative sign (the process is exothermic) if step 3 releases more energy than that required by steps 1 and 2. (b) ΔH_{soln} has a positive sign (the process is endothermic) if steps 1 and 2 require more energy than is released in step 3. (If the energy changes for steps 1 and 2 equal that for step 3, then ΔH_{soln} is zero.)

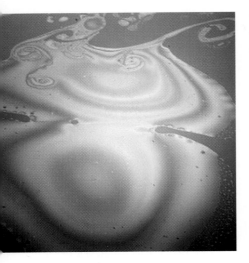

Gasoline floating on water. Because gasoline is nonpolar, it is immiscible with water.

Molecular Models: H₂O, NaCl

negligible. However, ΔH_2 will be large and positive because it takes considerable energy to overcome the hydrogen bonding forces among the water molecules to expand the solvent. Thus ΔH_{soln} will be large and positive because of the ΔH_1 and ΔH_2 terms. Since a large amount of energy would have to be expended to form an oil–water solution, this process does not occur to any appreciable extent. These same arguments hold true for any nonpolar solute and polar solvent—the combination of a nonpolar solute and a highly polar solvent is not expected to produce a solution.

As a second case, let's consider the solubility of an ionic solute, such as sodium chloride, in water. Here the term ΔH_1 is large and positive because the strong ionic forces in the crystal must be overcome, and ΔH_2 is large and positive because hydrogen bonds must be broken in the water. Finally, ΔH_3 is large and negative because of the strong interactions between the ions and the water molecules. In fact, the exothermic and endothermic terms essentially cancel, as shown from the known values:

$$NaCl(s) \longrightarrow Na^+(g) + Cl^-(g) \qquad \Delta H_1 = 786 \text{ kJ/mol}$$
$$H_2O(l) + Na^+(g) + Cl^-(g) \longrightarrow Na^+(aq) + Cl^-(aq) \qquad \begin{aligned} \Delta H_{hyd} &= \Delta H_2 + \Delta H_3 \\ &= -783 \text{ kJ/mol} \end{aligned}$$

Here the **enthalpy (heat) of hydration** (ΔH_{hyd}) combines the terms ΔH_2 (for expanding the solvent) and ΔH_3 (for solvent–solute interactions). The heat of hydration represents the enthalpy change associated with the dispersal of a gaseous solute in water. Thus the heat of solution for dissolving sodium chloride is the sum of ΔH_1 and ΔH_{hyd}:

$$\Delta H_{soln} = 786 \text{ kJ/mol} - 783 \text{ kJ/mol} = 3 \text{ kJ/mol}$$

Note that ΔH_{soln} is small but positive; the dissolving process requires a small amount of energy. Then why is NaCl so soluble in water? The answer lies in nature's tendency toward disorder. That is, processes naturally run in the direction that leads to greater disorder. For example, imagine equal numbers of orange and yellow spheres separated by a partition, as shown in Fig. 11.3(a). If we remove the partition and shake the container, the spheres will mix [Fig. 11.3(b)], and no amount

Figure 11.3

(a) Orange and yellow spheres separated by a partition in a closed container. (b) The spheres after the partition is removed and the container has been shaken for some time.

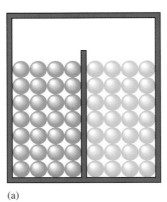

(a)

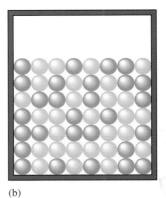

(b)

Table 11.3 The Energy Terms for Various Types of Solutes and Solvents

	ΔH_1	ΔH_2	ΔH_3	ΔH_{soln}	Outcome
Polar solvent, polar solute	Large	Large	Large, negative	Small	Solution forms
Polar solvent, nonpolar solute	Small	Large	Small	Large, positive	No solution forms
Nonpolar solvent, nonpolar solute	Small	Small	Small	Small	Solution forms
Nonpolar solvent, polar solute	Large	Small	Small	Large, positive	No solution forms

of shaking will cause them to return to the state of separated orange and yellow. Why? The mixed, or disordered, state is simply much more likely to occur (more probable) than the original separate, or ordered, state because there are many more ways of placing the spheres to give a mixed state than a separated state. This is a general principle. *One factor that favors a process is an increase in disorder.*

But energy considerations are also important. *Processes that require large amounts of energy tend not to occur.* Since dissolving 1 mole of solid NaCl requires only a small amount of energy, the solution forms, presumably because of the large increase in disorder occurring when the solute and solvent mix.

The various possible cases for solution formation are summarized in Table 11.3. Note that in two cases, polar–polar and nonpolar–nonpolar, the heat of solution is expected to be small. In these cases, the solution forms because of the increase in disorder. In the other cases (polar–nonpolar and nonpolar–polar), the heat of solution is expected to be large and positive, and the large quantity of energy required acts to prevent the solution from forming. Although this discussion has greatly oversimplified the complex driving forces for solubility, these ideas are a useful starting point for understanding the observation that *like dissolves like.*

The factors that act as driving forces for a process are discussed more fully in Chapter 16.

Sample Exercise 11.3 Differentiating Solvent Properties

Decide whether liquid hexane (C_6H_{14}) or liquid methanol (CH_3OH) is the more appropriate solvent for the substances grease ($C_{20}H_{42}$) and potassium iodide (KI).

Molecular Models: C_6H_{14}, CH_3OH, $C_{20}H_{42}$

Solution

Hexane is a nonpolar solvent because it contains C—H bonds. Thus hexane will work best for the nonpolar solute grease. Methanol has an O—H group that makes it significantly polar. Thus it will serve as the better solvent for the ionic solid KI.

See Exercises 11.39 through 11.42.

11.3 Factors Affecting Solubility

Structure Effects

In the last section we saw that solubility is favored if the solute and solvent have similar polarities. Since it is the molecular structure that determines polarity, there should be a definite connection between structure and solubility. Vitamins provide an excellent example of the relationship among molecular structure, polarity, and solubility.

Recently, there has been considerable publicity about the pros and cons of consuming large quantities of vitamins. For example, large doses of vitamin C have been advocated to combat various illnesses, including the common cold. Vitamin E has been extolled as a youth-preserving elixir and a protector against the carcinogenic (cancer-causing) effects of certain chemicals. However, there are possible detrimental effects from taking large amounts of some vitamins, depending on their solubilities.

Molecular Models: vitamins A and C

Vitamins can be divided into two classes: *fat-soluble* (vitamins A, D, E, and K) and *water-soluble* (vitamins B and C). The reason for the differing solubility characteristics can be seen by comparing the structures of vitamins A and C (Fig. 11.4). Vitamin A, composed mostly of carbon and hydrogen atoms that have similar electronegativities, is virtually nonpolar. This causes it to be soluble in nonpolar materials such as body fat, which is also largely composed of carbon and hydrogen, but not soluble in polar solvents such as water. On the other hand, vitamin C has many polar O—H and C—O bonds, making the molecule polar and thus water-soluble.

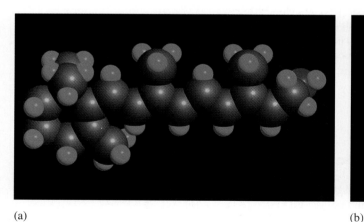

(a)

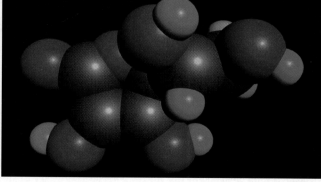

(b)

Figure 11.4

The molecular structures of (a) vitamin A (nonpolar, fat-soluble) and (b) vitamin C (polar, water-soluble). (c) The circles indicate polar bonds. Note that vitamin C contains far more polar bonds than vitamin A.

(c)

We often describe nonpolar materials such as vitamin A as *hydrophobic* (water-fearing) and polar substances such as vitamin C as *hydrophilic* (water-loving).

Because of their solubility characteristics, the fat-soluble vitamins can build up in the fatty tissues of the body. This has both positive and negative effects. Since these vitamins can be stored, the body can tolerate for a time a diet deficient in vitamins A, D, E, or K. Conversely, if excessive amounts of these vitamins are consumed, their buildup can lead to the illness *hypervitaminosis*.

In contrast, the water-soluble vitamins are excreted by the body and must be consumed regularly. This fact was first recognized when the British navy discovered that scurvy, a disease often suffered by sailors, could be prevented if the sailors regularly ate fresh limes (which are a good source of vitamin C) when aboard ship (hence the name "limey" for the British sailor).

Pressure Effects

While pressure has little effect on the solubilities of solids or liquids, it does significantly increase the solubility of a gas. Carbonated beverages, for example, are always bottled at high pressures of carbon dioxide to ensure a high concentration of carbon dioxide in the liquid. The fizzing that occurs when you open a can of soda results from the escape of gaseous carbon dioxide because under these conditions the pressure of CO_2 above the solution is now much lower than that used in the bottling process.

The increase in gas solubility with pressure can be understood from Fig. 11.5. Figure 11.5(a) shows a gas in equilibrium with a solution; that is, the gas molecules are entering and leaving the solution at the same rate. If the pressure is suddenly increased [Fig. 11.5(b)], the number of gas molecules per unit volume increases, and the gas enters the solution at a higher rate than it leaves. As the concentration of dissolved gas increases, the rate of the escape of the gas also increases until a new equilibrium is reached [Fig. 11.5(c)], where the solution contains more dissolved gas than before.

Carbonation in a bottle of soda.

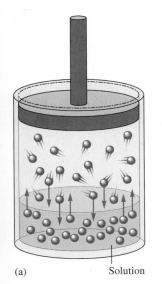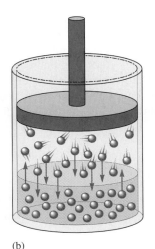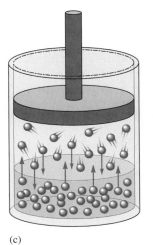

(a)   Solution   (b)   (c)

Figure 11.5

(a) A gaseous solute in equilibrium with a solution. (b) The piston is pushed in, which increases the pressure of the gas and the number of gas molecules per unit volume. This causes an increase in the rate at which the gas enters the solution, so the concentration of dissolved gas increases. (c) The greater gas concentration in the solution causes an increase in the rate of escape. A new equilibrium is reached.

CHEMICAL IMPACT

Hydrogen Beer

ONE OF THE most bizarre products to come along in years is a Japanese beer that has hydrogen gas dissolved in it. The novel beverage produced by the Asaka Beer Corporation contains a mixture of carbon dioxide and hydrogen. Reports indicate that the beer bottle caps have safety valves to relieve excess pressure and the beer is packed in concrete-lined crates for shipping to guard against explosions.

Why would anyone buy beer with hydrogen gas dissolved in it? Apparently it is used by singers in karaoke bars to help them hit high notes. Due to its low molar mass, when hydrogen is breathed, it causes the voice to be raised to a higher pitch because of the low density of the gas surrounding the vocal cords. A similar effect occurs when deep sea divers use a helium–oxygen mixture in their "air" tanks. A very dangerous offshoot of the hydrogen beer craze in Japan is the trick of blowing flames from the mouth using a cigarette as an ignition source. Asaka says it will not market the beer in the United States "due to legal complications."

The relationship between gas pressure and the concentration of dissolved gas is given by **Henry's law:**

$$P = kC$$

William Henry (1774–1836), a close friend of John Dalton, formulated his law in 1801.

where P represents the partial pressure of the gaseous solute above the solution, C represents the concentration of the dissolved gas, and k is a constant characteristic of a particular solution. In words, Henry's law states that *the amount of a gas dissolved in a solution is directly proportional to the pressure of the gas above the solution.*

Henry's law is obeyed most accurately for dilute solutions of gases that do not dissociate in or react with the solvent. For example, Henry's law is obeyed by oxygen gas in water, but it does *not* correctly represent the behavior of gaseous hydrogen chloride in water because of the dissociation reaction

Henry's law holds only when there is no chemical reaction between the solute and solvent.

$$HCl(g) \xrightarrow{H_2O} H^+(aq) + Cl^-(aq)$$

Sample Exercise 11.4 Calculations Using Henry's Law

A certain soft drink is bottled so that a bottle at 25°C contains CO_2 gas at a pressure of 5.0 atm over the liquid. Assuming that the partial pressure of CO_2 in the atmosphere is 4.0×10^{-4} atm, calculate the equilibrium concentrations of CO_2 in the soda both before and after the bottle is opened. The Henry's law constant for CO_2 in aqueous solution is 32 L · atm/mol at 25°C.

Solution

We can write Henry's law for CO_2 as

$$P_{CO_2} = k_{CO_2} C_{CO_2}$$

where $k_{CO_2} = 32$ L · atm/mol. In the *unopened* bottle, $P_{CO_2} = 5.0$ atm and

$$C_{CO_2} = \frac{P_{CO_2}}{k_{CO_2}} = \frac{5.0 \text{ atm}}{32 \text{ L} \cdot \text{atm/mol}} = 0.16 \text{ mol/L}$$

In the *opened* bottle, the CO_2 in the soda eventually reaches equilibrium with the atmospheric CO_2, so $P_{CO_2} = 4.0 \times 10^{-4}$ atm and

$$C_{CO_2} = \frac{P_{CO_2}}{k_{CO_2}} = \frac{4.0 \times 10^{-4} \text{ atm}}{32 \text{ L} \cdot \text{atm/mol}} = 1.2 \times 10^{-5} \text{ mol/L}$$

Note the large change in concentration of CO_2. This is why soda goes "flat" after being open for a while.

See Exercises 11.45 and 11.46.

Temperature Effects (for Aqueous Solutions)

Everyday experiences of dissolving substances such as sugar may lead you to think that solubility always increases with temperature. This is not the case. The dissolving of a solid occurs *more rapidly* at higher temperatures, but the amount of solid that can be dissolved may increase or decrease with increasing temperature. The effect of temperature on the solubility in water of several solids is shown in Fig. 11.6. Note that although the solubility of most solids in water increases with temperature, the solubilities of some substances (such as sodium sulfate and cerium sulfate) decrease with increasing temperature.

Predicting the temperature dependence of solubility is very difficult. For example, although there is some correlation between the sign of ΔH°_{soln} and the variation of solubility with temperature, important exceptions exist.* The only sure way to determine the temperature dependence of a solid's solubility is by experiment.

ΔH°_{soln} refers to the formation of a 1.0 M ideal solution and is not necessarily relevant to the process of dissolving a solid in a saturated solution. Thus ΔH°_{soln} is of limited use in predicting the variation of solubility with temperature.

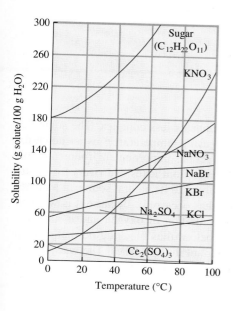

Figure 11.6

The solubilities of several solids as a function of temperature. Note that while most substances become more soluble in water with increasing temperature, sodium sulfate and cerium sulfate become less soluble.

* For more information see R. S. Treptow, "Le Châtelier's Principle Applied to the Temperature Dependence of Solubility," *J. Chem. Ed.* **61** (1984): 499.

CHEMICAL IMPACT

The Lake Nyos Tragedy

Lake Nyos in Cameroon.

ON AUGUST 21, 1986, a cloud of gas suddenly boiled from Lake Nyos in Cameroon, killing nearly 2000 people. Although at first it was speculated that the gas was hydrogen sulfide, it now seems clear it was carbon dioxide. What would cause Lake Nyos to emit this huge, suffocating cloud of CO_2? Although the answer may never be known for certain, many scientists believe that the lake suddenly "turned over," bringing to the surface water that contained huge quantities of dissolved carbon dioxide. Lake Nyos is a deep lake that is thermally stratified: Layers of warm, less dense water near the surface float on the colder, denser water layers near the lake's bottom. Under normal conditions the lake stays this way; there is little mixing among the different layers. Scientists believe that over hundreds or thousands of years, carbon dioxide gas had seeped into the cold water at the lake's bottom and dissolved in great amounts because of the large pressure of CO_2 present (in accordance with Henry's law). For some reason on August 21, 1986, the lake apparently suffered an overturn, possibly due to wind or to unusual cooling of the lake's surface by monsoon clouds. This caused water that was greatly supersaturated with CO_2 to reach the surface and release tremendous quantities of gaseous CO_2 that suffocated thousands of humans and animals before they knew what hit them—a tragic, monumental illustration of Henry's law.

Since 1986 the scientists studying Lake Nyos and nearby Lake Monoun have observed a rapid recharging of the CO_2 levels in the deep waters of these lakes, causing concern that another deadly gas release could occur at any time. Apparently the only way to prevent such a disaster is to pump away the CO_2-charged deep water in the two lakes. Scientists at a conference to study this problem in 1994 recommended such a solution, but it has not yet been funded by Cameroon.

The behavior of gases dissolving in water appears less complex. The solubility of a gas in water typically decreases with increasing temperature,* as is shown for several cases in Fig. 11.7. This temperature effect has important environmental implications because of the widespread use of water from lakes and rivers for industrial cooling. After being used, the water is returned to its natural source at a higher than ambient temperature (**thermal pollution** has occurred). Because it is warmer, this water contains less than the normal concentration of oxygen and is also less dense; it tends to "float" on the colder water below, thus blocking normal oxygen absorption. This effect can be especially important in deep lakes. The warm upper layer can seriously decrease the amount of oxygen available to aquatic life in the deeper layers of the lake.

* The opposite behavior is observed for most nonaqueous solvents.

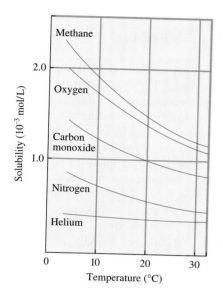

Figure 11.7

The solubilities of several gases in water as a function of temperature at a constant pressure of 1 atm of gas above the solution.

The decreasing solubility of gases with increasing temperature is also responsible for the formation of *boiler scale*. As we will see in more detail in Chapter 14, the bicarbonate ion is formed when carbon dioxide is dissolved in water containing the carbonate ion:

$$CO_3^{2-}(aq) + CO_2(aq) + H_2O(l) \longrightarrow 2HCO_3^-(aq)$$

When the water also contains Ca^{2+} ions, this reaction is especially important—calcium bicarbonate is soluble in water, but calcium carbonate is insoluble. When the water is heated, the carbon dioxide is driven off. In order for the system to replace the lost carbon dioxide, the reverse reaction occurs:

$$2HCO_3^-(aq) \longrightarrow H_2O(l) + CO_2(aq) + CO_3^{2-}(aq)$$

This reaction, however, also increases the concentration of carbonate ions, causing solid calcium carbonate to form. This solid is the boiler scale that coats the walls of containers such as industrial boilers and tea kettles. Boiler scale reduces the efficiency of heat transfer and can lead to blockage of pipes (see Fig. 11.8).

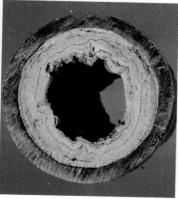

Figure 11.8

A pipe with accumulated mineral deposits. The lengthwise section (left) shows the formation of scale. The cross section (right) clearly indicates the reduction in pipe capacity.

11.4 *The Vapor Pressures of Solutions*

Liquid solutions have physical properties significantly different from those of the pure solvent, a fact that has great practical importance. For example, we add antifreeze to the water in a car's cooling system to prevent freezing in winter and boiling in summer. We also melt ice on sidewalks and streets by spreading salt. These preventatives work because of the solute's effect on the solvent's properties.

A nonvolatile solute has no tendency to escape from solution into the vapor phase.

To explore how a nonvolatile solute affects a solvent, we will consider the experiment represented in Fig. 11.9, in which a sealed container encloses a beaker containing an aqueous sulfuric acid solution and a beaker containing pure water. Gradually, the volume of the sulfuric acid solution increases and the volume of the pure water decreases. Why? We can explain this observation if the vapor pressure of the pure solvent is greater than that of the solution. Under these conditions, the pressure of vapor necessary to achieve equilibrium with the pure solvent is greater than that required to reach equilibrium with the aqueous acid solution. Thus, as the pure solvent emits vapor to attempt to reach equilibrium, the aqueous sulfuric acid solution absorbs vapor to try to lower the vapor pressure toward its equilibrium value. This process results in a net transfer of water from the pure water through the vapor phase to the sulfuric acid solution. The system can only reach an equilibrium vapor pressure when all the water is transferred to the solution. This experiment is just one of many observations indicating that the presence of a *nonvolatile solute lowers the vapor pressure of a solvent.*

The process described here is quite slow, taking several weeks to complete.

The presence of a nonvolatile solute reduces the tendency of solvent molecules to escape.

We can account for this behavior in terms of the simple model shown in Fig. 11.10. The dissolved nonvolatile solute decreases the number of solvent molecules per unit volume. Thus it lowers the number of solvent molecules at the surface, and it should proportionately lower the escaping tendency of the solvent molecules. For example, in a solution consisting of half nonvolatile solute molecules and half solvent molecules, we might expect the observed vapor pressure to be half that of the pure solvent, since only half as many molecules can escape. In fact, this is what is observed.

Figure 11.9

An aqueous solution and pure water in a closed environment. (a) Initial stage. (b) After a period of time, the water is transferred to the solution.

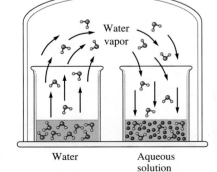

(a)

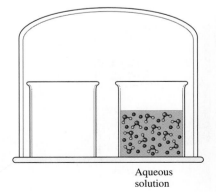

(b)

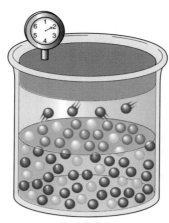

Pure solvent

Solution with a
nonvolatile solute

Figure 11.10
The presence of a nonvolatile
solute inhibits the escape of solvent molecules from the liquid
and so lowers the vapor pressure
of the solvent.

Detailed studies of the vapor pressures of solutions containing nonvolatile solutes were carried out by François M. Raoult (1830–1901). His results are described by the equation known as **Raoult's law:**

$$P_{soln} = \chi_{solvent}P^0_{solvent}$$

where P_{soln} is the observed vapor pressure of the solution, $\chi_{solvent}$ is the mole fraction of solvent, and $P^0_{solvent}$ is the vapor pressure of the pure solvent. Note that for a solution of half solute and half solvent molecules, $\chi_{solvent}$ is 0.5, so the vapor pressure of the solution is half that of the pure solvent. On the other hand, for a solution in which three-fourths of the solution molecules are solvent, $\chi_{solvent} = \frac{3}{4} = 0.75$, and $P_{soln} = 0.75P^0_{solvent}$. The idea is that the nonvolatile solute simply dilutes the solvent.

Raoult's law is a linear equation of the form $y = mx + b$, where $y = P_{soln}$, $x = \chi_{solvent}$, $m = P^0_{solvent}$, and $b = 0$. Thus a plot of P_{soln} versus $\chi_{solvent}$ gives a straight line with a slope equal to $P^0_{solvent}$, as shown in Fig. 11.11.

Raoult's law states that the vapor pressure of a solution is directly proportional to the mole fraction of solvent present.

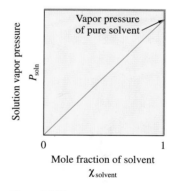

Figure 11.11
For a solution that obeys Raoult's law, a plot of P_{soln} versus $\chi_{solvent}$ gives a straight line.

Sample Exercise 11.5 Calculating the Vapor Pressure of a Solution

Calculate the expected vapor pressure at 25°C for a solution prepared by dissolving 158.0 g of common table sugar (sucrose, molar mass = 342.3 g/mol) in 643.5 cm³ of water. At 25°C, the density of water is 0.9971 g/cm³ and the vapor pressure is 23.76 torr.

Solution

We will use Raoult's law in the form

$$P_{soln} = \chi_{H_2O}P^0_{H_2O}$$

To calculate the mole fraction of water in the solution, we must first determine the number of moles of sucrose:

$$\text{Moles of sucrose} = 158.0 \text{ g sucrose} \times \frac{1 \text{ mol sucrose}}{342.3 \text{ g sucrose}}$$

$$= 0.4616 \text{ mol sucrose}$$

To determine the moles of water present, we first convert volume to mass using the density:

$$643.5 \text{ cm}^3 \text{ H}_2\text{O} \times \frac{0.9971 \text{ g H}_2\text{O}}{\text{cm}^3 \text{ H}_2\text{O}} = 641.6 \text{ g H}_2\text{O}$$

The number of moles of water is therefore

$$641.6 \text{ g H}_2\text{O} \times \frac{1 \text{ mol H}_2\text{O}}{18.01 \text{ g H}_2\text{O}} = 35.63 \text{ mol H}_2\text{O}$$

The mole fraction of water in the solution is

$$\chi_{\text{H}_2\text{O}} = \frac{\text{mol H}_2\text{O}}{\text{mol H}_2\text{O} + \text{mol sucrose}} = \frac{35.63 \text{ mol}}{35.63 \text{ mol} + 0.4616 \text{ mol}}$$

$$= \frac{35.63 \text{ mol}}{36.09 \text{ mol}} = 0.9873$$

Then $\quad\quad P_{\text{soln}} = \chi_{\text{H}_2\text{O}} P^0_{\text{H}_2\text{O}} = (0.9873)(23.76 \text{ torr}) = 23.46 \text{ torr}$

Thus the vapor pressure of water has been lowered from 23.76 torr in the pure state to 23.46 torr in the solution. The vapor pressure has been lowered by 0.30 torr.

See Exercises 11.47 and 11.48.

The lowering of vapor pressure depends on the number of solute particles present in the solution.

The phenomenon of the lowering of the vapor pressure gives us a convenient way to "count" molecules and thus provides a means for experimentally determining molar masses. Suppose a certain mass of a compound is dissolved in a solvent and the vapor pressure of the resulting solution is measured. Using Raoult's law, we can determine the number of moles of solute present. Since the mass of this number of moles is known, we can calculate the molar mass.

We also can use vapor pressure measurements to characterize solutions. For example, 1 mole of sodium chloride dissolved in water lowers the vapor pressure approximately twice as much as expected because the solid has two ions per formula unit, which separate when it dissolves. Thus vapor pressure measurements can give valuable information about the nature of the solute after it dissolves.

CHEMICAL IMPACT

Spray Power

PRODUCTS IN AEROSOL cans are widely used in our society. We use hairsprays, mouth sprays, shaving cream, whipped cream, spray paint, spray cleaners, and many others. As in the case of most consumer products, chemistry plays an important role in making aerosol products work.

An aerosol is a mixture of small particles (solids or liquids) dispersed in some sort of medium (a gas or a liquid). An inspection of the ingredients in an aerosol can reveals a long list of chemical substances, all of which fall into one of three categories: (1) an active ingredient, (2) an inactive ingredient, or (3) a propellant. The active ingredients perform the functions for which the product was purchased (for example, the resins in hairspray). It is very important that the contents of an aerosol can are chemically compatible. If an undesired chemical reaction were to occur inside the can, it is likely that the product would be unable to perform its function. The inactive ingredients serve to keep the product properly mixed and prevent chemical reactions within the can prior to application. The propellant delivers the product out of the can.

Most aerosol products contain liquefied hydrocarbon propellants* such as propane (C_5H_{12}) and butane (C_4H_{10}). While these molecules are extremely flammable, they are excellent propellants, and they also help to disperse and mix the components of the aerosol can as they are delivered. These propellants have critical temperatures above room temperature, which means that the intermolecular forces among their molecules are strong enough to form a liquid when pressure is applied. In the highly pressurized aerosol can, the liquid phase of

Insecticide is sprayed from an aerosol can.

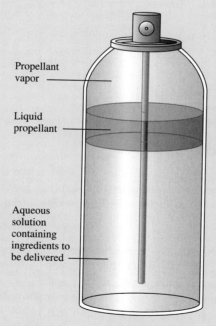

An aerosol can for delivery of an active ingredient dissolved in an aqueous solution.

the propellant is in equilibrium with the gaseous phase of the propellant in the head space of the can. The ability of the propellant to maintain this equilibrium is the key to how the aerosol can works. All aerosol cans are constructed in a similar way (see accompanying diagram). At the top of the can is a valve (acts to open and seal the can) and an actuator (to open the valve). Pushing the actuator opens the valve, and the propellant gas escapes through a long tube (the dip tube) that extends from the bottom of the can. With the valve open, the propellant, at a greater pressure than the atmosphere, escapes through the dip tube, carrying the active ingredient(s) with it. The rapidly expanding gas propels the contents from the can and in some instances (for example, shaving cream, carpet shampoo, etc.) produces a foam. After each use, the remaining propellant in the can reestablishes equilibrium between the liquid and gaseous phases, keeping the pressure constant within the can as long as sufficient propellant remains. The trick is to have the active and inactive ingredients and the propellant run out at the same time. Given the nature of the most common propellants, you can understand the warning about not putting the "empty" cans in a fire.

*For foods delivered by aerosol cans, propane and butane are obviously not appropriate propellants. For substances such as whipped cream, the propellant N_2O is often used.

Propellant vapor

Liquid propellant

Aqueous solution containing ingredients to be delivered

Sample Exercise 11.6 Calculating the Vapor Pressure of a Solution Containing Ionic Solute

Predict the vapor pressure of a solution prepared by mixing 35.0 g solid Na_2SO_4 (molar mass = 142 g/mol) with 175 g water at 25°C. The vapor pressure of pure water at 25°C is 23.76 torr.

Solution

First, we need to know the mole fraction of H_2O.

$$n_{H_2O} = 175 \text{ g } H_2O \times \frac{1 \text{ mol } H_2O}{18.0 \text{ g } H_2O} = 9.72 \text{ mol } H_2O$$

$$n_{Na_2SO_4} = 35.0 \text{ g } Na_2SO_4 \times \frac{1 \text{ mol } Na_2SO_4}{142 \text{ g } Na_2SO_4} = 0.246 \text{ mol } Na_2SO_4$$

It is essential to recognize that when 1 mole of solid Na_2SO_4 dissolves, it produces 2 mol Na^+ ions and 1 mol SO_4^{2-} ions. Thus the number of solute particles present in this solution is three times the number of moles of solute dissolved:

$$n_{solute} = 3(0.246) = 0.738 \text{ mol}$$

$$\chi_{H_2O} = \frac{n_{H_2O}}{n_{solute} + n_{H_2O}} = \frac{9.72 \text{ mol}}{0.738 \text{ mol} + 9.72 \text{ mol}} = \frac{9.72 \text{ mol}}{10.458} = 0.929$$

Now we can use Raoult's law to predict the vapor pressure:

$$P_{soln} = \chi_{H_2O}P^0_{H_2O} = (0.929)(23.76 \text{ torr}) = 22.1 \text{ torr}$$

See Exercise 11.50.

Nonideal Solutions

So far we have assumed that the solute is nonvolatile and so does not contribute to the vapor pressure over the solution. However, for liquid–liquid solutions where both components are volatile, a modified form of Raoult's law applies:

$$P_{TOTAL} = P_A + P_B = \chi_A P^0_A + \chi_B P^0_B$$

where P_{TOTAL} represents the total vapor pressure of a solution containing A and B, χ_A and χ_B are the mole fractions of A and B, P^0_A and P^0_B are the vapor pressures of pure A and pure B, and P_A and P_B are the partial pressures resulting from molecules of A and of B in the vapor above the solution (see Fig. 11.12).

A liquid–liquid solution that obeys Raoult's law is called an **ideal solution.** Raoult's law is to solutions what the ideal gas law is to gases. As with gases, ideal behavior for solutions is never perfectly achieved but is sometimes closely approached. Nearly ideal behavior is often observed when the solute–solute, solvent–solvent, and solute–solvent interactions are very similar. That is, in solutions where the solute and solvent are very much alike, the solute simply acts to dilute the solvent. However, if the solvent has a special affinity for the solute, such as if hydrogen bonding occurs, the tendency of the solvent molecules to escape will be

Strong solute–solvent interaction gives a vapor pressure lower than that predicted by Raoult's law.

Figure 11.12

When a solution contains two volatile components, both contribute to the total vapor pressure. Note that in this case the solution contains equal numbers of the components ○ and ○ but the vapor contains more ○ than ○. This means that component ○ is more volatile (has a higher vapor pressure as a pure liquid) than component ○

lowered more than expected. The observed vapor pressure will be *lower* than the value predicted by Raoult's law; there will be a *negative deviation from Raoult's law.*

When a solute and solvent release large quantities of energy in the formation of a solution, that is, when ΔH_{soln} is large and negative, we can assume that strong interactions exist between the solute and solvent. In this case we expect a negative deviation from Raoult's law, because both components will have a lower escaping tendency in the solution than in the pure liquids. This behavior is illustrated by an acetone–water solution, where the molecules can hydrogen bond effectively:

$$CH_3 \overset{\displaystyle CH_3}{\underset{\displaystyle CH_3}{\diagdown}} C=O\text{---}H-O \overset{\displaystyle H}{\diagup}$$
$$\delta- \quad \delta+$$

Molecular Models: acetone, C_2H_5OH, C_6H_{14}

In contrast, if two liquids mix endothermically, this indicates that the solute–solvent interactions are weaker than the interactions among the molecules in the pure liquids. More energy is required to expand the liquids than is released when the liquids are mixed. In this case the molecules in the solution have a higher tendency to escape than expected, and *positive* deviations from Raoult's law are observed (see Fig. 11.13). An example of this case is provided by a solution of ethanol and hexane, whose Lewis structures are as follows:

$$\begin{array}{cc} \overset{H}{\underset{H}{\overset{|}{\underset{|}{C}}}}\overset{H}{\underset{H}{\overset{|}{\underset{|}{C}}}} & \\ H-C-C-\overset{..}{\underset{..}{O}}-H \qquad & H-C-C-C-C-C-C-H \end{array}$$

Ethanol   Hexane

The polar ethanol and the nonpolar hexane molecules are not able to interact effectively. Thus the enthalpy of solution is positive, as is the deviation from Raoult's law.

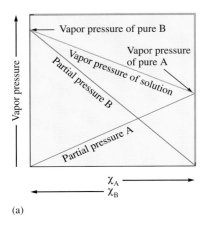

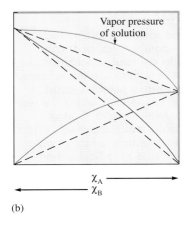

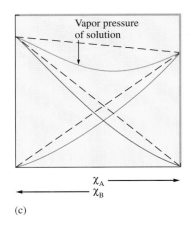

(a)

(b)

(c)

Figure 11.13

Vapor pressure for a solution of two volatile liquids. (a) The behavior predicted for an ideal liquid–liquid solution by Raoult's law. (b) A solution for which P_{TOTAL} is larger than the value calculated from Raoult's law. This solution shows a positive deviation from Raoult's law. (c) A solution for which P_{TOTAL} is smaller than the value calculated from Raoult's law. This solution shows a negative deviation from Raoult's law.

Molecular Models: C_6H_6, $C_6H_5CH_3$

Finally, for a solution of very similar liquids, such as benzene and toluene,

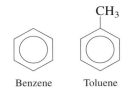

Benzene   Toluene

the enthalpy of solution is very close to zero, and thus the solution closely obeys Raoult's law (ideal behavior).

A summary of the behavior of various types of solutions is given in Table 11.4.

Table 11.4 Summary of the Behavior of Various Types of Solutions

Interactive Forces Between Solute (A) and Solvent (B) Particles	ΔH_{soln}	ΔT for Solution Formation	Deviation from Raoult's Law	Example
A ↔ A, B ↔ B ≡ A ↔ B	Zero	Zero	None (ideal solution)	Benzene–toluene
A ↔ A, B ↔ B < A ↔ B	Negative (exothermic)	Positive	Negative	Acetone–water
A ↔ A, B ↔ B > A ↔ B	Positive (endothermic)	Negative	Positive	Ethanol–hexane

Sample Exercise 11.7 Calculating the Vapor Pressure of a Solution Containing Two Liquids

A solution is prepared by mixing 5.81 g acetone (C_3H_6O, molar mass = 58.1 g/mol) and 11.9 g chloroform ($HCCl_3$, molar mass = 119.4 g/mol). At 35°C, this solution has a total vapor pressure of 260. torr. Is this an ideal solution? The vapor pressures of pure acetone and pure chloroform at 35°C are 345 and 293 torr, respectively.

Solution

To decide whether or not this solution behaves ideally, we first calculate the expected vapor pressure using Raoult's law:

Molecular Models: acetone, chloroform

$$P_{TOTAL} = \chi_A P_A^0 + \chi_C P_C^0$$

where A stands for acetone and C stands for chloroform. The calculated value can then be compared with the observed vapor pressure.

First, we must calculate the number of moles of acetone and chloroform:

$$5.81 \text{ g acetone} \times \frac{1 \text{ mol acetone}}{58.1 \text{ g acetone}} = 0.100 \text{ mol acetone}$$

$$11.9 \text{ g chloroform} \times \frac{1 \text{ mol chloroform}}{119 \text{ g chloroform}} = 0.100 \text{ mol chloroform}$$

Since the solution contains equal numbers of moles of acetone and chloroform, that is,

$$\chi_A = 0.500 \quad \text{and} \quad \chi_C = 0.500$$

the expected vapor pressure is

$$P_{TOTAL} = (0.500)(345 \text{ torr}) + (0.500)(293 \text{ torr}) = 319 \text{ torr}$$

Comparing this value with the observed pressure of 260. torr shows that the solution does not behave ideally. The observed value is lower than that expected. This negative deviation from Raoult's law can be explained in terms of the following dipole–dipole interaction:

Acetone — Chloroform

which lowers the tendency of these molecules to escape from the solution.

See Exercises 11.57 and 11.58.

11.5 Boiling-Point Elevation and Freezing-Point Depression

The relationships between vapor pressure and changes of state were discussed in Section 10.8.

In the preceding section we saw how a solute affects the vapor pressure of a liquid solvent. Because changes of state depend on vapor pressure, the presence of a solute also affects the freezing point and boiling point of a solvent. Freezing-point depression, boiling-point elevation, and osmotic pressure (discussed in Section 11.6) are called **colligative properties.** As we will see, they are grouped together because they depend only on the number, and not on the identity, of the solute particles in an ideal solution. Because of their direct relationship to the number of solute particles, the colligative properties are very useful for characterizing the nature of a solute after it is dissolved in a solvent and for determining molar masses of substances.

Boiling-Point Elevation

Normal boiling point was defined in Section 10.8.

The normal boiling point of a liquid occurs at the temperature where the vapor pressure is equal to 1 atmosphere. We have seen that a nonvolatile solute lowers the vapor pressure of the solvent. Therefore, such a solution must be heated to a higher temperature than the boiling point of the pure solvent to reach a vapor pressure of 1 atmosphere. This means that *a nonvolatile solute elevates the boiling point of the solvent.* Figure 11.14 shows the phase diagram for an aqueous solution containing a nonvolatile solute. Note that the liquid/vapor line is shifted to higher temperatures than those for pure water.

As you might expect, the magnitude of the boiling-point elevation depends on the concentration of the solute. The change in boiling point can be represented by the equation

$$\Delta T = K_b m_{\text{solute}}$$

where ΔT is the boiling-point elevation, or the difference between the boiling point of the solution and that of the pure solvent, K_b is a constant that is characteristic of the solvent and is called the **molal boiling-point elevation constant,** and m_{solute} is the *molality* of the solute in the solution.

Values of K_b for some common solvents are given in Table 11.5. The molar mass of a solute can be determined from the observed boiling-point elevation, as shown in Sample Exercise 11.8.

Figure 11.14

Phase diagrams for pure water (red lines) and for an aqueous solution containing a nonvolatile solute (blue lines). Note that the boiling point of the solution is higher than that of pure water. Conversely, the freezing point of the solution is lower than that of pure water. The effect of a nonvolatile solute is to extend the liquid range of a solvent.

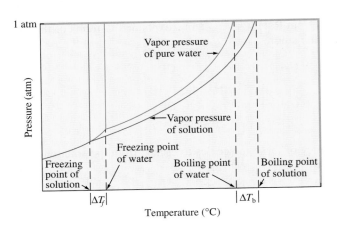

Table 11.5 Molal Boiling-Point Elevation Constants (K_b) and Freezing-Point Depression Constants (K_f) for Several Solvents

Solvent	Boiling Point (°C)	K_b (°C · kg/mol)	Freezing Point (°C)	K_f (°C · kg/mol)
Water (H$_2$O)	100.0	0.51	0	1.86
Carbon tetrachloride (CCl$_4$)	76.5	5.03	−22.99	30.
Chloroform (CHCl$_3$)	61.2	3.63	−63.5	4.70
Benzene (C$_6$H$_6$)	80.1	2.53	5.5	5.12
Carbon disulfide (CS$_2$)	46.2	2.34	−111.5	3.83
Ethyl ether (C$_4$H$_{10}$O)	34.5	2.02	−116.2	1.79
Camphor (C$_{10}$H$_{16}$O)	208.0	5.95	179.8	40.

Sample Exercise 11.8 *Calculating the Molar Mass by Boiling-Point Elevation*

A solution was prepared by dissolving 18.00 g glucose in 150.0 g water. The resulting solution was found to have a boiling point of 100.34°C. Calculate the molar mass of glucose. Glucose is a molecular solid that is present as individual molecules in solution.

Solution

We make use of the equation

$$\Delta T = K_b m_{solute}$$

where

$$\Delta T = 100.34°C - 100.00°C = 0.34°C$$

From Table 11.5, for water $K_b = 0.51$. The molality of this solution then can be calculated by rearranging the boiling-point elevation equation to give

$$m_{solute} = \frac{\Delta T}{K_b} = \frac{0.34°C}{0.51°C \cdot kg/mol} = 0.67 \text{ mol/kg}$$

The solution was prepared using 0.1500 kg water. Using the definition of molality, we can find the number of moles of glucose in the solution.

$$m_{solute} = 0.67 \text{ mol/kg} = \frac{\text{mol solute}}{\text{kg solvent}} = \frac{n_{glucose}}{0.1500 \text{ kg}}$$

$$n_{glucose} = (0.67 \text{ mol/kg})(0.1500 \text{ kg}) = 0.10 \text{ mol}$$

Thus 0.10 mol glucose has a mass of 18.00 g, and 1.0 mol glucose has a mass of 180 g (10 × 18.00 g). The molar mass of glucose is 180 g/mol.

See Exercise 11.60.

Melting point and *freezing point* both refer to the temperature where the solid and liquid coexist.

Freezing-Point Depression

When a solute is dissolved in a solvent, the freezing point of the solution is lower than that of the pure solvent. Why? Recall that the vapor pressures of ice and liquid water are the same at 0°C. Suppose a solute is dissolved in water. The resulting solution will not freeze at 0°C because *the water in the solution has a lower vapor pressure than that of pure ice.* No ice will form under these conditions. However, the vapor pressure of ice decreases more rapidly than that of liquid water as the temperature decreases. Therefore, as the solution is cooled, the vapor pressure of the ice and that of the liquid water in the solution will eventually become equal. The temperature at which this occurs is the new freezing point of the solution and is below 0°C. The freezing point has been *depressed.*

We can account for this behavior in terms of the simple model shown in Fig. 11.15. The presence of the solute lowers the rate at which molecules in the liquid return to the solid state. Thus, for an aqueous solution, only the liquid state is found at 0°C. As the solution is cooled, the rate at which water molecules leave the solid ice decreases until this rate and the rate of formation of ice become equal and equilibrium is reached. This is the freezing point of the water in the solution.

Because a solute lowers the freezing point of water, compounds such as sodium chloride and calcium chloride are often spread on streets and sidewalks to prevent ice from forming in freezing weather. Of course, if the outside temperature is lower than the freezing point of the resulting salt solution, ice forms anyway. So this procedure is not effective at extremely cold temperatures.

The solid/liquid line for an aqueous solution is shown on the phase diagram for water in Fig. 11.14. Since the presence of a solute elevates the boiling point and depresses the freezing point of the solvent, adding a solute has the effect of extending the liquid range.

The equation for freezing-point depression is analogous to that for boiling-point elevation:

$$\Delta T = K_f m_{solute}$$

where ΔT is the freezing-point depression, or the difference between the freezing point of the pure solvent and that of the solution, and K_f is a constant that is characteristic of a particular solvent and is called the **molal freezing-point depression constant.** Values of K_f for common solvents are listed in Table 11.5.

Like the boiling-point elevation, the observed freezing-point depression can be used to determine molar masses and to characterize solutions.

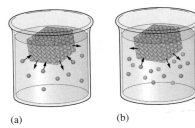

Figure 11.15

(a) Ice in equilibrium with liquid water. (b) Ice in equilibrium with liquid water containing a dissolved solute (shown in pink).

Crystals of rock salt causing ice to melt.

Sample Exercise 11.9 *Freezing-Point Depression*

What mass of ethylene glycol ($C_2H_6O_2$, molar mass = 62.1 g/mol), the main component of antifreeze, must be added to 10.0 L water to produce a solution for use in a car's radiator that freezes at $-10.0°F$ ($-23.3°C$)? Assume the density of water is exactly 1 g/mL.

Solution

The freezing point must be lowered from 0°C to $-23.3°C$. To determine the molality of ethylene glycol needed to accomplish this, we can use the equation

$$\Delta T = K_f m_{solute}$$

where $\Delta T = 23.3°C$ and $K_f = 1.86$ (from Table 11.5). Solving for the molality gives

$$m_{solute} = \frac{\Delta T}{K_f} = \frac{23.3°C}{1.86°C \cdot kg/mol} = 12.5 \text{ mol/kg}$$

0.56

This means that 12.5 mol ethylene glycol must be added per kilogram of water. We have 10.0 L, or 10.0 kg, of water. Therefore, the total number of moles of ethylene glycol needed is

$$\frac{12.5 \text{ mol}}{kg} \times 10.0 \text{ kg} = 1.25 \times 10^2 \text{ mol}$$

The mass of ethylene glycol needed is

$$1.25 \times 10^2 \text{ mol} \times \frac{62.1 \text{ g}}{mol} = 7.76 \times 10^3 \text{ g (or 7.76 kg)}$$

See Exercises 11.63 and 11.64.

The addition of antifreeze lowers the freezing point of water in a car's radiator.

Sample Exercise 11.10 Determining Molar Mass by Freezing-Point Depression

A chemist is trying to identify a human hormone, which controls metabolism, by determining its molar mass. A sample weighing 0.546 g was dissolved in 15.0 g benzene, and the freezing-point depression was determined to be 0.240°C. Calculate the molar mass of the hormone.

Solution

From Table 11.5, K_f for benzene is $5.12°C \cdot kg/mol$, so the molality of the hormone is

$$m_{hormone} = \frac{\Delta T}{K_f} = \frac{0.240°C}{5.12°C \cdot kg/mol} = 4.69 \times 10^{-2} \text{ mol/kg}$$

13.75   0.56

The moles of hormone can be obtained from the definition of molality:

$$4.69 \times 10^{-2} \text{ mol/kg} = m_{solute} = \frac{\text{mol hormone}}{0.0150 \text{ kg benzene}}$$

or

$$\text{mol hormone} = \left(4.69 \times 10^{-2}\frac{\text{mol}}{kg}\right)(0.0150 \text{ kg}) = 7.04 \times 10^{-4} \text{ mol}$$

0.0050 mol

Since 0.546 g hormone was dissolved, 7.04×10^{-4} mol hormone has a mass of 0.546 g, and

$$\frac{0.546 \text{ g}}{7.04 \times 10^{-4} \text{ mol}} = \frac{x \text{ g}}{1.00 \text{ mol}}$$

$$x = 776 \text{ g/mol}$$

Thus the molar mass of the hormone is 776 g/mol.

See Exercises 11.65 and 11.66.

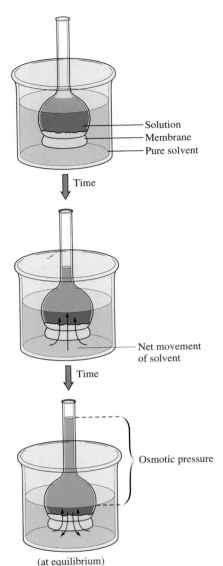

Figure 11.16

A tube with a bulb on the end that is covered by a semipermeable membrane. The solution is inside the tube and is bathed in the pure solvent. There is a net transfer of solvent molecules into the solution until the hydrostatic pressure equalizes the solvent flow in both directions.

11.6 Osmotic Pressure

Osmotic pressure, another of the colligative properties, can be understood from Fig. 11.16. A solution and pure solvent are separated by a **semipermeable membrane,** which allows *solvent but not solute* molecules to pass through. As time passes, the volume of the solution increases and that of the solvent decreases. This flow of solvent into the solution through the semipermeable membrane is called **osmosis.** Eventually the liquid levels stop changing, indicating that the system has reached equilibrium. Because the liquid levels are different at this point, there is a greater hydrostatic pressure on the solution than on the pure solvent. This excess pressure is called the **osmotic pressure.**

We can take another view of this phenomenon, as illustrated in Fig. 11.17. Osmosis can be prevented by applying a pressure to the solution. *The minimum pressure that stops the osmosis is equal to the osmotic pressure of the solution.* A simple model to explain osmotic pressure can be constructed as shown in Fig. 11.18. The membrane allows only solvent molecules to pass through. However, the initial rates of solvent transfer to and from the solution are not the same. The solute particles interfere with the passage of solvent, so the rate of transfer is slower from the solution to the solvent than in the reverse direction. Thus there is a net transfer of solvent molecules into the solution, which causes the solution volume to increase. As the solution level rises in the tube, the resulting pressure exerts an extra "push" on the solvent molecules in the solution, forcing them back through the membrane. Eventually, enough pressure develops so that the solvent transfer becomes equal in both directions. At this point, equilibrium is achieved and the levels stop changing.

Osmotic pressure can be used to characterize solutions and determine molar masses, as can the other colligative properties, but osmotic pressure is particularly useful because a small concentration of solute produces a relatively large osmotic pressure.

Experiments show that the dependence of the osmotic pressure on solution concentration is represented by the equation

$$\pi = MRT$$

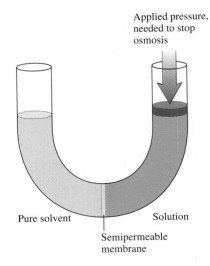

Figure 11.17

The normal flow of solvent into the solution (osmosis) can be prevented by applying an external pressure to the solution. The minimum pressure required to stop the osmosis is equal to the osmotic pressure of the solution.

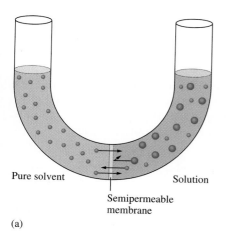
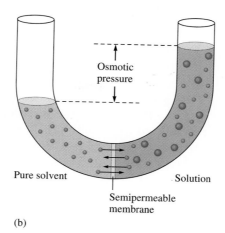

(a)

(b)

Figure 11.18

(a) A pure solvent and its solution (containing a nonvolatile solute) are separated by a semipermeable membrane through which solvent molecules (blue) can pass but solute molecules (green) cannot. The rate of solvent transfer is greater from solvent to solution than from solution to solvent. (b) The system at equilibrium, where the rate of solvent transfer is the same in both directions.

where π is the osmotic pressure in atmospheres, M is the molarity of the solution, R is the gas law constant, and T is the Kelvin temperature.

A molar mass determination using osmotic pressure is illustrated in Sample Exercise 11.11.

Sample Exercise 11.11 Determining Molar Mass from Osmotic Pressure

To determine the molar mass of a certain protein, 1.00×10^{-3} g of it was dissolved in enough water to make 1.00 mL of solution. The osmotic pressure of this solution was found to be 1.12 torr at 25.0°C. Calculate the molar mass of the protein.

Solution

We use the equation

$$\pi = MRT$$

In this case we have

$$\pi = 1.12 \text{ torr} \times \frac{1 \text{ atm}}{760 \text{ torr}} = 1.47 \times 10^{-3} \text{ atm}$$

$$R = 0.08206 \text{ L} \cdot \text{atm/K} \cdot \text{mol}$$

$$T = 25.0 + 273 = 298 \text{ K} \quad \checkmark$$

Note that the osmotic pressure must be converted to atmospheres because of the units of R.

Solving for M gives

$$M = \frac{1.47 \times 10^{-3} \text{ atm}}{(0.08206 \text{ L} \cdot \text{atm/K} \cdot \text{mol})(298 \text{ K})} = 6.01 \times 10^{-5} \text{ mol/L}$$

Since 1.00×10^{-3} g protein was dissolved in 1 mL solution, the mass of protein per liter of solution is 1.00 g. The solution's concentration is 6.01×10^{-5} mol/L. This concentration is produced from 1.00×10^{-3} g protein per milliliter, or 1.00 g/L. Thus 6.01×10^{-5} mol protein has a mass of 1.00 g and

$$\frac{1.00 \text{ g}}{6.01 \times 10^{-5} \text{ mol}} = \frac{x \text{ g}}{1.00 \text{ mol}}$$

$$x = 1.66 \times 10^4 \text{ g}$$

The molar mass of the protein is 1.66×10^4 g/mol. This molar mass may seem very large, but it is relatively small for a protein.

See Exercise 11.68.

Measurements of osmotic pressure generally give much more accurate molar mass values than those from freezing-point or boiling-point changes.

In osmosis, a semipermeable membrane prevents transfer of *all* solute particles. A similar phenomenon, called **dialysis,** occurs at the walls of most plant and animal cells. However, in this case the membrane allows transfer of both solvent molecules and *small* solute molecules and ions. One of the most important applications of dialysis is the use of artificial kidney machines to purify the blood. The blood is passed through a cellophane tube, which acts as the semipermeable membrane. The tube is immersed in a dialyzing solution (see Fig. 11.19). This "washing" solution contains the same concentrations of ions and small molecules as blood but has none of the waste products normally removed by the kidneys. The resulting dialysis (movement of waste molecules into the washing solution) cleanses the blood.

Impure blood in

Purified blood out

Essential ions and molecules remain in blood

Dialyzing solution

Waste products dialyze out into the washing solution

Figure 11.19

Representation of the functioning of an artificial kidney.

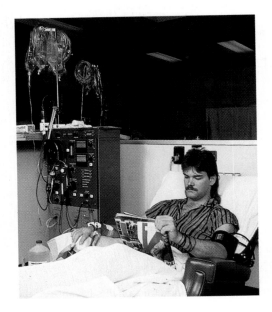

Patient undergoing dialysis.

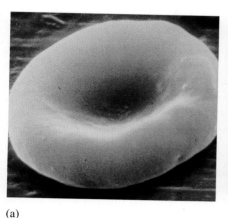
(a)

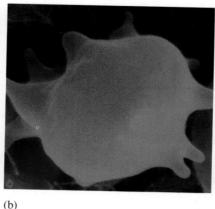
(b)

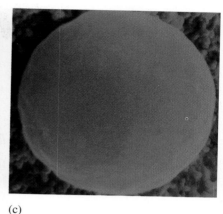
(c)

Red blood cells in three stages of osmosis. (a) The normal shape of a red blood cell. (b) This cell has shrunk because water moved out of it by osmosis. (c) This cell is swollen with water that has moved into it by osmosis.

Solutions that have identical osmotic pressures are said to be **isotonic solutions.** Fluids administered intravenously must be isotonic with body fluids. For example, if red blood cells are bathed in a hypertonic solution, which is a solution having an osmotic pressure higher than that of the cell fluids, the cells will shrivel because of a net transfer of water out of the cells. This phenomenon is called *crenation.* The opposite phenomenon, called *hemolysis,* occurs when cells are bathed in a hypotonic solution, a solution with an osmotic pressure lower than that of the cell fluids. In this case, the cells rupture because of the flow of water into the cells.

We can use the phenomenon of crenation to our advantage. Food can be preserved by treating its surface with a solute that gives a solution that is hypertonic to bacteria cells. Bacteria on the food then tend to shrivel and die. This is why salt can be used to protect meat and sugar can be used to protect fruit.

The brine used in pickling causes the cucumbers to shrivel.

Sample Exercise 11.12 *Isotonic Solutions*

What concentration of sodium chloride in water is needed to produce an aqueous solution isotonic with blood ($\pi = 7.70$ atm at 25°C)?

Solution

We can calculate the molarity of the solute from the equation

$$\pi = MRT \quad \text{or} \quad M = \frac{\pi}{RT}$$

$$M = \frac{7.70 \text{ atm}}{(0.08206 \text{ L} \cdot \text{atm/K} \cdot \text{mol})(298 \text{ K})} = 0.315 \text{ mol/L}$$

This represents the total molarity of solute particles. But NaCl gives two ions per formula unit. Therefore, the concentration of NaCl needed is $\frac{0.315 \, M}{2} = 0.1575 \, M = 0.158 \, M$. That is,

$$NaCl \longrightarrow Na^+ + Cl^-$$

$$\underset{0.1575\ M}{} \quad \underset{0.1575\ M}{\underline{\qquad}} \quad \underset{0.1575\ M}{\underline{\qquad}}$$

$$0.315\ M$$

See Exercise 11.70.

Reverse Osmosis

If a solution in contact with pure solvent across a semipermeable membrane is subjected to an external pressure larger than its osmotic pressure, **reverse osmosis** occurs. The pressure will cause a net flow of solvent from the solution to the solvent, as shown in Fig. 11.20. In reverse osmosis, the semipermeable membrane acts as a "molecular filter" to remove solute particles. This fact is applicable to the **desalination** (removal of dissolved salts) of seawater, which is highly hypertonic to body fluids and thus is not drinkable.

As the population of the sun belt areas of the United States increases, more demand will be placed on the limited supplies of fresh water there. One obvious source of fresh water is from the desalination of seawater. Various schemes have been suggested, including solar evaporation, reverse osmosis, and even a plan for towing icebergs from Antarctica. The problem, of course, is that all the available processes are expensive. However, as water shortages increase, desalination is becoming necessary. For example, the first full-time public desalination plant in the United States has just started operations on Catalina Island, just off the coast of California (see Fig. 11.21). This plant, which can produce 132,000 gallons of drinkable water from the Pacific Ocean every day, operates by reverse osmosis. Powerful pumps, developing over 800 lb/in^2 of pressure, are employed to force seawater through synthetic semipermeable membranes.

Catalina Island's plant may be just the beginning. The city of Santa Barbara opened a $40 million desalination plant in 1992 that can produce 8 million gallons of drinking water a day, and other plants are in the planning stages.

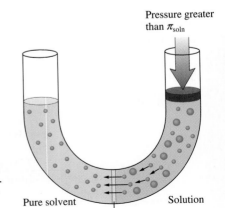

Figure 11.20

Reverse osmosis. A pressure greater than the osmotic pressure of the solution is applied, which causes a net flow of solvent molecules (blue) from the solution to the pure solvent. The solute molecules (green) remain behind.

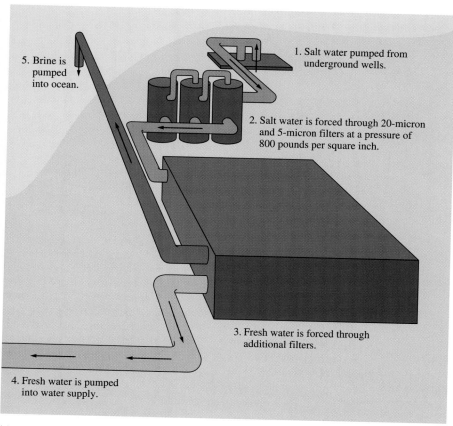

5. Brine is pumped into ocean.

1. Salt water pumped from underground wells.

2. Salt water is forced through 20-micron and 5-micron filters at a pressure of 800 pounds per square inch.

3. Fresh water is forced through additional filters.

4. Fresh water is pumped into water supply.

(a)

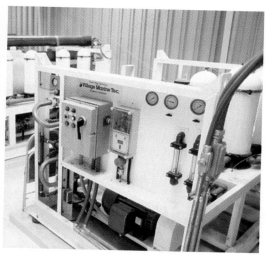

(b)

Figure 11.21

(a) Residents of Santa Catalina Island off the coast of southern California are benefiting from a new desalination plant that can supply 132,000 gallons a day, or one-third of the island's daily needs. (b) Machinery in the desalination plant for Catalina Island.

CHEMICAL IMPACT

The Drink of Champions—Water*

IN 1965, THE University of Florida football team, the Gators, participated in a research program to test a sports drink formula containing a mixture of carbohydrates and electrolytes. The drink was used to help prevent dehydration caused by extreme workouts in the hot Florida climate. The Gators' success that season was in part attributed to their use of the sports drink formula. In 1967, a modified form of this formula was marketed with the name Gatorade. Today, Gatorade leads sales in sports drinks, but many other brands have entered a market where annual sales exceed $700 million!

During moderate to high-intensity exercise, glycogen (a fuel reserve that helps maintain normal body processes) can be depleted within 60 to 90 minutes. Blood sugar levels drop as the glycogen reserves are used up, and lactic acid (a by-product of glucose metabolism) builds up in muscle tissue causing fatigue and muscle cramps. Muscles also generate a large amount of heat that must be dissipated. Water, which has a large specific heat capacity, is used to take heat away from these muscles. Sweating and evaporative cooling help the body maintain a constant temperature, but at a huge cost. During a high-intensity workout in hot

For healthy athletes, drinking water during exercise may be as effective as drinking sports drinks.

weather, anywhere from 1 to 3 quarts of water can be lost from sweating per hour. Sweating away more than 2% of your body weight—a quart for every 100 pounds—can put a large stress on the heart, increasing body temperature and decreasing performance. Excessive sweating also results in the loss of sodium and potassium ions—two very important electrolytes that are present in the fluids inside and outside cells.

All the major sports drinks contain three main ingredients—carbohydrates in the form of simple sugars such as sucrose,

glucose, and fructose; electrolytes, including sodium and potassium ions; and water. Because these are the three major substances lost through sweating, good scientific reasoning suggests that drinking sports drinks should improve performance. But just how effectively do sports drinks deliver on their promises?

Recent studies have confirmed that athletes who eat a balanced diet and drink plenty of water are just as well off as those who consume sports drinks. A sports drink may have only one advantage over drinking water—it tastes better than water to most athletes. And if a drink tastes better, it will encourage more consumption, thus keeping cells hydrated.

Since most of the leading sports drinks contain the same ingredients in similar concentrations, taste may be the single most important factor in choosing your drink. If you are not interested in any particular sports drink, drink plenty of water. The key to quality performance is to keep your cells hydrated.

*Adapted with permission from "Sports Drinks: Don't Sweat the Small Stuff," by Tim Graham, *ChemMatters*, February 1999, p.11.

A small-scale, manually operated reverse osmosis desalinator has been developed by the U.S. Navy to provide fresh water on life rafts. Potable water can be supplied by this desalinator at the rate of 1.25 gallons of water per hour—enough to keep 25 people alive. This compact desalinator, which weighs only 10 pounds, can now replace the bulky cases of fresh water formerly stored in Navy life rafts.

11.7 Colligative Properties of Electrolyte Solutions

As we have seen previously, the colligative properties of solutions depend on the total concentration of solute particles. For example, a 0.10 m glucose solution shows a freezing-point depression of 0.186°C:

$$\Delta T = K_f m = (1.86°C \cdot kg/mol)(0.100 \text{ mol/kg}) = 0.186°C$$

On the other hand, a 0.10 m sodium chloride solution should show a freezing-point depression of 0.37°C, since the solution is 0.10 m Na^+ ions and 0.10 m Cl^- ions. Therefore, the solution contains a total of 0.20 m solute particles, and $\Delta T = (1.86°C \cdot kg/mol)(0.20 \text{ mol/kg}) = 0.37°C$.

The relationship between the moles of solute dissolved and the moles of particles in solution is usually expressed using the **van't Hoff factor i**:

$$i = \frac{\text{moles of particles in solution}}{\text{moles of solute dissolved}}$$

The *expected* value for i can be calculated for a salt by noting the number of ions per formula unit. For example, for NaCl, i is 2; for K_2SO_4, i is 3; and for $Fe_3(PO_4)_2$, i is 5. These calculated values assume that when a salt dissolves, it completely dissociates into its component ions, which then move around independently. This assumption is not always true. For example, the freezing-point depression observed for 0.10 m NaCl is 1.87 times that for 0.10 m glucose rather than twice as great. That is, for a 0.10 m NaCl solution the observed value for i is 1.87 rather than 2. Why? The best explanation is that **ion pairing** occurs in solution (see Fig. 11.22). At a given instant a small percentage of the sodium and chloride ions are paired and thus count as a single particle. In general, ion pairing is most important in concentrated solutions. As the solution becomes more dilute, the ions are farther apart and less ion pairing occurs. For example, in a 0.0010 m NaCl solution, the observed value of i is 1.97, which is very close to the expected value.

Ion pairing occurs to some extent in all electrolyte solutions. Table 11.6 shows expected and observed values of i for a given concentration of various electrolytes. Note that the deviation of i from the expected value tends to be greatest where the ions have multiple charges. This is expected because ion pairing ought to be most important for highly charged ions.

The colligative properties of electrolyte solutions are described by including the van't Hoff factor in the appropriate equation. For example, for changes in freezing and boiling points, the modified equation is

$$\Delta T = imK$$

Dutch chemist J. H. van't Hoff (1852–1911) received the first Nobel Prize in chemistry in 1901.

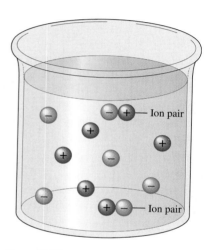

Figure 11.22

In an aqueous solution a few ions aggregate, forming ion pairs that behave as a unit.

Table 11.6 Expected and Observed Values of the van't Hoff Factor for 0.05 m Solutions of Several Electrolytes		
Electrolyte	i (expected)	i (observed)
NaCl	2.0	1.9
$MgCl_2$	3.0	2.7
$MgSO_4$	2.0	1.3
$FeCl_3$	4.0	3.4
HCl	2.0	1.9
Glucose*	1.0	1.0

*A nonelectrolyte shown for comparison.

where K represents the freezing-point depression or boiling-point elevation constant for the solvent.

For the osmotic pressure of electrolyte solutions, the equation is

$$\pi = iMRT$$

Sample Exercise **11.13** *Osmotic Pressure*

The observed osmotic pressure for a 0.10 M solution of $Fe(NH_4)_2(SO_4)_2$ at 25°C is 10.8 atm. Compare the expected and experimental values for i.

Solution

The ionic solid $Fe(NH_4)_2(SO_4)_2$ dissociates in water to produce 5 ions:

$$Fe(NH_4)_2(SO_4)_2 \xrightarrow{H_2O} Fe^{2+} + 2NH_4^+ + 2SO_4^{2-}$$

Thus the expected value for i is 5. We can obtain the experimental value for i by using the equation for osmotic pressure:

$$\pi = iMRT \qquad \text{or} \qquad i = \frac{\pi}{MRT}$$

where $\pi = 10.8$ atm, $M = 0.10$ mol/L, $R = 0.08206$ L · atm/K · mol, and $T = 25 + 273 = 298$ K. Substituting these values into the equation gives

$$i = \frac{\pi}{MRT} = \frac{10.8 \text{ atm}}{(0.10 \text{ mol/L})(0.08206 \text{ L · atm/K · mol})(298 \text{ K})} = 4.4$$

The experimental value for i is less than the expected value, presumably because of ion pairing.

See Exercises 11.75 through 11.77.

11.8 Colloids

Mud can be suspended in water by vigorous stirring. When the stirring stops, most of the particles rapidly settle out, but even after several days some of the smallest particles remain suspended. Although undetected in normal lighting, their presence can be demonstrated by shining a beam of intense light through the suspension. The beam is visible from the side because the light is scattered by the suspended particles (Fig. 11.23). In a true solution, on the other hand, the beam is invisible from the side because the individual ions and molecules dispersed in the solution are too small to scatter visible light.

The scattering of light by particles is called the **Tyndall effect** and is often used to distinguish between a suspension and a true solution.

CHEMICAL IMPACT

Organisms and Ice Formation

THE ICE-COLD waters of the polar oceans are teeming with fish that seem immune to freezing. One might think that these fish have some kind of antifreeze in their blood. However, studies show that they are protected from freezing in a very different way from the way antifreeze protects our cars. As we have seen in this chapter, solutes such as sugar, salt, and ethylene glycol lower the temperature at which the solid and liquid phases of water can coexist. However, the fish could not tolerate high concentrations of solutes in their blood because of the osmotic pressure effects. Instead, they are protected by proteins in their blood. These proteins allow the water in the bloodstream to be supercooled—exist below 0°C—without forming ice. They apparently coat the surface of each tiny ice crystal, as soon as it begins to form, preventing it from growing to a size that would cause biologic damage.

Although it might at first seem surprising, this research on polar fish has at-

An Antarctic fish, Chaerophalus aceratus.

tracted the attention of ice cream manufacturers. Premium quality ice cream is smooth; it does not have large ice crystals in it. The makers of ice cream would like to incorporate these polar fish proteins, or molecules that behave similarly, into ice cream to prevent the growth of ice crystals during storage.

Fruit and vegetable growers have a similar interest: They also want to prevent ice formation that damages their crops during an unusual cold wave. However, this is a very different kind of problem than keeping polar fish from freezing. Many types of fruits and vegetables are colonized by bacteria that manufacture a protein that *encourages* freezing by acting as a nucleating agent to start an ice crystal. Chemists have identified the offending protein in the bacteria and the gene that is responsible for making it. They have learned to modify the genetic material of these bacteria in a way that removes their ability to make the protein that encourages ice crystal formation. If testing shows that these modified bacteria have no harmful effects on the crop or the environment, the original bacteria strain will be replaced with the new form so that ice crystals will not form so readily when a cold snap occurs.

A suspension of tiny particles in some medium is called a **colloidal dispersion,** or a **colloid.** The suspended particles are single large molecules or aggregates of molecules or ions ranging in size from 1 to 1000 nm. Colloids are classified according to the states of the dispersed phase and the dispersing medium. Table 11.7 summarizes various types of colloids.

What stabilizes a colloid? Why do the particles remain suspended rather than forming larger aggregates and precipitating out? The answer is complicated, but the main factor seems to be *electrostatic repulsion.* A colloid, like all other macroscopic substances, is electrically neutral. However, when a colloid is placed in an electric field, the dispersed particles all migrate to the same electrode and thus must all have the same charge. How is this possible? The center of a colloidal particle (a tiny ionic crystal, a group of molecules, or a single large molecule) attracts from the medium a layer of ions, all of the same charge. This group of ions, in turn, attracts another layer of oppositely charged ions, as shown in Fig. 11.24. Because the colloidal particles all have an outer layer of ions with the same charge, they repel each other and do not easily aggregate to form particles that are large enough to precipitate.

Figure 11.23
The Tyndall effect.

Table 11.7 Types of Colloids

Examples	Dispersing Medium	Dispersed Substance	Colloid Type
Fog, aerosol sprays	Gas	Liquid	Aerosol
Smoke, airborne bacteria	Gas	Solid	Aerosol
Whipped cream, soap suds	Liquid	Gas	Foam
Milk, mayonnaise	Liquid	Liquid	Emulsion
Paint, clays, gelatin	Liquid	Solid	Sol
Marshmallow, polystyrene foam	Solid	Gas	Solid foam
Butter, cheese	Solid	Liquid	Solid emulsion
Ruby glass	Solid	Solid	Solid sol

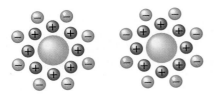

Figure 11.24

A representation of two colloidal particles. In each the center particle is surrounded by a layer of positive ions, with negative ions in the outer layer. Thus, although the particles are electrically neutral, they still repel each other because of their outer negative layer of ions.

The destruction of a colloid, called **coagulation,** usually can be accomplished either by heating or by adding an electrolyte. Heating increases the velocities of the colloidal particles, causing them to collide with enough energy that the ion barriers are penetrated and the particles can aggregate. Because this is repeated many times, the particle grows to a point where it settles out. Adding an electrolyte neutralizes the adsorbed ion layers. This is why clay suspended in rivers is deposited where the river reaches the ocean, forming the deltas characteristic of large rivers like the Mississippi. The high salt content of the seawater causes the colloidal clay particles to coagulate.

The removal of soot from smoke is another example of the coagulation of a colloid. When smoke is passed through an electrostatic precipitator (Fig. 11.25), the suspended solids are removed. The use of precipitators has produced an immense improvement in the air quality of heavily industrialized cities.

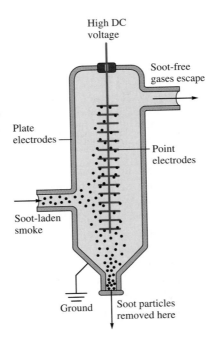

Figure 11.25

The Cottrell precipitator installed in a smokestack. The charged plates attract the colloidal particles because of their ion layers and thus remove them from the smoke.

For Review

Summary

Solution composition can be described in terms of molarity (the moles of solute per liter of solution), mass percent (the ratio of grams of solute to grams of solution multiplied by 100), mole fraction (the moles of a given component per total number of moles of all components of the solution), or molality (the moles of solute per kilogram of solvent).

Normality is defined as the number of equivalents per liter of solution. The definition of an equivalent depends on the reaction taking place in the solution. For an acid–base reaction, the equivalent is the mass of acid (or base) that can furnish (or accept) exactly 1 mole of protons. For an oxidation–reduction reaction, the equivalent is the quantity of reducing (or oxidizing) agent that can furnish (or accept) 1 mole of electrons.

The enthalpy of solution ΔH_{soln} is the enthalpy change accompanying solution formation. It can be broken down into terms expressing energies associated with overcoming interactions between solute particles and interactions between solvent particles (endothermic processes) and a term expressing energies associated with the interactions between solute and solvent particles (an exothermic process).

Various factors affect solubility. Molecular structure determines the polarity of a molecule. Polar molecules tend to be soluble in polar solvents, and nonpolar molecules tend to be soluble in nonpolar solvents. Pressure has little effect on the solubility of liquids or solids, but increased pressure increases the solubility of gases. Henry's law, which applies to gases that do not react chemically with the solvent, states that the concentration of a gaseous solute in a solvent is directly proportional to the partial pressure of the same gas above the solution. An increase in temperature decreases the solubility of a gas in water, but the effect of temperature on the solubility of a solid in water varies with the identity of the solid.

The vapor pressure of a solution containing a nonvolatile solute is always less than the vapor pressure of the pure solvent, because the presence of the solute decreases the number of solvent molecules per unit volume and thus proportionately lowers the escaping tendency of the solvent molecules. Raoult's law states that the vapor pressure of a solution is directly proportional to the mole fraction of the solvent. Raoult's law holds for an ideal solution. However, if a solute has a special affinity for the solvent, nonideal behavior is seen in the form of a negative deviation from Raoult's law (a lower vapor pressure than is predicted).

The colligative properties of solutions, which depend on the number of solute particles present, include boiling-point elevation, freezing-point depression, and osmotic pressure. Because a nonvolatile solute lowers the freezing point and raises the boiling point, it extends the liquid range of the solvent.

Osmosis occurs when a pure solvent and its solution are separated by a semipermeable membrane that prevents the passage of solute molecules. Under these circumstances, solvent molecules flow from the solvent into the solution. Osmotic pressure, the exact pressure that must be applied to a solution to prevent osmosis, is directly related to the molarity of the solution. Reverse osmosis occurs when an external pressure larger than the solution's osmotic pressure is applied. The effect is to cause a net flow of solvent from the solution into the pure solvent.

Key Terms

Section 11.1
molarity
mass percent
mole fraction
molality
normality

Section 11.2
enthalpy (heat) of solution
enthalpy (heat) of hydration

Section 11.3
Henry's law
thermal pollution

Section 11.4
Raoult's law
ideal solution

Section 11.5
colligative properties
molal boiling-point elevation
 constant
molal freezing-point depression
 constant

Section 11.6
semipermeable membrane
osmosis
osmotic pressure
dialysis
isotonic solution
reverse osmosis
desalination

Section 11.7
van't Hoff factor
ion pairing

Section 11.8
Tyndall effect
colloid (colloidal dispersion)
coagulation

To describe the colligative properties of electrolyte solutions, the number of ions must be taken into account by use of the van't Hoff factor i. Because of ion pairing, the experimental value for i is often significantly less than the expected value.

A colloid is a suspension of tiny particles in solution. Colloids are stabilized because of the electrostatic repulsions between the ion layers surrounding the individual particles. A colloid can be coagulated by heating or by adding an electrolyte.

In-Class Discussion Questions

These questions are designed to be considered by groups of students in class. Often these questions work well for introducing a particular topic in class.

1. Consider Fig. 11.9. According to the caption and picture, water seems to go from one beaker to another.
   a. Explain why this occurs.
   b. The explanation in the text uses terms such as *vapor pressure* and *equilibrium*. Explain what these have to do with the phenomenon. For example, what is coming to equilibrium?
   c. Does all the water end up in the second beaker?
   d. Is water evaporating from the beaker containing the solution? If so, is the rate of evaporation increasing, decreasing, or staying constant?
   Draw pictures to illustrate your explanations.

2. Once again, consider Fig. 11.9. Suppose instead of having a nonvolatile solute in the solvent in one beaker, the two beakers contain different volatile liquids. That is, suppose one beaker contains liquid A ($P_{vap} = 50$ torr) and the other beaker contains liquid B ($P_{vap} = 100$ torr). Explain what happens as time passes. How is this similar to the first case (shown in the figure)? How is it different?

3. Assume that you place a freshwater plant into a saltwater solution and examine it under a microscope. What happens to the plant cells? What if you placed a saltwater plant in pure water? Explain. Draw pictures to illustrate your explanations.

4. How does ΔH_{soln} relate to deviations from Raoult's law? Explain.

5. You have read that adding a solute to a solvent can both increase the boiling point and decrease the freezing point. A friend of yours explains it to you like this: "The solute and solvent can be like salt in water. The salt gets in the way of freezing in that it blocks the water molecules from joining together. The salt acts like a strong bond holding the water molecules together so that it is harder to boil." What do you say to your friend?

6. You drop an ice cube (made from pure water) into a saltwater solution at 0°C. Explain what happens and why.

7. Using the phase diagram for water and Raoult's law, explain why salt is spread on the roads in winter (even when it is below freezing).

8. You and your friend are each drinking cola from separate 2-L bottles. Both colas are equally carbonated. You are able to drink 1 L of cola, but your friend can drink only about half a liter. You each close the bottles and place them in the refrigerator. The next day when you each go to get the colas, whose will be more carbonated and why?

A blue question or exercise number indicates that the answer to that question or exercise appears at the back of this book and a solution appears in the *Solutions Guide*.

Solution Review

If you have trouble with these exercises, review Sections 4.1 to 4.3 in Chapter 4.

9. A solution is prepared by dissolving 125 g sucrose ($C_{12}H_{22}O_{11}$) in enough water to produce 1.00 L solution. What is the molarity of this solution?

10. What mass of sodium oxalate ($Na_2C_2O_4$) is needed to prepare 0.250 L of a 0.100 M solution?

11. A solution is prepared by diluting 25.00 mL of a 0.308 M solution of $NiCl_2$ to a final volume of 0.500 L. What is the concentration of nickel chloride in this solution? What are the concentrations of nickel ions and chloride ions in this solution?

12. A solution contains 1.06×10^{-3} M $Ca(NO_3)_2$.
   a. What are the molar concentrations of calcium cations and nitrate anions in this solution?
   b. What is the mass (in grams) of the Ca^{2+} ions in 1.0 mL of this solution?
   c. How many nitrate ions are there in 1.0×10^{-6} L (1.0 μL) of this solution?

13. What volume of 0.25 M HCl solution must be diluted to prepare 1.00 L of 0.040 M HCl?

14. Write equations showing the ions present after the following strong electrolytes are dissolved in water.
   a. HNO_3 d. $SrBr_2$ g. NH_4NO_3
   b. Na_2SO_4 e. $KClO_4$ h. $CuSO_4$
   c. $Al(NO_3)_3$ f. NH_4Br i. $NaOH$

Questions

15. Is molarity or molality dependent on temperature? Explain your answer. Why is molality, and not molarity, used in the

equations describing freezing-point depression and boiling-point elevation?

16. What specific feature of chemical substances do we refer to when we say that "like dissolves like"?

17. Define the terms *hydrophobic* and *hydrophilic*.

18. Rationalize the temperature dependence of the solubility of a gas in water in terms of the kinetic molecular theory.

19. In terms of intermolecular forces, what factors give rise to positive and negative deviations from Raoult's law?

20. If a solution shows positive deviations from Raoult's law, would you expect it to have a higher or lower boiling point than if it were ideal? Why?

21. When pure methanol is mixed with water, the resulting solution feels warm. Would you expect this solution to be ideal? Explain.

22. Why is the observed freezing-point depression for electrolyte solutions sometimes less than the calculated value? Is the discrepancy greater for concentrated or dilute solutions?

23. Before refrigeration was common, many foods were preserved by salting them heavily, and many fruits were preserved by mixing them with a large amount of sugar (fruit preserves). How do salt and sugar act as preservatives?

24. Distinguish between a strong electrolyte and a weak electrolyte. How can colligative properties be used to distinguish between strong and weak electrolytes?

25. The Tyndall effect is often used to distinguish between a colloidal suspension and a true solution. Explain.

26. Detergent molecules can stabilize the emulsion of oil in water as well as remove dirt from soiled clothes. A typical detergent is sodium dodecylsulfate, or SDS, and it has a formula of $CH_3(CH_2)_{10}CH_2SO_4^-Na^+$. In aqueous solution, SDS suspends oil or dirt by forming small aggregates of detergent anions called *micelles*. Propose a structure for micelles.

Exercises

In this section similar exercises are paired.

Concentration of Solutions

27. A solution is prepared by dissolving 50.0 g cesium chloride (CsCl) in 50.0 g water. The volume of the solution is 63.3 mL. Calculate the mass percent, molarity, molality, and mole fraction of the cesium chloride.

28. An aqueous antifreeze solution is 40.0% ethylene glycol ($C_2H_6O_2$) by mass. The density of the solution is 1.05 g/cm³. Calculate the molality, molarity, and mole fraction of the ethylene glycol.

29. Common commercial acids and bases are aqueous solutions with the following properties:

	Density (g/cm³)	Mass Percent of Solute
Hydrochloric acid	1.19	38
Nitric acid	1.42	70.
Sulfuric acid	1.84	95
Acetic acid	1.05	99
Ammonia	0.90	28

Calculate the molarity, molality, and mole fraction of each of the preceding reagents.

30. In lab you need to prepare at least 100 mL of each of the following solutions. Explain how you would proceed using the given information.
   a. 2.0 *m* KCl in water (density of H_2O = 1.00 g/cm³)
   b. 15% NaOH by mass in water (*d* = 1.00 g/cm³)
   c. 25% NaOH by mass in CH_3OH (*d* = 0.79 g/cm³)
   d. 0.10 mole fraction of $C_6H_{12}O_6$ in water (*d* = 1.00 g/cm³)

31. A solution is prepared by mixing 25 mL pentane (C_5H_{12}, *d* = 0.63 g/cm³) with 45 mL hexane (C_6H_{14}, *d* = 0.66 g/cm³). Assuming that the volumes add on mixing, calculate the mass percent, mole fraction, molality, and molarity of the pentane.

32. A bottle of wine contains 12.5% ethanol by volume. The density of ethanol (C_2H_5OH) is 0.789 g/cm³. Calculate the concentration of ethanol in wine in terms of mass percent and molality.

33. A 1.37 *M* solution of citric acid ($H_3C_6H_5O_7$) in water has a density of 1.10 g/cm³. Calculate the mass percent, molality, mole fraction, and normality of the citric acid. Citric acid has three acidic protons.

34. Calculate the molarity and mole fraction of acetone in a 1.00 *m* solution of acetone (CH_3COCH_3) in ethanol (C_2H_5OH). (Density of acetone = 0.788 g/cm³; density of ethanol = 0.789 g/cm³.) Assume that the volumes of acetone and ethanol add.

Energetics of Solutions and Solubility

35. The lattice energy* of KCl is −715 kJ/mol, and the enthalpy of hydration is −684 kJ/mol. Calculate the enthalpy of solution per mole of solid KCl. Describe the process to which this enthalpy change applies.

36. a. Use the following data to calculate the enthalpy of hydration for calcium chloride and calcium iodide.

	Lattice Energy*	ΔH_{soln}
$CaCl_2(s)$	−2247 kJ/mol	−46 kJ/mol
$CaI_2(s)$	−2059 kJ/mol	−104 kJ/mol

* Lattice energy was defined in Chapter 8 as the energy change for the process $M^+(g) + X^-(g) \rightarrow MX(s)$.

b. Based on your answers to part a, which ion, Cl^- or I^-, is more strongly attracted to water?

37. Although $Al(OH)_3$ is insoluble in water, NaOH is very soluble. Explain in terms of lattice energies.*

38. The high melting points of ionic solids indicate that a lot of energy must be supplied to separate the ions from one another. How is it possible that the ions can separate from one another when soluble ionic compounds are dissolved in water, often with essentially no temperature change?

39. Which solvent, water or carbon tetrachloride, would you choose to dissolve each of the following?
  a. CO_2 **d.** $HC_2H_3O_2$
  b. NH_4NO_3 **e.** $CH_3CH_2CH_2CH_2CH_3$
  c. $CH_3\underset{\underset{O}{\|}}{C}CH_3$

40. Which solvent, water or hexane (C_6H_{14}), would you choose to dissolve each of the following?
  a. NaCl   **c.** octane (C_8H_{18})
  b. HF   **d.** $(NH_4)_2SO_4$

41. What factors cause one solute to be more strongly attracted to water than another? For each of the following pairs, predict which substance would be more soluble in water.
  a. CH_3CH_2OH or $CH_3CH_2CH_3$
  b. $CHCl_3$ or CCl_4
  c. CH_3CH_2OH or $CH_3(CH_2)_{14}CH_2OH$

42. For each of the following pairs, predict which substance would be more soluble in water.
  a. NH_3 or PH_3
  b. CH_3CN or CH_3CH_3
  c. $CH_3\underset{\underset{O}{\|}}{C}-OH$ or $CH_3-\underset{\underset{O}{\|}}{C}-OCH_3$

43. Rationalize the trend in water solubility for the following simple alcohols:

Alcohol	Solubility (g/100 g H₂O at 20°C)
Methanol, CH_3OH	Soluble in all proportions
Ethanol, CH_3CH_2OH	Soluble in all proportions
Propanol, $CH_3CH_2CH_2OH$	Soluble in all proportions
Butanol, $CH_3(CH_2)_2CH_2OH$	8.14
Pentanol, $CH_3(CH_2)_3CH_2OH$	2.64
Hexanol, $CH_3(CH_2)_4CH_2OH$	0.59
Heptanol, $CH_3(CH_2)_5CH_2OH$	0.09

*See footnote on page 553.

44. The solubility of benzoic acid ($HC_7H_5O_2$),

is 0.34 g/100 mL in water at 25°C and is 10.0 g/100 mL in benzene (C_6H_6) at 25°C. Rationalize this solubility behavior. (*Hint:* Benzoic acid forms a dimer in benzene.) Would benzoic acid be more or less soluble in a 0.1 *M* NaOH solution than it is in water? Explain.

45. The solubility of nitrogen in water is 8.21×10^{-4} mol/L at 0°C when the N_2 pressure above water is 0.790 atm. Calculate the Henry's law constant for N_2 in units of L · atm/mol for Henry's law in the form $P = kC$, where C is the gas concentration in mol/L. Calculate the solubility of N_2 in water when the partial pressure of nitrogen above water is 1.10 atm at 0°C.

46. In Exercise 103 in Chapter 5, the pressure of CO_2 in a bottle of sparkling wine was calculated assuming that the CO_2 was insoluble in water. This was a bad assumption. Redo this problem by assuming that CO_2 obeys Henry's law. Use the data given in that problem to calculate the partial pressure of CO_2 in the gas phase and the solubility of CO_2 in the wine at 25°C. The Henry's law constant for CO_2 is 32 L · atm/mol at 25°C with Henry's law in the form $P = kC$, where C is the concentration of the gas in mol/L.

Vapor Pressures of Solutions

47. A solution is prepared by mixing 50.0 g glucose ($C_6H_{12}O_6$) with 600.0 g water. What is the vapor pressure of this solution at 25°C? (At 25°C the vapor pressure of pure water is 23.8 torr. Glucose is a nonelectrolyte.)

48. The vapor pressure of a solution containing 53.6 g glycerin ($C_3H_8O_3$) in 133.7 g ethanol (C_2H_5OH) is 113 torr at 40°C. Calculate the vapor pressure of pure ethanol at 40°C assuming that glycerin is a nonvolatile, nonelectrolyte solute in ethanol.

49. At a certain temperature, the vapor pressure of pure benzene (C_6H_6) is 0.930 atm. A solution was prepared by dissolving 10.0 g of a nondissociating, nonvolatile solute in 78.11 g of benzene at that temperature. The vapor pressure of the solution was found to be 0.900 atm. Assuming the solution behaves ideally, determine the molar mass of the solute.

50. A solution of sodium chloride in water has a vapor pressure of 19.6 torr at 25°C. What is the mole fraction of NaCl in this solution? What would be the vapor pressure of this solution at 45°C? The vapor pressure of pure water is 23.8 torr at 25°C and 71.9 torr at 45°C.

51. Pentane (C_5H_{12}) and hexane (C_6H_{14}) form an ideal solution. At 25°C the vapor pressures of pentane and hexane are 511 and 150. torr, respectively. A solution is prepared by mixing

25 mL pentane (density, 0.63 g/mL) with 45 mL hexane (density, 0.66 g/mL).
a. What is the vapor pressure of the resulting solution?
b. What is the composition by mole fraction of pentane in the vapor that is in equilibrium with this solution?

52. A solution is prepared by mixing 0.0300 mol CH_2Cl_2 and 0.0500 mol CH_2Br_2 at 25°C. Assuming the solution is ideal, calculate the composition of the vapor (in terms of mole fractions) at 25°C. At 25°C, the vapor pressures of pure CH_2Cl_2 and pure CH_2Br_2 are 133 and 11.4 torr, respectively.

53. What is the composition of a methanol (CH_3OH)–propanol ($CH_3CH_2CH_2OH$) solution that has a vapor pressure of 174 torr at 40°C? At 40°C, the vapor pressures of pure methanol and pure propanol are 303 and 44.6 torr, respectively. Assume the solution is ideal.

54. Benzene and toluene form an ideal solution. Consider a solution of benzene and toluene prepared at 25°C. Assuming the mole fractions of benzene and toluene in the vapor phase are equal, calculate the composition of the solution. At 25°C the vapor pressures of benzene and toluene are 95 and 28 torr, respectively.

55. Which of the following will have the lowest total vapor pressure at 25°C?
a. pure water (vapor pressure = 23.8 torr at 25°C)
b. a solution of glucose in water with $X_{C_6H_{12}O_6} = 0.01$
c. a solution of sodium chloride in water with $X_{NaCl} = 0.01$
d. a solution of methanol in water with $X_{CH_3OH} = 0.2$ (Consider the vapor pressure of both methanol [143 torr at 25°C] and water.)

56. Which of the choices in Exercise 55 has the highest vapor pressure?

57. A solution is made by mixing 50.0 g acetone (CH_3COCH_3) and 50.0 g methanol (CH_3OH). What is the vapor pressure of this solution at 25°C? What is the composition of the vapor expressed as a mole fraction? Assume ideal solution and gas behavior. (At 25°C the vapor pressures of pure acetone and pure methanol are 271 and 143 torr, respectively.) The actual vapor pressure of this solution is 161 torr. Explain any discrepancies.

58. The vapor pressures of several solutions of water–propanol ($CH_3CH_2CH_2OH$) were determined at various compositions, with the following data collected at 45°C:

X_{H_2O}	Vapor pressure (torr)
0	74.0
0.15	77.3
0.37	80.2
0.54	81.6
0.69	80.6
0.83	78.2
1.00	71.9

a. Are solutions of water and propanol ideal? Explain.
b. Predict the sign of ΔH_{soln} for water–propanol solutions.
c. Are the interactive forces between propanol and water molecules weaker than, stronger than, or equal to the interactive forces between the pure substances? Explain.
d. Which of the solutions in the data would have the lowest normal boiling point?

Colligative Properties

59. A solution is prepared by dissolving 4.9 g sucrose ($C_{12}H_{22}O_{11}$) in 175 g water. Calculate the boiling point of this solution. Sucrose is a nonelectrolyte.

60. A 2.00-g sample of a large biomolecule was dissolved in 15.0 g of carbon tetrachloride. The boiling point of this solution was determined to be 77.85°C. Calculate the molar mass of the biomolecule. For carbon tetrachloride, the boiling-point constant is 5.03°C · kg/mol, and the boiling point of pure carbon tetrachloride is 76.50°C.

61. What mass of glycerin ($C_3H_8O_3$), a nonelectrolyte, must be dissolved in 200.0 g water to give a solution with a freezing point of −1.50°C?

62. The freezing point of t-butanol is 25.50°C and K_f is 9.1°C · kg/mol. Usually t-butanol absorbs water on exposure to air. If the freezing point of a 10.0-g sample of t-butanol is 24.59°C, how many grams of water are present in the sample?

63. Calculate the freezing point and boiling point of an antifreeze solution that is 50.0% by mass of ethylene glycol ($HOCH_2CH_2OH$) in water. Ethylene glycol is a nonelectrolyte.

64. What volume of ethylene glycol ($C_2H_6O_2$), a nonelectrolyte, must be added to 15.0 L of water to produce an antifreeze solution with a freezing point of −30.0°C? What is the boiling point of this solution? (The density of ethylene glycol is 1.11 g/cm³, and the density of water is 1.00 g/cm³.)

65. A 0.350-g sample of a large biomolecule was dissolved in 15.0 g of chloroform, and the freezing-point depression was determined to be 0.240°C. Calculate the molar mass of the biomolecule (K_f for chloroform is 4.70°C · kg/mol).

66. Anthraquinone contains only carbon, hydrogen, and oxygen and has an empirical formula of C_7H_4O. The freezing point of camphor is lowered by 22.3°C when 1.32 g anthraquinone is dissolved in 11.4 g camphor. Determine the molecular formula of anthraquinone.

67. a. Calculate the freezing-point depression and osmotic pressure at 25°C of an aqueous solution containing 1.0 g/L of a protein (molar mass = 9.0×10^4 g/mol) if the density of the solution is 1.0 g/cm³.
b. Considering your answer to part a, which colligative property, freezing-point depression or osmotic pressure, would be better used to determine the molar masses of large molecules? Explain.

68. A 20.0-mg sample of a protein is dissolved in water to make 25.0 mL of solution. The osmotic pressure of the solution is 0.56 torr at 25°C. What is the molar mass of the protein?

69. If the human eye has an osmotic pressure of 8.00 atm at 25°C, what concentration of solute particles in water will provide an isotonic eyedrop solution (a solution with equal osmotic pressure)?

70. How would you prepare 1.0 L of an aqueous solution of sodium chloride having an osmotic pressure of 15 atm at 22°C?

Properties of Electrolyte Solutions

71. Consider the following solutions:

0.010 m Na_3PO_4 in water
0.020 m $CaBr_2$ in water
0.020 m KCl in water
0.020 m HF in water (HF is a weak acid.)

   a. Assuming complete dissociation of the soluble salts, which solution(s) would have the same boiling point as 0.040 m $C_6H_{12}O_6$ in water? $C_6H_{12}O_6$ is a nonelectrolyte.
   b. Which solution would have the highest vapor pressure at 28°C?
   c. Which solution would have the largest freezing-point depression?

72. From the following:

pure water
solution of $C_{12}H_{22}O_{11}$ (m = 0.01) in water
solution of NaCl (m = 0.01) in water
solution of $CaCl_2$ (m = 0.01) in water

choose the one with the
   a. highest freezing point.   **d.** lowest boiling point.
   b. lowest freezing point.   **e.** highest osmotic pressure.
   c. highest boiling point.

73. Calculate the freezing point and the boiling point of each of the following aqueous solutions. (Assume complete dissociation.)
   a. 0.050 m $MgCl_2$
   b. 0.050 m $FeCl_3$

74. A water desalination plant is set up near a salt marsh containing water that is 0.10 M NaCl. Calculate the minimum pressure that must be applied at 20.°C to purify the water by reverse osmosis. Assume NaCl is completely dissociated.

75. Use the following data for three aqueous solutions of $CaCl_2$ to calculate the apparent value of the van't Hoff factor.

Molality	Freezing-Point Depression (°C)
0.0225	0.110
0.0910	0.440
0.278	1.330

76. Calculate the freezing point and the boiling point of each of the following solutions using the observed van't Hoff factors in Table 11.6.
   a. 0.050 m $MgCl_2$ **b.** 0.050 m $FeCl_3$

77. Calculate the osmotic pressure at 25°C of a 0.50 M solution of $Ca(NO_3)_2$ in water. (Assume that i = 3.0.) Would you expect the measured osmotic pressure of 0.50 M $Ca(NO_3)_2$ to be higher or lower than the value you calculated? Explain.

78. In the winter of 1994, record low temperatures were registered throughout the United States. For example, in Champaign, Illinois, a record low of $-29°F$ was registered. At this temperature can salting icy roads with $CaCl_2$ be effective in melting the ice?
   a. Assume i = 3.00 for $CaCl_2$.
   b. Assume the average value of i from Exercise 75.
   (The solubility of $CaCl_2$ in cold water is 74.5 g per 100.0 g of water.)

Additional Exercises

79. In a coffee-cup calorimeter, 1.60 g of NH_4NO_3 was mixed with 75.0 g of water at an initial temperature of 25.00°C. After dissolution of the salt, the final temperature of the calorimeter contents was 23.34°C.
   a. Assuming the solution has a heat capacity of 4.18 J/g · °C, and assuming no heat loss to the calorimeter, calculate the enthalpy of solution (ΔH_{soln}) for the dissolution of NH_4NO_3 in units of kJ/mol.
   b. If the enthalpy of hydration for NH_4NO_3 is -630. kJ/mol, calculate the lattice energy of NH_4NO_3.

80. In flushing and cleaning columns used in liquid chromatography to remove adsorbed contaminants, a series of solvents is used. Hexane (C_6H_{14}), chloroform ($CHCl_3$), methanol (CH_3OH), and water are passed through the column in that order. Rationalize the order in terms of intermolecular forces and the mutual solubility (miscibility) of the solvents.

81. Most gases are sparingly soluble in water. For example, a liter of water saturated with oxygen gas at room temperature contains only 0.05 g of O_2. Conversely, ammonia gas can dissolve in water to produce a 15 M solution. Why is ammonia gas so much more soluble in water than oxygen gas?

82. Is Henry's law valid for the solubility of CO_2 in a 0.1 M NaOH solution? *Hint:* $CO_2 + OH^- \rightarrow HCO_3^-$.

83. At 25°C, the vapor in equilibrium with a solution containing carbon disulfide and acetonitrile has a total pressure of 263 torr and is 85.5 mole percent carbon disulfide. What is the mole fraction of carbon disulfide in the solution? At 25°C, the vapor pressure of carbon disulfide is 375 torr. Assume the solution and vapor exhibit ideal behavior.

84. The molar mass of a nonelectrolyte is 58.0 g/mol. Compute the boiling point of a solution containing 24.0 g of this compound and 600. g of water if the barometric pressure is such that pure water boils at 99.725°C.

85. An unknown compound contains only carbon, hydrogen, and oxygen. Combustion analysis of the compound gives mass percents of 31.57% C and 5.30% H. The molar mass is determined by measuring the freezing-point depression of an aqueous solution. A freezing point of $-5.20°C$ is recorded for a solution made by dissolving 10.56 g of the compound in 25.0 g water. Determine the empirical formula, molar mass, and molecular formula of the compound. Assume that the compound is a nonelectrolyte.

86. Consider the following:

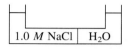

    What would happen to the level of liquid in the two arms if the semipermeable membrane separating the two liquids were permeable to
    a. H_2O only?   **b.** H_2O, Na^+, and Cl^-?

87. Consider an aqueous solution containing sodium chloride that has a density of 1.01 g/mL. Assume the solution behaves ideally. The freezing point of this solution at 1.0 atm is $-1.28°C$. Calculate the percent composition of this solution (by mass).

Challenge Problems

88. An aqueous solution is 1.00% NaCl by mass and has a density of 1.071 g/cm^3 at 25°C. The observed osmotic pressure of this solution is 7.83 atm at 25°C.
    a. What fraction of the moles of NaCl in this solution exist as ion pairs?
    b. Calculate the freezing point that would be observed for this solution.

89. The vapor in equilibrium with a pentane–hexane solution at 25°C has a mole fraction of pentane equal to 0.15 at 25°C. What is the mole fraction of pentane in the solution? (See Exercise 51 for the vapor pressures of the pure liquids.)

90. A forensic chemist is given a white solid that is suspected of being pure cocaine ($C_{17}H_{21}NO_4$, molar mass = 303.35 g/mol). She dissolves 1.22 ± 0.01 g of the solid in 15.60 ± 0.01 g benzene. The freezing point is lowered by 1.32 ± 0.04°C.
    a. What is the molar mass of the substance? Assuming that the percent uncertainty in the calculated molar mass is the same as the percent uncertainty in the temperature change, calculate the uncertainty in the molar mass.
    b. Could the chemist unequivocally state that the substance is cocaine? For example, is the uncertainty small enough to distinguish cocaine from codeine ($C_{18}H_{21}NO_3$, molar mass = 299.36 g/mol)?
    c. Assuming that the absolute uncertainties in the measurements of temperature and mass remain unchanged, how could the chemist improve the precision of her results?

91. A 1.60-g sample of a mixture of naphthalene ($C_{10}H_8$) and anthracene ($C_{14}H_{10}$) is dissolved in 20.0 g benzene (C_6H_6). The freezing point of the solution is 2.81°C. What is the composi-

tion as mass percent of the sample mixture? The freezing point of benzene is 5.51°C, and K_f is 5.12°C · kg/mol.

92. A solid consists of a mixture of $NaNO_3$ and $Mg(NO_3)_2$. When 6.50 g of the solid is dissolved in 50.0 g water, the freezing point is lowered by 5.40°C. What is the composition, by mass, of the solid?

93. Formic acid (HCO_2H) is a monoprotic acid that ionizes only partially in aqueous solutions. A 0.10 M formic acid solution is 4.2% ionized. Assuming that the molarity and molality of the solution are the same, calculate the freezing point and the boiling point of 0.10 M formic acid.

94. In some regions of the southwest United States, the water is very hard. For example, in Las Cruces, New Mexico, the tap water contains about 560 μg of dissolved solids per milliliter. Reverse osmosis units are marketed in this area to soften water. A typical unit exerts a pressure of 8.0 atm and can produce 45 L of water per day.
    a. Assuming all of the dissolved solids are $MgCO_3$ and assuming a temperature of 27°C, what total volume of water must be processed to produce 45 L of pure water?
    b. Would the same system work for purifying seawater? (Assume seawater is 0.60 M NaCl.)

Marathon Problem*

This problem is designed to incorporate several concepts and techniques into one situation. Marathon Problems can be used in class by groups of students to help facilitate problem-solving skills.

95. Using the following information, identify the strong electrolyte whose general formula is

$$M_x(A)_y \cdot zH_2O$$

    Ignore the effect of interionic attractions in the solution.
    a. A^{n-} is a common oxyanion. When 30.0 mg of the anhydrous sodium salt containing this oxyanion (Na_nA, where n = 1, 2, or 3) is reduced, 15.26 mL of 0.02313 M reducing agent is required to react completely with the Na_nA present. Assume a 1:1 mole ratio in the reaction.
    b. The cation is derived from a silvery white metal that is relatively expensive. The metal itself crystallizes in a body-centered cubic unit cell and has an atomic radius of 198.4 pm. The solid, pure metal has a density of 5.243 g/cm^3. The oxidation number of M in the strong electrolyte in question is +3.
    c. When 33.45 mg of the compound is present (dissolved) in 10.0 mL of aqueous solution at 25°C, the solution has an osmotic pressure of 558 torr.

* This Marathon Problem was developed by James H. Burness, Penn State University, York Campus. Reprinted with permission from the *Journal of Chemical Education*, Vol. 68, No. 11, 1991, pp. 919–922; copyright © 1991, Division of Chemical Education, Inc.

Chemical Kinetics

*T*he applications of chemistry focus largely on chemical reactions, and the commercial use of a reaction requires knowledge of several of its characteristics, including its stoichiometry, energetics, and rate. A reaction is defined by its reactants and products, whose identity must be learned by experiment. Once the reactants and products are known, the equation for the reaction can be written and balanced, and stoichiometric calculations can be carried out. Another very important characteristic of a reaction is its spontaneity. Spontaneity refers to the *inherent tendency* for the process to occur; however, it implies nothing about speed. *Spontaneous does not mean fast.* There are many spontaneous reactions that are so slow that no apparent reaction occurs over a period of weeks or years at normal temperatures. For example, there is a strong inherent tendency for gaseous hydrogen and oxygen to combine, that is,

$$2H_2(g) + O_2(g) \longrightarrow 2H_2O(l)$$

but in fact the two gases can coexist indefinitely at 25°C. Similarly, the gaseous reactions

$$H_2(g) + Cl_2(g) \longrightarrow 2HCl(g)$$
$$N_2(g) + 3H_2(g) \longrightarrow 2NH_3(g)$$

are both highly likely to occur from a thermodynamic standpoint, but we observe no reactions under normal conditions. In addition, the process of changing diamond to graphite is spontaneous but is so slow that it is not detectable.

To be useful, reactions must occur at a reasonable rate. To produce the 20 million tons of ammonia needed each year for fertilizer, we cannot simply mix nitrogen and hydrogen gases at 25°C and wait for them to react. It is not enough to understand the stoichiometry and thermodynamics of a reaction; we also must understand the factors that govern the rate of

A computer simulation of a porous aluminophosphate sheet, a potential solid-state catalyst. The atoms are indicated by colors: aluminum (yellow), phosphorus (light purple), oxygen (red), carbon (green), and nitrogen (blue).

The energy required for athletic exertion, the breaching of an Orca whale, and the combustion of fuel in a race car all result from chemical reactions.

the reaction. The area of chemistry that concerns reaction rates is called **chemical kinetics.**

One of the main goals of chemical kinetics is to understand the steps by which a reaction takes place. This series of steps is called the *reaction mechanism*. Understanding the mechanism allows us to find ways to facilitate the reaction. For example, the Haber process for the production of ammonia requires high temperatures to achieve commercially feasible reaction rates. However, even higher temperatures (and more cost) would be required without the use of iron oxide, which speeds up the reaction.

In this chapter we will consider the main ideas of chemical kinetics. We will explore rate laws, reaction mechanisms, and simple models for chemical reactions.

12.1 Reaction Rates

To introduce the concept of the rate of a reaction, we will consider the decomposition of nitrogen dioxide, a gas that causes air pollution. Nitrogen dioxide decomposes to nitric oxide and oxygen as follows:

$$2NO_2(g) \longrightarrow 2NO(g) + O_2(g)$$

Suppose in a particular experiment we start with a flask of nitrogen dioxide at 300°C and measure the concentrations of nitrogen dioxide, nitric oxide, and oxygen as the nitrogen dioxide decomposes. The results of this experiment are summarized in Table 12.1, and the data are plotted in Fig. 12.1.

Note from these results that the concentration of the reactant (NO_2) decreases with time and the concentrations of the products (NO and O_2) increase with time (see Fig. 12.2). Chemical kinetics deals with the speed at which these changes occur. The speed, or *rate,* of a process is defined as the change in a given quantity over a specific period of time. For chemical reactions, the quantity that changes is the amount or concentration of a reactant or product. So the **reaction rate** of a chemical reaction is defined as the *change in concentration of a reactant or product per unit time:*

$$\text{Rate} = \frac{\text{concentration of A at time } t_2 - \text{concentration of A at time } t_1}{t_2 - t_1}$$

$$= \frac{\Delta[A]}{\Delta t}$$

where A is the reactant or product being considered, and the square brackets indicate concentration in mol/L. As usual, the symbol Δ indicates a *change* in a given quantity. Note that a change can be positive (increase) or negative (decrease), thus leading to a positive or negative reaction rate by this definition. However, for convenience, we will always define the rate as a positive quantity, as we will see.

The kinetics of air pollution is discussed in Section 12.8.

Molecular Models: NO_2, NO, O_2

[A] means concentration of A in mol/L.

Table 12.1 Concentrations of Reactant and Products as a Function of Time for the Reaction $2NO_2(g) \rightarrow 2NO(g) + O_2(g)$ (at 300°C)

Time (±1 s)	Concentration (mol/L)		
	NO_2	NO	O_2
0	0.0100	0	0
50	0.0079	0.0021	0.0011
100	0.0065	0.0035	0.0018
150	0.0055	0.0045	0.0023
200	0.0048	0.0052	0.0026
250	0.0043	0.0057	0.0029
300	0.0038	0.0062	0.0031
350	0.0034	0.0066	0.0033
400	0.0031	0.0069	0.0035

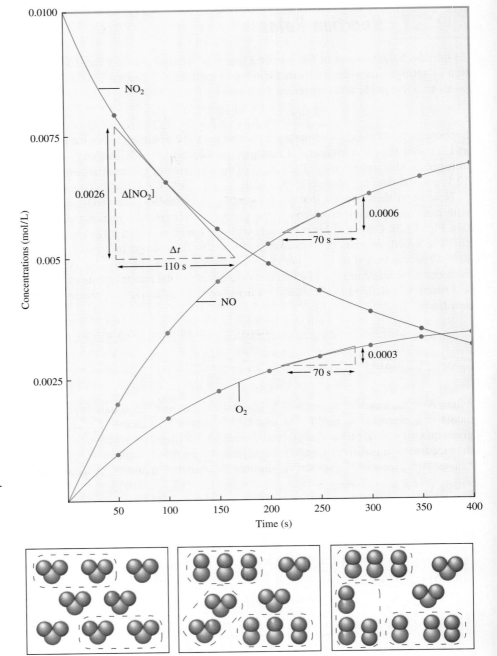

Figure 12.1
Starting with a flask of nitrogen dioxide at 300°C, the concentrations of nitrogen dioxide, nitric oxide, and oxygen are plotted versus time.

Figure 12.2
Representation of the reaction $2NO_2(g) \rightarrow 2NO(g) + O_2(g)$. (a) The reaction at the very beginning ($t = 0$). (b) and (c) As time passes, NO_2 is converted to NO and O_2.

Now let us calculate the average rate at which the concentration of NO_2 changes over the first 50 seconds of the reaction using the data given in Table 12.1.

$$\frac{\text{Change in } [NO_2]}{\text{Time elapsed}} = \frac{\Delta[NO_2]}{\Delta t}$$

$$= \frac{[NO_2]_{t=50} - [NO_2]_{t=0}}{50. \text{ s} - 0 \text{ s}}$$

$$= \frac{0.0079 \text{ mol/L} - 0.0100 \text{ mol/L}}{50. \text{ s}}$$

$$= -4.2 \times 10^{-5} \text{ mol/L} \cdot \text{s}$$

Note that since the concentration of NO_2 decreases with time, $\Delta[NO_2]$ is a negative quantity. Because it is customary to work with *positive* reaction rates, we define the rate of this particular reaction as

$$\text{Rate} = -\frac{\Delta[NO_2]}{\Delta t}$$

Since the concentrations of reactants always decrease with time, any rate expression involving a reactant will include a negative sign. The average rate of this reaction from 0 to 50 seconds is then

$$\text{Rate} = -\frac{\Delta[NO_2]}{\Delta t}$$

$$= -(-4.2 \times 10^{-5} \text{ mol/L} \cdot \text{s})$$

$$= 4.2 \times 10^{-5} \text{ mol/L} \cdot \text{s}$$

The average rates for this reaction during several other time intervals are given in Table 12.2. *Note that the rate is not constant but decreases with time.* The rates given in Table 12.2 are *average rates* over 50-second time intervals. The value of the rate at a particular time (the **instantaneous rate**) can be obtained by computing the slope of a line tangent to the curve at that point. Figure 12.1 shows a tangent drawn at $t = 100$ seconds. The *slope* of this line gives the rate at $t = 100$ seconds as follows:

Appendix 1.3 reviews slopes of straight lines.

$$\text{Slope of the tangent line} = \frac{\text{change in } y}{\text{change in } x}$$

$$= \frac{\Delta[NO_2]}{\Delta t}$$

But

$$\text{Rate} = -\frac{\Delta[NO_2]}{\Delta t}$$

Table 12.2 Average Rate (in mol/L · s) of Decomposition of Nitrogen Dioxide as a Function of Time*	
$-\dfrac{\Delta[NO_2]}{\Delta t}$	*Time Period (s)*
4.2×10^{-5}	$0 \rightarrow 50$
2.8×10^{-5}	$50 \rightarrow 100$
2.0×10^{-5}	$100 \rightarrow 150$
1.4×10^{-5}	$150 \rightarrow 200$
1.0×10^{-5}	$200 \rightarrow 250$
*Note that the *rate* decreases with time.*	

Therefore,

$$\text{Rate} = -(\text{slope of the tangent line})$$

$$= -\left(\frac{-0.0026 \text{ mol/L}}{110 \text{ s}}\right)$$

$$= 2.4 \times 10^{-5} \text{ mol/L} \cdot \text{s}$$

So far we have discussed the rate of this reaction only in terms of the reactant. The rate also can be defined in terms of the products. However, in doing so we must take into account the coefficients in the balanced equation for the reaction, because the stoichiometry determines the relative rates of consumption of reactants and generation of products. For example, in the reaction we are considering,

$$2NO_2(g) \longrightarrow 2NO(g) + O_2(g)$$

both the reactant NO_2 and the product NO have a coefficient of 2, so NO is produced at the same rate as NO_2 is consumed. We can verify this from Fig. 12.1. Note that the curve for NO is the same shape as the curve for NO_2, except that it is inverted, or flipped over. This means that, at any point in time, the slope of the tangent to the curve for NO will be the negative of the slope to the curve for NO_2. (Verify this at the point $t = 100$ seconds on both curves.) In the balanced equation, the product O_2 has a coefficient of 1, which means it is produced half as fast as NO, since NO has a coefficient of 2. That is, the rate of NO production is twice the rate of O_2 production.

We also can verify this fact from Fig. 12.1. For example, at $t = 250$ seconds,

$$\text{Slope of the tangent to the NO curve} = \frac{6.0 \times 10^{-4} \text{ mol/L}}{70. \text{ s}}$$

$$= 8.6 \times 10^{-6} \text{ mol/L} \cdot \text{s}$$

$$\text{Slope of the tangent to the } O_2 \text{ curve} = \frac{3.0 \times 10^{-4} \text{ mol/L}}{70. \text{ s}}$$

$$= 4.3 \times 10^{-6} \text{ mol/L} \cdot \text{s}$$

The slope at $t = 250$ seconds on the NO curve is twice the slope of that point on the O_2 curve, showing that the rate of production of NO is twice that of O_2.

The rate information can be summarized as follows:

Rate of consumption of NO_2	=	rate of production of NO	=	2(rate of production of O_2)
$-\dfrac{\Delta[NO_2]}{\Delta t}$	=	$\dfrac{\Delta[NO]}{\Delta t}$	=	$2\left(\dfrac{\Delta[O_2]}{\Delta t}\right)$

We have seen that the rate of a reaction is not constant, but that it changes with time. This is so because the concentrations change with time (Fig. 12.1).

Because the reaction rate changes with time, and because the rate is different (by factors that depend on the coefficients in the balanced equation) depending on which reactant or product is being studied, we must be very specific when we describe a rate for a chemical reaction.

12.2 Rate Laws: An Introduction

Chemical reactions are *reversible.* In our discussion of the decomposition of nitrogen dioxide, we have so far considered only the *forward reaction,* as shown here:

$$2NO_2(g) \longrightarrow 2NO(g) + O_2(g)$$

However, the *reverse reaction* also can occur. As NO and O_2 accumulate, they can react to re-form NO_2:

$$O_2(g) + 2NO(g) \longrightarrow 2NO_2(g)$$

When gaseous NO_2 is placed in an otherwise empty container, initially the dominant reaction is

$$2NO_2(g) \longrightarrow 2NO(g) + O_2(g)$$

and the change in the concentration of NO_2 ($\Delta[NO_2]$) depends only on the forward reaction. However, after a period of time, enough products accumulate so that the reverse reaction becomes important. Now $\Delta[NO_2]$ depends on the *difference in the rates of the forward and reverse reactions.* This complication can be avoided if we study the rate of a reaction under conditions where the reverse reaction makes only a negligible contribution. Typically, this means that we must study a reaction at a point soon after the reactants are mixed, before the products have had time to build up to significant levels.

If we choose conditions where the reverse reaction can be neglected, the *reaction rate will depend only on the concentrations of the reactants.* For the decomposition of nitrogen dioxide, we can write

$$\text{Rate} = k[NO_2]^n \qquad (12.1)$$

Such an expression, which shows how the rate depends on the concentrations of reactants, is called a **rate law.** The proportionality constant k, called the **rate constant,** and n, called the **order** of the reactant, must both be determined by experiment. The order of a reactant can be an integer (including zero) or a fraction. For the relatively simple reactions we will consider in this book, the orders will often be positive integers.

Note two important points about Equation (12.1):

1. The concentrations of the products do not appear in the rate law because the reaction rate is being studied under conditions where the reverse reaction does not contribute to the overall rate.

2. The value of the exponent n must be determined by experiment; it cannot be written from the balanced equation.

Before we go further we must define exactly what we mean by the term *rate* in Equation (12.1). In Section 12.1 we saw that reaction rate means a change in concentration per unit time. However, which reactant or product concentration do we choose in defining the rate? For example, for the decomposition of NO_2 to produce O_2 and NO considered in Section 12.1, we could define the rate in terms of any of these three species. However, since O_2 is produced only half as fast as NO, we must be careful to specify which species we are talking about in a given case. For instance, we might choose to define the reaction rate in terms of the consumption of NO_2:

$$\text{Rate} = -\frac{\Delta[NO_2]}{\Delta t} = k[NO_2]^n$$

On the other hand, we could define the rate in terms of the production of O_2:

$$\text{Rate}' = \frac{\Delta[O_2]}{\Delta t} = k'[NO_2]^n$$

When forward and reverse reaction rates are equal, there will be no changes in the concentrations of reactants or products. This is called *chemical equilibrium* and is discussed fully in Chapter 13.

Note that because $2NO_2$ molecules are consumed for every O_2 molecule produced,

$$\text{Rate} = 2 \times \text{rate}'$$

or

$$k[NO_2]^n = 2k'[NO_2]^n$$

and

$$k = 2 \times k'$$

Thus the value of the rate constant depends on how the rate is defined.

In this text we will always be careful to define exactly what is meant by the rate for a given reaction so that there will be no confusion about which specific rate constant is being used.

Types of Rate Laws

Notice that the rate law we have used to this point expresses rate as a function of concentration. For example, for the decomposition of NO_2 we have defined

$$\text{Rate} = -\frac{\Delta[NO_2]}{\Delta t} = k[NO_2]^n$$

which tells us (once we have determined the value of n) exactly how the rate depends on the concentration of the reactant, NO_2. A rate law that expresses how the *rate depends on concentration* is technically called the **differential rate law,** but it is often simply called the **rate law.** Thus when we use the term *the rate law* in this text, we mean the expression that gives the rate as a function of concentration.

A second kind of rate law, the **integrated rate law,** also will be important in our study of kinetics. The integrated rate law expresses how the *concentrations depend on time.* Although we will not consider the details here, a given differential rate law is always related to a certain type of integrated rate law, and vice versa. That is, if we determine the differential rate law for a given reaction, we automatically know the form of the integrated rate law for the reaction. This means that once we determine experimentally either type of rate law for a reaction, we also know the other one.

Which rate law we choose to determine by experiment often depends on what types of data are easiest to collect. If we can conveniently measure how the rate changes as the concentrations are changed, we can readily determine the differential (rate/concentration) rate law. On the other hand, if it is more convenient to measure the concentration as a function of time, we can determine the form of the integrated (concentration/time) rate law. We will discuss how rate laws are actually determined in the next several sections.

Why are we interested in determining the rate law for a reaction? How does it help us? It helps us because we can work backward from the rate law to infer the steps by which the reaction occurs. Most chemical reactions do not take place in a single step but result from a series of sequential steps. To understand a chemical reaction, we must learn what these steps are. For example, a chemist who is designing an insecticide may study the reactions involved in the process of insect growth to see what type of molecule might interrupt this series of reactions. Or an industrial chemist may be trying to make a given reaction occur faster. To accomplish this, he or she must know which step is slowest, because it is that step that must be speeded up. Thus a chemist is usually not interested in a rate law for its own sake but because of what it reveals about the steps by which a reaction occurs. We will develop a process for finding the reaction steps in this chapter.

The name *differential rate law* comes from a mathematical term. We will regard it simply as a label. The terms *differential rate law* and *rate law* will be used interchangeably in this text.

Rate Laws: A Summary

- There are two types of rate laws.
  1. The *differential rate law* (often called simply the *rate law*) shows how the rate of a reaction depends on concentrations.
  2. The *integrated rate law* shows how the concentrations of species in the reaction depend on time.
- Because we typically consider reactions only under conditions where the reverse reaction is unimportant, our rate laws will involve only concentrations of reactants.
- Because the differential and integrated rate laws for a given reaction are related in a well-defined way, the experimental determination of *either* of the rate laws is sufficient.
- Experimental convenience usually dictates which type of rate law is determined experimentally.
- Knowing the rate law for a reaction is important mainly because we can usually infer the individual steps involved in the reaction from the specific form of the rate law.

12.3 Determining the Form of the Rate Law

The first step in understanding how a given chemical reaction occurs is to determine the *form* of the rate law. That is, we need to determine experimentally the power to which each reactant concentration must be raised in the rate law. In this section we will explore ways to obtain the differential rate law for a reaction. First, we will consider the decomposition of dinitrogen pentoxide in carbon tetrachloride solution:

$$2N_2O_5(soln) \longrightarrow 4NO_2(soln) + O_2(g)$$

Molecular Models: N_2O_5, NO_2, O_2

Data for this reaction at 45°C are listed in Table 12.3 and plotted in Fig. 12.3. In this reaction the oxygen gas escapes from the solution and thus does not react with the nitrogen dioxide, so we do not have to be concerned about the effects of the reverse reaction at any time over the life of the reaction. That is, the reverse reaction is negligible at all times over the course of this reaction.

Evaluation of the reaction rates at concentrations of N_2O_5 of 0.90 *M* and 0.45 *M*, by taking the slopes of the tangents to the curve at these points (see Fig. 12.3), yields the following data:

$[N_2O_5]$	Rate $(mol/L \cdot s)$
0.90 *M*	5.4×10^{-4}
0.45 *M*	2.7×10^{-4}

Table 12.3 Concentration/Time Data for the Reaction $2N_2O_5(soln) \rightarrow 4NO_2(soln) + O_2(g)$ (at 45°C)

$[N_2O_5]$ (mol/L)	Time (s)
1.00	0
0.88	200
0.78	400
0.69	600
0.61	800
0.54	1000
0.48	1200
0.43	1400
0.38	1600
0.34	1800
0.30	2000

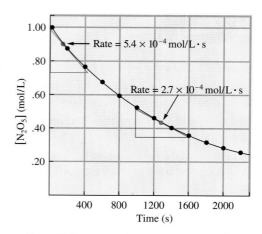

Figure 12.3
A plot of the concentration of N_2O_5 as a function of time for the reaction $2N_2O_5(soln) \rightarrow 4NO_2(soln) + O_2(g)$ (at 45°C). Note that the reaction rate at $[N_2O_5] = 0.90$ *M* is twice that at $[N_2O_5] = 0.45$ *M*.

Note that when $[N_2O_5]$ is halved, the rate is also halved. This means that the rate of this reaction depends on the concentration of N_2O_5 to the *first power*. In other words, the (differential) rate law for this reaction is

$$\text{Rate} = -\frac{\Delta[N_2O_5]}{\Delta t} = k[N_2O_5]^1 = k[N_2O_5]$$

First order: rate = $k[A]$. Doubling the concentration of A doubles the reaction rate.

Thus the reaction is *first order* in N_2O_5. Note that for this reaction the order is *not* the same as the coefficient of N_2O_5 in the balanced equation for the reaction. This reemphasizes the fact that the order of a particular reactant must be obtained by *observing* how the reaction rate depends on the concentration of that reactant.

We have seen that by determining the instantaneous rate at two different reactant concentrations, the rate law for the decomposition of N_2O_5 is shown to have the form

$$\text{Rate} = -\frac{\Delta[A]}{\Delta t} = k[A]$$

where A represents N_2O_5.

Method of Initial Rates

The value of the initial rate is determined for each experiment at the same value of t as close to $t = 0$ as possible.

 Video: Reaction Rate and Concentration

One common method for experimentally determining the form of the rate law for a reaction is the **method of initial rates.** The **initial rate** of a reaction is the instantaneous rate determined just after the reaction begins (just after $t = 0$). The idea is to determine the instantaneous rate before the initial concentrations of reactants have changed significantly. Several experiments are carried out using different initial concentrations, and the initial rate is determined for each run. The results are then compared to see how the initial rate depends on the initial concentrations. This allows the form of the rate law to be determined. We will illustrate the method of initial rates using the following equation:

Table 12.4 Initial Rates from Three Experiments for the Reaction
$NH_4^+(aq) + NO_2^-(aq) \rightarrow N_2(g) + 2H_2O(l)$

Experiment	Initial Concentration of NH_4^+	Initial Concentration of NO_2^-	Initial Rate (mol/L · s)
1	0.100 M	0.0050 M	1.35×10^{-7}
2	0.100 M	0.010 M	2.70×10^{-7}
3	0.200 M	0.010 M	5.40×10^{-7}

$$NH_4^+(aq) + NO_2^-(aq) \longrightarrow N_2(g) + 2H_2O(l)$$

Table 12.4 gives initial rates obtained from three experiments involving different initial concentrations of reactants. The general form of the rate law for this reaction is

$$\text{Rate} = -\frac{\Delta[NH_4^+]}{\Delta t} = k[NH_4^+]^n[NO_2^-]^m$$

We can determine the values of n and m by observing how the initial rate depends on the initial concentrations of NH_4^+ and NO_2^-. In Experiments 1 and 2, where the initial concentration of NH_4^+ remains the same but the initial concentration of NO_2^- doubles, the observed initial rate also doubles. Since

$$\text{Rate} = k[NH_4^+]^n[NO_2^-]^m$$

we have for Experiment 1

$$\text{Rate} = 1.35 \times 10^{-7} \text{ mol/L} \cdot \text{s} = k(0.100 \text{ mol/L})^n(0.0050 \text{ mol/L})^m$$

and for Experiment 2

$$\text{Rate} = 2.70 \times 10^{-7} \text{ mol/L} \cdot \text{s} = k(0.100 \text{ mol/L})^n(0.010 \text{ mol/L})^m$$

The ratio of these rates is

$$\frac{\text{Rate 2}}{\text{Rate 1}} = \underbrace{\frac{2.70 \times 10^{-7} \text{ mol/L} \cdot \text{s}}{1.35 \times 10^{-7} \text{ mol/L} \cdot \text{s}}}_{2.00} = \frac{\cancel{k(0.100 \text{ mol/L})^n}(0.010 \text{ mol/L})^m}{\cancel{k(0.100 \text{ mol/L})^n}(0.0050 \text{ mol/L})^m}$$

$$= \frac{(0.010 \text{ mol/L})^m}{(0.0050 \text{ mol/L})^m} = (2.0)^m$$

Thus

$$\frac{\text{Rate 2}}{\text{Rate 1}} = 2.00 = (2.0)^m$$

Rates 1, 2, and 3 were determined at the same value of t (very close to $t = 0$).

which means the value of m is 1. The rate law for this reaction is first order in the reactant NO_2^-.

A similar analysis of the results for Experiments 2 and 3 yields the ratio

$$\frac{\text{Rate 3}}{\text{Rate 2}} = \frac{5.40 \times 10^{-7} \text{ mol/L} \cdot \text{s}}{2.70 \times 10^{-7} \text{ mol/L} \cdot \text{s}} = \frac{(0.200 \text{ mol/L})^n}{(0.100 \text{ mol/L})^n}$$

$$= 2.00 = \left(\frac{0.200}{0.100}\right)^n = (2.00)^n$$

The value of n is also 1.

We have shown that the values of n and m are both 1 and the rate law is

$$\text{Rate} = k[\text{NH}_4^+][\text{NO}_2^-]$$

This rate law is first order in both NO_2^- and NH_4^+. Note that it is merely a coincidence that n and m have the same values as the coefficients of NH_4^+ and NO_2^- in the balanced equation for the reaction.

The **overall reaction order** is the sum of n and m. For this reaction, $n + m = 2$. The reaction is second order overall.

The value of the rate constant k can now be calculated using the results of *any* of the three experiments shown in Table 12.4. From the data for Experiment 1, we know that

$$\text{Rate} = k[\text{NH}_4^+][\text{NO}_2^-]$$

$$1.35 \times 10^{-7} \text{ mol/L} \cdot \text{s} = k(0.100 \text{ mol/L})(0.0050 \text{ mol/L})$$

Then

$$k = \frac{1.35 \times 10^{-7} \text{ mol/L} \cdot \text{s}}{(0.100 \text{ mol/L})(0.0050 \text{ mol/L})} = 2.7 \times 10^{-4} \text{ L/mol} \cdot \text{s}$$

> Overall reaction order is the sum of the orders for the various reactants.

Sample Exercise **12.1** *Determining a Rate Law*

The reaction between bromate ions and bromide ions in acidic aqueous solution is given by the equation

$$\text{BrO}_3^-(aq) + 5\text{Br}^-(aq) + 6\text{H}^+(aq) \longrightarrow 3\text{Br}_2(l) + 3\text{H}_2\text{O}(l)$$

Table 12.5 gives the results from four experiments. Using these data, determine the orders for all three reactants, the overall reaction order, and the value of the rate constant.

Table 12.5 The Results from Four Experiments to Study the Reaction $\text{BrO}_3^-(aq) + 5\text{Br}^-(aq) + 6\text{H}^+(aq) \rightarrow 3\text{Br}_2(l) + 3\text{H}_2\text{O}(l)$

Experiment	Initial Concentration of BrO_3^- (mol/L)	Initial Concentration of Br^- (mol/L)	Initial Concentration of H^+ (mol/L)	Measured Initial Rate (mol/L · s)
1	0.10	0.10	0.10	8.0×10^{-4}
2	0.20	0.10	0.10	1.6×10^{-3}
3	0.20	0.20	0.10	3.2×10^{-3}
4	0.10	0.10	0.20	3.2×10^{-3}

Solution

The general form of the rate law for this reaction is

$$\text{Rate} = k[\text{BrO}_3^-]^n[\text{Br}^-]^m[\text{H}^+]^p$$

We can determine the values of n, m, and p by comparing the rates from the various experiments. To determine the value of n, we use the results from Experiments 1 and 2, in which only $[\text{BrO}_3^-]$ changes:

$$\frac{\text{Rate 2}}{\text{Rate 1}} = \frac{1.6 \times 10^{-3} \text{ mol/L} \cdot \text{s}}{8.0 \times 10^{-4} \text{ mol/L} \cdot \text{s}} = \frac{k(0.20 \text{ mol/L})^n(0.10 \text{ mol/L})^m(0.10 \text{ mol/L})^p}{k(0.10 \text{ mol/L})^n(0.10 \text{ mol/L})^m(0.10 \text{ mol/L})^p}$$

$$2.0 = \left(\frac{0.20 \text{ mol/L}}{0.10 \text{ mol/L}}\right)^n = (2.0)^n$$

Thus n is equal to 1.

To determine the value of m, we use the results from Experiments 2 and 3, in which only $[Br^-]$ changes:

$$\frac{\text{Rate 3}}{\text{Rate 2}} = \frac{3.2 \times 10^{-3} \text{ mol/L} \cdot \text{s}}{1.6 \times 10^{-3} \text{ mol/L} \cdot \text{s}} = \frac{k(0.20 \text{ mol/L})^n(0.20 \text{ mol/L})^m(0.10 \text{ mol/L})^p}{k(0.20 \text{ mol/L})^n(0.10 \text{ mol/L})^m(0.10 \text{ mol/L})^p}$$

$$2.0 = \left(\frac{0.20 \text{ mol/L}}{0.10 \text{ mol/L}}\right)^m = (2.0)^m$$

Thus m is equal to 1.

To determine the value of p, we use the results from Experiments 1 and 4, in which $[BrO_3^-]$ and $[Br^-]$ are constant but $[H^+]$ differs:

$$\frac{\text{Rate 4}}{\text{Rate 1}} = \frac{3.2 \times 10^{-3} \text{ mol/L} \cdot \text{s}}{8.0 \times 10^{-4} \text{ mol/L} \cdot \text{s}} = \frac{k(0.10 \text{ mol/L})^n(0.10 \text{ mol/L})^m(0.20 \text{ mol/L})^p}{k(0.10 \text{ mol/L})^n(0.10 \text{ mol/L})^m(0.10 \text{ mol/L})^p}$$

$$4.0 = \left(\frac{0.20 \text{ mol/L}}{0.10 \text{ mol/L}}\right)^p$$

$$4.0 = (2.0)^p = (2.0)^2$$

Thus p is equal to 2.

The rate of this reaction is first order in BrO_3^- and Br^- and second order in H^+. The overall reaction order is $n + m + p = 4$.

The rate law can now be written

$$\text{Rate} = k[BrO_3^-][Br^-][H^+]^2$$

The value of the rate constant k can be calculated from the results of any of the four experiments. For Experiment 1, the initial rate is 8.0×10^{-4} mol/L $\cdot$ s and $[BrO_3^-] = 0.100 \ M$, $[Br^-] = 0.10 \ M$, and $[H^+] = 0.10 \ M$. Using these values in the rate law gives

$$8.0 \times 10^{-4} \text{ mol/L} \cdot \text{s} = k(0.10 \text{ mol/L})(0.10 \text{ mol/L})(0.10 \text{ mol/L})^2$$

$$8.0 \times 10^{-4} \text{ mol/L} \cdot \text{s} = k(1.0 \times 10^{-4} \text{ mol}^4/\text{L}^4)$$

$$k = \frac{8.0 \times 10^{-4} \text{ mol/L} \cdot \text{s}}{1.0 \times 10^{-4} \text{ mol}^4/\text{L}^4} = 8.0 \text{ L}^3/\text{mol}^3 \cdot \text{s}$$

CHECK

Verify that the same value of k can be obtained from the results of the other experiments.

See Exercises 12.23 through 12.26.

12.4 The Integrated Rate Law

The rate laws we have considered so far express the rate as a function of the reactant concentrations. It is also useful to be able to express the reactant concentrations as a function of time, given the (differential) rate law for the reaction. In this section we show how this is done.

We will proceed by first looking at reactions involving a single reactant:

$$aA \longrightarrow products$$

all of which have a rate law of the form

$$Rate = -\frac{\Delta[A]}{\Delta t} = k[A]^n$$

We will develop the integrated rate laws individually for the cases $n = 1$ (first order), $n = 2$ (second order), and $n = 0$ (zero order).

First-Order Rate Laws

For the reaction

$$2N_2O_5(soln) \longrightarrow 4NO_2(soln) + O_2(g)$$

we have found that the rate law is

$$Rate = -\frac{\Delta[N_2O_5]}{\Delta t} = k[N_2O_5]$$

Since the rate of this reaction depends on the concentration of N_2O_5 to the first power, it is a **first-order reaction.** This means that if the concentration of N_2O_5 in a flask were suddenly doubled, the rate of production of NO_2 and O_2 also would double. This rate law can be put into a different form using a calculus operation known as integration, which yields the expression

$$\ln[N_2O_5] = -kt + \ln[N_2O_5]_0$$

Appendix 1.2 contains a review of logarithms.

where ln indicates the natural logarithm, t is the time, $[N_2O_5]$ is the concentration of N_2O_5 at time t, and $[N_2O_5]_0$ is the initial concentration of N_2O_5 (at $t = 0$, the start of the experiment). Note that such an equation, called the *integrated rate law,* expresses the *concentration of the reactant as a function of time.*

For a chemical reaction of the form

$$aA \longrightarrow products$$

where the kinetics are first order in $[A]$, the rate law is

$$Rate = -\frac{\Delta[A]}{\Delta t} = k[A]$$

and the **integrated first-order rate law** is

$$\ln[A] = -kt + \ln[A]_0 \tag{12.2}$$

There are several important things to note about Equation (12.2):

1. The equation shows how the concentration of A depends on time. If the initial concentration of A and the rate constant k are known, the concentration of A at any time can be calculated.

An integrated rate law relates concentration to reaction time.

2. Equation (12.2) is of the form $y = mx + b$, where a plot of y versus x is a straight line with slope m and intercept b. In Equation (12.2),

$$y = \ln[A] \qquad x = t \qquad m = -k \qquad b = \ln[A]_0$$

Thus, for a first-order reaction, plotting the natural logarithm of concentration versus time always gives a straight line. This fact is often used to test whether a reaction is first order or not. For the reaction

For a first-order reaction, a plot of $\ln[A]$ versus t is always a straight line.

$$aA \longrightarrow \text{products}$$

the *reaction is first order in A if a plot of ln[A] versus t is a straight line.* Conversely, if this plot is not a straight line, the reaction is not first order in A.

3. This integrated rate law for a first-order reaction also can be expressed in terms of a *ratio* of [A] and $[A]_0$ as follows:

$$\ln\left(\frac{[A]_0}{[A]}\right) = kt$$

Sample Exercise 12.2 *First-Order Rate Laws I*

The decomposition of N_2O_5 in the gas phase was studied at constant temperature.

$$2N_2O_5(g) \longrightarrow 4NO_2(g) + O_2(g)$$

The following results were collected:

$[N_2O_5]$ (mol/L)	Time (s)
0.1000	0
0.0707	50
0.0500	100
0.0250	200
0.0125	300
0.00625	400

Using these data, verify that the rate law is first order in $[N_2O_5]$, and calculate the value of the rate constant, where the rate $= -\Delta[N_2O_5]/\Delta t$.

Solution

We can verify that the rate law is first order in $[N_2O_5]$ by constructing a plot of $\ln[N_2O_5]$ versus time. The values of $\ln[N_2O_5]$ at various times are given in the table on the next page, and the plot of $\ln[N_2O_5]$ versus time is shown in Fig. 12.4.

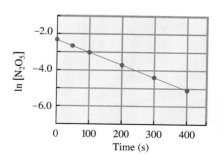

Figure 12.4
A plot of $\ln[N_2O_5]$ versus time.

$\ln[N_2O_5]$	Time (s)
−2.303	0
−2.649	50
−2.996	100
−3.689	200
−4.382	300
−5.075	400

The fact that the plot is a straight line confirms that the reaction is first order in N_2O_5, since it follows the equation $\ln[N_2O_5] = -kt + \ln[N_2O_5]_0$.

Since the reaction is first order, the slope of the line equals $-k$, where

$$\text{Slope} = \frac{\text{change in } y}{\text{change in } x} = \frac{\Delta y}{\Delta x} = \frac{\Delta(\ln[N_2O_5])}{\Delta t}$$

Since the first and last points are exactly on the line, we will use these points to calculate the slope:

$$\text{Slope} = \frac{-5.075 - (-2.303)}{400.\ \text{s} - 0\ \text{s}} = \frac{-2.772}{400.\ \text{s}} = -6.93 \times 10^{-3}\ \text{s}^{-1}$$

$$k = -(\text{slope}) = 6.93 \times 10^{-3}\ \text{s}^{-1}$$

See Exercise 12.29.

Sample Exercise 12.3 *First-Order Rate Laws II*

Using the data given in Sample Exercise 12.2, calculate $[N_2O_5]$ at 150 s after the start of the reaction.

Solution

We know from Sample Exercise 12.2 that $[N_2O_5] = 0.0500$ mol/L at 100 s and $[N_2O_5] = 0.0250$ mol/L at 200 s. Since 150 s is halfway between 100 and 200 s, it is tempting to assume that we can simply use an arithmetic average to obtain $[N_2O_5]$ at that time. This is incorrect because it is $\ln[N_2O_5]$, not $[N_2O_5]$, that is directly proportional to t. To calculate $[N_2O_5]$ after 150 s, we use Equation (12.2):

$$\ln[N_2O_5] = -kt + \ln[N_2O_5]_0$$

where $t = 150.$ s, $k = 6.93 \times 10^{-3}\ \text{s}^{-1}$ (as determined in Sample Exercise 12.2), and $[N_2O_5]_0 = 0.1000$ mol/L.

$$\ln([N_2O_5])_{t=150} = -(6.93 \times 10^{-3}\ \text{s}^{-1})(150.\ \text{s}) + \ln(0.100)$$
$$= -1.040 - 2.303 = -3.343$$
$$[N_2O_5]_{t=150} = \text{antilog}(-3.343) = 0.0353\ \text{mol/L}$$

The antilog operation means to exponentiate (see Appendix 1.2).

Note that this value of $[N_2O_5]$ is *not* halfway between 0.0500 and 0.0250 mol/L.

See Exercise 12.29.

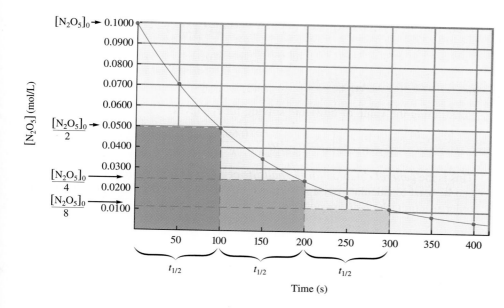

Figure 12.5

A plot of $[N_2O_5]$ versus time for the decomposition reaction of N_2O_5.

Half-Life of a First-Order Reaction

The time required for a reactant to reach half its original concentration is called the **half-life of a reactant** and is designated by the symbol $t_{1/2}$. For example, we can calculate the half-life of the decomposition reaction discussed in Sample Exercise 12.2. The data plotted in Fig. 12.5 show that the half-life for this reaction is 100 seconds. We can see this by considering the following numbers:

$[N_2O_5](mol/L)$	t (s)		
0.100	0		
0.0500	100	$\Delta t = 100$ s;	$\dfrac{[N_2O_5]_{t=100}}{[N_2O_5]_{t=0}} = \dfrac{0.050}{0.100} = \dfrac{1}{2}$
0.0250	200	$\Delta t = 100$ s;	$\dfrac{[N_2O_5]_{t=200}}{[N_2O_5]_{t=100}} = \dfrac{0.025}{0.050} = \dfrac{1}{2}$
0.0125	300	$\Delta t = 100$ s;	$\dfrac{[N_2O_5]_{t=300}}{[N_2O_5]_{t=200}} = \dfrac{0.0125}{0.0250} = \dfrac{1}{2}$

Note that it *always* takes 100 seconds for $[N_2O_5]$ to be halved in this reaction.

A general formula for the half-life of a first-order reaction can be derived from the integrated rate law for the general reaction

$$aA \longrightarrow products$$

If the reaction is first order in $[A]$,

$$\ln\left(\frac{[A]_0}{[A]}\right) = kt$$

By definition, when $t = t_{1/2}$,

$$[A] = \frac{[A]_0}{2}$$

Then, for $t = t_{1/2}$, the integrated rate law becomes

$$\ln\left(\frac{[A]_0}{[A]_0/2}\right) = kt_{1/2}$$

or

$$\ln(2) = kt_{1/2}$$

Substituting the value of $\ln(2)$ and solving for $t_{1/2}$ gives

$$t_{1/2} = \frac{0.693}{k} \tag{12.3}$$

For a first-order reaction, $t_{1/2}$ is independent of the initial concentration.

This is the *general equation for the half-life of a first-order reaction.* Equation (12.3) can be used to calculate $t_{1/2}$ if k is known or k if $t_{1/2}$ is known. Note that for a first-order reaction, *the half-life does not depend on concentration.*

Sample Exercise 12.4 Half-Life for First-Order Reaction

A certain first-order reaction has a half-life of 20.0 minutes.

a. Calculate the rate constant for this reaction.
b. How much time is required for this reaction to be 75% complete?

Solution

a. Solving Equation (12.3) for k gives

$$k = \frac{0.693}{t_{1/2}} = \frac{0.693}{20.0 \text{ min}} = 3.47 \times 10^{-2} \text{ min}^{-1}$$

b. We use the integrated rate law in the form

$$\ln\left(\frac{[A]_0}{[A]}\right) = kt$$

If the reaction is 75% complete, 75% of the reactant has been consumed, leaving 25% in the original form:

$$\frac{[A]}{[A]_0} \times 100 = 25$$

This means that

$$\frac{[A]}{[A]_0} = 0.25 \quad \text{or} \quad \frac{[A]_0}{[A]} = \frac{1}{0.25} = 4.0$$

Then

$$\ln\left(\frac{[A]_0}{[A]}\right) = \ln(4.0) = kt = \left(\frac{3.47 \times 10^{-2}}{\text{min}}\right)t$$

and

$$t = \frac{\ln(4.0)}{\dfrac{3.47 \times 10^{-2}}{\text{min}}} = 40. \text{ min}$$

Thus it takes 40. minutes for this particular reaction to reach 75% completion.

Let's consider another way of solving this problem using the definition of half-life. After one half-life the reaction has gone 50% to completion. If the initial concentration were 1.0 mol/L, after one half-life the concentration would be 0.50 mol/L. One more half-life would produce a concentration of 0.25 mol/L. Comparing 0.25 mol/L with the original 1.0 mol/L shows that 25% of the reactant is left after two half-lives. This is a general result. (What percentage of reactant remains after three half-lives?) Two half-lives for this reaction is 2(20.0 min), or 40.0 min, which agrees with the preceding answer.

See Exercises 12.30 and 12.37 through 12.40.

Second-Order Rate Laws

For a general reaction involving a single reactant, that is,

$$aA \longrightarrow products$$

that is second order in A, the rate law is

$$Rate = -\frac{\Delta[A]}{\Delta t} = k[A]^2 \qquad (12.4)$$

The **integrated second-order rate law** has the form

$$\frac{1}{[A]} = kt + \frac{1}{[A]_0} \qquad (12.5)$$

Second order: rate $= k[A]^2$. Doubling the concentration of A quadruples the reaction rate; tripling the concentration of A increases the rate by nine times.

Note the following characteristics of Equation (12.5):

1. A plot of $1/[A]$ versus t will produce a straight line with a slope equal to k.
2. Equation (12.5) shows how [A] depends on time and can be used to calculate [A] at any time t, provided k and $[A]_0$ are known.

For second-order reactions, a plot of $1/[A]$ versus t will be linear.

When one half-life of the second-order reaction has elapsed ($t = t_{1/2}$), by definition,

$$[A] = \frac{[A]_0}{2}$$

Equation (12.5) then becomes

$$\frac{1}{\dfrac{[A]_0}{2}} = kt_{1/2} + \frac{1}{[A]_0}$$

$$\frac{2}{[A]_0} - \frac{1}{[A]_0} = kt_{1/2}$$

$$\frac{1}{[A]_0} = kt_{1/2}$$

Solving for $t_{1/2}$ gives *the expression for the half-life of a second-order reaction:*

$$t_{1/2} = \frac{1}{k[A]_0} \qquad (12.6)$$

When two identical molecules combine, the resulting molecule is called a *dimer*.

Sample Exercise 12.5 Determining Rate Laws

Butadiene reacts to form its dimer according to the equation

$$2C_4H_6(g) \longrightarrow C_8H_{12}(g)$$

The following data were collected for this reaction at a given temperature:

[C₄H₆] (mol/L)	Time (±1 s)
0.01000	0
0.00625	1000
0.00476	1800
0.00370	2800
0.00313	3600
0.00270	4400
0.00241	5200
0.00208	6200

a. Is this reaction first order or second order?
b. What is the value of the rate constant for the reaction?
c. What is the half-life for the reaction under the conditions of this experiment?

Solution

a. To decide whether the rate law for this reaction is first order or second order, we must see whether the plot of $\ln[C_4H_6]$ versus time is a straight line (first order) or the plot of $1/[C_4H_6]$ versus time is a straight line (second order). The data necessary to make these plots are as follows:

t (s)	$\dfrac{1}{[C_4H_6]}$	$\ln[C_4H_6]$
0	100	−4.605
1000	160	−5.075
1800	210	−5.348
2800	270	−5.599
3600	320	−5.767
4400	370	−5.915
5200	415	−6.028
6200	481	−6.175

The resulting plots are shown in Fig. 12.6. Since the $\ln[C_4H_6]$ versus t plot [Fig. 12.6(a)] is not a straight line, the reaction is *not* first order. The reaction is, however, second order, as shown by the linearity of the $1/[C_4H_6]$ versus t plot [Fig. 12.6(b)]. Thus we can now write the rate law for this second-order reaction:

$$\text{Rate} = -\frac{\Delta[C_4H_6]}{\Delta t} = k[C_4H_6]^2$$

b. For a second-order reaction, a plot of $1/[C_4H_6]$ versus t produces a straight line of slope k. In terms of the standard equation for a straight line, $y = mx + b$,

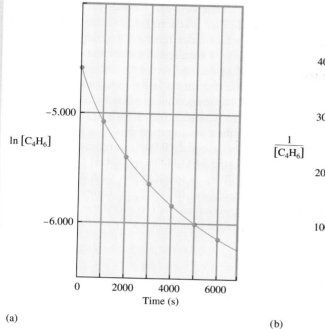

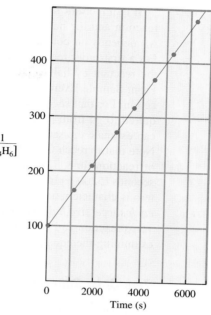

Figure 12.6

(a) A plot of $\ln[C_4H_6]$ versus t. (b) A plot of $1/[C_4H_6]$ versus t.

we have $y = 1/[C_4H_6]$ and $x = t$. Thus the slope of the line can be expressed as follows:

$$\text{Slope} = \frac{\Delta y}{\Delta x} = \frac{\Delta\left(\frac{1}{[C_4H_6]}\right)}{\Delta t}$$

Using the points at $t = 0$ and $t = 6200$, we can find the rate constant for the reaction:

$$k = \text{slope} = \frac{(481 - 100) \text{ L/mol}}{(6200. - 0) \text{ s}} = \frac{381}{6200.} \text{ L/mol} \cdot \text{s} = 6.14 \times 10^{-2} \text{ L/mol} \cdot \text{s}$$

c. The expression for the half-life of a second-order reaction is

$$t_{1/2} = \frac{1}{k[A]_0}$$

In this case $k = 6.14 \times 10^{-2}$ L/mol $\cdot$ s (from part b) and $[A]_0 = [C_4H_6]_0 = 0.01000$ M (the concentration at $t = 0$). Thus

$$t_{1/2} = \frac{1}{(6.14 \times 10^{-2} \text{ L/mol} \cdot \text{s})(1.000 \times 10^{-2} \text{ mol/L})} = 1.63 \times 10^3 \text{ s}$$

The initial concentration of C_4H_6 is halved in 1630 s.

See Exercises 12.31, 12.32, 12.41, and 12.42.

For a second-order reaction, $t_{1/2}$ is dependent on $[A]_0$. For a first-order reaction, $t_{1/2}$ is independent of $[A]_0$.

It is important to recognize the difference between the half-life for a first-order reaction and the half-life for a second-order reaction. For a second-order reaction, $t_{1/2}$ depends on both k and $[A]_0$; for a first-order reaction, $t_{1/2}$ depends only on k. For a first-order reaction, a constant time is required to reduce the concentration of the reactant by half, and then by half again, and so on, as the reaction proceeds. From Sample Exercise 12.5 we can see that this is *not* true for a second-order reaction. For that second-order reaction, we found that the first half-life (the time required to go from $[C_4H_6] = 0.010\ M$ to $[C_4H_6] = 0.0050\ M$) is 1630 seconds. We can estimate the second half-life from the concentration data as a function of time. Note that to reach $0.0024\ M$ C_4H_6 (approximately $0.0050/2$) requires 5200 seconds of reaction time. Thus to get from $0.0050\ M$ C_4H_6 to $0.0024\ M$ C_4H_6 takes 3570 seconds ($5200 - 1630$). The second half-life is much longer than the first. This pattern is characteristic of second-order reactions. In fact, *for a second-order reaction, each successive half-life is double the preceding one* (provided the effects of the reverse reaction can be ignored, as we are assuming here). Prove this to yourself by examining the equation $t_{1/2} = 1/(k[A]_0)$.

For each successive half-life, $[A]_0$ is halved. Since $t_{1/2} = 1/k[A]_0$, $t_{1/2}$ doubles.

Zero-Order Rate Laws

Most reactions involving a single reactant show either first-order or second-order kinetics. However, sometimes such a reaction can be a **zero-order reaction.** The rate law for a zero-order reaction is

$$\text{Rate} = k[A]^0 = k(1) = k$$

A zero-order reaction has a constant rate.

For a zero-order reaction, the rate is constant. It does not change with concentration as it does for first-order or second-order reactions.

The **integrated rate law for a zero-order reaction** is

$$[A] = -kt + [A]_0 \tag{12.7}$$

In this case a plot of $[A]$ versus t gives a straight line of slope $-k$, as shown in Fig. 12.7.

The expression for the half-life of a zero-order reaction can be obtained from the integrated rate law. By definition, $[A] = [A]_0/2$ when $t = t_{1/2}$, so

$$\frac{[A]_0}{2} = -kt_{1/2} + [A]_0$$

or

$$kt_{1/2} = \frac{[A]_0}{2k}$$

Solving for $t_{1/2}$ gives

$$t_{1/2} = \frac{[A]_0}{2k} \tag{12.8}$$

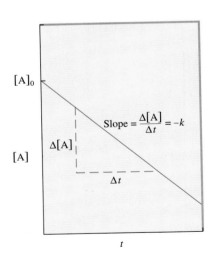

Figure 12.7

A plot of $[A]$ versus t for a zero-order reaction.

Zero-order reactions are most often encountered when a substance such as a metal surface or an enzyme is required for the reaction to occur. For example, the decomposition reaction

$$2N_2O(g) \longrightarrow 2N_2(g) + O_2(g)$$

occurs on a hot platinum surface. When the platinum surface is completely covered with N_2O molecules, an increase in the concentration of N_2O has no effect on the

Molecular Models: N_2O, N_2, O_2

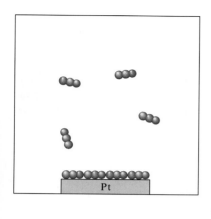

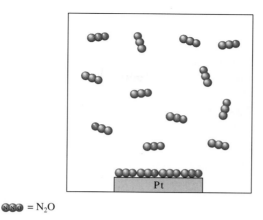

(a)

(b)

$= N_2O$

Figure 12.8
The decomposition reaction
$2N_2O(g) \rightarrow 2N_2(g) + O_2(g)$
takes place on a platinum surface. Although $[N_2O]$ is twice as
great in (b) as in (a), the rate of
decomposition of N_2O is the
same in both cases because the
platinum surface can accommodate only a certain number of
molecules. As a result, this reaction is zero order.

rate, since only those N_2O molecules on the surface can react. Under these conditions, *the rate is a constant* because it is controlled by what happens on the platinum surface rather than by the total concentration of N_2O, as illustrated in Fig.
12.8. This reaction also can occur at high temperatures with no platinum surface
present, but under these conditions, it is not zero order.

Integrated Rate Laws for Reactions with More Than One Reactant

So far we have considered the integrated rate laws for simple reactions with only
one reactant. Special techniques are required to deal with more complicated reactions. Let's consider the reaction

$$BrO_3^-(aq) + 5Br^-(aq) + 6H^+(aq) \longrightarrow 3Br_2(l) + 3H_2O(l)$$

Molecular Models: BrO_3^-, Br_2

From experimental evidence we know that the rate law is

$$Rate = -\frac{\Delta[BrO_3^-]}{\Delta t} = k[BrO_3^-][Br^-][H^+]^2$$

Suppose we run this reaction under conditions where $[BrO_3^-]_0 = 1.0 \times 10^{-3} M$,
$[Br^-]_0 = 1.0 M$, and $[H^+]_0 = 1.0 M$. As the reaction proceeds, $[BrO_3^-]$ decreases
significantly, but because the Br^- ion and H^+ ion concentrations are so large initially, relatively little of these two reactants is consumed. Thus $[Br^-]$ and $[H^+]$
remain *approximately constant*. In other words, under the conditions where the
Br^- ion and H^+ ion concentrations are much larger than the BrO_3^- ion concentration,
we can assume that throughout the reaction

$$[Br^-] = [Br^-]_0 \quad \text{and} \quad [H^+] = [H^+]_0$$

This means that the rate law can be written

$$Rate = k[Br^-]_0[H^+]_0^2[BrO_3^-] = k'[BrO_3^-]$$

where, since $[Br^-]_0$ and $[H^+]_0$ are constant,

$$k' = k[Br^-]_0[H^+]_0^2$$

The rate law

$$\text{Rate} = k'[\text{BrO}_3{}^-]$$

is first order. However, since this law was obtained by simplifying a more complicated one, it is called a **pseudo-first-order rate law.** Under the conditions of this experiment, a plot of $\ln[\text{BrO}_3{}^-]$ versus t will give a straight line where the slope is equal to $-k'$. Since $[\text{Br}^-]_0$ and $[\text{H}^+]_0$ are known, the value of k can be calculated from the equation

$$k' = k[\text{Br}^-]_0[\text{H}^+]_0{}^2$$

which can be rearranged to give

$$k = \frac{k'}{[\text{Br}^-]_0[\text{H}^+]_0{}^2}$$

Note that the kinetics of complicated reactions can be studied by observing the behavior of one reactant at a time. If the concentration of one reactant is much smaller than the concentrations of the others, then the amounts of those reactants present in large concentrations will not change significantly and can be regarded as constant. The change in concentration with time of the reactant present in a relatively small amount can then be used to determine the order of the reaction in that component. This technique allows us to determine rate laws for complex reactions.

12.5 Rate Laws: A Summary

In the last several sections we have developed the following important points:

1. To simplify the rate laws for reactions, we have always assumed that the rate is being studied under conditions where only the forward reaction is important. This produces rate laws that contain only reactant concentrations.

2. There are two types of rate laws.
   a. The *differential rate law* (often called the *rate law*) shows how the rate depends on the concentrations. The forms of the rate laws for zero-order, first-order, and second-order kinetics of reactions with single reactants are shown in Table 12.6.
   b. The *integrated rate law* shows how concentration depends on time. The integrated rate laws corresponding to zero-order, first-order, and second-order kinetics of one-reactant reactions are given in Table 12.6.

3. Whether we determine the differential rate law or the integrated rate law depends on the type of data that can be collected conveniently and accurately. Once we have experimentally determined either type of rate law, we can write the other for a given reaction.

4. The most common method for experimentally determining the differential rate law is the method of initial rates. In this method several experiments are run at different initial concentrations and the instantaneous rates are determined for each at the same value of t (as close to $t = 0$ as possible). The point is to evaluate the rate before the concentrations change significantly from the initial values. From a comparison of the initial rates and the initial concentrations the dependence of the rate on the concentrations of various reactants can be obtained—that is, the order in each reactant can be determined.

Table 12.6 Summary of the Kinetics for Reactions of the Type $aA \rightarrow$ Products That Are Zero, First, or Second Order in [A]

	Order		
	Zero	*First*	*Second*
Rate law:	Rate $= k$	Rate $= k[A]$	Rate $= k[A]^2$
Integrated rate law:	$[A] = -kt + [A]_0$	$\ln[A] = -kt + \ln[A]_0$	$\dfrac{1}{[A]} = kt + \dfrac{1}{[A]_0}$
Plot needed to give a straight line:	[A] versus t	$\ln[A]$ versus t	$\dfrac{1}{[A]}$ versus t
Relationship of rate constant to the slope of straight line:	Slope $= -k$	Slope $= -k$	Slope $= k$
Half-life:	$t_{1/2} = \dfrac{[A]_0}{2k}$	$t_{1/2} = \dfrac{0.693}{k}$	$t_{1/2} = \dfrac{1}{k[A]_0}$

5. To experimentally determine the integrated rate law for a reaction, concentrations are measured at various values of t as the reaction proceeds. Then the job is to see which integrated rate law correctly fits the data. Typically this is done visually by ascertaining which type of plot gives a straight line. A summary for one-reactant reactions is given in Table 12.6. Once the correct straight-line plot is found, the correct integrated rate law can be chosen and the value of k obtained from the slope. Also, the (differential) rate law for the reaction can then be written.

6. The integrated rate law for a reaction that involves several reactants can be treated by choosing conditions such that the concentration of only one reactant varies in a given experiment. This is done by having the concentration of one reactant small compared with the concentrations of all the others, causing a rate law such as

$$\text{Rate} = k[A]^n[B]^m[C]^p$$

to reduce to

$$\text{Rate} = k'[A]^n$$

where $k' = k[B]_0^m[C]_0^p$ and $[B]_0 \gg [A]_0$ and $[C]_0 \gg [A]_0$. The value of n is obtained by determining whether a plot of [A] versus t is linear ($n = 0$), a plot of $\ln[A]$ versus t is linear ($n = 1$), or a plot of $1/[A]$ versus t is linear ($n = 2$). The value of k' is determined from the slope of the appropriate plot. The values of m, p, and k can be found by determining the value of k' at several different concentrations of B and C.

12.6 *Reaction Mechanisms*

Most chemical reactions occur by a *series of steps* called the **reaction mechanism.** To understand a reaction, we must know its mechanism, and one of the main purposes for studying kinetics is to learn as much as possible about the steps involved

Figure 12.9

A molecular representation of the elementary steps in the reaction of NO_2 and CO.

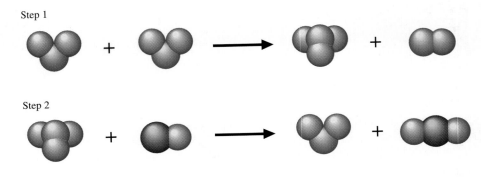

Step 1

Step 2

in a reaction. In this section we explore some of the fundamental characteristics of reaction mechanisms.

Consider the reaction between nitrogen dioxide and carbon monoxide:

$$NO_2(g) + CO(g) \longrightarrow NO(g) + CO_2(g)$$

The rate law for this reaction is known from experiment to be

$$\text{Rate} = k[NO_2]^2$$

A balanced equation does not tell us how the reactants become products.

As we will see below, this reaction is more complicated than it appears from the balanced equation. This is quite typical; the balanced equation for a reaction tells us the reactants, the products, and the stoichiometry but gives no direct information about the reaction mechanism.

For the reaction between nitrogen dioxide and carbon monoxide, the mechanism is thought to involve the following steps:

$$NO_2(g) + NO_2(g) \xrightarrow{k_1} NO_3(g) + NO(g)$$

$$NO_3(g) + CO(g) \xrightarrow{k_2} NO_2(g) + CO_2(g)$$

An intermediate is formed in one step and used up in a subsequent step and so is never seen as a product.

where k_1 and k_2 are the rate constants of the individual reactions. In this mechanism, gaseous NO_3 is an **intermediate,** a species that is neither a reactant nor a product but that is formed and consumed during the reaction sequence. This reaction is illustrated in Fig. 12.9.

Each of these two reactions is called an **elementary step,** *a reaction whose rate law can be written from its molecularity.* **Molecularity** is defined as the number of species that must collide to produce the reaction indicated by that step. A reaction involving one molecule is called a **unimolecular step.** Reactions involving the collision of two and three species are termed **bimolecular** and **termolecular,** respectively. Termolecular steps are quite rare, because the probability of three molecules colliding simultaneously is very small. Examples of these three types of elementary steps and the corresponding rate laws are shown in Table 12.7. Note from Table 12.7 that the rate law for an elementary step follows *directly* from the molecularity of that step. For example, for a bimolecular step the rate law is always second order, either of the form $k[A]^2$ for a step with a single reactant or of the form $k[A][B]$ for a step involving two reactants.

The prefix uni- means one, bi- means two, and ter- means three.

A unimolecular elementary step is always first order, a bimolecular step is always second order, and so on.

We can now define a reaction mechanism more precisely. It is a *series of elementary steps that must satisfy two requirements:*

Table 12.7 Examples of Elementary Steps

Elementary Step	Molecularity	Rate Law
A → products	Unimolecular	Rate = $k[A]$
A + A → products	Bimolecular	Rate = $k[A]^2$
(2A → products)		
A + B → products	Bimolecular	Rate = $k[A][B]$
A + A + B → products	Termolecular	Rate = $k[A]^2[B]$
(2A + B → products)		
A + B + C → products	Termolecular	Rate = $k[A][B][C]$

1. The sum of the elementary steps must give the overall balanced equation for the reaction.

2. The mechanism must agree with the experimentally determined rate law.

To see how these requirements are applied, we will consider the mechanism given above for the reaction of nitrogen dioxide and carbon monoxide. First, note that the sum of the two steps gives the overall balanced equation:

$$NO_2(g) + NO_2(g) \longrightarrow NO_3(g) + NO(g)$$
$$NO_3(g) + CO(g) \longrightarrow NO_2(g) + CO_2(g)$$

$$\overline{\cancel{NO_2}(g) + NO_2(g) + \cancel{NO_3}(g) + CO(g) \longrightarrow \cancel{NO_3}(g) + NO(g) + \cancel{NO_2}(g) + CO_2(g)}$$

Overall reaction: $NO_2(g) + CO(g) \longrightarrow NO(g) + CO_2(g)$

The first requirement for a correct mechanism is met. To see whether the mechanism meets the second requirement, we need to introduce a new idea: the **rate-determining step.** Multistep reactions often have one step that is much slower than all the others. Reactants can become products only as fast as they can get through this slowest step. That is, the overall reaction can be no faster than the slowest, or rate-determining, step in the sequence. An analogy for this situation is the pouring of water rapidly into a container through a funnel. The water collects in the container at a rate that is essentially determined by the size of the funnel opening and not by the rate of pouring.

A reaction is only as fast as its slowest step.

Which is the rate-determining step in the reaction of nitrogen dioxide and carbon monoxide? Let's *assume* that the first step is rate-determining and the second step is relatively fast:

$$NO_2(g) + NO_2(g) \longrightarrow NO_3(g) + 0NO(g) \quad \text{Slow (rate-determining)}$$
$$NO_3(g) + CO(g) \longrightarrow NO_2(g) + CO_2(g) \quad \text{Fast}$$

What we have really assumed here is that the formation of NO_3 occurs much more slowly than its reaction with CO. The rate of CO_2 production is then controlled by the rate of formation of NO_3 in the first step. Since this is an elementary step, we can write the rate law from the molecularity. The bimolecular first step has the rate law

$$\text{Rate of formation of } NO_3 = \frac{\Delta[NO_3]}{\Delta t} = k_1[NO_2]^2$$

Video: Oscillating Reaction

Since the overall reaction rate can be no faster than the slowest step,

$$\text{Overall rate} = k_1[NO_2]^2$$

Note that this rate law agrees with the experimentally determined rate law given earlier. The mechanism we assumed on the previous page satisfies the two requirements stated earlier and *may* be the correct mechanism for the reaction.

How does a chemist deduce the mechanism for a given reaction? The rate law is always determined first. Then, using chemical intuition and following the two rules given on the previous page, the chemist constructs possible mechanisms and tries, with further experiments, to eliminate those that are least likely. *A mechanism can never be proved absolutely.* We can only say that a mechanism that satisfies the two requirements is *possibly* correct. Deducing mechanisms for chemical reactions can be difficult and requires skill and experience. We will only touch on this process in this text.

Sample Exercise 12.6 Reaction Mechanisms

The balanced equation for the reaction of the gases nitrogen dioxide and fluorine is

$$2NO_2(g) + F_2(g) \longrightarrow 2NO_2F(g)$$

The experimentally determined rate law is

$$\text{Rate} = k[NO_2][F_2]$$

A suggested mechanism for this reaction is

$$NO_2 + F_2 \xrightarrow{k_1} NO_2F + F \quad \text{Slow}$$

$$F + NO_2 \xrightarrow{k_2} NO_2F \qquad \text{Fast}$$

Is this an acceptable mechanism? That is, does it satisfy the two requirements?

Solution

The first requirement for an acceptable mechanism is that the sum of the steps should give the balanced equation:

$$
\begin{array}{r}
NO_2 + F_2 \longrightarrow NO_2F + F \\
F + NO_2 \longrightarrow NO_2F \\
\hline
2NO_2 + F_2 + \cancel{F} \longrightarrow 2NO_2F + \cancel{F}
\end{array}
$$

Overall reaction: $2NO_2 + F_2 \longrightarrow 2NO_2F$

The first requirement is met.

The second requirement is that the mechanism must agree with the experimentally determined rate law. Since the proposed mechanism states that the first step is rate-determining, the overall reaction rate must be that of the first step. The first step is bimolecular, so the rate law is

$$\text{Rate} = k_1[NO_2][F_2]$$

This has the same form as the experimentally determined rate law. The proposed mechanism is acceptable because it satisfies both requirements. (Note that we have not proved that it is *the correct* mechanism.)

See Exercises 12.47 and 12.48.

12.7 A Model for Chemical Kinetics

Exploration: Transition States and Activation Energy

How do chemical reactions occur? We already have given some indications. For example, we have seen that the rates of chemical reactions depend on the concentrations of the reacting species. The initial rate for the reaction

$$aA + bB \longrightarrow products$$

can be described by the rate law

$$Rate = k[A]^n[B]^m$$

where the order of each reactant depends on the detailed reaction mechanism. This explains why reaction rates depend on concentration. But what about some of the other factors affecting reaction rates? For example, how does temperature affect the speed of a reaction?

We can answer this question qualitatively from our experience. We have refrigerators because food spoilage is retarded at low temperatures. The combustion of wood occurs at a measurable rate only at high temperatures. An egg cooks in boiling water much faster at sea level than in Leadville, Colorado (elevation 10,000 ft), where the boiling point of water is approximately 90°C. These observations and others lead us to conclude that *chemical reactions speed up when the temperature is increased.* Experiments have shown that virtually all rate constants show an exponential increase with absolute temperature, as represented in Fig. 12.10.

In this section we discuss a model used to account for the observed characteristics of reaction rates. This model, called the **collision model,** is built around the central idea that *molecules must collide to react.* We have already seen how this assumption explains the concentration dependence of reaction rates. Now we need to consider whether this model can account for the observed temperature dependence of reaction rates.

The kinetic molecular theory of gases predicts that an increase in temperature raises molecular velocities and so increases the frequency of collisions between molecules. This idea agrees with the observation that reaction rates are greater at higher temperatures. Thus there is qualitative agreement between the collision model and experimental observations. However, it is found that the rate of reaction is much smaller than the calculated collision frequency in a collection of gas particles. This must mean that *only a small fraction of the collisions produces a reaction.* Why?

This question was first addressed in the 1880s by Svante Arrhenius. He proposed the existence of a *threshold energy,* called the **activation energy,** that must be overcome to produce a chemical reaction. Such a proposal makes sense, as we can see by considering the decomposition of BrNO in the gas phase:

$$2BrNO(g) \longrightarrow 2NO(g) + Br_2(g)$$

In this reaction two Br—N bonds must be broken and one Br—Br bond must be formed. Breaking a Br—N bond requires considerable energy (243 kJ/mol), which must come from somewhere. The collision model postulates that the energy comes from the kinetic energies possessed by the reacting molecules before the collision. This kinetic energy is changed into potential energy as the molecules are distorted during a collision to break bonds and rearrange the atoms into the product molecules.

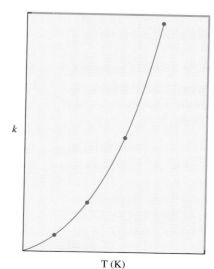

k

T (K)

Figure 12.10

A plot showing the exponential dependence of the rate constant on absolute temperature. The exact temperature dependence of k is different for each reaction. This plot represents the behavior of a rate constant that doubles for every increase in temperature of 10 K.

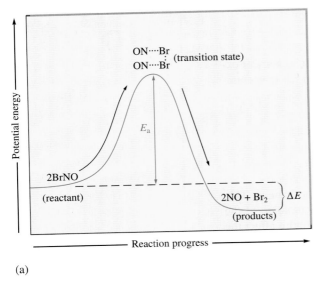

(a)

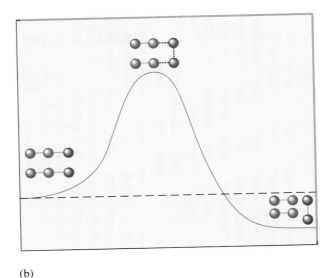

(b)

Molecular Models: BrNO, NO, Br₂

Figure 12.11

(a) The change in potential energy as a function of reaction progress for the reaction $2BrNO \rightarrow 2NO + Br_2$. The activation energy E_a represents the energy needed to disrupt the BrNO molecules so that they can form products. The quantity ΔE represents the net change in energy in going from reactant to products. (b) A molecular representation of the reaction.

We can envision the reaction progress as shown in Fig. 12.11. The arrangement of atoms found at the top of the potential energy "hill," or barrier, is called the **activated complex,** or **transition state.** The conversion of BrNO to NO and Br₂ is exothermic, as indicated by the fact that the products have lower potential energy than the reactant. However, ΔE has no effect on the rate of the reaction. Rather the rate depends on the size of the activation energy E_a.

The main point here is that a certain minimum energy is required for two BrNO molecules to "get over the hill" so that products can form. This energy is furnished by the energy of the collision. A collision between two BrNO molecules with small kinetic energies will not have enough energy to get over the barrier. At a given temperature only a certain fraction of the collisions possesses enough energy to be effective (to result in product formation).

We can be more precise by recalling from Chapter 5 that a distribution of velocities exists in a sample of gas molecules. Therefore, a distribution of collision energies also exists, as shown in Fig. 12.12 for two different temperatures. Figure 12.12 also shows the activation energy for the reaction in question. Only collisions with energy greater than the activation energy are able to react (get over the barrier). At the lower temperature, T_1, the fraction of effective collisions is quite small. However, as the temperature is increased to T_2, the fraction of collisions with the required activation energy increases dramatically. When the temperature is doubled, the fraction of effective collisions much more than doubles. In fact, the fraction of effective collisions increases *exponentially* with temperature. This is encouraging for our theory; remember that rates of reactions are observed to increase exponentially with temperature. Arrhenius postulated that the number of collisions having an energy greater than or equal to the activation energy is given by the expression:

The higher the activation energy, the slower is the reaction at a given temperature.

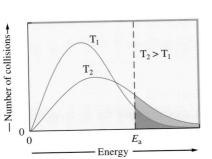

Figure 12.12

Plot showing the number of collisions with a particular energy at T_1 and T_2, where $T_2 > T_1$.

Number of collisions with the activation energy

$$= \text{(total number of collisions)} e^{-E_a/RT}$$

where E_a is the activation energy, R is the universal gas constant, and T is the Kelvin temperature. The factor $e^{-E_a/RT}$ represents the fraction of collisions with energy E_a or greater at temperature T.

We have seen that not all molecular collisions are effective in producing chemical reactions because a minimum energy is required for the reaction to occur. There is, however, another complication. Experiments show that the *observed reaction rate is considerably smaller than the rate of collisions with enough energy to surmount the barrier.* This means that many collisions, even though they have the required energy, still do not produce a reaction. Why not?

The answer lies in the **molecular orientations** during collisions. We can illustrate this using the reaction between two BrNO molecules, as shown in Fig. 12.13. Some collision orientations can lead to reaction, and others cannot. Therefore, we must include a correction factor to allow for collisions with nonproductive molecular orientations.

To summarize, two requirements must be satisfied for reactants to collide successfully (to rearrange to form products):

1. The collision must involve enough energy to produce the reaction; that is, the collision energy must equal or exceed the activation energy.

2. The relative orientation of the reactants must allow formation of any new bonds necessary to produce products.

Taking these factors into account, we can represent the rate constant as

$$k = zp e^{-E_a/RT}$$

where z is the collision frequency, p is called the **steric factor** (always less than 1) and reflects the fraction of collisions with effective orientations, and $e^{-E_a/RT}$

Food and other supplies on Ross Island left by the 1910 Scott expedition to the South Pole. The low temperatures that prevail in this region greatly slow the reactions that cause spoilage and corrosion.

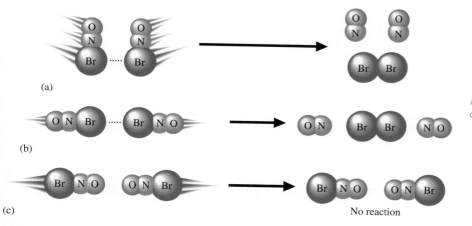

Animation: The Gas Phase Reaction of NO and Cl_2

Figure 12.13

Several possible orientations for a collision between two BrNO molecules. Orientations (a) and (b) can lead to a reaction, but orientation (c) cannot.

A snowy tree cricket. The frequency of a cricket's chirps depends on the temperature of the cricket.

represents the fraction of collisions with sufficient energy to produce a reaction. This expression is most often written in form

$$k = Ae^{-E_a/RT} \tag{12.9}$$

which is called the **Arrhenius equation.** In this equation, A replaces zp and is called the **frequency factor** for the reaction.

Taking the natural logarithm of each side of the Arrhenius equation gives

$$\ln(k) = -\frac{E_a}{R}\left(\frac{1}{T}\right) + \ln(A) \tag{12.10}$$

Equation (12.10) is a linear equation of the type $y = mx + b$, where $y = \ln(k)$, $m = -E_a/R = $ slope, $x = 1/T$, and $b = \ln(A) = $ intercept. Thus, for a reaction where the rate constant obeys the Arrhenius equation, a plot of $\ln(k)$ versus $1/T$ gives a straight line. The slope and intercept can be used to determine, respectively, the values of E_a and A characteristic of that reaction. The fact that most rate constants obey the Arrhenius equation to a good approximation indicates that the collision model for chemical reactions is physically reasonable.

Sample Exercise 12.7 *Determining Activation Energy I*

The reaction

$$2N_2O_5(g) \longrightarrow 4NO_2(g) + O_2(g)$$

was studied at several temperatures, and the following values of k were obtained:

$k\ (s^{-1})$	$T\ (°C)$
2.0×10^{-5}	20
7.3×10^{-5}	30
2.7×10^{-4}	40
9.1×10^{-4}	50
2.9×10^{-3}	60

Calculate the value of E_a for this reaction.

Solution

To obtain the value of E_a, we need to construct a plot of $\ln(k)$ versus $1/T$. First, we must calculate values of $\ln(k)$ and $1/T$, as shown below:

$T\ (°C)$	$T\ (K)$	$1/T\ (K)$	$k\ (s^{-1})$	$\ln(k)$
20	293	3.41×10^{-3}	2.0×10^{-5}	-10.82
30	303	3.30×10^{-3}	7.3×10^{-5}	-9.53
40	313	3.19×10^{-3}	2.7×10^{-4}	-8.22
50	323	3.10×10^{-3}	9.1×10^{-4}	-7.00
60	333	3.00×10^{-3}	2.9×10^{-3}	-5.84

The plot of $\ln(k)$ versus $1/T$ is shown in Fig. 12.14, where the slope

$$\frac{\Delta\ln(k)}{\Delta\left(\dfrac{1}{T}\right)}$$

is found to be -1.2×10^4 K. The value of E_a can be determined by solving the following equation:

$$\text{Slope} = -\frac{E_a}{R}$$

$$E_a = -R(\text{slope}) = -(8.3145 \text{ J/K} \cdot \text{mol})(-1.2 \times 10^4 \text{ K})$$
$$= 1.0 \times 10^5 \text{ J/mol}$$

Thus the value of the activation energy for this reaction is 1.0×10^5 J/mol.

See Exercises 12.53 and 12.54.

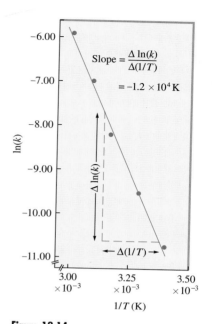

Figure 12.14

Plot of $\ln(k)$ versus $1/T$ for the reaction $2N_2O_5(g) \rightarrow 4NO_2(g) + O_2(g)$. The value of the activation energy for this reaction can be obtained from the slope of the line, which equals $-E_a/R$.

The most common procedure for finding E_a for a reaction involves measuring the rate constant k at several temperatures and then plotting $\ln(k)$ versus $1/T$, as shown in Sample Exercise 12.7. However, E_a also can be calculated from the values of k at only two temperatures by using a formula that can be derived as follows from Equation (12.10).

At temperature T_1, where the rate constant is k_1,

$$\ln(k_1) = -\frac{E_a}{RT_1} + \ln(A)$$

At temperature T_2, where the rate constant is k_2,

$$\ln(k_2) = -\frac{E_a}{RT_2} + \ln(A)$$

Subtracting the first equation from the second gives

$$\ln(k_2) - \ln(k_1) = \left[-\frac{E_a}{RT_2} + \ln(A)\right] - \left[-\frac{E_a}{RT_1} + \ln(A)\right]$$

$$= -\frac{E_a}{RT_2} + \frac{E_a}{RT_1}$$

And

$$\ln\left(\frac{k_2}{k_1}\right) = \frac{E_a}{R}\left(\frac{1}{T_1} - \frac{1}{T_2}\right) \tag{12.11}$$

Therefore, the values of k_1 and k_2 measured at temperatures T_1 and T_2 can be used to calculate E_a, as shown in Sample Exercise 12.8.

Sample Exercise 12.8 *Determining Activation Energy II*

The gas-phase reaction between methane and diatomic sulfur is given by the equation

$$CH_4(g) + 2S_2(g) \longrightarrow CS_2(g) + 2H_2S(g)$$

At 550°C the rate constant for this reaction is 1.1 L/mol · s, and at 625°C the rate constant is 6.4 L/mol · s. Using these values, calculate E_a for this reaction.

Solution

The relevant data are shown in the following table:

k (L/mol · s)	T (°C)	T (K)
1.1 = k_1	550	823 = T_1
6.4 = k_2	625	898 = T_2

Substituting these values into Equation (12.11) gives

$$\ln\left(\frac{6.4}{1.1}\right) = \frac{E_a}{8.3145 \text{ J/K} \cdot \text{mol}}\left(\frac{1}{823 \text{ K}} - \frac{1}{898 \text{ K}}\right)$$

Solving for E_a gives

$$E_a = \frac{(8.3145 \text{ J/K} \cdot \text{mol})\ln\left(\frac{6.4}{1.1}\right)}{\left(\frac{1}{823 \text{ K}} - \frac{1}{898 \text{ K}}\right)}$$

$$= 1.4 \times 10^5 \text{ J/mol}$$

See Exercises 12.55 through 12.58.

12.8 Catalysis

We have seen that the rate of a reaction increases dramatically with temperature. If a particular reaction does not occur fast enough at normal temperatures, we can speed it up by raising the temperature. However, sometimes this is not feasible. For example, living cells can survive only in a rather narrow temperature range, and the human body is designed to operate at an almost constant temperature of 98.6°F. But many of the complicated biochemical reactions keeping us alive would be much too slow at this temperature without intervention. We exist only because the body contains many substances called **enzymes,** which increase the rates of these reactions. In fact, almost every biologically important reaction is assisted by a specific enzyme.

Although it is possible to use higher temperatures to speed up commercially important reactions, such as the Haber process for synthesizing ammonia, this is very expensive. In a chemical plant an increase in temperature means significantly increased costs for energy. The use of an appropriate catalyst allows a reaction to proceed rapidly at a relatively low temperature and can therefore hold down production costs.

A **catalyst** is *a substance that speeds up a reaction without being consumed itself.* Just as virtually all vital biologic reactions are assisted by enzymes (biologic catalysts), almost all industrial processes also involve the use of catalysts. For example, the production of sulfuric acid uses vanadium(V) oxide, and the Haber process uses a mixture of iron and iron oxide.

How does a catalyst work? Remember that for each reaction a certain energy barrier must be surmounted. How can we make a reaction occur faster without raising the temperature to increase the molecular energies? The solution is to provide a new pathway for the reaction, one with a *lower activation energy*. This is what a catalyst does, as is shown in Fig. 12.15. Because the catalyst allows the reaction to occur with a lower activation energy, a much larger fraction of collisions is effective at a given temperature, and the reaction rate is increased. This effect is illustrated in Fig. 12.16. Note from this diagram that although a catalyst lowers the activation energy E_a for a reaction, it does not affect the energy difference ΔE between products and reactants.

Catalysts are classified as homogeneous or heterogeneous. A **homogeneous catalyst** is one that is *present in the same phase as the reacting molecules*. A **heterogeneous catalyst** exists *in a different phase*, usually as a solid.

Heterogeneous Catalysis

Heterogeneous catalysis most often involves gaseous reactants being adsorbed on the surface of a solid catalyst. **Adsorption** refers to the collection of one substance on the surface of another substance; *absorption* refers to the penetration of one substance into another. Water is *absorbed* by a sponge.

An important example of heterogeneous catalysis occurs in the hydrogenation of unsaturated hydrocarbons, compounds composed mainly of carbon and hydrogen with some carbon–carbon double bonds. Hydrogenation is an important industrial process used to change unsaturated fats, occurring as oils, to saturated fats (solid shortenings such as Crisco) in which the C=C bonds have been converted to C—C bonds through addition of hydrogen.

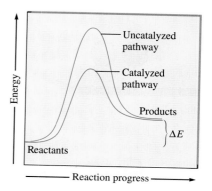

Figure 12.15

Energy plots for a catalyzed and an uncatalyzed pathway for a given reaction.

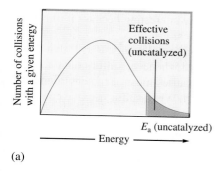

(a)

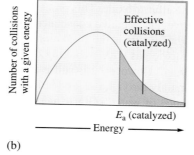

(b)

Figure 12.16

Effect of a catalyst on the number of reaction-producing collisions. Because a catalyst provides a reaction pathway with a lower activation energy, a much greater fraction of the collisions is effective for the catalyzed pathway (b) than for the uncatalyzed pathway (a) (at a given temperature). This allows reactants to become products at a much higher rate, even though there is no temperature increase.

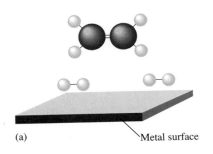

(a)

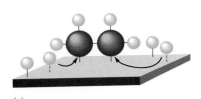

(b)

Metal surface

(c)

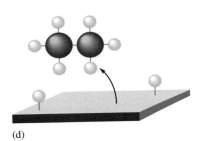

(d)

● Carbon

○ Hydrogen

Molecular Models: C₂H₄, C₂H₆

Figure 12.17
Heterogeneous catalysis of the hydrogenation of ethylene. (a) The reactants above the metal surface. (b) Hydrogen is adsorbed onto the metal surface, forming metal–hydrogen bonds and breaking the H—H bonds. The π bond in ethylene is broken and metal–carbon bonds are formed during adsorption. (c) The adsorbed molecules and atoms migrate toward each other on the metal surface, forming new C—H bonds. (d) The C atoms in ethane (C_2H_6) have completely saturated bonding capacities and so cannot bind strongly to the metal surfaces. The C_2H_6 molecule thus escapes.

A simple example of hydrogenation involves ethylene:

$$\underset{\text{Ethylene}}{\underset{H}{\overset{H}{}}C=C\underset{H}{\overset{H}{}}}(g) + H_2(g) \rightarrow \underset{\text{Ethane}}{H-\overset{H}{\underset{H}{C}}-\overset{H}{\underset{H}{C}}-H}(g)$$

This reaction is quite slow at normal temperatures, mainly because the strong bond in the hydrogen molecule results in a large activation energy for the reaction. However, the reaction rate can be greatly increased by using a solid catalyst of platinum, palladium, or nickel. The hydrogen and ethylene adsorb on the catalyst surface, where the reaction occurs. The main function of the catalyst apparently is to allow formation of metal–hydrogen interactions that weaken the H—H bonds and facilitate the reaction. The mechanism is illustrated in Fig. 12.17.

Typically, heterogeneous catalysis involves four steps:

1. Adsorption and activation of the reactants
2. Migration of the adsorbed reactants on the surface
3. Reaction of the adsorbed substances
4. Escape, or *desorption,* of the products

Heterogeneous catalysis also occurs in the oxidation of gaseous sulfur dioxide to gaseous sulfur trioxide. This process is especially interesting because it illustrates both positive and negative consequences of chemical catalysis.

The negative side is the formation of damaging air pollutants. Recall that sulfur dioxide, a toxic gas with a choking odor, is formed whenever sulfur-containing fuels are burned. However, it is sulfur trioxide that causes most of the environmental damage, mainly through the production of acid rain. When sulfur trioxide combines with a droplet of water, sulfuric acid is formed:

$$H_2O(l) + SO_3(g) \longrightarrow H_2SO_4(aq)$$

This sulfuric acid can cause considerable damage to vegetation, buildings and statues, and fish populations.

Sulfur dioxide is *not* rapidly oxidized to sulfur trioxide in clean, dry air. Why, then, is there a problem? The answer is catalysis. Dust particles and water droplets catalyze the reaction between SO_2 and O_2 in the air.

On the positive side, the heterogeneous catalysis of the oxidation of SO_2 is used to advantage in the manufacture of sulfuric acid, where the reaction of O_2 and SO_2 to form SO_3 is catalyzed by a solid mixture of platinum and vanadium(V) oxide.

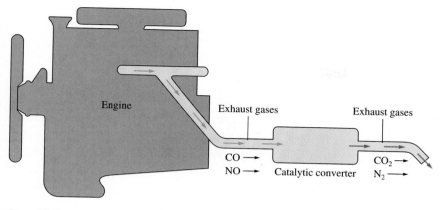

Figure 12.18

The exhaust gases from an automobile engine are passed through a catalytic converter to minimize environmental damage.

Heterogeneous catalysis is also utilized in the catalytic converters in automobile exhaust systems. The exhaust gases, containing compounds such as nitric oxide, carbon monoxide, and unburned hydrocarbons, are passed through a converter containing beads of solid catalyst (see Fig. 12.18). The catalyst promotes the conversion of carbon monoxide to carbon dioxide, hydrocarbons to carbon dioxide and water, and nitric oxide to nitrogen gas to lessen the environmental impact of the exhaust gases. However, this beneficial catalysis can, unfortunately, be accompanied by the unwanted catalysis of the oxidation of SO_2 to SO_3, which reacts with the moisture present to form sulfuric acid.

Because of the complex nature of the reactions that take place in the converter, a mixture of catalysts is used. The most effective catalytic materials are transition metal oxides and noble metals such as palladium and platinum.

CHEMICAL IMPACT

Automobiles: Air Purifiers?

OUTLANDISH AS IT may seem, a new scheme has been proposed to turn automobiles into air purifiers, devouring the pollutants ozone and carbon monoxide. Engelhard Corporation, an Iselin, New Jersey, company that specializes in the manufacture of catalytic converters for automotive exhaust systems, has developed a catalyst that decomposes ozone to oxygen and converts carbon monoxide to carbon dioxide. Engelhard proposes to paint the catalyst on automobile radiators and air-conditioner compressors where fans draw large volumes of air for cooling purposes. The catalyst works well at the warm temperatures present on the surfaces of these devices. The idea is to let cars destroy pollutants using nothing but the catalyst and waste radiator heat.

It's an intriguing idea. The residents of Los Angeles drive nearly 300 million miles a day. At that rate, they could process a lot of air.

CHEMICAL IMPACT

Enzymes: Nature's Catalysts

THE MOST IMPRESSIVE examples of homogeneous catalysis occur in nature, where the complex reactions necessary for plant and animal life are made possible by enzymes. Enzymes are large molecules specifically tailored to facilitate a given type of reaction. Usually enzymes are proteins, an important class of biomolecules constructed from α-amino acids that have the general structure

where R represents any one of 20 different substituents. These amino acid molecules can be "hooked together" to form a *polymer* (a word meaning "many parts") called a *protein*. The general structure of a protein can be represented as follows:

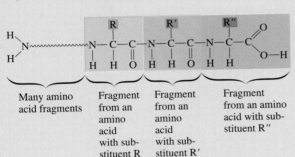

| Many amino acid fragments | Fragment from an amino acid with substituent R | Fragment from an amino acid with substituent R′ | Fragment from an amino acid with substituent R″ |

Since specific proteins are needed by the human body, the proteins in food must be broken into their constituent amino acids, which are then used to construct new proteins in the body's cells. The reaction in which a protein is broken down one amino acid at a time is shown in Fig. 12.19. Note that in this reaction a water molecule reacts with a protein molecule to produce an amino acid and a new protein containing one less amino acid. Without the enzymes found in human cells, this reaction would be much too slow to be useful. One of these enzymes is *carboxypeptidase-A*, a zinc-containing protein (Fig. 12.20).

Carboxypeptidase-A captures the protein to be acted on (called the *substrate*) in a special groove and positions the substrate so that the end is in the active site, where the catalysis occurs (Fig. 12.21). Note that the Zn^{2+} ion bonds to the oxygen of the C=O (carbonyl) group. This polarizes the electron density in the carbonyl group, allowing the neighboring C—N bond to be broken much more easily. When the reaction is completed, the remaining portion of the substrate protein and the newly formed amino acid are released by the enzyme.

The process just described for carboxypeptidase-A is characteristic of the behavior of other enzymes. Enzyme catalysis can be represented by the series of reactions shown below:

$$E + S \longrightarrow E \cdot S$$
$$E \cdot S \longrightarrow E + P$$

Figure 12.19

The removal of the end amino acid from a protein by reaction with a molecule of water. The products are an amino acid and a new, smaller protein.

Water molecule

Protein

Amino acid

New protein

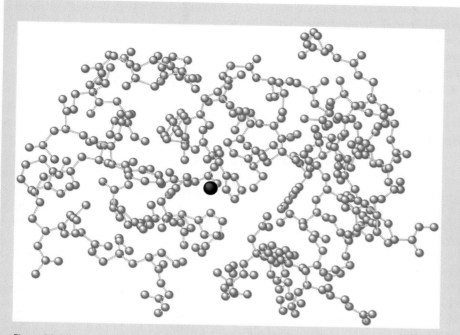

Figure 12.20

The structure of the enzyme carboxypeptidase-A, which contains 307 amino acids.

Figure 12.21

Protein–substrate interaction. The substrate is shown in black and red, with the red representing the terminal amino acid. Blue indicates side chains from the enzyme that help bind the substrate.

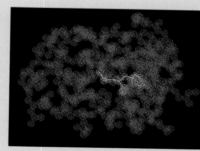

where E represents the enzyme, S represents the substrate, E · S represents the enzyme–substrate complex, and P represents the products. The enzyme and substrate form a complex, where the reaction occurs. The enzyme then releases the product and is ready to repeat the process. The most amazing thing about enzymes is their efficiency. Because an enzyme plays its catalytic role over and over and very rapidly, only a tiny amount of enzyme is required. This makes the isolation of enzymes for study quite difficult.

One consequence of the widespread use of catalytic converters has been the need to remove lead from gasoline. Tetraethyl lead was used for more than 50 years as a very effective "octane booster" owing to its antiknocking characteristics. However, lead quickly destroys much of a converter's catalytic efficiency. This poisoning effect, along with the serious adverse health effects of lead, has necessitated the removal of lead from gasoline. This has caused a search for other antiknock additives and the redesign of engines to run on lower-octane gasoline.

Homogeneous Catalysis

A homogeneous catalyst exists in the same phase as the reacting molecules. There are many examples in both the gas and liquid phases. One such example is the unusual catalytic behavior of nitric oxide toward ozone. In the troposphere, that part of the atmosphere closest to earth, nitric oxide catalyzes ozone production. However, in the upper atmosphere it catalyzes the decomposition of ozone. Both these effects are unfortunate environmentally.

In the lower atmosphere, NO is produced in any high-temperature combustion process where N_2 is present. The reaction

$$N_2(g) + O_2(g) \longrightarrow 2NO(g)$$

is very slow at normal temperatures because of the very strong $N \equiv N$ and $O = O$ bonds. However, at elevated temperatures, such as those found in the internal combustion engines of automobiles, significant quantities of NO form. Some of this NO is converted back to N_2 in the catalytic converter, but significant amounts escape into the atmosphere to react with oxygen:

$$2NO(g) + O_2(g) \longrightarrow 2NO_2(g)$$

In the atmosphere, NO_2 can absorb light and decompose as follows:

$$NO_2(g) \xrightarrow{\text{Light}} NO(g) + O(g)$$

The oxygen atom is very reactive and can combine with oxygen molecules to form ozone:

$$O_2(g) + O(g) \longrightarrow O_3(g)$$

Ozone is a powerful oxidizing agent that can react with other air pollutants to form substances irritating to the eyes and lungs, and is itself very toxic.

In this series of reactions, nitric oxide is acting as a true catalyst because it assists the production of ozone without being consumed itself. This can be seen by summing the reactions:

Although O_2 is represented here as the oxidizing agent for NO, the actual oxidizing agent is probably some type of peroxide compound produced by reaction of oxygen with pollutants. The direct reaction of NO and O_2 is very slow.

$$
\begin{aligned}
NO(g) + \tfrac{1}{2}O_2(g) &\longrightarrow NO_2(g) \\
NO_2(g) &\xrightarrow{\text{Light}} NO(g) + O(g) \\
O_2(g) + O(g) &\longrightarrow O_3(g) \\
\hline
\tfrac{3}{2}O_2(g) &\longrightarrow O_3(g)
\end{aligned}
$$

In the upper atmosphere, the presence of nitric oxide has the opposite effect—the depletion of ozone. The series of reactions involved is

$$
\begin{aligned}
NO(g) + O_3(g) &\longrightarrow NO_2(g) + O_2(g) \\
O(g) + NO_2(g) &\longrightarrow NO(g) + O_2(g) \\
\hline
O(g) + O_3(g) &\longrightarrow 2O_2(g)
\end{aligned}
$$

Nitric oxide is again catalytic, but here its effect is to change O_3 to O_2. This is a potential problem because O_3, which absorbs ultraviolet light, is necessary to protect us from the harmful effects of this high-energy radiation. That is, we want O_3 in the upper atmosphere to block ultraviolet radiation from the sun but not in the lower atmosphere, where we would have to breathe it and its oxidation products.

The ozone layer is also threatened by *Freons,* a group of stable, noncorrosive compounds, until recently, used as refrigerants and as propellants in aerosol cans. The most commonly used substance of this type was Freon-12 (CCl_2F_2). The chemical inertness of Freons makes them valuable but also creates a problem, since they remain in the environment a long time. Eventually, they migrate into the upper atmosphere to be decomposed by high-energy light. Among the decomposition products are chlorine atoms:

$$CCl_2F_2(g) \xrightarrow{\text{Light}} CClF_2(g) + Cl(g)$$

These chlorine atoms can catalyze the decomposition of ozone:

$$\begin{array}{r}
Cl(g) + O_3(g) \longrightarrow ClO(g) + O_2(g) \\
O(g) + ClO(g) \longrightarrow Cl(g) + O_2(g) \\
\hline
O(g) + O_3(g) \longrightarrow 2O_2(g)
\end{array}$$

The problem of Freons has been brought into strong focus by the discovery of a mysterious "hole" in the ozone layer in the stratosphere over Antarctica. Studies performed there to find the reason for the hole have found unusually high levels of chlorine monoxide (ClO). This strongly implicates the Freons in the atmosphere as being responsible for the ozone destruction.

Because they pose environmental problems, Freons have been banned by international agreement. Substitute compounds are now being used.

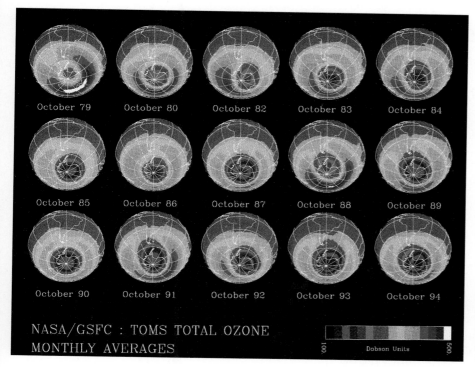

The ozone concentrations over Antarctica as measured by the Total Ozone Mapping Spectrometer (TOMS). A purple color indicates low ozone concentration.

For Review

Key Terms

chemical kinetics

Section 12.1
reaction rate
instantaneous rate

Section 12.2
rate law
rate constant
order
(differential) rate law
integrated rate law

Section 12.3
method of initial rates
initial rate
overall reaction order

Section 12.4
first-order reaction
integrated first-order rate law
half-life of a reactant
integrated second-order rate law
zero-order reaction
integrated zero-order rate law
pseudo-first-order rate law

Section 12.6
reaction mechanism
intermediate
elementary step
molecularity
unimolecular step
bimolecular step
termolecular step
rate-determining step

Section 12.7
collision model
activation energy
activated complex (transition state)
molecular orientations
steric factor
Arrhenius equation
frequency factor

Section 12.8
enzyme
catalyst
homogeneous catalyst
heterogeneous catalyst
adsorption

Summary

Even though a chemical reaction may have a strong tendency to occur thermodynamically, it is not necessarily fast. Chemical kinetics is the study of the factors that control the rates of chemical reactions. The reaction rate is defined as the change in concentration of a reactant or product per unit of time. Kinetic measurements are usually made under conditions where the reverse reaction is insignificant. Then only the forward reaction is important in determining the rate.

There are two kinds of rate laws: the differential rate law (or just rate law) and the integrated rate law. The rate law for a reaction of the type

$$aA \longrightarrow \text{products}$$

describes the dependence of the rate on the concentration of A:

$$\text{Rate} = -\frac{\Delta[A]}{\Delta t} = k[A]^n$$

where k is called the rate constant and n is the order of the reaction in A. The rate is defined as the negative of $\Delta[A]/\Delta t$ because [A] is decreasing (as the reactants are used up in the reaction). The value for n (the order) cannot be determined from the balanced equation for the reaction but must be found experimentally. For a first-order reaction n is 1 and the rate $= k[A]$. For a second-order reaction n is 2 and the rate $= k[A]^2$. For a zero-order reaction n is 0 and the rate $= k$.

A common experimental method for determining the rate law is the method of initial rates in which several runs are carried out with different initial concentrations, and the rate is measured for each at a value of t close to $t = 0$.

An integrated rate law expresses reactant concentrations as a function of time. The integrated rate law for a first-order reaction is

$$\ln[A] = -kt + \ln[A]_0$$

where $[A]_0$ is the initial concentration of A. Thus we can calculate [A] at any time, given $[A]_0$ and k. For a reaction that shows first-order kinetics, a plot of ln[A] versus time is a straight line.

The half-life ($t_{1/2}$) of a reaction is the time required for a reactant to reach half of its original concentration. For first-order reactions the half-life is independent of concentration:

$$t_{1/2} = \frac{0.693}{k}$$

The integrated rate law for a second-order reaction is

$$\frac{1}{[A]} = kt + \frac{1}{[A]_0}$$

Consequently, if a plot of 1/[A] versus time for a given reaction is a straight line, then the rate must be second order in A. For second-order kinetics, the half-life is dependent on both k and $[A]_0$:

$$t_{1/2} = \frac{1}{k[A]_0}$$

The integrated rate law for a zero-order reaction is

$$[A] = -kt + [A]_0$$

and the half-life is

$$t_{1/2} = \frac{[A]_0}{2k}$$

For a reaction with several reactants, the overall reaction order is the sum of the individual orders. We can determine the orders for this type of reaction by making the concentration of a particular reactant small in comparison to those of the other reactants.

A reaction mechanism is a series of elementary steps by which a given reaction occurs. The rate law for each step can be written from its molecularity, that is, the number of species that must collide to produce the reaction indicated by that step. A unimolecular step is always first order, and a bimolecular step is always second order.

For a mechanism to be acceptable, the sum of the elementary steps must give the overall balanced equation for the reaction, and the mechanism must give a rate law that agrees with the experimentally determined rate law. Multistep reactions often have one step that is much slower than the others. This is called the rate-determining step, since the overall rate of the reaction is limited by the rate of this step.

Chemical kinetics can be described by the collision model, which assumes that molecules must collide to react. In terms of this model, a certain threshold energy called the activation energy E_a must be overcome for a collision to produce a chemical reaction. E_a is the energy needed to rearrange the bonds in the molecules to form products. Both the rate of a reaction and the effect of temperature on the rate depend on the size of E_a.

Molecular orientation during a collision is also important, since not every collision will have the molecules aligned in an effective way. The factors affecting k can be described by the Arrhenius equation

$$k = Ae^{-E_a/RT}$$

where A is a factor reflecting collision frequency and molecular orientation and $e^{-E_a/RT}$ represents the fraction of collisions with sufficient energy to produce a reaction. The value of E_a can be determined by measuring values of k at two or more temperatures.

A catalyst is a substance that speeds up a reaction without being consumed. A catalyst operates by providing a lower energy pathway for the reaction in question. Enzymes are biologic catalysts. A homogeneous catalyst is present in the same phase as the reacting molecules, and a heterogeneous catalyst exists in a different phase.

In-Class Discussion Questions*

These questions are designed to be considered by groups of students in class. Often these questions work well for introducing a particular topic in class.

1. Define *stability* from both a kinetic and thermodynamic perspective. Give examples to show the differences in these concepts.

2. Describe at least two experiments you could perform to determine a rate law.

3. Make a graph of [A] versus time for zero-, first-, and second-order reactions. From these graphs, compare successive half-lives.

4. How does temperature affect k, the rate constant? Explain.

5. Consider the following statements: "In general, the rate of a chemical reaction increases a bit at first because it takes awhile for the reaction to get 'warmed up.' After that, however, the rate of the reaction decreases because its rate is dependent on the concentrations of the reactants, and these are decreasing." Indicate everything that is correct in these statements, and indicate everything that is incorrect. Correct the incorrect statements and explain.

* In the Questions and the Exercises, the term *rate law* always refers to the differential rate law.

6. For the reaction $A + B \longrightarrow C$, explain at least two ways in which the rate law could be zero order in chemical A.

7. A friend of yours states, "A balanced equation tells us how chemicals interact. Therefore, we can determine the rate law directly from the balanced equation." What do you tell your friend?

8. Provide a conceptual rationale for the differences in the half-lives of zero-, first-, and second-order reactions.

A blue question or exercise number indicates that the answer to that question or exercise appears at the back of this book and a solution appears in the *Solutions Guide*.

Questions*

9. Distinguish among the initial rate, average rate, and instantaneous rate of a chemical reaction. Which of these rates usually has the largest value?

10. Define each of the following.
  a. elementary step
  b. reaction mechanism
  c. rate-determining step

11. Why is the rate of a reaction affected by each of the following?
  a. frequency of collisions
  b. kinetic energy of collisions
  c. orientation of collisions

12. Define what is meant by unimolecular and bimolecular steps. Why are termolecular steps infrequently seen in chemical reactions?

13. Define each of the following.
  a. homogeneous catalyst
  b. heterogeneous catalyst

14. Why does a catalyst increase the rate of a chemical reaction?

15. Would a given reaction have the same rate law for both a catalyzed and an uncatalyzed pathway? Explain.

16. Hydrogen reacts explosively with oxygen. However, a mixture of H_2 and O_2 can exist indefinitely at room temperature. Explain why H_2 and O_2 do not react under these conditions.

17. Each of the statements given below is false. Explain why.
  a. The activation energy of a reaction depends on the overall energy change (ΔE) for the reaction.
  b. The rate law for a reaction can be deduced from examination of the overall balanced equation for the reaction.
  c. Most reactions occur by one-step mechanisms.

18. For the reaction

$$2H_2(g) + 2NO(g) \longrightarrow N_2(g) + 2H_2O(g)$$

*See footnote on page 601.

the observed rate law is

$$\text{Rate} = k[NO]^2[H_2]$$

Which of the changes listed below would affect the value of the rate constant k?
  a. increasing the partial pressure of hydrogen gas
  b. changing the temperature
  c. using an appropriate catalyst

Exercises*

In this section similar exercises are paired.

Reaction Rates

19. Consider the reaction

$$4PH_3(g) \longrightarrow P_4(g) + 6H_2(g)$$

If, in a certain experiment, over a specific time period, 0.0048 mol PH_3 is consumed in a 2.0-L container each second of reaction, what are the rates of production of P_4 and H_2 in this experiment?

20. In the Haber process for the production of ammonia,

$$N_2(g) + 3H_2(g) \longrightarrow 2NH_3(g)$$

what is the relationship between the rate of production of ammonia and the rate of consumption of hydrogen?

21. What are the units for each of the following if the concentrations are expressed in moles per liter and the time in seconds?
  a. rate of a chemical reaction
  b. rate constant for a zero-order rate law
  c. rate constant for a first-order rate law
  d. rate constant for a second-order rate law
  e. rate constant for a third-order rate law

22. The rate law for the reaction

$$Cl_2(g) + CHCl_3(g) \longrightarrow HCl(g) + CCl_4(g)$$

is $\qquad \text{Rate} = k[Cl_2]^{1/2}[CHCl_3]$

What are the units for k, assuming time in seconds and concentration in mol/L?

Rate Laws from Experimental Data: Initial Rates Method

23. The reaction

$$2NO(g) + Cl_2(g) \longrightarrow 2NOCl(g)$$

was studied at $-10°C$. The following results were obtained where

$$\text{Rate} = -\frac{\Delta[Cl_2]}{\Delta t}$$

$[NO]_0$ (mol/L)	$[Cl_2]_0$ (mol/L)	Initial Rate (mol/L · min)
0.10	0.10	0.18
0.10	0.20	0.36
0.20	0.20	1.45

a. What is the rate law?
b. What is the value of the rate constant?

24. The reaction

$$2I^-(aq) + S_2O_8{}^{2-}(aq) \longrightarrow I_2(aq) + 2SO_4{}^{2-}(aq)$$

was studied at 25°C. The following results were obtained where

$$\text{Rate} = -\frac{\Delta[S_2O_8{}^{2-}]}{\Delta t}$$

$[I^-]_0$ (mol/L)	$[S_2O_8{}^{2-}]_0$ (mol/L)	Initial Rate (mol/L · s)
0.080	0.040	12.5×10^{-6}
0.040	0.040	6.25×10^{-6}
0.080	0.020	6.25×10^{-6}
0.032	0.040	5.00×10^{-6}
0.060	0.030	7.00×10^{-6}

a. Determine the rate law.
b. Calculate a value for the rate constant for each experiment and an average value for the rate constant.

25. The decomposition of nitrosyl chloride was studied:

$$2NOCl(g) \rightleftharpoons 2NO(g) + Cl_2(g)$$

The following data were obtained where

$$\text{Rate} = -\frac{\Delta[NOCl]}{\Delta t}$$

$[NOCl]_0$ (molecules/cm³)	Initial Rate (molecules/cm³ · s)
3.0×10^{16}	5.98×10^4
2.0×10^{16}	2.66×10^4
1.0×10^{16}	6.64×10^3
4.0×10^{16}	1.06×10^5

a. What is the rate law?
b. Calculate the rate constant.
c. Calculate the rate constant for the concentrations given in moles per liter.

26. The reaction

$$I^-(aq) + OCl^-(aq) \longrightarrow IO^-(aq) + Cl^-(aq)$$

was studied, and the following data were obtained:

$[I^-]_0$ (mol/L)	$[OCl^-]_0$ (mol/L)	Initial Rate (mol/L · s)
0.12	0.18	7.91×10^{-2}
0.060	0.18	3.95×10^{-2}
0.030	0.090	9.88×10^{-3}
0.24	0.090	7.91×10^{-2}

a. What is the rate law?
b. Calculate the rate constant.

27. The rate of the reaction between hemoglobin (Hb) and carbon monoxide (CO) was studied at 20°C. The following data were collected with all concentration units in μmol/L. (A hemoglobin concentration of 2.21 μmol/L is equal to 2.21 $\times$ 10^{-6} mol/L.)

$[Hb]_0$ (μmol/L)	$[CO]_0$ (μmol/L)	Initial Rate (μmol/L · s)
2.21	1.00	0.619
4.42	1.00	1.24
4.42	3.00	3.71

a. Determine the orders of this reaction with respect to Hb and CO.
b. Determine the rate law.
c. Calculate the value of the rate constant.
d. What would be the initial rate for an experiment with $[Hb]_0 = 3.36\ \mu$mol/L and $[CO]_0 = 2.40\ \mu$mol/L?

28. The following data were obtained for the reaction

$$2ClO_2(aq) + 2OH^-(aq)$$
$$\longrightarrow ClO_3{}^-(aq) + ClO_2{}^-(aq) + H_2O(l)$$

where

$$\text{Rate} = -\frac{\Delta[ClO_2]}{\Delta t}$$

$[ClO_2]_0$ (mol/L)	$[OH^-]_0$ (mol/L)	Initial Rate (mol/L · s)
0.0500	0.100	5.75×10^{-2}
0.100	0.100	2.30×10^{-1}
0.100	0.0500	1.15×10^{-1}

a. Determine the rate law and the value of the rate constant.
b. What would be the initial rate for an experiment with $[ClO_2]_0 = 0.175$ mol/L and $[OH^-]_0 = 0.0844$ mol/L?

Integrated Rate Laws

29. The decomposition of hydrogen peroxide was studied, and the following data were obtained at a particular temperature:

Time (s)	$[H_2O_2]$ (mol/L)
0	1.00
120 ± 1	0.91
300 ± 1	0.78
600 ± 1	0.59
1200 ± 1	0.37
1800 ± 1	0.22
2400 ± 1	0.13
3000 ± 1	0.082
3600 ± 1	0.050

Assuming that

$$\text{Rate} = -\frac{\Delta[H_2O_2]}{\Delta t}$$

determine the rate law, the integrated rate law, and the value of the rate constant. Calculate the $[H_2O_2]$ at 4000. s after the start of the reaction.

30. A certain reaction has the following general form:

$$aA \longrightarrow bB$$

At a particular temperature and $[A]_0 = 2.00 \times 10^{-2} M$, concentration versus time data were collected for this reaction, and a plot of $\ln[A]$ versus time resulted in a straight line with a slope value of -2.97×10^{-2} min^{-1}.
  a. Determine the rate law, the integrated rate law, and the value of the rate constant for this reaction.
  b. Calculate the half-life for this reaction.
  c. How much time is required for the concentration of A to decrease to $2.50 \times 10^{-3} M$?

31. The rate of the reaction

$$NO_2(g) + CO(g) \longrightarrow NO(g) + CO_2(g)$$

depends only on the concentration of nitrogen dioxide below 225°C. At a temperature below 225°C, the following data were collected:

Time (s)	$[NO_2]$ (mol/L)
0	0.500
1.20×10^3	0.444
3.00×10^3	0.381
4.50×10^3	0.340
9.00×10^3	0.250
1.80×10^4	0.174

Determine the rate law, the integrated law, and the value of the rate constant. Calculate the $[NO_2]$ at 2.70×10^4 s after the start of the reaction.

32. A certain reaction has the following general form:

$$aA \longrightarrow bB$$

At a particular temperature and $[A]_0 = 2.80 \times 10^{-3} M$, concentration versus time data were collected for this reaction, and a plot of $1/[A]$ versus time resulted in a straight line with a slope value of $+3.60 \times 10^{-2}$ L/mol · s.
  a. Determine the rate law, the integrated rate law, and the value of the rate constant for this reaction.
  b. Calculate the half-life for this reaction.
  c. How much time is required for the concentration of A to decrease to $7.00 \times 10^{-4} M$?

33. The decomposition of ethanol (C_2H_5OH) on an alumina (Al_2O_3) surface

$$C_2H_5OH(g) \longrightarrow C_2H_4(g) + H_2O(g)$$

was studied at 600 K. Concentration versus time data were collected for this reaction, and a plot of [A] versus time resulted in a straight line with a slope value of -4.00×10^{-5} mol/L · s.
  a. Determine the rate law, the integrated rate law, and the value of the rate constant for this reaction.
  b. If the initial concentration of C_2H_5OH was $1.25 \times 10^{-2} M$, calculate the half-life for this reaction.
  c. How much time is required for all the $1.25 \times 10^{-2} M$ C_2H_5OH to decompose?

34. The reaction

$$A \longrightarrow B + C$$

is known to be zero order in A and to have a rate constant of 5.0×10^{-2} mol/L · s at 25°C. An experiment was run at 25°C where $[A]_0 = 1.0 \times 10^{-3} M$.
  a. Write the integrated rate law for this reaction.
  b. Calculate the half-life for the reaction.
  c. Calculate the concentration of B after 5.0×10^{-3} s has elapsed.

35. The dimerization of butadiene

$$2C_4H_6(g) \longrightarrow C_8H_{12}(g)$$

was studied at 500. K, and the following data were obtained:

Time (s)	$[C_4H_6]$ (mol/L)
195	1.6×10^{-2}
604	1.5×10^{-2}
1246	1.3×10^{-2}
2180	1.1×10^{-2}
6210	0.68×10^{-2}

Assuming that

$$\text{Rate} = -\frac{\Delta[C_4H_6]}{\Delta t}$$

determine the form of the rate law, the integrated rate law, and the rate constant for this reaction. (These are actual experimental data, so they may not give a perfectly straight line.)

36. The rate of the reaction

$$O(g) + NO_2(g) \longrightarrow NO(g) + O_2(g)$$

was studied at a certain temperature.
a. In the first set of experiments, NO_2 was in large excess, at a concentration of 1.0×10^{13} molecules/cm³ with the following data collected:

Time (s)	[O] (atoms/cm³)
0	5.0×10^9
1.0×10^{-2}	1.9×10^9
2.0×10^{-2}	6.8×10^8
3.0×10^{-2}	2.5×10^8

What is the order of the reaction with respect to oxygen atoms?
b. The reaction is known to be first order with respect to NO_2. Determine the overall rate law and the value of the rate constant.

37. A certain first-order reaction is 45.0% complete in 65 s. What are the rate constant and the half-life for this process?
38. The radioactive isotope ^{32}P decays by first-order kinetics and has a half-life of 14.3 days. How long does it take for 95.0% of a sample of ^{32}P to decay?

39. A first-order reaction is 38.5% complete in 480. s.
a. Calculate the rate constant.
b. What is the value of the half-life?
c. How long will it take for the reaction to go to 25%, 75%, and 95% completion?
40. The rate law for the decomposition of phosphine (PH_3) is

$$\text{Rate} = -\frac{\Delta[PH_3]}{\Delta t} = k[PH_3]$$

It takes 120. s for 1.00 M PH_3 to decrease to 0.250 M. How much time is required for 2.00 M PH_3 to decrease to a concentration of .350 M?

41. It took 143 s for 50.0% of a particular substance to decompose. If the initial concentration was 0.060 M and the decomposition reaction follows second-order kinetics, what is the value of the rate constant?
42. The rate law for the reaction

$$2NOBr(g) \longrightarrow 2NO(g) + Br_2(g)$$

at some temperature is

$$\text{Rate} = -\frac{\Delta[NOBr]}{\Delta t} = k[NOBr]^2$$

a. If the half-life for this reaction is 2.00 s when $[NOBr]_0 = 0.900$ M, calculate the value of k for this reaction.
b. How much time is required for the concentration of NOBr to decrease to 0.100 M?

43. In 6 M HCl the complex ion $Ru(NH_3)_6^{3+}$ has a half-life of 14 h at 25°C. Under these conditions, how long will it take for the $[Ru(NH_3)_6^{3+}]$ to decrease to 12.5% of its initial value? (Assume first-order kinetics.)
44. For the reaction A $\rightarrow$ products, successive half-lives are observed to be 10.0, 20.0, and 40.0 min for an experiment in which $[A]_0 = 0.10$ M. Calculate the concentration of A at the following times.
a. 80.0 min
b. 30.0 min

Reaction Mechanisms

45. Write the rate laws for the following elementary reactions.
a. $CH_3NC(g) \rightarrow CH_3CN(g)$
b. $O_3(g) + NO(g) \rightarrow O_2(g) + NO_2(g)$
46. Write the rate laws for the following elementary reactions.
a. $O_3(g) \rightarrow O_2(g) + O(g)$
b. $O_3(g) + O(g) \rightarrow 2O_2(g)$

47. A proposed mechanism for a reaction is

$C_4H_9Br \longrightarrow C_4H_9^+ + Br^-$	Slow
$C_4H_9^+ + H_2O \longrightarrow C_4H_9OH_2^+$	Fast
$C_4H_9OH_2^+ + H_2O \longrightarrow C_4H_9OH + H_3O^+$	Fast

Write the rate law expected for this mechanism. What is the overall balanced equation for the reaction? What are the intermediates in the proposed mechanism?
48. The mechanism for the reaction of nitrogen dioxide with carbon monoxide to form nitric oxide and carbon dioxide is thought to be

$NO_2 + NO_2 \longrightarrow NO_3 + NO$	Slow
$NO_3 + CO \longrightarrow NO_2 + CO_2$	Fast

Write the rate law expected for this mechanism. What is the overall balanced equation for the reaction?

Temperature Dependence of Rate Constants and the Collision Model

49. For the reaction profile on the following page, indicate
a. the positions of reactants and products.
b. the activation energy.
c. ΔE for the reaction.

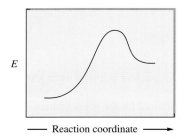

— Reaction coordinate —→

50. Draw a rough sketch of the energy profile for each of the following cases:
a. $\Delta E = +10$ kJ/mol, $E_a = 25$ kJ/mol
b. $\Delta E = -10$ kJ/mol, $E_a = 50$ kJ/mol
c. $\Delta E = -50$ kJ/mol, $E_a = 50$ kJ/mol

51. The activation energy for the reaction

$$NO_2(g) + CO(g) \longrightarrow NO(g) + CO_2(g)$$

is 125 kJ/mol, and ΔE for the reaction is -216 kJ/mol. What is the activation energy for the reverse reaction [$NO(g) + CO_2(g) \longrightarrow NO_2(g) + CO(g)$]?

52. For a certain process, the activation energy is greater for the forward reaction than for the reverse reaction. Does this reaction have a positive or negative value for ΔE?

53. Experimental values for the temperature dependence of the rate constant for the gas-phase reaction

$$NO + O_3 \longrightarrow NO_2 + O_2$$

are as follows:

T (K)	k (L/mol · s)
195	1.08×10^9
230.	2.95×10^9
260.	5.42×10^9
298	12.0×10^9
369	35.5×10^9

Make the appropriate graph using these data, and determine the activation energy for this reaction.

54. The reaction

$$(CH_3)_3CBr + OH^- \longrightarrow (CH_3)_3COH + Br^-$$

in a certain solvent is first order with respect to $(CH_3)_3CBr$ and zero order with respect to OH^-. In several experiments, the rate constant k was determined at different temperatures. A plot of $\ln(k)$ versus $1/T$ was constructed resulting in a straight line with a slope value of -1.10×10^4 K and y-intercept of 33.5. Assume k has units of s^{-1}.
a. Determine the activation energy for this reaction.
b. Determine the value of the frequency factor A.
c. Calculate the value of k at 25°C.

55. At 25°C the first-order rate constant for a reaction is 2.0×10^3 s^{-1}. The activation energy is 15.0 kJ/mol. What is the value of the rate constant at 75°C?

56. A first-order reaction has rate constants of 4.6×10^{-2} s^{-1} and 8.1×10^{-2} s^{-1} at 0°C and 20.°C, respectively. What is the value of the activation energy?

57. A certain reaction has an activation energy of 54.0 kJ/mol. As the temperature is increased from 22°C to a higher temperature, the rate constant increases by a factor of 7.00. Calculate the higher temperature.

58. Chemists commonly use a rule of thumb that an increase of 10 K in temperature doubles the rate of a reaction. What must the activation energy be for this statement to be true for a temperature increase from 25 to 35°C?

Catalysts

59. One mechanism for the destruction of ozone in the upper atmosphere is

$$O_3(g) + NO(g) \longrightarrow NO_2(g) + O_2(g) \quad \text{Slow}$$
$$NO_2(g) + O(g) \longrightarrow NO(g) + O_2(g) \quad \text{Fast}$$
Overall reaction: $O_3(g) + O(g) \longrightarrow 2O_2(g)$

a. Which species is a catalyst?
b. Which species is an intermediate?
c. E_a for the uncatalyzed reaction

$$O_3(g) + O(g) \longrightarrow 2O_2$$

is 14.0 kJ. E_a for the same reaction when catalyzed is 11.9 kJ. What is the ratio of the rate constant for the catalyzed reaction to that for the uncatalyzed reaction at 25°C? Assume that the frequency factor A is the same for each reaction.

60. One of the concerns about the use of Freons is that they will migrate to the upper atmosphere, where chlorine atoms can be generated by the following reaction:

$$CCl_2F_2 \xrightarrow{h\nu} CF_2Cl + Cl$$
Freon-12

Chlorine atoms can act as a catalyst for the destruction of ozone. The activation energy for the reaction

$$Cl + O_3 \longrightarrow ClO + O_2$$

is 2.1 kJ/mol. Which is the more effective catalyst for the destruction of ozone, Cl or NO? (See Exercise 59.)

61. Assuming that the mechanism for the hydrogenation of C_2H_4 given in Section 12.8 is correct, would you predict that the product of the reaction of C_2H_4 with D_2 would be CH_2D—CH_2D or CHD_2—CH_3? How could the reaction of C_2H_4 with D_2 be used to confirm the mechanism for the hydrogenation of C_2H_4 given in Section 12.8.

62. The decomposition of NH_3 to N_2 and H_2 was studied on two surfaces:

Surface	E_a (kJ/mol)
W	163
Os	197

Without a catalyst, the activation energy is 335 kJ/mol.

a. Which surface is the better heterogeneous catalyst for the decomposition of NH_3? Why?

b. How many times faster is the reaction at 298 K on the W surface compared with the reaction with no catalyst present? Assume that the frequency factor A is the same for each reaction.

c. The decomposition reaction on the two surfaces obeys a rate law of the form

$$Rate = k \frac{[NH_3]}{[H_2]}$$

How can you explain the inverse dependence of the rate on the H_2 concentration?

Additional Exercises

63. The reaction

$$2NO(g) + O_2(g) \longrightarrow 2NO_2(g)$$

was studied, and the following data were obtained where

$$Rate = -\frac{\Delta[O_2]}{\Delta t}$$

$[NO]_0$ (molecules/cm^3)	$[O_2]_0$ (molecules/cm^3)	Initial Rate (molecules/cm$^3 \cdot$ s)
1.00×10^{18}	1.00×10^{18}	2.00×10^{16}
3.00×10^{18}	1.00×10^{18}	1.80×10^{17}
2.50×10^{18}	2.50×10^{18}	3.13×10^{17}

What would be the initial rate for an experiment where $[NO]_0 = 6.21 \times 10^{18}$ molecules/cm^3 and $[O_2]_0 = 7.36 \times 10^{18}$ molecules/cm^3?

64. Consider the hypothetical reaction

$$A + B + 2C \longrightarrow 2D + 3E$$

where the rate law is

$$Rate = -\frac{\Delta[A]}{\Delta t} = k[A][B]^2$$

An experiment is carried out where $[A]_0 = 1.0 \times 10^{-2}$ M, $[B]_0 = 3.0$ M, and $[C]_0 = 2.0$ M. The reaction is started, and after 8.0 seconds, the concentration of A is 3.8×10^{-3} M.

a. Calculate k for this reaction.

b. Calculate the half-life for this experiment.

c. Calculate the concentration of A after 13.0 seconds.

d. Calculate the concentration of C after 13.0 seconds.

65. Sulfuryl chloride (SO_2Cl_2) decomposes to sulfur dioxide (SO_2) and chlorine (Cl_2) by reaction in the gas phase. The following pressure data were obtained when a sample containing 5.00×10^{-2} mol sulfuryl chloride was heated to 600. K in a 5.00×10^{-1} L container.

Time (hours):	0.00	1.00	2.00	4.00	8.00	16.00
$P_{SO_2Cl_2}$ (atm):	4.93	4.26	3.52	2.53	1.30	0.34

Defining the rate as $-\dfrac{\Delta[SO_2Cl_2]}{\Delta t}$,

a. determine the value of the rate constant for the decomposition of sulfuryl chloride at 600. K.

b. what is the half-life of the reaction?

c. what fraction of the sulfuryl chloride remains after 20.0 h?

66. At 620. K, butadiene dimerizes at a moderate rate. The following data were obtained in an experiment involving this reaction:

t (s)	$[C_4H_6]$ (mol/L)
0.	0.01000
1000.	0.00629
2000.	0.00459
3000.	0.00361

a. Determine the order of the reaction in butadiene.

b. Use the results from this problem and Exercise 35 to calculate the activation energy for the dimerization of butadiene.

67. The rate constant for the gas-phase decomposition of N_2O_5,

$$N_2O_5 \longrightarrow 2NO_2 + \tfrac{1}{2}O_2$$

has the following temperature dependence:

$T(K)$	$k(s^{-1})$
338	4.9×10^{-3}
318	5.0×10^{-4}
298	3.5×10^{-5}

Make the appropriate graph using these data, and determine the activation energy for this reaction.

68. The mechanisms shown below have been proposed to explain the kinetics of the reaction considered in Question 18. Which of the following are acceptable mechanisms? Explain.

Mechanism I:

$$2H_2(g) + 2NO(g) \longrightarrow N_2(g) + 2H_2O(g)$$

Mechanism II:

$$H_2(g) + NO(g) \longrightarrow H_2O(g) + N(g) \quad \text{Slow}$$
$$N(g) + NO(g) \longrightarrow N_2(g) + O(g) \quad \text{Fast}$$
$$H_2(g) + O(g) \longrightarrow H_2O(g) \quad \text{Fast}$$

Mechanism III:

$$H_2(g) + 2NO(g) \longrightarrow N_2O(g) + H_2O(g) \quad \text{Slow}$$
$$N_2O(g) + H_2(g) \longrightarrow N_2(g) + H_2O(g) \quad \text{Fast}$$

69. For enzyme-catalyzed reactions that follow the mechanism

$$E + S \rightleftharpoons E \cdot S$$
$$E \cdot S \rightleftharpoons E + P$$

a graph of the rate as a function of [S], the concentration of the substrate, has the following appearance:

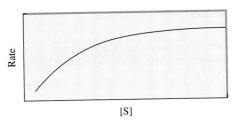

[S]

Note that at higher substrate concentrations the rate no longer changes with [S]. Suggest a reason for this.

70. The activation energy of a certain uncatalyzed biochemical reaction is 50.0 kJ/mol. In the presence of a catalyst at 37°C, the rate constant for the reaction increases by a factor of 2.50×10^3 as compared with the uncatalyzed reaction. Assuming the frequency factor A is the same for both the catalyzed and uncatalyzed reactions, calculate the activation energy for the catalyzed reaction.

Challenge Problems

71. A study was made of the effect of the hydroxide concentration on the rate of the reaction

$$I^-(aq) + OCl^-(aq) \longrightarrow IO^-(aq) + Cl^-(aq)$$

The following data were obtained:

$[I^-]_0$ (mol/L)	$[OCl^-]_0$ (mol/L)	$[OH^-]_0$ (mol/L)	Initial Rate (mol/L · s)
0.0013	0.012	0.10	9.4×10^{-3}
0.0026	0.012	0.10	18.7×10^{-3}
0.0013	0.0060	0.10	4.7×10^{-3}
0.0013	0.018	0.10	14.0×10^{-3}
0.0013	0.012	0.050	18.7×10^{-3}
0.0013	0.012	0.20	4.7×10^{-3}
0.0013	0.018	0.20	7.0×10^{-3}

Determine the rate law and the value of the rate constant for this reaction.

72. Two isomers (A and B) of a given compound dimerize as follows:

$$2A \xrightarrow{k_1} A_2$$

$$2B \xrightarrow{k_2} B_2$$

Both processes are known to be second order in reactant, and k_1 is known to be 0.250 L/mol · s at 25°C. In a particular experiment A and B were placed in separate containers at 25°C, where $[A]_0 = 1.00 \times 10^{-2}$ M and $[B]_0 = 2.50 \times 10^{-2}$ M. It was found that after each reaction had progressed for 3.00 min, $[A] = 3.00[B]$. In this case the rate laws are defined as

$$\text{Rate} = -\frac{\Delta[A]}{\Delta t} = k_1[A]^2$$

$$\text{Rate} = -\frac{\Delta[B]}{\Delta t} = k_2[B]^2$$

a. Calculate the concentration of A_2 after 3.00 min.
b. Calculate the value of k_2.
c. Calculate the half-life for the experiment involving A.

73. The reaction

$$NO(g) + O_3(g) \longrightarrow NO_2(g) + O_2(g)$$

was studied by performing two experiments. In the first experiment the rate of disappearance of NO was followed in the presence of a large excess of O_3. The results were as follows ([O_3] remains effectively constant at 1.0×10^{14} molecules/cm³):

Time (ms)	[NO] (molecules/cm³)
0	6.0×10^8
100 ± 1	5.0×10^8
500 ± 1	2.4×10^8
700 ± 1	1.7×10^8
1000 ± 1	9.9×10^7

In the second experiment [NO] was held constant at 2.0×10^{14} molecules/cm³. The data for the disappearance of O_3 are as follows:

Time (ms)	[O_3] (molecules/cm³)
0	1.0×10^{10}
50 ± 1	8.4×10^9
100 ± 1	7.0×10^9
200 ± 1	4.9×10^9
300 ± 1	3.4×10^9

a. What is the order with respect to each reactant?
b. What is the overall rate law?
c. What is the value of the rate constant from each set of experiments?

$$\text{Rate} = k'[NO]^x \qquad \text{Rate} = k''[O_3]^y$$

d. What is the value of the rate constant for the overall rate law?

$$\text{Rate} = k[NO]^x[O_3]^y$$

74. Most reactions occur by a series of steps. The energy profile for a certain reaction that proceeds by a two-step mechanism is

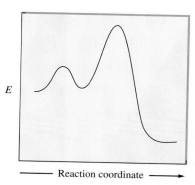

On the energy profile, indicate
a. The positions of reactants and products.
b. The activation energy for the overall reaction.
c. ΔE for the reaction.
d. Which point on the plot represents the energy of the intermediate in the two-step reaction?
e. Which step in the mechanism for this reaction is rate determining, the first or the second step? Explain.

75. Experiments have shown the average frequency of chirping of individual snowy tree crickets (*Oecanthus fultoni*) to be 178 min^{-1} at 25.0°C, 126 min^{-1} at 20.3°C, and 100. min^{-1} at 17.3°C.
a. What is the apparent activation energy of the reaction that controls the chirping?
b. What chirping rate would be expected at 15.0°C?
c. Compare the observed rates and your calculated rate from part b to the rule of thumb that the Fahrenheit temperature is 42 plus 0.80 times the number of chirps in 15 s.

76. The decomposition of $NO_2(g)$ occurs by the following bimolecular elementary reaction:

$$2NO_2(g) \longrightarrow 2NO(g) + O_2(g)$$

The rate constant at 273 K is 2.3×10^{-12} L/mol · s, and the activation energy is 111 kJ/mol. How long will it take for the concentration of $NO_2(g)$ to decrease from an initial partial pressure of 2.5 atm to 1.5 atm at 500. K? Assume ideal gas behavior.

Marathon Problem

This problem is designed to incorporate several concepts and techniques into one situation. Marathon Problems can be used in class by groups of students to help facilitate problem-solving skills.

77. Consider the following reaction:

$$CH_3X + Y \longrightarrow CH_3Y + X$$

At 25°C, the following two experiments were run, yielding the following data:

Experiment 1: $[Y]_0 = 3.0\ M$

[CH$_3$X]	Time (h)
$7.08 \times 10^{-3}\ M$	1.0
$4.52 \times 10^{-3}\ M$	1.5
$2.23 \times 10^{-3}\ M$	2.3
$4.76 \times 10^{-4}\ M$	4.0
$8.44 \times 10^{-5}\ M$	5.7
$2.75 \times 10^{-5}\ M$	7.0

Experiment 2: $[Y]_0 = 4.5\ M$

[CH$_3$X]	Time (h)
$4.50 \times 10^{-3}\ M$	0
$1.70 \times 10^{-3}\ M$	1.0
$4.19 \times 10^{-4}\ M$	2.5
$1.11 \times 10^{-4}\ M$	4.0
$2.81 \times 10^{-5}\ M$	5.5

Experiments also were run at 85°C. The value of the rate constant at 85°C was found to be 7.88×10^8 (with the time in units of hours), where $[CH_3X]_0 = 1.0 \times 10^{-2}\ M$ and $[Y]_0 = 3.0\ M$.
a. Determine the rate law and the value of k for this reaction at 25°C.
b. Determine the half-life at 85°C.
c. Determine E_a for the reaction.
d. Given that the C—X bond energy is known to be about 325 kJ/mol, suggest a mechanism that explains the results in parts a and c.

Chemical Equilibrium

Contents

*I*n doing stoichiometry calculations we assumed that reactions proceed to completion, that is, until one of the reactants runs out. Many reactions *do* proceed essentially to completion. For such reactions it can be assumed that the reactants are quantitatively converted to products and that the amount of limiting reactant that remains is negligible. On the other hand, there are many chemical reactions that stop far short of completion. An example is the dimerization of nitrogen dioxide:

$$NO_2(g) + NO_2(g) \longrightarrow N_2O_4(g)$$

The reactant, NO_2, is a dark brown gas, and the product, N_2O_4, is a colorless gas. When NO_2 is placed in an evacuated, sealed glass vessel at 25°C, the initial dark brown color decreases in intensity as it is converted to colorless N_2O_4. However, even over a long period of time, the contents of the reaction vessel do not become colorless. Instead, the intensity of the brown color eventually becomes constant, which means that the concentration of NO_2 is no longer changing. This is illustrated on the molecular level in Fig. 13.1. This observation is a clear indication that the reaction has stopped short of completion. In fact, the system has reached **chemical equilibrium,** *the state where the concentrations of all reactants and products remain constant with time.*

Any chemical reactions carried out in a closed vessel will reach equilibrium. For some reactions the equilibrium position so favors the products that the reaction appears to have gone to completion. We say that the equilibrium position for such reactions lies *far to the right* (in the direction of the products). For example, when gaseous hydrogen and oxygen are mixed in stoichiometric quantities and react to form water vapor, the reaction proceeds essentially to completion. The amounts of the reactants that remain when the system reaches equilibrium are so tiny as to be negligible. By contrast, some reactions occur only to a slight extent. For

---

The effect of temperature on the endothermic, aqueous equilibrium:

$$\underset{\text{Pink}}{Co(H_2O)_6^{2+}} + 4Cl^- \rightleftharpoons \underset{\text{Blue}}{CoCl_4^{2-}} + 6H_2O$$

The violet solution in the center is at 25°C and contains significant quantities of both pink $Co(H_2O)_6^{2+}$ and blue $CoCl_4^{2-}$. When the solution is cooled, it turns pink because the equilibrium is shifted to the left. Heating the solution favors the blue $CoCl_4^{2-}$ ions.

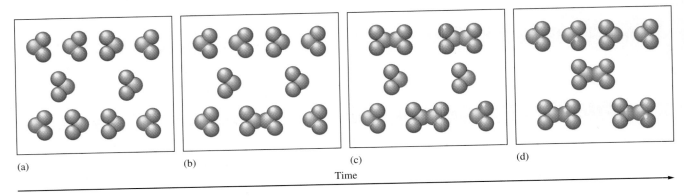

(a) (b) (c) (d)

Time

Molecular Models: NO_2, N_2O_4

Figure 13.1
A molecular representation of the reaction $2NO_2(g) \rightarrow N_2O_4(g)$ over time in a closed vessel. Note that the numbers of NO_2 and N_2O_4 in the container become constant (c and d) after sufficient time has passed.

example, when solid CaO is placed in a closed vessel at 25°C, the decomposition to solid Ca and gaseous O_2 is virtually undetectable. In cases like this, the equilibrium position is said to lie *far to the left* (in the direction of the reactants).

In this chapter we will discuss how and why a chemical system comes to equilibrium and the characteristics of equilibrium. In particular, we will discuss how to calculate the concentrations of the reactants and products present for a given system at equilibrium.

Exploration: Equilibrium

13.1 *The Equilibrium Condition*

Since no changes occur in the concentrations of reactants or products in a reaction system at equilibrium, it may appear that everything has stopped. However, this is not the case. On the molecular level, there is frantic activity. Equilibrium is not static but is a highly *dynamic* situation. The concept of chemical equilibrium is analogous to the flow of cars across a bridge connecting two island cities. Suppose the traffic flow on the bridge is the same in both directions. It is obvious that there is motion, since one can see the cars traveling back and forth across the bridge, but the number of cars in each city is not changing because equal numbers of cars are entering and leaving. The result is no *net* change in the car population.

Equilibrium is a dynamic situation.

To see how this concept applies to chemical reactions, consider the reaction between steam and carbon monoxide in a closed vessel at a high temperature where the reaction takes place rapidly:

Molecular Models: H_2O, CO, H_2, CO_2

$$H_2O(g) + CO(g) \rightleftharpoons H_2(g) + CO_2(g)$$

Assume that the same number of moles of gaseous CO and gaseous H_2O are placed in a closed vessel and allowed to react. The plots of the concentrations of reactants and products versus time are shown in Fig. 13.2. Note that since CO and H_2O were originally present in equal molar quantities, and since they react in a 1:1 ratio, the concentrations of the two gases are always equal. Also, since H_2 and CO_2 are formed in equal amounts, they are always present in the same concentrations.

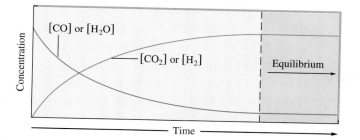

Figure 13.2 is a profile of the progress of the reaction. When CO and H_2O are mixed, they immediately begin to react to form H_2 and CO_2. This leads to a decrease in the concentrations of the reactants, but the concentrations of the products, which were initially at zero, are increasing. Beyond a certain time, indicated by the dashed line in Fig. 13.2, the concentrations of reactants and products no longer change—equilibrium has been reached. Unless the system is somehow disturbed, no further changes in concentrations will occur. Note that although the equilibrium position lies far to the right, the concentrations of reactants never go to zero; the reactants will always be present in small but constant concentrations. This is shown on the microscopic level in Fig. 13.3.

What would happen to the gaseous equilibrium mixture of reactants and products represented in Fig. 13.3, parts (c) and (d), if we injected some $H_2O(g)$ into the box? To answer this question, we need to be sure we understand the equilibrium condition: The concentrations of reactants and products remain constant at equilibrium because the forward and reverse reaction rates are equal. If we inject some H_2O molecules, what will happen to the forward reaction: $H_2O + CO \rightarrow H_2 + CO_2$? It will speed up because more H_2O molecules means more collisions between H_2O and CO molecules. This in turn will form more products and will cause the reverse reaction $H_2O + CO \leftarrow H_2 + CO_2$ to speed up. Thus the system will change until the forward and reverse reaction rates again become equal. Will this new equilibrium position contain more or fewer product molecules than are shown in Fig. 13.3(c) and (d)? Think about this carefully. If you are not sure of the answer now, keep reading. We will consider this type of situation in more detail later in this chapter.

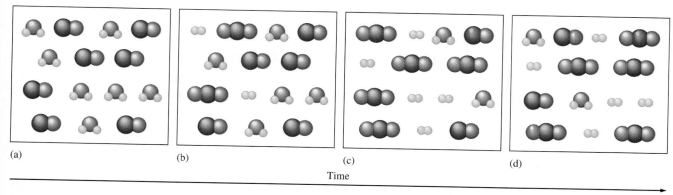

(a)　　　　　　　(b)　　　　　　　(c)　　　　　　　(d)

Time

Figure 13.3

(a) H_2O and CO are mixed in equal numbers and begin to react (b) to form CO_2 and H_2. After time has passed, equilibrium is reached (c) and the numbers of reactant and product molecules then remain constant over time (d).

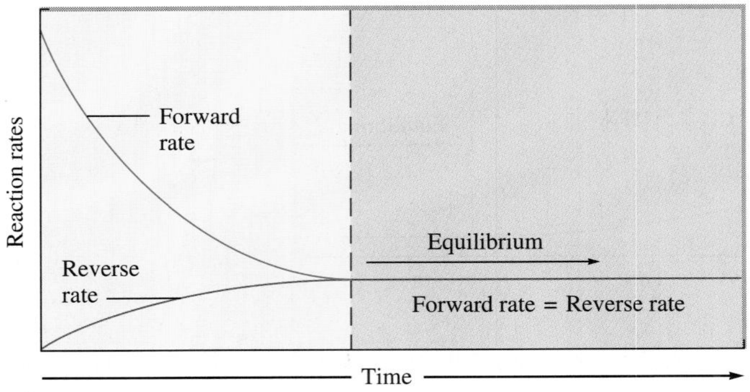

Figure 13.4

The changes with time in the rates of forward and reverse reactions for $H_2O(g) + CO(g) \rightleftharpoons H_2(g) + CO_2(g)$ when equimolar quantities of $H_2O(g)$ and $CO(g)$ are mixed. The rates do not change in the same way with time because the forward reaction has a much larger rate constant than the reverse reaction.

Why does equilibrium occur? We have seen in Chapter 12 that molecules react by colliding with one another, and the more collisions, the faster is the reaction. This is why reaction rates depend on concentrations. In this case the concentrations of H_2O and CO are lowered by the forward reaction:

$$H_2O + CO \longrightarrow H_2 + CO_2$$

As the concentrations of the reactants decrease, the forward reaction slows down (Fig. 13.4). As in the bridge traffic analogy, there is also a reverse direction:

$$H_2O + CO \longleftarrow H_2 + CO_2$$

Initially in this experiment no H_2 and CO_2 were present, and this reverse reaction could not occur. However, as the forward reaction proceeds, the concentrations of H_2 and CO_2 build up, and the rate of the reverse reaction increases (Fig. 13.4) as the forward reaction slows down. Eventually, the concentrations reach levels where the rate of the forward reaction equals the rate of the reverse reaction. The system has reached equilibrium.

The equilibrium position of a reaction—left, right, or somewhere in between—is determined by many factors: the initial concentrations, the relative energies of the reactants and products, and the relative degree of "organization" of the reactants and products. Energy and organization come into play because nature tries to achieve minimum energy and maximum disorder, as we will show in detail in Chapter 16. For now, we will simply view the equilibrium phenomenon in terms of the rates of opposing reactions.

A double arrow ($\rightleftharpoons$) is used to show that a reaction can occur in either direction.

The relationship between equilibrium and thermodynamics is explored in Section 16.8.

The Characteristics of Chemical Equilibrium

To explore the important characteristics of chemical equilibrium, we will consider the synthesis of ammonia from elemental nitrogen and hydrogen:

$$N_2(g) + 3H_2(g) \rightleftharpoons 2NH_3(g)$$

 Molecular Models: N_2, H_2, NH_3

This process is of great commercial value because ammonia is an important fertilizer for the growth of corn and other crops. Ironically, this beneficial process was discovered in Germany just before World War I in a search for ways to produce nitrogen-based explosives. In the course of this work, German chemist Fritz Haber (1868–1934) pioneered the large-scale production of ammonia.

The United States produces about 20 million tons of ammonia annually.

When gaseous nitrogen, hydrogen, and ammonia are mixed in a closed vessel at 25°C, no apparent change in the concentrations occurs over time, regardless of the original amounts of the gases. Why? There are two possible reasons why the concentrations of the reactants and products of a given chemical reaction remain unchanged when mixed.

1. The system is at chemical equilibrium.
2. The forward and reverse reactions are so slow that the system moves toward equilibrium at a rate that cannot be detected.

The second reason applies to the nitrogen, hydrogen, and ammonia mixture at 25°C. As we saw in Chapters 8 and 9, the N_2 molecule has a very strong triple bond (941 kJ/mol) and thus is very unreactive. Also, the H_2 molecule has an unusually strong single bond (432 kJ/mol). Therefore, mixtures of N_2, H_2, and NH_3 at 25°C can exist with no apparent change over long periods of time, unless a catalyst is introduced to speed up the forward and reverse reactions. Under appropriate conditions, the system does reach equilibrium, as shown in Fig. 13.5. Note that because of the reaction stoichiometry, H_2 disappears three times as fast as N_2 does and NH_3 forms twice as fast as N_2 disappears.

Molecules with strong bonds produce large activation energies and tend to react slowly at 25°C.

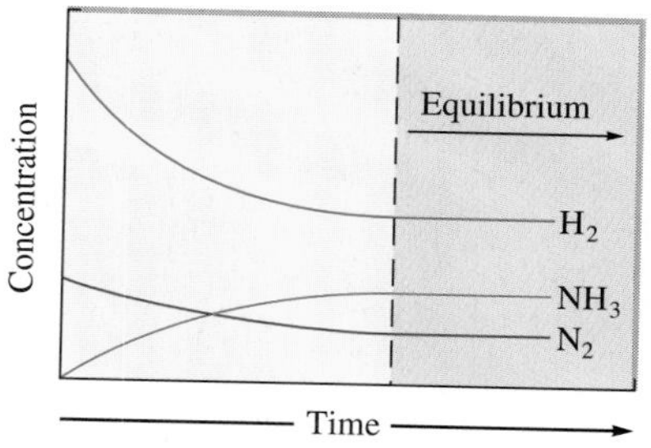

Figure 13.5
A concentration profile for the reaction $N_2(g) + 3H_2(g) \rightleftharpoons 2NH_3(g)$ when only $N_2(g)$ and $H_2(g)$ are mixed initially.

13.2 The Equilibrium Constant

Science is fundamentally empirical—it is based on experiment. The development of the equilibrium concept is typical. From their observations of many chemical reactions, two Norwegian chemists, Cato Maximilian Guldberg (1836–1902) and Peter Waage (1833–1900), proposed in 1864 the **law of mass action** as a general description of the equilibrium condition. Guldberg and Waage postulated that for a reaction of the type

The law of mass action is based on experimental observation.

$$jA + kB \rightleftharpoons lC + mD$$

where A, B, C, and D represent chemical species and j, k, l, and m are their coefficients in the balanced equation, the law of mass action is represented by the following **equilibrium expression:**

$$K = \frac{[C]^l[D]^m}{[A]^j[B]^k}$$

The square brackets indicate the concentrations of the chemical species *at equilibrium,* and K is a constant called the **equilibrium constant.**

Sample Exercise 13.1 *Writing Equilibrium Expressions*

Write the equilibrium expression for the following reaction:

$$4NH_3(g) + 7O_2(g) \rightleftharpoons 4NO_2(g) + 6H_2O(g)$$

Solution

Applying the law of mass action gives

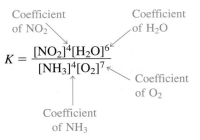

$$K = \frac{[NO_2]^4[H_2O]^6}{[NH_3]^4[O_2]^7}$$

Coefficient of NO_2

Coefficient of H_2O

Coefficient of O_2

Coefficient of NH_3

The square brackets indicate concentration in units of mol/L.

See Exercise 13.19.

The value of the equilibrium constant at a given temperature can be calculated if we know the equilibrium concentrations of the reaction components, as illustrated in Sample Exercise 13.2.

It is very important to note at this point that the equilibrium constants are customarily given without units. The reason for this is beyond the scope of this text, but it involves corrections for the nonideal behavior of the substances taking part in the reaction. When these corrections are made, the units cancel out and the corrected K has no units. Thus we will not use units for K in this text.

Sample Exercise 13.2 Calculating the Values of K

The following equilibrium concentrations were observed for the Haber process at 127°C:

$$[NH_3] = 3.1 \times 10^{-2} \text{ mol/L}$$
$$[N_2] = 8.5 \times 10^{-1} \text{ mol/L}$$
$$[H_2] = 3.1 \times 10^{-3} \text{ mol/L}$$

a. Calculate the value of K at 127°C for this reaction.

b. Calculate the value of the equilibrium constant at 127°C for the reaction

$$2NH_3(g) \rightleftharpoons N_2(g) + 3H_2(g)$$

c. Calculate the value of the equilibrium constant at 127°C for the reaction given by the equation

$$\tfrac{1}{2}N_2(g) + \tfrac{3}{2}H_2(g) \rightleftharpoons NH_3(g)$$

Solution

a. The balanced equation for the Haber process is

$$N_2(g) + 3H_2(g) \rightleftharpoons 2NH_3(g)$$

Thus
$$K = \frac{[NH_3]^2}{[N_2][H_2]^3} = \frac{(3.1 \times 10^{-2})^2}{(8.5 \times 10^{-1})(3.1 \times 10^{-3})^3}$$
$$= 3.8 \times 10^4$$

Note that K is written without units.

b. This reaction is written in the reverse order from the equation given in part a. This leads to the equilibrium expression

$$K' = \frac{[N_2][H_2]^3}{[NH_3]^2}$$

which is the reciprocal of the expression used in part a. Therefore,

$$K' = \frac{[N_2][H_2]^3}{[NH_3]^2} = \frac{1}{K} = \frac{1}{3.8 \times 10^4} = 2.6 \times 10^{-5}$$

c. We use the law of mass action:

$$K'' = \frac{[NH_3]}{[N_2]^{1/2}[H_2]^{3/2}}$$

If we compare this expression to that obtained in part a, we see that since

$$\frac{[NH_3]}{[N_2]^{1/2}[H_2]^{3/2}} = \left(\frac{[NH_3]^2}{[N_2][H_2]^3}\right)^{1/2}$$

$$K'' = K^{1/2}$$

Thus

$$K'' = K^{1/2} = (3.8 \times 10^4)^{1/2} = 1.9 \times 10^2$$

See Exercises 13.21 and 13.23 through 13.26.

We can draw some important conclusions from the results of Sample Exercise 13.2. For a reaction of the form

$$j\text{A} + k\text{B} \rightleftharpoons l\text{C} + m\text{D}$$

the equilibrium expression is

$$K = \frac{[C]^l[D]^m}{[A]^j[B]^k}$$

If this reaction is reversed, then the new equilibrium expression is

$$K' = \frac{[A]^j[B]^k}{[C]^l[D]^m} = \frac{1}{K}$$

If the original reaction is multiplied by some factor n to give

$$nj\text{A} + nk\text{B} \rightleftharpoons nl\text{C} + nm\text{D}$$

the equilibrium expression becomes

$$K'' = \frac{[C]^{nl}[D]^{nm}}{[A]^{nj}[B]^{nk}} = K^n$$

We Can Summarize These Conclusions About the Equilibrium Expression as Follows:

- The equilibrium expression for a reaction is the reciprocal of that for the reaction written in reverse.
- When the balanced equation for a reaction is multiplied by a factor n, the equilibrium expression for the new reaction is the original expression raised to the nth power. Thus $K_{new} = (K_{original})^n$.
- K values are customarily written without units.

The law of mass action applies to solution and gaseous equilibria.

A cross section showing how anhydrous ammonia is injected into the soil to act as a fertilizer.

For a reaction at a given temperature, there are many equilibrium positions but only one value for K.

The law of mass action is widely applicable. It correctly describes the equilibrium behavior of an amazing variety of chemical systems in solution and in the gas phase. Although, as we will see later, corrections must be applied in certain cases, such as for concentrated aqueous solutions and for gases at high pressures, the law of mass action provides a remarkably accurate description of all types of chemical equilibria.

Consider again the ammonia synthesis reaction. The equilibrium constant K always has the same value at a given temperature. At 500°C the value of K is 6.0×10^{-2}. Whenever N_2, H_2, and NH_3 are mixed together at this temperature, the system will always come to an equilibrium position such that

$$\frac{[NH_3]^2}{[N_2][H_2]^3} = 6.0 \times 10^{-2}$$

This expression has the same value at 500°C, *regardless of the amounts of the gases that are mixed together initially.*

Although the special ratio of products to reactants defined by the equilibrium expression is constant for a given reaction system at a given temperature, the *equilibrium concentrations will not always be the same.* Table 13.1 gives three sets of data for the synthesis of ammonia, showing that even though the individual sets of equilibrium concentrations are quite different for the different situations, the *equilibrium constant, which depends on the ratio of the concentrations, remains the same* (within experimental error). Note that subscript zeros indicate initial concentrations.

Each *set of equilibrium concentrations* is called an **equilibrium position.** It is essential to distinguish between the equilibrium constant and the equilibrium positions for a given reaction system. There is only *one* equilibrium constant for a particular system at a particular temperature, but there are an *infinite* number of equilibrium positions. The specific equilibrium position adopted by a system depends on the initial concentrations, but the equilibrium constant does not.

Table 13.1 Results of Three Experiments for the Reaction $N_2(g) + 3H_2(g) \rightleftharpoons 2NH_3(g)$			
Experiment	*Initial Concentrations*	*Equilibrium Concentrations*	$K = \dfrac{[NH_3]^2}{[N_2][H_2]^3}$
I	$[N_2]_0 = 1.000\ M$ $[H_2]_0 = 1.000\ M$ $[NH_3]_0 = 0$	$[N_2] = 0.921\ M$ $[H_2] = 0.763\ M$ $[NH_3] = 0.157\ M$	$K = 6.02 \times 10^{-2}$
II	$[N_2]_0 = 0$ $[H_2]_0 = 0$ $[NH_3]_0 = 1.000\ M$	$[N_2] = 0.399\ M$ $[H_2] = 1.197\ M$ $[NH_3] = 0.203\ M$	$K = 6.02 \times 10^{-2}$
III	$[N_2]_0 = 2.00\ M$ $[H_2]_0 = 1.00\ M$ $[NH_3]_0 = 3.00\ M$	$[N_2] = 2.59\ M$ $[H_2] = 2.77\ M$ $[NH_3] = 1.82\ M$	$K = 6.02 \times 10^{-2}$

Sample Exercise 13.3 *Equilibrium Positions*

The following results were collected for two experiments involving the reaction at 600°C between gaseous sulfur dioxide and oxygen to form gaseous sulfur trioxide:

Experiment 1		Experiment 2	
Initial	Equilibrium	Initial	Equilibrium
$[SO_2]_0 = 2.00\ M$	$[SO_2] = 1.50\ M$	$[SO_2]_0 = 0.500\ M$	$[SO_2] = 0.590\ M$
$[O_2]_0 = 1.50\ M$	$[O_2] = 1.25\ M$	$[O_2]_0 = 0$	$[O_2] = 0.0450\ M$
$[SO_3]_0 = 3.00\ M$	$[SO_3] = 3.50\ M$	$[SO_3]_0 = 0.350\ M$	$[SO_3] = 0.260\ M$

Show that the equilibrium constant is the same in both cases.

Solution

The balanced equation for the reaction is

$$2SO_2(g) + O_2(g) \rightleftharpoons 2SO_3(g)$$

From the law of mass action,

$$K = \frac{[SO_3]^2}{[SO_2]^2[O_2]}$$

For Experiment 1,

$$K_1 = \frac{(3.50)^2}{(1.50)^2(1.25)} = 4.36$$

For Experiment 2,

$$K_2 = \frac{(0.260)^2}{(0.590)^2(0.0450)} = 4.32$$

The value of K is constant, within experimental error.

See Question 13.13.

13.3 *Equilibrium Expressions Involving Pressures*

So far we have been describing equilibria involving gases in terms of concentrations. Equilibria involving gases also can be described in terms of pressures. The relationship between the pressure and the concentration of a gas can be seen from the ideal gas equation:

$$PV = nRT \quad \text{or} \quad P = \left(\frac{n}{V}\right)RT = CRT$$

The ideal gas equation was discussed in Section 5.3.

where C equals n/V, or the number of moles n of gas per unit volume V. Thus C represents the *molar concentration of the gas.*

For the ammonia synthesis reaction, the equilibrium expression can be written in terms of concentrations, that is,

$$K = \frac{[NH_3]^2}{[N_2][H_2]^3} = \frac{C_{NH_3}^2}{(C_{N_2})(C_{H_2}^3)} = K_c$$

or in terms of the *equilibrium partial pressures of the gases,* that is,

$$K_p = \frac{P_{NH_3}^2}{(P_{N_2})(P_{H_2}^3)}$$

Both the symbols K and K_c are used commonly for an equilibrium constant in terms of concentrations. We will always use K in this book. The symbol K_p represents an equilibrium constant in terms of partial pressures.

K involves concentrations; K_p involves pressures. In some books, the symbol K_c is used instead of K.

Sample Exercise 13.4 Calculating Values of K_p

The reaction for the formation of nitrosyl chloride

$$2NO(g) + Cl_2(g) \rightleftharpoons 2NOCl(g)$$

was studied at 25°C. The pressures at equilibrium were found to be

$$P_{NOCl} = 1.2 \text{ atm}$$
$$P_{NO} = 5.0 \times 10^{-2} \text{ atm}$$
$$P_{Cl_2} = 3.0 \times 10^{-1} \text{ atm}$$

Calculate the value of K_p for this reaction at 25°C.

Solution

For this reaction,

$$K_p = \frac{P_{NOCl}^2}{(P_{NO_2})^2(P_{Cl_2})} = \frac{(1.2)^2}{(5.0 \times 10^{-2})^2(3.0 \times 10^{-1})}$$
$$= 1.9 \times 10^3$$

See Exercises 13.27 and 13.28.

The relationship between K and K_p for a particular reaction follows from the fact that for an ideal gas, $C = P/RT$. For example, for the ammonia synthesis reaction,

$$K = \frac{[NH_3]^2}{[N_2][H_2]^3} = \frac{C_{NH_3}^2}{(C_{N_2})(C_{H_2}^3)}$$

$P = CRT$

or

$C = \dfrac{P}{RT}$

$$= \frac{\left(\dfrac{P_{NH_3}}{RT}\right)^2}{\left(\dfrac{P_{N_2}}{RT}\right)\left(\dfrac{P_{H_2}}{RT}\right)^3} = \frac{P_{NH_3}^2}{(P_{N_2})(P_{H_2}^3)} \times \frac{\left(\dfrac{1}{RT}\right)^2}{\left(\dfrac{1}{RT}\right)^4}$$

$$= \frac{P_{NH_3}^2}{(P_{N_2})(P_{H_2}^3)}(RT)^2$$
$$= K_p(RT)^2$$

However, for the synthesis of hydrogen fluoride from its elements,

$$H_2(g) + F_2(g) \rightleftharpoons 2HF(g)$$

the relationship between K and K_p is given by

$$K = \frac{[HF]^2}{[H_2][F_2]} = \frac{C_{HF}^2}{(C_{H_2})(C_{F_2})}$$

$$= \frac{\left(\dfrac{P_{HF}}{RT}\right)^2}{\left(\dfrac{P_{H_2}}{RT}\right)\left(\dfrac{P_{F_2}}{RT}\right)} = \frac{P_{HF}^2}{(P_{H_2})(P_{F_2})}$$

$$= K_p$$

Thus, for this reaction, K is equal to K_p. This equality occurs because the sum of the coefficients on either side of the balanced equation is identical, so the terms in RT cancel out. In the equilibrium expression for the ammonia synthesis reaction, the sum of the powers in the numerator is different from that in the denominator, and K does not equal K_p.

For the general reaction

$$jA + kB \rightleftharpoons lC + mD$$

the relationship between K and K_p is

$$K_p = K(RT)^{\Delta n}$$

where Δn is the sum of the coefficients of the *gaseous* products minus the sum of the coefficients of the *gaseous* reactants. This equation is quite easy to derive from the definitions of K and K_p and the relationship between pressure and concentration. For the preceding general reaction,

$$K_p = \frac{(P_C^l)(P_D^m)}{(P_A^j)(P_B^k)} = \frac{(C_C \times RT)^l(C_D \times RT)^m}{(C_A \times RT)^j(C_B \times RT)^k}$$

$$= \frac{(C_C^l)(C_D^m)}{(C_A^j)(C_B^k)} \times \frac{(RT)^{l+m}}{(RT)^{j+k}} = K(RT)^{(l+m)-(j+k)}$$

$$= K(RT)^{\Delta n}$$

where $\Delta n = (l + m) - (j + k)$, the difference in the sums of the coefficients for the gaseous products and reactants.

Δn always involves products minus reactants.

Sample Exercise 13.5 *Calculating K from K_p*

Using the value of K_p obtained in Sample Exercise 13.4, calculate the value of K at 25°C for the reaction

$$2NO(g) + Cl_2(g) \rightleftharpoons 2NOCl(g)$$

Solution

From the value of K_p, we can calculate K using

$$K_p = K(RT)^{\Delta n}$$

where $T = 25 + 273 = 298$ K and

$$\Delta n = 2 - (2 + 1) = -1$$

Sum of product coefficients ↗   ↖ Sum of reactant coefficients

$$\Delta n \downarrow$$

Thus

$$K_p = K(RT)^{-1} = \frac{K}{RT}$$

and

$$K = K_p(RT)$$
$$= (1.9 \times 10^3)(0.08206)(298)$$
$$= 4.6 \times 10^4$$

See Exercises 13.29, 13.30, and 13.35.

13.4 Heterogeneous Equilibria

So far we have discussed equilibria only for systems in the gas phase, where all reactants and products are gases. These are **homogeneous equilibria.** However, many equilibria involve more than one phase and are called **heterogeneous equilibria.** For example, the thermal decomposition of calcium carbonate in the commercial preparation of lime occurs by a reaction involving both solid and gas phases:

$$CaCO_3(s) \rightleftharpoons CaO(s) + CO_2(g)$$
$$\uparrow$$
$$\text{Lime}$$

Lime is among the top five chemicals manufactured in the United States in terms of the amount produced.

Straightforward application of the law of mass action leads to the equilibrium expression

$$K' = \frac{[CO_2][CaO]}{[CaCO_3]}$$

The concentrations of pure liquids and solids are constant.

However, experimental results show that the *position of a heterogeneous equilibrium does not depend on the amounts of pure solids or liquids present* (see Fig. 13.6). The fundamental reason for this behavior is that the concentrations of pure solids and liquids cannot change. Thus the equilibrium expression for the decomposition of solid calcium carbonate might be represented as

$$K' = \frac{[CO_2]C_1}{C_2}$$

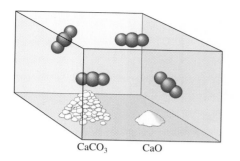

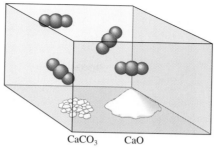

Figure 13.6
The position of the equilibrium $CaCO_3(s) \rightleftharpoons CaO(s) + CO_2(g)$ does not depend on the amounts of $CaCO_3(s)$ and $CaO(s)$ present.

where C_1 and C_2 are constants representing the concentrations of the solids CaO and $CaCO_3$, respectively. This expression can be rearranged to give

$$\frac{C_2 K'}{C_1} = K = [CO_2]$$

We can generalize from this result as follows: If pure solids or pure liquids are involved in a chemical reaction, their concentrations *are not included in the equilibrium expression* for the reaction. This simplification occurs *only* with pure solids or liquids, not with solutions or gases, since in these last two cases the concentrations can vary.

For example, in the decomposition of liquid water to gaseous hydrogen and oxygen,

$$2H_2O(l) \rightleftharpoons 2H_2(g) + O_2(g)$$

where $\quad K = [H_2]^2[O_2] \quad$ and $\quad K_p = (P_{H_2}{}^2)(P_{O_2})$

water is not included in either equilibrium expression because it is a pure liquid. However, if the reaction were carried out under conditions where the water is a gas rather than a liquid, that is,

$$2H_2O(g) \rightleftharpoons 2H_2(g) + O_2(g)$$

then $\quad K = \dfrac{[H_2]^2[O_2]}{[H_2O]^2} \quad$ and $\quad K_p = \dfrac{(P_{H_2}{}^2)(P_{O_2})}{P_{H_2O}{}^2}$

because the concentration or pressure of water vapor can change.

Sample Exercise 13.6 *Equilibrium Expressions for Heterogeneous Equilibria*

Write the expressions for K and K_p for the following processes:

a. The decomposition of solid phosphorus pentachloride to liquid phosphorus trichloride and chlorine gas.
b. Deep blue solid copper(II) sulfate pentahydrate is heated to drive off water vapor to form white solid copper(II) sulfate.

Hydrated copper(II) sulfate on the left. Water applied to anhydrous copper(II) sulfate, on the right, forms the hydrated compound.

Solution

a. The reaction is

$$PCl_5(s) \rightleftharpoons PCl_3(l) + Cl_2(g)$$

The equilibrium expressions are

$$K = [Cl_2] \quad \text{and} \quad K_p = P_{Cl_2}$$

In this case neither the pure solid PCl_5 nor the pure liquid PCl_3 is included in the equilibrium expressions.

b. The reaction is

$$CuSO_4 \cdot 5H_2O(s) \rightleftharpoons CuSO_4(s) + 5H_2O(g)$$

The equilibrium expressions are

$$K = [H_2O]^5 \quad \text{and} \quad K_p = P_{H_2O}^5$$

The solids are not included.

See Exercises 13.31 and 13.32.

13.5 Applications of the Equilibrium Constant

Knowing the equilibrium constant for a reaction allows us to predict several important features of the reaction: the tendency of the reaction to occur (but not the speed of the reaction), whether or not a given set of concentrations represents an equilibrium condition, and the equilibrium position that will be achieved from a given set of initial concentrations.

To introduce some of these ideas, we will first consider the reaction

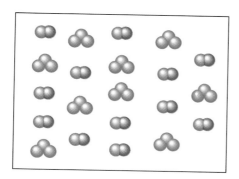

where ⊙ and ⊙ represent two different types of atoms. Assume that this reaction has an equilibrium constant equal to 16.

In a given experiment, the two types of molecules are mixed together in the following amounts:

After the system reacts and comes to equilibrium, what will the system look like? We know that at equilibrium the ratio

$$\frac{(N_{\text{⊙⊙}})(N_{\text{⊙⊙}})}{(N_{\text{⊙⊙}})(N_{\text{⊙⊙}})} = 16$$

must be satisfied, where each N represents the number of molecules of each type. We originally have 9 ⊙⊙ molecules and 12 ⊙⊙ molecules. As a place to start, let's just assume that 5 ⊙⊙ molecules disappear for the system to reach equilibrium. Since equal numbers of the ⊙⊙ and ⊙⊙ molecules react, this means that 5 ⊙⊙ molecules also will disappear. This also means that 5 ⊙⊙ molecules and 5 ⊙⊙ molecules will be formed. We can summarize as follows:

Initial Conditions	**New Conditions**
9 ⊙⊙ molecules	$9 - 5 = 4$ ⊙⊙ molecules
12 ⊙⊙ molecules	$12 - 5 = 7$ ⊙⊙ molecules
0 ⊙⊙ molecules	$0 + 5 = 5$ ⊙⊙ molecules
0 ⊙⊙ molecules	$0 + 5 = 5$ ⊙⊙ molecules

Do the new conditions represent equilibrium for this reaction system? We can find out by taking the ratio of the numbers of molecules:

$$\frac{(N_{\text{⊙⊙}})(N_{\text{⊙⊙}})}{(N_{\text{⊙⊙}})(N_{\text{⊙⊙}})} = \frac{(5)(5)}{(4)(7)} = 0.9$$

Thus this is not an equilibrium position because the ratio is not 16, as required for equilibrium. In which direction must the system move to achieve equilibrium? Since the observed ratio is smaller than 16, we must increase the numerator and decrease the denominator: The system needs to move to the right (toward more products) to achieve equilibrium. That is, more than 5 of the original reactant molecules must disappear to reach equilibrium for this system. How can we find the correct number? Since we do not know the number of molecules that need to disappear to reach equilibrium, let's call this number x. Now we can set up a table similar to the one we used above:

Initial Conditions

9 ⚛ molecules x ⚛ disappear

12 ⚭ molecules x ⚭ disappear

0 ⚛ molecules x ⚛ form

0 ⚭ molecules x ⚭ form

Equilibrium Conditions

$9 - x$ ⚛ molecules

$12 - x$ ⚭ molecules

x ⚛ molecules

x ⚭ molecules

For the system to be at equilibrium, we know that the following ratio must be satisfied:

$$\frac{(N_{⚭})(N_{⚛})}{(N_{⚛})(N_{⚭})} = 16 = \frac{(x)(x)}{(9-x)(12-x)}$$

The easiest way to solve for x here is by trial and error. From our previous discussion we know that x is greater than 5. Also, we know that it must be less than 9 because we have only 9 ⚛ molecules to start. We can't use all of them or we will have a zero in the denominator, which causes the ratio to be infinitely large. By trial and error, we find that $x = 8$ because

$$\frac{(x)(x)}{(9-x)(12-x)} = \frac{(8)(8)}{(9-8)(12-8)} = \frac{64}{4} = 16$$

The equilibrium mixture can be pictured as follows:

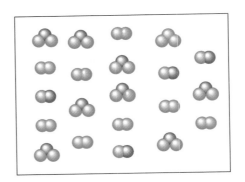

Note that it contains 8 ⚭ molecules, 8 ⚛ molecules, 1 ⚛ molecule, and 4 ⚭ molecules as required.

This pictorial example should help you understand the fundamental ideas of equilibrium. Now we will proceed to a more systematic quantitative treatment of chemical equilibrium.

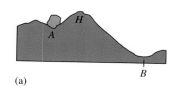

(a)

The Extent of a Reaction

The inherent tendency for a reaction to occur is indicated by the magnitude of the equilibrium constant. A value of K much larger than 1 means that at equilibrium the reaction system will consist of mostly products—the equilibrium lies to the right. Another way of saying this is that reactions with very large equilibrium constants go essentially to completion. On the other hand, a very small value of K means that the system at equilibrium will consist of mostly reactants—the equilibrium position is far to the left. The given reaction does not occur to any significant extent.

It is important to understand that *the size of K and the time required to reach equilibrium are not directly related.* The time required to achieve equilibrium depends on the reaction rate, which is determined by the size of the activation energy. The size of K is determined by thermodynamic factors such as the difference in energy between products and reactants. This difference is represented in Fig. 13.7 and will be discussed in detail in Chapter 16.

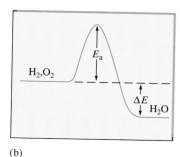

(b)

Reaction Quotient

When the reactants and products of a given chemical reaction are mixed, it is useful to know whether the mixture is at equilibrium or, if not, the direction in which the system must shift to reach equilibrium. If the concentration of one of the reactants or products is zero, the system will shift in the direction that produces the missing component. However, if all the initial concentrations are nonzero, it is more difficult to determine the direction of the move toward equilibrium. To determine the shift in such cases, we use the **reaction quotient Q.** The reaction quotient is obtained by applying the law of mass action using *initial concentrations* instead of equilibrium concentrations. For example, for the synthesis of ammonia

$$N_2(g) + 3H_2(g) \rightleftharpoons 2NH_3(g)$$

the expression for the reaction quotient is

$$Q = \frac{[NH_3]_0^2}{[N_2]_0[H_2]_0^3}$$

where the subscript zeros indicate initial concentrations.

To determine in which direction a system will shift to reach equilibrium, we compare the values of Q and K. There are three possible cases:

1. *Q is equal to K.* The system is at equilibrium; no shift will occur.

2. *Q is greater than K.* In this case, the ratio of initial concentrations of products to initial concentrations of reactants is too large. To reach equilibrium, a net change of products to reactants must occur. The system *shifts to the left,* consuming products and forming reactants, until equilibrium is achieved.

3. *Q is less than K.* In this case, the ratio of initial concentrations of products to initial concentrations of reactants is too small. The *system must shift to the right,* consuming reactants and forming products, to attain equilibrium.

Figure 13.7

(a) A physical analogy illustrating the difference between thermodynamic and kinetic stabilities. The boulder is thermodynamically more stable (lower potential energy) in position B than in position A but cannot get over the hump H. (b) The reactants H_2 and O_2 have a strong tendency to form H_2O. That is, H_2O has lower energy than H_2 and O_2. However, the large activation energy E_a prevents the reaction at 25°C. In other words, the magnitude of K for the reaction depends on ΔE, but the reaction rate depends on E_a.

Sample Exercise 13.7 Using the Reaction Quotient

For the synthesis of ammonia at 500°C, the equilibrium constant is 6.0×10^{-2}. Predict the direction in which the system will shift to reach equilibrium in each of the following cases:

a. $[NH_3]_0 = 1.0 \times 10^{-3} M$; $[N_2]_0 = 1.0 \times 10^{-5} M$; $[H_2]_0 = 2.0 \times 10^{-3} M$
b. $[NH_3]_0 = 2.00 \times 10^{-4} M$; $[N_2]_0 = 1.50 \times 10^{-5} M$; $[H_2]_0 = 3.54 \times 10^{-1} M$
c. $[NH_3]_0 = 1.0 \times 10^{-4} M$; $[N_2]_0 = 5.0 M$; $[H_2]_0 = 1.0 \times 10^{-2} M$

Solution

a. First we calculate the value of Q:

$$Q = \frac{[NH_3]_0^2}{[N_2]_0[H_2]_0^3} = \frac{(1.0 \times 10^{-3})^2}{(1.0 \times 10^{-5})(2.0 \times 10^{-3})^3}$$

$$= 1.3 \times 10^7$$

Since $K = 6.0 \times 10^{-2}$, Q is much greater than K. To attain equilibrium, the concentrations of the products must be decreased and the concentrations of the reactants increased. The system will shift to the left:

$$N_2 + 3H_2 \longleftarrow 2NH_3$$

b. We calculate the value of Q:

$$Q = \frac{[NH_3]_0^2}{[N_2]_0[H_2]_0^3} = \frac{(2.00 \times 10^{-4})^2}{(1.50 \times 10^{-5})(3.54 \times 10^{-1})^3}$$

$$= 6.01 \times 10^{-2}$$

In this case $Q = K$, so the system is at equilibrium. No shift will occur.
c. The value of Q is

$$Q = \frac{[NH_3]_0^2}{[N_2]_0[H_2]_0^3} = \frac{(1.0 \times 10^{-4})^2}{(5.0)(1.0 \times 10^{-2})^3}$$

$$= 2.0 \times 10^{-3}$$

Here Q is less than K, so the system will shift to the right to attain equilibrium by increasing the concentration of the product and decreasing the reactant concentrations:

$$N_2 + 3H_2 \longrightarrow 2NH_3$$

See Exercises 13.37 through 13.40.

Calculating Equilibrium Pressures and Concentrations

A typical equilibrium problem involves finding the equilibrium concentrations (or pressures) of reactants and products, given the value of the equilibrium constant and the initial concentrations (or pressures). However, since such problems sometimes become complicated mathematically, we will develop useful strategies for solving them by considering cases for which we know one or more of the equilibrium concentrations (or pressures).

Sample Exercise 13.8 Calculating Equilibrium Pressures I

Dinitrogen tetroxide in its liquid state was used as one of the fuels on the lunar lander for the NASA Apollo missions. In the gas phase it decomposes to gaseous nitrogen dioxide:

$$N_2O_4(g) \rightleftharpoons 2NO_2(g)$$

Consider an experiment in which gaseous N_2O_4 was placed in a flask and allowed to reach equilibrium at a temperature where $K_p = 0.133$. At equilibrium, the pressure of N_2O_4 was found to be 2.71 atm. Calculate the equilibrium pressure of $NO_2(g)$.

Solution

We know that the equilibrium pressures of the gases NO_2 and N_2O_4 must satisfy the relationship

$$K_p = \frac{P_{NO_2}^2}{P_{N_2O_4}} = 0.133$$

Since we know $P_{N_2O_4}$, we can simply solve for P_{NO_2}:

$$P_{NO_2}^2 = K_p(P_{N_2O_4}) = (0.133)(2.71) = 0.360$$

Therefore,
$$P_{NO_2} = \sqrt{0.360} = 0.600$$

See Exercises 13.41 and 13.42.

Sample Exercise 13.9 Calculating Equilibrium Pressures II

At a certain temperature a 1.00-L flask initially contained 0.298 mol $PCl_3(g)$ and 8.70×10^{-3} mol $PCl_5(g)$. After the system had reached equilibrium, 2.00×10^{-3} mol $Cl_2(g)$ was found in the flask. Gaseous PCl_5 decomposes according to the reaction

$$PCl_5(g) \rightleftharpoons PCl_3(g) + Cl_2(g)$$

Calculate the equilibrium concentrations of all species and the value of K.

Solution

The equilibrium expression for this reaction is

$$K = \frac{[Cl_2][PCl_3]}{[PCl_5]}$$

To find the value of K, we must calculate the equilibrium concentrations of all species and then substitute these quantities into the equilibrium expression. The best method for finding the equilibrium concentrations is to begin with the initial concentrations, which we will define as the concentrations before any shift toward equilibrium has occurred. We will then modify these initial concentrations appropriately to find the equilibrium concentrations.

The initial concentrations are

$$[Cl_2]_0 = 0$$

$$[PCl_3]_0 = \frac{0.298 \text{ mol}}{1.00 \text{ L}} = 0.298 \ M$$

$$[PCl_5]_0 = \frac{8.70 \times 10^{-3} \text{ mol}}{1.00 \text{ L}} = 8.70 \times 10^{-3} \ M$$

Next we find the change required to reach equilibrium. Since no Cl_2 was initially present but $2.00 \times 10^{-3} \ M \ Cl_2$ is present at equilibrium, 2.00×10^{-3} mol PCl_5 must have decomposed to form 2.00×10^{-3} mol Cl_2 and 2.00×10^{-3} mol PCl_3. In other words, to reach equilibrium, the reaction shifted to the right:

$$PCl_5(g) \longrightarrow PCl_3(g) + Cl_2(g)$$
$$2.00 \times 10^{-3} \text{ mol} \longrightarrow 2.00 \times 10^{-3} \text{ mol} + 2.00 \times 10^{-3} \text{ mol}$$

Net amount of PCl_5 decomposed

Net amounts of products formed

Now we apply this change to the initial concentrations to obtain the equilibrium concentrations:

$$[Cl_2] = \underset{[Cl_2]_0}{0} + \frac{2.00 \times 10^{-3} \text{ mol}}{1.00 \text{ L}} = 2.00 \times 10^{-3} \ M$$

$$[PCl_3] = \underset{[PCl_3]_0}{0.298 \ M} + \frac{2.00 \times 10^{-3} \text{ mol}}{1.00 \text{ L}} = 0.300 \ M$$

$$[PCl_5] = \underset{[PCl_5]_0}{8.70 \times 10^{-3} \ M} - \frac{2.00 \times 10^{-3} \text{ mol}}{1.00 \text{ L}} = 6.70 \times 10^{-3} \ M$$

These equilibrium concentrations can now be used to find K:

$$K = \frac{[Cl_2][PCl_3]}{[PCl_5]} = \frac{(2.00 \times 10^{-3})(0.300)}{6.70 \times 10^{-3}}$$
$$= 8.96 \times 10^{-2}$$

See Exercises 13.43 through 13.46.

Sometimes we are not given any of the equilibrium concentrations (or pressures), only the initial values. Then we must use the stoichiometry of the reaction to express concentrations (or pressures) at equilibrium in terms of the initial values. This is illustrated in Sample Exercise 13.10.

Sample Exercise 13.10 Calculating Equilibrium Concentrations I

Carbon monoxide reacts with steam to produce carbon dioxide and hydrogen. At 700 K the equilibrium constant is 5.10. Calculate the equilibrium concentrations of all species if 1.000 mol of each component is mixed in a 1.000-L flask.

Solution

The balanced equation for the reaction is

$$CO(g) + H_2O(g) \rightleftharpoons CO_2(g) + H_2(g)$$

and

$$K = \frac{[CO_2][H_2]}{[CO][H_2O]} = 5.10$$

Next we calculate the initial concentrations:

$$[CO]_0 = [H_2O]_0 = [CO_2]_0 = [H_2]_0 = \frac{1.000 \text{ mol}}{1.000 \text{ L}} = 1.000 \ M$$

Is the system at equilibrium, and if not, which way will it shift to reach the equilibrium position? These questions can be answered by calculating Q:

$$Q = \frac{[CO_2]_0[H_2]_0}{[CO]_0[H_2O]_0} = \frac{(1.000 \text{ mol/L})(1.000 \text{ mol/L})}{(1.000 \text{ mol/L})(1.000 \text{ mol/L})} = 1.000$$

Since Q is less than K, the system is not at equilibrium initially but must shift to the right.

What are the equilibrium concentrations? As before, we start with the initial concentrations and modify them to obtain the equilibrium concentrations. We must ask this question: How much will the system shift to the right to attain the equilibrium condition? In Sample Exercise 13.9 the change needed for the system to reach equilibrium was given. However, in this case we do not have this information.

Since the required change in concentrations is unknown at this point, we will define it in terms of x. Let's assume that x mol/L CO must react for the system to reach equilibrium. This means that the initial concentration of CO will decrease by x mol/L:

$$
\begin{array}{ccc}
[CO] & = & [CO]_0 & - & x \\
\uparrow & & \uparrow & & \uparrow \\
\text{Equilibrium} & & \text{Initial} & & \text{Change}
\end{array}
$$

Since each CO molecule reacts with one H_2O molecule, the concentration of water vapor also must decrease by x mol/L:

$$[H_2O] = [H_2O]_0 - x$$

As the reactant concentrations decrease, the product concentrations increase. Since all the coefficients are 1 in the balanced reaction, 1 mol CO reacting with 1 mol H_2O will produce 1 mol CO_2 and 1 mol H_2. Or in the present case, to reach equilibrium, x mol/L CO will react with x mol/L H_2O to give an additional x mol/L CO_2 and x mol/L H_2:

$$xCO + xH_2O \longrightarrow xCO_2 + xH_2$$

Thus the initial concentrations of CO_2 and H_2 will increase by x mol/L:

$$[CO_2] = [CO_2]_0 + x$$
$$[H_2] = [H_2]_0 + x$$

Now we have all the equilibrium concentrations defined in terms of the initial concentrations and the change x:

Initial Concentration (mol/L)	Change (mol/L)	Equilibrium Concentration (mol/L)
$[CO]_0 = 1.000$	$-x$	$1.000 - x$
$[H_2O]_0 = 1.000$	$-x$	$1.000 - x$
$[CO_2]_0 = 1.000$	$+x$	$1.000 + x$
$[H_2]_0 = 1.000$	$+x$	$1.000 + x$

Note that the sign of x is determined by the direction of the shift. In this example, the system shifts to the right, so the product concentrations increase and the reactant concentrations decrease. Also note that because the coefficients in the balanced equation are all 1, the magnitude of the change is the same for all species.

Now since we know that the equilibrium concentrations must satisfy the equilibrium expression, we can find the value of x by substituting these concentrations into the expression

$$K = 5.10 = \frac{[CO_2][H_2]}{[CO][H_2O]} = \frac{(1.000 + x)(1.000 + x)}{(1.000 - x)(1.000 - x)} = \frac{(1.000 + x)^2}{(1.000 - x)^2}$$

Since the right side of the equation is a perfect square, the solution of the problem can be simplified by taking the square root of both sides:

$$\sqrt{5.10} = 2.26 = \frac{1.000 + x}{1.000 - x}$$

Multiplying and collecting terms gives

$$x = 0.387 \text{ mol/L}$$

Thus the system shifts to the right, consuming 0.387 mol/L CO and 0.387 mol/L H_2O and forming 0.387 mol/L CO_2 and 0.387 mol/L H_2.

Now the equilibrium concentrations can be calculated:

$$[CO] = [H_2O] = 1.000 - x = 1.000 - 0.387 = 0.613 \ M$$
$$[CO_2] = [H_2] = 1.000 + x = 1.000 + 0.387 = 1.387 \ M$$

CHECK

These values can be checked by substituting them back into the equilibrium expression to make sure they give the correct value for K:

$$K = \frac{[CO_2][H_2]}{[CO][H_2O]} = \frac{(1.387)^2}{(0.613)^2} = 5.12$$

This result is the same as the given value of K (5.10) within round-off error, so the answer must be correct.

See Exercise 13.47.

Sample Exercise 13.11 Calculating Equilibrium Concentrations II

Assume that the reaction for the formation of gaseous hydrogen fluoride from hydrogen and fluorine has an equilibrium constant of 1.15×10^2 at a certain temperature. In a particular experiment, 3.000 mol of each component was added to a 1.500-L flask. Calculate the equilibrium concentrations of all species.

Solution

The balanced equation for the reaction is

$$H_2(g) + F_2(g) \rightleftharpoons 2HF(g)$$

The equilibrium expression is

$$K = 1.15 \times 10^2 = \frac{[HF]^2}{[H_2][F_2]}$$

We first calculate the initial concentrations:

$$[HF]_0 = [H_2]_0 = [F_2]_0 = \frac{3.000 \text{ mol}}{1.500 \text{ L}} = 2.000 \, M$$

Then we find the value of Q:

$$Q = \frac{[HF]_0^2}{[H_2]_0[F_2]_0} = \frac{(2.000)^2}{(2.000)(2.000)} = 1.000$$

Since Q is much less than K, the system must shift to the right to reach equilibrium.

What change in the concentrations is necessary? Since this is presently unknown, we will define the change needed in terms of x. Let x equal the number of moles per liter of H_2 consumed to reach equilibrium. The stoichiometry of the reaction shows that x mol/L F_2 also will be consumed and $2x$ mol/L HF will be formed:

$$H_2(g) \quad + \quad F_2(g) \quad \longrightarrow \quad 2HF(g)$$
$$x \text{ mol/L} + x \text{ mol/L} \longrightarrow 2x \text{ mol/L}$$

Now the equilibrium concentrations can be expressed in terms of x:

Initial Concentration (mol/L)	Change (mol/L)	Equilibrium Concentration (mol/L)
$[H_2]_0 = 2.000$ $[F_2]_0 = 2.000$ $[HF]_0 = 2.000$	$-x$ $-x$ $+2x$	$[H_2] = 2.000 - x$ $[F_2] = 2.000 - x$ $[HF] = 2.000 + 2x$

These concentrations can be represented in a shorthand table as follows:

	$H_2(g)$	$+$	$F_2(g)$	$\rightleftharpoons$	$2HF(g)$
Initial:	2.000		2.000		2.000
Change:	$-x$		$-x$		$+2x$
Equilibrium:	$2.000 - x$		$2.000 - x$		$2.000 + 2x$

To solve for x, we substitute the equilibrium concentrations into the equilibrium expression:

$$K = 1.15 \times 10^2 = \frac{[HF]^2}{[H_2][F_2]} = \frac{(2.000 + 2x)^2}{(2.000 - x)^2}$$

The right side of this equation is a perfect square, so taking the square root of both sides gives

$$\sqrt{1.15 \times 10^2} = \frac{2.000 + 2x}{2.000 - x}$$

which yields $x = 1.528$. The equilibrium concentrations can now be calculated:

$$[H_2] = [F_2] = 2.000 \ M - x = 0.472 \ M$$
$$[HF] = 2.000 \ M + 2x = 5.056 \ M$$

CHECK

Checking these values by substituting them into the equilibrium expression gives

$$\frac{[HF]^2}{[H_2][F_2]} = \frac{(5.056)^2}{(0.472)^2} = 1.15 \times 10^2$$

which agrees with the given value of K.

See Exercise 13.48.

13.6 Solving Equilibrium Problems

We have already considered most of the strategies needed to solve equilibrium problems. The typical procedure for analyzing a chemical equilibrium problem can be summarized as follows:

Procedure for Solving Equilibrium Problems

- Write the balanced equation for the reaction.
- Write the equilibrium expression using the law of mass action.
- List the initial concentrations.
- Calculate Q, and determine the direction of the shift to equilibrium.
- Define the change needed to reach equilibrium, and define the equilibrium concentrations by applying the change to the initial concentrations.
- Substitute the equilibrium concentrations into the equilibrium expression, and solve for the unknown.
- Check your calculated equilibrium concentrations by making sure they give the correct value of K.

So far we have been careful to choose systems in which we can solve for the unknown by taking the square root of both sides of the equation. However, this type of system is not really very common, and we must now consider a more typical problem. Suppose for a synthesis of hydrogen fluoride from hydrogen and fluorine, 3.000 mol H_2 and 6.000 mol F_2 are mixed in a 3.000-L flask. Assume that the equilibrium constant for the synthesis reaction at this temperature is 1.15×10^2. We calculate the equilibrium concentration of each component as follows:

STEP 1

We begin, as usual, by writing the balanced equation for the reaction:

$$H_2(g) + F_2(g) \rightleftharpoons 2HF(g)$$

STEP 2

The equilibrium expression is

$$K = 1.15 \times 10^2 = \frac{[HF]^2}{[H_2][F_2]}$$

STEP 3

The initial concentrations are

$$[H_2]_0 = \frac{3.000 \text{ mol}}{3.000 \text{ L}} = 1.000 \ M$$

$$[F_2]_0 = \frac{6.000 \text{ mol}}{3.000 \text{ L}} = 2.000 \ M$$

$$[HF]_0 = 0$$

STEP 4

There is no need to calculate Q because no HF is present initially, and we know that the system must shift to the right to reach equilibrium.

STEP 5

If we let x represent the number of moles per liter of H_2 consumed to reach equilibrium, we can represent the equilibrium concentrations as follows:

Initial Concentration (mol/L)	Change (mol/L)	Equilibrium Concentration (mol/L)
$[H_2]_0 = 1.000$	$-x$	$[H_2] = 1.000 - x$
$[F_2]_0 = 2.000$	$-x$	$[F_2] = 2.000 - x$
$[HF]_0 = 0$	$+2x$	$[HF] = 0 + 2x$

Or in shorthand form:

	$H_2(g)$	$+$	$F_2(g)$	$\rightleftharpoons$	$2HF(g)$
Initial:	1.000		2.000		0
Change:	$-x$		$-x$		$+2x$
Equilibrium:	$1.000 - x$		$2.000 - x$		$2x$

STEP 6

Substituting the equilibrium concentrations into the equilibrium expression gives

$$K = 1.15 \times 10^2 = \frac{[HF]^2}{[H_2][F_2]} = \frac{(2x)^2}{(1.000 - x)(2.000 - x)}$$

Since the right side of this equation is not a perfect square, we cannot take the square root of both sides, but must use some other procedure.

First, do the indicated multiplication:

$$(1.000 - x)(2.000 - x)(1.15 \times 10^2) = (2x)^2$$

or $\quad (1.15 \times 10^2)x^2 - 3.000(1.15 \times 10^2)x + 2.000(1.15 \times 10^2) = 4x^2$

and collect terms

$$(1.11 \times 10^2)x^2 - (3.45 \times 10^2)x + 2.30 \times 10^2 = 0$$

This is a quadratic equation of the general form

$$ax^2 + bx + c = 0$$

Use of the quadratic formula is explained in Appendix 1.4.

where the roots can be obtained from the quadratic formula:

$$x = \frac{-b \pm \sqrt{b^2 - 4ac}}{2a}$$

In this example, $a = 1.11 \times 10^2$, $b = -3.45 \times 10^2$, and $c = 2.30 \times 10^2$. Substituting these values into the quadratic formula gives two values for x:

$$x = 2.14 \text{ mol/L} \quad \text{and} \quad x = 0.968 \text{ mol/L}$$

Both these results cannot be valid (since a *given* set of initial concentrations leads to only *one* equilibrium position). How can we choose between them? Since the expression for the equilibrium concentration of H_2 is

$$[H_2] = 1.000 \ M - x$$

the value of x cannot be 2.14 mol/L (because subtracting 2.14 M from 1.000 M gives a negative concentration of H_2, which is physically impossible). Thus the correct value for x is 0.968 mol/L, and the equilibrium concentrations are as follows:

$$[H_2] = 1.000 \ M - 0.968 \ M = 3.2 \times 10^{-2} \ M$$
$$[F_2] = 2.000 \ M - 0.968 \ M = 1.032 \ M$$
$$[HF] = 2(0.968 \ M) = 1.936 \ M$$

STEP 7

We can check these concentrations by substituting them into the equilibrium expression:

$$\frac{[HF]^2}{[H_2][F_2]} = \frac{(1.936)^2}{(3.2 \times 10^{-2})(1.032)} = 1.13 \times 10^2$$

This value is in close agreement with the given value for K (1.15×10^2), so the calculated equilibrium concentrations are correct.

This procedure is further illustrated for a problem involving pressures in Sample Exercise 13.12.

Sample Exercise 13.12 Calculating Equilibrium Pressures

Assume that gaseous hydrogen iodide is synthesized from hydrogen gas and iodine vapor at a temperature where the equilibrium constant is 1.00×10^2. Suppose HI at 5.000×10^{-1} atm, H_2 at 1.000×10^{-2} atm, and I_2 at 5.000×10^{-3} atm are mixed in a 5.000-L flask. Calculate the equilibrium pressures of all species.

Solution

The balanced equation for this process is

$$H_2(g) + I_2(g) \rightleftharpoons 2HI(g)$$

and the equilibrium expression in terms of pressure is

$$K_p = \frac{P_{HI}^2}{(P_{H_2})(P_{I_2})} = 1.00 \times 10^2$$

The given initial pressures are

$$P_{HI}^0 = 5.000 \times 10^{-1} \text{ atm}$$
$$P_{H_2}^0 = 1.000 \times 10^{-2} \text{ atm}$$
$$P_{I_2}^0 = 5.000 \times 10^{-3} \text{ atm}$$

The value of Q for this system is

$$Q = \frac{(P_{HI}^0)^2}{(P_{H_2}^0)(P_{I_2}^0)} = \frac{(5.000 \times 10^{-1} \text{ atm})^2}{(1.000 \times 10^{-2} \text{ atm})(5.000 \times 10^{-3} \text{ atm})} = 5.000 \times 10^3$$

Since Q is greater than K, the system will shift to the left to reach equilibrium.

So far we have used moles or concentrations in stoichiometric calculations. However, it is equally valid to use pressures for a gas-phase system at constant temperature and volume because in this case pressure is directly proportional to the number of moles:

$$P = n\left(\frac{RT}{V}\right) \quad \longleftarrow \text{Constant if constant } T \text{ and } V$$

Thus we can represent the change needed to achieve equilibrium in terms of pressures.

Let x be the change in pressure (in atm) of H_2 as the system shifts left toward equilibrium. This leads to the following equilibrium pressures:

Initial Pressure (atm)	Change (atm)	Equilibrium Pressure (atm)
$P_{HI}^0 = 5.000 \times 10^{-1}$	$-2x$	$P_{HI} = 5.000 \times 10^{-1} - 2x$
$P_{H_2}^0 = 1.000 \times 10^{-2}$	$+x$	$P_{H_2} = 1.000 \times 10^{-2} + x$
$P_{I_2}^0 = 5.000 \times 10^{-3}$	$+x$	$P_{I_2} = 5.000 \times 10^{-3} + x$

Or in shorthand form:

	$H_2(g)$	$+$	$I_2(g)$	$\rightleftharpoons$	$2HI(g)$
Initial:	1.000×10^{-2}		5.000×10^{-3}		5.000×10^{-1}
Change:	$+x$		$+x$		$-2x$
Equilibrium:	$1.000 \times 10^{-2} + x$		$5.000 \times 10^{-3} + x$		$5.000 \times 10^{-1} - 2x$

Substitution into the equilibrium expression gives

$$K_p = \frac{(P_{HI})^2}{(P_{H_2})(P_{I_2})} = \frac{(5.000 \times 10^{-1} - 2x)^2}{(1.000 \times 10^{-2} + x)(5.000 \times 10^{-3} + x)}$$

Multiplying and collecting terms yield the quadratic equation where $a = 9.60 \times 10^1$, $b = 3.5$, and $c = -2.45 \times 10^{-1}$:

$$(9.60 \times 10^1)x^2 + 3.5x - (2.45 \times 10^{-1}) = 0$$

From the quadratic formula, the correct value for x is $x = 3.55 \times 10^{-2}$ atm. The equilibrium pressures can now be calculated from the expressions involving x:

$$P_{HI} = 5.000 \times 10^{-1} \text{ atm} - 2(3.55 \times 10^{-2}) \text{ atm} = 4.29 \times 10^{-1} \text{ atm}$$
$$P_{H_2} = 1.000 \times 10^{-2} \text{ atm} + 3.55 \times 10^{-2} \text{ atm} = 4.55 \times 10^{-2} \text{ atm}$$
$$P_{I_2} = 5.000 \times 10^{-3} \text{ atm} + 3.55 \times 10^{-2} \text{ atm} = 4.05 \times 10^{-2} \text{ atm}$$

CHECK

$$\frac{P_{HI}^2}{P_{H_2} \cdot P_{I_2}} = \frac{(4.29 \times 10^{-1})^2}{(4.55 \times 10^{-2})(4.05 \times 10^{-2})} = 99.9$$

This agrees with the given value of K (1.00×10^2), so the calculated equilibrium concentrations are correct.

See Exercises 13.49 through 13.52.

Treating Systems That Have Small Equilibrium Constants

We have seen that fairly complicated calculations are often necessary to solve equilibrium problems. However, under certain conditions, simplifications are possible that greatly reduce the mathematical difficulties. For example, gaseous NOCl decomposes to form the gases NO and Cl_2. At 35°C the equilibrium constant is 1.6×10^{-5}. In an experiment in which 1.0 mol NOCl is placed in a 2.0-L flask, what are the equilibrium concentrations?

The balanced equation is

$$2NOCl(g) \rightleftharpoons 2NO(g) + Cl_2(g)$$

and

$$K = \frac{[NO]^2[Cl_2]}{[NOCl]^2} = 1.6 \times 10^{-5}$$

The initial concentrations are

$$[NOCl]_0 = \frac{1.0 \text{ mol}}{2.0 \text{ L}} = 0.50 \ M \qquad [NO]_0 = 0 \qquad [Cl_2]_0 = 0$$

Since there are no products initially, the system will move to the right to reach equilibrium. We will define x as the change in concentration of Cl_2 needed to reach equilibrium. The changes in the concentrations of NOCl and NO can then be obtained from the balanced equation:

$$2NOCl(g) \longrightarrow 2NO(g) + Cl_2(g)$$
$$2x \longrightarrow 2x + x$$

The concentrations can be summarized as follows:

Initial Concentration (mol/L)	Change (mol/L)	Equilibrium Concentration (mol/L)
$[NOCl]_0 = 0.50$	$-2x$	$[NOCl] = 0.50 - 2x$
$[NO]_0 = 0$	$+2x$	$[NO] = 0 + 2x = 2x$
$[Cl_2]_0 = 0$	$+x$	$[Cl_2] = 0 + x = x$

Or in shorthand form:

	$2NOCl(g)$	$\rightleftharpoons$	$2NO(g)$	$+$	$Cl_2(g)$
Initial:	0.50		0		0
Change:	$-2x$		$+2x$		$+x$
Equilibrium:	$0.50 - 2x$		$2x$		x

The equilibrium concentrations must satisfy the equilibrium expression

$$K = 1.6 \times 10^{-5} = \frac{[NO]^2[Cl_2]}{[NOCl]^2} = \frac{(2x)^2(x)}{(0.50 - 2x)^2}$$

Multiplying and collecting terms will give an equation with terms containing x^3, x^2, and x, which requires complicated methods to solve directly. However, we can avoid this situation by recognizing that since K is so small (1.6×10^{-5}), the system will not proceed far to the right to reach equilibrium. That is, x *represents a relatively small number*. The consequence of this fact is that the term $(0.50 - 2x)$ can be approximated by 0.50. That is, when x is small,

$$0.50 - 2x \approx 0.50$$

Making this approximation allows us to simplify the equilibrium expression:

Approximations can simplify complicated math, but their validity should be checked carefully.

$$1.6 \times 10^{-5} = \frac{(2x)^2(x)}{(0.50 - 2x)^2} \approx \frac{(2x)^2(x)}{(0.50)^2} = \frac{4x^3}{(0.50)^2}$$

Solving for x^3 gives

$$x^3 = \frac{(1.6 \times 10^{-5})(0.50)^2}{4} = 1.0 \times 10^{-6}$$

and $x = 1.0 \times 10^{-2}$.

How valid is this approximation? If $x = 1.0 \times 10^{-2}$, then

$$0.50 - 2x = 0.50 - 2(1.0 \times 10^{-2}) = 0.48$$

The difference between 0.50 and 0.48 is 0.02, or 4% of the initial concentration of NOCl, a relatively small discrepancy that will have little effect on the outcome. That is, since $2x$ is very small compared with 0.50, the value of x obtained in the approximate solution should be very close to the exact value. We use this approximate value of x to calculate the equilibrium concentrations:

$$[NOCl] = 0.50 - 2x \approx 0.50 \ M$$
$$[NO] = 2x = 2(1.0 \times 10^{-2} \ M) = 2.0 \times 10^{-2} \ M$$
$$[Cl_2] = x = 1.0 \times 10^{-2} \ M$$

CHECK

$$\frac{[NO]^2[Cl_2]}{[NOCl]^2} = \frac{(2.0 \times 10^{-2})^2(1.0 \times 10^{-2})}{(0.50)^2} = 1.6 \times 10^{-5}$$

Since the given value of K is 1.6×10^{-5}, these calculated concentrations are correct.

This problem was much easier to solve than it appeared at first because the *small value of K and the resulting small shift to the right to reach equilibrium allowed simplification*.

13.7 Le Châtelier's Principle

It is important to understand the factors that control the *position* of a chemical equilibrium. For example, when a chemical is manufactured, the chemists and chemical engineers in charge of production want to choose conditions that favor the desired product as much as possible. That is, they want the equilibrium to lie far to the right. When Fritz Haber was developing the process for the synthesis of ammonia, he did extensive studies on how temperature and pressure affect the equilibrium concentration of ammonia. Some of his results are given in Table 13.2. Note

Table 13.2 The Percent by Mass of NH_3 at Equilibrium in a Mixture of N_2, H_2, and NH_3 as a Function of Temperature and Total Pressure*

Temperature (°C)	Total Pressure		
	300 atm	400 atm	500 atm
400	48% NH_3	55% NH_3	61% NH_3
500	26% NH_3	32% NH_3	38% NH_3
600	13% NH_3	17% NH_3	21% NH_3

*Each experiment was begun with a 3:1 mixture of H_2 and N_2.

Blue anhydrous cobalt(II) chloride and pink hydrated cobalt(II) chloride. Since the reaction $CoCl_2(s) + 6H_2O(g) \rightarrow CoCl_2 \cdot 6H_2O(s)$ is shifted to the right by water vapor, $CoCl_2$ is often used in novelty devices to detect humidity.

that the equilibrium amount of NH_3 increases with an increase in pressure but decreases as the temperature is increased. Thus the amount of NH_3 present at equilibrium is favored by conditions of low temperature and high pressure.

However, this is not the whole story. Carrying out the process at low temperatures is not feasible because then the reaction is too slow. Even though the equilibrium tends to shift to the right as the temperature is lowered, the attainment of equilibrium would be much too slow at low temperatures to be practical. This emphasizes once again that we must study both the thermodynamics and the kinetics of a reaction before we really understand the factors that control it.

We can qualitatively predict the effects of changes in concentration, pressure, and temperature on a system at equilibrium by using **Le Châtelier's principle,** which states that *if a change is imposed on a system at equilibrium, the position of the equilibrium will shift in a direction that tends to reduce that change.* Although this rule sometimes oversimplifies the situation, it works remarkably well.

The Effect of a Change in Concentration

To see how we can predict the effect of change in concentration on a system at equilibrium, we will consider the ammonia synthesis reaction. Suppose there is an equilibrium position described by these concentrations:

$$[N_2] = 0.399 \ M \qquad [H_2] = 1.197 \ M \qquad [NH_3] = 0.202 \ M$$

What will happen if 1.000 mol/L N_2 is suddenly injected into the system? We can answer this question by calculating the value of Q. The concentrations before the system adjusts are

$$[N_2]_0 = 0.399 \ M + 1.000 \ M = 1.399 \ M$$

Added N_2

$$[H_2]_0 = 1.197 \ M$$
$$[NH_3]_0 = 0.202 \ M$$

Note we are labeling these as "initial concentrations" because the system is no longer at equilibrium. Then

$$Q = \frac{[NH_3]_0^2}{[N_2]_0[H_2]_0^3} = \frac{(0.202)^2}{(1.399)(1.197)^3} = 1.70 \times 10^{-2}$$

Shifting the $N_2O_4(g) \rightarrow 2NO_2(g)$ equilibrium by changing the temperature. (a) At 100°C the flask is definitely reddish brown due to a large amount of NO_2 present. (b) At 0°C the equilibrium is shifted toward colorless $N_2O_4(g)$.

The system shifts in the direction that compensates for the imposed change.

Since we are not given the value of K, we must calculate it from the first set of equilibrium concentrations:

$$K = \frac{[NH_3]^2}{[N_2][H_2]^3} = \frac{(0.202)^2}{(0.399)(1.197)^3} = 5.96 \times 10^{-2}$$

As we might have expected, Q is less than K because the concentration of N_2 was increased.

The system will shift to the right to come to the new equilibrium position. Rather than do the calculations, we simply summarize the results:

Equilibrium Position I		Equilibrium Position II
$[N_2] = 0.399\ M$	$\xrightarrow[\text{of N}_2\text{ added}]{1.000\ \text{mol/L}}$	$[N_2] = 1.348\ M$
$[H_2] = 1.197\ M$		$[H_2] = 1.044\ M$
$[NH_3] = 0.202\ M$		$[NH_3] = 0.304\ M$

Note from these data that the equilibrium position does in fact shift to the right: The concentration of H_2 decreases, the concentration of NH_3 increases, and of course, since nitrogen is added, the concentration of N_2 shows an increase relative to the amount present in the original equilibrium position. (However, notice that the nitrogen showed a decrease relative to the amount present immediately after addition of the 1.000 mol N_2.)

We can understand this shift by thinking about reaction rates. When we add N_2 molecules to the system, the number of collisions between N_2 and H_2 will increase, thus increasing the rate of the forward reaction and in turn increasing the rate of formation of NH_3 molecules. More NH_3 molecules will in turn lead to a higher rate for the reverse reaction. Eventually, the forward and reverse reaction rates will again become equal, and the system will reach its new equilibrium position.

We can predict this shift qualitatively by using Le Châtelier's principle. Since the change imposed is the addition of nitrogen, Le Châtelier's principle predicts that the system will shift in a direction that consumes nitrogen. This reduces the effect of the addition. Thus Le Châtelier's principle correctly predicts that adding nitrogen will cause the equilibrium to shift to the right (see Fig. 13.8).

If ammonia had been added instead of nitrogen, the system would have shifted to the left to consume ammonia. So another way of stating Le Châtelier's principle is to say that *if a component (reactant or product) is added to a reaction system at equilibrium (at constant T and P or constant T and V), the equilibrium position will shift in the direction that lowers the concentration of that component. If a component is removed, the opposite effect occurs.*

Sample Exercise 13.13 *Using Le Châtelier's Principle I*

Arsenic can be extracted from its ores by first reacting the ore with oxygen (called *roasting*) to form solid As_4O_6, which is then reduced using carbon:

$$As_4O_6(s) + 6C(s) \rightleftharpoons As_4(g) + 6CO(g)$$

Predict the direction of the shift of the equilibrium position in response to each of the following changes in conditions.

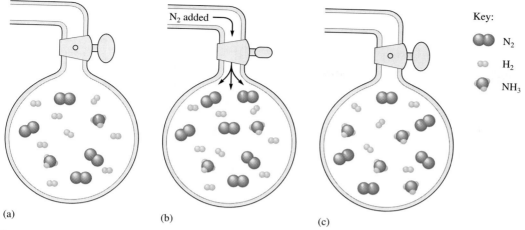

Key:

N$_2$

H$_2$

NH$_3$

(a)

(b)

(c)

N$_2$ added

Figure 13.8

(a) The initial equilibrium mixture of N$_2$, H$_2$, and NH$_3$. (b) Addition of N$_2$. (c) The new equilibrium position for the system containing more N$_2$ (due to addition of N$_2$), less H$_2$, and more NH$_3$ than in (a).

a. Addition of carbon monoxide

b. Addition or removal of carbon or tetraarsenic hexoxide (As$_4$O$_6$)

c. Removal of gaseous arsenic (As$_4$)

Solution

a. Le Châtelier's principle predicts that the shift will be away from the substance whose concentration is increased. The equilibrium position will shift to the left when carbon monoxide is added.

b. Since the amount of a pure solid has no effect on the equilibrium position, changing the amount of carbon or tetraarsenic hexoxide will have no effect.

c. If gaseous arsenic is removed, the equilibrium position will shift to the right to form more products. In industrial processes, the desired product is often continuously removed from the reaction system to increase the yield.

See Exercise 13.59.

The Effect of a Change in Pressure

Basically, there are three ways to change the pressure of a reaction system involving gaseous components:

1. Add or remove a gaseous reactant or product.

2. Add an inert gas (one not involved in the reaction).

3. Change the volume of the container.

We have already considered the addition or removal of a reactant or product. When an inert gas is added, there is no effect on the equilibrium position. *The addition of*

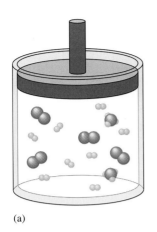
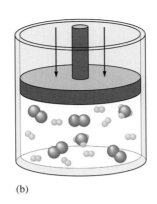
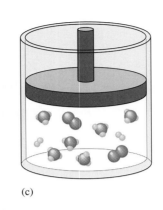
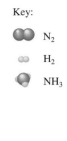

(a)　　　　　　　(b)　　　　　　　(c)

Figure 13.9
(a) A mixture of $NH_3(g)$, $N_2(g)$, and $H_2(g)$ at equilibrium. (b) The volume is suddenly decreased. (c) The new equilibrium position for the system containing more NH_3 and less N_2 and H_2. The reaction $N_2(g) + 3H_2(g) \rightleftharpoons 2NH_3(g)$ shifts to the right (toward the side with fewer molecules) when the container volume is decreased.

Animation: Equilibrium Decomposition of N_2O_4

an inert gas increases the total pressure but has no effect on the concentrations or partial pressures of the reactants or products. That is, in this case the added molecules do not participate in the reaction in any way and thus cannot affect the equilibrium in any way. Thus the system remains at the original equilibrium position.

When the volume of the container is changed, the concentrations (and thus the partial pressures) of both reactants and products are changed. We could calculate Q and predict the direction of the shift. However, for systems involving gaseous components, there is an easier way: We focus on the volume. The central idea is that *when the volume of the container holding a gaseous system is reduced, the system responds by reducing its own volume. This is done by decreasing the total number of gaseous molecules in the system.*

To see that this is true, we can rearrange the ideal gas law to give

$$V = \left(\frac{RT}{P}\right)n$$

or at constant T and P,

$$V \propto n$$

That is, at constant temperature and pressure, the volume of a gas is directly proportional to the number of moles of gas present.

Suppose we have a mixture of the gases nitrogen, hydrogen, and ammonia at equilibrium (Fig. 13.9). If we suddenly reduce the volume, what will happen to the equilibrium position? The reaction system can reduce its volume by reducing the number of molecules present. This means that the reaction

$$N_2(g) + 3H_2(g) \rightleftharpoons 2NH_3(g)$$

will shift to the right, since in this direction four molecules (one of nitrogen and three of hydrogen) react to produce two molecules (of ammonia), thus *reducing the total number of gaseous molecules present.* The new equilibrium position will be

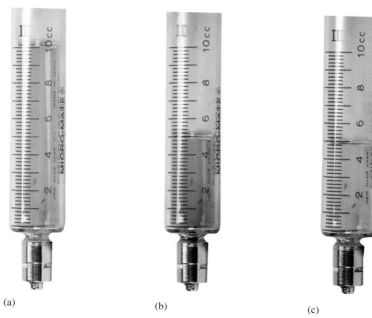

(a)   (b)   (c)

(a) Brown $NO_2(g)$ and colorless $N_2O_4(g)$ in equilibrium in a syringe. (b) The volume is suddenly decreased, giving a greater concentration of both N_2O_4 and NO_2 (indicated by the darker brown color). (c) A few seconds after the sudden volume decrease, the color is much lighter brown as the equilibrium shifts the brown $NO_2(g)$ to colorless $N_2O_4(g)$ as predicted by Le Châtelier's principle, since in the equilibrium

$$2NO_2(g) \rightleftharpoons N_2O_4(g)$$

the product side has the smaller number of molecules.

further to the right than the original one. That is, the equilibrium position will shift toward the side of the reaction involving the smaller number of gaseous molecules in the balanced equation.

The opposite is also true. When the container volume is increased, the system will shift so as to increase its volume. An increase in volume in the ammonia synthesis system will produce a shift to the left to increase the total number of gaseous molecules present.

Sample Exercise 13.14 Using Le Châtelier's Principle II

Predict the shift in equilibrium position that will occur for each of the following processes when the volume is reduced.

a. The preparation of liquid phosphorus trichloride by the reaction

$$P_4(s) + 6Cl_2(g) \rightleftharpoons 4PCl_3(l)$$

b. The preparation of gaseous phosphorus pentachloride according to the equation

$$PCl_3(g) + Cl_2(g) \rightleftharpoons PCl_5(g)$$

c. The reaction of phosphorus trichloride with ammonia:

$$PCl_3(g) + 3NH_3(g) \rightleftharpoons P(NH_2)_3(g) + 3HCl(g)$$

Solution

a. Since P_4 and PCl_3 are a pure solid and a pure liquid, respectively, we need to consider only the effect of the change in volume on Cl_2. The volume is decreased, so the position of the equilibrium will shift to the right, since the reactant side contains six gaseous molecules and the product side has none.

b. Decreasing the volume will shift the given reaction to the right, since the product side contains only one gaseous molecule while the reactant side has two.

c. Both sides of the balanced reaction equation have four gaseous molecules. A change in volume will have no effect on the equilibrium position. There is no shift in this case.

See Exercise 13.60.

The Effect of a Change in Temperature

It is important to realize that although the changes we have just discussed may alter the equilibrium *position,* they do not alter the equilibrium *constant.* For example, the addition of a reactant shifts the equilibrium position to the right but has no effect on the value of the equilibrium constant; the new equilibrium concentrations satisfy the original equilibrium constant.

The effect of temperature on equilibrium is different, however, because *the value of K changes with temperature.* We can use Le Châtelier's principle to predict the direction of the change.

The synthesis of ammonia from nitrogen and hydrogen is exothermic. We can represent this by treating energy as a product:

$$N_2(g) + 3H_2(g) \rightleftharpoons 2NH_3(g) + 92 \text{ kJ}$$

Of course, energy is not a chemical product of this reaction, but thinking of it in this way makes it easy to apply Le Châtelier's principle.

If energy is added to this system at equilibrium by heating it, Le Châtelier's principle predicts that the shift will be in the direction that consumes energy, that is, to the left. Note that this shift decreases the concentration of NH_3 and increases the concentrations of N_2 and H_2, thus *decreasing the value of K.* The experimentally observed change in K with temperature for this reaction is indicated in Table 13.3. The value of K decreases with increased temperature, as predicted.

On the other hand, for an endothermic reaction, such as the decomposition of calcium carbonate,

$$556 \text{ kJ} + CaCO_3(s) \rightleftharpoons CaO(s) + CO_2(g)$$

an increase in temperature will cause the equilibrium to shift to the right and the value of K to increase.

In summary, to use Le Châtelier's principle to describe the effect of a temperature change on a system at equilibrium, treat energy as a reactant (in an endothermic process) or as a product (in an exothermic process), and predict the direction of the shift in the same way as when an actual reactant or product is added or removed. Although Le Châtelier's principle cannot predict the size of the change in K, it does correctly predict the direction of the change.

Sample Exercise 13.15 *Using Le Châtelier's Principle III*

For each of the following reactions, predict how the value of K changes as the temperature is increased.

a. $N_2(g) + O_2(g) \rightleftharpoons 2NO(g)$ $\Delta H° = 181$ kJ
b. $2SO_2(g) + O_2(g) \rightleftharpoons 2SO_3(g)$ $\Delta H° = -198$ kJ

Solution

a. This is an endothermic reaction, as indicated by the positive value for $\Delta H°$. Energy can be viewed as a reactant, and K increases (the equilibrium shifts to the right) as the temperature is increased.
b. This is an exothermic reaction (energy can be regarded as a product). As the temperature is increased, the value of K decreases (the equilibrium shifts to the left).

See Exercises 13.61 through 13.66.

We have seen how Le Châtelier's principle can be used to predict the effect of several types of changes on a system at equilibrium. To summarize these ideas, Table 13.4 shows how various changes affect the equilibrium position of the endothermic reaction

$$N_2O_4(g) \rightleftharpoons 2NO_2(g) \qquad \Delta H° = 58 \text{ kJ}$$

Table 13.3 Observed Value of K for the Ammonia Synthesis Reaction as a Function of Temperature*

Temperature (K)	K
500	90
600	3
700	0.3
800	0.04

*For this exothermic reaction, the value of K decreases as the temperature increases, as predicted by Le Châtelier's principle.

Table 13.4 Shifts in the Equilibrium Position for the Reaction $58 \text{ kJ} + N_2O_4(g) \rightleftharpoons 2NO_2(g)$

Change	Shift
Addition of $N_2O_4(g)$	Right
Addition of $NO_2(g)$	Left
Removal of $N_2O_4(g)$	Left
Removal of $NO_2(g)$	Right
Addition of He(g)	None
Decrease container volume	Left
Increase container volume	Right
Increase temperature	Right
Decrease temperature	Left

For Review

Summary

For stoichiometry calculations, we assume that reactions run to completion. However, when a chemical reaction is carried out in a closed vessel, the system achieves chemical equilibrium, the state where the concentrations of both reactants and products remain constant over time. Although a particular equilibrium concentration may be small, it is never zero. Equilibrium is a highly dynamic state; reactants are converted continually to products, and vice versa, as molecules collide with each other. At equilibrium the rates of the forward and reverse reactions are equal.

The law of mass action is a general description of the equilibrium condition. It states that for a reaction of the type

$$jA + kB \rightleftharpoons lC + mD$$

the equilibrium expression is given by

$$K = \frac{[C]^l[D]^m}{[A]^j[B]^k}$$

where K is the equilibrium constant.

For each reaction system at a given temperature, there is only one value for the equilibrium constant but an infinite number of possible equilibrium positions. An equilibrium position is defined by a particular set of concentrations (equilibrium concentrations) that satisfies the equilibrium expression. The specific equilibrium position attained by a system depends on the initial concentrations. An equilibrium position never depends on the amount of a pure liquid or a pure solid, and therefore, these substances are not included in the equilibrium expression.

For a gas-phase reaction, equilibrium positions also can be described in terms of partial pressures. K_p, the equilibrium constant in terms of pressures, is related to K as follows:

$$K_p = K(RT)^{\Delta n}$$

where Δn is the sum of the coefficients of the gaseous products minus the sum of the coefficients of the gaseous reactants.

Homogeneous equilibria involve reactions where all reactants and products are in the same phase. However, many systems involve different phases, and their equilibria are described as heterogeneous.

The value of K allows us to predict the inherent tendency of a reaction to occur. A small value of K means that the equilibrium position lies far to the left, and therefore the reaction will not occur to any great extent. A large value of K means that the reaction will go essentially to completion—the equilibrium position lies far to the right. However, the value of K gives no information concerning how rapidly equilibrium will be achieved.

The reaction quotient Q applies the law of mass action to initial rather than equilibrium concentrations. We compare Q to K to determine in which direction a chemical system will shift to reach equilibrium. If Q is equal to K, the system is already at equilibrium; if Q is less than K, the system will shift to the right to reach equilibrium; if Q is greater than K, the system will shift to the left to reach equilibrium.

To find the concentrations that characterize a given equilibrium position, it is usually best to start with the given initial concentrations (or pressures), define the change needed to reach equilibrium, and apply this change to the initial concentrations (or pressures) to define the equilibrium concentrations (or pressures).

Le Châtelier's principle allows us to predict qualitatively the effects of changes in concentration, pressure, and temperature on a system at equilibrium. This principle states that if a change is imposed, the equilibrium position will shift in a direction that tends to compensate for the imposed change.

In-Class Discussion Questions

These questions are designed to be considered by groups of students in class. Often these questions work well for introducing a particular topic in class.

1. Consider an equilibrium mixture of four chemicals (A, B, C, and D, all gases) reacting in a closed flask according to the equation:

$$A + B \rightleftharpoons C + D$$

   a. You add more A to the flask. How does the concentration of each chemical compare to its original concentration after equilibrium is reestablished? Justify your answer.
   b. You have the original set-up at equilibrium, and add more D to the flask. How does the concentration of each chemical compare to its original concentration after equilibrium is reestablished? Justify your answer.

2. The boxes shown below represent a set of initial conditions for the reaction:

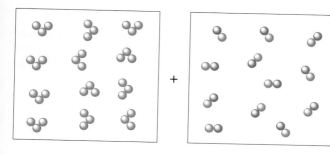

   Draw a quantitative molecular picture that shows what this system looks like after the reactants are mixed in one of the boxes and the system reaches equilibrium. Support your answer with calculations.

3. For the reaction, $H_2(g) + I_2(g) \rightleftharpoons 2HI(g)$, consider two possibilities: (a) you mix 0.5 mol of each reactant, allow the system to come to equilibrium, and then add another mole of H_2 and allow the system to reach equilibrium again, or (b) you mix 1.5 mol H_2 and 0.5 mol I_2 and allow the system to reach equilibrium. Will the final equilibrium mixture be different for the two procedures? Explain.

4. Given the reaction, $A(g) + B(g) \rightleftharpoons C(g) + D(g)$, consider the following situations:
   i. You have 1.3 M A and 0.8 M B initially.
   ii. You have 1.3 M A, 0.8 M B, and 0.2 M C initially.
   iii. You have 2.0 M A and 0.8 M B initially.

Order the preceding situations in terms of increasing equilibrium concentration of D. Explain your order. Then give the order in terms of increasing equilibrium concentration of B and explain.

5. Consider the reaction $A(g) + 2B(g) \rightleftharpoons C(g) + D(g)$ in a 1.0-L rigid flask. Answer the following questions for each situation (a–d):
   i. Estimate a range (as small as possible) for the requested substance. For example, [A] could be between 95 M and 100 M.
   ii. Explain how you decided on the limits for the estimated range.
   iii. Indicate what other information would enable you to narrow your estimated range.
   iv. Compare the estimated concentrations for a through d, and explain any differences.
   a. If at equilibrium [A] = 1 M, and then 1 mol C is added, estimate the value for [A] once equilibrium is reestablished.
   b. If at equilibrium [B] = 1 M, and then 1 mol C is added, estimate the value for [B] once equilibrium is reestablished.
   c. If at equilibrium [C] = 1 M, and then 1 mol C is added, estimate the value for [C] once equilibrium is reestablished.
   d. If at equilibrium [D] = 1 M, and then 1 mol C is added, estimate the value for [D] once equilibrium is reestablished.

6. Consider the reaction $A(g) + B(g) \rightleftharpoons C(g) + D(g)$. A friend asks the following: "I know we have been told that if a mixture of A, B, C, and D is at equilibrium and more of A is added, more C and D will form. But how can more C and D form if we do not add more B?" What do you tell your friend?

7. Consider the following statements: "Consider the reaction $A(g) + B(g) \rightleftharpoons C(g)$, for which at equilibrium [A] = 2 M, [B] = 1 M, and [C] = 4 M. To a 1-L container of the system at equilibrium you add 3 moles of B. A possible equilibrium condition is [A] = 1 M, [B] = 3 M, and [C] = 6 M because in both cases $K = 2$." Indicate everything that is correct in these statements and everything that is incorrect. Correct the incorrect statements, and explain.

8. Le Châtelier's principle is stated (Section 13.7) as follows: "If a change is imposed on a system at equilibrium, the position of the equilibrium will shift in a direction that tends to reduce that change." The system $N_2 + 3H_2 \rightleftharpoons 2NH_3$ is used as an example in which the addition of nitrogen gas at equilibrium results in a decrease in H_2 concentration and an increase in NH_3 concentration. In the experiment the volume is assumed to be constant. On the other hand, if N_2 is added to the reaction system in a container with a piston so that the pressure can be held constant, the amount of NH_3 actually could decrease and the concentration of H_2 would increase as equilibrium is reestablished. Explain how this can happen. Also, if you consider this same system at equilibrium, the addition of an inert gas, holding the pressure constant, *does* affect the equilibrium position. Explain why the addition of an inert gas to this system in a rigid container does not affect the equilibrium position.

A blue question or exercise number indicates that the answer to that question or exercise appears at the back of this book and a solution appears in the *Solutions Guide*.

Questions

9. Characterize a system at chemical equilibrium with respect to each of the following.
   a. the rates of the forward and reverse reactions
   b. the overall composition of the reaction mixture

10. Is the following statement true or false? "Reactions with large equilibrium constants are very fast." Explain.

11. Distinguish between the terms *equilibrium constant* and *equilibrium position*.

12. Distinguish between the terms *equilibrium constant* and *reaction quotient*.

13. There is only one value of the equilibrium constant for a particular system at a particular temperature, but there is an infinite number of equilibrium positions. Explain.

14. The magnitude of the equilibrium constant is related to the tendency of a reaction to occur. Explain.

15. Changing the pressure in a rigid reaction vessel by changing the volume may shift the position of a gas-phase equilibrium, whereas changing the pressure by adding an inert gas will not. Why?

16. How will the equilibrium position of a gas-phase reaction be affected by changing the volume of the reaction vessel? Are there reactions that will not have their equilibria shifted by a change in volume? Explain.

Exercises

In this section similar exercises are paired.

Characteristics of Chemical Equilibria

17. Consider the following reaction:

$$H_2O(g) + CO(g) \rightleftharpoons H_2(g) + CO_2(g)$$

Amounts of H_2O, CO, H_2, and CO_2 are put into a flask so that the composition corresponds to an equilibrium position. If the CO placed in the flask is labeled with radioactive ^{14}C, will ^{14}C be found only in CO molecules for an indefinite period of time? Explain.

18. Consider the same reaction as in Exercise 17. In one experiment 1.0 mol $H_2O(g)$ and 1.0 mol CO(g) are put into a flask and heated to 350°C. In a second experiment 1.0 mol $H_2(g)$ and 1.0 mol $CO_2(g)$ are put into another flask with the same volume as the first. This mixture is also heated to 350°C. After equilibrium is reached, will there be any difference in the composition of the mixtures in the two flasks?

The Equilibrium Constant

19. Write the equilibrium expression (K) for each of the following gas-phase reactions.
    a. $N_2(g) + O_2(g) \rightarrow 2NO(g)$
    b. $N_2O_4(g) \rightleftharpoons 2NO_2(g)$
    c. $SiH_4(g) + 2Cl_2(g) \rightleftharpoons SiCl_4(g) + 2H_2(g)$
    d. $2PBr_3(g) + 3Cl_2(g) \rightleftharpoons 2PCl_3(g) + 3Br_2(g)$

20. Write the equilibrium expression (K_p) for each reaction in Exercise 19.

21. At a given temperature, $K = 1.3 \times 10^{-2}$ for the reaction

$$N_2(g) + 3H_2(g) \rightleftharpoons 2NH_3(g)$$

Calculate values of K for the following reactions at this temperature.
    a. $\frac{1}{2}N_2(g) + \frac{3}{2}H_2(g) \rightleftharpoons NH_3(g)$
    b. $2NH_3(g) \rightleftharpoons N_2(g) + 3H_2(g)$
    c. $NH_3(g) \rightleftharpoons \frac{1}{2}N_2(g) + \frac{3}{2}H_2(g)$
    d. $2N_2(g) + 6H_2(g) \rightleftharpoons 4NH_3(g)$

22. For the reaction

$$H_2(g) + Br_2(g) \rightleftharpoons 2HBr(g)$$

$K_p = 3.5 \times 10^4$ at 1495 K. What is the value of K_p for the following reactions at 1495 K?
    a. $HBr(g) \rightleftharpoons \frac{1}{2}H_2(g) + \frac{1}{2}Br_2(g)$
    b. $2HBr(g) \rightleftharpoons H_2(g) + Br_2(g)$
    c. $\frac{1}{2}H_2(g) + \frac{1}{2}Br_2(g) \rightleftharpoons HBr(g)$

23. At high temperatures, elemental nitrogen and oxygen react with each other to form nitrogen monoxide:

$$N_2(g) + O_2(g) \rightleftharpoons 2NO(g)$$

Suppose the system is analyzed at a particular temperature, and the equilibrium concentrations are found to be $[N_2] = 0.041\ M$, $[O_2] = 0.0078\ M$, and $[NO] = 4.7 \times 10^{-4}\ M$. Calculate the value of K for the reaction.

24. For the reaction

$$N_2(g) + 3Cl_2(g) \rightleftharpoons 2NCl_3(g)$$

an analysis of an equilibrium mixture is performed at a certain temperature. It is found that $[NCl_3(g)] = 1.9 \times 10^{-1}\ M$, $[N_2(g)] = 1.4 \times 10^{-3}\ M$, and $[Cl_2(g)] = 4.3 \times 10^{-4}\ M$. Calculate K for the reaction at this temperature.

25. At a particular temperature, a 3.00-L flask contains 3.50 mol HI, 4.10 mol H_2, and 0.30 mol I_2 in equilibrium. Calculate K at this temperature for the reaction

$$H_2(g) + I_2(g) \rightleftharpoons 2HI(g)$$

26. At a particular temperature a 2.00-L flask at equilibrium contains 2.80×10^{-4} mol N_2, 2.50×10^{-5} mol O_2, and 2.00×10^{-2} mol N_2O. Calculate K at this temperature for the reaction

$$2N_2(g) + O_2(g) \rightleftharpoons 2N_2O(g)$$

27. The following equilibrium pressures at a certain temperature were observed for the reaction

$$2NO_2(g) \rightleftharpoons 2NO(g) + O_2(g)$$

$$P_{NO_2} = 0.55 \text{ atm}$$
$$P_{NO} = 6.5 \times 10^{-5} \text{ atm}$$
$$P_{O_2} = 4.5 \times 10^{-5} \text{ atm}$$

Calculate the value for the equilibrium constant K_p at this temperature.

28. The following equilibrium pressures were observed at a certain temperature for the reaction

$$N_2(g) + 3H_2(g) \rightleftharpoons 2NH_3(g)$$

$$P_{NH_3} = 3.1 \times 10^{-2} \text{ atm}$$
$$P_{N_2} = 8.5 \times 10^{-1} \text{ atm}$$
$$P_{H_2} = 3.1 \times 10^{-3} \text{ atm}$$

Calculate the value for the equilibrium constant K_p at this temperature.

29. At 25°C, $K = 3.7 \times 10^9$ for the reaction

$$CO(g) + Cl_2(g) \rightleftharpoons COCl_2(g)$$

Calculate K_p at this temperature.

30. At 1100 K, $K_p = 0.25$ for the reaction

$$2SO_2(g) + O_2(g) \rightleftharpoons 2SO_3(g)$$

What is the value of K at this temperature?

31. Write expressions for K for the following reactions.
 a. $P_4(s) + 5O_2(g) \rightleftharpoons P_4O_{10}(s)$
 b. $NH_4NO_3(s) \rightleftharpoons N_2O(g) + 2H_2O(g)$
 c. $CO_2(g) + NaOH(s) \rightleftharpoons NaHCO_3(s)$
 d. $S_8(s) + 8O_2(g) \rightleftharpoons 8SO_2(g)$

32. Write expressions for K_p for the following reactions.
 a. $2Fe(s) + \frac{3}{2}O_2(g) \rightleftharpoons Fe_2O_3(s)$
 b. $CO_2(g) + MgO(s) \rightleftharpoons MgCO_3(s)$
 c. $C(s) + H_2O(g) \rightleftharpoons CO(g) + H_2(g)$
 d. $4KO_2(s) + 2H_2O(g) \rightleftharpoons 4KOH(s) + 3O_2(g)$

33. Consider the following reaction at a certain temperature:

$$4Fe(s) + 3O_2(g) \rightleftharpoons 2Fe_2O_3(s)$$

An equilibrium mixture contains 1.0 mol Fe, 1.0×10^{-3} mol O_2, and 2.0 mol Fe_2O_3 all in a 2.0-L container. Calculate the value of K for this reaction.

34. In a study of the reaction

$$3Fe(s) + 4H_2O(g) \rightleftharpoons Fe_3O_4(s) + 4H_2(g)$$

at 1200 K it was observed that when the equilibrium partial pressure of water vapor is 15.0 torr, that total pressure at equilibrium is 36.3 torr. Calculate the value of K_p for this reaction at 1200 K. *Hint:* Apply Dalton's law of partial pressures.

35. For which of the reactions in Exercise 19 is K_p equal to K?

36. For which reactions in Exercises 31 and 32 is K_p equal to K?

Equilibrium Calculations

37. The equilibrium constant, K, is 2.4×10^3 at a certain temperature for the reaction

$$2NO(g) \rightleftharpoons N_2(g) + O_2(g)$$

For which of the following sets of conditions is the system at equilibrium? For those that are not at equilibrium, in which direction will the system shift?
 a. A 1.0-L flask contains 0.024 mol NO, 2.0 mol N_2, and 2.6 mol O_2.
 b. A 2.0-L flask contains 0.032 mol NO, 0.62 mol N_2, and 4.0 mol O_2.
 c. A 3.0-L flask contains 0.060 mol NO, 2.4 mol N_2, and 1.7 mol O_2.

38. The equilibrium constant, K_p, is 2.4×10^3 at a certain temperature for the reaction

$$2NO(g) \rightleftharpoons N_2(g) + O_2(g)$$

For which of the following sets of conditions is the system at equilibrium? For those that are not at equilibrium, in which direction will the system shift?
 a. $P_{NO} = 0.010$ atm, $P_{N_2} = 0.11$ atm, $P_{O_2} = 2.0$ atm
 b. $P_{NO} = 0.0078$ atm, $P_{N_2} = 0.36$ atm, $P_{O_2} = 0.67$ atm
 c. $P_{NO} = 0.0062$ atm, $P_{N_2} = 0.51$ atm, $P_{O_2} = 0.18$ atm

39. At 900°C, $K_p = 1.04$ for the reaction

$$CaCO_3(s) \rightleftharpoons CaO(s) + CO_2(g)$$

At a low temperature, dry ice (solid CO_2), calcium oxide, and calcium carbonate are introduced into a 50.0-L reaction chamber. The temperature is raised to 900°C, resulting in the dry ice converting to gaseous CO_2. For the following mixtures, will the initial amount of calcium oxide increase, decrease, or remain the same as the system moves toward equilibrium at 900°C?
 a. 655 g $CaCO_3$, 95.0 g CaO, $P_{CO_2} = 2.55$ atm
 b. 780 g $CaCO_3$, 1.00 g CaO, $P_{CO_2} = 1.04$ atm
 c. 0.14 g $CaCO_3$, 5000 g CaO, $P_{CO_2} = 1.04$ atm
 d. 715 g $CaCO_3$, 813 g CaO, $P_{CO_2} = 0.211$ atm

40. Ethyl acetate is synthesized in a nonreacting solvent (not water) according to the following reaction:

$$CH_3CO_2H + C_2H_5OH \rightleftharpoons CH_3CO_2C_2H_5 + H_2O$$

Acetic acid   Ethanol   Ethyl acetate

$$K = 2.2$$

For the following mixtures (a–d), will the concentration of H_2O increase, decrease, or remain the same as equilibrium is established?
 a. $[CH_3CO_2C_2H_5] = 0.22$ M, $[H_2O] = 0.10$ M, $[CH_3CO_2H] = 0.010$ M, $[C_2H_5OH] = 0.010$ M

b. $[CH_3CO_2C_2H_5] = 0.22\ M$, $[H_2O] = 0.0020\ M$, $[CH_3CO_2H] = 0.0020\ M$, $[C_2H_5OH] = 0.10\ M$

c. $[CH_3CO_2C_2H_5] = 0.88\ M$, $[H_2O] = 0.12\ M$, $[CH_3CO_2H] = 0.044\ M$, $[C_2H_5OH] = 6.0\ M$

d. $[CH_3CO_2C_2H_5] = 4.4\ M$, $[H_2O] = 4.4\ M$, $[CH_3CO_2H] = 0.88\ M$, $[C_2H_5OH] = 10.0\ M$

e. What must the concentration of water be for a mixture with $[CH_3CO_2C_2H_5] = 2.0\ M$, $[CH_3CO_2H] = 0.10\ M$, $[C_2H_5OH] = 5.0\ M$ to be at equilibrium?

f. Why is water included in the equilibrium expression for this reaction?

41. The equilibrium constant, K, for the reaction

$$H_2(g) + F_2(g) \rightleftharpoons 2HF(g)$$

has the value 2.1×10^3 at a particular temperature. When the system is analyzed at equilibrium at this temperature, the concentrations of $H_2(g)$ and $F_2(g)$ are both found to be $0.0021\ M$. What is the concentration of $HF(g)$ in the equilibrium system under these conditions?

42. The reaction

$$H_2(g) + I_2(g) \rightleftharpoons 2HI(g)$$

has $K_p = 45.9$ at 763 K. A particular equilibrium mixture at that temperature contains gaseous HI at a partial pressure of 4.00 atm and hydrogen gas at a partial pressure of 0.200 atm. What is the partial pressure of I_2?

43. A 1.00-L flask was filled with 2.00 mol gaseous SO_2 and 2.00 mol gaseous NO_2 and heated. After equilibrium was reached, it was found that 1.30 mol gaseous NO was present. Assume that the reaction

$$SO_2(g) + NO_2(g) \rightleftharpoons SO_3(g) + NO(g)$$

occurs under these conditions. Calculate the value of the equilibrium constant, K, for this reaction.

44. A sample of $S_8(g)$ is placed in an otherwise empty rigid container at 1325 K at an initial pressure of 1.00 atm, where it decomposes to $S_2(g)$ by the reaction

$$S_8(g) \rightleftharpoons 4S_2(g)$$

At equilibrium, the partial pressure of S_8 is 0.25 atm. Calculate K_p for this reaction at 1325 K.

45. At a particular temperature, 12.0 mol of SO_3 is placed into a 3.0-L rigid container, and the SO_3 dissociates by the reaction

$$2SO_3(g) \rightleftharpoons 2SO_2(g) + O_2(g)$$

At equilibrium, 3.0 mol of SO_2 is present. Calculate K for this reaction.

46. At a certain temperature, 4.0 mol NH_3 is introduced into a 2.0-L container, and the NH_3 partially dissociates by the reaction

$$2NH_3(g) \rightleftharpoons N_2(g) + 3H_2(g)$$

At equilibrium, 2.0 mol NH_3 remains. What is the value of K for this reaction?

47. At a particular temperature, $K = 3.75$ for the reaction

$$SO_2(g) + NO_2(g) \rightleftharpoons SO_3(g) + NO(g)$$

If all four gases had initial concentrations of $0.800\ M$, calculate the equilibrium concentrations of the gases.

48. At a particular temperature, $K = 1.00 \times 10^2$ for the reaction

$$H_2(g) + I_2(g) \rightleftharpoons 2HI(g)$$

In an experiment, 1.00 mol H_2, 1.00 mol I_2, and 1.00 mol HI are introduced into a 1.00-L container. Calculate the concentrations of all species when equilibrium is reached.

49. At 2200°C, $K_p = 0.050$ for the reaction

$$N_2(g) + O_2(g) \rightleftharpoons 2NO(g)$$

What is the partial pressure of NO in equilibrium with N_2 and O_2 that were placed in a flask at initial pressures of 0.80 and 0.20 atm, respectively?

50. At 25°C, $K = 0.090$ for the reaction

$$H_2O(g) + Cl_2O(g) \rightleftharpoons 2HOCl(g)$$

Calculate the concentrations of all species at equilibrium for each of the following cases.

a. 1.0 g H_2O and 2.0 g Cl_2O are mixed in a 1.0-L flask.

b. 1.0 mol pure HOCl is placed in a 2.0-L flask.

51. At 1100 K, $K_p = 0.25$ for the reaction

$$2SO_2(g) + O_2(g) \rightleftharpoons 2SO_3(g)$$

Calculate the equilibrium partial pressures of SO_2, O_2, and SO_3 produced from an initial mixture in which $P_{SO_2} = P_{O_2} = 0.50$ atm and $P_{SO_3} = 0$. (Hint: Use the method of successive approximations to solve, as discussed in Appendix 1.4.)

52. At a particular temperature, $K_p = 0.25$ for the reaction

$$N_2O_4(g) \rightleftharpoons 2NO_2(g)$$

a. A flask containing only N_2O_4 at an initial pressure of 4.5 atm is allowed to reach equilibrium. Calculate the equilibrium partial pressures of the gases.

b. A flask containing only NO_2 at an initial pressure of 9.0 atm is allowed to reach equilibrium. Calculate the equilibrium partial pressures of the gases.

c. From your answers to parts a and b, does it matter from which direction an equilibrium position is reached?

53. At 35°C, $K = 1.6 \times 10^{-5}$ for the reaction

$$2NOCl(g) \rightleftharpoons 2NO(g) + Cl_2(g)$$

Calculate the concentrations of all species at equilibrium for each of the following original mixtures.

a. 2.0 mol pure NOCl in a 2.0-L flask

b. 1.0 mol NOCl and 1.0 mol NO in a 1.0-L flask

c. 2.0 mol NOCl and 1.0 mol Cl_2 in a 1.0-L flask

54. At a particular temperature, $K = 4.0 \times 10^{-7}$ for the reaction

$$N_2O_4(g) \rightleftharpoons 2NO_2(g)$$

In an experiment, 1.0 mol N_2O_4 is placed in a 10.0-L vessel. Calculate the concentrations of N_2O_4 and NO_2 when this reaction reaches equilibrium.

55. At a particular temperature, $K = 2.0 \times 10^{-6}$ for the reaction

$$2CO_2(g) \rightleftharpoons 2CO(g) + O_2(g)$$

If 2.0 mol CO_2 is initially placed into a 5.0-L vessel, calculate the equilibrium concentrations of all species.

56. Lexan is a plastic used to make compact discs, eyeglass lenses, and bullet-proof glass. One of the compounds used to make Lexan is phosgene ($COCl_2$), an extremely poisonous gas. Phosgene decomposes by the reaction

$$COCl_2(g) \rightleftharpoons CO(g) + Cl_2(g)$$

for which $K_p = 6.8 \times 10^{-9}$ at 100°C. If pure phosgene at an initial pressure of 1.0 atm decomposes, calculate the equilibrium pressures of all species.

57. A sample of solid ammonium chloride was placed in an evacuated container and then heated so that it decomposed to ammonia gas and hydrogen chloride gas. After heating, the partial pressure of NH_3 in the container was found to be 2.2 atm. Calculate K_p at this temperature for the decomposition reaction

$$NH_4Cl(s) \rightleftharpoons NH_3(g) + HCl(g)$$

58. At 25°C, $K_p = 2.9 \times 10^{-3}$ for the reaction

$$NH_4OCONH_2(s) \rightleftharpoons 2NH_3(g) + CO_2(g)$$

In an experiment carried out at 25°C, a certain amount of NH_4OCONH_2 is placed in an evacuated container and allowed to come to equilibrium. Calculate the equilibrium partial pressures of NH_3 and CO_2.

Le Châtelier's Principle

59. Suppose the reaction system

$$UO_2(s) + 4HF(g) \rightleftharpoons UF_4(g) + 2H_2O(g)$$

has already reached equilibrium. Predict the effect that each of the following changes has on the equilibrium position. Tell whether the equilibrium will shift to the right, will shift to the left, or will not be affected.
a. Additional $UO_2(s)$ is added to the system.
b. The reaction is performed in a glass reaction vessel; $HF(g)$ attacks and reacts with glass.
c. Water vapor is removed.

60. Predict the shift in the equilibrium position that will occur for each of the following reactions when the volume of the reaction container is increased.

a. $N_2(g) + 3H_2(g) \rightleftharpoons 2NH_3(g)$
b. $PCl_5(g) \rightleftharpoons PCl_3(g) + Cl_2(g)$
c. $H_2(g) + F_2(g) \rightleftharpoons 2HF(g)$
d. $COCl_2(g) \rightleftharpoons CO(g) + Cl_2(g)$
e. $CaCO_3(s) \rightleftharpoons CaO(s) + CO_2(g)$

61. An important reaction in the commercial production of hydrogen is

$$CO(g) + H_2O(g) \rightleftharpoons H_2(g) + CO_2(g)$$

How will this system at equilibrium shift in each of the five following cases?
a. Gaseous carbon dioxide is removed.
b. Water vapor is added.
c. The pressure is increased by adding helium gas.
d. The temperature is increased (the reaction is exothermic).
e. The pressure is increased by decreasing the volume of the reaction container.

62. What will happen to the number of moles of SO_3 in equilibrium with SO_2 and O_2 in the reaction

$$2SO_3(g) \rightleftharpoons 2SO_2(g) + O_2(g) \qquad \Delta H° = 197 \text{ kJ}$$

in each of the following cases?
a. Oxygen gas is added.
b. The pressure is increased by decreasing the volume of the reaction container.
c. The pressure is increased by adding argon gas.
d. The temperature is decreased.
e. Gaseous sulfur dioxide is removed.

63. In which direction will the position of the equilibrium

$$2HI(g) \rightleftharpoons H_2(g) + I_2(g)$$

be shifted for each of the following changes?
a. $H_2(g)$ is added.
b. $I_2(g)$ is removed.
c. $HI(g)$ is removed.
d. Some $Ar(g)$ is added.
e. The volume of the container is doubled.
f. The temperature is decreased (the reaction is exothermic).

64. Hydrogen for use in ammonia production is produced by the reaction

$$CH_4(g) + H_2O(g) \xrightleftharpoons[750°C]{\text{Ni catalyst}} CO(g) + 3H_2(g)$$

What will happen to a reaction mixture at equilibrium if
a. $H_2O(g)$ is removed?
b. the temperature is increased (the reaction is endothermic)?
c. an inert gas is added?
d. $CO(g)$ is removed?
e. the volume of the container is tripled?

65. The reaction to prepare methanol from hydrogen and carbon monoxide

$$CO(g) + 2H_2(g) \rightleftharpoons CH_3OH(g)$$

is exothermic. If you wanted to use this reaction for producing methanol commercially, would high or low temperatures favor a maximum yield?

66. Ammonia is produced by the Haber process, in which nitrogen and hydrogen are reacted directly using an iron mesh impregnated with oxides as a catalyst. For the reaction

$$N_2(g) + 3H_2(g) \rightleftharpoons 2NH_3(g)$$

equilibrium constants (K_p values) as a function of temperature are

300°C, 4.34×10^{-3}
500°C, 1.45×10^{-5}
600°C, 2.25×10^{-6}

Is the reaction exothermic or endothermic?

Additional Exercises

67. Calculate a value for the equilibrium constant for the reaction

$$O_2(g) + O(g) \rightleftharpoons O_3(g)$$

given

$$NO_2(g) \overset{h\nu}{\rightleftharpoons} NO(g) + O(g)$$
$$K = 6.8 \times 10^{-49}$$

$$O_3(g) + NO(g) \rightleftharpoons NO_2(g) + O_2(g)$$
$$K = 5.8 \times 10^{-34}$$

Hint: When reactions are added together, the equilibrium expressions are multiplied.

68. At 25°C, $K_p \approx 1 \times 10^{-31}$ for the reaction

$$N_2(g) + O_2(g) \rightleftharpoons 2NO(g)$$

a. Calculate the concentration of NO, in molecules/cm^3, that can exist in equilibrium in air at 25°C. In air, $P_{N_2} = 0.8$ atm and $P_{O_2} = 0.2$ atm.
b. Typical concentrations of NO in relatively pristine environments range from 10^8 to 10^{10} molecules/cm^3. Why is there a discrepancy between these values and your answer to part a?

69. An initial mixture of nitrogen gas and hydrogen gas is reacted in a rigid container at a certain temperature by the reaction

$$3H_2(g) + N_2(g) \rightleftharpoons 2NH_3(g)$$

At equilibrium, the concentrations are $[H_2] = 5.0$ M, $[N_2] = 8.0$ M, and $[NH_3] = 4.0$ M. What were the concentrations of nitrogen gas and hydrogen gas that were reacted initially?

70. At a certain temperature, $K = 9.1 \times 10^{-4}$ for the reaction

$$FeSCN^{2+}(aq) \rightleftharpoons Fe^{3+}(aq) + SCN^-(aq)$$

Calculate the concentrations of Fe^{3+}, SCN^-, and $FeSCN^{2+}$ in a solution that is initially 2.0 M $FeSCN^{2+}$.

71. For the reaction

$$PCl_5(g) \rightleftharpoons PCl_3(g) + Cl_2(g)$$

at 600. K, the equilibrium constant, K_p, is 11.5. Suppose that 2.450 g of PCl_5 is placed in an evacuated 500.-mL bulb, which is then heated to 600. K.

a. What would be the pressure of PCl_5 if it did not dissociate?
b. What is the partial pressure of PCl_5 at equilibrium?
c. What is the total pressure in the bulb at equilibrium?
d. What is the degree of dissociation of PCl_5 at equilibrium?

72. The gas arsine, AsH_3, decomposes as follows:

$$2AsH_3(g) \rightleftharpoons 2As(s) + 3H_2(g)$$

In an experiment at a certain temperature, pure $AsH_3(g)$ was placed in an empty, rigid, sealed flask at a pressure of 392.0 torr. After 48 hours the pressure in the flask was observed to be constant at 488.0 torr.

a. Calculate the equilibrium pressure of $H_2(g)$.
b. Calculate K_p for this reaction.

73. For the following reaction at a certain temperature

$$H_2(g) + F_2(g) \rightleftharpoons 2HF(g)$$

it is found that the equilibrium concentrations in a 5.00-L rigid container are $[H_2] = 0.0500$ M, $[F_2] = 0.0100$ M, and $[HF] = 0.400$ M. If 0.200 mol of F_2 is added to this equilibrium mixture, calculate the concentrations of all gases once equilibrium is reestablished.

74. Novelty devices for predicting rain contain cobalt(II) chloride and are based on the following equilibrium:

$$\underset{\text{Purple}}{CoCl_2(s)} + 6H_2O(g) \rightleftharpoons \underset{\text{Pink}}{CoCl_2 \cdot 6H_2O(s)}$$

What color will such an indicator be if rain is imminent?

75. Chromium(VI) forms two different oxyanions, the orange dichromate ion, $Cr_2O_7^{2-}$, and the yellow chromate ion, CrO_4^{2-}. The equilibrium reaction between the two ions is

$$Cr_2O_7^{2-}(aq) + H_2O(l) \rightleftharpoons 2CrO_4^{2-}(aq) + 2H^+(aq)$$

Explain why orange dichromate solutions turn yellow when sodium hydroxide is added.

76. The synthesis of ammonia gas from nitrogen gas and hydrogen gas represents a classic case in which a knowledge of kinetics and equilibrium was used to make a desired chemical reaction economically feasible. Explain how each of the following conditions helps to maximize the yield of ammonia.

   a. running the reaction at an elevated temperature
   b. removing the ammonia from the reaction mixture as it forms
   c. using a catalyst
   d. running the reaction at high pressure

Challenge Problems

77. At 35°C, $K = 1.6 \times 10^{-5}$ for the reaction

$$2NOCl(g) \rightleftharpoons 2NO(g) + Cl_2(g)$$

If 2.0 mol NO and 1.0 mol Cl_2 are placed into a 1.0-L flask, calculate the equilibrium concentrations of all species.

78. Nitric oxide and bromine at initial partial pressures of 98.4 and 41.3 torr, respectively, were allowed to react at 300. K. At equilibrium the total pressure was 110.5 torr. The reaction is

$$2NO(g) + Br_2(g) \rightleftharpoons 2NOBr(g)$$

   a. Calculate the value of K_p.
   b. What would be the partial pressures of all species if NO and Br_2, both at an initial partial pressure of 0.30 atm, were allowed to come to equilibrium at this temperature?

79. At 25°C, $K_p = 5.3 \times 10^5$ for the reaction

$$N_2(g) + 3H_2(g) \rightleftharpoons 2NH_3(g)$$

When a certain partial pressure of $NH_3(g)$ is put into an otherwise empty rigid vessel at 25°C, equilibrium is reached when 50.0% of the original ammonia has decomposed. What was the original partial pressure of ammonia before any decomposition occurred?

80. Consider the reaction

$$P_4(g) \longrightarrow 2P_2(g)$$

where $K_p = 1.00 \times 10^{-1}$ at 1325 K. In an experiment where $P_4(g)$ was placed into a container at 1325 K, the equilibrium mixture of $P_4(g)$ and $P_2(g)$ has a total pressure of 1.00 atm. Calculate the equilibrium pressures of $P_4(g)$ and $P_2(g)$. Calculate the fraction (by moles) of $P_4(g)$ that has dissociated to reach equilibrium.

81. The partial pressures of an equilibrium mixture of $N_2O_4(g)$ and $NO_2(g)$ are $P_{N_2O_4} = 0.34$ atm and $P_{NO_2} = 1.20$ atm at a certain temperature. The volume of the container is doubled. Find the partial pressures of the two gases when a new equilibrium is established.

82. At 125°C, $K_p = 0.25$ for the reaction

$$2NaHCO_3(s) \rightleftharpoons Na_2CO_3(s) + CO_2(g) + H_2O(g)$$

A 1.00-L flask containing 10.0 g $NaHCO_3$ is evacuated and heated to 125°C.

   a. Calculate the partial pressures of CO_2 and H_2O after equilibrium is established.
   b. Calculate the masses of $NaHCO_3$ and Na_2CO_3 present at equilibrium.
   c. Calculate the minimum container volume necessary for all of the $NaHCO_3$ to decompose.

Marathon Problem*

This problem is designed to incorporate several concepts and techniques into one situation. Marathon Problems can be used in class by groups of students to help facilitate problem-solving skills.

83. Consider the reaction

$$A(g) + B(g) \rightleftharpoons C(g)$$

for which $K = 1.30 \times 10^2$. Assume that 0.406 mol $C(g)$ is placed in the cylinder represented below. The temperature is 300.0 K, and the barometric pressure on the piston (which is assumed to be massless and frictionless) is constant at 1.00 atm. The original volume (before the 0.406 mol $C(g)$ begins to decompose) is 10.00 L. What is the volume in the cylinder at equilibrium?

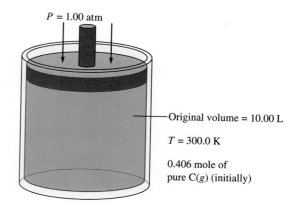

$P = 1.00$ atm

Original volume = 10.00 L

$T = 300.0$ K

0.406 mole of pure $C(g)$ (initially)

*This Marathon Problem was developed by James H. Burness, Penn State University, York Campus. Reprinted with permission from the *Journal of Chemical Education*, Vol. 68, No. 11, 1991, pp. 919–922; copyright © 1991, Division of Chemical Education, Inc.

CHAPTER 14

Acids and Bases

In this chapter we reencounter two very important classes of compounds, acids and bases. We will explore their interactions and apply the fundamentals of chemical equilibria discussed in Chapter 13 to systems involving proton-transfer reactions.

Acid–base chemistry is important in a wide variety of everyday applications. There are complex systems in our bodies that carefully control the acidity of our blood, since even small deviations may lead to serious illness and death. The same sensitivity exists in other life forms. If you have ever had tropical fish or goldfish, you know how important it is to monitor and control the acidity of the water in the aquarium.

Acids and bases are also important in industry. For example, the vast quantity of sulfuric acid manufactured in the United States each year is needed to produce fertilizers, polymers, steel, and many other materials.

The influence of acids on living things has assumed special importance in the United States, Canada, and Europe in recent years as a result of the phenomenon of acid rain (see the Chemical Impact in Chapter 5). This problem is complex and has diplomatic and economic overtones that make it all the more difficult to solve.

Contents

Lemons, limes, and oranges contain citric acid.

14.1 *The Nature of Acids and Bases*

Don't taste chemicals!

Acids and bases were first discussed in Section 4.2.

Acids were first recognized as a class of substances that taste sour. Vinegar tastes sour because it is a dilute solution of acetic acid; citric acid is responsible for the sour taste of a lemon. Bases, sometimes called *alkalis,* are characterized by their bitter taste and slippery feel. Commercial preparations for unclogging drains are highly basic.

The first person to recognize the essential nature of acids and bases was Svante Arrhenius. Based on his experiments with electrolytes, Arrhenius postulated that *acids produce hydrogen ions in aqueous solution, while bases produce hydroxide ions.* At the time, the **Arrhenius concept** of acids and bases was a major step forward in quantifying acid–base chemistry, but this concept is limited because it applies only to aqueous solutions and allows for only one kind of base—the hydroxide ion. A more general definition of acids and bases was suggested by the Danish chemist Johannes Brønsted (1879–1947) and the English chemist Thomas Lowry (1874–1936). In terms of the **Brønsted–Lowry model,** *an acid is a proton (H^+) donor, and a base is a proton acceptor.* For example, when gaseous HCl dissolves in water, each HCl molecule donates a proton to a water molecule and so qualifies as a Brønsted–Lowry acid. The molecule that accepts the proton, in this case water, is a Brønsted–Lowry base.

To understand how water can act as a base, we need to remember that the oxygen of the water molecule has two unshared electron pairs, either of which can form a covalent bond with an H^+ ion. When gaseous HCl dissolves, the following reaction occurs:

$$H\!-\!\overset{..}{O}\!:\ +\ H\!-\!\overset{..}{\underset{..}{Cl}}\!:\ \longrightarrow\ \left[H\!-\!\overset{..}{O}\!-\!H\right]^+ +\ \left[\overset{..}{\underset{..}{:Cl:}}\right]^-$$
$$\overset{\displaystyle|}{H} \qquad\qquad\qquad\qquad \overset{\displaystyle|}{H}$$

Common household substances that contain acids and bases. Vinegar is a dilute solution of acetic acid. Drain cleaners contain strong bases such as sodium hydroxide.

Note that the proton is transferred from the HCl molecule to the water molecule to form H_3O^+, which is called the **hydronium ion.** This reaction is represented in Fig. 14.1 using molecular models.

The general reaction that occurs when an acid is dissolved in water can best be represented as

$$HA(aq) + H_2O(l) \rightleftharpoons H_3O^+(aq) + A^-(aq) \qquad (14.1)$$

Acid   Base   Conjugate   Conjugate
                          acid   base

Recall that (*aq*) means the substance is hydrated.

This representation emphasizes the significant role of the polar water molecule in pulling the proton from the acid. Note that the **conjugate base** is everything that remains of the acid molecule after a proton is lost. The **conjugate acid** is formed when the proton is transferred to the base. A **conjugate acid–base pair** consists of two substances related to each other by the donating and accepting of a single proton. In Equation (14.1) there are two conjugate acid–base pairs: HA and A^- and H_2O and H_3O^+. This reaction is represented by molecular models in Fig. 14.2.

It is important to note that Equation (14.1) really represents *a competition for the proton between the two bases H_2O and A^-.* If H_2O is a much stronger base than A^-, that is, if H_2O has a much greater affinity for H^+ than does A^-, the equilibrium position will be far to the right; most of the acid dissolved will be in the ionized form. Conversely, if A^- is a much stronger base than H_2O, the equilibrium position will lie far to the left. In this case most of the acid dissolved will be present at equilibrium as HA.

The equilibrium expression for the reaction given in Equation (14.1) is

$$K_a = \frac{[H_3O^+][A^-]}{[HA]} = \frac{[H^+][A^-]}{[HA]} \qquad (14.2)$$

Molecular Models: H_2O, HCl, H_3O^+

where K_a is called the **acid dissociation constant.** Both $H_3O^+(aq)$ and $H^+(aq)$ are commonly used to represent the hydrated proton. In this book we will often use simply H^+, but you should remember that it is hydrated in aqueous solutions.

In Chapter 13 we saw that the concentration of a pure solid or a pure liquid is always omitted from the equilibrium expression. In a dilute solution we can assume that the concentration of liquid water remains essentially constant when an acid is dissolved. Thus the term $[H_2O]$ is not included in Equation (14.2), and the equilibrium expression for K_a has the same form as that for the simple dissociation into ions:

$$HA(aq) \rightleftharpoons H^+(aq) + A^-(aq)$$

You should not forget, however, that water plays an important role in causing the acid to ionize.

In this chapter we will always represent an acid as simply dissociating. This does not mean we are using the Arrhenius model for acids. Since water does not affect the equilibrium position, it is simply easier to leave it out of the acid dissociation reaction.

Note that K_a is the equilibrium constant for the reaction in which a proton is removed from HA to form the conjugate base A^-. We use K_a to represent *only* this type of reaction. Knowing this, you can write the K_a expression for any acid, even one that is totally unfamiliar to you. As you do Sample Exercise 14.1, focus on the definition of the reaction corresponding to K_a.

Sample Exercise 14.1 Acid Dissociation (Ionization) Reactions

Write the simple dissociation (ionization) reaction (omitting water) for each of the following acids.

a. Hydrochloric acid (HCl)
b. Acetic acid ($HC_2H_3O_2$)
c. The ammonium ion (NH_4^+)
d. The anilinium ion ($C_6H_5NH_3^+$)
e. The hydrated aluminum(III) ion $[Al(H_2O)_6]^{3+}$

Solution

a. $HCl(aq) \rightleftharpoons H^+(aq) + Cl^-(aq)$
b. $HC_2H_3O_2(aq) \rightleftharpoons H^+(aq) + C_2H_3O_2^-(aq)$
c. $NH_4^+(aq) \rightleftharpoons H^+(aq) + NH_3(aq)$
d. $C_6H_5NH_3^+(aq) \rightleftharpoons H^+(aq) + C_6H_5NH_2(aq)$
e. Although this formula looks complicated, writing the reaction is simple if you concentrate on the meaning of K_a. Removing a proton, which can come only from one of the water molecules, leaves one OH^- and five H_2O molecules attached to the Al^{3+} ion. So the reaction is

$$Al(H_2O)_6^{3+}(aq) \rightleftharpoons H^+(aq) + Al(H_2O)_5OH^{2+}(aq)$$

See Exercises 14.27 and 14.28.

The Brønsted–Lowry model is not limited to aqueous solutions; it can be extended to reactions in the gas phase. For example, we discussed the reaction between gaseous hydrogen chloride and ammonia when we studied diffusion (Section 5.7):

$$NH_3(g) + HCl(g) \rightleftharpoons NH_4Cl(s)$$

In this reaction, a proton is donated by the hydrogen chloride to the ammonia, as shown by these Lewis structures:

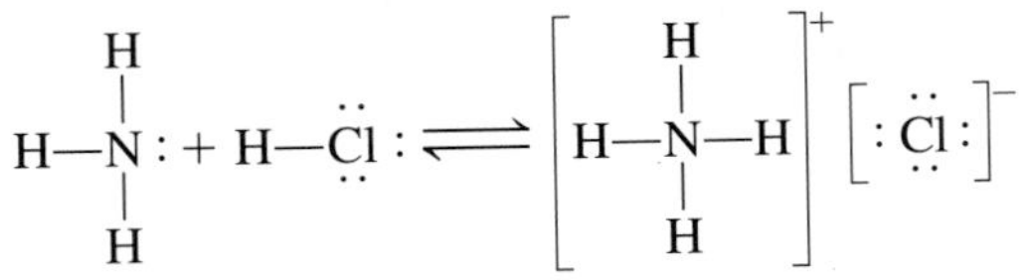

Note that this is not considered an acid–base reaction according to the Arrhenius concept. See Fig. 14.3 for a molecular representation of this reaction.

Figure 14.3
The reaction of NH_3 with HCl to form NH_4^+ and Cl^-.

14.2 Acid Strength

The strength of an acid is defined by the equilibrium position of its dissociation (ionization) reaction:

$$HA(aq) + H_2O(l) \rightleftharpoons H_3O^+(aq) + A^-(aq)$$

A **strong acid** is one for which *this equilibrium lies far to the right.* This means that almost all the original HA is dissociated (ionized) at equilibrium [see Fig. 14.4(a)]. There is an important connection between the strength of an acid and that of its conjugate base. *A strong acid yields a weak conjugate base*—one that has a low affinity for a proton. A strong acid also can be described as an acid whose conjugate base is a much weaker base than water (see Fig. 14.5). In this case the water molecules win the competition for the H^+ ions.

Conversely, a **weak acid** is one for which *the equilibrium lies far to the left.* Most of the acid originally placed in the solution is still present as HA at equilibrium. That is, a weak acid dissociates only to a very small extent in aqueous solution [see Fig. 14.4(b)]. In contrast to a strong acid, a weak acid has a conjugate base that is a much stronger base than water. In this case a water molecule is not very successful in pulling an H^+ ion from the conjugate base. *A weak acid yields a relatively strong conjugate base.*

Exploration: Weak and Strong Acids

A strong acid has a weak conjugate base.

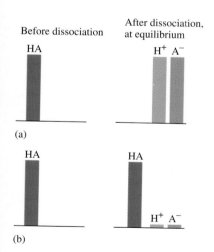

Before dissociation

After dissociation, at equilibrium

(a)

(b)

Figure 14.4
Graphic representation of the behavior of acids of different strengths in aqueous solution. (a) A strong acid. (b) A weak acid.

Figure 14.5
The relationship of acid strength and conjugate base strength for the reaction

$$HA(aq) + H_2O(l) \rightleftharpoons H_3O^+(aq) + A^-(aq)$$
$$\text{Acid} \qquad\qquad\qquad \text{Conjugate base}$$

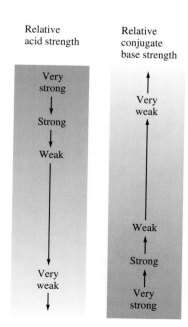

Table 14.1 Various Ways to Describe Acid Strength

Property	Strong Acid	Weak Acid
K_a value	K_a is large	K_a is small
Position of the dissociation (ionization) equilibrium	Far to the right	Far to the left
Equilibrium concentration of H^+ compared with original concentration of HA	$[H^+] \approx [HA]_0$	$[H^+] \ll [HA]_0$
Strength of conjugate base compared with that of water	A^- much weaker base than H_2O	A^- much stronger base than H_2O

≪ means much less than.
≫ means much greater than.

The various ways of describing the strength of an acid are summarized in Table 14.1. Strong and weak acids are represented pictorially in Fig. 14.6.

The common strong acids are sulfuric acid [$H_2SO_4(aq)$], hydrochloric acid [$HCl(aq)$], nitric acid [$HNO_3(aq)$], and perchloric acid [$HClO_4(aq)$]. Sulfuric acid is actually a **diprotic acid,** an acid having two acidic protons. The acid H_2SO_4 is a strong acid, virtually 100% dissociated (ionized) in water:

$$H_2SO_4(aq) \longrightarrow H^+(aq) + HSO_4^-(aq)$$

Perchloric acid can explode if handled improperly.

Molecular Models: H_2SO_4, HSO_4^-, HCl, HNO_3, $HClO_4$, H_3PO_4, HNO_2, HOCl, $HC_2H_3O_2$, C_6H_5COOH

Appendix 5.1 contains a table of K_a values.

but the HSO_4^- ion is a weak acid:

$$HSO_4^-(aq) \rightleftharpoons H^+(aq) + SO_4^{2-}(aq)$$

Most acids are **oxyacids,** in which the acidic proton is attached to an oxygen atom. The strong acids mentioned above, except hydrochloric acid, are typical examples. Many common weak acids, such as phosphoric acid (H_3PO_4), nitrous acid (HNO_2),

Sulfuric acid
(H_2SO_4)

Nitric acid
(HNO_3)

Perchloric acid
($HClO_4$)

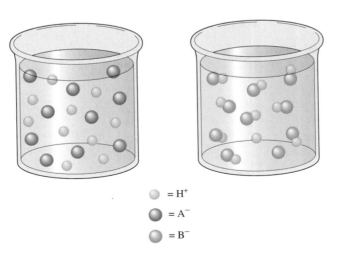

= H^+
= A^-
= B^-

Figure 14.6
(a) A strong acid HA is completely ionized in water.
(b) A weak acid HB exists mostly as undissociated HB molecules in water.

Table 14.2 Values of K_a for Some Common Monoprotic Acids

Formula	Name	Value of K_a*
HSO_4^-	Hydrogen sulfate ion	1.2×10^{-2}
$HClO_2$	Chlorous acid	1.2×10^{-2}
$HC_2H_2ClO_2$	Monochloracetic acid	1.35×10^{-3}
HF	Hydrofluoric acid	7.2×10^{-4}
HNO_2	Nitrous acid	4.0×10^{-4}
$HC_2H_3O_2$	Acetic acid	1.8×10^{-5}
$[Al(H_2O)_6]^{3+}$	Hydrated aluminum(III) ion	1.4×10^{-5}
HOCl	Hypochlorous acid	3.5×10^{-8}
HCN	Hydrocyanic acid	6.2×10^{-10}
NH_4^+	Ammonium ion	5.6×10^{-10}
HOC_6H_5	Phenol	1.6×10^{-10}

*The units of K_a are customarily omitted.

Increasing acid strength

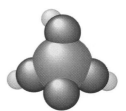

Phosphoric acid
(H_3PO_4)

Nitrous acid
(HNO_2)

Hypochlorous acid
(HOCl)

and hypochlorous acid (HOCl), are also oxyacids. **Organic acids,** those with a carbon atom backbone, commonly contain the **carboxyl group:**

$$-C\!\!\begin{array}{c} \nwarrow O \\ \searrow O-H \end{array}$$

Acids of this type are usually weak. Examples are acetic acid (CH_3COOH), often written $HC_2H_3O_2$, and benzoic acid (C_6H_5COOH). Note that the remainder of the hydrogens in these molecules are not acidic—they do not form H^+ in water.

There are some important acids in which the acidic proton is attached to an atom other than oxygen. The most significant of these are the hydrohalic acids HX, where X represents a halogen atom.

Table 14.2 contains a list of common **monoprotic acids** (those having *one* acidic proton) and their K_a values. Note that the strong acids are not listed. When a strong acid molecule such as HCl, for example, is placed in water, the position of the dissociation equilibrium

$$HCl(aq) + H_2O(l) \rightleftharpoons H^+(aq) + Cl^-(aq)$$

lies so far to the right that [HCl] cannot be measured accurately. This prevents an accurate calculation of K_a:

$$K_a = \frac{[H^+][Cl^-]}{[HCl]}$$

↖ Very small and highly uncertain

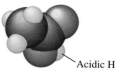

Acidic H

Acetic acid
(CH_3CO_2H)

Benzoic acid
($C_6H_5CO_2H$)

Sample Exercise 14.2 *Relative Base Strength*

Using Table 14.2, arrange the following species according to their strength as bases: H_2O, F^-, Cl^-, NO_2^-, and CN^-.

Animation: Neutralization of a Strong Acid by a Strong Base

Solution

Remember that water is a stronger base than the conjugate base of a strong acid but a weaker base than the conjugate base of a weak acid. This leads to the following order:

$$Cl^- < H_2O < \text{conjugate bases of weak acids}$$

Weakest bases ⟶ Strongest bases

We can order the remaining conjugate bases by recognizing that the strength of an acid is *inversely* related to the strength of its conjugate base. Since from Table 14.2 we have

$$K_a \text{ for HF} > K_a \text{ for HNO}_2 > K_a \text{ for HCN}$$

the base strengths increase as follows:

$$F^- < NO_2^- < CN^-$$

The combined order of increasing base strength is

$$Cl^- < H_2O < F^- < NO_2^- < CN^-$$

See Exercises 14.33 through 14.36.

Water as an Acid and a Base

A substance is said to be **amphoteric** if it can behave either as an acid or as a base. Water is the most common **amphoteric substance.** We can see this clearly in the **autoionization** of water, which involves the transfer of a proton from one water molecule to another to produce a hydroxide ion and a hydronium ion:

$$H_2O + H_2O \rightleftharpoons H_3O^+ + OH^-$$
acid(1) base(1) acid(2) base(2)

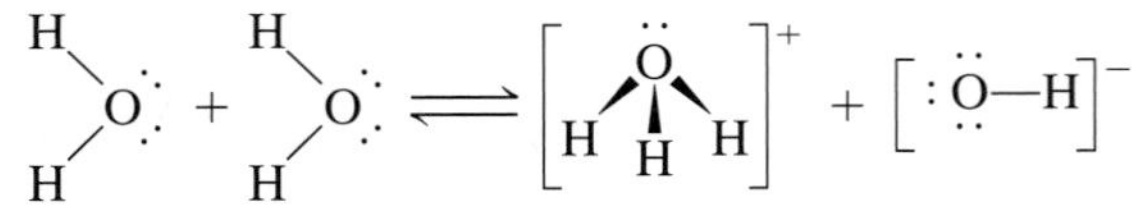

In this reaction, also illustrated in Fig. 14.7, one water molecule acts as an acid by furnishing a proton, and the other acts as a base by accepting the proton.

Autoionization can occur in other liquids besides water. For example, in liquid ammonia the autoionization reaction is

Molecular Models: H_2O, H_3O^+, OH^-, NH_3, NH_4^+

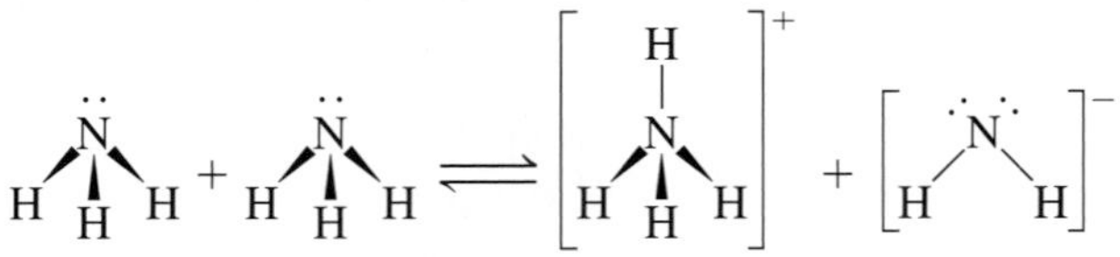

The autoionization reaction for water

$$2H_2O(l) \rightleftharpoons H_3O^+(aq) + OH^-(aq)$$

Figure 14.7

Two water molecules react to form H_3O^+ and OH^-.

leads to the equilibrium expression

$$K_w = [H_3O^+][OH^-] = [H^+][OH^-]$$

where K_w, called the **ion-product constant** (or the **dissociation constant** for water), always refers to the autoionization of water.

Experiment shows that at 25°C,

$$[H^+] = [OH^-] = 1.0 \times 10^{-7}\ M$$

which means that at 25°C

$$K_w = [H^+][OH^-] = (1.0 \times 10^{-7})(1.0 \times 10^{-7})$$
$$= 1.0 \times 10^{-14}$$

$K_w = [H^+][OH^-]$
$= 1.0 \times 10^{-14}$

It is important to recognize the meaning of K_w. In any aqueous solution at 25°C, *no matter what it contains,* the product of $[H^+]$ and $[OH^-]$ must always equal 1.0×10^{-14}. There are three possible situations:

1. A neutral solution, where $[H^+] = [OH^-]$.
2. An acidic solution, where $[H^+] > [OH^-]$.
3. A basic solution, where $[OH^-] > [H^+]$.

In each case, however, at 25°C,

$$K_w = [H^+][OH^-] = 1.0 \times 10^{-14}$$

Sample Exercise 14.3 *Calculating [H⁺] and [OH⁻]*

Calculate $[H^+]$ or $[OH^-]$ as required for each of the following solutions at 25°C, and state whether the solution is neutral, acidic, or basic.

a. $1.0 \times 10^{-5}\ M\ OH^-$
b. $1.0 \times 10^{-7}\ M\ OH^-$
c. $10.0\ M\ H^+$

Solution

a. $K_w = [H^+][OH^-] = 1.0 \times 10^{-14}$. Since $[OH^-]$ is $1.0 \times 10^{-5}\ M$, solving for $[H^+]$ gives

$$[H^+] = \frac{1.0 \times 10^{-14}}{[OH^-]} = \frac{1.0 \times 10^{-14}}{1.0 \times 10^{-5}} = 1.0 \times 10^{-9}\ M$$

Since $[OH^-] > [H^+]$, the solution is basic.

b. As in part a, solving for $[H^+]$ gives

$$[H^+] = \frac{1.0 \times 10^{-14}}{[OH^-]} = \frac{1.0 \times 10^{-14}}{1.0 \times 10^{-7}} = 1.0 \times 10^{-7}\ M$$

Since $[H^+] = [OH^-]$, the solution is neutral.

Animation: Self-Ionization of Water to Form H⁺ and OH⁻ in Equilibrium

c. Solving for $[OH^-]$ gives

$$[OH^-] = \frac{1.0 \times 10^{-14}}{[H^+]} = \frac{1.0 \times 10^{-14}}{10.0} = 1.0 \times 10^{-15} \, M$$

Since $[H^+] > [OH^-]$, the solution is acidic.

See Exercises 14.37 and 14.38.

Since K_w is an equilibrium constant, it varies with temperature. The effect of temperature is considered in Sample Exercise 14.4.

Sample Exercise **14.4** *Autoionization of Water*

At 60°C, the value of K_w is 1×10^{-13}.

a. Using Le Châtelier's principle, predict whether the reaction

$$2H_2O(l) \rightleftharpoons H_3O^+(aq) + OH^-(aq)$$

is exothermic or endothermic.

b. Calculate $[H^+]$ and $[OH^-]$ in a neutral solution at 60°C.

Solution

a. K_w *increases* from 1×10^{-14} at 25°C to 1×10^{-13} at 60°C. Le Châtelier's principle states that if a system at equilibrium is heated, it will adjust to consume energy. Since the value of K_w increases with temperature, we must think of energy as a reactant, and so the process must be endothermic.

b. At 60°C,

$$[H^+][OH^-] = 1 \times 10^{-13}$$

For a neutral solution,

$$[H^+] = [OH^-] = \sqrt{1 \times 10^{-13}} = 3 \times 10^{-7} \, M$$

See Exercise 14.39.

14.3 *The pH Scale*

The pH scale is a compact way to represent solution acidity.

Appendix 1.2 has a review of logs.

Because $[H^+]$ in an aqueous solution is typically quite small, the **pH scale** provides a convenient way to represent solution acidity. The pH is a log scale based on 10, where

$$pH = -\log[H^+]$$

Thus for a solution where

$$[H^+] = 1.0 \times 10^{-7} \, M$$

$$pH = -(-7.00) = 7.00$$

At this point we need to discuss significant figures for logarithms. The rule is that *the number of decimal places in the log is equal to the number of significant figures in the original number.* Thus

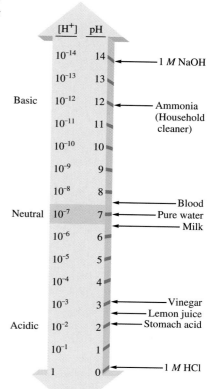

$$\overset{\overset{\text{2 significant figures}}{\frown}}{[H^+] = 1.0 \times 10^{-9}\ M}$$

$$\underset{\underset{\text{2 decimal places}}{\smile}}{pH = 9.00}$$

Similar log scales are used for representing other quantities; for example,

$$pOH = -\log[OH^-]$$

$$pK = -\log K$$

Since pH is a log scale based on 10, *the pH changes by 1 for every power of 10 change in [H⁺].* For example, a solution of pH 3 has an H⁺ concentration 10 times that of a solution of pH 4 and 100 times that of a solution of pH 5. Also note that because pH is defined as $-\log[H^+]$, *the pH decreases as [H⁺] increases.* The pH scale and the pH values for several common substances are shown in Fig. 14.8.

The pH of a solution is usually measured using a pH meter, an electronic device with a probe that can be inserted into a solution of unknown pH. The probe contains an acidic aqueous solution enclosed by a special glass membrane that allows migration of H⁺ ions. If the unknown solution has a different pH from the solution in the probe, an electric potential results, which is registered on the meter (see Fig. 14.9).

Figure 14.8

The pH scale and pH values of some common substances.

The pH meter is discussed more fully in Section 17.4.

Sample Exercise 14.5 *Calculating pH and pOH*

Calculate pH and pOH for each of the following solutions at 25°C.
a. $1.0 \times 10^{-3}\ M\ OH^-$
b. $1.0\ M\ H^+$

Solution

a.

$$[H^+] = \frac{K_w}{[OH^-]} = \frac{1.0 \times 10^{-14}}{1.0 \times 10^{-3}} = 1.0 \times 10^{-11}\ M$$

$$pH = -\log[H^+] = -\log(1.0 \times 10^{-11}) = 11.00$$

$$pOH = -\log[OH^-] = -\log(1.0 \times 10^{-3}) = 3.00$$

b.

$$[OH^-] = \frac{K_w}{[H^+]} = \frac{1.0 \times 10^{-14}}{1.0} = 1.0 \times 10^{-14}\ M$$

$$pH = -\log[H^+] = -\log(1.0) = 0.00$$

$$pOH = -\log[OH^-] = -\log(1.0 \times 10^{-14}) = 14.00$$

See Exercises 14.41 and 14.42.

Figure 14.9

pH meters are used to measure acidity.

It is useful to consider the log form of the expression

$$K_w = [H^+][OH^-]$$

That is,

$$\log K_w = \log[H^+] + \log[OH^-]$$

or

$$-\log K_w = -\log[H^+] - \log[OH^-]$$

Thus

$$pK_w = pH + pOH \qquad (14.3)$$

Since $K_w = 1.0 \times 10^{-14}$,

$$pK_w = -\log(1.0 \times 10^{-14}) = 14.00$$

Thus, for *any* aqueous solution at 25°C, pH and pOH add up to 14.00:

$$pH + pOH = 14.00 \qquad (14.4)$$

Sample Exercise 14.6 Calculating pH

The pH of a sample of human blood was measured to be 7.41 at 25°C. Calculate pOH, $[H^+]$, and $[OH^-]$ for the sample.

Solution

Since pH + pOH = 14.00,

$$pOH = 14.00 - pH = 14.00 - 7.41 = 6.59$$

To find $[H^+]$ we must go back to the definition of pH:

$$pH = -\log[H^+]$$

Thus

$$7.41 = -\log[H^+] \quad \text{or} \quad \log[H^+] = -7.41$$

We need to know the *antilog* of -7.41. As shown in Appendix 1.2, taking the antilog is the same as exponentiation; that is,

$$\text{antilog}(n) = 10^n$$

There are different methods for carrying out the antilog operation on various calculators. The most common are the $\boxed{Y^X}$ key and the two-key $\boxed{INV}$ $\boxed{LOG}$ sequence. Consult the user's manual for your calculator to find out how to do the antilog operation.

Since pH = $-\log[H^+]$,

$$-pH = \log[H^+]$$

and $[H^+]$ can be calculated by taking the antilog of $-pH$:

$$[H^+] = \text{antilog}(-pH)$$

In the present case,

$$[H^+] = \text{antilog}(-pH) = \text{antilog}(-7.41) = 10^{-7.41} = 3.9 \times 10^{-8}$$

Similarly, $[OH^-] = \text{antilog}(-pOH)$, and

$$[OH^-] = \text{antilog}(-6.59) = 10^{-6.59} = 2.6 \times 10^{-7} \, M$$

See Exercises 14.43 through 14.46.

Now that we have considered all the fundamental definitions relevant to acid–base solutions, we can proceed to a quantitative description of the equilibria present in these solutions. The main reason that acid–base problems sometimes seem difficult is that a typical aqueous solution contains many components, so the problems tend to be complicated. However, you can deal with these problems successfully if you use the following general strategies:

- *Think chemistry.* Focus on the solution components and their reactions. It will almost always be possible to choose one reaction that is the most important.

- *Be systematic.* Acid–base problems require a step-by-step approach.

- *Be flexible.* Although all acid–base problems are similar in many ways, important differences do occur. Treat each problem as a separate entity. Do not try to force a given problem into matching any you have solved before. Look for both the similarities and the differences.

- *Be patient.* The complete solution to a complicated problem cannot be seen immediately in all its detail. Pick the problem apart into its workable steps.

- *Be confident.* Look within the problem for the solution, and let the problem guide you. Assume that you can think it out. Do not rely on memorizing solutions to problems. In fact, memorizing solutions is usually detrimental because you tend to try to force a new problem to be the same as one you have seen before. *Understand and think; don't just memorize.*

14.4 Calculating the pH of Strong Acid Solutions

When we deal with acid–base equilibria, *we must focus on the solution components and their chemistry.* For example, what species are present in a 1.0 M solution of HCl? Since hydrochloric acid is a strong acid, we assume that it is completely dissociated. Thus, although the label on the bottle says 1.0 M HCl, the solution contains virtually no HCl molecules. Typically, container labels indicate the substance(s) used to make up the solution but do not necessarily describe the solution components after dissolution. Thus a 1.0 M HCl solution contains H^+ and Cl^- ions rather than HCl molecules.

The next step in dealing with aqueous solutions is to determine which components are significant and which can be ignored. We need to focus on the **major species,** those solution components present in relatively large amounts. In 1.0 M HCl, for example, the major species are H^+, Cl^-, and H_2O. Since this is a very

Common Strong Acids
$HCl(aq)$
$HNO_3(aq)$
$H_2SO_4(aq)$
$HClO_4(aq)$

acidic solution, OH^- is present only in tiny amounts and is classed as a minor species. In attacking acid–base problems, the importance of *writing the major species in the solution* as the first step cannot be overemphasized. *This single step is the key to solving these problems successfully.*

Always write the major species present in the solution.

To illustrate the main ideas involved, let us calculate the pH of 1.0 M HCl. We first list the major species: H^+, Cl^-, and H_2O. Since we want to calculate the pH, we will focus on those major species that can furnish H^+. Obviously, we must consider H^+ from the dissociation of HCl. However, H_2O also furnishes H^+ by autoionization, which is often represented by the simple dissociation reaction

$$H_2O(l) \rightleftharpoons H^+(aq) + OH^-(aq)$$

The H^+ from the strong acid drives the equilibrium $H_2O \rightleftharpoons H^+ + OH^-$ to the left.

However, is autoionization an important source of H^+ ions? In pure water at 25°C, $[H^+]$ is 10^{-7} M. In 1.0 M HCl solution, the water will produce even less than 10^{-7} M H^+, since by Le Châtelier's principle the H^+ from the dissociated HCl will drive the position of the water equilibrium to the left. Thus the amount of H^+ contributed by water is negligible compared with the 1.0 M H^+ from the dissociation of HCl. Therefore, we can say that $[H^+]$ in the solution is 1.0 M. The pH is then

$$pH = -\log[H^+] = -\log(1.0) = 0$$

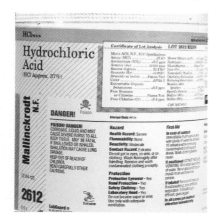

The label on a bottle of concentrated hydrochloric acid.

In pure water, only 10^{-7} M H^+ is produced.

Sample Exercise 14.7 pH of Strong Acids

a. Calculate the pH of 0.10 M HNO_3.
b. Calculate the pH of 1.0×10^{-10} M HCl.

Solution

a. Since HNO_3 is a strong acid, the major species in solution are

$$H^+, \quad NO_3^-, \quad \text{and} \quad H_2O$$

The concentration of HNO_3 is virtually zero, since the acid completely dissociates in water. Also, $[OH^-]$ will be very small because the H^+ ions from the acid will drive the equilibrium

$$H_2O(l) \rightleftharpoons H^+(aq) + OH^-(aq)$$

to the left. That is, this is an acidic solution where $[H^+] \gg [OH^-]$, so $[OH^-] \ll 10^{-7}$ M. The sources of H^+ are

1. H^+ from HNO_3 (0.10 M)

2. H^+ from H_2O

The number of H^+ ions contributed by the autoionization of water will be very small compared with the 0.10 M contributed by the HNO_3 and can be neglected. Since the dissolved HNO_3 is the only important source of H^+ ions in this solution,

$$[H^+] = 0.10 \ M \quad \text{and} \quad pH = -\log(0.10) = 1.00$$

b. Normally, in an aqueous solution of HCl the major species are H^+, Cl^-, and H_2O. However, in this case the amount of HCl in solution is so small that it has no effect; the only major species is H_2O. Thus the pH will be that of pure water, or pH = 7.00.

See Exercises 14.47 through 14.50.

14.5 Calculating the pH of Weak Acid Solutions

Since a weak acid dissolved in water can be viewed as a prototype of almost any equilibrium occurring in aqueous solution, we will proceed carefully and systematically. Although some of the procedures we develop here may seem unnecessary, they will become essential as the problems become more complicated. We will develop the necessary strategies by calculating the pH of a 1.00 M solution of HF ($K_a = 7.2 \times 10^{-4}$).

The first step, as always, is to *write the major species in the solution*. From its small K_a value, we know that hydrofluoric acid is a weak acid and will be dissociated only to a slight extent. Thus, when we write the major species, the hydrofluoric acid will be represented in its dominant form, as HF. The major species in solution are HF and H_2O.

The next step (since this is a pH problem) is to decide which of the major species can furnish H^+ ions. Actually, both major species can do so:

First, *always* write the major species present in the solution.

Molecular Model: HF

$$HF(aq) \rightleftharpoons H^+(aq) + F^-(aq) \qquad K_a = 7.2 \times 10^{-4}$$
$$H_2O(l) \rightleftharpoons H^+(aq) + OH^-(aq) \qquad K_w = 1.0 \times 10^{-14}$$

In aqueous solutions, however, typically one source of H^+ can be singled out as dominant. By comparing K_a for HF with K_w for H_2O, we see that hydrofluoric acid, although weak, is still a much stronger acid than water. Thus we will assume that hydrofluoric acid will be the dominant source of H^+. We will ignore the tiny contribution by water.

Therefore, it is the dissociation of HF that will determine the equilibrium concentration of H^+ and hence the pH:

$$HF(aq) \rightleftharpoons H^+(aq) + F^-(aq)$$

The equilibrium expression is

$$K_a = 7.2 \times 10^{-4} = \frac{[H^+][F^-]}{[HF]}$$

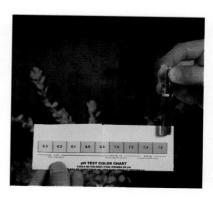

pH testing helps to monitor the acidity content of an aquarium.

To solve the equilibrium problem, we follow the procedures developed in Chapter 13 for gas-phase equilibria. First, we list the initial concentrations, the *concentrations before the reaction of interest has proceeded to equilibrium*. Before any HF dissociates, the concentrations of the species in the equilibrium are

$$[HF]_0 = 1.00 \ M \qquad [F^-]_0 = 0 \qquad [H^+]_0 = 10^{-7} \ M \approx 0$$

(Note that the zero value for $[H^+]_0$ is an approximation, since we are neglecting the H^+ ions from the autoionization of water.)

The next step is to determine the change required to reach equilibrium. Since some HF will dissociate to come to equilibrium (but this amount is presently unknown), we let x be the change in the concentration of HF that is required to achieve equilibrium. That is, we assume that x mol/L HF will dissociate to produce x mol/L H^+ and x mol/L F^- as the system adjusts to its equilibrium position. Now the equilibrium concentrations can be defined in terms of x:

$$[HF] = [HF]_0 - x = 1.00 - x$$
$$[F^-] = [F^-]_0 + x = 0 + x = x$$
$$[H^+] = [H^+]_0 + x \approx 0 + x = x$$

Substituting these equilibrium concentrations into the equilibrium expression gives

$$K_a = 7.2 \times 10^{-4} = \frac{[H^+][F^-]}{[HF]} = \frac{(x)(x)}{1.00 - x}$$

This expression produces a quadratic equation that can be solved using the quadratic formula, as for the gas-phase systems in Chapter 13. However, since K_a for HF is so small, HF will dissociate only slightly, and x is expected to be small. This will allow us to simplify the calculation. If x is very small compared to 1.00, the term in the denominator can be approximated as follows:

$$1.00 - x \approx 1.00$$

The equilibrium expression then becomes

$$7.2 \times 10^{-4} = \frac{(x)(x)}{1.00 - x} \approx \frac{(x)(x)}{1.00}$$

which yields

$$x^2 \approx (7.2 \times 10^{-4})(1.00) = 7.2 \times 10^{-4}$$
$$x \approx \sqrt{7.2 \times 10^{-4}} = 2.7 \times 10^{-2}$$

The validity of an approximation should always be checked.

How valid is the approximation that $[HF] = 1.00\ M$? Because this question will arise often in connection with acid–base equilibrium calculations, we will consider it carefully. *The validity of the approximation depends on how much accuracy we demand for the calculated value of $[H^+]$.* Typically, the K_a values for acids are known to an accuracy of only about $\pm 5\%$. It is reasonable therefore to apply this figure when determining the validity of the approximation

$$[HA]_0 - x \approx [HA]_0$$

We will use the following test. First, we calculate the value of x by making the approximation

$$K_a = \frac{x^2}{[HA]_0 - x} \approx \frac{x^2}{[HA]_0}$$

where

$$x^2 \approx K_a[HA]_0 \quad \text{and} \quad x \approx \sqrt{K_a[HA]_0}$$

We then compare the sizes of x and $[HA]_0$. If the expression

$$\frac{x}{[HA]_0} \times 100\%$$

is less than or equal to 5%, the value of x is small enough that the approximation

$$[HA]_0 - x \approx [HA]_0$$

will be considered valid.

In our example,

$$x = 2.7 \times 10^{-2} \text{ mol/L}$$
$$[HA]_0 = [HF]_0 = 1.00 \text{ mol/L}$$

and $$\frac{x}{[HA]_0} \times 100 = \frac{2.7 \times 10^{-2}}{1.00} \times 100\% = 2.7\%$$

The approximation we made is considered valid, and the value of x calculated using that approximation is acceptable. Thus

$$x = [H^+] = 2.7 \times 10^{-2} \, M \quad \text{and} \quad pH = -\log(2.7 \times 10^{-2}) = 1.57$$

This problem illustrates all the important steps for solving a typical equilibrium problem involving a weak acid. These steps are summarized as follows:

Solving Weak Acid Equilibrium Problems

- List the major species in the solution.
- Choose the species that can produce H^+, and write balanced equations for the reactions producing H^+.
- Using the values of the equilibrium constants for the reactions you have written, decide which equilibrium will dominate in producing H^+.
- Write the equilibrium expression for the dominant equilibrium.
- List the initial concentrations of the species participating in the dominant equilibrium.
- Define the change needed to achieve equilibrium; that is, define x.
- Write the equilibrium concentrations in terms of x.
- Substitute the equilibrium concentrations into the equilibrium expression.
- Solve for x the "easy" way; that is, by assuming that $[HA]_0 - x \approx [HA]_0$.
- Use the 5% rule to verify whether the approximation is valid.
- Calculate $[H^+]$ and pH.

The K_a values for various weak acids are given in Table 14.2 and in Appendix 5.1.

We use this systematic approach in Sample Exercise 14.8.

Sample Exercise **14.8** *The pH of Weak Acids*

The hypochlorite ion (OCl^-) is a strong oxidizing agent often found in household bleaches and disinfectants. It is also the active ingredient that forms when swimming pool water is treated with chlorine. In addition to its oxidizing abilities, the hypochlorite ion has a relatively high affinity for protons (it is a much stronger base than Cl^-, for example) and forms the weakly acidic hypochlorous acid (HOCl, $K_a = 3.5 \times 10^{-8}$). Calculate the pH of a 0.100 M aqueous solution of hypochlorous acid.

Solution

STEP 1

We list the major species. Since HOCl is a weak acid and remains mostly undissociated, the major species in a 0.100 M HOCl solution are

$$HOCl \quad \text{and} \quad H_2O$$

STEP 2

Both species can produce H^+:

$$HOCl(aq) \rightleftharpoons H^+(aq) + OCl^-(aq) \qquad K_a = 3.5 \times 10^{-8}$$
$$H_2O(l) \rightleftharpoons H^+(aq) + OH^-(aq) \qquad K_w = 1.0 \times 10^{-14}$$

STEP 3

Since HOCl is a significantly stronger acid than H_2O, it will dominate in the production of H^+.

STEP 4

We therefore use the following equilibrium expression:

$$K_a = 3.5 \times 10^{-8} = \frac{[H^+][OCl^-]}{[HOCl]}$$

STEP 5

The initial concentrations appropriate for this equilibrium are

$$[HOCl]_0 = 0.100 \ M$$
$$[OCl^-]_0 = 0$$
$$[H^+]_0 \approx 0 \qquad \text{(We neglect the contribution from } H_2O.)$$

STEP 6

Since the system will reach equilibrium by the dissociation of HOCl, let x be the amount of HOCl (in mol/L) that dissociates in reaching equilibrium.

STEP 7

The equilibrium concentrations in terms of x are

$$[HOCl] = [HOCl]_0 - x = 0.100 - x$$
$$[OCl^-] = [OCl^-]_0 + x = 0 + x = x$$
$$[H^+] = [H^+]_0 + x \approx 0 + x = x$$

STEP 8

Substituting these concentrations into the equilibrium expression gives

Swimming pool water must be frequently tested for pH and chlorine content.

$$K_a = 3.5 \times 10^{-8} = \frac{(x)(x)}{0.100 - x}$$

STEP 9

Since K_a is so small, we can expect a small value for x. Thus we make the approximation $[HA]_0 - x \approx [HA]_0$, or $0.100 - x \approx 0.100$, which leads to the expression

$$K_a = 3.5 \times 10^{-8} = \frac{x^2}{0.100 - x} \approx \frac{x^2}{0.100}$$

Solving for x gives

$$x = 5.9 \times 10^{-5}$$

STEP 10

The approximation $0.100 - x \approx 0.100$ must be validated. To do this, we compare x to $[HOCl]_0$:

$$\frac{x}{[HA]_0} \times 100 = \frac{x}{[HOCl]_0} \times 100 = \frac{5.9 \times 10^{-5}}{0.100} \times 100 = 0.059\%$$

Since this value is much less than 5%, the approximation is considered valid.

STEP 11

We calculate $[H^+]$ and pH:

$$[H^+] = x = 5.9 \times 10^{-5} \, M \quad \text{and} \quad pH = 4.23$$

See Exercises 14.55 through 14.58.

The pH of a Mixture of Weak Acids

Sometimes a solution contains two weak acids of very different strengths. This case is considered in Sample Exercise 14.9. Note that the steps are again followed (though not labeled).

The same systematic approach applies to all solution equilibria.

Sample Exercise 14.9 *The pH of Weak Acid Mixtures*

Calculate the pH of a solution that contains 1.00 M HCN ($K_a = 6.2 \times 10^{-10}$) and 5.00 M HNO$_2$ ($K_a = 4.0 \times 10^{-4}$). Also calculate the concentration of cyanide ion (CN$^-$) in this solution at equilibrium.

Solution

Since HCN and HNO$_2$ are both weak acids and are largely undissociated, the major species in the solution are:

$$HCN, \quad HNO_2, \quad \text{and} \quad H_2O$$

All three of these components produce H^+:

$$HCN(aq) \rightleftharpoons H^+(aq) + CN^-(aq) \qquad K_a = 6.2 \times 10^{-10}$$
$$HNO_2(aq) \rightleftharpoons H^+(aq) + NO_2^-(aq) \qquad K_a = 4.0 \times 10^{-4}$$
$$H_2O(l) \rightleftharpoons H^+(aq) + OH^-(aq) \qquad K_w = 1.0 \times 10^{-14}$$

A mixture of three acids might lead to a very complicated problem. However, the situation is greatly simplified by the fact that even though HNO_2 is a weak acid, it is much stronger than the other two acids present (as revealed by the K values). Thus HNO_2 can be assumed to be the dominant producer of H^+, and we will focus on the equilibrium expression

$$K_a = 4.0 \times 10^{-4} = \frac{[H^+][NO_2^-]}{[HNO_2]}$$

The initial concentrations, the definition of x, and the equilibrium concentrations are as follows:

Initial Concentration (mol/L)		Equilibrium Concentration (mol/L)
$[HNO_2]_0 = 5.00$ $[NO_2^-]_0 = 0$ $[H^+]_0 \approx 0$	$\xrightarrow{x \text{ mol/L } HNO_2 \atop \text{dissociates}}$	$[HNO_2] = 5.00 - x$ $[NO_2^-] = x$ $[H^+] = x$

It is often convenient to represent these concentrations in the following short-hand form (called an ICE table):

	$HNO_2(aq)$	$\rightleftharpoons$	$H^+(aq)$	+	$NO_2^-(aq)$
Initial:	5.00		0		0
Change:	$-x$		$+x$		$+x$
Equilibrium:	$5.00 - x$		x		x

Substituting the equilibrium concentrations in the equilibrium expression and making the approximation that $5.00 - x = 5.00$ give

$$K_a = 4.0 \times 10^{-4} = \frac{(x)(x)}{5.00 - x} \approx \frac{x^2}{5.00}$$

We solve for x:

$$x = 4.5 \times 10^{-2}$$

Using the 5% rule, we show that the approximation is valid:

$$\frac{x}{[HNO_2]_0} \times 100 = \frac{4.5 \times 10^{-2}}{5.00} \times 100 = 0.90\%$$

Therefore,

$$[H^+] = x = 4.5 \times 10^{-2} \, M \quad \text{and} \quad pH = 1.35$$

We also want to calculate the equilibrium concentration of cyanide ion in this solution. The CN^- ions in this solution come from the dissociation of HCN:

$$HCN(aq) \rightleftharpoons H^+(aq) + CN^-(aq)$$

Although the position of this equilibrium lies far to the left and does not contribute *significantly* to $[H^+]$, HCN is the *only source* of CN^-. Thus we must consider the extent of the dissociation of HCN to calculate $[CN^-]$. The equilibrium expression for the preceding reaction is

$$K_a = 6.2 \times 10^{-10} = \frac{[H^+][CN^-]}{[HCN]}$$

We know $[H^+]$ for this solution from the results of the first part of the problem. It is important to understand that *there is only one kind of H^+ in this solution.* It does not matter from which acid the H^+ ions originate. The equilibrium $[H^+]$ we need to insert into the HCN equilibrium expression is 4.5×10^{-2} M, even though the H^+ was contributed almost entirely from the dissociation of HNO_2. What is [HCN] at equilibrium? We know $[HCN]_0 = 1.00$ M, and since K_a for HCN is so small, a negligible amount of HCN will dissociate. Thus

$$[HCN] = [HCN]_0 - \text{amount of HCN dissociated} \approx [HCN]_0 = 1.00 \ M$$

Since $[H^+]$ and [HCN] are known, we can find $[CN^-]$ from the equilibrium expression:

$$K_a = 6.2 \times 10^{-10} = \frac{[H^+][CN^-]}{[HCN]} = \frac{(4.5 \times 10^{-2})[CN^-]}{1.00}$$

$$[CN^-] = \frac{(6.2 \times 10^{-10})(1.00)}{4.5 \times 10^{-2}} = 1.4 \times 10^{-8} \ M$$

Note the significance of this result. Since $[CN^-] = 1.4 \times 10^{-8}$ M and HCN is the only source of CN^-, this means that only 1.4×10^{-8} mol/L of HCN dissociated. This is a very small amount compared with the initial concentration of HCN, which is exactly what we would expect from its very small K_a value, and [HCN] = 1.00 M as assumed.

See Exercises 14.63 and 14.64.

Percent Dissociation

It is often useful to specify the amount of weak acid that has dissociated in achieving equilibrium in an aqueous solution. The **percent dissociation** is defined as follows:

Percent dissociation is also known as percent ionization.

$$\text{Percent dissociation} = \frac{\text{amount dissociated (mol/L)}}{\text{initial concentration (mol/L)}} \times 100\% \qquad (14.5)$$

For example, we found earlier that in a 1.00 M solution of HF, $[H^+] = 2.7 \times 10^{-2}$ M. To reach equilibrium, 2.7×10^{-2} mol/L of the original 1.00 M HF dissociates, so

$$\text{Percent dissociation} = \frac{2.7 \times 10^{-2} \text{ mol/L}}{1.00 \text{ mol/L}} \times 100\% = 2.7\%$$

For a given weak acid, the percent dissociation increases as the acid becomes more dilute. For example, the percent dissociation of acetic acid ($HC_2H_3O_2$, $K_a = 1.8 \times 10^{-5}$) is significantly greater in a 0.10 M solution than in a 1.0 M solution, as demonstrated in Sample Exercise 14.10.

Sample Exercise 14.10 *Calculating Percent Dissociation*

Calculate the percent dissociation of acetic acid ($K_a = 1.8 \times 10^{-5}$) in each of the following solutions.

a. 1.00 M $HC_2H_3O_2$
b. 0.100 M $HC_2H_3O_2$

Solution

a. Since acetic acid is a weak acid, the major species in this solution are $HC_2H_3O_2$ and H_2O. Both species are weak acids, but acetic acid is a much stronger acid than water. Thus the dominant equilibrium will be

$$HC_2H_3O_2(aq) \rightleftharpoons H^+(aq) + C_2H_3O_2^-(aq)$$

and the equilibrium expression is

$$K_a = 1.8 \times 10^{-5} = \frac{[H^+][C_2H_3O_2^-]}{[HC_2H_3O_2]}$$

The initial concentrations, definition of x, and equilibrium concentrations are as follows:

Initial Concentration (mol/L)		Equilibrium Concentration (mol/L)
$[HC_2H_3O_2]_0 = 1.00\ M$	$\xrightarrow{\ x\ \text{mol/L}\ HC_2H_3O_2\ }$	$[HC_2H_3O_2] = 1.00 - x$
$[C_2H_3O_2^-]_0 = 0$	dissociates	$[C_2H_3O_2^-] = x$
$[H^+]_0 \approx 0$		$[H^+] = x$

The corresponding ICE table is:

	$HC_2H_3O_2(aq)$	$\rightleftharpoons$	$H^+(aq)$	$+$	$C_2H_3O_2^-(aq)$
Initial:	1.00		0		0
Change:	$-x$		x		x
Equilibrium:	$1.00 - x$		x		x

Inserting the equilibrium concentrations into the equilibrium expression and making the usual approximation that x is small compared with $[HA]_0$ give

$$K_a = 1.8 \times 10^{-5} = \frac{[H^+][C_2H_3O_2^-]}{[HC_2H_3O_2]} = \frac{(x)(x)}{1.00 - x} \approx \frac{x^2}{1.00}$$

Thus

$$x^2 \approx 1.8 \times 10^{-5} \quad \text{and} \quad x \approx 4.2 \times 10^{-3}$$

The approximation $1.00 - x \approx 1.00$ is valid by the 5% rule (check this yourself), so

$$[H^+] = x = 4.2 \times 10^{-3}\ M$$

CHEMICAL IMPACT

Household Chemistry

COMMON HOUSEHOLD BLEACH is an aqueous solution containing approximately 5% sodium hypochlorite, a potent oxidizing agent that can react with and decolorize chemicals that cause stains. Bleaching solutions are manufactured by dissolving chlorine gas in a sodium hydroxide solution to give the reaction

$$Cl_2(g) + 2OH^-(aq) \rightleftharpoons$$
$$OCl^-(aq) + Cl^-(aq) + H_2O(l)$$

As long as the pH of this solution is maintained above 8, the OCl^- ion is the pre-

dominant chlorine-containing species. However, if the solution is made acidic (the $[OH^-]$ lowered), elemental chlorine (Cl_2) is favored, and since Cl_2 is much less soluble in water than is sodium hypochlorite, Cl_2 gas is suddenly evolved from the solution. This is why labels on bottles of bleach carry warnings about mixing the bleach with other cleaning solutions. For example, toilet bowl cleaners usually contain acids such as H_3PO_4 or HSO_4^- and have pH values around 2. Mixing toilet bowl cleaner with bleach

can lead to a very dangerous evolution of chlorine gas.

On the other hand, if bleach is mixed with a cleaning agent containing ammonia, the chlorine and ammonia react to produce chloramines, such as NH_2Cl, $NHCl_2$, and NCl_3. These compounds produce acrid fumes that can cause respiratory distress.

The percent dissociation is

$$\frac{[H^+]}{[HC_2H_3O_2]_0} \times 100 = \frac{4.2 \times 10^{-3}}{1.00} \times 100\% = 0.42\%$$

b. This is a similar problem, except that in this case $[HC_2H_3O_2] = 0.100\ M$. Analysis of the problem leads to the expression

$$K_a = 1.8 \times 10^{-5} = \frac{[H^+][C_2H_3O_2^-]}{[HC_2H_3O_2]} = \frac{(x)(x)}{0.100 - x} \approx \frac{x^2}{0.100}$$

Thus

$$x = [H^+] = 1.3 \times 10^{-3}\ M$$

and

$$\text{Percent dissociation} = \frac{1.3 \times 10^{-3}}{0.10} \times 100\% = 1.3\%$$

See Exercises 14.65 through 14.68.

The results in Sample Exercise 14.10 show two important facts. The concentration of H^+ ion at equilibrium is smaller in the 0.10 M acetic acid solution than in the 1.0 M acetic acid solution, as we would expect. However, the percent dissociation is significantly greater in the 0.10 M solution than in the 1.0 M solution. This is a general result. *For solutions of any weak acid HA, $[H^+]$ decreases as $[HA]_0$ decreases, but the percent dissociation increases as $[HA]_0$ decreases.* This phenomenon can be explained as follows.

The more dilute the weak acid solution, the greater is the percent dissociation.

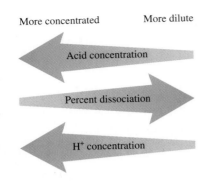

Figure 14.10
The effect of dilution on the percent dissociation and [H⁺] of a weak acid solution.

Consider the weak acid HA with the initial concentration $[HA]_0$, where at equilibrium

$$[HA] = [HA]_0 - x \approx [HA]_0$$
$$[H^+] = [A^-] = x$$

Thus
$$K_a = \frac{[H^+][A^-]}{[HA]} \approx \frac{(x)(x)}{[HA]_0}$$

Now suppose enough water is added suddenly to dilute the solution by a factor of 10. The new concentrations before any adjustment occurs are

$$[A^-]_{new} = [H^+]_{new} = \frac{x}{10}$$

$$[HA]_{new} = \frac{[HA]_0}{10}$$

and Q, the reaction quotient, is

$$Q = \frac{\left(\dfrac{x}{10}\right)\left(\dfrac{x}{10}\right)}{\dfrac{[HA]_0}{10}} = \frac{1(x)(x)}{10[HA]_0} = \frac{1}{10}K_a$$

Since Q is less than K_a, the system must adjust to the right to reach the new equilibrium position. Thus the percent dissociation increases when the acid is diluted. This behavior is summarized in Fig. 14.10. In Sample Exercise 14.11 we see how the percent dissociation can be used to calculate the K_a value for a weak acid.

Sample Exercise 14.11 *Calculating Kₐ from Percent Dissociation*

Lactic acid ($HC_3H_5O_3$) is a waste product that accumulates in muscle tissue during exertion, leading to pain and a feeling of fatigue. In a 0.100 *M* aqueous solution, lactic acid is 3.7% dissociated. Calculate the value of K_a for this acid.

Solution

From the small value for the percent dissociation, it is clear that $HC_3H_5O_3$ is a weak acid. Thus the major species in the solution are the undissociated acid and water:

$$HC_3H_5O_3 \quad \text{and} \quad H_2O$$

However, even though $HC_3H_5O_3$ is a weak acid, it is a much stronger acid than water and will be the dominant source of H^+ in the solution. The dissociation reaction is

$$HC_3H_5O_3(aq) \rightleftharpoons H^+(aq) + C_3H_5O_3^-(aq)$$

and the equilibrium expression is

$$K_a = \frac{[H^+][C_3H_5O_3^-]}{[HC_3H_5O_3]}$$

The initial and equilibrium concentrations are as follows:

Initial Concentration		Equilibrium Concentration
$[HC_3H_5O_3]_0 = 0.10\ M$		$[HC_3H_5O_3] = 0.10 - x$
$[C_3H_5O_3^-]_0 = 0$	$\xrightarrow[\substack{HC_3H_5O_3 \\ \text{dissociates}}]{x\ mol/L}$	$[C_3H_5O_3^-] = x$
$[H^+]_0 \approx 0$		$[H^+] = x$

The change needed to reach equilibrium can be obtained from the percent dissociation and Equation (14.5). For this acid,

$$\text{Percent dissociation} = 3.7\% = \frac{x}{[HC_3H_5O_3]_0} \times 100\% = \frac{x}{0.10} \times 100\%$$

and

$$x = \frac{3.7}{100}(0.10) = 3.7 \times 10^{-3}\ \text{mol/L}$$

Now we can calculate the equilibrium concentrations:

$$[HC_3H_5O_3] = 0.10 - x = 0.10\ M \qquad \text{(to the correct number of significant figures)}$$
$$[C_3H_5O_3^-] = [H^+] = x = 3.7 \times 10^{-3}\ M$$

These concentrations can now be used to calculate the value of K_a for lactic acid:

$$K_a = \frac{[H^+][C_3H_5O_3^-]}{[HC_3H_5O_3]} = \frac{(3.7 \times 10^{-3})(3.7 \times 10^{-3})}{0.10} = 1.4 \times 10^{-4}$$

See Exercises 14.69 and 14.70.

Strenuous exercise causes a buildup of lactic acid in muscle tissues.

14.6 Bases

According to the Arrhenius concept, a base is a substance that produces OH^- ions in aqueous solution. According to the Brønsted–Lowry model, a base is a proton acceptor. The bases sodium hydroxide (NaOH) and potassium hydroxide (KOH) fulfill both criteria. They contain OH^- ions in the solid lattice and, behaving as strong electrolytes, dissociate completely when dissolved in aqueous solution:

In a basic solution at 25°C, pH > 7.

$$NaOH(s) \longrightarrow Na^+(aq) + OH^-(aq)$$

leaving virtually no undissociated NaOH. Thus a 1.0 M NaOH solution really contains 1.0 M Na^+ and 1.0 M OH^-. Because of their complete dissociation, NaOH and KOH are called **strong bases** in the same sense as we defined strong acids.

All the hydroxides of the Group 1A elements (LiOH, NaOH, KOH, RbOH, and CsOH) are strong bases, but only NaOH and KOH are common laboratory reagents, because the lithium, rubidium, and cesium compounds are expensive. The alkaline earth (Group 2A) hydroxides—$Ca(OH)_2$, $Ba(OH)_2$, and $Sr(OH)_2$—are also strong bases. For these compounds, two moles of hydroxide ion are produced for every mole of metal hydroxide dissolved in aqueous solution.

The alkaline earth hydroxides are not very soluble and are used only when the solubility factor is not important. In fact, the low solubility of these bases can sometimes be an advantage. For example, many antacids are suspensions of metal hydroxides, such as aluminum hydroxide and magnesium hydroxide. The low solubility of these compounds prevents a large hydroxide ion concentration that would harm the tissues of the mouth, esophagus, and stomach. Yet these suspensions furnish plenty of hydroxide ion to react with the stomach acid, since the salts dissolve as this reaction proceeds.

Calcium hydroxide, $Ca(OH)_2$, often called **slaked lime,** is widely used in industry because it is inexpensive and plentiful. For example, slaked lime is used in scrubbing stack gases to remove sulfur dioxide from the exhaust of power plants and factories. In the scrubbing process a suspension of slaked lime is sprayed into the stack gases to react with sulfur dioxide gas according to the following steps:

$$SO_2(g) + H_2O(l) \rightleftharpoons H_2SO_3(aq)$$
$$Ca(OH)_2(aq) + H_2SO_3(aq) \rightleftharpoons CaSO_3(s) + 2H_2O(l)$$

Slaked lime is also widely used in water treatment plants for softening hard water, which involves the removal of ions, such as Ca^{2+} and Mg^{2+}, that hamper the action of detergents. The softening method most often employed in water treatment plants is the **lime–soda process,** in which *lime* (CaO) and *soda ash* (Na_2CO_3) are added to the water. As we will see in more detail later in this chapter, the CO_3^{2-} ion reacts with water to produce the HCO_3^- ion. When the lime is added to the water, it forms slaked lime, that is,

$$CaO(s) + H_2O(l) \longrightarrow Ca(OH)_2(aq)$$

which then reacts with the HCO_3^- ion from the added soda ash and a Ca^{2+} ion in the hard water to produce calcium carbonate:

$$Ca(OH)_2(aq) + Ca^{2+}(aq) + 2HCO_3^-(aq) \longrightarrow 2CaCO_3(s) + 2H_2O(l)$$

From hard water

Thus, for every mole of $Ca(OH)_2$ consumed, 1 mole of Ca^{2+} is removed from the hard water, thereby softening it. Some hard water naturally contains bicarbonate ions. In this case, no soda ash is needed—simply adding the lime produces the softening.

Calculating the pH of a strong base solution is relatively simple, as illustrated in Sample Exercise 14.12.

Calcium carbonate is also used in scrubbing, as discussed in Section 5.9.

Molecular Models: SO_2, H_2O, H_2SO_3

Video: Limewater

Sample Exercise 14.12 The pH of Strong Bases

Calculate the pH of a 5.0×10^{-2} M NaOH solution.

Solution

The major species in this solution are

$$\underbrace{Na^+, \quad OH^-,}_{\text{From NaOH}} \quad \text{and} \quad H_2O$$

Although autoionization of water also produces OH^- ions, the pH will be dominated by the OH^- ions from the dissolved NaOH. Thus, in the solution,

$$[OH^-] = 5.0 \times 10^{-2} \, M$$

and the concentration of H^+ can be calculated from K_w:

$$[H^+] = \frac{K_w}{[OH^-]} = \frac{1.0 \times 10^{-14}}{5.0 \times 10^{-2}} = 2.0 \times 10^{-13} \, M$$

$$pH = 12.70$$

Note that this is a basic solution for which

$$[OH^-] > [H^+] \quad \text{and} \quad pH > 7$$

The added OH^- from the salt has shifted the water autoionization equilibrium

$$H_2O(l) \rightleftharpoons H^+(aq) + OH^-(aq)$$

to the left, significantly lowering $[H^+]$ compared with that in pure water.

See Exercises 14.81 through 14.84.

Many types of proton acceptors (bases) do not contain the hydroxide ion. However, when dissolved in water, these substances increase the concentration of hydroxide ion because of their reaction with water. For example, ammonia reacts with water as follows:

A base does not have to contain hydroxide ion.

$$NH_3(aq) + H_2O(l) \rightleftharpoons NH_4^+(aq) + OH^-(aq)$$

The ammonia molecule accepts a proton and thus functions as a base. Water is the acid in this reaction. Note that even though the base ammonia contains no hydroxide ion, it still increases the concentration of hydroxide ion to yield a basic solution.

Bases such as ammonia typically have at least one unshared pair of electrons that is capable of forming a bond with a proton. The reaction of an ammonia molecule with a water molecule can be represented as follows:

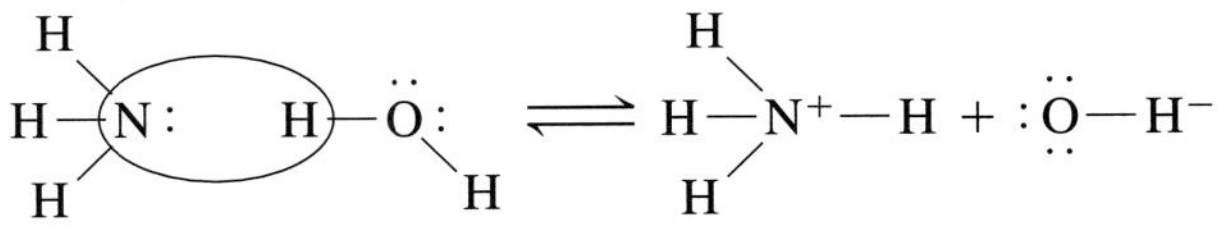

There are many bases like ammonia that produce hydroxide ion by reaction with water. In most of these bases, the lone pair is located on a nitrogen atom. Some examples are

Molecular Models: CH_3NH_2, $(CH_3)_2NH$, $(CH_3)_3N$, C_5H_5N

| Methylamine | Dimethylamine | Trimethylamine | Ethylamine | Pyridine |

CHEMICAL IMPACT

Amines

WE HAVE SEEN that many bases have nitrogen atoms with one lone pair and can be viewed as substituted ammonia molecules, with the general formula $R_xNH_{(3-x)}$. Compounds of this type are called **amines**. Amines are widely distributed in animals and plants, and complex amines often serve as messengers or regulators. For example, in the human nervous system, there are two amine stimulants, *norepinephrine* and *adrenaline*.

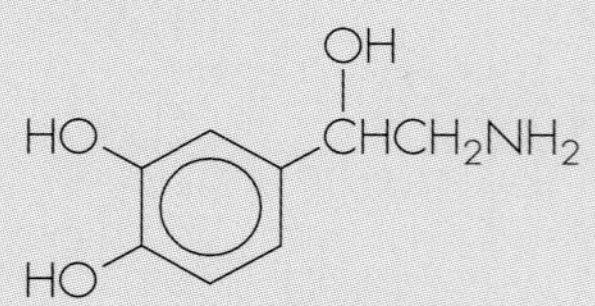

Norepinephrine

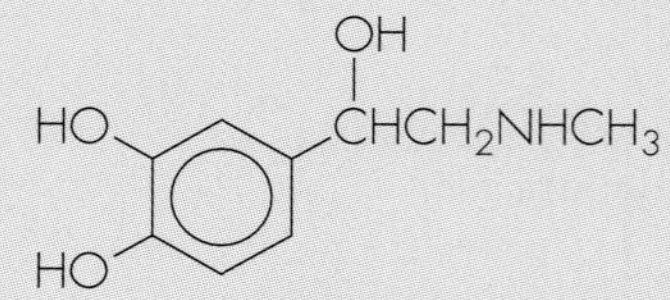

Adrenaline

Ephedrine, widely used as a decongestant, was a known drug in China over 2000 years ago. Indians in Mexico and the Southwest have used the hallucinogen *mescaline*, extracted from the peyote cactus, for centuries.

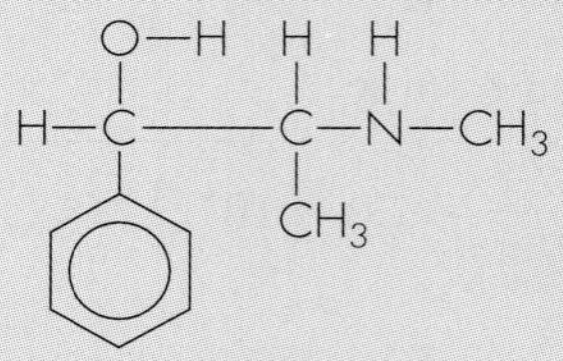

Ephedrine

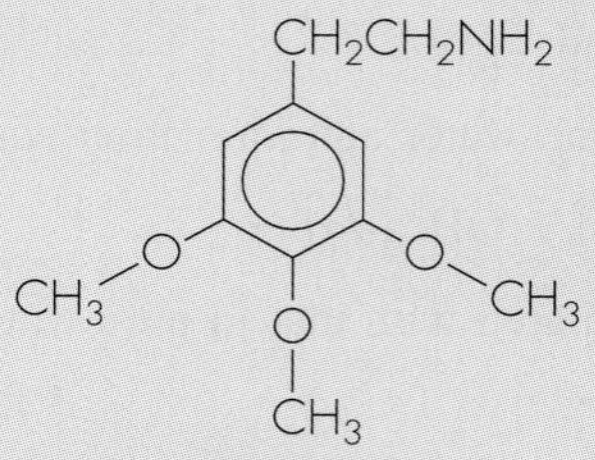

Mescaline

Many other drugs, such as codeine and quinine, are amines, but they are usually not used in their pure amine forms. Instead, they are treated with an acid to become acid salts. An example of an acid salt is ammonium chloride, obtained by the reaction

$$NH_3 + HCl \longrightarrow NH_4Cl$$

Amines also can be protonated in this way. The resulting acid salt, written as AHCl (where A represents the amine), contains AH^+ and Cl^-. In general, the acid salts are more stable and more sol-

Peyote cactus growing on a rock.

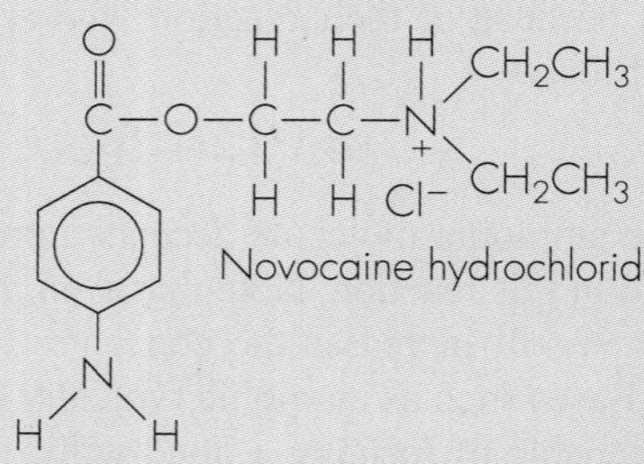

uble in water than the parent amines. For instance, the parent amine of the well-known local anesthetic *novocaine* is insoluble in water, whereas the acid salt is much more soluble.

Novocaine hydrochloride

 Molecular Models: norepinephrine, ephedrine, adrenaline, mescaline, novocaine

Note that the first four bases can be thought of as substituted ammonia molecules with hydrogen atoms replaced by methyl (CH_3) or ethyl (C_2H_5) groups. The pyridine molecule is like benzene

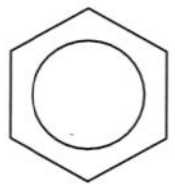

except that a nitrogen atom replaces one of the carbon atoms in the ring. The general reaction between a base B and water is given by

Table 14.3 Values of K_b for Some Common Weak Bases

Name	Formula	Conjugate Acid	K_b
Ammonia	NH_3	NH_4^+	1.8×10^{-5}
Methylamine	CH_3NH_2	$CH_3NH_3^+$	4.38×10^{-4}
Ethylamine	$C_2H_5NH_2$	$C_2H_5NH_3^+$	5.6×10^{-4}
Aniline	$C_6H_5NH_2$	$C_6H_5NH_3^+$	3.8×10^{-10}
Pyridine	C_5H_5N	$C_5H_5NH^+$	1.7×10^{-9}

Video: Ammonia Fountain

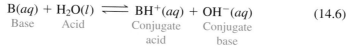

$$B(aq) + H_2O(l) \rightleftharpoons BH^+(aq) + OH^-(aq) \qquad (14.6)$$

Base   Acid   Conjugate   Conjugate
acid   base

The equilibrium constant for this general reaction is

$$K_b = \frac{[BH^+][OH^-]}{[B]}$$

Appendix 5.3 contains a table of K_b values.

where K_b *always refers to the reaction of a base with water to form the conjugate acid and the hydroxide ion.*

Bases of the type represented by B in Equation (14.6) compete with OH^-, a very strong base, for the H^+ ion. Thus their K_b values tend to be small (for example, for ammonia, $K_b = 1.8 \times 10^{-5}$), and they are called **weak bases.** The values of K_b for some common weak bases are listed in Table 14.3.

Typically, pH calculations for solutions of weak bases are very similar to those for weak acids, as illustrated by Sample Exercises 14.13 and 14.14.

Refer to the steps for solving weak acid equilibrium problems. Use the same systematic approach for weak base equilibrium problems.

Sample Exercise 14.13 The pH of Weak Bases I

Calculate the pH for a 15.0 M solution of NH_3 ($K_b = 1.8 \times 10^{-5}$).

Molecular Models: $CH_3NH_3^+$, $CH_3CH_2NH_2$, $CH_3CH_2NH_3^+$

Solution

Since ammonia is a weak base, as can be seen from its small K_b value, most of the dissolved NH_3 will remain as NH_3. Thus the major species in solution are

$$NH_3 \quad \text{and} \quad H_2O$$

Both these substances can produce OH^- according to the reactions

$$NH_3(aq) + H_2O(l) \rightleftharpoons NH_4^+(aq) + OH^-(aq) \qquad K_b = 1.8 \times 10^{-5}$$
$$H_2O(l) \rightleftharpoons H^+(aq) + OH^-(aq) \qquad K_w = 1.0 \times 10^{-14}$$

However, the contribution from water can be neglected, since $K_b \gg K_w$. The equilibrium for NH_3 will dominate, and the equilibrium expression to be used is

$$K_b = 1.8 \times 10^{-5} = \frac{[NH_4^+][OH^-]}{[NH_3]}$$

The appropriate concentrations are

Initial Concentration (mol/L)		Equilibrium Concentration (mol/L)
$[NH_3]_0 = 15.0$	x mol/L	$[NH_3] = 15.0 - x$
$[NH_4^+]_0 = 0$	$\xrightarrow{\text{NH}_3 \text{ reacts with}}$	$[NH_4^+] = x$
$[OH^-]_0 \approx 0$	H_2O to reach equilibrium	$[OH^-] = x$

In terms of an ICE table, these concentrations are:

	$NH_3(aq)$	$+$	$H_2O(l)$	$\rightleftharpoons$	$NH_4^+(aq)$	$+$	$OH^-(aq)$
Initial:	15.0		—		0		0
Change:	$-x$		—		$+x$		$+x$
Equilibrium:	$15.0 - x$		—		x		x

Substituting the equilibrium concentrations into the equilibrium expression and making the usual approximation gives

$$K_b = 1.8 \times 10^{-5} = \frac{[NH_4^+][OH^-]}{[NH_3]} = \frac{(x)(x)}{15.0 - x} \approx \frac{x^2}{15.0}$$

Thus

$$x \approx 1.6 \times 10^{-2}$$

The 5% rule validates the approximation (check it yourself), so

$$[OH^-] = 1.6 \times 10^{-2} \ M$$

Since we know that K_w must be satisfied for this solution, we can calculate $[H^+]$ as follows:

$$[H^+] = \frac{K_w}{[OH^-]} = \frac{1.0 \times 10^{-14}}{1.6 \times 10^{-2}} = 6.3 \times 10^{-13} \ M$$

Therefore,

$$pH = -\log(6.3 \times 10^{-13}) = 12.20$$

See Exercises 14.87 and 14.88.

Sample Exercise 14.13 illustrates how a typical weak base equilibrium problem should be solved. Note two additional important points:

A table of K_b values for bases is also given in Appendix 5.3.

1. We calculated $[H^+]$ from K_w and then calculated the pH, but another method is available. The pOH could have been calculated from $[OH^-]$ and then used in Equation (14.3):

$$pK_w = 14.00 = pH + pOH$$
$$pH = 14.00 - pOH$$

2. In a 15.0 M NH_3 solution, the equilibrium concentrations of NH_4^+ and OH^- are each 1.6×10^{-2} M. Only a small percentage,

$$\frac{1.6 \times 10^{-2}}{15.0} \times 100\% = 0.11\%$$

of the ammonia reacts with water. Bottles containing 15.0 M NH_3 solution are often labeled 15.0 M NH_4OH, but as you can see from these results, 15.0 M NH_3 is actually a much more accurate description of the solution contents.

Sample Exercise 14.14 The pH of Weak Bases II

Calculate the pH of a 1.0 M solution of methylamine ($K_b = 4.38 \times 10^{-4}$).

Solution

Since methylamine (CH_3NH_2) is a weak base, the major species in solution are

$$CH_3NH_2 \quad \text{and} \quad H_2O$$

Both are bases; however, water can be neglected as a source of OH^-, so the dominant equilibrium is

$$CH_3NH_2(aq) + H_2O(l) \rightleftharpoons CH_3NH_3^+(aq) + OH^-(aq)$$

and $\quad K_b = 4.38 \times 10^{-4} = \dfrac{[CH_3NH_3^+][OH^-]}{[CH_3NH_2]}$

The concentrations are as follows:

Initial Concentration (mol/L)		Equilibrium Concentration (mol/L)
$[CH_3NH_2]_0 = 1.0$ $[CH_3NH_3^+]_0 = 0$ $[OH^-]_0 \approx 0$	x mol/L CH_3NH_2 reacts with H_2O to reach equilibrium $\longrightarrow$	$[CH_3NH_2] = 1.0 - x$ $[CH_3NH_3^+] = x$ $[OH^-] = x$

The ICE table is:

	$CH_3NH_2(aq)$	+	$H_2O(l)$	$\rightleftharpoons$	$CH_3NH_3^+(aq)$	+	$OH^-(aq)$
Initial:	1.0		—		0		0
Change:	$-x$		—		$+x$		$+x$
Equilibrium:	$1.0 - x$		—		x		x

Substituting the equilibrium concentrations in the equilibrium expression and making the usual approximation give

$$K_b = 4.38 \times 10^{-4} = \frac{[CH_3NH_3^+][OH^-]}{[CH_3NH_2]} = \frac{(x)(x)}{1.0 - x} \approx \frac{x^2}{1.0}$$

and $\quad x \approx 2.1 \times 10^{-2}$

The approximation is valid by the 5% rule, so

$$[OH^-] = x = 2.1 \times 10^{-2} \ M$$
$$pOH = 1.68$$
$$pH = 14.00 - 1.68 = 12.32$$

See Exercises 14.89 and 14.90.

14.7 Polyprotic Acids

Molecular Models: H_2CO_3, H_3PO_4

Some important acids, such as sulfuric acid (H_2SO_4) and phosphoric acid (H_3PO_4), can furnish more than one proton and are called **polyprotic acids.** A polyprotic acid always dissociates in a *stepwise* manner, one proton at a time. For example, the diprotic (two-proton) acid carbonic acid (H_2CO)$_3$, which is so important in maintaining a constant pH in human blood, dissociates in the following steps:

$$H_2CO_3(aq) \rightleftharpoons H^+(aq) + HCO_3^-(aq) \qquad K_{a_1} = \frac{[H^+][HCO_3^-]}{[H_2CO_3]} = 4.3 \times 10^{-7}$$

$$HCO_3^-(aq) \rightleftharpoons H^+(aq) + CO_3^{2-}(aq) \qquad K_{a_2} = \frac{[H^+][CO_3^{2-}]}{[HCO_3^-]} = 5.6 \times 10^{-11}$$

The successive K_a values for the dissociation equilibria are designated K_{a_1} and K_{a_2}. Note that the conjugate base HCO_3^- of the first dissociation equilibrium becomes the acid in the second step.

Carbonic acid is formed when carbon dioxide gas is dissolved in water. In fact, the first dissociation step for carbonic acid is best represented by the reaction

$$CO_2(aq) + H_2O(l) \rightleftharpoons H^+(aq) + HCO_3^-(aq)$$

since relatively little H_2CO_3 actually exists in solution. However, it is convenient to consider CO_2 in water as H_2CO_3 so that we can treat such solutions using the familiar dissociation reactions for weak acids.

Phosphoric acid is a **triprotic acid** (three protons) that dissociates in the following steps:

$$H_3PO_4(aq) \rightleftharpoons H^+(aq) + H_2PO_4^-(aq) \quad K_{a_1} = \frac{[H^+][H_2PO_4^-]}{[H_3PO_4]} = 7.5 \times 10^{-3}$$

$$H_2PO_4^-(aq) \rightleftharpoons H^+(aq) + HPO_4^{2-}(aq) \quad K_{a_2} = \frac{[H^+][HPO_4^{2-}]}{[H_2PO_4^-]} = 6.2 \times 10^{-8}$$

$$HPO_4^{2-}(aq) \rightleftharpoons H^+(aq) + PO_4^{3-}(aq) \quad K_{a_3} = \frac{[H^+][PO_4^{3-}]}{[HPO_4^{2-}]} = 4.8 \times 10^{-13}$$

For a typical weak polyprotic acid,

$$K_{a_1} > K_{a_2} > K_{a_3}$$

That is, the acid involved in each step of the dissociation is successively weaker, as shown by the stepwise dissociation constants given in Table 14.4. These values indicate that the loss of a second or third proton occurs less readily than loss of the

Table 14.4 Stepwise Dissociation Constants for Several Common Polyprotic Acids

Name	Formula	K_{a_1}	K_{a_2}	K_{a_3}
Phosphoric acid	H_3PO_4	7.5×10^{-3}	6.2×10^{-8}	4.8×10^{-13}
Arsenic acid	H_3AsO_4	5×10^{-3}	8×10^{-8}	6×10^{-10}
Carbonic acid	H_2CO_3	4.3×10^{-7}	5.6×10^{-11}	
Sulfuric acid	H_2SO_4	Large	1.2×10^{-2}	
Sulfurous acid	H_2SO_3	1.5×10^{-2}	1.0×10^{-7}	
Hydrosulfuric acid*	H_2S	1.0×10^{-7}	$\sim 10^{-19}$	
Oxalic acid	$H_2C_2O_4$	6.5×10^{-2}	6.1×10^{-5}	
Ascorbic acid (vitamin C)	$H_2C_6H_6O_6$	7.9×10^{-5}	1.6×10^{-12}	

*The K_{a_2} value for H_2S is very uncertain. Because it is so small, the K_{a_2} value is very difficult to measure accurately.

A table of K_a values for polyprotic acids is also given in Appendix 5.2.

first proton. This is not surprising; as the negative charge on the acid increases, it becomes more difficult to remove the positively charged proton.

Although we might expect the pH calculations for solutions of polyprotic acids to be complicated, the most common cases are surprisingly straightforward. To illustrate, we will consider a typical case, phosphoric acid, and a unique case, sulfuric acid.

Phosphoric Acid

Phosphoric acid is typical of most polyprotic acids in that the successive K_a values are very different. For example, the ratios of successive K_a values (from Table 14.4) are

$$\frac{K_{a_1}}{K_{a_2}} = \frac{7.5 \times 10^{-3}}{6.2 \times 10^{-8}} = 1.2 \times 10^5$$

$$\frac{K_{a_2}}{K_{a_3}} = \frac{6.2 \times 10^{-8}}{4.8 \times 10^{-13}} = 1.3 \times 10^5$$

Molecular Models: H_3PO_4, $H_2PO_4^-$, HPO_4^{2-}, PO_4^{3-}

Thus the relative acid strengths are

$$H_3PO_4 \gg H_2PO_4^- \gg HPO_4^{2-}$$

This means that in a solution prepared by dissolving H_3PO_4 in water, *only the first dissociation step makes an important contribution to $[H^+]$*. This greatly simplifies the pH calculations for phosphoric acid solutions, as is illustrated in Sample Exercise 14.15.

For a typical polyprotic acid in water, only the first dissociation step is important in determining the pH.

Sample Exercise 14.15 *The pH of a Polyprotic Acid*

Calculate the pH of a 5.0 M H_3PO_4 solution and the equilibrium concentrations of the species H_3PO_4, $H_2PO_4^-$, HPO_4^{2-}, and PO_4^{3-}.

Solution

The major species in solution are

$$H_3PO_4 \quad \text{and} \quad H_2O$$

None of the dissociation products of H_3PO_4 is written, since the K_a values are all so small that they will be minor species. The dominant equilibrium is the dissociation of H_3PO_4:

$$H_3PO_4(aq) \rightleftharpoons H^+(aq) + H_2PO_4^-(aq)$$

where

$$K_{a_1} = 7.5 \times 10^{-3} = \frac{[H^+][H_2PO_4^-]}{[H_3PO_4]}$$

The concentrations are as follows:

Initial Concentration (mol/L)		*Equilibrium* Concentration (mol/L)
$[H_3PO_4]_0 = 5.0$	x mol/L	$[H_3PO_4] = 5.0 - x$
$[H_2PO_4^-]_0 = 0$	H_3PO_4	$[H_2PO_4^-] = x$
$[H^+]_0 \approx 0$	dissociates	$[H^+] = x$

The ICE table is:

	$H_3PO_4(aq)$	$\rightleftharpoons$	$H^+(aq)$	$+$	$H_2PO_4^-(aq)$
Initial:	5.0		0		0
Change:	$-x$		$+x$		$+x$
Equilibrium:	$5.0 - x$		x		x

Substituting the equilibrium concentrations into the expression for K_{a_1} and making the usual approximation give

$$K_{a_1} = 7.5 \times 10^{-3} = \frac{[H^+][H_2PO_4^-]}{[H_3PO_4]} = \frac{(x)(x)}{5.0 - x} \approx \frac{x^2}{5.0}$$

Thus

$$x \approx 1.9 \times 10^{-1}$$

Since 1.9×10^{-1} is less than 5% of 5.0, the approximation is acceptable, and

$$[H^+] = x = 0.19 \ M$$
$$pH = 0.72$$

So far we have determined that

$$[H^+] = [H_2PO_4^-] = 0.19 \ M$$

and

$$[H_3PO_4] = 5.0 - x = 4.8 \ M$$

The concentration of HPO_4^{2-} can be obtained by using the expression for K_{a_2}:

$$K_{a_2} = 6.2 \times 10^{-8} = \frac{[H^+][HPO_4^{2-}]}{[H_2PO_4^-]}$$

where

$$[H^+] = [H_2PO_4^-] = 0.19 \ M$$

Thus
$$[HPO_4^{2-}] = K_{a_2} = 6.2 \times 10^{-8} \ M$$

To calculate $[PO_4^{3-}]$, we use the expression for K_{a_3} and the values of $[H^+]$ and $[HPO_4^{2-}]$ calculated previously:

$$K_{a_3} = \frac{[H^+][PO_4^{3-}]}{[HPO_4^{2-}]} = 4.8 \times 10^{-13} = \frac{0.19[PO_4^{3-}]}{(6.2 \times 10^{-8})}$$

$$[PO_4^{3-}] = \frac{(4.8 \times 10^{-13})(6.2 \times 10^{-8})}{0.19} = 1.6 \times 10^{-19} \ M$$

These results show that the second and third dissociation steps do not make an important contribution to $[H^+]$. This is apparent from the fact that $[HPO_4^{2-}]$ is $6.2 \times 10^{-8} \ M$, which means that only 6.2×10^{-8} mol/L $H_2PO_4^-$ has dissociated. The value of $[PO_4^{3-}]$ shows that the dissociation of HPO_4^{2-} is even smaller. We must, however, use the second and third dissociation steps to calculate $[HPO_4^{2-}]$ and $[PO_4^{3-}]$, since these steps are the only sources of these ions.

See Exercises 14.99 and 14.100.

Sulfuric Acid

Sulfuric acid is unique among the common acids in that it is *a strong acid in its first dissociation step and a weak acid in its second step:*

$$H_2SO_4(aq) \longrightarrow H^+(aq) + HSO_4^-(aq) \qquad K_{a_1} \text{ is very large}$$
$$HSO_4^-(aq) \rightleftharpoons H^+(aq) + SO_4^{2-}(aq) \qquad K_{a_2} = 1.2 \times 10^{-2}$$

Molecular Models: H_2SO_4, HSO_4^-, SO_4^{2-}

Sample Exercise 14.16 illustrates how to calculate the pH for sulfuric acid solutions.

Sample Exercise 14.16 *The pH of Sulfuric Acid*

Calculate the pH of a 1.0 M H_2SO_4 solution.

Solution

The major species in the solution are

$$H^+, \quad HSO_4^-, \quad \text{and} \quad H_2O$$

where the first two ions are produced by the complete first dissociation step of H_2SO_4. The concentration of H^+ in this solution will be at least 1.0 M, since this amount is produced by the first dissociation step of H_2SO_4. We must now answer this question: Does the HSO_4^- ion dissociate enough to produce a significant contribution to the concentration of H^+? This question can be answered by calculating the equilibrium concentrations for the dissociation reactions of HSO_4^-:

$$HSO_4^-(aq) \rightleftharpoons H^+(aq) + SO_4^{2-}(aq)$$

where
$$K_{a_2} = 1.2 \times 10^{-2} = \frac{[H^+][SO_4^{2-}]}{[HSO_4^-]}$$

The concentrations are as follows:

Initial Concentration (mol/L)		Equilibrium Concentration (mol/L)
$[HSO_4^-]_0 = 1.0$ $[SO_4^{2-}]_0 = 0$ $[H^+]_0 = 1.0$	x mol/L HSO_4^- dissociates $\longrightarrow$ to reach equilibrium	$[HSO_4^-] = 1.0 - x$ $[SO_4^{2-}] = x$ $[H^+] = 1.0 + x$

The ICE table is:

	$HSO_4^-(aq)$	$\rightleftharpoons$	$H^+(aq)$	$+$	$SO_4^{2-}(aq)$
Initial:	1.0		1.0		0
Change:	$-x$		$+x$		$+x$
Equilibrium:	$1.0 - x$		$1.0 + x$		x

Note that $[H^+]_0$ is not equal to zero, as it usually is for a weak acid, because the first dissociation step has already occurred. Substituting the equilibrium concentrations into the expression for K_{a_2} and making the usual approximation give

$$K_{a_2} = 1.2 \times 10^{-2} = \frac{[H^+][SO_4^{2-}]}{[HSO_4^-]} = \frac{(1.0 + x)(x)}{1.0 - x} \approx \frac{(1.0)(x)}{(1.0)}$$

Thus
$$x \approx 1.2 \times 10^{-2}$$

Since 1.2×10^{-2} is 1.2% of 1.0, the approximation is valid according to the 5% rule. Note that x is not equal to $[H^+]$ in this case. Instead,

$$[H^+] = 1.0 \ M + x = 1.0 \ M + (1.2 \times 10^{-2}) \ M$$
$$= 1.0 \ M \quad \text{(to the correct number of significant figures)}$$

Thus the dissociation of HSO_4^- does not make a significant contribution to the concentration of H^+, and

$$[H^+] = 1.0 \ M \quad \text{and} \quad pH = 0.00$$

See Exercise 14.101.

Only in dilute H_2SO_4 solutions does the second dissociation step contribute significantly to $[H^+]$.

Sample Exercise 14.16 illustrates the most common case for sulfuric acid in which only the first dissociation makes an important contribution to the concentration of H^+. In solutions more dilute than 1.0 M (for example, 0.10 M H_2SO_4), the dissociation of HSO_4^- is important, and solving the problem requires use of the quadratic formula, as shown in Sample Exercise 14.17.

Sample Exercise 14.17 The pH of Sulfuric Acid

Calculate the pH of a 1.00×10^{-2} M H_2SO_4 solution.

Solution

The major species in solution are

$$H^+, \quad HSO_4^-, \quad and \quad H_2O$$

Proceeding as in Sample Exercise 14.16, we consider the dissociation of HSO_4^-, which leads to the following concentrations:

Initial Concentration (mol/L)		Equilibrium Concentration (mol/L)
$[HSO_4^-]_0 = 0.0100$	x mol/L HSO_4^-	$[HSO_4^-] = 0.0100 - x$
$[SO_4^{2-}]_0 = 0$	dissociates	$[SO_4^{2-}] = x$
$[H^+]_0 = 0.0100$	to reach equilibrium	$[H^+] = 0.0100 + x$
↑ From dissociation of H_2SO_4		

Substituting the equilibrium concentrations into the expression for K_{a_2} gives

$$1.2 \times 10^{-2} = K_{a_2} = \frac{[H^+][SO_4^{2-}]}{[HSO_4^-]} = \frac{(0.0100 + x)(x)}{(0.0100 - x)}$$

If we make the usual approximation, then $0.0100 + x \approx 0.0100$ and $0.0100 - x \approx 0.0100$, and we have

$$1.2 \times 10^{-2} = \frac{(0.0100 + x)(x)}{(0.0100 - x)} \approx \frac{(0.0100)x}{(0.0100)}$$

The calculated value of x is

$$x = 1.2 \times 10^{-2} = 0.012$$

This value is larger than 0.010, clearly a ridiculous result. Thus we cannot make the usual approximation and must instead solve the quadratic equation. The expression

$$1.2 \times 10^{-2} = \frac{(0.0100 + x)(x)}{(0.0100 - x)}$$

leads to $\qquad (1.2 \times 10^{-2})(0.0100 - x) = (0.0100 + x)(x)$

$$(1.2 \times 10^{-4}) - (1.2 \times 10^{-2})x = (1.0 \times 10^{-2})x + x^2$$

$$x^2 + (2.2 \times 10^{-2})x - (1.2 \times 10^{-4}) = 0$$

This equation can be solved using the quadratic formula

$$x = \frac{-b \pm \sqrt{b^2 - 4ac}}{2a}$$

where $a = 1$, $b = 2.2 \times 10^{-2}$, and $c = -1.2 \times 10^{-4}$. Use of the quadratic formula gives one negative root (which cannot be correct) and one positive root,

$$x = 4.5 \times 10^{-3}$$

Thus $\quad\quad\quad\quad$ $[H^+] = 0.0100 + x = 0.0100 + 0.0045 = 0.0145$

and $\quad\quad\quad\quad\quad\quad\quad\quad$ pH $= 1.84$

Note that in this case the second dissociation step produces about half as many H^+ ions as the initial step does.

This problem also can be solved by successive approximations, a method illustrated in Appendix 1.4.

See Exercise 14.102.

Characteristics of Weak Polyprotic Acids

1. Typically, successive K_a values are so much smaller than the first value that only the first dissociation step makes a significant contribution to the equilibrium concentration of H^+. This means that the calculation of the pH for a solution of a typical weak polyprotic acid is identical to that for a solution of a weak monoprotic acid.

2. Sulfuric acid is unique in being a strong acid in its first dissociation step and a weak acid in its second step. For relatively concentrated solutions of sulfuric acid (1.0 M or higher), the large concentration of H^+ from the first dissociation step represses the second step, which can be neglected as a contributor of H^+ ions. For dilute solutions of sulfuric acid, the second step does make a significant contribution, and the quadratic equation must be used to obtain the total H^+ concentration.

14.8 Acid–Base Properties of Salts

Salt is simply another name for *ionic compound*. When a salt dissolves in water, we assume that it breaks up into its ions, which move about independently, at least in dilute solutions. Under certain conditions, these ions can behave as acids or bases. In this section we explore such reactions.

Salts That Produce Neutral Solutions

Recall that the conjugate base of a strong acid has virtually no affinity for protons in water. This is why strong acids completely dissociate in aqueous solution. Thus, when anions such as Cl^- and NO_3^- are placed in water, they do not combine with H^+ and have no effect on the pH. Cations such as K^+ and Na^+ from strong bases have no affinity for H^+, nor can they produce H^+, so they too have no effect on the pH of an aqueous solution. *Salts that consist of the cations of strong bases and the anions of strong acids have no effect on [H⁺] when dissolved in water.* This means that aqueous solutions of salts such as KCl, NaCl, NaNO$_3$, and KNO$_3$ are neutral (have a pH of 7).

The salt of a strong acid and a strong base gives a neutral solution.

Salts That Produce Basic Solutions

In an aqueous solution of sodium acetate (NaC$_2$H$_3$O$_2$), the major species are

$$Na^+, \quad C_2H_3O_2^-, \quad and \quad H_2O$$

Molecular Models: C$_2$H$_3$O$_2^-$, HC$_2$H$_3$O$_2$

What are the acid–base properties of each component? The Na$^+$ ion has neither acid nor base properties. The C$_2$H$_3$O$_2^-$ ion is the conjugate base of acetic acid, a weak acid. This means that C$_2$H$_3$O$_2^-$ has a significant affinity for a proton and is a base. Finally, water is a weakly amphoteric substance.

The pH of this solution will be determined by the C$_2$H$_3$O$_2^-$ ion. Since C$_2$H$_3$O$_2^-$ is a base, it will react with the best proton donor available. In this case, water is the *only* source of protons, and the reaction between the acetate ion and water is

$$C_2H_3O_2^-(aq) + H_2O(l) \rightleftharpoons HC_2H_3O_2(aq) + OH^-(aq) \qquad (14.7)$$

Note that this reaction, which yields a base solution, involves a *base reacting with water to produce hydroxide ion and a conjugate acid.* We have defined K_b as the equilibrium constant for such a reaction. In this case,

$$K_b = \frac{[HC_2H_3O_2][OH^-]}{[C_2H_3O_2^-]}$$

The value of K_a for acetic acid is well known (1.8×10^{-5}). But how can we obtain the K_b value for the acetate ion? The answer lies in the relationships among K_a, K_b, and K_w. Note that when the expression for K_a for acetic acid is multiplied by the expression for K_b for the acetate ion, the result is K_w:

$$K_a \times K_b = \frac{[H^+][C_2H_3O_2^-]}{[HC_2H_3O_2]} \times \frac{[HC_2H_3O_2][OH^-]}{[C_2H_3O_2^-]} = [H^+][OH^-] = K_w$$

This is a very important result. For any weak acid and its conjugate base,

$$K_a \times K_b = K_w$$

Thus, when either K_a or K_b is known, the other can be calculated. For the acetate ion,

$$K_b = \frac{K_w}{K_a \text{ (for HC}_2\text{H}_3\text{O}_2)} = \frac{1.0 \times 10^{-14}}{1.8 \times 10^{-5}} = 5.6 \times 10^{-10}$$

This is the K_b value for the reaction described by Equation (14.7). Note that it is obtained from the K_a value of the parent weak acid, in this case acetic acid. The sodium acetate solution is an example of an important general case. *For any salt whose cation has neutral properties (such as Na$^+$ or K$^+$) and whose anion is the conjugate base of a weak acid, the aqueous solution will be basic.* The K_b value for the anion can be obtained from the relationship $K_b = K_w/K_a$. Equilibrium calculations of this type are illustrated in Sample Exercise 14.18.

A basic solution is formed if the anion of the salt is the conjugate base of a weak acid.

Sample Exercise 14.18 *Salts as Weak Bases*

Calculate the pH of a 0.30 M NaF solution. The K_a value for HF is 7.2×10^{-4}.

Solution

The major species in solution are

$$Na^+, \quad F^-, \quad \text{and} \quad H_2O$$

Since HF is a weak acid, the F^- ion must have a significant affinity for protons, and the dominant reaction will be

$$F^-(aq) + H_2O(l) \rightleftharpoons HF(aq) + OH^-(aq)$$

which yields the K_b expression

$$K_b = \frac{[HF][OH^-]}{[F^-]}$$

The value of K_b can be calculated from K_w and the K_a value for HF:

$$K_b = \frac{K_w}{K_a \text{ (for HF)}} = \frac{1.0 \times 10^{-14}}{7.2 \times 10^{-4}} = 1.4 \times 10^{-11}$$

The concentrations are as follows:

Initial Concentration (mol/L)		Equilibrium Concentration (mol/L)
$[F^-]_0 = 0.30$ $[HF]_0 = 0$ $[OH^-]_0 \approx 0$	$\xrightarrow[\text{H}_2\text{O to reach}]{\substack{x \text{ mol/L} \\ \text{reacts with}}} \atop \text{equilibrium}$	$[F^-] = 0.30 - x$ $[HF] = x$ $[OH^-] = x$

Thus

$$K_b = 1.4 \times 10^{-11} = \frac{[HF][OH^-]}{[F^-]} = \frac{(x)(x)}{0.30 - x} \approx \frac{x^2}{0.30}$$

and

$$x \approx 2.0 \times 10^{-6}$$

The approximation is valid by the 5% rule, so

$$[OH^-] = x = 2.0 \times 10^{-6} \; M$$
$$pOH = 5.69$$
$$pH = 14.00 - 5.69 = 8.31$$

As expected, the solution is basic.

See Exercise 14.107.

Base Strength in Aqueous Solution

To emphasize the concept of base strength, let us consider the basic properties of the cyanide ion. One relevant reaction is the dissociation of hydrocyanic acid in water:

$$HCN(aq) + H_2O(l) \rightleftharpoons H_3O^+(aq) + CN^-(aq) \qquad K_a = 6.2 \times 10^{-10}$$

Since HCN is such a weak acid, CN^- appears to be a *strong* base, showing a very high affinity for H^+ *compared to H_2O*, with which it is competing. However, we also need to look at the reaction in which cyanide ion reacts with water:

$$CN^-(aq) + H_2O(l) \rightleftharpoons HCN(aq) + OH^-(aq)$$

where
$$K_b = \frac{K_w}{K_a} = \frac{1.0 \times 10^{-14}}{6.2 \times 10^{-10}} = 1.6 \times 10^{-5}$$

In this reaction CN^- appears to be a weak base; the K_b value is only 1.6×10^{-5}. What accounts for this apparent difference in base strength? The key idea is that in the reaction of CN^- with H_2O, *CN^- is competing with OH^- for H^+, instead of competing with H_2O*, as it does in the HCN dissociation reaction. These equilibria show the following relative base strengths:

$$OH^- > CN^- > H_2O$$

Similar arguments can be made for other "weak" bases, such as ammonia, the acetate ion, the fluoride ion, and so on.

Salts That Produce Acidic Solutions

Some salts produce acidic solutions when dissolved in water. For example, when solid NH_4Cl is dissolved in water, NH_4^+ and Cl^- ions are present, with NH_4^+ behaving as a weak acid:

$$NH_4^+(aq) \rightleftharpoons NH_3(aq) + H^+(aq)$$

The Cl^- ion, having virtually no affinity for H^+ in water, does not affect the pH of the solution.

In general, *salts in which the anion is not a base and the cation is the conjugate acid of a weak base produce acidic solutions.*

Sample Exercise 14.19 *Salts as Weak Acids I*

Calculate the pH of a 0.10 M NH_4Cl solution. The K_b value for NH_3 is 1.8×10^{-5}.

Solution

The major species in solution are

$$NH_4^+, \quad Cl^-, \quad \text{and} \quad H_2O$$

Note that both NH_4^+ and H_2O can produce H^+. The dissociation reaction for the NH_4^+ ion is

$$NH_4^+(aq) \rightleftharpoons NH_3(aq) + H^+(aq)$$

for which
$$K_a = \frac{[NH_3][H^+]}{[NH_4^+]}$$

Note that although the K_b value for NH_3 is given, the reaction corresponding to K_b is not appropriate here, since NH_3 is not a major species in the solution. Instead, the given value of K_b is used to calculate K_a for NH_4^+ from the relationship

$$K_a \times K_b = K_w$$

Thus $\quad K_a \text{ (for NH}_4{}^+) = \dfrac{K_w}{K_b \text{ (for NH}_3)} = \dfrac{1.0 \times 10^{-14}}{1.8 \times 10^{-5}} = 5.6 \times 10^{-10}$

Although $NH_4{}^+$ is a very weak acid, as indicated by its K_a value, it is stronger than H_2O and thus will dominate in the production of H^+. Thus we will focus on the dissociation reaction of $NH_4{}^+$ to calculate the pH in this solution.

We solve the weak acid problem in the usual way:

Initial *Concentration (mol/L)*		*Equilibrium* *Concentration (mol/L)*
$[NH_4{}^+]_0 = 0.10$	x mol/L $NH_4{}^+$ dissociation	$[NH_4{}^+] = 0.10 - x$
$[NH_3]_0 = 0$	$\longrightarrow$	$[NH_3] = x$
$[H^+]_0 \approx 0$	to reach equilibrium	$[H^+] \approx x$

Thus

$$5.6 \times 10^{-10} = K_a = \dfrac{[H^+][NH_3]}{[NH_4{}^+]} = \dfrac{(x)(x)}{0.10 - x} \approx \dfrac{x^2}{0.10}$$

$$x \approx 7.5 \times 10^{-6}$$

The approximation is valid by the 5% rule, so

$$[H^+] = x = 7.5 \times 10^{-6} \, M \quad \text{and} \quad pH = 5.13$$

See Exercise 14.108.

Molecular Models: $Al(H_2O)_6{}^{3+}$, $Al(H_2O)_5OH^{2+}$

A second type of salt that produces an acidic solution is one that contains a *highly charged metal ion*. For example, when solid aluminum chloride ($AlCl_3$) is dissolved in water, the resulting solution is significantly acidic. Although the Al^{3+} ion is not itself a Brønsted–Lowry acid, the hydrated ion $Al(H_2O)_6{}^{3+}$ formed in water is a weak acid:

$$Al(H_2O)_6{}^{3+}(aq) \rightleftharpoons Al(OH)(H_2O)_5{}^{2+}(aq) + H^+(aq)$$

Section 14.9 contains a further discussion of the acidity of hydrated ions.

The high charge on the metal ion polarizes the O—H bonds in the attached water molecules, making the hydrogens in these water molecules more acidic than those in free water molecules. Typically, the higher the charge on the metal ion, the stronger the acidity of the hydrated ion.

Sample Exercise 14.20 *Salts as Weak Acids II*

Calculate the pH of a 0.010 M $AlCl_3$ solution. The K_a value for $Al(H_2O)_6{}^{3+}$ is 1.4×10^{-5}.

Solution

The major species in solution are

$$Al(H_2O)_6^{3+}, \quad Cl^-, \quad \text{and} \quad H_2O$$

Since the $Al(H_2O)_6^{3+}$ ion is a stronger acid than water, the dominant equilibrium is

$$Al(H_2O)_6^{3+}(aq) \rightleftharpoons Al(OH)(H_2O)_5^{2+}(aq) + H^+(aq)$$

and

$$1.4 \times 10^{-5} = K_a = \frac{[Al(OH)(H_2O)_5^{2+}][H^+]}{[Al(H_2O)_6^{3+}]}$$

This is a typical weak acid problem, which we can solve with the usual procedure:

Initial Concentration (mol/L)		Equilibrium Concentration (mol/L)
$[Al(H_2O)_6^{3+}]_0 = 0.010$ $[Al(OH)(H_2O)_5^{2+}]_0 = 0$ $[H^+]_0 \approx 0$	$\xrightarrow[\substack{\text{dissociates} \\ \text{to reach} \\ \text{equilibrium}}]{\substack{x \text{ mol/L} \\ Al(OH_2)_6^{3+}}}$	$[Al(H_2O)_6^{3+}] = 0.010 - x$ $[Al(OH)(H_2O)_5^{2+}] = x$ $[H^+] = x$

Thus

$$1.4 \times 10^{-5} = K_a = \frac{[Al(OH)(H_2O)_5^{2+}][H^+]}{[Al(H_2O)_6^{3+}]} = \frac{(x)(x)}{0.010 - x} \approx \frac{x^2}{0.010}$$

$$x \approx 3.7 \times 10^{-4}$$

Since the approximation is valid by the 5% rule,

$$[H^+] = x = 3.7 \times 10^{-4} \ M \quad \text{and} \quad pH = 3.43$$

See Exercises 14.113 and 14.114.

So far we have considered salts in which only one of the ions has acidic or basic properties. For many salts, such as ammonium acetate ($NH_4C_2H_3O_2$), both ions can affect the pH of the aqueous solution. Because the equilibrium calculations for these cases can be quite complicated, we will consider only the qualitative aspects of such problems. We can predict whether the solution will be basic, acidic, or neutral by comparing the K_a value for the acidic ion with the K_b value for the basic ion. If the K_a value for the acidic ion is larger than the K_b value for the basic ion, the solution will be acidic. If the K_b value is larger than the K_a value, the solution will be basic. Equal K_a and K_b values mean a neutral solution. These facts are summarized in Table 14.5.

Sample Exercise 14.21 *The Acid–Base Properties of Salts*

Predict whether an aqueous solution of each of the following salts will be acidic, basic, or neutral.

a. $NH_4C_2H_3O_2$ **b.** NH_4CN **c.** $Al_2(SO_4)_3$

Table 14.5 Qualitative Prediction of pH for Solutions of Salts for Which Both Cation and Anion Have Acidic or Basic Properties

$K_a > K_b$	pH < 7 (acidic)
$K_b > K_a$	pH > 7 (basic)
$K_a = K_b$	pH $= 7$ (neutral)

Solution

a. The ions in solution are NH_4^+ and $C_2H_3O_2^-$. As we mentioned previously, K_a for NH_4^+ is 5.6×10^{-10} and K_b for $C_2H_3O_2^-$ is 5.6×10^{-10}. Thus K_a for NH_4^+ is equal to K_b for $C_2H_3O_2^-$, and the solution will be neutral (pH = 7).

b. The solution will contain NH_4^+ and CN^- ions. The K_a value for NH_4^+ is 5.6×10^{-10} and

$$K_b \text{ (for } CN^-) = \frac{K_w}{K_a \text{ (for HCN)}} = 1.6 \times 10^{-5}$$

Since K_b for CN^- is much larger than K_a for NH_4^+, CN^- is a much stronger base than NH_4^+ is an acid. This solution will be basic.

c. The solution will contain $Al(H_2O)_6^{3+}$ and SO_4^{2-} ions. The K_a value for $Al(H_2O)_6^{3+}$ is 1.4×10^{-5}, as given in Sample Exercise 14.20. We must calculate K_b for SO_4^{2-}. The HSO_4^- ion is the conjugate acid of SO_4^{2-}, and its K_a value is K_{a_2} for sulfuric acid, or 1.2×10^{-2}. Therefore,

$$K_b \text{ (for } SO_4^{2-}) = \frac{K_w}{K_{a_2} \text{ (for sulfuric acid)}}$$

$$= \frac{1.0 \times 10^{-14}}{1.2 \times 10^{-2}} = 8.3 \times 10^{-13}$$

This solution will be acidic, since K_a for $Al(H_2O)_6^{3+}$ is much greater than K_b for SO_4^{2-}.

See Exercises 14.115 and 14.116.

The acid–base properties of aqueous solutions of various salts are summarized in Table 14.6.

Table 14.6 Acid–Base Properties of Various Types of Salts

Type of Salt	Examples	Comment	pH of Solution
Cation is from strong base; anion is from strong acid	KCl, KNO_3, $NaCl$, $NaNO_3$	Neither acts as an acid or a base	Neutral
Cation is from strong base; anion is from weak acid	$NaC_2H_3O_2$, KCN, NaF	Anion acts as a base; cation has no effect on pH	Basic
Cation is conjugate acid of weak base; anion is from strong acid	NH_4Cl, NH_4NO_3	Cation acts as acid; anion has no effect on pH	Acidic
Cation is conjugate acid of weak base; anion is conjugate base of weak acid	$NH_4C_2H_3O_2$, NH_4CN	Cation acts as an acid; anion acts as a base	Acidic if $K_a > K_b$, basic if $K_b > K_a$, neutral if $K_a = K_b$
Cation is highly charged metal ion; anion is from strong acid	$Al(NO_3)_3$, $FeCl_3$	Hydrated cation acts as an acid; anion has no effect on pH	Acidic

14.9 The Effect of Structure on Acid–Base Properties

We have seen that when a substance is dissolved in water, it produces an acidic solution if it can donate protons and produces a basic solution if it can accept protons. What structural properties of a molecule cause it to behave as an acid or as a base?

Any molecule containing a hydrogen atom is potentially an acid. However, many such molecules show no acidic properties. For example, molecules containing C—H bonds, such as chloroform ($CHCl_3$) and nitromethane (CH_3NO_2), do not produce acidic aqueous solutions because a C—H bond is both strong and nonpolar and thus there is no tendency to donate protons. On the other hand, although the H—Cl bond in gaseous hydrogen chloride is slightly stronger than a C—H bond, it is much more polar, and this molecule readily dissociates when dissolved in water.

Thus there are two main factors that determine whether a molecule containing an X—H bond will behave as a Brønsted–Lowry acid: the strength of the bond and the polarity of the bond.

To explore these factors let's consider the relative acid strengths of the hydrogen halides. The bond polarities vary as shown

$$H—F > H—Cl > H—Br > H—I$$

$\uparrow$ Most polar $\uparrow$ Least polar

because electronegativity decreases going down the group. Based on the high polarity of the H—F bond, we might expect hydrogen fluoride to be a very strong acid. In fact, among HX molecules, HF is the only weak acid ($K_a = 7.2 \times 10^{-4}$) when dissolved in water. The H—F bond is unusually strong, as shown in Table 14.7, and thus is difficult to break. This contributes significantly to the reluctance of the HF molecules to dissociate in water.

Another important class of acids are the oxyacids, which as we saw in Section 14.2 characteristically contain the grouping H—O—X. Several series of oxyacids are listed with their K_a values in Table 14.8. Note from these data that for a given series the acid strength increases with an increase in the number of oxygen atoms attached to the central atom. For example, in the series containing chlorine and a varying number of oxygen atoms, HOCl is a weak acid, but the acid strength is successively greater as the number of oxygen atoms increases. This happens because

Further aspects of acid strengths are discussed in Section 19.7.

Table 14.7 Bond Strengths and Acid Strengths for Hydrogen Halides

H—X Bond	Bond Strength (kJ/mol)	Acid Strength in Water
H—F	565	Weak
H—Cl	427	Strong
H—Br	363	Strong
H—I	295	Strong

Table 14.8 Several Series of Oxyacids and Their K_a Values

Oxyacid	Structure	K_a Value
$HClO_4$	$H-O-Cl$ (with O above, O to right, O below)	Large ($\sim 10^7$)
$HClO_3$	$H-O-Cl$ (with O above, O below)	~ 1
$HClO_2$	$H-O-Cl-O$	1.2×10^{-2}
$HClO$	$H-O-Cl$	3.5×10^{-8}
H_2SO_4	$H-O-S$ (with $O-H$ above, O to right, O below)	Large
H_2SO_3	$H-O-S$ (with $O-H$ above, O below)	1.5×10^{-2}
HNO_3	$H-O-N$ (with O above, O below)	Large
HNO_2	$H-O-N-O$	4.0×10^{-4}

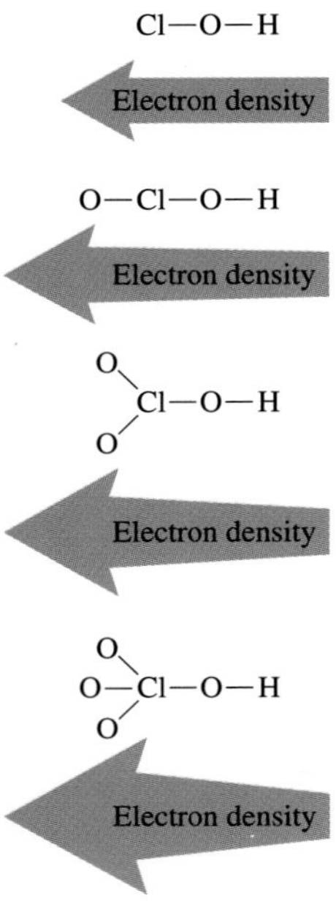

Figure 14.11

The effect of the number of attached oxygens on the O—H bond in a series of chlorine oxyacids. As the number of oxygen atoms attached to the chlorine atom increases, they become more effective at withdrawing electron density from the O—H bond, thereby weakening and polarizing it. This increases the tendency for the molecule to produce a proton, and so its acid strength increases.

the very electronegative oxygen atoms are able to draw electrons away from the chlorine atom and the O—H bond, as shown in Fig. 14.11. The net effect is to both polarize and weaken the O—H bond; this effect is more important as the number of attached oxygen atoms increases. This means that a proton is most readily produced by the molecule with the largest number of attached oxygen atoms ($HClO_4$).

This type of behavior is also observed for hydrated metal ions. Earlier in this chapter we saw that highly charged metal ions such as Al^{3+} produce acidic solutions. The acidity of the water molecules attached to the metal ion is increased by the attraction of electrons to the positive metal ion:

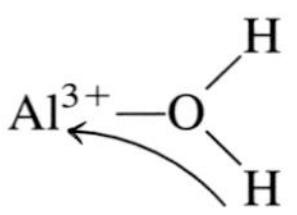

$$Al^{3+} \longleftarrow O \begin{matrix} H \\ H \end{matrix}$$

The greater the charge on the metal ion, the more acidic the hydrated ion becomes.

For acids containing the H—O—X grouping, the greater the ability of X to draw electrons toward itself, the greater is the acidity of the molecule. Since the electronegativity of X reflects its ability to attract the electrons involved in bonding, we might expect acid strength to depend on the electronegativity of X. In fact, there is an excellent correlation between the electronegativity of X and the acid strength for oxyacids, as shown in Table 14.9.

Table 14.9 Comparison of Electronegativity of X and K_a Value for a Series of Oxyacids

Acid	X	Electronegativity of X	K_a for Acid
HOCl	Cl	3.0	4×10^{-8}
HOBr	Br	2.8	2×10^{-9}
HOI	I	2.5	2×10^{-11}
HOCH$_3$	CH$_3$	2.3 (for carbon in CH$_3$)	$\sim 10^{-15}$

14.10 Acid–Base Properties of Oxides

We have just seen that molecules containing the grouping H—O—X can behave as acids and that the acid strength depends on the electron-withdrawing ability of X. But substances with this grouping also can behave as bases if the hydroxide ion instead of a proton is produced. What determines which behavior will occur? The answer lies mainly in the nature of the O—X bond. If X has a relatively high electronegativity, the O—X bond will be covalent and strong. When the compound containing the H—O—X grouping is dissolved in water, the O—X bond will remain intact. It will be the polar and relatively weak H—O bond that will tend to break, releasing a proton. On the other hand, if X has a very low electronegativity, the O—X bond will be ionic and subject to being broken in polar water. Examples are the ionic substances NaOH and KOH that dissolve in water to give the metal cation and the hydroxide ion.

A compound containing the H—O—X group will produce an acidic solution in water if the O—X bond is strong and covalent. If the O—X bond is ionic, the compound will produce a basic solution in water.

We can use these principles to explain the acid–base behavior of oxides when they are dissolved in water. For example, when a covalent oxide such as sulfur trioxide is dissolved in water, an acidic solution results because sulfuric acid is formed:

$$SO_3(g) + H_2O(l) \longrightarrow H_2SO_4(aq)$$

The structure of H_2SO_4 is shown in the margin. In this case, the strong, covalent O—S bonds remain intact and the H—O bonds break to produce protons. Other common covalent oxides that react with water to form acidic solutions are sulfur dioxide, carbon dioxide, and nitrogen dioxide, as shown by the following reactions:

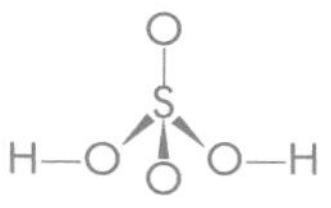

$$SO_2(g) + H_2O(l) \longrightarrow H_2SO_3(aq)$$
$$CO_2(g) + H_2O(l) \longrightarrow H_2CO_3(aq)$$
$$2NO_2(g) + H_2O(l) \longrightarrow HNO_3(aq) + HNO_2(aq)$$

Thus, when a covalent oxide dissolves in water, an acidic solution forms. These oxides are called **acidic oxides.**

On the other hand, when an ionic oxide dissolves in water, a basic solution results, as shown by the following reactions:

$$CaO(s) + H_2O(l) \longrightarrow Ca(OH)_2(aq)$$
$$K_2O(s) + H_2O(l) \longrightarrow 2KOH(aq)$$

These reactions can be explained by recognizing that the oxide ion has a high affinity for protons and reacts with water to produce hydroxide ions:

$$O^{2-}(aq) + H_2O(l) \longrightarrow 2OH^-(aq)$$

Thus the most ionic oxides, such as those of the Group 1A and 2A metals, produce basic solutions when they are dissolved in water. As a result, these oxides are called **basic oxides.**

14.11 The Lewis Acid–Base Model

We have seen that the first successful conceptualization of acid–base behavior was proposed by Arrhenius. This useful but limited model was replaced by the more general Brønsted–Lowry model. An even more general model for acid–base behavior was suggested by G. N. Lewis in the early 1920s. A **Lewis acid** is an *electron-pair acceptor*, and a **Lewis base** is an *electron-pair donor*. Another way of saying this is that a Lewis acid has an empty atomic orbital that it can use to accept (share) an electron pair from a molecule that has a lone pair of electrons (Lewis base). The three models for acids and bases are summarized in Table 14.10.

Note that Brønsted–Lowry acid–base reactions (proton donor–proton acceptor reactions) are encompassed by the Lewis model. For example, the reaction between a proton and an ammonia molecule, that is,

can be represented as a reaction between an electron-pair acceptor (H^+) and an electron-pair donor (NH_3). The same holds true for a reaction between a proton and a hydroxide ion:

The Lewis model encompasses the Brønsted–Lowry model, but the reverse is not true.

The real value of the Lewis model for acids and bases is that it covers many reactions that do not involve Brønsted–Lowry acids. For example, consider the gas-phase reaction between boron trifluoride and ammonia.

Table 14.10 Three Models for Acids and Bases		
Model	*Definition of Acid*	*Definition of Base*
Arrhenius	H^+ producer	OH^- producer
Brønsted–Lowry	H^+ donor	H^+ acceptor
Lewis	Electron-pair acceptor	Electron-pair donor

CHEMICAL IMPACT

Self-Destructing Paper

THE NEW YORK City Public Library has 88 miles of bookshelves, and on 36 miles of these shelves the books are quietly disintegrating between their covers. In fact, it is estimated that 40% of the books in the major research collections in the United States will soon be too fragile to handle.

The problem results from the acidic paper widely used in printing books in the past century. Ironically, books from the eighteenth, seventeenth, sixteenth, and even fifteenth century are in much better shape. Gutenberg Bibles contain paper that is in remarkably good condition. In those days, paper was made by hand from linen or rags, but in the nineteenth century, the demand for cheap paper skyrocketed. Paper manufacturers found that paper could be made economically, by machine, using wood pulp. To size the paper (that is, fill in microscopic holes to lower absorption of moisture and prevent seeping or spreading of inks), alum $[Al_2(SO_4)_3]$ was added in large amounts. Because the hydrated aluminum ion $[Al(H_2O)_6^{3+}]$ is an acid ($K_a \approx 10^{-5}$), paper manufactured using alum is quite acidic. Over time this acidity causes the paper fibers to disintegrate; the pages of books fall apart when they are used.

One could transfer the contents of the threatened books to microfilm, but that would be a very slow and expensive process. Can the books be chemically treated to neutralize the acid and stop the deterioration? Yes. In fact, you know enough chemistry at this point to design the treatment patented in 1936 by Otto Schierholz. He dipped individual pages in solutions of alkaline earth bicarbonate salts ($Mg(HCO_3)_2$, $Ca(HCO_3)_2$, etc.). The HCO_3^- ions present in these solutions react with the H^+ in the paper to give CO_2 and H_2O. This treatment works well and is used today to preserve especially important works, but it is slow and labor-intensive.

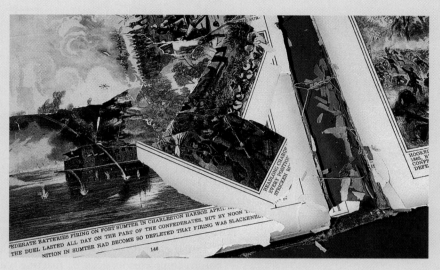

A book ravaged by the decomposition of acidic paper.

It would be much more economical if large numbers of books could be treated at one time without disturbing the bindings. However, soaking entire books in an aqueous solution is out of the question. A logical question then is: Are there gaseous bases that could be used to neutralize the acid? Certainly; the organic amines (general formula, RNH_2) are bases, and those with low molar masses are gases under normal conditions. Experiments in which books were treated using ammonia, butylamine ($CH_3CH_2CH_2CH_2NH_2$), and other amines have shown that the method works, but only for a short time. The amines do enter the paper and neutralize the acid, but being volatile, they gradually evaporate, leaving the paper in its original acidic condition.

A much more effective treatment involves diethylzinc [$(CH_3CH_2)_2Zn$], which boils at 117°C and 1 atm. Diethylzinc (DEZ) reacts with oxygen or water to produce ZnO as follows:

$$(CH_3CH_2)_2Zn(g) + 7O_2(g) \longrightarrow ZnO(s) + 4CO_2(g) + 5H_2O(g)$$

$$(CH_3CH_2)_2Zn(g) + H_2O(g) \longrightarrow ZnO(s) + 2CH_3CH_3(g)$$

The solid zinc oxide produced in these reactions is deposited among the paper fibers, and being a basic oxide, it neutralizes the acid present as shown in the equation

$$ZnO + 2H^+ \longrightarrow Zn^{2+} + H_2O$$

One major problem is that DEZ ignites spontaneously on contact with air. Therefore, this treatment must be carried out in a chamber filled mainly with $N_2(g)$, where the amount of O_2 present can be rigorously controlled. The pressure in the chamber must be maintained well below one atmosphere both to lower the boiling point of DEZ and to remove excess moisture from the book's pages. Several major DEZ fires have slowed its implementation as a book preservative. However, the Library of Congress has designed a new DEZ treatment plant that includes a chamber large enough for approximately 9000 books to be treated at one time.

Figure 14.12
The $Al(H_2O)_6^{3+}$ ion.

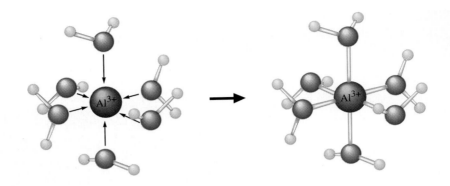

Molecular Model: H_3NBF_3

Here the electron-deficient BF_3 molecule (there are only six electrons around the boron) completes its octet by reacting with NH_3, which has a lone pair of electrons. In fact, as mentioned in Chapter 8, the electron deficiency of boron trifluoride makes it very reactive toward any electron-pair donor. That is, it is a strong Lewis acid.

The hydration of a metal ion, such as Al^{3+}, also can be viewed as a Lewis acid–base reaction:

Here the Al^{3+} ion accepts one electron pair from each of six water molecules to form $Al(H_2O)_6^{3+}$ (see Fig. 14.12).

In addition, the reaction between a covalent oxide and water to form a Brønsted–Lowry acid can be defined as a Lewis acid–base reaction. An example is the reaction between sulfur trioxide and water:

Note that as the water molecule attaches to sulfur trioxide, a proton shift occurs to form sulfuric acid.

Sample Exercise 14.22 Lewis Acids and Bases

For each reaction, identify the Lewis acid and base.

a. $Ni^{2+}(aq) + 6NH_3(aq) \longrightarrow Ni(NH_3)_6^{2+}(aq)$
b. $H^+(aq) + H_2O(aq) \rightleftharpoons H_3O^+(aq)$

Solution

a. Each NH_3 molecule donates an electron pair to the Ni^{2+} ion:

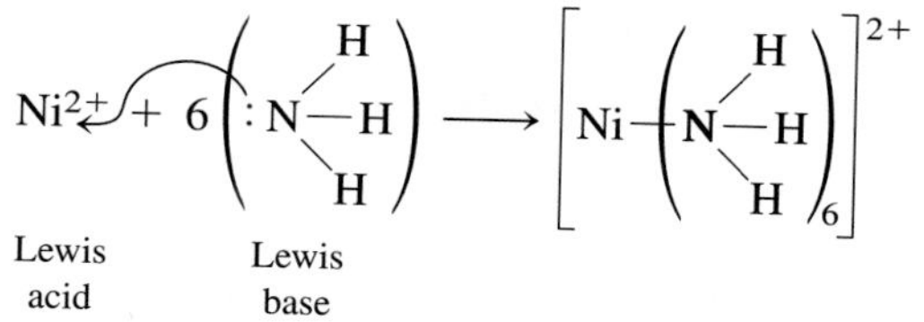

The nickel(II) ion is the Lewis acid, and ammonia is the Lewis base.
b. The proton is the Lewis acid and the water molecule is the Lewis base:

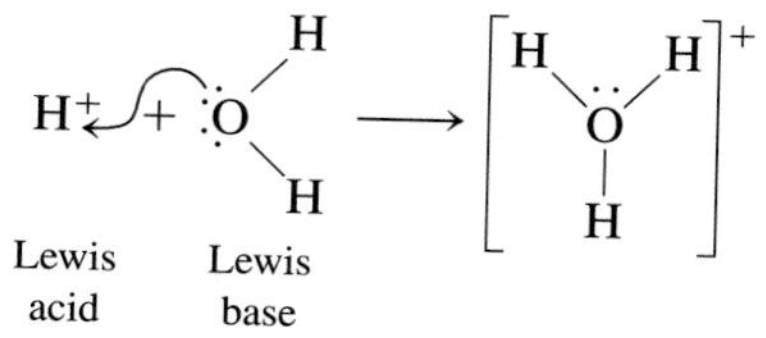

See Exercises 14.123 and 14.124.

14.12 Strategy for Solving Acid–Base Problems: A Summary

In this chapter we have encountered many different situations involving aqueous solutions of acids and bases, and in the next chapter we will encounter still more. In solving for the equilibrium concentrations in these aqueous solutions, it is tempting to create a pigeonhole for each possible situation and to memorize the procedures necessary to deal with that particular case. This approach is just not practical and usually leads to frustration: Too many pigeonholes are required—there seems to be an infinite number of cases. But you can handle any case successfully by taking a systematic, patient, and thoughtful approach. When analyzing an acid–base equilibrium problem, do *not* ask yourself how a memorized solution can be used to solve the problem. Instead, ask this question: *What are the major species in the solution and what is their chemical behavior?*

The most important part of doing a complicated acid–base equilibrium problem is the analysis you do at the beginning of a problem.

What major species are present?

Does a reaction occur that can be assumed to go to completion?

What equilibrium dominates the solution?

Let the problem guide you. Be patient.

The following steps outline a general strategy for solving problems involving acid–base equilibria.

Solving Acid–Base Problems

STEP 1

List the major species in solution.

STEP 2

Look for reactions that can be assumed to go to completion, for example, a strong acid dissociating or H^+ reacting with OH^-.

STEP 3

For a reaction that can be assumed to go to completion:
a. Determine the concentration of the products.
b. Write down the major species in solution after the reaction.

STEP 4

Look at each major component of the solution and decide if it is an acid or a base.

STEP 5

Pick the equilibrium that will control the pH. Use known values of the dissociation constants for the various species to help decide on the dominant equilibrium.
a. Write the equation for the reaction and the equilibrium expression.
b. Compute the initial concentrations (assuming the dominant equilibrium has not yet occurred, that is, no acid dissociation, etc.).
c. Define x.
d. Compute the equilibrium concentrations in terms of x.
e. Substitute the concentrations into the equilibrium expression, and solve for x.
f. Check the validity of the approximation.
g. Calculate the pH and other concentrations as required.

Although these steps may seem somewhat cumbersome, especially for simpler problems, they will become increasingly helpful as the aqueous solutions become more complicated. If you develop the habit of approaching acid–base problems systematically, the more complex cases will be much easier to manage.

For Review

Summary

In this chapter we have developed several models of acid–base behavior and have applied fundamental equilibrium principles to calculate the pH values for solutions of acids and bases.

Arrhenius postulated that acids produce H^+ ions in solutions and bases produce OH^- ions. The Brønsted–Lowry model is more general: An acid is a proton donor, and a base is a proton acceptor. Water acts as a Brønsted–Lowry base when it accepts a proton from an acid to form a hydronium ion:

$$\underset{\text{Acid}}{HA(aq)} + \underset{\text{Base}}{H_2O(l)} \rightleftharpoons \underset{\substack{\text{Conjugate} \\ \text{acid}}}{H_3O^+(aq)} + \underset{\substack{\text{Conjugate} \\ \text{base}}}{A^-(aq)}$$

A conjugate base is everything that remains of the acid molecule after the proton is lost. A conjugate acid is formed when a proton is transferred to the base. Two substances related in this way are called a conjugate acid–base pair.

The equilibrium expression for the dissociation of an acid in water is

$$K_a = \frac{[H^+][A^-]}{[HA]}$$

where H_3O^+ is simplified to H^+, $[H_2O]$ is not included because it is assumed to be constant, and K_a is called the acid dissociation constant. The strength of an acid is defined by the position of the dissociation (ionization) equilibrium. A small value of K_a denotes a weak acid, one that does not dissociate to any great extent in aqueous solution. A strong acid is one for which the dissociation equilibrium lies far to the right—the K_a value is very large.

Strong acids such as nitric, hydrochloric, sulfuric, and perchloric acids have weak conjugate bases, which have a low affinity for a proton. The strength of an acid is inversely related to the strength of its conjugate base.

Water is an amphoteric substance—it can behave either as an acid or as a base. The autoionization of water demonstrates this property, since one water molecule transfers a proton to another water molecule to produce a hydronium ion and a hydroxide ion:

$$2H_2O(l) \rightleftharpoons H_3O^+(aq) + OH^-(aq)$$

This leads to the expression

$$K_w = [H^+][OH^-]$$

where K_w is called the ion-product constant. It has been experimentally shown that at 25°C in pure water $[H^+] = [OH^-] = 1.0 \times 10^{-7}\ M$. Thus, at 25°C,

$$K_w = 1.0 \times 10^{-14}$$

In an acidic solution, $[H^+]$ is greater than $[OH^-]$. In a basic solution, $[OH^-]$ is greater than $[H^+]$. In a neutral solution, $[H^+]$ is equal to $[OH^-]$.

To describe $[H^+]$ in aqueous solutions, we often use the pH scale, where

$$pH = -\log[H^+]$$

Key Terms

Section 14.1
Arrhenius concept
Brønsted–Lowry model
hydronium ion
conjugate base
conjugate acid
conjugate acid–base pair
acid dissociation constant

Section 14.2
strong acid
weak acid
diprotic acid
oxyacids
organic acids
carboxyl group
monoprotic acid
amphoteric substance
autoionization
ion-product (dissociation) constant

Section 14.3
pH scale

Section 14.4
major species

Section 14.5
percent dissociation

Section 14.6
strong bases
slaked lime
lime–soda process
weak base
amine

Section 14.7
polyprotic acid
triprotic acid

Section 14.8
salt

Section 14.10
acidic oxide
basic oxide

Section 14.11
Lewis acid
Lewis base

Since pH is a log scale based on 10, the pH changes by 1 for every change by a power of 10 in $[H^+]$. Because pH is defined as $-\log[H^+]$, the pH decreases as $[H^+]$ increases.

The percent dissociation of a weak acid is defined as follows:

$$\text{Percent dissociation} = \frac{\text{amount dissociated (mol/L)}}{\text{initial concentration (mol/L)}} \times 100\%$$

This is another measure of the strength of an acid: The larger the percent dissociation, the stronger is the acid. As $[HA]_0$ decreases, $[H^+]$ decreases, but the percent dissociation increases. That is, dilution causes an increase in the percent dissociation.

Strong bases are hydroxide salts, such as NaOH or KOH, that dissociate completely in water. Bases do not have to contain the hydroxide ion; they can be species that remove a proton from water, producing the hydroxide ion. For example, ammonia is a base because it can accept a proton from water:

$$NH_3(aq) + H_2O(l) \rightleftharpoons NH_4^+(aq) + OH^-(aq)$$

The equilibrium expression is

$$K_b = \frac{[NH_4^+][OH^-]}{[NH_3]}$$

where K_b always refers to a reaction in which a base reacts with water to produce the conjugate acid and hydroxide ion. Because bases like ammonia must compete with the hydroxide ion for the proton, values of K_b for these bases are typically much less than 1, and these substances are called weak bases.

A polyprotic acid is an acid with more than one acidic proton, which dissociates in a stepwise fashion with a K_a value for each step. Typically, for a weak polyprotic acid,

$$K_{a_1} > K_{a_2} > K_{a_3}$$

Sulfuric acid is unique in that it is a strong acid in the first dissociation step and a weak acid in the second step.

Salts can exhibit neutral, acidic, or basic properties when dissolved in water. Salts that contain the cations of strong bases and the anions of strong acids produce neutral aqueous solutions. A basic solution is produced when the dissolved salt has a neutral cation and an anion that is the conjugate base of a weak acid. An acidic solution is produced when the dissolved salt has a neutral anion and a cation that is the conjugate acid of a weak base. Acidic solutions are also produced by salts containing a highly charged metal cation. For example, the hydrated ion $Al(H_2O)_6^{3+}$ is a weak acid.

Most substances that function as acids or bases contain the H—O—X grouping. Molecules where the O—X is a strong covalent bond tend to behave as acids, especially when X is highly electronegative, because the H—O bond is polarized and weakened. When X has low electronegativity (if X is a metal, for example), the O—X bond tends to be ionic and hydroxide ions form when these substances are dissolved in water.

The Lewis model for acids and bases generalizes the concept of acid–base behavior in terms of electron pairs. A Lewis acid is an electron-pair acceptor, and a Lewis base is an electron-pair donor. The value of the Lewis model is that it covers many reactions that do not involve Brønsted–Lowry acids and bases.

In-Class Discussion Questions

These questions are designed to be considered by groups of students in class. Often these questions work well for introducing a particular topic in class.

1. Consider two beakers of pure water at different temperatures. How do their pH values compare? Which is more acidic? more basic? Explain.

2. Differentiate between the terms *strength* and *concentration* as they apply to acids and bases. When is HCl strong? weak? concentrated? dilute? Answer the same questions for ammonia. Is the conjugate base of a weak acid a strong base?

3. Sketch two graphs: (a) percent dissociation for weak acid HA versus the initial concentration of HA ($[HA]_0$) and (b) H^+ concentration versus $[HA]_0$. Explain both.

4. Consider a solution prepared by mixing a weak acid HA and HCl. What are the major species? Explain what is occurring in solution. How would you calculate the pH? What if you added NaA to this solution? then added NaOH?

5. Explain why salts can be acidic, basic, or neutral, and show examples. Do this without specific numbers.

6. Consider two separate aqueous solutions: one of a weak acid HA and one of HCl. Assuming you started with 10 molecules of each:
   a. Draw a picture of what each solution looks like at equilibrium.
   b. What are the major species in each beaker?
   c. From your pictures, calculate the K_a values of each acid.
   d. Order the following from the strongest to the weakest base: H_2O, A^-, Cl^-. Explain your order.

7. You are asked to calculate the H^+ concentration in a solution of NaOH(aq). Because sodium hydroxide is a base, can we say there is no H^+, since having H^+ would imply that the solution is acidic?

8. Consider a solution prepared by mixing a weak acid HA, HCl, and NaA. Which of the following statements best describes what happens?
   a. The H^+ from the HCl reacts completely with the A^- from the NaA. Then, the HA dissociates somewhat.
   b. The H^+ from the HCl reacts somewhat with the A^- from the NaA to make HA, while the HA is dissociating. Eventually you have equal amounts of everything.
   c. The H^+ from the HCl reacts somewhat with the A^- from the NaA to make HA while the HA is dissociating. Eventually all the reactions have equal rates.
   d. The H^+ from the HCl reacts completely with the A^- from the NaA. Then the HA dissociates somewhat until "too much" H^+ and A^- are formed, so the H^+ and A^- react to form HA, etc. Eventually equilibrium is reached.
   Justify your choice, and for choices you did not pick, explain what is wrong with them.

9. Consider a solution formed by mixing 100.0 mL of 0.10 M HA ($K_a = 1.0 \times 10^{-6}$), 100.00 mL of 0.10 M NaA, and 100.0 mL of 0.10 M HCl. In calculating the pH for the final solution, you would make some assumptions about the order in which various reactions occur to simplify the calculations. State these assumptions. Does it matter whether or not the reactions actually occur in the assumed order? Explain.

10. A certain sodium compound is dissolved in water to liberate Na^+ ions and a certain negative ion. What evidence would you look for to determine whether the anion is behaving as an acid or a base? How could you tell whether the anion is a strong base? Explain how the anion could behave simultaneously as an acid and a base.

11. Acids and bases can be thought of as chemical opposites (acids are proton donors, and bases are proton acceptors). Therefore, one might think that $K_a = 1/K_b$. Why isn't this the case? What is the relationship between K_a and K_b? Prove it with a derivation.

12. Consider two solutions of the salts NaX(aq) and NaY(aq) at equal concentrations. What would you need to know in order to determine which solution has the higher pH? Explain how you would decide (perhaps even provide a sample calculation).

13. What is meant by *pH*? True or false, a strong acid solution always has a lower pH than a weak acid solution. Explain.

14. Why is the pH of water at 25°C equal to 7.00?

15. Can the pH of a solution be negative? Explain.

A blue question or exercise number indicates that the answer to that question or exercise appears at the back of this book and a solution appears in the *Solutions Guide.*

Questions

16. Define each of the following using the Arrhenius model.
   a. strong acid   c. weak acid
   b. strong base   d. weak base

17. Define each of the following.
   a. Arrhenius acid
   b. Brønsted–Lowry acid
   c. Lewis acid
   Which of the definitions is most general? Write reactions to justify your answer.

18. Why is H_3O^+ the strongest acid and OH^- the strongest base that can exist in significant amounts in aqueous solutions?

19. Give the conditions for a neutral solution at 25°C, in terms of $[H^+]$, pH, and the relationship between $[H^+]$ and $[OH^-]$.

20. How many significant figures are there in the numbers: 10.78, 6.78, 0.78? If these were pH values, to how many significant figures can you express the $[H^+]$? Explain any discrepancies between your answers to the two questions.

21. The presence of what element most commonly results in basic properties for an organic compound?

22. For oxyacids, how does acid strength depend on
    a. strength of the bond to the acidic hydrogen atom?
    b. electronegativity of the element bonded to the oxygen atom that bears the acidic hydrogen?
    c. the number of oxygen atoms?

23. How does the strength of a conjugate base depend on the factors listed in Question 22?

24. In terms of orbitals and electron arrangements, what must be present for a molecule or an ion to act as a Lewis acid? What must be present for a molecule or an ion to act as a Lewis base?

25. Consider the reaction of acetic acid in water

    $$CH_3CO_2H(aq) + H_2O(l) \rightleftharpoons CH_3CO_2^-(aq) + H_3O^+(aq)$$

    where $K_a = 1.8 \times 10^{-5}$.
    a. Which two bases are competing for the proton?
    b. Which is the stronger base?
    c. In light of your answer to b, why do we classify the acetate ion ($CH_3CO_2^-$) as a weak base? Use an appropriate reaction to justify your answer.

26. In general, as base strength increases, conjugate acid strength decreases. Explain why the conjugate acid of the weak base NH_3 is a weak acid.

Exercises

In this section similar exercises are paired.

Nature of Acids and Bases

27. Write balanced equations that describe the following reactions.
    a. the dissociation of perchloric acid in water
    b. the dissociation of propanoic acid ($CH_3CH_2CO_2H$) in water
    c. the dissociation of ammonium ion in water

28. Write the dissociation reaction and the corresponding K_a equilibrium expression for each of the following acids in water.
    a. $HC_2H_3O_2$ b. $Co(H_2O)_6^{3+}$ c. $CH_3NH_3^+$

29. For each of the following aqueous reactions, identify the acid, the base, the conjugate base, and the conjugate acid.
    a. $HF + H_2O \rightleftharpoons F^- + H_3O^+$
    b. $H_2SO_4 + H_2O \rightleftharpoons H_3O^+ + HSO_4^-$
    c. $HSO_4^- + H_2O \rightleftharpoons SO_4^{2-} + H_3O^+$

30. For each of the following aqueous reactions, identify the acid, the base, the conjugate base, and the conjugate acid.
    a. $Al(H_2O)_6^{3+} + H_2O \rightleftharpoons H_3O^+ + Al(H_2O)_5(OH)^{2+}$
    b. $H_2O + HONH_3^+ \rightleftharpoons HONH_2 + H_3O^+$
    c. $HOCl + C_6H_5NH_2 \rightleftharpoons OCl^- + C_6H_5NH_3^+$

31. Classify each of the following as a strong acid or a weak acid in aqueous solution.

    a. HNO_2 c. HCl
    b. HNO_3 d. HF

32. Classify each of the following as a strong acid or a weak acid in aqueous solution.
    a. $HClO_4$ c. H_2SO_4
    b. $HOCl$ d. HSO_4^-

33. Use Table 14.2 to order the following from the strongest to the weakest acid.

    $$H_2O, \quad HNO_3, \quad HOCl, \quad NH_4^+$$

34. Use Table 14.2 to order the following from the strongest to the weakest base.

    $$H_2O, \quad NO_3^-, \quad OCl^-, \quad NH_3$$

35. You may need Table 14.2 to answer the following questions.
    a. Which is the stronger acid, HCl or H_2O?
    b. Which is the stronger acid, H_2O or HNO_2?
    c. Which is the stronger acid, HCN or HOC_6H_5?

36. You may need Table 14.2 to answer the following questions.
    a. Which is the stronger base, Cl^- or H_2O?
    b. Which is the stronger base, H_2O or NO_2^-?
    c. Which is the stronger base, CN^- or $OC_6H_5^-$?

Autoionization of Water and the pH Scale

37. Calculate the $[OH^-]$ of each of the following solutions at 25°C. Identify each solution as neutral, acidic, or basic.
    a. $[H^+] = 1.0 \times 10^{-7} M$ c. $[H^+] = 1.9 \times 10^{-11} M$
    b. $[H^+] = 6.7 \times 10^{-4} M$ d. $[H^+] = 2.3 M$

38. Calculate the $[H^+]$ of each of the following solutions at 25°C. Identify each solution as neutral, acidic, or basic.
    a. $[OH^-] = 3.6 M$ c. $[OH^-] = 2.2 \times 10^{-3} M$
    b. $[OH^-] = 9.7 \times 10^{-9} M$ d. $[OH^-] = 1.0 \times 10^{-7} M$

39. Values of K_w as a function of temperature are as follows:

Temperature (°C)	K_w
0	1.14×10^{-15}
25	1.00×10^{-14}
35	2.09×10^{-14}
40.	2.92×10^{-14}
50.	5.47×10^{-14}

    a. Is the autoionization of water exothermic or endothermic?
    b. Calculate $[H^+]$ and $[OH^-]$ in a neutral solution at 50°C.

40. At 40°C, the value of K_w is 2.92×10^{-14}.
    a. Calculate the $[H^+]$ and $[OH^-]$ in pure water at 40°C.
    b. What is the pH of pure water at 40°C?
    c. If the hydroxide ion concentration in a solution is 0.10 M, what is the pH at 40°C?

41. Calculate the pH and pOH of the solutions in Exercise 37.

42. Calculate the pH and pOH of the solutions in Exercise 38.

43. Calculate $[H^+]$ and $[OH^-]$ for each solution at 25°C. Identify each solution as neutral, acidic, or basic.
   a. pH = 7.40 (the normal pH of blood)
   b. pH = 15.3
   c. pH = −1.0
   d. pH = 3.20
   e. pOH = 5.0
   f. pOH = 9.60

44. Calculate $[H^+]$ and $[OH^-]$ for each solution at 25°C. Identify each solution as neutral, acidic, or basic.
   a. pH = −0.42   **d.** pOH = 14.30
   b. pH = 3.42   **e.** pOH = 9.67
   c. pH = 10.67   **f.** pOH = 1.15

45. The pH of a sample of milk is 6.77 at 25°C. Calculate the pOH, $[H^+]$, and $[OH^-]$ for this sample. Is milk acidic or basic?

46. The pOH of a sample of baking soda dissolved in water is 5.74 at 25°C. Calculate the pH, $[H^+]$, and $[OH^-]$ for this sample. Is the solution acidic or basic?

Solutions of Acids

47. What are the major species present in 0.250 M solutions of each of the following acids? Calculate the pH of each of these solutions.
   a. HCl   **b.** HBr (a strong acid)

48. What are the major species present in 0.250 M solutions of each of the following acids? Calculate the pH of each of these solutions.
   a. $HClO_4$ **b.** HNO_3

49. Calculate the pH of each of the following solutions of a strong acid in water.
   a. 0.10 M HCl   **c.** 1.0×10^{-11} M HCl
   b. 5.0 M HCl

50. Calculate the pH of each of the following solutions of a strong acid in water.
   a. 5.6×10^{-3} M $HClO_4$ **c.** 8.1×10^{-10} M $HClO_4$
   b. 2.0 M $HClO_4$

51. A solution is prepared by adding 50.0 mL of 0.050 M HCl to 150.0 mL of 0.10 M HNO_3. Calculate the concentrations of all species in this solution.

52. A solution is prepared by mixing 90.0 mL of 5.00 M HCl and 30.0 mL of 8.00 M HNO_3. Water is then added until the final volume is 1.00 L. Calculate $[H^+]$, $[OH^-]$, and the pH for this solution.

53. Calculate the concentration of an aqueous HCl solution that has pH = 2.50.

54. Calculate the concentration of an aqueous HNO_3 solution that has pH = 5.10.

55. What are the major species present in 0.250 M solutions of each of the following acids? Calculate the pH of each of these solutions.
   a. HNO_2 **b.** CH_3CO_2H $(HC_2H_3O_2)$

56. What are the major species present in 0.250 M solutions of each of the following acids? Calculate the pH of each of these solutions.
   a. HOC_6H_5 **b.** HCN

57. Using the K_a values given in Table 14.2, calculate the concentrations of all species present and the pH of a 1.5 M HOCl solution.

58. A solution with a total volume of 250.0 mL is prepared by diluting 20.0 mL of glacial acetic acid with water. Calculate $[H^+]$ and the pH of this solution. Assume that glacial acetic acid is pure liquid acetic acid with a density of 1.05 g/cm^3.

59. Calculate the concentration of all species present and the pH of a 0.020 M HF solution.

60. Calculate the pH of a 0.20 M solution of iodic acid (HIO_3, $K_a = 0.17$).

61. Calculate the pH of a 0.50 M solution of chlorous acid ($HClO_2$, $K_a = 1.2 \times 10^{-2}$).

62. Monochloroacetic acid, $HC_2H_2ClO_2$, is a skin irritant that is used in "chemical peels" intended to remove the top layer of dead skin from the face and ultimately improve the complexion. The value of K_a for monochloroacetic acid is 1.35×10^{-3}. Calculate the pH of a 0.10 M solution of monochloroacetic acid.

63. Calculate the pH of a solution containing a mixture of 0.10 M HCl and 0.10 M HOCl.

64. Calculate the pH of a solution that contains 1.0 M HF and 1.0 M HOC_6H_5. Also calculate the concentration of $OC_6H_5^-$ in this solution at equilibrium.

65. Calculate the percent dissociation of the acid in each of the following solutions.
   a. 0.50 M acetic acid
   b. 0.050 M acetic acid
   c. 0.0050 M acetic acid
   d. Use Le Châtelier's principle to explain why percent dissociation increases as the concentration of a weak acid decreases.
   e. Even though the percent dissociation increases from solutions a to c, the $[H^+]$ decreases. Explain.

66. Using the K_a values in Table 14.2, calculate the percent dissociation in a 0.20 M solution of each of the following acids.
   a. nitric acid (HNO_3)
   b. nitrous acid (HNO_2)
   c. phenol (HOC_6H_5)
   d. How is percent dissociation of an acid related to the K_a value for the acid (assuming equal initial concentrations of acids)?

67. For propanoic acid ($HC_3H_5O_2$, $K_a = 1.3 \times 10^{-5}$), calculate the [H^+], pH, and percent dissociation for a 0.10 M solution.

68. Calculate the percent dissociation for a 0.22 M solution of chlorous acid ($HClO_2$, $K_a = 1.2 \times 10^{-2}$).

69. A 0.15 M solution of a weak acid is 3.0% dissociated. Calculate K_a.

70. In a 0.100 M solution of HF, the percent dissociation is 8.1%. Calculate K_a.

71. The pH of a 0.063 M solution of hypobromous acid (HOBr but usually written HBrO) is 4.95. Calculate K_a.

72. Trichloroacetic acid (CCl_3CO_2H) is a corrosive acid that is used to precipitate proteins. The pH of a 0.050 M solution of trichloroacetic acid is the same as the pH of a 0.040 M $HClO_4$ solution. Calculate K_a for trichloroacetic acid.

73. A solution of formic acid (HCOOH, $K_a = 1.8 \times 10^{-4}$) has a pH of 2.70. Calculate the initial concentration of formic acid in this solution.

74. One mole of a weak acid HA was dissolved in 2.0 L of water. After the system had come to equilibrium, the concentration of HA was found to be 0.45 M. Calculate K_a for HA.

Solutions of Bases

75. Write the reaction and the corresponding K_b equilibrium expression for each of the following substances acting as bases in water.
    a. NH_3 b. C_5H_5N

76. Write the reaction and the corresponding K_b equilibrium expression for each of the following substances acting as bases in water.
    a. aniline, $C_6H_5NH_2$ b. dimethylamine, $(CH_3)_2NH$

77. Use Table 14.3 to help order the following bases from strongest to weakest.

$$NO_3^-, \quad H_2O, \quad NH_3, \quad C_5H_5N$$

78. Use Table 14.3 to help order the following acids from strongest to weakest.

$$HNO_3, \quad H_2O, \quad NH_4^+, \quad C_5H_5NH^+$$

79. Use Table 14.3 to help answer the following questions.
    a. Which is the stronger base, NO_3^- or NH_3?
    b. Which is the stronger base, H_2O or NH_3?
    c. Which is the stronger base, OH^- or NH_3?
    d. Which is the stronger base, NH_3 or CH_3NH_2?

80. Use Table 14.3 to help answer the following questions.
    a. Which is the stronger acid, HNO_3 or NH_4^+?
    b. Which is the stronger acid, H_2O or NH_4^+?
    c. Which is the stronger acid, NH_4^+ or $CH_3NH_3^+$?

81. Calculate the pH of the following solutions.
    a. 0.10 M NaOH   c. 2.0 M NaOH
    b. 1.0×10^{-10} M NaOH

82. Calculate the pH of the following solutions.
    a. 0.0062 M $Sr(OH)_2$
    b. 0.75 M $Sr(OH)_2$
    c. 5.0×10^{-10} M $Sr(OH)_2$

83. What are the major species present in 0.150 M solutions of each of the following bases?
    a. KOH   b. $Ca(OH)_2$
    What is [OH^-] and the pH of each of these solutions?

84. What are the major species present in the following mixtures of bases?
    a. 0.050 M NaOH and 0.050 M LiOH
    b. 0.0010 M $Ba(OH)_2$ and 0.020 M RbOH
    What is [OH^-] and the pH of each of these solutions?

85. Calculate the concentration of an aqueous KOH solution that has pH = 10.50.

86. Calculate the concentration of an aqueous $Ba(OH)_2$ that has pH = 10.50.

87. What are the major species present in a 0.150 M NH_3 solution? Calculate the [OH^-] and the pH of this solution.

88. For the reaction of hydrazine (N_2H_4) in water,

$$H_2NNH_2(aq) + H_2O(l) \rightleftharpoons H_2NNH_3^+(aq) + OH^-(aq)$$

K_b is 3.0×10^{-6}. Calculate the concentrations of all species and the pH of a 2.0 M solution of hydrazine in water.

89. Calculate [OH^-], [H^+], and the pH of 0.20 M solutions of each of the following amines.
    a. Triethylamine [$(C_2H_5)_3N$, $K_b = 4.0 \times 10^{-4}$]
    b. Hydroxylamine ($HONH_2$, $K_b = 1.1 \times 10^{-8}$)

90. Calculate [OH^-], [H^+], and the pH of 0.20 M solutions of each of the following amines (the K_b values are found in Table 14.3).
    a. Aniline   b. Pyridine

91. Calculate the pH of a 0.20 M $C_2H_5NH_2$ solution ($K_b = 5.6 \times 10^{-4}$).

92. Calculate the pH of a 0.050 M $(C_2H_5)_2NH$ solution ($K_b = 1.3 \times 10^{-3}$).

93. Calculate the percent ionization in each of the following solutions.
    a. 0.10 M NH_3 b. 0.010 M NH_3

94. Calculate the percent ionization in each of the following solutions (see Table 14.3 for K_b values).
    a. 0.10 M hydroxylamine ($HONH_2$, $K_b = 1.1 \times 10^{-8}$)
    b. 0.10 M methylamine (CH_3NH_2)

95. Codeine ($C_{18}H_{21}NO_3$) is a derivative of morphine that is used as an analgesic, narcotic, or antitussive. It was once commonly used in cough syrups but is now available only by prescription because of its addictive properties. If the pH of a 1.7×10^{-3} M solution of codeine is 9.59, calculate K_b.

96. The pH of a 1.00×10^{-3} M solution of pyrrolidine is 10.82. Calculate K_b.

$$CH_2 - CH_2$$
$$| \quad |$$
$$CH_2 \quad CH_2$$
$$\backslash \quad /$$
$$NH$$

Pyrrolidine

Polyprotic Acids

97. Write out the stepwise K_a reactions for the diprotic acid H_2SO_3.

98. Write out the stepwise K_a reactions for citric acid ($H_3C_6H_5O_7$), a triprotic acid.

99. Using the K_a values in Table 14.4 and only the first dissociation step, calculate the pH of 0.10 M solutions of each of the following polyprotic acids.
a. H_3PO_4 b. H_2CO_3

100. Arsenic acid (H_3AsO_4) is a triprotic acid with $K_{a_1} = 5 \times 10^{-3}$, $K_{a_2} = 8 \times 10^{-8}$, and $K_{a_3} = 6 \times 10^{-10}$. Calculate $[H^+]$, $[OH^-]$, $[H_3AsO_4]$, $[H_2AsO_4^-]$, $[HAsO_4^{2-}]$, and $[AsO_4^{3-}]$ in a 0.20 M arsenic acid solution.

101. Calculate the pH of a 2.0 M H_2SO_4 solution.

102. Calculate the pH of a 5.0×10^{-3} M solution of H_2SO_4.

Acid–Base Properties of Salts

103. Arrange the following 0.10 M solutions in order of most acidic to most basic.

KOH, KCl, KCN, NH_4Cl, HCl

104. Arrange the following 0.10 M solutions in order of most acidic to most basic.

$Ca(NO_3)_2$, $NaNO_2$, HNO_3, NH_4NO_3, $Ca(OH)_2$

105. Given that the K_a value for acetic acid is 1.8×10^{-5} and the K_a value for hypochlorous acid is 3.5×10^{-8}, which is the stronger base, OCl^- or $C_2H_3O_2^-$?

106. The K_b values for ammonia and methylamine are 1.8×10^{-5} and 4.4×10^{-4}, respectively. Which is the stronger acid, NH_4^+ or $CH_3NH_3^+$?

107. Sodium azide (NaN_3) is sometimes added to water to kill bacteria. Calculate the concentration of all species in a 0.010 M solution of NaN_3. The K_a value for hydrazoic acid (HN_3) is 1.9×10^{-5}.

108. Calculate the concentrations of all species present in a 0.25 M solution of ethylammonium chloride ($C_2H_5NH_3Cl$).

109. Calculate the pH of each of the following solutions.
a. 0.10 M CH_3NH_3Cl b. 0.050 M NaCN

110. Calculate the pH of each of the following solutions.
a. 0.12 M KNO_2 c. 0.40 M NH_4ClO_4
b. 0.45 M NaOCl

111. An unknown salt is either NaCN, $NaC_2H_3O_2$, NaF, NaCl, or NaOCl. When 0.100 mol of the salt is dissolved in 1.00 L of

water, the pH of the solution is 8.07. What is the identity of the salt?

112. Consider a solution of an unknown salt having the general formula BHCl, where B is one of the weak bases in Table 14.3. A 0.10 M solution of the unknown salt has a pH of 5.82. What is the actual formula of the salt?

113. Calculate the pH of a 0.050 M $Al(NO_3)_3$ solution. The K_a value for $Al(H_2O)_6^{3+}$ is 1.4×10^{-5}.

114. Calculate the pH of a 0.10 M $CoCl_3$ solution. The K_a value for $Co(H_2O)_6^{3+}$ is 1.0×10^{-5}.

115. Are solutions of the following salts acidic, basic, or neutral? For those that are not neutral, write balanced chemical equations for the reactions causing the solution to be acidic or basic. The relevant K_a and K_b values are found in Tables 14.2 and 14.3.
a. $NaNO_3$ c. $C_5H_5NHClO_4$ e. KOCl
b. $NaNO_2$ d. NH_4NO_2 f. NH_4OCl

116. Are solutions of the following salts acidic, basic, or neutral? For those that are not neutral, write balanced equations for the reactions causing the solution to be acidic or basic. The relevant K_a and K_b values are found in Tables 14.2 and 14.3.
a. KCl   c. CH_3NH_3Cl e. NH_4F
b. $NH_4C_2H_3O_2$ d. KF   f. CH_3NH_3CN

Relationships Between Structure and Strengths of Acids and Bases

117. Place the species in each of the following groups in order of increasing acid strength. Explain the order you chose for each group.
a. HIO_3, $HBrO_3$ c. HOCl, HOI
b. HNO_2, HNO_3 d. H_3PO_4, H_3PO_3

118. Place the species in each of the following groups in order of increasing base strength. Give your reasoning in each case.
a. IO_3^-, BrO_3^- b. NO_2^-, NO_3^- c. OCl^-, OI^-

119. Place the species in each of the following groups in order of increasing acid strength.
a. H_2O, H_2S, H_2Se (bond energies: H—O, 467 kJ/mol; H—S, 363 kJ/mol; H—Se, 276 kJ/mol)
b. CH_3CO_2H, FCH_2CO_2H, F_2CHCO_2H, F_3CCO_2H
c. NH_4^+, $HONH_3^+$
d. NH_4^+, PH_4^+ (bond energies: N—H, 391 kJ/mol; P—H, 322 kJ/mol)
Give reasons for the orders you chose.

120. Using your results from Exercise 119, place the species in each of the following groups in order of increasing base strength.
a. OH^-, SH^-, SeH^- b. NH_3, PH_3 c. NH_3, $HONH_2$

121. Will the following oxides give acidic, basic, or neutral solutions when dissolved in water? Write reactions to justify your answers.
a. CaO   b. SO_2 c. Cl_2O

122. Will the following oxides give acidic, basic, or neutral solutions when dissolved in water? Write reactions to justify your answers.
  a. Li_2O **b.** CO_2 **c.** SrO

Lewis Acids and Bases

123. Identify the Lewis acid and the Lewis base in each of the following reactions.
  a. $B(OH)_3(aq) + H_2O(l) \rightleftharpoons B(OH)_4^-(aq) + H^+(aq)$
  b. $Ag^+(aq) + 2NH_3(aq) \rightleftharpoons Ag(NH_3)_2^+(aq)$
  c. $BF_3(g) + F^-(aq) \rightleftharpoons BF_4^-(aq)$
124. Identify the Lewis acid and the Lewis base in each of the following reactions.
  a. $Fe^{3+}(aq) + 6H_2O(l) \rightleftharpoons Fe(H_2O)_6^{3+}(aq)$
  b. $H_2O(l) + CN^-(aq) \rightleftharpoons HCN(aq) + OH^-(aq)$
  c. $HgI_2(s) + 2I^-(aq) \rightleftharpoons HgI_4^{2-}(aq)$

125. Aluminum hydroxide is an amphoteric substance. It can act as either a Brønsted–Lowry base or a Lewis acid. Write a reaction showing $Al(OH)_3$ acting as a base toward H^+ and as an acid toward OH^-.
126. Zinc hydroxide is an amphoteric substance. Write equations that describe $Zn(OH)_2$ acting as a Brønsted–Lowry base toward H^+ and as a Lewis acid toward OH^-.

127. Would you expect Fe^{3+} or Fe^{2+} to be the stronger Lewis acid? Explain.
128. Use the Lewis acid–base model to explain the following reaction.

$$CO_2(g) + H_2O(l) \longrightarrow H_2CO_3(aq)$$

Additional Exercises

129. A 10.0-mL sample of an HCl solution has a pH of 2.000. What volume of water must be added in order to change the pH to 4.000?
130. Thallium(I) hydroxide is a strong base used in the synthesis of some organic compounds. Calculate the pH of a solution containing 2.48 g TlOH per liter.
131. Derive an expression for the relationship between pK_a and pK_b for a conjugate acid–base pair. $(pK = -\log K.)$
132. At 25°C, a saturated solution of benzoic acid $(K_a = 6.4 \times 10^{-5})$ has a pH of 2.80. Calculate the water solubility of benzoic acid in moles per liter.
133. Quinine $(C_{20}H_{24}N_2O_2)$ is an important alkaloid derived from cinchona bark. It is used as an antimalarial drug. For quinine $pK_{b_1} = 5.1$ and $pK_{b_2} = 9.7$ $(pK_b = -\log K_b)$. One gram of quinine will dissolve in 1900.0 mL of water. Calculate the pH of a saturated aqueous solution of quinine. Consider only the aqueous reaction $Q + H_2O \rightleftharpoons QH^+ + OH^-$ described by pK_{b_1} where Q = quinine.
134. Phosphoric acid is a common ingredient in traditional cola drinks. It is added to provide the drinks with a pleasantly tart

taste. Although phosphoric acid is a triprotic acid, its protons are lost one at a time. Assuming that in cola drinks the concentration of phosphoric acid is 0.007 *M*, calculate the pH in this solution.

135. Acrylic acid $(CH_2=CHCO_2H)$ is a precursor for many important plastics. K_a for acrylic acid is 5.6×10^{-5}.
  a. Calculate the pH of a 0.10 *M* solution of acrylic acid.
  b. Calculate the percent dissociation of a 0.10 *M* solution of acrylic acid.
  c. Calculate the pH of a 0.050 *M* solution of sodium acrylate $(NaC_3H_3O_2)$.

136. A 0.20 *M* sodium chlorobenzoate $(NaC_7H_4ClO_2)$ solution has a pH of 8.65. Calculate the pH of a 0.20 *M* chlorobenzoic acid $(HC_7H_4ClO_2)$ solution.

137. The equilibrium constant K_a for the reaction

$$Fe(H_2O)_6^{3+}(aq) + H_2O(l)$$
$$\rightleftharpoons Fe(H_2O)_5(OH)^{2+}(aq) + H_3O^+(aq)$$

is 6.0×10^{-3}.
  a. Calculate the pH of a 0.10 *M* solution of $Fe(H_2O)_6^{3+}$.
  b. Will a 1.0 *M* solution of iron(II) nitrate have a higher or lower pH than a 1.0 *M* solution of iron(III) nitrate? Explain.

138. Rank the following 0.10 *M* solutions in order of increasing pH.
  a. HI, HF, NaF, NaI
  b. NH_4Br, HBr, KBr, NH_3
  c. $C_6H_5NH_3NO_3$, $NaNO_3$, NaOH, HOC_6H_5, KOC_6H_5, $C_6H_5NH_2$, HNO_3

139. Is an aqueous solution of $NaHSO_4$ acidic, basic, or neutral? What reaction occurs with water? Calculate the pH of a 0.10 *M* solution of $NaHSO_4$.

140. Calculate $[CO_3^{2-}]$ in a 0.010 *M* solution of CO_2 in water (H_2CO_3). If all the CO_3^{2-} in this solution comes from the reaction

$$HCO_3^-(aq) \rightleftharpoons H^+(aq) + CO_3^{2-}(aq)$$

what percent of the H^+ ions in the solution are a result of the dissociation of HCO_3^-? When acid is added to a solution of sodium hydrogen carbonate $(NaHCO_3)$, vigorous bubbling occurs. How is this reaction related to the existence of carbonic acid (H_2CO_3) molecules in aqueous solution?

141. Hemoglobin (abbreviated Hb) is a protein that is responsible for the transport of oxygen in the blood of mammals. Each hemoglobin molecule contains four iron atoms that are the binding sites for O_2 molecules. The oxygen binding is pH dependent. The relevant equilibrium reaction is

$$HbH_4^{4+}(aq) + 4O_2(g) \rightleftharpoons Hb(O_2)_4(aq) + 4H^+(aq)$$

Use Le Châtelier's principle to answer the following.
  a. What form of hemoglobin, HbH_4^{4+} or $Hb(O_2)_4$, is favored in the lungs? What form is favored in the cells?

b. When a person hyperventilates, the concentration of CO_2 in the blood is decreased. How does this affect the oxygen-binding equilibrium? How does breathing into a paper bag help to counteract this effect?

c. When a person has suffered a cardiac arrest, injection of a sodium bicarbonate solution is given. Why is this necessary?

142. Calculate the value for the equilibrium constant for each of the following aqueous reactions.

a. $NH_3 + H_3O^+ \rightleftharpoons NH_4^+ + H_2O$
b. $NO_2^- + H_3O^+ \rightleftharpoons HNO_2 + H_2O$
c. $NH_4^+ + OH^- \rightleftharpoons NH_3 + H_2O$
d. $HNO_2 + OH^- \rightleftharpoons H_2O + NO_2^-$

143. Students are often surprised to learn that organic acids, such as acetic acid, contain —OH groups. Actually, all oxyacids contain hydroxyl groups. Sulfuric acid, usually written as H_2SO_4, has the structural formula $SO_2(OH)_2$, where S is the central atom. Identify the acids whose structural formulas are shown below. Why do they behave as acids, while NaOH and KOH are bases?

a. $SO(OH)_2$ **c.** $HPO(OH)_2$
b. $ClO_2(OH)$

Challenge Problems

144. The pH of 1.0×10^{-8} M hydrochloric acid is not 8.00. The correct pH can be calculated by considering the relationship between the molarities of the three principal ions in the solution (i.e., H^+, Cl^-, and OH^-). These molarities can be calculated from algebraic equations that can be derived from the considerations given below.

a. The solution is electrically neutral.
b. The hydrochloric acid can be assumed to be 100% ionized.
c. The product of the molarities of the hydronium ions and the hydroxide ions must equal K_w.

Calculate the pH of a 1.0×10^{-8} HCl solution.

145. Calculate the pH of a 1.0×10^{-7} M solution of NaOH in water.

146. Consider 50.0 mL of a solution of weak acid HA ($K_a = 1.00 \times 10^{-6}$), which has a pH of 4.000. What volume of water must be added to make the pH = 5.000?

147. Making use of the assumptions we ordinarily make in calculating the pH of an aqueous solution of a weak acid, calculate the pH of a 1.0×10^{-6} M solution of hypobromous acid (HBrO, $K_a = 2 \times 10^{-9}$). What is wrong with your answer? Why is it wrong? Without trying to solve the problem, tell what has to be included to solve the problem correctly.

148. Concentrated NaOH is added dropwise to 1.0 L of a 0.10 M solution of iodic acid (HIO_3) until the pH is 1.20. Calculate $[HIO_3]$ and $[IO_3^-]$ in this solution assuming the volume remains constant ($K_a = 1.7 \times 10^{-1}$).

149. Calculate $[OH^-]$ in a solution obtained by adding 0.0100 mol of solid NaOH to 1.00 L of 15.0 M NH_3.

150. A certain acid, HA, has a vapor density of 5.11 g/L when in the gas phase at a temperature of 25°C and a pressure of 1.00 atm. When 1.50 g of this acid is dissolved in enough water to make 100.0 mL of solution, the pH is found to be 1.80. Calculate K_a for the acid.

151. Consider the species PO_4^{3-}, HPO_4^{2-}, and $H_2PO_4^-$. Each ion can act as a base in water. Determine the K_b value for each of these species. Which species is the strongest base?

152. a. The principal equilibrium in a solution of $NaHCO_3$ is

$$HCO_3^-(aq) + HCO_3^-(aq) \rightleftharpoons H_2CO_3(aq) + CO_3^{2-}(aq)$$

Calculate the value of the equilibrium constant for this reaction.

b. At equilibrium, what is the relationship between $[H_2CO_3]$ and $[CO_3^{2-}]$?

c. Using the equilibrium

$$H_2CO_3(aq) \rightleftharpoons 2H^+(aq) + CO_3^{2-}(aq)$$

derive an expression for the pH of the solution in terms of K_{a_1} and K_{a_2} using the result from part b.

d. What is the pH of a solution of $NaHCO_3$?

Marathon Problem*

This problem is designed to incorporate several concepts and techniques into one situation. Marathon Problems can be used in class by groups of students to help facilitate problem-solving skills.

153. Captain Kirk, of the Starship *Enterprise*, has been told by his superiors that only a chemist can be trusted with the combination to the safe containing the dilithium crystals that power the ship. The combination is the pH of solution A, described below, followed by the pH of solution C. (Example: If the pH of solution A is 3.47 and that of solution C is 8.15, then the combination to the safe is 3-47-8-15.) The chemist must determine the combination using only the information below (all solutions are at 25°C):

Solution A is 50.0 mL of a 0.100 M solution of the weak monoprotic acid HX.

Solution B is a 0.0500 M solution of the salt NaX. It has a pH of 10.02.

Solution C is made by adding 15.0 mL of 0.250 M KOH to solution A.

What is the combination to the safe?

*This Marathon Problem was developed by James H. Burness, Penn State University, York Campus. Reprinted with permission from the *Journal of Chemical Education*, Vol. 68, No. 11, 1991, pp. 919–922; copyright © 1991, Division of Chemical Education, Inc.

CHAPTER 15

Applications of Aqueous Equilibria

Contents

Much important chemistry, including almost all the chemistry of the natural world, occurs in aqueous solution. We have already introduced one very significant class of aqueous equilibria, acid–base reactions. In this chapter we consider more applications of acid–base chemistry and introduce two additional types of aqueous equilibria, those involving the solubility of salts and those involving the formation of complex ions.

The interplay of acid–base, solubility, and complex ion equilibria is often important in natural processes, such as the weathering of minerals, the uptake of nutrients by plants, and tooth decay. For example, limestone ($CaCO_3$) will dissolve in water made acidic by dissolved carbon dioxide:

$$CO_2(aq) + H_2O(l) \rightleftharpoons H^+(aq) + HCO_3^-(aq)$$
$$H^+(aq) + CaCO_3(s) \rightleftharpoons Ca^{2+}(aq) + HCO_3^-(aq)$$

This two-step process and its reverse account for the formation of limestone caves and the stalactites and stalagmites found therein. In the forward direction of the process, the acidic water (containing carbon dioxide) dissolves the underground limestone deposits, thereby forming a cavern. The reverse process occurs as the water drips from the ceiling of the cave, and the carbon dioxide is lost to the air. This causes solid calcium carbonate to form, producing stalactites on the ceiling and stalagmites where the drops hit the cave floor.

Before we consider the other types of aqueous equilibria, we will deal with acid–base equilibria in more detail.

Stalactites are formed when carbonate minerals dissolve in ground water acidified by carbon dioxide and then solidify when the water evaporates.

ACID–BASE EQUILIBRIA

15.1 Solutions of Acids or Bases Containing a Common Ion

In Chapter 14 we were concerned with calculating the equilibrium concentrations of species (particularly H^+ ions) in solutions containing an acid or a base. In this section we discuss solutions that contain not only the weak acid HA but also its salt NaA. Although this appears to be a new type of problem, we will see that this case can be handled rather easily using the procedures developed in Chapter 14.

Suppose we have a solution containing the weak acid hydrofluoric acid (HF, $K_a = 7.2 \times 10^{-4}$) and its salt sodium fluoride (NaF). Recall that when a salt dissolves in water, it breaks up completely into its ions—it is a strong electrolyte:

$$NaF(s) \xrightarrow{H_2O(l)} Na^+(aq) + F^-(aq)$$

Since hydrofluoric acid is a weak acid and only slightly dissociated, the major species in the solution are HF, Na^+, F^-, and H_2O. The **common ion** in this solution is F^-, since it is produced by both hydrofluoric acid and sodium fluoride. What effect does the presence of the dissolved sodium fluoride have on the dissociation equilibrium of hydrofluoric acid?

To answer this question, we compare the extent of dissociation of hydrofluoric acid in two different solutions, the first containing 1.0 M HF and the second containing 1.0 M HF and 1.0 M NaF. By Le Châtelier's principle, we would expect the dissociation equilibrium for HF

$$HF(aq) \rightleftharpoons H^+(aq) + F^-(aq)$$

in the second solution to be *driven to the left by the presence of F^- ions from the NaF.* Thus the extent of dissociation of HF will be *less* in the presence of dissolved NaF:

$$HF(aq) \rightleftharpoons H^+(aq) + F^-(aq)$$

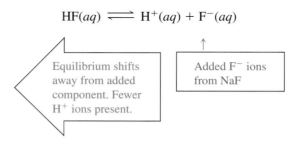

Equilibrium shifts away from added component. Fewer H^+ ions present.

Added F^- ions from NaF

The common ion effect is an application of Le Châtelier's principle.

The shift in equilibrium position that occurs because of the addition of an ion already involved in the equilibrium reaction is called the **common ion effect.** This effect makes a solution of NaF and HF less acidic than a solution of HF alone.

The common ion effect is quite general. For example, solid NH_4Cl added to a 1.0 M NH_3 solution produces additional ammonium ions:

$$NH_4Cl(s) \xrightarrow{H_2O} NH_4^+(aq) + Cl^-(aq)$$

and this causes the position of the ammonia–water equilibrium to shift to the left:

$$NH_3(aq) + H_2O(l) \rightleftharpoons NH_4^+(aq) + OH^-(aq)$$

This reduces the equilibrium concentration of OH^- ions.

The common ion effect is also important in solutions of polyprotic acids. The production of protons by the first dissociation step greatly inhibits the succeeding dissociation steps, which, of course, also produce protons, the common ion in this case. We will see later in this chapter that the common ion effect is also important in dealing with the solubility of salts.

Equilibrium Calculations

The procedures for finding the pH of a solution containing a weak acid or base plus a common ion are very similar to the procedures, which we covered in Chapter 14, for solutions containing the acids or bases alone. For example, in the case of a weak acid, the only important difference is that the initial concentration of the anion A^- is not zero in a solution that also contains the salt NaA. Sample Exercise 15.1 illustrates a typical example using the same general approach we developed in Chapter 14.

Sample Exercise 15.1 Acidic Solutions Containing Common Ions

In Section 14.5 we found that the equilibrium concentration of H^+ in a 1.0 M HF solution is 2.7×10^{-2} M, and the percent dissociation of HF is 2.7%. Calculate $[H^+]$ and the percent dissociation of HF in a solution containing 1.0 M HF ($K_a = 7.2 \times 10^{-4}$) and 1.0 M NaF.

Solution

As the aqueous solutions we consider become more complex, it is more important than ever to be systematic and to *focus on the chemistry* occurring in the solution before thinking about mathematical procedures. The way to do this is *always* to write the major species first and consider the chemical properties of each one.

In a solution containing 1.0 M HF and 1.0 M NaF, the major species are

$$HF, \quad F^-, \quad Na^+, \quad and \quad H_2O$$

We know that Na^+ ions have neither acidic nor basic properties and that water is a very weak acid (or base). Therefore, the important species are HF and F^-, which participate in the acid dissociation equilibrium that controls $[H^+]$ in this solution. That is, the position of the equilibrium

$$HF(aq) \rightleftharpoons H^+(aq) + F^-(aq)$$

will determine $[H^+]$ in the solution. The equilibrium expression is

$$K_a = \frac{[H^+][F^-]}{[HF]} = 7.2 \times 10^{-4}$$

The important concentrations are shown in the following table.

	Initial Concentration (mol/L)		Equilibrium Concentration (mol/L)
$[HF]_0 = 1.0$ (from dissolved HF) $[F^-]_0 = 1.0$ (from dissolved NaF) $[H^+]_0 = 0$ (neglect contribution from H_2O)		$\xrightarrow[\text{dissociates}]{x \text{ mol/L HF}}$	$[HF] = 1.0 - x$ $[F^-] = 1.0 + x$ $[H^+] = x$

Note that $[F^-]_0 = 1.0\ M$ because of the dissolved sodium fluoride and that at equilibrium $[F^-] > 1.0\ M$ because when the acid dissociates it produces F^- as well as H^+. Then

$$K_a = 7.2 \times 10^{-4} = \frac{[H^+][F^-]}{[HF]} = \frac{(x)(1.0 + x)}{1.0 - x} \approx \frac{(x)(1.0)}{1.0}$$

(since x is expected to be small).

Solving for x gives

$$x = \frac{1.0}{1.0}(7.2 \times 10^{-4}) = 7.2 \times 10^{-4}$$

Noting that x is small compared to 1.0, we conclude that this result is acceptable. Thus

$$[H^+] = x = 7.2 \times 10^{-4}\ M \qquad \text{(The pH is 3.14.)}$$

The percent dissociation of HF in this solution is

$$\frac{[H^+]}{[HF]_0} \times 100 = \frac{7.2 \times 10^{-4}\ M}{1.0\ M} \times 100 = 0.072\%$$

Compare these values for $[H^+]$ and percent dissociation of HF with those for a 1.0 M HF solution, where $[H^+] = 2.7 \times 10^{-2}\ M$ and the percent dissociation is 2.7%. The large difference shows clearly that the presence of the F^- ions from the dissolved NaF greatly inhibits the dissociation of HF. The position of the acid dissociation equilibrium has been shifted to the left by the presence of F^- ions from NaF.

See Exercises 15.25 and 15.26.

15.2   Buffered Solutions

Learning Module: Buffers

The most important application of acid–base solutions containing a common ion is for buffering. A **buffered solution** is one that *resists a change in its pH* when either hydroxide ions or protons are added. The most important practical example of a buffered solution is our blood, which can absorb the acids and bases produced in biologic reactions without changing its pH. A constant pH for blood is vital because cells can survive only in a very narrow pH range.

A buffered solution may contain a *weak* acid and its salt (for example, HF and NaF) or a *weak* base and its salt (for example, NH_3 and NH_4Cl). By choosing the appropriate components, a solution can be buffered at virtually any pH.

In treating buffered solutions in this chapter, we will start by considering the equilibrium calculations. We will then use these results to show how buffering works. That is, we will answer the question: How does a buffered solution resist changes in pH when an acid or a base is added?

As you do the calculations associated with buffered solutions, keep in mind that these are merely solutions containing weak acids or bases, and the procedures required are the same ones we have already developed. Be sure to use the systematic approach introduced in Chapter 14.

> The most important buffering system in the blood involves HCO_3^- and H_2CO_3.

> The systematic approach developed in Chapter 14 for weak acids and bases applies to buffered solutions.

Sample Exercise 15.2 *The pH of a Buffered Solution I*

A buffered solution contains 0.50 *M* acetic acid ($HC_2H_3O_2$, $K_a = 1.8 \times 10^{-5}$) and 0.50 *M* sodium acetate ($NaC_2H_3O_2$). Calculate the pH of this solution.

> Notice as you do this problem that it is exactly like examples you have seen in Chapter 14.

Solution

The major species in the solution are

$$HC_2H_3O_2, \quad Na^+, \quad C_2H_3O_2^-, \quad \text{and} \quad H_2O$$

↑	↑	↑	↑
Weak acid	Neither acid nor base	Base (conjugate base of $HC_2H_3O_2$)	Very weak acid or base

> Molecular Models: $HC_2H_3O_2$, $C_2H_3O_2^-$

Examination of the solution components leads to the conclusion that the acetic acid dissociation equilibrium, which involves both $HC_2H_3O_2$ and $C_2H_3O_2^-$, will control the pH of the solution:

$$HC_2H_3O_2(aq) \rightleftharpoons H^+(aq) + C_2H_3O_2^-(aq)$$

$$K_a = 1.8 \times 10^{-5} = \frac{[H^+][C_2H_3O_2^-]}{[HC_2H_3O_2]}$$

The concentrations are as follows:

Initial Concentration (mol/L)		Equilibrium Concentration (mol/L)
$[HC_2H_3O_2]_0 = 0.50$ $[C_2H_3O_2^-]_0 = 0.50$ $[H^+]_0 \approx 0$	$\xrightarrow[\text{dissociates to reach equilibrium}]{x \text{ mol/L of } HC_2H_3O_2}$	$[HC_2H_3O_2] = 0.50 - x$ $[C_2H_3O_2^-] = 0.50 + x$ $[H^+] = x$

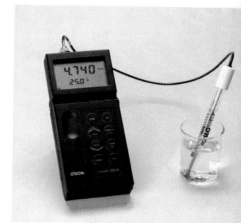

A digital pH meter shows the pH of the buffered solution to be 4.740.

Then

$$K_a = 1.8 \times 10^{-5} = \frac{[\text{H}^+][\text{C}_2\text{H}_3\text{O}_2^-]}{[\text{HC}_2\text{H}_3\text{O}_2]} = \frac{(x)(0.50 + x)}{0.50 - x} \approx \frac{(x)(0.50)}{0.50}$$

and

$$x \approx 1.8 \times 10^{-5}$$

The approximations are valid (by the 5% rule), so

$$[\text{H}^+] = x = 1.8 \times 10^{-5} \; M \qquad \text{and} \qquad \text{pH} = 4.74$$

See Exercises 15.33 and 15.34.

Sample Exercise 15.3 pH Changes in Buffered Solutions

Calculate the change in pH that occurs when 0.010 mol solid NaOH is added to 1.0 L of the buffered solution described in Sample Exercise 15.2. Compare this pH change with that which occurs when 0.010 mol solid NaOH is added to 1.0 L of water.

Solution

Since the added solid NaOH will completely dissociate, the major species in solution *before any reaction occurs* are $\text{HC}_2\text{H}_3\text{O}_2$, Na^+, $\text{C}_2\text{H}_3\text{O}_2^-$, OH^-, and H_2O. Note that the solution contains a relatively large amount of the very strong base hydroxide ion, which has a great affinity for protons. The best source of protons is the acetic acid, and the reaction that will occur is

$$\text{OH}^- + \text{HC}_2\text{H}_3\text{O}_2 \longrightarrow \text{H}_2\text{O} + \text{C}_2\text{H}_3\text{O}_2^-$$

Although acetic acid is a weak acid, the hydroxide ion is such a strong base that the reaction above will *proceed essentially to completion* (until the OH^- ions are consumed).

The best approach to this problem involves two distinct steps: (1) assume that the reaction goes to completion, and carry out the stoichiometric calculations, and then (2) carry out the equilibrium calculations.

1. *The stoichiometry problem.* The stoichiometry for the reaction is shown below.

	$\text{HC}_2\text{H}_3\text{O}_2$	$+$	OH^-	$\longrightarrow$	$\text{C}_2\text{H}_3\text{O}_2^-$	$+$	H_2O
Before reaction:	1.0 L × 0.50 M = 0.50 mol		0.010 mol		1.0 L × 0.50 M = 0.50 mol		
After reaction:	0.50 − 0.010 = 0.49 mol		0.010 − 0.010 = 0 mol		0.50 + 0.010 = 0.51 mol		

Note that 0.010 mol $\text{HC}_2\text{H}_3\text{O}_2$ has been converted to 0.010 mol $\text{C}_2\text{H}_3\text{O}_2^-$ by the added OH^-.

2. *The equilibrium problem.* After the reaction between OH^- and $\text{HC}_2\text{H}_3\text{O}_2$ is complete, the major species in solution are

$$\text{HC}_2\text{H}_3\text{O}_2, \quad \text{Na}^+, \quad \text{C}_2\text{H}_3\text{O}_2^-, \quad \text{and} \quad \text{H}_2\text{O}$$

The dominant equilibrium involves the dissociation of acetic acid.

This problem is then very similar to that in Sample Exercise 15.2. The only difference is that the addition of 0.010 mol OH^- has consumed some $HC_2H_3O_2$ and produced some $C_2H_3O_2^-$, yielding the following concentrations:

Initial Concentration (mol/L)		Equilibrium Concentration (mol/L)
$[HC_2H_3O_2]_0 = 0.49$	x mol/L	$[HC_2H_3O_2] = 0.49 - x$
$[C_2H_3O_2^-]_0 = 0.51$	$\xrightarrow{\ HC_2H_3O_2\ }$	$[C_2H_3O_2^-] = 0.51 + x$
$[H^+]_0 \approx 0$	dissociates	$[H^+] = x$

Or, in shorthand notation, we have:

	$HC_2H_3O_2(aq)$	$\rightleftharpoons$	$H^+(aq)$	$+$	$C_2H_3O_2^-(aq)$
Initial:	0.49		0		0.51
Change:	$-x$		$+x$		$+x$
Equilibrium:	$0.49 - x$		x		$0.51 + x$

Note that the initial concentrations are defined after the reaction with OH^- is complete but before the system adjusts to equilibrium. Following the usual procedure gives

$$K_a = 1.8 \times 10^{-5} = \frac{[H^+][C_2H_3O_2^-]}{[HC_2H_3O_2]} = \frac{(x)(0.51 + x)}{0.49 - x} \approx \frac{(x)(0.51)}{0.49}$$

and

$$x \approx 1.7 \times 10^{-5}$$

The approximations are valid (by the 5% rule), so

$$[H^+] = x = 1.7 \times 10^{-5} \quad \text{and} \quad pH = 4.76$$

The change in pH produced by the addition of 0.01 mol OH^- to this buffered solution is then

$$\underset{\underset{\text{New solution}}{\uparrow}}{4.76} \quad - \quad \underset{\underset{\text{Original solution}}{\uparrow}}{4.74} \quad = +0.02$$

The pH increased by 0.02 pH units.

Now compare this with what happens when 0.01 mol solid NaOH is added to 1.0 L water to give 0.01 M NaOH. In this case $[OH^-] = 0.01\ M$ and

$$[H^+] = \frac{K_w}{[OH^-]} = \frac{1.0 \times 10^{-14}}{1.0 \times 10^{-2}} = 1.0 \times 10^{-12}$$

$$pH = 12.00$$

Thus the change in pH is

$$\underset{\underset{\text{New solution}}{\uparrow}}{12.00} \quad - \quad \underset{\underset{\text{Pure water}}{\uparrow}}{7.00} \quad = +5.00$$

The increase is 5.00 pH units. Note how well the buffered solution resists a change in pH as compared with pure water.

See Exercises 15.35 and 15.36.

(top) Pure water at pH 7.000. (bottom) When 0.01 mol NaOH is added to 1.0 L of pure water, the pH jumps to 12.000.

Sample Exercises 15.2 and 15.3 represent typical buffer problems that involve all the concepts that you need to know to handle buffered solutions containing weak acids. Pay special attention to the following points:

1. Buffered solutions are simply solutions of weak acids or bases containing a common ion. The pH calculations on buffered solutions require exactly the same procedures introduced in Chapter 14. *This is not a new type of problem.*

2. When a strong acid or base is added to a buffered solution, it is best to deal with the stoichiometry of the resulting reaction first. After the stoichiometric calculations are completed, then consider the equilibrium calculations. This procedure can be presented as follows:

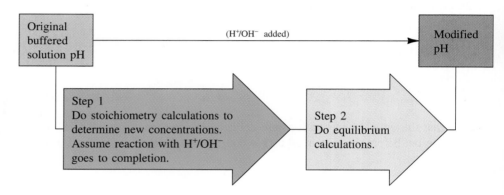

Buffering: How Does It Work?

Sample Exercises 15.2 and 15.3 demonstrate the ability of a buffered solution to absorb hydroxide ions without a significant change in pH. *But how does a buffer work?* Suppose a buffered solution contains relatively large quantities of a weak acid HA and its conjugate base A^-. When hydroxide ions are added to the solution, since the weak acid represents the best source of protons, the following reaction occurs:

$$OH^- + HA \longrightarrow A^- + H_2O$$

The net result is that OH^- ions are not allowed to accumulate but are replaced by A^- ions.

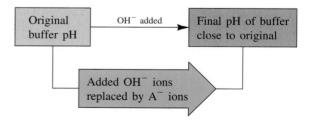

The stability of the pH under these conditions can be understood by examining the equilibrium expression for the dissociation of HA:

$$K_a = \frac{[H^+][A^-]}{[HA]}$$

or, rearranging,
$$[H^+] = K_a \frac{[HA]}{[A^-]}$$

In other words, the *equilibrium concentration of H$^+$, and thus the pH, is determined by the ratio [HA]/[A$^-$].* When OH$^-$ ions are added, HA is converted to A$^-$, and the ratio [HA]/[A$^-$] decreases. However, *if the amounts of HA and A$^-$ originally present are very large compared with the amount of OH$^-$ added,* the change in the [HA]/[A$^-$] ratio will be small.

In a buffered solution the pH is governed by the ratio [HA]/[A$^-$].

In Sample Exercises 15.2 and 15.3,

$$\frac{[HA]}{[A^-]} = \frac{0.50}{0.50} = 1.0 \qquad \text{Initially}$$

$$\frac{[HA]}{[A^-]} = \frac{0.49}{0.51} = 0.96 \qquad \text{After adding 0.01 mol/L OH}^-$$

The change in the ratio [HA]/[A$^-$] is very small. Thus the [H$^+$] and the pH remain essentially constant.

The essence of buffering, then, is that [HA] and [A$^-$] are large compared with the amount of OH$^-$ added. Thus, when the OH$^-$ is added, the concentrations of HA and A$^-$ change, but only by small amounts. Under these conditions, the [HA]/[A$^-$] ratio and thus the [H$^+$] remain virtually constant.

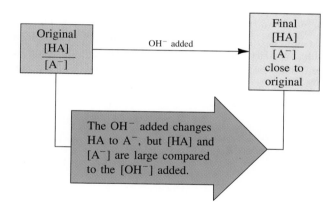

Similar reasoning applies when protons are added to a buffered solution of a weak acid and a salt of its conjugate base. Because the A$^-$ ion has a high affinity for H$^+$, the added H$^+$ ions react with A$^-$ to form the weak acid:

$$H^+ + A^- \longrightarrow HA$$

and free H$^+$ ions do not accumulate. In this case there will be a net change of A$^-$ to HA. However, if [A$^-$] and [HA] are large compared with the [H$^+$] added, little change in the pH will occur.

The form of the acid dissociation equilibrium expression

$$[H^+] = K_a \frac{[HA]}{[A^-]} \qquad (15.1)$$

is often useful for calculating [H$^+$] in a buffered solution, since [HA] and [A$^-$] are known. For example, to calculate [H$^+$] in a buffered solution containing 0.10 *M* HF

($K_a = 7.2 \times 10^{-4}$) and 0.30 M NaF, we simply substitute into Equation (15.1):

$$[H^+] = (7.2 \times 10^{-4}) \overset{\text{[HF]}}{\underset{K_a}{\frac{0.10}{0.30}}} = 2.4 \times 10^{-4}\ M$$

Another useful form of Equation (15.1) can be obtained by taking the negative log of both sides:

$$-\log[H^+] = -\log(K_a) - \log\left(\frac{[HA]}{[A^-]}\right)$$

That is,
$$pH = pK_a - \log\left(\frac{[HA]}{[A^-]}\right)$$

or, where inverting the log term reverses the sign:

$$pH = pK_a + \log\left(\frac{[A^-]}{[HA]}\right) = pK_a + \log\left(\frac{[\text{base}]}{[\text{acid}]}\right) \tag{15.2}$$

This log form of the expression for K_a is called the **Henderson–Hasselbalch equation** and is useful for calculating the pH of solutions when the ratio $[HA]/[A^-]$ is known.

For a particular buffering system (acid–conjugate base pair), all solutions that have the same ratio $[A^-]/[HA]$ will have the same pH. For example, a buffered solution containing 5.0 M $HC_2H_3O_2$ and 3.0 M $NaC_2H_3O_2$ will have the same pH as one containing 0.050 M $HC_2H_3O_2$ and 0.030 M $NaC_2H_3O_2$. This can be shown as follows:

System	$[A^-]/[HA]$
5.0 M $HC_2H_3O_2$ and 3.0 M $NaC_2H_3O_2$	$\dfrac{3.0\ M}{5.0\ M} = 0.60$
0.050 M $HC_2H_3O_2$ and 0.030 M $NaC_2H_3O_2$	$\dfrac{0.030\ M}{0.050\ M} = 0.60$

Therefore,

$$pH = pK_a + \log\left(\frac{[C_2H_3O_2^-]}{[HC_2H_3O_2]}\right) = 4.74 + \log(0.60) = 4.74 - 0.22 = 4.52$$

Note that in using this equation we have assumed that the equilibrium concentrations of A^- and HA are equal to the initial concentrations. That is, we are assuming the validity of the approximations

$$[A^-] = [A^-]_0 + x \approx [A^-]_0 \quad \text{and} \quad [HA] = [HA]_0 - x \approx [HA]_0$$

where x is the amount of acid that dissociates. Since the initial concentrations of HA and A^- are relatively large in a buffered solution, this assumption is generally acceptable.

Sample Exercise 15.4 *The pH of a Buffered Solution II*

Calculate the pH of a solution containing 0.75 M lactic acid ($K_a = 1.4 \times 10^{-4}$) and 0.25 M sodium lactate. Lactic acid ($HC_3H_5O_3$) is a common constituent of biologic systems. For example, it is found in milk and is present in human muscle tissue during exertion.

Solution

The major species in solution are

$$HC_3H_5O_3, \quad Na^+, \quad C_3H_5O_3^-, \quad \text{and} \quad H_2O$$

Since Na^+ has no acid–base properties and H_2O is a weak acid or base, the pH will be controlled by the lactic acid dissociation equilibrium:

$$HC_3H_5O_3(aq) \rightleftharpoons H^+(aq) + C_3H_5O_3^-(aq)$$

$$K_a = \frac{[H^+][C_3H_5O_3^-]}{[HC_3H_5O_3]} = 1.4 \times 10^{-4}$$

Since $[HC_3H_5O_3]_0$ and $[C_3H_5O_3^-]_0$ are relatively large,

$$[HC_3H_5O_3] \approx [HC_3H_5O_3]_0 = 0.75 \ M$$

and

$$[C_3H_5O_3^-] \approx [C_3H_5O_3^-]_0 = 0.25 \ M$$

Thus, using the rearranged K_a expression, we have

$$[H^+] = K_a\frac{[HC_3H_5O_3]}{[C_3H_5O_3^-]} = (1.4 \times 10^{-4})\frac{(0.75 \ M)}{(0.25 \ M)} = 4.2 \times 10^{-4} \ M$$

and

$$pH = -\log(4.2 \times 10^{-4}) = 3.38$$

Alternatively, we could use the Henderson–Hasselbalch equation:

$$pH = pK_a + \log\left(\frac{[C_3H_5O_3^-]}{[HC_3H_5O_3]}\right) = 3.85 + \log\left(\frac{0.25 \ M}{0.75 \ M}\right) = 3.38$$

See Exercises 15.39 through 15.41.

Buffered solutions also can be formed from a weak base and the corresponding conjugate acid. In these solutions, the weak base B reacts with any H^+ added:

$$B + H^+ \longrightarrow BH^+$$

and the conjugate acid BH^+ reacts with any added OH^-:

$$BH^+ + OH^- \longrightarrow B + H_2O$$

The approach needed to perform pH calculations for these systems is virtually identical to that used above. This makes sense because, as is true of all buffered solutions, a weak acid (BH^+) and a weak base (B) are present. A typical case is illustrated in Sample Exercise 15.5.

Sample Exercise 15.5 The pH of a Buffered Solution III

A buffered solution contains 0.25 M NH_3 ($K_b = 1.8 \times 10^{-5}$) and 0.40 M NH_4Cl. Calculate the pH of this solution.

Solution

The major species in solution are

$$NH_3, \quad \underbrace{NH_4{}^+, \quad Cl^-,}_{\text{From the dissolved } NH_4Cl} \quad \text{and} \quad H_2O$$

Since Cl^- is such a weak base and water is a weak acid or base, the important equilibrium is

$$NH_3(aq) + H_2O(l) \rightleftharpoons NH_4{}^+(aq) + OH^-(aq)$$

and

$$K_b = 1.8 \times 10^{-5} = \frac{[NH_4{}^+][OH^-]}{[NH_3]}$$

The appropriate concentrations are as follows:

Initial Concentration (mol/L)		Equilibrium Concentration (mol/L)
$[NH_3]_0 = 0.25$		$[NH_3] = 0.25 - x$
$[NH_4{}^+]_0 = 0.40$	$\xrightarrow[\text{reacts with } H_2O]{x \text{ mol/L } NH_3}$	$[NH_4{}^+] = 0.40 + x$
$[OH^-] \approx 0$		$[OH^-] = x$

Then

$$K_b = 1.8 \times 10^{-5} = \frac{[NH_4{}^+][OH^-]}{[NH_3]} = \frac{(0.40 + x)(x)}{0.25 - x} \approx \frac{(0.40)(x)}{0.25}$$

and

$$x \approx 1.1 \times 10^{-5}$$

The approximations are valid (by the 5% rule), so

$$[OH^-] = x = 1.1 \times 10^{-5}$$
$$pOH = 4.95$$
$$pH = 14.00 - 4.95 = 9.05$$

This case is typical of a buffered solution in that the initial and equilibrium concentrations of buffering materials are essentially the same.

ALTERNATIVE SOLUTION

There is another way of looking at this problem. Since the solution contains relatively large quantities of *both* $NH_4{}^+$ and NH_3, we can use the equilibrium

$$NH_3(aq) + H_2O(l) \rightleftharpoons NH_4{}^+(aq) + OH^-(aq)$$

to calculate $[OH^-]$ and then calculate $[H^+]$ from K_w as we have just done. Or we can use the dissociation equilibrium for $NH_4{}^+$, that is,

$$NH_4^+(aq) \rightleftharpoons NH_3(aq) + H^+(aq)$$

to calculate $[H^+]$ directly. *Either choice will give the same answer,* since the same equilibrium concentrations of NH_3 and NH_4^+ must satisfy both equilibria.

We can obtain the K_a value for NH_4^+ from the given K_b value for NH_3, since $K_a \times K_b = K_w$:

$$K_a = \frac{K_w}{K_b} = \frac{1.0 \times 10^{-14}}{1.8 \times 10^{-5}} = 5.6 \times 10^{-10}$$

Then, using the Henderson–Hasselbalch equation, we have

$$pH = pK_a + \log\left(\frac{[\text{base}]}{[\text{acid}]}\right)$$

$$= 9.25 + \log\left(\frac{0.25\ M}{0.40\ M}\right) = 9.25 - 0.20 = 9.05$$

See Exercises 15.42 and 15.43.

Sample Exercise 15.6 Adding Strong Acid to a Buffered Solution I

Calculate the pH of the solution that results when 0.10 mol gaseous HCl is added to 1.0 L of the buffered solution from Sample Exercise 15.5.

Solution

Before any reaction occurs, the solution contains the following major species:

$$NH_3, \quad NH_4^+, \quad Cl^-, \quad H^+, \quad \text{and} \quad H_2O$$

What reaction can occur? We know that H^+ will not react with Cl^- to form HCl. In contrast to Cl^-, the NH_3 molecule has a great affinity for protons (this is demonstrated by the fact that NH_4^+ is such a weak acid $[K_a = 5.6 \times 10^{-10}]$). Thus NH_3 will react with H^+ to form NH_4^+:

Remember: Think about the chemistry first. Ask yourself if a reaction will occur among the major species.

$$NH_3(aq) + H^+(aq) \longrightarrow NH_4^+(aq)$$

Since this reaction can be assumed to go essentially to completion to form the very weak acid NH_4^+, we will do the stoichiometry calculations before we consider the equilibrium calculations. That is, we will let the reaction run to completion and then consider the equilibrium.

The stoichiometry calculations for this process are shown below.

	NH_3	+	H^+	$\longrightarrow$	NH_4^+
Before reaction:	(1.0 L)(0.25 M) = 0.25 mol		0.10 mol ↑ Limiting reactant		(1.0 L)(0.40 M) = 0.40 mol
After reaction:	0.25 − 0.10 = 0.15 mol		0		0.40 + 0.10 = 0.50 mol

After the reaction goes to completion, the solution contains the major species

$$NH_3, \quad NH_4^+, \quad Cl^-, \quad and \quad H_2O$$

and

$$[NH_3]_0 = \frac{0.15 \text{ mol}}{1.0 \text{ L}} = 0.15 \ M$$

$$[NH_4^+]_0 = \frac{0.50 \text{ mol}}{1.0 \text{ L}} = 0.50 \ M$$

We can use the Henderson–Hasselbalch equation, where

$$[Base] = [NH_3] \approx [NH_3]_0 = 0.15 \ M$$
$$[Acid] = [NH_4^+] \approx [NH_4^+]_0 = 0.50 \ M$$

Then

$$pH = pK_a + \log\left(\frac{[NH_3]}{[NH_4^+]}\right)$$

$$= 9.25 + \log\left(\frac{0.15 \ M}{0.50 \ M}\right) = 9.25 - 0.52 = 8.73$$

Note that the addition of HCl only slightly decreases the pH, as we would expect in a buffered solution.

See Exercise 15.44.

Summary of the Most Important Characteristics of Buffered Solutions

- Buffered solutions contain relatively large concentrations of a weak acid and the corresponding weak base. They can involve a weak acid HA and the conjugate base A^- or a weak base B and the conjugate acid BH^+.
- When H^+ is added to a buffered solution, it reacts essentially to completion with the weak base present:

$$H^+ + A^- \longrightarrow HA \quad or \quad H^+ + B \longrightarrow BH^+$$

- When OH^- is added to a buffered solution, it reacts essentially to completion with the weak acid present:

$$OH^- + HA \longrightarrow A^- + H_2O \quad or \quad OH^- + BH^+ \longrightarrow B + H_2O$$

- The pH in the buffered solution is determined by the ratio of the concentrations of the weak acid and weak base. As long as this ratio remains virtually constant, the pH will remain virtually constant. This will be the case as long as the concentrations of the buffering materials (HA and A^- or B and BH^+) are large compared with the amounts of H^+ or OH^- added.

15.3 Buffer Capacity

The **buffering capacity** of a buffered solution represents the amount of protons or hydroxide ions the buffer can absorb without a significant change in pH. A buffer with a large capacity contains large concentrations of buffering components and so can absorb a relatively large amount of protons or hydroxide ions and show little pH change. *The pH of a buffered solution is determined by the ratio [A⁻]/[HA]. The capacity of a buffered solution is determined by the magnitudes of [HA] and [A⁻].*

A buffer with a large capacity contains large concentrations of the buffering components.

Sample Exercise 15.7 *Adding Strong Acid to a Buffered Solution II*

Calculate the change in pH that occurs when 0.010 mol gaseous HCl is added to 1.0 L of each of the following solutions:

Solution A: 5.00 M $HC_2H_3O_2$ and 5.00 M $NaC_2H_3O_2$
Solution B: 0.050 M $HC_2H_3O_2$ and 0.050 M $NaC_2H_3O_2$

For acetic acid, $K_a = 1.8 \times 10^{-5}$.

Solution

For both solutions the initial pH can be determined from the Henderson–Hasselbalch equation:

$$pH = pK_a + \log\left(\frac{[C_2H_3O_2^-]}{[HC_2H_3O_2]}\right)$$

In each case, $[C_2H_3O_2^-] = [HC_2H_3O_2]$. Therefore, the initial pH for both A and B is

$$pH = pK_a + \log(1) = pK_a = -\log(1.8 \times 10^{-5}) = 4.74$$

After the addition of HCl to each of these solutions, the major species *before any reaction occurs* are

$$HC_2H_3O_2, \quad Na^+, \quad C_2H_3O_2^-, \quad \underbrace{H^+, \quad Cl^-}, \quad \text{and} \quad H_2O$$

From the added HCl

Will any reactions occur among these species? Note that we have a relatively large quantity of H^+, which will readily react with any effective base. We know that Cl^- will not react with H^+ to form HCl in water. However, $C_2H_3O_2^-$ will react with H^+ to form the weak acid $HC_2H_3O_2$:

$$H^+(aq) + C_2H_3O_2^-(aq) \longrightarrow HC_2H_3O_2(aq)$$

Because $HC_2H_3O_2$ is a weak acid, we assume that this reaction runs to completion; the 0.010 mol of added H^+ will convert 0.010 mol $C_2H_3O_2^-$ to 0.010 mol $HC_2H_3O_2$.

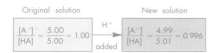

Original solution → New solution

$\dfrac{[A^-]}{[HA]} = \dfrac{5.00}{5.00} = 1.00$ ─H⁺ added→ $\dfrac{[A^-]}{[HA]} = \dfrac{4.99}{5.01} = 0.996$

For solution A (since the solution volume is 1.0 L, the number of moles equals the molarity), the following calculations apply:

	H^+	$+$	$C_2H_3O_2{}^-$	$\longrightarrow$	$HC_2H_3O_2$
Before reaction:	0.010 M		5.00 M		5.00 M
After reaction:	0		4.99 M		5.01 M

The new pH can be obtained by substituting the new concentrations into the Henderson–Hasselbalch equation:

$$pH = pK_a + \log\left(\frac{[C_2H_3O_2{}^-]}{[HC_2H_3O_2]}\right)$$

$$= 4.74 + \log\left(\frac{4.99}{5.01}\right) = 4.74 - 0.0017 = 4.74$$

There is virtually no change in pH for solution A when 0.010 mol gaseous HCl is added.

For solution B, the following calculations apply:

Original solution → New solution

$\dfrac{[A^-]}{[HA]} = \dfrac{.050}{.050} = 1.0$ ─H⁺ added→ $\dfrac{[A^-]}{[HA]} = \dfrac{0.040}{0.060} = 0.67$

	H^+	$+$	$C_2H_3O_2{}^-$	$\longrightarrow$	$HC_2H_3O_2$
Before reaction:	0.010 M		0.050 M		0.050 M
After reaction:	0		0.040 M		0.060 M

The new pH is

$$pH = 4.74 + \log\left(\frac{0.040}{0.060}\right)$$

$$= 4.74 - 0.18 = 4.56$$

Although the pH change for solution B is small, a change did occur, which is in contrast to solution A.

These results show that solution A, which contains much larger quantities of buffering components, has a much higher buffering capacity than solution B.

See Exercises 15.45 and 15.46.

We have seen that the pH of a buffered solution depends on the ratio of the concentrations of buffering components. When this ratio is least affected by added protons or hydroxide ions, the solution is the most resistant to a change in pH. To find the ratio that gives optimal buffering, let's suppose we have a buffered solution containing a large concentration of acetate ion and only a small concentration of acetic acid. Addition of protons to form acetic acid will produce a relatively large *percent* change in the concentration of acetic acid and so will produce a relatively large change in the ratio $[C_2H_3O_2{}^-]/[HC_2H_3O_2]$ (see Table 15.1). Similarly, if hydroxide ions are added to remove some acetic acid, the percent change in the concentration of acetic acid is again large. The same effects are seen if the initial concentration of acetic acid is large and that of acetate ion is small.

Table 15.1 Change in $[C_2H_3O_2^-]/[HC_2H_3O_2]$ for Two Solutions When 0.01 mol H^+ Is Added to 1.0 L of Each

Solution	$\left(\dfrac{[C_2H_3O_2^-]}{[HC_2H_3O_2]}\right)_{orig}$	$\left(\dfrac{[C_2H_3O_2^-]}{[HC_2H_3O_2]}\right)_{new}$	Change	Percent Change
A	$\dfrac{1.00\ M}{1.00\ M} = 1.00$	$\dfrac{0.99\ M}{1.01\ M} = 0.98$	$1.00 \rightarrow 0.98$	2.00%
B	$\dfrac{1.00\ M}{0.01\ M} = 100$	$\dfrac{0.99\ M}{0.02\ M} = 49.5$	$100 \rightarrow 49.5$	50.5%

Solution A

Solution B

Because large changes in the ratio $[A^-]/[HA]$ will produce large changes in pH, we want to avoid this situation for the most effective buffering. This type of reasoning leads us to the general conclusion that optimal buffering occurs when [HA] is equal to $[A^-]$. It is for this condition that the ratio $[A^-]/[HA]$ is most resistant to change when H^+ or OH^- is added to the buffered solution. This means that when choosing the buffering components for a specific application, we want $[A^-]/[HA]$ to equal 1. It follows that since

$$pH = pK_a + \log\left(\frac{[A^-]}{[HA]}\right) = pK_a + \log(1) = pK_a$$

the *pK$_a$ of the weak acid to be used in the buffer should be as close as possible to the desired pH.* For example, suppose we need a buffered solution with a pH of 4.00. The most effective buffering will occur when [HA] is equal to $[A^-]$. From the Henderson–Hasselbalch equation,

$$pH = pK_a + \log\left(\frac{[A^-]}{[HA]}\right)$$

4.00 is wanted

Ratio = 1 for most effective buffer

That is, $4.00 = pK_a + \log(1) = pK_a + 0$ and $pK_a = 4.00$

Thus the best choice of a weak acid is one that has $pK_a = 4.00$ or $K_a = 1.0 \times 10^{-4}$.

Sample Exercise 15.8 *Preparing a Buffer*

A chemist needs a solution buffered at pH 4.30 and can choose from the following acids (and their sodium salts):

a. chloroacetic acid ($K_a = 1.35 \times 10^{-3}$)
b. propanoic acid ($K_a = 1.3 \times 10^{-5}$)
c. benzoic acid ($K_a = 6.4 \times 10^{-5}$)
d. hypochlorous acid ($K_a = 3.5 \times 10^{-8}$)

Calculate the ratio $[HA]/[A^-]$ required for each system to yield a pH of 4.30. Which system will work best?

Solution

A pH of 4.30 corresponds to

$$[H^+] = 10^{-4.30} = \text{antilog}(-4.30) = 5.0 \times 10^{-5} \, M$$

Since K_a values rather than pK_a values are given for the various acids, we use Equation (15.1)

$$[H^+] = K_a \frac{[HA]}{[A^-]}$$

rather than the Henderson–Hasselbalch equation. We substitute the required $[H^+]$ and K_a for each acid into Equation (15.1) to calculate the ratio $[HA]/[A^-]$ needed in each case.

Acid	$[H^+] = K_a \dfrac{[HA]}{[A^-]}$	$\dfrac{[HA]}{[A^-]}$
a. Chloroacetic	$5.0 \times 10^{-5} = 1.35 \times 10^{-3}\left(\dfrac{[HA]}{[A^-]}\right)$	3.7×10^{-2}
b. Propanoic	$5.0 \times 10^{-5} = 1.3 \times 10^{-5}\left(\dfrac{[HA]}{[A^-]}\right)$	3.8
c. Benzoic	$5.0 \times 10^{-5} = 6.4 \times 10^{-5}\left(\dfrac{[HA]}{[A^-]}\right)$	0.78
d. Hypochlorous	$5.0 \times 10^{-5} = 3.5 \times 10^{-8}\left(\dfrac{[HA]}{[A^-]}\right)$	1.4×10^{3}

Since $[HA]/[A^-]$ for benzoic acid is closest to 1, the system of benzoic acid and its sodium salt will be the best choice among those given for buffering a solution at pH 4.3. This example demonstrates the principle that the optimal buffering system has a pK_a value close to the desired pH. The pK_a for benzoic acid is 4.19.

See Exercises 15.49 and 15.50.

15.4 Titrations and pH Curves

As we saw in Chapter 4, a titration is commonly used to determine the amount of acid or base in a solution. This process involves a solution of known concentration (the titrant) delivered from a buret into the unknown solution until the substance being analyzed is just consumed. The stoichiometric (equivalence) point is often signaled by the color change of an indicator. In this section we will discuss the pH changes that occur during an acid–base titration. We will use this information later to show how an appropriate indicator can be chosen for a particular titration.

The progress of an acid–base titration is often monitored by plotting the pH of the solution being analyzed as a function of the amount of titrant added. Such a plot is called a **pH curve** or **titration curve.**

Strong Acid–Strong Base Titrations

The net ionic reaction for a strong acid–strong base titration is

$$H^+(aq) + OH^-(aq) \longrightarrow H_2O(l)$$

To compute $[H^+]$ at a given point in the titration, we must determine the amount of H^+ that remains at that point and divide by the total volume of the solution. Before we proceed, we need to consider a new unit, which is especially convenient for titrations. Since titrations usually involve small quantities (burets are typically graduated in milliliters), the mole is inconveniently large. Therefore, we will use the **millimole** (abbreviated **mmol**), which, as the prefix indicates, is a thousandth of a mole:

$$1 \text{ mmol} = \frac{1 \text{ mol}}{1000} = 10^{-3} \text{ mol}$$

So far we have defined molarity only in terms of moles per liter. We can now define it in terms of *millimoles per milliliter*, as shown below:

$$\text{Molarity} = \frac{\text{mol solute}}{\text{L solution}} = \frac{\dfrac{\text{mol solute}}{1000}}{\dfrac{\text{L solution}}{1000}} = \frac{\text{mmol solute}}{\text{mL solution}}$$

A 1.0 M solution thus contains 1.0 mole of solute per liter of solution or, *equivalently*, 1.0 millimole of solute per milliliter of solution. Just as we obtain the number of moles of solute from the product of the volume in liters and the molarity, we obtain the number of millimoles of solute from the product of the volume in milliliters and the molarity:

$$\text{Number of mmol} = \text{volume (in mL)} \times \text{molarity}$$

Case Study: Strong Acid–Strong Base Titration

We will illustrate the calculations involved in a strong acid–strong base titration by considering the titration of 50.0 mL of 0.200 M HNO_3 with 0.100 M NaOH. We will calculate the pH of the solution at selected points during the course of the titration, where specific volumes of 0.100 M NaOH have been added.

A. No NaOH has been added.

Since HNO_3 is a strong acid (is completely dissociated), the solution contains the major species

$$H^+, \quad NO_3^-, \quad \text{and} \quad H_2O$$

and the pH is determined by the H^+ from the nitric acid. Since 0.200 M HNO_3 contains 0.200 M H^+,

$$[H^+] = 0.200 \ M \quad \text{and} \quad \text{pH} = 0.699$$

B. 10.0 mL of 0.100 M NaOH has been added.

In the mixed solution *before any reaction occurs*, the major species are

$$H^+, \quad NO_3^-, \quad Na^+, \quad OH^-, \quad \text{and} \quad H_2O$$

---

1 millimole = 1×10^{-3} mol

1 mL = 1×10^{-3} L

$$\frac{\text{mmol}}{\text{mL}} = \frac{\text{mol}}{\text{L}} = M$$

Animation: Neutralization of a Strong Acid by a Strong Base

Note that large quantities of both H^+ and OH^- are present. The 1.00 mmol (10.0 mL $\times$ 0.100 M) of added OH^- will react with 1.00 mmol H^+ to form water:

	H^+	$+$	OH^-	$\longrightarrow$	H_2O
Before reaction:	50.0 mL $\times$ 0.200 M = 10.0 mmol		10.0 mL $\times$ 0.100 M = 1.00 mmol		
After reaction:	10.0 − 1.00 = 9.0 mmol		1.00 − 1.00 = 0		

After the reaction, the solution contains

$$H^+, \quad NO_3^-, \quad Na^+, \quad \text{and} \quad H_2O \text{ (the } OH^- \text{ ions have been consumed)}$$

and the pH will be determined by the H^+ remaining:

The final solution volume is the sum of the original volume of HNO_3 and the volume of added NaOH.

$$[H^+] = \frac{\text{mmol } H^+ \text{ left}}{\text{volume of solution (mL)}} = \frac{9.0 \text{ mmol}}{(50.0 + 10.0) \text{ mL}} = 0.15 \, M$$

Original volume of HNO_3 solution / Volume of NaOH added

$$pH = -\log(0.15) = 0.82$$

C. 20.0 mL (total) of 0.100 M NaOH has been added.

We consider this point from the perspective that a total of 20.0 mL NaOH has been added to the *original* solution, rather than that 10.0 mL has been added to the solution from point B. It is best to go back to the original solution each time so that a mistake made at an earlier point does not show up in each succeeding calculation. As before, the added OH^- will react with H^+ to form water:

	H^+	$+$	OH^-	$\longrightarrow$	H_2O
Before reaction:	50.0 mL $\times$ 0.200 M = 10.0 mmol		20.0 mL $\times$ 0.100 M = 2.00 mmol		
After reaction:	10.0 − 2.00 = 8.00 mmol		2.00 − 2.00 = 0 mmol		

After the reaction

$$[H^+] = \frac{8.00 \text{ mmol}}{(50.0 + 20.0) \text{ mL}} = 0.11 \, M \quad \text{(H^+ remaining)}$$

$$pH = 0.942$$

D. 50.0 mL (total) of 0.100 M NaOH has been added.

Proceeding exactly as for points B and C, the pH is found to be 1.301.

E. 100.0 mL (total) of 0.100 M NaOH has been added.

At this point the amount of NaOH that has been added is

$$100.0 \text{ mL} \times 0.100 \, M = 10.0 \text{ mmol}$$

Equivalence (stoichiometric) point: The point in the titration where an amount of base has been added to exactly react with all the acid originally present.

The original amount of nitric acid was

$$50.0 \text{ mL} \times 0.200 \text{ } M = 10.0 \text{ mmol}$$

Enough OH^- has been added to react exactly with the H^+ from the nitric acid. This is the **stoichiometric point,** or **equivalence point,** of the titration. At this point the major species in solution are

$$Na^+, \quad NO_3^-, \quad \text{and} \quad H_2O$$

Since Na^+ has no acid or base properties and NO_3^- is the anion of the strong acid HNO_3 and is therefore a very weak base, neither NO_3^- nor Na^+ affects the pH, and the solution is neutral (the pH is 7.00).

F. 150.0 mL (total) of 0.100 M NaOH has been added.

The stoichiometric calculations for the titration reaction are as follows:

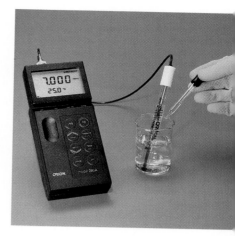

When 100.0 mL of 0.100 M sodium hydroxide is added to 50.0 mL of 0.200 M nitric acid, the equivalence (stoichiometric) point of the strong acid–strong base titration is reached, and the solution is neutral (pH = 7).

	H^+	$+$	OH^-	$\longrightarrow$	H_2O
Before reaction:	$50.0 \text{ mL} \times 0.200 \text{ } M$ $= 10.0$ mmol		$150.0 \text{ mL} \times 0.100 \text{ } M$ $= 15.0$ mmol		
After reaction:	$10.0 - 10.0$ $= 0$ mmol		$15.0 - 10.0$ $= 5.0$ mmol		

$$\uparrow$$
$$\text{Excess } OH^- \text{ added}$$

Now OH^- is *in excess* and will determine the pH:

$$[OH^-] = \frac{\text{mmol } OH^- \text{ in excess}}{\text{volume (mL)}} = \frac{5.0 \text{ mmol}}{(50.0 + 150.0) \text{ mL}} = \frac{5.0 \text{ mmol}}{200.0 \text{ mL}} = 0.025 \text{ } M$$

Since $[H^+][OH^-] = 1.0 \times 10^{-14}$,

$$[H^+] = \frac{1.0 \times 10^{-14}}{2.5 \times 10^{-2}} = 4.0 \times 10^{-13} \text{ } M \quad \text{and} \quad \text{pH} = 12.40$$

G. 200.0 mL (total) of 0.100 M NaOH has been added.

Proceeding as for point F, the pH is found to be 12.60.

The results of these calculations are summarized by the pH curve shown in Fig. 15.1. Note that the pH changes very gradually until the titration is close to the equivalence point, where a dramatic change occurs. This behavior is due to the fact that early in the titration there is a relatively large amount of H^+ in the solution, and the addition of a given amount of OH^- thus produces a small change in pH. However, near the equivalence point $[H^+]$ is relatively small, and the addition of a small amount of OH^- produces a large change.

The pH curve in Fig. 15.1, typical of the titration of a strong acid with a strong base, has the following characteristics:

Before the equivalence point, $[H^+]$ (and hence the pH) can be calculated by dividing the number of millimoles of H^+ remaining by the total volume of the solution in millimeters.

At the equivalence point, the pH is 7.00.

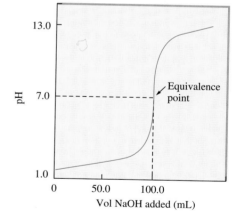

Figure 15.1

The pH curve for the titration of 50.0 mL of 0.200 M HNO_3 with 0.100 M NaOH. Note that the equivalence point occurs at 100.0 mL of NaOH added, the point where exactly enough OH^- has been added to react with all the H^+ originally present. The pH of 7 at the equivalence point is characteristic of a strong acid–strong base titration.

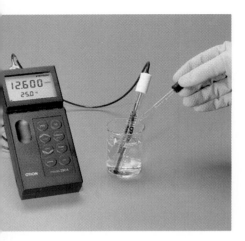

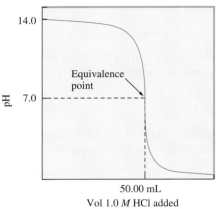

Figure 15.2
The pH curve for the titration of 100.0 mL of 0.50 M NaOH with 1.0 M HCl. The equivalence point occurs at 50.00 mL of HCl added, since at this point 5.0 mmol H^+ has been added to react with the original 5.0 mmol OH^-.

After 200.0 mL of 0.100 M NaOH is added to 50.0 mL of 0.200 M nitric acid, the pH reaches a value of 12.600.

After the equivalence point, $[OH^-]$ can be calculated by dividing the number of millimoles of excess OH^- by the total volume of the solution. Then $[H^+]$ is obtained from K_w.

The titration of a strong base with a strong acid requires reasoning very similar to that used above, except, of course, that OH^- is in excess before the equivalence point and H^+ is in excess after the equivalence point. The pH curve for the titration of 100.0 mL of 0.50 M NaOH with 1.0 M HCl is shown in Fig. 15.2.

Titrations of Weak Acids with Strong Bases

We have seen that since strong acids and strong bases are completely dissociated, the calculations to obtain the pH curves for titrations involving the two are quite straightforward. However, when the acid being titrated is a weak acid, there is a major difference: To calculate $[H^+]$ after a certain amount of strong base has been added, we must deal with the weak acid dissociation equilibrium. We have dealt with this same situation earlier in this chapter when we treated buffered solutions. Calculation of the pH curve for a titration of a weak acid with a strong base really amounts to a series of buffer problems. In performing these calculations it is very important to remember that even though the acid is weak, it *reacts essentially to completion* with hydroxide ion, a very strong base.

Calculating the pH curve for a weak acid–strong base titration involves a two-step procedure:

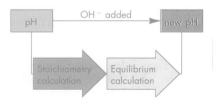

STEP 1

A stoichiometry problem. The reaction of hydroxide ion with the weak acid is assumed to run to completion, and the concentrations of the acid *remaining* and the conjugate base *formed* are determined.

STEP 2

An equilibrium problem. The position of the weak acid equilibrium is determined, and the pH is calculated.

Treat the stoichiometry and equilibrium problems separately.

It is *essential* to do these steps *separately*. Note that the procedures necessary to do these calculations have all been used before.

Case Study: Weak Acid–Strong Base Titration

As an illustration, we will consider the titration of 50.0 mL of 0.10 M acetic acid ($HC_2H_3O_2$, $K_a = 1.8 \times 10^{-5}$) with 0.10 M NaOH. As before, we will calculate the pH at various points representing volumes of added NaOH.

A. No NaOH has been added.

This is a typical weak acid calculation of the type introduced in Chapter 14. The pH is 2.87. (Check this yourself.)

B. 10.0 mL of 0.10 M NaOH has been added.

The major species in the mixed solution *before any reaction takes place* are

$$HC_2H_3O_2, \quad OH^-, \quad Na^+, \quad \text{and} \quad H_2O$$

The strong base OH^- will react with the strongest proton donor, which in this case is $HC_2H_3O_2$.

The Stoichiometry Problem

	OH^-	$+$	$HC_2H_3O_2$	$\longrightarrow$	$C_2H_3O_2^-$	$+$	H_2O
Before reaction:	10 mL $\times$ 0.10 M = 1.0 mmol		50.0 mL $\times$ 0.10 M = 5.0 mmol		0 mmol		
After reaction:	1.0 − 1.0 = 0 mmol ↑ Limiting reactant		5.0 − 1.0 = 4.0 mmol		1.0 mmol ↑ Formed by the reaction		

You are again doing exactly the same type of calculation already considered in Chapter 14.

The Equilibrium Problem   We examine the major components left in the solution *after the reaction takes place* to decide on the dominant equilibrium. The major species are

$$HC_2H_3O_2, \quad C_2H_3O_2^-, \quad Na^+, \quad \text{and} \quad H_2O$$

Since $HC_2H_3O_2$ is a much stronger acid than H_2O, and since $C_2H_3O_2^-$ is the conjugate base of $HC_2H_3O_2$, the pH will be determined by the position of the acetic acid dissociation equilibrium:

$$HC_2H_3O_2(aq) \rightleftharpoons H^+(aq) + C_2H_3O_2^-(aq)$$

where

$$K_a = \frac{[H^+][C_2H_3O_2^-]}{[HC_2H_3O_2]}$$

We follow the usual steps to complete the equilibrium calculations:

Initial Concentration		Equilibrium Concentration
$[HC_2H_3O_2]_0 = \dfrac{4.0 \text{ mmol}}{(50.0 + 10.0) \text{ mL}} = \dfrac{4.0}{60.0}$		$[HC_2H_3O_2] = \dfrac{4.0}{60.0} - x$
$[C_2H_3O_2^-]_0 = \dfrac{1.0 \text{ mmol}}{(50.0 + 10.0) \text{ mL}} = \dfrac{1.0}{60.0}$	$\xrightarrow[\text{dissociates}]{x \text{ mmol/mL} \atop HC_2H_3O_2}$	$[C_2H_3O_2^-] = \dfrac{1.0}{60.0} + x$
$[H^+]_0 \approx 0$		$[H^+] = x$

The initial concentrations are defined after the reaction with OH^- has gone to completion but before any dissociation of $HC_2H_3O_2$ occurs.

Therefore,

$$1.8 \times 10^{-5} = K_a = \frac{[H^+][C_2H_3O_2^-]}{[HC_2H_3O_2]} = \frac{x\left(\dfrac{1.0}{60.0} + x\right)}{\dfrac{4.0}{60.0} - x} \approx \frac{x\left(\dfrac{1.0}{60.0}\right)}{\dfrac{4.0}{60.0}} = \left(\dfrac{1.0}{4.0}\right)x$$

Note that the approximations made are well within the 5% rule.

$$x = \left(\frac{4.0}{1.0}\right)(1.8 \times 10^{-5}) = 7.2 \times 10^{-5} = [H^+] \quad \text{and} \quad pH = 4.14$$

C. 25.0 mL (total) of 0.10 M NaOH has been added.

The procedure here is very similar to that used at point B and will only be summarized briefly. The stoichiometry problem is summarized as follows:

	OH^-	$+$	$HC_2H_3O_2$	$\longrightarrow$	$C_2H_3O_2^-$	$+$	H_2O
Before reaction:	25.0 mL × 0.10 M = 2.5 mmol		50.0 mL × 0.10 M = 5.0 mmol		0 mmol		
After reaction:	2.5 − 2.5 = 0		5.0 − 2.5 = 2.5 mmol		2.5 mmol		

After the reaction, the major species in solution are

$$HC_2H_3O_2, \quad C_2H_3O_2^-, \quad Na^+, \quad \text{and} \quad H_2O$$

The equilibrium that will control the pH is

$$HC_2H_3O_2(aq) \rightleftharpoons H^+(aq) + C_2H_3O_2^-(aq)$$

and the pertinent concentrations are as follows:

Initial Concentration		*Equilibrium Concentration*
$[HC_2H_3O_2]_0 = \dfrac{2.5 \text{ mmol}}{(50.0 + 25.0) \text{ mL}}$	$\xrightarrow[\substack{HC_2H_3O_2 \\ \text{dissociates}}]{x \text{ mmol/mL}}$	$[HC_2H_3O_2] = \dfrac{2.5}{75.0} - x$
$[C_2H_3O_2^-]_0 = \dfrac{2.5 \text{ mmol}}{(50.0 + 25.0) \text{ mL}}$		$[C_2H_3O_2^-] = \dfrac{2.5}{75.0} + x$
$[H^+]_0 \approx 0$		$[H^+] = x$

Therefore,

$$1.8 \times 10^{-5} = K_a = \frac{[H^+][C_2H_3O_2^-]}{[HC_2H_3O_2]} = \frac{x\left(\dfrac{2.5}{75.0} + x\right)}{\dfrac{2.5}{75.0} - x} \approx \frac{x\left(\dfrac{2.5}{75.0}\right)}{\dfrac{2.5}{75.0}}$$

$$x = 1.8 \times 10^{-5} = [H^+] \quad \text{and} \quad pH = 4.74$$

This is a special point in the titration because it is *halfway to the equivalence point*. The original solution, 50.0 mL of 0.10 M $HC_2H_3O_2$, contained 5.0 mmol $HC_2H_3O_2$. Thus 5.0 mmol OH^- is required to reach the equivalence point. That is, 50 mL NaOH is required, since

$$(50.0 \text{ mL})(0.10 \text{ } M) = 5.0 \text{ mmol}$$

After 25.0 mL NaOH has been added, half the original $HC_2H_3O_2$ has been converted to $C_2H_3O_2^-$. At this point in the titration $[HC_2H_3O_2]_0$ is equal to $[C_2H_3O_2^-]_0$. We can neglect the effect of dissociation; that is,

$$[HC_2H_3O_2] = [HC_2H_3O_2]_0 - x \approx [HC_2H_3O_2]_0$$
$$[C_2H_3O_2] = [C_2H_3O_2^-]_0 + x \approx [C_2H_3O_2^-]_0$$

At this point, half the acid has been used up, so

$$[HC_2H_3O_2] = [C_2H_3O_2^-]$$

The expression for K_a at the halfway point is

$$K_a = \frac{[H^+][C_2H_3O_2^-]}{[HC_2H_3O_2]} = \frac{[H^+][C_2H_3O_2^-]_0}{[HC_2H_3O_2]_0} = [H^+]$$

Equal at the
halfway point

Then, *at the halfway point* in the titration,

$$[H^+] = K_a \quad \text{and} \quad pH = pK_a$$

D. 40.0 mL (total) of 0.10 M NaOH has been added.

The procedures required here are the same as those used for points B and C. The pH is 5.35. (Check this yourself.)

E. 50.0 mL (total) of 0.10 M NaOH has been added.

This is the equivalence point of the titration; 5.0 mmol OH^- has been added, which will just react with the 5.0 mmol $HC_2H_3O_2$ originally present. At this point the solution contains the major species

$$Na^+, \quad C_2H_3O_2^-, \quad \text{and} \quad H_2O$$

Note that the solution contains $C_2H_3O_2^-$, which is a base. Remember that a base wants to combine with a proton, and the only source of protons in this solution is water. Thus the reaction will be

$$C_2H_3O_2^-(aq) + H_2O(l) \rightleftharpoons HC_2H_3O_2(aq) + OH^-(aq)$$

This is a *weak base* reaction characterized by K_b:

$$K_b = \frac{[HC_2H_3O_2][OH^-]}{[C_2H_3O_2^-]} = \frac{K_w}{K_a} = \frac{1.0 \times 10^{-14}}{1.8 \times 10^{-5}} = 5.6 \times 10^{-10}$$

The relevant concentrations are as follows:

Initial Concentration (before any $C_2H_3O_2^-$ reacts with H_2O)		Equilibrium Concentration
$[C_2H_3O_2^-]_0 = \dfrac{5.0 \text{ mmol}}{(50.0 + 50.0) \text{ mL}}$ $= 0.050\ M$	$\xrightarrow[\text{with } H_2O]{\begin{array}{c} x \text{ mmol/mL} \\ C_2H_3O_2^- \text{ reacts} \end{array}}$	$[C_2H_3O_2^-] = 0.050 - x$
$[OH^-]_0 \approx 0$		$[OH^-] = x$
$[HC_2H_3O_2]_0 = 0$		$[HC_2H_3O_2] = x$

Therefore,

$$5.6 \times 10^{-10} = K_b = \frac{[HC_2H_3O_2][OH^-]}{[C_2H_3O_2^-]} = \frac{(x)(x)}{0.050 - x} \approx \frac{x^2}{0.050}$$

$$x \approx 5.3 \times 10^{-6}$$

The approximation is valid (by the 5% rule), so

$$[OH^-] = 5.3 \times 10^{-6} \ M$$

and

$$[H^+][OH^-] = K_w = 1.0 \times 10^{-14}$$

$$[H^+] = 1.9 \times 10^{-9} \ M$$

$$pH = 8.72$$

The pH at the equivalence point of a titration of a weak acid with a strong base is always greater than 7.

This is another important result: *The pH at the equivalence point of a titration of a weak acid with a strong base is always greater than 7.* This is so because the anion of the acid, which remains in solution at the equivalence point, is a base. In contrast, for the titration of a strong acid with a strong base, the pH at the equivalence point is 7.0, because the anion remaining in this case is *not* an effective base.

F. 60.0 mL (total) of 0.10 M NaOH has been added.

At this point, excess OH^- has been added. The stoichiometric calculations are as follows:

	OH^-	$+$	$HC_2H_3O_2$	$\longrightarrow$	$C_2H_3O_2^-$	$+$	H_2O
Before reaction:	60.0 mL $\times$ 0.10 M = 6.0 mmol		50.0 mL $\times$ 0.10 M = 5.0 mmol		0 mmol		
After reaction:	6.0 − 5.0 = 1.0 mmol in excess		5.0 − 5.0 = 0		5.0 mmol		

After the reaction is complete, the solution contains the major species

$$Na^+, \quad C_2H_3O_2^-, \quad OH^-, \quad \text{and} \quad H_2O$$

There are two bases in this solution, OH^- and $C_2H_3O_2^-$. However, $C_2H_3O_2^-$ is a weak base compared with OH^-. Therefore, the amount of OH^- produced by reaction of $C_2H_3O_2^-$ with H_2O will be small compared with the excess OH^- already in solution. You can verify this conclusion by looking at point E, where only $5.3 \times 10^{-6} \ M \ OH^-$ was produced by $C_2H_3O_2^-$. The amount in this case will be even smaller, since the excess OH^- will push the K_b equilibrium to the left.

Thus the pH is determined by the excess OH^-:

$$[OH^-] = \frac{\text{mmol of } OH^- \text{ in excess}}{\text{volume (in mL)}} = \frac{1.0 \ \text{mmol}}{(50.0 + 60.0) \ \text{mL}}$$

$$= 9.1 \times 10^{-3} \ M$$

and

$$[H^+] = \frac{1.0 \times 10^{-14}}{9.1 \times 10^{-3}} = 1.1 \times 10^{-12} \ M$$

$$pH = 11.96$$

G. 75.0 mL (total) of 0.10 M NaOH has been added.

The procedure needed here is very similar to that for point F. The pH is 12.30. (Check this yourself.)

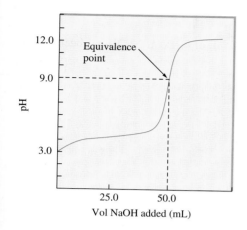

Figure 15.3

The pH curve for the titration of 50.0 mL of 0.100 M HC$_2$H$_3$O$_2$ with 0.100 M NaOH. Note that the equivalence point occurs at 50.0 mL of NaOH added, where the amount of added OH$^-$ exactly equals the original amount of acid. The pH at the equivalence point is greater than 7.0 because the C$_2$H$_3$O$_2^-$ ion present at this point is a base and reacts with water to produce OH$^-$.

The pH curve for this titration is shown in Fig. 15.3. It is important to note the differences between this curve and that in Fig. 15.1. For example, the shapes of the plots are quite different before the equivalence point, although they are very similar after that point. (The shapes of the strong and weak acid curves are the same after the equivalence points because excess OH$^-$ controls the pH in this region in both cases.) Near the beginning of the titration of the weak acid, the pH increases more rapidly than it does in the strong acid case. It levels off near the halfway point and then increases rapidly again. The leveling off near the halfway point is caused by buffering effects. Earlier in this chapter we saw that optimal buffering occurs when [HA] is equal to [A$^-$]. This is exactly the case at the halfway point of the titration. As we can see from the curve, the pH changes least rapidly in this region of the titration.

The other notable difference between the curves for strong and weak acids is the value of the pH at the equivalence point. For the titration of a strong acid, the equivalence point occurs at pH 7. For the titration of a weak acid, the pH at the equivalence point is greater than 7 because of the basicity of the conjugate base of the weak acid.

It is important to understand that the equivalence point in an acid–base titration is *defined by the stoichiometry, not by the pH.* The equivalence point occurs when enough titrant has been added to react exactly with all the acid or base being titrated.

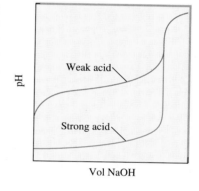

The equivalence point is defined by the stoichiometry, not by the pH.

Sample Exercise 15.9 *Titration of a Weak Acid*

Hydrogen cyanide gas (HCN), a powerful respiratory inhibitor, is highly toxic. It is a very weak acid ($K_a = 6.2 \times 10^{-10}$) when dissolved in water. If a 50.0-mL sample of 0.100 M HCN is titrated with 0.100 M NaOH, calculate the pH of the solution

a. after 8.00 mL of 0.100 M NaOH has been added.
b. at the halfway point of the titration.
c. at the equivalence point of the titration.

Solution

a. *The stoichiometry problem.* After 8.00 mL of 0.100 M NaOH has been added, the following calculations apply:

	HCN	+	OH$^-$	$\longrightarrow$	CN$^-$	+ H$_2$O
Before reaction:	50.0 mL × 0.100 M = 5.00 mmol		8.00 mL × 0.100 M = 0.800 mmol		0 mmol	
After reaction:	5.00 − 0.800 = 4.20 mmol		0.800 − 0.800 = 0		0.800 mmol	

The equilibrium problem. Since the solution contains the major species

$$HCN, \quad CN^-, \quad Na^+, \quad \text{and} \quad H_2O$$

the position of the acid dissociation equilibrium

$$HCN(aq) \rightleftharpoons H^+(aq) + CN^-(aq)$$

will determine the pH.

Initial Concentration		*Equilibrium Concentration*
$[HCN]_0 = \dfrac{4.2 \text{ mmol}}{(50.0 + 8.0) \text{ mL}}$	x mmol/mL	$[HCN] = \dfrac{4.2}{58.0} - x$
$[CN^-]_0 = \dfrac{0.800 \text{ mmol}}{(50.0 + 8.0) \text{ mL}}$	$\xrightarrow{\begin{array}{c}\text{HCN}\\\text{dissociates}\end{array}}$	$[CN^-] = \dfrac{0.80}{58.0} + x$
$[H^+]_0 \approx 0$		$[H^+] = x$

Substituting the equilibrium concentrations into the expression for K_a gives

The approximations made here are well within the 5% rule.

$$6.2 \times 10^{-10} = K_a = \frac{[H^+][CN^-]}{[HCN]} = \frac{x\left(\dfrac{0.80}{58.0} + x\right)}{\dfrac{4.2}{58.0} - x} \approx \frac{x\left(\dfrac{0.80}{58.0}\right)}{\left(\dfrac{4.2}{58.0}\right)} = x\left(\frac{0.80}{4.2}\right)$$

$$x = 3.3 \times 10^{-9} \ M = [H^+] \quad \text{and} \quad pH = 8.49$$

b. *At the halfway point of the titration.* The amount of HCN originally present can be obtained from the original volume and molarity:

$$50.0 \text{ mL} \times 0.100 \ M = 5.00 \text{ mmol}$$

Thus the halfway point will occur when 2.50 mmol OH$^-$ has been added:

$$\text{Volume of NaOH (in mL)} \times 0.100 \ M = 2.50 \text{ mmol OH}^-$$

or   Volume of NaOH = 25.0 mL

As was pointed out previously, at the halfway point [HCN] is equal to [CN$^-$] and pH is equal to pK_a. Thus, after 25.0 mL of 0.100 M NaOH has been added,

$$pH = pK_a = -\log(6.2 \times 10^{-10}) = 9.21$$

c. *At the equivalence point.* The equivalence point will occur when a total of 5.00 mmol OH$^-$ has been added. Since the NaOH solution is 0.100 M, the equivalence point occurs when 50.0 mL NaOH has been added. This amount will form 5.00 mmol CN^-. The major species in solution at the equivalence point are

$$CN^-, \quad Na^+, \quad \text{and} \quad H_2O$$

Thus the reaction that will control the pH involves the basic cyanide ion extracting a proton from water:

$$CN^-(aq) + H_2O(l) \rightleftharpoons HCN(aq) + OH^-(aq)$$

and $\quad K_b = \dfrac{K_w}{K_a} = \dfrac{1.0 \times 10^{-14}}{6.2 \times 10^{-10}} = 1.6 \times 10^{-5} = \dfrac{[HCN][OH^-]}{[CN^-]}$

Initial Concentration		Equilibrium Concentration
$[CN^-]_0 = \dfrac{5.00 \text{ mmol}}{(50.0 + 50.0) \text{ mL}}$ $= 5.00 \times 10^{-2} M$	*x* mmol/mL of CN^- reacts with H_2O	$[CN^-] = (5.00 \times 10^{-2}) - x$
$[HCN]_0 = 0$	$\longrightarrow$	$[HCN] = x$
$[OH^-]_0 \approx 0$		$[OH^-] = x$

Substituting the equilibrium concentrations into the expression for K_b and solving in the usual way gives

$$[OH^-] = x = 8.9 \times 10^{-4}$$

Then, from K_w, we have

$$[H^+] = 1.1 \times 10^{-11} \quad \text{and} \quad pH = 10.96$$

See Exercises 15.59, 15.61, and 15.62.

The amount of acid present, not its strength, determines the equivalence point.

Two important conclusions can be drawn from a comparison of the titration of 50.0 mL of 0.1 *M* acetic acid covered earlier in this section and that of 50.0 mL of 0.1 *M* hydrocyanic acid analyzed in Sample Exercise 15.9. First, the same amount of 0.1 *M* NaOH is required to reach the equivalence point in both cases. The fact that HCN is a much weaker acid than $HC_2H_3O_2$ has no bearing on the amount of base required. It is the *amount* of acid, not its strength, that determines the equivalence point. Second, the pH value at the equivalence point *is* affected by the acid strength. For the titration of acetic acid, the pH at the equivalence point is 8.72; for the titration of hydrocyanic acid, the pH at the equivalence point is 10.96. This difference occurs because the CN^- ion is a much stronger base than the $C_2H_3O_2^-$ ion. Also, the pH at the halfway point of the titration is much higher for HCN than for $HC_2H_3O_2$, again because of the greater base strength of the CN^- ion (or equivalently, the smaller acid strength of HCN).

The strength of a weak acid has a significant effect on the shape of its pH curve. Figure 15.4 shows pH curves for 50-mL samples of 0.10 *M* solutions of various acids titrated with 0.10 *M* NaOH. Note that the equivalence point occurs in each case when the same volume of 0.10 *M* NaOH has been added but that the shapes of the curves are dramatically different. The weaker the acid, the greater is the pH

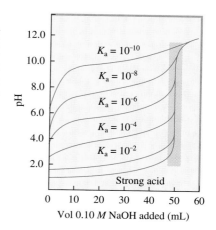

Figure 15.4

The pH curves for the titrations of 50.0-mL samples of 0.10 *M* acids with various K_a values with 0.10 *M* NaOH.

value at the equivalence point. In particular, note that the vertical region that surrounds the equivalence point becomes shorter as the acid being titrated becomes weaker. We will see in the next section that the choice of an indicator is more limited for such a titration.

Besides being used to analyze for the amount of acid or base in a solution, titrations also can be used to determine the values of equilibrium constants, as shown in Sample Exercise 15.10.

Calculation of K_a

Sample Exercise 15.10 *Calculating* K_a

A chemist has synthesized a monoprotic weak acid and wants to determine its K_a value. To do so, the chemist dissolves 2.00 mmol of the solid acid in 100.0 mL water and titrates the resulting solution with 0.0500 M NaOH. After 20.0 mL NaOH has been added, the pH is 6.00. What is the K_a value for the acid?

Solution

The stoichiometry problem. We represent the monoprotic acid as HA. The stoichiometry for the titration reaction is shown below.

2.00 mmol HA

↓ add OH⁻

1.00 mmol HA
1.00 mmol A⁻

	HA	+	OH⁻	⟶	A⁻	+	H₂O
Before reaction:	2.00 mmol		20.0 mL × 0.0500 M = 1.00 mmol		0 mmol		
After reaction:	2.00 − 1.00 = 1.00 mmol		1.00 − 1.00 = 0		1.00 mmol		

The equilibrium problem. After the reaction the solution contains the major species

$$HA, \quad A^-, \quad Na^+, \quad and \quad H_2O$$

The pH will be determined by the equilibrium

$$HA(aq) \rightleftharpoons H^+(aq) + A^-(aq)$$

for which
$$K_a = \frac{[H^+][A^-]}{[HA]}$$

Initial Concentration	Equilibrium Concentration
$[HA]_0 = \dfrac{1.00 \text{ mmol}}{(100.0 + 20.0) \text{ mL}}$ $= 8.33 \times 10^{-3} \ M$	$[HA] = 8.33 \times 10^{-3} - x$
$[A^-] = \dfrac{1.00 \text{ mmol}}{(100.0 + 20.0) \text{ mL}}$ $= 8.33 \times 10^{-3} \ M$	$[A^-] = 8.33 \times 10^{-3} + x$
$[H^+]_0 \approx 0$	$[H^+] = x$

x mmol/mL HA dissociates →

Note that x is known here because the pH at this point is known to be 6.00. Thus

$$x = [H^+] = \text{antilog}(-pH) = 1.0 \times 10^{-6} \, M$$

Substituting the equilibrium concentrations into the expression for K_a allows calculation of the K_a value:

$$
\begin{aligned}
K_a &= \frac{[H^+][A^-]}{[HA]} = \frac{x(8.33 \times 10^{-3} + x)}{(8.33 \times 10^{-3}) - x} \\
&= \frac{(1.0 \times 10^{-6})(8.33 \times 10^{-3} + 1.0 \times 10^{-6})}{(8.33 \times 10^{-3}) - (1.0 \times 10^{-6})} \\
&\approx \frac{(1.0 \times 10^{-6})(8.33 \times 10^{-3})}{8.33 \times 10^{-3}} = 1.0 \times 10^{-6}
\end{aligned}
$$

There is an easier way to think about this problem. The original solution contained 2.00 mmol of HA, and since 20.0 mL of added 0.0500 M NaOH contains 1.0 mmol OH^-, this is the halfway point in the titration (where [HA] is equal to [A$^-$]). Thus

$$[H^+] = K_a = 1.0 \times 10^{-6}$$

See Exercise 15.67.

Titrations of Weak Bases with Strong Acids

Titrations of weak bases with strong acids can be treated using the procedures we introduced previously. As always, you should *think first about the major species in solution* and decide whether a reaction occurs that runs essentially to completion. If such a reaction does occur, let it run to completion and do the stoichiometric calculations. Finally, choose the dominant equilibrium and calculate the pH.

Case Study: Weak Base–Strong Acid Titration

The calculations involved for the titration of a weak base with a strong acid will be illustrated by the titration of 100.0 mL of 0.050 M NH$_3$ with 0.10 M HCl.

Before the addition of any HCl.

1. Major species:

$$NH_3 \quad \text{and} \quad H_2O$$

   NH$_3$ is a base and will seek a source of protons. In this case H$_2$O is the only available source.

2. No reactions occur that go to completion, since NH$_3$ cannot readily take a proton from H$_2$O. This is evidenced by the small K_b value for NH$_3$.

3. The equilibrium that controls the pH involves the reaction of ammonia with water:

$$NH_3(aq) + H_2O(l) \rightleftharpoons NH_4^+(aq) + OH^-(aq)$$

   Use K_b to calculate [OH$^-$]. Although NH$_3$ is a weak base (compared with OH$^-$), it produces much more OH$^-$ in this reaction than is produced from the autoionization of H$_2$O.

Before the equivalence point.

1. Major species (before any reaction occurs):

$$NH_3, \quad \underbrace{H^+, \quad Cl^-,}_{\substack{\text{From added} \\ \text{HCl}}} \quad \text{and} \quad H_2O$$

2. The NH_3 will react with H^+ from the added HCl:

$$NH_3(aq) + H^+(aq) \rightleftharpoons NH_4^+(aq)$$

This reaction proceeds essentially to completion because the NH_3 readily reacts with a free proton. This case is much different from the previous case, where H_2O was the only source of protons. The stoichiometric calculations are then carried out using the known volume of 0.10 M HCl added.

3. After the reaction of NH_3 with H^+ is run to completion, the solution contains the following major species:

$$NH_3, \quad \underset{\substack{\uparrow \\ \text{Formed in} \\ \text{titration reaction}}}{NH_4^+}, \quad Cl^-, \quad \text{and} \quad H_2O$$

Note that the solution contains NH_3 and NH_4^+, and the equilibria involving these species will determine $[H^+]$. You can use either the dissociation reaction of NH_4^+

$$NH_4^+(aq) \rightleftharpoons NH_3(aq) + H^+(aq)$$

or the reaction of NH_3 with H_2O

$$NH_3(aq) + H_2O(l) \rightleftharpoons NH_4^+(aq) + OH^-(aq)$$

At the equivalence point.

1. By definition, the equivalence point occurs when all the original NH_3 is converted to NH_4^+. Thus the major species in solution are

$$NH_4^+, \quad Cl^-, \quad \text{and} \quad H_2O$$

2. No reactions occur that go to completion.

3. The dominant equilibrium (the one that controls the $[H^+]$) will be the dissociation of the weak acid NH_4^+, for which

$$K_a = \frac{K_w}{K_b \text{ (for NH}_3)}$$

Beyond the equivalence point.

1. Excess HCl has been added, and the major species are

$$H^+, \quad NH_4^+, \quad Cl^-, \quad \text{and} \quad H_2O$$

2. No reaction occurs that goes to completion.

3. Although NH_4^+ will dissociate, it is such a weak acid that $[H^+]$ will be determined simply by the excess H^+:

$$[H^+] = \frac{\text{mmol } H^+ \text{ in excess}}{\text{mL solution}}$$

Table 15.2 Summary of Results for the Titration of 100.0 mL 0.050 M NH$_3$ with 0.10 M HCl

Volume of 0.10 M HCl Added (mL)	[NH$_3$]$_0$	[NH$_4^+$]$_0$	[H$^+$]	pH
0	0.05 M	0	1.1×10^{-11} M	10.96
10.0	$\dfrac{4.0 \text{ mmol}}{(100 + 10) \text{ mL}}$	$\dfrac{1.0 \text{ mmol}}{(100 + 10) \text{ mL}}$	1.4×10^{-10} M	9.85
25.0*	$\dfrac{2.5 \text{ mmol}}{(100 + 25) \text{ mL}}$	$\dfrac{2.5 \text{ mmol}}{(100 + 25) \text{ mL}}$	5.6×10^{-10} M	9.25
50.0†	0	$\dfrac{5.0 \text{ mmol}}{(100 + 50) \text{ mL}}$	4.3×10^{-6} M	5.36
60.0‡	0	$\dfrac{5.0 \text{ mmol}}{(100 + 60) \text{ mL}}$	$\dfrac{1.0 \text{ mmol}}{160 \text{ mL}}$ $= 6.2 \times 10^{-3}$ M	2.21

* Halfway point
† Equivalence point
‡ [H$^+$] determined by the 1.0 mmol of excess H$^+$

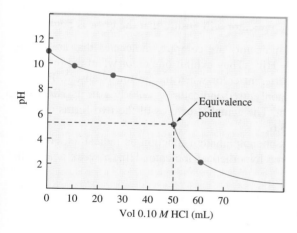

Figure 15.5

The pH curve for the titration of 100.0 mL of 0.050 M NH$_3$ with 0.10 M HCl. Note the pH at the equivalence point is less than 7, since the solution contains the weak acid NH$_4^+$.

The results of these calculations are shown in Table 15.2. The pH curve is shown in Fig. 15.5.

15.5 Acid–Base Indicators

There are two common methods for determining the equivalence point of an acid–base titration:

1. Use a pH meter (see Fig. 14.4) to monitor the pH and then plot the titration curve. The center of the vertical region of the pH curve indicates the equivalence point (for example, see Figs. 15.1 through 15.5).

Methyl orange indicator is yellow in basic solution and red in acidic solution.

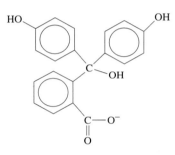

(Colorless acid form, HIn)

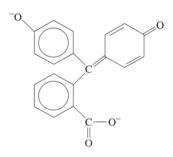

(Pink base form, In⁻)

Figure 15.6

The acid and base forms of the indicator phenolphthalein. In the acid form (HIn), the molecule is colorless. When a proton (plus H_2O) is removed to give the base form (In⁻), the color changes to pink.

 Molecular Models: phenolphthalein (acidic), phenolphthalein (basic)

2. Use an **acid–base indicator,** which marks the end point of a titration by changing color. Although the *equivalence point of a titration, defined by the stoichiometry, is not necessarily the same as the end point* (where the indicator changes color), careful selection of the indicator will ensure that the error is negligible.

The most common acid–base indicators are complex molecules that are themselves weak acids (represented by HIn). They exhibit one color when the proton is attached to the molecule and a different color when the proton is absent. For example, **phenolphthalein,** a commonly used indicator, is colorless in its HIn form and pink in its In⁻, or basic, form. The actual structures of the two forms of phenolphthalein are shown in Fig. 15.6.

To see how molecules such as phenolphthalein function as indicators, consider the following equilibrium for some hypothetical indicator HIn, a weak acid with $K_a = 1.0 \times 10^{-8}$.

$$HIn(aq) \rightleftharpoons H^+(aq) + In^-(aq)$$
$$\text{Red} \qquad\qquad\qquad \text{Blue}$$

$$K_a = \frac{[H^+][In^-]}{[HIn]}$$

By rearranging, we get

$$\frac{K_a}{[H^+]} = \frac{[In^-]}{[HIn]}$$

Suppose we add a few drops of this indicator to an acidic solution whose pH is 1.0 ($[H^+] = 1.0 \times 10^{-1}$). Then

$$\frac{K_a}{[H^+]} = \frac{1.0 \times 10^{-8}}{1.0 \times 10^{-1}} = 10^{-7} = \frac{1}{10,000,000} = \frac{[In^-]}{[HIn]}$$

This ratio shows that the predominant form of the indicator is HIn, resulting in a red solution. As OH⁻ is added to this solution in a titration, $[H^+]$ decreases and the equilibrium shifts to the right, changing HIn to In⁻. At some point in a titration,

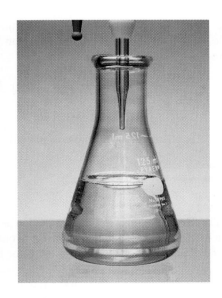

The indicator phenolphthalein is pink in basic solution and colorless in acidic solution.

enough of the In⁻ form will be present in the solution so that a purple tint will be noticeable. That is, a color change from red to reddish purple will occur.

The end point is defined by the change in color of the indicator. The equivalence point is defined by the reaction stoichiometry.

How much In⁻ must be present for the human eye to detect that the color is different from the original one? For most indicators, about a tenth of the initial form must be converted to the other form before a new color is apparent. We will assume, then, that in the titration of an acid with a base, the color change will occur at a pH where

$$\frac{[\text{In}^-]}{[\text{HIn}]} = \frac{1}{10}$$

Sample Exercise 15.11 *Indicator Color Change*

Bromthymol blue, an indicator with a K_a value of 1.0×10^{-7}, is yellow in its HIn form and blue in its In⁻ form. Suppose we put a few drops of this indicator in a strongly acidic solution. If the solution is then titrated with NaOH, at what pH will the indicator color change first be visible?

Solution

For bromthymol blue,

$$K_a = 1.0 \times 10^{-7} = \frac{[\text{H}^+][\text{In}^-]}{[\text{HIn}]}$$

We assume that the color change is visible when

$$\frac{[\text{In}^-]}{[\text{HIn}]} = \frac{1}{10}$$

(a)

(b)

(c)

Figure 15.7

(a) Yellow acid form of bromthymol blue; (b) a greenish tint is seen when the solution contains 1 part blue and 10 parts yellow; (c) blue basic form.

That is, we assume that we can see the first hint of a greenish tint (yellow plus a little blue) when the solution contains 1 part blue and 10 parts yellow (see Fig. 15.7). Thus

$$K_a = 1.0 \times 10^{-7} = \frac{[H^+](1)}{10}$$

$$[H^+] = 1.0 \times 10^{-6} \quad \text{or} \quad pH = 6.00.$$

The color change is first visible at pH 6.00.

See Exercises 15.69 and 15.70.

The Henderson–Hasselbalch equation is very useful in determining the pH at which an indicator changes color. For example, application of Equation (15.2) to the K_a expression for the general indicator HIn yields

$$pH = pK_a + \log\left(\frac{[In^-]}{[HIn]}\right)$$

where K_a is the dissociation constant for the acid form of the indicator (HIn). Since we assume that the color change is visible when

$$\frac{[In^-]}{[HIn]} = \frac{1}{10}$$

we have the following equation for determining the pH at which the color change occurs:

$$pH = pK_a + \log(\tfrac{1}{10}) = pK_a - 1$$

For bromthymol blue ($K_a = 1 \times 10^{-7}$, or $pK_a = 7$), the pH at the color change is

$$pH = 7 - 1 = 6$$

as we calculated in Sample Exercise 15.11.

When a basic solution is titrated, the indicator HIn will initially exist as In^- in solution, but as acid is added, more HIn will be formed. In this case the color change will be visible when there is a mixture of 10 parts In^- and 1 part HIn. That is, a color change from blue to blue-green will occur (see Fig. 15.7) due to the presence of some of the yellow HIn molecules. This color change will be first visible when

$$\frac{[In^-]}{[HIn]} = \frac{10}{1}$$

Note that this is the reciprocal of the ratio for the titration of an acid. Substituting this ratio into the Henderson–Hasselbalch equation gives

$$pH = pK_a + \log(\tfrac{10}{1}) = pK_a + 1$$

For bromthymol blue ($pK_a = 7$), we have a color change at

$$pH = 7 + 1 = 8$$

In summary, when bromthymol blue is used for the titration of an acid, the starting form will be HIn (yellow), and the color change occurs at a pH of about 6. When bromthymol blue is used for the titration of a base, the starting form is In^- (blue), and the color change occurs at a pH of about 8. Thus the useful pH range for bromthymol blue is

$$pK_a \text{ (bromthymol blue)} \pm 1 = 7 \pm 1$$

or from 6 to 8. This is a general result. For a typical acid–base indicator with dissociation constant K_a, the color transition occurs over a range of pH values given by $pK_a \pm 1$. The useful pH ranges for several common indicators are shown in Fig. 15.8.

When we choose an indicator for a titration, we want the indicator end point (where the color changes) and the titration equivalence point to be as close as possible. Choosing an indicator is easier if there is a large change in pH near the equivalence point of the titration. The dramatic change in pH near the equivalence point in a strong acid–strong base titration (Figs. 15.1 and 15.2) produces a sharp end point; that is, the complete color change (from the acid-to-base or base-to-acid colors) usually occurs over one drop of added titrant.

What indicator should we use for the titration of 100.00 mL of 0.100 M HCl with 0.100 M NaOH? We know that the equivalence point occurs at pH 7.00. In the initially acidic solution, the indicator will be predominantly in the HIn form. As OH^- ions are added, the pH increases rather slowly at first (see Fig. 15.1) and then rises rapidly at the equivalence point. This sharp change causes the indicator dissociation equilibrium

$$HIn \rightleftharpoons H^+ + In^-$$

to shift suddenly to the right, producing enough In^- ions to give a color change. Since we are titrating an acid, the indicator is predominantly in the acid form initially. Therefore, the first observable color change will occur at a pH where

$$\frac{[In^-]}{[HIn]} = \frac{1}{10}$$

Thus
$$pH = pK_a + \log(\tfrac{1}{10}) = pK_a - 1$$

If we want an indicator that changes color at pH 7, we can use this relationship to find the pK_a value for a suitable indicator:

$$pH = 7 = pK_a - 1 \quad \text{or} \quad pK_a = 7 + 1 = 8$$

Thus an indicator with a pK_a value of 8 ($K_a = 1 \times 10^{-8}$) changes color at about pH 7 and is ideal for marking the end point for a strong acid–strong base titration.

How crucial is it for a strong acid–strong base titration that the indicator change color exactly at pH 7? We can answer this question by examining the pH change near the equivalence point of the titration of 100 mL of 0.10 M HCl and 0.10 M NaOH. The data for a few points at or near the equivalence point are shown in Table 15.3. Note that in going from 99.99 to 100.01 mL of added NaOH solution (about half of a drop), the pH changes from 5.3 to 8.7—a very dramatic change. This behavior leads to the following general conclusions about indicators for a strong acid–strong base titration:

Indicator color changes will be sharp, occurring with the addition of a single drop of titrant.

There is a wide choice of suitable indicators. The results will agree within one drop of titrant, using indicators with end points as far apart as pH 5 and pH 9 (see Fig. 15.9).

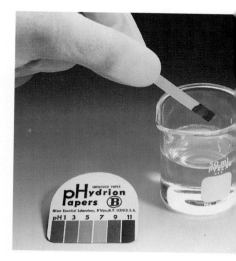

Universal indicator paper can be used to estimate the pH of a solution.

Table 15.3 Selected pH Values Near the Equivalence Point in the Titration of 100.0 mL of 0.10 M HCl with 0.10 M NaOH

NaOH Added (mL)	pH
99.99	5.3
100.00	7.0
100.01	8.7

Figure 15.8

The useful pH ranges for several common indicators. Note that most indicators have a useful range of about two pH units, as predicted by the expression $pK_a \pm 1$.

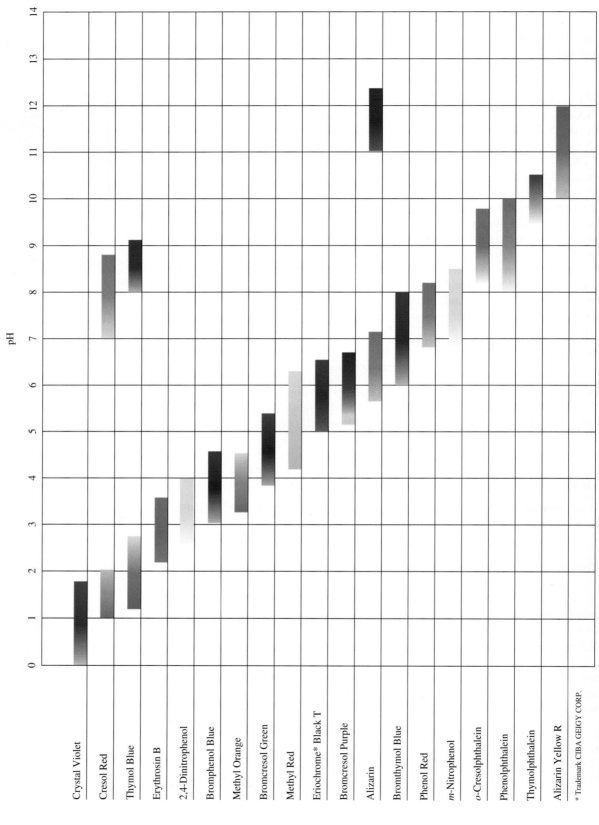

The pH ranges shown are approximate. Specific transition ranges depend on the indicator solvent chosen.

* Trademark CIBA GEIGY CORP.

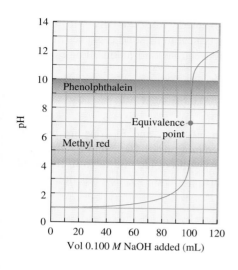

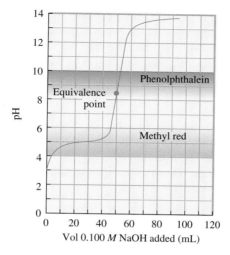

Figure 15.9 (left)

The pH curve for the titration of 100.0 mL of 0.10 M HCl with 0.10 M NaOH. Note that the end points of phenolphthalein and methyl red occur at virtually the same amounts of added NaOH.

Figure 15.10 (right)

The pH curve for the titration of 50 mL of 0.1 M $HC_2H_3O_2$ with 0.1 M NaOH. Phenolphthalein will give an end point very close to the equivalence point of the titration. Methyl red would change color well before the equivalence point (so the end point would be very different from the equivalence point) and would not be a suitable indicator for this titration.

The titration of weak acids is somewhat different. Figure 15.4 shows that the weaker the acid being titrated, the smaller is the vertical area around the equivalence point. This allows much less flexibility in choosing the indicator. We must choose an indicator whose useful pH range has a midpoint as close as possible to the pH at the equivalence point. For example, we saw earlier that in the titration of 0.1 M $HC_2H_3O_2$ with 0.1 M NaOH the pH at the equivalence point is 8.7 (see Fig. 15.3). A good indicator choice would be phenolphthalein, since its useful pH range is 8 to 10. Thymol blue also would be acceptable, but methyl red would not. The choice of an indicator is illustrated graphically in Fig. 15.10.

SOLUBILITY EQUILIBRIA

15.6 Solubility Equilibria and the Solubility Product

Solubility is a very important phenomenon. The fact that substances such as sugar and table salt dissolve in water allows us to flavor foods easily. The fact that calcium sulfate is less soluble in hot water than in cold water causes it to coat tubes in boilers, reducing thermal efficiency. Tooth decay involves solubility: When food lodges between the teeth, acids form that dissolve tooth enamel, which contains a mineral called *hydroxyapatite,* $Ca_5(PO_4)_3OH$. Tooth decay can be reduced by treating teeth with fluoride (see Chemical Impact, p. 778). Fluoride replaces the hydroxide in hydroxyapatite to produce the corresponding fluorapatite, $Ca_5(PO_4)_3F$, and calcium fluoride, CaF_2, both of which are less soluble in acids than the original enamel. Another important consequence of solubility involves the use of a suspension of barium sulfate to improve the clarity of X rays of the gastrointestinal tract. The very low solubility of barium sulfate, which contains the toxic ion Ba^{2+}, makes ingestion of the compound safe.

Adding F^- to drinking water is controversial. See Bette Hileman, "Fluoridation of Water," *Chem. Eng. News,* Aug. 1, 1988, p. 26.

In this section we consider the equilibria associated with solids dissolving to form aqueous solutions. We will assume that when a typical ionic solid dissolves in water, it dissociates completely into separate hydrated cations and anions. For example, calcium fluoride dissolves in water as follows:

$$CaF_2(s) \xrightarrow{\text{H}_2\text{O}} Ca^{2+}(aq) + 2F^-(aq)$$

For simplicity, we will ignore the effects of ion associations in these solutions.

When the solid salt is first added to the water, no Ca^{2+} and F^- ions are present. However, as the dissolution proceeds, the concentrations of Ca^{2+} and F^- increase, making it more and more likely that these ions will collide and re-form the solid phase. Thus two competing processes are occurring: the dissolution reaction and its reverse:

$$Ca^{2+}(aq) + 2F^-(aq) \longrightarrow CaF_2(s)$$

Ultimately, dynamic equilibrium is reached:

$$CaF_2(s) \rightleftharpoons Ca^{2+}(aq) + 2F^-(aq)$$

At this point no more solid dissolves (the solution is said to be *saturated*).

We can write an equilibrium expression for this process according to the law of mass action:

$$K_{sp} = [Ca^{2+}][F^-]^2$$

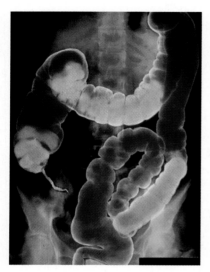

An X ray of the lower gastrointestinal tract using barium sulfate.

where $[Ca^{2+}]$ and $[F^-]$ are expressed in mol/L. The constant K_{sp} is called the **solubility product constant** or simply the **solubility product** for the equilibrium expression.

Since CaF_2 is a pure solid, it is not included in the equilibrium expression. The fact that the amount of excess solid present does not affect the position of the solubility equilibrium might seem strange at first; more solid means more surface area exposed to the solvent, which would seem to result in greater solubility. This is not the case, however. When the ions in solution re-form the solid, they do so on the surface of the solid. Thus doubling the surface area of the solid not only doubles the rate of dissolving, it also doubles the rate of re-formation of the solid. The amount of excess solid present therefore has no effect on the equilibrium position. Similarly, although either increasing the surface area by grinding up the solid or stirring the solution speeds up the attainment of equilibrium, neither procedure changes the amount of solid dissolved at equilibrium. Neither the amount of excess solid nor the size of the particles present will shift the *position* of the solubility equilibrium.

Pure liquids and pure solids are never included in an equilibrium expression (Section 13.4).

It is very important to distinguish between the *solubility* of a given solid and its *solubility product*. The solubility product is an *equilibrium constant* and has only *one* value for a given solid at a given temperature. Solubility, on the other hand, is an *equilibrium position*. In pure water at a specific temperature a given salt has a particular solubility. On the other hand, if a common ion is present in the solution, the solubility varies according to the concentration of the common ion. However, in all cases the product of the ion concentrations must satisfy the K_{sp} expression. The K_{sp} values at 25°C for many common ionic solids are listed in Table 15.4. The units are customarily omitted.

Solving solubility equilibria problems requires many of the same procedures we have used to deal with acid–base equilibria, as illustrated in Sample Exercises 15.12 and 15.13.

Video: Supersaturated Sodium Acetate

K_{sp} is an equilibrium constant; solubility is an equilibrium position.

Table 15.4 K_{sp} Values at 25°C for Common Ionic Solids

Ionic Solid	K_{sp} (at 25°C)	Ionic Solid	K_{sp} (at 25°C)	Ionic Solid	K_{sp} (at 25°C)
Fluorides		Hg_2CrO_4*	2×10^{-9}	$Co(OH)_2$	2.5×10^{-16}
BaF_2	2.4×10^{-5}	$BaCrO_4$	8.5×10^{-11}	$Ni(OH)_2$	1.6×10^{-16}
MgF_2	6.4×10^{-9}	Ag_2CrO_4	9.0×10^{-12}	$Zn(OH)_2$	4.5×10^{-17}
PbF_2	4×10^{-8}	$PbCrO_4$	2×10^{-16}	$Cu(OH)_2$	1.6×10^{-19}
SrF_2	7.9×10^{-10}			$Hg(OH)_2$	3×10^{-26}
CaF_2	4.0×10^{-11}	**Carbonates**		$Sn(OH)_2$	3×10^{-27}
		$NiCO_3$	1.4×10^{-7}	$Cr(OH)_3$	6.7×10^{-31}
Chlorides		$CaCO_3$	8.7×10^{-9}	$Al(OH)_3$	2×10^{-32}
$PbCl_2$	1.6×10^{-5}	$BaCO_3$	1.6×10^{-9}	$Fe(OH)_3$	4×10^{-38}
$AgCl$	1.6×10^{-10}	$SrCO_3$	7×10^{-10}	$Co(OH)_3$	2.5×10^{-43}
Hg_2Cl_2*	1.1×10^{-18}	$CuCO_3$	2.5×10^{-10}		
		$ZnCO_3$	2×10^{-10}	**Sulfides**	
Bromides		$MnCO_3$	8.8×10^{-11}	MnS	2.3×10^{-13}
$PbBr_2$	4.6×10^{-6}	$FeCO_3$	2.1×10^{-11}	FeS	3.7×10^{-19}
$AgBr$	5.0×10^{-13}	Ag_2CO_3	8.1×10^{-12}	NiS	3×10^{-21}
Hg_2Br_2*	1.3×10^{-22}	$CdCO_3$	5.2×10^{-12}	CoS	5×10^{-22}
		$PbCO_3$	1.5×10^{-15}	ZnS	2.5×10^{-22}
Iodides		$MgCO_3$	6.8×10^{-6}	SnS	1×10^{-26}
PbI_2	1.4×10^{-8}	Hg_2CO_3*	9.0×10^{-15}	CdS	1.0×10^{-28}
AgI	1.5×10^{-16}			PbS	7×10^{-29}
Hg_2I_2*	4.5×10^{-29}	**Hydroxides**		CuS	8.5×10^{-45}
		$Ba(OH)_2$	5.0×10^{-3}	Ag_2S	1.6×10^{-49}
Sulfates		$Sr(OH)_2$	3.2×10^{-4}	HgS	1.6×10^{-54}
$CaSO_4$	6.1×10^{-5}	$Ca(OH)_2$	1.3×10^{-6}		
Ag_2SO_4	1.2×10^{-5}	$AgOH$	2.0×10^{-8}	**Phosphates**	
$SrSO_4$	3.2×10^{-7}	$Mg(OH)_2$	8.9×10^{-12}	Ag_3PO_4	1.8×10^{-18}
$PbSO_4$	1.3×10^{-8}	$Mn(OH)_2$	2×10^{-13}	$Sr_3(PO_4)_2$	1×10^{-31}
$BaSO_4$	1.5×10^{-9}	$Cd(OH)_2$	5.9×10^{-15}	$Ca_3(PO_4)_2$	1.3×10^{-32}
		$Pb(OH)_2$	1.2×10^{-15}	$Ba_3(PO_4)_2$	6×10^{-39}
Chromates		$Fe(OH)_2$	1.8×10^{-15}	$Pb_3(PO_4)_2$	1×10^{-54}
$SrCrO_4$	3.6×10^{-5}				

*Contains Hg_2^{2+} ions. $K = [Hg_2^{2+}][X^-]^2$ for Hg_2X_2 salts, for example.

Sample Exercise 15.12 Calculating K_{sp} from Solubility I

Copper(I) bromide has a measured solubility of 2.0×10^{-4} mol/L at 25°C. Calculate its K_{sp} value.

Solution

In this experiment the solid was placed in contact with water. Thus, before any reaction occurred, the system contained solid CuBr and H_2O. The process that occurs is the dissolving of CuBr to form the separated Cu^+ and Br^- ions:

$$CuBr(s) \rightleftharpoons Cu^+(aq) + Br^-(aq)$$

where

$$K_{sp} = [Cu^+][Br^-]$$

Initially, the solution contains no Cu^+ or Br^-, so the initial concentrations are

$$[Cu^+]_0 = [Br^-]_0 = 0$$

The equilibrium concentrations can be obtained from the measured solubility of CuBr, which is 2.0×10^{-4} mol/L. This means that 2.0×10^{-4} mol solid CuBr dissolves per 1.0 L of solution to come to equilibrium with the excess solid. The reaction is

$$CuBr(s) \longrightarrow Cu^+(aq) + Br^-(aq)$$

Thus

2.0×10^{-4} mol/L CuBr(s)
$$\longrightarrow 2.0 \times 10^{-4} \text{ mol/L } Cu^+(aq) + 2.0 \times 10^{-4} \text{ mol/L } Br^-(aq)$$

We can now write the equilibrium concentrations:

$$[Cu^+] = [Cu^+]_0 + \text{change to reach equilibrium}$$
$$= 0 + 2.0 \times 10^{-4} \text{ mol/L}$$

and
$$[Br^-] = [Br^-]_0 + \text{change to reach equilibrium}$$
$$= 0 + 2.0 \times 10^{-4} \text{ mol/L}$$

These equilibrium concentrations allow us to calculate the value of K_{sp} for CuBr:

$$K_{sp} = [Cu^+][Br^-] = (2.0 \times 10^{-4} \text{ mol/L})(2.0 \times 10^{-4} \text{ mol/L})$$
$$= 4.0 \times 10^{-8} \text{ mol}^2/\text{L}^2 = 4.0 \times 10^{-8}$$

The units for K_{sp} values are usually omitted.

See Exercise 15.81.

Sample Exercise 15.13 *Calculating K_{sp} from Solubility II*

Calculate the K_{sp} value for bismuth sulfide (Bi_2S_3), which has a solubility of 1.0×10^{-15} mol/L at 25°C.

Solution

The system initially contains H_2O and solid Bi_2S_3, which dissolves as follows:

$$Bi_2S_3(s) \rightleftharpoons 2Bi^{3+}(aq) + 3S^{2-}(aq)$$

Therefore, $$K_{sp} = [Bi^{3+}]^2[S^{2-}]^3$$

Since no Bi^{3+} and S^{2-} ions were present in solution before the Bi_2S_3 dissolved,

$$[Bi^{3+}]_0 = [S^{2-}]_0 = 0$$

Thus the equilibrium concentrations of these ions will be determined by the amount of salt that dissolves to reach equilibrium, which in this case is 1.0×10^{-15} mol/L. Since each Bi_2S_3 unit contains $2Bi^{3+}$ and $3S^{2-}$ ions:

1.0×10^{-15} mol/L $Bi_2S_3(s)$
$$\longrightarrow 2(1.0 \times 10^{-15} \text{ mol/L}) Bi^{3+}(aq) + 3(1.0 \times 10^{-15} \text{ mol/L}) S^{2-}(aq)$$

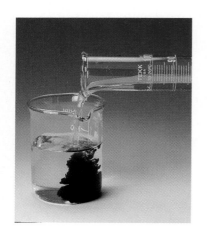

Precipitation of bismuth sulfide.

Sulfide is a very basic anion and really exists in water as HS^-. We will not consider this complication.

The equilibrium concentrations are

$$[Bi^{3+}] = [Bi^{3+}]_0 + \text{change} = 0 + 2.0 \times 10^{-15} \text{ mol/L}$$
$$[S^{2-}] = [S^{2-}]_0 + \text{change} = 0 + 3.0 \times 10^{-15} \text{ mol/L}$$

Then

$$K_{sp} = [Bi^{3+}]^2[S^{2-}]^3 = (2.0 \times 10^{-15})^2(3.0 \times 10^{-15})^3 = 1.1 \times 10^{-73}$$

See Exercises 15.82 through 15.84.

Solubilities must be expressed in mol/L in K_{sp} calculations.

We have seen that the experimentally determined solubility of an ionic solid can be used to calculate its K_{sp} value.* The reverse is also possible: The solubility of an ionic solid can be calculated if its K_{sp} value is known.

Sample Exercise 15.14 Calculating Solubility from K_{sp}

The K_{sp} value for copper(II) iodate, $Cu(IO_3)_2$, is 1.4×10^{-7} at 25°C. Calculate its solubility at 25°C.

Solution

The system initially contains H_2O and solid $Cu(IO_3)_2$, which dissolves according to the following equilibrium:

$$Cu(IO_3)_2(s) \rightleftharpoons Cu^{2+}(aq) + 2IO_3^-(aq)$$

Therefore,

$$K_{sp} = [Cu^{2+}][IO_3^-]^2$$

To find the solubility of $Cu(IO_3)_2$, we must find the equilibrium concentrations of the Cu^{2+} and IO_3^- ions. We do this in the usual way by specifying the initial concentrations (before any solid has dissolved) and then defining the change required to reach equilibrium. Since in this case we do not know the solubility, we will assume that x mol/L of the solid dissolves to reach equilibrium. The 1:2 stoichiometry of the salt means that

$$x \text{ mol/L } Cu(IO_3)_2(s) \longrightarrow x \text{ mol/L } Cu^{2+}(aq) + 2x \text{ mol/L } IO_3^-(aq)$$

The concentrations are as follows:

Initial Concentration (mol/L) (Before Any $Cu(IO_3)_2$ Dissolves)		Equilibrium Concentration (mol/L)
$[Cu^{2+}]_0 = 0$ $[IO_3^-]_0 = 0$	$\xrightarrow[\text{to reach}]{\substack{x \text{ mol/L} \\ \text{dissolves} \\ \text{equilibrium}}}$	$[Cu^{2+}] = x$ $[IO_3^-] = 2x$

---

* This calculation assumes that all the dissolved solid is present as separated ions. In some cases, such as $CaSO_4$, large numbers of ion pairs exist in solution, so this method yields an incorrect value for K_{sp}.

Substituting the equilibrium concentrations into the expression for K_{sp} gives

$$1.4 \times 10^{-7} = K_{sp} = [Cu^{2+}][IO_3^-]^2 = (x)(2x)^2 = 4x^3$$

Then

$$x = \sqrt[3]{3.5 \times 10^{-8}} = 3.3 \times 10^{-3} \text{ mol/L}$$

Thus the solubility of solid $Cu(IO_3)_2$ is 3.3×10^{-3} mol/L.

See Exercises 15.85 and 15.86.

Relative Solubilities

A salt's K_{sp} value gives us information about its solubility. However, we must be careful in using K_{sp} values to predict the *relative* solubilities of a group of salts. There are two possible cases:

1. The salts being compared produce the same number of ions. For example, consider

$$
\begin{array}{ll}
\text{AgI}(s) & K_{sp} = 1.5 \times 10^{-16} \\
\text{CuI}(s) & K_{sp} = 5.0 \times 10^{-12} \\
\text{CaSO}_4(s) & K_{sp} = 6.1 \times 10^{-5}
\end{array}
$$

Each of these solids dissolves to produce two ions:

$$\text{Salt} \rightleftharpoons \text{cation} + \text{anion}$$
$$K_{sp} = [\text{cation}][\text{anion}]$$

If x is the solubility in mol/L, then at equilibrium

$$[\text{Cation}] = x$$
$$[\text{Anion}] = x$$
$$K_{sp} = [\text{cation}][\text{anion}] = x^2$$
$$x = \sqrt{K_{sp}} = \text{solubility}$$

Therefore, in this case we can compare the solubilities for these solids by comparing the K_{sp} values:

$$\underset{\substack{\text{Most soluble;} \\ \text{largest } K_{sp}}}{\text{CaSO}_4(s)} > \text{CuI}(s) > \underset{\substack{\text{Least soluble;} \\ \text{smallest } K_{sp}}}{\text{AgI}(s)}$$

2. The salts being compared produce different numbers of ions. For example, consider

$$
\begin{array}{ll}
\text{CuS}(s) & K_{sp} = 8.5 \times 10^{-45} \\
\text{Ag}_2\text{S}(s) & K_{sp} = 1.6 \times 10^{-49} \\
\text{Bi}_2\text{S}_3(s) & K_{sp} = 1.1 \times 10^{-73}
\end{array}
$$

Because these salts produce different numbers of ions when they dissolve, the K_{sp} values cannot be compared *directly* to determine relative solubilities. In fact, if we calculate the solubilities (using the procedure in Sample Exercise 15.14), we obtain the results summarized in Table 15.5. The order of solubilities is

$$\underset{\text{Most soluble}}{\text{Bi}_2\text{S}_3(s)} > \text{Ag}_2\text{S}(s) > \underset{\text{Least soluble}}{\text{CuS}(s)}$$

Table 15.5 Calculated Solubilities for CuS, Ag$_2$S, and Bi$_2$S$_3$ at 25°C		
Salt	K_{sp}	Calculated Solubility (mol/L)
CuS	8.5×10^{-45}	9.2×10^{-23}
Ag$_2$S	1.6×10^{-49}	3.4×10^{-17}
Bi$_2$S$_3$	1.1×10^{-73}	1.0×10^{-15}

which is opposite to the order of the K_{sp} values.

Remember that relative solubilities can be predicted by comparing K_{sp} values *only* for salts that produce the same total number of ions.

Common Ion Effect

So far we have considered ionic solids dissolved in pure water. We will now see what happens when the water contains an ion in common with the dissolving salt. For example, consider the solubility of solid silver chromate (Ag$_2$CrO$_4$, $K_{sp} = 9.0 \times 10^{-12}$) in a 0.100 M solution of AgNO$_3$. Before any Ag$_2$CrO$_4$ dissolves, the solution contains the major species Ag$^+$, NO$_3^-$, and H$_2$O, with solid Ag$_2$CrO$_4$ on the bottom of the container. Since NO$_3^-$ is not found in Ag$_2$CrO$_4$, we can ignore it. The relevant initial concentrations (before any Ag$_2$CrO$_4$ dissolves) are

$$[Ag^+]_0 = 0.100 \ M \ \text{(from the dissolved AgNO}_3)$$
$$[CrO_4^{2-}]_0 = 0$$

The system comes to equilibrium as the solid Ag$_2$CrO$_4$ dissolves according to the reaction

$$Ag_2CrO_4(s) \rightleftharpoons 2Ag^+(aq) + CrO_4^{2-}(aq)$$

for which

$$K_{sp} = [Ag^+]^2[CrO_4^{2-}] = 9.0 \times 10^{-12}$$

We assume that x mol/L of Ag$_2$CrO$_4$ dissolves to reach equilibrium, which means that

$$x \ \text{mol/L Ag}_2\text{CrO}_4(s) \longrightarrow 2x \ \text{mol/L Ag}^+(aq) + x \ \text{mol/L CrO}_4^{2-}$$

Now we can specify the equilibrium concentrations in terms of x:

$$[Ag^+] = [Ag^+]_0 + \text{change} = 0.100 + 2x$$
$$[CrO_4^{2-}] = [CrO_4^{2-}]_0 + \text{change} = 0 + x = x$$

Substituting these concentrations into the expression for K_{sp} gives

$$9.0 \times 10^{-12} = [Ag^+]^2[CrO_4^{2-}] = (0.100 + 2x)^2(x)$$

The mathematics required here appear to be complicated, since the multiplication of terms on the right-hand side produces an expression that contains an x^3 term. However, as is usually the case, we can make simplifying assumptions. Since the K_{sp} value for Ag$_2$CrO$_4$ is small (the position of the equilibrium lies far to the left), x is expected to be small compared with 0.100 M. Therefore, $0.100 + 2x \approx 0.100$, which allows simplification of the expression:

$$9.0 \times 10^{-12} = (0.100 + 2x)^2(x) \approx (0.100)^2(x)$$

A potassium chromate solution being added to aqueous silver nitrate, forming silver chromate.

Then
$$x \approx \frac{9.0 \times 10^{-12}}{(0.100)^2} = 9.0 \times 10^{-10} \text{ mol/L}$$

Since x is much less than 0.100 M, the approximation is valid (by the 5% rule). Thus

Solubility of Ag_2CrO_4 in 0.100 M $AgNO_3$ = x = 9.0×10^{-10} mol/L

and the equilibrium concentrations are

$$[Ag^+] = 0.100 + 2x = 0.100 + 2(9.0 \times 10^{-10}) = 0.100 \text{ } M$$
$$[CrO_4^{2-}] = x = 9.0 \times 10^{-10} \text{ } M$$

Now we compare the solubilities of Ag_2CrO_4 in pure water and in 0.100 M $AgNO_3$:

Solubility of Ag_2CrO_4 in pure water = 1.3×10^{-4} mol/L

Solubility of Ag_2CrO_4 in 0.100 M $AgNO_3$ = 9.0×10^{-10} mol/L

Note that the solubility of Ag_2CrO_4 is much less in the presence of Ag^+ ions from $AgNO_3$. This is another example of the common ion effect. The solubility of a solid is lowered if the solution already contains ions common to the solid.

Sample Exercise 15.15 *Solubility and Common Ions*

Calculate the solubility of solid CaF_2 ($K_{sp} = 4.0 \times 10^{-11}$) in a 0.025 M NaF solution.

Solution

Before any CaF_2 dissolves, the solution contains the major species Na^+, F^-, and H_2O. The solubility equilibrium for CaF_2 is

$$CaF_2(s) \rightleftharpoons Ca^{2+}(aq) + 2F^-(aq)$$

and
$$K_{sp} = 4.0 \times 10^{-11} = [Ca^{2+}][F^-]^2$$

Initial Concentration (mol/L) *(Before Any CaF_2 Dissolves)*		*Equilibrium Concentration (mol/L)*
$[Ca^{2+}]_0 = 0$ $[F^-]_0 = 0.025 \text{ } M$ ↗ From 0.025 M NaF	x mol/L CaF_2 dissolves $\xrightarrow{\text{to reach}}$ equilibrium	$[Ca^{2+}] = x$ $[F^-] = 0.025 + 2x$ ↗ ↗ From NaF From CaF_2

Substituting the equilibrium concentrations into the expression for K_{sp} gives

$$K_{sp} = 4.0 \times 10^{-11} = [Ca^{2+}][F^-]^2 = (x)(0.025 + 2x)^2$$

Assuming that $2x$ is negligible compared with 0.025 (since K_{sp} is small) gives

$$4.0 \times 10^{-11} \approx (x)(0.025)^2$$
$$x \approx 6.4 \times 10^{-8}$$

The approximation is valid (by the 5% rule), and

$$\text{Solubility} = x = 6.4 \times 10^{-8} \text{ mol/L}$$

Thus 6.4×10^{-8} mol solid CaF_2 dissolves per liter of the 0.025 M NaF solution.

See Exercises 15.91 through 15.94.

pH and Solubility

The pH of a solution can greatly affect a salt's solubility. For example, magnesium hydroxide dissolves according to the equilibrium

$$Mg(OH)_2(s) \rightleftharpoons Mg^{2+}(aq) + 2OH^-(aq)$$

Addition of OH^- ions (an increase in pH) will, by the common ion effect, force the equilibrium to the left, decreasing the solubility of $Mg(OH)_2$. On the other hand, an addition of H^+ ions (a decrease in pH) increases the solubility, because OH^- ions are removed from solution by reacting with the added H^+ ions. In response to the lower concentration of OH^-, the equilibrium position moves to the right. This is why a suspension of solid $Mg(OH)_2$, known as *milk of magnesia,* dissolves as required in the stomach to combat excess acidity.

This idea also applies to salts with other types of anions. For example, the solubility of silver phosphate (Ag_3PO_4) is greater in acid than in pure water because the PO_4^{3-} ion is a strong base that reacts with H^+ to form the HPO_4^{2-} ion. The reaction

$$H^+ + PO_4^{3-} \longrightarrow HPO_4^{2-}$$

occurs in acidic solution, thus lowering the concentration of PO_4^{3-} and shifting the solubility equilibrium

$$Ag_3PO_4(s) \rightleftharpoons 3Ag^+(aq) + PO_4^{3-}(aq)$$

to the right. This, in turn, increases the solubility of silver phosphate.

Silver chloride (AgCl), however, has the same solubility in acid as in pure water. Why? Since the Cl^- ion is a very weak base (that is, HCl is a very strong acid), no HCl molecules are formed. Thus the addition of H^+ to a solution containing Cl^- does not affect $[Cl^-]$ and has no effect on the solubility of a chloride salt.

The general rule is that if the anion X^- is an effective base—that is, if HX is a weak acid—the salt MX will show increased solubility in an acidic solution. Examples of common anions that are effective bases are OH^-, S^{2-}, CO_3^{2-}, $C_2O_4^{2-}$, and CrO_4^{2-}. Salts containing these anions are much more soluble in an acidic solution than in pure water.

As mentioned at the beginning of this chapter, one practical result of the increased solubility of carbonates in acid is the formation of huge limestone caves such as Mammoth Cave in Kentucky or Carlsbad Caverns in New Mexico. Carbon dioxide dissolved in groundwater makes it acidic, increasing the solubility of calcium carbonate and eventually producing huge caverns. As the carbon dioxide escapes to the air, the pH of the dripping water goes up and the calcium carbonate precipitates, forming stalactites and stalagmites.

15.7 Precipitation and Qualitative Analysis

So far we have considered solids dissolving in solutions. Now we will consider the reverse process—the formation of a solid from solution. When solutions are mixed, various reactions can occur. We have already considered acid–base reactions in some detail. In this section we show how to predict whether a precipitate will form when two solutions are mixed. We will use the **ion product,** which is defined just like the expression for K_{sp} for a given solid except that *initial concentrations are used* instead of equilibrium concentrations. For solid CaF_2, the expression for the ion product Q is written

$$Q = [Ca^{2+}]_0[F^-]_0^2$$

If we add a solution containing Ca^{2+} ions to a solution containing F^- ions, a precipitate may or may not form, depending on the concentrations of these ions in the resulting mixed solution. To predict whether precipitation will occur, we consider the relationship between Q and K_{sp}.

Q is used here in a very similar way to the use of the reaction quotient in Chapter 13.

If Q is greater than K_{sp}, precipitation occurs and will continue until the concentrations are reduced to the point that they satisfy K_{sp}.

If Q is less than K_{sp}, no precipitation occurs.

Sample Exercise 15.16 Determining Precipitation Conditions

A solution is prepared by adding 750.0 mL of 4.00×10^{-3} M $Ce(NO_3)_3$ to 300.0 mL of 2.00×10^{-2} M KIO_3. Will $Ce(IO_3)_3$ ($K_{sp} = 1.9 \times 10^{-10}$) precipitate from this solution?

Solution

First, we calculate $[Ce^{3+}]_0$ and $[IO_3^-]_0$ in the mixed solution before any reaction occurs:

$$[Ce^{3+}]_0 = \frac{(750.0 \text{ mL})(4.00 \times 10^{-3} \text{ mmol/mL})}{(750.0 + 300.0) \text{ mL}} = 2.86 \times 10^{-3} \text{ M}$$

$$[IO_3^-]_0 = \frac{(300.0 \text{ mL})(2.00 \times 10^{-2} \text{ mmol/mL})}{(750.0 + 300.0) \text{ mL}} = 5.71 \times 10^{-3} \text{ M}$$

The ion product for $Ce(IO_3)_3$ is

For $Ce(IO_3)_3(s)$, $K_{sp} = [Ce^{3+}][IO_3^-]^3$.

$$Q = [Ce^{3+}]_0[IO_3^-]_0^3 = (2.86 \times 10^{-3})(5.71 \times 10^{-3})^3 = 5.32 \times 10^{-10}$$

Since Q is greater than K_{sp}, $Ce(IO_3)_3$ will precipitate from the mixed solution.

See Exercises 15.97 and 15.98.

Sometimes we want to do more than simply predict whether precipitation will occur; we may want to calculate the equilibrium concentrations in the solution after precipitation occurs. For example, let us calculate the equilibrium concentrations of Pb^{2+} and I^- ions in a solution formed by mixing 100.0 mL of 0.0500 M $Pb(NO_3)_2$ and 200.0 mL of 0.100 M NaI. First, we must determine whether solid PbI_2 ($K_{sp} = 1.4 \times 10^{-8}$) forms when the solutions are mixed. To do so, we need to calculate $[Pb^{2+}]_0$ and $[I^-]_0$ before any reaction occurs:

$$[Pb^{2+}]_0 = \frac{\text{mmol } Pb^{2+}}{\text{mL solution}} = \frac{(100.0 \text{ mL})(0.0500 \text{ mmol/mL})}{300.0 \text{ mL}} = 1.67 \times 10^{-2} \ M$$

$$[I^-]_0 = \frac{\text{mmol } I^-}{\text{mL solution}} = \frac{(200.0 \text{ mL})(0.100 \text{ mmol/mL})}{300.0 \text{ mL}} = 6.67 \times 10^{-2} \ M$$

The ion product for PbI_2 is

$$Q = [Pb^{2+}]_0[I^-]_0^2 = (1.67 \times 10^{-2})(6.67 \times 10^{-2})^2 = 7.43 \times 10^{-5}$$

Since Q is greater than K_{sp}, a precipitate of PbI_2 will form.

Since the K_{sp} for PbI_2 is quite small (1.4×10^{-8}), only very small quantities of Pb^{2+} and I^- can coexist in aqueous solution. In other words, when Pb^{2+} and I^- are mixed, most of these ions will precipitate out as PbI_2. That is, the reaction

$$Pb^{2+}(aq) + 2I^-(aq) \longrightarrow PbI_2(s)$$

(which is the reverse of the dissolution reaction) goes essentially to completion.

If, when two solutions are mixed, a reaction occurs that goes virtually to completion, it is essential to do the stoichiometry calculations before considering the equilibrium calculations. Therefore, in this case we let the system go completely in the direction toward which it tends. Then we will let it adjust back to equilibrium. If we let Pb^{2+} and I^- react to completion, we have the following concentrations:

> The equilibrium constant for formation of solid PbI_2 is $1/K_{sp}$, or 7×10^7, so this equilibrium lies far to the right.

	Pb^{2+}	+	$2I^-$	$\longrightarrow$	PbI_2
Before reaction:	(100.0 mL)(0.0500 M) = 5.00 mmol		(200.0 mL)(0.100 M) = 20.0 mmol		The amount of PbI_2 formed does
After reaction:	0 mmol		20.0 − 2(5.00) = 10.0 mmol		not influence the equilibrium.

> In this reaction 10 mmol I^- is in excess.

Next we must allow the system to adjust to equilibrium. At equilibrium $[Pb^{2+}]$ is not actually zero because the reaction does not go quite to completion. The best way to think about this is that once the PbI_2 is formed, a very small amount redissolves to reach equilibrium. Since I^- is in excess, the PbI_2 is dissolving into a solution that contains 10.0 mmol I^- per 300.0 mL of solution, or $3.33 \times 10^{-2} \ M \ I^-$.

We could state this problem as follows: What is the solubility of solid PbI_2 in a $3.33 \times 10^{-2} \ M$ NaI solution? The lead iodide dissolves according to the equation

$$PbI_2(s) \rightleftharpoons Pb^{2+}(aq) + 2I^-(aq)$$

The concentrations are as follows:

Initial Concentration (mol/L)		Equilibrium Concentration (mol/L)
$[Pb^{2+}]_0 = 0$ $[I^-]_0 = 3.33 \times 10^{-2}$	$\xrightarrow[\text{dissolves}]{\substack{x \text{ mol/L} \\ PbI_2(s)}}$	$[Pb^{2+}] = x$ $[I^-] = 3.33 \times 10^{-2} + 2x$

Substituting into the expression for K_{sp} gives

$$K_{sp} = 1.4 \times 10^{-8} = [Pb^{2+}][I^-]^2 = (x)(3.33 \times 10^{-2} + 2x)^2 \approx (x)(3.33 \times 10^{-2})^2$$

Then
$$[Pb^{2+}] = x = 1.3 \times 10^{-5} \; M$$
$$[I^-] = 3.33 \times 10^{-2} \; M$$

Note that $3.33 \times 10^{-2} \gg 2x$, so the approximation is valid. These Pb^{2+} and I^- concentrations thus represent the equilibrium concentrations present in a solution formed by mixing 100.0 mL of 0.0500 M $Pb(NO_3)_2$ and 200.0 mL of 0.100 M NaI.

Sample Exercise 15.17 Precipitation

A solution is prepared by mixing 150.0 mL of 1.00×10^{-2} M $Mg(NO_3)_2$ and 250.0 mL of 1.00×10^{-1} M NaF. Calculate the concentrations of Mg^{2+} and F^- at equilibrium with solid MgF_2 ($K_{sp} = 6.4 \times 10^{-9}$).

Solution

The first step is to determine whether solid MgF_2 forms. To do this, we need to calculate the concentrations of Mg^{2+} and F^- in the mixed solution and find Q:

For $MgF_2(s)$, $K_{sp} = [Mg^{2+}][F^-]^2$.

$$[Mg^{2+}]_0 = \frac{\text{mmol } Mg^{2+}}{\text{mL solution}} = \frac{(150.0 \text{ mL})(1.00 \times 10^{-2} \; M)}{400.0 \text{ mL}} = 3.75 \times 10^{-3} \; M$$

$$[F^-]_0 = \frac{\text{mmol } F^-}{\text{mL solution}} = \frac{(250.0 \text{ mL})(1.00 \times 10^{-1} \; M)}{400.0 \text{ mL}} = 6.25 \times 10^{-2} \; M$$

$$Q = [Mg^{2+}]_0[F^-]_0^2 = (3.75 \times 10^{-3})(6.25 \times 10^{-2})^2 = 1.46 \times 10^{-5}$$

Since Q is greater than K_{sp}, solid MgF_2 will form.

The next step is to run the precipitation reaction to completion:

	Mg^{2+}	$+$	$2F^-$	$\longrightarrow$	$MgF_2(s)$
Before reaction:	$(150.0)(1.00 \times 10^{-2})$ $= 1.50$ mmol		$(250.0)(1.00 \times 10^{-1})$ $= 25.0$ mmol		
After reaction:	$1.50 - 1.50 = 0$		$25.0 - 2(1.50)$ $= 22.0$ mmol		

Note that excess F^- remains after the precipitation reaction goes to completion. The concentration is

$$[F^-]_{\text{excess}} = \frac{22.0 \text{ mmol}}{400.0 \text{ mL}} = 5.50 \times 10^{-2} \; M$$

Although we have assumed that the Mg^{2+} is completely consumed, we know that $[Mg^{2+}]$ will not be zero at equilibrium. We can compute the equilibrium $[Mg^{2+}]$ by letting MgF_2 redissolve to satisfy the expression for K_{sp}. How much MgF_2 will dissolve in a 5.50×10^{-2} M NaF solution? We proceed as usual:

$$MgF_2(s) \rightleftharpoons Mg^{2+}(aq) + 2F^-(aq)$$
$$K_{sp} = [Mg^{2+}][F^-]^2 = 6.4 \times 10^{-9}$$

Initial Concentration (mol/L)		Equilibrium Concentration (mol/L)
$[Mg^{2+}]_0 = 0$ $[F^-]_0 = 5.50 \times 10^{-2}$	$\xrightarrow[\text{dissolves}]{\substack{x \text{ mol/L} \\ MgF_2(s)}}$	$[Mg^{2+}] = x$ $[F^-] = 5.50 \times 10^{-2} + 2x$

$$
\begin{aligned}
K_{sp} = 6.4 \times 10^{-9} &= [Mg^{2+}][F^-]^2 \\
&= (x)(5.50 \times 10^{-2} + 2x)^2 \approx (x)(5.50 \times 10^{-2})^2 \\
[Mg^{2+}] = x &= 2.1 \times 10^{-6} \ M \\
[F^-] &= 5.50 \times 10^{-2} \ M
\end{aligned}
$$

The approximations made here fall within the 5% rule.

See Exercises 15.99 and 15.100.

Selective Precipitation

Mixtures of metal ions in aqueous solution are often separated by **selective precipitation,** that is, by using a reagent whose anion forms a precipitate with only one or a few of the metal ions in the mixture. For example, suppose we have a solution containing both Ba^{2+} and Ag^+ ions. If NaCl is added to the solution, AgCl precipitates as a white solid, but since $BaCl_2$ is soluble, the Ba^{2+} ions remain in solution.

Sample Exercise 15.18 Selective Precipitation

A solution contains $1.0 \times 10^{-4} \ M \ Cu^+$ and $2.0 \times 10^{-3} \ M \ Pb^{2+}$. If a source of I^- is added gradually to this solution, will PbI_2 ($K_{sp} = 1.4 \times 10^{-8}$) or CuI ($K_{sp} = 5.3 \times 10^{-12}$) precipitate first? Specify the concentration of I^- necessary to begin precipitation of each salt.

Solution

For PbI_2, the K_{sp} expression is

$$1.4 \times 10^{-8} = K_{sp} = [Pb^{2+}][I^-]^2$$

Since $[Pb^{2+}]$ in this solution is known to be $2.0 \times 10^{-3} \ M$, the greatest concentration of I^- that can be present without causing precipitation of PbI_2 can be calculated from the K_{sp} expression:

$$1.4 \times 10^{-8} = [Pb^{2+}][I^-]^2 = (2.0 \times 10^{-3})[I^-]^2$$
$$[I^-] = 2.6 \times 10^{-3} \ M$$

Any I^- in excess of this concentration will cause solid PbI_2 to form.

Similarly, for CuI, the K_{sp} expression is

$$5.3 \times 10^{-12} = K_{sp} = [Cu^+][I^-] = (1.0 \times 10^{-4})[I^-]$$

and

$$[I^-] = 5.3 \times 10^{-8} \ M$$

A concentration of I^- in excess of $5.3 \times 10^{-8} \ M$ will cause formation of solid CuI.

As I^- is added to the mixed solution, CuI will precipitate first, since the $[I^-]$ required is less. Therefore, Cu^+ would be separated from Pb^{2+} using this reagent.

See Exercises 15.101 and 15.102.

We can compare K_{sp} values to find relative solubilities because FeS and MnS produce the same number of ions in solution.

Since metal sulfide salts differ dramatically in their solubilities, the sulfide ion is often used to separate metal ions by selective precipitation. For example, consider a solution containing a mixture of $10^{-3} \ M \ Fe^{2+}$ and $10^{-3} \ M \ Mn^{2+}$. Since FeS ($K_{sp} = 3.7 \times 10^{-19}$) is much less soluble than MnS ($K_{sp} = 2.3 \times 10^{-13}$), careful addition of S^{2-} to the mixture will precipitate Fe^{2+} as FeS, leaving Mn^{2+} in solution.

One real advantage of the sulfide ion as a precipitating reagent is that because it is basic, its concentration can be controlled by regulating the pH of the solution. H_2S is a diprotic acid that dissociates in two steps:

$$H_2S \rightleftharpoons H^+ + HS^- \qquad K_{a_1} = 1.0 \times 10^{-7}$$
$$HS^- \rightleftharpoons H^+ + S^{2-} \qquad K_{a_2} \approx 10^{-19}$$

Note from the small K_{a_2} value that S^{2-} ions have a high affinity for protons. In an acidic solution (large $[H^+]$), $[S^{2-}]$ will be relatively small, since under these conditions the dissociation equilibria will lie far to the left. On the other hand, in basic solutions $[S^{2-}]$ will be relatively large, since the very small value of $[H^+]$ will pull both equilibria to the right, producing S^{2-}.

This means that the most insoluble sulfide salts, such as CuS ($K_{sp} = 8.5 \times 10^{-45}$) and HgS ($K_{sp} = 1.6 \times 10^{-54}$), can be precipitated from an acidic solution, leaving the more soluble ones, such as MnS ($K_{sp} = 2.3 \times 10^{-13}$) and NiS ($K_{sp} = 3 \times 10^{-21}$), still dissolved. The manganese and nickel sulfides can then be precipitated by making the solution slightly basic. This procedure is diagrammed in Fig. 15.11.

Qualitative Analysis

The classic scheme for **qualitative analysis** of a mixture containing all the common cations (listed in Fig. 15.12) involves first separating them into five major groups based on solubilities. (These groups are not directly related to the groups of the periodic table.) Each group is then treated further to separate and identify the individual ions. We will be concerned here only with separation of the major groups.

Group I—Insoluble chlorides

When dilute aqueous HCl is added to a solution containing a mixture of the common cations, only Ag^+, Pb^{2+}, and Hg_2^{2+} will precipitate out as insoluble chlorides. All other chlorides are soluble and remain in solution. The Group I precipitate is removed, leaving the other ions in solution for treatment with sulfide ion.

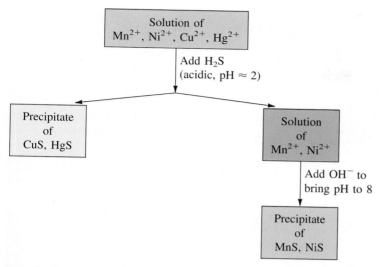

Figure 15.11

The separation of Cu^{2+} and Hg^{2+} from Ni^{2+} and Mn^{2+} using H_2S. At a low pH, $[S^{2-}]$ is relatively low and only the very insoluble HgS and CuS precipitate. When OH^- is added to lower $[H^+]$, the value of $[S^{2-}]$ increases, and MnS and NiS precipitate.

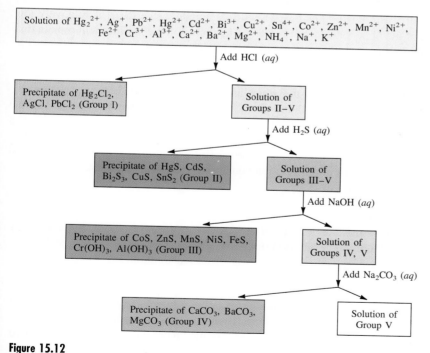

Figure 15.12

A schematic diagram of the classic method for separating the common cations by selective precipitation.

(top) Flame test for potassium.
(bottom) Flame test for sodium.

From left to right, cadmium sulfide, chromium(III) hydroxide, aluminum hydroxide, and nickel(II) hydroxide.

Group II—Sulfides insoluble in acid solution

After the insoluble chlorides are removed, the solution is still acidic, since HCl was added. If H_2S is added to this solution, only the most insoluble sulfides (those of Hg^{2+}, Cd^{2+}, Bi^{3+}, Cu^{2+}, and Sn^{4+}) will precipitate, since $[S^{2-}]$ is relatively low because of the high concentration of H^+. The more soluble sulfides will remain dissolved under these conditions, and the precipitate of the insoluble salt is removed.

Group III—Sulfides insoluble in basic solution

The solution is made basic at this stage, and more H_2S is added. As we saw earlier, a basic solution produces a higher $[S^{2-}]$, which leads to precipitation of the more soluble sulfides. The cations precipitated as sulfides at this stage are Co^{2+}, Zn^{2+}, Mn^{2+}, Ni^{2+}, and Fe^{2+}. If any Cr^{3+} and Al^{3+} ions are present, they also will precipitate, but as insoluble hydroxides (remember the solution is now basic). The precipitate is separated from the solution containing the rest of the ions.

Group IV—Insoluble carbonates

At this point, all the cations have been precipitated except those from Groups 1A and 2A of the periodic table. The Group 2A cations form insoluble carbonates and can be precipitated by the addition of CO_3^{2-}. For example, Ba^{2+}, Ca^{2+}, and Mg^{2+} form solid carbonates and can be removed from the solution.

Group V—Alkali metal and ammonium ions

The only ions remaining in solution at this point are the Group 1A cations and the NH_4^+ ion, all of which form soluble salts with the common anions. The Group 1A cations are usually identified by the characteristic colors they produce when heated in a flame. These colors are due to the emission spectra of these ions.

The qualitative analysis scheme for cations based on the selective precipitation procedure described above is summarized in Fig. 15.12.

COMPLEX ION EQUILIBRIA

15.8 Equilibria Involving Complex Ions

A **complex ion** is a charged species consisting of a metal ion surrounded by *ligands*. A ligand is simply a Lewis base—a molecule or ion having a lone electron pair that can be donated to an empty orbital on the metal ion to form a covalent bond. Some common ligands are H_2O, NH_3, Cl^-, and CN^-. The number of ligands attached to a metal ion is called the *coordination number*. The most common coordination numbers are 6, for example, in $Co(H_2O)_6^{2+}$ and $Ni(NH_3)_6^{2+}$; 4, for example, in $CoCl_4^{2-}$ and $Cu(NH_3)_4^{2+}$; and 2, for example, in $Ag(NH_3)_2^+$; but others are known.

The properties of complex ions will be discussed in more detail in Chapter 20. For now, we will just look at the equilibria involving these species. Metal ions add ligands one at a time in steps characterized by equilibrium constants called **formation constants** or **stability constants.** For example, when solutions containing Ag^+ ions and NH_3 molecules are mixed, the following reactions take place:

$$Ag^+ + NH_3 \rightleftharpoons Ag(NH_3)^+ \qquad K_1 = 2.1 \times 10^3$$
$$Ag(NH_3)^+ + NH_3 \rightleftharpoons Ag(NH_3)_2^+ \qquad K_2 = 8.2 \times 10^3$$

Molecular Model: $Ag(NH_3)_2^+$

where K_1 and K_2 are the formation constants for the two steps. In a solution containing Ag^+ and NH_3, all the species NH_3, Ag^+, $Ag(NH_3)^+$, and $Ag(NH_3)_2^+$ exist at equilibrium. Calculating the concentrations of all these components can be complicated. However, usually the total concentration of the ligand is much larger than the total concentration of the metal ion, and approximations can greatly simplify the problems.

For example, consider a solution prepared by mixing 100.0 mL of 2.0 M NH_3 with 100.0 mL of 1.0×10^{-3} M $AgNO_3$. *Before any reaction occurs,* the mixed solution contains the major species Ag^+, NO_3^-, NH_3, and H_2O. What reaction or reactions will occur in this solution? From our discussions of acid–base chemistry, we know that one reaction is

$$NH_3(aq) + H_2O(l) \rightleftharpoons NH_4^+(aq) + OH^-(aq)$$

However, we are interested in the reaction between NH_3 and Ag^+ to form complex ions, and since the position of the preceding equilibrium lies far to the left (K_b for NH_3 is 1.8×10^{-5}), we can neglect the amount of NH_3 used up in the reaction with water. Therefore, before any complex ion formation, the concentrations in the mixed solution are

$$[Ag^+]_0 = \frac{(100.0 \text{ mL})(1.0 \times 10^{-3} \text{ } M)}{(200.0 \text{ mL})} = 5.0 \times 10^{-4} \text{ } M$$

Total volume

$$[NH_3]_0 = \frac{(100.0 \text{ mL})(2.0 \text{ } M)}{(200.0 \text{ mL})} = 1.0 \text{ } M$$

As mentioned already, the Ag^+ ion reacts with NH_3 in a stepwise fashion to form $AgNH_3^+$ and then $Ag(NH_3)_2^+$:

$$Ag^+ + NH_3 \rightleftharpoons Ag(NH_3)^+ \qquad K_1 = 2.1 \times 10^3$$
$$Ag(NH_3)^+ + NH_3 \rightleftharpoons Ag(NH_3)_2^+ \qquad K_2 = 8.2 \times 10^3$$

Since both K_1 and K_2 are large, and since there is a large excess of NH_3, *both reactions can be assumed to go essentially to completion.* This is equivalent to writing the net reaction in the solution as follows:

$$Ag^+ + 2NH_3 \longrightarrow Ag(NH_3)_2^+$$

The relevant stoichiometric calculations are as follows:

	Ag^+	$+$	$2NH_3$	$\longrightarrow$	$Ag(NH_3)_2^+$
Before reaction:	$5.0 \times 10^{-4}\ M$		$1.0\ M$		0
After reaction:	0		$1.0 - 2(5.0 \times 10^{-4}) \approx 1.0\ M$		$5.0 \times 10^{-4}\ M$

Twice as much NH_3 as Ag^+ is required

Note that in this case we have used molarities when performing the stoichiometry calculations and we have assumed this reaction to be complete, using all the original Ag^+ to form $Ag(NH_3)_2^+$. In reality, a *very small amount* of the $Ag(NH_3)_2^+$ formed will dissociate to produce small amounts of $Ag(NH_3)^+$ and Ag^+. However, since the amount of $Ag(NH_3)_2^+$ dissociating will be so small, we can safely assume that $[Ag(NH_3)_2^+]$ is $5.0 \times 10^{-4}\ M$ at equilibrium. Also, we know that since so little NH_3 has been consumed, $[NH_3]$ is $1.0\ M$ at equilibrium. We can use these concentrations to calculate $[Ag^+]$ and $[Ag(NH_3)^+]$ using the K_1 and K_2 expressions.

To calculate the equilibrium concentration of $Ag(NH_3)^+$, we use

$$K_2 = 8.2 \times 10^3 = \frac{[Ag(NH_3)_2^+]}{[Ag(NH_3)^+][NH_3]}$$

since $[Ag(NH_3)_2^+]$ and $[NH_3]$ are known. Rearranging and solving for $[Ag(NH_3)^+]$ give

$$[Ag(NH_3)^+] = \frac{[Ag(NH_3)_2^+]}{K_2[NH_3]} = \frac{5.0 \times 10^{-4}}{(8.2 \times 10^3)(1.0)} = 6.1 \times 10^{-8}\ M$$

Now the equilibrium concentration of Ag^+ can be calculated using K_1:

$$K_1 = 2.1 \times 10^3 = \frac{[Ag(NH_3)^+]}{[Ag^+][NH_3]} = \frac{6.1 \times 10^{-8}}{[Ag^+](1.0)}$$

$$[Ag^+] = \frac{6.1 \times 10^{-8}}{(2.1 \times 10^3)(1.0)} = 2.9 \times 10^{-11}\ M$$

So far we have assumed that $Ag(NH_3)_2^+$ is the dominant silver-containing species in solution. Is this a valid assumption? The calculated concentrations are

$$[Ag(NH_3)_2{}^+] = 5.0 \times 10^{-4} \ M$$
$$[Ag(NH_3){}^+] = 6.1 \times 10^{-8} \ M$$
$$[Ag^+] = 2.9 \times 10^{-11} \ M$$

These values clearly support the conclusion that

$$[Ag(NH_3)_2{}^+] \gg [Ag(NH_3){}^+] \gg [Ag^+]$$

Thus the assumption that $[Ag(NH_3)_2{}^+]$ is the dominant Ag^+-containing species is valid, and the calculated concentrations are correct.

This analysis shows that although complex ion equilibria have many species present and look complicated, the calculations are actually quite straightforward, especially if the ligand is present in large excess.

Essentially all the Ag^+ ions originally present end up in $Ag(NH_3)_2{}^+$.

Sample Exercise 15.19 *Complex Ions*

Molecular Model: $Ag(S_2O_3)_2{}^{3-}$

Calculate the concentrations of Ag^+, $Ag(S_2O_3){}^-$, and $Ag(S_2O_3)_2{}^{3-}$ in a solution prepared by mixing 150.0 mL of $1.00 \times 10^{-3} \ M \ AgNO_3$ with 200.0 mL of 5.00 $M \ Na_2S_2O_3$. The stepwise formation equilibria are

$$Ag^+ + S_2O_3{}^{2-} \rightleftharpoons Ag(S_2O_3){}^- \qquad K_1 = 7.4 \times 10^8$$
$$Ag(S_2O_3){}^- + S_2O_3{}^{2-} \rightleftharpoons Ag(S_2O_3)_2{}^{3-} \qquad K_2 = 3.9 \times 10^4$$

Solution

The concentrations of the ligand and metal ion in the mixed solution *before any reaction occurs* are

$$[Ag^+]_0 = \frac{(150.0 \ \text{mL})(1.00 \times 10^{-3} \ M)}{(150.0 \ \text{mL} + 200.0 \ \text{mL})} = 4.29 \times 10^{-4} \ M$$

$$[S_2O_3{}^{2-}]_0 = \frac{(200.0 \ \text{mL})(5.00 \ M)}{(150.0 \ \text{mL} + 200.0 \ \text{mL})} = 2.86 \ M$$

Since $[S_2O_3{}^{2-}]_0 \gg [Ag^+]_0$, and since K_1 and K_2 are large, both formation reactions can be assumed to go to completion, and the net reaction in the solution is as follows:

	Ag^+	$+$	$2S_2O_3{}^{2-}$	$\longrightarrow$	$Ag(S_2O_3)_2{}^{3-}$
Before reaction:	$4.29 \times 10^{-4} \ M$		$2.86 \ M$		0
After reaction:	~ 0		$2.86 - 2(4.29 \times 10^{-4})$ $\approx 2.86 \ M$		$4.29 \times 10^{-4} \ M$

Note that Ag^+ is limiting and that the amount of $S_2O_3{}^{2-}$ consumed is negligible. Also note that since all these species are in the same solution, the molarities can be used to do the stoichiometry problem.

Of course, the concentration of Ag^+ is not zero at equilibrium, and there is some $Ag(S_2O_3){}^-$ in the solution. To calculate the concentrations of these species,

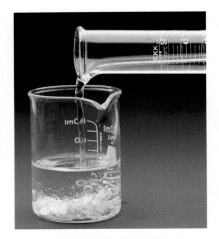

(top) Aqueous ammonia is added to silver chloride (white). (bottom) Silver chloride, insoluble in water, dissolves to form $Ag(NH_3)_2^+(aq)$ and $Cl^-(aq)$.

we must use the K_1 and K_2 expressions. We can calculate the concentration of $Ag(S_2O_3)^-$ from K_2:

$$3.9 \times 10^4 = K_2 = \frac{[Ag(S_2O_3)_2{}^{3-}]}{[Ag(S_2O_3)^-][S_2O_3{}^{2-}]} = \frac{4.29 \times 10^{-4}}{[Ag(S_2O_3)^-](2.86)}$$

$$[Ag(S_2O_3)^-] = 3.8 \times 10^{-9} \, M$$

We can calculate $[Ag^+]$ from K_1:

$$7.4 \times 10^8 = K_1 = \frac{[Ag(S_2O_3)^-]}{[Ag^+][S_2O_3{}^{2-}]} = \frac{3.8 \times 10^{-9}}{[Ag^+](2.86)}$$

$$[Ag^+] = 1.8 \times 10^{-18} \, M$$

These results show that $[Ag(S_2O_3)_2{}^{3-}] \gg [Ag(S_2O_3)^-] \gg [Ag^+]$

Thus the assumption is valid that essentially all the original Ag^+ is converted to $Ag(S_2O_3)_2{}^{3-}$ at equilibrium.

See Exercises 15.107 and 15.108.

Complex Ions and Solubility

Often ionic solids that are very nearly water-insoluble must be dissolved somehow in aqueous solutions. For example, when the various qualitative analysis groups are precipitated out, the precipitates must be redissolved to separate the ions within each group. Consider a solution of cations that contains Ag^+, Pb^{2+}, and Hg_2^{2+}, among others. When dilute aqueous HCl is added to this solution, the Group I ions will form the insoluble chlorides $AgCl$, $PbCl_2$, and Hg_2Cl_2. Once this mixed precipitate is separated from the solution, it must be redissolved to identify the cations individually. How can this be done? We know that some solids are more soluble in acidic than in neutral solutions. What about chloride salts? For example, can $AgCl$ be dissolved by using a strong acid? The answer is no, because Cl^- ions have virtually no affinity for H^+ ions in aqueous solution. The position of the dissolution equilibrium

$$AgCl(s) \rightleftharpoons Ag^+(aq) + Cl^-(aq)$$

is not affected by the presence of H^+.

How can we pull the dissolution equilibrium to the right, even though Cl^- is an extremely weak base? The key is to lower the concentration of Ag^+ in solution by forming complex ions. For example, Ag^+ reacts with excess NH_3 to form the stable complex ion $Ag(NH_3)_2^+$. As a result, $AgCl$ is quite soluble in concentrated ammonia solutions. The relevant reactions are

$$
\begin{aligned}
AgCl(s) &\rightleftharpoons Ag^+ + Cl^- & K_{sp} &= 1.6 \times 10^{-10} \\
Ag^+ + NH_3 &\rightleftharpoons Ag(NH_3)^+ & K_1 &= 2.1 \times 10^3 \\
Ag(NH_3)^+ + NH_3 &\rightleftharpoons Ag(NH_3)_2{}^+ & K_2 &= 8.2 \times 10^3
\end{aligned}
$$

The Ag^+ ion produced by dissolving solid $AgCl$ combines with NH_3 to form $Ag(NH_3)_2^+$, which causes more $AgCl$ to dissolve, until the point at which

$$[Ag^+][Cl^-] = K_{sp} = 1.6 \times 10^{-10}$$

Here $[Ag^+]$ refers only to the Ag^+ ion that is present as a separate species in solution. It is *not* the total silver content of the solution, which is

$$[Ag]_{\text{total dissolved}} = [Ag^+] + [Ag(NH_3)^+] + [Ag(NH_3)_2^+]$$

For reasons discussed in the previous section, virtually all the Ag^+ from the dissolved AgCl ends up in the complex ion $Ag(NH_3)_2^+$. Thus we can represent the dissolving of solid AgCl in excess NH_3 by the equation

$$AgCl(s) + 2NH_3(aq) \rightleftharpoons Ag(NH_3)_2^+(aq) + Cl^-(aq)$$

Since this equation is the *sum of the three stepwise reactions* given above, the equilibrium constant for the reaction is the product of the constants for the three reactions. (Demonstrate this to yourself by multiplying together the three expressions for K_{sp}, K_1, and K_2.) The equilibrium expression is

When reactions are added, the equilibrium constant for the overall process is the product of the constants for the individual reactions.

$$K = \frac{[Ag(NH_3)_2^+][Cl^-]}{[NH_3]^2}$$

$$= K_{sp} \times K_1 \times K_2 = (1.6 \times 10^{-10})(2.1 \times 10^3)(8.2 \times 10^3) = 2.8 \times 10^{-3}$$

Using this expression, we will now calculate the solubility of solid AgCl in a 10.0 M NH_3 solution. If we let x be the solubility (in mol/L) of AgCl in the solution, we can then write the following expressions for the equilibrium concentrations of the pertinent species:

$$[Cl^-] = x$$

x mol/L of AgCl dissolves to produce x mol/L of Cl^- and x mol/L of $Ag(NH_3)_2^+$

$$[Ag(NH_3)_2^+] = x$$

$$[NH_3] = 10.0 - 2x$$

Formation of x mol/L of $Ag(NH_3)_2^+$ requires $2x$ mol/L of NH_3, since each complex ion contains two NH_3 ligands

Substituting these concentrations into the equilibrium expression gives

$$K = 2.8 \times 10^{-3} = \frac{[Ag(NH_3)_2^+][Cl^-]}{[NH_3]^2} = \frac{(x)(x)}{(10.0 - 2x)^2} = \frac{x^2}{(10.0 - 2x)^2}$$

No approximations are necessary here. Taking the square root of both sides of the equation gives

$$\sqrt{2.8 \times 10^{-3}} = \frac{x}{10.0 - 2x}$$

$$x = 0.48 \text{ mol/L} = \text{solubility of AgCl}(s) \text{ in } 10.0 \ M \ NH_3$$

Thus the solubility of AgCl in 10.0 M NH_3 is much greater than its solubility in pure water, which is

$$\sqrt{K_{sp}} = 1.3 \times 10^{-5} \text{ mol/L}$$

In this chapter we have considered two strategies for dissolving a water-insoluble ionic solid. If the *anion* of the solid is a good base, the solubility is greatly increased by acidifying the solution. In cases where the anion is not sufficiently basic, the ionic solid often can be dissolved in a solution containing a ligand that forms stable complex ions with its *cation*.

Sometimes solids are so insoluble that combinations of reactions are needed to dissolve them. For example, to dissolve the extremely insoluble HgS ($K_{sp} = 10^{-54}$),

CHEMICAL IMPACT

The Chemistry of Teeth

IF DENTAL CHEMISTRY continues to progress at the present rate, tooth decay may soon be a thing of the past. Cavities are holes that develop in tooth enamel, which is composed of the mineral hydroxyapatite, $Ca_5(PO_4)_3OH$. Recent research has shown that there is constant dissolving and re-forming of the tooth mineral in the saliva at the tooth's surface. Demineralization (dissolving of tooth enamel) is mainly caused by weak acids in the saliva created by bacteria as they metabolize carbohydrates in food. (The solubility of $Ca_5(PO_4)_3OH$ in acidic saliva should come as no surprise to you if you understand how pH affects the solubility of a salt with basic anions.)

In the first stages of tooth decay, parts of the tooth surface become porous and spongy and develop swiss-cheese–like holes that, if untreated, eventually turn into cavities (see photo). However, recent results indicate that if the affected tooth is bathed in a solution containing appropriate amounts of Ca^{2+}, PO_4^{3-}, and F^-, it remineralizes. Because the F^- replaces OH^- in the tooth mineral ($Ca_5(PO_4)_3OH$ is changed to $Ca_5(PO_4)_3F$), the remineralized area is more resistant to future decay, since fluoride is a weaker base than

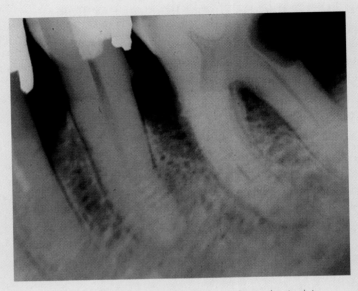

X-ray photo showing decay (dark area) on the molar (right).

hydroxide ion. In addition, it has been shown that the presence of Sr^{2+} in the remineralizing fluid significantly increases resistance to decay.

If these results hold up under further study, the work of dentists will change dramatically. Dentists will be much more involved in preventing damage to teeth than in repairing damage that has already occurred. One can picture the routine use of a remineralization rinse that will repair problem areas before they become cavities. Dental drills could join leeches as a medical anachronism.

it is necessary to use a mixture of concentrated HCl and concentrated HNO_3, called *aqua regia*. The H^+ ions in the aqua regia react with the S^{2-} ions to form H_2S, and Cl^- reacts with Hg^{2+} to form various complex ions, including $HgCl_4^{2-}$. In addition, NO_3^- oxidizes S^{2-} to elemental sulfur. These processes lower the concentrations of Hg^{2+} and S^{2-} and thus promote the solubility of HgS.

Since the solubility of many salts increases with temperature, simple heating is sometimes enough to make a salt sufficiently soluble. For example, earlier in this section we considered the mixed chloride precipitates of the Group I ions—$PbCl_2$, AgCl, and Hg_2Cl_2. The effect of temperature on the solubility of $PbCl_2$ is such that we can precipitate $PbCl_2$ with cold aqueous HCl and then redissolve it by heating the solution to near boiling. The silver and mercury(I) chlorides remain precipitated, since they are not significantly soluble in hot water. However, solid AgCl can be

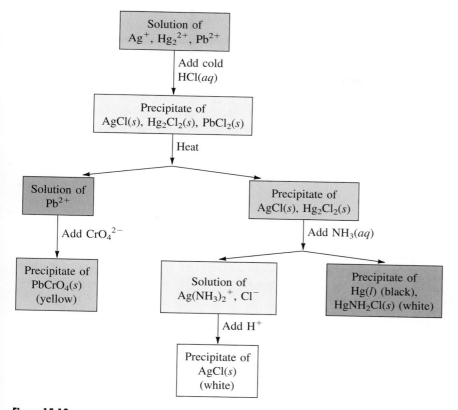

Figure 15.13

The separation of the Group I ions in the classic scheme of qualitative analysis.

dissolved using aqueous ammonia. The solid Hg_2Cl_2 reacts with NH_3 to form a mixture of elemental mercury and $HgNH_2Cl$:

$$Hg_2Cl_2(s) + 2NH_3(aq) \longrightarrow HgNH_2Cl(s) + Hg(l) + NH_4^+(aq) + Cl^-(aq)$$
$$\text{White} \qquad \text{Black}$$

The mixed precipitate appears gray. This is an oxidation–reduction reaction in which one mercury(I) ion in Hg_2Cl_2 is oxidized to Hg^{2+} in $HgNH_2Cl$ and the other mercury(I) ion is reduced to Hg, or elemental mercury.

The treatment of the Group I ions is summarized in Fig. 15.13. Note that the presence of Pb^{2+} is confirmed by adding CrO_4^{2-}, which forms bright yellow lead(II) chromate ($PbCrO_4$). Also note that H^+ added to a solution containing $Ag(NH_3)_2^+$ reacts with the NH_3 to form NH_4^+, destroying the $Ag(NH_3)_2^+$ complex. Silver chloride then re-forms:

$$2H^+(aq) + Ag(NH_3)_2^+(aq) + Cl^-(aq) \longrightarrow 2NH_4^+(aq) + AgCl(s)$$

Note that the qualitative analysis of cations by selective precipitation involves all the types of reactions we have discussed and represents an excellent application of the principles of chemical equilibrium.

For Review

Summary

When a weak acid HA and its salt NaA are dissolved in the same aqueous solution, a buffering effect is observed. A buffered solution is one that resists a change in pH when either hydroxide ions or protons are added. A buffer may contain a weak acid and its salt or a weak base and its salt. In a buffered solution the pH is governed by the ratio $[A^-]/[HA]$. The Henderson–Hasselbalch equation gives the relationship between pH, pK_a, and the ratio $[A^-]/[HA]$:

$$pH = pK_a + \log\left(\frac{[A^-]}{[HA]}\right)$$

The capacity of a buffer depends on the amounts of HA and A^- present. Buffering results because the relatively large amounts of HA and A^- cause the ratio $[A^-]/[HA]$ to be almost constant when H^+ or OH^- is added. Optimal buffering results when [HA] is equal to $[A^-]$.

The progress of an acid–base titration is often monitored by plotting the pH of the solution versus the volume of added titrant to give a pH curve or titration curve. Strong acid–strong base titrations have a very sharp change in pH near the stoichiometric, or equivalence, point, the point at which the original acid (or base) in the solution has been exactly consumed by the titrant base (or acid). When a weak acid is titrated with a strong base, the shape of the titration curve is quite different. Initially, the curve rises sharply; then it levels off because of the buffering effects of the weak acid and salt mixture. At the equivalence point of a titration of a weak acid with a strong base, the pH is greater than 7 because of the basicity of the conjugate base of the weak acid. For a titration of a weak base with a strong acid, the pH at the equivalence point is always less than 7 because of the acidity of the conjugate acid of the weak base. For a strong acid–strong base titration, the pH at the equivalence point equals 7. The equivalence point of a titration is determined by stoichiometry, not by pH.

Another way of following an acid–base titration is by the use of an indicator that marks the end point by changing color. Most commonly used indicators are themselves weak acids and exist in two forms, HIn and In^-, that exhibit different colors. For most indicators, the ratio of the minor form to the major form must be $\frac{1}{10}$ before a color change is apparent. The goal in choosing an indicator is to have the equivalence point and the end point coincide.

The principles of equilibrium also can be applied when a solid dissolves in water. The solubility product K_{sp} is an equilibrium constant defined by the law of mass action. Solubility is an equilibrium position. The K_{sp} value for a salt can be determined by measuring its solubility. The solubility of a salt can be calculated if its K_{sp} value is known.

Addition of an ion common to a salt will push the dissolution equilibrium to the left, reducing the salt's solubility. This is known as the common ion effect. The solubility of a salt MX that is only slightly soluble in pure water can be increased if the solubility equilibrium

$$MX(s) \rightleftharpoons M^+(aq) + X^-(aq)$$

can be shifted to the right by lowering $[M^+]$ or $[X^-]$. If X^- is a good base, addition of H^+ will form HX and lower $[X^-]$, thus increasing the salt's solubility. The equilibrium concentration of M^+ can be lowered by adding a ligand to form complex ions with it.

We can predict whether a precipitate will form when two solutions are mixed by using the ion product Q, which is defined just like K_{sp} except that initial concentrations of the ions are used. If Q is greater than K_{sp}, the salt will precipitate.

Mixtures of ions can be separated by selective precipitation, a process in which reagents are added to precipitate single ions or small groups of ions.

In-Class Discussion Questions

These questions are designed to be considered by groups of students in class. Often these questions work well for introducing a particular topic in class.

1. What are the major species in solution after $NaHSO_4$ is dissolved in water? What happens to the pH of the solution as more $NaHSO_4$ is added? Why? Would the results vary if baking soda ($NaHCO_3$) were used instead?

2. A friend asks the following: "Consider a buffered solution made up of the weak acid HA and its salt NaA. If a strong base like NaOH is added, the HA reacts with the OH^- to form A^-. Thus the amount of acid (HA) is decreased, and the amount of base (A^-) is increased. Analogously, adding HCl to the buffered solution forms more of the acid (HA) by reacting with the base (A^-). Thus how can we claim that a buffered solution resists changes in the pH of the solution?" How would you explain buffering to this friend?

3. Mixing together solutions of acetic acid and sodium hydroxide can make a buffered solution. Explain. How does the amount of each solution added change the effectiveness of the buffer? Would a buffer solution made by mixing HCl and NaOH be effective? Explain.

4. Sketch two pH curves, one for the titration of a weak acid with a strong base and one for a strong acid with a strong base. How are they similar? How are they different? Account for the similarities and the differences.

5. Sketch a pH curve for the titration of a weak acid (HA) with a strong base (NaOH). List the major species and explain how you would go about calculating the pH of the solution at various points, including the halfway point and the equivalence point.

6. Devise as many ways as you can to experimentally determine the K_{sp} value of a solid. Explain why each of these would work.

7. You are browsing through the *Handbook of Hypothetical Chemistry* when you come across a solid that is reported to have a K_{sp} value of zero in water at 25°C. What does this mean?

8. A friend tells you: "The constant K_{sp} of a salt is called the solubility product constant and is calculated from the concentrations of ions in the solution. Thus, if salt A dissolves to a greater extent than salt B, salt A must have a higher K_{sp} than salt B." Do you agree with your friend? Explain.

9. Explain the following phenomenon: You have a test tube with about 20 mL of silver nitrate solution. Upon adding a few drops of sodium chromate solution, you notice a red solid forming in a relatively clear solution. Upon adding a few drops of a sodium chloride solution to the same test tube, you notice a white solid and a pale yellow solution. Use the K_{sp} values in the book to support your explanation, and include the balanced reactions.

10. What happens to the K_{sp} value of a solid as the temperature of the solution changes? Consider both increasing and decreasing temperatures, and explain your answer.

11. Which is more likely to dissolve in an acidic solution, silver sulfide or silver chloride? Why?

12. You have two salts, AgX and AgY, with very similar K_{sp} values. You know that the K_a value for HX is much greater than the K_a value for HY. Which salt is more soluble in an acidic solution? Explain.

A blue question or exercise number indicates that the answer to that question or exercise appears at the back of this book and a solution appears in the *Solutions Guide*.

Questions

13. What is meant by a *common ion*? How does the presence of a common ion affect an equilibrium such as

$$HNO_2(aq) \rightleftharpoons H^+(aq) + NO_2^-(aq)$$

14. What components must be present in order to have a buffered solution? For what purposes are buffers used? What is meant by the *capacity* of a buffer? How do the following buffers differ in capacity? How do they differ in pH?

0.01 *M* acetic acid/0.01 *M* sodium acetate
0.1 *M* acetic acid/0.1 *M* sodium acetate
1.0 *M* acetic acid/1.0 *M* sodium acetate

15. Is it necessary that the concentration of the weak acid and weak base in a buffered solution be equal? Explain.

16. Show that the pH at the halfway point of the titration of a weak acid with a strong base is equal to pK_a. Is it possible to determine the K_a of a weak acid from data at points other than the halfway point of a titration?

17. Is it possible for the indicator thymol blue to contain only a single —CO_2H group and no other acidic or basic functional group? Explain.

18. Define the equivalence (stoichiometric) point and the end point of a titration. Why does one choose an indicator so that the two points coincide? Is it necessary that the pH of the two points be within ±0.01 pH unit of each other? Explain.

19. Why does an indicator change from its acid to its base color over a range of pH values?

20. Under what circumstances can the relative solubilities of two salts be compared by directly comparing values of their solubility products?

Exercises

In this section similar exercises are paired.

Buffers

21. Write reactions to show how a solution containing acetic acid and sodium acetate acts as a buffer when a strong acid or base is added.

22. A buffer is made by dissolving NH_4Cl and NH_3 in water. Write equations to show how this buffer neutralizes added H^+ and OH^-.

23. Calculate the pH of each of the following solutions.
    a. 0.100 M propanoic acid ($HC_3H_5O_2$, $K_a = 1.3 \times 10^{-5}$)
    b. 0.100 M sodium propanoate ($NaC_3H_5O_2$)
    c. Pure H_2O
    d. A mixture containing 0.100 M $HC_3H_5O_2$ and 0.100 M $NaC_3H_5O_2$

24. Calculate the pH of each of the following solutions.
    a. 0.100 M $HONH_2$ ($K_b = 1.1 \times 10^{-8}$)
    b. 0.100 M $HONH_3Cl$
    c. pure H_2O
    d. a mixture containing 0.100 M $HONH_2$ and 0.100 M $HONH_3Cl$

25. Compare the percent dissociation of the acid in Exercise 23a with the percent dissociation of the acid in Exercise 23d. Explain the large difference in percent dissociation of the acid.

26. Compare the percent ionization of the base in Exercise 24a with the percent ionization of the base in Exercise 24d. Explain any differences.

27. Calculate the pH after 0.020 mol HCl is added to 1.00 L of each of the four solutions in Exercise 23.

28. Calculate the pH after 0.020 mol HCl is added to 1.00 L of each of the four solutions in Exercise 24.

29. Calculate the pH after 0.020 mol NaOH is added to 1.00 L of each of the four solutions in Exercise 23.

30. Calculate the pH after 0.020 mol NaOH is added to 1.00 L of each of the solutions in Exercise 24.

31. Which of the solutions in Exercise 23 shows the least change in pH upon the addition of acid or base? Explain.

32. Which of the solutions in Exercise 24 is a buffered solution?

33. Calculate the pH of a solution that is 1.00 M HNO_2 and 1.00 M $NaNO_2$.

34. Calculate the pH of a solution that is 0.60 M HF and 1.00 M KF.

35. Calculate the pH after 0.10 mol of NaOH is added to 1.00 L of the solution in Exercise 33.

36. Calculate the pH after 0.10 mol of NaOH is added to 1.00 L of the solution in Exercise 34.

37. Calculate the pH after 0.20 mol of HCl is added to 1.00 L of the solution in Exercise 33.

38. Calculate the pH after 0.20 mol of HCl is added to 1.00 L of the solution in Exercise 34.

39. A buffered solution is made by adding 75.0 g sodium acetate to 500.0 mL of a 0.64 M solution of acetic acid. What is the pH of the final solution? (Assume no volume change.)

40. A buffered solution is made by adding 50.0 g NH_4Cl to 1.00 L of a 0.75 M solution of NH_3. Calculate the pH of the final solution.

41. Calculate the pH of each of the following buffered solutions.
    a. 0.10 M acetic acid/0.25 M sodium acetate
    b. 0.25 M acetic acid/0.10 M sodium acetate
    c. 0.080 M acetic acid/0.20 M sodium acetate
    d. 0.20 M acetic acid/0.080 M sodium acetate

42. Calculate the pH of each of the following buffered solutions.
    a. 0.50 M $C_2H_5NH_2$/0.25 M $C_2H_5NH_3Cl$
    b. 0.25 M $C_2H_5NH_2$/0.50 M $C_2H_5NH_3Cl$
    c. 0.50 M $C_2H_5NH_2$/0.50 M $C_2H_5NH_3Cl$

43. Calculate the pH of a solution that is 0.50 M CH_3NH_2 and 0.70 M CH_3NH_3Cl.

44. Calculate the pH after 0.10 mol of NaOH is added to 1.0 L of the solution in Exercise 43. Also calculate the pH after 0.10 mol of HCl is added to 1.0 L of the solution in Exercise 43.

45. Calculate the pH after 0.010 mol gaseous HCl is added to 250.0 mL of each of the following buffered solutions.

a. 0.050 M NH$_3$/0.15 M NH$_4$Cl

b. 0.50 M NH$_3$/1.50 M NH$_4$Cl

Do the two original buffered solutions differ in their pH or their capacity? What advantage is there in having a buffer with a greater capacity?

46. Calculate the pH after 0.15 mol solid NaOH is added to 1.00 L of each of the following buffered solutions.

a. 0.050 M propanoic acid (HC$_3$H$_5$O$_2$, $K_a = 1.3 \times 10^{-5}$)/0.080 M sodium propanoate

b. 0.50 M propanoic acid/0.80 M sodium propanoate

c. Is the solution in part a still a buffered solution after the NaOH has been added? Explain.

47. Consider a solution that contains both C$_5$H$_5$N and C$_5$H$_5$NHNO$_3$. Calculate the ratio [C$_5$H$_5$N]/[C$_5$H$_5$NH$^+$] if the solution has the following pH values.

a. pH = 4.50

b. pH = 5.00

c. pH = 5.23

d. pH = 5.50

48. a. Carbonate buffers are important in regulating the pH of blood at 7.40. What is the concentration ratio of CO$_2$ (usually written H$_2$CO$_3$) to HCO$_3^-$ in blood at pH = 7.40?

$$H_2CO_3(aq) \rightleftharpoons HCO_3^-(aq) + H^+(aq) \qquad K_a = 4.3 \times 10^{-7}$$

b. Phosphate buffers are important in regulating the pH of intracellular fluids at pH values generally between 7.1 and 7.2. What is the concentration ratio of H$_2$PO$_4^-$ to HPO$_4^{2-}$ in intracellular fluid at pH = 7.15?

$$H_2PO_4^-(aq) \rightleftharpoons HPO_4^{2-}(aq) + H^+(aq)$$
$$K_a = 6.2 \times 10^{-8}$$

c. Why is a buffer composed of H$_3$PO$_4$ and H$_2$PO$_4^-$ ineffective in buffering the pH of intracellular fluid?

$$H_3PO_4(aq) \rightleftharpoons H_2PO_4^-(aq) + H^+(aq)$$
$$K_a = 7.5 \times 10^{-3}$$

49. Consider the acids in Table 14.2. Which acid would be the best choice for preparing a pH = 7.00 buffer? Explain how to make 1.0 L of this buffer.

50. Consider the bases in Table 14.3. Which base would be the best choice for preparing a pH = 5.00 buffer? Explain how to make 1.0 L of this buffer.

51. Which of the following mixtures would result in buffered solutions when 1.0 L of each of the two solutions are mixed?

a. 0.1 M KOH and 0.1 M CH$_3$NH$_3$Cl

b. 0.1 M KOH and 0.2 M CH$_3$NH$_2$

c. 0.2 M KOH and 0.1 M CH$_3$NH$_3$Cl

d. 0.1 M KOH and 0.2 M CH$_3$NH$_3$Cl

52. Which of the following mixtures would result in a buffered solution when 1.0 L of each of the two solutions are mixed?

a. 0.2 M HNO$_3$ and 0.4 M NaNO$_3$

b. 0.2 M HNO$_3$ and 0.4 M HF

c. 0.2 M HNO$_3$ and 0.4 M NaF

d. 0.2 M HNO$_3$ and 0.4 M NaOH

53. How many moles of NaOH must be added to 1.0 L of 2.0 M HC$_2$H$_3$O$_2$ to produce a solution buffered at each pH?

a. pH = pK_a

b. pH = 4.00

c. pH = 5.00

54. Calculate the number of moles of HCl(g) that must be added to 1.0 L of 1.0 M NaC$_2$H$_3$O$_2$ to produce a solution buffered at each pH?

a. pH = pK_a

b. pH = 4.20

c. pH = 5.00

Acid–Base Titrations

55. Consider the titration of a generic weak acid HA with a strong base that gives the following titration curve:

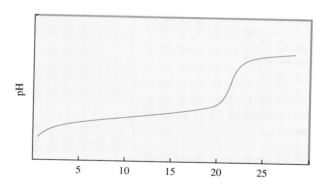

On the curve, indicate the points that correspond to the following:

a. the stoichiometric (equivalence) point

b. the region with maximum buffering

c. pH = pK_a

d. pH depends only on [HA]

e. pH depends only on [A$^-$]

f. pH depends only on the amount of excess strong base added

56. Sketch the titration curve for the titration of a generic weak base B with a strong acid. The titration reaction is

$$B + H^+ \rightleftharpoons BH^+$$

On this curve, indicate the points that correspond to the following:

a. the stoichiometric (equivalence) point

b. the region with maximum buffering

c. pH = pK_a
d. pH depends only on [B]
e. pH depends only on [BH^+]
f. pH depends only on the amount of excess strong acid added

57. Consider the titration of 40.0 mL of 0.200 M $HClO_4$ by 0.100 M KOH. Calculate the pH of the resulting solution after the following volumes of KOH have been added.
    a. 0.0 mL
    b. 10.0 mL
    c. 40.0 mL
    d. 80.0 mL
    e. 100.0 mL

58. Consider the titration of 80.0 mL of 0.100 M $Sr(OH)_2$ by 0.400 M HCl. Calculate the pH of the resulting solution after the following volumes of HCl have been added.
    a. 0.0 mL
    b. 20.0 mL
    c. 30.0 mL
    d. 40.0 mL
    e. 80.0 mL

59. Consider the titration of 100.0 mL of 0.200 M acetic acid ($K_a = 1.8 \times 10^{-5}$) by 0.100 M KOH. Calculate the pH of the resulting solution after the following volumes of KOH have been added.
    a. 0.0 mL
    b. 50.0 mL
    c. 100.0 mL
    d. 150.0 mL
    e. 200.0 mL
    f. 250.0 mL

60. Consider the titration of 100.0 mL of 0.100 M H_2NNH_2 ($K_b = 3.0 \times 10^{-6}$) by 0.200 M HNO_3. Calculate the pH of the resulting solution after the following volumes of HNO_3 have been added.
    a. 0.0 mL
    b. 20.0 mL
    c. 25.0 mL
    d. 40.0 mL
    e. 50.0 mL
    f. 100.0 mL

61. A 25.0-mL sample of 0.100 M lactic acid ($HC_3H_5O_3$, $pK_a = 3.86$) is titrated with 0.100 M NaOH solution. Calculate the pH after the addition of 0.0 mL, 4.0 mL, 8.0 mL, 12.5 mL, 20.0 mL, 24.0 mL, 24.5 mL, 24.9 mL, 25.0 mL, 25.1 mL, 26.0 mL, 28.0 mL, and 30.0 mL of the NaOH. Plot the results of your calculations as pH versus milliliters of NaOH added.

62. Repeat the procedure in Exercise 61, but for the titration of 25.0 mL of 0.100 M propanoic acid ($HC_3H_5O_2$, $K_a = 1.3 \times 10^{-5}$) with 0.100 M KOH.

63. Repeat the procedure in Exercise 61, but for the titration of 25.0 mL of 0.100 M NH_3 ($K_b = 1.8 \times 10^{-5}$) with 0.100 M HCl.

64. Repeat the procedure in Exercise 61, but for the titration of 25.0 mL of 0.100 M pyridine with 0.100 M hydrochloric acid (K_b for pyridine is 1.7×10^{-9}). Do not do the points at 24.9 and 25.1 mL.

65. Calculate the pH at the halfway point and at the equivalence point for each of the following titrations.
    a. 100.0 mL of 0.10 M $HC_7H_5O_2$ ($K_a = 6.4 \times 10^{-5}$) titrated by 0.10 M NaOH
    b. 100.0 mL of 0.10 M $C_2H_5NH_2$ ($K_b = 5.6 \times 10^{-4}$) titrated by 0.20 M HNO_3
    c. 100.0 mL of 0.50 M HCl titrated by 0.25 M NaOH

66. In the titration of 50.0 mL of 1.0 M methylamine, CH_3NH_2 ($K_b = 4.4 \times 10^{-4}$), with 0.50 M HCl, calculate the pH under the following conditions.
    a. after 50.0 mL of 0.50 M HCl has been added
    b. at the stoichiometric point

67. A sample of a certain monoprotic weak acid was dissolved in water and titrated with 0.125 M NaOH, requiring 16.00 mL to reach the equivalence point. During the titration, the pH after adding 2.00 mL of NaOH was 6.912. Calculate K_a for the weak acid.

68. A sample of an ionic compound NaA, where A^- is the anion of a weak acid, was dissolved in enough water to make 100.0 mL of solution and was then titrated with 0.100 M HCl. After 500.0 mL of HCl was added, the pH was measured and found to be 5.00. The experimenter found that 1.00 L of 0.100 M HCl was required to reach the stoichiometric point of the titration.
    a. What is the K_b value for A^-?
    b. Calculate the pH of the solution at the stoichiometric point of the titration.

Indicators

69. Two drops of indicator HIn ($K_a = 1.0 \times 10^{-9}$), where HIn is yellow and In^- is blue, are placed in 100.0 mL of 0.10 M HCl.
    a. What color is the solution initially?
    b. The solution is titrated with 0.10 M NaOH. At what pH will the color change (yellow to greenish yellow) occur?
    c. What color will the solution be after 200.0 mL of NaOH has been added?

70. Methyl red has the following structure:

$$K_a = 5.0 \times 10^{-6}$$

It undergoes a color change from red to yellow as a solution gets more basic. Calculate an approximate pH range for which methyl red is useful. What is the color change and the pH at the color change when a weak acid is titrated with a strong base using methyl red as an indicator? What is the color change and the pH at the color change when a weak base is titrated with a strong acid using methyl red as an indicator? For which of these two types of titrations is methyl red a possible indicator?

71. Which of the indicators in Fig. 15.8 could be used for the titrations in Exercises 57 and 59?

72. Which of the indicators in Fig. 15.8 could be used for the titrations in Exercises 58 and 60?

73. Which of the indicators in Fig. 15.8 could be used for the titrations in Exercises 61 and 63?

74. Which of the indicators in Fig. 15.8 could be used for the titrations in Exercises 62 and 64?

75. Estimate the pH of a solution in which crystal violet is yellow and methyl orange is red. (See Fig. 15.8.)

76. Estimate the pH of a solution in which bromcresol green is blue and thymol blue is yellow. (See Fig. 15.8.)

77. A solution has a pH of 7.0. What would be the color of the solution if each of the following indicators were added? (See Fig. 15.8.)
   a. thymol blue
   b. bromthymol blue
   c. methyl red
   d. crystal violet

78. A solution has a pH of 4.5. What would be the color of the solution if each of the following indicators were added? (See Fig. 15.8.)
   a. methyl orange
   b. alizarin
   c. bromcresol green
   d. phenolphthalein

Solubility Equilibria

79. Write balanced equations for the dissolution reactions and the corresponding solubility product expressions for each of the following solids.
   a. $AgC_2H_3O_2$
   b. $Al(OH)_3$
   c. $Ca_3(PO_4)_2$

80. Write balanced equations for the dissolution reactions and the corresponding solubility product expressions for each of the following solids.
   a. Ag_2CO_3
   b. $Ce(IO_3)_3$
   c. BaF_2

81. Use the following data to calculate the K_{sp} value for each solid.
   a. The solubility of CaC_2O_4 is 4.8×10^{-5} mol/L.
   b. The solubility of BiI_3 is 1.32×10^{-5} mol/L.

82. Use the following data to calculate the K_{sp} value for each solid.
   a. The solubility of $Pb_3(PO_4)_2$ is 6.2×10^{-12} mol/L.
   b. The solubility of Li_2CO_3 is 7.4×10^{-2} mol/L.

83. The concentration of Pb^{2+} in a solution saturated with $PbBr_2(s)$ is 2.14×10^{-2} M. Calculate K_{sp} for $PbBr_2$.

84. The concentration of Ag^+ in a solution saturated with $Ag_2C_2O_4(s)$ is 2.2×10^{-4} M. Calculate K_{sp} for $Ag_2C_2O_4$.

85. Calculate the solubility of each of the following compounds in moles per liter. Ignore any acid–base properties.
   a. Ag_3PO_4, $K_{sp} = 1.8 \times 10^{-18}$
   b. $CaCO_3$, $K_{sp} = 8.7 \times 10^{-9}$
   c. Hg_2Cl_2, $K_{sp} = 1.1 \times 10^{-18}$ (Hg_2^{2+} is the cation in solution.)

86. Calculate the solubility of each of the following compounds in moles per liter. Ignore any acid–base properties.
   a. PbI_2, $K_{sp} = 1.4 \times 10^{-8}$
   b. $CdCO_3$, $K_{sp} = 5.2 \times 10^{-12}$
   c. $Sr_3(PO_4)_2$, $K_{sp} = 1 \times 10^{-31}$

87. Calculate the molar solubility of $Co(OH)_3$, $K_{sp} = 2.5 \times 10^{-43}$.

88. Calculate the molar solubility of $Mg(OH)_2$, $K_{sp} = 8.9 \times 10^{-12}$.

89. For each of the following pairs of solids, determine which solid has the smallest molar solubility.
   a. $CaF_2(s)$, $K_{sp} = 4.0 \times 10^{-11}$, or $BaF_2(s)$, $K_{sp} = 2.4 \times 10^{-5}$
   b. $Ca_3(PO_4)_2(s)$, $K_{sp} = 1.3 \times 10^{-32}$, or $FePO_4(s)$, $K_{sp} = 1.0 \times 10^{-22}$

90. For each of the following pairs of solids, determine which solid has the smallest molar solubility.
   a. FeC_2O_4, $K_{sp} = 2.1 \times 10^{-7}$, or $Cu(IO_4)_2$, $K_{sp} = 1.4 \times 10^{-7}$
   b. Ag_2CO_3, $K_{sp} = 8.1 \times 10^{-12}$, or $Mn(OH)_2$, $K_{sp} = 2 \times 10^{-13}$

91. Calculate the solubility (in moles per liter) of $Fe(OH)_3$ ($K_{sp} = 4 \times 10^{-38}$) in each of the following.
   a. Water
   b. A solution buffered at pH = 5.0
   c. A solution buffered at pH = 11.0

92. The K_{sp} for silver sulfate (Ag_2SO_4) is 1.2×10^{-5}. Calculate the solubility of silver sulfate in each of the following.
   a. water
   b. 0.10 M $AgNO_3$
   c. 0.20 M K_2SO_4

93. Calculate the solubility of solid $Ca_3(PO_4)_2$ ($K_{sp} = 1.3 \times 10^{-32}$) in a 0.20 M Na_3PO_4 solution.

94. The solubility of $Ce(IO_3)_3$ in a 0.20 M KIO_3 solution is 4.4×10^{-8} mol/L. Calculate K_{sp} for $Ce(IO_3)_3$.

95. Which of the substances in Exercises 85 and 86 show increased solubility as the pH of the solution becomes more acidic? Write equations for the reactions that occur to increase the solubility.

96. For which salt in each of the following groups will the solubility depend on pH?
   a. AgF, $AgCl$, $AgBr$
   b. $Pb(OH)_2$, $PbCl_2$
   c. $Sr(NO_3)_2$, $Sr(NO_2)_2$
   d. $Ni(NO_3)_2$, $Ni(CN)_2$

97. Will a precipitate form when 75.0 mL of 0.020 M $BaCl_2$ and 125 mL of 0.040 M Na_2SO_4 are mixed together?

98. Will a precipitate form when 100.0 mL of 0.020 M $Pb(NO_3)_2$ is added to 100.0 mL of 0.020 M $NaCl$?

99. Calculate the final concentrations of $K^+(aq)$, $C_2O_4{}^{2-}(aq)$, $Ba^{2+}(aq)$, and $Br^-(aq)$ in a solution prepared by adding 0.100 L of 0.200 M $K_2C_2O_4$ to 0.150 L of 0.250 M $BaBr_2$. (For BaC_2O_4, $K_{sp} = 2.3 \times 10^{-8}$.)

100. A solution is prepared by mixing 50.0 mL of 0.10 M $Pb(NO_3)_2$ with 50.0 mL of 1.0 M KCl. Calculate the concentrations of Pb^{2+} and Cl^- at equilibrium. K_{sp} for $PbCl_2(s)$ is 1.6×10^{-5}.

101. A solution contains 1.0×10^{-5} M Na_3PO_4. What is the minimum concentration of $AgNO_3$ that would cause precipitation of solid Ag_3PO_4 ($K_{sp} = 1.8 \times 10^{-18}$)?

102. A solution contains 0.25 M $Ni(NO_3)_2$ and 0.25 M $Cu(NO_3)_2$. Can the metal ions be separated by slowly adding Na_2CO_3? Assume that for successful separation 99% of the metal ion must be precipitated before the other metal ion begins to precipitate, and assume no volume change on addition of Na_2CO_3.

Complex Ion Equilibria

103. Write equations for the stepwise formation of each of the following complex ions.
   a. $Co(NH_3)_6{}^{2+}$
   b. $Ag(NH_3)_2{}^+$

104. Write equations for the stepwise formation of each of the following complex ions.
   a. $Ni(CN)_4{}^{2-}$
   b. $Mn(C_2O_4)_2{}^{2-}$

105. When aqueous KI is added gradually to mercury(II) nitrate, an orange precipitate forms. Continued addition of KI causes the precipitate to dissolve. Write balanced equations to explain these observations. (*Hint:* Hg^{2+} reacts with I^- to form $HgI_4{}^{2-}$.)

106. As sodium chloride solution is added to a solution of silver nitrate, a white precipitate forms. Ammonia is added to the mixture and the precipitate dissolves. When potassium bromide solution is then added, a pale yellow precipitate appears. When a solution of sodium thiosulfate is added, the yellow precipitate dissolves. Finally, potassium iodide is added to the solution and a yellow precipitate forms. Write reactions for all the changes mentioned above. What conclusions can you draw concerning the sizes of the K_{sp} values for $AgCl$, $AgBr$, and AgI?

107. The overall formation constant for $HgI_4{}^{2-}$ is 1.0×10^{30}. That is,

$$1.0 \times 10^{30} = \frac{[HgI_4{}^{2-}]}{[Hg^{2+}][I^-]^4}$$

What is the concentration of Hg^{2+} in 500.0 mL of a solution that was originally 0.010 M Hg^{2+} and 0.78 M I^-? The reaction is

$$Hg^{2+}(aq) + 4I^-(aq) \rightleftharpoons HgI_4{}^{2-}(aq)$$

108. A solution is formed by mixing 50.0 mL of 10.0 M NaX with 50.0 mL of 2.0×10^{-3} M $CuNO_3$. Assume that Cu(I) forms complex ions with X^- as follows:

$$Cu^+(aq) + X^-(aq) \rightleftharpoons CuX(aq) \qquad K_1 = 1.0 \times 10^2$$
$$CuX(aq) + X^-(aq) \rightleftharpoons CuX_2{}^-(aq) \qquad K_2 = 1.0 \times 10^4$$
$$CuX_2{}^-(aq) + X^-(aq) \rightleftharpoons CuX_3{}^{2-}(aq) \qquad K_3 = 1.0 \times 10^3$$

with an overall reaction

$$Cu^+(aq) + 3X^-(aq) \rightleftharpoons CuX_3{}^{2-}(aq) \qquad K = 1.0 \times 10^9$$

Calculate the following concentrations at equilibrium.
   a. $CuX_3{}^{2-}$
   b. $CuX_2{}^-$
   c. Cu^+

109. The copper(I) ion forms a chloride salt that has $K_{sp} = 1.2 \times 10^{-6}$. Copper(I) also forms a complex ion with Cl^-:

$$Cu^+(aq) + 2Cl^-(aq) \rightleftharpoons CuCl_2{}^-(aq) \qquad K = 8.7 \times 10^4$$

   a. Calculate the solubility of copper(I) chloride in pure water. (Ignore $CuCl_2{}^-$ formation for part a.)
   b. Calculate the solubility of copper(I) chloride in 0.10 M $NaCl$.

110. Solutions of sodium thiosulfate are used to dissolve unexposed AgBr ($K_{sp} = 5.0 \times 10^{-13}$) in the developing process for black-and-white film. What mass of AgBr can dissolve in 1.00 L of 0.500 M $Na_2S_2O_3$? Ag^+ reacts with $S_2O_3{}^{2-}$ to form a complex ion:

$$Ag^+(aq) + 2S_2O_3^{2-}(aq) \rightleftharpoons$$
$$Ag(S_2O_3)_2^{3-}(aq) \qquad K = 2.9 \times 10^{13}$$

111. Silver(I) chloride dissolves readily in 2 M NH_3 but is quite insoluble in 2 M NH_4NO_3. Explain.

112. The solubility of copper(II) hydroxide in water can be increased by adding either the base NH_3 or the acid HNO_3. Explain. Would added NH_3 or HNO_3 have the same effect on the solubility of silver acetate or silver chloride? Explain.

Additional Exercises

113. Derive an equation analogous to the Henderson–Hasselbalch equation but relating pOH and pK_b of a buffered solution composed of a weak base and its conjugate acid, such as NH_3 and NH_4^+.

114. a. Calculate the pH of a buffered solution that is 0.100 M in $C_6H_5CO_2H$ (benzoic acid, $K_a = 6.4 \times 10^{-5}$) and 0.100 M in $C_6H_5CO_2Na$.

b. Calculate the pH after 20.0% (by moles) of the benzoic acid is converted to benzoate anion by addition of base. Use the dissociation equilibrium

$$C_6H_5CO_2H(aq) \rightleftharpoons C_6H_5CO_2^-(aq) + H^+(aq)$$

to calculate the pH.

c. Do the same as in part b, but use the following equilibrium to calculate the pH:

$$C_6H_5CO_2^-(aq) + H_2O(l) \rightleftharpoons C_6H_5CO_2H(aq) + OH^-(aq)$$

d. Do your answers in parts b and c agree? Explain.

115. You have the following reagents on hand:

Solids (pK_a of Acid Form Is Given)	Solutions
Benzoic acid (4.19)	5.0 M HCl
Sodium acetate (4.74)	1.0 M acetic acid (4.74)
Potassium fluoride (3.14)	2.6 M NaOH
Ammonium chloride (9.26)	1.0 M HOCl (7.46)

What combinations of reagents would you use to prepare buffers at the following pH values?
a. 3.0
b. 4.0
c. 5.0
d. 7.0
e. 9.0

116. Tris(hydroxymethyl)aminomethane, commonly called TRIS or Trizma, is often used as a buffer in biochemical studies. Its buffering range is pH 7 to 9, and K_b is 1.19×10^{-6} for the aqueous reaction

$$(HOCH_2)_3CNH_2 + H_2O \rightleftharpoons (HOCH_2)_3CNH_3^+ + OH^-$$
$$\text{TRIS} \qquad\qquad \text{TRISH}^+$$

a. What is the optimal pH for TRIS buffers?
b. Calculate the ratio [TRIS]/[TRISH$^+$] at pH = 7.00 and at pH = 9.00.
c. A buffer is prepared by diluting 50.0 g TRIS base and 65.0 g TRIS hydrochloride (written as TRISHCl) to a total volume of 2.0 L. What is the pH of this buffer? What is the pH after 0.50 mL of 12 M HCl is added to a 200.0-mL portion of the buffer?

117. An aqueous solution contains dissolved NH_4Cl and NH_3. The concentration of NH_3 is 0.500 M, and the pH is 8.95.
a. Calculate the equilibrium concentration of NH_4^+.
b. Calculate the pH after 4.00 g of NaOH(s) is added to 1.00 L of this solution. (Neglect any volume changes.)

118. Calculate the value of the equilibrium constant for each of the following reactions in aqueous solution.
a. $HC_2H_3O_2 + OH^- \rightleftharpoons C_2H_3O_2^- + H_2O$
b. $C_2H_3O_2^- + H^+ \rightleftharpoons HC_2H_3O_2$
c. $HCl + NaOH \rightleftharpoons NaCl + H_2O$

119. How many moles of HCl(g) must be added to 1.0 L of 2.0 M NaOH to achieve a pH of 0.00? (Neglect any volume changes.)

120. Repeat the procedure in Exercise 61, but for the titration of 25.0 mL of 0.100 M HNO_3 with 0.100 M NaOH.

121. The active ingredient in aspirin is acetylsalicylic acid. A 2.51-g sample of acetylsalicylic acid required 27.36 mL of 0.5106 M NaOH for complete reaction. Addition of 13.68 mL of 0.5106 M HCl to the flask containing the aspirin and the sodium hydroxide produced a mixture with pH = 3.48. Find the molar mass of acetylsalicylic acid and its K_a value. State any assumptions you must make to reach your answer.

122. Potassium hydrogen phthalate, known as KHP (molar mass = 204.22 g/mol), can be obtained in high purity and is used to determine the concentration of solutions of strong bases by the reaction

$$HP^-(aq) + OH^-(aq) \longrightarrow H_2O(l) + P^{2-}(aq)$$

If a typical titration experiment begins with about 0.5 g KHP and has a final volume of about 100 mL, what would be an appropriate indicator to use? The pK_a for HP$^-$ is 5.51.

123. The K_{sp} of hydroxyapatite, $Ca_5(PO_4)_3OH$, is 6.8×10^{-37}. Calculate the solubility of hydroxyapatite in pure water in moles per liter. How is the solubility of hydroxyapatite affected by adding acid? When hydroxyapatite is treated with fluoride, the mineral fluorapatite, $Ca_5(PO_4)_3F$, forms. The K_{sp} of this substance is 1×10^{-60}. Calculate the solubility of fluorapatite in water. How do these calculations provide a rationale for the fluoridation of drinking water?

124. In the chapter discussion of precipitate formation, we ran the precipitation reaction to completion and then let some of the precipitate redissolve to get back to equilibrium. To see why, redo Sample Exercise 15.17, where

Initial Concentration (mol/L)	Equilibrium Concentration (mol/L)
$[Mg^{2+}]_0 = 3.75 \times 10^{-3}$ $[F^-]_0 = 6.25 \times 10^{-2}$	
$\xrightarrow[\text{reacts to form} \atop MgF_2]{y \text{ mol/L } Mg^{2+}}$	$[Mg^{2+}] = 3.75 \times 10^{-3} - y$ $[F^-] = 6.25 \times 10^{-2} - 2y$

125. Calculate the concentration of Pb^{2+} in each of the following.
   a. a saturated solution of $Pb(OH)_2$, $K_{sp} = 1.2 \times 10^{-15}$
   b. a saturated solution of $Pb(OH)_2$ buffered at pH = 13.00
   c. Ethylenediaminetetraacetate ($EDTA^{4-}$) is used as a complexing agent in chemical analysis and has the following structure:

$$\begin{array}{c} ^-O_2C-CH_2 \\ ^-O_2C-CH_2 \end{array} N-CH_2-CH_2-N \begin{array}{c} CH_2-CO_2^- \\ CH_2-CO_2^- \end{array}$$

Ethylenediaminetetraacetate

Solutions of $EDTA^{4-}$ are used to treat heavy metal poisoning by removing the heavy metal in the form of a soluble complex ion. The complex ion virtually eliminates the heavy metal ions from reacting with biochemical systems. The reaction of $EDTA^{4-}$ with Pb^{2+} is

$$Pb^{2+}(aq) + EDTA^{4-}(aq) \rightleftharpoons PbEDTA^{2-}(aq)$$
$$K = 1.1 \times 10^{18}$$

Consider a solution with 0.010 mol $Pb(NO_3)_2$ added to 1.0 L of an aqueous solution buffered at pH = 13.00 and containing 0.050 M Na_4EDTA. Does $Pb(OH)_2$ precipitate from this solution?

Challenge Problems

126. Another way to treat data from a pH titration is to graph the absolute value of the change in pH per change in milliliters added versus milliliters added ($\Delta pH/\Delta mL$ versus mL added). Make this graph using your results from Exercise 61. What advantage might this method have over the traditional method for treating titration data?

127. A buffer is made using 45.0 mL of 0.750 M $HC_3H_5O_2$ ($K_a = 1.3 \times 10^{-5}$) and 55.0 mL of 0.700 M $NaC_3H_5O_2$. What volume of 0.10 M NaOH must be added to change the pH of the original buffer solution by 2.5%?

128. A 0.400 M solution of ammonia was titrated with hydrochloric acid to the equivalence point, where the total volume was 1.50 times the original volume. At what pH does the equivalence point occur?

129. What volume of 0.0100 M NaOH must be added to 1.00 L of 0.0500 M HOCl to achieve a pH of 8.00?

130. Consider a solution formed by mixing 50.0 mL of 0.100 M H_2SO_4, 30.0 mL of 0.100 M HOCl, 25.0 mL of 0.200 M NaOH, 25.0 mL of 0.100 M $Ca(OH)_2$, and 10.0 mL of 0.150 M KOH. Calculate the pH of this solution.

131. Malonic acid ($HO_2CCH_2CO_2H$) is a diprotic acid. In the titration of malonic acid with NaOH, stoichiometric points occur at pH = 3.9 and 8.8. A 25.00-mL sample of malonic acid of unknown concentration is titrated with 0.0984 M NaOH, requiring 31.50 mL of the NaOH solution to reach the phenolphthalein end point. Calculate the concentration of malonic acid in the unknown solution.

132. A few drops of each of the indicators shown in the accompanying table were placed in separate portions of a 1.0 M solution of a weak acid, HX. The results are shown in the last column of the table. What is the approximate pH of the solution containing HX? Calculate the approximate value of K_a for HX.

Indicator	Color of HIn	Color of In$^-$	pK$_a$ of HIn	HX
Bromphenol blue	Yellow	Blue	4.0	Blue
Bromcresol purple	Yellow	Purple	6.0	Yellow
Bromcresol green	Yellow	Blue	4.8	Green
Alizarin	Yellow	Red	6.5	Yellow

133. **a.** Calculate the molar solubility of SrF_2 in water, ignoring the basic properties of F^-. (For SrF_2, $K_{sp} = 7.9 \times 10^{-10}$.)
   b. Would the measured molar solubility of SrF_2 be greater than or less than the value calculated in part a? Explain.
   c. Calculate the molar solubility of SrF_2 in a solution buffered at pH = 2.00. (K_a for HF is 7.2×10^{-4}.)

Marathon Problem*

This problem is designed to incorporate several concepts and techniques into one situation. Marathon Problems can be used in class by groups of students to help facilitate problem-solving skills.

134. A 225-mg sample of a diprotic acid is dissolved in enough water to make 250. mL of solution. The pH of this solution is 2.06. A saturated solution of calcium hydroxide ($K_{sp} = 5.5 \times 10^{-6}$) is prepared by adding excess calcium hydroxide to pure water and then removing the undissolved solid by filtration. Enough of the calcium hydroxide solution is added to the solution of the acid to reach the second equivalence point. The pH at the second equivalence point (as determined by a pH meter) is 7.96. The first dissociation constant for the acid (K_{a_1}) is 5.90×10^{-2}. Assume that the volumes of the solutions are additive, all solutions are at 25°C, and that K_{a_1} is at least 1000 times greater than K_{a_2}.

a. Calculate the molar mass of the acid.

b. Calculate the second dissociation constant for the acid (K_{a_2}).

* This Marathon Problem was developed by James H. Burness, Penn State University, York Campus. Reprinted with permission from the *Journal of Chemical Education,* Vol. 68, No. 11, 1991, pp. 919–922; copyright © 1991, Division of Chemical Education, Inc.

CHAPTER 16

Spontaneity, Entropy, and Free Energy

Contents

The *first law of thermodynamics* is a statement of the law of conservation of energy: Energy can be neither created nor destroyed. In other words, *the energy of the universe is constant*. Although the total energy is constant, the various forms of energy can be interchanged in physical and chemical processes. For example, if you drop a book, some of the initial potential energy of the book is changed to kinetic energy, which is then transferred to the atoms in the air and the floor as random motion. The net effect of this process is to change a given quantity of potential energy to exactly the same quantity of thermal energy. Energy has been converted from one form to another, but the same quantity of energy exists before and after the process.

Now let's consider a chemical example. When methane is burned in excess oxygen, the major reaction is

$$CH_4(g) + 2O_2(g) \longrightarrow CO_2(g) + 2H_2O(g) + \text{energy}$$

This reaction produces a quantity of energy, which is released as heat. This energy flow results from the lowering of the potential energy stored in the bonds of CH_4 and O_2 as they react to form CO_2 and H_2O. This is illustrated in Fig. 16.1. Potential energy has been converted to thermal energy, but the energy content of the universe has remained constant in accordance with the first law of thermodynamics.

Molecular Models: CH_4, O_2, CO_2, H_2O

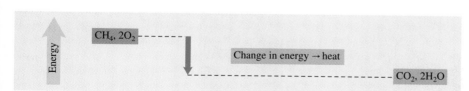

Figure 16.1

When methane and oxygen react to form carbon dioxide and water, the products have lower potential energy than the reactants. This change in potential energy results in energy flow (heat) to the surroundings.

Solid carbon dioxide (dry ice), when placed in water, causes violent bubbling as gaseous CO_2 is released. The "fog" is moisture condensed from the cold air.

The first law of thermodynamics is used mainly for energy bookkeeping, that is, to answer such questions as

How much energy is involved in the change?

Does energy flow into or out of the system?

What form does the energy finally assume?

The first law of thermodynamics: The energy of the universe is constant.

Although the first law of thermodynamics provides the means for accounting for energy, it gives no hint as to *why* a particular process occurs in a given direction. This is the main question to be considered in this chapter.

16.1 *Spontaneous Processes and Entropy*

Spontaneous does not mean fast.

A process is said to be *spontaneous* if it *occurs without outside intervention.* **Spontaneous processes** may be fast or slow. As we will see in this chapter, thermodynamics can tell us the *direction* in which a process will occur but can say nothing about the *speed* of the process. As we saw in Chapter 12, the rate of a reaction depends on many factors, such as activation energy, temperature, concentration, and catalysts, and we were able to explain these effects using a simple collision model. In describing a chemical reaction, the discipline of chemical kinetics focuses on the pathway between reactants and products; thermodynamics considers only the initial and final states and does not require knowledge of the pathway between reactants and products (see Fig. 16.2).

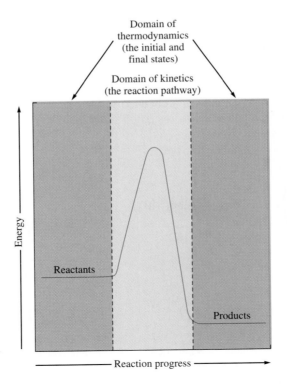

Figure 16.2

The rate of a reaction depends on the pathway from reactants to products; this is the domain of kinetics. Thermodynamics tells us whether or not a reaction is spontaneous based only on the properties of the reactants and products. The predictions of thermodynamics do not require knowledge of the pathway between reactants and products.

In summary, thermodynamics lets us predict whether a process will occur but gives no information about the amount of time required for the process. For example, according to the principles of thermodynamics, a diamond should change spontaneously to graphite. The fact that we do not observe this process does not mean the prediction is wrong; it simply means the process is very slow. Thus we need both thermodynamics and kinetics to describe reactions fully.

To explore the idea of spontaneity, consider the following physical and chemical processes:

A ball rolls down a hill but never spontaneously rolls back up the hill.

If exposed to air and moisture, steel rusts spontaneously. However, the iron oxide in rust does not spontaneously change back to iron metal and oxygen gas.

A gas fills its container uniformly. It never spontaneously collects at one end of the container.

Heat flow always occurs from a hot object to a cooler one. The reverse process never occurs spontaneously.

Wood burns spontaneously in an exothermic reaction to form carbon dioxide and water, but wood is not formed when carbon dioxide and water are heated together.

At temperatures below 0°C, water spontaneously freezes, and at temperatures above 0°C, ice spontaneously melts.

What thermodynamic principle will provide an explanation of why, under a given set of conditions, each of these diverse processes occurs in one direction and never in the reverse? In searching for an answer, we could explain the behavior of a ball on a hill in terms of gravity. But what does gravity have to do with the rusting of a nail or the freezing of water? Early developers of thermodynamics thought that exothermicity might be the key—that a process would be spontaneous if it were exothermic. Although this factor does appear to be important, since many sponta-

Plant materials burn to form carbon dioxide and water.

neous processes are exothermic, it is not the total answer. For example, the melting of ice, which occurs spontaneously at temperatures greater than 0°C, is an endothermic process.

What common characteristic causes the processes listed above to be spontaneous in one direction only? After many years of observation, scientists have concluded that the characteristic common to all spontaneous processes is an increase in a property called **entropy,** denoted by the symbol S. *The driving force for a spontaneous process is an increase in the entropy of the universe.*

What is entropy? Although there is no simple definition that is completely accurate, *entropy can be viewed as a measure of randomness or disorder.* The natural progression of things is from order to disorder, from lower entropy to higher entropy. You only have to think about the condition of your room to be convinced of this. Your room naturally tends to get messy (disordered), because an ordered room requires everything to be in its place. There are simply many more ways for things to be out of place than for them to be in their places.

As another example, suppose you have a deck of playing cards ordered in some particular way. You throw these cards into the air and pick them all up at random. Looking at the new sequence of the cards, you would be very surprised to find that it matched the original order. Such an event would be possible, but *very improbable.* There are billions of ways for the deck to be disordered, but only one way to be ordered according to your definition. Thus the chances of picking the cards up out of order are much greater than the chance of picking them up in order. It is natural for disorder to increase.

Entropy is a thermodynamic function that describes the *number of arrangements* (positions and/or energy levels) that are *available to a system* existing in a given state. Entropy is closely associated with probability. The key concept is that the more ways a particular state can be achieved, the greater is the likelihood (probability) of finding that state. In other words, *nature spontaneously proceeds toward the states that have the highest probabilities of existing.* This conclusion is not surprising at all. The difficulty comes in connecting this concept to real-life processes. For example, what does the spontaneous rusting of steel have to do with probability? Understanding the connection between entropy and spontaneity will allow us to answer such questions. We will begin to explore this connection by considering a very simple process, the expansion of an ideal gas into a vacuum, as represented in Fig. 16.3. Why is this process spontaneous? The driving force is probability. Because there are more ways of having the gas evenly spread throughout the container than there are ways for it to be in any other possible state, the gas spontaneously attains the uniform distribution.

To understand this conclusion, we will greatly simplify the system and consider some of the possible arrangements of only four gas molecules in the two-bulbed container (Fig. 16.4). How many ways can each arrangement (state) be achieved? Arrangement I can be achieved in only one way—all the molecules must be in one end. Arrangement II can be achieved in four ways, as shown in Table 16.1. Each configuration that gives a particular arrangement is called a *microstate.* Arrangement I has one microstate, and arrangement II has four microstates. Arrangement III can be achieved in six ways (six microstates), as shown in Table 16.1. *Which arrangement is most likely to occur?* The one that can be achieved in the greatest number of ways. Thus arrangement III is most probable. The relative probabilities of arrangements III, II, and I are 6 : 4 : 1. We have discovered an important principle: The probability of occurrence of a particular arrangement (state) depends on the number of ways (microstates) in which that arrangement can be achieved.

A disordered pile of playing cards.

Probability refers to likelihood.

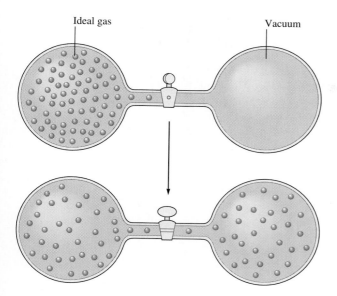

Figure 16.3

The expansion of an ideal gas into an evacuated bulb.

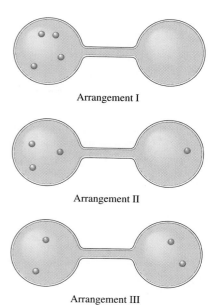

Arrangement I

Arrangement II

Arrangement III

Figure 16.4

Three possible arrangements (states) of four molecules in a two-bulbed flask.

The consequences of this principle are dramatic for large numbers of molecules. One gas molecule in the flask in Fig. 16.4 has one chance in two of being in the left bulb. We say that the probability of finding the molecule in the left bulb is $\frac{1}{2}$. For two molecules in the flask, there is one chance in two of finding each molecule in the left bulb, so there is one chance in four ($\frac{1}{2} \times \frac{1}{2} = \frac{1}{4}$) that *both* molecules will be in the left bulb. As the number of molecules increases, the relative probability of

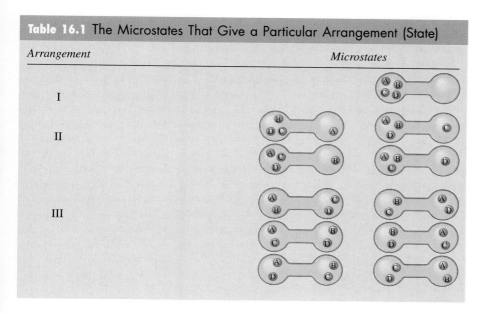

Table 16.1 The Microstates That Give a Particular Arrangement (State)

Arrangement	Microstates
I	
II	
III	

For two molecules in the flask, there are four possible microstates:

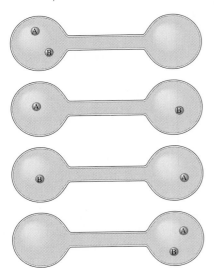

Thus there is one chance in four of finding

Table 16.2 Probability of Finding All the Molecules in the Left Bulb as a Function of the Total Number of Molecules

Number of Molecules	Relative Probability of Finding All Molecules in the Left Bulb
1	$\dfrac{1}{2}$
2	$\dfrac{1}{2} \times \dfrac{1}{2} = \dfrac{1}{2^2} = \dfrac{1}{4}$
3	$\dfrac{1}{2} \times \dfrac{1}{2} \times \dfrac{1}{2} = \dfrac{1}{2^3} = \dfrac{1}{8}$
5	$\dfrac{1}{2} \times \dfrac{1}{2} \times \dfrac{1}{2} \times \dfrac{1}{2} \times \dfrac{1}{2} = \dfrac{1}{2^5} = \dfrac{1}{32}$
10	$\dfrac{1}{2^{10}} = \dfrac{1}{1024}$
n	$\dfrac{1}{2^n} = \left(\dfrac{1}{2}\right)^n$
6×10^{23} (1 mole)	$\left(\dfrac{1}{2}\right)^{6 \times 10^{23}} \approx 10^{-(2 \times 10^{23})}$

finding all of them in the left bulb decreases, as shown in Table 16.2. For 1 mole of gas, the probability of finding all the molecules in the left bulb is so small that this arrangement would "never" occur.

Thus a gas placed in one end of a container will spontaneously expand to fill the entire vessel evenly because, for a large number of gas molecules, there is a huge number of microstates in which equal numbers of molecules are in both ends. On the other hand, the opposite process,

although not impossible, is *highly* improbable, since only one microstate leads to this arrangement. Therefore, this process does not occur spontaneously.

The type of probability we have been considering in this example is called **positional probability** because it depends on the number of configurations in space (positional microstates) that yield a particular state. A gas expands into a vacuum to give a uniform distribution because the expanded state has the highest positional probability, that is, the largest entropy, of the states available to the system.

Positional probability is also illustrated by changes of state. In general, positional entropy increases in going from solid to liquid to gas. A mole of a substance has a much smaller volume in the solid state than it does in the gaseous state. In the solid state, the molecules are close together, with relatively few positions available to them; in the gaseous state, the molecules are far apart, with many more positions

Solid, liquid, and gaseous states were compared in Chapter 10.

available to them. The liquid state is closer to the solid state than it is to the gaseous state in these terms. We can summarize these comparisons as follows:

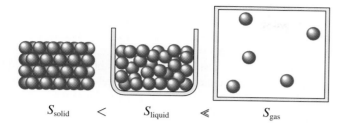

$$S_{\text{solid}} \quad < \quad S_{\text{liquid}} \quad \ll \quad S_{\text{gas}}$$

Solids are more ordered than liquids or gases and thus have lower entropy.

Positional entropy is also very important in the formation of solutions. In Chapter 11 we saw that solution formation is favored by the natural tendency for substances to mix. We can now be more precise. The entropy change associated with the mixing of two pure substances is expected to be positive. An increase in entropy is expected because there are many more microstates for the mixed condition than for the separated condition. This effect is due principally to the increased volume available to a given "particle" after mixing occurs. For example, when two liquids are mixed to form a solution, the molecules of each liquid have more available volume and thus more available positions. Therefore, the increase in positional entropy associated with mixing favors the formation of solutions.

The tendency to mix is due to the increased volume available to the particles of each component of the mixture. For example, when two liquids are mixed, the molecules of each liquid have more available volume and thus more available positions.

Sample Exercise 16.1 *Positional Entropy*

For each of the following pairs, choose the substance with the higher positional entropy (per mole) at a given temperature.

a. Solid CO_2 and gaseous CO_2
b. N_2 gas at 1 atm and N_2 gas at 1.0×10^{-2} atm

Solution

a. Since a mole of gaseous CO_2 has the greater volume by far, the molecules have many more available positions than in a mole of solid CO_2. Thus gaseous CO_2 has the higher positional entropy.
b. A mole of N_2 gas at 1×10^{-2} atm has a volume 100 times that (at a given temperature) of a mole of N_2 gas at 1 atm. Thus N_2 gas at 1×10^{-2} atm has the higher positional entropy.

See Exercises 16.21 and 16.22.

Sample Exercise 16.2 *Predicting Entropy Changes*

Predict the sign of the entropy change for each of the following processes.

a. Solid sugar is added to water to form a solution.
b. Iodine vapor condenses on a cold surface to form crystals.

Solution

a. The sugar molecules become randomly dispersed in the water when the solution forms and thus have access to a larger volume and a larger number of possible positions. The positional disorder is increased, and there will be an increase in entropy. ΔS is positive, since the final state has a larger entropy than the initial state, and $\Delta S = S_{final} - S_{initial}$.

b. Gaseous iodine is forming a solid. This process involves a change from a relatively large volume to a much smaller volume, which results in lower positional disorder. For this process ΔS is negative (the entropy decreases).

See Exercises 16.23 and 16.24.

16.2 Entropy and the Second Law of Thermodynamics

The total energy of the universe is constant, but the entropy is increasing.

We have seen that processes are spontaneous when they result in an increase in disorder. Nature always moves toward the most probable state available to it. We can state this principle in terms of entropy: *In any spontaneous process there is always an increase in the entropy of the universe.* This is the **second law of thermodynamics.** Contrast this with the first law of thermodynamics, which tells us that the energy of the universe is constant. Energy is conserved in the universe, but entropy is not. In fact, the second law can be paraphrased as follows: *The entropy of the universe is increasing.*

As in Chapter 6, we find it convenient to divide the universe into a system and the surroundings. Thus we can represent the change in the entropy of the universe as

$$\Delta S_{univ} = \Delta S_{sys} + \Delta S_{surr}$$

where ΔS_{sys} and ΔS_{surr} represent the changes in entropy that occur in the system and surroundings, respectively.

To predict whether a given process will be spontaneous, we must know the sign of ΔS_{univ}. If ΔS_{univ} is positive, the entropy of the universe increases, and the process is spontaneous in the direction written. If ΔS_{univ} is negative, the process is spontaneous in the *opposite* direction. If ΔS_{univ} is zero, the process has no tendency to occur, and the system is at equilibrium. To predict whether a process is spontaneous, we must consider the entropy changes that occur both in the system and in the surroundings and then take their sum.

Sample Exercise 16.3 *The Second Law*

In a living cell, large molecules are assembled from simple ones. Is this process consistent with the second law of thermodynamics?

Solution

To reconcile the operation of an order-producing cell with the second law of thermodynamics, we must remember that ΔS_{univ}, not ΔS_{sys}, must be positive for a

Fresh-water green algae.

CHEMICAL IMPACT

Entropy: An Organizing Force?

IN THIS TEXT we have emphasized the meaning of the second law of thermodynamics—that the entropy of the universe is always increasing. Although the results of all our experiments support this conclusion, this does not mean that order cannot appear spontaneously in a given part of the universe. The best example of this phenomenon involves the assembly of cells in living organisms. Of course, when a process that creates an ordered system is examined in detail, it is found that other parts of the process involve an increase in disorder such that the sum of all the entropy changes is positive. In fact, scientists are now finding that the search for maximum entropy in one part of a system can be a powerful force for organization in another part of the system.

To understand how entropy can be an organizing force, look at the accompanying figure. In a system containing large and small "balls" as shown in the figure, the small balls can "herd" the large balls into clumps in the corners and near the walls. This clears out the maximum space

for the small balls so that they can move more freely, thus maximizing the entropy of the system, as demanded by the second law of thermodynamics.

In essence, the ability to maximize entropy by sorting different-sized objects creates a kind of attractive force, called a *depletion*, or *excluded-volume*, *force*. These "entropic forces" operate for objects in the size range of approximately 10^{-8} to approximately 10^{-6} m. For entropy-induced ordering to occur, the particles must be constantly jostling each other and must be constantly agitated by

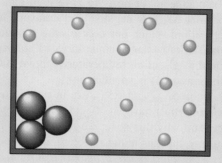

solvent molecules, thus making gravity unimportant.

There is increasing evidence that entropic ordering is important in many biological systems. For example, this phenomenon seems to be responsible for the clumping of sickle-cell hemoglobin in the presence of much smaller proteins that act as the "smaller balls." Entropic forces also have been linked to the clustering of DNA in cells without nuclei, and Allen Minton of the National Institutes of Health in Bethesda, Maryland, is studying the role of entropic forces in the binding of proteins to cell membranes.

Entropic ordering also appears in nonbiological settings, especially in the ways polymer molecules clump together. For example, polymers added to paint to improve the flow characteristics of the paint actually caused it to coagulate because of depletion forces.

Thus, as you probably have concluded already, entropy is a complex issue. As entropy drives the universe to its ultimate death of maximum chaos, it provides some order along the way.

process to be spontaneous. A process for which ΔS_{sys} is negative can be spontaneous if the associated ΔS_{surr} is both larger and positive. The operation of a cell is such a process.

See Questions 16.11 and 16.13.

16.3 The Effect of Temperature on Spontaneity

To explore the interplay of ΔS_{sys} and ΔS_{surr} in determining the sign of ΔS_{univ}, we will first discuss the change of state for one mole of water from liquid to gas,

$$H_2O(l) \longrightarrow H_2O(g)$$

considering the water to be the system and everything else the surroundings.

What happens to the entropy of water in this process? A mole of liquid water (18 grams) has a volume of approximately 18 mL. A mole of gaseous water at 1 atmosphere and 100°C occupies a volume of approximately 31 liters. Clearly, there are many more positions available to the water molecules in a volume of 31 L than in 18 mL, and the vaporization of water is favored by this increase in positional probability. That is, for this process the entropy of the system increases; ΔS_{sys} has a positive sign.

What about the entropy change in the surroundings? Although we will not prove it here, entropy changes in the surroundings are determined primarily by the flow of energy into or out of the system as heat. To understand this, suppose an exothermic process transfers 50 J of energy as heat to the surroundings, where it becomes thermal energy, that is, kinetic energy associated with the random motions of atoms. Thus this flow of energy into the surroundings increases the random motions of atoms there and thereby increases the entropy of the surroundings. The sign of ΔS_{surr} is positive. When an endothermic process occurs in the system, it produces the opposite effect. Heat flows from the surroundings to the system, and the random motions of the atoms in the surroundings decrease, decreasing the entropy of the surroundings. The vaporization of water is an endothermic process. Thus, for this change of state, ΔS_{surr} is negative.

Remember it is the sign of ΔS_{univ} that tells us whether the vaporization of water is spontaneous or not. We have seen that ΔS_{sys} is positive and favors the process and that ΔS_{surr} is negative and unfavorable. Thus the components of ΔS_{univ} are in opposition. Which one controls the situation? The answer *depends on the temperature.* We know that at a pressure of 1 atmosphere, water changes spontaneously from liquid to gas at all temperatures above 100°C. Below 100°C, the opposite process (condensation) is spontaneous.

Since ΔS_{sys} and ΔS_{surr} are in opposition for the vaporization of water, the temperature must have an effect on the relative importance of these two terms. To understand why this is so, we must discuss in more detail the factors that control the entropy changes in the surroundings. The central idea is that *the entropy changes in the surroundings are primarily determined by heat flow.* An exothermic process in the system increases the entropy of the surroundings, because the resulting energy flow increases the random motions in the surroundings. This means that exothermicity is an important driving force for spontaneity. In earlier chapters we have seen that a system tends to undergo changes that lower its energy. We now understand the reason for this tendency. When a system at constant temperature moves to a lower energy, the energy it gives up is transferred to the surroundings, leading to an increase in entropy there.

The significance of exothermicity as a driving force *depends on the temperature at which the process occurs.* That is, the magnitude of ΔS_{surr} depends on the temperature at which the heat is transferred. We will not attempt to prove this fact here. Instead, we offer an analogy. Suppose that you have $50 to give away. Giving it to a millionaire would not create much of an impression—a millionaire has money to spare. However, to a poor college student, $50 would represent a significant sum and would be received with considerable joy. The same principle can be applied to energy transfer via the flow of heat. If 50 J of energy is transferred to the surroundings, the impact of that event depends greatly on the temperature. If the temperature of the surroundings is very high, the atoms there are in rapid motion. The 50 J of energy will not make a large percent change in these motions. On the other hand, if 50 J of energy is transferred to the surroundings at a very low temperature,

In an endothermic process, heat flows from the surroundings into the system. In an exothermic process, heat flows into the surroundings from the system.

where atomic motion is slow, the energy will cause a large percent change in these motions. *The impact of the transfer of a given quantity of energy as heat to or from the surroundings will be greater at lower temperatures.*

For our purposes, there are two important characteristics of the entropy changes that occur in the surroundings:

1. *The sign ΔS_{surr} depends on the direction of the heat flow.* At constant temperature, an exothermic process in the system causes heat to flow into the surroundings, increasing the random motions and thus the entropy of the surroundings. For this case, ΔS_{surr} is positive. The opposite is true for an endothermic process in a system at constant temperature. Note that although the driving force described here really results from the change in entropy, it is often described in terms of energy: Nature tends to seek the lowest possible energy.

In a process occurring at constant temperature, the tendency for the system to lower its energy results from the positive value of ΔS_{surr}.

2. *The magnitude of ΔS_{surr} depends on the temperature.* The transfer of a given quantity of energy as heat produces a much greater percent change in the randomness of the surroundings at a low temperature than it does at a high temperature. Thus ΔS_{surr} depends directly on the quantity of heat transferred and inversely on temperature. In other words, the tendency for the system to lower its energy becomes a more important driving force at lower temperatures.

$$\begin{matrix}\text{Driving force} \\ \text{provided by} \\ \text{the energy flow} \\ \text{(heat)}\end{matrix} = \begin{matrix}\text{magnitude of the} \\ \text{entropy change of} \\ \text{the surroundings}\end{matrix} = \frac{\text{quantity of heat (J)}}{\text{temperature (K)}}$$

These ideas are summarized as follows:

$$\text{Exothermic process:} \qquad \Delta S_{surr} = +\frac{\text{quantity of heat (J)}}{\text{temperature (K)}}$$

$$\text{Endothermic process:} \qquad \Delta S_{surr} = -\frac{\text{quantity of heat (J)}}{\text{temperature (K)}}$$

Exothermic process:
ΔS_{surr} = positive

Endothermic process:
ΔS_{surr} = negative

We can express ΔS_{surr} in terms of the change in enthalpy ΔH for a process occurring at constant pressure, since

$$\text{Heat flow (constant } P\text{)} = \text{change in enthalpy} = \Delta H$$

Recall that ΔH consists of two parts: a sign and a number. The *sign* indicates the direction of flow, where a plus sign means into the system (endothermic) and a minus sign means out of the system (exothermic). The *number* indicates the quantity of energy.

When no subscript is present, the quantity (for example, ΔH) refers to the system.

Combining all these concepts produces the following definition of ΔS_{surr} for a reaction that takes place under conditions of constant temperature (in kelvins) and pressure:

$$\Delta S_{surr} = -\frac{\Delta H}{T}$$

The minus sign is necessary because the sign of ΔH is determined with respect to the reaction system, and this equation expresses a property of the surroundings. This means that if the reaction is exothermic, ΔH has a negative sign, but since heat flows into the surroundings, ΔS_{surr} is positive.

The minus sign changes the point of view from the system to the surroundings.

The mineral stibnite contains Sb_2S_3.

Sample Exercise 16.4 Determining ΔS_{surr}

In the metallurgy of antimony, the pure metal is recovered via different reactions, depending on the composition of the ore. For example, iron is used to reduce antimony in sulfide ores:

$$Sb_2S_3(s) + 3Fe(s) \longrightarrow 2Sb(s) + 3FeS(s) \qquad \Delta H = -125 \text{ kJ}$$

Carbon is used as the reducing agent for oxide ores:

$$Sb_4O_6(s) + 6C(s) \longrightarrow 4Sb(s) + 6CO(g) \qquad \Delta H = 778 \text{ kJ}$$

Calculate ΔS_{surr} for each of these reactions at 25°C and 1 atm.

Solution

We use

$$\Delta S_{surr} = -\frac{\Delta H}{T}$$

where

$$T = 25 + 273 = 298 \text{ K}$$

For the sulfide ore reaction,

$$\Delta S_{surr} = -\frac{-125 \text{ kJ}}{298 \text{ K}} = 0.419 \text{ kJ/K} = 419 \text{ J/K}$$

Note that ΔS_{surr} is positive, as it should be, since this reaction is exothermic and heat flow occurs to the surroundings, increasing the randomness of the surroundings.

For the oxide ore reaction,

$$\Delta S_{surr} = -\frac{778 \text{ kJ}}{298} = -2.61 \text{ kJ/K} = -2.61 \times 10^3 \text{ J/K}$$

In this case ΔS_{surr} is negative because heat flow occurs from the surroundings to the system.

See Exercises 16.25 and 16.26.

We have seen that the spontaneity of a process is determined by the entropy change it produces in the universe. We also have seen that ΔS_{univ} has two components, ΔS_{sys} and ΔS_{surr}. If for some process both ΔS_{sys} and ΔS_{surr} are positive, then ΔS_{univ} is positive, and the process is spontaneous. If, on the other hand, both ΔS_{sys} and ΔS_{surr} are negative, the process does not occur in the direction indicated but is spontaneous in the opposite direction. Finally, if ΔS_{sys} and ΔS_{surr} have opposite signs, the spontaneity of the process depends on the sizes of the opposing terms. These cases are summarized in Table 16.3.

We can now understand why spontaneity is often dependent on temperature and thus why water spontaneously freezes below 0°C and melts above 0°C. The term ΔS_{surr} is temperature-dependent. Since

Table 16.3 Interplay of ΔS_{sys} and ΔS_{surr} in Determining the Sign of ΔS_{univ}			
Signs of Entropy Changes			
ΔS_{sys}	ΔS_{surr}	ΔS_{univ}	*Process Spontaneous?*
+	+	+	Yes
−	−	−	No (reaction will occur in opposite direction)
+	−	?	Yes, if ΔS_{sys} has a larger magnitude than ΔS_{surr}
−	+	?	Yes, if ΔS_{surr} has a larger magnitude than ΔS_{sys}

$$\Delta S_{surr} = -\frac{\Delta H}{T}$$

at constant pressure, the value of ΔS_{surr} changes markedly with temperature. The magnitude of ΔS_{surr} will be very small at high temperatures and will increase as the temperature decreases. That is, exothermicity is most important as a driving force at low temperatures.

16.4 *Free Energy*

So far we have used ΔS_{univ} to predict the spontaneity of a process. However, another thermodynamic function is also related to spontaneity and is especially useful in dealing with the temperature dependence of spontaneity. This function is called the **free energy,** which is symbolized by G and defined by the relationship

$$G = H - TS$$

where H is the enthalpy, T is the Kelvin temperature, and S is the entropy.

For a process that occurs at constant temperature, the change in free energy (ΔG) is given by the equation

$$\Delta G = \Delta H - T\Delta S$$

Note that all quantities here refer to the system. From this point on we will follow the usual convention that when no subscript is included, the quantity refers to the system. To see how this equation relates to spontaneity, we divide both sides of the equation by $-T$ to produce

$$-\frac{\Delta G}{T} = -\frac{\Delta H}{T} + \Delta S$$

The symbol G for free energy honors Josiah Willard Gibbs (1839–1903), who was professor of mathematical physics at Yale University from 1871 to 1903. He laid the foundations of many areas of thermodynamics, particularly as they apply to chemistry.

Remember that at constant temperature and pressure

$$\Delta S_{surr} = -\frac{\Delta H}{T}$$

So we can write

$$-\frac{\Delta G}{T} = -\frac{\Delta H}{T} + \Delta S = \Delta S_{surr} + \Delta S = \Delta S_{univ}$$

We have shown that

$$\Delta S_{univ} = -\frac{\Delta G}{T} \qquad \text{at constant } T \text{ and } P$$

This result is very important. It means that a process carried out at constant temperature and pressure will be spontaneous only if ΔG is negative. That is, *a process (at constant T and P) is spontaneous in the direction in which the free energy decreases* ($-\Delta G$ means $+\Delta S_{univ}$).

Now we have two functions that can be used to predict spontaneity: the entropy of the universe, which applies to all processes, and free energy, which can be used for processes carried out at constant temperature and pressure. Since so many chemical reactions occur under the latter conditions, free energy is the more useful to chemists.

Let's use the free energy equation to predict the spontaneity of the melting of ice:

$$H_2O(s) \longrightarrow H_2O(l)$$

for which $\Delta H° = 6.03 \times 10^3$ J/mol and $\Delta S° = 22.1$ J/K · mol

The superscript degree symbol (°) indicates all substances are in their standard states.

Results of the calculations of ΔS_{univ} and $\Delta G°$ at $-10°C$, $0°C$, and $10°C$ are shown in Table 16.4. These data predict that the process is spontaneous at $10°C$; that is, ice melts at this temperature because ΔS_{univ} is positive and $\Delta G°$ is negative. The opposite is true at $-10°C$, where water freezes spontaneously.

Why is this so? The answer lies in the fact that ΔS_{sys} ($\Delta S°$) and ΔS_{surr} oppose each other. The term $\Delta S°$ favors the melting of ice because of the increase in positional entropy, and ΔS_{surr} favors the freezing of water because it is an exothermic

To review the definitions of standard states, see page 260.

Table 16.4 Results of the Calculation of ΔS_{univ} and $\Delta G°$ for the Process $H_2O(s) \rightarrow H_2O(l)$ at $-10°C$, $0°C$, and $10°C$*

T (°C)	T (K)	$\Delta H°$ (J/mol)	$\Delta S°$ (J/K · mol)	$\Delta S_{surr} = -\dfrac{\Delta H°}{T}$ (J/K · mol)	$\Delta S_{univ} = \Delta S° + \Delta S_{surr}$ (J/K · mol)	$T\Delta S°$ (J/mol)	$\Delta G° = \Delta H° - T\Delta S°$ (J/mol)
-10	263	6.03×10^3	22.1	-22.9	-0.8	5.81×10^3	$+2.2 \times 10^2$
0	273	6.03×10^3	22.1	-22.1	0	6.03×10^3	0
10	283	6.03×10^3	22.1	-21.3	$+0.8$	6.25×10^3	-2.2×10^2

*Note that at 10°C, $\Delta S°$ (ΔS_{sys}) controls, and the process occurs even though it is endothermic. At $-10°C$, the magnitude of ΔS_{surr} is larger than that of $\Delta S°$, so the process is spontaneous in the opposite (exothermic) direction.

Table 16.5 Various Possible Combinations of ΔH and ΔS for a Process and the Resulting Dependence of Spontaneity on Temperature

Case	Result
ΔS positive, ΔH negative	Spontaneous at all temperatures
ΔS positive, ΔH positive	Spontaneous at high temperatures (where exothermicity is relatively unimportant)
ΔS negative, ΔH negative	Spontaneous at low temperatures (where exothermicity is dominant)
ΔS negative, ΔH positive	Process not spontaneous at *any* temperature (reverse process is spontaneous at *all* temperatures)

Note that although ΔH and ΔS are somewhat temperature dependent, it is a good approximation to assume they are constant over a relatively small temperature range.

process. At temperatures below 0°C, the change of state occurs in the exothermic direction because ΔS_{surr} is larger in magnitude than ΔS_{sys}. But above 0°C the change occurs in the direction in which ΔS_{sys} is favorable, since in this case ΔS_{sys} is larger in magnitude than ΔS_{surr}. At 0°C the *opposing tendencies just balance,* and the two states coexist; there is no driving force in either direction. An equilibrium exists between the two states of water. Note that ΔS_{univ} is equal to 0 at 0°C.

We can reach the same conclusions by examining $\Delta G°$. At −10°C, $\Delta G°$ is positive because the $\Delta H°$ term is larger than the $T\Delta S°$ term. The opposite is true at 10°C. At 0°C, $\Delta H°$ is equal to $T\Delta S°$ and $\Delta G°$ is equal to 0. This means that solid H_2O and liquid H_2O have the same free energy at 0°C ($\Delta G° = G_{liquid} - G_{solid}$), and the system is at equilibrium.

We can understand the temperature dependence of spontaneity by examining the behavior of ΔG. For a process occurring at constant temperature and pressure,

$$\Delta G = \Delta H - T\Delta S$$

If ΔH and ΔS favor opposite processes, spontaneity will depend on temperature in such a way that the exothermic direction will be favored at low temperatures. For example, for the process

$$H_2O(s) \longrightarrow H_2O(l)$$

ΔH is positive and ΔS is positive. The natural tendency for this system to lower its energy is in opposition to its natural tendency to increase its positional randomness. At low temperatures, ΔH dominates, and at high temperatures, ΔS dominates. The various possible cases are summarized in Table 16.5.

Sample Exercise 16.5 *Free Energy and Spontaneity*

At what temperatures is the following process spontaneous at 1 atm?

$$Br_2(l) \longrightarrow Br_2(g)$$

$$\Delta H° = 31.0 \text{ kJ/mol} \quad \text{and} \quad \Delta S° = 93.0 \text{ J/K} \cdot \text{mol}$$

What is the normal boiling point of liquid Br_2?

Solution

The vaporization process will be spontaneous at all temperatures where $\Delta G°$ is negative. Note that $\Delta S°$ favors the vaporization process because of the increase in positional entropy, and $\Delta H°$ favors the *opposite* process, which is exothermic. These opposite tendencies will exactly balance at the boiling point of liquid Br_2, since at this temperature liquid and gaseous Br_2 are in equilibrium ($\Delta G° = 0$). We can find this temperature by setting $\Delta G° = 0$ in the equation

$$\Delta G° = \Delta H° - T\Delta S°$$

$$0 = \Delta H° - T\Delta S°$$

$$\Delta H° = T\Delta S°$$

Then

$$T = \frac{\Delta H°}{\Delta S°} = \frac{3.10 \times 10^4 \text{ J/mol}}{93.0 \text{ J/K} \cdot \text{mol}} = 333 \text{ K}$$

At temperatures above 333 K, $T\Delta S°$ has a larger magnitude than $\Delta H°$, and $\Delta G°$ (or $\Delta H° - T\Delta S°$) is negative. Above 333 K, the vaporization process is spontaneous; the opposite process occurs spontaneously below this temperature. At 333 K, liquid and gaseous Br_2 coexist in equilibrium. These observations can be summarized as follows (the pressure is 1 atm in each case):

1. $T > 333$ K. The term $\Delta S°$ controls. The increase in entropy when liquid Br_2 is vaporized is dominant.

2. $T < 333$ K. The process is spontaneous in the direction in which it is exothermic. The term $\Delta H°$ controls.

3. $T = 333$ K. The opposing driving forces are just balanced ($\Delta G° = 0$), and the liquid and gaseous phases of bromine coexist. This is the normal boiling point.

See Exercises 16.29 through 16.32.

16.5 Entropy Changes in Chemical Reactions

The second law of thermodynamics tells us that a process will be spontaneous if the entropy of the universe increases when the process occurs. We saw in Section 16.4 that for a process at constant temperature and pressure, we can use the change in free energy of the system to predict the sign of ΔS_{univ} and thus the direction in which it is spontaneous. So far we have applied these ideas only to physical processes, such as changes of state and the formation of solutions. However, the main business of chemistry is studying chemical reactions, and therefore, we want to apply the second law to reactions.

First, we will consider the entropy changes accompanying chemical reactions that occur under conditions of constant temperature and pressure. As for the other types of processes we have considered, the entropy changes in the *surroundings* are determined by the heat flow that occurs as the reaction takes place. However, the entropy changes in the *system* (the reactants and products of the reaction) are determined by positional probability.

For example, in the ammonia synthesis reaction

$$N_2(g) + 3H_2(g) \longrightarrow 2NH_3(g)$$

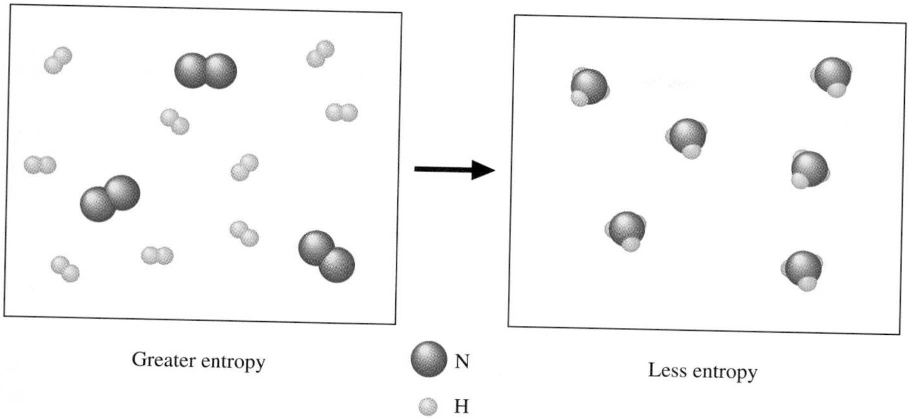

Molecular Models: N_2, H_2, NH_3, O_2, NO, H_2O

| Greater entropy | N | Less entropy |

H

four reactant molecules become two product molecules, lowering the number of independent units in the system, which leads to less positional disorder. *Fewer molecules mean fewer possible configurations.* To help clarify this, consider a special container with a million compartments, each large enough to hold a hydrogen molecule. Thus there are a million ways one H_2 molecule can be placed in this container. But suppose we break the H—H bond and place the two independent H atoms in the same container. A little thought will convince you that there are *many* more than a million ways to place the two separate atoms. The number of arrangements possible for the two independent atoms is much greater than the number for the molecule. Thus for the process

$$H_2 \longrightarrow 2H$$

positional entropy increases.

Does positional entropy increase or decrease when the following reaction takes place?

$$4NH_3(g) + 5O_2(g) \longrightarrow 4NO(g) + 6H_2O(g)$$

In this case 9 gaseous molecules are changed to 10 gaseous molecules, and the positional entropy increases. There are more independent units as products than as reactants. In general, when a reaction involves gaseous molecules, *the change in positional entropy is dominated by the relative numbers of molecules of gaseous reactants and products.* If the number of molecules of the gaseous products is greater than the number of molecules of the gaseous reactants, positional entropy typically increases, and ΔS will be positive for the reaction.

Sample Exercise 16.6 *Predicting the Sign of* $\Delta S°$

Predict the sign of $\Delta S°$ for each of the following reactions.

a. The thermal decomposition of solid calcium carbonate:

$$CaCO_3(s) \longrightarrow CaO(s) + CO_2(g)$$

b. The oxidation of SO_2 in air:

$$2SO_2(g) + O_2(g) \longrightarrow 2SO_3(g)$$

Solution

a. Since in this reaction a gas is produced from a solid reactant, the positional entropy increases, and $\Delta S°$ is positive.
b. Here three molecules of gaseous reactants become two molecules of gaseous products. Since the number of gas molecules decreases, positional entropy decreases, and $\Delta S°$ is negative.

See Exercises 16.33 and 16.34.

In thermodynamics it is the *change* in a certain function that is usually important. The change in enthalpy determines if a reaction is exothermic or endothermic at constant pressure. The change in free energy determines if a process is spontaneous at constant temperature and pressure. It is fortunate that changes in thermodynamic functions are sufficient for most purposes, since absolute values for many thermodynamic characteristics of a system, such as enthalpy or free energy, cannot be determined.

However, we can assign absolute entropy values. Consider a solid at 0 K, where molecular motion virtually ceases. If the substance is a perfect crystal, its internal arrangement is absolutely regular [see Fig. 16.5(a)]. There is only *one way* to achieve this perfect order: Every particle must be in its place. For example, with N coins there is only one way to achieve the state of all heads. Thus a perfect crystal represents the lowest possible entropy; that is, *the entropy of a perfect crystal at 0 K is zero.* This is a statement of the **third law of thermodynamics.**

As the temperature of a perfect crystal is increased, the random vibrational motions increase, and disorder increases within the crystal [see Fig. 16.5(b)]. Thus the entropy of a substance increases with temperature. Since S is zero for a perfect crystal at 0 K, the entropy value for a substance at a particular temperature can be calculated by knowing the temperature dependence of entropy. (We will not show such calculations here.)

The *standard entropy values* $S°$ of many common substances at 298 K and 1 atm are listed in Appendix 4. From these values you will see that the entropy of a substance does indeed increase in going from solid to liquid to gas. One especially interesting feature of this table is the very low $S°$ value for diamond. The structure of diamond is highly ordered, with each carbon strongly bound to a tetrahedral arrangement of four other carbon atoms (see Section 10.5, Fig. 10.22). This type of structure

A perfect crystal at 0 K is an unattainable ideal, taken as a standard but never actually observed.

The standard entropy values represent the increase in entropy that occurs when a substance is heated from 0 K to 298 K at 1 atm pressure.

Figure 16.5

(a) A perfect crystal of hydrogen chloride at 0 K; the dipolar HCl molecules are represented by (+ −). The entropy is zero ($S = 0$) for this perfect crystal at 0 K.
(b) As the temperature rises above 0 K, lattice vibrations allow some dipoles to change their orientations, producing some disorder and an increase in entropy ($S > 0$).

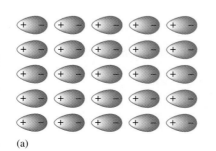 (a)

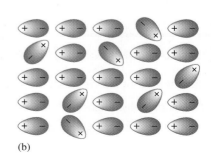 (b)

allows very little disorder and has a very low entropy, even at 298 K. Graphite has a slightly higher entropy because its layered structure allows for a little more disorder.

Molecular Models: diamond, graphite, HCl

Because *entropy is a state function of the system* (it is not pathway-dependent), the entropy change for a given chemical reaction can be calculated by taking the difference between the standard entropy values of products and those of the reactants:

$$\Delta S^\circ_{reaction} = \Sigma n_p S^\circ_{products} - \Sigma n_r S^\circ_{reactants}$$

where, as usual, Σ represents the sum of the terms. It is important to note that entropy is an extensive property (it depends on the amount of substance present). This means that the number of moles of a given reactant (n_r) or product (n_p) must be taken into account.

Sample Exercise 16.7 Calculating ΔS°

Calculate ΔS° at 25°C for the reaction

$$2NiS(s) + 3O_2(g) \longrightarrow 2SO_2(g) + 2NiO(s)$$

given the following standard entropy values:

Substance	S° (J/K · mol)
$SO_2(g)$	248
$NiO(s)$	38
$O_2(g)$	205
$NiS(s)$	53

Solution

Since

$$\Delta S^\circ = \Sigma n_p S^\circ_{products} - \Sigma n_r S^\circ_{reactants}$$
$$= 2S^\circ_{SO_2(g)} + 2S^\circ_{NiO(s)} - 2S^\circ_{NiS(s)} - 3S^\circ_{O_2(s)}$$
$$= 2 \text{ mol} \left(248 \frac{J}{K \cdot mol}\right) + 2 \text{ mol} \left(38 \frac{J}{K \cdot mol}\right)$$
$$-2 \text{ mol} \left(53 \frac{J}{K \cdot mol}\right) - 3 \text{ mol} \left(205 \frac{J}{K \cdot mol}\right)$$
$$= 496 \text{ J/K} + 76 \text{ J/K} - 106 \text{ J/K} - 615 \text{ J/K}$$
$$= -149 \text{ J/K}$$

We would expect ΔS° to be negative because the number of gaseous molecules decreases in this reaction.

See Exercise 16.37.

Sample Exercise 16.8 Calculating ΔS°

Calculate ΔS° for the reduction of aluminum oxide by hydrogen gas:

$$Al_2O_3(s) + 3H_2(g) \longrightarrow 2Al(s) + 3H_2O(g)$$

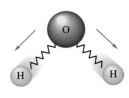

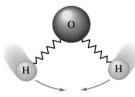

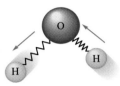

Vibrations

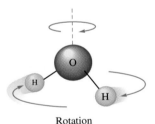

Rotation

Figure 16.6
The H_2O molecule can vibrate and rotate in several ways, some of which are shown here. This freedom of motion leads to a higher entropy for water than for a substance like hydrogen, a simple diatomic molecule with fewer possible motions.

Use the following standard entropy values:

Substance	$S°$ (J/K · mol)
$Al_2O_3(s)$	51
$H_2(g)$	131
$Al(s)$	28
$H_2O(g)$	189

Solution

$$\Delta S° = \Sigma n_p S°_{products} - \Sigma n_r S°_{reactants}$$
$$= 2S°_{Al(s)} + 3S°_{H_2O(g)} - 3S°_{H_2(g)} - S°_{Al_2O_3(s)}$$
$$= 2 \text{ mol} \left(28 \frac{J}{K \cdot mol}\right) + 3 \text{ mol} \left(189 \frac{J}{K \cdot mol}\right)$$
$$-3 \text{ mol} \left(131 \frac{J}{K \cdot mol}\right) - 1 \text{ mol} \left(51 \frac{J}{K \cdot mol}\right)$$
$$= 56 \text{ J/K} + 567 \text{ J/K} - 393 \text{ J/K} - 51 \text{ J/K}$$
$$= 179 \text{ J/K}$$

See Exercises 16.38 through 16.40.

The reaction considered in Sample Exercise 16.8 involves 3 moles of hydrogen gas on the reactant side and 3 moles of water vapor on the product side. Would you expect ΔS to be large or small for such a case? We have assumed that ΔS depends on the relative numbers of molecules of gaseous reactants and products. Based on this assumption, ΔS should be near zero for this reaction. However, ΔS is large and positive. Why is this so? The large value for ΔS results from the difference in the entropy values for hydrogen gas and water vapor. The reason for this difference can be traced to the difference in molecular structure. Because it is a nonlinear, triatomic molecule, H_2O has more rotational and vibrational motions (see Fig. 16.6) than does the diatomic H_2 molecule. Thus the standard entropy value for $H_2O(g)$ is greater than that for $H_2(g)$. Generally, *the more complex the molecule, the higher is the standard entropy value.*

16.6 *Free Energy and Chemical Reactions*

For chemical reactions we are often interested in the **standard free energy change** ($\Delta G°$), *the change in free energy that will occur if the reactants in their standard states are converted to the products in their standard states.* For example, for the ammonia synthesis reaction at 25°C,

$$N_2(g) + 3H_2(g) \rightleftharpoons 2NH_3(g) \qquad \Delta G° = -33.3 \text{ kJ} \qquad (16.1)$$

This $\Delta G°$ value represents the change in free energy when 1 mol nitrogen gas at 1 atm reacts with 3 mol hydrogen gas at 1 atm to produce 2 mol gaseous NH_3 at 1 atm.

It is important to recognize that the standard free energy change for a reaction is not measured directly. For example, we can measure heat flow in a calorimeter to determine $\Delta H°$, but we cannot measure $\Delta G°$ this way. The value of $\Delta G°$ for the ammonia synthesis in Equation (16.1) was *not* obtained by mixing 1 mol N_2 and 3 mol H_2 in a flask and measuring the change in free energy as 2 mol NH_3 formed. For one thing, if we mixed 1 mol N_2 and 3 mol H_2 in a flask, the system would go to equilibrium rather than to completion. Also, we have no instrument that measures free energy. However, while we cannot directly measure $\Delta G°$ for a reaction, we can calculate it from other measured quantities, as we will see later in this section.

Why is it useful to know $\Delta G°$ for a reaction? As we will see in more detail later in this chapter, knowing the $\Delta G°$ values for several reactions allows us to compare the relative tendency of these reactions to occur. The more negative the value of $\Delta G°$, the further a reaction will go to the right to reach equilibrium. We must use standard-state free energies to make this comparison because free energy varies with pressure or concentration. Thus, to get an accurate comparison of reaction tendencies, we must compare all reactions under the same pressure or concentration conditions. We will have more to say about the significance of $\Delta G°$ later.

> The value of $\Delta G°$ tells us nothing about the rate of a reaction, only its eventual equilibrium position.

There are several ways to calculate $\Delta G°$. One common method uses the equation

$$\Delta G° = \Delta H° - T\Delta S°$$

which applies to a reaction carried out at constant temperature. For example, for the reaction

$$C(s) + O_2(g) \longrightarrow CO_2(g)$$

the values of $\Delta H°$ and $\Delta S°$ are known to be -393.5 kJ and 3.05 J/K, respectively, and $\Delta G°$ can be calculated at 298 K as follows:

$$\Delta G° = \Delta H° - T\Delta S°$$
$$= -3.935 \times 10^5 \text{ J} - (298 \text{ K})(3.05 \text{ J/K})$$
$$= -3.944 \times 10^5 \text{ J}$$
$$= -394.4 \text{ kJ (per mole of CO}_2)$$

Sample Exercise 16.9 Calculating $\Delta H°$, $\Delta S°$, and $\Delta G°$

Consider the reaction

$$2SO_2(g) + O_2(g) \longrightarrow 2SO_3(g)$$

carried out at 25°C and 1 atm. Calculate $\Delta H°$, $\Delta S°$, and $\Delta G°$ using the following data:

Substance	$\Delta H_f°$ (kJ/mol)	S° (J/K · mol)
$SO_2(g)$	-297	248
$SO_3(g)$	-396	257
$O_2(g)$	0	205

Solution

The value of $\Delta H°$ can be calculated from the enthalpies of formation using the equation we discussed in Section 6.4:

$$\Delta H° = \Sigma n_p \Delta H°_{f \text{ (products)}} - \Sigma n_r \Delta H°_{f \text{ (reactants)}}$$

Then
$$\Delta H° = 2\Delta H°_{f\,(SO_3(g))} - 2\Delta H°_{f\,(SO_2(g))} - \Delta H°_{f\,(O_2(g))}$$
$$= 2 \text{ mol}(-396 \text{ kJ/mol}) - 2 \text{ mol}(-297 \text{ kJ/mol}) - 0$$
$$= -792 \text{ kJ} + 594 \text{ kJ}$$
$$= -198 \text{ kJ}$$

The value of $\Delta S°$ can be calculated using the standard entropy values and the equation discussed in Section 16.5:

$$\Delta S° = \Sigma n_p S°_{\text{products}} - \Sigma n_r S°_{\text{reactants}}$$

Thus

$$\Delta S° = 2S°_{SO_3(g)} - 2S°_{SO_2(g)} - S°_{O_2(g)}$$
$$= 2 \text{ mol}(257 \text{ J/K} \cdot \text{mol}) - 2 \text{ mol}(248 \text{ J/K} \cdot \text{mol}) - 1 \text{ mol}(205 \text{ J/K} \cdot \text{mol})$$
$$= 514 \text{ J/K} - 496 \text{ J/K} - 205 \text{ J/K}$$
$$= -187 \text{ J/K}$$

We would expect $\Delta S°$ to be negative because three molecules of gaseous reactants give two molecules of gaseous products.

The value of $\Delta G°$ can now be calculated from the equation

$$\Delta G° = \Delta H° - T\Delta S°$$
$$= -198 \text{ kJ} - (298 \text{ K})\left(-187 \frac{J}{K}\right)\left(\frac{1 \text{ kJ}}{1000 \text{ J}}\right)$$
$$= -198 \text{ kJ} + 55.7 \text{ kJ} = -142 \text{ kJ}$$

See Exercises 16.45 and 16.46.

A second method for calculating ΔG for a reaction takes advantage of the fact that, like enthalpy, *free energy is a state function*. Therefore, we can use procedures for finding ΔG that are similar to those for finding ΔH using Hess's law.

To illustrate this method for calculating the free energy change, we will obtain $\Delta G°$ for the reaction

$$2CO(g) + O_2(g) \longrightarrow 2CO_2(g) \tag{16.2}$$

from the following data:

$$2CH_4(g) + 3O_2(g) \longrightarrow 2CO(g) + 4H_2O(g) \qquad \Delta G° = -1088 \text{ kJ} \tag{16.3}$$
$$CH_4(g) + 2O_2(g) \longrightarrow CO_2(g) + 2H_2O(g) \qquad \Delta G° = -801 \text{ kJ} \tag{16.4}$$

Note that $CO(g)$ is a reactant in Equation (16.2). This means that Equation (16.3) must be reversed, since $CO(g)$ is a product in that reaction as written. When a reaction is reversed, the sign of $\Delta G°$ is also reversed. In Equation (16.4), $CO_2(g)$ is a product, as it is in Equation (16.2), but only one molecule of CO_2 is formed. Thus Equation (16.4) must be multiplied by 2, which means the $\Delta G°$ value for Equation (16.4) also must be multiplied by 2. Free energy is an extensive property, since it is defined by two extensive properties, H and S.

Reversed Equation (16.3)

$$2CO(g) + 4H_2O(g) \longrightarrow 2CH_4(g) + 3O_2(g) \qquad \Delta G° = -(-1088 \text{ kJ})$$

$2 \times$ Equation (16.4)

$$\frac{2CH_4(g) + 4O_2(g) \longrightarrow 2CO_2(g) + 4H_2O(g) \qquad \Delta G° = 2(-801 \text{ kJ})}{2CO(g) + O_2(g) \longrightarrow 2CO_2(g)} \qquad \begin{aligned} \Delta G° &= -(-1088 \text{ kJ}) \\ &\quad + 2(-801 \text{ kJ}) \\ &= -514 \text{ kJ} \end{aligned}$$

This example shows that the ΔG values for reactions are manipulated in exactly the same way as the ΔH values.

Sample Exercise 16.10 *Calculating $\Delta G°$*

Using the following data (at 25°C)

$$C_{diamond}(s) + O_2(g) \longrightarrow CO_2(g) \qquad \Delta G° = -397 \text{ kJ} \qquad (16.5)$$
$$C_{graphite}(s) + O_2(g) \longrightarrow CO_2(g) \qquad \Delta G° = -394 \text{ kJ} \qquad (16.6)$$

calculate $\Delta G°$ for the reaction

$$C_{diamond}(s) \longrightarrow C_{graphite}(s)$$

Solution

We reverse Equation (16.6) to make graphite a product, as required, and then add the new equation to Equation (16.5):

$$C_{diamond}(s) + O_2(g) \longrightarrow CO_2(g) \qquad\qquad \Delta G° = -397 \text{ kJ}$$

Reversed Equation (16.6)

$$\frac{CO_2(g) \longrightarrow C_{graphite}(s) + O_2(g) \qquad \Delta G° = -(-394 \text{ kJ})}{C_{diamond}(s) \longrightarrow C_{graphite}(s)} \qquad \begin{aligned} \Delta G° &= -397 \text{ kJ} + 394 \text{ kJ} \\ &= -3 \text{ kJ} \end{aligned}$$

Since $\Delta G°$ is negative for this process, diamond should spontaneously change to graphite at 25°C and 1 atm. However, the reaction is so slow under these conditions that we do not observe the process. This is another example of kinetic rather than thermodynamic control of a reaction. We can say that diamond is kinetically stable with respect to graphite even though it is thermodynamically unstable.

See Exercises 16.49 and 16.50.

A diamond anvil cell used to study materials at very high pressures.

In Sample Exercise 16.10 we saw that the process

$$C_{diamond}(s) \longrightarrow C_{graphite}(s)$$

is spontaneous but very slow at 25°C and 1 atm. The reverse process can be made to occur at high temperatures and pressures. Diamond has a more compact structure and thus a higher density than graphite, so exerting very high pressure causes it to become thermodynamically favored. If high temperatures are also used to make the process fast enough to be feasible, diamonds can be made from graphite. The conditions usually used involve temperatures greater than 1000°C and pressures of about 10^5 atm. About half of all industrial diamonds are made this way.

A third method for calculating the free energy change for a reaction uses standard free energies of formation. The **standard free energy of formation** (ΔG_f°) of a substance is defined as the *change in free energy that accompanies the formation of 1 mole of that substance from its constituent elements with all reactants and products in their standard states.* For the formation of glucose ($C_6H_{12}O_6$), the appropriate reaction is

$$6C(s) + 6H_2(g) + 3O_2(g) \longrightarrow C_6H_{12}O_6(s)$$

The standard free energy associated with this process is called the *free energy of formation of glucose.* Values of the standard free energy of formation are useful in calculating ΔG° for specific chemical reactions using the equation

$$\Delta G^\circ = \Sigma n_p \Delta G_{f\,(products)}^\circ - \Sigma n_r \Delta G_{f\,(reactants)}^\circ$$

Values of ΔG_f° for many common substances are listed in Appendix 4. Note that, analogous to the enthalpy of formation, *the standard free energy of formation of an element in its standard state is zero.* Also note that the number of moles of each reactant (n_r) and product (n_p) must be used when calculating ΔG° for a reaction.

> The standard state of an element is its most stable state of 25°C and 1 atm.

> Calculating ΔG° is very similar to calculating ΔH°, as shown in Section 6.4.

Sample Exercise 16.11 *Calculating* ΔG°

Methanol is a high-octane fuel used in high-performance racing engines. Calculate ΔG° for the reaction

$$2CH_3OH(g) + 3O_2(g) \longrightarrow 2CO_2(g) + 4H_2O(g)$$

given the following free energies of formation:

Substance	ΔG_f° (kJ/mol)
$CH_3OH(g)$	-163
$O_2(g)$	0
$CO_2(g)$	-394
$H_2O(g)$	-229

Solution

We use the equation

$$\Delta G^\circ = \Sigma n_p \Delta G^\circ_{f \text{ (products)}} - \Sigma n_r \Delta G^\circ_{f \text{ (reactants)}}$$
$$= 2\Delta G^\circ_{f \text{ (CO}_2(g))} + 4\Delta G^\circ_{f \text{ (H}_2\text{O}(g))} - 3\Delta G^\circ_{f \text{ (O}_2(g))} - 2\Delta G^\circ_{f \text{ (CH}_3\text{OH}(g))}$$
$$= 2 \text{ mol}(-394 \text{ kJ/mol}) + 4 \text{ mol}(-229 \text{ kJ/mol}) - 3(0) - 2 \text{ mol}(-163 \text{ kJ/mol})$$
$$= -1378 \text{ kJ}$$

The large magnitude and the negative sign of ΔG° indicate that this reaction is very favorable thermodynamically.

See Exercises 16.51 through 16.53.

Sample Exercise 16.12 *Free Energy and Spontaneity*

A chemical engineer wants to determine the feasibility of making ethanol (C_2H_5OH) by reacting water with ethylene (C_2H_4) according to the equation

$$C_2H_4(g) + H_2O(l) \longrightarrow C_2H_5OH(l)$$

Is this reaction spontaneous under standard conditions?

Solution

To determine the spontaneity of this reaction under standard conditions, we must determine ΔG° for the reaction. We can do this using standard free energies of formation at 25°C from Appendix 4:

$$\Delta G^\circ_{f \text{ (C}_2\text{H}_5\text{OH}(l))} = -175 \text{ kJ/mol}$$
$$\Delta G^\circ_{f \text{ (H}_2\text{O}(l))} = -237 \text{ kJ/mol}$$
$$\Delta G^\circ_{f \text{ (C}_2\text{H}_4(g))} = 68 \text{ kJ/mol}$$

Then
$$\Delta G^\circ = \Delta G^\circ_{f \text{ (C}_2\text{H}_5\text{OH}(l))} - \Delta G^\circ_{f \text{ (H}_2\text{O}(l))} - \Delta G^\circ_{f \text{ (C}_2\text{H}_4(g))}$$
$$= -175 \text{ kJ} - (-237 \text{ kJ}) - 68 \text{ kJ}$$
$$= -6 \text{ kJ}$$

Thus the process is spontaneous under standard conditions at 25°C.

See Exercise 16.54.

Although the reaction considered in Sample Exercise 16.12 is spontaneous, other features of the reaction must be studied to see if the process is feasible. For example, the chemical engineer will need to study the kinetics of the reaction to determine whether it is fast enough to be useful and, if it is not, whether a catalyst can be found to enhance the rate. In doing these studies, the engineer must remember that ΔG° depends on temperature:

$$\Delta G^\circ = \Delta H^\circ - T\Delta S^\circ$$

Thus, if the process must be carried out at high temperatures to be fast enough to be feasible, ΔG° must be recalculated at that temperature from the ΔH° and ΔS° values for the reaction.

16.7 *The Dependence of Free Energy on Pressure*

In this chapter we have seen that a system at constant temperature and pressure will proceed spontaneously in the direction that lowers its free energy. This is why reactions proceed until they reach equilibrium. As we will see later in this section, *the equilibrium position represents the lowest free energy value available to a particular reaction system.* The free energy of a reaction system changes as the reaction proceeds, because free energy is dependent on the pressure of a gas or on the concentration of species in solution. We will deal only with the pressure dependence of the free energy of an ideal gas. The dependence of free energy on concentration can be developed using similar reasoning.

To understand the pressure dependence of free energy, we need to know how pressure affects the thermodynamic functions that comprise free energy, that is, enthalpy and entropy (recall that $G = H - TS$). For an ideal gas, enthalpy is not pressure-dependent. However, entropy *does* depend on pressure because of its dependence on volume. Consider 1 mole of an ideal gas at a given temperature. At a volume of 10.0 L, the gas has many more positions available for its molecules than if its volume is 1.0 L. The positional entropy is greater in the larger volume. In summary, at a given temperature for 1 mole of ideal gas

$$S_{\text{large volume}} > S_{\text{small volume}}$$

or, since pressure and volume are inversely related,

$$S_{\text{low pressure}} > S_{\text{high pressure}}$$

We have shown qualitatively that the entropy and therefore the free energy of an ideal gas depend on its pressure. Using a more detailed argument, which we will not consider here, it can be shown that

$$G = G° + RT \ln(P)$$

where $G°$ is the free energy of the gas at a pressure of 1 atm, G is the free energy of the gas at a pressure of P atm, R is the universal gas constant, and T is the Kelvin temperature.

To see how the change in free energy for a reaction depends on pressure, we will consider the ammonia synthesis reaction

$$N_2(g) + 3H_2(g) \longrightarrow 2NH_3(g)$$

See Appendix 1.2 to review logarithms.

In general, $\Delta G = \Sigma n_p G_{\text{products}} - \Sigma n_r G_{\text{reactants}}$

For this reaction $\Delta G = 2G_{NH_3} - G_{N_2} - 3G_{H_2}$

where
$$G_{NH_3} = G°_{NH_3} + RT \ln(P_{NH_3})$$
$$G_{N_2} = G°_{N_2} + RT \ln(P_{N_2})$$
$$G_{H_2} = G°_{H_2} + RT \ln(P_{H_2})$$

Substituting these values into the equation gives

$$\Delta G = 2[G°_{NH_3} + RT \ln(P_{NH_3})] - [G°_{N_2} + RT \ln(P_{N_2})] - 3[G°_{H_2} + RT \ln(P_{H_2})]$$
$$= 2G°_{NH_3} - G°_{N_2} - 3G°_{H_2} + 2RT \ln(P_{NH_3}) - RT \ln(P_{N_2}) - 3RT \ln(P_{H_2})$$
$$= \underbrace{(2G°_{NH_3} - G°_{N_2} - 3G°_{H_2})}_{\Delta G° \text{ reaction}} + RT[2 \ln(P_{NH_3}) - \ln(P_{N_2}) - 3 \ln(P_{H_2})]$$

The first term (in parentheses) is $\Delta G°$ for the reaction. Thus we have

$$\Delta G = \Delta G°_{reaction} + RT[2 \ln(P_{NH_3}) - \ln(P_{N_2}) - 3 \ln(P_{H_2})]$$

and since

$$2 \ln(P_{NH_3}) = \ln(P_{NH_3}^2)$$

$$-\ln(P_{N_2}) = \ln\left(\frac{1}{P_{N_2}}\right)$$

$$-3 \ln(P_{H_2}) = \ln\left(\frac{1}{P_{H_2}^3}\right)$$

the equation becomes

$$\Delta G = \Delta G° + RT \ln\left(\frac{P_{NH_3}^2}{(P_{N_2})(P_{H_2}^3)}\right)$$

But the term

$$\frac{P_{NH_3}^2}{(P_{N_2})(P_{H_2}^3)}$$

is the reaction quotient Q discussed in Section 13.5. Therefore, we have

$$\Delta G = \Delta G° + RT \ln(Q)$$

where Q is the reaction quotient (from the law of mass action), T is the temperature (K), R is the gas law constant and is equal to 8.3145 J/K · mol, $\Delta G°$ is the free energy change for the reaction with all reactants and products at a pressure of 1 atm, and ΔG is the free energy change for the reaction for the specified pressures of reactants and products.

Sample Exercise 16.13 *Calculating ΔG°*

One method for synthesizing methanol (CH_3OH) involves reacting carbon monoxide and hydrogen gases:

$$CO(g) + 2H_2(g) \longrightarrow CH_3OH(l)$$

Calculate ΔG at 25°C for this reaction where carbon monoxide gas at 5.0 atm and hydrogen gas at 3.0 atm are converted to liquid methanol.

Solution

To calculate ΔG for this process, we use the equation

$$\Delta G = \Delta G° + RT \ln(Q)$$

We must first compute $\Delta G°$ from standard free energies of formation (see Appendix 4). Since

$$\Delta G°_{f\,(CH_3OH(l))} = -166 \text{ kJ}$$
$$\Delta G°_{f\,(H_2(g))} = 0$$
$$\Delta G°_{f\,(CO(g))} = -137 \text{ kJ}$$
$$\Delta G° = -166 \text{ kJ} - (-137 \text{ kJ}) - 0 = -29 \text{ kJ} = -2.9 \times 10^4 \text{ J}$$

Note that this is the value of $\Delta G°$ for the reaction of 1 mol CO with 2 mol H_2 to produce 1 mol CH_3OH. We might call this the value of $\Delta G°$ for one "round" of the reaction or for one mole of the reaction. Thus the $\Delta G°$ value might better be written as -2.9×10^4 J/mol of reaction, or -2.9×10^4 J/mol rxn.

We can now calculate ΔG using

$$\Delta G° = -2.9 \times 10^4 \text{ J/mol rxn}$$

$$R = 8.3145 \text{ J/K} \cdot \text{mol}$$

$$T = 273 + 25 = 298 \text{ K}$$

$$Q = \frac{1}{(P_{CO})(P_{H_2}{}^2)} = \frac{1}{(5.0)(3.0)^2} = 2.2 \times 10^{-2}$$

Note in this case that ΔG is defined for "one mole of the reaction," that is, for 1 mol $CO(g)$ reacting with 2 mol $H_2(g)$ to form 1 mol $CH_3OH(l)$. Thus ΔG, $\Delta G°$, and $RT \ln(Q)$ all have units of J/mol of reaction. In this case the units of R are actually J/K · mol of reaction, although they are usually not written this way.

Note that the pure liquid methanol is not included in the calculation of Q. Then

$$\begin{aligned}\Delta G &= \Delta G° + RT \ln(Q) \\ &= (-2.9 \times 10^4 \text{ J/mol rxn}) + (8.3145 \text{ J/K} \cdot \text{mol rxn})(298 \text{ K}) \ln(2.2 \times 10^{-2}) \\ &= (-2.9 \times 10^4 \text{ J/mol rxn}) - (9.4 \times 10^3 \text{ J/mol rxn}) = -3.8 \times 10^4 \text{ J/mol rxn} \\ &= -38 \text{ kJ/mol rxn}\end{aligned}$$

Note that ΔG is significantly more negative than $\Delta G°$, implying that the reaction is more spontaneous at reactant pressures greater than 1 atm. We might expect this result from Le Châtelier's principle.

See Exercises 16.55 and 16.56.

The Meaning of ΔG for a Chemical Reaction

In this section we have learned to calculate ΔG for chemical reactions under various conditions. For example, in Sample Exercise 16.13 the calculations show that the formation of $CH_3OH(l)$ from $CO(g)$ at 5.0 atm reacting with $H_2(g)$ at 3.0 atm is spontaneous. What does this result mean? Does it mean that if we mixed 1.0 mol $CO(g)$ and 2.0 mol $H_2(g)$ together at pressures of 5.0 and 3.0 atm, respectively, that 1.0 mol $CH_3OH(l)$ would form in the reaction flask? The answer is no. This answer may surprise you in view of what has been said in this section. It is true that 1.0 mol $CH_3OH(l)$ has a lower free energy than 1.0 mol $CO(g)$ at 5.0 atm plus 2.0 mol $H_2(g)$ at 3.0 atm. However, when $CO(g)$ and $H_2(g)$ are mixed under these conditions, there is *an even lower free energy available to this system than 1.0 mol pure $CH_3OH(l)$*. For reasons we will discuss shortly, *the system can achieve the lowest possible free energy by going to equilibrium, not by going to completion*. At the equilibrium position, some of the $CO(g)$ and $H_2(g)$ will remain in the reaction flask. So even though 1.0 mol pure $CH_3OH(l)$ is at a lower free energy than 1.0 mol $CO(g)$ and 2.0 mol $H_2(g)$ at 5.0 and 3.0 atm, respectively, the reaction system will stop short of forming 1.0 mol $CH_3OH(l)$. The reaction stops short of completion because the equilibrium mixture of $CH_3OH(l)$, $CO(g)$, and $H_2(g)$ exists at the lowest possible free energy available to the system.

To illustrate this point, we will explore a mechanical example. Consider balls rolling down the two hills shown in Fig. 16.7. Note that in both cases point B has a lower potential energy than point A.

In Fig. 16.7(a) the ball will roll to point B. This diagram is analogous to a phase change. For example, at 25°C ice will spontaneously change completely to liquid

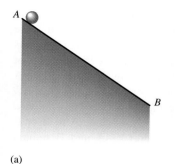

(a)

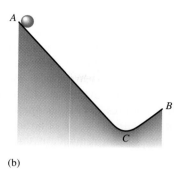

(b)

Figure 16.7

Schematic representations of balls rolling down two types of hills.

water, because the latter has the lowest free energy. In this case liquid water is the only choice. There is no intermediate substance with lower free energy.

The situation is different for a chemical reaction system, as illustrated in Fig. 16.7(b). In Fig. 16.7(b) the ball will not get to point *B* because there is a lower potential energy at point *C*. Like the ball, a chemical system will seek the *lowest possible* free energy, which, for reasons we will discuss below, is the equilibrium position.

Therefore, although the value of ΔG for a given reaction system tells us whether the products or reactants are favored under a given set of conditions, it does not mean that the system will proceed to pure products (if ΔG is negative) or remain at pure reactants (if ΔG is positive). Instead, the system will spontaneously go to the equilibrium position, the lowest possible free energy available to it. In the next section we will see that the value of $\Delta G°$ for a particular reaction tells us exactly where this position will be.

16.8 *Free Energy and Equilibrium*

When the components of a given chemical reaction are mixed, they will proceed, rapidly or slowly depending on the kinetics of the process, to the equilibrium position. In Chapter 13 we defined the equilibrium position as the point at which the forward and reverse reaction rates are equal. In this chapter we look at equilibrium from a thermodynamic point of view, and we find that the **equilibrium point** *occurs at the lowest value of free energy available to the reaction system*. As it turns out, the two definitions give the same equilibrium state, which must be the case for both the kinetic and thermodynamic models to be valid.

To understand the relationship of free energy to equilibrium, let's consider the following simple hypothetical reaction:

$$A(g) \rightleftharpoons B(g)$$

where 1.0 mole of gaseous A is initially placed in a reaction vessel at a pressure of 2.0 atm. The free energies for A and B are diagramed as shown in Fig. 16.8(a). As A reacts to form B, the total free energy of the system changes, yielding the following results:

$$\text{Free energy of A} = G_A = G_A° + RT \ln(P_A)$$
$$\text{Free energy of B} = G_B = G_B° + RT \ln(P_B)$$
$$\text{Total free energy of system} = G = G_A + G_B$$

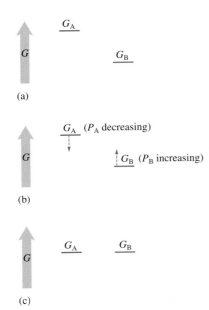

Figure 16.8

(a) The initial free energies of A and B. (b) As A(g) changes to B(g), the free energy of A decreases and that of B increases. (c) Eventually, pressures of A and B are achieved such that $G_A = G_B$, the equilibrium position.

For the reaction A(g) $\rightleftharpoons$ B(g), the pressure is constant during the reaction, since the same number of gas molecules is always present.

As A changes to B, G_A will decrease because P_A is decreasing [Fig. 16.8(b)]. In contrast, G_B will increase because P_B is increasing. The reaction will proceed to the right as long as the total free energy of the system decreases (as long as G_B is less than G_A). At some point the pressures of A and B reach the values P_A^e and P_B^e that make G_A equal to G_B. *The system has reached equilibrium* [Fig. 16.8(c)]. Since A at pressure P_A^e and B at pressure P_B^e have the same free energy (G_A equals G_B), ΔG is zero for A at pressure P_A^e changing to B at pressure P_B^e. *The system has reached minimum free energy.* There is no longer any driving force to change A to B or B to A, so the system remains at this position (the pressures of A and B remain constant).

Suppose that for the experiment described above the plot of free energy versus the mole fraction of A reacted is defined as shown in Fig. 16.9(a). In this experiment, minimum free energy is reached when 75% of A has been changed to B. At this point, the pressure of A is 0.25 times the original pressure, or

$$(0.25)(2.0 \text{ atm}) = 0.50 \text{ atm}$$

The pressure of B is

$$(0.75)(2.0 \text{ atm}) = 1.5 \text{ atm}$$

Since this is the equilibrium position, we can use the equilibrium pressures to calculate a value for K for the reaction in which A is converted to B at this temperature:

$$K = \frac{P_B^e}{P_A^e} = \frac{1.5 \text{ atm}}{0.50 \text{ atm}} = 3.0$$

Exactly the same equilibrium point would be achieved if we placed 1.0 mol pure B(g) in the flask at a pressure of 2.0 atm. In this case B would change to A until equilibrium ($G_B = G_A$) is reached. This is shown in Fig. 16.9(b).

The overall free energy curve for this system is shown in Fig. 16.9(c). Note that any mixture of A(g) and B(g) containing 1.0 mol (A plus B) at a total pressure of 2.0 atm will react until it reaches the minimum in the curve.

In summary, when substances undergo a chemical reaction, the reaction proceeds to the minimum free energy (equilibrium), which corresponds to the point where

$$G_{\text{products}} = G_{\text{reactants}} \quad \text{or} \quad \Delta G = G_{\text{products}} - G_{\text{reactants}} = 0$$

We can now establish a quantitative relationship between free energy and the value of the equilibrium constant. We have seen that

$$\Delta G = \Delta G° + RT \ln(Q)$$

and at equilibrium ΔG equals 0 and Q equals K.

So
$$\Delta G = 0 = \Delta G° + RT \ln(K)$$

or
$$\Delta G° = -RT \ln(K)$$

We must note the following characteristics of this very important equation.

Case 1: $\Delta G° = 0$. When $\Delta G°$ equals zero for a particular reaction, the free energies of the reactants and products are equal when all components are in the standard states (1 atm for gases). The system is at equilibrium when the pressures of all reactants and products are 1 atm, which means that K equals 1.

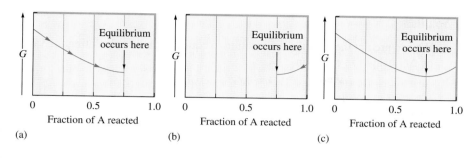

Figure 16.9
(a) The change in free energy to reach equilibrium, beginning with 1.0 mol A(g) at $P_A = 2.0$ atm. (b) The change in free energy to reach equilibrium, beginning with 1.0 mol B(g) at $P_B = 2.0$ atm. (c) The free energy profile for A(g) $\rightleftharpoons$ B(g) in a system containing 1.0 mol (A plus B) at $P_{TOTAL} = 2.0$ atm. Each point on the curve corresponds to the total free energy of the system for a given combination of A and B.

Case 2: $\Delta G° < 0$. In this case $\Delta G°$ ($G°_{products} - G°_{reactants}$) is negative, which means that

$$G°_{products} < G°_{reactants}$$

If a flask contains the reactants and products, all at 1 atm, the system will *not* be at equilibrium. Since $G°_{products}$ is less than $G°_{reactants}$, the system will adjust to the right to reach equilibrium. In this case K will be *greater than 1,* since the pressures of the products at equilibrium will be greater than 1 atm and the pressures of the reactants at equilibrium will be less than 1 atm.

Case 3: $\Delta G° > 0$. Since $\Delta G°$ ($G°_{products} - G°_{reactants}$) is positive,

$$G°_{reactants} < G°_{products}$$

If a flask contains the reactants and products, all at 1 atm, the system will *not* be at equilibrium. In this case the system will adjust to the left (toward the reactants, which have a lower free energy) to reach equilibrium. The value of K will be *less than 1,* since at equilibrium the pressures of the reactants will be greater than 1 atm and the pressures of the products will be less than 1 atm.

These results are summarized in Table 16.6. The value of K for a specific reaction can be calculated from the equation

$$\Delta G° = -RT \ln(K)$$

as is shown in Sample Exercises 16.14 and 16.15.

Table 16.6 Qualitative Relationship Between the Change in Standard Free Energy and the Equilibrium Constant for a Given Reaction

$\Delta G°$	K
$\Delta G° = 0$	$K = 1$
$\Delta G° < 0$	$K > 1$
$\Delta G° > 0$	$K < 1$

Sample Exercise 16.14 *Free Energy and Equilibrium I*

Consider the ammonia synthesis reaction

$$N_2(g) + 3H_2(g) \rightleftharpoons 2NH_3(g)$$

where $\Delta G° = -33.3$ kJ per mole of N_2 consumed at 25°C. For each of the following mixtures of reactants and products at 25°C, predict the direction in which the system will shift to reach equilibrium.

a. $P_{NH_3} = 1.00$ atm, $P_{N_2} = 1.47$ atm, $P_{H_2} = 1.00 \times 10^{-2}$ atm
b. $P_{NH_3} = 1.00$ atm, $P_{N_2} = 1.00$ atm, $P_{H_2} = 1.00$ atm

Solution

a. We can predict the direction of reaction to equilibrium by calculating the value of ΔG using the equation

$$\Delta G = \Delta G° + RT \ln(Q)$$

The units of ΔG, $\Delta G°$, and $RT \ln(Q)$ all refer to the balanced reaction with all amounts expressed in moles. We might say that the units are joules per "mole of reaction," although only the "per mole" is indicated for R (as is customary).

where $\quad Q = \dfrac{P_{NH_3}^{\ 2}}{(P_{N_2})(P_{H_2}^{\ 3})} = \dfrac{(1.00)^2}{(1.47)(1.00 \times 10^{-2})^3} = 6.80 \times 10^5$

$T = 25 + 273 = 298\ K$

$R = 8.3145\ J/K \cdot mol$

and

$$\Delta G° = -33.3\ kJ/mol = -3.33 \times 10^4\ J/mol$$

Then

$$\Delta G = (-3.33 \times 10^4\ J/mol) + (8.3145\ J/K \cdot mol)(298\ K)\ \ln(6.8 \times 10^5)$$
$$= (-3.33 \times 10^4\ J/mol) + (3.33 \times 10^4\ J/mol) = 0$$

Since $\Delta G = 0$, the reactants and products have the same free energies at these partial pressures. The system is already at equilibrium, and no shift will occur.

b. The partial pressures given here are all 1.00 atm, which means that the system is in the standard state. That is,

$$\Delta G = \Delta G° + RT \ln(Q) = \Delta G° + RT \ln\dfrac{(1.00)^2}{(1.00)(1.00)^3}$$
$$= \Delta G° + RT \ln(1.00) = \Delta G° + 0 = \Delta G°$$

For this reaction at 25°C,

$$\Delta G° = -33.3\ kJ/mol$$

The negative value for $\Delta G°$ means that in their standard states the products have a lower free energy than the reactants. Thus the system will move to the right to reach equilibrium. That is, K is greater than 1.

See Exercise 16.57.

Sample Exercise **16.15** *Free Energy and Equilibrium II*

The overall reaction for the corrosion (rusting) of iron by oxygen is

$$4Fe(s) + 3O_2(g) \rightleftharpoons 2Fe_2O_3(s)$$

Using the following data, calculate the equilibrium constant for this reaction at 25°C.

Substance	$\Delta H_f°$ (kJ/mol)	$S°$ (J/K · mol)
$Fe_2O_3(s)$	-826	90
$Fe(s)$	0	27
$O_2(g)$	0	205

Solution

To calculate K for this reaction, we will use the equation

$$\Delta G^\circ = -RT \ln(K)$$

We must first calculate ΔG° from

$$\Delta G^\circ = \Delta H^\circ - T\Delta S^\circ$$

where

$$
\begin{aligned}
\Delta H^\circ &= 2\Delta H^\circ_{f\,(Fe_2O_3(s))} - 3\Delta H^\circ_{f\,(O_2(g))} - 4\Delta H^\circ_{f\,(Fe(s))} \\
&= 2 \text{ mol}(-826 \text{ kJ/mol}) - 0 - 0 \\
&= -1652 \text{ kJ} = -1.652 \times 10^6 \text{ J} \\
\Delta S^\circ &= 2S^\circ_{Fe_2O_3} - 3S^\circ_{O_2} - 4S^\circ_{Fe} \\
&= 2 \text{ mol}(90 \text{ J/K} \cdot \text{mol}) - 3 \text{ mol}(205 \text{ J/K} \cdot \text{mol}) - 4 \text{ mol}(27 \text{ J/K} \cdot \text{mol}) \\
&= -543 \text{ J/K}
\end{aligned}
$$

and $T = 273 + 25 = 298 \text{ K}$

Then $\Delta G^\circ = \Delta H^\circ - T\Delta S^\circ = (-1.652 \times 10^6 \text{ J}) - (298 \text{ K})(-543 \text{ J/K})$
$$= -1.490 \times 10^6 \text{ J}$$

and

$$\Delta G^\circ = -RT \ln(K) = -1.490 \times 10^6 \text{ J} = -(8.3145 \text{ J/K} \cdot \text{mol})(298 \text{ K}) \ln(K)$$

Thus
$$\ln(K) = \frac{1.490 \times 10^6}{2.48 \times 10^3} = 601$$

and
$$K = e^{601}$$

In terms of base 10,
$$K = 10^{261}$$

This is a very large equilibrium constant. The rusting of iron is clearly very favorable from a thermodynamic point of view.

See Exercises 16.59 and 16.60.

Formation of rust on bare steel is a spontaneous process.

The Temperature Dependence of K

In Chapter 13 we used Le Châtelier's principle to predict qualitatively how the value of K for a given reaction would change with a change in temperature. Now we can specify the quantitative dependence of the equilibrium constant on temperature from the relationship

$$\Delta G^\circ = -RT \ln(K) = \Delta H^\circ - T\Delta S^\circ$$

We can rearrange this equation to give

$$\ln(K) = -\frac{\Delta H^\circ}{RT} + \frac{\Delta S^\circ}{R} = -\frac{\Delta H^\circ}{R}\left(\frac{1}{T}\right) + \frac{\Delta S^\circ}{R}$$

Note that this is a linear equation of the form $y = mx + b$, where $y = \ln(K)$, $m = -\Delta H^\circ/R = $ slope, $x = 1/T$, and $b = \Delta S^\circ/R = $ intercept. This means that if values of

K for a given reaction are determined at various temperatures, a plot of $\ln(K)$ versus $1/T$ will be linear, with slope $-\Delta H°/R$ and intercept $\Delta S°/R$. This result assumes that both $\Delta H°$ and $\Delta S°$ are independent of temperature over the temperature range considered. This assumption is a good approximation over a relatively small temperature range.

16.9   Free Energy and Work

One of the main reasons we are interested in physical and chemical processes is that we want to use them to do work for us, and we want this work done as efficiently and economically as possible. We have already seen that at constant temperature and pressure, the sign of the change in free energy tells us whether a given process is spontaneous or not. This is very useful information because it prevents us from wasting effort on a process that has no inherent tendency to occur. Although a thermodynamically favorable chemical reaction may not occur to any appreciable extent because it is too slow, it makes sense in this case to try to find a catalyst to speed up the reaction. On the other hand, if the reaction is prevented from occurring by its thermodynamic characteristics, we would be wasting our time looking for a catalyst.

In addition to its qualitative usefulness (telling us whether a process is spontaneous), the change in free energy is important quantitatively because it can tell us how much work can be done with a given process. In fact, the *maximum possible useful work obtainable from a process at constant temperature and pressure is equal to the change in free energy:*

$$w_{max} = \Delta G$$

Note that "PV work" is not counted as useful work here.

This relationship explains why this function is called the *free* energy. Under certain conditions, ΔG for a spontaneous process represents the energy that is *free to do useful work*. On the other hand, for a process that is not spontaneous, the value of ΔG tells us the minimum amount of work that must be *expended* to make the process occur.

Knowing the value of ΔG for a process thus gives us valuable information about how close the process is to 100% efficiency. For example, when gasoline is burned in a car's engine, the work produced is about 20% of the maximum work available.

For reasons we will only briefly introduce in this book, the amount of work we actually obtain from a spontaneous process is *always* less than the maximum possible amount.

To explore this idea more fully, let's consider an electric current flowing through the starter motor of a car. The current is generated from a chemical change in a battery, and we can calculate ΔG for the battery reaction and so determine the energy available to do work. Can we use all this energy to do work? No, because a current flowing through a wire causes frictional heating, and the greater the current, the greater the heat. This heat represents wasted energy—it is not useful for running the starter motor. We can minimize this energy waste by running very low currents through the motor circuit. However, zero current flow would be necessary to eliminate frictional heating entirely, and we cannot derive any work from the motor if no current flows. This represents the difficulty in which nature places us. Using a

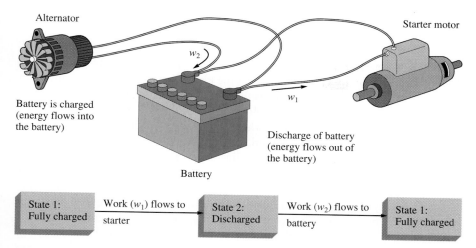

Figure 16.10

A battery can do work by sending current to a starter motor. The battery can then be recharged by forcing current through it in the opposite direction. If the current flow in both processes is infinitesimally small, $w_1 = w_2$. This is a *reversible process*. But if the current flow is finite, as it would be in any real case, $w_2 > w_1$. This is an *irreversible process* (the *universe is different* after the cyclic process occurs). All real processes are irreversible.

process to do work requires that some of the energy be wasted, and usually the faster we run the process, the more energy we waste.

Achieving the maximum work available from a spontaneous process can occur only via a hypothetical pathway. Any real pathway wastes energy. If we could discharge the battery infinitely slowly by an infinitesimal current flow, we would achieve the maximum useful work. Also, if we could then recharge the battery using an infinitesimally small current, exactly the same amount of energy would be used to return the battery to its original state. After we cycle the battery in this way, the universe (the system and surroundings) is exactly the same as it was before the cyclic process. This is a **reversible process** (see Fig. 16.10).

However, if the battery is discharged to run the starter motor and then recharged using a *finite* current flow, as is the case in reality, *more* work will always be required to recharge the battery than the battery produces as it discharges. This means that even though the battery (the system) has returned to its original state, the surroundings have not, because the surroundings had to furnish a net amount of work as the battery was cycled. The *universe is different* after this cyclic process is performed, and this function is called an **irreversible process.** *All real processes are irreversible.*

In general, after any real cyclic process is carried out in a system, the surroundings have less ability to do work and contain more thermal energy. In other words, *in any real cyclic process in the system, work is changed to heat in the surroundings, and the entropy of the universe increases.* This is another way of stating the second law of thermodynamics.

Thus thermodynamics tells us the work potential of a process and then tells us that we can never achieve this potential. In this spirit, thermodynamicist Henry Bent has paraphrased the first two laws of thermodynamics as follows:

First law: You can't win, you can only break even.

Second law: You can't break even.

When energy is used to do work, it becomes less organized and less concentrated and thus less useful.

The ideas we have discussed in this section are applicable to the energy crisis that will probably increase in severity over the next 25 years. The crisis is obviously not one of supply; the first law tells us that the universe contains a constant supply of energy. The problem is the availability of *useful* energy. *As we use energy, we degrade its usefulness.* For example, when gasoline reacts with oxygen in the combustion reaction, the change in potential energy results in heat flow. Thus the energy concentrated in the bonds of the gasoline and oxygen molecules ends up *spread* over the surroundings as thermal energy, where it is much more difficult to harness for useful work. This is a way in which the entropy of the universe increases: Concentrated energy becomes spread out—more disordered and less useful. Thus the crux of the energy problem is that we are rapidly consuming the concentrated energy found in fossil fuels. It took millions of years to concentrate the sun's energy in these fuels, and we will consume these same fuels in a few hundred years. Thus we must use these energy sources as wisely as possible.

For Review

Key Terms

Section 16.1
spontaneous process
entropy
positional probability

Section 16.2
second law of thermodynamics

Section 16.4
free energy

Section 16.5
third law of thermodynamics

Section 16.6
standard free energy change
standard free energy of formation

Section 16.8
equilibrium point (thermodynamic definition)

Section 16.9
reversible process
irreversible process

Summary

The first law of thermodynamics, which states that the energy of the universe is constant, gives us no clue as to why a particular process occurs in a given direction. A process is said to be spontaneous if it occurs without outside intervention. The driving force for a spontaneous process is described in terms of entropy (S). Entropy is a thermodynamic function that can be viewed as a measure of randomness, or disorder. It describes the number of arrangements (positions and/or energy levels) available to a system existing in a given state. Nature spontaneously proceeds toward states that have the highest probabilities of occurring. The second law of thermodynamics states that for any spontaneous process there is always an increase in the entropy of the universe. Using entropy, thermodynamics predicts the direction in which a process will occur. However, it cannot predict the rate at which the process will occur; this must be done using the principles of kinetics.

We can predict whether a process is spontaneous by considering the entropy changes that occur in the system and the surroundings:

$$\Delta S_{univ} = \Delta S_{sys} + \Delta S_{surr}$$

For a process at constant temperature and pressure, ΔS_{sys} is dominated by changes in positional entropy, and ΔS_{surr} is determined by heat flow:

$$\Delta S_{surr} = -\frac{\Delta H}{T}$$

The sign of ΔS_{surr} depends on the direction of the heat flow: ΔS_{surr} is positive for an exothermic process and negative for an endothermic process. The magnitude of ΔS_{surr}, however, depends on both the quantity of energy that flows as heat and the temperature at which the energy is transferred. Thus the significance of exothermicity as a driving force for a process depends on the temperature at which the process occurs.

For a chemical reaction, entropy changes in the system are dominated by the change in the number of gaseous molecules. Fewer gaseous molecules on the product side means a decrease in entropy, and vice versa. Molecular structure also plays a role. In general, a complex molecule has a higher standard entropy than a simpler one.

The third law of thermodynamics states that the entropy of a perfect crystal at 0 K is zero. Above this temperature the molecules will begin to vibrate, and disorder will occur.

Free energy (G) is a thermodynamic function defined by the relationship

$$G = H - TS$$

A process occurring at constant temperature and pressure is spontaneous in the direction in which the free energy decreases.

The standard free energy change ($\Delta G°$) is the change in free energy that will occur if the reactants in their standard states are converted to the products in their standard states. Since free energy is a state function, we can use procedures similar to those used with Hess's law to calculate $\Delta G°$, for example,

$$\Delta G° = \Sigma n_p \Delta G°_f \text{ (products)} - \Sigma n_r \Delta G°_f \text{ (reactants)}$$

where $\Delta G°_f$, the standard free energy of formation of a substance, is the change in free energy accompanying the formation of one mole of that substance from its constituent elements with all reactants and products in their standard states. The standard free energy of formation of an element in its standard state is zero.

Free energy depends on pressure according to the equation

$$G = G° + RT \ln(P)$$

The ΔG value for a reaction at conditions other than standard conditions can be calculated from

$$\Delta G = \Delta G° + RT \ln(Q)$$

where Q is the reaction quotient.

The equilibrium position for a chemical reaction occurs where the free energy is the minimum value available to the system. The relationship between $\Delta G°$ and the equilibrium constant K is

$$\Delta G° = -RT \ln(K)$$

When $\Delta G°$ is equal to zero, the system is at equilibrium with the products and reactants in their standard states ($K = 1$). When $\Delta G°$ is less than zero, then $G°_{products}$ is less than $G°_{reactants}$, and the system will adjust to the right from standard conditions to attain equilibrium (K is greater than 1). When $\Delta G°$ is greater than zero, $G°_{reactants}$ is less than $G°_{products}$, and the system will shift to the left from standard conditions to attain equilibrium (K is less than 1).

The maximum possible useful work obtainable from a process at constant temperature and pressure is equal to the change in free energy:

$$w_{max} = \Delta G$$

In any real process, the actual work obtained is less than w_{max}. When energy is used to do work, the total energy of the universe remains constant, but it is rendered less useful. After being used to do work, concentrated energy is spread out in the surroundings as thermal energy, and this is the crux of our energy problem.

In-Class Discussion Questions

These questions are designed to be considered by groups of students in class. Often these questions work well for introducing a particular topic in class.

1. For the process $A(l) \rightarrow A(g)$, which direction is favored by energy randomness? positional randomness? Explain your answers. If you wanted to favor the process as written, would you raise or lower the temperature of the system? Explain.

2. For a liquid, which would you expect to be larger, ΔS_{fusion} or $\Delta S_{evaporation}$? Why?

3. Gas A_2 reacts with gas B_2 to form gas AB at a constant temperature. The bond energy of AB is much greater than that of either reactant. What can be said about the sign of ΔH? ΔS_{surr}? ΔS? Explain how potential energy changes for this process. Explain how random kinetic energy changes during the process.

4. What types of experiments can be carried out to determine if a reaction is spontaneous? Does spontaneity have any relationship to the final equilibrium position of a reaction? Explain.

5. A friend tells you, "Free energy G and pressure P are related by the equation $G = G° + RT \ln(P)$. Also, G is related to the equilibrium constant K in that when $G_{products} = G_{reactants}$, the system is at equilibrium. Therefore, it must be true that a system is at equilibrium when all the pressures are equal." Do you agree with this friend? Explain.

6. You remember that $\Delta G°$ is related to $RT \ln(K)$ but cannot remember if it's $RT \ln(K)$ or $-RT \ln(K)$. Realizing what $\Delta G°$ and K mean, how can you figure out the correct sign?

A blue question or exercise number indicates that the answer to that question or exercise appears at the back of this book and a solution appears in the *Solutions Guide*.

Questions

7. Define what is meant by a *spontaneous process*.

8. Define *entropy*.

9. Describe how the following changes affect the positional entropy of a substance.
   a. increase in volume of a gas at constant T
   b. increase in temperature of a gas at constant V
   c. increase in pressure of a gas at constant T

10. Define the following:
   a. *system*
   b. *surroundings*

11. The synthesis of glucose directly from CO_2 and H_2O and the synthesis of proteins directly from amino acids are both nonspontaneous processes under standard conditions. Yet it is necessary for these to occur in order for life to exist. In light of the second law of thermodynamics, how can life exist?

12. If you calculate a value for $\Delta G°$ for a reaction using the values of $\Delta G_f°$ in Appendix 4 and get a negative number, is it correct to say that the reaction is always spontaneous?

13. When the environment is contaminated by a toxic or potentially toxic substance (for example, from a chemical spill or the use of insecticides), the substance tends to disperse. How is this consistent with the second law of thermodynamics? In terms of the second law, which requires the least work: cleaning the environment after it has been contaminated or trying to prevent the contamination before it occurs? Explain.

14. Of the functions ΔH, ΔS, and ΔG, which has the strongest dependence on temperature?

15. Discuss the relationship between w_{max} and the magnitude and sign of the free energy change for a reaction. Also discuss w_{max} for real processes.

16. High temperatures are favorable to a reaction kinetically but may be unfavorable to a reaction thermodynamically. Explain.

Exercises

In this section similar exercises are paired.

Spontaneity, Entropy, and the Second Law of Thermodynamics: Free Energy

17. Which of the following processes are spontaneous?
   a. Salt dissolves in H_2O.
   b. A clear solution becomes a uniform color after a few drops of dye are added.
   c. Iron rusts.
   d. You clean your bedroom.

18. Which of the following processes are spontaneous?
   a. A house is built.
   b. A satellite is launched into orbit.
   c. A satellite falls back to earth.
   d. The kitchen gets cluttered.

19. Consider the following energy levels, each capable of holding two objects:

$E = 2$ kJ _____
$E = 1$ kJ _____
$E = 0$ XX

Draw all the possible arrangements of the two identical particles (represented by X) in the three energy levels. What total energy is most likely, that is, occurs the greatest number of times? Assume that the particles are indistinguishable from each other.

20. In rolling two dice, what *total* number is the most likely to occur? Is there an energy reason why this number is favored? Would energy have to be spent to increase the probability of getting a particular number (that is, to cheat)?

21. Choose the compound with the greatest positional entropy in each case.
  a. 1 mol H_2 (at STP) or 1 mol H_2 (at 100°C, 0.5 atm)
  b. 1 mol N_2 (at STP) or 1 mol N_2 (at 100 K, 2.0 atm)
  c. 1 mol $H_2O(s)$ (at 0°C) or 1 mol $H_2O(l)$ (at 20°C)

22. Choose the substance with the greater positional entropy in each case.
  a. 1 mol He (at 500°C, 1 atm) or 1 mol He (at 500°C, 2 atm)
  b. 1 mol He (at STP) or 1 mol He (at 200 K, 2 atm)
  c. 1 mol He(s) (at 0 K) or 1 mol He(g) (at 5 K)

23. Which of the following involve an increase in the entropy of the system?
  a. melting of a solid
  b. sublimation
  c. freezing

24. Which of the following involve an increase in the entropy of the system?
  a. mixing
  b. separation
  c. boiling

25. Predict the sign ΔS_{surr} for the following processes.
  a. $H_2O(l) \rightarrow H_2O(g)$
  b. $CO_2(g) \rightarrow CO_2(s)$

26. Calculate ΔS_{surr} for the following reactions at 25°C and 1 atm.
  a. $C_3H_8(g) + 5O_2(g) \rightarrow 3CO_2(g) + 4H_2O(l)$
    $\Delta H° = -2221$ kJ
  b. $2NO_2(g) \rightarrow 2NO(g) + O_2(g)$ $\Delta H° = 112$ kJ

27. Given the values of ΔH and ΔS, which of the following changes will be spontaneous at constant T and P?
  a. $\Delta H = +25$ kJ, $\Delta S = +5.0$ J/K, $T = 300.$ K
  b. $\Delta H = +25$ kJ, $\Delta S = +100.$ J/K, $T = 300.$ K
  c. $\Delta H = -10.$ kJ, $\Delta S = +5.0$ J/K, $T = 298$ K
  d. $\Delta H = -10.$ kJ, $\Delta S = -40.$ J/K, $T = 200.$ K

28. At what temperatures will the following processes be spontaneous?
  a. $\Delta H = -18$ kJ and $\Delta S = -60.$ J/K
  b. $\Delta H = +18$ kJ and $\Delta S = +60.$ J/K
  c. $\Delta H = +18$ kJ and $\Delta S = -60.$ J/K
  d. $\Delta H = -18$ kJ and $\Delta S = +60.$ J/K

29. The boiling point of chloroform ($CHCl_3$) is 61.7°C. The enthalpy of vaporization is 31.4 kJ/mol. Calculate the entropy of vaporization.

30. For mercury, the enthalpy of vaporization is 58.51 kJ/mol and the entropy of vaporization is 92.92 J/K · mol. What is the normal boiling point of mercury?

31. For ammonia (NH_3), the enthalpy of fusion is 5.65 kJ/mol and the entropy of fusion is 28.9 J/K · mol.
  a. Will $NH_3(s)$ spontaneously melt at 200. K?
  b. What is the approximate melting point of ammonia?

32. The melting point of tungsten is the second highest among the elements (only that of carbon is higher). The melting point of tungsten is 3680 K, and the enthalpy of fusion is 35.2 kJ/mol. What is the entropy of fusion?

Chemical Reactions: Entropy Changes and Free Energy

33. Predict the sign of $\Delta S°$ for each of the following changes.
  a.

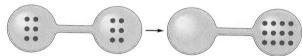

  b. $AgCl(s) \rightarrow Ag^+(aq) + Cl^-(aq)$
  c. $2H_2(g) + O_2(g) \rightarrow 2H_2O(l)$
  d. $H_2O(l) \rightarrow H_2O(g)$

34. Predict the sign of $\Delta S°$ for each of the following changes.
  a. $Na(s) + \frac{1}{2}Cl_2(g) \rightarrow NaCl(s)$
  b. $N_2(g) + 3H_2(g) \rightarrow 2NH_3(g)$
  c. $NaCl(s) \rightarrow Na^+(aq) + Cl^-(aq)$
  d. $NaCl(s) \rightarrow NaCl(l)$

35. For each of the following pairs of substances, which substance has the greater value of S at 25°C?
  a. $C_{graphite}(s)$ or $C_{diamond}(s)$
  b. $C_2H_5OH(l)$ or $C_2H_5OH(g)$
  c. $CO_2(s)$ or $CO_2(g)$

36. For each of the following pairs, which substance has the greater value of S?
  a. N_2O (at 0 K) or He (at 10 K)
  b. $N_2O(g)$ (at 1 atm, 25°C) or He(g) (at 1 atm, 25°C)
  c. $H_2O(s)$ (at 0°C) or $H_2O(l)$ (at 0°C)

37. Predict the sign of $\Delta S°$ and then calculate $\Delta S°$ for each of the following reactions.
  a. $2H_2S(g) + SO_2(g) \rightarrow 3S_{rhombic}(s) + 2H_2O(g)$
  b. $2SO_3(g) \rightarrow 2SO_2(g) + O_2(g)$
  c. $Fe_2O_3(s) + 3H_2(g) \rightarrow 2Fe(s) + 3H_2O(g)$

38. Predict the sign of $\Delta S°$ and then calculate $\Delta S°$ for each of the following reactions.
  a. $H_2(g) + \frac{1}{2}O_2(g) \rightarrow H_2O(l)$
  b. $N_2(g) + 3H_2(g) \rightarrow 2NH_3(g)$
  c. $HCl(g) \rightarrow H^+(aq) + Cl^-(aq)$

39. For the reaction

$$C_2H_2(g) + 4F_2(g) \longrightarrow 2CF_4(g) + H_2(g)$$

$\Delta S°$ is equal to -358 J/K. Use this value and data from Appendix 4 to calculate the value of $S°$ for $CF_4(g)$.

40. For the reaction

$$2Al(s) + 3Br_2(l) \longrightarrow 2AlBr_3(s)$$

$\Delta S°$ is equal to -144 J/K. Use this value and data from Appendix 4 to calculate the value of $S°$ for solid aluminum bromide.

41. It is quite common for a solid to change from one structure to another at a temperature below its melting point. For example, sulfur undergoes a phase change from the rhombic crystal structure to the monoclinic crystal form at temperatures above 95°C.
  a. Predict the signs of ΔH and ΔS for the process $S_{rhombic} \rightarrow$ $S_{monoclinic}$.
  b. Which form of sulfur has the more ordered crystalline structure?

42. When most biologic enzymes are heated they lose their catalytic activity. The change

$$\text{Original enzyme} \longrightarrow \text{new form}$$

that occurs on heating is endothermic and spontaneous. Is the structure of the original enzyme or its new form more ordered? Explain.

43. For the reaction

$$2O(g) \longrightarrow O_2(g)$$

  a. predict the signs of ΔH and ΔS.
  b. would the reaction be more spontaneous at high or low temperatures?

44. Hydrogen cyanide is produced industrially by the following exothermic reaction:

$$2NH_3(g) + 3O_2(g) + 2CH_4(g) \xrightarrow[\text{Pt-Rh}]{1000°C}$$
$$2HCN(g) + 6H_2O(g)$$

Is the high temperature needed for thermodynamic or kinetic reasons?

45. From data in Appendix 4, calculate $\Delta H°$, $\Delta S°$, and $\Delta G°$ for each of the following reactions at 25°C.
  a. $CH_4(g) + 2O_2(g) \rightarrow CO_2(g) + 2H_2O(g)$
  b. $6CO_2(g) + 6H_2O(l) \rightarrow C_6H_{12}O_6(s) + 6O_2(g)$
  Glucose
  c. $P_4O_{10}(s) + 6H_2O(l) \rightarrow 4H_3PO_4(s)$
  d. $HCl(g) + NH_3(g) \rightarrow NH_4Cl(s)$

46. For the reaction at 298 K,

$$2NO_2(g) \rightleftharpoons N_2O_4(g)$$

the values of $\Delta H°$ and $\Delta S°$ are -58.03 kJ and -176.6 J/K, respectively. What is the value of $\Delta G°$ at 298 K? Assuming that $\Delta H°$ and $\Delta S°$ do not depend on temperature, at what temperature is $\Delta G° = 0$? Is $\Delta G°$ negative above or below this temperature?

47. Using data from Appendix 4, calculate $\Delta H°$, $\Delta S°$, and $\Delta G°$ for the following reactions that produce acetic acid:

$$CH_4(g) + CO_2(g) \rightarrow CH_3\overset{\displaystyle O}{\overset{\displaystyle \|}{C}}\text{—OH}(l)$$

$$CH_3OH(g) + CO(g) \rightarrow CH_3\overset{\displaystyle O}{\overset{\displaystyle \|}{C}}\text{—OH}(l)$$

Which reaction would you choose as a commercial method for producing acetic acid (CH_3CO_2H) at standard conditions? What temperature conditions would you choose for the reaction? Assume $\Delta H°$ and $\Delta S°$ do not depend on temperature.

48. Consider two reactions for the production of ethanol:

$$C_2H_4(g) + H_2O(g) \longrightarrow CH_3CH_2OH(l)$$
$$C_2H_6(g) + H_2O(g) \longrightarrow CH_3CH_2OH(l) + H_2(g)$$

Which would be the more thermodynamically feasible at standard conditions? Why?

49. Given the following data

$$S(s) + \tfrac{3}{2}O_2(g) \longrightarrow SO_3(g) \qquad \Delta G° = -371 \text{ kJ}$$
$$2SO_2(g) + O_2(g) \longrightarrow 2SO_3(g) \qquad \Delta G° = -142 \text{ kJ}$$

calculate $\Delta G°$ for the reaction

$$S(s) + O_2(g) \longrightarrow SO_2(g)$$

50. Given the following data:

$$2C_6H_6(l) + 15O_2(g) \longrightarrow 12CO_2(g) + 6H_2O(l)$$
$$\Delta G° = -6399 \text{ kJ}$$
$$C(s) + O_2(g) \longrightarrow CO_2(g) \qquad \Delta G° = -394 \text{ kJ}$$
$$H_2(g) + \tfrac{1}{2}O_2(g) \longrightarrow H_2O(l) \qquad \Delta G° = -237 \text{ kJ}$$

calculate $\Delta G°$ for the reaction

$$6C(s) + 3H_2(g) \longrightarrow C_6H_6(l)$$

51. For the reaction

$$SF_4(g) + F_2(g) \longrightarrow SF_6(g)$$

the value of $\Delta G°$ is -374 kJ. Use this value and data from Appendix 4 to calculate the value of $\Delta G_f°$ for $SF_4(g)$.

52. The value of $\Delta G°$ for the reaction

$$2C_4H_{10}(g) + 13O_2(g) \longrightarrow 8CO_2(g) + 10H_2O(l)$$

is -5490. kJ. Use this value and data from Appendix 4 to calculate the standard free energy of formation for $C_4H_{10}(g)$.

53. Use ΔG_f° values in Appendix 4 to calculate ΔG° for the reaction

$$4PH_3(g) + 8O_2(g) \longrightarrow P_4O_{10}(s) + 6H_2O(l)$$

54. Consider the reaction

$$2POCl_3(g) \longrightarrow 2PCl_3(g) + O_2(g)$$

   a. Calculate ΔG° for this reaction. The ΔG_f° values for $POCl_3(g)$ and $PCl_3(g)$ are -502 kJ/mol and $-270.$ kJ/mol, respectively.
   b. Is this reaction spontaneous under standard conditions at 298 K?
   c. The value of ΔS° for this reaction is 179 J/K. At what temperatures is this reaction spontaneous at standard conditions? Assume that ΔH° and ΔS° do not depend on temperature.

Free Energy: Pressure Dependence and Equilibrium

55. Using data from Appendix 4, calculate ΔG for the reaction

$$NO(g) + O_3(g) \longrightarrow NO_2(g) + O_2(g)$$

   for these conditions:

$$T = 298 \text{ K}$$
$$P_{NO} = 1.00 \times 10^{-6} \text{ atm}, \ P_{O_3} = 2.00 \times 10^{-6} \text{ atm}$$
$$P_{NO_2} = 1.00 \times 10^{-7} \text{ atm}, \ P_{O_2} = 1.00 \times 10^{-3} \text{ atm}$$

56. Using data from Appendix 4, calculate ΔG for the reaction

$$2H_2S(g) + SO_2(g) \rightleftharpoons 3S_{rhombic}(s) + 2H_2O(g)$$

   for the following conditions at 25°C:

$$P_{H_2S} = 1.0 \times 10^{-4} \text{ atm}$$
$$P_{SO_2} = 1.0 \times 10^{-2} \text{ atm}$$
$$P_{H_2O} = 3.0 \times 10^{-2} \text{ atm}$$

57. Consider the reaction

$$2NO_2(g) \rightleftharpoons N_2O_4(g)$$

   For each of the following mixtures of reactants and products at 25°C, predict the direction in which the reaction will shift to reach equilibrium.
   a. $P_{NO_2} = P_{N_2O_4} = 1.0$ atm
   b. $P_{NO_2} = 0.21$ atm, $P_{N_2O_4} = 0.50$ atm
   c. $P_{NO_2} = 0.29$ atm, $P_{N_2O_4} = 1.6$ atm

58. Using data from Appendix 4, calculate ΔH°, ΔS°, and K (at 298 K) for the synthesis of ammonia by the Haber process:

$$N_2(g) + 3H_2(g) \rightleftharpoons 2NH_3(g)$$

   Calculate ΔG for this reaction under the following conditions (assume an uncertainty of ± 1 in all quantities):

   a. $T = 298$ K, $P_{N_2} = P_{H_2} = 200$ atm, $P_{NH_3} = 50$ atm
   b. $T = 298$ K, $P_{N_2} = 200$ atm, $P_{H_2} = 600$ atm, $P_{NH_3} = 200$ atm

59. One of the reactions that destroys ozone in the upper atmosphere is

$$NO(g) + O_3(g) \rightleftharpoons NO_2(g) + O_2(g)$$

   Using data from Appendix 4, calculate ΔG° and K (at 298 K) for this reaction.

60. Consider the reaction

$$H_2(g) + Cl_2(g) \rightleftharpoons 2HCl(g)$$

   a. Calculate ΔH°, ΔS°, ΔG°, and K (at 298 K) using data in Appendix 4.
   b. If $H_2(g)$, $Cl_2(g)$, and $HCl(g)$ are placed in a flask such that the pressure of each gas is 1 atm, in which direction will the system shift to reach equilibrium at 25°C?

61. Consider the autoionization of water at 25°C:

$$H_2O(l) \rightleftharpoons H^+(aq) + OH^-(aq) \qquad K_w = 1.00 \times 10^{-14}$$

   a. Calculate ΔG° for this process at 25°C.
   b. At 40.°C, $K_w = 2.92 \times 10^{-14}$. Calculate ΔG° at 40.°C.

62. The Ostwald process for the commercial production of nitric acid involves three steps:

$$4NH_3(g) + 5O_2(g) \xrightarrow[825°C]{Pt} 4NO(g) + 6H_2O(g)$$
$$2NO(g) + O_2(g) \longrightarrow 2NO_2(g)$$
$$3NO_2(g) + H_2O(l) \longrightarrow 2HNO_3(l) + NO(g)$$

   a. Calculate ΔH°, ΔS°, ΔG°, and K (at 298 K) for each of the three steps in the Ostwald process (see Appendix 4).
   b. Calculate the equilibrium constant for the first step at 825°C, assuming ΔH° and ΔS° do not depend on temperature.
   c. Is there a thermodynamic reason for the high temperature in the first step assuming standard conditions?

63. Consider the following reaction at 800. K:

$$N_2(g) + 3F_2(g) \longrightarrow 2NF_3(g)$$

   An equilibrium mixture contains the following partial pressures: $P_{N_2} = 0.021$ atm, $P_{F_2} = 0.063$ atm, $P_{NF_3} = 0.48$ atm. Calculate ΔG° for the reaction at 800. K.

64. Consider the following reaction at 298 K:

$$2SO_2(g) + O_2(g) \longrightarrow 2SO_3(g)$$

   An equilibrium mixture contains $O_2(g)$ and $SO_3(g)$ at partial pressures of 0.50 atm and 2.0 atm, respectively. Using data from Appendix 4, determine the equilibrium partial pressure of SO_2 in the mixture.

65. Using the relationship

$$\ln(K) = -\frac{\Delta H°}{RT} + \frac{\Delta S°}{R}$$

show that for a system at equilibrium, the equilibrium will shift to the right for an endothermic process when the temperature is increased.

66. Use the equation in Exercise 65 to determine $\Delta H°$ and $\Delta S°$ for the autoionization of water:

$$H_2O(l) \rightleftharpoons H^+(aq) + OH^-(aq)$$

$T(°C)$	K_w
0	1.14×10^{-15}
25	1.00×10^{-14}
35	2.09×10^{-14}
40.	2.92×10^{-14}
50.	5.47×10^{-14}

Additional Exercises

67. A green plant synthesizes glucose by photosynthesis, as shown in the reaction

$$6CO_2(g) + 6H_2O(l) \longrightarrow C_6H_{12}O_6(s) + 6O_2(g)$$

Animals use glucose as a source of energy:

$$C_6H_{12}O_6(s) + 6O_2(g) \longrightarrow 6CO_2(g) + 6H_2O(l)$$

If we were to assume that both these processes occur to the same extent in a cyclic process, what thermodynamic property must have a nonzero value?

68. The lines from T. S. Eliot's "The Hollow Men" (V)

. . . this is the way the world ends—
not with a bang, but a whimper

have been said by some to describe the eventual heat death of the universe. Comment on this view.
(Excerpt from "The Hollow Men" in *Collected Poems 1909–1962*, by T. S. Eliot, copyright © 1936 by Harcourt Brace, Inc.; copyright © 1963, 1964 by T. S. Eliot. Reprinted by permission of Harcourt Brace & Company and Faber & Faber, Ltd.)

69. Human DNA contains almost twice as much information as is needed to code for all the substances produced in the body. Likewise, the digital data sent from *Voyager II* contained one redundant bit out of every two bits of information. The Hubble space telescope transmits three redundant bits for every bit of information. How is entropy related to the transmission of information? What do you think is accomplished by having so many redundant bits of information in both DNA and the space probes?

70. Calculate the entropy change for the vaporization of liquid methane and liquid hexane using the following data.

	Boiling Point (1 atm)	ΔH_{vap}
Methane	112 K	8.20 kJ/mol
Hexane	342 K	28.9 kJ/mol

Compare the molar volume of gaseous methane at 112 K with that of gaseous hexane at 342 K. How do the differences in molar volume affect the values of ΔS_{vap} for these liquids?

71. Elemental sulfur can exist in two crystalline forms, rhombic and monoclinic. Calculate the temperature for the conversion of monoclinic sulfur to rhombic sulfur given the following data:

	$\Delta H_f°$ (kJ/mol)	$S°$ (J/K · mol)
S (rhombic)	0	31.73
S (monoclinic)	0.30	32.55

72. Consider the following reaction:

$$H_2O(g) + Cl_2O(g) \rightleftharpoons 2HOCl(g) \qquad K_{298} = 0.090$$

For $Cl_2O(g)$,

$$\Delta G_f° = 97.9 \text{ kJ/mol}$$
$$\Delta H_f° = 80.3 \text{ kJ/mol}$$
$$S° = 266.1 \text{ J/K · mol}$$

a. Calculate $\Delta G°$ for the reaction using the equation $\Delta G° = -RT \ln(K)$.
b. Use bond energy values (Table 8.4) to estimate $\Delta H°$ for the reaction.
c. Use the results from parts a and b to estimate $\Delta S°$ for the reaction.
d. Estimate $\Delta H_f°$ and $S°$ for HOCl(g).
e. Estimate the value of K at 500. K.
f. Calculate ΔG at 25°C when $P_{H_2O} = 18$ torr, $P_{Cl_2O} = 2.0$ torr, and $P_{HOCl} = 0.10$ torr.

73. Carbon monoxide is toxic because it binds much more strongly to the iron in hemoglobin than does O_2. The equilibrium constant for the binding of CO is about two hundred times that for the binding of O_2. That is, for the reactions

$$\text{(heme)Fe} + O_2 \underset{}{\overset{K_{O_2}}{\rightleftharpoons}} \text{(heme)Fe} - O_2$$

$$(heme)Fe + CO \xrightleftharpoons{K_{CO}} (heme)Fe - CO$$

$K_{CO}/K_{O_2} = 2.1 \times 10^2$. Calculate the difference in $\Delta G°$ for the binding of CO and O_2 to hemoglobin at 25°C.

74. Using the following data, calculate the value of K_{sp} for $Ba(NO_3)_2$, one of the *least* soluble of the common nitrate salts.

Species	$\Delta G_f°$
$Ba^{2+}(aq)$	-561 kJ/mol
$NO_3^-(aq)$	-109 kJ/mol
$Ba(NO_3)_2(s)$	-797 kJ/mol

75. In the text the following equation was derived

$$\Delta G = \Delta G° + RT \ln(Q)$$

for gaseous reactions where the quantities in Q were expressed in units of pressure. We also can use units of mol/L for the quantities in Q, specifically for aqueous reactions. With this in mind, consider the reaction

$$HF(aq) \rightleftharpoons H^+(aq) + F^-(aq)$$

for which $K_a = 7.2 \times 10^{-4}$ at 25°C. Calculate ΔG for the reaction under the following conditions at 25°C.
a. $[HF] = [H^+] = [F^-] = 1.0 \ M$
b. $[HF] = 0.98 \ M, [H^+] = [F^-] = 2.7 \times 10^{-2} \ M$
c. $[HF] = [H^+] = [F^-] = 1.0 \times 10^{-5} \ M$
d. $[HF] = [F^-] = 0.27 \ M, [H^+] = 7.2 \times 10^{-4} \ M$
e. $[HF] = 0.52 \ M, [F^-] = 0.67 \ M, [H^+] = 1.0 \times 10^{-3} \ M$
Based on the calculated ΔG values, in what direction will the reaction shift to reach equilibrium for each of the five sets of conditions?

76. Many biochemical reactions that occur in cells require relatively high concentrations of potassium ion (K^+). The concentration of K^+ in muscle cells is about 0.15 M. The concentration of K^+ in blood plasma is about 0.0050 M. The high internal concentration in cells is maintained by pumping K^+ from the plasma. How much work must be done to transport 1.0 mol K^+ from the blood to the inside of a muscle cell at 37°C, normal body temperature? When 1.0 mol K^+ is transferred from blood to the cells, do any other ions have to be transported? Why or why not?

77. Cells use the hydrolysis of adenosine triphosphate, abbreviated as ATP, as a source of energy. Symbolically, this reaction can be written as

$$ATP(aq) + H_2O(l) \longrightarrow ADP(aq) + H_2PO_4^-(aq)$$

where ADP represents adenosine diphosphate. For this reaction, $\Delta G° = -30.5$ kJ/mol.

a. Calculate K at 25°C.
b. If all the free energy from the metabolism of glucose

$$C_6H_{12}O_6(s) + 6O_2(g) \longrightarrow 6CO_2(g) + 6H_2O(l)$$

goes into forming ATP from ADP, how many ATP molecules can be produced for every molecule of glucose?

78. One reaction that occurs in human metabolism is

$$HO_2CCH_2CH_2CHCO_2H(aq) + NH_3(aq) \rightleftharpoons$$
$$\underset{NH_2}{|}$$

Glutamic acid

$$H_2NCCH_2CH_2CHCO_2H(aq) + H_2O(l)$$
$$\overset{O}{\underset{NH_2}{\|}}$$

Glutamine

For this reaction $\Delta G° = 14$ kJ at 25°C.
a. Calculate K for this reaction at 25°C.
b. In a living cell this reaction is coupled with the hydrolysis of ATP. (See Exercise 77.) Calculate $\Delta G°$ and K at 25°C for the following reaction:

$$Glutamic \ acid(aq) + ATP(aq) + NH_3(aq) \rightleftharpoons$$
$$Glutamine(aq) + ADP(aq) + H_2PO_4^-(aq)$$

79. Monochloroethane (C_2H_5Cl) can be produced by the direct reaction of ethane gas (C_2H_6) with chlorine gas or by the reaction of ethylene gas (C_2H_4) with hydrogen chloride gas. The second reaction gives almost a 100% yield of pure C_2H_5Cl at a rapid rate without catalysis. The first method requires light as an energy source or the reaction would not occur. Yet $\Delta G°$ for the first reaction is considerably more negative than $\Delta G°$ for the second reaction. Explain how this can be so.

80. Consider the reaction

$$Fe_2O_3(s) + 3H_2(g) \longrightarrow 2Fe(s) + 3H_2O(g)$$

Assuming $\Delta H°$ and $\Delta S°$ do not depend on temperature, calculate the temperature where $K = 1.00$ for this reaction.

Challenge Problems

81. Using data from Appendix 4, calculate $\Delta H°$, $\Delta G°$, and K (at 298 K) for the production of ozone from oxygen:

$$3O_2(g) \rightleftharpoons 2O_3(g)$$

At 30 km above the surface of the earth, the temperature is about 230. K and the partial pressure of oxygen is about 1.0×10^{-3} atm. Estimate the partial pressure of ozone in equilibrium with oxygen at 30 km above the earth's surface. Is it reasonable to assume that the equilibrium between oxygen and ozone is maintained under these conditions? Explain.

82. Entropy can be calculated by a relationship proposed by Ludwig Boltzmann:

$$S = k \ln(W)$$

where $k = 1.38 \times 10^{-23}$ J/K and W is the number of ways a particular state can be obtained. (This equation is engraved on Boltzmann's tombstone.) Calculate S for the three arrangements of particles in Table 16.1.

83. a. Using the free energy profile for a simple one-step reaction, show that at equilibrium $K = k_f/k_r$, where k_f and k_r are the rate constants for the forward and reverse reactions. *Hint:* Use the relationship $\Delta G° = -RT \ln(K)$ and represent k_f and k_r using the Arrhenius equation ($k = Ae^{-E_a/RT}$).

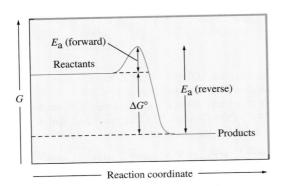

b. Why is the following statement false? "A catalyst can increase the rate of a forward reaction but not the rate of the reverse reaction."

84. Consider the reaction

$$H_2(g) + Br_2(g) \rightleftharpoons 2HBr(g)$$

where $\Delta H° = -103.8$ kJ/mol. In a particular experiment, equal moles of $H_2(g)$ at 1.00 atm and $Br_2(g)$ at 1.00 atm were mixed in a 1.00 L flask at 25°C and allowed to reach equilibrium. Then the molecules of H_2 at equilibrium were counted using a very sensitive technique, and 1.10×10^{13} molecules were found. For this reaction, calculate the values of K, $\Delta G°$, and $\Delta S°$.

85. Consider the system

$$A(g) \longrightarrow B(g)$$

at 25°C.
a. Assuming that $G_A° = 8996$ J/mol and $G_B° = 11,718$ J/mol, calculate the value of the equilibrium constant for this reaction.
b. Calculate the equilibrium pressures that result if 1.00 mol A(g) at 1.00 atm and 1.00 mol B(g) at 1.00 atm are mixed at 25°C.
c. Show by calculations that $\Delta G = 0$ at equilibrium.

86. The equilibrium constant for a certain reaction decreases from 8.84 to 3.25×10^{-2} when the temperature increases from 25°C to 75°C. Estimate the temperature where $K = 1.00$ for this reaction. Estimate the value of $\Delta S°$ for this reaction. *Hint:* Manipulate the equation in Exercise 65.

87. If wet silver carbonate is dried in a stream of hot air, the air must have a certain concentration level of carbon dioxide to prevent silver carbonate from decomposing by the reaction

$$Ag_2CO_3(s) \rightleftharpoons Ag_2O(s) + CO_2(g)$$

$\Delta H°$ for this reaction is 79.14 kJ/mol in the temperature range of 25 to 125°C. Given that the partial pressure of carbon dioxide in equilibrium with pure solid silver carbonate is 6.23×10^{-3} torr at 25°C, calculate the partial pressure of CO_2 necessary to prevent decomposition of Ag_2CO_3 at 110.°C. *Hint:* Manipulate the equation in Exercise 65.

Marathon Problem

This problem is designed to incorporate several concepts and techniques into one situation. Marathon Problems can be used in class by groups of students to help facilitate problem-solving skills.

88. Impure nickel, refined by smelting sulfide ores in a blast furnace, can be converted into metal from 99.90% to 99.99% purity by the Mond process. The primary reaction involved in the Mond process is

$$Ni(s) + 4CO(g) \rightleftharpoons Ni(CO)_4(g)$$

a. Without referring to Appendix 4, predict the sign of $\Delta S°$ for the above reaction. Explain.
b. The spontaneity of the above reaction is temperature dependent. Predict the sign of ΔS_{surr} for this reaction. Explain.
c. For $Ni(CO)_4(g)$, $\Delta H_f° = -607$ kJ/mol and $S° = 417$ J/K · mol at 298 K. Using these values and data in Appendix 4, calculate $\Delta H°$ and $\Delta S°$ for the above reaction.
d. Calculate the temperature at which $\Delta G° = 0$ ($K = 1$) for the above reaction, assuming that $\Delta H°$ and $\Delta S°$ do not depend on temperature.
e. The first step of the Mond process involves equilibrating impure nickel with CO(g) and $Ni(CO)_4(g)$ at about 50°C. The purpose of this step is to convert as much nickel as possible into the gas phase. Calculate the equilibrium constant for the above reaction at 50.°C.
f. In the second step of the Mond process, the gaseous $Ni(CO)_4$ is isolated and heated to 227°C. The purpose of this step is to deposit as much nickel as possible as pure solid (the reverse of the above reaction). Calculate the equilibrium constant for the above reaction at 227°C.

g. Why is temperature increased for the second step of the Mond process?

h. The Mond process relies on the volatility of $Ni(CO)_4$ for its success. Only pressures and temperatures at which $Ni(CO)_4$ is a gas are useful. A recently developed variation of the Mond process carries out the first step at higher pressures and a temperature of 152°C. Estimate the maximum pressure of $Ni(CO)_4(g)$ that can be attained before the gas will liquefy at 152°C. The boiling point for $Ni(CO)_4$ is 42°C and the enthalpy of vaporization is 29.0 kJ/mol. (*Hint:* The phase change reaction and the corresponding equilibrium expression are

$$Ni(CO)_4(l) \rightleftharpoons Ni(CO)_4(g) \qquad K = P_{Ni(CO)_4}$$

$Ni(CO)_4(g)$ will liquefy when the pressure of $Ni(CO)_4$ is greater than the K value.)

Electrochemistry

Contents

*E*lectrochemistry constitutes one of the most important interfaces between chemistry and everyday life. Every time you start your car, turn on your calculator, look at your digital watch, or listen to a radio at the beach, you are depending on electrochemical reactions. Our society sometimes seems to run almost entirely on batteries. Certainly the advent of small, dependable batteries along with silicon-chip technology has made possible the tiny calculators, tape recorders, and clocks that we take for granted.

Electrochemistry is important in other less obvious ways. For example, the corrosion of iron, which has tremendous economic implications, is an electrochemical process. In addition, many important industrial materials such as aluminum, chlorine, and sodium hydroxide are prepared by electrolytic processes. In analytical chemistry, electrochemical techniques employ electrodes that are specific for a given molecule or ion, such as H^+ (pH meters), F^-, Cl^-, and many others. These increasingly important methods are used to analyze for trace pollutants in natural waters or for the tiny quantities of chemicals in human blood that may signal the development of a specific disease.

Electrochemistry is best defined as *the study of the interchange of chemical and electrical energy*. It is primarily concerned with two processes that involve oxidation–reduction reactions: the generation of an electric current from a spontaneous chemical reaction and the opposite process, the use of a current to produce chemical change.

A nickel half-electroplated with copper.

17.1 Galvanic Cells

Exploration: Electrochemistry

Balancing half-reactions is discussed in Section 4.10.

Molecular Model: MnO_4^-

As we discussed in detail in Section 4.9, an **oxidation–reduction (redox) reaction** involves a transfer of electrons from the **reducing agent** to the **oxidizing agent.** Recall that **oxidation** involves a *loss of electrons* (an increase in oxidation number) and that **reduction** involves a *gain of electrons* (a decrease in oxidation number).

To understand how a redox reaction can be used to generate a current, let's consider the reaction between MnO_4^- and Fe^{2+}:

$$8H^+(aq) + MnO_4^-(aq) + 5Fe^{2+}(aq) \longrightarrow Mn^{2+}(aq) + 5Fe^{3+}(aq) + 4H_2O(l)$$

In this reaction, Fe^{2+} is oxidized and MnO_4^- is reduced; electrons are transferred from Fe^{2+} (the reducing agent) to MnO_4^- (the oxidizing agent).

It is useful to break a redox reaction into **half-reactions,** one involving oxidation and one involving reduction. For the reaction above, the half-reactions are

Reduction: $8H^+ + MnO_4^- + 5e^- \longrightarrow Mn^{2+} + 4H_2O$

Oxidation: $5(Fe^{2+} \longrightarrow Fe^{3+} + e^-)$

The multiplication of the second half-reaction by 5 indicates that this reaction must occur five times for each time the first reaction occurs. The balanced overall reaction is the sum of the half-reactions.

When MnO_4^- and Fe^{2+} are present in the same solution, the electrons are transferred directly when the reactants collide. Under these conditions, no useful work is obtained from the chemical energy involved in the reaction, which instead is released as heat. How can we harness this energy? The key is to separate the oxidizing agent from the reducing agent, thus requiring the electron transfer to occur through a wire. The current produced in the wire by the electron flow can then be directed through a device, such as an electric motor, to provide useful work.

For example, consider the system illustrated in Fig. 17.1. If our reasoning has been correct, electrons should flow through the wire from Fe^{2+} to MnO_4^-. However, when we construct the apparatus as shown, no flow of electrons is apparent. Why? Careful observation shows that when we connect the wires from the two compartments, current flows for an instant and then ceases. The current stops flowing because of charge buildups in the two compartments. If electrons flowed from the right to the left compartment in the apparatus as shown, the left compartment (receiving electrons) would become negatively charged, and the right compartment (losing electrons) would become positively charged. Creating a charge separation

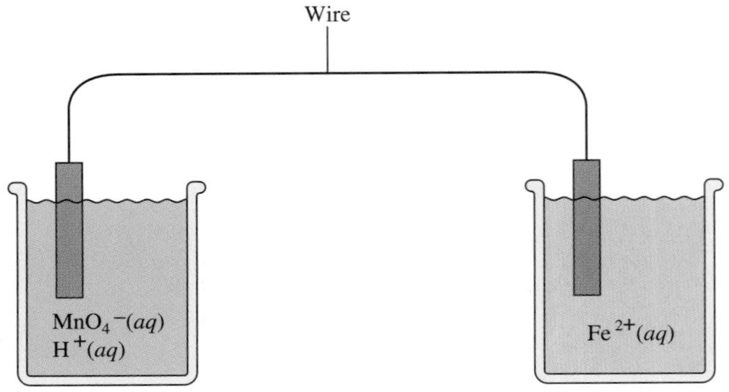

Wire

Figure 17.1

Schematic of a method to separate the oxidizing and reducing agents of a redox reaction. (The solutions also contain counterions to balance the charge.)

$MnO_4^-(aq)$
$H^+(aq)$

$Fe^{2+}(aq)$

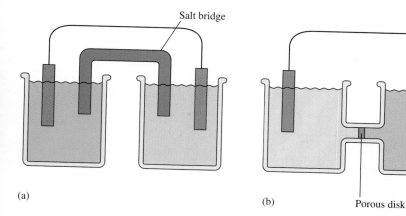

Figure 17.2

Galvanic cells can contain a salt bridge as in (a) or a porous-disk connection as in (b). A salt bridge contains a strong electrolyte held in a Jello-like matrix. A porous disk contains tiny passages that allow hindered flow of ions.

of this type requires a large amount of energy. Thus sustained electron flow cannot occur under these conditions.

However, we can solve this problem very simply. The solutions must be connected so that ions can flow to keep the net charge in each compartment zero. This connection might involve a **salt bridge** (a U-tube filled with an electrolyte) or a **porous disk** in a tube connecting the two solutions (see Fig. 17.2). Either of these devices allows ion flow without extensive mixing of the solutions. When we make the provision for ion flow, the circuit is complete. Electrons flow through the wire from reducing agent to oxidizing agent, and ions flow from one compartment to the other to keep the net charge zero.

We now have covered all the essential characteristics of a **galvanic cell,** *a device in which chemical energy is changed to electrical energy.* (The opposite process is called *electrolysis* and will be considered in Section 17.7.)

The reaction in an electrochemical cell occurs at the interface between the electrode and the solution where the electron transfer occurs. The electrode compartment in which *oxidation* occurs is called the **anode;** the electrode compartment in which *reduction* occurs is called the **cathode** (see Fig. 17.3).

> A galvanic cell uses a spontaneous redox reaction to produce a current that can be used to do work.

> Oxidation occurs at the anode. Reduction occurs at the cathode.

Cell Potential

A galvanic cell consists of an oxidizing agent in one compartment that pulls electrons through a wire from a reducing agent in the other compartment. The "pull,"

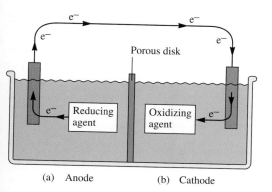

(a) Anode (b) Cathode

Figure 17.3

An electrochemical process involves electron transfer at the interface between the electrode and the solution. (a) The species in the solution acting as the reducing agent supplies electrons to the anode. (b) The species in the solution acting as the oxidizing agent receives electrons from the cathode.

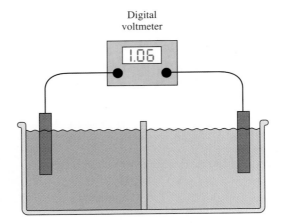

Digital
voltmeter

1.06

Figure 17.4

Digital voltmeters draw only a negligible current and are convenient to use.

A volt is 1 joule of work per coulomb of charge transferred: $1\ V = 1\ J/C$.

or driving force, on the electrons is called the **cell potential** ($\mathscr{E}_{cell}$), or the **electromotive force** (emf) of the cell. The unit of electrical potential is the **volt** (abbreviated V), which is defined as 1 joule of work per coulomb of charge transferred.

How can we measure the cell potential? One possible instrument is a crude **voltmeter,** which works by drawing current through a known resistance. However, when current flows through a wire, the frictional heating that occurs wastes some of the potentially useful energy of the cell. A traditional voltmeter will therefore measure a potential that is less than the maximum cell potential. The key to determining the maximum potential is to do the measurement under conditions of zero current so that no energy is wasted. Traditionally, this has been accomplished by inserting a variable-voltage device (powered from an external source) in *opposition* to the cell potential. The voltage on this instrument (called a **potentiometer**) is adjusted until no current flows in the cell circuit. Under such conditions, the cell potential is equal in magnitude and opposite in sign to the voltage setting of the potentiometer. This value represents the *maximum* cell potential, since no energy is wasted heating the wire. More recently, advances in electronic technology have allowed the design of *digital voltmeters* that draw only a negligible amount of current (see Fig. 17.4). Since these instruments are more convenient to use, they have replaced potentiometers in the modern laboratory.

17.2 Standard Reduction Potentials

The name *galvanic cell* honors Luigi Galvani (1737–1798), an Italian scientist generally credited with the discovery of electricity. These cells are sometimes called *voltaic cells* after Alessandro Volta (1745–1827), another Italian, who first constructed cells of this type around 1800.

The reaction in a galvanic cell is always an oxidation–reduction reaction that can be broken down into two half-reactions. It would be convenient to assign a potential to *each* half-reaction so that when we construct a cell from a given pair of half-reactions we can obtain the cell potential by summing the half-cell potentials. For example, the observed potential for the cell shown in Fig. 17.5(a) is 0.76 V, and the cell reaction* is

$$2H^+(aq) + Zn(s) \longrightarrow Zn^{2+}(aq) + H_2(g)$$

---

*In this text we will follow the convention of indicating the physical states of the reactants and products only in the overall redox reaction. For simplicity, half-reactions will *not* include the physical states.

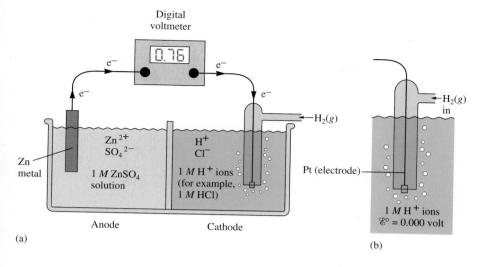

Figure 17.5

(a) A galvanic cell involving the reactions $Zn \rightarrow Zn^{2+} + 2e^-$ (at the anode) and $2H^+ + 2e^- \rightarrow H_2$ (at the cathode) has a potential of 0.76 V. (b) The standard hydrogen electrode where $H_2(g)$ at 1 atm is passed over a platinum electrode in contact with 1 M H^+ ions. This electrode process (assuming ideal behavior) is arbitrarily assigned a value of exactly zero volts.

For this cell, the anode compartment contains a zinc metal electrode with Zn^{2+} and SO_4^{2-} ions in aqueous solution. The anode reaction is the oxidation half-reaction:

$$Zn \longrightarrow Zn^{2+} + 2e^-$$

The zinc metal, in producing Zn^{2+} ions that go into solution, is giving up electrons, which flow through the wire. For now, we will assume that all cell components are in their standard states, so in this case the solution in the anode compartment will contain 1 M Zn^{2+}. The cathode reaction of this cell is the reduction half-reaction:

$$2H^+ + 2e^- \longrightarrow H_2$$

The cathode consists of a platinum electrode (used because it is a chemically inert conductor) in contact with 1 M H^+ ions and bathed by hydrogen gas at 1 atm. Such an electrode, called the **standard hydrogen electrode,** is shown in Fig. 17.5(b).

Although we can measure the *total* potential of this cell (0.76 V), there is no way to measure the potentials of the individual electrode processes. Thus, if we want potentials for the half-reactions (half-cells), we must arbitrarily divide the total cell potential. For example, if we assign the reaction

$$2H^+ + 2e^- \longrightarrow H_2$$

where

$$[H^+] = 1 \; M \quad \text{and} \quad P_{H_2} = 1 \text{ atm}$$

a potential of exactly zero volts, then the reaction

$$Zn \longrightarrow Zn^{2+} + 2e^-$$

will have a potential of 0.76 V because

$$\mathscr{E}^\circ_{cell} = \mathscr{E}^\circ_{H^+ \rightarrow H_2} + \mathscr{E}^\circ_{Zn \rightarrow Zn^{2+}}$$
$$\uparrow \qquad\qquad \uparrow \qquad\qquad \uparrow$$
$$0.76 \text{ V} \qquad 0 \text{ V} \qquad\; 0.76 \text{ V}$$

where the superscript $^\circ$ indicates that *standard states* are employed. In fact, by setting the standard potential for the half-reaction $2H^+ + 2e^- \rightarrow H_2$ equal to zero, we can assign values to all other half-reactions.

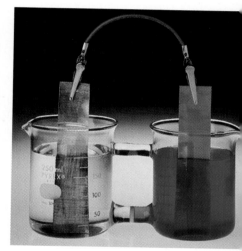

Copper being plated onto the copper metal cathode on the right, and zinc dissolving from the zinc metal anode on the left. Note the porous disk in the tube connecting the two solutions, which allows the ion flow to balance the electron flow through the wire.

Animation: Electrochemical Half-Reactions in a Galvanic Cell

Standard states were discussed in Section 6.4.

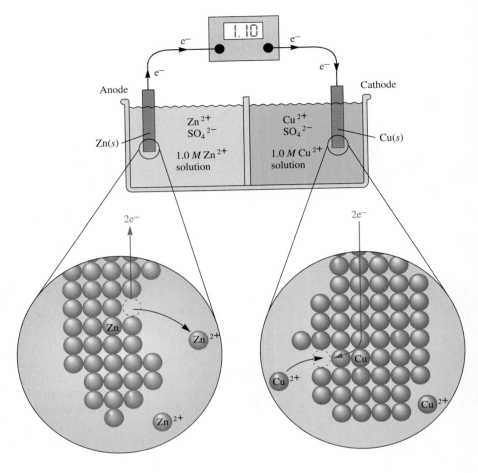

Figure 17.6

A galvanic cell involving the half-reactions Zn → Zn^{2+} + 2e$^-$ (anode) and Cu^{2+} + 2e$^-$ → Cu (cathode), with $\mathscr{E}^\circ_{cell}$ = 1.10 V.

For example, the measured potential for the cell shown in Fig. 17.6 is 1.10 V. The cell reaction is

$$Zn(s) + Cu^{2+}(aq) \longrightarrow Zn^{2+}(aq) + Cu(s)$$

which can be divided into the half-reactions

Anode: Zn $\longrightarrow$ Zn^{2+} + 2e$^-$

Cathode: Cu^{2+} + 2e$^-$ $\longrightarrow$ Cu

Then

$$\mathscr{E}^\circ_{cell} = \mathscr{E}^\circ_{Zn \rightarrow Zn^{2+}} + \mathscr{E}^\circ_{Cu^{2+} \rightarrow Cu}$$

Since $\mathscr{E}^\circ_{Zn \rightarrow Zn^{2+}}$ was earlier assigned a value of 0.76 V, the value of $\mathscr{E}^\circ_{Cu^{2+} \rightarrow Cu}$ must be 0.34 V because

$$1.10 \text{ V} = 0.76 \text{ V} + 0.34 \text{ V}$$

The scientific community has universally accepted the half-reaction potentials based on the assignment of zero volts to the process 2H$^+$ + 2e$^-$ → H$_2$ (under standard conditions where ideal behavior is assumed). However, before we can use these

The standard hydrogen potential is the reference potential against which all half-reaction potentials are assigned.

Table 17.1 Standard Reduction Potentials at 25°C (298 K) for Many Common Half-Reactions

Half-Reaction	$\mathscr{E}°$ (V)	Half-Reaction	$\mathscr{E}°$ (V)
$F_2 + 2e^- \rightarrow 2F^-$	2.87	$O_2 + 2H_2O + 4e^- \rightarrow 4OH^-$	0.40
$Ag^{2+} + e^- \rightarrow Ag^+$	1.99	$Cu^{2+} + 2e^- \rightarrow Cu$	0.34
$Co^{3+} + e^- \rightarrow Co^{2+}$	1.82	$Hg_2Cl_2 + 2e^- \rightarrow 2Hg + 2Cl^-$	0.27
$H_2O_2 + 2H^+ + 2e^- \rightarrow 2H_2O$	1.78	$AgCl + e^- \rightarrow Ag + Cl^-$	0.22
$Ce^{4+} + e^- \rightarrow Ce^{3+}$	1.70	$SO_4^{2-} + 4H^+ + 2e^- \rightarrow H_2SO_3 + H_2O$	0.20
$PbO_2 + 4H^+ + SO_4^{2-} + 2e^- \rightarrow PbSO_4 + 2H_2O$	1.69	$Cu^{2+} + e^- \rightarrow Cu^+$	0.16
$MnO_4^- + 4H^+ + 3e^- \rightarrow MnO_2 + 2H_2O$	1.68	$2H^+ + 2e^- \rightarrow H_2$	0.00
$2e^- + 2H^+ + IO_4^- \rightarrow IO_3^- + H_2O$	1.60	$Fe^{3+} + 3e^- \rightarrow Fe$	−0.036
$MnO_4^- + 8H^+ + 5e^- \rightarrow Mn^{2+} + 4H_2O$	1.51	$Pb^{2+} + 2e^- \rightarrow Pb$	−0.13
$Au^{3+} + 3e^- \rightarrow Au$	1.50	$Sn^{2+} + 2e^- \rightarrow Sn$	−0.14
$PbO_2 + 4H^+ + 2e^- \rightarrow Pb^{2+} + 2H_2O$	1.46	$Ni^{2+} + 2e^- \rightarrow Ni$	−0.23
$Cl_2 + 2e^- \rightarrow 2Cl^-$	1.36	$PbSO_4 + 2e^- \rightarrow Pb + SO_4^{2-}$	−0.35
$Cr_2O_7^{2-} + 14H^+ + 6e^- \rightarrow 2Cr^{3+} + 7H_2O$	1.33	$Cd^{2+} + 2e^- \rightarrow Cd$	−0.40
$O_2 + 4H^+ + 4e^- \rightarrow 2H_2O$	1.23	$Fe^{2+} + 2e^- \rightarrow Fe$	−0.44
$MnO_2 + 4H^+ + 2e^- \rightarrow Mn^{2+} + 2H_2O$	1.21	$Cr^{3+} + e^- \rightarrow Cr^{2+}$	−0.50
$IO_3^- + 6H^+ + 5e^- \rightarrow \frac{1}{2}I_2 + 3H_2O$	1.20	$Cr^{3+} + 3e^- \rightarrow Cr$	−0.73
$Br_2 + 2e^- \rightarrow 2Br^-$	1.09	$Zn^{2+} + 2e^- \rightarrow Zn$	−0.76
$VO_2^+ + 2H^+ + e^- \rightarrow VO^{2+} + H_2O$	1.00	$2H_2O + 2e^- \rightarrow H_2 + 2OH^-$	−0.83
$AuCl_4^- + 3e^- \rightarrow Au + 4Cl^-$	0.99	$Mn^{2+} + 2e^- \rightarrow Mn$	−1.18
$NO_3^- + 4H^+ + 3e^- \rightarrow NO + 2H_2O$	0.96	$Al^{3+} + 3e^- \rightarrow Al$	−1.66
$ClO_2 + e^- \rightarrow ClO_2^-$	0.954	$H_2 + 2e^- \rightarrow 2H^-$	−2.23
$2Hg^{2+} + 2e^- \rightarrow Hg_2^{2+}$	0.91	$Mg^{2+} + 2e^- \rightarrow Mg$	−2.37
$Ag^+ + e^- \rightarrow Ag$	0.80	$La^{3+} + 3e^- \rightarrow La$	−2.37
$Hg_2^{2+} + 2e^- \rightarrow 2Hg$	0.80	$Na^+ + e^- \rightarrow Na$	−2.71
$Fe^{3+} + e^- \rightarrow Fe^{2+}$	0.77	$Ca^{2+} + 2e^- \rightarrow Ca$	−2.76
$O_2 + 2H^+ + 2e^- \rightarrow H_2O_2$	0.68	$Ba^{2+} + 2e^- \rightarrow Ba$	−2.90
$MnO_4^- + e^- \rightarrow MnO_4^{2-}$	0.56	$K^+ + e^- \rightarrow K$	−2.92
$I_2 + 2e^- \rightarrow 2I^-$	0.54	$Li^+ + e^- \rightarrow Li$	−3.05
$Cu^+ + e^- \rightarrow Cu$	0.52		

values to calculate cell potentials, we need to understand several essential characteristics of half-cell potentials.

Video: Galvanic Cells

The accepted convention is to give the potentials of half-reactions as *reduction* processes; for example:

$$2H^+ + 2e^- \longrightarrow H_2$$
$$Cu^{2+} + 2e^- \longrightarrow Cu$$
$$Zn^{2+} + 2e^- \longrightarrow Zn$$

The $\mathscr{E}°$ values corresponding to reduction half-reactions with all solutes at 1 *M* and all gases at 1 atm are called **standard reduction potentials.** Standard reduction potentials for the most common half-reactions are given in Table 17.1 and Appendix 5.5.

All half-reactions are given as reduction processes in standard tables.

Combining two half-reactions to obtain a balanced oxidation–reduction reaction often requires two manipulations:

When a half-reaction is reversed, the sign of $\mathscr{E}°$ is reversed.

1. One of the reduction half-reactions must be reversed (since redox reactions must involve a substance being oxidized and a substance being reduced), which means that the *sign* of the potential for the reversed half-reaction also must be *reversed*.

2. Since the number of electrons lost must equal the number gained, the half-reactions must be multiplied by integers as necessary to achieve the balanced equation. However, the *value of $\mathscr{E}°$ is not changed* when a half-reaction is multiplied by an integer. Since a standard reduction potential is an *intensive property* (it does not depend on how many times the reaction occurs), the potential is *not* multiplied by the integer required to balance the cell reaction.

When a half-reaction is multiplied by an integer, $\mathscr{E}°$ remains the same.

Consider a galvanic cell based on the redox reaction

$$Fe^{3+}(aq) + Cu(s) \longrightarrow Cu^{2+}(aq) + Fe^{2+}(aq)$$

The pertinent half-reactions are

$$Fe^{3+} + e^- \longrightarrow Fe^{2+} \qquad \mathscr{E}° = 0.77 \text{ V} \qquad (1)$$
$$Cu^{2+} + 2e^- \longrightarrow Cu \qquad \mathscr{E}° = 0.34 \text{ V} \qquad (2)$$

To balance the cell reaction and calculate the standard cell potential, reaction (2) must be reversed:

$$Cu \longrightarrow Cu^{2+} + 2e^- \qquad -\mathscr{E}° = -0.34 \text{ V}$$

Note the change in sign for the $\mathscr{E}°$ value. Now, since each Cu atom produces two electrons but each Fe^{3+} ion accepts only one electron, reaction (1) must be multiplied by 2:

$$2Fe^{3+} + 2e^- \longrightarrow 2Fe^{2+} \qquad \mathscr{E}° = 0.77 \text{ V}$$

Note that $\mathscr{E}°$ is not changed in this case.

Now we can obtain the balanced cell reaction by summing the appropriately modified half-reactions:

$$Cu \longrightarrow Cu^{2+} + 2e^- \qquad\qquad -\mathscr{E}° = -0.34 \text{ V}$$
$$2Fe^{3+} + 2e^- \longrightarrow 2Fe^{2+} \qquad\qquad \mathscr{E}° = 0.77 \text{ V}$$

Cell reaction: $\quad Cu(s) + 2Fe^{3+}(aq) \longrightarrow Cu^{2+}(aq) + 2Fe^{2+}(aq) \qquad \mathscr{E}°_{cell} = -0.34 \text{ V} + 0.77 \text{ V}$
$$= 0.43 \text{ V}$$

Sample Exercise 17.1 *Galvanic Cells*

a. Consider a galvanic cell based on the reaction

$$Al^{3+}(aq) + Mg(s) \longrightarrow Al(s) + Mg^{2+}(aq)$$

The half-reactions are

$$Al^{3+} + 3e^- \longrightarrow Al \qquad \mathscr{E}° = -1.66 \text{ V} \qquad (1)$$
$$Mg^{2+} + 2e^- \longrightarrow Mg \qquad \mathscr{E}° = -2.37 \text{ V} \qquad (2)$$

Give the balanced cell reaction and calculate $\mathscr{E}°$ for the cell.

b. A galvanic cell is based on the reaction

$$MnO_4^-(aq) + H^+(aq) + ClO_3^-(aq) \longrightarrow ClO_4^-(aq) + Mn^{2+}(aq) + H_2O(l)$$

The half-reactions are

$$MnO_4^- + 5e^- + 8H^+ \longrightarrow Mn^{2+} + 4H_2O \qquad \mathscr{E}° = 1.51 \text{ V} \qquad (1)$$
$$ClO_4^- + 2H^+ + 2e^- \longrightarrow ClO_3^- + H_2O \qquad \mathscr{E}° = 1.19 \text{ V} \qquad (2)$$

Give the balanced cell reaction and calculate $\mathscr{E}°$ for the cell.

Solution

a. The half-reaction involving magnesium must be reversed:

$$Mg \longrightarrow Mg^{2+} + 2e^- \qquad -\mathscr{E}° = -(-2.37 \text{ V}) = 2.37 \text{ V}$$

Also, since the two half-reactions involve different numbers of electrons, they must be multiplied by integers as follows:

$$\begin{array}{ll} 2(Al^{3+} + 3e^- \longrightarrow Al) & \mathscr{E}° = -1.66 \text{ V} \\ \underline{3(Mg \longrightarrow Mg^{2+} + 2e^-)} & \underline{-\mathscr{E}° = 2.37 \text{ V}} \\ 2Al^{3+}(aq) + 3Mg(s) \longrightarrow 2Al(s) + 3Mg^{2+}(aq) & \mathscr{E}°_{cell} = -1.66 \text{ V} + 2.37 \text{ V} \\ & \phantom{\mathscr{E}°_{cell}} = 0.71 \text{ V} \end{array}$$

b. Half-reaction (2) must be reversed, and both half-reactions must be multiplied by integers to make the number of electrons equal:

$$\begin{array}{ll} 2(MnO_4^- + 5e^- + 8H^+ \longrightarrow Mn^{2+} + 4H_2O) & \mathscr{E}° = 1.51 \text{ V} \\ \underline{5(ClO_3^- + H_2O \longrightarrow ClO_4^- + 2H^+ + 2e^-)} & \underline{-\mathscr{E}° = -1.19 \text{ V}} \\ 2MnO_4^-(aq) + 6H^+(aq) + 5ClO_3^-(aq) \longrightarrow 2Mn^{2+}(aq) + 3H_2O(l) + 5ClO_4^-(aq) & \mathscr{E}°_{cell} = 1.51 \text{ V} - 1.19 \text{ V} \\ & \phantom{\mathscr{E}°_{cell}} = 0.32 \text{ V} \end{array}$$

See Exercises 17.27 and 17.28.

Line Notation

We now will introduce a handy line notation used to describe electrochemical cells. In this notation the anode components are listed on the left and the cathode components are listed on the right, separated by double vertical lines (indicating the salt bridge or porous disk). For example, the line notation for the cell described in Sample Exercise 17.1(a) is

$$Mg(s) \,|\, Mg^{2+}(aq) \,||\, Al^{3+}(aq) \,|\, Al(s)$$

In this notation a phase difference (boundary) is indicated by a single vertical line. Thus, in this case, vertical lines occur between the solid Mg metal and the Mg^{2+} in aqueous solution and between solid Al and Al^{3+} in aqueous solution. Also note that the substance constituting the anode is listed at the far left and the substance constituting the cathode is listed at the far right.

For the cell described in Sample Exercise 17.1(b), all the components involved in the oxidation–reduction reaction are ions. Since none of these dissolved ions can serve as an electrode, a nonreacting (inert) conductor must be used. The usual choice is platinum. Thus, for the cell described in Sample Exercise 17.1(b), the line notation is

$$Pt(s) \,|\, ClO_3^-(aq), ClO_4^-(aq), H^+(aq) \,||\, H^+(aq), MnO_4^-(aq), Mn^{2+}(aq) \,|\, Pt(s)$$

Complete Description of a Galvanic Cell

Next we want to consider how to describe a galvanic cell fully, given just its half-reactions. This description will include the cell reaction, the cell potential, and the physical setup of the cell. Let's consider a galvanic cell based on the following half-reactions:

$$Fe^{2+} + 2e^- \longrightarrow Fe \qquad\qquad \mathscr{E}° = -0.44 \text{ V}$$
$$MnO_4^- + 5e^- + 8H^+ \longrightarrow Mn^{2+} + 4H_2O \qquad \mathscr{E}° = 1.51 \text{ V}$$

In a working galvanic cell, one of these reactions must run in reverse. Which one?

We can answer this question by considering the sign of the potential of a working cell: *A cell will always run spontaneously in the direction that produces a positive cell potential.* Thus, in the present case, it is clear that the half-reaction involving iron must be reversed, since this choice leads to a positive cell potential:

A galvanic cell runs spontaneously in the direction that gives a positive value for $\mathscr{E}_{cell}$.

$$Fe \longrightarrow Fe^{2+} + 2e^- \qquad\qquad -\mathscr{E}° = 0.44 \text{ V}$$
$$MnO_4^- + 5e^- + 8H^+ \longrightarrow Mn^{2+} + 4H_2O \qquad \mathscr{E}° = 1.51 \text{ V}$$

where
$$\mathscr{E}°_{cell} = 0.44 \text{ V} + 1.51 \text{ V} = 1.95 \text{ V}$$

The balanced cell reaction is obtained as follows:

$$5(Fe \longrightarrow Fe^{2+} + 2e^-)$$
$$2(MnO_4^- + 5e^- + 8H^+ \longrightarrow Mn^{2+} + 4H_2O)$$
$$\overline{2MnO_4^-(aq) + 5Fe(s) + 16H^+(aq) \longrightarrow 5Fe^{2+}(aq) + 2Mn^{2+}(aq) + 8H_2O(l)}$$

Now consider the physical setup of the cell, shown schematically in Fig. 17.7. In the left compartment the active components in their standard states are pure metallic iron (Fe) and 1.0 M Fe^{2+}. The anion present depends on the iron salt used. In this compartment the anion does not participate in the reaction but simply balances the charge. The half-reaction that takes place at this electrode is

$$Fe \longrightarrow Fe^{2+} + 2e^-$$

which is an oxidation reaction, so this compartment is the anode. The electrode consists of pure iron metal.

In the right compartment the active components in their standard states are 1.0 M MnO_4^-, 1.0 M H^+, and 1.0 M Mn^{2+}, with appropriate unreacting ions (often called *counterions*) to balance the charge. The half-reaction in this compartment is

$$MnO_4^- + 5e^- + 8H^+ \longrightarrow Mn^{2+} + 4H_2O$$

which is a reduction reaction, so this compartment is the cathode. Since neither MnO_4^- nor Mn^{2+} ions can serve as the electrode, a nonreacting conductor such as platinum must be employed.

The next step is to determine the direction of electron flow. In the left compartment the half-reaction involves the oxidation of iron:

$$Fe \longrightarrow Fe^{2+} + 2e^-$$

In the right compartment the half-reaction is the reduction of MnO_4^-:

$$MnO_4^- + 5e^- + 8H^+ \longrightarrow Mn^{2+} + 4H_2O$$

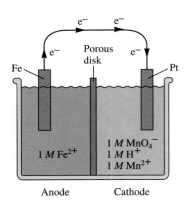

Figure 17.7

The schematic of a galvanic cell based on the half-reactions:

$$Fe \longrightarrow Fe^{2+} + 2e^-$$
$$MnO_4^- + 5e^- + 8H^+ \longrightarrow$$
$$Mn^{2+} + 4H_2O$$

Thus the electrons flow from Fe to MnO_4^- in this cell, or from the anode to the cathode, as is always the case. The line notation for this cell is

$$Fe(s) \,|\, Fe^{2+}(aq) \,||\, MnO_4^-(aq), \, Mn^{2+}(aq) \,|\, Pt(s)$$

A complete description of a galvanic cell usually includes four items:

- The cell potential (always positive for a galvanic cell) and the balanced cell reaction.
- The direction of electron flow, obtained by inspecting the half-reactions and using the direction that gives a positive $\mathscr{E}_{cell}$.
- Designation of the anode and cathode.
- The nature of each electrode and the ions present in each compartment. A chemically inert conductor is required if none of the substances participating in the half-reaction is a conducting solid.

Sample Exercise 17.2 *Description of a Galvanic Cell*

Describe completely the galvanic cell based on the following half-reactions under standard conditions:

$$Ag^+ + e^- \longrightarrow Ag \qquad \mathscr{E}° = 0.80 \text{ V} \qquad (1)$$
$$Fe^{3+} + e^- \longrightarrow Fe^{2+} \qquad \mathscr{E}° = 0.77 \text{ V} \qquad (2)$$

Solution

Item 1

Since a positive $\mathscr{E}_{cell}°$ value is required, reaction (2) must run in reverse:

$$
\begin{array}{lll}
Ag^+ + e^- \longrightarrow Ag & \mathscr{E}° = & 0.80 \text{ V} \\
Fe^{2+} \longrightarrow Fe^{3+} + e^- & -\mathscr{E}° = & -0.77 \text{ V} \\
\hline
\text{Cell reaction: } Ag^+(aq) + Fe^{2+}(aq) \longrightarrow Fe^{3+}(aq) + Ag(s) & \mathscr{E}_{cell}° = & 0.03 \text{ V}
\end{array}
$$

Item 2

Since Ag^+ receives electrons and Fe^{2+} loses electrons in the cell reaction, the electrons will flow from the compartment containing Fe^{2+} to the compartment containing Ag^+.

Item 3

Oxidation occurs in the compartment containing Fe^{2+} (electrons flow from Fe^{2+} to Ag^+). Hence this compartment functions as the anode. Reduction occurs in the compartment containing Ag^+, so this compartment functions as the cathode.

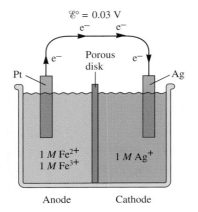

Figure 17.8

Schematic diagram for the galvanic cell based on the half-reactions

$$Ag^+ + e^- \longrightarrow Ag$$
$$Fe^{2+} \longrightarrow Fe^{3+} + e^-$$

Item 4

The electrode in the Ag/Ag^+ compartment is silver metal, and an inert conductor, such as platinum, must be used in the Fe^{2+}/Fe^{3+} compartment. Appropriate counterions are assumed to be present. The diagram for this cell is shown in Fig. 17.8. The line notation for this cell is

$$Pt(s) \,|\, Fe^{2+}(aq), Fe^{3+}(aq) \,||\, Ag^+(aq) \,|\, Ag(s)$$

See Exercises 17.29 and 17.30.

17.3 Cell Potential, Electrical Work, and Free Energy

So far we have considered electrochemical cells in a very practical fashion without much theoretical background. The next step will be to explore the relationship between thermodynamics and electrochemistry.

The work that can be accomplished when electrons are transferred through a wire depends on the "push" (the thermodynamic driving force) behind the electrons. This driving force (the emf) is defined in terms of a *potential difference* (in volts) between two points in the circuit. Recall that a volt represents a joule of work per coulomb of charge transferred:

$$emf = \text{potential difference (V)} = \frac{\text{work (J)}}{\text{charge (C)}}$$

Thus 1 joule of work is produced or required (depending on the direction) when 1 coulomb of charge is transferred between two points in the circuit that differ by a potential of 1 volt.

In this book, *work is viewed from the point of view of the system.* Thus work flowing out of the system is indicated by a minus sign. When a cell produces a current, the cell potential is positive, and the current can be used to do work—to run a motor, for instance. Thus the cell potential $\mathscr{E}$ and the work w have opposite signs:

$$\mathscr{E} = \frac{-w}{q} \quad \begin{array}{l} \leftarrow \text{Work} \\ \leftarrow \text{Charge} \end{array}$$

Therefore,
$$-w = q\mathscr{E}$$

From this equation it can be seen that the maximum work in a cell would be obtained at the maximum cell potential:

$$-w_{max} = q\mathscr{E}_{max} \quad \text{or} \quad w_{max} = -q\mathscr{E}_{max}$$

Work is never the maximum possible if any current is flowing.

However, there is a problem. To obtain electrical work, current must flow. When current flows, some energy is inevitably wasted through frictional heating, and the maximum work is not obtained. This reflects the important general principle introduced in Section 16.9: *In any real, spontaneous process some energy is always wasted—the actual work realized is always less than the calculated maximum.* This is a consequence of the fact that the entropy of the universe must increase in any spontaneous process. Recall from Section 16.9 that the only process from which maximum work could be realized is the hypothetical reversible process. For a galvanic cell this would involve an infinitesimally small current flow and thus an infinite amount of time to do the work. Even though we can never achieve the maximum work through the actual discharge of a galvanic cell, we can measure the maximum potential. There is negligible current flow when a cell potential is measured with a potentiometer or an efficient digital voltmeter. No current flow implies no waste of energy, so the potential measured is the maximum.

Although we can never actually realize the maximum work from a cell reaction, the value for it is still useful in evaluating the efficiency of a real process based on the cell reaction. For example, suppose a certain galvanic cell has a maximum potential (at zero current) of 2.50 V. In a particular experiment 1.33 moles of electrons were passed through this cell at an average actual potential of 2.10 V. The actual work done is

$$w = -q\mathscr{E}$$

where $\mathscr{E}$ represents the actual potential difference at which the current flowed (2.10 V or 2.10 J/C) and q is the quantity of charge in coulombs transferred. The charge on 1 mole of electrons is a constant called the **faraday** (abbreviated F), which has the value *96,485 coulombs of charge per mole of electrons*. Thus q equals the number of moles of electrons times the charge per mole of electrons:

$$q = nF = 1.33 \text{ mol } e^- \times 96{,}485 \text{ C/mol } e^-$$

Then, for the experiment above, the actual work is

$$\begin{aligned} w &= -q\mathscr{E} = -(1.33 \text{ mol } e^- \times 96{,}485 \text{ C/mol } e^-) \times (2.10 \text{ J/C}) \\ &= -2.69 \times 10^5 \text{ J} \end{aligned}$$

For the maximum possible work, the calculation is similar, except that the maximum potential is used:

$$\begin{aligned} w_{max} &= -q\mathscr{E} \\ &= -\left(1.33 \text{ mol } e^- \times 96{,}485 \frac{\text{C}}{\text{mol } e^-}\right)\left(2.50 \frac{\text{J}}{\text{C}}\right) \\ &= -3.21 \times 10^5 \text{ J} \end{aligned}$$

Thus, in its actual operation, the efficiency of this cell is

$$\frac{w}{w_{max}} \times 100\% = \frac{-2.69 \times 10^5 \text{ J}}{-3.21 \times 10^5 \text{ J}} \times 100\% = 83.8\%$$

Next we want to relate the potential of a galvanic cell to free energy. In Section 16.9 we saw that for a process carried out at constant temperature and pressure, the change in free energy equals the maximum useful work obtainable from that process:

$$w_{max} = \Delta G$$

For a galvanic cell,

$$w_{max} = -q\mathscr{E}_{max} = \Delta G$$

Since

$$q = nF$$

we have

$$\Delta G = -q\mathscr{E}_{max} = -nF\mathscr{E}_{max}$$

Michael Faraday lecturing at the Royal Institution before Prince Albert and others (1855). The faraday was named in honor of Michael Faraday (1791–1867), an Englishman who may have been the greatest experimental scientist of the nineteenth century. Among his many achievements were the invention of the electric motor and generator and the development of the principles of electrolysis.

From now on the subscript on $\mathscr{E}_{max}$ will be deleted, with the understanding that any potential given in this book is the maximum potential. Thus

$$\Delta G = -nF\mathscr{E}$$

For standard conditions,

$$\Delta G° = -nF\mathscr{E}°$$

This equation states that *the maximum cell potential is directly related to the free energy difference between the reactants and the products in the cell*. This relationship is important because it provides an experimental means to obtain ΔG for a reaction. It also confirms that a galvanic cell will run in the direction that gives a positive value for $\mathscr{E}_{cell}$; a positive $\mathscr{E}_{cell}$ value corresponds to a negative ΔG value, which is the condition for spontaneity.

Sample Exercise 17.3 *Calculating ΔG° for a Cell Reaction*

Using the data in Table 17.1, calculate $\Delta G°$ for the reaction

$$Cu^{2+}(aq) + Fe(s) \longrightarrow Cu(s) + Fe^{2+}(aq)$$

Is this reaction spontaneous?

Solution

The half-reactions are

$$
\begin{array}{lr}
Cu^{2+} + 2e^- \longrightarrow Cu & \mathscr{E}° = 0.34 \text{ V} \\
Fe \longrightarrow Fe^{2+} + 2e^- & -\mathscr{E}° = 0.44 \text{ V} \\
\hline
Cu^{2+} + Fe \longrightarrow Fe^{2+} + Cu & \mathscr{E}°_{cell} = 0.78 \text{ V}
\end{array}
$$

We can calculate $\Delta G°$ from the equation

$$\Delta G° = -nF\mathscr{E}°$$

Since two electrons are transferred per atom in the reaction, 2 moles of electrons are required per mole of reactants and products. Thus $n = 2$ mol e^-, $F = 96{,}485$ C/mol e^-, and $\mathscr{E}° = 0.78$ V $= 0.78$ J/C. Therefore,

$$\Delta G° = -(2 \text{ mol } e^-)\left(96{,}485\frac{C}{\text{mol } e^-}\right)\left(0.78\frac{J}{C}\right)$$

$$= -1.5 \times 10^5 \text{ J}$$

The process is spontaneous, as indicated by both the negative sign of $\Delta G°$ and the positive sign of $\mathscr{E}°_{cell}$.

This reaction is used industrially to deposit copper metal from solutions resulting from the dissolving of copper ores.

See Exercises 17.37 through 17.40.

Sample Exercise 17.4 *Predicting Spontaneity*

Using the data from Table 17.1, predict whether 1 M HNO_3 will dissolve gold metal to form a 1 M Au^{3+} solution.

Solution

The half-reaction for HNO_3 acting as an oxidizing agent is

$$NO_3^- + 4H^+ + 3e^- \longrightarrow NO + 2H_2O \qquad \mathscr{E}° = 0.96 \text{ V}$$

The reaction for the oxidation of solid gold to Au^{3+} ions is

$$Au \longrightarrow Au^{3+} + 3e^- \qquad -\mathscr{E}° = -1.50 \text{ V}$$

The sum of these half-reactions gives the required reaction:

$$Au(s) + NO_3^-(aq) + 4H^+(aq) \longrightarrow Au^{3+}(aq) + NO(g) + 2H_2O(l)$$

and
$$\mathscr{E}°_{cell} = 0.96 \text{ V} - 1.50 \text{ V} = -0.54 \text{ V}$$

Since the $\mathscr{E}°$ value is negative, the process will *not* occur under standard conditions. That is, gold will not dissolve in 1 M HNO_3 to give 1 M Au^{3+}. In fact, a mixture (1:3 by volume) of concentrated nitric and hydrochloric acids, called *aqua regia,* is required to dissolve gold.

See Exercises 17.49 and 17.50.

17.4 Dependence of Cell Potential on Concentration

So far we have described cells under standard conditions. In this section we consider the dependence of the cell potential on concentration. Under standard conditions (all concentrations 1 M), the cell with the reaction

$$Cu(s) + 2Ce^{4+}(aq) \longrightarrow Cu^{2+}(aq) + 2Ce^{3+}(aq)$$

has a potential of 1.36 V. What will the cell potential be if $[Ce^{4+}]$ is greater than 1.0 M? This question can be answered qualitatively in terms of Le Châtelier's principle. An increase in the concentration of Ce^{4+} will favor the forward reaction and thus increase the driving force on the electrons. The cell potential will increase. On the other hand, an increase in the concentration of a product (Cu^{2+} or Ce^{3+}) will oppose the forward reaction, thus decreasing the cell potential.

These ideas are illustrated in Sample Exercise 17.5.

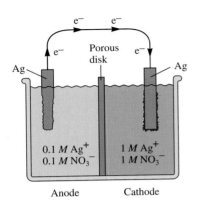

Figure 17.9

A concentration cell that contains a silver electrode and aqueous silver nitrate in both compartments. Because the right compartment contains 1 M Ag^+ and the left compartment contains 0.1 M Ag^+, there will be a driving force to transfer electrons from left to right. Silver will be deposited on the right electrode, thus lowering the concentration of Ag^+ in the right compartment. In the left compartment the silver electrode dissolves (producing Ag^+ ions) to raise the concentration of Ag^+ in solution.

Sample Exercise 17.5 The Effects of Concentration on $\mathscr{E}$

For the cell reaction

$$2Al(s) + 3Mn^{2+}(aq) \longrightarrow 2Al^{3+}(aq) + 3Mn(s) \qquad \mathscr{E}^\circ_{cell} = 0.48 \text{ V}$$

predict whether $\mathscr{E}_{cell}$ is larger or smaller than $\mathscr{E}^\circ_{cell}$ for the following cases.

a. $[Al^{3+}] = 2.0 \text{ } M$, $[Mn^{2+}] = 1.0 \text{ } M$
b. $[Al^{3+}] = 1.0 \text{ } M$, $[Mn^{2+}] = 3.0 \text{ } M$

Solution

a. A product concentration has been raised above 1.0 M. This will oppose the cell reaction and will cause $\mathscr{E}_{cell}$ to be less than $\mathscr{E}^\circ_{cell}$ ($\mathscr{E}_{cell} < 0.48$ V).
b. A reactant concentration has been increased above 1.0 M, and $\mathscr{E}_{cell}$ will be greater than $\mathscr{E}^\circ_{cell}$ ($\mathscr{E}_{cell} > 0.48$ V).

See Exercise 17.55.

Concentration Cells

Because cell potentials depend on concentration, we can construct galvanic cells where both compartments contain the same components but at different concentrations. For example, in the cell in Fig. 17.9, both compartments contain aqueous $AgNO_3$, but with different molarities. Let's consider the potential of this cell and the direction of electron flow. The half-reaction relevant to both compartments of this cell is

$$Ag^+ + e^- \longrightarrow Ag \qquad \mathscr{E}^\circ = 0.80 \text{ V}$$

If the cell had 1 M Ag^+ in both compartments,

$$\mathscr{E}^\circ_{cell} = 0.80 \text{ V} - 0.80 \text{ V} = 0 \text{ V}$$

However, in the cell described here, the concentrations of Ag^+ in the two compartments are 1 M and 0.1 M. Because the concentrations of Ag^+ are unequal, the half-cell potentials will not be identical, and the cell will exhibit a positive voltage. In which direction will the electrons flow in this cell? The best way to think about this question is to recognize that nature will try to equalize the concentrations of Ag^+ in the two compartments. This can be done by transferring electrons from the compartment containing 0.1 M Ag^+ to the one containing 1 M Ag^+ (left to right in Fig. 17.9). This electron transfer will produce more Ag^+ in the left compartment and consume Ag^+ (to form Ag) in the right compartment.

A cell in which both compartments have the same components but at different concentrations is called a **concentration cell**. The difference in concentration is the only factor that produces a cell potential in this case, and the voltages are typically small.

Sample Exercise 17.6 Concentration Cells

Determine the direction of electron flow and designate the anode and cathode for the cell represented in Fig. 17.10.

Solution

The concentrations of Fe^{2+} ion in the two compartments can (eventually) be equalized by transferring electrons from the left compartment to the right. This will cause Fe^{2+} to be formed in the left compartment, and iron metal will be deposited (by reducing Fe^{2+} ions to Fe) on the right electrode. Since electron flow is from left to right, oxidation occurs in the left compartment (the anode) and reduction occurs in the right (the cathode).

See Exercise 17.56.

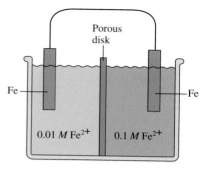

Figure 17.10

A concentration cell containing iron electrodes and different concentrations of Fe^{2+} ion in the two compartments.

The Nernst Equation

The dependence of the cell potential on concentration results directly from the dependence of free energy on concentration. Recall from Chapter 16 that the equation

$$\Delta G = \Delta G° + RT \ln(Q)$$

where Q is the reaction quotient, was used to calculate the effect of concentration on ΔG. Since $\Delta G = -nF\mathscr{E}$ and $\Delta G° = -nF\mathscr{E}°$, the equation becomes

$$-nF\mathscr{E} = -nF\mathscr{E}° + RT \ln(Q)$$

Dividing each side of the equation by $-nF$ gives

$$\mathscr{E} = \mathscr{E}° - \frac{RT}{nF} \ln(Q) \qquad (17.1)$$

Equation (17.1), which gives the relationship between the cell potential and the concentrations of the cell components, is commonly called the **Nernst equation,** after the German chemist Walther Hermann Nernst (1864–1941).

The Nernst equation is often given in a form that is valid at 25°C:

$$\mathscr{E} = \mathscr{E}° - \frac{0.0591}{n} \log(Q)$$

Using this relationship, we can calculate the potential of a cell in which some or all of the components are not in their standard states.

For example, $\mathscr{E}°_{cell}$ is 0.48 V for the galvanic cell based on the reaction

$$2Al(s) + 3Mn^{2+}(aq) \longrightarrow 2Al^{3+}(aq) + 3Mn(s)$$

Consider a cell in which

$$[Mn^{2+}] = 0.50 \ M \quad \text{and} \quad [Al^{3+}] = 1.50 \ M$$

The cell potential at 25°C for these concentrations can be calculated using the Nernst equation:

$$\mathscr{E}_{cell} = \mathscr{E}°_{cell} - \frac{0.0591}{n} \log(Q)$$

Nernst was one of the pioneers in the development of electrochemical theory and is generally given credit for first stating the third law of thermodynamics. He won the Nobel Prize in chemistry in 1920.

We know that

$$\mathscr{E}^\circ_{cell} = 0.48 \text{ V}$$

and

$$Q = \frac{[Al^{3+}]^2}{[Mn^{2+}]^3} = \frac{(1.50)^2}{(0.50)^3} = 18$$

Since the half-reactions are

Oxidation: $2Al \longrightarrow 2Al^{3+} + 6e^-$

Reduction: $3Mn^{2+} + 6e^- \longrightarrow 3Mn$

we know that

$$n = 6$$

Thus

$$\mathscr{E}_{cell} = 0.48 - \frac{0.0591}{6} \log(18)$$

$$= 0.48 - \frac{0.0591}{6}(1.26) = 0.48 - 0.01 = 0.47 \text{ V}$$

Note that the cell voltage decreases slightly because of the nonstandard concentrations. This change is consistent with the predictions of Le Châtelier's principle (see Sample Exercise 17.5). In this case, since the reactant concentration is lower than 1.0 *M* and the product concentration is higher than 1.0 *M*, $\mathscr{E}_{cell}$ is less than $\mathscr{E}^\circ_{cell}$.

The potential calculated from the Nernst equation is the maximum potential before any current flow has occurred. As the cell discharges and current flows from anode to cathode, the concentrations will change, and as a result, $\mathscr{E}_{cell}$ will change. In fact, *the cell will spontaneously discharge until it reaches equilibrium,* at which point

$$Q = K \text{ (the equilibrium constant)} \quad \text{and} \quad \mathscr{E}_{cell} = 0$$

A "dead" battery is one in which the cell reaction has reached equilibrium, and there is no longer any chemical driving force to push electrons through the wire. In other words, *at equilibrium, the components in the two cell compartments have the same free energy,* and $\Delta G = 0$ for the cell reaction at the equilibrium concentrations. The cell no longer has the ability to do work.

Sample Exercise 17.7 *The Nernst Equation*

Describe the cell based on the following half-reactions:

$$VO_2^+ + 2H^+ + e^- \longrightarrow VO^{2+} + H_2O \qquad \mathscr{E}^\circ = 1.00 \text{ V} \qquad (1)$$

$$Zn^{2+} + 2e^- \longrightarrow Zn \qquad \mathscr{E}^\circ = -0.76 \text{ V} \qquad (2)$$

where

$$T = 25°C$$

$$[VO_2^+] = 2.0 \text{ M}$$

$$[H^+] = 0.50 \text{ M}$$

$$[VO^{2+}] = 1.0 \times 10^{-2} \text{ M}$$

$$[Zn^{2+}] = 1.0 \times 10^{-1} \text{ M}$$

Solution

The balanced cell reaction is obtained by reversing reaction (2) and multiplying reaction (1) by 2:

$2 \times$ reaction (1)	$2VO_2^+ + 4H^+ + 2e^- \longrightarrow 2VO^{2+} + 2H_2O$	$\mathscr{E}° = 1.00$ V
Reaction (2) reversed	$Zn \longrightarrow Zn^{2+} + 2e^-$	$-\mathscr{E}° = 0.76$ V
Cell reaction:	$2VO_2^+(aq) + 4H^+(aq) + Zn(s) \longrightarrow 2VO^{2+}(aq) + 2H_2O(l) + Zn^{2+}(aq)$	$\mathscr{E}°_{cell} = 1.76$ V

Since the cell contains components at concentrations other than 1 M, we must use the Nernst equation, where $n = 2$ (since two electrons are transferred), to calculate the cell potential. At 25°C we can use the equation

$$\mathscr{E} = \mathscr{E}°_{cell} - \frac{0.0591}{n} \log(Q)$$

$$= 1.76 - \frac{0.0591}{2} \log\left(\frac{[Zn^{2+}][VO^{2+}]^2}{[VO_2^+]^2[H^+]^4}\right)$$

$$= 1.76 - \frac{0.0591}{2} \log\left(\frac{(1.0 \times 10^{-1})(1.0 \times 10^{-2})^2}{(2.0)^2(0.50)^4}\right)$$

$$= 1.76 - \frac{0.0591}{2} \log(4 \times 10^{-5}) = 1.76 + 0.13 = 1.89 \text{ V}$$

The cell diagram is given in Fig. 17.11.

See Exercises 17.61 through 17.64.

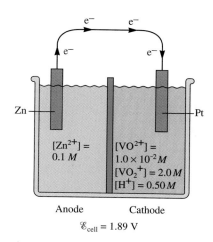

$[Zn^{2+}] = 0.1\,M$
$[VO^{2+}] = 1.0 \times 10^{-2}\,M$
$[VO_2^+] = 2.0\,M$
$[H^+] = 0.50\,M$

Anode   Cathode

$\mathscr{E}_{cell} = 1.89$ V

Figure 17.11
Schematic diagram of the cell described in Sample Exercise 17.7.

Ion-Selective Electrodes

Because the cell potential is sensitive to the concentrations of the reactants and products involved in the cell reaction, measured potentials can be used to determine the concentration of an ion. A pH meter (see Fig. 14.4) is a familiar example of an instrument that measures concentration using an observed potential. The pH meter has three main components: a standard electrode of known potential, a special **glass electrode** that changes potential depending on the concentration of H^+ ions in the solution into which it is dipped, and a potentiometer that measures the potential between the electrodes. The potentiometer reading is automatically converted electronically to a direct reading of the pH of the solution being tested.

The glass electrode (see Fig. 17.12) contains a reference solution of dilute hydrochloric acid in contact with a thin glass membrane. The electrical potential of the glass electrode depends on the difference in $[H^+]$ between the reference solution and the solution into which the electrode is dipped. Thus the electrical potential varies with the pH of the solution being tested.

Electrodes that are sensitive to the concentration of a particular ion are called **ion-selective electrodes,** of which the glass electrode for pH measurement is just one example. Glass electrodes can be made sensitive to such ions as Na^+, K^+, or NH_4^+ by changing the composition of the glass. Other ions can be detected if an appropriate crystal replaces the glass membrane. For example, a crystal of lanthanum(III) fluoride (LaF_3) can be used in an electrode to measure $[F^-]$. Solid silver sulfide (Ag_2S) can be used to measure $[Ag^+]$ and $[S^{2-}]$. Some of the ions that can be detected by ion-selective electrodes are listed in Table 17.2.

Table 17.2 Some Ions Whose Concentrations Can Be Detected by Ion-Selective Electrodes

Cations	Anions
H^+	Br^-
Cd^{2+}	Cl^-
Ca^{2+}	CN^-
Cu^{2+}	F^-
K^+	NO_3^-
Ag^+	S^{2-}
Na^+	

Figure 17.12
A glass electrode contains a reference solution of dilute hydrochloric acid in contact with a thin glass membrane in which a silver wire coated with silver chloride has been embedded. When the electrode is dipped into a solution containing H^+ ions, the electrode potential is determined by the difference in $[H^+]$ between the two solutions.

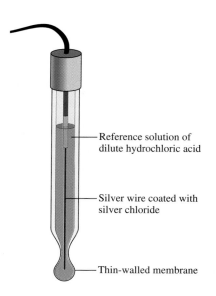
— Reference solution of dilute hydrochloric acid

— Silver wire coated with silver chloride

— Thin-walled membrane

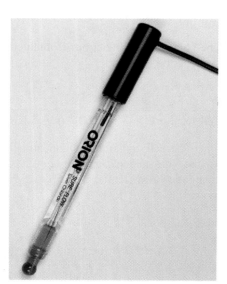

Calculation of Equilibrium Constants for Redox Reactions

The quantitative relationship between $\mathscr{E}°$ and $\Delta G°$ allows calculation of equilibrium constants for redox reactions. For a cell at equilibrium,

$$\mathscr{E}_{cell} = 0 \quad \text{and} \quad Q = K$$

Applying these conditions to the Nernst equation valid at 25°C,

$$\mathscr{E} = \mathscr{E}° - \frac{0.0591}{n} \log (Q)$$

gives

$$0 = \mathscr{E}° - \frac{0.0591}{n} \log (K)$$

or

$$\log (K) = \frac{n\mathscr{E}°}{0.0591} \qquad \text{at 25°C}$$

Molecular Models: $S_4O_6{}^{2-}$, $S_2O_3{}^{2-}$

Sample Exercise 17.8 Equilibrium Constants from Cell Potentials

For the oxidation–reduction reaction

$$S_4O_6{}^{2-}(aq) + Cr^{2+}(aq) \longrightarrow Cr^{3+}(aq) + S_2O_3{}^{2-}(aq)$$

the appropriate half-reactions are

$$S_4O_6{}^{2-} + 2e^- \longrightarrow 2S_2O_3{}^{2-} \qquad \mathscr{E}° = 0.17 \text{ V} \qquad (1)$$
$$Cr^{3+} + e^- \longrightarrow Cr^{2+} \qquad \mathscr{E}° = -0.50 \text{ V} \qquad (2)$$

Balance the redox reaction, and calculate $\mathscr{E}°$ and K (at 25°C).

Solution

To obtain the balanced reaction, we must reverse reaction (2), multiply it by 2, and add it to reaction (1):

2 × reaction (2) reversed	$2(Cr^{2+} \longrightarrow Cr^{3+} + e^-)$	$-\mathscr{E}° = -(-0.50)$ V
Reaction (1)	$S_4O_6^{2-} + 2e^- \longrightarrow 2S_2O_3^{2-}$	$\mathscr{E}° = 0.17$ V
Cell reaction:	$2Cr^{2+}(aq) + S_4O_6^{2-}(aq) \longrightarrow 2Cr^{3+}(aq) + 2S_2O_3^{2-}(aq)$	$\mathscr{E}° = 0.67$ V

In this reaction, 2 moles of electrons are transferred for every unit of reaction that is, for every 2 mol Cr^{2+} reacting with 1 mol $S_4O_6^{2-}$ to form 2 mol Cr^{3+} and 2 mol $S_2O_3^{2-}$. Thus $n = 2$. Then

$$\log(K) = \frac{n\mathscr{E}°}{0.0591} = \frac{2(0.67)}{0.0591} = 22.6$$

The value of K is found by taking the antilog of 22.6:

$$K = 10^{22.6} = 4 \times 10^{22}$$

This very large equilibrium constant is not unusual for a redox reaction.

See Exercises 17.69 through 17.72.

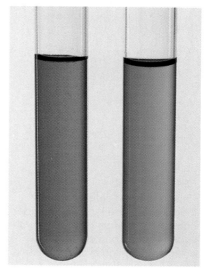

The blue solution contains Cr^{2+} ions, and the green solution contains Cr^{3+} ions.

17.5 Batteries

A **battery** is a galvanic cell or, more commonly, a group of galvanic cells connected in series, where the potentials of the individual cells add to give the total battery potential. Batteries are a source of direct current and have become an essential source of portable power in our society. In this section we examine the most common types of batteries. Some new batteries currently being developed are described at the end of the chapter.

Lead Storage Battery

Since about 1915 when self-starters were first used in automobiles, the **lead storage battery** has been a major factor in making the automobile a practical means of transportation. This type of battery can function for several years under temperature extremes from $-30°F$ to $120°F$ and under incessant punishment from rough roads.

In this battery, lead serves as the anode, and lead coated with lead dioxide serves as the cathode. Both electrodes dip into an electrolyte solution of sulfuric acid. The electrode reactions are

Anode reaction:	$Pb + HSO_4^- \longrightarrow PbSO_4 + H^+ + 2e^-$
Cathode reaction:	$PbO_2 + HSO_4^- + 3H^+ + 2e^- \longrightarrow PbSO_4 + 2H_2O$
Cell reaction:	$Pb(s) + PbO_2(s) + 2H^+(aq) + 2HSO_4^-(aq) \longrightarrow 2PbSO_4(s) + 2H_2O(l)$

The typical automobile lead storage battery has six cells connected in series. Each cell contains multiple electrodes in the form of grids (Fig. 17.13) and produces

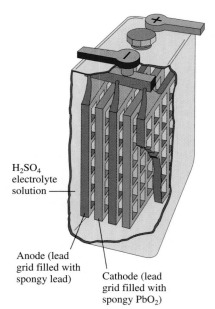

H₂SO₄ electrolyte solution

Anode (lead grid filled with spongy lead)

Cathode (lead grid filled with spongy PbO₂)

Figure 17.13

One of the six cells in a 12-V lead storage battery. The anode consists of a lead grid filled with spongy lead, and the cathode is a lead grid filled with lead dioxide. The cell also contains 38% (by mass) sulfuric acid.

approximately 2 V, to give a total battery potential of about 12 V. Note from the cell reaction that sulfuric acid is consumed as the battery discharges. This lowers the density of the electrolyte solution from its initial value of about 1.28 g/cm^3 in the fully charged battery. As a result, the condition of the battery can be monitored by measuring the density of the sulfuric acid solution. The solid lead sulfate formed in the cell reaction during discharge adheres to the grid surfaces of the electrodes. The battery is recharged by forcing current through the battery in the opposite direction to reverse the cell reaction. A car's battery is continuously charged by an alternator driven by the automobile engine.

An automobile with a dead battery can be "jump-started" by connecting its battery to the battery in a running automobile. This process can be dangerous, however, because the resulting flow of current causes electrolysis of water in the dead battery, producing hydrogen and oxygen gases (see Section 17.7 for details). Disconnecting the jumper cables after the disabled car starts causes an arc that can ignite the gaseous mixture. If this happens, the battery may explode, ejecting corrosive sulfuric acid. This problem can be avoided by connecting the ground jumper cable to a part of the engine remote from the battery. Any arc produced when this cable is disconnected will then be harmless.

Traditional types of storage batteries require periodic "topping off" because the water in the electrolyte solution is depleted by the electrolysis that accompanies the charging process. Recent types of batteries have electrodes made of an alloy of calcium and lead that inhibits the electrolysis of water. These batteries can be sealed, since they require no addition of water.

It is rather amazing that in the 85 years in which lead storage batteries have been used, no better system has been found. Although a lead storage battery does provide excellent service, it has a useful lifetime of 3 to 5 years in an automobile. While it might seem that the battery could undergo an indefinite number of discharge/charge cycles, physical damage from road shock and chemical side-reactions eventually cause it to fail.

Other Batteries

The calculators, electronic watches, portable radios, and tape players that are so familiar to us are all powered by small, efficient batteries. The common **dry cell battery** was invented more than 100 years ago by George Leclanché (1839–1882), a French chemist. In its *acid version,* the dry cell battery contains a zinc inner case that acts as the anode and a carbon rod in contact with a moist paste of solid MnO_2, solid NH_4Cl, and carbon that acts as the cathode (Fig. 17.14). The half-reactions are complex but can be approximated as follows:

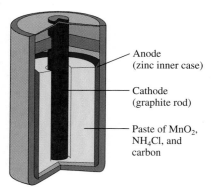

Anode (zinc inner case)

Cathode (graphite rod)

Paste of MnO₂, NH₄Cl, and carbon

Figure 17.14

A common dry cell battery.

Anode reaction: $$Zn \longrightarrow Zn^{2+} + 2e^-$$
Cathode reaction: $$2NH_4^+ + 2MnO_2 + 2e^- \longrightarrow Mn_2O_3 + 2NH_3 + H_2O$$

This cell produces a potential of about 1.5 V.

In the *alkaline version* of the dry cell battery, the solid NH_4Cl is replaced with KOH or NaOH. In this case the half-reactions can be approximated as follows:

Anode reaction: $$Zn + 2OH^- \longrightarrow ZnO + H_2O + 2e^-$$
Cathode reaction: $$2MnO_2 + H_2O + 2e^- \longrightarrow Mn_2O_3 + 2OH^-$$

CHEMICAL IMPACT

Thermophotovoltaics: Electricity from Heat

A PHOTOVOLTAIC CELL transforms the energy of sunlight into an electric current. These devices are used to power calculators, electric signs in rural areas, experimental cars, and an increasing number of other devices. But what happens at night or on cloudy days? Usually photovoltaic power sources employ a battery as a reserve energy source when light levels are low.

Now there is an emerging technology, called *thermophotovoltaics* (TPV), that uses a heat source instead of the sun for energy. These devices can operate at night or on an overcast day without a battery. Although TPV devices could use many different sources of heat, the examples currently under development use a propane burner. To produce an electric current, the radiant heat from the burner is used to excite a "radiator," a device that emits infrared (IR) radiation when heated. The emitted IR radiation then falls on a "converter," which is a semiconductor that contains p–n junctions. The IR radiation excites electrons from valence bands to conduction bands in the semiconductor so that the electrons can flow as a current. A schematic of a TPV generator is illustrated in the accompanying diagram.

TPV technology has advanced recently because researchers have found that it is possible to use radiators such as silicon carbide, which can operate at relatively low temperatures (approximately 1000°C), with III–V semiconductor converters such as gallium antimonide (GSb) or gallium arsenide (GaAs). While development work continues on many fronts, the first commercial TPV product is being marketed by JX Crystals of Issaquah, Washington. The product—Midnight Sun—is a propane-powered TPV generator that can produce 30 watts of electricity and is intended for use on boats to charge the batteries that power naviga-

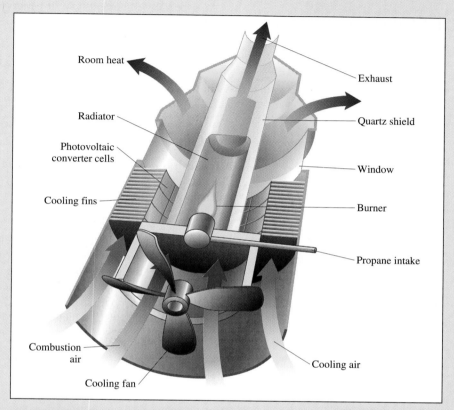

Diagram of a TPV generator.

tion and other essential equipment. Although at $3000 the TPV generator is more expensive than a conventional diesel-powered generator, Midnight Sun is silent and more reliable because it has no moving parts.

Although TPV technology is still in its infancy, it has many possible uses. The utilization of industrial waste heat—generated by glass and steel manufacturing and other industries—could establish a huge market for TPV. For example, two-thirds of the energy used in the manufacture of glass ends up as waste heat. If a significant quantity of this now wasted energy could be used to produce elec-

tricity, this would have tremendous fiscal implications.

Another promising application of TPV technology is for cars with hybrid energy sources. For example, an experimental electric car built at Western Washington University uses a 10-kw TPV generator to supplement the batteries that serve as the main power source.

Projections indicate that TPV devices could account for $500 million in sales by 2005, mainly by substituting TPV generators for small diesel-powered generators used on boats and by the military in the field. It appears that this technology has a hot future.

The alkaline dry cell lasts longer mainly because the zinc anode corrodes less rapidly under basic conditions than under acidic conditions.

Other types of useful batteries include the *silver cell,* which has a Zn anode and a cathode that employs Ag_2O as the oxidizing agent in a basic environment. *Mercury cells,* often used in calculators, have a Zn anode and a cathode involving HgO as the oxidizing agent in a basic medium (see Fig. 17.15).

An especially important type of battery is the *nickel–cadmium battery,* in which the electrode reactions are

Anode reaction: $\qquad Cd + 2OH^- \longrightarrow Cd(OH)_2 + 2e^-$

Cathode reaction: $\qquad NiO_2 + 2H_2O + 2e^- \longrightarrow Ni(OH)_2 + 2OH^-$

As in the lead storage battery, the products adhere to the electrodes. Therefore, a nickel–cadmium battery can be recharged an indefinite number of times.

Fuel Cells

A **fuel cell** is *a galvanic cell for which the reactants are continuously supplied.* To illustrate the principles of fuel cells, let's consider the exothermic redox reaction of methane with oxygen:

$$CH_4(g) + 2O_2(g) \longrightarrow CO_2(g) + 2H_2O(g) + \text{energy}$$

Usually the energy from this reaction is released as heat to warm homes and to run machines. However, in a fuel cell designed to use this reaction, the energy is used to produce an electric current: The electrons flow from the reducing agent (CH_4) to the oxidizing agent (O_2) through a conductor.

The U.S. space program has supported extensive research to develop fuel cells. The Apollo missions used a fuel cell based on the reaction of hydrogen and oxygen to form water:

$$2H_2(g) + O_2(g) \longrightarrow 2H_2O(l)$$

Batteries for electronic watches are, by necessity, very tiny.

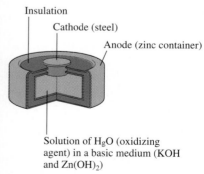

Insulation

Cathode (steel)

Anode (zinc container)

Solution of HgO (oxidizing agent) in a basic medium (KOH and $Zn(OH)_2$)

Figure 17.15

A mercury battery of the type used in small calculators.

A schematic of a fuel cell that employs this reaction is shown in Fig. 17.16. The half-reactions are

Anode reaction: $\qquad 2H_2 + 4OH^- \longrightarrow 4H_2O + 4e^-$

Cathode reaction: $\quad 4e^- + O_2 + 2H_2O \longrightarrow 4OH^-$

A cell of this type weighing about 500 pounds has been designed for space vehicles, but neither this nor any other type of fuel cell is practical enough for general use as a source of portable power. Current research on portable electrochemical power sources seems mainly focused on rechargeable storage batteries with high power-to-weight ratios.

Fuel cells are finding some use, however, as permanent power sources. For example, a power plant built in New York City contains stacks of hydrogen–oxygen fuel cells, which can be rapidly put on-line in response to fluctuating power demands. The hydrogen gas is obtained by decomposing the methane in natural gas. A plant of this type also has been constructed in Tokyo.

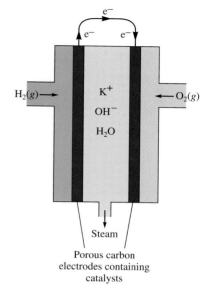

Figure 17.16

Schematic of the hydrogen–oxygen fuel cell.

17.6 *Corrosion*

Corrosion can be viewed as the process of returning metals to their natural state—the ores from which they were originally obtained. Corrosion involves oxidation of the metal. Since corroded metal often loses its structural integrity and attractiveness, this spontaneous process has great economic impact. Approximately one-fifth of the iron and steel produced annually is used to replace rusted metal.

Metals corrode because they oxidize easily. Table 17.1 shows that, with the exception of gold, those metals commonly used for structural and decorative purposes all have standard reduction potentials less positive than that of oxygen gas. When any of these half-reactions is reversed (to show oxidation of the metal) and combined with the reduction half-reaction for oxygen, the result is a positive $\mathscr{E}°$ value. Thus the oxidation of most metals by oxygen is spontaneous (although we cannot tell from the potential how fast it will occur).

In view of the large difference in reduction potentials between oxygen and most metals, it is surprising that the problem of corrosion does not completely prevent the use of metals in air. However, most metals develop a thin oxide coating, which tends to protect their internal atoms against further oxidation. The metal that best demonstrates this phenomenon is aluminum. With a reduction potential of -1.7 V, aluminum should be easily oxidized by O_2. According to the apparent thermodynamics of the reaction, an aluminum airplane could dissolve in a rainstorm. The fact that this very active metal can be used as a structural material is due to the formation of a thin, adherent layer of aluminum oxide (Al_2O_3), more properly represented as $Al_2(OH)_6$, which greatly inhibits further corrosion. The potential of the "passive," oxide-coated aluminum is -0.6 V, a value that causes it to behave much like a noble metal.

Iron also can form a protective oxide coating. This is not an infallible shield against corrosion, however; when steel is exposed to oxygen in moist air, the oxide that forms tends to scale off and expose new metal surfaces to corrosion.

The corrosion products of noble metals such as copper and silver are complex and affect the use of these metals as decorative materials. Under normal atmospheric

Some metals, such as copper, gold, silver, and platinum, are relatively difficult to oxidize. These are often called *noble metals*.

conditions, copper forms an external layer of greenish copper carbonate called *patina. Silver tarnish* is silver sulfide (Ag_2S), which in thin layers gives the silver surface a richer appearance. Gold, with a positive standard reduction potential of 1.50 V, significantly larger than that for oxygen (1.23 V), shows no appreciable corrosion in air.

Corrosion of Iron

Since steel is the main structural material for bridges, buildings, and automobiles, controlling its corrosion is extremely important. To do this, we must understand the corrosion mechanism. Instead of being a direct oxidation process as we might expect, the corrosion of iron is an electrochemical reaction, as shown in Fig. 17.17.

Steel has a nonuniform surface because the chemical composition is not completely homogeneous. Also, physical strains leave stress points in the metal. These nonuniformities cause areas where the iron is more easily oxidized (*anodic regions*) than it is at others (*cathodic regions*). In the anodic regions each iron atom gives up two electrons to form the Fe^{2+} ion:

$$Fe \longrightarrow Fe^{2+} + 2e^-$$

The electrons that are released flow through the steel, as they do through the wire of a galvanic cell, to a cathodic region, where they react with oxygen:

$$O_2 + 2H_2O + 4e^- \longrightarrow 4OH^-$$

The Fe^{2+} ions formed in the anodic regions travel to the cathodic regions through the moisture on the surface of the steel, just as ions travel through a salt bridge in a galvanic cell. In the cathodic regions Fe^{2+} ions react with oxygen to form rust, which is hydrated iron(III) oxide of variable composition:

$$4Fe^{2+}(aq) + O_2(g) + (4 + 2n)H_2O(l) \longrightarrow 2Fe_2O_3 \cdot nH_2O(s) + 8H^+(aq)$$
$$\text{Rust}$$

Because of the migration of ions and electrons, rust often forms at sites that are remote from those where the iron dissolved to form pits in the steel. The degree of

A rusty shipwreck.

Figure 17.17

The electrochemical corrosion of iron.

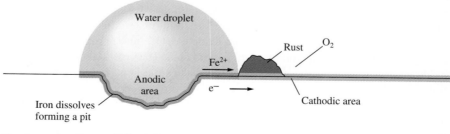

Water droplet

Rust O_2

Fe^{2+}

Anodic area

e^-

Iron dissolves forming a pit

Cathodic area

(Anode reaction: $Fe \longrightarrow Fe^{2+} + 2e^-$)   (Cathode reaction: $O_2 + 2H_2O + 4e^- \longrightarrow 4OH^-$)

CHEMICAL IMPACT

Paint That Stops Rust—Completely

TRADITIONALLY, PAINT HAS provided the most economical method for protecting steel against corrosion. However, as people who live in the Midwest know well, paint cannot prevent a car from rusting indefinitely. Eventually, flaws develop in the paint that allow the ravages of rusting to take place.

This situation may soon change. Chemists at Glidden Research Center in Ohio have developed a paint called Rustmaster Pro that worked so well to prevent rusting in its initial tests that the scientists did not believe their results. Steel coated with the new paint showed no signs of rusting after an astonishing 10,000 hours of exposure in a salt spray chamber at 38°C.

Rustmaster is a water-based polymer formulation that prevents corrosion in two different ways. First, the polymer layer that cures in air forms a barrier impenetrable to both oxygen and water vapor. Second, the chemicals in the coating react with the steel surface to produce an interlayer between the metal and the polymer coating. This interlayer is a complex mineral called *pyroaurite* that contains cations of the form $[M_{1-x}Z_x(OH)_2]^{x+}$, where M is a 2+ ion (Mg^{2+}, Fe^{2+}, Zn^{2+}, Co^{2+}, or Ni^{2+}), Z is a 3+ ion (Al^{3+}, Fe^{3+}, Mn^{3+}, Co^{3+}, or Ni^{3+}), and x is a number between 0 and 1. The anions in pyroaurite are typically CO_3^{2-}, Cl^-, and/or SO_4^{2-}.

This pyroaurite interlayer is the real secret of the paint's effectiveness. Because the corrosion of steel has an electrochemical mechanism, motion of ions must be possible between the cathodic and anodic areas on the surface of the steel for rusting to occur. However, the pyroaurite interlayer grows into the neighboring polymer layer, thus preventing this crucial movement of ions. In effect, this layer prevents corrosion in the same way that removing the salt bridge prevents current from flowing in a galvanic cell.

In addition to having an extraordinary corrosion-fighting ability, Rustmaster yields an unusually small quantity of volatile solvents as it dries. A typical paint can produce from 1 to 5 kg of volatiles per gallon; Rustmaster produces only 0.05 kg. This paint may signal a new era in corrosion prevention.

---

hydration of the iron oxide affects the color of the rust, which may vary from black to yellow to the familiar reddish brown.

The electrochemical nature of the rusting of iron explains the importance of moisture in the corrosion process. Moisture must be present to act as a kind of salt bridge between anodic and cathodic regions. Steel does not rust in dry air, a fact that explains why cars last much longer in the arid Southwest than in the relatively humid Midwest. Salt also accelerates rusting, a fact all too easily recognized by car owners in the colder parts of the United States, where salt is used on roads to melt snow and ice. The severity of rusting is greatly increased because the dissolved salt on the moist steel surface increases the conductivity of the aqueous solution formed there and thus accelerates the electrochemical corrosion process. Chloride ions also form very stable complex ions with Fe^{3+}, and this factor tends to encourage the dissolving of the iron, again accelerating the corrosion.

Prevention of Corrosion

Prevention of corrosion is an important way of conserving our natural resources of energy and metals. The primary means of protection is the application of a coating, most commonly paint or metal plating, to protect the metal from oxygen and moisture. Chromium and tin are often used to plate steel (see Section 17.8) because they oxidize to form a durable, effective oxide coating. Zinc, also used to coat steel in a

Refurbishing the Lady

THE RESTORATION OF the Statue of Liberty in New York harbor represents a fascinating blend of science, technology, and art. The statue consists of copper sheets attached to a framework of iron, which had become so weakened by corrosion during 100 years of exposure to the elements that the statue was in danger of collapsing.

Gustave Eiffel, who designed the ingenious support structure, knew from experience that if the copper touched the iron framework, the more active iron would corrode very rapidly. Why does this happen? It is apparent from the reduction potentials

$$Cu^{2+} + 2e^- \longrightarrow Cu$$
$$\mathscr{E}° = 0.34 \text{ V}$$
$$Fe^{2+} + 2e^- \longrightarrow Fe$$
$$\mathscr{E}° = -0.44 \text{ V}$$

that Cu^{2+} will spontaneously oxidize iron. However, as with many electrochemical processes, the situation is more complex than it first appears. Since we are talking about two metal strips touching each other, the question is: Where do the Cu^{2+} ions (the oxidizing agents) come from? In fact, research on this process suggests that the copper simply acts as a conductor for electrons and that the oxidizing agent is not Cu^{2+} at all but probably O_2 or oxides of N or S.

Whatever the mechanism, Eiffel attempted to combat the corrosion problem by inserting asbestos pads between the copper sheets and the frame. However, this idea did not work, probably because copper is such a good conductor that any contact between the two metals anywhere on the statue totally thwarted the effect of the insulation. In fact, the iron framework was found to be so corroded it had to be completely replaced with stainless steel, which is much more corrosion-resistant.

Stainless steel has its own problems, however. In being bent to achieve the intricate shapes needed, the steel bars often became brittle. Flexibility was restored by heating each bar to a very high temperature using a current of 30,000 amperes and then cooling the bar suddenly. (See Section 20.9, for more on the heat treatment of steel.) Unfortunately, this process also destroyed the resistance to corrosion of the stainless steel. That resistance had to be restored by soaking the bars in nitric acid, an oxidizing acid that re-forms the protective oxide coating removed by heating the stainless steel.

Another problem faced by the restorers was the removal of layers of coal tar and paint, which had been applied in vain attempts to protect the statue's interior. Although the iron could be cleaned by blasting with aluminum oxide powder, the more fragile copper sheets required a gentler treatment. The restorers discovered that liquid nitrogen (77 K) cracked the paint and caused it to peel off. The coal-tar layer under the paint was removed by blasting with baking soda ($NaHCO_3$), a substance sometimes used by museum curators for polishing dinosaur bones. Although this worked very well, it created another chemical problem: Where the baking soda seeped between the seams in the copper plates onto the exterior, the statue turned from green to light blue when it rained. After this phenomenon was observed for the first time, workers stationed on the exterior scaffolding immediately cleaned off any leaking $NaHCO_3$.

One of the most interesting aspects of the chemistry of the Statue of Liberty is the green patina on its surface. Copper metal exposed to the atmosphere changes from its bright reddish brown metallic luster first to an almost black color and then to the familiar green patina. The initial blackening is due mainly to the formation of copper oxide and copper sulfide. The green patina that then forms consists of thin layers of two types of basic copper sulfates: brochantite, $CuSO_4 \cdot 3Cu(OH)_2$, and antlerite, $CuSO_4 \cdot 2Cu(OH)_2$. Crystals of these compounds

The Statue of Liberty in New York harbor.

seem to be cemented onto the copper surface by organic molecules from the air.

In recent years, large areas of the statue's left side have been observed to darken as if the patina were being removed. Scientists speculated that this may be the result of acid rain that converts brochantite to the more soluble antlerite, which is then washed off by rainwater.

To make any new copper sheets look like the old ones, the restorers transplanted the patina from a weathered piece of copper to the new surface. Applying acetone, an organic solvent, to the weathered surface and scraping with an abrasive cloth caused tiny flakes of patina to fall off. These flakes, applied to the new copper, attached themselves permanently in one to three weeks of exposure to the atmosphere.

The restoration of the Statue of Liberty made use of the latest advances in chemistry as well as facts known to most general chemistry students. It's an example of the fascinating and varied problems faced by chemists in their profession.

Suggested Reading

Ivars Peterson. "Lessons Learned from a Lady," *Science News* 130 (1986): 392.

process called **galvanizing,** forms a mixed oxide-carbonate coating. Since zinc is a more active metal than iron, as the potentials for the oxidation half-reactions show:

$$Fe \longrightarrow Fe^{2+} + 2e^- \qquad -\mathscr{E}° = 0.44 \text{ V}$$
$$Zn \longrightarrow Zn^{2+} + 2e^- \qquad -\mathscr{E}° = 0.76 \text{ V}$$

any oxidation that occurs dissolves zinc rather than iron. Recall that the reaction with the most positive standard potential has the greatest thermodynamic tendency to occur. Thus zinc acts as a "sacrificial" coating on steel.

Alloying is also used to prevent corrosion. *Stainless steel* contains chromium and nickel, both of which form oxide coatings that change steel's reduction potential to one characteristic of the noble metals. In addition, a new technology is now being developed to create surface alloys. That is, instead of forming a metal alloy such as stainless steel, which has the same composition throughout, a cheaper carbon steel is treated by ion bombardment to produce a thin layer of stainless steel or other desirable alloy on the surface. In this process, a "plasma" or "ion gas" of the alloying ions is formed at high temperatures and is then directed onto the surface of the metal.

Cathodic protection is a method most often employed to protect steel in buried fuel tanks and pipelines. An active metal, such as magnesium, is connected by a wire to the pipeline or tank to be protected [Fig. 17.18(a)]. Because the magnesium is a better reducing agent than iron, electrons are furnished by the magnesium rather than by the iron, keeping the iron from being oxidized. As oxidation occurs, the magnesium anode dissolves, and so it must be replaced periodically. Ships' hulls are protected in a similar way by attaching bars of titanium metal to the steel hull [Fig. 17.18(b)]. In salt water the titanium acts as the anode and is oxidized instead of the steel hull (the cathode).

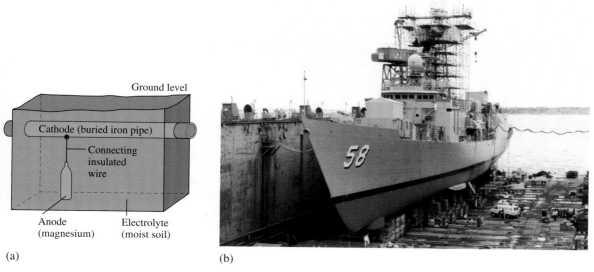

(a)   (b)

Figure 17.18

(a) Cathodic protection of an underground pipe. (b) Cathodic protection is also used to prevent corrosion of the hulls of ships, such as this one belonging to the U.S. Navy.

17.7 *Electrolysis*

An electrolytic cell uses electrical energy to produce a chemical change that would otherwise not occur spontaneously.

A galvanic cell produces current when an oxidation–reduction reaction proceeds spontaneously. A similar apparatus, an **electrolytic cell,** uses electrical energy to produce chemical change. The process of **electrolysis** involves *forcing a current through a cell to produce a chemical change for which the cell potential is negative;* that is, electrical work causes an otherwise nonspontaneous chemical reaction to occur. Electrolysis has great practical importance; for example, charging a battery, producing aluminum metal, and chrome plating an object are all done electrolytically.

To illustrate the difference between a galvanic cell and an electrolytic cell, consider the cell shown in Fig. 17.19(a) as it runs spontaneously to produce 1.10 V. In this *galvanic* cell the reaction at the anode is

$$Zn \longrightarrow Zn^{2+} + 2e^-$$

whereas at the cathode the reaction is

$$Cu^{2+} + 2e^- \longrightarrow Cu$$

Figure 17.19(b) shows an external power source forcing electrons through the cell in the *opposite* direction to that in (a). This requires an external potential greater than 1.10 V, which must be applied in opposition to the natural cell potential. This device is an *electrolytic cell.* Notice that since electron flow is opposite in the two cases, the anode and cathode are reversed between (a) and (b). Also, ion flow through the salt bridge is opposite in the two cells.

Now we will consider the stoichiometry of electrolytic processes, that is, *how much chemical change occurs with the flow of a given current for a specified time.* Suppose we wish to determine the mass of copper that is plated out when a current of 10.0 amps (an **ampere** [amp], abbreviated A, is *1 coulomb of charge per second*) is passed for 30.0 minutes through a solution containing Cu^{2+}. *Plating* means depositing the neutral metal on the electrode by reducing the metal ions in solution. In this case each Cu^{2+} ion requires two electrons to become an atom of copper metal:

$1\ A = 1\ C/s$

$$Cu^{2+}(aq) + 2e^- \longrightarrow Cu(s)$$

This reduction process will occur at the cathode of the electrolytic cell.

To solve this stoichiometry problem, we need the following steps:

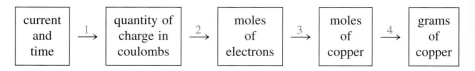

STEP 1

Since an amp is a coulomb of charge per second, we multiply the current by the time in seconds to obtain the total coulombs of charge passed into the Cu^{2+} solution at the cathode:

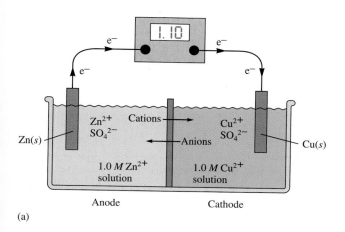

(a)

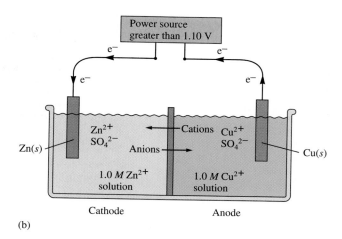

(b)

Figure 17.19

(a) A standard galvanic cell based on the spontaneous reaction

$$Zn + Cu^{2+} \longrightarrow Zn^{2+} + Cu$$

(b) A standard electrolytic cell. A power source forces the reaction $Cu + Zn^{2+} \rightarrow Cu^{2+} + Zn$ to occur.

$$Coulombs \ of \ charge \ = amps \times seconds = \frac{C}{s} \times s$$

$$= 10.0 \ \frac{C}{s} \times 30.0 \ min \times 60.0 \ \frac{s}{min}$$

$$= 1.80 \times 10^4 \ C$$

STEP 2

Since 1 mole of electrons carries a charge of 1 faraday, or 96,485 coulombs, we can calculate the number of moles of electrons required to carry 1.80×10^4 coulombs of charge:

$$1.80 \times 10^4 \ C \times \frac{1 \ mol \ e^-}{96,485 \ C} = 1.87 \times 10^{-1} \ mol \ e^-$$

This means that 0.187 mole of electrons flowed into the Cu^{2+} solution.

STEP 3

Each Cu^{2+} ion requires two electrons to become a copper atom. Thus each mole of electrons produces $\frac{1}{2}$ mole of copper metal:

$$1.87 \times 10^{-1} \ mol \ e^- \times \frac{1 \ mol \ Cu}{2 \ mol \ e^-} = 9.35 \times 10^{-2} \ mol \ Cu$$

STEP 4

We now know the moles of copper metal plated onto the cathode, and we can calculate the mass of copper formed:

$$9.35 \times 10^{-2} \ mol \ Cu \times \frac{63.546 \ g}{mol \ Cu} = 5.94 \ g \ Cu$$

Sample Exercise 17.9 Electroplating

Sample Exercise 17.9 describes only the half-cell of interest. There also must be an anode at which oxidation is occurring.

How long must a current of 5.00 A be applied to a solution of Ag^+ to produce 10.5 g silver metal?

Solution

In this case, we must use the steps given earlier in reverse:

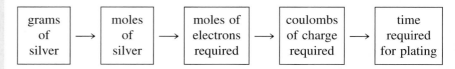

$$10.5 \text{ g Ag} \times \frac{1 \text{ mol Ag}}{107.868 \text{ g Ag}} = 9.73 \times 10^{-2} \text{ mol Ag}$$

Each Ag^+ ion requires one electron to become a silver atom:

$$Ag^+ + e^- \longrightarrow Ag$$

Thus 9.73×10^{-2} mol of electrons is required, and we can calculate the quantity of charge carried by these electrons:

$$9.73 \times 10^{-2} \text{ mol e}^- \times \frac{96,485 \text{ C}}{\text{mol e}^-} = 9.39 \times 10^3 \text{ C}$$

The 5.00 A (5.00 C/s) of current must produce 9.39×10^3 C of charge. Thus

$$\left(5.00\frac{C}{s}\right) \times (\text{time, in s}) = 9.39 \times 10^3 \text{ C}$$

$$\text{Time} = \frac{9.39 \times 10^3}{5.00}\text{s} = 1.88 \times 10^3 \text{ s} = 31.3 \text{ min}$$

See Exercises 17.79 through 17.82.

Electrolysis of Water

We have seen that hydrogen and oxygen combine spontaneously to form water and that the accompanying decrease in free energy can be used to run a fuel cell to produce electricity. The reverse process, which is of course nonspontaneous, can be forced by electrolysis:

Anode reaction:	$2H_2O \longrightarrow O_2 + 4H^+ + 4e^-$	$-\mathscr{E}° = -1.23$ V
Cathode reaction:	$4H_2O + 4e^- \longrightarrow 2H_2 + 4OH^-$	$\mathscr{E}° = -0.83$ V
Net reaction:	$6H_2O \longrightarrow 2H_2 + O_2 + 4(\underbrace{H^+ + OH^-}_{4H_2O})$	$\mathscr{E}° = -2.06$ V

or

$$2H_2O \longrightarrow 2H_2 + O_2$$

Note that these potentials assume an anode chamber with 1 M H^+ and a cathode chamber with 1 M OH^-. In pure water, where $[H^+] = [OH^-] = 10^{-7}$ M, the potential for the overall process is -1.23 V.

In practice, however, if platinum electrodes connected to a 6-V battery are dipped into pure water, no reaction is observed because pure water contains so few ions that only a negligible current can flow. However, addition of even a small amount of a soluble salt causes an immediate evolution of bubbles of hydrogen and oxygen, as illustrated in Fig. 17.20.

Video: Electrolysis of Water

Electrolysis of Mixtures of Ions

Suppose a solution in an electrolytic cell contains the ions Cu^{2+}, Ag^+, and Zn^{2+}. If the voltage is initially very low and is gradually turned up, in which order will the metals be plated out onto the cathode? This question can be answered by looking at the standard reduction potentials of these ions:

$$Ag^+ + e^- \longrightarrow Ag \qquad \mathscr{E}° = 0.80 \text{ V}$$
$$Cu^{2+} + 2e^- \longrightarrow Cu \qquad \mathscr{E}° = 0.34 \text{ V}$$
$$Zn^{2+} + 2e^- \longrightarrow Zn \qquad \mathscr{E}° = -0.76 \text{ V}$$

Remember that the more *positive* the $\mathscr{E}°$ value, the more the reaction has a tendency to proceed in the direction indicated. Of the three reactions listed, the reduction of Ag^+ occurs most easily, and the order of oxidizing ability is

$$Ag^+ > Cu^{2+} > Zn^{2+}$$

This means that silver will plate out first as the potential is increased, followed by copper, and finally zinc.

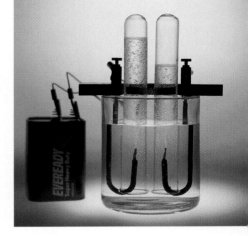

Figure 17.20
The electrolysis of water produces hydrogen gas at the cathode (on the right) and oxygen gas at the anode (on the left).

Sample Exercise 17.10 Relative Oxidizing Abilities

An acidic solution contains the ions Ce^{4+}, VO_2^+, and Fe^{3+}. Using the $\mathscr{E}°$ values listed in Table 17.1, give the order of oxidizing ability of these species and predict which one will be reduced at the cathode of an electrolytic cell at the lowest voltage.

Solution

The half-reactions and $\mathscr{E}°$ values are

$$Ce^{4+} + e^- \longrightarrow Ce^{3+} \qquad\qquad \mathscr{E}° = 1.70 \text{ V}$$
$$VO_2^+ + 2H^+ + e^- \longrightarrow VO^{2+} + H_2O \qquad \mathscr{E}° = 1.00 \text{ V}$$
$$Fe^{3+} + e^- \longrightarrow Fe^{2+} \qquad\qquad \mathscr{E}° = 0.77 \text{ V}$$

The order of oxidizing ability is therefore

$$Ce^{4+} > VO_2^+ > Fe^{3+}$$

The Ce^{4+} ion will be reduced at the lowest voltage in an electrolytic cell.

See Exercises 17.91 and 17.92.

CHEMICAL IMPACT

The Chemistry of Sunken Treasure

WHEN THE GALLEON *Atocha* was destroyed on a reef by a hurricane in 1622, it was bound for Spain carrying approximately 47 tons of copper, gold, and silver from the New World. The bulk of the treasure was silver bars and coins packed in wooden chests. When treasure hunter Mel Fisher salvaged the silver in 1985, corrosion and marine growth had transformed the shiny metal into something that looked like coral. Restoring the silver to its original condition required an understanding of the chemical changes that had occurred in 350 years of being submerged in the ocean. Much of this chemistry we have already considered at various places in this text.

As the wooden chests containing the silver decayed, the oxygen supply was depleted, favoring the growth of certain bacteria that use the sulfate ion rather than oxygen as an oxidizing agent to generate energy. As these bacteria consume sulfate ions, they release hydrogen sulfide gas that reacts with silver to form black silver sulfide:

$$2Ag(s) + H_2S(aq) \longrightarrow Ag_2S(s) + H_2(g)$$

Thus, over the years, the surface of the silver became covered with a tightly adhering layer of corrosion, which fortunately protected the silver underneath and thus prevented total conversion of the silver to silver sulfide.

Another change that took place as the wood decomposed was the formation of carbon dioxide. This shifted the equilibrium that is present in the ocean,

$$CO_2(aq) + H_2O(l) \rightleftharpoons HCO_3^-(aq) + H^+$$

to the right, producing higher concentrations of HCO_3^-. In turn, the HCO_3^- reacted with Ca^{2+} ions present in the seawater to form calcium carbonate:

$$Ca^{2+}(aq) + HCO_3^-(aq) \rightleftharpoons CaCO_3(s) + H^+(aq)$$

Calcium carbonate is the main component of limestone. Thus, over time, the corroded silver coins and bars became encased in limestone.

Both the limestone formation and the corrosion had to be dealt with. Since $CaCO_3$ contains the basic anion CO_3^{2-}, acid dissolves limestone:

$$2H^+(aq) + CaCO_3(s) \longrightarrow Ca^{2+}(aq) + CO_2(g) + H_2O(l)$$

Soaking the mass of coins in a buffered acidic bath for several hours allowed the individual pieces to be separated, and the black Ag_2S on the surfaces was revealed. An abrasive could not be used to remove this corrosion; it would have destroyed the details of the engraving—a very valuable feature of the coins to a historian or a collector—and it would have washed away some of the silver. Instead,

Silver coins and tankards salvaged from the wreck of the *Atocha.*

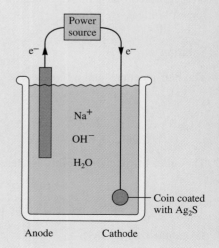

the corrosion reaction was reversed through electrolytic reduction. The coins were connected to the cathode of an electrolytic cell in a dilute sodium hydroxide solution as represented in the figure.

As electrons flow, the Ag^+ ions in the silver sulfide are reduced to silver metal:

$$Ag_2S + 2e^- \longrightarrow Ag + S^{2-}$$

As a by-product, bubbles of hydrogen gas from the reduction of water form on the surface of the coins:

$$2H_2O + 2e^- \longrightarrow H_2(g) + 2OH^-$$

The agitation caused by the bubbles loosens the flakes of metal sulfide and helps clean the coins.

These procedures have made it possible to restore the treasure to very nearly its condition when the *Atocha* sailed many years ago.

The principle described in this section is very useful, but it must be applied with some caution. For example, in the electrolysis of an aqueous solution of sodium chloride, we should be able to use $\mathscr{E}°$ values to predict the products. Of the major species in the solution (Na^+, Cl^-, and H_2O), only Cl^- and H_2O can be readily oxidized. The half-reactions (written as oxidization processes) are

$$2Cl^- \longrightarrow Cl_2 + 2e^- \qquad -\mathscr{E}° = -1.36 \text{ V}$$
$$2H_2O \longrightarrow O_2 + 4H^+ + 4e^- \qquad -\mathscr{E}° = -1.23 \text{ V}$$

Since water has the more positive potential, we would expect to see O_2 produced at the anode because it is easier (thermodynamically) to oxidize H_2O than Cl^-. Actually, this does not happen. As the voltage is increased in the cell, the Cl^- ion is the first to be oxidized. A much higher potential than expected is required to oxidize water. The voltage required in excess of the expected value (called the *overvoltage*) is much greater for the production of O_2 than for Cl_2, which explains why chlorine is produced first.

The causes of overvoltage are very complex. Basically, the phenomenon is caused by difficulties in transferring electrons from the species in the solution to the atoms on the electrode across the electrode–solution interface. Because of this situation, $\mathscr{E}°$ values must be used cautiously in predicting the actual order of oxidation or reduction of species in an electrolytic cell.

17.8 *Commercial Electrolytic Processes*

The chemistry of metals is characterized by their ability to donate electrons to form ions. Because metals are typically such good reducing agents, most are found in nature in *ores,* mixtures of ionic compounds often containing oxide, sulfide, and silicate anions. The noble metals, such as gold, silver, and platinum, are more difficult to oxidize and are often found as pure metals.

Production of Aluminum

Aluminum is one of the most abundant elements on earth, ranking third behind oxygen and silicon. Since aluminum is a very active metal, it is found in nature as its oxide in an ore called *bauxite* (named after Les Baux, France, where it was discovered in 1821). Production of aluminum metal from its ore proved to be more

Figure 17.21

Charles Martin Hall (1863–1914) was a student at Oberlin College in Ohio when he first became interested in aluminum. One of his professors commented that anyone who could manufacture aluminum cheaply would make a fortune, and Hall decided to give it a try. The 21-year-old Hall worked in a wooden shed near his house with an iron frying pan as a container, a blacksmith's forge as a heat source, and galvanic cells constructed from fruit jars. Using these crude galvanic cells, Hall found that he could produce aluminum by passing a current through a molten Al_2O_3/Na_3AlF_6 mixture. By a strange coincidence, Paul Heroult, a Frenchman who was born and died in the same years as Hall, made the same discovery at about the same time.

difficult than production of most other metals. In 1782 Lavoisier recognized aluminum to be a metal "whose affinity for oxygen is so strong that it cannot be overcome by any known reducing agent." As a result, pure aluminum metal remained unknown. Finally, in 1854 a process was found for producing metallic aluminum using sodium, but aluminum remained a very expensive rarity. In fact, it is said that Napoleon III served his most honored guests with aluminum forks and spoons, while the others had to settle for gold and silver utensils.

The breakthrough came in 1886 when two men, Charles M. Hall in the United States and Paul Heroult in France, almost simultaneously discovered a practical electrolytic process for producing aluminum (see Fig. 17.21). The key factor in the *Hall–Heroult process* is the use of molten cryolite (Na_3AlF_6) as the solvent for the aluminum oxide.

Electrolysis is possible only if ions can move to the electrodes. A common method for producing ion mobility is dissolving the substance to be electrolyzed in water. This is not possible in the case of aluminum because water is more easily reduced than Al^{3+}, as the following standard reduction potentials show:

$$Al^{3+} + 3e^- \longrightarrow Al \qquad \mathscr{E}° = -1.66 \text{ V}$$
$$2H_2O + 2e^- \longrightarrow H_2 + 2OH^- \qquad \mathscr{E}° = -0.83 \text{ V}$$

Thus aluminum metal cannot be plated out of an aqueous solution of Al^{3+}.

Ion mobility also can be produced by melting the salt. But the melting point of solid Al_2O_3 is much too high (2050°C) to allow practical electrolysis of the molten oxide. A mixture of Al_2O_3 and Na_3AlF_6, however, has a melting point of 1000°C, and the resulting molten mixture can be used to obtain aluminum metal electrolytically. Because of this discovery by Hall and Heroult, the price of aluminum plunged (see Table 17.3), and its use became economically feasible.

Bauxite is not pure aluminum oxide (called *alumina*); it also contains the oxides of iron, silicon, and titanium, and various silicate materials. To obtain the pure hydrated alumina ($Al_2O_3 \cdot nH_2O$), the crude bauxite is treated with aqueous sodium hydroxide. Being amphoteric, alumina dissolves in the basic solution:

$$Al_2O_3(s) + 2OH^-(aq) \longrightarrow 2AlO_2^-(aq) + H_2O(l)$$

Table 17.3 The Price of Aluminum over the Past Century

Date	Price of Aluminum ($/lb)*
1855	100,000
1885	100
1890	2
1895	0.50
1970	0.30
1980	0.80
1990	0.74

*Note the precipitous drop in price after the discovery of the Hall–Heroult process.

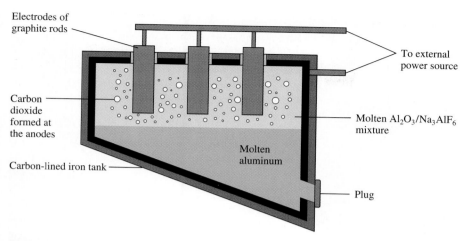

Electrodes of graphite rods

To external power source

Carbon dioxide formed at the anodes

Molten Al_2O_3/Na_3AlF_6 mixture

Carbon-lined iron tank

Molten aluminum

Plug

Figure 17.22

A schematic diagram of an electrolytic cell for producing aluminum by the Hall–Heroult process. Because molten aluminum is more dense than the mixture of molten cryolite and alumina, it settles to the bottom of the cell and is drawn off periodically. The graphite electrodes are gradually eaten away and must be replaced from time to time. The cell operates at a current flow of up to 250,000 A.

The other metal oxides, which are basic, remain as solids. The solution containing the aluminate ion (AlO_2^-) is separated from the sludge of the other oxides and is acidified with carbon dioxide gas, causing the hydrated alumina to reprecipitate:

$$2CO_2(g) + 2AlO_2^-(aq) + (n + 1)H_2O(l) \longrightarrow 2HCO_3^-(aq) + Al_2O_3 \cdot nH_2O(s)$$

The purified alumina is then mixed with cryolite and melted, and the aluminum ion is reduced to aluminum metal in an electrolytic cell of the type shown in Fig. 17.22. Because the electrolyte solution contains a large number of aluminum-containing ions, the chemistry is not completely clear. However, the alumina probably reacts with the cryolite anion as follows:

$$Al_2O_3 + 4AlF_6^{3-} \longrightarrow 3Al_2OF_6^{2-} + 6F^-$$

The electrode reactions are thought to be

Cathode reaction:
$$AlF_6^{3-} + 3e^- \longrightarrow Al + 6F^-$$

Anode reaction:
$$2Al_2OF_6^{2-} + 12F^- + C \longrightarrow 4AlF_6^{3-} + CO_2 + 4e^-$$

Molecular Model: AlF_6^{3-}

The overall cell reaction can be written as

$$2Al_2O_3 + 3C \longrightarrow 4Al + 3CO_2$$

The aluminum produced in this electrolytic process is 99.5% pure. To be useful as a structural material, aluminum is alloyed with metals such as zinc (used for trailer and aircraft construction) and manganese (used for cooking utensils, storage tanks, and highway signs). The production of aluminum consumes about 5% of all the electricity used in the United States.

Figure 17.23
Ultrapure copper sheets that serve as the cathodes are lowered between slabs of impure copper that serve as the anodes into a tank containing an aqueous solution of copper sulfate ($CuSO_4$). It takes about four weeks for the anodes to dissolve and for the pure copper to be deposited on the cathodes.

Electrorefining of Metals

Purification of metals is another important application of electrolysis. For example, impure copper from the chemical reduction of copper ore is cast into large slabs that serve as the anodes for electrolytic cells. Aqueous copper sulfate is the electrolyte, and thin sheets of ultrapure copper function as the cathodes (see Fig. 17.23).

The main reaction at the anode is

$$Cu \longrightarrow Cu^{2+} + 2e^-$$

Other metals such as iron and zinc are also oxidized from the impure anode:

$$Zn \longrightarrow Zn^{2+} + 2e^-$$
$$Fe \longrightarrow Fe^{2+} + 2e^-$$

Noble metal impurities in the anode are not oxidized at the voltage used; they fall to the bottom of the cell to form a sludge, which is processed to remove the valuable silver, gold, and platinum.

The Cu^{2+} ions from the solution are deposited onto the cathode

$$Cu^{2+} + 2e^- \longrightarrow Cu$$

producing copper that is 99.95% pure.

Metal Plating

Metals that readily corrode can often be protected by the application of a thin coating of a metal that resists corrosion. Examples are "tin" cans, which are actually steel cans with a thin coating of tin, and chrome-plated steel bumpers for automobiles.

An object can be plated by making it the cathode in a tank containing ions of the plating metal. The silver plating of a spoon is shown schematically in Fig. 17.24(b). In an actual plating process, the solution also contains ligands that form

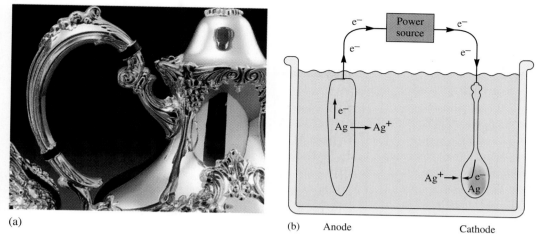

(a)   (b)   Anode   Cathode

Figure 17.24

(a) A silver-plated teapot. Silver plating is often used to beautify and protect cutlery and items of table service. (b) Schematic of the electroplating of a spoon. The item to be plated is the cathode, and the anode is a silver bar. Silver is plated out at the cathode: $Ag^+ + e^- \rightarrow Ag$. Note that a salt bridge is not needed here because Ag^+ ions are involved at both electrodes.

complexes with the silver ion. By lowering the concentration of Ag^+ in this way, a smooth, even coating of silver is obtained.

Electrolysis of Sodium Chloride

Sodium metal is mainly produced by the electrolysis of molten sodium chloride. Because solid NaCl has a rather high melting point (800°C), it is usually mixed with solid $CaCl_2$ to lower the melting point to about 600°C. The mixture is then electrolyzed in a **Downs cell,** as illustrated in Fig. 17.25, where the reactions are

Anode reaction: $\qquad 2Cl^- \longrightarrow Cl_2 + 2e^-$

Cathode reaction: $\qquad Na^+ + e^- \longrightarrow Na$

Addition of a nonvolatile solute lowers the melting point of the solvent, molten NaCl in this case.

At the temperatures in the Downs cell, the sodium is liquid and is drained off, then cooled, and cast into blocks. Because it is so reactive, sodium must be stored in an inert solvent, such as mineral oil, to prevent its oxidation.

Electrolysis of aqueous sodium chloride (brine) is an important industrial process for the production of chlorine and sodium hydroxide. In fact, this process is the second largest consumer of electricity in the United States, after the production of aluminum. Sodium is not produced in this process under normal circumstances because H_2O is more easily reduced than Na^+, as the standard reduction potentials show:

$$Na^+ + e^- \longrightarrow Na \qquad\qquad \mathscr{E}° = -2.71 \text{ V}$$
$$2H_2O + 2e^- \longrightarrow H_2 + 2OH^- \qquad \mathscr{E}° = -0.83 \text{ V}$$

Hydrogen, not sodium, is produced at the cathode.

For the reasons we discussed in Section 17.7, chlorine gas is produced at the anode. Thus the electrolysis of brine produces hydrogen and chlorine:

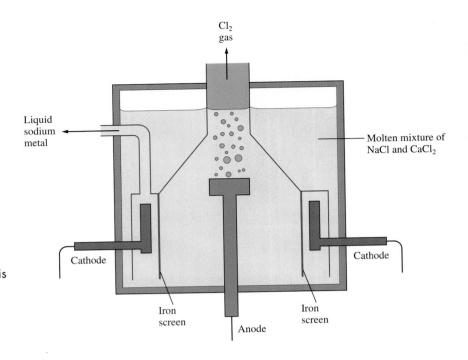

Figure 17.25
The Downs cell for the electrolysis of molten sodium chloride. The cell is designed so that the sodium and chlorine produced cannot come into contact with each other to re-form NaCl.

Anode reaction: $\qquad$ $2Cl^- \longrightarrow Cl_2 + 2e^-$

Cathode reaction: $\quad 2H_2O + 2e^- \longrightarrow H_2 + 2OH^-$

It leaves a solution containing dissolved NaOH and NaCl.

The contamination of the sodium hydroxide by NaCl can be virtually eliminated using a special **mercury cell** for electrolyzing brine (see Fig. 17.26). In this cell, mercury is the conductor at the cathode, and because hydrogen gas has an extremely high overvoltage with a mercury electrode, Na^+ is reduced instead of H_2O. The resulting sodium metal dissolves in the mercury, forming a liquid alloy, which is then pumped to a chamber where the dissolved sodium reacts with water to produce hydrogen:

$$2Na(s) + 2H_2O(l) \longrightarrow 2Na^+(aq) + 2OH^-(aq) + H_2(g)$$

Relatively pure solid NaOH can be recovered from the aqueous solution, and the regenerated mercury is then pumped back to the electrolysis cell. This process, called the **chlor–alkali process,** was the main method for producing chlorine and sodium hydroxide in the United States for many years. However, because of the environmental problems associated with the mercury cell, it has been largely displaced in the chlor–alkali industry by other technologies. In the United States, nearly 75 percent of the chlor–alkali production is now carried out in diaphragm cells. In a diaphragm cell the cathode and anode are separated by a diaphragm that allows passage of H_2O molecules, Na^+ ions, and to a limited extent, Cl^- ions. The diaphragm does not allow OH^- ions to pass through it. Thus the H_2 and OH^- formed at the cathode are kept separate from the Cl_2 formed at the anode. The major disadvantage of this process is that the aqueous effluent pumped from the cathode compartment contains a mixture of sodium hydroxide and unreacted sodium chloride, which must be separated if pure sodium hydroxide is a desired product.

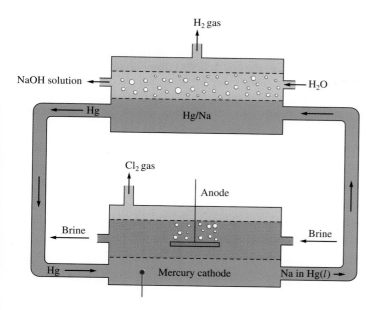

Figure 17.26

The mercury cell for production of chlorine and sodium hydroxide. The large overvoltage required to produce hydrogen at a mercury electrode means that Na$^+$ ions are reduced rather than water. The sodium formed dissolves in the liquid mercury and is pumped to a chamber where it reacts with water.

In the past 30 years, a new process has been developed in the chlor–alkali industry that employs a membrane to separate the anode and cathode compartments in brine electrolysis cells. The membrane is superior to a diaphragm because the membrane is impermeable to anions. Only cations can flow through the membrane. Because neither Cl$^-$ nor OH$^-$ ions can pass through the membrane separating the anode and cathode compartments, NaCl contamination of the NaOH formed at the cathode does not occur. Although membrane technology is now just becoming prominent in the United States, it is the dominant method for chlor–alkali production in Japan.

For Review

Summary

Electrochemistry is the study of the interchange of chemical and electrical energy that occurs through oxidation–reduction (redox) reactions, in which electrons are transferred from a reducing agent to an oxidizing agent. Oxidation is the loss of electrons, and reduction is the gain of electrons. It is useful to break a redox reaction into half-reactions, one involving oxidation and one involving reduction.

When a redox reaction occurs in solution, the electrons are transferred directly, and no useful work can be obtained from the chemical energy involved in the reaction. However, if the oxidizing agent is physically separated from the reducing agent so that the electrons must flow through a wire from one to the other, the chemical energy can produce useful work. A galvanic cell is a device in which chemical energy is transformed to electrical energy. The opposite process, where electrical

Key Terms

electrochemistry

Section 17.1
oxidation–reduction (redox)
  reaction
reducing agent
oxidizing agent
oxidation
reduction
half-reactions
salt bridge

energy is used to produce chemical change, is called electrolysis and is accomplished in an electrolytic cell by forcing current through the cell.

Oxidation occurs at the anode of a cell; reduction occurs at the cathode. The driving force on the electrons is called the cell potential ($\mathscr{E}_{cell}$). A galvanic cell always runs in the direction that gives a positive value for $\mathscr{E}_{cell}$. Standard reduction potentials are assigned to half-reactions written as reduction processes by arbitrarily assigning a potential of zero volts to the half-reaction $2H^+ + 2e^- \rightarrow H_2$ under standard conditions.

The unit of electrical potential is the volt (V), defined as a joule of work per coulomb of charge:

$$\mathscr{E} \ (V) = \frac{-\text{work (J)}}{\text{charge (C)}} = \frac{-w}{q}$$

where the sign for work is determined from the point of view of the system (cell). The maximum work can be calculated from the equation

$$-w_{max} = q\mathscr{E}_{max}$$

where $\mathscr{E}_{max}$ represents the cell potential when no current flows. Actual work is always less than the maximum possible work, since energy is wasted through frictional heating when a current flows through a wire.

For a process carried out at constant temperature and pressure, the change in free energy equals the maximum useful work obtainable from that process:

$$\Delta G = w_{max} = -q\mathscr{E}_{max} = -nF\mathscr{E}$$

where F (the faraday) is the charge of 1 mole of electrons (96,485 coulombs) and n is the number of moles of electrons transferred in the reaction.

A concentration cell is a galvanic cell in which both compartments have the same components but at different concentrations. The electrons flow in the direction that tends to equalize the concentrations.

The Nernst equation gives the relationship between the cell potential and the concentrations of the cell components:

$$\mathscr{E} = \mathscr{E}° - \frac{RT}{nF} \ln (Q)$$

When the cell is at 25°C, the Nernst equation can be written

$$\mathscr{E} = \mathscr{E}° - \frac{0.0591}{n} \log (Q)$$

When the cell is at equilibrium, $Q = K$ and $\mathscr{E}_{cell} = 0$. Thus the Nernst equation can be used to calculate the values of equilibrium constants for oxidation–reduction reactions.

A battery is a galvanic cell or group of cells connected in series, which serves as a source of direct current. The lead storage battery has a lead anode, a cathode of lead coated with PbO_2, and an electrolyte of sulfuric acid. Dry cell batteries do not have liquid electrolytes but have a moist paste of either solid manganese dioxide, carbon, and ammonium chloride (the acid version) or potassium hydroxide or sodium hydroxide (the alkaline version). A case of zinc acts as the anode, and a carbon rod acts as the electrode for the cathode reaction.

Fuel cells are galvanic cells in which the reactants are continuously supplied. For example, a hydrogen–oxygen fuel cell is based on the reaction of hydrogen and oxygen gases to form water.

Corrosion involves the oxidation of metals to form mainly oxides and sulfides. Some metals, such as aluminum, form a thin protective coating of oxide that inhibits further corrosion. The corrosion of iron is an electrochemical process; different parts of the iron surface form anodic and cathodic regions. The Fe^{2+} ions formed in the anodic regions migrate through the moisture on the iron surface to the cathodic regions, and the electrons flow through the metal to the cathodic regions, where they react with oxygen in the air. Corrosion can be prevented by coating the iron with paint or a layer of a metal such as chromium, tin, or zinc; by alloying; and by cathodic protection.

Aluminum is commercially produced by the electrolysis of a molten alumina–cryolite mixture in the Hall–Heroult process. Metals such as copper can be refined electrolytically. The chlor–alkali process is used to manufacture chlorine and sodium hydroxide by electrolysis.

In-Class Discussion Questions

These questions are designed to be considered by groups of students in class. Often these questions work well for introducing a particular topic in class.

1. Sketch a galvanic cell, and explain how it works. Look at Figs. 17.1 and 17.2. Explain what is occurring in each container and why the cell in Fig. 17.2 "works" but the one in Fig. 17.1 does not.

2. In making a specific galvanic cell, explain how one decides on the electrodes and the solutions to use in the cell.

3. You want to "plate out" nickel metal from a nickel nitrate solution onto a piece of metal inserted into the solution. Should you use copper or zinc? Explain.

4. A copper penny can be dissolved in nitric acid but not in hydrochloric acid. Using reduction potentials from the book, show why this is so. What are the products of the reaction? Newer pennies contain a mixture of zinc and copper. What happens to the zinc in the penny when placed in nitric acid? hydrochloric acid? Support your explanations with data from the book, and include balanced equations for all reactions.

5. Sketch a cell that forms iron metal from iron(II) while changing chromium metal to chromium(III). Calculate the voltage, show the electron flow, label the anode and cathode, and balance the overall cell equation.

6. Which of the following is the best reducing agent: F_2, H_2, Na, Na^+, F^-? Explain. Order as many of these species as possible from the best to the worst oxidizing agent. Why can't you order all of them? From Table 17.1 choose the species that is the best oxidizing agent. Choose the best reducing agent. Explain.

7. You are told that metal A is a better reducing agent than metal B. What, if anything, can be said about A^+ and B^+? Explain.

8. Explain the following relationships: ΔG and w, cell potential and w, cell potential and ΔG, cell potential and Q. Using these relationships, explain how you could make a cell in which both electrodes are the same metal and both solutions con-

tain the same compound, but at different concentrations. Why does such a cell run spontaneously?

9. Explain why cell potentials are not multiplied by the coefficients in the balanced redox equation. (Use the relationship between ΔG and cell potential to do this.)

10. What is the difference between $\mathscr{E}$ and $\mathscr{E}°$? When is $\mathscr{E}$ equal to zero? When is $\mathscr{E}°$ equal to zero? (Consider "regular" galvanic cells as well as concentration cells.)

11. Suppose you make a cell using silver and zinc electrodes. What happens to $\mathscr{E}$ as the concentration of Zn^{2+} is increased? as the concentration of Ag^+ is increased? What happens to $\mathscr{E}°$ in these cases?

12. Look up the reduction potential for Fe^{3+} to Fe^{2+}. Look up the reduction potential for Fe^{2+} to Fe. Finally, look up the reduction potential for Fe^{3+} to Fe. You should notice that adding the reduction potentials for the first two does not give the potential for the third. Why not? Show how you can use the first two potentials to calculate the third potential.

A blue question or exercise number indicates that the answer to that question or exercise appears at the back of this book and a solution appears in the *Solutions Guide*.

Review of Oxidation–Reduction Reactions

If you have trouble with these exercises, you should review Sections 4.9 and 4.10.

13. Define *oxidation* and *reduction* in terms of both change in oxidation number and electron loss or gain.

14. Assign oxidation numbers to all the atoms in each of the following.

a. HNO_3	**e.** $MgSO_4$	**i.** $Na_2C_2O_4$
b. $CuCl_2$	**f.** Ag	**j.** CO_2
c. O_2	**g.** $PbSO_4$	**k.** $(NH_4)_2Ce(SO_4)_3$
d. H_2O_2	**h.** PbO_2	**l.** Cr_2O_3

15. Specify which of the following equations represent oxidation–reduction reactions, and indicate the oxidizing agent, the reducing agent, the species being oxidized, and the species being reduced.
    a. $CH_4(g) + H_2O(g) \rightarrow CO(g) + 3H_2(g)$
    b. $2AgNO_3(aq) + Cu(s) \rightarrow Cu(NO_3)_2(aq) + 2Ag(s)$
    c. $Zn(s) + 2HCl(aq) \rightarrow ZnCl_2(aq) + H_2(g)$
    d. $2H^+(aq) + 2CrO_4^{2-}(aq) \rightarrow Cr_2O_7^{2-}(aq) + H_2O(l)$

16. Balance each of the following equations by the half-reaction method for the pH conditions specified.
    a. $Cr(s) + NO_3^-(aq) \rightarrow Cr^{3+}(aq) + NO(g)$ (acidic)
    b. $Al(s) + MnO_4^-(aq) \rightarrow Al^{3+}(aq) + Mn^{2+}(aq)$ (acidic)
    c. $CH_3OH(aq) + Ce^{4+}(aq) \rightarrow CO_2(aq) + Ce^{3+}(aq)$
    (acidic)
    d. $PO_3^{3-}(aq) + MnO_4^-(aq) \rightarrow PO_4^{3-}(aq) + MnO_2(s)$
    (basic)
    e. $Mg(s) + OCl^-(aq) \rightarrow Mg(OH)_2(s) + Cl^-(aq)$ (basic)
    f. $H_2CO(aq) + Ag(NH_3)_2^+(aq)$
    $\rightarrow HCO_3^-(aq) + Ag(s) + NH_3(aq)$ (basic)

Questions

17. Explain the difference between a galvanic and an electrolytic cell.

18. Why is it necessary to use a salt bridge or a porous disk in a galvanic cell?

19. Define the following.
    a. cathode
    c. oxidation half-reaction
    b. anode
    d. reduction half-reaction

20. Describe each of the following.
    a. purification of a metal by electrolysis
    b. cathodic protection

21. What happens to $\mathcal{E}_{cell}$ as a battery discharges? Does a battery represent a system at equilibrium? Explain. What is $\mathcal{E}_{cell}$ when a battery reaches equilibrium?

22. Why isn't the value of the cell potential multiplied by the same integer used to multiply a half-reaction in balancing the equation for a cell reaction?

23. How do fuel cells and batteries differ?

24. Explain how moisture and salt can increase the severity of corrosion. Give three methods by which metals are protected against corrosion.

Exercises

In this section similar exercises are paired.

Galvanic Cells, Cell Potentials, Standard Reduction Potentials, and Free Energy

25. Sketch the galvanic cells based on the following overall reactions. Show the direction of electron flow and identify the cathode and anode. Give the overall balanced reaction. As-

sume that all concentrations are 1.0 M and that all partial pressures are 1.0 atm.
    a. $Cr^{3+}(aq) + Cl_2(g) \rightleftharpoons Cr_2O_7^{2-}(aq) + Cl^-(aq)$
    b. $Cu^{2+}(aq) + Mg(s) \rightleftharpoons Mg^{2+}(aq) + Cu(s)$

26. Sketch the galvanic cells based on the following overall reactions. Show the direction of electron flow, the direction of ion migration through the salt bridge, and identify the cathode and anode. Give the overall balanced reaction. Assume that all concentrations are 1.0 M and that all partial pressures are 1.0 atm.
    a. $IO_3^-(aq) + Fe^{2+}(aq) \rightleftharpoons Fe^{3+}(aq) + I_2(aq)$
    b. $Zn(s) + Ag^+(aq) \rightleftharpoons Zn^{2+}(aq) + Ag(s)$

27. Calculate $\mathcal{E}°$ values for the galvanic cells in Exercise 25.

28. Calculate $\mathcal{E}°$ values for the galvanic cells in Exercise 26.

29. Sketch the galvanic cells based on the following half-reactions. Show the direction of electron flow, show the direction of ion migration through the salt bridge, and identify the cathode and anode. Give the overall balanced reaction, and determine $\mathcal{E}°$ for the galvanic cells. Assume that all concentrations are 1.0 M and that all partial pressures are 1.0 atm.
    a. $Cl_2 + 2e^- \rightarrow 2Cl^-$ $\mathcal{E}° = 1.36$ V
       $Br_2 + 2e^- \rightarrow 2Br^-$ $\mathcal{E}° = 1.09$ V
    b. $MnO_4^- + 8H^+ + 5e^- \rightarrow Mn^{2+} + 4H_2O$ $\mathcal{E}° = 1.51$ V
       $IO_4^- + 2H^+ + 2e^- \rightarrow IO_3^- + H_2O$ $\mathcal{E}° = 1.60$ V

30. Sketch the galvanic cells based on the following half-reactions. Show the direction of electron flow, show the direction of ion migration through the salt bridge, and identify the cathode and anode. Give the overall balanced reaction, and determine $\mathcal{E}°$ for the galvanic cells. Assume that all concentrations are 1.0 M and that all partial pressures are 1.0 atm.
    a. $H_2O_2 + 2H^+ + 2e^- \rightarrow 2H_2O$ $\mathcal{E}° = 1.78$ V
       $O_2 + 2H^+ + 2e^- \rightarrow H_2O_2$ $\mathcal{E}° = 0.68$ V
    b. $Mn^{2+} + 2e^- \rightarrow Mn$ $\mathcal{E}° = -1.18$ V
       $Fe^{3+} + 3e^- \rightarrow Fe$ $\mathcal{E}° = -0.036$ V

31. Give the standard line notation for each cell in Exercises 25 and 29.

32. Give the standard line notation for each cell in Exercises 26 and 30.

33. Give the balanced cell reaction and determine $\mathcal{E}°$ for the galvanic cells based on the following half-reactions. Standard reduction potentials are found in Table 17.1.
    a. $Cu^{2+} + e^- \rightarrow Cu^+$
       $Au^{3+} + 3e^- \rightarrow Au$
    b. $Cd^{2+} + 2e^- \rightarrow Cd$
       $VO_2^+ + 2H^+ + e^- \rightarrow VO^{2+} + H_2O$

34. Give the balanced cell reaction and determine $\mathcal{E}°$ for the galvanic cells based on the following half-reactions. Standard reduction potentials are found in Table 17.1.
    a. $Cr_2O_7^{2-} + 14H^+ + 6e^- \rightarrow 2Cr^{3+} + 7H_2O$
       $H_2O_2 + 2H^+ + 2e^- \rightarrow 2H_2O$
    b. $2H^+ + 2e^- \rightarrow H_2$
       $Al^{3+} + 3e^- \rightarrow Al$

35. Calculate $\mathscr{E}°$ values for the following cells. Which reactions are spontaneous as written (under standard conditions)? Balance the reactions that are not already balanced. Standard reduction potentials are found in Table 17.1.
  a. $2Ag^+(aq) + Cu(s) \rightleftharpoons Cu^{2+}(aq) + 2Ag(s)$
  b. $Zn^{2+}(aq) + Ni(s) \rightleftharpoons Ni^{2+}(aq) + Zn(s)$

36. Calculate $\mathscr{E}°$ values for the following cells. Which reactions are spontaneous as written (under standard conditions)? Balance the reactions. Standard reduction potentials are found in Table 17.1.
  a. $MnO_4^-(aq) + I^-(aq) \rightleftharpoons I_2(aq) + Mn^{2+}(aq)$
  b. $MnO_4^-(aq) + F^-(aq) \rightleftharpoons F_2(g) + Mn^{2+}(aq)$

37. Calculate $\Delta G°$ at 25°C for the reactions in Exercises 25 and 29.

38. Calculate $\Delta G°$ at 25°C for the reactions in Exercises 26 and 30.

39. Chlorine dioxide (ClO_2), which is produced by the reaction

$$2NaClO_2(aq) + Cl_2(g) \rightarrow 2ClO_2(g) + 2NaCl(aq)$$

has been tested as a disinfectant for municipal water treatment. Using data from Table 17.1, calculate $\mathscr{E}°$ and $\Delta G°$ at 25°C for the production of ClO_2.

40. The amount of manganese in steel is determined by changing it to permanganate ion. The steel is first dissolved in nitric acid, producing Mn^{2+} ions. These ions are then oxidized to the deeply colored MnO_4^- ions by periodate ion (IO_4^-) in acid solution.
  a. Complete and balance an equation describing each of the above reactions.
  b. Calculate $\mathscr{E}°$ and $\Delta G°$ at 25°C for each reaction.

41. Calculate the maximum amount of work that can be obtained from the galvanic cells at standard conditions in Exercise 33.

42. Calculate the maximum amount of work that can be obtained from the galvanic cells at standard conditions in Exercise 34.

43. Estimate $\mathscr{E}°$ for the half-reaction

$$2H_2O + 2e^- \rightarrow H_2 + 2OH^-$$

given the following values of $\Delta G_f°$:

$$H_2O(l) = -237 \text{ kJ/mol}$$
$$H_2(g) = 0.0$$
$$OH^-(aq) = -157 \text{ kJ/mol}$$
$$e^- = 0.0$$

Compare this value of $\mathscr{E}°$ with the value of $\mathscr{E}°$ given in Table 17.1.

44. Calculate $\mathscr{E}°$ for the reaction

$$CH_3OH(l) + \tfrac{3}{2}O_2(g) \longrightarrow CO_2(g) + 2H_2O(l)$$

using values of $\Delta G_f°$ in Appendix 4.

45. The equation $\Delta G° = -nF\mathscr{E}°$ also can be applied to half-reactions. For the half-reaction

$$Ag^+ + e^- \longrightarrow Ag \qquad \mathscr{E}° = 0.80 \text{ V}$$

calculate the value of $\Delta G_f°$ for $Ag^+(aq)$. ($\Delta G_f°$ for $e^- = 0$.)

46. Use standard reduction potentials to estimate $\Delta G_f°$ for $Fe^{2+}(aq)$ and $Fe^{3+}(aq)$. ($\Delta G_f°$ for $e^- = 0$.)

47. Using data from Table 17.1, place the following in order of increasing strength as oxidizing agents (all under standard conditions).

$$Cd^{2+}, \quad IO_3^-, \quad K^+, \quad H_2O, \quad AuCl_4^-, \quad I_2$$

48. Using data from Table 17.1, place the following in order of increasing strength as reducing agents (all under standard conditions).

$$Cr^{3+}, \quad H_2, \quad Zn, \quad Li, \quad F^-, \quad Fe^{2+}$$

49. Answer the following questions using data from Table 17.1 (all under standard conditions).
  a. Is $H^+(aq)$ capable of oxidizing $Cu(s)$ to $Cu^{2+}(aq)$?
  b. Is $H^+(aq)$ capable of oxidizing $Mg(s)$?
  c. Is $Fe^{3+}(aq)$ capable of oxidizing $I^-(aq)$?
  d. Is $Fe^{3+}(aq)$ capable of oxidizing $Br^-(aq)$?

50. Answer the following questions using data from Table 17.1 (all under standard conditions).
  a. Is $H_2(g)$ capable of reducing $Ag^+(aq)$?
  b. Is $H_2(g)$ capable of reducing $Ni^{2+}(aq)$?
  c. Is $Fe^{2+}(aq)$ capable of reducing $VO_2^+(aq)$?
  d. Is $Fe^{2+}(aq)$ capable of reducing $Cr^{3+}(aq)$ to $Cr^{2+}(aq)$?

51. Consider only the species (at standard conditions)

$$Na^+, \quad Cl^-, \quad Ag^+, \quad Ag, \quad Zn^{2+}, \quad Zn, \quad Pb$$

in answering the following questions. Give reasons for your answers. (Use data from Table 17.1.)
  a. Which is the strongest oxidizing agent?
  b. Which is the strongest reducing agent?
  c. Which species can be oxidized by $SO_4^{2-}(aq)$ in acid?
  d. Which species can be reduced by $Al(s)$?

52. Consider only the species (at standard conditions)

$$Ce^{4+}, \quad Ce^{3+}, \quad Fe^{2+}, \quad Fe^{3+}, \quad Fe, \quad Mg^{2+}, \quad Mg, \quad Ni^{2+}, \quad Sn$$

in answering the following questions. Give reasons for your answers. (Use data from Table 17.1.)
  a. Which is the strongest oxidizing agent?
  b. Which is the strongest reducing agent?
  c. Will iron dissolve in a 1.0 M solution of Ce^{4+}?
  d. Which of the species can be oxidized by $H^+(aq)$?
  e. Which of the species can be reduced by $H_2(g)$?

53. Use the table of standard reduction potentials (Table 17.1) to pick a reagent that is capable of each of the following oxidations (under standard conditions in acidic solution).

a. Oxidize Br^- to Br_2 but not oxidize Cl^- to Cl_2

b. Oxidize Mn to Mn^{2+} but not oxidize Ni to Ni^{2+}

54. Use the table of standard reduction potentials (Table 17.1) to pick a reagent that is capable of each of the following reductions (under standard conditions in acidic solution).

a. Reduce Cu^{2+} to Cu but not reduce Cu^{2+} to Cu^+.

b. Reduce Br_2 to Br^- but not reduce I_2 to I^-.

The Nernst Equation

55. A galvanic cell is based on the following half-reactions at 25°C:

$$Ag^+ + e^- \longrightarrow Ag$$
$$H_2O_2 + 2H^+ + 2e^- \longrightarrow 2H_2O$$

Predict whether $\mathscr{E}_{cell}$ is larger or smaller than $\mathscr{E}^\circ_{cell}$ for the following cases.

a. $[Ag^+] = 1.0\ M$, $[H_2O_2] = 2.0\ M$, $[H^+] = 2.0\ M$

b. $[Ag^+] = 2.0\ M$, $[H_2O_2] = 1.0\ M$, $[H^+] = 1.0 \times 10^{-7}\ M$

56. Consider the concentration cell in Fig. 17.10. If the Fe^{2+} concentration in the right compartment is changed from 0.1 M to $1 \times 10^{-7}\ M$ Fe^{2+}, predict the direction of electron flow, and designate the anode and cathode compartments.

57. Calculate $\mathscr{E}_{cell}$ for the galvanic cells in Exercise 55.

58. Calculate $\mathscr{E}_{cell}$ for the concentration cell described in Exercise 56. (Assume $T = 25°C$.)

59. Consider the concentration cell shown below. Calculate the cell potential at 25°C when the concentration of Ag^+ in the compartment on the right is the following.

a. 1.0 M

b. 2.0 M

c. 0.10 M

d. $4.0 \times 10^{-5}\ M$

e. Calculate the potential when both solutions are 0.10 M in Ag^+.

For each case, also identify the cathode, the anode, and the direction in which electrons flow.

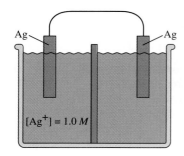

60. Consider a concentration cell similar to the one shown in Exercise 59, except that both electrodes are made of Ni and in the left-hand compartment $[Ni^{2+}] = 1.0\ M$. Calculate

the cell potential at 25°C when the concentration of Ni^{2+} in the compartment on the right has each of the following values.

a. 1.0 M

b. 2.0 M

c. 0.10 M

d. $4.0 \times 10^{-5}\ M$

e. Calculate the potential when both solutions are 2.5 M in Ni^{2+}.

For each case, also identify the cathode, anode, and the direction in which electrons flow.

61. Can permanganate ion oxidize Fe^{2+} to Fe^{3+} at 25°C under the following conditions?

$$[Mn^{2+}] = 1 \times 10^{-6}\ M$$
$$[MnO_4^-] = 0.01\ M$$
$$[Fe^{2+}] = 1 \times 10^{-3}\ M$$
$$[Fe^{3+}] = 1 \times 10^{-6}\ M$$
$$pH = 4.0$$

62. The overall reaction in the lead storage battery is

$$Pb(s) + PbO_2(s) + 2H^+(aq) + 2HSO_4^-(aq)$$
$$\longrightarrow 2PbSO_4(s) + 2H_2O(l)$$

Calculate $\mathscr{E}$ at 25°C for this battery when $[H_2SO_4] = 4.5\ M$, that is, $[H^+] = [HSO_4^-] = 4.5\ M$. At 25°C, $\mathscr{E}^\circ = 2.04$ V for the lead storage battery.

63. Consider the cell described below:

$$Zn\,|\,Zn^{2+}(1.00\ M)\,||\,Cu^{2+}(1.00\ M)\,|\,Cu$$

Calculate the cell potential after the reaction has operated long enough for the $[Zn^{2+}]$ to have changed by 0.20 mol/L. (Assume $T = 25°C$.)

64. Consider the cell described below:

$$Al\,|\,Al^{3+}\,(1.00\ M)\,||\,Pb^{2+}\,(1.00\ M)\,|\,Pb$$

Calculate the cell potential after the reaction has operated long enough for the $[Al^{3+}]$ to have changed by 0.60 mol/L. (Assume $T = 25°C$.)

65. An electrochemical cell consists of a standard hydrogen electrode and a copper metal electrode.

a. What is the potential of the cell at 25°C if the copper electrode is placed in a solution in which $[Cu^{2+}] = 2.5 \times 10^{-4}\ M$?

b. The copper electrode is placed in a solution of unknown $[Cu^{2+}]$. The measured potential at 25°C is 0.195 V. What is $[Cu^{2+}]$? (Assume Cu^{2+} is reduced.)

66. An electrochemical cell consists of a nickel metal electrode immersed in a solution with $[Ni^{2+}] = 1.0\ M$ separated by a porous disk from an aluminum metal electrode.

a. What is the potential of this cell at 25°C if the aluminum electrode is placed in a solution in which $[Al^{3+}] = 7.2 \times 10^{-3}\ M$?

b. When the aluminum electrode is placed in a certain solution in which $[Al^{3+}]$ is unknown, the measured cell potential at 25°C is 1.62 V. Calculate $[Al^{3+}]$ in the unknown solution. (Assume Al is oxidized.)

67. An electrochemical cell consists of a standard hydrogen electrode and a copper metal electrode. If the copper electrode is placed in a solution of 0.10 M NaOH that is saturated with $Cu(OH)_2$, what is the cell potential at 25°C? (For $Cu(OH)_2$, $K_{sp} = 1.6 \times 10^{-19}$.)

68. An electrochemical cell consists of a nickel metal electrode immersed in a solution with $[Ni^{2+}] = 1.0\ M$ separated by a porous disk from an aluminum metal electrode immersed in a solution with $[Al^{3+}] = 1.0\ M$. Sodium hydroxide is added to the aluminum compartment causing $Al(OH)_3(s)$ to precipitate. After precipitation of $Al(OH)_3$ has ceased, the concentration of OH^- is $1.0 \times 10^{-4}\ M$ and the measured cell potential is 1.82 V. Calculate the K_{sp} value for $Al(OH)_3$.

$$Al(OH)_3(s) \rightleftharpoons Al^{3+}(aq) + 3OH^-(aq) \quad K_{sp} = ?$$

69. Calculate K at 25°C for the reactions in Exercises 25 and 29.
70. Calculate K at 25°C for the reactions in Exercises 26 and 30.

71. Under standard conditions, what reaction occurs, if any, when each of the following operations are performed?
a. Crystals of I_2 are added to a solution of NaCl.
b. Cl_2 gas is bubbled into a solution of NaI.
c. A silver wire is placed in a solution of $CuCl_2$.
d. An acidic solution of $FeSO_4$ is exposed to air.
For the reactions that occur, write a balanced equation and calculate $\mathscr{E}°$, $\Delta G°$, and K at 25°C.

72. A disproportionation reaction involves a substance that acts as both an oxidizing and reducing agent, producing higher and lower oxidation states of the same element in the products. Which of the following disproportionation reactions are spontaneous under standard conditions? Calculate $\Delta G°$ and K at 25°C for those reactions that are spontaneous under standard conditions.
a. $2Cu^+(aq) \rightarrow Cu^{2+}(aq) + Cu(s)$
b. $3Fe^{2+}(aq) \rightarrow 2Fe^{3+}(aq) + Fe(s)$
c. $HClO_2(aq) \rightarrow ClO_3^-(aq) + HClO(aq)$ (unbalanced)
Use the half-reactions

$$ClO_3^- + 3H^+ + 2e^- \longrightarrow HClO_2 + H_2O$$
$$\mathscr{E}° = 1.21\text{ V}$$

$$HClO_2 + 2H^+ + 2e^- \longrightarrow HClO + H_2O$$
$$\mathscr{E}° = 1.65\text{ V}$$

73. Consider the galvanic cell based on the following half-reactions:

$$Zn^{2+} + 2e^- \longrightarrow Zn \quad \mathscr{E}° = -0.76\text{ V}$$
$$Fe^{2+} + 2e^- \longrightarrow Fe \quad \mathscr{E}° = -0.44\text{ V}$$

a. Determine the overall cell reaction and calculate $\mathscr{E}°_{cell}$.
b. Calculate $\Delta G°$ and K for the cell reaction at 25°C.
c. Calculate $\mathscr{E}_{cell}$ at 25°C when $[Zn^{2+}] = 0.10\ M$ and $[Fe^{2+}] = 1.0 \times 10^{-5}\ M$.

74. Consider the galvanic cell based on the following half-reactions:

$$Au^{3+} + 3e^- \longrightarrow Au \quad \mathscr{E}° = 1.50\text{ V}$$
$$Tl^+ + e^- \longrightarrow Tl \quad \mathscr{E}° = -0.34\text{ V}$$

a. Determine the overall cell reaction and calculate $\mathscr{E}°_{cell}$.
b. Calculate $\Delta G°$ and K for the cell reaction at 25°C.
c. Calculate $\mathscr{E}_{cell}$ at 25°C when $[Au^{3+}] = 1.0 \times 10^{-2}\ M$ and $[Tl^+] = 1.0 \times 10^{-4}\ M$.

75. Cadmium sulfide (CdS) is used in some semiconductor applications. Calculate the value of the solubility product (K_{sp}) for CdS given the following standard reduction potentials:

$$CdS + 2e^- \longrightarrow Cd + S^{2-} \quad \mathscr{E}° = -1.21\text{ V}$$
$$Cd^{2+} + 2e^- \longrightarrow Cd \quad \mathscr{E}° = -0.402\text{ V}$$

76. For the following half-reaction, $\mathscr{E}° = -2.07$ V:

$$AlF_6^{3-} + 3e^- \longrightarrow Al + 6F^-$$

Using data from Table 17.1, calculate the equilibrium constant at 25°C for the reaction

$$Al^{3+}(aq) + 6F^-(aq) \rightleftharpoons AlF_6^{3-}(aq)$$

77. Calculate $\mathscr{E}°$ for the following half-reaction:

$$AgI(s) + e^- \longrightarrow Ag(s) + I^-$$

(*Hint:* Reference the K_{sp} value for AgI and the standard reduction potential for Ag^+.)

78. The solubility product for $CuI(s)$ is 1.1×10^{-12}. Calculate the value of $\mathscr{E}°$ for the half-reaction

$$CuI + e^- \longrightarrow Cu + I^-$$

Electrolysis

79. How long will it take to plate out each of the following with a current of 100.0 A?
a. 1.0 kg Al from aqueous Al^{3+}
b. 1.0 g Ni from aqueous Ni^{2+}
c. 5.0 mol Ag from aqueous Ag^+

80. The electrolysis of BiO^+ produces pure bismuth. How long would it take to produce 10.0 g of Bi by the electrolysis of a BiO^+ solution using a current of 25.0 A?

81. What mass of each of the following substances can be produced in 1.0 hour with a current of 15 A?

a. Co from aqueous Co^{2+}
b. Hf from aqueous Hf^{4+}
c. I_2 from aqueous KI
d. Cr from molten CrO_3

82. What mass of chromium metal can be produced in 1.00 h by the electrolysis of a $K_2Cr_2O_7$ solution using a current of 15.0 A?

83. Electrolysis of a molten metal chloride (MCl_3) using a current of 6.50 A for 1397 seconds deposits 1.41 g of the metal at the cathode. What is the metal?

84. It took 74.6 seconds for a 2.50-A current to plate 0.1086 g of a metal from a solution containing M^{2+} ions. What is the metal?

85. What volume of F_2 gas, at 25°C and 1.00 atm, is produced when molten KF is electrolyzed by a current of 10.0 A for 2.00 hours? What mass of potassium metal is produced? At which electrode does each reaction occur?

86. What volumes of $H_2(g)$ and $O_2(g)$ at STP are produced from the electrolysis of water by a current of 2.50 A in 15.0 minutes?

87. One of the few industrial-scale processes that produce organic compounds electrochemically is used by the Monsanto Company to produce 1,4-dicyanobutane. The reduction reaction is

$$2CH_2{=}CHCN + 2H^+ + 2e^- \longrightarrow NC{-}(CH_2)_4{-}CN$$

The $NC{-}(CH_2)_4{-}CN$ is then chemically reduced using hydrogen gas to $H_2N{-}(CH_2)_6{-}NH_2$, which is used in the production of nylon. What current must be used to produce 150. kg of $NC{-}(CH_2)_4{-}CN$ per hour?

88. A single Hall–Heroult cell (as shown in Fig. 17.22) produces about 1 ton of aluminum in 24 hours. What current must be used to accomplish this?

89. It took 2.30 minutes using a current of 2.00 A to plate out all the silver from 0.250 L of a solution containing Ag^+. What was the original concentration of Ag^+ in the solution?

90. A solution containing Pt^{4+} is electrolyzed with a current of 4.00 A. How long will it take to plate out 99% of the platinum in 0.50 L of a 0.010 M solution of Pt^{4+}?

91. A solution at 25°C contains 1.0 M Cd^{2+}, 1.0 M Ag^+, 1.0 M Au^{3+}, and 1.0 M Ni^{2+} in the cathode compartment of an electrolytic cell. Predict the order in which the metals will plate out as the voltage is gradually increased.

92. A solution at 25°C is 1.0 M in Cu^{2+} and 0.010 M in Ag^+. Which metal will be plated on the cathode first as the voltage is gradually increased when this solution is electrolyzed? (*Hint:* Use the Nernst equation to calculate $\mathscr{E}$ for each half-reaction.)

93. What reactions take place at the cathode and the anode when each of the following is electrolyzed?
a. molten $NiBr_2$
b. molten AlF_3
c. molten CrI_3

94. What reactions take place at the cathode and the anode when each of the following is electrolyzed? (Assume standard conditions.)
a. 1.0 M $NiBr_2$ solution
b. 1.0 M AlF_3 solution
c. 1.0 M CrI_3 solution

95. In the electrolysis of an aqueous solution of Na_2SO_4, what reactions occur at the anode and the cathode? (Assume standard conditions.)

	$\mathscr{E}°$
$S_2O_8^{2-} + 2e^- \longrightarrow 2SO_4^{2-}$	2.01 V
$O_2 + 4H^+ + 4e^- \longrightarrow 2H_2O$	1.23 V
$2H_2O + 2e^- \longrightarrow H_2 + 2OH^-$	-0.83 V
$Na^+ + e^- \longrightarrow Na$	-2.71 V

96. What reactions occur at the anode and the cathode when an acidic aqueous solution of $FeSO_4$ is electrolyzed? (Assume standard conditions.)

Additional Exercises

97. The saturated calomel electrode, abbreviated SCE, is often used as a reference electrode in making electrochemical measurements. The SCE is composed of mercury in contact with a saturated solution of calomel (Hg_2Cl_2). The electrolyte solution is saturated KCl. $\mathscr{E}_{SCE}$ is $+0.242$ V relative to the standard hydrogen electrode. Calculate the potential for each of the following galvanic cells containing a saturated calomel electrode and the given half-cell components at standard conditions. In each case, indicate whether the SCE is the cathode or the anode. Standard reduction potentials are found in Table 17.1.
a. $Cu^{2+} + 2e^- \longrightarrow Cu$
b. $Fe^{3+} + e^- \longrightarrow Fe^{2+}$
c. $AgCl + e^- \longrightarrow Ag + Cl^-$
d. $Al^{3+} + 3e^- \longrightarrow Al$
e. $Ni^{2+} + 2e^- \longrightarrow Ni$

98. Consider the following half-reactions:

$Pt^{2+} + 2e^- \longrightarrow Pt$	$\mathscr{E}° = 1.188$ V
$PtCl_4^{2-} + 2e^- \longrightarrow Pt + 4Cl^-$	$\mathscr{E}° = 0.755$ V
$NO_3^- + 4H^+ + 3e^- \longrightarrow NO + 2H_2O$	$\mathscr{E}° = 0.96$ V

Explain why platinum metal will dissolve in aqua regia (a mixture of hydrochloric and nitric acids) but not in either concentrated nitric or concentrated hydrochloric acid individually.

99. Consider the standard galvanic cell based on the following half-reactions

$$Cu^{2+} + 2e^- \longrightarrow Cu$$
$$Ag^+ + e^- \longrightarrow Ag$$

The electrodes in this cell are Ag(s) and Cu(s). Does the cell potential increase, decrease, or remain the same when the following changes occur to the standard cell?
a. $CuSO_4(s)$ is added to the copper half-cell compartment (assume no volume change).
b. $NH_3(aq)$ is added to the copper half-cell compartment. *Hint:* Cu^{2+} reacts with NH_3 to form $Cu(NH_3)_4^{2+}(aq)$.
c. NaCl(s) is added to the silver half-cell compartment. *Hint:* Ag^+ reacts with Cl^- to form AgCl(s).
d. Water is added to both half-cell compartments until the volume of solution is doubled.
e. The silver electrode is replaced with a platinum electrode.

$$Pt^{2+} + 2e^- \longrightarrow Pt \quad \mathscr{E}° = 1.19 \text{ V}$$

100. A standard galvanic cell is constructed so that the overall cell reaction is

$$2Al^{3+}(aq) + 3M(s) \longrightarrow 3M^{2+}(aq) + 2Al(s)$$

where M is an unknown metal. If $\Delta G° = -411$ kJ for the overall cell reaction, identify the metal used to construct the standard cell.

101. The black silver sulfide discoloration of silverware can be removed by heating the silver article in a sodium carbonate solution in an aluminum pan. The reaction is

$$3Ag_2S(s) + 2Al(s) \rightleftharpoons 6Ag(s) + 3S^{2-}(aq) + 2Al^{3+}(aq)$$

a. Using data in Appendix 4, calculate $\Delta G°$, K, and $\mathscr{E}°$ for the above reaction at 25°C. (For $Al^{3+}(aq)$, $\Delta G_f° = -480$ kJ/mol.)
b. Calculate the value of the standard reduction potential for the following half-reaction:

$$2e^- + Ag_2S(s) \longrightarrow 2Ag(s) + S^{2-}(aq)$$

102. In 1973 the wreckage of the Civil War ironclad USS *Monitor* was discovered near Cape Hatteras, North Carolina. (The *Monitor* and the CSS *Virginia* [formerly the USS *Merrimack*] fought the first battle between iron-armored ships.) In 1987 investigations were begun to see if the ship could be salvaged. It was reported in *Time* (June 22, 1987) that scientists were considering adding sacrificial anodes of zinc to the rapidly corroding metal hull of the *Monitor*. Describe how attaching zinc to the hull would protect the *Monitor* from further corrosion.

103. Will corrosion be a greater problem under acidic or basic conditions?

104. When aluminum foil is placed in hydrochloric acid, nothing happens for the first 30 seconds or so. This is followed by vigorous bubbling and the eventual disappearance of the foil. Explain these observations.

105. A patent attorney has asked for your advice concerning the merits of a patent application that describes a single aqueous galvanic cell capable of producing a 12-V potential. Comment.

106. The overall reaction and equilibrium constant value for a hydrogen–oxygen fuel cell at 298 K is

$$2H_2(g) + O_2(g) \longrightarrow 2H_2O(l) \quad K = 1.28 \times 10^{83}$$

a. Calculate $\mathscr{E}°$ and $\Delta G°$ at 298 K for the fuel cell reaction.
b. Predict the signs of $\Delta H°$ and $\Delta S°$ for the fuel cell reaction.
c. As temperature increases, does the maximum amount of work obtained from the fuel cell reaction increase, decrease, or remain the same? Explain.

107. What is the maximum work that can be obtained from a hydrogen–oxygen fuel cell at standard conditions that produces 1.00 kg of water at 25°C? Why do we say that this is the maximum work that can be obtained? What are the advantages and disadvantages in using fuel cells rather than the corresponding combustion reactions to produce electricity?

108. The overall reaction and standard cell potential at 25°C for the rechargeable nickel–cadmium alkaline battery is

$$Cd(s) + NiO_2(s) + 2H_2O(l) \longrightarrow Ni(OH)_2(s) + Cd(OH)_2(s)$$
$$\mathscr{E}° = 1.10 \text{ V}$$

For every mole of Cd consumed in the cell, what is the maximum useful work that can be obtained at standard conditions?

109. Use standard reduction potentials in Table 17.1 to explain why the ionic compound $AgCl_2$ is unstable.

110. In the electrolysis of a sodium chloride solution, what volume of $H_2(g)$ is produced in the same time it takes to produce 257 L of $Cl_2(g)$, with both volumes measured at 50.°C and 2.50 atm?

111. An aqueous solution of an unknown salt of ruthenium is electrolyzed by a current of 2.50 A passing for 50.0 minutes. If 2.618 g Ru is produced at the cathode, what is the charge on the ruthenium ions in solution?

112. It takes 15 kWh (kilowatthours) of electrical energy to produce 1.0 kg of aluminum metal from aluminum oxide by the Hall–Heroult process. Compare this to the amount of energy necessary to melt 1.0 kg of aluminum metal. Why is it economically feasible to recycle aluminum cans? (The enthalpy of fusion for aluminum metal is 10.7 kJ/mol [1 watt = 1 J/s].)

Challenge Problems

113. Combine the equations

$$\Delta G° = -nF\mathscr{E}° \quad \text{and} \quad \Delta G° = \Delta H° - T\Delta S°$$

to derive an expression for $\mathscr{E}°$ as a function of temperature. Describe how one can graphically determine $\Delta H°$ and $\Delta S°$

from measurements of $\mathscr{E}°$ at different temperatures, assuming that $\Delta H°$ and $\Delta S°$ do not depend on temperature. What property would you look for in designing a reference half-cell that would produce a potential relatively stable with respect to temperature?

114. The overall reaction in the lead storage battery is

$$Pb(s) + PbO_2(s) + 2H^+(aq) + 2HSO_4^-(aq)$$
$$\longrightarrow 2PbSO_4(s) + 2H_2O(l)$$

a. For the cell reaction $\Delta H° = -315.9$ kJ and $\Delta S° = 263.5$ J/K. Calculate $\mathscr{E}°$ at $-20.°C$. Assume $\Delta H°$ and $\Delta S°$ do not depend on temperature.

b. Calculate $\mathscr{E}$ at $-20.°C$ when $[HSO_4^-] = [H^+] = 4.5$ M.

c. Consider your answer to Exercise 62. Why does it seem that batteries fail more often on cold days than on warm days?

115. Consider a concentration cell that has both electrodes made of some metal M. Solution A in one compartment of the cell contains 1.0 M M^{2+}. Solution B in the other cell compartment has a volume of 1.00 L. At the beginning of the experiment, 0.0100 mol of $M(NO_3)_2$ and 0.0100 mol of Na_2SO_4 are dissolved in solution B (ignore volume changes), where the reaction

$$M^{2+}(aq) + SO_4^{2-}(aq) \rightleftharpoons MSO_4(s)$$

occurs. After precipitation of MSO_4 is complete, the cell potential is found to be 0.44 V at 25°C. Assuming that no other redox process occurs in the cell other than the concentration cell process, calculate the value of K_{sp} for MSO_4 at 25°C.

116. A zinc–copper battery is constructed as follows at 25°C:

$$Zn\,|\,Zn^{2+}(0.10\ M)\,||\,Cu^{2+}(2.50\ M)\,|\,Cu$$

The mass of each electrode is 200. g.

a. Calculate the cell potential when this battery is first connected.

b. Calculate the cell potential after 10.0 A of current has flowed for 10.0 h. (Assume each half-cell contains 1.00 L of solution.)

c. Calculate the mass of each electrode after 10.0 h.

d. How long can this battery deliver a current of 10.0 A before it goes dead?

117. A galvanic cell is based on the following half-reactions:

$$Fe^{2+} + 2e^- \longrightarrow Fe(s) \qquad \mathscr{E}° = -0.440\ V$$
$$2H^+ + 2e^- \longrightarrow H_2(g) \qquad \mathscr{E}° = 0.000\ V$$

where the iron compartment contains an iron electrode and $[Fe^{2+}] = 1.00 \times 10^{-3}\ M$ and the hydrogen compartment contains a platinum electrode, $P_{H_2} = 1.00$ atm, and a weak acid, HA, at an initial concentration of 1.00 M. If the observed cell potential is 0.333 V at 25°C, calculate the K_a value for the weak acid HA.

118. Consider a cell based on the following half-reactions:

$$Au^{3+} + 3e^- \longrightarrow Au \qquad \mathscr{E}° = 1.50\ V$$
$$Fe^{3+} + e^- \longrightarrow Fe^{2+} \qquad \mathscr{E}° = 0.77\ V$$

a. Draw this cell under standard conditions, labeling the anode, the cathode, the direction of electron flow, and the concentrations, as appropriate.

b. When enough NaCl(s) is added to the compartment containing gold to make the $[Cl^-] = 0.10$ M, the cell potential is observed to be 0.31 V. Assume that Au^{3+} is reduced and assume that the reaction in the compartment containing gold is

$$Au^{3+}(aq) + 4Cl^-(aq) \rightleftharpoons AuCl_4^-(aq)$$

Calculate the value of K for this reaction at 25°C.

119. The measurement of pH using a glass electrode obeys the Nernst equation. The typical response of a pH meter at 25.00°C is given by the equation

$$\mathscr{E}_{meas} = \mathscr{E}_{ref} + 0.05916\ pH$$

where $\mathscr{E}_{ref}$ contains the potential of the reference electrode and all other potentials that arise in the cell that are not related to the hydrogen ion concentration. Assume that $\mathscr{E}_{ref} = 0.250$ V and that $\mathscr{E}_{meas} = 0.480$ V.

a. What is the uncertainty in the values of pH and $[H^+]$ if the uncertainty in the measured potential is ± 1 mV (± 0.001 V)?

b. To what accuracy must the potential be measured for the uncertainty in pH to be ± 0.02 pH unit?

Marathon Problem*

This problem is designed to incorporate several concepts and techniques into one situation. Marathon Problems can be used in class by groups of students to help facilitate problem-solving skills.

120. The addition of aqueous ammonia to the cathode compartment of the cell described below reduces the cell potential. Likewise, addition of aqueous ammonia to the anode compartment increases the cell potential.

$$Zn(s)\,|\,Zn^{2+}(aq)\,||\,Cu^{2+}(aq)\,|\,Cu(s)$$

*This Marathon Problem was developed by James H. Burness, Penn State University, York Campus. Reprinted with permission from the *Journal of Chemical Education*, Vol. 68, No. 11, 1991, pp. 919–922; copyright © 1991. Division of Chemical Education, Inc.

Assume that $[Cu^{2+}(aq)]_0 = [Zn^{2+}(aq)]_0 = 0.10\ M$ and that both Cu^{2+} and Zn^{2+} form very stable complexes with ammonia (overall formation constants $> 10^{10}$), each with a coordination number of 4.

a. Show how to estimate the ratio of the overall formation constant for $[Zn(NH_3)_4]^{2+}$ to the overall formation constant for $[Cu(NH_3)_4]^{2+}$ if the cell potential is observed to be 0.96 V after adding equal amounts (assume a large excess) of 6 M NH_3 to each compartment (assume that $T = 298$ K).

b. Which of the two transition metal complexes is more thermodynamically stable? How much more stable is it than the other complex?

CHAPTER *18*

The Representative Elements: Groups 1A Through 4A

So far in this book we have covered the major principles and explored the most important models of chemistry. In particular, we have seen that the chemical properties of the elements can be explained very successfully by the quantum mechanical model of the atom. In fact, the most convincing evidence of that model's validity is its ability to relate the observed periodic properties of the elements to the number of valence electrons in their atoms.

We have learned many properties of the elements and their compounds, but we have not discussed in detail the relationship between the chemical properties of a particular element and its position on the periodic table. In this chapter and the next we will explore the chemical similarities and differences among the elements in the several groups of the periodic table and will try to interpret these data using the quantum mechanical model of the atom. In the process we will illustrate a great variety of chemical properties and further demonstrate the practical importance of chemistry.

Potassium reacts vigorously with water.

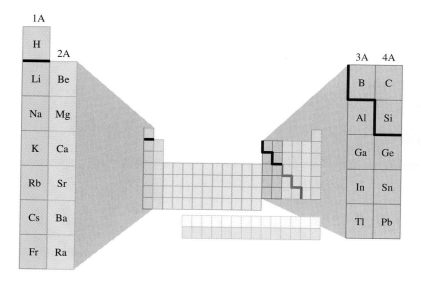

18.1   A Survey of the Representative Elements

The traditional form of the periodic table is shown in Fig. 18.1. Recall that the **representative elements,** whose chemical properties are determined by the valence-level *s* and *p* electrons, are designated Groups 1A through 8A. The **transition metals,** in the center of the table, result from the filling of *d* orbitals. The elements that correspond to the filling of the 4*f* and 5*f* orbitals are listed separately as the **lanthanides** and **actinides,** respectively.

The heavy black line in Fig. 18.1 divides the metals from the nonmetals. Some elements just on either side of this line, such as silicon and germanium, exhibit both metallic and nonmetallic properties and are often called **metalloids** or **semimetals.** The fundamental chemical difference between a metal and a nonmetal is that metals tend to lose their valence electrons to form *cations,* usually with the valence-electron configuration of the noble gas from the preceding period, and nonmetals tend to gain electrons to form *anions* that exhibit the electron configuration of the noble gas in the same period. Metallic character is observed to increase going down a given group, which is consistent with the trends in ionization energy, electron affinity, and electronegativity discussed earlier (see Sections 7.13 and 8.2).

Metallic character increases going down a group in the periodic table.

Atomic Size and Group Anomalies

Although the chemical properties of the members of a group show many similarities, there are also important differences. In fact, the relatively large increase in atomic radius in going from the first to the second member of a group causes the first element to show properties that are often quite different from the others. Consequently, hydrogen, beryllium, boron, carbon, nitrogen, oxygen, and fluorine all have some properties that distinguish them from the other members of their groups. For example, in Group 1A hydrogen is a nonmetal and lithium is a very active metal. This extreme difference results primarily from the very large difference in the atomic radii of hydrogen and lithium, as shown in Fig. 18.2. The small hydrogen atom has

Figure 18.1

The periodic table. The elements in the A groups are the representative elements. The elements shown in pink are called *transition metals*. The dark line approximately divides the nonmetals from the metals. The elements that have both metallic and nonmetallic properties (semimetals) are shaded in blue.

a much greater attraction for electrons than do the larger members of Group 1A and forms covalent bonds with nonmetals; the other members of Group 1A lose their valence electrons to nonmetals to form 1+ cations in ionic compounds.

This effect of size is also evident in other groups. For example, the oxides of the metals in Group 2A are all quite basic except for the first member of the series; beryllium oxide (BeO) is amphoteric. Recall from Section 14.10 that the basicity of an oxide depends on its ionic character. Ionic oxides contain the O^{2-} ion, which reacts with water to form two OH^- ions. All the oxides of the Group 2A metals are highly ionic except for beryllium oxide, which has considerable covalent character. The small Be^{2+} ion can effectively polarize the electron "cloud" of the O^{2-} ion, producing significant electron sharing. We see the same pattern in Group 3A, where only the small boron atom behaves as a nonmetal, or sometimes as a semimetal, and aluminum and the other members are active metals.

In Group 4A the effect of size is reflected in the dramatic differences between the chemistry of carbon and that of silicon. The chemistry of carbon is dominated by molecules containing chains of C—C bonds, but silicon compounds mainly contain Si—O bonds rather than Si—Si bonds. Carbon forms a wide variety of stable compounds with strong C—C single bonds. Silicon also forms compounds with chains of Si—Si bonds, but these compounds are much more reactive than the corresponding carbon compounds. The reasons for the difference in reactivity between the carbon and silicon compounds are quite complex but are likely related to the differences in the sizes of the carbon and silicon atoms.

Carbon and silicon differ markedly in their abilities to form π bonds. As we discussed in Section 9.1, carbon dioxide is composed of discrete CO_2 molecules with the Lewis structure

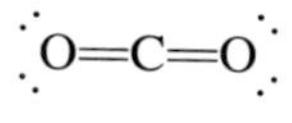

$$\ddot{\ddot{O}}=C=\ddot{\ddot{O}}$$

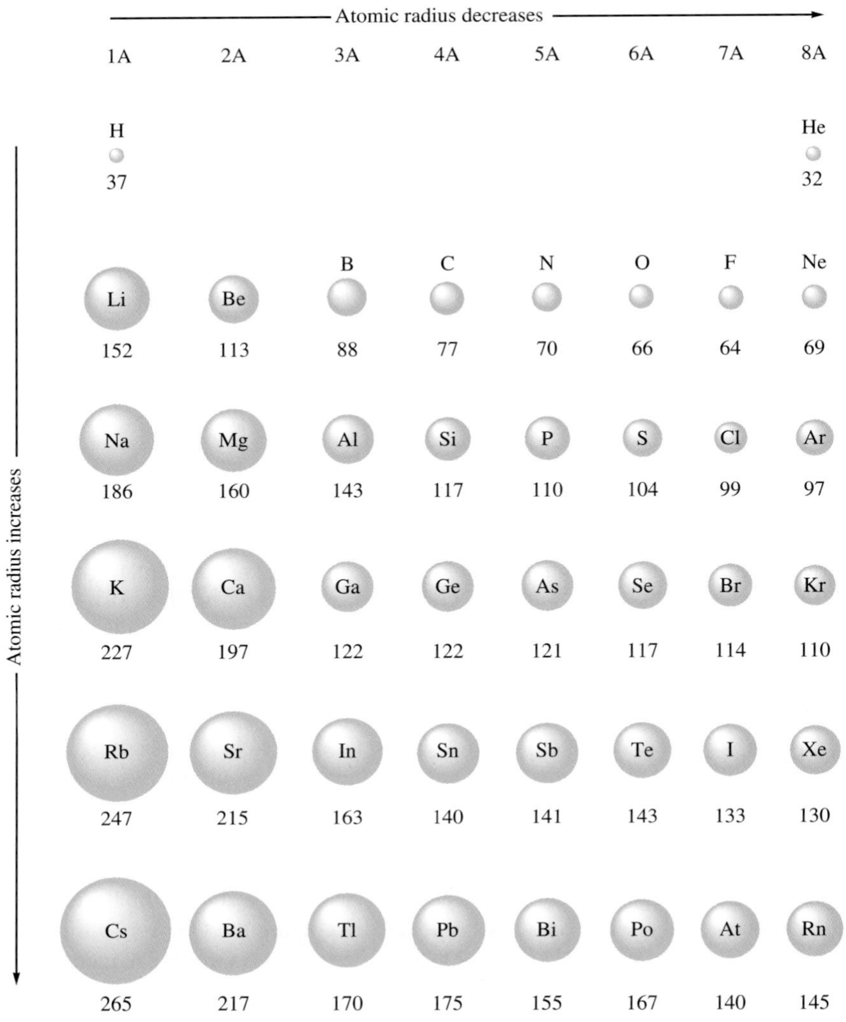

Figure 18.2
The atomic radii of some atoms in picometers.

Molecular Models: $(SiO_2)_n$, N_2, P_4, O_2, S_8, F_2

where the carbon and oxygen atoms achieve the [Ne] configuration by forming π bonds. In contrast, the structure of silica (empirical formula SiO_2) is based on SiO_4 tetrahedra with Si—O—Si bridges, as shown in Fig. 18.3. The silicon $3p$ valence orbitals do not overlap very effectively with the smaller oxygen $2p$ orbitals to form π bonds; therefore, discrete SiO_2 molecules with the Lewis structure

$$\ddot{O}\!\!=\!\!Si\!\!=\!\!\ddot{O}\!:$$

are not stable. Instead, the silicon atoms achieve a noble gas configuration by forming several Si—O single bonds.

The importance of π bonding for the relatively small elements of the second period also explains the different elemental forms of the members of Groups 5A and 6A. For example, elemental nitrogen consists of very stable N_2 molecules with the Lewis structure

$$:N\!\!\equiv\!\!N:$$

Elemental phosphorus forms larger aggregates of atoms, the simplest being the tetrahedral P_4 molecules found in white phosphorus (see Fig. 19.12). Like silicon atoms, the relatively large phosphorus atoms do not form strong π bonds and prefer to achieve a noble gas configuration by forming single bonds to several other phosphorus atoms. In contrast, its very strong π bonds make the N_2 molecule the most stable form of elemental nitrogen. Similarly, in Group 6A the most stable form of elemental oxygen is the O_2 molecule with a double bond, but the larger sulfur atom forms bigger aggregates, such as the cyclic S_8 molecule (see Fig. 19.16), which contains only single bonds.

The relatively large change in size in going from the first to second member of a group also has important consequences for the Group 7A elements. For example, fluorine has a smaller electron affinity than chlorine. This reversal of the expected trend can be attributed to the small fluorine $2p$ orbitals, which result in unusually large electron repulsions. The relative weakness of the bond in the F_2 molecule can be explained in terms of the repulsions among the lone pairs, shown in the Lewis structure:

$$: \overset{..}{\underset{..}{F}} {-} \overset{..}{\underset{..}{F}} :$$

The small size of the fluorine atoms allows close approach of the lone pairs, which leads to much greater repulsions than are found in the Cl_2 molecule with its much larger atoms.

Abundance and Preparation

Table 18.1 shows the distribution of elements in the earth's crust, oceans, and atmosphere. The major element is, of course, oxygen, which is found in the atmosphere as O_2, in the oceans in H_2O, and in the earth's crust primarily in silicate and carbonate minerals. The second most abundant element, silicon, is found throughout the earth's crust in the silica and silicate minerals that form the basis of most sand, rocks, and soil. The most abundant metals, aluminum and iron, are found in ores in which they are combined with nonmetals, most commonly oxygen. One notable fact revealed by Table 18.1 is the small incidence of most transition metals. Since many of these relatively rare elements are assuming increasing importance in

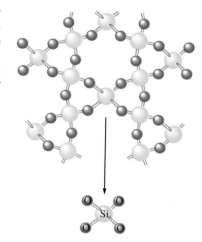

Figure 18.3

The structure of quartz, which has the empirical formula SiO_2. Note that the structure is based on interlocking SiO_4 tetrahedra, where each oxygen atom is shared by two silicon atoms.

Sand dunes in Monument Valley, Arizona.

Table 18.1 Distribution (Mass Percent) of the 18 Most Abundant Elements in the Earth's Crust, Oceans, and Atmosphere

Element	Mass Percent	Element	Mass Percent
Oxygen	49.2	Chlorine	0.19
Silicon	25.7	Phosphorus	0.11
Aluminum	7.50	Manganese	0.09
Iron	4.71	Carbon	0.08
Calcium	3.39	Sulfur	0.06
Sodium	2.63	Barium	0.04
Potassium	2.40	Nitrogen	0.03
Magnesium	1.93	Fluorine	0.03
Hydrogen	0.87	All others	0.49
Titanium	0.58		

Table 18.2 Abundance of Elements in the Human Body

Major Elements	Mass Percent	Trace Elements (in alphabetical order)
Oxygen	65.0	Arsenic
Carbon	18.0	Chromium
Hydrogen	10.0	Cobalt
Nitrogen	3.0	Copper
Calcium	1.4	Fluorine
Phosphorus	1.0	Iodine
Magnesium	0.50	Manganese
Potassium	0.34	Molybdenum
Sulfur	0.26	Nickel
Sodium	0.14	Selenium
Chlorine	0.14	Silicon
Iron	0.004	Vanadium
Zinc	0.003	

our high-technology society, it is possible that the control of transition metal ores may ultimately have more significance for world politics than the control of petroleum supplies.

The distribution of elements in living materials is very different from that found in the earth's crust. Table 18.2 shows the relative abundance of elements in the human body. Oxygen, carbon, hydrogen, and nitrogen form the basis for all biologically important molecules. The other elements, even though they are found in relatively small amounts, are often crucial for life. For example, zinc is found in over 150 different biomolecules in the human body.

Only about one-fourth of the elements occur naturally in the free state. Most are found in a combined state. The *process of obtaining a metal from its ore* is called **metallurgy.** Since the metals in ores are found in the form of cations, the chemistry of *metallurgy always involves reduction of the ions to the elemental metal (with an oxidation state of zero).* A variety of reducing agents can be used, but carbon is the usual choice because of its wide availability and relatively low cost. As we will see in Chapter 20, carbon is the primary reducing agent in the production of steel. Carbon also can be used to produce tin and lead from their oxides:

$$2SnO(s) + C(s) \xrightarrow{\text{Heat}} 2Sn(s) + CO_2(g)$$

$$2PbO(s) + C(s) \xrightarrow{\text{Heat}} 2Pb(s) + CO_2(g)$$

Hydrogen gas also can be used as a reducing agent for metal oxides, as in the production of tin:

$$SnO(s) + H_2(g) \xrightarrow{\text{Heat}} Sn(s) + H_2O(g)$$

Electrolysis is often used to reduce the most active metals. In Chapter 17 we considered the electrolytic production of aluminum metal. The alkali metals are also produced by electrolysis, usually of their molten halide salts.

The preparation of nonmetals varies widely. Elemental nitrogen and oxygen are usually obtained from the **liquefaction** of air, which is based on the principle that a real gas cools when it expands. After each expansion, part of the cooler gas is compressed, while the rest is used to carry away the heat of the compression. The

Metallurgy is discussed in more detail in Chapter 20.

Carbon is the cheapest and most readily available industrial reducing agent for metallic ions.

compressed gas is then allowed to expand again. This cycle is repeated many times. Eventually, the remaining gas becomes cold enough to form the liquid state. Because liquid nitrogen and liquid oxygen have different boiling points, they can be separated by the distillation of liquid air. Both substances are important industrial chemicals, ranking in the top five in terms of the amounts manufactured in the United States. Hydrogen can be obtained from the electrolysis of water, but more commonly it is obtained from the decomposition of the methane in natural gas. Sulfur is found underground in its elemental form and is recovered using the Frasch process (see Section 19.6). The halogens are obtained by oxidation of the anions from halide salts (see Section 19.7).

The preparation of sulfur and the halogens is discussed in Chapter 19.

18.2 *The Group 1A Elements*

The Group 1A elements with their ns^1 valence-electron configurations are all very active metals (they lose their valence electrons very readily), except for hydrogen, which behaves as a nonmetal. We will discuss the chemistry of hydrogen in the next section. Many of the properties of the **alkali metals** have been described previously (see Section 7.13). The sources and methods of preparation of pure alkali metals are given in Table 18.3. The ionization energies, standard reduction potentials, ionic radii, and melting points for the alkali metals are listed in Table 18.4. Lepidolite, shown in Fig. 18.4, is composed of pure alkali metals.

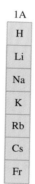

Several properties of the alkali metals are given in Table 7.8.

Table 18.3 Sources and Methods of Preparation of the Pure Alkali Metals

Element	Source	Method of Preparation
Lithium	Silicate minerals such as spodumene, $LiAl(Si_2O_6)$	Electrolysis of molten LiCl
Sodium	NaCl	Electrolysis of molten NaCl
Potassium	KCl	Electrolysis of molten KCl
Rubidium	Impurity in lepidolite, $Li_2(F,OH)_2Al_2(SiO_3)_3$	Reduction of RbOH with Mg and H_2
Cesium	Pollucite $(Cs_4Al_4Si_9O_{26} \cdot H_2O)$ and an impurity in lepidolite (see Fig. 18.4)	Reduction of CsOH with Mg and H_2

Figure 18.4

Lepidolite is composed mainly of lithium, aluminum, silicon, and oxygen, but it also contains significant amounts of rubidium and cesium.

Table 18.4 Selected Physical Properties of the Alkali Metals

Element	Ionization Energy (kJ/mol)	Standard Reduction Potential (V) for $M^+ + e^- \rightarrow M$	Radius of M^+ (pm)	Melting Point (°C)
Lithium	520	−3.05	60	180
Sodium	495	−2.71	95	98
Potassium	419	−2.92	133	63
Rubidium	409	−2.99	148	39
Cesium	382	−3.02	169	29

In Section 7.13 we saw that the alkali metals all react vigorously with water to release hydrogen gas:

$$2M(s) + 2H_2O(l) \longrightarrow 2M^+(aq) + 2OH^-(aq) + H_2(g)$$

We will reconsider this process briefly because it illustrates several important concepts. Based on the ionization energies, we might expect lithium to be the weakest of the alkali metals as a reducing agent in water. However, the standard reduction potentials indicate that it is the strongest. This reversal results mainly from the very large energy of hydration of the small Li^+ ion. Because of its relatively high charge density, the Li^+ ion very effectively attracts water molecules. A large quantity of energy is released in the process, favoring the formation of the Li^+ ion and making lithium a strong reducing agent in aqueous solution.

We also saw in Section 7.13 that lithium, although it is the strongest reducing agent, reacts more slowly with water than does sodium or potassium. From the discussions in Chapters 12 and 16, we know that the *equilibrium position* for a reaction (in this case indicated by the $\mathscr{E}°$ values) is controlled by thermodynamic factors but that the *rate* of a reaction is controlled by kinetic factors. There is *no* direct connection between these factors. Lithium reacts more slowly with water than does sodium or potassium because as a solid it has a higher melting point than either of them. It does not become molten from the heat of reaction with water as sodium and potassium do, and thus it has a smaller area of contact with the water.

The relative ease with which the alkali metals lose electrons to form M^+ cations means that they react with nonmetals to form ionic compounds. Although we might expect the alkali metals to react with oxygen to form regular oxides of the general formula M_2O, lithium is the only one that does so in the presence of excess oxygen gas:

$$4Li(s) + O_2(g) \longrightarrow 2Li_2O(s)$$

Sodium forms solid Na_2O if the oxygen supply is limited, but in excess oxygen it forms *sodium peroxide:*

$$2Na(s) + O_2(g) \longrightarrow Na_2O_2(s)$$

Sodium peroxide contains the basic O_2^{2-} anion and reacts with water to form hydrogen peroxide and hydroxide ions:

$$Na_2O_2(s) + 2H_2O(l) \longrightarrow 2Na^+(aq) + H_2O_2(aq) + 2OH^-(aq)$$

Hydrogen peroxide is a strong oxidizing agent often used as a bleach for hair and as a disinfectant.

Potassium, rubidium, and cesium react with oxygen to produce **superoxides** of the general formula MO_2, which contains the O_2^- anion. For example, potassium reacts with oxygen as follows:

$$K(s) + O_2(g) \longrightarrow KO_2(s)$$

The superoxides release oxygen gas in reactions with water or carbon dioxide:

$$2MO_2(s) + 2H_2O(l) \longrightarrow 2M^+(aq) + 2OH^-(aq) + O_2(g) + H_2O_2(aq)$$
$$4MO_2(s) + 2CO_2(g) \longrightarrow 2M_2CO_3(s) + 3O_2(g)$$

Hydrogen peroxide has the Lewis structure

Molecular Model: H_2O_2

Table 18.5 Types of Compounds Formed by the Alkali Metals with Oxygen

General Formula	Name	Examples
M_2O	Oxide	Li_2O, Na_2O
M_2O_2	Peroxide	Na_2O_2
MO_2	Superoxide	KO_2, RbO_2, CsO_2

This chemistry makes superoxides very useful in the self-contained breathing apparatuses used by firefighters. These "airpacks" are also used as emergency equipment in labs and production facilities in case toxic fumes are released.

The types of compounds formed by the alkali metals with oxygen are summarized in Table 18.5.

Lithium is the only alkali metal that reacts with gaseous nitrogen to form a **nitride salt** containing the N^{3-} anion:

$$6Li(s) + N_2(g) \longrightarrow 2Li_3N(s)$$

Table 18.6 summarizes some important reactions of the alkali metals.

The alkali metal ions are very important for the proper functioning of biologic systems, such as nerves and muscles, and Na^+ and K^+ ions are present in all body cells and fluids. In human blood plasma the concentrations are

$$[Na^+] \approx 0.15 \, M \quad \text{and} \quad [K^+] \approx 0.005 \, M$$

For the fluids *inside* the cells the concentrations are reversed:

$$[Na^+] \approx 0.005 \, M \quad \text{and} \quad [K^+] \approx 0.16 \, M$$

Airpacks are an essential source of oxygen for firefighters.

Since the concentrations are so different inside and outside the cells, an elaborate mechanism is needed to transport Na^+ and K^+ ions through the cell membranes.

Recently, studies have been carried out concerning the role of the Li^+ ion in the human brain, and lithium carbonate has been used extensively in the treatment of manic-depressive patients. The Li^+ ion apparently affects the levels of neurotransmitters, molecules that assist the transmission of messages along the nerve networks. Incorrect concentrations of these molecules can lead to depression or mania.

Table 18.6 Selected Reactions of the Alkali Metals

Reaction	Comment
$2M + X_2 \rightarrow 2MX$	X_2 = any halogen molecule
$4Li + O_2 \rightarrow 2Li_2O$	Excess oxygen
$2Na + O_2 \rightarrow Na_2O_2$	
$M + O_2 \rightarrow MO_2$	M = K, Rb, or Cs
$2M + S \rightarrow M_2S$	
$6Li + N_2 \rightarrow 2Li_3N$	Li only
$12M + P_4 \rightarrow 4M_3P$	
$2M + H_2 \rightarrow 2MH$	
$2M + 2H_2O \rightarrow 2MOH + H_2$	
$2M + 2H^+ \rightarrow 2M^+ + H_2$	Violent reaction!

Sodium reacts violently with chlorine.

Sample Exercise 18.1 *Predicting Reaction Products*

Predict the products formed by the following reactants.

a. $Li_3N(s)$ and $H_2O(l)$
b. $KO_2(s)$ and $H_2O(l)$

Solution

a. Solid Li_3N contains the N^{3-} anion, which has a strong attraction for three H^+ ions to form NH_3. Thus the reaction is

$$Li_3N(s) + 3H_2O(l) \longrightarrow NH_3(g) + 3Li^+(aq) + 3OH^-(aq)$$

b. Solid KO_2 is a superoxide that characteristically reacts with water to produce O_2, H_2O_2, and OH^-:

$$2KO_2(s) + 2H_2O(l) \longrightarrow 2K^+(aq) + 2OH^-(aq) + O_2(g) + H_2O_2(aq)$$

See Exercises 18.19 and 18.20.

18.3 Hydrogen

Under ordinary conditions of temperature and pressure, hydrogen is a colorless, odorless gas composed of H_2 molecules. Because of its low molar mass and non-polarity, hydrogen has a very low boiling point ($-253°C$) and melting point ($-260°C$). Hydrogen gas is highly flammable, and mixtures of air containing from 18% to 60% hydrogen by volume are explosive. In a common lecture demonstra-

 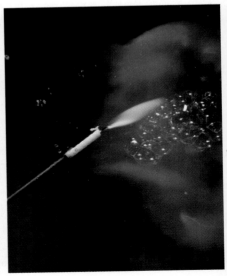

(left) Hydrogen gas being used to blow soap bubbles. (right) As the bubbles float upward, they are lighted using a candle on a long pole. The orange flame is due to the heat from the reaction of hydrogen with the oxygen in the air that excites sodium ions in the soap solution.

tion hydrogen and oxygen gases are bubbled into soapy water. The resulting bubbles can be ignited with a candle on a long stick, giving a loud explosion.

The major industrial source of hydrogen gas is the reaction of methane and water at high temperatures (800–1000°C) and high pressures (10–50 atm) with a metallic catalyst, often nickel:

$$CH_4(g) + H_2O(g) \xrightarrow[\text{Catalyst}]{\text{Heat, pressure}} CO(g) + 3H_2(g)$$

Large quantities of hydrogen are also formed as a by-product of gasoline production, in which hydrocarbons with high molar masses are broken down (*cracked*) to produce smaller molecules more suitable for use as a motor fuel (see Section 22.4).

Very pure hydrogen can be produced by electrolysis of water (see Section 17.7), but this method is currently not economically feasible for large-scale production because of the relatively high cost of electricity.

The major industrial use of hydrogen is in the production of ammonia by the Haber process. Large quantities of hydrogen are also used for hydrogenating unsaturated vegetable oils (those containing carbon–carbon double bonds) to produce solid shortenings that are saturated (containing carbon–carbon single bonds):

The catalysis of this process was discussed in Section 12.8.

Chemically, hydrogen behaves as a typical nonmetal, forming covalent compounds with other nonmetals and forming salts with very active metals. Binary compounds containing hydrogen are called **hydrides,** of which there are three classes. The **ionic** (or **saltlike**) **hydrides** are formed when hydrogen combines with the most active metals, those from Groups 1A and 2A. Examples are LiH and CaH_2, which can best be characterized as containing hydride ions (H^-) and metal cations. Because the presence of two electrons in the small $1s$ orbital produces large electron–electron repulsions and the nucleus only has a $1+$ charge, the hydride ion is a strong reducing agent (easily loses electrons). For example, when ionic hydrides are placed in water, a violent reaction takes place. This reaction results in the formation of hydrogen gas, as seen in the equation

$$LiH(s) + H_2O(l) \longrightarrow H_2(g) + Li^+(aq) + OH^-(aq)$$

Covalent hydrides are formed when hydrogen combines with other nonmetals. We have encountered many of these compounds already: HCl, CH_4, NH_3, H_2O, and so on. The most important covalent hydride is water. The polarity of the H_2O molecule leads to many of water's unusual properties. Water has a much higher boiling point than is expected from its molar mass. It has a large heat of vaporization and a large heat capacity, both of which make it a very useful coolant. Water has a higher density as a liquid than as a solid. This is due to the open structure of ice, which results from maximizing the hydrogen bonding (see Fig. 18.5). Because water is an excellent solvent for ionic and polar substances, it provides an effective medium for life processes. In fact, water is one of the few covalent hydrides that is nontoxic to organisms.

Boiling points of covalent hydrides are discussed in Section 10.1.

Figure 18.5
The structure of ice, showing the hydrogen bonding.

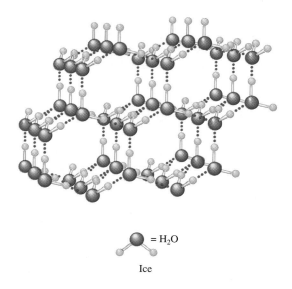

= H_2O

Ice

The third class of hydrides, the **metallic (or interstitial) hydrides,** are formed when transition metal crystals are treated with hydrogen gas. The hydrogen molecules dissociate at the metal's surface, and the small hydrogen atoms migrate into the crystal structure to occupy holes, or interstices. These metal–hydrogen mixtures are more like solid solutions than true compounds. Palladium can absorb about *900 times* its own volume of hydrogen gas. In fact, hydrogen can be purified by placing it under slight pressure in a vessel containing a thin wall of palladium. The hydrogen diffuses into and through the metal wall, leaving the impurities behind.

Although hydrogen can react with transition metals to form compounds of constant composition, most of the interstitial hydrides have variable compositions (often called *nonstoichiometric compositions*) with formulas such as $LaH_{2.76}$ and $VH_{0.56}$. The compositions of the nonstoichiometric hydrides vary with the length of exposure of the metal to hydrogen gas and other factors.

When interstitial hydrides are heated, much of the absorbed hydrogen is expelled as hydrogen gas. Because of this behavior, these materials offer possibilities for storing hydrogen for use as a portable fuel. The internal combustion engines in current automobiles can burn hydrogen gas with little modification, but storage of enough hydrogen to provide an acceptable mileage range remains a problem. One possible solution might be to use a fuel tank containing a porous solid that includes a transition metal into which the hydrogen gas could be pumped to form the interstitial hydride. The hydrogen gas could then be released as required by the engine.

See Section 6.6 for a discussion of the feasibility of using hydrogen gas as a fuel.

2A
Be
Mg
Ca
Sr
Ba
Ra

18.4 The Group 2A Elements

The Group 2A elements (with valence-electron configuration ns^2) are very reactive, losing their two valence electrons to nonmetals to form ionic compounds containing M^{2+} cations. These elements are commonly called the **alkaline earth metals** because of the basicity of their oxides:

An amphoteric oxide displays both acidic and basic properties.

$$MO(s) + H_2O(l) \longrightarrow M^{2+}(aq) + 2OH^-(aq)$$

Table 18.7 Selected Physical Properties, Sources, and Methods of Preparation for the Group 2A Elements

Element	Radius of M^{2+} (pm)	Ionization Energy (kJ/mol) First	Ionization Energy (kJ/mol) Second	$\mathscr{E}°(V)$ for $M^{2+} + 2e^- \rightarrow M$	Source	Method of Preparation
Beryllium	~30	900	1760	−1.70	Beryl $(Be_3Al_2Si_6O_{18})$	Electrolysis of molten $BeCl_2$
Magnesium	65	738	1450	−2.37	Magnesite $(MgCO_3)$, dolomite $(MgCO_3 \cdot CaCO_3)$, carnallite $(MgCl_2 \cdot KCl \cdot 6H_2O)$	Electrolysis of molten $MgCl_2$
Calcium	99	590	1146	−2.76	Various minerals containing $CaCO_3$	Electrolysis of molten $CaCl_2$
Strontium	113	549	1064	−2.89	Celestite $(SrSO_4)$, strontianite $(SrCO_3)$	Electrolysis of molten $SrCl_2$
Barium	135	503	965	−2.90	Baryte $(BaSO_4)$, witherite $(BaCO_3)$	Electrolysis of molten $BaCl_2$
Radium	140	509	979	−2.92	Pitchblende (1 g of Ra/7 tons of ore)	Electrolysis of molten $RaCl_2$

Only beryllium oxide (BeO) also shows some acidic properties, such as dissolving in aqueous solutions containing hydroxide ions:

$$BeO(s) + 2OH^-(aq) + H_2O(l) \longrightarrow Be(OH)_4^{2-}(aq)$$

The more active alkaline earth metals react with water as the alkali metals do, producing hydrogen gas:

$$M(s) + 2H_2O(l) \longrightarrow M^{2+}(aq) + 2OH^-(aq) + H_2(g)$$

Calcium, strontium, and barium react vigorously at 25°C. The less easily oxidized beryllium and magnesium show no observable reaction with water at 25°C, although magnesium reacts with boiling water. Table 18.7 summarizes various properties, sources, and preparations of the alkaline earth metals.

The heavier alkaline earth metals react with nitrogen or hydrogen at high temperatures to produce ionic nitride or hydride salts, for example:

$$3Ca(s) + N_2(g) \longrightarrow Ca_3N_2(s)$$
$$Ca(s) + H_2(g) \longrightarrow CaH_2(s)$$

Magnesium, strontium, and barium form similar compounds. Beryllium hydride cannot be formed by direct combination of the elements but can be prepared by the following reaction:

$$BeCl_2 + 2LiH \longrightarrow BeH_2 + 2LiCl$$

Hydrogen bridges between the beryllium atoms produce a polymeric structure for BeH$_2$, as shown in Fig. 18.6. The localized electron model describes this bonding by assuming only one electron pair is available to bind each Be—H—Be cluster. This is called a *three-center bond*, since one electron pair is shared among three

Calcium metal reacting with water to form bubbles of hydrogen gas.

Molecular Models: $Be(OH)_4^{2-}$, $BeCl_2$, $(BeCl_2)_n$, BeH_2, $(BeH_2)_n$, H_3NBeCl_2

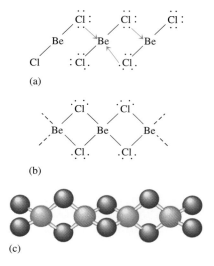

Figure 18.6

The structure of solid BeH_2.

(a)

(b)

(c)

Figure 18.7

(a) Solid $BeCl_2$ can be visualized as being formed from many $BeCl_2$ molecules, where lone pairs on the chlorine atoms are used to bond to the beryllium atoms in adjacent $BeCl_2$ molecules. (b) The extended structure of solid $BeCl_2$. (c) The ball-and-stick model of the extended structure.

atoms. Three-center bonds also have been postulated to explain the bonding in other electron-deficient compounds (compounds in which there are fewer electron pairs than bonds) such as the boron hydrides (see Section 18.5).

As we saw in Section 18.1, the small size and relatively high electronegativity of the beryllium atom cause its bonds to be more covalent than is usual for a metal. For example, beryllium chloride with the Lewis structure

$$: \ddot{Cl}-Be-\ddot{Cl} :$$

exists as a linear molecule, as predicted by the VSEPR model. The Be—Cl bonds are covalent, and beryllium is best described as being sp hybridized. Since the beryllium atom in $BeCl_2$ is very electron-deficient (only four valence electrons surround it), it is very reactive toward electron-pair donors (Lewis bases) such as ammonia:

Table 18.8 Selected Reactions of the Group 2A Elements

Reaction	Comment
$M + X_2 \rightarrow MX_2$	X_2 = any halogen molecule
$2M + O_2 \rightarrow 2MO$	Ba gives BaO_2 as well
$M + S \rightarrow MS$	
$3M + N_2 \rightarrow M_3N_2$	High temperatures
$6M + P_4 \rightarrow 2M_3P_2$	High temperatures
$M + H_2 \rightarrow MH_2$	M = Ca, Sr, or Ba; high temperatures; Mg at high pressure
$M + 2H_2O \rightarrow M(OH)_2 + H_2$	M = Ca, Sr, or Ba
$M + 2H^+ \rightarrow M^{2+} + H_2$	
$Be + 2OH^- + 2H_2O \rightarrow Be(OH)_4^{2-} + H_2$	

The Dolomite mountains in Italy.

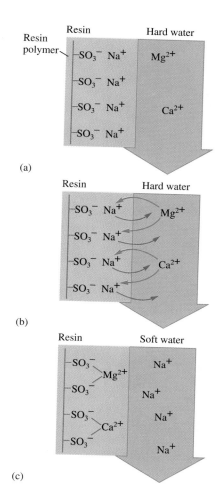

(a)

(b)

(c)

Figure 18.8

(a) A schematic representation of a typical cation-exchange resin. (b) and (c) When hard water is passed over the cation-exchange resin, the Ca^{2+} and Mg^{2+} bind to the resin.

As a solid, $BeCl_2$ achieves an octet of electrons around each beryllium atom by forming an extended structure containing Be in a tetrahedral environment, as shown in Fig. 18.7. The lone pairs on the chlorine atoms are used to form Be—Cl bonds.

The alkaline earth metals have great practical importance. Calcium and magnesium ions are essential for human life. Calcium is found primarily in the structural minerals comprising bones and teeth; magnesium (as the Mg^{2+} ion) plays a vital role in metabolism and muscle functions. Also, magnesium is commonly used to produce the bright light for photographic flash units from its reaction with oxygen:

$$2Mg(s) + O_2(g) \longrightarrow 2MgO(s) + \text{light}$$

Because magnesium metal has a relatively low density and moderate strength, it is a useful structural material, especially if alloyed with aluminum.

Table 18.8 summarizes some important reactions of the alkaline earth metals.

Relatively large concentrations of Ca^{2+} and Mg^{2+} ions are often found in natural water supplies. These ions in this **hard water** interfere with the action of detergents and form precipitates with soap. In Section 14.6 we saw that Ca^{2+} is often removed by precipitation as $CaCO_3$ in large-scale water softening. In individual homes Ca^{2+}, Mg^{2+}, and other cations are removed by **ion exchange**. An **ion-exchange resin** consists of large molecules (polymers) that have many ionic sites. A **cation-exchange resin** is represented schematically in Fig. 18.8(a), showing Na^+ ions bound ionically to the SO_3^- groups that are covalently attached to the resin polymer. When hard water is passed over the resin, Ca^{2+} and Mg^{2+} bind to the resin in place of Na^+, which is released into the solution [Fig. 18.8(b)]. Replacing Mg^{2+} and Ca^{2+} by Na^+ [Fig. 18.8(c)] "softens" the water because the sodium ions interfere much less with the action of soaps and detergents.

Sample Exercise **18.2** *Electrolytic Production of Magnesium*

Calculate the amount of time required to produce 1.00×10^3 kg of magnesium metal by the electrolysis of molten $MgCl_2$ using a current of 1.00×10^2 A.

Solution

The reaction for plating magnesium is

$$Mg^{2+} + 2e^- \longrightarrow Mg$$

which means that 2 moles of electrons are required for each mole of Mg produced. The number of moles of magnesium in 1.00×10^3 kg is

$$1.00 \times 10^3 \text{ kg} \times \frac{1000 \text{ g}}{\text{kg}} \times \frac{1 \text{ mol Mg}}{24.31 \text{ g}} = 4.11 \times 10^4 \text{ mol Mg}$$

Thus $\quad \dfrac{2 \text{ mol e}^-}{1 \text{ mol Mg}} \times 4.11 \times 10^4 \text{ mol Mg} = 8.22 \times 10^4 \text{ mol e}^-$

Using the faraday (96,485 C/mol e$^-$), we can calculate the coulombs of charge:

$$8.22 \times 10^4 \text{ mol e}^- \times \frac{96,485 \text{ C}}{\text{mol e}^-} = 7.93 \times 10^9 \text{ C}$$

Since an ampere is a coulomb of charge per second, we can now calculate the time required:

$$\frac{7.93 \times 10^9 \text{ C}}{1.00 \times 10^2 \text{ C/s}} = 7.93 \times 10^7 \text{ s} \quad \text{or} \quad 918 \text{ days}$$

See Exercises 18.31 and 18.32.

Video: Dry Ice and Magnesium

3A
B
Al
Ga
In
Tl

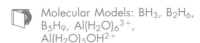

Molecular Models: BH_3, B_2H_6, B_5H_9, $Al(H_2O)_6^{3+}$, $Al(H_2O)_5OH^{2+}$

18.5 *The Group 3A Elements*

The Group 3A elements (valence-electron configuration ns^2np^1) generally show the increase in metallic character in going down the group that is characteristic of the representative elements. Some physical properties, sources, and methods of preparation for the Group 3A elements are summarized in Table 18.9.

Boron is a nonmetal, and most of its compounds are covalent. The most interesting compounds of boron are the covalent hydrides called **boranes.** We might expect BH_3 to be the simplest hydride, since boron has three valence electrons to share with three hydrogen atoms. However, this compound is unstable, and the simplest known member of the series is diborane (B_2H_6), with the structure shown in Fig. 18.9(a). In this molecule the terminal B—H bonds are normal covalent bonds, each involving one electron pair. The bridging bonds are three-center bonds similar to those in solid BeH_2. Another interesting borane contains the square pyramidal B_5H_9 molecule [Fig. 18.9(b)], which has four three-center bonds around the base of the

Table 18.9 Selected Physical Properties, Sources, and Methods of Preparation for the Group 3A Elements

Element	Radius of M^{3+} (pm)	Ionization Energy (kJ/mol)	$\mathscr{E}°$ (V) for $M^{3+} + 3e^- \rightarrow M$	Sources	Method of Preparation
Boron	20	798	—	Kernite, a form of borax ($Na_2B_4O_7 \cdot 4H_2O$)	Reduction by Mg or H_2
Aluminum	51	581	−1.71	Bauxite (Al_2O_3)	Electrolysis of Al_2O_3 in molten Na_3AlF_6
Gallium	62	577	−0.53	Traces in various minerals	Reduction with H_2 or electrolysis
Indium	81	556	−0.34	Traces in various minerals	Reduction with H_2 or electrolysis
Thallium	95	589	0.72	Traces in various minerals	Electrolysis

pyramid. Because the boranes are extremely electron-deficient, they are highly re-active. The boranes react very exothermically with oxygen and were once evaluated as potential fuels for rockets in the U.S. space program.

Aluminum, the most abundant metal on earth, has metallic physical properties, such as high thermal and electrical conductivities and a lustrous appearance, but its bonds to nonmetals are significantly covalent. This covalency is responsible for the amphoteric nature of Al_2O_3, which dissolves in acidic or basic solution, and for the acidity of $Al(H_2O)_6^{3+}$ (see Section 14.8):

$$Al(H_2O)_6^{3+}(aq) \rightleftharpoons Al(OH)(H_2O)_5^{2+}(aq) + H^+(aq)$$

One especially interesting property of *gallium* is its unusually low melting point at 29.8°C, which is in contrast to the 660°C melting point of aluminum. Gallium's boiling point is approximately 2400°C. This gives gallium the largest liquid range of any metal, which makes it useful for thermometers, especially to measure high temperatures. Gallium, like water, expands when it freezes. The chemistry of gal-lium is quite similar to that of aluminum. For example, Ga_2O_3 is amphoteric.

The chemistry of *indium* is similar to that of aluminum and gallium except that compounds containing the 1+ ion are known, such as InCl and In_2O, in addition to those with the more common 3+ ion.

Gallium metal has such a low melting point (30°C) that it melts from the heat of a hand.

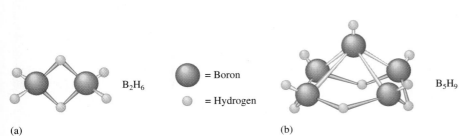

(a) B_2H_6 = Boron   = Hydrogen   (b) B_5H_9

Figure 18.9

(a) The structure of B_2H_6 with its two three-center B—H—B bridg-ing bonds and four "normal" B—H bonds. (b) The structure of B_5H_9. There are five "normal" B—H bonds to terminal hydro-gens and four three-center bridg-ing bonds around the base.

Table 18.10 Selected Reactions of the Group 3A Elements

Reaction	Comment
$2M + 3X_2 \rightarrow 2MX_3$	X_2 = any halogen molecule; Tl gives TlX as well, but no TlI_3
$4M + 3O_2 \rightarrow 2M_2O_3$	High temperatures; Tl gives Tl_2O as well
$2M + 3S \rightarrow M_2S_3$	High temperatures; Tl gives Tl_2S as well
$2M + N_2 \rightarrow 2MN$	M = Al only
$2M + 6H^+ \rightarrow 2M^{3+} + 3H_2$	M = Al, Ga, or In; Tl gives Tl^+
$2M + 2OH^- + 6H_2O \rightarrow 2M(OH)_4^- + 3H_2$	M = Al or Ga

The chemistry of *thallium* is completely metallic. For example, Tl_2O_3 is a basic oxide. Both the +1 and +3 oxidation states are quite common for thallium; Tl_2O_3, Tl_2O, $TlCl_3$, and $TlCl$ are all well-known compounds. The tendency for the heavier members of Group 3A to exhibit the +1 as well as the expected +3 oxidation state is often called the **inert-pair effect.** This effect is also found in Group 4A, where lead and tin exhibit both +4 and +2 oxidation states.

Table 18.10 summarizes some important reactions of the Group 3A elements.

The practical importance of the Group 3A elements centers on aluminum. Since the discovery of the electrolytic production process by Hall and Heroult (see Section 17.8), aluminum has become a highly important structural material in a wide variety of applications from aircraft bodies to bicycle components. Aluminum is especially valuable because it has a high strength-to-weight ratio and because it protects itself from corrosion by developing a tough, adherent oxide coating.

The explanation for the inert-pair effect is very complex, involving a relativistic treatment of the atom, and will not be considered here.

Aluminum is used in airplane construction.

18.6 The Group 4A Elements

4A

C
Si
Ge
Sn
Pb

Group 4A (with the valence-electron configuration ns^2np^2) contains two of the most important elements on earth: carbon, the fundamental constituent of the molecules necessary for life, and silicon, which forms the basis of the geologic world. The change from nonmetallic to metallic properties seen in Group 3A is also apparent in going down Group 4A from carbon, a typical nonmetal, to silicon and germanium, usually considered semimetals, to the metals tin and lead. Table 18.11 summarizes some physical properties, sources, and methods of preparation for the elements in this group.

All the Group 4A elements can form four covalent bonds to nonmetals, for example: CH_4, SiF_4, $GeBr_4$, $SnCl_4$, and $PbCl_4$. In each of these tetrahedral molecules, the central atom is described as sp^3 hybridized by the localized electron model. All these compounds, except those of carbon, can react with Lewis bases to form two additional covalent bonds. For example, $SnCl_4$, which is a fuming liquid (bp = 114°C), can add two chloride ions:

$$SnCl_4 + 2Cl^- \longrightarrow SnCl_6^{2-}$$

Carbon compounds cannot react in this way because of the small atomic size of carbon and because there are no d orbitals on carbon to accommodate the extra electrons, as there are on the other elements in the group.

We have seen that carbon also differs markedly from the other members of Group 4A in its ability to form π bonds. This accounts for the completely different structures and properties of CO_2 and SiO_2. Note from Table 18.12 that C—C bonds and Si—O bonds are stronger than Si—Si bonds. This partly explains why the chemistry of carbon is dominated by C—C bonds, whereas that of silicon is dominated by Si—O bonds.

Carbon occurs in the earth's crust in two allotropic forms—graphite and diamond. In addition, new forms of elemental carbon, including buckminsterfullerene (C_{60}) and other related substances, have recently been characterized. The structures of graphite and diamond are given in Section 10.5.

Molecular Models: CH_4, SiF_4, $GeBr_4$, $SnCl_4$, $SnCl_6^{2-}$, CO_2, $(SiO_2)_n$, CO, C_2H_5OH, $C_6H_{12}O_6$

Although graphite is thermodynamically more stable than diamond, the transformation of diamond to graphite is not observed under normal conditions.

Fullerenes have been discovered recently by geologists in ancient rocks in Russia.

Table 18.11 Selected Physical Properties, Sources, and Methods of Preparation for the Group 4A Elements

Element	Electronegativity	Melting Point (°C)	Boiling Point (°C)	Sources	Method of Preparation
Carbon	2.5	3727 (sublimes)	—	Graphite, diamond, petroleum, coal	—
Silicon	1.8	1410	2355	Silicate minerals, silica	Reduction of K_2SiF_6 with Al, or reduction of SiO_2 with Mg
Germanium	1.8	937	2830	Germanite (mixture of copper, iron, and germanium sulfides)	Reduction of GeO_2 with H_2 or C
Tin	1.8	232	2270	Cassiterite (SnO_2)	Reduction of SnO_2 with C
Lead	1.9	327	1740	Galena (PbS)	Roasting of PbS with O_2 to form PbO_2 and then reduction with C

Table 18.12 Strengths of C—C, Si—Si, and Si—O Bonds	
Bond	Bond Energy (kJ/mol)
C—C	347
Si—Si	340
Si—O	452

Carbon monoxide (CO), one of three oxides of carbon, is an odorless, colorless, and toxic gas formed as a by-product of the combustion of carbon-containing compounds when there is a limited oxygen supply. Incidents of carbon monoxide poisoning are especially common in the winter in cold areas of the world when blocked furnace vents limit the availability of oxygen. The bonding in carbon monoxide, which has the Lewis structure

$$:C{\equiv}O:$$

is described in terms of *sp* hybridized carbon and oxygen atoms that interact to form one σ and two π bonds.

Carbon dioxide, a linear molecule with the Lewis structure

$$\ddot{O}{=}C{=}\ddot{O}$$

has an *sp* hybridized carbon atom, and is a product of human and animal respiration and of the combustion of fossil fuels. It is also produced by fermentation, a process by which the sugar in fruits and grains is changed to ethanol (C_2H_5OH) and carbon dioxide (see Section 22.5):

$$C_6H_{12}O_6(aq) \xrightarrow{\text{Enzymes}} 2C_2H_5OH(aq) + 2CO_2(g)$$
$$\text{Glucose}$$

Carbon dioxide dissolves in water to produce an acidic solution:

$$CO_2(aq) + H_2O(l) \rightleftharpoons H^+(aq) + HCO_3^-(aq)$$

Carbon suboxide, the third carbon oxide, is a linear molecule with the Lewis structure

$$\ddot{O}{=}C{=}C{=}C{=}\ddot{O}$$

which contains *sp* hybridized carbon atoms.

Molecular Models: C_3O_2, $Pb(C_2H_5)_4$

Silicon, the second most abundant element in the earth's crust, is a semimetal found widely distributed in silica and silicates (see Section 10.5). Approximately 85% of the earth's crust is composed of these substances. Although silicon is found in some steel and aluminum alloys, its major use is in semiconductors for electronic devices (see the Chemical Impact on page 498).

Germanium, a relatively rare element, is a semimetal used mainly in the manufacture of semiconductors for transistors and similar electronic devices.

Tin is a soft silvery metal that can be rolled into thin sheets (tin foil) and has been used for centuries in various alloys such as bronze (~20% Sn and ~80% Cu), solder (~33% Sn and ~67% Pb), and pewter (~85% Sn, ~7% Cu, ~6% Bi, and ~2% Sb). Tin exists as three allotropes: *white tin,* stable at normal temperatures; *gray tin,* stable at temperatures below 13.2°C; and *brittle tin,* found at temperatures above 161°C. When tin is exposed to low temperatures, it gradually changes to the powdery gray tin and crumbles away; this process is known as *tin disease.*

The compositions of these alloys vary significantly. For example, the tin content of bronze varies from 5% to 30%, and the tin content of pewter is often as high as 95%.

The major current use for tin is as a protective coating for steel, especially for cans used as food containers. The thin layer of tin, applied electrolytically, forms a protective oxide coating that prevents further corrosion.

Tin forms compounds in the +2 and +4 oxidation states. For example, all the possible tin(II) and tin(IV) halides are known. The tin(IV) halides, except for SnF_4, are all relatively volatile (see Table 18.13) and generally behave much more like molecular than ionic compounds. This is no doubt due to the high charge-to-radius

Table 18.13 Boiling Points of the Tin(IV) Halides	
Compound	Boiling Point (°C)
SnF_4	705 (sublimes)
$SnCl_4$	114
$SnBr_4$	202
SnI_4	364

CHEMICAL IMPACT

Concrete Learning

CONCRETE HAS LITERALLY paved the way for civilization over the past 5000 years, tracing its roots to the ancient Egyptians. At a cost of about a penny per pound, concrete is ubiquitous in today's world—used in houses, factories, roads, dams, cooling towers, pipes, skyscrapers, and countless other places. In the United States alone there are an estimated $6 trillion worth of concrete-based structures.

Most concretes are based on Portland cement, patented in 1824 by an English bricklayer named J. Aspdin and so named because it forms a product that resembles the natural limestone on the Isle of Portland in England. Portland cement is a powder containing a mixture of calcium silicates [Ca_2SiO_4 (26%) and Ca_3SiO_5 (51%)], calcium aluminate [$Ca_3Al_2O_6$ (11%)], and calcium iron aluminate [$Ca_4Al_2Fe_2O_{10}$ (1%)]. Portland cement is made from a mixture of limestone, sand, shale, clay, and gypsum ($CaSO_4 \cdot 2H_2O$). When the cement is mixed with sand, gravel, and water, it turns into a muddy substance that eventually hardens into the familiar concrete that finds so many uses in our world. The

hardening of concrete occurs not through drying but through hydration. The material becomes dry and hard as the water is consumed in building the complex silicate structures present in cured concrete. Although many of the details of this process are poorly understood, the main "glue" that holds the components of concrete together is calcium silicate hydrate, which forms a three-dimensional network mainly responsible for concrete's strength.

Despite its strength when newly produced, concrete contains pockets of air and water dispersed throughout, making it porous and subject to deterioration. Thus, despite all the advantages of concrete, it cracks and deteriorates seriously over time.

Much research is now being carried out to improve the durability of concrete. Most of these efforts are directed toward lowering the porosity of concrete and making it less brittle. One group of additives aimed at solving this problem consists of molecules with carbon atom backbones that have sulfate groups attached. These so-called superplasticizers allow the formation of concrete using much less water, and these chemicals have doubled

the strength of ready-mix concrete over the past 20 years.

Researchers also have found that the properties of concrete can be greatly improved by adding fibers of various kinds, including those made of steel, glass, and carbon-based polymers. One type of fiber concrete—called *slurry infiltrated fiber concrete* (SIFCON), which is tough enough to be used to make missile silos and can be formed into complex shapes—may be especially useful for structures in earthquake-prone areas.

Other efforts to improve concrete center on replacing Portland cement with other binders such as carbon-based polymers. Although these polymer-based concretes will burn and do lose their shapes at high temperatures, they are much more resistant to the effects of water, acids, and salts than those made with Portland cement.

Despite the fact that most concrete now used is very similar to that used by the Romans to build the Pantheon, progress is being made, and revolutionary improvements may be just around the corner.

---

ratio that would be characteristic of Sn^{4+} if it existed. Thus, instead of containing Sn^{4+} and X^- ions, the tin(IV) halides contain covalent Sn—X bonds. The Sn^{4+} ion almost certainly does not exist in these or any other known compounds. The compound SnF_4 is relatively nonvolatile, not because it contains Sn^{4+} and F^- ions, but because it consists of a mixture of SnF_6^{2-} and SnF_2^{2+} ions.

The tin(II) halides are much less volatile than the corresponding tin(IV) compounds; in fact, they are probably ionic, containing Sn^{2+} and X^- ions. Tin(II) chloride in aqueous solution is commonly used as a reducing agent. Tin(II) fluoride (stannous fluoride) was formerly added to toothpaste to help prevent tooth decay.

Lead is easily obtained from its ore, galena (PbS). Because lead melts at such a low temperature, it may have been the first pure metal obtained from its ore. We know that lead was used as early as 3000 B.C. by the Egyptians and was later used by the Romans to make eating utensils, glazes on pottery, and even intricate plumbing systems. Lead is very toxic, however. In fact, the Romans had so much contact

A Persian bronze bottle used to hold eye makeup, circa the first century B.C.

Lead(II) oxide, known as litharge.

Roman baths such as these in Bath, England, used lead pipes for water.

with lead that it may have contributed to the demise of their civilization. Analysis of bones from that era shows significant levels of lead.

Although lead poisoning has been known since at least the second century B.C., the incidences of this problem have been relatively isolated. However, the widespread use of tetraethyl lead, $(C_2H_5)_4Pb$, as an antiknock agent in gasoline increased the lead levels in our environment in the twentieth century. Concern about the effects of this lead pollution has caused the U.S. government to require the gradual replacement of the lead in gasoline with other antiknock agents. The largest commercial use of lead (about 1.3 million tons annually) is for electrodes in the lead storage batteries used in automobiles (see Section 17.5).

Lead forms compounds in the +2 and +4 oxidation states. The lead(II) halides, all of which are known, exhibit ionic properties and thus can be assumed to contain Pb^{2+} ions. Only PbF_4 and $PbCl_4$ are known among the possible lead(IV) halides, presumably because lead(IV) oxidizes bromide and iodide ions to give the lead(II) halide and the free halogen:

$$PbX_4 \longrightarrow PbX_2 + X_2$$

Lead(IV) chloride decomposes in this fashion at temperatures above 100°C.

Yellow lead(II) oxide, known as *litharge*, is widely used to glaze ceramic ware. Lead(IV) oxide does not exist in nature, but a substance with the formula $PbO_{1.9}$ can be produced in the laboratory by oxidation of lead(II) compounds in basic solution. The nonstoichiometric nature of this compound is caused by defects in the crystal structure. The crystal has some vacancies in positions where there should be oxide ions. These imperfections in the crystal (lattice defects) make lead(IV) oxide an electrical conductor, since the oxide ions can jump from hole to hole. This makes possible the use of lead(IV) oxide as an electrode (the cathode) in the lead storage battery.

Table 18.14 summarizes some important reactions of the Group 4A elements.

Table 18.14 Selected Reactions of the Group 4A Elements	
Reaction	*Comment*
$M + 2X_2 \rightarrow MX_4$	X_2 = any halogen molecule; M = Ge or Sn; Pb gives PbX_2
$M + O_2 \rightarrow MO_2$	M = Ge or Sn; high temperatures; Pb gives PbO or Pb_3O_4
$M + 2H^+ \rightarrow M^{2+} + H_2$	M = Sn or Pb

For Review

Summary

The representative elements have chemical properties determined by their valence s and p electrons. Although the chemical properties of the members of a group are similar in many ways, there is usually a dramatic difference between the first member and the rest of the group due to size variations. For example, hydrogen in Group 1A is much smaller than lithium and forms covalent bonds because it has a much greater attraction for electrons than do the larger members of Group 1A. The first member of a group forms the strongest π bonds, causing elemental nitrogen and oxygen to exist as N_2 and O_2 molecules, while phosphorus and sulfur exist as P_4 and S_8 molecules.

The most abundant element is oxygen, followed by silicon. The most abundant metals are aluminum and iron, which are found as ores in which they are combined with nonmetals, most commonly oxygen.

The Group 1A elements have the valence-electron configuration ns^1 and lose the one electron readily to form M^+ ions, except for hydrogen, which is a nonmetal. The alkali metals all react vigorously with water to form M^+ and OH^- ions and hydrogen gas. With oxygen they form a series of oxides. The regular oxide is formed by lithium (Li_2O). Sodium forms the peroxide Na_2O_2 in excess oxygen, and potassium, rubidium, and cesium form the superoxides of general formula MO_2.

Hydrogen can form covalent compounds with other nonmetals and can form salts with very active metals. Hydrogen's binary compounds are called hydrides. Ionic hydrides are formed when hydrogen combines with the Group 1A and Group 2A metals. The hydride ion (H^-) is a strong reducing agent. Covalent hydrides are formed when hydrogen combines with other nonmetals. Metallic hydrides are formed when hydrogen atoms migrate into transition metal crystals.

The Group 2A elements (with the valence-electron configuration ns^2) are called the alkaline earth metals because of the basicity of their oxides. Only the smallest (first) member of the group, beryllium, has an amphoteric oxide. The alkaline earth metals react less vigorously with water than do the alkali metals, beryllium and magnesium showing no reaction at all at 25°C. The heavier alkaline earth metals form ionic nitrides and hydrides. Solid BeH_2 is a polymeric compound that contains three-center bonds in which one electron pair is shared among three atoms.

Hard water contains Ca^{2+} and Mg^{2+} ions, which can be removed by precipitation of $CaCO_3$ or by ion-exchange resins. These polymeric molecules have many ionic sites, usually with Na^+ ions bound to them. When hard water is passed over the resin, the Ca^{2+} and Mg^{2+} ions replace Na^+ on the resin, and are removed from the water.

The Group 3A elements (with the valence-electron configuration ns^2np^1) show increasing metallic character going down the group. Boron is a nonmetal that forms covalent hydrides called boranes; these are highly electron-deficient with three-center bonds and are therefore very reactive. Aluminum, a metal, has some covalent characteristics, as do gallium and indium. The chemistry of thallium is completely metallic.

The Group 4A elements (with the valence-electron configuration ns^2np^2) also show a change from nonmetallic to metallic properties in going down the group. However, all these elements can form covalent bonds to nonmetals. The MX_4

Key Terms

Section 18.1
representative elements
transition metals
lanthanides
actinides
metalloids (semimetals)
metallurgy
liquefaction

Section 18.2
alkali metals
superoxide
nitride salt

Section 18.3
hydride
ionic (saltlike) hydride
covalent hydride
metallic (interstitial) hydride

Section 18.4
alkaline earth metals
hard water
ion exchange
ion-exchange resin
cation-exchange resin

Section 18.5
boranes
inert-pair effect

compounds, except those of carbon, can react with Lewis bases to form two additional covalent bonds; CX_4 compounds cannot react in this way because carbon has no $2d$ orbitals and the $3d$ orbitals are too high in energy to be used.

A blue question or exercise number indicates that the answer to that question or exercise appears at the back of this book and a solution appears in the *Solutions Guide*.

Questions

1. Although the earth was formed from the same interstellar material as the sun, there is little elemental hydrogen (H_2) in the earth's atmosphere. Explain.

2. List two major industrial uses of hydrogen.

3. Name the three types of hydrides. How do they differ?

4. Many lithium salts are hygroscopic (absorb water), whereas the corresponding salts of the other alkali metals are not. Explain.

5. What evidence supports putting hydrogen in Group 1A of the periodic table? In some periodic tables hydrogen is listed separately from any of the groups. In what ways is hydrogen unlike a typical Group 1A element?

6. Describe how potassium superoxide is used in a self-contained breathing apparatus.

7. All the Group 1A and 2A metals are produced by electrolysis of molten salts. Why?

8. How do the acidities of the aqueous solutions of the alkaline earth metal ions (M^{2+}) change in going down the group?

9. Why is graphite a good lubricant? What advantages does it have over grease- or oil-based lubricants?

10. What are some of the structural differences between quartz and amorphous SiO_2?

11. Why are the tin(IV) halides more volatile than the tin(II) halides?

12. What type of semiconductor is formed when a Group 3A element is added as an impurity to Si or Ge?

13. Diagonal relationships in the periodic table exist as well as the vertical relationships. For example, Be and Al are similar in some of their properties as are B and Si. Rationalize why these diagonal relationships hold for properties such as size, ionization energy, and electron affinity.

14. What is the inert-pair effect? How is it important in the properties of thallium and lead?

Exercises

In this section similar exercises are paired.

Group 1A Elements

15. Hydrogen is produced commercially by the reaction of methane with steam:

$$CH_4(g) + H_2O(g) \rightleftharpoons CO(g) + 3H_2(g)$$

a. Calculate $\Delta H°$ and $\Delta S°$ for this reaction (use the data in Appendix 4).

b. What temperatures will favor product formation at standard conditions? Assume $\Delta H°$ and $\Delta S°$ do not depend on temperature.

16. The major industrial use of hydrogen is in the production of ammonia by the Haber process:

$$3H_2(g) + N_2(g) \rightarrow 2NH_3(g)$$

a. Using data from Appendix 4, calculate $\Delta H°$, $\Delta S°$, and $\Delta G°$ for the Haber process reaction.

b. Is the reaction spontaneous at standard conditions?

c. At what temperatures is the reaction spontaneous at standard conditions? Assume $\Delta H°$ and $\Delta S°$ do not depend on temperature.

17. Name each of the following compounds.
   a. Li_2O
   b. KO_2
   c. Na_2O_2

18. Write the formula for each of the following compounds.
   a. lithium nitride
   b. potassium carbonate
   c. rubidium hydroxide
   b. sodium hydride

19. Complete and balance the following reactions.
   a. $Li_2O(s) + H_2O(l) \rightarrow$
   b. $Na_2O_2(s) + H_2O(l) \rightarrow$
   c. $LiH(s) + H_2O(l) \rightarrow$
   d. $KO_2(s) + H_2O(l) \rightarrow$

20. Write balanced equations describing the reaction of lithium metal with each of the following: O_2, S_8, Cl_2, P_4, H_2, H_2O, and HCl.

21. Lithium reacts with acetylene in liquid ammonia to produce LiC_2H (lithium acetylide, $LiC\equiv CH$) and hydrogen gas. Write a balanced equation for this reaction. What type of reaction is this?

22. Show how the reaction of NaH with water

$$NaH(s) + H_2O(l) \longrightarrow Na^+(aq) + OH^-(aq) + H_2(g)$$

can be described as both an oxidation–reduction and an acid–base reaction.

Group 2A Elements

23. Name each of the following compounds.
   a. $MgCO_3$ b. $BaSO_4$ c. $Sr(OH)_2$

24. Write the formula for each of the following compounds.
  a. calcium nitride
  b. beryllium chloride
  c. barium hydride

25. Magnesium nitride and magnesium phosphide are expected to react with water in a fashion similar to lithium nitride. Write equations describing the reactions of magnesium nitride and magnesium phosphide with water.

26. Write balanced equations describing the reaction of Sr with each of the following: O_2, S_8, Cl_2, P_4, H_2, H_2O, and HCl.

27. Predict the geometry about beryllium in the compound Cl_2BeNH_3. What hybrid orbitals are predicted for beryllium and nitrogen in this compound? What type of acid is $BeCl_2$?

28. Would you expect $BeCl_2NH_3$ or another compound to form from the reaction of $BeCl_2$ with an excess of ammonia? Draw Lewis structures of other products that might be produced.

29. The U.S. Public Health Service recommends the fluoridation of water as a means for preventing tooth decay. The recommended concentration is 1 mg F^- per liter. The presence of calcium ions in hard water can precipitate the added fluoride. What is the maximum molarity of calcium ions in hard water if the fluoride concentration is at the USPHS recommended level? (K_{sp} for $CaF_2 = 4.0 \times 10^{-11}$)

30. Slaked lime, $Ca(OH)_2$, is used to soften hard water by removing calcium ions from hard water through the reaction

$$Ca(OH)_2(aq) + Ca^{2+}(aq) + 2HCO_3^-(aq) \longrightarrow$$
$$2CaCO_3(s) + 2H_2O(l)$$

Although $CaCO_3(s)$ is considered insoluble, some of it does dissolve in aqueous solutions. Calculate the molar solubility of $CaCO_3$ in water ($K_{sp} = 8.7 \times 10^{-9}$).

31. What mass of barium is produced when molten $BaCl_2$ is electrolyzed by a current of 2.50×10^5 A for 6.00 hours?

32. Electrolysis of an alkaline earth metal chloride using a current of 5.00 A for 748 seconds deposits 0.471 g of metal at the cathode. What is the identity of the alkaline earth metal chloride?

Group 3A Elements

33. Name each of the following compounds.
  a. In_2O
  b. In_2O_3
  c. BF_3

34. Write the formula for each of the following compounds.
  a. aluminum sulfate
  b. indium(III) chloride
  c. thallium(I) oxide

35. Boron hydrides were once evaluated for possible use as rocket fuels. Complete and balance the following equation for the combustion of diborane.

$$B_2H_6 + O_2 \longrightarrow B(OH)_3$$

36. Elemental boron is produced by reduction of boron oxide with magnesium to give boron and magnesium oxide. Write a balanced equation for this reaction.

37. Ga_2O_3 is an amphoteric oxide, and In_2O_3 is a basic oxide. Write equations for the reactions that illustrate these properties.

38. Aluminum hydroxide is amphoteric and will dissolve in both acidic and basic solutions. Write balanced chemical equations representing each process.

39. Write equations describing the reactions of Ga with each of the following: F_2, O_2, S_8, N_2, and HCl.

40. Write a balanced equation describing the reaction of aluminum metal with concentrated aqueous sodium hydroxide.

Group 4A Elements

41. Draw Lewis structures for CF_4, GeF_4, and GeF_6^{2-}. Predict the molecular structure (including bond angles), and give the expected hybridization of the central atom in these three substances. Explain why CF_6^{2-} does not form.

42. Carbon and sulfur form compounds with the formulas CS_2 and C_3S_2. Draw Lewis structures and predict the shapes of these two compounds.

43. Elemental silicon was not isolated until 1823 when J. J. Berzelius succeeded in reducing K_2SiF_6 with molten potassium.
  a. Write a balanced equation for this reaction.
  b. Describe the bonding in K_2SiF_6.

44. Write equations describing the reactions of Sn with each of the following: Cl_2, O_2, and HCl.

45. Why are people advised not to drink hot tap water if their plumbing contains lead solder?

46. Calculate the solubility of $Pb(OH)_2$ ($K_{sp} = 1.2 \times 10^{-15}$) in water. Is $Pb(OH)_2$ more or less soluble in acidic solutions? Explain.

47. Name each of the following compounds.
  a. CCl_4
  b. $SiCl_4$
  c. $PbCl_2$
  d. $SnCl_2$

48. Write the formula for each of the following compounds.
  a. carbon monoxide
  b. silicon dioxide
  c. tin(IV) sulfide
  d. lead(II) sulfide

49. The resistivity (a measure of electrical resistance) of graphite is $(0.4 \text{ to } 5.0) \times 10^{-4}$ ohm · cm in the basal plane. (The basal plane is the plane of the six-membered rings of carbon atoms.) The resistivity is 0.2 to 1.0 ohm · cm along the axis perpendicular to the plane. The resistivity of diamond is 10^{14} to 10^{16} ohm · cm and is independent of direction. How can you account for this behavior in terms of the structures of graphite and diamond?

50. Silicon carbide (SiC) is an extremely hard substance. Propose a structure for SiC.

Additional Exercises

51. Calculate $\Delta H°$ for the reaction

$$2K(s) + 2H_2O(l) \longrightarrow 2KOH(aq) + H_2(g)$$

A 5.00-g chunk of potassium is dropped into 1.00 kg of water at 24.0°C. What is the final temperature of the water after the preceding reaction occurs? Assume that all the heat is used to raise the temperature of the water, and assume that the specific heat capacity of the solution is 4.18 J/°C · g. (Never run this reaction. It is very dangerous; it bursts into flame!)

52. Predict the structure of BeF_2 in the gas phase. What structure would you predict for $BeF_2(s)$?

53. In the 1950s and 1960s, several nations conducted tests of nuclear warheads in the atmosphere. It was customary following each test to monitor the concentration of strontium-90 (a radioactive isotope of strontium) in milk. Why would strontium-90 tend to accumulate in milk?

54. The compound $BeSO_4 \cdot 4H_2O$ cannot be dehydrated easily by heating. It dissolves in water to give an acidic solution. Explain these observations.

55. The compound $AlCl_3$ is quite volatile and appears to exist as a dimer in the gas phase. Propose a structure for this dimer.

56. Assume that element 113 is produced. What is the expected electron configuration for element 113? What oxidation states would be exhibited by element 113 in its compounds?

57. Calculate the pH of a 0.050 M $Al(NO_3)_3$ solution. The K_a value for $Al(H_2O)_6^{3+}$ is 1.4×10^{-5}.

58. The compound with the formula TlI_3 is a black solid. Given the following standard reduction potentials:

$$Tl^{3+} + 2e^- \longrightarrow Tl^+ \quad \mathscr{E}° = +1.25 \text{ V}$$
$$I_3^- + 2e^- \longrightarrow 3I^- \quad \mathscr{E}° = +0.55 \text{ V}$$

would you formulate this compound as thallium(III) iodide or thallium(I) triiodide?

59. How could you determine experimentally whether the compound Ga_2Cl_4 contains two gallium(II) ions or one gallium(I) and one gallium(III) ion? (*Hint:* Consider the electron configurations of the three possible ions.)

60. Tricalcium aluminate, an important component of Portland cement, is 44.4% calcium and 20.0% aluminum by mass. The remainder is oxygen.
    a. Calculate the empirical formula of tricalcium aluminate.
    b. The structure of tricalcium aluminate was not determined until 1975. The aluminate anion ($Al_6O_{18}^{18-}$) has the following structure:

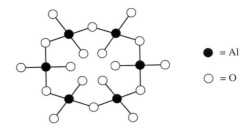

What is the molecular formula of tricalcium aluminate?
    c. How would you describe the bonding in the $Al_6O_{18}^{18-}$ anion?

61. In Exercise 103 in Chapter 5, the pressure of CO_2 in a bottle of sparkling wine was calculated assuming that the CO_2 was insoluble in water. This was a bad assumption. Redo this problem by assuming CO_2 obeys Henry's law. Use the data given in that problem to calculate the partial pressure of CO_2 in the gas phase and the solubility of CO_2 in the wine at 25°C. The Henry's law constant for CO_2 is 32 L · atm/mol at 25°C with Henry's law in the form $P = kC$, where C is the concentration of the gas in mol/L.

62. What is the mole ratio of lead(II) to lead(IV) in red lead (Pb_3O_4)?

63. Which Group 4A elements are capable of reducing H^+ to H_2? Write balanced equations describing the reactions.

Challenge Problems

64. a. Many biochemical reactions that occur in cells require relatively high concentrations of potassium ion (K^+). The concentration of K^+ in muscle cells is about 0.15 M. The concentration of K^+ in blood plasma is about 0.0050 M. The high internal concentration in cells is maintained by pumping K^+ from the plasma. How much work must be done to transport 1.0 mol of K^+ from the blood to the inside of a muscle cell at 37°C (normal body temperature)?
    b. When 1.0 mol of K^+ is transferred from blood to the cells, do any other ions have to be transported? Why or why not?
    c. Cells use the hydrolysis of adenosine triphosphate, abbreviated ATP, as a source of energy. Symbolically, this reaction can be represented as

$$ATP(aq) + H_2O(l) \longrightarrow ADP(aq) + H_2PO_4^-(aq)$$

where ADP represents adenosine diphosphate. For this reaction at 37°C, $K = 1.7 \times 10^5$. How many moles of ATP must be hydrolyzed to provide the energy for the transport of 1.0 mol of K^+? Assume standard conditions for the ATP hydrolysis reaction.

65. EDTA is used as a complexing agent in chemical analysis. Solutions of EDTA, usually containing the disodium salt Na_2H_2EDTA, are also used to treat heavy metal poisoning. The equilibrium constant for the following reaction is 1.0×10^{23}:

$$Pb^{2+}(aq) + H_2EDTA^{2-}(aq) \rightleftharpoons PbEDTA^{2-}(aq) + 2H^+(aq)$$

$$EDTA^{4-} = \begin{array}{c} ^-O_2C-CH_2 \\ ^-O_2C-CH_2 \end{array} N-CH_2-CH_2-N \begin{array}{c} CH_2-CO_2^- \\ CH_2-CO_2^- \end{array}$$

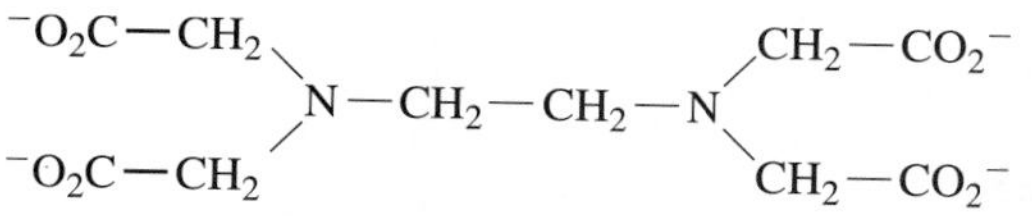

Ethylenediaminetetraacetate

Calculate the $[Pb^{2+}]$ at equilibrium in a solution originally 0.0010 M in Pb^{2+}, 0.050 M in H_2EDTA^{2-}, and buffered at pH = 6.00.

66. The compounds CCl_4 and H_2O do not react with each other. On the other hand, silicon tetrachloride reacts with water according to the equation

$$SiCl_4(l) + 2H_2O(l) \longrightarrow SiO_2(s) + 4HCl(aq)$$

Discuss the importance of thermodynamics and kinetics in the reactivity of water with $SiCl_4$ as compared with its lack of reactivity with CCl_4.

67. One reason suggested to account for the instability of long chains of silicon atoms is that the decomposition involves the transition state shown below:

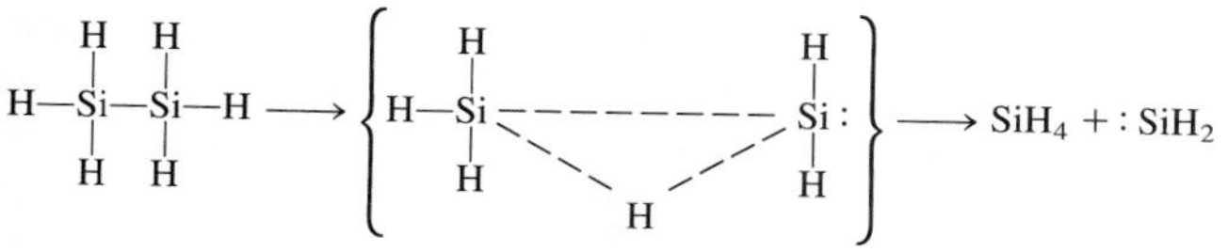

The activation energy for such a process is 210 kJ/mol, which is less than either the Si—Si or Si—H energy. Why would a similar mechanism not be expected to be very important in the decomposition of long carbon chains?

68. From the information on the temperature stability of white and gray tin given in this chapter, which form would you expect to have the more ordered structure?

Marathon Problem

This problem is designed to incorporate several concepts and techniques into one situation. Marathon Problems can be used in class by groups of students to help facilitate problem-solving skills.

69. Use the symbols of the elements described in the following clues to fill in the blanks that spell out the name of a famous American scientist. Although this scientist was better known as a physicist than as a chemist, the Philadelphia institute that bears his name does include a biochemistry research facility.

$$\underline{} \quad \underline{} \quad \underline{} \, \underline{} \, \underline{} \, \underline{} \, \underline{} \, \underline{}$$
  (1)   (2)   (3)   (4)   (5) (6)   (7)

(1) The oxide of this metal is amphoteric.
(2) You might be surprised to learn that a binary compound of sodium with this element has the formula NaX_3, a compound used in airbags.
(3) This alkali metal is radioactive.
(4) This element is the alkali metal with the least negative standard reduction potential. Write its symbol in reverse order.
(5) Potash is an oxide of this alkali metal.
(6) This is the only alkali metal that reacts directly with nitrogen to make a binary compound with formula M_3N.
(7) This element is the first in Group 3A for which the +1 oxidation state is exhibited in stable compounds. Use only the second letter of its symbol.

CHAPTER 19

The Representative Elements: Groups 5A Through 8A

Contents

*I*n Chapter 18 we saw that vertical groups of elements tend to show similar chemical characteristics because they have identical valence-electron configurations. Generally, metallic character increases going down a group, as the valence electrons are found farther from the nucleus. Also, recall that the most dramatic change in properties occurs after the first group member, mainly because the most dramatic change in size occurs between the first and second group members.

As we proceed from Group 1A to Group 7A, the elements change from active metals (electron donors) to strong nonmetals (electron acceptors). Thus it is not surprising that the middle groups show the most varied chemistry: Some group members behave principally as metals, others behave mainly as nonmetals, and some show both tendencies. The elements in Groups 5A and 6A show great chemical variety and form many compounds of considerable practical value. The halogens (Group 7A) are nonmetals that are also found in many everyday substances such as household bleach, photographic films, and "automatic" sunglasses. The elements in Group 8A (the noble gases) are most useful in their elemental forms, but their ability to form compounds, discovered only within the past 40 years, has provided important tests for the theories of chemical bonding.

In this chapter we give an overview of the elements in Groups 5A through 8A, concentrating on the chemistry of the most important elements in these groups: nitrogen, phosphorus, oxygen, sulfur, and the halogens.

The carnivorous pitcher plant "eats" insects to utilize the nitrogen held in the insect tissue.

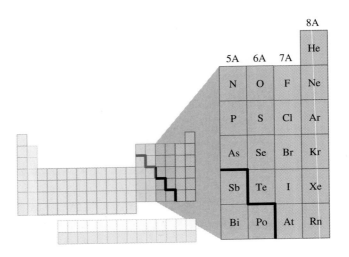

19.1   *The Group 5A Elements*

The Group 5A elements (with the valence-electron configuration ns^2np^3) are prepared as shown in Table 19.1, and they show remarkably varied chemical properties. As usual, metallic character increases going down the group, as is apparent from the electronegativity values (Table 19.1). *Nitrogen* and *phosphorus* are nonmetals that can gain three electrons to form $3-$ anions in salts with active metals, for example, magnesium nitride (Mg_3N_2) and beryllium phosphide (Be_3P_2). The chemistry of these two important elements is discussed in the next two sections.

Table 19.1 Selected Physical Properties, Sources, and Methods of Preparation for the Group 5A Elements

Element	Electro-negativity	Sources	Method of Preparation
Nitrogen	3.0	Air	Liquefaction of air
Phosphorus	2.1	Phosphate rock ($Ca_3(PO_4)_2$)	$2Ca_3(PO_4)_2 + 6SiO_2 \rightarrow$ $6CaSiO_3 + P_4O_{10}$
		Fluorapatite ($Ca_5(PO_4)_3F$)	$P_4O_{10} + 10C \rightarrow$ $4P + 10CO$
Arsenic	2.0	Arsenopyrite (Fe_3As_2, FeS)	Heating arsenopyrite in the absence of air
Antimony	1.9	Stibnite (Sb_2S_3)	Roasting Sb_2S_3 in air to form Sb_2O_3 and then reduction with carbon
Bismuth	1.9	Bismite (Bi_2O_3), bismuth glance (Bi_2S_3)	Roasting Bi_2S_3 in air to form Bi_2O_3 and then reduction with carbon

Bismuth and *antimony* tend to be metallic, readily losing electrons to form cations. Although these elements have five valence electrons, so much energy is required to remove all five that no ionic compounds containing Bi^{5+} or Sb^{5+} ions are known. Three pentahalides (BiF_5, $SbCl_5$, and SbF_5) are known, but these are molecular rather than ionic compounds. The fact that no other pentahalides of these elements are known no doubt results from the strong oxidizing ability of bismuth and antimony in the +5 oxidation state. In fact, BiF_5 is an excellent fluorinating agent, readily decomposing to bismuth trifluoride and fluorine:

Molecular Models: BiF_5, $SbCl_5$, SbF_5

$$BiF_5 \longrightarrow BiF_3 + F_2$$

Salts containing the Bi^{3+} or Sb^{3+} ions, such as $Sb_2(SO_4)_3$ and $Bi(NO_3)_3$, are quite common. When these salts are dissolved in water, the resulting hydrated cations are very acidic. For example, the reaction of the Bi^{3+} ion with water can be represented as

$$Bi^{3+}(aq) + H_2O(l) \longrightarrow BiO^+(aq) + 2H^+(aq)$$

where BiO^+ is called the *bismuthyl ion.* If chloride ion is added to this solution, a white salt, bismuthyl chloride ($BiOCl$), precipitates. Antimony exhibits similar chemistry in aqueous solution.

The Group 5A elements can form molecules or ions that involve three, five, or six covalent bonds to the Group 5A atom. Examples involving three single bonds are NH_3, PH_3, NF_3, and $AsCl_3$. Each of these molecules has a lone pair of electrons (and thus can behave as a Lewis base) and a pyramidal shape as predicted by the VSEPR model (see Fig. 19.1).

All the Group 5A elements except nitrogen can form molecules with five covalent bonds (of general formula MX_5). Nitrogen cannot form such molecules because of its small size and lack of available *d* orbitals. The MX_5 molecules have a trigonal bipyramidal shape (see Fig. 19.1) as predicted by the VSEPR model, and the central atom is described as dsp^3 hybridized. The MX_5 molecules can accept an additional electron pair to form ionic species containing six covalent bonds. An example is

Molecular Models: PF_3, PF_5, $PF_6{}^-$, PCl_3, $PCl_4{}^+$, PCl_5, $PCl_6{}^-$, P_4, As_4, Sb_4

$$PF_5 + F^- \longrightarrow PF_6{}^-$$

where the $PF_6{}^-$ anion has an octahedral shape (see Fig. 19.1) and the phosphorus atom is described as d^2sp^3 hybridized.

Although the MX_5 molecules have a trigonal bipyramidal structure in the gas phase, the solids of many of these compounds contain the ions $MX_4{}^+$ and $MX_6{}^-$ (Fig. 19.2), where the $MX_4{}^+$ cation is tetrahedral (the atom represented by M is described as sp^3 hybridized) and the $MX_6{}^-$ anion is octahedral (the atom represented by M is described as d^2sp^3 hybridized). Examples are PCl_5, which in the solid state contains $PCl_4{}^+$ and $PCl_6{}^-$, and AsF_3Cl_2, which in the solid state contains $AsCl_4{}^+$ and $AsF_6{}^-$.

As discussed in Section 18.1, the ability of the Group 5A elements to form π bonds decreases dramatically after nitrogen. This explains why elemental nitrogen exists as N_2 molecules, whereas the other elements in the group exist as larger aggregates containing single bonds. For example, in the gas phase, the elements phosphorus, arsenic, and antimony consist of P_4, As_4, and Sb_4 molecules, respectively.

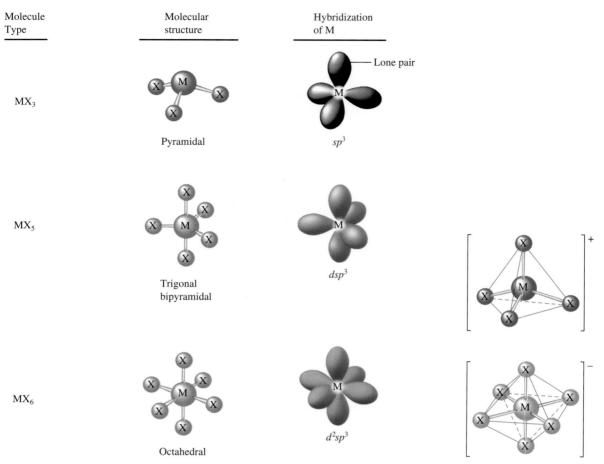

Molecule Type	Molecular structure	Hybridization of M
MX$_3$	Pyramidal	sp^3 (Lone pair)
MX$_5$	Trigonal bipyramidal	dsp^3
MX$_6$	Octahedral	d^2sp^3

Figure 19.1
The molecules of the types MX$_3$, MX$_5$, and MX$_6$ formed by Group 5A elements.

Figure 19.2
The structures of the tetrahedral MX$_4^+$ and octahedral MX$_6^-$ ions.

19.2 *The Chemistry of Nitrogen*

At the earth's surface, virtually all elemental nitrogen exists as the N$_2$ molecule with its very strong triple bond (941 kJ/mol). Because of this high bond strength, the N$_2$ molecule is so unreactive that it can coexist with most other elements under normal conditions without undergoing any appreciable reaction. This property makes nitrogen gas very useful as a medium for experiments involving substances that react with oxygen or water. Such experiments can be done using an inert-atmosphere box of the type shown in Fig. 19.3.

The strength of the triple bond in the N$_2$ molecule is important both thermodynamically and kinetically. Thermodynamically, the great stability of the N≡N bond

At the Center for Disease Control in Atlanta, Georgia, a worker checks samples stored in a liquid nitrogen tank.

means that most binary compounds containing nitrogen decompose exothermically to the elements, for example:

$$N_2O(g) \longrightarrow N_2(g) + \tfrac{1}{2}O_2(g) \qquad \Delta H° = -82 \text{ kJ}$$
$$NO(g) \longrightarrow \tfrac{1}{2}N_2(g) + \tfrac{1}{2}O_2(g) \qquad \Delta H° = -90 \text{ kJ}$$
$$NO_2(g) \longrightarrow \tfrac{1}{2}N_2(g) + O_2(g) \qquad \Delta H° = -34 \text{ kJ}$$
$$N_2H_4(g) \longrightarrow N_2(g) + 2H_2(g) \qquad \Delta H° = -95 \text{ kJ}$$
$$NH_3(g) \longrightarrow \tfrac{1}{2}N_2(g) + \tfrac{3}{2}H_2(g) \qquad \Delta H° = +46 \text{ kJ}$$

Molecular Models: N_2O, NO, NO_2, N_2H_4, NH_3

Figure 19.3

An inert-atmosphere box used when working with oxygen- or water-sensitive materials. The box is filled with an inert gas such as nitrogen, and work is done through the ports fitted with large rubber gloves.

Of these compounds, only ammonia is thermodynamically more stable than its component elements. That is, only for ammonia is energy required (endothermic process, positive value of $\Delta H°$) to decompose the molecule to its elements. For the remaining molecules, energy is released when decomposition to the elements occurs as a result of the great stability of N_2.

Molecular Models: nitroglycerin, trinitrofoluene

The importance of the thermodynamic stability of N_2 can be seen clearly in the power of nitrogen-based explosives, such as nitroglycerin ($C_3H_5N_3O_9$), which has the structure

Figure 19.4
Chemical explosives are used to demolish a building in Miami, Florida.

When ignited or subjected to sudden impact, nitroglycerin decomposes very rapidly and exothermically:

$$4C_3H_5N_3O_9(l) \longrightarrow 6N_2(g) + 12CO_2(g) + 10H_2O(g) + O_2(g) + \text{energy}$$

An explosion occurs; that is, large volumes of gas are produced in a fast, highly exothermic reaction. Note that 4 moles of liquid nitroglycerin produce 29 (6 + 12 + 10 + 1) moles of gaseous products. This alone produces a large increase in volume. However, also note that the products, including N_2, are very stable molecules with strong bonds. Their formation is therefore accompanied by the release of large quantities of energy as heat, which increases the gaseous volume. The hot, rapidly expanding gases produce a pressure surge and damaging shock wave.

Pure nitroglycerin is quite dangerous because it explodes with little provocation. However, in 1867 the Swedish inventor Alfred Nobel found that if nitroglycerin is absorbed in porous silica, it can be handled quite safely. This tremendously important explosive (see Fig. 19.4), which he called *dynamite*, earned Nobel a great fortune, which he subsequently used to establish the Nobel Prizes.

Most high explosives are organic compounds that, like nitroglycerin, contain nitro ($-NO_2$) groups and produce nitrogen and other gases as products. Another example is *trinitrotoluene*, or TNT, a solid at normal temperatures, which decomposes as follows:

$$2C_7H_5N_3O_6(s) \longrightarrow 12CO(g) + 5H_2(g) + 3N_2(g) + 2C(s) + \text{energy}$$

Note that 2 moles of solid TNT produce 20 moles of gaseous products plus energy.

Sample Exercise *19.1*   *Decomposition of NH₄NO₂*

When ammonium nitrite is heated, it decomposes to nitrogen gas and water. Calculate the volume of N_2 gas produced from 1.00 g of solid NH_4NO_2 at 250°C and 1.00 atm.

Solution

The decomposition reaction is

$$NH_4NO_2(s) \xrightarrow{\text{Heat}} N_2(g) + 2H_2O(g)$$

Using the molar mass of NH_4NO_2 (64.05 g/mol), we first calculate the moles of NH_4NO_2:

$$1.00 \text{ g } NH_4NO_2 \times \frac{1 \text{ mol } NH_4NO_2}{64.05 \text{ g } NH_4NO_2} = 1.56 \times 10^{-2} \text{ mol } NH_4NO_2$$

Since 1 mol N_2 is produced for each mole of NH_4NO_2, 1.56×10^{-2} mol N_2 will be produced in the given experiment. We can calculate the volume of N_2 from the ideal gas law:

$$PV = nRT$$

In this case we have

$$P = 1.00 \text{ atm}$$
$$n = 1.56 \times 10^{-2} \text{ mol}$$
$$R = 0.08206 \text{ L} \cdot \text{atm/K} \cdot \text{mol}$$
$$T = 250 + 273 = 523 \text{ K}$$

and the volume of N_2 is

$$V = \frac{nRT}{P} = \frac{(1.56 \times 10^{-2} \text{ mol})\left(0.08206 \dfrac{\text{L} \cdot \text{atm}}{\text{K} \cdot \text{mol}}\right)(523 \text{ K})}{1.00 \text{ atm}}$$

$$= 0.670 \text{ L}$$

See Exercises 19.17 and 19.18.

The effect of bond strength on the kinetics of reactions involving the N_2 molecule is illustrated by the synthesis of ammonia from nitrogen and hydrogen, a reaction we have discussed many times before. Because a large quantity of energy is required to disrupt the $N{\equiv}N$ bond, the ammonia synthesis reaction has a negligible rate at room temperature, even though the equilibrium constant is very large ($K \approx 10^6$) at 25°C. Of course, the most direct way to increase the rate is to raise the temperature, but since the reaction is very exothermic, that is,

$$N_2(g) + 3H_2(g) \longrightarrow 2NH_3(g) \qquad \Delta H° = -92 \text{ kJ}$$

the value of K decreases significantly with a temperature increase (at 500°C, $K \approx 10^{-2}$).

Obviously, the kinetics and the thermodynamics of this reaction are in opposition. A compromise must be reached: high pressure to force the equilibrium to the right and high temperature to produce a reasonable rate. The **Haber process** for manufacturing ammonia illustrates this compromise (see Fig. 19.5). The process is carried out at a pressure of about 250 atm and a temperature of approximately 400°C. Even higher temperatures would be required except that a catalyst, consisting of a

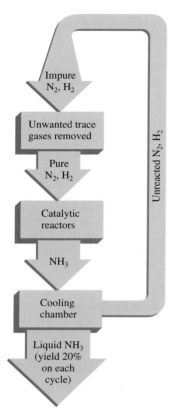

Figure 19.5

A schematic diagram of the Haber process for the manufacture of ammonia.

solid iron oxide mixed with small amounts of potassium oxide and aluminum oxide, is used to facilitate the reaction.

Nitrogen is essential to living systems. The problem with nitrogen is not one of supply—we are surrounded by it—but of changing it from inert N_2 molecules to a form usable by plants and animals. The process of transforming N_2 to other nitrogen-containing compounds is called **nitrogen fixation.** The Haber process is one example of nitrogen fixation. The ammonia produced can be applied to the soil as a fertilizer, since plants can readily employ the nitrogen in ammonia to make the nitrogen-containing biomolecules essential for their growth.

Nitrogen fixation also results from the high-temperature combustion process in automobile engines. The nitrogen in the air drawn into the engine reacts at a significant rate with oxygen to form nitric oxide (NO), which further reacts with oxygen from the air to form nitrogen dioxide (NO_2). This nitrogen dioxide, which is an important contributor to photochemical smog in many urban areas (see Section 12.8), eventually reacts with moisture in the air and reaches the soil to form nitrate salts, which are plant nutrients.

Nitrogen fixation also occurs naturally. For example, lightning provides the energy to disrupt N_2 and O_2 molecules in the air, producing highly reactive nitrogen and oxygen atoms that attack other N_2 and O_2 molecules to form nitrogen oxides that eventually become nitrates. Although lightning traditionally has been credited with forming about 10% of the total fixed nitrogen, recent studies indicate that lightning may account for as much as half the fixed nitrogen available on earth. Another natural nitrogen fixation process is provided by bacteria that reside in the root nodules of plants such as beans, peas, and alfalfa. These **nitrogen-fixing bacteria** readily allow the conversion of nitrogen to ammonia and other nitrogen-containing compounds useful to plants. The efficiency of these bacteria is intriguing: They produce ammonia at soil temperature and 1 atm of pressure, whereas the Haber process requires severe conditions of 400°C and 250 atm. For obvious reasons, researchers are studying these bacteria intensively.

When plants and animals die, they decompose, and the elements they consist of are returned to the environment. In the case of nitrogen, the return of the element to the atmosphere as nitrogen gas, called **denitrification,** is carried out by bacteria

Nodules on the roots of pea plants contain nitrogen-fixing bacteria.

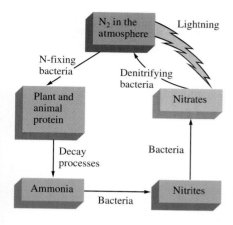

Figure 19.6

The nitrogen cycle. To be used by plants and animals, nitrogen must be converted from N_2 to nitrogen-containing compounds, such as nitrates, ammonia, and proteins. The nitrogen is returned to the atmosphere by natural decay processes.

that change nitrates to nitrogen. The complex **nitrogen cycle** is summarized in Fig. 19.6. It has been estimated that as much as 10 million tons per year more nitrogen is currently being fixed by natural and human processes than is being returned to the atmosphere. This fixed nitrogen is accumulating in the soil, lakes, rivers, and oceans, where it can promote the growth of algae and other undesirable organisms.

Nitrogen Hydrides

By far the most important hydride of nitrogen is **ammonia** (NH_3). A toxic, colorless gas with a pungent odor, ammonia is manufactured in huge quantities (~30 billion pounds per year), mainly for use in fertilizers.

The pyramidal ammonia molecule (see Fig. 19.1) has a lone pair of electrons on the nitrogen atom and polar N—H bonds. This structure leads to a high degree of intermolecular interaction by hydrogen bonding in the liquid state and produces an unusually high boiling point ($-33.4°C$) for a substance of such low molar mass. Note, however, that the hydrogen bonding in liquid ammonia is clearly not as important as that in liquid water, which has about the same molar mass but a much higher boiling point. The water molecule has two polar bonds involving hydrogen and two lone pairs—the right combination for optimal hydrogen bonding—in contrast to the one lone pair and three polar bonds of the ammonia molecule.

As we saw in Chapter 14, ammonia behaves as a base and reacts with acids to produce ammonium salts, for example,

$$NH_3(g) + HCl(g) \longrightarrow NH_4Cl(s)$$

A second nitrogen hydride of major importance is **hydrazine** (N_2H_4). The Lewis structure of hydrazine is

indicating that each nitrogen atom should be sp^3 hybridized with bond angles close to 109.5 degrees (the tetrahedral angle), since the nitrogen atom is surrounded by four electron pairs. The observed structure with bond angles of 112 degrees (see Fig. 19.7) agrees reasonably well with these predictions. Hydrazine, a colorless

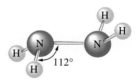

Figure 19.7

The molecular structure of hydrazine (N_2H_4). This arrangement minimizes the repulsion between the lone pairs on the nitrogen atoms by placing them on opposite sides.

liquid with an ammonia-like odor, freezes at 2°C and boils at 113.5°C. This boiling point is quite high for a compound with a molar mass of 32 g/mol; this suggests that considerable hydrogen bonding must occur among the polar hydrazine molecules.

Hydrazine is a powerful reducing agent that has been used widely as a rocket propellant. For example, its reaction with oxygen is highly exothermic:

$$N_2H_4(l) + O_2(g) \longrightarrow N_2(g) + 2H_2O(g) \qquad \Delta H° = -622 \text{ kJ}$$

Since hydrazine also reacts vigorously with the halogens, fluorine is often used instead of oxygen as the oxidizer in rocket engines. Substituted hydrazines, where one or more of the hydrogen atoms are replaced by other groups, are also useful rocket fuels. For example, monomethylhydrazine,

is used with the oxidizer dinitrogen tetroxide (N_2O_4) to power the U.S. space shuttle orbiter. The reaction is

$$5N_2O_4(l) + 4N_2H_3(CH_3)(l) \longrightarrow 12H_2O(g) + 9N_2(g) + 4CO_2(g)$$

Because of the large number of gaseous molecules produced and the exothermic nature of this reaction, a very high thrust per mass of fuel is achieved. The reaction is also self-starting—it begins immediately when the fuels are mixed—which is a useful property for rocket engines that must be started and stopped frequently.

Molecular Model: $N_2H_3CH_3$

The space shuttle Endeavor being launched from the Kennedy Space Center in Florida. The space shuttle orbiter uses monomethylhydrazine mixed with an oxidizer as fuel.

Sample Exercise 19.2 Heats of Reaction from Bond Energies

Using the bond energies in Table 8.4, calculate the approximate value of ΔH for the reaction between gaseous monomethylhydrazine and dinitrogen tetroxide:

$$5N_2O_4(g) + 4N_2H_3(CH_3)(g) \longrightarrow 12H_2O(g) + 9N_2(g) + 4CO_2(g)$$

The bonding in N_2O_4 is described by resonance structures that predict that the N—O bonds are intermediate in strength between single and double bonds (assume an average N—O bond energy of 440 kJ/mol).

Solution

To calculate ΔH for this reaction, we must compare the energy necessary to break the bonds of the reactants and the energy released by formation of the bonds in the products:

Breaking bonds requires energy (positive sign), and forming bonds releases energy (negative sign). As summarized in the following table,

$$\Delta H = (21.1 \times 10^3 \text{ kJ}) - (26.1 \times 10^3 \text{ kJ}) = -5.0 \times 10^3 \text{ kJ}$$

The reaction is highly exothermic.

Bonds Broken	Energy Required (kJ/mol)		Bonds Formed	Energy Released (kJ/mol)	
$5 \times 4 = 20$ N$=$O	$20 \times 440 =$	8.8×10^3	$12 \times 2 = 24$ O—H	$24 \times 467 =$	1.12×10^4
$5 + 4 = 9$ N—N	$9 \times 160 =$	1.4×10^3	9 N$\equiv$N	$9 \times 941 =$	8.5×10^3
$4 \times 3 = 12$ N—H	$12 \times 391 =$	4.7×10^3	$4 \times 2 = 8$ C$=$O	$8 \times 799 =$	6.4×10^3
$4 \times 3 = 12$ C—H	$12 \times 413 =$	5.0×10^3			
$4 \times 1 = 4$ C—N	$4 \times 305 =$	1.2×10^3			
Total		21.1×10^3	Total		26.1×10^3

See Exercises 19.19 and 19.20.

The use of hydrazine as a rocket propellant is a rather specialized application. The main industrial use of hydrazine is as a "blowing" agent in the manufacture of plastics. Hydrazine decomposes to form nitrogen gas, which causes foaming in the liquid plastic, which results in a porous texture. Another major use of hydrazine is in the production of agricultural pesticides. Of the many hundreds of hydrazine derivatives (substituted hydrazines) that have been tested, 40 are used as fungicides, herbicides, insecticides, and plant growth regulators.

The manufacture of hydrazine involves the oxidation of ammonia by the hypochlorite ion in basic solution:

$$2NH_3(aq) + OCl^-(aq) \longrightarrow N_2H_4(aq) + Cl^-(aq) + H_2O(l)$$

Although this reaction looks straightforward, the actual process involves many steps and requires high pressure, high temperature, and catalysis to optimize the yield of hydrazine in the face of many competing reactions.

Nitrogen Oxides

Nitrogen forms a series of oxides in which it has an oxidation state from $+1$ to $+5$, as shown in Table 19.2.

Dinitrogen monoxide (N_2O), more commonly called *nitrous oxide* or "laughing gas," has an inebriating effect and has been used as a mild anesthetic by dentists. Because of its high solubility in fats, nitrous oxide is used widely as a propellant in aerosol cans of whipped cream. It is dissolved in the liquid in the can at high pressure and forms bubbles that produce foaming as the liquid is released from the can. A significant amount of N_2O exists in the atmosphere, mostly produced by soil microorganisms, and its concentration appears to be gradually increasing. Because it can strongly absorb infrared radiation, nitrous oxide plays a small but probably significant role in controlling the earth's temperature in the same way that atmospheric carbon dioxide and water vapor do (see the discussion of the greenhouse effect in Section 6.5). Some scientists fear that the rapid decrease of tropical rain forests

Blowing agents such as hydrazine, which forms nitrogen gas on decomposition, are used to produce porous plastics like these styrofoam products.

Molecular Models: NH₃, N₂H₄, N₂O, N₂O₃, N₂O₄, N₂O₅, HNO₃

Table 19.2 Some Common Nitrogen Compounds

Oxidation State of Nitrogen	Compound	Formula	Lewis Structure*
−3	Ammonia	NH_3	H—N̈—H with H below
−2	Hydrazine	N_2H_4	H—N̈—N̈—H with H, H below
−1	Hydroxylamine	NH_2OH	H—N̈—Ö—H with H below
0	Nitrogen	N_2	:N≡N:
+1	Dinitrogen monoxide (nitrous oxide)	N_2O	:N̈=N=Ö:
+2	Nitrogen monoxide (nitric oxide)	NO	:N̈=Ö:
+3	Dinitrogen trioxide	N_2O_3	O₂N—N=O structure
+4	Nitrogen dioxide	NO_2	:Ö—N̈=O
+5	Nitric acid	HNO_3	:Ö—N—Ö—H with =O below

*In some cases, additional resonance structures are needed to fully describe the electron distribution.

resulting from development in countries such as Brazil will significantly affect the rate of production of N_2O by soil organisms and thus will have important effects on the earth's temperature.

In the laboratory, nitrous oxide is prepared by the thermal decomposition of ammonium nitrate:

$$NH_4NO_3(s) \xrightarrow{\text{Heat}} N_2O(g) + 2H_2O(g)$$

This experiment must be done carefully because ammonium nitrate can explode. In fact, one of the greatest industrial disasters in U.S. history occurred in 1947 in Texas, when a ship loaded with ammonium nitrate for use as fertilizer exploded and killed nearly 600 people.

Nitrogen monoxide (NO), commonly called *nitric oxide,* is a colorless gas under normal conditions that can be produced in the laboratory by reaction of 6 *M* nitric acid with copper metal:

$$8H^+(aq) + 2NO_3^-(aq) + 3Cu(s) \longrightarrow 3Cu^{2+}(aq) + 4H_2O(l) + 2NO(g)$$

When this reaction is run in the air, the nitric oxide is immediately oxidized to brown nitrogen dioxide (NO_2).

Do *not* attempt this experiment unless you have the proper safety equipment.

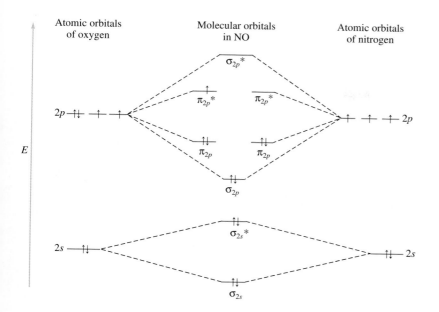

Figure 19.8

The molecular orbital energy-level diagram for nitric oxide (NO). The bond order is 2.5, or $(8 - 3)/2$.

Although nitric oxide is toxic when inhaled, it has been shown to be produced in certain tissues of the human body, where it behaves as a neurotransmitter. Current research indicates that nitric oxide plays a role in regulating blood pressure, blood clotting, and the muscle changes that allow erection of the penis in males.

Since the NO molecule has an odd number of electrons, it is most conveniently described in terms of the molecular orbital model. The molecular orbital energy-level diagram is shown in Fig. 19.8. Note that the NO molecule is paramagnetic and should have a bond order of 2.5, a prediction that is supported by experimental observations. Since the NO molecule has one high-energy electron, it is not surprising that it can be rather easily oxidized to form NO^+, the *nitrosyl ion*. Because an antibonding electron is removed in going from NO to NO^+, the ion should have a stronger bond (the predicted bond order is 3) than the molecule. This is borne out by experiment. The bond lengths and bond energies for nitric oxide and the nitrosyl ion are shown in Table 19.3. The nitrosyl ion is formed when nitric oxide and nitrogen dioxide are dissolved in concentrated sulfuric acid:

$$NO(g) + NO_2(g) + 3H_2SO_4(aq) \longrightarrow 2NO^+(aq) + 3HSO_4^-(aq) + H_3O^+(aq)$$

The ionic compound $NO^+HSO_4^-$ can be isolated from this solution.

A copper penny reacts with nitric acid to produce NO gas, which is immediately oxidized in air to brown NO_2.

Table 19.3 Comparison of the Bond Lengths and Bond Energies for Nitric Oxide and the Nitrosyl Ion

	NO	NO$^+$
Bond length (pm)	115	109
Bond energy (kJ/mol)	630	1020
Bond order (predicted by MO model)	2.5	3

CHEMICAL IMPACT

Nitrous Oxide: Laughing Gas That Propels Whipped Cream and Cars

NITROUS OXIDE (N_2O), more properly called *dinitrogen monoxide,* is a compound with many interesting uses. It was discovered in 1772 by Joseph Priestly (who is also given credit for discovering oxygen gas), and its intoxicating effects were noted almost immediately. In 1798, the 20-year-old Humphry Davy became director of the Pneumatic Institute, which was set up to investigate the medical effects of various gases. Davy tested the effects of N_2O on himself, reporting that after inhaling 16 quarts of the gas in 7 minutes, he became "absolutely intoxicated."

Over the next century "laughing gas," as nitrous oxide became known, was developed as an anesthetic, particularly for dental procedures. Nitrous oxide is still used as an anesthetic, although it has been largely replaced by more modern drugs.

One major use of nitrous oxide today is as the propellant in cans of "instant" whipped cream. The high solubility of N_2O in the whipped cream mixture makes it an excellent candidate for pressurizing the cans of whipping cream.

Another current use of nitrous oxide is to produce "instant horsepower" for hot rods and street racers. Because the reaction of N_2O with O_2 to form NO actually absorbs heat, this reaction has a cooling effect when placed in the fuel mixture in an automobile engine. This cooling effect lowers combustion temperatures, thus allowing the fuel–air mixture to be significantly more dense (the density of a gas is inversely proportional to temperature). This effect can produce a burst of additional power in excess of 200 horsepower. Because engines are not designed to run steadily at such high power levels, the nitrous oxide is injected from a tank when extra power is desired.

Nitric oxide is thermodynamically unstable and decomposes to nitrous oxide and nitrogen dioxide:

$$3NO(g) \longrightarrow N_2O(g) + NO_2(g)$$

Nitrogen dioxide (NO_2) is also an odd-electron molecule and has a V-shaped structure. The brown, paramagnetic NO_2 molecule readily dimerizes to form dinitrogen tetroxide,

$$2NO_2(g) \rightleftharpoons N_2O_4(g)$$

which is diamagnetic and colorless. The value of the equilibrium constant is ~1 for this process at 55°C, and since the dimerization is exothermic, K decreases as the temperature increases.

Production of NO_2 by power plants and automobiles leads to smog (see Section 12.8).

Sample Exercise 19.3 Molecular Orbital Description of NO⁻

Use the molecular orbital model to predict the bond order and magnetism of the NO⁻ ion.

Solution

Using the energy-level diagram for the NO molecule in Fig. 19.8, we can see that NO⁻ has one more antibonding electron than NO. Thus there will be unpaired electrons in the two π_{2p}^* orbitals, and NO^- will be paramagnetic with a bond order of $(8-4)/2$, or 2. Note that the bond in the NO^- ion is weaker than that in the NO molecule.

See Exercises 19.23 and 19.24.

The least common of the nitrogen oxides are *dinitrogen trioxide* (N_2O_3), a blue liquid that readily dissociates into gaseous nitric oxide and nitrogen dioxide, and *dinitrogen pentoxide* (N_2O_5), which under normal conditions is a solid that is best viewed as a mixture of NO_2^+ and NO_3^- ions. Although N_2O_5 molecules do exist in the gas phase, they readily dissociate to nitrogen dioxide and oxygen:

$$2N_2O_5(g) \rightleftharpoons 4NO_2(g) + O_2(g)$$

This reaction follows first-order kinetics, as was discussed in Section 12.4.

Oxyacids of Nitrogen

Nitric acid is an important industrial chemical (almost 10 million tons are produced annually) used in the manufacture of many products, such as nitrogen-based explosives and ammonium nitrate for use as fertilizer.

Nitric acid is produced commercially by the oxidation of ammonia in the **Ostwald process** (see Fig. 19.9). In the first step of this process, ammonia is oxidized to nitric oxide:

$$4NH_3(g) + 5O_2(g) \longrightarrow 4NO(g) + 6H_2O(g) \qquad \Delta H° = -905 \text{ kJ}$$

Although this reaction is highly exothermic, it is very slow at 25°C. There is also a side reaction between nitric oxide and ammonia:

$$4NH_3(g) + 6NO(g) \longrightarrow 5N_2(g) + 6H_2O(g)$$

which is particularly undesirable because it traps the nitrogen as very unreactive N_2 molecules. To speed up the desired reaction and minimize the effects of the competing reaction, the ammonia oxidation is carried out using a catalyst of a platinum–rhodium alloy heated to 900°C. Under these conditions, there is a 97% conversion of the ammonia to nitric oxide.

In the second step, nitric oxide reacts with oxygen to produce nitrogen dioxide:

$$2NO(g) + O_2(g) \longrightarrow 2NO_2(g) \qquad \Delta H° = -113 \text{ kJ}$$

This oxidation reaction has a rate that *decreases* with increasing temperature. Because of this very unusual behavior, the reaction is carried out at ~25°C and is kept at this temperature by cooling with water.

The third step in the Ostwald process is the absorption of nitrogen dioxide by water:

$$3NO_2(g) + H_2O(l) \longrightarrow 2HNO_3(aq) + NO(g) \qquad \Delta H° = -139 \text{ kJ}$$

The gaseous NO produced in this reaction is recycled to be oxidized to NO_2. The aqueous nitric acid from this process is about 50% HNO_3 by mass, which can be increased to 68% by distillation to remove some of the water. The maximum

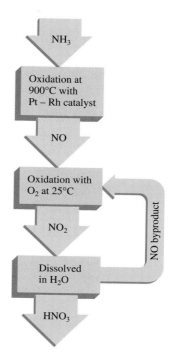

Figure 19.9

The Ostwald process.

Molecular Model: HNO_3

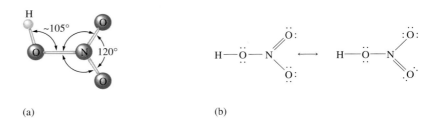

(a) (b)

Figure 19.10

(a) The molecular structure of HNO_3. (b) The resonance structures of HNO_3.

An azeotrope is a solution that, like a pure liquid, distills at a constant temperature without a change in composition.

concentration attainable this way is 68% because nitric acid and water form an *azeotrope* at this concentration. The solution can be further concentrated to 95% HNO_3 by treatment with concentrated sulfuric acid, which strongly absorbs water; H_2SO_4 is often used as a dehydrating (water-removing) agent.

Nitric acid is a colorless, fuming liquid (bp = 83°C) with a pungent odor; it decomposes in sunlight via the following reaction:

$$4HNO_3(l) \xrightarrow{h\nu} 4NO_2(g) + 2H_2O(l) + O_2(g)$$

As a result, nitric acid turns yellow as it ages because of the dissolved nitrogen dioxide. The common laboratory reagent known as concentrated nitric acid is 15.9 M HNO_3 (70.4% HNO_3 by mass) and is a very strong oxidizing agent. The resonance structures and molecular structure of HNO_3 are shown in Fig. 19.10. Note that the hydrogen is bound to an oxygen atom rather than to nitrogen, as the formula suggests.

Nitric acid reacts with metal oxides, hydroxides, and carbonates and with other ionic compounds containing basic anions to form nitrate salts. For example,

$$Ca(OH)_2(s) + 2HNO_3(aq) \longrightarrow Ca(NO_3)_2(aq) + 2H_2O(l)$$

Nitrate salts are generally very soluble in water.

Nitrous acid (HNO_2) is a weak acid,

$$HNO_2(aq) \rightleftharpoons H^+(aq) + NO_2^-(aq) \qquad K_a = 4.0 \times 10^{-4}$$

that forms pale yellow nitrite (NO_2^-) salts. In contrast to nitrates, which are often used as explosives, nitrites are quite stable even at high temperatures. Nitrites are usually prepared by bubbling equal numbers of moles of nitric oxide and nitrogen dioxide into the appropriate aqueous solution of a metal hydroxide, for example,

$$NO(g) + NO_2(g) + 2NaOH(aq) \longrightarrow 2NaNO_2(aq) + H_2O(l)$$

19.3 *The Chemistry of Phosphorus*

Although phosphorus lies directly below nitrogen in Group 5A of the periodic table, its chemical properties are significantly different from those of nitrogen. The differences arise mainly from four factors: nitrogen's ability to form much stronger π bonds, the greater electronegativity of nitrogen, the larger size of the phosphorus atom, and the availability of empty valence d orbitals on phosphorus.

(a)

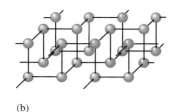
(b)

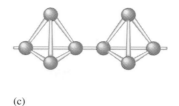
(c)

Figure 19.11
(a) The P_4 molecule found in white phosphorus. (b) The crystalline network structure of black phosphorus. (c) The chain structure of red phosphorus.

The chemical differences are apparent in the elemental forms of nitrogen and phosphorus. In contrast to the diatomic form of elemental nitrogen, which is stabilized by strong π bonds, there are several solid forms of phosphorus, all containing aggregates of atoms. *White phosphorus,* which contains discrete tetrahedral P_4 molecules [see Fig. 19.11(a)], is very reactive and bursts into flames on contact with air (it is said to be *pyrophoric*). To prevent this, white phosphorus is commonly stored under water. White phosphorus is quite toxic, and the P_4 molecules are very damaging to tissue, particularly the cartilage and bones of the nose and jaw. The much less reactive forms known as *black phosphorus* and *red phosphorus* are network solids (see Section 10.5). Black phosphorus has a regular crystalline structure [Fig. 19.11(b)], but red phosphorus is amorphous and is thought to consist of chains of P_4 units [Fig. 19.11(c)]. Red phosphorus can be obtained by heating white phosphorus in the absence of air at 1 atm. Black phosphorus is obtained from either white or red phosphorus by heating at high pressures.

Even though phosphorus has a lower electronegativity than nitrogen, it will form phosphides (ionic substances containing the P^{3-} anion) such as Na_3P and Ca_3P_2. Phosphide salts react vigorously with water to produce *phosphine* (PH_3), a toxic, colorless gas:

$$2Na_3P(s) + 6H_2O(l) \longrightarrow 2PH_3(g) + 6Na^+(aq) + 6OH^-(aq)$$

Phosphine is analogous to ammonia, although it is a much weaker base ($K_b \approx 10^{-26}$) and much less soluble in water. Because phosphine has a relatively small affinity for protons, phosphonium (PH_4^+) salts are very uncommon and not very stable—only PH_4I, PH_4Cl, and PH_4Br are known.

Phosphine has the Lewis structure

$$\left[H-\overset{\cdot\cdot}{\underset{\underset{H}{|}}{P}}-H \right]$$

and a pyramidal molecular structure, as we would predict from the VSEPR model. However, it has bond angles of 94 degrees, rather than 107 degrees, as found in the ammonia molecule. The reasons for this are complex, and we will simply regard phosphine as an exception to the simple version of the VSEPR model that we use.

Molecular Models: P_4, PH_3, PH_4^+

Molecular Models: P_4O_6, P_4O_{10}

Phosphorus Oxides and Oxyacids

Phosphorus reacts with oxygen to form oxides in which it has oxidation states of $+5$ and $+3$. The oxide P_4O_6 is formed when elemental phosphorus is burned in a limited supply of oxygen, and P_4O_{10} is produced when the oxygen is in excess.

CHEMICAL IMPACT

Phosphorus: An Illuminating Element

THE ELEMENTAL FORM of phosphorus was discovered by accident in 1669 by German alchemist Henning Brand when he heated dried urine with sand (alchemists often investigated the chemistry of body fluids in an attempt to better understand the "stuff of life"). When Brand passed the resulting vapors through water, he was able to isolate the form of elemental phosphorus known as *white phosphorus* (contains P_4 molecules). The name *phosphorus* is derived from the Latin *phos*, meaning "light," and *phorus*, meaning "bearing." It seems that when Brand stored the solid white phosphorus in a sealed bottle, it glowed in the dark! This effect—a glow that persists even after the light source has been removed—came to be called *phosphorescence*. Interestingly, the term phosphorescence is derived from the name of an element that really does not phosphoresce. The glow that Brand saw actually was the result of a reaction of oxygen from the air on the surface of white phosphorus. If isolated completely from air, phosphorus does not glow in the dark after being irradiated.

After its discovery, phosphorus became quite a novelty in the seventeenth century. People would deposit a film of phosphorus on their faces and hands so that they would glow in the dark.* This fascination was short-lived—painful, slow-healing burns result from the spontaneous reaction of phosphorus with oxygen from the air.

The phosphorus in safety matches helps ignite the flame in the match.

The greatest consumer use of phosphorus compounds concerns the chemistry of matches. Two kinds of matches are currently available—strike-anywhere matches and safety matches. Both types of matches use phosphorus (in different forms) to help initiate a flame at the match head. The chemistry of matches is quite interesting. The tip of a strike-anywhere match is made from a mixture of powdered glass, binder, and tetraphosphorus trisulfide (P_4S_3). When the match is struck, friction ignites the combustion reaction of P_4S_3:

$$P_4S_3(s) + 6O_2(g) \longrightarrow P_4O_6(g) + 3SO_2(g)$$

The heat from this reaction causes an oxidizing agent such as potassium chlorate to decompose:

$$2KClO_3(s) \longrightarrow 2KCl(s) + 3O_2(g)$$

which in turn causes solid sulfur to melt and react with oxygen, producing sulfur dioxide and more heat. This then ignites a paraffin wax that helps to "light" the wooden stem of the match.

The chemistry of a safety match is quite similar, but the location of the reactants is different. The phosphorus needed to initiate all the reactions is found on the striking surface of the box. Thus, in theory, a safety match is able to ignite only when used with the box. For a safety match, the striking surface contains red phosphorus, which is easily converted to white phosphorus by the friction of the match head on the striking surface. White phosphorus ignites spontaneously in air and generates enough heat to initiate all the other reactions to ignite the match stem.

$$4P \text{ (red)} + \text{energy (friction)} \longrightarrow$$
$$P_4(s)\text{(white)} + 5O_2(g) \longrightarrow$$
$$P_4O_{10}(s) + \text{heat}$$

*An interesting reference to white phosphorus can be found in the Sherlock Holmes mystery, *The Hound of the Baskervilles*, where a large dog was coated with white phosphorus to scare Baskerville family members to death.

These oxides, as shown in Fig. 19.12, can be pictured as being constructed by adding oxygen atoms to the fundamental P_4 structure. The intermediate states, P_4O_7, P_4O_8, and P_4O_9, which contain one, two, and three terminal oxygen atoms, respectively, are also known.

Tetraphosphorus decoxide (P_4O_{10}), which was formerly represented as P_2O_5, has a great affinity for water and thus is a powerful dehydrating agent. For example, it can be used to convert HNO_3 and H_2SO_4 to their parent oxides, N_2O_5 and SO_3, respectively.

When tetraphosphorus decoxide dissolves in water, **phosphoric acid** (H_3PO_4), also called **orthophosphoric acid,** is produced:

The terminal oxygens are the non-bridging oxygen atoms.

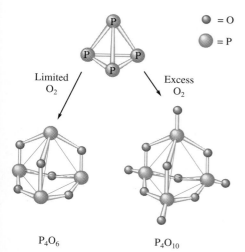

Figure 19.12
The structures of P_4O_6 and P_4O_{10}.

$$P_4O_{10}(s) + 6H_2O(l) \longrightarrow 4H_3PO_4(aq)$$

Pure phosphoric acid is a white solid that melts at 42°C. Aqueous phosphoric acid is a much weaker acid ($K_{a_1} \approx 10^{-2}$) than nitric acid or sulfuric acid and is a poor oxidizing agent.

Phosphate minerals are the main source of phosphoric acid. Unlike nitrogen, phosphorus is found in nature exclusively in a combined state, principally as the PO_4^{3-} ion in phosphate rock, which is mainly calcium phosphate, $Ca_3(PO_4)_2$, and fluorapatite, $Ca_5(PO_4)_3F$. Fluorapatite can be converted to phosphoric acid by grinding up the phosphate rock and forming a slurry with sulfuric acid:

$$Ca_5(PO_4)_3F(s) + 5H_2SO_4(aq) + 10H_2O(l)$$
$$\longrightarrow HF(aq) + 5CaSO_4 \cdot 2H_2O(s) + 3H_3PO_4(aq)$$

(A similar reaction can be written for the conversion of calcium phosphate.) The solid product $CaSO_4 \cdot 2H_2O$, called *gypsum,* is used to manufacture wallboard for the construction of buildings.

The process just described, called the *wet process,* produces only impure phosphoric acid. In another procedure, phosphate rock, sand (SiO_2), and coke are heated in an electric furnace to form white phosphorus:

$$12Ca_5(PO_4)_3F + 43SiO_2 + 90C \longrightarrow 9P_4 + 90CO + 20(3CaO \cdot 2SiO_2) + 3SiF_4$$

The white phosphorus obtained is burned in air to form tetraphosphorus decoxide, which is then combined with water to give phosphoric acid.

Phosphoric acid easily undergoes **condensation reactions,** where a molecule of water is eliminated in the joining of two molecules of acid:

The mineral hydroxyapatite, $Ca_5(PO_4)_3OH$, the principal component of tooth enamel, can be converted to fluorapatite by reaction with fluoride. Fluoride ions added to drinking water and toothpaste help prevent tooth decay because fluorapatite is less soluble in the acids of the mouth than hydroxyapatite.

$$\text{H—O—P—O—H} \quad \text{H—O—P—O—H} \longrightarrow \text{H—O—P—O—P—O—H} + H_2O$$

The product ($H_4P_2O_7$) is called *pyrophosphoric acid.* Further heating produces polymers, such as *tripolyphosphoric acid* ($H_5P_3O_{10}$), which has the structure

Molecular Model: $H_4P_2O_7$, $H_5P_3O_{10}$

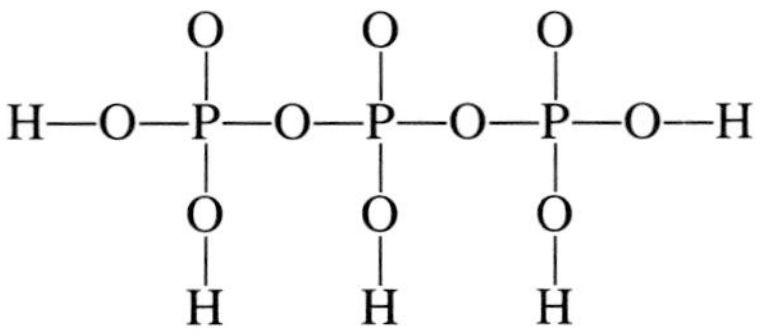

$$\text{H}-\text{O}-\overset{\displaystyle \text{O}}{\underset{\displaystyle \text{H}}{\overset{|}{\underset{|}{\text{P}}}}}-\text{O}-\overset{\displaystyle \text{O}}{\underset{\displaystyle \text{H}}{\overset{|}{\underset{|}{\text{P}}}}}-\text{O}-\overset{\displaystyle \text{O}}{\underset{\displaystyle \text{H}}{\overset{|}{\underset{|}{\text{P}}}}}-\text{O}-\text{H}$$

The sodium salt of tripolyphosphoric acid is widely used in detergents because the $P_3O_{10}^{5-}$ anion can form complexes with metal ions such as Mg^{2+} and Ca^{2+}, which would otherwise interfere with detergent action.

Sample Exercise 19.4 *Structure of Phosphoric Acid*

What are the molecular structure and the hybridization of the central atom of the phosphoric acid molecule?

Solution

In the phosphoric acid molecule, the hydrogen atoms are attached to oxygens, and the Lewis structure is as shown below. Thus the phosphorus atom is surrounded by four effective pairs, which are arranged tetrahedrally. The atom is described as sp^3 hybridized.

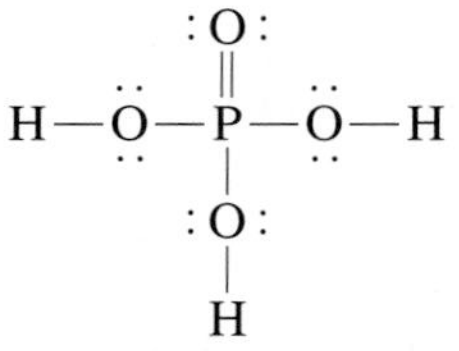

Lewis structure

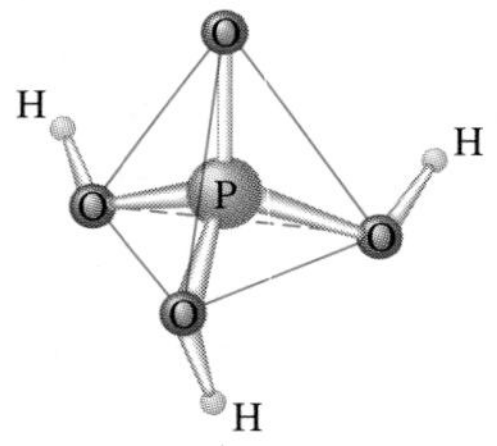

See Exercises 19.27 and 19.28.

When P_4O_6 is placed in water, **phosphorous acid** (H_3PO_3) is formed [Fig. 19.13(a)]. Although the formula suggests a triprotic acid, phosphorous acid is a *diprotic* acid. The hydrogen atom bonded directly to the phosphorus atom is not acidic in aqueous solution; only those hydrogen atoms bonded to the oxygen atoms in H_3PO_3 can be released as protons.

A third oxyacid of phosphorus is *hypophosphorous acid* (H_3PO_2) [Fig. 19.13(b)], which is a monoprotic acid.

Phosphorus in Fertilizers

Phosphorus is essential for plant growth. Although most soil contains large amounts of phosphorus, it is often present as insoluble minerals, which makes it inaccessi-

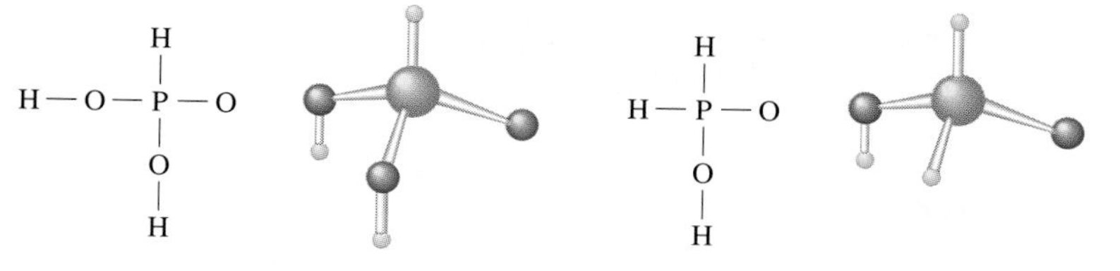

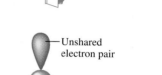

(a)

(b)

Figure 19.13

(a) The structure of phosphorous acid (H_3PO_3). (b) The structure of hypophosphorous acid (H_3PO_2).

ble to plants. Soluble phosphate fertilizers are manufactured by treating phosphate rock with sulfuric acid to make **superphosphate of lime,** a mixture of $CaSO_4 \cdot 2H_2O$ and $Ca(H_2PO_4)_2 \cdot H_2O$. If phosphate rock is treated with phosphoric acid, $Ca(H_2PO_4)_2$, or *triple phosphate,* is produced. The reaction of ammonia and phosphoric acid gives *ammonium dihydrogen phosphate* ($NH_4H_2PO_4$), a very efficient fertilizer because it furnishes both phosphorus and nitrogen.

Molecular Models: H_3PO_3, H_3PO_2, H_3PO_4

Phosphorus Halides

Phosphorus forms all possible halides of the general formulas PX_3 and PX_5, with the exception of PI_5. The PX_3 molecule has the expected pyramidal structure [Fig. 19.14(a)]. Under normal conditions of temperature and pressure, PF_3 is a colorless gas, PCl_3 is a liquid (bp = 74°C), PBr_3 is a liquid (bp = 175°C), and PI_3 is an unstable red solid (mp = 61°C). All the PX_3 compounds react with water to produce phosphorous acid:

$$PX_3 + 3H_2O(l) \longrightarrow H_3PO_3(aq) + 3HX(aq)$$

In the gaseous and liquid states, the PX_5 compounds have molecules with a trigonal bipyramidal structure [Fig. 19.14(b)]. However, PCl_5 and PBr_5 form ionic solids: Solid PCl_5 contains a mixture of octahedral PCl_6^- ions and tetrahedral PCl_4^+ ions, and solid PBr_5 appears to consist of PBr_4^+ and Br^- ions.

The PX_5 compounds react with water to form phosphoric acid:

$$PX_5 + 4H_2O(l) \longrightarrow H_3PO_4(aq) + 5HX(aq)$$

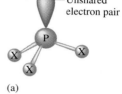

Unshared electron pair

(a)

(b)

Figure 19.14

Structures of the phosphorus halides. (a) The PX_3 compounds have pyramidal molecules. (b) The gaseous and liquid phases of the PX_5 compounds are composed of trigonal bipyramidal molecules.

19.4 *The Group 6A Elements*

Although in Group 6A (Table 19.4) there is the usual tendency for metallic properties to increase going down the group, none of the Group 6A elements (valence-electron configuration n^2np^4) behaves as a typical metal. The most common chemical behavior of a Group 6A atom is to achieve a noble gas electron configuration by adding two electrons to become a 2− anion in ionic compounds with metals. In fact, for most metals, the oxides and sulfides constitute the most common minerals.

The Group 6A elements can form covalent bonds with other nonmetals. For example, they combine with hydrogen to form a series of covalent hydrides of the general formula H_2X. Those members of the group that have valence *d* orbitals available (all except oxygen) commonly form molecules in which they are surrounded by more than eight electrons. Examples are SF_4, SF_6, TeI_4, and $SeBr_4$.

6A

O
S
Se
Te
Po

Molecular Models: SF_4, SF_6, TeI_4, $SeBr_4$

Table 19.4 Selected Physical Properties, Sources, and Methods of Preparation for the Group 6A Elements

Element	Electro-negativity	Radius of X^{2-} (pm)	Source	Method of Preparation
Oxygen	3.5	140	Air	Distillation from liquid air
Sulfur	2.5	184	Sulfur deposits	Melted with hot water and pumped to the surface
Selenium	2.4	198	Impurity in sulfide ores	Reduction of H_2SeO_4 with SO_2
Tellurium	2.1	221	Nagyagite (mixed sulfide and telluride)	Reduction of ore with SO_2
Polonium	2.0	230	Pitchblende	

The two heaviest members of Group 6A can lose electrons to form cations. Although they do not lose all six valence electrons because of the high energies that would be required, tellurium and polonium appear to exhibit some chemistry involving their 4+ cations. However, the chemistry of these Group 6A cations is much more limited than that of the Group 5A elements bismuth and antimony.

In recent years there has been a growing interest in the chemistry of selenium, an element found throughout the environment in trace amounts. Selenium's toxicity has long been known, but recent medical studies have shown an *inverse* relationship between the incidence of cancer and the selenium levels in soil. It has been suggested that the resulting greater dietary intake of selenium by people living in areas of relatively high levels of selenium somehow furnishes protection from cancer. These studies are only preliminary, but selenium is known to be physiologically important (it is involved in the activity of vitamin E and certain enzymes) and selenium deficiency has been shown to be connected to the occurrence of congestive heart failure. Also of importance is the fact that selenium (along with tellurium) is a semiconductor and therefore finds some application in the electronics industry.

Polonium was discovered in 1898 by Marie and Pierre Curie in their search for the sources of radioactivity in pitchblende. Polonium has 27 isotopes and is highly toxic and very radioactive. It has been suggested that the isotope ^{210}Po, a natural contaminant of tobacco and an α-particle emitter (see Section 21.1), might be at least partly responsible for the incidence of cancer in smokers.

19.5 The Chemistry of Oxygen

It is hard to overstate the importance of oxygen, the most abundant element in and near the earth's crust. Oxygen is present in the atmosphere in oxygen gas and ozone; in soil and rocks in oxide, silicate, and carbonate minerals; in the oceans in water; and in our bodies in water and in a myriad of molecules. In addition, most of the energy we need to live and to run our civilization comes from the exothermic reactions of oxygen and carbon-containing molecules.

The most common elemental form of oxygen (O_2) constitutes 21% of the volume of the earth's atmosphere. Since nitrogen has a lower boiling point than oxygen, nitrogen can be boiled away from liquid air, leaving oxygen and small amounts of argon, another component of air. Liquid oxygen is a pale blue liquid that freezes at $-219°C$ and boils at $-183°C$. The paramagnetism of the O_2 molecule can be demonstrated by pouring liquid oxygen between the poles of a strong magnet, where it "sticks" as it boils away (see Fig. 9.40). The paramagnetism of the O_2 molecule can be accounted for by the molecular orbital model (see Fig. 9.39), which also explains its bond strength.

The other form of elemental oxygen is **ozone** (O_3), a molecule that can be represented by the resonance structures

Molecular Models: O_2, O_3

The bond angle in the O_3 molecule is 117 degrees, in reasonable agreement with the prediction of the VSEPR model (three effective pairs require a trigonal planar arrangement). That the bond angle is slightly less than 120 degrees can be explained by concluding that more space is required for the lone pair than for the bonding pairs.

Ozone can be prepared by passing an electric discharge through pure oxygen gas. The electrical energy disrupts the bonds in some O_2 molecules to give oxygen atoms, which react with other O_2 molecules to form O_3. Ozone is much less stable than oxygen at 25°C and 1 atm. For example, $K \approx 10^{-57}$ for the equilibrium

$$3O_2(g) \rightleftharpoons 2O_3(g)$$

A pale blue, highly toxic gas, ozone is a much more powerful oxidizing agent than oxygen. Because of its oxidizing ability, ozone is being considered as a replacement for chlorine in municipal water purification. Chlorine leaves residues of chloro compounds, such as chloroform ($CHCl_3$), which may cause cancer after long-term exposure. Although ozone effectively kills the bacteria in water, one problem with **ozonolysis** is that the water supply is not protected against recontamination, since virtually no ozone remains after the initial treatment. In contrast, for chlorination, significant residual chlorine remains after treatment.

The oxidizing ability of ozone can be highly detrimental, especially when it is formed in the pollution from automobile exhausts (see Section 5.9).

Ozone exists naturally in the upper atmosphere of the earth. The *ozone layer* is especially important because it absorbs ultraviolet light and thus acts as a screen to prevent this radiation, which can cause skin cancer, from penetrating to the earth's surface. When an ozone molecule absorbs this energy, it splits into an oxygen molecule and an oxygen atom:

$$O_3 \xrightarrow{h\nu} O_2 + O$$

If the oxygen molecule and atom collide, they will not stay together as ozone unless a "third body," such as a nitrogen molecule, is present to help absorb the energy released in the bond formation. The third body absorbs the energy as kinetic energy; its temperature is increased. Therefore, the energy originally absorbed as ultraviolet radiation is eventually changed to thermal energy. Thus the ozone prevents the harmful high-energy ultraviolet light from reaching the earth.

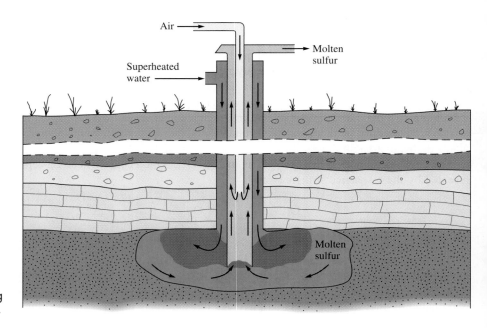

Figure 19.15

The Frasch process for recovering sulfur from underground deposits.

19.6 The Chemistry of Sulfur

Sulfur is found in nature both in large deposits of the free element and in widely distributed ores, such as galena (PbS), cinnabar (HgS), pyrite (FeS_2), gypsum ($CaSO_4 \cdot 2H_2O$), epsomite ($MgSO_4 \cdot 7H_2O$), and glauberite ($Na_2SO_4 \cdot CaSO_4$).

About 60% of the sulfur produced in the United States comes from the underground deposits of elemental sulfur found in Texas and Louisiana. This sulfur is recovered using the **Frasch process** developed by Herman Frasch in the 1890s. Superheated water is pumped into the deposit to melt the sulfur (mp = 113°C), which is then forced to the surface by air pressure (see Fig. 19.15). The remaining 40% of sulfur produced in the United States is either a by-product of the purification of fossil fuels before combustion to prevent pollution or from the sulfur dioxide (SO_2) scrubbed from the exhaust gases when sulfur-containing fuels are burned.

In contrast to oxygen, elemental sulfur exists as S_2 molecules only in the gas phase at high temperatures. Because sulfur atoms form much stronger σ bonds than π bonds, S_2 is less stable at 25°C than larger aggregates such as S_6 and S_8 rings and S_n chains (Fig. 19.16). The most stable form of sulfur at 25°C and 1 atm is

The scrubbing of sulfur dioxide from exhaust gases was discussed in Section 5.9.

Figure 19.16

(a) The S_8 molecule. (b) Chains of sulfur atoms in viscous liquid sulfur. The chains may contain as many as 10,000 atoms.

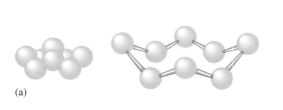
(a)

(b)

called *rhombic sulfur* [see Fig. 19.17(a)], which contains stacked S_8 rings. If rhombic sulfur is melted and heated to 120°C, it forms *monoclinic sulfur* as it cools slowly [Fig. 19.17(b)]. This form also contains S_8 rings, but the rings are stacked differently than they are in rhombic sulfur.

As sulfur is heated beyond its melting point, a relatively nonviscous liquid containing S_8 rings forms initially. With continued heating, the liquid becomes highly viscous as the rings first break and then link up to form long chains. Further heating lowers the viscosity because the long chains are broken down as the energetic sulfur atoms break loose. If the liquid is suddenly cooled, a substance called *plastic sulfur,* which contains S_n chains and has rubberlike qualities, is formed. Eventually, this form reverts back to the more stable S_8 rings.

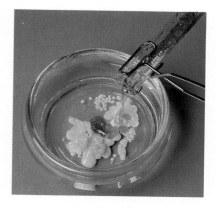

Pouring liquid sulfur into water to produce plastic sulfur.

Sulfur Oxides

From its position below oxygen in the periodic table, we might expect the simplest stable oxide of sulfur to have the formula SO. However, *sulfur monoxide,* which can be produced in small amounts when gaseous sulfur dioxide (SO_2) is subjected to an electrical discharge, is very unstable. The difference in the stabilities of the O_2 and SO molecules probably reflects the stronger π bonding between oxygen atoms than between sulfur and oxygen atoms.

Sulfur burns in air with a bright blue flame to give *sulfur dioxide* (SO_2), a colorless gas with a pungent odor, which condenses to a liquid at −10°C and 1 atm. Sulfur dioxide is a very effective antibacterial agent and is often used to preserve stored fruit. Its structure is given in Fig. 19.18.

Molecular Models: S_8, SO_2, SO_3

Sulfur dioxide reacts with oxygen to produce *sulfur trioxide* (SO_3):

$$2SO_2(g) + O_2(g) \longrightarrow 2SO_3(g)$$

However, this reaction is very slow in the absence of a catalyst. One of the mysteries during early research on air pollution was how the sulfur dioxide produced from the combustion of sulfur-containing fuels is so rapidly converted to sulfur

(a)

(b)

Figure 19.17

(a) Crystals of rhombic sulfur. (b) Crystals of monoclinic sulfur.

(left) A sulfur deposit. (right) Melted sulfur obtained from underground deposits by the Frasch process.

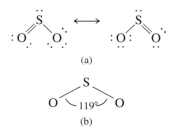

Figure 19.18

(a) Two of the resonance structures for SO_2. (b) SO_2 is a bent molecule with a 119-degree bond angle, as predicted by the VSEPR model.

trioxide. It is now known that dust and other particles can act as heterogeneous catalysts for this process (see Section 12.8). In the preparation of sulfur trioxide for the manufacture of sulfuric acid, a platinum or vanadium(V) oxide (V_2O_5) catalyst is used, and the reaction is carried out at ~500°C, even though this temperature decreases the value of the equilibrium constant for this exothermic reaction.

The bonding in the SO_3 molecule is usually described in terms of the resonance structures shown in Fig. 19.19. The molecule is trigonal planar, as predicted by the VSEPR model. Sulfur trioxide is a corrosive gas with a choking odor that forms white fumes of sulfuric acid when it reacts with moisture in the air. Thus sulfur trioxide and nitrogen dioxide, which reacts with water to form a mixture of nitrous and nitric acids, are the major culprits in the formation of acid rain.

Sulfur trioxide condenses to a colorless liquid at 44.5°C and freezes at 16.8°C to give three solid forms, one containing S_3O_9 rings and the other two containing $(SO_3)_x$ chains (Fig. 19.20).

Oxyacids of Sulfur

Sulfur dioxide dissolves in water to form an acidic solution. The reaction is often represented as

$$SO_2(g) + H_2O(l) \longrightarrow H_2SO_3(aq)$$

Figure 19.19

(a) Three of the resonance structures of SO_3. (b) A resonance structure with three double bonds. (c) SO_3 is a planar molecule with 120-degree bond angles.

where H_2SO_3 is called *sulfurous acid*. However, very little H_2SO_3 actually exists in the solution. The major form of sulfur dioxide in water is SO_2, and the acid dissociation equilibria are best represented as

$$SO_2(aq) + H_2O(l) \rightleftharpoons H^+(aq) + HSO_3^-(aq) \qquad K_{a_1} = 1.5 \times 10^{-2}$$
$$HSO_3^-(aq) \rightleftharpoons H^+(aq) + SO_3^{2-}(aq) \qquad K_{a_2} = 1.0 \times 10^{-7}$$

This situation is analogous to the behavior of carbon dioxide in water (see Section 14.7). Although H_2SO_3 cannot be isolated, salts of SO_3^{2-} (*sulfites*) and HSO_3^- (*hydrogen sulfites*) are well known.

Sulfur trioxide reacts violently with water to produce the diprotic acid **sulfuric acid**:

$$SO_3(g) + H_2O(l) \longrightarrow H_2SO_4(aq)$$

Manufactured in greater amounts than any other chemical, sulfuric acid is usually produced by the *contact process,* which is described at the end of Chapter 3. About 60% of the sulfuric acid manufactured in the United States is used to produce fertilizers from phosphate rock (see Section 19.3). The other 40% is used in lead storage batteries and in petroleum refining, in steel manufacturing, and for various purposes in most of the chemical industries.

Because sulfuric acid has a high affinity for water, it is often used as a dehydrating agent. Gases that do not react with sulfuric acid, such as oxygen, nitrogen, and carbon dioxide, are often dried by bubbling them through concentrated solutions of the acid. Sulfuric acid is such a powerful dehydrating agent that it will remove hydrogen and oxygen from a substance in a 2:1 ratio even when the substance contains no molecular water. For example, concentrated sulfuric acid reacts vigorously with common table sugar (sucrose), leaving a charred mass of carbon (see Fig. 19.21):

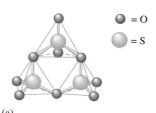

(a)

(b)

Figure 19.20

Different structures for solid SO_3. (a) S_3O_9 rings. (b) $(SO_3)_x$ chains. In both cases the sulfur atoms are surrounded by a tetrahedral arrangement of oxygen atoms.

(a)

(b)

(c)

Figure 19.21

(a) A beaker of sucrose (table sugar). (b) Concentrated sulfuric acid reacts with the sucrose to produce a column of carbon (c), accompanied by an intense burnt-sugar odor.

$$C_{12}H_{22}O_{11}(s) + 11H_2SO_4(conc) \longrightarrow 12C(s) + 11H_2SO_4 \cdot H_2O(l)$$
Sucrose

The preparation of sulfur trioxide provides an example of the compromise that often must be made between thermodynamics and kinetics.

Sulfuric acid is a moderately strong oxidizing agent, especially at high temperatures. Hot concentrated sulfuric acid oxidizes bromide or iodide ions to elemental bromine or iodine, for example,

$$2I^-(aq) + 3H_2SO_4(aq) \longrightarrow I_2(aq) + SO_2(aq) + 2H_2O(l) + 2HSO_4^-(aq)$$

Hot sulfuric acid attacks copper metal:

$$Cu(s) + 2H_2SO_4(aq) \longrightarrow CuSO_4(aq) + 2H_2O(l) + SO_2(aq)$$

The cold acid does not react with copper.

Other Compounds of Sulfur

The acidic properties of sulfuric acid solutions are discussed in Section 14.7.

Molecular Models: H_2SO_3, H_2SO_4, H_2S, HSO_3^-, HSO_4^-

Sulfur reacts with both metals and nonmetals to form a wide variety of compounds in which it has a +6, +4, +2, 0, or −2 oxidation state (see Table 19.5). The −2 oxidation state occurs in the metal sulfides and in *hydrogen sulfide* (H_2S), a toxic, foul-smelling gas that acts as a diprotic acid when dissolved in water. Hydrogen sulfide is a strong reducing agent in aqueous solution, producing a milky looking suspension of finely divided sulfur as one of the products. For example, hydrogen sulfide reacts with chlorine in aqueous solution as follows:

$$H_2S(g) + Cl_2(aq) \longrightarrow 2H^+(aq) + 2Cl^-(aq) + S(s)$$

Milky suspension of sulfur

The prefix *thio* means "sulfur."

Sulfur also forms the **thiosulfate ion** ($S_2O_3^{2-}$), which has the Lewis structure

$$\left[\begin{array}{c} :\ddot{O}: \\ | \\ :\ddot{O}-S-\ddot{S}: \\ | \\ :\ddot{O}: \end{array}\right]^{2-}$$

Note that this anion can be viewed as a sulfate ion in which one of the oxygen atoms has been replaced by sulfur, which is reflected in the name *thio*sulfate. The thiosulfate ion can be formed by heating sulfur with a sulfite salt in aqueous solution:

Table 19.5 Common Compounds of Sulfur with Various Oxidation States

Oxidation State of Sulfur	Compounds
+6	SO_3, H_2SO_4, SO_4^{2-}, SF_6
+4	SO_2, HSO_3^-, SO_3^{2-}, SF_4
+2	SCl_2
0	S_8 and all other forms of elemental sulfur
−2	H_2S, S^{2-}

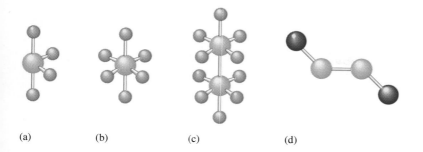

(a)   (b)   (c)   (d)

Figure 19.22
The structures of (a) SF_4, (b) SF_6, (c) S_2F_{10}, and (d) S_2Cl_2.

Molecular Models: SO_3^{2-}, $S_2O_3^{2-}$, $S_4O_6^{2-}$, S_2F_{10}, S_2Cl_2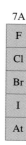

$$S(s) + SO_3^{2-}(aq) \longrightarrow S_2O_3^{2-}(aq)$$

One important use of thiosulfate ion is in photography, where $S_2O_3^{2-}$ dissolves solid silver bromide by forming a complex with the Ag^+ ion (see the Chemical Impact in Section 19.7). Thiosulfate ion is also a good reducing agent and is often used to analyze for iodine:

$$2S_2O_3^{2-}(aq) + I_2(aq) \longrightarrow S_4O_6^{2-}(aq) + 2I^-(aq)$$

where $S_4O_6^{2-}$ is called the *tetrathionate ion.*

Sulfur reacts with the halogens to form a variety of compounds, such as S_2Cl_2, SF_4, SF_6, and S_2F_{10}. The structures of these molecules are shown in Fig. 19.22.

19.7 *The Group 7A Elements*

In our coverage of the representative elements, we have progressed from groups of metallic elements (Groups 1A and 2A), through groups in which the lighter members are nonmetals and the heavier members are metals (Groups 3A, 4A, and 5A), to a group of all nonmetals (Group 6A—although some might prefer to call polonium a metal). The Group 7A elements, the **halogens** (with the valence-electron configuration ns^2np^5), are also all nonmetals whose properties generally vary smoothly going down the group. The only notable exceptions are the unexpectedly low values for the electron affinity of fluorine and the bond energy of the F_2 molecule (see Section 18.1). Table 19.6 summarizes the trends in some physical properties of the halogens.

Because of their high reactivities, the halogens are not found as the free elements in nature. Instead, they are found as halide ions (X^-) in various minerals and in seawater (see Table 19.7).

Although astatine is a member of Group 7A, its chemistry is of no practical importance because all its known isotopes are radioactive. The longest-lived isotope, ^{210}At, has a half-life of only 8.3 hours.

The halogens, particularly fluorine, have very high electronegativity values (Table 19.6). They tend to form polar covalent bonds with other nonmetals and ionic bonds with metals in their lower oxidation states. When a metal ion is in a higher oxidation state, such as $+3$ or $+4$, the metal–halogen bonds are polar covalent ones. For example, $TiCl_4$ and $SnCl_4$ are both covalent compounds that are liquids under normal conditions.

7A
F
Cl
Br
I
At

Table 19.6 Trends in Selected Physical Properties of the Group 7A Elements

Element	Electro-negativity	Radius of X^- (pm)	$\mathscr{E}°$ (V) for $X_2 + 2e \rightarrow 2X^-$	Bond Energy of X_2 (kJ/mol)
Fluorine	4.0	136	2.87	154
Chlorine	3.0	181	1.36	239
Bromine	2.8	185	1.09	193
Iodine	2.5	216	0.54	149
Astatine	2.2	—	—	—

Table 19.7 Some Physical Properties, Sources, and Methods of Preparation for the Group 7A Elements

Element	Color and State	Percentage of Earth's Crust	Melting Point (°C)	Boiling Point (°C)	Sources	Method of Preparation
Fluorine	Pale yellow gas	0.07	−220	−188	Fluorospar (CaF_2), cryolite (Na_3AlF_6), fluorapatite ($Ca_5(PO_4)_3F$)	Electrolysis of molten KHF_2
Chlorine	Yellow-green gas	0.14	−101	−34	Rock salt (NaCl), halite (NaCl), sylvite (KCl)	Electrolysis of aqueous NaCl
Bromine	Red-brown liquid	2.5×10^{-4}	−7.3	59	Seawater, brine wells	Oxidation of Br^- by Cl_2
Iodine	Violet-black solid	3×10^{-5}	113	184	Seaweed, brine wells	Oxidation of I^- by electrolysis or MnO_2

Hydrogen Halides

The hydrogen halides can be prepared by a reaction of the elements:

$$H_2(g) + X_2(g) \longrightarrow 2HX(g)$$

This reaction occurs with explosive vigor when fluorine and hydrogen are mixed. On the other hand, hydrogen and chlorine can coexist with little apparent reaction for relatively long periods in the dark. However, ultraviolet light causes an explosively fast reaction, and this is the basis of a popular lecture demonstration, the "hydrogen–chlorine cannon." Bromine and iodine also react with hydrogen, but more slowly.

The hydrogen halides also can be prepared by treating halide salts with acid. For example, hydrogen fluoride and hydrogen chloride can be prepared as follows:

$$CaF_2(s) + H_2SO_4(aq) \longrightarrow CaSO_4(s) + 2HF(g)$$
$$2NaCl(s) + H_2SO_4(aq) \longrightarrow Na_2SO_4(s) + 2HCl(g)$$

Sulfuric acid is capable of oxidizing Br^- to Br_2 and I^- to I_2 and so cannot be used to prepare hydrogen bromide and hydrogen iodide. However, phosphoric acid, a nonoxidizing acid, can be used to treat bromides and iodides to form the corresponding hydrogen halides.

CHEMICAL IMPACT

Photography

IN BLACK-AND-white photography, light from an object is focused onto a special paper containing an emulsion of solid silver bromide. Silver salts turn dark when exposed to light because the radiant energy stimulates the transfer of an electron to the Ag^+ ion, forming an atom of elemental silver. When photographic paper (film) is exposed to light, the areas exposed to the brightest light form the most silver atoms. The next step is the application of a chemical reducing agent to the film, a process called *developing*. The real advantage of silver-based films is that the silver atoms already present from exposure to light catalyze the reduction of millions of Ag^+ ions in the immediate vicinity in the developing process. Thus the effect of exposure to light is greatly intensified in this chemical reduction process. Once the image has been developed, the unchanged solid silver bromide must be removed so that the film is

Positive and negative images.

no longer light-sensitive and the image is fixed. A solution of sodium thiosulfate (called *hypo*) is used in this *fixing process*:

$$AgBr(s) + 2S_2O_3{}^{2-}(aq)$$
$$\longrightarrow Ag(S_2O_3)_2{}^{3-}(aq) + Br^-(aq)$$

After the excess silver bromide is dissolved and washed away, the fixed image (the *negative*) is ready to produce the positive print. By shining light through the negative onto a fresh sheet of film and repeating the developing and fixing processes, a black-and-white photograph can be produced.

Some physical properties of the hydrogen halides are listed in Table 19.8. Note the very high boiling point for hydrogen fluoride, which results from extensive hydrogen bonding among the very polar HF molecules (Fig. 19.23). Fluoride ion has such a high affinity for protons that in concentrated aqueous solutions of hydrogen fluoride, the ion $[F\text{—}H\text{—}F]^-$ exists, in which an H^+ ion is centered between two F^- ions.

When dissolved in water, the hydrogen halides behave as acids, and all except hydrogen fluoride are completely dissociated. Because water is a much stronger base than Cl^-, Br^-, or I^- ion, the acid strengths of HCl, HBr, and HI cannot be differentiated in water. However, in a less basic solvent, such as glacial (pure) acetic acid, the acids show different strengths of the order

$$\underset{\substack{\text{Strongest}\\\text{acid}}}{\text{H—I}} > \text{H—Br} > \underset{\substack{\text{Weakest}\\\text{acid}}}{\text{H—Cl} \gg \text{H—F}}$$

To see why hydrogen fluoride is the only weak acid in water among the HX molecules, let's consider the dissociation equilibrium

$$HX(aq) \rightleftharpoons H^+(aq) + X^-(aq)$$

where

$$K_a = \frac{[H^+][X^-]}{[HX]}$$

Chlorine, bromine, and iodine.

A candle burning in an atmosphere of Cl₂(g). The exothermic reaction, which involves breaking C—C and C—H bonds in the wax and forming C—Cl bonds in their places, produces enough heat to make the gases in the region incandescent (a flame results).

Table 19.8 Some Physical Properties of the Hydrogen Halides

HX	Melting Point (°C)	Boiling Point (°C)	H—X Bond Energy (kJ/mol)
HF	−83	20	565
HCl	−114	−85	427
HBr	−87	−67	363
HI	−51	−35	295

from a thermodynamic point of view. Recall that acid strength is reflected by the magnitude of K_a—a small K_a value means a weak acid. Also recall that the value of an equilibrium constant depends on the standard free energy change for the reaction as follows:

$$\Delta G° = -RT \ln(K)$$

As $\Delta G°$ becomes more negative, K becomes larger; a *decrease* in free energy favors a given reaction. As we saw in Chapter 16, free energy depends on enthalpy, entropy, and temperature. For a process at constant temperature,

$$\Delta G° = \Delta H° - T\Delta S°$$

Thus, to explain the various acid strengths of the hydrogen halides, we must focus on the factors that determine $\Delta H°$ and $\Delta S°$ for the acid dissociation reaction.

What energy terms are important in determining $\Delta H°$ for the dissociation of HX in water? (Keep in mind that large positive contributions to the value of $\Delta H°$ will tend to make $\Delta G°$ more highly positive, K_a smaller, and the acid weaker.) One important factor is certainly the H—X bond strength. Note from Table 19.8 that the H—F bond is much stronger than the other H—X bonds. This factor tends to make HF a weaker acid than the others.

Another important contribution to $\Delta H°$ is the enthalpy of hydration (see Section 11.2) of X^- (see Table 19.9). As we would expect, the smallest of the halide ions, F^-, has the most negative value—its hydration is the most exothermic. This term favors the dissociation of HF into its ions more so than it does for the other HX molecules.

When H₂O molecules cluster around an ion, an ordering effect occurs, and $\Delta S°_{hyd}$ is negative.

So far we have two conflicting factors: The large HF bond energy tends to make HF a weaker acid than the other hydrogen halides, but the enthalpy of hydration favors the dissociation of HF more than that of the others. In comparing data for HF and HCl, the difference in bond energy (138 kJ/mol) is slightly smaller than the difference in the enthalpies of hydration for the anions (144 kJ/mol). If these were the *only* important factors, HF should be a stronger acid than HCl because the large enthalpy of hydration of F^- more than makes up the large HF bond strength.

As it turns out, the *deciding factor is entropy.* Note from Table 19.9 that the entropy of hydration for F^- is much more negative than for the other halides because of the high degree of ordering that occurs as the water molecules associate with the small F^- ion. Remember that a negative change in entropy is unfavorable. Thus, although the enthalpy of hydration favors dissociation of HF, the *entropy* of hydration strongly opposes it.

Figure 19.23

The hydrogen bonding among HF molecules in liquid hydrogen fluoride.

Table 19.9 The Enthalpies and Entropies of Hydration for the Halide Ions

$$X^-(g) \xrightarrow{H_2O} X^-(aq)$$

X^-	$\Delta H°$ (kJ/mol)	$\Delta S°$ (J/K · mol)
F^-	−510	−159
Cl^-	−366	−96
Br^-	−334	−81
I^-	−291	−64

Hydration becomes more exothermic as the charge density of an ion increases. Thus, for ions of a given charge, the smallest is most strongly hydrated.

Stomach acid is 0.1 M HCl.

This Steuben glass design was etched using hydroflouric acid.

When all these factors are taken into account, $\Delta G°$ for the dissociation of HF in water is positive; that is, K_a is small. In contrast, $\Delta G°$ for dissociation of the other HX molecules in water is negative (K_a is large). This example illustrates the complexity of the processes that occur in aqueous solutions and the importance of entropy effects in that medium.

In practical terms, **hydrochloric acid** is the most important of the **hydrohalic acids,** the aqueous solutions of the hydrogen halides. About 3 million tons of hydrochloric acid are produced annually for use in cleaning steel before galvanizing and in the manufacture of many other chemicals.

Hydrofluoric acid is used to etch glass by reacting with the silica in glass to form the volatile gas SiF_4:

$$SiO_2(s) + 4HF(aq) \longrightarrow SiF_4(g) + 2H_2O(l)$$

Oxyacids and Oxyanions

All the halogens except fluorine combine with various numbers of oxygen atoms to form a series of oxyacids, as shown in Table 19.10. The strengths of these acids vary in direct proportion to the number of oxygen atoms attached to the halogen, as we discussed in Section 14.9.

Table 19.10 The Known Oxyacids of the Halogens*

Oxidation State of Halogen	Fluorine	Chlorine	Bromine	Iodine*	General Name of Acids	General Name of Salts
+1	HOF	HOCl	HOBr	HOI	Hypohalous acid	Hypohalites, MOX
+3	**	HOClO	**	**	Halous acid	Halites, MXO₂
+5	**	HOClO₂	HOBrO₂	HOIO₂	Halic acid	Halates, MXO₃
+7	**	HOClO₃	HOBrO₃	HOIO₃	Perhalic acid	Perhalates, MXO₄

*Iodine also forms $H_4I_2O_9$ (mesodiperiodic acid) and H_5IO_6 (paraperiodic acid).

**Compound is unknown.

The only member of the chlorine series that has been obtained in the pure state is *perchloric acid* ($HOClO_3$), a strong acid and powerful oxidizing agent. Because perchloric acid reacts explosively with many organic materials, it must be handled with great caution. The other oxyacids of chlorine are known only in solution, although salts containing their anions are well known (Fig. 19.24).

Hypochlorous acid (HOCl) is formed when chlorine gas is dissolved in cold water:

$$Cl_2(aq) + H_2O(l) \rightleftharpoons HOCl(aq) + H^+(aq) + Cl^-(aq)$$

Note that in this reaction chlorine is both oxidized (from 0 in Cl_2 to +1 in HOCl) and reduced (from 0 in Cl_2 to −1 in Cl^-). Such a reaction, *where a given element is both oxidized and reduced,* is called a **disproportionation reaction.** Hypochlorous acid and its salts are strong oxidizing agents, and solutions of them are widely used as household bleaches and disinfectants.

Chlorate salts, such as $KClO_3$, are also strong oxidizing agents and are used as weed killers and as oxidizers in fireworks (see Chapter 7) and explosives.

Fluorine forms only one oxyacid, hypofluorous acid (HOF), but at least two oxides. When fluorine gas is bubbled into a dilute solution of sodium hydroxide, the compound *oxygen difluoride* (OF_2) is formed:

$$4F_2(g) + 3H_2O(l) \longrightarrow 6HF(aq) + OF_2(g) + O_2(g)$$

The name for OF_2 is *oxygen difluoride* rather than difluorine oxide because fluorine has a higher electronegativity than oxygen and thus is named as if it were an anion.

Molecular Models: HOF, HOCl, HOBr, $HClO_3$

Oxygen difluoride is a pale yellow gas (bp = −145°C), which is a strong oxidizing agent. The oxide *dioxygen difluoride* (O_2F_2) is an orange solid that can be prepared by passing an electric discharge through an equimolar mixture of fluorine and oxygen gases:

$$F_2(g) + O_2(g) \xrightarrow{\text{Electric discharge}} O_2F_2(s)$$

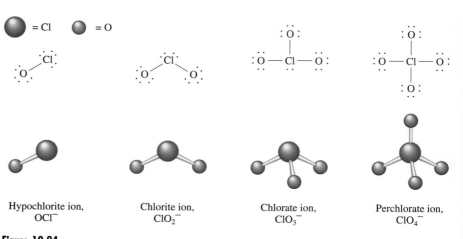

Hypochlorite ion, OCl^-

Chlorite ion, ClO_2^-

Chlorate ion, ClO_3^-

Perchlorate ion, ClO_4^-

Figure 19.24

The structures of the oxychloro anions.

Sample Exercise 19.5 *Bonding Description of* OF_2

Give the Lewis structure, molecular structure, and hybridization of the oxygen atom for OF_2.

Solution

The OF_2 molecule has 20 valence electrons and the Lewis structure is

The four effective pairs around the oxygen are arranged tetrahedrally. Therefore, the oxygen atom is sp^3 hybridized. The molecule is bent (V-shaped), and the bond angle is predicted to be smaller than 109.5 degrees because of the lone-pair repulsions.

See Exercise 19.35.

Other Halogen Compounds

The halogens react readily with most nonmetals to form a variety of compounds, some of which are shown in Table 19.11 on the following page.

Halogens react with each other to form **interhalogen compounds** with the general formula AB_n, where n is typically 1, 3, 5, or 7 and A is the larger of the two halogens. The structures of these compounds (see Fig. 19.25) are predicted accurately by the VSEPR model. The interhalogens are volatile, highly reactive compounds that act as strong oxidizing agents. They react readily with water, forming the halide ion of the more electronegative halogen and the hypohalous acid of the less electronegative halogen; for example,

$$ICl(s) + H_2O(l) \longrightarrow H^+(aq) + Cl^-(aq) + HOI(aq)$$

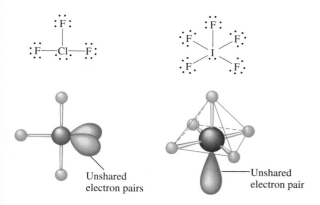

(a) ClF_3 is "T-shaped" (b) IF_5 is square pyramidal

Figure 19.25

The idealized structures of the interhalogens ClF_3 and IF_5. In reality, the lone pairs cause the bond angles to be slightly less than 90 degrees.

Table 19.11 Some Compounds of the Halogens with Nonmetals

Compounds with Group 3A Nonmetals	Compounds with Group 4A Nonmetals	Compounds with Group 5A Nonmetals	Compounds with Group 6A Nonmetals	Compounds with Group 7A Nonmetals
BX_3 (X = F,Cl,Br,I)	CX_4 (X = F,Cl,Br,I)	NX_3 (X = F,Cl,Br,I)	OF_2	ICl
BF_4^-		N_2F_4	O_2F_2	IBr
	SiF_4		OCl_2	BrF
	SiF_6^{2-}	PX_3 (X = F,Cl,Br,I)	OBr_2	BrCl
	$SiCl_4$	PF_5		ClF
		PCl_5	SF_2	
	GeF_4	PBr_5	SCl_2	ClF_3
	GeF_6^{2-}		S_2F_2	BrF_3
	$GeCl_4$	AsF_3	S_2Cl_2	ICl_3
		AsF_5	SF_4	IF_3
			SCl_4	
		SbF_3	SF_6	ClF_5
		SbF_5		BrF_5
			SeF_4	IF_5
			SeF_6	
			$SeCl_2$	IF_7
			$SeCl_4$	
			$SeBr_4$	
			TeF_4	
			TeF_6	
			$TeCl_4$	
			$TeBr_4$	
			TeI_4	

The halogens react with carbon to form many commercially important compounds. Especially significant are a group of polymers, or long-chain compounds (see Section 22.6), made from ethylene molecules:

For example, the compound perfluoroethylene

can react with itself to give the polymer

CHEMICAL IMPACT

Automatic Sunglasses

SUNGLASSES CAN BE troublesome. It seems they are always getting lost or sat on. One solution to this problem for people who wear glasses is photochromic glass—glass that darkens in response to intense light. Recall that glass is a complex, noncrystalline material that is composed of polymeric silicates (see Chapter 10). Of course, glass transmits visible light—its transparency is its most useful property.

Glass can be made photochromic by adding tiny silver chloride crystals that get trapped in the glass matrix as the glass solidifies. Silver chloride has the unusual property of darkening when struck by light—the property that makes the silver halide salts so useful for photographic films. This darkening occurs because light causes an electron transfer from Cl^- to Ag^+ in the silver chloride crystal, forming a silver atom and a chlorine atom. The silver atoms formed in this way tend to migrate to the surface of the silver chloride crystal, where they aggregate to form a tiny crystal of silver metal, which is opaque to light.

In photography the image defined by the grains of silver is fixed by chemical treatment so that it remains permanent. However, in photochromic glass this process must be reversible—the glass must

Glasses with photosensitive lenses. The right lens has been exposed to light and the left one has not.

become fully transparent again when the person goes back indoors. The secret to the reversibility of photochromic glass is the presence of Cu^+ ions. The added Cu^+ ions serve two important functions. First, they reduce the Cl atoms formed in the light-induced reaction. This prevents them from escaping from the crystal:

$$Ag^+ + Cl^- \xrightarrow{h\nu} Ag + Cl$$
$$Cl + Cu^+ \longrightarrow Cu^{2+} + Cl^-$$

Second, when the exposure to intense light ends (the person goes indoors), the Cu^{2+} ions migrate to the surface of the silver chloride crystal, where they accept

electrons from silver atoms as the tiny crystal of silver atoms disintegrates:

$$Cu^{2+} + Ag \longrightarrow Cu^+ + Ag^+$$

The Ag^+ ions are re-formed in this way, then return to their places in the silver chloride crystal, making the glass transparent once again.

Typical photochromic glass decreases to about 20% transmittance (transmits 20% of the light that strikes it) in strong sunlight, and then over a period of a few minutes returns to about 80% transmittance indoors (normal glass has 92% transmittance).

or *Teflon,* a substance with high thermal stability and resistance to chemical attack, used as a coating in many different applications.

Molecular Models: ClF_3, ClF_5

The **Freons,** compounds of the general formula CCl_xF_{4-x}, are very stable compounds that were used as coolant fluids in refrigerators and air conditioners for many years but are now being replaced by more environmentally friendly substances.

Chlorine is found in many other useful carbon compounds. For example, the molecule called *vinyl chloride,* can be polymerized to form *polyvinyl chloride,* or PVC:

Chlorine is also found in many pesticides.

Bromine is used in silver bromide–based photographic films. It is also used to make NaBr and KBr, two chemicals used in sedatives and soporifics (sleeping aids). Bromine-containing compounds are also used as flame retardants for cloth (see Section 22.7).

8A

| He |
| Ne |
| Ar |
| Kr |
| Xe |
| Rn |

19.8 The Group 8A Elements

The Group 8A elements, the **noble gases,** are characterized by filled s and p valence orbitals (electron configuration of $2s^2$ for helium and ns^2np^6 for the others). Because of this, these elements are very unreactive. In fact, no noble gas compounds were known 40 years ago. Selected properties of the Group 8A elements are summarized in Table 19.12.

Helium was identified by its characteristic emission spectrum as a component of the sun before it was found on earth. The major sources of helium on earth are natural gas deposits, where helium was formed from α-particle decay of radioactive elements. The α particle is a helium nucleus that can easily pick up electrons from the environment to form a helium atom. Although helium forms no compounds, it is an important substance that is used as a coolant, as a pressurizing gas for rocket fuels, as a diluent in the gases used for deep-sea diving and spaceship atmospheres, and as the gas in lighter-than-air airships (blimps).

Like helium, *neon* and *argon* form no compounds but are used extensively. For example, neon is employed in luminescent lighting (neon signs), and argon is used to provide the noncorrosive atmosphere in incandescent light bulbs, which prolongs the life of the tungsten filament.

Of the Group 8A elements, only *krypton* and *xenon* have been observed to form chemical compounds. The first of these was prepared in 1962 by Neil Bartlett, an English chemist who used $Xe(g)$ and $PtF_6(g)$ to make the ionic compound with the empirical formula $XePtF_6$.

Less than a year after Barlett's report of $XePtF_6$, a group at Argonne National Laboratory near Chicago prepared xenon tetrafluoride by reaction of xenon and fluorine gases in a nickel reaction vessel at 400°C and 6 atm:

$$Xe(g) + 2F_2(g) \longrightarrow XeF_4(s)$$

Xenon tetrafluoride forms stable colorless crystals. Two other xenon fluorides, XeF_2 and XeF_6, were synthesized by the group at Argonne, and a highly explosive xenon oxide (XeO_3) also was found. The xenon fluorides react with water to form hydrogen fluoride and oxycompounds; for example:

The airship Spirit of Akron *providing TV coverage of an Ohio State vs. Michigan football game.*

Table 19.12 Selected Properties of Group 8A Elements

Element	Melting Point (°C)	Boiling Point (°C)	Atmospheric Abundance (% by Volume)	Examples of Compounds
Helium	−270	−269	5×10^{-4}	None
Neon	−249	−246	1×10^{-3}	None
Argon	−189	−186	9×10^{-1}	None
Krypton	−157	−153	1×10^{-4}	KrF_2
Xenon	−112	−107	9×10^{-6}	XeF_4, XeO_3, XeF_6

$$XeF_6(s) + 3H_2O(l) \longrightarrow XeO_3(aq) + 6HF(aq)$$
$$XeF_6(s) + H_2O(l) \longrightarrow XeOF_4(aq) + 2HF(g)$$

In the past 40 years, other xenon compounds have been prepared, for example, XeO_4 (explosive), XeO_2F_4, XeO_2F_2, and XeO_3F_2. These compounds contain discrete molecules with covalent bonds between the xenon and the other atoms. The structures of some of these xenon compounds are summarized in Fig. 19.26. A few compounds of krypton, such as KrF_2 and KrF_4, also have been observed. There is evidence that radon also reacts with fluorine, but the radioactivity of radon makes its chemistry very difficult to study.

Molecular Models: XeF_2, XeF_4, XeF_6, XeO_3, XeO_4, XeO_3F_2, $XeOF_4$

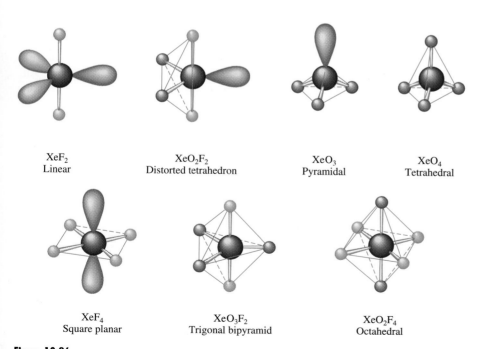

| XeF_2 Linear | XeO_2F_2 Distorted tetrahedron | XeO_3 Pyramidal | XeO_4 Tetrahedral |

| XeF_4 Square planar | XeO_3F_2 Trigonal bipyramid | XeO_2F_4 Octahedral |

Figure 19.26
The structures of several known xenon compounds.

Sample Exercise 19.6 The Structure of XeF₆

Use the VSEPR model to predict whether XeF$_6$ has an octahedral structure.

Solution

The XeF$_6$ molecule contains 50 [8 + 6(7)] valence electrons and the Lewis structure is

$$
\begin{array}{c}
:\!\ddot{F}\; :\!\ddot{F}\!: \;\; \ddot{F}: \\
\diagdown \;\; | \;\; \diagup \\
:\!Xe\!: \\
\diagup \;\; | \;\; \diagdown \\
:\!\ddot{F}\; :\!\ddot{F}\!: \;\; \ddot{F}:
\end{array}
$$

The xenon atom has seven pairs of electrons around it (one lone pair and six bonding pairs), one more pair than can be accommodated in an octahedral arrangement. Thus XeF$_6$ will not have an octahedral structure, but should be distorted from this geometry by the extra electron pair. There is experimental evidence that the structure of XeF$_6$ is not octahedral.

See Exercises 19.41 and 19.42.

For Review

Key Terms

Section 19.2
Haber process
nitrogen fixation
nitrogen-fixing bacteria
denitrification
nitrogen cycle
ammonia
hydrazine
nitric acid
Ostwald process

Section 19.3
phosphoric (orthophosphoric) acid
condensation reactions
phosphorous acid
superphosphate of lime

Section 19.5
ozone
ozonolysis

Section 19.6
Frasch process

Summary

The Group 5A elements show remarkably varied chemical properties. Nitrogen and phosphorus are nonmetals and can form 3− anions in salts with active metals. Antimony and bismuth tend to be metallic, although no ionic compounds with their 5+ ions are known. The compounds containing bismuth(V) or antimony(V) are molecular rather than ionic. All the Group 5A members except nitrogen form molecules with five covalent bonds. The ability of these elements to form π bonds decreases dramatically after nitrogen. Thus phosphorus, arsenic, and antimony exist in the gas phase as aggregates of more than two atoms.

The strength of the triple bond in the N$_2$ molecule is of great importance both thermodynamically and kinetically. Most binary nitrogen-containing compounds decompose exothermically to the elements, a fact that explains the power of nitrogen-based explosives.

The nitrogen cycle is composed of a series of steps describing how nitrogen is cycled in the natural environment. One step involves the transformation of nitrogen gas in the atmosphere into nitrogen-containing compounds useful to plants, a process called nitrogen fixation. The Haber process is one example of nitrogen fixation; another is provided by nitrogen-fixing bacteria in the root nodules of certain plants. Denitrification is the reverse process—the release of nitrogen gas back into the atmosphere.

Ammonia, the most important nitrogen hydride, has pyramidal molecules with polar bonds. Hydrazine (N$_2$H$_4$) is a powerful reducing agent. Nitrogen forms a series of oxides in which it has an oxidation state ranging from 1 to 5; the most important are nitric oxide and nitrogen dioxide. Nitric acid (HNO$_3$) is an important strong acid made by the Ostwald process, in which ammonia is first oxidized to nitric oxide, which is then oxidized to nitrogen dioxide, which is dissolved in water to form nitric acid. Nitrous acid (HNO_2) is a weak acid.

Phosphorus exists in three elemental forms: white, black, and red. Although it has a lower electronegativity than nitrogen, phosphorus forms the P^{3-} anion in phosphides. Phosphine (PH_3) has a structure analogous to that of ammonia but with bond angles close to 90°. Phosphorus reacts with oxygen to form P_4O_6 (oxidation state of +3) and P_4O_{10} (oxidation state of +5). When P_4O_{10} dissolves in water, it forms phosphoric acid (H_3PO_4), a weak acid. Phosphoric acid readily undergoes condensation reactions, giving up water molecules to form polymeric acids.

The Group 6A elements show the usual tendency of increasing metallic properties going down the group. However, none behave as typical metals. Most commonly, these elements achieve noble gas configurations by adding two electrons to form 2− anions. Group 6A elements also can form covalent bonds with other nonmetals.

Oxygen exists in two elemental forms, O_2 and ozone (O_3), a V-shaped molecule. Ozone is a powerful oxidizing agent with important environmental implications.

Sulfur also exists in two elemental forms, rhombic and monoclinic, both of which contain stacks of S_8 rings. Sulfur occurs in nature both as the free element and in ores as sulfides and sulfates. Sulfur forms three oxides. Sulfur monoxide (SO) is unstable. When sulfur dioxide (SO_2) is dissolved in water, sulfurous acid (H_2SO_3) forms, which is analogous in many respects to carbonic acid as a weak acid. Sulfur trioxide (SO_3) dissolves in water to form sulfuric acid (H_2SO_4), an extremely important industrial chemical and a strong acid that is a powerful dehydrating agent. Sulfur forms a variety of compounds in which it has a +6, +4, +2, 0, or −2 oxidation state.

The Group 7A elements, the halogens, are all nonmetals. The halogens form hydrogen halides (HX) that behave as strong acids in water, except for hydrogen fluoride. Hydrofluoric acid is a weak acid because of the strong H—F bond and because the entropy of hydration for the F^- ion is much more negative than it is for the other halide ions. The oxyacids of the halogens become stronger as the number of oxygen atoms attached to the halogen increases. Interhalogens are compounds of two different halogens. Halogen–carbon compounds are important industrially; examples are Teflon, PVC, and the Freons.

The noble gases of Group 8A are characterized by filled valence shells and are generally unreactive. Krypton, xenon, and radon do, however, form compounds with the highly electronegative atoms fluorine and oxygen.

sulfuric acid
thiosulfate ion

Section 19.7
halogens
hydrochloric acid
hydrohalic acids
disproportionation reaction
interhalogen compounds
Freons

Section 19.8
noble gases

A blue question or exercise number indicates that the answer to that question or exercise appears at the back of this book and a solution appears in the *Solutions Guide.*

Questions

1. What trade-offs must be made between kinetics and thermodynamics in the Haber process for the production of ammonia? How did the discovery of an appropriate catalyst make the process feasible?

2. White phosphorus is much more reactive than black or red phosphorus. Explain.

3. In many natural waters, nitrogen and phosphorus are the least abundant nutrients available for plant life. Some waters that become polluted from agricultural runoff or municipal sewage become infested with algae. The algae consume most of the dissolved oxygen in the water, and fish life dies off as a result. Describe how these events are chemically related.

4. Ozone is desirable in the upper atmosphere and undesirable in the lower atmosphere. A dictionary states that ozone has the scent of a fresh spring day. How can these seemingly conflicting statements be reconciled in terms of the chemical properties of ozone?

5. Describe the structural changes that occur when plastic sulfur becomes brittle.

6. Sulfur dissolves in an aqueous solution that contains sulfide ion. Sulfur will then precipitate from this solution if nitric acid is added. Explain.

7. Give two reasons why F_2 is the most reactive of the halogens.

8. Explain why HF is a weak acid, whereas HCl, HBr, and HI are all strong acids.

9. Although He is the second most abundant element in the universe, it is very rare on earth. Why?

10. The noble gases were among the latest elements discovered; their existence was not predicted by Mendeleev when he published his first periodic table. Explain. In chemistry textbooks written before 1962 the noble gases were referred to as the inert gases. Why do we no longer use this term?

Exercises

In this section similar exercises are paired.

Group 5A Elements

11. The oxyanion of nitrogen in which it has the highest oxidation state is the nitrate ion (NO_3^-). The corresponding oxyanion of phosphorus is PO_4^{3-}. The NO_4^{3-} ion is known but not very stable. The PO_3^- ion is not known. Account for these differences in terms of the bonding in the four anions.

12. In each of the following pairs of substances, one is stable and known, the other is unstable. For each pair, choose the stable substance, and explain why the other is unstable.
    a. NF_5 or PF_5 b. AsF_5 or AsI_5 c. NF_3 or NBr_3

13. Complete and balance each of the following reactions.
    a. The decomposition of solid ammonium nitrate.
    b. The decomposition of gaseous dinitrogen pentoxide.
    c. The reaction between solid potassium phosphide and water.
    d. The reaction between liquid phosphorus tribromide and water.
    e. The reaction between aqueous ammonia and aqueous sodium hypochlorite.

14. Arsenic reacts with oxygen to form oxides that react with water in a manner analogous to that of the phosphorus oxides. Write balanced chemical equations describing the reaction of arsenic with oxygen and the reaction of the resulting oxide with water.

15. Given the information about N_2O_5 in Section 19.2, draw possible Lewis structures for this molecule in the gas phase.

16. Lewis structures can be used to understand why some molecules react in certain ways. Write the Lewis structure for the reactants and products in the reactions described below.
    a. Nitrogen dioxide dimerizes to produce dinitrogen tetroxide.
    b. Boron trifluoride accepts a pair of electrons from ammonia, forming BF_3NH_3.
    Give a possible explanation for why these two reactions occur.

17. In a recent year, production of ammonia in the United States totaled 27.37×10^9 lb. Assuming 100% yield, calculate the volumes of N_2 and H_2 measured at STP required to produce this much ammonia by the reaction

$$N_2(g) + 3H_2(g) \longrightarrow 2NH_3(g)$$

18. Air bags are activated when a severe impact causes a steel ball to compress a spring and electrically ignite a detonator cap. This causes sodium azide (NaN_3) to decompose explosively according to the following reaction:

$$2NaN_3(s) \longrightarrow 2Na(s) + 3N_2(g)$$

How many moles of $NaN_3(s)$ must be reacted to inflate an air bag to 70.0 L at STP?

19. Write an equation for the reaction of hydrazine with fluorine gas to produce nitrogen gas and hydrogen fluoride gas. Estimate ΔH for this reaction using bond energies from Table 8.4.

20. Hydrazine (N_2H_4) is used as a fuel in liquid-fueled rockets. When hydrazine reacts with oxygen gas, nitrogen gas and water are produced. Write a balanced equation and use bond energies from Table 8.4 to estimate ΔH for this reaction.

21. Many oxides of nitrogen have positive values for the standard free energy of formation. Using NO as an example, explain why this is the case.

22. Using data from Appendix 4 calculate $\Delta H°$, $\Delta S°$, and $\Delta G°$ for the reaction

$$N_2(g) + O_2(g) \longrightarrow 2NO(g)$$

Why does NO form in an automobile engine but then does not readily decompose back to N_2 and O_2 in the atmosphere?

23. Compare the Lewis structures with the molecular orbital view of the bonding in NO, NO^+, and NO^-. Account for any discrepancies between the two models.

24. The energy to break a particular bond is not always constant. It takes about 200 kJ/mol less energy to break the N—Cl bond in NOCl as compared with NCl_3:

$$NOCl \longrightarrow NO + Cl \qquad \Delta H° = 158 \text{ kJ/mol}$$
$$NCl_3 \longrightarrow NCl_2 + Cl \qquad \Delta H° = 375 \text{ kJ/mol}$$

Why is there such a great discrepancy in the apparent N—Cl bond energies? *Hint:* Consider what happens to the nitrogen–oxygen bond in the first reaction.

25. Predict the relative acid strengths of the following compounds.
    a. H_3PO_4 and H_3PO_3 b. H_3PO_4, $H_2PO_4^-$, HPO_4^{2-}

26. Trisodium phosphate (TSP) is an effective grease remover. Like many cleaners, TSP acts as a base in water. Write a balanced equation to account for this behavior.

27. Isohypophosphonic acid ($H_4P_2O_6$) and diphosphonic acid ($H_4P_2O_5$) are tri- and diprotic acids, respectively. Draw Lewis structures for these acids that are consistent with these facts.

28. One of the most strongly acidic solutions known is a mixture of antimony pentafluoride (SbF_5) and fluorosulfonic acid (HSO_3F). The dominant equilibria are

$$SbF_5 + HSO_3F \rightleftharpoons F_5SbOSO_2FH$$
$$F_5SbOSO_2FH + HSO_3F \rightleftharpoons H_2SO_3F^+ + F_5SbOSO_2F^-$$

a. Draw Lewis structures for all the species shown in the preceding reactions. Predict the hybridization of the central Sb and S atoms in each structure.

b. This *superacid* solution is capable of protonating (adding H^+ to) virtually every known organic compound. What is the active protonating agent in the superacid solution?

Group 6A Elements

29. Use bond energies to estimate the maximum wavelength of light that will cause the reaction

$$O_3 \xrightarrow{h\nu} O_2 + O$$

30. The xerographic (dry writing) process was invented in 1938 by C. Carlson. In xerography, an image is produced on a photoconductor by exposing it to light. Selenium is commonly used, since its conductivity increases three orders of magnitude upon exposure to light in the range from 400 to 500 nm. What color light should be used to cause selenium to become conductive? (See Figure 7.2.)

31. Complete and balance each of the following reactions.
   a. The reaction between sulfur dioxide gas and oxygen gas.
   b. The reaction between sulfur trioxide gas and water.
   c. The reaction between aqueous sodium thiosulfate and aqueous iodine.
   d. The reaction between copper metal and aqueous hot sulfuric acid.

32. Write a balanced equation describing the reduction of H_2SeO_4 by SO_2 to produce selenium.

33. For each of the following, write the Lewis structure(s), predict the molecular structure (including bond angles), and give the expected hybridization of the central atom.
   a. SO_3^{2-} **c.** SCl_2 **e.** TeF_6
   b. O_3 **d.** $SeBr_4$

34. The teflate anion ($OTeF_5^-$) often acts like a halide ion. For example, $P(OTeF_5)_3$ has a structure similar to that of PF_3. Draw Lewis structures for $OTeF_5^-$ and $P(OTeF_5)_3$.

Group 7A Elements

35. Write the Lewis structure for O_2F_2. Predict the bond angles and hybridization of the two central oxygen atoms. Assign oxidation states and formal charges to the atoms in O_2F_2. The compound O_2F_2 is a vigorous and potent oxidizing and fluorinating agent. Are oxidation states or formal charges more useful in accounting for these properties of O_2F_2?

36. For each of the following, write the Lewis structure(s), predict the molecular structure (including bond angles), and give the expected hybridization of the central atom.
   a. Freon-12 (CCl_2F_2)   **c.** iodine trichloride
   b. perchloric acid   **d.** bromine pentafluoride

37. Complete and balance each of the following reactions.

a. $BaCl_2(s) + H_2SO_4(aq) \longrightarrow$ **c.** $SiO_2(s) + HF(aq) \longrightarrow$
b. $BrF(s) + H_2O(l) \longrightarrow$

38. Hypofluorous acid is the most recently prepared of the halogen oxyacids. Weighable amounts were first obtained in 1971 by M. H. Studies and E. N. Appelman using the fluorination of ice. Hypofluorous acid is exceedingly unstable, decomposing spontaneously (with a half-life of 30 min) to HF and O_2 in a Teflon container at room temperature. It reacts rapidly with water to produce HF, H_2O_2, and O_2. In dilute acid, H_2O_2 is the major product; in dilute base, O_2 is the major product.
   a. Write balanced equations for the reactions described above.
   b. Assign oxidation states to the elements in hypofluorous acid. Does this suggest why hypofluorous acid is so unstable?

39. Hydrazine is somewhat toxic. Use the half-reactions shown below to explain why household bleach (highly alkaline solution of sodium hypochlorite) should not be mixed with household ammonia or glass cleansers that contain ammonia.

$$ClO^- + H_2O + 2e^- \longrightarrow 2OH^- + Cl^- \qquad \mathscr{E}° = 0.90 \text{ V}$$
$$N_2H_4 + 2H_2O + 2e^- \longrightarrow 2NH_3 + 2OH^-$$
$$\mathscr{E}° = -0.10 \text{ V}$$

40. What is a disproportionation reaction? Use the following reduction potentials

$$ClO_3^- + 3H^+ + 2e^- \longrightarrow HClO_2 + H_2O \qquad \mathscr{E}° = 1.21 \text{ V}$$
$$HClO_2 + 2H^+ + 2e^- \longrightarrow HClO + H_2O \qquad \mathscr{E}° = 1.65 \text{ V}$$

to predict whether $HClO_2$ will disproportionate.

Group 8A Elements

41. The xenon halides and oxides are isoelectronic with many other compounds and ions containing halogens. Give a molecule or ion in which iodine is the central atom that is isoelectronic with each of the following.
   a. xenon tetroxide   **d.** xenon tetrafluoride
   b. xenon trioxide   **e.** xenon hexafluoride
   c. xenon difluoride

42. For each of the following, write the Lewis structure(s), predict the molecular structure (including bond angles), and give the expected hybridization of the central atom.
   a. KrF_2 **c.** XeO_2F_2
   b. KrF_4 **d.** XeO_2F_4

43. Xenon difluoride has proven to be a versatile fluorinating agent. For example, in the reaction

$$C_6H_6(l) + XeF_2(g) \longrightarrow C_6H_5F(l) + Xe(g) + HF(g)$$

the by-products Xe and HF are easily removed, leaving pure C_6H_5F. Xenon difluoride is stored in an inert atmosphere free from oxygen and water. Why is this necessary?

44. Using the data in Table 19.12, calculate the mass of argon at 25°C and 1.0 atm in a room 10.0 m × 10.0 m × 10.0 m. How many Ar atoms are in this room? How many Ar atoms do you inhale in one breath (approximately 2 L) of air at 25°C and 1.0 atm? Argon gas is inert, so it poses no serious health risks. However, if significant amounts of radon were inhaled into the lungs, lung cancer is a possible result. Explain the health-risk differences between argon gas and radon gas.

Additional Exercises

45. The compound NF_3 is quite stable, but NCl_3 is very unstable (NCl_3 was first synthesized in 1811 by P. L. Dulong, who lost three fingers and an eye studying its properties). The compounds NBr_3 and NI_3 are unknown, although the explosive compound $NI_3 \cdot NH_3$ is known. Account for the instability of these halides of nitrogen.

46. The N_2O molecule is linear and polar.
    a. On the basis of this experimental evidence, which arrangement, NNO or NON, is correct? Explain your answer.
    b. On the basis of your answer in part a above, write the Lewis structure of N_2O (including resonance forms). Give the formal charge on each atom and the hybridization of the central atom.
    c. How would the multiple bonding in $:N≡N—\ddot{O}:$ be described in terms of orbitals?

47. Oxidation of the cyanide ion produces the stable cyanate ion, OCN^-. The fulminate ion, CNO^-, on the other hand, is very unstable. Fulminate salts explode when struck; $Hg(CNO)_2$ is used in blasting caps. Write the Lewis structures and assign formal charges for the cyanate and fulminate ions. Why is the fulminate ion so unstable?

48. Write balanced equations for the reactions described in Table 19.1 for the production of Bi and Sb.

49. Bacterial digestion is an economical method of sewage treatment. The reaction

$$5CO_2(g) + 55NH_4^+(aq) + 76O_2(g) \xrightarrow{\text{Bacteria}}$$
$$C_5H_7O_2N(s) + 54NO_2^-(aq) + 52H_2O(l) + 109H^+(aq)$$
Bacterial tissue

   is an intermediate step in the conversion of the nitrogen in organic compounds into nitrate ions. How much bacterial tissue is produced in a treatment plant for every 1.0×10^4 kg of wastewater containing 3.0% NH_4^+ ions by mass? Assume that 95% of the ammonium ions are consumed by the bacteria.

50. Write the Lewis structures for the $AsCl_4^+$ and $AsCl_6^-$ ions. What type of reaction (acid–base, oxidation–reduction, etc.) is the following?

$$2AsCl_5(g) \longrightarrow AsCl_4AsCl_6(s)$$

51. What experiment can be done to verify that bismuthyl chloride (BiOCl) is composed of BiO^+ and Cl^- ions and not Bi^+ and OCl^- ions? *Hint:* OCl^- is capable of oxidizing I^- to I_2.

52. An unknown element is a nonmetal and has a valence electron configuration of ns^2np^4.

a. How many valence electrons does this element have?
b. What are some possible identities for this element?
c. What is the formula of the compound this element would form with lithium?
d. Would this element have a larger or smaller radius than barium?
e. Would this element have a greater or smaller ionization energy than fluorine?

53. The structure of TeF_5^- is

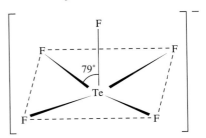

   Draw a complete Lewis structure for TeF_5^-, and explain the distortion from the ideal square pyramidal structure.

54. Photogray lenses contain small embedded crystals of solid silver chloride. Silver chloride is light-sensitive because of the reaction

$$AgCl(s) \xrightarrow{h\nu} Ag(s) + Cl$$

   Small particles of metallic silver cause the lenses to darken. In the lenses this process is reversible. When the light is removed, the reverse reaction occurs. However, when pure white silver chloride is exposed to sunlight it darkens; the reverse reaction does not occur in the dark.
    a. How do you explain this difference?
    b. Photogray lenses do become permanently dark in time. How do you account for this?

Challenge Problems

55. Use bond energies (Table 8.4) to show that the preferred products for the decomposition of N_2O_3 are NO_2 and NO rather than O_2 and N_2O. (The N—O single bond energy is 201 kJ/mol.) *Hint:* Consider the reaction kinetics.

56. Sodium tripolyphosphate ($Na_5P_3O_{10}$) is used in many synthetic detergents to soften the water by complexing Mg^{2+} and Ca^{2+} ions. It also increases the efficiency of surfactants (wetting agents) that lower a liquid's surface tension. The K value for the formation of $MgP_3O_{10}^{3-}$ is 4.0×10^8. The reaction is

$$Mg^{2+} + P_3O_{10}^{5-} \rightleftharpoons MgP_3O_{10}^{3-}$$

   Calculate the concentration of Mg^{2+} in a solution that was originally 50. ppm of Mg^{2+} (50. mg/L of solution) after 40. g $Na_5P_3O_{10}$ is added to 1.0 L of the solution.

57. One pathway for the destruction of ozone in the upper atmosphere is

$$O_3(g) + NO(g) \longrightarrow NO_2(g) + O_2(g) \quad \text{Slow}$$
$$NO_2(g) + O(g) \longrightarrow NO(g) + O_2(g) \quad \text{Fast}$$

Overall reaction: $O_3(g) + O(g) \longrightarrow 2O_2(g)$

a. Which species is a catalyst?
b. Which species is an intermediate?
c. The activation energy E_a for the uncatalyzed reaction

$$O_3(g) + O(g) \longrightarrow 2O_2(g)$$

is 14.0 kJ. E_a for the same reaction when catalyzed by the presence of NO is 11.9 kJ. What is the ratio of the rate constant for the catalyzed reaction to that for the uncatalyzed reaction at 25°C? Assume that the frequency factor A is the same for each reaction.

d. One of the concerns about the use of Freons is that they will migrate to the upper atmosphere, where chlorine atoms can be generated by the reaction

$$\underset{\text{Freon-12}}{CCl_2F_2} \xrightarrow{h\nu} CF_2Cl + Cl$$

Chlorine atoms also can act as a catalyst for the destruction of ozone. The first step of a proposed mechanism for chlorine-catalyzed ozone destruction is

$$Cl(g) + O_3(g) \longrightarrow ClO(g) + O_2(g) \quad \text{Slow}$$

Assuming a two-step mechanism, propose the second step in the mechanism and give the overall balanced equation.

e. The activation energy for Cl-catalyzed destruction of ozone is 2.1 kJ/mol. Estimate the efficiency with which Cl atoms destroy ozone as compared with NO molecules at 25°C. Assume that the frequency factor A is the same for each catalyzed reaction and assume similar rate laws for each catalyzed reaction.

58. Using data from Appendix 4, calculate $\Delta H°$, $\Delta G°$, and K_p (at 298 K) for the production of ozone from oxygen:

$$3O_2(g) \rightleftharpoons 2O_3(g)$$

At 30 km above the surface of the earth, the temperature is about 230. K, and the partial pressure of oxygen is about 1.0×10^{-3} atm. Estimate the partial pressure of ozone in equilibrium with oxygen at 30 km above the earth's surface. Is it reasonable to assume that the equilibrium between oxygen and ozone is maintained under these conditions? Explain.

Marathon Problem

This problem is designed to incorporate several concepts and techniques into one situation. Marathon Problems can be used in class by groups of students to help facilitate problem-solving skills.

59. Captain Kirk has set a trap for the Klingons who are threatening an innocent planet. He has sent small groups of fighter rockets to sites that are invisible to Klingon radar and put a decoy in the open. He calls this the "fishhook" strategy. Mr. Spock has sent a coded message to the chemists on the fighters to tell the ships what to do next. The outline of the message is

— —   — —   · — — — —
(1) (2)   (3)   (4)   (5)   (6)

— — — — —   — — — — —
(7)   (8) (9)   (10) (11) (12) (10) (11)

Fill in the blanks of the message using the following clues.

(1) Symbol of the halogen whose hydride has the second highest boiling point in the series of HX compounds that are hydrogen halides.

(2) Symbol of the halogen that is the only hydrogen halide, HX, that is a weak acid in aqueous solution.

(3) Symbol of the element whose existence on the sun was known before its existence on earth was discovered.

(4) Symbol of the element whose presence can interfere with the qualitative analysis for Pb^{2+}, Hg_2^{2+}, and Ag^+. When chloride ions are added to an aqueous solution of this metal ion, a white precipitate forms with formula MOCl.

(5) Symbol of the Group 6A element that, like selenium, is a semiconductor.

(6) Symbol for the element known in rhombic and monoclinic forms.

(7) Symbol for the element that exists as diatomic molecules in a yellow-green gas when not combined with another element; its silver, lead, and mercury(I) salts are white and insoluble in water.

(8) Symbol for the most abundant element in and near the earth's crust.

(9) Symbol for the element that seems to give some protection against cancer when a diet rich in this element is consumed.

(10) Symbol for the only noble gas besides xenon that has been shown to form compounds under some circumstances (write the symbol backward and split the letters as shown).

(11) Symbol for the toxic element that, like phosphorus and antimony, forms tetrameric molecules when uncombined with other elements (split the letters of the symbol as shown).

(12) Symbol for the element that occurs as an inert component of air but is a very prominent part of fertilizers and explosives.

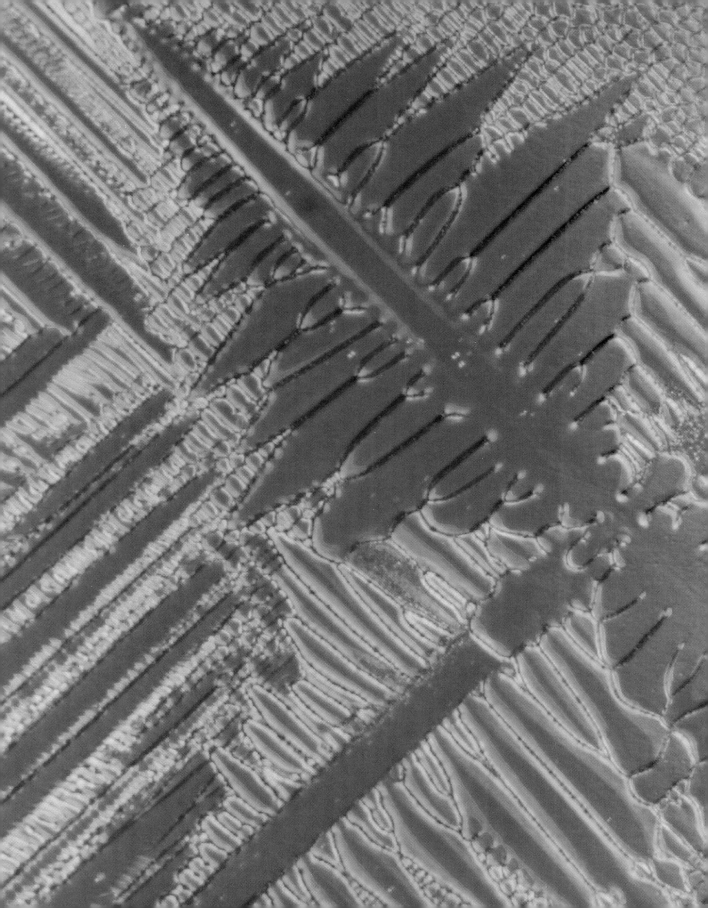

CHAPTER 20

Transition Metals and Coordination Chemistry

*T*ransition metals have many uses in our society. Iron is used for steel; copper for electrical wiring and water pipes; titanium for paint; silver for photographic paper; manganese, chromium, vanadium, and cobalt as additives to steel; platinum for industrial and automotive catalysts; and so on.

One indication of the importance of transition metals is the great concern shown by the U.S. government for continuing the supply of these elements. In recent years the United States has been a net importer of about 60 "strategic and critical" minerals, including cobalt, manganese, platinum, palladium, and chromium. All these metals play a vital role in the U.S. economy and defense, and approximately 90% of the required amounts must be imported (see Table 20.1).

In addition to being important in industry, transition metal ions also play a vital role in living organisms. For example, complexes of iron provide for the transport and storage of oxygen, molybdenum and iron compounds are catalysts in nitrogen fixation, zinc is found in more than 150 biomolecules in humans, copper and iron play a crucial role in the respiratory cycle, and cobalt is found in essential biomolecules such as vitamin B_{12}.

In this chapter we explore the general properties of transition metals, paying particular attention to the bonding, structure, and properties of the complex ions of these metals.

An optical micrograph of the dendritic structure that forms during the solidification of a certain type of stainless steel.

Table 20.1 Some Transition Metals Important to the U.S. Economy and Defense

Metal	Uses	Percentage Imported
Chromium	Stainless steel (especially for parts exposed to corrosive gases and high temperatures)	~91%
Cobalt	High-temperature alloys in jet engines, magnets, catalysts, drill bits	~93%
Manganese	Steelmaking	~97%
Platinum and palladium	Catalysts	~87%

20.1 The Transition Metals: A Survey

General Properties

One striking characteristic of the representative elements is that their chemistry changes markedly across a given period as the number of valence electrons changes. The chemical similarities occur mainly within the vertical groups. In contrast, *the transition metals show great similarities within a given period as well as within a*

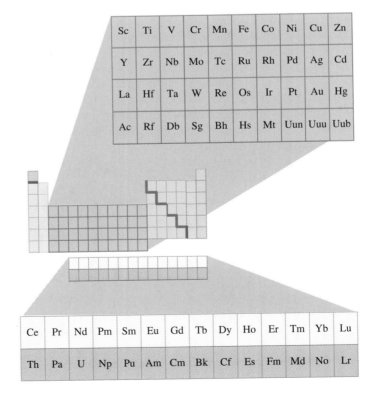

Sterling silver candlesticks and bowl from Japan.

given vertical group. This difference occurs because the last electrons added for transition metals are inner electrons: d electrons for the d-block transition metals and f electrons for the lanthanides and actinides. These inner d and f electrons cannot participate as easily in bonding as can the valence s and p electrons. Thus the chemistry of the transition elements is not affected as greatly by the gradual change in the number of electrons as is the chemistry of the representative elements.

Group designations are traditionally given on the periodic table for the d-block transition metals (see Fig. 20.1). However, these designations do not relate as directly to the chemical behavior of these elements as they do for the representative elements (the A groups), so we will not use them.

As a class, the transition metals behave as typical metals, possessing metallic luster and relatively high electrical and thermal conductivities. Silver is the best conductor of heat and electric current. However, copper is a close second, which explains copper's wide use in the electrical systems of homes and factories.

Despite their many similarities, the transition metals do vary considerably in certain properties. For example, tungsten has a melting point of 3400°C and is used for filaments in light bulbs; mercury is a liquid at 25°C. Some transition metals such as iron and titanium are hard and strong and make very useful structural materials; others such as copper, gold, and silver are relatively soft. The chemical reactivity of the transition metals also varies significantly. Some react readily with oxygen to form oxides. Of these metals, some, such as chromium, nickel, and cobalt, form oxides that adhere tightly to the metallic surface, protecting the metal from further oxidation. Others, such as iron, form oxides that scale off, constantly exposing new metal to the corrosion process. On the other hand, the noble metals—primarily gold, silver, platinum, and palladium—do not readily form oxides.

In forming ionic compounds with nonmetals, the transition metals exhibit several typical characteristics:

d-block transition elements

Sc	Ti	V	Cr	Mn	Fe	Co	Ni	Cu	Zn
Y	Zr	Nb	Mo	Tc	Ru	Rh	Pd	Ag	Cd
La*	Hf	Ta	W	Re	Os	Ir	Pt	Au	Hg
Ac†	Rf	Db	Sg	Bh	Hs	Mt	Uun	Uuu	Uub

f-block transition elements

*Lanthanides	Ce	Pr	Nd	Pm	Sm	Eu	Gd	Tb	Dy	Ho	Er	Tm	Yb	Lu
†Actinides	Th	Pa	U	Np	Pu	Am	Cm	Bk	Cf	Es	Fm	Md	No	Lr

Figure 20.1
The position of the transition elements on the periodic table. The *d*-block elements correspond to filling the 3*d*, 4*d*, 5*d*, or 6*d* orbitals. The inner transition metals correspond to filling the 4*f* (lanthanides) or 5*f* (actinides) orbitals.

More than one oxidation state is often found. For example, iron combines with chlorine to form $FeCl_2$ and $FeCl_3$.

The cations are often **complex ions,** species where *the transition metal ion is surrounded by a certain number of ligands* (molecules or ions that behave as Lewis bases). For example, the compound $[Co(NH_3)_6]Cl_3$ contains the $Co(NH_3)_6^{3+}$ cation and Cl^- anions.

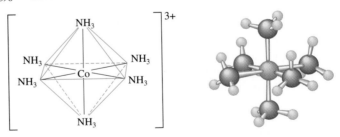

The Co $(NH_3)_6^{3+}$ ion

Molecular Model: Co(NH₃)₆³⁺

Most compounds are colored, because the transition metal ion in the complex ion can absorb visible light of specific wavelengths.

Many compounds are paramagnetic (they contain unpaired electrons).

In this chapter we will concentrate on the **first-row transition metals** (scandium through zinc) because they are representative of the other transition series and because they have great practical significance. Some important properties of these elements are summarized in Table 20.2 and are discussed in the next section.

(clockwise from upper left) Calcite stalactites colored by traces of iron. Quartz is often colored by the presence of transition metals such as Mn, Fe, and Ni. Wulfenite contains $PbMoO_4$. Rhodochrosite is a mineral containing $MnCO_3$.

Electron Configurations

The electron configurations of the first-row transition metals were discussed in Section 7.11. The $3d$ orbitals begin to fill after the $4s$ orbital is complete, that is, after calcium ($[Ar]4s^2$). The first transition metal, *scandium,* has one electron in the $3d$ orbitals; the second, *titanium,* has two; and the third, *vanadium,* has three. We would expect *chromium,* the fourth transition metal, to have the electron configuration $[Ar]4s^23d^4$. However, the actual configuration is $[Ar]4s^13d^5$, which shows a half-filled $4s$ orbital and a half-filled set of $3d$ orbitals (one electron in each of the five $3d$ orbitals). It is tempting to say that the configuration results because half-filled "shells" are especially stable. Although there are some reasons to think that this explanation might be valid, it is an oversimplification. For instance, tungsten, which is in the same vertical group as chromium, has the configuration $[Xe]6s^24f^{14}5d^4$, where half-filled s and d shells are not found. There are several similar cases.

Basically, the chromium configuration occurs because the energies of the $3d$ and $4s$ orbitals are very similar for the first-row transition elements. We saw in Section 7.11 that when electrons are placed in a set of degenerate orbitals, they first occupy each orbital singly to minimize electron repulsions. Since the $4s$ and $3d$ orbitals are virtually degenerate in the chromium atom, we would expect the configuration

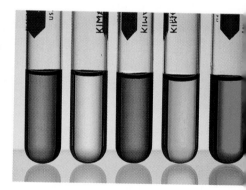

(from left to right) Aqueous solutions containing the metal ions Co^{2+}, Mn^{2+}, Cr^{3+}, Fe^{3+}, and Ni^{2+}.

Chromium has the electron configuration $[Ar]4s^13d^5$.

A set of orbitals with the same energy is said to be *degenerate.*

$$4s \uparrow \qquad 3d \uparrow \uparrow \uparrow \uparrow \uparrow$$

rather than

$$4s \uparrow\downarrow \qquad 3d \uparrow \uparrow \uparrow \uparrow \underline{}$$

Table 20.2 Selected Properties of the First-Row Transition Metals

	Scandium	Titanium	Vanadium	Chromium	Manganese	Iron	Cobalt	Nickel	Copper	Zinc
Atomic number	21	22	23	24	25	26	27	28	29	30
Electron configuration*	$4s^2 3d^1$	$4s^2 3d^2$	$4s^2 3d^3$	$4s^1 3d^5$	$4s^2 3d^5$	$4s^2 3d^6$	$4s^2 3d^7$	$4s^2 3d^8$	$4s^1 3d^{10}$	$4s^2 3d^{10}$
Atomic radius (pm)	162	147	134	130	135	126	125	124	128	138
Ionization energies (eV/atom)										
First	6.54	6.82	6.74	6.77	7.44	7.87	7.86	7.64	7.73	9.39
Second	12.80	13.58	14.65	16.50	15.64	16.18	17.06	18.17	20.29	17.96
Third	24.76	27.49	29.31	30.96	33.67	30.65	33.50	35.17	36.83	39.72
Reduction potential† (V)	−2.08	−1.63	−1.2	−0.91	−1.18	−0.44	−0.28	−0.23	+0.34	−0.76
Common oxidation states	+3	+2,+3, +4	+2,+3, +4,+5	+2,+3, +6	+2,+3, +4,+7	+2,+3	+2,+3	+2	+1,+2	+2
Melting point (°C)	1397	1672	1710	1900	1244	1530	1495	1455	1083	419
Density (g/cm³)	2.99	4.49	5.96	7.20	7.43	7.86	8.9	8.90	8.92	7.14
Electrical conductivity‡	—	2	3	10	2	17	24	24	97	27

*Each atom has an argon inner-core configuration.
†For the reduction process $M^{2+} + 2e^- \rightarrow M$ (except for scandium, where the ion is Sc^{3+}).
‡Compared with an arbitrarily assigned value of 100 for silver.

since the second arrangement has greater electron–electron repulsions and thus a higher energy.

Copper has the electron configuration $[Ar]4s^1 3d^{10}$.

The only other unexpected configuration among the first-row transition metals is that of copper, which is $[Ar]4s^1 3d^{10}$ rather than the expected $[Ar]4s^2 3d^9$.

In transition metal *ions*, the 3d orbitals are lower in energy than the 4s orbitals.

In contrast to the neutral transition metals, where the 3d and 4s orbitals have very similar energies, the *energy of the 3d orbitals in transition metal ions is significantly less than that of the 4s orbital.* This means that the electrons remaining after the ion is formed occupy the 3d orbitals, since they are lower in energy. *First-row transition metal ions do not have 4s electrons.* For example, manganese has the configuration $[Ar]4s^2 3d^5$, while that of Mn^{2+} is $[Ar]3d^5$. The neutral titanium atom has the configuration $[Ar]4s^2 3d^2$, while that of Ti^{3+} is $[Ar]3d^1$.

Oxidation States and Ionization Energies

The transition metals can form a variety of ions by losing one or more electrons. The common oxidation states of these elements are shown in Table 20.2. Note that for the first five metals the maximum possible oxidation state corresponds to the

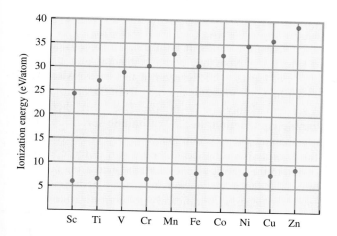

Figure 20.2

Plots of the first (red dots) and third (blue dots) ionization energies for the first-row transition metals.

loss of all the $4s$ and $3d$ electrons. For example, the maximum oxidation state of chromium ($[Ar]4s^1 3d^5$) is +6. Toward the right end of the period, the maximum oxidation states are not observed; in fact, the 2+ ions are the most common. The higher oxidation states are not seen for these metals because the $3d$ orbitals become lower in energy as the nuclear charge increases, and the electrons become increasingly difficult to remove. From Table 20.2 we see that ionization energy increases gradually going from left to right across the period. However, the third ionization energy (when an electron is removed from a $3d$ orbital) increases faster than the first ionization energy, clear evidence of the significant decrease in the energy of the $3d$ orbitals going across the period (see Fig. 20.2).

Standard Reduction Potentials

When a metal acts as a *reducing agent,* the half-reaction is

$$M \longrightarrow M^{n+} + ne^-$$

This is the reverse of the conventional listing for half-reactions in tables. Thus, to rank the transition metals in order of reducing ability, it is most convenient to reverse the reactions and the signs given in Table 20.2. The metal with the most positive potential is then the best reducing agent. The transition metals are listed in order of reducing ability in Table 20.3.

Since $\mathscr{E}°$ is zero for the process

$$2H^+ + 2e^- \longrightarrow H_2$$

all the metals except copper can reduce H^+ ions to hydrogen gas in 1 M aqueous solutions of strong acid:

$$M(s) + 2H^+(aq) \longrightarrow H_2(g) + M^{2+}(aq)$$

As Table 20.3 shows, the reducing abilities of the first-row transition metals generally decrease going from left to right across the period. Only chromium and zinc do not follow this trend.

Table 20.3 Relative Reducing Abilities of the First-Row Transition Metals in Aqueous Solution

Reaction	Potential (V)
$Sc \rightarrow Sc^{3+} + 3e^-$	2.08
$Ti \rightarrow Ti^{2+} + 2e^-$	1.63
$V \rightarrow V^{2+} + 2e^-$	1.2
$Mn \rightarrow Mn^{2+} + 2e^-$	1.18
$Cr \rightarrow Cr^{2+} + 2e^-$	0.91
$Zn \rightarrow Zn^{2+} + 2e^-$	0.76
$Fe \rightarrow Fe^{2+} + 2e^-$	0.44
$Co \rightarrow Co^{2+} + 2e^-$	0.28
$Ni \rightarrow Ni^{2+} + 2e^-$	0.23
$Cu \rightarrow Cu^{2+} + 2e^-$	−0.34

Reducing ability →

The 4d and 5d Transition Series

In comparing the 3*d*, 4*d*, and 5*d* transition series, it is instructive to consider the atomic radii of these elements (Fig. 20.3). Note that there is a general, although not regular, decrease in size going from left to right for each of the series. Also note that although there is a significant increase in radius in going from the 3*d* to the 4*d* metals, the 4*d* and 5*d* metals are remarkably similar in size. This latter phenomenon is the result of the **lanthanide contraction.** In the **lanthanide series,** consisting of the elements between lanthanum and hafnium (see Fig. 20.1), electrons are filling the 4*f* orbitals. Since the 4*f* orbitals are buried in the interior of these atoms, the additional electrons do not add to the atomic size. In fact, the increasing nuclear charge (remember that a proton is added to the nucleus for each electron) causes the radii of the lanthanide elements to decrease significantly going from left to right. This lanthanide contraction just offsets the normal increase in size due to going from one principal quantum level to another. Thus the 5*d* elements, instead of being significantly larger than the 4*d* elements, are almost identical to them in size. This leads to a great similarity in the chemistry of the 4*d* and 5*d* elements in a given vertical group. For example, the chemical properties of hafnium and zirconium are remarkably similar, and they always occur together in nature. Their separation, which is probably more difficult than the separation of any other pair of elements, often requires fractional distillation of their compounds.

In general, the differences between the 4*d* and 5*d* elements in a group increase gradually going from left to right. For example, niobium and tantalum are also quite similar, but less so than zirconium and hafnium.

Although generally less well known than the 3*d* elements, the 4*d* and 5*d* transition metals have certain very useful properties. For example, zirconium and zirconium oxide (ZrO_2) have great resistance to high temperatures and are used, along with niobium and molybdenum alloys, for space vehicle parts that are exposed to high temperatures during reentry into the earth's atmosphere. Niobium and molybdenum are also important alloying materials for certain types of steel. Tantalum, which has a high resistance to attack by body fluids, is often used for replacement of bones. The *platinum group metals*—ruthenium, osmium, rhodium, iridium, palladium, and platinum—are all quite similar and are widely used as catalysts for many types of industrial processes.

Niobium was originally called *columbium* and is still occasionally referred to by that name.

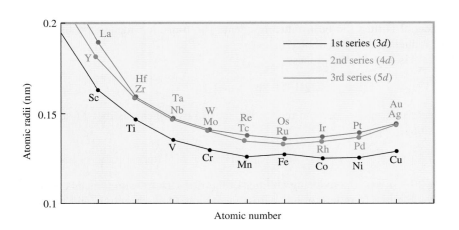

Figure 20.3

Atomic radii of the 3*d*, 4*d*, and 5*d* transition series.

20.2 The First-Row Transition Metals

We have seen that the transition metals are similar in many ways but also show important differences. We will now explore some of the specific properties of each of the 3d transition metals.

Scandium is a rare element that exists in compounds mainly in the +3 oxidation state, for example, in $ScCl_3$, Sc_2O_3, and $Sc_2(SO_4)_3$. The chemistry of scandium strongly resembles that of the lanthanides, with most of its compounds being colorless and diamagnetic. This is not surprising; as we will see in Section 20.6, the color and magnetism of transition metal compounds usually arise from the d electrons on the metal ion, and Sc^{3+} has no d electrons. Scandium metal, which can be prepared by electrolysis of molten $ScCl_3$, is not widely used because of its rarity, but it is found in some electronic devices, such as high-intensity lamps.

Titanium is widely distributed in the earth's crust (0.6% by mass). Because of its relatively low density and high strength, titanium is an excellent structural material, especially in jet engines, where light weight and stability at high temperatures are required. Nearly 5000 kg of titanium alloys are used in each engine of a Boeing 747 jetliner. In addition, the resistance of titanium to chemical attack makes it a useful material for pipes, pumps, and reaction vessels in the chemical industry.

The most familiar compound of titanium is no doubt responsible for the white color of this paper. Titanium dioxide, or more correctly, *titanium(IV) oxide* (TiO_2), is a highly opaque substance used as the white pigment in paper, paint, linoleum, plastics, synthetic fibers, whitewall tires, and cosmetics (sunscreens, for example). Approximately 700,000 tons are used annually in these and other products. Titanium(IV) oxide is widely dispersed in nature, but the main ores are rutile (impure TiO_2) and ilmenite ($FeTiO_3$). Rutile is processed by treatment with chlorine to form volatile $TiCl_4$, which is separated from the impurities and burned to form TiO_2:

$$TiCl_4(g) + O_2(g) \longrightarrow TiO_2(s) + 2Cl_2(g)$$

Ilmenite is treated with sulfuric acid to form a soluble sulfate:

$$FeTiO_3(s) + 2H_2SO_4(aq) \longrightarrow Fe^{2+}(aq) + TiO^{2+}(aq) + 2SO_4^{2-}(aq) + 2H_2O(l)$$

When this aqueous mixture is allowed to stand, under vacuum, solid $FeSO_4 \cdot 7H_2O$ forms first and is removed. The mixture is then heated, and the insoluble titanium(IV) oxide hydrate ($TiO_2 \cdot H_2O$) forms. The water of hydration is driven off by heating to form pure TiO_2:

$$TiO_2 \cdot H_2O(s) \xrightarrow{\text{Heat}} TiO_2(s) + H_2O(g)$$

In its compounds, titanium is most often found in the +4 oxidation state. Examples are TiO_2 and $TiCl_4$, the latter a colorless liquid (bp = 137°C) that fumes in moist air to produce TiO_2:

$$TiCl_4(l) + 2H_2O(l) \longrightarrow TiO_2(s) + 4HCl(g)$$

Titanium(III) compounds can be produced by reduction of the +4 state. In aqueous solution, Ti^{3+} exists as the purple $Ti(H_2O)_6^{3+}$ ion, which is slowly oxidized to titanium(IV) by air. Titanium(II) is not stable in aqueous solution but does exist in the solid state in compounds such as TiO and the dihalides of general formula TiX_2.

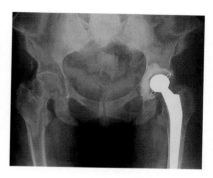

An X ray of a patient who has had a hip replacement. The normal hip joint is on the left; the hip joint constructed from tantalum metal is on the right.

Molecular Model: $TiCl_4$

$Ti(H_2O)_6^{3+}$ is purple in solution.

Vanadium is widely spread throughout the earth's crust (0.02% by mass). It is used mostly in alloys with other metals such as iron (80% of vanadium is used in steel) and titanium. Vanadium(V) oxide (V_2O_5) is used as an industrial catalyst in the production of materials such as sulfuric acid.

The manufacture of sulfuric acid was discussed at the end of Chapter 3.

Pure vanadium can be obtained from the electrolytic reduction of fused salts, such as VCl_2, to produce a metal similar to titanium that is steel gray, hard, and corrosion resistant. Often the pure element is not required for alloying. For example, *ferrovanadium*, produced by the reduction of a mixture of V_2O_5 and Fe_2O_3 with aluminum, is added to iron to form *vanadium steel*, a hard steel used for engine parts and axles.

The most common oxidation state for vanadium is +5.

The principal oxidation state of vanadium is +5, found in compounds such as the orange V_2O_5 (mp = 650°C) and the colorless VF_5 (mp = 19.5°C). The oxidation states from +5 to +2 all exist in aqueous solution (see Table 20.4). The higher oxidation states, +5 and +4, do not exist as hydrated ions of the type $V^{n+}(aq)$ because the highly charged ion causes the attached water molecules to be very acidic. The H^+ ions are lost to give the oxycations VO_2^+ and VO^{2+}. The hydrated V^{3+} and V^{2+} ions are easily oxidized and thus can function as reducing agents in aqueous solution.

Table 20.4 Oxidation States and Species for Vanadium in Aqueous Solution

Oxidation State of Vanadium	Species in Aqueous Solution
+5	VO_2^+ (yellow)
+4	VO^{2+} (blue)
+3	$V^{3+}(aq)$ (blue-green)
+2	$V^{2+}(aq)$ (violet)

Although *chromium* is relatively rare, it is a very important industrial material. The chief ore of chromium is chromite ($FeCr_2O_4$), which can be reduced by carbon to give *ferrochrome*,

$$FeCr_2O_4(s) + 4C(s) \longrightarrow \underbrace{Fe(s) + 2Cr(s)}_{\text{Ferrochrome}} + 4CO(g)$$

which can be added directly to iron in the steelmaking process. Chromium metal, which is often used to plate steel, is hard and brittle and maintains a bright surface by developing a tough invisible oxide coating.

Chromium commonly forms compounds in which it has the oxidation state +2, +3, or +6, as shown in Table 20.5. The Cr^{2+} (chromous) ion is a powerful reducing agent in aqueous solution. In fact, traces of O_2 in other gases can be removed by bubbling through a Cr^{2+} solution:

$$4Cr^{2+}(aq) + O_2(g) + 4H^+(aq) \longrightarrow 4Cr^{3+}(aq) + 2H_2O(l)$$

The chromium(VI) species are excellent oxidizing agents, especially in acidic solution, where chromium(VI) as the dichromate ion ($Cr_2O_7^{2-}$) is reduced to the Cr^{3+} ion:

$$Cr_2O_7^{2-}(aq) + 14H^+(aq) + 6e^- \longrightarrow 2Cr^{3+}(aq) + 7H_2O(l) \qquad \mathscr{E}° = 1.33 \text{ V}$$

The oxidizing ability of the dichromate ion is strongly pH-dependent, increasing as $[H^+]$ increases, as predicted by Le Châtelier's principle. In basic solution, chromium(VI) exists as the chromate ion, a much less powerful oxidizing agent:

$$CrO_4^{2-}(aq) + 4H_2O(l) + 3e^- \longrightarrow Cr(OH)_3(s) + 5OH^-(aq) \qquad \mathscr{E}° = -0.13 \text{ V}$$

The structures of the $Cr_2O_7^{2-}$ and CrO_4^{2-} ions are shown in Fig. 20.4.

Red chromium(VI) oxide (CrO_3) dissolves in water to give a strongly acidic, red-orange solution:

$$2CrO_3(s) + H_2O(l) \longrightarrow 2H^+(aq) + Cr_2O_7^{2-}(aq)$$

Table 20.5 Typical Chromium Compounds

Oxidation State of Chromium	Examples of Compounds (X = halogen)
+2	CrX_2
+3	CrX_3
	Cr_2O_3 (green)
	$Cr(OH)_3$ (blue-green)
+6	$K_2Cr_2O_7$ (orange)
	Na_2CrO_4 (yellow)
	CrO_3 (red)

CHEMICAL IMPACT

Titanium Makes Great Bicycles

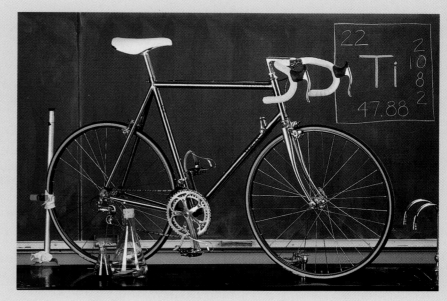

A titanium bicycle.

ONE OF THE most interesting characteristics of the world of bicycling is the competition among various frame materials. Bicycle frames are now built from steel, aluminum, carbon fiber composites, and titanium, with each material having advantages and disadvantages. Steel is strong, economical, adaptable, and (unfortunately) "rustable." Aluminum is light and stiff but has relatively low fatigue limits (resistance to repeated stresses). Carbon fiber composites have amazing strength-to-mass ratios and have shock- and vibration-dampening properties superior to any metal; however, they are very expensive. Titanium has a density approximately 43% less than that of steel, a yield strength (when alloyed with metals such as aluminum and tin) that is 30% greater than that of steel, an extraordinary resistance to fatigue, and a high resistance to corrosion, but it is expensive and difficult to work.

Of all these materials, titanium gives the bicycle that fanatics seem to love the most. After their first ride on a bicycle with a titanium frame, most experienced cyclists find themselves shaking their heads and searching hard for the right words to describe the experience. Typically, the word magic is used a great deal in the ensuing description.

The magic of titanium results from its combination of toughness, stretchability, and resilience. A bicycle that is built stiff to resist pedaling loads usually responds by giving a harsh, uncomfortable ride. A titanium bike is very stiff against high pedaling torques, but it seems to transmit much less road shock than bikes made of competitive materials. Why titanium excels in dampening vibrations is not entirely clear. Despite titanium's significantly lower density than steel, shock waves travel more slowly in titanium than in steel. Whatever the explanation for its shock-absorbing abilities, titanium pro-

vides three things that cyclists find crucial: light weight, stiffness, and a smooth ride—magic.

Titanium is quite abundant in the earth's crust, ranking ninth of all the elements and second among the transition elements. The metallurgy of titanium presents special challenges. Carbon, the reducing agent most commonly used to obtain metals from their oxide ores, cannot be used because it forms intractable interstitial carbides with titanium. These carbides are extraordinarily hard and have melting points close to 3000°C. However, if chlorine gas is used in conjunction with carbon to treat the ore, volatile $TiCl_4$ is formed, which can be distilled off and then reduced with magnesium or sodium at approximately 1000°C to form a titanium "sponge." This sponge is then ground up, cleaned with aqua regia (a 1:3 mixture of concentrated HNO_3 and concentrated HCl),

melted under a blanket of inert gas (to prevent reaction with oxygen), and cast into ingots. Titanium, a lustrous, silvery metal with a high melting point (1667°C), crystallizes in a hexagonal closest packed structure. Because titanium tends to become quite brittle when trace impurities such as C, N, and O are present, it must be fabricated with great care.

Titanium's unusual ability to stretch makes it hard to machine. It tends to push away even from a very sharp cutting blade, giving a rather unpredictable final dimension. Also, because titanium is embrittled by reaction with oxygen, all welding operations must be carried out under a shielding gas such as argon.

However, the bicycle that results is worth all these difficulties. One woman described a titanium bicycle as "the one God rides on Sunday."

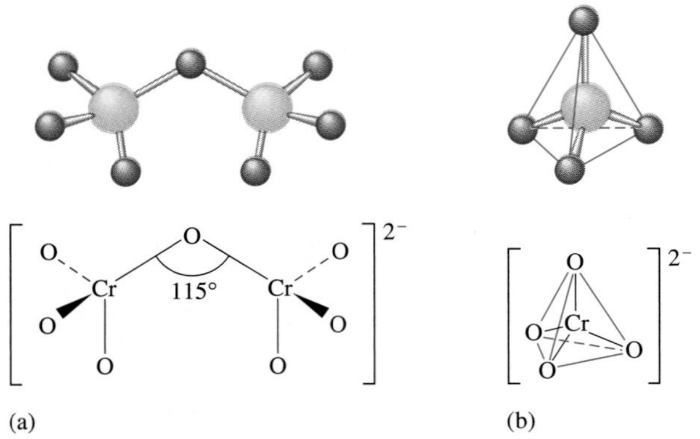

Figure 20.4

The structures of the chromium(VI) anions: (a) $Cr_2O_7^{2-}$, which exists in acidic solution, and (b) CrO_4^{2-}, which exists in basic solution.

(a)

(b)

It is possible to precipitate bright orange dichromate salts, such as $K_2Cr_2O_7$, from these solutions. When made basic, the solution turns yellow, and chromate salts such as Na_2CrO_4 can be obtained. A mixture of chromium(VI) oxide and concentrated sulfuric acid, commonly called *cleaning solution,* is a powerful oxidizing medium that can remove organic materials from analytical glassware, yielding a very clean surface.

Manganese is relatively abundant (0.1% of the earth's crust), although no significant sources are found in the United States. The most common use of manganese is in the production of an especially hard steel used for rock crushers, bank vaults, and armor plate. One interesting source of manganese is from *manganese nodules* found on the ocean floor. These roughly spherical "rocks" contain mixtures of manganese and iron oxides as well as smaller amounts of other metals such as cobalt, nickel, and copper. Apparently, the nodules were formed at least partly by the action of marine organisms. Because of the abundance of these nodules, there is much interest in developing economical methods for their recovery and processing.

Manganese can exist in all oxidation states from $+2$ to $+7$, although $+2$ and $+7$ are the most common. Manganese(II) forms an extensive series of salts with all the common anions. In aqueous solution Mn^{2+} forms $Mn(H_2O)_6^{2+}$, which has a light pink color. Manganese(VII) is found in the intensely purple permanganate ion (MnO_4^-). Widely used as an analytical reagent in acidic solution, the MnO_4^- ion behaves as a strong oxidizing agent, with the manganese becoming Mn^{2+}:

$$MnO_4^-(aq) + 8H^+(aq) + 5e^- \longrightarrow Mn^{2+}(aq) + 4H_2O(l) \qquad \mathscr{E}° = 1.51 \text{ V}$$

Several typical compounds of manganese are shown in Table 20.6.

Iron is the most abundant heavy metal (4.7% of the earth's crust) and the most important to our civilization. It is a white, lustrous, not particularly hard metal that is very reactive toward oxidizing agents. For example, in moist air it is rapidly oxidized by oxygen to form rust, a mixture of iron oxides.

The chemistry of iron mainly involves its $+2$ and $+3$ oxidation states. Typical compounds are shown in Table 20.7. In aqueous solutions iron(II) salts are generally light green because of the presence of $Fe(H_2O)_6^{2+}$. Although the $Fe(H_2O)_6^{3+}$ ion is colorless, aqueous solutions of iron(III) salts are usually yellow to brown in color due to the presence of $Fe(OH)(H_2O)_5^{2+}$, which results from the acidity of $Fe(H_2O)_6^{3+}$ ($K_a = 6 \times 10^{-3}$):

$$Fe(H_2O)_6^{3+}(aq) \rightleftharpoons Fe(OH)(H_2O)_5^{2+}(aq) + H^+(aq)$$

Oxidation State of Manganese	Examples of Compounds
+2	Mn(OH)$_2$ (pink)
	MnS (salmon)
	MnSO$_4$ (reddish)
	MnCl$_2$ (pink)
+4	MnO$_2$ (dark brown)
+7	KMnO$_4$ (purple)

Table 20.6 Some Compounds of Manganese in Its Most Common Oxidation States

Oxidation State of Iron	Examples of Compounds
+2	FeO (black)
	FeS (brownish black)
	FeSO$_4 \cdot$ 7H$_2$O (green)
	K$_4$Fe(CN)$_6$ (yellow)
+3	FeCl$_3$ (brownish black)
	Fe$_2$O$_3$ (reddish brown)
	K$_3$Fe(CN)$_6$ (red)
	Fe(SCN)$_3$ (red)
+2, +3 (mixture)	Fe$_3$O$_4$ (black)
	KFe[Fe(CN)$_6$] (deep blue, "Prussian blue")

Table 20.7 Typical Compounds of Iron

Although *cobalt* is relatively rare, it is found in ores such as smaltite (CoAs$_2$) and cobaltite (CoAsS) in large enough concentrations to make its production economically feasible. Cobalt is a hard, bluish white metal mainly used in alloys such as stainless steel and stellite, an alloy of iron, copper, and tungsten that is used in surgical instruments.

The chemistry of cobalt involves mainly its +2 and +3 oxidation states, although compounds containing cobalt in the 0, +1, or +4 oxidation state are known. Aqueous solutions of cobalt(II) salts contain the Co(H$_2$O)$_6^{2+}$ ion, which has a characteristic rose color. Cobalt forms a wide variety of coordination compounds, many of which will be discussed in later sections of this chapter. Some typical cobalt compounds are shown in Table 20.8.

Nickel, which ranks twenty-fourth in elemental abundance in the earth's crust, is found in ores, where it is combined mainly with arsenic, antimony, and sulfur. Nickel metal, a silvery white substance with high electrical and thermal conductivities, is quite resistant to corrosion and is often used for plating more active metals. Nickel is also widely used in the production of alloys such as steel.

Molecular Model: Ni(H$_2$O)$_6^{2+}$

Nickel in compounds is almost exclusively in the +2 oxidation state. Aqueous solutions of nickel(II) salts contain the Ni(H$_2$O)$_6^{2+}$ ion, which has a characteristic emerald green color. Coordination compounds of nickel(II) will be discussed later in this chapter. Some typical nickel compounds are shown in Table 20.9.

Copper, widely distributed in nature in ores containing sulfides, arsenides, chlorides, and carbonates, is valued for its high electrical conductivity and its resistance to corrosion. It is widely used for plumbing, and 50% of all copper produced

An aqueous solution containing the Ni²⁺ ion.

Copper roofs and bronze statues, such as the Statue of Liberty (see Chemical Impact on page 864), turn green in air because $Cu_3(OH)_4SO_4$ and $Cu_4(OH)_6SO_4$ form.

Table 20.8 Typical Compounds of Cobalt

Oxidation State	Examples of Compounds
+2	$CoSO_4$ (dark blue)
	$[Co(H_2O)_6]Cl_2$ (pink)
	$[Co(H_2O)_6](NO_3)_2$ (red)
	CoS (black)
	CoO (greenish brown)
+3	CoF_3 (brown)
	Co_2O_3 (charcoal)
	$K_3[Co(CN)_6]$ (yellow)
	$[Co(NH_3)_6]Cl_3$ (yellow)

Table 20.9 Typical Compounds of Nickel

Oxidation State of Nickel	Examples of Compounds
+2	$NiCl_2$ (yellow)
	$[Ni(H_2O)_6]Cl_2$ (green)
	NiO (greenish black)
	NiS (black)
	$[Ni(H_2O)_6]SO_4$ (green)
	$[Ni(NH_3)_6](NO_3)_2$ (blue)

annually is used for electrical applications. Copper is a major constituent in several well-known alloys (see Table 20.10).

Although copper is not highly reactive (it will not reduce H^+ to H_2, for example), the reddish metal does slowly corrode in air, producing the characteristic green *patina* consisting of basic copper sulfate

$$3Cu(s) + 2H_2O(l) + SO_2(g) + 2O_2(g) \longrightarrow Cu_3(OH)_4SO_4$$

Basic copper sulfate

and other similar compounds.

The chemistry of copper principally involves the +2 oxidation state, but many compounds containing copper(I) are also known. Aqueous solutions of copper(II) salts are a characteristic bright blue color due to the presence of the $Cu(H_2O)_6^{2+}$ ion. Table 20.11 lists some typical copper compounds.

Although trace amounts of copper are essential for life, copper in large amounts is quite toxic; copper salts are used to kill bacteria, fungi, and algae. For example,

Table 20.10 Alloys Containing Copper

Alloy	Composition (% by Mass in Parentheses)
Brass	Cu (20–97), Zn (2–80), Sn (0–14), Pb (0–12), Mn (0–25)
Bronze	Cu (50–98), Sn (0–35), Zn (0–29), Pb (0–50), P (0–3)
Sterling silver	Cu (7.5), Ag (92.5)
Gold (18-karat)	Cu (5–15), Au (75), Ag (10–20)
Gold (14-karat)	Cu (12–28), Au (58), Ag (4–30)

paints containing copper are used on ship hulls to prevent fouling by marine organisms.

Widely dispersed in the earth's crust, *zinc* is mainly refined from sphalerite (ZnS), which often occurs with galena (PbS). Zinc is a white, lustrous, very active metal that behaves as an excellent reducing agent and tarnishes rapidly. About 90% of the zinc produced is used for galvanizing steel. Zinc forms colorless salts in the +2 oxidation state.

Table 20.11 Typical Compounds of Copper

Oxidation State of Copper	Examples of Compounds
+1	Cu_2O (red)
	Cu_2S (black)
	$CuCl$ (white)
+2	CuO (black)
	$CuSO_4 \cdot 5H_2O$ (blue)
	$CuCl_2 \cdot 2H_2O$ (green)
	$[Cu(H_2O)_6](NO_3)_2$ (blue)

20.3 Coordination Compounds

Transition metal ions characteristically form coordination compounds, which are usually colored and often paramagnetic. A **coordination compound** typically consists of a *complex ion,* a transition metal ion with its attached ligands (see Section 15.8), and **counterions,** anions or cations as needed to produce a compound with no net charge. The substance $[Co(NH_3)_5Cl]Cl_2$ is a typical coordination compound. The brackets indicate the composition of the complex ion, in this case $Co(NH_3)_5Cl^{2+}$, and the two Cl^- counterions are shown outside the brackets. Note that in this compound one Cl^- acts as a ligand along with the five NH_3 molecules. In the solid state this compound consists of the large $Co(NH_3)_5Cl^{2+}$ cations and twice as many Cl^- anions, all packed together as efficiently as possible. When dissolved in water, the solid behaves like any ionic solid; the cations and anions are assumed to separate and move about independently:

$$[Co(NH_3)_5Cl]Cl_2(s) \xrightarrow{H_2O} Co(NH_3)_5Cl^{2+}(aq) + 2Cl^-(aq)$$

Coordination compounds have been known since about 1700, but their true nature was not understood until the 1890s when a young Swiss chemist named Alfred Werner (1866–1919) proposed that transition metal ions have two types of valence (combining ability). One type of valence, which Werner called the *secondary valence,* refers to the ability of a metal ion to bind to Lewis bases (ligands) to form complex ions. The other type, the *primary valence,* refers to the ability of the metal ion to form ionic bonds with oppositely charged ions. Thus Werner explained that the compound, originally written as $CoCl_3 \cdot 5NH_3$, was really $[Co(NH_3)_5Cl]Cl_2$, where the Co^{3+} ion has a primary valence of 3, satisfied by the three Cl^- ions, and a secondary valence of 6, satisfied by the six ligands (five NH_3 and one Cl^-). We now call the primary valence the **oxidation state** and the secondary valence the **coordination number,** which reflects the number of bonds formed between the metal ion and the ligands in the complex ion.

Molecular Model: $Co(NH_3)_5Cl^{2+}$

Coordination Number

The number of bonds formed by metal ions to ligands in complex ions varies from two to eight depending on the size, charge, and electron configuration of the transition metal ion. As shown in Table 20.12, 6 is the most common coordination number, followed closely by 4, with a few metal ions showing a coordination number of 2. Many metal ions show more than one coordination number, and there is really no simple way to predict what the coordination number will be in a particular case. The typical geometries for the various common coordination numbers are shown in

Coordination number	Geometry
2	 Linear
4	Tetrahedral Square planar
6	Octahedral

Figure 20.5

The ligand arrangements for coordination numbers 2, 4, and 6.

Molecular Models: en, dien, EDTA

Table 20.12 Typical Coordination Numbers for Some Common Metal Ions					
M^+	Coordination Numbers	M^{2+}	Coordination Numbers	M^{3+}	Coordination Numbers
Cu^+	2, 4	Mn^{2+}	4, 6	Sc^{3+}	6
Ag^+	2	Fe^{2+}	6	Cr^{3+}	6
Au^+	2, 4	Co^{2+}	4, 6	Co^{3+}	6
		Ni^{2+}	4, 6		
		Cu^{2+}	4, 6	Au^{3+}	4
		Zn^{2+}	4, 6		

Fig. 20.5. Note that six ligands produce an octahedral arrangement around the metal ion. Four ligands can form either a tetrahedral or a square planar arrangement, and two ligands give a linear structure.

Ligands

A **ligand** is a *neutral molecule or ion having a lone electron pair that can be used to form a bond to a metal ion*. The formation of a metal–ligand bond therefore can be described as the interaction between a Lewis base (the ligand) and a Lewis acid (the metal ion). The resulting bond is often called a **coordinate covalent bond.**

A *ligand that can form one bond to a metal ion* is called a **monodentate ligand,** or a **unidentate ligand** (from root words meaning "one tooth"). Examples of unidentate ligands are shown in Table 20.13.

Some ligands have more than one atom with a lone electron pair that can be used to bond to a metal ion. Such ligands are said to be **chelating ligands, or chelates** (from the Greek word *chele* for "claw"). A ligand that can form two bonds to a metal ion is called a **bidentate ligand.** A very common bidentate ligand is ethylenediamine (abbreviated en), which is shown coordinating to a metal ion in Fig. 20.6(a). Note the relationship between this ligand and the unidentate ligand ammonia [Fig. 20.6(b)]. Oxalate, another typical bidentate ligand, is shown in Table 20.13.

Ligands that can form more than two bonds to a metal ion are called *polydentate ligands*. Some ligands can form as many as six bonds to a metal ion. The best known example is ethylenediaminetetraacetate (abbreviated EDTA), which is shown in Table 20.13. This ligand virtually surrounds the metal ion (Fig. 20.7), coordinating through six atoms (a *hexadentate ligand*). As might be expected from the large number of coordination sites, EDTA forms very stable complex ions with most metal ions and is used as a "scavenger" to remove toxic heavy metals such as lead from the human body. It is also used as a reagent to analyze solutions for their metal ion content. EDTA is found in countless consumer products, such as soda, beer, salad dressings, bar soaps, and most cleaners. In these products EDTA ties up trace metal ions that would otherwise catalyze decomposition and produce unwanted precipitates.

Some even more complicated ligands are found in biologic systems, where metal ions play crucial roles in catalyzing reactions, transferring electrons, and transporting and storing oxygen. A discussion of these complex ligands will follow in Section 20.8.

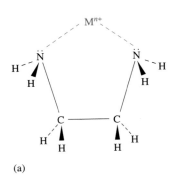

(a)

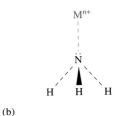

(b)

Figure 20.6

(a) The bidentate ligand ethylenediamine can bond to the metal ion through the lone pair on each nitrogen atom, thus forming two coordinate covalent bonds.
(b) Ammonia is a monodentate ligand.

Table 20.13 Some Common Ligands

Type	Examples
Unidentate/monodentate	H_2O CN^- SCN^- (thiocyanate) X^- (halides) NH_3 NO_2^- (nitrite) OH^-

Bidentate	Oxalate 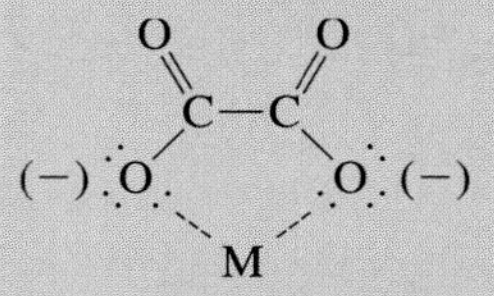 Ethylenediamine (en) 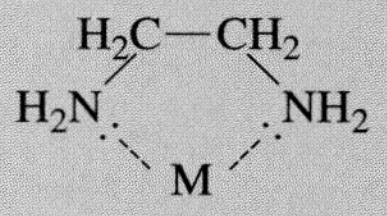
Polydentate	Diethylenetriamine (dien) $H_2N-(CH_2)_2-NH-(CH_2)_2-NH_2$ Three coordinating atoms Ethylenediaminetetraacetate (EDTA) Six coordinating atoms

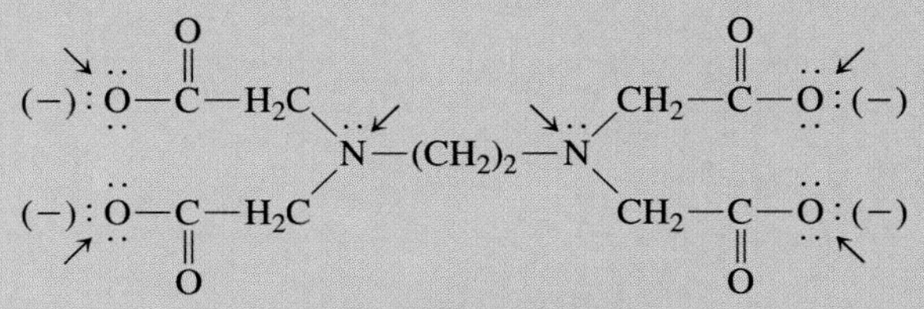

Nomenclature

In Werner's lifetime, no system was used to name coordination compounds. Names of the compounds were commonly based on colors and names of discoverers. As the field expanded and more coordination compounds were identified, an orderly system of nomenclature became necessary. A simplified version of this system is summarized by the following rules.

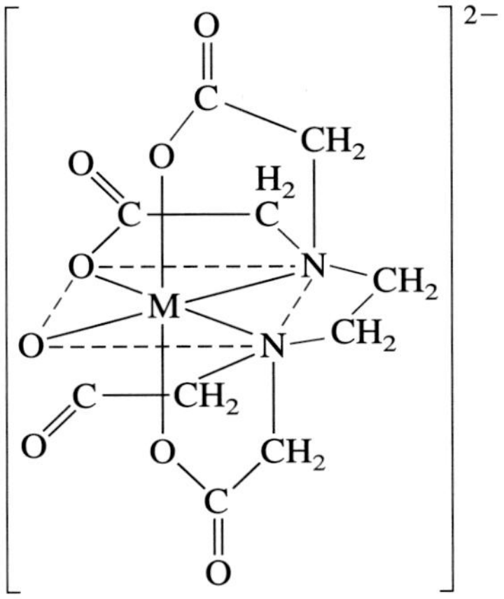

Rules for Naming Coordination Compounds

- As with any ionic compound, *the cation is named before the anion.*
- In naming a complex ion, *the ligands are named before the metal ion.*
- In naming ligands, *an o is added to the root name of an anion.* For example, the halides as ligands are called *fluoro, chloro, bromo,* and *iodo*; hydroxide is *hydroxo*; cyanide is *cyano*; etc. *For a neutral ligand the name of the molecule is used,* with the exception of H_2O, NH_3, CO, and NO, as illustrated in Table 20.14.

Figure 20.7

The coordination of EDTA with a 2+ metal ion.

Table 20.14 Names of Some Common Unidentate Ligands

Neutral Molecules	
Aqua	H_2O
Ammine	NH_3
Methylamine	CH_3NH_2
Carbonyl	CO
Nitrosyl	NO

Anions	
Fluoro	F^-
Chloro	Cl^-
Bromo	Br^-
Iodo	I^-
Hydroxo	OH^-
Cyano	CN^-

Table 20.15 Latin Names Used for Some Metal Ions in Anionic Complex Ions

Metal	Name in an Anionic Complex
Iron	Ferrate
Copper	Cuprate
Lead	Plumbate
Silver	Argentate
Gold	Aurate
Tin	Stannate

- *The prefixes mono-, di-, tri-, tetra-, penta-, and hexa- are used to denote the number of simple ligands.* The prefixes *bis-, tris-, tetrakis-,* etc., are also used, especially for more complicated ligands or ones that already contain *di-, tri-,* etc.
- *The oxidation state of the central metal ion is designated by a Roman numeral in parentheses.*
- *When more than one type of ligand is present, they are named alphabetically.** Prefixes do not affect the order.
- *If the complex ion has a negative charge, the suffix -ate is added to the name of the metal.* Sometimes the Latin name is used to identify the metal (see Table 20.15).

The application of these rules is shown in Sample Exercise 20.1.

Sample Exercise 20.1 *Naming Coordination Compounds I*

Give the systematic name for each of the following coordination compounds.

a. $[Co(NH_3)_5Cl]Cl_2$
b. $K_3Fe(CN)_6$
c. $[Fe(en)_2(NO_2)_2]_2SO_4$

Solution

a. To determine the oxidation state of the metal ion, we examine the charges of all ligands and counterions. The ammonia molecules are neutral and the chloride ions each have a $1-$ charge, so the cobalt ion must have a $3+$ charge to produce a neutral compound. Thus cobalt has the oxidation state $+3$, and we use cobalt(III) in the name.

   The ligands include one Cl^- ion and five NH_3 molecules. The chloride ion is designated as *chloro,* and each ammonia molecule is designated *ammine.* The prefix *penta-* indicates that there are five NH_3 ligands present. The name of the complex cation is therefore pentaamminechlorocobalt(III). Note that the ligands are named alphabetically, disregarding the prefix. Since the counterions are chloride ions, the compound is named as a chloride salt:

$$\underbrace{\text{Pentaamminechlorocobalt(III)}}_{\text{Cation}} \underbrace{\text{chloride}}_{\text{Anion}}$$

---

*In an older system the negatively charged ligands were named first, then neutral ligands, with positively charged ligands named last. We will follow the newer convention in this text.

b. First, we determine the oxidation state of the iron by considering the other charged species. The compound contains three K^+ ions and six CN^- ions. Therefore, the iron must carry a charge of 3+, giving a total of six positive charges to balance the six negative charges. The complex ion present is thus $Fe(CN)_6^{3-}$. The cyanide ligands are each designated *cyano,* and the prefix *hexa-* indicates that six are present. Since the complex ion is an anion, we use the Latin name *ferrate.* The oxidation state is indicated by (III) at the end of the name. The anion name is therefore hexacyanoferrate(III). The cations are K^+ ions, which are simply named potassium. Putting this together gives the name

$$\underbrace{\text{Potassium}}_{\text{Cation}}\ \underbrace{\text{hexacyanoferrate(III)}}_{\text{Anion}}$$

(The common name of this compound is potassium ferricyanide.)

c. We first determine the oxidation state of the iron by looking at the other charged species: four NO_2^- ions and one SO_4^{2-} ion. The ethylenediamine is neutral. Thus the two iron ions must carry a total positive charge of six to balance the six negative charges. This means that each iron has a +3 oxidation state and is designated as iron(III).

Since the name ethylenediamine already contains *di,* we use *bis-* instead of *di-* to indicate the two en ligands. The name for NO_2^- as a ligand is *nitro,* and the prefix *di-* indicates the presence of two NO_2^- ligands. Since the anion is sulfate, the compound's name is

$$\underbrace{\text{Bis(ethylenediamine)dinitroiron(III)}}_{\text{Cation}}\ \underbrace{\text{sulfate}}_{\text{Anion}}$$

Because the complex ion is a cation, the Latin name for iron is not used.

See Exercises 20.33 through 20.36.

(top) An aqueous solution of $[Co(NH_3)_5Cl]Cl_2$. (bottom) Solid $K_3Fe(CN)_6$.

Sample Exercise 20.2 *Naming Coordination Compounds II*

Given the following systematic names, give the formula of each coordination compound.

a. Triamminebromoplatinum(II) chloride
b. Potassium hexafluorocobaltate(III)

Solution

a. *Triammine* signifies three ammonia ligands, and *bromo* indicates one bromide ion as a ligand. The oxidation state of platinum is +2, as indicated by the

CHEMICAL IMPACT

Alfred Werner: Coordination Chemist

DURING THE EARLY and middle parts of the nineteenth century, chemists prepared a large number of colored compounds containing transition metals and other substances such as ammonia, chloride ion, cyanide ion, and water. These compounds were very interesting to chemists who were trying to understand the nature of bonding (Dalton's atomic theory of 1808 was very new at this time), and many theories were suggested to explain these substances. The most widely accepted early theory was the *chain theory*, championed by Sophus Mads Jorgensen (1837–1914), professor of chemistry at the University of Copenhagen. The chain theory got its name from the postulate that metal ammine* complexes contain chains of NH_3 molecules. For example, Jorgensen proposed the structure

$$Co\begin{matrix} NH_3-Cl \\ NH_3-NH_3-NH_3-NH_3-Cl \\ NH_3-Cl \end{matrix}$$

*Ammine is the name for NH_3 as a ligand.

for the compound $Co(NH_3)_6Cl_3$. In the late nineteenth century this theory was used in classrooms around the world to explain the nature of metal–ammine compounds.

However, in 1890, a young Swiss chemist named Alfred Werner, who had just obtained a Ph.D. in the field of organic chemistry, became so interested in these compounds that he apparently even dreamed about them. In the middle of one night Werner awoke realizing that he had the correct explanation for the constitution of these compounds. Writing furiously the rest of that night and into the late afternoon of the following day, he constructed a scientific paper containing his now famous *coordination theory*. This model postulates an octahedral arrangement of ligands around the Co^{3+} ion, producing the $Co(NH_3)_6^{3+}$ complex ion with three Cl^- ions as counterions. Thus Werner's picture of $Co(NH_3)_6Cl_3$ varied greatly from the chain theory.

In his paper on the coordination theory, Werner explained not only the metal–ammine compounds but also most of the other known transition metal com-

pounds, and the importance of his contribution was recognized immediately. He was appointed professor at the University of Zurich, where he spent the rest of his life studying coordination compounds and refining his theory. Alfred Werner was a confident, impulsive man of seemingly boundless energy, who was known for his inspiring lectures, his intolerance of incompetence (he once threw a chair at a student who performed poorly on an oral exam), and his intuitive scientific brilliance. For example, he was the first to show that stereochemistry is a general phenomenon, not one exhibited only by carbon, as was previously thought. He also recognized and named many types of isomerism.

In 1913, for his work on coordination chemistry and stereochemistry, Werner became the fourteenth Nobel Prize winner in chemistry and the first Swiss chemist to be so honored. Werner's work is even more remarkable when one realizes that his ideas preceded by many years any real understanding of the nature of covalent bonds.

Roman numeral II. Thus the complex ion is $[Pt(NH_3)_3Br]^+$. One chloride ion is needed to balance the 1+ charge of this cation. The formula of the compound is $[Pt(NH_3)_3Br]Cl$. Note that brackets enclose the complex ion.

b. The complex ion contains six fluoride ligands attached to a Co^{3+} ion to give CoF_6^{3-}. Note that the *-ate* ending indicates that the complex ion is an anion. The cations are K^+ ions, and three are required to balance the 3− charge on the complex ion. Thus the formula is $K_3[CoF_6]$.

See Exercises 20.37 and 20.38.

20.4 Isomerism

When two or more species have the same formula but different properties, they are said to be **isomers.** Although isomers contain exactly the same types and numbers of atoms, the arrangements of the atoms differ, and this leads to different properties. We will consider two main types of isomerism: **structural isomerism,** where the isomers contain the same atoms but one or more bonds differ, and **stereoisomerism,** where all the bonds in the isomers are the same but the spatial arrangements of the atoms are different. Each of these classes also has subclasses (see Fig. 20.8), which we will now consider.

Structural Isomerism

The first type of structural isomerism we will consider is **coordination isomerism,** in which the composition of the complex ion varies. For example, $[Cr(NH_3)_5SO_4]Br$ and $[Cr(NH_3)_5Br]SO_4$ are coordination isomers. In the first case, SO_4^{2-} is coordinated to Cr^{3+}, and Br^- is the counterion; in the second case, the roles of these ions are reversed.

Another example of coordination isomerism is the $[Co(en)_3][Cr(ox)_3]$ and $[Cr(en)_3][Co(ox)_3]$ pair, where ox represents the oxalate ion, a bidentate ligand shown in Table 20.13.

In a second type of structural isomerism, **linkage isomerism,** the composition of the complex ion is the same, but the point of attachment of at least one of the ligands differs. Two ligands that can attach to metal ions in different ways are thiocyanate (SCN^-), which can bond through lone electron pairs on the nitrogen or the sulfur atom, and the nitrite ion (NO_2^-), which can bond through lone electron pairs

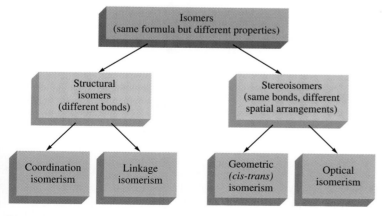

Figure 20.8
Some classes of isomers.

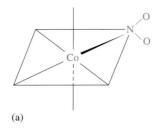

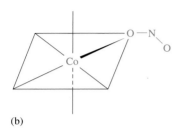

(a)

(b)

Figure 20.9

As a ligand, NO_2^- can bond to a metal ion (a) through a lone pair on the nitrogen atom or (b) through a lone pair on one of the oxygen atoms.

on the nitrogen or the oxygen atom. For example, the following two compounds are linkage isomers:

$$[Co(NH_3)_4(NO_2)Cl]Cl$$
Tetraamminechloronitrocobalt(III) chloride
(yellow)

$$[Co(NH_3)_4(ONO)Cl]Cl$$
Tetraamminechloronitritocobalt(III) chloride
(red)

In the first case, the NO_2^- ligand is called *nitro* and is attached to Co^{3+} through the nitrogen atom; in the second case, the NO_2^- ligand is called *nitrito* and is attached to Co^{3+} through an oxygen atom (see Fig. 20.9).

Stereoisomerism

Stereoisomers have the same bonds but different spatial arrangements of the atoms. One type, **geometrical isomerism**, or *cis–trans* **isomerism**, occurs when atoms or groups of atoms can assume different positions around a rigid ring or bond. An important example is the compound $Pt(NH_3)_2Cl_2$, which has a square planar structure. The two possible arrangements of the ligands are shown in Fig. 20.10. In the *trans* **isomer,** the ammonia molecules are across (*trans*) from each other. In the *cis* **isomer,** the ammonia molecules are next (*cis*) to each other.

Geometrical isomerism also occurs in octahedral complex ions. For example, the compound $[Co(NH_3)_4Cl_2]Cl$ has *cis* and *trans* isomers (Fig. 20.11).

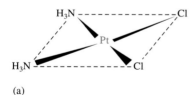

(a)

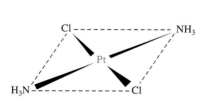

(b)

Figure 20.10

(a) The *cis* isomer of $Pt(NH_3)_2Cl_2$ (yellow). (b) The *trans* isomer of $Pt(NH_3)_2Cl_2$ (pale yellow).

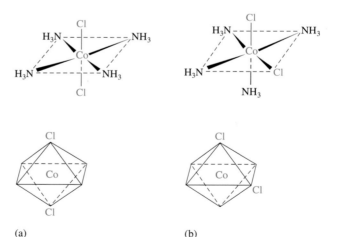

(a)

(b)

Figure 20.11

(a) The *trans* isomer of $[Co(NH_3)_4Cl_2]^+$. The chloride ligands are directly across from each other. (b) The *cis* isomer of $[Co(NH_3)_4Cl_2]^+$. The chloride ligands in this case share an edge of the octahedron. Because of their different structures, the *trans* isomer of $[Co(NH_3)_4Cl_2]Cl$ is green and the *cis* isomer is violet.

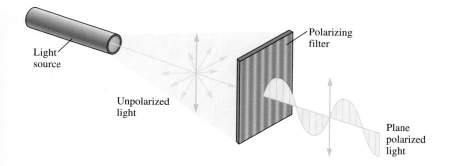

Figure 20.12

Unpolarized light consists of waves vibrating in many different planes (indicated by the arrows). The polarizing filter blocks all waves except those vibrating in a given plane.

A second type of stereoisomerism is called **optical isomerism** because the isomers have opposite effects on plane-polarized light. When light is emitted from a source such as a glowing filament, the oscillating electric fields of the photons in the beam are oriented randomly, as shown in Fig. 20.12. If this light is passed through a polarizer, only the photons with electric fields oscillating in a single plane remain, constituting *plane-polarized light.*

In 1815, a French physicist, Jean Biot (1774–1862), showed that certain crystals could rotate the plane of polarization of light. Later it was found that solutions of certain compounds could do the same thing (see Fig. 20.13). Louis Pasteur (1822–1895) was the first to understand this behavior. In 1848 he noted that solid sodium ammonium tartrate ($NaNH_4C_4H_4O_4$) existed as a mixture of two types of crystals, which he painstakingly separated with tweezers. Separate solutions of these two types of crystals rotated plane-polarized light in exactly opposite directions. This led to a connection between optical activity and molecular structure.

We now realize that optical activity is exhibited by molecules that have *nonsuperimposable mirror images.* Your hands are nonsuperimposable mirror images (Fig. 20.15). The two hands are related like an object and its mirror image; one hand cannot be turned to make it identical to the other. Many molecules show this same

Molecular Models: $Co(NH_3)_4(NO_2)Cl^+$, $Co(NH_3)_4(ONO)Cl^+$, $Pt(NH_3)_2Cl_2$ *cis* and *trans*

Molecular Models: $Co(NH_3)_4Cl_2^+$ *cis* and *trans*

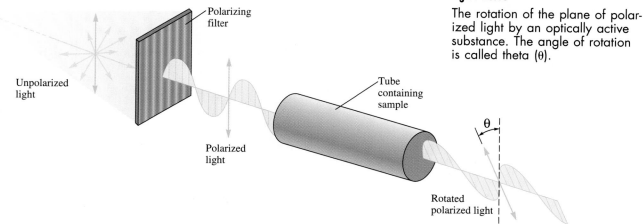

Figure 20.13

The rotation of the plane of polarized light by an optically active substance. The angle of rotation is called theta (θ).

CHEMICAL IMPACT

The Importance of Being cis

SOME OF THE most important advancements of science are the results of accidental discoveries, for example, penicillin, Teflon, and the sugar substitutes cyclamate and aspartame. Another important chance discovery occurred in 1964, when a group of scientists using platinum electrodes to apply an electric field to a colony of *E. coli* bacteria noticed that the bacteria failed to divide but continued to grow, forming long fibrous cells. Further study revealed that cell division was inhibited by small concentrations of *cis*-Pt(NH₃)₂Cl₂ and *cis*-

$Pt(NH_3)_2Cl_4$ formed electrolytically in the solution.

Cancerous cells multiply very rapidly because cell division is uncontrolled. Thus these and similar platinum complexes were evaluated as *antitumor agents*, which inhibit the division of cancer cells. The results showed that *cis*-Pt(NH₃)₂Cl₂ was active against a wide variety of tumors, including testicular and ovarian tumors, which are very resistant to treatment by more traditional methods. However, although the *cis* complex showed significant antitumor activity, the

corresponding *trans* complex had no effect on tumors. This shows the importance of isomerism in biologic systems. When drugs are synthesized, great care must be taken to obtain the correct isomer.

Although *cis*-Pt(NH₃)₂Cl₂ has proven to be a valuable drug, unfortunately it has some troublesome side effects, the most serious being kidney damage. As a result, the search continues for even more effective antitumor agents. Promising candidates are shown in Fig. 20.14. Note that they are all *cis* complexes.

Figure 20.14

Some *cis* complexes of platinum and palladium that show significant antitumor activity. It is thought that the *cis* complexes work by losing two adjacent ligands and forming coordinate covalent bonds to adjacent bases on a DNA molecule.

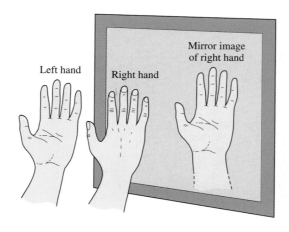

Figure 20.15

A human hand exhibits a nonsuperimposable mirror image. Note that the mirror image of the right hand (while identical to the left hand) cannot be turned in any way to make it identical to (superimposable on) the actual right hand.

feature, for example, the complex ion $[Co(en)_3]^{3+}$ shown in Fig. 20.16. Objects that have nonsuperimposable mirror images are said to be **chiral** (from the Greek word *cheir,* meaning "hand").

The isomers of $[Co(en)_3]^{3+}$ (Fig. 20.17) are nonsuperimposable mirror images called **enantiomers,** which rotate plane-polarized light in opposite directions and are thus optical isomers. The isomer that rotates the plane of light to the right (when viewed down the beam of oncoming light) is said to be *dextrorotatory,* designated by *d.* The isomer that rotates the plane of light to the left is *levorotatory* (*l*). An equal mixture of the *d* and *l* forms in solution, called a *racemic mixture,* does not rotate the plane of the polarized light at all because the two opposite effects cancel.

Molecular Models: Co(en)$_2$Cl$_2$$^+$ *cis* and *trans*

Geometrical isomers are not necessarily optical isomers. For instance, the *trans* isomer of $[Co(en)_2Cl_2]^+$ shown in Fig. 20.17 is identical to its mirror image. Since this isomer is superimposable on its mirror image, it does not exhibit optical isomerism and is not chiral. On the other hand, *cis*-$[Co(en)_2Cl_2]^+$ is *not* superimposable on its mirror image; a pair of enantiomers exists for this complex ion (the *cis* isomer is chiral).

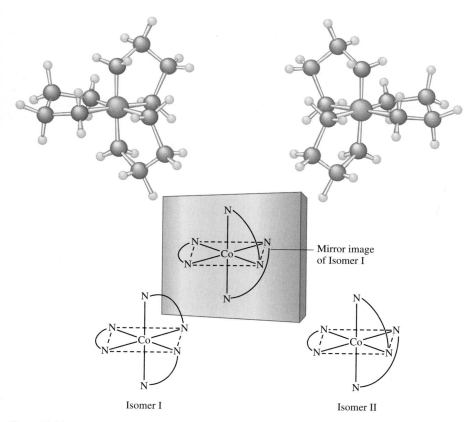

Isomer I   Mirror image of Isomer I   Isomer II

Figure 20.16

Isomers I and II of Co(en)$_3$$^{3+}$ are mirror images (the image of I is identical to II) that cannot be superimposed. That is, there is no way that I can be turned in space so that it is the same as II.

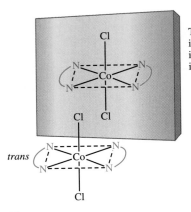

The *trans* isomer and its mirror image are identical. They are not isomers of each other.

(a)

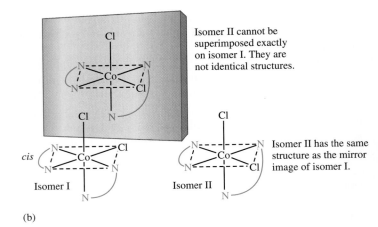

Isomer II cannot be superimposed exactly on isomer I. They are not identical structures.

Isomer II has the same structure as the mirror image of isomer I.

(b)

Figure 20.17

(a) The *trans* isomer of $Co(en)_2Cl_2^+$ and its mirror image are identical (superimposable). (b) The *cis* isomer of $Co(en)_2Cl_2^+$ and its mirror image are not superimposable and are thus a pair of optical isomers.

Most important biomolecules are chiral, and their reactions are highly structure dependent. For example, a drug can have a particular effect because its molecules can bind to chiral molecules in the body. In order to bind correctly, however, the correct optical isomer of the drug must be administered. Just as the right hand of one person requires the right hand of another to perform a handshake, a given isomer in the body requires a specific isomer of the drug to bind together. Because of this, the syntheses of drugs, which are usually very complicated molecules, must be carried out in a way that produces the correct "handedness," a requirement that greatly adds to the synthetic difficulties.

Sample Exercise 20.3 *Geometrical and Optical Isomerism*

Does the complex ion $[Co(NH_3)Br(en)_2]^{2+}$ exhibit geometrical isomerism? Does it exhibit optical isomerism?

Solution

The complex ion exhibits geometrical isomerism because the ethylenediamine ligands can be across from or next to each other:

The *cis* isomer of the complex ion also exhibits optical isomerism because its mirror images

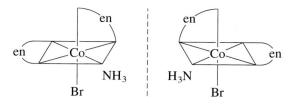

cannot be turned in any way to make them superimposable. Thus these mirror-image isomers of the *cis* complex are shown to be enantiomers that will rotate plane-polarized light in opposite directions.

See Exercises 20.45 and 20.46.

20.5 Bonding in Complex Ions: The Localized Electron Model

In Chapters 8 and 9 we considered the localized electron model, a very useful model for describing the bonding in molecules. Recall that a central feature of this model is the formation of hybrid atomic orbitals that are used to share electron pairs to form σ bonds between atoms. This same model can be used to account for the bonding in complex ions, but there are two important points to keep in mind:

1. The VSEPR model for predicting structure generally *does not work for complex ions*. However, we can safely assume that a complex ion with a coordination number of 6 will have an octahedral arrangement of ligands, and complexes with two ligands will be linear. On the other hand, complex ions with a coordination number of 4 can be either tetrahedral or square planar, and there is no completely reliable way to predict which will occur in a particular case.

2. The interaction between a metal ion and a ligand can be viewed as a Lewis acid–base reaction with the ligand donating a lone pair of electrons to an *empty* orbital of the metal ion to form a coordinate covalent bond:

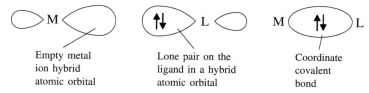

Empty metal ion hybrid atomic orbital — Lone pair on the ligand in a hybrid atomic orbital — Coordinate covalent bond

The hybrid orbitals used by the metal ion depend on the number and arrangement of the ligands. For example, accommodating the lone pairs from the six

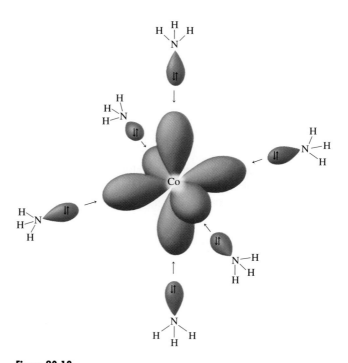

Figure 20.18

A set of six d^2sp^3 hybrid orbitals on Co^{3+} can accept an electron pair from each of six NH_3 ligands to form the $Co(NH_3)_6^{3+}$ ion.

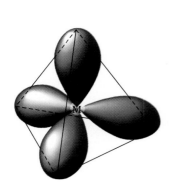

Tetrahedral ligand arrangement; sp^3 hybridization

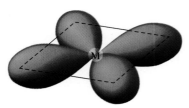

Square planar ligand arrangement; dsp^2 hybridization

Linear ligand arrangement; sp hybridization

Figure 20.19

The hybrid orbitals required for tetrahedral, square planar, and linear complex ions. The metal ion hybrid orbitals are empty, and the metal ion bonds to the ligands by accepting lone pairs.

ammonia molecules in the octahedral $Co(NH_3)_6^{3+}$ ion requires a set of six empty hybrid atomic orbitals in an octahedral arrangement. As we discussed in Section 9.1, an octahedral set of orbitals is formed by the hybridization of two d, one s, and three p orbitals to give a set of six d^2sp^3 orbitals (see Fig. 20.18).

The hybrid orbitals required on a metal ion in a four-coordinate complex depends on whether the structure is tetrahedral or square planar. For a tetrahedral arrangement of ligands, an sp^3 hybrid set is required (see Fig. 20.19). For example, in the tetrahedral $CoCl_4^{2-}$ ion, the Co^{2+} can be described as sp^3 hybridized. A square planar arrangement of ligands requires a dsp^2 hybrid orbital set on the metal ion (see Fig. 20.19). For example, in the square planar $Ni(CN)_4^{2-}$ ion, the Ni^{2+} is described as dsp^2 hybridized.

A linear complex requires two hybrid orbitals 180 degrees from each other. This arrangement is given by an sp hybrid set (see Fig. 20.19). Thus, in the linear $Ag(NH_3)_2^{+}$ ion, the Ag^+ can be described as sp hybridized.

Although the localized electron model can account in a general way for metal–ligand bonds, it is rarely used today because it cannot readily account for important properties of complex ions, such as magnetism and color. Thus we will not pursue the model any further.

20.6 The Crystal Field Model

The main reason the localized electron model cannot fully account for the properties of complex ions is that it gives no information about how the energies of the d orbitals are affected by complex ion formation. This is critical because, as we will see, the color and magnetism of complex ions result from changes in the energies of the metal ion d orbitals caused by the metal–ligand interactions.

The **crystal field model** focuses on the energies of the d orbitals. In fact, this model is not so much a bonding model as it is an attempt to account for the colors and magnetic properties of complex ions. In its simplest form, the crystal field model assumes that the ligands can be approximated by *negative point charges* and that metal–ligand bonding is *entirely ionic*.

Octahedral Complexes

We will illustrate the fundamental principles of the crystal field model by applying it to an octahedral complex. Figure 20.20 shows the orientation of the $3d$ orbitals relative to an octahedral arrangement of point-charge ligands. The important thing to note is that two of the orbitals, d_{z^2} and $d_{x^2-y^2}$, point their lobes *directly at* the point-charge ligands and three of the orbitals, d_{xz}, d_{yz}, and d_{xy}, point their lobes *between* the point charges.

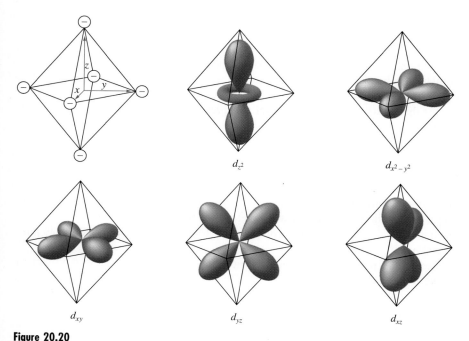

Figure 20.20

An octahedral arrangement of point-charge ligands and the orientation of the $3d$ orbitals.

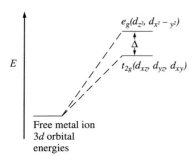

Figure 20.21

The energies of the 3d orbitals for a metal ion in an octahedral complex. The 3d orbitals are degenerate (all have the same energy) in the free metal ion. In the octahedral complex the orbitals are split into two sets as shown. The difference in energy between the two sets is designated as Δ (delta).

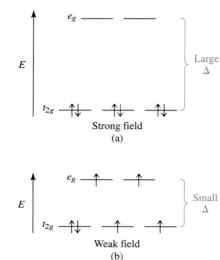

Figure 20.22

Possible electron arrangements in the split 3d orbitals in an octahedral complex of Co^{3+} (electron configuration $3d^6$). (a) In a strong field (large Δ value), the electrons fill the t_{2g} set first, giving a diamagnetic complex. (b) In a weak field (small Δ value), the electrons occupy all five orbitals before any pairing occurs.

To understand the effect of this difference, we need to consider which type of orbital is lower in energy. Because the negative point-charge ligands repel negatively charged electrons, the electrons will first fill the d orbitals farthest from the ligands to minimize repulsions. In other words, the d_{xz}, d_{yz}, and d_{xy} orbitals (known as the t_{2g} set) are at a *lower energy* in the octahedral complex than are the d_{z^2} and $d_{x^2-y^2}$ orbitals (the e_g set). This is shown in Fig. 20.21. The negative point-charge ligands increase the energies of all the d orbitals. However, the orbitals that point at the ligands are raised in energy more than those that point between the ligands.

It is this **splitting of the 3d orbital energies** (symbolized by Δ) that explains the color and magnetism of complex ions of the first-row transition metal ions. For example, in an octahedral complex of Co^{3+} (a metal ion with six 3d electrons), there are two possible ways to place the electrons in the split 3d orbitals (Fig. 20.22). If the splitting produced by the ligands is very large, a situation called the **strong-field case,** the electrons will pair in the lower-energy t_{2g} orbitals. This gives a *diamagnetic* complex in which all the electrons are paired. On the other hand, if the splitting is small (the **weak-field case**), the electrons will occupy all five orbitals before pairing occurs. In this case the complex has four unpaired electrons and is *paramagnetic.*

The crystal field model allows us to account for the differences in the magnetic properties of $Co(NH_3)_6^{3+}$ and CoF_6^{3-}. The $Co(NH_3)_6^{3+}$ ion is known to be diamagnetic and thus corresponds to the strong-field case, also called the **low-spin case,** since it yields the *minimum* number of unpaired electrons. In contrast, the CoF_6^{3-} ion, which is known to have four unpaired electrons, corresponds to the weak-field case, also known as the **high-spin case,** since it gives the *maximum* number of unpaired electrons.

Sample Exercise 20.4 Crystal Field Model I

The $Fe(CN)_6^{3-}$ ion is known to have one unpaired electron. Does the CN^- ligand produce a strong or weak field?

Solution

Since the ligand is CN^- and the overall complex ion charge is $3-$, the metal ion must be Fe^{3+}, which has a $3d^5$ electron configuration. The two possible arrangements of the five electrons in the d orbitals split by the octahedrally arranged ligands are

The strong-field case gives one unpaired electron, which agrees with the experimental observation. The CN^- ion is a strong-field ligand toward the Fe^{3+} ion.

See Exercises 20.49 and 20.50.

From studies of many octahedral complexes, we can arrange ligands in order of their ability to produce d-orbital splitting. A partial listing of ligands in this **spectrochemical series** is

$$CN^- > NO_2^- > en > NH_3 > H_2O > OH^- > F^- > Cl^- > Br^- > I^-$$

Strong-field ligands (large Δ) .... Weak-field ligands (small Δ)

The ligands are arranged in order of decreasing Δ values toward a given metal ion.

It also has been observed that *the magnitude of Δ for a given ligand increases as the charge on the metal ion increases.* For example, NH_3 is a weak-field ligand toward Co^{2+} but acts as a strong-field ligand toward Co^{3+}. This makes sense; as the metal ion charge increases, the ligands will be drawn closer to the metal ion because of the increased charge density. As the ligands move closer, they cause greater splitting of the d orbitals and produce a larger Δ value.

Sample Exercise 20.5 Crystal Field Model II

Predict the number of unpaired electrons in the complex ion $[Cr(CN)_6]^{4-}$.

Solution

The net charge of $4-$ means that the metal ion present must be Cr^{2+} ($-6 + 2 = -4$), which has a $3d^4$ electron configuration. Since CN^- is a strong-field ligand (see the spectrochemical series), the correct crystal field diagram for $[Cr(CN)_6]^{4-}$ is

The complex ion will have two unpaired electrons. Note that the CN^- ligand produces such a large splitting that all four electrons will occupy the t_{2g} set even though two of the electrons must be paired in the same orbital.

See Exercises 20.51 and 20.52.

We have seen how the crystal field model can account for the magnetic properties of octahedral complexes. The same model also can explain the colors of these complex ions. For example, $Ti(H_2O)_6^{3+}$, an octahedral complex of Ti^{3+}, which has a $3d^1$ electron configuration, is violet because it absorbs light in the middle of the visible region of the spectrum (see Fig. 20.23). When a substance absorbs certain wavelengths of light in the visible region, the color of the substance is determined by the wavelengths of visible light that remain. We say that the substance exhibits the color *complementary* to those absorbed. The $Ti(H_2O)_6^{3+}$ ion is violet because it absorbs light in the yellow-green region, thus letting red light and blue light pass, which gives the observed violet color. This is shown schematically in Fig. 20.24. Table 20.16 shows the general relationship between the wavelengths of visible light absorbed and the approximate color observed.

The reason that the $Ti(H_2O)_6^{3+}$ ion absorbs a specific wavelength of visible light can be traced to the transfer of the lone d electron between the split d orbitals, as shown in Fig. 20.25. A given photon of light can be absorbed by a molecule only if the wavelength of the light provides exactly the energy needed by the molecule. Or, in other words, the wavelength absorbed is determined by the relationship

$$\Delta E = \frac{hc}{\lambda}$$

where ΔE represents the energy spacing in the molecule (we have used simply Δ in this chapter) and λ represents the wavelength of light needed. Because the d-orbital

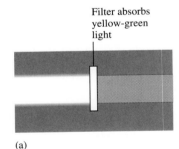

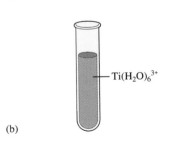

(a)

(b)

Figure 20.24

(a) When white light shines on a filter that absorbs in the yellow-green region, the emerging light is violet. (b) Because the complex ion $Ti(H_2O)_6^{3+}$ absorbs yellow-green light, a solution of it is violet.

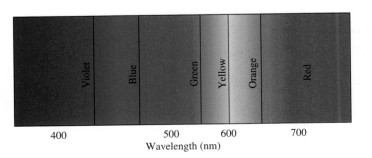

Figure 20.23

The visible spectrum.

Table 20.16 Approximate Relationship of Wavelength of Visible Light Absorbed to Color Observed

Absorbed Wavelength in nm (Color)	Observed Color
400 (violet)	Greenish yellow
450 (blue)	Yellow
490 (blue-green)	Red
570 (yellow-green)	Violet
580 (yellow)	Dark blue
600 (orange)	Blue
650 (red)	Green

Table 20.17 Several Octahedral Complexes of Cr^{3+} and Their Colors

Isomer	Color
$[Cr(H_2O)_6]Cl_3$	Violet
$[Cr(H_2O)_5Cl]Cl_2$	Blue-green
$[Cr(H_2O)_4Cl_2]Cl$	Green
$[Cr(NH_3)_6]Cl_3$	Yellow
$[Cr(NH_3)_5Cl]Cl_2$	Purple
$[Cr(NH_3)_4Cl_2]Cl$	Violet

$$E$$

Ground state of $Ti(H_2O)_6^{3+}$

Excited state of $Ti(H_2O)_6^{3+}$

Figure 20.25

The complex ion $Ti(H_2O)_6^{3+}$ can absorb visible light in the yellow-green region to transfer the lone d electron from the t_{2g} to the e_g set.

Video: Flame Tests

splitting in most octahedral complexes corresponds to the energies of photons in the visible region, octahedral complex ions are usually colored.

Since the ligands coordinated to a given metal ion determine the size of the d-orbital splitting, the color changes as the ligands are changed. This occurs because a change in Δ means a change in the wavelength of light needed to transfer electrons between the t_{2g} and e_g orbitals. Several octahedral complexes of Cr^{3+} and their colors are listed in Table 20.17.

Other Coordination Geometries

Using the same principles developed for octahedral complexes, we will now consider complexes with other geometries. For example, Fig. 20.26 shows a tetrahedral arrangement of point charges in relation to the $3d$ orbitals of a metal ion. There are two important facts to note:

1. None of the $3d$ orbitals "point at the ligands" in the tetrahedral arrangement, as the $d_{x^2-y^2}$ and d_{z^2} orbitals do in the octahedral case. Thus the tetrahedrally arranged ligands do not differentiate the d orbitals as much in the tetrahedral as in the octahedral case. That is, the difference in energy between the split d orbitals will be significantly less in tetrahedral complexes. Although we will not derive it here, the tetrahedral splitting is $\frac{4}{9}$ that of the octahedral splitting for a given ligand and metal ion:

$$\Delta_{tet} = \tfrac{4}{9}\Delta_{oct}$$

Solutions of $[Cr(NH_3)_6]Cl_3$ (yellow) and $[Cr(NH_3)_5Cl]Cl_2$ (purple).

CHEMICAL IMPACT

Transition Metal Ions Lend Color to Gems

THE BEAUTIFUL PURE color of gems, so valued by cultures everywhere, arises from trace transition metal ion impurities in minerals that would otherwise be colorless. For example, the stunning red of a ruby, the most valuable of all gemstones, is caused by Cr^{3+} ions, which replace about 1% of the Al^{3+} ions in the mineral corundum, which is a form of aluminum oxide (Al_2O_3) that is nearly as hard as diamond. In the corundum structure the Cr^{3+} ions are surrounded by six oxide ions at the vertices of an octahedron. This leads to the characteristic octahedral splitting of chromium's $3d$ orbitals, such that the Cr^{3+} ions absorb strongly in the blue-violet and yellow-green regions of the visible spectrum but transmit red light to give the characteristic ruby color. (On the other hand, if some of the Al^{3+} ions in corundum are replaced by a mixture of Fe^{2+}, Fe^{3+}, and Ti^{4+} ions, the gem is a sapphire with its brilliant blue color; or if some of the Al^{3+} ions are replaced by Fe^{3+} ions, the stone is a yellow topaz.)

Emeralds are derived from the mineral beryl, which is a beryllium aluminum silicate (empirical formula $3BeO \cdot Al_2O_3 \cdot 6SiO_2$). When some of the Al^{3+} ions in beryl are replaced by Cr^{3+} ions, the characteristic green color of emerald results. In this environment the splitting of

the Cr^{3+} $3d$ orbitals causes it to strongly absorb yellow and blue-violet light and to transmit green light.

A gem closely related to ruby and emerald is alexandrite, named after Alexander II of Russia. This gem is based on the mineral chrysoberyl, a beryllium aluminate with the empirical formula $BeO \cdot Al_2O_3$ in which approximately 1% of the Al^{3+} ions are replaced by Cr^{3+} ions. In the chrysoberyl environment Cr^{3+} absorbs strongly in the yellow region of the spectrum. Alexandrite has the interesting property of changing colors depending on the light source. When the first alexandrite stone was discovered deep in a mine in the Russian Ural Mountains in 1831, it appeared to be a deep red color in the firelight of the miners' lamps. However, when the stone was brought to the surface, its color was blue. This seemingly magical color change occurs because the firelight of a miner's helmet is rich in the yellow and red wavelengths of the visible spectrum but does not contain much blue. Absorption of the yellow by the stone produces a reddish color. However, daylight has much more intensity in the blue region than firelight. Thus the extra blue in the light transmitted by the stone gives it bluish color in daylight.

Alexandrite, a gem closely related to ruby and emerald.

Once the structure of a natural gem is known, it is usually not very difficult to make the gem artificially. For example, rubies and sapphires are made on a large scale by fusing $Al(OH)_3$ with the appropriate transition metal salts at approximately 1200°C to make the "doped" corundum. With these techniques gems of astonishing size can be manufactured: Rubies as large as 10 lb and sapphires up to 100 lb have been synthesized. Smaller synthetic stones produced for jewelry are virtually identical to the corresponding natural stones, and it takes great skill for a gemologist to tell the difference.

Figure 20.26

(a) Tetrahedral and octahedral arrangements of ligands shown inscribed in cubes. Note that in the two types of arrangements, the point charges occupy opposite parts of the cube; the octahedral point charges are at the centers of the cube faces, and the tetrahedral point charges occupy opposite corners of the cube.
(b) The orientations of the $3d$ orbitals relative to the tetrahedral set of point charges.

(a)

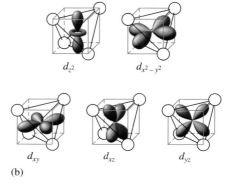

(b)

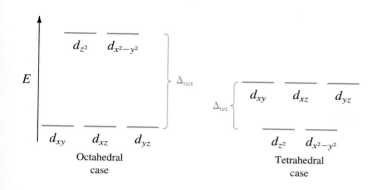

Figure 20.27

The crystal field diagrams for octahedral and tetrahedral complexes. The relative energies of the sets of d orbitals are reversed. For a given type of ligand, the splitting is much larger for the octahedral complex ($\Delta_{oct} > \Delta_{tet}$) because in this arrangement the d_{z^2} and $d_{x^2-y^2}$ point their lobes directly at the point charges and are thus relatively high in energy.

2. Although not exactly pointing at the ligands, the d_{xy}, d_{xz}, and d_{yz} orbitals are closer to the point charges than are the d_{z^2} and $d_{x^2-y^2}$ orbitals. This means that the tetrahedral d-orbital splitting will be opposite to that for the octahedral arrangement. The two arrangements are contrasted in Fig. 20.27. Because the d-orbital splitting is relatively small for the tetrahedral case, the weak-field case (high-spin case) *always* applies. There are no known ligands powerful enough to produce the strong-field case in a tetrahedral complex.

Sample Exercise 20.6 *Crystal Field Model III*

Solution

Give the crystal field diagram for the tetrahedral complex ion $CoCl_4^{2-}$.

The complex ion contains Co^{2+}, which has a $3d^7$ electron configuration. The splitting of the d orbitals will be small, since this is a tetrahedral complex, giving the high-spin case with three unpaired electrons.

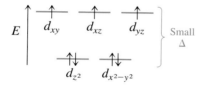

See Exercises 20.55 through 20.57.

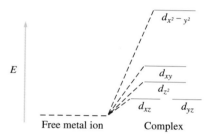

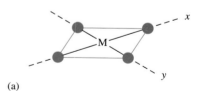

(a)

The crystal field model also applies to square planar and linear complexes. The crystal field diagrams for these cases are shown in Fig. 20.28. The ranking of orbitals in these diagrams can be explained by considering the relative orientations of

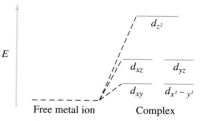

Figure 20.28

(a) The crystal field diagram for a square planar complex oriented in the xy plane with ligands along the x and y axes. The position of the d_{z^2} orbital is higher than those of the d_{xz} and d_{yz} orbitals because of the "doughnut" of electron density in the xy plane. The actual position of d_{z^2} is somewhat uncertain and varies in different square planar complexes. (b) The crystal field diagram for a linear complex where the ligands lie along the z axis.

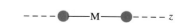

(b)

the point charges and the orbitals. The diagram in Fig. 20.27 for the octahedral arrangement can be used to obtain these orientations. We can obtain the square planar complex by removing the two point charges along the z axis. This will greatly lower the energy of d_{z^2}, leaving only $d_{x^2-y^2}$, which points at the four remaining ligands as the highest-energy orbital. We can obtain the linear complex from the octahedral arrangement by leaving the two ligands along the z axis and removing the four in the xy plane. This means that only the d_{z^2} points at the ligands and is highest in energy.

20.7 The Biologic Importance of Coordination Complexes

The ability of metal ions to coordinate with and release ligands and to easily undergo oxidation and reduction makes them ideal for use in biologic systems. For example, metal ion complexes are used in humans for the transport and storage of oxygen, as electron-transfer agents, as catalysts, and as drugs. Most of the first-row transition metals are essential for human health, as is summarized in Table 20.18. We will concentrate on iron's role in biologic systems, since several of its coordination complexes have been studied extensively.

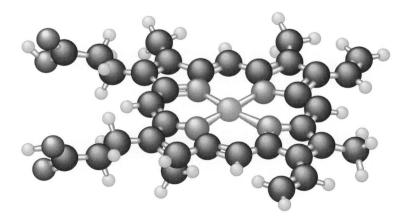

Figure 20.29

The heme complex, in which an Fe^{2+} ion is coordinated to four nitrogen atoms of a planar porphyrin ligand.

Table 20.18 The First-Row Transition Metals and Their Biologic Significance

First-Row Transition Metal	Biologic Function(s)
Scandium	None known.
Titanium	None known.
Vanadium	None known in humans.
Chromium	Assists insulin in the control of blood sugar; may also be involved in the control of cholesterol.
Manganese	Necessary for a number of enzymatic reactions.
Iron	Component of hemoglobin and myoglobin; involved in the electron-transport chain.
Cobalt	Component of vitamin B_{12}, which is essential for the metabolism of carbohydrates, fats, and proteins.
Nickel	Component of the enzymes urease and hydrogenase.
Copper	Component of several enzymes; assists in iron storage; involved in the production of color pigments of hair, skin, and eyes.
Zinc	Component of insulin and many enzymes.

Iron plays a central role in almost all living cells. In mammals, the principal source of energy comes from the oxidation of carbohydrates, proteins, and fats. Although oxygen is the oxidizing agent for these processes, it does not react directly with these molecules. Instead, the electrons from the breakdown of these nutrients are passed along a complex chain of molecules, called the *respiratory chain,* eventually reaching the O_2 molecule. The principal electron-transfer molecules in the respiratory chain are iron-containing species called **cytochromes,** consisting of two main parts: an iron complex called **heme** and a protein. The structure of the heme complex is shown in Fig. 20.29. Note that it contains an iron ion (it can be either Fe^{2+} or Fe^{3+}) coordinated to a rather complicated planar ligand called a **porphyrin.** As a class, porphyrins all contain the same central ring structure but have different substituent groups at the edges of the rings. The various porphyrin molecules act as tetradentate ligands for many metal ions, including iron, cobalt, and magnesium. In fact, *chlorophyll,* a substance essential to the process of photosynthesis, is a magnesium–porphyrin complex of the type shown in Fig. 20.30.

A protein is a large molecule assembled from amino acids, which have the general structure in which R represents various groups.

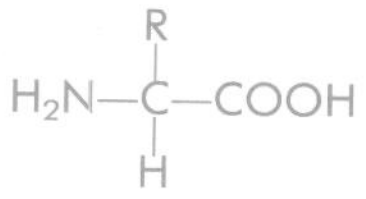

$$H_2N-\underset{\underset{H}{|}}{\overset{\overset{R}{|}}{C}}-COOH$$

Molecular Models: heme, chlorophyll

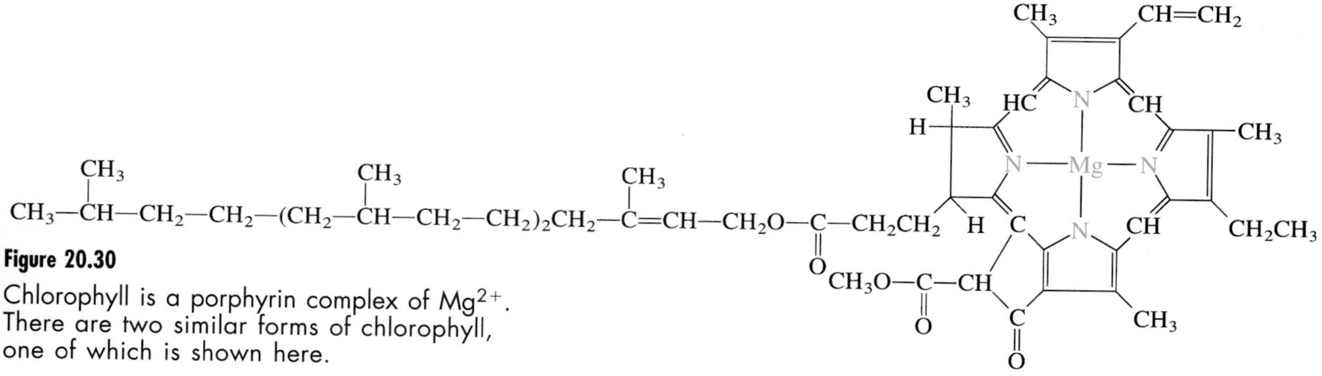

Figure 20.30

Chlorophyll is a porphyrin complex of Mg^{2+}. There are two similar forms of chlorophyll, one of which is shown here.

CHEMICAL IMPACT

The Danger of Mercury*

IN AUGUST 1989, four family members from Lincoln Park, Michigan, died under mysterious circumstances. All four victims had severe tissue damage to the esophagus and lungs, which led doctors to suspect exposure to some type of caustic chemical. Subsequently, local police and fire investigators discovered a crude laboratory in the basement that was used to recover valuable silver from stolen dental amalgams. A dental amalgam is a metal alloy that a dentist uses to fill a tooth. The alloy typically contains silver, tin, copper, and zinc dissolved in liquid mercury. The mixture is placed in a cavity, where it hardens, resulting in a standard "filling."

One of the victims worked at a manufacturing facility for amalgams and was stealing some of the products. At home in his crude lab he heated the amalgam to drive off the mercury (which vaporized at relatively low temperatures) so that he could recover the silver that was left behind. In the process, the colorless, odorless, tasteless mercury vapor entered the ductwork of the home, which was contaminated with mercury at levels 1500 times normal—levels certain to result in

death to those exposed. In fact, postmortem analysis revealed extreme levels of mercury in the vital organs of all four victims. Mercury vapor was the silent killer.

The toxicity of mercury varies significantly depending on the route of entry into the body. Inhalation is the most dangerous route because mercury vapor entering the lungs quickly passes across the lung–blood barrier and into the bloodstream, where it can interfere with normal blood chemistry. One of the reactions that takes place in the blood is the decomposition of hydrogen peroxide (a metabolic waste product) by the enzyme peroxidase:

$$2H_2O_2 \xrightarrow{\text{Peroxidase}} 2H_2O + O_2$$

When elemental mercury enters the bloodstream, it reacts with hydrogen peroxide in the presence of peroxidase to produce mercury(II) oxide and water:

$$Hg + H_2O_2 \xrightarrow{\text{Peroxidase}} HgO + H_2O$$

If this conversion to mercury(II) occurs within vital tissues, the mercury(II) cation can

denature proteins, inhibit enzyme activity, and disrupt cell membranes. Death often results from respiratory or kidney failure.

If mercury is so toxic, how can it be used in dental fillings? Surprisingly, unlike elemental mercury in the vapor form, mercury bound as a solid in a dental amalgam presents little, if any, risk. Because the mercury is not mobile, even in the harsh environment of the human mouth, the American Dental Association has determined it to be a minimal health risk to dental patients. Even if a filling loosens and is accidentally swallowed, it is passed through the digestive system and excreted before it can pose any risk. The mercury that the four victims in this story were exposed to resulted from heating the amalgam in a smelting furnace, thus vaporizing the mercury and exposing the occupants of the house to the most hazardous route of entry—inhalation.

*Reprinted with permission from "Nightmare on White Street," by Tim Graham as it appeared in *ChemMatters*, December 1996. Copyright © 1996, American Chemical Society.

In addition to participating in the transfer of electrons from nutrients to oxygen, iron also plays a principal role in the transport and storage of oxygen in mammalian blood and tissues. Oxygen is stored in a molecule called **myoglobin,** which consists of a heme complex and a protein in a structure very similar to that of the cytochromes. In myoglobin, the Fe^{2+} ion is coordinated to four nitrogen atoms of the porphyrin ring and to a nitrogen atom of the protein chain, as shown in Fig. 20.31. Since Fe^{2+} is normally six-coordinate, this leaves one position open for attachment of an O_2 molecule.

One especially interesting feature of myoglobin is that it involves an O_2 molecule attaching directly to Fe^{2+}. However, if gaseous O_2 is bubbled into an aqueous solution containing heme, the Fe^{2+} is immediately oxidized to Fe^{3+}. This oxidation of the Fe^{2+} in heme does not happen in myoglobin. This fact is of crucial importance because Fe^{3+} does not form a coordinate covalent bond with O_2, and myo-

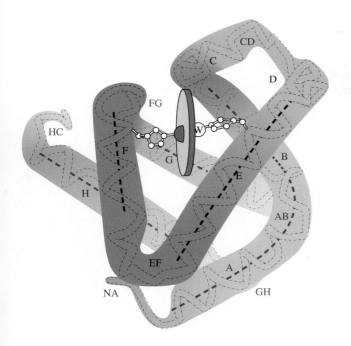

Figure 20.31

A representation of the myoglobin molecule. The Fe^{2+} ion is coordinated to four nitrogen atoms in the porphyrin of the heme (represented by the disk in the figure) and on nitrogen from the protein chain. This leaves a sixth coordination position (indicated by the W) available for an oxygen molecule.

globin would not function if the bound Fe^{2+} could be oxidized. Since the Fe^{2+} in the "bare" heme complex can be oxidized, it must be the protein that somehow prevents the oxidation. How? Based on much research, the answer seems to be that the oxidation of Fe^{2+} to Fe^{3+} involves an oxygen bridge between two iron ions (the circles indicate the ligands):

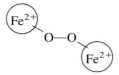

The bulky protein around the heme group in myoglobin prevents two molecules from getting close enough to form the oxygen bridge, and so oxidation of the Fe^{2+} is prevented.

The transport of O_2 in the blood is carried out by **hemoglobin,** a molecule consisting of four myoglobin-like units, as shown in Fig. 20.32. Each hemoglobin can therefore bind four O_2 molecules to form a bright red diamagnetic complex. The diamagnetism occurs because oxygen is a strong-field ligand toward Fe^{2+}, which has a $3d^6$ electron configuration. When the oxygen molecule is released, water molecules occupy the sixth coordination position around each Fe^{2+}, giving a bluish paramagnetic complex (H_2O is a weak-field ligand toward Fe^{2+}) that gives venous blood its characteristic bluish tint.

Hemoglobin dramatically demonstrates how sensitive the function of a biomolecule is to its structure. In certain people, in the synthesis of the proteins needed for hemoglobin, an improper amino acid is inserted into the protein in two places. This

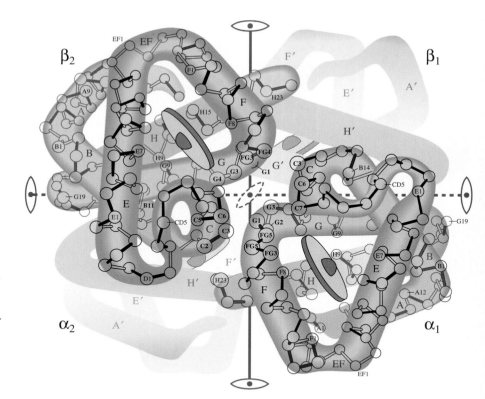

Figure 20.32

A representation of the hemoglobin structure. There are two slightly different types of protein chains (α and β). Each hemoglobin has two α chains and two β chains, each with a heme complex near the center. Thus each hemoglobin molecule can complex with four O_2 molecules.

may not seem very serious, since there are several hundred amino acids present. However, because the incorrect amino acid has a nonpolar substituent instead of the polar one found on the proper amino acid, the hemoglobin drastically changes its shape. The red blood cells are then sickle-shaped rather than disk-shaped, as shown in Fig. 20.33. The misshapen cells can aggregate, causing clogging of tiny capillaries. This condition, known as *sickle cell anemia,* is the subject of intense research.

Our knowledge of the workings of hemoglobin allows us to understand the effects of high altitudes on humans. The reaction between hemoglobin and oxygen can be represented by the following equilibrium:

$$\text{Hb}(aq) + 4O_2(g) \rightleftharpoons \text{Hb}(O_2)_4(aq)$$
$$\qquad\text{Hemoglobin} \qquad\qquad\qquad \text{Oxyhemoglobin}$$

At high altitudes, where the oxygen content of the air is lower, the position of this equilibrium will shift to the left, according to Le Châtelier's principle. Because less oxyhemoglobin is formed, fatigue, dizziness, and even a serious illness called *high-altitude sickness* can result. One way to combat this problem is to use supplemental oxygen, as most high-altitude mountain climbers do. However, this is impractical for people who live at high elevations. In fact, the human body adapts to the lower oxygen concentrations by making more hemoglobin, causing the equilibrium to shift back to the right. Someone moving from Chicago to Boulder, Colorado (5300 feet), would notice the effects of the new altitude for a couple of weeks, but as the hemoglobin level increased, the effects would disappear. This change is called *high-altitude acclimatization,* which explains why athletes who want to compete at high elevations should practice there for several weeks prior to the event.

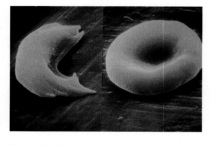

Figure 20.33

A normal red blood cell (right) and a sickle cell (left), both magnified 18,000 times.

CHEMICAL IMPACT

Supercharged Blood

The 1998 Tour de France.

DURING THE 1964 Winter Olympics in Innsbruck, Austria, a Finn named Eero Maentyranta won three gold medals in cross-country skiing and immediately became a national hero. His success was due in no small part to the fact that his blood carried 25% to 50% more hemoglobin than the average man's blood. Maentyranta suffered from a rare genetic disorder that results in unusually elevated levels of red blood cells. This extra oxygen-carrying capacity lends itself to increased stamina and endurance, certainly an advantage in the rigorous sport of cross-country skiing. Several years later, geneticists at the University of Helsinki determined that the disorder was due to a mutation of a protein responsible for red blood cell production called the *erythropoietin receptor* (EPO-R). The mutation, which was common in the Maentyranta family, resulted in a protein that was missing 70 amino acids (out of 550). This mutation deleted the portion of the protein that contained the "off switch" for red blood cell production.

Since the discovery of EPO's role in red blood cell production, genetic engineers have been able to synthesize EPO by bioengineering techniques. The protein, marketed in the United States by Amgen of Thousand Oaks, California, is used by kidney dialysis, AIDS, and cancer patients to boost red blood cell production. It has become biotechnology's biggest revenue producer, with over $1 billion in annual sales.

While the potential benefits of this protein are obvious, the potential for abuse may be even greater. The Tour de France, thought by many to be the world's greatest endurance race, was rocked in 1998 by controversy when several riders (including three race favorites) were ex-

pelled from the race over allegations of blood doping with the red blood cell–enchancing hormone EPO. EPO has become the drug of choice for many endurance athletes trying to gain an unfair advantage because it is metabolized quickly and, being identical to the body's own EPO, it is almost impossible to detect by blood or urine analysis. But the hazards are great. Endurance athletes are especially at risk from abuse of EPO due to extreme water loss during the athletic competition, which, when coupled with elevated levels of EPO, results in an extreme thickening of the blood. This puts an obvious strain on the heart. Since EPO became available in 1986, several world-class athletes (mostly bicyclists and

distance runners) have died under mysterious circumstances thought to be associated with abuse of EPO. Because of the widespread abuse of EPO, new methods of detection are being put in place to limit its impact on organized sports and its participants.

The advantage that Eero Maentyranta gained in the 1964 Olympics was the result of a disorder that he had lived with for his entire life. His body had become accustomed to operating with elevated levels of hemoglobin, and it became a natural advantage. Synthetic EPO holds much promise for those suffering conditions that result in hemoglobin deficiency. But as a performance-enhancing drug, EPO's advantages come with enormous risk.

Sherpa and Balti porters are acclimatized to high elevations such as those around the K2 mountain peak in Pakistan.

Our understanding of the biologic role of iron also allows us to explain the toxicities of substances such as carbon monoxide and the cyanide ion. Both CO and CN^- are very good ligands toward iron and so can interfere with the normal workings of the iron complexes in the body. For example, carbon monoxide has about 200 times the affinity for the Fe^{2+} in hemoglobin as oxygen does. The resulting stable complex, **carboxyhemoglobin,** prevents the normal uptake of O_2, thus depriving the body of needed oxygen. Asphyxiation can result if enough carbon monoxide is present in the air. The mechanism for the toxicity of the cyanide ion is somewhat different. Cyanide coordinates strongly to cytochrome oxidase, an iron-containing cytochrome enzyme that catalyzes the oxidation–reduction reactions of certain cytochromes. The coordinated cyanide thus prevents the electron-transfer process and rapid death results. Because of its behavior, cyanide is called a *respiratory inhibitor.*

20.8   Metallurgy and Iron and Steel Production

In the preceding section we saw the importance of iron in biologic systems. Of course, iron is also very important in many other ways in our world. In this section we will discuss the isolation of metals from their natural sources and the formulation of metals into useful materials, with special emphasis on the role of iron.

Metals are very important for structural applications, electrical wires, cooking utensils, tools, decorative items, and many other purposes. However, because the main chemical characteristic of a metal is its ability to give up electrons, almost all metals in nature are found in ores, combined with nonmetals such as oxygen, sulfur, and the halogens. To recover and use these metals, we must separate them from their ores and reduce the metal ions. Then, because most metals are unsuitable for use in the pure state, we must form alloys that have the desired properties. The

Table 20.19 Common Minerals Found in Ores

Anion	Examples
None (free metal)	Au, Ag, Pt, Pd, Rh, Ir, Ru
Oxide	Fe_2O_3 (hematite)
	Fe_3O_4 (magnetite)
	Al_2O_3 (bauxite)
	SnO_2 (cassiterite)
Sulfide	PbS (galena)
	ZnS (sphalerite)
	FeS_2 (pyrite)
	HgS (cinnabar)
	Cu_2S (chalcocite)
Chloride	NaCl (rock salt)
	KCl (sylvite)
	$KCl \cdot MgCl_2$ (carnalite)
Carbonate	$FeCO_3$ (siderite)
	$CaCO_3$ (limestone)
	$MgCO_3$ (magnesite)
	$MgCO_3 \cdot CaCO_3$ (dolomite)
Sulfate	$CaSO_4 \cdot 2H_2O$ (gypsum)
	$BaSO_4$ (barite)
Silicate	$Be_3Al_2Si_6O_{18}$ (beryl)
	$Al_2(Si_2O_8)(OH)_4$ (kaolinite)
	$LiAl(SiO_3)_2$ (spondumene)

Figure 20.34

A schematic diagram of a cyclone separator. The ore is pulverized and blown into the separator. The more dense mineral particles are thrown toward the walls by centrifugal force and fall down the funnel. The lighter particles (gangue) tend to stay closer to the center and are drawn out through the top by the stream of air.

process of separating a metal from its ore and preparing it for use is known as **metallurgy.** The steps in this process are typically

1. Mining
2. Pretreatment of the ore
3. Reduction to the free metal
4. Purification of the metal (refining)
5. Alloying

An ore can be viewed as a mixture containing **minerals** (relatively pure metal compounds) and **gangue** (sand, clay, and rock). Some typical minerals are listed in Table 20.19. Although silicate minerals are the most common in the earth's crust, they are typically very hard and difficult to process, making metal extraction relatively expensive. Therefore, other ores are used when available.

After mining, an ore must be treated to remove the gangue and to concentrate the mineral. The ore is first pulverized and then processed in a variety of devices, including cyclone separators (see Fig. 20.34), inclined vibrating tables, and flotation tanks.

In the **flotation process,** the crushed ore is fed into a tank containing a water–oil–detergent mixture. Because of the difference in the surface characteristics of the mineral particles and the silicate rock particles, the oil wets the mineral particles. A stream of air blown through the mixture causes tiny bubbles to form on the oil-covered pieces, which then float to the surface, where they can be skimmed off.

A steel mill in Brazil.

After the mineral has been concentrated, it is often chemically altered in preparation for the reduction step. For example, nonoxide minerals are often converted to oxides before reduction. Carbonates and hydroxides can be converted by simple heating:

$$CaCO_3(s) \xrightarrow{\text{Heat}} CaO(s) + CO_2(g)$$

$$Mg(OH)_2(s) \xrightarrow{\text{Heat}} MgO(s) + H_2O(g)$$

Sulfide minerals can be converted to oxides by heating in air at temperatures below their melting points, a process called **roasting:**

$$2ZnS(s) + 3O_2(g) \xrightarrow{\text{Heat}} 2ZnO(s) + 2SO_2(g)$$

As we have seen earlier, sulfur dioxide causes severe problems if released into the atmosphere, and modern roasting operations collect this gas and use it in the manufacture of sulfuric acid.

The method chosen to reduce the metal ion to the free metal, a process called **smelting,** depends on the affinity of the metal ion for electrons. Some metals are good enough oxidizing agents that the free metal is produced in the roasting process. For example, the roasting reaction for cinnabar is

$$HgS(s) + O_2(g) \xrightarrow{\text{Heat}} Hg(l) + SO_2(g)$$

where the Hg^{2+} is reduced by electrons donated by the S^{2-} ion, which is then further oxidized by O_2 to form SO_2.

The roasting of a more active metal produces the metal oxide, which must be reduced to obtain the free metal. The most common reducing agents are coke (impure carbon), carbon monoxide, and hydrogen. The following are some common examples of the reduction process:

$$Fe_2O_3(s) + 3CO(g) \xrightarrow{\text{Heat}} 2Fe(l) + 3CO_2(g)$$

$$WO_3(s) + 3H_2(g) \xrightarrow{\text{Heat}} W(l) + 3H_2O(g)$$

$$ZnO(s) + C(s) \xrightarrow{\text{Heat}} Zn(l) + CO(g)$$

The most active metals, such as aluminum and the alkali metals, must be reduced electrolytically, usually from molten salts (see Section 17.8).

The metal obtained in the reduction step is invariably impure and must be refined. The methods of refining include electrolytic refining (see Section 17.8), oxidation of impurities (as for iron, see below), and distillation of low-boiling metals such as mercury and zinc. One process used when highly pure metals are needed is **zone refining.** In this process a bar of the impure metal travels through a heater (see Fig. 20.35), which causes melting and recrystallizing of the metal as the bar cools.

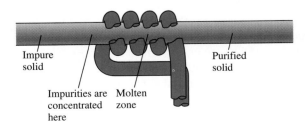

Figure 20.35

A schematic representation of zone refining.

Impure
solid

Purified
solid

Impurities are   Molten
concentrated   zone
here

Purification of the metal occurs because as the crystal re-forms, the metal ions are likely to fit much better in the crystal lattice than are the atoms of impurities. Thus the impurities tend to be excluded and carried to the end of the bar. Several repetitions of this process give a very pure metal bar.

Hydrometallurgy

The metallurgical processes we have considered so far are usually called **pyrometallurgy** (*pyro* means "at high temperatures"). These traditional methods require large quantities of energy and have two other serious problems: atmospheric pollution (mainly by sulfur dioxide) and relatively high costs that make treatment of low-grade ores economically unfeasible.

In the past hundred years, a different process, **hydrometallurgy** (*hydro* means "water"), has been employed to extract metals from ores by use of aqueous chemical solutions, a process called **leaching.** The first two uses of hydrometallurgy were for the extraction of gold from low-grade ores and for the production of aluminum oxide, or alumina, from bauxite, an aluminum-bearing ore.

Gold is sometimes found in ores in the elemental state, but it usually occurs in relatively small concentrations. A process called **cyanidation** treats the crushed ore with an aqueous cyanide solution in the presence of air to dissolve the gold by forming the complex ion $Au(CN)_2^-$:

$$4Au(s) + 8CN^-(aq) + O_2(g) + 2H_2O(l) \longrightarrow 4Au(CN)_2^-(aq) + 4OH^-(aq)$$

Pure gold is then recovered by reaction of the solution of $Au(CN)_2^-$ with zinc powder to reduce Au^+ to Au:

$$2Au(CN)_2^-(aq) + Zn(s) \longrightarrow 2Au(s) + Zn(CN)_4^{2-}(aq)$$

The extraction of alumina from bauxite (the Bayer process) leaches the ore with sodium hydroxide at high temperatures and pressures to dissolve the amphoteric aluminum oxide:

$$Al_2O_3(s) + 2OH^-(aq) \longrightarrow 2AlO_2^-(aq) + H_2O(l)$$

This process leaves behind solid impurities such as SiO_2, Fe_2O_3, and TiO_2, which are not appreciably soluble in basic solution. After the solid impurities are removed, the pH of the solution is lowered, causing the pure aluminum oxide to re-form. It is then electrolyzed to produce aluminum metal (see Section 17.8).

As illustrated by these processes, hydrometallurgy involves two distinct steps: *selective leaching* of a given metal ion from the ore and recovery of the metal ion from the solution by *selective precipitation* as an ionic compound.

The leaching agent can simply be water if the metal-containing compound is a water-soluble chloride or sulfate. However, most commonly, the metal is present in a water-insoluble substance that must somehow be dissolved. The leaching agents used in such cases are usually aqueous solutions containing acids, bases, oxidizing agents, salts, or some combination of these. Often the dissolving process involves the formation of complex ions. For example, when an ore containing water-insoluble lead sulfate is treated with an aqueous sodium chloride solution, the soluble complex ion $PbCl_4^{2-}$ is formed:

$$PbSO_4(s) + 4Na^+(aq) + 4Cl^-(aq) \longrightarrow 4Na^+(aq) + PbCl_4^{2-}(aq) + SO_4^{2-}(aq)$$

Formation of a complex ion also occurs in the cyanidation process for the recovery of gold. However, since the gold is present in the ore as particles of metal, it must first be oxidized by oxygen to produce Au^+, which then reacts with CN^-

Table 20.20 Examples of Methods for Recovery of Metal Ions from Leaching Solutions

Method		Examples
Precipitation of a salt		$Cu^{2+}(aq) + S^{2-}(aq) \longrightarrow CuS(s)$
		$Cu^+(aq) + HCN(aq) \longrightarrow CuCN(s) + H^+(aq)$
Reduction	Chemical	$\begin{cases} Au^+(aq) + Fe^{2+}(aq) \longrightarrow Au(s) + Fe^{3+}(aq) \\ Cu^{2+}(aq) + Fe(s) \longrightarrow Cu(s) + Fe^{2+}(aq) \\ Ni^{2+}(aq) + H_2(g) \longrightarrow Ni(s) + 2H^+(aq) \end{cases}$
	Electrolytic	$\begin{cases} Cu^{2+}(aq) + 2e^- \longrightarrow Cu(s) \\ Al^{3+}(aq) + 3e^- \longrightarrow Al(s) \end{cases}$
Reduction plus precipitation		$2Cu^{2+}(aq) + 2Cl^-(aq) + H_2SO_3(aq) + H_2O(l) \longrightarrow$ $2CuCl(s) + 3H^+(aq) + HSO_4^-(aq)$

Precipitation reactions are discussed in Section 15.7.

to form the soluble $Au(CN)_2^-$ species. Thus, in this case, the leaching process involves a combination of oxidation and complexation.

Sometimes just oxidation is used. For example, insoluble zinc sulfide can be converted to soluble zinc sulfate by pulverizing the ore and suspending it in water to form a slurry through which oxygen is bubbled:

$$ZnS(s) + 2O_2(g) \longrightarrow Zn^{2+}(aq) + SO_4^{2-}(aq)$$

One advantage of hydrometallurgy over the traditional processes is that sometimes the leaching agent can be pumped directly into the ore deposits in the earth. For example, aqueous sodium carbonate (Na_2CO_3) can be injected into uranium-bearing ores to form water-soluble complex carbonate ions.

Recovering the metal ions from the leaching solution involves forming an insoluble solid containing the metal ion to be recovered. This step may involve addition of an anion to form an insoluble salt, reduction to the solid metal, or a combination of reduction and precipitation of a salt. Examples of these processes are shown in Table 20.20. Because of its suitability for treating low-grade ores economically and without significant pollution, hydrometallurgy is becoming more popular for recovering many important metals such as copper, nickel, zinc, and uranium.

The Metallurgy of Iron

Iron is present in the earth's crust in many types of minerals. *Iron pyrite* (FeS_2) is widely distributed but is not suitable for production of metallic iron and steel because it is almost impossible to remove the last traces of sulfur. The presence of sulfur makes the resulting steel too brittle to be useful. *Siderite* ($FeCO_3$) is a valuable iron mineral that can be converted to iron oxide by heating. The iron oxide minerals are *hematite* (Fe_2O_3), the more abundant, and *magnetite* (Fe_3O_4, really $FeO \cdot Fe_2O_3$). *Taconite* ores contain iron oxides mixed with silicates and are more difficult to process than the others. However, taconite ores are being increasingly used as the more desirable ores are consumed.

To concentrate the iron in iron ores, advantage is taken of the natural magnetism of Fe_3O_4 (hence its name, *magnetite*). The Fe_3O_4 particles can be separated from the gangue by magnets. The ores that are not magnetic are often converted to Fe_3O_4;

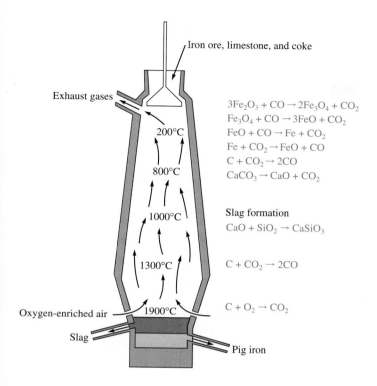

Iron ore, limestone, and coke

Exhaust gases

200°C

800°C

1000°C

1300°C

1900°C

Oxygen-enriched air

Slag

Pig iron

$$3Fe_2O_3 + CO \rightarrow 2Fe_3O_4 + CO_2$$
$$Fe_3O_4 + CO \rightarrow 3FeO + CO_2$$
$$FeO + CO \rightarrow Fe + CO_2$$
$$Fe + CO_2 \rightarrow FeO + CO$$
$$C + CO_2 \rightarrow 2CO$$
$$CaCO_3 \rightarrow CaO + CO_2$$

Slag formation
$$CaO + SiO_2 \rightarrow CaSiO_3$$

$$C + CO_2 \rightarrow 2CO$$

$$C + O_2 \rightarrow CO_2$$

Figure 20.36

The blast furnace used in the production of iron.

hematite is partially reduced to magnetite, while siderite is first converted to FeO thermally, then oxidized to Fe_2O_3, and then reduced to Fe_3O_4:

$$FeCO_3(s) \xrightarrow{\text{Heat}} FeO(s) + CO_2(g)$$

$$4FeO(s) + O_2(g) \longrightarrow 2Fe_2O_3(s)$$

$$3Fe_2O_3(s) + C(s) \longrightarrow 2Fe_3O_4(s) + CO(g)$$

Sometimes the nonmagnetic ores are concentrated by flotation processes.

The most commonly used reduction process for iron takes place in the **blast furnace** (Fig. 20.36). The raw materials required are concentrated iron ore, coke, and limestone (which serves as a *flux* to trap impurities). The furnace, which is approximately 25 feet in diameter, is charged from the top with a mixture of iron ore, coke, and limestone. A very strong blast (~350 mi/h) of hot air is injected at the bottom, where the oxygen reacts with the carbon in the coke to form carbon monoxide, the reducing agent for the iron. The temperature of the charge increases as it travels down the furnace, with reduction of the iron to iron metal occurring in steps:

$$3Fe_2O_3 + CO \longrightarrow 2Fe_3O_4 + CO_2$$

$$Fe_3O_4 + CO \longrightarrow 3FeO + CO_2$$

$$FeO + CO \longrightarrow Fe + CO_2$$

Iron can reduce carbon dioxide,

$$Fe + CO_2 \longrightarrow FeO + CO$$

so complete reduction of the iron occurs only if the carbon dioxide is destroyed by adding excess coke:

$$CO_2 + C \longrightarrow 2CO$$

The limestone ($CaCO_3$) in the charge loses carbon dioxide, or *calcines,* in the hot furnace and combines with silica and other impurities to form **slag,** which is mostly molten calcium silicate, $CaSiO_3$,

$$CaO + SiO_2 \longrightarrow CaSiO_3$$

and alumina (Al_2O_3). The slag floats on the molten iron and is skimmed off. The gas that escapes from the top of the furnace contains carbon monoxide, which is combined with air to form carbon dioxide. The energy released in this exothermic reaction is collected in a heat exchanger and used in heating the furnace.

The iron collected from the blast furnace, called **pig iron,** is quite impure. It contains ~90% iron, ~5% carbon, ~2% manganese, ~1% silicon, ~0.3% phosphorus, and ~0.04% sulfur (from impurities in the coke). The production of 1 ton of pig iron requires approximately 1.7 tons of iron ore, 0.5 ton of coke, 0.25 ton of limestone, and 2 tons of air.

Iron oxide also can be reduced in a **direct reduction furnace,** which operates at much lower temperatures (1300–2000°F) than a blast furnace and produces a solid "sponge iron" rather than molten iron. Because of the milder reaction conditions, the direct reduction furnace requires a higher grade of iron ore (with fewer impurities) than that used in a blast furnace. The iron from the direct reduction furnace is called *DRI (directly reduced iron)* and contains ~95% iron, with the balance mainly silica and alumina.

Production of Steel

Steel is an alloy and can be classified as **carbon steel,** which contains up to about 1.5% carbon, or **alloy steel,** which contains carbon plus other metals such as Cr, Co, Mn, and Mo. The wide range of mechanical properties associated with steel is determined by its chemical composition and by the heat treatment of the final product.

The production of iron from its ore is fundamentally a reduction process, but the conversion of iron to steel is basically an oxidation process in which unwanted impurities are eliminated. Oxidation is carried out in various ways, but the two most common are the open hearth process and the basic oxygen process.

In the oxidation reactions of steelmaking, the manganese, phosphorus, and silicon in the impure iron react with oxygen to form oxides, which in turn react with appropriate fluxes to form slag. Sulfur enters the slag primarily as sulfides, and excess carbon forms carbon monoxide or carbon dioxide. The flux chosen depends on the major impurities present. If manganese is the chief impurity, an acidic flux of silica is used:

$$MnO(s) + SiO_2(s) \xrightarrow{\text{Heat}} MnSiO_3(l)$$

If the main impurity is silicon or phosphorus, a basic flux, usually lime (CaO) or magnesia (MgO), is needed to give reactions such as

$$SiO_2(s) + MgO(s) \xrightarrow{\text{Heat}} MgSiO_3(l)$$

$$P_4O_{10}(s) + 6CaO(s) \xrightarrow{\text{Heat}} 2Ca_3(PO_4)_2(l)$$

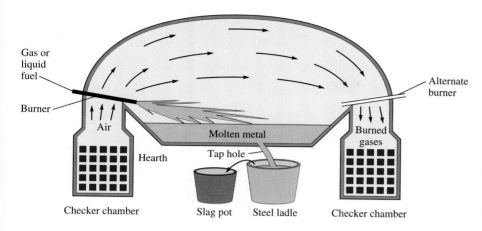

Figure 20.37

A schematic diagram of the open hearth process for steel-making. The checker chambers contain bricks that absorb heat from gases passing over the molten charge. The flow of air and gases is reversed periodically.

Whether an acidic or a basic slag will be needed is a factor that must be considered when a furnace is constructed so that its refractory linings will be compatible with the slag. Silica bricks would deteriorate quickly in the presence of basic slag, and magnesia or lime bricks would dissolve in acid slag.

The **open hearth process** (Fig. 20.37) uses a dishlike container that holds 100 to 200 tons of molten iron. An external heat source is required to keep the iron molten, and a concave roof over the container reflects heat back toward the iron surface. A blast of air or oxygen is passed over the surface of the iron to react with impurities. Silicon and manganese are oxidized first and enter the slag, followed by oxidation of carbon to carbon monoxide, which causes agitation and foaming of the molten bath. The exothermic oxidation of carbon raises the temperature of the bath, causing the limestone flux to calcine:

$$CaCO_3 \xrightarrow{\text{Heat}} CaO + CO_2$$

The resulting lime floats to the top of the molten mixture (an event called the *lime boil*), where it combines with phosphates, sulfates, and silicates. Next comes the refining process, which involves continued oxidation of carbon and other impurities. Because the melting point increases as the carbon content decreases, the bath temperatures must be increased during this phase of the operation. If the carbon content falls below that desired in the final product, coke or pig iron may be added.

The final composition of the steel is "fine-tuned" after the charge is poured. For example, aluminum is sometimes added at this stage to remove trace amounts of oxygen via the reaction

$$4Al + 3O_2 \longrightarrow 2Al_2O_3$$

Alloying metals such as vanadium, chromium, titanium, manganese, and nickel are also added to give the steel the properties needed for a specific application.

The processing of a batch of steel by the open hearth process is quite slow, taking up to 8 hours. The **basic oxygen process** is much faster. Molten pig iron and scrap iron are placed in a barrel-shaped container (Fig. 20.38) that can hold as much as 300 tons of material. A high-pressure blast of oxygen is directed at the surface of the molten iron, oxidizing impurities in a manner very similar to that used in the open hearth process. Fluxes are added after the oxygen blow begins. One advantage of this process is that the exothermic oxidation reactions proceed so rapidly that they produce enough heat to raise the temperature nearly to the boiling point of iron

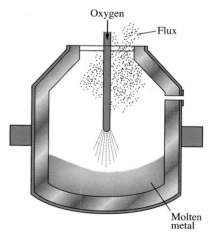

Figure 20.38

The basic oxygen process for steelmaking.

Table 20.21 Percent Composition and Uses of Various Types of Steel

Type of Steel	% Carbon	% Manganese	% Phosphorus	% Sulfur	% Silicon	% Nickel	% Chromium	% Other	Uses
Plain carbon	≤1.35	≤1.65	≤0.04	≤0.05	≤0.60	—	—	—	Sheet steel, tools
High-strength (low-alloy)	≤0.25	≤1.65	≤0.04	≤0.05	0.15–0.9	0.4–1	0.3–1.3	Cu (0.2–0.6) Sb (0.01–0.08) V (0.01–0.08)	Transportation equipment, structural beams
Alloy	≤1.00	≤3.50	≤0.04	≤0.05	0.15–2.0	0.25–10.0	0.25–4.0	Mo (0.08–4.0) V (0–0.2) W (0–18) Co (0–5)	Automobile and aircraft engine parts
Stainless	0.03–1.2	1.0–10	0.04–0.06	≤0.03	1–3	1–22	4.0–27	—	Engine parts, steam turbine parts, kitchen utensils
Silicon	—	—	—	—	0.5–5.0	—	—	—	Electric motors and transformers

without an external heat source. Also, at these high temperatures only about an hour is needed to complete the oxidation processes.

The **electric arc method,** which was once used only for small batches of specialty steels, is being utilized more and more in the steel industry. In this process an electric arc between carbon electrodes is used to melt the charge. This means that no fuel-borne impurities are added to the steel, since no fuel is needed. Also, higher temperatures are possible than in the open hearth or basic oxygen processes, and this leads to more effective removal of sulfur and phosphorus impurities. Oxygen is added in this process so that the oxide impurities in the steel can be controlled effectively.

Heat Treatment of Steel

Refer to Section 10.3 for a review of packing and crystal lattices.

One way of producing the desired physical properties in steel is by controlling the chemical composition (see Table 20.21). Another method for tailoring the properties of steel involves heat treatment. Pure iron exists in two different crystalline forms, depending on the temperature. At any temperature below 912°C, iron has a body-centered cubic structure and is called α-iron. Between 912°C and 1394°C, iron has a face-centered cubic structure called *austentite,* or γ-iron. At 1394°C, iron changes to δ-iron, a body-centered cubic structure identical to α-iron.

When iron is alloyed with carbon, which fits into holes among the iron atoms to form the interstitial alloy *carbon steel,* the situation becomes even more complex. For example, the temperature at which α-iron changes to austentite is lowered by about 200°C. Also, at high temperatures iron and carbon react by an endothermic reversible reaction to form an iron carbide called *cementite:*

$$3Fe + C + \underset{\text{(Heat)}}{energy} \rightleftharpoons \underset{\text{Cementite}}{Fe_3C}$$

By Le Châtelier's principle, we can predict that cementite will become more stable relative to iron and carbon as the temperature is increased. This is the observed result.

Thus steel is really a mixture of iron metal in one of its crystal forms, carbon, and cementite. The proportions of these components are very important in determining the physical properties of steel.

When steel is heated to temperatures in the region of 1000°C, much of the carbon is converted to cementite. If the steel is then allowed to cool slowly, the equilibrium shown above shifts to the left, and small crystals of carbon precipitate, giving a steel that is relatively ductile. If the cooling is very rapid, the equilibrium does not have time to adjust. The cementite is trapped, and the steel has a high cementite content, making it quite brittle. The proportions of carbon crystals and cementite can be "fine-tuned" to give the desired properties by heating to intermediate temperatures followed by rapid cooling, a process called **tempering.** The rate of heating and cooling determines not only the amounts of cementite present but also the size of its crystals and the form of crystalline iron present.

For Review

Summary

For the first-row transition metals (scandium through zinc), the last electrons occupy the 3d orbitals. Because electrons in these inner orbitals cannot participate as easily in bonding as can electrons in valence s and p orbitals, the chemistry of the transition elements is not greatly affected by the gradual change in the number of electrons. As a class, these elements have metallic physical and chemical properties. In forming ionic compounds with nonmetals, the transition metals exhibit several typical characteristics: More than one oxidation state is often found, the cations often are complex ions, and most compounds are colored and many are paramagnetic.

First-row transition metal ions can form a variety of ions by losing one or more of their electrons. The maximum possible oxidation state for a given element corresponds to the loss of all the 4s and 3d electrons, but toward the right end of the period the maximum possible oxidation state is not seen. Rather, 2+ ions become the most common because the 3d electrons become increasingly difficult to remove.

Transition metals typically form coordination compounds, which consist of a complex ion (a transition metal ion with attached ligands) and counterions (anions or cations to produce a solid with no net charge). A ligand (a Lewis base) is a neutral molecule or ion having a lone pair of electrons that can be shared with an empty orbital on a metal ion (a Lewis acid) to form a coordinate covalent bond. The coordination number is the number of bonds formed by the metal ion to its ligands and can range from 2 to 8 depending on the size, charge, and electron configuration of the metal ion. A coordination number of 6 means an octahedral arrangement of ligands about the central metal ion; 2 means a linear arrangement, and 4 means either a planar or a tetrahedral arrangement.

Ligands can form one bond (unidentate), two bonds (bidentate), or as many as six bonds to the metal ion. Ligands that can bond to a metal ion through more than one atom are called chelates. For example, ethylenediamine (en) is bidentate, and EDTA is hexadentate (forms six bonds).

Key Terms

Section 20.1
complex ion
first-row transition metals
lanthanide contraction
lanthanide series

Section 20.3
coordination compound
counterion
oxidation state
coordination number
ligand
coordinate covalent bond
monodentate (unidentate) ligand
chelating ligand (chelate)
bidentate ligand

Section 20.4
isomers
structural isomerism
stereoisomerism
coordination isomerism
linkage isomerism
geometrical (*cis–trans*)
  isomerism
trans isomer
cis isomer
optical isomerism
chiral
enantiomers

When two or more species have the same formula but different properties, they are called isomers. Structural isomers contain the same atoms but one or more different bonds. Coordination isomerism is a type of structural isomerism in which the composition of the coordination sphere around the metal varies. In linkage isomerism, the composition of the coordination spheres is the same, but the point of attachment of at least one of the ligands differs.

In stereoisomerism, the isomers have the same bonds but different spatial arrangements. For example, in geometric isomerism, atoms or groups can assume different relative positions in the coordination sphere around the metal. When two identical ligands lie across from each other, the isomer is *trans;* two ligands located next to each other produce the *cis* isomer.

A second type of stereoisomerism is optical isomerism, which is exhibited by molecules that have nonsuperimposable mirror images, that is, by chiral molecules. The pair of isomers, called enantiomers, rotate plane-polarized light in equal but opposite directions.

Bonding in complex ions can be described in terms of the localized electron model. However, even though this model can account for the bonding in complex ions by use of hybrid orbitals, it does not account for important properties such as magnetism and color. The crystal field model is much more successful at accounting for these properties by focusing on the energies of the *d* orbitals of the metal ion. To predict the effects ligands will have on the energies of the *d* orbitals, the ligands are approximated as negative point charges and the metal–ligand bonding is assumed to be completely ionic. The effect of the point charges in an octahedral complex ion is to split the 3*d* orbitals into two groups with different energies. If the splitting is large (the strong-field case), the electrons pair in the lower-energy orbitals before any jump the energy gap. If the splitting is small (the weak-field case), the electrons occupy all five *d* orbitals singly before pairing occurs. Ligands can be arranged according to their ability to produce splitting, the spectrochemical series.

The crystal field model also accounts for the colors of complex ions. When a substance absorbs a certain wavelength of light in the visible region, its color is determined by the wavelengths of visible light that remain unabsorbed. Complex ions can absorb light as they transfer electrons between the split *d* orbitals. The relationship between the wavelength of light absorbed (λ) and the magnitude of the splitting (Δ) is given by

$$\Delta = \frac{hc}{\lambda}$$

Coordination complexes are vitally important in the chemistry of biologic systems, with iron having special importance in electron-transfer processes and the transport and storage of oxygen.

The process of separating a metal from its ore and preparing it for use is known as metallurgy. An ore is a mixture of minerals (relatively pure metal compounds) and gangue (sand, clay, and rock). Minerals can be concentrated by various methods before being processed. Minerals are often converted to the metal oxides (roasted) before the metal ion is reduced in a process called smelting.

Hydrometallurgy extracts metals from ores using aqueous chemical solutions in a process called leaching. An example of this is cyanidation, in which gold is leached with an aqueous cyanide solution.

Iron is often concentrated from iron ore by magnetic methods. The most commonly used reduction process for iron takes place in the blast furnace. The raw materials required are concentrated iron ore, coke, and limestone (which serves as a flux to trap impurities). The iron oxide (Fe_2O_3) is reduced by carbon monoxide to iron metal. The impure product, pig iron, is about 90% iron. Another process using the direct reduction furnace, which yields sponge iron, is coming into increased use.

Steel is a carbon-containing alloy of iron that is manufactured by oxidizing the impurities in pig iron or sponge iron in either the open hearth process or the basic oxygen process. Other metals are often added to form alloy steels.

In-Class Discussion Questions

These questions are designed to be considered by groups of students in class. Often these questions work well for introducing a particular topic in class.

1. You isolate a compound with the formula $PtCl_4 \cdot 2KCl$. From electrical conductance tests of an aqueous solution of the compound, you find that three ions per formula unit are present, and you also notice that addition of $AgNO_3$ does not cause a precipitate. Give the formula for this compound that shows the complex ion present. Explain your findings. Name this compound.

2. Both $Ni(NH_3)_4^{2+}$ and $Ni(CN)_4^{2-}$ have four ligands. The first is paramagnetic, and the second is diamagnetic. Are the complex ions tetrahedral or square planar? Explain.

3. Which is more likely to be paramagnetic, $Fe(CN)_6^{4-}$ or $Fe(H_2O)_6^{2+}$? Explain.

4. A metal ion in a high-spin octahedral complex has two more unpaired electrons than the same ion does in a low-spin octahedral complex. Name some possible metal ions for which this would be true.

A blue question or exercise number indicates that the answer to that question or exercise appears at the back of this book and a solution appears in the *Solutions Guide*.

Questions

5. Define each of the following.
   a. ligand   c. bidentate
   b. chelate   d. complex ion

6. What must a ligand have in order to bond to a metal?

7. What do we mean when we say that a bond is a coordinate covalent bond?

8. How would transition metal ions be classified using the Lewis definition of acids and bases?

9. Define each of the following and give examples.
   a. isomers   e. linkage isomers
   b. structural isomers   f. geometrical isomers
   c. stereoisomers   g. optical isomers
   d. coordination isomers

10. Define each of the following.
   a. weak-field ligand
   b. strong-field ligand
   c. low-spin complex
   d. high-spin complex

11. Compounds of copper(II) are generally colored, but compounds of copper(I) are not. Explain. Would you expect $Cd(NH_3)_4Cl_2$ to be colored? Explain.

12. Compounds of Sc^{3+} are not colored, but those of Ti^{3+} and V^{3+} are. Explain.

13. Why are virtually all tetrahedral complexes "high spin"?

14. Why are CN^- and CO toxic to humans?

15. Oxalic acid is often used to remove rust stains. What properties of oxalic acid allow it to do this?

16. Why do transition metal ions often have several oxidation states, while representative metals generally have only one?

17. What is the lanthanide contraction? How does the lanthanide contraction affect the properties of the $4d$ and $5d$ transition metals?

18. Define and give an example of each of the following.
   a. roasting   d. leaching
   b. smelting   e. gangue
   c. flotation

19. What are the advantages and disadvantages of hydrometallurgy?

20. Describe the process by which a metal is purified by zone refining.

Exercises

In this section similar exercises are paired.

Transition Metals

21. Write electron configurations for the following metals.
   a. Ni   b. Cd   c. Zr   d. Os

22. Write electron configurations for the following metals.
   a. Sc   b. Ru   c. Ir   d. Mn

23. Write electron configurations for the following ions.
   a. Ni^{2+} c. Zr^{3+} and Zr^{4+}
   b. Cd^{2+} d. Os^{2+} and Os^{3+}

24. Write electron configurations for the following ions.
   a. Sc^{3+} c. Ir^+, Ir^{3+}
   b. Ru^{2+}, Ru^{3+} d. Mn^{2+}

25. Write electron configurations for each of the following.
   a. Ti, Ti^{2+}, Ti^{4+}
   b. Re, Re^{2+}, Re^{3+}
   c. Ir, Ir^{2+}, Ir^{3+}

26. Write electron configurations for each of the following.
   a. Cr, Cr^{2+}, Cr^{3+}
   b. Cu, Cu^+, Cu^{2+}
   c. V, V^{2+}, V^{3+}

27. Molybdenum is obtained both as a by-product of copper mining and from direct mining (primary deposits are in the Rocky Mountains in Colorado). In both cases it is obtained as MoS_2, which is then converted to MoO_3. The MoO_3 can be used directly in the production of stainless steel for high-speed tools, which accounts for about 85% of the molybdenum used.
    a. Name MoS_2 and MoO_3.
    b. What is the oxidation state of Mo in each compound in part a?

28. Titanium dioxide, the most widely used white pigment, occurs naturally but is often colored by the presence of impurities. The chloride process is often used in purifying rutile, a mineral form of titanium dioxide.
    a. Show that the unit cell for rutile, shown below, conforms to the formula TiO_2. (*Hint:* Recall the discussion in Sections 10.4 and 10.7.)

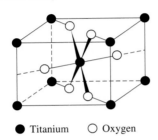

● Titanium   ○ Oxygen

    b. The reactions for the chloride process are

$$2TiO_2(s) + 3C(s) + 4Cl_2(g) \xrightarrow{950°C}$$
$$2TiCl_4(g) + CO_2(g) + 2CO(g)$$

$$TiCl_4(g) + O_2(g) \xrightarrow{1000–1400°C} TiO_2(s) + 2Cl_2(g)$$

Assign oxidation states to the elements in both reactions. Which elements are being reduced, and which are being oxidized? Identify the oxidizing agent and the reducing agent in each reaction.

Coordination Compounds

29. When aqueous KI is added gradually to mercury(II) nitrate, an orange precipitate forms. Continued addition of KI causes the precipitate to dissolve. Write balanced equations to explain these observations. (*Hint:* Hg^{2+} reacts with I^- to form HgI_4^{2-}.)

30. When an aqueous solution of KCN is added to a solution containing Ni^{2+} ions, a precipitate forms, which redissolves on addition of more KCN solution. Write reactions describing what happens in this solution. (*Hint:* CN^- is a Brønsted–Lowry base [$K_b \approx 10^{-5}$] and a Lewis base.)

31. Consider aqueous solutions of the following coordination compounds: $Co(NH_3)_6I_3$, $Pt(NH_3)_4I_4$, Na_2PtI_6, and $Cr(NH_3)_4I_3$. If aqueous $AgNO_3$ is added to separate beakers containing solutions of each coordination compound, how many moles of AgI will precipitate per mole of transition metal present? Assume that each transition metal ion forms an octahedral complex.

32. A coordination compound of cobalt(III) contains four ammonia molecules, one sulfate ion, and one chloride ion. Addition of aqueous $BaCl_2$ solution to an aqueous solution of the compound gives no precipitate. Addition of aqueous $AgNO_3$ to an aqueous solution of the compound produces a white precipitate. Propose a structure for this coordination compound.

33. Name the following complex ions.
    a. $Ru(NH_3)_5Cl^{2+}$ c. $Mn(NH_2CH_2CH_2NH_2)_3^{2+}$
    b. $Fe(CN)_6^{4-}$ d. $Co(NH_3)_5NO_2^{2+}$

34. Name the following complex ions.
    a. $Ni(CN)_4^{2-}$ c. $Fe(C_2O_4)_3^{3-}$
    b. $Cr(NH_3)_4Cl_2^{+}$ d. $Co(SCN)_2(H_2O)_4^{+}$

35. Name the following coordination compounds.
    a. $[Co(NH_3)_6]Cl_2$ d. $K_4[PtCl_6]$
    b. $[Co(H_2O)_6]I_3$ e. $[Co(NH_3)_5Cl]Cl_2$
    c. $K_2[PtCl_4]$ f. $[Co(NH_3)_3(NO_2)_3]$

36. Name the following coordination compounds.
    a. $[Cr(H_2O)_5Br]Br_2$
    b. $Na_3[Co(CN)_6]$
    c. $[Fe(NH_2CH_2CH_2NH_2)_2(NO_2)_2]Cl$
    d. $[Pt(NH_3)_4I_2][PtI_4]$

37. Give formulas for the following.
    a. potassium tetrachlorocobaltate(II)
    b. aquatricarbonylplatinum(II) bromide
    c. sodium dicyanobis(oxalato)ferrate(III)
    d. triamminechloroethylenediaminechromium(III) iodide

38. Give formulas for the following complex ions.
    a. tetrachloroferrate(III) ion
    b. pentaammineaquaruthenium(III) ion
    c. tetracarbonyldihydroxochromium(III) ion
    d. amminetrichloroplatinate(II) ion

39. Draw geometrical isomers of each of the following complex ions.
    a. $[Co(C_2O_4)_2(H_2O)_2]^-$ c. $[Ir(NH_3)_3Cl_3]$
    b. $[Pt(NH_3)_4I_2]^{2+}$ d. $[Cr(en)(NH_3)_2I_2]^+$

40. Draw structures of each of the following.
    a. *cis*-dichloroethylenediamineplatinum(II)
    b. *trans*-dichlorobis(ethylenediamine)cobalt(II)
    c. *cis*-tetraamminechloronitrocobalt(III) ion
    d. *trans*-tetraamminechloronitritocobalt(III) ion
    e. *trans*-diaquabis(ethylenediamine)copper(II) ion

41. Amino acids can act as ligands toward transition metal ions. The simplest amino acid is glycine ($NH_2CH_2CO_2H$). Draw a structure of the glycinate anion ($NH_2CH_2CO_2^-$) acting as a bidentate ligand. Draw the structural isomers of the square planar complex $Cu(NH_2CH_2CO_2)_2$.

42. The carbonate ion (CO_3^{2-}) can act as either a monodentate or a bidentate ligand. Draw a picture of CO_3^{2-} coordinating to a metal ion as a bidentate and as a monodentate ligand.

43. Which of the following ligands are capable of linkage isomerism? Explain your answer.

SCN^-, N_3^-, NO_2^-, $NH_2CH_2CH_2NH_2$, OCN^-, I^-

44. Draw all geometrical and linkage isomers of $Co(NH_3)_4(NO_2)_2$.

45. Acetylacetone, abbreviated acacH, is a bidentate ligand. It loses a proton and coordinates as $acac^-$, as shown below, where M is a transition metal:

Which of the following complexes are optically active: *cis*-$Cr(acac)_2(H_2O)_2$, *trans*-$Cr(acac)_2(H_2O)_2$, and $Cr(acac)_3$?

46. Draw all geometrical isomers of $Pt(CN)_2Br_2(H_2O)_2$. Which of these isomers has an optical isomer? Draw the various optical isomers.

Bonding, Color, and Magnetism in Coordination Compounds

47. Draw the *d*-orbital splitting diagrams for the octahedral complex ions of each of the following.
  a. Fe^{2+} (high and low spin)
  b. Fe^{3+} (high spin)
  c. Ni^{2+}

48. Draw the *d*-orbital splitting diagrams for the octahedral complex ions of each of the following.
  a. Zn^{2+}
  b. Co^{2+} (high and low spin)
  c. Ti^{3+}

49. The CrF_6^{4-} ion is known to have four unpaired electrons. Does the F^- ligand produce a strong or weak field?

50. The $Co(NH_3)_6^{3+}$ ion is diamagnetic, but $Fe(H_2O)_6^{2+}$ is paramagnetic. Explain.

51. How many unpaired electrons are in the following complex ions?
  a. $Ru(NH_3)_6^{2+}$ (low-spin case) **c.** $V(en)_3^{3+}$
  b. $Ni(H_2O)_6^{2+}$

52. The complex ion $Fe(CN)_6^{3-}$ is paramagnetic with one unpaired electron. The complex ion $Fe(SCN)_6^{3-}$ has five unpaired electrons. Where does SCN^- lie in the spectrochemical series relative to CN^-?

53. The compound $[Cr(H_2O)_6]Cl_3$ is violet, $[Cr(H_2O)_4Cl_2]Cl$ is green, and $[Cr(NH_3)_6]Cl_3$ is yellow. Predict the predominant color of light absorbed by each compound. Which compound absorbs light with the shorter wavelength? Predict in which compound Δ is greater, and rank the ligands Cl^-, H_2O, and NH_3 in order of ligand field strength. Do your conclusions agree with the spectrochemical series?

54. Consider the complex ions $Co(NH_3)_6^{3+}$, $Co(CN)_6^{3-}$, and CoF_6^{3-}. The wavelengths of absorbed electromagnetic radiation for these compounds (in no specific order) are 770 nm,

440 nm, and 290 nm. Match the complex ion to the wavelength of absorbed electromagnetic radiation.

55. The wavelength of absorbed electromagnetic radiation for $CoBr_4^{2-}$ is 3.4×10^{-6} m. Will the complex ion $CoBr_6^{4-}$ absorb electromagnetic radiation having a wavelength longer or shorter than 3.4×10^{-6} m? Explain.

56. Tetrahedral complexes of Co^{2+} are quite common. Use a *d*-orbital splitting diagram to rationalize the stability of Co^{2+} tetrahedral complex ions.

57. How many unpaired electrons are present in the tetrahedral ion $FeCl_4^-$?

58. The complex ion $PdCl_4^{2-}$ is diamagnetic. Propose a structure for $PdCl_4^{2-}$.

Metallurgy

59. A blast furnace is used to reduce iron oxides to elemental iron. The reducing agent for this reduction process is carbon monoxide.
  a. Given the following data:

$$Fe_2O_3(s) + 3CO(g) \longrightarrow 2Fe(s) + 3CO_2(g)$$
$$\Delta H° = -23 \text{ kJ}$$
$$3Fe_2O_3(s) + CO(g) \longrightarrow 2Fe_3O_4(s) + CO_2(g)$$
$$\Delta H° = -39 \text{ kJ}$$
$$Fe_3O_4(s) + CO(g) \longrightarrow 3FeO(s) + CO_2(g)$$
$$\Delta H° = 18 \text{ kJ}$$

determine $\Delta H°$ for the reaction

$$FeO(s) + CO(g) \longrightarrow Fe(s) + CO_2(g)$$

  b. The CO_2 produced in a blast furnace during the reduction process actually can oxidize iron into FeO. In order to eliminate this reaction, excess coke is added to convert CO_2 into CO by the reaction

$$CO_2(g) + C(s) \longrightarrow 2CO(g)$$

Using data from Appendix 4, determine $\Delta H°$ and $\Delta S°$ for this reaction. Assuming $\Delta H°$ and $\Delta S°$ do not depend on temperature, at what temperature is the conversion reaction of CO_2 into CO spontaneous at standard conditions?

60. What roles do kinetics and thermodynamics play in the effect that the following reaction has on the properties of steel?

$$3Fe + C \rightleftharpoons Fe_3C$$

Additional Exercises

61. Ammonia and potassium iodide solutions are added to an aqueous solution of $Cr(NO_3)_3$. A solid is isolated (compound A), and the following data are collected:
  i. When 0.105 g of compound A was strongly heated in excess O_2, 0.0203 g of CrO_3 was formed.
  ii. In a second experiment it took 32.93 mL of 0.100 *M* HCl to titrate completely the NH_3 present in 0.341 g of compound A.

iii. Compound A was found to contain 73.53% iodine by mass.

iv. The freezing point of water was lowered by 0.64°C when 0.601 g of compound A was dissolved in 10.00 g of H_2O ($K_f = 1.86$°C · kg/mol).

What is the formula of the compound? What is the structure of the complex ion present? (*Hints:* Cr^{3+} is expected to be six-coordinate, with NH_3 and possibly I^- as ligands. The I^- ions will be the counterions if needed.)

62. In the production of printed circuit boards for the electronics industry, a 0.60-mm layer of copper is laminated onto an insulating plastic board. Next, a circuit pattern made of a chemically resistant polymer is printed on the board. The unwanted copper is removed by chemical etching, and the protective polymer is finally removed by solvents. One etching reaction is

$$[Cu(NH_3)_4]Cl_2(aq) + 4NH_3(aq) + Cu(s)$$
$$\longrightarrow 2[Cu(NH_3)_4]Cl(aq)$$

a. Is this reaction an oxidation–reduction process? Explain.

b. A plant needs to manufacture 10,000 printed circuit boards, each 8.0×16.0 cm in area. An average of 80.% of the copper is removed from each board (density of copper = 8.96 g/cm³). What masses of $[Cu(NH_3)_4]Cl_2$ and NH_3 are needed to do this? Assume 100% yield.

63. How many bonds could each of the following chelates form with a metal ion?

a. acetylacetone(acacH)

$$CH_3-\overset{O}{\overset{\|}{C}}-CH_2-\overset{O}{\overset{\|}{C}}-CH_3$$

b. diethylenetriamine

$$NH_2-CH_2-CH_2-NH-CH_2-CH_2-NH_2$$

c. salen

d. porphine

64. Until the discoveries of Werner, it was thought that carbon had to be present in a compound for it to be optically active. Werner prepared the following compound containing OH^- ions as bridging groups and separated the optical isomers.

a. Draw structures of the two optically active isomers of this compound.

b. What are the oxidation states of the cobalt ions?

c. How many unpaired electrons are present if the complex is the low-spin case?

65. The complex ion $Ru(phen)_3^{2+}$ has been used as a probe for the structure of DNA. (Phen is a bidentate ligand.)

a. What type of isomerism is found in $Ru(phen)_3^{2+}$?

b. $Ru(phen)_3^{2+}$ is diamagnetic (as are all complex ions of Ru^{2+}). Draw the crystal field diagram for the d orbitals in this complex ion.

Phen = 1,10-phenanthroline =

66. A compound related to acetylacetone is 1,1,1-trifluoroacetyl-acetone (abbreviated Htfa):

$$CF_3\overset{O}{\overset{\|}{C}}CH_2\overset{O}{\overset{\|}{C}}CH_3$$

Htfa forms complexes in a manner similar to acetylacetone. (See Exercise 45.) Both Be^{2+} and Cu^{2+} form complexes with tfa^- having the formula $M(tfa)_2$. Two isomers are formed for each metal complex.

a. The Be^{2+} complexes are tetrahedral. Draw the two isomers of $Be(tfa)_2$. What type of isomerism is exhibited by $Be(tfa)_2$?

b. The Cu^{2+} complexes are square planar. Draw the two isomers of $Cu(tfa)_2$. What type of isomerism is exhibited by $Cu(tfa)_2$?

67. Would it be better to use octahedral Ni^{2+} complexes or octahedral Cr^{2+} complexes to determine whether a given ligand is a strong-field or weak-field ligand by measuring the number of unpaired electrons? How else could the relative ligand field strengths be determined?

Challenge Problems

68. Impure nickel, refined by smelting sulfide ores in a blast furnace, can be converted into metal from 99.90% to 99.99% purity by the Mond process. The primary reaction involved in the Mond process is

$$Ni(s) + 4CO(g) \rightleftharpoons Ni(CO)_4(g)$$

a. Without referring to Appendix 4, predict the sign of $\Delta S°$ for the preceding reaction. Explain.

b. The spontaneity of the preceding reaction is temperature-dependent. Predict the sign of ΔS_{surr} for this reaction. Explain.

c. For $Ni(CO)_4(g)$, $\Delta H_f^\circ = -607$ kJ/mol and $S^\circ = 417$ J/K·mol at 298 K. Using these values and data in Appendix 4, calculate ΔH° and ΔS° for the preceding reaction.

d. Calculate the temperature at which $\Delta G^\circ = 0$ ($K = 1$) for the preceding reaction, assuming that ΔH° and ΔS° do not depend on temperature.

e. The first step of the Mond process involves equilibrating impure nickel with $CO(g)$ and $Ni(CO)_4(g)$ at about 50°C. The purpose of this step is to convert as much nickel as possible into the gas phase. Calculate the equilibrium constant for the preceding reaction at 50.°C.

f. In the second step of the Mond process, the gaseous $Ni(CO)_4$ is isolated and heated at 227°C. The purpose of this step is to deposit as much nickel as possible as pure solid (the reverse of the preceding reaction). Calculate the equilibrium constant for the above reaction at 227°C.

g. Why is temperature increased for the second step of the Mond process?

69. Consider the following data:

$$Co^{3+} + e^- \longrightarrow Co^{2+} \qquad \mathscr{E}^\circ = 1.82 \text{ V}$$
$$Co^{2+} + 3en \longrightarrow Co(en)_3^{2+} \qquad K = 1.5 \times 10^{12}$$
$$Co^{3+} + 3en \longrightarrow Co(en)_3^{3+} \qquad K = 2.0 \times 10^{47}$$

where en = ethylenediamine.

a. Calculate $\mathscr{E}^\circ$ for the half-reaction

$$Co(en)_3^{3+} + e^- \longrightarrow Co(en)_3^{2+}$$

b. Based on your answer to part a, which is the stronger oxidizing agent, Co^{3+} or $Co(en)_3^{3+}$?

c. Use the crystal field model to rationalize the result in part b.

70. Henry Taube, 1983 Nobel Prize winner in chemistry, has studied the mechanisms of the oxidation–reduction reactions of transition metal complexes. In one experiment he and his students studied the following reaction:

$$Cr(H_2O)_6^{2+}(aq) + Co(NH_3)_5Cl^{2+}(aq)$$
$$\longrightarrow Cr(III) \text{ complexes} + Co(II) \text{ complexes}$$

Chromium(III) and cobalt(III) complexes are substitutionally inert (no exchange of ligands) under conditions of the experiment. Chromium(II) and cobalt(II) complexes can exchange ligands very rapidly. One of the products of the reaction is $Cr(H_2O)_5Cl^{2+}$. Is this consistent with the reaction proceeding through formation of $(H_2O)_5Cr—Cl—Co(NH_3)_5$ as an intermediate? Explain.

71. Chelating ligands often form more stable complex ions than the corresponding monodentate ligands with the same donor atoms. For example,

$$Ni^{2+}(aq) + 6NH_3(aq) \rightleftharpoons Ni(NH_3)_6^{2+}(aq)$$
$$K = 3.2 \times 10^8$$
$$Ni^{2+}(aq) + 3en(aq) \rightleftharpoons Ni(en)_3^{2+}(aq) \qquad K = 1.6 \times 10^{18}$$
$$Ni^{2+}(aq) + penten(aq) \rightleftharpoons Ni(penten)^{2+}(aq)$$
$$K = 2.0 \times 10^{19}$$

where en is ethylenediamine and penten is

This increased stability is called the *chelate effect*. Based on bond energies, would you expect the enthalpy changes for the above reactions to be very different? What is the order (from least favorable to most favorable) of the entropy changes for the above reactions? How do the values of the formation constants correlate with ΔS°? How can this be used to explain the chelate effect?

72. Qualitatively draw the crystal field splitting of the d orbitals in a trigonal planar complex ion. (Let the z axis be perpendicular to the plane of the complex.)

73. Qualitatively draw the crystal field splitting for a trigonal bipyramidal complex ion. (Let the z axis be perpendicular to the trigonal plane.)

74. a. Calculate the molar solubility of AgBr in pure water. K_{sp} for AgBr is 5.0×10^{-13}.

b. Calculate the molar solubility of AgBr in $3.0\,M$ NH_3. The overall formation constant for $Ag(NH_3)_2^+$ is 1.7×10^7, that is,

$$Ag^+(aq) + 2NH_3(aq) \longrightarrow Ag(NH_3)_2^+(aq)$$
$$K = 1.7 \times 10^7.$$

c. Compare the calculated solubilities from parts a and b. Explain any differences.

d. What mass of AgBr will dissolve in 250.0 mL of $3.0\,M$ NH_3?

e. What effect does adding HNO_3 have on the solubilities calculated in parts a and b?

Marathon Problem

This problem is designed to incorporate several concepts and techniques into one situation. Marathon Problems can be used in class by groups of students to help facilitate problem-solving skills.

75. There are three salts that contain complex ions of chromium and have the molecular formula $CrCl_3 \cdot 6H_2O$. Treating 0.27 g of the first salt with a strong dehydrating agent resulted in a mass loss of 0.036 g. Treating 270 mg of the second salt with the same dehydrating agent resulted in a mass loss of 18 mg. The third salt did not lose any mass when treated with the same dehydrating agent. Addition of excess aqueous silver nitrate to 100.0-mL portions of 0.100 M solutions of each salt resulted in the formation of different masses of silver chloride; one solution yielded 1430 mg AgCl; another, 2870 mg AgCl; the third, 4300 mg AgCl. Two of the salts are green and one is violet.

Suggest probable structural formulas for these salts, defending your answer on the basis of the preceding observations. State which salt is most likely to be violet. Would a study of the magnetic properties of the salts be helpful in determining the structural formulas? Explain.

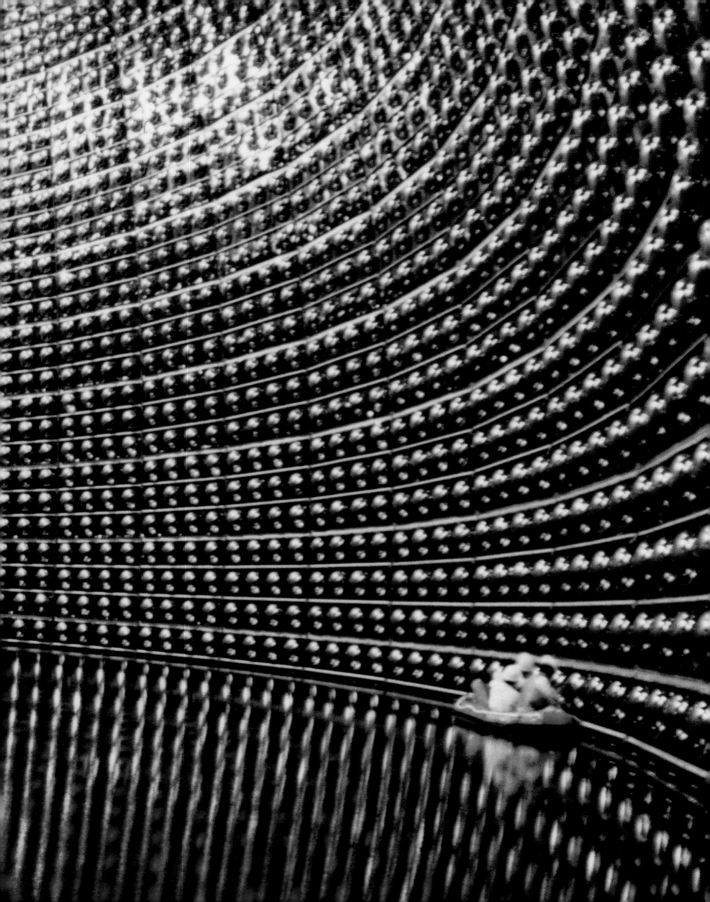

The Nucleus: A Chemist's View

Since the chemistry of an atom is determined by the number and arrangement of its electrons, the properties of the nucleus are not of primary importance to chemists. In the simplest view, the nucleus provides the positive charge to bind the electrons in atoms and molecules. However, a quick reading of any daily newspaper will show you that the nucleus and its properties have an important impact on our society. This chapter considers those aspects of the nucleus about which everyone should have some knowledge.

Several aspects of the nucleus are immediately impressive: its very small size, its very large density, and the magnitude of the energy that holds it together. The radius of a typical nucleus appears to be about 10^{-13} cm. This can be compared to the radius of a typical atom, which is on the order of 10^{-8} cm. A visualization will help you appreciate the small size of the nucleus: If the nucleus of the hydrogen atom were the size of a Ping-Pong ball, the electron in the $1s$ orbital would be, on average, 0.5 kilometer (0.3 mile) away. The density of the nucleus is equally impressive—approximately 1.6×10^{14} g/cm^3. A sphere of nuclear material the size of a Ping-Pong ball would have a mass of 2.5 *billion tons!* In addition, the energies involved in nuclear processes are typically millions of times larger than those associated with normal chemical reactions. This fact makes nuclear processes very attractive for feeding the voracious energy appetite of our civilization.

Atomos, the Greek root of the word *atom,* means "indivisible." It was originally believed that the atom was the ultimate indivisible particle of which all matter was composed. However, as we discussed in Chapter 2, Lord Rutherford showed in 1911 that the atom is not homogeneous, but rather has a dense, positively charged center surrounded by electrons. Subsequently, scientists have learned that the nucleus of the atom can be subdivided into particles called **neutrons** and **protons**. In fact, in the past two decades it has become apparent that even the protons and neutrons are composed of smaller particles called *quarks.*

Workers inside the Super-Kamiokande detector in Japan.

The atomic number Z is the number of protons in a nucleus; the mass number A is the sum of protons and neutrons in a nucleus.

For most purposes, the nucleus can be regarded as a collection of **nucleons** (neutrons and protons), and the internal structures of these particles can be ignored. As we discussed in Chapter 2, the number of protons in a particular nucleus is called the **atomic number** (Z), and the sum of the neutrons and protons is the **mass number** (A). Atoms that have identical atomic numbers but different mass number values are called **isotopes.** However, we usually do not use the singular form *isotope* to refer to a particular member of a group of isotopes. Rather, we use the term *nuclide*. A **nuclide** is a unique atom, represented by the symbol

$$^A_Z X$$

The term *isotopes* refers to a group of nuclides with the same atomic number. Each individual atom is properly called a *nuclide*, not an isotope.

where X represents the symbol for a particular element. For example, the following nuclides constitute the isotopes of carbon: carbon-12 ($^{12}_6C$), carbon-13 ($^{13}_6C$), and carbon-14 ($^{14}_6C$).

21.1 Nuclear Stability and Radioactive Decay

Nuclear stability is the central topic of this chapter and forms the basis for all the important applications related to nuclear processes. Nuclear stability can be considered from both a kinetic and a thermodynamic point of view. **Thermodynamic stability,** as we will use the term here, refers to the potential energy of a particular nucleus as compared with the sum of the potential energies of its component protons and neutrons. We will use the term **kinetic stability** to describe the probability that a nucleus will undergo decomposition to form a different nucleus—a process called **radioactive decay.** We will consider radioactivity in this section.

Many nuclei are radioactive; that is, they decompose, forming another nucleus and producing one or more particles. An example is carbon-14, which decays as follows:

$$^{14}_6C \longrightarrow ^{14}_7N + ^{\ 0}_{-1}e$$

where $^{\ 0}_{-1}e$ represents an electron, which is called a **beta particle,** or **β particle,** in nuclear terminology. This equation is typical of those representing radioactive decay in that both A and Z must be conserved. That is, the Z values must give the same sum on both sides of the equation ($6 = 7 - 1$), as must the A values ($14 = 14 + 0$).

Of the approximately 2000 known nuclides, only 279 are stable with respect to radioactive decay. Tin has the largest number of stable isotopes—10.

It is instructive to examine how the numbers of neutrons and protons in a nucleus are related to its stability with respect to radioactive decay. Figure 21.1 shows a plot of the positions of the stable nuclei as a function of the number of protons (Z) and the number of neutrons (A − Z). The stable nuclides are said to reside in the **zone of stability.**

The following are some important observations concerning radioactive decay:

All nuclides with 84 or more protons are unstable with respect to radioactive decay.

Light nuclides are stable when Z equals A − Z, that is, when the neutron/proton ratio is 1. However, for heavier elements the neutron/proton ratio required for stability is greater than 1 and increases with Z.

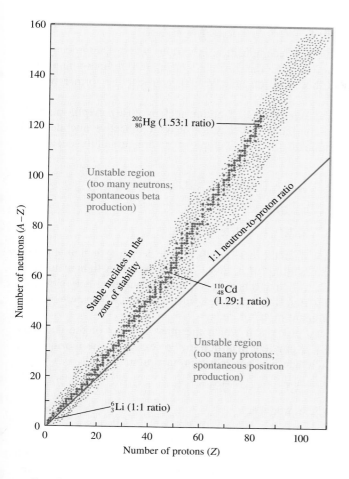

Figure 21.1

The zone of stability. The red dots indicate the nuclides that *do not* undergo radioactive decay. Note that as the number of protons in a nuclide increases, the neutron/proton ratio required for stability also increases.

Certain combinations of protons and neutrons seem to confer special stability. For example, nuclides with even numbers of protons and neutrons are more often stable than those with odd numbers, as shown by the data in Table 21.1.

There are also certain specific numbers of protons or neutrons that produce especially stable nuclides. These *magic numbers* are 2, 8, 20, 28, 50, 82, and 126. This behavior parallels that for atoms in which certain numbers of electrons (2, 10, 18, 36, 54, and 86) produce special chemical stability (the noble gases).

Table 21.1 Number of Stable Nuclides Related to Numbers of Protons and Neutrons

Number of Protons	Number of Neutrons	Number of Stable Nuclides	Examples
Even	Even	168	$^{12}_{6}C$, $^{16}_{8}O$
Even	Odd	57	$^{13}_{6}C$, $^{47}_{22}Ti$
Odd	Even	50	$^{19}_{9}F$, $^{23}_{11}Na$
Odd	Odd	4	$^{2}_{1}H$, $^{6}_{3}Li$

Note: Even numbers of protons and neutrons seem to favor stability.

Types of Radioactive Decay

Radioactive nuclei can undergo decomposition in various ways. These decay processes fall into two categories: those that involve a change in the mass number of the decaying nucleus and those that do not. We will consider the former type of process first.

α-particle production involves a change in A for the decaying nucleus; β-particle production has no effect on A.

An **alpha particle,** or **α particle,** is a helium nucleus ($^4_2$He). **Alpha-particle production** is a very common mode of decay for heavy radioactive nuclides. For example, $^{238}_{92}$U, the predominant (99.3%) isotope of natural uranium, decays by α-particle production:

$$^{238}_{92}\text{U} \longrightarrow {}^4_2\text{He} + {}^{234}_{90}\text{Th}$$

Another α-particle producer is $^{230}_{90}$Th:

$$^{230}_{90}\text{Th} \longrightarrow {}^4_2\text{He} + {}^{226}_{88}\text{Ra}$$

Another decay process in which the mass number of the decaying nucleus changes is **spontaneous fission,** the splitting of a heavy nuclide into two lighter nuclides with similar mass numbers. Although this process occurs at an extremely slow rate for most nuclides, it is important in some cases, such as for $^{254}_{98}$Cf, where spontaneous fission is the predominant mode of decay.

The most common decay process in which the mass number of the decaying nucleus remains constant is **β-particle production.** For example, the thorium-234 nuclide produces a β particle and is converted to protactinium-234:

$$^{234}_{90}\text{Th} \longrightarrow {}^{234}_{91}\text{Pa} + {}^{\ 0}_{-1}\text{e}$$

Iodine-131 is also a β-particle producer:

$$^{131}_{53}\text{I} \longrightarrow {}^{\ 0}_{-1}\text{e} + {}^{131}_{54}\text{Xe}$$

The β particle is assigned the mass number 0, since its mass is tiny compared with that of a proton or neutron. Because the value of Z is -1 for the β particle, the atomic number for the new nuclide is greater by 1 than for the original nuclide. Thus *the net effect of β-particle production is to change a neutron to a proton.* We therefore expect nuclides that lie above the zone of stability (those nuclides whose neutron/proton ratios are too high) to be β-particle producers.

It should be pointed out that although the β particle is an electron, the emitting nucleus does not contain electrons. As we shall see later in this chapter, a given quantity of energy (which is best regarded as a form of matter) can become a particle (another form of matter) under certain circumstances. The unstable nuclide creates an electron as it releases energy in the decay process. The electron thus results from the decay process rather than being present before the decay occurs. Think of this as somewhat like talking: Words are not stored inside us but are formed as we speak. Later in this chapter we will discuss in more detail this very interesting phenomenon where matter in the form of particles and matter in the form of energy can interchange.

A **gamma ray,** or **γ ray,** refers to a high-energy photon. Frequently, γ-ray production accompanies nuclear decays and particle reactions, such as in the α-particle decay of $^{238}_{92}$U:

$$^{238}_{92}\text{U} \longrightarrow {}^4_2\text{He} + {}^{234}_{90}\text{Th} + 2\,{}^0_0\gamma$$

where two γ rays of different energies are produced in addition to the α particle. The emission of γ rays is one way a nucleus with excess energy (in an excited nuclear state) can relax to its ground state.

Table 21.2 Various Types of Radioactive Processes Showing the Changes That Take Place in the Nuclides

Process	Change in A	Change in Z	Change in Neutron/Proton Ratio	Example
β-particle (electron) production	0	+1	Decrease	$^{227}_{89}\text{Ac} \longrightarrow {}^{227}_{90}\text{Th} + {}^{0}_{-1}\text{e}$
Positron production	0	−1	Increase	$^{13}_{7}\text{N} \longrightarrow {}^{13}_{6}\text{C} + {}^{0}_{1}\text{e}$
Electron capture	0	−1	Increase	$^{73}_{33}\text{As} + {}^{0}_{-1}\text{e} \longrightarrow {}^{73}_{32}\text{Ge}$
α-particle production	−4	−2	Increase	$^{210}_{84}\text{Po} \longrightarrow {}^{206}_{82}\text{Pb} + {}^{4}_{2}\text{He}$
γ-ray production	0	0	—	Excited nucleus $\longrightarrow$ ground state nucleus $+ {}^{0}_{0}\gamma$
Spontaneous fission	—	—	—	$^{254}_{98}\text{Cf} \longrightarrow$ lighter nuclides + neutrons

Positron production occurs for nuclides that are below the zone of stability (those nuclides whose neutron/proton ratios are too small). The positron is a particle with the same mass as the electron but opposite charge. An example of a nuclide that decays by positron production is sodium-22:

$$^{22}_{11}\text{Na} \longrightarrow {}^{0}_{1}\text{e} + {}^{22}_{10}\text{Ne}$$

Note that *the net effect is to change a proton to a neutron,* causing the product nuclide to have a higher neutron/proton ratio than the original nuclide.

Besides being oppositely charged, the positron shows an even more fundamental difference from the electron: It is the *antiparticle* of the electron. When a positron collides with an electron, the particulate matter is changed to electromagnetic radiation in the form of high-energy photons:

$$-{}^{0}_{1}\text{e} + {}^{0}_{1}\text{e} \longrightarrow 2\,{}^{0}_{0}\gamma$$

This process, which is characteristic of matter–antimatter collisions, is called *annihilation* and is another example of the interchange of the forms of matter.

Electron capture is a process in which one of the inner-orbital electrons is captured by the nucleus, as illustrated by the process

$$^{201}_{80}\text{Hg} + \underset{\text{Inner-orbital electron}}{{}^{0}_{-1}\text{e}} \longrightarrow {}^{201}_{79}\text{Au} + {}^{0}_{0}\gamma$$

This reaction would have been of great interest to the alchemists, but unfortunately it does not occur at a rate that would make it a practical means for changing mercury to gold. Gamma rays are always produced along with electron capture to release excess energy. The various types of radioactive decay are summarized in Table 21.2.

Sample Exercise 21.1 Nuclear Equations I

Write balanced equations for each of the following processes.

a. $^{11}_{6}\text{C}$ produces a positron.

b. $^{214}_{83}\text{Bi}$ produces a β particle.

c. $^{237}_{93}\text{Np}$ produces an α particle.

Solution

a. We must find the product nuclide represented by $^{A}_{Z}X$ in the following equation:

$$^{11}_{6}C \longrightarrow {}^{0}_{1}e + {}^{A}_{Z}X$$

$$\uparrow$$
$$\text{Positron}$$

We can find the identity of $^{A}_{Z}X$ by recognizing that the total of the Z and A values must be the same on both sides of the equation. Thus for X, Z must be $6 - 1 = 5$ and A must be $11 - 0 = 11$. Therefore, $^{A}_{Z}X$ is $^{11}_{5}B$. (The fact that Z is 5 tells us that the nuclide is boron.) Thus the balanced equation is

$$^{11}_{6}C \longrightarrow {}^{0}_{1}e + {}^{11}_{5}B$$

b. Knowing that a β particle is represented by $_{-1}^{0}e$ and that Z and A are conserved, we can write

$$^{214}_{83}Bi \longrightarrow {}^{0}_{-1}e + {}^{214}_{84}X$$

so $^{A}_{Z}X$ must be $^{214}_{84}Po$.

c. Since an α particle is represented by $^{4}_{2}He$, the balanced equation must be

$$^{237}_{93}Np \longrightarrow {}^{4}_{2}He + {}^{233}_{91}Pa$$

See Exercises 21.9 and 21.10.

Sample Exercise 21.2 *Nuclear Equations II*

In each of the following nuclear reactions, supply the missing particle.

a. $^{195}_{79}Au + ? \rightarrow {}^{195}_{78}Pt$
b. $^{38}_{19}K \rightarrow {}^{38}_{18}Ar + ?$

Solution

a. Since A does not change and Z decreases by 1, the missing particle must be an electron:

$$^{195}_{79}Au + {}^{0}_{-1}e \longrightarrow {}^{195}_{78}Pt$$

This is an example of electron capture.

b. To conserve Z and A, the missing particle must be a positron:

$$^{38}_{19}K \longrightarrow {}^{38}_{18}Ar + {}^{0}_{1}e$$

Thus potassium-38 decays by positron production.

See Exercises 21.11 and 21.12.

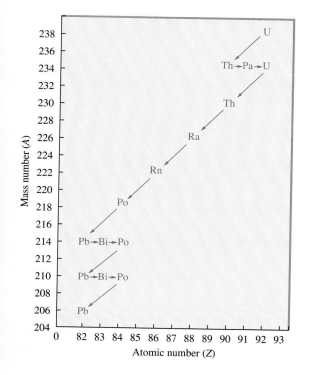

Figure 21.2
The decay series from $^{238}_{92}U$ to $^{206}_{82}Pb$. Each nuclide in the series except $^{206}_{82}Pb$ is unstable, and the successive transformations (shown by the arrows) continue until $^{206}_{82}Pb$ is finally formed. Note that horizontal arrows indicate processes where A is unchanged, while diagonal arrows signify that both A and Z change.

Often a radioactive nucleus cannot reach a stable state through a single decay process. In such a case, a **decay series** occurs until a stable nuclide is formed. A well-known example is the decay series that starts with $^{238}_{92}U$ and ends with $^{206}_{82}Pb$, as shown in Fig. 21.2. Similar series exist for $^{235}_{92}U$:

$$^{235}_{92}U \xrightarrow[\text{decays}]{\text{Series of}} {}^{207}_{82}Pb$$

and for $^{232}_{90}Th$:

$$^{232}_{90}Th \xrightarrow[\text{decays}]{\text{Series of}} {}^{208}_{82}Pb$$

21.2 *The Kinetics of Radioactive Decay*

In a sample containing radioactive nuclides of a given type, each nuclide has a certain probability of undergoing decay. Suppose that a sample of 1000 atoms of a certain nuclide produces 10 decay events per hour. This means that over the span of an hour, 1 out of every 100 nuclides will decay. Given that this probability of decay is characteristic for this type of nuclide, we could predict that a 2000-atom sample would give 20 decay events per hour. Thus, for radioactive nuclides, the **rate of decay,** which is the negative of the change in the number of nuclides per unit time

$$\left(-\frac{\Delta N}{\Delta t}\right)$$

Rates of reaction are discussed in Chapter 12.

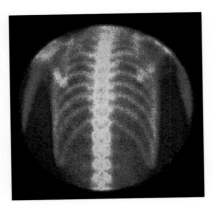

The image of a bone scan of a normal chest (posterior view). Radioactive technetium-99m is injected into the patient and is then concentrated in bones, allowing a physician to look for abnormalities such as might be caused by cancer.

is directly proportional to the number of nuclides N in a given sample:

$$\text{Rate} = -\frac{\Delta N}{\Delta t} \propto N$$

The negative sign is included because the number of nuclides is decreasing. We now insert a proportionality constant k to give

$$\text{Rate} = -\frac{\Delta N}{\Delta t} = kN$$

This is the rate law for a first-order process, as we saw in Chapter 12. As shown in Section 12.4, the integrated first-order rate law is

$$\ln\left(\frac{N}{N_0}\right) = -kt$$

where N_0 represents the original number of nuclides (at $t = 0$) and N represents the number *remaining* at time t.

Half-Life

The **half-life** ($t_{1/2}$) of a radioactive sample is defined as the time required for the number of nuclides to reach half the original value ($N_0/2$). We can use this definition in connection with the integrated first-order rate law (as we did in Section 12.4) to produce the following expression for $t_{1/2}$:

$$t_{1/2} = \frac{\ln(2)}{k} = \frac{0.693}{k}$$

Thus, if the half-life of a radioactive nuclide is known, the rate constant can be easily calculated, and vice versa.

Sample Exercise 21.3   *Kinetics of Nuclear Decay I*

Technetium-99m is used to form pictures of internal organs in the body and is often used to assess heart damage. The *m* for this nuclide indicates an excited nuclear state that decays to the ground state by gamma emission. The rate constant for decay of $^{99m}_{43}\text{Tc}$ is known to be 1.16×10^{-1}/h. What is the half-life of this nuclide?

Solution

The half-life can be calculated from the expression

$$t_{1/2} = \frac{0.693}{k} = \frac{0.693}{1.16 \times 10^{-1}\text{/h}}$$

$$= 5.98 \text{ h}$$

Thus it will take 5.98 h for a given sample of technetium-99m to decrease to half the original number of nuclides.

See Exercises 21.19 and 21.20.

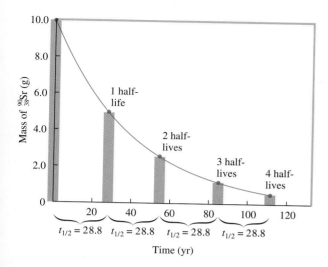

Figure 21.3

The decay of a 10.0-g sample of strontium-90 over time. Note that the half-life is a constant 28.8 years.

As we saw in Section 12.4, the half-life for a first-order process is constant. This is shown for the β-particle decay of strontium-90 in Fig. 21.3; it takes 28.8 years for each halving of the amount of $^{90}_{38}Sr$. Contamination of the environment with $^{90}_{38}Sr$ poses serious health hazards because of the similar chemistry of strontium and calcium (both are in Group 2A). Strontium-90 in grass and hay is incorporated into cow's milk along with calcium and is then passed on to humans, where it lodges in the bones. Because of its relatively long half-life, it persists for years in humans, causing radiation damage that may lead to cancer.

The harmful effects of radiation will be discussed in Section 21.7.

Sample Exercise 21.4 *Kinetics of Nuclear Decay II*

The half-life of molybdenum-99 is 67.0 h. How much of a 1.000-mg sample of $^{99}_{42}Mo$ is left after 335 h?

Solution

The easiest way to solve this problem is to recognize that 335 h represents five half-lives for $^{99}_{42}Mo$:

$$335 = 5 \times 67.0$$

We can sketch the change that occurs, as is shown in Fig. 21.4. Thus, after 335 h, 0.031 mg $^{99}_{42}Mo$ remains.

See Exercise 21.21.

The half-lives of radioactive nuclides vary over a tremendous range. For example, $^{144}_{60}Nd$ has a half-life of 5×10^{15} years, while $^{214}_{84}Po$ has a half-life of 2×10^{-4} second. To give you some perspective on this, the half-lives of the nuclides in the $^{238}_{92}U$ decay series are given in Table 21.3.

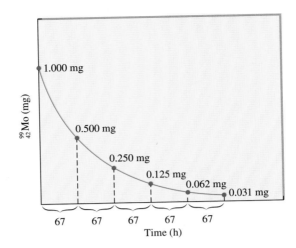

Figure 21.4

The change in the amount of $^{99}_{42}\text{Mo}$ with time ($t_{1/2} = 67$ h).

Table 21.3 The Half-Lives of Nuclides in the $^{238}_{92}\text{U}$ Decay Series

Nuclide	Particle Produced	Half-Life
Uranium-238 ($^{238}_{92}\text{U}$)	α	4.51×10^9 years
Thorium-234 ($^{234}_{90}\text{Th}$)	β	24.1 days
Protactinium-234 ($^{234}_{91}\text{Pa}$)	β	6.75 hours
Uranium-234 ($^{234}_{92}\text{U}$)	α	2.48×10^5 years
Thorium-230 ($^{230}_{90}\text{Th}$)	α	8.0×10^4 years
Radium-226 ($^{226}_{88}\text{Ra}$)	α	1.62×10^3 years
Radon-222 ($^{222}_{86}\text{Rn}$)	α	3.82 days
Polonium-218 ($^{218}_{84}\text{Po}$)	α	3.1 minutes
Lead-214 ($^{214}_{82}\text{Pb}$)	β	26.8 minutes
Bismuth-214 ($^{214}_{83}\text{Bi}$)	β	19.7 minutes
Polonium-214 ($^{214}_{84}\text{Po}$)	α	1.6×10^{-4} second
Lead-210 ($^{210}_{82}\text{Pb}$)	β	20.4 years
Bismuth-210 ($^{210}_{83}\text{Bi}$)	β	5.0 days
Polonium-210 ($^{210}_{84}\text{Po}$)	α	138.4 days
Lead-206 ($^{206}_{82}\text{Pb}$)	—	Stable

CHEMICAL IMPACT

Stellar Nucleosynthesis

HOW DID ALL the matter around us originate? The scientific answer to this question is a theory called *stellar nucleosynthesis*, literally, the formation of nuclei in stars.

Many scientists believe that our universe originated as a cloud of neutrons that became unstable and produced an immense explosion, giving this model its name—*the big bang theory*. The model postulates that, following the initial explosion, neutrons decomposed into protons and electrons,

$$_0^1n \longrightarrow {}_1^1H + {}_{-1}^0e$$

which eventually recombined to form clouds of hydrogen. Over the eons, gravitational forces caused many of these hydrogen clouds to contract and heat up sufficiently to reach temperatures where proton fusion was possible, which released large quantities of energy. When the tendency to expand due to the heat from fusion and the tendency to contract due to the forces of gravity are balanced, a stable young star such as our sun can be formed.

Eventually, when the supply of hydrogen is exhausted, the core of the star will again contract with further heating until temperatures are reached where fusion of helium nuclei can occur, leading to the formation of $_6^{12}C$ and $_8^{16}O$ nuclei. In turn,

Image of a portion of the Cygnus Loop supernova remnant, taken by the Hubble space telescope.

when the supply of helium nuclei runs out, further contraction and heating will occur, until fusion of heavier nuclei takes place. This process occurs repeatedly, forming heavier and heavier nuclei until iron nuclei are formed. Because the iron nucleus is the most stable of all, energy is required to fuse iron nuclei. This endothermic fusion process cannot furnish energy to sustain the star, and therefore it cools to a small, dense *white dwarf*.

The evolution just described is characteristic of small and medium-sized stars. Much larger stars, however, become unstable at some time during their evolution and undergo a *supernova explosion*. In this explosion, some medium-mass nuclei are fused to form heavy elements. Also, some light nuclei capture neutrons. These neutron-rich nuclei then produce β particles, increasing their atomic number with each event. This eventually leads to heavy nuclei. In fact, almost all nuclei heavier than iron are thought to originate from supernova explosions. The debris of a supernova explosion thus contains a large variety of elements and might eventually form a solar system such as our own.

Although other theories for the origin of matter have been suggested, there is much evidence to support the big bang theory, and it continues to be widely accepted.

For more information see V. E. Viola, "Formation of the chemical elements and the evolution of our universe," *J. Chem. Ed.* **67** (1990): 723.

21.3 Nuclear Transformations

In 1919 Lord Rutherford observed the first **nuclear transformation,** *the change of one element into another.* He found that by bombarding $_7^{14}N$ with α particles, the nuclide $_8^{17}O$ could be produced:

$$_7^{14}N + {}_2^4He \longrightarrow {}_8^{17}O + {}_1^1H$$

Figure 21.5

A schematic diagram of a cyclotron. The ion is introduced in the center and is pulled back and forth between the hollow D-shaped electrodes by constant reversals of the electric field. Magnets above and below these electrodes produce a spiral path that expands as the particle velocity increases. When the particle has sufficient speed, it exits the accelerator and is directed at the target nucleus.

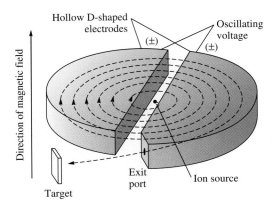

Fourteen years later, Irene Curie and her husband Frederick Joliot observed a similar transformation from aluminum to phosphorus

$$^{27}_{13}\text{Al} + {}^{4}_{2}\text{He} \longrightarrow {}^{30}_{15}\text{P} + {}^{1}_{0}\text{n}$$

where ${}^{1}_{0}\text{n}$ represents a neutron.

Over the years, many other nuclear transformations have been achieved, mostly using **particle accelerators,** which, as the name reveals, are devices used to give particles very high velocities. Because of the electrostatic repulsion between the target nucleus and a positive ion, accelerators are needed when positive ions are used as bombarding particles. The particle, accelerated to a very high velocity, can overcome the repulsion and penetrate the target nucleus, thus effecting the transformation. A schematic diagram of one type of particle accelerator, the **cyclotron,** is shown in Fig. 21.5. The ion is introduced at the center of the cyclotron and is accelerated in an expanding spiral path by use of alternating electric fields in the presence of a magnetic field. The **linear accelerator** illustrated in Fig. 21.6 employs changing electric fields to achieve high velocities on a linear pathway.

In addition to positive ions, neutrons are often employed as bombarding particles to effect nuclear transformations. Because neutrons are uncharged and thus not repelled electrostatically by a target nucleus, they are readily absorbed by many nuclei, leading to new nuclides. The most common source of neutrons for this purpose is a fission reactor (see Section 21.6).

By using neutron and positive-ion bombardment, scientists have been able to extend the periodic table. Prior to 1940, the heaviest known element was uranium ($Z = 92$), but in 1940, neptunium ($Z = 93$) was produced by neutron bombardment of ${}^{238}_{92}\text{U}$. The process initially gives ${}^{239}_{92}\text{U}$, which decays to ${}^{239}_{93}\text{Np}$ by β-particle production:

$$^{238}_{92}\text{U} + {}^{1}_{0}\text{n} \longrightarrow {}^{239}_{92}\text{U} \xrightarrow[t_{1/2} = 23 \text{ min}]{} {}^{239}_{93}\text{Np} + {}^{0}_{-1}\text{e}$$

Figure 21.6

Schematic diagram of a linear accelerator, which uses a changing electric field to accelerate a positive ion along a linear path. As the ion leaves the source, the odd-numbered tubes are negatively charged, and the even-numbered tubes are positively charged. The positive ion is thus attracted into tube 1. As the ion leaves tube 1, the tube polarities are reversed. Now tube 1 is positive, repelling the positive ion, and tube 2 is negative, attracting the positive ion. This process continues, eventually producing high particle velocity.

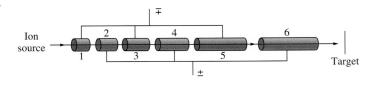

Table 21.4 Syntheses of Some of the Transuranium Elements

Element	Neutron Bombardment	Half-Life
Neptunium (Z = 93)	$^{238}_{92}U + ^{1}_{0}n \longrightarrow ^{239}_{93}Np + ^{0}_{-1}e$	2.35 days ($^{239}_{93}Np$)
Plutonium (Z = 94)	$^{239}_{93}Np \longrightarrow ^{239}_{94}Pu + ^{0}_{-1}e$	24,400 years ($^{239}_{94}Pu$)
Americium (Z = 95)	$^{239}_{94}Pu + 2\,^{1}_{0}n \longrightarrow ^{241}_{94}Pu \longrightarrow ^{241}_{95}Am + ^{0}_{-1}e$	458 years ($^{241}_{95}Am$)

Element	Positive-Ion Bombardment	Half-Life
Curium (Z = 96)	$^{239}_{94}Pu + ^{4}_{2}He \longrightarrow ^{242}_{96}Cm + ^{1}_{0}n$	163 days ($^{242}_{96}Cm$)
Californium (Z = 98)	$^{242}_{96}Cm + ^{4}_{2}He \longrightarrow ^{245}_{98}Cf + ^{1}_{0}n$ or $^{238}_{92}U + ^{12}_{6}C \longrightarrow ^{246}_{98}Cf + 4\,^{1}_{0}n$	44 minutes ($^{245}_{98}Cf$)
Element 104	$^{249}_{98}Cf + ^{12}_{6}C \longrightarrow ^{257}_{104}X + 4\,^{1}_{0}n$	
Element 105	$^{249}_{98}Cf + ^{15}_{7}N \longrightarrow ^{260}_{105}X + 4\,^{1}_{0}n$	
Element 106	$^{249}_{98}Cf + ^{18}_{8}O \longrightarrow ^{263}_{106}X + 4\,^{1}_{0}n$	

In the years since 1940, the elements with atomic numbers 93 through 112, called the **transuranium elements,**[*] have been synthesized. Many of these elements have very short half-lives, as shown in Table 21.4. As a result, only a few atoms of some have ever been formed. This of course makes the chemical characterization of these elements extremely difficult.

21.4 *Detection and Uses of Radioactivity*

Although various instruments measure radioactivity levels, the most familiar of them is the **Geiger–Müller counter,** or **Geiger counter** (see Fig. 21.7). This instrument takes advantage of the fact that the high-energy particles from radioactive decay

Geiger counters are often called *survey meters* in industry.

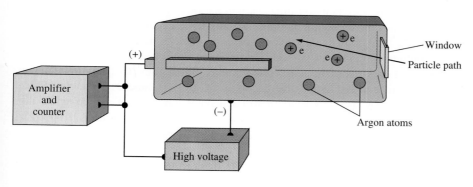

Figure 21.7

A schematic representation of a Geiger–Müller counter. The high-energy radioactive particle enters the window and ionizes argon atoms along its path. The resulting ions and electrons produce a momentary current pulse, which is amplified and counted.

*For more information, see G. B. Kauffman, "Beyond uranium," *Chem. Eng. News* (Nov. 19, 1990): 18.

processes produce ions when they travel through matter. The probe of the Geiger counter is filled with argon gas, which can be ionized by a rapidly moving particle as illustrated below. This reaction is demonstrated by the equation:

$$Ar(g) \xrightarrow[\text{particle}]{\text{High-energy}} Ar^+(g) + e^-$$

Normally, a sample of argon gas will not conduct a current when an electrical potential is applied. However, the formation of ions and electrons produced by the passage of the high-energy particle allows a momentary current to flow. Electronic devices detect this current flow, and the number of these events can be counted. Thus the decay rate of the radioactive sample can be determined.

Another instrument often used to detect levels of radioactivity is a **scintillation counter,** which takes advantage of the fact that certain substances, such as zinc sulfide, give off light when they are struck by high-energy radiation. A photocell senses the flashes of light that occur as the radiation strikes and thus measures the number of decay events per unit of time.

Dating by Radioactivity

Archeologists, geologists, and others involved in reconstructing the ancient history of the earth rely heavily on radioactivity to provide accurate dates for artifacts and rocks. A method that has been very important for dating ancient articles made from wood or cloth is **radiocarbon dating,** or **carbon-14 dating,** a technique originated in the 1940s by Willard Libby, an American chemist who received a Nobel Prize for his efforts in this field.

Radiocarbon dating is based on the radioactivity of the nuclide $^{14}_{6}C$, which decays via β-particle production:

$$^{14}_{6}C \longrightarrow _{-1}^{0}e + {}^{14}_{7}N$$

Carbon-14 is continuously produced in the atmosphere when high-energy neutrons from space collide with nitrogen-14:

$$^{14}_{7}N + {}^{1}_{0}n \longrightarrow {}^{14}_{6}C + {}^{1}_{1}H$$

Thus carbon-14 is continuously produced by this process, and it continuously decomposes through β-particle production. Over the years, the rates for these two processes have become equal, and like a participant in a chemical reaction at equilibrium, the amount of $^{14}_{6}C$ that is present in the atmosphere remains approximately constant.

Carbon-14 can be used to date wood and cloth artifacts because the $^{14}_{6}C$, along with the other carbon isotopes in the atmosphere, reacts with oxygen to form carbon dioxide. A living plant consumes carbon dioxide in the photosynthesis process and incorporates the carbon, including $^{14}_{6}C$, into its molecules. As long as the plant lives, the $^{14}_{6}C/^{12}_{6}C$ ratio in its molecules remains the same as in the atmosphere because of the continuous uptake of carbon. However, as soon as a tree is cut to make a wooden bowl or a flax plant is harvested to make linen, the $^{14}_{6}C/^{12}_{6}C$ ratio begins to decrease because of the radioactive decay of $^{14}_{6}C$ (the $^{12}_{6}C$ nuclide is stable). Since the half-life of $^{14}_{6}C$ is 5730 years, a wooden bowl found in an archeological dig showing a $^{14}_{6}C/^{12}_{6}C$ ratio that is half that found in currently living trees is approximately 5730 years old. This reasoning assumes that the current $^{14}_{6}C/^{12}_{6}C$ ratio is the same as that found in ancient times.

Dendrochronologists, scientists who date trees from annual growth rings, have used data collected from long-lived species of trees, such as bristlecone pines and

Brigham Young researcher Scott Woodward taking a bone sample for carbon-14 dating at an archeological site in Egypt.

Radioactive nuclides are often called *radionuclides.* Carbon dating is based on the radionuclide $^{14}_{6}C$.

The $^{14}_{6}C/^{12}_{6}C$ ratio is the basis for carbon-14 dating.

sequoias, to show that the $^{14}_{6}C$ content of the atmosphere has changed significantly over the ages. These data have been used to derive correction factors that allow very accurate dates to be determined from the observed $^{14}_{6}C/^{12}_{6}C$ ratio in an artifact, especially for artifacts 10,000 years old or less. Recent measurements of uranium/thorium ratios in ancient coral indicate that dates in the 20,000- to 30,000-year range may have errors as large as 3000 years. As a result, efforts are now being made to recalibrate the $^{14}_{6}C$ dates over this period.

Sample Exercise 21.5 ^{14}C Dating

The remnants of an ancient fire in a cave in Africa showed a $^{14}_{6}C$ decay rate of 3.1 counts per minute per gram of carbon. Assuming that the decay rate of $^{14}_{6}C$ in freshly cut wood (corrected for changes in the $^{14}_{6}C$ content of the atmosphere) is 13.6 counts per minute per gram of carbon, calculate the age of the remnants. The half-life of $^{14}_{6}C$ is 5730 years.

Solution

The key to solving this problem is to realize that the decay rates given are directly proportional to the number of $^{14}_{6}C$ nuclides present. Radioactive decay follows first-order kinetics:

$$\text{Rate} = kN$$

Thus

A dendrochronologist cutting a section from a dead tree in South Africa.

$$\frac{3.1 \text{ counts/min} \cdot \text{g}}{13.6 \text{ counts/min} \cdot \text{g}} = \underbrace{\frac{\text{rate at time } t}{\text{rate at time } 0}}_{} = \frac{kN}{kN_0} \begin{array}{l} \text{Number of nuclides} \\ \text{present at time } t \\ \\ \text{Number of nuclides} \\ \text{present at time } 0 \end{array}$$

$$= \frac{N}{N_0} = 0.23$$

We can now use the integrated first-order rate law:

$$\ln\left(\frac{N}{N_0}\right) = -kt$$

where

$$k = \frac{0.693}{t_{1/2}} = \frac{0.693}{5730 \text{ years}}$$

to solve for t, the time elapsed since the campfire:

$$\ln\left(\frac{N}{N_0}\right) = \ln(0.23) = -\left(\frac{0.693}{5730 \text{ years}}\right)t$$

Solving this equation gives $t = 12,000$ years; the campfire in the cave occurred about 12,000 years ago.

See Exercises 21.27 and 21.28.

One drawback of radiocarbon dating is that a fairly large piece of the object (from a half to several grams) must be burned to form carbon dioxide, which is then analyzed for radioactivity. Another method for counting $^{14}_6C$ nuclides avoids destruction of a significant portion of a valuable artifact. This technique, requiring only about 10^{-3} g, uses a mass spectrometer (see Chapter 3), in which the carbon atoms are ionized and accelerated through a magnetic field that deflects their path. Because of their different masses, the various ions are deflected by different amounts and can be counted separately. This allows a very accurate determination of the $^{14}_6C/^{12}_6C$ ratio in the sample.

In their attempts to establish the geologic history of the earth, geologists have made extensive use of radioactivity. For example, since $^{238}_{92}U$ decays to the stable $^{206}_{82}Pb$ nuclide, the ratio of $^{206}_{82}Pb$ to $^{238}_{92}U$ in a rock can, under favorable circumstances, be used to estimate the age of the rock.

Because the half-life of $^{238}_{92}U$ is very long compared with those of the other members of the decay series (see Table 21.3) to reach $^{206}_{82}Pb$, the number of nuclides present in intermediate stages of decay is negligible. That is, once a $^{238}_{92}U$ nuclide starts to decay, it reaches $^{206}_{82}Pb$ relatively fast.

Sample Exercise 21.6 Dating by Radioactivity

A rock containing $^{238}_{92}U$ and $^{206}_{82}Pb$ was examined to determine its approximate age. Analysis showed the ratio of $^{206}_{82}Pb$ atoms to $^{238}_{92}U$ atoms to be 0.115. Assuming that no lead was originally present, that all the $^{206}_{82}Pb$ formed over the years has remained in the rock, and that the number of nuclides in intermediate stages of decay between $^{238}_{92}U$ and $^{206}_{82}Pb$ is negligible, calculate the age of the rock. The half-life of $^{238}_{92}U$ is 4.5×10^9 years.

Solution

This problem can be solved using the integrated first-order rate law:

$$\ln\left(\frac{N}{N_0}\right) = -kt = -\left(\frac{0.693}{4.5 \times 10^9 \text{ years}}\right)t$$

where N/N_0 represents the ratio of $^{238}_{92}U$ atoms now found in the rock to the number present when the rock was formed. We are assuming that each $^{206}_{82}Pb$ nuclide present must have come from decay of a $^{238}_{92}U$:

$$^{238}_{92}U \longrightarrow {}^{206}_{82}Pb$$

Thus

| Number of $^{238}_{92}U$ atoms originally present | = | number of $^{206}_{82}Pb$ atoms now present | + | number of $^{238}_{92}U$ atoms now present |

$$\frac{\text{Atoms of } ^{206}_{82}Pb \text{ now present}}{\text{Atoms of } ^{238}_{92}U \text{ now present}} = 0.115 = \frac{0.115}{1.000} = \frac{115}{1000}$$

Think carefully about what this means. For every 1115 $^{238}_{92}U$ atoms originally present in the rock, 115 have been changed to $^{206}_{82}Pb$ and 1000 remain as $^{238}_{92}U$. Thus

$$\frac{N}{N_0} = \frac{\overbrace{^{238}_{92}U}^{\text{Now present}}}{\underbrace{^{206}_{82}Pb + {}^{238}_{92}U}_{^{238}_{92}U \text{ originally present}}} = \frac{1000}{1115} = 0.8969$$

$$\ln\left(\frac{N}{N_0}\right) = \ln(0.8969) = -\left(\frac{0.693}{4.5 \times 10^9 \text{ years}}\right)t$$
$$t = 7.1 \times 10^8 \text{ years}$$

This is the approximate age of the rock. It was formed sometime in the Cambrian period.

See Exercises 21.29 and 21.30.

Medical Applications of Radioactivity

Although the rapid advances of the medical sciences in recent decades are due to many causes, one of the most important has been the discovery and use of **radiotracers,** radioactive nuclides that can be introduced into organisms in food or drugs and whose pathways can be *traced* by monitoring their radioactivity. For example, the incorporation of nuclides such as $^{14}_{6}C$ and $^{32}_{15}P$ into nutrients has produced important information about metabolic pathways.

Iodine-131 has proved very useful in the diagnosis and treatment of illnesses of the thyroid gland. Patients drink a solution containing small amounts of $Na^{131}I$, and the uptake of the iodine by the thyroid gland is monitored with a scanner (see Fig. 21.8).

Thallium-201 can be used to assess the damage to the heart muscle in a person who has suffered a heart attack, because thallium is concentrated in healthy muscle tissue. Technetium-99m is also taken up by normal heart tissue and is used for damage assessment in a similar way.

Radiotracers provide sensitive and noninvasive methods for learning about biologic systems, for detection of disease, for monitoring the action and effectiveness of drugs, and for early detection of pregnancy, and their usefulness should continue to grow. Some useful radiotracers are listed in Table 21.5.

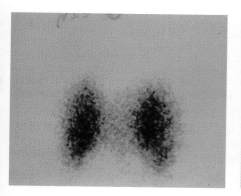
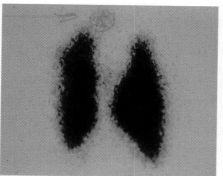
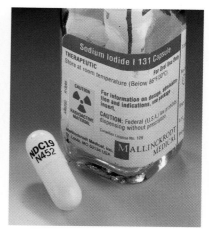

Figure 21.8

After consumption of $Na^{131}I$, the patient's thyroid is scanned for radioactivity levels to determine the efficiency of iodine absorption. (left) A normal thyroid. (right) An enlarged thyroid.

A pellet containing radioactive ^{131}I.

Table 21.5 Some Radioactive Nuclides, with Half-Lives and Medical Applications as Radiotracers

Nuclide	Half-Life	Area of the Body Studied
^{131}I	8.1 days	Thyroid
^{59}Fe	45.1 days	Red blood cells
^{99}Mo	67 hours	Metabolism
^{32}P	14.3 days	Eyes, liver, tumors
^{51}Cr	27.8 days	Red blood cells
^{87}Sr	2.8 hours	Bones
^{99m}Tc	6.0 hours	Heart, bones, liver, and lungs
^{133}Xe	5.3 days	Lungs
^{24}Na	14.8 hours	Circulatory system

21.5 Thermodynamic Stability of the Nucleus

We can determine the thermodynamic stability of a nucleus by calculating the change in potential energy that would occur if that nucleus were formed from its constituent protons and neutrons. For example, let's consider the hypothetical process of forming a $^{16}_{8}O$ nucleus from eight neutrons and eight protons:

$$8\,^{1}_{0}n + 8\,^{1}_{1}H \longrightarrow\ ^{16}_{8}O$$

The energy change associated with this process can be calculated by comparing the sum of the masses of eight protons and eight neutrons with that of the oxygen nucleus:

$$\text{Mass of } (8\,^{1}_{0}n + 8\,^{1}_{1}H) = 8(1.67493 \times 10^{-24}\text{ g}) + 8(1.67262 \times 10^{-24}\text{ g})$$

$$\underset{\text{Mass of }^{1}_{0}n}{\uparrow} \qquad\qquad \underset{\text{Mass of }^{1}_{1}H}{\uparrow}$$

$$= 2.67804 \times 10^{-23}\text{ g}$$

$$\text{Mass of }^{16}_{8}O \text{ nucleus} = 2.65535 \times 10^{-23}\text{ g}$$

The difference in mass for one nucleus is

$$\text{Mass of }^{16}_{8}O - \text{mass of } (8\,^{1}_{0}n + 8\,^{1}_{1}H) = -2.269 \times 10^{-25}\text{ g}$$

The difference in mass for formation of 1 mole of $^{16}_{8}O$ nuclei is therefore

$$(-2.269 \times 10^{-25}\text{ g/nucleus})(6.022 \times 10^{23}\text{ nuclei/mol}) = -0.1366\text{ g/mol}$$

Thus 0.1366 g of mass would be lost if 1 mole of oxygen-16 were formed from protons and neutrons. What is the reason for this difference in mass, and how can this information be used to calculate the energy change that accompanies this process?

The answers to these questions can be found in the work of Albert Einstein. As we discussed in Section 7.2, Einstein's theory of relativity showed that energy should be considered a form of matter. His famous equation

Energy is a form of matter.

$$E = mc^2$$

where c is the speed of light, gives the relationship between a quantity of energy and its mass. When a system gains or loses energy, it also gains or loses a quantity of mass, given by E/c^2. Thus the mass of a nucleus is less than that of its component nucleons because the process is so exothermic.

Einstein's equation in the form

$$\text{Energy change} = \Delta E = \Delta mc^2$$

where Δm is the change in mass, or the **mass defect,** can be used to calculate ΔE for the hypothetical formation of a nucleus from its component nucleons.

The energy changes associated with normal chemical reactions are small enough that the corresponding mass changes are not detectable.

Sample Exercise 21.7   *Nuclear Binding Energy I*

Calculate the change in energy if 1 mol $^{16}_{8}O$ nuclei were formed from neutrons and protons.

Solution

We have already calculated that 0.1366 g of mass would be lost in the hypothetical process of assembling 1 mol $^{16}_{8}O$ nuclei from the component nucleons. We can calculate the change in energy for this process from

$$\Delta E = \Delta mc^2$$

where

$$c = 3.00 \times 10^8 \text{ m/s} \quad \text{and} \quad \Delta m = -0.1366 \text{ g/mol} = -1.366 \times 10^{-4} \text{ kg/mol}$$

Thus

$$\Delta E = (-1.366 \times 10^{-4} \text{ kg/mol})(3.00 \times 10^8 \text{ m/s})^2 = -1.23 \times 10^{13} \text{ J/mol}$$

The negative sign for the ΔE value indicates that the process is exothermic. Energy, and thus mass, is lost from the system.

See Exercises 21.31 through 21.33.

The energy changes observed for nuclear processes are extremely large compared with those observed for chemical and physical changes. Thus nuclear processes constitute a potentially valuable energy resource.

The thermodynamic stability of a particular nucleus is normally represented as energy released per nucleon. To illustrate how this quantity is obtained, we will continue to consider $^{16}_{8}O$. First, we calculate ΔE per nucleus by dividing the molar value from Sample Exercise 21.7 by Avogadro's number:

$$\Delta E \text{ per } ^{16}_{8}O \text{ nucleus} = \frac{-1.23 \times 10^{13} \text{ J/mol}}{6.022 \times 10^{23} \text{ nuclei/mol}} = -2.04 \times 10^{-11} \text{ J/nucleus}$$

In terms of a more convenient energy unit, a million electronvolts (MeV), where

$$1 \text{ MeV} = 1.60 \times 10^{-13} \text{ J}$$

$$\Delta E \text{ per } ^{16}_{8}O \text{ nucleus} = (-2.04 \times 10^{-11} \text{ J/nucleus})\left(\frac{1 \text{ MeV}}{1.60 \times 10^{-13} \text{ J}}\right)$$

$$= -1.28 \times 10^2 \text{ MeV/nucleus}$$

Next, we can calculate the value of ΔE per nucleon by dividing by A, the sum of neutrons and protons:

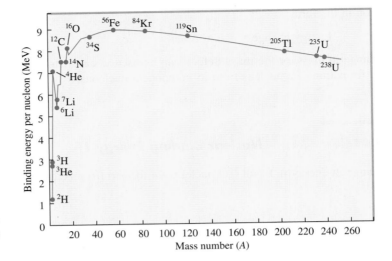

Figure 21.9

The binding energy per nucleon as a function of mass number. The most stable nuclei are at the top of the curve. The most stable nucleus is $^{56}_{26}$Fe.

$$\Delta E \text{ per nucleon for } ^{16}_{8}\text{O} = \frac{-1.28 \times 10^2 \text{ MeV/nucleus}}{16 \text{ nucleons/nucleus}}$$

$$= -7.98 \text{ MeV/nucleon}$$

This means that 7.98 MeV of energy per nucleon would be *released* if $^{16}_{8}$O were formed from neutrons and protons. The energy required to *decompose* this nucleus into its components has the same numeric value but with a positive sign (since energy is required). This is called the **binding energy** per nucleon for $^{16}_{8}$O.

The values of the binding energy per nucleon for the various nuclides are shown in Fig. 21.9. Note that the most stable nuclei (those requiring the largest energy per nucleon to decompose the nucleus) occur at the top of the curve. The most stable nucleus known is $^{56}_{26}$Fe, which has a binding energy per nucleon of 8.79 MeV.

Sample Exercise 21.8 *Nuclear Binding Energy II*

Calculate the binding energy per nucleon for the $^4_2$He nucleus (atomic masses: $^4_2$He = 4.0026 amu; $^1_1$H = 1.0078 amu).

Solution

First, we must calculate the mass defect (Δm) for $^4_2$He. Since atomic masses (which include the electrons) are given, we must decide how to account for the electron mass:

$$4.0026 = \text{mass of } ^4_2\text{He atom} = \text{mass of } ^4_2\text{He nucleus} + 2m_e$$

Electron mass

$$1.0078 = \text{mass of } ^1_1\text{H atom} = \text{mass of } ^1_1\text{H nucleus} + m_e$$

Thus, since a $^4_2$He nucleus is "synthesized" from two protons and two neutrons, we see that

Since atomic masses include the masses of the electrons, to obtain the mass of a given atomic nucleus from its atomic mass, we must subtract the mass of the electrons.

$$\Delta m = \underbrace{(4.0026 - 2m_e)}_{\substack{\text{Mass of } {}^4_2\text{He} \\ \text{nucleus}}} - [\underbrace{2(1.0078 - m_e)}_{\substack{\text{Mass of } {}^1_1\text{H} \\ \text{nucleus (proton)}}} + \underbrace{2(1.0087)}_{\substack{\text{Mass of} \\ \text{neutron}}}]$$

$$= 4.0026 - 2m_e - 2(1.0078) + 2m_e - 2(1.0087)$$

$$= 4.0026 - 2(1.0078) - 2(1.0087)$$

$$= -0.0304 \text{ amu}$$

Note that in this case the electron mass cancels out in taking the difference. This will always happen in this type of calculation if the atomic masses are used both for the nuclide of interest and for ${}^1_1\text{H}$. Thus 0.0304 amu of mass is *lost* per ${}^4_2\text{He}$ nucleus formed.

The corresponding energy change can be calculated from

$$\Delta E = \Delta mc^2$$

where

$$\Delta m = -0.0304 \frac{\text{amu}}{\text{nucleus}} = \left(-0.0304 \frac{\text{amu}}{\text{nucleus}}\right)\left(1.66 \times 10^{-27} \frac{\text{kg}}{\text{amu}}\right)$$

$$= -5.04 \times 10^{-29} \frac{\text{kg}}{\text{nucleus}}$$

and

$$c = 3.00 \times 10^8 \text{ m/s}$$

Thus

$$\Delta E = \left(-5.04 \times 10^{-29} \frac{\text{kg}}{\text{nucleus}}\right)\left(3.00 \times 10^8 \frac{\text{m}}{\text{s}}\right)^2$$

$$= -4.54 \times 10^{-12} \text{ J/nucleus}$$

This means that 4.54×10^{-12} J of energy is *released* per nucleus formed and that 4.54×10^{-12} J would be required to decompose the nucleus into the constituent neutrons and protons. Thus the binding energy (BE) per nucleon is

$$\text{BE per nucleon} = \frac{4.54 \times 10^{-12} \text{ J/nucleus}}{4 \text{ nucleons/nucleus}}$$

$$= 1.14 \times 10^{-12} \text{ J/nucleon}$$

$$= \left(1.14 \times 10^{-12} \frac{\text{J}}{\text{nucleon}}\right)\left(\frac{1 \text{ MeV}}{1.60 \times 10^{-13} \text{ J}}\right)$$

$$= 7.13 \text{ MeV/nucleon}$$

See Exercises 21.34 through 21.36.

21.6 Nuclear Fission and Nuclear Fusion

The graph shown in Fig. 21.9 has very important implications for the use of nuclear processes as sources of energy. Recall that energy is released, that is, ΔE is negative, when a process goes from a less stable to a more stable state. The higher a nuclide is on the curve, the more stable it is. This means that two types of nuclear processes will be exothermic (see Fig. 21.10):

1. Combining two light nuclei to form a heavier, more stable nucleus. This process is called **fusion.**

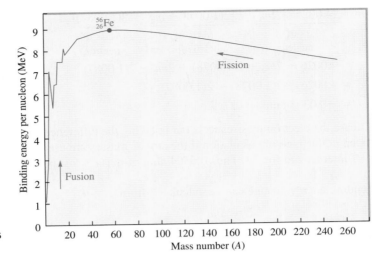

Figure 21.10

Both fission and fusion produce more stable nuclides and are thus exothermic.

2. Splitting a heavy nucleus into two nuclei with smaller mass numbers. This process is called **fission.**

Because of the large binding energies involved in holding the nucleus together, both these processes involve energy changes more than a million times larger than those associated with chemical reactions.

Nuclear Fission

Nuclear fission was discovered in the late 1930s when $^{235}_{92}U$ nuclides bombarded with neutrons were observed to split into two lighter elements:

$$^{1}_{0}n + ^{235}_{92}U \longrightarrow ^{141}_{56}Ba + ^{92}_{36}Kr + 3\ ^{1}_{0}n$$

This process, shown schematically in Fig. 21.11, releases 3.5×10^{-11} J of energy per event, which translates to 2.1×10^{13} J per mole of $^{235}_{92}U$. Compare this figure with that for the combustion of methane, which releases only 8.0×10^{5} J of energy per mole. The fission of $^{235}_{92}U$ produces about 26 million times more energy than the combustion of methane.

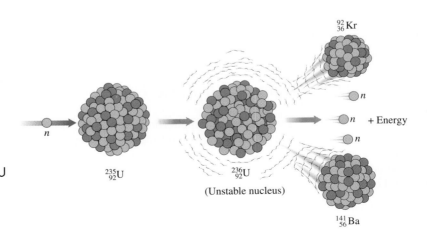

Figure 21.11

On capturing a neutron, the $^{235}_{92}U$ nucleus undergoes fission to produce two lighter nuclides, free neutrons (typically three), and a large amount of energy.

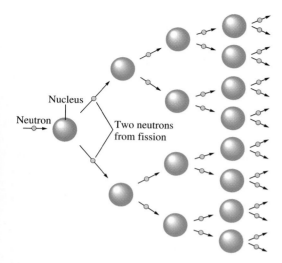

Figure 21.12

Representation of a fission process in which each event produces two neutrons, which can go on to split other nuclei, leading to a self-sustaining chain reaction.

The process shown on the preceding page is only one of the many fission reactions that $^{235}_{92}$U can undergo. Another is

$$^{1}_{0}n + ^{235}_{92}U \longrightarrow ^{137}_{52}Te + ^{97}_{40}Zr + 2\,^{1}_{0}n$$

In fact, over 200 different isotopes of 35 different elements have been observed among the fission products of $^{235}_{92}$U.

In addition to the product nuclides, neutrons are also produced in the fission reactions of $^{235}_{92}$U. This makes it possible to have a self-sustaining fission process—a **chain reaction** (see Fig. 21.12). In order for the fission process to be self-sustaining, at least one neutron from each fission event must go on to split another nucleus. If, on average, *less than one* neutron causes another fission event, the process dies out and the reaction is said to be **subcritical**. If *exactly one* neutron from each fission event causes another fission event, the process sustains itself at the same level and is said to be **critical**. If *more than one* neutron from each fission event causes another fission event, the process rapidly escalates and the heat buildup causes a violent explosion. This situation is described as **supercritical**.

To achieve the critical state, a certain mass of fissionable material, called the **critical mass,** is needed. If the sample is too small, too many neutrons escape before they have a chance to cause a fission event, and the process stops. This is illustrated in Fig. 21.13.

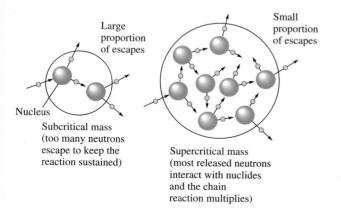

Large proportion of escapes

Small proportion of escapes

Nucleus

Subcritical mass (too many neutrons escape to keep the reaction sustained)

Supercritical mass (most released neutrons interact with nuclides and the chain reaction multiplies)

Figure 21.13

If the mass of fissionable material is too small, most of the neutrons escape before causing another fission event, and the process dies out.

Uranium oxide (refined uranium).

During World War II, an intense research effort called the Manhattan Project was carried out by the United States to build a bomb based on the principles of nuclear fission. This program produced the fission bombs that were used with devastating effects on the cities of Hiroshima and Nagasaki in 1945. Basically, a fission bomb operates by suddenly combining subcritical masses of fissionable material to form a supercritical mass, thereby producing an explosion of incredible intensity.

Nuclear Reactors

Because of the tremendous energies involved, it seemed desirable to develop the fission process as an energy source to produce electricity. To accomplish this, reactors were designed in which controlled fission can occur. The resulting energy is used to heat water to produce steam to run turbine generators, in much the same way that a coal-burning power plant generates energy. A schematic diagram of a nuclear power plant is shown in Fig. 21.14.

In the **reactor core,** shown in Fig. 21.15, uranium that has been enriched to approximately 3% $^{235}_{92}U$ (natural uranium contains only 0.7% $^{235}_{92}U$) is housed in cylinders. A **moderator** surrounds the cylinders to slow down the neutrons so that the uranium fuel can capture them more efficiently. **Control rods,** composed of substances that absorb neutrons, are used to regulate the power level of the reactor. The reactor is designed so that should a malfunction occur, the control rods are automatically inserted into the core to stop the reaction. A liquid (usually water) is circulated through the core to extract the heat generated by the energy of fission; the energy can then be passed on via a heat exchanger to water in the turbine system.

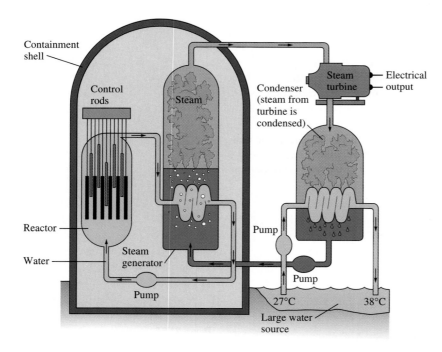

Figure 21.14

A schematic diagram of a nuclear power plant.

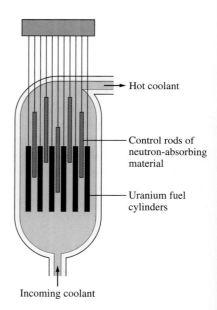

Figure 21.15

A schematic of a reactor core. The position of the control rods determines the level of energy production by regulating the amount of fission taking place.

CHEMICAL IMPACT

Nuclear Power: Could It Stage a Comeback?

AS EVERYONE KNOWS, nuclear power has been a very controversial issue in the United States over the past 35 years. Safety issues and cost, along with the attendant political sensitivities, have stalled the growth of nuclear power. However, this situation might change. The intense concern about the warming effects of the carbon dioxide produced by fossil fuels, the uncertain rate of progress in harnessing solar energy, and innovative reactor designs may lead to a resurgence of interest in fission-powered nuclear plants.

Indeed, the French have demonstrated that nuclear power can be economically and politically feasible. France, which uses breeder reactors to provide most of its electricity, has an excellent safety record and is pioneering new methods for the storage of radioactive wastes.

In the United States, experiments at Argonne National Laboratory in Illinois indicate that a new generation of breeder reactors can be developed that will be inherently safer than the pressurized boiling-water reactors now in use. This research also shows that these reactors can be cost competitive with coal-fired power plants. The reactor under investigation at Argonne, called an *integral fast reactor (IFR)*, is quite different from the current reactors used in power plants. The key differences are that (1) the IFR uses liquid sodium instead of water as the coolant, (2) the IFR uses its fuel much more efficiently and, in fact, breeds new fissionable fuel as it runs, and (3) the IFR produces only a fraction of the radioactive wastes produced by current reactors. Because the boiling point of sodium is near 900°C, the liquid sodium does not need to be under pressure to prevent boiling, as is required for the water in current power reactors. This greatly lessens the chance of a very rapid loss of coolant should a leak develop. Liquid sodium has other advantages over water, such as not being corrosive to steel. Also, the use of sodium as a coolant allows for much faster neutrons than are possible in present water-cooled reactors. These fast neutrons produce extra power and greatly reduce the radioactive waste from the reactor, because they cause the fission (and thus the destruction) of many radioactive products of the fission process.

In addition, the IFR uses a new type of fuel element, which is an alloy of uranium, plutonium, and zirconium. Because these new metal fuel elements conduct heat so much more efficiently than the ceramic fuel elements now commonly in use, lower core temperatures are possible. Also, these metal fuel elements allow electrochemical reprocessing, which leads to very efficient recycling of usable fuel. This means that virtually all the initial uranium fuel is eventually consumed. In contrast, present-day reactors consume only a small percentage of the original uranium; the rest is removed with the radioactive fission products. Because the fuel recycling for the IFR does not require a large facility, it can be done at the reactor site, thus eliminating the transportation of large amounts of radioactive materials.

If development goes as smoothly as projected, the IFR may be providing safe, economical power in the near future while adding no carbon dioxide or other pollutants to the atmosphere.

Although the concentration of $^{235}_{92}U$ in the fuel elements is not great enough to allow a supercritical mass to develop in the core, a failure of the cooling system can lead to temperatures high enough to melt the core. As a result, the building housing the core must be designed to contain the core even if meltdown occurs. A great deal of controversy now exists about the efficiency of the safety systems in nuclear power plants. Accidents such as the one at the Three Mile Island facility in Pennsylvania in 1979 and in Chernobyl,[*] Ukraine, in 1986 have led many people to question the wisdom of continuing to build fission-based power plants.

Breeder Reactors

One potential problem facing the nuclear power industry is the supply of $^{235}_{92}U$. Some scientists have suggested that we have nearly depleted those uranium deposits rich

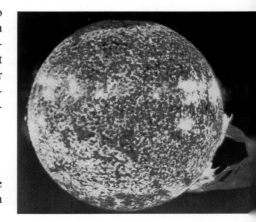

Skylab ultraviolet picture of the sun.

*See C. A. Atwood, "Chernobyl—What happened?" *J. Chem. Ed.* **65** (1988): 1037.

CHEMICAL IMPACT

Nuclear Waste Disposal

OUR SOCIETY HAS not had an impressive record for safe disposal of industrial wastes. We have polluted our water and air, and some land areas have become virtually uninhabitable because of the improper burial of chemical wastes. As a result, many people are wary about the radioactive wastes from nuclear reactors. The potential threats of cancer and genetic mutations make these materials especially frightening.

Because of its controversial nature, no nuclear waste generated over the past 45 years has been permanently disposed of. However, in 1982 the U.S. Congress passed the Nuclear Waste Policy Act, which established a timetable for choosing and preparing sites for deep underground disposal of radioactive materials. The program is being funded by a tax of 0.1% per kilowatt hour on electricity generated by nuclear power.

The tentative disposal plan calls for the incorporation of the spent nuclear fuel into blocks of borosilicate glass that will be packed in corrosion-resistant metal containers and then buried in a deep, stable rock formation (see figure).

There are indications that this method will isolate the waste until the radioactivity decays to safe levels. One reassuring indication comes from the natural fission "reactor" at Oklo in Gabon, Africa. Initiated about 2 billion years ago when uranium in ore deposits there formed a critical mass, the "reactor" produced fission and fusion products for several thousand years. Although some of these products have migrated away from the site in the intervening 2 billion years, most have stayed in place. Another indication of the possible success of underground isolation is the disposal program carried out at Oak Ridge National Laboratory over the past 25 years. In this program, the waste has been ground up; mixed with cement, fly ash, and clay; and injected at high

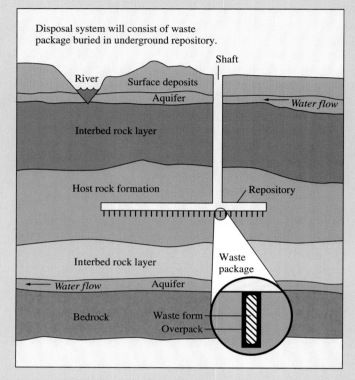

A schematic diagram of the tentative plan for deep underground isolation of nuclear waste.   Reproduced with permission from *Chemical Engineering News*, July 18, 1983, 61(29), p. 30. Copyright © 1983, American Chemical Society.

pressures into a shale bed 1000 feet underground. This method of injection causes fractures in the rock into which the liquid waste seeps and then solidifies. Monitoring of the wastes has shown little movement of radioactivity. Although this procedure has worked well, the materials involved are not nearly as radioactive as those from power plants, for which this method is not thought suitable. However, this experiment has demonstrated that such wastes can be immobilized.

Choosing the waste repository sites is an especially sensitive issue. Many states

have resisted the plan, but Congress has the power to override a state's disapproval. In fact, Congress amended the Nuclear Waste Policy Act in 1987 to make Yucca Mountain in Nevada the primary potential site. Studies are now being carried out to evaluate the feasibility of this site as a safe repository for nuclear waste.

In a related situation, the Department of Energy (DOE) is preparing the Waste Isolation Pilot Plant (WIPP) near Carlsbad, New Mexico, for the long-term storage of defense-related nuclear waste. This storage facility is sited 2150 feet below the surface in salt beds that have remained stable and free of groundwater for about 225 million years, according to studies by the DOE. In the next stages of the testing of WIPP, the DOE will store several thousand drums of waste, which will be monitored for effects such as gas formation.

An alternative to permanent isolation of spent nuclear fuel is monitored, retrievable storage. This method has an advantage since, if reprocessing to remove potentially useful materials such as plutonium becomes feasible, the wastes are still accessible. The argument for this plan is that the technologies and alternatives available to society a few hundred years from now may be so different from those of the present that these wastes could become valuable resources. At the present time, isolation of the wastes seems the most likely event; even so, these underground deposits may become plutonium mines in the future.

enough in $^{235}_{92}U$ to make production of fissionable fuel economically feasible. Because of this possibility, **breeder reactors** have been developed, in which fissionable fuel is actually produced while the reactor runs. In the breeder reactors now being studied, the major component of natural uranium, nonfissionable $^{238}_{92}U$, is changed to fissionable $^{239}_{94}Pu$. The reaction involves absorption of a neutron, followed by production of two β particles:

$$^1_0n + {}^{238}_{92}U \longrightarrow {}^{239}_{92}U$$

$$^{239}_{92}U \longrightarrow {}^{239}_{93}Np + {}^{\ 0}_{-1}e$$

$$^{239}_{93}Np \longrightarrow {}^{239}_{94}Pu + {}^{\ 0}_{-1}e$$

As the reactor runs and $^{235}_{92}U$ is split, some of the excess neutrons are absorbed by $^{238}_{92}U$ to produce $^{239}_{94}Pu$. The $^{239}_{94}Pu$ is then separated out and used to fuel another reactor. Such a reactor thus "breeds" nuclear fuel as it operates.

Although breeder reactors are now used in France, the United States is proceeding slowly with their development because of their controversial nature. One problem involves the hazards in handling plutonium, which flames on contact with air and is very toxic.

Fusion

Large quantities of energy are also produced by the fusion of two light nuclei. In fact, stars produce their energy through nuclear fusion. Our sun, which presently consists of 73% hydrogen, 26% helium, and 1% other elements, gives off vast quantities of energy from the fusion of protons to form helium:

$$^1_1H + {}^1_1H \longrightarrow {}^2_1H + {}^0_1e$$

$$^1_1H + {}^2_1H \longrightarrow {}^3_2He$$

$$^3_2He + {}^3_2He \longrightarrow {}^4_2He + 2\,{}^1_1H$$

$$^3_2He + {}^1_1H \longrightarrow {}^4_2He + {}^0_1e$$

Intense research is underway to develop a feasible fusion process because of the ready availability of many light nuclides (deuterium, ^2_1H, in seawater, for example) that can serve as fuel in fusion reactors. The major stumbling block is that high temperatures are required to initiate fusion. The forces that bind nucleons together to form a nucleus are effective only at *very small* distances ($\sim 10^{-13}$ cm). Thus, for two protons to bind together and thereby release energy, they must get very close together. But protons, because they are identically charged, repel each other

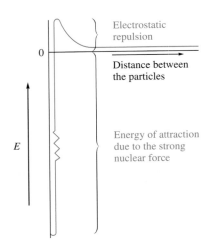

Figure 21.16
A plot of energy versus the separation distance for two $_1^2$H nuclei. The nuclei must have sufficient velocities to get over the electrostatic repulsion "hill" and get close enough for the nuclear binding forces to become effective, thus "fusing" the particles into a new nucleus and releasing large quantities of energy. The binding force is at least 100 times the electrostatic repulsion.

The ozone layer is discussed in Section 19.5.

electrostatically. This means that in order to get two protons (or two deuterons) close enough to bind together (the nuclear binding force is *not* electrostatic), they must be "shot" at each other at speeds high enough to overcome the electrostatic repulsion.

The electrostatic repulsion forces between two $_1^2$H nuclei are so great that a temperature of 4×10^7 K is required to give them velocities large enough to cause them to collide with sufficient energy that the nuclear forces can bind the particles together and thus release the binding energy. This situation is represented in Fig. 21.16.

Currently, scientists are studying two types of systems to produce the extremely high temperatures required: high-powered lasers and heating by electric currents. At present, many technical problems remain to be solved, and it is not clear which method will prove more useful or when fusion might become a practical energy source. However, there is still hope that fusion will be a major energy source sometime in the future.

21.7 Effects of Radiation

Everyone knows that being hit by a train is very serious. The problem is the energy transfer involved. In fact, any source of energy is potentially harmful to organisms. Energy transferred to cells can break chemical bonds and cause malfunctioning of the cell systems. This fact is behind the concern about the ozone layer in the earth's upper atmosphere, which screens out high-energy ultraviolet radiation from the sun. Radioactive elements, which are sources of high-energy particles, are also potentially hazardous, although the effects are usually quite subtle. The reason for the subtlety of radiation damage is that even though high-energy particles are involved, the quantity of energy actually deposited in tissues *per event* is quite small. However, the resulting damage is no less real, although the effects may not be apparent for years.

Radiation damage to organisms can be classified as somatic or genetic damage. **Somatic damage** is damage to the organism itself, resulting in sickness or death. The effects may appear almost immediately if a massive dose of radiation is received; for smaller doses, damage may appear years later, usually in the form of cancer. **Genetic damage** is damage to the genetic machinery, which produces malfunctions in the offspring of the organism.

The biologic effects of a particular source of radiation depend on several factors:

1. *The energy of the radiation.* The higher the energy content of the radiation, the more damage it can cause. Radiation doses are measured in **rads** (which is short for *r*adiation *a*bsorbed *d*ose), where 1 rad corresponds to 10^{-2} J of energy deposited per kilogram of tissue.

2. *The penetrating ability of the radiation.* The particles and rays produced in radioactive processes vary in their abilities to penetrate human tissue: γ rays are highly penetrating, β particles can penetrate approximately 1 cm, and α particles are stopped by the skin.

3. *The ionizing ability of the radiation.* Extraction of electrons from biomolecules to form ions is particularly detrimental to their functions. The ionizing ability of radiation varies dramatically. For example, γ rays penetrate very deeply but cause only occasional ionization. On the other hand, α particles, although not very penetrating, are very effective at causing ionization and produce a dense

Table 21.6 Effects of Short-Term Exposures to Radiation

Dose (rem)	Clinical Effect
0–25	Nondetectable
25–50	Temporary decrease in white blood cell counts
100–200	Strong decrease in white blood cell counts
500	Death of half the exposed population within 30 days after exposure

trail of damage. Thus ingestion of an α-particle producer, such as plutonium, is particularly damaging.

4. *The chemical properties of the radiation source.* When a radioactive nuclide is ingested into the body, its effectiveness in causing damage depends on its residence time. For example, $^{85}_{36}Kr$ and $^{90}_{38}Sr$ are both β-particle producers. However, since krypton is chemically inert, it passes through the body quickly and does not have much time to do damage. Strontium, being chemically similar to calcium, can collect in bones, where it may cause leukemia and bone cancer.

Because of the differences in the behavior of the particles and rays produced by radioactive decay, both the energy dose of the radiation and its effectiveness in causing biologic damage must be taken into account. The **rem** (which is short for *r*oentgen *e*quivalent for *m*an) is defined as follows:

$$\text{Number of rems} = (\text{number of rads}) \times \text{RBE}$$

where RBE represents the relative effectiveness of the radiation in causing biologic damage.

Table 21.6 shows the physical effects of short-term exposure to various doses of radiation, and Table 21.7 gives the sources and amounts of radiation exposure for a typical person in the United States. Note that natural sources contribute about twice as much as human activities to the total exposure. However, although the nuclear industry contributes only a small percentage of the total exposure, the major controversy associated with nuclear power plants is the *potential* for radiation hazards. These arise mainly from two sources: accidents allowing the release of radioactive materials and improper disposal of the radioactive products in spent fuel elements. The radioactive products of the fission of $^{235}_{92}U$, although only a small percentage of the total products, have half-lives of several hundred years and remain dangerous for a long time. Various schemes have been advanced for the disposal of these wastes. The one that seems to hold the most promise is the incorporation of the wastes into ceramic blocks and the burial of these blocks in geologically stable formations. At present, however, no disposal method has been accepted, and nuclear wastes continue to accumulate in temporary storage facilities.

Even if a satisfactory method for permanent disposal of nuclear wastes is found, there will continue to be concern about the effects of exposure to low levels of radiation. Exposure is inevitable from natural sources such as cosmic rays and radioactive minerals, and many people are also exposed to low levels of radiation from reactors, radioactive tracers, or diagnostic X rays. Currently, we have little reliable information on the long-term effects of low-level exposure to radiation.

Table 21.7 Typical Radiation Exposures for a Person Living in the United States (1 millirem = 10^{-3} rem)

	Exposure (millirems/year)
Cosmic radiation	50
From the earth	47
From building materials	3
In human tissues	21
Inhalation of air	5
Total from natural sources	126
X-ray diagnosis	50
Radiotherapy	10
Internal diagnosis/ therapy	1
Nuclear power industry	0.2
TV tubes, industrial wastes, etc.	2
Radioactive fallout	4
Total from human activities	67
Total	193

Disposal of nuclear wastes is discussed in the Chemical Impact on page 1046.

CHEMICAL IMPACT

Nuclear Physics: An Introduction

NUCLEAR PHYSICS IS concerned with the fundamental nature of matter. The central focuses of this area of study are the relationship between a quantity of energy and its mass, given by $E = mc^2$, and the fact that matter can be converted from one form (energy) to another (particulate) in particle accelerators. Collisions between high-speed particles have produced a dazzling array of new particles—hundreds of them. These events can best be interpreted as conversions of kinetic energy into particles. For example, a collision of sufficient energy between a proton and a neutron can produce four particles: two protons, one antiproton, and a neutron:

$$_1^1H + _0^1n \longrightarrow 2\,_1^1H + _{-1}^1H + _0^1n$$

where $_{-1}^1H$ is the symbol for an *antiproton*, which has the same mass as a proton but the opposite charge. This process is a little like throwing one baseball at a very high speed into another and having the energy of the collision converted into two additional baseballs.

The results of such accelerator experiments have led scientists to postulate the existence of three types of forces important in the nucleus: the *strong force*, the *weak force*, and the *electromagnetic force*. Along with the *gravitational force*, these forces are thought to account for all types of interactions found in matter. These forces are believed to be generated by the exchange of particles between the interacting pieces of matter. For example, gravitational forces are thought to be carried by particles called *gravitons*. The electromagnetic force (the classical electrostatic force between charged particles) is assumed to be exerted through the exchange of *photons*. The strong force, not charge-related and effective only at very short distances ($\sim 10^{-13}$ cm), is postulated to involve the exchange of particles called *gluons*. The weak force is 100 times weaker than the strong force and seems to be exerted through the exchange of two types of large particles, the W (has a mass 70 times the proton mass) and the Z (has a mass 90 times the proton mass).

The particles discovered have been classified into several categories. Three of the most important classes are as follows:

1. *Hadrons* are particles that respond to the strong force and have internal structure.

2. *Leptons* are particles that do not respond to the strong force and have no internal structure.

3. *Quarks* are particles with no internal structure that are thought to be the fundamental constituents of hadrons. Neutrons and protons are hadrons that are thought to be composed of three quarks each.

The world of particle physics appears mysterious and complicated. For example, particle physicists have discovered new properties of matter they call "color," "charm," and "strangeness" and have pos-

(left) An aerial view of Fermilab, a high-energy particle accelerator in Batavia, Illinois. (right) The accelerator tunnel at Fermilab.

tulated conservation laws involving these properties. This area of science is extremely important because it should help us to understand the interactions of matter in a more elegant and unified way. For example, the classification of force into four categories is probably necessary only because we do not understand the true nature of forces. All forces may be special cases of a single, all-pervading force field that governs all of nature. In fact, Einstein spent the last 30 years of his life looking for a way to unify the gravitational and electromagnetic forces—without success. Physicists may now be on the verge of accomplishing what Einstein failed to do.

Although the practical aspects of the work in nuclear physics are not yet totally apparent, a more fundamental understanding of the way nature operates could lead to presently undreamed-of devices for energy production and communication, which could revolutionize our lives.

Two models of radiation damage, illustrated in Fig. 21.17, have been proposed: the *linear model* and the *threshold model*. The linear model postulates that damage from radiation is proportional to the dose, even at low levels of exposure. Thus any exposure is dangerous. The threshold model, on the other hand, assumes that no significant damage occurs below a certain exposure, called the *threshold exposure*. Note that if the linear model is correct, radiation exposure should be limited to a bare minimum (ideally at the natural levels). If the threshold model is correct, a certain level of radiation exposure beyond natural levels can be tolerated. Most scientists feel that since there is little evidence available to evaluate these models, it is safest to assume that the linear hypothesis is correct and to minimize radiation exposure.

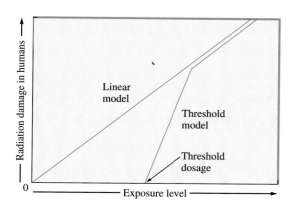

Figure 21.17

The two models for radiation damage. In the linear model, even a small dosage causes a proportional risk. In the threshold model, risk begins only after a certain dosage.

For Review

Summary

The stability of the nucleus, which is composed of neutrons and protons, can be considered from kinetic and thermodynamic points of view. Nuclei that are kinetically unstable decompose into more stable nuclei by radioactive decay, which can involve production of an α particle ($^4_2$He), which changes both A and Z, production of a β particle ($^0_{-1}$e), which increases Z, or production of a positron ($^0_1$e), which decreases Z. High-energy photons called γ rays also can be produced.

A radioactive nuclide may undergo a number of decay events, called a decay series, until a stable nuclide is formed. Radioactive decay follows first-order kinetics. The half-life of a radioactive sample is the time required for the amount of the nuclide to reach half the original amount. The transuranium elements, those coming after uranium in the periodic table, can be synthesized by particle bombardment of uranium or heavier elements.

Radiocarbon dating uses the ratio $^{14}_{6}C/^{12}_{6}C$ to date any object containing carbon from living sources.

The thermodynamic stability of the nucleus involves a comparison of the energy of the nucleus to that of its component nucleons. When a system gains or loses energy, it also gains or loses a quantity of mass, given by the relationship $E = mc^2$. The change in mass, called the mass defect, can be obtained by comparing the nuclear mass to the sum of the masses of the component nucleons and can be used to calculate the energy of formation of a nucleus from its nucleons. The binding energy is the energy required to decompose the nucleus into protons and neutrons.

Nuclear fusion is the process of combining two light nuclei to form a heavier, more stable nucleus. Fission is the splitting of a heavy nucleus into two lighter nuclei. Nuclear reactors now in use employ controlled fission.

Radiation damage can cause either direct damage to living organisms or genetic damage to the organism's offspring. The biologic effects of radiation depend on the energy, the penetrating ability, and the ionizing ability of the radiation, and on the chemical properties of the radiation source.

A blue question or exercise number indicates that the answer to that question or exercise appears at the back of this book and a solution appears in the *Solutions Guide.*

Questions

1. Define *fission* and *fusion.* What types of nuclei are likely to undergo each process?

2. When nuclei undergo nuclear transformations, γ rays of characteristic frequencies are observed. How does this fact, along with other information in the chapter on nuclear stability, suggest that a quantum mechanical model may apply to the nucleus?

3. What assumptions must be made and what problems arise in using carbon-14 dating?

4. How could a radioactive nuclide be used to demonstrate that chemical equilibrium is a dynamic process?

5. There is a trend in the United States toward using coal-fired power plants to generate electricity rather than building new nuclear fission power plants. Is the use of coal-fired power plants without risk? Make a list of the risks to society from the use of each type of power plant.

6. Fusion processes are more likely to occur for lighter elements, while fission processes are more likely to occur for heavier elements. Explain.

7. Why are elevated temperatures necessary to initiate fusion reactions but not fission reactions?

8. What are the purposes of the moderator and of the control rods in a fission reactor?

Exercises

In this section similar exercises are paired.

Radioactive Decay and Nuclear Transformations

9. Write balanced equations for each of the processes described below.
   a. Chromium-51, which targets the spleen and is used as a tracer in studies of red blood cells, decays by electron capture.
   b. Iodine-131, used to treat hyperactive thyroid glands, decays by producing a β particle.

10. Write balanced equations for each of the processes described below.
   a. Phosphorus-32, which accumulates in the liver, decays by β-particle production.
   b. Uranium-235, which is used in atomic bombs, decays initially by α-particle production.

11. Write an equation describing the radioactive decay of each of the following nuclides. (The particle produced is shown in

parentheses, except for electron capture, where an electron is a reactant.)

a. ^{68}Ga (electron capture) **c.** ^{212}Fr (α)
b. ^{62}Cu (positron) **d.** ^{129}Sb (β)

12. In each of the following nuclear reactions, supply the missing particle.

a. ^{73}Ga $\rightarrow$ ^{73}Ge + ? **c.** ^{205}Bi $\rightarrow$ ^{205}Pb + ?
b. ^{192}Pt $\rightarrow$ ^{188}Os + ? **d.** ^{241}Cm + ? $\rightarrow$ ^{241}Am

13. The radioactive isotope ^{242}Cm decays by a series of α-particle and β-particle productions, taking ^{242}Cm through many transformations to end up as ^{206}Pb. In the complete decay series, how many α particles and β particles are produced?

14. One type of commercial smoke detector contains a minute amount of radioactive americium-241 (^{241}Am), which decays by α-particle production. The α particles ionize molecules in the air, allowing it to conduct an electric current. When smoke particles enter, the conductivity of the air is changed and the alarm buzzes.

a. Write the equation for the decay of $^{241}_{95}$Am by α-particle production.
b. The complete decay of ^{241}Am involves successively α, α, β, α, α, β, α, α, α, β, α, and β production. What is the final stable nucleus produced in this decay series?
c. Identify the 11 intermediate nuclides.

15. There are four stable isotopes of iron with mass numbers 54, 56, 57, and 58. There are also two radioactive isotopes: iron-53 and iron-59. Predict modes of decay for these two isotopes. (See Table 21.2.)

16. The only stable isotope of fluorine is fluorine-19. Predict possible modes of decay for fluorine-21, fluorine-18, and fluorine-17.

17. In 1994 it was proposed that element 106 be named seaborgium, Sg, in honor of Glenn T. Seaborg, discoverer of the transuranium elements.

a. ^{263}Sg was produced by the bombardment of ^{249}Cf with a beam of ^{18}O nuclei. Complete and balance an equation for this reaction.
b. ^{263}Sg decays by α emission. What is the other product resulting from the α decay of ^{263}Sg?

18. Many elements have been synthesized by bombarding relatively heavy atoms with high-energy particles in particle accelerators. Complete the following nuclear reactions, which have been used to synthesize elements.

a. _____ + $^4_2$He $\rightarrow$ $^{243}_{97}$Bk + $^1_0$n
b. $^{238}_{92}$U + $^{12}_6$C $\rightarrow$ _____ + 6 $^1_0$n
c. $^{249}_{98}$Cf + _____ $\rightarrow$ $^{260}_{105}$Db + 4 $^1_0$n
d. $^{249}_{98}$Cf + $^{10}_5$B $\rightarrow$ $^{257}_{103}$Lr + _____

Kinetics of Radioactive Decay

19. The rate constant for a certain radioactive nuclide is 1.0×10^{-3} h^{-1}. What is the half-life of this nuclide?

20. Determine the rate of decay (in decay events per second) from 1.00 mol of radioactive nuclides with each of the following half-lives: 12,000 years, 12 h, 12 s.

21. Cobalt-60 is commonly used as a source of β particles. How long does it take for 87.5% of a sample of cobalt-60 to decay (the half-life is 5.26 years)?

22. Radioactive copper-64 decays with a half-life of 12.8 days.

a. What is the value of k in s^{-1}?
b. A sample contains 28.0 mg ^{64}Cu. How many decay events will be produced in the first second? Assume the atomic mass of ^{64}Cu is 64.0.
c. A chemist obtains a fresh sample of ^{64}Cu and measures its radioactivity. She then determines that to do an experiment, the radioactivity cannot fall below 25% of the initial measured value. How long does she have to do the experiment?

23. Phosphorus-32 is a commonly used radioactive nuclide in biochemical research, particularly in studies of nucleic acids. The half-life of phosphorus-32 is 14.3 days. What mass of phosphorus-32 is left from an original sample of 175 mg of Na$_3{}^{32}$PO$_4$ after 35.0 days? Assume the atomic mass of ^{32}P is 32.0.

24. The curie (Ci) is a commonly used unit for measuring nuclear radioactivity: 1 curie of radiation is equal to 3.7×10^{10} decay events per second (the number of decay events from 1 g of radium in 1 s).

a. What mass of Na$_2{}^{38}$SO$_4$ has an activity of 10.0 mCi? Sulfur-38 has an atomic mass of 38.0 and a half-life of 2.87 h.
b. How long does it take for 99.99% of a sample of sulfur-38 to decay?

25. The first atomic explosion was detonated in the desert north of Alamogordo, New Mexico, on July 16, 1945. What fraction of the strontium-90 ($t_{1/2} = 28.8$ years) originally produced by that explosion still remains as of July 16, 2000?

26. Iodine-131 is used in the diagnosis and treatment of thyroid disease and has a half-life of 8.1 days. If a patient with thyroid disease consumes a sample of Na^{131}I containing 10 μg of ^{131}I, how long will it take for the amount of ^{131}I to decrease to 1/100 of the original amount?

27. A living plant contains approximately the same fraction of carbon-14 as in atmospheric carbon dioxide. Assuming that the observed rate of decay of carbon-14 from a living plant is 13.6 counts per minute per gram of carbon, how many counts per minute per gram of carbon will be measured from a 15,000-year-old sample? Will radiocarbon dating work well for small samples of 10 mg or less? (For ^{14}C, $t_{1/2} = 5730$ years.)

28. At a flea market, you've found a very interesting painting done in the style of Rembrandt's "dark period" (1642–1672). You suspect that you really do not have a genuine Rembrandt, but you take it to the local university for testing. Living wood shows a carbon-14 activity of 15.3 counts per minute per gram. Your painting showed a carbon-14 activity of 15.1 counts per minute per gram. Could it be a genuine Rembrandt?

29. A rock contains 0.688 mg of ^{206}Pb for every 1.000 mg of ^{238}U present. Assuming that no lead was originally present, that all the ^{206}Pb formed over the years has remained in the rock, and that the number of nuclides in intermediate stages of decay between ^{238}U and ^{206}Pb is negligible, calculate the age of the rock. (For ^{238}U, $t_{1/2} = 4.5 \times 10^9$ years.)

30. The mass ratios of ^{40}Ar to ^{40}K also can be used to date geologic materials. Potassium-40 decays by two processes:

$$^{40}_{19}\text{K} + ^{0}_{-1}\text{e} \longrightarrow ^{40}_{18}\text{Ar} \quad (10.7\%) \qquad t_{1/2} = 1.27 \times 10^9 \text{ years}$$

$$^{40}_{19}\text{K} \longrightarrow ^{40}_{20}\text{Ca} + ^{0}_{-1}\text{e} \quad (89.3\%)$$

a. Why are ^{40}Ar/^{40}K ratios used to date materials rather than ^{40}Ca/^{40}K ratios?

b. What assumptions must be made using this technique?

c. A sedimentary rock has a ^{40}Ar/^{40}K ratio of 0.95. Calculate the age of the rock.

d. How will the measured age of a rock compare to the actual age if some ^{40}Ar escaped from the sample?

Energy Changes in Nuclear Reactions

31. The sun radiates 3.9×10^{23} J of energy into space every second. What is the rate at which mass is lost from the sun?

32. The earth receives 1.8×10^{14} kJ/s of solar energy. What mass of solar material is converted to energy over a 24-h period to provide the daily amount of solar energy to the earth? What mass of coal would have to be burned to provide the same amount of energy? (Coal releases 32 kJ of energy per gram when burned.)

33. Many transuranium elements, such as plutonium-232, have very short half-lives. (For ^{232}Pu, the half-life is 36 minutes.) However, some, like protactinium-231 (half-life $= 3.34 \times 10^4$ years), have relatively long half-lives. Use the masses given below to calculate the change in energy when one mol of ^{232}Pu nuclei and one mol of ^{231}Pa nuclei are each formed from their respective number of protons and neutrons.

Atom or Particle	Atomic Mass
Neutron	1.67493×10^{-24} g
Proton	1.67262×10^{-24} g
Electron	9.10939×10^{-28} g
Pu-232	3.85285×10^{-22} g
Pa-231	3.83616×10^{-22} g

(Since the masses of ^{232}Pu and ^{231}Pa are atomic masses, they each include the mass of the electrons present. The mass of the nucleus will be the atomic mass minus the mass of the electrons.)

34. The atomic mass of zinc-66 is 65.9260. What is the mass of the zinc-66 nucleus? Calculate the total binding energy per mole of zinc-66.

35. Calculate the binding energy in J/nucleon for carbon-12 (atomic mass 12.0000) and uranium-235 (atomic mass 235.0439). The atomic mass of $^{1}_{1}$H is 1.00782 amu and the mass of a neutron is 1.00866 amu. The most stable nucleus known is ^{56}Fe. Would the binding energy per nucleon for ^{56}Fe be larger or smaller than that of ^{12}C or ^{235}U? Explain.

36. Calculate the binding energy per nucleon for $^{2}_{1}$H and $^{3}_{1}$H. The atomic masses are $^{2}_{1}$H, 2.01410, and $^{3}_{1}$H, 3.01605.

37. Calculate the amount of energy released per gram of hydrogen nuclei reacted for the following reaction. The atomic masses are $^{1}_{1}$H, 1.00782 amu, $^{2}_{1}$H, 2.01410 amu, and an electron, 5.4858×10^{-4} amu. (*Hint:* Think carefully about how to account for the electron mass.)

$$^{1}_{1}\text{H} + ^{1}_{1}\text{H} \longrightarrow ^{2}_{1}\text{H} + ^{0}_{+1}\text{e}$$

38. The easiest fusion reaction to initiate is

$$^{2}_{1}\text{H} + ^{3}_{1}\text{H} \longrightarrow ^{4}_{2}\text{He} + ^{1}_{0}\text{n}$$

Calculate the energy released per $^{4}_{2}$He nucleus produced and per mole of $^{4}_{2}$He produced. The atomic masses are $^{2}_{1}$H, 2.01410, $^{3}_{1}$H, 3.01605, and $^{4}_{2}$He, 4.00260. The masses of the electron and neutron are 5.4858×10^{-4} and 1.00866 amu, respectively.

Detection, Uses, and Health Effects of Radiation

39. The typical response of a Geiger–Müller tube is shown below. Explain the shape of this curve.

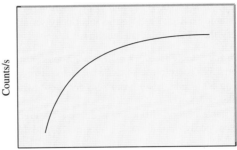

Disintegrations/s from sample

40. When using a Geiger–Müller counter to measure radioactivity, it is necessary to maintain the same geometrical orientation between the sample and the Geiger–Müller tube in order to compare different measurements. Why?

41. Photosynthesis in plants can be represented by the following overall reaction:

$$6\text{CO}_2(g) + 6\text{H}_2\text{O}(l) \xrightarrow{\text{Light}} \text{C}_6\text{H}_{12}\text{O}_6(s) + 6\text{O}_2(g)$$

Algae grown in water containing some ^{18}O (in H$_2$^{18}O) evolve oxygen gas with the same isotopic composition as the oxygen in the water. When algae growing in water containing only ^{16}O were furnished carbon dioxide containing ^{18}O, no ^{18}O was found to be evolved from the oxygen gas produced. What conclusions about photosynthesis can be drawn from these experiments?

42. Consider the following reaction to produce methyl acetate:

$$\text{CH}_3\text{OH} + \text{CH}_3\overset{\overset{\text{O}}{\|}}{\text{C}}\text{OH} \longrightarrow \text{CH}_3\overset{\overset{\text{O}}{\|}}{\text{C}}\text{OCH}_3 + \text{H}_2\text{O}$$

Methyl acetate

When this reaction is carried out with CH_3OH containing oxygen-18, the water produced does not contain oxygen-18. Explain.

43. Which do you think would be the greater health hazard: the release of a radioactive nuclide of Sr or a radioactive nuclide of Xe into the environment? Assume the amount of radioactivity is the same in each case. Explain your answer on the basis of the chemical properties of Sr and Xe. Why are the chemical properties of a radioactive substance important in assessing its potential health hazards?

44. Consider the following information:
  i. The layer of dead skin on our bodies is sufficient to protect us from most α-particle radiation.
  ii. Plutonium is an α-particle producer.
  iii. The chemistry of Pu^{4+} is similar to that of Fe^{3+}.
  iv. Pu oxidizes readily to Pu^{4+}.
  Why is plutonium one of the most toxic substances known?

Additional Exercises

45. Predict whether each of the following nuclides are stable or unstable (radioactive). If the nuclide is unstable, predict the type of radioactivity you would expect it to exhibit.
  a. $^{45}_{19}K$ **b.** $^{56}_{26}Fe$ **c.** $^{20}_{11}Na$ **d.** $^{194}_{81}Tl$

46. A proposed system for storing nuclear wastes involves storing the radioactive material in caves or deep mine shafts. One of the most toxic nuclides that must be disposed of is plutonium-239, which is produced in breeder reactors and has a half-life of 24,100 years. A suitable storage place must be geologically stable long enough for the activity of plutonium-239 to decrease to 0.1% of its original value. How long is this for plutonium-239?

47. The tritium (^3H) activity in rainwater is 5.5 counts per minute per 100. g of water. If you own a 40.-year-old bottle of wine, what approximate tritium activity would be expected in 100. g of that wine? (The half-life of ^3H is 12.3 years.)

48. A positron and an electron can annihilate each other on colliding, producing energy as photons:

$$^{0}_{-1}e + {}^{0}_{+1}e \longrightarrow 2\,^{0}_{0}\gamma$$

Assuming that both γ rays have the same energy, calculate the wavelength of the electromagnetic radiation produced.

49. A small atomic bomb releases energy equivalent to the detonation of 20,000 tons of TNT; a ton of TNT releases 4×10^9 J of energy when exploded. Using 2×10^{13} J/mol as the energy released by fission of ^{235}U, approximately what mass of ^{235}U undergoes fission in this atomic bomb?

Challenge Problems

50. Many metals become brittle when subjected to intense radiation from radioactive materials. Explain this observation. How might this fact affect the design of nuclear reactors?

51. A 0.10-cm^3 sample of a solution containing a radioactive nuclide (5.0×10^3 counts per minute per milliliter) is injected into a rat. Several minutes later 1.0 cm^3 of blood is removed. The blood shows 48 counts per minute of radioactivity. Calculate the volume of blood in the rat. What assumptions must be made in performing this calculation?

52. Zirconium is one of the few metals that retains its structural integrity upon exposure to radiation. The fuel rods in most nuclear reactors therefore are often made of zirconium. Answer the following questions about the redox properties of zirconium based on the half-reaction

$$ZrO_2 \cdot H_2O + H_2O + 4e^- \longrightarrow Zr + 4OH^-$$
$$\mathscr{E}° = -2.36\text{ V}$$

  a. Is zirconium metal capable of reducing water to form hydrogen gas at standard conditions?
  b. Write a balanced equation for the reduction of water by zirconium.
  c. Calculate $\mathscr{E}°$, $\Delta G°$, and K for the reduction of water by zirconium metal.
  d. The reduction of water by zirconium occurred during the accidents at Three Mile Island in 1979. The hydrogen produced was successfully vented and no chemical explosion occurred. If 1.00×10^3 kg of Zr reacts, what mass of H_2 is produced? What volume of H_2 at 1.0 atm and 1000.°C is produced?
  e. At Chernobyl in 1986, hydrogen was produced by the reaction of superheated steam with the graphite reactor core:

$$C(s) + H_2O(g) \longrightarrow CO(g) + H_2(g)$$

  It was not possible to prevent a chemical explosion at Chernobyl. In light of this, do you think it was a correct decision to vent the hydrogen and other radioactive gases into the atmosphere at Three Mile Island? Explain.

53. In addition to the process described in the text, a second process called the *carbon–nitrogen cycle* occurs in the sun:

$$^{1}_{1}H + {}^{12}_{6}C \longrightarrow {}^{13}_{7}N + {}^{0}_{0}\gamma$$
$$^{13}_{7}N \longrightarrow {}^{13}_{6}C + {}^{0}_{+1}e$$
$$^{1}_{1}H + {}^{13}_{6}C \longrightarrow {}^{14}_{7}N + {}^{0}_{0}\gamma$$
$$^{1}_{1}H + {}^{14}_{7}N \longrightarrow {}^{15}_{8}O + {}^{0}_{0}\gamma$$
$$^{15}_{8}O \longrightarrow {}^{15}_{7}N + {}^{0}_{+1}e$$
$$^{1}_{1}H + {}^{15}_{7}N \longrightarrow {}^{12}_{6}C + {}^{4}_{2}He + {}^{0}_{0}\gamma$$

Overall reaction: $4\,^{1}_{1}H \longrightarrow {}^{4}_{2}He + 2\,^{0}_{+1}e$

  a. What is the catalyst in this process?
  b. What nucleons are intermediates?
  c. How much energy is released per mole of hydrogen nuclei in the overall reaction? (The atomic masses of $^{1}_{1}H$ and $^{4}_{2}He$ are 1.00782 and 4.00260, respectively.)

Appendixes

Appendix One Mathematical Procedures

A1.1 Exponential Notation

The numbers characteristic of scientific measurements are often very large or very small; thus it is convenient to express them using powers of 10. For example, the number 1,300,000 can be expressed as 1.3×10^6, which means multiply 1.3 by 10 six times, or

$$1.3 \times 10^6 = 1.3 \times \underbrace{10 \times 10 \times 10 \times 10 \times 10 \times 10}_{10^6 = 1 \text{ million}}$$

Note that each multiplication by 10 moves the decimal point one place to the right:

$$1.3 \times 10 = 13.$$
$$13 \times 10 = 130.$$
$$130 \times 10 = 1300.$$

Thus the easiest way to interpret the notation 1.3×10^6 is that it means move the decimal point in 1.3 to the right six times:

$$1.3 \times 10^6 = 1\underbrace{3\,0\,0\,0\,0\,0}_{1\ 2\ 3\ 4\ 5\ 6} = 1,300,000$$

Using this notation, the number 1985 can be expressed as 1.985×10^3. Note that the usual convention is to write the number that appears before the power of 10 as a number between 1 and 10. To end up with the number 1.985, which is between 1 and 10, we had to move the decimal point three places to the left. To compensate for that, we must multiply by 10^3, which says that to get the intended number we start with 1.985 and move the decimal point three places to the right; that is:

$$1.985 \times 10^3 = 1\underbrace{9\,8\,5}_{1\ 2\ 3}$$

Some other examples are given below.

Number	Exponential Notation
5.6	5.6×10^0 or 5.6×1
39	3.9×10^1
943	9.43×10^2
1126	1.126×10^3

So far we have considered numbers greater than 1. How do we represent a number such as 0.0034 in exponential notation? We start with a number between 1 and 10 and *divide* by the appropriate power of 10:

$$0.0034 = \frac{3.4}{10 \times 10 \times 10} = \frac{3.4}{10^3} = 3.4 \times 10^{-3}$$

Division by 10 moves the decimal point one place to the *left*. Thus the number

$$0.\underset{7\ 6\ 5\ 4\ 3\ 2\ 1}{0\ 0\ 0\ 0\ 0\ 1}\ 4$$

can be written as 1.4×10^{-7}.

To summarize, we can write any number in the form

$$N \times 10^{\pm n}$$

where N is between 1 and 10 and the exponent n is an integer. If the sign preceding n is positive, it means the decimal point in N should be moved n places to the right. If a negative sign precedes n, the decimal point in N should be moved n places to the left.

Multiplication and Division

When two numbers expressed in exponential notation are multiplied, the initial numbers are multiplied and the exponents of 10 are added:

$$(M \times 10^m)(N \times 10^n) = (MN) \times 10^{m+n}$$

For example (to two significant figures, as required),

$$(3.2 \times 10^4)(2.8 \times 10^3) = 9.0 \times 10^7$$

When the numbers are multiplied, if a result greater than 10 is obtained for the initial number, the decimal point is moved one place to the left and the exponent of 10 is increased by 1:

$$(5.8 \times 10^2)(4.3 \times 10^8) = 24.9 \times 10^{10}$$
$$= 2.49 \times 10^{11}$$
$$= 2.5 \ \times 10^{11} \qquad \text{(two significant figures)}$$

Division of two numbers expressed in exponential notation involves normal division of the initial numbers and *subtraction* of the exponent of the divisor from that of the dividend. For example,

$$\frac{4.8 \times 10^8}{\underbrace{2.1 \times 10^3}_{\text{Divisor}}} = \frac{4.8}{2.1} \times 10^{(8-3)} = 2.3 \times 10^5$$

If the initial number resulting from the division is less than 1, the decimal point is moved one place to the right and the exponent of 10 is decreased by 1. For example,

$$\frac{6.4 \times 10^3}{8.3 \times 10^5} = \frac{6.4}{8.3} \times 10^{(3-5)} = 0.77 \times 10^{-2}$$
$$= 7.7 \times 10^{-3}$$

Addition and Subtraction

To add or subtract numbers expressed in exponential notation, *the exponents of the numbers must be the same.* For example, to add 1.31×10^5 and 4.2×10^4, we must rewrite one number so that the exponents of both are the same. The number 1.31×10^5 can be written 13.1×10^4, since moving the decimal point one place to the right can be compensated for by decreasing the exponent by 1. Now we can add the numbers:

$$\begin{array}{r} 13.1 \times 10^4 \\ + \ 4.2 \times 10^4 \\ \hline 17.3 \times 10^4 \end{array}$$

In correct exponential notation the result is expressed as 1.73×10^5.

To perform addition or subtraction with numbers expressed in exponential notation, only the initial numbers are added or subtracted. The exponent of the result is the same as those of the numbers being added or subtracted. To subtract 1.8×10^2 from 8.99×10^3, we write

$$\begin{array}{r} 8.99 \times 10^3 \\ - \ 0.18 \times 10^3 \\ \hline 8.81 \times 10^3 \end{array}$$

Powers and Roots

When a number expressed in exponential notation is taken to some power, the initial number is taken to the appropriate power and the exponent of 10 is multiplied by that power:

$$(N \times 10^n)^m = N^m \times 10^{m \cdot n}$$

For example,[*]

$$\begin{aligned}
(7.5 \times 10^2)^3 &= 7.5^3 \times 10^{3 \cdot 2} \\
&= 422 \times 10^6 \\
&= 4.22 \times 10^8 \\
&= 4.2 \ \times 10^8 \qquad \text{(two significant figures)}
\end{aligned}$$

When a root is taken of a number expressed in exponential notation, the root of the initial number is taken and the exponent of 10 is divided by the number representing the root:

$$\sqrt{N \times 10^n} = (N \times 10^n)^{1/2} = \sqrt{N} \times 10^{n/2}$$

For example, $$(2.9 \times 10^6)^{1/2} = \sqrt{2.9} \times 10^{6/2}$$
$$= 1.7 \times 10^3$$

Because the exponent of the result must be an integer, we may sometimes have to change the form of the number so that the power divided by the root equals an integer, for example:

$$\begin{aligned}
\sqrt{1.9 \times 10^3} = (1.9 \times 10^3)^{1/2} &= (0.19 \times 10^4)^{1/2} \\
&= \sqrt{0.19} \times 10^2 \\
&= 0.44 \times 10^2 \\
&= 4.4 \times 10^1
\end{aligned}$$

[*]Refer to the instruction booklet for your calculator for directions concerning how to take roots and powers of numbers.

In this case, we moved the decimal point one place to the left and increased the exponent from 3 to 4 to make $n/2$ an integer.

The same procedure is followed for roots other than square roots, for example:

$$\sqrt[3]{6.9 \times 10^5} = (6.9 \times 10^5)^{1/3} = (0.69 \times 10^6)^{1/3}$$
$$= \sqrt[3]{0.69} \times 10^2$$
$$= 0.88 \times 10^2$$
$$= 8.8 \times 10^1$$

and

$$\sqrt[3]{4.6 \times 10^{10}} = (4.6 \times 10^{10})^{1/3} = (46 \times 10^9)^{1/3}$$
$$= \sqrt[3]{46} \times 10^3$$
$$= 3.6 \times 10^3$$

A1.2 Logarithms

A logarithm is an exponent. Any number N can be expressed as follows:

$$N = 10^x$$

For example,

$$1000 = 10^3$$
$$100 = 10^2$$
$$10 = 10^1$$
$$1 = 10^0$$

The common, or base 10, logarithm of a number is the power to which 10 must be taken to yield the number. Thus, since $1000 = 10^3$,

$$\log 1000 = 3$$

Similarly,

$$\log 100 = 2$$
$$\log 10 = 1$$
$$\log 1 = 0$$

For a number between 10 and 100, the required exponent of 10 will be between 1 and 2. For example, $65 = 10^{1.8129}$; that is, $\log 65 = 1.8129$. For a number between 100 and 1000, the exponent of 10 will be between 2 and 3. For example, $650 = 10^{2.8129}$ and $\log 650 = 2.8129$.

A number N greater than 0 and less than 1 can be expressed as follows:

$$N = 10^{-x} = \frac{1}{10^x}$$

For example,

$$0.001 = \frac{1}{1000} = \frac{1}{10^3} = 10^{-3}$$

$$0.01 = \frac{1}{100} = \frac{1}{10^2} = 10^{-2}$$

$$0.1 = \frac{1}{10} = \frac{1}{10^1} = 10^{-1}$$

Thus

$$\log 0.001 = -3$$
$$\log 0.01 = -2$$
$$\log 0.1 = -1$$

Although common logs are often tabulated, the most convenient method for obtaining such logs is to use an electronic calculator. On most calculators the number is first entered and then the log key is punched. The log of the number then appears in the display.* Some examples are given below. You should reproduce these results on your calculator in order to be sure that you can find common logs correctly.

Number	Common Log
36	1.56
1849	3.2669
0.156	−0.807
1.68×10^{-5}	−4.775

Note that the number of digits after the decimal point in a common log is equal to the number of significant figures in the original number.

Since logs are simply exponents, they are manipulated according to the rules for exponents. For example, if $A = 10^x$ and $B = 10^y$, then their product is

$$A \cdot B = 10^x \cdot 10^y = 10^{x+y}$$

and

$$\log AB = x + y = \log A + \log B$$

For division, we have

$$\frac{A}{B} = \frac{10^x}{10^y} = 10^{x-y}$$

and

$$\log \frac{A}{B} = x - y = \log A - \log B$$

For a number raised to a power, we have

$$A^n = (10^x)^n = 10^{nx}$$

and

$$\log A^n = nx = n \log A$$

It follows that

$$\log \frac{1}{A^n} = \log A^{-n} = -n \log A$$

or, for $n = 1$,

$$\log \frac{1}{A} = -\log A$$

When a common log is given, to find the number it represents, we must carry out the process of exponentiation. For example, if the log is 2.673, then $N = 10^{2.673}$. The process of exponentiation is also called taking the antilog, or the inverse logarithm. This operation is usually carried out on calculators in one of two ways. The majority of calculators require that the log be entered first and then the keys $\boxed{\text{INV}}$ and $\boxed{\text{LOG}}$ pressed in succession. For example, to find $N = 10^{2.673}$ we enter 2.673 and then press $\boxed{\text{INV}}$ and $\boxed{\text{LOG}}$. The number 471 will be displayed; that is, $N = 471$.

*Refer to the instruction booklet for your calculator for the exact sequence to obtain logarithms.

Some calculators have a $\boxed{10^x}$ key. In that case, the log is entered first and then the $\boxed{10^x}$ key is pressed. Again, the number 471 will be displayed.

Natural logarithms, another type of logarithm, are based on the number 2.7183, which is referred to as e. In this case, a number is represented as $N = e^x = 2.7183^x$. For example:

$$N = 7.15 = e^x$$

$$\ln 7.15 = x = 1.967$$

To find the natural log of a number using a calculator, the number is entered and then the $\boxed{\ln}$ key is pressed. Use the following examples to check your technique for finding natural logs with your calculator:

Number (e^x)	Natural Log(x)
784	6.664
1.61×10^3	7.384
1.00×10^{-7}	-16.118
1.00	0

If a natural logarithm is given, to find the number it represents, exponentiation to the base e(2.7183) must be carried out. With many calculators this is done using a key marked $\boxed{e^x}$ (the natural log is entered, with the correct sign, and then the $\boxed{e^x}$ key is pressed). The other common method for exponentiation to base e is to enter the natural log and then press the $\boxed{\text{INV}}$ and $\boxed{\ln}$ keys in succession. The following examples will help you check your technique.

$\ln N(x)$	$N(e^x)$
3.256	25.9
-5.169	5.69×10^{-3}
13.112	4.95×10^5

Since natural logarithms are simply exponents, they are also manipulated according to the mathematical rules for exponents given above for common logs.

A1.3 Graphing Functions

In interpreting the results of a scientific experiment, it is often useful to make a graph. If possible, the function to be graphed should be in a form that gives a straight line. The equation for a straight line (a *linear equation*) can be represented by the general form

$$y = mx + b$$

where y is the *dependent variable*, x is the *independent variable*, m is the *slope*, and b is the *intercept* with the y axis.

To illustrate the characteristics of a linear equation, the function $y = 3x + 4$ is plotted in Fig. A.1. For this equation $m = 3$ and $b = 4$. Note that the y intercept occurs when $x = 0$. In this case the intercept is 4, as can be seen from the equation ($b = 4$).

The slope of a straight line is defined as the ratio of the rate of change in y to that in x:

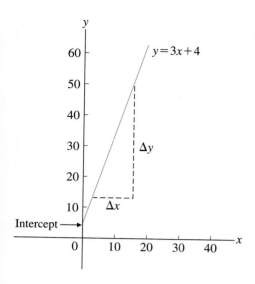

Figure A.1
Graph of the linear equation
$y = 3x + 4$.

$$m = \text{slope} = \frac{\Delta y}{\Delta x}$$

For the equation $y = 3x + 4$, y changes three times as fast as x (since x has a coefficient of 3). Thus the slope in this case is 3. This can be verified from the graph. For the triangle shown in Fig. A.1,

$$\Delta y = 34 - 10 = 24 \quad \text{and} \quad \Delta x = 10 - 2 = 8$$

Thus

$$\text{Slope} = \frac{\Delta y}{\Delta x} = \frac{24}{8} = 3$$

The preceding example illustrates a general method for obtaining the slope of a line from the graph of that line. Simply draw a triangle with one side parallel to the y axis and the other parallel to the x axis as shown in Fig. A.1. Then determine the lengths of the sides to give Δy and Δx, respectively, and compute the ratio $\Delta y / \Delta x$.

Sometimes an equation that is not in standard form can be changed to the form $y = mx + b$ by rearrangement or mathematical manipulation. An example is the equation $k = Ae^{-E_a/RT}$ described in Section 12.7, where A, E_a, and R are constants; k is the dependent variable; and $1/T$ is the independent variable. This equation can be changed to standard form by taking the natural logarithm of both sides,

$$\ln k = \ln Ae^{-E_a/RT} = \ln A + \ln e^{-E_a/RT} = \ln A - \frac{E_a}{RT}$$

noting that the log of a product is equal to the sum of the logs of the individual terms and that the natural log of $e^{-E_a/RT}$ is simply the exponent $-E_a/RT$. Thus, in standard form, the equation $k = Ae^{-E_a/RT}$ is written

$$\underset{y}{\ln k} = \underset{m}{-\frac{E_a}{R}} \underset{x}{\left(\frac{1}{T}\right)} + \underset{b}{\ln A}$$

A plot of $\ln k$ versus $1/T$ (see Fig. A.2) gives a straight line with slope $-E_a/R$ and intercept $\ln A$.

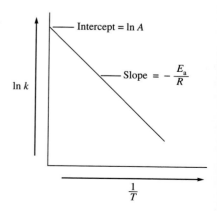

Figure A.2
Graph of $\ln k$ versus $1/T$.

Table A.1 Some Useful Linear Equations in Standard Form

Equation $(y = mx + b)$	What Is Plotted $(y$ vs. $x)$	Slope (m)	Intercept (b)	Section in Text
$[A] = -kt + [A]_0$	$[A]$ vs. t	$-k$	$[A]_0$	12.4
$\ln[A] = -kt + \ln[A]_0$	$\ln[A]$ vs. t	$-k$	$\ln[A]_0$	12.4
$\dfrac{1}{[A]} = kt + \dfrac{1}{[A]_0}$	$\dfrac{1}{[A]}$ vs. t	k	$\dfrac{1}{[A]_0}$	12.4
$\ln P_{vap} = -\dfrac{\Delta H_{vap}}{R}\left(\dfrac{1}{T}\right) + C$	$\ln P_{vap}$ vs. $\dfrac{1}{T}$	$-\dfrac{\Delta H_{vap}}{R}$	C	10.8

Other linear equations that are useful in the study of chemistry are listed in standard form in Table A.1.

A1.4 Solving Quadratic Equations

A *quadratic equation,* a polynomial in which the highest power of x is 2, can be written as

$$ax^2 + bx + c = 0$$

One method for finding the two values of x that satisfy a quadratic equation is to use the *quadratic formula:*

$$x = \frac{-b \pm \sqrt{b^2 - 4ac}}{2a}$$

where a, b, and c are the coefficients of x^2 and x and the constant, respectively. For example, in determining $[H^+]$ in a solution of 1.0×10^{-4} M acetic acid the following expression arises:

$$1.8 \times 10^{-5} = \frac{x^2}{1.0 \times 10^{-4} - x}$$

which yields

$$x^2 + (1.8 \times 10^{-5})x - 1.8 \times 10^{-9} = 0$$

where $a = 1$, $b = 1.8 \times 10^{-5}$, and $c = -1.8 \times 10^{-9}$. Using the quadratic formula, we have

$$x = \frac{-b \pm \sqrt{b^2 - 4ac}}{2a}$$

$$= \frac{-1.8 \times 10^{-5} \pm \sqrt{3.24 \times 10^{-10} - (4)(1)(-1.8 \times 10^{-9})}}{2(1)}$$

$$= \frac{-1.8 \times 10^{-5} \pm \sqrt{3.24 \times 10^{-10} + 7.2 \times 10^{-9}}}{2}$$

$$= \frac{-1.8 \times 10^{-5} \pm \sqrt{7.5 \times 10^{-9}}}{2}$$

$$= \frac{-1.8 \times 10^{-5} \pm 8.7 \times 10^{-5}}{2}$$

Thus
$$x = \frac{6.9 \times 10^{-5}}{2} = 3.5 \times 10^{-5}$$

and
$$x = \frac{-10.5 \times 10^{-5}}{2} = -5.2 \times 10^{-5}$$

Note that there are two roots, as there always will be, for a polynomial in x^2. In this case x represents a concentration of H^+ (see Section 14.3). Thus the positive root is the one that solves the problem, since a concentration cannot be a negative number.

A second method for solving quadratic equations is by *successive approximations,* a systematic method of trial and error. A value of x is guessed and substituted into the equation everywhere x (or x^2) appears, except for one place. For example, for the equation

$$x^2 + (1.8 \times 10^{-5})x - 1.8 \times 10^{-9} = 0$$

we might guess $x = 2 \times 10^{-5}$. Substituting that value into the equation gives

$$x^2 + (1.8 \times 10^{-5})(2 \times 10^{-5}) - 1.8 \times 10^{-9} = 0$$

or
$$x^2 = 1.8 \times 10^{-9} - 3.6 \times 10^{-10} = 1.4 \times 10^{-9}$$

Thus
$$x = 3.7 \times 10^{-5}$$

Note that the guessed value of $x(2 \times 10^{-5})$ is not the same as the value of x that is calculated (3.7×10^{-5}) after inserting the estimated value. This means that $x = 2 \times 10^{-5}$ is not the correct solution, and we must try another guess. We take the calculated value (3.7×10^{-5}) as our next guess:

$$x^2 + (1.8 \times 10^{-5})(3.7 \times 10^{-5}) - 1.8 \times 10^{-9} = 0$$
$$x^2 = 1.8 \times 10^{-9} - 6.7 \times 10^{-10} = 1.1 \times 10^{-9}$$

Thus
$$x = 3.3 \times 10^{-5}$$

Now we compare the two values of x again:

$$\text{Guessed:} \quad x = 3.7 \times 10^{-5}$$
$$\text{Calculated:} \quad x = 3.3 \times 10^{-5}$$

These values are closer but not close enough. Next we try 3.3×10^{-5} as our guess:

$$x^2 + (1.8 \times 10^{-5})(3.3 \times 10^{-5}) - 1.8 \times 10^{-9} = 0$$
$$x^2 = 1.8 \times 10^{-9} - 5.9 \times 10^{-10} = 1.2 \times 10^{-9}$$

Thus
$$x = 3.5 \times 10^{-5}$$

Again we compare:

$$\text{Guessed:} \quad x = 3.3 \times 10^{-5}$$
$$\text{Calculated:} \quad x = 3.5 \times 10^{-5}$$

Next we guess $x = 3.5 \times 10^{-5}$ to give

$$x^2 + (1.8 \times 10^{-5})(3.5 \times 10^{-5}) - 1.8 \times 10^{-9} = 0$$
$$x^2 = 1.8 \times 10^{-9} - 6.3 \times 10^{-10} = 1.2 \times 10^{-9}$$

Thus
$$x = 3.5 \times 10^{-5}$$

Now the guessed value and the calculated value are the same; we have found the correct solution. Note that this agrees with one of the roots found with the quadratic formula in the first method above.

To further illustrate the method of successive approximations, we will solve Sample Exercise 14.17 using this procedure. In solving for $[H^+]$ for 0.010 M H_2SO_4, we obtain the following expression:

$$1.2 \times 10^{-2} = \frac{x(0.010 + x)}{0.010 - x}$$

which can be rearranged to give

$$x = (1.2 \times 10^{-2})\left(\frac{0.010 - x}{0.010 + x}\right)$$

We will guess a value for x, substitute it into the right side of the equation, and then calculate a value for x. In guessing a value for x, we know it must be less than 0.010, since a larger value will make the calculated value for x negative and the guessed and calculated values will never match. We start by guessing $x = 0.005$.

The results of the successive approximations are shown in the following table:

Trial	Guessed Value for x	Calculated Value for x
1	0.0050	0.0040
2	0.0040	0.0051
3	0.00450	0.00455
4	0.00452	0.00453

Note that the first guess was close to the actual value and that there was oscillation between 0.004 and 0.005 for the guessed and calculated values. For trial 3, an average of these values was used as the guess, and this led rapidly to the correct value (0.0045 to the correct number of significant figures). Also, note that it is useful to carry extra digits until the correct value is obtained. That value can then be rounded off to the correct number of significant figures.

The method of successive approximations is especially useful for solving polynomials containing x to a power of 3 or higher. The procedure is the same as for quadratic equations: Substitute a guessed value for x into the equation for every x term but one, and then solve for x. Continue this process until the guessed and calculated values agree.

A1.5 Uncertainties in Measurements

Like all the physical sciences, chemistry is based on the results of measurements. Every measurement has an inherent uncertainty, so if we are to use the results of measurements to reach conclusions, we must be able to estimate the sizes of these uncertainties.

For example, the specification for a commercial 500-mg acetaminophen (the active painkiller in Tylenol) tablet is that each batch of tablets must contain 450 to 550 mg of acetaminophen per tablet. Suppose that chemical analysis gave the following results for a batch of acetaminophen tablets: 428 mg, 479 mg, 442 mg, and 435 mg. How can we use these results to decide if the batch of tablets meets the specification? Although the details of how to draw such conclusions from measured data are beyond the scope of this text, we will consider some aspects of how this is done. We will focus here on the types of experimental uncertainty, the expression of experimental results, and a simplified method for estimating experimental uncertainty when several types of measurement contribute to the final result.

Types of Experimental Error

There are two types of experimental uncertainty (error). A variety of names are applied to these types of errors:

$$\text{Precision} \longleftrightarrow \text{random error} \quad \equiv \text{indeterminate error}$$
$$\text{Accuracy} \longleftrightarrow \text{systematic error} \equiv \text{determinate error}$$

The difference between the two types of error is well illustrated by the attempts to hit a target shown in Fig. 1.7 in Chapter 1.

Random error is associated with every measurement. To obtain the last significant figure for any measurement, we must always make an estimate. For example, we interpolate between the marks on a meter stick, a buret, or a balance. The precision of replicate measurements (repeated measurements of the same type) reflects the size of the random errors. Precision refers to the reproducibility of replicate measurements.

The accuracy of a measurement refers to how close it is to the true value. An inaccurate result occurs as a result of some flaw (systematic error) in the measurement: the presence of an interfering substance, incorrect calibration of an instrument, operator error, etc. The goal of chemical analysis is to eliminate systematic error, but random errors can only be minimized. In practice, an experiment is almost always done in order to find an unknown value (the true value is not known—someone is trying to obtain that value by doing the experiment). In this case the precision of several replicate determinations is used to assess the accuracy of the result. The results of the replicate experiments are expressed as an average (which we assume is close to the true value) with an error limit that gives some indication of how close the average value may be to the true value. The error limit represents the uncertainty of the experimental result.

Expression of Experimental Results

If we perform several measurements, such as for the analysis for acetaminophen in painkiller tablets, the results should express two things: the average of the measurements and the size of the uncertainty.

There are two common ways of expressing an average: the mean and the median. The mean ($\overline{x}$) is the arithmetic average of the results, or

$$\text{Mean} = \overline{x} = \sum_{i=1}^{n} \frac{x_i}{n} = \frac{x_1 + x_2 + \cdots + x_n}{n}$$

where Σ means take the sum of the values. The mean is equal to the sum of all the measurements divided by the number of measurements. For the acetaminophen results given previously, the mean is

$$\overline{x} = \frac{428 + 479 + 442 + 435}{4} = 446 \text{ mg}$$

The median is the value that lies in the middle among the results. Half the measurements are above the median and half are below the median. For results of 465 mg, 485 mg, and 492 mg, the median is 485 mg. When there is an even number of results, the median is the average of the two middle results. For the acetaminophen results, the median is

$$\frac{442 + 435}{2} = 438 \text{ mg}$$

There are several advantages to using the median. If a small number of measurements is made, one value can greatly affect the mean. Consider the results for the analysis of acetaminophen: 428 mg, 479 mg, 442 mg, and 435 mg. The mean is 446 mg, which is larger than three of the four weights. The median is 438 mg, which lies near the three values that are relatively close to one another.

In addition to expressing an average value for a series of results, we must also express the uncertainty. This usually means expressing either the precision of the measurements or the observed range of the measurements. The range of a series of measurements is defined by the smallest value and the largest value. For the analytical results on the acetaminophen tablets, the range is from 428 mg to 479 mg. Using this range, we can express the results by saying that the true value lies between 428 mg and 479 mg. That is, we can express the amount of acetaminophen in a typical tablet as 446 ± 33 mg, where the error limit is chosen to give the observed range (approximately).

The most common way to specify precision is by the standard deviation, s, which for a small number of measurements is given by the formula

$$s = \left[\frac{\sum_{i=1}^{n} (x_i - \bar{x})^2}{n - 1} \right]^{1/2}$$

where x_i is an individual result, $\bar{x}$ is the average (either mean or median), and n is the total number of measurements. For the acetaminophen example, we have

$$s = \left[\frac{(428 - 446)^2 + (479 - 446)^2 + (442 - 446)^2 + (435 - 446)^2}{4 - 1} \right]^{1/2} = 23$$

Thus we can say the amount of acetaminophen in the typical tablet in the batch of tablets is 446 mg with a sample standard deviation of 23 mg. Statistically this means that any additional measurement has a 68% probability (68 chances out of 100) of being between 423 mg (446 − 23) and 469 mg (446 + 23). Thus the standard deviation is a measure of the precision of a given type of determination.

The standard deviation gives us a means of describing the precision of a given type of determination using a series of replicate results. However, it is also useful to be able to estimate the precision of a procedure that involves several measurements by combining the precisions of the individual steps. That is, we want to answer the following question: How do the uncertainties propagate when we combine the results of several different types of measurements? There are many ways to deal with the propagation of uncertainty. We will discuss only one simple method here.

A Simplified Method for Estimating Experimental Uncertainty

To illustrate this method, we will consider the determination of the density of an irregularly shaped solid. In this determination we make three measurements. First, we measure the mass of the object on a balance. Next, we must obtain the volume of the solid. The easiest method for doing this is to partially fill a graduated cylinder with a liquid and record the volume. Then we add the solid and record the volume again. The difference in the measured volumes is the volume of the solid. We can then calculate the density of the solid from the equation

$$D = \frac{M}{V_2 - V_1}$$

where M is the mass of the solid, V_1 is the initial volume of liquid in the graduated cylinder, and V_2 is the volume of liquid plus solid. Suppose we get the following results:

$$M = 23.06 \text{ g}$$
$$V_1 = 10.4 \text{ mL}$$
$$V_2 = 13.5 \text{ mL}$$

The calculated density is

$$\frac{23.06 \text{ g}}{13.5 \text{ mL} - 10.4 \text{ mL}} = 7.44 \text{ g/mL}$$

Now suppose that the precision of the balance used is ± 0.02 g and that the volume measurements are precise to ± 0.05 mL. How do we estimate the uncertainty of the density? We can do this by assuming a worst case. That is, we assume the largest uncertainties in all measurements, and see what combinations of measurements will give the largest and smallest possible results (the greatest range). Since the density is the mass divided by the volume, the largest value of the density will be that obtained using the largest possible mass and the smallest possible volume:

Largest possible mass = 23.06 + .02

$$D_{max} = \frac{23.08}{13.45 - 10.45} = 7.69 \text{ g/mL}$$

Smallest possible V_2 Largest possible V_1

The smallest value of the density is

Smallest possible mass

$$D_{min} = \frac{23.04}{13.35 - 10.35} = 7.20 \text{ g/mL}$$

Largest possible V_2 Smallest possible V_1

Thus the calculated range is from 7.20 to 7.69 and the average of these values is 7.44. The error limit is the number that gives the high and low range values when added and subtracted from the average. Therefore, we can express the density as 7.44 ± 0.25 g/mL, which is the average value plus or minus the quantity that gives the range calculated by assuming the largest uncertainties.

Analysis of the propagation of uncertainties is useful in drawing qualitative conclusions from the analysis of measurements. For example, suppose that we obtained the above results for the density of an unknown alloy and we want to know if it is one of the following alloys:

Alloy A: $D = 7.58$ g/mL
Alloy B: $D = 7.42$ g/mL
Alloy C: $D = 8.56$ g/mL

We can safely conclude that the alloy is not C. But the values of the densities for alloys A and B are both within the inherent uncertainty of our method. To distinguish between A and B, we need to improve the precision of our determination: The obvious choice is to improve the precision of the volume measurement.

The worst case method is very useful in estimating uncertainties when the results of several measurements are combined to calculate a result. We assume the maximum uncertainty in each measurement and calculate the minimum and maximum possible result. These extreme values describe the range and thus the error limit.

Appendix Two The Quantitative Kinetic Molecular Model

We have seen that the kinetic molecular model successfully accounts for the properties of an ideal gas. This appendix will show in some detail how the postulates of the kinetic molecular model lead to an equation corresponding to the experimentally obtained ideal gas equation.

Recall that the particles of an ideal gas are assumed to be volumeless, to have no attraction for each other, and to produce pressure on their container by colliding with the container walls.

Suppose there are n moles of an ideal gas in a cubical container with sides each of length L. Assume each gas particle has a mass m and that it is in rapid, random, straight-line motion colliding with the walls, as shown in Fig. A.3. The collisions will be assumed to be *elastic*—no loss of kinetic energy occurs. We want to compute the force on the walls from the colliding gas particles and then, since pressure is force per unit area, to obtain an expression for the pressure of the gas.

Before we can derive the expression for the pressure of a gas, we must first discuss some characteristics of velocity. Each particle in the gas has a particular velocity u that can be divided into components u_x, u_y, and u_z, as shown in Fig. A.4. First, using u_x and u_y and the Pythagorean theorem, we can obtain u_{xy} as shown in Fig. A.4(c):

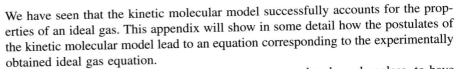

$$u_{xy}^2 = u_x^2 + u_y^2$$

Hypotenuse of   Sides of
right triangle   right triangle

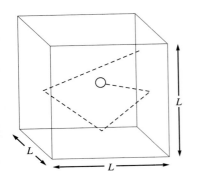

Figure A.3

An ideal gas particle in a cube whose sides are of length L. The particle collides elastically with the walls in a random, straight-line motion.

Then, constructing another triangle as shown in Fig. A.4(c), we find

$$u^2 = u_{xy}^2 + u_z^2$$

or

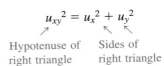

$$u^2 = u_x^2 + u_y^2 + u_z^2$$

Now let's consider how an "average" gas particle moves. For example, how often does this particle strike the two walls of the box that are perpendicular to the x axis? It is important to realize that only the x component of the velocity affects the particle's impacts on these two walls, as shown in Fig. A.5(a). The larger the x component of the velocity, the faster the particle travels between these two walls, and the more impacts per unit of time it will make on these walls. Remember, the pressure of the gas is due to these collisions with the walls.

The collision frequency (collisions per unit of time) with the two walls that are perpendicular to the x axis is given by

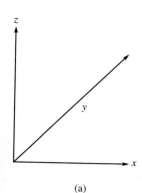

(a)

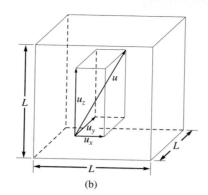

(b)

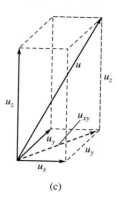

(c)

Figure A.4

(a) The Cartesian coordinate axes.

(b) The velocity of u of any gas particle can be broken down into three mutually perpendicular components, u_x, u_y, and u_z. This can be represented as a rectangular solid with sides u_x, u_y, and u_z and body diagonal u.

(c) In the xy plane,
$$u_x^2 + u_y^2 = u_{xy}^2$$
by the Pythagorean theorem. Since u_{xy} and u_x are also perpendicular,
$$u^2 = u_{xy}^2 + u_z^2 = u_x^2 + u_y^2 + u_z^2$$

$$(\text{Collision frequency})_x = \frac{\text{velocity in the } x \text{ direction}}{\text{distance between the walls}}$$

$$= \frac{u_x}{L}$$

Next, what is the force of a collision? Force is defined as mass times acceleration (change in velocity per unit of time):

$$F = ma = m\left(\frac{\Delta u}{\Delta t}\right)$$

where F represents force, a represents acceleration, Δu represents a change in velocity, and Δt represents a given length of time.

Since we assume that the particle has constant mass, we can write

$$F = \frac{m\Delta u}{\Delta t} = \frac{\Delta(mu)}{\Delta t}$$

The quantity mu is the momentum of the particle (momentum is the product of mass and velocity), and the expression $F = \Delta(mu)/\Delta t$ implies that force is the change in momentum per unit of time. When a particle hits a wall perpendicular to the x axis, as shown in Fig. A.5(b), an elastic collision results in an *exact reversal* of the x component of velocity. That is, the *sign,* or direction, of u_x reverses when the particle collides with one of the walls perpendicular to the x axis. Thus the final momentum is the *negative,* or opposite, of the initial momentum. Remember that an elastic collision means that there is no change in the *magnitude* of the velocity. The change in momentum in the x direction is then

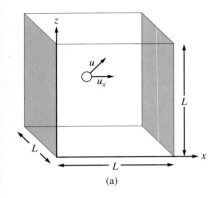

(a)

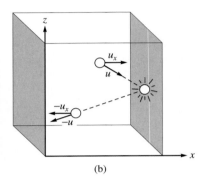

(b)

Figure A.5

(a) Only the x component of the gas particle's velocity affects the frequency of impacts on the shaded walls, the walls that are perpendicular to the x axis. (b) For an elastic collision, there is an exact reversal of the x component of the velocity and of the total velocity. The change in momentum (final − initial) is then

$$-mu_x - mu_x = -2mu_x$$

Change in momentum $= \Delta(mu_x) =$ final momentum − initial momentum

$$= \underset{\substack{\nearrow \\ \text{Final} \\ \text{momentum} \\ \text{in } x \text{ direction}}}{-mu_x} \underset{\substack{\nwarrow \\ \text{Initial} \\ \text{momentum} \\ \text{in } x \text{ direction}}}{-\; mu_x}$$

$$= -2mu_x$$

But we are interested in the force the gas particle exerts on the walls of the box. Since we know that every action produces an equal but opposite reaction, the change in momentum with respect to the wall on impact is $-(-2mu_x)$, or $2mu_x$.

Recall that since force is the change in momentum per unit of time,

$$\text{Force}_x = \frac{\Delta(mu_x)}{\Delta t}$$

for the walls perpendicular to the x axis.

This expression can be obtained by multiplying the change in momentum per impact by the number of impacts per unit of time:

$$\text{Force}_x = \underset{\substack{\nearrow \\ \text{Change in momentum} \\ \text{per impact}}}{(2mu_x)} \underset{\substack{\nwarrow \\ \text{Impacts per} \\ \text{unit of time}}}{\left(\frac{u_x}{L}\right)} = \text{change in momentum per unit of time}$$

That is,

$$\text{Force}_x = \frac{2mu_x^2}{L}$$

So far we have considered only the two walls of the box perpendicular to the x axis. We can assume that the force on the two walls perpendicular to the y axis is given by

$$\text{Force}_y = \frac{2mu_y^2}{L}$$

and that on the two walls perpendicular to the z axis by

$$\text{Force}_z = \frac{2mu_z^2}{L}$$

Since we have shown that

$$u^2 = u_x^2 + u_y^2 + u_z^2$$

the total force on the box is

$$\text{Force}_{\text{TOTAL}} = \text{force}_x + \text{force}_y + \text{force}_z$$

$$= \frac{2mu_x^2}{L} + \frac{2mu_y^2}{L} + \frac{2mu_z^2}{L}$$

$$= \frac{2m}{L}(u_x^2 + u_y^2 + u_z^2) = \frac{2m}{L}(u^2)$$

Now since we want the average force, we use the average of the square of the velocity $(\overline{u^2})$ to obtain

$$\overline{\text{Force}}_{\text{TOTAL}} = \frac{2m}{L}(\overline{u^2})$$

Next, we need to compute the pressure (force per unit of area)

$$\text{Pressure due to "average" particle} = \frac{\overline{\text{force}}_{\text{TOTAL}}}{\text{area}_{\text{TOTAL}}}$$

$$= \frac{\dfrac{2m\overline{u^2}}{L}}{6L^2} = \frac{m\overline{u^2}}{3L^3}$$

The 6 sides   Area of
of the cube   each side

Since the volume V of the cube is equal to L^3, we can write

$$\text{Pressure} = P = \frac{m\overline{u^2}}{3V}$$

So far we have considered the pressure on the walls due to a single, "average" particle. Of course, we want the pressure due to the entire gas sample. The number of particles in a given gas sample can be expressed as follows:

$$\text{Number of gas particles} = nN_A$$

where n is the number of moles and N_A is Avogadro's number.

The total pressure on the box due to n moles of a gas is therefore

$$P = nN_A \frac{m\overline{u^2}}{3V}$$

Next we want to express the pressure in terms of the kinetic energy of the gas molecules. Kinetic energy (the energy due to motion) is given by $\frac{1}{2}mu^2$, where m is the mass and u the velocity. Since we are using the average of the velocity squared ($\overline{u^2}$), and since $m\overline{u^2} = 2(\frac{1}{2}m\overline{u^2})$, we have

$$P = \left(\frac{2}{3}\right) \frac{nN_A(\frac{1}{2}m\overline{u^2})}{V}$$

or

$$\frac{PV}{n} = \left(\frac{2}{3}\right) N_A(\tfrac{1}{2}m\overline{u^2})$$

Thus, based on the postulates of the kinetic molecular model, we have been able to derive an equation that has the same form as the ideal gas equation,

$$\frac{PV}{n} = RT$$

This agreement between experiment and theory supports the validity of the assumptions made in the kinetic molecular model about the behavior of gas particles, at least for the limiting case of an ideal gas.

Appendix Three Spectral Analysis

Although volumetric and gravimetric analyses are still very commonly used, spectroscopy is the technique most often used for modern chemical analysis. *Spectroscopy* is the study of electromagnetic radiation emitted or absorbed by a given chemical species. Since the quantity of radiation absorbed or emitted can be related

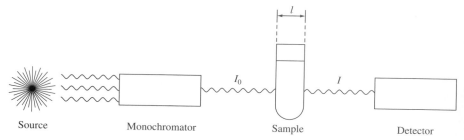

Figure A.6

A schematic diagram of a simple spectrophotometer. The source emits all wavelengths of visible light, which are dispersed using a prism or grating and then focused, one wavelength at a time, onto the sample. The detector compares the intensity of the incident light (I_0) to the intensity of the light after it has passed through the sample (I).

to the quantity of the absorbing or emitting species present, this technique can be used for quantitative analysis. There are many spectroscopic techniques, since electromagnetic radiation spans a wide range of energies to include X rays, ultraviolet, infrared, and visible light, and microwaves, to name a few of its familiar forms. However, we will consider here only one procedure, which is based on the absorption of visible light.

If a liquid is colored, it is because some component of the liquid absorbs visible light. In a solution the greater the concentration of the light-absorbing substance, the more light is absorbed, and the more intense the color of the solution.

The quantity of light absorbed by a substance can be measured by a *spectrophotometer,* shown schematically in Fig. A.6. This instrument consists of a source that emits all wavelengths of light in the visible region (wavelengths of ~400 to 700 nm); a monochromator, which selects a given wavelength of light; a sample holder for the solution being measured; and a detector, which compares the intensity of incident light I_0 to the intensity of light after it has passed through the sample I. The ratio I/I_0, called the *transmittance,* is a measure of the fraction of light that passes through the sample. The amount of light absorbed is given by the *absorbance A,* where

$$A = -\log \frac{I}{I_0}$$

The absorbance can be expressed by the *Beer–Lambert law:*

$$A = \epsilon l c$$

where ϵ is the molar absorptivity or the molar extinction coefficient (in L/mol · cm), l is the distance the light travels through the solution (in cm), and c is the concentration of the absorbing species (in mol/L). The Beer–Lambert law is the basis for using spectroscopy in quantitative analysis. If ϵ and l are known, measuring A for a solution allows us to calculate the concentration of the absorbing species in the solution.

Suppose we have a pink solution containing an unknown concentration of $Co^{2+}(aq)$ ions. A sample of this solution is placed in a spectrophotometer, and the absorbance is measured at a wavelength where ϵ for $Co^{2+}(aq)$ is known to be

12 L/mol · cm. The absorbance A is found to be 0.60. The width of the sample tube is 1.0 cm. We want to determine the concentration of $Co^{2+}(aq)$ in the solution. This problem can be solved by a straightforward application of the Beer–Lambert law,

$$A = \epsilon l c$$

where
$$A = 0.60$$

$$\epsilon = \frac{12 \text{ L}}{\text{mol} \cdot \text{cm}}$$

$$l = \text{light path} = 1.0 \text{ cm}$$

Solving for the concentration gives

$$c = \frac{A}{\epsilon l} = \frac{0.60}{\left(12 \dfrac{\text{L}}{\text{mol} \cdot \text{cm}}\right)(1.0 \text{ cm})} = 5.0 \times 10^{-2} \text{ mol/L}$$

To obtain the unknown concentration of an absorbing species from the measured absorbance, we must know the product ϵl, since

$$c = \frac{A}{\epsilon l}$$

We can obtain the product ϵl by measuring the absorbance of a solution of *known* concentration, since

Measured using a
↙ spectrophotometer

$$\epsilon l = \frac{A}{c}$$

↖ Known from making up
the solution

However, a more accurate value of the product ϵl can be obtained by plotting A versus c for a series of solutions. Note that the equation $A = \epsilon l c$ gives a straight line with slope ϵl when A is plotted against c.

For example, consider the following typical spectroscopic analysis. A sample of steel from a bicycle frame is to be analyzed to determine its manganese content. The procedure involves weighing out a sample of the steel, dissolving it in strong acid, treating the resulting solution with a very strong oxidizing agent to convert all the manganese to permanganate ion (MnO_4^-), and then using spectroscopy to determine the concentration of the intensely purple MnO_4^- ions in the solution. To do this, however, the value of ϵl for MnO_4^- must be determined at an appropriate wavelength. The absorbance values for four solutions with known MnO_4^- concentrations were measured to give the following data:

Solution	Concentration of MnO_4^- (mol/L)	Absorbance
1	7.00×10^{-5}	0.175
2	1.00×10^{-4}	0.250
3	2.00×10^{-4}	0.500
4	3.50×10^{-4}	0.875

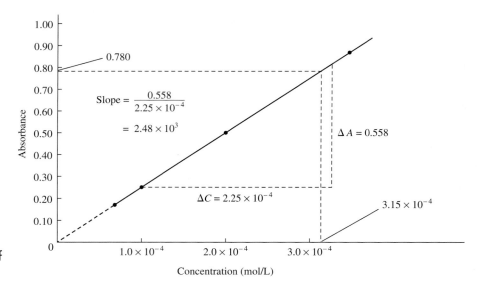

Figure A.7

A plot of absorbance versus concentration of MnO_4^- in a series of solutions of known concentration.

A plot of absorbance versus concentration for the solutions of known concentration is shown in Fig. A.7. The slope of this line (change in A/change in c) is 2.48×10^3 L/mol. This quantity represents the product ϵl.

A sample of the steel weighing 0.1523 g was dissolved and the unknown amount of manganese was converted to MnO_4^- ions. Water was then added to give a solution with a final volume of 100.0 mL. A portion of this solution was placed in a spectrophotometer, and its absorbance was found to be 0.780. Using these data, we want to calculate the percent manganese in the steel. The MnO_4^- ions from the manganese in the dissolved steel sample show an absorbance of 0.780. Using the Beer–Lambert law, we calculate the concentration of MnO_4^- in this solution:

$$c = \frac{A}{\epsilon l} = \frac{0.780}{2.48 \times 10^3 \text{ L/mol}} = 3.15 \times 10^{-4} \text{ mol/L}$$

There is a more direct way for finding c. Using a graph such as that in Fig. A.7 (often called a *Beer's law plot*), we can read the concentration that corresponds to $A = 0.780$. This interpolation is shown by dashed lines on the graph. By this method, $c = 3.15 \times 10^{-4}$ mol/L, which agrees with the value obtained above.

Recall that the original 0.1523-g steel sample was dissolved, the manganese was converted to permanganate, and the volume was adjusted to 100.0 mL. We now know that the $[MnO_4^-]$ in that solution is 3.15×10^{-4} M. Using this concentration, we can calculate the total number of moles of MnO_4^- in that solution:

$$\text{mol of } MnO_4^- = 100.0 \text{ mL} \times \frac{1 \text{ L}}{1000 \text{ mL}} \times 3.15 \times 10^{-4} \frac{\text{mol}}{\text{L}}$$
$$= 3.15 \times 10^{-5} \text{ mol}$$

Since each mole of manganese in the original steel sample yields a mole of MnO_4^-, that is,

$$1 \text{ mol of Mn} \xrightarrow{\text{Oxidation}} 1 \text{ mol of } MnO_4^-$$

the original steel sample must have contained 3.15×10^{-5} mol of manganese. The mass of manganese present in the sample is

$$3.15 \times 10^{-5} \text{ mol of Mn} \times \frac{54.938 \text{ g of Mn}}{1 \text{ mol of Mn}} = 1.73 \times 10^{-3} \text{ g of Mn}$$

Since the steel sample weighed 0.1523 g, the present manganese in the steel is

$$\frac{1.73 \times 10^{-3} \text{ g of Mn}}{1.523 \times 10^{-1} \text{ g of sample}} \times 100 = 1.14\%$$

This example illustrates a typical use of spectroscopy in quantitative analysis. The steps commonly involved are as follows:

1. Preparation of a calibration plot (a Beer's law plot) by measuring the absorbance values of a series of solutions with known concentrations.

2. Measurement of the absorbance of the solution of unknown concentration.

3. Use of the calibration plot to determine the unknown concentration.

Appendix Four Selected Thermodynamic Data

Note: All values are assumed precise to at least ±1.

Substance and State	ΔH_f° (kJ/mol)	ΔG_f° (kJ/mol)	S° (J/K · mol)	Substance and State	ΔH_f° (kJ/mol)	ΔG_f° (kJ/mol)	S° (J/K · mol)
Aluminum				**Calcium**			
Al(s)	0	0	28	Ca(s)	0	0	41
Al$_2$O$_2$(s)	−1676	−1582	51	CaC$_2$(s)	−63	−68	70
Al(OH)$_3$(s)	−1277			CaCO$_3$(s)	−1207	−1129	93
AlCl$_3$(s)	−704	−629	111	CaO(s)	−635	−604	40
Barium				Ca(OH)$_2$(s)	−987	−899	83
Ba(s)	0	0	67	Ca$_3$(PO$_4$)$_2$(s)	−4126	−3890	241
BaCO$_3$(s)	−1219	−1139	112	CaSO$_4$(s)	−1433	−1320	107
BaO(s)	−582	−552	70	CaSiO$_3$(s)	−1630	−1550	84
Ba(OH)$_2$(s)	−946			**Carbon**			
BaSO$_4$(s)	−1465	−1353	132	C(s) (graphite)	0	0	6
Beryllium				C(s) (diamond)	2	3	2
Be(s)	0	0	10	CO(g)	−110.5	−137	198
BeO(s)	−599	−569	14	CO$_2$(g)	−393.5	−394	214
Be(OH)$_2$(s)	−904	−815	47	CH$_4$(g)	−75	−51	186
Bromine				CH$_3$OH(g)	−201	−163	240
Br$_2$(l)	0	0	152	CH$_3$OH(l)	−239	−166	127
Br$_2$(g)	31	3	245	H$_2$CO(g)	−116	−110	219
Br$_2$(aq)	−3	4	130	HCOOH(g)	−363	−351	249
Br$^-$(aq)	−121	−104	82	HCN(g)	135.1	125	202
HBr(g)	−36	−53	199	C$_2$H$_2$(g)	227	209	201
Cadmium				C$_2$H$_4$(g)	52	68	219
Cd(s)	0	0	52	CH$_3$CHO(g)	−166	−129	250
CdO(s)	−258	−228	55	C$_2$H$_5$OH(l)	−278	−175	161
Cd(OH)$_2$(s)	−561	−474	96	C$_2$H$_6$(g)	−84.7	−32.9	229.5
CdS(s)	−162	−156	65	C$_3$H$_6$(g)	20.9	62.7	266.9
CdSO$_4$(s)	−935	−823	123	C$_3$H$_8$(g)	−104	−24	270

(continued)

Appendix Four (continued)

Substance and State	ΔH_f° (kJ/mol)	ΔG_f° (kJ/mol)	S° (J/K · mol)	Substance and State	ΔH_f° (kJ/mol)	ΔG_f° (kJ/mol)	S° (J/K · mol)
Carbon, *continued*				Iron			
$C_2H_4O(g)$				$Fe(s)$	0	0	27
(ethylene oxide)	−53	−13	242	$Fe_3C(s)$	21	15	108
$CH_2{=}CHCN(g)$	185.0	195.4	274	$Fe_{0.95}O(s)$ (wustite)	−264	−240	59
$CH_3COOH(l)$	−484	−389	160	FeO	−272	−255	61
$C_6H_{12}O_6(s)$	−1275	−911	212	$Fe_3O_4(s)$ (magnetite)	−1117	−1013	146
CCl_4	−135	−65	216	$Fe_2O_3(s)$ (hematite)	−826	−740	90
Chlorine				$FeS(s)$	−95	−97	67
$Cl_2(g)$	0	0	223	$FeS_2(s)$	−178	−166	53
$Cl_2(aq)$	−23	7	121	$FeSO_4(s)$	−929	−825	121
$Cl^-(aq)$	−167	−131	57	Lead			
$HCl(g)$	−92	−95	187	$Pb(s)$	0	0	65
Chromium				$PbO_2(s)$	−277	−217	69
$Cr(s)$	0	0	24	$PbS(s)$	−100	−99	91
$Cr_2O_3(s)$	−1128	−1047	81	$PbSO_4(s)$	−920	−813	149
$CrO_3(s)$	−579	−502	72	Magnesium			
Copper				$Mg(s)$	0	0	33
$Cu(s)$	0	0	33	$MgCO_3(s)$	−1113	−1029	66
$CuCO_3(s)$	−595	−518	88	$MgO(s)$	−602	−569	27
$Cu_2O(s)$	−170	−148	93	$Mg(OH)_2(s)$	−925	−834	64
$CuO(s)$	−156	−128	43	Manganese			
$Cu(OH)_2(s)$	−450	−372	108	$Mn(s)$	0	0	32
$CuS(s)$	−49	−49	67	$MnO(s)$	−385	−363	60
Fluorine				$Mn_3O_4(s)$	−1387	−1280	149
$F_2(g)$	0	0	203	$Mn_2O_3(s)$	−971	−893	110
$F^-(aq)$	−333	−279	−14	$MnO_2(s)$	−521	−466	53
$HF(g)$	−271	−273	174	$MnO_4^-(aq)$	−543	−449	190
Hydrogen				Mercury			
$H_2(g)$	0	0	131	$Hg(l)$	0	0	76
$H(g)$	217	203	115	$Hg_2Cl_2(s)$	−265	−211	196
$H^+(aq)$	0	0	0	$HgCl_2(s)$	−230	−184	144
$OH^-(aq)$	−230	−157	−11	$HgO(s)$	−90	−59	70
$H_2O(l)$	−286	−237	70	$HgS(s)$	−58	−49	78
$H_2O(g)$	−242	−229	189	Nickel			
Iodine				$Ni(s)$	0	0	30
$I_2(s)$	0	0	116	$NiCl_2(s)$	−316	−272	107
$I_2(g)$	62	19	261	$NiO(s)$	−241	−213	38
$I_2(aq)$	23	16	137	$Ni(OH)_2(s)$	−538	−453	79
$I^-(aq)$	−55	−52	106	$NiS(s)$	−93	−90	53

Appendix Four (continued)

Substance and State	ΔH_f° (kJ/mol)	ΔG_f° (kJ/mol)	S° (J/K · mol)
Nitrogen			
$N_2(g)$	0	0	192
$NH_3(g)$	−46	−17	193
$NH_3(aq)$	−80	−27	111
$NH_4^+(aq)$	−132	−79	113
$NO(g)$	90	87	211
$NO_2(g)$	34	52	240
$N_2O(g)$	82	104	220
$N_2O_4(g)$	10	98	304
$N_2O_4(l)$	−20	97	209
$N_2O_5(s)$	−42	134	178
$N_2H_4(l)$	51	149	121
$N_2H_3CH_3(l)$	54	180	166
$HNO_3(aq)$	−207	−111	146
$HNO_3(l)$	−174	−81	156
$NH_4ClO_4(s)$	−295	−89	186
$NH_4Cl(s)$	−314	−203	96
Oxygen			
$O_2(g)$	0	0	205
$O(g)$	249	232	161
$O_3(g)$	143	163	239
Phosphorus			
$P(s)$ (white)	0	0	41
$P(s)$ (red)	−18	−12	23
$P(s)$ (black)	−39	−33	23
$P_4(g)$	59	24	280
$PF_5(g)$	−1578	−1509	296
$PH_3(g)$	5	13	210
$H_3PO_4(s)$	−1279	−1119	110
$H_3PO_4(l)$	−1267	—	—
$H_3PO_4(aq)$	−1288	−1143	158
$P_4O_{10}(s)$	−2984	−2698	229
Potassium			
$K(s)$	0	0	64
$KCl(s)$	−436	−408	83
$KClO_3(s)$	−391	−290	143
$KClO_4(s)$	−433	−304	151
$K_2O(s)$	−361	−322	98
$K_2O_2(s)$	−496	−430	113
$KO_2(s)$	−283	−238	117
$KOH(s)$	−425	−379	79
$KOH(aq)$	−481	−440	.9.20

Substance and State	ΔH_f° (kJ/mol)	ΔG_f° (kJ/mol)	S° (J/K · mol)
Silicon			
$SiO_2(s)$ (quartz)	−911	−856	42
$SiCl_4(l)$	−687	−620	240
Silver			
$Ag(s)$	0	0	43
$Ag^+(aq)$	105	77	73
$AgBr(s)$	−100	−97	107
$AgCN(s)$	146	164	84
$AgCl(s)$	−127	−110	96
$Ag_2CrO_4(s)$	−712	−622	217
$AgI(s)$	−62	−66	115
$Ag_2O(s)$	−31	−11	122
$Ag_2S(s)$	−32	−40	146
Sodium			
$Na(s)$	0	0	51
$Na^+(aq)$	−240	−262	59
$NaBr(s)$	−360	−347	84
$Na_2CO_3(s)$	−1131	−1048	136
$NaHCO_3(s)$	−948	−852	102
$NaCl(s)$	−411	−384	72
$NaH(s)$	−56	−33	40
$NaI(s)$	−288	−282	91
$NaNO_2(s)$	−359		
$NaNO_3(s)$	−467	−366	116
$Na_2O(s)$	−416	−377	73
$Na_2O_2(s)$	−515	−451	95
$NaOH(s)$	−427	−381	64
$NaOH(aq)$	−470	−419	50
Sulfur			
$S(s)$ (rhombic)	0	0	32
$S(s)$ (monoclinic)	0.3	0.1	33
$S^{2-}(aq)$	33	86	−15
$S_8(g)$	102	50	431
$SF_6(g)$	−1209	−1105	292
$H_2S(g)$	−21	−34	206
$SO_2(g)$	−297	−300	248
$SO_3(g)$	−396	−371	257
$SO_4^{2-}(aq)$	−909	−745	20
$H_2SO_4(l)$	−814	−690	157
$H_2SO_4(aq)$	−909	−745	20

(continued)

Appendix Four (continued)

Substance and State	ΔH_f° (kJ/mol)	ΔG_f° (kJ/mol)	S° (J/K · mol)	Substance and State	ΔH_f° (kJ/mol)	ΔG_f° (kJ/mol)	S° (J/K · mol)
Tin				Xenon			
Sn(s) (white)	0	0	52	Xe(g)	0	0	170
Sn(s) (gray)	−2	0.1	44	XeF$_2$(g)	−108	−48	254
SnO(s)	−285	−257	56	XeF$_4$(s)	−251	−121	146
SnO$_2$(s)	−581	−520	52	XeF$_6$(g)	−294		
Sn(OH)$_2$(s)	−561	−492	155	XeO$_3$(s)	402		
Titanium				Zinc			
TiCl$_4$(g)	−763	−727	355	Zn(s)	0	0	42
TiO$_2$(s)	−945	−890	50	ZnO(s)	−348	−318	44
Uranium				Zn(OH)$_2$(s)	−642		
U(s)	0	0	50	ZnS(s) (wurtzite)	−193		
UF$_6$(s)	−2137	−2008	228	ZnS(s) (zinc blende)	−206	−201	58
UF$_6$(g)	−2113	−2029	380	ZnSO$_4$(s)	−983	−874	120
UO$_2$(s)	−1084	−1029	78				
U$_3$O$_8$(s)	−3575	−3393	282				
UO$_3$(s)	−1230	−1150	99				

Appendix Five Equilibrium Constants and Reduction Potentials

A5.1 Values of K_a for Some Common Monoprotic Acids

Name	Formula	Value of K_a
Hydrogen sulfate ion	HSO$_4^-$	1.2×10^{-2}
Chlorous acid	HClO$_2$	1.2×10^{-2}
Monochloracetic acid	HC$_2$H$_2$ClO$_2$	1.35×10^{-3}
Hydrofluoric acid	HF	7.2×10^{-4}
Nitrous acid	HNO$_2$	4.0×10^{-4}
Formic acid	HCO$_2$H	1.8×10^{-4}
Lactic acid	HC$_3$H$_5$O$_3$	1.38×10^{-4}
Benzoic acid	HC$_7$H$_5$O$_2$	6.4×10^{-5}
Acetic acid	HC$_2$H$_3$O$_2$	1.8×10^{-5}
Hydrated aluminum(III) ion	[Al(H$_2$O)$_6$]$^{3+}$	1.4×10^{-5}
Propanoic acid	HC$_3$H$_5$O$_2$	1.3×10^{-5}
Hypochlorous acid	HOCl	3.5×10^{-8}
Hypobromous acid	HOBr	2×10^{-9}
Hydrocyanic acid	HCN	6.2×10^{-10}
Boric acid	H$_3$BO$_3$	5.8×10^{-10}
Ammonium ion	NH$_4^+$	5.6×10^{-10}
Phenol	HOC$_6$H$_5$	1.6×10^{-10}
Hypoiodous acid	HOI	2×10^{-11}

A5.2 Stepwise Dissociation Constants for Several Common Polyprotic Acids

Name	Formula	K_{a_1}	K_{a_2}	K_{a_3}
Phosphoric acid	H_3PO_4	7.5×10^{-3}	6.2×10^{-8}	4.8×10^{-13}
Arsenic acid	H_3AsO_4	5×10^{-3}	8×10^{-8}	6×10^{-10}
Carbonic acid	H_2CO_3	4.3×10^{-7}	5.6×10^{-11}	
Sulfuric acid	H_2SO_4	Large	1.2×10^{-2}	
Sulfurous acid	H_2SO_3	1.5×10^{-2}	1.0×10^{-7}	
Hydrosulfuric acid	H_2S	1.0×10^{-7}	$\sim 10^{-19}$	
Oxalic acid	$H_2C_2O_4$	6.5×10^{-2}	6.1×10^{-5}	
Ascorbic acid (vitamin C)	$H_2C_6H_6O_6$	7.9×10^{-5}	1.6×10^{-12}	
Citric acid	$H_3C_6H_5O_7$	8.4×10^{-4}	1.8×10^{-5}	4.0×10^{-6}

A5.3 Values of K_b for Some Common Weak Bases

Name	Formula	Conjugate Acid	K_b
Ammonia	NH_3	NH_4^+	1.8×10^{-5}
Methylamine	CH_3NH_2	$CH_3NH_3^+$	4.38×10^{-4}
Ethylamine	$C_2H_5NH_2$	$C_2H_5NH_3^+$	5.6×10^{-4}
Diethylamine	$(C_2H_5)_2NH$	$(C_2H_5)_2NH_2^+$	1.3×10^{-3}
Triethylamine	$(C_2H_5)_3N$	$(C_2H_5)_3NH^+$	4.0×10^{-4}
Hydroxylamine	$HONH_2$	$HONH_3^+$	1.1×10^{-8}
Hydrazine	H_2NNH_2	$H_2NNH_3^+$	3.0×10^{-6}
Aniline	$C_6H_5NH_2$	$C_6H_5NH_3^+$	3.8×10^{-10}
Pyridine	C_5H_5N	$C_5H_5NH^+$	1.7×10^{-9}

A5.4 K_{sp} Values at 25°C for Common Ionic Solids

Ionic Solid	K_{sp} (at 25°C)	Ionic Solid	K_{sp} (at 25°C)	Ionic Solid	K_{sp} (at 25°C)
Fluorides		Hg_2CrO_4*	2×10^{-9}	$Co(OH)_2$	2.5×10^{-16}
BaF_2	2.4×10^{-5}	$BaCrO_4$	8.5×10^{-11}	$Ni(OH)_2$	1.6×10^{-16}
MgF_2	6.4×10^{-9}	Ag_2CrO_4	9.0×10^{-12}	$Zn(OH)_2$	4.5×10^{-17}
PbF_2	4×10^{-8}	$PbCrO_4$	2×10^{-16}	$Cu(OH)_2$	1.6×10^{-19}
SrF_2	7.9×10^{-10}			$Hg(OH)_2$	3×10^{-26}
CaF_2	4.0×10^{-11}	Carbonates		$Sn(OH)_2$	3×10^{-27}
		$NiCO_3$	1.4×10^{-7}	$Cr(OH)_3$	6.7×10^{-31}
Chlorides		$CaCO_3$	8.7×10^{-9}	$Al(OH)_3$	2×10^{-32}
$PbCl_2$	1.6×10^{-5}	$BaCO_3$	1.6×10^{-9}	$Fe(OH)_3$	4×10^{-38}
$AgCl$	1.6×10^{-10}	$SrCO_3$	7×10^{-10}	$Co(OH)_3$	2.5×10^{-43}
Hg_2Cl_2*	1.1×10^{-18}	$CuCO_3$	2.5×10^{-10}		
		$ZnCO_3$	2×10^{-10}	Sulfides	
Bromides		$MnCO_3$	8.8×10^{-11}	MnS	2.3×10^{-13}
$PbBr_2$	4.6×10^{-6}	$FeCO_3$	2.1×10^{-11}	FeS	3.7×10^{-19}
$AgBr$	5.0×10^{-13}	Ag_2CO_3	8.1×10^{-12}	NiS	3×10^{-21}
Hg_2Br_2*	1.3×10^{-22}	$CdCO_3$	5.2×10^{-12}	CoS	5×10^{-22}
		$PbCO_3$	1.5×10^{-15}	ZnS	2.5×10^{-22}
Iodides		$MgCO_3$	1×10^{-5}	SnS	1×10^{-26}
PbI_2	1.4×10^{-8}	Hg_2CO_3*	9.0×10^{-15}	CdS	1.0×10^{-28}
AgI	1.5×10^{-16}			PbS	7×10^{-29}
Hg_2I_2*	4.5×10^{-29}	Hydroxides		CuS	8.5×10^{-45}
		$Ba(OH)_2$	5.0×10^{-3}	Ag_2S	1.6×10^{-49}
Sulfates		$Sr(OH)_2$	3.2×10^{-4}	HgS	1.6×10^{-54}
$CaSO_4$	6.1×10^{-5}	$Ca(OH)_2$	1.3×10^{-6}		
Ag_2SO_4	1.2×10^{-5}	$AgOH$	2.0×10^{-8}	Phosphates	
$SrSO_4$	3.2×10^{-7}	$Mg(OH)_2$	8.9×10^{-12}	Ag_3PO_4	1.8×10^{-18}
$PbSO_4$	1.3×10^{-8}	$Mn(OH)_2$	2×10^{-13}	$Sr_3(PO_4)_2$	1×10^{-31}
$BaSO_4$	1.5×10^{-9}	$Cd(OH)_2$	5.9×10^{-15}	$Ca_3(PO_4)_2$	1.3×10^{-32}
		$Pb(OH)_2$	1.2×10^{-15}	$Ba_3(PO_4)_2$	6×10^{-39}
Chromates		$Fe(OH)_2$	1.8×10^{-15}	$Pb_3(PO_4)_2$	1×10^{-54}
$SrCrO_4$	3.6×10^{-5}				

*Contains Hg_2^{2+} ions. $K_{sp} = [Hg_2^{2+}][X^-]^2$ for Hg_2X_2 salts.

A5.5 Standard Reduction Potentials at 25°C (298 K) for Many Common Half-Reactions

Half-Reaction	$\mathscr{E}°$ (V)	Half-Reaction	$\mathscr{E}°$ (V)
$F_2 + 2e^- \rightarrow 2F^-$	2.87	$O_2 + 2H_2O + 4e^- \rightarrow 4OH^-$	0.40
$Ag^{2+} + e^- \rightarrow Ag^+$	1.99	$Cu^{2+} + 2e^- \rightarrow Cu$	0.34
$Co^{3+} + e^- \rightarrow Co^{2+}$	1.82	$Hg_2Cl_2 + 2e^- \rightarrow 2Hg + 2Cl^-$	0.34
$H_2O_2 + 2H^+ + 2e^- \rightarrow 2H_2O$	1.78	$AgCl + e^- \rightarrow Ag + Cl^-$	0.22
$Ce^{4+} + e^- \rightarrow Ce^{3+}$	1.70	$SO_4^{2-} + 4H^+ + 2e^- \rightarrow H_2SO_3 + H_2O$	0.20
$PbO_2 + 4H^+ + SO_4^{2-} + 2e^- \rightarrow PbSO_4 + 2H_2O$	1.69	$Cu^{2+} + e^- \rightarrow Cu^+$	0.16
$MnO_4^- + 4H^+ + 3e^- \rightarrow MnO_2 + 2H_2O$	1.68	$2H^+ + 2e^- \rightarrow H_2$	0.00
$2e^- + 2H^+ + IO_4^- \rightarrow IO_3^- + H_2O$	1.60	$Fe^{3+} + 3e^- \rightarrow Fe$	-0.036
$MnO_4^- + 8H^+ + 5e^- \rightarrow Mn^{2+} + 4H_2O$	1.51	$Pb^{2+} + 2e^- \rightarrow Pb$	-0.13
$Au^{3+} + 3e^- \rightarrow Au$	1.50	$Sn^{2+} + 2e^- \rightarrow Sn$	-0.14
$PbO_2 + 4H^+ + 2e^- \rightarrow Pb^{2+} + 2H_2O$	1.46	$Ni^{2+} + 2e^- \rightarrow Ni$	-0.23
$Cl_2 + 2e^- \rightarrow 2Cl^-$	1.36	$PbSO_4 + 2e^- \rightarrow Pb + SO_4^{2-}$	-0.35
$Cr_2O_7^{2-} + 14H^+ + 6e^- \rightarrow 2Cr^{3+} + 7H_2O$	1.33	$Cd^{2+} + 2e^- \rightarrow Cd$	-0.40
$O_2 + 4H^+ + 4e^- \rightarrow 2H_2O$	1.23	$Fe^{2+} + 2e^- \rightarrow Fe$	-0.44
$MnO_2 + 4H^+ + 2e^- \rightarrow Mn^{2+} + 2H_2O$	1.21	$Cr^{3+} + e^- \rightarrow Cr^{2+}$	-0.50
$IO_3^- + 6H^+ + 5e^- \rightarrow \frac{1}{2}I_2 + 3H_2O$	1.20	$Cr^{3+} + 3e^- \rightarrow Cr$	-0.73
$Br_2 + 2e^- \rightarrow 2Br^-$	1.09	$Zn^{2+} + 2e^- \rightarrow Zn$	-0.76
$VO_2^+ + 2H^+ + e^- \rightarrow VO^{2+} + H_2O$	1.00	$2H_2O + 2e^- \rightarrow H_2 + 2OH^-$	-0.83
$AuCl_4^- + 3e^- \rightarrow Au + 4Cl^-$	0.99	$Mn^{2+} + 2e^- \rightarrow Mn$	-1.18
$NO_3^- + 4H^+ + 3e^- \rightarrow NO + 2H_2O$	0.96	$Al^{3+} + 3e^- \rightarrow Al$	-1.66
$ClO_2 + e^- \rightarrow ClO_2^-$	0.954	$H_2 + 2e^- \rightarrow 2H^-$	-2.23
$2Hg^{2+} + 2e^- \rightarrow Hg_2^{2+}$	0.91	$Mg^{2+} + 2e^- \rightarrow Mg$	-2.37
$Ag^+ + e^- \rightarrow Ag$	0.80	$La^{3+} + 3e^- \rightarrow La$	-2.37
$Hg_2^{2+} + 2e^- \rightarrow 2Hg$	0.80	$Na^+ + e^- \rightarrow Na$	-2.71
$Fe^{3+} + e^- \rightarrow Fe^{2+}$	0.77	$Ca^{2+} + 2e^- \rightarrow Ca$	-2.76
$O_2 + 2H^+ + 2e^- \rightarrow H_2O_2$	0.68	$Ba^{2+} + 2e^- \rightarrow Ba$	-2.90
$MnO_4^- + e^- \rightarrow MnO_4^{2-}$	0.56	$K^+ + e^- \rightarrow K$	-2.92
$I_2 + 2e^- \rightarrow 2I^-$	0.54	$Li^+ + e^- \rightarrow Li$	-3.05
$Cu^+ + e^- \rightarrow Cu$	0.52		

Appendix Six SI Units and Conversion Factors

Length

SI unit: meter (m)

1 meter	= 1.0936 yards
1 centimeter	= 0.39370 inch
1 inch	= 2.54 centimeters (exactly)
1 kilometer	= 0.62137 mile
1 mile	= 5280 feet
	= 1.6093 kilometers
1 angstrom	= 10^{-10} meter
	= 100 picometers

Mass

SI unit: kilogram (kg)

1 kilogram	= 1000 grams
	= 2.2046 pounds
1 pound	= 453.59 grams
	= 0.45359 kilogram
	= 16 ounces
1 ton	= 2000 pounds
	= 907.185 kilograms
1 metric ton	= 1000 kilograms
	= 2204.6 pounds
1 atomic mass unit	= 1.66056×10^{-27} kilograms

Volume

SI unit: cubic meter (m³)

1 liter	= 10^{-3} m^3
	= 1 dm^3
	= 1.0567 quarts
1 gallon	= 4 quarts
	= 8 pints
	= 3.7854 liters
1 quart	= 32 fluid ounces
	= 0.94633 liter

Temperature

SI unit: kelvin (K)

0 K	= $-273.15°$C
	= $-459.67°$F
K	= °C + 273.15
°C	= $\frac{5}{9}$(°F $-$ 32)
°F	= $\frac{9}{5}$(°C) + 32

Energy

SI unit: joule (J)

1 joule	= 1 kg $\cdot$ m^2/s^2
	= 0.23901 calorie
	= 9.4781×10^{-4} btu (British thermal unit)
1 calorie	= 4.184 joules
	= 3.965×10^{-3} btu
1 btu	= 1055.06 joules
	= 252.2 calories

Pressure

SI unit: pascal (Pa)

1 pascal	= 1 N/m^2
	= 1 kg/m $\cdot$ s^2
1 atmosphere	= 101.325 kilopascals
	= 760 torr (mmHg)
	= 14.70 pounds per square inch
1 bar	= 10^5 pascals

Glossary

Accuracy the agreement of a particular value with the true value. (1.4)

Acid a substance that produces hydrogen ions in solution; a proton donor. (2.8; 4.2; 4.8)

Acid–base indicator a substance that marks the end point of an acid–base titration by changing color. (15.5)

Acid dissociation constant (K_a) the equilibrium constant for a reaction in which a proton is removed from an acid by H_2O to form the conjugate base and H_3O^+. (14.1)

Acid rain a result of air pollution by sulfur dioxide. (5.9)

Acidic oxide a covalent oxide that dissolves in water to give an acidic solution. (14.10)

Actinide series a group of 14 elements following actinium in the periodic table, in which the $5f$ orbitals are being filled. (7.11; 18.1)

Activated complex (transition state) the arrangement of atoms found at the top of the potential energy barrier as a reaction proceeds from reactants to products. (12.7)

Activation energy the threshold energy that must be overcome to produce a chemical reaction. (12.7)

Addition polymerization a type of polymerization in which the monomers simply add together to form the polymer, with no other products. (22.6)

Addition reaction a reaction in which atoms add to a carbon–carbon multiple bond. (22.2)

Adsorption the collection of one substance on the surface of another. (12.8)

Air pollution contamination of the atmosphere, mainly by the gaseous products of transportation and production of electricity. (5.9)

Alcohol an organic compound in which the hydroxyl group is a substituent on a hydrocarbon. (22.5)

Aldehyde an organic compound containing the carbonyl group bonded to at least one hydrogen atom. (22.5)

Alkali metal a Group 1A metal. (2.7; 18.2)

Alkaline earth metal a Group 2A metal. (2.7; 18.4)

Alkane a saturated hydrocarbon with the general formula C_nH_{2n+2}. (22.1)

Alkene an unsaturated hydrocarbon containing a carbon–carbon double bond. The general formula is C_nH_{2n}. (22.2)

Alkyne an unsaturated hydrocarbon containing a triple carbon–carbon bond. The general formula is C_nH_{2n-2}. (22.2)

Alloy a substance that contains a mixture of elements and has metallic properties. (10.4)

Alloy steel a form of steel containing carbon plus other metals such as chromium, cobalt, manganese, and molybdenum. (20.8)

Alpha (α) particle a helium nucleus. (21.1)

Alpha particle production a common mode of decay for radioactive nuclides in which the mass number changes. (21.1)

Amine an organic base derived from ammonia in which one or more of the hydrogen atoms are replaced by organic groups. (14.6; 22.5)

α-Amino acid an organic acid in which an amino group and an R group are attached to the carbon atom next to the carboxyl group. (23.1)

Amorphous solid a solid with considerable disorder in its structure. (10.3)

Ampere the unit of electric current equal to one coulomb of charge per second. (17.7)

Amphoteric substance a substance that can behave either as an acid or as a base. (14.2)

Angular momentum quantum number (ℓ) the quantum number relating to the shape of an atomic orbital, which can assume any integral value from 0 to $n - 1$ for each value of n. (7.6)

Anion a negative ion. (2.6)

Anode the electrode in a galvanic cell at which oxidation occurs. (17.1)

Antibonding molecular orbital an orbital higher in energy than the atomic orbitals of which it is composed. (9.2)

Aqueous solution a solution in which water is the dissolving medium or solvent. (4)

Aromatic hydrocarbon one of a special class of cyclic unsaturated hydrocarbons, the simplest of which is benzene. (22.3)

Arrhenius concept a concept postulating that acids produce hydrogen ions in aqueous solution, while bases produce hydroxide ions. (14.1)

Arrhenius equation the equation representing the rate constant as $k = Ae^{-E_a/RT}$, where A represents the product of the collision frequency and the steric factor, and $e^{-E_a/RT}$ is the fraction of collisions with sufficient energy to produce a reaction. (12.7)

Atactic chain a polymer chain in which the substituent groups such as CH_3 are randomly distributed along the chain. (22.7)

Atmosphere the mixture of gases that surrounds the earth's surface. (5.9)

Atomic number the number of protons in the nucleus of an atom. (2.5)

Atomic radius half the distance between the nuclei in a molecule consisting of identical atoms. (7.12)

Atomic solid a solid that contains atoms at the lattice points. (10.3)

Atomic weight the weighted average mass of the atoms in a naturally occurring element. (2.3)

Aufbau principle the principle stating that as protons are added one by one to the nucleus to build up the elements, electrons are similarly added to hydrogen-like orbitals. (7.11)

Autoionization the transfer of a proton from one molecule to another of the same substance. (14.2)

Avogadro's law equal volumes of gases at the same temperature and pressure contain the same number of particles. (5.2)

Avogadro's number the number of atoms in exactly 12 grams of pure ^{12}C, equal to 6.022×10^{23}. (3.2)

Ball-and-stick model a molecular model that distorts the sizes of atoms but shows bond relationships clearly. (2.6)

Band model a molecular model for metals in which the electrons are assumed to travel around the metal crystal in molecular orbitals formed from the valence atomic orbitals of the metal atoms. (10.4)

Barometer a device for measuring atmospheric pressure. (5.1)

Base a substance that produces hydroxide ions in aqueous solution, a proton acceptor. (4.8)

Base dissociation constant (K_b) the equilibrium constant for the reaction of a base with water to produce the conjugate acid and hydroxide ion. (14.6)

Basic oxide an ionic oxide that dissolves in water to produce a basic solution. (14.10)

Basic oxygen process a process for producing steel by oxidizing and removing the impurities in iron using a high-pressure blast of oxygen. (20.8)

Battery a group of galvanic cells connected in series. (17.5)

Beta (β) particle an electron produced in radioactive decay. (21.1)

Beta particle production a decay process for radioactive nuclides in which the mass number remains constant and the atomic number changes. The net effect is to change a neutron to a proton. (21.1)

Bidentate ligand a ligand that can form two bonds to a metal ion. (20.3)

Bilayer a portion of the cell membrane consisting of phospholipids with their nonpolar tails in the interior and their polar heads interfacing with the polar water molecules. (23.4)

Bimolecular step a reaction involving the collision of two molecules. (12.6)

Binary compound a two-element compound. (2.8)

Binding energy (nuclear) the energy required to decompose a nucleus into its component nucleons. (21.5)

Biochemistry the study of the chemistry of living systems. (23)

Biomolecule a molecule responsible for maintaining and/or reproducing life. (23)

Blast furnace a furnace in which iron oxide is reduced to iron metal by using a very strong blast of hot air to produce carbon monoxide from coke, and then using this gas as a reducing agent for the iron. (20.8)

Bond energy the energy required to break a given chemical bond. (8.1)

Bond length the distance between the nuclei of the two atoms connected by a bond; the distance where the total energy of a diatomic molecule is minimal. (8.1)

Bond order the difference between the number of bonding electrons and the number of antibonding electrons, divided by two. It is an index of bond strength. (9.2)

Bonding molecular orbital an orbital lower in energy than the atomic orbitals of which it is composed. (9.2)

Bonding pair an electron pair found in the space between two atoms. (8.9)

Borane a covalent hydride of boron. (18.5)

Boyle's law the volume of a given sample of gas at constant temperature varies inversely with the pressure. (5.2)

Breeder reactor a nuclear reactor in which fissionable fuel is produced while the reactor runs. (21.6)

Brønsted–Lowry model a model proposing that an acid is a proton donor, and a base is a proton acceptor. (14.1)

Buffer capacity the ability of a buffered solution to absorb protons or hydroxide ions without a significant change in pH; determined by the magnitudes of [HA] and [A$^-$] in the solution. (15.3)

Buffered solution a solution that resists a change in its pH when either hydroxide ions or protons are added. (15.2)

Calorimetry the science of measuring heat flow. (6.2)

Capillary action the spontaneous rising of a liquid in a narrow tube. (10.2)

Carbohydrate a polyhydroxyl ketone or polyhydroxyl aldehyde or a polymer composed of these. (23.2)

Carbon steel an alloy of iron containing up to about 1.5% carbon. (20.8)

Carboxyhemoglobin a stable complex of hemoglobin and carbon monoxide that prevents normal oxygen uptake in the blood. (20.7)

Carboxyl group the —COOH group in an organic acid. (14.2; 22.5)

Carboxylic acid an organic compound containing the carboxyl group; an acid with the general formula RCOOH. (22.5)

Catalyst a substance that speeds up a reaction without being consumed. (12.8)

Cathode the electrode in a galvanic cell at which reduction occurs. (17.1)

Cathode rays the "rays" emanating from the negative electrode (cathode) in a partially evacuated tube; a stream of electrons. (2.4)

Cathodic protection a method in which an active metal, such as magnesium, is connected to steel in order to protect it from corrosion. (17.6)

Cation a positive ion. (2.6)

Cell potential (electromotive force) the driving force in a galvanic cell that pulls electrons from the reducing agent in one compartment to the oxidizing agent in the other. (17.1)

Ceramic a nonmetallic material made from clay and hardened by firing at high temperature; it contains minute silicate crystals suspended in a glassy cement. (10.5)

Chain reaction (nuclear) a self-sustaining fission process caused by the production of neutrons that proceed to split other nuclei. (21.6)

Charles's law the volume of a given sample of gas at constant pressure is directly proportional to the temperature in kelvins. (5.2)

Chelating ligand (chelate) a ligand having more than one atom with a lone pair that can be used to bond to a metal ion. (20.3)

Chemical bond the force or, more accurately, the energy, that holds two atoms together in a compound. (2.6)

Chemical change the change of substances into other substances through a reorganization of the atoms; a chemical reaction. (1.9)

Chemical equation a representation of a chemical reaction showing the relative numbers of reactant and product molecules. (3.6)

Chemical equilibrium a dynamic reaction system in which the concentrations of all reactants and products remain constant as a function of time. (13)

Chemical formula the representation of a molecule in which the symbols for the elements are used to indicate the types of atoms present and subscripts are used to show the relative numbers of atoms. (2.6)

Chemical kinetics the area of chemistry that concerns reaction rates. (12)

Chemical stoichiometry the calculation of the quantities of material consumed and produced in chemical reactions. (3)

Chirality the quality of having nonsuperimposable mirror images. (20.4)

Chlor–alkali process the process for producing chlorine and sodium hydroxide by electrolyzing brine in a mercury cell. (17.8)

Chromatography the general name for a series of methods for separating mixtures by employing a system with a mobile phase and a stationary phase. (1.9)

Coagulation the destruction of a colloid by causing particles to aggregate and settle out. (11.8)

Codons organic bases in sets of three that form the genetic code. (23.2)

Colligative properties properties of a solution that depend only on the number, and not on the identity, of the solute particles. (11.5)

Collision model a model based on the idea that molecules must collide to react; used to account for the observed characteristics of reaction rates. (12.7)

Colloid (colloidal dispersion) a suspension of particles in a dispersing medium. (11.8)

Combustion reaction the vigorous and exothermic reaction that takes place between certain substances, particularly organic compounds, and oxygen. (22.1)

Common ion effect the shift in an equilibrium position caused by the addition or presence of an ion involved in the equilibrium reaction. (15.1)

Complete ionic reaction an equation that shows all substances that are strong electrolytes as ions. (4.6)

Complex ion a charged species consisting of a metal ion surrounded by ligands. (15.8; 20.1)

Compound a substance with constant composition that can be broken down into elements by chemical processes. (1.9)

Concentration cell a galvanic cell in which both compartments contain the same components, but at different concentrations. (17.4)

Condensation the process by which vapor molecules reform a liquid. (10.8)

Condensation polymerization a type of polymerization in which the formation of a small molecule, such as water, accompanies the extension of the polymer chain. (22.6)

Condensation reaction a reaction in which two molecules are joined, accompanied by the elimination of a water molecule. (19.3)

Condensed states of matter liquids and solids. (10.1)

Conduction bands the molecular orbitals that can be occupied by mobile electrons, which are free to travel throughout a metal crystal to conduct electricity or heat. (10.4)

Conjugate acid the species formed when a proton is added to a base. (14.1)

Conjugate acid–base pair two species related to each other by the donating and accepting of a single proton. (14.1)

Conjugate base what remains of an acid molecule after a proton is lost. (14.1)

Continuous spectrum a spectrum that exhibits all the wavelengths of visible light. (7.3)

Control rods rods in a nuclear reactor composed of substances that absorb neutrons. These rods regulate the power level of the reactor. (21.6)

Coordinate covalent bond a metal–ligand bond resulting from the interaction of a Lewis base (the ligand) and a Lewis acid (the metal ion). (20.3)

Coordination compound a compound composed of a complex ion and counter ions sufficient to give no net charge. (20.3)

Coordination isomerism isomerism in a coordination compound in which the composition of the coordination sphere of the metal ion varies. (20.4)

Coordination number the number of bonds formed between the metal ion and the ligands in a complex ion. (20.3)

Copolymer a polymer formed from the polymerization of more than one type of monomer. (22.6)

Core electron an inner electron in an atom; one not in the outermost (valence) principal quantum level. (7.11)

Corrosion the process by which metals are oxidized in the atmosphere. (17.6)

Coulomb's law $E = 2.31 \times 10^{-19} \left(\dfrac{Q_1 Q_2}{r} \right)$, where E is the energy of interaction between a pair of ions, expressed in joules; r is the distance between the ion centers in nm; and Q_1 and Q_2 are the numerical ion charges. (8.1)

Counterions anions or cations that balance the charge on the complex ion in a coordination compound. (20.3)

Covalent bonding a type of bonding in which electrons are shared by atoms. (2.6; 8.1)

Cracking a process whereby large molecules of petroleum components are broken down to smaller ones by breaking carbon–carbon bonds. (22.4)

Critical mass the mass of fissionable material required to produce a self-sustaining chain reaction. (21.6)

Critical point the point on a phase diagram at which the temperature and pressure have their critical values; the end point of the liquid–vapor line. (10.9)

Critical pressure the minimum pressure required to produce liquefaction of a substance at the critical temperature. (10.9)

Critical reaction (nuclear) a reaction in which exactly one neutron from each fission event causes another fission event, thus sustaining the chain reaction. (21.6)

Critical temperature the temperature above which vapor cannot be liquefied no matter what pressure is applied. (10.9)

Crosslinking the existence of bonds between adjacent chains in a polymer, thus adding strength to the material. (22.7)

Crystal field model a model used to explain the magnetism and colors of coordination complexes through the splitting of the d orbital energies. (20.6)

Crystalline solid a solid with a regular arrangement of its components. (10.3)

Cubic closest packed (ccp) structure a solid modeled by the closest packing of spheres with an *abcabc* arrangement of layers; the unit cell is face-centered cubic. (10.4)

Cyanidation a process in which crushed gold ore is treated with an aqueous cyanide solution in the presence of air to dissolve the gold. Pure gold is recovered by reduction of the ion to the metal. (20.8)

Cyclotron a type of particle accelerator in which an ion introduced at the center is accelerated in an expanding spiral path by the use of alternating electrical fields in the presence of a magnetic field. (21.3)

Cytochromes a series of iron-containing species composed of heme and a protein. Cytochromes are the principal electron-transfer molecules in the respiratory chain. (20.7)

Dalton's law of partial pressures for a mixture of gases in a container, the total pressure exerted is the sum of the pressures that each gas would exert if it were alone. (5.5)

Degenerate orbitals a group of orbitals with the same energy. (7.7)

Dehydrogenation reaction a reaction in which two hydrogen atoms are removed from adjacent carbons of a saturated hydrocarbon, giving an unsaturated hydrocarbon. (22.1)

Delocalization the condition where the electrons in a molecule are not localized between a pair of atoms but can move throughout the molecule. (8.9)

Denaturation the breaking down of the three-dimensional structure of a protein resulting in the loss of its function. (23.1)

Denitrification the return of nitrogen from decomposed matter to the atmosphere by bacteria that change nitrates to nitrogen gas. (19.2)

Density a property of matter representing the mass per unit volume. (1.8)

Deoxyribonucleic acid (DNA) a huge nucleotide polymer having a double helical structure with complementary bases on the two strands. Its major functions are protein synthesis and the storage and transport of genetic information. (23.3)

Desalination the removal of dissolved salts from an aqueous solution. (11.6)

Dialysis a phenomenon in which a semipermeable membrane allows transfer of both solvent molecules and small solute molecules and ions. (11.6)

Diamagnetism a type of magnetism, associated with paired electrons, that causes a substance to be repelled from the inducing magnetic field. (9.3)

Differential rate law an expression that gives the rate of a reaction as a function of concentrations; often called the rate law. (12.2)

Diffraction the scattering of light from a regular array of points or lines, producing constructive and destructive interference. (7.2)

Diffusion the mixing of gases. (5.7)

Dilution the process of adding solvent to lower the concentration of solute in a solution. (4.3)

Dimer a molecule formed by the joining of two identical monomers. (22.6)

Dipole–dipole attraction the attractive force resulting when polar molecules line up so that the positive and negative ends are close to each other. (10.1)

Dipole moment a property of a molecule whose charge distribution can be represented by a center of positive charge and a center of negative charge. (8.3)

Direct reduction furnace a furnace in which iron oxide is reduced to iron metal using milder reaction conditions than in a blast furnace. (20.8)

Disaccharide a sugar formed from two monosaccharides joined by a glycoside linkage. (23.2)

Disproportionation reaction a reaction in which a given element is both oxidized and reduced. (19.7)

Distillation a method for separating the components of a liquid mixture that depends on differences in the ease of vaporization of the components. (1.9)

Disulfide linkage an S—S bond that stabilizes the tertiary structure of many proteins. (23.1)

Double bond a bond in which two pairs of electrons are shared by two atoms. (8.8)

Downs cell a cell used for electrolyzing molten sodium chloride. (17.8)

Dry cell battery a common battery used in calculators, watches, radios, and tape players. (17.5)

Dual nature of light the statement that light exhibits both wave and particulate properties. (7.2)

Effusion the passage of a gas through a tiny orifice into an evacuated chamber. (5.7)

Elastomer a material that recovers its shape after a deforming force is removed. (22.7)

Electrical conductivity the ability to conduct an electric current. (4.2)

Electrochemistry the study of the interchange of chemical and electrical energy. (17)

Electrolysis a process that involves forcing a current through a cell to cause a nonspontaneous chemical reaction to occur. (17.7)

Electrolyte a material that dissolves in water to give a solution that conducts an electric current. (4.2)

Electrolytic cell a cell that uses electrical energy to produce a chemical change that would otherwise not occur spontaneously. (17.7)

Electromagnetic radiation radiant energy that exhibits wavelike behavior and travels through space at the speed of light in a vacuum. (7.1)

Electron a negatively charged particle that moves around the nucleus of an atom. (2.4)

Electron affinity the energy change associated with the addition of an electron to a gaseous atom. (7.12)

Electron capture a process in which one of the inner-orbital electrons in an atom is captured by the nucleus. (21.1)

Electron sea model a model for metals postulating a regular array of cations in a "sea" of electrons. (10.4)

Electron spin quantum number a quantum number representing one of the two possible values for the electron spin; either $+\frac{1}{2}$ or $-\frac{1}{2}$. (7.8)

Electronegativity the tendency of an atom in a molecule to attract shared electrons to itself. (8.2)

Element a substance that cannot be decomposed into simpler substances by chemical or physical means. (1.9)

Elementary step a reaction whose rate law can be written from its molecularity. (12.6)

$E = mc^2$ Einstein's equation proposing that energy has mass; E is energy, m is mass, and c is the speed of light. (7.2)

Empirical formula the simplest whole number ratio of atoms in a compound. (3.5)

Enantiomers isomers that are nonsuperimposable mirror images of each other. (20.4)

Endpoint the point in a titration at which the indicator changes color. (4.8)

Endothermic refers to a reaction where energy (as heat) flows into the system. (6.1)

Energy the capacity to do work or to cause heat flow. (6.1)

Enthalpy a property of a system equal to $E + PV$, where E is the internal energy of the system, P is the pressure of the system, and V is the volume of the system. At constant pressure the change in enthalpy equals the energy flow as heat. (6.2)

Enthalpy (heat) of fusion the enthalpy change that occurs to melt a solid at its melting point. (10.8)

Entropy a thermodynamic function that measures randomness or disorder. (16.1)

Enzyme a large molecule, usually a protein, that catalyzes biological reactions. (12.8; 23.1)

Equilibrium point (thermodynamic definition) the position where the free energy of a reaction system has its lowest possible value. (16.8)

Equilibrium constant the value obtained when equilibrium concentrations of the chemical species are substituted in the equilibrium expression. (13.2)

Equilibrium expression the expression (from the law of mass action) obtained by multiplying the product concentrations and dividing by the multiplied reactant concentrations, with each concentration raised to a power represented by the coefficient in the balanced equation. (13.2)

Equilibrium position a particular set of equilibrium concentrations. (13.2)

Equivalence point (stoichiometric point) the point in a titration when enough titrant has been added to react exactly with the substance in solution being titrated. (4.9; 15.4)

Essential elements the elements definitely known to be essential to human life. (23)

Ester an organic compound produced by the reaction between a carboxylic acid and an alcohol. (22.5)

Exothermic refers to a reaction where energy (as heat) flows out of the system. (6.1)

Exponential notation expresses a number as $N \times 10^M$, a convenient method for representing a very large or very small number and for easily indicating the number of significant figures. (1.5)

Faraday a constant representing the charge on one mole of electrons; 96,485 coulombs. (17.3)

Fat (glyceride) an ester composed of glycerol and fatty acids. (23.4)

Fatty acid a long-chain carboxylic acid. (23.4)

Feedstock the portion of petroleum used as the raw material in a petrochemical plant; it varies from heavy hydrocarbons to light ones. (22.4)

Fermentation (as in winemaking) the conversion of sugar to ethanol using yeast. (22.5)

Filtration a method for separating the components of a mixture containing a solid and a liquid. (1.9)

First law of thermodynamics the energy of the universe is constant; same as the law of conservation of energy. (6.1)

Fission the process of using a neutron to split a heavy nucleus into two nuclei with smaller mass numbers. (21.6)

Flotation process a method of separating the mineral particles in an ore from the gangue that depends on the greater wettability of the mineral pieces. (20.8)

Formal charge the charge assigned to an atom in a molecule or polyatomic ion derived from a specific set of rules. (8.12)

Formation constant (stability constant) the equilibrium constant for each step of the formation of a complex ion by the addition of an individual ligand to a metal ion or complex ion in aqueous solution. (15.8)

Fossil fuel coal, petroleum, or natural gas; consists of carbon-based molecules derived from decomposition of once-living organisms. (6.5)

Frasch process the recovery of sulfur from underground deposits by melting it with hot water and forcing it to the surface by air pressure. (19.6)

Free energy a thermodynamic function equal to the enthalpy (H) minus the product of the entropy (S) and the Kelvin temperature (T); $G = H - TS$. Under certain conditions the change in free energy for a process is equal to the maximum useful work. (16.4)

Free radical a species with an unpaired electron. (22.6)

Frequency the number of waves (cycles) per second that pass a given point in space. (7.1)

Fuel cell a galvanic cell for which the reactants are continuously supplied. (17.5)

Functional group an atom or group of atoms in hydrocarbon derivatives that contains elements in addition to carbon and hydrogen. (22.5)

Fusion the process of combining two light nuclei to form a heavier, more stable nucleus. (21.6)

Galvanic cell a device in which chemical energy from a spontaneous redox reaction is changed to electrical energy that can be used to do work. (17.1)

Galvanizing a process in which steel is coated with zinc to prevent corrosion. (17.6)

Gamma (γ) ray a high-energy photon. (21.1)

Gangue the impurities (such as clay or sand) in an ore. (20.8)

Geiger–Müller counter (Geiger counter) an instrument that measures the rate of radioactive decay based on the ions and electrons produced as a radioactive particle passes through a gas-filled chamber. (21.4)

Gene a given segment of the DNA molecule that contains the code for a specific protein. (23.3)

Geometric (cis–trans) isomerism isomerism in which atoms or groups of atoms can assume different positions around a rigid ring or bond. (20.4; 22.2)

Glass an amorphous solid obtained when silica is mixed with other compounds, heated above its melting point, and then cooled rapidly. (10.5)

Glass electrode an electrode for measuring pH from the potential difference that develops when it is dipped into an aqueous solution containing H^+ ions. (17.4)

Glycosidic linkage a C—O—C bond formed between the rings of two cyclic monosaccharides by the elimination of water. (23.2)

Graham's law of effusion the rate of effusion of a gas is inversely proportional to the square root of the mass of its particles. (5.7)

Greenhouse effect a warming effect exerted by the earth's atmosphere (particularly CO_2 and H_2O) due to thermal energy retained by absorption of infrared radiation. (6.5)

Ground state the lowest possible energy state of an atom or molecule. (7.4)

Group (of the periodic table) a vertical column of elements having the same valence electron configuration and showing similar properties. (2.7)

Haber process the manufacture of ammonia from nitrogen and hydrogen, carried out at high pressure and high temperature with the aid of a catalyst. (3.9; 19.2)

Half-life (of a radioactive sample) the time required for the number of nuclides in a radioactive sample to reach half of the original value. (21.2)

Half-life (of a reaction) the time required for a reactant to reach half of its original concentration. (12.4)

Half-reactions the two parts of an oxidation-reduction reaction, one representing oxidation, the other reduction. (4.10; 17.1)

Halogen a Group 7A element. (2.7; 19.7)

Halogenation the addition of halogen atoms to unsaturated hydrocarbons. (22.2)

Hard water water from natural sources that contains relatively large concentrations of calcium and magnesium ions. (18.4)

Heat energy transferred between two objects due to a temperature difference between them. (6.1)

Heat capacity the amount of energy required to raise the temperature of an object by one degree Celsius. (6.2)

Heat of fusion the enthalpy change that occurs to melt a solid at its melting point. (10.8)

Heat of hydration the enthalpy change associated with placing gaseous molecules or ions in water; the sum of the energy needed to expand the solvent and the energy released from the solvent–solute interactions. (11.2)

Heat of solution the enthalpy change associated with dissolving a solute in a solvent; the sum of the energies needed to expand both solvent and solute in a solution and the energy released from the solvent–solute interactions. (11.2)

Heat of vaporization the energy required to vaporize one mole of a liquid at a pressure of one atmosphere. (10.8)

Heating curve a plot of temperature versus time for a substance where energy is added at a constant rate. (10.8)

Heisenberg uncertainty principle a principle stating that there is a fundamental limitation to how precisely both the position and momentum of a particle can be known at a given time. (7.5)

Heme an iron complex. (20.7)

Hemoglobin a biomolecule composed of four myoglobin-like units (proteins plus heme) that can bind and transport four oxygen molecules in the blood. (20.7)

Henderson–Hasselbalch equation an equation giving the relationship between the pH of an acid–base system and the concentrations of base and acid: $pH = pK_a + \log\left(\frac{[\text{base}]}{[\text{acid}]}\right)$. (15.2)

Henry's law the amount of a gas dissolved in a solution is directly proportional to the pressure of the gas above the solution. (11.3)

Hess's law in going from a particular set of reactants to a particular set of products, the enthalpy change is the same whether the reaction takes place in one step or in a series of steps; in summary, enthalpy is a state function. (6.3)

Heterogeneous equilibrium an equilibrium involving reactants and/or products in more than one phase. (13.4)

Hexagonal closest packed (hcp) structure a structure composed of closest packed spheres with an *ababab* arrangement of layers; the unit cell is hexagonal. (10.4)

Homogeneous equilibrium an equilibrium system where all reactants and products are in the same phase. (13.4)

Homopolymer a polymer formed from the polymerization of only one type of monomer. (22.6)

Hund's rule the lowest energy configuration for an atom is the one having the maximum number of unpaired electrons allowed by the Pauli exclusion principle in a particular set of degenerate orbitals, with all unpaired electrons having parallel spins. (7.11)

Hybrid orbitals a set of atomic orbitals adopted by an atom in a molecule different from those of the atom in the free state. (9.1)

Hybridization a mixing of the native orbitals on a given atom to form special atomic orbitals for bonding. (9.1)

Hydration the interaction between solute particles and water molecules. (4.1)

Hydride a binary compound containing hydrogen. The hydride ion, H^-, exists in ionic hydrides. The three classes of hydrides are covalent, interstitial, and ionic. (18.3)

Hydrocarbon a compound composed of carbon and hydrogen. (22.1)

Hydrocarbon derivative an organic molecule that contains one or more elements in addition to carbon and hydrogen. (22.5)

Hydrogen bonding unusually strong dipole–dipole attractions that occur among molecules in which hydrogen is bonded to a highly electronegative atom. (10.1)

Hydrogenation reaction a reaction in which hydrogen is added, with a catalyst present, to a carbon–carbon multiple bond. (22.2)

Hydrohalic acid an aqueous solution of a hydrogen halide. (19.7)

Hydrometallurgy a process for extracting metals from ores by use of aqueous chemical solutions. Two steps are involved: selective leaching and selective precipitation. (20.8)

Hydronium ion the H_3O^+ ion; a hydrated proton. (14.1)

Hypothesis one or more assumptions put forth to explain the observed behavior of nature. (1.2)

Ideal gas law an equation of state for a gas, where the state of the gas is its condition at a given time; expressed by $PV = nRT$, where P = pressure, V = volume, n = moles of the gas, R = the universal gas constant, and T = absolute temperature. This equation expresses behavior approached by real gases at high T and low P. (5.3)

Ideal solution a solution whose vapor pressure is directly proportional to the mole fraction of solvent present. (11.4)

Indicator a chemical that changes color and is used to mark the end point of a titration. (4.8; 15.5)

Inert pair effect the tendency for the heavier Group 3A elements to exhibit the $+1$ as well as the expected $+3$ oxidation states, and Group 4A elements to exhibit the $+2$ as well as the $+4$ oxidation states. (18.5)

Inhibition (of combustion) the process whereby a polymer is made flame-retardant by interrupting the cycle of combustion. (22.7)

Integrated rate law an expression that shows the concentration of a reactant as a function of time. (12.2)

Interhalogen compound a compound formed by the reaction of one halogen with another. (19.7)

Intermediate a species that is neither a reactant nor a product but that is formed and consumed in the reaction sequence. (12.6)

Intermolecular forces relatively weak interactions that occur between molecules. (10.1)

Internal energy a property of a system that can be changed by a flow of work, heat or both; $\Delta E = q + w$, where ΔE is the change in the internal energy of the system, q is heat, and w is work. (6.1)

Ion an atom or a group of atoms that has a net positive or negative charge. (2.6)

Ion exchange (water softening) the process in which an ion-exchange resin removes unwanted ions (for example, Ca^{2+} and Mg^{2+}) and replaces them with Na^+ ions, which do not interfere with soap and detergent action. (18.4)

Ion pairing a phenomenon occurring in solution when oppositely charged ions aggregate and behave as a single particle. (11.7)

Ion-product (dissociation) constant (K_w) the equilibrium constant for the auto-ionization of water; $K_w = [H^+][OH^-]$. At $25°C$, K_w equals 1.0×10^{-14}. (14.2)

Ion-selective electrode an electrode sensitive to the concentration of a particular ion in solution. (17.4)

Ionic bonding the electrostatic attraction between oppositely charged ions. (2.6; 8.1)

Ionic compound (binary) a compound that results when a metal reacts with a nonmetal to form a cation and an anion. (8.1)

Ionic solid (salt) a solid containing cations and anions that dissolves in water to give a solution containing the separated ions which are mobile and thus free to conduct electrical current. (2.6; 10.3)

Irreversible process any real process. When a system undergoes the changes State 1 → State 2 → State 1 by any real pathway, the universe is different than before the cyclic process took place in the system. (16.9)

Isoelectronic ions ions containing the same number of electrons. (8.4)

Isomers species with the same formula but different properties. (20.4)

Isotactic chain a polymer chain in which the substituent groups such as CH_3 are all arranged on the same side of the chain. (22.7)

Isotonic solutions solutions having identical osmotic pressures. (11.6)

Isotopes atoms of the same element (the same number of protons) with different numbers of neutrons. They have identical atomic numbers but different mass numbers. (2.5; 21)

Ketone an organic compound containing the carbonyl group

bonded to two carbon atoms. (22.5)

Kinetic energy ($\frac{1}{2}mv^2$) energy due to the motion of an object; dependent on the mass of the object and the square of its velocity. (6.1)

Kinetic molecular theory (KMT) a model that assumes that an ideal gas is composed of tiny particles (molecules) in constant motion. (5.6)

Lanthanide contraction the decrease in the atomic radii of the lanthanide series elements, going from left to right in the periodic table. (20.1)

Lanthanide series a group of fourteen elements following lanthanum in the periodic table, in which the $4f$ orbitals are being filled. (7.11; 18.1; 20.1)

Lattice a three-dimensional system of points designating the positions of the centers of the components of a solid (atoms, ions, or molecules). (10.3)

Lattice energy the energy change occurring when separated gaseous ions are packed together to form an ionic solid. (8.5)

Law of conservation of energy energy can be converted from one form to another but can be neither created nor destroyed. (6.1)

Law of conservation of mass mass is neither created nor destroyed. (1.2; 2.2)

Law of definite proportions a given compound always contains exactly the same proportion of elements by mass. (2.2)

Law of mass action a general description of the equilibrium condition; it defines the equilibrium constant expression. (13.2)

Law of multiple proportions a law stating that when two elements form a series of compounds, the ratios of the masses of the second element that combine with one gram of the first element can always be reduced to small whole numbers. (2.2)

Leaching the extraction of metals from ores using aqueous chemical solutions. (20.8)

Lead storage battery a battery (used in cars) in which the anode is lead, the cathode is lead coated with lead dioxide, and the electrolyte is a sulfuric acid solution. (17.5)

Le Châtelier's principle if a change is imposed on a system at equilibrium, the position of the equilibrium will shift in a direction that tends to reduce the effect of that change. (13.7)

Lewis acid an electron-pair acceptor. (14.11)

Lewis base an electron-pair donor. (14.11)

Lewis structure a diagram of a molecule showing how the valence electrons are arranged among the atoms in the molecule. (8.10)

Ligand a neutral molecule or ion having a lone pair of electrons that can be used to form a bond to a metal ion; a Lewis base. (20.1)

Lime–soda process a water-softening method in which lime and soda ash are added to water to remove calcium and magnesium ions by precipitation. (14.6)

Limiting reactant (limiting reagent) the reactant that is completely consumed when a reaction is run to completion. (3.9)

Line spectrum a spectrum showing only certain discrete wavelengths. (7.3)

Linear accelerator a type of particle accelerator in which a changing electrical field is used to accelerate a positive ion along a linear path. (21.3)

Linkage isomerism isomerism involving a complex ion where the ligands are all the same but the point of attachment of at least one of the ligands differs. (20.4)

Lipids water-insoluble substances that can be extracted from cells by nonpolar organic solvents. (23.4)

Liquefaction the transformation of a gas into a liquid. (18.1)

Localized electron (LE) model a model which assumes that a molecule is composed of atoms that are bound together by sharing pairs of electrons using the atomic orbitals of the bound atoms. (8.9)

Lock-and-key model a model for the mechanism of enzyme activity postulating that the shapes of the substrate and the enzyme are such that they fit together as a key fits a specific lock. (23.1)

London dispersion forces the forces, existing among noble gas atoms and nonpolar molecules, that involve an accidental dipole that induces a momentary dipole in a neighbor. (10.1)

Lone pair an electron pair that is localized on a given atom; an electron pair not involved in bonding. (8.9)

Magnetic quantum number m_ℓ, the quantum number relating to the orientation of an orbital in space relative to the other orbitals with the same ℓ quantum number. It can have integral values between ℓ and $-\ell$, including zero. (7.6)

Main-group (representative) elements elements in the groups labeled 1A, 2A, 3A, 4A, 5A, 6A, 7A, and 8A in the periodic table. The group number gives the sum of the valence s and p electrons. (7.11; 18.1)

Major species the components present in relatively large amounts in a solution. (14.3)

Manometer a device for measuring the pressure of a gas in a container. (5.1)

Mass the quantity of matter in an object. (1.3)

Mass defect the change in mass occurring when a nucleus is formed from its component nucleons. (21.5)

Mass number the total number of protons and neutrons in the atomic nucleus of an atom. (2.5; 21)

Mass percent the percent by mass of a component of a mixture (11.1) or of a given element in a compound. (3.4)

Mass spectrometer an instrument used to determine the relative masses of atoms by the deflection of their ions on a magnetic field. (3.1)

Matter the material of the universe. (1.9)

Messenger RNA (mRNA) a special RNA molecule built in the cell nucleus that migrates into the cytoplasm and participates in protein synthesis. (23.3)

Metal an element that gives up electrons relatively easily and is lustrous, malleable, and a good conductor of heat and electricity. (2.7)

Metalloenzyme an enzyme containing a metal ion at its active site. (23.1)

Metalloids (semimetals) elements along the division line in the periodic table between metals and nonmetals. These elements exhibit both metallic and nonmetallic properties. (7.13; 18.1)

Metallurgy the process of separating a metal from its ore and preparing it for use. (18.1; 20.8)

Micelles aggregates of fatty acid anions having their hydrophobic tails in the interior and their polar heads pointing outward to interact with the polar water molecules. (23.4)

Millimeters of mercury (mmHg) a unit of pressure, also called a torr, 760 mm Hg = 760 torr = 101,325 Pa = 1 standard atmosphere. (5.1)

Mineral a relatively pure compound as found in nature. (20.8)

Mixture a material of variable composition that contains two or more substances. (1.8)

Model (theory) a set of assumptions put forth to explain the observed behavior of matter. The models of chemistry usually involve assumptions about the behavior of individual atoms or molecules. (1.2)

Moderator a substance used in a nuclear reactor to slow down the neutrons. (21.6)

Molal boiling-point elevation constant a constant characteristic of a particular solvent that gives the change in boiling point as a function of solution molality; used in molecular weight determinations. (11.5)

Molal freezing-point depression constant a constant characteristic of a particular solvent that gives the change in freezing point as a function of the solution molality; used in molecular weight determinations (11.5)

Molality the number of moles of solute per kilogram of solvent in a solution. (11.1)

Molar heat capacity the energy required to raise the temperature of one mole of a substance by one degree Celsius. (6.2)

Molar mass the mass in grams of one mole of molecules or formula units of a substance; also called *molecular weight*. (3.3)

Molar volume the volume of one mole of an ideal gas; equal to 22.42 liters at STP. (5.4)

Molarity moles of solute per volume of solution in liters. (4.3; 11.1)

Mole (mol) the number equal to the number of carbon atoms in exactly 12 grams of pure ^{12}C: Avogadro's number. One mole represents 6.022×10^{23} units. (3.2)

Mole fraction the ratio of the number of moles of a given component in a mixture to the total number of moles in the mixture. (5.5; 11.1)

Mole ratio (stoichiometry) the ratio of moles of one substance to moles of another substance in a balanced chemical equation. (3.8)

Molecular equation an equation representing a reaction in solu-

tion showing the reactants and products in undissociated form, whether they are strong or weak electrolytes. (4.6)

Molecular formula the exact formula of a molecule, giving the types of atoms and the number of each type. (3.5)

Molecular orbital (MO) model a model that regards a molecule as a collection of nuclei and electrons, where the electrons are assumed to occupy orbitals much as they do in atoms, but having the orbitals extend over the entire molecule. In this model the electrons are assumed to be delocalized rather than always located between a given pair of atoms. (9.2; 10.4)

Molecular orientations (kinetics) orientations of molecules during collisions, some of which can lead to reaction while others cannot. (12.7)

Molecular solid a solid composed of neutral molecules at the lattice points. (10.3)

Molecular structure the three-dimensional arrangement of atoms in a molecule. (8.13)

Molecular weight the mass in grams of one mole of molecules or formula units of a substance; the same as molar mass. (3.3)

Molecularity the number of species that must collide to produce the reaction represented by an elementary step in a reaction mechanism. (12.6)

Molecule a bonded collection of two or more atoms of the same or different elements. (2.6)

Monodentate (unidentate) ligand a ligand that can form one bond to a metal ion. (20.3)

Monoprotic acid an acid with one acidic proton. (14.2)

Monosaccharide (simple sugar) a polyhydroxy ketone or aldehyde containing from three to nine carbon atoms. (23.2)

Myoglobin an oxygen-storing biomolecule consisting of a heme complex and a proton. (20.7)

Natural law a statement that expresses generally observed behavior. (1.2)

Nernst equation an equation relating the potential of an electrochemical cell to the concentrations of the cell components;

$$\mathscr{E} = \mathscr{E}° - \frac{0.0591}{n} \log(Q) \text{ at } 25°C \qquad (17.4)$$

Net ionic equation an equation for a reaction in solution, where strong electrolytes are written as ions, showing only those components that are directly involved in the chemical change. (4.6)

Network solid an atomic solid containing strong directional covalent bonds. (10.5)

Neutralization reaction an acid–base reaction. (4.8)

Neutron a particle in the atomic nucleus with mass virtually equal to the proton's but with no charge. (2.5; 21)

Nitride salt a compound containing the N^{3-} anion. (18.2)

Nitrogen cycle the conversion of N_2 to nitrogen-containing compounds, followed by the return of nitrogen gas to the atmosphere by natural decay processes. (19.2)

Nitrogen fixation the process of transforming N_2 to nitrogen-containing compounds useful to plants. (19.2)

Nitrogen-fixing bacteria bacteria in the root nodules of plants that can convert atmospheric nitrogen to ammonia and other nitrogen-containing compounds useful to plants. (19.2)

Noble gas a Group 8A element. (2.7; 19.8)

Node an area of an orbital having zero electron probability. (7.7)

Nonelectrolyte a substance which, when dissolved in water, gives a nonconducting solution. (4.2)

Nonmetal an element not exhibiting metallic characteristics. Chemically, a typical nonmetal accepts electrons from a metal. (2.7)

Normal boiling point the temperature at which the vapor pressure of a liquid is exactly one atmosphere. (10.8)

Normal melting point the temperature at which the solid and liquid states have the same vapor pressure under conditions where the total pressure on the system is one atmosphere. (10.8)

Normality the number of equivalents of a substance dissolved in a liter of solution. (11.1)

Nuclear atom an atom having a dense center of positive charge (the nucleus) with electrons moving around the outside. (2.4)

Nuclear transformation the change of one element into another. (21.3)

Nucleon a particle in an atomic nucleus, either a neutron or a proton. (21)

Nucleotide a monomer of the nucleic acids composed of a five-carbon sugar, a nitrogen-containing base, and phosphoric acid. (23.3)

Nucleus the small, dense center of positive charge in an atom. (2.4)

Nuclide the general term applied to each unique atom; represented by $^A_Z X$, where X is the symbol for a particular element. (21)

Octet rule the observation that atoms of nonmetals tend to form the most stable molecules when they are surrounded by eight electrons (to fill their valence orbitals). (8.10)

Open hearth process a process for producing steel by oxidizing and removing the impurities in molten iron using external heat and a blast of air or oxygen. (20.8)

Optical isomerism isomerism in which the isomers have opposite effects on plane-polarized light. (20.4)

Orbital a specific wave function for an electron in an atom. The square of this function gives the probability distribution for the electron. (7.5)

d-**Orbital splitting** a splitting of the *d* orbitals of the metal ion in a complex such that the orbitals pointing at the ligands have higher energies than those pointing between the ligands. (20.6)

Order (of reactant) the positive or negative exponent, determined by experiment, of the reactant concentration in a rate law. (12.2)

Organic acid an acid with a carbon-atom backbone; often contains the carboxyl group. (14.2)

Organic chemistry the study of carbon-containing compounds (typically chains of carbon atoms) and their properties. (22)

Osmosis the flow of solvent into a solution through a semipermeable membrane. (11.6)

Osmotic pressure (π) the pressure that must be applied to a solution to stop osmosis; $\pi = MRT$. (11.6)

Ostwald process a commercial process for producing nitric acid by the oxidation of ammonia. (19.2)

Oxidation an increase in oxidation state (a loss of electrons). (4.9; 17.1)

Oxidation–reduction (redox) reaction a reaction in which one or more electrons are transferred. (4.9; 17.1)

Oxidation states a concept that provides a way to keep track of electrons in oxidation–reduction reactions according to certain rules. (4.9; 20.3)

Oxidizing agent (electron acceptor) a reactant that accepts electrons from another reactant. (4.9; 17.1)

Oxyacid an acid in which the acidic proton is attached to an oxygen atom. (14.2)

Ozone O_3, the form of elemental oxygen in addition to the much more common O_2. (19.5)

Paramagnetism a type of induced magnetism, associated with unpaired electrons, that causes a substance to be attracted into the inducing magnetic field. (9.3)

Partial pressures the independent pressures exerted by different gases in a mixture. (5.5)

Particle accelerator a device used to accelerate nuclear particles to very high speeds. (21.3)

Pascal the SI unit of pressure; equal to newtons per meter squared. (5.1)

Pauli exclusion principle in a given atom no two electrons can have the same set of four quantum numbers. (7.8)

Peptide linkage the bond resulting from the condensation reaction between amino acids; represented by:

$$\underset{\substack{|\\ -C-N- \\ |}}{\overset{\substack{O \quad H\\ \| \quad |}}{}} \qquad (23.1)$$

Percent dissociation the ratio of the amount of a substance that is dissociated at equilibrium to the initial concentration of the substance in a solution, multiplied by 100. (14.5)

Percent yield the actual yield of a product as a percentage of the theoretical yield. (3.9)

Periodic table a chart showing all the elements arranged in columns with similar chemical properties. (2.7)

Petrochemicals chemicals obtained from petroleum either by steam cracking or as by-products of refinery operations. They serve as raw materials for the chemical industry. (22.4)

pH curve (titration curve) a plot showing the pH of a solution being analyzed as a function of the amount of titrant added. (15.4)

pH scale a log scale based on 10 and equal to $-\log[H^+]$; a convenient way to represent solution acidity. (14.3)

Phase diagram a convenient way of representing the phases of a substance in a closed system as a function of temperature and pressure. (10.9)

Phenyl group the benzene molecule minus one hydrogen atom. (22.3)

Phospholipids esters of glycerol containing two fatty acids and a phosphate group. Having nonpolar tails and polar heads, they tend to form bilayers in aqueous solution. (23.4)

Photochemical smog air pollution produced by the action of light on oxygen, nitrogen oxides, and unburned fuel from auto exhaust to form ozone and other pollutants. (5.9)

Photon a quantum of electromagnetic radiation. (7.2)

Physical change a change in the form of a substance, but not in its chemical composition; chemical bonds are not broken in a physical change. (1.9)

Pi (π) bond a covalent bond in which parallel *p* orbitals share an electron pair occupying the space above and below the line joining the atoms. (9.1)

Planck's constant the constant relating the change in energy for a system to the frequency of the electromagnetic radiation absorbed or emitted; equal to 6.626×10^{-34} J s. (7.2)

Polar covalent bond a covalent bond in which the electrons are not shared equally because one atom attracts them more strongly than the other. (8.1)

Polar molecule a molecule that has a permanent dipole moment. (4.1)

Polyatomic ion an ion containing a number of atoms. (2.6)

Polyelectronic atom an atom with more than one electron. (7.9)

Polymer a large, usually chainlike molecule built from many small molecules (monomers). (22.6)

Polymerization a process in which many small molecules (monomers) are joined together to form a large molecule. (22.2; 22.4; 22.7)

Polypeptide a polymer formed from amino acids joined together by peptide linkages. (23.1)

Polyprotic acid an acid with more than one acidic proton. It dissociates in a stepwise manner, one proton at a time. (14.7)

Porous disk a disk in a tube connecting two different solutions in a galvanic cell that allows ion flow without extensive mixing of the solutions. (17.1)

Porphyrin a planar ligand with a central ring structure and various substituent groups at the edges of the ring. (20.7)

Positional probability a type of probability that depends on the number of arrangements in space that yield a particular state. (16.1)

Positron production a mode of nuclear decay in which a particle is formed having the same mass as an electron but opposite charge. The net effect is to change a proton to a neutron. (21.1)

Potential energy energy due to position or composition. (6.1)

Precipitation reaction a reaction in which an insoluble substance forms and separates from the solution. (4.5)

Precision the degree of agreement among several measurements of the same quantity; the reproducibility of a measurement. (1.4)

Primary structure (of a protein) the order (sequence) of amino acids in the protein chain. (23.1)

Principal quantum number (n) the quantum number relating to the size and energy of an orbital; it can have any positive integer value. (7.6)

Probability distribution the square of the wave function indicating the probability of finding an electron at a particular point in space. (7.5)

Product a substance resulting from a chemical reaction. It is shown to the right of the arrow in a chemical equation. (3.6)

Protein a natural high-molecular-weight polymer formed by condensation reactions between amino acids. (23.1)

Proton a positively charged particle in an atomic nucleus. (2.5; 21)

Pure substance a substance with constant composition. (1.9)

Pyrometallurgy recovery of a metal from its ore by treatment at high temperatures. (20.8)

Quantization the concept that energy can occur only in discrete units called *quanta*. (7.2)

Rad a unit of radiation dosage corresponding to 10^{-2} J of energy deposited per kilogram of tissue (from *r*adiation *a*bsorbed *d*ose). (21.7)

Radioactive decay (radioactivity) the spontaneous decomposition of a nucleus to form a different nucleus. (2.4; 21.1)

Radiocarbon dating (carbon-14 dating) a method for dating ancient wood or cloth based on the rate of radioactive decay of the nuclide $^{14}_{6}C$. (21.4)

Radiotracer a radioactive nuclide, introduced into an organism for diagnostic purposes, whose pathway can be traced by monitoring its radioactivity. (21.4)

Random error an error that has an equal probability of being high or low. (1.4)

Raoult's law the vapor pressure of a solution is directly proportional to the mole fraction of solvent present. (11.4)

Rate constant the proportionality constant in the relationship between reaction rate and reactant concentrations. (12.2)

Rate of decay the change in the number of radioactive nuclides in a sample per unit time. (21.2)

Rate-determining step the slowest step in a reaction mechanism, the one determining the overall rate. (12.6)

Rate law (differential rate law) an expression that shows how the rate of reaction depends on the concentration of reactants. (12.2)

Reactant a starting substance in a chemical reaction. It appears to the left of the arrow in a chemical equation. (3.6)

Reaction mechanism the series of elementary steps involved in a chemical reaction. (12.6)

Reaction quotient Q a quotient obtained by applying the law of mass action to initial concentrations rather than to equilibrium concentrations. (13.5)

Reaction rate the change in concentration of a reactant or product per unit time. (12.1)

Reactor core the part of a nuclear reactor where the fission reaction takes place. (21.6)

Reducing agent (electron donor) a reactant that donates electrons to another substance to reduce the oxidation state of one of its atoms. (4.9; 17.1)

Reduction a decrease in oxidation state (a gain of electrons). (4.9; 17.1)

Rem a unit of radiation dosage that accounts for both the energy of the dose and its effectiveness in causing biological damage (from *r*oentgen *e*quivalent for *m*an). (21.7)

Resonance a condition occurring when more than one valid Lewis structure can be written for a particular molecule. The actual electronic structure is not represented by any one of the Lewis structures but by the average of all of them. (8.12)

Reverse osmosis the process occurring when the external pressure on a solution causes a net flow of solvent through a semipermeable membrane from the solution to the solvent. (11.6)

Reversible process a cyclic process carried out by a hypothetical pathway, which leaves the universe exactly the same as it was before the process. No real process is reversible. (16.9)

Ribonucleic acid (RNA) a nucleotide polymer that transmits the genetic information stored in DNA to the ribosomes for protein synthesis. (23.3)

Roasting a process of converting sulfide minerals to oxides by heating in air at temperatures below their melting points. (20.8)

Root mean square velocity the square root of the average of the squares of the individual velocities of gas particles. (5.6)

Salt an ionic compound. (14.8)

Salt bridge a U-tube containing an electrolyte that connects the two compartments of a galvanic cell, allowing ion flow without extensive mixing of the different solutions. (17.1)

Scientific method the process of studying natural phenomena, involving observations, forming laws and theories, and testing of theories by experimentation. (1.1)

Scintillation counter an instrument that measures radioactive decay by sensing the flashes of light produced in a substance by the radiation. (21.4)

Second law of thermodynamics in any spontaneous process, there is always an increase in the entropy of the universe. (16.2)

Secondary structure (of a protein) the three-dimensional structure of the protein chain (for example, α-helix, random coil, or pleated sheet). (23.1)

Selective precipitation a method of separating metal ions from an aqueous mixture by using a reagent whose anion forms a precipitate with only one or a few of the ions in the mixture. (4.7; 15.7)

Semiconductor a substance conducting only a slight electrical current at room temperature, but showing increased conductivity at higher temperatures. (10.5)

Semipermeable membrane a membrane that allows solvent but not solute molecules to pass through. (11.6)

SI units International System of units based on the metric system and units derived from the metric system. (1.2)

Side chain (of amino acid) the hydrocarbon group on an amino acid represented by H, CH_3, or a more complex substituent. (23.1)

Sigma (σ) bond a covalent bond in which the electron pair is shared in an area centered on a line running between the atoms. (9.1)

Significant figures the certain digits and the first uncertain digit of a measurement. (1.4)

Silica the fundamental silicon-oxygen compound, which has the empirical formula SiO_2, and forms the basis of quartz and certain types of sand. (10.5)

Silicates salts that contain metal cations and polyatomic silicon-oxygen anions that are usually polymeric. (10.5)

Single bond a bond in which one pair of electrons is shared by two atoms. (8.8)

Smelting a metallurgical process that involves reducing metal ions to the free metal. (20.8)

Solubility the amount of a substance that dissolves in a given volume of solvent at a given temperature. (4.2)

Solubility product constant the constant for the equilibrium expression representing the dissolving of an ionic solid in water. (15.6)

Solute a substance dissolved in a liquid to form a solution. (4.2; 11.1)

Solution a homogeneous mixture. (1.9)

Solvent the dissolving medium in a solution. (4.2)

Somatic damage radioactive damage to an organism resulting in its sickness or death. (21.7)

Space-filling model a model of a molecule showing the relative sizes of the atoms and their relative orientations. (2.6)

Specific heat capacity the energy required to raise the temperature of one gram of a substance by one degree Celsius. (6.2)

Spectator ions ions present in solution that do not participate directly in a reaction. (4.6)

Spectrochemical series a listing of ligands in order based on their ability to produce d-orbital splitting. (20.6)

Spontaneous fission the spontaneous splitting of a heavy nuclide into two lighter nuclides. (21.1)

Spontaneous process a process that occurs without outside intervention. (16.1)

Standard atmosphere a unit of pressure equal to 760 mm Hg. (5.1)

Standard enthalpy of formation the enthalpy change that accompanies the formation of one mole of a compound at 25°C from its elements, with all substances in their standard states at that temperature. (6.4)

Standard free energy change the change in free energy that will occur for one unit of reaction if the reactants in their standard states are converted to products in their standard states. (16.6)

Standard free energy of formation the change in free energy that accompanies the formation of one mole of a substance from its constituent elements with all reactants and products in their standard states. (16.6)

Standard hydrogen electrode a platinum conductor in contact with 1 M H^+ ions and bathed by hydrogen gas at one atmosphere. (17.2)

Standard reduction potential the potential of a half-reaction under standard state conditions, as measured against the potential of the standard hydrogen electrode. (17.2)

Standard solution a solution whose concentration is accurately known. (4.3)

Standard state a reference state for a specific substance defined according to a set of conventional definitions. (6.4)

Standard temperature and pressure (STP) the condition 0°C and 1 atmosphere of pressure. (5.4)

Standing wave a stationary wave as on a string of a musical instrument; in the wave mechanical model, the electron in the hydrogen atom is considered to be a standing wave. (7.5)

State function (property) a property that is independent of the pathway. (6.1)

States of matter the three different forms in which matter can exist; solid, liquid, and gas. (1.9)

Steam cracking a process whereby hydrocarbon molecules are broken into small fragments by steam at very high temperatures. (22.4)

Stereoisomerism isomerism in which all the bonds in the isomers are the same but the spatial arrangements of the atoms are different. (20.4)

Steric factor the factor (always less than one) that reflects the fraction of collisions with orientations that can produce a chemical reaction. (12.7)

Steroid one of a class of lipids with a characteristic fused carbon-ring structure that includes cholesterol, hormones, and bile acids. (23.4)

Stoichiometric quantities quantities of reactants mixed in exactly the correct amounts so that all are used up at the same time. (3.9)

Strong acid an acid that completely dissociates to produce an H^+ ion and the conjugate base. (4.2; 14.2)

Strong base a metal hydroxide salt that completely dissociates into its ions in water. (4.2; 14.6)

Strong electrolyte a material which, when dissolved in water, gives a solution that conducts an electric current very efficiently. (4.2)

Structural formula the representation of a molecule in which the relative positions of the atoms are shown and the bonds are indicated by lines. (2.6)

Structural isomerism isomerism in which the isomers contain the same atoms but one or more bonds differ. (20.4; 22.1)

Subcritical reaction (nuclear) a reaction in which less than one neutron causes another fission event and the process dies out. (21.6)

Sublimation the process by which a substance goes directly from the solid to the gaseous state without passing through the liquid state. (10.8)

Subshell a set of orbitals with a given azimuthal quantum number. (7.6)

Substitution reaction (hydrocarbons) a reaction in which an atom, usually a halogen, replaces a hydrogen atom in a hydrocarbon. (22.1)

Supercooling the process of cooling a liquid below its freezing point without its changing to a solid. (10.8)

Supercritical reaction (nuclear) a reaction in which more than one neutron from each fission event causes another fission event. The process rapidly escalates to a violent explosion. (21.6)

Superheating the process of heating a liquid above its boiling point without its boiling. (10.8)

Superoxide a compound containing the O_2^- anion. (18.2)

Surface tension the resistance of a liquid to an increase in its surface area. (10.2)

Surfactant a wetting agent, such as soap, that assists water in wetting and suspending nonpolar materials. (23.4)

Surroundings everything in the universe surrounding a thermodynamic system. (6.1)

Syndiotactic chain a polymer chain in which the substituent groups such as CH_3 are arranged on alternate sides of the chain. (22.7)

Syngas synthetic gas, a mixture of carbon monoxide and hydrogen, obtained by coal gasification. (6.6)

System (thermodynamic) that part of the universe on which attention is to be focused. (6.1)

Systematic error an error that always occurs in the same direction. (1.4)

Tempering a process in steel production that fine-tunes the proportions of carbon crystals and cementite by heating to intermediate temperatures followed by rapid cooling. (20.8)

Termolecular step a reaction involving the simultaneous collision of three molecules. (12.6)

Tertiary structure (of a protein) the overall shape of a protein, long and narrow or globular, maintained by different types of intramolecular interactions. (23.1)

Theoretical yield the maximum amount of a given product that can be formed when the limiting reactant is completely consumed. (3.9)

Theory a set of assumptions put forth to explain some aspect of the observed behavior of matter. (1.2)

Thermal pollution the oxygen-depleting effect on lakes and rivers of using water for industrial cooling and returning it to its natural source at a higher temperature. (11.3)

Thermodynamics the study of energy and its interconversions. (6.1)

Thermodynamic stability (nuclear) the potential energy of a particular nucleus as compared to the sum of the potential energies of its component protons and neutrons. (21.1)

Thermoplastic polymer a substance that when molded to a certain shape under appropriate conditions can later be remelted. (22.7)

Thermoset polymer a substance that when molded to a certain shape under pressure and high temperatures cannot be softened again or dissolved. (22.7)

Third law of thermodynamics the entropy of a perfect crystal at 0 K is zero. (16.5)

Titration a technique in which one solution is used to analyze another. (4.8)

Torr another name for millimeter of mercury (mm Hg). (5.1)

Trace elements metals present only in trace amounts in the human body but essential for the action of many enzymes. (23)

Transfer RNA (tRNA) a small RNA fragment that finds specific amino acids and attaches them to the protein chain as dictated by the codons in mRNA. (23.3)

Transition metals several series of elements in which inner orbitals (*d* or *f* orbitals) are being filled. (7.11; 18.1)

Transuranium elements the elements beyond uranium that are made artificially by particle bombardment. (21.3)

Triple bond a bond in which three pairs of electrons are shared by two atoms. (8.8)

Triple point the point on a phase diagram at which all three states of a substance are present. (10.9)

Tyndall effect the scattering of light by particles in a suspension. (11.8)

Uncertainty (in measurement) the characteristic that any measurement involves estimates and cannot be exactly reproduced. (1.4)

Unimolecular step a reaction step involving only one molecule. (12.6)

Unit cell the smallest repeating unit of a lattice. (10.3)

Unit factor method an equivalence statement between units used for converting from one unit to another. (1.6)

Universal gas constant the combined proportionality constant in the ideal gas law; 0.08206 L · atm/K · mol or 8.3145 J/K · mol. (5.3)

Valence electrons the electrons in the outermost principal quantum level of an atom. (7.11)

Valence shell electron pair repulsion (VSEPR) model a model whose main postulate is that the structure around a given atom in a molecule is determined principally by minimizing electron-pair repulsions. (8.13)

van der Waals's equation a mathematical expression for describing the behavior of real gases. (5.8)

van't Hoff factor the ratio of moles of particles in solution to moles of solute dissolved. (11.7)

Vapor pressure the pressure of the vapor over a liquid at equilibrium. (10.8)

Vaporization (evaporization) the change in state that occurs when a liquid evaporates to form a gas. (10.8)

Viscosity the resistance of a liquid to flow. (10.2)

Volt the unit of electrical potential defined as one joule of work per coulomb of charge transferred. (17.1)

Voltmeter an instrument that measures cell potential by drawing electric current through a known resistance. (17.1)

Volumetric analysis a process involving titration of one solution with another. (4.8)

Vulcanization a process in which sulfur is added to rubber and the mixture is heated, causing crosslinking of the polymer chains and thus adding strength to the rubber. (22.7)

Wave function a function of the coordinates of an electron's position in three-dimensional space that describes the properties of the electron. (7.5)

Wave mechanical model a model for the hydrogen atom in which the electron is assumed to behave as a standing wave. (7.5)

Wavelength the distance between two consecutive peaks or troughs in a wave. (7.1)

Wax an ester similar to a fat or a phospholipid but containing a monohydroxy alcohol instead of glycerol. (23.4)

Weak acid an acid that dissociates only slightly in aqueous solution. (4.2; 14.2)

Weak base a base that reacts with water to produce hydroxide ions to only a slight extent in aqueous solution. (4.2; 14.6)

Weak electrolyte a material which, when dissolved in water, gives a solution that conducts only a small electric current. (4.2)

Weight the force exerted on an object by gravity. (1.3)

Work force acting over a distance. (6.1)

X-ray diffraction a technique for establishing the structure of crystalline solids by directing X rays of a single wavelength at a crystal and obtaining a diffraction pattern from which interatomic spaces can be determined. (10.3)

Zone of nuclear stability the area encompassing the stable nuclides on a plot of their positions as a function of the number of protons and the number of neutrons in the nucleus. (21.1)

Zone refining a metallurgical process for obtaining a highly pure metal that depends on continuously melting the impure material and recrystallizing the pure metal. (20.8)

Answers to Selected Exercises

The answers listed here are from the *Complete Solutions Guide,* in which rounding is carried out at each intermediate step in a calculation in order to show the correct number of significant figures for that step. Therefore, an answer given here may differ in the last digit from the result obtained by carrying extra digits throughout the entire calculation and rounding at the end (the procedure you should follow).

Chapter 1

17. No, it is useful whenever a systematic approach of observation and hypothesis testing can be used. **19.** Precision is related to how many significant figures one can associate with a measurement. Consider weighing an object on three different balances with the following results: 11 g; 11.25 g; 11.2456 g. Since the assumed uncertainty in all measurements is ±1 in the last digit, then the uncertainty of the three balances are ±1 g, ±0.01 g, and ±0.0001 g, respectively. The balance with the smallest uncertainty is the balance with the most significant figures associated with the measurement, which is also the balance that is assumed most precise. **21.** Chemical changes involve the making and breaking of chemical forces (bonds). Physical changes do not. The identity of a substance changes after a chemical change, but not after a physical change. **23. a.** Inexact; **b.** Exact; **c.** Exact; 36 in/yd × 2.54 cm/in × 1 m/100 cm = 0.9144 m/yd (All conversion factors used are exact.) **d.** Inexact; the announced attendance is generally the number of tickets sold, not the number who were actually in the stadium. Some people who paid may not have gone, some may sneak in without paying, etc. **e.** Exact; **f.** Inexact **25. a.** 2; **b.** 4; **c.** 4; **d.** 4; **e.** 3; **f.** 3; **g.** 4; **h.** 7 **27. a.** 3.13×10^2; **b.** 3.13×10^{-4}; **c.** 3.13×10^7; **d.** 3.13×10^{-1}; **e.** 3.13×10^{-2}. **29. a.** 102.623; **b.** 236.2; **c.** 3.0814; **d.** 4.67 **31. a.** 467; **b.** 0.24; **c.** 33.04; **d.** 75; **e.** 0.12; **f.** 0.21; **g.** 4.9; **h.** 0.01 **33. a.** 84.3 mm; **b.** 2.41 m; **c.** 2.945×10^{-5} cm; **d.** 14.45 km; **e.** 2.353×10^5 mm; **f.** 0.9033 μm **35.** 1×10^{-1} nm; 1×10^2 pm **37. a.** 8 lb and 9.9 oz; $20\frac{1}{4}$ in; **b.** 4.0×10^4 km, 4.0×10^7 m; **c.** 1.2×10^{-2} m³, 12 L, 730 in³, 0.42 ft³ **39. a.** 4.00×10^2 rods; 10.0 furlongs; 2.01×10^3 m; 2.01 km; **b.** 8390.0 rods; 209.75 furlongs; 42,195 m; 42.195 km **41. a.** 0.373 kg, 0.822 lb; **b.** 31.1 g, 156 carats; **c.** 19.3 cm³ **43.** The Intercity-225, with a top speed of 140. mi/h, is faster. **45.** The spouse's car, with 33 mi/gal, has the better gas mileage. **47.** 39.2°C, 312.4 K **49.** 77°F, 298 K **51.** 69.1 ± 0.2°F **53.** 2.70×10^3 kg/m³, 169 lb/ft³ **55.** 1×10^6 g/cm³ **57.** 0.28 cm³ **59.** 3.8 g/cm³ **61. a.** Both are the same mass; **b.** 1.0 mL mercury; **c.** Both are the same mass; **d.** 1.0 L benzene **63.** Solid: own volume, own shape, does not flow. Liquid: own volume, takes shape of container, flows. Gas: takes volume and shape of container, flows **65. a.** Pure; **b.** Mixture; **c.** Mixture; **d.** Pure; **e.** Mixture; **f.** Pure; **g.** Mixture; **h.** Mixture; **i.** Pure; Iron and uranium are elements. Water and table salt are compounds. **67.** 15 to 22 mg acetaminophen per kilogram of body weight **69.** 477 L **71.** 1.0×10^5 bags **73. a.** 351.3 K; 173°F; **b.** 248 K; −13°F; **c.** 0 K; −459°F; **d.** 1074 K; 1470°F **75.** 7×10^5 kg **77.** Since d_{cube} is between 5.15 g/cm³ and 5.25 g/cm³ and d_{sphere} is between 5.08 g/cm³ and 5.18 g/cm³, then we cannot decisively say if they are the same or different. The data are not precise enough to say. **79.** 0.40 ± 0.03 oz/in³ **81.** 8.5 ± 0.5 g/cm³ **83.** In a subtraction, the result gets smaller, but the un-

certainties are added. If the two numbers are very close, the uncertainty may be larger than the result. **85.** $d_{old} = 8.8$ g/cm³, $d_{new} = 7.17$ g/cm³; $d_{new}/d_{old} = mass_{new}/mass_{old} = 0.81$; The difference in mass is accounted for by the difference in the alloy used (if the assumptions are correct). **87. a.** One possibility is that rope B is not attached to anything and rope A and rope C are connected via a pair of pulleys and/or gears; **b.** Try to pull rope B out of the box. Measure the distance moved by C for a given movement of A. Hold either A or C firmly while pulling on the other rope.

Chapter 2

15. a. Atoms have mass and are neither destroyed nor created by chemical reactions. Therefore, mass is neither created nor destroyed by chemical reactions. Mass is conserved. **b.** The composition of a substance depends on the number and kinds of atoms that form it. **c.** Compounds of the same elements differ only in the numbers of atoms of the elements forming them, i.e., NO, N_2O, NO_2. **17.** Deflection of cathode rays by magnetic and electric fields led to the conclusion that they were negatively charged. The cathode ray was produced at the negative electrode and repelled by the negative pole of the applied electric field. **19.** The atomic number of an element is equal to the number of protons in the nucleus of an atom of that element. The mass number is the sum of the number of protons and neutrons in the nucleus. The atomic mass is the actual mass of a particular isotope (including electrons). As we will see in Chapter 3, the average mass of an atom is taken from a measurement made on a large number of atoms. The average atomic mass value is listed in the periodic table. **21.** A compound will always contain the same numbers (and types) of atoms. A given amount of hydrogen will react only with a specific amount of oxygen. Any excess oxygen will remain unreacted. **23. a.** The composition of a substance depends on the number of atoms of each element making up the compound (depends on the formula of the compound) and not on the composition of the mixture from which it was formed. **b.** Avogadro's hypothesis implies that volume ratios are equal to molecule ratios at constant temperature and pressure. $H_2(g) + Cl_2(g) \rightarrow 2 HCl(g)$; from the balanced equation, the volume of HCl produced will be twice the volume of H_2 (or Cl_2) reacted. **25.** The F to S mass ratios are simple whole numbers, 1:2:3. **27.** O, 7.94; Na, 22.8; Mg, 11.9; O and Mg are incorrect by a factor of ≈2; correct formulas are H_2O, Na_2O, and MgO. **29.** Using $r = 5 \times 10^{-14}$ cm, $d_{nucleus} = 3 \times 10^{15}$ g/cm³; using $r = 1 \times 10^{-8}$ cm, $d_{atom} = 0.4$ g/cm³ **31.** 37 **33.** Gold: Au, silver: Ag, mercury: Hg, potassium: K, iron: Fe, antimony: Sb, tungsten: W. **35.** Fluorine: F, chlorine: Cl, bromine: Br, sulfur: S, oxygen: O, phosphorus: P. **37.** Sn: tin, Pt: platinum, Co: cobalt, Ni: nickel, Mg: magnesium, Ba: barium, K: potassium. **39.** The noble gases are He, Ne, Ar, Kr, Xe, and Rn (helium, neon, argon, krypton, xenon, and radon). All isotopes of radon are radioactive. **41. a.** 8; **b.** 8; **c.** 18; **d.** 5 **43. a.** 94 p, 144 n; **b.** 29 p, 36 n; **c.** 24 p, 28 n; **d.** 2 p, 2 n; **e.** 27 p, 33 n; **f.** 24 p, 30 n **45.** $^{19}_{9}F$ **47.** $^{151}_{63}Eu^{3+}$ **49.** $^{34}_{16}S^{2-}$ **51.** $^{75}_{33}As^{3+}$, 30 e; $^{128}_{52}Te^{2-}$, 52 p, 76 n, 2−; $^{32}_{16}S$, 0; $^{204}_{81}Ti^{+}$, 80 e; $^{195}_{78}Pt$, 78 p, 117 n, 78 e, 0 **53.** Metals: Mg, Ti, Au, Bi, Ge, Eu, Am; Nonmetals: Si, B, At, Rn, Br **55.** a, d **57.** Metallic character increases down a group. **59. a.** lose, Na⁺; **b.** lose, Sr²⁺; **c.** lose, Ba²⁺; **d.** gain, I⁻; **e.** lose, Al³⁺; **f.** gain, S²⁻ **61. a.** sodium chloride; **b.** rubidium oxide; **c.** calcium sulfide; **d.** aluminum iodide **63. a.** chromium(VI) oxide; **b.** chromium(III) oxide; **c.** aluminum oxide; **d.** sodium hydride; **e.** calcium bromide; **f.** zinc chloride **65. a.** potassium perchlorate; **b.** calcium phosphate; **c.** aluminum sulfate; **d.** lead(II) nitrate **67. a.** nitrogen triiodide; **b.** phosphorus trichloride; **c.** sulfur difluoride; **d.** dinitrogen tetrafluoride **69. a.** copper(I) iodide; **b.** copper(II) iodide; **c.** cobalt(II) iodide; **d.** sodium carbonate; **e.** sodium hydrogen carbonate or sodium bicarbonate; **f.** tetrasulfur tetranitride; **g.** sulfur hexafluoride; **h.** sodium hypochlorite; **i.** barium chromate; **j.** ammonium nitrate **71. a.** CsBr; **b.** BaSO₄; **c.** NH₄Cl; **d.** ClO; **e.** SiCl₄; **f.** ClF₃; **g.** BeO; **h.** MgF₂ **73. a.** Na₂O; **b.** Na₂O₂; **c.** KCN; **d.** Cu(NO₃)₂; **e.** SiCl₄; **f.** PbS; **g.** PbS₂; **h.** CuCl; **i.** GaAs (from the positions in the periodic table, Ga³⁺ and As³⁻ are the predicted ions); **j.** CdSe; **k.** ZnS **75.** No difference since both should have the same chemical composition. **77. a.** lead(II) acetate; **b.** copper(II) sulfate; **c.** calcium oxide; **d.** magnesium sulfate; **e.** magnesium hydroxide; **f.** calcium sulfate; **g.** dinitrogen monoxide or nitrous oxide (common) **79.** All contain 12 hydrogen atoms. **81. a.** Ca₃N₂; calcium nitride; **b.** K₂O; potassium oxide; **c.** RbF; rubidium fluoride; **d.** MgS; magnesium sulfide; **e.** BaI₂; barium iodide; **f.** Al₂Se₃; aluminum selenide; **g.** Cs₃P; cesium phosphide; **h.** InBr₃; indium(III) bromide (In forms compounds with +1 and +3 ions. You would predict a +3 ion from the position of In in the periodic table.) **83.** Cu, Ag, and Au **85.** The ratio of the masses of R that combines with 1.00 g Q is 3:1, as expected by the law of multiple proportions. R₃Q is the formula of the first compound. **87. a.** The compounds are isomers of each other. Isomers are compounds with the same formula but the atoms are attached differently, resulting in different properties. **b.** When wood burns, most of the solid material is converted to gases, which escape. **c.** Atoms are not an indivisible particle. Atoms are composed of electrons, neutrons, and protons. **d.** The two hydride samples contain different isotopes of either hydrogen and/or lithium. Isotopes may have different masses but have similar chemical properties.

Chapter 3

19. The molecular formula gives the actual number of atoms of each element in a molecule (or formula unit) of a compound. The empirical formula gives the simplest whole-number ratio of atoms of each element in a molecule. The molecular formula is a whole number multiple of the empirical formula. If that multiplier is one, the molecular and empirical formulas are the same. **21.** 24.31 amu **23.** 35.46 amu; Cl **25.** 48% ¹⁵¹Eu and 52% ¹⁵³Eu **27.** There are three peaks in the mass spectrum, each 2 mass units apart. This is consistent with two isotopes, differing in mass by two mass units. **29.** 4.64 × 10⁻²⁰ g Fe **31.** 1.00 × 10²² atoms C **33.** Al₂O₃, 101.96 g/mol; Na₃AlF₆, 209.95 g/mol **35. a.** 17.03 g/mol; **b.** 32.05 g/mol; **c.** 252.08 g/mol **37. a.** 0.0587 mol NH₃; **b.** 0.0312 mol N₂H₄; **c.** 3.97 × 10⁻³ mol (NH₄)₂Cr₂O₇ **39. a.** 85.2 g NH₃; **b.** 160. g N₂H₄; **c.** 1260 g (NH₄)₂Cr₂O₇ **41. a.** 70.1 g N; **b.** 140. g N; **c.** 140. g N

43. a. 3.54 × 10²² molecules NH₃; **b.** 1.88 × 10²² molecules N₂H₄; **c.** 2.39 × 10²¹ molecules (NH₄)₂Cr₂O₇ **45. a.** 3.54 × 10²² atoms N; **b.** 3.76 × 10²² atoms N; **c.** 4.78 × 10²¹ atoms N **47.** 176.12 g/mol; 2.839 × 10⁻³ mol; 1.710 × 10²¹ molecules **49. a.** 1.661 × 10⁻²² mol; **b.** 5.549 mol; **c.** 2.491 × 10⁻²² mol **51. a.** 1.40 × 10⁻² g N₂; **b.** 8.41 × 10⁻² g N₂; **c.** 4.2 × 10³ g N₂; **d.** 4.653 × 10⁻²³ g N₂; **e.** 5.60 × 10⁻¹⁴ g N₂; **f.** 5.04 × 10⁻¹⁰ g N₂; **g.** 1.4 × 10⁻⁷ g N₂ **53. a.** 294.30 g/mol; **b.** 3.40 × 10⁻² mol; **c.** 459 g; **d.** 1.0 × 10¹⁹ molecules; **e.** 4.9 × 10²¹ atoms; **f.** 4.9 × 10⁻¹³ g; **g.** 4.887 × 10⁻²² g **55.** CdS, 77.79% Cd; CdSe, 58.73% Cd; CdTe, 46.83% Cd **57.** 13.35% Y, 41.22% Ba, 28.62% Cu, 16.81% O **59.** C₁₂H₂₂O₁₁ < C₈H₁₀N₄O₂ < C₂H₅OH **61.** 1360 g/mol **63. a.** 39.99% C, 6.713% H, 53.30% O; **b.** 40.00% C, 6.714% H, 53.29% O; **c.** 40.00% C, 6.714% H, 53.29% O (all the same except for rounding differences) **65. a.** C₃H₄O₃; **b.** CH; **c.** CH; **d.** P₂O₅; **e.** CH₂O; **f.** CH₂O **67.** TiO₂ **69.** compound I: HgO; compound II: Hg₂O **71.** NO₂, N₂O₄ **73.** CH, C₆H₆ **75.** C₃H₈ **77.** C₃H₄, C₉H₁₂ **79. a.** 4Fe(s) + 3O₂(g) → 2Fe₂O₃(s); **b.** Ca(s) + 2H₂O(l) → Ca(OH)₂(aq) + H₂(g); **c.** Ba(OH)₂(aq) + H₂SO₄(aq) → BaSO₄(s) + 2H₂O(l) **81. a.** Cu(s) + 2AgNO₃(aq) → 2Ag(s) + Cu(NO₃)₂(aq); **b.** Zn(s) + 2HCl(aq) → ZnCl₂(aq) + H₂(g); **c.** Au₂S₃(s) + 3H₂(g) → 2Au(s) + 3H₂S(g); **83. a.** C₁₂H₂₂O₁₁(s) + 12O₂(g) → 12CO₂(g) + 11H₂O(g); **b.** 2C₆H₆(l) + 15O₂(g) → 12CO₂(g) + 6H₂O(g); **c.** 4Fe(s) + 3O₂(g) → 2Fe₂O₃(s); **d.** 2C₄H₁₀(g) + 13O₂(g) → 8CO₂(g) + 10H₂O(g); **e.** 4FeO(s) + O₂(g) → 2Fe₂O₃(s) **85. a.** SiO₂(s) + 2C(s) → Si(s) + 2CO(g); **b.** SiCl₄(l) + 2Mg(s) → Si(s) + 2MgCl₂(s); **c.** Na₂SiF₆(s) + 4Na(s) → Si(s) + 6NaF(s) **87.** Pb(NO₃)₂(aq) + H₃AsO₄(aq) → PbHAsO₄(s) + 2HNO₃(aq) **89.** 6.51 g Cr₂O₃, 1.20 g N₂, 3.09 g H₂O **91.** 4.355 kg **93.** 7.2 ×10⁴ g coke **95. a.** 65.01% Pt; 9.337% N; 2.015% H; 23.63% Cl; **b.** 72.3 g Pt(NH₃)₂Cl₂; 35.9 g KCl **97. a.** stoichiometric mixture; **b.** I₂; **c.** Mg; **d.** Mg; **e.** stoichiometric mixture; **f.** I₂; **g.** stoichiometric mixture; **h.** I₂; **i.** Mg **99. a.** 2.4 g; **b.** 1.7 g S₈ unreacted **101.** 1300 g CaSO₄, 630 g H₃PO₄ **103.** 82.8% **105.** 59 g AlBr₃ (theoretical), 85% **107.** Mn, 54.94 amu **109.** 9.25 × 10²² H atoms **111.** 28.1 amu **113.** 1.12 × 10⁶ g **115. a.** Al; **b.** Al; **c.** Al; **d.** Al; **e.** Al; **f.** Al **117.** 86.2% **119.** C₂₀H₃₀O **121.** C₇H₅N₃O₆ **123.** 1.8 × 10⁶ g Cu(NH₃)₄Cl₂; 5.9 × 10⁵ g NH₃ **125.** 207 amu, Pb **127.** Al₂Se₃ **129.** 40.% Cu₂O, 60.% CuO

Chapter 4

9. Solubility refers to how much dissolves. Electrolyte refers to whether or not ions are produced. **11. a.** NaBr → Na⁺ + Br⁻; **b.** MgCl₂ → Mg²⁺ + 2Cl⁻; **c.** Al(NO₃)₃ → Al³⁺ + 3NO₃⁻; **d.** (NH₄)₂SO₄ → 2NH₄⁺ + SO₄²⁻; **e.** HI → H⁺ + I⁻; **f.** FeSO₄ → Fe²⁺ + SO₄²⁻; **g.** KMnO₄ → K⁺ + MnO₄⁻; **h.** HClO₄ → H⁺ + ClO₄⁻; **i.** NH₄C₂H₃O₂ → NH₄⁺ + C₂H₃O₂⁻ **13.** CaCl₂(s) → Ca²⁺(aq) + 2Cl⁻(aq) **15. a.** 0.2677 M; **b.** 1.255 × 10⁻³ M; **c.** 8.065 × 10⁻³ M **17. a.** $M_{Ca^{2+}}$ = 0.15 M, M_{Cl^-} = 0.30 M; **b.** $M_{Al^{3+}}$ = 0.26 M, $M_{NO_3^-}$ = 0.78 M; **c.** M_{K^+} = 0.50 M, $M_{Cr_2O_7^{2-}}$ = 0.25 M; **d.** $M_{Al^{3+}}$ = 4.0 × 10⁻³ M, $M_{SO_4^{2-}}$ = 6.0 × 10⁻³ M **19.** 100.0 mL of 0.30 M AlCl₃ **21.** 41.7 mL **23. a.** Place 20.0 g NaOH in a 2-L volumetric flask; add water to dissolve the NaOH and fill to the mark.

b. Add 500. mL of the 1.00 M NaOH stock solution to a 2-L volumetric flask; fill to the mark with water. **c.** As in a, instead using 38.8 g K_2CrO_4. **d.** As in b, instead using 114 mL of 1.75 M K_2CrO_4 stock solution. **25.** $M_{NH_4^+} = 0.272\,M$, $M_{SO_4^{2-}} = 0.136\,M$ **27.** $5.94 \times 10^{-8}\,M$ steroid **29. a.** $BaSO_4(s)$; **b.** $PbCl_2(s)$; **c.** $Ag_3PO_4(s)$; **d.** $Fe(OH)_3(s)$ **31. a.** $BaCl_2(aq) + Na_2SO_4(aq) \rightarrow BaSO_4(s) + 2NaCl(aq)$; $Ba^{2+}(aq) + 2Cl^-(aq) + 2Na^+(aq) + SO_4^{2-}(aq) \rightarrow BaSO_4(s) + 2Na^+(aq) + 2Cl^-(aq)$; $Ba^{2+}(aq) + SO_4^{2-}(aq) \rightarrow BaSO_4(s)$; **b.** $Pb(NO_3)_2(aq) + 2KCl(aq) \rightarrow PbCl_2(s) + 2KNO_3(aq)$; $Pb^{2+}(aq) + 2NO_3^-(aq) + 2K^+(aq) + 2Cl^-(aq) \rightarrow PbCl_2(s) + 2K^+(aq) + 2NO_3^-(aq)$; $Pb^{2+}(aq) + 2Cl^-(aq) \rightarrow PbCl_2(s)$; **c.** $3AgNO_3(aq) + Na_3PO_4(aq) \rightarrow Ag_3PO_4(s) + 3NaNO_3(aq)$; $3Ag^+(aq) + 3NO_3^-(aq) + 3Na^+(aq) + PO_4^{3-}(aq) \rightarrow Ag_3PO_4(s) + 3Na^+(aq) + 3NO_3^-(aq)$; $3Ag^+(aq) + PO_4^{3-}(aq) \rightarrow Ag_3PO_4(s)$; **d.** $3NaOH(aq) + Fe(NO_3)_3(aq) \rightarrow Fe(OH)_3(s) + 3NaNO_3(aq)$; $3Na^+(aq) + 3OH^-(aq) + Fe^{3+}(aq) + 3NO_3^-(aq) \rightarrow Fe(OH)_3(s) + 3Na^+(aq) + 3NO_3^-(aq)$; $Fe^{3+}(aq) + 3OH^-(aq) \rightarrow Fe(OH)_3(s)$ **33. a.** $Ag^+(aq) + I^-(aq) \rightarrow AgI(s)$; **b.** $Cu^{2+}(aq) + S^{2-}(aq) \rightarrow CuS(s)$; **c.** $Co^{2+}(aq) + 2OH^-(aq) \rightarrow Co(OH)_2(s)$; **d.** No reaction **35. a.** $Ba^{2+}(aq) + SO_4^{2-}(aq) \rightarrow BaSO_4(s)$; **b.** $Pb^{2+}(aq) + 2Cl^-(aq) \rightarrow PbCl_2(s)$; **c.** No reaction; **d.** No reaction; **e.** $Cu^{2+}(aq) + 2OH^-(aq) \rightarrow Cu(OH)_2(s)$ **37.** Three possibilities are: addition of K_2SO_4 solution to give a white ppt. of $PbSO_4$; addition of NaCl to give a white ppt. of $PbCl_2$; addition of K_2CrO_4 solution to give a bright yellow ppt. of $PbCrO_4$ **39.** 0.146 g **41.** 0.520 g $Al(OH)_3$ **43. a.** $2KOH(aq) + Mg(NO_3)_2(aq) \rightarrow Mg(OH)_2(s) + 2KNO_3(aq)$; **b.** $Mg(OH)_2(s)$; **c.** 0.583 g; **d.** 0.100 M K^+, 0.200 M NO_3^-, $5.00 \times 10^{-2}\,M$ Mg^{2+} **45. a.** $2HClO_4(aq) + Mg(OH)_2(s) \rightarrow Mg(ClO_4)_2(aq) + 2H_2O(l)$; $2H^+(aq) + 2ClO_4^-(aq) + Mg(OH)_2(s) \rightarrow Mg^{2+}(aq) + 2ClO_4^-(aq) + 2H_2O(l)$; $2H^+(aq) + Mg(OH)_2(s) \rightarrow Mg^{2+}(aq) + 2H_2O(l)$; **b.** $HCN(aq) + NaOH(aq) \rightarrow NaCN(aq) + H_2O(l)$; $HCN(aq) + Na^+(aq) + OH^-(aq) \rightarrow Na^+(aq) + CN^-(aq) + H_2O(l)$; $HCN(aq) + OH^-(aq) \rightarrow H_2O(l) + CN^-(aq)$; **c.** $HCl(aq) + NaOH(aq) \rightarrow NaCl(aq) + H_2O(l)$; $H^+(aq) + Cl^-(aq) + Na^+(aq) + OH^-(aq) \rightarrow Na^+(aq) + Cl^-(aq) + H_2O(l)$; $H^+(aq) + OH^-(aq) \rightarrow H_2O(l)$ **47. a.** $KOH(aq) + HNO_3(aq) \rightarrow H_2O(l) + KNO_3(aq)$; $K^+(aq) + OH^-(aq) + H^+(aq) + NO_3^-(aq) \rightarrow H_2O(l) + K^+(aq) + NO_3^-(aq)$; $OH^-(aq) + H^+(aq) \rightarrow H_2O(l)$; **b.** $Ba(OH)_2(aq) + 2HCl(aq) \rightarrow 2H_2O(l) + BaCl_2(aq)$; $Ba^{2+}(aq) + 2OH^-(aq) + 2H^+(aq) + 2Cl^-(aq) \rightarrow Ba^{2+}(aq) + 2Cl^-(aq) + 2H_2O(l)$; $OH^-(aq) + H^+(aq) \rightarrow H_2O(l)$; **c.** $3HClO_4(aq) + Fe(OH)_3(s) \rightarrow 3H_2O(l) + Fe(ClO_4)_3(aq)$; $3H^+(aq) + 3ClO_4^-(aq) + Fe(OH)_3(s) \rightarrow 3H_2O(l) + Fe^{3+}(aq) + 3ClO_4^-(aq)$; $3H^+(aq) + Fe(OH)_3(s) \rightarrow 3H_2O(l) + Fe^{3+}(aq)$ **49. a.** 100. mL; **b.** 66.7 mL; **c.** 50.0 mL **51.** Basic, 0.250 M NO_3^-, 2.50 M Na^+, 2.25 M OH^- **53.** 0.102 M **55.** 0.4178 g **57. a.** K, +1; O, −2; **b.** Ni, +4; O, −2; **c.** Fe, +2; **d.** H, +1; O, −2; N, −3; P, +5; **e.** P, +3; O, −2; **f.** O, −2; Fe, $+\frac{8}{3}$; **g.** O, −2; F, −1; Xe, +6; **h.** S, +4; F, −1; **i.** C, +2; O, −2; **j.** Na, +1; O, −2; C, +3 **59.** OCl^-, +1; ClO_2^-, +3; ClO_3^-, +5; ClO_4^-, +7

61.

Redox?	Oxidizing Agent	Reducing Agent	Substance Oxidized	Substance Reduced
a. Yes	O_2	CH_4	CH_4 (C)	O_2 (O)
b. Yes	HCl	Zn	Zn	HCl (H)
c. No	—	—	—	—
d. Yes	O_3	NO	NO (N)	O_3 (O)
e. Yes	H_2O_2	H_2O_2	H_2O_2 (O)	H_2O_2 (O)
f. Yes	CuCl	CuCl	CuCl (Cu)	CuCl (Cu)

63. a. $Zn + 2HCl \rightarrow Zn^{2+} + H_2 + 2Cl^-$; **b.** $2H^+ + 3I^- + ClO^- \rightarrow I_3^- + Cl^- + H_2O$; **c.** $7H_2O + 4H^+ + 3As_2O_3 + 4NO_3^- \rightarrow 4NO + 6H_3AsO_4$; **d.** $16H^+ + 2MnO_4^- + 10Br^- \rightarrow 5Br_2 + 2Mn^{2+} + 8H_2O$; **e.** $8H^+ + 3CH_3OH + Cr_2O_7^{2-} \rightarrow 2Cr^{3+} + 3CH_2O + 7H_2O$ **65. a.** $2H_2O + Al + MnO_4^- \rightarrow Al(OH)_4^- + MnO_2$; **b.** $2OH^- + Cl_2 \rightarrow Cl^- + ClO^- + H_2O$; **c.** $OH^- + H_2O + NO_2^- + 2Al \rightarrow NH_3 + 2AlO_2^-$ **67.** $4NaCl + 2H_2SO_4 + MnO_2 \rightarrow 2Na_2SO_4 + MnCl_2 + Cl_2 + 2H_2O$ **69.** 0.942 M **71. a.** $2AgNO_3(aq) + BaCl_2(aq) \rightarrow 2AgCl(s) + Ba(NO_3)_2(aq)$, $2Ag^+(aq) + 2NO_3^-(aq) + Ba^{2+}(aq) + 2Cl^-(aq) \rightarrow 2AgCl(s) + Ba^{2+}(aq) + 2NO_3^-(aq)$, $Ag^+(aq) + Cl^-(aq) \rightarrow AgCl(s)$; **b.** NR **c.** $(NH_4)_2S(aq) + FeCl_2(aq) \rightarrow FeS(s) + 2NH_4Cl(aq)$, $2NH_4^+(aq) + S^{2-}(aq) + Fe^{2+}(aq) + 2Cl^-(aq) \rightarrow FeS(s) + 2NH_4^+(aq) + 2Cl^-(aq)$, $Fe^{2+}(aq) + S^{2-}(aq) \rightarrow FeS(s)$; **d.** $K_2CO_3(aq) + CuSO_4(aq) \rightarrow CuCO_3(s) + K_2SO_4(aq)$, $2K^+(aq) + CO_3^{2-}(aq) + Cu^{2+}(aq) + SO_4^{2-}(aq) \rightarrow CuCO_3(s) + 2K^+(aq) + SO_4^{2-}(aq)$, $Cu^{2+}(aq) + CO_3^{2-}(aq) \rightarrow CuCO_3(s)$ **73. a.** No; no element shows a change in oxidation number; **b.** 3.7 g Fe_2O_3 **75.** 63.74% **77.** 4.03% **79. a.** 0.8393 M; **b.** 5.010% **81.** $C_6H_8O_6$ **83. a.** All three reactions are oxidation–reduction reactions; **b.** For reaction one, O_2 is the oxidizing agent and NH_3 is the reducing agent. For reaction two, O_2 is the oxidizing agent and NO is the reducing agent. For reaction three, NO_2 is both the oxidizing agent and the reducing agent. **85.** Fe^{2+} will react with MnO_4^- (purple) producing Fe^{3+} and Mn^{2+} (almost colorless). There is no reaction between MnO_4^- and Fe^{3+}. **87. a.** 24.8% Co, 29.7% Cl, 5.09% H, 40.4% O; **b.** $CoCl_2 \cdot 6H_2O$; **c.** $CoCl_2 \cdot 6H_2O(aq) + 2AgNO_3(aq) \rightarrow 2AgCl(s) + Co(NO_3)_2(aq) + 6H_2O(l)$, $CoCl_2 \cdot 6H_2O(aq) + 2NaOH(aq) \rightarrow Co(OH)_2(s) + 2NaCl(aq) + 6H_2O(l)$, $4Co(OH)_2(s) + O_2(g) \rightarrow 2Co_2O_3(s) + 4H_2O(l)$ **89.** 0.123 g SO_4^{2-}, 60.0% SO_4^{2-}; 61% K_2SO_4 and 39% Na_2SO_4 **91.** $CaCO_3(s) + H_2SO_4(aq) \rightarrow CaSO_4(aq) + H_2O(l) + CO_2(g)$ **93. a.** $MgO(s) + 2HCl(aq) \rightarrow MgCl_2(aq) + H_2O(l)$, $Mg(OH)_2(s) + 2HCl(aq) \rightarrow MgCl_2(aq) + 2H_2O(l)$, $Al(OH)_3(s) + 3HCl(aq) \rightarrow AlCl_3(aq) + 3H_2O(l)$; **b.** MgO **95.** Citric acid has three acidic hydrogens per citric acid molecule. **97.** $0.0257 \pm 0.0007\,M$ **99.** Weigh out between 4.24 and 4.32 g KIO_3, recording the mass to the nearest milligram or 0.1 mg. Dissolve the KIO_3 in water in a 1-L volumetric flask and dilute with water to the mark on the flask.

Chapter 5

17. At constant n and T, $nRT = $ constant, so $PV = k$ (Boyle's law). At constant P and n, $V = nRT/P = kT$ (Charles's law). **19.** For an ideal gas, the PV product should equal a constant value at any pressure. The plot for Ne appears closest to the ideal plot. **21.** Graham's law of effusion can be used. Determine the relative effusion rate of the unknown gas to some known gas; then use Graham's law to determine the molar mass of the unknown. The ideal gas law also can be used to determine the molar mass. The appropriate form to use is molar mass = dRT/P. If the density, temperature, and pressure of the gas are known, then the molar mass can be calculated. **23. a.** 3.6×10^3 mm Hg; **b.** 3.6×10^3 torr; **c.** 4.9×10^5 Pa; **d.** 71 psi **25.** 65 torr, 8.7×10^3 Pa, 8.6×10^{-2} atm **27. a.** 642 torr, 0.845 atm; 8.56×10^4 Pa; **b.** 975 torr; 1.28 atm; 1.30×10^5 Pa; **c.** 517 torr; 850. torr **29.** 0.972 atm **31.** 44.8 L **33. a.** 14.0 L; **b.** 4.72×10^{-2} mol; **c.** 678 K; **d.** 133 atm **35.** 0.449 mol **37. a.** 69.6 K; **b.** 32.3 atm **39.** The balloon will burst. **41.** 33.5 MPa **43.** 5.1×10^4 torr **45.** The volume of the balloon increases from 1.00 L to 2.82 L, so the change in volume is 1.82 L. **47.** 0.27 g **49.** 307 L **51.** 1.5×10^7 g Fe, 2.6×10^7 g 98% H_2SO_4 **53.** 2.47 mol H_2O **55. a.** $2CH_4(g) + 2NH_3(g) + 3O_2(g) \rightarrow 2HCN(g) + 6H_2O(g)$; **b.** 13.3 L **57.** 42.1 g/mol, C_3H_6 **59.** 5.77 g/L ($SiCl_4$), 4.60 g/L ($SiHCl_3$) **61.** 1.1 atm, $P_{CO_2} = 1.1$ atm, $P_{TOTAL} = 2.1$ atm **63.** $P_{H_2} = 317$ torr, $P_{N_2} = 50.7$ torr, $P_{TOTAL} = 368$ torr **65. a.** $\chi_{CH_4} = 0.412$, $\chi_{O_2} = 0.588$; **b.** 0.161 mol; **c.** 1.06 g CH_4, 3.03 g O_2 **67.** 0.286 g **69.** 18.0% **71.** 3.40×10^3 J/mol (273 K); 6.81×10^3 J/mol (546 K) **73.** 652 m/s (273 K); 921 m/s (546 K) **75.** No, there is a distribution of energies. **77.** Both the average kinetic energy and the average velocity will increase with an increase in temperature. **79. a.** All the same; **b.** Flask C **81.** NO **83.** The relative rates of effusion of $^{12}C^{16}O$, $^{12}C^{17}O$, and $^{12}C^{18}O$ are 1.04, 1.02, and 1.00. Advantage: CO_2 isn't as toxic as CO. Disadvantages: Can get a mixture of oxygen isotopes in CO_2, thus some species would effuse at about the same rate. **85. a.** 12.24 atm; **b.** 12.13 atm; **c.** The ideal gas law is high by 0.91%. **87.** 5×10^{-7} atm, 1×10^{13} molecules/cm^3 **89.** 0.4 mL **91.** $2NO_2(g) + H_2O(l) \rightarrow HNO_3(aq) + HNO_2(aq)$; $SO_3(g) + H_2O(l) \rightarrow H_2SO_4(aq)$

93. a.

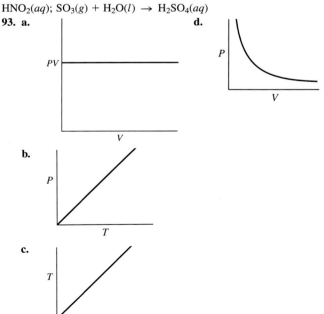

b.

c.

d.

e.

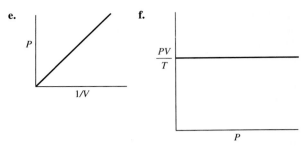

f.

95. $MnCl_4$ **97.** 1490 **99.** $P_{He} = 45.0$ torr, $P_{Ne} = 85.9$ torr, $P_{Ar} = 93.8$ torr, $P_{TOTAL} = 224.7$ torr **101.** 24 torr **103.** 490 atm **105.** 12.6 g/L **107.** N_2H_4 **109.** 13.3% N **111.** The pressure will increase because H_2 will effuse into container A faster than air will escape. **113.** CO_2 **115.** 13.4% CaO, 86.6% BaO **117. a.** 8.7×10^3 L air/min; **b.** $\chi_{CO} = 0.0017$, $\chi_{CO_2} = 0.032$, $\chi_{O_2} = 0.13$, $\chi_{N_2} = 0.77$, $\chi_{H_2O} = 0.067$ **119. a.** 1.01×10^4 g; **b.** 6.65×10^4 g; **c.** 8.7×10^3 g **121. a.** 0.19 torr; **b.** 6.6×10^{15} molecules CO/cm^3

Chapter 6

9. A coffee-cup calorimeter is at constant pressure. The heat at constant P equals ΔH. A bomb calorimeter is at constant volume. The heat at constant V equals ΔE. **11.** Al. Al has a higher heat capacity and a lower density than Fe. The same amount of heat could be dissipated by a smaller mass of Al. **13.** A function whose change depends only on the initial and final states and not on the pathway from the initial to the final state. If H and E were not state functions, the law of conservation of energy (first law) would not be true. **15.** Standard enthalpies of formation provide a reference point, allowing ΔH comparisons. **17.** 150 J **19.** 1.0 kg object with velocity of 2.0 m/s. **21. a.** 36 kJ; **b.** 35 kJ; **c.** −85 kJ; **d.** all **23.** 16 kJ **25.** 10. L · atm = 1.0×10^3 J **27.** $q = 30.9$ kJ, $w = -12.4$ kJ, $\Delta E = 18.5$ kJ **29.** exothermic; heat is evolved. **31. a.** endothermic; **b.** exothermic; **c.** exothermic; **d.** endothermic **33. a.** 2.54×10^3 kJ; **b.** 7.4×10^3 kJ; **c.** 693 kJ **35.** 4400 g C_3H_8 **37. a.** 54.9 kJ; **b.** 24.3 J/mol · °C **39.** 0.129 J/g · °C, 26.7 J/mol · °C **41.** 311 K **43.** 0.25 J/g · °C **45.** −66 kJ/mol **47.** 39.2°C **49.** 2.05 kJ/°C **51.** −220.8 kJ **53.** −296.1 kJ **55.** −233 kJ **57.** 28.4 kJ **59.** The enthalpy change for the formation of one mole of a compound from its elements, with all substances in their standard states. $Na(s) + \frac{1}{2}Cl_2(g) \rightarrow NaCl(s)$; $H_2(g) + \frac{1}{2}O_2(g) \rightarrow H_2O(l)$; $6C_{graphite}(s) + 6H_2(g) + 3O_2(g) \rightarrow C_6H_{12}O_6(s)$; $Pb(s) + S(s) + 2O_2(g) \rightarrow PbSO_4(s)$ **61. a.** −940. kJ; **b.** −265 kJ; **c.** −176 kJ **63. a.** −908 kJ, −112 kJ, −140. kJ; **b.** $12NH_3(g) + 21O_2(g) \rightarrow 8HNO_3(aq) + 4NO(g) + 14H_2O(g)$, exothermic **65.** −2677 kJ **67.** −169 kJ/mol **69.** 132 kJ **71.** For $C_3H_8(g)$, −50.37 kJ/g vs. −47.7 kJ/g for octane. Because of the low boiling point of propane, there are extra safety hazards associated with using the necessary high-pressure compressed gas tanks. **73.** 1.05×10^5 L **75.** The system does work on the surroundings for reactions (a), (d), and (f). The surroundings does work on the system for reactions (b) and (e). No work is done by reaction (c). **77.** −13.2 kJ **79.** −390. kJ, 30.0°C **81.** 6.66 kJ/°C **83.** 1.65 kJ/°C, −25.2 kJ/g, −3830 kJ/mol **85.** white phosphorus **87. a.** −361 kJ; **b.** −199 kJ; **c.** −227 kJ; **d.** −112 kJ **89. a.** $C_{12}H_{22}O_{11}(s) + 12O_2(g) \rightarrow 12CO_2(g) + 11H_2O(l)$; **b.** −5630 kJ; **c.** −5630 kJ **91.** 37 m^2 **93.** 1×10^4 steps

Chapter 7

15. Planck found it necessary to assume quantized energies to explain the radiation that heated bodies emit. Einstein's analysis of the photoelectric effect. **17.** Particles with very small mass, which generally have large velocities. **19. a.** A discrete bundle of light energy; **b.** A number describing a discrete state of an electron; **c.** The lowest energy state; **d.** An allowed energy state higher than the ground state **21.** Spatial orientation **23.** A surface where the probability of finding an electron is zero. **25.** No, the spin is a convenient model. Since we cannot locate or "see" the electron, we cannot see if it is spinning. **27.** When atoms interact with each other, it will be the outermost (valence) electrons that are involved in those interactions. In addition, how tightly the nucleus holds the outermost electrons determines atomic size and ionization energy. **29.** If one more electron is added to a half-filled subshell, electron–electron repulsions will increase. **31.** As electrons are removed, the nuclear charge exerted on the remaining electrons increases. Since the remaining electrons are "held" more strongly by the nucleus, the energy required to remove these electrons increases. **33.** For hydrogen, all orbitals with the same value of n have the same energy. For polyatomic atoms/ions, the energy of the orbitals also depends on ℓ. Since there are more nondegenerate energy levels for polyatomic atoms/ions as compared with hydrogen, then there are many more possible electronic transitions resulting in more complicated line spectra. **35.** Yes, the maximum number of unpaired electrons in any configuration corresponds to a minimum in electron–electron repulsions. **37.** 3.84×10^{14} s^{-1} **39.** 3.0×10^{10} s^{-1}, 2.0×10^{-23} J/photon, 12 J/mol **41.** 427.7 nm **43.** 276 nm **45. a.** 1.5×10^{-6} nm; **b.** 4.4×10^{-25} nm **47.** 2.4 nm **49. a.** 656.7 nm; **b.** 486.4 nm; **c.** 121.6 nm

51.

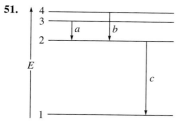

53. $n = 1 \rightarrow n = 5$, $\lambda = 95.00$ nm; $n = 2 \rightarrow n = 6$, $\lambda = 410.4$ nm; visible light has sufficient energy for the $n = 2 \rightarrow n = 6$ transition but does not have sufficient energy for the $n = 1 \rightarrow n = 5$ transition. **55.** $n = 1$, 91.20 nm; $n = 2$, 364.8 nm **57.** 5.79×10^5 nm; Δx much larger than atom **59.** $n = 1, 2, 3, \ldots$; $\ell = 0, 1, 2, \ldots (n - 1)$; $m_\ell = -\ell, \ldots, -2, -1, 0, 1, 2, \ldots, +\ell$. **61. b.** ℓ must be $< n$; **d.** For $\ell = 0$, $m_\ell = 0$ only **63.** ψ^2 gives the probability of finding the electron at that point. **65.** 3; 1; 5; 25; 16 **67. a.** 32; **b.** 8; **c.** 25; **d.** 10; **e.** 6 **69.** Si: $1s^2 2s^2 2p^6 3s^2 3p^2$ or [Ne]$3s^2 3p^2$; Ga: $1s^2 2s^2 2p^6 3s^2 3p^6 4s^2 3d^{10} 4p^1$ or [Ar]$4s^2 3d^{10} 4p^1$; As: [Ar]$4s^2 3d^{10} 4p^3$; Ge: [Ar]$4s^2 3d^{10} 4p^2$; Al: [Ne]$3s^2 3p^1$; Cd: [Kr]$5s^2 4d^{10}$; S: [Ne]$3s^2 3p^4$; Se: [Ar]$4s^2 3d^{10} 4p^4$ **71.** Sc: $1s^2 2s^2 2p^6 3s^2 3p^6 4s^2 3d^1$; Fe: $1s^2 2s^2 2p^6 3s^2 3p^6 4s^2 3d^6$; P: $1s^2 2s^2 2p^6 3s^2 3p^3$; Cs: $1s^2 2s^2 2p^6 3s^2 3p^6 4s^2 3d^{10} 4p^6 5s^2 4d^{10} 5p^6 6s^1$; Eu: $1s^2 2s^2 2p^6 3s^2 3p^6 4s^2 3d^{10} 4p^6 5s^2 4d^{10} 5p^6 6s^2 4f^6 5d^1$ (Actual: [Xe]$6s^2 4f^7$); Pt: $1s^2 2s^2 2p^6 3s^2 3p^6 4s^2 3d^{10} 4p^6 5s^2 4d^{10} 5p^6 6s^2 4f^{14} 5d^8$ (Actual: [Xe]$6s^1 4f^{14} 5d^9$); Xe: $1s^2 2s^2 2p^6 3s^2 3p^6 4s^2 3d^{10} 4p^6 5s^2 4d^{10} 5p^6$ **73.** Cr, Cu, Nb, Mo, Tc, Ru, Rh, Pd, Ag, Pt, Au **75. a.** F, $1s^2 2s^2 2p^5$; **b.** K, [Ar]$4s^1$; **c.** Be, $1s^2 2s^2$; Mg, [Ne]$3s^2$; Ca, [Ar]$4s^2$; **d.** In, [Kr]$5s^2 4d^{10} 5p^1$; **e.** C, $1s^2 2s^2 2p^2$; Si, [Ne]$3s^2 3p^2$; **f.** 118, [Rn] $7s^2 5f^{14} 6d^{10} 7p^6$

77.

B: $1s^2 2s^2 2p^1$

	n	ℓ	m_ℓ	m_s
$1s$	1	0	0	$+\frac{1}{2}$
$1s$	1	0	0	$-\frac{1}{2}$
$2s$	2	0	0	$+\frac{1}{2}$
$2s$	2	0	0	$-\frac{1}{2}$
$2p$	2	1	-1	$+\frac{1}{2}$

N: $1s^2 2s^2 2p^3$

	n	ℓ	m_ℓ	m_s
$1s$	1	0	0	$+\frac{1}{2}$
$1s$	1	0	0	$-\frac{1}{2}$
$2s$	2	0	0	$+\frac{1}{2}$
$2s$	2	0	0	$-\frac{1}{2}$
$2p$	2	1	-1	$+\frac{1}{2}$
$2p$	2	1	0	$+\frac{1}{2}$
$2p$	2	1	$+1$	$+\frac{1}{2}$

For boron, there are six possibilities for the $2p$ electron. For nitrogen, all the $2p$ electrons could have $m_s = -\frac{1}{2}$. **79.** none; an excited state; energy released **81.** Zn(0) < Cu(1) < Ni(2) < Co(3) < Fe(4) < Mn(5) < Cr(6) **83. a.** Be < Mg < Ca; **b.** Xe < I < Te; **c.** Ge < Ga < In **85. a.** Ca < Mg < Be; **b.** Te < I < Xe; **c.** In < Ga < Ge **87. a.** Li; **b.** P; **c.** O$^+$; **d.** Cl; **e.** Cu **89. a.** [Rn]$7s^2 5f^{14} 6d^4$; **b.** W; **c.** Using Sg as a symbol for element 106, SgO$_3$ and SgO$_4^{2-}$ probably would form (similar to Cr). **91.** P(g) $\rightarrow$ P$^+$(g) + e$^-$ **93.** Se is an exception to the general ionization trend. There are extra electron–electron repulsions in Se because two electrons are in the same $4p$ orbital, resulting in a lower ionization energy than expected. **95. a.** C, Br; **b.** N, Ar; **c.** C, Br **97. a.** Se < S; **b.** I < Br < F < Cl **99.** Electron–electron repulsions are much greater in O$^-$ than S$^-$ because the electron goes into a smaller $2p$ orbital vs. the larger $3p$ orbital on sulfur, resulting in a more favorable (more exothermic) E.A. for sulfur. **101. a.** -1445 kJ/mol; **b.** -580 kJ/mol **103.** potassium peroxide, K$_2$O$_2$; K^{2+} unstable **105.** 6.582×10^{14} s^{-1}; 4.361×10^{-19} J **107. a.** lithium nitride, Li$_3$N; **b.** sodium bromide, NaBr; **c.** potassium sulfide, K$_2$S **109. a.** 4Li(s) + O$_2$(g) $\rightarrow$ 2Li$_2$O(s); **b.** 2K(s) + S(s) $\rightarrow$ K$_2$S(s) **111.** 386 nm **113.** $\lambda = 4.104 \times 10^{-5}$ cm so violet light is emitted. **115. a.** n; **b.** n and ℓ **117. a.** 20; **b.** 18; **c.** 10; **d.** 24 **119.** element 119: [Rn]$7s^2 5f^{14} 6d^{10} 7p^6 8s^1$ **121.** Valence electrons are easier to remove than inner-core electrons. The large difference in energy between I_2 and I_3 indicates that this element has two valence electrons. The element is most likely an alkaline earth metal because alkaline earth metals have two valence electrons. **123.** The noble gases are an exception. The noble gases have large ionization energies but have endothermic electron affinities. Noble gases have a stable arrangement of electrons. Adding an electron disrupts this stable arrangement, resulting in unfavorable electron affinities. **125. a.** 146 kJ; **b.** 407 kJ; **c.** 1117 kJ; **d.** 1524 kJ **127.** The ionization energy refers to the removal of the electron from the atom in the gas phase. The work function refers to the removal of an electron from the solid. **129.** 4 **131.** For $r = a_0$ and $\theta = 0°$, $\psi^2 = 2.46 \times 10^{28}$. For $r = a_0$ and $\theta = 90°$, $\psi^2 = 0$. As expected, the xy plane is a node for the $2p_z$, atomic orbital. **133. a.**

1						2	
3						4	
5	6	7	8	9	10	11	12
13	14	15	16	17	18	19	20

b. 2, 4, 12, and 20; **c.** There are many possibilities. One example of each formula is XY = 1 + 11, XY$_2$ = 6 + 11, X$_2$Y = 1 + 10, XY$_3$ = 7 + 11, and X$_2$Y$_3$ = 7 + 10; **d.** 6; **e.** 0; **f.** 18 **135. a.** As we remove succeeding electrons, the electron being removed is closer to the nucleus and there are fewer electrons left repelling it. The remaining electrons are more strongly attracted to the nucleus and it takes more energy to remove these electrons. **b.** For I_4, we begin removing an electron with $n = 2$. For I_3, we removed an electron with $n = 3$. In going from $n = 3$ to $n = 2$ there is a big jump in ionization energy because the $n = 2$ electrons (inner core) are much closer to the nucleus on the average than the $n = 3$ electrons (valence electrons). Since the $n = 2$ electrons are closer to the nucleus, they are held more tightly and require a much larger amount of energy to remove them. **c.** Al^{4+}; the electron affinity for Al^{4+} is ΔH for the reaction

$$Al^{4+}(g) + e^- \longrightarrow Al^{3+}(g) \qquad \Delta H = -I_4 = -11,600 \text{ kJ/mol}$$

d. The greater the number of electrons, the greater the size. So

$$Al^{4+} < Al^{3+} < Al^{2+} < Al^+ < Al$$

Chapter 8
13. a. Electronegativity: the ability of an atom in a molecule to attract electrons to itself. Electron affinity: the energy change for $M(g) + e^- \rightarrow M^-(g)$. Electron affinity deals with isolated atoms in the gas phase. **b.** Covalent bond: sharing of electron pair(s); polar covalent bond: unequal sharing of electron pair(s). **c.** Ionic bond: electrons are no longer shared, as in a covalent bond. Instead, there is a complete transfer of electron(s) from one atom to another to form ions. **15.** H_2O and NH_3 have lone pair electrons on the central atoms. These lone pair electrons require more space than the bonding electrons, which tends to compress the angles between the bonding pairs. The bond angle for H_2O is the smallest because oxygen has two lone pairs on the central atom and the bond angle is compressed more than in NH_3, where N has only one lone pair. **17.** 1. polar bonds; 2. a structure such that the bond dipoles of the polar bonds do not cancel **19. a.** $C < N < O$; **b.** $Se < S < Cl$; **c.** $Sn < Ge < Si$; **d.** $Tl < Ge < S$ **21. a.** Ge—F; **b.** P—Cl; **c.** S—F; **d.** Ti—Cl **23.** Order of E.N. from Fig. 8.3: **a.** C (2.5) < N (3.0) < O (3.5), same; **b.** Se (2.4) < S (2.5) < Cl (3.0), same; **c.** Si = Ge = Sn (1.8), different; **d.** Tl (1.8) = Ge (1.8) < S (2.5), different. Most polar bonds using actual E.N. values; **a.** Si—F and Ge—F equal polarity (Ge—F predicted); **b.** P—Cl (same as predicted); **c.** S—F (same as predicted); **d.** Ti—Cl (same as predicted). **25.** F—H > O—H > N—H > C—H > P—H **27.** Rb^+ and Se^{2-}: $[Ar]4s^23d^{10}4p^6$; Ba^{2+} and I^-: $[Kr]5s^24d^{10}5p^6$ **29. a.** Mg^{2+}: $1s^22s^22p^6$; K^+: $1s^22s^22p^63s^23p^6$; Al^{3+}: $1s^22s^22p^6$; **b.** N^{3-}, O^{2-}, and F^-: $1s^22s^22p^6$; Te^{2-}: $[Kr]5s^24d^{10}5p^6$ **31. a.** Sc^{3+}; **b.** Te^{2-}; **c.** Ce^{4+}, Ti^{4+}; **d.** Ba^{2+} **33.** Some possibilities are N^{3-}, O^{2-}, F^-, Na^+, Mg^{2+}, and Al^{3+}. $Al^{3+} < Mg^{2+} < Na^+ < F^- < O^{2-} < N^{3-}$ **35. a.** $Cu > Cu^+ > Cu^{2+}$; **b.** $Pt^{2+} > Pd^{2+} > Ni^{2+}$; **c.** $O^{2-} > O^- > O$; **d.** $La^{3+} > Eu^{3+} > Gd^{3+} > Yb^{3+}$; **e.** $Te^{2-} > I^- > Cs^+ > Ba^{2+} >$ La^{3+} **37. a.** Li_3N (lithium nitride); **b.** Ga_2O_3 (gallium oxide); **c.** $RbCl$ (rubidium chloride); **d.** BaS (barium sulfide) **39. a.** $NaCl$, Na^+ smaller than K^+; **b.** LiF, F^- smaller than Cl^-; **c.** MgO, O^{2-} greater charge than OH^-; **d.** $Fe(OH)_3$, Fe^{3+} greater charge than Fe^{2+}; **e.** Na_2O, O^{2-} greater charge than Cl^-; **f.** MgO, Mg^{2+} smaller than Ba^{2+}, and O^{2-} smaller than S^{2-}. **41.** $\Delta H^\circ_f = -412 \text{ kJ/mol}$ **43.** The lattice energy for $Mg^{2+}O^{2-}$ will be much more exothermic than for Mg^+O^-. **45.** Ca^{2+} has greater charge than Na^+, and Se^{2-} is smaller than Te^{2-}. Since charge differences affect lattice energy values more than size differences, we expect the trend from most exothermic to least exothermic to be:

$$\begin{array}{cccc} CaSe & > CaTe & > Na_2Se & > Na_2Te \\ (-2862) & (-2721) & (-2130) & (-2095) \end{array}$$

47. a. -183 kJ; **b.** -109 kJ **49.** -42 kJ **51.** -1276 kJ **53.** -203 kJ **55.** 146 kJ/mol **57. a.** Using standard enthalpies of formation, $\Delta H^\circ = -184$ kJ vs. -183 kJ from bond energies; **b.** Using standard enthalpies of formation, $\Delta H = -92$ kJ vs. -109 kJ from bond energies. Bond energies give a reasonably good estimate for ΔH, especially when all reactants and products are gases. **59. a.** Using SF_4 data: $D_{SF} = 342.5$ kJ/mol. Using SF_6 data: $D_{SF} = 327.0$ kJ/mol. **b.** The S—F bond energy in the table is 327 kJ/mol. The value in the table was based on the S—F bond in SF_6. **c.** $S(g)$ and $F(g)$ are not the most stable forms of the elements at 25°C. The most stable forms are $S_8(s)$ and $F_2(g)$; $\Delta H^\circ_f = 0$ for these two species. **61.** 388.2 kJ/mol vs. 391 kJ/mol in text

63. a. $H-C\equiv N:$ **b.** $H-\overset{\displaystyle H}{\underset{\displaystyle H}{P}}-H$ **c.**

d.

e.

f. $:\!\overset{..}{\underset{..}{F}}\!-\!\overset{..}{\underset{..}{Se}}\!-\!\overset{..}{\underset{..}{F}}\!:$

g. $\overset{..}{\underset{..}{O}}=C=\overset{..}{\underset{..}{O}}$ **h.** $\overset{..}{\underset{..}{O}}=\overset{..}{\underset{..}{O}}$ **i.** $H-\overset{..}{\underset{..}{Br}}:$

65.

PF_5

BeH_2 $H-Be-H$

BH_3

Br_3^- $[:\!\overset{..}{\underset{..}{Br}}-\overset{..}{\underset{..}{Br}}-\overset{..}{\underset{..}{Br}}\!:]^-$

SF_4

XeF_4

ClF_5

SF_6

67. a. NO_2^- $\left[\overset{..}{\underset{..}{O}}=N-\overset{..}{\underset{..}{O}}\!:\right]^- \longleftrightarrow \left[:\!\overset{..}{\underset{..}{O}}-N=\overset{..}{\underset{..}{O}}\right]^-$

NO_3^-

b.

$$OCN^- \quad \left[:\ddot{O}-C\equiv N: \right]^- \leftrightarrow \left[:\ddot{O}=C=\ddot{N}: \right]^- \leftrightarrow \left[:O\equiv C-\ddot{N}: \right]^- ;$$

$$SCN^- \quad \left[:\ddot{S}-C\equiv N: \right]^- \leftrightarrow \left[:\ddot{S}=C=\ddot{N}: \right]^- \leftrightarrow \left[:S\equiv C-\ddot{N}: \right]^- ;$$

$$N_3^- \quad \left[:\ddot{N}-N\equiv N: \right]^- \leftrightarrow \left[:\ddot{N}=N=\ddot{N}: \right]^- \leftrightarrow \left[:N\equiv N-\ddot{N}: \right]^-$$

69.

71. With resonance all carbon–carbon bonds are equivalent (we indicate this with a circle in the ring), giving three different structures:

Localized double bonds give four unique structures.
73. N_2 (triple bond) $< N_2F_2$ (double bond) $< N_2F_4$ (single bond)
75. The structure

obeys the octet rule but has a +1 formal charge on the most electronegative element (fluorine) and a negative formal charge on a much less electronegative element (boron). The BF_3 structure with just three single bonds to the F atoms has a formal charge of zero on all atoms.
77. **a.–f.** and **h.** all have similar Lewis structures:

g. ClO_3^-

Formal charges: **a.** +1; **b.** +2; **c.** +3; **d.** +1; **e.** +2; **f.** +4;
g. +2; **h.** +1
79. [63] **a.** linear, 180°; **b.** trigonal pyramid, < 109.5°; **c.** tetrahedral, 109.5°; **d.** tetrahedral, 109.5°; **e.** trigonal planar, 120°; **f.** V-shaped, <109.5°; **g.** linear, 180°; **h.** and **i.** linear, no bond angle in diatomic molecules; [67] **a.** NO_2^-: V-shaped, ~120°; NO_3^-: trigonal planar, 120°; **b.** all are linear, 180° **81.** Br_3^-: linear; ClF_3 and BrF_3: T-shaped; SF_4: see-saw **83.** **a.** trigonal planar; 120°; **b.** V-shaped; ~120° **85.** **a.** linear; 180°; **b.** T-shaped; ~90°;

c. see-saw; ~90° and ~120°; **d.** trigonal bipyramid; 90° and 120°
87. SeO_2 (bond dipoles do not cancel each other out in SeO_2)
89. ICl_3 and TeF_4 (bond dipoles do not cancel each other out in ICl_3 and TeF_4)

91. a. OCl_2 V-shaped, polar

KrF_2 Linear, nonpolar

BeH_2 $H-Be-H$ Linear, nonpolar

SO_2 V-shaped, polar

(one other resonance structure possible)

b. SO_3 Trigonal planar, nonpolar

(Two other resonance structures possible)

NF_3 Trigonal pyramid, polar

IF_3 T-shaped, polar

c. CF_4 Tetrahedral, nonpolar

SeF_4 See-saw, polar

KrF_4 Square planar, nonpolar

d. IF_5 Square pyramid, polar

AsF_5 Trigonal bipyramid, nonpolar

93.

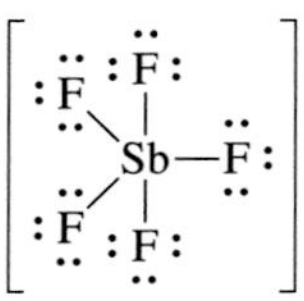

Trigonal bipyramid, nonpolar

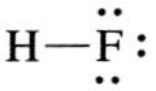

Linear, polar

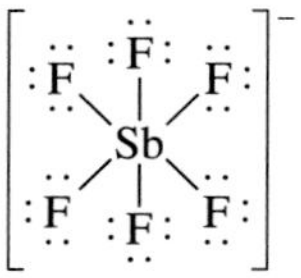

Octahedral 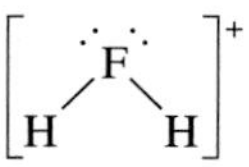   V-shaped

95. The polar bonds are symmetrically arranged about the central atoms, and all the individual bond dipoles cancel to give no net dipole moment for each molecule, i.e., the molecules are nonpolar. **97. a.** radius: $Mg^{2+} < Na^+ < F^- < O^{2-}$, I.E.: $O^{2-} < F^- < Na^+ < Mg^{2+}$; **b.** radius: $Ca^{2+} < P^{3-}$, I.E.: $P^{3-} < Ca^{2+}$; **c.** radius: $K^+ < Cl^- < S^{2-}$, I.E.: $S^{2-} < Cl^- < K^+$ **99. a.** $Na^+(g) + Cl^-(g) \rightarrow NaCl(s)$; **b.** $NH_4^+(g) + Br^-(g) \rightarrow NH_4Br(s)$; **c.** $Mg^{2+}(g) + S^{2-}(g) \rightarrow MgS(s)$; **d.** $O_2(g) \rightarrow 2O(g)$

101. CO_3^{2-}:

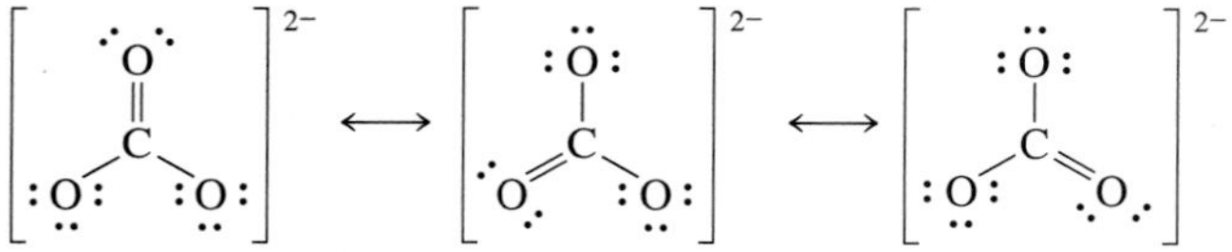

HCO_3^-

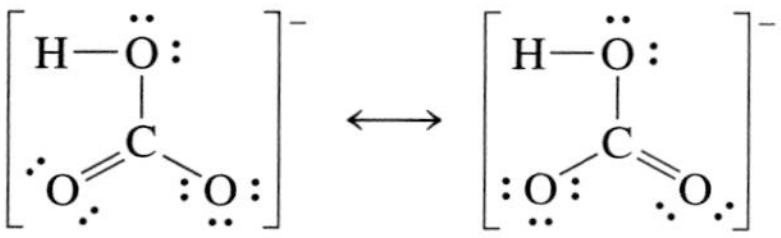

H_2CO_3

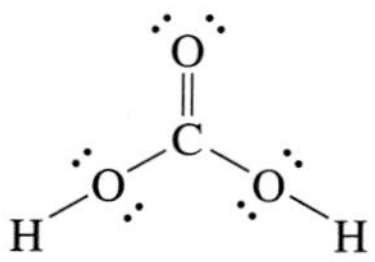

$\Delta H = -83$ kJ; the carbon–oxygen double bond in CO_2 is stronger than two carbon–oxygen single bonds in H_2CO_3.

103. a. NO_2: 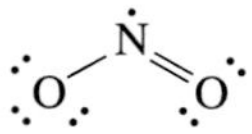 + other resonance structures

N_2O_4 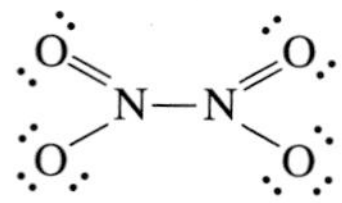 + other resonance structures

Since NO_2 has an odd number of valence electrons, it is impossible to satisfy the octet rule for NO_2. By dimerizing to form N_2O_4, the unpaired electron on two NO_2 molecules can pair up, giving a compound that can have a valid Lewis structure. Odd electron species are generally very reactive species.

b.

BF_3

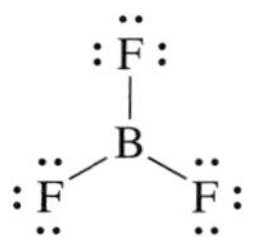

NH_3

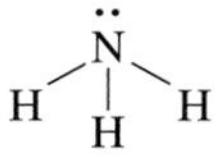

BF_3NH_3

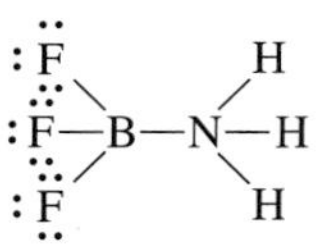

BF_3 can be considered electron deficient. Boron has only six electrons around it. By forming BF_3NH_3, the boron atom satisfies the octet rule by sharing electrons in four single bonds. **105.** The general structure of the trihalide ions is:

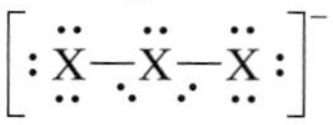

Bromine and iodine are large enough and have low-energy, empty d orbitals to accommodate the expanded octet. Fluorine is small and its valence shell contains only $2s$ and $2p$ orbitals (4 orbitals) and cannot expand its octet. The d orbitals in F are $3d$; they are too high in energy compared with $2s$ and $2p$ to be used. **107.** Yes, each structure has the same number of effective pairs around the central atom. (We count a multiple bond as a single group of electrons.) **109. a.** $\approx 120°$

b.

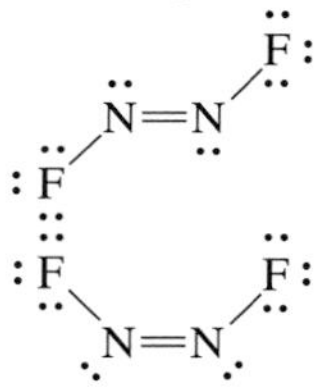

Nonpolar

Polar

111. The CO bond is polar, while the N_2 bond is nonpolar. This may lead to a greater reactivity. **113.** 540 ± 50 kJ **115. a.** The most likely structures are:

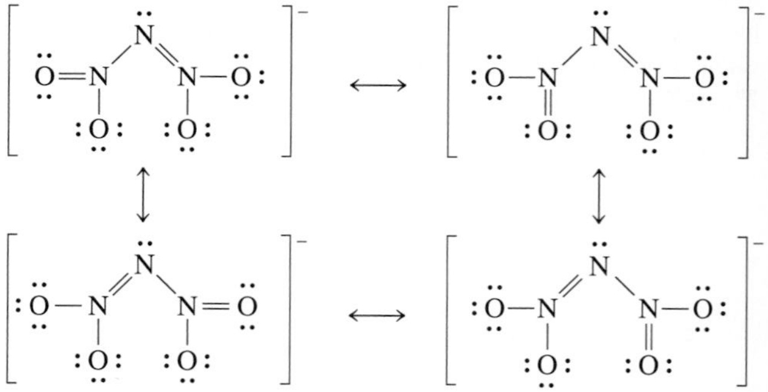

There are other possible resonance structures, but these are most likely. **b.** The NNN and all ONN and ONO bond angles should be about 120°. **117. a.** Two possible structures exist; each has a T-shaped molecular structure:

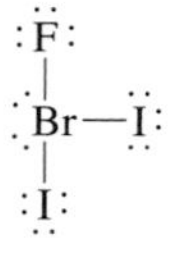

90° bond angle between I atoms 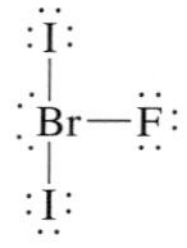   180° bond angle between I atoms

b. Three possible structures exist; each has a see-saw molecular structure.

90° bond angle between O atoms | 180° bond angle between O atoms | 120° bond angle between O atoms

c. Three possible structures exist; each has a square pyramid molecular structure.

One F atom is 180° from lone pair. | Both F atoms are 90° from lone pair and 90° from each other. | Both F atoms are 90° from lone pair and 180° from each other.

119. $:N=N=O: \longleftrightarrow :N\equiv N-O: \longleftrightarrow :N-N\equiv O:$

$\quad\quad -1\ \ +1\ \ 0 \quad\quad\quad 0\ \ +1\ \ -1 \quad\quad\quad -2\ \ +1\ \ +1$

We should eliminate N—N≡O, since it has a formal charge of +1 on the most electronegative element (O). This is consistent with the observation that the N—N bond is between a double and triple bond and that the N—O bond is between a single and double bond.

Chapter 9

7. Bond energy is proportional to bond order. Bond length is inversely proportional to bond order. Bond energy and length can be measured. **9.** Paramagnetic: Unpaired electrons are present. Measure the mass of a substance in the presence and absence of a magnetic field. A substance with unpaired electrons will be attracted by the magnetic field, giving an apparent increase in mass in the presence of the field. Greater number of unpaired electrons will give greater attraction and greater observed mass increase.

11. H_2O:

H_2O has a tetrahedral arrangement of the electron pairs about the O atom that requires sp^3 hybridization. Two of the sp^3 hybrid orbitals are used to form bonds to the two hydrogen atoms, and the other two sp^3 hybrid orbitals hold the two lone pairs on oxygen.

13. H_2CO:

The central carbon atom has a trigonal planar arrangement of the electron pairs that requires sp^2 hybridization. Two of the sp^2 hybrid orbitals are used to form the two bonds to hydrogen. The other sp^2 hybrid orbital forms the σ bond to oxygen. The unchanged (unhybridized) p orbital on carbon is used to form the π bond between carbon and oxygen. **15.** [63] **a.** sp; **b.** sp^3; **c.** sp^3; **d.** sp^3; **e.** sp^2; **f.** sp^3; **g.** sp; **h.** each O is sp^2 hybridized; **i.** Br is sp^3 hybridized [67] **a.** NO_2^-, sp^2; NO_3^-, sp^2; **b.** All are sp hybridized. **17.** PF_5, dsp^3; BeH_2, sp; BH_3, sp^2; Br_3^-, dsp^3; SF_4, dsp^3; XeF_4, d^2sp^3; ClF_5, d^2sp^3;

SF_6, d^2sp^3 **19.** All are sp^2. **21.** All are dsp^3. **23. a.** tetrahedral, 109.5°, sp^3, nonpolar

b. trigonal pyramid, ≈109.5°, sp^3, polar

c. V-shaped, ≈109.5°, sp^3, polar

d. trigonal planar, 120°, sp^2, nonpolar

e. linear, 180°, sp, nonpolar

H—Be—H

f. $a ≈ 120°$, see-saw, dsp^3, polar
$b ≈ 90°$

g. $a = 90°$, trigonal bipyramid, dsp^3, nonpolar
$b = 120°$

h. linear, 180°, dsp^3, nonpolar

i. square planar, 90°, d^2sp^3, nonpolar

j. octahedral, 90°, d^2sp^3, nonpolar

k. square pyramid, ≈90°; d^2sp^3, polar

l. T-shaped, ≈90°, dsp^3, polar

25. The π bond forces all six atoms into the same plane.
27. Biacetyl

All CCO angles are 120°. The six atoms are not in the same plane.
11σ and 2π
Acetoin

angle a $= 120°$, angle b $= 109.5°$, 13 σ and 1 π bond
29. To complete the Lewis structure, add lone pairs to complete octets for each atom. **a.** 6; **b.** 4; **c.** The center N in $-N{=}N{=}N$ group; **d.** 33 σ; **e.** 5 π; **f.** 180°; **g.** $\approx 109.5°$; **h.** sp^3

31.

a. The two nitrogens in the ring with double bonds are sp^2 hybridized. The other three nitrogens are sp^3 hybridized. **b.** The five carbon atoms in the ring with one nitrogen are all sp^3 hybridized. The four carbon atoms in the other ring with double bonds are all sp^2 hybridized. **c.** Angles a and b: $\approx 109.5°$; angles c, d, and e: $\approx 120°$; **d.** 31 σ bonds; **e.** 3 π bonds   **33. a.** H_2^+, H_2, H_2^-; **b.** He_2^{2+} and He_2^+
35. a. $(\sigma_{2s})^2$; B.O. $= 1$; diamagnetic (0 unpaired electrons); **b.** $(\sigma_{2s})^2(\sigma_{2s}^*)^2(\pi_{2p})^4$; B.O. $= 2$; diamagnetic (0 unpaired electrons); **c.** $(\sigma_{2s})^2 (\sigma_{2s}^*)^2 (\sigma_{2p})^2 (\pi_{2p})^4 (\pi_{2p}^*)^2$; B.O. $= 2$; paramagnetic (2 unpaired electrons)   **37.** O_2^+: $(\sigma_{2s})^2 (\sigma_{2s}^*)^2 (\sigma_{2p})^2 (\pi_{2p})^4 (\pi_{2p}^*)^1$; B.O. $= 2.5$; 1 unpaired electron; O_2: $(\sigma_{2s})^2 (\sigma_{2s}^*)^2 (\sigma_{2p})^2 (\pi_{2p})^4 (\pi_{2p}^*)^2$; B.O. $= 2$; 2 unpaired electrons; O_2^-: $(\sigma_{2s})^2 (\sigma_{2s}^*)^2 (\sigma_{2p})^2 (\pi_{2p})^4 (\pi_{2p}^*)^3$; B.O. $= 1.5$; 1 unpaired electron; O_2^{2-}: $(\sigma_{2s})^2 (\sigma_{2s}^*)^2 (\sigma_{2p})^2 (\pi_{2p})^4 (\pi_{2p}^*)^4$; B.O. $= 1$; 0 unpaired electrons; bond energy: $O_2^{2-} < O_2^- < O_2 < O_2^+$; bond length: $O_2^+ < O_2 < O_2^- < O_2^{2-}$.
39. C_2^{2-} has 10 valence electrons. $[:C{\equiv}C:]^{2-}$; sp hybrid orbitals used; $(\sigma_{2s})^2(\sigma_{2s}^*)^2(\pi_{2p})^4(\sigma_{2p})^2$; B.O. $= 3$. Both give the same picture, a triple bond composed of one σ and two π bonds. Both predict the ion to be diamagnetic.   **41. a.** $(\sigma_{2s})^2(\sigma_{2s}^*)^2(\pi_{2p})^4(\sigma_{2p})^2$; B.O. $= 3$; dia-

magnetic; **b.** $(\sigma_{2s})^2(\sigma_{2s}^*)^2(\pi_{2p})^4(\sigma_{2p})^1$; B.O. $= 2.5$; paramagnetic; **c.** $(\sigma_{2s})^2(\sigma_{2s}^*)^2(\pi_{2p})^4$; B.O. $= 2$; diamagnetic   **43.** bond length: CO $<$ CO$^+$ $<$ CO^{2+}; bond energy: CO^{2+} $<$ CO$^+$ $<$ CO
45.

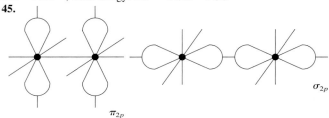

47. a. The electrons would be closer to F on the average. The F atom is more electronegative than the H atom, and the $2p$ orbital of F is lower in energy than the $1s$ orbital of H; **b.** The bonding MO would have more fluorine $2p$ character because it is closer in energy to the fluorine $2p$ orbital; **c.** The antibonding MO would place more electron density closer to H and would have a greater contribution from the higher-energy hydrogen $1s$ atomic orbital.   **49.** O_3 and NO_2^- have identical Lewis structures, so we need to discuss only one of them. The Lewis structure for O_3 is

Localized electron model: The central oxygen atom is sp^2 hybridized, which is used to form the two σ bonds and hold the lone pair of electrons. An unchanged (unhybridized) p atomic orbital forms the π bond with the neighboring oxygen atoms. The π bond resonates between the two positions. Molecular orbital model: There are two localized σ bonds and a π bond that is delocalized over the entire surface of the molecule. The delocalized π bond results from overlap of a p atomic oribtal on each oxygen atom in O_3.

51. a. Trigonal pyramid; sp^3

b. Tetrahedral; sp^3

c. See-saw; dsp^3

d. T-shaped, dsp^3

e. Trigonal bipyramid; dsp^3

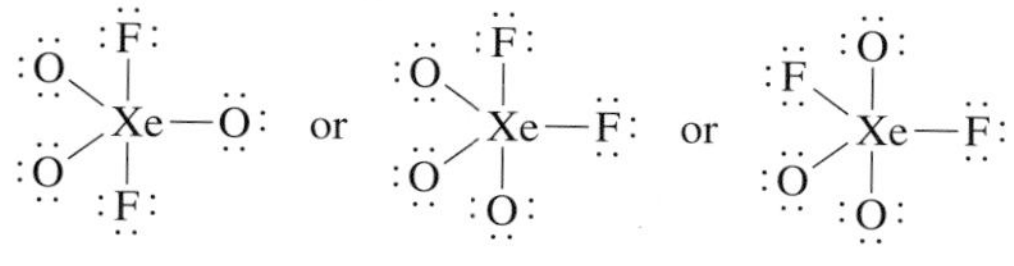

(Three Lewis structures of Xe with O and F atoms: XeO_3F_2 type structures shown "or ... or")

53.

(Lewis structure of an aromatic ring compound with C—H, C—O—H, CH substituents, and an N in the ring, drawn as a resonance pair connected by a double-headed arrow)

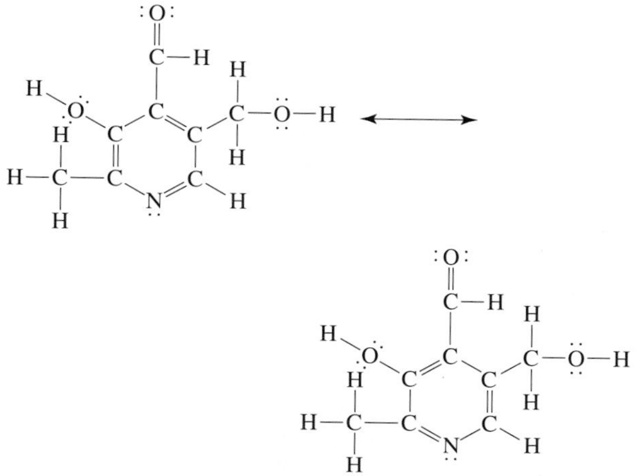

a. 20 σ bonds; 4 π bonds (The electrons in the 3 π bonds in the ring are delocalized.) **b.** angles a, c, and g: $\approx 109.5°$; angles b, d, e, and f: $\approx 120°$; **c.** 6 sp^2 carbons; **d.** 4 sp^3 atoms; **e.** Yes, the π electrons in the ring are delocalized. The atoms in the ring are all sp^2 hybridized. This leaves a p orbital perpendicular to the plane of the ring from each atom. Overlap of all six of these p orbitals results in a π molecular orbital system where the electrons are delocalized above and below the plane of the ring (similar to benzene in Fig. 9.48 of the text).

55. a. $COCl_2$ Trigonal planar, polar, 120°, sp^2

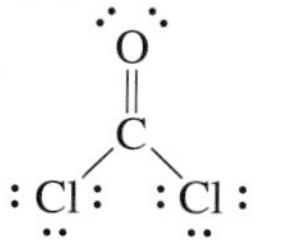

(Lewis structure: O double bonded to C, with two Cl atoms)

b. N_2F_2

can also be

(Two Lewis structures of N_2F_2: Polar and Nonpolar)

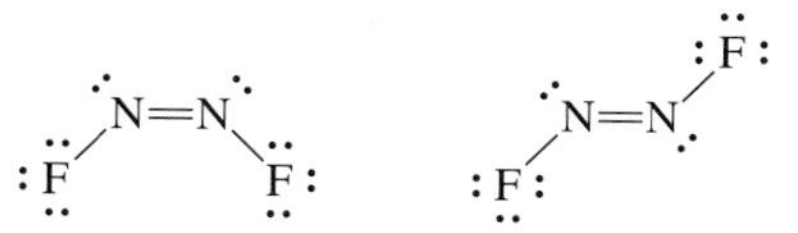

Polar   Nonpolar

V-shaped about both N atoms, $\approx 120°$, sp^2

These are distinctly different molecules.

c. COS

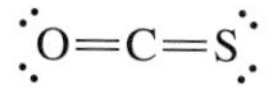

$O{=}C{=}S$ Linear, polar, 180°, sp

d. ICl_3

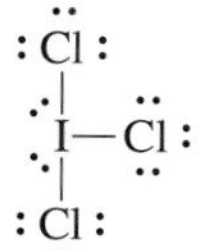

(Lewis structure of ICl_3, T-shaped)

T-shaped, polar, $\approx 90°$, dsp^3

57. a. The NNO structure is correct. From the Lewis structures we would predict both NNO and NON to be linear, but NON would be nonpolar. NNO is polar.

b.

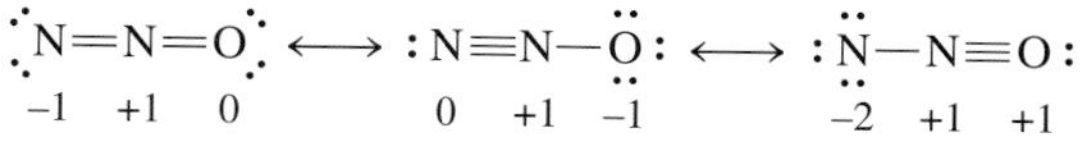

$$:N{=}N{=}O: \longleftrightarrow :N{\equiv}N{-}O: \longleftrightarrow :N{-}N{\equiv}O:$$

    -1 $+1$ 0 0 $+1$ -1 -2 $+1$ $+1$ Formal charges

The central N is sp hybridized. We can probably ignore the third resonance structure on the basis of formal charge. **c.** sp hybrid orbitals on the center N overlap with atomic orbitals (or hybrid orbitals) on the other two atoms to form two σ bonds. The remaining p orbitals on the center N overlap with p orbitals on the other N to form two π bonds. **59.** N_2: $(\sigma_{2s})^2(\sigma_{2s}{}^*)^2(\pi_{2p})^4(\sigma_{2p})^2$ in ground state, B.O. = 3, diamagnetic; 1st excited state: $(\sigma_{2s})^2(\sigma_{2s}{}^*)^2(\pi_{2p})^4(\sigma_{2p})^1(\pi_{2p}{}^*)^1$, B.O. = 2, paramagnetic (two unpaired electrons) **61. a.** No, some atoms are attached differently; **b.** Structure 1: All N = sp^3, all C = sp^2; structure 2: All C and N = sp^2; **c.** The first structure with the carbon–oxygen double bonds is slightly more stable.
63. a. NCN^{2-}:

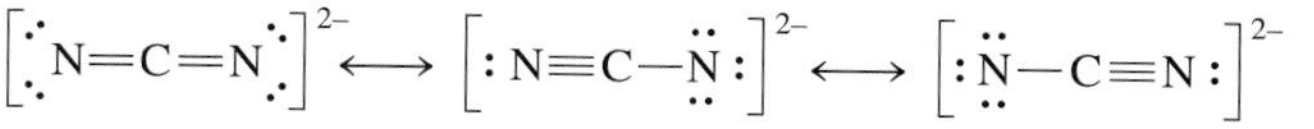

$$\left[:N{=}C{=}N:\right]^{2-} \longleftrightarrow \left[:N{\equiv}C{-}N:\right]^{2-} \longleftrightarrow \left[:N{-}C{\equiv}N:\right]^{2-}$$

H_2NCN:

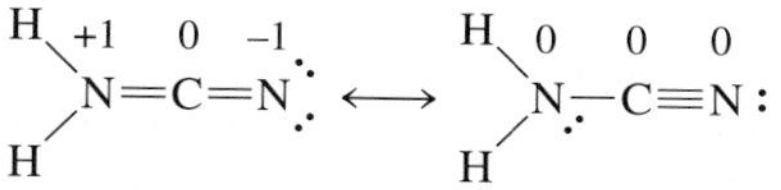

(Two resonance structures of H_2NCN with formal charges +1, 0, −1 and 0, 0, 0)

Favored by formal charge

Dicyandiamide:

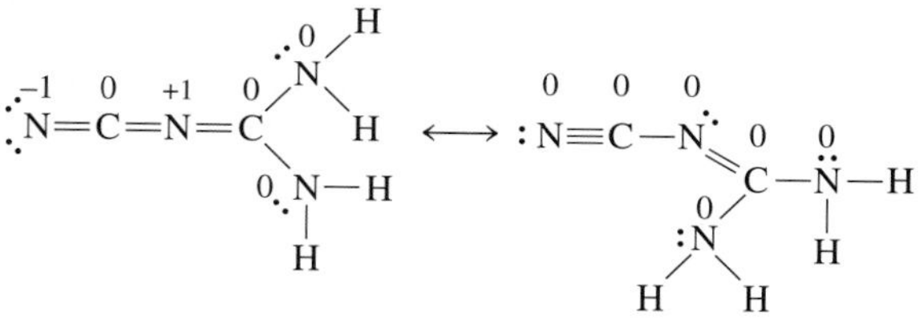

(Two resonance structures of dicyandiamide with formal charges; second favored by formal charge)

Favored by formal charge

Melamine:

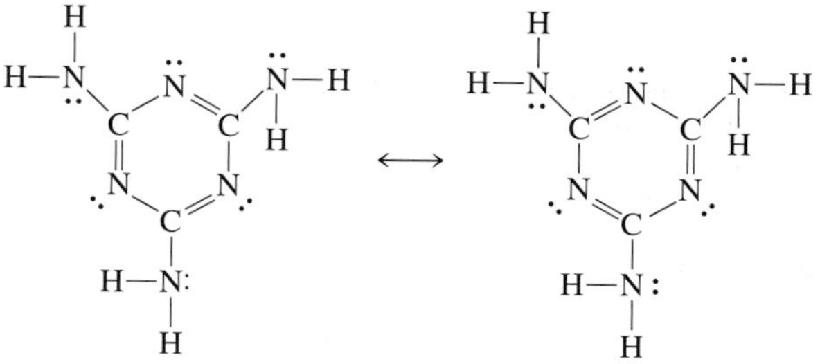

(Two resonance structures of melamine, a triazine ring with three NH_2/NH substituents, connected by a double-headed arrow)

b. NCN^{2-}: C is sp hybridized. Cannot predict hybrids for N's (different for each resonance structure). For the remaining compounds, we will predict hybrids for the favored resonance structures only.

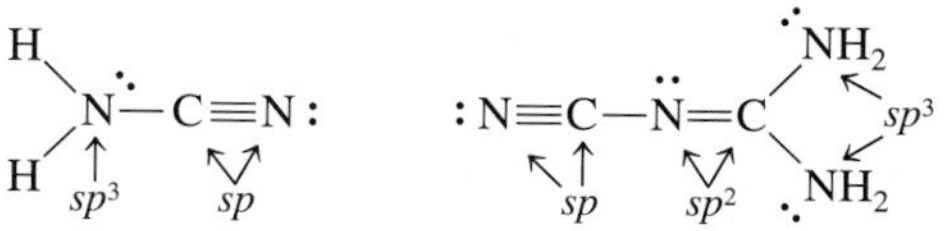

(Structures showing hybridization labels: H_2NCN with sp^3 N and sp C; dicyandiamide with sp, sp^2, sp^3 labels on NH_2)

Melamine: N in NH_2 groups are all sp^3 hybridized. Atoms in ring are all sp^2 hybridized; **c.** NCN^{2-}: 2 σ and 2 π bonds; H_2NCN: 4 σ and 2 π bonds; dicyandiamide: 9 σ and 3 π bonds; melamine: 15 σ and 3 π bonds; **d.** The π system forces the ring to be planar just as the benzene ring is planar. **e.** The structure

$$:N\equiv C-\overset{\cdot\cdot}{N}$$

(Lewis structure: $:N\equiv C-\overset{\cdot\cdot}{N}$ connected to C which bonds to $\overset{\cdot\cdot}{N}-H$ with H, and to $:\overset{\cdot\cdot}{N}$ with H and H)

is the most important because it has three different CN bonds. This structure is also favored on the basis of formal charge. **65. a.** 25-nm light has sufficient energy to ionize N and N_2 and to break the triple bond in N_2. Thus, N_2, N_2^+, N, and N^+ will all be present, assuming excess N_2. **b.** 85.33 nm $< \lambda \leq 127$ nm; **c.** The ionization energy of a substance is the energy it takes to completely remove an electron. N_2: $(\sigma_{2s})^2(\sigma_{2s}^*)^2(\pi_{2p})^4(\sigma_{2p})^2$; the electron removed from N_2 is in the σ_{2p} molecular orbital, which is lower in energy than the $2p$ atomic orbital from which the electron in atomic nitrogen is removed. Since the electron removed from N_2 is lower in energy than the electron removed in N, then the ionization energy of N_2 is greater than the ionization energy of N. **67.** Both reactions apparently involve only the breaking of the N—Cl bond. However, in the reaction $ONCl \rightarrow NO + Cl$ some energy is released in forming the stronger NO bond, lowering the value of ΔH. Therefore, the apparent N—Cl bond energy is artificially low for this reaction. The first reaction involves only the breaking of the N—Cl bond.

Chapter 10

13. London dispersion forces (LD forces) < dipole–dipole < H bonding < metallic bonding, covalent network, ionic. Yes, there is considerable overlap. Consider some of the examples in Exercise 10.94. Benzene (only LD forces) has a higher boiling point than acetone (dipole–dipole). Also, there is even more overlap of the stronger forces (metallic, covalent, and ionic). **15.** As the strengths of intermolecular forces increase, surface tension, viscosity, melting point, and boiling point increase, while the vapor pressure decreases. **17. a.** *Polarizability* of an atom refers to the ease of distorting the electron cloud. It also can refer to distorting the electron clouds in molecules or ions. *Polarity* refers to the presence of a permanent dipole moment in a molecule. **b.** London dispersion forces are present in all substances. LDF can be referred to as accidental dipole-induced dipole forces. Dipole–dipole forces involve the attraction of molecules with permanent dipoles for each other. **c.** *inter:* between; *intra:* within. For example, in Br_2 the covalent bond is an intramolecular force, holding the two Br atoms together in the molecule. The much weaker London dispersion forces are intermolecular forces of attraction, which hold different Br_2 molecules together in the liquid phase. **19.** Atoms have an approximately spherical shape. It is impossible to pack spheres together without some empty space between the spheres. **21.** As the intermolecular forces increase, the critical temperature increases. **23. a.** crystalline solid: long range order; amorphous solid: no long range order; **b.** ionic solid: contains ions held together by ionic bonding; molecular solid: contains discrete covalently bonded molecules held together in the solid by weaker forces (LDF, dipole, or hydrogen bonds); **c.** molecular solid: discrete molecules; covalent network solid: no discrete molecules. A covalent network is like a giant molecule. The intermolecular forces are the covalent bonds between the atoms. **d.** metallic solid: contains delocalized electrons; excellent conductor of electricity; covalent network: localized electrons, insulator or semiconductor **25.** No, an example is common glass, which is primarily amorphous SiO_2 (a

covalent network solid) as compared with ice (a crystalline solid held together by weaker H bonds). The intermolecular forces in the amorphous solid in this case are stronger than those in the crystalline solid. Whether or not a solid is amorphous or crystalline depends on the long range order in the solid and not on the strengths of the intermolecular forces. **27. a.** As the temperature is increased, more electrons in the valence band have sufficient kinetic energy to jump to the conduction bands. **b.** A photon is absorbed by an electron, which then goes from the valence band to the conduction band. **c.** An impurity either adds electrons at an energy near that of the conduction band (n-type) or creates holes (unfilled energy levels) at an energy in the previously filled molecular orbitals (p-type). **29. a.** condensation: vapor $\rightarrow$ liquid; **b.** evaporation: liquid $\rightarrow$ vapor; **c.** sublimation: solid $\rightarrow$ vapor; **d.** A supercooled liquid is a liquid at a temperature below its freezing point. **31. a.** As intermolecular forces increase, the rate of evaporation decreases. **b.** increase T: increase rate; **c.** increase surface area: increase rate **33.** The phase change, $H_2O(g) \rightarrow H_2O(l)$ releases heat that can cause additional damage. Also steam can be at a temperature much greater than 100°C. **35. a.** LD (London dispersion); **b.** dipole, LD; **c.** hydrogen bonding, LD; **d.** ionic; **e.** LD; **f.** dipole, LD; **g.** ionic **37. a.** OCS; **b.** PF_3; **c.** SF_2; **d.** SO_2 **39. a.** Neopentane is more compact than *n*-pentane, producing less area of contact between neopentane molecules, leading to weaker London dispersion forces and a lower boiling point. **b.** Ethanol exhibits H bonding; dimethyl ether does not. **c.** HF exhibits H bonding; **d.** LiCl, ionic, HCl, weaker dipole forces; **e.** *n*-Pentane is larger and so has stronger LD forces; **f.** Dimethyl ether has dipole forces in addition to LD forces. **41. a.** HCl has dipole forces in addition to LD forces; **b.** NaCl, stronger ionic forces; **c.** I_2, larger molecule so stronger LD forces; **d.** N_2, smallest nonpolar compound present, has weakest LD forces; **e.** CH_4, smallest nonpolar compound present, has weakest LD forces; **f.** HF, can form relatively strong hydrogen bonding interactions, unlike the other compounds; **g.** $CH_3CH_2CH_2OH$, unlike others, has relatively strong hydrogen bonding. **43.** H_2O is attracted to glass while Hg is not. Convex (like Hg in glass) **45.** The structure of H_2O_2 produces greater hydrogen bonding than water. Long chains of hydrogen bonded H_2O_2 molecules then get tangled together. **47.** 3.13 Å **49.** 1.54 g/cm^3 **51.** 22.68 g/cm^3 **53.** edge, 328 pm; radius, 142 pm **55.** 74.06% **57.** Dope with a Group 5A element (P, As). **59.** p-type **61.** 5.0×10^2 nm **63.** NaCl: $4Na^+$, $4Cl^-$; CsCl: $1Cs^+$, $1Cl^-$; ZnS: $4Zn^{2+}$, $4S^{2-}$; TiO_2: $2Ti^{4+}$, $4O^{2-}$ **65.** CoF_2 **67.** MF_2 **69.** From density data, 421 pm; from ionic radii data, 410. pm; the two values agree within 3%. **71. a.** CO_2: molecular; **b.** SiO_2: covalent network; **c.** Si: atomic, covalent network; **d.** CH_4: molecular; **e.** Ru: atomic, metallic; **f.** I_2: molecular; **g.** KBr: ionic; **h.** H_2O: molecular; **i.** NaOH: ionic; **j.** U: atomic, metallic; **k.** $CaCO_3$: ionic; **l.** PH_3: molecular **73. a.** The unit cell consists of Ni at the cube corners and Ti at the body center or Ti at the cube corners and Ni at the body center. **b.** NiTi; **c.** Both have a coordination number of 8. **75.** $CaTiO_3$; six oxygens around each Ti **77. a.** $YBa_2Cu_3O_9$; **b.** The structure of this superconductor material is based on the second perovskite structure. The $YBa_2Cu_3O_9$ structure is three of these cubic perovskite unit cells stacked on top of each other. The oxygen atoms are in the same places, Cu takes the place of Ti, and two Ca atoms are replaced by Ba and one Ca atom is replaced by Y. **c.** $YBa_2Cu_3O_7$ **79.** Li, 158 kJ/mol; Mg, 139 kJ/mol. Bonding is stronger in Li. **81.** 89°C **83.** 2.56×10^{-3} torr

85.

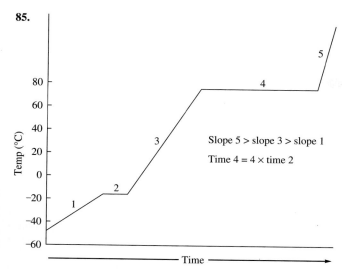

Slope 5 > slope 3 > slope 1

Time 4 = 4 × time 2

87. 1680 kJ **89.** 1490 g **91.** A: solid; B: liquid; C: vapor; D: solid + vapor; E: solid + liquid + vapor (triple point); F: liquid + vapor; G: liquid + vapor (critical point); H: vapor; the first dashed line (at the lower temperature) is the normal melting point, and the second dashed line is the normal boiling point. The solid phase is denser. **93.** $C_{25}H_{52}$ has the stronger intermolecular forces because it has the higher boiling point. Even though $C_{25}H_{52}$ is nonpolar, it is so large that its London dispersion forces are much stronger than the sum of the London dispersion forces and hydrogen bonding interactions found in H_2O.

95.

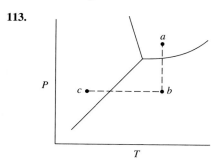

97. 0.229 nm **99.** If TiO_2 conducts electricity as a liquid, then it would be ionic. **101.** The student neglected to consider the enthalpy change that occurs at the melting point, called the *enthalpy of fusion.* **103.** 4.65 kg/h **105.** 46.7 kJ/mol; 90% **107.** The solids with high melting points (NaCl, $MgCl_2$, NaF, MgF_2, AlF_3) are all ionic solids. $SiCl_4$, SiF_4, Cl_2, F_2, PF_5, and SF_6 are nonpolar covalent molecules with LD forces. PCl_3 and SCl_2 are polar molecules with LD and dipole forces. In these 8 molecular substances the intermolecular forces are weak and the melting points low. $AlCl_3$ is intermediate. The melting point indicates there are stronger forces present than in the nonmetal halides, but not as strong as for an ionic solid. $AlCl_3$ illustrates a gradual transition from ionic to covalent bonding; from an ionic solid to discrete molecules. **109.** $TiO_{1.182}$ or $Ti_{0.8462}$ O; 63.7% Ti^{2+}, 36.3% Ti^{3+} **111.** 6.58 g/cm³

113.

As *P* is lowered, we go from *a* to *b* on the phase diagram. The water boils. The evaporation of the water is endothermic and the water is cooled (*b* → *c*), forming some ice. If the pump is left on, the ice will sublime until none is left. This is the basis of freeze drying.

Chapter 11

9. 0.365 *M* **11.** 1.54×10^{-2} *M* $NiCl_2$, Ni^{2+}: 1.54×10^{-2} *M*; Cl^-: 3.08×10^{-2} *M* **13.** 0.16 L **15.** Since volume is temperature-dependent and mass is not, then molarity is temperature-dependent and molality is temperature-independent. In determining ΔT_f and ΔT_b, we are interested in how some temperature depends on composition. Thus we do not want our expression of composition to also be dependent on temperature. **17.** hydrophobic: water hating; hydrophilic: water loving **19.** Negative deviation: Solute–solvent attractions are stronger than attractions in pure substances. Positive deviation: Solute–solvent attractions are weaker than in pure substances. **21.** No. For ideal solution, $\Delta H_{soln} = 0$ **23.** The osmotic pressure inside bacteria cells is less than outside the cell causing the cells to dehydrate and die. **25.** The Tyndall effect is the scattering of light by particles. Colloids scatter light, and true solutions do not scatter light. **27.** 50.0%, 4.69 *M*, 5.94 *m*, 9.68×10^{-2} **29.** HCl: 12 *M*, 17 *m*, 0.23; HNO_3: 16 *M*, 37 *m*, 0.39; H_2SO_4: 18 *M*, 200 *m*, 0.76; $HC_2H_3O_2$: 17 *M*, 2000 *m*, 0.96; NH_3: 15 *M*, 23 *m*, 0.29 **31.** 35%; 0.39; 7.3 *m*; 3.1 *M* **33.** 23.9%; 1.6 *m*, 0.028, 4.11 *N* **35.** $KCl(s) \rightarrow K^+(aq) + Cl^-(aq)$ $\Delta H_{soln} = 31$ kJ/mol **37.** The attraction of water molecules for Al^{3+} and OH^- cannot overcome the larger lattice energy of $Al(OH)_3$. **39.** Water will dissolve polar solutes (c and d) and ionic solutes (b). Carbon tetrachloride will dissolve nonpolar solutes (a and e). **41.** Ability to form hydrogen bonding interactions, ability to break up into ions, and polarity are some factors affecting solute solubility. **a.** CH_3CH_2OH; **b.** $CHCl_3$; **c.** CH_3CH_2OH **43.** As the length of the hydrocarbon chain increases, the solubility decreases because the nonpolar hydrocarbon chain interacts poorly with the polar water molecules. **45.** 962 L · atm/mol; 1.14×10^{-3} mol/L **47.** 23.6 torr **49.** 3.0×10^2 g/mol **51. a.** 290 torr; **b.** 0.69 **53.** $\chi_{methanol} = \chi_{propanol} = 0.500$ **55.** solution c **57.** $P_{ideal} = 188.6$ torr; $\chi_{acetone} = 0.512$, $\chi_{methanol} = 0.488$; since the actual vapor pressure of the solution is smaller than the ideal vapor pressure, then this solution exhibits a negative deviation from Raoult's law. This occurs when solute–solvent attractions are stronger than for the pure substances. **59.** 100.042°C **61.** 14.8 g $C_3H_8O_3$ **63.** $T_f = -29.9°C$, $T_b = 108.2°C$ **65.** 456 g/mol **67. a.** $\Delta T = 2.0 \times 10^{-5}°C$, $\pi = 0.20$ torr; **b.** Osmotic pressure is better for determining the molar mass of large molecules. A temperature change of $10^{-5}°C$ is very difficult to measure. A change in height of a column of mercury by 0.2 mm is not as hard to measure precisely. **69.** 0.327 *M* **71. a.** 0.010 *m* Na_3PO_4 and 0.020 *m* KCl; **b.** 0.020 *m* HF; **c.** 0.020 *m* $CaBr_2$ **73. a.** $T_f = -0.28°C$; $T_b = 100.077°C$; **b.** $T_f = -0.37°C$; $T_b = 100.10°C$ **75.** 2.63 (0.0225 *m*), 2.60 (0.0910 *m*), 2.57 (0.278 *m*); $i_{average} = 2.60$ **77.** 37 atm; the osmotic pressure should be lower due to ion pairing. **79. a.** 26.6 kJ/mol; **b.** -657 kJ/mol **81.** NH_3 is capable of forming hydrogen bonding interactions with water, while O_2 is a nonpolar substance. **83.** 0.600 **85.** $C_2H_4O_3$; 151 g/mol (exp.); 152.10 g/mol (calc.); $C_4H_8O_6$ **87.** 1.97% NaCl **89.** 0.050 **91.** 44% naphthalene, 56% anthracene **93.** $-0.20°C$, 100.056°C

Chapter 12

9. For a generic reaction A → B, an instantaneous rate is the slope of a tangent line to the graph of [A] versus time (or [B] versus time). We can determine an instantaneous rate at any time. The instantaneous rate at $t \approx 0$ is called the *initial rate.* Since a tangent line generally has the greatest slope at $t \approx 0$ versus tangent lines at other times, then the initial rate would have the largest rate value. The average rate is the change in concentration of a reactant or product per some time period ($\Delta[A]/\Delta t$); an average rate is determined over some time period while an instantaneous rate is determined at one specific time. **11. a.** The greater the frequency of collisions, the greater is the opportunity for molecules to react, and hence the greater is the rate. **b.** Chemical reactions involve the making and breaking of chemical bonds. The kinetic energy of the collisions can be used to break bonds. So, as the kinetic energy of the collisions increases, the rate increases. **c.** For a reaction to occur, it is the reactive portion of each molecule that must be involved in a collision. Only some of all the possible collisions have the correct orientation to convert from reactants to products. **13. a.** A homogeneous catalyst is in the same phase as the reactants. **b.** A heterogeneous catalyst is in a different phase than the reactants. The catalyst is usually a solid, although a catalyst in a liquid phase can act as a heterogeneous catalyst for some gas phase reactions. **15.** No, the catalyzed reaction has a different mechanism and hence most likely a different rate law. **17. a.** They are independent of each other. **b.** The rate law can only be determined from experiment. **c.** Most reactions occur by a multiple series of steps. **19.** P_4: 6.0×10^{-4} mol/L·s; H_2: 3.6×10^{-3} mol/L·s **21. a.** mol/L·s; **b.** mol/L·s; **c.** s^{-1}; **d.** L/mol·s; **e.** $L^2/mol^2 \cdot s$ **23. a.** rate = $k[NO]^2[Cl_2]$; **b.** 1.8×10^2 $L^2/mol^2 \cdot min$ **25. a.** rate = $k[NOCl]^2$; **b.** 6.6×10^{-29} $cm^3/molecules \cdot s$; **c.** 4.0×10^{-8} L/mol·s **27. a.** first order in Hb and first order in CO; **b.** rate = $k[Hb][CO]$; **c.** 0.280 L/μmol·s; **d.** 2.26 μmol/L·s **29.** rate = $k[H_2O_2]$; $\ln[H_2O_2] = -kt + \ln[H_2O_2]_0$; $k = 8.3 \times 10^{-4} s^{-1}$; 0.037 M **31.** rate = $k[NO_2]^2$; $\frac{1}{[NO_2]} = kt + \frac{1}{[NO_2]_0}$; $k = 2.08 \times 10^{-4}$ L/mol·s; 0.131 M **33. a.** rate = k; $[C_2H_5OH] = -kt + [C_2H_5OH]_0$; since slope = $-k$, then $k = 4.00 \times 10^{-5}$ mol/L·s; **b.** 156 s; **c.** 313 s **35.** rate = $k[C_4H_6]^2$; $\frac{1}{[C_4H_6]} = kt + \frac{1}{[C_4H_6]_0}$; $k = 1.4 \times 10^{-2}$ L/mol·s **37.** $9.2 \times 10^{-3} s^{-1}$; 75 s **39. a.** $1.01 \times 10^{-3} s^{-1}$; **b.** 686 s; **c.** 280 s (25%); 1.4×10^3 s (75%); 3×10^3 s (95%) **41.** 0.12 L/mol·s **43.** 42 hours **45. a.** rate = $k[CH_3NC]$; **b.** rate = $k[O_3][NO]$ **47.** Rate = $k[C_4H_9Br]$; $C_4H_9Br + 2H_2O \rightarrow C_4H_9OH + Br^- + H_3O^+$; the intermediates are $C_4H_9^+$ and $C_4H_9OH_2^+$. **49.**

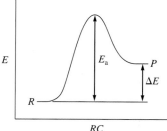

51. 341 kJ/mol **53.** A plot of $\ln(k)$ vs. $1/T$ is linear with slope equal to $-E_a/R = -1.35 \times 10^3$ K. $E_a = 11.2$ kJ/mol **55.** 4.8×10^3 s^{-1} **57.** 51°C **59. a.** NO; **b.** NO_2; **c.** 2.3 **61.** $CH_2D{-}CH_2D$ should be the product. If the mechanism is possible, then the reaction must be $C_2H_4 + D_2 \rightarrow CH_2DCH_2D$. If we got this product, then we could conclude that this is a possible mechanism. If we got some other product, e.g., CH_3CHD_2, then we would conclude that the mechanism is wrong. Even though this mechanism correctly predicts the products of the reaction, we cannot say conclusively that this is the correct mechanism; we might be able to conceive of other mechanisms that would

give the same product as our proposed one. **63.** 5.68×10^{18} molecules/cm^3·s **65. a.** 0.168 h^{-1} = 4.67×10^{-5} s^{-1}; **b.** 4.13 h; **c.** 0.0347 (3.47%) **67.** A graph of ln k versus $1/T$ is linear with slope = $-E_a/R = -1.2 \times 10^4$ K. $E_a = 1.0 \times 10^2$ kJ/mol **69.** At high [S], the enzyme is completely saturated with substrate. Once the enzyme is completely saturated, the rate of decomposition of ES can no longer increase, and the overall rate remains constant. **71.** rate = $\frac{k[I^-][OCl^-]}{[OH^-]}$; $k = 6.0 \times 10^1$ s^{-1} **73. a.** first order with respect to both reactants; **b.** rate = $k[NO][O_3]$; **c.** $k' = 1.8$ s^{-1}; $k'' = 3.6$ s^{-1}; **d.** $k = 1.8 \times 10^{-14}$ molecules/cm^3·s **75. a.** 53.9 kJ/mol; **b.** 83 chirps/min; **c.** The rule of thumb is accurate to about ±1°F.

Chapter 13

9. a. The rates of the forward and reverse reactions are equal. **b.** There is no net change in the composition. **11.** The equilibrium constant is a number that tells us the relative concentrations (pressures) of reactants and products at equilibrium. An equilibrium position is a set of concentrations that satisfy the equilibrium constant expression. More than one equilibrium position can satisfy the same equilibrium constant expression. **13.** The equilibrium position depends on the initial concentrations of an experiment. Since there are an infinite number of initial conditions, then there are an infinite number of equilibrium positions. However, each one of these infinite equilibrium positions will always give the same value for the equilibrium constant. **15.** When we change the pressure by adding an unreactive gas, we do not change the partial pressure of any of the substances in equilibrium with each other. In this case the equilibrium will not shift. If we change the pressure by changing the volume, we will change the partial pressures of all the substances in equilibrium by the same factor. If there are unequal numbers of gaseous particles on the two sides of the equation, the equilibrium will shift. **17.** No, equilibrium is a dynamic process. Both the forward and reverse reactions are occurring at equilibrium, just at equal rates. Thus the forward and reverse reactions will distribute ^{14}C atoms between CO and CO_2. **19. a.** $K = \frac{[NO]^2}{[N_2][O_2]}$; **b.** $K = \frac{[NO_2]^2}{[N_2O_4]}$; **c.** $K = \frac{[SiCl_4][H_2]^2}{[SiH_4][Cl_2]^2}$; **d.** $K = \frac{[PCl_3]^2[Br_2]^3}{[PBr_3]^2[Cl_2]^3}$

21. a. 0.11; **b.** 77; **c.** 8.8; **d.** 1.7×10^{-4} **23.** 6.9×10^{-4} **25.** 10. **27.** 6.3×10^{-13} **29.** 1.5×10^8 **31. a.** $K = \frac{1}{[O_2]^5}$; **b.** $K = [N_2O][H_2O]^2$; **c.** $K = \frac{1}{[CO_2]}$; **d.** $K = \frac{[SO_2]^8}{[O_2]^8}$ **33.** 8.0×10^9 **35.** $K_p = K$ for the reactions a, c, and d since $\Delta n = 0$ for these reactions. **37. a.** $Q > K$, so reaction shifts left to reach equilibrium. **b.** $Q = K$, so reaction is at equilibrium. **c.** $Q < K$, so reaction shifts right to reach equilibrium. **39. a.** decrease; **b.** no change; **c.** no change; **d.** increase **41.** 0.096 M **43.** 3.4 **45.** 0.056 **47.** $[SO_3] = [NO] = 1.06$ M; $[SO_2] = [NO_2] = 0.54$ M **49.** 7.8×10^{-2} atm **51.** $P_{SO_2} = 0.38$ atm; $P_{O_2} = 0.44$ atm; $P_{SO_3} = 0.12$ atm **53. a.** [NO] = 0.032 M, $[Cl_2] = 0.016$ M, [NOCl] = 1.0 M; **b.** [NO] = [NOCl] = 1.0 M, $[Cl_2] = 1.6 \times 10^{-5}$ M; **c.** [NO] = 8.0×10^{-3} M, $[Cl_2] = 1.0$ M, [NOCl] = 2.0 M **55.** $[CO_2] = 0.39$ M, [CO] = 8.6×10^{-3} M, $[O_2] = 4.3 \times 10^{-3}$ M **57.** 4.8 **59. a.** no effect; **b.** shifts left; **c.** shifts right **61. a.** right **b.** right; **c.** no effect; **d.** left; **e.** no effect **63. a.** left; **b.** right; **c.** left; **d.** no effect; **e.** no effect; **f.** right **65.** low temperatures **67.** 2.6×10^{81} **69.** $[N_2]_0 = 10.0$ M; $[H_2]_0 = 11.0 M$ **71. a.** 1.16 atm; **b.** 0.10 atm; **c.** 2.22 atm; **d.** 91.4%

73. $[H_2] = [F_2] = 0.0251\ M$; $[HF] = 0.450\ M$ **75.** Added OH^- reacts with H^+ to produce H_2O. As H^+ is removed, the reaction shifts right to produce more H^+ and $CrO_4{}^{2-}$. Since more $CrO_4{}^{2-}$ is produced, then the solution turns yellow. **77.** $[NOCl] = 2.0\ M$, $[NO] = 0.050\ M$, $[Cl_2] = 0.025\ M$ **79.** 2.1×10^{-3} atm **81.** $P_{NO_2} = 0.704$ atm, $P_{N_2O_4} = 0.12$ atm

Chapter 14

17. a. Arrhenius acid: produce H^+ in water; **b.** Brønsted–Lowry acid: proton (H^+) donor; **c.** Lewis acid: electron pair acceptor; the Lewis definition is most general. The Lewis definition can apply to all Arrhenius and Brønsted–Lowry acids; H^+ has an empty $1s$ orbital and forms bonds to all bases by accepting a pair of electrons from the base. In addition, the Lewis definition incorporates other reactions not typically considered acid–base reactions, e.g., $BF_3(g) + NH_3(g) \rightarrow F_3B{-}NH_3(s)$. NH_3 is something we usually consider a base, and it is in this reaction using the Lewis definition; NH_3 donates a pair of electrons to form the N—B bond. **19.** $[H^+] = [OH^-] = 1.0 \times 10^{-7}\ M$, pH = 7.00 **21.** Nitrogen **23. a.** stronger bond = stronger base; **b.** greater electronegativity = weaker base; **c.** more oxygen atoms = weaker base **25. a.** H_2O and $CH_3CO_2{}^-$; **b.** $CH_3CO_2{}^-$, since the equilibrium favors acetic acid ($K_a < 1$); **c.** Acetate ion is a better base than water and produces basic solutions in water. When we put acetate ion into solution as the only major basic species, the reaction is

$$CH_3CO_2{}^- + H_2O \rightleftharpoons CH_3CO_2H + OH^-$$

Now the competition is between $CH_3CO_2{}^-$ and OH^- for the proton. Hydroxide ion is the strongest base possible in water. The above equilibrium favors acetate plus water resulting in a K_b value less than one. Those species we specifically call weak bases ($10^{-14} < K_b < 1$) lie between H_2O and OH^- in base strength. Weak bases are stronger bases than water but are weaker bases than OH^-. **27. a.** $HClO_4(aq) + H_2O(l) \rightarrow H_3O^+(aq) + ClO_4{}^-(aq)$ or $HClO_4(aq) \rightarrow H^+(aq) + ClO_4{}^-(aq)$; water is commonly omitted from K_a reactions. **b.** $CH_3CH_2CO_2H(aq) \rightleftharpoons H^+(aq) + CH_3CH_2CO_2{}^-(aq)$; **c.** $NH_4{}^+(aq) \rightleftharpoons H^+(aq) + NH_3(aq)$

29.

Acid	Base	Conjugate Base of Acid	Conjugate Acid of Base
a. HF	H_2O	F^-	H_3O^+
b. H_2SO_4	H_2O	$HSO_4{}^-$	H_3O^+
c. $HSO_4{}^-$	H_2O	$SO_4{}^{2-}$	H_3O^+

31. a. weak acid; **b.** strong acid; **c.** strong acid; **d.** weak acid **33.** $HNO_3 > HOCl > NH_4{}^+ > H_2O$ **35. a.** HCl; **b.** HNO_2; **c.** HCN since it has a larger K_a value. **37. a.** $1.0 \times 10^{-7}\ M$; neutral; **b.** $1.5 \times 10^{-11}\ M$; acidic; **c.** $5.3 \times 10^{-4}\ M$; basic; **d.** $4.3 \times 10^{-15}\ M$; acidic **39. a.** endothermic; **b.** $[H^+] = [OH^-] = 2.34 \times 10^{-7}\ M$ **41. a.** pH = pOH = 7.00; **b.** pH = 3.17; pOH = 10.83; **c.** pH = 10.72; pOH = 3.28; **d.** pH = -0.36; pOH = 14.36 **43. a.** $[H^+] = 4.0 \times 10^{-8}\ M$; $[OH^-] = 2.5 \times 10^{-7}\ M$; basic; **b.** $[H^+] = 5 \times 10^{-16}\ M$; $[OH^-] = 20\ M$; basic; **c.** $[H^+] = 10\ M$; $[OH^-] = 1 \times 10^{-15}\ M$; acidic; **d.** $[H^+] = 6.3 \times 10^{-4}\ M$; $[OH^-] = 1.6 \times 10^{-11}\ M$; acidic; **e.** $[H^+] = 1 \times 10^{-9}\ M$; $[OH^-] = 1 \times 10^{-5}\ M$; basic; **f.** $[H^+] = 4.0 \times 10^{-5}\ M$; $[OH^-] = 2.5 \times 10^{-10}\ M$; acidic **45.** pOH = 7.23, $[H^+] = 1.7 \times 10^{-7}\ M$, $[OH^-] = 5.9 \times 10^{-8}\ M$, acidic **47. a.** H^+, Cl^-, H_2O; 0.602; **b.** H^+, Br^-, H_2O; 0.602 **49. a.** 1.00; **b.** -0.70;

c. 7.00 **51.** $[H^+] = 0.088\ M$, $[OH^-] = 1.1 \times 10^{-13}\ M$, $[Cl^-] = 0.013\ M$, $[NO_3{}^-] = 0.075\ M$ **53.** $3.2 \times 10^{-3}\ M$ **55. a.** HNO_2 and H_2O, 2.00; **b.** $HC_2H_3O_2$ and H_2O, 2.68 **57.** $[HOCl] = 1.5\ M$; $[H^+] = [OCl^-] = 2.3 \times 10^{-4}\ M$; $[OH^-] = 4.3 \times 10^{-11}\ M$; pH = 3.64 **59.** $[H^+] = [F^-] = 3.5 \times 10^{-3}\ M$, $[OH^-] = 2.9 \times 10^{-12}\ M$, $[HF] = 0.017\ M$, 2.46 **61.** 1.14 **63.** 1.00 **65. a.** 0.60%; **b.** 1.9%; **c.** 5.8%; **d.** Dilution shifts equilibrium to the side with the greater number of particles (% dissociation increases). **e.** $[H^+]$ also depends on initial concentration of weak acid. **67.** $1.1 \times 10^{-3}\ M$, 2.96, 1.1% **69.** 1.4×10^{-4} **71.** 1.9×10^{-9} **73.** $0.024\ M$
75. a. $NH_3(aq) + H_2O(l) \rightleftharpoons NH_4{}^+(aq) + OH^-(aq)$

$$K_b = \frac{[NH_4{}^+][OH^-]}{[NH_3]};$$

b. $C_5H_5N(aq) + H_2O(l) \rightleftharpoons C_5H_5NH^+(aq) + OH^-(aq)$

$$K_b = \frac{[C_5H_5NH^+][OH^-]}{[C_5H_5N]}$$

77. $NH_3 > C_5H_5N > H_2O > NO_3{}^-$ **79. a.** NH_3; **b.** NH_3; **c.** OH^-; **d.** CH_3NH_2 **81. a.** 13.00; **b.** 7.00; **c.** 14.30 **83. a.** K^+, OH^-, and H_2O, 0.150 M, 13.176; **b.** Ca^{2+}, OH^-, and H_2O, 0.300 M, 13.477 **85.** $3.2 \times 10^{-4}\ M$ **87.** NH_3 and H_2O, $1.6 \times 10^{-3}\ M$, 11.20 **89. a.** $[OH^-] = 8.9 \times 10^{-3}\ M$, $[H^+] = 1.1 \times 10^{-12}\ M$, 11.96; **b.** $[OH^-] = 4.7 \times 10^{-5}\ M$, $[H^+] = 2.1 \times 10^{-10}\ M$, 9.68 **91.** 12.00 **93. a.** 1.3%; **b.** 4.2% **95.** 9.2×10^{-7}
97. $H_2SO_3(aq) \rightleftharpoons HSO_3{}^-(aq) + H^+(aq)$ $\quad K_{a_1}$ reaction
$\quad\quad HSO_3{}^-(aq) \rightleftharpoons SO_3{}^{2-}(aq) + H^+(aq)$ $\quad K_{a_2}$ reaction
99. a. 1.62; **b.** 3.68 **101.** -0.30 **103.** HCl > NH_4Cl > KCl > KCN > KOH **105.** OCl^- **107.** $[HN_3] = [OH^-] = 2.3 \times 10^{-6}\ M$, $[Na^+] = 0.010\ M$, $[N_3{}^-] = 0.010\ M$, $[H^+] = 4.3 \times 10^{-9}\ M$ **109. a.** 5.82; **b.** 10.95 **111.** NaF **113.** 3.08 **115. a.** neutral; **b.** basic; $NO_2{}^- + H_2O \rightleftharpoons HNO_2 + OH^-$; **c.** acidic; $C_5H_5NH^+ \rightleftharpoons C_5H_5N + H^+$; **d.** acidic since $NH_4{}^+$ is a stronger acid than $NO_2{}^-$ is a base; $NH_4{}^+ \rightleftharpoons NH_3 + H^+$; $NO_2{}^- + H_2O \rightleftharpoons HNO_2 + OH^-$; **e.** basic; $OCl^- + H_2O \rightleftharpoons HOCl + OH^-$; **f.** basic since OCl^- is a stronger base than $NH_4{}^+$ is an acid; $OCl^- + H_2O \rightleftharpoons HOCl + OH^-$, $NH_4{}^+ \rightleftharpoons NH_3 + H^+$ **117. a.** $HIO_3 < HBrO_3$; as the electronegativity of the central atom increases, acid strength increases. **b.** $HNO_2 < HNO_3$; as the number of oxygen atoms attached to the central atom increases, acid strength increases. **c.** $HOI < HOCl$; same reasoning as in part a. **d.** $H_3PO_3 < H_3PO_4$; same reasoning as in part b. **119. a.** $H_2O < H_2S < H_2Se$; acid strength increases as bond energy decreases. **b.** $CH_3CO_2H < FCH_2CO_2H < F_2CHCO_2H < F_3CCO_2H$; as the electronegativity of the neighboring atoms increases, acid strength increases. **c.** $NH_4{}^+ < HONH_3{}^+$; same reasoning as in part b. **d.** $NH_4{}^+ < PH_4{}^+$; same reasoning as in part a. **121. a.** basic; $CaO(s) + H_2O(l) \rightarrow Ca(OH)_2(aq)$; **b.** acidic; $SO_2(g) + H_2O(l) \rightarrow H_2SO_3(aq)$; **c.** acidic; $Cl_2O(g) + H_2O(l) \rightarrow 2HOCl(aq)$ **123. a.** $B(OH)_3$, acid; H_2O, base; **b.** Ag^+, acid; NH_3, base; **c.** BF_3, acid; F^-, base **125.** $Al(OH)_3(s) + 3H^+(aq) \rightarrow Al^{3+}(aq) + 3H_2O(l)$; $Al(OH)_3(s) + OH^-(aq) \rightarrow Al(OH)_4{}^-(aq)$ **127.** Fe^{3+}; because it is smaller with a greater positive charge, Fe^{3+} will be more strongly attracted to a lone pair of electrons from a Lewis base. **129.** 990 mL H_2O **131.** $K_a \times K_b = K_w$, $-\log(K_a \times K_b) = -\log(K_w)$, $-\log K_a - \log K_b = -\log K_w$, $pK_a + pK_b = pK_w$ **133.** 10.0 **135. a.** 2.62; **b.** 2.4%; **c.** 8.48 **137. a.** 1.66; **b.** Fe^{2+} ions will produce a less acidic solution (higher pH) due to the lower charge on Fe^{2+} as compared with Fe^{3+}. As the charge on a metal ion increases, acid strength of the hydrated ion increases. **139.** acidic; $HSO_4{}^- \rightleftharpoons SO_4{}^{2-} + H^+$; 1.54 **141. a.** $Hb(O_2)_4$ in lungs, $HbH_4{}^{4+}$ in cells;

b. Decreasing $[CO_2]$ will decrease $[H^+]$, favoring $Hb(O_2)_4$ formation. Breathing into a bag raises $[CO_2]$. **c.** $NaHCO_3$ lowers the acidity from accumulated CO_2. **143. a.** H_2SO_3; **b.** $HClO_3$; **c.** H_3PO_3; $NaOH$ and KOH are ionic compounds composed of either Na^+ or K^+ cations and OH^- anions. When soluble ionic compounds dissolve in water, they form the ions from which they are formed. The acids in this problem are all covalent compounds. When these acids dissolve in water, the covalent bond between oxygen and hydrogen breaks to form H^+ ions. **145.** 7.20. **147.** 7.4; when an acid is added to water, the pH cannot be basic. Must account for the autoionization of water. **149.** 0.022 M **151.** PO_4^{3-}, $K_b = 0.021$; HPO_4^{2-}, $K_b = 1.6 \times 10^{-7}$; $H_2PO_4^-$, $K_b = 1.3 \times 10^{-12}$; from the K_b values, PO_4^{3-} is the strongest base.

Chapter 15

13. A common ion is an ion that appears in an equilibrium reaction but came from a source other than that reaction. Addition of a common ion (H^+ or NO_2^-) to the reaction $HNO_2 \rightleftharpoons H^+ + NO_2^-$ will drive the equilibrium to the left as predicted by Le Châtelier's principle. **15.** No, as long as there are both a weak acid and a weak base present, the solution will be buffered. If the concentrations are the same, the buffer will have the same capacity toward both added H^+ and OH^-. **17.** No, since there are three colored forms, there must be two proton transfer reactions. Thus there must be at least two acidic protons in the acid (orange) form of thymol blue. **19.** The two forms of an indicator are different colors. To see only one color, that form must be in tenfold excess or greater over the other. When the ratio of the two forms is less than 10, both colors are present. To go from $[HIn]/[In^-] = 10$ to $[HIn]/[In^-] = 0.1$ requires a change of 2 pH units as the indicator changes from the acid color to the base color. **21.** When strong acid or strong base is added to an acetic acid–sodium acetate mixture, the strong acid/base is neutralized. The reaction goes to completion. The strong acid/base is replaced with a weak acid/base:

$$H^+(aq) + CH_3CO_2^-(aq) \rightarrow$$
$$CH_3CO_2H(aq); \quad OH^-(aq) + CH_3CO_2H(aq) \rightarrow$$
$$CH_3CO_2^-(aq) + H_2O(l)$$

23. a. 2.96; **b.** 8.94; **c.** 7.00; **d.** 4.89 **25.** 1.1% vs. $1.3 \times 10^{-2}\%$ dissociated; the presence of $C_3H_5O_2^-$ in solution 23d greatly inhibits the dissociation of $HC_3H_5O_2$. This is called the *common ion effect*. **27. a.** 1.70; **b.** 5.49; **c.** 1.70; **d.** 4.71 **29. a.** 4.29; **b.** 12.30; **c.** 12.30; **d.** 5.07 **31.** solution d; solution d is a buffer solution that resists pH changes. **33.** 3.40 **35.** 3.48 **37.** 3.22 **39.** 5.20 **41. a.** 5.14; **b.** 4.34; **c.** 5.14; **d.** 4.34 **43.** 10.49 **45. a.** 7.97; **b.** 8.73; both solutions have an initial pH = 8.77. The two solutions differ in their buffer capacity. Solution b with the larger concentrations has the greater capacity to resist pH change. **47. a.** 0.19; **b.** 0.59; **c.** 1.0; **d.** 1.9 **49.** HOCl; there are many possibilities. One possibility is a solution with [HOCl] = 1.0 M and [NaOCl] = 0.35 M. **51.** solution d **53. a.** 1.0 mol; **b.** 0.30 mol; **c.** 1.3 mol **55. a.** ~22 mL base added; **b.** buffer region is from ~1 mL to ~21 mL base added. The maximum buffering region would be from ~5 mL to ~17 mL of base added with the halfway point to equivalence (~11 mL) as the best buffer point. **c.** ~11 mL base added; **d.** 0 mL base added; **e.** ~22 mL base added (the stoichiometric point); **f.** any point after the stoichiometric point (volume base added > ~22 mL) **57. a.**

0.699; **b.** 0.854; **c.** 1.301; **d.** 7.00; **e.** 12.15 **59. a.** 2.72; **b.** 4.26; **c.** 4.74; **d.** 5.22; **e.** 8.79; **f.** 12.15

61.

Volume (mL)	pH
0.0	2.43
4.0	3.14
8.0	3.53
12.5	3.86
20.0	4.46
24.0	5.24
24.5	5.6
24.9	6.3
25.0	8.28
25.1	10.3
26.0	11.29
28.0	11.75
30.0	11.96

See *Solutions Guide* for pH plot.

63.

Volume (mL)	pH
0.0	11.11
4.0	9.97
8.0	9.58
12.5	9.25
20.0	8.65
24.0	7.87
24.5	7.6
24.9	6.9
25.0	5.28
25.1	3.7
26.0	2.71
28.0	2.24
30.0	2.04

See *Solutions Guide* for pH plot.

65. a. 4.19, 8.45; **b.** 10.74; 5.96; **c.** 0.89, 7.00 **67.** 1.74×10^{-8} **69. a.** yellow; **b.** 8.0; **c.** blue **71.** Phenol red is one possible indicator for the titration in Exercise 57. Phenolphthalein is one possible indicator for the titration in Exercise 59. **73.** Phenolphthalein is one possible indicator for Exercise 61. Bromcresol green is one possible indicator for Exercise 63. **75.** pH < 0.5 **77. a.** yellow; **b.** green; **c.** yellow; **d.** blue **79. a.** $AgC_2H_3O_2(s) \rightleftharpoons Ag^+(aq) + C_2H_3O_2^-(aq)$; $K_{sp} = [Ag^+][C_2H_3O_2^-]$; **b.** $Al(OH)_3(s) \rightleftharpoons Al^{3+}(aq) + 3OH^-(aq)$; $K_{sp} = [Al^{3+}][OH^-]^3$; **c.** $Ca_3(PO_4)_2(s) \rightleftharpoons 3Ca^{2+}(aq) + 2PO_4^{3-}(aq)$; $K_{sp} = [Ca^{2+}]^3[PO_4^{3-}]^2$ **81. a.** 2.3×10^{-9}; **b.** 8.20×10^{-19} **83.** 3.92×10^{-5} **85. a.** 1.6×10^{-5} mol/L; **b.** 9.3×10^{-5} mol/L; **c.** 6.5×10^{-7} mol/L **87.** 2.5×10^{-22} mol/L **89. a.** CaF_2; **b.** $FePO_4$ **91. a.** 4×10^{-17} mol/L; **b.** 4×10^{-11} mol/L; **c.** 4×10^{-29} mol/L **93.** 2.3×10^{-11} mol/L **95.** If the anion in the salt can act as a base in water, then the solubility of the salt will increase as the solution becomes more acidic. Added H^+ will react with the base, forming the conjugate acid. As the basic anion is removed, more of the salt will dissolve to replenish the basic anion. The salts with basic anions are Ag_3PO_4, $CaCO_3$, $CdCO_3$, and $Sr_3(PO_4)_2$. Hg_2Cl_2 and PbI_2 do not have any pH dependence because Cl^- and I^- are terrible bases (the conjugate bases of strong acids).

$$Ag_3PO_4(s) + H^+(aq) \rightarrow 3Ag^+(aq) + HPO_4^{2-}(aq) \xrightarrow{\text{excess } H^+}$$
$$3Ag^+(aq) + H_3PO_4(aq)$$

$CaCO_3(s) + H^+(aq) \rightarrow Ca^{2+}(aq) + HCO_3^-(aq) \xrightarrow{\text{excess } H^+}$
$\quad Ca^{2+}(aq) + H_2CO_3(aq) [H_2O(l) + CO_2(g)]$

$CdCO_3(s) + H^+(aq) \rightarrow Cd^{2+}(aq) + HCO_3^-(aq) \xrightarrow{\text{excess } H^+}$
$\quad Cd^{2+}(aq) + H_2CO_3(aq) [H_2O(l) + CO_2(g)]$

$Sr_3(PO_4)_2(s) + 2H^+(aq) \rightarrow 3Sr^{2+}(aq) + 2HPO_4^{2-}(aq) \xrightarrow{\text{excess } H^+}$
$\quad 3Sr^{2+}(aq) + 2H_3PO_4(aq)$

97. yes; $Q = 1.9 \times 10^{-4} > K_{sp}$ **99.** $[K^+] = 0.160$ M, $[C_2O_4^{2-}] = 3.3 \times 10^{-7}$ M, $[Ba^{2+}] = 0.0700$ M, $[Br^-] = 0.300$ M **101.** $[Ag^+] > 5.6 \times 10^{-5}$ M

103. a.

$Co^{2+} +$	$NH_3 \rightleftharpoons CoNH_3^{2+}$		K_1
$CoNH_3^{2+} +$	$NH_3 \rightleftharpoons Co(NH_3)_2^{2+}$		K_2
$Co(NH_3)_2^{2+} +$	$NH_3 \rightleftharpoons Co(NH_3)_3^{2+}$		K_3
$Co(NH_3)_3^{2+} +$	$NH_3 \rightleftharpoons Co(NH_3)_4^{2+}$		K_4
$Co(NH_3)_4^{2+} +$	$NH_3 \rightleftharpoons Co(NH_3)_5^{2+}$		K_5
$Co(NH_3)_5^{2+} +$	$NH_3 \rightleftharpoons Co(NH_3)_6^{2+}$		K_6

$$Co^{2+} + 6NH_3 \rightleftharpoons Co(NH_3)_6^{2+}$$

b.

$Ag^+ + NH_3 \rightleftharpoons AgNH_3^+$	K_1
$AgNH_3^+ + NH_3 \rightleftharpoons Ag(NH_3)_2^+$	K_2

$$Ag^+ + 2NH_3 \rightleftharpoons Ag(NH_3)_2^+$$

105. $Hg^{2+}(aq) + 2I^-(aq) \rightarrow HgI_2(s)$ (orange precipitate); $HgI_2(s) + 2I^-(aq) \rightarrow HgI_4^{2-}(aq)$ (soluble complex ion) **107.** 3.3×10^{-32} M **109. a.** 1.1×10^{-3} mol/L; **b.** 9.1×10^{-3} mol/L **111.** In 2.0 M NH_3, the soluble complex ion $Ag(NH_3)_2^+$ forms, which increases the solubility of AgCl. The reaction is $AgCl(s) + 2NH_3 \rightleftharpoons Ag(NH_3)_2^+ + Cl^-$. In 2.0 M NH_4NO_3, NH_3 is formed only by the dissociation of the weak acid NH_4^+. There is not enough NH_3 produced by this reaction to dissolve AgCl. **113.** pOH = $pK_b + \log\dfrac{[\text{acid}]}{[\text{base}]}$ **115. a.** potassium fluoride + HCl; **b.** benzoic acid + NaOH; **c.** acetic acid + sodium acetate; **d.** HOCl + NaOH; **e.** ammonium chloride + NaOH **117. a.** 1.0 M; **b.** 9.1 **119.** 3.0 mol **121.** 180. g/mol; 3.3×10^{-4}; assume acetylsalicylic acid is a weak monoprotic acid. **123.** 2.7×10^{-5} mol/L; the solubility of hydroxyapatite will increase as a solution gets more acidic, since both phosphate and hydroxide can react with H^+. 6×10^{-8} mol/L; the hydroxyapatite in the tooth enamel is converted to the less soluble fluorapatite by fluoride-treated water. The less soluble fluorapatite will then be more difficult to dissolve, making teeth less susceptible to decay. See Chemical Impact on "Chemistry of Teeth." **125. a.** 6.7×10^{-6} mol/L; **b.** 1.2×10^{-13} mol/L; **c.** $Pb(OH)_2(s)$ will not form since $Q < K_{sp}$ **127.** 49 mL **129.** 3.9 L **131.** 0.0620 M **133. a.** 5.8×10^{-4} mol/L; **b.** Greater; F^- is a weaker base ($K_b = 1.4 \times 10^{-11}$), so some of the F^- is removed by reaction with water. As F^- is removed, more SrF_2 will dissolve; **c.** 3.5×10^{-3} mol/L

Chapter 16

7. A spontaneous process is one that occurs without any outside intervention. **9. a.** increase; **b.** no change; **c.** decrease **11.** Living organisms need an external energy source to produce the necessary "ordering." **13.** The more widely something is dispersed, the greater the disorder and the greater the work needed to overcome the disorder. It would be more advantageous to prevent contamination of the environment rather than clean it up later. **15.** $w_{max} = \Delta G$; when ΔG

is negative, the magnitude of ΔG is equal to the maximum possible useful work obtainable from the process (at constant T and P). When ΔG is positive, the magnitude of ΔG is equal to the minimum amount of work that must be expended to make the process spontaneous. Due to waste energy (heat) in any real process, the amount of useful work obtainable from a spontaneous process is always less than w_{max}, and for a nonspontaneous reaction, an amount of work greater than w_{max} must be applied to make the process spontaneous. **17.** a, b, c **19.** We draw all of the possible arrangements of the two particles in the three levels.

2 kJ	—	—	X	—	X	XX
1 kJ	—	X	—	XX	X	—
0 kJ	XX	X	X	—	—	—
Total $E =$	0 kJ	1 kJ	2 kJ	2 kJ	3 kJ	4 kJ

The most likely total energy is 2 kJ. **21. a.** H_2 at 100°C and 0.5 atm; **b.** N_2 at STP; **c.** $H_2O(l)$ **23.** a, b **25. a.** negative; **b.** positive **27.** $\Delta G < 0$ for b, c, d **29.** 93.8 J/K · mol **31. a.** yes ($\Delta G < 0$); **b.** 196 K **33. a.** negative; **b.** positive; **c.** negative; **d.** positive **35. a.** $C_{graphite}(s)$; **b.** $C_2H_5OH(g)$; **c.** $CO_2(g)$ **37. a.** negative, −186 J/K; **b.** positive, 187 J/K; **c.** hard to predict since $\Delta n = 0$.; 138 J/K **39.** 262 J/K · mol **41. a.** ΔH and ΔS are both positive; **b.** $S_{rhombic}$ **43. a.** ΔH and ΔS are both negative; **b.** low temperatures **45. a.** $\Delta H° = -803$ kJ, $\Delta S° = -4$ J/K, $\Delta G° = -802$ kJ; **b.** $\Delta H° = 2802$ kJ, $\Delta S° = -262$ J/K, $\Delta G° = 2880.$ kJ; **c.** $\Delta H° = -416$ kJ, $\Delta S° = -209$ J/K, $\Delta G° = -354$ kJ; **d.** $\Delta H° = -176$ kJ, $\Delta S° = -284$ J/K, $\Delta G° = -91$ kJ **47.** $CH_4(g) + CO_2(g) \rightarrow CH_3CO_2H(l)$, $\Delta H° = -16$ kJ, $\Delta S° = -240.$ J/K, $\Delta G° = 56$ kJ; $CH_3OH(g) + CO(g) \rightarrow CH_3CO_2H(l)$, $\Delta H° = -173$ kJ, $\Delta S° = -278$ J/K, $\Delta G° = -90.$ kJ; the second reaction is preferred. It should be run at temperatures below 622 K. **49.** −300. kJ **51.** −731 kJ/mol **53.** −4172 kJ **55.** −188 kJ **57. a.** shifts right; **b.** no shift since the reaction is at equilibrium; **c.** shifts left **59.** $\Delta G° = -198$ kJ, $K = 5.07 \times 10^{34}$ **61. a.** 79.9 kJ/mol; **b.** 81.1 kJ/mol **63.** −71 kJ/mol **65.** If we graph ln K vs. $1/T$, we get a straight line ($y = mx + b$). For an endothermic process, the slope is negative (m = slope = $-\Delta H°/R$).

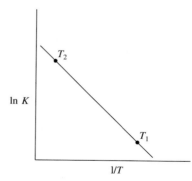

As we increase the temperature from T_1 to T_2 ($1/T_2 < 1/T_1$), we can see that ln K and, hence, K increases. A larger value of K means some more reactants can be converted to products (reaction shifts right).

67. ΔS_{univ} **69.** The introduction of mistakes is an effect of entropy. The purpose of redundant information is to provide a control to check the "correctness" of the transmitted information. **71.** 370 K **73.** $\Delta G°_{CO} - \Delta G°_{O_2} = -13$ kJ/mol **75. a.** 1.8×10^4 J/mol; shifts left; **b.** 0; no shift since at equilibrium; **c.** -1.1×10^4 J/mol; shifts right; **d.** 0; no shift since at equilibrium; **e.** 2×10^3 J/mol; shifts left **77. a.** 2.22×10^5; **b.** 94.3 **79.** The light source for the first reaction is necessary in order to increase the rate of the reaction. The rate of a reaction is independent of ΔG. When considering if a reaction will occur, thermodynamics and kinetics must both be considered. **81.** $\Delta H° = 286$ kJ; $\Delta G° = 326$ kJ; $K = 7.22 \times 10^{-58}$; $P_{O_3} = 3.3 \times 10^{-41}$ atm; This partial pressure represents one molecule of ozone per 9.5×10^{17} L of air. Equilibrium is probably not maintained under the conditions because the concentration of ozone is not large enough to maintain equilibrium. **83. a.** Since $k_f = A \exp \left(\dfrac{-E_a}{RT} \right)$ and $k_r = A \exp \left(\dfrac{-(E_a - \Delta G°)}{RT} \right)$, then $\dfrac{k_f}{k_r} = \exp \left(\dfrac{-E_a}{RT} + \dfrac{(E_a - \Delta G°)}{RT} \right) = \exp \left(\dfrac{-\Delta G°}{RT} \right)$. Since $K = \exp \left(\dfrac{-\Delta G°}{RT} \right)$, then $K = \dfrac{k_f}{k_r}$. **b.** A catalyst increases the value of the rate constant (increases rate) by lowering the activation energy. In order for the equilibrium constant K to remain constant, both k_f and k_r must increase by the same factor. Therefore, a catalyst must increase the rate of both the forward and the reverse reactions. **85. a.** 0.333; **b.** $P_A = 1.50$ atm; $P_B = 0.50$ atm; **c.** $\Delta G = \Delta G° + RT \ln(P_B/P_A) = 2722$ J $- 2722$ J $= 0$ **87.** at least 7.5 torr

Chapter 17

13. Oxidation: increase in oxidation number, loss of electrons; reduction: decrease in oxidation number, gain of electrons **15.** Reactions a, b, and c are oxidation–reduction reactions.

Oxidizing Agent	Reducing Agent	Substance Oxidized	Substance Reduced
a. H_2O	CH_4	$CH_4(C)$	$H_2O(H)$
b. $AgNO_3$	Cu	Cu	$AgNO_3(Ag)$
c. HCl	Zn	Zn	HCl(H)

17. In a galvanic cell a spontaneous reaction occurs, producing an electric current. In an electrolytic cell electricity is used to force a reaction to occur that is not spontaneous. **19. a.** cathode: where reduction occurs; **b.** anode: where oxidation occurs; **c.** oxidation half-reaction: e^- are products; **d.** reduction half-reaction: e^- are reactants **21.** As a battery discharges, $\mathscr{E}_{cell}$ decreases, eventually reaching zero. A charged battery is not at equilibrium. At equilibrium, $\mathscr{E}_{cell} = 0$ and $\Delta G = 0$. We get no work out of an equilibrium system. A battery is useful to us because it can do work as it approaches equilibrium. **23.** Both fuel cells and batteries are galvanic cells. However, fuel cells, unlike batteries, have the reactants continuously supplied and can produce a current indefinitely. **25.** See Figure 17.2 of the text for a typical galvanic cell. The anode compartment contains the oxidation half-reaction compounds/ions, and the cathode compartment contains the reduction half-reaction compounds/ions. The electrons flow from the anode to the cathode. For each of the following answers, all solutes are 1.0 M and all gases are at 1.0 atm. **a.** $7H_2O(l) + 2Cr^{3+}(aq) + 3Cl_2(g) \rightarrow Cr_2O_7^{2-}(aq) + 6Cl^-(aq) + 14H^+(aq)$; cathode: Pt electrode; Cl_2 bubbled into solution, Cl^- in solution; anode: Pt electrode; Cr^{3+}, H^+, and $Cr_2O_7^{2-}$ in solution; **b.** $Cu^{2+}(aq) + Mg(s) \rightarrow Cu(s) + Mg^{2+}(aq)$; cathode: Cu electrode; Cu^{2+} in solution; anode: Mg electrode; Mg^{2+} in solution **27. a.** 0.03 V; **b.** 2.71 V **29.** See Exercise 25 for a description of a galvanic cell. For each of the following answers, all solutes are 1.0 M and all gases are at 1.0 atm. **a.** $Cl_2(g) + 2Br^-(aq) \rightarrow Br_2(aq) + 2Cl^-(aq)$ $\mathscr{E}° = 0.27$ V; cathode: Pt electrode; $Cl_2(g)$ bubbled in, Cl^- in solution; anode: Pt electrode; Br_2 and Br^- in solution; **b.** $3H_2O(l) + 5IO_4^-(aq) + 2Mn^{2+}(aq) \rightarrow 5IO_3^-(aq) + 2MnO_4^-(aq) + 6H^+(aq)$ $\mathscr{E}° = 0.09$ V; cathode: Pt electrode; IO_4^-, IO_3^-, and H_2SO_4 (as a source of H^+) in solution; an-

ode: Pt electrode; Mn^{2+}, MnO_4^-, and H_2SO_4 in solution **31.** 25a. $Pt \mid Cr^{3+}$ (1.0 M), H^+ (1.0 M), $Cr_2O_7^{2-}$ (1.0 M) $\| Cl_2$ (1.0 atm) $\mid Cl^-$ (1.0 M) $\mid Pt$; 25b. $Mg \mid Mg^{2+}$ (1.0 M) $\| Cu^{2+}$ (1.0 M) $\mid Cu$; 29a. $Pt \mid Br^-$ (1.0 M), Br_2 (1.0 M) $\| Cl_2$ (1.0 atm) $\mid Cl^-$ (1.0 M) $\mid Pt$; 29b. $Pt \mid Mn^{2+}$ (1.0 M), MnO_4^- (1.0 M), H^+ (1.0 M) $\| IO_4^-$ (1.0 M), IO_3^- (1.0 M), H^+(1.0 M) $\mid Pt$ **33. a.** $Au^{3+}(aq) + 3Cu^+(aq) \rightarrow 3Cu^{2+}(aq) + Au(s)$ $\mathscr{E}° = 1.34$V; **b.** $2VO_2^+(aq) + 4H^+(aq) + Cd(s) \rightarrow Cd^{2+}(aq) + 2VO^{2+}(aq) + 2H_2O(l)$ $\mathscr{E}° = 1.40$ V **35. a.** $\mathscr{E}° = 0.46$ V, spontaneous; **b.** $\mathscr{E}° = -0.53$ V, not spontaneous **37.** 25a. -20 kJ; 25b. -523 kJ; 29a. -52 kJ; 29b. -90 kJ **39.** $\mathscr{E}° = 0.41$ V, $\Delta G° = -79$ kJ **41.** 33a. -388 kJ; 33b. -270. kJ **43.** -0.829 V (calculated), -0.83 V (table) **45.** 77 kJ/mol **47.** $K^+ < H_2O < Cd^{2+} < I_2 < AuCl_4^- < IO_3^-$ **49. a.** no; **b.** yes; **c.** yes; **d.** no **51. a.** Ag^+, largest $\mathscr{E}°$; **b.** Zn, largest $-\mathscr{E}°$; **c.** Zn and Pb, $\mathscr{E}°_{cell} > 0$; **d.** Ag^+ and Zn^{2+}, $\mathscr{E}°_{cell} > 0$. **53. a.** $Cr_2O_7^{2-}$, O_2, MnO_2, IO_3^-; **b.** $PbSO_4$, Cd^{2+}, Fe^{2+}, Cr^{3+}, Zn^{2+}, H_2O **55. a.** larger; **b.** smaller **57. a.** 1.01 V; **b.** 0.55 V **59.** Electron flow is always from the anode to the cathode. For the cells with a nonzero cell potential, we will identify the cathode, which means the other compartment is the anode. **a.** 0; **b.** 0.018 V; compartment with $[Ag^+] = 2.0$ M is cathode; **c.** 0.059 V; compartment with $[Ag^+] = 1.0$ M is cathode; **d.** 0.26 V; compartment with $[Ag^+] = 1.0$ M is cathode; **e.** 0 **61.** yes **63.** 1.09 V **65. a.** 0.23 V; **b.** 1.2×10^{-5} M **67.** 0.16 V, copper is oxidized. **69.** 25a. 1×10^3; 25b. 5.12×10^{91}; 29a. 1.4×10^9; 29b. 2×10^{15} **71. a.** no reaction; **b.** $Cl_2(g) + 2I^-(aq) \rightarrow I_2(s) + 2Cl^-(aq)$ $\mathscr{E}°_{cell} = 0.82$ V, $\Delta G° = -160$ kJ; $K = 5.6 \times 10^{27}$; **c.** no reaction; **d.** $4Fe^{2+}(aq) + 4H^+(aq) + O_2(g) \rightarrow 4Fe^{3+}(aq) + 2H_2O(l)$ $\mathscr{E}°_{cell} = 0.46$ V; $\Delta G° = -180$ kJ; $K = 1.3 \times 10^{31}$; **73. a.** $Zn(s) + Fe^{2+}(aq) \rightarrow Zn^{2+}(aq) + Fe(s)$ $\mathscr{E}° = 0.32$ V; **b.** $\Delta G° = -62$ kJ, $K = 6.8 \times 10^{10}$; **c.** 0.20 V **75.** 3.9×10^{-28} **77.** -0.14 V **79. a.** 30. hours; **b.** 33 s; **c.** 1.3 hours **81. a.** 16 g; **b.** 25 g; **c.** 71 g; **d.** 4.9 g **83.** Sc **85.** 9.12 L F_2 (anode), 29.2 g K (cathode) **87.** 7.44×10^4 A **89.** 1.14×10^{-2} M **91.** Au followed by Ag followed by Ni followed by Cd **93. a.** cathode: $Ni^{2+} + 2e^- \rightarrow Ni$; anode: $2Br^- \rightarrow Br_2 + 2e^-$; **b.** cathode: $Al^{3+} + 3e^- \rightarrow Al$; anode: $2F^- \rightarrow F_2 + 2e^-$; **c.** cathode: $Cr^{3+} + 3e^- \rightarrow Cr$; anode: $2I^- \rightarrow I_2 + 2e^-$ **95.** cathode: $2H_2O + 2e^- \rightarrow H_2 + 2OH^-$; anode: $2H_2O \rightarrow O_2 + 4H^+ + 4e^-$ **97. a.** 0.10V, SCE is anode; **b.** 0.53 V, SCE is anode; **c.** 0.02 V, SCE is cathode; **d.** 1.90 V, SCE is cathode; **e.** 0.47 V, SCE is cathode **99. a.** decrease; **b.** increase; **c.** decrease; **d.** decrease; **e.** same **101. a.** $\Delta G° = -582$ kJ; $K = 3.45 \times 10^{102}$; $\mathscr{E}° = 1.01$ V; **b.** -0.65 V; **103.** acidic conditions **105.** The claim is impossible. The strongest oxidizing agent and reducing agent when combined only give $\mathscr{E}°$ of about 6 V. **107.** $w_{max} = -13,200$ kJ; the work done can be no larger than the free energy change. If the process were reversible all of the free energy released would go into work, but this does not occur in any real process. Fuel cells are more efficient in converting chemical energy to electrical energy; they are also less massive. Major disadvantage: They are expensive. **109.** $AgCl_2$ would be composed of Ag^{2+} and Cl^- ions. From standard reduction potentials, Ag^{2+} can spontaneously oxidize Cl^- into Cl_2, making $AgCl_2$ unstable. **111.** $+3$

113. $\mathscr{E}° = \dfrac{T\Delta S°}{nF} - \dfrac{\Delta H°}{nF}$; if we graph $\mathscr{E}°$ vs. T, we should get a straight line ($y = mx + b$). The slope of the line is equal to $\Delta S°/nF$ and the y-intercept is equal to $-\Delta H°/nF$. $\mathscr{E}°$ will have little temperature dependence for cell reactions with $\Delta S°$ close to zero. **115.** 1.7×10^{-30} **117.** 2.39×10^{-7} **119. a.** ± 0.02 pH units; $\pm 6 \times 10^{-6}$ M H^+; **b.** ± 0.001 V

Chapter 18

1. The gravity of the earth cannot keep H_2 in the atmosphere. **3.** Ionic, covalent, and metallic (or interstitial). The ionic and covalent hydrides are true compounds that differ in the type of bonding. The interstitial hydrides are more like solid solutions of hydrogen and a transition metal and have variable content. **5.** Hydrogen forms many compounds in which its oxidation state is $+1$. On the other hand hydrogen forms diatomic H_2 molecules and is a nonmetal, while the Group 1A elements are metals. Hydrogen forms the hydride anion H^-; the Group 1A metals do not form stable anions. **7.** They must be produced in the absence of materials (H_2O, O_2) that are capable of oxidizing them. **9.** The planes of carbon atoms slide easily. Graphite is not volatile so the lubricant will not be lost when used in a high vacuum environment. **11.** The bonds in SnX_4 compounds generally have covalent character, and the SnX_4 molecules interact by dispersion forces. SnX_2 compounds are ionic. **13.** Size decreases from left to right and increases going down. So going one element right and one element down would result in a similar size for the two elements diagonal to each other. The ionization energies will also be similar for the diagonal elements. Electron affinities are harder to predict, but the similar size and ionization energies would lead to similar properties. **15. a.** $\Delta H° = 207$ kJ, $\Delta S° = 216$ J/K; **b.** $T > 958$ K **17. a.** Lithium oxide; **b.** Potassium superoxide; **c.** Sodium peroxide; **19. a.** $Li_2O(s) + H_2O(l) \rightarrow 2LiOH(aq)$; **b.** $Na_2O_2(s) + 2H_2O(l) \rightarrow 2NaOH(aq) + H_2O_2(aq)$; **c.** $LiH(s) + H_2O(l) \rightarrow H_2(g) + LiOH(aq)$; **d.** $2KO_2(s) + 2H_2O(l) \rightarrow 2KOH(aq) + O_2(g) + H_2O_2(aq)$ **21.** $2Li(s) + 2C_2H_2(g) \rightarrow 2LiC_2H(s) + H_2(g)$; oxidation–reduction **23. a.** Magnesium carbonate; **b.** Barium sulfate; **c.** Strontium hydroxide; **25.** $Mg_3N_2(s) + 6H_2O(l) \rightarrow 2NH_3(g) + 3Mg^{2+}(aq) + 6OH^-(aq)$; $Mg_3P_2(s) + 6H_2O(l) \rightarrow 2PH_3(g) + 3Mg^{2+}(aq) + 6OH^-(aq)$ **27.** Trigonal planar; Be, sp^2; N, sp^3; Lewis acid **29.** 2×10^{-2} M **31.** 3.84×10^6 g Ba **33. a.** Indium(I) oxide; **b.** Indium(III) oxide; **c.** Boron trifluoride **35.** $B_2H_6(g) + 3O_2(g) \rightarrow 2B(OH)_3(s)$ **37.** $In_2O_3(s) + 6H^+(aq) \rightarrow 2In^{3+}(aq) + 3H_2O(l)$; $In_2O_3(s) + OH^-(aq) \rightarrow$ no reaction; $Ga_2O_3(s) + 6H^+(aq) \rightarrow 2Ga^{3+}(aq) + 3H_2O(l)$; $Ga_2O_3(s) + 2OH^-(aq) + 3H_2O(l) \rightarrow 2Ga(OH)_4^-(aq)$ **39.** $2Ga(s) + 3F_2(g) \rightarrow 2GaF_3(s)$; $4Ga(s) + 3O_2(g) \rightarrow 2Ga_2O_3(s)$; $16Ga(s) + 3S_8(s) \rightarrow 8Ga_2S_3(s)$; $2Ga(s) + N_2(g) \rightarrow 2GaN(s)$; $2Ga(s) + 6HCl(aq) \rightarrow 2GaCl_3(aq) + 3H_2(g)$

41.

Tetrahedral; 109.5°; sp^3 Tetrahedral; 109.5°; sp^3 Octahedral; 90°; d^2sp^3

In order to form CF_6^{2-}, carbon would have to expand its octet of electrons. Carbon compounds do not expand their octet because of the small atomic size of carbon and because there are no low energy d orbitals on carbon to accommodate the extra electrons. **43. a.** $K_2SiF_6(s) + 4K(l) \rightarrow Si(s) + 6KF(s)$; **b.** The bonding is ionic between K^+ and SiF_6^{2-} ions and covalent between Si and F in the octahedral SiF_6^{2-} anion. **45.** Lead is very toxic. As the temperature of the water increases, the solubility of Pb will increase. Drinking hot tap water from pipes containing lead solder could result in higher Pb concentrations in the body. **47. a.** Carbon tetrachloride; **b.** Silicon tetrachloride; **c.** Lead(II) chloride; **d.** Tin(II) chloride **49.** The π electrons are free to move in graphite, thus giving it a greater conductivity (lower resistance). The electrons have the greatest mobility within the sheets of carbon atoms. Electrons in diamond are not mobile (high resistance). The structure of diamond is uniform in all directions; thus there is no directional dependence of the resistivity. **51.** $-390.$ kJ; 30.0°C **53.** Strontium and calcium are both alkaline earth metals, so both have similar chemical properties. Since milk is a good source of calcium, strontium could replace some calcium in milk without much difficulty.

55.

57. 3.08 **59.** If the compound contained Ga(II) it would be paramagnetic and if the compound contained Ga(I) and Ga(III), it would be diamagnetic. Paramagnetic compounds have an apparent greater mass in a magnetic field. **61.** 59 atm in the gas phase; 2.8 mol CO_2/L in the wine **63.** Sn and Pb; $Sn(s) + 2H^+(aq) \rightarrow Sn^{2+}(aq) + H_2(g)$; $Pb(s) + 2H^+(aq) \rightarrow Pb^{2+}(aq) + H_2(g)$ **65.** 2.0×10^{-37} M **67.** Carbon is much smaller than Si and cannot form a fifth bond in the transition state.

Chapter 19

1. The reaction $N_2(g) + 3H_2(g) \rightarrow 2NH_3(g)$ is exothermic. Thus K decreases as the temperature increases. Lower temperatures are favored for maximum yield of ammonia. However, at lower temperatures the rate is slow; without a catalyst the rate is too slow for the process to be feasible. The discovery of a catalyst increased the rate of reaction at a lower temperature favored by thermodynamics. **3.** Pollutants provide nitrogen and phosphorus nutrients, causing the algae to grow, which consumes oxygen, causing fish to die. **5.** Plastic sulfur has long S_n chains that break down into S_8 rings. **7.** Fluorine is the most electronegative element; the F_2 bond is very weak. **9.** Helium, which does not combine with other elements, has a low mass and easily escaped the earth's gravitational pull as the planet was formed. **11.** Nitrogen's small size does not provide room for all four oxygen atoms, making NO_4^{3-} unstable. Phosphorus is larger so PO_4^{3-} is more stable. To form NO_3^-, a pi bond must form. Phosphorus doesn't form strong pi bonds as readily as nitrogen. **13. a.** $NH_4NO_3(s) \xrightarrow{\text{Heat}} N_2O(g) + 2H_2O(g)$; **b.** $2N_2O_5(g) \rightarrow 4NO_2(g) + O_2(g)$; **c.** $2K_3P(s) + 6H_2O(l) \rightarrow 2PH_3(g) + 6KOH(aq)$; **d.** $PBr_3(l) + 3H_2O(l) \rightarrow H_3PO_3(aq) + 3HBr(aq)$; **e.** $2NH_3(aq) + NaOCl(aq) \rightarrow N_2H_4(aq) + NaCl(aq) + H_2O(l)$; **15.** In the solid state: NO_2^+ and NO_3^-; in the gas phase: molecular N_2O_5

17. 8.170×10^{12} L N_2, 2.451×10^{13} L H_2 **19.** $N_2H_4(l) + 2F_2(g) \rightarrow 4HF(g) + N_2(g)$; -1169 kJ **21.** $\frac{1}{2}N_2(g) + \frac{1}{2}O_2(g) \rightarrow NO(g)$ $\Delta G° = \Delta G°_{f(NO)}$; NO (and some other oxides of nitrogen) have weaker bonds as compared with the triple bond of N_2 and the double bond of O_2. Because of this, NO (and some other oxides of nitrogen) has a higher (positive) standard free energy of formation as compared to the relatively stable N_2 and O_2 molecules.

23.

M.O.		Bond order	# unpaired e$^-$
	NO	2.5	1
	NO$^+$	3	0
	NO$^-$	2	2

Lewis NO$^+$ $[:N\equiv O:]^+$

NO $\cdot\ddot{N}=\ddot{O}: \longleftrightarrow :\ddot{N}=\ddot{O}\cdot \longleftrightarrow :\ddot{N}\dot{=}\ddot{O}\cdot$

NO$^-$ $\left[:\ddot{N}=\ddot{O}:\right]^-$

Lewis structures are not adequate for NO and NO$^-$. The M.O. model gives correct results for all three species. For NO, Lewis structures fail for odd electron species. For NO$^-$, Lewis structures fail to predict that NO$^-$ is paramagnetic. **25. a.** $H_3PO_4 > H_3PO_3$; **b.** $H_3PO_4 > H_2PO_4^- > HPO_4^{2-}$ **27.** The acidic protons are attached to oxygen.

$H_4P_2O_6$ $H_4P_2O_5$

29. 821 nm **31. a.** $2SO_2(g) + O_2(g) \rightarrow 2SO_3(g)$; **b.** $SO_3(g) + H_2O(l) \rightarrow H_2SO_4(aq)$; **c.** $2Na_2S_2O_3(aq) + I_2(aq) \rightarrow Na_2S_4O_6(aq) + 2NaI(aq)$; **d.** $Cu(s) + 2H_2SO_4(aq) \rightarrow CuSO_4(aq) + 2H_2O(l) + SO_2(aq)$

33. a.

Trigonal pyramid; $\approx 109.5°$; sp^3

b.

V-shaped; $\approx 120°$; sp^2

c.

V-shaped; $\approx 109.5°$; sp^3

d.

See-saw; $a \approx 120°$, $b \approx 90°$; dsp^3

e.

Octahedral; $90°$; d^2sp^3

35. From the following Lewis structure, each oxygen atom has a tetrahedral arrangement of electron pairs. Therefore, bond angles $\approx 109.5°$, and each O is sp^3 hybridized.

Formal charge:	0	0	0	0
Oxidation state:	-1	$+1$	$+1$	-1

Oxidation states are more useful. We are forced to assign $+1$ as the oxidation state for oxygen. Oxygen is very electronegative, and $+1$ is not a stable oxidation state for this element. **37. a.** $BaCl_2(s) + H_2SO_4(aq) \rightarrow BaSO_4(s) + 2HCl(g)$; **b.** $BrF(s) + H_2O(l) \rightarrow HF(aq) + HOBr(aq)$; **c.** $SiO_2(s) + 4HF(aq) \rightarrow SiF_4(g) + 2H_2O(l)$ **39.** ClO^- can oxide NH_3 to the somewhat toxic N_2H_4. **41. a.** IO_4^-; **b.** IO_3^-; **c.** IF_2^-; **d.** IF_4^-; **e.** IF_6^- **43.** XeF_2 can react with oxygen to produce explosive xenon oxides and oxyfluorides. **45.** As the halogen atoms get larger, it becomes more difficult to fit three halogens around the small N.

47.

| Formal charge: | 0 | 0 | -1 | | -1 | 0 | 0 | | $+1$ | 0 |

| Formal charge: | -2 | $+1$ | 0 | | -1 | $+1$ | -1 | | -3 | $+1$ |

All the resonance structures for fulminate involve greater formal charges than in cyanate, making fulminate more reactive (less stable). **49.** 32 kg bacterial tissue **51.** Hypochlorite can act as an oxidizing agent. For example, it is capable of oxidizing I^- to I_2. If a solution containing I^- turns brown when BiOCl is added, then BiOCl is bismuth(I) hypochlorite. The brown color indicates production of I_2. If the solution doesn't change color, then it is bismuthylchloride.

53.

The lone pair of electrons around Te exerts a stronger repulsion than the bonding pairs, pushing the four square planar F's away from the lone pair.

55. For the reaction

the activation energy must in some way involve the breaking of a nitrogen–nitrogen single bond. For the reaction

at some point nitrogen–oxygen bonds must be broken. N—N single bonds (160 kJ/mol) are weaker than N—O single bonds (201 kJ/mol). In addition, resonance structures indicate that there is more double bond character in the N—O bonds than in the N—N bond. Thus NO_2 and NO are preferred by kinetics because of the lower activation energy. **57. a.** NO; **b.** NO_2; **c.** $k_{cat}/k_{un} = 2.3$; **d.** $ClO(g) + O(g) \rightarrow O_2(g) + Cl(g)$; $O_3(g) + O(g) \rightarrow 2O_2(g)$; **e.** The Cl-catalyzed reaction is roughly 52 times faster (more efficient) than the NO-catalyzed reaction.

Chapter 20

5. a. ligand: species that donates a pair of electrons to form a covalent bond to a metal ion (a Lewis base); **b.** chelate: ligand that can form more than one bond; **c.** bidentate: ligand that forms two bonds; **d.** complex ion: metal ion plus ligands **7.** Both shared electrons originally come from a ligand. **9. a.** isomers: species with the same formulas but different properties (see text for examples of the following types of isomers); **b.** structural isomers: isomers that have one or more bonds that are different; **c.** stereoisomers: isomers that contain the same bonds but differ in how the atoms are arranged in space; **d.** coordination isomers: structural isomers that differ in the atoms that make up the complex ion; **e.** linkage isomers: structural isomers that differ in how one or more ligands are attached to the transition metal; **f.** geometrical isomers: (*cis–trans* isomerism) stereoisomers that differ in the positions of atoms with respect to a rigid ring, bond, or each other; **g.** optical isomers: stereoisomers that are non-superimposable mirror images of each other; that is, they are different in the same way that our left and right hands are different. **11.** Cu^{2+} is d^9; Cu^+ is d^{10}. Color results from electron transfer between split d orbitals. This cannot occur for the filled d orbitals in Cu^+. Cd^{2+}, like Cu^+, is also d^{10}. We would not expect $Cd(NH_3)_4Cl_2$ to be colored due to the filled d orbitals of Cd^{2+}. **13.** The d-orbital splitting in tetrahedral complexes is less than one-half the d-orbital splitting in octahedral complexes. There are no known ligands powerful enough to produce the strong-field case; hence all tetrahedral complexes are weak field or high spin. **15.** A soluble complex ion forms: $Fe_2O_3(s) + 6H_2C_2O_4(aq) \rightarrow 2Fe(C_2O_4)_3{}^{3-}(aq) + 3H_2O(l) + 6H^+(aq)$ **17.** There is a steady decrease in the atomic radii of the lanthanide elements, going from left to right. As a result, the properties of the $4d$ and $5d$ elements in each group are very similar because of the similar sizes of atoms and ions. **19.** Advantages: low energy cost, less air pollution; disadvantage: chemicals used are expensive **21. a.** Ni: $[Ar]4s^2 3d^8$; **b.** Cd: $[Kr]5s^2 4d^{10}$; **c.** Zr: $[Kr]5s^2 4d^2$; **d.** Os: $[Xe]6s^2 4f^{14}5d^6$ **23. a.** Ni^{2+}: $[Ar]3d^8$; **b.** Cd^{2+}: $[Kr]4d^{10}$; **c.** Zr^{3+}: $[Kr]4d^1$; Zr^{4+}: $[Kr]$; **d.** Os^{2+}: $[Xe]4f^{14}5d^6$; Os^{3+}: $[Xe]4f^{14}5d^5$ **25. a.** Ti: $[Ar]4s^2 3d^2$; Ti^{2+}: $[Ar]3d^2$; Ti^{4+}: $[Ne]3s^2 3p^6$ or $[Ar]$; **b.** Re: $[Xe]6s^2 4f^{14}5d^5$; Re^{2+}: $[Xe]4f^{14}5d^5$; Re^{3+}: $[Xe]4f^{14}5d^4$; **c.** Ir: $[Xe]6s^2 4f^{14}5d^7$; Ir^{2+}: $[Xe]4f^{14}5d^7$; Ir^{3+}: $[Xe]4f^{14}5d^6$ **27. a.** Molybdenum(IV) sulfide, molybdenum(VI) oxide; **b.** $+4$, $+6$ **29.** $Hg^{2+}(aq) + 2I^-(aq) \rightarrow HgI_2(s)$ (orange precipitate); $HgI_2(s) + 2I^-(aq) \rightarrow HgI_4{}^{2-}(aq)$ (soluble complex ion) **31.** $[Co(NH_3)_6]I_3$: 3 mol AgI; $[Pt(NH_3)_4I_2]I_2$: 2 mol AgI; $Na_2[PtI_6]$: 0 mol AgI; $[Cr(NH_3)_4I_2]I$: 1 mol AgI. **33. a.** pentaamminechlororuthenium(III) ion; **b.** hexacyanoferrate(II) ion; **c.** tris(ethylenediamine)manganese(II) ion; **d.** pentaamminenitrocobalt(III) ion **35. a.** hexaamminecobalt(II) chloride; **b.** hexaaquacobalt(III) iodide; **c.** potassium tetrachloroplatinate(II); **d.** potassium hexachloroplatinate(II); **e.** pentaamminechlorocobalt(III) chloride; **f.** triamminetrinitrocobalt(III) **37. a.** $K_2[CoCl_4]$; **b.** $[Pt(H_2O)(CO)_3]Br_2$; **c.** $Na_3[Fe(CN)_2(C_2O_4)_2]$; **d.** $[Cr(NH_3)_3Cl(H_2NCH_2CH_2NH_2)]I_2$

39. a.

cis   *trans*

b.

cis   *trans*

c.

cis   *trans*

d.

$en = N \frown N = NH_2CH_2CH_2NH_2$

41.

and

43. SCN^-, $NO_2{}^-$, and OCN^- can form linkage isomers; all are able to bond to the metal ion in two different ways. **45.** $Cr(acac)_3$ and *cis*-$Cr(acac)_2(H_2O)_2$ are optically active. **47. a.** Fe^{2+}

High spin   Low spin

b. Fe^{3+} **c.** Ni^{2+}

High spin

49. weak field **51. a.** 0; **b.** 2; **c.** 2 **53.** $[Cr(H_2O)_6]Cl_3$ absorbs yellow-green light; $[Cr(H_2O)_4Cl_2]Cl$ absorbs red light; $[Cr(NH_3)_6]Cl_3$ absorbs blue light. $[Cr(NH_3)_6]Cl_3$ absorbs the shorter wavelength of light, so Δ is larger for $[Cr(NH_3)_6]Cl_3$ because energy and wavelength of light are inversely related. From the wavelengths of light absorbed by the various compounds, NH_3 is a stronger field ligand than H_2O, which is a stronger field ligand than Cl. This is consistent with the spectrochemical series. **55.** $CoBr_4{}^{2-}$ is a tetrahedral complex ion, while $CoBr_6{}^{4-}$ is an octahedral complex ion. Since tetrahedral d-orbital splitting is less than one-half the octahedral d-orbital splitting, the octahedral complex ion ($CoBr_6{}^{4-}$) will absorb higher-energy light, which will have a shorter wavelength than 3.4×10^{-6} m ($E = hc/\lambda$). **57.** 5 **59. a.** -11 kJ; **b.** $\Delta H^\circ = 172.5$ kJ; $\Delta S^\circ = 176$ J/K; $T > 980$. K

61. $[Cr(NH_3)_5I]I_2$; octahedral **63. a.** 2; **b.** 3; **c.** 4; **d.** 4 **65. a.** optical isomerism
b.

67. Octahedral Cr^{2+} complexes should be used. Cr^{2+}: $[Ar]3d^4$; High-spin (weak-field) Cr^{2+} complexes have four unpaired electrons and low-spin (strong-field) Cr^{2+} complexes have two unpaired electrons. Ni^{2+}: $[Ar]3d^8$; Octahedral Ni^{2+} complexes will always have two unpaired electrons, whether high or low spin. Therefore, Ni^{2+} complexes cannot be used to distinguish weak- from strong-field ligands by examining magnetic properties. Alternatively, the ligand field strengths can be measured using visible spectra. Either Cr^{2+} or Ni^{2+} complexes can be used for this method. **69. a.** -0.26 V; **b.** From standard reduction potentials, Co^{3+} ($\mathscr{E}° = 1.82$ V) is a much stronger oxidizing agent than $Co(en)_3^{3+}$ ($\mathscr{E}° = -0.26$ V); **c.** In aqueous solution, Co^{3+} forms the hydrated transition metal complex, $Co(H_2O)_6^{3+}$. In both complexes, $Co(H_2O)_6^{3+}$ and $Co(en)_3^{3+}$, cobalt exists as Co^{3+}, which has 6 d electrons. If we assume a strong-field case for each complex ion, then the d-orbital splitting diagram for each has the six electrons paired in the lower-energy t_{2g} orbitals. When each complex ion gains an electron, the electron enters the higher-energy e_g orbitals. Since en is a stronger field ligand than H_2O, then the d-orbital splitting is larger for $Co(en)_3^{3+}$, and it takes more energy to add an electron to $Co(en)_3^{3+}$ than to $Co(H_2O)_6^{3+}$. Therefore, it is more favorable for $Co(H_2O)_6^{3+}$ to gain an electron than for $Co(en)_3^{3+}$ to gain an electron. **71.** No, since in all three cases six bonds are formed between Ni^{2+} and nitrogen. So ΔH values should be similar. $\Delta S°$ for formation of the complex ion is most negative for $6NH_3$ molecules reacting with a metal ion (7 independent species become 1). For penten reacting with a metal ion, 2 independent species become 1, so $\Delta S°$ is the least negative. Thus the chelate effect occurs because the more bonds a chelating agent can form to the metal, the more favorable $\Delta S°$ is for the formation of the complex ion, and the larger the formation constant.
73.

Chapter 21

1. Fission: splitting a heavy nucleus into two lighter nuclei; fusion: combining two light nuclei to form a heavier nucleus. Fusion is more likely for elements lighter than Fe; fission is more likely for elements heavier than Fe. **3.** Assume ^{14}C level is constant or can be determined at the time the object died. Constant ^{14}C level is a poor assumption and accounting for variation is complicated. Also, some of the material must be destroyed. **5.** No, coal-fired power plants also pose risks. A partial list of risks:

Coal	Nuclear
Air pollution	Radiation exposure to workers
Coal mine accidents	Disposal of wastes
Health risks to miners (black lung disease)	Meltdown
	Terrorists
	Public fear

7. For fusion a collision of sufficient energy must occur between two positively charged particles to initiate the reaction. This requires high temperatures. In fission, an electrically neutral neutron collides with the positively charged nucleus. This has a much lower activation

energy. **9. a.** $^{51}_{24}Cr + ^{0}_{-1}e \rightarrow ^{51}_{23}V$; **b.** $^{131}_{53}I \rightarrow ^{0}_{-1}e + ^{131}_{54}Xe$ **11. a.** $^{68}_{31}Ga + ^{0}_{-1}e \rightarrow ^{68}_{30}Zn$; **b.** $^{62}_{29}Cu \rightarrow ^{0}_{+1}e + ^{62}_{28}Ni$; **c.** $^{212}_{87}Fr \rightarrow ^{4}_{2}He + ^{208}_{85}At$; **d.** $^{129}_{51}Sb \rightarrow ^{0}_{-1}e + ^{129}_{52}Te$ **13.** 9 $^{4}_{2}He$; 4 $^{0}_{-1}e$ **15.** $^{53}_{26}Fe$ has too many protons. It will undergo positron production, electron capture, and/or alpha-particle production. $^{59}_{26}Fe$ has too many neutrons and will undergo beta-particle production. (See Table 21.2 of the text.) **17. a.** $^{249}_{98}Cf + ^{18}_{8}O \rightarrow ^{263}_{106}Sg + 4^{1}_{0}n$; **b.** $^{259}_{104}Rf$ **19.** 690 hours **21.** 15.8 yr **23.** 6.22 mg ^{32}P remains **25.** 0.267 **27.** 2.3 counts per minute per gram of C. No; for a 10.-mg C sample, it would take roughly 40 min to see a single disintegration. This is too long to wait, and the background radiation would probably be much greater than the ^{14}C activity. Thus ^{14}C dating is not practical for very small samples. **29.** 3.8×10^9 yr **31.** 4.3×10^6 kg/s **33.** ^{232}Pu, -1.715×10^{14} J/mol; ^{231}Pa, -1.714×10^{14} J/mol **35.** ^{12}C: 1.23×10^{-12} J/nucleon; ^{235}U: 1.2155×10^{-12} J/nucleon; since ^{56}Fe is the most stable known nucleus, then the binding energy per nucleon for ^{56}Fe would be larger than that of ^{12}C or ^{235}U. (See Fig. 21.9 of the text.) **37.** -2.0×10^{10} J/g of hydrogen nuclei **39.** The Geiger–Müller tube has a certain response time. After the gas in the tube ionizes to produce a "count," some time must elapse for the gas to return to an electrically neutral state. The response of the tube levels off because at high activities radioactive particles are entering the tube faster than the tube can respond to them. **41.** All evolved $O_2(g)$ comes from water. **43.** Strontium. Xe is chemically unreactive and not readily incorporated into the body. Sr can be easily oxidized to Sr^{2+}. Strontium is in the same family as calcium and could be absorbed and concentrated in the body in a fashion similar to Ca^{2+}. The chemical properties determine where radioactive material may be concentrated in the body or how easily it may be excreted. **45. a.** unstable; beta production; **b.** stable; **c.** unstable; positron production or electron capture; **d.** unstable, positron production, electron capture, or alpha production. **47.** 0.58 counts per minute per 100. g **49.** 900 g ^{235}U **51.** Assuming that (1) the radionuclide is long lived enough that no significant decay occurs during the time of the experiment, and (2) the total activity is uniformly distributed only in the rat's blood; $V = 10$. mL. **53. a.** $^{12}_{6}C$; **b.** ^{13}N, ^{13}C, ^{14}N, ^{15}O, and ^{15}N; **c.** -5.950×10^{11} J/mol ^1H

Photo Credits

Chapter 1 p. xxiv: Chuck Davis/Tony Stone Images; p. 2, Chris Sharp/Photo Researchers, Inc.; p. 3, Courtesy, Agricultural Research Service/USDA; p. 5, Corbis-Bettmann; p. 8, Jay Freis/The Image Bank; p. 9, Courtesy, Mettler-Toledo; p. 14, Sean Brady; p. 24, Peter Steiner/The Stock Market; p. 25, Richard Megna/Fundamental Photographs; p. 26, Richard Nowitz; p. 28, Ken O'Donoghue; p. 29 (top, left), Sean Brady; p. 29 (top, right), Ken Kay/Fundamental Photographs; p. 29 (bottom), Kristen Brochmann/Fundamental Photographs. **Chapter 2** pp. 38 and iii, Brian Brake/Photo Researchers, Inc.; p. 40, Roald Hoffmann/Cornell University; p. 41, Paul Souders/Tony Stone Images; p. 42, (Detail) *Antoine Laurent Lavoisier and His Wife* by Jacques Louis David. The Metropolitan Museum of Art, Purchase, Mr. and Mrs. Charles Wrightsman Gift, in honor of Everett Fahy, 1977; p. 43, Reproduced by permission, Manchester Literary and Philosophical Society; p. 45, The Granger Collection; p. 47 (top), The Cavendish Laboratory; p. 47 (bottom), Richard Megna/Fundamental Photographs; p. 48, Roger Du Buisson/The Stock Market; p. 50, Bob Daemmrich/Stock, Boston; p. 51, Topham Picture Library/The Image Works; p. 56 (top, photo a), Ken O'Donoghue; p. 56 (top, photos b, c, d), Sean Brady; p. 56 (bottom, left), Frank Cox; p. 56 (bottom, right), Ken O'Donoghue; p. 58 (top, right), Andrew Syred/Tony Stone Images; p. 58 (center), Ken O'Donoghue; p. 58 (bottom), William E. Ferguson; p. 60, Tom Pantages; p. 63, Sean Brady; p. 65, Richard Megna/Fundamental Photographs. **Chapter 3** p. 78, Ken Karp; p. 80, Geoff Tompkinson/Science Photo Library/Photo Researchers, Inc.; p. 81, Sean Brady; p. 82, Tom Pantages; p. 83, Ken O'Donoghue; p. 86 (top), Sean Brady; p. 86 (bottom), Tom Pantages; p. 90, Kenneth Lorenzen; p. 93, Phil Degginger/Tony Stone Images; p. 94 (both), Ken O'Donoghue; p. 96 (left, center), Ken O'Donoghue; p. 96 (right), Sean Brady; p. 97, Ken O'Donoghue; p. 98, Ken O'Donoghue; p. 99, Frank Cox; pp. 102 and iv, Sean Brady; p. 105 (both), Ken O'Donoghue; p. 110, NASA; p. 111, Eric Fordham; p. 112, Grant Heilman Photography; p. 119, Focus on Sports. **Chapter 4** p. 130, Richard Megna/Fundamental Photographs; p. 132, Tim Alt/Digital Art; p. 135 (all), Ken O'Donoghue; p. 138, The Swedish Royal Academy of Sciences; p. 140, Sean Brady; p. 142, Courtesy, Robert Mondavi Winery; p. 143, Ken O'Donoghue; p. 144, Image courtesy of Caliper Technologies Corporation; p. 147, Richard Megna/Fundamental Photographs; p. 150, Sean Brady; p. 151, Sean Brady; p. 152, Sean Brady; p. 162 (all), Richard Megna/Fundamental Photographs; p. 165 (far left, far right), Sean Brady; p. 165 (two center photos), Ken O'Donoghue; p. 167, Richard Megna/Fundamental Photographs; p. 168, Sean Brady; p. 170, Sean Brady; p. 172, Stephen Studd/Tony Stone Images; p. 175 (both), Sean Brady. **Chapter 5** p. 188, Photo by Jean-Francois Luy with the kind authorization of Breitling SA; p. 190 (both) Ken O'Donoghue; p. 194, Nick Nicholson/The Image Bank; p. 197, Ken O'Donoghue; p. 201, Runk/Schoenberger/Grant Heilman Photography; p. 209, Courtesy, Ford Motor Corporation; p. 211, Tom Stack/Tom Stack & Associates; p. 216 (all), Ken O'Donoghue; p. 220, U.S. Department of Energy; p. 221, Ken O'Donoghue; p. 227 (both), The Field Museum, Chicago, IL; p. 228, David Woodfall/Tony Stone Images. **Chapter 6** p. 240, Al Francekevich/The Stock Market; pp. 243 and v, Chuck Keeler Jr./The Stock Market; p. 248, Mark E. Gibson/Visuals Unlim-

ited; p. 254, E.R. Degginger; p. 255, Jack Field/Rapho/Photo Researchers, Inc.; p. 257, Argonne National Laboratory; p. 261, Sean Brady; p. 266, Richard Megna/Fundamental Photographs; p. 269, Stephanie S. Ferguson; p. 271, Goddard Space Flight Center; p. 272, Lee Rentz/Bruce Coleman, Inc.; p. 274, F. Westmorland/Photo Researchers, Inc.; p. 277, Ken O'Donoghue; p. 278, Robert E. Lyons/Photo/Nats; p. 279, Courtesy, National Biodiesel Board, Inc. **Chapter 7** p. 290, Philip Habib/Tony Stone Images; p. 292, David B. Fleetham/Tony Stone Images; p. 294 (top), Ken O'Donoghue; p. 294 (bottom), Donald Clegg; p. 297, Corbis-Bettmann; p. 298 (top), Ken O'Donoghue; p. 298 (bottom), Robert P. Carr/Bruce Coleman, Inc.; p. 300, David Lokey/Comstock; p. 302, Emilio Segre Visuals Archives; p. 304, Bob Burch/Bruce Coleman, Inc.; p. 317 (top), Image Select/Art Resource, NY; p. 317 (bottom), *Annalen der Chemie und Pharmacie*, VIII, Supplementary Volume for 1872; p. 318, David Parker/Photo Researchers, Inc.; p. 320, Sean Brady; p. 321 (top), Sean Brady; p. 321 (bottom), Ken O'Donoghue; p. 322, Leslie Zumdahl; p. 336, Sean Brady; p. 337, Gabe McDonald/VisualsUnlimited. **Chapter 8** p. 348, Ken Eward/Photo Researchers, Inc.; p. 350 (left), Sean Brady; p. 350 (right), Runk/Schoenberger/Grant Heilman Photography; p. 357 (top, center), Ken O'Donoghue; p. 357 (bottom), Sean Brady; p. 360, Courtesy, Aluminum Company of America; p. 363, Sean Brady; p. 369, Ken O'Donoghue; p. 371, Will & Deni McIntyre/Photo Researchers, Inc.; p. 377, Courtesy, The Bancroft Library/University of California, Berkeley; p. 396 (all), Ken O'Donoghue; pp. 397 and v, Argonne National Laboratory; p. 402, Kenneth Lorenzen. **Chapter 9** p. 414, Dr. Jeremy Burgess/Science Photo Library/Photo Researchers, Inc.; p. 424, Ken O'Donoghue; p. 432, Sean Brady; p. 437, Donald Clegg. **Chapter 10** p. 450, David Job/Tony Stone Images; p. 456 (left, center), Sean Brady; p. 456 (right), Ray Massey/Tony Stone Images; p. 458 (both), Brian Parker/Tom Stack & Associates; pp. 465 and vi, Sean Brady; p. 468, Chip Clark; p. 469, Courtesy, RMS Titanic, Inc. All rights reserved; p. 472 (top), Ken Eward/Photo Researchers, Inc.; p. 472 (bottom), IBM Corporation; p. 474 (top), Richard Pasley/Stock, Boston; p. 474 (bottom), Mathias Oppersdorff/Photo Researchers, Inc.; p. 475, Courtesy, LiquidMetal Golf; p. 478 (top), Sean Brady; p. 478 (bottom, left), Ken O'Donoghue; p. 478 (bottom, right), Richard Megna/Fundamental Photographs; p. 489, Stephen Frisch/Stock, Boston; p. 496, Chris Noble/Tony Stone Images; p. 501, Courtesy, Norsk Hydro. **Chapter 11** p. 512, Charles Derby/Photo Researchers, Inc.; p. 517, Sean Brady; p. 518, Betty Anne Schreiber/Animals, Animals; p. 520, E.R. Degginger; p. 522 (both), Frank Cox; p. 523, Sean Brady; p. 526, T. Orban/Sygma; p. 527 (both), Betz/Visuals Unlimited; p. 531, David Young-Wolkfe/PhotoEdit; p. 538, Sean Brady; p. 539, Leslie Zumdahl; p. 542, Visuals Unlimited; p. 543 (left), Stanley Flagler/Visuals Unlimited; p. 543 (center, right), David M. Phillips/Visuals Unlimited; p. 545, Courtesy, Southern California Electric; p. 546, Sean Brady; p. 549 (top), Doug Allan/Animals, Animals; p. 549 (bottom), Stephen Frisch. **Chapter 12** p. 558, Professor Sir John Neurig Thomas/Royal Institution of Great Britain; p. 560 (top, left), Bob Daemmrich/Stock, Boston; pp. 560 (top, right) and vii, Thomas H. Brakefield/The Stock Market; p. 560 (bottom, left), Tom Stillo/Omni-Photo Communications; p. 560 (bottom, right), E. Bordis/Leo de Wys; p. 589, Keven

Index

SUPPLEMENTAL
MATERIAL

Taken from
CHEMICAL PRINCIPLES
Fourth Edition

STEVEN S. ZUMDAHL

Supplemental Material taken from Chemical Principles, Fourth Edition:

Although other technologies are now coming into use for this purpose, gaseous diffusion has played an important role in the enrichment of uranium for use in nuclear reactors. Natural uranium is mostly $^{238}_{92}U$, which cannot be fissioned to produce energy. It contains only about 0.7% of the fissionable nuclide $^{235}_{92}U$. For uranium to be useful as a nuclear fuel, the relative amount of $^{235}_{92}U$ must be increased to about 3%. In the gas diffusion enrichment process, the natural uranium (containing $^{238}_{92}U$ and a small amount of $^{235}_{92}U$) reacts with fluorine to form a mixture of $^{238}UF_6$ and $^{235}UF_6$. Because these molecules have slightly different masses, they will have slightly different velocities at a given temperature, which allows them to be separated by a multistage diffusion process. To understand how this process works, imagine a series of chambers separated by semiporous walls that allow passage of some UF_6 molecules but prevent bulk flow of gas. In effect, each porous wall acts much like a tiny hole in an effusion cell. Assume that the UF_6 from natural uranium is placed in chamber 1. Thus chamber 1 contains 99.3% $^{238}UF_6$ and 0.7% $^{235}UF_6$ (that is, 993 molecules of $^{238}UF_6$ for every 7 molecules of $^{235}UF_6$). Some molecules of this UF_6 diffuse through the semiporous barrier into chamber 2, which was initially empty. Because of its smaller mass, $^{235}UF_6$, which has a slightly greater velocity than $^{238}UF_6$, diffuses at a slightly greater rate. Thus chamber 2 will contain a ratio of $^{235}UF_6$ to $^{238}UF_6$ that is slightly greater than 7 to 993.

Although the process is called **gaseous diffusion**, because the chambers are separated by barriers that effectively allow only individual UF_6 molecules to pass through, it behaves like an effusion process. Thus we can find the actual ratio of the two types of UF_6 in chamber 2 from Graham's law:

$$\frac{\text{Diffusion rate for }^{235}UF_6}{\text{Diffusion rate for }^{238}UF_6} = \sqrt{\frac{\text{Mass}(^{238}UF_6)}{\text{Mass}(^{235}UF_6)}}$$

$$= \sqrt{\frac{352.05 \text{ g/mol}}{349.03 \text{ g/mol}}}$$

$$= 1.0043$$

We can use this factor to calculate the ratio of $^{235}UF_6/^{238}UF_6$ in chamber 2:

$$\underset{\text{Chamber 2}}{\frac{^{235}UF_6}{^{238}UF_6}} = 1.0043 \times \underset{\text{Chamber 1}}{\frac{^{235}UF_6}{^{238}UF_6}} = 1.0043\left(\frac{7}{993}\right)$$

$$= 1.0043(7.0493 \times 10^{-3})$$

$$= 7.0797 \times 10^{-3}$$

Figure 5.20
Uranium-enrichment converters from the Paducah gaseous diffusion plant in Kentucky.

This very slight increase represents a change from the ratio of 70,493 $^{235}UF_6$ molecules per 10,000,000 $^{238}UF_6$ molecules in chamber 1 to the ratio of 70,797 $^{235}UF_6$ molecules per 10,000,000 $^{238}UF_6$ molecules in chamber 2.

This enrichment process (in $^{235}UF_6$) continues as the slightly enriched gas in chamber 2 diffuses into chamber 3 and is again enriched by a factor of 1.0043. The same process is repeated until sufficient enrichment occurs. Obviously, this process will take many stages. For example, to calculate the number of steps required to enrich from 0.700% ^{235}U to 3.00% ^{235}U, we have the following equation:

$$\underbrace{\frac{0.700 \; ^{235}UF_6}{99.3 \; ^{238}UF_6}}_{\text{Original ratio}} \times (1.0043)^N = \underbrace{\frac{3.00 \; ^{235}UF_6}{97.0 \; ^{238}UF_6}}_{\text{Desired ratio}}$$

where N represents the number of stages. This equation follows from the fact that each stage produces an enrichment by the factor 1.0043. Thus

$$(\text{Original ratio}) \times \underset{\substack{\text{First} \\ \text{stage}}}{1.0043} \times \underset{\substack{\text{Second} \\ \text{stage}}}{1.0043} \times \underset{\substack{\text{Third} \\ \text{stage}}}{1.0043} \times \cdots = \text{final ratio}$$

Solving the above equation for N yields 345. Thus we predict that 345 stages are required to obtain the desired enrichment.

Although we have greatly oversimplified* the actual enrichment process here, this discussion gives you an idea of how it is accomplished. A photo of actual diffusion cells is shown in Fig. 5.20.

Recall from Chapter 5 that for an ideal gas

$$(KE)_{avg} = \tfrac{3}{2}RT$$

where $(KE)_{avg}$ represents the average, random, translational energy for 1 mole of gas at a given temperature T (in Kelvins). The only way to change the kinetic energy of an ideal gas is to change its temperature. The energy ("heat") required to change the energy of 1 mole of an ideal gas by ΔT is

$$\text{Energy ("heat") required} = \tfrac{3}{2}R\Delta T$$

Note that for a temperature change of 1 K ($\Delta T = 1$), the energy required is $\tfrac{3}{2}R$.

The **molar heat capacity** of a substance is defined as the energy required to raise the temperature of 1 mole of that substance by 1 K. Thus we might conclude that the molar heat capacity of an ideal gas is $\tfrac{3}{2}R$. However, we will have to qualify this conclusion when we consider the implications of the PV work that can occur when a gas is heated.

Heating an Ideal Gas at Constant Volume

For an ideal gas, work occurs only when its volume changes. Thus, if a gas is heated at constant volume, the pressure increases but no work occurs.

When an ideal gas is heated in a rigid container in which no change in volume occurs, there can be no PV work ($\Delta V = 0$). Under these conditions all the energy that flows into the gas is used to increase the translational energies of the gas molecules. Thus C_v, the molar heat capacity of an ideal gas *at constant volume*, is $\tfrac{3}{2}R$, the result anticipated in the above discussion:

$$C_v = \tfrac{3}{2}R = \begin{array}{l}\text{"heat" required to change the temperature} \\ \text{of 1 mol of gas by 1 K at constant volume}\end{array}$$

Heating an Ideal Gas at Constant Pressure

When an ideal gas is heated at constant pressure, its volume increases and PV work occurs. Thus, when a gas is heated at constant pressure, energy must be supplied both to change the translational energy of the gas and to provide the work the gas does as it expands:

$$\text{Energy required} = \text{"heat"} = \begin{array}{c}\text{energy needed} \\ \text{to change the} \\ \text{translational energy}\end{array} + \begin{array}{c}\text{energy needed to} \\ \text{do the } PV \text{ work}\end{array}$$

The heat needed to increase the translational energy is $\tfrac{3}{2}R$, as we concluded above.

The *quantity* of work done as the gas expands by ΔV is $P\Delta V$. Using the ideal gas law, we see that

$$P\Delta V = nR\Delta T = R\Delta T \qquad \text{(per mole)}$$

Thus for a 1 K change in temperature ($\Delta T = 1$ K) the work is R, so

$$\begin{array}{l}\text{Heat required to increase the temperature} \\ \text{of 1 mol of gas by 1 K (constant } P)\end{array} = \tfrac{3}{2}R + R = \tfrac{5}{2}R$$

$$= C_v + R = C_p$$

$$C_v = \tfrac{3}{2}R$$
$$C_p = \tfrac{5}{2}R = C_v + R$$

Therefore, we have shown that C_p, the molar heat capacity of an ideal gas at constant pressure, is $\tfrac{5}{2}R$ or $C_v + R$.

Heating a Polyatomic Gas

We have established that for an ideal gas the molar heat capacity at constant volume is $\tfrac{3}{2}R$. This value of C_v assumes that an ideal gas consists of "particles" that have no structure. That is, we assume that the particles are monatomic (consisting of a single atom). Monatomic real gases, such as helium, have measured values of C_v very close to $\tfrac{3}{2}R$. However, gases such as SO_2 and $CHCl_3$ that contain polyatomic molecules have observed values for C_v that are significantly greater than $\tfrac{3}{2}R$. For example, the value of C_v for SO_2 is almost $4R$ at 25°C. This larger value for C_v results because polyatomic molecules absorb energy to excite rotational and vibrational motions in addition to translational motions. That is, at 25°C the molecules in such a gas are rotating, and the atoms in the molecule are vibrating, as if the bonds were springs.

As a polyatomic gas is heated, the gas molecules absorb energy to increase their rotational and vibrational motions as well as to move through space (translate) at higher speeds. Recall from our previous discussions that the temperature of a monatomic ideal gas is an index of the average random *translational* energy of the gas. Thus, when a gas is heated, the temperature only increases to the extent that the translational energies of the molecules increase. Any energy that is absorbed to increase the vibrational and rotational energies does not contribute directly to the translational kinetic energy; so for a gas that consists of diatomic or polyatomic molecules, much of the heat absorbed is used in processes that do not directly increase the temperature. Thus its heat capacity (the energy required to change its *temperature* by 1 K) is greater than $\tfrac{3}{2}R$.

C_v is greater than $\tfrac{3}{2}R$ for a gas in which the individual particles are molecules, because some of the energy added via heat flow is "stored" in motions that do not directly raise the temperature of the gas.

Note that the elevated value of C_v for a gas whose particles are molecules is not caused by nonideal behavior. That is, it does not depend on whether the gas obeys the ideal gas law. Rather, it is simply that the internal structure of the molecules enables them to absorb energy for processes other than translational motions.

Recall that C_p is greater than C_v because of the work done by the heated gas as it expands at constant pressure. Thus, if we assume that a given polyatomic gas obeys the ideal gas law, the expression

$$C_p = C_v + R$$

can be used to calculate C_p if the value of C_v for the gas is known.

The observed heat capacities of several gases are shown in Table 9.1. Notice that the monatomic gases have values of C_v equal to $\tfrac{3}{2}R$ (12.47 J K^{-1} mol^{-1}). Note also that as the molecules become more complex (more atoms), C_v increases. This result is expected because the presence of more atoms means that more nontranslational motions are available to absorb energy. Finally, notice that in all cases $C_p - C_v = R$, as expected for gases that closely obey the ideal gas law.

Heating a Gas: Energy and Enthalpy

Recall that the average translational energy of an ideal gas E is given by the expression

$$E = \tfrac{3}{2}RT \qquad \text{(per mole)}$$

Table 9.1   Molar Heat Capacities of Various Gases at 298 K

Gas	$C_v\left(\dfrac{J}{K\ mol}\right)$	$C_p\left(\dfrac{J}{K\ mol}\right)$	$C_p - C_v$
He, Ne, Ar	12.47	20.80	8.33
H_2	20.54	28.86	8.32
N_2	20.71	29.03	8.32
N_2O	30.38	38.70	8.32
CO_2	28.95	37.27	8.32
C_2H_6	44.60	52.92	8.32

for a monatomic ideal gas. The energy of an ideal gas can be changed only by changing the temperature:

$$\Delta E = \tfrac{3}{2}R\Delta T \qquad \text{(per mole)}$$

Note that this expression corresponds to

$$\Delta E = C_v\Delta T \qquad \text{(per mole)}$$

or

$$\Delta E = nC_v\Delta T \qquad (n \text{ moles})$$

The constant-volume heat capacity appears in this expression because when a gas is heated at constant volume, all the input energy (heat) goes toward increasing E (no heat is needed to do work).

On the other hand, when a gas is heated at constant pressure, the volume changes and work occurs. In this case (for n moles of gas),

$$\text{“Heat” required} = q_p = nC_p\Delta T$$
$$= n(C_v + R)\Delta T$$
$$= \underbrace{nC_v\Delta T}_{\Delta E} + \underbrace{nR\Delta T}_{P\Delta V\ =\ \text{work required}}$$

Notice that although this process is carried out at constant pressure, ΔE is still given by $nC_v\Delta T$. This result seems contradictory at first glance, but actually it makes good sense. Because E for an ideal gas depends only on T (it does not depend on pressure or volume, for example), $\Delta E = nC_v\Delta T$ when an ideal gas is heated whether the process occurs at constant volume or constant pressure.

Next, consider the change in enthalpy when a gas is heated. Recall that by definition

$$H = E + PV$$

Thus, in general, a change in enthalpy is given by the expression

$$\Delta H = \Delta E + \Delta(PV)$$

which (using the ideal gas law) becomes

$$\Delta H = \Delta E + \Delta(nRT) = \Delta E + nR\Delta T$$

for a sample of ideal gas containing n moles. Substituting $\Delta E = nC_v\Delta T$, we have

$$\Delta H = nC_v\Delta T + nR\Delta T$$
$$= n(C_v + R)\Delta T = nC_p\Delta T$$

Note that we have shown that

$$\Delta H = nC_p\Delta T$$

even though we have not assumed constant pressure (or volume). Thus we have shown that for an ideal gas we can always use the expression $nC_p\Delta T$ to calculate the change in enthalpy when n moles of an ideal gas is heated, regardless of any conditions on pressure or volume.

Again, it may seem contradictory that C_p appears in this expression for ΔH even though the pressure may or may not be constant in the process. However, note that the enthalpy ($H = E + PV$) of an ideal gas depends on E and the product PV. We have seen that E depends directly on T, and from the ideal gas law we can easily show that PV depends directly on T ($PV = nRT$) for a given sample of ideal gas (containing n moles). Thus both the energy E and the enthalpy H of an ideal gas depend only on T, not on P or V (individually):

$$E \propto T \quad \text{and} \quad H \propto T$$

For energy (E) the proportionality constant is C_v (per mole), and for enthalpy (H) the proportionality constant is C_p (per mole).

In considering these ideas, we must distinguish among q, ΔH, and ΔE. In the calculation of the heat flow for an ideal gas the equation

$$q = nC\Delta T$$

applies where C_v or C_p is used depending on the conditions. In contrast, $\Delta H = nC_p\Delta T$ and $\Delta E = nC_v\Delta T$ for a temperature change of an ideal gas regardless of whether pressure or volume (or neither) is constant. Also, note that the heat flow equals ΔE at constant volume ($\Delta E = q_v$) but the heat flow equals ΔH at constant pressure ($\Delta H = q_p$). These results are summarized in Table 9.2.

We will illustrate these concepts in Example 9.2.

The only way to change H and E for an ideal gas is to change the temperature of the gas. Thus, for any process involving *an ideal gas at constant temperature*, $\Delta H = 0$ and $\Delta E = 0$.

Table 9.2   Thermodynamic Properties of an Ideal Gas

Expression	Application
$C_v = \frac{3}{2}R$	Monatomic ideal gas
$C_v > \frac{3}{2}R$	Polyatomic ideal gas (value must be measured experimentally)
$C_p = C_v + R$	All ideal gases
$C_p = \frac{5}{2}R = \frac{3}{2}R + R$	Monatomic ideal gas
$C_p > \frac{5}{2}R$	Polyatomic ideal gas (specific value depends on the value of C_v)
$\Delta E = nC_v\Delta T$	All ideal gases
$\Delta H = nC_p\Delta T$	All ideal gases

Example 9.2

Consider 2.00 mol of a monatomic ideal gas that is taken from state A (P_A = 2.00 atm, V_A = 10.0 L) to state B (P_B = 1.00 atm, V_B = 30.0 L) by two different pathways:

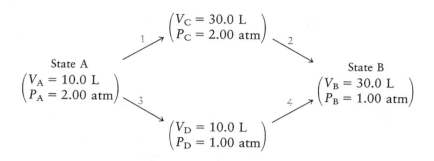

Calculate q, w, ΔE, and ΔH for both pathways.

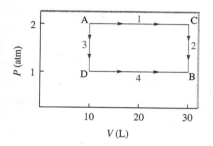

Figure 9.5

Summary of the two pathways discussed in Example 9.2.

Solution

Before we do any calculations, it is useful to summarize the processes described above by using the "PV diagram" shown in Fig. 9.5.

Step 1

Notice from Fig. 9.5 that this step corresponds to an expansion from 10.0 to 30.0 L at a constant pressure of 2.00 atm. This process must occur by heating the gas to produce some temperature change ΔT (not specified in the given data). From the ideal gas law we know that

$$P\Delta V = nR\Delta T$$

In this case ΔV = 30.0 L − 10.0 L, so

$$P\Delta V = (2.00 \text{ atm})(20.0 \text{ L}) = 4.00 \times 10^1 \text{ L atm}$$

or if we convert to joules,

$$P\Delta V = 4.00 \times 10^1 \text{ L atm} \times \frac{101.3 \text{ J}}{\text{L atm}} = 4.05 \times 10^3 \text{ J}$$

It follows that

$$\Delta T = \frac{P\Delta V}{nR} = \frac{4.05 \times 10^3 \text{ J}}{nR}$$

We know that $w = -P\Delta V$, and because in this case the gas expands against a constant external pressure of 2.00 atm, we have

$$w_1 = -(2.00 \text{ atm})(30.0 \text{ L} - 10.0 \text{ L}) = -4.00 \times 10^1 \text{ L atm}$$
$$= -4.05 \times 10^3 \text{ J}$$

Also, in this case (constant P)

$$q_1 = q_p = nC_p\Delta T$$

$$= n\left(\frac{5}{2}R\right)\left(\frac{4.05 \times 10^3 \text{ J}}{nR}\right) = 1.01 \times 10^4 \text{ J}$$

(Note that the signs of w and q are as expected: The gas expands, so work flows out of the system; the gas is heated, so heat flows into the system.)
    We can calculate ΔE_1 and ΔH_1 as follows:

$$\Delta E_1 = nC_v\Delta T = n\left(\frac{3}{2}R\right)\left(\frac{4.05 \times 10^3 \text{ J}}{nR}\right) = 6.08 \times 10^3 \text{ J}$$

$$\Delta H_1 = nC_p\Delta T = n\left(\frac{5}{2}R\right)\left(\frac{4.05 \times 10^3 \text{ J}}{nR}\right) = 1.01 \times 10^4 \text{ J}$$

Note that in this case $q_1(q_p)$ equals ΔH_1, as expected, because this process is carried out at constant pressure.

Step 2

In this step the gas pressure decreases from 2.00 atm to 1.00 atm at constant volume. This step must correspond to the cooling of the gas by a quantity ΔT, which we can find from the ideal gas law:

$$\Delta PV = nR\Delta T$$

$$\Delta T = \frac{\Delta PV}{nR} = \frac{(1.00 \text{ atm} - 2.00 \text{ atm})(30.0 \text{ L})}{nR}$$

$$= \frac{-30.0 \text{ L atm}}{nR} = \frac{-3.04 \times 10^3 \text{ J}}{nR}$$

Note that ΔT is negative, as expected for a cooling process.
    Because in this step $\Delta V = 0$, thus $w_2 = 0$. In this case

$$q_2 = q_v = nC_v\Delta T = n\left(\frac{3}{2}R\right)\left(\frac{-3.04 \times 10^3 \text{ J}}{nR}\right)$$

$$= -4.56 \times 10^3 \text{ J}$$

Also,

$$\Delta E_2 = nC_v\Delta T = n\left(\frac{3}{2}R\right)\left(\frac{-3.04 \times 10^3 \text{ J}}{nR}\right)$$

$$= -4.56 \times 10^3 \text{ J} = q_v$$

and

$$\Delta H_2 = nC_p\Delta T = n\left(\frac{5}{2}R\right)\left(\frac{-3.04 \times 10^3 \text{ J}}{nR}\right)$$

$$= -7.60 \times 10^3 \text{ J}$$

Notice that in this case $q_2 = q_v = \Delta E$, as expected for a constant-volume process.
    Using similar reasoning, we can compute the required quantities for steps 3 and 4.

Step 3

$$\Delta T = \frac{\Delta PV}{nR} = \frac{(-1.00 \text{ atm})(10.0 \text{ L})}{nR} = \frac{-10.0 \text{ L atm}}{nR}$$

$$= \frac{-1.01 \times 10^3 \text{ J}}{nR}$$

$$w_3 = 0 \qquad (\Delta V = 0)$$

$$q_3 = q_v = nC_v\Delta T = n\left(\frac{3}{2}R\right)\left(\frac{-1.01 \times 10^3 \text{ J}}{nR}\right)$$

$$= -1.52 \times 10^3 \text{ J}$$

$$\Delta E_3 = q_v = -1.52 \times 10^3 \text{ J}$$

$$\Delta H_3 = nC_p\Delta T = n\left(\frac{5}{2}R\right)\left(\frac{-1.01 \times 10^3 \text{ J}}{nR}\right) = -2.53 \times 10^3 \text{ J}$$

Step 4

$$\Delta T = \frac{P\Delta V}{nR} = \frac{(1.00 \text{ atm})(20.0 \text{ L})}{nR} = \frac{20.0 \text{ L atm}}{nR}$$

$$= \frac{2.03 \times 10^3 \text{ J}}{nR}$$

$$w_4 = -P\Delta V = -(1.00 \text{ atm})(20.0 \text{ L}) = -20.0 \text{ L atm}$$

$$= -2.03 \times 10^3 \text{ J}$$

$$q_4 = q_p = nC_p\Delta T = n\left(\frac{5}{2}R\right)\left(\frac{2.03 \times 10^3 \text{ J}}{nR}\right)$$

$$= 5.08 \times 10^3 \text{ J}$$

$$\Delta E_4 = nC_v\Delta T = n\left(\frac{3}{2}R\right)\left(\frac{2.03 \times 10^3 \text{ J}}{nR}\right)$$

$$= 3.05 \times 10^3 \text{ J}$$

$$\Delta H_4 = nC_p\Delta T = n\left(\frac{5}{2}R\right)\left(\frac{2.03 \times 10^3 \text{ J}}{nR}\right)$$

$$= 5.08 \times 10^3 \text{ J} = q_p$$

Summary

- Pathway one (steps 1 and 2):

$$q_{one} = q_1 + q_2 = 1.01 \times 10^4 \text{ J} - 4.56 \times 10^3 \text{ J}$$

$$= 5.5 \times 10^3 \text{ J}$$

$$w_{one} = w_1 + w_2 = -4.05 \times 10^3 \text{ J}$$

$$q_{one} + w_{one} = 1.5 \times 10^3 \text{ J} = \Delta E_{one}$$

$$\Delta H_{one} = \Delta H_1 + \Delta H_2$$

$$= 1.01 \times 10^4 \text{ J} - 7.60 \times 10^3 \text{ J}$$

$$= 2.5 \times 10^3 \text{ J}$$

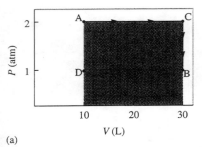

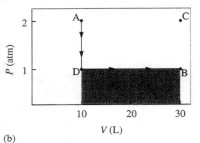

(a)

(b)

Figure 9.6

The magnitude of the work for pathway one (a) and pathway two (b) are shown by the colored areas: $|w| = |P\Delta V|$.

- Pathway two (steps 3 and 4):

$$q_{two} = q_3 + q_4 = -1.52 \times 10^3 \text{ J} + 5.08 \times 10^3 \text{ J}$$
$$= 3.56 \times 10^3 \text{ J}$$
$$w_{two} = w_3 + w_4 = -2.03 \times 10^3 \text{ J}$$
$$q_{two} + w_{two} = 3.55 \times 10^3 \text{ J} - 2.03 \times 10^3 \text{ J}$$
$$= 1.52 \times 10^3 \text{ J} = \Delta E_{two}$$
$$\Delta H_{two} = \Delta H_3 + \Delta H_4$$
$$= -2.53 \times 10^3 \text{ J} + 5.08 \times 10^3 \text{ J}$$
$$= 2.55 \times 10^3 \text{ J}$$

Notice from the results of Example 9.2 that the work and heat are different for the two pathways between states A and B. For example, in pathway one the expansion (by 20.0 L) is carried out at a pressure of 2.00 atm, and in pathway two the expansion (by 20.0 L) is carried out at 1.00 atm. Thus, since $|w| = |P\Delta V|$, twice as much work is obtained by way of pathway one as via pathway two. This result is shown graphically in Fig. 9.6, where the darker areas represent $|P\Delta V|$. These results again emphasize that heat and work are both pathway-dependent. On the other hand, note that the sum of q and w is the same for both pathways (within round-off differences). This is expected. Recall that

$$\Delta E = q + w$$

and that E is a state function. Note also that the overall ΔH value for pathway one equals that for pathway two (within rounding errors) as expected, because enthalpy is a state function as well.

The next important development in the knowledge of atomic structure came when Albert Einstein (see Fig. 12.5) proposed that electromagnetic radiation is itself quantized. Einstein suggested that electromagnetic radiation can be viewed as a stream of "particles" now called **photons.** The energy of each photon is given by the expression

G. N. Lewis (see Section 13.10) actually coined the term "photon" in 1926.

$$E_{\text{photon}} = h\nu = \frac{hc}{\lambda}$$

where h is Planck's constant, ν is the frequency of the radiation, and λ is the wavelength of the radiation.

Einstein arrived at this conclusion through his analysis of the **photoelectric effect** (for which he later was awarded the Nobel Prize). The photoelectric effect refers to the phenomenon in which electrons are emitted from the surface of a metal when light strikes it. The following observations characterize the photoelectric effect.

1. Studies in which the frequency of the light is varied show that no electrons are emitted by a given metal below a specific threshold frequency ν_0.

2. For light with frequency lower than the threshold frequency, no electrons are emitted regardless of the intensity of the light.

3. For light with frequency greater than the threshold frequency, the number of electrons emitted increases with the intensity of the light.

4. For light with frequency greater than the threshold frequency, the kinetic energy of the emitted electrons increases linearly with the frequency of the light.

Figure 12.5   Albert Einstein (1879–1955) was born in Germany. Nothing in his early development suggested genius; even at the age of 9 he did not speak clearly, and his parents feared that he might have a handicap. When asked what profession Einstein should follow, his school principal replied, "It doesn't matter; he'll never make a success of anything." When he was 10, Einstein entered the Luitpold Gymnasium (high school), which was typical of German schools of that time in being harshly disciplinarian. There he developed a deep suspicion of authority and a skepticism that encouraged him to question and doubt—valuable qualities in a scientist. In 1905, while a patent clerk in Switzerland, Einstein published a paper explaining the photoelectric effect via the quantum theory. For this revolutionary thinking he received a Nobel Prize in 1921. Highly regarded by this time, he worked in Germany until 1933, when Hitler's persecution of the Jews forced him to come to the United States. He worked at the Institute for Advanced Study at Princeton University until his death in 1955.

Einstein was undoubtedly the greatest physicist of our age. Even if someone else had derived the theory of relativity, his other work would have ensured his ranking as the second greatest physicist of his time. Our concepts of space and time were radically changed by ideas he first proposed when he was 26 years old. From then until the end of his life, he attempted unsuccessfully to find a single unifying theory that would explain all physical events.

These observations can be explained by assuming that electromagnetic radiation is quantized (consists of photons), and that the threshold frequency represents the minimum energy required to remove the electron from the metal's surface.

Minimum energy required to remove an electron $= E_0 = h\nu_0$

Because a photon with energy less than E_0 ($\nu < \nu_0$) cannot remove an electron, light with a frequency less than the threshold frequency produces no electrons. On the other hand, for light where $\nu > \nu_0$, the energy in excess of that required to remove the electron is given to the electron as kinetic energy (KE):

$$\text{KE}_{\text{electron}} = \tfrac{1}{2}mv^2 = h\nu - h\nu_0$$

| Mass of electron | Velocity of electron | Energy of incident photon | Energy required to remove electron from metal's surface |

Because in this picture the intensity of light is a measure of the number of photons present in a given part of the beam, a greater intensity means that more photons are available to release electrons (as long as $\nu > \nu_0$ for the radiation).

At about the same time that Einstein was performing his analysis of the photoelectric effect, he was also constructing the theory of special relativity. In connection with this work Einstein derived the famous equation

$$E = mc^2$$

which he published in 1905. This equation points out the close relationship between energy and mass. In fact, we have learned that mass is a form of energy. When a system loses energy, it also loses mass. This result is more apparent if we rearrange the equation to the following form:

$$m = \frac{E}{c^2} \quad \leftarrow \text{Energy}$$

Mass   Speed of light

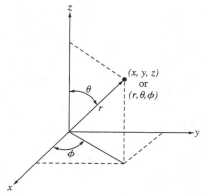

Figure 12.15

The spherical polar coordinate system.

7.7X   The Wave Equation for the Hydrogen Atom

Unlike the particle in a one-dimensional box, the electron of the hydrogen atom moves in three dimensions and has potential energy, because of its attraction to the positive nucleus at the atom's center. These differences can be easily accounted for by including the second derivatives with respect to all three of the Cartesian coordinates and by inserting a term that specifies the dependence of the electron's potential energy on its position in space.

Because it is more convenient mathematically, the coordinate system is changed from Cartesian to spherical polar coordinates (see Fig. 12.15) before the Schrödinger equation is solved. In the system of spherical polar coordinates a given point in space, specified by values of the Cartesian coordinates x, y, and z, is described by specific values of r, θ, and ϕ.

In the spherical polar coordinate system the wave function $\psi(r, \theta, \phi)$ can be written as a product of one function depending on r, one depending on θ, and one depending on ϕ:

$$\psi(r, \theta, \phi) = R(r)\Theta(\theta)\Phi(\phi)$$

This separation of variables allows an exact solution to the Schrödinger equation

$$\hat{H}\psi = E\psi$$

for the hydrogen atom.

In spherical polar coordinates the potential energy (in cgs units) of the electron is

$$V(r) = -\frac{(Ze)(e)}{r}$$

To convert the potential energy from cgs units to SI units (joules), the expression shown must be multiplied by $1/4\pi\epsilon_0$, where ϵ_0 (the permittivity of the vacuum) is 8.854×10^{-12} C^2/J m.

where Ze represents the nuclear charge ($Z = 1$ for the hydrogen atom). As with the particle in a box, when the Schrödinger equation for the hydrogen atom is solved and the boundary conditions are applied, a series of wave functions is obtained, each function corresponding to a particular energy. In contrast to the particle in a one-dimensional box, where one quantum number emerges from the mathematics, the three-dimensional hydrogen atom gives rise to three quantum numbers.

The boundary conditions, which differ in some important aspects from those of the particle in the box because of the very different nature of the physical system, will not be discussed here.

The conventional symbols for these quantum numbers are as follows:

n the *principal quantum number*
ℓ the *angular momentum quantum number*
m_ℓ the *magnetic quantum number*

We will have more to say in succeeding sections about what values these quantum numbers can assume and their physical meanings.

The mathematics of wave mechanics leads to the following expression for the allowed energies of hydrogen's electron:

$$E_n = -\frac{Z^2}{n^2}\left(\frac{me^4}{8\epsilon_0^2h^2}\right) = -2.178 \times 10^{-18} \text{ J}\left(\frac{Z^2}{n^2}\right)$$

where $Z = 1$ for hydrogen and where n can assume only integer values (1, 2, 3, . . .). Several characteristics of this equation are worth emphasizing. First, note that the energy of the electron depends only on the principal quantum number (this is true only for one-electron species). Also note that because n is restricted to integer values, hydrogen's electron can assume only discrete energy values—the energy levels are quantized. Finally, note that this is exactly the same equation for energy as obtained in the Bohr model.

So that you have an idea of what they look like, the first few wave functions for hydrogen are shown in Table 12.1 on the next page, along with the three quantum numbers n, ℓ, and m_ℓ.

When we solve the Schrödinger equation for the hydrogen atom, some of the solutions contain complex numbers (that is, they contain $i = \sqrt{-1}$). Because it is more convenient physically to deal with orbitals that contain only real numbers, the complex orbitals are usually combined (added and subtracted) to remove the complex portions. For example, the p_x and p_y orbitals shown in Table 12.1 are combinations of the complex orbitals that correspond

Table 12.1   Solutions of the Schrödinger Wave Equation for a One-Electron Atom

n	ℓ	m_ℓ	Orbital	Solution
1	0	0	$1s$	$\psi_{1s} = \dfrac{1}{\sqrt{\pi}}\left(\dfrac{Z}{a_0}\right)^{3/2} e^{-\sigma}$
2	0	0	$2s$	$\psi_{2s} = \dfrac{1}{4\sqrt{2\pi}}\left(\dfrac{Z}{a_0}\right)^{3/2} (2-\sigma)e^{-\sigma/2}$
2	1	0	$2p_z$	$\psi_{2p_z} = \dfrac{1}{4\sqrt{2\pi}}\left(\dfrac{Z}{a_0}\right)^{3/2} \sigma e^{-\sigma/2}\cos\theta$
2	1	± 1	$\begin{cases}2p_x \\[2em] 2p_y\end{cases}$	$\psi_{2p_x} = \dfrac{1}{4\sqrt{2\pi}}\left(\dfrac{Z}{a_0}\right)^{3/2} \sigma e^{-\sigma/2}\sin\theta\cos\phi$ $\psi_{2p_y} = \dfrac{1}{4\sqrt{2\pi}}\left(\dfrac{Z}{a_0}\right)^{3/2} \sigma e^{-\sigma/2}\sin\theta\sin\phi$
3	0	0	$3s$	$\psi_{3s} = \dfrac{1}{81\sqrt{3\pi}}\left(\dfrac{Z}{a_0}\right)^{3/2} (27-18\sigma+2\sigma^2)e^{-\sigma/3}$
3	1	0	$3p_z$	$\psi_{3p_z} = \dfrac{\sqrt{2}}{81\sqrt{\pi}}\left(\dfrac{Z}{a_0}\right)^{3/2} (6\sigma-\sigma^2)e^{-\sigma/3}\cos\theta$
3	1	± 1	$\begin{cases}3p_x \\[2em] 3p_y\end{cases}$	$\psi_{3p_x} = \dfrac{\sqrt{2}}{81\sqrt{\pi}}\left(\dfrac{Z}{a_0}\right)^{3/2} (6\sigma-\sigma^2)e^{-\sigma/3}\sin\theta\cos\phi$ $\psi_{3p_y} = \dfrac{\sqrt{2}}{81\sqrt{\pi}}\left(\dfrac{Z}{a_0}\right)^{3/2} (6\sigma-\sigma^2)e^{-\sigma/3}\sin\theta\sin\phi$
3	2	0	$3d_{z^2}$	$\psi_{3d_{z^2}} = \dfrac{1}{81\sqrt{6\pi}}\left(\dfrac{Z}{a_0}\right)^{3/2} \sigma^2 e^{-\sigma/3}(3\cos^2\theta-1)$
3	2	± 1	$\begin{cases}3d_{xz} \\[2em] 3d_{yz}\end{cases}$	$\psi_{3d_{xz}} = \dfrac{\sqrt{2}}{81\sqrt{\pi}}\left(\dfrac{Z}{a_0}\right)^{3/2} \sigma^2 e^{-\sigma/3}\sin\theta\cos\theta\cos\phi$ $\psi_{3d_{yz}} = \dfrac{\sqrt{2}}{81\sqrt{\pi}}\left(\dfrac{Z}{a_0}\right)^{3/2} \sigma^2 e^{-\sigma/3}\sin\theta\cos\theta\sin\phi$
3	2	± 2	$\begin{cases}3d_{xy} \\[2em] 3d_{x^2-y^2}\end{cases}$	$\psi_{3d_{xy}} = \dfrac{1}{81\sqrt{2\pi}}\left(\dfrac{Z}{a_0}\right)^{3/2} \sigma^2 e^{-\sigma/3}\sin^2\theta\sin 2\phi$ $\psi_{3d_{x^2-y^2}} = \dfrac{1}{81\sqrt{2\pi}}\left(\dfrac{Z}{a_0}\right)^{3/2} \sigma^2 e^{-\sigma/3}\sin^2\theta\cos 2\phi$

Note: $\sigma = Zr/a_0$ where $Z = 1$ for hydrogen; $a_0 = \epsilon_0 h^2/\pi m e^2 = 5.29 \times 10^{-11}$ m.

to values of m_ℓ of $+1$ and -1. These orbitals are indicated with a brace in Table 12.1. The last four d orbitals listed are also obtained by combination of complex orbitals, as indicated by braces in Table 12.1.

9.6   Orbitals: Human Inventions

In the treatment of the bonding and structure in molecules we have stressed that the descriptions we have given are models—and simple ones, at that. These models are extraordinarily valuable because they provide pictures in our minds of what molecules might look like and how they might behave. This helps us decide what questions to ask (what experiments to do) as we try to understand more completely the complicated behavior of matter. However, as valuable as these pictures are, we must remember that they greatly oversimplify a very complex situation. We must realize that these models can give us a rather superficial view that is often highly misleading.

For example, after all of the talk about orbitals in the last several chapters, you probably have the distinct impression that orbitals actually exist. The truth is, they do not—at least not in the physical sense. Orbitals are mathematical functions—solutions to a modified Schrödinger equation (the changes made to allow separation into independent electron equations).

Thus orbitals are mathematical tools we use to describe atoms and molecules. However, they have no physical reality in the sense that if you could look at a water molecule, you would probably not "see" anything like the pictures we have shown in this book. These pictures merely help us visualize the theoretical information we have accumulated for water.

We should also make clear that much more sophisticated treatments of atoms and molecules than we have considered here do exist and are carried out quite routinely by chemists who specialize in this area. These quantum mechanical calculations involve many fewer approximations than are made to obtain the models we have discussed here. However, although these treatments produce accurate mathematical descriptions of atomic and molecular properties, they are usually very difficult to interpret physically.

In contrast, the simple, highly pictorial models we have considered in this text are extremely useful because they help us do first-order chemical thinking and organize the information about matter that we gather from experiments. For example, there is a great deal of experimental evidence to suggest that methane has a tetrahedral structure. We have seen that the VSEPR model predicts this structure and that sp^3 hybrid orbitals on the carbon atom are consistent with this structure. Of course, this does not mean that methane really has four localized pairs of electrons, all with the same energy. In fact, the electrons in methane are delocalized and do not all have the same energy. However, the fact that methane is more complicated than these models indicate does not destroy the usefulness of the models. They still help us greatly as we organize the vast amount of information we collect about molecules. For example, chemists have learned to expect certain behaviors of "sp^3 carbon atoms" no matter what molecule contains them. A similar statement also applies to "sp^2 carbon atoms," "sp carbon atoms," and so on.

There is another point that should be made in connection with the theories of atoms and molecules. Even the experts in the field disagree (sometimes violently) about what the mathematical descriptions of atoms and molecules mean.* And even the most fundamental ideas about bonding that we have discussed in this text are subject to controversy. The point here is not to present these more complex concepts but to make sure that you appreciate the nature of models and that you recognize the difference between the information learned about matter from experiments and the information learned from theories. Because matter is so complex, we often tailor our theories to explain a limited area of nature so as to keep the theories simple enough to understand and use. However, it is very dangerous to assume that such a limited theory can then be used in a wider sense. We must be very careful to

---

*References to some interesting and provocative papers on this subject follow. These articles are probably too sophisticated to be read with great understanding now, but you can try to read them and then put copies of them in your files to be reread as your knowledge of chemistry increases. They raise some interesting questions.

Linus Pauling, "The Nature of the Chemical Bond—1992," *J. Chem. Ed.* **69** (1992): 519.
J. F. Ogilvie, "The Nature of the Chemical Bond—1990," *J. Chem. Ed.* **67** (1990): 280.
Michael Laing, "No Rabbit Ears on Water," *J. Chem. Ed.* **64** (1987): 124.
R. Bruce Martin, "Localized and Spectroscopic Orbitals: Squirrel Ears on Water," *J. Chem. Ed.* **65** (1988): 688.

ask proper questions of our theories or we face the danger of being greatly misled.

9.7 Molecular Spectroscopy

Spectroscopy can be defined as the study of the interaction of electromagnetic radiation with matter. We have already discussed the emission spectrum of the hydrogen atom (Chapter 12) and the importance of the information it provides about hydrogen's quantized energy levels. Spectroscopy is also very useful for the study of molecules. Molecules can absorb electromagnetic radiation to furnish energy for many different processes, all which have quantized energy levels. For example, a molecule can absorb or emit a photon and go from a lower electronic energy state to a higher electronic energy state, or vice versa. This so-called *electronic transition* can be described approximately as a change from one electron arrangement (a particular configuration of electrons in the molecular orbitals) to another. Typically, electronic transitions require photons in the ultraviolet or visible regions of the spectrum. In addition to undergoing electronic transitions, molecules can undergo vibrational and rotational energy transitions. For example, the atoms in a molecule vibrate around their equilibrium positions, giving rise to quantized vibrational energy levels whose spacings correspond to the energies of photons in the infrared region of the electromagnetic spectrum. Molecules also rotate and have quantized rotational energy levels whose spacings correspond to the energies of photons in the microwave region. In fact, it is the rotational excitation of the water molecules in food and the transfer of this energy to other molecules that form the basis for microwave cooking.

A schematic representation of two molecular electronic states with the accompanying vibrational and rotational energy levels is given in Fig. 14.52. Note that each electronic energy level has a set of quantized vibrational states and that each vibrational state has a set of rotational states.

Depending on the energy of the photons interacting with it, a molecule can undergo a pure rotational transition (change rotational levels but remain in the same vibrational and electronic states), a vibrational transition that may also involve a simultaneous rotational transition (see Fig. 14.52), or an electronic transition that may involve a simultaneous vibrational and/or rotational change. The details of the geometric structure and electronic structure of the molecule determine exactly what types of transitions can occur. We will not deal with these issues here because they are beyond the scope of this text.

Rotational Spectroscopy

The spacings of the quantized rotational energy levels for a molecule depend on its molecular structure. Therefore, the experimental determination of a molecule's rotational energy-level spacings provides information about its structure. That is, determination of the specific photons of microwave radiation that a given molecule absorbs yields direct information about the rotational energy spacings. This in turn gives information about the details of the

Figure 14.52

A schematic representation of two electronic energy levels in a molecule, with the vibrational (in red) and rotational (in blue) energy levels shown for each electronic state. Note that rotational changes are lowest in energy, followed by vibrational changes and then electronic changes, which require the highest-energy photons.

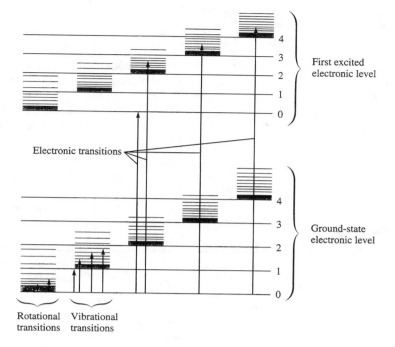

molecule's structure. For example, for a linear molecule the energies of the rotational states are given by the formula

$$E_J = \frac{\hbar^2}{2I} J(J + 1)$$

where J = the rotational quantum number, which can assume only integer values and zero ($J = 0, 1, 2, 3, \ldots$)

        $\hbar$ = Planck's constant divided by 2π

        I = the moment of inertia of the molecule

For a diatomic molecule containing atoms with masses m_1 and m_2, the moment of inertia is given by the relationship

$$I = \mu R_e^2$$

where μ = reduced mass = $\dfrac{m_1 m_2}{m_1 + m_2}$

R_e = average (equilibrium) bond length

If the energy of the photon necessary to promote a diatomic molecule from E_0 ($J = 0$) to E_1 ($J = 1$) is determined, the value of I for the molecule can be calculated, which, in turn, allows the calculation of R_e. Thus the rotational spectrum of a diatomic molecule provides an accurate method for measuring its average bond length.

The analysis of the rotational spectra for polyatomic molecules is more complex but also can provide accurate details of molecular structure.

Vibrational Spectroscopy

As we have seen, a molecule can be approximated as a collection of atoms held together by bonds. In describing the vibrations in a molecule, we can compare the bond between a given pair of atoms to a spring attached to two masses. As the atoms move apart in a vibrational motion, the bond, like a spring, provides a restoring force that pulls the atoms back toward each other. The atoms vibrate back and forth about the average bond distance R_e, which leads to quantized energy levels given by the expression

$$E_v = h\nu_0 \left(v + \tfrac{1}{2}\right)$$

where

ν_0 = the characteristic frequency of the vibration

v = the vibrational quantum number, which can assume only the values 0, 1, 2, 3, . . .

Notice that the vibrational energy is not zero when $v = 0$. The energy $h\nu_0/2$ corresponding to $v = 0$ is the zero-point energy of the molecule.

One very important use of vibrational spectroscopy, which involves energy transitions in the infrared (IR) region of the spectrum, is to assist in the identification of an unknown molecule. The infrared (IR) spectrum of a molecule is typically represented as a plot of the energy transmitted versus the *wave number* of the radiation. The wave number for electromagnetic radiation is the reciprocal of the wavelength in centimeters. This provides a conveniently sized unit commonly used in plotting infrared spectra. A typical spectrum is shown in Fig. 14.53. Note that regions of the spectrum where the energy transmitted is small correspond to regions where the molecule has absorbed a large quantity of this radiation.

A particular bonded pair of atoms has a characteristic vibrational frequency (wave number) that is relatively insensitive to its molecular environment. Thus a vibration that appears in the IR spectrum at that characteristic wave number provides good evidence that this particular atom pair is present in the molecule. For example, a C—H pair in a molecule will always show a vibration at about 3000 cm^{-1} (the range of wave numbers is actually about 2750–3150 cm^{-1}, depending on the specific molecular environment). On the other hand,

Figure 14.53

The infrared spectrum of CH_2Cl_2. (Note that the wave number scale changes on this spectrum at 2000 cm^{-1}.)

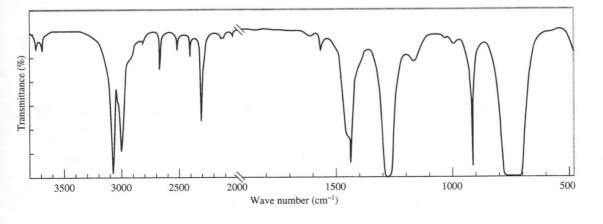

the O—H group in a molecule will show a vibration at about 3600 cm^{-1}. Likewise, a carbonyl group

$$\diagdown\!\!\!\diagup C\!\!=\!\!O$$

always shows a distinctively shaped vibrational band at about 1700 cm^{-1}, a carbon–carbon double bond

$$\diagdown\!\!\!\diagup C\!\!=\!\!C\diagup\!\!\!\diagdown$$

shows a vibration at about 1650 cm^{-1}, and so on. Therefore, the IR spectrum of a molecule can be a great aid in identifying what atom groupings are present in a molecule and thus can provide valuable information for identifying a specific molecule.

Electronic Spectroscopy

The electronic spectrum of a molecule, which typically occurs in the ultraviolet or visible region of the electromagnetic spectrum, provides information about the spacings of the electronic energy levels in the molecule. The electronic spectrum, a plot of the quantity of radiation absorbed versus the wavelength of the radiation, shows peaks (maxima) at wavelengths where the photons have an energy that matches an energy gap in the molecule.

Often when a molecule absorbs a photon, the resulting excited state is much more chemically reactive than is the molecule in its ground state. The study of

A science student at Lehigh University adjusting an electron spectroscopy unit used for chemical analysis.

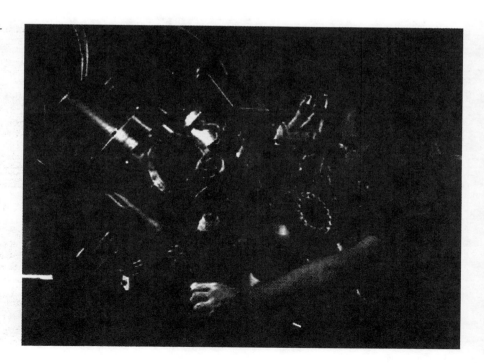

the chemistry of these electronically excited molecules is called *photochemistry*. A particularly important area of photochemistry concerns the study of the reactions that occur in the earth's atmosphere. For example, photochemical smog depends to an important extent on the photodecomposition of nitrogen dioxide to form very reactive oxygen atoms that combine with oxygen molecules in the air to form ozone, which then goes on to react with other pollutants. Ironically, the problems of ozone *depletion* in the upper atmosphere also result from a photochemical reaction—in this case, the photodecomposition of chlorofluorocarbons such as CF_2Cl_2 to produce reactive chlorine atoms, which catalyze ozone decomposition. We will discuss this situation in more detail in Chapter 15.

Lasers, which will be discussed in more detail in Chapter 16, have assumed a very important role in electronic spectroscopy in recent years, both because they can deliver large quantities of energy at very precise wavelengths and because the power can be delivered in very short bursts—on the order of only 10^{-12} second (one picosecond) in duration. This allows the excitation of molecules with an ultrashort pulse of energy, after which the molecule can be observed as it decays back to the ground state by various pathways, many of which take place on the picosecond time scale.

In this section we have touched on only three types of spectroscopy. There are many other types, some dealing with the properties of the nucleus, some dealing with the surface properties of solids, some dealing with the various types of emissions by excited molecules, and so on. Spectroscopy is one of the most powerful tools available to the scientist.

How does a chemist deduce the mechanism for a given reaction? The rate law is always determined first. Then using chemical intuition and following the two rules given above, the chemist constructs a possible mechanism. Until recently, we could not prove a mechanism absolutely. We could only say that a mechanism that satisfies the two requirements is *possibly* correct.

Recent advances in spectroscopy, however, such as those pioneered by Professor Ahmed Zewail (see "Femtochemistry" on page 689), have provided the means for identifying mechanisms exactly. Deducing the mechanism for a chemical reaction is difficult; it requires skill and experience. We will only touch on this process in this text.

12.6X Mechanisms with Fast Forward and Reverse First Steps

A common type of reaction mechanism is one involving a first step in which *both* the forward and reverse reactions are very fast compared with the reactions in the second step. An example of this type of mechanism is that for the decomposition of ozone to oxygen. The balanced reaction is

$$2O_3(g) \longrightarrow 3O_2(g)$$

The observed rate law is

$$\text{Rate} = k\frac{[O_3]^2}{[O_2]}$$

Note that this rate law is unusual in that it contains the concentration of a *product*. The mechanism proposed for this process is

$$O_3 \underset{k_{-1}}{\overset{k_1}{\rightleftharpoons}} O_2 + O$$

$$O + O_3 \xrightarrow{k_2} 2O_2$$

The double arrows in the first step indicate that both the forward and reverse reactions are important. They have the rate constants k_1 and k_{-1}, respectively.

For this mechanism we will assume that *both* the forward and reverse reactions of the first step are very fast compared with the reaction in the second step. This means that the second step is rate determining. Therefore, the rate for the overall reaction is equal to the rate of the second step:

$$\text{Rate} = k_2[O][O_3]$$

This rate law does not have the same form as the experimentally determined rate law. For one thing, it contains the concentration of the intermediate, an oxygen atom. We can remove [O] and obtain a rate law that agrees with the experiment results by making an additional assumption. We assume that the rates of the forward and reverse reactions in the first step are equal. That is, we assume that the initial reversible fast step is at equilibrium. This makes sense because the rates of both the forward and reverse reactions for the first step are so much faster than the rate of the second step. For the first step

$$\text{Rate of forward reaction} = k_1[O_3]$$

and

$$\text{Rate of reverse reaction} = k_{-1}[O_2][O]$$

At equilibrium we have

$$k_1[O_3] = k_{-1}[O_2][O]$$

We solve for [O]:

$$[O] = \frac{k_1[O_3]}{k_{-1}[O_2]}$$

Now we substitute the expression for [O] into the rate law for the second step:

$$\text{Rate} = k_2[O][O_3] = k_2\left(\frac{k_1[O_3]}{k_{-1}[O_2]}\right)[O_3] = \frac{k_2k_1[O_3]^2}{k_{-1}[O_2]}$$

$$= k\frac{[O_3]^2}{[O_2]}$$

where k is a composite constant representing k_2k_1/k_{-1}.

This rate law, *derived* by postulating the two elementary steps and making assumptions about the relative rates of these steps, agrees with the experimental rate law. Since this mechanism (the elementary steps *plus* the assumptions) also gives the correct overall stoichiometry, it is an acceptable mechanism for the decomposition of ozone to oxygen.

The second step is relatively slow because of the very small concentration of O_3 molecules.

Example 15.7

The gas-phase reaction of chlorine with chloroform is described by the equation

$$Cl_2(g) + CHCl_3(g) \longrightarrow HCl(g) + CCl_4(g)$$

The rate law determined from experiment has a noninteger order:

$$\text{Rate} = k[Cl_2]^{1/2}[CHCl_3]$$

A proposed mechanism for this reaction follows:

$$Cl_2(g) \underset{k_{-1}}{\overset{k_1}{\rightleftharpoons}} 2Cl(g) \qquad \text{Both fast with equal rates (fast equilibrium)}$$

$$Cl(g) + CHCl_3(g) \xrightarrow{k_2} HCl(g) + CCl_3(g) \qquad \text{Slow}$$

$$CCl_3(g) + Cl(g) \xrightarrow{k_3} CCl_4(g) \qquad \text{Fast}$$

Is this an acceptable mechanism for the reaction?

Solution

Two questions must be answered. First, does the mechanism give the correct overall stoichiometry? Adding the three steps does yield the correct balanced equation:

$$Cl_2(g) \rightleftharpoons 2Cl(g)$$
$$Cl(g) + CHCl_3(g) \longrightarrow HCl(g) + CCl_3(g)$$
$$CCl_3(g) + Cl(g) \longrightarrow CCl_4(g)$$

$$\overline{Cl_2(g) + \cancel{Cl}(g) + CHCl_3(g) + \cancel{CCl_3}(g) + \cancel{Cl}(g) \longrightarrow 2\cancel{Cl}(g) + HCl(g) + \cancel{CCl_3}(g) + CCl_4(g)}$$

Overall reaction: $Cl_2(g) + CHCl_3(g) \longrightarrow HCl(g) + CCl_4(g)$

Second, does the mechanism agree with the observed rate law? Since the overall reaction rate is determined by the rate of the slowest step,

$$\text{Overall rate} = \text{rate of second step} = k_2[Cl][CHCl_3]$$

Since the chlorine atom is an intermediate, we must find a way to eliminate [Cl] in the rate law. This can be done by recognizing that since the first step is at equilibrium, its forward and reverse rates are equal:

$$k_1[Cl_2] = k_{-1}[Cl]^2$$

Solving for $[Cl]^2$ gives

$$[Cl]^2 = \frac{k_1[Cl_2]}{k_{-1}}$$

Taking the square root of both sides yields

$$[Cl] = \left(\frac{k_1}{k_{-1}}\right)^{1/2} [Cl_2]^{1/2}$$

and

$$\text{Rate} = k_2[Cl][CHCl_3] = k_2\left(\frac{k_1}{k_{-1}}\right)^{1/2} [Cl_2]^{1/2}[CHCl_3] = k[Cl_2]^{1/2}[CHCl_3]$$

where

$$k = k_2 \left(\frac{k_1}{k_{-1}} \right)^{1/2}$$

The rate law derived from the mechanism agrees with the experimentally observed rate law. This mechanism satisfies the two requirements and thus is an acceptable mechanism.

12.6Y   The Steady-State Approximation

In the simplest reaction mechanisms one particular step is usually rate determining. However, it is not unusual in complex, multistep reaction mechanisms for different steps to be rate determining under different sets of conditions.

In cases where a specific rate-determining step cannot be chosen, an analysis called the **steady-state approximation** is often used. The central feature of this method is the assumption that the concentration of any intermediate remains constant as the reaction proceeds. An intermediate is neither a reactant nor a product but something that is formed and then consumed as the reaction proceeds.

For example, the reaction between nitric oxide and hydrogen,

$$2NO(g) + H_2(g) \longrightarrow N_2O(g) + H_2O(g)$$

may proceed via the following mechanism:

1. $2NO \underset{k_{-1}}{\overset{k_1}{\rightleftharpoons}} N_2O_2$

2. $N_2O_2 + H_2 \overset{k_2}{\longrightarrow} N_2O + H_2O$

In this mechanism the intermediate is N_2O_2. To apply the steady-state approximation to this mechanism, we assume the concentration of N_2O_2 remains constant. That is,

$$\frac{d[N_2O_2]}{dt} = 0$$

Next, we will identify the steps that produce N_2O_2 and those that consume N_2O_2 and write the rate law for each. Then we will apply the condition that the concentration of N_2O_2 is constant by setting the total rate of production of N_2O_2 equal to the total rate of consumption of N_2O_2. That is, if

Rate of production of N_2O_2 = rate of consumption of N_2O_2

then

$$\frac{d[N_2O_2]}{dt} = 0$$

Rate of Production of N_2O_2

In this mechanism N_2O_2 is produced only in the forward part of the first elementary step,

$$2NO \overset{k_1}{\longrightarrow} N_2O_2$$

and the rate law for this step is

$$\frac{d[N_2O_2]}{dt} = k_1[NO]^2$$

Rate of Consumption of N_2O_2

In this mechanism N_2O_2 is consumed in the reverse part of the first step,

$$2NO \xleftarrow{k_{-1}} N_2O_2$$

and in the second step,

$$N_2O_2 + H_2 \xrightarrow{k_2} N_2O + H_2O$$

The rate laws for these steps are

$$-\frac{d[N_2O_2]}{dt} = k_{-1}[N_2O_2] \qquad \text{and} \qquad -\frac{d[N_2O_2]}{dt} = k_2[N_2O_2][H_2]$$

The Steady-State Condition

Now we equate the rates of production and consumption of N_2O_2:

$$k_1[NO]^2 = k_{-1}[N_2O_2] + k_2[N_2O_2][H_2]$$

$$\underbrace{\qquad}_{\text{Rate of production}} \qquad \underbrace{\qquad}_{\text{Total rate of consumption}}$$

The Rate Law for the Overall Reaction

Next, we will write the rate law for the overall reaction,

$$2NO + H_2 \longrightarrow N_2O + H_2O$$

We can do this in several ways, depending on which reactant or product we use to represent the rate. In this case we will choose the decomposition of H_2 to define the rate:

$$\text{Rate of reaction} = -\frac{d[H_2]}{dt}$$

Note that H_2 is consumed only in the second step of the mechanism:

$$N_2O_2 + H_2 \xrightarrow{k_2} N_2O + H_2O$$

Thus the rate law is

$$-\frac{d[H_2]}{dt} = k_2[N_2O_2][H_2]$$

However, this is not the final form of the rate law for the overall reaction because it contains the concentration of an intermediate. We can remove this concentration from the rate law by solving the steady-state expression

$$k_1[NO]^2 = k_{-1}[N_2O_2] + k_2[N_2O_2][H_2]$$

for $[N_2O_2]$:

$$[N_2O_2] = \frac{k_1[NO]^2}{k_{-1} + k_2[H_2]}$$

We substitute this expression into the rate law,

$$\text{Rate} = -\frac{d[H_2]}{dt} = k_2[N_2O_2][H_2]$$

to give

$$\text{Rate} = -\frac{d[H_2]}{dt} = k_2[H_2]\left(\frac{k_1[NO]^2}{k_{-1} + k_2[H_2]}\right)$$

or

$$\text{Rate} = -\frac{d[H_2]}{dt} = \frac{k_2k_1[H_2][NO]^2}{k_{-1} + k_2[H_2]}$$

This is the overall rate law for the proposed mechanism based on the steady-state analysis. Note that this rate law is quite complicated, which is common for rate laws obtained by assuming steady-state conditions. The usual practice for testing the validity of a complicated rate law involves choosing concentration conditions that produce a simpler form of the rate law. For example, if the reaction between NO and H_2 is studied under conditions where the concentration of H_2 is large enough so that

$$k_2[H_2] \gg k_{-1}$$

then the full rate law

$$\frac{k_2k_1[H_2][NO]^2}{k_{-1} + k_2[H_2]}$$

reduces to

$$\frac{k_2k_1[H_2][NO]^2}{k_2[H_2]} = k_1[NO]^2$$

Thus, at sufficiently high concentrations of H_2, the reaction should show second-order dependence on the concentration of nitric oxide, if the suggested mechanism is valid.

On the other hand, at low concentrations of H_2, such that

$$k_{-1} \gg k_2[H_2]$$

the rate law reduces to the form

$$\text{Rate} = \frac{k_2k_1}{k_{-1}}[H_2][NO]^2 = k[H_2][NO]^2$$

Studies of the reaction under these conditions should show first-order dependence on $[H_2]$, as well as second-order dependence on [NO], if the suggested mechanism is valid.

The ideas we have developed above for a specific mechanism can be generalized as follows.

Summary: Analyzing a Mechanism Using the Steady-State Approximation

1. Write the proposed mechanism (the elementary steps).

2. Construct a steady-state expression for each intermediate I by applying the criterion

$$\frac{d[\text{I}]}{dt} = 0$$

which means that

Rate of production of I = rate of consumption of I

This condition is implemented by identifying each step that produces or consumes I and writing the appropriate rate law for each. The sum of the rate laws that produce I are then set equal to the sum of the rate laws that consume I.

3. From the steady-state approximation for each intermediate I_1, I_2, . . ., solve for $[I_1]$, $[I_2]$, ...

4. Construct the rate law for the overall reaction in terms of one of the reactants or products. The decision about which reactant or product to use in constructing the rate law is based on convenience.

5. Use the expressions from Step 3 for $[I_1]$, $[I_2]$, . . . to substitute for the concentrations of intermediates found in the rate law for Step 4. The goal is to obtain an overall rate law that contains only reactant and/or product concentrations.

14.8X Strong Acid Solutions in Which Water Contributes to the H⁺ Concentration

Although in a typical strong acid solution (for example, 0.1 M HCl) the $[H^+]$ is determined by the amount of strong acid present, there are circumstances in which the contribution of water must be taken into account. For example, consider a 1.0×10^{-7} M HNO_3 solution. For this very dilute solution the strong acid and the water make comparable contributions to $[H^+]$ at equilibrium. Because the H^+ from HNO_3 will affect the position of the water equilibrium, the total $[H^+]$ in this solution will not be simply 1.0×10^{-7} M +

1.0×10^{-7} $M = 2.0 \times 10^{-7}$ M. Rather, $[H^+]$ will be between 1.0×10^{-7} M and 2.0×10^{-7} M. We can calculate the exact $[H^+]$ by using the principle of charge balance:

$$[\text{Positive charge}] = [\text{negative charge}]$$

In this case we have

$$[H^+] = [NO_3^-] + [OH^-]$$

which, from $K_w = [H^+][OH^-]$, can be written as

$$[H^+] = [NO_3^-] + \frac{K_w}{[H^+]} \qquad \text{or} \qquad \frac{[H^+]^2 - K_w}{[H^+]} = [NO_3^-]$$

The fact that the solution contains 1.0×10^{-7} M HNO_3 means that $[NO_3^-]$ $= 1.0 \times 10^{-7}$ M. Inserting this value, we can solve the above equation to give $[H^+] = 1.6 \times 10^{-7}$ M.

This approach applies for any strong acid (although it is unnecessary for more typical concentrations). It can also be adapted to calculate the pH of a very dilute strong base solution. (Try your hand at this problem by calculating the pH of a 5.0×10^{-8} M KOH solution.)

16.1X The Isothermal Expansion and Compression of an Ideal Gas

In this section we will lay the groundwork for several fundamental concepts of thermodynamics by considering the isothermal expansion and compression of an ideal gas. An **isothermal process** is one in which the temperatures of the system and the surroundings remain constant at all times. Recall that the energy of an ideal gas can be changed only by changing its temperature. Therefore, for any isothermal process *involving an ideal gas*,

$$\Delta E = 0$$

and since

$$\Delta E = q + w = 0$$

then

$$q = -w$$

To illustrate the work and heat effects that accompany the expansion or compression of an ideal gas, consider the apparatus shown in Fig. 10.5. Assume that the pulley is frictionless and that the cable and pan have zero mass.

Initially, assume that the gas occupies a volume V_1 at pressure P_1, where P_1 is just balanced by a mass M_1 on the pan. Thus

$$P_1 = \frac{\text{force}}{\text{area}} = \frac{M_1 g}{A}$$

where A is the area of the piston and g is the gravitational constant. Thus state 1 of the gas is defined by P_1, V_1, n, and T, where n and T remain constant as the expansion occurs.

Figure 10.5

A device for the isothermal expansion/compression of an ideal gas.

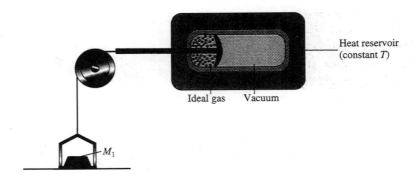

Heat reservoir (constant T)

Ideal gas   Vacuum

M_1

One-Step Expansion—No Work

If mass M_1 is removed from the pan, the gas will expand, moving the piston to the right end of the cylinder. After expansion the gas occupies a volume $V_2 = 4V_1$ and pressure $P_2 = P_1/4$.

When the process goes from state 1 (P_1, V_1) to state 2 ($P_1/4$, $4V_1$) with no mass on the pan, no heat flows into or out of the gas because T is constant and no work is done (no mass is lifted). Thus work = $w_0 = 0$. This is called a *free expansion*.

P_{external} (the pressure against which the gas expands) is zero in a free expansion.

One-Step Expansion

Now consider an experiment with the gas initially at state 1 where the mass M_1 is replaced by a mass $M_1/4$. The gas will now expand against the pressure (P_{external}):

$$P_{\text{ex}} = \frac{\left(\frac{M_1}{4}\right)g}{A} = \frac{P_1}{4}$$

The mass is lifted and the gas expands until the pressure is $P_1/4$. The new volume is $4V_1$. In this case work is performed:

$$|\text{Work}| = |w_1| = \left(\frac{M_1}{4}\right)gh$$

where h is the *change* in height of the mass.

This work can also be expressed in terms of the external pressure (P_{ex}) on the gas as it expands and the change in volume (ΔV). Recall from Chapter 9 that

$$w = -P_{\text{ex}}\Delta V$$

In this expansion the magnitude (absolute value) of the work is

$$|w_1| = P_{\text{ex}}\Delta V = \frac{P_1}{4}(V_2 - V_1) = \frac{P_1}{4}(4V_1 - V_1) = \frac{3}{4}P_1V_1$$

Since in this case work flows out of the system into the surroundings, the correct sign is

$$w_1 = -P_{\text{ex}}\Delta V = -\tfrac{3}{4}P_1V_1$$

Two-Step Expansion

Next, we will expand the gas in two steps by using two different weights on the pan. First, we put a weight with mass $M_1/2$ on the pan. In this case

$$P_{\text{ex}} = \frac{\left(\frac{M_1}{2}\right)g}{A} = \frac{P_1}{2}$$

and the gas expands until $P_2 = P_1/2$ and $V_2 = 2V_1$. The magnitude of the work is

$$|w_2'| = \frac{P_1}{2}(V_2 - V_1) = \frac{P_1}{2}(2V_1 - V_1) = \frac{P_1V_1}{2}$$

Figure 10.6

The *PV* diagram for a two-step expansion.

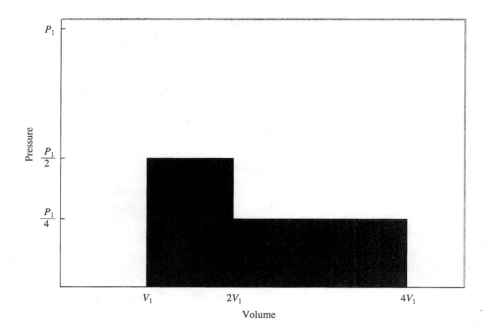

Next, replace the mass $M_1/2$ with a mass $M_1/4$. The gas expands again until $P_3 = P_1/4$ and $V_3 = 4V_1$. The quantity of work in this step is

$$|w_2''| = \frac{P_1}{4}(4V_1 - 2V_1) = \frac{P_1 V_1}{2}$$

The total quantity of work in this two-step expansion is

$$|w_2| = \frac{P_1 V_1}{2} + \frac{P_1 V_1}{2} = P_1 V_1$$

With its correct sign $w_2 = -P_1 V_1$. This process is diagramed in Fig. 10.6. Note that $|w_2| > |w_1| > |w_0|$, even though in each case the gas is taken from state 1 (P_1, V_1) to state 2 $(P_1/4, 4V_1)$. This result illustrates a property of work we have discussed before: Work is pathway-dependent—it is not a state function.

Six-Step Expansion

Next, we will consider the expansion of the gas from state 1 to state 2 in six steps, using several masses between M_1 and $M_1/4$. This process is summarized in Fig. 10.7. In this case $|w_6|$, which is the sum of these six steps, is clearly greater than $|w_2|$.

Infinite-Step Expansion

If one continues to increase the number of steps, the magnitude of w_n (for an n-step process),

$$|w_n| = \sum_{i=1}^{n} P_i \Delta V_i$$

continues to increase.

Now we consider the limiting case—a process in which P_{ex} is changed by infinitesimally small increments. This case corresponds to the use of an in-

Figure 10.7

The *PV* diagram for a six-step expansion.

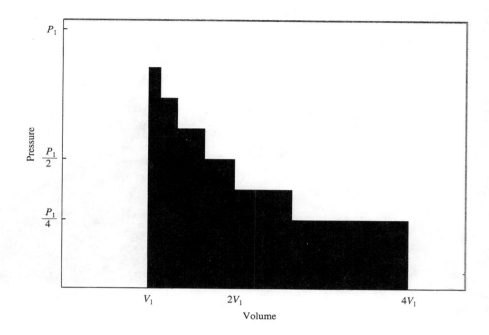

finite number of weights, each differing from the previous one by an infinitesimally small mass. Under these conditions the successive volume changes become infinitesimally small (dV), and the process requires an infinite number of steps. The mathematical operation needed to sum the steps in this instance is the integral

$$|\text{Work}| = \int_{V_1}^{V_2} P_{ex}dV$$

The diagram corresponding to this process is given in Fig. 10.8 on page 406.

It is important to recognize that when the expansion of the gas is carried out in an infinite number of steps, the *external pressure is always almost exactly equal to the pressure produced by the gas*. That is, at any given time P_{ex} is only less than $P_{gas}(= P)$ by an infinitesimally small amount dP. Thus one can assume that at any point in the process $P \approx P_{ex}$.

A process like this one, carried out so that the system is always at equilibrium, is called a *reversible process*. The expansions described earlier that were carried out in a finite number of steps were not done reversibly, because in these processes P_{ex} was smaller than P by a finite amount during each step. We will have more to say presently about what the term *reversible* means in this context.

Since $P_{ex} \approx P_{gas} = P$ in the reversible expansion, by use of the ideal gas law,

$$P_{ex} \approx P = \frac{nRT}{V}$$

and

$$|\text{Total work}|^* = |w_\infty| = |w_{rev}| = \int_{V_1}^{V_2} \frac{nRT\ dV}{V}$$

---

*In these calculations we deal with the magnitude, for convenience. Actually, for the expansion of a gas the work has a negative sign.

Figure 10.8

The *PV* diagram for the reversible expansion.

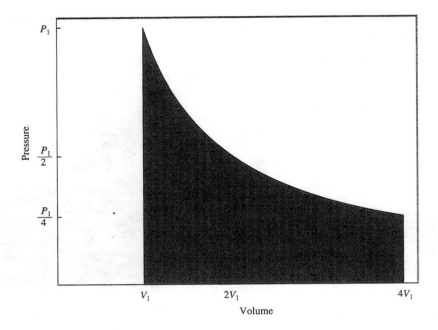

Since n and T are held constant in this experiment,

$$|w_{rev}| = nRT \int_{V_1}^{V_2} \frac{dV}{V} = nRT(\ln V_2 - \ln V_1) = nRT \ln\left(\frac{V_2}{V_1}\right)$$

In this specific experiment $V_2 = 4V_1$. Therefore,

$$|w_{rev}| = nRT \ln 4 = 1.4nRT$$

And since $P_1 V_1 = nRT$,

$$|w_{rev}| = 1.4P_1 V_1$$

for this particular expansion.

Note that as the number of steps in the expansion increases, the amount of work the gas performs also increases. The maximum work that a given amount of gas can perform in going from V_1 to V_2 at constant temperature occurs in the reversible expansion. Thus

$$|w_{max}| = |w_{rev}| = nRT \ln\left(\frac{V_2}{V_1}\right)$$

for the isothermal expansion of n moles of an ideal gas.

In doing this hypothetical experiment, we have assumed that the gas behaves ideally. When a given amount of an ideal gas expands at constant temperature, the internal energy of the gas remains constant; that is, $\Delta E = 0$. As mentioned above, this condition means that $q = -w$. Thus a quantity of energy q (equal in magnitude to w) flows into the gas (as heat) as the expansion occurs, and the work (w) is performed. Therefore, the surroundings furnished the energy (through heat flow) necessary to perform the work.

Since work flows out of the system in the reversible expansion, it has a negative sign:

$$w_{\text{rev}} = -nRT \ln\left(\frac{V_2}{V_1}\right)$$

and

$$q_{\text{rev}} = -w_{\text{rev}} = nRT \ln\left(\frac{V_2}{V_1}\right)$$

The Isothermal Compression of an Ideal Gas

Now let's consider the opposite experiment: compressing a gas at pressure $P_1/4$ and volume $4V_1$ to pressure P_1 and volume V_1. This experiment can be done in one step or a number of steps.

One-Step Compression

Initially, the gas is at pressure $P_1/4$ and volume $4V_1$. When mass M_1 is placed on the pan, the gas will be rapidly compressed to the state described by P_1 and V_1. To see how this process works, consider the diagram for the gas at $P_1/4$ and $4V_1$ (Fig. 10.9). We raise the mass M_1 to the pan, which then causes the gas to be compressed to P_1 and V_1 as the pan returns to the original level.

The work performed to recompress the gas is equal to the work performed to lift the weight up to the pan. It also can be expressed in terms of $P_{\text{ex}}\Delta V$:

$$|w_1'| = M_1 gh = P_1 \Delta V = P_1(4V_1 - V_1) = 3P_1 V_1$$

Two-Step Compression

We can compress the gas in two steps. For example, a mass $M_1/2$ is lifted onto the pan, and after the gas has been partially compressed, M_1 is put onto the pan in place of $M_1/2$ to finish the compression. In this case the total work required for the compression is

$$|w_2'| = \frac{P_1}{2}(4V_1 - 2V_1) + P_1(2V_1 - V_1) = 2P_1 V_1$$

Figure 10.9

The situation before the one-step compression.

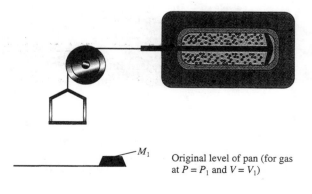

M_1

Original level of pan (for gas at $P = P_1$ and $V = V_1$)

Infinite-Step Compression

Notice that in compressing the gas isothermally, as the number of steps increases, the work required to compress the gas decreases.

If we compress the gas in an infinite number of steps (in which, at all times, $P_{ex} \approx P$), the work required is

$$|w'_\infty| = \int_{V_1}^{V_2} P dV = nRT \ln\left(\frac{V_2}{V_1}\right)$$

$$= nRT \ln\left(\frac{V_1}{4V_1}\right) = 1.4 P_1 V_1$$

Because $P_{ex} \approx P$ throughout the process, this is a *reversible* compression. In this case w has a positive sign, because we are performing work on the system. Thus, in the reversible, isothermal compression of the gas, $w'_\infty = 1.4 P_1 V_1$; and since $\Delta E = 0$,

$$q_\infty = -w'_\infty = -1.4 P_1 V_1$$

As the gas is compressed reversibly and isothermally, it releases $1.4 P_1 V_1$ (L atm) of energy as heat to the surroundings. In other words, the same quantity of energy flows into the gas as work and flows out of the gas as heat to produce no net change in E as the compression occurs.

In general terms, for a reversible compression from V_1 to V_2,

$$w_{rev} = -q_{rev} = -nRT \ln\left(\frac{V_2}{V_1}\right)$$

or in terms of pressures,

$$w_{rev} = -q_{rev} = -nRT \ln\left(\frac{P_1}{P_2}\right)$$

Note that since this process is a compression ($V_2 < V_1$), $\ln(V_2/V_1)$ has a negative sign, making w_{rev} positive and q_{rev} negative, as expected.

Summary

We summarize the results of these expansion and compression experiments in Table 10.3. The most important conclusion that can be drawn from these results can be stated as follows: Only when the expansion and compression *are both done reversibly* (by an infinite number of steps) is the universe the same after the cyclic process (the expansion and the subsequent compression of the gas back to its original state). That is, only for the reversible processes is the heat absorbed during expansion exactly equal to the heat released during compression. In all the processes carried out using a finite number of steps, more heat is released into the surroundings than is absorbed in the comparable expansion (same number of steps).

For example, in the one-step expansion and compression the net work done is

$$w_{net} = \underset{\uparrow}{-0.75 P_1 V_1} + \underset{\uparrow}{3 P_1 V_1} = 2.25 P_1 V_1$$
$$\text{Expansion} \quad \text{Compression}$$

and the net heat flow is $-2.25 P_1 V_1$.

Table 10.3   Summary of the Isothermal Expansion and Compression Experiments

	Number of Steps	w	q
Expansion (constant T)	0 (no mass)	0	0
	1	$-0.75P_1V_1$	$0.75P_1V_1$
	2	$-1P_1V_1$	$1P_1V_1$
	4	$-1.16P_1V_1$	$1.16P_1V_1$
	∞	$-1.4P_1V_1$	$1.4P_1V_1$
Compression (constant T)	1	$3P_1V_1$	$-3P_1V_1$
	2	$2P_1V_1$	$-2P_1V_1$
	4	$1.67P_1V_1$	$-1.67P_1V_1$
	∞	$1.4P_1V_1$	$-1.4P_1V_1$

In terms of the *system* this one-step expansion/compression is cyclic. That is, the system starts at state 1 before the expansion process and ends up back at state 1 after the compression process. However, although the system is returned to the same state in this cyclic expansion–compression process, the *surroundings* are not the same. In fact, we might say that in the surroundings "work has been changed to heat." In this one-step cyclic process, $2.25P_1V_1$ (L atm) of work is changed to $2.25P_1V_1$ (L atm) of heat (thermal energy) in the surroundings. This amount represents the net extra work required to lift the weights onto the pan to compress the gas, compared with the work that was obtained as the gas expanded.

This is a general result. In any finite-step, cyclic expansion–compression process "work is always converted to heat":

$$\text{Work} \longrightarrow \text{Heat}$$

Ordered energy   Disordered energy

This result applies whenever the process is carried out in a nonreversible (irreversible) manner. In other words, in an *irreversible* cyclic process more work must be input to the system than the system produces. In all the finite gas compressions the work required is greater than $1.4P_1V_1$, which is the maximum work available from the expansion.

Of course, all real processes are irreversible, because they cannot be carried out in an infinite number of steps without taking an infinite amount of time. In other words, *all real processes are irreversible* (in a thermodynamic sense).

Another important conclusion to be drawn from the above example is that the *maximum work obtainable from the gas occurs when the expansion is carried out reversibly* ($w_{\text{max}} = w_{\text{rev}}$). This result is always true for PV work, as well as for any other type of work, such as electrical work performed by an electrochemical cell. We will examine this latter example in the next chapter.

The final point that this experiment reemphasizes is that work and heat are pathway-dependent and thus are not state functions. Energy, on the other hand, is a state function. In each of these isothermal expansions and compressions between (P_1, V_1) and $(P_1/4, 4V_1)$, ΔE is always zero, regardless of the number of steps, since T is constant.

All real processes are irreversible.

The maximum work corresponds to the reversible expansion.

Page Numbers of Some Important Tables

Physical Constants

Constant	Symbol	Value
Atomic mass unit	amu	1.66054×10^{-27} kg
Avogadro's number	N	6.02214×10^{23} mol^{-1}
Bohr radius	a_0	5.292×10^{-11} m
Boltzmann constant	k	1.38066×10^{-23} J/K
Charge of an electron	e	1.60218×10^{-19} C
Faraday constant	F	96,485 C/mol
Gas constant	R	8.31451 J/K · mol
		0.08206 L · atm/K · mol
Mass of an electron	m_e	9.10939×10^{-31} kg
		5.48580×10^{-4} amu
Mass of a neutron	m_n	1.67493×10^{-27} kg
		1.00866 amu
Mass of a proton	m_p	1.67262×10^{-27} kg
		1.00728 amu
Planck's constant	h	6.62608×10^{-34} J · s
Speed of light	c	2.99792458×10^8 m/s